THE
ALL ENGLAND
LAW REPORTS
1983

Volume 1

Editor
PETER HUTCHESSON LL M
Barrister, New Zealand

Assistant Editor
BROOK WATSON
of Lincoln's Inn, Barrister
and of the New South Wales Bar

Consulting Editor
WENDY SHOCKETT
of Gray's Inn, Barrister

London
BUTTERWORTHS

ENGLAND	Butterworth & Co (Publishers) Ltd
	88 Kingsway, **London** WC2B 6AB
AUSTRALIA	Butterworths Pty Ltd, **Sydney, Melbourne,**
	Brisbane, Adelaide and **Perth**
CANADA	Butterworth & Co (Canada) Ltd, **Toronto**
	Butterworth & Co (Western Canada) Ltd, **Vancouver**
NEW ZEALAND	Butterworths of New Zealand Ltd, **Wellington**
SINGAPORE	Butterworth & Co (Asia) Pte Ltd, **Singapore**
SOUTH AFRICA	Butterworth Publishers (Pty) Ltd, **Durban**
USA	Mason Publishing Co, **St Paul**, Minnesota
	Butterworth Legal Publishers, **Seattle**, Washington,
	Boston, Massachusetts and **Austin**, Texas
	D & S Publishers, **Clearwater**, Florida

©

Butterworth & Co (Publishers) Ltd

1983

ISBN 0 406 85147 6

Typeset by CCC, printed and bound in Great Britain by William Clowes (Beccles) Limited, Beccles and London

House of Lords

The Lord High Chancellor: Lord Hailsham of St Marylebone

Lords of Appeal in Ordinary

Lord Diplock
Lord Fraser of Tullybelton
Lord Keith of Kinkel
Lord Scarman
Lord Roskill

Lord Bridge of Harwich
Lord Brandon of Oakbrook
Lord Brightman
Lord Templeman

Court of Appeal

The Lord High Chancellor

The Lord Chief Justice of England: Lord Lane
(President of the Criminal Division)

The Master of the Rolls: Sir John Francis Donaldson
(President of the Civil Division)

The President of the Family Division: Sir John Lewis Arnold

The Vice-Chancellor: Sir Robert Edgar Megarry

Lords Justices of Appeal

Sir John Frederick Eustace Stephenson
Sir Frederick Horace Lawton
Sir George Stanley Waller
Sir James Roualeyn Hovell-Thurlow-
 Cumming-Bruce
Sir Edward Walter Eveleigh
Sir Desmond James Conrad Ackner
Sir Robin Horace Walford Dunn
Sir Peter Raymond Oliver
Sir Tasker Watkins VC

Sir Patrick McCarthy O'Connor
Sir William Hugh Griffiths
Sir Michael John Fox
Sir Michael Robert Emanuel Kerr
Sir John Douglas May
Sir Christopher John Slade
Sir Francis Brooks Purchas
Sir Robert Lionel Archibald Goff
Sir George Brian Hugh Dillon

Chancery Division

The Lord High Chancellor

The Vice-Chancellor

Sir Peter Harry Batson Woodroffe Foster
Sir John Norman Keates Whitford
Sir Ernest Irvine Goulding
Sir Raymond Henry Walton
Sir Nicolas Christopher Henry Browne-
Wilkinson
Sir John Evelyn Vinelott

Sir Martin Charles Nourse
Sir Douglas William Falconer
Sir Jean-Pierre Frank Eugene Warner
Sir Peter Leslie Gibson
Sir David Herbert Mervyn Davies
Sir Jeremiah LeRoy Harman

Queen's Bench Division

The Lord Chief Justice of England

Sir John Thompson
(retired 16 December 1982)
Sir Joseph Donaldson Cantley
Sir Hugh Eames Park
Sir Bernard Caulfield
Sir Hilary Gwynne Talbot
Sir William Lloyd Mars-Jones
Sir Ralph Kilner Brown
Sir Peter Henry Rowley Bristow
Sir Hugh Harry Valentine Forbes
Sir Neil Lawson
(retired 8 April 1983)
Sir David Powell Croom-Johnson
Sir Leslie Kenneth Edward Boreham
Sir Alfred William Michael Davies
Sir John Dexter Stocker
Sir Kenneth George Illtyd Jones
Sir Haydn Tudor Evans
Sir Peter Richard Pain
Sir Kenneth Graham Jupp
Sir Stephen Brown
Sir Roger Jocelyn Parker
Sir Ralph Brian Gibson
Sir Walter Derek Thornley Hodgson
Sir James Peter Comyn
Sir Anthony John Leslie Lloyd
Sir Frederick Maurice Drake
Sir Brian Thomas Neill

Sir Michael John Mustill
Sir Barry Cross Sheen
Sir David Bruce McNeill
Sir Harry Kenneth Woolf
Sir Christopher James Saunders French
Sir Thomas Patrick Russell
Sir Peter Edlin Webster
Sir Thomas Henry Bingham
Sir Iain Derek Laing Glidewell
Sir Henry Albert Skinner
Sir Peter Murray Taylor
Sir Murray Stuart-Smith
Sir Christopher Stephen Thomas Jonathan
Thayer Staughton
Sir Donald Henry Farquharson
Sir Anthony James Denys McCowan
Sir Iain Charles Robert McCullough
Sir Hamilton John Leonard
Sir Alexander Roy Asplan Beldam
Sir David Cozens-Hardy Hirst
Sir John Stewart Hobhouse
Sir Michael Mann
Sir Andrew Peter Leggatt
Sir Michael Patrick Nolan
Sir Oliver Bury Popplewell
(appointed 6 January 1983)
Sir William Alan Macpherson
(appointed 11 April 1983)

Family Division

The President of the Family Division

Sir John Brinsmead Latey
Sir Alfred Kenneth Hollings
Sir Charles Trevor Reeve
Dame Rose Heilbron
Sir Brian Drex Bush
Sir Alfred John Balcombe
Sir John Kember Wood
Sir Ronald Gough Waterhouse

Sir John Gervase Kensington Sheldon
Sir Thomas Michael Eastham
Dame Margaret Myfanwy Wood Booth
Sir Anthony Leslie Julian Lincoln
Dame Ann Elizabeth Oldfield Butler-Sloss
Sir Anthony Bruce Ewbank
Sir John Douglas Waite
Sir Anthony Barnard Hollis

CITATION

These reports are cited thus:

[1983] 1 All ER

REFERENCES

These reports contain references to the following major works of legal reference described in the manner indicated below.

Halsbury's Laws of England

The reference 39 Halsbury's Laws (3rd edn) 860, para 1303 refers to paragraph 1303 on page 860 of volume 39 of the third edition, and the reference 26 Halsbury's Laws (4th edn) para 577 refers to paragraph 577 on page 296 of volume 26 of the fourth edition of Halsbury's Laws of England.

Halsbury's Statutes of England

The reference 5 Halsbury's Statutes (3rd edn) 302 refers to page 302 of volume 5 of the third edition of Halsbury's Statutes of England.

The Digest

References are to the blue band replacement volumes and the green band reissue volumes of The Digest (formerly the English and Empire Digest), and to the continuation volumes.

The reference 47 Digest (Repl) 781, 25 refers to case number 25 on page 781 of Digest Blue Band Replacement Volume 47.

The reference 36(2) Digest (Reissue) 764, 1398 refers to case number 1398 on page 764 of Digest Green Band Reissue Volume 36(2).

The reference Digest (Cont Vol E) 640, 2392a refers to case number 2392a on page 640 of Digest Continuation Volume E.

Halsbury's Statutory Instruments

The reference 20 Halsbury's Statutory Instruments (4th reissue) 302 refers to page 302 of the fourth reissue of volume 20 of Halsbury's Statutory Instruments; references to subsequent reissues are similar.

Cases reported in volume 1

Digest of cases reported in volume 1

CORRIGENDA

[1983] 1 All ER

p 72. **Pirelli General Cable Works Ltd v Oscar Faber & Partners (a firm).** Line *b*3 should read:
'... It seems to me that, *except* perhaps where the advice...'

p 416. **Clark v MacLennan.** Line *g*1 should read '... The *plaintiff's* disability...'

The Despina GK

b QUEEN'S BENCH DIVISION (ADMIRALTY COURT)
SHEEN J
24 JUNE, 9 JULY 1982

Admiralty – Jurisdiction – Action in rem – Arrest – Enforcement of foreign judgment – Claim for damages for loss of cargo – Cargo owners obtaining final judgment against shipowners by
c *proceedings in rem in foreign court – Ship released from arrest on shipowner putting up security – Shipowner paying only part of judgment debt – Ship entering English port – Whether cargo owners entitled to bring action in rem in English court against ship to enforce judgment of foreign court – Whether cargo owners having right to arrest ship in England.*

Cargo belonging to the plaintiffs was lost at sea while it was being carried in the
d shipowners' vessel. When the vessel arrived in a Swedish port, the plaintiffs brought an action in rem in the Swedish Admiralty Court, claiming damages from the shipowners for the loss of the cargo. The vessel was arrested but was released shortly after when the shipowners put up security. The Swedish court gave judgment for the plaintiffs and ordered the shipowners to pay a specified sum to the plaintiffs. The shipowners paid only part of that sum and later, when the vessel entered an English port, the plaintiffs issued a
e writ in rem in the English Admiralty Court, claiming the balance outstanding under the Swedish judgment, and applied for a warrant for her arrest. The vessel still belonged to the same shipowners. The question arose whether the court had jurisdiction to issue the warrant since the vessel had already been arrested once in respect of the proceedings in Sweden and her owners had put up security there to secure her release from the action.

f **Held** – The English Admiralty Court had a duty, founded on international comity, to enforce a decree of a foreign Admiralty court, and a judgment creditor who obtained a final judgment against a shipowner by proceeding in rem in a foreign admiralty court could bring an action in rem in the English Admiralty Court to enforce the decree of the foreign court if it was necessary to complete the execution of that judgment, provided, however, that at the time of the vessel's arrest she was still the property of the judgment
g debtor. Accordingly, the English court had jurisdiction to issue the warrant for the arrest of the shipowner's vessel (see p 3 c and p 5 f g, post).

Dicta of Sir Robert Phillimore in *The City of Mecca* (1879) 5 PD at 30, 32–33 applied.
The Kalamazoo (1851) 15 Jur 885 and *The Point Breeze* [1928] P 135 distinguished.

h **Notes**
For the extent of judgments in rem on maritime liens, see 35 Halsbury's Laws (3rd edn) 782, para 1203, and for cases on the subject, see 42 Digest (Repl) 1083–1084, 8956–8965.

Cases referred to in judgment
j *Alletta, The* [1974] 1 Lloyd's Rep 40.
City of Mecca, The (1879) 5 PD 28; *on appeal* (1881) 6 PD 106, CA, 1(1) Digest (Reissue) 304, 1841.
Gemma, The [1899] P 285, [1895–99] All ER Rep 596, CA, 1(1) Digest (Reissue) 369, 2532.
Kalamazoo, The (1851) 15 Jur 885, 1(1) Digest (Reissue) 300, 1803.
Point Breeze, The [1928] P 135, 1(1) Digest 295, 1768.

Case also cited
Freedom, The (1871) LR 3 A & E 495.

Appeal
On 23 June 1982 the plaintiffs, New Hampshire Insurance Co, issued a writ in rem against the vessel Despina GK, claiming outstanding sums due to them from her owners, Despinoula Shipping Inc of Piraeus, under a judgment in rem in the Swedish Admiralty Court, which had not been completely satisfied, and applied ex parte for a warrant for her arrest. When the Admiralty Registrar refused to issue the writ, the plaintiffs appealed to the court. The appeal, which was argued solely by the plaintiffs, was heard in chambers, but judgment was given by Sheen J in open court. The facts are set out in the judgment.

Jeffrey Gruder for the plaintiffs.

At the conclusion of the argument Sheen J announced that, for reasons to be given later, the appeal would be allowed and a warrant for the arrest of the ship would issue.

9 July. The following judgment was delivered.

SHEEN J. The Despina GK is a dry cargo ship of 9,411 gross register tonnage. She is owned by Despinoula Shipping Incorporated of Piraeus and is registered in Monrovia. At the relevant time she was on time charter to Lelakis Shipping Ltd of Piraeus, and sub-chartered to a Belgian company, Getradco, for a voyage from Antwerp to Mogadishu on which she carried, amongst other cargo, 710 tons of skimmed milk powder. In November 1975 the plaintiffs learned that their cargo had been dumped at sea. They wished to claim damages from the owners of the Despina GK. In 1976 the plaintiffs found the Despina GK in a Swedish port. Accordingly they commenced an action in the Admiralty Court of Stockholm and arrested the Despina GK on 15 May 1976. On 17 November 1978 the Stockholm District Court Division 8 gave judgment for the plaintiffs in the following terms:

'The District Court rules that the shipping company shall pay New Hampshire immediately 2,410,188 Dutch guilders or the equivalent sum in Swedish currency at the highest exchange rate on the date of payment plus interest on this sum in accordance with section 6 of the Interest Act from 19 May 1976 until payment in full is made. The District Court awards New Hampshire a maritime lien on the vessel DESPINA G.K. for this their claim.'

The District Court also made an order for costs in favour of the plaintiffs. On 12 June 1979 that judgment was amended by the Appeal Court Division 5. The ruling of the Appeal Court was:

'The Appeal Court amends the decision of the District Court only to the extent that the Appeal Court declares that the amounts including interest in respect of the lawsuit proper and the legal costs, which the District Court ordered the shipping company to pay to New Hampshire, will not be levied on any property of the shipping company other than the vessel DESPINA G.K.'

On 19 December 1979 the Swedish Supreme Court upheld the decision of the Appeal Court. The final judgment ordered the owners of the Despina GK to pay the sums set out in the statement of claim indorsed on the writ herein, namely (i) 2,410,188 Dutch guilders or the equivalent sum in Swedish currency at the highest exchange rate on the date of payment plus interest thereon in accordance with s 6 of the 1975 Swedish Interest Act, (ii) 198,191 Swedish kroner plus interest thereon at 6% from the date of judgment in respect of costs before the Stockholm District Court, (iii) 41,135 Swedish kroner plus interest thereon at 6% from 12 June 1979 in respect of costs before the Court of Appeal

a Division 5, (iv) 3,000 Swedish kroner plus interest thereon at 6% from 19 December
1979.

That judgment was obtained against Despinoula Shipping Inc, who have paid US
$1,425,000. They are still indebted to the plaintiffs under the judgment in a sum not less
than US $200,000. That company were still the owners of the Despina GK when the writ
herein was issued on 23 June 1982, claiming the sums outstanding on the judgment of
the Swedish Admiralty Court. The Despina GK had then entered a port within the
b jurisdiction of this court. The plaintiffs applied for a warrant of arrest. The Admiralty
registrar refused to issue a warrant. This is an appeal from that refusal. It is right that I
should say at the outset that on this appeal I have had the advantage of reading a second
affidavit sworn by Mr S R Curtis, which was not before the Admiralty Registrar. The
contents of the later affidavit and the exhibits thereto make it clear that the Swedish
proceedings were proceedings in rem, which was an aspect of the case on which the
c Admiralty registrar was not satisfied on the evidence before him.

After hearing the submissions made by counsel on behalf of the plaintiffs, I ordered
that a warrant of arrest be issued. In consequence of my order the Despina GK was
arrested at Immingham on 24 June 1982. Her owners did not apply to have the warrant
of arrest set aside. They came to terms with the plaintiffs, who then consented to the
release of the ship on 29 June 1982. I stress, therefore, that I have only heard argument
d on behalf of the plaintiffs. That argument was presented with characteristic skill and care
by counsel for the plaintiffs. As the point raised seems to me to be of interest to
practitioners I decided to state the reasons for my decision in open court.

Section 20(1) of the Supreme Court Act 1981 provides:

'The Admiralty jurisdiction of the High Court shall be as follows, that is to
say . . . (c) any other Admiralty jurisdiction which it had immediately before the
e commencement of this Act.'

That takes one back to s 1 of the Administration of Justice Act 1956, which provides:

'(1) The Admiralty jurisdiction of the High Court shall be as follows, that is to
say jurisdiction to hear and determine any of the following questions or
claims . . . together with any other jurisdiction which either was vested in the High
f Court of Admiralty immediately before the date of the commencement of the
Supreme Court of Judicature Act 1873 . . . or is conferred by or under an Act which
came into operation on or after that date on the High Court as being a court with
Admiralty jurisdiction . . .'

Counsel for the plaintiffs relies on this residual jurisdiction and in particular on the
g decision of Sir Robert Phillimore in The City of Mecca (1879) 5 PD 28. In that case the
question to be decided was whether the Admiralty Court of this country can and ought
to enforce the judgment of a foreign admiralty court by a proceeding in rem. Sir Robert
Phillimore said (at 30):

'It appears to be expedient to make two preliminary observations. First, I express
h my opinion that whatever authority upon this subject was incident to the Court of
Admiralty before the Judicature Act belongs to this Court now. Secondly, that this
Court has always exercised a jurisdiction founded upon international comity with
respect to the execution of the sentences of foreign admiralty courts. I proceed to
consider the authorities on this subject in their chronological order, as it is important
to show that the duty of the Admiralty Court in England to enforce the decree of a
j foreign admiralty court has been steadily recognised for a great number of years.'

Then, after reference to a number of authorities and to well-known works on
Admiralty law, Sir Robert Phillimore continued (at 32–33):

'A consideration of these authorities, and the principle on which they rest, leads
me to the conclusion that it is the duty of one admiralty court, a duty arising from

the international comity, to enforce the decree of another upon a subject over which the latter had jurisdiction . . . I am of opinion that it is the duty of this Court to act as auxiliary to the Portuguese Court and to complete the execution of justice, which, owing to the departure of the ship, was necessarily left unfinished by that Court. In other words, it is my duty to place the English Court in the position of the Portuguese Court after its sentence has been given against the defendants.'

The action which was heard in Portugal arose out of a collision which resulted in the sinking of the plaintiffs' ship Insulano. That collision created a maritime lien on the City of Mecca in favour of the owners of Insulano. A proceeding for the enforcement of a maritime lien is a proceeding in rem. Such an action was instituted in Portugal but, for reasons which are not stated in the report of that case, the City of Mecca left Lisbon without giving security. Her owners appeared to the proceedings and contested them. Sir Robert Phillimore assumed that the action in Portugal was an action in rem. He said (at 33): 'This Court is now called upon to be an aidant to the enforcement of a judgment in rem, given by a Portuguese Court.' The writ in the action in England was indorsed in the following terms:

'The plaintiffs' claim is upon a judgment of the Tribunal of Commerce of Lisbon, by which the Court determined that the *City of Mecca* was alone to blame for a collision, and ordered the defendants to pay to the plaintiffs the loss sustained by them by reason of the said collision, and the plaintiffs claim 25,000l.'

Counsel drew my attention to, and relied on, a comment made by D R Thomas in his book *Maritime Liens* (1980) p 330, para 591, which said:

'A beneficiary of a foreign judgment *in rem* is therefore in the same position as a maritime lienee [sic, meaning, I think, lienor] for he may pursue the *res* into whosoever's hands it may pass.'

If that statement were accurate, there could be no doubt that the plaintiffs have a right to arrest the Despina GK to enforce their maritime lien. I do not regard it as a correct statement. There is nothing in the judgment of Sir Robert Phillimore to support it. On the contrary, the judge starts with the elementary proposition that a collision such as there was in that case creates a maritime lien (see 5 PD 28 at 33). If he had taken the view that the plaintiffs, as beneficiaries of a foreign judgment, had a maritime lien over the City of Mecca, he would have said so in terms. That was part of the argument of counsel for the plaintiffs. In truth, the cause of action arising out of the collision merged in the judgment. The court was called on to aid in enforcing that judgment.

The decision of Sir Robert Phillimore was reversed on appeal. In the Court of Appeal ((1881) 6 PD 106) Jessel MR stressed that the facts which were proved before that court were different from the facts on which judgment had been given by Sir Robert Phillimore. It appeared from a further affidavit that the action in the Portuguese court was a personal action and this court has no jurisdiction to enforce by proceedings in rem a judgment given in a personal action. Nothing was said in the Court of Appeal which in any way undermined the principle on which Sir Robert Phillimore decided the case, or his statement as to the duty of one Admiralty court to enforce the decree of another.

The main argument against the issuing of a warrant for the arrest of the Despina GK in England is that when she was arrested in Sweden her owners put up security and thereby, in effect, purchased her freedom from arrest. Thus in *The Kalamazoo* (1851) 15 Jur 885 at 886 Dr Lushington said:

'It is perfectly competent to take bail to the full value; but the effect of taking bail is to release the ship in that action altogether. It would be perfectly absurd to contend that you could arrest a ship, take bail to any amount, and afterwards arrest her again for the same cause of action. The bail represents the ship, and when a ship is once released upon bail she is altogether released from that action.'

a This was followed in *The Point Breeze* [1928] P 135. That case arose out of a collision
between a French ship and the American ship Point Breeze. Two days after the collision
bail was asked for in the sum of £3,500. Then after a writ was issued against the Point
Breeze, solicitors acting on behalf of her owners accepted service and gave an undertaking
to put up bail. After judgment was given the plaintiffs asked for additional bail in the
sum of £3,000. They arrested the Point Breeze at Southampton for that amount. The
defendants by motion sought to set aside the warrant of arrest. It was held by Bateson J
b that they were entitled to have the arrest set aside. He indorsed the words of Dr
Lushington in *The Kalamazoo* which I have set out above and said ([1928] P 135 at 142):

> 'The only right to arrest in a damage case is that which the party claiming has got
> by a maritime lien, and a maritime lien follows the ship into other people's hands.
> The position of people who have ships that have been released on bail—if I were to
> allow this arrest to stand—might be very unfortunate.'

c
There is, of course, a distinction between those claims which give rise to a maritime
lien and which may, therefore, be enforced against the ship notwithstanding a change of
ownership and those claims which may only be enforced by an action in rem if the
person who would be liable in personam is still the owner of the ship at the time when
the writ is issued.
d Likewise, there is the further distinction between an action in rem which may be
brought in the High Court against the ship, and execution of a judgment obtained in
such an action. In *The Gemma* [1899] P 285, [1895–99] All ER Rep 596 the Court of
Appeal held that the owners of a foreign vessel had, by appearing in an action in rem,
rendered themselves personally liable. Accordingly, if the amount of bail given for the
release of the ship was insufficient to satisfy the judgment the balance outstanding could
e be enforced by a writ of fieri facias against any of the defendants' goods and chattels,
including the released vessel if she came within the jurisdiction.
This distinction was recognised by Mocatta J in *The Alletta* [1974] 1 Lloyd's Rep 40.
The plaintiffs sought to rearrest a ship after judgment and after that ship had been sold
to new owners. Mocatta J held that the plaintiffs' right of arrest was lost because the cause
of action had become merged in the judgment. He applied the principle laid down in
f *The Kalamazoo* (1851) 15 Jur 885 and followed in *The Point Breeze* [1928] P 135. But he
distinguished the judgment of Sir Robert Phillimore in *The City of Mecca* (1879) 5 PD 28.
A judgment creditor who has obtained a final judgment against a shipowner by
proceeding in rem in a foreign admiralty court can bring an action in rem in this court
against that ship to enforce the decree of the foreign court if that is necessary to complete
the execution of that judgment, provided that the ship is the property of the judgment
g debtor at the time when she is arrested.

Order accordingly.

Solicitors: *Ince & Co* (for the plaintiffs).

N P Metcalfe Esq   Barrister.

R v Seisdon Justices, ex parte Dougan

QUEEN'S BENCH DIVISION
O'CONNOR LJ AND COMYN J
26, 27 JULY 1982

Magistrates – Jurisdiction – Reopening case to rectify mistake etc – Trial of information adjourned – Accused receiving no notice of date of adjourned hearing – Magistrates under statutory duty not to proceed unless satisfied that notice had been served on accused – Magistrates convicting accused in his absence without considering whether there was proof of service of notice on him – Whether magistrates having jurisdiction to order rehearing of case – Whether magistrates functi officio as soon as conviction announced – Magistrates' Courts Act 1980, ss 10, 142 – Magistrates' Courts Rules 1981, rr 15, 99.

The applicant was summoned to appear before magistrates on 16 July 1981 to answer to an information charging him with a driving offence. He notified the magistrates' court that he intended to plead not guilty and the trial was adjourned, under s 10(1)[a] of the Magistrates' Courts Act 1980, to 10 September 1981. Under r 15[b] of the Magistrates' Courts Rules 1981 notice of the date of the adjourned hearing was required to be served on the applicant in the manner prescribed by r 99[c] of those rules and, by s 10(2) of the 1980 Act, the hearing could not proceed on the new date unless the magistrates were satisfied that such notice had been served. Under r 99(2) (as applied by r 15(2)) service of the notice on the applicant could not be treated as proved unless it was shown that the notice had come to his knowledge. The applicant received no notification of the date of the adjourned hearing and so did not appear before the magistrates on 10 September 1981. On that date the magistrates, without considering whether he had received the notice, convicted him on the basis of the prosecution evidence. When the applicant learned of the conviction he informed the magistrates' court of the reason for his absence and the magistrates decided that the case should be relisted for hearing on 11 March 1982. When the case came on for hearing on that date the magistrates were advised by their clerk that they were functi officio as soon as they had announced the applicant's conviction on 10 September 1981 and accordingly they had no power to rehear the case. The case was adjourned sine die so that the applicant could apply to the Queen's Bench Division for the appropriate relief by way of judicial review. He applied for an order of certiorari to quash the conviction on the grounds (i) that the magistrates had been wrong to convict him in his absence without proof that he had received notice of the hearing on 10 September 1981 and (ii) alternatively, that they had no power to set aside the conviction and direct a rehearing under s 142(2)[d] of the 1980 Act because the 28-day time limit prescribed by s 142(4) for the exercise of that power had expired.

Held – (1) If the applicant had been properly served with notice of the date of the adjourned hearing, the proceedings on 10 September 1981 would not have been a nullity and accordingly the magistrates would have been functi officio in view of the fact that they had not exercised their power under s 142(2) of the 1980 Act to direct a rehearing within the period prescribed by s 142(4), and the appropriate remedy would then be an order of certiorari to quash the conviction, leaving the information valid so that the prosecution could still proceed (see p 10 f and p 11 e, post).

(2) However, the purported trial of the applicant on 10 September 1981 was a nullity because of the magistrates' failure to comply with the requirements of the 1980 Act and

---

a   Section 10, so far as material, is set out at p 8 g h, post
b   Rule 15 is set out at p 8 j, post
c   Rule 99, so far as material, is set out at p 9 a to c, post
d   Section 142, so far as material, is set out at p 10 d e, post

the 1981 rules as to proof of service of the notice. In consequence there was no conviction,
a with the result that the magistrates were entitled to relist the case for hearing. Since there
was no conviction to be quashed the appropriate remedy was a declaration in the
appropriate terms rather than an order of certiorari (see p 9 *d e*, p 10 *f g* and p 11 *d* to *f*,
post); *R v Marsham, ex p Pethick Lawrence* [1911–13] All ER Rep 639, *R v Essex Justices, ex
p Final* [1962] 3 All ER 924 and *R v Uxbridge Justices, ex p Clark* [1968] 2 All ER 992
considered.

b

Notes
For certiorari to quash orders of justices, see 11 Halsbury's Laws (4th edn) 1529, and for
cases on the subject, see 14(1) Digest (Reissue) 440, 458, 3780, 3897, 16 Digest (Reissue)
434, 4792, 4793, and 33 Digest (Reissue) 158, 1212–1228.
    For the Magistrates' Courts Act 1980, ss 10, 142, see 50(2) Halsbury's Statutes (3rd edn)
c 1452, 1563.

Cases referred to in judgments
R v Essex Justices, ex p Final [1962] 3 All ER 924, [1963] 2 QB 816, [1962] 2 WLR 38, DC,
    33 Digest (Reissue) 158, 1216.
R v Manchester Justices, ex p Lever [1937] 3 All ER 4, [1937] 2 KB 96, DC, 14(1) Digest
d (Reissue) 440, 3780.
R v Marsham, ex p Pethick Lawrence [1912] 2 KB 362, [1911–13] All ER Rep 639, DC,
    14(1) Digest (Reissue) 458, 3897.
R v Uxbridge Justices, ex p Clark [1968] 2 All ER 992, DC, 16 Digest (Reissue) 434, 4793.
R v Willesden Justices, ex p Utley [1947] 2 All ER 838, [1948] 1 KB 397, DC, 16 Digest
    (Reissue) 434, 4792.
e

Application for judicial review
Derek Dougan applied, with the leave of Stephen Brown J granted on 4 May 1982, for an
order of certiorari to bring up and quash his conviction, on 10 September 1981, by the
respondents, the Seisdon justices, of driving a motor vehicle on a restricted road at a speed
exceeding 30 mph, contrary to the Road Traffic Regulation Act 1967, ss 71(1) and 78A.
f The facts are set out in the judgment of O'Connor LJ.

David Barnard for the applicant.
The respondents did not appear.

Cur adv vult
g
27 July. The following judgments were delivered.

O'CONNOR LJ. By leave of the single judge, the applicant moves for judicial review
of a conviction imposed on him by magistrates sitting in the petty sessional division of
Seisdon in Staffordshire on 10 September 1981.
h   The matter arises in this way. As a result of information duly laid, the applicant was
summoned on 11 June 1981 for an offence of driving a motor vehicle in excess of the
speed limit in a built-up area. He consulted his solicitors, and notified the court of his
intention to plead not guilty. The summons had a return date of 16 July 1981. The
solicitors also communicated with the court and told them of the applicant's intention to
plead not guilty and, as was the custom of that court, a new date for the hearing was
j fixed.
    The justices, on 16 July, adjourned the case until 10 September 1981. Unfortunately,
neither the applicant nor the solicitors received notice of the date of the adjourned
hearing. On 10 September nobody was present. The prosecution, however, were present,
and the justices, in the absence of the defendant, convicted him, but adjourned sentence
on him until 8 October 1981.

A few days later, when the solicitors learned of the conviction, they complained that no notice of the date of the hearing had been received. In the result, the justices decided to relist the case for hearing and a series of dates were listed, which for various reasons are not relevant. Finally, the case was listed on 11 March 1982. By that date, the justices had acquired a new clerk, and the clerk was of the opinion, and so told the applicant's solicitors, that the justices were functi officio and had no power to rehear the case. In order that that issue could be decided, proceedings were adjourned sine die to enable the applicant to apply to this court for the appropriate relief by way of judicial review.

At the hearing before us, the justices have not appeared and no affidavit has been filed on their behalf.

The grounds for the application, which was seeking an order of certiorari to quash the conviction on 10 September, were that the information would remain alive, and the effect of quashing the conviction would be to enable the prosecution, if they so wished, to proceed with the case, and the defendant to enter his plea of not guilty and be heard and have the case decided.

Counsel for the applicant put forward the ground that in the absence of any proof that the notice of the hearing had been received by the applicant or the solicitors acting on his behalf, the justices were wrong in proceeding to convict the applicant on 10 September 1981. The alternative which is submitted is that they purported to vary their decision by seeking to set aside the conviction, an act which they had no power to do.

These were arguments in the alternative, and it is necessary for the court to look closely at the relevant sections of the Magistrates' Courts Act and the Magistrates' Courts Rules to see what the position really is.

Section 11 of the 1980 Act provides:

'(1) Subject to the provisions of this Act, where at the time and place appointed for the trial or adjourned trial of an information the prosecutor appears but the accused does not, the court may proceed in his absence.

(2) Where a summons has been issued, the court shall not begin to try the information in the absence of the accused unless either it is proved to the satisfaction of the court, on oath or in such other manner as may be prescribed, that the summons was served on the accused within what appears to the court to be a reasonable time before the trial or adjourned trial or the accused has appeared on a previous occasion to answer to the information . . .'

Section 10 of the 1980 Act provides:

'(1) A magistrates' court may at any time, whether before or after beginning to try an information, adjourn the trial, and may do so, notwithstanding anything in this Act, when composed of a single justice.

(2) The court may when adjourning either fix the time and place at which the trial is to be resumed, or, unless it remands the accused, leave the time and place to be determined later by the court; but the trial shall not be resumed at that time and place unless the court is satisfied that the parties had had adequate notice thereof . . .'

Rule 15 of the Magistrates' Courts Rules 1981, SI 1981/552, which came into force on 6 July 1981, provides:

'(1) Where in the absence of the accused a magistrates' court adjourns the trial of an information, the clerk of the court shall give to the accused notice in writing of the time and place at which the trial is to be resumed.

(2) Service of the notice required to be given by paragraph (1) may be effected in any manner in which service of a summons may be effected under paragraph (1) or (3) of rule 99 and paragraph (2) of that rule shall apply to the proof of service of the notice as it applies to the proof of service of a summons in respect of the offence charged in the information.'

Turning to r 99, para (1) thereof provides:

a
'Service of a summons issued by a justice of the peace on a person other than a corporation may be effected—(a) by delivering it to the person to whom it is directed; or (b) by leaving it for him with some person at his last known or usual place of abode; or (c) by sending it by post in a letter addressed to him at his last known or usual place of abode.'

The next paragraph, which is the most important one in this case, provides:

b
'(2) If the person summoned fails to appear, service of a summons in manner authorised by sub-paragraph (b) or (c) of paragraph (1) shall not be treated as proved unless it is proved that the summons came to his knowledge; and for that purpose any letter or other communication purporting to be written by him or on his behalf in such terms as reasonably to justify the inference that the summons came to his knowledge shall be admissible as evidence of that fact; Provided that this paragraph shall not apply to any summons in respect of a summary offence served in the manner authorised by the said sub-paragraph (c) in a registered letter or by recorded delivery service.'

c

In reading para (2) of r 99, as applied by para (2) of r 15, for 'summons' one must substitute 'notice of adjournment', that being written notice of the adjourned case.

It was, therefore, incumbent on the justices, before proceeding with the trial in the
d absence of the applicant and with the knowledge that it was his intention to plead not guilty, to satisfy themselves that not only the letter had been sent by the court, but that it had been received. We understand from counsel for the applicant that that course was never taken, and we have to proceed on the basis that it was not done, and that that was the ground on which the justices decided in their wisdom to relist the case for hearing.

As it is said that the position of the justices was that they were functi officio and could
e not take such a course, some difficulties, which have arisen many times over a number of years, occur. We start by looking at R v Marsham, ex p Pethick Lawrence [1912] 2 KB 362, [1911–13] All ER Rep 639. In that case the applicant was convicted by a metropolitan magistrate of assaulting a constable in the execution of his duty, but by some inadvertence, the constable who was assaulted gave his evidence at the hearing of the trial without being sworn. Later that day, the magistrates' attention was drawn to this defect and,
f presumably with everybody still in his presence, he heard the case again, but that time round he had the constable sworn.

The defendant was convicted. Certiorari was moved for, on the ground that the magistrate had no power to rehear the case as he had done. The court held that as the first proceedings were a nullity, he had got the power and they refused to grant the writ. That is one line of authority.

g
The ordinary rule, which was exemplified in 1963, is that as soon as justices have announced a conviction, so far as that is concerned, they are functi officio. R v Essex Justices, ex p Final [1962] 3 All ER 924, [1963] 2 QB 816, was put before the court. In that case an information was laid, charging the defendant with attempting to use a motor vehicle, parts of which were in a condition likely to cause danger, contrary to the regulations of the Motor Vehicles (Construction and Use) Regulations 1955, SI 1955/482.
h There was a plea of not guilty, and the issue was whether or not the parts were likely to cause danger. The justices convicted, but after announcing the conviction, further matters were argued. The result was that they decided to change their minds and dismiss the information. On application for an order of certiorari to quash the dismissal, and an order of mandamus for the conviction and fine to be registered, the court held that since they announced their decision, they were functi officio and therefore had no power or
j jurisdiction, either statutory or inherent, to substitute the acquittal for the conviction or vice versa. In that case R v Marsham, ex p Pethick Lawrence [1912] 2 KB 362, [1911–13] All ER Rep 639 was considered, but I will return to that in a moment.

The difficulties created by the lack of power in justices to vary their decision are exemplified by R v Essex Justices, ex p Final [1962] 3 All ER 924, [1963] 2 QB 816 and also by R v Uxbridge Justices, ex p Clark [1968] 2 All ER 992.

In *Ex p Clark* the justices passed a sentence of six months' imprisonment on the defendant, but they ought, under the legislation in force at the time, to have suspended *a* that sentence. They were in error because they had misunderstood a previous sentence served by the defendant while he was in the army. It was held by the court that they had no power to suspend the sentence; they were functi officio as soon as they had passed the sentence.

That was a matter which seemed to need remedy, and remedy is to be found in the Criminal Justice Act 1972, s 41 as amended, which is now s 142 of the Magistrates' Courts *b* Act 1980. The position in *Ex p Clark* is really corrected by s 142(1). It provides:

> Subject to subsection (4) below, a magistrates' court may vary or rescind a sentence or other order imposed or made by it when dealing with an offender; and it is hereby declared that this power extends to replacing a sentence or order which for any reason appears to be invalid by another which the court has power to impose or make. *c*

The trouble which arose in *Ex p Final* is corrected by s 142(2), which provides:

> 'Where a person is found guilty by a magistrates' court in a case in which he has pleaded not guilty or the court has proceeded in his absence under section 11(1) above, and it subsequently appears to the court that it would be in the interests of justice that the case should be heard again by different justices, the court may, *d* subject to subsection (4) below, so direct.'

Subsection (4) provides:

> 'The powers conferred by subsections (1) and (2) above shall be exercisable only within the period of 28 days beginning with the day on which the sentence or order was imposed or made or the person was found guilty, as the case may be . . .' *e*

Therefore, if in the present case the justices were functi officio, the only power they had was that which they might have exercised under s 142. They did not do so, and the advice of the justices' clerk in March 1982 would be valid and the appropriate remedy would be certiorari to quash the conviction and leave the information valid so that the prosecution could still proceed if they saw fit. *f*

In my judgment, that is not the position. The proceedings on 10 September 1981 were a nullity. That is shown by Lord Parker CJ's judgment in *Ex p Clark* [1968] 2 All ER 992, where he said:

> 'This court is quite satisfied that the justices were in fact functus officio and that the present case comes within the line of cases of which *R. v. Willesden Justices, Ex p. Utley* ([1947] 2 All ER 838, [1948] 1 KB 397) is one, rather than the case to *g* which the justices refer of *R. v. Marsham, Ex p. Pethick Lawrence* ([1912] 2 KB 362, [1911–13] All ER Rep 639), the reason being that in the former case there had been a perfectly proper hearing, whereas in the latter case the hearing itself had been a nullity.'

Lord Parker CJ recognised that *Ex p Pethick Lawrence* could not be applied in that case, *h* because as it was a nullity the magistrate had the power to do what he did.

In *Ex p Final* [1962] 3 All ER 924, [1963] 2 QB 816 Lord Parker CJ relied on *R v Manchester Justices, ex p Lever* [1937] 3 All ER 4, [1937] 2 KB 96. I need only refer to that case in order to say that again was an example where there had been a conviction in the absence of the accused, but the report showed that the summons had been properly served, so that the point that is raised in the present case was not before the court. In that *j* case it was held that the justices were functi officio.

In *Ex p Final* [1962] 3 All ER 924 at 927, [1963] 2 QB 816 at 823, Salmon J, agreeing with the order proposed, had this to say:

> 'It is quite plain on authority that once a decision by magistrates is announced in open court, that decision so announced amounts either to an acquittal or to a

a
conviction, as the case may be. Once the magistrates have convicted or acquitted, they are functi officio and cannot alter their decision. The only apparent exception to that rule is in the sort of case which is exemplified by *R. v. Marsham, Ex p. Pethick Lawrence* ([1912] 2 KB 362, [1911–13] All ER Rep 639). In that case, after the magistrate had convicted, it was discovered that one of the witnesses called had not been sworn.

b
When the magistrates' attention was drawn to the circumstances to which I have referred, he said, in effect, that there had been a mis-trial, and he heard the case all over again. The accused was convicted. When the case came to this court, it was decided that the magistrate had not fallen into any error because the first so-called trial was a nullity. Accordingly, there had been no conviction and there was nothing to prevent the magistrate from hearing the case according to law. I say that *Marsham's* case is only an apparent exception to the rule to which I have referred, because in that case and in cases of that kind the original proceedings are a nullity,

c
and the magistrate is merely going on to try a case which has never been tried.'

In my judgment, those words exactly fit the position in the present case. Because of the failure to comply with the provisions of the 1980 Act and the 1981 rules, the purported trial on 10 September 1981 was a nullity and the justices were entitled to do what they proposed to do, namely to make provisions to hear the case again. That being the position, the proper remedy in this court, under RSC Ord 53, which now enables the

d
court to grant a declaration rather than quash the conviction, because there was no conviction to quash, would be to grant a declaration that the proceedings of 10 September 1981 were a nullity and the justices are free to restore the case for hearing according to the law.

e
COMYN J. I agree. The hearing and the conviction on 10 September 1981 were a nullity in my view for want of proof of service. Proof of service is something which is a widespread requirement in our law, and is a specific requirement in regard to the justices.

I agree that the result is that the hearing was a nullity and that the appropriate remedy is not by an order of certiorari, but to declare the proceedings to be what they were, and are, that is to say a nullity.

f
Certiorari refused. Declaration granted that the proceedings on 10 September 1981 were a nullity and that the justices might hear and determine the case on due application by the prosecution.

Solicitors: *Pitt & Cooksey*, Bridgnorth (for the applicant).

Raina Levy   Barrister.

Bradshaw v Ewart-James   a

QUEEN'S BENCH DIVISION
LORD LANE CJ AND WOOLF J
8, 29 JUNE 1982

Shipping – Collision regulations – Observance – Liability for infringement – Liability of master –
Navigation of ship delegated to duly certificated officer of the watch – Infringement of collision b
regulations caused by act or omission of officer of the watch – Master not present on bridge at time
of infringement and having no knowledge of infringement – Whether infringement of collision
regulations an offence of strict liability – Whether master guilty of an offence – Merchant Shipping
Act 1894, s 419(2).

On its true construction s 419(2)ᵃ of the Merchant Shipping Act 1894 (which provides c
that, if an infringement of the collision regulationsᵇ is caused by the wilful default of the
master or owner of a ship that master or that owner shall be guilty of an offence) does not
create an offence of strict liability, and accordingly the master of a ship is not guilty of
'wilful default' and is hence not guilty of an offence under s 419(2) if the collision
regulations have been infringed and if (i) he has not personally committed any act or d
omission which has resulted in the infringement, (ii) at the time of the infringement he
was not present on the bridge and the ship was being navigated by a duly certificated
officer of the watch, (iii) the infringement occurred as a result of the acts or omissions of
that officer of the watch and (iv) at the time the infringement occurred the master had
no actual personal knowledge of that infringement (see p 16 c to e, post).

Dictum of Lord Reid in *Vane v Yiannopoullos* [1964] 3 All ER at 822–823 applied. e

Notes
For offences of strict liability, see 11 Halsbury's Laws (4th edn) para 18.
For criminal liability for the acts of others, see ibid paras 51–55, and for cases on the
subject, see 14(1) Digest (Reissue) 25–30, 73–111.
For the offence of disobedience to the collision regulations, see 35 Halsbury's Laws (3rd f
edn) 594, para 874, and for a case on the subject, see 42 Digest (Repl) 819, 5948.
For the Merchant Shipping Act 1894, s 419, see 31 Halsbury's Statutes (3rd edn) 284.
For the Collision Regulations and Distress Signals Order 1977, Sch 1, see 20 Halsbury's
Statutory Instruments (4th reissue) 133.

Cases referred to in judgment   g
Howker v Robinson [1972] 2 All ER 786, [1973] QB 178, [1972] 3 WLR 234, DC, 30 Digest
(Reissue) 105, 763.
Lady Gwendolen, The, Arthur Guinness, Son & Co (Dublin) Ltd v mv Freshfield (owners) [1965]
2 All ER 283, [1965] P 294, [1965] 3 WLR 91, Digest (Cont Vol B) 653, 5948.
Police Comrs v Cartman [1896] 1 QB 655, DC, 30 Digest (Reissue) 102, 749.
R v Winson [1968] 1 All ER 197, [1969] 1 QB 371, [1968] 2 WLR 113, CA, 8(2) Digest h
(Reissue) 639 153.
Vane v Yiannopoullos [1964] 3 All ER 820, [1965] AC 486, [1964] 3 WLR 1218, HL, 30
Digest (Reissue) 105, 767.

Cases also cited
Hodge v Higgins [1980] 2 Lloyd's Rep 589, DC.   j
R v Lowe [1973] 1 All ER 805, [1973] QB 702, CA.

---

a   Section 419(2), so far as material, is set out at p 14 a b, post
b   Ie the International Regulations for Preventing Collisions at Sea 1972 set out in Sch 1 to the
    Collision Regulations and Distress Signals Order 1977

Case stated

a Henry Bradshaw, acting for and on behalf of the Secretary of State for Trade, appealed by way of case stated by the Kent justices acting in and for the petty sessional division of Ramsgate in respect of their adjudication as a magistrates' court at Ramsgate on 16 February 1982 whereby they dismissed an information preferred by the appellant against the respondent, Alan Ewart-James, that, at sea in the English Channel on 26 August 1980, the respondent, being the master of the motor vessel NF Tiger which was crossing

b traffic lanes, failed to cross as nearly as practicable at right angles to the general direction of traffic flow, contrary to ss 418, 419 and 680 of the Merchant Shipping Act 1894 and r 10(c) of the International Regulations for Preventing Collisions at Sea 1972. The facts are set out in the judgment of the court.

Richard Aikens for the appellant.
c Jervis Kay for the respondent.

Cur adv vult

29 June. The following judgment of the court was delivered.

d

LORD LANE CJ. This appeal by way of case stated by the justices for the petty sessional division of Ramsgate raises the question of the nature and extent of the criminal liability of a master of a ship for an infringement of the International Regulations for Preventing Collisions at Sea 1972 (which are set out in Sch 1 to the Collision Regulations and Distress Signals Order 1977, SI 1977/982), which are regulations which are made for

e the prevention of collisions at sea.

The respondent was the master of the motor vessel Tiger and an information was preferred against him on behalf of the Secretary of State for Trade alleging that he—

'At sea in the English Channel on the 26th day of August, 1980 being the Master of the Motor Vessel "N.F. Tiger" which was crossing traffic lanes failed to cross as nearly as practicable at right angles to the general direction of traffic flow, contrary

f to Sections 418, 419 and 680 of the Merchant Shipping Act, 1894, and Rule 10 (c) of the Collision Regulations and Distress Signals Order, 1977,'

The facts admitted and found by the justices can be shortly stated.

On 26 August 1980 the respondent was the master of the motor vessel which was at sea in the English Channel. At 0255 GMT the respondent was on the bridge and ordered

g a course to be steered which with the prevailing tide would have resulted in the vessel crossing the traffic lanes in accordance with r 10(c). About five minutes later the respondent handed over the watch to his chief officer, who was a qualified master mariner, and left the bridge (probably to visit the passenger areas), returning approximately 30 to 45 minutes later. While the respondent was away from the bridge the vessel sailed on a course which was in breach of r 10(c) of the collision regulations.

h However, it was not established to the satisfaction of the justices that the respondent had knowledge of the infringement or that he had been deliberately negligent and the justices dismissed the information. In reaching this decision the justices rejected the submission which had been made to them on behalf of the Secretary of State for Trade that, if the court were satisfied that the vessel had crossed the traffic lane in contravention of r 10(c) and that the respondent was at the time of the contravention the master in

j command of the ship, he must be found guilty of the offence charged as the master could not avoid responsibility by delegating his statutory duty to the chief officer.

Whether this submission of the appellant is right or not primarily depends on the construction of the relevant statutory provisions. These are contained in s 419 of the Merchant Shipping Act 1894. It is not necessary to read the whole of that section. It suffices if we set out sub-ss (1) to (3), which read:

'(1) All owners and masters of ships shall obey the collision regulations, and shall
not carry or exhibit any other lights, or use any other fog signals, than such as are   *a*
required by those regulations.

(2) If an infringement of the collision regulations is caused by the wilful default
of the master or owner of the ship, that master or owner shall, in respect of each
offence, be liable [to a penalty as specified in the Merchant Shipping Act 1979, Sch
6, Part VII, para 5, which amends this subsection].

(3) If any damage to person or property arises from the non-observance by any   *b*
ship of any of the collision regulations, the damage shall be deemed to have been
occasioned by the wilful default of the person in charge of the deck of the ship at
the time, unless it is shown to the satisfaction of the court that the circumstances of
the case made a departure from the regulation necessary.'

It is sub-s (2) which creates the criminal offence. Bearing in mind that it applies to an   *c*
infringement 'caused by the wilful default of the master', it would at first sight appear
surprising if the master had been guilty of a criminal offence, because it was clearly the
view of the justices that the infringement of the collision regulations, which had
admittedly occurred, was not due to any fault on the part of the master. However, the
argument which has been advanced on behalf of the appellant has made it clear that the
point raised in this case is one of substance which is by no means easy to resolve.   *d*

The first step in the argument turns on s 419(1). It is argued that this subsection creates
an absolute obligation on the master to comply with the regulations of the type
contravened and that it would be no answer to an allegation of breach of this obligation
for the master to say he had delegated the obligation to another member of the crew.
This first step in the argument seems to us to be correct. The language used in sub-s (1) is
in accord with such an interpretation and bearing in mind the obligation is a civil   *e*
obligation the result is in no way surprising. Furthermore, this interpretation of s 419(1)
is consistent with the judgments of the Court of Appeal in *The Lady Gwendolen, Arthur
Guinness, Son & Co (Dublin) Ltd v mv Freshfield (owners)* [1965] 2 All ER 283, [1965] P 294.

The second stage in the argument is the contention of the appellant that the 'default of
the master' referred to in sub-s (2) is the breach of the obligation under sub-s (1) and, just
as the master cannot avoid his obligation under sub-s (1) by delegating, so he cannot   *f*
escape liability under sub-s (2) by delegating. It is this step which causes the difficulty
and we will have to return to it.

The third stage in the argument is to construe the word 'wilful' as being synonymous
with the word 'conscious', so that what is required is a conscious default and, what is
more, a conscious default either by the master or, if he had delegated the matter to
someone else, the conscious default of the person to whom the obligation had been   *g*
delegated. If the other stages in the argument are correct, then we would be prepared to
accept this stage as being accurate.

The final stage in the argument depends on the difficulties which would be caused in
enforcing a breach of the regulations if the master can escape responsibility by delegating.
It is submitted that it cannot have been Parliament's intention that if a breach of the
obligations is committed as here by a chief officer no criminal proceedings can be   *h*
brought, whereas if the breach were personally committed by the master criminal
proceedings can be brought.

The appellant supports his submission on the second stage of the argument by relying
on those cases which have over the years established that in certain areas of the law,
particularly in the licensing field in respect of the unlawful supply of alcohol, criminal
liability cannot be avoided by delegating to others. The court was referred to *R v Winson*   *j*
[1978] 1 All ER 197, [1969] 1 QB 371 and *Howker v Robinson* [1972] 2 All ER 786, [1973]
QB 178. These cases make it clear that in the licensing field, even in relation to offences
expressly requiring knowledge, a master can be criminally liable for contraventions of
the licensing laws by servants to whom the master has delegated his duties. The reasoning
for this approach being adopted in licensing and similar cases is made clear by Bristow J
in *Howker v Robinson* [1972] 2 All ER 786 at 788-789, [1973] 1 QB 178 at 181:

a   'It is a general rule of English law that an accused person cannot be convicted unless he has a guilty mind. An exception to this rule is where Parliament by statute creates an absolute offence. Whether Parliament has done so is to be decided on the construction of the statutory provision concerned. An example of such an absolute offence is s 13 of the Licensing Act 1872 which made it an offence for a licensee to supply liquor to an intoxicated person: see *Police Comrs v Cartman* [1896] 1 QB 655.

b   Where Parliament, as in s 169(1) of the 1964 Act, prohibits someone from doing something "knowingly" it is clear that an absolute offence has not been created, but a canon of construction of the provisions of the Licensing Acts has grown up in the courts that where the statute provides that the licensee shall not do something knowingly, and he does not, as the justices found in this case, in fact know that the thing is being done, nevertheless if he has delegated his control of the premises to the person who does the thing, he cannot get out of the responsibilities and duties

c   attached to the licence, and the knowledge of this delegate is imputed to him.'

This reasoning, so well established in licensing cases, has been the subject of criticism. There is no difficulty in making a master responsible for the defaults of his servant in cases of absolute liability because then no question of mens rea arises. Where, however, the offence is one involving mens rea, it is unsatisfactory to treat the master as having mens rea when in fact he had no such thing and it was his servant who had the necessary
d   state of mind.

The establishing of criminal liability in consequence of delegation was considered by the House of Lords in *Vane v Yiannopoullos* [1964] 3 All ER 820, [1965] AC 486. Both Lord Reid and Lord Evershed were obviously unhappy about the delegation principle but felt that it was so well established in the licensing and similar fields that it was too late to do anything about it. Lord Morris and Lord Hodson in their speeches made it
e   clear that they were not prepared to extend the principle based on delegation to a new provision in the licensing legislation. Lord Donovan expressed his views with characteristic conciseness in this way ([1964] 3 All ER 820 at 832, [1965] AC 486 at 511–512):

f   'The rule that there may be liability in certain cases on an otherwise innocent licensee, if he has delegated sufficient control of the premises to the person who actually commits the offence, but no liability if he has delegated insufficient control, is a rule which so far I have failed to spell out of any Act of Parliament cited to us. In the present case it is, fortunately, not necessary to pronounce on its validity. Like my noble and learned friend, I think that the case can and should be decided on the language of s. 22(1)(a) alone: since it is sufficiently clear by itself not to need elucidation by reference to the outside aids to which the appellant has been obliged
g   to resort. If a decision that "knowingly" means "knowingly" will make the provision difficult to enforce, the remedy lies with the legislature.'

As was pointed out in the judgment in *R v Winson*, the views expressed in the speeches in that case were obiter on the question of criminal liability arising from delegation. However when considering whether or not it is right to extend the principle to areas of
h   the law where it has not previously been applied the greatest respect must be paid to what was said by their Lordships in that case. Furthermore, although Bristow J applied the principle in *Howker v Robinson* [1972] 2 All ER 786, [1973] 1 QB 178, he did not like the principle, saying ([1972] 2 All ER 786 at 791, [1973] 1 QB 178 at 184):

j   'For my part I would like to think that if there had been an appeal in *Winson's* case it might have been discovered that the law after all did not really drive the court to a result, to borrow, the words of Lord Reid [in *Vane v Yiannopoullos* [1964] 3 All ER 820 at 822–823, [1965] AC 486 at 486]—"so contrary to the ordinary principles of construction and to the fundamental principle that an accused person cannot be convicted without proof of mens rea, unless from a consideration of the terms of the statute and other relevant circumstances it clearly appears that that must have been the intention of Parliament." When Parliament says in s 169 that the holder of

the licence or his servant shall not knowingly sell intoxicating liquor to a person
under 18, can it really have been its intention that either should be convicted when   *a*
it is proved that he did not know?'

There has been no decision so far as is known applying the principle of delegation to
prosecutions under s 419(2) of the Merchant Shipping Act 1894, notwithstanding the
long period the offence created by that subsection has been in existence. The offence
created by the subsection is a serious one and for a master of a ship to have a conviction
of causing an infringement of collision regulations by wilful default on his record is   *b*
bound to have a most prejudicial effect on his future career.

The offence, pursuant to s 680(1)(*a*), is punishable with a fine and up to two years'
imprisonment. In view of the contrast between the wording of s 419(1) and s 419(2) it
was clearly intended that, whereas there should be an absolute civil obligation, the
criminal offence should not be an absolute offence. As Lord Reid said in *Vane v*   *c*
Yiannopoullos [1964] 3 All ER 820 at 822–823, [1965] AC 486 at 496:

> 'I doubt whether any authority however strong would justify your lordships
> reaching a result so contrary to the ordinary principles of construction and to the
> fundamental principle that an accused person cannot be convicted without proof of
> mens rea, unless from a consideration of the terms of the statute and other relevant
> circumstances it clearly appears that that must have been the intention of Parliament.'   *d*

There is no clear indication with regard to s 419(2) of the Merchant Shipping Act 1894
that Parliament intended that a master could be convicted although he personally had no
mens rea. In the absence of that clear indication it would be wrong to apply the principle
of delegation to s 419(2). It is appreciated that this decision could make enforcement
more difficult. However, once it is accepted that sub-s (2) does not create an absolute
offence, there are bound to be difficulties in enforcement but, bearing in mind that this   *e*
is the first time this problem has come before this court in relation to this Act, it is
difficult to believe that the problem in practice will be great. The respondent contended
that there would be in most circumstances other offences which would be appropriate
which would justify proceedings against the actual offender and this may well be the
case. Even if this is not the position, as Lord Donovan said, the remedy lies with the   *f*
legislature.

It follows that this appeal should be dismissed.

Appeal dismissed.

The court refused leave to appeal to the House of Lords but certified, under s 1(2) of the
Administration of Justice Act 1960, that the following point of law of general public importance,
was involved in the decision: whether a master of a ship could be held guilty of 'wilful default' and
so be held guilty of an offence under s 419(2) of the Merchant Shipping Act 1894 in circumstances
when (i) the master had not personally committed any act or omission which resulted in an
infringement of the collision regulations, (ii) at the time of the infringement of the collision
regulations, the master was not present on the bridge and the vessel was being navigated by a duly
certificated officer of the watch, (iii) the collision regulations were infringed as a result of the acts
or omissions of that officer of the watch, (iv) at the time the infringement of the collision regulations
occurred the master had no actual personal knowledge of such infringement.

Solicitors: *Treasury Solicitor*; *Ingledew Brown Bennison & Garrett* (for the respondent).

Jacqueline Charles   Barrister.

a

Acrecrest Ltd v W S Hattrell & Partners (a firm) and another

COURT OF APPEAL, CIVIL DIVISION

STEPHENSON, DONALDSON LJJ AND SIR DAVID CAIRNS

22, 23, 24 JUNE, 22 JULY 1982

b

Negligence – Duty to take care – Statutory powers – Local authority – Building operations – Duty of care owed to building owner – Duty of care to supervise building works – Developer employing builder to erect building – Local authority inspector inspecting foundations – Inspector's instructions regarding depth of foundations carried out – Instructions not complying with building regulations – Foundations inadequate for site – Subsequent damage occurring to building after

c *occupation – Whether local authority owing duty of care to building owner – Whether negligence of building owner the source of his own loss – Whether building owner's opportunities for inspection and control removing him from scope of local authority's duty of care.*

In 1971 the plaintiffs, a land development company, employed a firm of architects to design, and a firm of builders to build, a block of flats. The architects' specifications required the foundations to be built to a depth of 3 ft 6 in. A building inspector from

d the local authority which had responsibility for the inspection and approval of the building works inspected the foundation trenches and found tree roots in part of the site. He thereupon gave instructions that in that part of the site the foundations were to be dug to a depth of 5 ft but that elsewhere they need only be to a depth of between 3 ft 6 in and 4 ft. The building was completed in accordance with the inspector's requirements,

e but in fact those requirements were inadequate and not in accordance with the Building Regulations 1965, which required foundations to be constructed to a depth sufficient to safeguard the building against damage by swelling or shrinking of the subsoil. In 1973, after the flats were let on long leases and occupied by tenants, cracks appeared in the building as a result of swelling in the subsoil and 'heave' in the foundations. The plaintiffs brought proceedings against the architects for negligence and breach of contract. The

f architects admitted that the foundations should have been designed to a uniform depth of 5 ft and that they were negligent and in breach of contract, but they issued a third party notice against the local authority, claiming contribution amounting to an indemnity, on the grounds that the authority was under a duty to exercise its powers of inspection and approval with proper care and skill and that the damage to the plaintiffs was caused by the authority's negligence. The plaintiffs joined the local authority as a

g defendant to the action. At the trial of the action the plaintiffs obtained judgment by consent against the architects and were granted leave to discontinue against the local authority. However, the architects continued their third party proceedings against the local authority, in effect taking over the plaintiffs' claim against the authority, in order to establish that the authority was liable to the plaintiffs in tort for the same damage for which the architects were liable and thereby liable to indemnify the architects. The judge

h held that the architects were entitled to a 25% contribution from the local authority, the architects being 75% responsible for the plaintiffs' damage. The local authority appealed, contending that it owed no duty of care to the plaintiffs in connection with the building works because (i) although the authority might owe a duty of care to owners or occupiers the plaintiffs were neither but were instead owners who had employed builders who had developed the land by erecting the defective building and were therefore in the same

j position as a builder-owner whose own negligence had caused the loss and to whom the authority would not, as a matter of law, owe a duty of care, (ii) the plaintiffs themselves were in breach of a duty to comply with the 1965 regulations and that breach excluded them from the scope of any duty owed by the local authority, and (iii) it had not caused the damage suffered by the plaintiffs since the plaintiffs had not relied on the building inspector's requirements to establish the safety of the foundations.

Held – The appeal would be dismissed for the following reasons—

(1) A local authority, when exercising its statutory power to inspect the foundations *a* of a building to ensure that they complied with the building regulations, owed a duty of care to an owner who employed builders to build a building, provided the owner's negligence was not the source of his own loss. The duty owed was the same as that owed by the local authority to future owners and existing and future occupiers. Furthermore, a building owner who was in breach of his statutory duty to comply with the building regulations because he relied on his architect or the local authority's building inspector *b* to ensure that the regulations were complied with could not be described as being so negligent as to be the source of his own loss. However, although a building owner who was not negligent fell within the ambit of the local authority's duty of care, the scope of that duty might well be restricted or affected by questions of causation (ie whether the building inspector's negligence caused the damage) and contributory negligence (ie whether the building owner's opportunities for inspection and control made him *c* responsible for the loss), but the mere fact that the building owner had opportunities for inspection and control or that he had employed architects and builders as independent contractors did not remove him from the class of persons who were reasonably likely to be affected by the local authority's negligence. It followed that the local authority owed the plaintiffs a prima facie duty of care and, since the loss suffered by the plaintiffs had not been caused by their own negligence, they were not excluded from such duty of care *d* (see p 24 j to p 25 h, p 26 a to e, p 27 c, p 29 h j, p 31 b d, p 32 c j and p 33 b to d and g, post); dicta of Lord Wilberforce and Lord Salmon in *Anns v Merton London Borough* [1977] 2 All ER at 504, 511 explained.

(2) Since the foundations were laid in accordance with and because of the requirements of the local authority's inspector, there was a sufficient causal link between his negligence and the damage to the plaintiffs for the architects, who were liable to the plaintiffs for *e* the same damage, to be entitled to a contribution from the local authority. Furthermore, the court would not, in the circumstances, interfere with assessment of the proportion of the contribution made by the trial judge (see p 26 e f, p 27 b c, p 31 j to p 32 c and p 33 d to g, post).

f

Notes

For negligence in relation to statutory functions and the duty to take care, see 34 Halsbury's Laws (4th edn) paras 4–7, and for cases on the subject, see 36(1) Digest (Reissue) 17–55, 34–177.

Cases referred to in judgments   *g*

Anns v Merton London Borough [1977] 2 All ER 492, [1978] AC 728, [1977] 2 WLR 1024, HL, Digest (Cont Vol E) 449, 99b.

Donoghue (or M'Alister) v Stevenson [1932] AC 562, [1932] All ER Rep 1, HL, 36(1) Digest (Reissue) 144, 562.

Dutton v Bognor Regis United Building Co Ltd [1972] 1 All ER 462, [1972] 1 QB 373, [1972] 2 WLR 299, CA, 36(1) Digest (Reissue) 30, 98.   *h*

Eames London Estates v North Hertfordshire DC (1980) 259 EG 491.

Hedley Byrne & Co Ltd v Heller & Partners Ltd [1963] 2 All ER 575, [1964] AC 465, [1963] 3 WLR 101, HL, 36(1) Digest (Reissue) 24, 84.

Home Office v Dorset Yacht Co Ltd [1970] 2 All ER 294, [1970] AC 1004, [1970] 2 WLR 1140, HL, 36(1) Digest (Reissue) 27, 93.

Sparham-Souter v Town and Country Developments (Essex) Ltd [1976] 2 All ER 65, [1976] *j* QB 858, [1976] 2 WLR 493, CA, 32 Digest (Reissue) 507, 3865.

Cases also cited

Batty v Metropolitan Property Realizations Ltd [1978] 2 All ER 445, [1978] QB 554, CA.

a *Harris (John) & Son v Demolition & Roading Contractors (NZ) Ltd* [1979] 2 NZLR 166, NZ
SC.
Ingram v United Automobile Services Ltd [1943] 2 All ER 71, [1943] KB 612, CA.
McLoughlin v O'Brian [1982] 2 All ER 298, [1982] 2 WLR 982, HL.
Worlock v Saws (a firm) (1981) 260 EG 920.

Appeal
b The second defendants, Harrow London Borough Council (the local authority), appealed
against the order of Sir Douglas Frank QC, sitting as a deputy judge of the Queen's Bench
Division on 8 August 1979, assessing their contribution for liability in negligence to the
plaintiffs, Acrecrest Ltd, at 25%, in third party proceedings brought against the local
authority by the first defendants, W S Hattrell & Partners (a firm) (the architects). The
facts are set out in the judgment of Stephenson LJ.

c
Gerald Moriarty QC and *John Tackaberry QC* for the local authority.
Christopher Bathurst QC and *Richard Fernyhough* for the architects.

Cur adv vult

d 22 July. The following judgments were delivered.

STEPHENSON LJ. The plaintiffs, Acrecrest Ltd, own land in Spencer Road in the
London Borough of Harrow. They developed the land by building on it ten 2-storey flats
and garages. They did not themselves build the flats, but in 1971 employed builders, of
whom we know nothing except that the plantiffs did not think them worth suing, and
architects, whom they did think worth suing and have sued successfully, and who are
e the first defendants, W S Hattrell & Partners.
The flats and garages were built in 1972 and let by the plaintiffs to tenants on long
leases. In 1973 cracks began to appear in the buildings, the tenants made claims against
the plaintiffs and in 1976 the plaintiffs brought proceedings against the architects for
negligence and breach of contract. The cause of the trouble was undoubtedly, as in other
f cases which have come before the courts, the foundations. These had been inspected in
the course of the work by an inspector employed by the local authority, the London
Borough of Harrow, who are the second defendants. In January 1972 the architects
claimed contribution amounting to an indemnity from the authority by a third party
notice under the Law Reform (Married Women and Tortfeasors) Act 1935. The plaintiffs
joined the authority as a defendant and in September 1977 the authority served defences
g to the plaintiffs' claim.
The plaintiffs' action against the two of them came on for trial before Sir Douglas
Frank QC, sitting as a deputy judge of the Queen's Bench Division, in July 1979. After
the first week the plaintiffs obtained judgment by consent against the architects for
£67,500 and leave to discontinue against the authority. That left the architects' claim for
contribution against the authority, on which the judge decided that the architects should
h recover not the whole sum for which the plaintiffs had settled their claim against them,
but 25% of it, the architects themselves being 75% responsible in respect of the plaintiffs'
damage.
It is against that order for contribution that the authority appeals to this court,
contending either that the authority owed no duty to the plaintiffs, or that if they did
their admitted breach of duty made a nil contribution to the plaintiffs' damage and
should be reduced from 25% to a lower minimal figure, or nothing.
j
The second of these questions seems to me, with all respect to counsel who argued it
for the appellant authority, unarguable; but the first question is one of general interest
and importance to building owners and local authorities, on which we have heard far-
reaching submissions by counsel for the authority and counsel for the respondent
architects.

The facts are not in dispute. The soil of the building site was clay. There were trees growing on the site and near the site; on the site fruit trees which had to be removed, near the site poplars which were pollarded and elm trees which were soon to die of Dutch elm disease.

The first specification prepared by the architects and the builders provided for strip foundations 1,070 mm or 3 ft 6 in deep. In order to reduce the cost of the works the plaintiffs asked the builders to alter the specified foundations by substituting 914 mm or 3 ft deep strip foundations for the buildings, and 500 × 300 mm strip foundations beneath 114 mm load-bearing walls. Informed of this request, the architects sent the builders articles of agreement in the standard form and a revised specification, the relevant part of which reads:

'05.   Strip foundations of flats to be concrete, 750 × 300 mm mass, load-bearing walls. Depth from ground to beneath underside to be 914 mm or as required by the Building Inspector.

06.   Strip foundations of garage outer walls to be 450 × 150 mm mass concrete. Depth from ground to underside to be 610 mm or as required by the Building Inspector.'

In cl 05 the words 'as required by the Building Inspector' were struck through. It is common ground that the purpose of striking through those words was not that the building inspector's instructions were to be disobeyed but to ensure that if the building inspector required wider or deeper foundations the builder would be paid for them.

In the first week of 1972 building began and on 7 January a building inspector employed by the authority, in response to notice from the builders, inspected the foundation trenches and, finding tree roots, gave instructions to the builder that in part of the site the foundations were to be dug to a depth of 5 ft minimum, but elsewhere they were to be at depths of 3 ft 6 in to 4 ft. Neither the builders nor the inspector gave evidence, and these instructions were inferred from documents before the judge and accepted. The same is true of the judge's conclusion that extra work to the foundations, as required by the inspector, was done by the builders and paid for in the sum of about £220. There is no challenge to the judge's further finding that the architects knew of the inspector's requirements and authorised the builders to comply with them.

Unhappily the inspector's requirements were inadequate and did not comply with the relevant building regulations, namely the Building Regulations 1965, SI 1965/1373. Those regulations were made by the Minister of Public Buildings and Works under, inter alia, s 61 of the Public Health Act 1936, as amended by, inter alia, s 4 of the Public Health Act 1961, and take the place of byelaws formerly made by local authorities. Regulation D3, as applied to the erection of these buildings by reg A5, provides:

'The foundations of a building shall—(a) safely sustain and transmit to the ground the combined dead load and imposed load in such a manner as not to cause any settlement or other movement which would impair the stability of, or cause damage to, the whole or any part of the building or of any adjoining building or works; and (b) be taken down to such a depth, or be so constructed, as to safeguard the building against damage by swelling, shrinking or freezing of the subsoil.'

The plaintiffs' case, as originally pleaded against both defendants and as supported by expert evidence, was that this clay subsoil had shrunk and caused settlement; but the defendants' experts' evidence, which the judge accepted, was that the cracks were caused by swelling of the subsoil, or 'heave', caused by the clay absorbing water which had previously been absorbed by the trees removed from the site and the elms near the site when they were alive and healthy, and by the poplars near the site before they were pollarded. This alternative explanation was covered by a reamendment of the plaintiffs' statement of claim, and it made no difference to the liability of either defendant whether the buildings were forced up or subsided. For the architects in their amended defence admitted—

a
'that having regard to the number, nature and position of trees on the site the first defendants [the architects] ought to have designed the building with uniform foundations to a depth of 5 feet and that they were in breach of contract and negligent in designing foundations of lesser depth.'

The authority did not admit liability in either of their defences, or even in the reamendments of their defences to the third party notice which the judge apparently did not allow (the tape and counsel's recollection are equally unable to provide certainty on

b
the point); but the judge found that the architects' partner responsible had specified foundations 3 ft 6 in deep instead of the conventional 3 ft because he recognised the risks inherent in a London clay subsoil planted with trees, and he concluded that the authority's inspector did not take reasonable care, in the context of building reg D3, in that 'he would have required the foundations to be 5 feet deep all round' if he had complied with reg D3(b). And that conclusion, challenged in the notice of appeal, was accepted before

c
us without argument.

Many other grounds of appeal appearing in that notice have not been pursued and I hope I do counsel for the local authority (the second defendants) no injustice if I confine this judgment to the grounds under the first head which are lettered A, C, D, E and J, namely that—

d
'The learned judge erred in law—

(A) In holding that the second defendant owed a duty of care to the plaintiff in connection with the execution of building works by or on behalf of the plaintiff at all; alternatively that such a duty is owed where the plaintiff instructs a firm of architects to design and supervise the execution of the relevant building works . . .

(C) In refusing to hold that the plaintiff was itself under a statutory duty to

e
comply with the building regulations;

(D) In refusing to hold that the negligence of the plaintiff's architects was attributable to the plaintiff for the purposes of establishing the existence or ambit of any such duty of care;

(E) In failing to give any or any sufficient weight to the existence of both a statutory and a contractual duty on the part of the contractor employed by the

f
plaintiff to comply with the building regulations . . .

(J) In holding that as between the first and second defendants the second defendant's share of the liability should be apportioned as high as 25%.'

The first of those grounds raises the first question, the last ground the second question to be decided in this appeal. The other grounds relate to the first question, which I shall proceed to consider first.

g
The judge expressed his opinion about the statutory duty of the plaintiffs and the builders as follows:

'In my judgment it matters not whether the plaintiffs had such a duty because, even if they had, I can find no reason for thereby excusing the council from exercising reasonable care. Although it seems clear from *Dutton v Bognor Regis United*

h
Building Co Ltd [1972] 1 All ER 462, [1972] 1 QB 373 and *Anns v Merton London Borough* [1977] 2 All ER 492, [1978] AC 728 that the lessees have a remedy against the plaintiffs, I do not find anything in the Public Health Acts or the building regulations which imposes a duty on the building owner as such, although it may be, in certain circumstances as for example where the owner is also the builder, that he would be liable to penalties or other sanctions for failing to comply with the

j
building regulations. However, in my judgment none of these considerations go to the question of the duty on the council to take reasonable care.'

I shall have to refer later to these cases, but for present purposes I would only say that the builder, whether he is the owner or a contractor employed by the owner, is beyond doubt under a duty, both statutory and contractual, to comply with the regulations, but I do not find it necessary to decide whether the plaintiffs, as owners who were not themselves the builders, were under a statutory duty to comply with the regulations; I shall assume for the purposes of this appeal that they were.

The contractual duty of the builders is contained in cl 4(1) of the printed conditions subject to which they agreed to carry out the works under the articles of agreement already mentioned. The clause provides:

'(1) The contractor shall comply with and give all notices required by any Act of Parliament, any instrument rule or order made under any Act of Parliament, or any regulation or byelaw of any local authority or of any statutory undertaker which has any jurisdiction with regard to the works or with whose system the same are or will be connected. The contractor before making any variation from the contract drawings or the specification necessitated by such compliance shall give to the architect a written notice specifying and giving the reason for such variation and the architect may issue instructions in regard thereto. If within seven days of having given the said written notice the contractor does not receive any instructions in regard to the matters therein specified, he shall proceed with the work conforming to the Act of Parliament, instrument, rule, order, regulation or byelaw in question and any variation thereby necessitated shall be deemed to be a variation required by the architect.

(2) The contractor shall pay and indemnify the employer against liability in respect of any fees or charges (including any rates or taxes) legally demandable under any Act of Parliament, any instrument, rule or order made under any Act of Parliament, or any regulation or byelaw of any local authority or of any statutory undertaker in respect of the works. Provided that the amount of any such fees or charges (including any rates or taxes) shall be added to the Contract sum . . .'

I need not read the rest of the condition.

Clause 18 contains the builders' agreement to indemnify the plaintiffs in very comprehensive terms.

Section 4(6) of the Public Health Act 1961 provides:

'If a person contravenes or fails to comply with any provision contained in building regulations he shall be liable to a fine not exceeding one hundred pounds and to a further fine not exceeding ten pounds for each day on which the default continues after he is convicted.'

Regulation A9 of the Building Regulations 1965 deals with the giving of notices and the deposit of particulars and plans. It provides:

'(1) Any person who intends to—(a) erect any building; or (b) make any structural alteration of or extension to a building; or (c) (subject to paragraphs (2) and (3) of this regulation) execute any works or instal any fittings in connection with a building; or (d) make any material change of use of a building, shall, if any provisions of these regulations apply to such operation or such change of use, give notices and deposit plans, sections, specifications and written particulars in accordance with the relevant rules of Schedule 2.'

I need not read the rest of the regulation.

Regulation A10 deals with the giving of notice of commencement and completion of contract stages of work by a builder who is defined as meaning 'any person carrying out or intending to carry out any such operation as is referred to in A9(1)(a), (b) and (c) to which any of these regulations apply'.

There is no preliminary regulation such as is to be found in reg 3 of the Construction (General Provisions) Regulations 1961, SI 1961/1580, specifying whose duty it shall be to comply with this or that regulation. Regulation A5 of the Building Regulations 1965 simply says: '. . . Parts A to L inclusive of these regulations shall apply to the erection of any building not under former control.' Though the plaintiffs and the builders are clearly under the duties imposed by regs A9 and A10 respectively, and both appear to be liable to a fine for contravening or failing to comply with any of these regulations, there may

be some limitation on the person liable which might exempt the plaintiffs from liability
a   to comply with reg D3(b), although it could not exempt the builders from liability: see
Anns v Merton London Borough [1977] 2 All ER 492 at 504, [1978] AC 728 at 759. However
that may be, I shall assume that both were under a duty to comply with that regulation,
the builders' duty being contractual as well as statutory.

On this basis did the authority owe a duty of care to the plaintiffs?

For the architects to succeed in recovering any contribution from the authority there
b   must be such a duty. If there is none, the authority is not a tortfeasor liable in respect of
the damage suffered by the plaintiffs, whether as a joint tortfeasor with the architects or
otherwise, and the appeal must be allowed. The architects as a tortfeasor liable in respect
of that damage can only recover from such another tortfeasor if he has done the plaintiffs
a legal wrong resulting in the same damage: see the Law Reform (Married Women and
Tortfeasors) Act 1935, s 6(1)(c).

c   On this question the judge said:

'The first question I have to decide is whether the council owed a duty to the
plaintiffs. [Counsel for the council] submitted that the duty owed by the council is
to such persons whose health or safety would be affected; that is the rationale in
Anns v Merton London Borough [1977] 2 All ER 492, [1978] AC 728. He argued that
d   the philosophy underlying that decision was that historically there was no duty on
local authorities in such cases but the court found a duty emanating from the Public
Health Acts and accordingly there is only a duty to an owner or occupier whose
health or safety is likely to be affected. Certainly in both *Anns* and *Dutton v Bognor
Regis United Building Co Ltd* [1972] 1 All ER 462, [1972] 1 QB 373 the plaintiffs were
occupiers as purchasers in one case of a freehold and in the other of a long lease, and
Lord Wilberforce in the former case appeared to be considering whether there was
e   a duty towards owners and occupiers whose health and safety is likely to be affected
(see [1977] 2 All ER 492 at 500ff, [1978] AC 728 at 753ff). Moreover, he said in
terms that no duty is owed to a negligent building owner, the source of his own loss
(see [1977] 2 All ER 492 at 504, [1978] AC 728 at 758). I am bound to say that I
found this part of the case difficult because I could not distinguish in law the rights
of a builder who intended to occupy a house and of one whose intention was to sell.
f   However, I have come to the conclusion that no such distinction was drawn in the
Anns case and that the only exception which Lord Wilberforce intended to make
was in the case where the cause of the damage resulted from the builder's negligence;
that is, ex turpi causa. It would indeed be odd if a negligent builder could look to a
local authority to insure him against his own negligence. In this case it is not alleged
that the plaintiffs were negligent and accordingly I hold, following the *Anns* case,
g   that the building inspector was under a duty to take reasonable care to secure that
the building complied with the building regulations.'

In *Dutton's* case this court affirmed the decision of Cusack J that a local authority
exercising its statutory power under the Public Health Acts by inspecting the foundations
of a building to see if they complied with regulations made under those Acts owed a duty
h   to a subsequent owner occupying the building to take reasonable care to see that the
building complied with those regulations. The plaintiff occupied the house and was in
fact a purchaser at second hand from an owner who had himself built the house. She
settled her claim against the builder-owner and succeeded in her claim against the local
authority. In the *Anns* case a number of occupiers of flats under long leases from the
owner who had built them sued the builder-owner and the local authority in respect of
j   damage from defective foundations and, on appealing to the House of Lords on a
different point from a decision of this court following *Dutton's* case, were given leave to
file a supplementary petition raising the question whether *Dutton's* case was rightly
decided and whether the local authority owed such a duty of reasonable care. Some of
the plaintiffs were original lessees, others were assignees. All were occupiers. The builder-
owners put in no defence to their claims. The House of Lords held that there was such a
duty owed to the plaintiffs in respect of damage to their property.

The question for their Lordships' decision was whether the duty was owed by the local authority *to the plaintiffs*, and it was so stated by Lord Wilberforce (see [1977] 2 All ER 492 at 498, 505, [1978] AC 728 at 751, 760). And the plaintiffs in that case, and in *Dutton's* case were all occupiers, though Mrs Dutton was both owner and occupier, as were the plaintiffs in *Sparham-Souter v Town and Country Developments (Essex) Ltd* [1976] 2 All ER 65, [1976] QB 858, whose similar claims against builder-owners and a local authority had been held by this court not to be statute-barred. So at the time when the House of Lords decided the *Anns* case the position of owners and tenants who were occupiers, and the position of owners who were also the builders, had been considered by the courts, but they had not considered the position of an owner who was, like the plaintiffs in the present case, neither the builder of the defective building nor an occupier of it, but employed a builder to develop his land by erecting the defective building. Of the similar cases decided since *Anns* to which we were referred, only one case at first instance (not reported in the law reports) decided that an owner could recover damages from a local authority. In *Eames London Estates Ltd v North Hertfordshire DC* 259 EG 491, a decision of his Honour Judge Fay QC given on 31 October 1980, the plaintiffs were both tenants and owners, but holding the defective premises from earlier holders. This, therefore, is the first case in which the position of a building owner as distinguished from a builder-owner has to be considered in relation to a local authority's negligence in this class of case.

But the position of both was raised in argument in the *Anns* case and Lord Wilberforce refers more than once to the duty owed *to owners or occupiers* (see [1977] 2 All ER 492 at 496, 504, [1978] AC 728 at 749, 758), and *owners and occupiers* (see [1977] 2 All ER 492 at 499–500, [1978] AC 728 at 752–754). In the *Anns* case it was argued by counsel for the local authority that the decisions of the Court of Appeal in *Dutton's* case and the *Anns* case were that the duty was owed to present and future owners and occupiers (see [1978] AC 728 at 735, 737). Counsel for the lessees urged the House to limit the duty to the facts of the case (at 740), but apparently raised the problem of the duty owed to and by the negligent 'owner-builder' who was guilty of contributory negligence or the author of his own harm, and distinguished him from the 'building owner' who was not responsible for the negligence of a competent builder employed by him (at 745); that was answered by counsel in reply (at 748). That led Lord Wilberforce to state that the duty is owed to owners or occupiers, 'not of course to a negligent building owner, the source of his own loss' (see [1977] 2 All ER 492 at 504, [1978] AC 728 at 758). So also Lord Salmon, after stating the question (see [1977] 2 All ER 492 at 507, [1978] AC 728 at 763) as:

'did the inspector, acting on behalf of the council, owe a duty to future tenants to use reasonable care and skill in order to discover whether the foundations conformed with the approved plans and with the byelaws?'

and having answered it by holding it was owed to the future tenants and occupiers (see [1977] 2 All ER 492 at 511, [1978] AC 728 at 767), stated that—

'any damage caused by negligence should be borne by those responsible for the negligence rather than by the innocents who suffer from it.'

Reading this in the light of Lord Salmon's later comments on the negligence of a contractor who was also a landowner (see [1977] 2 All ER 492 at 512, [1978] AC 728 at 768), I take him to have been agreeing with Lord Wilberforce in his opinion that the local authority's duty could be owed to a building owner employing a negligent builder. Neither of their Lordships was directly concerned with such an owner but only with a subsequent occupier, and it was unnecessary to decide whether the local authority owed the duty to anybody but an occupier who did not own the freehold and was in no way responsible as building owner or as owner-builder or a builder. Moreover it would be wrong to construe the reported argument of counsel like a statute. The judgments of Lord Wilberforce, however, do not, if I may respectfully say so, use language loosely or add unnecessary words, and when he says that the duty is owed to occupiers and owners, he includes owners who are not occupiers, and I see no reason to restrict owners to those

who hold long leases from building owners. When he excludes the negligent building
a owner who is the source of his own loss, I read his speech as meaning what it expresses
and necessarily implies. If no duty is owed to any building owner, why exclude the
negligent building owner from its scope? Why not exclude the building owner without
qualifying words? I therefore conclude that Lord Wilberforce, with whom Lord Diplock
and Lord Simon agreed, was not accepting counsel's invitation to limit the duty to the
facts of the case, but was defining judicially the scope of the duty to include building
b owners and owners who were not in occupation when their property suffered damage.

We are accordingly bound to hold that the duty of the authority is owed to the
plaintiffs in the present case unless they are excluded by the exception. Were they
'negligent' building owners, and so negligent that they were 'the source of their own loss'
and therefore cannot recover even part of their damage? Or were they 'innocents' like
the plaintiffs in the *Anns* case?

c The authority contended that the plaintiffs' failure to comply with the building
regulations constitutes the negligence and guilt necessary to exclude them and they are
in this respect no better off than the owner-builder. To that the plaintiffs reply that
unlike the owner-builder the duty to comply with the relevant regulations is not imposed
on them but on the builder. Assuming, as I have said that I shall assume for the purposes
of this appeal, that the duty to comply with reg D3(*b*) may rest on the building owner
d who employs a builder, and an architect, as well as on the builder, the plaintiffs are not,
in my judgment, excluded from the duty owed by the authority.

Again I base my decision on the language of Lord Wilberforce. He excludes a negligent
building owner, not a building owner in breach of statutory duty; he excludes a negligent
building owner who is the source of his own loss, not a building owner who is in breach
of a statutory duty which he has relied on a competent builder to perform under the
e supervision of an architect and to some extent of the authority's inspector. I would not
describe such a building owner as either negligent or so negligent as to be the source of
his own loss, and therefore unable to recover from any of those who are obviously
negligent and responsible for the damage caused to him, any contribution towards it.
That is the kind of building owner to whom Lord Wilberforce's words indirectly refer
and they do not catch the plaintiffs. They would, in my judgment, catch a building
f owner who, knowing the requirements of the inspector or of the building regulations,
chooses to flout them. Here the plaintiffs did request 3 ft deep foundations, but did not
insist on preferring their own judgment to others'; they in fact acted to some extent on
the inspector's advice and complied with his requirements. I agree with the submission
of counsel for the authority that the original building owner, even if he is not his own
builder, is in a better position than any subsequent owner to control the work of building
g and to prevent its being done in a negligent manner or in a manner which contravenes
the building regulations. He is not as 'innocent' as an occupier or subsequent owner of
responsibility for defects in the building. But the fact that he has opportunities of
inspection and control denied to his tenants or assignees does not, in my judgment, make
him 'volens' or his cause of action 'turpis', or by itself exclude him from the scope of the
authority's duty.

h It is not without significance that when resisting an occupier's claim in *Dutton's* case
[1972] 1 All ER 462, [1972] 1 QB 373 the local authority's counsel argued that their duty
was owed to the building owner, and that in pleading the present claim the authority's
counsel has not at any stage included in their defence a plea of contributory negligence
on the part of the plaintiffs themselves or on the part of the architects as servants or
agents of the plaintiffs for whose negligence they are vicariously responsible.

j Counsel for the authority accordingly had difficulty in relying on the allegation in his
notice of appeal that the negligence of the plaintiffs' architects was attributable to the
plaintiffs; but he called attention to para 17 of the authority's defence, which alleged that
the plaintiffs' loss and damage flowed from the breach by the plaintiffs themselves of
their duties and/or by reason of the architects' failure to discharge their duties, and he did
rely on the architects' advice and supervision as intervening to break the chain of
causation between the inspector's breach of duty and the plaintiffs' loss, and as negativing

both the proximity necessary to create a duty owed by the authority to the plaintiffs
under the principle in *Donoghue v Stevenson* [1932] AC 562, [1932] All ER Rep 1 and the   *a*
reliance on the inspector's advice necessary to create the duty under the principle of
Hedley Byrne & Co Ltd v Heller & Partners Ltd [1963] 2 All ER 575, [1964] AC 465. But in
my judgment the original building owner can properly rely on his architect and builder
to design and erect buildings which are not defective through want of reasonable care
and skill or through failure to comply with building regulations or the local authority's
instructions; and he does not, by employing them as independent contractors, remove   *b*
himself from the class of those who are reasonably likely to be directly affected by the
authority's negligence or breach of statutory duty.

Developers in the plaintiffs' position are therefore in a relationship to the authority in
which a prima facie duty of care arises and the question is 'whether there are any
considerations which might negative or reduce or limit the scope of the duty or the class
of person to whom it is owed or the damages to which a breach of it may give rise' so as   *c*
to exclude them or the damages arising from their having to repair the damage to these
flats or compensating their lessees: see the classic statement of Lord Wilberforce in the
Anns case [1977] 2 All ER 492 at 498, [1978] AC 728 at 751–752. I can find no
consideration which excludes the plaintiffs from recovering these damages from the
authority, and the authority are consequently tortfeasors liable in respect of them. To
have one owner claiming damages, instead of a multiplicity of occupiers, is a consideration   *d*
in favour of *including* the plaintiffs and their damages.

It was suggested that any compensation paid by the plaintiffs to their lessees would not
be recoverable in law and so neither the architects nor the authority could be liable to the
plaintiffs in respect of it. But there was no evidence of the nature of the damage in respect
of which the architects had paid £67,500 and the point does not avail the authority.

I would accordingly reject the submission that the authority owed no duty to the   *e*
plaintiffs, and I have therefore to consider the question of contribution, on which I have
at the outset indicated my opinion.

I can see no ground for interfering with the judge's apportionment of responsibility
between the architects and the authority and reducing the lesser responsibility of the
latter.

The judge expressed his view on this question shortly as follows: *f*

'[Counsel for the architects] argued that the building inspector, being particularly
concerned with foundations, should be expected to have a deeper knowledge of the
subject than an architect. He said that the building inspector was more closely in
touch with local conditions such as the load-bearing capacity of the subsoil and the
effect of trees in that area. I do not accept that that is the right approach to this   *g*
matter. As [counsel for the council] said, it was the architects' basic design that was
at fault, the fons et origo of the damage; they took on the job and should not have
done so unless they were competent to do it. The architects were employed and paid
to design and supervise the work and it was their duty to see that it was done
properly. They should and did make preliminary inquiries as to the loading capacity
of the subsoil, and they should have been and were aware of the trees. In my   *h*
judgment the primary responsibility for what happened rests with the architects
and, accordingly, I assess the council's contribution at 25%.'

It is submitted against that conclusion that the architects were not less expert but
better qualified than the inspector in judging what the subsoil and the trees required in
the way of foundations. I do not think the judge was unfair to the authority in refusing   *j*
to attribute either to the inspector or to the architects knowledge of the dangers of Dutch
elm disease which another department of the authority might possess, and in finding
that neither the architects nor the inspector were negligent in failing to take the disease
into account. The judge heard unchallenged evidence that the architects could not at the
time when they designed the building and specified the foundations have reasonably

a foreseen the possibility of the disease and of heave in consequence, but he said that they were admittedly negligent in not specifying foundations 5 ft deep and the inspector negligent in not requiring them to be 5 ft deep all round. Yet he attributed the lion's share of blame to the architects, as did Judge Fay in the *Eames* case (1980) 259 EG 491. What was wrong in not going further in favour of the authority at the architects' expense? All that could be said was that the architects were working for profit, the authority and its inspector for the public and the safety of others, and the inspector's

b requirements in fact reduced the damage which would have resulted from the architects' negligence in providing for even shallower foundations than the inspector required.

I cannot find in either of these considerations, or any other circumstance, a reason for absolving the authority altogether from liability for damage resulting from their inspector's carelessness. Indeed, the safety of buildings requires the co-operation of owners, builders, architects and such inspectors, and putting the matter at its lowest, I see

c no objection in justice or in equity to imposing some liability to contribute something on the authority responsible for a negligent inspector, even at the suit of a negligent architect.

I would accordingly dismiss the appeal and affirm the judge's judgment. His assessment of 75% : 25% will stand, as will his order that the assessment of damages will take place before a circuit judge assigned to official referees' business.

d

DONALDSON LJ (read by Sir David Cairns). Counsel for the authority, the appellants, submits that it is very odd if architects can look to local authorities to insure them against the consequences of their negligence. I agree that it would indeed be odd, but odd or not, right or wrong, this is not what the learned judge decided. In order to make this good, I

e fear that I must cover a small part of the ground already covered by Stephenson LJ.

This is not an action in which the architects claim damages from the local authority. It is not an action in which the architects need to, or do, allege that the local authority owed them any duty or were in breach of that duty. It is an action by Acrecrest (the plaintiffs) against two defendants, their architects, W S Hattrell & Partners, and the local authority, the London Borough of Harrow. The plaintiffs were landowners who

f employed Hattrells as architects, and Eric R Mayne (Bucks) Ltd as builders, to construct 10 flats and garages at Spencer Road, Harrow Weald, Middlesex within the area of the local authority. Original owners of a building may be their own builders (owner-builders) or they may employ others to build (building owners). Their intentions may be to occupy the building themselves, to let it to others or to sell it, or a combination of these intentions where the building is one fit for multiple occupation. The plaintiffs did not in

g fact intend to occupy any part of the building. They intended to, and did, retain ownership, letting the flats and garages to tenants who occupied them.

The basis of the plaintiffs' claim against the architects was, in substance, that they were negligent in the design and supervision of the construction of the foundations which were not 'taken down to such a depth, or so constructed, as to safeguard the building against damage by swelling, shrinking or freezing of the subsoil'. I have no doubt that

h the architects were under a duty to exercise all reasonable skill and care in their design and supervision and that in the circumstances of this case they would be in breach of that duty if the foundations did not have these characteristics. I have used quotation marks solely because reg D3(b) of the Building Regulations 1965, SI 1965/1373, uses those words in relation to its requirement for foundations.

The basis of the plaintiffs' claim against the local authority was that they failed to

j detect or to warn or advise the plaintiffs of the deficiencies in the foundation design, and required the builders to increase the depth of the foundations in some places instead of requiring a similar increase throughout.

The plaintiffs claimed a declaration against both the architects and the local authority that they were entitled to be indemnified in respect of (a) the cost of making good damage to the building and (b) all sums which they might be liable to pay to the tenants.

In the course of the proceedings the architects submitted to judgment for £67,500
and certain costs, but how this sum was calculated, if indeed it was calculated, has never
been revealed. Certainly it is impossible to say how it was divided as between the
platintiffs' alleged liability to their tenants and their loss as owners of the flats. At the
same time the plaintiffs sought and obtained leave to discontinue their action against the
local authority, all questions of costs being reserved.

The position thus reached was that the architects had submitted to judgment in favour
of the plaintiffs and no decision had been reached on whether or not the local authority
was also liable. This sets the scene for the present proceedings in which the architects, in
effect, resurrected the plaintiffs' claim against the local authority which they have
prosecuted with vigour. They have not adopted this course in order to claim any damages
to which the plaintiffs would have been entitled if the plaintiffs had sued the local
authority to judgment. They have adopted it in order to establish that the local authority,
if sued, would have been liable to the plaintiffs in tort in respect of the same damage as
that for which they are liable in tort and thus put themselves in a position to claim
contribution towards their own liability to the plaintiffs under s 6(1)(c) of the Law
Reform (Married Women and Tortfeasors) Act 1935. They succeeded before the judge
and obtained an order for a 25% contribution. The local authority now appeals both on
liability and on the quantum of contribution. So far as liability is concerned, the issue is
thus quite simple: if the plaintiffs had displayed more stamina, would they have
succeeded in establishing the liability of the local authority? In so formulating the issue,
I make no criticism of the plaintiffs: they had got as much as they wanted or at least as
much as they thought that they could get.

The judge found that the local authority's building inspector failed on this occasion to
exercise the appropriate standard of care, and this finding is accepted. The issue can
therefore be further refined. It is not the broad issue of the local authority's liability to
the plaintiffs, but the somewhat narrower issue of whether the local authority owed the
plaintiffs any duty of care and, if so, whether the admitted breach of any such duty
caused the damage of which the plaintiffs complained.

Anns v Merton London Borough [1977] 2 All ER 492, [1978] AC 728 establishes that local
authorities whose function is to enforce the building regulations in their district owe a
duty of care in private law to those who will occupy a building at the time at which the
condition of that building becomes such as to create a present or imminent danger to the
health or safety of the occupiers. In the *Anns* case all the plaintiffs were occupiers under
long leases, two as original lessees and the remainder as assignees. The freehold owners,
occupying the same position as the plaintiffs, found themselves as first defendants, and
no question arose as to the local authority's duty towards them or as to contribution
between defendants. In the present case, the occupiers have not claimed against the local
authority. Had they done so they would no doubt have succeeded, but the basis of their
claim and its amount would have been different from that of the plaintiffs (Acrecrest) as
freehold owners. Accordingly, the occupier's rights against the local authority are
irrelevant.

The leading speech, with which Lord Diplock and Lord Simon agreed, was given by
Lord Wilberforce. He explained the approach to a determination of whether a duty of
care arises in the following terms ([1977] 2 All ER 492 at 498, [1978] AC 728 at 751):

'Through the trilogy of cases in this House, *Donoghue v Stevenson* [1932] AC 562,
[1932] All ER Rep 1, *Hedley Byrne & Co Ltd v Heller & Partners Ltd* [1963] 2 All ER
575, [1964] AC 465, and *Home Office v Dorset Yacht Co Ltd* [1970] 2 All ER 294,
[1970] AC 1004, the position has now been reached that in order to establish that a
duty of care arises in a particular situation, it is not necessary to bring the facts of
that situation within those of previous situations in which a duty of care has been
held to exist. Rather the question has to be approached in two stages. First one has
to ask whether, as between the alleged wrongdoer and the person who has suffered
damage there is a sufficient relationship of proximity or neighbourhood such that,
in the reasonable contemplation of the former, carelessness on his part may be likely

to cause damage to the latter, in which case a prima facie duty of care arises.
a   Secondly, if the first question is answered affirmatively, it is necessary to consider
whether there are any considerations which ought to negative or to reduce or limit
the scope of the duty or the class of person to whom it is owed or the damages to
which a breach of it may give rise (see the *Dorset Yacht* case [1970] 2 All ER 294 at
297–298, [1970] AC 1004 at 1027, per Lord Reid).'

Lord Wilberforce then went on to review 'the factual relationship between the council
b   and owners and occupiers of new dwellings constructed in their area' and to consider the
relevant provisions of the Public Health Act 1936. In the context of the present appeal,
the relevant statutory provisions are those of the Public Health Acts 1936 and 1961,
together with the Building Regulations 1965, which have replaced local building
byelaws, but it is not suggested that this updating affects the issue. Lord Wilberforce
concluded ([1977] 2 All ER 492 at 500, [1978] AC 728):
c
'It must be in the reasonable contemplation not only of the builder but also of the
local authority that failure to comply with the byelaws' requirement as to
foundations may give rise to a hidden defect which in the future may cause damage
to the building affecting the safety and health of owners and occupiers. And as the
building is intended to last, the class of owners and occupiers likely to be affected
d   cannot be limited to those who go in immediately after construction.'

Lord Wilberforce then explained that although a situation of 'proximity' existed
between 'the council and owners and occupiers' of the houses, the council's duty could
not be based on the 'neighbourhood' principle alone and that a plaintiff complaining of
negligence must prove not only a breach of the common law duty of care, but also that
the action of the local authority was not within the terms of a discretion bona fide
e   exercised. On the facts in the instant appeal, this qualification is not material, since if the
duty exists, it was admittedly broken.
Summarising his conclusions as to whom the duty is owed, Lord Wilberforce said
([1977] 2 All ER 492 at 504, [1978] AC 728 at 758):

'There is, in my opinion, no difficulty about this. A reasonable man in the
f   position of the inspector must realise that if the foundations are covered in without
adequate depth or strength as required by the byelaws, injury to safety or health
may be suffered by the owners or occupiers of the house. The duty is owed to them,
not of course to a negligent building owner, the source of his own loss. I would
leave open the case of users, who might themselves have a remedy against the
occupier under the Occupiers' Liability Act 1957. A right of action can only be
g   conferred on an owner or occupier, who is such when the damage occurs . . . This
disposes of the possible objection that an endless, indeterminate class of potential
plaintiffs may be called into existence.'

It will be seen that, in the passages which I have quoted, Lord Wilberforce on no less
than four occasions refers to 'owners and occupiers' and twice, where the context was
disjunctive, to 'owners or occupiers'. Counsel for the authority submitted that Lord
h   Wilberforce may not have applied his mind to a distinction between the non-occupying
owner and the occupier, whether or not also an owner. This I cannot accept. In
considering the nature of the damages recoverable, he expressly included damage to the
dwelling house itself, a matter which would primarily affect the owner or the occupier
qua owner. In my judgment, Lord Wilberforce was deciding that prima facie the duty
extended to occupiers, and was expressing the opinion that prima facie it also extended
j   to owners. I say 'prima facie' because counsel for the authority has submitted that even if
he is wrong in his broader submission, the duty does not extend to *all* occupiers or to *all*
owners and it is to this submission that I must now turn.
In the run up to the decision in the *Anns* case, local authorities were arguing that if,
which was denied, they owed any duty to those who suffered as a result of a negligent
failure to enforce the building regulations, their duty of care was limited to the building

owner, and possibly to the first purchaser if he could show reliance on the council's approval. This is apparent from the report of counsel's argument in *Dutton's* case [1972] **a** 1 QB 373 at 383. The same argument was put forward in *Sparham-Souter v Town and Country Developments (Essex) Ltd* [1976] QB 858 at 862. The *Anns* case itself was concerned only with limitation both at first instance and in the Court of Appeal, but when it reached the House of Lords the appellants were granted special leave to widen the issues so as, in effect, to appeal against the decision in *Dutton's* case. Again counsel for the local authority argued that the duty was restricted to those who have an interest in the land **b** and buildings at the time when it was completed (see [1978] AC 728 at 738). I mention this because the speeches in the *Anns* case were delivered against the background of a tacit acceptance that (a) if the duty was owed to occupiers, a fortiori it was owed to owners; and (b) if the duty was owed to subsequent owners or occupiers, a fortiori it was owed to original owners or occupiers. However, counsel for the authority is fully entitled now to reverse the trend, and we have to consider whether the House of Lords, in **c** concentrating on occupiers and on subsequent owners or occupiers, has overlooked some limitation on the duty as regards owners or original owners.

In terms of a proximity test, it is clear that original owners have a stronger claim than subsequent owners. Accordingly, the argument of counsel for the authority has to be, and is, based on other grounds. They are (a) that the original building owner or builder-owner, unlike a subsequent owner or occupier, has an opportunity of approving the **d** design of the foundations and inspecting the foundations themselves during the course of construction, and accordingly there is in law no causal connection between any negligence on the part of the building inspector and the damage to the buildings, and (b) that as a matter of public policy no duty is owed to someone who is himself subject to a primary duty to comply with the building regulations by a local authority whose function is the secondary one of enforcing those regulations. As it was put in argument, **e** 'the policeman owes no duty to the burglar to prevent him breaking and entering'.

Let me first deal with causation. I can conceive of a case in which the building owner or builder-owner deliberately sets out to deceive a negligent building inspector. In such circumstances the building owners or builder-owner's claim would fail, either because of his inability to prove a causal connection between his loss and the negligence of the building inspector, or because of the application of the principle of volenti non fit injuria, **f** or because of the application of the principle ex turpi causa non oritur actio, or for all three reasons. I can also conceive of a case in which a building owner or builder-owner exercised his own judgment and, for example, built with 2 ft foundations notwithstanding that the building inspector had negligently required 3 ft foundations when what was really called for were 5 ft foundations. He too would be unable to recover because there was no causal connection between the damage and the negligence of the building **g** inspector. But that is not this case. Here the plaintiffs concluded a contract with the builder which specified 3 ft foundations for the flats, required the builder to comply with the building regulations and provided that any additional work involved in such compliance over and above the cost of 3 ft foundations should be treated as a variation (see cl 4 of the Standard Form of Building Contract, Private Edition Without Quantities (1963 edn with July 1971 revision)). The building inspector gave negligent advice and **h** the builder accepted and followed that advice.

Next, the question of public policy. There is apparently no decision by the courts on who is required to comply with reg D3 of the Building Regulations 1965. In terms it appears to operate in rem: 'the foundations of a building shall . . .' Section 4(6) of the Public Health Act 1961, makes it clear that someone has to comply, but not whom:

'If a person contravenes or fails to comply with any provision contained in **j** building regulations, he shall be liable to a fine . . .'

For present purposes I am content to assume, without deciding, that everyone whose actions lead to a breach of the building regulations is liable to a fine and that in the present case the plaintiffs, the builders and the architects were so liable. Counsel for the authority submits that there can be no duty owed by the local authority to those who have acted in breach of the building regulations. I do not accept this argument. If it were

a correct, an employee who committed an offence under the Factories Acts could never recover against his employer who had failed to take all reasonable steps to prevent the contravention, and that is not the law.

In my judgment, the local authority's duty of care extends to the building owner and the builder-owner to the same extent as to future owners and present and future occupiers. The difference in the position of the building owner or builder-owner is not

b in the ambit of the duty, but in the fact that they may have more difficulty in proving a causal connection between the damage and the building inspector's negligence and may also be faced with allegations of contributory negligence which may partially or even wholly defeat their claim. This, I think, is what Lord Wilberforce meant when in the *Anns* case [1977] 2 All ER 492 at 504, [1978] AC 728 at 758 he said:

c 'The duty is owed to them [the owners or occupiers of the house], not of course to the negligent building owner, the source of his own loss.'

If the building owner's negligence was the effective source of his loss, he would fail on the ground that there was a break in the chain of causation or on the ground that it was just and equitable that the damages recoverable should be reduced to nothing, having regard to the building owner's share in the responsibility for the damage (see s 1(1) of the

d Law Reform (Contributory Negligence) Act 1945).

For these reasons I consider that the local authority owed the plaintiffs a duty of care, the breach of which is admitted, and that that breach caused the plaintiffs some loss for which the local authority would have been liable if sued by the plaintiffs.

This brings me back to the fact that we are concerned with contribution proceedings. The essence of such proceedings is that the plaintiff (P) could have successfully sued two

e actual or potential defendants (D1 and D2) to judgment in respect of the same damage and that both claims would have been founded in tort. Questions of causation arise only as between P and D1 and between P and D2. If there is a break in the chain of causation between P and D2, D1 will have no claim to contribution because D2 is neither a joint nor a fellow tortfeasor. If there is such a break between P and D1, D1 will be under no liability and so should have no need for contribution. He will also fail to qualify as a

f tortfeasor. If, nevertheless, D1 has settled P's claim, he will fail in his claim for contribution on the footing that he is not a tortfeasor and is not liable in respect of the relevant damage.

Questions of contributory negligence similarly arise primarily between P and whichever of the defendants is seeking contribution from the other, because his claim is for contribution to *his* liability to P and any contributory negligence on the part of P will

g have reduced the liability in respect of which contribution is sought. I say 'primarily' because I can conceive of two situations in which a court considering a claim for contribution between D1 and D2 might be concerned with P's contributory negligence. The first is if P has conducted himself differently towards D1 and D2, so that, for example, his loss is £1,000 but D1's liability is only £250 (75% contributory negligence by P) whereas D2 is liable for the full amount. If D2 claimed contribution, I can see it

h being argued with force that it could not be just and equitable that D1's contribution should exceed £250 and that it should probably be considerably less. The second qualification or complication arises where D1 is claiming contribution from D2 and D1's liability to P is founded both in contract and in tort. Assuming, as I do, that the Law Reform (Contributory Negligence) Act 1945 does not apply to claims in contract, P may achieve a judgment against D1 for £1,000 damages, but on investigation it may appear

j that whilst this was correct as a judgment based on breach of contract, it would have been reduced to, say, £600 if based on tort, since there would have been a 40% discount for contributory negligence. D1 can only claim contribution towards the £600 liability.

So far as I can see, none of these complications arise, or if they do arise they have not been raised as issues in this case. Causation is clearly established as between the plaintiffs and the architects, and as between the plaintiffs and the local authority, and neither has raised any issue of contributory negligence against the plaintiffs. Accordingly, in my judgment the architects, who are admittedly liable to the plaintiffs in tort for the same damage for which the local authority, if sued, would have been found liable also in tort, *a* are in principle entitled to contribution from the local authority.

This brings me to the appeal as to the amount of that contribution. Counsel for the authority frankly accepts that this court will not interfere in the absence of some clear error of principle on the part of the trial judge. He has therefore sought to persuade us that it is not just or equitable that, having regard to the architects' share in the responsibility for the damage, the local authority should make *any* contribution. In *b* support of this submission he says that the architect is, or should be, a highly skilled professional man; his duty was not only to use all reasonable skill to ensure that his client's building complied with the building regulations, but also, if this be different, to ensure that it would be immune to the effects of subsidence or heave. Putting it another way, he submits that the responsibility of the architects for this damage is so great that the responsibility of the local authority pales into insignificance. For my part, I can see *c* no error in principle in fixing the rate of contribution by the local authority at 25%.

For these reasons I too would dismiss the appeal.

SIR DAVID CAIRNS. The plaintiffs, as building owners of flats on a plot of land in the London Borough of Harrow, claimed damages against two defendants, their architects and the local authority. Against the architects it was alleged that they were negligent in *d* the design of the foundations of the flats. Against the local authority it was alleged that through their building inspector they were negligent in approving the design of the foundations and in failing to require them to be taken to a uniform depth. The plaintiffs alleged that by reason of the deficiencies of the foundations, the flats, when built, were unstable so that extensive remedial work was necessary, and that claims had been made against the plaintiffs by their tenants. The plaintiffs accordingly claimed damages against *e* each defendant, and the architects claimed under s 6 of the Law Reform (Married Women and Tortfeasors) Act 1935 contribution amounting to an indemnity from the local authority.

At the trial before Sir Douglas Frank QC, sitting as a deputy judge of the Queen's Bench Division, the architects admitted liability to the plaintiffs and submitted to judgment. By leave of the judge the plaintiffs discontinued their claim against the local *f* authority. At the end of the trial of the issues between the architects and the local authority the judge upheld the claim to contribution, but only to the extent of 25%. The local authority appeal to this court contending that *no* order for contribution should have been made, or that the contribution should be nil or a nominal sum.

The grounds of appeal relied on at the hearing were all matters of law and the local authority's main contentions may be summarised as follows. (1) The local authority *g* owed no duty of care to the plaintiffs (a) because the plaintiffs were not occupiers; (b) because the plaintiffs were themselves in breach of statutory duty under the building regulations; (c) because the negligence of their architects was attributable to them; (d) because they did not rely on the building inspector's requirements. (2) The contribution should be nothing, or a nominal sum (a) because the primary cause of the damage was the negligence of the architects, and the local authority were merely 'policing' the *h* scheme; (b) because the architects were engaged in activities for profit whereas the local authority were acting for the benefit of the public for no reward; (c) the requirements of the building inspector did not increase the damage but reduced it, and so it would be unjust that they should have to pay anything to the architects.

In my judgment all these contentions fail for the following reasons:

(1) (a) There is no logical reason why the duty of care should be owed only to occupiers. *j* The building owner is in proximity to the building inspector. If by reason of that inspector's negligence the building is insecurely supported by its foundations so as to be dangerous to the health or safety of people living in it, the value of the building to the building owner is thereby reduced, and if he pays to have remedial work done or reimburses tenants who have had it done, he has suffered damage from the negligence of

the inspector, for which it is just that he should be compensated. It is much more
a convenient, in relation to a block of flats, that the building owner should be able to claim
against the local authority than that each tenant or purchaser from him of a separate flat
should be left to pursue his own right of action. In *Anns v Merton London Borough* [1977]
2 All ER 492 at 500, 504, [1978] AC 728 at 753, 758 Lord Wilberforce refers to 'owners
and/or occupiers'. He says (see [1977] 2 All ER 492 at 504, [1978] AC 728 at 758) that the
duty is not owed to 'a negligent building owner, the source of his own loss'. This assumes
b that the duty of care is owed to a building owner who is not negligent.

(1) (b) Assuming that a building owner who is not himself the builder is in breach of
building regulations when his builder infringes them, I cannot accept that this excludes
him from the category of persons to whom the duty of care is owed. It is obvious that
the building owner will often in practice be ignorant of the provisions of the regulations
and will quite properly leave it to others to see that the regulations are complied with.
c Unless he was actually conscious that the work was being done illegally, he could not
sensibly be regarded as one who was 'a negligent building owner, the source of his own
loss'.

(1) (c) There is no good reason why the negligence of architects, who are independent
contractors, should be attributed to the building owners.

(1) (d) On the facts here it is clear that the foundations were laid in accordance with
d the requirements of the building inspector and because of his requirements. That is quite
enough to form the causal link between his negligence and the damage to the plaintiffs.

(2) (a) It was because the judge regarded the negligence of the architects as the primary
cause of the damage that he assessed the local authority's contribution at 25% and not
50%. The analogy of 'policing' is misleading: the local authority's function (at least in a
case such as the present one) is not that of restraining a wrongdoer from persisting in his
e wrongdoing, but is rather that of co-operating with the builder and the architects to see
that the law is obeyed and that the building is safely erected. I cannot see that in such
circumstances the proportion either of blameworthiness or of causative potency can be
said to be overwhelmingly higher for the architects than for the local authority.

(2) (b) I can see no more reason why the difference of function of the architects and the
local authority should affect the assessment of contribution than it would if an accident
f was caused by the negligence of the drivers of one of the architects' motor cars and one
of the local authority's refuse-collecting vehicles.

(2) (c) The fact that the requirements of the building inspector reduced the damage is
not a reason for saying that the local authority should make *no* contribution to the
plaintiffs' damages. Admittedly both defendants were negligent and if the building
inspector had not been negligent the plaintiffs would probably have suffered no damage,
g certainly they would have suffered less.

Taking into account all the matters relied on by the local authority in respect of
apportionment, I find it impossible to say that the judge's assessment was so much too
favourable to the architects as to justify this court in interfering with it.

For these reasons I also would dismiss the appeal.

h   *Appeal dismissed. Leave to appeal to the House of Lords refused.*

Solicitors: *Barlow Lyde & Gilbert* (for the local authority); *Reynolds Porter Chamberlain* (for
the architects).

Sophie Craven   Barrister.

Paal Wilson & Co A/S v Partenreederei Hannah Blumenthal

The Hannah Blumenthal

HOUSE OF LORDS

LORD DIPLOCK, LORD KEITH OF KINKEL, LORD ROSKILL, LORD BRANDON OF OAKBROOK AND LORD BRIGHTMAN

27, 28 OCTOBER, 2 DECEMBER 1982

Arbitration – Practice – Want of prosecution – Inordinate and inexcusable delay – Delay making satisfactory arbitration impossible – Rescission – Frustration – Repudiation – Whether implied agreement to abandon arbitration agreement – Whether mutual delay can constitute repudiation by one party of arbitration agreement – Whether agreement frustrated because delay making satisfactory arbitration impossible – Whether one party can rely on frustration when there is mutual delay.

In 1969 the sellers agreed to sell a vessel to the buyers under a contract which provided that any dispute arising out of the sale was to be settled by arbitration in London by a single arbitrator or, if the parties could not agree on a single arbitrator, by three arbitrators, one appointed by each party and one appointed by an outside body. In 1972 the buyers informed the sellers that they had a number of complaints about the vessel and some months later commenced arbitration proceedings by appointing an arbitrator. The sellers also appointed an arbitrator, but a third arbitrator was never appointed. In 1974 the buyers delivered their points of claim alleging that the sellers had made a false representation or warranty prior to the execution of the contract regarding the vessel's speed and engine performance. Four months later the sellers delivered their defence in which they denied the claim. In the period from the delivery of the defence in 1974 until July 1980 when the buyers proposed that a date of hearing be fixed there was a lengthy delay in the process of discovery and in the progress of the arbitration generally. However, throughout that period there was an intermittent exchange of letters between the two sides in which each side pressed the other for production of the relevant log books. Nevertheless by July 1980, some 11 years after the sale, there had occurred over 7 years' delay in the arbitration. When the buyers proposed, in July 1980, that a date of hearing be fixed for the arbitration, the sellers issued a writ seeking, inter alia, a declaration that the arbitration agreement had been discharged by the buyers' repudiation of it or by frustration or by mutual rescission arising out of an agreement by the parties to abandon the agreement. The judge held (i) that on the evidence there was no agreement to abandon the agreement and (ii) that he was bound by House of Lords authority to hold that because both parties were under a mutual obligation to prevent delay and to keep the arbitration moving it was not open to the sellers to do nothing themselves and then rely on the buyers' delay as being a repudiation of the arbitration agreement. The judge went on, however, to hold that the length of delay was such that the arbitration agreement had been frustrated because a fair trial of the issues was no longer possible, and he granted a declaration to that effect. The buyers appealed to the Court of Appeal, which held (i) that the judge had been right to hold that there had been no abandonment of the arbitration agreement, (ii) that since the buyers had never taken any initiative to bring the delay to an end so as to bring any duty of mutual co-operation into play the sellers were entitled to rely on the buyers' delay as amounting to repudiation, and (iii) that since the delay was such as to make a fair trial impossible and the sellers had not been responsible for the delay the agreement to arbitrate had been frustrated. The Court of Appeal accordingly dismissed the buyers' appeal. The buyers appealed to the

House of Lords on the repudiation and frustration issues and the sellers cross-appealed on
a   the abandonment issue.

Held – The appeal would be allowed and the cross-appeal dismissed for the following
reasons—
(1) Where delay in proceeding with an arbitration was caused by breaches by both
claimant and respondent of the mutual obligations to one another to avoid delay, it was
b   not open to either party to rely on the other's conduct as amounting to repudiation.
Furthermore, the fact that the parties were under a mutual obligation to keep the
arbitration moving meant that neither party could claim that delay by the other party
had frustrated the agreement to arbitrate (see p 43 j, p 44 b c, p 48 a to c, p 50 b c, p 52 d
e, p 54 f j and p 55 c, post); Bremer Vulkan Schiffbau Und Maschinenfabrik v South India
Shipping Corp [1981] 1 All ER 289 explained.
c   (2) In any event, the two essential prerequisites for a contract to be held to be frustrated
were (a) that there was some outside event or extraneous change of situation which was
not foreseen or provided for by the parties at the time of making the contract and which
either made it impossible for the contract to be performed at all or rendered its
performance radically different from that which the parties contemplated when entering
into the contract and (b) that the outside event or extraneous change of situation and the
d   consequences thereof occurred without the fault or default of either party. On the facts,
there had been no outside event or external change of situation affecting the performance
of the agreement to refer disputes to arbitration, and, since both parties were under a
mutual obligation to keep the arbitration moving and both were in breach of that
obligation, the delay could not be said to have arisen without the fault or default of either
party. Accordingly, the mutual obligation on both parties to apply to the arbitrators for
e   directions to put an end to any delay effectively prevented the sellers from relying on the
buyers' delay to assert that the arbitration agreement was either repudiated or frustrated,
even though a satisfactory trial of the issues was no longer possible (see p 44 e f, p 45 a to
d, p 47 b c, p 48 a to c, p 51 d e and j to p 52 e and p 54 f j, post); Bremer Vulkan Schiffbau
Und Maschinenfabrik v South India Shipping Corp [1981] 1 All ER 289 applied.
(3) Since the doctrine of abandonment depended on the formation of a contract of
f   abandonment (to which the normal rules of contract applied, including the necessity for
consensus ad idem between the parties), the sellers had to show either (a) that an implied
agreement to abandon the contract to arbitrate was to be inferred from the parties'
conduct or (b) that the buyers' conduct as evinced to the sellers was such as to lead the
sellers reasonably to believe that the buyers had abandoned the contract to arbitrate (even
though that may not have been the buyers' actual intention) and that the sellers had
g   significantly altered their position in reliance on that belief. Furthermore (per Lord
Brightman), in the latter case the sellers were required to produce evidence not only of
what the buyers did or omitted to do, to the knowledge of the sellers, which entitled the
sellers to assume that the contract was agreed to be abandoned, but also of what the sellers
themselves did or omitted to do, whether or not to the knowledge of the buyers, which
showed that the sellers had assumed that the contract was agreed to be abandoned. Since
h   there had been intermittent exchanges between the parties during the period of delay
from 1974 onwards the sellers were unable to show that the buyers' conduct was such as
to induce in the minds of the sellers a reasonable belief that the buyers had abandoned
the arbitration agreement or that the sellers had acted on any such belief (see p 47 d e and
g to p 48 c and f to p 49 c and g to p 50 a, p 52 d e, p 54 f j and p 55 g to p 56 b, post);
André & Cie SA v Marine Transocean Ltd, The Splendid Sun [1981] 2 All ER 993 considered.
j   Per curiam. The mutual obligation on both parties to an arbitration to keep the
arbitration moving is not merely a matter of each party co-operating with any initiative
taken by the other but a positive obligation imposed on each party to take the initiative
himself, with or without the co-operation of the other party (see p 45 g h, p 48 a to c, p 52
d e and p 54 f j, post).
Decision of the Court of Appeal [1982] 3 All ER 394 reversed.

Notes

For termination of an arbitration agreement, see 2 Halsbury's Laws (4th edn) paras 547–554, and for cases on the subject, see 3 Digest (Reissue) 104–118, 545–646.

For the doctrine of frustration, see 9 Halsbury's Laws (4th edn) paras 450–453, and for cases on the subject, see 12 Digest (Reissue) 482–511, 3426–3535.

For repudiation of contract, see 9 Halsbury's Laws (4th edn) paras 546–549, and for cases on the subject, see 12 Digest (Reissue) 411–416, 3032–3049.

Cases referred to in opinions

Allen v Sir Alfred McAlpine & Sons Ltd, Bostic v Bermondsey and Southwark Group Hospital Management Committee, Sternberg v Hammond [1968] 1 All ER 543, [1968] 2 QB 229, [1968] 2 WLR 336, CA, Digest (Cont Vol C) 1091, 2262b.

André & Cie SA v Marine Transocean Ltd, The Splendid Sun [1981] 2 All ER 993, [1981] QB 694, [1981] 3 WLR 43, CA.

Bell v Lever Bros Ltd [1932] AC 161, [1931] All ER Rep 1, HL, 35 Digest (Repl) 23, 140.

Birkett v James [1977] 2 All ER 801, [1978] AC 297, [1977] 3 WLR 38, HL, Digest (Cont Vol E) 666, 2698b.

Bremer Vulkan Schiffbau Und Maschinenfabrik v South India Shipping Corp [1981] 1 All ER 289, [1981] AC 909, [1981] 2 WLR 14, HL; rvsg [1980] 1 All ER 420, [1981] AC 909, [1980] 2 WLR 905, CA; on appeal from [1979] 3 All ER 194, [1981] AC 909, [1979] 3 WLR 471.

Central London Property Trust Ltd v High Trees House Ltd (1946) [1956] 1 All ER 256, [1947] KB 130, 21 Digest (Reissue) 9, 53.

Chancery Lane Safe Deposit and Offices Co Ltd v IRC [1966] 1 All ER 1, [1966] AC 5, [1966] 2 WLR 251, HL, 28(1) Digest (Reissue) 278, 924.

Constantine (Joseph) Steamship Line Ltd v Imperial Smelting Corp Ltd, The Kingswood [1941] 2 All ER 165, [1942] AC 154, HL, 12 Digest (Reissue) 482, 3428.

Crawford v A E A Prowting Ltd [1972] 1 All ER 1199, [1973] 1 QB 1, [1972] 2 WLR 749, 3 Digest (Reissue) 116, 637.

Davis Contractors Ltd v Fareham UDC [1956] 2 All ER 145, [1956] AC 696, [1956] 3 WLR 37, HL, 12 Digest (Reissue) 507, 3518.

Donoghue (or M'Alister) v Stevenson [1932] AC 562, [1932] All ER Rep 1, HL, 36(1) Digest (Reissue) 144, 562.

Fitzleet Estates Ltd v Cherry (Inspector of Taxes) [1977] 3 All ER 996, [1977] 1 WLR 1345, HL, Digest (Cont Vol E) 291, 923a.

Heyman v Darwins Ltd [1942] 1 All ER 337, [1942] AC 356, HL, 3 Digest (Reissue) 88, 453.

Hong Kong Fir Shipping Co Ltd v Kawasaki Kisen Kaisha Ltd [1962] 1 All ER 474, [1962] 2 QB 26, [1962] 2 WLR 474, CA, 41 Digest (Repl) 363, 1553.

Johanna Oldendorff, The, E L Oldendorff & Co GbmH v Tradax Export SA [1973] 3 All ER 148, [1974] AC 479, [1973] 3 WLR 382, HL, Digest (Cont Vol D) 828, 2543a.

Jones v Secretary of State for Social Services, Hudson v Secretary of State for Social Services [1972] 1 All ER 145, [1972] AC 944, [1972] 2 WLR 210, HL, Digest (Cont Vol D) 683, 4585b.

Knuller (Publishing, Printing and Promotions) Ltd v DPP [1972] 2 All ER 898, [1973] AC 435, [1972] 3 WLR 143, HL, 14(1) Digest (Reissue) 140, 966.

Maritime National Fish Ltd v Ocean Trawlers Ltd [1935] AC 524, [1935] All ER Rep 86, 12 Digest (Reissue) 428, 3100.

Pearl Mill Co v Ivy Tannery Co [1919] 1 KB 78, [1918–19] All ER Rep 702, DC, 12 Digest (Reissue) 435, 3132.

Photo Production Ltd v Securicor Transport Ltd [1980] 1 All ER 556, [1980] AC 827, [1980] 2 WLR 283, HL.

R v Cunningham [1981] 2 All ER 863, [1982] AC 566, [1981] 3 WLR 223, HL.

Shaw v DPP [1961] 2 All ER 446, [1962] AC 220, [1961] 2 WLR 897, HL, 14(1) Digest (Reissue) 139, 965.

a *Sociedad Financiera de Bienes Raices SA v Agrimpex Hungarian Trading Co for Agricultural
   Products, The Aello* [1960] 2 All ER 578, [1961] AC 135, [1960] 3 WLR 145, HL, 41
   Digest (Repl) 333, 1304.

Appeal

The defendants, Partenreederei Hannah Blumenthal (the buyers), appealed by leave of
the Court of Appeal against the decision of the Court of Appeal (Lord Denning MR and
Kerr LJ, Griffiths LJ dissenting) ([1982] 3 All ER 394, [1982] 3 WLR 49) on 26 March
b 1982 dismissing their appeal against the decision of Staughton J ([1982] 1 All ER 197,
   [1981] 3 WLR 823) on 7 July 1981 granting the plaintiffs, Paal Wilson & Co A/S (the
   sellers), a declaration that an arbitration agreement contained in a contract dated 23
   September 1969 between the buyers and the sellers for sale of the vessel Pinto (later
   renamed the Hannah Blumenthal) was discharged by frustration. The sellers, by their
   cross-appeal sought to uphold the decision of the Court of Appeal on the alternative
c ground that the contract had been abandoned by mutual consent. The facts are set out in
   the opinion of Lord Brandon.

   Mark Saville QC and *Timothy Wormington* for the buyers.
   David Johnson QC and *Jonathan Sumption* for the sellers.

d Their Lordships took time for consideration.

   2 December. The following opinions were delivered.

   LORD DIPLOCK. My Lords, since the speech to be delivered by my noble and learned
   friend Lord Brandon will be the principal speech in this appeal, I have asked him, with
e the agreement of all your Lordships, that it should be delivered first. Such observations
   as I shall myself be making are intended to be supplementary to and in amplification of
   some parts of it; and I understand that those to be made by my noble and learned friends
   Lord Roskill and Lord Brightman are intended by them to be regarded in the same light.

   LORD BRANDON OF OAKBROOK. My Lords, your Lordships have before you
f an appeal from a judgment of the Court of Appeal (Lord Denning MR and Kerr LJ,
   Griffiths LJ dissenting) ([1982] 3 All ER 394, [1982] 3 WLR 49) affirming a judgment of
   Staughton J in an action in the Commercial Court ([1982] 1 All ER 197, [1981] 3 WLR
   823). The question raised by the appeal is of a general character and of great importance
   to arbitrators and commercial practitioners. It can be formulated in this way. Suppose
   that two parties to a contract have agreed to refer a dispute arising out of it to arbitration,
g and subsequently there is such prolonged delay by either or both parties in preparing for
   the arbitration and bringing it to a hearing that it becomes no longer possible for the
   arbitrator or arbitrators concerned to decide the case satisfactorily. In those circumstances,
   is the result in law that the agreement to refer is frustrated, so that neither party has
   either the duty or the right to proceed further with the reference, and that, if either
   should wish to do so, he should be restrained by injunction from so acting? Both
h Staughton J at first instance and the Court of Appeal by a majority on appeal from him
   have given an affirmative answer to that question, have held that the agreement to refer
   which is the subject matter of the present action has been frustrated by the delay of one
   or both the parties and have granted an injunction against the claimants restraining them
   from proceeding further with the reference. The original appellants, with the leave of
   the Court of Appeal, now appeal to your Lordships' House against that decision.
j   Your Lordships also have before you a cross-appeal by the original respondents. That
   cross-appeal raises a further question, which is not of a general character but which
   depends on the particular facts of the present case. The further question is this: on the
   assumption that the decision of the courts below on the first question referred to above
   was wrong, so that, on a true view of the law, the agreement to refer in the present case
   was not frustrated, was the conduct of the parties nevertheless of such a character as to

lead to the inference that they impliedly consented with each other to abandon that agreement? It was held by Staughton J, and unanimously by the Court of Appeal, that no such mutual consent to abandon the agreement to refer could properly be inferred from the conduct of the parties. The original respondents cross-appeal against that further decision.

The original appellants and cross-respondents are Partenreederei Hannah Blumenthal, a West German concern, whom I shall call 'the buyers'. The original respondents and cross-appellants are Paal Wilson & Co A/S, a Norwegian company, whom I shall call 'the sellers'. The matter arises out of a written contract, entitled 'Memorandum of Agreement' and dated 23 September 1969, for the sale of a ship by the sellers to the buyers. The ship's name before the sale was Pinto; she was renamed after the sale Hannah Blumenthal. The contract of sale of the ship contained the following, among other, provisions:

'Section 4. The Sellers shall provide for inspection of the Vessel . . . about 27th September 1969 and the Buyers shall undertake the inspection without undue delay to the Vessel . . .

Section 8 . . . The Sellers shall, at the time of delivery, hand to the Buyers all classification certificates . . . as well as all plans which may be in Sellers' possession. The same applies to log books, unless otherwise agreed.

Section 11 . . . the Vessel with everything belonging to her shall be delivered and taken over as she is at the time of delivery, after which the Sellers shall have no responsibility for possible faults or deficiencies of any description . . .

Section 15. If any dispute should arise in connection with the interpretation and fulfilment of this contract, same shall be decided by arbitration in the city of LONDON and shall be referred to a single Arbitrator to be appointed by the parties hereto. If the parties cannot agree upon the appointment of the single Arbitrator, the dispute shall be settled by three Arbitrators, each party appointing one Arbitrator, the third being appointed by The Baltic and International Maritime Conference in Copenhagen . . .'

The contract of sale contained no provision of any kind relating to the rpm or speed of the ship in service. It was duly carried out and the property in the ship was transferred from the sellers to the buyers, who proceeded to operate her with the new name referred to above.

On 28 January 1972 Messrs Holman Fenwick & Willan (Holmans), London solicitors acting for the buyers, wrote to the sellers asking them for delivery of the ship's deck and engine log books in accordance with section 8 of the contract of sale. By letter dated 15 March 1972 the sellers informed Holmans that the log books were with their Protection and Indemnity Associations, the London Steam-Ship Owners' Mutual Insurance Association Ltd and Assuranceforeningen Skuld. On 5 April 1972 A Bilbrough & Co Ltd (Bilbroughs), the managers of the former association, wrote to the West of England Ship Owners Mutual Insurance Association (London) Ltd, in their capacity as insurers of the buyers, saying that Skuld had sent such log books of the ship as they had in their possession to Bilbroughs.

In the following months the buyers notified the sellers, either directly or through agents, that they had a claim against them in respect of the speed of the ship, and the sellers, again directly or through agents, rejected such claim, with the result that a dispute between the parties in connection with the contract of sale had come into being.

During the course of August 1972, after the parties had been unable to agree on a single arbitrator for the settlement of the dispute, the buyers appointed Mr Ralph Kingsley as their arbitrator, and notice of such appointment was given to Bilbroughs as agents for the sellers. At the same time Bilbroughs were asked to give inspection of the ship's predelivery log books. On 1 September 1972 Bilbroughs wrote refusing to comply with this request on the ground that the buyers were not entitled to such inspection until discovery in the arbitration.

Between December 1972 and February 1973 Messrs Sinclair Roche & Temperley (Sinclairs), London solicitors acting for the sellers, appointed Mr Cedric Barclay as the

sellers' arbitrator, and gave notice of such appointment to Holmans. No steps, however,
a were taken by either party separately, or both parties together, then or at any later time,
to effect the appointment of a third arbitrator by the Baltic and International Maritime
Conference in Copenhagen, as provided for in section 15 of the contract of sale.

Between February 1973 and February 1974 Holmans and Sinclairs exchanged a
considerable number of letters relating to the nature of the buyers' claim and the
production for inspection of the ship's predelivery log books. This correspondence proved
b inconclusive and on 22 February 1974 Holmans served on Sinclairs the buyers' points of
claim in the arbitration. These made it clear that the buyers founded their case on alleged
representations, both oral and written, made by the buyers or their agents before the
conclusion of the written contract of sale, and not on any express or implied terms of that
contract. On 26 June 1974 Sinclairs served on Holmans the sellers' points of defence in
the arbitration, which consisted substantially of a denial of all the relevant averments in
c the buyers' points of claim. In September 1974 Sinclairs sought and obtained from
Holmans consent to amendment of the points of defence.

By November 1974 the pleadings in the arbitration could reasonably be regarded as
closed. A suggestion had earlier been made by Holmans that it might be necessary for
the buyers to serve points of reply, but no such further pleadings had by then been
served. The stage was accordingly set for discovery of documents by both parties. In fact,
d however, there was a lengthy delay in the process of discovery, so much so that it was not
until 15 September 1977 that Holmans served on Sinclairs the buyers' list of documents.
Subsequently there was a further prolonged exchange of letters between the solicitors on
either side, in the course of which Holmans pressed Sinclairs to serve the sellers' list of
documents, and to agree a timetable for the further conduct of the arbitration. There
was much delay on the sellers' side during this period, and it was not until 12 May 1978
e that Sinclairs ultimately served on Holmans the sellers' list of documents, subject to a
reservation about other documents not so far translated into English.

The documents set out in the sellers' list did not, extraordinary as it may seem having
regard to the nature of the buyers' claim and the history of the matter, include any of the
ship's predelivery log books, and not surprisingly Holmans immediately wrote to
Sinclairs complaining of this vital omission. Between 17 May 1978 and 15 November
f 1978 a further exchange of letters took place between Holmans and Sinclairs in the
course of which Holmans were pressing their request for discovery of the ship's
predelivery log books and of other documents which Sinclairs had informed them should
be added to the sellers' list, and Sinclairs, in addition to stalling on those requests,
themselves pressed Holmans for discovery of the ship's post-delivery log books. On 14
September 1978 Holmans supplied to Sinclairs copies of translations of the ship's post-
g delivery log books, and repeated once again their request for production of the ship's
predelivery log books. On 16 November 1978 Holmans at long last received these log
books from Sinclairs.

Between December 1978 and February 1979 Holmans were in correspondence with a
marine expert with a view to his examining and reporting on the ship's log books in
relation to the buyers' claim for mispresentation by the sellers of the ship's service speed.
h In February 1980 Holmans received their expert's first report and in June 1980 his second
report. On 30 July 1980 Holmans sent to Sinclairs the two reports prepared by their
expert, saying that they strongly supported the buyers' case and invited them to agree a
date for the hearing of the arbitration.

On 5 August 1980 Sinclairs, galvanised into action no doubt by the receipt of the
expert's reports, and Holmans' assertion that they strongly supported the buyers' case,
j wrote to Holmans saying that they were going to apply to the court for an order that the
buyers' claim should be struck out for want of prosecution. On 14 August 1980 Sinclairs
wrote a further letter to Holmans in which they purported to accept the buyers' conduct
in connection with the arbitration as amounting to a repudiation by the buyers of the
agreement to refer the dispute between the parties to arbitration, and claimed that that
agreement had thereby been discharged.

On 19 August 1980 Sinclairs issued a writ on behalf of the sellers against the buyers in
the Commercial Court. The writ was indorsed on the reverse with points of claim, by

which the sellers claimed against the buyers the following items of relief: (1) a declaration
that the arbitration agreement in the contract of sale had been discharged by reason of
repudiation of it by the buyers accepted as such by the sellers; (2) an injunction restraining
the buyers from taking any further action in pursuance of that agreement; (3) an order
dismissing the buyers' claim for want of prosecution; (4) damages limited to the sellers'
costs in the reference; alternatively (5) a declaration that, if the arbitration agreement was
still subsisting, the arbitrators had power to strike out the buyers' claims for want of
prosecution.

So far as those points of claim are concerned, I think it right to make two observations
in passing. First, even on the most favourable view of the sellers' case, it could not be
contended that the whole of the arbitration agreement contained in s 15 of the contract
of sale had been discharged; at best, from the sellers' point of view, it could only be
contended that the agreement to refer the particular dispute between the parties which
had arisen had been discharged in the manner alleged. Second, since no third arbitrator
had been appointed as required by s 15, it is difficult to see how the court could possibly
have made the alternative declaration asked for in (5) above.

Following the service of the writ various interlocutory applications were made by both
parties. The buyers applied twice to have the sellers' claims struck out as disclosing no
cause of action. The sellers also applied twice to amend their points of claim. Directions
were given for trial of the action on affidavit evidence alone, any further pleadings and
discovery of documents to be dispensed with. It was further decided that the various
interlocutory applications referred to above should be dealt with immediately before the
trial of the action, the date for which was then or later fixed as 6 June 1981. In the result,
before the trial, which occupied both 6 and 7 July 1981, was begun, the buyers'
applications to have the sellers' claims struck out were dismissed, and the sellers were
given leave to amend item (1) of their claim by adding to the existing contention that
the arbitration agreement had been discharged by the sellers' acceptance of the buyers'
repudiation of it the further contentions that it had in the alternative been discharged
either by frustration or by an agreement between the parties to abandon it.

My Lords, Staughton J at first instance and all three members of the Court of Appeal
on appeal from him were of the opinion that there had been such inordinate delay by
the buyers and the sellers in their preparation for the arbitration and the bringing of it to
a hearing that a fair trial of the dispute between the parties was no longer possible. There
was, in my view, ample material on which the two courts below could properly reach
this conclusion, and it would, I apprehend, only be in very rare cases that your Lordships'
House would see fit to disturb a concurrent conclusion of that kind. Even if that
consideration were to be disregarded, however, I think it right to say, after a careful
examination of the extensive delays which admittedly occurred in this case, that I should
have no hesitation in reaching the same conclusion on the matter concerned as was
reached in the two courts below. I would only say that I should prefer to substitute, for
the concept that a fair trial would be impossible, the similar, but as it seems to me more
accurate, concept that a satisfactory trial would be impossible, and I approach the primary
question raised by the original appeal on that basis.

My Lords, it is not possible to explain and understand the manner in which the present
case was dealt with in the two courts below without first referring in some detail to the
history and outcome of an earlier case in which attempts were made by respondents in
an arbitration to bring the reference of a dispute to a summary end on the ground of
inordinate and inexcusable delay by the claimants in prosecuting their claim. That earlier
case is *Bremer Vulkan Schiffbau Und Maschinenfabrik v South India Shipping Corp* [1981] 1 All
ER 289, [1981] AC 909, and the present case is in a number of senses a sequel to it.

Bremer Vulkan was tried at first instance by Donaldson J (see [1979] 3 All ER 194,
[1981] AC 909). He found that the claimants in an arbitration between the parties (the
defendants in the action) had been guilty of inordinate and inexcusable delay in
prosecuting their claim to the serious detriment of the respondents (the plaintiffs in the
action), and that, if the claim had been brought in an action instead of an arbitration and

the same delays had occurred, the court would have exercised its undoubted jurisdiction
a to dismiss the action for want of prosecution in accordance with the principles laid down
in *Allen v Sir Alfred McAlpine & Sons Ltd* [1968] 1 All ER 543, [1968] 2 QB 229. The judge
further held that, in these circumstances, it was open to the plaintiffs to bring the
reference to arbitration concerned to a summary end in one or other of two different
ways. First, the plaintiffs could apply to the arbitrator himself to dismiss the claim for
want of prosecution, and the arbitrator would then have the same power as the court to
b do so. Second, there was to be implied in the agreement to refer a term that each party
would use his best endeavours to bring the matter to a speedy conclusion; the inordinate
and inexcusable delay of the defendants in prosecuting their claim was so serious a breach
of that implied term as to amount to a repudiation of the agreement to refer; and the
plaintiffs, by accepting that repudiation as such, were entitled to treat that agreement as
discharged by breach. The court could then protect the plaintiffs' position by granting
c an injunction against the defendants restraining them from taking any further step in
the arbitration. It is to be observed that, in so far as Donaldson J held that an arbitrator
himself has the power to dismiss a claim for want of prosecution, he was disagreeing
with and declining to follow an earlier decision to the contrary effect of Bridge J, in
Crawford v A E A Prowting Ltd [1972] 1 All ER 1199, [1973] QB 1.

The judgment of Donaldson J in *Bremer Vulkan* was substantially upheld by the Court
d of Appeal (Lord Denning MR, Roskill and Cumming-Bruce LJJ) (see [1980] 1 All ER
420, [1981] AC 909), although with some variations in the precise grounds of decision.
Lord Denning MR held, contrary to the view of Donaldson J, and in accordance with the
earlier decision of Bridge J referred to above, that an arbitrator himself had no power to
dismiss a claim for want of prosecution. He took the view, however, that the court, in
the exercise of its jurisdiction to supervise arbitrations, did have such power. He also
e supported the view of Donaldson J that a claimant in an arbitration was under an implied
obligation to use reasonable dispatch, that if a claimant failed to comply with that
obligation to such an extent as to make a fair hearing of the dispute impossible, and
thereby to frustrate the whole purpose of the arbitration, the respondent was entitled to
accept such conduct as a repudiation of the agreement to refer and to treat such agreement
as at an end, and, further, that the court could protect a claimant's position in such a case
f by the grant of an injunction.

Roskill LJ also held that an arbitrator himself has no power to strike out a claim for
want of prosecution. As regards the issue of accepted repudiation, he did not agree with
the view of Donaldson J about the term to be implied in an agreement to refer. He
agreed that some term was to be implied, but formulated it as an obligation on a claimant
not to be guilty of such delay as would frustrate the whole purpose of the arbitration. He
g found that the claimant in that case had been guilty of such delay, so that the respondent
was entitled to treat the agreement to refer as discharged by breach and have the
protection of an injunction from the court.

Cumming-Bruce LJ agreed with both Lord Denning MR and Roskill LJ that the appeal
should be dismissed on the grounds given by them. He went on to state in express terms
his view that the principles laid down in *Allen v Sir Alfred McAlpine & Sons Ltd* were as
h relevant to arbitrations as to actions.

The defendants brought a further appeal from the judgment of the Court of Appeal to
your Lordships' House, which by a majority allowed the appeal. The reasoning on which
the majority founded their decision was fully expounded in the speech of Lord Diplock.
He laid much stress on the contractual nature of an agreement to refer a dispute to
arbitration and disagreed strongly with the view much relied on by the two courts below
j that, because actions and arbitrations were alike adversarial in character, the same
principles which applied to the summary dismissal of an action on the ground of
inordinate and inexcusable delay in its prosecution by the plaintiff applied equally to the
summary dismissal of a claim in an arbitration on the ground of similar delay in its
prosecution by a claimant.

It is not possible, in a short compass, to summarise the whole effect of the speech of

Lord Diplock in *Bremer Vulkan*. Nor do I think it is necessary for me to do so, for it seems to me that it is sufficient to quote two important passages from it, which afford powerful *a* guidance in the decision of the present appeal.

In the first passage Lord Diplock said ([1981] 1 All ER 289 at 301, [1981] AC 909 at 985–986):

'I turn then to consider what the mutual obligations of the parties are in a private arbitration. By appointing a sole arbitrator pursuant to a private arbitration agreement which does not specify expressly or by reference any particular procedural *b* rules, the parties make the arbitrator the master of the procedure to be followed in the arbitration. Apart from a few statutory requirements under the Arbitration Act 1950, which are not relevant to the instant case, he has a complete discretion to determine how the arbitration is to be conducted from the time of his appointment to the time of his award, so long as the procedure he adopts does not offend the rules of natural justice. The contractual obligation which the parties assume to one *c* another in relation to the procedure to be followed in the arbitration unless a contrary intention is expressed in the arbitration agreement is that which is stated in s 12(1) of the Act, viz: "... parties to the reference, and all persons claiming through them respectively, shall, subject to any legal objection, submit to be examined by the arbitrator or umpire, on oath or affirmation, in relation to the matters in dispute, and shall, subject as aforesaid, produce before the arbitrator or *d* umpire all documents within their possession or power respectively which may be required or called for, *and do all other things which during the proceedings on the reference the arbitrator or umpire may require*." No doubt in some arbitrations of a kind with which those who act on behalf of the parties in the conduct of the arbitration are familiar both claimant and respondent may carry out voluntarily some of all of the preliminary steps needed to prepare the matter for the hearing by the arbitrator, *e* and do so without seeking and obtaining any prior direction from him; but, if what is done voluntarily by way of preparation is done so tardily that it threatens to delay the hearing to a date when there will be a substantial risk that justice cannot be done, it is in my view a necessary implication from their having agreed that the arbitrator shall resolve their dispute that both parties, respondent as well as claimant, are under a mutual obligation to one another to join in applying to the arbitrator *f* for appropriate directions to put an end to the delay. Even if an application to the arbitrator for directions in such circumstances were a matter of right only and not, as I think it is, a mutual obligation, it provides a remedy to the party which thinks that the proceedings are not progressing fast enough voluntarily, which renders unnecessary the implication in the arbitration agreement of any such term as was suggested by Donaldson J or Roskill LJ.' (Lord Diplock's emphasis.) *g*

In the second passage Lord Diplock said ([1981] 1 All ER 289 at 302, [1981] AC 909 at 987–988):

'In the instant case, however, as in *Crawford v A E A Prowting Ltd* [1972] 1 All ER 1199, [1973] QB 1, the respondents, Bremer Vulkan, were content to allow the claimants, South India, to carry out voluntarily the preparation of detailed points of *h* claim. They never made an application for directions to the arbitrator and none were made by him. For failure to apply for such directions before so much time had elapsed that there was a risk that a fair trial of the dispute would not be possible, both claimant and respondent were in my view in breach of their contractual obligations to one another; and neither can rely on the other's breach as giving him a right to treat the primary obligations of each to continue with the reference as *j* brought to an end. Respondents in private arbitrations are not entitled to let sleeping dogs lie and then complain that they did not bark.'

I have described the history and outcome of *Bremer Vulkan* in some detail for this reason. The members of both the courts below made no secret of the fact that they regretted the decision of your Lordships' House in that case. Being of that mind the trial a   judge and the majority in the Court of Appeal were at pains to reach a conclusion on the present case which their deeply held convictions led them to believe that both justice and good sense demanded, despite the obstacles which they recognised at first sight that the *Bremer Vulkan* decision put in their way.

The conclusion which they reached was, as I indicated earlier, that, because there had been such inordinate delay by one or both of the parties to the arbitration in preparing for it and bringing it to a hearing that a fair trial of the issues raised in it was no longer

b   possible, the agreement of the parties to refer the dispute which has arisen between them to arbitration had been frustrated, and that the claimants should accordingly be restrained by injunction from proceeding with it further. Griffiths LJ on the other hand, in his dissenting judgment, while making it abundantly clear that his distaste for the decision of your Lordships' House in *Bremer Vulkan* was no less than that of the other judges concerned, reached what was for him the unhappy conclusion that to hold that the

c   agreement to refer had been frustrated for the reasons given by the majority could not be reconciled with the reasoning on which that decision was founded.

The reasoning of Lord Denning MR can be summarised as follows. First, he held that the views expressed by Lord Diplock in *Bremer Vulkan*, that the parties to an agreement to refer a dispute between them to arbitration owed to one another a mutual obligation to apply to the arbitrator for directions to prevent inordinate delay (the mutual obligation

d   concept), did not form part of the ratio decidendi in that case, and were wrong. Second, that, since this was so, the *Bremer Vulkan* case did not form an obstacle to holding that an agreement to refer a dispute to arbitration could be repudiated by inordinate and inexcusable delay by the claimant. Third, and alternatively, inordinate delay by a claimant could frustrate, and in the present case in fact had frustrated, the agreement to refer.

e   The reasoning of Kerr LJ went like this. First, he accepted, unlike Lord Denning MR, that Lord Diplock's mutual obligation concept did form part of the ratio decidendi in *Bremer Vulkan*. Second, he recognised that, since that was so, inordinate and inexcusable delay by a claimant could not, without some additional factor or factors, amount to a repudiation by such claimant of an agreement to refer. But, third, he said that there was nothing in the decision of your Lordships' House in *Bremer Vulkan* to prevent the court

f   from treating delay, of such a length as to make the fair trial of an arbitration no longer possible, as causing frustration of an agreement to refer, and that, on the facts of the present case, such frustration had occurred.

Griffiths LJ, in his dissenting judgment, expressed views which accorded substantially with the first two steps in the reasoning of Kerr LJ set out above. He went on, however, to express his further view that it was not open to the Court of Appeal, in the light of

g   your Lordships' decision in *Bremer Vulkan*, to hold that an agreement to refer a dispute to arbitration could be frustrated by delay alone, and in particular by delay which was caused, not by an external event or circumstances outside the control of the parties, but solely by their own conduct of the reference.

In the light of this necessarily compressed analysis of the reasoning of the three members of the Court of Appeal, two issues emerge for your Lordships' decision in

h   relation to the first and general question raised by this appeal. The first issue is whether Lord Diplock's mutual obligation concept in *Bremer Vulkan* formed part of the ratio decidendi of that case. The second issue is whether, if it did, it was open to the majority of the Court of Appeal to hold that, on the facts of the present case, the agreement to refer the dispute between the parties to arbitration had been discharged by frustration, so as to entitle the sellers to an injunction restraining the buyers from taking any further

j   step in that reference.

So far as the first question is concerned, I entertain no doubt whatever that Lord Diplock's mutual obligation concept formed an essential part of the ratio decidendi of *Bremer Vulkan* in your Lordship's House. That this is so is, in my opinion, made crystal clear by the words used by him in the second of the two passages from his speech which I quoted earlier, and which I shall now, in order to make good my opinion, venture to quote once again.

'For failure to apply for such directions before so much time had elapsed that there was a risk that a fair trial of the dispute would not be possible, both claimant and respondent were in my view in breach of their contractual obligations to one another; and neither can rely on the other's breach as giving him a right to treat the primary obligation of each to continue with the reference as brought to an end.'

The Court of Appeal in *Bremer Vulkan* had held that the claimant had been guilty of such inordinate and inexcusable delay in proceeding with the reference there concerned as to amount to a repudiation of the agreement to refer, that the respondents were entitled to accept, and had accepted, that repudiation as such, and that the agreement to refer had accordingly been discharged by breach. What Lord Diplock was saying was that, since the delay concerned was the consequence of breaches on the part of both the claimant and the respondent of their mutual obligation owed to one another, neither could rely on the other's conduct as amounting to repudiation. It necessarily follows that Lord Diplock's mutual obligation concept was an essential part of the ratio decidendi of the *Bremer Vulkan* case in your Lordships' House.

So far as the second issue is concerned there can be no doubt that an agreement to refer a dispute to arbitration can in theory, like any other contract, be discharged by frustration. Lord Diplock expressly recognised this in his speech in *Bremer Vulkan* [1981] 1 All ER 289 at 297, [1981] AC 909 at 980. Before this can happen, however, the usual requirements necessary to give rise to frustration of a contract must be present. What those requirements are appears clearly from the various pronouncements of high authority on the doctrine of frustration of contract conveniently gathered together by Griffiths LJ in his dissenting judgment in this case (see [1982] 3 All ER 394 at 406–407, [1982] 3 WLR 49 at 64–65).

Those pronouncements, which I do not consider that it is necessary for me to quote again myself, show that there are two essential factors which must be present in order to frustrate a contract. The first essential factor is that there must be some outside event or extraneous change of situation, not foreseen or provided for by the parties at the time of contracting, which either makes it impossible for the contract to be performed at all, or at least renders its performance something radically different from what the parties contemplated when they entered into it. The second essential factor is that the outside event or extraneous change of situation concerned, and the consequences of either in relation to the performance of the contract, must have occurred without either the fault or the default of either party to the contract.

It was contended for the sellers that the courts have never defined with precision the meaning of the expression 'default' in this context. In this connection reliance was placed on the observations of Viscount Simon LC in *Joseph Constantine Steamship Line Ltd v Imperial Smelting Corp Ltd, The Kingswood* [1941] 2 All ER 165 at 173, [1942] AC 154 at 166, where he said:

'... I do not think that the ambit of "default" as an element disabling the plea of frustration to prevail has as yet been precisely and finally determined. "Self-induced" frustration, as illustrated by the two decided cases already quoted, involves deliberate choice, and those cases amount to saying that a man cannot ask to be excused by reason of frustration if he has purposely so acted as to bring it about. "Default" is a much wider term, and in many commercial cases dealing with frustration is treated as equivalent to negligence. Yet in cases of frustration of another class, arising in connection with a contract for personal performance, it has not, I think, been laid down that, if the personal incapacity is due to want of care, the plea fails. Some day it may have to be finally determined whether a *prima donna* is excused by complete loss of voice from an executory contract to sing if it is proved that her condition was caused by her carelessness in not changing her wet clothes after being out in the rain. The implied term in such a case may turn out to be that the fact of supervening physical incapacity dissolves the contract without inquiring further into its cause, provided, of course, that it has not been deliberately induced in order to get out of the engagement.'

I turn now to consider whether what I have described as being, on the authorities, the
a two factors essential to the frustration of a contract are present in this case. As to that, I
agree with Griffiths LJ that neither such factor is present. In the first place there has been
in this case no outside event or external change of situation affecting the performance of
the agreement to refer at all, and no one, as far as I can see, has been able to put forward
an argument that there has. In the second place the state of affairs relied on as causing
frustration is delay by one or both of the parties of such a length as to make a fair, or as I
b prefer to call it satisfactory, trial of the dispute between the parties no longer possible.
That delay, however, on the facts as I have stated them earlier, was clearly itself caused by
the failure of both parties to comply with what your Lordships' House in *Bremer Vulkan*
decided was their mutual contractual obligation owed to one another, namely (after
taking the necessary steps to have a third arbitrator appointed) to apply to the full arbitral
tribunal as then constituted for directions to prevent the very delay which is now sought
c to be relied on by the sellers as having frustrated the agreement to refer.

Whatever may be the precise ambit of the expression 'default' in this context, and
whether it would or would not apply to the case of the prima donna postulated by
Viscount Simon LC in the part of his speech in *Joseph Constantine Steamship Line Ltd v
Imperial Smelting Corp Ltd*, which I quoted above, it is not, in my view, necessary to
determine. It is not necessary because I entertain no doubt whatever that the conduct of
d the parties in the present case, in failing to comply with what this House has held to be
their mutual contractual obligation to one another, comes fairly and squarely within
such expression.

Kerr LJ avoided this last conclusion by interpreting Lord Diplock's mutual obligation
concept in a special manner, as explained by him in his judgment (see [1982] 3 All ER
394 at 410–411, [1982] 3 WLR 49 at 69–70). He said, in effect, that the only obligation
e of the parties under the decision of your Lordships' House in *Bremer Vulkan* was to co-
operate with each other, that no question of co-operating or failing to co-operate could
arise unless and until one or other of the parties took the initiative, that the only party
obliged to take the initiative was the one by whom, at any given stage of the proceedings,
the next step fell to be taken, that, while it was open to the other party to take the
initiative, he was not in breach of his obligation to co-operate by not doing so, and that,
f on that analysis of the obligations imposed on the parties, the sellers could not be regarded
as having broken theirs. In my opinion, this analysis of the parties' obligations under the
decision of your Lordships' House in *Bremer Vulkan* is, with all respect to Kerr LJ, based
on far too narrow and restricted an interpretation of the relevant passages in the speech
of Lord Diplock in *Bremer Vulkan* which I quoted earlier. The whole thrust of Lord
Diplock's speech in those passages is, to my mind, that, whenever there is a possibility of
g such delay by either side occurring as would create a risk of a fair or satisfactory trial
becoming no longer possible, both parties are under a joint and several obligation to
apply to the arbitrator or arbitrators for directions to put an end to such delay. On this
interpretation of what Lord Diplock said the question of its being the obligation of the
one party or the other to take the initiative does not arise: each party is obliged to take
the initiative, with the co-operation of the other if it is forthcoming, without it if it is
h not.

It was contended for the sellers that this was a case in which it would be right for your
Lordships' House to exercise the freedom conferred on it by the practice statement (see
Note [1966] 3 All ER 77, [1966] 1 WLR 1234) to depart from its previous decision in
Bremer Vulkan. In support of this contention four main points were put forward. The
first point was the obvious regret of the two lower courts at the decision, and the
j consequent efforts of the trial judge and the majority of the Court of Appeal in the
present case to find a way round it if they could possibly do so. The second point
concerned the observations of Griffiths LJ (see [1982] 3 All ER 394 at 404, [1982] 3 WLR
49 at 61). He there said that, if he had not had the advantage of reading Lord Diplock's
speech in *Bremer Vulkan*, he would have fallen into the same error as the judge of first
instance, the Court of Appeal and the two of their Lordships who dissented in this House
in that case. It would, he continued, have appeared to him to be wholly divorced from

reality and the expectation of commercial men that those facing claims should be under
the same obligation to keep such claims moving against them as was imposed on those *a*
making them. The third point was that the decision, if carried to its logical conclusion,
would lead to situations arising in which, although a satisfactory trial of a reference was
no longer possible, that reference must nevertheless still proceed to trial. The fourth
point was that, since actions and arbitrations were alike adversarial in character, the same
principles with regard to inordinate and inexcusable delay were expected by commercial
men to apply, and should as a matter of justice and common sense apply, equally to both. *b*

Guidance on the circumstances in which it would or would not be right for this House
to depart from a previous decision, albeit a majority one, is to be found in the speech of
Lord Wilberforce in *Fitzleet Estates Ltd v Cherry (Inspector of Taxes)* [1977] 3 All ER 996 at
999, [1977] 1 WLR 1345 at 1349:

> 'There is therefore nothing left to the taxpayer but to contend, as it frankly does,
> that the 1966 decision [*Chancery Lane Safe Deposit and Offices Co Ltd v IRC* [1966] 1 *c*
> All ER 1, [1966] AC 85] is wrong. This contention means, when interpreted, that
> three or more of your Lordships ought to take the view which appealed then to the
> minority. My Lords, in my firm opinion, the 1966 Practice Statement (*Note* [1966]
> 3 All ER 77, [1966] 1 WLR 1234) was never intended to allow and should not be
> considered to allow such a course. Nothing could be more undesirable, in fact, than
> to permit litigants, after a decision has been given by this House with all appearance *d*
> of finality, to return to this House in the hope that a differently constituted
> committee might be persuaded to take the view which its predecessors rejected.
> True that the earlier decision was by a majority: I say nothing as to its correctness or
> as to the validity of the reasoning by which it was supported. That there were two
> eminently possible views is shown by the support for each by at any rate two
> members of the House. But doubtful issues have to be resolved and the law knows *e*
> no better way of resolving them than by the considered majority opinion of the
> ultimate tribunal. It requires much more than doubts as to the correctness of such
> opinion to justify departing from it.'

My Lords, that guidance should, in my view, be followed and acted on in the present
case. I express no opinion one way or another as to the conclusion which I might have *f*
reached if I had been a member of the committee which decided the *Bremer Vulkan* case.
It is sufficient to say that that decision was reached by what Lord Wilberforce described
as the best way of resolving doubtful issues known to the law, and that no special or
unusual circumstances have been put forward as justifying a departure from it.

Dealing specifically with the four points put forward by the sellers to which I referred
above, I would say this. With regard to the first point, the fact that a decision of your *g*
Lordships' House is so unpopular with members of courts below that they are led to seek
a way to get round it if they can reflects greater credit on their independence of mind
than on their loyalty to the established and indispensable principle of judicial precedent.
With regard to the second point, it is not difficult to understand the reaction of Griffiths
LJ, and of solicitors and others concerned in arbitrations, that it seems hard on a party
against whom a claim is being made to be obliged himself to ensure that his opponent *h*
proceeds with it with proper dispatch. Against that it is to be remembered that the
primary object sought to be achieved by parties who have agreed to refer a dispute
between them to arbitration is that the dispute should be decided on its merits by the
arbitral process which they have chosen with reasonable speed, and not that it shall end
up, after inordinate and inexcusable delay, by not being decided on its merits by that
process at all. With regard to the third point, I do not consider that the consequence *j*
flows from the premise. If a claimant is guilty of inordinate and inexcusable delay in the
prosecution of a reference to arbitration, the respondent can and should apply to the
arbitrator to give peremptory directions to the claimant to end the delay; then, if the
claimant fails to comply with such directions, the arbitrator can apply to the court under
s 5 of the Arbitration Act 1979 for power to dismiss the claim for want of prosecution.

a With regard to the fourth point, that illustrates very well the situation, described by Lord Wilberforce in the passage from his speech in *Fitzleet Estates Ltd v Cherry (Inspector of Taxes)* which I quoted above, where two eminently possible views of a question may be taken, where a decision between them has to be made by the best method known to the law, and where, once such decision has been made, it must for the future be followed and acted on without the risk of its being later held to have been wrong and departed from on that account. In this connection I would lay stress on what is generally accepted

b to be the special need for certainty, consistency and continuity in the field of commercial law.

For the reasons which I have given, my opinion on the first and general question raised by the appeal is this: that neither of the two factors essential for the frustration of the agreement to refer are present in this case; that the decision of the judge of first instance and of the majority of the Court of Appeal that such frustration occurred should be

c reversed; and that the dissenting judgment of Griffiths LJ that no such frustration took place should be upheld.

I pass now to the further question raised by the cross-appeal. That question is, as I indicated earlier, whether, assuming (contrary to the decisions of the courts below) that the agreement to refer in the present case was not frustrated, the conduct of the parties was nevertheless of such a character as to lead to the inference that they impliedly

d consented with each other to abandon that agreement.

The question whether a contract has been abandoned or not is one of fact. That being so, it would, I think, be sufficient, for the purposes of the present case, to say that there are concurrent findings of fact by both the courts below against the sellers on that question, that it is not the practice of your Lordships' House to interfere with such concurrent findings of fact save in exceptional circumstances which are not here present,

e and that the cross-appeal fails on that ground alone.

Because the question of the abandonment of a contract is, however, of some general importance, I consider that it may be helpful to examine the matter, as it arises in the present case, somewhat further. For this purpose it is, I think, necessary to make some additions to the history of the parties' conduct in relation to the reference which I set out earlier. The additional facts which I regard, for reasons which will become apparent later,

f as necessary to state are these. According to the affidavit of Mr Fitzpatrick, a solicitor employed by Sinclairs, sworn on 16 December 1980, that firm was still seeking to trace, and obtain evidence from, witnesses whom it might be necessary to call on the hearing of the arbitration as late as November 1979, February 1980 and November 1980.

The concept of the implied abandonment of a contract as a result of the conduct of the parties to it is well established in law: see *Chitty on Contracts* (23rd edn, 1968) vol 1, para

g 1231 and cases there cited. Where A seeks to prove that he and B have abandoned a contract in this way, there are two ways in which A can put his case. The first way is by showing that the conduct of each party, as evinced to the other party and acted on by him, leads necessarily to the inference of an implied agreement between them to abandon the contract. The second method is by showing that the conduct of B, as evinced towards A, has been such as to lead A reasonably to believe that B has abandoned the contract,

h even though it has not in fact been B's intention to do so, and that A has significantly altered his position in reliance on that belief. The first method involves actual abandonment by both A and B. The second method involves the creation by B of a situation in which he is estopped from asserting, as against A, that he, B, has not abandoned the contract (see *Pearl Mill Co Ltd v Ivy Tannery Co Ltd* [1919] 1 KB 78, [1918–19] All ER Rep 702).

j On whichever of the two bases of abandonment discussed above the sellers seek to reply in the present case, it seems to me that they are bound to fail. As I indicated above, Sinclairs, as the sellers' solicitors, were still, in November 1979, February 1980 and even as late as November 1980, trying to trace, and obtain evidence from, witnesses who might be called at the hearing of the arbitration. Even if it could fairly be said (which I do not think that it can) that the buyers' prolonged delays from 1974 onwards were such as to induce in the minds of the sellers or their solicitors a reasonable belief that the buyers had abandoned the agreement to refer, Sinclairs' continuing conduct with regard *a* to tracing, and obtaining evidence from, witnesses referred to above makes it impossible for the sellers to say that they acted on any such belief, or that they altered their position significantly in reliance on it.

For the reasons which I have given I would allow the buyers' original appeal and dismiss the sellers' cross-appeal, with costs against the sellers in either case.

b

LORD DIPLOCK. My Lords, the facts in this appeal and cross-appeal (in which I shall refer to the parties as 'the buyers' and 'the sellers' respectively) are sufficiently stated in the speech of my noble and learned friend Lord Brandon. I agree with and adopt his reasons for allowing this appeal; but, as author of the speech which constitutes the ratio decidendi of this House in *Bremer Vulkan Schiffbau Und Maschinenfabrik v South India* *c* *Shipping Corp* [1981] 1 All ER 289, [1981] AC 909, it may not be inappropriate for me, in support of his reasoning, to add my own somewhat more detailed analysis of the concept of rescission of contract by abandonment and of the legal nature of the obligations assumed by the parties to a commercial contract under an arbitration clause contained in it.

In my view the decision of the majority of the Court of Appeal in the instant case, *d* from which Griffiths LJ dissented, can only be upheld either (a) by holding that the agreement resulting from the submission of particular disputes that had arisen between the buyers and the sellers to arbitration under the arbitration clause in the sale agreement (which I will call 'the arbitration agreement') had been abandoned or (b) by overruling the decision of this House in *Bremer Vulkan*.

I will deal first with abandonment and in doing so, and later in dealing with the *e* obligations assumed by the parties under an arbitration clause in a commercial contract, I shall use the expressions 'primary and secondary obligations' under a contract in the sense that I used them in *Photo Production Ltd v Securicor Transport Ltd* [1980] 1 All ER 556, [1980] AC 827 and in *Bremer Vulkan* itself. Since I shall be dealing with bipartite synallagmatic contracts only, I will leave the adjectives to be understood whenever I speak of 'contract'.

Abandonment of a contract (the former contract) which is still executory, ie one in *f* which at least one primary obligation of one or other of the parties remains unperformed, is effected by the parties entering into a new contract (the contract of abandonment) by which each party promises the other to release that other party from further performance of any primary obligations on his part under the former contract then remaining unperformed, without such non-performance giving rise to any substituted secondary *g* obligation under the former contract to pay damages.

It is the latter part of the promise by each party, ie the release of the other party from all further secondary as well as primary obligations, that distinguishes the legal concept of abandonment of the former contract from the extinction of unperformed primary obligations of both parties under the former contract by fundamental breach of a primary obligation (or breach of condition) by one of them, followed by the election of the party *h* not in breach to put an end to all primary obligations of both parties under the former contract remaining unperformed. Unlike the contract of abandonment, this leaves the secondary obligations under the former contract of the party who committed the breach enforceable against him by the other party.

To the formation of the contract of abandonment, the ordinary principles of the English law of contract apply. To create a contract by exchange of promises between two *j* parties where the promise of each party constitutes the consideration for the promise of the other what is necessary is that the intention of each *as it has been communicated to and understood by the other* (even though that which has been communicated does not represent the actual state of mind of the communicator) should coincide. That is what English lawyers mean when they resort to the latin phrase consensus ad idem and the words that

I have italicised are essential to the concept of consensus ad idem, the lack of which
a prevents the formation of a binding contract in English law.

Thus if A (the offeror) makes a communication to B (the offeree), whether in writing,
orally or by conduct, which, in the circumstances at the time the communication was
received, (1) B, if he were a reasonable man, would understand as stating A's intention to
act or refrain from acting in some specified manner if B will promise on his part to act or
refrain from acting in some manner also specified in the offer, and (2) B does in fact
b understand A's communication to mean this, and in his turn makes to A a communication
conveying his willingness so to act or to refrain from acting which mutatis mutandis
satisfies the same two conditions as respects A, the consensus ad idem essential to the
formation of a contract in English law is complete.

The rule that neither party can rely on his own failure to communicate accurately to
the other party his own real intention by what he wrote or said or did, as negativing the
c consensus ad idem, is an example of a general principle of English law that injurious
reliance on what another person did may be a source of legal rights against him. I use the
broader expression 'injurious reliance' in preference to 'estoppel' so as to embrace all
circumstances in which A can say to B, 'You led me reasonably to believe that you were
assuming particular legally enforceable obligations to me', of which promissory or *High
Trees* estoppel (see *Central London Property Trust Ltd v High Trees House Ltd* (1946) [1956]
d 1 All ER 256, [1947] KB 130) affords another example, whereas 'estoppel', in the strict
sense of the term, is an exclusionary rule of evidence, though it may operate so as to affect
substantive legal rights inter partes.

In the instant case, as in most cases where abandonment of a former contract is relied
on, the contract of abandonment of the arbitration agreement is said by the sellers to
have been created by the conduct of the parties, consisting of their common inaction,
e after the buyers' letter of 12 December 1979. Where the inference that a reasonable man
would draw from the prolonged failure by the claimant in an arbitration procedure is
that the claimant is willing to consent to the abandonment of the agreement to submit
the dispute to arbitration and the respondent did in fact draw such inference and by his
own inaction thereafter indicated his own consent to its abandonment in similar fashion
to the claimant and was so understood by the claimant, the court would be right in
f treating the arbitration agreement as having been terminated by abandonment. In *André
& Cie SA v Marine Transocean Ltd, The Splendid Sun* [1981] 2 All ER 993, [1981] 1 QB 694
all three members of the Court of Appeal drew such an inference from the conduct of
both parties in the arbitration. That case was, in my view, rightly decided, though not
for reasons other than those which were given by Eveleigh and Fox LJJ.

The facts in the instant case, however, are very different from those of *The Splendid
g Sun*. As my noble and learned friends Lord Brandon and Lord Brightman both point out,
they are inconsistent with any actual belief on the part of the sellers that the buyers had
agreed to abandon the arbitration before their letter of 30 July 1980, which stated their
intention of continuing with it.

Your Lordships were urged to hold that the absence of any actual belief on the part of
the sellers did not matter so long as someone in the sellers' position could not unreasonably
h have drawn the inference from the apparent inaction of the buyers that they had
abandoned the arbitration at some date between their letter of 12 December 1979, when
they were manifestly treating the arbitration as being still alive, and 30 July 1980, when
they wrote to the sellers forwarding their expert's report and asking for a hearing date
for the arbitration to be fixed. The absence of actual belief on the sellers' part that the
buyers had abandoned the arbitration, however, would mean that there had in fact been
j no injurious reliance by the sellers; and to treat that ingredient of consensus ad idem as
unnecessary would introduce into the law of contract a novel heresy which your
Lordships should, in my view, be vigilant to reject.

Applying the orthodox concept of termination of contract by abandonment, neither
the trial judge nor any member of the Court of Appeal was prepared to hold that the
sellers were entitled to succeed on this ground; and even if your Lordships yourselves felt

some doubt on this issue, which I myself do not, I agree with my noble and learned friends that your Lordships would hesitate long before upsetting the unanimous decision a of the judges in the lower courts on what, on a proper application of the law of contract, is essentially a question of fact.

In considering the question of abandonment, I found of great assistance the tabulated chronology of events which the parties agreed and tendered to your Lordships after the cases had been prepared. Your Lordships may feel that such a chronology would be welcome and time saving in many other appeals, particularly if lodged before the start of b the hearing.

My Lords, as respect the propriety of this House declining to follow its own recent decision in *Bremer Vulkan* I have nothing to add to what is said on this topic by my noble and learned friends Lord Roskill, Lord Brandon and Lord Brightman. Even if I had been persuaded, as unrepentantly I have not, that of the two eminently possible views in *Bremer Vulkan* the majority of the House, speaking through me, made the worse and not c the better choice, I would none the less agree with my Lords that in the interests of legal certainty we should abide by it.

I turn finally to the question whether it is possible to escape the consequences of the decision in *Bremer Vulkan* by resorting to the doctrine of frustration of the arbitration agreement as Staughton J and the majority of the Court of Appeal (Lord Denning MR and Kerr LJ) thought that they could do; and on this aspect of the case I think it helpful d to start by analysing the legal characteristics of an arbitration clause in a commercial contract.

The first characteristic is that which was established by this House in *Heyman v Darwins Ltd* [1942] 1 All ER 337, [1942] AC 356. An arbitration clause is collateral to the main contract in which it is incorporated and it gives rise to collateral primary and secondary obligations of its own. Those collateral obligations survive the termination (whether by e fundamental breach, breach of condition or frustration) of all primary obligations assumed by the parties under the other clauses in the main contract. In saying this I do no more than paraphrase, in the nomenclature I adopted in *Photo Production Ltd v Securicor Transport Ltd* [1980] 1 All ER 556, [1980] AC 827, what was said by Lord Macmillan in *Heyman v Darwins Ltd* [1942] 1 All ER 337 at 347, [1942] AC 356 at 374.

The second characteristic of an arbitration clause is that the primary obligations that it f creates are subject to conditions subsequent. The clause comes into operation so as to impose primary obligations on the parties to the contract only on the occurrence of a combination of future events which may or may not occur, viz (1) the coming into existence of a dispute between the parties as to their primary or secondary obligations under the main contract and (2) the invoking of the arbitration clause by a party to the contract (the claimant) who desires to obtain the resolution of that dispute by the g procedure for which the arbitration clause provides. It follows from this latter condition subsequent that the arbitration clause may be brought into operation by the claimant at any time before the expiry of the limitation period applicable to the breach of primary obligation under the main contract by the other party (the respondent) of which he complains.

The third characteristic is that the subject matter of an arbitration agreement is not a h thing that is susceptible of physical destruction. It is an agreement by the parties (1) to embark on and follow a joint course of action (viz the procedure for which the arbitration clause provides), for the purpose of obtaining from a third party, the arbitrator or arbitral tribunal, a decision of the dispute, and (2) to abide by that decision.

In order to determine whether the primary obligations of the parties under an arbitration clause, once it has been brought into operation, have been terminated by j frustration, one must first consider whether the occurrence of the event relied on as the frustrating event has rendered the further performance by both parties of their primary obligations under the arbitration clause 'a thing radically different from that which was undertaken' by each when the arbitration clause was brought into operation, as Lord Radcliffe put it in *Davis Contractors Ltd v Fareham UDC* [1956] 2 All ER 145 at 160, [1956]

AC 696 at 729, or as I ventured to put it myself in *Hong Kong Fir Shipping Co Ltd v*
a *Kawasaki Kisen Kaisha Ltd* [1962] 1 All ER 474 at 485, [1962] 2 QB 26 at 66:
   '. . . does the occurrence of the event deprive the party who has further
   undertakings [sc primary obligations] still to perform of substantially the whole
   benefit which it was the intention of the parties as expressed in the contract that he
   should obtain as the consideration for performing those undertakings?'

My Lords, I accept, as I understand all your Lordships do in common with Staughton J
b and all three members of the Court of Appeal, that, during the parties' delay in proceeding
with the arbitration, events have occurred which would involve so substantial a risk that
a 'fair trial' of the issues in the arbitration could not be had, if the arbitration proceedings
had been an action in a court of law, that the court in the exercise of its inherent power
to prevent abuse of its own process by procrastination would be justified in striking out
the action for want of prosecution, on the principles approved by the Court of Appeal in
c *Allen v Sir Alfred McAlpine & Sons Ltd* [1968] 1 All ER 543, [1968] 2 QB 229. What puts
what in that case was described as the 'fairness' of the trial in jeopardy by procrastination
is the difficulty that the decider of fact, in the instant case the arbitral tribunal and in the
McAlpine case the judge, would encounter in ascertaining with any reasonable degree of
certainty what actually happened many years before. Like my noble and learned friend
Lord Brandon, I would substitute 'satisfactory trial' for the expression 'fair trial' which I
d myself used in the *McAlpine* case.

There seem to me to be two reasons, each of them decisive, why inability to obtain a
'satisfactory trial' because of the difficulty which the arbitral tribunal will encounter in
ascertaining the true facts, even if caused by delay in the proceedings, is not capable in
law of bringing an arbitration agreement to an end by frustration.

In the first place, it is the nature of the event that determines whether its occurrence
e deprives the party who has further primary obligations to perform under the arbitration
agreement of substantially the whole benefit which it was the intention of the parties
that he should obtain as consideration for performing those further primary obligations.
As my noble and learned friend Lord Roskill points out, events creating difficulty in
ascertaining what were the true facts may, without default by either party to the
arbitration agreement, occur at any time after those facts came into existence. Witnesses
f may die or disappear, documents or physical evidence may be lost or be destroyed even
before and at any time, however short, after the arbitration clause has been brought into
operation; and that this is a possibility is well known to the parties when the contract
containing the arbitration clause is entered into. In particular, events making it virtually
impossible for the arbitrator to be confident that he had been able at the hearing to
ascertain the true facts might well occur before the expiry of the limitation period. If the
g mere fact that because important evidence has become unavailable it has become virtually
impossible for the arbitrator to be confident that he has been able to ascertain the true
facts relevant in the dispute were sufficient to terminate the arbitration agreement by
frustration, the termination would take place by operation of law independently of the
wishes of the parties as soon as that evidence became unavailable. If this took place, as
well it might, before the expiry of the limitation period, the claimant in the frustrated
h arbitration would then be at liberty to make the same claim in an action in a court of
law, despite the fact that, at the hearing of the action, the judge would experience the
same difficulty in ascertaining the true facts as the arbitrator would have experienced
(see *Birkett v James* [1977] 2 All ER 801, [1978] AC 297).

My Lords, these considerations make it, in my view, quite impossible to say that the
continuance of arbitration proceedings after it has become virtually impossible that at
j the hearing the arbitrator can be confident that he has been able to ascertain the true
facts, is a thing radically different from that which was undertaken by the parties when
they incorporated the arbitration clause in the main contract or when the submission of
the particular dispute to arbitration was made. Such virtual impossibility would for this
reason be incapable of qualifying as a frustrating event, even if it had come about without
default by either party.

My Lords, as regards the second decisive reason why in the instant case frustration cannot be relied on by the sellers as having put an end to the arbitration agreement, I *a* have little to add to what is said on this matter in the speech by my noble and learned friend Lord Brandon, and also in the dissenting judgment of Griffiths LJ where there can be found a judicious selection of the most pertinent citations from the numerous authorities in this well-ploughed field of law. Of these citations, that which applies most aptly to the circumstances of the instant case is the statement of Lord Wright in *Maritime National Fish Ltd v Ocean Trawlers Ltd* [1935] AC 524 at 530, [1935] All ER Rep 86 at 89: *b* 'The essence of "frustration" is that it should not be due to the act or election of the party.' In the instant case the continuing deterioration, during the period of delay, in the amount and quality of evidence which could be made available to the arbitral tribunal when the hearing eventually takes place constitutes the events of which the cumulative effect by August 1980 is relied on as amounting to frustration of the arbitration agreement. The delay, so far as it was not justified to enable proper preparation for the hearing to be made *c* by both parties, could have been put to an end by the sellers by taking steps available to them in the arbitration proceedings. That they elected not to do so would, in my view, be sufficient in itself to debar them from relying on frustration; a fortiori when their election not to do so was a breach of a primary obligation on their part under the arbitrating agreement.

So for the reasons given by Lord Brandon supplemented by what is said by others of *d* your Lordships and by what I myself have said above, I would allow this appeal.

LORD KEITH OF KINKEL. My Lords, I have had the advantage of reading in draft the speech to be delivered by my noble and learned friend Lord Brandon. I agree with it, and for the reasons he gives I too would allow the appeal and dismiss the cross-appeal.

e

LORD ROSKILL. My Lords, counsel for the sellers contended, as an alternative to his main submission that the majority judgments in the Court of Appeal were correct and should be upheld, that this House should not follow the decision given less than two years ago in *Bremer Vulkan Schiffbau Und Maschinenfabrik v South India Shipping Corp* [1981] 1 All ER 289, [1981] AC 909. Your Lordships may think that logically this submission *f* should precede the other since, were the House now to accept as correct not the view which then prevailed but the view of the Court of Appeal and of two of your Lordships, my noble and learned friends Lord Fraser and Lord Scarman, in the *Bremer Vulkan* case, there can be little doubt that, on the concurrent findings both of Staughton J and of all the members of the Court of Appeal in the present case, had these proceedings been by way of action and not of arbitration, they would have been struck out for want of *g* prosecution, and an injunction would issue to stay the progress of this arbitration.

In support of this submission it was urged that this House should avail itself of the 1966 practice direction (*Note* [1966] 3 All ER 77, [1966] 1 WLR 1234). The principal reasons were said to be two. First, reliance was placed on the unanimity of the criticisms of the *Bremer Vulkan* decision in the lower courts and in particular the criticism of the rejection by this House of the view that such delay as would justify the dismissal of an *h* action for want of prosecution could amount to repudiation of the agreement to arbitrate. Second, it was said that to impose on a respondent to an arbitration a duty to proceed diligently with that arbitration, parallel with a similar duty on a claimant, 'flew in the face of the practice and understanding of lawyers and commercial men' (I quote the actual words used by counsel) and resulted in arbitrations proceeding to hearing even though the issues could not be determined 'fairly'.

My Lords, it will be convenient to dispose of this last point at once. The adverb 'fairly' *j* has been frequently used in the context of what is called a 'fair hearing'. It is said that a hearing cannot be 'fair' if witnesses or documents who or which might have been available at an earlier date are no longer available. But this risk is inherent in all litigation and all arbitrations. Even at an early date a witness may die or become unavailable for some other reason and documents may be destroyed. Sometimes witnesses are available

to parties but not to the court since, for what is thought to be good reason under our
a adversarial system, they are not called and available documents may not be put in
evidence. To say that in those circumstances the trial or the hearing of the arbitration is
'not fair' is, with respect, a misuse of that word. I agree with my noble and learned friend
Lord Brandon that the better phrase is 'not satisfactory'. Every tribunal must do its best
with the material placed before it. But no tribunal can add to that material however
much it may wish to do so; and if in the end the result is 'not satisfactory' the blame lies
b not with the tribunal but with the parties. In such an event I do not think the result can
be said to be 'unfair'.

My Lords, the contention that the result of the decision in the *Bremer Vulkan* case 'flew
in the face of the practice and understanding of lawyers and commercial men' requires
consideration. Kerr LJ spoke of the *Bremer Vulkan* case as having been 'received with the
greatest concern, not only in the City and the Temple, but also abroad . . .' (see [1982] 3
c All ER 394 at 409, [1982] 3 WLR 49 at 67).

My Lords, it would no doubt have been convenient to many had the contrary view
prevailed. But, with all respect, the language both of the submission and of the learned
Lord Justice is difficult to accept in its entirety since it was not until the decision of
Donaldson J at first instance in the *Bremer Vulkan* case [1979] 3 All ER 194, [1981] AC
909 on 10 April 1979 that it had been held, or, it seems, previously suggested, that stale
d arbitrations could be stopped by injunction. It had, it seems, not occurred to anyone to
advance this submission, notwithstanding that some six years earlier Bridge J had held in
Crawford v A E A Prowting Ltd [1972] 1 All ER 1199, [1973] QB 1 that an arbitrator had
no power to dismiss an arbitration for want of prosecution. Indeed, my recollection is
that in the Court of Appeal in the *Bremer Vulkan* case [1980] 1 All ER 420, [1981] AC 909
(I was a member of that court) one of the main arguments against the view which there
e found favour was the novelty of the procedure which the plaintiffs in that action had
adopted.

If the language which I have ventured to criticise means no more than that until the
decision in the *Bremer Vulkan* case in this House it was the practice of lawyers and of
commercial men to allow arbitrations, and in particular arbitrations where a claimant's
prospects of success seemed slight, to drift lethargically along with the respondent hoping
f that in consequence the claim might be dropped, this is no doubt true. Some solicitors
and especially those acting for plaintiffs had been accustomed to similar inaction in
personal injury cases. The decision of the Court of Appeal in *Allen v Sir Alfred McAlpine
& Sons Ltd* [1968] 1 All ER 543, [1968] 2 QB 229 put an end to that practice, much to the
alarm of those who had previously been guilty of adopting it. If the decision in this
House in the *Bremer Vulkan* case, if not now departed from, stops arbitrations being
g allowed to drift into inactivity I do not think that the decision is to be criticised on that
ground alone.

My Lords, I turn to consider the first reason which was advanced for urging that the
decision in the *Bremer Vulkan* case should now be departed from. This submission when
analysed amounts to no more than that this House, which by a majority rejected the
conclusion of Donaldson J and the Court of Appeal, should now, less than two years later,
h say that the reasoning which led to that conclusion was wrong and that the reasons which
appealed to the Court of Appeal and two of my noble and learned friends in this House
should now be held to be the law.

I have reread all the judgments and speeches in the *Bremer Vulkan* case. It is apparent
from their perusal that there were two possible views of the correct analysis of the nature
of an arbitration agreement. One commanded the greater numerical support. The other
j commanded the support of the majority in this House. The law of this country is
determined in this way and it was the latter view which prevailed. There are many cases
where the common law of this country has been similarly determined. Two well-known
examples are *Donoghue v Stevenson* [1932] AC 562, [1932] All ER Rep 1 and *Bell v Lever
Bros Ltd* [1932] AC 161, [1931] All ER Rep 1. Each decision was subjected to considerable
contemporary criticism. Each has stood the test of time and the former has been widely
regarded as a milestone in the development of the law of negligence.

Naturally, counsel for the respondents drew your Lordships' attention to a number of cases where the possible review of an earlier decision of this House has been considered. In *The Johanna Oldendorff, E L Oldendorff & Co GmbH v Tradax Export SA* [1973] 3 All ER 148, [1974] AC 479 this House departed from its earlier decision by a majority in *Sociedad Financiera de Bienes Raices SA v Agrimpex Hungarian Trading Co for Agricultural Products, The Aello* [1960] 2 All ER 578, [1961] AC 135. But that departure took place because of the practical difficulties to which the earlier decision had given rise: see the observations of Lord Reid and of Lord Diplock ([1973] 3 All ER 148 at 156, 179, [1974] AC 479 at 535, 561). On the other hand, in *Knuller (Publishing, Printing and Promotions) Ltd v DPP* [1972] 2 All ER 898, [1973] AC 435 this House by a majority declined to review the earlier decision in *Shaw v DPP* [1961] 2 All ER 446, [1962] AC 220. Lord Reid who had dissented in *Shaw's* case and 12 years later still thought that the decision of the majority wrong (see [1972] 2 All ER 898 at 903, [1973] AC 435 at 455) firmly refused to permit the majority decision to be reconsidered even though Lord Diplock dissented on two grounds, first, that *Shaw's* case was wrongly decided and, second, that in a criminal case where the liberty of the subject was involved the House should be vigilant to correct what Lord Diplock regarded as an earlier mistake.

None of these considerations presently arise. No useful purpose will be served by reviewing other decisions where the House has or has not departed from earlier decisions. I see nothing in the present case which would bring it within Lord Reid's statement of principle in *Jones v Secretary of State for Social Services* [1972] 1 All ER 145 at 149, [1972] AC 944 at 966. I respectfully echo what Lord Reid there said, that cases where the 1966 practice direction ([1966] 3 All ER 77, [1966] 1 WLR 1234) should or should not apply cannot be categorised.

In commercial law it is essential that the law should be certain. Your Lordships have recently reasserted this principle on a number of occasions, notably in cases arising from the alleged wrongful withdrawal of time chartered ships for supposedly unpunctual payment of hire. To review the *Bremer Vulkan* decision would create not certainty but uncertainty. Were your Lordships to yield to the sellers' submissions a few years have only to elapse and other litigants might hope to persuade a differently constituted appellate committee once again to reconsider the position and to restore the *Bremer Vulkan* decision to its present role.

My Lords, it follows that, since I agree with all your Lordships on the critical issue in this appeal, namely that the majority judgments in the Court of Appeal, in seeking to distinguish the *Bremer Vulkan* decision, depart from fundamental principles regarding the law of frustration and thus cannot be supported, this appeal must be allowed. I would only add that, if it be said that the refusal of your Lordships' House to reconsider the *Bremer Vulkan* decision weakens the abilities of arbitrators or of the courts to dispose of stale arbitrations, I question whether that is in truth so. In the first place there may well be cases such as *André & Cie SA v Marine Transocean Ltd, The Splendid Sun* [1981] 2 All ER 993, [1981] 1 QB 694 where the conduct of the parties is such that the only possible inference is that the agreement to arbitrate has been rescinded by mutual consent. On that ground *The Splendid Sun* was in my view plainly rightly decided, though I agree with Fox LJ that the doctrine of frustration was not available in that case. It was sought to advance the same argument in the instant case, but in my view both courts below were right in rejecting it. There is no evidence of implied mutual recission. Second, s 5 of the Arbitration Act 1979 confers drastic powers which can and no doubt will from time to time be properly used by arbitrators and umpires to avoid delay and to dispose of stale arbitrations.

LORD BRIGHTMAN. My Lords, I am in agreement with your Lordships, and I wish to add only a few words of emphasis of my own.

I turn first to the sellers' invitation that this House should depart from the conclusion which it reached less than two years ago in *Bremer Vulkan Schiffbau Und Maschinenfabrik v South India Shipping Corp* [1981] 1 All ER 289, [1981] AC 909. That is an invitation which I would unhesitatingly decline. Nothing has occurred since January 1981 in the field of

arbitration to warrant such an inroad into the principle of stare decisis, described in *R v*
a   *Cunningham* [1981] 2 All ER 863 at 870, [1982] AC 566 at 581 as 'the indispensable
foundation of the use by your Lordships of the appellate jurisdiction of the House and its
normal practice'. I appreciate that the decision in the *Bremer Vulkan* case may have caused
alarm and despondency to respondents in moribund arbitration cases, by encouraging
the attempted resuscitation of stale claims. But that is a transitory consequence of the
decision. So far as the future is concerned, the decision introduces a sense of urgency into
b   arbitration proceedings which is just as commendable there as it is in court proceedings.
I would have thought that the parties themselves would welcome the incentive for speed
which the *Bremer Vulkan* decision injects into their cases. I appreciate that some busy
professional people may find this irksome, because speed tends to increase the weight of
an overload of work, while deferment may sometimes ease the burden. This is a
disadvantage to professional people which must be accepted. I cannot see that it is
c   remotely unjust or unfair to tell respondents that, if they suffer claimants to delay, they
will lose the right to complain of that delay.

I turn to the alleged abandonment of the arbitration. Although the claimant's delay
does not of itself confer any right on the respondent to call a halt to the arbitration, it
may lead to an inference that the submission of the dispute to arbitration has been
abandoned by mutual agreement and thus prevent the claimant reviving the proceedings.
d   *André & Cie SA v Marine Transocean Ltd, The Splendid Sun* [1981] 2 All ER 993, [1981] QB
694 is an example. In the instant case the sellers' submission that the arbitration
agreement ought to be treated as abandoned by mutual consent was, in my opinion,
rightly rejected by the trial judge and by the Court of Appeal. Your Lordships may feel
that it would not be appropriate to reconsider this aspect of the case, which depends on
the inference to be drawn from the admitted primary facts, and on which both the lower
e   courts were in agreement. I wish, however, to touch briefly on this topic to correct what
I believe is a fallacy in the sellers' case. Under the heading 'Rescission by mutual
agreement—"abandonment"' the sellers make this submission:

'An agreement may be discharged by its being tacitly abandoned by both parties.
Tacit abandonment may be inferred from a sufficient delay. The question is whether
"the proper inference to be drawn was that each party was justified in assuming that
f   the matter was off altogether" . . . Since the test is an objective one the question is
what inferences would a reasonable person in the position of the [sellers] draw from
the delay which had occurred [between October 1978 and the end of July 1980].'

The statement with which I quarrel, because it is incomplete, is 'the test is an objective
one'. The test in my opinion is not wholly objective.
g   The basis of 'tacit abandonment by both parties', to use the phraseology of the sellers'
case, is that the primary facts are such that it ought to be inferred that the contract to
arbitrate the particular dispute was rescinded by the mutual agreement of the parties. To
entitle the sellers to rely on abandonment, they must show that the buyers so conducted
themselves as to entitle the sellers to assume, *and that the sellers did assume*, that the
contract was agreed to be abandoned sub silentio. The evidence which is relevant to that
h   inquiry will consist of or include: (1) what the buyers did or omitted to do *to the knowledge*
of the sellers. Excluded from consideration will be the acts of the buyers of which the
sellers were ignorant, because those acts will have signalled nothing to the sellers and
cannot have founded or fortified any assumption on the part of the sellers; (2) what the
sellers did or omitted to do, *whether or not to the knowledge of the buyers*. These facts
evidence the state of mind of the sellers, and therefore the validity of the assertion by the
j   sellers that they assumed that the contract was agreed to be abandoned. The state of mind
of the buyers is irrelevant to a consideration of what the sellers were entitled to assume.
The state of mind of the sellers is vital to what the sellers in fact assumed.

In the instant case there is a period of 21 months which contains the acts and omissions
relied on by the sellers. During that period there were five communications from buyers
to sellers. Those communications can be relied on by the buyers to counter the submission
that the sellers were entitled to assume that the contract to arbitrate had been abandoned

by the buyers. There were during the same period four additional acts on the part of the buyers inconsistent with an intention on their part to rescind the arbitration agreement, *a* of which the sellers were ignorant. The buyers cannot rely on those acts. Per contra, there were two important steps taken by the sellers, without the knowledge of the buyers, inconsistent with the proposition that the sellers assumed the arbitration was abandoned. This evidence, though going to the state of mind of the sellers and signalling nothing to the buyers, is admissible and in the instant case decisive.

I also found of great assistance the tabulated chronology of events which the parties *b* agreed and tendered to your Lordships after the cases had been prepared.

Appeal allowed ; cross-appeal dismissed.

Solicitors: *Holman Fenwick & Willan* (for the buyers); *Sinclair Roche & Temperley* (for the sellers). *c*

Mary Rose Plummer   Barrister.

R v Pigg *d*

HOUSE OF LORDS
LORD FRASER OF TULLYBELTON, LORD SCARMAN, LORD BRIDGE OF HARWICH, LORD BRANDON OF OAKBROOK AND LORD TEMPLEMAN
17 NOVEMBER, 9 DECEMBER 1982

Jury – Majority verdict – Statement of number of assenting and dissenting jurors – Number of *e* *dissenting jurors – Failure to comply with requirement that number of dissenting jurors be stated by foreman in open court – Validity of verdict – Whether mandatory to state number of dissenting jurors – Whether failure to comply with requirement rendering verdict nugatory – Juries Act 1974, s 17(3).*

At the trial of the appellant on two charges of attempted rape the jury of twelve jurors *f* were unable to reach a unanimous verdict in respect of the first charge. Following a majority direction by the judge the jury then returned a majority verdict of guilty. The clerk of the court asked the foreman of the jury how many agreed on the verdict and how many dissented. The foreman replied, 'Ten agreed'. The clerk then said: 'Ten agreed to two of you.' The judge accepted that verdict. The jury returned a unanimous verdict of guilty in respect of the second charge. The appellant was convicted of both charges *g* and sentenced. He successfully appealed against conviction to the Court of Appeal in respect of the first charge on the grounds that the verdict was void because the foreman had failed to state in open court the number of jurors who dissented, contrary to s 17(3)[a] of the Juries Act 1974 which required that a majority verdict of guilty should not be accepted by the court unless the foreman stated in open court 'the number of jurors who respectively agreed to and dissented from the verdict'. The Crown appealed to the House *h* of Lords.

Held – Although compliance with the requirement of s 17(3) of the 1974 Act that the foreman of the jury state in open court the number of jurors who respectively agreed to and dissented from the verdict was mandatory before a judge could accept a majority verdict of guilty, the precise form of words used by the clerk of the court when asking *j* the foreman the number who agreed and dissented and by the foreman when replying did not constitute an essential part of that requirement. All that was necessary was that the words used by the clerk and the foreman made it clear to an ordinary person how the

a   Section 17(3) is set out at p 58 j, post

jury was divided. Where there were twelve jurors the requirements of s 17(3) were
a satisfied if the foreman of the jury, on being asked how many jurors agreed with the
verdict, answered that ten agreed. It was then a necessary and inevitable inference which
would be obvious to any ordinary person that two disagreed. The Crown's appeal would
accordingly be allowed (see p 57 *f* to *h*, p 62 *a* to *j* and p 63 *b c*, post).
     R v Reynolds [1981] 3 All ER 849 overruled.
     Practice Direction [1967] 3 All ER 137 approved.
b   Decision of the Court of Appeal [1982] 2 All ER 591 reversed.

Notes

For majority verdicts, see 11 Halsbury's Laws (4th edn) paras 317–319, and for cases on
the subject, see 30 Digest (Reissue) 336–337, 513–524.
     For the Juries Act 1974, s 17, see 44 Halsbury's Statutes (3rd edn) 576.

c
Cases referred to in opinions

Practice Direction [1967] 3 All ER 137, [1967] 1 WLR 1198, CA, 30 Digest (Reissue) 336,
515.
R v Barry [1975] 2 All ER 760, [1975] 1 WLR 1190, CA, Digest (Cont Vol D) 573, 524a.
R v Reynolds [1981] 3 All ER 849, CA.

d
Appeal

The Crown appealed by leave of the Court of Appeal against the decision of the Court of
Appeal, Criminal Division (Lord Lane CJ, Talbot and McCowan JJ) ([1982] 2 All ER 591,
[1982] 1 WLR 762) given on 5 February 1982 quashing the conviction of the respondent,
Stephen Pigg, on a charge of attempted rape at the Crown Court at York before his
Honour Judge Bennett QC and a jury on 6 March 1981. The facts are set out in the
e opinion of Lord Brandon.

Peter Charlesworth for the Crown.
Paul Worsley for the respondent.

Their Lordships took time for consideration.
f
9 December. The following opinions were delivered.

LORD FRASER OF TULLYBELTON. My Lords, I have had the advantage of
reading in draft the speech of my noble and learned friend Lord Brandon. I agree with
it, and for the reasons given by him I would answer the certified question in the negative
g and allow the appeal.

LORD SCARMAN. My Lords, I have had the advantage of reading in draft the speech
to be delivered by my noble and learned friend Lord Brandon. I agree with it, and for
the reasons he gives I would allow the Crown's appeal.

h **LORD BRIDGE OF HARWICH.** My Lords, for the reasons given in the speech to
be delivered by my noble and learned friend Lord Brandon, with which I agree, I would
answer the certified question in the negative and allow the appeal.

LORD BRANDON OF OAKBROOK. My Lords, this is an appeal from a judgment
of the Court of Appeal, Criminal Division (Lord Lane CJ, Talbot and McCowan JJ)
pursuant to leave given by that court to the Crown to appeal to your Lordships' House
j on a point of law certified by that court to be of general public importance.
     The point of law so certified is in these terms:

> 'Whether it is necessary in order to comply with the terms of section 17(3) of the
> Juries Act 1974 for the foreman of the jury, having stated in open court the number
> agreeing to the verdict, to go on to state the number of those dissenting.'

The case for the Crown is that the question should be answered in the negative; the case for the respondent is that it should be answered in the affirmative.

My Lords, until 1 October 1967 it was only possible for a defendant tried on indictment in criminal proceedings to be found either guilty or not guilty on the unanimous verdict of the jury. On 27 July 1967 the Criminal Justice Act 1967 was passed, and on 1 October 1967, s 13 of that Act, which provided for the first time for majority verdicts of juries in criminal proceedings, came into force.

Section 13 of the 1967 Act provided:

'(1) Subject to the following provisions of this section, the verdict of a jury in criminal proceedings need not be unanimous if—(a) in a case where there are not less than eleven jurors, ten of them agree on the verdict; and (b) in a case where there are ten jurors, nine of them agree on the verdict; and a verdict authorised by this subsection is hereafter in this section referred to as a "majority verdict".

(2) A court shall not accept a majority verdict of guilty unless the foreman of the jury has stated in open court the number of jurors who respectively agreed to and dissented from the verdict.

(3) A court shall not accept a majority verdict unless it appears to the court that the jury have had not less than two hours for deliberation or such longer period as the court thinks reasonable having regard to the nature and complexity of the case.'

On 31 July 1967, in anticipation of the coming into force of s 13 of the 1967 Act, Lord Parker CJ, presiding over a division of the Court of Appeal, Criminal Division, issued in open court a practice direction for the guidance of judges in the application of that section (see [1967] 3 All ER 137, [1967] 1 WLR 1198). It deals first with the way in which a judge should direct a jury in an effort to obtain from them a unanimous verdict if possible. Later it deals with the situation which may arise when, despite all encouragement to reach a unanimous verdict, and more than one retirement of the jury for that purpose, the jury finally returns into court having found itself unable to do so. In that situation the Practice Direction recommends a specific procedure, in the form of questions by the clerk of the court to the foreman of the jury and answers by the foreman to such questions, to be followed. This procedure is explained in para 3 of the direction ([1967] 3 All ER 137 at 138, [1967] 1 WLR 1198 at 1200):

'When the jury finally return they should be asked (i) Have at least ten (or nine as the case may be) of you agreed on your verdict? If "Yes", (ii) What is your verdict? Please only answer "Guilty" or "Not Guilty". (iii) (a) If "Not Guilty"—accept the verdict without more ado. (b) If "Guilty"—is it the verdict of you all or by a majority? (iv) If "Guilty" by a majority, how many of you agreed to the verdict and how many dissented?'

Section 13 of the 1967 Act was later repealed by s 22(4) and Sch 3 of the Juries Act 1974. In s 17 of the 1974 Act provision was made for majority verdicts of juries in civil, as well as in criminal, proceedings. Because of this, the form of s 17 of the 1974 Act differs in a number of respects from that of the 1967 Act. So far as majority verdicts in criminal proceedings are concerned, however, no alteration of substance was effected by that change of form. In particular s 17(3) of the 1974 Act, which replaced s 13(2) of the 1967 Act, contained only a minor alteration of wording to take account of the creation, between 1967 and 1974, of the Crown Court system.

The essential provisions of s 17 of the 1974 Act, with the changes of form and wording to which I have just referred, are these:

'(1) Subject to subsections (3) and (4) below, the verdict of a jury in proceedings in the Crown Court . . . need not be unanimous if—(a) in a case where there are not less than eleven jurors, ten of them agree on the verdict; and (b) in a case where there are ten jurors, nine of them agree on the verdict . . .

(3) The Crown Court shall not accept a verdict of guilty by virtue of subsection (1) above unless the foreman of the jury has stated in open court the number of jurors who respectively agreed to and dissented from the verdict . . .'

a It is against that background of s 13 of the 1967 Act, the Practice Direction of 31 July 1967 ([1967] 3 All ER 137, [1967] 1 WLR 1198) and s 17 of the 1974 Act, that I turn to the facts and circumstances giving rise to the instant appeal.

Over a number of days preceding 6 March 1981 the respondent, Stephen Pigg, was tried at the Crown Court at Leeds before his Honour Judge Bennett QC and a jury of 12 on an indictment containing a number of counts relating to various sexual and other offences alleged to have been committed by him on 16 September 1980 against two *b* young girls aged 15 and 17 respectively.

For the purposes of this appeal the only material count is count 1 which reads:

'STATEMENT OF OFFENCE

Rape contrary to Section 1(1) Sexual Offences Act 1956.

c
PARTICULARS OF OFFENCE

STEPHEN PIGG on the 16th day of September, 1980 had unlawful sexual intercourse with Beverley Jane Horrill, who at the time of the said intercourse did not consent to it . . .'

d In his summing up the judge correctly directed the jury that it was open to them, in relation to this count, if they were not satisfied that the respondent had committed the full offence of rape as charged, but were nevertheless satisfied that he had committed the lesser offence of attempted rape, to bring in a verdict of not guilty of rape but guilty of attempted rape.

The jury were given by the judge ample directions with regard to the desirability of their reaching a unanimous verdict if possible, and were afforded by him proper time, in *e* accordance with s 17(4) of the 1974 Act, for deliberation in order to achieve that aim. Despite this, the jury were unable to reach a unanimous verdict, after which the judge gave them an impeccable direction with regard to their power to return a majority verdict. The jury then retired for further deliberation, and, on their subsequent return to court, the following exchange took place between the clerk of the court on the one hand and the foreman of the jury on the other:
f
'*The clerk.* Would the foreman please stand? Mr Foreman, would you answer my first question either yes or no only? Members of the jury, have at least ten of you agreed on a verdict? *The foreman.* Yes.

The clerk. On the charge of rape, do you find the accused guilty or not guilty? *The foreman.* Not guilty.

g *The clerk.* On the charge of attempted rape, do you find him guilty or not guilty? *The foreman.* Guilty.

The clerk. Is that the verdict of you all, or by a majority? *The foreman.* By a majority.

The clerk. How many of you agreed to the verdict and how many dissented? *The foreman.* Ten agreed.

h *The clerk.* Ten agreed to two of you.'

According to the transcript the foreman said nothing in reply to the clerk's last statement, either by way of agreement or by way of disagreement.

The judge, having listened to this exchange between the clerk of the court and the foreman of the jury, accepted what had been said by the latter as a majority verdict of guilty of attempted rape on count 1, and he later passed a sentence of five years' *j* imprisonment on the respondent in respect of that offence. The respondent was also convicted and sentenced on certain other counts in the indictment. For the purposes of this appeal, however, nothing turns on these further matters.

The respondent subsequently appealed to the Court of Appeal, Criminal Division (see [1982] 2 All ER 591, [1982] 1 WLR 762) against, inter alia, his conviction of attempted rape on count 1. One of the grounds of appeal against that conviction on which his counsel relied was that what had been said by the foreman of the jury in the exchange between him and the clerk of the court, which I have quoted in full above, did not comply with the requirement for the acceptance by a judge of a majority verdict of guilty prescribed by s 17(3) of the 1974 Act.

The argument for the respondent advanced to the Court of Appeal, Criminal Division, and again to your Lordships on this appeal, was extremely simple, and can be summarised in this way. First, until 1967 a defendant in criminal proceedings tried on indictment could only have been convicted on the unanimous verdict of the jury. Second, the introduction for the first time of majority verdicts by the 1967 Act made a substantial inroad into the protection which the previous need for unanimity had given him. Third, the legislature had been at considerable pains in s 13(2) and (3) of the 1967 Act, and later in s 17(3) and (4) of the 1974 Act, to hedge about the acceptance of a majority verdict of guilty with clear and unambiguous requirements. Fourth, it must be presumed to have been the intention of the legislature, in prescribing those clear and unambiguous requirements, designed expressly for the protection of a defendant, that they should be complied with to the letter. Fifth, in the present case the requirement prescribed by s 17(3) of the 1974 Act had not been complied with to the letter, in that, while the foreman of the jury had stated in open court that ten of the jury agreed to the majority verdict of guilty, he did not also state the number who dissented from it. Sixth, it was immaterial that any numerate person could readily infer, from the foreman's statement that ten of the jury agreed to the verdict, that the number who dissented from it was two, since s 17(3), by its express terms, required the latter number to be stated as well as the former, and did not leave it to be inferred by any process of reasoning, however simple for a numerate person such process might be.

The argument advanced for the Crown, both in the Court of Appeal, Criminal Division, and before your Lordships on this appeal, was also simple. It was that s 17(3) of the 1974 Act should be given a broad, commonsense interpretation as requiring only that any ordinary person in the court, hearing what the foreman of the jury said in answer to the questions put to him by the clerk of the court, should be able to understand without difficulty the number of the jury who agreed with a majority verdict of guilty and the number who dissented from it. It was therefore, immaterial, so far as compliance with the requirement of s 17(3) of the 1974 Act was concerned, that the foreman of the jury in the present case, having stated expressly in open court the number of the jury who agreed to the verdict, did not then go on to state expressly also the number of the jury who dissented from the verdict, but left that number to be inferred by the application of the simplest of arithmetic.

The Court of Appeal, Criminal Division, consisted, as I indicated earlier, of Lord Lane CJ, Talbot and McCowan JJ. The judgment of the court was delivered by Lord Lane CJ. As will become apparent when I quote from the judgment later, the court obviously regarded the ground of appeal in relation to count 1 discussed above as highly technical and wholly without merit; and it is clear that, if it had not considered itself bound by the authority of a previous decision of the Court of Appeal, Criminal Division, to do otherwise, it would have rejected that ground of appeal out of hand. The court did, however, consider itself so bound, as I think it was, and for that reason, and that reason alone, felt obliged to treat the ground of appeal in question as valid, and to quash the respondent's conviction on count 1 accordingly.

The previous decision of the Court of Appeal, Criminal Division, by which that court in the present case considered itself to be bound is R v Reynolds [1981] 3 All ER 849, where the court consisted of Shaw LJ, Tudor Evans and Sheldon JJ. The relevant facts of that case were, for all practical purposes, indistinguishable from those of the present case. Everything went correctly until the crucial exchange between the clerk of the court and the foreman of the jury with regard to the return of a majority verdict of guilty. The exchange which followed in that case took this form (at 850–851):

> 'The clerk. Is that the verdict of you all or by a majority? The foreman. By a majority.
> The clerk. How many agreed and how many opposed? The foreman. Ten agreed.'

Nothing more was said, either by the clerk to the foreman or by the foreman to the clerk.
a   Substantially the same arguments were advanced on either side in that case as have
been advanced in the present case. Judgment was reserved and the judgment of the court
was later delivered by Shaw LJ. In that judgment it was held that the omission by the
foreman of the jury to state expressly in open court, not only the number of the jury
who agreed to the verdict, but also the number who dissented from it, constituted a
failure to comply with the requirement of s 17(3) of the 1974 Act, that, in those
b   circumstances, the judge was wrong to accept the verdict and that the conviction of the
defendant which followed on such acceptance was therefore bad in law and must be
quashed.

Shaw LJ, after quoting s 17(3) of the 1974 Act, said ([1981] 3 All ER 849 at 851):

'The requirement could not be more explicit or stated in more peremptory terms
. . . The requirement that where there is a majority verdict the foreman of a jury
c   should state in open court how many dissented is neither more nor less imperative
than stating how many agreed. It was argued in the present case that, since the
foreman had stated in open court that ten agreed, it was superfluous to go further.
The number who dissented became a matter of the simplest arithmetic. This is a
fallacious argument. As has been said already, s 17, like its precursor, is in
peremptory and mandatory terms. Its insistence on requiring a statement in open
d   court by the foreman of how many dissented is to preclude a verdict being accepted
where ten had agreed but one or both of the remaining jurors had not formed a
final view at all. On hearing the foreman say that two dissented, that one or those
two would have the opportunity of demurring publicly to the foreman's assertion.
Otherwise, the verdict might operate against a defendant when only ten of the jury
had made up their minds one way or the other. The statutory requirements are
e   plainly stated and they must be meticulously followed if a majority verdict is to be
legitimately accepted. It is the duty of the presiding judge to see that they are
followed. In the present case, counsel very properly sought to alert the judge to the
irregularity but his intervention was regrettably ignored. The irregularity is fatal as
no verdict was properly taken, and it is irrelevant to consider the application of the
proviso to s 2(1) of the Criminal Appeal Act 1968.'

f   Lord Lane CJ, in the judgment of the court delivered by him in the present case, after
quoting all or most of the passage from the judgment delivered by Shaw LJ in R v
Reynolds which I have quoted above, made the following comments ([1982] 2 All ER 591
at 595, [1982] 1 WLR 762 at 766–767):

'It seems to us, if we may respectfully say so, that the reasoning in that case was
g   possibly open to a certain amount of doubt. It is said that the requirement of a
statement being made in open court by the foreman of how many dissented is to
preclude a verdict being accepted when ten had agreed but one or both of the
remaining jurors had not formed a final view at all. It seems to us that, if one or two
jurors have not formed a final view at all, they are of necessity dissenting from the
view of the other ten who have made up their minds. Perhaps that is a carping
h   criticism but it occurs to this court that that must be the case, otherwise a jury could
never return a majority verdict if one or two of their number refused to take part in
the discussion at all and refused to express a view. That seems to be a very strange
result and certainly not one which is envisaged by the Juries Act 1974. However, it
is plain that we are bound by that authority and it is plain, accordingly, that there
was a breach of that authority which states it as a mandatory requirement. It may
j   be that the matter should be considered elsewhere but it does seem to us that it is
highly unlikely that Parliament should intend that the validity of a verdict should
depend on the following of a precise formula of words. No doubt it is highly
desirable and necessary that the foreman should himself state in open court that ten
of the jury, in a case where there is a full complement of twelve, are agreed on the
prisoner's guilt. That should be mandatory. But to say that it is other than

discretionary that he should go on to say how many dissented seems to us to be bordering on the absurd. In the event we have no alternative save to quash this *a* conviction.'

My Lords, it is not, and cannot be, in doubt that compliance with the requirement for the acceptance by a judge of a majority verdict of guilty of a jury prescribed by s 17(3) of the 1974 Act is, in general, mandatory in nature. That conclusion is the only possible one having regard to the language of that subsection. If authority for it is needed, it is to be found in *R v Barry* [1975] 2 All ER 760, [1975] 1 WLR 1190, a decision on s 13(2) of the *b* 1967 Act. In that case the judge accepted a majority verdict of guilty without the foreman of the jury even being asked to state, let alone stating, either the number of the jury who agreed to the verdict or the number who dissented from it. On appeal by the defendant to the Court of Appeal, Criminal Division (Roskill LJ, Croom-Johnson and Stocker JJ) it was held that the requirement prescribed by s 13(2) of the 1967 Act, like the requirement prescribed by s 17(3), was mandatory in nature, and that, since that requirement had *c* been wholly disregarded, the verdict could not be allowed to stand.

It is not enough, however, in order to decide the point of law which is before your Lordships, to say simply that compliance with the requirement for the acceptance by a judge of a majority verdict prescribed by s 17(3) of the 1974 Act is mandatory. It is necessary to go on to consider what, on a true construction of that subsection, constitutes or does not constitute compliance with that requirement. With regard to that, it is quite *d* clear that if, in the case of a majority verdict of guilty, the foreman of the jury makes no statement in open court either of the number of jurors who agreed to the verdict, or of the number of those who dissented from it, as in *R v Barry*, the requirement is not complied with and the judge cannot lawfully accept the verdict. On the other hand it seems to me that the criticisms made by Lord Lane CJ in the present case of the reasoning of Shaw LJ in *R v Reynolds* are fully justified. If one or two members of a jury do not *e* agree to a majority verdict of guilty, then, ex hypothesi, they dissent from it: whether they have made up their minds that the defendant is not guilty, or whether, for one reason or another, they have failed or been unable to reach a final conclusion on the matter at all, is immaterial. Their position is perfectly expressed by the well-known saying in the New Testament: 'He that is not with me is against me.'

Once the reasoning of Shaw LJ in *R v Reynolds* is shown to be unsound, the major basis *f* of the decision goes. One is left with what seems to me to be the overwhelming argument, in a case where there are twelve jurors, that, if the foreman of the jury states no more than that the number agreeing to the verdict is ten, it is nevertheless a necessary and inevitable inference, obvious to any ordinary person, that the number dissenting from the verdict is two. True it is that the foreman of the jury has not said so in terms as s 17(3) of the 1974 Act, interpreted literally, requires. In my opinion, however, it is the *g* substance of the requirement prescribed by s 17(3) which has to be complied with, and the precise form of words by which such compliance is achieved, so long as the effect is clear, is not material. In a case where there are twelve jurors, once the foreman has stated in open court that ten of them agreed to the verdict, it becomes immediately obvious to any ordinary person that the remaining two jurors did not agree to the verdict, ie that they dissented from it. I agree entirely with Lord Lane CJ that it would be bordering on *h* the absurd, indeed I would go further and say that it would be absurd, to hold that, in circumstances of the kind just mentioned, the requirement prescribed by s 17(3) of the 1974 Act was not complied with because the foreman did not go on to state in express words that the number of the jury dissenting from the verdict was two.

In short, compliance with the requirement of s 17(3) of the 1974 Act is mandatory before a judge can accept a majority verdict of guilty; but the precise form of words used *j* by the clerk of the court when asking questions of the foreman of the jury, and the precise form of words used by the latter in answer to such questions, as long as they make it clear to an ordinary person how the jury was divided, do not constitute any essential part of that requirement.

a It was not suggested, and could not sensibly have been suggested, that the form of questions by the clerk and answers by the foreman envisaged in the Practice Direction of 31 July 1967 was itself mandatory. It is the terms of the relevant statutory provision, now s 17(3) of the 1974 Act, which govern the matter, and I have already expressed my opinion as to what the correct interpretation of that subsection should be.

b My Lords, for the reasons which I have given, I would give a negative answer to the question of law certified by the Court of Appeal, Criminal Division and allow the Crown's appeal accordingly.

I would only add this, that, while I am of opinion that the question of law as certified should be answered in the negative, and that the form of questions and answers recommended by the Practice Direction is not of itself mandatory, I nevertheless consider that it would be helpful, as a matter of good practice, if that form, or, some form close to it, were to be used in all criminal cases in which the giving by the jury of a majority c verdict of guilty arises.

LORD TEMPLEMAN. My Lords, for the reasons given by my noble and learned friend Lord Brandon, I would answer the certified question in the negative and allow the appeal.

d *Appeal allowed.*

Solicitors: *Iliffe & Edwards*, agents for *Thorpe & Co*, Scarborough (for the Crown); *Campbell Hooper Wright & Supperstone*, agents for *Atha Summers & Co*, Scarborough (for the respondent).

Mary Rose Plummer   Barrister.

Practice Note   *a*

QUEEN'S BENCH DIVISION
LORD LANE CJ, TALBOT AND MCCOWAN JJ
6 DECEMBER 1982

Contempt of court – Publications concerning legal proceedings – Postponement of publication – *b*
Prohibition of publication of name or other matter in connection with proceedings – Orders –
Practice – Contents of orders – Permanent record of orders to be kept – Notice to press –
Responsibility of editors and reporters – Contempt of Court Act 1981, ss 4(2), 11.

LORD LANE CJ made the following statement at the sitting of the court: Under
s 4(2) of the Contempt of Court Act 1981, a court may, where it appears necessary for
avoiding a substantial risk of prejudice to the administration of justice in the proceedings *c*
before it or in any others pending or imminent, order that publication of any report of
the proceedings or part thereof be postponed for such period as the court thinks necessary
for that purpose. Section 11 of the 1981 Act provides that a court may prohibit the
publication of any name or other matter in connection with the proceedings before it
which (having power to do so) it has allowed to be withheld from the public. *d*

It is necessary to keep a permanent record of such orders for later reference. For this
purpose all orders made under s 4(2) must be formulated in precise terms, having regard
to the decision of *R v Horsham Justices, ex p Farquharson* [1982] 2 All ER 269, [1982] QB
762, and orders under both sections must be committed to writing either by the judge
personally or by the clerk of the court under the judge's directions. An order must state
(a) its precise scope, (b) the time at which it shall cease to have effect, if appropriate, and *e*
(c) the specific purpose of making the order.

Courts will normally give notice to the press in some form that an order has been
made under either section of the 1981 Act and court staff should be prepared to answer
any inquiry about a specific case, but it is, and will remain, the responsibility of those
reporting cases, and their editors, to ensure that no breach of any order occurs and the
onus rests with them to make inquiry in any case of doubt. *f*

N P Metcalfe Esq   Barrister.

a Pirelli General Cable Works Ltd v Oscar Faber & Partners (a firm)

HOUSE OF LORDS

LORD FRASER OF TULLYBELTON, LORD SCARMAN, LORD BRIDGE OF HARWICH, LORD BRANDON OF OAKBROOK AND LORD TEMPLEMAN

b 8, 9 NOVEMBER, 9 DECEMBER 1982

Limitation of action – When time begins to run – Actions in tort – Accrual of cause of action – Negligence – Damage – Lapse of time between negligent act and occurrence of damage – Action against consultant engineers in respect of negligent design of chimney – Cracks occurring in chimney more than six years before action brought – Writ issued within six years of date when
c *cracks could reasonably have been discovered – Whether limitation period running from date when damage occurred or when damage could reasonably have been discovered.*

In March 1969 the defendants, a firm of consulting engineers, advised the plaintiffs on the design and erection of a boiler flue chimney at their works. The chimney was *d* installed by specialist sub-contractors. However, the defendants were negligent in the design of the chimney and damage in the form of cracks occurred in the chimney. The damage was not discovered by the plaintiffs until November 1977. In October 1978 the plaintiffs issued a writ against the defendants claiming damages for negligence in relation to the design of the chimney. The judge found that the damage, in the form of cracks at the top of the chimney, could not have occurred later than April 1970. The judge further *e* held that the plaintiffs could not with reasonable diligence have discovered the damage before October 1972 and that the cause of action accrued when the plaintiffs and not the building suffered damage and that the plaintiffs only suffered damage when they discovered or ought with reasonable diligence to have discovered the damage. The judge accordingly held that the cause of action had accrued within the six-year limitation period and that the plaintiffs were entitled to judgment. The defendants appealed to the *f* Court of Appeal contending that the action was time-barred. The Court of Appeal dismissed the appeal and the defendants appealed to the House of Lords.

Held – A cause of action in tort for negligence in the design or workmanship of a building accrued at the date when physical damage occurred to the building, e g by the *g* formation of cracks, as a result of a defect, whether or not the damage could have been discovered with reasonable diligence at that date by the plaintiff. It followed therefore that the plaintiffs' claim was time-barred because the cause of action accrued in April 1970 when damage, in the form of cracks at the top of the chimney, came into existence. The appeal would therefore be allowed (see p 70 *f g* and p 72 *f g* and *j* to p 73 *b*, post).

Cartledge v E Jopling & Sons Ltd [1963] 1 All ER 341 applied.
h *Sparham-Souter v Town and Country Developments (Essex) Ltd* [1976] 2 All ER 65 overruled.

Per curiam. Where the defective property is owned by successive owners, the duty of care of the builder is owed to the owners as a class, and if time runs against one owner it also runs against all his successors in title (see p 71 *j* and p 72 *g* and *j* to p 73 *b*, post).

Davie v New Merton Board Mills Ltd [1959] 1 All ER 346 distinguished.

j

Notes

For when a limitation period begins to run, see 28 Halsbury's Laws (4th edn) paras 622–623, and for cases on the subject, see 32 Digest (Reissue) 486–487, 503–509, 3737–3745, 3842–3869.

Cases referred to in opinions

Anns v Merton London Borough [1977] 2 All ER 492, [1978] AC 728, [1977] 2 WLR 1024,   **a**
HL, Digest (Cont Vol E) 449, 99b.
Bagot v Stevens Scanlan & Co Ltd [1964] 3 All ER 577, [1966] 1 QB 197, [1964] 3 WLR
1162, 7 Digest (Reissue) 458, 2632.
Cartledge v E Jopling & Sons Ltd [1963] 1 All ER 341, [1963] AC 758, [1963] 2 WLR 210,
HL, 32 Digest (Reissue) 503, 3844.
Darley Main Colliery Co v Mitchell (1886) 11 App Cas 127, [1886–90] All ER Rep 449, HL,   **b**
32 Digest (Reissue) 504, 3846.
Davie v New Merton Board Mills Ltd [1959] 1 All ER 346, [1959] AC 604, [1959] 2 WLR
331, HL, 34 Digest (Repl) 253, 1836.
Dennis v Charnwood BC [1982] 3 All ER 486, [1982] 3 WLR 1064, CA.
Dutton v Bognor Regis United Building Co Ltd [1972] 1 All ER 462, [1972] 1 QB 373, [1972]
2 WLR 299, CA, 36(1) Digest (Reissue) 30, 98.   **c**
Forster v Outred & Co [1982] 2 All ER 753, [1982] 1 WLR 86, CA.
Higgins v Arfon BC [1975] 2 All ER 589, [1975] 1 WLR 524, 32 Digest (Reissue) 507, 3864.
Howell v Young (1826) 5 B & C 259, [1824–34] All ER Rep 377, 32 Digest (Reissue) 506,
3857.
Miliangos v George Frank (Textiles) Ltd [1975] 3 All ER 801, [1976] AC 443, [1975] 3 WLR
758, HL, Digest (Cont Vol D) 571, 678b.   **d**
Practice Note [1966] 3 All ER 77, [1966] 1 WLR 1234.
Sparham-Souter v Town and Country Developments (Essex) Ltd [1976] 2 All ER 65, [1976]
QB 858, [1976] 2 WLR 493, CA, 32 Digest (Reissue) 507, 3865.

Appeal
The defendants, Oscar Faber & Partners (a firm), appealed by leave of the Court of Appeal,   **e**
against the decision of the Court of Appeal (Ormrod, Dunn LJJ and Sir Sebag Shaw) on 3
February 1982 dismissing an appeal by the defendants against the judgment of his
Honour Judge Stabb QC sitting as official referee dated 1 August 1980 whereby he gave
judgment for the respondents, the plaintiffs Pirelli General Cable Works Ltd, on the issue
of liability in an action in which the plaintiffs claimed damages for negligence and/or
breach of contract by the defendants as consulting engineers in relation to the design of a   **f**
boiler flue chimney constructed for the plaintiffs in about 1969 at their premises at
Western Esplanade, Southampton. The Court of Appeal dismissed the appeal on the
ground that it was bound by its decision in *Sparham-Souter v Town and Country
Developments (Essex) Ltd* [1976] 2 All ER 65, [1976] QB 858 to hold that the claim in
negligence was not time-barred. Before the trial judge the plaintiffs had conceded that
their claim in contract was time-barred. The facts are set out in the opinion of Lord   **g**
Fraser.

Desmond Wright QC and *Jeremy Storey* for the defendants.
Patrick Garland QC and *John Dyson QC* for the plaintiffs.

Their Lordships took time for consideration.   **h**

9 December. The following opinions were delivered.

LORD FRASER OF TULLYBELTON. My Lords, this appeal raises once again the
question of whether time can begin to run, for the purpose of the Limitation Acts, in an
action founded on negligence in the design or workmanship of a building, at a date   **j**
before damage to the building has been discovered, or ought with reasonable diligence
to have been discovered, by the plaintiff. The writ in this action was issued on 17 October
1978. The appellants (defendants) are a firm of consulting engineers. In or about March
1969 they were engaged by the respondents (plaintiffs) to advise them in relation to the
building of a new services block at the plaintiffs' works at Southampton. The new block

included a chimney about 160 feet high. It was designed and supplied by a nominated
a sub-contractor, now in liquidation, but the judge found that the defendants had accepted
responsibility for the design and his finding is not now challenged. The chimney was
made of pre-cast concrete, and had four flues. Unfortunately the concrete used for the
refractory inner lining was partly made of a relatively new material, called lytag, which
was unsuitable for the purpose. Cracks developed and eventually the chimney had to be
partly demolished and replaced.

b   The plaintiffs originally sued for damages both for breach of contract and for tort, but
they accepted that their claim for breach of contract was time-barred and their claim is
now confined to tort. The judge held that the defendants had been negligent in passing
the design and his decision in that respect also is not challenged. The chimney was built
during June and July 1969. Damage, in the form of cracks near the top of the chimney,
must have occurred not later than April 1970, more than eight years before the writ was
c issued. The damage was not discovered by the plaintiffs until November 1977, and the
judge found that the defendants had not established that the plaintiffs ought, with
reasonable diligence, to have discovered the damage before October 1972, that is six years
before the writ was issued. I shall hereafter use the expression 'date of discoverability' to
mean the date on which the damage was actually discovered, or the date on which it
ought with reasonable diligence to have been discovered, whichever is the earlier. For
d reasons which will appear, the judge held that the date at which the plaintiffs' cause of
action accrued was the date of discoverability and, as that date was not more than six
years before the writ was issued, he held that the action was not time-barred.

All the judge's findings of fact are now accepted by both parties and the sole issue
between them is on the question of law as to the date at which a cause of action accrued.
The plaintiffs maintain that the judge came to the right conclusion on that matter and
e that the action is not time-barred. The defendants maintain that the cause of action
accrued more than six years before the writ was issued. They suggest three possible dates
as the date of accrual. The earliest suggested date is that on which the plaintiffs acted in
reliance on the defendants' advice to instal the chimney, which was bound to be defective
and eventually to fall down unless previously demolished. They did not fix this date
precisely but it must have been between March and June 1969, well outside the limitation
f period. The second suggested date is that on which the building of the chimney was
completed, namely July 1969. The third is that on which cracks occurred, namely April
1970. These three dates are all more than six years before the issue of the writ, which as
already mentioned, was 17 October 1978. If any of them is the correct date, the action is
time-barred.

The Act which applies in this case is the Limitation Act 1939, as amended. It has been
g repealed and replaced by the Limitation Act 1980 but the relevant provision remains
substantially unchanged. It is the following provision in s 2 of the 1939 Act:

> '(1) The following actions shall not be brought after the expiration of six years
> from the date on which the cause of action accrued, that is to say:—(a) actions
> founded on simple contract or on tort . . .'

h
As already mentioned, the findings of fact made by his Honour Judge Stabb QC, sitting
as official referee are now all accepted. He held as a matter of law that he was bound by
the decision of the Court of Appeal in *Sparham-Souter v Town and Country Developments
(Essex) Ltd* [1976] 2 All ER 65, [1976] 1 QB 858 to decide that the action was not time-
barred. He expressed his reason with admirable brevity and lucidity in the following
words:
j
> '. . . I regard the Court of Appeal in *Sparham-Souter* as having laid down that the
> cause of action, in negligence cases such as this, arises when the plaintiff and not the
> building suffers damage, and that the plaintiff only suffers damage when he
> discovers, or ought with reasonable diligence to have discovered, damage to the
> building. This decision seems to have been applied by the House of Lords in *Anns v*

Merton London Borough [1977] 2 All ER 492, [1978] AC 728, and I certainly regard it as binding on me.'

The Court of Appeal also felt bound by its own decision in *Sparham-Souter* and by the decision of this House in *Anns* and it gave leave to appeal to this House without going fully into the law. Ormrod LJ in a short judgment, with which Dunn LJ and Sir Sebag Shaw agreed, explained why the leapfrog procedure had not been used.

My Lords, it was decided by this House in *Cartledge v E Jopling & Sons Ltd* [1963] 1 All ER 341 at 343, [1963] AC 758 at 771–772 that, in the words of Lord Reid:

'. . . a cause of action accrues as soon as a wrongful act has caused personal injury beyond what can be regarded as negligible, even when that injury is unknown to and cannot be discovered by the sufferer; and that further injury arising from the same act at a later date does not give rise to a further cause of action.'

Lord Reid went on, however, to say:

'It appears to me to be unreasonable and unjustifiable in principle that a cause of action should be held to accrue before it is possible to discover any injury and therefore before it is possible to raise any action. If this were a matter governed by the common law I would hold that a cause of action ought not to be held to accrue until either the injured person has discovered the injury or it would be possible for him to discover it if he took such steps as were reasonable in the circumstances. The common law ought never to produce a wholly unreasonable result, nor ought existing authorities to be read so literally as to produce such a result in circumstances never contemplated when they were decided. But the present question depends on statute, the Limitation Act, 1939, and s. 26 of that Act appears to me to make it impossible to reach the result which I have indicated. That section makes special provisions where fraud or mistake is involved: it provides that time shall not begin to run until the fraud has been or could with reasonable diligence have been discovered. Fraud here has been given a wide interpretation but obviously it could not be extended to cover this case. The necessary implication from that section is that, where fraud or mistake is not involved, time begins to run whether or not the damage could be discovered. So the mischief in the present case can only be prevented by further legislation.'

All the other members of the House who took part in deciding that appeal expressed similar reluctance or regret at being obliged to decide as they did. Thus Lord Pearce said that the argument of counsel for the plaintiff in that case—

'would produce a result according with common sense and would avoid the harshness and absurdity of a limitation that in many cases must bar a plaintiff's cause of action before he knows or ought to have known that he has one.'

(See [1963] 1 All ER 341 at 348, [1963] AC 758 at 778.)

Although *Cartledge v Jopling* was a case of personal injuries, the plaintiffs did not dispute that the principle of the decision was applicable in the present case. In that respect the plaintiffs were in my opinion exercising a wise discretion because the decision in *Cartledge v Jopling* depended mainly on the necessary implication from s 26 of the 1939 Act, and s 26 is not limited to claims for personal injuries. Indeed, fraud or mistake are much more likely to be in issue where the plaintiff is claiming for damage to property than for personal injuries. Moreover, Lord Pearce seems to have regarded the two types of claim as being subject to the same rules. In the course of his speech ([1963] 1 All ER 341 at 350, [1963] AC 758 at 780), he relied on the observations of Lord Halsbury in *Darley Main Colliery Co v Mitchell* (1886) 11 App Cas 127 at 132, [1886–90] All ER Rep 449 at 451 as follows:

'No one will think of disputing the proposition that for one cause of action you must recover all damages incident to it by law once and for ever. A house that has

a   received a shock may not at once shew all the damage done to it, but it is damaged
none the less then to the extent that it is damaged, and the fact that the damage only
manifests itself later on by stages does not alter the fact that the damage is there; and
so of the more complex mechanism of the human frame, the damage is done in a
railway accident, the whole machinery is injured, though it may escape the eye or
even the consciousness of the sufferer at the time; the later stages of suffering are
but the manifestations of the original damage done and consequent upon the injury
b   originally sustained.'

Cartledge v Jopling was decided by your Lordships' House on 16 January 1963. Later
the same year Parliament passed the Limitation Act 1963, which received the royal assent
on 31 July 1963, and was evidently passed to deal with the mischief disclosed by Cartledge
v Jopling. It extended the time limit for raising of actions for damages where material
facts of a decisive character were outside the knowledge of the plaintiff until after the
c   action would normally have been time-barred, but it applied only to actions for damages
consisting of or including personal injuries. It must, therefore, be taken that Parliament
deliberately left the law unchanged so far as actions for damages of other sorts was
concerned. It is, therefore, not surprising that until the decision in Sparham-Souter such
authority as exists is to the effect that in cases of latent defects to buildings, the cause of
action accrues and the damage occurs when the defective work is done, even if that was
d   before the date of discoverability. In Bagot v Stevens Scanlan & Co Ltd [1964] 3 All ER 577
at 579, [1966] 1 QB 197 at 203, Diplock LJ said that damage from breach of duty by an
architect in failing to see that the drains for a new house were properly built must have
occurred when they were improperly built. But that was obiter dictum and I mention it
only because it was relied on by Lord Denning MR in Dutton v Bognor Regis United Building
Co Ltd [1972] 1 All ER 462, [1972] 1 QB 373. Dutton was an action by the owner of a
e   building against a local authority for the negligence of one of their servants in inspecting
the foundations of the building. The question of limitation arose only as part of an
argument on behalf of the defendants, to the effect that if they were liable they would be
exposed to endless claims. Lord Denning MR quoted from the opinion of Diplock LJ in
Bagot and said ([1972] 1 All ER 462 at 474, [1972] 1 QB 373 at 396): 'The damage was
done when the foundations were badly constructed'. That was, I think, also obiter
f   dictum. In any event, it would not necessarily identify the beginning of the limitation
period in the present action against the architects, because Lord Denning MR went on to
say that, although the local authority would be protected by a six-year limitation, the
builder might not be because he might be guilty of concealed fraud by covering up his
own bad work, so that the period of limitation would not begin to run until the fraud
was discovered. Sachs LJ ([1972] 1 All ER 462 at 482, [1972] 1 QB 373 at 405)
g   distinguished Bagot, and expressed no concluded view as to when a cause of action in
negligence would arise. Nor did Stamp LJ, the third member of the court.

The obiter dicta of Diplock LJ in Bagot and Lord Denning MR in Dutton were applied
by Mars-Jones J in Higgins v Arfon BC [1975] 2 All ER 589, [1975] 1 WLR 524, when he
held an action against a local authority to be time-barred.

But in Sparham-Souter the Court of Appeal took a different view and said that, where a
h   house is built with inadequate foundations, the cause of action does not accrue until such
time as the plaintiff discovers that the bad work has done damage, or ought, with
reasonable diligence to have discovered it. Lord Denning MR expressly recanted his
dictum in Dutton. The limitation question was tried as a preliminary issue, on which the
facts as pleaded had to be assumed to be true. The latest act of negligence pleaded was
j   less than six years before the issue of the writ, so that, once again, the observations as to
the date on which the cause of action accrued were, strictly speaking, obiter. The main
reason for the view of the Court of Appeal was that, until the owner had discovered the
defective state of the property, he could resell it at a full price, and, if he did so, he would
suffer no damage (see [1976] 2 All ER 65 at 76, 79–80, [1976] QB 858 at 875, 880 per
Roskill and Geoffrey Lane LJJ). Geoffrey Lane LJ contrasted the position of the building
owner in Sparham-Souter with that of the injured person in Cartledge v Jopling and said:

'There is no proper analogy between this situation [sc the situation in *Sparham-Souter*] and the type of situation exemplified in *Cartledge v E Jopling & Sons Ltd* where   *a*
a plaintiff due to the negligence of the defendants suffers physical bodily injury
which at the outset and for many years thereafter may be clinically unobservable.
In those circumstances clearly damage is done to the plaintiff and the cause of action
accrues from the moment of the first injury, albeit undetected and undetectable.
That is not so where the negligence has caused unobservable damage not to the
plaintiff's body but to his house. He can get rid of his house before any damage is   *b*
suffered. Not so with his body.'

My Lords, I find myself with the utmost respect unable to agree with that argument.
It seems to me that there is a true analogy between a plaintiff whose body has, unknown
to him, suffered injury by inhaling particles of dust, and a plaintiff whose house has
unknown to him sustained injury because it was built with inadequate foundations or of
unsuitable materials. Just as the owner of the house may sell the house before the damage   *c*
is discovered, and may suffer no financial loss, so the man with the injured body may die
before pneumoconiosis becomes apparent, and he also may suffer no financial loss. But
in both cases they have a damaged article when, but for the defendant's negligence, they
would have had a sound one. Lord Pearce in *Cartledge v Jopling* [1963] 1 All ER 341 at
349, [1963] AC 758 at 778–779 showed how absurd it would be to hold that the plaintiff's   *d*
knowledge of the state of his lungs could be the decisive factor. He said:

'It would be impossible to hold that while the x-ray photographs are being taken
he cannot yet have suffered any damage to his body but that immediately the result
of them is told to him, he has from that moment suffered damage. It is for the
judge or jury to decide when a man has suffered any actionable harm and in
borderline cases it is a question of degree.'   *e*

It seems to me that exactly the same can rightly be said of damage to property.
I think, with all respect to Geoffrey Lane LJ, that there is an element of confusion
between *damage* to the plaintiff's body and latent *defect* in the foundations of a building.
Unless the defect is very gross, it may never lead to any damage to all to the building. It
would be analogous to a predisposition or natural weakness in the human body which   *f*
may never develop into disease or injury. The plaintiff's cause of action will not accrue
until *damage* occurs, which will commonly consist of cracks coming into existence as a
result of the defect even though the cracks or the defect may be undiscovered and
undiscoverable. There may perhaps be cases where the defect is so gross that the building
is doomed from the start, and where the owner's cause of action will accrue as soon as it
is built, but it seems unlikely that such a defect would not be discovered within the
limitation period. Such cases, if they exist, would be exceptional.   *g*
For the reasons I have tried to explain I do not find the distinction between personal
injuries and damage to property drawn in the *Sparham-Souter* case convincing. I observe
that in *Dennis v Charnwood BC* [1982] 3 All ER 486 at 492, 495, [1982] 3 WLR 1064 at
1071, 1075, Templeman LJ referred to the distinction as 'delicate and surprising' and
Lawton LJ found reconciling *Sparham-Souter* with the reasoning in *Cartledge v Jopling* as   *h*
'difficult'. I agree.
Part of the plaintiffs' argument in favour of the date of discoverability as the date when
the right of action accrued was that that date could be ascertained objectively. In my
opinion that is by no means necessarily correct. In the present case, for instance, the
judge held that the plaintiffs as owners of a new chimney, built in 1969, had no duty to
inspect the top of it for cracks in spring 1970. But if they had happened to sell their
works at that time, it is quite possible that the purchaser might have had such a duty to   *j*
inspect and, if so, that would have been the date of discoverability. That appears to me to
show that the date of discoverability may depend on events which have nothing to do
with the nature or extent of the damage.
Counsel for the plaintiffs argued that in *Anns v Merton London Borough* Lord Wilberforce,
and the other members of this House who agreed with his speech, had approved of the

a observations in *Sparham-Souter* to the effect that the discoverability date was the date when the cause of action accrued. But I do not so read Lord Wilberforce's speech. He simply narrated the conflict between the cases of *Dutton* and *Sparham-Souter* without indicating any preference (see [1977] 2 All ER 492 at 497, [1978] AC 728 at 750). He posed the question 'When does the cause of action arise?' and he answered it as follows ([1977] 2 All ER 492 at 505, [1978] AC 728 at 760):

b   'In my respectful opinion the Court of Appeal was right when, in *Sparham-Souter v Town and Country Developments (Essex) Ltd*, it abjured the view that the cause of action arose immediately on delivery, ie conveyance of the defective house. It can only arise when the state of the building is such that there is present or imminent danger to the health or safety of persons occupying it.'

The only express approval in that passage is to the Court of Appeal's decision that the
c cause of action did *not* arise immediately the defective house was conveyed. His Lordship did not say, nor in my opinion did he imply, that the date of discoverability was the date when the cause of action accrued. The date which he regarded as material (when there is 'present or imminent danger . . . health or safety') was, of course, related to the particular duty resting on the defendants as the local authority, which was different from the duty resting on the builders or architects, but I see nothing to indicate that Lord Wilberforce
d regarded the date of discoverability of the damage as having any relevance. He was not considering the question of discoverability, no doubt because the main issue in the appeal by the time it reached this House was whether any duty at all was incumbent on the local authority (see [1977] 2 All ER 492 at 498, [1978] AC 728 at 751). Three other noble and learned Lords expressed agreement with Lord Wilberforce. Only Lord Salmon delivered a separate reasoned speech and he clearly considered that the cause of action could arise
e before damage was discovered or discoverable, although he recognised that proof might be difficult. He said ([1977] 2 All ER 492 at 514, [1978] AC 728 at 771):

    'Whether it is possible to prove that damage to the building had occurred *four years before it manifested itself* is another matter, but it can only be decided by evidence.' (My emphasis.)

f Neither Lord Salmon nor the other Lords seem to have considered that they were dissenting from the majority view on that matter. In these circumstances I do not think that the majority in *Anns* are to be taken as having approved the discoverability test applied in *Sparham-Souter*.

There is one other matter on which I am, with the utmost respect, unable to agree with the reasoning in *Sparham-Souter*. Both Roskill and Geoffrey Lane LJJ held that the
g earliest moment at which time could begin to run against each successive owner of the defective property was when he bought, or agreed to buy, it (see [1976] 2 All ER 65 at 75, 79, [1976] QB 858 at 875, 880). If that is right, it would mean that if the property happened to be owned by several owners in quick succession, each owning it for less than six years, the date when action would be time barred might be postponed indefinitely. Indeed, Geoffrey Lane LJ expressly recognised that the period of limitation might be
h postponed indefinitely, and he accepted that result as—

    'less obnoxious than the alternative, which is that a house owner may be deprived of his remedy against a negligent defendant by the arbitrary imposition of a limitation period which started to run before the damage caused by the defendant could even be detected.'

j (See [1976] 2 All ER 65 at 80, [1976] QB 858 at 881.)
    While I see the force of that view I cannot agree that it is one which is open to me to accept. I think the true view is that the duty of the builder and of the local authority is owed to owners of the property as a class, and that if time runs against one owner, it also runs against all his successors in title. No owner in the chain can have a better claim than his predecessor in title. The position of successive owners of property is, in my opinion,

to be contrasted with that of workers in a case such as *Davie v New Merton Board Mills Ltd* [1959] 1 All ER 346, [1959] AC 604, where a separate duty of care is owed by the maker *a* of a machine to each worker who uses it, and a new worker is not a successor in title to a former holder of his job.

Counsel for the defendants submitted that the fault of his clients in advising on the design of the chimney was analogous to that of a solicitor who gives negligent advice on law, which results in the client suffering damage and a right of action accruing when the client acts on the advice (see *Howell v Young* (1826) 5 B & C 259, [1824–34] All ER Rep *b* 377 and *Forster v Outred & Co* [1982] 2 All ER 753, [1982] 1 WLR 86). It is not necessary for the present purpose to decide whether that submission is well founded, but as at present advised, I do not think it is. It seems to me that, except perhaps where the advice of an architect or consulting engineer leads to the erection of a building which is so defective as to be doomed from the start, the cause of action accrues only when physical *c* damage occurs to the building. In the present case that was April 1970 when, as found by the judge, cracks must have occurred at the top of the chimney, even though that was before the date of discoverability. I am respectfully in agreement with Lord Reid's view expressed in *Cartledge v Jopling* that such a result appears to be unreasonable and contrary to principle, but I think the law is now so firmly established that only Parliament can alter it. Postponement of the accrual of the cause of action until the date of discoverability may involve the investigation of facts many years after their occurrence (see, for example, *d* *Dennis v Charnwood*) with possible unfairness to the defendant, unless a final longstop date is prescribed, as in ss 6 and 7 of the Prescription and Limitation (Scotland) Act 1973. If there is any question of altering this branch of the law, this is, in my opinion, a clear case where any alteration should be made by legislation, and not by judicial decision, because this is, in the words of Lord Simon in *Miliangos v George Frank (Textiles) Ltd* [1975] 3 All ER 801 at 823, [1976] AC 443 at 480, 'a decision which demands a far wider *e* range of review than is available to courts following our traditional and valuable adversary system—the sort of review compassed by an interdepartmental committee.' I express the hope that Parliament will soon take action to remedy the unsatisfactory state of the law on this subject.

I would hold that the cause of action accrued in spring 1970 when damage, in the form of cracks near the top of the chimney, must have come into existence. I avoid *f* saying that cracks 'appeared' because that might seem to imply that they had been observed at that time. The action is, therefore, time-barred and I would allow the appeal. We were told that parties had reached agreement as to costs, and there should therefore be no order on that matter.

g

LORD SCARMAN. My Lords, I agree that the law is now as set out in the speech of my noble and learned friend Lord Fraser. But it is no matter for pride. It must be, as Lord Reid said in *Cartledge v E Jopling & Sons Ltd* [1963] 1 All ER 341, [1961] AC 758 and quoted by my noble and learned friend in his speech, unjustifiable in principle that a cause of action should be held to accrue before it is possible to discover any injury (or damage). A law which produces such a result, as Lord Pearce, also quoted by my noble *h* and learned friend, said in the same case, is harsh and absurd.

It is tempting to suggest that, in accordance with the practice statement 26 July 1966 (see *Note* [1966] 3 All ER 77, [1966] 1 WLR 1234), the House might consider it right to depart from the decision in *Cartledge v Jopling*. But the reform needed is not the substitution of a new principle or rule of law for an existing one but a detailed set of provisions to replace existing statute law. The true way forward is not by departure from *j* precedent but by amending legislation. Fortunately reform may be expected, since the Lord Chancellor has already referred the problem of latent damage and date of accrual of cause of action to his Law Reform Committee.

Accordingly, for the reasons given by my noble and learned friend, I would allow the appeal.

LORD BRIDGE OF HARWICH. My Lords, for the reasons given in the speech of
a my noble and learned friend Lord Fraser, with which I fully agree, I would allow this
appeal.

LORD BRANDON OF OAKBROOK. My Lords, I have had the advantage of
reading in advance the speech prepared by my noble and learned friend Lord Fraser. I
agree with it, and for the reasons which he gives I would allow the appeal.

b
LORD TEMPLEMAN. My Lords, for the reasons given by my noble and learned
friend Lord Fraser, I too would allow the appeal.

Appeal allowed.

c Solicitors: *Beale & Co* (for the defendants); *Herbert Oppenheimer Nathan & Vandyk* (for the
plaintiffs).

Mary Rose Plummer   Barrister.

d

Trustees of Henry Smith's Charity v Willson and others

e COURT OF APPEAL, CIVIL DIVISION
ORMROD, GRIFFITHS AND SLADE LJJ
10, 12, 28 MAY 1982

*Rent restriction – Subtenancy – Unlawful subtenancy – Tenant covenanting not to let premises
for more than six months without landlord's consent – Tenant subletting premises on periodic
f monthly tenancy for indefinite period – Whether subtenancy for a period exceeding six months –
Whether landlord's consent required – Rent Act 1977, s 137.*

*Rent restriction – Possession – Breach of covenant – Waiver – Statutory tenant unlawfully
subletting premises – Landlord's agent knowing of unlawful subletting but sending demand for
rent to statutory tenant – Whether rent demand amounting to waiver of landlord's right to seek
g possession for breach of covenant – Rent Act 1977, s 3(3).*

By a lease the landlords demised a flat for a term of eight years from 29 September 1971
at a rent specified in the lease. The lease contained a covenant by the tenant not to assign
or underlet or otherwise part with possession of the premises without the landlords'
written consent but with the proviso that the landlords' consent was not required for a
h furnished subletting 'for a term not exceeding six calendar months in any one year'. In
April 1977 the then tenant assigned the residue of the term to the first defendant's wife.
A few days before the expiry of the contractual term on 29 September 1979 the wife
lawfully assigned the residue of the lease to her husband, the first defendant. Accordingly,
on the expiry of the contractual term the first defendant became a statutory tenant of the
flat within the Rent Act 1977. On 6 June 1980 the first defendant, without obtaining the
j landlords' consent, entered into a transaction with the third defendant by which, in
return for the payment of a substantial premium, he sublet the flat and furnishings to
the third defendant at a rent of £75 a month payable in advance on the first day of each
month. The first defendant indicated to the third defendant that the flat was now hers
and that he had no intention of returning to it. On the same day the third defendant and
the second defendant took possession of the flat. On 18 September 1980 the landlord's

agents became aware of the circumstances in which the second and third defendants
were occupying the flat and took the view that their occupation was unlawful. However, *a*
despite instructions being issued within the firm of agents not to demand or accept any
further rent for the flat, the firm sent a rent demand on 22 September addressed to the
first defendant's wife at the flat (mistakenly believing her still to be the tenant) demanding
the rent due on 29 September for the preceding quarter and also seven days' future rent.
There was no evidence that the demand ever reached the first defendant. In February
1981 the landlords commenced possession proceedings against all three defendants, *b*
contending that they were entitled to possession against the first defendant because his
statutory tenancy had ceased on 6 June 1980 and that they were entitled to possession
against the second and third defendants because (i) the subletting to the third defendant
was unlawful since the first defendant, having ceased to occupy the flat on 6 June 1980,
had no title to make the subletting and (ii) the subletting was in breach of the covenant
in the lease (which it was conceded was a contractual term of the lease imported into the *c*
first defendant's statutory tenancy). The judge made an order for possession against the
first defendant but refused to make possession orders against the second and third
defendants because, although he held that the third defendant's subtenancy was unlawful,
he further held that the landlords had waived that unlawfulness by sending the rent
demand on 22 September 1980, with the consequence that the third defendant was a
lawful subtenant within s 137(2)*ᵃ* of the 1977 Act who was entitled under that subsection *d*
to be treated as the landlords' tenant. The landlords appealed. The second and third
defendants submitted (i) that the subletting was a lawful subletting within s 137(2)
because, being a periodic, monthly subletting, it was for 'a term not exceeding six . . .
months in any one year', within the proviso to the covenant in the lease, and therefore
the landlords' consent was not required, and (ii) alternatively, that the demand for rent
sent on 22 September 1980 was an unequivocal act affirming the first defendant's *e*
statutory tenancy which thereby converted the third defendant's subtenancy into a
lawful tenancy within s 137(2).

Held – The landlords' appeal would be allowed for the following reasons—
   (1) Since the purpose of the covenant and proviso thereto in the lease was to restrict
the lessee's right to sublet the flat without consent to a subletting for the short and *f*
definite period of six months, a subletting fell within the proviso only if it was a
subletting for a fixed term of not more than six months. Accordingly, the proviso did
not include a periodic, monthly subtenancy for an indefinite period. It followed that the
landlords' consent to the subletting had been required and that at its inception the
subletting had been an unlawful subletting which did not come within s 137(2) of the
1977 Act (see p 81 *g h*, p 82 *d* to *j*, p 86 *g* to *j*, p 87 *d e* and *j* and p 88 *a*, post); *Hammond v* *g*
Farrow [1904] 2 KB 332 considered.
   (2) Furthermore, since by virtue of s 3(3)*ᵇ* of the 1977 Act a statutory tenancy
continued until it was terminated by notice by the tenant or by a court order, and since
the landlord was entitled to demand rent so long as the statutory tenancy continued, a
mere demand for future rent made with knowledge that the statutory tenancy had in
fact ceased and that the statutory tenant had granted an unlawful subtenancy did not *h*
amount to an election by the landlord to treat the subtenancy as lawful, since the landlord
was entitled to demand rent from the statutory tenant until the statutory tenancy was
properly terminated. In any event such a demand was at most an equivocal act. It
followed that the demand for future rent by the plaintiffs' agents on 22 September 1980
was not an unequivocal affirmation of the first defendant's statutory tenancy or of the
lawfulness of the third defendant's subtenancy and did not amount to a waiver by the *j*
landlords of their right to claim subsequently that the statutory tenancy had been
terminated on 6 June 1980 or that the subtenancy was unlawful. Moreover, since there
was no evidence that the demand had ever reached the first defendant, who was the

a   Section 137(2) is set out on p 77 *b*, post
b   Section 3(3) is set out at p 85 *h*, post

statutory tenant, it could not in any event have sufficed to support such a waiver (see
a p 85 a to d and g to p 86 j, p 87 g and j and p 88 a, post); Carter v Green [1950] 1 All ER
627 and David Blackstone Ltd v Burnetts (West End) Ltd [1973] 3 All ER 782 distinguished.

Per Ormrod LJ. Section 137 of the 1977 Act clearly contemplates that a statutory
tenant can validly sublet the whole of a dwelling house and create the legal relationship
of a statutory tenancy between the landlord and the subtenant (see p 87 a, post).

b **Notes**
For statutory tenancies, see 27 Halsbury's Laws (4th edn) paras 591–593, for the lawfulness
of a subtenancy granted by a statutory tenant, see ibid para 695, and for cases on the
subject, see 31(2) Digest (Reissue) 1025–1030, 8123–8174.

For the Rent Act 1977, ss 3, 137, see 47 Halsbury's Statutes (3rd edn) 399, 539.

c **Cases referred to in judgments**
Blackstone (David) Ltd v Burnetts (West End) Ltd [1973] 3 All ER 782, [1973] 1 WLR 1487,
    Digest (Cont Vol D) 587, 6997a.
Carter v Green [1950] 1 All ER 627, [1950] 2 KB 76, CA, 31(2) Digest (Reissue) 1101,
    8558.
Central Estates (Belgravia) Ltd v Woolgar (No 2) [1972] 3 All ER 610, [1972] 1 WLR 1048,
d   CA, 31(2) Digest (Reissue) 827, 6866.
Hammond v Farrow [1904] 2 KB 332, DC, 31(1) Digest (Reissue) 124, 1017.
Milmo v Carreras [1946] 1 All ER 288, [1946] KB 306, CA, 31(1) Digest (Reissue) 183,
    1531.
Muspratt v Johnston [1963] 2 All ER 339, [1963] 2 QB 383, [1963] 2 WLR 1153, CA, 31(2)
    Digest (Reissue) 1105, 8580.
e Oak Property Co Ltd v Chapman [1947] 2 All ER 1, [1947] KB 886, CA, 31(2) Digest
    (Reissue) 1101, 8556.
Roe v Russell [1928] 2 KB 117, [1928] All ER Rep 262, CA, 31(2) Digest (Reissue) 1029,
    8167.

Appeal
f The plaintiffs, the Trustees of Henry Smith's Charity, the landlords of premises known
as Flat 9, 11 Onslow Gardens, South Kensington, London SW7, appealed against the
judgment of his Honour Judge Corcoran given in the West London County Court on 18
November 1981 dismissing the plaintiffs' claim for possession of the premises against the
second and third defendants, Robert Spraggon and Pamela Rosemary Blakeney but
granting an order for possession against the first defendant, Simon James Willson. The
g facts are set out in the judgment of Slade LJ.

A Seys Llewellyn for the plaintiffs.
John Male for the second and third defendants.
The first defendant did not appear.

h   Cur adv vult

28 May. The following judgments were delivered.

SLADE LJ (giving the first judgment at the invitation of Ormrod LJ). This is an appeal
by the trustees of Henry Smith's Charity against an order made by his Honour Judge
j Corcoran on 19 November 1981 in the West London County Court in a possession action.
The appellants were the plaintiffs in the proceedings. The three defendants were
respectively Mr Willson, Mr Spraggon and Mrs Blakeney. The action concerned premises
known at Flat 9, 11 Onslow Square, South Kensington, London, which I will call 'the
flat'. By his order the judge made an order for possession of the flat in favour of the
plaintiffs against Mr Willson, but refused to make an order for possession in their favour

against Mr Spraggon and Mrs Blakeney. The plaintiffs now appeal against this refusal. Though the notice of appeal is addressed to all three defendants, Mr Willson has not been *a* represented before this court; Mr Spraggon and Mrs Blakeney are the only effective defendants and have appeared by the same counsel.

The relevant facts are more or less common ground and, I think, may be sufficiently summarised as follows. By a lease dated 13 January 1972 (the lease), the trustees of Henry Smith's Charity demised the flat to a Mr Neale for a term of eight years from 29 September 1971 at the rent therein specified, which was to be payable quarterly in *b* arrears. By cl 3(24) of the lease the tenant covenanted with the landlords in the following terms:

'Not to assign mortgage charge underlet or otherwise part with possession of the whole of the premises to any person or persons without the previous consent in writing of the landlords or their Treasurer for the time being (such consent not to be unreasonably withheld in the case of any respectable and responsible person or *c* persons), PROVIDED that no such consent shall be required for a furnished sub-letting for a term not exceeding six calendar months in any one year.'

Clause 3(25) obliged the tenant, inter alia, within one calendar month of any assignment or subletting of the tenant's interest to give particulars thereof and to produce the instrument effecting the same to the landlords. Clause 5 contained a common form *d* proviso for re-entry in the event of non-payment of rent or any breach of any of the tenant's other covenants.

On 29 April 1977 the residue of the term was assigned to Mrs Willson, the first defendant's wife. A few days before 29 September 1979 Mrs Willson assigned the residue of the term to Mr Willson. It is not disputed that the plaintiffs gave their licence to this assignment, though the correspondence suggests that formal notification of it was not *e* given to them until about 19 September 1980. The validity of the assignment has not been questioned on this appeal.

On 29 September 1979, the contractual term under the lease having expired, Mr Willson became a 'statutory tenant' of the flat, within the meaning of s 2 of the Rent Act 1977 (the 1977 Act).

At this point in this judgment, I think it may assist clarity if I embark on a brief *f* excursion into the law. The nature of the right or interest of a statutory tenant is 'that of a personal right of possession on the terms partly of the original contract of tenancy and partly derived from the statutes': see *Oak Property Co Ltd v Chapman* [1947] 2 All ER 1 at 3, [1947] KB 886 at 894 per Somervell LJ, who was in that case delivering the judgment of the court prepared by Evershed LJ.

It follows from the personal nature of a statutory tenancy that it cannot be assigned *g* (see for example the *Oak Property* case [1947] 2 All ER 1 at 3, [1947] KB 886 at 894; *Roe v Russell* [1928] 2 KB 117 at 126, 134, 139, [1928] 2 All ER Rep 262 at 264, 267–268, 270 per Scrutton, Sargant LJJ and Eve J). Paragraph 13(1) of Sch 1 to the 1977 Act contains a provision which enables an agreement in writing to be made between a statutory tenant and a person proposing to occupy the house with the effect that the new occupier is deemed to be the statutory tenant of the dwelling as from the agreed transfer date. But *h* para 13(2) specifically provides that such an agreement shall not have effect unless the landlord is a party thereto. Furthermore para 14(1) renders it an offence for any person to require the payment of any pecuniary consideration for entering into such an agreement.

Somervell LJ in the *Oak Property* case [1947] 2 All ER 1 at 3–4, [1947] KB 886 at 894 observed that, as a matter of principle and logic, it would appear at first sight necessarily *j* to follow that a subtenancy, whether of the whole or any part of the premises, granted by a statutory tenant must, no less than an assignment, fail to confer on the grantee any such estate in the property. As he pointed out in that case, however, such a wide proposition would not be correct in law. It is well established by decisions of this court, including the *Oak Property* case itself, and *Roe v Russell* [1928] 2 KB 117, [1928] 2 All ER

Rep 262 that a 'lawful' subletting of *part of* the demised premises, by a person who
a himself retains the status of a statutory tenant at the date of the subletting, is effectual to
confer on the subtenant the rights specified in what is now s 137(2) of the 1977 Act. This
subsection provides:

> 'Where a statutorily protected tenancy of a dwelling-house is determined, either
> as a result of an order for possession or for any other reason, any sub-tenant to whom
> the dwelling-house or any part of it has been lawfully sublet shall, subject to this
b > Act, be deemed to become the tenant of the landlord on the same terms as if the
> tenant's statutorily protected tenancy has continued.'

Whether this subsection is ever capable of affording protection to a sublessee of the
whole demised premises is a more doubtful question, to which I shall briefly revert later
in this judgment. I now resume the narrative of facts.
c   On 6 June 1980 Mr Willson entered into a transaction with Mrs Blakeney in relation
to the flat. So far as it was evidenced by any documents, this transaction was recorded
only in a letter dated 6 June 1980 written by Mr Willson to Mrs Blakeney, and in an
inventory of furniture referred to in that letter. The letter read:

> 'Dear Mrs. Blakeney,
d >   I confirm that I am happy to offer you the entire accommodation of the furnished
> flat at no. 9, 11 Onslow Square, SW7, at a newly registered rent of £75·00 per
> calendar month, plus rates, service charge, electricity, gas and telephone. The rent is
> to be paid to me in advance on the first day of each month. You may move into this
> flat on June 6th 1980. You will not be allowed to sublet or keep pets, except for a
> budgerigar. If you wish to accept this offer and move into the flat on the above
e > terms, please sign the attached copy of this letter and return it to me. I would also
> like you to sign an inventory which I am preparing.
>
> > Yours sincerely,
> > S. WILLSON'

It is now common ground that Mrs Blakeney also signed a copy of this letter. On the
face of it, this letter embodied the whole transaction. But this was far from the case. First,
f possibly appreciating the legal restrictions on his rights as a statutory tenant which I have
already mentioned, Mr Willson did not in his letter refer to the fact that Mrs Blakeney
had paid, or was to pay him the sum of £13,450 as consideration for the transaction.
Second, the letter did not reflect the fact that Mr Willson told her that he had no intention
to return to the flat and was giving up his occupation forever. I refer to some important
findings of fact made by the judge in this context, when he said as follows:
g
> 'I think it is important to rehearse what the third defendant said she was told by
> the first defendant when he agreed to let the flat to her and at and before the time
> she paid him the £13,450. She asked the first defendant: "If I wish to sell this flat in
> years to come would it be all right?"; to which she says the first defendant replied:
> "It is your flat. You do what you like." Therefore she said: "I thought I had the flat.
h > I thought it was mine to do what I wanted with it. We [she and her friend the
> second defendant] thought we had the place ad infinitum paying all that money.
> We thought it was his place to sell to us." Further, she says: "The first defendant said
> he had no intention to return to it; none whatsoever. From the moment he signed
> the agreement he was giving up occupation for ever." The third defendant also said
> that prior to her making the agreement with the first defendant on 6 June 1980 she
j > had no contact with the plaintiffs or their managing agents. The first defendant did
> not inform her, nor did she ask him, the name of his landlords or of the terms on
> which he held the lease of the flat or whether he was a contractual or a statutory
> tenant. He did not show her, nor did she ask to see the lease or agreement under
> which he held the flat as a tenant. She says she made no such inquiries nor did she
> consult a solicitor because she employed an estate agent and thought that would be

enough. Perhaps significantly she said: "I understand that I had purchased the statutory tenancy of the flat." That indicates someone must have disclosed to her the *a* fact that the first defendant was a statutory tenant. She also said that the first defendant said he had no intention to return to the flat and was giving up occupation "forever". Had she taken advice or been properly advised that should have set the alarm bells ringing. I accept the third defendant's evidence as to all these matters. There is no evidence to contradict it and further, it seems to be more consistent with the probabilities of the situation than not.'   *b*

None of these findings of fact have been challenged on the present appeal.

On 6 June 1980 Mr Willson gave up possession of the flat. On the same day Mrs Blakeney took possession of it with Mr Spraggon. He was not a party to the arrangement with Mr Willson. It is common ground that his defence to this appeal must stand or fall with that of Mrs Blakeney.   *c*

The judge made the following further findings of fact:

'I find on the evidence that the first defendant had no intention to return to the flat at least on or after 6 June 1980 and the probability is he had formed such intention earlier than this and did not leave any visible signs of an intention to return. He left some furniture in the flat. It was a furnished subletting. Against that however, he sublet the whole at a very high premium of £13,450 and at a rent *d* of £75 per month and in addition the third defendant had to pay the first defendant the rates and service charges. At that time the first defendant's rent was £132·50 a quarter and the service charge was £23·75. The first defendant did not retain any part for his personal belongings or clothing; he gave no indication that the third defendant was to be a "caretaker" for him or that he intended to return to occupy it as his residence within a reasonable time. He did not, for example, give written *e* notice to the third defendant that possession might be recovered under the Rent Act 1977, Sch 15, Case 11, nor is there any evidence on which the court may consider it just and equitable to dispense with that requirement, eg a subletting for a fixed term (eg 6 months) with a clear indication by the first defendant that he would require possession at the expiration of the term. In any event the first defendant has not brought proceedings for possession against the third defendant nor has he filed *f* a defence or appeared in these proceedings. I find also on the evidence that the first defendant did not seek or obtain the consent of the plaintiffs to sublet the flat to the third defendant and contrary to cl 3(25) of the original lease and he did not notify them of the subletting.'

At all material times the plaintiffs' properties in Onslow Square and the neighbourhood *g* were managed by Messrs Cluttons. A partner in that firm, Mr Cullum, had overall responsibility for that management. Soon after 6 June 1980, Messrs Cluttons became aware of the occupation of the flat by Mrs Blakeney and Mr Spraggon. It is, however, common ground that until 18 September 1980 the plaintiffs had no sufficient knowledge of the circumstances of the occupation to support a waiver of any unlawfulness which it might involve. On 18 September 1980, Mr Cullum had a meeting with Mr Willson, *h* with a view to clarifying the position. It is also common ground that, at that meeting, the plaintiffs through Mr Cullum acquired knowledge sufficient to support a waiver of any unlawfulness involved in the occupation, if their subsequent acts sufficed to constitute a waiver.

As a result of what he learned at this meeting, Mr Cullum considered that an immediate instruction should be given to his firm not to demand or accept any further *j* rent in respect of the flat for the time being. He gave such instruction on 19 September 1980. However it seems that it did not immediately reach the person in his firm actually responsible for sending out the rent demands. On 22 September 1980, a demand for the rent for the flat due on 29 September in respect of the preceding quarter, and also certain accumulated arrears, was sent by Cluttons. The judge described it as having been sent 'to the first defendant'. In fact, as the demand itself shows, it was addressed to Mrs Willson

rather than Mr Willson. The reason for this would appear to be the delay in notifying
a the plaintiffs of the assignment of the term in favour of Mr Willson. The judge seems to
have assumed that this demand in due course reached Mr Willson, but it is common
ground that there is no evidence that it did.

The plaintiffs primary contention is and has at all material times been that the so-
called underletting in favour of Mrs Blakeney was wholly unlawful. In case this primary
contention was wrong, however, and having regard to the form of the proviso to cl 3(24)
b of the lease, the plaintiffs allowed six months from 6 June 1980 to elapse before issuing
proceedings for possession.

On 15 January 1981 the plaintiffs' solicitors wrote to Mr Willson's solicitors referring
to their application to register the assignment to him. They said that it had come to the
plaintiffs' attention that the flat had been illegally sublet in breach of cl 3(24) of the lease
and that, in the circumstances, they were not prepared to entertain any application for
c registration of the assignment to Mr Willson. They gave warning of the plaintiffs'
intention to institute proceedings. Proceedings were duly instituted by them against all
three defendants. On 19 November 1981 the judge gave his decision and made an order
of the nature which I have outlined at the beginning of this judgment.

Before him, the plaintiffs contended that they were entitled to possession of the flat
against Mr Willson on the grounds, inter alia, that his statutory tenancy ceased on 6 June
d 1980, when he ceased to occupy the flat as his residence, and that he had sublet the flat to
Mrs Blakeney without obtaining their consent. Section 98(1) of the 1977 Act precludes
the court from making an order for possession of a dwelling house which is still subject
to a statutory tenancy—

e
> 'unless the court considers it reasonable to make such an order and either—(a) the
> court is satisfied that suitable alternative accommodation is available for the tenant
> or will be available for him when the order in question takes effect, or (b) the
> circumstances are as specified in any of the Cases in Part 1 of Schedule 15 to this
> Act.'

Case 6, so far as material for present purposes, provides as follows:

f
> 'Where, without the consent of the landlord, the tenant has at any time after . . .
> (d) 8th December 1965, in the case of any other tenancy, assigned or sublet the
> whole of the dwelling-house or sublet part of the dwelling-house, the remainder
> being already sublet.'

The judge made an immediate order for possession against Mr Willson, on the grounds
that he no longer occupied the flat as his residence and further or alternatively under
g Case 6 on the grounds that Mr Willson had sublet the whole flat without the landlords'
consent and that in all the circumstances it was reasonable to do so. This part of his
decision is not challenged.

Before him the defence of Mrs Blakeney and Mr Spraggon to the plaintiffs' claim was
founded on s 137(2) of the 1977 Act, which I have already quoted. The definition of
'statutorily protected tenancy' in sub-s (4) of that section includes a statutory tenancy. It
h was submitted in effect to the judge, as it has been submitted to this court, that though
Mr Willson's statutory tenancy has been determined, Mrs Blakeney is a 'sub-tenant to
whom the dwelling-house . . . has been lawfully sublet', within the meaning of s 137(2),
and that accordingly, by virtue of the subsection, she is deemed to have become the
tenant of the plaintiffs on the same terms as if Mr Willson's statutory tenancy had
continued.

These submissions are entirely founded on the contention that there has been a 'lawful'
subletting. Before this court, and I understand also before the court below, counsel for
the plaintiffs sought to refute this contention essentially on three grounds, namely (1)
that, on the evidence, Mr Willson had already lost his status as statutory tenant before he
entered into the transaction with Mrs Blakeney, because he had already abandoned the
flat as his home, (2) that, even if Mr Willson had not lost his status as statutory tenant
before he entered into this transaction, a statutory tenant, such as Mr Willson was, cannot

ever grant an effective subtenancy of *the whole* of the demised premises, (3) that, even if
the first two of those grounds were ill-founded, any subletting of the flat in favour of Mrs **a**
Blakeney was on any footing unlawful, because it was in breach of cl 3(24) of the lease.

The judge rejected the third of these submissions, having regard to the construction
which he placed on the proviso to cl 3(24). Nevertheless he came to the following
conclusion:

> 'The statutory tenant, by ceasing to occupy the whole premises as his residence **b**
> with no intention of returning and leaving no visible signs of such an intention, had
> no right of possession of or interest in the premises and had no rights as a statutory
> tenant. The first defendant had no title to pass, therefore the third defendant cannot
> be said to have derived title under the statutory tenant. Accordingly in my judgment
> the "sub-tenancy" is not a "lawful sub-tenancy" and is ineffectual in law and legally
> ineffective to confer on the "sub-tenant" any right under s 137(2).'
>   **c**

For these reasons, if he had not found for them on the subsequent issue of waiver, the
judge would have decided the case against Mrs Blakeney and Mr Spraggon.

It is not entirely clear to me whether he was accepting the first or second of the three
submissions made on behalf of the plaintiffs in this context. In relation to the first of
them, there is an element of ambiguity in his findings. For example, early in his
judgment, having said that about 6 June the first defendant sublet the whole of the flat **d**
to the third defendant, he went on to say that the first defendant 'either had or thereupon
ceased to occupy the flat as his residence.' Similarly at a later point in his judgment, he
expressed the view that the first defendant lost his status 'at or before' the time when he
sublet the whole of the flat. In relation to the second of the three submissions he pointed
to the views of writers and editors of well-known textbooks on the Rent Acts, who appear
to consider that a statutory tenant cannot ever grant an effective subtenancy of the whole **e**
of the demised premises (see, for example, Megarry *The Rent Acts* (10th edn, 1967) p 455;
Woodfall's Law of Landlord and Tenant (28th edn, 1978) vol 3, para 3-0207; 27 Halsbury's
Laws (4th edn) para 695, n 1).

I think that substantial support for these views of the textbook writers is to be gathered
from the decisions of this court in *Roe v Russell* [1928] 2 KB 117, [1928] 2 All ER Rep 262
and *Oak Property Co Ltd v Chapman* [1947] 2 All ER 1, [1947] KB 886, to which the judge **f**
referred. Nevertheless, as he appreciated, I do not think that these cases can be regarded
as direct authority on the point. The conceptual difficulties involved in treating a person
as deriving a valid title as subtenant from a statutory tenant, when the tenant is giving
up possession of the whole, as opposed to only part of, the premises are all the greater.
For an essential feature of a statutory tenancy is that it continues only 'if and so long as
[the tenant] occupies the dwelling-house as his residence' (see s 2(1)(*a*) of the 1977 Act). **g**
A fortiori, in the present case, there are conceptual difficulties involved in treating Mrs
Blakeney as deriving a valid title as subtenant from the statutory tenant, Mr Willson,
when the evidence seems to show that he was not only giving up possession of the whole
flat to her, but had no intention ever to return to it.

On the other side, it is fair to point out that there are certain provisions in the 1977
Act which could be taken as indicating that in certain circumstances a statutory tenant **h**
may lawfully sublet the whole of the premises; the use of the phrase 'the dwelling-house
or any part of it' in s 137(2) itself and in the immediately preceding subsection, may be
thought to lend some support to this view. I hope that counsel will not think it
disrespectful to their careful and interesting arguments on these points if I do not attempt
to grapple further with these conceptual problems. I think there is another quite short
and simple reason why, on any footing, a negative answer must be given to the crucial **j**
question whether the flat has been 'lawfully sublet' to Mrs Blakeney, within the meaning
of s 137(2) of the 1977 Act.

It is common ground that premises cannot be treated as having been 'lawfully sublet'
within this meaning, if the statutory tenant disposed of them to the alleged sublessee in
breach of an express prohibition in his original contract of tenancy. Any such prohibition

would, I think, inevitably be one of the contractual terms imported by s 3(1) of the 1977
a Act into Mr Willson's statutory tenancy. Accordingly, in order to show that the flat was
'lawfully sublet' to her, Mrs Blakeney has to show that the transaction concluded between
her and Mr Willson on 4 June 1980 did not constitute a breach of cl 3(24) of the lease. It
is manifest that the transaction, effected, as it was, without the plaintiffs' consent, must
have constituted such a breach, unless it fell within the proviso which states that:

b   '... no such consent shall be required for a furnished sub-letting for a term not
          exceeding six calendar months in any one year'.

Counsel for the second and third defendants has submitted that the transaction did
indeed constitute a furnished subletting 'for a term not exceeding six calendar months'
within the meaning of the proviso.

When this transaction is looked at as a whole, and not merely by reference to the
c document signed by the two parties, I, for my part, am doubtful whether it constituted
a 'subletting' at all. The judge said that he must construe the agreement actually entered
into between Mr Willson and Mrs Blakeney as disclosed in the document of 6 June 1980
signed by them, and that he could not go behind that document. With respect to him, I
think this cannot be correct. For reasons which I have already given, that document only
incorporated part of the whole transaction. In my judgment the court can and should
d ascertain the terms of this transaction by reference not only to the document itself, but
also the evidence given by Mrs Blakeney as to what was agreed orally between her and
Mr Willson, at the time when she agreed to take the flat and pay him £13,450. In the
light of this evidence, which the judge accepted, I think it reasonably clear that the
transaction was in substance one under which, in consideration of a premium, Mr
Willson was to make an outright disposition of his entire interest in the flat, such as it
e was, reserving no kind of reversion. At least in relation to a contractual tenancy, the rule
is that—

          'where a lessee, by a document in the form of a sub-lease, divests himself of
          everything that he has got (which he must necessarily do if he is transferring to his
          so-called sub-lessee an estate as great as, or purporting to be greater than, his own)
          he from that moment is a stranger to the land, in the sense that the relationship of
f   landlord and tenant, in respect of tenure, cannot any longer exist between him and
          the so-called sub-lessee.'

(See Milmo v Carreras [1946] 1 All ER 288 at 290, [1946] 1 KB 306 at 310–311 per Lord
Greene MR.)

I am doubtful whether a transaction entered into by a statutory tenant, under which
g he purports to make what is in substance an outright disposition of his interest in favour
of another, reserving no reversion to himself, can accurately be said to constitute a
'subletting' within the ordinary meaning of words.

I leave this point open, however, since I am satisfied that, even on the assumption that
the disposition by Mr Willson constituted a 'furnished subletting', it was not a 'furnished
subletting for a term not exceeding six calendar months in any one year', within the
h proviso to cl 3(24) of the lease.

Counsel for the second and third defendants referred to the provision in the document
of 6 June 1980 which required Mrs Blakeney to pay a monthly rent of £75 in advance
on the first day of each month. He submitted that this gave rise to a monthly periodic
subtenancy. He pointed out that there was no evidence that there had been any previous
subletting by Mr Willson during the preceding 12 months. He submitted that a monthly
j periodic subletting constitutes 'a sub-letting for a term not exceeding six calendar
months'. He pointed out that s 205(1)(xxvii) of the Law of Property Act 1925, which
contains a definition of the phrase 'term of years absolute' for the purpose of that Act,
goes on to provide that in this definition the expression 'term of years' includes 'a term
for less than a year or for a year or years and a fraction of a year or from year to year', so
that it is capable of including a periodic tenancy. He referred to the decision in Hammond

v Farrow [1904] 2 KB 332. In that case an order for payment of the amount of a poor-
rate had been made against a man who held certain premises merely as a weekly tenant. *a*
He claimed the benefit of certain relief afforded by s 2 of the Poor Rate Assessment and
Collection Act 1869. The question whether he was entitled to this relief depended on
whether he was an 'occupier' of the nature referred to in s 1, that is to say an 'occupier of
any rateable hereditament let to him for a term not exceeding three months'. The court,
having regard to the objects of the 1869 Act, held that he was. Lord Alverstone CJ said
(at 334–335):   *b*

> 'It is contended for the respondent that, because the tenancy may, in the absence
> of notice determining it, possibly continue for a longer period than three months, it
> is not one of the tenancies contemplated by s. 2 of the Act. In my opinion that
> argument is not sound. We are dealing with an Act one of the objects of which was
> to assist occupiers of small means holding premises on short terms. I do not think
> that it was intended to deprive a weekly tenant of the benefit of s. 2 merely because *c*
> he might be permitted by his landlord to continue as a weekly tenant for a period
> exceeding three months. In my opinion, in order to deprive a tenant of the benefit
> of s. 2, it is necessary to shew that he has by virtue of the letting an absolute right as
> against his landlord to occupy the premises for more than three months.'

I do not doubt that in a proper context the phrase 'a term not exceeding three months', *d*
or any other stated period of months, would be capable of including a periodic tenancy;
and in *Hammond v Farrow* [1904] 2 KB 332, the 1869 Act clearly provided such a context.
In my judgment, however, there is no rule of construction which requires the relevant
phrase to be read in this way in the present case. I think that, in the context of the proviso
to cl 3(24) of the lease and having regard to its obvious purpose, which was to restrict the
lessee's rights to sublet to underlettings for a short definite term, it is clear that the phrase *e*
'a term not exceeding six calendar months in any one year' means a *fixed* term not
exceeding six calendar months. Any other construction would have rendered the
covenant in cl 3(24) practically useless from the landlords' point of view, since it would
have enabled tenant and subtenant, without the landlords' consent, to enter into a
collusive arrangement for a periodic subtenancy, on the implicit understanding that
neither side would serve notice of termination for many years. I should add that the *f*
validity or otherwise of a disposition by the tenant without the landlords' consent, having
regard to cl 3(24) must, I think, be determined as at the date of the grant and cannot
depend on the length of time for which the term lasts in the subsequent events which
happen.

I do not think that the extended definition of a 'term of years' in s 205(1)(xxvii) of the
Law of Property Act 1925 assists the second and third defendants. Indeed rather the *g*
reverse. The very inclusion of this definition in the subsection suggests that the legislature
considered that, without it, the phrase 'term of years' would or might not include a
periodic tenancy.

For these reasons, even assuming in favour of the plaintiffs that the transaction effected
by Mr Willson in favour of the second and third defendants on 6 June 1980 constituted a
subletting, I conclude that it did not fall within the proviso to cl 3(24) of the lease. *h*
Accordingly, albeit by a very different route, I reach the same conclusion as did the judge
on one important aspect of the case, namely that, at least at the inception of that
transaction, the flat was not 'lawfully sublet' within the meaning of s 137(2) of the 1977
Act.

It remains to consider the question whether the plaintiffs by sending to the flat,
through their agents, on 22 September 1980, a demand for rent, which included about *j*
seven days' future rent, must be deemed to have waived the unlawfulness of the original
subtenancy of Mrs Blakeney, so as to render it a 'lawful' one and to enable her to rely
successfully on s 137(2) of the 1977 Act. This was the ground on which the judge
ultimately decided the case in favour of the second and third defendants. As I have
already indicated, there is no challenge to his finding of fact that, by 22 September 1980,
the plaintiffs had sufficient knowledge of the circumstances to support a waiver. The

disputed question is whether or not the mere serving of this one rent demand had this
a effect.

The doctrine of waiver, as applying to contractual tenancies, was summarised in the
judgment of this court delivered by Somervell LJ in the *Oak Property* case [1947] 2 All
ER 1 at 5–6, [1947] KB 886 at 898 in the following terms:

> 'By the common law, which tended to construe forfeiture provisions as effective
b to render leases voidable and not void, a landlord was bound, as soon as he was fully
> aware of a non-continuing breach of covenant by the tenant entitling the landlord
> to avoid the lease, to elect at once for or against avoidance, and to notify the tenant
> if he made the former election. On this principle acceptance of any rent accrued due
> after the landlord's knowledge of the tenant's breach was regarded necessarily as
> inconsistent with an election to avoid the lease and consistent only with its
> affirmance.'

c

Somervell LJ, however, then observed that the principles of the common law cannot
wholly apply to a statutory tenancy. He said ([1947] 2 All ER 1 at 6, [1947] KB 886 at
898–899):

> 'In the first place, the landlord of a statutory tenant has no right to avoid the
> tenancy: his only right is to invoke the jurisdiction of the court to make an order
d for possession, and the tenancy continues until at least the date of the order.
> Secondly—and consequentially—the obligation of the tenant to pay rent and the
> right of the landlord to accept it continues notwithstanding the breach of covenant
> and notwithstanding the landlord's election to invoke the court's jurisdiction, and
> the issue by him of his summons pursuant to his election. In our judgment,
e therefore, it may fairly be said that the acceptance of rent by a landlord after
> knowledge of a non-continuing breach of covenant by a tenant entitling the landlord
> to go to the court is not so unequivocal an act of affirmance of the tenancy as is
> acceptance of rent in like circumstances from a contractual tenant.'

Somervell LJ went on to point out that in some circumstances the acceptance of rent by
a landlord, after acquiring knowledge of circumstances giving rise to a claim for
f possession, may constitute an act of affirmance of even a statutory tenancy. In this context
he drew a distinction between cases where there has been an unqualified acceptance of
rent and cases where the acceptance has been a qualified one. He said ([1947] 2 All ER 1
at 6, [1947] KB 886 at 899):

> '. . . we are strongly inclined to think that the strict common law rule in regard
g to a qualified acceptance of rent is not applicable to a statutory tenancy and that a
> qualified acceptance of rent from a statutory tenant is not necessarily fatal to the
> landlord's rights to seek an order for possession.'

In the end, however, on the particular facts of the *Oak Property* case [1947] 2 All ER 1
at 7, [1947] KB 886 at 900 the court came to the conclusion that:

> '. . . as a question of fact, the acts of the landlords amounted, and were understood
h by the tenant to amount, to such an unequivocal affirmance of the sub-tenancy that
> they must be taken to have waived their statutory rights and condoned the absence
> of consent.'

In *Carter v Green* [1950] 1 All ER 627, [1950] 2 KB 76, a tenant of property holding
under a contractual tenancy, before her tenancy became statutory, sublet a part of the
j premises without the landlord's prior written consent and in breach of the tenancy
agreement. Later, after the tenancy had become statutory, the landlord, with knowledge
of the breach, accepted rent without qualification. The conclusion of Cohen LJ, delivering
the judgment of this court ([1950] 1 All ER 627 at 631–632, [1950] 2 KB 76 at 85) was:

> 'In these circumstances it seems to us that the position is that the judge has found
> that the plaintiff knew of the sub-letting before Jan. 1, 1948, and it is plain from the

evidence that he received substantial payments of rent without in any way qualifying
his receipt thereof between that date and Oct. 6, 1948. We think, therefore, that we *a*
are bound to conclude that, even if the sub-demise was originally unlawful, the
landlord had waived the illegality before he commenced the present action and thus
the sub-tenancy had become a lawful sub-tenancy.'

Earlier in his judgment Cohen LJ, having quoted the passage from the judgment of
Somervell LJ in the Oak Property case (see [1947] 2 All ER 1 at 6, [1947] KB 886 at 899)
which I have already read, said ([1950] 1 All ER 627 at 631, [1950] 2 KB 76 at 84):   *b*

'From this passage we infer that what the court meant was that an unqualified
acceptance of rent is as much as affirmance of the statutory tenancy as it would be
in the case of a common law tenancy, but that if the acceptance of rent is qualified,
it would be a question of fact for the county court judge to determine whether that
qualified acceptance must be treated in all the circumstances as an unequivocal act *c*
of affirmance of the tenancy.'

On a superficial reading of this particular sentence from the judgment in *Carter v
Green*, it might appear that it is an absolute rule of law that an acceptance of rent with
knowledge of the relevant facts, which is not accompanied by an express qualification,
necessarily and in all cases must be regarded as affirmance of a statutory tenancy. But I
do not think that this is a correct interpretation of this sentence. In my judgment all that *d*
it is intended to do, when read in its context, is to give broad guidance to judges of first
instance when reaching their decision on the facts. In the end, the question whether or
not an acceptance of rent has operated as a waiver of the landlord's rights to recover
possession in any given case of a statutory tenancy must, in my opinion, be a question of
fact, as I think the passage of the judgment of the court in the *Oak Property* case (see
[1947] 2 All ER 1 at 7, [1947] KB 886 at 900) clearly indicates. Support for this view is, I *e*
think to be found in a short passage from the judgment of Lord Denning MR in *Muspratt
v Johnston* [1963] 2 All ER 339 at 341, [1963] 2 QB 383 at 393 which I will cite, though it
was not cited in argument in the present case:

'We have been referred to the cases on waiver, particularly *Carter* v. *Green* ([1950]
1 All ER 627, [1950] 2 KB 76), and I think the result of them is that in these Rent *f*
Act cases, there is not a waiver of an unlawful sub-letting from the mere acceptance
of rent or the mere failure to write out a qualification at once. There has to be such
a degree of acquiescence that a consent to a sub-letting can be inferred. I think this
case is very near the line, but on the whole I think there is just sufficient evidence
from which the judge could infer a waiver, and I am not disposed to differ from his
finding on it.'   *g*

The *Oak Property* case [1947] 2 All ER 1, [1947] KB 886 and *Carter v Green* [1950] 1
All ER 627, [1950] 2 KB 76 were both cases where the landlord had actually accepted
rent. There has been no acceptance of rent by the plaintiffs in the present case since they
learned of Mrs Blakeney's and Mr Spraggon's occupation of the flat. Nevertheless, in
David Blackstone Ltd v Burnetts (West End) Ltd [1973] 3 All ER 782, [1973] 1 WLR 1487 *h*
Swanwick J held, in relation to a contractual tenancy, that an unambiguous demand for
future rent in advance amounts in law to an election and constitutes a waiver of the right
of forfeiture, if, at the time when the demand is made, the landlord has sufficient
knowledge of the facts to put him to his election. In that case Swanwick J pointed out
that the researches of counsel had failed to find any direct authority on the question (see
[1973] 3 All ER 782 at 790, [1973] 1 WLR 1487 at 1496). Likewise in the present case no *j*
authority on the point binding on this court has been cited, either in relation to a
contractual tenancy or in relation to a statutory tenancy.

I think that the substance of the able argument of counsel for the first and second
defendants on the question of waiver can be summarised in the five following
propositions, though this was not the precise form in which he presented the point: (1)
The decision in the *David Blackstone* case was a correct decision and the principle there

applied by Swanwick J should be applied mutatis mutandis to a statutory tenancy. (2)
a Accordingly, the unambiguous and unqualified demand for future rent sent by the
plaintiffs to the flat on 22 September 1980 must be treated as an unequivocal act of
affirmance of Mr Willson's statutory tenancy. (3) The mere fact that the rent demand
was dispatched owing to something going amiss in Messrs Cluttons' internal arrangements
would not by itself avail the plaintiffs (see *Central Estates (Belgravia) Ltd v Woolgar (No 2)*
[1972] 3 All ER 610 at 613, 617, [1972] 1 WLR 1048 at 1051, 1055 per Lord Denning
b MR and Buckley LJ. (4) Likewise, the mere fact that the clerk who sent the demand for
future rent may not have intended to waive the unlawful subletting on behalf of his
principals is also irrelevant. The effect in law of an act relied on as constituting a waiver
in such circumstances must be considered objectively, without regard to the landlord's
actual state of mind (see *Central Estates (Belgravia) Ltd v Woolgar (No 2)* [1972] 3 All ER
610 at 614, 616, [1972] 1 WLR 1048 at 1052, 1054 per Lord Denning MR and Buckley
c LJ. (5) Accordingly, as in *Carter v Green* [1950] 1 All ER 627, [1950] 2 KB 76, the sending
of the rent demand converted what had previously been the unlawful subtenancy of Mrs
Blakeney to a lawful subtenancy.

As I read his judgment, the judge decided the case in favour of the second and third
defendants substantially on the basis of these five propositions.

I would accept the third and fourth of them. I am also content to accept that the
d dispatch by the landlord and receipt by the tenant of an unambiguous and unqualified
demand for future rent will, in the case of a contractual tenancy, ordinarily constitute an
affirmation of its continuance. In the *Central Estates* case [1972] 3 All ER 610 at 616,
[1972] 1 WLR 1048 at 1054 Buckley LJ explained the relevant principle thus:

> 'If the landlord by word or deed manifests to the tenant by an unequivocal act a
> concluded decision to elect in a particular manner, he will be bound by such an
e > election. If he chooses to do something such as demanding or receiving rent which
> can only be done consistently with the existence of a certain state of affairs, namely,
> the continuance of the lease or tenancy in operation, he cannot thereafter be heard
> to say that that state of affairs did not then exist.'

In the case of a contractual tenancy, it can no doubt ordinarily be said that an
f unqualified demand for future rent can only be delivered consistently with its future
continuance. As Swanwick J observed in the *David Blackstone* case [1973] 3 All ER 782 at
792, [1973] 1 WLR 1487 at 1498:

> 'To my perhaps simple mind there is a fundamental inconsistency between
> contending that a lease has been determined and demanding rent on the basis of its
> future continuance.'

g The present case is in my opinion plainly distinguishable on its facts. It cannot, in my
opinion, fairly be said that on 22 September 1980 the plaintiffs demanded rent on the
basis of the future continuance of the statutory tenancy of Mr Willson. Nor could their
demand reasonably have been interpreted as being made on this basis. Section 3(3) of the
Rent Act 1977 provides:

h > 'Subject to section 5 of the Protection from Eviction Act 1977 (under which at
> least 4 weeks' notice to quit is required), a statutory tenant of a dwelling-house shall
> be entitled to give up possession of the dwelling-house if, and only if, he gives such
> notice as would have been required under the provisions of the original contract of
> tenancy, or, if no notice would have been so required, on giving not less than 3
> months' notice.'

j Mr Willson had not given the plaintiffs any notice as required by this section. They were
therefore entitled to look to him for payment of the quarter's rent due on 29 September
1980, even though they may be taken to have known that he had given up possession of
the flat and ceased to be statutory tenant thereof on 6 June 1980. In these circumstances
I am, with all respect to him, unable to agree with the view expressed by the judge in
regard to the demand for rent dated 22 September 1980, when he said:

'In the ordinary course of events, a tenant receiving the demand would think he
had to do what was stated in that demand. The demand for future rent coming a
within a few days of his meeting with the landlord's agents, he might be pardoned
for thinking that the landlords had elected to waive the unlawfulness of his breach
otherwise why have they made an unqualified demand for future rent?'

The answer to this question, I think, is that the plaintiffs were entitled to demand this
rent from Mr Willson, whether or not the statutory tenancy had determined on 6 June
1980, because of s 3(3) of the 1977 Act. There was therefore, in my opinion, no necessary b
inconsistency between a single demand for the rent for that quarter and a subsequent
claim that the statutory tenancy had determined on 6 June 1980. The case is plainly
distinguishable on its facts from *Carter v Green* [1950] 1 All ER 627, [1950] 2 KB 76, if
only because in that case the landlord had accepted rent with full knowledge of the
subletting on about six separate occasions, before he attempted to claim that the
subletting was unlawful, so that a waiver of the illegality was the obvious inference.   c

If this reasoning is correct, it is alone sufficient to dispose of the defendants' submissions
based on waiver. In my judgment, however, there is another, no less conclusive answer
to these submissions. Though the judge seems to have assumed that the demand for rent
dated 22 September 1980 addressed to Mrs Willson and sent to the flat, in due course
reached Mr Willson, it is common ground that there was no clear evidence before him
to support any finding of fact to this effect. The most that counsel for the second and d
third defendants could do in this context was to point to certain other correspondence
which appeared to have been forwarded from the flat to Mr Willson, and to invite the
court to infer that the rent demand would have been similarly forwarded. On the
available evidence, I think it impossible to make any such inference; it would be no more
than mere conjecture.

If therefore, as I conclude, there is no evidence that the rent demand ever reached Mr   e
Willson, I do not see how it can possibly suffice to support a waiver. It is the actual
communication, rather than the preparation, of the rent demand which would have to
be relied on for this purpose. An uncommunicated rent demand, which ex hypothesi
will not have caused the tenant to change his position in any way, must in my opinion
be capable of withdrawal by the landlord at any time before it has been received by the
tenant. For this further or alternative reason, I think that the defence based on waiver   f
must fail.

It follows that in my judgment the second and third defendants have failed to
discharge the onus which must fall on them of showing that they or one of them are
lawful subtenants of the plaintiffs. The demand for seven days future rent mistakenly
sent by the plaintiffs' agents on 22 September 1980 did not in my opinion operate to
confer this status on them and there is no evidence that the plaintiffs did or said anything g
else which could possibly be said to have constituted a recognition of such status.

In the result, though I have considerable sympathy with Mr Spraggon and Mrs
Blakeney, I would allow the appeal and make an order for delivery of possession of the
flat by Mr Spraggon and Mrs Blakeney to the plaintiffs within 28 days, or within such
extended time as may be sought by them, and that these two defendants pay the plaintiffs'
costs of the action and of the appeal. Finally I would like to express my gratitude to   h
counsel on both sides for their arguments in this difficult case.

ORMROD LJ. I have come to the same conclusion. At the end of the very able
argument on both sides in this case, my provisional opinion was that the conceptual j
difficulties involved in the proposition of counsel for the second and third defendants
that a statutory tenant, whose intention was never to reoccupy the premises, could sublet
the whole, were so great that it could not be supported. On further consideration I think
that it is a mistake to try to impress common law concepts on to the legal relationships
created by the Rent Act. Words like 'tenant' and 'sublet' are so familiar to us in their
common law sense that it is not easy to accept that their meaning in the Rent Act is not

a the same. The incidents of a statutory tenancy must, therefore, be collected from the provisions of the Act itself.

Section 137 of the Rent Act 1977 clearly contemplates that a statutory tenant can validly 'sublet' the whole dwellinghouse and create the legal relationship of statutory tenancy between the landlord and the subtenant. Subsection (4) expressly extends sub-ss (1) and (2) to statutory tenants. Section 98, with Sch 15, Case 6, shows that a statutory tenant can 'sublet' the whole without giving the landlord an absolute right to possession
b against him, notwithstanding that he no longer satisfies the definition of a statutory tenant in s 2(1), because he has ceased to occupy the premises. The landlord, under s 98, must still show that it is reasonable to make an order for possession. Similarly, s 3(3) provides that the statutory tenancy continues unless the tenant gives a notice of appropriate length to determine it, even when he is not occupying, and not intending to reoccupy the premises.

c The only real issue in this case is, therefore, whether the defendants, Mr Spraggon and Mrs Blakeney can bring themselves within the terms of s 137(2), ie whether they can show that the flat was 'lawfully sublet' to them by Mr Willson. It is common ground that 'lawfully' means in accordance with the provisions of cl 3(24) of the original lease. No permission was obtained from the landlords, so the only question is whether this subletting was within the proviso to this clause. For the reasons given by Slade LJ, I am
d satisfied that a subletting for an indefinite period on a periodic tenancy is not within the proviso. The concluding words 'in any one year' are wholly inconsistent with anything other than a tenancy for a fixed term. Only a furnished tenancy for a fixed term of less than six months is within the proviso. It follows that the letting of the flat to Mrs Blakeney on 6 June 1980 on a monthly tenancy was a breach of cl 3(24) and, therefore, unlawful.

e Counsel for the second and third defendants, however, in a valiant argument, which found favour with the judge below, contends that the plaintiffs have waived their right to eject his clients by sending a demand for rent addressed to Mrs Willson, with full knowledge of the unlawful subletting, notwithstanding that there is no evidence that this demand was ever communicated to Mr Willson, and was due to an administrative error in the office of the plaintiffs' agents.

f Waiver is another common law concept which has a limited application to the statutory relationships created by the Rent Act. At common law it refers, essentially, to waiver of the landlord's right of forfeiture, as evidenced by an act or acts consistent only with an election to treat the contractual relationship as continuing. In the statutory relationship the landlord has no right of forfeiture and no choice. The statutory tenancy continues until it is determined by notice by the tenant or by order of the court. The
g landlord is entitled to demand the rent so long as the statutory tenancy continues. A mere demand for rent, therefore, is not an act consistent only with an election to treat the subletting as lawful. At most in this context it is equivocal. Nor does it affect the landlord's claim for possession under Case 6, which does not depend on proof of a breach of the tenancy agreement, although a breach might make the court marginally more inclined to hold that it was reasonable to make an order for possession. This would, of
h course, depend on the true facts relating to the demand, and not on the presumption which underlies the decision in *David Blackstone Ltd v Burnetts (West End) Ltd* [1973] 3 All ER 782, [1973] 1 WLR 1487. I cannot think that an undelivered demand for rent could affect in any way the rights of the landlord and tenant, nor is there any evidence from which it could properly be inferred that the plaintiffs, in this case, had consented to the subletting of the flat to Mrs Blakeney.

j The result, I am sorry to say, is a disaster for Mr Spraggon and Mrs Blakeney, for whom I have much sympathy. If the evidence in the court below is true, they have been the victim of a wicked trick, or grave negligence, or both, although their own naivety in not taking legal advice has contributed to their misfortune. One can only hope that they may be able to obtain redress in other proceedings for the loss of the protected tenancy in their former flat, and the sum of £13,450, which they have paid to Mr Willson. I agree that the appeal must be allowed.

GRIFFITHS LJ. For the reasons given by Ormrod and Slade LJJ, I also agree that this
appeal must be allowed.

Appeal allowed.

Solicitors: *Warrens* (for the plaintiffs); *Wilde Sapte* (for the second and third defendants).

Bebe Chua   Barrister.

Casson and another v University of Aston in Birmingham

VISITOR OF THE UNIVERSITY OF ASTON IN BIRMINGHAM
LORD HAILSHAM OF ST MARYLEBONE LC ON BEHALF OF THE VISITOR
26 NOVEMBER 1982

*University – Visitor – Modern university – Jurisdiction of visitor – Contract – Petitioner applying
for and offered place to study particular course – Petitioner accepting offer – University unable
to mount course and offering petitioner place in alternative course – Petitioner accepting new offer
and admitted to university to study alternative course – Petitioner seeking damages for breach of
contract – Petitioner alleging university withdrew original offer in breach of contract – Whether
visitor having jurisdiction to hear petition alleging breach of contract by university – Whether
visitor having jurisdiction to hear petition from stranger to university – Whether petition
misconceived.*

*Corporation – Visitor – Jurisdiction – Damages – Moneys wrongfully withheld from member of
foundation or had and received to his use or impressed with trust in his favour – Whether visitor
having jurisdiction to order payment of money to member.*

The two petitioners applied for admission to a university for the purpose of taking a
course in human communication which was listed in the university's undergraduate
prospectus for the year 1981–82. Both applications were accepted, the acceptance taking
the form of an offer of a place for the purpose of studying the course of human
communication which in each case was accepted by the petitioners. In the event the
university was unable to mount the course, but it offered the petitioners a place in the
university to take a choice of alternative courses. The petitioners accepted that offer and
were admitted to the university to study a course of human psychology. In October 1981
the petitioners brought actions against the university in the county court for damages
for breach of contract arising out of the university's late and wrongful retraction of its
offer to the petitioners to study human communication. The registrar struck out the
proceedings and his decision was upheld by the judge, who declined jurisdiction on the
ground that the matter was properly within the exclusive jurisdiction of the visitor of
the university. In May 1982 the petitioners petitioned the university's visitor, seeking
similar relief to that claimed in the county court. Although one petitioner had terminated
her course in March 1982, it was accepted that both petitioners remained members of
the university.

Held – The petitions would be dismissed for the following reasons—
   (1) A visitor of a foundation had no jurisdiction in any matter governed by the
common law, and, once a relationship with the foundation had been established which
was governed by the general laws of the realm over which the visitor could have no
jurisdiction, the visitor was wholly excluded from considering any question concerning
that relationship. Since the relationship of contract was governed by the general laws of
the realm, the visitor had no jurisdiction over contracts entered into with the foundation,
and the fact that the other contracting party was also a member of the foundation did

not have the effect of excluding the jurisdiction of the courts and putting the matter
a exclusively within the visitor's authority (see p 91 *c* to *f* and p 92 *c*, post).

(2) Assuming that prior to the petitioners' admission to the university there was a
contractual relationship between the petitioners and the university, any late and wrongful
retraction by the university of its offer to the petitioners to study human communication
took place prior to their admission to the university (and therefore while they were
strangers to it) and sounded in contract or in nothing. Accordingly, since a visitor had no
b jurisdiction over contracts made between a corporation or a member of a corporation of
which he was the visitor and a stranger who was outside the corporation, the petitions
were fundamentally misconceived and the visitor had no jurisdiction to hear them (see
p 91 *d f* to *h* and p 92 *c*, post).

(3) In any event the acceptance by the petitioners of membership of the university on
terms different from those of the alleged contract and the action of the parties in acting
c on that acceptance effectively substituted the new obligations for the old and put an end
to any rights of either party under the old contracts either by novation, variation or
estoppel (see p 91 *d h j* and p 92 *c*, post).

Per Lord Hailsham LC. It may be that a visitor has the power to order the payment of
money wrongfully withheld from a member of a foundation or had and received to his
use or, less probably, impressed with a trust in his favour. But to order what is in effect a
d payment in respect of damages is in effect to create a new type of compensation sounding
neither in contract nor in tort, and in the absence of any special provision in the charter
or statutes of the foundation would be wholly outside the functions or powers of the
visitor (see p 91 *j* to p 92 *b*, post).

Notes

e For visitors of modern universities, see 15 Halsbury's Laws (4th edn) para 284, and for
cases on the subject, see 19 Digest (Reissue) 570–571, 4256–4265.

For the nature of visitatorial power and a visitor's powers and jurisdiction, see 5
Halsbury's Laws (4th edn) paras 872, 879–884, and for cases on the subject, see 8(1) Digest
(Reissue) 452–453, 456, 2020–2030, 2078–2089.

f **Petitions**

Clare Casson and Amanda Elaine O'Brien, by separate petitions dated 18 May 1982 and
addressed to the visitor of the University of Aston in Birmingham, sought as against the
university the following relief: (1) a hearing at which the petitioners could present to the
visitor their grievance against the university; (2) compensation for the university's alleged
late and wrongful retraction of its offers to the petitioners to study the course of human
g communication listed in the undergraduate prospectus issued by the university for the
year 1981–82; and (3) costs. In the absence of the appointment of a visitor of the
university pursuant to the power reserved to Her Majesty by cl 28 of the university's
royal charter dated 22 April 1966, the visitatorial power in relation to the university was
and remained vested in Her Majesty, and accordingly by permission and command of
Her Majesty the Lord Chancellor of Great Britain undertook the burden of determining
h the petitions in exercise of Her Majesty's visitatorial powers. The facts essential to the
determination of the dispute appearing sufficiently from the petitions, from the
university's answers thereto dated 30 June 1982, from the petitioners' replies dated 13
October 1982 and from certain other available documents, and not being significantly or
relevantly in dispute, the Lord Chancellor did not direct an oral hearing or take oral
evidence. The facts are set out in the determination.

j
26 November. The following determination was made.

LORD HAILSHAM OF ST MARYLEBONE LC. 1. The University of Aston
in Birmingham (hereinafter referred to as 'the university') was incorporated by royal
charter dated 22 April 1966, scheduling the statutes of the university as the second
schedule to the said charter.

2. By cl 28 of the said charter Her Majesty reserved to herself, her heirs and successors the right to appoint a visitor of the university in circumstances more particularly defined *a* in the said clause. No such appointment has in fact been made and in consequence the visitatorial power in relation to the university is and remains vested in Her Majesty.

3. In accordance with normal constitutional usage, and for the purposes of the present dispute, by permission and command of Her Majesty, I, the Right Honourable Quintin McGarel, Lord Hailsham of St Marylebone, Lord Chancellor of Great Britain, have undertaken the burden of determining the above-named petitions in exercise of Her *b* Majesty's visitatorial powers.

4. The two above-named petitions are each dated 18 May 1982. The university delivered separate answers to the said petitions, each dated 30 June 1982. The two petitioners delivered replies to the said petitions each dated 13 October 1982. In addition to these documents, and their respective annexures, for the purposes of the present determination, I have taken into account a letter dated 3 June 1982 written to the Lord *c* Chancellor's Department on behalf of the said petitioners by Messrs Robin Thompson & Partners, the solicitors to the petitioners, and the purported copy of the judgment more particularly referred to in para 8 of this determination.

5. Since the facts essential to the determination of this dispute appear sufficiently from the above documents, and do not appear to be significantly or relevantly in dispute, I do not find it necessary to direct an oral hearing or to take oral evidence. *d*

6. Both petitions arise out of similar facts. The undergraduate prospectus issued by the University for the year 1981–82 listed a course entitled Human Communication, and both petitioners applied for admission to the university for the purpose of taking this course. Both applications were accepted by the university, in the case of the petitioner O'Brien unconditionally, in the case of the petitioner Casson on conditions which, in the event, were fulfilled. The acceptance took the form of an offer of a place for the purpose *e* of studying the course on Human Communication which in each case was accepted by the petitioners.

7. In the events which happened the university found itself unable to mount the course (described by the university as 'the B.Sc. Behavioural Science Course on which you have been offered a place'), but in each case offered the petitioners a place in the university to take a choice of alternative courses. In each case the petitioner concerned accepted this *f* offer and was in fact admitted to the university to study a course referred to as Human Psychology. The documents show that the petitioner O'Brien remains an undergraduate member of the university (presumably studying this course), and is therefore, both now and at the time of the petition, a member of the university. Although the petition of the petitioner Casson describes herself as 'an undergraduate member of the University', para 6 of her reply shows that she terminated her course on 19 March 1982 with the result *g* that 'it will take me one extra year to graduate'. Since the university does not contend to the contrary I assume, however, that she remains a member of the university for the purposes of her petition.

8. In October 1981 both petitioners appeared to have sued the university in the Birmingham County Court for damages for breach of contract arising out of the above matters. In the event it appears that the proceedings were struck out by the registrar, and *h* that on appeal on 16 February 1982 his Honour Judge Toyn upheld the decision of the registrar, but gave leave to appeal to the Court of Appeal. This does not appear to have been pursued. I have not available to me a complete record of the proceedings in the Birmingham County Court, but I have read what purports to be a copy of the judgment declining jurisdiction, on the ground that the matters arising are properly within the exclusive jurisdiction of the visitor. The essence of the judgment as recorded is confirmed *j* by the letter of 3 June 1982 above referred to from the petitioners' solicitors. Having read it with interest and care I do not feel bound to say more than that, in so far as it is inconsistent with what follows, I respectfully disagree with it. I do not regard myself as bound by the decision.

9. It is, perhaps, unfortunate that none of the parties to this dispute have referred to

the exhaustive and up-to-date article by Dr Peter M Smith 'The Exclusive Jurisdiction of
a   the University Visitor' (1981) 97 LQR 610. If they had, I believe much trouble would
have been avoided.

10. The two petitions are each founded on an alleged contract between the respective
petitioners before they became members of the university to provide instruction in
accordance with the terms of the original prospectus. The existence of this contract is
denied by the university.

b   11. Apart from a request for a 'hearing at which I can present to the Visitor my
grievance against the University' the only prayer for substantive relief in the petitions is
a prayer for 'compensation from the University for its late and wrongful retraction of
their offer to me to study human communication', and a prayer for costs. I agree,
however, with Dr Smith that a visitor can have no jurisdiction in any matter governed
by the common law, eg contract (see 97 LQR 610 at 615). I regard each of the petitions
c   as claims for damages for breach of a contract entered into before the petitioners became
members of the university and for nothing else. For the purposes of argument I assume
(without deciding since the matter is contentious) that, had the university refused to
accept the petitioners as members of the university, it might have been possible for the
visitor to direct the admission of the petitioners, but, as they were in fact admitted, albeit
by agreement with the petitioners for a different course, and both parties presumably
d   acted on the faith of this agreement, I do not find anything within the jurisdiction of the
visitor disclosed by the petition. I also agree with Dr Smith when he writes (at 642),
though in a slightly different context:

'. . . once a relationship has been established which is governed by the general
laws of the realm over which the visitor can have no jurisdiction, the visitor is
wholly excluded from considering any question concerning that relationship. There
e   does not seem to be any good reason why this reasoning should not be equally
applicable to the relationship of contract which is likewise governed by the general
laws of the realm. The visitor can have no jurisdiction over such contracts, and by
analogy with the trust situation, it would appear that the fact that a contracting
party is also a member of the corporation will not have the effect of excluding the
jurisdiction of the courts and putting the matter exclusively within the visitor's
f   authority.'

12. Assuming in favour of the petitioners (but without deciding) that prior to their
admission to the university there was a contractual relationship between the petitioners
and the university, any 'late and wrongful retraction' (on which the only claim for
substantive relief is based) took place prior to the admission of the petitioners to the
g   university and either sounds in contract or in nothing. I refer also to the proposition in
Dr Smith's article (with which I also agree) that '. . . the visitor has no jurisdiction over
contracts made between the body, or member of the body of which he is visitor, and a
stranger who is outside the foundation' (cf 97 LQR 610 at 637 and passim). The matters
complained of in both petitions, if they give rise to complaints at all, occurred at a
moment of time when the petitioners were wholly 'outside the foundation of the
h   University', and therefore strangers to it.

13. Even if I were wrong about this I would hold that the acceptance by the petitioners
of membership of the university on terms different from those of the alleged contract,
and the action of both parties in acting on that acceptance (in the case of the petitioner
Casson at least until March 1982 and in the case of the petitioner O'Brien apparently up
to the present), effectively substituted the new obligations for the old and put an end to
j   any rights of either party under the old contract either by novation, variation or estoppel.

14. I must add this. As I have said, the only substantive prayer for relief in this case is
a monetary claim for compensation in the nature of damages. After considerable research,
I have been unable to find any precedent in the long history of visitatorial powers in
which a visitor has made such an order and in my view he has no such power. It may be,
though I do not so decide, that a visitor has the power to order the payment of moneys

wrongfully withheld from a member of a foundation or had and received to his use or, less probably, impressed with a trust in his favour. But to order what is in effect a *a* payment in respect of damages is in effect to create a new type of compensation sounding neither in contract nor in tort. This could only be done by statute and in my view in the absence of any special provision in the charter or statutes of the foundation is wholly outside the functions or powers of a visitor.

15. The only order capable of being made by the visitor would be to order the university to mount a special course of the original specification for the benefit of the *b* petitioners. This is not asked for and would in any event be out of the question, owing to the time which has elapsed and the events which have supervened. In any event I would have regarded the mounting of such a course as a matter within the unfettered discretion of the university authorities assuming them to be acting within their powers and in good faith (see the proposition and authorities in 5 Halsbury's Laws (4th edn) para 882). In the event I determine and decide that both these petitions are fundamentally misconceived *c* and therefore stand to be dismissed.

Petitions dismissed.

Solicitors: *Robin Thompson & Partners,* Birmingham (for the petitioners); *Johnson & Co,* Birmingham (for the university).   *d*

Mary Rose Plummer   Barrister.

Lloyds Bank Ltd v City of London Corp   *e*

COURT OF APPEAL, CIVIL DIVISION
CUMMING-BRUCE, TEMPLEMAN AND O'CONNOR LJJ
23, 24 JUNE, 7 JULY 1982

Landlord and tenant – Business premises – Application for new tenancy – Withdrawal of *f* *application – Leave to discontinue proceedings – Terms on which leave should be given – Tenants entitled to compensation on withdrawal of application – Landlords withdrawing opposition to grant of new tenancy before tenants deciding to seek leave to withdraw application – Whether court in giving leave to discontinue should impose condition that tenants should not pursue claim for compensation – Landlord and Tenant Act 1954, s 37(1) – RSC Ord 21, r 3(1).*

g
In February 1980 the tenants of certain business premises served on the landlords a request under s 26 of the Landlord and Tenant Act 1954 for a new tenancy to begin on 25 December 1980. In March 1980 the landlords served a counter-notice under s 26(6) stating that they would oppose the grant of a new tenancy on the ground set out in s 30(1)(*f*) of the 1954 Act, namely that on the termination of the existing tenancy they intended to redevelop the premises. In June 1980 the tenants applied to the court for a *h* new tenancy under s 24 of the 1954 Act. Concurrently they investigated the possibility of moving to other premises in case the landlords succeeded in opposing the new tenancy and the court failed to make an order for a new tenancy. In July the landlords informed the tenants that they were withdrawing their opposition. In August the tenants decided that, because there was still a risk that the landlords might wish to redevelop the premises at a future date, they would vacate them on the termination of the existing tenancy and *j* move to other accommodation which they had found. They notified the landlords of their decision and applied to the High Court under RSC Ord 21, r 3(1)[a] for leave to discontinue their application for a new tenancy. The landlords contended that leave to

---

a   Rule 3(1), so far as material, is set out at p 96 *j*, post

discontinue should be given only on condition that the tenants undertook to waive their
right to claim compensation under s 37(1)[b] of the 1954 Act on quitting the premises,
because if leave to discontinue were not granted and the tenants were required to proceed
with the application they would not be able to claim compensation. The landlords
submitted that by withdrawing their opposition to the new tenancy before the tenants
decided to withdraw their application the landlords had made certain that they would
not have had to pay compensation if the tenants' application had continued and that the
court ought not to deprive them of that advantage. The tenants contended that it would
be unjust to make the grant of leave conditional on their foregoing their right to claim
compensation.

Held – (1) Once a landlord served a counter-notice based on any ground set out in
s 30(1)(e) to (g) of the 1954 Act he had no right both to recover possession of the demised
premises and also to avoid payment of compensation, because by serving the counter-
notice he presented the tenant with a choice between the doubtful possibility of a new
tenancy and the certainty of compensation under s 37 of that Act, and if, after the tenant
had decided to apply for a new tenancy, the landlord withdrew his opposition he could
not avoid paying compensation if the tenant's application was subsequently withdrawn
(see p 94 b c and p 99 b to j, post); Stahlschmidt v Walford (1879) 4 QBD 217 and Covell
Matthews & Partners v French Wools Ltd [1978] 2 All ER 800 distinguished; Young, Austen
& Young Ltd v British Medical Association [1977] 2 All ER 884 disapproved.

(2) Where a tenant applied to the court for leave to withdraw his application for a new
tenancy after the landlord had withdrawn his opposition to the grant of a new tenancy,
the court when exercising its discretion under RSC Ord 21, r 3(1) would give the tenant
leave to do so unconditionally unless there was evidence that the landlord had been
prejudiced by delay or events which had occurred between the date when the landlord
withdrew his opposition and the date when he was informed that the tenant no longer
wished to proceed with the application. Since there was no evidence that the landlords
had been so prejudiced, the tenants would be given unconditional leave to withdraw
their application (see p 94 b c and p 99 j to p 100 c e and g, post).

Notes
For compensation where the application to the court for a new tenancy has been
withdrawn, see 27 Halsbury's Laws (4th edn) paras 518–519.

For leave to discontinue, see ibid para 492, and for cases on the subject, see 51 Digest
(Repl) 572–574, 2057–2082.

For the Landlord and Tenant Act 1954, ss 24, 26, 30, 37, see 18 Halsbury's Statutes
(3rd edn) 557, 561, 565, 576.

Cases referred to in judgment
Cardshops Ltd v John Lewis Properties Ltd [1982] 3 All ER 746, [1982] 3 WLR 803, CA.
Covell Matthews & Partners v French Wools Ltd [1977] 2 All ER 591, [1977] 1 WLR 876;
    affd [1978] 2 All ER 800, [1978] 1 WLR 1477, CA, Digest (Cont Vol E) 378, 7824a.
Stahlschmidt v Walford (1879) 4 QBD 217, 51 Digest (Repl) 573, 2062.
Stream Properties Ltd v Davis [1972] 2 All ER 746, [1972] 1 WLR 645, Digest (Reissue)
    959, 7772.
Young, Austen & Young Ltd v British Medical Association [1977] 2 All ER 884, [1977] 1 WLR
    881, Digest (Cont Vol E) 378, 7824b.

Appeal
The Corporation of the City of London (the landlords) appealed against an order of Slade
J, dated 22 May 1981, whereby he gave Lloyds Bank Ltd (the tenants) leave to discontinue
proceedings under Part II of the Landlord and Tenant Act 1954 for the grant of a new

---

b   Section 37(1), so far as material, is set out at p 96 a b, post

tenancy of 3 Broad Street Place, London EC2. The facts are set out in the judgment of
Templeman LJ.   a

Michael Essayan QC and Michael Segal for the landlords.
Jonathan Gaunt for the tenants.

                                                                           Cur adv vult
                                                                                        b
7 July. The following judgments were delivered.

CUMMING-BRUCE LJ. O'Connor LJ is unable to be present today. He has authorised
me to say that, like myself, he has had the advantage of reading the judgment which
Templeman LJ is about to deliver and he agrees with that judgment. I also agree with it
and would ask Templeman LJ to deliver his judgment.   c

TEMPLEMAN LJ. This is an appeal by the defendant landlords, the Corporation of
the City of London, against the decision of Slade J delivered on 22 May 1981, whereby
he gave leave to the plaintiff tenants, Lloyds Bank Ltd, to discontinue proceedings under
Part II of the Landlord and Tenant Act 1954 for the grant of a new tenancy. The judge
rejected the landlords' submission that leave should only be granted to the tenants to d
discontinue their proceedings provided they abandoned any claim for compensation
under the Act. The landlords appeal to this court.
     The tenants were in occupation of part of 3 Broad Street Place, London, as the Finsbury
Circus branch of their banking business under the terms of a lease which was expressed
to expire by effluxion of time on 18 December 1980. By s 23 of the 1954 Act the tenancy
could not come to an end unless terminated by a landlord's notice under s 25 or by a   e
tenant's request for a new tenancy under s 26.
     In January 1980 the tenants made inquiries to ascertain whether the landlords would
grant a new tenancy or whether they would oppose the grant of a new tenancy. The
tenants were unable to clarify the position. The tenants brought matters to a head by a
notice dated 8 February 1980 whereby they requested the grant of a new tenancy to
begin on 25 December 1980 for a term of 14 years at an annual rent of £20,000.   f
     If a landlord is not willing for a new tenancy to be granted he must under s 26(6),
within two months after receiving the tenant's request, give a counter-notice stating on
which of the grounds mentioned in s 30 of the 1954 Act he would oppose an application
to the court for a new tenancy.
     On 31 March 1980 the landlords served a counter-notice pursuant to s 26(6) intimating
that the landlords would oppose the grant of a new tenancy on the grounds mentioned   g
in s 30(1)(f).
     There are seven grounds on which a landlord may successfully oppose the grant of a
new tenancy under s 30(1) of the 1954 Act. Grounds (a), (b) and (c) relate to the conduct
of the tenant and, for example, debar the tenant from obtaining a new tenancy if he has
been found guilty of substantial breaches of covenant. Ground (d) debars the tenant from
a new tenancy if the landlord offers suitable alternative accommodation. Grounds (e),   h
(f), and (g) relate to the wishes of the landlord. In particular, ground (f), on which the
landlords relied in the present case in their counter-notice, enables the landlord
successfully to oppose the grant of a new tenancy if the landlord intends to demolish or
reconstruct or redevelop the premises and cannot do so without obtaining possession.
     By ss 24(1) and 29 a tenant who has made a request for a new tenancy may, not less
than two nor more than four months after the making of the request, apply to the court   j
for a new tenancy. By s 64 the effect of an application to the court is to continue the
existing tenancy, so far as is necessary, until three months after the date on which the
tenant's application to the court for a new tenancy is finally disposed of. The tenants in
the present case applied to the court for a new tenancy on 5 June 1980.
     On 26 June 1980 Master Dyson ordered that the question whether the landlords'

opposition to the grant of a new tenancy was well founded should be tried as a preliminary issue and he directed discovery.

On 14 July 1980 representatives of the landlords informed the tenants that the landlords would abandon their opposition to the grant of a new tenancy. A formal letter to this effect was sent on 17 July 1980.

From January 1980 onwards the tenants were uncertain whether they would be able to continue in the premises. From 31 March 1980 onwards it was doubtful, in view of the landlords' notice of opposition under s 30(1)(f), whether the tenants would be able to continue in the premises. The tenants, therefore, investigated alternatives. Those investigations resulted in a decision a fortnight after the landlords had changed their minds and withdrawn their opposition to the grant of a new tenancy. On 29 July 1980, as appears from a file note of the tenants, the joint general manager of the tenants decided 'that we would not renew the Lease and that some time in the spring the branch would close and that the business would be amalgamated with Stock Exchange branch. This proposal is to be put to Committee very shortly and the full instruction shall be issued to us shortly after.' This decision was confirmed and the tenants' solicitors were so informed by a letter dated 7 August 1980. This letter from the estates manager of the tenants advised that:

'. . . our General Managers' Committee has agreed to the closure of Finsbury Circus Branch, with the work being transferred to vacant accommodation in our Stock Exchange Branch. This matter is still rather confidential, as the staff of the branches concerned have not yet been told, but I feel that we should now make an approach to the City Corporation. The position is that it is anticipated the transfer can be effected by April, 1981, and we are therefore likely to want an extension on our existing Lease for, say, six months. I have not yet had terms quoted to me by the City Corporation for the granting of a new Lease and I would like you, please, to write to them on this matter. I would suggest that we should advise them that, in view of our uncertainty as to whether a new Lease would be granted, consideration was given as to any alternative action we could take to protect the Bank's interest. We can say that it has now been found possible to transfer the business to another branch and, under the circumstances, we will be prepared to give vacant possession, so that the Landlords can carry out their refurbishment without the complication of a sitting tenant.'

The tenants did not communicate their decision of August 1980 to the landlords immediately because of the need for confidentiality. The landlords remained under the impression that the tenants were still seeking a new tenancy until 20 October 1980. The Comptroller and City Solicitor was then informed by the tenants' solicitors that:

'Our clients have instructed us that your opposition earlier this year to their request for the grant of a new tenancy of their Branch premises in the building caused their General Management to consider the continued presence of the Branch in the building and, as a result, our clients will, in fact, be vacating the premises in the Spring of next year. Would you please confirm that on vacating the premises our clients will be paid the statutory compensation to which they are entitled under Section 37 of the 1954 Act.'

Apart from acknowledgments there was no reply to this letter or to reminders and on 23 January 1981 the tenants' solicitors wrote to the City Solicitor saying:

'Our clients will be ceasing business at the premises at about the end of next month and they will be finally vacating the premises about a month after that. Accordingly, we consider that our clients' proceedings should now be withdrawn by mutual consent . . . Our clients are entitled to statutory compensation of an amount equal to twice the rateable value of their premises.'

Section 37 of the 1954 Act as amended by the Law of Property Act 1969, s 11, provides

that, where a tenant applies to the court under s 24 of the 1954 Act for a new tenancy
and the court is precluded from making an order for the grant of a new tenancy by
reason of any of the grounds specified in paras (e), (f) and (g) of s 30(1)—

> 'or where no other ground is specified in the landlord's notice . . . under section
> 26(6) . . . than those specified in the said paragraphs (e), (f) and (g) and either no
> application under the said section 24 is made or such an application is withdrawn,
> then . . . the tenant shall be entitled on quitting the holding to recover from the
> landlord by way of compensation an amount [which in the case of business premises
> occupied for the past 14 years shall be twice the rateable value].'

In the present case the tenants applied to the court under s 24 for a new tenancy. The
landlords served a counter-notice opposing the grant of a new tenancy on the grounds
specified in s 30(1)(f) and on no other grounds. The tenants propose to withdraw their
application for a new tenancy. The tenants claim compensation of two years' rateable
value amounting to the agreed sum of £65,776.

The City Solicitor replied on 30 January 1981:

> 'At the present moment the Corporation are not willing to consent to the
> withdrawal of your Clients action . . . as certain points must be cleared up before
> this step can be taken. Firstly the question of interim rent must be dealt with as this
> is due from your Clients to the Corporation and before I am able to expand on this
> point, I must take instructions with regard to the rate at which this is due . . . I am
> again taking instructions with regard to the second matter, namely any compensation
> payable to your Clients by the Corporation.'

On 9 March 1981 the landlords issued a summons in the tenants' proceedings for a
new tenancy asking under s 24A of the 1954 Act for the court 'to determine a rent which
it would be reasonable for the tenant to pay while the tenancy continues by virtue of
section 24' of the Act. The interim rent would have been payable from 18 December
1980 if the landlords had taken the step of issuing their summons on or before that date.
The landlords did not, however, issue a summons until 9 March 1981 and, under the
provisions of s 24A as construed in *Stream Properties Ltd v Davis* [1972] 2 All ER 746,
[1972] 1 WLR 645, the interim rent became payable from 9 March 1981, the date of the
landlord's summons, until the existing tenancy ends under s 64 of the 1954 Act, three
months after the date on which the tenants' application to the court for a new tenancy
was finally disposed of.

On 24 March 1981 the landlords wrote to the tenants' solicitors, saying:

> 'I note that your clients wish to vacate the premises on March 31st next. I am
> prepared to consent to an application by your clients to discontinue the proceedings
> which at present stand adjourned, provided that [the tenants undertook not to seek
> compensation under section 37 of the Landlord and Tenant Act 1954, undertook to
> pay interim rent until a date for vacating the premises was agreed between the
> parties or was ascertained by reference to an order of the court and undertook to pay
> an appropriate sum for dilapidations].'

These terms were not acceptable to the tenant. On 31 March 1981 the tenants vacated
the premises. The landlords have not yet resumed possession.

On 6 April 1981 the tenants issued a motion for leave to discontinue their proceedings
for a new tenancy. RSC Ord 21, r 3, provides that, with exceptions not here material, a
party may not discontinue an action, whether begun by writ or otherwise, without the
leave of the court, which may order the action to be discontinued 'on such terms as to
costs, the bringing of a subsequent action or otherwise as it thinks just.'

The tenants' application for leave to discontinue their proceedings for a new tenancy
came before Slade J and the landlords submitted that the tenants should only be allowed
to discontinue their application for a new tenancy on condition that they undertook not
to apply for compensation under s 37.

On 22 May 1981 Slade J in a reserved judgment gave reasons for giving the tenants unconditional leave to discontinue and for his refusal to make that leave conditional on the tenants abandoning their claim for compensation. He ordered that the landlords' application for an interim rent should continue as a counter-claim and he ordered that the tenants' proceedings for a new tenancy be discontinued. The tenants were ordered to pay the landlords' costs of the tenants' proceedings down to and including 23 January 1981.

If the order of Slade J of 22 May 1981 is the date when the tenants' application for a new tenancy 'is finally disposed of' then by s 64 the existing tenancy will terminate on 22 August 1981. If the tenants' proceedings are only finally disposed of by appellate proceedings then the existing tenancy will terminate three months after the date of final disposal of those proceedings. In this court the landlords, appealing against the decision of Slade J, have submitted that the tenants should only be allowed to discontinue their proceedings for a new tenancy on terms that they waive any compensation under the 1954 Act. The landlords further submit that the tenants should pay all the costs of the tenants' proceedings for a new tenancy and that the tenants are liable to pay an interim rent from 9 March 1981 and until the termination of the existing tenancy. The landlords are agreeable to any formula which will establish the order of Slade J as the final disposition of the tenants' proceedings for a new tenancy, a formula which will entitle the landlords to an interim rent from 9 March 1981 until 22 August 1981, that is to say three months after Slade J made his order dated 22 May 1981.

On the present wording of s 37 of the 1954 Act as amended the tenants are entitled to compensation if they withdraw their application for a new tenancy. The section provides for compensation if a landlord serves a notice opposing the grant of a new tenancy on the ground of s 30(1)(f) and the tenant either makes no application for a new tenancy or withdraws his application. But, as counsel on behalf of the landlords pointed out, the tenants cannot withdraw their application without leave and the question is whether, in the exercise of its discretion under RSC Ord 21, r 3, the court should allow the tenants to withdraw their application without imposing terms on the tenants.

Section 37 of the 1954 Act as originally enacted only provided compensation where the court dismissed a tenant's application for a new tenancy because the landlord had established a ground of opposition within s 30(1)(e), (f) or (g). The tenant could not claim compensation if he withdrew his application. The 1954 Act was amended by the Law of Property Act 1969 so as to enable a tenant to claim compensation if the landlord served a counter-notice and the tenant either did not apply to the court at all or, after making an application, withdrew that application before it came on for hearing before the court. One object of the amendment was to save the time and expense involved in initiating or continuing an application to the court, an application in which the tenant no longer had any confidence in the face of the landlord's counter-notice, but an application which the tenant was compelled to continue in order to obtain compensation when the court ultimately refused his application. Counsel for the landlords submitted that the amendment was never intended to allow a tenant to claim compensation if he withdraws his application for a new tenancy after the landlord has withdrawn his opposition to the grant of a new tenancy.

If the tenant proceeds with his application after the landlord has withdrawn his opposition, the tenant will be entitled to an order for a new tenancy; by s 36(2) the tenant can apply within 14 days from the order for the order to be revoked and can thus refuse to take up the new tenancy, but in that event no provision is made for the tenant to receive compensation. Counsel for the landlords submitted that the discretion conferred on the court by RSC Ord 21, r 3, should be exercised so as to preserve to the landlords the advantage they had already gained. The landlords, he said, obtained an advantage in July 1980 when they abandoned their opposition to the grant of a new tenancy and thus made it certain that, if the tenants continued with their application for a new tenancy, the landlords could not be obliged to pay compensation.

Counsel for the landlords submitted that authority established the principle that the

court, in the judicial exercise of its discretion under Ord 21, r 3, would not deprive the
landlords of the advantage which they had gained when they changed their minds in *a*
July 1980 and decided no longer to oppose the grant of a new tenancy before the tenants
in turn changed their minds in August 1980 and decided to withdraw their application
for a new tenancy. Whitford J accepted a similar submission in *Young, Austen & Young
Ltd v British Medical Association* [1977] 2 All ER 884, [1977] 1 WLR 881 and only allowed
the tenants to discontinue an application for a new tenancy on their undertaking not to
pursue their claim to compensation under s 37.   *b*

Counsel for the tenants referred to two anomalies which arise if, in the exercise of the
discretion conferred by Ord 21, r 3, the court is only prepared to grant leave to the
tenants to discontinue their proceedings for a new tenancy provided they abandon their
claim for compensation.

If a tenant serves a request for a new tenancy and the landlord serves a counter-notice
opposing the grant of a new tenancy and the landlord withdraws his opposition within *c*
four months after the tenant's request, it is open to the tenant also to change his mind
and to forfeit his right to a new tenancy by making no application to the court for a new
tenancy within the prescribed four months' period. In this unlikely combination of
events, s 37 as amended provides for compensation to be paid to the tenant. The landlord
will lose the advantage which, it is said, he obtains by withdrawing his opposition to the
grant of a new tenancy before the tenant decides to abandon his application. I agree with *d*
counsel for the landlords that this result follows because in the circumstances Ord 21, r 3,
has no application.

Similarly, in the county court, which has jurisdiction under Part II of the 1954 Act as
amended, where the rateable value of the demised premises does not exceed £5,000,
there is no rule which confers on the county court the discretion which is to be found in
Ord 21, r 3. A tenant may withdraw his application to the county court for a new tenancy *e*
without leave and cannot be deprived of the claim to compensation under s 37 if he
withdraws his application, even if the landlords have withdrawn their opposition to the
grant of a new tenancy before the tenant decides to withdraw his application for a new
tenancy. Again, in those circumstances, the landlord will lose the advantage which
counsel for the landlords claims. But I agree with him that the absence of a discretion in
the county court does not assist the High Court in the exercise of its undoubted discretion *f*
under Ord 21, r 3.

He referred to authority in support of his submission that the landlords should not be
deprived of the advantage which they gained when in July 1980 they withdrew their
opposition to the grant of a new tenancy. In *Stahlschmidt v Walford* (1879) 4 QBD 217 the
court refused to allow a plaintiff to discontinue an action in which an arbitrator had
found facts adverse to the plaintiff in a case stated. The advantage in that case consisted *g*
of findings of fact which the defendant had established and it would have been unjust to
enable the plaintiff to dispute those findings in a fresh action.

In my judgment, that decision is of no assistance in the present circumstances where
the landlords claim an advantage as a result of the accidental and fortuitous fact that they
changed their minds in July 1980 before the tenants changed their minds in August
1980. In *Stahlschmidt v Walford* (1879) 4 QBD 217 at 219 it was held by Cockburn CJ that *h*
the defendant was 'in justice entitled to the fruits of these proceedings, and we ought not
to interfere to deprive him of them'. In the present case the landlords did not become
entitled to the fruits of any proceedings. They abandoned their opposition to the tenants
culling the fruits of their proceedings for a new tenancy shortly before the tenants
concluded that the fruits were not worth culling. In the same case (1879) 4 QBD 217 at
219 Mellor J said that the discretion exercisable to impose terms on the withdrawal of *j*
proceedings 'must be exercised within certain limitations, and so as not to take away
from the defendant any advantage to which he is fairly and reasonably entitled'. In *Covell
Matthews & Partners v French Wools Ltd* [1977] 2 All ER 591 at 594, [1977] 1 WLR 876 at
879, approved by the Court of Appeal in [1978] 2 All ER 800, [1978] 1 WLR 1477,
Graham J echoed the words of Mellor J and said that 'the defendant is not to be deprived

of some advantage which he has already gained in the litigation'. In the present case the
landlords did not gain an advantage by the litigation or at all. In July 1980 the landlords
abandoned the right to prevent the tenants obtaining a new tenancy. The landlords in
July 1980 could not foresee and were not entitled to the advantage of regaining possession
of the property without payment of compensation. The landlords seek an advantage
which will only accrue to them if the court now imposes terms on the tenants, namely
the advantage of recovering demised premises without payment of compensation.

I therefore reject counsel for the landlords' ingenious submission which in effect
meant that the landlords would be entitled to the best of both worlds because the
landlords withdrew their opposition before the tenants withdrew their application.

In my judgment, where a landlord serves a counter-notice based on grounds within
s 30(1)(e), (f) or (g), he is asserting a right to inflict loss or damage on the tenant by
requiring the tenant to quit the premises. The counter-notice creates difficulties for the
tenants who cannot know whether the landlord will succeed in his opposition or not.
The prudent tenant must, therefore, cast around for alternative courses open to him if he
is obliged to quit the premises and must then decide whether it is safer to adopt one of
those alternative courses or to take the risks inherent in proceeding with an application
for a new tenancy. The tenant's difficulties do not disappear if the landlord withdraws
his opposition. In the present case the landlords, by their counter-notice in March 1980,
asserted that they intended to carry out redevelopment on the premises and required
possession for that purpose. The withdrawal by the landlords in July 1980 of their
opposition on these grounds left alive the possibility that the landlords remained anxious
to redevelop and would be able to prevail on the court to grant a new tenancy to the
tenants of a short duration or a tenancy which could be determined by the landlords as
soon as they were in a position to carry out works of redevelopment. When a landlord
serves a counter-notice under s 30(1)(e), (f) or (g) he brings to bear influence and pressure
on the tenant to consider the advisability of quitting the premises. That pressure and
influence are not removed as soon as the landlord withdraws his opposition. By then the
tenant will, in most cases, have made investigations and inquiries which he would not
have made if the landlord had not served a counter-notice in the first place. The prudent
tenant must consider his alternatives and will have reason to fear that his days of
occupation are numbered and will not be reassured by the withdrawal of the landlord's
opposition to the grant of a new tenancy.

In my judgment, a landlord who serves a counter-notice opposing the grant of a new
tenancy under s 30(1)(e), (f) or (g) presents the tenant with a choice between the doubtful
possibility of a new tenancy or the certainty of compensation under s 37. Once such a
counter-notice is served, the landlord has no right both to recover the demised premises
and to avoid payment of compensation.

It is not right to treat the tenant as being in no different or worse position than he
would have occupied if the landlord had never served a counter-notice.

In the present case it is not just to deprive the tenants of compensation because of the
accident that the landlords in July 1980 completed their inquiries and investigations
which satisfied them that they could not, or no longer wished to, persist in opposing the
grant of a new tenancy, whereas it was not until August 1980 that the tenants completed
inquiries and investigations which satisfied them that, having regard to the landlords'
conduct or to other factors, the tenants no longer wished to persist in their application
for a new tenancy. If the tenants had repented of their application to the court in June
1980 before the landlords repented of their counter-notice in July 1980 the tenants would
clearly have been entitled to compensation. I do not accept that the fact that the landlords
happened to repent one month before the tenants enables the landlords, who made
themselves liabile to pay compensation by serving a counter-notice, now to recover
possession of the demised premises without compensation.

In my judgment, when a tenant applies for leave to discontinue an application for a
new tenancy, the correct judicial principle which the court ought to apply in considering
the exercise of its discretion under RSC Ord 21, r 3, involves the court in inquiring

whether the landlord has been prejudiced. The fact that the landlord will be obliged to pay compensation is not in itself evidence of prejudice because the 1954 Act provides for compensation to be paid if the landlord has served the counter-notice. The tenant should be allowed unconditionally to withdraw his application for a new tenancy even if the landlord has withdrawn his counter-notice, unless the landlord has been prejudiced by the delay or by the events which have occurred between the date when the landlord withdrew his opposition to the grant of a new tenancy and the date when the landlord is informed that the tenant does not propose to proceed with his application for a new tenancy.

There is no evidence that the landlords in the present case suffered because they were not informed in June or July 1980 that the tenants would not persist in their application for a new tenancy. The landlords have been in no hurry to recover possession and could not have hoped in practice to recover possession before the tenants were willing to vacate the premises on 31 March 1981. The landlords were informed in October 1980 of the tenants' intentions and it would have been a simple matter for the landlords to have arranged with the tenants for the landlords to take possession of the demised premises on 31 March 1981 when the tenants vacated the premises without prejudice to the outcome of the disputes between the landlords and the tenants over the right to compensation and over interim rent. The landlords could have applied for an interim rent to take effect after 18 December 1980 but they neglected to do so until 9 March 1981. After the tenants vacated the premises on 31 March 1981 the landlords allowed the premises to lie idle and are now in a position to demand rent from the tenants at a rate determined by the court pursuant to s 24A for the period from 9 March 1981 until 22 August 1981. It does not appear to me that the landlords have suffered from the delay and it was open to them to bring the delay to an end and to recover possession at any time on or after 31 March 1981. I cannot see, therefore, that the landlords have suffered and I would dismiss the appeal. It follows that I would also disapprove of the decision of Whitford J in *Young, Austen & Young Ltd v British Medical Association* [1977] 2 All ER 884, [1977] 1 WLR 881.

By the Local Government, Planning and Land Act 1980, s 193, and Sch 33, para 4, the provisions of s 37 of the 1954 Act were amended so as to permit the Secretary of State by statutory instrument to prescribe that a multiple of the rateable value of the demised premises should be the amount of compensation payable by the landlord. By the Landlord and Tenant Act 1954 (Appropriate Multiplier) Regulations 1981, SI 1981/69, which came into force on 25 March 1981, the minister prescribed 2¼ as the appropriate multiplier. In the present case, and notwithstanding the decision of this court in *Cardshops Ltd v John Lewis Properties Ltd* [1982] 3 All ER 746, [1982] 3 WLR 803, the tenants have agreed to limit their claims to compensation to twice the rateable value.

Accordingly, on the tenants' undertaking not to require payment of compensation in excess of twice the rateable value of the premises and on the landlords' undertaking not to require payment of any rent for any period after 22 August 1981, I would dismiss the appeal.

Appeal dismissed. Leave to appeal to the House of Lords refused. Compensation to be payable and interim rent to cease to be payable from 22 August 1981.

Solicitors: *Comptroller and City Solicitor*; *Cameron Markby* (for the tenants).

Henrietta Steinberg   Barrister.

Ailsa Craig Fishing Co Ltd v Malvern Fishing Co Ltd and another et e contra

HOUSE OF LORDS

LORD WILBERFORCE, LORD ELWYN-JONES, LORD SALMON, LORD FRASER OF TULLYBELTON AND LORD LOWRY

21, 22 OCTOBER, 26 NOVEMBER 1981

Contract – Construction – Exception clause – Liability limited in amount – Complete failure to perform contract – Whether defendant entitled to rely on limitation clause when he has totally failed to perform contractual services.

The appellants were the owners of a fishing boat which sank on 31 December 1971 while berthed in Aberdeen harbour. The vessel was a complete loss. At the time the respondents, a security company, were required by a contract made with a fishing boat owners' association of which the appellants were a member to provide a security service in the harbour. In particular, the respondents were required to provide a continuous security cover for the appellants' vessel. However, condition 2(a) of the security service contract provided that the respondents' liability was to be totally excluded in certain circumstances, while condition 2(f) of the contract stated that in the event of the respondents incurring liability 'for any loss or damage of whatever nature arising out of ... or [the] failure in [the] provision of the services' contracted for, such liability was to be limited to £1,000 in respect of any claim arising from a duty assumed by the respondents and £10,000 for the consequences of any incident involving liability by the respondents. The appellants brought an action in Scotland against the respondents claiming damages. At first instance the judge held that the appellants' loss had been caused by negligence and breach of contract on the part of the respondents and assessed damages in favour of the appellants at some £55,000. The respondents appealed to the Court of Session, conceding that they had been negligent and in breach of contract but contending that their liability was excluded or limited by the terms of condition 2(f). The court allowed the appeal, holding that the respondents' liability was limited under condition 2(f) to £1,000 even though there had been a total failure by the respondents to perform the contract. The appellants appealed to the House of Lords, contending (i) that condition 2(f) could not apply because there had been a total failure by the respondents to perform the contract, (ii) that condition 2 as a whole was inconsistent in that it purported both to exclude liability and to limit liability, and (iii) that condition 2(f) was by itself inconsistent in that it was not clear whether liability would be limited to £1,000 or £10,000 in any particular case.

Held – The appeal would be dismissed for the following reasons—

(1) The issue of whether a condition in a contract limiting liability was effective depended on the construction of the condition in the context of the contract as a whole. Furthermore, although a limitation clause had to be clearly and unambiguously expressed in order to be effective and was to be construed contra proferentem, the relevant words were, if possible, to be given their natural, plain meaning. Thus a limitation clause was not to be construed as rigidly and strictly as an exclusion clause since an agreed limitation of liability was more likely to accord with the true intention of the parties (having regard to the amount of the potential loss in relation to the sum paid for the service contracted to be rendered) than an exclusion of all liability (see p 102 *j* to p 103 *a*, p 104 *d e*, p 105 *h* to p 106 *a* and p 107 *h j*, post); *W & S Pollock & Co v Macrae* 1922 SC (HL) 192 explained.

(2) On its true construction condition 2(f) was effective in limiting the respondents' liability to £1,000 because (a) it applied not only where there was a partial failure to perform the contracted services but also where there was a total failure to perform the

services, (b) the validity of condition 2(f) was unaffected by any inconsistency with
condition 2(a), which purported to exclude all liability, since the fact that such   *a*
inconsistency might cast doubt on the validity of the exclusion clause did not necessarily
mean that condition 2(f) which limited liability, was invalid, and (c) the limitation of the
respondents' liability to £10,000 only applied where there was more than one claim
arising out of the same incident, whereas the respondents' liability in fact arose out of a
single claim, for which the limit of liability was £1,000 (see p 103 g h, p 104 b to e and
p 107 a b and d to j, post).

b

Notes
For exclusion clauses and limitation clauses in contracts, see 9 Halsbury's Laws (4th edn)
paras 363–365.

Cases referred to in opinions
Canada Steamship Lines Ltd v R [1952] 1 All ER 305, [1952] AC 192, PC, 11 Digest (Reissue)
    697, 213.
Mechans Ltd v Highland Marine Charters Ltd 1964 SC 48, CS, Digest (Cont Vol B) 635,
    1121a.
Pollock (W & S) & Co v Macrae 1922 SC (HL) 192, 39 Digest (Repl) 578, 566.
Smith v UMB Chrysler (Scotland) Ltd 1978 SC (HL) 1.

c

d

Consolidated appeals
In consolidated appeals the pursuers, Ailsa Craig Fishing Co Ltd, appealed with leave of
the Court of Session granted on 13 November 1980 against two interlocutors of the First
Division of the Court of Session (the Lord President (Lord Emslie), Lord Cameron and
Lord Dunpark) dated 13 November 1980 allowing in part reclaiming motions by the   *e*
respondents, the second defenders Securicor (Scotland) Ltd, against interlocutors of the
Lord Ordinary (Wylie) dated 6 April 1979 and 9 May 1981 allowing claims for damages
brought in two separate actions, namely (i) an action commenced on 21 December 1973·
by the appellants against the first defenders, Malvern Fishing Co Ltd, and the respondents
in respect of the sinking of the appellants' motor trawler Strathallan, and (ii) an action
commenced on 25 September 1973 by the first defenders against the appellants in respect   *f*
of the sinking of the first defenders' motor trawler George Craig and in which the
appellants joined the respondents as third parties. The facts are set out in the judgment
of Lord Fraser.

A Malcolm Morison QC and *W A Nimmo Smith* (both of the Scottish Bar) for the appellants.
Richard Yorke QC, Kenneth H Osborne QC and *P H Brodie* (both of the Scottish Bar) with   *g*
    him, for the respondents.

Their Lordships took time for consideration.

26 November. The following opinions were delivered.

h

LORD WILBERFORCE. My Lords, the only questions for decision in these appeals
are (i) whether the liability of the respondents, Securicor (Scotland) Ltd, under a short-
term contract made on 31 December 1971, has been effectively limited by a special
condition in that contract, and if so (ii) whether the applicable limit is £1,000 or £10,000.
    Whether a condition limiting liability is effective or not is a question of construction
of that condition in the context of the contract as a whole. If it is to exclude liability for   *j*
negligence, it must be most clearly and unambiguously expressed, and, in such a contract
as this, must be construed contra proferentem. I do not think that there is any doubt so
far. But I venture to add one further qualfication, or at least clarification: one must not
strive to create ambiguities by strained construction, as I think the appellants have striven
to do. The relevant words must be given, if possible, their natural, plain meaning.
Clauses of limitation are not regarded by the courts with the same hostility as clauses of

exclusion; this is because they must be related to other contractual terms, in particular to
a the risks to which the defending party may be exposed, the remuneration which he
receives and possibly also the opportunity of the other party to insure.

It is clear, on the findings of the Lord Ordinary (Wylie), that the respondents were
negligent as well as in material breach of their contractual obligations. The negligence
consisted in a total or partial failure to provide the service contracted for, viz 'continuous
security cover for your [the appellants'] vessels from 1900 hours on 31/12/71 until 0700
b hours on 5/1/72' over the increased area specified in the contract. It is arguable, in my
opinion, that the failure was not total, in that some security against some risks was
provided, though not that which was necessary to prevent the actual damage which
occurred. But I do not think that it makes a difference as regards the applicability of the
clause of limitation whether this is right or not, and since their Lordships in the Inner
House were of opinion that the failure was total, I will proceed on the assumption that
c this was so.

The clause of limitation was as follows (condition 2(f) of the special conditions of the
contract):

> 'If, pursuant to the provisions set out herein, any liability on the part of the
> Company shall arise (whether under the express or implied terms of this Contract,
> or at Common Law, or in any other way) to the customer for any loss or damage of
d > whatever nature arising out of or connected with the provision of, or purported
> provision of, or failure in provision of, the services covered by this Contract, such
> liability shall be limited to the payment by the Company by way of damages of a
> sum [alternatives are then stated to which I shall refer later].'

This clause is on the face of it clear. It refers to failure in provision of the services covered
e by the contract. There is no warrant as a matter of construction for reading 'failure' as
meaning 'partial failure', i e as excluding 'total failure' and there is no warrant in authority
for so reading the word as a matter of law. I am clearly of opinion that *W & S Pollock &
Co v Macrae* 1922 SC (HL) 192 is no such authority, and if the later case of *Mechans Ltd v
Highland Marine Charters Ltd* 1964 SC 48 so decided it ought in my view not to be
followed.

f The appellants tried to find an ambiguity in this clause in three ways.

(1) First they relied on the finding of the Lord Ordinary, with which the Inner House
generally agreed, that there was such an inconsistency between the provisions of condition
2(a), excluding liability, and those of condition 2(f) as to create uncertainty as to the
meaning of the former condition. It was this inconsistency which led the courts below
to conclude against the validity of the exclusion clause. So it was argued the same
g inconsistency and the doubts engendered by it must invalidate condition 2(f). But this is
transparently fallacious. Because cl A casts doubt on the meaning of cl B, it does not
follow at all that the converse is true and that cl B casts doubt on the meaning of cl A.
Clause B must be looked at on its own, and may turn out to be perfectly clear. A similar
argument was presented as to an inconsistency between condition 2(f) and condition 4(i)
and, in my opinion, fails for the same reason.

h (2) It was contended that the initial words 'If, pursuant to the provisions set out herein'
are ambiguous and that their ambiguity invalidates the whole subclause. But I accept on
this the conclusion of Lord Dunpark that the words are 'open to construction' and I agree
on the construction which he prefers. The possibility of construction of a clause does not
amount to ambiguity: that disappears after the court has pronounced the meaning.

(3) There is an inconsistency between cll (i)(a) and (b) of condition 2(f) so that it is
j impossible to arrive at a figure of limitation clearly expressed. Therefore, it is said, no
limitation has effectively been made. I reproduce these clauses:

> '(i) in the case of all services other than the Special Delivery Service (a) Not
> exceeding £1,000 in respect of any one claim arising from any duty assumed by the
> Company which involves the operation, testing, examination, or inspection of the
> operational condition of any machine, plant or equipment in or about the customer's
> premises, or which involves the provision of any service not solely related to the

prevention or detection of fire or theft; (b) Not exceeding a maximum of £10,000 for the consequences of any incident involving fire theft or any other cause of liability in the Company under the terms thereof; and further provided that the total liability of the Company shall not in any circumstances exceed the sum of £10,000 in respect of all and any incidents arising during any consecutive period of twelve months.'

For my part I find these conditions, though intricate, perfectly clear. Clause (a) limits any one claim; cl (b) limits any aggregate of claims which are the consequences of any one incident; the proviso limits the total liability of Securicor in respect of incidents arising in any period of 12 months. The conditions may overlap, in the sense that more than one may apply: they may give rise to difficulty, e g if the total liability is exhausted early in the 12 months period, and other claims arise. But I cannot find any ambiguity in them, notably in relation to the present case. And this answers the second question. I have no doubt that cl (a) applies so as to limit individual claims to £1,000 each. There is no question here of applying cl (b). For these reasons I would dismiss the appeals.

LORD ELWYN-JONES. My Lords, I have had the advantage of reading in draft the speeches of my noble and learned friends Lord Wilberforce and Lord Fraser. For the reasons they have given I would refuse the appeal and I agree that the respondents must have their costs in this House.

LORD SALMON. My Lords, I have had the advantage of reading the speeches of my noble and learned friends Lord Wilberforce and Lord Fraser. Although I consider that Securicor's contract was deplorably drafted, I agree for the reasons stated by my noble and learned friends that the appeal must be dismissed.

LORD FRASER OF TULLYBELTON. My Lords, the only surviving issue in these appeals is whether the respondents (Securicor) have succeeded in limiting their liability under a contract between themselves and the Aberdeen Fishing Vessel Owners' Association Ltd (the association) who were acting on behalf of a number of owners of fishing vessels, including the appellants. Nothing turns on the fact that the appellants were not themselves a party to the contract and I shall proceed as if the contract had been made with them.

The appellants were the owners of the fishing vessel Strathallan which sank while berthed in Aberdeen Harbour on 31 December 1971, at a time when Securicor were bound, under the contract with the association, to provide security cover in the harbour. Her gallows fouled the vessel moored next to her on the starboard side, called the George Craig, which also sank. Both vessels became total losses. Two actions were then raised. In one the appellants claimed damages from the owners of George Craig as first defenders and from Securicor as second defenders. In the other the owners of the George Craig claimed damages from the appellants, who brought in Securicor as a third party. The Lord Ordinary (Wylie) held that the loss of both vessels had been caused by breach of contract and negligence on the part of Securicor. He found them liable to the appellants in damages for the loss of the Strathallan, and found them liable to relieve the appellants of their full liability to the owners of the George Craig for the loss of that vessel. He assessed the damages in each case at a little over £55,000. The Lord Ordinary rejected arguments on behalf of Securicor to the effect that their liability was either wholly excluded, or limited in amount, by the terms of their contract. Securicor reclaimed against the Lord Ordinary's judgment but they did not contest his findings of breach of contract and negligence. Their contention on the reclaiming motion was solely that their liability had been either excluded or limited by the terms of the contract. The First Division of the Court of Session (the Lord President (Lord Emslie), Lord Cameron and Lord Dunpark) allowed the reclaiming motion in part, holding that liability had been limited in amount but that it had not been excluded. The appellants now appeal to your Lordships' House against that decision in so far as it held that liability had been limited.

In order to appreciate the contentions of the parties, it is necessary to refer briefly to the circumstances in which the contract came to be made. Until 31 December 1971 Securicor had for some months been providing a security service for vessels of owners represented by the association. They did so under a contract dated 12 May 1971, under which the service was limited to vessels berthed at the Albert Quay in Aberdeen Harbour, and operated only during the nights and at weekends. The main object was to prevent intruders from boarding unmanned vessels and damaging them or stealing from them. Early on 31 December an official of the association realised that the service would not be adequate for the New Year period, partly because there were many more vessels than usual in the harbour and partly because they would be remaining there for several days. Owing to the unusual number of vessels they could not all be berthed at Albert Quay, where security patrols were already provided during certain hours, and some of them would have to be berthed at the Fish Market/Commercial Quay (the Fish Market area). The quay in the Fish Market area was of open structure, and there was a special risk that vessels might slide under the deck of the quay and become caught or 'snubbed' by the bow. The risk arose especially on a rising tide. That was just what happened to the appellants' vessel, the Strathallan, during the evening of 31 December 1971, and caused her to sink taking the George Craig with her. As Securicor accept the Lord Ordinary's findings of fault against them, it is unnecessary to refer in greater detail to the events of that evening. Securicor also accept the decision of the First Division that the liability was not wholly excluded by the contract.

The question whether Securicor's liability has been limited falls to be answered by construing the terms of the contract in accordance with the ordinary principles applicable to contracts of this kind. The argument for limitation depends on certain special conditions attached to the contract prepared on behalf of Securicor and put forward in their interest. There is no doubt that such conditions must be construed strictly against the proferens, in this case Securicor, and that in order to be effective they must be 'most clearly and unambiguously expressed': see *W & S Pollock & Co v Macrae* 1922 SC (HL) 192 at 199 per Lord Dunedin. *Pollock v Macrae* was a decision on an exclusion clause but in so far as it emphasised the need for clarity in clauses to be construed contra proferentem it is in my opinion relevant to the present case also. It has sometimes apparently been regarded as laying down, as a proposition of law, that a condition excluding liability can never have any application where there has been a total breach of contract, but I respectfully agree with the Lord President (Lord Emslie) who said in his opinion in the present case that that was a misunderstanding of *Pollock v Macrae*. *Pollock v Macrae* was followed by the Second Division in *Mechans Ltd v Highland Marine Charters Ltd* 1964 SC 48 and there are passages in the judgments in that case which might seem to treat *Pollock v Macrae* as having laid down some such general proposition of law, although it is not clear that they were so intended. If they were I would regard them as being erroneous. *Mechans v Highland Marine Charters Ltd* appears to have been relied on by counsel for the appellants before the Second Division, but was not relied on in this House.

There are later authorities which lay down very strict principles to be applied when considering the effect of clauses of exclusion or of indemnity: see particularly the Privy Council case of *Canada Steamship Lines Ltd v R* [1952] 1 All ER 305 at 310, [1952] AC 192 at 208, where Lord Morton, delivering the advice of the Board, summarised the principles in terms which have recently been applied by this House in *Smith v UMB Chrysler (Scotland) Ltd* 1978 SC (HL) 1. In my opinion these principles are not applicable in their full rigour when considering the effect of conditions merely limiting liability. Such conditions will of course be read contra proferentem and must be clearly expressed, but there is no reason why they should be judged by the specially exacting standards which are applied to exclusion and indemnity clauses. The reason for imposing such standards on these conditions is the inherent improbability that the other party to a contract including such a condition intended to release the proferens from a liability that would otherwise fall on him. But there is no such high degree of improbability that he would agree to a limitation of the liability of the proferens, especially when, as explained in condition 4(i) of the present contract, the potential losses that might be caused by the negligence of the proferens or its servants are so great in proportion to the sums that can reasonably be charged for the services contracted for. It is enough in the present case that *a* the condition must be clear and unambiguous.

The contract was arranged during the morning of 31 December 1971 in some haste. It is set out on a form partly printed and partly filled in in ink, which is headed 'Temporary Contract or Contract Change Request' and in which the association 'request Securicor Ltd. to carry out the services detailed below subject to the Special Conditions printed overleaf'. The form requested 'continuous security cover for your [sic] vessels *b* from 19.00 hours on 31/12/71 until 07.00 hours on 5/1/72' and stated that the area covered was to be extended to include the Fish Market area. Nothing turns on that part of the contract but I should mention that the appellants contended that this temporary contract, so long as it was in operation, entirely superseded the contract of 12 May 1971 and was the sole measure of parties' rights and obligations to one another. Having regard to condition 8 of the special conditions, I see no reason to question that contention. *c*

The 'special conditions of contract' were elaborate and are applied to services of several types. So far as this appeal is concerned, the part which is most directly applicable is condition 2, and especially para (f) of that condition. Condition 2(f) is in the following terms:

'If, pursuant to the provisions set out herein, any liability on the part of the Company shall arise (whether under the express or implied terms of this Contract *d* or at Common Law, or in any other way) to the customer for any loss or damage of whatever nature arising out of or connected with the provision of, or purported provision of, or failure in provision of, the services covered by this Contract, such liability shall be limited to the payment by the Company by way of damages of a sum: (i) In the case of all services other than the Special Delivery Service (a) Not exceeding £1,000 in respect of any one claim arising from any duty assumed by the *e* Company which involves the operation, testing, examination, or inspection of the operational condition of any machine, plant or equipment in or about the customer's premises, or which involves the provision of any service not solely related to the prevention or detection of fire or theft; (b) Not exceeding a maximum of £10,000 for the consequences of any incident involving fire, theft or any other cause of liability in the Company under the terms hereof; and further provided that the total *f* liability of the Company shall not in any circumstances exceed the sum of £10,000 in respect of all and any incidents arising during any consecutive period of twelve months . . .'

On behalf of the appellants it was argued that condition 2(f), even if apparently clear in its own terms, is not applicable when read in the context of the contract as a whole, *g* where there has been a total failure to perform the services contracted for or what is sometimes called a total failure of contract, and that this was such a case. It was said that condition 2(f) must be qualified by the opening words of condition 2 and of para (a) of that condition which show that liability can only arise for some fault in the course of providing the services contracted for, and not where there has been a total failure to provide the service. I cannot accept that submission, because condition 2(f) expressly *h* states that it applies to liability arising out of 'the provision of, or purported provision of, or *failure* in provision of' the services contracted for. If this submission had not been so persuasively presented, I would have thought it to be unarguable in face of the provisions of para (f).

The learned judges of the First Division found that this was a case of total failure or total breach of contract, in the sense of Lord Dunedin's speech in *Pollock v Macrae*. As *j* that is the finding most favourable to the appellants on this part of the case it is not now material to consider whether this is strictly a case of total failure. If the question had been material at this stage I would have wished to give it further consideration, because there is no suggestion that the security cover was not duly maintained during the evening of 31 December 1971 in the Albert Dock area, which was part of the area covered by the temporary contract, and I think there is much to be said for the view that the contract was performed in part. But it is not necessary to come to a decision on that point.

A further argument for the appellants was that condition 2(f) applied only to liability
a which arose 'pursuant to' the provisions of the contract, and that 'pursuant to' meant 'in
accordance with the express provisions of the contract'. This meaning was said to be
emphasised by the first sentence of condition 4(iii). But that argument fails, in my
opinion, if for no other reason than that condition 2(f) itself proclaims unambiguously
that it applies to liability which shall arise under the 'express or implied' terms of the
contract. Next, the appellants argued that there is an inconsistency between condition
b 2(a) which purports to exclude liability altogether and condition 2(f) which purports to
limit the amount of liability in certain cases. The existence of that inconsistency was one
of the reasons for the First Division's decision that the exclusion clause was lacking in
clarity, and counsel for the appellants sought to apply the same argument in reverse to
the limitation clause. But the argument is in my opinion unsound. It is one thing to say,
as the First Division did, that when you find a provision for limiting liability coming
c after a provision which is capable of being read as excluding liability altogether, the
limitation provision casts doubt on the meaning of the earlier one. But it is quite a
different thing to say that the inconsistency casts doubt on the meaning of the limitation
clause. If the exclusion clause had succeeded in its purpose, the limitation might have
been unnecessary, but its meaning as a sort of long stop is, in my opinion clear, and is not
affected by the existence of the exclusion clause.

d   A separate argument was advanced to the effect that condition 2(f) was confused and
uncertain in itself because the provisions of cll (i)(a) and (b) did not make it clear whether
the limit of liability in any particular case was £1,000 or £10,000. Perhaps the intention
of cll (a) and (b) may not be immediately clear on first reading to a person unfamiliar
with provisions of this sort, but a very little consideration is enough to show, in my
opinion, that the meaning is that explained by the learned judges of the First Division.
e Clause (a) relates to any *claim* arising in any of the ways there mentioned and it limits the
liability of Securicor to £1,000 for each claim. Clause (b) relates to any one *incident* and
limits their liability to £10,000 in respect of each incident. The two provisions overlap
but they are in no way inconsistent. For example, in the present case the owner of each
of the vessels has a separate claim which, if the clause is applicable, will be limited to
£1,000. But both claims arise out of one incident, and if there had been more than ten
f claims for £1,000 each arising out of the same incident, the total liability of Securicor
would have been limited to £10,000. That meaning is in my view clear and unambiguous
and I reject this argument.

Having considered these particular criticisms of condition 2(f) the question remains
whether in its context it is sufficiently clear and unambiguous to receive effect in limiting
the liability of Securicor for its own negligence or that of its employees. In my opinion it
g is. It applies to any liability 'whether under the express or implied terms of this contract,
or at common law, or in any other way'. Liability at common law is undoubtedly wide
enough to cover liability including the negligence of the proferens itself, so that even
without relying on the final words 'any other way', I am clearly of opinion that the
negligence of Securicor is covered.

For these reasons I would refuse the appeal. The respondents must have their costs in
h this House.

LORD LOWRY. My Lords, I have had the opportunity of reading in draft the speeches
of my noble and learned friends, Lord Wilberforce and Lord Fraser. There is nothing
which I can usefully add, since I entirely agree with their reasoning and conclusions and
with the order proposed. I, too, would dismiss the appeal.

j   *Appeal dismissed.*

Solicitors: *Holman Fenwick & Willan*, agents for *Boyd Jameson & Young WS*, Leith (for the
appellants); *Hextall Erskine & Co*, agents for *Strathern & Blair WS*, Edinburgh (for the
respondents).

Mary Rose Plummer   Barrister.

George Mitchell (Chesterhall) Ltd v Finney Lock Seeds Ltd

COURT OF APPEAL, CIVIL DIVISION
LORD DENNING MR, OLIVER AND KERR LJJ
26, 27, 28, 29 JULY, 29 SEPTEMBER 1982

Contract – Condition – Incorporation in contract – Trade usage – Oral contract in course of trade – Contract for supply of seed – Seed supplied with invoice purporting to limit supplier's liability – Common form clause – Whether clause limiting liability forming part of contract.

Contract – Fundamental breach – Effect on clause limiting liability – Construction of exclusion clause – Whether exclusion clause inoperative because of fundamental breach.

Sale of goods – Implied condition as to merchantable quality – Exclusion of implied term – Unfair contract term – Whether fair and reasonable for seller to rely on clause limiting liability for supplying goods not of merchantable quality – Sale of Goods Act 1979, s 55.

By an oral agreement made in December 1973 the defendants, who were seed merchants, agreed to supply the plaintiffs, who were farmers who had dealt with the defendants for some years, with 30 lb of Dutch winter cabbage seed at a cost of £192. The seed was delivered in February 1974 together with an invoice in common form and of long standing in the seed trade which contained a clause purporting to limit the liability of the defendants in the event of the seed proving to be defective to replacing the defective seed or refunding the purchase price thereof and further purporting to 'exclude all liability for any loss or damage arising from the use of any seeds or plants supplied by us and for any consequential loss or damage arising out of such use . . . or for any other loss or damage whatsoever'. The plaintiffs planted some 63 acres using the seed supplied by the defendants. However, unknown to the plaintiffs and as a result of the negligence of the defendants' employees, the seed supplied was not of the variety agreed to be supplied and furthermore was, in the event, unmerchantable. The crop was a failure and had to be ploughed in, and consequently the plaintiffs lost a year's production from the 63 acres. The plaintiffs brought an action against the defendants claiming damages of £61,513 for breach of contract. The defendants contended that they were entitled to rely on the clause in the invoice to limit their liability. The plaintiffs contended (i) that the clause could only be treated as an implied term of the oral contract and that since it was inconsistent with an express term as to the seed to be supplied it was not part of the contract and therefore could not be relied on by the defendants, (ii) that on its true construction the clause did not apply to the breach in question because the seed which had been delivered was not cabbage seed in any accepted sense of the term and (iii) that it would not be fair or reasonable for the defendants to rely on it and therefore, by virtue of s 55(4)[a] set out in para 11 of Sch 1 to the Sale of Goods Act 1979, it was unenforceable. The judge held that, assuming the clause to be a contractual term, it could not exempt the defendants from liability because on its true construction it did not apply where what was delivered was wholly different in kind from that ordered. The judge accordingly awarded the plaintiffs the damages sought plus interest. The defendants appealed. On the appeal the plaintiffs further contended that the exemption clause did not apply because there had been a fundamental breach of the contract.

Held – The appeal would be dismissed for the following reasons—
    (1) The clause limiting liability formed part of the contract since it was a common trade term which had been used in earlier transactions and the plaintiffs were aware of its existence. Accordingly, the issue remained whether on its true construction the clause

---

a   Section 55(4), so far as material, is set out at p 120 j, post

protected the defendants against liability (see p 112 *c d*, p 117 *j*, p 118 *a*, p 122 *c* and
a p 126 *g*, post); *J Evans & Son (Portsmouth) Ltd v Andrea Merzario Ltd* [1976] 2 All ER 930
distinguished.

(2) The plaintiffs could not rely on fundamental breach in order to render the
exclusion clause inoperative because the doctrine of fundamental breach was not a rule
of law. Whatever the nature of a breach, an exemption clause did not terminate or cease
to have effect, but instead remained to be construed along with the rest of the contract in
b order to decide whether the parties intended that its terms should apply to the breach in
question. The words of the clause were to be given their plain, natural meaning and the
court was not entitled to place on an exclusion clause a strained construction for the
purpose of rejecting it. However (per Oliver and Kerr LJJ), clauses which purported to
exclude all liability were to be construed more narrowly than those which sought to
limit liability (see p 114 *g h*, p 117 *j*, p 118 *f* to p 119 *c*, p 120 *a b*, p 122 *h* to p 123 *g*,
c p 124 *b c* and p 126 *g*, post); *Suisse Atlantique Société d'Armement Maritime SA v NV
Rotterdamsche Kolen Centrale* [1966] 2 All ER 61, *Photo Production Ltd v Securicor Transport
Ltd* [1980] 1 All ER 556 and *Ailsa Craig Fishing Co Ltd v Malvern Fishing Co Ltd* [1983] 1
All ER 101 followed; *Glynn & Co v Margetson* [1891–4] All ER Rep 693, *London and North
Western Rly Co v Neilson* [1922] All ER Rep 395 and *Atlantic Shipping and Trading Co v
Louis Dreyfus & Co* [1922] All ER Rep 559 explained.

d (3) The defendants, by delivering seed which was not seed in any commercial sense,
were in breach of an express term of the contract that the seed supplied would be Dutch
winter cabbage seed and of the conditions implied into the contract by s 13(1)[b] of, and
s 14(2)[c] as set out in para 5 of Sch 1 to, the 1979 Act that the seed supplied would
correspond to its contractual description and that it would be of merchantable quality.
Those breaches could not have occurred without negligence on the part of the defendants.
e Accordingly (Lord Denning MR dissenting), on its true construction the limitation clause
did not exempt the defendants from liability because there was nothing in it which
protected them from the consequences of their own negligence and (per Oliver LJ)
because what was delivered was wholly different in kind from that which the plaintiffs
had ordered (see p 117 *h j*, p 119 *e* to *j*, p 120 *f g*, p 124 *g h*, p 125 *a* to *d* and p 126 *g*, post);
Canada Steamship Lines Ltd v R [1952] 1 All ER 305 followed; *Joseph Travers & Sons Ltd v
f Cooper* [1914–15] All ER Rep 104 and *Gibaud v Great Eastern Rly Co* [1921] All ER Rep
35 approved.

(4) The agreement was subject to s 55(4) as set out in para 11 of Sch 1 to the 1979 Act
and, applying s 55(4), it would not be fair or reasonable to permit the defendants to rely
on the clause because they were best able to insure against the risk of such loss, all the
fault lay with them and they had imposed the term unilaterally and without negotiation
g (see p 117 *a d h j*, p 118 *a*, p 121 *c* to *f* and p 125 *f* to p 126 *d* and *g*, post); *R W Green Ltd v
Cade Bros Farm* [1978] 1 Lloyd's Rep 662 distinguished.

Per Lord Denning MR. Quite apart from the provisions of s 55 of the 1979 Act it is a
general principle that the court will not permit a party to rely on an exemption or
limitation clause in circumstances in which it would not be fair or reasonable to allow
reliance on it (see p 115 *b*, post).

h Per Kerr LJ. If the expression 'fundamental breach' is to be retained in any context
whatever, it should be confined to cases of anticipatory breach (see p 123 *a* to *c*, post).

Notes

For the incorporation of exclusions clause in contracts, for the construction of exclusion
clauses and for the effect of breach of contract on exclusion clauses, see 9 Halsbury's Laws
j (4th edn) paras 367–380.

For the Sale of Goods Act 1979, s 13, see 49 Halsbury's Statutes (3rd edn) 1113, and for

---

b Section 13(1), so far as material, provides: 'Where there is a contract for the sale of goods by
   description, there is an implied condition that the goods will correspond with the description.'
c Section 14(2), so far as material, provides: 'Where the seller sells goods in the course of a business,
   there is an implied condition that the goods supplied under the contract are of merchantable
   quality . . .'

ss 14 and 55 of that Act (as set out in paras 5 and 11 of Sch 1 thereto), see ibid 1153 and
1155. Sections 14 and 55 as set out in Sch 1 are the relevant provisions for contracts made   a
between 18 May 1973 and, in the case of s 14, a day to be appointed, and, in the case of
s 55, 1 February 1978. For contracts made after the day to be appointed (in the case of
s 14) and after 1 February 1978 (in the case of s 55) the relevant provisions are ss 14 and
55 of the 1979 Act itself.

Cases referred to in judgments   b
Ailsa Craig Fishing Co Ltd v Malvern Fishing Co Ltd [1983] 1 All ER 101, HL.
Alderslade v Hendon Laundry Ltd [1945] 1 All ER 244, [1945] KB 189, CA, 3 Digest
    (Reissue) 469, 3116.
Atlantic Shipping and Trading Co v Louis Dreyfus & Co [1922] 2 AC 250, [1922] All ER Rep
    559, HL, 12 Digest (Reissue) 310, 2243.
Bank of Australasia v Clan Line Steamers Ltd [1916] 1 KB 39, CA, 41 Digest (Repl) 362,   c
    1548.
Canada Steamship Lines Ltd v R [1952] 1 All ER 305, [1952] AC 192, PC, 11 Digest (Reissue)
    697, 213.
Conemsco Ltd v Contrapol Ltd [1981] CA Bound Transcript 536.
Cunard Steamship Co Ltd v Buerger [1927] AC 1, [1926] All ER Rep 103, HL, 41 Digest
    (Repl) 385, 1732.   d
Evans (J) & Son (Portsmouth) Ltd v Andrea Merzario Ltd [1976] 2 All ER 930, [1976] 1
    WLR 1078, CA, Digest (Cont Vol E) 552, 1509.
Gibaud v Great Eastern Rly Co [1921] 2 KB 426, [1921] All ER Rep 35, CA, 3 Digest
    (Reissue) 455, 3032.
Gillespie Bros & Co Ltd v Roy Bowles Transport Ltd [1973] 1 All ER 193, [1973] QB 400,
    [1972] 3 WLR 1003, CA.   e
Glynn v Margetson & Co [1893] AC 351, [1891–4] All ER Rep 693, HL, 17 Digest (Reissue)
    401, 1645, 8(1) Digest (Reissue) 53, 300.
Green (R W) Ltd v Cade Bros Farm [1978] 1 Lloyd's Rep 602, Digest (Cont Vol E) 520,
    1015a.
Hain Steamship Co Ltd v Tate & Lyle Ltd [1936] 2 All ER 597, HL, 41 Digest (Repl) 385,
    1737.   f
Harbutt's Plasticine Ltd v Wayne Tank and Pump Co Ltd [1970] 1 All ER 225, [1970] 1 QB
    447, [1970] 2 WLR 198, CA, 12 Digest (Reissue) 475, 3407.
Karsales (Harrow) Ltd v Wallis [1956] 2 All ER 866, [1956] 1 WLR 936, CA, 26 Digest
    (Reissue) 772, 5238.
Lamport & Holt Lines Ltd v Coubro & Scrutton (M & I) Ltd, The Raphael [1982] 2 Lloyd's
    Rep 42, CA.   g
L'Estrange v F Graucob Ltd [1934] 2 KB 394, [1934] All ER Rep 16, 12 Digest (Reissue) 78,
    415.
Levison v Patent Steam Carpet Cleaning Co Ltd [1977] 3 All ER 498, [1978] QB 69, [1977] 3
    WLR 90, CA.
London and North Western Rly Co v Neilson [1922] 2 AC 263, [1922] All ER Rep 395, HL,
    8(1) Digest (Reissue) 61, 359.   h
Photo Production Ltd v Securicor Transport Ltd [1980] 1 All ER 556, [1980] AC 827, [1980]
    2 WLR 283, HL; *rvsg* [1978] 3 All ER 146, [1978] 1 WLR 856, CA.
Pollock (W & S) & Co v Macrae 1922 SC (HL) 192, HL, 39 Digest (Repl) 578, 566.
Smeaton Hanscomb & Co Ltd v Sassoon I Setty Son & Co (No 1) [1953] 2 All ER 1471, [1953]
    1 WLR 1468, 39 Digest (Repl) 582, 1046.
Suisse Atlantique Société d'Armement Maritime SA v NV Rotterdamsche Kolen Centrale [1966]   j
    2 All ER 61, [1967] 1 AC 361, [1966] 2 WLR 944, HL, Digest (Cont Vol B) 652, 2413a.
Sze Hai Tong Bank Ltd v Rambler Cycle Co Ltd [1959] 3 All ER 182, [1959] AC 576, [1959]
    3 WLR 214, PC, 41 Digest (Repl) 441, 2226.
Thompson v London Midland and Scottish Rly Co [1930] 1 KB 41, [1929] All ER Rep 474,
    CA, 8(1) Digest (Reissue) 120, 711.

a   *Travers (Joseph) & Sons Ltd v Cooper* [1915] 1 KB 73, [1914–15] All ER Rep 104, CA, 3
Digest (Reissue) 438, 2967.
Wathes (Western) Ltd v Austins (Menswear) Ltd [1976] 1 Lloyd's Rep 14, CA.

Cases also cited

Angelia, The, Trade and Transport Inc v Iino Kaiun Kaisha Ltd [1973] 2 All ER 144, [1973] 1
WLR 210.

b   *Vigers Bros v Sanderson Bros* [1901] 1 KB 608.

Appeal

The defendants, Finney Lock Seeds Ltd, appealed against the judgment of Parker J ([1981]
1 Lloyd's Rep 476) given on 10 December 1980 whereby he awarded the plaintiffs,
George Mitchell (Chesterhall) Ltd, damages of £61,513·78 together with interest of

c   £30,756·00 in the plaintiffs' claim against the defendants for breach of contract. The
facts are set out in the judgment of Lord Denning MR.

Patrick Twigg for the plaintiffs.
Mark Waller QC and *Mordecai Levene* for the defendants.

Cur adv vult

d
29 September. The following judgments were delivered.

LORD DENNING MR.

In outline

Many of you know Lewis Carroll's *Through the Looking-Glass*. In it there are these words

e   (ch 4):

      '"The time has come," the Walrus said,
       "To talk of many things:
       Of shoes—and ships—and sealing wax—
       Of cabbages—and kings . . ."'

f   Today it is not 'of cabbages and kings', but of cabbages and whatnots. Some farmers,
called George Mitchell (Chesterhall) Ltd, ordered 30 lb of cabbage seed. It was supplied.
It looked just like cabbage seed. No one could say it was not. The farmers planted it over
63 acres. Six months later there appeared out of the ground a lot of loose green leaves.
They looked like cabbage leaves but they never turned in. They had no hearts. They
were not 'cabbages' in our common parlance because they had no hearts. The crop was

g   useless for human consumption. Sheep or cattle might eat it if hungry enough. It was
commercially useless. The price of the seed was £192. The loss to the farmers was over
£61,000. They claimed damages from the seed merchants, Finney Lock Seeds Ltd. The
judge awarded them that sum with interest. The total comes to nearly £100,000.

     The seed merchants appeal to this court. They say that they supplied the seed on a
printed clause by which their liability was limited to the cost of the seed, that is £192.

h   They rely much on two recent cases in the House of Lords: *Photo Production Ltd v Securicor
Transport Ltd* [1980] 1 All ER 556, [1980] AC 827 and *Ailsa Craig Fishing Co Ltd v Malvern
Fishing Co Ltd* [1983] 1 All ER 101 (the two *Securicor* cases).

In detail

     The farmers' farm land is in the maritime belt of the East Lothian, almost at sea level.

j   The soil is very fertile. It has very mild winters with no frosts. It is about the one place in
the country where Dutch winter cabbage can be grown successfully. It is sown in the
spring and transplanted in the summer. It grows very slowly and stands throughout the
winter in the fields. It is harvested from February onwards. It is a hard, dense, heavy
cabbage which captures the market at a time when there is very little other greenstuff
available.

For the last 25 years these farmers, and other farmers in the maritime belt, have got their seed from Finneys who get it from Holland. Finneys had a representative, Mr Wing. He called on the farmers each year. At Christmas 1973 he came. They gave him an order by word of mouth for 30 lb of Finneys Late Dutch Special Cabbage Seed. There was no order in writing. In February 1974 the seeds arrived. The invoice gave the date of despatch as 14 February 1974:

'30 lbs Cabbage Finneys Late Dutch Special £192·00 . . . IMPORTANT.—For Seeds Act statutory declarations, Conditions of Sale etc., see reverse.'

Then on the back there were in small printed many conditions of sale. Included in them was the clause relied on by Finneys. They say that their liability was limited to the return of the price, £192, and that they are not liable for the £61,000 claimed.

Are the conditions part of the contract?
The farmers were aware that the sale was subject to some conditions of sale. All seed merchants have conditions of sale. They were on the back of the catalogue. They were also on the back of the invoice each year. So it would seem that the farmers were bound at common law by the terms of them. The inference from the course of dealing would be that the farmers had accepted the conditions as printed, even though they had never read them and did not realise that they contained a limitation on liability.

But, in view of modern developments, it is to be noticed that the conditions were not negotiated at all between any representative bodies. They were not negotiated by the National Farmers' Union. They were introduced by the seed merchants by putting them in their catalogue and invoice, and never objected to by the farmers.

It is also to be noticed that the farmers never thought of insuring against any breach of contract by the seedsmen. It would be difficult to get any quotation. It might be possible for the seed merchants to insure themselves, something in the nature of a product liability insurance. Some seed merchants do so.

The printed condition here
The limitation clause here is of long standing in the seed trade. It has been in use for many years. The material part of it is as follows:

'All Seeds, Bulbs, Corms, Tubers, Roots, Shrubs, Trees and Plants (hereinafter referred to as "Seeds or Plants") offered for sale or sold by us to which the Seeds Act 1920 or the Plant Varieties and Seeds Act 1964 as the case may be and the Regulations thereunder apply have been tested in accordance with the provisions of the same. In the event of any seeds or plants sold or agreed to be sold by us not complying with the express terms of the contract of sale or with any representation made by us or by any duly authorised agent or representative on our behalf prior to, at the time of, or in any such contract, or any seeds or plants proving defective in varietal purity *we will, at our option, replace the defective seeds or plants, free of charge to the buyer or will refund all payments made to us by the buyer in respect of the defective seeds or plants and this shall be the limit of our obligation. We hereby exclude all liability for any loss or damage arising from the use of any seeds or plants supplied by us and for any consequential loss or damage arising out of such use* or any failure in the performance of or any defect in any seeds or plants supplied by us *or for any other loss or damage whatsoever save for, at our option, liability for any such replacement or refund as aforesaid.* In accordance with the established custom of the Seed Trade any express or implied condition, statement or warranty, statutory or otherwise, not stated in these Conditions is hereby excluded. *The price of any seeds or plants sold or offered for sale by us is based upon the foregoing limitations upon our liability. The price of such seeds or plants would be much greater if a more extensive liability were required to be undertaken by us.*' (My emphasis.)

The natural meaning
There was much discussion before us as to the construction of that condition. I am much impressed by the words I have emphasised. Taking the clause in its natural plain

meaning, I think it is effective to limit the liability of the seed merchants to a return of
a the money or replacement of the seeds. The explanation they give seems fair enough.
They say that it is so as to keep the price low, and that if they were to undertake any
greater liability the price would be much greater.

After all, the seed merchants did supply seeds. True, they were the wrong kind
altogether. But they were seeds. On the natural interpretation, I think the condition is
sufficient to limit the seed merchants to a refund of the price paid or replacement of the
b seeds.

The hostile meaning

Before the decisions of the House of Lords in the two *Securicor* cases, I would have been
inclined to decide the case as the judge did. I would have been 'hostile' to the clause. I
would have said that the goods supplied here were different *in kind* from those that were
c ordered, and that the seed merchants could not avail themselves of the limitation clause.
But in the light of the House of Lords cases, I think that that approach is not available.

I am particularly impressed by the words of Lord Wilberforce in the *Ailsa Craig* case
[1983] 1 All ER 101 at 102–103, where he said:

> '. . . one must not strive to create ambiguities by strained construction, as I think
> *d* the appellants have striven to do. The relevant words must be given, if possible,
> their natural, plain meaning. Clauses of limitation are not regarded by the courts
> with the same hostility as clauses of exclusion; this is because they must be related
> to other contractual terms, in particular to the risks to which the defending party
> may be exposed, the remuneration which he receives and possibly also the
> opportunity of the other party to insure.'

e To my mind these two cases have revolutionised our approach to exemption clauses.
In order to explain their importance, I propose to take you through the story.

The heyday of freedom of contract

None of you nowadays will remember the trouble we had, when I was called to the
Bar, with exemption clauses. They were printed in small print on the back of tickets and
f order forms and invoices. They were contained in catalogues or timetables. They were
held to be binding on any person who took them without objection. No one ever did
object. He never read them or knew what was in them. No matter how unreasonable
they were, he was bound. All this was done in the name of 'freedom of contract'. But the
freedom was all on the side of the big concern which had the use of the printing press.
No freedom for the little man who took the ticket or order form or invoice. The big
g concern said, 'Take it or leave it.' The little man had no option but to take it. The big
concern could and did exempt itself from liability in its own interest without regard to
the little man. It got away with it time after time. When the courts said to the big
concern, 'You must put it in clear words,' the big concern had no hesitation in doing so.
It knew well that the little man would never read the exemption clauses or understand
them.

h It was a bleak winter for our law of contract. It is illustrated by two cases, *Thompson v
London Midland and Scottish Rly Co* [1930] 1 KB 41, [1929] All ER Rep 474 (in which there
was exemption from liability, not on the ticket, but only in small print at the back of the
timetable, and the company were held not liable) and *L'Estrange v F Graucob Ltd* [1934] 2
KB 394, [1934] All ER Rep 16 (in which there was complete exemption in small print at
the bottom of the order form, and the company were held not liable).

j ### The secret weapon

Faced with this abuse of power, by the strong against the weak, by the use of the small
print of the conditions, the judges did what they could to put a curb on it. They still had
before them the idol, 'freedom of contract'. They still knelt down and worshipped it, but
they concealed under their cloaks a secret weapon. They used it to stab the idol in the
back. This weapon was called 'the true construction of the contract'. They used it with

great skill and ingenuity. They used it so as to depart from the natural meaning of the words of the exemption clause and to put on them a strained and unnatural construction. *a* In case after case, they said that the words were not strong enough to give the big concern exemption from liability, or that in the circumstances the big concern was not entitled to rely on the exemption clause. If a ship deviated from the contractual voyage, the owner could not rely on the exemption clause. If a warehouseman stored the goods in the wrong warehouse, he could not pray in aid the limitation clause. If the seller supplied goods different in kind from those contracted for, he could not rely on any exemption *b* from liability. If a shipowner delivered goods to a person without production of the bill of lading, he could not escape responsibility by reference to an exemption clause. In short, whenever the wide words, in their natural meaning, would give rise to an unreasonable result, the judges either rejected them as repugnant to the main purpose of the contract or else cut them down to size in order to produce a reasonable result. This is illustrated by these cases in the House of Lords: *Glynn v Margetson & Co* [1893] AC 351, *c* [1891–4] All ER Rep 693, *London and North Western Rly Co v Neilson* [1922] 2 AC 263, [1922] All ER Rep 395, *Cunard Steamship Co Ltd v Buerger* [1927] AC 1, [1926] All ER Rep 103; and by these in the Privy Council: *Canada Steamship Lines Ltd v R* [1952] 1 All ER 305, [1952] AC 192, *Sze Hai Tong Bank Ltd v Rambler Cycle Co Ltd* [1959] 3 All ER 182, [1959] AC 576; and innumerable cases in the Court of Appeal, culminating in *Levison v Patent Steam Carpet Cleaning Co Ltd* [1977] 3 All ER 498, [1978] QB 69. But when the *d* clause was itself reasonable and gave rise to a reasonable result, the judges upheld it, at any rate when the clause did not exclude liability entirely but only limited it to a reasonable amount. So, where goods were deposited in a cloakroom or sent to a laundry for cleaning, it was quite reasonable for the company to limit their liability to a reasonable amount, having regard to the small charge made for the service. These are illustrated by *Gibaud v Great Eastern Rly Co* [1921] 2 KB 426, [1921] All ER Rep 35, *Alderslade v Hendon* *e* *Laundry Ltd* [1945] 1 All ER 244, [1945] KB 189 and *Gillespie Bros & Co Ltd v Roy Bowles Transport Ltd* [1973] 1 All ER 193, [1973] QB 400.

Fundamental breach
     No doubt had ever been cast thus far by anyone. But doubts arose when in this court, in a case called *Karsales (Harrow) Ltd v Wallis* [1956] 2 All ER 866, [1956] 1 WLR 936, we *f* ventured to suggest that if the big concern was guilty of a breach which went to the 'very root' of the contract, sometimes called a 'fundamental breach', or at other times a 'total failure' of its obligations, then it could not rely on the printed clause to exempt itself from liability. This way of putting it had been used by some of the most distinguished names in the law, such as Lord Dunedin in *W & S Pollock & Co v Macrae* 1922 SC (HL) 192 Lord Atkin and Lord Wright in *Hain Steamship Co Ltd v Tate & Lyle Ltd* [1936] 2 All *g* ER 597 at 603, 601, 607–608 and Devlin J in *Smeaton Hanscomb & Co Ltd v Sassoon I Setty Son & Co (No 1)* [1953] 2 All ER 1471 at 1473, [1953] 1 WLR 1468 at 1470. But we did make a mistake, in the eyes of some, in elevating it, by inference, into a 'rule of law'. That was too rude an interference with the idol of 'freedom of contract'. We ought to have used the secret weapon. We ought to have said that in each case, on the 'true construction of the contract' in that case, the exemption clause did not avail the party *h* where he was guilty of a fundamental breach or a breach going to the root. That is the lesson to be learnt from the 'indigestible' speeches in *Suisse Atlantique Société d'Armement Maritime SA v NV Rotterdamsche Kolen Centrale* [1966] 2 All ER 61, [1967] 1 AC 361. They were all obiter dicta. The House were dealing with an agreed damages clause and not an exemption clause and the point had never been argued in the courts below at all. It is noteworthy that the House did not overrule a single decision of the Court of Appeal. *j* Lord Wilberforce appears to have approved them (see [1966] 2 All ER 61 at 92–93, [1967] 1 AC 361 at 433). At any rate, he cast no doubt on the actual decision in any case.

The change in climate
     In 1969 there was a change in climate. Out of winter into spring. It came with the first report of the Law Commission on Exemption Clauses in Contracts (Law Com no 24)

which was implemented in the Supply of Goods (Implied Terms) Act 1973. In 1975

a there was a further change. Out of spring into summer. It came with their second report on Exemption Clauses (Law Com no 69) which was implemented by the Unfair Contract Terms Act 1977. No longer was the big concern able to impose whatever terms and conditions it liked in a printed form, no matter how unreasonable they might be. These reports showed most convincingly that the courts could and should only enforce them if they were fair and reasonable in themselves and it was fair and reasonable to allow the

b big concern to rely on them. So the idol of 'freedom of contract' was shattered. In cases of personal injury or death, it was not permissible to exclude or restrict liability at all. In consumer contracts any exemption clause was subject to the test of reasonableness.

These reports and statutes have influenced much the thinking of the judges. At any rate, they·influenced me as you will see if you read *Gillespie Bros & Co Ltd v Roy Bowles Transport Ltd* [1973] 1 All ER 193 at 200, [1973] 1 QB 400 at 416 and *Photo Production Ltd*

c *v Securicor Transport Ltd* [1978] 3 All ER 146 at 153, [1978] 1 WLR 856 at 865:

> 'Thus we reach, after long years, the principle which lies behind all our striving: the court will not allow a party to rely on an exemption or limitation clause in circumstances in which it would not be fair or reasonable to allow reliance on it; and, in considering whether it is fair and reasonable, the court will consider whether
> *d*   it was in a standard form, whether there was equality of bargaining power, the nature of the breach, and so forth.'

The effect of the changes

What is the result of all this? To my mind it heralds a revolution in our approach to exemption clauses; not only where they exclude liability altogether and also where they limit liability; not only in the specific categories in the Unfair Contract Terms Act 1977,

e but in other contracts too. Just as in other fields of law we have done away with the multitude of cases on 'common employment', 'last opportunity', 'invitees' and 'licensees' and so forth, so also in this field we should do away with the multitude of cases on exemption clauses. We should no longer have to go through all kinds of gymnastic contortions to get round them. We should no longer have to harass our students with the study of them. We should set about meeting a new challenge. It is presented by the

f test of reasonableness.

The two Securicor cases

The revolution is exemplified by the recent two *Securicor* cases in the House of Lords (*Photo Production Ltd v Securicor Transport Ltd* [1980] 1 All ER 556, [1980] AC 827 and *Ailsa Craig Fishing Co Ltd v Malvern Fishing Co Ltd* [1983] 1 All ER 101). In each of them

g the Securicor company provided a patrolman to keep watch on premises so as to see that they were safe from intruders. They charged very little for the service. In the *Photo Production* case it was a factory with a lot of paper in it. The patrolman set light to it and burnt down the factory. In the *Ailsa Craig* case it was a quay at Aberdeen where ships were berthed. The patrolman went off for the celebrations on New Year's Eve. He left the ships unattended. The tide rose. A ship rose with it. Its bow got 'snubbed' under the

h deck of the quay. It sank. In each case the owners were covered by insurance. The factory owners had their fire insurance. The shipowners had their hull insurance. In each case the Securicor company relied on a limitation clause. Under it they were protected from liability beyond a limit which was quite reasonable and their insurance cover was limited accordingly. The issue in practical terms was: which of the insurers should bear the loss? The question in legal terms in each case was whether Securicor could avail themselves of

j the limitation clause. In each case the House held that they could.

In the first case the House made it clear that the doctrine of 'fundamental breach' was no longer applicable. They replaced it by the test of reasonableness. That was the test applied by the trial judge MacKenna J which I myself quoted with approval (see [1978] 3 All ER 146 at 154, [1978] 1 WLR 856 at 865). He said:

> 'Condition 1, as I construe it, is, I think, a reasonable provision . . . Either the

owner of the premises, or the person providing the service, must bear the risk. Why should the parties not agree to its being borne by the [owner of the premises]? He is *a* certain to be insured against fire and theft, and is better able to judge the cover needed than the party providing the service . . . That is only another way of shifting the risk from the party who provides the service to the party who receives it. There is, as I have said, nothing unreasonable, nothing impolitic, in such a contract.'

His judgment was approved by the House of Lords, who themselves held that the limitation clause was valid because it was a reasonable way of opportioning the risks, as *b* between the insurers on either side. I would set out two passages to prove it. Lord Wilberforce said ([1980] 1 All ER 556 at 564, [1980] AC 827 at 846):

'Securicor undertook to provide a service of periodical visits for a very modest charge which works out at 26p per visit. It did not agree to provide equipment. It would have no knowledge of the value of Photo Productions' factory; that, and the *c* efficacy of their fire precautions, would be known to Photo Productions. In these circumstances nobody could consider it unreasonable that as between these two equal parties the risk assumed by Securicor should be a modest one, and that Photo Productions should carry the substantial risk of damage or destruction.'

And Lord Diplock said ([1980] 1 All ER 556 at 568, [1980] AC 827 at 851):
d

'For the reasons given by Lord Wilberforce it seems to me that this apportionment of the risk of the factory being damaged or destroyed by the injurious act of an employee of Securicor while carrying out a visit to the factory is one which reasonable businessmen in the position of Securicor and Photo Productions might well think was the most economical. An analogous apportionment of risk is provided for by the Hague Rules in the case of goods carried by sea under bills of *e* lading.'

I do hope, however, that we shall not often have to consider the new-found analysis of contractual obligations into 'primary obligations', 'secondary obligations', 'general secondary obligations' and 'anticipatory secondary obligations'. No doubt it is logical enough, but it is too esoteric altogether. It is fit only for the rarified atmosphere of the House of Lords. Not at all for the chambers of the practitioner. Let alone for the student *f* at the university.

In the second case the House made a distinction between clauses which excluded liability altogether, and those which only limited liability to a certain sum. Exclusion clauses were to be construed strictly contra proferentem, whereas limitation clauses were to be construed naturally. This must be because a limitation clause is more likely to be reasonable than an exclusion clause. If you go by the plain, natural meaning of the words *g* (as you should do) there is nothing to choose between them. As Lord Sumner said fifty years ago in *Atlantic Shipping and Trading Co v Louis Dreyfus & Co* [1922] 2 AC 250 at 260, [1922] All ER Rep 559 at 563:

'There is no difference in principle between words which save them from having to pay at all and words which save them from paying as much as they would *h* otherwise have had to pay.'

If you read the speeches in the *Ailsa Craig* case, it does look as if the House of Lords were relying on the reasonableness of the limitation clause. They held it was applicable even though the failure of the Securicor company was a 'total failure' to provide the service contracted for. They also said, obiter, that they would construe an exclusion clause much more strictly, just as was done in the old cases decided in the winter time. But I *j* would suggest that the better reason is because it would not be fair or reasonable to allow the propounder of them to rely on them in the circumstances of the case.

The Supply of Goods (Implied Terms) Act 1973
In any case the contract for these cabbage seeds was governed by s 4 of the Supply of Goods (Implied Terms) Act 1973: see now s 55(4) as set out in para 11 of Sch 1 to the Sale

of Goods Act 1979. That section says that in the case of a contract of sale of goods any
a   term 'is . . . not enforceable to the extent that it is shown that it would not be fair or
reasonable to allow reliance on the term'. That provision is exactly in accord with the
principle which I have advocated above. So the ultimate question, to my mind, in this
case is just this: to what extent would it be fair or reasonable to allow the seed merchants
to rely on the limitation clause?

b   *Fair and reasonable*
There is only one case in the books so far on this point. It is *R W Green Ltd v Cade Bros
Farm* [1978] 1 Lloyd's Rep 602. There Griffiths J held that it was fair and reasonable for
seed potato merchants to rely on a limitation clause which limited their liability to the
contract price of the potatoes. That case was very different from the present. The terms
had been evolved over twenty years. The judge said (at 607): 'They are therefore not
c   conditions imposed by the strong upon the weak; but are rather a set of trading terms
upon which both sides are apparently content to do business.' The judge added (at 608):
'No moral blame attaches to either party; neither of them knew, nor could be expected
to know, that the potatoes were infected.' In that case the judge held that the clause was
fair and reasonable and that the seed merchants were entitled to rely on it.
Our present case is very much on the borderline. There is this to be said in favour of
d   the seed merchants. The price of this cabbage seed was small: £192. The damages
claimed are high: £61,000. But there is this to be said on the other side. The clause was
not negotiated between persons of equal bargaining power. It was inserted by the seed
merchants in their invoices without any negotiation with the farmers.
To this I would add that the seed merchants rarely, if ever, invoked the clause. Their
very frank director said: 'The trade does not stand on the strict letter of the clause . . .
e   Almost invariably when a customer justifiably complains, the trade pays something
more than a refund.' The papers contain many illustrations where the clause was not
invoked and a settlement was reached.
Next, I would point out that the buyers had no opportunity at all of knowing or
discovering that the seed was not cabbage seed, whereas the sellers could and should have
known that it was the wrong seed altogether. The buyers were not covered by insurance
f   against the risk. Nor could they insure. But, as to the seed merchants, the judge said
([1981] 1 Lloyd's Rep 476 at 480):

> 'I am entirely satisfied that it is possible for seedsmen to insure against this risk. I
> am entirely satisfied that the cost of so doing would not materially raise the price of
> seeds on the market. I am entirely satisfied that the protection of this clause for the
> purposes of protecting against the very rare case indeed, such as the present, is not
g   > reasonably required. If and in so far as it may be necessary to consider the matter, I
> am also satisfied that it is possible for seedsmen to test seeds before putting them on
> to the market.'

To that I would add this further point. Such a mistake as this could not have happened
without serious negligence on the part of the seed merchants themselves or their Dutch
h   suppliers. So serious that it would not be fair to enable them to escape responsibility for
it.
In all the circumstances I am of opinion that it would not be fair or reasonable to allow
the seed merchants to rely on the clause to limit their liability.
I would dismiss the appeal accordingly.

j   **OLIVER LJ.** I agree that this appeal fails. Before the judge and on the hearing of the
appeal the plaintiffs argued that the exclusion clause, which forms the bedrock of the
defendants' defence, forms no part of the contract between the parties either because,
having regard to the fact that the contract was negotiated orally and without any express
reference to the clause, it could not be implied so as to qualify an express term, namely
that the seed sold was 'Finneys Late Dutch Special', or because, since the clause purports
to exclude, inter alia, the statutory implied condition as to the seller's title, the effect of

s 55(3) of the Sale of Goods Act 1979 and Sch 1 to the Sale of Goods Act 1979 is to render
it void in toto. Although the judge found it unnecessary to deal specifically with these   a
arguments, they are fully dealt with in the judgment of Kerr LJ, which I have had the
advantage of reading in draft. For myself I need only say that I wholly concur in the
reasons which he gives for rejecting both arguments. I turn therefore to the principal
point at issue, namely that of the construction of the relevant clause.

At the trial the judge dealt with the case on the basis of a concession made by counsel
then appearing for the defendants that they could not rely on the limitation clause in the   b
contract if what had been delivered was seed quite other than that contracted for, for
instance beetroot seed or carrot seed, and that it was a sine qua non of his successful
reliance on the clause that what the defendants had delivered was cabbage seed. On this
footing, the issue was simply one of fact: was this or was it not cabbage seed? The judge's
finding of fact, which was based on the evidence of the defendants' own witnesses, was
that this seed was not cabbage seed in any accepted sense of the term. It was not, in any   c
commercial sense, even vegetable seed, and accordingly it followed that the clause
conferred no protection on the defendant.

In this court, counsel for the defendants makes no such concession. He accepts that
what was delivered was not, in any commercial sense, cabbage seed but, he argues, it was
literally seed, useless seed, but nevertheless seed, and accordingly the protecting clause is,
as a matter of construction, sufficiently wide to protect the defendants from any claim   d
beyond the return of the price which, it is common ground, has never been paid.   ·

Now it is clear that the breach of contract which admittedly occurred was a breach of
such a nature as to constitute, using the expression used in the authorities prior to *Suisse
·Atlantique Société d'Armement Maritime SA v NV Rottendamsche Kolen Centrale* [1966] 2 All
ER 61, [1967] 1 AC 361, 'a fundamental breach'. To deliver as winter cabbage seed
something that was not even vegetable seed in any commercial sense clearly went to the   e
very root of the contract, and counsel for the plaintiffs argues that, even in the light of
Suisse Atlantique and the two subsequent decisions of the House of Lords in *Photo Production
Ltd v Securicor Transport Ltd* [1980] 1 All ER 556, [1980] AC 827 and *Ailsa Craig Fishing
Co Ltd v Malvern Co Ltd* [1983] 1 All ER 101, that remains a fatal objection to the
application of the clause. It is therefore necessary to analyse those cases in order to see
whether, as counsel for the plaintiffs contends, there still remains anything of what used   f
to be termed 'the fundamental breach rule'. The propositions which emerge from the
trilogy of cases mentioned appear to me to be the following.

(1) There is no rule of law that the effect of a fundamental breach of contract, whether
or not accepted by the innocent party as a repudiation, is to preclude reliance on an
exclusion clause in the contract inserted for the protection of the party in breach.

(2) The effect of an exclusion clause has to be ascertained simply by construing the   g
contract as a whole. What has to be determined is whether, as a matter of construction,
the clause applies to excuse or limit liability for the particular breach which has occurred,
whether 'fundamental' or otherwise.

(3) There is a presumption that any breach of the primary obligations of the contract
will result in continuing secondary obligation on the party in breach to pay compensation
for the breach. A clause in the contract excluding, modifying or limiting that secondary   h
obligation is, therefore, to be construed restrictively and contra proferentem. (I add in
parenthesis that, with deference to Lord Denning MR, I find the analysis adopted by
Lord Diplock in the *Photo Production* case a helpful one, so long as it is borne in mind that
the purpose of a contract is performance and not the grant of an option to pay damages.)

(4) The contract has to be construed as a whole, for the exclusion clause is part of an
entire contract and may, as a matter of construction, be an essential factor in determining   j
the extent of the primary obligation. Thus, for instance, the *Photo Production* case was not
a case of a clause excluding liability for a fundamental breach of the contract but of a
clause which, on its true construction, demonstrated that there had been no breach at all
of the primary obligation, which was simply to exercise reasonable care.

(5) Since such clauses may not only modify or limit the secondary obligation to pay
damages for breach but may also show the extent of the primary obligation, a clause

totally excluding liability tends to be construed more restrictively than a clause merely

a limiting damages payable for breach, for a total exclusion of liability, if widely construed, might lead to the conclusion that there was no primary obligation at all and thus no contract. This is to say no more than that, when it is called on to construe a commercial document clearly intended by both parties to have contractual force, the court will lean against a construction which leads to an absurdity.

(6) Where the language used is unclear or susceptible fairly of more than one

b construction, the court will construe it in the manner which appears more likely to give effect to what must have been the common intention of the parties when they contracted. But, where, even construing the contract contra proferentum and allowing for the presumption of the continuance of a secondary obligation to pay damages for breach of the primary contractual duty, the language of the contract is clear and is fairly susceptible of only one meaning, the court is not entitled to place on an exclusion clause a strained

c construction for the purpose of rejecting it.

The contractual document in the instant case consists simply of the invoice which described the subject matter of the sale as 'Finneys Late Dutch Special' and the conditions appearing on the reverse side which contained a number of terms most of which are immaterial in this case. The only material condition for present purposes is the exclusion clause the terms of which have already been referred to in the judgment of Lord Denning

d MR. It begins with a representation that all seeds etc offered or sold by the defendants and to which the provisions of the Seeds Act 1920 or the Plant Varieties and Seeds Act 1964 apply have been tested in accordance with the statutory provisions. Thereafter the clause, so far as material, divides into three sections. The first of these limits the liability of the vendors to replacement or refund of the price in the event of any seeds 'sold or agreed to be sold by us' (a) not complying with the express terms of the contract, (b) not

e complying with any representation made or (c) proving defective in varietal purity. Counsel for the defendants argues that this is a clear and unambiguous limitation on liability for exactly the type of breach which has occurred here. It was an express term of the contract (see the invoice) that the seed sold should be Finneys Late Dutch Special. The seed delivered was not Finneys Late Dutch Special. It was something else and therefore did not comply with an express term of the contract. This is attractively simple but it is

f not, in my judgment, correct. The clause applies only to seeds 'sold or agreed to be sold' and, however this is approached, it seems to me that it can only relate to goods which actually were the subject matter of a contract between vendor and purchaser. What was delivered to the plaintiffs simply was not a fulfilment of the contract, even a defective fulfilment, any more than delivery of a motor bicycle would be a fulfilment of a contract for the sale of a car. When the clause refers to 'express terms' of the contract it is, in my

g judgment, referring to express terms applicable to those goods to which the contract relates, and I, for my part, find it impossible to read the clause sensibly as if it said 'in the event of the goods sold or agreed to be sold by us not being the goods agreed to be sold by us'. The clause, in other words, assumes that the primary obligation has been fulfilled to the extent of delivering the goods which the vendor has agreed to sell, but seeks to limit the vendor's liability under the secondary obligation which arises if those goods

h prove, in breach of an express term or representation, to be defective. The discharge of that obligation is limited to replacing 'the *defective* seeds or plants' or to refunding payments made in respect of 'the *defective* seeds or plants'. A motor bicycle delivered in purported fulfilment of a contract to sell a car is not a defective car. It is simply something which does not fall within the contract at all. For my part, therefore, I do not find that what I may call the first part of the condition assists the defendants.

j The matter does not, however, end there. The second part of the condition is directed to the total exclusion of any liability for consequential loss arising from the use of the goods sold. Now one starts from the position that the parties can hardly be thought rationally to have been contracting on the footing that a farmer about to dedicate a substantial acreage of land to the commercial growing of seed supplied by a seedsman assumes the risk that the seedsman will supply him with something bearing no resemblance at all to what he is contracting to buy. If, therefore, the contract is to lay

that risk on him, it can only do so if it is clearly expressed in terms which compulsively
lead to the conclusion that what prima facie is an irrational intention was nevertheless *a*
the true intention of the parties. One has, therefore, to ask the question whether the
words used so clearly exclude liability for the type of breach that has occurred here that
they are not fairly susceptible of any other meaning. In so far as there is any 'rule'
applicable here it is simply a rule of construction that a provision intended to give
exemption from the consequences of a fundamental breach of the contract must, if it is
to be accorded the effect intended, be expressed in clear and unambiguous terms (see the *b*
speech of Viscount Dilhorne in *Suisse Atlantique* [1966] 2 All ER 61 at 67, [1967] 1 AC
361 at 392). Is there anything on the face of this document which clearly indicates that
the seller was excluding not just liability for loss arising from the use of Finneys Late
Dutch Special which proves in some way to be defective but all liability arising from the
use of something delivered as Finneys Late Dutch Special but which is not in fact even
vegetable seed in any commercial sense? Speaking for myself, I do not consider that the *c*
words used in this clause are sufficiently clear and unambiguous to exclude such a
liability. The second part of the conditions is, as it seems to me, merely a supplement to
the first part. The first part having limited the liability in respect of the matters there
mentioned, the second part goes on, by way of clarification, to exclude any liability for
any consequential damage in respect of the same matters beyond the amount of the
limited liability. Counsel for the defendants relies on the words 'any seeds or plants *d*
supplied by us' as words of sufficient width to cover not only seeds and plants of the type
agreed to be sold but any seeds or plants of any type which may in fact be delivered to
and used by the purchaser so long as they are literally 'supplied by us'. I agree that the
words are capable of being so construed, but in the context of the contract as a whole I do
not consider that that is the only meaning of which they are fairly susceptible. Anyone
reading the clause would, I think, relate those words to the seeds and plants which were *e*
the subject matter of the contract for sale and would greet with some surprise the news
that they were intended to cover a case where what had been supplied was wholly
different in kind from what had been ordered.

In my judgment, therefore, the judge was right when he said that it would be making
commercial nonsense of the contract to suggest that either party can have intended that
it was to operate in the circumstances of this case, and I would dismiss the appeal for this *f*
reason.

If, however, this be too bold a view of construction, then in any event I entirely agree
with the analysis of Kerr LJ. I can find nothing in the clause which clearly protects or
could have been intended to protect the sellers against the consequences of their own
negligence. Such a bargain is, of course, possible if the parties are content to use words
which clearly point to such a conclusion, but it would, in my judgment, require *g*
something very much more precise and unequivocal than we have here before such a
conclusion could be justified.

On the view that I take it is not strictly necessary to decide the further point which
arises as regards the fairness and reasonableness of the clause, if enforceable. For the sake
of completeness I should refer to the third section of the exclusion clause, which provides:

> 'In accordance with the established custom of the Seed Trade any express or *h*
> implied condition, statement or warranty, statutory or otherwise, not stated in these
> Conditions, is hereby excluded.'

It is common ground that, the contract having been entered into prior to 1 February
1978, it is subject to the substituted s 55 contained in Sch 1 to the Sale of Goods Act 1979,
sub-s (4) of which provides (so far as material): *j*

> 'In the case of a contract of sale of goods, any term of that . . . contract exempting
> from all or any of the provisions of section 13, 14 or 15 above . . . is . . . not
> enforceable to the extent that it is shown that it would not be fair or reasonable to
> allow reliance on the term.'

Subsection (9) extends this to terms which, whilst not referring in terms to the exclusion
of the provisions of ss 13, 14 and 15, have a similar operation.

a The judge found as a fact that it would have been possible for the defendants to insure against the risk of loss in the circumstances of this case without materially raising the price of seed and he expressed himself as satisfied that the protection of this clause for the purpose of protecting against the very rare case such as the present was not reasonably required. The defendants attack the judge's finding of fact because, they say, the evidence showed only that a very limited form of cover had been inquired for, restricted to a relatively small amount in total for all claims in any one year. They also rely on the

b decision of Griffiths J in *R W Green Ltd v Cade Bros Farm* [1978] 1 Lloyd's Rep 602, where a similar exclusion clause was held to be reasonable in the case of potato seed which, through an undetectable defect, failed to crop properly. That case, however, although valuable as an exemplar of the sort of circumstances which need to be considered, was a case on its own facts, and there are here a number of facts which seem to me to point strongly to the conclusion that it would not be reasonable to permit the defendants to

c rely on the clause. I mention only a few. In the first place, whilst it may be true that the evidence did not show that the insurance market had been tested beyond the point of a policy to provide a limited protection, it was clear that some insurance was possible which would have covered the relevant risk. It has to be borne in mind that what the clause was seeking to do was not to limit the risk to an amount conveniently insurable but to exclude liability altogether. Secondly, it was a clause unilaterally imposed. Thirdly,

d the loss for which the protection of the clause was being invoked, was not one which, as in *R W Green Ltd v Cade Bros Farm*, involved no fault on the part of the vendor. There was here no significant risk of the wrong seed being delivered except for negligence on the part of someone in the defendants' organisation and such negligence was admitted by the evidence of the defendants' own witness.

The question is not whether there are not circumstances in which a clause such as this

e may be fair and reasonable but whether, in the circumstances, it would be fair and reasonable to allow reliance on it. It may well be, I do not know, that in this trade it may be reasonable for a vendor so to protect himself against undiscoverable defects, arising without fault, in the material which he supplies. But, even assuming this to be so, it does not at all follow that it would be fair and reasonable to permit such a clause to be relied on in order to protect a vendor against a claim by the purchaser arising out of the vendor's

f own negligence. The judge left the point open. For my part I would be prepared, were it necessary to do so, to hold that reliance on the clause in the instant case would not be fair and reasonable.

KERR LJ. The facts have already been fully stated, and I therefore only summarise them briefly for the purpose of defining the issues which arise on this appeal.

g The contract, made orally in February 1974, was for the supply of 30 lb of cabbage seed described as 'Finneys Late Dutch Special'. It was common ground that this was 'winter' and not 'autumn' cabbage seed. Subject to the effect of the exemption clause in the conditions of sale as discussed hereafter, the contract accordingly incorporated the following material express and implied terms. First, an express term that the seed supplied would be Dutch winter cabbage seed. Second, a number of conditions implied

h by what is now the Sale of Goods Act 1979, subject to certain qualifications which were not yet in force in 1974 and which appear from Sch 1 to that Act. For present purposes it is sufficient to summarise these as (i) a condition implied by s 13(1) that the seed supplied would correspond with its contractual description and (ii) a condition implied by s 14(2) that the seed supplied would be of merchantable quality.

As events turned out, all of these terms were broken, due to a combination of the

j following circumstances. First, the defendants' Dutch suppliers delivered to the defendants what was described as, and purported to be, autumn seed, but, due to negligence on the part of employees of the defendants, this delivery was wrongly entered in the defendants' books under a description denoting winter seed, and was supplied to the plaintiffs as winter seed in purported fulfilment of the contract. At that point there was accordingly a breach of the express term, and of the implied condition that the seed supplied would correspond with its contractual description. Second, due to some unexplained act or omission on the part of the Dutch suppliers, the seed was in fact unmerchantable even as autumn seed. It was cabbage seed of a sort, in the sense that it was capable of germination, transplantation and of growing plants of a cabbage variety. a But the resulting plants were not merchantable as cabbages, or even fit for animal consumption, and ultimately had to be ploughed in.

Against this background I then turn to the exemption clause on which everything depends. The relevant part consists of six sentences, which have already been set out in the judgment of Lord Denning MR and I therefore do not repeat them. The two issues which arise on this appeal are (a) whether on its true construction the clause protects the b defendants against liability for the breaches summarised above and (b) if so, whether it would nevertheless not be fair or reasonable to allow them to rely on the clause, having regard to s 55 of the Sale of Goods Act 1979 as modified by para 11 of Sch 1 to that Act.

Before discussing both of these issues it is necessary to mentioned two preliminary points. First, it was common ground that the contract was made against the background of the exemption clause in the sense that, subject to its legal effect, the clause formed part c of the bargain made by the parties. The plaintiffs agreed that they knew of its existence, and that it had for many years been accepted in the trade that all sales of seed were made subject to its terms, without the need for any express stipulation to this effect. However, counsel for the plaintiffs made two submissions in this regard. First, that, since the clause was not expressly mentioned between the parties, it could only form part of the terms of the contract by implication, but that, on this basis, it fell to be ignored, since its effect d was to contradict the express terms of the contract. In support of this argument he relied on the decision of this court in *J Evans & Son (Portsmouth) Ltd v Andrea Merzario Ltd* [1976] 2 All ER 930, [1976] 1 WLR 1078. But that case has no application here; it concerned an express and specific oral promise whose effect could not be cut down by subsequently incorporated inconsistent printed terms. This has nothing to do with the situation in the present case. Second, counsel for the plaintiffs submitted that the clause e was wholly void by virtue of s 55(3) in Sch 1 to the 1979 Act, because its fourth sentence (beginning 'In accordance with the established custom of the Seed Trade . . .') purported to exclude all conditions implied by statute, including s 12 of the 1979 Act concerning the implied condition as to the seller's title. I cannot accept this submission either. Even allowing for the fact that we are dealing with an exemption clause which has to be strictly construed, it seems to me that a reasonable and businesslike construction, which gives f full effect to s 55(3), is that the clause is void to the extent that it purports to exempt the defendants from the condition implied by s 12, but no further.

I then turn to the construction and effect of the clause. In this connection it is first necessary briefly to summarise the present state of the law on 'fundamental breach' in the light of the recent decisions of the House of Lords in *Photo Production Ltd v Securicor Transport Ltd* [1980] 1 All ER 556, [1980] AC 827 and *Ailsa Craig Fishing Co Ltd v Malvern* g *Fishing Co Ltd* [1983] 1 All ER 101. I will refer to these for convenience as the *Photo Production* and *Ailsa Craig* cases, and the crucial question concerns their effect on various dicta on 'fundamental breach' which are to be found in the speeches in *Suisse Atlantique Société d'Armement Maritime SA v NV Rotterdamsche Kolen Centrale* [1966] 2 All ER 61, [1967] AC 361. In that case, it should be remembered, the House of Lords was (perhaps unfortunately) discussing 'fundamental breach' in general terms, and not by reference to h any specific exempting provision. (I use the term 'exempting' throughout in the wide sense of s 55(9) as set out in para 11 of Sch 1 to the Sale of Goods Act 1979.)

Beginning with the *Photo Production* case, it is in my view perfectly clear that this has wholly laid to rest the doctrine of 'fundamental breach' in one respect at least. It has abrogated the supposed rule, exemplified most signally by the decisions of this court in *Harbutt's Plasticine Ltd v Wayne Tank and Pump Co Ltd* [1970] 1 All ER 225, [1970] 1 QB j 447 and *Wathes (Western) Ltd v Austins (Menswear) Ltd* [1976] 1 Lloyd's Rep 14, that a breach which can be described as fundamental, or a breach of one of the terms of the contract which can be so described, causes any exemption clause to cease to be applicable and capable of being relied on, and, further, that this is so whether the innocent party treats the breach as a repudiation of the entire contract or whether it affirms the contract. It is now clear law that, whatever the nature of the breach, an exemption clause can never 'terminate' or 'cease to have effect', but remains to be construed in order to decide

whether or not the parties intended that its terms should apply to the breach in question.
a Thus, such commonly used expressions as 'the defendants cannot rely on the clause' must
now be treated as suspect, unless they mean no more than that the clause, on its true
construction, does not apply to the breach in question. Further, as pointed out by Lord
Diplock in the *Photo Production* case [1980] 1 All ER 556 at 566, [1980] AC 827 at 849, if
the expression 'fundamental' is to be retained in any context whatever, it should be
confined to cases of anticipatory breach, ie to breaches which entitle the innocent party
b to treat the contract as at an end and to absolve him from any further performance of its
terms, but not in any context which bears on the continuing effect of an exemption
clause.

However, while it is clear that to this extent the doctrine of 'fundamental breach' was
unsound and has disappeared, it is less clear whether it still survives in some sense as a
rule of construction. In my view this is not so. Rules of construction are not rules of law;
c they are merely guidelines to the presumed intention of the parties in the light of the
events which have occurred. Provided that the words used do not go so far as, in effect,
to absolve one party from any contractual obligation whatever, so as to reduce a so-called
contract to a mere declaration of intent without imposing any binding obligation, all
provisions of a contract, including all exemption clauses however wide, fall to be
construed and to be applied if, on their true construction, it is clear that the parties
d intended them to apply to the situation in question. Thus, to take an example which has
virtually become a cliché, if there is a contract for the sale of apples or of cheese, but the
contract goes on to provide, clearly and expressly, that the seller is to be under no liability
in damages if he delivers pears or chalk instead, then there is in my view no rule of law
or of construction which disentitles the seller from relying on that provisions if he in fact
delivers pears or chalk. The buyer's only remedy in such cases, as it seems to me, is to
e invoke the new statutory provisions, if these are applicable, which enable the court to
hold that such a provision, or the seller's reliance on it, would not be fair or reasonable,
eg s 55 in Sch 1 to the Sale of Goods Act 1979 or the Unfair Contract Terms Act 1977.
The only principle, though in my view it is also no more than a guide to construction,
which the *Ailsa Craig* case has engrafted on the decision in the *Photo Production* case, is
that exemption clauses which provide for a limitation, as opposed to a total exclusion, of
f liability are more likely to be construed to protect the party in default, because an agreed
limitation of liability may well be more likely to be consonant with the intention of the
parties in the event of a breach than an exclusion of all liability. However, this again is
only a guideline to construction.

Counsel for the plaintiffs has strenuously contended that any analysis on the lines
indicated above flies in the face of almost innumerable authorities. But I am in no way
g persuaded that this is so. I do not propose to go through all the cases cited to us, but
merely to refer briefly to five decisions of the House of Lords on which he mainly relied.
First, *Glynn v Margetson & Co* [1893] AC 351 at 357, [1891–4] All ER Rep 693 at 696, one
of the deviation cases, where the speech of Lord Halsbury included the oft-quoted
dictum:

h 'Looking at the whole of the instrument, and seeing what one must regard . . . as
its main purpose, one must reject words, indeed whole provisions, if they are
inconsistent with what one assumes to be the main purpose of the contract.'

This, as it seems to me, lays down no rule of law but merely a guideline to construction.
Furthermore, the decisions in the deviation cases were all based in part on extra-
contractual obligations, stemming from the law of bailment, underlying and additional
j to the express obligations undertaken by a bailee, with the result that the express terms
of the contract have usually been held incapable of qualifying such underlying obligations.
This is illustrated, for instance, by the remarks of Lord Atkinson in *London and North
Western Rly Co v Neilson* [1922] 2 AC 263 at 273, [1972] All ER Rep 395 at 400, on which
counsel for the plaintiffs also relied. Similar considerations apply to the implied obligation
of seaworthiness in a contract of affreightment, as illustrated by *Atlantic Shipping and
Trading Co Ltd v Louis Dreyfus & Co* [1922] 2 AC 250, [1922] All ER Rep 395, the next
decision of the House of Lords on which counsel for the plaintiffs relied. It was there

held that an express exemption clause in a charterparty could not impinge on the *implied* underlying obligation of seaworthiness. However, it is also to be noted that the House of Lords there upheld a similar provision which, on its true construction, was effective to qualify an *express* undertaking of seaworthiness, by approving the decision of this court in *Bank of Australasia v Clan Line Steamers Ltd* [1916] 1 KB 39. So, again, it was a question of construction, not the application of any rule of law. Next, counsel for the plaintiffs relied on the decision of the House of Lords in *W & S Pollock & Co v Macrae* 1922 SC (HL) 192, but in the *Ailsa Craig* case both Lord Wilberforce and Lord Fraser made it clear that that decision was no authority contrary to what I have sought to indicate above. Finally, counsel for the plaintiff relied on various passages in the *Suisse Atlantique* case, in particular on a passage in the speech of Lord Wilberforce ([1966] 2 All ER 61 at 92–93, [1967] 1 AC 361 at 433) under the heading 'Supply of a different article'. This passage was quoted by Parker J in his judgment in the present case and formed its main basis (see [1981] 1 Lloyd's Rep 476). However, for the reasons already stated, in my view this also did no more than to indicate a guideline for construction, not a rule of law, which must now be viewed in the light of the speeches of Lord Wilberforce himself and of Lord Diplock in the *Photo Production* case.

I then turn to the present exemption clause against this background. Parker J did not consider or analyse its terms in any way in his judgment, because he treated the clause as being ipso facto incapable of application to a breach which involved the double gravamen of a supply of (a) the wrong kind of seed and (b) of seed which was unmerchantable. In my judgment, and for the reasons already explained, I respectfully consider that this approach must now be regarded as wrong in principle. Thus, a clause on the following lines would clearly have protected the defendants: 'In the event of our supplying seed which, due to the negligence of our suppliers or of our own employees, turns out to be seed of the wrong kind and/or to be unmerchantable, we shall be under no liability other than to refund the contract price.'

The real difficulty, as it seems to me, and on which my mind has wavered a great deal, is whether the actual terms of this clause are sufficiently clear to have this effect. Its provisions certainly go a very long way. The defendants' limitation of liability, by restricting this to a refund of the price of the seed, appears to me at first sight to cover the following breaches in toto: (i) a breach of the express obligation to supply Dutch winter cabbage seed (see the second sentence of the clause beginning 'In the event of any seeds or plants . . .'); (ii) a breach of the condition implied by s 13(1) of the Sale of Goods Act 1979 that the seed supplied should correspond with its contractual description (see the fourth sentence to which I have already referred); and (iii) a breach of the condition implied by s 14(2) of the 1979 Act that the seed supplied should be of merchantable quality (also by virtue of the fourth sentence). As to these, I am doubtful about (i) for the reasons stated by Oliver LJ. However, the point which has finally tipped the balance of my mind in any event is that all these breaches could have arisen without negligence on the part of the defendants, but there is nothing in the clause which protects the defendants against the consequences of their own negligence. Despite the width of the third sentence (beginning 'We hereby exclude . . .') I do not think that this can be construed as having this effect. In this connection I would apply the well-known passage from the judgment of the Privy Council delivered by Lord Morton in *Canada Steamship Lines Ltd v R* [1952] 1 All ER 305 at 310, [1952] AC 192 at 208 to which Lord Fraser also made reference in the *Ailsa Craig* case.

This passage can be paraphrased as follows. (1) If the contract contains an express exemption from the consequence of negligence for which the party in default would otherwise be responsible, then effect must be given to it. (2) If there is no express reference to negligence, then the court must consider whether the words used are nevertheless wide enough, in their ordinary meaning, to cover loss or damage due to negligence; but any doubt in this connection must be resolved against the defaulting party. (3) However, even if the words used are wide enough for this purpose, the court must consider whether liability for the loss or damage in question may arise on some ground other than that of negligence, which ground is not so fanciful or remote that the party in default cannot be supposed to have desired protection against it.

a Applying these guidelines to the present clause, it clearly does not satisfy (1), since negligence is nowhere mentioned. In my view it also fails to satisfy (2); in this regard the position might well have been different if the magic words 'howsoever caused' had qualified the words 'loss or damage' in the third sentence: see eg *Joseph Travers & Sons Ltd v Cooper* [1915] 1 KB 73 at 101, [1914–15] All ER Rep 104 at 115 and *Gibaud v Great Eastern Rly Co* [1921] 2 KB 426 at 437, [1921] All ER Rep 35 at 40. However, even if this be wrong, I think that guideline (3) would still apply, since it seems perfectly consistent
b with the intention of both parties that the sellers should be protected if, but only if, the delivery of the wrong and/or of unmerchantable seed should occur without negligence on their part. It is true that, in the *Ailsa Craig* case, Lord Fraser appears to have qualified these guidelines to some extent where an exemption clause limits, but does not wholly exclude, liability, particularly in a context such as the fifth and sixth sentences of the present clause which draw attention to the business reasons for the inclusion of the clause.
c But his remarks were made in relation to a clause worded in unusually strong terms, covering 'any loss or damage of whatever nature arising out of or connected with the provision of, or purported provision of, or failure in provision of, the services covered by this contract'. In my view the wording of the present clause does not go as far as this. Since the type, nature and characteristics of any seeds may be wholly unascertainable by a supplier (unless he himself tests them to full growth), it seems to me that the present
d clause can perfectly sensibly be restricted to cases where the seed supplied turns out to be of the wrong kind, and/or to be unmerchantable, without any fault on the part of the seller, but that the parties are not to be taken to have intended that its wording should also apply if, as in the present case, the buyer's losses would not have occurred if the seller had not been negligent.

I would accordingly hold that the defendants are not protected by the clause in the
e present case, because the plaintiffs would not have suffered this disaster if there had not been negligence on the part of the defendants' staff, and because the clause does not require to be construed so as to cover cases where the buyer's loss has been caused, at any rate in part, by the seller's negligence.

However, even if this be wrong, I would unhesitatingly also decide this case in favour of the plaintiffs on the ground that it would not be fair or reasonable to allow the
f defendants to rely on this clause, by applying s 55(4) and (5) in Sch 1 to the Sale of Goods Act 1979. In this regard the balance of fairness and reasonableness appears to me to be overwhelmingly on the side of the plaintiffs, and I will only mention some of the most material facts in this connection.

The plaintiffs have suffered a loss of some £61,000 in terms of money; and in terms of time and labour the productivity of over 60 acres has been wasted for over a year. There
g was nothing whatever which the plaintiffs could have done to avoid this. As between them and the defendants all the fault lay admittedly on the side of the defendants. Further, farmers do not, and cannot be expected to, insure against this kind of disaster; but suppliers of seeds can. We were referred to a 'Wrong Variety of Seed Indemnity Insurance Scheme', set up under the auspices of the United Kingdom Agricultural Supply Trade Association Ltd (UKASTA), which provides an annual cover of £20,000. Although
h this particular scheme stipulates the exercise of due diligence on the part of the supplier, I am not persuaded that liability for rare events of this kind cannot be adequately insured against. Nor am I persuaded that the cost of such cover would add significantly to the cost of the seed. Further, although the present exemption clause has been in existence for many decades, the evidence shows that it was never negotiated. In effect, it was simply imposed by the suppliers, and no seed can in practice be bought otherwise than subject
j to its terms. To limit the suppliers' liability to the price of the seed in all cases, as against the magnitude of the losses which farmers can incur in rare disasters of this kind, appears to me to be a grossly disproportionate and unreasonable allocation of the respective risks. Furthermore, the evidence clearly shows that the clause is not relied on 'to the letter' in practice, and that neither the suppliers nor the farmers expect it to be applied literally. Its existence merely provides a basis for the negotiation of mutually acceptable settlements. Thus, we were told that there had been some inconclusive negotiations in the present case, though no figures were mentioned. However, these negotiations do not

matter, since the defendants are now seeking to uphold the clause to the letter. It is on
this basis that we have to decide whether reliance on the clause would be fair or　*a*
reasonable, and in my view the answer is clearly that it would not be.

Furthermore, to my mind there is another, overriding, consideration. It seems to me
that this new legislation, the modified version of s 55 of the Sale of Goods Act 1979 and
the Unfair Contract Terms Act 1977, was designed for exempting provisions whose
meaning is clear. Thus, one of the matters to be taken into account in judging fairness
and reasonableness (under s 55(5)(c)) is 'whether the buyer knew or ought reasonably to　*b*
have known of the . . . extent of the term . . .'. But we have had several days of argument
about the meaning and effect of the present clause, and it is already clear to what extent
opinions may differ about it. I do not think that this is the kind of situation for which
this legislation was designed. It was designed for exempting provisions whose meaning
is plain. Thus, if the present clause had been headed, for instance, 'Supply of wrong or
unmerchantable seed, whether by negligence or otherwise', the defendants' case in　*c*
relation to fairness and reasonableness would to that extent be strengthened. The effect
of the parties' bargain would then be plain. But businessmen do not choose to make plain
the meaning of the 'small print' which they use, and often do not themselves know what
it really means. In that event they must take the consequences of the uncertainty which
their 'small print' has created; and uncertainty involves unfairness to the other side.
Perhaps the effect of this new legislation will bring about a welcome change in this　*d*
respect. But so long as the meaning and effect of such provisions remains shrouded in
obscurity unless and until determined by the courts (and to many minds even thereafter),
I think that the courts should hold that reliance on such provisions would in any event
be unfair and unreasonable.

Finally, I must briefly refer to *R W Green Ltd v Cade Bros Farm* [1978] 1 Lloyd's Rep
602, on which counsel strongly relied on behalf of the defendants. In that case, seed　*e*
potatoes had been sold subject to the standard form of conditions of the National
Association of Seed Potato Merchants. These included a time limit for claims, and they
also limited the supplier's liability to refunding the contract price. The potatoes were
suffering from a virus which was undetectable by either party. Griffiths J held that the
exempting provision protected the sellers and that it was neither unfair nor unreasonable
for them to rely on it. In the latter regard he used language suggesting that he was　*f*
merely exercising a discretion, but I do not think that this was his intention. As stated by
this court in *Conemsco Ltd v Contrapol Ltd* [1981] CA Bound Transcript 536, a determination
under s 55 or under the Unfair Contract Terms Act 1977 constitutes a decision, of mixed
fact and law, and not merely the exercise of a discretion. But that case was very different
from the present. In particular, no blame attached to either party, and the standard
condition had been negotiated within the trade. There was also no basis for argument　*g*
about its meaning and effect. Further, there was evidence that the buyers could have
purchased seed certified by inspectors from the Ministry of Agriculture at a small extra
charge, whereas it was accepted on behalf of the defendants in the present case that there
was nothing equivalent which the plaintiffs could have done. I therefore do not think
that that case assists the defendants here in any way.

Accordingly, I would dismiss this appeal. I should add that since writing this judgment　*h*
I have seen a report of the decision of this court in *Lamport & Holt Lines Ltd v Coubro &
Scrutton (M & I) Ltd, The Raphael* [1982] 2 Lloyd's Rep 42, in which *Canada Steamship Lines
Ltd v R* [1952] 1 All ER 305, [1952] AC 192 was discussed in relation to a different
exemption clause. However, it does not seem to me that this affects the analysis of the
present clause as explained above.

Appeal dismissed. Leave to appeal to the House of Lords refused.

9 December. The Appeal Committee of the House of Lords granted the defendants leave to appeal.

Solicitors: *Davidson Doughty & Co* (for the defendants); *McKenna & Co* (for the plaintiffs).

Diana Procter　Barrister.

a   # Johns v Martin Simms (Cheltenham) Ltd

QUEEN'S BENCH DIVISION AT BRISTOL
LAWSON J
25 FEBRUARY 1982

b   *Building – Building operations – Fencing of machinery – Dangerous parts of machinery –
Radiator fan in excavator – Employee injured by blade on radiator fan while repairing excavator
at end of day's work – Radiator fan unfenced in breach of regulations – Whether excavator in
'use' when accident occurring – Construction (General Provisions) Regulations 1961, reg 3(1).*

The plaintiff was employed as an excavator driver by the defendants, who carried on a
plant hire business. In March 1976 the plaintiff was required by the defendants to use an
c   excavator to put stone and hardcore over a building site. In the course of doing that work
the plaintiff noticed that diesel fuel was leaking from the excavator. It was the plaintiff's
normal practice and part of his day's work to carry out maintenance work on the vehicle
when he finished work for the day. Accordingly, when he finished the day's active work
he decided to check on the fuel leak and for that purpose opened the engine cowling and
made adjustments to the bolts on the piping of the fuel system. He then started the
d   engine and looked to see whether those adjustments had solved the problem. In doing so
his hand got caught by a blade on the rotating fan at the rear of the radiator and his hand
was injured. The rotating fan was a dangerous part of the machinery which formed part
of the plant and it was not securely fenced as required by reg 42[a] of the Construction
(General Provisions) Regulations 1961. The plaintiff brought an action against the
defendants claiming damages, inter alia, for breach of statutory duty. The defendants
e   contended that they were not liable because the machinery was not at 'work' or in 'use' at
the time of the accident within reg 3(1)[b] and therefore reg 42 did not apply.

Held – The words 'works' and 'uses' in reg 3 of the 1961 regulations embraced not only
the commercial or industrial operation of a machine for its designed purpose but also
f   any operation of it for any purpose which involved activation of the machinery itself.
Since it was part of the normal use of the excavator that it should be subject to ordinary
maintenance and adjustment and that it should be daily inspected and checked and any
necessary adjustments made, it was in 'use' within reg 3(1) when the accident occurred
and the defendants were liable under reg 42 of the 1961 regulations (see p 130 *a b d e* and
f g, post).
Smith v W & J R Watson Ltd 1977 JC 52 followed.

g   ## Notes
For general provisions as to safety in building operations and duty to fence dangerous
machinery, see 20 Halsbury's Laws (4th edn) paras 662, 670.
    For the Construction (General Provisions) Regulations 1961, regs 2, 3, 42, see 8
Halsbury's Statutory Instruments (3rd reissue) 247–248, 260.

h   ## Case referred to in judgment
Smith v W & J R Watson Ltd 1977 JC 52.

Case also cited
Baxter v Central Electricity Generating Board [1964] 2 All ER 815, [1965] 1 WLR 200.

j   ## Action
By a writ issued on 9 October 1978 the plaintiff, Brian Keith Johns, brought an action
against the defendants, Martin Simms (Cheltenham) Ltd, claiming damages for personal

---

a   Regulation 42, so far as material, is set out at p 129 *j*, post
b   Regulation 3(1), so far as material, is set out at p 129 *h*, post

injuries arising out of an accident sustained by the plaintiff in the course of his
employment with the defendants on 22 March 1976 caused by the breach of statutory   *a*
duty laid on the defendants by reg 42 of Construction (General Provisions) Regulations
1961 and/or negligence of the defendants, their servants or agents. The facts are set out
in the judgment of Lawson J.

Philip Naughton for the plaintiff.
John Royce for the defendants.   *b*

LAWSON J. By writ issued on 9 October 1978 the plaintiff claims against the
defendants who were at the material time and still are his employers, damages for
personal injuries which the plaintiff sustained in an accident whilst he was working for
the defendants on 22 March 1976.

I find that the facts are as follows. The plaintiff was at the time of the accident and he   *c*
still is, and had been for a number of years, since about 1968, employed by the defendants
who are plant hire contractors and who operate a plant hire business which involves their
owning and hiring out machines which are used in the building and engineering
construction industry, and hiring them out, anyhow on this occasion, with the use of the
driver, which is a form of arrangement in plant hire.

The plaintiff is a man who was first employed as a farm labourer or agricultural   *d*
labourer, in the course of which he became acquainted with the use of agricultural
machinery, and he joined the defendants as a driver of a construction plant in June 1968
when he was aged about 25. He had many years experience with the defendants of
driving various types of plant, including the particular type of plant that he was using on
the day of the accident, that is to say, a Massey-Ferguson 450S excavator

At the time of the accident the plaintiff and his excavator were certainly engaged in   *e*
building operations within the meaning of the Construction (General Provision)
Regulations 1961, SI 1961/1580, because the work they were undertaking was part of
the construction of, I think, an additional building or annexe to certain premises known
as the Churchdown Club.

The plaintiff did his normal day's operations on that day which was to put stone or
hardcore to form over site for a building extension at this club, and at the end of that   *f*
operation and as part of his day's work in accordance with his normal practice he was
going to see that his excavator was in satisfactory working order and was prepared ready
for use on the following day.

I should interpose that this particular excavator had, a week or so before the accident
happened, been found to have a leaking exhaust, and this had been reported to Mr Simms
who is the responsible officer of the defendants (I think it is his company) and I think it   *g*
was decided that this machine should be set on one side and not used until the necessary
repairs to the flexible metal tubing which was the part from which the exhaust fumes
were leaking had been replaced; but on the morning of the accident this excavator was
required for a job in the course of these building operations and I find that the plaintiff
told Mr Simms he was going to take the excavator down and use it for these operations,
notwithstanding that no repair to the flexible tubing part of the exhaust had been carried   *h*
out, and nothing more was said about the matter.

As the plaintiff was doing the job he observed that there was some leakage of diesel oil,
which was the fuel by which this excavator was operated, so accordingly at the end of the
day's active work in dealing with the over-laying and providing for the over site of the
building extension, the plaintiff decided that he would check on the fuel leak, and for
that purpose he got out of his cab and he opened the engine cowling and proceeded to   *j*
see if he could find where the leak was coming from. He did that with the engine
running.

I am quite satisfied that having decided with the engine running certain adjustments
needed to be made to bolts on the piping of the fuel system he got into his cab and turned
the engine off. He then proceeded to make the adjustments he thought were necessary,

and he did so with the engine cowling, of course, being open but the engine not running
at the time. Having done his adjustments he then returned to his cab and started the
engine running and came back to look into the engine, the cowling still open, to see
whether the leaking fuel and the problem of the fuel leak had been solved.

Whilst he was so engaged, unfortunately in some way or other, his left hand got
caught by a blade on the fan which is at the rear of the radiator of the motor of the
excavator, and his hand was injured.

The plaintiff's case was based on three grounds. First, it was submitted that he was
overcome by the leaking fumes from the exhaust, and his level of consciousness and
concentration was therefore lowered and this provided the explanation as to how his
hand got into a position which it would normally not get into at all so that it could be
injured by the blade from the fan.

So far as that is concerned, the plaintiff was an extremely frank and honest witness,
and although he was pressed, and indeed I pressed him fairly hard about this, whether he
could recall any feeling of muzziness or dizziness or lack of clarity, he could not
remember feeling like that at all, and in fact the operations he did before, during and
after he had made his adjustments to the fuel lines rather contra-indicate that he was at
any stage overcome to any extent by fumes. I agree it is a possibility but of course in
order to establish that cause of action (and had he established it there is no doubt there
would have been a prima facie liability on the defendants because a machine with a
defective exhaust is something which is a potentially dangerous thing because it emits
fumes), the plaintiff has to satisfy me that it is more likely than not that this was the
cause of his accident, and I am not so satisfied. I do not think it comes higher than a
possibility here. The engine cowling was open at all relevant times and the plaintiff
himself was actually standing in the open air and not in an enclosed space, and it seems
to me that the probabilities are against the exhaust fumes having overcome him to any
extent.

The second point which was put on his behalf was that the blades of the fan behind
the radiator within the space of the motor of this excavator were protruding beyond the
circular frame which surrounds them as shown in the photographs before me. In the
course of his evidence he said one of the plates seemed to have got a bit twisted and
protruded a little beyond the others. Unfortunately I have had no evidence from an
expert who examined this machine after the accident, and the plaintiff's recollection of
the twisted plate does not relate to the time of the accident or a time before it but relates
to something which he observed later, and therefore he fails to satisfy me on balance of
probability that his injury was caused by a disrotated blade on the fan.

The other ground on which the plaintiff claims damages is for breach of the statutory
duty which is laid on the defendants by the Construction (General Provisions) Regulations
1961. Regulation 2(1)(b) of those regulations says that they apply to building operations
undertaken by way of trade or business, and these certainly were building operations
undertaken by way of trade or business. Regulation 3(1) provides:

> '. . . it shall be the duty of every contractor, and every employer of workmen,
> who erects, installs, works or uses any plant or equipment to which any of the
> provisions of Regulations . . . 42 . . . applies, to erect, install, work or use any such
> plant or equipment in a manner which complies with those provisions.'

Regulation 42, which was covered by the part of reg 3 which I have read, provides:

> '. . . every dangerous part of other machinery [that is to say, machinery other than
> prime movers and transmission machinery] (whether or not driven by mechanical
> power) shall be securely fenced unless it is in such a position or of such construction
> as to be as safe to every person employed or working on the site of the operations or
> works as it would be if it were securely fenced.'

There is not the slightest doubt that this rotating fan was a dangerous part of the
machinery which formed part of the plant, and it was not securely fenced as it very

simply and easily could have been, and the only question really here, there being prima facie a breach of reg 42, and this is the only question as it seems to me in dispute under *a* the regulations, is: was this plant at work or was it in use at the time when the accident occurred?

Without reference to any authority and just applying ordinary common sense to the situation I would have thought that it was in use. It was part of the normal use of this plant that it should be subject to ordinary maintenance and adjustment, and it is part of the normal use of construction plant that it should be daily inspected, checked and any *b* necessary adjustments made, but I am persuaded that this is the right view by the decision of the High Court of Justiciary in *Smith v W & J R Watson Ltd* 1977 JC 52. This was a case where the defendants had been tried and the sheriff had ruled in the course of the trial that the machine which was being cleaned at the relevant time, the time of the accident, was not being used for the purpose of these same regulations.

Now on appeal there was a strong court, which the Lord Justice-General (Emslie), Lord *c* Cameron and Lord Johnston, and the court held that the sheriff was wrong in ruling as he had ruled, and this was a cause. The accident happened when the machine was being cleaned and not actually working at working operation. I quote from the judgment of the court (at 56):

> 'The words "works or uses" accordingly embrace not only the commercial or industrial operation of a machine for its designed purpose but any operation thereof *d* for whatever purpose which involves the activation of the machine itself.'

Clearly this was a case which falls squarely within the principle which leads to that discretion which I have cited. It therefore follows, with the duty under reg 42 being an absolute duty, that the defendants are liable.

The defendants contend that the plaintiff was guilty of contributory negligence, and it *e* is said he must have been careless because he should not have got his hand in such a position as it would come into contact with the rotating fan.

I take the view that there is no evidence which would justify me in taking the view that the plaintiff was failing to take any proper care for his own safety, because this is the sort of accident which can happen by inadvertence and that is one of the reasons why the regulations made under this statute are made, because workmen who are concentrating *f* on doing a job may inadvertently get their hands in a position of danger by reason of a dangerous part of the machine, and that is why the law requires the dangerous part to be fenced. It therefore follows that I find this accident is wholly the responsibility of the defendants and the plaintiff is not guilty of any negligence on his own part. [His Lordship then referred to the severe multiple injuries sustained by the plaintiff to his left hand described in three medical reports and having regard to those injuries and their effect on *g* the plaintiff's prospects of employment he awarded the plaintiff general damages of £7,750, comprising £5,250 for pain, suffering and loss of amenities, and £2,500 for loss of his prospects on the open labour market, and agreed special damages of £107·69.]

Judgment for plaintiff.

Solicitors: *Rowberry Morris*, Gloucester (for the plaintiff); *Sansbury Hill & Co*, Bristol (for the defendants).

Mary Rose Plummer   Barrister.

Practice Direction

CHANCERY DIVISION

Land – Summary proceedings for possession – Procedure – Adjournment to judge – Appointment before master not required – RSC Ord 113.

Practice – Title of proceedings – Approved methods.

Practice – Chambers proceedings – Master's powers – Monetary limit – Increase of limit.

Practice – Motion – Adjournment – Chancery Division – Agreed adjournment – Procedure.

Costs – Taxation – Review of taxation – Procedure – Chancery Division.

Practice – Chancery Division – Affidavit – Office copies – Normally no longer required.

Practice – Chambers proceedings – Appeal from master – Appeal to judge in chambers – Procedure – RSC Ord 58, r 1.

Practice – Summons for directions – Chancery Division – Timetable no longer required.

1. *Possession under RSC Ord 113*
As from January 1983 it will no longer be necessary under RSC Ord 113 to take an appointment before the master prior to adjournment to the judge. The plaintiff should stamp and issue the originating summons in room 157, and the date for hearing before a judge in chambers will be inserted in the body of the summons, giving at least five clear days between the date of issue and the date of hearing. The affidavits in support of the originating summons are filed in room 157.

The Practice Direction of 31 July 1970 ([1970] 3 All ER 240, [1970] 1 WLR 1250) is revoked as from 1 January 1983.

2. *Title to proceedings*
The general rule is that the title should contain only the parties to the proceedings, but there are two exceptions: (1) where the proceedings relate to the administration of an estate or a probate action they should be entitled 'In the estate of *AB* deceased'; and (2) where the proceedings relate to the construction of a document they should be entitled 'In the matter of [*describe document briefly*] dated   between *AB* and *CD*'. Parties should be named by their initials and surnames only; and if there are numerous parties, it will usually suffice to state that the document is made 'between *AB* and others'. If there is more than one document, only the main or first document need be referred to.

If proceedings are under an Act of Parliament, the Act no longer need be mentioned in the title but should be referred to in the body of the writ or originating summons.

Paragraph (1) of the Practice Note of 18 June 1959 ([1959] 2 All ER 629, [1959] 1 WLR 743) is hereby revoked.

3. *Masters' jurisdiction*
The masters' powers under para 3(b), (l)(ii) and (m) of the Practice Direction of 18 December 1974 ([1975] 1 All ER 255, [1975] 1 WLR 129), as varied by the Practice Direction of 22 July 1977 ([1977] 3 All ER 121, [1977] 1 WLR 1019), are now extended to cases in which the amount does not exceed £30,000.

4. *Agreed adjournment of motions*
The procedure for adjourning motions by consent has now been extended to cases in which an undertaking to the court has been given and that undertaking is to be continued unchanged. The Practice Note of 17 April 1976 ([1976] 2 All ER 198, [1976] 1 WLR 441), as modified by para 18 of the Practice Direction of 29 July 1982 ([1982] 3 All ER 124, [1982] 1 WLR 1189), is varied accordingly. Applications may be made either

personally at room 180 or by post. Adjournments on which an undertaking to the court is to be varied or a new undertaking is to be given must still be dealt with in court.

5. *Review of taxation*
Application for a review of taxation is made by ordinary summons in the proceedings in which the taxation has been ordered (see RSC Ord 62, r 35(3)). The summons should identify the item or items of the bill disputed and the amounts allowed. The summons should be issued in the Chancery Registry (room 156) for hearing before a judge in chambers on a day and time to be fixed. The summons must be served within three days after issue.

The court file will be sent to the Chief Clerk of the Taxing Office who will arrange for the necessary documents to be lodged, for the appointment of assessors, if required, and for the date of hearing of the summons; and he will notify the assessors and the parties of the date fixed. The Practice Direction of the Chief Master of 4 April 1962 ([1962] 2 All ER 128, [1962] 1 WLR 580), as amended the Practice Direction of 22 May 1968 ([1968] 2 All ER 635, [1968] 1 WLR 1144), set out in *The Supreme Court Practice 1982* vol 1, p 1075, para 62/35/2 is hereby revoked.

6. *Affidavit evidence*
Office copies of affidavits are normally no longer required for use either in court or in chambers, and para 1 (apart from the last sub-paragraph) of the Practice Direction of 22 May 1969 ([1969] 2 All ER 639, [1969] 1 WLR 974) is hereby revoked. If office copies of an affidavit are required, they may be obtained from room 157.

7. *Appeals from masters*
In place of the former procedure for a litigant who is dissatisfied with a decision of a master to require the summons to be adjourned to a judge, there is now a right of appeal from the master to a judge in chambers under RSC Ord 58, r 1, as amended. The appeal is brought by a notice of appeal, stating the grounds of appeal, and this is issued out of room 157. The appellant opens the appeal, but, even if the appeal is against only part of the master's order, the whole of the summons is treated as being before the judge, who will make such order on it as he thinks fit.

8. *Timetables*
The party setting down an action need no longer supply a timetable of the proceedings, since all the information will now be available on the court file. Paragraphs 4 and 6 of the Practice Direction of 4 February 1977 ([1977] 1 All ER 543, [1977] 1 WLR 198) are therefore revoked.

By direction of the Vice-Chancellor.

30 December 1982

EDMUND HEWARD
Chief Master.

Clark (Inspector of Taxes) v Oceanic Contractors Inc

HOUSE OF LORDS

LORD SCARMAN, LORD WILBERFORCE, LORD EDMUND-DAVIES, LORD LOWRY AND LORD ROSKILL

11, 12, 13 OCTOBER, 16 DECEMBER 1982

Income tax – Pay as you earn system – Deduction of tax by employer – Failure to deduct tax – Foreign employer – Employees employed in United Kingdom sector of North Sea – Employees paid in US dollars by cheques sent from abroad – Employees liable to Sch E tax – Employer having branch or agency in United Kingdom and liable to corporation tax – Whether employer to be required to deduct PAYE tax from wages or salaries paid to employees working in United Kingdom sector of North Sea – Whether legislation requiring collection of PAYE tax having extra-territorial effect – Whether employer having sufficient 'tax presence' in United Kingdom to require it to collect PAYE tax – Income and Corporation Taxes Act 1970, s 204 – Finance Act 1973, s 38(4)(6)

A non-resident overseas company engaged in pipe laying and platform construction in the North Sea employed some 400 workers on its barges and other vessels based at Antwerp. The company carried on its operations in various locations throughout the world, some of which were in the United Kingdom sector of the North Sea and were 'designated areas' under the Continental Shelf Act 1964. The company also maintained establishments in the United Kingdom and deducted PAYE tax in respect of employees employed at those establishments. However, employees who were employed in the United Kingdom sector of the North Sea were paid in US dollars free of United Kingdom tax by cheques sent by post from the company's administrative headquarters in Brussels. The employees were liable to tax under Sch E in respect of their earnings in that sector. The Crown claimed that the company was required by s 204[a] of the Income and Corporation Taxes Act 1970 to deduct PAYE tax payable under Sch E from wages and salaries paid to its employees who worked in the United Kingdom sector of the North Sea. The Crown took the view that s 204 contained no territorial limitation on the duty arising on making any payment of income assessable to tax under Sch E that 'income tax shall ... be deducted or repaid by the person making the payment'. The Special Commissioners allowed an appeal by the company against the Crown's claim. On appeal by the Crown the judge upheld the Crown's claim. On appeal by the company, the Court of Appeal held that, although s 204 was in general terms, Parliament could not have intended to cast on a foreigner who was not resident in the United Kingdom the role of tax collector for the Revenue and therefore s 204 was to be presumed not to have extra-territorial effect. The Crown appealed, contending (i) that whenever Sch E applied to a taxpayer's income s 204 imposed a duty on the employer to deduct and account for PAYE tax payable under Sch E even when the taxpayer's work was performed and paid for outside the United Kingdom and the employer was not resident in or connected with the United Kingdom, (ii) that emoluments earned in the United Kingdom sector of the North Sea which were required by s 38(6)[b] of the Finance Act 1973 to be treated as emoluments earned in the United Kingdom 'for the purposes of income tax' were required to be so treated for all purposes of income tax, including the collection of tax, (iii) that the company had a sufficient 'tax presence' by virtue of its United Kingdom operations and address for service to justify the imposition of liability under s 204 and (iv) that it was to be implied from the fact that the company was, by virtue of s 38(4)[c] of

---

a   Section 204, so far as material, is set out at p 142 c d, post

b   Section 38(6) provides: 'Any emoluments from an office or employment in respect of duties performed in a designated area in connection with exploration or exploitation activities shall be treated for the purposes of income tax as emoluments in respect of duties performed in the United Kingdom.'

c   Section 38(4) is set out at p 143 a, post

the 1973 Act, liable for capital gains tax and corporation tax that it was subject to United Kingdom tax legislation generally, including the liability to deduct and account for *a* PAYE tax payable under Sch E.

Held – (1) Although s 204 of the 1970 Act was expressed in general and unqualified terms, it was subject to the general principle that English legislation was primarily territorial. Accordingly, s 204 could not, by itself, be construed as having worldwide extra-territorial effect so as to apply generally to a foreign employer resident abroad who *b* paid an employee in foreign currency abroad in respect of work done abroad. In particular, since the United Kingdom sector of the North Sea, although a 'designated area' under the 1964 Act, was not part of the United Kingdom, s 204 could not apply by virtue of any extra-territorial effect to the company's employees employed in that sector. Furthermore, although the Sch E charge was extended to the British sector of the North Sea by s 38(6) of the 1973 Act and although Sch E contained express territorial limitations, *c* those could not be the only limitations to which s 204 was subject, because the practical impossibility of making unco-operative foreign employers who made taxable payments outside the United Kingdom comply with s 204 presupposed that s 204 was subject to other territorial limitations. Moreover, the effect of s 38(6) of the 1973 Act was not to extend liability under s 204 of the 1970 Act to cover a non-resident foreign company making payments abroad to employees working in the United Kingdom sector of the *d* North Sea because s 38(6) was merely concerned with the imposition of tax whereas s 204 was concerned with the collection of tax (see p 137 *j*, p 139 *g* to *j*, p 140 *c d h j*, p 142 *d*, p 143 *f g*, p 146 *h j*, p 147 *b c g h*, p 149 *a* to *e* and p 150 *g h*, post); *Re Sawers, ex p Blain* [1874–80] All ER Rep 708, dicta of Lord Herschell in *Colquhoun v Brooks* [1886–90] All ER Rep at 1067, of the Earl of Halsbury LC in *Cooke v Charles A Vogeler Co* [1900–3] All ER Rep at 662 and of Viscount Simonds in *Government of India, Ministry of Finance* *e* *(Revenue Division) v Taylor* [1955] 1 All ER at 295 applied.

(2) (Lord Edmund-Davies and Lord Lowry dissenting) Having regard to the rule against extra-territorial effect, it was to be implied that s 204 only applied where an employer had a 'tax presence' in the United Kingdom, since the employer by making himself subject to United Kingdom jurisdiction had made effective collection of tax possible. The company had, by its trading operations within the United Kingdom and in *f* the United Kingdom sector of the North Sea and its assumption of liability to corporation tax under s 38(4) of the 1973 Act by virtue of having a 'branch or agency' in the United Kingdom, a sufficient tax presence in the United Kingdom for s 204 to apply. The company was therefore liable under s 204 to deduct and account for PAYE tax payable under Sch E from wages and salaries paid to its employees who worked in the United Kingdom sector of the North Sea. The Crown's appeal would therefore be allowed (see *g* p 141 *e* to *h*, p 145 *e* and p 150 *g h*, post).

Notes

For the collection of PAYE tax, see 23 Halsbury's Laws (4th edn) paras 714ff, and for the taxation of emoluments in respect of duties performed in a designated area, see ibid para 1364.

For the Income and Corporation Taxes Act, s 204, see 33 Halsbury's Statutes (3rd edn) 285.

For the Finance Act 1973, s 38, see 43 ibid 1438.

Cases referred to in opinions

A-G of the Province of Alberta v Huggard Assets Ltd [1953] 2 All ER 951, [1953] AC 420, [1952] 2 WLR 768, PC, 8(2) Digest (Reissue) 782, 500.

Cail v Papayanni, The Amalia (1863) 1 Moo PCCNS 471, 15 ER 778.

Colquhoun v Brooks (1889) 14 App Cas 493, [1886–90] All ER Rep 1063, HL, 44 Digest (Repl) 265, 906.

Colquhoun v Heddon (1890) 25 QBD 129, CA, 44 Digest (Repl) 277, 1052.

---

d Section 246, so far as material, is set out at p 143 *c* to *e*, post

Cooke v Charles A Vogeler Co [1901] AC 102, [1900–3] All ER Rep 660, HL, 44 Digest
a   (Repl) 277, 1061.
De Beers Consolidated Mines Ltd v Howe (Surveyor of Taxes) [1906] AC 455, HL, 28(1) Digest
(Reissue) 366, 1339.
Government of India, Ministry of Finance (Revenue Division) v Taylor [1955] 1 All ER 292,
[1955] AC 491, [1955] 2 WLR 303, HL, 11 Digest (Reissue) 341, 8.
National Bank of Greece SA v Westminster Bank Exor and Trustee Co (Channel Islands) Ltd
b   [1971] 1 All ER 233, [1971] AC 945, [1971] 2 WLR 105, HL.
Sawers, Re, ex p Blain (1879) 12 Ch D 522, [1874–80] All ER Rep 708, CA, 11 Digest
(Reissue) 340, 1.
Tuck & Sons v Priester (1887) 19 QBD 629, CA, 44 Digest (Reissue) 324, 1583.
Vestey v IRC (Nos 1 and 2) [1979] 3 All ER 976, [1980] AC 1148, [1979] 3 WLR 915, HL,
Digest (Cont Vol E) 307, 1584a.

c
Appeal
The Crown appealed against an order of the Court of Appeal (Lawton, Brightman and
Fox LJJ) ([1982] STC 66) reversing the decision of Dillon J ([1980] STC 656) allowing the
Crown's appeal by way of case stated against the determination of the Commissioners for
the Special Purposes of the Income Tax Acts allowing an appeal by Oceanic Contractors
d   Inc (Oceanic) against the claim by the Crown that Oceanic was required by s 204 of the
Income and Corporation Taxes Act 1970 to deduct tax in accordance with regulations
made under that section from emoluments paid to employees engaged to work on barges
in the United Kingdom sector of the North Sea. The facts are set out in the opinion of
Lord Scarman.

e   *D C Potter QC* and *Robert Carnwath* for the Crown.
F Heyworth Talbot QC, John Gardiner QC and *Roger C Thomas* for Oceanic.

Their Lordships took time for consideration.

f   16 December. The following opinions were delivered.

LORD SCARMAN. My Lords, in this appeal the Crown seeks to have restored the
determination of the inspector of taxes that tax amounting to £2,033,254 is payable by
the respondent corporation (Oceanic) under reg 26 of the PAYE regulations (Income Tax
(Employments) Regulations 1973, SI 1973/334) for the year 1977–78. The issue is of
g   great practical importance to the Revenue and to Oceanic: it is also one of some legal
difficulty. The issue turns on the true construction of s 204 of the Income and Corporation
Taxes Act 1970, the section which imposes the PAYE obligation.
Oceanic is a foreign corporation registered in Panama; it is not resident in the United
Kingdom for the purposes of income tax. Its operations are worldwide and include the
provision of technical services and equipment to those who are engaged in the exploration
h   and exploitation of the oil and gas resources of the North Sea. The issue in the appeal is
whether Oceanic can be required to operate the PAYE procedure for tax collection in
respect of the wages and salaries of those of its work force whom it employs in the United
Kingdom sector of the North Sea. It is conceded that the emoluments of these employees
are assessable to British income tax under Sch E. Is that, by itself, enough to impose on
Oceanic the PAYE obligation? The Crown submits that it is. If, however, it is not, the
j   Crown's alternative submission is that Oceanic has, by reason of its operations and trading
activities in the United Kingdom and in the North Sea, a sufficient presence in, or
connection with, the United Kingdom to justify the Revenue's requirement that it
operate PAYE in respect of the earnings of the personnel it employs in the United
Kingdom sector of the North Sea.
To these submissions Oceanic makes reply as follows: in its submission, the anomalies
and enforcement problems arising from an attempt to impose the PAYE obligation on a
non-resident corporation paying emoluments abroad to persons who are working outside

the United Kingdom are such that, even though those emoluments be (as they may well
be) assessable to tax under Sch E, Parliament cannot have intended to impose on the   *a*
employer the duties of deduction and collection of tax formulated in s 204 and the PAYE
regulations: the section must be subject to an implied territorial limitation which would
exclude its operation in such circumstances.

The Special Commissioners upheld Oceanic's submission. Dillon J ([1980] STC 656),
while he rejected the Crown's first submission because of its 'world-wide' implications
which he could not conceive Parliament intended and which he held to be inconsistent   *b*
with the general rule that an Act of Parliament only applies to transactions within the
United Kingdom, upheld the Crown's second submission, finding in s 38(6) of the
Finance Act 1973 (which it will be necessary to consider later) a sufficient link with the
United Kingdom to justify the imposition of the PAYE obligation in respect of
emoluments arising from duties performed in the United Kingdom sector of the North
Sea. He reversed, therefore, the determination of the Special Commissioners in favour of   *c*
Oceanic.

The Court of Appeal reversed the judge (see [1982] STC 66). They considered s 38(6)
of the 1973 Act on which the judge relied, to be a charging provision affording no
guidance as to the collecting liability imposed by s 204. They accepted Oceanic's
submission that some territorial limitation must be placed on the s 204 liability. They
refrained, however, from formulating the limitation. It was, in Brightman LJ's view,   *d*
unnecessary to say more than that it must exclude a non-resident corporation making
payments in circumstances such as those of this case.

The facts have been lucidly set out by the Special Commissioners and summarised by
Dillon J at the beginning of his judgment. It will suffice to mention specifically only the
following. (1) Oceanic is not resident for income tax purposes in the United Kingdom.
(2) It has, however, a design office at Wembley, a platform fabrication yard near Inverness,   *e*
and a branch at Aberdeen providing skilled services in connection with its North Sea
activities. It operates PAYE in respect of employees at these establishments. (3) It accepts
that it has a place of business within Great Britain and is liable to corporation tax on
profits from its activities in the United Kingdom and in the United Kingdom sector of
the North Sea, all of which are taxed as a single trade. It is an overseas company to which
s 407 of the Companies Act 1948 applies. It has complied with the requirements of the   *f*
section and has an address for service in Wembley. (4) The operating base for its North
Sea activities is the port of Antwerp; the headquarters of its North Sea division are at
Brussels. Its North Sea activities consist of installation and maintenance of platforms and
the laying of pipelines in the United Kingdom and Norwegian sectors of the North Sea,
for which purpose it operates barges out of Antwerp. (5) The work force employed on
these operations was in 1977–78 several hundred strong (approximately four hundred in   *g*
1977) of whom approximately 60% were United Kingdom nationals. They had written
contracts not governed by English law. They were paid (in US dollars) and employed
outside the United Kingdom.

The statutes

The Continental Shelf Act 1964 makes provision for the exploration and exploitation   *h*
of the natural resources of the continental shelf outside territorial waters. Its purpose is
to give effect to certain provisions of the Geneva Convention on the High Seas (Cmnd
584). The Act recognises that the United Kingdom sector of the North Sea continental
shelf is not part of the United Kingdom (see s 1(1)). The Act provides that areas of the
continental shelf outside territorial waters may be designated by Order in Council as
areas within which the United Kingdom may exercise rights of exploration and   *j*
exploitation (see s 1(7)). Certain areas of the North Sea, compendiously described in these
proceedings as 'the UK sector of the North Sea' have been so designated.

Consequential on the 1964 Act, s 38 of the Finance Act 1973 made provision for the
territorial extension of the charge to income tax, capital gains tax, and corporation tax.
Section 38(1) provides that the territorial sea of the United Kingdom shall for tax purposes
be deemed to be part of the United Kingdom. Designated areas under the 1964 Act,
which are by definition beyond the territorial sea, are not part of the United Kingdom.

The section, however, extends the application of some of our tax laws to these areas. In
a particular, s 38(4) provides that profits or gains arising to any person not resident in the
United Kingdom from exploration or exploitation activities carried on in the United
Kingdom or in a designated area shall for the purposes of corporation tax or capital gains
tax be treated as the profits or gains of a trade carried on in the United Kingdom through
a branch or agency. The subsection brings such a person within s 246 of the Income and
Corporation Taxes Act 1970, thereby recognising a 'tax presence' in the United Kingdom
b of a non-resident corporation if it be engaged by way of trade in exploration or
exploitation activities in designated areas. Section 38(6) brings within the charge to
income tax emoluments from an office or employment in respect of duties performed in
a designated area: they are to be treated for the purposes of income tax as emoluments in
respect of duties performed in the United Kingdom. In other words, they are chargeable
to income tax under Sch E. The effect of the section is, therefore: (1) that a non-resident
c corporation, which, like Oceanic, is engaged by way of trade in exploration or exploitation
activities in the United Kingdom sector of the North Sea, is liable to corporation tax and
capital gains tax in respect of the profits and gains of its trade there; and (2) that its
employees engaged in the United Kingdom sector are liable to tax under Sch E in respect
of their earnings in the sector. Non-resident corporations and their employees are,
therefore, in certain very important respects subject to British tax laws in respect of their
d activities in the United Kingdom sector of the North Sea.

I turn now to the Income and Corporation Taxes Act 1970. Put very briefly, liability
to tax depends, as it always has, on the location of the source from which the taxable
income is derived or the residence of the person whose income is to be taxed. If either
the source of income or the residence of the owner of the income is in the United
Kingdom, the income is liable to tax. The combination of this principle of income tax
e law with the provisions of s 38(6) of the 1973 Act results in persons, whether or not
resident in the United Kingdom, who are paid emoluments in respect of duties performed
in the United Kingdom sector of the North Sea, being liable to income tax in respect of
those emoluments.

For the purposes of this appeal, the critical sections of the Income and Corporation
Taxes Act 1970 are ss 181 and 204, which provide for the charging and collection of
f income tax under Sch E, and s 246, which imposes a corporation tax liability on a non-
resident corporation in respect of the profits of a trade carried on through a branch or
agency within the United Kingdom. Again, it is to be noted that a tax liability can arise
in the case of non-resident persons where the income, profit, or gains arise from activities
carried on within the United Kingdom.

Sections 181 and 204 bear directly on the issue of this appeal. Section 181, as amended
g by s 21 of the Finance Act 1974, provides for the Sch E charge to income tax. Tax under
the schedule is charged in respect of emoluments falling under one or more of three
cases: Case I, where the employee is resident and ordinarily resident in the United
Kingdom; Case II, in respect of duties performed in the United Kingdom where the
person is not resident (or not ordinarily resident) in the United Kingdom); Case III, in
respect of emoluments received in the United Kingdom by a person there resident. The
h Sch E charge is, therefore, not limited to the income of United Kingdom residents but is
imposed on non-residents in respect of duties performed in the United Kingdom.

Section 204 imposes the PAYE system of tax collection in respect of any income
assessable under Sch E. On the making of any payment on account of such income, the
payer is to deduct the tax (s 204(1)). The Board of Inland Revenue is to make regulations
with respect to the assessment, charge, collection and recovery of Sch E tax; and these
i regulations may include (as, indeed, the regulations made most assuredly do) provision
for (a) requiring the payer to make deduction according to tax tables prepared by the
board, (b) the production for inspection of relevant documents and records and (c) the
collection and recovery of the tax to be deducted. Criminal sanctions and penalties for
failure to comply with PAYE obligations arise under s 98 of the Taxes Management Act
1970.

Section 204 is general in terms. It contains no express territorial limitation on the
extent of the obligation it imposes. In particular, it is silent as to the place of payment,

the currency in which payment is made, the residence of the person making payment, and the place of the contract pursuant to which the payments are made. It contains only *a* two express limitations on the extent of the liability it imposes: (1) the PAYE obligation arises when the payment is made; and (2) it arises only in respect of income assessable under Sch E.

It is plain from the terms of s 204 and its position as the first section in the chapter dealing with the assessment, collection and recovery of Sch E tax that Parliament intended PAYE to be the primary method of Sch E tax collection. Provision is, however, *b* made by s 205 and reg 50 of the Income Tax (Employments) Regulations 1973 for direct assessment on and collection from the employee at the option either of the Board of Inland Revenue or the employee.

To conclude this summary of the relevant statutory provisions, two propositions of law may be said to emerge with clarity: (1) residence is not a necessary condition of tax liability if there be otherwise a sufficient connection between the source of the income, *c* profit or gain and the United Kingdom; and (2) s 204, silent itself as to the territorial extent of the obligation it imposes, is a machinery section for the collection of Sch E tax under Cases I and II. Case III is excluded because its charge arises on the receipt of income, whereas s 204 operates on a person making a payment as and when he makes the payment. Subject, therefore, to the exclusion of Case III, s 204 applies whenever a payment is made on account of income, unless it be necessary to imply some limitation *d* not expressed in Sch E itself.

I would add that a review of the statutory provisions amply justifies Dillon J's comment ([1980] STC 656 at 669, [1981] 1 WLR 59 at 66) that—

's 204 must apply where the duties of the office or employment are carried out within the United Kingdom, whether the employer is foreign or not and whatever method be adopted for paying the emoluments for those duties.'   *e*

The principle of construction

The question being, therefore, whether there is to be implied into s 204 a territorial limitation further to those expressed in Sch E, it becomes necessary to consider what principle of law would justify such an implication.

It is well-settled law that English legislation is primarily territorial: see *Re Sawers, ex p* *f* *Blain* (1879) 12 Ch D 522 at 528, [1874–80] All ER Rep 708 at 711 per Brett LJ. The principle was recognised and formulated (admittedly in language which now has echoes of a world which has departed) by the Court of Appeal in *Ex p Blain* and was commented on with approval by the Earl of Halsbury LC in *Cooke v Charles A Vogeler Co* [1901] AC 102 at 107, [1900–3] All ER Rep 660 at 662. Two passages from the judgments in *Blain's* case are directly relevant to the issue in this case. First, a passage from the judgment of *g* James LJ ((1879) 12 Ch D 522 at 526, [1874–80] All ER Rep 708 at 709). He referred to the—

'broad, general, universal principle that English legislation, unless the contrary is expressly enacted or so plainly implied as to make it the duty of an English Court to give effect to an English statute, is applicable only to English subjects or to foreigners *h* who by coming into this country, whether for a long or a short time, have made themselves during that time subject to English jurisdiction . . . But, if a foreigner remains abroad, if he has never come into this country at all, it seems to me impossible to imagine that the English Legislature could have ever intended to make such a man subject to particular English legislation.'

And, second, a passage from the judgment of Cotton LJ ((1879) 12 Ch D 522 at 531–532, *j* [1874–80] All ER Rep 708 at 713):

'. . . all laws of the English Parliament must be territorial—territorial in this sense, that they apply to and bind all subjects of the Crown who come within the fair interpretation of them, and also all aliens who come to this country, and who, during the time they are here, do any act which, on a fair interpretation of the statute as regards them, comes within its provisions . . . If he is resident here a   temporarily, and does an act which comes within the intent and purview of a statute, he, as regards that statute, as does every alien who comes here in regard to all the laws of this realm, submits himself to the law, and must be dealt with accordingly. As regards an Englishman, a subject of the British Crown, it is not necessary that he shall give jurisdiction, because he is bound by the Act by reason of his being a British subject, though, of course, in the case of a British subject not resident here, it may be a question on the construction of the Act of Parliament

b   whether that which, if he had been resident here, would have brought him within the Act, has that effect when he is not resident here.'

Put into the language of today, the general principle being there stated is simply that, unless the contrary is expressly enacted or so plainly implied that the courts must give effect to it, United Kingdom legislation is applicable only to British subjects or to foreigners who by coming to the United Kingdom, whether for a short or long time,

c   have made themselves subject to British jurisdiction. Two points would seem to be clear: first, that the principle is a rule of construction only and, second, that it contemplates mere presence within the jurisdiction as sufficient to attract the application of British legislation. Certainly there is no general principle that the legislation of the United Kingdom is applicable only to British subjects or persons resident here. Merely to state such a proposition is to manifest its absurdity. Presence, not residence, is the test.

d   But, of course, the Income Tax Acts impose their own territorial limits. Parliament recognises the almost universally accepted principle that fiscal legislation is not enforceable outside the limits of the territorial sovereignty of the kingdom. Fiscal legislation is, no doubt, drafted in the knowledge that it is the practice of nations not to enforce the fiscal legislation of other nations. But, in the absence of any clear indications to the contrary, it does not necessarily follow that Parliament has in its fiscal legislation

e   intended any territorial limitation other than that imposed by such unenforceability: see *Government of India v Taylor* [1955] 1 All ER 292 at 295, [1955] AC 491 at 503. Indeed, British tax liability has never been exclusively limited to British subjects and foreigners resident within the jurisdiction. As long ago as 1889 Lord Herschell in the well-known case of *Colquhoun v Brooks* (1889) 14 App Cas 493 at 504, [1886–90] All ER Rep 1063 at 1067 summarised the income tax position in one sentence (which received the approval

f   of this House in *National Bank of Greece SA v Westminster Bank Exor and Trustee Co (Channel Islands) Ltd* [1971] 1 All ER 233 at 236, [1971] AC 945 at 954):

'The Income Tax Acts, however, themselves impose a territorial limit; either that from which the taxable income is derived must be situate in the United Kingdom or the person whose income is to be taxed must be resident there.'

g   In the light of these general considerations, I now turn to consider the issue of this appeal. The PAYE obligation is the primary means established by law for the collection of tax charged under Sch E. Section 204, which imposes the obligation, is the first section in the chapter dealing with the assessment, collection and recovery of Sch E tax. In seeking the territorial limitations to which the liability imposed by the section is subject,

h   it makes sense, therefore, at the outset of the search to consider the section in its Sch E context. It is a section tied to the schedule: its machinery of collection is available only in respect of Sch E tax. And Sch E has its own express territorial limitations. The operation of s 204 is, therefore, subject to them; that is to say, however, no more than that the PAYE obligation can arise only in respect of emoluments charged to tax under the schedule. The possibility that s 204 may have to be read subject to further limitation

j   remains.
    The section itself contains no express territorial limitation. More particularly, it imposes the PAYE obligation on making a payment on account of Sch E emoluments without any limitation as to place of payment, the currency in which it is made or the residence of the payer. Is it then necessary to imply any further limitation? And, if any is to be implied, what is it to be?
    The persuasiveness of the Crown's submission lies in the attractive robe of logicality which it wears. How can it be necessary to write into the section any territorial limitation

other than the two specified in the two Sch E Cases to which s 204 by its language plainly applies? To this question Oceanic makes answer that it is inconceivable that Parliament should have intended the PAYE obligation to be imposed on a foreign employer in respect of the emoluments paid outside the United Kingdom in a foreign currency to a person engaged in duties wholly performed outside the United Kingdom. Yet, if the Crown is right, the garb of logicality which it claims for its submission conceals extraordinarily far-reaching and anomalous consequences. How can the PAYE duties be enforced? How can the system be made to work? How can it be supervised? How can the necessary documents be obtained for inspection by the Revenue, unless the foreign corporation is compliant? It all adds up to a practical impossibility of enforcing or monitoring the system against an unco-operative employer outside the United Kingdom making payments outside the United Kingdom.

The difficulties are such that I have reached the conclusion that the judge and the Court of Appeal were right to hold that some limitation other than those specified in Sch E must be implied into s 204. It is perfectly true, as counsel for the Crown urged, that there are situations where our tax laws recognise the existence of a tax liability even though the tax is not collectable and the tax obligation is unenforceable. But, in my view, the problems of construing s 204 so as to extend the duty it imposes to all income assessable under Cases I and II of Sch E and the anomaly of the theoretical subjection of unco-operative foreigners outside the United Kingdom to the penalties of non-compliance compel the conclusion that there must be some further limitation implied.

I turn now to the alternative and narrower submission of the Crown. The Court of Appeal did not answer the question as to the extent of the s 204 liability. In the words of Brightman LJ ([1982] STC 66 at 75) they thought it—

'unnecessary to express a concluded view on this formulation of the s 204 liability. It is sufficient to say that Oceanic is not a UK company, or resident in the UK and does not make payments in this country to the employees of its North Sea Division, without considering whether it would make all the difference if, for example, Oceanic were an individual with British nationality.'

They did, however, reject Dillon J's view that the effect of s 38(6) of the 1973 Act was to extend the s 204 liability to cover a non-resident foreign company making payments abroad to employees engaged in performing duties in the United Kingdom sector of the North Sea.

The Crown has formulated its submission in this House somewhat differently from the way in which the judge reached his decision. The judge relied exclusively on s 38(6). The Crown, while adopting his view as to the importance of the subsection in establishing a link between the designated areas of the North Sea and the United Kingdom, did not, save perhaps by way of last resort, ask the House to treat the subsection as decisive in the interpretation of s 204. Their submission was that in all the circumstances Oceanic had a sufficient 'tax presence' in the United Kingdom to justify the imposition of the s 204 liability.

It will be convenient to state the view which I have reached as to the true effect of s 38(6) before considering the Crown's argument. I agree with the Court of Appeal. The effect of the subsection is merely to render income earned in respect of duties performed in the United Kingdom sector of the North Sea assessable under Sch E. Once the conclusion is reached that not all income assessable to Sch E is subject to collection by PAYE, it cannot be decisive as to the formulation of the s 204 liability. It remains, however, an important indication. It goes some way towards establishing a company's presence in the United Kingdom in that the duties performed by a company's employees in the United Kingdom sector of the North Sea are to be treated for the purposes of income tax as performed within the United Kingdom.

Is, then, the true limitation on the s 204 liability the presence within the United Kingdom of the person making the payment, even though he be non-resident and the payment be made outside the United Kingdom? The 'tax presence' concept was strongly attacked by counsel for Oceanic. He submitted that income tax law knows nothing of a　such a concept as determinant of tax liability. Presence is only relevant as evidence of residence, and Oceanic is admitted to be a non-resident corporation.

My Lords, I find nothing anomalous or contrary to principle in a 'tax presence' being the determinant of the s 204 liability. The Sch E charge to tax is not limited by reference to the residence of the employer paying the emoluments: it applies also to emoluments, wherever paid, in respect of duties performed in the United Kingdom. To imply into s 204 a limitation to employers resident in the United Kingdom would mean that a non-

b　resident employer of persons working in the United Kingdom and paid in this country could escape the PAYE obligation. This would mean that tax charged under Case II could not be collected by PAYE, even though there would in such circumstances be no practical difficulty in operating the system. Indeed, as your Lordships know, Oceanic itself operates PAYE in respect of personnel employed by it in the United Kingdom.

Schedule E contains the territorial limitations on the charge to tax. The only question

c　is to determine in what circumstances the tax may be collected by PAYE. This question can be answered by invoking an old principle, even though today it has a new name. The 'tax presence' for which the Crown contends signifies no more and no less than that the foreigner in question, ie the employer who makes the payment on account of wages or salary, has by coming into this country made himself subject to United Kingdom jurisdiction, or, as Cotton LJ in *Ex p Blain* put it, he has for the time being brought

d　himself within the allegiance of the legislating power.

My Lords, it has been repeatedly, and correctly, asserted in argument that this appeal is not concerned with the charge to tax. Indeed, it is conceded that the income, the tax on which the Revenue seeks to collect by PAYE, is chargeable under Sch E. Residence of the taxpayer is, of course, one of the factors determining chargeability to tax. But the present case is concerned with the territorial limitation to be implied into a section which

e　establishes a method of tax collection. The method is to require the person paying the income to deduct it from his payments and account for it to the Revenue. The only critical factor, so far as collection is concerned, is whether in the circumstances it can be made effective. A trading presence in the United Kingdom will suffice.

On the facts of this case a trading presence is made out. For the purposes of corporation tax Oceanic, it is agreed, carries on a trade in the United Kingdom which includes its

f　operations in the United Kingdom sector of the North Sea. For the purpose of this trade it employs a workforce in that sector, whose earnings are assessable to British income tax. Finally, Oceanic does have an address for service in the United Kingdom. It is not the least surprising that the Special Commissioners concluded that in Oceanic's case there would be no practical difficulties in operating PAYE. For these reasons I conclude that Oceanic by its trading operations within the United Kingdom and in the United

g　Kingdom sector of the North Sea has subjected itself to the liability to operate PAYE in respect of those emoluments of its employees which are by s 38(6) of the 1973 Act chargeable to British income tax. Oceanic must, therefore, operate PAYE in respect of those emoluments.

For these reasons I would allow the appeal and restore the order of the judge. Oceanic must pay the Crown's costs in your Lordships' House, in the Court of Appeal and before

h　the judge.

LORD WILBERFORCE. My Lords, the issue in this appeal is whether the respondent corporation (Oceanic) is obliged to operate the United Kingdom PAYE system of tax collection by deducting tax from the wages of those of its employees who are engaged in exploration or exploitation activities in the United Kingdom sector of the North Sea.

j　Oceanic is a foreign company incorporated in Panama; it is wholly controlled by the United States company whose main place of business is in the State of Louisiana. It claims that because it is neither a United Kingdom company nor 'resident' in the United Kingdom it is not obliged to operate the PAYE system.

The Special Commissioners have found a number of detailed facts concerning Oceanic's business and operations. It conducts certain operations in the United Kingdom at Wembley, Aberdeen and Inverness, but this appeal does not relate to the company's employees in those places. Its North Sea operations consist, inter alia, of pipe-laying both in the United Kingdom sector and in other sectors; they are controlled from Antwerp, Belgium. It employs United Kingdom nationals as well as citizens of other countries; some, if not all, of the former are resident and ordinarily resident in the United Kingdom. Though I do not think that these facts are material, they are, in fact, employed under contracts not governed by English or Scottish law; they are paid abroad and in foreign currency. It is not disputed that Oceanic's employees in the United Kingdom sector of the North Sea are liable to United Kingdom income tax under Sch E in respect of their pay for duties performed in that sector. But Oceanic contends that they are not liable to have tax deducted from their pay by their employer.

The statutory scheme of deduction of tax from wages took shape in the 1939–45 war, and was restated in the Income Tax Act 1952. The operative provision is now s 204(1) of the Income and Corporation Taxes Act 1970, which I reproduce:

'On the making of any payment of, or on account of, any income assessable to income tax under Schedule E, income tax shall, subject to and in accordance with regulations made by the Board under this section, be deducted or repaid by the person making the payment, notwithstanding that when the payment is made no assessment has been made in respect of the income and notwithstanding that the income is in whole or in part income for some year of assessment other than the year during which the payment is made.'

It is obvious that this section is expressed in general and unqualified terms sufficient to apply to Oceanic unless it can be qualified or cut down in some way. Section 204(2) provides for the making of regulations by the board with respect to the assessment, charge, collection and recovery of tax in respect of all income 'assessable thereto under Schedule E' and provides that any such regulations shall have effect notwithstanding anything in the Income Tax Acts. It is under this subsection that the now familiar tax tables are made applicable as regards deduction of tax. In the present connection it is important to notice that the regulations may provide for the production to and inspection by tax officers of wages sheets and other documents so that they may satisfy themselves that tax has been correctly deducted and accounted for. The Income Tax (Employments) Regulations 1973, SI 1973/334, are of an extremely detailed character amounting almost to a comprehensive code of provisions which, if the Revenue's contentions are correct, would have to be complied with by Oceanic. As regards records, it would be obliged (by reg 32) to produce at its premises all wages sheets, deduction cards and other documents and records whatsoever relating to the calculation or payment of the emoluments of its employees. By virtue of s 98 of the Taxes Management Act 1970, which expressly refers to these regulations, failure to comply with these obligations may attract a penalty.

The effect of all these provisions is (a) that income tax is imposed on wages, not primarily on the wage earner, (b) that the tax is collectable by deduction by the employer who then becomes a statutory debtor in respect of it to the Revenue, (c) that, as a fall-back, provision is made for direct assessment, where necessary, on the employee.

As to the United Kingdom sector of the North Sea, the legal position is as follows. Under the Continental Shelf Act 1964 an area may be designated by Order in Council as one in which rights with respect to the sea bed and subsoil of the North Sea and their natural resources may be exercised by the United Kingdom. The United Kingdom sector is an area which has been so designated; its designation does not, of course, make it part of the United Kingdom. However, there are statutory provisions regarding the application of United Kingdom income tax law in this area.

Under s 38(6) of the Finance Act 1973 any emoluments from employment in respect of duties there performed in connection with 'exploration or exploitation activities' (for this expression, see s 38(2)(b)) are to be treated for the purposes of income tax as emoluments in respect of duties performed in the United Kingdom. This admittedly applies to the activities of Oceanic, so that their employees in the sector are chargeable to income tax under Sch E, Case II in respect of their emoluments.

Section 38(4) of the same Act applies as regards the profits or gains of persons (including companies) operating in the area. I must quote it:

a

'Any profits or gains arising to any person not resident in the United Kingdom from exploration or exploitation activities carried on in the United Kingdom or in a designated area or from exploration or exploitation rights, and any gains accruing to such a person on the disposal of such rights shall, for the purposes of corporation tax or capital gains tax, be treated as profits or gains of a trade, or gains accruing on the disposal of assets used for the purposes of a trade, carried on by that person in the United Kingdom through a branch or agency.'

b

I regard this subsection as critical in this appeal. It quite clearly brings Oceanic within the net of United Kingdom corporation tax in respect of its profits from its activities (exploration or exploitation) in the United Kingdom sector. It does so by treating Oceanic as carrying on its trade through a branch or agency in the United Kingdom. This brings it within the taxing provision of s 246 of the 1970 Act which states the tax position of companies not resident in the United Kingdom. Again, I must cite sub-ss (1) and (2) of

c s 246:

'(1) A company not resident in the United Kingdom shall not be within the charge to corporation tax unless it carries on a trade in the United Kingdom through a branch or agency but, if it does so, it shall, subject to any exceptions provided for by the Corporation Tax Acts, be chargeable to corporation tax on all its chargeable

d profits wherever arising.

(2) For purposes of corporation tax the chargeable profits of a company not resident in the United Kingdom but carrying on a trade there through a branch or agency shall be—(a) any trading income arising directly or indirectly through or from the branch of agency, and any income from property or rights used by, or held by or for, the branch or agency (but so that this paragraph shall not include

e distributions received from companies resident in the United Kingdom) . . .'

The combination of s 246(2)(a) of the 1970 Act with s 38(4) of the 1973 Act clearly makes Oceanic chargeable to United Kingdom corporation tax in respect of the profits or gains of its North Sea operations and, since it has a registered address in the United Kingdom in compliance with s 407 of the Companies Act 1948, this tax can be enforced against it.

f

Returning to s 204 of the 1970 Act, Oceanic's contention is that although expressed in general terms, it must be limited in some way, limited, it suggests, by reference to the territorial principles of legislation. There is no doubt of the existence of such a general principle. 'English legislation is primarily territorial' (see per the Earl of Halsbury LC in *Cooke v Charles A Vogeler Co* [1901] AC 102 at 107, [1900–3] All ER Rep 660 at 662) or 'prima facie territorial' (per Brett LJ in *Re Sawers, ex p Blain* (1879) 12 Ch D 522 at 528,

g [1874–80] All ER Rep 708 at 711). And the principle was expanded in *Blain's* case 12 Ch D 522 at 526, [1874–80] All ER Rep 708 at 709 by James LJ in often quoted words. There is, he said—

'a broad, general, universal principle that English legislation, unless the contrary is expressly enacted or so plainly implied as to make it the duty of an English court

h to give effect to an English statute, is applicable only to English subjects or to foreigners who by coming into this country, whether for a long or a short time, have made themselves during that time subject to English jurisdiction . . . But, if a foreigner remains abroad, if he has never come into this country at all, it seems to me impossible to imagine that the English legislature could have ever intended to make such a man subject to particular English legislation.'

i

Lord Herschell applied this principle to income tax in *Colquhoun v Brooks* (1889) 14 App Cas 493 at 504, [1886–90] All ER Rep 1063 at 1067 in these words:

'The Income Tax Acts, however, themselves impose a territorial limit; either that from which the taxable income is derived must be situate in the United Kingdom or the person whose income is to be taxed must be resident there.'

This was a simple statement about liability to pay income tax and as such is still broadly correct. But since 1889 many extensions have been made in the law, and successive statutes must be examined to see what limit has been imposed in particular cases.   a

Oceanic contends, and the Court of Appeal has held, that the provisions regarding collection of tax by deduction from wages can never have been intended to apply to a foreign company, non-resident in the United Kingdom, which makes payments outside the United Kingdom.

In my opinion this contention is erroneous, because it is based on a mistaken application or understanding of the 'territorial principle'. That principle, which is really   b
a rule of construction of statutes expressed in general terms and which, as James LJ said, is a 'broad principle', requires an inquiry to be made as to the persons with respect to whom Parliament is presumed, in the particular case, to be legislating.

Who, it is to be asked, is within the legislative grasp, or intendment, of the statute under consideration? The contention being that, as regards companies, the statute cannot have been intended to apply to them if they are non-resident, one asks immediately: why   c
not?

As regards companies, non-residence in the United Kingdom is not the relevant criterion for freedom from corporation tax. That is not surprising given the difficulty of ascertaining where they do reside. The classic test, laid down judicially (and see s 482(7) of the 1970 Act for its adoption in a context other than the present), is where its central management and control actually resides or, in more homely language, where it really   d
keeps house and does its real business (see De Beers Consolidated Mines Ltd v Howe [1906] AC 455 per Lord Loreburn LC). That, with companies such as Oceanic, may be difficult to fix. So the tax legislation (s 246(1)) adopts the test of carrying on a trade in the United Kingdom through a branch or agency, and it taxes any trading income arising directly or indirectly through or from the branch or agency. The link with Oceanic is firmly made through s 38(4) of the Finance Act 1973. I quote at this point the finding of the   e
Special Commissioners ([1980] STC 656 at 657–658):

> 'Oceanic's operations extend throughout the world, including the Middle East, the Far East, Africa and Central and Southern America. Oceanic was not resident for tax purposes in the United Kingdom. It did, however, have a permanent establishment on the United Kingdom mainland and [ie but] was liable to United Kingdom corporation tax on its profits from activities in the United Kingdom and   f
the United Kingdom continental shelf, all of which were taxed as a single trade. It was an overseas company to which s 407 of the Companies Act 1948 applied and had complied with the requirements of that section. Its address for service in Great Britain was McDermott House, 140 Wembley Park Drive, Wembley.

So, the question one has to ask in relation to s 204 is this: why should not this section   g
apply to a company which, as regards the very activities to which the section relates, is itself made subject to United Kingdom tax legislation. Why not more particularly, when the employees to whom the question relates are employed on precisely those activities, so that the wages they are paid, which are treated as being in respect of duties performed in the United Kingdom, enter into the trading accounts of the company? To the answering of this question non-residence is quite immaterial, as, indeed, s 246 itself   h
shows; it disregards non-residence or, perhaps more accurately, it makes 'non-residence' a condition of liability and fastens on trading through a branch or agency. This provides a clear, and surely satisfactory, answer to the question of construction of s 204, so that this section only applies to those companies which are within the taxing provisions of s 246. As to such companies s 246 provides a convincing reason why Oceanic should be liable to operate the PAYE system. I should add that, as the company has an address for   j
service in the United Kingdom, the liability can be enforced against assets here.

This was the conclusion reached in the High Court by Dillon J by a process of similar, if not quite identical, reasoning to that which I have tried to express. I agree with it and would restore his judgment.

In this House, counsel for the Crown put forward an alternative argument. That was really his first choice, not, I suspect, because he considered it more persuasive, but because of the very attractive consequences for the Revenue which its success would entail. It was a   to say, quite boldly, that s 204 should be read according to its terms; that if (and he accepted this) some limitation ought to be imposed on it, on the 'territorial principle', that was sufficiently achieved through its link with Sch E of the Income and Corporation Taxes Act 1970, to which this section expressly refers. Schedule E itself contains a clear territorial test, or rather territorial tests: whether the employee 'is resident and ordinarily resident in the United Kingdom' (Case I) or his emoluments are 'in respect of duties performed in the United Kingdom' (Case II). So the reference in s 204 to Sch E has the

b   effect of introducing the necessary territorial principle into the section, which can, subject thereto, be given general application.

This is an ingenious argument which at one time attracted me. It has very far-reaching consequences, since it imposes on companies which, as regards their income, are not in any way subject to the United Kingdom tax laws, and which may not be capable of being served with process here, very extensive obligations, with sanctions attached to them.

c   Some of the consequences involved are painted in bright colours in the judgments of the Court of Appeal. Counsel for the Crown did not shrink from accepting these consequences, pointing out that in most cases they would simply be unenforceable and that there are parallels elsewhere in tax legislation for general provisions which in individual cases cannot be enforced.

Nevertheless I do shrink from them when there is a safer route to take; an

d   unenforceable obligation is still an obligation which may be onerous; the existence of it may have a deterrent effect on the employment of United Kingdon residents. I shrink from it all the more since I am not convinced that the argument for it is sound. The expressed limitation in s 204 to Sch E is a limitation as to its subject matter, ie it only applies to certain emoluments; it is a *necessary* condition for the section to apply that the emoluments should be taxable under Sch E. But it seems to me that it may leave open

e   the different question, which is what we are concerned with, namely to *whom* the section is to apply. The Sch E limitation may, in fact, not be a *sufficient* condition. I am therefore, as at present advised, unwilling to accept the argument.

I would allow the appeal.

LORD EDMUND-DAVIES. My Lords, this appeal relates to the construction of

f   s 204(1) of the Income and Corporation Taxes Act 1970, the relevant parts of which provide:

'On the making of any payment of, or on account of, any income assessable to income tax under Schedule E, income tax shall, subject to and in accordance with regulations made by the Board under this section, be deducted or repaid by the person making the payment...'

g   As far as the respondent corporation (Oceanic) is concerned, your Lordships are therefore not concerned with liability to be taxed, but with the quite different question of whether in the circumstances of this case they are under a duty to deduct income tax from emoluments assessable under Sch E paid by them to certain of their employees.

The relevant facts have been set out by Dillon J ([1980] STC 656 at 665–666) Lawton

h   LJ ([1982] STC 66 at 68) and by others of your Lordships, and I shall not repeat them. It is common ground that some of the employees of Oceanic in its North Sea division who worked on barges in the United Kingdom sector of the North Sea (a 'designated area' within s 38 of the Finance Act 1973) were assessable within Sch E.

The primary submission of the Crown in this appeal from the unanimous decision of the Court of Appeal is that those simple facts are in themselves sufficient to bring Oceanic

j   within s 204(1). The submission involves the rejection as irrelevant of the further facts that Oceanic is incorporated under the law of Panama and (as the Special Commissioners found) is not resident for tax purposes in the United Kingdom, and that the relevant payments of emoluments were made by Oceanic in Brussels in United States dollars by cheques drawn on their New York bank account.

My Lords, there are two rules or guides to the construction of s 204(1) which have to be borne in mind: (1) the rule relating to extra-territoriality and (2) the rule relating to penal statutes. As to (1), Dr Lushington said in *Cail v Papayanni*, *The Amalia* (1863) 1 Moo

PCCNS 471 at 474, 15 ER 778 at 779: '. . . the British Parliament has no proper authority to legislate for Foreigners out of its jurisdiction . . . unless the words of the Statute are *a* perfectly clear.' This statement of principle has been judicially followed on innumerable occasions. The important decision in *Re Sawers, ex p Blain* (1879) 12 Ch D 522, [1874–80] All ER Rep 708 has been closely considered below and by others of your Lordships, and it is therefore sufficient to recall also that in *A-G of the Province of Alberta v Huggard Assets Ltd* [1953] 2 All ER 951 at 956, [1953] AC 420 at 441 Lord Asquith said:

'An Act of the Imperial Parliament today, unless it provides otherwise, applies to *b* the whole of the United Kingdom and to nothing outside the United Kingdom: not even to the Channel Islands or the Isle of Man, let alone to a remote overseas colony or possession.'

As to (2), 'A citizen cannot be taxed unless he is designated in clear terms by a taxing Act as a taxpayer' (see *Vestey v IRC (Nos 1 and 2)* [1979] 3 All ER 976 at 984, [1980] AC *c* 1148 at 1172 per Lord Wilberforce). And in *Tuck & Sons v Priester* (1887) 19 QBD 629 at 638 Lord Esher MR said:

'If there is a reasonable interpretation which will avoid the penalty in any particular case, we must avoid that construction. If there are two reasonable constructions, we must give the more lenient one. That is the settled rule for penal sections.' *d*

My Lords, s 204 is a penal section, and the Crown here seeks to apply it extra-territorially, in the words of Brightman LJ, 'to a foreign employer, resident abroad, paying emoluments in foreign currency outside the United Kingdom to an employee in respect of duties performed outside the United Kingdom' (see [1982] STC 66 at 73). As to its penal nature, not only is s 204 part of a taxing statute, but the Income Tax (Employments) Regulations *e* 1973, SI 1973/334, made by the Board of Inland Revenue under the section, impose by reg 26 a narrow time limit within which the employer must pay over to the collector all the tax deducted by him from employees' emoluments; Reg 27 provides for the rendering by the employer of elaborate returns; reg 28 empowers the collector to sue the employer personally for the tax he was liable to deduct; and reg 32 obliges the employer to produce at his premises for inspection by an authorised officer all wages sheets, *f* deduction cards and other documents. Furthermore, s 98 of the Taxes Management Act 1970 provides for the imposition of monetary penalties in respect of failure to comply with any of the foregoing regulations, and s 100(7) empowers the commissioners to summon defaulters to appear before them at a specified time and place for summary hearing of informations laid against them. The duty of discharging the burden of deducting, while not impossible, could thus well prove onerous and expensive (for no *g* remuneration will be forthcoming), and the consequences of default are undoubtedly penal in character.

It is true that s 204 itself contains no express territorial limitation, but so to approach the problem is in my judgment wrong and irreconcilable with the observation of Lord Esher MR in *Colquhoun v Heddon* (1890) 25 QBD 129 at 135 that 'parliament (unless it expressly declares otherwise) when it uses general words is only dealing with persons or *h* things over which it has properly jurisdiction'. The proper approach is to ask whether it has been manifested that, despite the absence of express words giving the section an extra-territorial application, it can operate against Oceanic. My judgment is that it cannot, and that the contrary conclusion arrived at by adverting simply to the wide compass of the *charging* provisions contained in s 181 must be rejected. On this part of the appeal I am accordingly in respectful concurrence with my noble and learned friend Lord *j* Scarman.

The Crown then launch, in the alternative, a narrower attack on the decisions of the Special Commissioners and the Court of Appeal in favour of Oceanic. They assert, in effect, that it is unrealistic to regard Oceanic as merely a foreign company. They invoke the references in *Re Sawers, ex p Blain* (1879) 12 Ch D 522 at 526, 528, [1874–80] All ER Rep 708 at 709, 711 by James LJ to 'foreigners who by coming into this country, whether

for a long or a short time, having made themselves during that time subject to English
jurisdiction', and by Brett LJ in the same case to 'the subjects of other countries who for
the time being bring themselves within the allegiance of the legislating power', and then
attempt to demonstrate that Oceanic comes within those tests.

Relying solely on s 38(6) of the Finance Act 1973, Dillon J agreed with that submission.
It was expansively considered in the Court of Appeal and unanimously rejected. I
understand my noble and learned friend Lord Scarman to be of a like mind, and I
respectfully adopt his summation that 'Once the conclusion is reached that not all income
assessable to Sch E is subject to collection by PAYE, it [ie s 38(6)] cannot be decisive as to
the formulation of the s 204 liability'.

The majority of your Lordships are nevertheless of the opinion that this appeal should
be allowed. Accepting the finding of the Special Commissioners that Oceanic is not
resident in the United Kingdom, the opinion is expressed that this is immaterial, and
that it is sufficient if a company has a 'tax presence' here. My noble and learned friend
Lord Wilberforce regards s 38(4) of the Finance Act 1973 as 'critical in this appeal', but
the whole section makes purely charging provisions in respect of income tax, capital
gains tax and corporation tax, sub-s (4) having reference only to the two latter categories
of tax. Granted that the activities of Oceanic, with its design office at Wembley, its
fabrication yard near Inverness and its Aberdeen branch, constitute carrying on a trade
'in the United Kingdom through a branch or agency' within the meaning of the
subsection, I respectfully find it difficult to appreciate the bearing of that conclusion on
the application of s 204 of the 1970 Act to emoluments paid abroad to employees of the
North Sea division with headquarters in Brussels and an operational centre in Antwerp.
Nor am I assisted by the knowledge that Oceanic also comes within the provision as to
the charging of corporation tax contained in s 246 of that same Act, any more than I am
by the undoubted fact that this overseas company has complied with s 407 of the
Companies Act 1948 by having a London address for service.

My Lords, the concept of a 'taxable presence' was described by counsel for Oceanic as
'unknown to income tax law' and as 'appearing nowhere in the Income Tax Acts; though
it can have some significance in relation to residence, it is otherwise irrelevant'. No case
cited to this House has convinced me that this submission was wrong. And, even had
persuasion been induced, it would still not have served, in my judgment, to establish
that personal chargeability to tax has any rational or legal connection with a duty to make
deductions in respect of the chargeability of others. This would doubtless be highly
convenient to the Crown, but that is nothing to the point.

In these circumstances, I am not persuaded that the Court of Appeal arrived at a wrong
conclusion, and for my part I would therefore dismiss the appeal.

LORD LOWRY. My Lords, the facts and the relevant statutory provisions have been
set out in certain of your Lordships' speeches, which I have had the opportunity of
reading in draft, and in the judgments delivered in the court below. My conclusion
agrees with that of my noble and learned friend Lord Edmund-Davies which supports
the judgments of the Court of Appeal and the opinion of the Special Commissioners.
Having regard to the different opinions to which the facts have led this House and the
courts which have already considered the problem, I wish to state quite shortly the
reasons for my view.

The first argument presented to your Lordships by the Crown was that, whenever Sch
E applied to a taxpayer's income, s 204(1) of the Income and Corporation Taxes Act 1970
imposed a duty on the employer, whether individual or corporate, even when the
employer was not resident in or connected with the United Kingdom and the taxpayer's
work was performed and paid for outside the United Kingdom, of deducting the tax
which was payable and accounting for it to the Revenue.

This argument has not actually achieved acceptance at any judicial level, although, as
your Lordships' opinions confirm, it received an attentive hearing in this House and I,
too, confess to having been at one stage attracted by its simplicity.

According to the literal meaning of s 204(1), Oceanic is bound to operate PAYE, as claimed. In the ordinary way, therefore, Oceanic would have to produce a *special* argument based on the 1970 Act for saying that s 204(1) does not mean what it says. But *a* that is not so here, because Oceanic can rely on a *general* argument, which I shall refer to as the territorial principle, according to which there is a presumption against applying statutory provisions outside the United Kingdom to persons who are not resident there. The authorities illustrating the territorial principle, which is simply a rule of construction, have already been cited to and by your Lordships and I do not need to go over them again. Their effect, as seems to be accepted by the Crown, is to cast on the Crown the *b* burden of showing, by reference to express enactment or clear implication, that s 204(1) does apply. Thus, to distinguish the usual situation when one is confronted with the ordinary and natural meaning of words in a statute, the quest is not on behalf of Oceanic for a means of escape from the ordinary and natural meaning, but on behalf of the Crown for an indication to overcome expressly or by implication the territorial principle. The Crown claimed, and at first I thought the claim might be a good one, that the indication *c* in its favour was provided by s 181(1) of the 1970 Act, which gives *territorial* clues to the chargeability of the taxpayer under Sch E. But, on reflection, I cannot at all subscribe to the view that the presence of territorial provisions in s 181(1) relating to the income of taxpayers serves to destroy the implied limitations relating to their employers outside the United Kingdom which the territorial principle has imposed on s 204(1).

There is no other support for what Brightman LJ called 'The argument of the Crown *d* for a worldwide application of s 204' (see [1982] STC 66 at 74) which could offset the territorial principle; this appears clearly from your Lordships' speeches, the judgments of the Court of Appeal and Dillon J and the decision of the Special Commissioners. I would sum up my remarks on it by quoting the observations of Brightman LJ ([1982] STC 66 at 73):

'Oceanic has made payments of income assessable to income tax under Sch E. *e* Therefore in terms s 204 applies to the taxpayer company. But such a simplistic construction flies in the face of the principle, laid down notably in *Ex parte Blain* (1879) 12 Ch D 522 at 528, [1874–80] All ER Rep 708 at 711, and echoed in numerous later cases, that "English legislation is primarily territorial"; "a broad substantial rule" which Lord Halsbury LC said in *Cooke v Charles A Vogeler Co* [1901] AC 102 at 107, [1900–3] All ER Rep 660 at 662 he should be sorry to see departed *f* from.'

The Crown's second argument was, as my noble and learned friend Lord Scarman has put it, that Oceanic has, by reason of its operations and trading activities in the United Kingdom and in the North Sea, a sufficient presence in, or connection with, the United Kingdom to justify the Revenue's requirement that it operate PAYE in respect of the *g* earnings of the personnel it employs in the United Kingdom sector of the North Sea. Here again, my Lords, I would say that the reasons given by my noble and learned friend Lord Edmund-Davies for rejecting the Crown's first argument are equally cogent and formidable obstacles to accepting the second. I also respectfully consider that his further citations of authority are most persuasive.

Recalling that the United Kingdom sector is nowhere deemed to be part of the United *h* Kingdom, I remind myself that the framers and promoters of the tax legislation must be taken to know very well the high authority and long standing of the cases, including tax cases, on the territorial principle. That is the background against which to judge whether the legislature has made it clear that s 204(1) reaches Oceanic in the present case. And, once the territorial principle is admitted to be relevant, it is not a question of how or to what extent one can qualify or cut down the operation of s 204(1) but of how and to *j* what extent one can widen the operation of s 204(1) beyond the limited sphere of influence to which that principle has prima facie confined it.

If the Crown loses the 'worldwide' argument, I do not consider that the Crown can find a halfway house, or a safe anchorage in the North Sea, based on its alternative argument, and I can think of only three ways for it to present it.

(1) The first, my Lords, which has the attraction of simplicity and which, though not

specifically advanced by the Crown, was adopted by Dillon J, is to say that the words in
a s 38(6) of the 1973 Act, 'for the purposes of income tax', mean for all such purposes, so
that the subsection is viewed not only as a charging provision but as referring to the
purposes of tax collection. At this point I follow my noble and learned friend Lord
Edmund-Davies in adopting the statement of my noble and learned friend Lord Scarman
who expressed himself as agreeing with the Court of Appeal that—

'The effect of the subsection is merely to render income earned in respect of duties
b   performed in the United Kingdom sector of the North Sea assessable under Sch E.
Once the conclusion is reached that not all income assessable to Sch E is subject to
collection by PAYE, it cannot be decisive as to the formulation of the s 204 liability.'

I do not forget that Lord Scarman continued:

'It remains, however, an important indication. It goes some way towards
c   establishing a company's presence in the United Kingdom in that the duties
performed by a company's employees in the United Kingdom sector of the North
Sea are to be treated for the purposes of income tax as performed within the United
Kingdom.'

But I must respectfully insist that there is no in-between meaning to be assigned to the
words, 'for the purposes of income tax'. We must either accept the meaning preferred by
d Dillon J (in which case the Crown have no problem) or confine the purposes mentioned
in s 38(6) to those of assessment and chargeability.
My Lords, in my opinion s 38(6), which contains a clear echo of the words of Case II, is
neutral and does not provide the indication which the Crown needs in order to overcome
the territorial principle. This view has commended itself not only to the judges of the
Court of Appeal but, it seems, to your Lordships as well.
e   (2) The second way of putting the alternative argument is to say that Oceanic had a
sufficient 'tax presence' in the United Kingdom to justify imposing on it the duty of tax
collection under s 204 in respect of emoluments earned by its employees in the United
Kingdom sector of the North Sea. Your Lordships will recognise that this contention
accepts the operation of the territorial principle but seeks to say that it has been satisfied.
Counsel for Oceanic, in the course of a persuasive and cogent submission, ridiculed the
f concept of tax presence (in contrast to residence) as a means of attracting liability to the
company. His criticism went too far, in my respectful opinion; after all, the liability to
deduct tax in respect of the Wembley and Aberdeen employees does not depend on
residence. But the tax presence, to be effective, must be tax presence *in the United Kingdom*.
Let me therefore consider the nature of the alleged tax presence on which the Crown
relies.
g   I do not believe that anyone has suggested, or could credibly suggest, that the
employment of staff at Wembley, Aberdeen and Inverness or the furnishing of a United
Kingdom address for service would oblige an American company employing a United
Kingdom resident in New York to deduct PAYE tax, unless that company were already
liable to do so by virtue of the Crown's 'worldwide' argument; the tax presence, to be
effective, must be relevant to the income in question, and not merely coincidental. Nor
h is it logical to rely on the kind of tax presence I have mentioned for the purpose of
imposing on the company here the duty of deducting tax from United Kingdom sector
earnings, if that duty would not otherwise exist. Neither can s 38(6) be prayed in aid. As
your Lordships have seen, that provision simply requires earnings in a designated area
(ie the United Kingdom sector) to be treated *for the purposes of income tax* as emoluments
in respect of duties performed in the United Kingdom; but the designated area is not
j part of the United Kingdom, and an employer who is operating there cannot be said, in
the words of *Ex p Blain*, to have 'come to this country'.
I agree that residence is not the criterion of amenability to our laws, but, once that
criterion is rejected, a satisfactory alternative on the facts of each case must be found
before it can be validly argued that the territorial principle has been complied with. A
certain vagueness at this point of the Crown's otherwise precise and crisp submissions led

me to the conclusion that the tax presence relied on was specious. The Crown must still face the fact that, so far as the designated areas are concerned, Oceanic has not 'come into *a* the United Kingdom and thereby made itself subject to United Kingdom jurisdiction'.

(3) The third way of putting the Crown's alternative argument relies on s 38(4) of the 1973 Act and s 246 of the 1970 Act and has been clearly set out in the speech of my noble and learned friend Lord Wilberforce. As he says, s 38(4) brings the company within the net of United Kingdom corporation tax in respect of its profits from its activities in the United Kingdom sector. My noble and learned friend further points out that the liability *b* to corporation tax can be enforced against the company because it has a registered address in the United Kingdom in compliance with s 407 of the Companies Act 1948. It is not, of course, suggested that the need to have a registered address here has arisen from the activities in the United Kingdom sector. Lord Wilberforce also states, as I respectfully accept, that non-residence is not the relevant criterion for freedom from corporation tax. But, equally respectfully, I would observe that, failing residence, Parliament has *expressly* *c* enacted a test of chargeability, namely s 246, and has also *expressly*, by s 38(4), extended that chargeability to the designated areas. Therefore it is quite right that Oceanic is by s 38(4) made subject to United Kingdom tax legislation, specifically by making it liable for capital gains tax and corporation tax on profits or gains arising from activities in a designated area, but it does not, in my opinion, follow that Oceanic is thereby impliedly made liable to deduct Sch E tax under s 204(1) from the earnings of those whom it *d* employs in those activities. Furthermore, I do not consider that the Crown can, in support of this particular argument, soundly rely on Oceanic's United Kingdom address for service.

On this part of the case I would again express my respectful concurrence in everything which my noble and learned friend Lord Edmund-Davies has said. I believe that, as he observes, there is nothing to establish that personal chargeability (expressly imposed, I *e* may add) has any rational or legal connection with a duty (allegedly created by implication) to make deductions in respect of the chargeability of others. Indeed, I cannot see that the argument based on s 38(4), although different, is any stronger than that based on s 38(6).

Whichever branch of the argument one looks at, the same practical difficulties exist as were described in detail in the judgment of Lawton LJ. I agree that the difficulty, or even *f* the impossibility, of enforcement does not provide a bar to accepting the Crown's interpretation, but the making of that concession does not give the Crown a good case if they have not one already.

When I finally come back to reread the judgments of a distinguished Court of Appeal in the cold light of reason, I conclude that they cannot be faulted on any aspect of the case. *g*

Accordingly, my Lords, I would dismiss the appeal.

LORD ROSKILL. My Lords, I have had the advantage of reading in draft the speeches of my noble and learned friends Lord Scarman and Lord Wilberforce. Like them I would allow this appeal for the reasons which they give. Like my noble and learned friend Lord Wilberforce I was for a long time attracted, and I still am attracted, by the alternative *h* argument advanced by counsel for the Crown though I am very conscious of the consequences if that argument were accepted. I am still not wholly persuaded that that argument is unsound but like my noble and learned friend I shrink from accepting it when, as he states, a safer route exists. I therefore see no useful purpose in considering the alternative argument further.

j

Appeal allowed.

Solicitors: *Solicitor of Inland Revenue; Slaughter & May* (for Oceanic).

Mary Rose Plummer   Barrister.

Wicks v Firth (Inspector of Taxes)
Johnson v Firth (Inspector of Taxes)

HOUSE OF LORDS

LORD FRASER OF TULLYBELTON, LORD SCARMAN, LORD BRIDGE OF HARWICH, LORD BRANDON OF OAKBROOK AND LORD TEMPLEMAN

15, 16 NOVEMBER, 16 DECEMBER 1982

Income tax – Emoluments from office or employment – Benefits derived by directors and higher-paid employees from employment – Scholarship awarded to employee's child by employer – Whether award provided at cost of parent's employers – Whether award emolument of parent's employment – Whether award 'income arising from a scholarship' – Income and Corporation Taxes Act 1970, s 375(1) – Finance Act 1976, ss 61(1)(3), 72(3).

In 1977 a large public company established, and paid money to, an educational trust for the award of scholarships to children of employees of the company or of certain of its nominated subsidiaries for full-time study at universities or other comparable establishments. The award of the scholarships was at the discretion of the trustees. The company subsequently supplemented the initial trust fund by very large payments to enable the trustees to meet the demand for scholarships. The taxpayers, who were higher-paid employees of the company, were assessed to income tax for the year 1978–79 under Sch E in respect of scholarships awarded to their children as emoluments of their employment. The assessments on each taxpayer was made under s 61(1)[a] of the Finance Act 1976 on the basis that as a person 'employed in . . . higher-paid employment' there had 'by reason of his employment [been] provided for him, or . . . members of his family . . . [a] benefit'. The taxpayers appealed against the assessments to the Special Commissioners, contending that they were exempt from any charge to tax under s 61(1) because (i) the scholarships were not awarded 'by reason of' their employment and (ii) that the emoluments were income 'arising from a scholarship held by a person receiving full-time instruction at a university . . . or other educational establishment' within s 375(1)[b] of the Income and Corporation Taxes Act 1970. The Crown contended (i) that the awards were benefits provided by the company for the employees 'by reason of [their] employment' and (ii) that the charge to tax under s 61 of the 1976 Act was, by virtue of s 63(1)[c] of that Act on the 'cash equivalent of [the] benefit', and that it was impossible to equate that with 'income arising from a scholarship' within s 375(1) of the 1970 Act, for although the two might be the same in amount they were different in character, and that, accordingly, s 375(1) could not confer an exemption on a charge which arose under s 61. The Special Commissioners dismissed the taxpayers' appeals, holding (i) that the benefit of the awards was provided 'at [the] cost' of the company within s 61(3)[d] and accordingly was deemed to be received by the taxpayers 'by reason of [their] employment' by virtue of s 72(3)[e] of the 1976 Act and (ii) that the charge to tax under s 61 of the 1976 Act was on the cash equivalent of the benefit provided, which was to be treated as an emolument, and that a notional sum so treated was not 'income arising from a scholarship' within s 375(1) of the 1970 Act. The judge allowed an appeal by the taxpayers, holding that the scheme of assessing the cash equivalent of benefits under s 61 of the 1976 Act was aimed generally at benefits given not in cash but in kind, and was not intended to nullify or impair the unqualified exemption from tax conferred by s 375(1) of the 1970 Act on income arising from a scholarship, that exemption not being restricted to the

---

a   Section 61(1) is set out at p 156 *d e*, post
b   Section 375(1) is set out at p 153 *j* to p 154 *a*, post
c   Section 63(1) is set out at p 156 *h*, post
d   Section 61(3), so far as material, is set out at p 157 *a*, post
e   Section 72(3), so far as material, is set out at p 156 *j* to p 157 *a*, post

scholarship holder. The Crown appealed to the Court of Appeal, which allowed the appeal holding (i) that the scholarships were a benefit provided 'by reason of [the taxpayers'] employment' within s 61 of the 1976 Act and were, in any event, deemed by s 72(3) thereof to have been so provided since they had been provided 'at [the] cost' of the taxpayers' employer within s 61(3) and accordingly were to be treated as an emolument of the taxpayers' employment, and (ii) that the emoluments were not exempt from tax under s 375(1) of the 1970 Act because that section applied only to the income of the recipient of the scholarship. The taxpayers appealed to the House of Lords contending, inter alia, that the scholarships were not provided 'at [the] cost' of the company within s 61(3) of the 1976 Act but at the cost of the trust fund or the trustees.

Held – (1) The awards of the scholarships to the taxpayers' children were not benefits provided at the cost of the trust fund or the trustees but at the cost of the taxpayers' employer within the meaning of s 61(3) of the 1976 Act because the trustees were only performing fiduciary duties imposed on them by the company with moneys supplied by the company, and all the trust powers and discretions and other authorised activities of the trustees emanated from and were established and defined by the company, and, moreover, the identity and personality of the trustees could make no difference to the effect of s 61. Accordingly, by reason of s 72(3) of the 1976 Act, the benefit in each case was deemed to have been made by reason of the taxpayers' employment and the cash equivalent, or cost of providing the benefit, was therefore to be treated as an emolument of the taxpayers' employment (see p 153 b c g to j, p 155 e and p 157 e to h, post).

(2) (Lord Templeman dissenting) Where a notional sum was deemed by statute to be treated as the income of a taxpayer it was to be treated as his income for all purposes. Thus a notional sum which fell to be treated as the income of the taxpayer by virtue of s 61 of the 1976 Act was not prevented from being 'income' within s 375 of the 1970 Act. In the case of each taxpayer, the benefits to which s 61 applied was the scholarship awarded to his child and accordingly the cash equivalents of those benefits treated as the taxpayer's income under s 61 represented 'income arising from a scholarship' within s 375(1) of the 1970 Act. It followed that the taxpayers were not liable to tax in respect of the awards of scholarships to their children. The appeals would therefore be allowed (see p 153 d to g, p 154 b to f and j and p 155 e, post).

Decision of the Court of Appeal [1982] 2 All ER 9 reversed.

Notes

For the taxation of benefits received by reason of employment, see 23 Halsbury's Laws (4th edn) paras 694–696.

For scholarship income, see ibid para 1077.

For the Income and Corporation Taxes Act 1970, s 375, see 33 Halsbury's Statutes (3rd edn) 490.

For the Finance Act 1976, ss 61, 63, 72, see 46 ibid 1672, 1674, 1687.

Appeal

Malcolm James Wicks and Maurice Johnson (the taxpayers) appealed by leave of the Court of Appeal against the decision and order of the Court of Appeal (Oliver and Watkins LJJ, Lord Denning MR dissenting) ([1982] 2 All ER 9, [1982] Ch 355) on 13 November 1981 allowing an appeal by the Crown against the decision of Goulding J dated 6 November 1980 ([1981] 1 All ER 506, [1981] 1 WLR 475) allowing appeals by the taxpayers from a decision of the Commissioner for the Special Purposes of the Income Tax Acts dismissing the taxpayers' appeals against assessments to income tax under s 61(1) of the Finance Act 1976 in respect of scholarship awards paid to their children by the trustees of an educational trust established by the taxpayers' employers. The facts are set out in the opinion of Lord Templeman.

F Heyworth Talbot QC, Graham Aaronson QC and *Terence Mowschenson* for the taxpayers.
D C Potter QC and *Robert Carnwath* for the Crown.

Their Lordships took time for consideration.

a 16 December. The following opinions were delivered.

LORD FRASER OF TULLYBELTON. My Lords, the facts out of which these appeals arise are explained in the speech about to be delivered by my noble and learned friend Lord Templeman and I need not repeat them. The appeals raise two questions of
b law. The first is whether the benefits, consisting of awards to Martin Wicks and Christine Johnson, were provided 'at the cost of' Imperial Chemical Industries Ltd (ICI) in the sense of s 61(3) of the Finance Act 1976. ICI were the employers of the fathers of Martin and Christine. For the reasons explained by Lord Templeman I agree with him that the answer to that question is in the affirmative. It follows that, by reason of s 72(3) of the 1976 Act, the benefit in each case is deemed to have been made by reason of the father's
c employment, and therefore that the cash equivalent, or cost of providing the benefit, is to be treated as an emolument of the father's employment and chargeable to income tax under Sch E (see s 61(1)).

Like Lord Templeman I decline to be drawn into consideration of what is, in the circumstances of these appeals, the hypothetical question whether the benefit was provided by reason of the employment apart from the deeming provisions of s 72(3).
d The second question is whether the emoluments are exempt, on the ground that they are income 'arising from a scholarship' within the meaning of s 375(1) of the Income and Corporation Taxes Act 1970. I would answer that question also in the affirmative. I entirely agree with the reasons given by my noble and learned friend Lord Bridge for arriving at that result. I wish only to make a brief addition to the reasons which he has so well expressed. In the first place it seems to me that the contrary view depends on what I
e regard, with the utmost respect, as an unduly literal reading of s 61(1) of the 1976 Act and s 375(1) of the 1970 Act, which fails to give effect to the clear intention of Parliament expressed in s 375(1) that scholarship income should be exempt from income tax. In the second place, even reading the two sections literally, I do not think it is correct to describe the notional income created by s 61(1) as income 'arising from' an emolument. It is to be treated as an emolument of the employee, in this case the father of the scholar, and, like
f all emoluments, it necessarily *is* income: see s 183(1) of the 1970 Act. But I think that it arises from the scholarship awarded to the taxpayer's child.

For these reasons I would allow the appeal and restore the order of Goulding J.

LORD SCARMAN. My Lords, I have had the advantage of reading in draft the speeches delivered by my noble and learned friends Lord Fraser and Lord Bridge. I agree
g with them. For the reasons which they give I would allow the appeals.

LORD BRIDGE OF HARWICH. My Lords, I gratefully adopt the statement of the facts giving rise to these appeals in the speech to be delivered by my noble and learned friend Lord Templeman. I also agree with him that, for the reasons he gives, the awards made to Martin Wicks and Christine Johnson from the Imperial Chemical Industries
h Educational Trust were benefits provided at the cost of the appellant taxpayers' employers, within the meaning of s 61(3) of the Finance Act 1976. It follows that, in each case, by the application of s 72(3), the benefit was deemed to be provided by reason of the relevant taxpayer's employment and, therefore, by s 61(1), in the case of each taxpayer, an amount equal to the cash equivalent of the benefit was to be treated as emoluments of the employment, and accordingly chargeable to income tax under Sch E.
j The only difficult question raised by the appeals is that on which the judges who have already considered the case have been equally divided in opinion, viz whether s 375(1) of the Income and Corporation Taxes Act 1970 is capable of providing an exemption from the liability which s 61 of the Act of 1976 creates. Section 375(1) provides:

'Income arising from a scholarship held by a person receiving full-time instruction at a university, college, school or other educational establishment shall be exempt from income tax, and no account shall be taken of any such income in computing the amount of income for income tax purposes.'

It is common ground that the awards to Martin and Christine were 'scholarships' within the meaning of this provision. The argument for the taxpayers in favour of the exemption to which they claim to be entitled is, as Oliver LJ pointed out in the Court of Appeal, an engagingly simple one (see [1982] 2 All ER 9 at 15, [1982] Ch 355 at 368). The effect of s 61 of the 1976 Act is to attribute to the taxpayer a certain sum of money which is to be treated as part of his income for tax purposes. The fact that it is notional income of the taxpayer arising from a statutory fiction does not prevent it from being 'income' within the meaning of s 375. If one then asks what gives rise to this income, the answer must be the scholarship awarded to the taxpayer's child, for this is the benefit the provision of which brings into operation the machinery of s 61 of the 1976 Act. That which is treated as income under s 61 is accordingly income arising from a scholarship under s 375.

For myself I find the argument not only engagingly simple but also compelling. If there is a fallacy in it, I have been unable to detect it. I cannot see that the argument involves any straining of language beyond its natural meaning, and I should require to be persuaded that there were cogent reasons for denying the taxpayer an exemption to which, on the face of it, he appears to be entitled.

The commissioners' reason for deciding this point in favour of the Crown was thus expressed ([1981] 1 All ER 506 at 514):

'The charge under s 61 is on the cash equivalent of the benefit provided, not on the benefit itself. The cash equivalent is not of itself income but is to be treated as an emolument. A notional sum so treated is not, in our judgment, covered by the words "income arising from a scholarship".'

With respect, I cannot follow this reasoning. That which a statute deems to be income, whatever the precise language used to achieve that effect, can and should, in my opinion, be treated as income for all purposes. If it is income prima facie liable to bear tax, it is equally income prima facie eligible to qualify for any relevant exemption.

It appears that the primary consideration which weighed with Oliver LJ and the sole consideration which weighed with Watkins LJ on this point was that s 375 of the 1970 Act re-enacted without change s 28 of the Finance Act 1920, which was said to have been intended only to exempt from taxation scholarship income in the hands of the scholarship holder. I am content to assume that the original intent of the provision was so limited. The argument founded on this consideration, however, seems to me, with respect, to beg the question arising from the need to construe s 375 in the new statutory context created by the Finance Act 1976. The legislature, enacting the latter statute, had no need to provide an express exemption of scholarships from the fringe benefits to be taxed under Chapter II of the 1976 Act, if the language of s 375 of the 1970 Act, in its ordinary meaning, was already apt to provide such an exemption. The earlier limitation on the scope of s 375 is irrelevant to its operation and effect when read in conjunction with the charging provision of s 61 of the 1976 Act.

Oliver LJ also presents a more sophisticated version of the view expressed by the commissioners, on which I have already commented, and which I again find unconvincing (see [1982] 2 All ER 9 at 15–16, [1982] Ch 355 at 368). He further emphasises the wide definition of the 'benefits' to which s 61 applies and the limited range of exceptions. The language of s 61, however, cannot have intended that the sums required to be 'treated as emoluments of the employment, and accordingly chargeable to income tax under Schedule E', should be ineligible for any appropriate reliefs and exemptions made available by provisions to be found elsewhere in the general corpus of taxing legislation. For the reasons I have indicated, I think s 375 of the 1970 Act affords such an appropriate exemption.

I note that in a press release issued by the Inland Revenue in June 1978, of which the

relevant extract is quoted in the case stated (see [1981] 1 All ER 506 at 509), the Revenue,
a when announcing their intention to exact tax in cases such as those under appeal,
indicated that they would still treat as exempt scholarships awarded, from a fund open
to all, to scholars who happened to be the children of employees of the firm by which the
fund was financed. Yet, if the construction of the relevant provisions for which the
Crown contends is right, liability would arise equally in such cases. This is not a decisive
consideration, but in choosing between competing constructions of a taxing provision it
b is legitimate, I think, to incline against a construction which the Revenue are unwilling
to apply in its full rigour but feel they must mitigate by way of extra-statutory concession,
recognising, presumably, that in some cases their construction would operate to produce
a result which Parliament can hardly have intended.

Although I have expressed my reasons at some length, the point at issue is essentially a
very short one. But for the conflict of judicial opinion in the courts below I should have
c been content respectfully to adopt and indorse the view of Goulding J, who said, in
allowing the taxpayers' appeals from the commissioners ([1981] 1 All ER 506 at 519,
[1981] 1 WLR 475 at 483):

> '. . . I cannot think that Parliament, without giving an express indication, intended
> in effect to nullify or impair an unqualified exemption of this kind of scholarship
> income under s 375 by introducing, in relation to a very much wider class of benefit,
d > a scheme of assessing notional sums, that scheme (which is really in the nature of
> machinery) being necessary because in general the benefits aimed at are given not
> in cash but in kind.'

My Lords, I would allow the appeals and restore the order of Goulding J.

e **LORD BRANDON OF OAKBROOK.** My Lords, I have had the advantage of
reading in draft the speech prepared by my noble and learned friend Lord Bridge. I agree
with it and for the reasons which he gives I would allow the appeals.

LORD TEMPLEMAN. My Lords, these appeals raise two problems for consideration:
first, the construction of certain of the provisions of the Finance Act 1976 which levy
f income tax on directors and higher-paid employees in respect of fringe benefits and,
second, the scope and effect of s 375 of the Income and Corporation Taxes Act 1970
which confers exemption from income tax in respect of scholarships.

By a trust deed dated 13 January 1977 Imperial Chemicals Industries Ltd (ICI)
established a trust for the award of scholarships. Each scholarship holder must be a
student at a university or other comparable establishment and must be the child of an
g employee or officer of ICI, or of certain nominated subsidiaries of ICI, when the
scholarship is awarded.

By cl 2 of the trust deed the trustees appointed by the deed were directed to hold the
trust fund settled by ICI during a defined perpetuity period not exceeding 79 years on
trust to pay or apply capital or income—

h > 'in the award of Scholarships for the educational instruction of such of the
> Beneficiaries as the Trustees (being at least two in number) shall from time to time
> by writing under their hands in their absolute discretion resolve and direct.'

This trust in favour of the beneficiaries was subjected to a power for the trustees to pay
capital and income to any educational charities, and there was an ultimate trust for the
educational charities or the Charities Aid Foundation. These charitable trust provisions
j are not relevant to these appeals save that they ensured, and cl 20 of the deed expressly
confirmed, that no part of the trust fund or the income could thereafter enure for the
benefit of ICI.

Between 13 January 1977 and 30 September 1979 ICI contributed the aggregate sum
of £3,250,000 to the trust fund, and ICI have continued to make contributions. In the
year ending 30 September 1979 the trustees received £800,000 from ICI and made 2,683

awards, amounting in all to £823,933, out of capital receipts and reserves and out of
income earned. The policy of ICI as disclosed by the trust accounts appears to be to supply a
the trustees towards the end of each academic year with sufficient money to enable the
trustees to meet the demand for scholarships in the following year. The trustees exercise
their powers independently and without reference to ICI. It is the policy of the trustees
to see that all eligible applicants receive by way of scholarship basic awards which make
up the difference between the maintenance grants made by the local educational
authorities and the assessed maintenance requirements of the students, save for a sum of b
£300 which may then be made up by merit awards or hardship awards by the trustees.

Martin is the son of the appellant taxpayer Mr Wicks and Martin received a local
educational authority maintenance grant of £409 as a student of King's College,
Cambridge, the authority considering that Mr Wicks having regard to his income and
resources ought to contribute the balance of Martin's maintenance requirements of
£1,100. In November 1978 the trustees awarded Martin a scholarship of £600 made up c
of £400 basic award and £200 merit award. Christine Johnson, the daughter of the
appellant taxpayer, Mr Johnson, received a local educational maintenance grant of £542
as a student of the University of Newcastle upon Tyne and in November 1978 the trustees
awarded Christine a scholarship of £460 made up of £260 basic award and £200 merit
award.

Chapter II of Pt III of the Finance Act 1976 is entitled 'Benefits derived by Company d
Directors and others From their Employment'. Section 61(1) of the Act is in these terms:

> 'Where in any year a person is employed in director's or higher-paid employment
> and—(a) by reason of his employment there is provided for him, or for others being
> members of his family or household, any benefit to which this section applies; and
> (b) the cost of providing the benefit is not (apart from this section) chargeable to tax
> as his income, there is to be treated as emoluments of the employment, and e
> accordingly chargeable to income tax under Schedule E, an amount equal to
> whatever is the cash equivalent of the benefit.'

The appellant taxpayers, Mr Wicks and Mr Johnson, were both higher-paid employees
of ICI.

Section 61(2) provides as follows: f

> 'The benefits to which this section applies are living or other accommodation,
> entertainment, domestic or other services, and other benefits and facilities of
> whatsoever nature (whether or not similar to any of those mentioned above in this
> subsection)...'

The scholarships received by Martin and Christine were benefits as defined by s 61(2) g
and they were provided for members of the families of the appellant taxpayers, Mr Wicks
and Mr Johnson, within s 61(1).

Section 63(1) is in the following terms:

> 'The cash equivalent of any benefit chargeable to tax under section 61 above is an
> amount equal to the cost of the benefit, less so much (if any) of it as is made good by h
> the employee to those providing the benefit.'

The cost of the benefit was £600 in the case of Martin and £460 in the case of
Christine. It follows that, if Martin's scholarship was provided by reason of the
employment of Mr Wicks by ICI, then £600 must be treated as emoluments of that
employment and taxed accordingly. But as against that tax burden Mr Wicks is relieved
of the burden of finding £600 for the maintenance of Martin out of Mr Wicks's taxed j
income. Similarly, if Christine's scholarship was provided by reason of the employment
of Mr Johnson by ICI, £460 must be treated as emoluments of that employment and
taxed accordingly.

Section 72(3) provides, inter alia:

> '... all such provision as is mentioned in this Chapter which is made for an

employee, or for members of his family or household, by his employer, are deemed
to be paid to or made for him or them by reason of his employment.'

By s 61(3): '. . . the persons providing a benefit are those at whose cost the provision is
made.'

If, therefore, the benefit provided for Martin, namely his scholarship of £600, was
provided 'at the cost' of ICI, then such provision is deemed to be made by reason of the
employment of Martin's father, Mr Wicks, by ICI and to be treated as emoluments of
that employment charged to income tax under Sch E. Similarly if the benefit provided
for Christine, namely her scholarship of £460, was provided 'at the cost' of ICI, then such
provision is deemed to be made by reason of the employment of Christine's father, Mr
Johnson, by ICI and to be treated as emoluments of that employment subject to income
tax under Sch E.

On behalf of the taxpayers it was argued that the scholarships were not provided 'at
the cost' of ICI. The trust fund which financed the scholarship was settled by ICI but the
scholarships were provided at the cost of the trust fund or at the cost of the trustees.

In my opinion the scholarships were either provided at the cost of ICI or at the cost of
the trustees. They were not provided at the cost of the trust fund. Section 61(3) requires
an identification of 'the persons . . . at whose cost' the scholarship is provided. If the
person thus identified is the employer, then by virtue of s 72(3) the employee is charged
to tax under s 61(1). If the person thus identified is not the employer but is some third
party then the employee is only to be charged with tax under s 61(1) if the scholarship
was provided 'by reason of his employment', that is to say if there is a relevant connection
between the award of a scholarship and the employment. In the present case if the
scholarships were provided at the cost of ICI then liability under s 61(1) attaches to the
taxpayer employees. If the scholarships were provided at the cost of the trustees, then
liability under s 61(1) only attaches if the Revenue establish that the scholarships were
otherwise made 'by reason of the employment' of the appellant taxpayers by ICI.

In my opinion the scholarships were provided at the cost of ICI and not at the cost of
the trustees because the trustees with moneys supplied by ICI were only performing
fiduciary duties imposed on them by ICI. All the trust powers and discretions and other
authorised activities of the trustees emanate from and were established and defined by
ICI. The capital moneys necessary for the performance by the trustees of their functions
were provided by ICI. The income of the trust fund was sacrificed by ICI to the same
purpose. The trustees can only continue to award scholarships if ICI remain able and
willing to bear the cost of those scholarships. Martin and Christine could appropriately
thank the trustees for the awards of their scholarships but they could only thank ICI for
their generosity in meeting the cost of the scholarships. In those circumstances the
scholarships were provided at the cost of ICI.

There was no need for the appointment of independent trustees. By the trust deed ICI
could have declared themselves sole trustees of the trust fund on the irrevocable trusts
specified in the deed. In that event the scholarships must have been provided 'at the cost'
of ICI in default of any other candidate. But the identity and personality of the trustees
cannot make any difference to the effect of s 61. If the course of the scholarship payment
can be traced to the employer, then the benefit conferred by that payment is provided 'at
the cost' of the employer.

Your Lordships were invited by counsel for the taxpayers to express a view as to the
meaning of the expression 'by reason of his employment' for the purposes of s 61 and to
determine whether tax would have been chargeable if the true construction of s 61(3)
had been different from that which I have indicated. I do not feel tempted to accept this
invitation to decide a hypothetical question on the basis of a construction of the Act
which I have rejected. Whether a benefit provided at the cost of a third party is provided
by reason of his employment must depend on a variety of circumstances including the
source of the benefit and the relationship, rights and expectations of the employer, the
employee and the third party respectively. I decline to speculate.

If then the payment of the scholarship moneys to Martin and Christine requires sums

of £600 and £460 to be treated as emoluments of the employment by ICI of Mr Wicks
and Mr Johnson respectively chargeable to tax under Sch E by virtue of s 61 of the   a
Finance Act 1976, the question arises whether s 375 of the Income and Corporation Taxes
Act 1970 has the effect of exempting those sums from income tax.

Section 375 of the 1970 Act is in these terms:

'(1) Income arising from a scholarship held by a person receiving full-time
instruction at a university, college, school or other educational establishment shall
be exempt from income tax, and no account shall be taken of any such income in   b
computing the amount of income for income tax purposes.

(2) In this section "scholarship" includes an exhibition, bursary or any other
similar educational endowment . . .'

On behalf of the taxpayers it was submitted that s 61 of the 1976 Act creates a notional
remuneration which is additional income of the taxpayer employee. That income is   c
'income arising from a scholarship' within s 375 of the 1970 Act because the scholarship
is the cause, the subject matter and the measure of the income which is created and
which is taxed under s 61.

On behalf of the Crown it was submitted that the exemption afforded by s 375 only
applies to income of the scholarship holder. Alternatively, the exemption afforded by
s 375 does not affect income of a parent employee created by s 61 of the 1976 Act which   d
is income 'arising from an emolument' and not 'income arising from a scholarship'.

By s 61 a benefit provided at the cost of an employer for a child of a higher-paid
employee gives rise to a charge to income tax on the employee as though the employee
had received additional remuneration equal to the cost of the benefit. Section 61 assumes
that a benefit conferred on a child relieves the parent-employee of expenditure which the
employee would otherwise be obliged to meet or which the employee should wish to be   e
met. A benefit is not bestowed on a child against the wishes of the parent. A financial
benefit to a child relieves the pocket, or at any rate gladdens the heart, of the parent.
Expressly, and by implication, s 61 assumes that in many, most or all respects a benefit
conferred on a child is a benefit conferred on the parent not less valuable to the parent
than the benefit which the employee would have received if his remuneration had been
increased by his employer by the cost of the benefit.   f

For the purposes of s 61, the exact form of the benefit conferred on the child is
immaterial. The Act draws no distinction and there is no logical distinction between the
types of benefit provided. Payment by an employer of the cost of accommodation of a
child of an employee at a convalescent home, or the purchase of books and clothing and
equipment for a child, or a contribution to the maintenance of the child, which may or
may not take the form of a scholarship, all constitute benefits for the purposes of s 61 and
have the same effect as the provision of the convalescent accommodation for the employee   g
himself, or the provisions of clothing for the employee, or the purchase of a night club
or golf club subscription. All these benefits relieve the employee of expenditure which
he would be obliged to meet or which he would wish to be met. They all give rise to a
charge to tax on the employee under s 61. I am not concerned to approve or disapprove
the provision of fringe benefits, or to approve or disapprove the imposition of tax on
higher-paid employees in respect of fringe benefits. But s 61 is by no means as draconian   h
as junior counsel for the taxpayer lamented, and does not wholly discourage the provision
of fringe benefits. In the present case, for example, a contribution at the cost of the
employer to the maintenance of a child results in the higher-paid employee-parent being
taxed on the amount of that contribution, but he would be worse off if he found the
contribution to the child's maintenance himself out of his taxed income. The significance
of s 61 is that, rightly or wrongly, it treats any and every kind of benefit to a child as   j
being a benefit to the parent. Not only does s 61 deliberately apply to every conceivable
form of benefit at the cost of an employer which may be said to enure in any way to the
advantage of the employee, without exception, but it would be illogical to provide any
exception.

If the taxpayers are right in the present case, there is a special exemption from s 61.
a Their submission involves contradiction between s 61 of the 1976 Act and s 375 of the
1970 Act to be resolved in favour of the taxpayers. The contradiction arises because s 61,
according to the argument for the taxpayers, provides that income arising from a
scholarship shall be subject to income tax, whereas s 375 of the 1970 Act provides that
income arising from a scholarship shall be exempt from income tax. In my opinion no
such conflict arises because s 61 does not have the effect of taxing income arising from a
b scholarship. Section 61 provides that an amount equal to the cost of any benefit shall be
treated as emoluments of the employment, and chargeable to income tax accordingly
under Sch E. The income which arises under s 61 is the income of an emolument. The
income which is taxed under s 61 arises because the child of the higher-paid employee
receives a benefit at the cost of the employer and because the cost of the benefit is deemed
to be an emolument of the employee. The benefit to Martin, for example, is £600 being
c a contribution to his maintenance requirements. It so happens that this £600 is provided
as the result of a scholarship established by ICI, but it could equally have been an
allowance or grant made by ICI without falling within the definition of a scholarship. In
either event, the £600 which is taxed under s 61 is an amount equal to the cost of the
benefit, which amount is treated as an additional emolument received by the employee.
In my opinion that amount cannot fairly be described as 'income arising from a
d scholarship'. The only income which arises from a scholarship is the sum paid by the
trustees to the scholarship holder, Martin. That sum is not taxed by s 61, or at all. I am
unable to accept the view that income created by s 61, and arising from an emolument,
is at one and the same time, income arising from a scholarship under s 375. On behalf of
the taxpayers reliance was placed on a press release issued by the Revenue, and it was also
argued that, if the expression 'at the cost' is broadly construed in order to give rise to
e liability under s 61, the expression 'income arising from a scholarship' under s 375 should
also be broadly construed. In my opinion the press release is not relevant to statutory
construction, and the approach which I have adopted is neither broad nor narrow, but
merely gives effect to the words used by the legislature in ss 61 and 375.

On behalf of the taxpayers it was argued that s 61 is unfair because it would impose
tax on a higher-paid employee if his child received a scholarship from a charity established
f by the employer. That submission, if well founded, might dispose Parliament to exclude
from the ambit of s 61 benefits received from a charity. But it would be illogical for
Parliament to exclude from the ambit of s 61 a scholarship but not to exclude other
forms of benefit received from a charity. It would be even more illogical for Parliament
to exclude from the ambit of s 61 a scholarship which, as in the present case, is not
received from a charity while taxing a higher-paid employee in respect of all other
g benefits whether received from a charity or not. Section 375 does not exempt any
'benefit' from s 61, but exempts scholarship income from tax. Section 61 provides that,
for income tax purposes, Mr Wicks shall be deemed to have received from his employer,
ICI, an additional salary of £600, equal in amount to the sum of £600 provided for
Martin at the cost of ICI. An emolument is not a scholarship; and income arising from
an emolument is not income arising from a scholarship.

h For these reasons, and in agreement with the conclusion reached by Oliver LJ in the
Court of Appeal, I would dismiss these appeals.

Appeals allowed.

Solicitors: *V O White* (for the taxpayers); *Solicitor of Inland Revenue.*

Rengan Krishnan Esq   Barrister.

Practice Direction

CHANCERY DIVISION
FAMILY DIVISION

Sale of land – Sale by court – Estate agents and auctioneers – Scale of remuneration – Sales pursuant to orders of Chancery Division, Family Division, Court of Protection or divorce county courts.

1. The charges of estate agents and auctioneers selling freehold or leasehold property pursuant to orders of the Chancery Division, the Family Division, the Court of Protection or divorce county courts will normally be considered reasonable by the court if they do not exceed the rate of commission which that agent would normally charge on a sole agency basis, and they do not exceed 2½% of the sale price, exclusive of value added tax.

2. These charges are to include all commission, valuations, expenses and other disbursements, including making affidavits, the cost of advertising and all other work except surveys. The allowance for a survey will be at the court's discretion.

3. If (a) an agent's charges do not fall within the limits set out in para 1 or (b) there is a sale of any investment property, business property or farm property or (c) a property is sold in lots or by valuation, an application must be made to the court to authorise the fee to be charged.

4. The limits set out in paras 1 and 2 above do not apply to sales of property for patients of the Court of Protection where an agreement has been concluded with the estate agent before the jurisdiction of the court has been invoked.

5. In matrimonial cases, either where the party who has been condemned in these costs has not agreed to the increased rate or where the costs fall to be paid out of the legal aid fund, the higher charges will be subject to the discretion of the taxing officer.

6. This Practice Direction applies to all instructions for sale which are placed with estate agents and auctioneers after 1 January 1983.

The Practice Directions of 26 July 1972 ([1972] 3 All ER 256, [1972] 1 WLR 1431) and 18 October 1972 ([1972] 3 All ER 910, [1972] 1 WLR 1471) are hereby revoked.

By direction of the Vice-Chancellor and the President of the Family Division and with the concurrence of the Lord Chancellor.

E R HEWARD
Chief Chancery Master

A B McFARLANE
Master, Court of Protection

B P TICKLE
Senior Registrar, Family Division.

22 December 1982

Air Canada and others v Secretary of State for Trade and another (No 2)

Pan American World Airways Inc v British Airports Authority and another

QUEEN'S BENCH DIVISION

BINGHAM J

26, 27, 28, 29 APRIL, 6 MAY 1982

COURT OF APPEAL, CIVIL DIVISION

LORD DENNING MR, WATKINS AND FOX LJJ

28, 29, 30 JUNE, I, 2 JULY, 24 SEPTEMBER 1982

Discovery – Privilege – Production contrary to public interest – Class of documents – Documents relating to government policy – Communications between government ministers – Documents prepared for use of ministers in formulating government policy – Certificate on behalf of Crown claiming privilege from disclosure on ground of public interest – Production sought by plaintiffs in action seeking declaration that minister abused his powers – Requirements for establishing that disclosure or inspection necessary for due administration of justice – When court can override certificate – Whether disclosure necessary in public interest for due administration of justice – Whether person seeking production must prove that documents likely to assist his case – Whether sufficient to prove that documents likely to affect decision in case.

A nationalised undertaking, the British Airports Authority (BAA), fixed the landing charges at Heathrow Airport. BAA was under the statutory control of the Secretary of State for Trade who had power to give general, but not specific, directions to BAA regarding the conduct of its affairs. BAA wished to build two new air terminals and wished to meet the cost of them partly out of its reserve fund and partly by borrowing. The Secretary of State refused to allow BAA to fund the terminals in that manner and gave directions to BAA that it should meet the cost of the new terminals by increasing landing charges. BAA accordingly increased landing charges at Heathrow Airport by 35%. The plaintiffs, who were some 20 foreign airlines using Heathrow Airport and who considered the new charges to be excessive and unreasonable, brought an action against the Secretary of State seeking a declaration that he had acted unlawfully and ultra vires in giving such directions to BAA and alleging, inter alia, (i) that the Secretary of State had exercised his statutory powers over BAA for extraneous and ultra vires purposes, namely the political purpose of enforcing a government policy of reducing and containing public sector borrowing, and (ii) that in exercising his powers he had both taken into account extraneous considerations, namely the government's desire to reduce public sector borrowing, and failed to take into account such relevant considerations as the alleged fact that the increased charges were in breach of the United Kingdom's international obligations. On discovery of documents the Secretary of State produced to the plaintiffs the documents passing between him and BAA regarding the increased charges but refused the plaintiffs' request to produce another class of documents (the ministerial documents) which comprised communications passing between government ministers and the preparatory documents used by ministers at their meetings, and which related to the formulation of government policy regarding BAA and the limitation of public sector borrowing generally. It was admitted that the ministerial documents were relevant documents but the Secretary of State submitted that they were privileged from disclosure by virtue of public interest immunity. The Secretary of State tendered certificates on behalf of the Crown which constituted a valid claim for public interest immunity from disclosure in the interests of the proper functioning of government. However, the judge ordered that the ministerial documents be produced, subject to his prior inspection,

because, so he held, even if they were not likely to assist the plaintiffs' case, and might
even harm it, they would substantially assist the court to elicit the true facts regarding **a**
the plaintiffs' case and would thereby affect the court's decision, and that demonstrated a
sufficient public interest in the production of the documents (subject to their inspection)
on the ground of the due administration of justice to outweigh the public interest in
their non-disclosure. The Secretary of State appealed, contending that a party seeking
production of documents had to show that the documents were likely to assist his case.

Held – The Secretary of State's appeal would be allowed for the following reasons— **b**
(1) Although (Fox LJ assuming, without deciding) the court could override a certificate
given on behalf of the Crown claiming privilege from production of a document or class
of documents on the ground of public interest immunity if the disclosure of the
documents was necessary for the due administration of justice, the party seeking
disclosure on the ground of the public interest in the due administration of justice had **c**
to show, before the judge could proceed to balance the competing public interests or
inspect the documents, either that it was reasonably likely that the documents would
assist his case, or (per Watkins LJ) that they would put him on useful inquiry or would
damage the other side's case, and that he was not just entering on a 'fishing expedition'
for evidence to support his case. Furthermore, the due administration of justice did not
necessarily mean that the true facts regarding a case had to be elicited, since (per Fox LJ) **d**
the mere existence of the law of privilege postulated that material facts might be
withheld from production. Instead, whether the true facts were required to be elicited
from the other side in the interests of justice depended on the nature of the issue between
the parties and the burden of proof. In particular, in an action against a public authority
for a declaration that the authority had misused its powers, by analogy with an application
for judicial relief under RSC Ord 53, the plaintiff had to make out a prima facie case on
his own evidence without the aid of discovery from the public authority save in most **e**
exceptional cases (see p 179 f, p 180 b d e h, p 181 b to g, p 183 c to f, p 185 d, p 186 b c j, p
187 c to f and j to p 188 a j, and p 189 a to d, post); *Compagnie Financière et Commerciale du
Pacifique v Peruvian Guano Co* (1882) 11 QBD 55, *Conway v Rimmer* [1968] 1 All ER 874
and *Burmah Oil Co Ltd v Bank of England (A-G intervening)* [1979] 3 All ER 700 applied.
(2) Production of the ministerial documents was not justified in the interests of justice **f**
because (a) the certificate on behalf of the Secretary of State made out a very strong case
for immunity from disclosure, (b) the plaintiffs had failed to make out a prima facie case
on their own evidence, (c) the plaintiffs had not established that the ministerial documents
would be likely to assist their case, or put them on useful inquiry or damage the Secretary
of State's case, and (d) (per Watkins LJ) any abuse of power would emerge from the
documents passing between the Secretary of State and BAA which had already been **g**
produced to the plaintiffs. Accordingly, the plaintiffs had failed to demonstrate a
sufficient or any public interest in the disclosure or inspection of the documents, and
therefore the court could not override the certificate claiming immunity from disclosure
(see p 181 g to j, p 182 b to e, p 184 d to f h j, p 185 a to d, p 187 h j, p 188 h j and p 189 b
to d, post).
Per Lord Denning MR. Where a judge is minded to override a certificate on behalf of **h**
the Crown claiming public interest immunity from production for documents, he need
only first inspect the documents if the certificate is lacking in detail in regard to the
documents or is lacking in the reasons for the claim or if the competing public interests
are very evenly balanced. Before inspecting the documents, however, he should give the
minister an opportunity to appeal against the order that the documents be produced (see
p 182 a b, post).

j

Notes
For withholding documents on the ground of public interest and Crown privilege, see
13 Halsbury's Laws (4th edn) paras 86–91, and for cases on the subject, see 18 Digest
(Reissue) 154–160, 1265–1301.

Cases referred to in judgments

a   A-G v Mulholland, A-G v Foster [1963] 1 All ER 767, [1963] 2 QB 477, [1963] 2 WLR 658, CA, 22 Digest (Reissue) 459, 4588.

A-G v Newcastle-upon-Tyne Corp [1897] 2 QB 384, [1895–9] All ER Rep 747, CA, 18 Digest (Reissue) 28, 172.

Associated Provincial Picture Houses Ltd v Wednesbury Corp [1947] 2 All ER 680, [1948] 1 KB 223, CA, 45 Digest (Repl) 215, 189.

b   British Steel Corp v Granada Television Ltd [1981] 1 All ER 417, [1981] AC 1096, [1980] 3 WLR 774, Ch D, CA and HL.

Burmah Oil Co Ltd v Bank of England (A-G intervening) [1979] 3 All ER 700, [1980] AC 1090, [1979] 3 WLR 722, HL, Digest (Cont Vol E) 184, 1277a.

Campbell v Tameside BC [1982] 2 All ER 791, [1982] 3 WLR 74, CA.

Compagnie Financière et Commerciale du Pacifique v Peruvian Guano Co (1882) 11 QBD 55, c   CA, 18 Digest (Reissue) 81, 580.

Conway v Rimmer [1967] 2 All ER 1260, [1967] 1 WLR 1031, CA; rvsd [1968] 1 All ER 874, [1968] AC 910, [1968] 2 WLR 998, HL; subsequent proceedings [1968] 2 All ER 304, [1968] 2 WLR 1535, HL, 18 Digest (Reissue) 155, 1273.

Crompton (Alfred) Amusement Machines Ltd v Customs and Excise Comrs (No 2) [1973] 2 All ER 1169, [1974] AC 405, [1973] 3 WLR 268, HL, 18 Digest (Reissue) 102, 756.

d   D v National Society for the Prevention of Cruelty to Children [1977] 1 All ER 589, [1978] AC 171, [1977] 2 WLR 201, HL, Digest (Cont Vol E) 185, 1301b. .

Duncan v Cammell Laird & Co Ltd [1942] 1 All ER 587, [1942] AC 624, HL, 18 Digest (Reissue) 155, 1272.

Gashin v Liverpool City Council [1980] 1 WLR 1549, CA.

Home Office v Harman [1981] 2 All ER 349, [1981] QB 534, [1981] 2 WLR 310, CA; affd e   [1982] 1 All ER 532, [1982] 2 WLR 338, HL.

Lonrho Ltd v Shell Petroleum Co Ltd [1980] 1 WLR 627, HL.

Marks v Beyfus (1890) 25 QBD 494, CA, 22 Digest (Reissue) 432, 4297.

Neilson v Laugharne [1981] 1 All ER 829, [1981] QB 736, [1981] 2 WLR 537, CA.

Nixon v United States (1974) 418 US 683.

R v Lewes Justices, ex p Secretary of State for the Home Dept [1971] 2 All ER 1126, [1972] 1 f   QB 232, [1971] 2 WLR 1466, DC; affd in part sub nom Rogers v Secretary of State for the Home Dept, Gaming Board for GB v Rogers [1972] 2 All ER 1057, [1973] AC 388, [1972] 3 WLR 279, HL, 16 Digest (Reissue) 406, 4466.

Riddick v Thames Board Mills Ltd [1977] 3 All ER 677, [1977] QB 881, [1977] 3 WLR 63, CA, Digest (Cont Vol E) 180, 495b.

Sankey v Whitlam (1978) 53 ALJR 11.

g   Science Research Council v Nassé, BL Cars Ltd v Vyas [1979] 3 All ER 673, [1980] AC 1028, [1979] 3 WLR 762, HL, Digest (Cont Vol E) 186, 1301d.

Tamlin v Hannaford [1949] 2 All ER 327, [1950] 1 KB 18, CA, 11 Digest (Reissue) 682, 160.

Williams v Home Office [1981] 1 All ER 1151.

h   **Cases also cited**

Golden Chemical Products Ltd, Re (1976) Times, 10 December, DC.

Norwest Holst Ltd v Dept of Trade [1978] 3 All ER 280, [1978] Ch 201, CA.

IRC v National Federation of Self-Employed and Small Businesses Ltd [1981] 2 All ER 93, [1982] AC 617, HL.

Pan American World Airways Inc v Dept of Trade [1976] 1 Lloyds Rep 257, CA.

j   **Summons for production of documents**

By common points of claim served on 1 May 1981 and subsequently amended and re-served on 5 February 1982 the plaintiffs, who were 20 international airlines operating into and out of Heathrow airport, including Air Canada and Pan American World Airways Inc, sought as against the defendants, the Secretary of State for Trade and the

British Airports Authority (BAA) (1) a declaration against the Secretary of State that he
acted ultra vires and unlawfully in directing BAA to increase the user charges for *a*
Heathrow airport to fund the building of new terminals at Heathrow and Gatwick
airports, and (2) a declaration against BAA that the user charges were ultra vires and
unlawful and an injunction restraining BAA from imposing the charges. By a summons
dated 8 April 1982 the plaintiffs sought (i) an order requiring the Secretary of State to
produce for inspection certain documents enumerated in his list of documents comprising
(a) communications between government ministers or for their use at meetings (the *b*
category A documents) and (b) communications between senior officials of government
departments for the use of those who drew up documents for the ministers (the category
B documents), production of which was objected to in a certificate dated 26 June 1981 on
the ground that the documents in categories A and B belonged to a class production of
which would be injurious to the public interest, and (ii) inspection by the court of further
documents listed in the schedule to the certificate. The summons was heard in chambers *c*
but judgment was given by Bingham J in open court. The facts are set out in the
judgment.

Samuel Stamler QC and *Michael Crystal* for Air Canada.
Denis R M Henry QC, Christopher Bellamy and *Trevor Philipson* for Pan American World
    Airways Inc.
J M Chadwick QC, Simon D Brown and *Christopher Clarke* for the Secretary of State. *d*
Peter Scott QC and *Timothy Walker* for BAA.

Cur adv vult

6 May. The following judgment was delivered.

BINGHAM J. I have before me three summonses in this consolidated action, two on *e*
behalf of the plaintiffs and one on behalf of the defendants. A fourth summons, issued
by the defendants, has been withdrawn on terms which I will mention. One of the
summonses, concerned with public interest immunity, raises questions of general
interest and I am accordingly, at the request of the parties, giving judgment in open
court. *f*
    The plaintiffs in the action fall into two groups. The first group consists of 18
international airlines headed by Air Canada. I shall call them the Air Canada plaintiffs.
The second group will after amendment consist of Pan American World Airways Inc and
Trans World Airlines Inc. I shall call them the Pan American plaintiffs. The feature
which unifies all these plaintiffs, despite differences in other respects, is that they are all
airlines operating into and out of Heathrow airport and contend that they have been *g*
required to pay an unlawfully high price for doing so.
    There are two defendants. The first is the British Airports Authority (BAA), a statutory
body whose function is to own and manage a number of United Kingdom airports
including Heathrow. Its powers and duties are laid down in the Airports Authority Act
1975. The pleadings in the action contain an extensive summary of the relevant statutory
provisions and I need not attempt to repeat them here. It suffices to note that, although *h*
BAA has no express statutory powers to charge airlines for using Heathrow (or any other
airport, but I shall confine myself to Heathrow, with which this action is concerned) it is
accepted by all parties that an implied power to do so exists. It exercises this power by
issuing conditions of use, including aircraft charges, usually on an annual basis running
from 1 April of each year, but in 1979 there was a mid-year increase in November. The
charges are imposed for landing and take off, parking and runway movement, the rate *j*
of charge varying according to the weight of the aircraft and the number of passengers.
Further variations depend on whether the flight is domestic or international and on the
time of day and period of the year. In reliance on English statutory provisions, European
Community law, common law and international obligations undertaken by the United
Kingdom, the plaintiffs contend that any charges imposed by BAA should be fair, just
and reasonable, reasonably calculated to facilitate the discharge of BAA's duties under the

1975 Act and non-discriminatory. The plaintiffs also contend that BAA is bound to make
a Heathrow available to all operators (or all aircraft of other states party to the Chicago
Convention) on equal terms and conditions, and the Pan American plaintiffs rely on a
duty deriving from agreement with the United States to impose airport charges which
are just and reasonable, reflecting but not exceeding the full cost to BAA of providing
appropriate facilities and providing for a reasonable rate of return on assets after
depreciation.

b   The second defendant is the Secretary of State for Trade. He has certain powers and
duties under the 1975 Act, particularly in respect to financial matters. Where the United
Kingdom has undertaken obligations by international treaty, as by the Chicago
Convention and the Bermuda II agreement with the United States, it is said that he is the
minister responsible for seeing that these are honoured.

The case made by the plaintiffs against the defendants falls under four main heads.
c The first is referred to as the constitutional case. I shall have to return to this in more
detail later. For the moment it suffices to note its general character, as summarised in
para 22 of the rereamended points of claim:

d
      'The November 1979 and April 1980 increases in the user charges . . . were ultra
      vires the BAA and unlawful and not imposed in the proper exercise of its discretion
      under the 1975 Act but were substantially caused or contributed to by the ultra
      vires and unlawful directions, requirements or interference of the Secretary of State
      whose dominant purpose was the implementation of non-aviation related
      government policy (and particularly to achieve any reduction, whether temporary
      or otherwise in the public sector borrowing requirement) and who at no time paid
      any or any sufficient regard to his own powers and duties, the powers and duties of
      the BAA or the international obligations of the United Kingdom. The facts and
e   matters in support of these allegations are hereinafter set out . . .'

The second head, called the economic case, rests on the contention that BAA has imposed
charges which are much higher than are reasonable and than are justified to cover the
cost of providing appropriate facilities with a reasonable rate of return on assets after
depreciation. The third head, the Community law case, asserts that by its charges at
f Heathrow BAA has in breach of art 86 of the EEC Treaty abused a dominant position
and that the Secretary of State in breach of art 90 has maintained in force measures
having that effect. Fourthly, in the feather-bedding case, the Pan American plaintiffs
claim that BAA has so fixed its charges at Heathrow as to favour British carriers and in
particular British Airways to the unlawful prejudice of foreign carriers including
themselves. The relief claimed consists of declarations and damages and (against BAA)
g injunctions and orders for repayment of charges overpaid. This summary greatly
oversimplifies a very complex claim, with some consequent distortion, but I think it
gives an adequate outline for present purposes.

[His Lordship then considered the plaintiffs' summons to amend the common points
of claim. He gave leave to make certain amendments and dismissed a summons by BAA
for further and better particulars. His Lordship continued:]

h
*3. The plaintiffs' summons seeking production of documents for which the Secretary of State has
claimed public interest immunity*
      Since the decision in *Conway v Rimmer* [1968] 1 All ER 874, [1968] AC 910 the
question of public interest immunity has arisen on a number of occasions, most
importantly for present purposes in *Burmah Oil Co Ltd v Bank of England* [1979] 3 All ER
j 700, [1980] AC 1090. From the authorities, and that authority in particular, I derive the
following as the principles to be followed where it is sought to withhold documents on
the ground that they belong to a class such that their production would be injurious to
the public interest and where that claim is contested by a party to the litigation.

      1. The first task of the court is to peruse the certificate or document in which the
claim for public interest immunity is made in order to satisfy itself (a) that the class to
which the documents are said to belong is one recognised as capable of attracting public

interest immunity or is at least closely analogous to a recognised class, (b) that there is no reason to believe the documents do not fall within the class claimed, and (c) that the   *a* documents themselves and the basis of the claim to immunity have apparently been the subject of proper consideration by an appropriate person. If these conditions are met, in the absence of any contrary indication the court will treat the certificate or claim, not as conclusive, but as motivated by a concern for the public interest which (despite the inevitable difference of viewpoint) is as genuine as that of the court itself. In some cases the nature of the class will virtually conclude the matter (for example, where Cabinet   *b* papers or diplomatic dispatches are concerned) but such cases are the exception and are not those which in practice give rise to controversy.

2. If the court is satisfied that the party seeking to withhold the documents has made a valid claim for public interest immunity the next step is to determine whether the party seeking production is able to show a public interest in production. To do so, such party must show not only that the documents are relevant under the *Peruvian Guano* test   *c* (a condition which the claim for immunity itself assumes to be satisfied: see *Compagnie Financière et Commerciale du Pacifique v Peruvian Guano Co* (1882) 11 QBD 55) but that they are necessary for disposing fairly of the cause or matter or (to put it in a different way) are necessary for the due administration of justice: see the *Burmah Oil* case [1979] 3 All ER 700 at 708, 714, 718, 731, [1980] AC 1090 at 1113, 1121, 1125, 1141. If it appears to the court that the documents are likely to be necessary for the due administration of   *d* justice the court is confronted by a second aspect of the public interest, fit to be weighed in the balance against the first.

3. If the court is satisfied that there is a public interest both in production and in non-disclosure it must consider the relative substance of each claim with a view to forming a judgment whether, on balance, the public interest will be better served by the withholding of the documents or by their production. It might be concluded that in   *e* respect of some documents the claim for immunity, although properly made, was of relatively little weight (as in the *Burmah Oil* case [1979] 3 All ER 700 at 714, 720, [1980] AC 1090 at 1121, 1128). It might conversely emerge (as it did in the *Burmah Oil* case during argument in the House of Lords) that only very few of the documents were truly necessary for resolving the real issues in the action, and then the claim for immunity would have to be considered in relation to those documents. But the task of the court is   *f* to weigh the harm which production would cause to the business of government or public administration against the harm which non-disclosure would do to the just determination of the particular case and decide where the balance of public interest lies.

4. Where the court is of opinion that the balance of public interest lies clearly against production it will not inspect the documents on the off-chance that that conclusion might prove to be wrong if the documents were looked at. But the court may privately   *g* inspect the documents, certainly if it is provisionally inclined to order production (see *Conway v Rimmer* [1968] 1 All ER 874 at 888, 900, [1968] AC 910 at 953, 971) but also, it would seem, if careful consideration of the conflicting claims in the absence of the documents leaves the court subject to grave and disquieting doubts as to where the balance lies: see the *Burmah Oil* case [1979] 3 All ER 700 at 726, 734, [1980] AC 1090 at 1135, 1145. If provisionally inclined to order production the court would not ordinarily   *h* make that order without first inspecting the documents privately.

The first of these principles was not the subject of debate before me, although counsel of course had no opportunity to comment on my formulation of it. Counsel for the Pan American plaintiffs, whose argument was adopted by the Air Canada plaintiffs, accepted that a valid claim for immunity on recognised grounds was made on behalf of the Secretary of State. This was to be expected, since the certificate of the Permanent Secretary   *j* to the Department of Trade (dated 26 June 1981) is in almost exactly the same form (making allowance for the difference in subject matter) as that which was considered by the House of Lords in the *Burmah Oil* case. This makes it unnecessary to cite at length the terms of the certificate. The first two categories, A and B, in the earlier certificate are reproduced in this, the first relating to what may be loosely called ministerial documents, the second to documents of senior officials, in each case relating to the formulation of

government policy towards BAA, its borrowing powers, its capital expenditure, its
a landing fees and so on. The permanent secretary expresses the opinion that it is necessary
for the proper functioning of the public service that all the documents in question should
be withheld from production since they are documents, not of a routine nature, passing
at a high level and relating to the formulation of government policy on matters of major
economic importance to the United Kingdom. He does not think that the policy
considerations underlying the documents lack topical significance, since the question of
b landing fees at Heathrow is still a matter of active governmental consideration. All the
persons involved are still active in public life. In the permanent secretary's view it would
be against the public interest that documents revealing the process of providing for
ministers honest and candid advice on matters of high level policy should be subject to
disclosure. He also relies in particular on the well-known observations of Lord Reid in
Conway v Rimmer [1968] 1 All ER 874 at 888, [1968] AC 910 at 952 concerning the effect
c on the inner workings of the government machine of the public disclosure of documents
concerned with the making of policy. So one starts with a claim, admittedly good unless
displaced, that the documents be withheld from disclosure.

The argument between the parties begins with the second principle. Counsel for Pan
American would, I think, accept the principle much as I have put it but would add an
important rider: documents are necessary for the due administration of justice if they
d are highly material to significant issues in the action in the sense that they are likely to
affect the decision on them, irrespective of whether they are helpful or unhelpful towards
the party seeking production. Counsel for the Secretary of State challenged that approach.
In his submission it was necessary for a party seeking to show a public interest in
production to establish that the documents were likely to be of substantial help to him
in proving his claim; if it was just as probable that the documents would undermine his
e case or strengthen that of his opponent no public interest in production was shown. Both
parties relied on extracts from the speeches in *Burmah Oil*, counsel for Pan American
relying in particular on the question which their Lordships asked themselves, counsel for
the Secretary of State on the answers which they gave. I do not doubt that the submission
of counsel for the Secretary of State reflects the way in which the argument on this
question usually proceeds in practice. A party to adversarial proceedings will not press
f for production of documents unless he thinks they will help him, and where the claim
for immunity is made by his opponent in the litigation he may even suspect a desire to
suppress documents which his opponent knows to be potentially damaging or
embarrassing. But the concern of the court must surely be to ensure that the truth is
elicited, not caring whether the truth favours one party or the other but anxious that its
final decision should be grounded on a sure foundation of fact. Justice is as greatly
g affronted where a plaintiff is wrongly awarded relief as where he is wrongly denied it.
Where the claimant for immunity is not himself a party to the litigation, the court could
not, I think, concern itself wholly with the litigious advantage of the party seeking
production even if the other party could join in the challenge and declines to do so. I do
not think the principle is different where the party claiming immunity is himself a
litigant. In my judgment documents are necessary for fairly disposing of a cause or for
h the due administration of justice if they give substantial assistance to the court in
determining the facts on which the decision in the cause will depend. For reasons which
will become apparent hereafter when I consider the balance, I conclude that some of the
documents covered by this certificate are necessary in this sense. I am not sure that
counsel for the Secretary of State would seriously contest this if, contrary to his
submission, the test is as I have indicated. I therefore proceed on the assumption that
j there is a public interest both in production and in non-disclosure. I would just add this,
for the avoidance of doubt. It is not of course open to a party to plead a case consisting of
mere assertion and then seek discovery on the ground that there may be documents
which will enable him to found a case. The remedy is to attack the original pleading for
want of particularity. Nothing that I have said indicates that there should be a different
rule where public interest immunity is claimed and challenged than in any other case.

On the relative weight to be given to the competing public interests in this case the

parties are sharply divided. I begin by considering the grounds of the claim to public
interest immunity. In doing so I accept both the sincerity and the weight of the   *a*
permanent secretary's certificate and expression of opinion. It is plain that these are
documents passing at a very high level of government. They deal with the formulation,
not the implementation, of policy. They relate to matters of great economic importance
to the United Kingdom. They have an obvious bearing on a policy still in force and are
certainly not of mere historical significance. Counsel for the Secretary of State is, I think,
correct when he contends that documents as close as these to the inner processes of   *b*
government have never previously been ordered to be produced in any litigation. There
is furthermore great force in his submission that there are many proceedings in which
the basis of a minister's decision is the subject of attack, but in none of them have what
may be called his working papers been the subject of production. The consequences of
production in this case could be potentially far reaching. There are, however, points to
be made the other way. First of all, this is a class and not a contents claim. It is not,   *c*
therefore, suggested, as it might have been, that there is anything in the contents of these
documents which would embarrass Her Majesty's government in its relations with
foreign states or which, in the possession of a foreign corporation, could prove injurious
to any national interest. Secondly, the present context is not one in which the candour
argument, as it has come to be called, appears to me to have much force. That argument
is currently unfashionable and has been much disparaged. There are, in my view, some   *d*
contexts (as, for example, personal references for public appointments) where it could
have considerable public importance. But the present is not one of them. I cannot think
that the possibility of public scrutiny would adversely affect the quality of advice given
by officials or views expressed by ministers engaged in formulating national policy
concerning BAA's airports and the charges to be made for using them. Thirdly, this is, as
counsel for the Secretary of State readily accepted, important litigation and at its heart is   *e*
a carefully prepared and serious criticism of government policy. Captious that criticism
may be said by the defendants to be, but the extent to which it is ill-informed is naturally
affected by the extent to which relevant documents are available. And, lastly, one need
not be a radical advocate of government in the sunshine to feel that the protection
afforded to official documents in the past has perhaps been somewhat overgenerous.
So I turn to the other side of the public interest equation, the necessity for production   *f*
for the due administration of justice in this case. I must for this purpose consider in more
detail than I have so far done the plaintiffs' constitutional case, on which the success of
the plaintiffs' application must turn. In doing so I wish at the outset to pay tribute to the
common points of defence delivered on behalf of both defendants. These do not consist,
like most such documents, of denials of all material paragraphs in the points of claim
interspersed with occasional grudging admissions of the obvious, but set out the   *g*
defendants' case in very considerable detail. The pleading reflects great credit on counsel
who very ably drafted and settled the document and on those who instructed them. As a
result it is much easier than it might be to ascertain what the real issues are. There are, I
think, three strands in the plaintiffs' constitutional case which it is convenient to separate.
The first is an allegation that the Secretary of State imposed a financial target on BAA,
thereby arrogating to himself powers which he did not have and usurping the exercise   *h*
of a discretion not vested in him. The plaintiffs are able to point to statements emanating
from BAA and the Secretary of State which could be understood to mean that the
Secretary of State had himself set a target which BAA were to achieve. The defendants
admit that the Secretary of State was not entitled to impose a financial target on BAA but
they deny that he did so. There was, they say, consultation between the Secretary of State
and BAA concerning a financial target but no dictation by the one to the other. Now it is   *j*
obvious that this issue will turn on a close consideration of what passed between BAA
and the Secretary of State. Oral evidence may be important; even more so will be
correspondence, minutes of meetings and possibly even records of telephone calls. The
court will have to determine the true nature and effect of these exchanges. I would have
no doubt that these documents are crucial to the determination of this issue. I am,

however, told (and the list attached to the certificate bears this out) that no claim for
immunity has been made for any document containing or recording any exchange
between BAA and the Secretary of State. I have then to consider whether any purely
internal ministry documents, not recording an exchange with BAA, would probably be
necessary for deciding this issue. It is clearly possible that such documents might contain
useful material but I cannot regard it as likely and I think such documents would in any
event be peripheral to the main issue of what passed between the two. I do not consider,
therefore, that this strand of the plaintiffs' constitutional case raises any public interest in
production fit to be weighed against the permanent secretary's claim.

The second strand of the plaintiffs' constitutional case is the allegation that in
performing certain acts the Secretary of State acted with a purpose which was ultra vires
and contrary to his statutory powers and obligations: that, in a nutshell, he exercised his
powers for purposes other than those for which the powers were entrusted to him. It is
common ground that the Secretary of State had exchanges with BAA concerning a
financial target for BAA, that the Department of Trade informed BAA that the Treasury
were looking for savings of £20m from BAA either by way of increased charges or
postponement of less urgent investments, that prior to July 1979 the Secretary of State
required BAA not to borrow, or notified BAA that permission to borrow would be
refused, and that the Secretary of State approved BAA's charges which took effect in
November 1979, but only after an earlier scale had been submitted and commented on
by the department and a revised scale submitted. The plaintiffs allege that the Secretary
of State's dominant purpose in acting as he did was the purely domestic political purpose
of reducing and containing the public sector borrowing requirement and not any purpose
properly relating to the performance of BAA's duties under the 1975 Act. The Secretary
of State denies that this was his dominant purpose but says that, if it was, it properly
related to the exercise of his powers and the performance of BAA's duties under the 1975
Act. Elsewhere it is pleaded in the points of defence that the dominant purpose of the
Secretary of State at all material times was to secure the efficient use of the public
resources employed by BAA in accordance with stated government policy, that policy, as
I understand, including the principles set out in *The Nationalised Industries* (Cmnd 7131
(1978)).

The third strand in the plaintiffs' constitutional case is very close to the second. They
allege that the Secretary of State took account of considerations which he should not have
done (such as the government's desire to reduce the public sector borrowing requirement)
and failed to take account of considerations which he should have done (such as the
alleged fact that the proposed landing charges would render the United Kingdom in
breach of its international obligations under the Chicago Convention and the Bermuda
II Agreement). The Secretary of State in his pleading positively avers that in acting as he
did he did take account of BAA's powers under specified sections of the 1975 Act and
specified paragraphs of the Air Navigation Order, SI 1976/1783, of his own powers under
specified sections of the 1975 Act and a specified paragraph of the 1976 order, of the
former functions of the Board of Trade transferred to him, of his duties and his
accountability as one of Her Majesty's principal Secretaries of State; of BAA's common
law power to impose reasonable charges for the use of land which it owns, of his
obligations under the 1949 Act, and, finally, of the international obligations of the United
Kingdom, although in this last case he denies that he was bound to take these into
account save in so far as they had been incorporated by enactment into English law.

I must (in the absence of any application to strike out or any contrary submission) act
on the assumption that these last two strands of the plaintiffs' claim show a good cause of
action, that is that they plead facts which if fully established could entitle the plaintiffs to
relief. No doubt the documents passing between the Secretary of State and BAA, or
between one or other of these and the airlines or a third party, might throw some light
on the Secretary of State's dominant purpose and on what factors he did and did not take
into account. But the plaintiffs contend that these last two strands of their case are
directed not, like the first, to what passed between the two defendants but to the intention

with which and the manner in which policy was formulated by the Secretary of State. This is not, they contend, a case like *Burmah Oil* or *Williams v Home Office* [1981] 1 All ER 1151 in which the challenged documents are incidental to the central issue in the action; it is a case in which immunity is claimed for documents relating to the formulation of government policy when an attack on the formulation of that policy lies at the very heart of the plaintiffs' claim. If these documents are immune from production, the Secretary of State's averments as to his intentions and self-direction are likewise debarred from being the subject of oral evidence because that evidence could not properly be given without breaching the public interest alleged in withholding these matters from scrutiny. The result, so counsel for Pan American submitted, would be to render this part of the case incapable of judicial determination on the merits.

It is, of course, plain that a successful plea for public interest immunity may have that result: see, for example, *Marks v Beyfus* (1890) 2 QBD 494 or *R v Lewes Justice, ex p Secretary of State for the Home Dept* [1972] 2 All ER 1057 at 1060, [1973] AC 388 at 400. The likelihood of such a consequence is not in itself a conclusive objection to the claim. But it is a consequence which no court would welcome and in which, with a bona fide claim, it would not acquiesce unless (as in those two cases) the public interest in withholding the documents or the information was very weighty indeed.

In this case the problem of choosing between the competing claims presents itself to the court in an acute form. On the one hand is a claim for immunity properly made in respects of documents traditionally protected. On the other hand are bona fide plaintiffs who believe themselves to have suffered an injury which, they say, cannot be fully investigated without production of the documents. The conclusions to which I have come after most helpful argument on both sides are these.

1. I consider that some of these documents are very likely to be necessary for the just determination of the second and third issues in the plaintiffs' constitutional case. They are very likely to affect the outcome one way or the other. I do not think any court could be confident that its decision on those issues was grounded on a sure foundation of fact in the absence of the documents. The documents to which I refer are those in category A, the ministerial documents. I confine myself to those because these matters were plainly dealt with at a ministerial level and it is the Secretary of State's purpose and his self-direction which is important. No doubt, as the permanent secretary observed, decisions made by ministers are frequently preceded by discussions within and between departments, but it is the minister's thinking which is crucial here. If his thinking reflected official thinking as recorded in the category B documents, those documents would add nothing. If it differed, regard would be paid to his thinking, not theirs. In my judgment the plaintiffs demonstrate a public interest in production of the category A, but not the category B, documents.

2. If it were necessary for the plaintiffs (in accordance with the submission of counsel for the Secretary of State) to show a likelihood that the documents, if produced, would help them I could not on the material put before me conclude that they would do so. There are indications both ways. It would be wrong to guess. But I do not regard the chance that these documents will be helpful as at all speculative. The strong probability is, in my judgment, that they will be of great assistance in resolving these issues one way or the other, possibly even determinative.

3. I have already indicated what seems to me to be the strengths and weaknesses of the claim for immunity. I have also indicated what I see as the strength of the claim for production. What are the weaknesses of that claim? If I have correctly directed myself as to the proper test, and if I have correctly analysed the relevant issues between the parties, the only real weakness that I can see lies in the possibility that the documents, if produced, would take the matter no further than the defendants' admissions and the documents already produced. This possibility, although in my view unlikely, is one that can be met, as it was in *Burmah Oil*, by the court's inspection of the documents prior to production.

4. In all the circumstances of the present case I am provisionally of opinion that the damage to the public service which production of the documents would cause is likely to

be outweighed by the damage to the just disposal of this cause if they were withheld. I
am provisionally inclined to order production, and would accordingly inspect the
category A documents. At the very lowest, I would have grave and disquieting doubts as
to where the balance of public interest lies if I rejected the plaintiffs' claim for production
without inspection.

This conclusion makes it, I think, unnecessary to deal in detail with the fourth
principle which I expressed above. Counsel for the Secretary of State strongly urged that
great caution should be shown in exercising the power to inspect, contending that the
court should only inspect if satisfied that after inspection an order for production would
probably be regarded as appropriate. He relied on statements in *Conway v Rimmer* [1968]
1 All ER 874 at 888, 900, 904, 905, 908, 915–916, [1968] AC 910 at 953, 971, 978, 979,
983, 995 and very recent authority such as *Neilson v Laugharne* [1981] 1 All ER 829 at
836, [1981] QB 736 at 748. I unhesitatingly accept the need for caution. Inspection is not
something to be undertaken lightly. I am not quite sure that a majority of the House in
Burmah Oil favoured counsel for the Secretary of State's more stringent test of inspection
but I need not linger on that question since I find that standard to be satisfied here. In
reaching the decision to inspect I am not unmindful of the contention of counsel for the
Secretary of State that the floodgates would be opened to similar claims in many cases.
But the courts have ample powers to prevent orders being made in inappropriate cases,
and I also bear in mind the Johnsonian maxim that 'you must not neglect doing a thing
immediately good, from fear of remote evil'.

Counsel for the Secretary of State submitted, lastly, that if I were minded to inspect I
should not do so without offering the Secretary of State an opportunity to appeal before I
did so. He based this submission on Lord Keith's statement in the *Burmah Oil* case [1979]
3 All ER 700 at 729, [1980] AC 1090 at 1136, quoting Lord Reid in *Conway v Rimmer*
[1968] 1 All ER 874 at 914, [1968] AC 910 at 993, and on McNeill J's adoption of what
Lord Keith had said as reported in *Williams v Home Office* [1981] 1 All ER 1151 at 1154. I
would myself understand Lord Reid to be indicating the desirability of an opportunity
to appeal before production, not inspection, and I think that Lord Scarman in *Burmah Oil*
also understood him in that way. It may also be that Lord Keith's main concern was the
risk of irresponsible decisions to inspect being made at levels lower than the High Court.
But be that as it may, I would think it quite wrong to pre-empt the Secretary of State's
right to pursue this aspect of the matter by insisting on production before appeal. I have
indicated my opinion. It is as well that the question of a right to appeal before inspection
should be authoritatively resolved.

To the extent I have indicated I would, accordingly, allow the plaintiffs' application,
but I would grant the Secretary of State leave to appeal.

4. BAA's summons to strike out

BAA issued a summons to strike out certain parts of the plaintiffs' prayer for relief.
After some discussion it was agreed that this summons should be withdrawn on the basis
that any objection to the relief claimed by the plaintiffs would, if necessary, be argued at
the trial, it being understood that no concession has been made by the plaintiffs as to the
manner in which they put their claim. I should, however, record that while making no
concession counsel for Air Canada did advance as his primary contention that the claim
made by his clients was not a claim for mandamus, reserving the right, if that primary
contention were held to be wrong, to claim an order of mandamus. I shall forbear from
comment on this matter.

Application granted. Leave to appeal.

Solicitors: *Freshfields* (for Air Canada); *Slaughter & May* (for Pan American World Airways
Inc); *Treasury Solicitor*; *McKenna & Co* (for BAA).

K Mydeen Esq   Barrister.

Interlocutory appeal and cross-appeal

The Secretary of State appealed seeking an order that the documents in category A should *a*
not be produced or inspected by the court. The principal grounds of the appeal were (1)
that the judge was wrong in law in deciding that a public interest in the production of
documents on the ground of the due administration of justice, fit to be weighed against
a valid claim for public interest immunity in respect of the documents, was shown by
establishing merely that the documents were likely to affect the decision in the action on
significant issues, irrespective of whether it appeared that the documents would be likely *b*
to be helpful or unhelpful towards the party seeking production, and accordingly the
judge, having accepted that the documents were as likely to harm the plaintiffs' case as to
support it, erred in reaching the provisional conclusion that the category A documents
should be produced, and (2) that the judge wrongly concluded that there was a strong
probability that the category A documents would be of great assistance in resolving, and
possibly be determinative of, the second and third issues in the plaintiffs' constitutional *c*
claim in the action. The plaintiffs cross-appealed, contending that the judge wrongly
concluded (1) that the category A documents were not likely to be necessary for the just
determination of the first issue in the plaintiffs' constitutional claim and (2) that none of
the category B documents was likely to be necessary for the just determination of any of
the issues in the plaintiffs' constitutional claim. The facts are set out in the judgment of
Lord Denning MR. *d*

Simon D Brown for the Secretary of State.
Samuel Stamler QC and *Michael Crystal* for Air Canada.
Denis R M Henry QC and *Trevor Philipson* for Pan American World Airways Inc.
BAA did not appear.

e

Cur adv vult

24 September. The following judgments were delivered.

LORD DENNING MR. The call today is for more 'open government'. It is voiced
mainly by newsmen and critics and oppositions. They want to know all about the *f*
discussions that go on in the inner circles of government. They feel that policy-making
is the concern of everyone. So everyone should be told about it.

In our present case the demand for 'open government' comes from an unusual quarter.
It is made by the airlines of the world. They are much concerned about the policy of the
Secretary of State for Trade. They say that he has acted unlawfully and unreasonably.
They have sued him for it. They ask to see all the documents which led up to his policy *g*
decisions. Not only at ministerial level. But also at Cabinet level. The judge has ordered
the ministerial papers to be produced. The Secretary of State appeals to this court.

1. INTRODUCTORY

London's Heathrow is a great airport. It is one of the largest in the world. Aircraft of
all nations fly in and out continuously. They land and take off. They park and are housed, *h*
as occasion may require. They have to pay the prescribed charges for doing so. These
charges are fixed by a nationalised undertaking called the British Airports Authority
(BAA). It is a statutory corporation established by the Airports Authority Act 1975. It is
of the nature we described in *Tamlin v Hannaford* [1949] 2 All ER 327, [1950] 1 KB 18. It
has no shareholders. It has no subscribed capital. It borrows all the money it needs. Its
borrowings are guaranteed by the Treasury. It makes no profits. It owes money, but it *j*
cannot be made bankrupt. It cannot be wound up. It is very much a government
concern. The statute contains many provisions putting it under the control of the
Secretary of State.

In recent years Heathrow has become very severely congested. So much so that BAA
have made plans to relieve the congestion. They propose to make a new terminal 4 at

Heathrow and a new terminal 2 at Gatwick, and to make other considerable alterations. These will cost £500m–700m. BAA have to raise the money for it. In order to do so, they thought of using a reserve of £19m and borrowing the rest. But the Secretary of State put his foot down. He would not let BAA raise the money in that way. He thought that they should raise it by increasing the charges. That is what they did.

In 1979 BAA decided to increase the charges by 35%. The British airlines did not object. But the others did. Many airlines from abroad complained. They made an outcry about it. They said it was a gross overcharge. It was unfair and unreasonable. It was an abuse of a dominant position. It was discriminatory in favour of British carriers. It was unlawful.

Actions are brought

The airlines regarded the increase as so excessive that they have brought actions in the High Court. They desire to test the legality of the charges. The pleadings are very elaborate and complex. The statement of claim and particulars under it cover 217 pages. The defence and particulars under it cover 140 pages.

At this stage we are only concerned with a preliminary matter. It arises about the discovery of documents. The airlines wish to see the documents which led to the increase of charges at Heathrow. Many of these documents were at a very high level. Some were to and from ministers themselves. A few came before the Cabinet itself. The judge has ordered that those at ministerial level should be disclosed to the airlines, so that they can be used at the trial.

The Secretary of State appeals to this court together with BAA. He claims 'Crown privilege', now described as 'public interest immunity'. The Secretary of State says that it is in the public interest that these documents should be kept secret. They should not be disclosed for use at the trial. The airlines must do as best they can without them.

The issues in the case

On a question of discovery, it is necessary to determine what are the issues in the action. Discovery is only permitted of the documents in the possession or power of the party 'relating to any matter in question in the cause or matter': see RSC Ord 24, r 3(1). There are many matters in question in these actions, but for present purposes the only matter in question is what is called 'the constitutional case'.

2. THE CONSTITUTIONAL CASE

The airlines allege that the Secretary of State broke the rules of our constitution. They say that he gave directions to BAA which he had no power to give; that he was actuated by an ulterior motive and by irrelevant considerations. In order for these allegations to be understood, I must go into a little detail.

Financial target

Under the statute the Secretary of State has power to give the BAA 'directions of a general nature' as to how it should conduct its affairs, but not specific directions. The airlines allege that the Secretary of State gave BAA specific directions to attain the financial target of 6%, and that he had no power to do so.

This arises out of a white paper which the government issued in 1978. It dealt with the nationalised industries. It is Cmnd 7131. It showed that the government was determined to settle an overall 'financial target' for each industry. This target was expressed as a percentage return on the average net assets employed in the industry. Once the target was settled, it was to be announced to Parliament by the Secretary of State. He was also to tell Parliament the reasons for it.

In the case of BAA the Secretary of State on 26 February 1980 announced in the House of Commons:

'I have decided that a reasonable financial duty for the British Airports Authority

would be to achieve on average a rate of return of 6% per annum on net assets
revalued at current cost over the three financial years 1980/81 to 1982/83.'   *a*

I hope that the members of Parliament understood it. It needs an accountant to explain
it to me. I expect to you also. In ordinary language it means that BAA should ascertain
the value of its assets, not at their original cost years ago, but at their present cost if they
had to buy them afresh today. BAA should then aim to get a return of 6% on that value
each year. They should fix their charges so as to get that return.   *b*

Use of reserves

Before April 1979 BAA had done reasonably well. So well that it had put £19m into a
reserve. They were thinking of using it so as to meet some of the big capital expenditure
needed for the new terminals and so forth. The airlines allege that the Secretary of State
'froze' that sum and refused to allow BAA to make use of it.   *c*

Borrowing

Under the statute BAA had power to borrow money for its capital improvements
provided that the Secretary of State gave his consent. In February 1979 the Secretary of
State ordered BAA not to borrow any money. He told them that permission to borrow
would be refused.   *d*

The effect

This decision had a profound impact on the plans of BAA. But they were determined
to go ahead with the new terminals at Heathrow and Gatwick and their other
improvements. They felt it was necessary so as to cope with the traffic. The money had
to be raised somehow. The only way to do it was to make an overall increase of 35% on
the charges made to users. In their annual report for the year 1979–1980 the chairman   *e*
said: 'In order to set its prices at the right level to achieve the tough 6% financial target,
traffic charges were increased by 35%.' Note the chairman's word 'tough'. The airlines
suggest that BAA were directed to achieve that target without their consent.

What was behind it all

The airlines say that behind all the decisions of the Secretary of State there was this   *f*
broad policy consideration. The country was in a difficult economic position. Inflation
was rampant. The nationalised undertakings were borrowing too much money, which
the government had to underwrite. The government decided that borrowing in the
'public sector' had to be cut down. It had to be considered as a whole. In order to do this,
the profitable industries ought to subsidise the unprofitable industries. BAA was one of
the profitable industries. It should increase its charges so as to make the 'public sector' as   *g*
a whole more viable. The airlines say that this was an ulterior motive, and an irrelevant
consideration, which the Secretary of State ought not to have taken into account. He
should have considered BAA as a unit on its own, and not lumped it in with the other
nationalised industries as a part of the 'public sector'. The airlines suggest that if BAA
were considered on its own there was no need to increase the charges by anything like   *h*
35%.

3. THE THREE STRANDS

Such was the 'constitutional case' alleged by the airlines. The judge most helpfully
divided it into three strands.

The first strand   *j*

The judge described this as (see p 168, ante)—

'The first is an allegation that the Secretary of State *imposed* a financial target on
BAA, thereby arrogating to himself powers which he did not have and usurping the
exercise of a discretion not vested in him . . . The defendants admit that the Secretary

of State was not entitled to impose a financial target on BAA but they deny that he did so.' (My emphasis.)

On this issue it is plain that all the documents passing between the Secretary of State and BAA must be disclosed. Also all memoranda of meetings or telephone calls. These have been disclosed. No claim for immunity has been made in respect of them.

But a question arises as to the 'purely internal ministry documents'. These are the documents within the ministry, which do not record any exchanges between the minister and BAA, but are simply notes or memoranda by the clerks of the ministry passing between themselves. The judge refused to order them to be disclosed.

The second strand
The judge described this as (see p 169, ante)—

'The second strand of the plaintiffs' constitutional case is the allegation that in performing certain acts the Secretary of State acted with a purpose which was ultra vires and contrary to his statutory powers and obligations: that, in a nutshell, he exercised his powers for purposes other than those for which the powers were entrusted to him . . . The plaintiffs allege that the Secretary of State's dominant purpose in acting as he did was the purely domestic political purpose of reducing and containing the public sector borrowing requirement and not any purpose properly relating to the performance of BAA's duties under the 1975 Act.'

The third strand
The judge described this as (see p 169, ante)—

'The third strand in the plaintiffs' constitutional case is very close to the second. They allege that the Secretary of State took account of considerations which he should not have done (such as the government's desire to reduce the public sector borrowing requirement) and failed to take account of considerations which he should have done (such as the alleged fact that the proposed landing charges would render the United Kingdom in breach of its international obligations under the Chicago Convention and the Bermuda II Agreement).'

These two second and third strands stand together. They involve an inquiry into the 'purpose' of the Secretary of State and the considerations which he 'took into account'. Any documents are relevant which go to show what his purpose was, or what considerations he took into account. There are many of these documents. They are divided into two categories, A and B. The Secretary of State claims that they should not be disclosed on the ground that it would be contrary to the public interest.

Category A consists of communications at a high level between ministers or for the use of ministers at their meetings. These include the preparatory documents prepared for the use of ministers prior to their meetings. Category B consists of communications at a little lower level between senior officials of government departments, not for the use of ministers but for the use of those who draw up documents for ministers.

The Secretary of State claims 'public interest immunity' for both categories A and B. The judge held that category A should be disclosed (there was no immunity in respect of them) but that category B need not be disclosed. I must say that this seems a little odd to me. The documents at the higher level are to be disclosed: but those at a little lower level need not be.

Since the judge gave his decision, six more documents have been found. They were not in the possession of the Department of Trade. They were in the possession of the Cabinet office. Thus at the highest possible level. They are papers submitted to a Cabinet committee.

4. ILLUSTRATIONS
In order to illustrate the nature of the documents, I will pick out some samples:

At Cabinet level

'Number	Description of Document	Date
1	Memorandum by the Chief Secretary to the Treasury on Nationalised Industries Cash Limits for 1979/80 circulated as a paper for a Cabinet Committee	12 March 1979
2	Extract (section 4—at pages 9–11) from the minutes of a meeting of that Cabinet Committee chaired by the Prime Minister	15 March 1979
5	Cabinet Paper entitled Nationalised Industries Investment and Financing Review	9 July 1979
6	Note of a Cabinet discussion recording the Cabinet's decision on document 5 above	24 July 1979'

At ministerial level

'Category A

Number	Description of Document	Date
1	4 paragraphs from the Minutes of a meeting attended by the Chief Secretary to the Treasury (Mr. Biffen) the Secretary of State for Trade (Mr. Nott) and 7 officials of the Treasury and the Department of Trade	24 Sept. 1980
2	Letter S. Clinton Davis MP (Parliamentary Under Secretary of State, Department of Trade) to J. Barnett MP (Chief Secretary to the Treasury)	4 Sept. 1980
9	Copy letter Sir G. Howe MP (Chancellor of the Exchequer) to Sir K. Joseph MP (Secretary of State for Industry)	13 Feb. 1980
10	Letter J. Nott MP (Secretary of State for Trade) to Sir G. Howe MP	26 Feb. 1980
75	Discussion Paper prepared for Ministers entitled "British Airports Authority—Airport Charges"	Undated (1978)'

At official level

'Category B

Number	Description of Document	Date
242	Document entitled "Conclusions of a Meeting held in the Treasury on 9th November 1978"	
244	Note of a meeting between Officials of the Department of Trade and HM Treasury	11 April 1979
247	Document entitled "Nationalised Industries Capital Expenditure"	Undated
251	Background Note entitled "British Airports Authority—Airport User Charges"	Feb. 1980'

Those illustrations show that three government departments were concerned in this matter: the Treasury, the Department of Trade and the Department of Industry. The ministers in charge of those departments were 'briefed' by their officials. Those officials collected information from many sources and prepared papers on it to submit to ministers. The ministers attended a Cabinet committee at which decisions were taken.

5. THE CERTIFICATES

In order to claim 'Crown privilege' or 'public interest immunity', the practice is for a certificate to be given by a minister. It states his objection to disclosure and sets out the

reasons. In this case, however, this was not possible because the papers contained privately
a expressed opinions of ministers in a previous government; there is a long-standing and
important constitutional rule that ministers of a government formed by one party are
not allowed to see documents of a former government. So in the present case the
certificates were given by the permanent secretaries of the departments.

They were given by Sir Kenneth Clucas, the Permanent Secretary of the Board of
Trade, and his successor Mr Michael Franklin, and by Sir Robert Armstrong, the Secretary
b of the Cabinet. It is clear that they have given the most careful consideration to each of
the documents. They have described the nature of them and set out their reasons for
objecting. The certificate of Sir Robert Armstrong sets out the case so well that I set it out
for permanent record:

'3. The subject matter of all the documents is Government spending in relation
c   to the nationalised industries. The allocation of financial resources between the
various sectors in the economy is one of the most important of the functions of
government. Decisions about it affect the whole of national life. Inside this wider
framework the allocation of resources to nationalised industries is a very important
part of the allocation of resources in the public sector generally. Its importance is
evidenced in this case by the fact that it was referred to Cabinet.

d   4. In my opinion it is necessary in the national interest for the proper functioning
of government in this country that documents of this kind, being documents
relating to the formulation of issues of Government policy at the highest level,
namely Cabinet Committees and Cabinet, should be withheld from production.
The importance of confidentiality for the inner-workings of government at this
level has been widely recognised and I respectfully refer to the observations of Lord
e   Reid in Conway v. Rimmer ([1968] 1 All ER 874 at 888, [1968] AC 910 at 952). Since
that judgment the confidentiality of Cabinet proceedings has been considered by
two independent committees, the Franks Committee on section 2 of the Official
Secrets Act 1911 (Cmnd 5104) and the Radcliffe Committee on Ministerial Memoirs
(Cmnd 6386). Both reaffirmed without qualification the importance of preserving
the confidentiality of the proceedings in Cabinet and Cabinet Committees.

f   5. The policies under consideration in these documents are of recent date and
remain of topical significance. The question of landing fees at Heathrow continues
to be a sensitive issue and the persons involved in the earlier decision are still active
in public life.

6. In my capacity as Secretary of the Cabinet I am concerned to maintain the
confidentiality of the decision-making process in the Cabinet and its Committees
g   and the formulation of policy within them. That confidentiality may be prejudiced
not only by the disclosure of formal Cabinet Office documents but also of documents
within Departments dealing with the formulation of policy on subjects on which
decisions have been or will be taken in the Cabinet or its Committees. Discussions
in Cabinet Committees and in the Cabinet are made on the basis of papers prepared
within Departments which are circulated by the Cabinet Secretariat to the
h   Committees or to the Cabinet. The actual document, whether Cabinet Committee
paper or Cabinet paper, is normally drafted in the Department responsible for that
item, and the nature of its contents is likely to evidenced not only by those
departmental documents directly involved in its formulation, but also by other
documents leading to the establishment of a departmental view which is then
embodied in the paper submitted to Cabinet or Cabinet Committee for discussion,
j   and, in those departments not responsible for the paper, by briefs to their ministers
on the paper. Moreover, documents prepared for the Cabinet or Cabinet Committee
by one Department may well have been the subject of communication between
Departments at ministerial or official level. In the case of documents such as those
that are the subject of this certificate affecting nationalised industries with several
different sponsoring departments subject to numerous and differing political

pressures this will inevitably have been the case. For these reasons the confidentiality of the decision-making process of the Cabinet and its Committees may well be *a* prejudiced by the disclosure of such departmental and interdepartmental documents.

8. The discussion of policies by Cabinet Committees or the Cabinet itself is evidence that those policies are matters of the highest national importance. They remain so when being dealt with departmentally. I would respectfully agree with the remarks of Lord Reid in *Conway v. Rimmer* where he having dealt with the necessity for protecting "Cabinet Minutes and the like" from disclosure goes on to *b* add: "And that must, in my view, also apply to all documents concerned with policy making within departments including, it may be, minutes and the like by quite junior officials and correspondence with outside bodies." They are all part of the decision-making process which culminates at Cabinet or Cabinet Committee level.

9. I understand that oral evidence may be given in these proceedings. If oral evidence were sought to be given of the contents of any of the documents to the *c* production of which I have in this certificate objected, I would wish to object to such evidence on the same grounds as those hereinbefore set out in relation to the documents in question.'

I have read Sir Robert Armstrong's certificate because it is important that it should be permanently on record.

d

6. THE LAW

This brings me at long last to the law. Counsel for the Secretary of State told us that the government regarded this case as the most important since *Conway v Rimmer* [1968] 1 All ER 874, [1968] AC 910. I hope I shall be forgiven, therefore, if I go into it at some *e* length.

This is another branch of the law which has changed beyond recognition during my time. When I was at the Bar the Crown had a prerogative which was called 'Crown privilege'. The law said that the Crown was entitled to full discovery against the subject, but the subject as against the Crown was not entitled to any discovery at all. 'That is a prerogative of the Crown, part of the law of England': see *A-G v Newcastle-upon-Tyne Corp* *f* [1897] 2 QB 384 at 395, [1895–9] All ER Rep 747 at 750 per Rigby LJ. As a derivative of this prerogative, it was held that if a minister came to the courts and certified that it was contrary to the public interest that a document or a class of documents should be disclosed, that certificate was conclusive. The courts of law could not go behind the certificate. The documents were shut out altogether. No one could see them. In the nineteenth century this prerogative was carried so far that the Crown, through its *g* ministers, used to object to disclosing reports made by police officers on street accidents, or by naval officers on a collision at sea. These reports would have been of the greatest value in eliciting the true facts, but the courts were deprived of the use of them, by the *ipse dixit* of a minister or, if he was not available, by the permanent head of his department. This approach was upheld by the strongest House of Lords that could be mustered at the time: seven of them. It was in 1942 in *Duncan v Cammell Laird & Co Ltd* *h* [1942] 1 All ER 587, [1942] AC 624. The whole House said, in a single unanimous judgment, that the certificate was conclusive. They added, however, that the minister—

'ought not to take the responsibility of withholding production except in cases where the public interest would otherwise be damnified, e.g., where disclosure would be injurious to national defence, or to good diplomatic relations, or where the practice of keeping a class of documents secret is necessary for the proper *j* functioning of the public service. When these conditions are satisfied and the minister feels it is his duty to deny access to material which would otherwise be available, there is no question but that the public interest must be preferred to any private consideration.'

(See [1942] 1 All ER 587 at 595, [1942] AC 624 at 642–643.)

Five years later there came the Crown Proceedings Act 1947. It enabled actions to be
a brought against government departments. In s 28(1) it enabled orders to be made against
them for discovery. But there was an express proviso preserving Crown privilege as laid
down in *Duncan v Cammell Laird*. It said that this section shall be—

'without prejudice to any rule of law which authorises or requires the withholding
of any document or the refusal to answer any question on the ground that the
disclosure of the document or the answering of the question would be injurious to
b the public interest.'

After I became Master of the Rolls in 1962 we launched an attack on this 'Crown
privilege'. By good fortune or design the court was composed in three successive cases by
the same three of us. My brethren Harman and Salmon LJJ and myself. We were called
'the three musketeers'. Our attack made good progress. We shot down one certificate
c after another for some reason or other. We were much helped by some good marksmen
from the Commonwealth. But then we suffered a reverse. There came a fourth case. It
was *Conway v Rimmer* [1967] 2 All ER 1260, [1967] 1 WLR 1031. By chance and not by
design the court by that time was differently composed. It was Davies and Russell LJJ
and myself. I fought hard. But the other two brought up their reserves. They held that
they were bound by *Duncan v Cammell Laird*. 'The three musketeers' were driven back. I
d was taken prisoner. But then from over the hill there came, most unexpectedly, a relief
force. It was the House of Lords themselves, in *Conway v Rimmer* [1968] 1 All ER 874,
[1968] AC 910. The House declared that they were no longer bound by their previous
decisions. They held that the certificate of the minister was not conclusive. They held
that they could themselves examine the documents and see whether the disclosure would
be prejudicial to the public interest or not. They overruled the certificate in that case,
e and ordered production of the documents.
This decision of the House did not do away with the prerogative. It still remained
open to a minister of the Crown to give a certificate objecting to the disclosure of a
document or a class of documents on the ground that it would be prejudicial to the
public interest. Although the certificate is no longer conclusive, it is to be given great
weight. It is not to be overriden unless the court is of opinion that the disclosure of the
f documents is necessary for fairly disposing of the matter or, to put it another way,
necessary for the due administration of justice. That is the result, as I see it, of the four
cases in modern times in the House of Lords where the minister has given a certificate or
the equivalent. They are *R v Lewes Justices, ex p Secretary of State for the Home Dept* [1972]
2 All ER 1057, [1973] AC 388, *Alfred Crompton Amusement Machines Ltd v Customs and
Excise Comrs (No 2)* [1973] 2 All ER 1169, [1974] AC 405, *Burmah Oil Co Ltd v Bank of
g England* [1979] 3 All ER 700, [1980] AC 1090 and *Lonrho v Shell Petroleum Co Ltd* [1980] 1
WLR 627. In none of those cases was the certificate overruled. Several of their Lordships
said that the judges were to strike a balance between the public interest in the proper
functioning of the public service (ie the executive arm of government) and the public
interest in the administration of justice: see for instance Lord Pearson in the *Lewes Justices*
case [1972] 2 All ER 1057 at 1065, [1973] AC 388 at 406 and Lord Scarman in the *Burmah
h Oil* case [1979] 3 All ER 700 at 734, [1980] AC 1090 at 1145. But, in holding the balance,
the scales are tilted in favour of the certificate of the minister. If he has directed himself
rightly and has considered the documents rightly, with reasons which commend
themselves to the court, the court is very unlikely to overthrow it.
It is altogether different when the minister has not given a certificate or its equivalent.
Then no question of Crown privilege arises. The distinction appears from the many cases
j in recent years on confidential information. The courts have often had to balance the
public interest in preserving confidences against the public interest in the due
administration of justice. Sometimes the scales have come down in favour of maintaining
confidences completely, as in *D v National Society for the Prevention of Cruelty to Children*
[1977] 1 All ER 589, [1978] AC 171. At other times in maintaining them partially, as in
Science Research Council v Nassé [1979] 3 All ER 673, [1980] AC 1028. In the Court of
Appeal we have often had to do this balancing act. We have come down sometimes in

favour of preserving confidences (as in *Gaskin v Liverpool City Council* [1980] 1 WLR 1549 and *Neilson v Laugharne* [1981] 1 All ER 829, [1981] QB 736) and sometimes against them (as in *Campbell v Tameside BC* [1982] 2 All ER 791, [1982] 3 WLR 74).

7. OVERRIDING THE CERTIFICATE

There is no doubt that the court can override the certificate, but it should only do so when it is necessary in the interest of justice. It was done in the United States where the Supreme Court overrode the prerogative of President Nixon (see *Nixon v United States* (1974) 418 US 683), and in Australia where the High Court overrode the objections of the Commonwealth government (see *Sankey v Whitlam* (1978) 53 ALJR 11). It is similar to the rule about confidential communications when they are made to a clergyman, a banker or a medical man. This appears from the decision of the House of Lords in *British Steel Corp v Granada Television Ltd* [1981] 1 All ER 417, [1981] AC 1096, where their Lordships approved what I said in *A-G v Mulholland* [1963] 1 All ER 767 at 771, [1963] 2 QB 477 at 489–490:

'The judge will respect the confidences which each member of these honourable professions receives in the course of it, and will not direct him to answer unless not only it is relevant but also it is a proper and, indeed, necessary question in the course of justice to be put and answered.'

8. A LESSON FROM EXPERIENCE

A recent case teaches us to give great weight to the certificate of the minister, and not to override it except in extreme cases. In *Williams v Home Office* [1981] 1 All ER 1151 Mr Williams sued the Home Office for subjecting him to cruel and unusual punishment. He criticised the policy of a 'special control unit'. The Home Office had in their possession the minutes of high level policy meetings within the department. They claimed public interest immunity for them. McNeill J overruled their objection. He thought that there was a safeguard in that they could only be used for the purposes of the action: see *Riddick v Thames Board Mills* [1977] 3 All ER 677, [1977] QB 881. So the Home Office did disclose them. His decision was claimed by the advocates of 'open government' to be a 'legal milestone'. But the safeguard proved to be no safeguard at all. The documents were used by a journalist to make severe criticisms of ministers and of higher civil servants who could not answer back. When this was brought to our attention, I said: 'The "legal milestone" will have to be taken up and set back a bit': see *Home Office v Harman* [1981] 2 All ER 349 at 364, [1981] QB 534 at 558.

That case is a good illustration of the need for keeping high-level documents secret. Once they are let out of the bag, untold mischief may be done. It is no use relying on safeguards. The documents must not be let out of the bag at all. I trust that today we are setting back the 'legal milestone' to the place where it was before.

9. THE 'DUE ADMINISTRATION OF JUSTICE'

In all the cases it is said that the courts are required to have regard to the public interest in the 'due administration of justice'. But I would point out that this depends on the nature of the issue between the parties. In some cases it means simply ascertaining the truth, finding out what in fact happened, and then adjusting the rights and liabilities of the parties on the faith of it. That is how the judge regarded our present case. He said (see p 167, ante):

'... the concern of the court must surely be to ensure that the truth is elicited, not caring whether the truth favours one party or the other but anxious that its final decision should be grounded on a sure foundation of fact ... In my judgment documents are necessary for fairly disposing of a cause or for the due administration of justice if they give substantial assistance to the court in determining the facts on which the decision in the cause will depend.'

That is why he thought that the ministerial documents in category A should be disclosed. He said (see p 170, ante):

'I consider that some of these documents are very likely to be necessary for the just determination of the second and third issues in the plaintiffs' constitutional case. They are very likely to affect the outcome one way or the other. I do not think any court could be confident that its decision on those issues was grounded on a sure foundation of fact in the absence of the documents.'

10. I DIFFER FROM THE JUDGE

This is where I differ from the judge. The 'due administration of justice' does not always depend on eliciting the truth. It often depends on the burden of proof. Many times it requires the complainant to prove his case without any discovery from the other side.

Where a man is charged with a crime, no matter how serious or how minor it may be, the prosecution must prove the case against him without any disclosure from him of any documents that he has. When a public authority is accused of any abuse or misuse of its power, or any non-performance of its public duties (in proceedings for mandamus or certiorari or under RSC Ord 53), the accuser must make out his case without the help of any discovery save in most exceptional cases. No one has ever doubted the 'justice' of those proceedings. Now let us take the same accusation against a public authority but made in an action for a declaration. Does this different mode of procedure alter the 'justice' of the case? Ought not the rule of discovery to be the same whichever procedure is adopted? Then take legal professional privilege. A defendant may have made the most self-revealing statements to his lawyer. He may have given his whole case away to him. But 'justice' demands that this should not be disclosed to the other side. If the plaintiff fails to prove his case, for want of any admission by the defendant, no injustice is done to him. Even though the truth may not have been ascertained, no injustice is done. In these cases all that 'justice' requires is that there should be a fair determination of the case whatever the real truth may be. Likewise, when a plaintiff alleges that the defendant has done him some wrong, but has no evidence whatever to support it, he seeks to obtain it by making a 'fishing expedition'. He asks to see all the documents of the other side so as to see if he can get some evidence out of them. The court invariably refuses. It refuses because 'justice' requires that he should have some material to go on before he goes a-fishing.

So I hold that when we speak of the 'due administration of justice' this does not always mean ascertaining the truth of what happened. It often means that, as a matter of justice, the party must prove his case without any help from the other side. He must do it without discovery and without putting him into the box to answer questions.

11. APPLIED TO THIS CASE

I start with the certificate. It gives clear and cogent reasons for keeping these documents secret. It is because of the public interest in the proper functioning of the public service (ie the executive arm of government). I see no reason whatever for overriding the certificate. It is 'not necessary' in the interests of the due administration of justice. If the airlines have sufficient evidence to warrant their charges against the minister, they are in a strong position. They can put forward their evidence, and he will be in much difficulty in refuting it. He cannot himself refer to these documents nor can he give oral evidence about them or the conversations they record. But if the airlines have no, or no sufficient, evidence to warrant their charges against the minister, then they ought 'in justice' to lose their case. They should not be permitted to rove through these documents in order to see if they can discover something. The sight of them is 'not necessary for fairly disposing of the matter'. The airlines would be on a 'fishing expedition'. They would be hoping to catch a fish where none were rising to the fly. A forlorn hope as all fishermen know. If they have a grievance, but no evidence, they should get some member of Parliament to raise it in the House and move for papers. It is not a matter for the courts of law.

12. INSPECTION

Both in *Conway v Rimmer* and in *Burmah Oil v Bank of England* the House of Lords inspected the documents. In the one they ordered production; in the other they did not. It all depends on the certificate. If it describes documents in sufficient detail and gives *a* the reasons with sufficient clarity, that should be sufficient for the judge to refuse production without more ado. Inspection is only necessary where the certificate is lacking in detail or the reasons are not clearly or sufficiently expressed, or the scales are very evenly balanced. In that case, if the judge is minded to override the certificate and order production, he should inspect the documents before doing so. But even so, he should give the minister an opportunity to appeal as the judge did here. In *Conway v Rimmer* the *b* House thought that the report to the Director of Public Prosecutions was in the balance. In *Burmah Oil v Bank of England* the majority of their Lordships felt that they could not adequately perform the balancing exercise without inspecting the documents. In the present case I feel no doubt. I see no need for any inspection. The certificates are clear and convincing. They satisfy me that the documents in both categories A and B should not be disclosed.   *c*

13. CONCLUSION
I would pay tribute to the judgment of Bingham J. It is quite admirable. He is an acknowledged authority on the subject. He was engaged in many of the leading cases on it. So much so that I differ from him with much hesitation. If it were only on discretion, I would have accepted his view. But I differ because of his interpretation of the phrase *d* the 'due administration of justice'. He has interpreted it as meaning 'eliciting the true facts', whereas I interpret it as meaning the 'just decision of the case'. Those documents in categories A and B are not necessary for fairly disposing of the matter. They should not be disclosed. I would allow the appeal accordingly.

WATKINS LJ. The British Airports Authority (BAA) runs its vast undertaking at a *e* profit. It is one of the few industries in the public sector which does so. It has to a considerable extent, if not entirely so, to conduct itself as to conform to the provisions of the Airports Authority Act 1975, some of which confer powers on the Secretary of State designed to control that conduct in several ways.

In 1979 BAA decided to embark on improving the facilities for the world's airlines at Heathrow and elsewhere. This venture was calculated to cost something in the region of *f* £600m. BAA had at that time £19m in reserve. It determined to use this reserve to meet in part this cost and to provide the remainder from borrowings from the government and elsewhere. The Secretary of State refused to countenance this. He told BAA that it would have to maintain its reserves and pay the cost of any improved facilities that it wished to provide by increasing landing charges. So BAA kept its reserves, did not borrow money and increased the landing charges which it has an implied power to *g* impose by 35%.

The plaintiffs and many other foreign airlines strenuously object to the imposition of this substantial increase and by the present action seek to test the legality of its imposition. They maintain among other things that the intereference by the Secretary of State with BAA's proposed method of meeting the cost of improved facilities was unlawful. They say, and he denies, that he imposed a financial target on the BAA when he had no power, *h* discretionary or otherwise, to do so. Furthermore, in placing an embargo on borrowing, he was moved to do that by the then prevailing government economic policy, which was of general application in the public sector, whereas he should have confined himself strictly within the obligations and duties arising out of the 1975 Act. Use of such power was ultra vires and, so they say further, assuming he exercised any kind of discretion in the use of it, he exercised it wrongly, ie out of accord with what has become known as *j* the *Wednesbury* rule: see *Associated Provincial Pictures Houses Ltd v Wednesbury Corp* [1947] 2 All ER 680, [1948] 1 KB 223. The Secretary of State denies these allegations also. This has been called the plaintiffs' constitutional case. There are others which divide the parties, namely the economic, the Community law (BAA is said to be in breach of the EEC Treaty) and the feather-bedding cases, but with these we are not concerned.

I say no more of the origins of and the issues arising out of this action, seeing that Lord
Denning MR has already explained them in considerable and necessary detail. Needless
to say we are appealed to against Bingham J's decision, which is challenged by the
Secretary of State, to order production by him of public documents, the nature of which
has been amply disclosed. The judge has called this a provisional order because it is, as I
have said, subject to his prior inspection of these documents.

The Secretary of State claims public interest immunity in respect of them and, through
certificates placed before the court on his behalf, has explained his reasons why none of
the documents in contention should be produced for any purpose in relation to the
constitutional issue which alone has prompted the plaintiffs to seek discovery of them.
The plaintiffs accept that the claim for public interest immunity has been validly made
but contend that, in the interests of the due administration of justice, they have a superior
overriding claim to discovery of the documents, irrespective of whether they assist them.
They have already had discovery of relevant documents which passed between the
Secretary of State and BAA. That does not satisfy them. They want to enter and roam
about the cloisters of the Department of Trade and thereafter proceed as far as the Cabinet
Office. It is to this which the Secretary of State, not surprisingly, objects. It is plain, as the
judge found, that the documents they want to see have passed to and fro at a very high
level of government. I do not think there can be any doubt that, having regard also to
certificates which were not before the judge, but which we received, the Secretary of
State has made a formidable claim for immunity which cannot be easily overridden in
litigation of this kind. Nevertheless, the judge regarded the plaintiffs' claim as superior
and asserted that he was not concerned about which side, if any, discovery might assist.
The concern of the court, he said, was with the ascertainment of the truth because its
final decision should be grounded on a sure foundation of fact. I must confess to having
found this approach to discovery, however morally impeccable and desirable the purpose
of it may appear to be, novel in my experience in the adversarial scene in this kind of
litigation. Lord Denning MR has commented on it. I agree, generally speaking, with
what he has said and therefore say little more of it. So I pass to another consideration
strenuously argued before us.

In assessing the merits of the competing claims for and against discovery the judge
conducted a balancing exercise. He brought a judicial discretion to bear on the
formulation of his decision which is not lightly to be set aside.

In *Burmah Oil Co Ltd v Bank of England* [1979] 3 All ER 700 at 708, [1980] AC 1090 at
1113–1114 Lord Wilberforce said:

> 'I am therefore quite prepared to deal with this case on the basis that the courts
> may, in a suitable case, decide that a high level governmental public interest must
> give way to the interests of the administration of justice. But it must be clear what
> this involves. A claim for public interest immunity having been made, on manifestly
> solid grounds, it is necessary for those who seek to overcome it to demonstrate the
> existence of a counteracting interest calling for disclosure of particular documents.
> When this is demonstrated, but only then, may the court proceed to a balancing
> process. In *Conway v Rimmer* [1968] 1 All ER 874, [1968] AC 910 itself it was known
> that there were in existence probationary reports on the plaintiff as to which an
> obviously strong argument could be made that their disclosure was necessary if the
> plaintiff's claim were to have any hope of succeeding (in the end they turned out to
> be far from helpful to him), so the court had something very definite to go on which
> it could put into the scales against the (minor) public interest of not revealing
> routine reports.'

He went on to say, when referring to inspection of documents ([1979] 3 All ER 700 at
711, [1980] AC 1090 at 1117):

> 'As to principle, I cannot think that it is desirable that the courts should assume
> the task of inspection except in rare instances where a strong positive case is made

out, certainly not on a bare unsupported assertion by the party seeking production
that something to help him may be found, or on some unsupported, viz speculative, *a*
hunch of its own. In the first place it is necessary to draw a reasonably clear line
between the responsibility of Ministers on the one hand, and those of the courts on
the other. Each has its proper contribution to make towards solution of the problem
where the public interest lies; judicial review is not a "bonum in se", it is a part, and
a valuable one, of democratic government in which other responsibilities coexist.
Existing cases, from *Conway v Rimmer* onwards, have drawn this line carefully and *b*
suitably. It is for the Minister to define the public interest and the grounds on which
he considers that production would affect it. Similarly, the court, responsible for the
administration of justice, should, before it decides that the Minister's view must
give way, have something positive or identifiable to put into the scales. To override
the Minister's opinion by "amorphous" phrases, or unsupported contentions, would
be to do precisely what the courts will not countenance in the actions of Ministers.' *c*

Lord Wilberforce was in the minority in the *Burmah Oil* case but he said nothing in the
foregoing valuable quotations from his speech on the subject of the balancing of interests,
whether discovery generally or inspection of documents is being regarded, which does
not, I think, find universal acceptance.

The plaintiffs' arguments here for disclosure of the material documents when put *d*
under the microscope of critical examination seem to me to be very threadbare. They
have not, I think, pointed to any one of these documents successfully contending that it
is likely to assist their case.

Their cri de coeur is 'Who knows what we may find if we are given the opportunity to
search where we should like to?' They really do, in my judgment, fall into the category
of he who makes 'a bare unsupported assertion by the party seeking production that
something to help him may be found, or on some unsupported, viz speculative, hunch *e*
of its own'. They have produced nothing, in my view, positive or identifiable to put in
the scales. At any early stage in the argument I ventured to suggest that they had
embarked on a fishing expedition. The more I heard and have read and thought about
their claim since then, the more firmly entrenched I have become in that view.

In *Compagnie Financière et Commerciale du Pacifique v Peruvian Guano Co* (1882) 11 QBD *f*
55 at 63 Brett LJ, in regard to the contents of an affidavit of documents, stated:

'It seems to me that every document relates to the matters in question in the
action, which not only would be evidence upon any issue, but also which, it is
reasonable to suppose, contains information which *may*—not which *must*—either
directly or indirectly enable the party requiring the affidavit either to advance his
own case or to damage the case of his adversary. I have put in the words "either *g*
directly or indirectly," because, as it seems to me, a document can properly be said
to contain information which may enable the party requiring the affidavit either to
advance his own case or to damage the case of his adversary, if it is a document
which may fairly lead him to a train of inquiry, which may have either of these two
consequences . . .' (Brett LJ's emphasis.)
                                                                                        h
It is not suggested here that the Secretary of State has presented the plaintiffs with
other than a frank and full list of documents of the nature they have been requested to
produce. But when consideration is given to their claim to overbear the Secretary of
State's objection to produce them it seems to me that the plaintiffs have come nowhere
near establishing that there is any document in the list which may directly or indirectly
enable them to either advance their case or damage that of the defendants or to put them *j*
on to further useful inquiry. I observe in passing that there is no reference in the
guidance provided by Brett LJ to the need for ascertaining the truth in litigation. The
emphasis is, as I see it, on the gaining of assistance to improve the chance of discharging
the burden of proof which almost exclusively lies on a plaintiff to prove his case.
Discovery to this end can only be obtained in accordance with the rules of court.

If the judge, as I think with respect he did not and should have done, had regarded his task of balancing the interests along the lines I have been indicating, I think he would have come to a different conclusion.

Accordingly, he, in my opinion, exercised his discretion wrongly. It is, therefore, unnecessary to proceed to examine in the circumstances his somewhat perilous decision to inspect the documents by, for example, posing rhetorically such a question as, for example: 'Supposing he had on inspection found that the documents assisted the defendants and positively damaged the plaintiffs, would he then, against the defendants' will, have ordered them to be produced?' However, these and other interesting questions arising from the difficulties which confront a court when inspecting documents must lie in limbo in this appeal.

Finally, I wish to say that I am much persuaded by the argument of counsel for the Secretary of State that the constitutional case can satisfactorily and properly be examined and determined by the court on the documents already produced which passed between the Secretary of State and BAA. It seems to me that whether there has been an abuse of power by the Secretary of State will either emerge directly or by inference from those documents or not at all. If that be right there is nothing to be gained for the plaintiffs by their having a speculative look at papers from a higher level. They are not necessary for the due administration of justice and as such are more than likely to be surplusage and irrelevant.

For these reasons and for those provided by Lord Denning MR I, too, would allow this appeal.

FOX LJ. This appeal is concerned with the production of documents relating to very high levels of government. They are, to an important extent, what the judge called the 'working papers' of ministers of both the present and previous governments. The documents are of two categories. Category A consists of communications between, to and from ministers (including personal secretaries on their behalf), minutes, briefs and other documents for ministers and memoranda of meetings attended by them.

These documents relate to (a) the formulation of the policy of the previous government in relation to the policy of the British Airports Authority and the exercise of the Secretary of State's powers relating to borrowing under the Airports Authority Act 1975, having regard to that government's policy of trying to limit public sector borrowing, (b) the formulation of the policy of the present government regarding the limitation of public sector borrowing with particular reference to the exercise of the Secretary of State's powers to control the authority's borrowing and the effect of the authority's plans for capital expenditure, (c) the formulation of the policy of the present government regarding the authority's proposals for landing fees for 1980–81, (d) the formulation of the policy of the present government in the light of representations by MP's and various airlines using Heathrow.

The category B documents consist of communications between, to and from senior officials of various departments of state, memoranda of meetings of such officials and drafts prepared by them, all of which relate to the formulation of one or more aspects of the policy to which I have referred in relation to category A.

The category A and B documents are those to which the judgment of Bingham J relates. Since the judgment, certain further documents (which I will call 'the Cabinet documents') have come to light which are specified in the certificate made by Sir Robert Armstrong on 23 June 1982, a few days before the hearing of this appeal began. These documents are six in number. Two are papers submitted to a cabinet committee and the third an extract from a minute of that committee. The others are a paper submitted to the Cabinet, a note of the Cabinet's discussion regarding the Cabinet's decision on that paper, and a letter from the Chief Secretary to the Treasury to the Secretary of State for Energy which was copied to members of the Cabinet committee which I have mentioned as it dealt with the subject matter of their discussion. As I understand it, the plaintiffs' counsel, though without formal instructions on the matter, was not disposed to press for disclosure of the Cabinet documents. It is, therefore, the category A and B documents with which we are concerned.

It is not in dispute that the certificates claiming immunity, which have been tendered on behalf of the Crown, constitute valid claims for immunity on recognised grounds.

Under the general principles established in *Conway v Rimmer* [1968] 1 All ER 874, [1968] AC 910 and *Burmah Oil Co Ltd v Bank of England* [1979] 3 All ER 700, [1980] AC 1090, the court having been satisfied that the Crown has made a valid claim for immunity, the next question is whether the party seeking disclosure has shown that the disclosure of the documents is, in the language of RSC Ord 24, r 13, 'necessary . . . for disposing fairly of the cause or matter'. If the court is satisfied on those points, it must then consider the relative substance of the competing claims for disclosure and non-disclosure. There is a public interest in each: that is to say in the due administration of justice and in the preservation of the confidentiality of the documents in question.

There are passages in the speeches in the House of Lords in *Conway v Rimmer* which suggest that, with documents of the level of those with which the present case is concerned, no considerations relating to the administration of justice will prevail against the public interest in preventing disclosure. Thus Lord Reid said ([1968] 1 All ER 874 at 888, [1968] AC 910 at 952):

> 'I do not doubt that there are certain classes of documents which ought not to be disclosed whatever their content may be. Virtually everyone agrees that cabinet minutes and the like ought not to be disclosed until such time as they are only of historical interest; but I do not think that many people would give as the reason that premature disclosure would prevent candour in the cabinet. To my mind the most important reason is that such disclosure would create or fan ill-informed or captious public or political criticism. . . . That must in my view also apply to all documents concerned with policy making within departments including it may be minutes and the like by quite junior officials and correspondence with outside bodies.'

Lord Pearce said ([1968] 1 All ER 874 at 910, [1968] AC 910 at 987):

> 'Obviously production would never be ordered of fairly wide classes of documents at a high level. To take an extreme case, production would never be ordered of cabinet correspondence, letters or reports on appointments to offices of importance and the like . . .'

And Lord Upjohn said ([1968] 1 All ER 874 at 914, [1968] AC 910 at 993):

> 'No doubt there are many cases in which documents by their very nature fall into a class which requires protection such as, only by way of example, cabinet papers, foreign office despatches, the security of the State, high level inter-departmental minutes and correspondence . . .'

But *Burmah Oil* represents, perhaps, a more flexible approach: see the speeches of Lord Keith and Lord Scarman ([1979] 3 All ER 700 at 724–725, 733, [1980] AC 1090 at 1133–1134, 1144). Lord Wilberforce observed ([1979] 3 All ER 700 at 708, [1980] AC 1090 at 1113):

> 'It may well be arguable whether, when one is faced with a claim for immunity from production on "public interest" grounds, and when the relevant public interest is shown to be of a high, or the highest, level of importance, that'fact is of itself conclusive, and nothing which relates to the interest in the administration of justice can prevail against it.'

He went on to say that he was quite prepared to deal with the case—

> 'on the basis that the courts may, in a suitable case, decide that a high level governmental public interest must give way to the interests of the administration of justice.'

I will, for present purposes, assume the same basis.

Now, in dealing with the question whether the plaintiffs have demonstrated that the production of the documents is necessary for disposing fairly of the case or, put another way, for the due administration of justice, there is a fundamental difference of approach between the plaintiffs and the Secretary of State. The plaintiffs say that documents are necessary for the due administration of justice if they are material in the sense that they are likely to affect the decision on those issues irrespective of whether they are helpful or unhelpful to the party seeking production. The Secretary of State, on the other hand, says that the party seeking production must show that the documents are likely to assist his case. The judge accepted the plaintiffs' contention. 'Justice,' he said (see p 167, ante), 'is as greatly affronted where a plaintiff is wrongly awarded relief as where he is wrongly denied it.' That, in a broad sense, is true but, in relation to individual cases, it depends on what is meant by 'wrongly'. The issue here is whether disclosure is necessary for disposing fairly of the case. If a document supports the defendant's case and he lawfully chooses not to produce it, there is no affront to justice and no unfairness though it may cause him to lose a case which he could otherwise have won. To that extent, the result may be said to be 'wrong'. But the defendant has had his chance and he has chosen to place some other consideration above his interest in winning the action. The law does, in many cases, accept that material facts may be withheld from the scrutiny of the court. The mere existence of a law of privilege postulates that. And there are cases where a party to litigation decides, for reasons of delicacy or humanity, not to call a witness whose evidence is highly material to his case. In an adversarial system that is acceptable. The logic of the plaintiffs' contention, on the other hand, seems to result in this: that the more a document is likely to help the Secretary of State's case the more likely he is to be compelled to produce it or to submit to judgment. The alternative is that if, on inspection, a document is found wholly to support the case of the party resisting discovery he need not produce it. But, if that be so, then the idea of an even-handed inquiry to ascertain the true facts cannot really stand. In the circumstances, I do not feel able to accept the judge's approach on this point.

What, then, should be the approach of the court? As a preliminary to the consideration of that, I should refer to the nature of the plaintiffs' claim on the constitutional case (with which alone the present issue is concerned). There are, as the judge found, three threads in that. The first is that the Secretary of State imposed a financial target on the British Airports Authority. All communications between the minister and the authority have, however, been disclosed and I agree with the judge that it is unlikely that internal ministry documents would be material.

The second point is that the Secretary of State exercised his powers for purposes other than those for which they were given to him. The third thread, which is very similar to the second, is that the Secretary of State both took into account considerations which he ought not to have done and failed to take into account considerations which he should have considered. The judge decided that the category A documents (which are at ministerial, rather than merely departmental, level) but not the category B documents, were likely to affect the outcome one way or another. He distinguished the category A documents from the category B documents on the basis that it was the minister's thinking that was crucial. Accordingly, the judge decided that, thus far, a public interest was demonstrated in the production of the category A documents, but that he should inspect them before ordinary disclosure.

The judge's conclusion was, of course, based on the approach which I have already mentioned and with which I do not agree. The judge stated that, if it were necessary for the plaintiffs to show a likelihood that the documents, if produced, would help them, he could not, on the material available, conclude that they had done so. I agree with that, both in relation to the category A and the category B documents. The documents might help the plaintiffs or they might not. It is guesswork. What, then, is the court to do? Here are documents which are admittedly relevant and which might possibly contain material of consequence to the resolution of the plaintiffs' constitutional claim. Should the court look at them to see if they are of assistance? In my view, the court should not. I think that the party seeking disclosure should normally have to show that there is a

reasonable likelihood that the documents will assist his case. That is necessary to prevent
'fishing'. The mere fact that the documents are relevant cannot be sufficient. The *a*
documents will always be relevant in these cases, otherwise the question would not arise
at all; it would not be necessary to claim immunity. I refer on this problem to the
observations of Lord Edmund-Davies in *Burmah Oil Co Ltd v Bank of England* [1979] 3 All
ER 700 at 721, [1980] AC 1090 at 1129 where, after referring to a contention that the
proposition that, if the judge is in doubt, he should inspect the documents should not
apply where a 'class' claim to immunity is not challenged, he said: *b*

> 'I see no reason why this should be so, once it is postulated that the withheld
> "class" documents are "likely" to contain material substantially useful to the party
> seeking discovery. That qualification is necessary, for what is no more than a "fishing
> expedition" ought not to be advanced by the judge's having a peep to see whether
> they contain an attractive catch. But, provided such reservation is rigidly adhered
> to, a judicial peep seems to be justifiable in both cases and may, indeed, prove vital *c*
> in each if the judge is to be enabled to arrive at a just conclusion in the matter of
> discovery.'

As I have indicated, I do not think that it can be said that it is 'likely' or that there is a
'reasonable probability' that these documents will disclose material of assistance to the
plaintiffs. All that one can say is that it is possible that they might.   *d*
At this point I should refer to the Crown's case, as disclosed in the certificates, for
immunity. Broadly, it is this. All the documents (in both categories) relate to the
formulation of government policy at a high level involving matters of major economic
importance to the United Kingdom. The allocation of resources to the various sectors of
the economy is one of the most important of the functions of government. The
documents are in no way routine. The category A documents are intended for the *e*
guidance of or to record the views of the Secretary of State for Trade, the Chancellor of
the Exchequer, the Chief Secretary to the Treasury, and the Secretary of State for Industry.
The Secretary of the Cabinet, Sir Robert Armstrong, states that many of the category A
documents came into existence for the purpose either of preparing ministers for meetings
of the Cabinet or developing in detail decisions reached at Cabinet meetings or meetings
of Cabinet committees. In his opinion, the disclosure of such documents would gravely *f*
prejudice the confidentiality of the decision making process of the Cabinet and its
committees.
The category B documents, though passing at a lower level, all relate to policy decisions
to be taken at a higher level. Inevitably, decisions taken by ministers have to be preceded
by discussions within and between departments.
The policy considerations underlying the documents remain of topical significance *g*
'since the events giving rise to the actions took place recently and the question of landing
fees at Heathrow is still a matter of active governmental consideration' (see Sir Kenneth
Clucas's certificate of 26 June 1981). Sir Robert Armstrong in his certificate of 23 June
1982 states that the question of landing fees at Heathrow continues to be a sensitive issue.
The general ground of public interest on which the claim for immunity is made is
that set out in the passage from the speech of Lord Reid in *Conway v Rimmer* to which I *h*
have already referred.
It seems to me that the Crown makes out a very strong case that, in the interests of the
proper functioning of government and the public service, the confidentiality of these
documents should be preserved. Cabinet papers apart, it is difficult to imagine a much
stronger case in respect of 'class' documents. Accepting that such public interest may be
overriden by the public interest in the administration of justice, I do not think that the *j*
plaintiffs have demonstrated the existence of such an interest here. I am not satisfied that
the documents are likely to assist the plaintiffs' case or that a case for inspection is made
out. Nor, in general, does it seem to me that the interests of justice are likely to be
interfered with by refusing disclosure. The issue, substantially, is whether the plaintiffs
can establish that the Secretary of State took into account the wrong considerations or

acted for the wrong purpose so that his decision is assailable under the principles of *Associated Provincial Picture Houses Ltd v Wednesbury Corp* [1947] 2 All ER 680, [1948] 1 KB 223. It is not in dispute that the matter can properly be raised in this action, but it is the sort of issue which would normally be raised in an application under RSC Ord 53 on which discovery would not, in most cases, be ordered. If the complainant made out a prima facie case, either the minister would have to disclose his documents in order to meet it or submit to an order. Similarly here. The Secretary of State has made it clear during the argument that he does not intend to call any evidence on this part of the action. Consistently with his view as to the public interest in preserving the confidentiality of the ministerial discussions he cannot do so. He intends merely to assert that the plaintiffs' evidence shows no prima facie case entitling them to relief. Either the plaintiffs can show a prima facie case or they cannot. If they can they should succeed. If they cannot, I do not think that, in such a case as the present, where a very strong argument for immunity is made out, the public interest requires that the court should search the Crown's documents on the chance that something might be found to assist the plaintiffs' case. In short, I think that the Crown show a substantial public interest in preserving the confidentiality of the documents and no sufficient public interest in disclosure or inspection with a view to disclosure has been demonstrated. I would allow the appeal.

Appeal allowed. Plaintiffs' cross-appeal dismissed. Leave to appeal to House of Lords.

Solicitors: *Treasury Solicitor; Freshfields* (for Air Canada); *Slaughter & May* (for Pan American World Airways Inc).

Diana Procter   Barrister.

R v Fitzmaurice

COURT OF APPEAL, CRIMINAL DIVISION
O'CONNOR LJ, NEILL AND TAYLOR JJ
29 APRIL, 8 JULY 1982

Criminal law – Incitement – Commission of crime – Impossibility of committing crime – Defendant at father's request encouraging another to rob a woman – Defendant believing robbery would take place – Proposed robbery merely a device by the father to enable him to collect police reward for false information about a false bank raid – Whether defendant guilty of incitement to commit an offence – Whether impossibility of committing proposed offence preventing commission of incitement to commit the offence.

The appellant was asked by his father to find someone to rob a woman on her way to a bank by snatching wages from her. The appellant, believing the robbery was to take place, approached B, who was unemployed and in need of money, and encouraged him to take part in the proposed robbery. In fact the proposed robbery was a fiction invented by the father to enable him to collect reward money from the police for providing false information about a false robbery from a security van outside the bank supposedly planned for the time when the father pretended the woman would be approaching the bank carrying wages. The appellant was convicted of inciting B to commit robbery by robbing a woman near the bank. He appealed against the conviction, contending that at common law incitement to commit an offence could not be committed where it was impossible to commit the offence incited, and that, since the proposed robbery of the woman was fictitious, it was impossible to commit that robbery.

Held – (1) At common law incitement to commit an offence could not be committed where it was impossible to commit the offence alleged to have been incited because the common law regarding incitement in that circumstance was the same as the common law regarding the other inchoate offences of attempting to commit an offence and conspiracy to commit an offence, namely that those inchoate offences could not be committed where it was impossible to commit the complete offence. Accordingly, in the case of incitement at common law, it was necessary to analyse the evidence to decide the precise offence which the defendant was alleged to have incited and whether it was possible to commit that offence (see p 191 c, p 193 e to g and p 194 c to e, post); DPP v Nock [1978] 2 All ER 654 applied; dictum of Lord Scarman in DPP v Nock [1978] 2 All ER at 663 considered; R v McDonough (1962) 47 Cr App R 37 explained.

(2) Since at the time the appellant encouraged B to carry out the proposed robbery the appellant believed that there was to be a wages snatch from a woman on her way to the bank, and since it would have been possible for B to carry out such a robbery, the appellant had incited B to carry out an offence which it would have been possible rather than impossible for B to commit. It followed that the appellant had been rightly convicted. Accordingly, the appeal would be dismissed (see p 191 c and p 194 e to h, post).

Notes

For incitement to commit an offence, see 11 Halsbury's Laws (4th edn) para 57, and for cases on the subject, see 14(1) Digest (Reissue) 115–118, 770–794.

Cases referred to in judgment

DPP v Nock, DPP v Alsford [1978] 2 All ER 654, [1978] AC 979, [1978] 3 WLR 57, HL, Digest (Cont Vol E) 130, 842a.

Haggard v Mason [1976] 1 All ER 337, [1976] 1 WLR 187, DC, 15 Digest (Reissue) 1077, 9171.

Haughton v Smith [1973] 3 All ER 1109, [1975] AC 476, [1974] 2 WLR 1, HL, 14(1) Digest (Reissue) 113, 756.

R v Hendrickson and Tichner [1977] Crim LR 356, CA.

R v McDonough (1962) 47 Cr App R 37, CCA, 15 Digest (Reissue) 1366, 11,939.

Race Relations Board v Applin [1973] 2 All ER 1190, [1973] 1 QB 815, CA; affd [1974] 2 All ER 73, [1975] AC 259, HL, 2 Digest (Reissue) 317, 1786.

Cases also cited

A-G's Reference (No 1 of 1975) [1975] 2 All ER 684, [1975] QB 773, CA.

DPP for Northern Ireland v Maxwell [1978] 3 All ER 1140, [1978] 1 WLR 1350, HL.

R v Bainbridge [1959] 3 All ER 200, [1960] 1 QB 129, CCA.

R v Banks (1873) 12 Cox CC 393.

R v Bentley [1923] 1 KB 403, CCA.

R v Brown (1899) 63 JP 790.

R v Christian (1913) 78 JP 112.

R v Shephard [1919] 2 KB 125, [1918–19] All ER Rep 374, CAA.

R v Tyrrell [1894] 1 QB 710, [1891–4] All ER Rep 1215, CCR.

R v Whitehouse [1977] 3 All ER 737, [1977] QB 868, CA.

R v Woolf [1930] Transvaal Law Reports 823.

Appeal

On 22 July 1981 at the Central Criminal Court (his Honour Judge Gwyn Morris QC) the appellant, Robert Fitzmaurice, was convicted of unlawfully inciting Terence Bonham, James Brown and Steven Brown to commit robbery and was sentenced to 12 months' imprisonment. With leave of a single judge he appealed against the conviction on the grounds, inter alia, that the judge should have withdrawn the case from the jury because it was impossible to commit the crime incited (the robbery) and that the judge misdirected the jury by saying that it was irrelevant that it would have been impossible to commit the robbery. The facts are set out in the judgment of the court.

David Cocks QC and Linda Dobbs for the appellant.
Paul Purnell QC for the Crown.

At the conclusion of argument the court announced that the appeal would be dismissed for reasons to be given later.

8 July. The following judgment of the court was delivered.

NEILL J. On 22 July 1981 the appellant was convicted at the Central Criminal Court of unlawfully inciting three men, Terence Bonham, James Brown and Steven Brown, to commit robbery by robbing a woman at Bow. He was sentenced to 12 months' imprisonment. The appellant was charged with two other men, but the charges against them were not proceeded with because they had already pleaded guilty in January 1981 to a number of other counts in the same indictment and had each been sentenced to four years' imprisonment. One of these other two men was the appellant's father.

The appellant appealed against his conviction by leave of the single judge. On 29 April 1982 the appellant's appeal was dismissed by this court. We now give the reasons for the dismissal of the appeal.

The facts of the case were unusual. They have been set out in a convenient form in an agreed statement of facts as follows. (1) On 28 September 1978, Bonham, James Brown and Steven Brown were arrested in Bow, East London, in a green van. Bonham was the driver and the Browns were each armed with an imitation firearm. All had sleeve masks and there was a pickaxe handle in the van. (2) Bonham and the others believed that they were there to carry out a wages snatch from a woman walking from her place of work to the bank. A security van was due to visit the National Westminster Bank in Bow Road at this time, and police officers had received information from the appellant's father that a robbery on the security van had been planned. All three were subsequently charged with conspiracy to rob a person on the basis of their account that they were there to rob a woman of money on her way to the bank and not the security van. At their trial they pleaded guilty to the conspiracy count and were sentenced to imprisonment. (3) Subsequent investigations revealed that the three men were the victims of a trick by the appellant's father, and had been set up to carry out a robbery by him so that he and his accomplice, Skipp, could collect the reward money for informing the police of an intended raid on the security van. That information was false and the invention of the appellant's father. (4) The appellant's father asked the appellant if he could find someone to carry out a robbery. The appellant approached Bonham, informed him of the proposed robbery, describing it as a 'wages snatch'. The appellant brought Bonham to an address where the appellant's father outlined the plan. The plan was to snatch wages from a woman carrying money from a factory to a bank in Bow. The appellant offered to participate, but was excluded. Bonham agreed to the plan. Later Bonham, who had recruited the two Browns, visited Bow with the appellant's father, but not the appellant. They saw a woman, in fact Skipp's girlfriend, walking from the factory to the bank. She was carrying a bag. The following week the appellant's father took Bonham and the two Browns to Bow again and pointed out where the getaway car would be left. On the day appointed, Bonham and the others met at the appellant's house. Imitation guns and masks were distributed. Bonham and the others left the premises and were subsequently arrested. The appellant believed throughout that the robbery plan was genuine and agreed to accept £200 and a television for his part. (5) On 5 June 1981, Bonham had his conviction for conspiracy set aside by the Court of Appeal on the grounds that the crime which he had conspired to commit was impossible of fulfilment. O'Connor LJ said:

> 'However morally culpable, the truth is that these three men had been fraudulently induced to agree to commit a crime which could not be committed in the strict sense; they were themselves the victims of a different conspiracy to which they were not parties.'

In support of the appellant's appeal to this court, his counsel put forward two submissions: (a) that the trial judge had misdirected the jury as to the meaning of 'incitement'; and (b) that the appellant could not be guilty of inciting other men to commit a crime which in fact could not be committed.

On his first submission, counsel drew our attention to a passage in the summing up. The judge said:

'The word "incitement" is a word which is used in widely differing circumstances. A person can incite another to envy or hatred. A person can also be incited to loyalty and patriotism. Here, the charge is that the [appellant] incited Mr Bonham to commit a crime. Now, the original approach by the [appellant] to Mr Bonham is not denied. There is no dispute about the fact that the [appellant] approached Mr Bonham, and it was an approach to him to commit a crime. There is no question about that. The [appellant] does not deny that Mr Bonham was an old friend of his, and that he knew at the time that he was out of work and needed money. You may conclude that an approach to Mr Bonham in those circumstances by the [appellant], whether it was a suggestion, a proposal or a request, was an approach that embodied naturally the promise of reward, that if he engaged in the enterprise he would get money. That prospect, you may think, was the most persuasive factor in the approach. If you take that view, then clearly you may think that there was incitement to commit the crime, in the broad sense I have indicated.'

Counsel for the appellant criticised this passage on the basis that it provided an unsatisfactory and inadequate definition of incitement because the judge did not sufficiently instruct the jury as to the necessity of proof that the appellant had persuaded or encouraged the commission of the robbery. He submitted that there was a clear distinction between the mere procurement of a crime and incitement. Procuration, he said, did not necessarily involve any persuasion or counselling of a third party by the defendant to commit the crime. Similarly, said counsel, a person may be liable as an accessory before the fact, for example, by providing the tools for a crime, but, in the absence of any proof of persuasion to commit the crime, he will not be guilty of incitement. Counsel for the appellant drew our attention to a number of authorities including the decisions in *Race Relations Board v Applin* [1973] 2 All ER 1190, [1973] 1 QB 815 and *R v Hendrickson and Tichner* [1977] Crim LR 356. In addition we were provided with a full transcript of the judgment of Stephenson LJ in the *Hendrickson* case.

We have considered this submission in the context of the present case. In our judgment the judge gave a perfectly adequate definition to deal with the facts which the jury had to consider. We are satisfied that in some cases a person who is deputed to collect men together to take part in a crime may well not be guilty of incitement. For example, his role may be limited to informing certain named individuals that the planner of the enterprise would like to see them. But in the present case the judge could point to the fact that Bonham was out of work and needed money. The suggestion, proposal or request was accompanied by an implied promise of reward. Indeed, by using the words 'That proposal, you may think, was the most persuasive factor in the approach', the judge rightly focused the attention of the jury on the element of persuasion which it was necessary for the Crown to prove. We therefore see no reason to fault the judge's summing up in this respect.

The second submission of counsel for the appellant, however, is at first sight more formidable. Incitement is one of the three inchoate offences, incitement, conspiracy and attempt. Counsel argued that there was no logical basis for treating the three offences differently when considering their application in circumstances where the complete offence would be impossible to commit, and that therefore the court should apply the principles laid down by the House of Lords in the case of attempts in *Haughton v Smith* [1973] 3 All ER 1109, [1975] AC 476 and in the case of conspiracy in *DPP v Nock* [1978] 2 All ER 654, [1978] AC 979.

Counsel pointed to the fact that though the law as laid down by the House of Lords in those two cases had been altered by statute, by s 1(2) and s 5(1) of the Criminal Attempts Act 1981, there had been no change in the law relating to the offence of incitement. Accordingly, he said, the common law rule as to impossibility should be applied.

It is to be observed that the omission of the crime of incitement from the Criminal

Attempts Act 1981, followed the recommendations of the Law Commission in their
a Report published in 1980 (Law Com no 102) and was in accordance with the draft bill
set out in appendix A to that report. The Law Commission explained the omission of
incitement from the draft bill on the basis that in their view the House of Lords in *DPP
v Nock* was prepared to distinguish the law relating to incitement from that relating to
attempts: see paras 4.2 to 4.4. We have had to give careful attention to these paragraphs
in the Law Commission's report.

b   We have also had to consider with care the passage in the speech of Lord Scarman in
DPP v Nock which appears to have formed the basis for the decision by the Law
Commission to exclude incitement from their recommendations for change and from
their draft bill.

      In *DPP v Nock* [1978] 2 All ER 654 at 663, [1978] AC 979 at 999 Lord Scarman made
reference to two cases which had been cited to their Lordships. He said:

c   'Our attention was also drawn to two cases, on which it may be helpful to
       comment very briefly. In *R v McDonough* (1962) 47 Cr App R 37 the Court of
       Criminal Appeal held that an incitement to receive stolen goods was complete on
       the making of the incitement even though there were no stolen goods, perhaps
       even, no goods at all. In *Haggard v Mason* [1976] 1 All ER 337, [1976] 1 WLR 187
d   the Divisional Court held that the offence of offering to supply a controlled drug
       was committed, even though the drug in fact supplied was not a controlled drug.
       Neither of these cases infringes the principle of *Haughton v Smith* [1973] 3 All ER
       1109, [1975] AC 476; for in each, as was pointed out in *Haggard v Mason* [1976] 1
       All ER 337 at 339, [1976] 1 WLR 187 at 189 the offence was complete. In *R v
       McDonough* the actus reus was the making of the incitement and in *Haggard's* case it
e   was the making of the offer.'

      We have come to the conclusion that, on analysis, this passage in Lord Scarman's
speech does not support the proposition that cases of incitement are to be treated quite
differently at common law from cases of attempt or conspiracy. The decision in *Haggard
v Mason* related to the statutory offence of offering to supply a controlled drug and, as
Lord Scarman pointed out, the actus reus which the prosecution had to prove was the
f making of the offer. The explanation of *McDonough's* case, as it seems to us, is that though
there may have been no stolen goods or no goods at all which were available to be
received at the time of the incitement, the offence of incitement to receive stolen goods
could nevertheless be proved because it was not impossible that at the relevant time in
the future the necessary goods would be there.

      In our view, therefore, the right approach in a case of incitement is the same as that
g which was underlined by Lord Scarman in *DPP v Nock* when he considered the offence
of conspiracy. In every case it is necessary to analyse the evidence with care to decide the
precise offence which the defendant is alleged to have incited.

      In *DPP v Nock* [1978] 2 All ER 654 at 659–660, [1978] AC 979 at 995 Lord Scarman
said:

h   'The indictment makes plain that the Crown is alleging in this case a conspiracy
       to commit a crime, and no one has suggested that the particulars fail to disclose an
       offence known to the law. But the appellants submit, and it is not disputed by the
       Crown, that the agreement as proved was narrower in scope than the conspiracy
       charged. When the case was before the Court of Appeal, counsel on both sides
       agreed that the evidence went to prove that the appellants agreed together to obtain
j   cocaine by separating it from the other substance or substances contained in a
       powder which they had obtained from one of their co-defendants, a Mr Mitchell.
       They believed that the powder was a mixture of cocaine and lignocaine, and that
       they would be able to produce cocaine from it. In fact the powder was lignocaine
       hydrochloride, an anaesthetic used in dentistry, which contains no cocaine at all. It
       is impossible to produce, by separation or otherwise, cocaine from lignocaine . . .

The trial judge in his direction to the jury, and the Court of Appeal in their judgment dismissing the two appeals, treated this impossibility as an irrelevance. In their view the agreement was what mattered; and there was plain evidence of an agreement to produce cocaine, even though unknown to the two conspirators it could not be done. Neither the trial judge nor the Court of Appeal thought it necessary to carry their analysis of the agreement further. The trial judge described it simply as an agreement to produce cocaine. The Court of Appeal thought it enough that the prosecution had proved "an agreement to do an act which was forbidden by s 4 of the Misuse of Drugs Act 1971". Both descriptions are accurate, as far as they go. But neither contains any reference to the limited nature of the agreement proved: it was an agreement on a specific course of conduct with the object of producing cocaine, and limited to that course of conduct. Since it could not result in the production of cocaine, the two appellants by pursuing it could not commit the statutory offence of producing a controlled drug.'

In our view these words suggest the correct approach at common law to any inchoate offence. It is necessary in every case to decide on the evidence what was the course of conduct which was (as the case may be) incited or agreed or attempted. In some cases the evidence may establish that the persuasion by the inciter was in quite general terms whereas the subsequent agreement of the conspirators was directed to a specific crime and a specific target. In such cases where the committal of the specific offence is shown to be impossible it may be quite logical for the inciter to be convicted even though the alleged conspirators (if not caught by s 5 of the Criminal Attempts Act 1981) may be acquitted. On the other hand, if B and C agree to kill D, and A, standing beside B and C, though not intending to take any active part whatever in the crime, encourages them to do so, we can see no satisfactory reason, if it turns out later that D was already dead, why A should be convicted of incitement to murder whereas B and C at common law would be entitled to an acquittal on a charge of conspiracy. The crucial question is to establish on the evidence the course of conduct which the alleged inciter was encouraging.

We return to the facts of the instant case. Counsel for the appellant submitted that the 'crime' which Bonham and the two Browns were being encouraged to commit was a mere charade. The appellant's father was not planning a real robbery at all and therefore the appellant could not be found guilty of inciting the three men to commit it. In our judgment, however, the answer to counsel's argument is to be found in the facts which the Crown proved against the appellant. As was made clear by counsel on behalf of the Crown, the case against the appellant was based on the steps he took to recruit Bonham. At that stage the appellant believed that there was to be a wage snatch and he was encouraging Bonham to take part in it. As counsel put it: 'The appellant thought he was recruiting for a robbery not for a charade.' It is to be remembered that the particulars of offence in the indictment included the words 'by robbing a woman at Bow'. By no stretch of the imagination was that an impossible offence to carry out and it was that offence which the appellant was inciting Bonham to commit.

For these reasons, therefore, we are satisfied that the appellant was rightly convicted. The appeal is dismissed.

Appeal dismissed.

Solicitors: *Duthie Hart & Duthie, Plaistow* (for the appellant).

Dilys Tausz   Barrister.

R v Immigration Appeal Tribunal, ex parte Weerasuriya

QUEEN'S BENCH DIVISION (CROWN OFFICE LIST)
WEBSTER J
27 APRIL 1982

Immigration – Appeal – Evidence – Explanatory statement by Home Office of facts relating to Secretary of State's decision or action – Evidence of facts coming into existence after Secretary of State's decision – Whether Home Office statement a pleading or evidence in appeal – Whether adjudicator can admit evidence of facts occurring after Secretary of State's decision – Immigration Act 1971, s 19(1) – Immigration Appeal (Procedure) Rules 1972, r 8(1).

Where an appellant gives notice of appeal under Part II of the Immigration Act 1971 against a decision of the Secretary of State to refuse the appellant leave to enter the United Kingdom or to grant him only conditional leave to enter or to deport him as an overstayer, an explanatory statement of the facts made by the Home Office pursuant to r 8(1)[a] of the Immigration Appeals (Procedure) Rules 1972 is not merely a pleading setting out the Secretary of State's case but is evidence in the case which may be acted on as such by the immigration adjudicator and the Immigration Appeal Tribunal (see p 199 *j* to p 200 *b*, post).

Having regard to the jurisdiction of immigration adjudicators as set out in s 19(1)[b] of the 1971 Act, an appeal to an adjudicator is not an extension of the Secretary of State's administrative function in arriving at a decision but is instead a process for enabling the Secretary of State's decision to be reviewed. Accordingly, an adjudicator has no power to admit evidence of facts which came into existence after the Secretary of State made his decision (see p 202 *a b d e*, post).

Notes

For the procedure in immigration appeals, see 4 Halsbury's Laws (4th edn) paras 1024–1026.

For the Immigration Act 1971, s 19, see 41 Halsbury's Statutes (3rd edn) 40.

For the Immigration Appeals (Procedure) Rules 1972, r 8, see 2 Halsbury's Statutory Instruments (4th reissue) 29.

Cases referred to in judgment

Hadmor Productions Ltd v Hamilton [1982] 1 All ER 1042, [1982] 2 WLR 322, HL.
R v Immigration Appeal Tribunal, ex p Nathwani (23 February 1979, unreported), DC.

Application for judicial review

Jayantha Weerasuriya applied, with the leave of Forbes J given on 11 November 1981, for an order of certiorari to quash a decision of the Immigration Appeal Tribunal made on 4 August 1981 refusing the applicant leave to appeal from the decision of an adjudicator, made on 15 June 1981, refusing him leave to appeal against the Secretary of State's decision, made on 20 March 1981, that he should be deported. The facts are set out in the judgment.

Michael Beloff QC and *Raana Sheikh* for the applicant.
John Laws for the Secretary of State.

---

a   Rule 8(1) is set out at p 199 *a*, post
b   Section 19(1), so far as material, is set out at p 201 *d*, post

WEBSTER J. This is an application for judicial review by way of certiorari to quash a
decision of the Immigration Appeal Tribunal made on 4 August 1981 when that tribunal
refused the applicant leave to appeal against the decision of an adjudicator made on 15
June 1981.

The applicant in his appeal to the adjudicator was seeking to challenge the decision of
the Secretary of State made on 20 March 1981 to deport him on the ground that he was
an overstayer. His claim that he was entitled to stay in this country was based on a
marriage which, it is common ground, had occurred, to a woman who (I think this is
also common ground) is to be regarded as settled in this country. The point at issue
throughout has been whether that marriage was a real marriage or a marriage of
convenience. Those are the short issues.

I now turn to the history of the matter in a little bit more detail. The applicant is a
citizen of Sri Lanka and is, therefore, subject to the Immigration Act 1971 and the rules
made under it. He arrived in this country on 9 September 1974 when he was granted
permission to enter as a student with 12 months' leave. On 9 September 1975 that leave
was varied so as to expire at the end of May 1976, and some time during 1976 he was
given a further extension to remain as a student, which leave expired at the end of
September 1976. On 10 November 1976, whilst still in the United Kingdom, he married
a Miss Jarman, who was either a patrial or, in any event, as I have said, a woman who is
to be regarded as settled in the United Kingdom. On 12 November 1976, two days later,
he applied for an extension of his leave on the ground of that marriage.

The response to that application by the Secretary of State was made on 6 October 1977,
when leave was extended, on the basis of that marriage, to end in November 1977. At
that stage, therefore, no decision had been made by the Secretary of State whether or not
to regard the marriage as one of convenience. On 30 November 1977 the applicant
applied to have the conditions on his leave to enter removed, that is to say he applied to
be allowed to settle permanently in this country on the basis or in reliance on his
marriage. On 19 June 1978 that application was refused by the Secretary of State on the
grounds that the marriage was a marriage of convenience.

On 10 May 1979 the applicant appealed to the adjudicator against that refusal and that
appeal was dismissed. On 3 August 1979 he appealed to the Immigration Appeal
Tribunal for leave to appeal against the adjudicator's decision and that application was
dismissed. Nothing more of any materiality happened until 1981, although in December
1979 he made a fresh application for permanent settlement which was clearly
misconceived and rejected.

On 20 March 1981 the Secretary of State made his decision which is effectively the
subject matter of this application for judicial review because, on that date, he decided to
deport the applicant under s 3(5)(a) of the 1971 Act. On 15 June 1981 the adjudicator
refused the applicant leave to appeal against that decision. On 4 August 1981 the
Immigration Appeal Tribunal refused the applicant leave to appeal against that decision
of the adjudicator. It is that decision of the Immigration Appeal Tribunal of 4 August
1981 which is the subject matter of this application.

I now turn to the decisions of 1979 and 1981 in more detail taking, first, the relevant
parts of the 1979 decisions and the material facts which led to them. For the purposes of
the application which was made by the applicant in that year, which was ultimately
dismissed, the Home Office prepared, as is their usual practice, a written statement of
facts, which included the following. On 19 May 1978 immigration officers called at
Dingwalls Club, Camden Lock, and asked the manager if they could speak to the
applicant's wife. He said that she worked there, although he knew her in her maiden
name of Jarman. The applicant's wife's first comment when told that the immigration
officers wished to interview her was to say she had wondered how long it would take
them to catch up with her. She was questioned about her marriage to the applicant and
said she had married him in November 1976 to facilitate his remaining in the United
Kingdom. She said he had wished to remain there for a further two years rather than
return to Sri Lanka where he would have to marry someone of his parents' choice. She
said she had never lived with the applicant and had never officially used his name. She

was not wearing a wedding ring, and said that she would institute divorce proceedings
a when the two years mentioned by the applicant expired in November 1978.

On 24 May 1978 an immigration officer advised the Home Office that he had visited
an address which was the matrimonial home on five occasions between 22 January 1978
and 14 May 1978 in an endeavour to interview the applicant and his wife. On two
occasions the applicant was in, when he said that his marriage was subsisting and that he
and his wife were very happy. On each occasion the applicant's wife was not present
b although the applicant said that his wife was living with him. Items of women's clothing
and cosmetics were evident in the flat.

The statement on behalf of the Secretary of State concluded with the expression of
view by the Secretary of State that he was not satisfied 'that the marriage was not one of
convenience entered into primarily to obtain for the [applicant] his . . . settlement in the
United Kingdom . . .'

c In the adjudication on the applicant's appeal against that decision, the adjudicator, Mr
Farmer, referred to the fact that both the applicant and his wife had given evidence
before him. He referred to the applicant's evidence before him including evidence given
by him about his wife and, in particular, including his evidence that he and his wife
were not living together because their hours always clashed and they both liked their
jobs very much, but that he was hopeful of a reconciliation and they still saw each other.

d Dealing with the evidence given by the applicant's wife, he mentioned, amongst other
things, the fact that she had said that she and the applicant had split up about seven or
eight months either after the marriage or after the move to the matrimonial home,
which of the two is not clear but is immaterial. He also dealt with another matter in the
following terms. He said: 'She was interviewed by immigration officers in May 1978.
She told them that she had no intention of getting a divorce. She said that she was staying
e with friends as she could not stand one room. She did not tell them that she wondered
how long it would take for them to catch up with her. She did not tell them she had
married the [applicant] in November 1976 to facilitate his remaining in this country.'

At the conclusion of his adjudication he made a number of findings including, as his
third finding, the fact that he did not believe that either the applicant or his wife at any
stage had any intention of entering into a lasting marriage. He also found that it was
f common ground between the applicant and his witnesses that seven months after the
marriage it broke up, that he was most unimpressed by the way in which the applicant
and his witnesses gave their evidence, and that he did not believe that there was or ever
had been the slightest chance of reconciliation. So much for the decisions made in 1978
and 1979.

As to 1981, I should refer first to the decision of Mr Richards, the adjudicator who
g adjudicated on the applicant's appeal to him against the Home Secretary's decision to
deport him. Having set out some of the history of the matter, the adjudicator towards
the end of his decision said that at the hearing of the appeal the applicant had given
evidence, and had recounted the events leading to his marriage and those which followed,
matters which, the adjudicator observed, had already been adjudicated on. He referred
back to the adjudication which I have already just mentioned. He concluded that having
h considered the evidence as a whole and the submissions made on the applicant's behalf
he was not persuaded that it was shown that the decision was not in accordance with the
law and immigration rules; he did not find that the discretion should be exercised
differently and he dismissed the appeal.

Against that decision the applicant gave notice of application for leave to appeal.
Amongst the grounds of application were, as ground 1, that the applicant and his wife
j had been reconciled and resumed cohabitation. In ground 6 he relied on a retrospectivity
argument, which I will deal with in a moment. The Immigration Appeal Tribunal
dismissed that application for leave to appeal against the adjudicator's decision. I should
mention some of the terms of their decision. They said:

'The [applicant's] solicitors have submitted grounds of appeal and an affidavit
sworn by the [applicant's] wife to the effect that they are now reconciled and

cohabiting. If this is so it refers to matters subsequent to the decision appealed against and has no relevance to this appeal. In the opinion of the Tribunal there was   *a* sufficient evidence to support the adjudicator's findings of fact, which were not unreasonable, and he does not appear to have misdirected himself in any way as to the law or immigration rules.'

Later, having expressed the opinion that the determination of the appeal did not turn on any arguable point of law, they dismissed the application.

The Home Secretary's decision in question against which this series of appeals has been   *b* instituted, arises out of the application of para 143 of Statement of Changes in Immigration Rules (HC Paper (1979–80) no 394) which is in these terms.

'Deportation will normally be the proper course where the person has failed to comply with or has contravened a condition or has remained without authorisation. Full account is to be taken of all the relevant circumstances known to the Secretary   *c* of State, including those listed in paragraph 141, before a decision is reached.'

It is common ground that none of the circumstances listed in para 141 are material.

Counsel on behalf of the applicant submits that the decision of the Immigration Appeal Tribunal dismissing the application for leave to appeal was wrong for three reasons. The first of those reasons is that the relevant immigration rule which was in force on the date on which the application was made by the applicant to extend his leave   *d* on the ground of his marriage, namely 12 November 1976, was the rule contained in para 25 of Statement of Change in Immigration Rules for Control after Entry: Commonwealth Citizens (1974; Cmnd 5716) but that, wrongly as he submits, the rule which was applied in all decisions made subsequent to that date was the rule which succeeded that rule, which came into effect on, I think, 22 March 1977 and is contained in a House of Commons paper (HC Paper (1976–77) no 239). He concedes, however, that   *e* this point is not open to argument on his behalf in this court because the point has already been decided adversely to him by a full Divisional Court in *R v Immigration Appeal Tribunal, ex p Nathwani* (23 February 1979, unreported). He does not, therefore, pursue that argument (which is the retrospectivity argument which I mentioned earlier) further except for the purpose of noting that it has been raised.

The other grounds on which he relies are, first, that the adjudicator wrongly, in   *f* dismissing the applicant's appeal, relied on hearsay evidence or on evidence which was inadmissible or on which he should not have relied and, second, that he refused to admit fresh evidence as to facts which had come about since the date of the Secretary of State's decision and that, as he refused to admit that evidence because of an error of law, that refusal itself constitutes an error of law on the basis of which the Immigration Appeal Tribunal should have given the applicant leave to appeal.   *g*

I take, first of all, the submission that the tribunal should have given leave to appeal because the adjudicator acted on hearsay evidence or treated as evidence evidence which is not to be regarded as evidence at all. I have already referred to some passages from the decisions of both of the adjudicators and, as will be remembered, the second of the two adjudicators referred back to the adjudication made by the first one, Mr Farmer. I have already referred to the fact that Mr Farmer in his determination and reasons referred to   *h* the evidence given by the applicant and his wife, to an interview of the applicant's wife by immigration officers and to the adjudicator's conclusion that he was unimpressed by the way in which the applicant and his witnesses had given their evidence.

Counsel for the applicant is not suggesting that the adjudicator on that occasion was bound to accede or to accept the evidence of the applicant and his wife or other witnesses. But his submission is that, as is apparent from his reasons for his determination, the   *j* adjudicator did take into account and must have attached some weight to the material contained in the Home Office statement to which I have already referred. That statement, he submits, is not, as a matter of law, evidence. His argument runs thus. The statement by the Home Office was a statement which was made pursuant to r 8 of the Immigration Appeals (Procedure) Rules 1972, SI 1972/1684. Paragraph 1 of that rule provides:

a
'Subject to the provisions of paragraphs (2) and (3) below, the respondent in an appeal shall, as soon as practicable after notice of the appeal is given, prepare a written statement of the facts relating to the decision or action in question and the reasons therefor and take such steps as are necessary to ensure that the statement is referred to an adjudicator or the Tribunal as appropriate, and that a copy thereof is given to the appellant.'

b
Rule 29 of the same rules deals with evidence. Paragraph (1) is in these terms:

'An appellate authority may receive oral, documentary or other evidence of any fact which appears to the authority to be relevant to the appeal, notwithstanding that such evidence would be inadmissible in a court of law.'

c
The submission of counsel for the applicant on this point is very short. It is simply to this effect, that the explanatory statement provided for under r 8 does not constitute, and is not capable of constituting, evidence of any kind whether oral, documentary or otherwise, of any fact. It is, he says, in the nature of a pleading, giving notice to the appellant of the respondent's case on which the respondent will rely at the hearing of the appeal. The point is a very short one. Counsel on behalf of the Secretary of State submits that the explanatory statement is indeed evidence and is capable of constituting evidence.

d
He draws my attention not only to the provisions of para (1) of r 8 which I have already recited, but also to the provisions of paras (2) and (4). Paragraph (2) provides:

'It shall not be necessary for an immigration officer who is the respondent in an appeal to comply with the requirements of paragraph (1) above if he is of the opinion that it is not practicable to do so, having regard to the time available before the hearing of the appeal; [these are the words he emphasises] but he shall then, as

e
soon as practicable after notice of the appeal is given, give written notice to the appellate authority and the appellant that he is of that opinion and that a statement of the facts relating to the decision or action in question and the reasons therefor will be given orally at the hearing of the appeal.'

Paragraph (4) is in these terms:

f
'At the commencement of any hearing before an appellate authority, the authority shall give to the respondent an opportunity to amplify orally the written statement given in accordance with paragraph (1) above or, if no such written statement has been given, shall obtain from the respondent an oral statement of the facts relating to the decision or action in question and the reasons therefor.'

g
Moreover, he refers me back to para (1) of r 29, which I have already recited, and he submits that, even if counsel for the applicant's construction of the meaning and effect of the explanatory statement provided under r 8(1) is correct, none the less r 29(1) would give the appellate authority the power to receive that document as evidence, in which event, the discretion or power having been exercised to that effect, the document would constitute evidence. Counsel for the applicant agrees that that could be done although he says that were it to be done (it was not done in this case) there might be implications

h
which would follow which I need not enumerate.

In short, submits counsel for the Secretary of State, the explanatory statement is not, as counsel for the applicant submits, something in the nature of a pleading but is, and is capable of being, of itself, evidence. Whether it constitutes evidence without the exercise by the appellate authority of the power under r 29(1), depends primarily, as it seems to me, on the construction of para (1) of r 8 and, in particular, on the words in that

j
paragraph 'a written statement of the facts.' In construing those words it seems to me that I may, and indeed should, construe them in the context of the other paragraphs of that rule and, in particular, of the two paragraphs, (2) and (4), which I have already recited.

Taking into account the very words themselves, 'statement of the facts', and taking into account the contents of paras (2) and (4) of r 8, I am satisfied that that written statement of the facts does, of itself, constitute evidence for the purpose of these rules; indeed it is quite difficult to get any closer to an apt description of evidence in writing *a* than to describe it as a written statement of the facts.

The matter, as I have said, is a short one and permits of little elaboration. It is the case that statements of the facts by the Secretary of State have been used habitually and have been regarded as evidence, but although it is common ground that that has been the practice, and although I myself know it to have been the practice, I do not take that matter into account in deciding, as I do, that those written statements of facts or *b* explanatory statements constitute evidence for the purposes of the rules. So I decide the first point against counsel for the applicant.

I turn to the second point which relates to the refusal to give leave to appeal in reliance on the fresh evidence. The Secretary of State's decision was made on 20 March 1981. In July 1981 the applicant's wife swore a very short affidavit, no parts of which are of any, or of much, relevance except para 4 in which she swears to the fact that she and the *c* applicant were then reconciled and had resumed cohabitation. As appears from the determination reasons of the Immigration Appeal Tribunal, they refused leave to appeal in reliance on that matter because it referred to 'matters subsequent to the decision appealed against and has no relevance to this appeal'.

In order to consider this point one has, first of all, to consider r 18 of the Immigration Appeals (Procedure) Rules 1972 and, in particular, para (3) of that rule which provides: *d*

'In any proceedings on an appeal—(a) the Tribunal may, in its discretion, receive or decline to receive further evidence of which notice has been given in accordance with paragraph (2) above . . .'

Paragraph (2) above goes simply to the machinery for giving notice of such evidence. So it appears that the Immigration Appeal Tribunal has powers to receive evidence which *e* was not before the adjudicator. But the question is whether it, or the adjudicator, had power to consider evidence of facts which came into existence after the date of the decision made by the Home Secretary himself. Counsel for the applicant submits that both those appellate tribunals have that power and counsel for the Secretary of State submits that they have not.

In support of his submission counsel for the applicant relies on two passages from the *f* speech of Lord Diplock in *Hadmor Productions Ltd v Hamilton* [1982] 1 All ER 1042 at 1046, [1982] 2 WLR 322 at 325–326. In the first of those two passages Lord Diplock says this:

'Before adverting to the evidence that was before the judge and the additional evidence that was before the Court of Appeal, it is I think appropriate to remind your Lordships of the limited function of an appellate court in an appeal of this *g* kind. An interlocutory injunction is a discretionary relief and the discretion whether or not to grant it is vested in the High Court judge by whom the application for it is heard. On an appeal from the judge's grant or refusal of an interlocutory injunction the function of an appellate court, whether it be the Court of Appeal or your Lordships' House, is not to exercise an independent discretion of its own. It must defer to the judge's exercise of his discretion and must not interfere with it merely *h* on the ground that the members of the appellate court would have exercised the discretion differently. The function of the appellate court is initially [and I think counsel for the applicant would emphasise the word "initially"] one of review only. It may set aside the judge's exercise of his discretion on the ground that it was based on a misunderstanding of the law or of the evidence before him or on an inference that particular facts existed or did not exist, which, although it was one that might *j* legitimately have been drawn on the evidence that was before the judge [and this is the passage which he emphasises] can be demonstrated to be wrong by further evidence that has become available by the time of the appeal, or on the ground that there has been a change of circumstances after the judge made his order that would have justified his acceding to an application to vary it.'

The second passage is that in which Lord Diplock takes up the same point again where
a he says:

> 'The right approach by an appellate court is to examine the fresh evidence in
> order to see to what extent, if any, the facts disclosed by it invalidate the reasons
> given by the judge for his decision. Only if they do, is the appellate court entitled to
> treat the fresh evidence as constituting in itself a ground for exercising an original
b > discretion of its own to grant or withhold the interlocutory relief.'

So, submits counsel for the applicant, an appellate court of law in the High Court civil
jurisdiction, at any rate, has a power to take into account, on entertaining an appeal to it,
evidence of facts which have come into existence since the decision at first instance was
made. He submits that the powers given to the appellate tribunal under the Immigration
Act 1971, far from being narrower than the powers which an appellate court in the High
c Court civil jurisdiction has, are wider. He refers, as I must refer, to the provisions of s 19
of the 1971 Act which covers such appeals. Section 19 provides (and I quote it leaving
out immaterial words): ·

> '(1) . . . an adjudicator on an appeal to him under this Part of this Act—(a) shall
> allow the appeal if he considers—(i) that the decision or action against which the
> appeal is brought was not in accordance with the law or with any immigration rules
d > applicable to the case; or (ii) where the decision or action involved the exercise of a
> discretion by the Secretary of State or an officer, that the discretion should have been
> exercised differently . . .
> (2) For the purposes of subsection (1)(a) above the adjudicator may review any
> determination of a question of fact on which the decision or action was based . . .'

e As to appeals to the tribunal, s 20(1) provides:

> 'Subject to any requirement of rules of procedure as to leave to appeal, any party
> to an appeal to an adjudicator may, if dissatisfied with his determination thereon,
> appeal to the Appeal Tribunal, and the Tribunal may affirm the determination or
> make any other determination which could have been made by the adjudicator.'

f So, submits counsel for the applicant, not only the High Court but the appellate
tribunals constituted under the Act have power to take into account facts which have
come into existence since the date on which the initial decision, in this case that of the
Secretary of State, was made. ·

The submission of counsel for the Secretary of State is to the contrary effect and it is
that although, as I have already said, it is common ground that an appellate tribunal may
g take into account evidence which was not available at an earlier stage of the proceedings
in question, it may not take into account evidence of any fact which was not in existence
at the date when the Secretary of State made his decision. He relies, primarily as matters
of construction, on the use of the past tense in s 19(1)(a)(i) and (ii), and on the words, in
(ii), 'should have been exercised differently'.

If it were to be purely a question of construction I would be persuaded, I think, by that
h argument, namely that those words which I have just quoted would, if there were no
other assistance to be gained as to the answers to this question, be determinant of it in
favour of counsel for the Secretary of State. But it seems to me that there are other
considerations which reinforce that conclusion.

The decision which is effectively under appeal is the decision of the Secretary of State,
that is to say an administrative decision. In judgments on applications for judicial review
j of administrative decisions it has often been stated that the function of the court is not to
substitute its own decision for the decision of the department or tribunal under review.
Of course it is not possible to apply that principle directly to the appellate structure which
is attached to the Secretary of State's decision in this case and in similar cases; but it is, as
it seems to me, necessary to look at that appellate structure in order to ask oneself the
question whether that appellate structure has to be regarded as an extension of the

original administrative decision-making function or whether it is to be regarded as
simply a process for enabling that decision to be reviewed. As it seems to me it falls into *a*
the latter category rather than into the former category. The appellate tribunals are
provided for in Sch 5 to the 1971 Act. I need say no more than that there is no indication
anywhere in that schedule that those tribunals are vested with any of the administrative
powers or functions of the Secretary of State or his department.

That that conclusion is the right one, at least in the context of this particular case, is
perhaps well illustrated by the provisions of para 143 of HC Paper (1979–80) no 394 *b*
which I have already quoted. I emphasise the last sentence of that paragraph and repeat
it. It is in these terms:

> 'Full account is to be taken of all the relevant circumstances *known to the Secretary
> of State*, including those listed in paragraph 141, before a decision is reached.' (My
> emphasis.)

c

Counsel for the Secretary of State, at the conclusion of the argument, helpfully referred
me to the provisions of s 21 of the 1971 Act. It does not seem to me that those provisions
affect the conclusion I have reached either in one way or the other. It does seem to me
that the analogy, or what counsel for the applicant suggests is the analogy, of the
statement of principle given by Lord Diplock in *Hadmor's* case is not an apt analogy at all
because, for reasons which I need not elaborate, it seems to me that a court of law is a *d*
court of law at whatever stage in the legal hierarchy it sits; whereas, conversely, it does
not seem to me that either an adjudicator or an Immigration Appeal Tribunal is, or is to
be regarded as, the administrative person on whom, and on which only, is conferred, as I
understand it, the power to make the decision in question in this case and similar
administrative decisions.

Therefore, in my judgment, the adjudicator had no power to entertain or admit *e*
evidence which went to a fact which came into existence after the date of the Secretary
of State's decision. It follows that in my judgment the Immigration Appeal Tribunal
rightly refused to give the applicant leave to appeal against the adjudicator's decision on
the grounds that he had refused to admit that evidence.

Were I to be wrong on this question of law and if, as a matter of law, the adjudicator
had a discretion to admit that evidence, I, in the exercise of my discretion on this *f*
application, if the matter rested only on the exercise of my discretion would refuse to
exercise it in the applicant's favour because of the tenuous nature of the additional
evidence, particularly tenuous when seen in the light of the affidavit of Mr Fitzgerald
sworn on 24 February 1982 which, though not before the adjudicator or before the
tribunal, has been put before this court.

For all these reasons I dismiss this application.   *g*

Application dismissed.

Solicitors: M *Hetty & Co*, Kenton (for the applicant); *Treasury Solicitor.*

Sepala Munasinghe Esq   Barrister.

Re British Concrete Pipe Association

COURT OF APPEAL, CIVIL DIVISION
SIR JOHN DONALDSON MR, MAY AND ROBERT GOFF LJJ
17 NOVEMBER 1982

Restrictive trade practices – Contempt of court – Breach of undertaking given to court – Company giving undertaking to court in respect of agreement declared to be contrary to public interest – Company subsequently becoming wholly-owned subsidary of publicly-owned corporation – All assets, liabilities and obligations of company transferred by vesting order to corporation – Corporation entering into agreements in breach of undertaking given by company – Whether undertaking given to court forming part of 'obligations' transferred to corporation – Whether corporation in contempt of court – Iron and Steel Act 1969, s 8(1) – Steel Companies (Vesting) Order 1970, art 3.

In 1957 a company which was a member of a trade association entered into agreements which had the effect of restricting price competition. In 1965 the agreements were declared by the court to be contrary to the public interest. The court, instead of making an injunctive order, accepted an undertaking from the company that it would not enter into agreements to the like effect. In 1969, on the nationalisation of the steel industry, the company became a wholly-owned subsidiary of the British Steel Corp. By s 8(1)[a] of the Iron and Steel Act 1969 the minister had authority to make an order in respect of such a company vesting its 'property, rights, liabilities and obligations' in British Steel. A vesting order was duly made in respect of the company by virtue of art 3[b] of the Steel Companies (Vesting) Order 1970. Subsequently British Steel entered into two restrictive agreements which were in breach of the undertaking given to the court in 1965 by the company. The Director General of Fair Trading applied for leave to issue a writ of sequestration against British Steel for contempt of court. The Restrictive Practices Court held British Steel to be in contempt of court by breaching the undertaking given to the court in 1965. British Steel appealed, contending that s 8 of the 1969 Act and art 3 of the 1970 order, and in particular the word 'obligations' in those provisions, were to be given a sufficiently restricted meaning to exclude the transfer to British Steel of the undertaking given to the court by the company, and therefore, although the restrictive practices legislation required traders and manufacturers to register agreements which prima facie infringed the prohibition contained in the 1969 Act, British Steel were free to operate such an agreement unless and until it was declared by the court to be contrary to public interest.

Held – Applying the general rule of construction that the words of a statute were to be given their plain and natural meaning unless it was clear from the context that Parliament intended those words to have a different or more restricted meaning, the word 'obligations' in s 8 of the 1969 Act and art 3 of the 1970 order referred to an action which bound a person by oath, promise or contract to do or forbear something. That was an accurate description of the undertaking given to the court by the company and there was nothing in either s 8(1) of the 1969 Act or art 3 of the 1970 order which justified a different interpretation. It followed that the undertaking had been transferred to British Steel under the 1970 vesting order. The appeal would accordingly be dismissed (see p 205 *a* to *d*, p 206 *j* and p 207 *f* to *h*, post).

Nokes v Doncaster Amalgamated Collieries Ltd [1940] 3 All ER 549 distinguished.

Notes

For the Iron and Steel Act 1969, s 8, see 37 Halsbury's Statutes (3rd edn) 613.

---

a   Section 8(1) is set out at p 204 *h*, post
b   Article 3 is set out at p 204 *j*, post

Cases referred to in judgments

Nokes v Doncaster Amalgamated Collieries Ltd [1940] 3 All ER 549, [1940] AC 1014, HL, 10   *a*
Digest (Reissue) 1229, 7728.
Watkinson v Hollington [1943] 2 All ER 573, [1944] 1 KB 16, CA, 18 Digest (Reissue) 446,
1647.

Cases also cited

Cox v Hakes (1890) 15 App Cas 506, HL.   *b*
United Steel Co Ltd v Cullington [1940] 2 All ER 170, [1940] AC 812, HL.

Appeal

The British Steel Corp appealed against the decision of Mocatta J in the Restrictive
Practices Court on 17 December 1980 granting the application of the Director General of
Fair Trading for leave to issue a writ of sequestration on the property and assets of British   *c*
Steel for its contempt of court in failing to comply with an undertaking given by Stanton
& Staveley Ltd, a wholly-owned subsidiary of British Steel, to the court on 11 January
1965 that it would not, whether by itself, its agents or otherwise, enter into or make any
agreement to which Part I of the Restrictive Trade Practices Act 1956 applied which
undertaking was embodied in an order of the Restrictive Practices Court made on 11
January 1965. The facts are set out in the judgment of Sir John Donaldson MR.   *d*

David Kemp QC and *Richard Seymour* for British Steel.
Francis Ferris QC for the Director General of Fair Trading.

SIR JOHN DONALDSON MR. This is an appeal by the British Steel Corp against
a judgment of the Restrictive Practices Court given on 17 December 1980. The court   *e*
held British Steel to be in contempt of court by breaching an undertaking which had
been given to the court in January 1965, not by British Steel, but by Stanton & Staveley
Ltd.

At that time in 1965 Stanton & Staveley Ltd were members of the British Concrete
Pipe Association. As such they made an agreement which had the effect of restricting
price competition. They duly registered that agreement. It was selected for examination   *f*
by the registrar, brought before the court, and declared to be contrary to the public
interest. The court, instead of making an injunctive order, accepted an undertaking from
Stanton & Staveley Ltd and from others that they would not enter into agreements to the
like effect (I am paraphrasing the undertaking because its exact terms are immaterial for
present purposes).

British Steel came on the scene in 1969 when under s 8 of the Iron and Steel Act 1969   *g*
the minister was given power to transfer property from private steel companies. Section
8(1) of the 1969 Act is in these terms:

> 'The Minister may, with respect to a publicly-owned company which was in
> public ownership on 30th April 1969, by order (made by statutory instrument
> whereof a draft shall be laid before Parliament) vest all or any of its property, rights,   *h*
> liabilities and obligations in the Corporation; and an order under this section may
> contain provision for any matter for which it appears to the Minister requisite or
> expedient to make provision in connection with, or in consequence of, the vesting.'

That was followed by the Steel Companies (Vesting) Order 1970, SI 1970/430, which
provided by art 3:

> 'On the date on which this Order comes into operation [ie 29 March 1970] all the   *j*
> property, rights, liabilities and obligations of each scheduled company shall vest in
> the Corporation by virtue of this Order and without further assurance.'

Stanton & Staveley Ltd were, of course, one of the companies in the schedule; and it
was said by the registrar and upheld by the Restrictive Practices Court that the effect of

art 3 of the order, which follows the wording of s 8(1) of the 1969 Act, was to transfer to British Steel the burden of the undertaking which had been given to the court by Stanton & Staveley Ltd five years before.

The particular word relied on by the registrar is the word 'obligation'. The primary meaning given to that word by the *Oxford English Dictionary* is: 'The action of binding oneself by oath, promise, or contract to do or forbear something.' Indeed, binding oneself by oath or promise would appear to be a very accurate description of an undertaking given to the court. The word 'obligation' was also considered in *Watkinson v Hollington* [1943] 2 All ER 573 at 575, [1944] 1 KB 16 at 21 where Scott LJ adverted to this meaning and made it clear in his judgment that the word 'obligation' was not limited to a contractual obligation or the payment or non-payment of money but had this broader meaning, although it is true to say that he was dealing with the matter in quite a different context.

Counsel for British Steel submits that s 8 and art 3 of the 1970 order should be construed restrictively in this particular context so as not to transfer the burden of an undertaking given to the court. Our task, as I see it, is to construe the 1969 Act, and in so doing the prima facie rule is that words have their ordinary meaning. But that is subject to the qualification that if, giving words their ordinary meaning, we are faced with extraordinary results which cannot have been intended by Parliament, we then have to move on to a second stage in which we re-examine the words and see whether they must in all the circumstances have been intended by Parliament to have a different meaning or a more restricted meaning.

Counsel for the British Steel, pursuing that approach, has advanced seven main reasons for urging that s 8 and art 3 should be given a sufficiently restricted meaning to exclude the transfer of this undertaking. It is common ground between the parties that for practical purposes an undertaking to the court can be treated in the same way as an injunction.

The first point is this. Counsel for British Steel says that the restrictive practices legislation requires traders and manufacturers to register agreements which prima facie infringe the prohibitions contained in the 1969 Act, but they are free to operate such agreements unless and until they are declared by the court to be contrary to the public interest. In counsel's submission, if the registrar is correct in this case, Parliament has deprived British Steel of a fundamental freedom enjoyed by every British subject engaged in trade or commerce, namely the right to operate a restrictive agreement until such time as that particular agreement has been declared to be contrary to law.

I think the answer to that submission is really this, that price fixing is not inherently bad (it can be justified in some circumstances) and accordingly the restrictive practices legislation provides that, so long as you do not do it secretly and you register your agreement, you may go on with the agreement unless and until the court has examined it and has come to the conclusion that it is not one of the exceptional agreements which should be permitted, but there is no reason why that examination should take place again and again. This particular agreement and analogous agreements have been examined by the court, and in terms of public policy it is quite understandable that Parliament should have no inhibitions about legislating in such a way as to prevent that matter having to be relitigated.

Put in more homely language, what counsel for British Steel is really saying is that every dog is entitled to his bite before anything beastly shall happen to the dog, and British Steel have been deprived of the opportunity of having their first bite. If British Steel really want to have a bite and think that they could justify the bite, then their right course was to go back to the Restrictive Practices Court, make their case, and ask to be released from their undertaking; but that they have not done.

The second argument is this. Counsel for British Steel says that s 154 of the Companies Act 1929 contains similar words. That section provides:

'Where an application is made to the court . . . for the sanctioning of a compromise or arrangement . . . and it is shown to the court that the compromise or arrangement has been proposed for the purposes of or in connection with a scheme for the reconstruction of any company or companies or the amalgamation of any two or more companies, and that under the scheme the whole or any part of the undertaking or the property of any company concerned in the scheme (in this section referred to as "a transferor company") is to be transferred to another company (in this section referred to as "the transferee company"), the court may . . . by . . . order, make provision for all or any of the following matters:—(a) The transfer to the transferee company of the whole or any part of the undertaking and of the property or liabilities of any transferor company . . .'

And sub-s (4) provides:

'In this section the expression "property" includes property, rights and powers of every description, and the expression "liabilities" includes duties.'

That section was considered by the House of Lords in *Nokes v Doncaster Amalgamated Collieries Ltd* [1940] 3 All ER 549, [1940] AC 1014. Their Lordships decided that the wording of the section was not wide enough to authorise the transfer to a transferee company of a contract of personal services. That perhaps is not surprising when you consider that this section is concerned with sanctioning a compromise or arrangement reached between creditors and the company or between other companies. It is not a matter of public policy that these transfers should take place; it is a question of the court approving transfers for private reasons and, as was shown by the judgments in that case, there would have been considerable problems if it had extended to the transfer of contracts for personal service, since you might have, for example, the managing director of a very small company who was suddenly transferred and found himself the managing director of a vast conglomerate or vice versa. In any case, the wording is different. There is no reference to 'obligation' in that section. Indeed, s 8 of the 1969 Act uses much wider words; the lessons indicated by their Lordships in *Nokes v Doncaster Amalgamated Collieries Ltd* had obviously been learned by the minister, who in his statutory instrument made special provision to get over any possible difficulties which might arise from transferring contracts of employment: that provision is contained in art 4(1)(f) of the 1970 order.

Counsel's third point is that the minister could have used the powers in s 8 of the 1969 Act to transfer only the undertaking to the court. In other words, he could have used his powers to go round the country giving a bonus or Christmas present to all the private steel companies by removing the undertaking but leaving them with the whole of their businesses unfettered by the undertaking.

He may be right that on the literal working of the section the minister had that power; but, if it is any consolation to British Steel, for my part I have not the slightest doubt that had the minister done so and had there been an application to the Divisional Court on the basis that this was an abuse of power the applicant would have succeeded. There are many cases in which widely drawn authority given to a minister, if used literally and in a way in which nobody could conceivably have foreseen, can be shown to be an abuse of power, but of course it has not happened.

The fourth point made is that Stanton & Staveley Ltd are still in existence. They are still in existence largely I think because it was found on nationalisation that they owned some foreign shares and learned and distinguished counsel advised that it was not possible to nationalise a holding of foreign shares. So it is said that, as Stanton & Staveley Ltd are still in existence, they could start up in the pipe making business if they so wished and they would do so free of the undertaking.

I agree that that is an odd result, but I do not think that Parliament can be expected to cover every eventuality, and that is one of them. Parliament could of course have provided that the undertaking to the court should be divided into two and become two undertakings, but parliamentary counsel no doubt failed to foresee this interesting possibility and did not provide for it. I am quite unpersuaded by the fact that there is an anomaly to stray away from the natural meaning of the words.

The fifth point is analogous to the fourth point. It is said that the corporation could
a consent to the transfer back to Stanton & Staveley Ltd of the very assets which were
transferred by Parliament, and it is said that it has actually done so with some other
companies. So you would have had something analogous to bond washing in the sense
that the undertaking was transferred and then got left behind on the retransfer. Of
course, had that all been done in 1970, then questions of abuse of power would have
arisen. As it is, I cannot regard it as anything more than another form of the same
b anomaly to which I referred earlier.

The sixth point is that under this legislation, construed as the registrar would have it
construed and the court below has construed it, it would be possible for the corporation
to be in breach of the undertaking inadvertently. That no doubt is right. Where the
corporation is taking over a whole host of companies, they may not (they ought to but
they may not) be aware of what undertakings have been given. There cannot be all that
c number of undertakings given by steel companies to the court, but it is just possible that
the corporation might not know about them. If they did not know about an undertaking,
that would go to penalty and no doubt full effect would be given to any such excuse. But
it is not suggested in this case that they did not know. It is because they did know that
the penalty was substantial and is under appeal.

Lastly, it is said by counsel for British Steel that the most interesting possibility, and it
d is interesting, is that if Stanton & Staveley Ltd's undertaking had in fact covered an
activity which was being carried on by the corporation on vesting day, you might have
had an automatic contempt of court by operation of law. For my part I would like to
reserve the question of whether it is a contempt of court to be in instantaneous breach of
an undertaking to the court by operation of statute and without any possibility of
avoiding the breach. But it did not happen, and this must be speculation: I note that the
e minister had power under the second part of s 8(1) to make provision 'for any matter for
which it appears to the Minister requisite or expedient . . . in connection with, or in
consequence of, the vesting'. It would not have surprised me, and I do not think it would
have been ultra vires, if he had provided that the undertaking should transfer at a later
date than the rest of the property or otherwise somehow managed to cushion the blow
to the corporation so that they were not suddenly and overnight standing before the
f court pleading guilty to a contempt of court.

However that may be, it seems to me that the words were plain, that the undertaking
bound the corporation, and that there are no grounds for allowing this appeal which I
would dismiss.

MAY LJ. I too wish to reserve the last question to which Sir John Donaldson MR has
g referred, namely whether one could be put into contempt of court by the mere passing
of a statute. In all other respects I agree entirely with the judgment of Sir John Donaldson
MR and agree that this appeal should be dismissed.

ROBERT GOFF LJ. I also agree.

h *Appeal dismissed.*

Solicitors: *Bristows Cooke & Carpmael* (for British Steel); *Treasury Solicitor.*

Diana Procter   Barrister.

R v Immigration Appeal Tribunal, ex parte   *a*
Coomasaru

COURT OF APPEAL, CIVIL DIVISION
SIR JOHN DONALDSON MR, O'CONNOR AND DILLON LJJ
6, 15 OCTOBER 1982
                                                    b

Immigration – Leave to enter – Indefinite leave – Person who is settled in United Kingdom – Person ordinarily resident without restriction on period for which he can remain – Restriction – Immigrant's passport containing entry 'employed with Sri Lanka High Commission' – Passport stamped with unrestricted entry stamp – Whether immigrant having unrestricted right of entry – Whether period of entry restricted to period of employment with high commission – Whether *c* *immigrant given right of entry as member of diplomatic mission – Immigration Act 1971, ss 2(3)(d), 8(5).*

Immigration – Appeal – Conditions on which leave to enter granted – Rules regulating appeal – Immigration Act 1971, ss 13, 14.
                                                    d

The applicant, a citizen of Sri Lanka, came to the United Kingdom in 1973 as a visitor. Subsequently he was given leave to remain in the United Kingdom so long as he remained in the employment of the Sri Lanka High Commission, with whom he had obtained employment as a sub-warden at the Sri Lanka students' centre. The centre was not part of the Sri Lanka diplomatic mission. On two occasions in 1975 the applicant temporarily left the United Kingdom. On his readmission to the United Kingdom on 11   *e* May and 2 June 1975, the immigration officer, mistakenly believing that the applicant was a member of the Sri Lanka diplomatic mission and exempt from immigration control under s 8[a] of the Immigration Act 1971, gave him leave to re-enter without expressly imposing any restrictions on that leave, and stamped his passport with the ordinary unrestricted entry stamp. However, on the first occasion, on 11 May 1975, the immigration officer wrote in the passport below the entry stamp the words 'employed *f* with Sri Lanka [High Commission]' and on the second occasion, on 7 June 1975, the immigration officer accepted that those words in the passport were true and merely added the ordinary entry stamp beneath them. The applicant remained in the United Kingdom in the employment of the high commission until April or May 1978 when he again went abroad for a short period. He returned on 20 May 1978 and was initially refused readmission, but on 7 June 1978 he was granted conditional leave to enter for 12 *g* months and subject to the further restriction that he could only take employment as a warden at the Sri Lanka students' centre. On 10 August 1978 he applied to the Secretary of State for the conditions of leave to enter imposed on 7 June 1978 to be varied by the grant of indefinite leave to enter, on the grounds that when he was readmitted in May and June 1975 he was, in effect, given indefinite and unconditional leave to enter and remain and was thereafter 'settled in the United Kingdom', i e 'ordinarily resident there *h* without being subject . . . to any restriction on the period for which he [could] remain',

---

a Section 8, so far as material, provides:
    '(3) The provisions of this Act relating to those who are not patrial shall not apply to any person *j* so long as he is a member of a mission (within the meaning of the Diplomatic Privileges Act 1964) . . .
    (5) . . . a person is not to be regarded for purposes of this Act as having been settled in the United Kingdom . . . at any time when he was entitled to an exemption under subsection (3) above . . .'

a within s 2(3)(*d*)[b] of the 1971 Act. The Secretary of State refused to vary the conditions of leave to enter. The applicant's appeals against that decision to an adjudicator and to the appeal tribunal were dismissed. The applicant was refused leave to apply for an order of judicial review of the appeal tribunal's decision. He appealed to the Court of Appeal.

Held – The applicant could not claim that he was already settled in the United Kingdom prior to 20 May 1978, and the appeal would accordingly be dismissed for the following

b reasons—
  (1) The words 'employed with the Sri Lanka [High Commission]' written in his passport when he was readmitted in 1975 restricted the period for which he could remain in the United Kingdom, within s 2(3)(*d*) of the 1971 Act, since he was entitled to remain only so long as he was in the high commission's employment (see p 210 *f* to *j*, p 213 *c d* and p 214 *e f*, post).

c   (2) The applicant was not entitled to claim, on the basis of the entries made in his passport on his readmissions in 1975, that in May 1978 he was already settled in the United Kingdom, because those entries showed that he was being readmitted as a member of a diplomatic mission and, by virtue of s 8(5)[e] of the 1971 Act, that could not provide a basis for settlement in the United Kingdom. From the time of the applicant's 1975 readmissions until his departure from the United Kingdom in 1978 he had only

d enjoyed residence as, or under colour of being, a diplomat, and not independently thereof (see p 210 *f g*, p 213 *c d* and p 214 *f* to *j*, post).
  Discussion of a person's right of appeal under ss 13[c] and 14[d] of the 1971 Act against conditions imposed on his entry into the United Kingdom, and of which immigration rules the adjudicator or appeal tribunal should take into account when hearing the appeal (see p 212 *e* to *h* and p 213 *a* to *d* and *j*, post); *R v Immigration Appeal Tribunal, ex p Aisha*

e *Khatoon Ali* [1979–80] Imm AR 195 considered.

Notes
For entry and settlement of non-patrials, see 4 Halsbury's Laws (4th edn) para 976.
  For appeals against exclusion from the United Kingdom and against conditions of

f entry or stay, see ibid paras 1017–1018.
  For the Immigration Act 1971, ss 2, 8, 13, 14, see 41 Halsbury's Statutes (3rd edn) 17, 29, 34, 35.
  As from 1 January 1983 the 1971 Act was amended as regards the right of abode in the United Kingdom by the British Nationality Act 1981.
  As from 1 March 1980 the rules as to the practice to be followed in the administration

g of the 1971 Act for regulating entry into and the stay of persons in the United Kingdom are set out in the Statement of Changes in Immigration Rules (HC Paper (1979–80) no 394). Transitional provisions are contained in paras 157 to 162 thereof.

Cases referred to in the judgments
R v Immigration Appeal Tribunal, ex p Aisha Khatoon Ali [1979–80] Imm AR 195.

h *R v Secretary of State for the Home Dept, ex p Ram* [1979] 1 All ER 687, [1979] 1 WLR 148, Digest (Cont Vol E) 8, 1154c.

Cases also cited
Alexander v Immigration Appeal Tribunal [1982] 2 All ER 766, [1982] 1 WLR 1076, HL.

j   b   Section 2(3), so far as material, provides: '. . . (*d*) subject to section 8(5) below, references to a person being settled in the United Kingdom . . . are references to his being ordinarily resident there without being subject under the immigration laws to any restriction on the period for which he may remain.'
    c   Section 13, so far as material, is set out at p 211 *a*, post
    d   Section 14, so far as material, is set out at p 211 *b*, post

R v Immigration Appeal Tribunal, ex p Martin [1972] Imm AR 275.
R v Immigration Appeal Tribunal, ex p Prajapati (12 November 1981, unreported), QBD.
R v Immigration Appeal Tribunal, ex p Shaikh [1981] 3 All ER 29, [1981] 1 WLR 1107.

Application for leave to appeal
The applicant, Gilbert Coomasaru, sought leave to appeal against the refusal of Woolf J
hearing the Divisional Court list on 17 March 1981 to grant him leave to apply for an
order of judicial review of a decision of the Immigration Appeal Tribunal dated 2
December 1980 upholding the adjudicator's dismissal of the applicant's appeal against
the decision of the Secretary of State for Home Affairs, dated 5 February 1979, refusing
to vary the conditions on which the applicant was given leave to enter the United
Kingdom on 7 June 1978. In the course of the argument the Court of Appeal granted
the applicant leave to appeal and proceeded to determine the appeal. The grounds of
appeal were (1) that Woolf J misdirected himself as to the purport, effect and proper
construction of HC Paper (1972–73) no 79, (2) that the judge wrongly upheld the appeal
tribunal's decision that the applicant was not settled in the United Kingdom prior to 20
May 1978 and (3) that the judge accordingly wrongly failed to grant the applicant leave
to apply for an order of judicial review of the appeal tribunal's decision. The facts are set
out in the judgment of Dillon LJ.

Michael Beloff QC for the applicant.
Simon D Brown for the appeal tribunal.

Cur adv vult

15 October. The following judgments were delivered.

SIR JOHN DONALDSON MR. This appeal raises two distinct issues. The first is
whether the applicant was entitled to be admitted to this country as a returning resident.
The second is whether, if he was or claimed to be so entitled, he could appeal against the
restrictions imposed on his entry in June 1978.
    I have had the advantage of reading the judgment of Dillon LJ with which I agree.
Both for the purposes of the Immigration Act 1971 and for the purposes of the Statement
of Immigration Rules for Control on Entry: Commonwealth Citizens (HC Paper (1972–
73) no 79) a person is settled in the United Kingdom if he is ordinarily resident there
without being subject under the immigration laws to any restriction on the period for
which he may remain (see s 2(3)(d) of the 1971 Act). No immigration officer had
authority to grant the applicant diplomatic status, but the officer concerned with his
entry on 11 May 1975 was entitled to grant him permission to enter and remain so long
as he was employed with the Sri Lanka High Commission. This, as I see it, is precisely
what he did. It is true that it is an unusual form of permission, but for present purposes
that is immaterial. It is equally immaterial that in granting permission in this form the
officer thought that the applicant had diplomatic status and was exempt from control so
long as he retained that status. What matters is that this form of permission involved a
restriction on the period for which the applicant might remain, namely only so long as
he was employed with the Sri Lanka High Commission, and so prevented his acquiring
the status of one who is settled in the United Kingdom. Quite clearly the permission
given on 2 June 1975 was intended to reinstate the same restricted permission which had
become spent when the applicant left the country on 30 May 1975.
    The second issue, concerning the applicant's right of appeal, is one of general
importance. Part II of the Immigration Act 1971 provides successively in ss 13 to 17 for
five different species of appeal. The appeal is in the first instance to an adjudicator, whose

powers are set out in s 19 and there is a further right of appeal to the appeal tribunal under s 20.

Section 13 is concerned with appeals against exclusion from the United Kingdom: '... a person who is refused leave to enter the United Kingdom under this Act may appeal ...' This type of appeal suffers from the disadvantage from the point of view of the appellant that before he can exercise his right he must first leave the United Kingdom unless he held a current entry clearance permit or was a person named in a current work permit (s 13(3)). No such impediment exists in the case of an appeal under s 14, which is concerned with appeals against conditions attached to a leave to enter:

> '(1) ... a person who has a limited leave under this Act to enter or remain in the United Kingdom may appeal to an adjudicator against any variation of the leave (whether as regards duration or conditions), or against any refusal to vary it ...'

Sections 15, 16 and 17 are not material for present purposes.

The scheme of immigration control in respect of Commonwealth citizens operated in 1978 by means of two apparently distinct sets of rules. The first was entitled 'Statement of Immigration Rules for Control on Entry: Commonwealth Citizens' (HC Paper (1972–73) no 79) (the pre-entry rules). The second was entitled 'Statement of Immigration Rules for Control after Entry: Commonwealth Citizens' (HC Paper (1972–73) no 80) (the post-entry rules). As might be expected, the criteria applied in deciding whether or not a Commonwealth citizen should be allowed to enter the United Kingdom are quite different from those applied in deciding whether or not to vary the conditions applicable to a permit under which the Commonwealth citizen has already entered. In general the latter are designed to take account of changes in circumstances since that entry.

This dichotomy in rules for control and related appeals procedures makes sense until you get a situation in which a would-be immigrant is aggrieved at the conditions which are imposed at the time when he is permitted to enter. This is covered by para 70 of the pre-entry rules, which provides that:

> 'Where a passenger is admitted but is aggrieved by a time limit or condition imposed, or it is clear that it will leave him dissatisfied, it should be explained that his proper course is to apply to the Home Office for variation of his leave, and that he will have a right of appeal if variation is refused.'

The impartial observer, having read that rule, would no doubt say, 'How sensible. If an immigrant is permitted to enter as a visitor when he claims to have been entitled to some other and better status on entry or if he claims to have been entitled to stay for longer than the immigration officer was prepared to permit, it would be absurd to require him not only to treat his limited permission to enter as a refusal of permission to enter but also to leave the United Kingdom before he could appeal. Of course the scheme is that he can use his permission to enter, in accordance with its terms, renew his application for a better status and, if that is refused, appeal under s 14 on the basis that there has been a refusal to vary.'

'Not so', says counsel who has appeared on behalf of the appeal tribunal but is not unfamiliar with the views of the Home Office. 'There may be an unfortunate lacuna in the system, but the sad fact is that s 14 appeals are only concerned with variations which can be claimed on the basis of the post-entry rules, which are not concerned with what status should have been accorded to an immigrant on entry. The immigrant cannot use the s 14 route.' The impartial observer replies, 'Oh; I see. Then I assume that the immigrant can appeal under s 13 and, since he is already in the United Kingdom on the strength of a valid entry permit, he need not first leave the country.' 'Not so,' replies counsel for the appeal tribunal. 'If he wants to appeal under s 13, he must first leave the country, but I ought to warn you that such an appeal is bound to fail unless he not only leaves the country but also reapplies for entry and is refused. If he reapplies for entry and

is again given a limited permit to enter, he will be no better off than when he started.'
'Why?' asks the impartial observer. 'Well,' says counsel for the appeal tribunal, 's 13   *a*
appeals are against a refusal of entry and the immigrant whom we have been discussing
has not been refused entry. He has been permitted to enter, albeit on terms which are
less favourable than those to which he claims to be entitled.' At this point the impartial
observer asks counsel for the appeal tribunal to explain how para 70 of the pre-entry rules
is intended to operate, and counsel says that he will have to take instructions.

The plain fact is that either the s 14 appeal procedure can be used to challenge the   *b*
propriety of conditions imposed on entry or para 70 involves a very serious
misrepresentation by the Secretary of State. I prefer to accept the former alternative.

The interrelationship between s 13 and the pre-entry rules on the one hand and s 14
and the post-entry rules on the other was considered by a Divisional Court of the Queen's
Bench Division in *R v Immigration Appeal Tribunal, ex p Aisha Khatoon Ali* [1979–80] Imm
AR 195. There, as here, Mr Beloff appeared for the immigrant, but Mr Latham appeared   *c*
for the tribunal. The facts were slightly different and may have obscured the full
enormity of the Home Office's interpretation of para 70 of the pre-entry rules. It seems
that Mrs Ali had been told by the entry clearance office in Karachi that she was not
entitled to return to the United Kingdom for settlement and in consequence possibly
asked for and certainly accepted a visitor's entry permit. It was only after she had entered
that she thought to claim that she ought always to have been allowed to return for   *d*
settlement. The Divisional Court held that the two systems of control were quite separate,
that Mrs Ali, having entered, had to rely on the post-entry rules and that her complaints
related to the pre-entry rules and not to the post-entry rules. Mrs Ali was, as the Divisional
Court saw it, asking the Secretary of State to apply the pre-entry rules to someone in this
country and, whilst he had discretion to do so, his refusal to depart from the immigration
rules was not appealable (see s 19(2) of the 1971 Act).   *e*

For my part I accept that the s 13 appeal procedure is intended only for those who are
refused entry. I also accept that the s 14 appeal procedure is concerned with a variation
of leave to enter or a refusal to vary such leave. Where I part company with the appeal
tribunal and also, I think, with the Home Office and the decision of the Divisional Court
in *Ali*'s case is in relation to the rules to be applied on the hearing and determination of a
s 14 appeal. Although a s 14 appeal will always concern a variation of the conditions of   *f*
an entry permit or a refusal to vary those conditions, such an appeal can fall into either
of two quite different categories. The first category is a complaint that the Secretary of
State has failed to vary the conditions of an entry permit in the light of some change in
circumstances. The basis of any such complaint must always be that the provisions of the
post-entry rules have not been correctly applied. Accordingly the 'immigration rules
applicable to the case' referred to in s 19 of the 1971 Act, which gives the adjudicator   *g*
jurisdiction, are those contained in the post-entry rules. The second category is a
complaint that the entry permit was subject to conditions which could not be justified
under the terms of the pre-entry rules and a further complaint that the Secretary of State
has refused to put this error right. Here the 'immigration rules applicable to the case' are
those contained in the pre-entry rules.

If this is right, para 70 of the pre-entry rules not only makes sense, but affords the   *h*
immigrant the guidance which he needs. If it is not, para 70 is grossly misleading.

Counsel for the appeal tribunal asked us to hold that there can be no complaint about
a failure to apply the pre-entry rules correctly if the immigrant at the time of entry did
not ask for that to which he was entitled. I see the force of this from the point of view of
the Home Office. Immigration officers are busy people and if someone seeks admission
as a visitor, as Mrs Ali seems to have done, it is a little hard to criticise them for not   *j*
ferreting out the fact that the immigrant is entitled to something more. However,
looked at from the point of view of the immigrant, the point is not so attractive.
Immigrants do not always know what is their entitlement (Mrs Ali probably did not)
although I do not doubt that many of them are very well informed indeed.

I would reconcile these two points of view in this way. First, I would repudiate any suggestion that an immigration appeal necessarily involves any criticism of the immigration officer. He may merely not have appreciated the true facts. Second, I would draw a distinction between the case of an immigrant who always wanted the type of entry permit which he claims in the appeal, whether or not he asked for it at the time of entry, and one who, subsequent to entry, changed his mind. The latter is not in my view entitled to complain of the conditions attached to his entry permit or to seek a variation, unless he can bring himself within the post-entry rules. The former is entitled to do so in reliance on the pre-entry rules. On the facts of any particular case, the Secretary of State and, on appeal, the adjudicator and the Immigration Appeal Tribunal will take full account of the fact, if such it be, that when the immigrant entered the country he did not ask for the type of entry permit which he is now seeking and will demand an explanation in order to be satisfied that this is not merely a case of a change of intention.

In the light of our decision on the first issue, the second does not arise for decision in this appeal, but, bearing in mind its general importance, I have felt it right to express my view which I would have applied if the applicant had succeeded on the first issue.

O'CONNOR LJ. I have had the advantage of reading the judgments prepared by Sir John Donaldson MR and Dillon LJ. I agree with both judgments and for the reasons given would dismiss the appeal.

DILLON LJ. The applicant in this case, who is a citizen of Sri Lanka, seeks leave to appeal against the refusal of Woolf J, hearing the Divisional Court list to grant him leave to apply for an order for judicial review of a decision of the Immigration Tribunal dated 2 December 1980. That decision of the tribunal dismissed an appeal by the applicant against a determination of an adjudicator, Mr Healey, who in turn had dismissed an appeal by the applicant against a refusal by the Secretary of State, on 5 January 1979, to revoke or vary the conditions subject to which the applicant had been allowed to enter the United Kingdom in June 1978.

The applicant first came to the United Kingdom as a visitor in August 1973. He subsequently got the job of sub-warden of the Sri Lanka Students' Welfare Centre, but his right to remain in the United Kingdom continued to be only restricted and temporary. He left the United Kingdom on 11 May 1975 but returned and was readmitted on the same day. He left again on 30 May 1975 but returned and was readmitted on 2 June 1975. He then remained in the United Kingdom until April or May 1978, when he went abroad for a short period. He returned on 20 May 1978 and was initially refused readmission, but that was modified on 7 June 1978 when he was granted permission to enter for 12 months only subject to the further restriction that he could take no employment save as sub-warden of the Sri Lanka Students' Welfare Centre. He now no longer holds that employment.

The substance of the applicant's case is that on a true appreciation of what happened when he was readmitted on 11 May and 2 June 1975 he was granted, although not in express terms, unconditional leave to enter and remain in the United Kingdom. Therefore when he left the United Kingdom in 1978 for the trip from which he returned on 20 May 1978 he was, he says, already settled in the United Kingdom within the meaning of s 2(3)(d) of the Immigration Act 1971 and para 51 of the relevant immigration rules, the Statement of Immigration Rules for Control on Entry: Commonwealth Citizens (HC Paper (1972–73) no 79), and should have been readmitted unconditionally.

He is met in part by a procedural difficulty in that it is said, and in a previous case the Divisional Court has so held, that on a proper construction of the rules a person who objects to the conditions imposed on his entry to the United Kingdom where entry is allowed subject to conditions and is not refused outright has no right of appeal. As to that, I have had the advantage of reading the judgment of Sir John Donaldson MR and I entirely agree with him.

On the substance of the applicant's case, the position is very shortly this. When he was readmitted to the United Kingdom on 11 May 1975 the immigration officer, to whom he presented his passport, stamped the passport with the ordinary entry stamp and wrote below that stamp the words in brackets 'employed with Sri Lanka HC', meaning the Sri Lanka High Commission. It is common ground that the immigration officer did this because he had made a mistake, in no way induced by the applicant. The immigration officer had been shown a letter from the High Commissioner for Sri Lanka which referred to the applicant's appointment as sub-warden of the Sri Lanka Students' Welfare Centre, and he erroneously supposed that the applicant was entitled, because of that appointment, to diplomatic status, and, as a member of a mission within the meaning of the Diplomatic Privileges Act 1964, was exempt from immigration control: see s 8(3) of the Immigration Act 1971.

When the applicant presented himself for readmission the next time on 2 June 1975 the immigration officer stamped his passport with the ordinary entry stamp on the same page as and just below the reference to employment with the Sri Lanka High Commission. It is common ground that the immigration officer was simply following what his colleague had done on 11 May, and making the same mistake.

The applicant submits that he was granted unconditional and unrestricted permission to enter and remain in the United Kingdom in 1975, albeit by a mistake, and he further submits that he can rely on that permission now, although it was granted by mistake, since he did not induce the mistake. He relies on *R v Secretary of State for the Home Dept, ex p Ram* [1979] 1 All ER 687, [1979] 1 WLR 148. That case was, if I may say so, plainly correct on its facts, but it is distinguishable from the present case in that the stamp on Mr Ram's passport would expressly have said 'Leave to enter for an indefinite period' whereas the stamps on the applicant's passport are qualified by the words 'employed with Sri Lanka [High Commission]'.

Those words are in my judgment fatal to the applicant's contentions for two reasons. In the first place, they constitute, as I read them, a qualification of the permission to enter which is evidenced by the entry stamp. The applicant was granted permission to enter and remain in the United Kingdom only for so long as he should be employed with the Sri Lanka High Commission. That was a restriction on the period for which he might remain which prevents him from being settled in the United Kingdom within the meaning of the 1971 Act or the relevant immigration rules (HC Paper (1972–73) no 79).

In the second place, the applicant points to the 1975 entries in his passport in order to establish that he has been ordinarily resident, which means lawfully resident, in the United Kingdom. But he has to take the entries as a whole including the qualifying words and he is not entitled to be treated better than the Home Office have, on the face of his passport, treated him. Under s 8(5) of the 1971 Act residence as a diplomat cannot found a settlement in the United Kingdom, but from his readmissions in 1975 until his departure in 1978 the applicant only enjoyed residence in the United Kingdom as a diplomat or under colour of his being a diplomat and not independently of any actual or supposed diplomatic status. He cannot now claim to be settled here.

In the course of the argument this court granted the applicant leave to appeal. I would now dismiss his appeal.

Appeal dismissed. Leave to appeal to the House of Lords refused.

Solicitors: *Seifert Sedley & Co* (for the applicant); *Treasury Solicitor*.

Diana Procter   Barrister.

Hawkins v Harold A Russett Ltd

QUEEN'S BENCH DIVISION
O'CONNOR LJ AND COMYN J
26, 27 JULY, 12 OCTOBER 1982

Road traffic – Heavy motor vehicle – Overhang – Overall length – Permitted overhang exceeded when container clipped onto vehicle – Container acting as body of vehicle – Container easily detachable and transferable to other vehicles – Whether vehicle exceeding permitted overhang – Whether container part of vehicle – Motor Vehicles (Construction and Use) Regulations 1978, reg 58.

A heavy lorry belonging to the respondents, who were road hauliers, was designed to be used with a container clipped onto the bed of the lorry so as to act as the body of the lorry and provide the lorry's carrying capacity. The container was easily detachable from the bed of the lorry and was intended to be transferable to other vehicles in the course of the respondents' business. Without the container the overhang at the rear of the lorry was within the limits permitted by reg 58[a] of the Motor Vehicles (Construction and Use) Regulations 1978, but when the container was clipped on the overhang at the rear exceeded the limit permitted by reg 58. The respondents used the lorry with the container and were charged in an information with using a heavy vehicle on a road with a rear overhang exceeding the permitted overhang of such a vehicle, contrary to reg 58. The magistrates dismissed the information because they found that the container was part of the load being carried by the lorry and was not, for the purpose of reg 58, part of the vehicle itself. The prosecutor appealed.

Held – The body of a vehicle did not cease to be such merely because it was easily detachable from the vehicle, and accordingly the fact that a vehicle was so designed that its body comprised a detachable container did not mean that for the purpose of reg 58 of the 1978 regulations the container had to be treated as a container rather than as the body of the vehicle. The correct question when considering the overhang or overall length of a heavy vehicle of similar design to the respondents' lorry was whether the vehicle was fitted with a body. On the facts, the container attached to the respondents' lorry was the body of the vehicle and was not merely the load which the vehicle was carrying. It followed that the lorry's overhang with the container clipped on exceeded the permitted overhang of a heavy vehicle under reg 58. The appeal would therefore be allowed and the case remitted to the magistrates with a direction to convict the respondent (see p 217 *g h* and p 218 *c* to *f*, post).

Patterson v Redpath Bros Ltd [1979] 2 All ER 108 and *Bindley v Willett* [1981] RTR 19 applied.

Notes

For the overall length and overhang of a heavy motor vehicle, see 33 Halsbury's Laws (3rd edn) 422, 428, paras 694, 722, and for cases on excessive overall length of a vehicle, see 45 Digest (Repl) 76, 232–235.

Cases referred to in judgment

Andrews v H E Kershaw Ltd [1951] 2 All ER 764, [1952] 1 KB 70, DC, 45 Digest (Repl) 76, 232.
Bindley v Willett [1981] RTR 19, DC.
Guest Scottish Carriers Ltd v Trend [1967] 3 All ER 52, [1967] 1 WLR 1371, DC, Digest (Cont Vol C) 923, 235a.

---

a   Regulation 58, so far as material, is set out at p 217 *c*, post

Patterson v Redpath Bros Ltd [1979] 2 All ER 108, [1979] 1 WLR 553, DC, Digest (Cont Vol E) 578, 203a.

Cases also cited
Hughes (Claude) & Co (Carlisle) Ltd v Hyde [1963] 1 All ER 598, [1963] 2 QB 757, DC.
Marston Services Ltd v Police Authority (1934) 98 JP Jo 848.

Case stated
Peter Ronald Hawkins (the prosecutor) appealed by way of case stated by the justices for the County of Somerset acting in and for the petty sessional division of Taunton Deane in respect of their adjudication as a magistrates' court sitting at the Shire Hall, Taunton on 4 February 1982 on an information preferred against the respondents, Harold A Russett Ltd, a haulage company, alleging that on 28 April 1981 at Trull in Somerset the respondents used a vehicle on the M5 motorway which did not comply with reg 58 of the Motor Vehicles (Construction and Use) Regulations 1978, SI 1978/1017, in that the overhang of the vehicle at the rear exceeded the permitted overhang, contrary to the 1978 regulations and s 40(5) of the Road Traffic Act 1972, as amended. The justices found that the container which was secured to the bed of the lorry by clips but was detachable was part of the load and not part of the vehicle and dismissed the information. The question for the opinion of the High Court was whether the justices' conclusion that the container formed part of the load, and was not part of the vehicle for the purpose of reg 58 of the 1978 regulations, was correct. The facts are set out in the judgment of O'Connor LJ.

Ian Glen for the prosecutor.
David Griffiths for the respondents.

Cur adv vult

12 October. The following judgments were delivered.

O'CONNOR LJ (read by Comyn J). This is an appeal by case stated by the prosecution against the dismissal of an information by the justices for the petty sessional division of Taunton Deane.

The case shows that the respondents were alleged to have used a motor vehicle on the road in contravention of reg 58 of the Motor Vehicles (Construction and Use) Regulations 1978, SI 1978/1017, in that there was an excessive overhang at the rear. Regulation 58 provides a formula for controlling the overhang of the vehicle to the rear. This vehicle had no body in the conventional sense for it was designed to be used with a container clipped on to act as a body. Without a container clipped on, the vehicle complied with reg 58, but when a container was clipped on and if it formed part of the vehicle then there was an excessive overhang at the rear.

The question was whether the container when clipped on became part of the vehicle or was it part of the load. The justices found that it was part of the load and dismissed the information.

The justices found the following facts relevant to the issue:

'The vehicle was laden with jam, scaffolding and paper which was packed into a large rigid oblong container. This container was secured to the bed of the lorry by clips. The container was completely detachable and removable without disturbing the load. The container was not a specific part of this particular lorry being transferable quickly and easily to other similar vehicles. The respondent company traded as Premier Transport and was one of the largest haulage companies in the south-west of England. The entire transport fleet was containerised and the containers were transferred at frequent intervals to other vehicles during the ordinary course of business. The container in question was being used to carry items which were intended to be off-loaded at various separate places with the container in situ.'

Free of any statutory provision or authority I do not think there is any difficulty about answering the question whether this container was part of the vehicle or the load. In one sense the justices answer the question in their findings of fact when they said 'the vehicle was loaded with jam, scaffolding and paper . . . items which were intended to be off-loaded at various . . . places . . .' They did not say nor would anyone say 'the vehicle was loaded with a container'. Am I then driven to hold that contrary to common sense this clipped-on container was not part of the vehicle but was part of the load?

I start by considering the relevant Motor Vehicles (Construction and Use) Regulations 1978. The relevant part of reg 58 provides:

'The overhang of a heavy motor car shall not exceed 60 per cent. of the distance between the plane perpendicular to the longitudinal axis of the vehicle which passes through the centre or centres of the front wheel or wheels and the foremost vertical plane from which the overhang is to be measured as defined in Regulation 3 . . .'

'Overhang', as defined in reg 3, means the distance measured horizontally and parallel to the longitudinal axis of a vehicle between two vertical planes at right angles to that axis passing through the following two points, namely 'the rearmost point of the vehicle' and a forward point defined by reference to the rear axle of the vehicle.

So the search is for the 'rearmost point of the vehicle'. Regulation 9 places limits on the overall length of various types of vehicles. 'Overall length', as defined in reg 3, means—

'the length of a vehicle measured between vertical planes at right angles to the longitudinal axis of the vehicle and passing through the extreme projecting points thereof exclusive of—[there follow a number of excluded projections such as starting handles. The definition continues:] In ascertaining the extreme projecting points of a vehicle account shall be taken of any device or any receptacle on or attached to the vehicle which increases the carrying capacity of the vehicle unless—[(i) and (ii) deal with tailboards] (iii) it is a receptacle which is constructed or adapted for the purpose of being lifted on or off vehicles with goods or burden contained therein and is from time to time actually used for that purpose in the ordinary course of business.'

The respondents submit that these provisions show that a container such as the one used as a body in this case is not a part of the vehicle because if it were it would not be necessary to say that account should be taken of it and in any event it is excluded by para (iii) of the definition of 'overall length', the justices having found that from time to time it was removed from the vehicle in the ordinary course of business.

I cannot accept this submission. There is no evidence that this container 'increased the carrying capacity of the vehicle'; on the contrary, the evidence was that it provided the carrying capacity of the vehicle so that the exemption in para (iii) of the definition of 'overall length' is not operative. It is plainly desirable that 'rearmost point' for overhang should be the same as the 'extreme projecting point [to the rear]' for overall length. In *Patterson v Redpath Bros Ltd* [1979] 2 All ER 108, [1979] 1 WLR 553 this court held that a container was not an 'indivisible load' for the purposes of reg 9(1) but was part of the vehicle. Although the respondents relied on the last paragraph of the definition of 'overall length' no mention is made of it in the judgments, presumably on the ground that the vehicle was a special purpose vehicle designed and constructed to be fitted with the container in question.

In *Bindley v Willett* [1981] RTR 19 this court held that a container designed to be bolted to the flat platform of the vehicle but was not bolted was part of the vehicle for the purposes of reg 90(1) of the 1973 regulations (reg 97(1) of the 1978 regulations) as the justices had found.

In *Guest Scottish Carriers Ltd v Trend* [1967] 3 All ER 52, [1967] 1 WLR 1371, a tailboard case, this court held that the present definition of 'overall length' which first appeared in the 1964 regulations was designed to meet the difficulty expressed by the majority of the court in *Andrews v H E Kershaw Ltd* [1951] 2 All ER 764, [1952] 1 KB 70 and that the justices had correctly found the overhang excessive where the excess was created by a tailboard let down to horizontal and used to carry furniture. Lord Parker CJ was quite clear that the rearmost point of the vehicle for overhang should be the same as the extreme projecting point to the rear for overall length. He said so (see [1967] 3 All ER 52 at 55, [1967] 1 WLR 1371 at 1375). I do not get any help from the other authorities cited.

I have great sympathy with the justices, faced as they were with difficult regulations to construe and what may be thought to be conflicting cases. It is obvious that parts of a vehicle which are detachable do not cease to be parts of the vehicle, for example the wheels. The fact that the body of a vehicle is detachable does not justify referring to it as a 'container'. When overall length or overhang are in issue in a case such as the present, I think that the correct question to ask is: 'Is this vehicle fitted with a body?' The body of a vehicle does not cease to be a body because it can be detached with ease, laden or unladen and fitted to a sister chassis. This does not make the body 'a receptable on or attached to the vehicle . . .': it is part of the vehicle. On the facts of the present case as found by the justices, coupled with the sketch and photograph of the vehicle, the correct question can only receive one answer: 'This vehicle was fitted with a body.' It was not carrying a container; its body was loaded with jam etc; the overhang was excessive.

Very understandably the justices fell into error. I would allow the appeal and send the case back with a direction to convict.

COMYN J. So far as my own judgment is concerned, it is brief and I hope to the point. I agree and have nothing to add.

Appeal allowed ; case remitted to justices with direction to convict.

Solicitors: *Blyth Dutton Holloway*, agents for *R O M Lovibond*, Bristol (for the prosecutor); *Keary Stokes & White*, Corsham (for the respondents).

Raina Levy   Barrister.

Re C (a minor) (wardship: care order)

FAMILY DIVISION AT LIVERPOOL
BALCOMBE J
24 MARCH, 28 JUNE, 8 JULY 1982

Child – Care – Local authority – Wardship proceedings – Existing care order made in criminal proceedings by juvenile court – Whether jurisdiction to make care order in favour of local authority in wardship proceedings – Whether in child's interests to make care order in wardship proceedings – Whether care order in wardship proceedings superseding existing care order made by juvenile court – Family Law Reform Act 1969, s 7(2) – Children and Young Persons Act 1969, s 7(7).

In 1979 a child who had been made a ward of court in proceedings issued by his grandmother (who lived in Leeds) was placed by the court in the care and control of his father who lived in Norfolk. In October 1980, at the father's request, the child was received into the care of Norfolk County Council (Norfolk) on the ground that he was out of control. In January 1981 the child was found guilty in a Norfolk juvenile court of certain offences. The juvenile court, pursuant to s 7(7)[a] of the Children and Young Persons Act 1969, made a care order in respect of the child in favour of Norfolk. Norfolk then returned the child to his father for a trial period. The child ran away to Leeds to his grandmother and Norfolk then placed him with the grandmother for a trial period and asked Leeds City Council (Leeds) to exercise supervision over him on Norfolk's behalf. While in Leeds the child committed further offences and was sentenced to a period in a detention centre. Norfolk applied to the juvenile court to have the care order in its favour discharged on the ground that the order had proved ineffective and to continue it would be of no value. Leeds opposed the application, submitting that it would not be in the child's best interests to discharge the care order. The juvenile court refused to discharge the care order. When the child was released from the detention centre Norfolk again placed him with his grandmother in Leeds for a trial period but Leeds took the view that he ought to be placed in a local authority residential home and declined to supervise him while he was living with his grandmother. Norfolk could not adequately supervise him while he was in Leeds and in those circumstances the Official Solicitor, who was the child's guardian ad litem in the wardship proceedings, applied in the wardship proceedings for an interim care order to be made in favour of Leeds under s 7(2)[b] of the Family Law Reform Act 1969. Leeds submitted that, because there was an existing care order in favour of Norfolk which had been made by a juvenile court in the exercise of its criminal jurisdiction, a court exercising the civil jurisdiction of wardship could not interfere with that care order and therefore while the care order in favour of Norfolk subsisted the court had no jurisdiction to make a care order under s 7(2) of the Family Law Reform Act 1969. Leeds further submitted that, because the child was already in

---

a   Section 7(7), so far as material, provides: '. . . where a . . . young person is found guilty of any offence by or before any court, that court or the court to which his case is remitted shall have power—(a) if the offence is punishable in the case of an adult with imprisonment, to make a care order (other than an interim order) in respect of him . . . and, if it makes such an order as is mentioned in this subsection while another such order made by any court is in force in respect of the child or young person, shall also have power to discharge the earlier order . . .'

b   Section 7(2) provides: 'Where it appears to the court that there are exceptional circumstances making it impracticable or undesirable for a ward of court to be, or to continue to be, under the care of either of his parents or of any other individual the court may, if it thinks fit, make an order committing the care of the ward to a local authority; and thereupon Part III of the Child Care Act 1980 (which relates to the treatment of children in the care of a local authority) shall, subject to the next following subsection, apply as if the child had been received by the local authority into their care under section 2 of that Act.'

the care of Norfolk, the pre-conditions for making a care order under s 7(2) of the Family
Law Reform Act 1969 could not be satisfied, since it could not be shown that it was *a*
'impracticable or undesirable for [the child] to be ... under the care of either of his
parents or of any other individual'. Leeds also submitted that if the wardship court did
have jurisdiction to make a care order s 7(2) it should not, in the circumstances, exercise
it. Before hearing the application the judge discharged the care order in favour of the
father made in the wardship proceedings in 1979.

Held – (1) Since the aim of a court exercising wardship jurisdiction was to make an *b*
order which would protect, and be for the welfare of, the ward, the court could invoke
its jurisdiction under s 7(2) of the Family Law Reform Act 1969 to make an order
committing the care of a ward to a local authority if it was in the best interests of the
ward to do so, notwithstanding the existence of a care order made by a court exercising
criminal jurisdiction under s 7(7) of the Children and Young Persons Act 1969. *c*
Accordingly, the existence of the care order in favour of Norfolk made by the juvenile
court did not preclude the court from making a care order in favour of Leeds in the
wardship proceedings (see p 223 *j* to p 224 *d* and *f*, post); *Re D (a minor)* [1977] 3 All ER
481 and dictum of Lord Roskill in *A v Liverpool City Council* [1981] 2 All ER at 393
applied.

(2) Furthermore, the existence of the care order in favour of Norfolk did not prevent *d*
the pre-conditions for making a care order under s 7(2) of the Family Law Reform Act
1969 from being satisfied, since there were exceptional circumstances making it
impracticable and undesirable for the child to be under the care of 'any other individual',
namely his grandmother (see p 225 *a b*, post).

(3) Since it was impossible for Norfolk adequately to take direct care of the child while
he lived in Leeds, and since Leeds was no longer prepared to exercise supervision over *e*
him on behalf of Norfolk, it was in the interests of the child that the court should make
a care order under s 7(2) of the Family Law Reform Act 1969 in favour of Leeds.
Accordingly, the court would make such an order, which would supersede the care order
in favour of Norfolk (see p 225 *b* to *e*, post).

Notes *f*
For care and supervision orders in the wardship jurisdiction, see 24 Halsbury's Laws (4th
edn) para 596.
    For the imposition of a care order on a juvenile offender, see ibid para 898:13.
    For the Family Law Reform Act 1969, s 7, see 17 Halsbury's Statutes (3rd edn) 797.
    For the Children and Young Persons Act 1969, s 7, see 40 ibid 861.

g
Cases referred to in judgment
A v Liverpool City Council [1981] 2 All ER 385, [1982] AC 363, [1981] 2 WLR 948, HL.
D (a minor) (justices' decision: review), Re [1977] 3 All ER 481, [1977] Fam 158, [1977] 2
    WLR 1006, Digest (Cont Vol E) 326, 2247a.
H (a minor) (wardship: jurisdiction), Re [1978] 2 All ER 903, [1978] Fam 65, [1978] 2 WLR
    608, CA, Digest (Cont Vol E) 324, 2239b. *h*

Summons in wardship proceedings
The Official Solicitor applied as the guardian ad litem in wardship proceedings of a boy,
S, who had been made a ward of court in April 1979 in proceedings issued by his
grandmother as the plaintiff to which S and his parents were defendants, seeking an
order that S be given into the care and control of his grandmother, who lived in Leeds, *j*
with a supervision order in favour of Leeds City Council probation service. The questions
arose (i) whether the court had jurisdiction to make the order sought having regard to an
existing care order in respect of S in favour of Norfolk County Council made in January
1981 by the King's Lynn juvenile court under s 7(7) of the Children and Young Persons
Act 1969, (ii) if the court had jurisdiction despite the existing care order, whether it had

jurisdiction to make a care order in favour of Leeds City Council under s 7(2) of the Family Law Reform Act 1969 and (iii) if it had jurisdiction to make a care order under s 7(2) of the Family Law Reform Act 1969 whether that would be in the best interests of S. The application was heard and judgment was delivered in chambers at Liverpool. The case is reported by permission of Balcombe J. The facts are set out in the judgment.

D Peter Hunt for the Official Solicitor as guardian ad litem.
Sally Cahill for Leeds City Council.
Barbara Wootliff for the grandmother.
The parents and Norfolk County Council did not appear.

Cur adv vult

8 July. The following judgment was delivered.

BALCOMBE J. This is yet another case which raises the question of the relationship between the wardship jurisdiction of the High Court and the statutory provisions concerning children.

Two children, a boy and a girl, became wards of court on 6 April 1979 when an originating summons under the Law Reform (Miscellaneous Provisions) Act 1949 was issued by the plaintiff, their paternal grandmother. To that summons the father of the wards was the only defendant but, on 17 May 1979, I directed that the mother and the wards themselves should be added as defendants and that the Official Solicitor be invited to act as guardian ad litem of the wards. This invitation was duly accepted. On 25 October 1979 Waterhouse J gave care and control of the wards to their father and made a supervision order in favour of the probation service. On 24 March 1982 I discharged the order of 25 October 1979 giving care and control of the wards to their father. In the case of the girl I made a further supervision order in favour of the probation service and her position now occasions no difficulty. It is with the boy, S, that this case is concerned.

S was born on 28 October 1966, and so is now 15¾. When those proceedings started he was living with his paternal grandmother in Leeds and had done so since soon after his birth. The immediate cause of these proceedings was an occasion in March 1979, when S went to his father and stepmother at their home in a caravan on a site near King's Lynn, Norfolk. By the time the order of 25 October 1979 was made the father had moved to a caravan site at Boston, Lincolnshire, and it was to that home that S went in October 1979. The family moved to Leeds in March 1980, but left again in April 1980, and the probation service lost contact with them until October 1980 when they were traced to King's Lynn. During this period S ran away from home on several occasions and was invariably returned by the police. On 22 October 1980, S was received into the care of the Norfolk County Council (whom I will refer to as 'Norfolk') under s 1 of the Children Act 1948, the father having reported him as being beyond his control. S again ran away from the assessment centre where he had been placed, and was traced to Leeds and again absconded. He was eventually returned to King's Lynn and on 8 January 1981 appeared before the King's Lynn juvenile court charged with theft and taking a motor car without the owner's consent. On his being found guilty of these offences the juvenile court made a care order in favour of Norfolk pursuant to their powers under s 7(7) of the Children and Young Persons Act 1969. That care order is still in force.

Following the care order S was returned to his father 'home on trial', but ran away to Leeds. He was then placed with his grandmother 'home on trial', and Norfolk asked Leeds social services department to exercise their supervisory functions under the care order. S's disruptive behaviour continued, he refused to attend school and absconded more than once from the assessment centre, from the residential school in which he was placed, and from the hospital to which he was admitted when he suffered an injury. During the periods when he was on the run he committed criminal offences. On two occasions in November 1981 the Leeds magistrates' court certified that S was of so unruly

a character that he could not safely be committed to the care of a local authority and he
was placed at a remand centre. Eventually, on 4 December 1981, S appeared at Leeds
Crown Court charged with taking a motor car without the owner's consent, criminal
damage and driving whilst disqualified. He was found guilty and sentenced to three
months in a detention centre.

On 14 January 1982 (the day before S's discharge from the detention centre) Norfolk
applied to the King's Lynn juvenile court for the discharge of the care order made on 8
January 1981. The application was supported by a report from the social services
department of Norfolk which set out S's history in some detail, and concluded that the
care order had proved ineffective and that there was no value in its continuation. The
application was opposed by the Leeds City Council (whom I will refer to as 'Leeds'),
whose social services department also put in a report, submitting that the facts (which
were recited) indicated that S was still very much in need of the care and control afforded
by the care order, and that its revocation would not be in his best interests. The King's
Lynn juvenile court refused the application on the grounds, as set out in a letter to this
court from their clerk, that it appeared to that court that S was still in need of care and
control and the court was not satisfied that he would receive that care or control if the
order were discharged.

On 15 January 1982 S was discharged from the detention centre and was again placed
by Norfolk at 'home on trial' with his grandmother. The social services department of
Leeds was of the opinion that S continued to warrant residential care and informed
Norfolk that they would be unwilling to supervise S on the basis of his remaining in the
community with his grandmother. In consequence S has nominally been supervised by
Norfolk since January, but it is clearly impossible for that supervision to be adequate,
having regard to the distances involved.

It was in these circumstances that the Official Solicitor took out an application in the
wardship for an order that S be given into the care and control of his grandmother, with
a supervision order in favour of the probation service. This application came before me
on 24 March 1982. I was concerned to be satisfied that I had jurisdiction to make such an
order, having regard to the existing care order in favour of Norfolk. Assuming I had
jurisdiction, I was also concerned to be satisfied that such an order would be in S's best
interests, having regard to the opinion of Leeds referred to above, and I wished to be able,
if appropriate, to make an order under s 7(2) of the Family Law Reform Act 1969
committing the care of S to a local authority, that is Leeds. Accordingly I adjourned the
matter for further argument and directed that notice of the adjourned hearing be given
to Leeds under s 7(3) of the Family Law Reform Act 1969 incorporating by reference
s 43(2) of the Matrimonial Causes Act 1973; see also RSC Ord 90, r 11(1) and the
Matrimonial Causes Rules 1977, SI 1977/344, r 93(1). I also directed that notice of the
adjourned hearing be given to Norfolk.

The matter came back before me on 28 June 1982 when the Official Solicitor, Leeds
and the grandmother were all represented before me. Norfolk did not appear, nor did S's
father or mother. There was a further report before me from the social services
department of Leeds indicating that S's disruptive behaviour had continued since his
release from the detention centre in January. He has failed to attend school with any
degree of regularity and has been charged with further criminal offences, including
criminal damage, burglary and theft. On 15 June he was remanded by the Leeds juvenile
court to the local authority and is currently residing in a remand and assessment centre.

On the most recent hearing the contentions before me were as follows. (1) The Official
Solicitor asked me to make an interim care order in favour of Leeds. In view of the
present circumstances, he no longer submitted that care and control to the grandmother,
together with a supervision order, would be adequate. (2) Leeds submitted that there
should be no order in the wardship leaving S in the care of Norfolk under the order of
the King's Lynn juvenile court of 8 January 1981. (3) The grandmother submitted that I
should restore S to her care and control, with a supervision order in favour of Norfolk if
necessary.

In order to deal with these contentions I have to consider, first, what is the power of the court exercising jurisdiction in wardship to make an order for S's care, having regard to the existing order of the juvenile court? Second, assuming this court has the necessary power, what order does S's welfare require?

Although S was a ward of court before he came before the King's Lynn juvenile court, there is no question but that that court, in exercising its criminal jurisdiction, was able to make a care order under s 7(7) of the Children and Young Persons Act 1969. Any other result would gravely handicap a juvenile court dealing with a ward of court who commits a criminal offence. It necessarily follows that, so long as that care order remained in force, the operation of the pre-existing order of this court giving care and control of S to the father was suspended. That situation, in which two inconsistent orders of different courts relating to S were in existence at the same time, came to an end when I discharged the order giving care and control to the father on 24 March 1982.

It is also common ground that this court has no power to discharge the care order made by the King's Lynn juvenile court. That power is entrusted to the juvenile court under s 21(2) of the Children and Young Persons Act 1969. However, sub-s (2A) of that section provides that a juvenile court shall not make an order under sub-s (2) in the case of a person who has not attained the age of 18 and appears to the court to be in need of care and control unless the court is satisfied that, whether through the making of a supervision order or otherwise, he will receive that care and control. (It appears that it was because of this restriction that the King's Lynn juvenile court refused to discharge the care order.) It is also open to a court which makes a care order under s 7(7) of the Children and Young Persons Act 1969, while another such order made by any court is in force in respect of the young person, to discharge the earlier order. Thus if the court before which S comes on the charges currently pending against him were minded to make a care order in favour of Leeds, it would have power to discharge the care order in favour of Norfolk. I considered whether I should adjourn the further hearing of this application pending the decision on the current charges, but I am persuaded that this would not be a desirable course. S may be acquitted of the charges against him; alternatively, if he is convicted, having regard to his past record the juvenile court may commit him to the Crown Court with a view to a sentence of Borstal training. In either of these events the present problem would remain unresolved.

The real issue between the Official Solicitor on the one hand and Leeds on the other is whether I have the power, notwithstanding the existence of the care order in favour of Norfolk made by the King's Lynn juvenile court, to make a care order in favour of Leeds and, if I have that power, whether I should exercise it.

Counsel for Leeds submitted that a care order made under s 7(7) of the Children and Young Persons Act 1969 in respect of a young person who has been found guilty of an offence is in the nature of a punishment with which this court, exercising a civil jurisdiction, cannot and should not interfere. Indeed she went so far as to submit that the court exercising criminal jurisdiction could under that section discharge an earlier order made by this court in wardship. She based this latter submission on the following words in s 7(7): 'and, if it makes such an order as is mentioned in this subsection while another such order made by any court is in force in respect of the child or young person, shall also have power to discharge the earlier order'. '*Any* court', says counsel means what it says and includes the High Court. The point does not arise directly for decision in this case, but I am not convinced that the submission is correct. 'Such an order as is mentioned in this subsection' means a care order, a supervision order or an order on a parent or guardian to enter into a recognisance to take proper care of, and exercise proper control over, the young offender *made by a court exercising criminal jurisdiction by or before which the young person has been found guilty of an offence.* 'Another such order' is accordingly qualified in relation to the court which made the original order.

The primary submission of counsel for Leeds, that this court, exercising wardship jurisdiction, cannot make an order which is inconsistent with an order made by a court exercising criminal jurisdiction, is in my judgment contrary to a line of authority by which I am bound. In *Re D (a minor) (justices' decision : review)* [1977] 3 All ER 481, [1977] Fam 158 Dunn J held that it was open to the court to exercise its jurisdiction in wardship notwithstanding that the juvenile court had, in exercise of their powers under s 21(2) of the Children and Young Persons Act 1969, discharged a care order directing that the child should reside with his grandparents, and made a supervision order in favour of the London borough in whose area the grandparents resided. The fact that the care order in that case had originally been made under s 1(2)(a) of the Children and Young Persons Act 1969, that is as a result of care proceedings and not as the result of the conviction of a young offender, is in my judgment irrelevant. The philosophy behind s 7(7) of the Children and Young Persons Act 1969 is clearly that in the case of a juvenile offender punishment in the ordinary sense may not be appropriate, and the court is given power to make orders for the protection and welfare of the juvenile similar to those which it can make in care proceedings: see s 1(3) of the Children and Young Persons Act 1969. This is the aim which this court seeks to achieve in the exercise of its wardship jurisdiction. *Re D* has been approved (at any rate as to the issue of the exercise of jurisdiction in wardship) by the Court of Appeal in *Re H (a minor) (wardship jurisdiction)* [1978] 2 All ER 903 at 910, [1978] Fam 65 at 77 and by the House of Lords in *A v Liverpool City Council* [1981] 2 All ER 385 at 393, [1982] AC 363 at 379. Indeed, in both these cases there are passages which make it clear that this court can and should intervene in an appropriate case. I refer in particular to the passage in the speech of Lord Roskill in *A v Liverpool City Council* [1981] 2 All ER 385 at 393, [1982] AC 363 at 378:

'I venture to think that the decision [in *Re H*] can perhaps be better supported on the ground that the wardship jurisdiction of the court could properly be invoked in addition to the statutory jurisdiction of the local authority because it was only in this way that the result which was best in the paramount interest of the child could be achieved, the local authority and juvenile court being unable within the limits of their powers to achieve that result.'

See also Lord Wilberforce ([1981] 2 All ER 385 at 389, [1982] AC 363 at 373).

Accordingly in my judgment the existence of the care order made by the King's Lynn juvenile court in favour of Norfolk does not preclude my making a care order in favour of Leeds.

The existence of the care order in favour of Norfolk does, however, present a practical problem. Clearly it is undesirable that there should be in existence at the same time two inconsistent orders relating to the same child. Nevertheless the problem is not unique to this case. It has long been possible that the High Court or a divorce county court may make an order as to custody of, or access to, a child which is inconsistent with a pre-existing order made by a magistrates' court. Neither the High Court nor the county court has power to discharge a custody order made by a magistrates' court. It used to be the practice for the High Court or county court in these circumstances to require an undertaking from the parties to apply for the earlier order to be discharged. That practice has now ceased and the present practice, regulated by a Practice Note dated 18 June 1975 and issued by the President of the Family Division with the concurrence of the Lord Chancellor, is to give notice to the magistrates' court that its order has been superseded, even though the earlier order remains technically undischarged. See the Home Office Circular No 152 of 1975, the Registrar's Direction of 19 June 1975 and the Practice Note of 18 June 1975 set out in *Clarke Hall and Morrison on Children* (9th edn, 1977) p 1205. If I make a care order in favour of Leeds the position will be analogous to that contemplated by the Practice Note, although having regard to the financial consequences of a care order it will be preferable if Norfolk, or the Official Solicitor as representing S, then makes a further application to the King's Lynn juvenile court for the discharge of the care order in favour of Norfolk.

The other submission of counsel for Leeds was that because S is already in the care of Norfolk, the pre-conditions for the making of a care order under s 7(2) of the Family Law Reform Act 1969 cannot be satisfied. Those conditions are 'that there are exceptional circumstances making it impracticable or undesirable for a ward of court to be, or to continue to be, under the care of either of his parents or of any other individual'. I am satisfied that there are here exceptional circumstances, and that it is both impracticable and undesirable for S to be under the care of either of his parents. It is also undesirable that he should be under the care of the only other individual who has displayed any interest in him, namely the grandmother. In my judgment, therefore, there is no bar to my making a care order in favour of Leeds.

That leaves only the question whether it is in S's interests that I should make a care order in favour of Leeds. As to that I feel no doubt. So long as Leeds were prepared to act on behalf of Norfolk in exercising the latter's supervisory functions, it may be that it mattered little in whose favour the care order was made. But it is clearly impossible for Norfolk adequately to take direct care of a boy who currently lives in Leeds and who considers Leeds to be his home town. It may be that Leeds' real objection to the making of a care order in its favour is financial, but that cannot be allowed to take precedence over what S's welfare requires.

Accordingly I make an order committing the care of S to Leeds. This supersedes the existing care order in favour of Norfolk although, for the reasons I have already given, it is desirable that that order should be formally discharged. The Official Solicitor submitted that I should make only an interim care order in favour of Leeds in order that in due course there could be a full hearing on the merits. I can see no advantage in taking that course. At the moment it seems to me that a care order in favour of *a* local authority, and I have decided in favour of Leeds, is the only practicable order to make. Anything less is clearly inadequate for S's protection. If in due course any party is in a position to put forward a practicable alternative they will be free to do so. Any order relating to a ward of court is always open to review.

Order accordingly.

Solicitors: *Official Solicitor*; *James Rawnsley*, Leeds (for Leeds City Council); *Middlebrook Crotty & Co*, Leeds (for the grandmother).

Bebe Chua   Barrister.

Shah v Barnet London Borough Council and other appeals

HOUSE OF LORDS

LORD FRASER OF TULLYBELTON, LORD SCARMAN, LORD LOWRY, LORD ROSKILL AND LORD BRANDON OF OAKBROOK

26, 27, 28, 29 JULY, 14, 18, 19, 20, 21 OCTOBER, 16 DECEMBER 1982

Education – University – Grant for study – Local authority grant – Eligibility – Student entitled to grant from local authority for university study if ordinarily resident in United Kingdom for three years – Ordinarily resident – Education Act 1962, s 1 – Local Education Authority Awards Regulations 1979, reg 13.

Education – University – Grant for study – Local authority grant – Refusal – Judicial review – Remedy – Whether declaration appropriate remedy – Whether court should order certiorari and mandamus directed to local authority – Education Act 1962, s 1.

Education – University – Grant for study – Local authority grant – Application for grant – Refusal to grant mandatory award – Whether local authority required to consider granting discretionary award – Education Act 1962, s 1.

Statute – Construction – Construction by reference to policy – Purposive interpretation – Purposive interpretation only to be adopted where statute as a whole or permitted aids to interpretation containing expression of Parliament's purpose or policy.

Section 1(1)[a] of the Education Act 1962 imposed a duty on local education authorities to make grants for university study to students who were 'ordinarily resident' within their areas and who possessed the requisite educational qualifications for university study. However, by reg 13[b] of the Local Education Authority Awards Regulations 1979 an authority was not obliged to make a grant to an applicant who had not been 'ordinarily resident . . . in the United Kingdom' for the three years preceding the commencement of his course of study. The five applicants were foreign-born students who applied for, and were refused, local authority grants for their further education. The applicants had all been resident in the United Kingdom for the requisite period but in each case the local education authority claimed that they had not been 'ordinarily' resident. Four of the applicants had entered and remained in the United Kingdom with limited leave under student's entry certificates which included a condition that the student leave the country when he completed his studies. The other applicant, NS, had entered the United Kingdom with his parents when they were given indefinite leave to enter for the purposes of settlement in the United Kingdom. The Divisional Court granted an application by NS for orders of certiorari to quash the education authority's decision and of mandamus to compel the award of a grant to him but refused similar applications by two of the other applicants. The education authority in NS's case and the two applicants appealed. The remaining two applicants obtained leave to apply direct to the Court of Appeal for judicial review of the education authorities' refusal to award them grants. The Court of Appeal heard all the appeals and applications together, and held that an overseas student admitted to the United Kingdom to pursue a course of study was not resident in the United Kingdom for the purposes of everyday life or making a home and therefore was not 'ordinarily' resident for the purposes of s 1 of the 1962 Act and reg 13 of the 1979 regulations, interpreted against the background of the Immigration Act 1971. The Court of Appeal accordingly dismissed the appeals and applications by the four applicants and dismissed the appeal by the education authority in the case of NS. The applicants and the

---

a Section 1 is set out at p 230 *j* to p 231 *g*, post

b Regulation 13 is set out at p 231 *j* to p 232 *b*, post

education authority appealed to the House of Lords. On the appeal, the education authorities contended that the proper test of ordinary residence was the 'real home' test, namely the place where the applicant had his permanent home. One of the applicants, MS, contended that the education authority was under a duty when it refused him a mandatory award to go on to consider his application for a discretionary award.

Held – (1) The phrase 'ordinarily resident' in s 1 of the 1962 Act and reg 13 of the 1979 regulations was to be construed according to its natural and ordinary meaning without reference to the immigration legislation, since the material provisions of the 1962 Act and the 1979 regulations made no reference to any restriction on the awards of grants based on an applicant's place of origin, domicile or nationality. According to the natural and ordinary meaning of the phrase a person was 'ordinarily resident' in the United Kingdom if he habitually and normally resided lawfully in the United Kingdom from choice and for a settled purpose throughout the prescribed period, apart from temporary or occasional absences. Furthermore, a specific and limited purpose, such as education, could be a settled purpose. It was irrelevant that the applicant's permanent residence or 'real home' might be outside the United Kingdom or that his future intention or expectation might be to live outside the United Kingdom. Applying the natural and ordinary meaning of the phrase 'ordinarily resident', all five applicants had been ordinarily resident in the United Kingdom prior to commencing their university study (see p 229 *g*, p 231 *g h*, p 232 *c d* and *j* to p 233 *c*, p 234 *e* to *g*, p 235 *e* to *j*, p 236 *a* to *c* and *j* to p 237 *a*, p 238 *g* to p 239 *g*, and p 240 *h* to p 241 *a*, post); dicta of Viscount Cave LC in *Levene v IRC* [1928] All ER Rep at 750 and of Viscount Sumner in *IRC v Lysaght* [1928] All ER Rep at 580 applied; *Gout v Cimitian* [1922] 1 AC 105 and *Stransky v Stransky* [1954] 2 All ER 536 considered.

(2) Where the court granted a person relief by way of judicial review of a decision of a local education authority to refuse an application for an award under s 1 of the 1962 Act, the appropriate remedy was an order of certiorari quashing the refusal to make an award and an order of mandamus requiring the authority to reconsider the application. The court could not and should not make a declaration of the person's entitlement or right to an award or of the authority's duty to make an award, since that would usurp the authority's function. It followed that the applicants' appeals would be allowed and orders of certiorari and mandamus would go accordingly, and the local education authority's appeal would be dismissed (see p 229 *g*, p 233 *f g* and p 240 *d* to p 241 *a*, post).

Per curiam. (1) Where a student applies for an award under s 1 of the 1962 Act (or the equivalent provisions in the Education Act 1980) the application, unless it is expressly limited, is for a mandatory award under s 1(1) or, if that is refused, a discretionary award under s 1(4). Accordingly, if a local authority decides to refuse to grant a mandatory award it must then go on to consider whether to grant a discretionary award (see p 229 *g*, p 239 *h j* and p 240 *h* to p 241 *a*, post).

(2) Judges may not interpret legislation in the light of their own views as to policy. They may, however, adopt a purposive interpretation if they can find in the statute, read as a whole, or in material to which they are permitted by law to refer as aids to interpretation, an expression of Parliament's purpose or policy (see p 229 *g*, p 238 *f g* and p 240 *h* to p 241 *a*, post).

Decision of the Court of Appeal sub nom *R v Barnet London Borough Council, ex p Shah* [1982] 1 All ER 698 reversed.

Notes

For eligibility for mandatory awards by local education authorities for university study, see 15 Halsbury's Laws (4th edn) paras 240–258, and for cases on the subject, see 19 Digest (Reissue) 561–562, 4215–4216.

For the Education Act 1962, s 1, see 11 Halsbury's Statutes (3rd edn) 315.

As from 5 May 1980 s 1 of the 1962 Act was substituted by the Education Act 1980, s 19 and Sch 5.

As from 1 September 1981 reg 13 of the Local Education Authority Awards Regulations 1979 was replaced by reg 13 of the Education (Mandatory Awards) Regulations 1981, SI 1981/943.

Cases referred to in opinions

Abdul Manan, Re [1971] 2 All ER 1016, [1971] 1 WLR 859, CA, 2 Digest (Reissue) 198, *1151.*

Associated Provincial Picture Houses Ltd v Wednesbury Corp [1947] 2 All ER 680, [1948] 1 KB 223, CA, 45 Digest (Repl) 215, *189.*

Brutus v Cozens [1972] 2 All ER 1297, [1973] AC 854, [1972] 3 WLR 521, HL, 15 Digest (Reissue) 910, 7807.

Cicutti v Suffolk CC [1980] 3 All ER 689, [1981] 1 WLR 558.

Clarke v Insurance Office of Australia Ltd [1965] 1 Lloyd's Rep 308, 29 Digest (Reissue) 598, *5225.*

Gout v Cimitian [1922] 1 AC 105, PC, 2 Digest (Reissue) 226, *1257.*

IRC v Lysaght [1928] AC 234, [1928] All ER Rep 575, HL, 28(1) Digest (Reissue) 359, *1310.*

Levene v IRC [1928] AC 217, [1928] All ER Rep 746, HL, 28(1) Digest (Reissue) 359, *1309.*

Miesegaes v IRC (1957) 37 TC 493, CA, 28(1) Digest (Reissue) 360, *1314.*

Norris, Re, ex p Reynolds (1888) 5 Morr 111, CA, 4 Digest (Reissue) 26, *217.*

O'Reilly v Mackman [1982] 3 All ER 1124, [1982] 3 WLR 1096, HL.

P (G E) (an infant), Re [1964] 3 All ER 977, [1965] Ch 568, [1965] 2 WLR 1, CA, 28(2) Digest (Reissue) 917, *2257.*

R v Secretary of State for the Home Dept, ex p Margueritte [1982] 3 All ER 909, [1982] 3 WLR 754, CA.

Stransky v Stransky [1954] 2 All ER 536, [1954] P 428, [1954] 3 WLR 123, 11 Digest (Reissue) 355, *69.*

Conjoined appeals

Hamid Akbarali v Brent London Borough Council

Hamid Inayatali Akbarili applied, with leave of the Court of Appeal (Lord Denning MR, Eveleigh and Fox LJJ) given on 9 February 1981, direct to the Court of Appeal for judicial review by way of orders of certiorari to quash the decision of the respondent, Brent London Borough Council, on 1 August 1979 to refuse to grant the appellant a mandatory award under s 1 of the Education Act 1962 and mandamus to compel the council to reconsider his application. On 10 November 1981 the Court of Appeal (Lord Denning MR, Eveleigh and Templeman LJJ) ([1982] 1 All ER 698, [1982] QB 688) dismissed his application for judicial review. The appellant appealed by leave of the Court of Appeal to the House of Lords. The facts are set out in the opinion of Lord Scarman.

Abu Abdullah v Shropshire County Council

Abu Naim Mohammed Abdullah applied, with leave of the Court of Appeal (Lord Denning MR, Eveleigh and Fox LJJ) given on 9 February 1981, direct to the Court of Appeal for judicial review by way of orders of certiorari to quash the decision of the respondent, Shropshire County Council, on 14 June 1979 to refuse to grant the appellant a mandatory award under s 1 of the Education Act 1962 and mandamus to compel the council to reconsider his application. On 10 November 1981 the Court of Appeal ([1982] 1 All ER 698, [1982] QB 688) dismissed his application. The appellant appealed by leave of the Court of Appeal to the House of Lords. The facts are set out in the opinion of Lord Scarman.

Jitendra Shah v Barnet London Borough Council

Jitendra Umedchand Harakchand Shah appealed by leave of the Court of Appeal against the decision of the Court of Appeal (Lord Denning MR, Eveleigh and Templeman LJJ) ([1982] 1 All ER 698, [1982] QB 688) on 10 November 1981 dismissing his appeal against the judgment of the Divisional Court of the Queen's Bench Division (Ormrod LJ, Kilner Brown and McNeill JJ) ([1980] 3 All ER 679, [1982] QB 688) on 18 July 1980 dismissing the appellant's application for certiorari, mandamus and a declaration in respect of the decision of the respondent, Barnet London Borough Council, on 20 August 1979 to refuse to grant the appellant a mandatory award under s 1 of the Education Act 1962. The facts are set out in the opinion of Lord Scarman.

Madjid Shabpar v Barnet London Borough Council

Madjid Shabpar appealed by leave of the Court of Appeal against the decision of the Court of Appeal (Lord Denning MR, Eveleigh and Templeman LJJ) ([1982] 1 All ER 698, [1982] QB 688) on 10 November 1981 dismissing his appeal against the order of Hodgson J hearing the Divisional Court list on 21 July 1981 dismissing the appellant's application for judicial review by way of orders for certiorari and mandamus in respect of the decision of the respondent, Barnet London Borough Council, on 17 February 1979 to refuse to grant the appellant a mandatory award under s 1 of the Education Act 1962. The facts are set out in the opinion of Lord Scarman.

Nilish Shah v Barnet London Borough Council

Barnet London Borough Council appealed by leave of the Court of Appeal against the decision of the Court of Appeal (Lord Denning MR, Eveleigh and Templeman LJJ) ([1982] 1 All ER 698, [1982] QB 688) on 10 November 1981 dismissing the council's appeal against the judgment of the Divisional Court of the Queen's Bench Division (Ormrod LJ, Kilner Brown and McNeill JJ) ([1980] 3 All ER 679, [1982] QB 688) on 18 July 1980 granting the application of the respondent, Nilish Ramniklal Lalji Shah, for orders of certiorari and mandamus quashing the council's decision of 28 August 1979 to refuse to grant the respondent a mandatory award under s 1 of the Education Act 1962 and directing the council to reconsider his application for an award. The facts are set out in the opinion of Lord Scarman.

The appeals were conjoined by order of the House of Lords made on 22 April 1982.

Michael Beloff QC and *Judith Beale* for Akbarali and Abdullah.
Anthony Lester QC and *Judith Beale* for Jitendra Shah and Nilish Shah.
Anthony Lester QC and *K S Nathan* for Shabpar.
Anthony Scrivener QC and *Robin Barratt* for Barnet and Brent borough councils.
Elizabeth Appleby QC, Duncan Ouseley and *Stephen Aitchison* for Shropshire County Council.

Their Lordships took time for consideration.

16 December. The following opinions were delivered.

LORD FRASER OF TULLYBELTON. My Lords, I have had the advantage of reading in draft the speech of my noble and learned friend Lord Scarman. I agree with it and, for the reasons given by him, I would allow the appeals in all cases except in Nilish Shah's case.

LORD SCARMAN. My Lords, the detailed facts in these five appeals are succinctly stated in the judgments of the Court of Appeal, and need not be repeated. In four of the appeals an immigrant student is the appellant and a local education authority the respondent. In one, Nilish Shah's case, the roles are reversed. In each case the student had entered the United Kingdom some three years ago, or earlier, for the purpose of seeking an educational qualification by pursuing a course of study at some school or college, paying his own fees and relying on family resources for his maintenance. After obtaining his educational qualification, he applied to a local education authority for an award in respect of a first degree, or comparable, course of further education. In each case the application was refused. Each student has applied for judicial review on the ground that the local education authority had erred in law in reaching the conclusion that the student had failed to prove that he had been ordinarily resident in the United Kingdom throughout the three years preceding the first year of the course in question. It is common ground that to secure a mandatory award, ie one which it was the duty of the local education authority to bestow, the ordinary residence condition had to be met by these students. The students say that the local education authorities misdirected themselves in law in that they applied the wrong test in respect of ordinary residence. One student, Shabpar, has a further point. He alone has pursued to this House the case that the local education authority, having refused him a mandatory award, failed or refused to consider his alternative application for a discretionary award.

All five students are immigrants. None of them has the right of abode in the United Kingdom. None of them is a national of a member state of the European Communities. All needed leave to enter and to remain here: see s 3(1) of the Immigration Act 1971. Four of them entered as students with limited leave; one, Nilish Shah, entered with his parents for settlement and obtained indefinite leave. The limited leave included a condition that on completion of his studies the student would depart from the country, though, of course, it would be open to him to apply for an extension, in which event the Secretary of State could grant a limited or unlimited extension or refuse the application.

Two questions of law are common to all five appeals. The first, and more difficult, question is as to the meaning to be given in the context of the Education Acts to the words 'ordinarily resident in the United Kingdom'. The second question arises only if the first is answered in favour of the students and relates to the judicial remedy appropriate to these cases.

The cases of Nilish Shah and Jitendra Shah came before a Divisional Court (see [1980] 3 All ER 679, [1982] QB 688). Ormrod LJ delivered the considered judgment of the court, allowing Nilish's application for judicial review but dismissing Jitendra's. The distinguishing fact was that Nilish entered for settlement, whereas Jitendra was admitted for the purpose of study and given limited leave only. In other cases, all of them cases of limited leave, a Divisional Court refused judicial review. The Court of Appeal, after one hearing covering all five cases (and one other), upheld the Divisional Court's decision in favour of Nilish but dismissed the appeals of the other four applicants (see [1982] 1 All ER 698, [1982] QB 688). The Court of Appeal granted leave to appeal to your Lordships' House.

The Education Act 1944, s 81 required the Secretary of State to make regulations empowering local education authorities—

'for the purpose of enabling pupils to take advantage without hardship to themselves or their parents of any educational facilities available to them . . . (c) to grant scholarships . . . and other allowances in respect of pupils over compulsory school age, including pupils undergoing training as teachers.'

The section set no limit, imposed no restrictions by way of nationality, origin or sex. It was an integral part of an enlightened statute, the policy of which has governed educational provision ever since.

By 1962 immigration from the Commonwealth and elsewhere had become a factor in the life of British society: witness the Commonwealth Immigrants Act 1962.

In the same year and during the same session Parliament enacted the Education Act 1962.

It is inconceivable, and I refuse, therefore, to infer, that Parliament, in enacting the education statute, could have been unaware of the restrictions then being imposed for the first time on Commonwealth immigrants. The Act was, amongst other matters, 'to make further provision with respect to awards and grants by local education authorities'. Section 1 was as follows:

'(1) It shall be the duty of every local education authority, subject to and in accordance with regulations made under this Act, to bestow awards on persons who—(a) are ordinarily resident in the area of the authority, and (b) possess the requisite educational qualifications, in respect of their attendance at courses to which this section applies.
(2) This section shall apply to such full-time courses at universities, colleges or other institutions in Great Britain and Northern Ireland as may for the time being be designated by or under the regulations for the purposes of this section as being

first degree courses or comparable to first degree courses; and for the purposes of the preceding subsection the requisite educational qualifications, in relation to any course, shall be such as may be prescribed by or under the regulations, either generally or with respect to that course or a class of courses which includes that course.

(3) Regulations made for the purposes of subsection (1) of this section shall prescribe the conditions and exceptions subject to which the duty imposed by that subsection is to have effect, and the descriptions of payments to be made in pursuance of awards bestowed thereunder, and, with respect to each description of payments, shall—(a) prescribe the circumstances in which it is to be payable, and the amount of the payment or the scales or other provisions by reference to which that amount is to be determined, and (b) indicate whether the payment is to be obligatory or is to be at the discretion of the authority bestowing the award; and, subject to the exercise of any power conferred by the regulations to suspend or terminate awards, a local education authority by whom an award has been bestowed under subsection (1) of this section shall be under a duty, or shall have power, as the case may be, to make such payments as they are required or authorised to make in accordance with the regulations.

(4) Without prejudice to the duty imposed by subsection (1) of this section, a local education authority shall have power to bestow an award on any person in respect of his attendance at a course to which this section applies, where he is not eligible for an award under subsection (1) of this section in respect of that course.

(5) The provisions of subsection (3) of this section and of the regulations made in accordance with that subsection (except so much of those provisions as relates to the conditions and exceptions subject to which the duty imposed by subsection (1) of this section is to have effect) shall apply in relation to awards under the last preceding subsection as they apply in relation to awards under subsection (1) of this section.

(6) Notwithstanding anything in subsection (1) of this section, that subsection shall not have effect so as to require a local education authority—(a) to bestow awards in respect of any period beginning before the first day of September, nineteen hundred and sixty-two, or (b) to bestow an award on a person in respect of any course, if a scholarship, exhibition, bursary or other allowance granted to him in respect of that course is in force on that day by virtue of regulations made under paragraph (c) of section eighty-one of the Act of 1944.

(7) The reference in subsection (1) of this section to persons who are ordinarily resident in the area of a local education authority is a reference to persons who, in accordance with the provisions of the First Schedule to this Act, are to be treated as being so resident.'

The section imposed a duty on every local education authority to bestow awards ('mandatory', as they are called) on persons ordinarily resident in its area who possessed the requisite educational qualifications. It contained no restriction on the scope of the duty other than ordinary residence in the area of the local education authority and the education qualification. There was no hint of nationality, country of origin, or domicile as a condition of eligibility; but the duty was to be subject to and in accordance with regulations made under the Act.

Such regulations were, amongst other matters, to prescribe the conditions and exceptions subject to which the duty was to have effect. Regulations have been made from time to time; and they have always included an exception based on a requirement of three years' ordinary residence in the United Kingdom as a condition of eligibility for a mandatory award. The terms of the exception may be conveniently quoted from the Local Education Authority Awards Regulations 1979, SI 1979/889. Regulation 13 provides as follows:

'Other Exceptions
13. An authority shall not be under a duty to bestow an award in respect of a person's attendance at a course—(a) upon a person who has not been ordinarily

resident, throughout the three years preceding the first year of the course in question, in the United Kingdom or, in the case of such a person as is mentioned in Regulation 9(1)(b), has not been so resident in the European Economic Community; (b) upon a person who has, in the opinion of the authority, shown himself by his conduct to be unfitted to receive an award; (c) in the case of a course comparable to a first degree course, upon a person who does not possess a qualification specified by or under Schedule 5.'

The condition of three years' ordinary residence in the United Kingdom had featured in the earlier regulations (eg SI 1962/1689, reg 5; SI 1977/1307, reg 10; SI 1978/1097, reg 13). The extension to the European Economic Community was new in 1979.

Throughout the period 1962 to 1979 Parliament found it necessary to review the problem of immigration, passing the Commonwealth Immigrants Act 1968 and finally introducing a statutory code of immigration control, the Immigration Act 1971. Yet the education legislation, and the regulations made thereunder during this period, retained the three years' ordinary residence requirement without any hint of other restriction such as the applicants' place of origin or domicile or (save in one unimportant respect) nationality.

All the cases now under appeal, other than Shabpar's, fall to be considered under the 1962 Act and the 1979 regulations; Shabpar's case falls under the Education Act 1980 and its regulations, the Education (Mandatory Awards) Regulations 1980, SI 1980/974. Section 19 of that Act substitutes for ss 1 to 4 of and Sch 4 to the 1962 Act the provisions set out in its Sch 5. That schedule and reg 13 of the 1980 regulations retain the three years' ordinary residence requirement with the substitution of 'British Islands' for 'United Kingdom'.

To conclude this sketch of the relevant legislation I would draw attention to the availability of a discretionary award, if a student should fail to establish his entitlement to a mandatory award: see s 1(4) of the 1962 Act, re-enacted in para 1(b) of Sch 5 to the 1980 Act. Shabpar alleges that in his case the local education authority, having refused him a mandatory award, failed to consider whether he should have an award under this subsection.

A confusing feature of the legislation is that in the same sections and regulations it has endeavoured to deal with two entirely separate problems, namely: (1) an applicant's eligibility for a mandatory award, ie three years' ordinary residence in the United Kingdom (British Islands); and (2) the distribution of cost of such awards between local education authorities where doubt exists as to the local education area to which it may be said the applicant 'belongs', ie in which as between local education authorities he is to be treated as being ordinarily resident: see the Education (Miscellaneous Provisions) Act 1953, s 7.

The first question, being one of statutory interpretation, is legal in character; and it is related to an applicant's right. The second is administrative and fiscal, and, significantly, is ultimately for decision by the Secretary of State: see s 7(5) of the Education (Miscellaneous Provisions) Act 1953, repealed and replaced by s 31(3) of the Education Act 1980. Both the students and the local education authorities have, at certain stages of their elaborate submissions to your Lordships' House, endeavoured to pray in aid the provisions for 'recoupment', which is the statutory description of the fiscal problem, as indicating the meaning to be given to 'ordinary residence in the United Kingdom (British Islands)' in the context of an applicant's right to an award. But the problems are wholly distinct; one is justiciable, the other is not. If, as to which I offer no firm opinion, ordinary residence in an area of the local education authority has a special meaning when the distribution of the fiscal burden between local education authorities is being considered as a matter for the exercise of executive decision by the Secretary of State, it does not follow that such special meaning, whatever it be, is to be attributed to the term 'ordinarily resident . . . in the United Kingdom (British Islands)' when used as a criterion of an applicant's eligibility for an award.

Two questions of statutory interpretation, therefore, arise. The first is: what is the natural and ordinary meaning of 'ordinarily resident . . . in the United Kingdom' (it is

unnecessary to refer any further to the 1980 variant 'British Islands')? The second is: does
a the statute in the context of the relevant law against the background of which it was
enacted, or in the circumstances of today, including in particular the impact of the
Immigration Act 1971, compel one to substitute a special, and, if so, what, meaning to
the words 'ordinarily resident in the United Kingdom'?

For the reasons which I shall endeavour to develop I answer the two questions as
follows. The natural and ordinary meaning of the words has been authoritatively
b determined in this House in two tax cases reported in 1928 (see *Levene v IRC* [1928] AC
217, [1928] All ER Rep 746 and *IRC v Lysaght* [1928] AC 234, [1928] All ER Rep 575).
To the second question my answer is No. The 1962 Act and the regulations are to be
construed by giving to the words 'ordinarily resident in the United Kingdom' their
natural and ordinary meaning.

Ordinary residence is not a term of art in English law. But it embodies an idea of
c which Parliament has made increasing use in the statute law of the United Kingdom
since the beginning of the nineteenth century. The words have been a feature of the
Income Tax Acts since 1806. They were used in English family law when it was decided
to give a wife the right to petition for divorce notwithstanding the foreign domicile of
her husband: see the Matrimonial Causes Act 1950, s 18(1)(b). Ordinary or habitual
residence has, in effect, now supplanted domicile as the test of jurisdiction in family law;
d and, as Eveleigh LJ in the Court of Appeal reminded us (see [1982] 1 All ER 698 at 705,
[1982] QB 688 at 721–722), the concept is used in a number of twentieth century statutes,
including (very significantly) the Immigration Act 1971.

Though the meaning of ordinary words is, as Lord Reid observed in *Brutus v Cozens*
[1972] 2 All ER 1297 at 1299, [1973] AC 854 at 861, a question of fact, the meaning to
be attributed to enacted words is a question of law, being a matter of statutory
e interpretation. So in this case a question of law arises as to the meaning of 'ordinarily
resident in the United Kingdom', even though it arises only at a preliminary stage in the
process of determining a question of fact, namely whether the 'propositus' (in these
appeals, the student applicant) has established the fact of ordinary residence for the
prescribed period (ie three years immediately preceding the course in respect of which
he seeks an award). It is with this preliminary stage that the courts are concerned. If a
f local education authority gets the law right, or, as lawyers would put it, directs itself
correctly in law, the question of fact, ie has the student established the prescribed
residence? is for the authority, not the court, to decide. The merits of the application are
for the local education authority, subject only to judicial review to ensure that the
authority has proceeded according to the law.

The words 'ordinary residence' were considered by this House in two tax cases reported
g in 1928. In each, the House saw itself as seeking the natural and ordinary meaning of the
words. In *Levene v IRC* [1928] AC 217 at 225, [1928] All ER Rep 746 at 750 Viscount
Cave LC said:

> '... I think that [ordinary residence] connotes residence in a place with some
> degree of continuity and apart from accidental or temporary absences.'

h In *IRC v Lysaght* [1928] AC 234 at 243, [1928] All ER Rep 575 at 580 Viscount Sumner
said:

> 'I think the converse to "ordinarily" is "extraordinarily" and that part of the
> regular order of a man's life, adopted voluntarily and for settled purposes, is not
> "extraordinary".'

j In *Levene*'s case [1928] AC 217 at 232, [1928] All ER Rep 746 at 753–754 Lord Warrington
said:

> 'I do not attempt to give any definition of the word "resident". In my opinion it
> has no technical or special meaning for the purposes of the Income Tax Act.
> "Ordinarily resident" also seems to me to have no such technical or special meaning.
> In particular it is in my opinion impossible to restrict its connotation to its duration.
> A member of this House may well be said to be ordinarily resident in London

during the Parliamentary session and in the country during the recess. If it has any
definite meaning I should say it means according to the way in which a man's life is
usually ordered.'   *a*

It was urged on your Lordships by counsel for Brent and Barnet borough councils (but
not, as I understood her ultimate position, by counsel for Shropshire County Council)
that these two decisions of the House were authority only for a special meaning limited
to the Income Tax Acts. The converse is the case. The true reading of the speeches
delivered is that the House decided to construe the words in their tax context as bearing   *b*
their natural and ordinary meaning as words of common usage in the English language:
note particularly the words of Lord Warrington. In the present cases Lord Denning MR
adopted the same view of the natural and ordinary meaning of the words, for in his
judgment he said ([1982] 1 All ER 698 at 704, [1982] QB 688 at 720):

> 'Traditionally we ought simply to apply the natural and ordinary meaning of the   *c*
> two words "ordinarily resident" in the context of [the Education Act 1962] . . . If we
> were to do that here, I feel I would apply the test submitted by counsel for the Shahs.
> The words "ordinarily resident" mean that the person must be habitually and
> normally resident here, apart from temporary or occasional absences of long or short
> duration. On that test all [the] students would qualify for a mandatory award.'
>   *d*

Strictly, my Lords, it is unnecessary to go further into such case law as there is in search
of the natural and ordinary meaning of the words. In 1928 this House declared it in
general terms which were not limited to the Income Tax Acts. Lord Denning MR has
reaffirmed it in 1981, thus showing, if it were needed, that there has been no significant
change in the common meaning of the words between 1928 and now. If further evidence
of this fact is needed (for the meaning of ordinary words as a matter of common usage is   *e*
a question of fact), the dictionaries provide it: see, for instance, *Supplement to the Oxford
English Dictionary* vol 3 sv 'ordinarily' and 'resident'. I therefore accept the two tax cases
as authoritative guidance, displaceable only by evidence (which does not exist) of a
subsequent change in English usage. I agree with Lord Denning MR that in their natural
and ordinary meaning the words mean 'that the person must be habitually and normally
resident here, apart from temporary or occasional absences of long or short duration'.
The significance of the adverb 'habitually' is that it recalls two necessary features   *f*
mentioned by Lord Sumner in *Lysaght's* case, namely residence adopted voluntarily and
for settled purposes.

Accordingly, I do not lengthen a lengthy speech by a review of the decided cases, most
of which were examined by Templeman LJ in the Court of Appeal. The decision in each
depended on its own particular facts; and such dicta as can be culled from the reported
judgments must be read with that in mind. I note that in the nineteenth century
bankruptcy case *Re Norris, ex p Reynolds* (1888) 5 Morr 111 it was accepted that one   *g*
person could be ordinarily resident in two countries at the same time. This is, I have no
doubt, a significant feature of the words' ordinary meaning, for it is an important factor
distinguishing ordinary residence from domicile. *Miesegaes v IRC* (1957) 37 TC 493, *Re
P (G E) (an infant)* [1964] 3 All ER 977, [1965] Ch 568 and the Australian case of *Clarke v   *h*
Insurance Office of Australia Ltd* [1965] 1 Lloyd's Rep 308 appear to me to have been
correctly decided on their facts. They contain nothing to throw doubt on the views
expressed by the House in the two tax cases or the view of Lord Denning MR; and, if
they did, I would reject any proposition inconsistent with those views. Like Templeman
LJ in the Court of Appeal, I derive no help from *Cicutti v Suffolk CC* [1980] 3 All ER 689,
[1981] 1 WLR 558, where Sir Robert Megarry V-C would seem to have equated ordinary   *j*
residence with a domicile of choice, a dangerous confusion (which I think the Divisional
Court and the Court of Appeal did not succeed in wholly avoiding in these two cases).
Parliament has evinced a strong legislative preference for ordinary residence as a
jurisdictional substitute for domicile, and the choice must be respected by the courts.

Two cases call for a slightly more extended consideration. *Gout v Cimitian* [1922] 1 AC
105 preceded the two tax cases in your Lordships' House. It was a Privy Council case in
which an Ottoman subject had lived in Cairo from 1893 to 1913. In December 1913 he

went to Cyprus, where he rented a house. He was in Cyprus on 5 November 1914 and
a remained until October 1915, when he returned to Cairo. The question was whether he
was ordinarily resident in Cyprus on 5 November 1914. The Judicial Committee held
that he was, whether or not Cyprus was then his domicile. Lord Carson, who delivered
the opinion of the Board, said (at 110) that in the context of the relevant Order in Council
the words 'ordinarily resident' could not be interpreted as comparable with domicile but
must be given their usual and ordinary meaning.

b   The other case is *Stransky v Stransky* [1954] 2 All ER 536, [1954] P 428, on which
counsel for the local education authorities placed reliance in submitting that in
determining ordinary residence the test is the 'real home' of the propositus. A wife,
whose husband was domiciled abroad, was invoking s 18(1)(*b*) of the Matrimonial Causes
Act 1950 so that she could petition for divorce. The test of jurisdiction was ordinary
residence in England for three years preceding her petition. She had a flat in London
c where she resided, though during the three years she had spent substantial periods of
time (in all more than 15 months) in Munich, where her husband was. The case was
undefended; counsel for the Queen's Proctor submitted that her 'real home' was London,
notwithstanding her absences; and the judge adopted this description of her place of
abode in his judgment. I do not read the judgment of Karminski J as importing into
ordinary residence an intention to live in a place permanently or indefinitely; his
d problem was to determine whether her absences from London destroyed the degree of
continuity needed to establish ordinary residence. But, if he did hold that such an
intention was necessary, he would, in my view, have erred in law. For to have done so
would have been to import into the law that which, in its time, s 18(1)(*b*) of the 1950 Act
sought to exorcise (so far as wives were concerned), namely 'animus manendi', the
subjective test of domicile. In any event, any such error would be obiter dictum, since
e on the facts it was clear that the wife was ordinarily resident in England in the natural
and ordinary meaning of the words as explained in the *Levene* and *Lysaght* cases.

Unless, therefore, it can be shown that the statutory framework or the legal context in
which the words are used requires a different meaning, I unhesitatingly subscribe to the
view that 'ordinarily resident' refers to a man's abode in a particular place or country
which he has adopted voluntarily and for settled purposes as part of the regular order of
f his life for the time being, whether of short or long duration.

There is, of course, one important exception. If a man's presence in a particular place
or country is unlawful, eg in breach of the immigration laws, he cannot rely on his
unlawful residence as constituting ordinary residence (even though in a tax case the
Crown may be able to do so): see *Re Abdul Manan* [1971] 2 All ER 1016, [1971] 1 WLR
859 and *R v Secretary of State for the Home Dept, ex p Margueritte* [1982] 3 All ER 909,
g [1982] 3 WLR 754. There is, indeed, express provision to this effect in the Immigration
Act 1971, s 33(2). But even without this guidance I would conclude that it was wrong in
principle that a man could rely on his own unlawful act to secure an advantage which
could have been obtained if he had acted lawfully.

There are two, and no more than two, respects in which the mind of the propositus is
important in determining ordinary residence. The residence must be voluntarily
h adopted. Enforced presence by reason of kidnapping or imprisonment, or a Robinson
Crusoe existence on a desert island with no opportunity of escape, may be so
overwhelming a factor as to negative the will to be where one is.

And there must be a degree of settled purpose. The purpose may be one or there may
be several. It may be specific or general. All the law requires is that there is a settled
purpose. This is not to say that the propositus intends to stay where he is indefinitely;
j indeed his purpose, while settled, may be for a limited period. Education, business or
profession, employment, health, family or merely love of the place spring to mind as
common reasons for a choice of regular abode. And there may well be many others. All
that is necessary is that the purpose of living where one does has a sufficient degree of
continuity to be properly described as settled.

The legal advantage of adopting the natural and ordinary meaning, as accepted by the
House of Lords in 1928 and recognised by Lord Denning MR in this case, is that it results
in the proof of ordinary residence, which is ultimately a question of fact, depending

more on the evidence of matters susceptible of objective proof than on evidence as to state of mind. Templeman LJ emphasised in the Court of Appeal the need for a simple test for local education authorities to apply, and I agree with him. The ordinary and natural meaning of the words supplies one. For if there be proved a regular, habitual mode of life in a particular place, the continuity of which has persisted despite temporary absences, ordinary residence is established provided only it is adopted voluntarily and for a settled purpose.

An attempt has been made in this case to suggest that education cannot be a settled purpose. I have no doubt it can be. A man's settled purpose will be different at different ages. Education in adolescence or early adulthood can be as settled a purpose as a profession or business in later years. There will seldom be any difficulty in determining whether residence is voluntary or for a settled purpose; nor will inquiry into such questions call for any deep examination of the mind of the propositus.

The view which I have expressed was, however, rejected by the Divisional Court and by the Court of Appeal; and it is strenuously challenged by the local education authorities in argument in your Lordships' House. It is, therefore, necessary to state briefly the reasons which have led me to reject the views of the courts below and the submissions of the local education authorities.

The Brent and Barnet borough councils submit that the words 'ordinarily resident . . . in the United Kingdom', in the context of a student's eligibility for a mandatory award, denote the place where he has his home permanently or indefinitely, ie his permanent base or centre adopted for general purposes, eg family or career. This is the 'real home test'; it necessarily means that a person has at any one time only one ordinary residence, viz his 'real home'. And they accept that this was the test which they applied. In doing so, they followed guidance given to local education authorities by the Department of Education and Science circular letter of 27 January 1972.

The Shropshire County Council contends for a variant of this test, namely a person's residence, permanent or indefinite, where he lives as a member of the general community and not merely for a specific or limited purpose. This contention is very close to the view expressed by the Divisional Court. It is clear from the documents embodying its decision that this was the test which it applied.

Counsel for the local education authorities recognised, and, indeed, submitted, that it is a necessary consequence of the 'real home' test, or its variant, that a man can have only one ordinary residence at any one time. It was said on behalf of Brent and Barnet borough councils that this view was supported by the 'recoupment' provisions to which I have already referred. For the reasons already given I derive no assistance from those provisions. What is important is to note that the test is wholly inconsistent with the natural and ordinary meaning of the words as construed by this House in the two tax cases. Indeed it is, I believe, an unhappy echo of 'domicile', the rules for ascertaining which impose great difficulties of proof. In *Dicey and Morris on the Conflict of Laws* (8th edn, 1967) ch 8, p 78 one finds the comment that 'the notion which lies at the root of the concept of domicile is that of permanent home'. The long and notorious existence of this difficult concept in our law, dependent on a refined, subtle and frequently very expensive judicial investigation of the devious twists and turns of the mind of man, must have been known to Parliament when enacting the 1962 Act. The choice of ordinary residence for determining the test of eligibility for a mandatory award suggests to my mind a legislative intention not to impose on local education authorities who are entrusted with the duty of making mandatory awards the infinitely difficult, if not impossible, task of determining whether a student has established a permanent home in the United Kingdom. Further, the language of the regulation lays emphasis not on intention or expectation for the future which is implicit in the idea of permanence, but on immediately past events, namely the usual order of the applicant's way of life and the place where in fact he has lived during the three years preceding his projected course of further education. There are, therefore, powerful reasons for holding that by selecting ordinary residence Parliament intended local education authorities to address their minds to a test more objective and less subjective than domicile or the concept of 'real home' which is a reflection of it. If the words of the regulation are allowed to have their natural *a* and ordinary meaning, such intention will be fulfilled. I would add one further comment. By giving the words their natural and ordinary meaning one helps to prevent the growth and multiplication of refined and subtle distinctions in the law's use of common English words. Nothing is more confusing and more likely to bring the statute law into disrepute than a proliferation by judicial interpretation of special meanings, when Parliament has not expressly enacted any.

b One of the unusual features in this very unusual litigation is that the local education authorities in this House seek to support the conclusions but not the reasoning of the judgments in the Divisional Court and the Court of Appeal. Both courts relied on policy considerations and the impact of the Immigration Act 1971. If, and in so far as, either court relied (and Lord Denning MR certainly did) on the Immigration Act 1971 as an aid to the interpretation of the Education Act 1962 and the regulations made thereunder, no party represented in your Lordships' House has been prepared to support this line of argument. It is recognised that the only relevance of the 1971 Act is that it established immigration control, which may give rise to relevant facts, but no more, in determining whether in truth a man is ordinarily resident in the United Kingdom.

c If, and in so far as, either court relied on its own subjective ideas as to policy, the same is true. Counsel has not sought to say that this approach was correct.

The Divisional Court rejected in terms the 'real home' test but attached importance to *d* the purpose or reason for a person's presence in the United Kingdom (see [1980] 3 All ER 679, [1982] QB 688). In its view, there must be shown an intention to live here on a permanent basis as part of the general community; if a person's presence here was for a 'specific or limited purpose only', eg to pursue a course of study, he would not be ordinarily resident. This, it will be remembered, is also the way the Shropshire County Council has put its case.

e The court attached importance to the terms on which the immigration authority permitted the student to enter the country. 'His immigration status is not in itself conclusive but it justifies [the] inference' that he intends to stay only for a limited period (see [1980] 3 All ER 679 at 688, [1982] QB 688 at 704). And so, because Nilish Shah was admitted for settlement, he was held to be ordinarily resident; but, because Jitendra Shah was admitted only for the purpose of study, the local education authority was held to be *f* entitled to decide he was not eligible for a mandatory award. The court thought it was confirmed in its construction of the regulation—

> 'by the reflection that it is almost inconceivable that Parliament could have intended to bestow major awards for higher education, out of public funds, on persons permitted to enter this country on a temporary basis, solely for the purpose of engaging in courses of study at their own expense. Such an improbable result is *g* not to be accepted if it can properly be avoided.'

(See [1980] 3 All ER 679 at 688, [1982] QB 688 at 704.)

Three points emerge as of critical importance in the court's judgment. First, the emphasis laid on the purpose of the presence here; second, the reliance on 'immigration status'; and, third, the reliance on policy considerations derived not from the education *h* legislation itself but from the court's own view as to what Parliament could or could not have intended.

In the Court of Appeal all three judges also emphasised the importance of immigration status. Lord Denning MR believed '. . . we must abandon our traditional method of interpretation' and 'say what the meaning of the words "ordinarily resident" is in the context of the situation brought about by the Immigration Act 1971' (see [1982] 1 All *j* ER 698 at 704, [1982] QB 688 at 720–721). He also expressed himself as much influenced by the policy considerations which influenced the Divisional Court. In the result he decided the appeals according to the terms of each student's leave to enter the United Kingdom. If the student was granted indefinite leave (Nilish Shah) or possessed the right of abode, he would be ordinarily resident; but, if he had limited leave only, he would be 'shut out' from eligibility for a mandatory award.

Eveleigh LJ adopted the approach of the Divisional Court. He denied the relevance of the tax cases saying that 'When [a person] seeks to claim a benefit from the state . . . the

position will be different' (see [1982] 1 All ER 698 at 706, [1982] QB 688 at 722). He had
the immigration legislation in mind and, in effect, decided each case according to the
terms of the student's leave to enter the country. He alone of the judges dealt explicitly
with the claim for a discretionary award, holding that 'there is no obligation on an
authority to consider an application from the point of view of its discretionary power'
(see [1982] 1 All ER 698 at 707, [1982] QB 688 at 724).

Templeman LJ made one point of great importance, namely that the words must be
construed so as to enable local education authorities to establish without undue difficulty
eligibility for an award. But he also attached critical importance to policy considerations,
prefacing a long passage in his judgment on policy with the words: 'It is improbable that
the 1962 Act was intended to entitle overseas students to a mandatory award' (see [1982]
1 All ER 698 at 710, [1982] QB 688 at 727).

In the end he based his decision on the immigration status of the student and on his
view that 'ordinary residence' implies a home. A person 'will not become ordinarily
resident in the United Kingdom unless and until he becomes entitled to remain in the
United Kingdom indefinitely' (see [1982] 1 All ER 689 at 711, [1982] QB 688 at 729).
Finally, he summed up his view as follows ([1982] 1 All ER 698 at 714, [1982] QB 688 at
733):

> '. . . in the context and against the background of the Education Act 1962 overseas
> students, that is to say persons who are admitted to and are present only for the
> limited purpose of pursuing a course of study, are not ordinarily resident in the
> United Kingdom during their period of study.'

He found the simplicity, for which he was right to search, in immigration status.

My Lords, the basic error of law in the judgments below was the failure by all the
judges, save Lord Denning MR, to appreciate the authoritative guidance given by this
House in the *Levene* and *Lysaght* cases as to the natural and ordinary meaning of the words
'ordinarily resident'. They attached too much importance to the particular purpose of
the residence, and too little to the evidence of a regular mode of life adopted voluntarily
and for a *settled* purpose, whatever it be, whether study, business, work or pleasure. In so
doing, they were influenced by their own views of policy and by the immigration status
of the students.

The way in which they used policy was, in my judgment, an impermissible approach
to the interpretation of statutory language. Judges may not interpret statutes in the light
of their own views as to policy. They may, of course, adopt a purposive interpretation if
they can find in the statute read as a whole or in material to which they are permitted by
law to refer as aids to interpretation an expression of Parliament's purpose or policy. But
that is not this case. The Education Act's only guidance is the requirement contained in
the regulations that, to be eligible for a mandatory award, a student must have been
ordinarily resident in the United Kingdom for three years. There is no hint of any other
restriction, provided, of course, he has the educational qualifications and his conduct is
satisfactory.

Both courts also agreed in attaching decisive importance to what the Divisional Court
called 'the immigration status' of the student. 'Immigration status', unless it be that of
one who has no right to be here, in which event presence in the United Kingdom is
unlawful, means no more than the terms of a person's leave to enter as stamped on his
passport. This may or may not be a guide to a person's intention in establishing a
residence in this country; it certainly cannot be the decisive test, as in effect the courts
below have treated it. Moreover, in the context with which these appeals are concerned,
i e past residence, intention or expectations for the future, are not critical; what matters
is the course of living over the past three years.

A further error was their view that a specific limited purpose could not be the settled
purpose, which is recognised as an essential ingredient of ordinary residence. This was,
no doubt, because they discarded the guidance of the *Levene* and *Lysaght* cases. But it was
also a confusion of thought, for study can be as settled a purpose as business or pleasure.
And the notion of a permanent or indefinitely enduring purpose as an element in

a ordinary residence derives not from the natural and ordinary meaning of the words 'ordinarily resident' but from a confusion of it with domicile.

I therefore reject the conclusions and reasoning of the courts below. And I also reject the 'real home' test (and the variant of it) for which the local education authorities contended. In my view neither the test nor the variant is consistent with the natural and ordinary meaning of the words. And, once it is accepted that it is not legitimate to look to the 'recoupment' provisions of the Education Acts for guidance, there is nothing in

b the Acts to suggest that the words should bear any other than their natural and ordinary meaning. In particular, the Immigration Act 1971, passed some nine years after the Education Act 1962, gives no guidance to the interpretation of that Act. It cannot be permissible in the absence of a reference (express or necessarily to be implied) by one statute to the other to interpret an earlier Act by reference to a later Act. But, if it were permissible to refer to the Immigration Act 1971 as an aid in the interpretation of the

c education legislation, it would immediately become apparent that the Act uses 'ordinary residence' to denote something less than 'right of abode' and less even than 'settlement'. Indeed, it would seem to use the words in their natural and ordinary meaning: see ss 2(1)(c) and (3)(d), 7, 33(2), Sch 1, App A (the substituted s 5A(3) of the British Nationality Act 1948). The indications are, therefore, strong that the Immigration Act 1971 uses the words in their natural and ordinary meaning, though it is not, of course, necessary to

d decide the question in these appeals.

My Lords, it is, therefore, my view that local education authorities, when considering an application for a mandatory award, must ask themselves the question: has the applicant shown that he has habitually and normally resided in the United Kingdom from choice and for a settled purpose throughout the prescribed period, apart from temporary or occasional absences? If a local education authority asks this, the correct,

e question, it is then for it, and it alone, to determine whether as a matter of fact the applicant has shown such residence. An authority is not required to determine his 'real home', whatever that means; nor need any attempt be made to discover what his long-term future intentions or expectations are. The relevant period is not the future but one which has largely (or wholly) elapsed, namely that between the date of the commencement of his proposed course and the date of his arrival in the United Kingdom. The terms of

f an immigrant student's leave to enter and remain here may or may not throw light on the question; it will, however, be of little weight when put into the balance against the fact of continued residence over the prescribed period, unless the residence is itself a breach of the terms of his leave, in which event his residence, being unlawful, could not be ordinary.

I now turn to the student Shabpar's alternative case in relation to a discretionary grant.

g This case does not now arise for decision, but it does raise a question on which it was made clear local education authorities would welcome guidance. Eveleigh LJ, who alone of the appeal judges dealt with the power to grant a discretionary award, expressed the opinion that on an application for an award under s 1 of the Education Act 1962 there was no obligation on the authority to consider it 'from the point of view of its discretionary power' (see [1982] 1 All ER 698 at 707, [1982] QB 688 at 724). I cannot

h agree. When a student applies for an award under s 1 of the 1962 Act (or its modern equivalent) he is to be understood to be applying for one or other of the awards available under the section, ie mandatory under sub-s (1) or, if he fails, discretionary under sub-s (4). His application under the section, unless it be expressly limited to a mandatory award, which it was not in Shabpar's case and is in any event highly improbable, involves the duty to consider whether or not to make a discretionary award in the event of a

j failure to establish eligibility for a mandatory award. In my view, therefore, an application under s 1 of the 1962 Act, or its modern equivalent, requires, unless it be in terms a restricted application, the local education authority to consider the exercise of its discretion, if it has concluded that the applicant is not entitled to a mandatory award.

Finally, on this part of the case I must salute in passing, but without deciding, the interesting points made on behalf of the students by counsel for the Shahs and adopted by counsel for Akbarali and Abdullah, which were concerned with the possible impact

on these cases of European Community law and the European Convention for the
Protection of Human Rights and Fundamental Freedoms (Rome, 4 November 1950; TS
71 (1953); Cmd 8969). The points only arise for discussion if the House should be
disposed to favour the 'real home' test, or its variant, the limited purpose test, as
determinative of ordinary residence in the context of eligibility for a mandatory award.
I am not so disposed; and I do not understand counsel for the Shahs to suggest that either
the European Communities Act 1972 or the European convention contain any rule or
provision which should discourage the House from giving to the words 'ordinarily
resident' in the present context the natural and ordinary meaning recognised and adopted
by the House in 1928. I am, therefore, in duty bound to resist, as unnecessary, the
invitation to explore the fascinating vistas of legal speculation which counsel for the
Shahs has skilfully and temptingly opened to our view.

In the result, I am satisfied that the local education authorities misdirected themselves
in law. It is now settled law that an administrative or executive authority entrusted with
the exercise of a discretion must direct itself properly in law: see *Associated Provincial
Picture Houses Ltd v Wednesbury Corp* [1947] 2 All ER 680 at 682–683, [1948] 1 KB 223 at
229. The duty of decision entrusted to the local education authorities is a comparable
function. In truth, it is a stronger case for judicial review; for, if the applicant establishes
the facts required by law, he has a right to receive, and the local education authority a
duty to bestow, an award. It follows, therefore, that all the students have made out their
case for judicial review. The remedy available on judicial review is, however, discretionary
and a matter for the court: see *O'Reilly v Mackman* [1982] 3 All ER 1124, [1982] 3 WLR
1096. Nilish Shah, who succeeded before the Divisional Court and now has the local
education authority's appeal from that decision finally dismissed, was granted by the
Divisional Court an order of certiorari to quash the refusal of a mandatory award and an
order of mandamus to require the authority to reconsider his application for an award.
My Lords, I think this is the appropriate relief, for it avoids any semblance of the courts
assuming the function assigned by Parliament to the local education authorities, namely
the power to decide whether to make or to refuse an award. Counsel for the students did
suggest that declaratory relief was appropriate. Declarations are appropriate to declare an
entitlement or a right, or a duty. But this is exactly what the courts cannot, and must not
do, in these cases. It is not for the courts to say either that the students are entitled to an
award or that the authorities are under a duty to make an award. The function of the
court is to ensure due observance of the law; that is all. However, it suffices for the
purpose of the appeals, without exploring any further what is a developing branch of the
law, to say that certiorari and mandamus will do justice, in that their combined effect
will be to remit to the authorities the task of decision which the statute imposes on them.
In performing their task it will be their duty to follow the guidance as to the law now
given by your Lordships' House.

Accordingly, I would allow the appeals of Akbarali, Abdullah, Jitendra Shah and
Shabpar and propose that certiorari and mandamus should go to the authorities
concerned. Barnet's appeal in Nilish Shah's case is dismissed, the order made by the
Divisional Court being upheld. The students should have their costs here and below.
And there must be legal aid taxation in all five cases of the students' costs.

LORD LOWRY. My Lords, the legal and public interest of the points at issue in these
appeals and the excellence of the argument on each side offer an invitation to which it is
tempting to respond. I have, however, read in draft the speech of my noble and learned
friend Lord Scarman, which expresses so exactly and so elegantly my own view of the
matter that it would be pointless, even in this important case, for me to add anything.

I am therefore content to agree with my noble and learned friend's opinion, including
that part which refers to discretionary awards, and with the order which he has proposed.

LORD ROSKILL. My Lords, I have had the advantage of reading in draft the speech
of my noble and learned friend Lord Scarman. I agree with it in all respects. For the
reasons he gives I would allow the first four appeals and dismiss the appeal in the case of
Nilish Shah.

LORD BRANDON OF OAKBROOK. My Lords, I have had the advantage of reading in draft the speech prepared by my noble and learned friend Lord Scarman. I agree with it, and for the reasons which he gives would allow the first four appeals and dismiss the appeal in Nilish Shah's case.

Appeals of Akbarali, Abdullah, Jitendra Shah and Shabpar allowed; orders of certiorari and mandamus accordingly. Appeal of Barnet London Borough Council in Nilish Shah's case dismissed.

Solicitors: *Bindman & Partners* (for Akbarali and Abdullah); *Jaques & Co* (for Jitendra Shah and Nilish Shah); *E M Bennett*, Hendon (for Barnet London Borough Council); *Nicholls Christie & Crocker*, Uxbridge (for Shabpa); *Stephen R Forster*, Wembley (for Brent London Borough Council); *Sharpe Pritchard & Co*, agents for *R C Sawtell*, Shrewsbury (for Shropshire County Council).

Mary Rose Plummer   Barrister.

R v British Broadcasting Corp, ex parte Lavelle

QUEEN'S BENCH DIVISION (CROWN OFFICE LIST)
WOOLF J
21 JUNE, 2 JULY 1982

Judicial review – Availability of remedy – Certiorari – Declaration or injunction – Dismissal of employee – Disciplinary procedure for dismissal forming part of contract of employment – Whether relief by way of judicial review of dismissal available – Supreme Court Act 1981, s 31(1)(2) – RSC Ord 53, r 1(1)(a)(2).

Judicial review – Availability of remedy – Declaration or injunction – Relief sought in action begun by writ claiming declaration or injunction – Dismissal of employee – Disciplinary procedure for dismissal forming part of contract of employment – Criminal proceedings for theft pending against employee – Whether jurisdiction to interfere with dismissal by injunctive or declaratory relief – Whether pending criminal proceedings requiring proceedings under disciplinary procedure to be postponed until conclusion of criminal proceedings – RSC Ord 53, r 9(5).

The applicant was employed by the BBC as a tape examiner under a contract of employment which expressly included the BBC's staff regulations. The regulations contained a code of practice setting out the disciplinary procedure to be followed where misconduct was alleged against an employee. Under that procedure the BBC had to give an employee an opportunity to explain his conduct at a formal disciplinary interview before dismissing him for misconduct. The employee was entitled to be accompanied by a union or other representative at the interview. If, following the interview, the BBC decided to dismiss the employee under the code of practice he had a right to appeal against the dismissal to a BBC managing director or the head of establishment and then to the director-general of the BBC. In January 1982 the police found tapes belonging to the BBC at the applicant's home. The applicant was charged with theft and elected jury trial in the Crown Court. The BBC took the view that her removal of the tapes was misconduct which justified her dismissal from the BBC regardless of whether she was guilty of theft, and decided to conduct a disciplinary interview under the disciplinary procedure. The applicant was given only one hour's notice of the interview and consequently was unable to arrange for a union or other representative to accompany her. She herself attended the interview and gave an explanation for the removal of the tapes. Following the interview the BBC decided to dismiss her and gave her contractual notice terminating her employment as from 20 March 1982. The applicant consulted

her union and decided not to insist on her right to have been represented at the
disciplinary interview and that she would proceed to the next stage of the disciplinary   *a*
procedure by appealing against the dismissal to a managing director. However, she
requested the managing director to postpone hearing the appeal until the conclusion of
the criminal proceedings, on the ground that the hearing of the appeal would prejudice
her defence in the criminal proceedings. The managing director refused to delay the
appeal and, having heard it, confirmed the decision to dismiss the applicant. The
applicant gave notice that she intended to appeal to the director-general. She then applied   *b*
to the court under RSC Ord 53 for judicial review of the decision to dismiss her, seeking
(i) under Ord 53, r 1(1)(*a*)*ᵃ*, orders of certiorari to quash both the original decision to
dismiss her and the managing director's decision upholding that decision, and (ii) under
Ord 53, r 1(2), an injunction to stay the further appeal to the director-general until the
conclusion of the criminal proceedings, on the ground of prejudice to the applicant if the
appeal was heard before then. The applicant contended that certiorari should be granted   *c*
because the failure to give her adequate notice of the disciplinary interview was a breach
of natural justice and the managing director's refusal to postpone the hearing of the
appeal had prejudiced her defence in the criminal proceedings. At the hearing of the
application the parties agreed that if the court considered that judicial relief should not
be granted under Ord 53, r 1 the court should under Ord 53, r 9(5)*ᵇ* continue to hear the
proceedings as if the applicant had begun an action by writ seeking declarations regarding   *d*
the invalidity of the disciplinary interview and the managing director's refusal to
postpone hearing the appeal and an injunction against the director-general.

Held – The application would be refused for the following reasons—
     (1) Under RSC Ord 53, r 1(1), as confirmed by s 31(1)*ᶜ* of the Supreme Court Act 1981,
certiorari and the other prerogative remedies were only available to impugn a decision   *e*
of a tribunal which was performing a public duty, and were inappropriate to impugn a
decision of a domestic tribunal such as an employer's disciplinary tribunal. Similarly,
judicial review by way of an injunction or declaration under Ord 53, r 1(2), or s 31(2) of
the 1981 Act, although wider in ambit than relief by prerogative order, was nevertheless
confined to the review of activities of a public nature as opposed to those of a purely
private or domestic character. Since the disciplinary procedure under which the applicant   *f*
was dismissed arose out of her contract of employment and was purely private or
domestic in character, the applicant was not entitled to relief by way of certiorari under
Ord 53, r 1(1) or an injunction or declaration under Ord 53, r 1(2) (see p 248 *e f*, p 249 *b*
to *e* and p 255 *h*, post); dictum of Denning LJ in *Lee v Showmen's Guild of Great Britain*
[1952] 1 All ER at 1183 and *R v Criminal Injuries Compensation Board, ex p Lain* [1967] 2
All ER 770 applied.
     (2) On the question whether the court had jurisdiction to grant the applicant relief by   *g*

---

a   Rule 1(1) is set out at p 248 *b* to *d*, post
b   Rule 9(5) provides: 'Where the relief sought is a declaration, an injunction or damages and the
     Court considers that it should not be granted on an application for judicial review but might have
     been granted if it had been sought in an action begun by writ by the applicant at the time of
     making his application, the Court may, instead of refusing the application, order the proceedings   *h*
     to continue as if they had been begun by writ; and Order 28, rule 8, shall apply as if, in the case of
     an application made by motion, it had been made by summons.'
c   Section 31, so far as material, provides:
        '(1) An application to the High Court for one or more of the following forms of relief, namely—
     (*a*) an order of mandamus, prohibition or certiorari; (*b*) a declaration or injunction under subsection
     (2) . . . shall be made in accordance with rules of court by a procedure to be known as an application   *j*
     for judicial review.
        (2) A declaration may be made or an injunction granted under this subsection in any case where
     an application for judicial review, seeking that relief, has been made and the High Court considers
     that, having regard to—(*a*) the nature of the matters in respect of which relief may be granted by
     orders of mandamus, prohibition or certiorari; (*b*) the nature of the persons and bodies against
     whom relief may be granted by such orders; and (*c*) all the circumstances of the case, it would be
     just and convenient for the declaration to be made or the injunction to be granted as the case may
     be . . .'

way of an injunction or declaration under Ord 53, r 9(5), the court had no jurisdiction to interfere with an employee's dismissal in a pure master and servant situation where there was no protection of the employment beyond that afforded by the common law. However, where the employment was protected by, inter alia, the employer being required to observe procedural requirements outside the common law before dismissing the employee the court did have jurisdiction under Ord 53, r 9(5) to grant an injunction or declaration if the employer failed to observe the procedural requirements. Whether the employment was protected otherwise than by the common law was to be determined by examining the framework and context of the employment. Since the disciplinary procedure incorporated in the applicant's contract restricted the BBC's common law right of dismissal, the court had jurisdiction to grant the applicant relief under Ord 53, r 9(5) if in its discretion the court considered that such relief should be granted (see p 252 *b c* and p 253 *b c*, post); dicta of Lord Reid in *Ridge v Baldwin* [1963] 2 All ER at 71, of Lord Wilberforce in *Malloch v Aberdeen Corp* [1971] 2 All ER at 1294–1296 and of Buckley LJ in *Stevenson v United Road Transport Union* [1977] 2 All ER at 948–949 applied.

(3) However, on the facts, the court would not exercise its discretion to grant the applicant declarations or an injunction under RSC Ord 53, r 9(5) because (a) although the applicant had not been given adequate notice of the disciplinary interview, she had chosen not to insist on her rights to receive proper notice and to have a representative present at the interview, and (b) where criminal proceedings were pending against an employee the court would only require disciplinary proceedings in respect of the same matter to be postponed if there was a real risk that the disciplinary proceedings might cause a miscarriage of justice in the criminal proceedings, and on the facts no such risk arose (see p 255 *g h j* to p 256 *b f*, post); *Harris (Ipswich) Ltd v Harrison* [1978] ICR 1256 and *Jefferson v Bhetcha* [1979] 2 All ER 1108 applied.

Notes
For judicial remedies in general and for certiorari, injunctions and declaratory judgments in particular, see 1 Halsbury Laws (4th edn) paras 80–84, 147–149, 159, 168, 185, 186.

For the Supreme Court Act 1981, s 31, see 51 Halsbury's Statutes (3rd edn) 625.

Cases referred to in judgment
A-G v Butterworth [1962] 3 All ER 326, [1963] 1 QB 696, [1962] 3 WLR 819, CA, 16 Digest (Reissue) 52, *498*.

Breen v Amalgamated Engineering Union (now Amalgamated Engineering and Foundry Workers' Union) [1971] 1 All ER 1148, [1971] 2 QB 175, [1971] 2 WLR 742, CA, Digest (Cont Vol D) 954, *1249c*.

Carr v Alexander Russell Ltd [1975] IRLR 49, EAT; *affd* [1976] IRLR 220, CS.

Harris (Ipswich) Ltd v Harrison [1978] ICR 1256, EAT.

Jefferson v Bhetcha [1979] 2 All ER 1108, [1979] 1 WLR 898, CA, Digest (Cont Vol E) 670, *5404b*.

Lee v Showmen's Guild of Great Britain [1952] 1 All ER 1175, [1952] 2 QB 329, CA, 45 Digest (Repl) 541, *1221*.

Malloch v Aberdeen Corp [1971] 2 All ER 1278, [1971] 1 WLR 1578, HL, 19 Digest (Reissue) 548, *4128*.

R v Criminal Injuries Compensation Board, ex p Lain [1967] 2 All ER 770, [1967] 2 QB 864, [1967] 3 WLR 348, DC, 14(2) Digest (Reissue) 866, *7499*.

R v Darlington School Governors (1844) 6 QB 682, 115 ER 257, 19 Digest (Reissue) 556, *4182*.

R v Manchester Legal Aid Committee, ex p R A Brand & Co Ltd [1952] 1 All ER 480, [1952] 2 QB 413, DC, 5 Digest (Reissue) 1077, *8631*.

Ridge v Baldwin [1963] 2 All ER 66, [1964] AC 40, [1963] 2 WLR 935, HL, 37(1) Digest (Reissue) 331, *2132*.

Russell v Duke of Norfolk [1949] 1 All ER 109, CA, 12 Digest (Reissue) 706, *5446*.

Stevenson v United Road Transport Union [1977] 2 All ER 941, [1977] ICR 893, CA, Digest (Cont Vol E) 609, *1249ba*.

Tucker v British Museum (1967) Times, 8 December.
Vidyodaya University of Ceylon v Silva [1964] 3 All ER 865, [1965] 1 WLR 77, PC.
Vine v National Dock Labour Board [1956] 3 All ER 939, [1957] AC 488, [1957] 2 WLR
    106, HL, 30 Digest (Reissue) 208, *311*.
Wonder Heat Pty Ltd v Bishop [1960] VR 489, 1(1) Digest (Reissue) 78, *248*.

Application for judicial review
By an amended application dated 18 June 1982 Anne Marie Lavelle applied, with the
leave of McNeill J granted on 6 April 1982, for (1) an order prohibiting Mr Aubrey
Singer, managing director of the BBC's Radio Service, or any other representative of the
BBC, sitting as an appellate tribunal, from proceeding with the hearing of Miss Lavelle's
appeal against her dismissal on 20 March 1982 from her employment with the BBC,
until the determination of the trial in the Crown Court of a charge against her of theft of
16 recording tapes belonging to the BBC, valued at £96, or any subsequent appeal
therefrom, (2) an order of certiorari to quash the dismissal decision of 20 March 1982,
which followed a disciplinary interview with Miss Lavelle held by a member of the BBC
on 2 February 1982, (3) an order of certiorari to quash the decision on 6 April 1982 of Mr
Aubrey Singer to uphold the dismissal decision of 20 March 1982, and (4) an order
staying all proceedings on Miss Lavelle's further appeal to the director-general of the BBC
against her dismissal. The grounds of the application were that (1) it was prejudicial to
Miss Lavelle's defence in the criminal trial for theft for any appeal by her against her
dismissal to be held before the trial was determined and (2) Miss Lavelle was given
insufficient notice of the disciplinary interview held on 2 February 1982 to enable her to
arrange to be accompanied at the interview by a colleague or a trade union representative
and at the interview was not advised of her right to an adjournment of the interview to
enable her to arrange for a colleague or union representative to be present. The facts are
set out in the judgment.

William Evans for the applicant.
Andrew Caldecott for the BBC.

Cur adv vult

2 July. The following judgment was delivered.

WOOLF J. The applicant, Miss Anne Marie Lavelle, is employed by the BBC as a tape
examiner. By her application, as amended, she seeks orders of certiorari to quash a
decision which was taken to dismiss her from her employment with the BBC as a result
of the disciplinary interview which was conducted on 2 February 1982 and the decision
to uphold that dismissal which was made by the managing director of BBC Radio on 6
April 1982. The applicant had previously been seeking an order of prohibition, but as a
result of the passage of time since the application was made, an order of prohibition in
the terms in which it was sought would no longer serve any purpose.
    The application raises a number of points which are of general importance. The points
are: (1) whether judicial review is the appropriate procedure for an employee to adopt if
he wishes to challenge the legality of disciplinary proceedings conducted by his employers
into alleged misconduct; (2) whether the court has jurisdiction in the appropriate
proceedings to grant an injunction to restrain a disciplinary tribunal set up by an
employer to investigate alleged misconduct by an employee which would justify the
dismissal of that employee; (3) if there is such jurisdiction, whether it should be exercised
to stay the hearing before the disciplinary tribunal until after the conclusion of criminal
proceedings against the employee which raised the same issues as before the disciplinary
tribunal.
    In addition, it is necessary to consider whether in any event, on the facts, this is an
appropriate case in which to grant relief.
    The applicant's employment commenced on 21 April 1975. Initially her employment
was probationary, but it was confirmed the following year. A letter dated 16 April 1975

set out various terms and conditions. Condition 4 provided that her employment was to continue until determined by the appropriate period of notice. Condition 5 provided:

'The B.B.C. shall have the right to dismiss you summarily without compensation and without payment beyond your last day of service if you are guilty of any gross misconduct or neglect or refusal of duty or other serious breach of the terms of your employment and this dismissal shall be without prejudice to any claim that either party may have against the other or any breach of the terms of your employment.'

Condition 6 provides that the procedure for an appeal in the event of the applicant's employment being determined shall 'be as prescribed in the B.B.C. Regulations for the time being'. Condition 8 stated that the BBC regulations for the time being shall be deemed to form part of the applicant's contract of employment.

At the material time the disciplinary procedure was set out in staff instruction 366 of 24 May 1977 as amended. The staff instruction sets out the purpose of the disciplinary procedures as including ensuring—

'that the staff concerned have the opportunity to explain their actions at a formal disciplinary interview at which if they wish they may be accompanied by a Union or other representative.'

It recites the fact that the procedures comply with the official code of practice approved by Parliament and are concerned only with misconduct and are distinct from the appraisal of performance.

It is necessary for me to read out the relevant parts of the staff instructions.

'3. *Disciplinary Proceedings*: Where it appears that a member of staff has committed a breach of discipline which may warrant the imposition of a penalty listed in paragraph 5 below, he will be formally interviewed. The member of staff has the right to be accompanied, if he wishes, by his legal representative or a colleague, other than a practising lawyer, in order to assist him in expressing his case; to be available as a witness in case of any subsequent conflict as to what transpired at the interview; to confirm that the interview has been conducted fairly; and to request an adjournment if he believes this to be necessary.

3.1 *Preliminary Investigations*: The disciplinary interview may be preceded by such preliminary investigation as is needed to establish the facts. In cases where this involves questioning other members of staff besides those immediately concerned, the purpose of the questioning must be clearly explained at the outset. Any statements made at such interviews which could be used at a subsequent interview must be recorded formally, and the record countersigned. At the disciplinary interview it will be open to the member of staff whose conduct is being enquired into to challenge the accuracy of any information which may have been obtained in the course of a preliminary investigation.

3.2 *Arrangements for Disciplinary Interview*: Before the interview is held the member of staff will be notified in writing of: the place and time at which the interview is to be held; who is to conduct the interview and, where possible, who may accompany the person conducting it; the nature of the breach of discipline being enquired into; and his right to be accompanied at the interview by either an official Union representative, or, if he wishes, a colleague on the staff of the B.B.C., other than a practising lawyer. Reasonable arrangements will be made for allowing a postponement of the interview at the member of staff's request—if, for example, he needs time to make arrangements to be accompanied at the interview. If he does wish to exercise his right to be accompanied by an official Union representative or by a colleague, he should inform the interviewing officer in advance and say whether he will be accompanied . . .

3.4.1 *Procedure*: A disciplinary interview is not a trial and there are no formal procedural rules. The member of staff has the right: to be given full details of his alleged misconduct to enable him fully to understand the nature of the complaint against him; to have an adequate opportunity to explain his actions and put his own point of view. Witnesses will not normally be called, but if relevant facts are in dispute, and the member of staff claims that there is someone who can corroborate his story, the interview may be adjourned, either to allow the personnel officer or departmental manager conducting the inquiry to carry out such further investigations as he deems necessary, or to allow the member of staff to ascertain or verify facts relevant to his case.

3.4.2 An adjournment may also be allowed at the request of the Union representative or of the member of staff.

4. *Direction not to report for duty pending further instructions:* When a breach of discipline occurs, and if it seems to be essential in his own and/or the B.B.C.'s interests, the member of staff concerned may be directed to leave his place of work and not return to duty or enter B.B.C. premises pending further instructions. (Formal arrangements may, however, be made to allow him to enter B.B.C. premises for the specific purpose of gathering evidence relevant to the case). During this time he remains on full pay. The instruction may be given by the most senior manager or supervisor immediately available, but it must be reported to, and confirmed in writing, by the Head of Department or Personnel Officer concerned as soon as practicable. If the member of staff believes that the grounds on which he has been directed not to report for duty has been unreasonable and that he has suffered financial loss, he has the right, under S.I. 330 paragraph 6 to state a grievance. *Note:* For the purposes of this paragraph "full pay" means the pay staff would have received during an authorised absence from duty, e.g. during annual leave, bisque leave, compensatory leave, sick leave for more than three days etc., i.e.: for monthly staff, the normal basic salary plus any Shift, Irregular Hour, MP, Language or other continuing allowances for which they are elegible, but not Actuality, Penalty Payments or Extra Duty Pay; for Weekly staff as set out in the current Staff Instruction governing their condition of service.

5. *Penalties:* When misconduct has been established, one of the penalties set out below (in ascending order of severity) may be imposed. The imposition of any of those penalties is confirmed in writing to the member of staff and will be recorded on the staff file. Two copies of the record will be sent to the member of staff—one copy for his retention, the other to forward to his representative or union if he wishes. A penalty less severe than termination may be accompanied by a warning of the consequences of any repetition of the unsatisfactory conduct . . .

5.4 *Termination:* (i.e. dismissal with contractual notice) *Application:* Termination may be imposed as a consequence of a single act of serious misconduct, being then regarded as an alternative to summary dismissal (see 5.5 below). It may also be used where the misconduct is of a more general nature, such as a series of misdemeanours which are minor in themselves but which demonstrate the member of staff's inability to achieve the standards of discipline and behaviour expected of B.B.C. staff; but in such cases there will be a record of at least one previous formal warning or other disciplinary penalties. *Authorisation:* Head of Establishment with the prior agreement of staff administration.

5.5 *Summary Dismissal. Application:* Summary dismissal is reserved for cases of gross misconduct or neglect or refusal of duty or other serious breach of the terms of employment. Examples of the type of conduct which could lead to summary dismissal are: assault; dishonesty; negligence endangering life; gross dereliction of duty; persistent insobriety; and conviction for a grave offence inconsistent with the proper performance of the person's B.B.C. duties. Staff who are summarily dismissed are paid only up to the day on which they are dismissed, and they are not entitled to pay in lieu of notice or to security pay. *Authorisation:* D. Pers. or, in his absence, C.S.A.'

A right of appeal is given by para 7, and the procedure, so far as that is concerned, is now set out in staff instruction 372. This provides that in appropriate circumstances there is a right of appeal to the head of establishment, but if the decision appealed against was taken by the head of establishment to the managing director concerned, and also provides that if that appeal is rejected, the appellant may if he wishes further appeal to the director-general who has the right to delegate the case to the director of personnel in respect of both appeals. There is a right to appeal in person and for the appellant to be accompanied, if he wishes, by an official of a recognised trade union or another member of staff, excluding a practising lawyer. A member of the staff appealing against a determination, other than summary dismissal, remains on the payroll until his contractual notice has expired.

Staff instruction 372 sets out that under current legislation employees have certain rights of complaint to an industrial tribunal and that there can be no question of a member of the BBC management rejudging a matter which has been referred to such a statutory tribunal. Therefore, a member of the staff who makes an application to an industrial tribunal can thereafter have no further right of appeal under the internal procedures as regards that particular complaint.

On 25 January 1982 the police paid a visit to the address at which the applicant was living, for reasons wholly unconnected with these proceedings and because of information which had been provided to the police, which as far as I am aware, was absolutely without any foundation. However, while the police were at her address they found certain tapes which were the property of the BBC and because of this, in due course, the applicant was charged on 4 February 1982 with the theft of those tapes. She has elected trial by jury in respect of that charge, and it is anticipated that the hearing of the charge will be some time in about August 1982. The applicant intends to plead not guilty.

The BBC alleges that the removal of the tapes is, in itself, misconduct justifying dismissal irrespective of whether or not that removal amounts to theft. It was therefore decide to conduct a disciplinary interview into the removal of the tapes at 4 pm on 2 February 1982. Regrettably, the applicant was only given notice of that interview by letter dated 2 February 1982 which was handed to her at 3 pm, an hour before the interview was due to take place. The letter set out her right to be accompanied but not surprisingly, having only had such short notice, the applicant was unable to make arrangements to be accompanied. She did, however, attend and give her explanation as to what had happened to Mr Tink, the engineer in charge of technical services who conducted the disciplinary interview in the presence of the senior personnel officer (radio). I do not propose to indicate the explanation the applicant gave, bearing in mind the forthcoming criminal proceedings.

Following that disciplinary interview, by letter dated 17 February 1982 the applicant was given notice of the BBC's decision to terminate her service following contractual notice to take effect on 20 March 1982, the termination being for the removal of the tapes. The letter set out the right of appeal to the managing director (radio). Having consulted her trade union, the applicant decided to appeal and arrangements were made for that appeal to be held on 12 March 1982 by Mr Aubrey Singer, managing director of BBC radio with Mr A J K Austin, senior personnel officer (radio) in attendance. On 12 March 1982 the applicant attended before Mr Singer accompanied by Judith Blakeman, her trade union representative, and a request was made that the hearing of the appeal should be adjourned until after the conclusion of the criminal proceedings. Mr Singer then adjourned the appeal so that he could be advised whether it would be appropriate for the appeal to be heard before the hearing of the criminal proceedings. The BBC, having taken the advice of its solicitors, decided that it would be proper for the hearing to continue and it was therefore reconvened on 6 April. On that day an application for leave to move was made in these proceedings and leave was duly granted. However, no application for a stay or an injunction was made at that stage. At the reconvened hearing, again after taking advice, Mr Singer decided to proceed with the hearing notwithstanding that the application for judicial review had been made. The decision which Mr Singer came to was to uphold the previous decision.

The applicant then served a further notice of appeal on 23 April 1982 and that appeal was due to be heard on 23 June 1982 but has been adjourned to enable me to give this judgment. Part of the relief the applicant is now seeking is the stay of that further appeal until after the conclusion of the criminal proceedings.

Having recited the facts, it is now necessary for me to consider the points of general application to which I referred at the commencement of this judgment.

Is an application for judicial review the appropriate procedure?

RSC Ord 53, r 1, produced in 1977, sets out the cases appropriate for application for judicial review in these terms:

> '(1) An application for—(a) an order of mandamus, prohibition or certiorari, or (b) an injunction under section 9 of the Administration of Justice (Miscellaneous Provisions) Act 1938 restraining a person from acting in any office in which he is not entitled to act, shall be made by way of an application for judicial review in accordance with the provisions of this Order.
>
> (2) An application for a declaration or an injunction (not being an injunction mentioned in paragraph (1)(b)) may be made by way of an application for judicial review, and on such an application the Court may grant the declaration or injunction claimed if it considers that, having regard to—(a) the nature of the matters in respect of which relief may be granted by way of an order of mandamus, prohibition or certiorari, (b) the nature of the persons and bodies against whom relief may be granted by way of such an order, and (c) all the circumstances of the case, it would be just and convenient for the declaration or injunction to be granted on an application for judicial review.'

Rule 1 has since received statutory confirmation in almost identical terms in s 31 of the Supreme Court Act 1981. There is nothing in r 1 or s 31 which expressly extends the circumstances in which the prerogative remedies of mandamus, prohibition or certiorari are available. Those remedies were not previously available to enforce private rights but were what could be described as public law remedies. They were not appropriate, and in my view remain inappropriate remedies, for enforcing breaches of ordinary obligations owed by a master to his servant. An application for judicial review has not and should not be extended to a pure employment situation. Nor does it, in my view, make any difference that what is sought to be attacked is a decision of a domestic tribunal such as the series of disciplinary tribunals provided for by the BBC.

Support for this approach can be found in the judgment of Denning LJ in *Lee v Showmen's Guild of Great Britain* [1952] 1 All ER 1175 at 1183, [1952] 2 QB 329 at 346. That was a case where an action was brought and there was no application for a prerogative writ. Therefore what Denning LJ said is, strictly speaking, obiter. However, while he made it clear that a remedy by way of declaration and injunction could be available in respect of domestic tribunals, the remedy by certiorari does not lie in domestic tribunals.

The matter was dealt with very clearly by Lord Parker CJ in *R v Criminal Injuries Compensation Board, ex p Lain* [1967] 2 All ER 770 at 778, [1967] 2 QB 864 at 882 in a passage which I will read:

> 'The position as I see it is that the exact limits of the ancient remedy by way of certiorari have never been, and ought not to be, specifically defined. They have varied from time to time, being extended to meet changing conditions. At one time the writ only went to an inferior court. Later its ambit was extended to statutory tribunals determining a lis inter partes. Later again it extended to cases where there was no lis in the strict sense of the word, but where immediate or subsequent rights of a citizen were affected. The only constant limits throughout were that it was performing a public duty. Private or domestic tribunals have always been outside the scope of certiorari since their authority is derived solely from contract, that is from the agreement of the parties concerned. Finally, it is to be observed that the remedy has now been extended (see *R. v. Manchester Legal Aid Committee, Ex p. R. A.*

Brand & Co., Ltd. ([1952] 1 All ER 480, [1952] 2 QB 413), to cases in which the decision of an administrative officer is arrived at only after an inquiry or process of a judicial or quasi-judicial character. In such a case this court has jurisdiction to supervise that process. We have, as it seems to me, reached the position when the ambit of certiorari can be said to cover every case in which a body of persons, of a public as opposed to a purely private or domestic character, has to determine matters affecting subjects provided always that it has a duty to act judicially.'

Notwithstanding the present wording of Ord 53, r 1 and s 31 of the 1981 Act, the position remains the same and, if this application had been confined to an application for an order of certiorari, in my view there would have been no jurisdiction to make the order sought. However, in seeking a stay, the applicant is seeking, in effect, an injunction. The matter was argued before me on the basis that relief by way of an injunction was being sought on the application for judicial review. Paragraph (2) of r 1 of Ord 53 does not strictly confine applications for judicial review to cases where an order for mandamus, prohibition or certiorari could be granted. It merely requires that the court should have regard to the nature of the matter in respect of which such relief may be granted. However, although applications for judicial review are not confined to those cases where relief could be granted by way of prerogative order, I regard the wording of Ord 53, r 1(2) and sub-s (2) of s 31 of the 1981 Act as making it clear that the application for judicial review is confined to reviewing activities of a public nature as opposed to those of a purely private or domestic character. The disciplinary appeal procedure set up by the BBC depends purely on the contract of employment between the applicant and the BBC, and therefore it is a procedure of a purely private or domestic character.

Accordingly, it is my view that it was inappropriate to seek relief by way of judicial review in the circumstances of this case. However, when I indicated in the course of argument this could be my view, I also indicated that, if the parties were agreeable, I would be prepared to go on and consider the other issues so as to avoid the unnecessary expense and delay which would arise from the proceedings being aborted.

Power to proceed where a declaration or an injunction or damages is sought as if the action has begun by writ is provided for by Ord 53, r 9(5) and, accordingly, with the consent of the parties I will now consider the remaining issues on the basis that the action had been begun by writ. I turn therefore to the second point.

Has the court jurisdiction to grant an injunction?

It was contended on behalf of the BBC that in relation to the dismissal of a servant the ordinary courts would not interfere by way of injunction. There was no duty, in the case of tribunals under the disciplinary appeal procedure set up by the BBC, to act fairly which was enforcible by the courts. The procedure was purely domestic, and if it resulted in a wrongful dismissal, the remedy was the common law remedy of damages. In support of this contention I was referred to the speech of Lord Reid in *Ridge v Baldwin* [1963] 2 All ER 66 at 71, [1964] AC 40 at 65, a case concerning the chief constable of Brighton. Lord Reid said:

'So I shall deal first with cases of dismissal. These appear to fall into three classes, dismissal of a servant by his master, dismissal from an office held during pleasure, and dismissal from an office where there must be something against a man to warrant his dismissal. The law regarding master and servant is not in doubt. There cannot be specific performance of a contract of service and the master can terminate the contract with his servant at any time for any reason or for none. But if he does so in a manner not warranted by the contract he must pay damages for breach of contract. So the question in a pure case of master and servant does not at all depend on whether the master has heard the servant in his own defence: it depends on whether the facts emerging at the trial prove breach of contract. But this kind of case can resemble dismissal from an office where the body employing the man is under some statutory or other restriction as to the kind of contract which it can make with its servants, or the grounds on which it can dismiss them. The present case does not fall within this class because a chief constable is not the servant of the watch committee or indeed of anyone else.'

a

I was also referred to the decision of the House of Lords in *Malloch v Aberdeen Corp* [1971] 2 All ER 1278, [1971] 1 WLR 1578, which was the case concerning the dismissal of the Scottish teacher, a case in which Lord Reid also gave the first speech. He said ([1971] 2 All ER 1278 at 1282, [1971] 1 WLR 1578 at 1581):

'The first depends on a submission that the status of teachers in Scotland is simply *b* that of an ordinary servant. At common law a master is not bound to hear his servant before he dismisses him. He can act unreasonably or capriciously if he so chooses but the dismissal is valid. The servant has no remedy unless the dismissal is in breach of contract and then the servant's only remedy is damages for breach of contract.'

In that case Lord Reid then went on to distinguish the position of a teacher because he, *c* in effect, held a kind of office. The matter was also dealt with by Lord Wilberforce in a speech which I found particularly helpful and which I will accordingly read ([1971] 2 All ER 1278 at 1294–1296, [1971] 1 WLR 1578 at 1595–1597):

'What is the test of whether the appellant is entitled to a hearing, or to state his case? In the judgments in the courts below and also in argument at the Bar, this was *d* put largely in terms of the question whether the relation between the appellant and the education authority was that of master and servant, or was some other relation. If the appellant was merely a servant, then, it was said, the law is that he can be dismissed without a hearing; and his remedy lies only in damages. That the relationship between the appellant and the respondents was simply that of servant and master was the opinion of the Lord Ordinary, and the same approach is implicit *e* in the judgments of the Inner House. An alternative argument has been that as he could be dismissed at pleasure he could not demand to state his case. The argument that, once it is shown that the relevant relationship is that of master and servant, this is sufficient to exclude the requirements of natural justice is often found, in one form or another, in reported cases. These are two reasons behind it. The first is that, in master and servant cases, one is normally in the field of the common law of *f* contract inter partes, so that principles of administrative law, including those of natural justice, have no part to play. The second relates to the remedy: it is that in pure master and servant cases, the most that can be obtained is damages, if the dismissal is wrongful: no order for reinstatement can be made, so no room exists for such remedies as administrative law may grant, such as a declaration that the dismissal is void. I think there is validity in both of these arguments, but they, *g* particularly the first, must be carefully used. It involves the risk of a compartmental approach which, although convenient as a solvent, may lead to narrower distinctions that are appropriate to the broader issues of administrative law. A comparative list of situations in which persons have been held entitled or not entitled to a hearing, or to observation of rules of natural justice, according to the master and servant test, looks illogical and even bizarre. A specialist surgeon is denied protection which is *h* given to a hospital doctor; a university professor, as a servant, has been denied the right to be heard, a dock labourer and an undergraduate have been granted it; examples can be multiplied. [Then Lord Wilberforce cited a number of cases.] One may accept that if there are relationships in which all requirements of the observance of rules of natural justice are excluded (and I do not wish to assume that this is inevitably so), these must be confined to what have been called "pure master and *j* servant cases", which I take to mean cases in which there is no element of public employment or service, no support by statute, nothing in the nature of an office or a status which is capable of protection. If any of these elements exist, then, in my opinion, whatever the terminology used, and even though in some inter partes aspects the relationship may be called that of master and servant, there may be essential procedural requirements to be observed, and failure to observe them may

a   result in a dismissal being declared to be void. This distinction was, I think, clearly
perceived in two cases in this House. In *Vine v National Dock Labour Board* [1956] 3
All ER 939 at 944, [1957] AC 488 at 500, dealing with a registered dock labourer,
Viscount Kilmuir LC said that the situation was entirely different from the ordinary
master and servant case and referred to his status as a registered worker which he
was entitled to have secured. And Lord Keith said ([1956] 3 All ER 939 at 948,
[1957] AC 488 at 508): "This is not a straightforward relationship of master and
b   servant". The dock labour scheme gave the dock worker a status, supported by
statute. In *Ridge v Baldwin* [1963] 2 All ER 66 at 71, [1964] AC 40 at 65 Lord Reid
developed the point in an illuminating way. Cases of dismissal, he said, appear to
fall into three classes: first, there are pure master and servant cases—these are
governed by the law of contract and there is no right to be heard; but "this kind of
case can resemble dismissal from an office where the body employing the man is
under some statutory or other restriction as to the kind of contract which it can
c   make with its servants, or the grounds on which it can dismiss him"; secondly, there
are cases where an office is held at pleasure (I shall return to this category); and,
thirdly, there is the case where a man cannot be dismissed unless there is something
against him—in this he has a right to be heard. On the other hand, there are some
cases where the distinction has been lost sight of, and where the mere allocation of
d   the label—master and servant—has been thought decisive against an administrative
law remedy. One such, which I refer to because it may be thought to have some
relevance here, is *Vidyodaya University of Ceylon v Silva* [1964] 3 All ER 865, [1965] 1
WLR 77, concerned with a university professor, who was dismissed without a
hearing. He succeeded before the Supreme Court of Ceylon in obtaining an order
for certiorari to quash the decision of the university, but that judgment was set aside
e   by the Privy Council on the ground that the relation was that of master and servant
to which the remedy of certiorari had no application. It would not be necessary or
appropriate to disagree with the procedural or even the factual basis on which this
decision rests; but I must confess that I could not follow it in this country insofar as
it involves a denial of any remedy of administrative law to analogous employments.
Statutory provisions similar to those on which the employment tested would tend
f   to show, to my mind, in England or in Scotland, that it was one of a sufficiently
public character, or one partaking sufficiently of the nature of an office, to attract
appropriate remedies of administrative law. I come now to the present case. Its
difficulty lies in the fact that the appellant's appointment was held during pleasure,
so that he could be dismissed without any reason being assigned. There is little
authority on the question whether such persons have a right to be heard before
g   dismissal, either generally, or at least in a case where a reason is in fact given. The
case of *R v Darlington School Governors* (1844) 6 QB 682, 115 ER 257 was one where
by charter the governors had complete discretion to dismiss without hearing, so
complete that they were held not entitled to fetter it by by-law. It hardly affords a
basis for modern application any more than the more recent case of *Tucker v British
Museum* (1967) Times, 8 December decided on an Act of 1753. In *Ridge v Baldwin*
h   [1963] 2 All ER 66 at 71, [1964] AC 40 at 65 my noble and learned friend Lord Reid
said "It has always been held, I think rightly, that such an officer [sc one holding at
pleasure] has no right to be heard before being dismissed". As a general principle, I
respectfully agree; and I think it important not to weaken a principle which, for
reasons of public policy, applies, at least as a starting point, to so wide a range of the
public service. The difficulty arises when, as here, there are other incidents of the
j   employment laid down by statute, or regulations, or code of employment or
agreement. The rigour of the principle is often, in modern practice, mitigated for it
has come to be perceived that the very possibility of dismissal without reason being
given—action which may vitally affect a man's career or his pension—makes it all
the more important for him, in suitable circumstances, to be able to state his case
and, if denied the right to do so, to be able to have his dismissal declared void. So,
while the courts will necessarily respect the right, for good reasons of public policy,

to dismiss without assigned reasons, this should not, in my opinion, prevent them from examining the framework and context of the employment to see whether *a* elementary rights are conferred on him expressly or by necessary implication, and how far these extend.'

It will be observed from the concluding part of the speech which I have just read that Lord Wilberforce thought it necessary to have regard to the framework and context of the employment. When one has regard to the framework of this employment, one finds that the BBC has engrafted on to the ordinary principles of master and servant an *b* elaborate framework of appeals. This framework restricts the power of the BBC as an employer to terminate the employee's employment. It clearly presupposes that the employee should have more than one opportunity of being heard. It may be right, as was submitted, that the reason this is done is to avoid any question of the dismissal being regarded as being unfair. However, here I would adopt the argument advanced by counsel for the applicant that the employment protection legislation has substantially *c* changed the position at common law so far as dismissal is concerned. In appropriate circumstances the statute now provides that an industrial tribunal can order the reinstatement of an employee. It is true that the order cannot be specifically enforced. However, the existence of that power does indicate that even the ordinary contract of master and servant now has many of the attributes of an office, and the distinction which previously existed between pure cases of master and servant and cases where a person *d* holds an office are not longer clear.

I would respectfully here adopt a passage in the judgment of Buckley LJ in *Stevenson v United Road Transport Union* [1977] 2 All ER 941 at 948–949:

'Nor, in our judgment, can the union be said to have brought any improper pressure to bear on the plaintiff in relation to the appeal by means of the 1976 *e* disciplinary proceedings (distinguishing *Attorney-General v Butterworth* [1962] 3 All ER 326, [1963] 1 QB 696. We rejected the preliminary point and proceeded to hear the appeal on its merits. Counsel for the union has contended that the principles applicable here are those applicable to the dismissal of a servant by his master, where, as Lord Reid pointed out in *Ridge v Baldwin* [1963] 2 All ER 66 at 71, [1964] AC 40 at 65, the master is under no obligation to hear the servant in his own defence *f* (and see *Malloch v Aberdeen Corpn* [1971] 2 All ER 1278 at 1282, [1971] 1 WLR 1578 at 1581, per Lord Reid). Counsel for the union contends that there is no circumstance in this case which elevates the plaintiff's position to that of an officer whose tenure of his office or whose status as an officer cannot be terminated without his being given an opportunity to answer any charges made against him or any criticisms of him or of his conduct. In our opinion, it does not much help to solve the problem *g* to try to place the plaintiff in the category of a servant, on the one hand, or of an officer, on the other. It is true that in *Ridge v Baldwin* Lord Reid divided cases of dismissal into three classes: (1) dismissal of a servant by his master; (2) dismissal from an office held during pleasure, and (3) dismissal from an office when there must be something against a man to warrant his dismissal; but he goes on in the next paragraph to point out that, although in "a pure master and servant case" the *h* master need not hear the servant in his own defence, dismissal of a servant by a master can resemble dismissal from an office where the body embodying the man is under some statutory or other restriction as to the grounds on which it can dismiss its servants. Moreover, the problem is not confined to termination of contracts of employment. It may arise in relation to the termination or denial of a privilege, as in *Russell v Duke of Norfolk* [1949] 1 All ER 109, or of an office which does not *j* involve any contract of employment, as in *Breen v Amalgamated Engineering Union* [1971] 1 All ER 1148, [1971] 2 QB 175. In our judgment, a useful test can be formulated in this way. Where one party has a discretionary power to terminate the tenure or enjoyment by another of an employment or an office or a post or a privilege, is that power conditional on the party invested with the power being first satisfied on a particular point which involves investigating some matter on which

the other party ought in fairness to be heard or to be allowed to give his explanation
or put his case? If the answer to the question is Yes, then unless, before the power
purports to have been exercised, the condition has been satisfied after the other
party has been given a fair opportunity of being heard or of giving his explanation
or putting his case, the power will not have been well exercised.'

In this case it seems clear to me that the applicant had a right to be heard and that there
was a restriction as to the circumstances in which she could be dismissed. Although the
restriction was largely procedural, as the BBC contends, it did alter her rights substantially
from what they would have been at common law. In my view, this had the consequence
of making her contract of employment different from those referred to by Lord Reid
where in the past the sole remedy was one of damages. I have therefore come to the
conclusion that in the appropriate circumstances, in the case of employment of the nature
here being considered, the court can if necessary intervene by way of injunction, and
certainly by way of declaration.

*Should the courts intervene to stay proceedings before disciplinary tribunals because of pending
criminal proceedings?*

If an employee makes an application to a domestic tribunal to adjourn its proceedings
until after the conclusion of criminal proceedings on the basis that the continuation of
the disciplinary proceedings would prejudice criminal proceedings that application
should be sympathetically considered by the tribunal. If it comes to the conclusion that
the employee will suffer real prejudice if the domestic proceedings continue, then unless
there is a good reason for not doing so, the disciplinary proceedings should be adjourned.
However, if the disciplinary tribunal does not adjourn in such circumstances, should the
court intervene, and if so, in what circumstances?

Although I was not referred to any case dealing with disciplinary tribunals, I was
referred to two authorities which I regard as providing very considerable assistance, both
as to what the attitude of disciplinary tribunals should be and what the attitude of the
courts should be. The first case was *Jefferson v Bhetcha* [1979] 2 All ER 1108, [1979] 1
WLR 898. That case concerned the possible conflict between civil and criminal
proceedings in the courts. This is the passage in Megaw LJ's judgment which I find of
particular assistance ([1979] 2 All ER 1108 at 1112–1113, [1979] 1 WLR 898 at 904–
905):

> 'The reason given by Forbes J for granting the adjournment of the Ord 14
> application or the stay of the action (whichever it may have been) appears from the
> notes of judgment. Having referred to *Wonder Heat Pty Ltd v Bishop* [1960] VR 489
> which I have just mentioned, the judge went on: "Like the Australian judge, I take
> the view that if there be a good defence there is no harm in producing it. But that is
> not the law. The defendant is entitled to keep silent. That seems to me to be
> fundamental and that right is not to be eroded by a sidewing." As I understand it,
> the judge based his decision on the view that there is an established principle of law
> that, if criminal proceedings are pending against a defendant in respect of the same
> subject-matter, he, the defendant, is entitled to be excused from taking in the civil
> action any procedural step, which step would, in the ordinary way, be necessary or
> desirable for him to take in furtherance of his defence in the civil action, if that step
> would, or might, have the result of disclosing, in whole or in part, what his defence
> is, or is likely to be, in the criminal proceedings. Counsel for the defendant in this
> court submitted that that is the general rule which ought to be followed. He did
> not, as I understand it, submit that it was an invariable or inflexible rule which
> would deprive the court of any discretion if the matters which I have mentioned
> were established. With the view, if it were put forward, that this is an established
> principle of law, I would respectfully but firmly disagree. There is no such principle
> of law. There is no authority which begins to support it, other than, to a limited
> extent, *Wonder Heat Pty Ltd v Bishop*, which, with great respect, I should not be
> prepared to follow, if indeed it does purport to lay down such a principle. I do not

think that it does. I should be prepared to accept that the court which is competent
to control the proceedings in the civil action, whether it be a master, a judge, or this *a*
court, would have a discretion, under s 41 of the Supreme Court of Judicature
(Consolidation) Act 1925, to stay the proceedings, if it appeared to the court that
justice (the balancing of justice between the parties) so required, having regard to
the concurrent criminal proceedings, and taking into account the principle, which
applies in the criminal proceeding itself, of what is sometimes referred to as the
"right of silence" and the reason why that right, under the law as it stands, is a right *b*
of a defendant in criminal proceedings. But in the civil court it would be a matter
of discretion, and not of right. There is, I say again, in my judgment, no principle
of law that a plaintiff in a civil action is to be debarred from pursuing that action in
accordance with the normal rules for the conduct of civil actions merely because so
to do would, or might, result in the defendant, if he wished to defend the action,
having to disclose, by an affidavit under Ord 14, or in the pleading of his defence, *c*
or by way of discovery or otherwise, what his defence is or may be, in whole or in
part, with the result that he might be giving an indication of what his defence was
likely to be in the contemporaneous criminal proceedings. The protection which is
at present given to one facing a criminal charge (the so-called "right of silence") does
not extend to give the defendant as a matter of right the same protection in
contemporaneous civil proceedings. Counsel for the defendant, though he submitted *d*
that there was such a general principle, accepted that it was not a principle of
absolute and invariable application, but that there was a measure of discretion in the
court. He submitted, however, that in this case there ought here to be a stay of the
proceedings in the civil action until such time as the criminal proceedings have
come to a conclusion. In my judgment, while each case must be judged on its own
facts, the burden is on the defendant in the civil action to show that it is just and *e*
convenient that the plaintiff's ordinary rights of having his claim processed and
heard and decided should be interfered with. Of course, one factor to be taken into
account, and it may well be a very important factor, is whether there is a real danger
of the causing of injustice in the criminal proceedings. There may be cases (no doubt
there are) where that discretion should be exercised. In my view it would be wrong
and undesirable to attempt to define in the abstract what are the relevant factors. By *f*
way of example, a relevant factor telling in favour of a defendant might well be the
fact that the civil action, or some step in it, would be likely to obtain such publicity
as might sensibly be expected to reach, and to influence, persons who would or
might be jurors in criminal proceedings. It may be that, if the criminal proceedings
were likely to be heard in a very short time (such as was the fact in the *Wonder Heat*
case in the Victoria Supreme Court) it would be fair and sensible to postpone the *g*
hearing of the civil action. It might be that it could be shown, or inferred, that there
was some real, not merely notional, danger that the disclosure of the defence in the
civil action would, or might, lead to a potential miscarriage of justice in the criminal
proceedings, by, for example, enabling prosecution witnesses to prepare a fabrication
of evidence or by leading to inteference with witnesses or in some other way.'

Everything which Megaw LJ said in regard to civil proceedings, it seems to me, can be *h*
applied to disciplinary proceedings.

The other case from which I obtained assistance is *Harris (Ipswich) Ltd v Harrison* [1978]
ICR 1256. In that case Phillips J gave the judgment of the appeal tribunal. He said (at
1259–1260):

'[Counsel for the employers] submits that *Carr* v. *Alexander Russell Ltd* ([1975]
IRLR 49), upon which the industrial tribunal relied, similarly applied the wrong *j*
test, and that this error was followed in the Court of Session when that decision was
approved (see [1976] IRLR 220). We do not accept this criticism of *Carr* v. *Alexander
Russell Ltd.*, which seems to us to be in accordance with the general law as it has been
applied in England and Wales and in Scotland, and as it is now approved in the

Court of Appeal and possibly in the Court of Session. However, upon one point in the judgment in that case, we take a somewhat different view. In that case, both in the industrial tribunal and in the Court of Session, it is suggested to be improper after an employee has been arrested and charged with a criminal offence alleged to have been committed in the course of his employment, for the employer to seek to question him when the matter of dismissal is under consideration. While we can see that there are practical difficulties, and that care is necessary to do nothing to prejudice the subsequent trial, we do not think that there is anything in the law of England and Wales to prevent an employer in such circumstances before dismissing an employee from discussing the matter with the employee or his representative; indeed, it seems to us that it is proper to do so. What needs to be discussed is not so much the alleged offence as the action which the employer is proposing to take. It is often difficult for an employer to know what is best to do in a case of this kind, particularly where the employee elects to go for trial. Unfortunately it may be many months before the trial takes place, and it is often impractical for the employer to wait until the trial takes place before making some decision as to the future of the employee so far as his employment is concerned. At first sight those not familiar with the problem tend to say that it is wrong to dismiss the employee until his guilt has been established. Further experience shows that this is impractical. In the first place, quite apart from guilt, involvement in the alleged criminal offence often involves a serious breach of duty or discipline. The cashier charged with a till offence, guilty or not, is often undoubtedly in breach of company rules in the way in which the till has been operated. The employee who removes goods from the premises, guilty or not, is often in breach of company rules in taking his employer's goods from the premises without express permission; and it is irrelevant to that matter that a jury may be in doubt whether he intended to steal them. Such examples could be multiplied. What it is right to do will depend on the exact circumstances, including the employer's disciplinary code. Sometimes it may be right to dismiss the employee, sometimes to retain him, sometimes to suspend him on full pay, and sometimes to suspend him without pay. The size of the employer's business, the nature of that business and the number of employees are also relevant factors. It is impossible to lay down any hard and fast rule. It is all a matter for the judgment of the industrial tribunal.'

In the above passage from his judgment, Phillips J was dealing with the matter in the context of whether or not dismissal was unfair. However, his approach strongly suggests that there should be no automatic intervention by the court. Bearing in mind that, if the court does not intervene, the employee still has the choice whether to co-operate with the disciplinary proceedings or not, and the employee will still be entitled to contend that his dismissal was wrongful or unfair in the subsequent proceedings before the court or an industrial tribunal, it seems to me that while the court must have jurisdiction to intervene to prevent a serious injustice occurring, it will only do so in very clear cases in which the applicant can show that there is a real danger and not merely a notional danger that there would be a miscarriage of justice in the criminal proceedings if the court did not intervene.

Turning to apply the conclusions to which I have come to the facts of this case, I start from the position that the court cannot give the applicant relief by way of certiorari. As to the alternative remedies of an injunction or declaration, it is first necessary to consider what happened on 2 February 1982. It was not suggested that the applicant had proper notice of the meeting which was due to take place that day. That interview should have been conducted in accordance with the principles of natural justice, and the failure to give her proper notice could, with justification, be regarded as contravening those rules. However, subsequently, the applicant did consult her union and the decision was then made, while disapproving of what had happened, to go on with the next stage of the disciplinary proceedings. Indeed, it was only just prior to the commencement of the hearing of these proceedings that an attack was made on what happened on 2 February. Having chosen not to insist on her rights in respect of the meeting of 2 February, it would be wrong now to grant relief in respect of what then occurred. Of course, normally an employee is entitled to the benefit of each stage of the BBC's disciplinary procedure. A stage could, however, be omitted by agreement and equally an employee could waive a defect in a stage in the procedure even though that defect could otherwise fatally flaw that stage. I do not, therefore, consider that the applicant is entitled to any relief in respect of what happened on 2 February.

It is next necessary to consider what happened on 6 April 1982. The refusal of Mr Singer to adjourn resulted in no further explanation being given to him on the part of the applicant because the view was taken that to do so would involve revealing her defence. Assuming that this view was correct, was Mr Singer entitled to proceed? I conclude he was, if, after having considered the matter, he decided this was the appropriate course to take. In reaching his decision he was entitled to take into account not only the position of the applicant, but also of the BBC. The BBC was going to have to continue to pay the applicant until the appeal procedure was exhausted and if, as I am told, the trial is not to take place until the early part of August, any adjournment would have to be for a substantial time.

Furthermore, approaching the matter in the way indicated by Megaw LJ and Phillips J, I have considerable reservations whether or not there was any risk of a real injustice to the applicant in this case. The proceedings before Mr Singer were to be in private. The applicant had already on 2 February given a version of events which was presumably substantially true. Although a witness from the BBC was to be an important witness at the criminal trial, it is fanciful to suggest that he would fabricate his evidence to incriminate the applicant in some dishonest manner. Finally, the matters which are going to have to be proved in the criminal proceedings are much more extensive than those in the disciplinary proceedings. In disciplinary proceedings the removal of the tapes to where they were found would be sufficient to establish a disciplinary offence in the contention of the BBC.

If Mr Singer was, as I consider to be the case, entitled to refuse the adjournment, then there remains the final stage in the appeal procedure. So far as that is concerned, it seems to me that the position is basically the same as it was before Mr Singer. The question is largely one for the director of personnel. If he decides to proceed, having weighed up the various considerations, then he is at liberty to do so. The result therefore is that this application is refused. I would, however, conclude by acknowledging the very considerable assistance I have had from both counsel in the case.

Application refused.

Solicitors: *Hart Fortgang & Co* (for the applicant); *Rhory Robertson* (for the BBC).

Sepala Munasinghe   Barrister.

T R H Sampson Associates Ltd v British Railways Board

CHANCERY DIVISION

MICHAEL WHEELER QC SITTING AS A DEPUTY JUDGE OF THE HIGH COURT

24, 25, 26 MAY, 18 JUNE 1982

Railway – Accommodation works – Duty of railway authority to maintain works – Bridge over railway line – Owner of land adjoining railway conveying part of his land to railway authority for railway purposes – Railway authority covenanting to make and for ever maintain bridge over railway for owner's convenience – Adjoining land used for purposes of a brewery – Use of adjoining land altered after construction of bridge – Extent of railway authority's duty to maintain bridge thereafter – Whether bridge 'accommodation works' – Whether owner of adjoining land permitted to use bridge for purpose other than that contemplated by conveyance – Railway Clauses Consolidation Act 1845, s 68.

The plaintiffs' predecessors in title (the vendors) owned certain land which they used in connection with their brewery. In 1903 the vendors agreed to sell part of the land to the defendants' predecessors in title (the railway company) who required it to construct a railway. The land was conveyed by means of an indenture which stated in the recitals that the railway company had power under the Railway Clauses Consolidation Act 1845 to take and use the land for railway purposes. Under the indenture the railway company covenanted to 'make and for ever maintain the several works specified in the First Schedule [to the indenture] as Accommodation Works for the convenience of the adjoining lands of the Vendors'. The term 'accommodation works' was not defined either in the indenture or in the 1845 Act but the first schedule to the indenture was headed 'Accommodation Works' and provided, inter alia, for the construction of a strong bridge and properly stoned approach road over the vendors' adjoining land and that 'such bridge [was] to be maintained in good and sufficient repair by the Company'. The bridge and the approach road were duly constructed. Subsequently the vendors' adjoining land ceased to be used for the purposes of the brewery. At some later date the plaintiffs asked the defendants to repair the bridge in accordance with the covenant in the indenture, in order that they could use it for the purpose for which they currently wished to use the adjoining land. The defendants refused, stating that they were not liable under the covenant to maintain the bridge for the plaintiffs' current purpose. They claimed that the bridge was an 'accommodation work', for the purposes of s 68[a] of the 1845 Act, and that since s 68 merely imposed on a railway company an obligation to maintain for the accommodation of owners of lands adjoining the railway such bridges as were 'necessary for the purpose of making good any interruptions caused by the railway to the use of the lands through which the railway [was] made', they were only obliged to maintain the bridge for the purpose for which it was used at the time of its construction, ie in connection with the brewery. The plaintiffs contended that, on the true construction of the indenture, they had been given, through their predecessors in title, an unrestricted right to use the bridge at all times and for all purposes, and that accordingly the defendants were bound to maintain it so that it could be used for the purpose for which the plaintiffs required it. They brought an action against the defendants seeking, inter alia, a declaration to that effect.

Held – The bridge was an accommodation work for the purposes of s 68 of the 1845 Act but, although the plaintiffs did not have the general right of user which they claimed, their basic right to use the bridge was not restricted to the use to which the adjoining land was put in 1903 or which was or ought to have been contemplated by the parties to the indenture in 1903. The plaintiffs were entitled to alter the user of the bridge provided

---

a   Section 68, so far as material, is set out at p 260 *c* to *e*, post

the change of user did not impose an additional burden on the defendants. A declaration would accordingly be made to that effect (see p 258 *h j*, p 263 *c*, p 266 *d* to *j* and p 267 *a b*, post).

Great Western Rly Co v Talbot [1902] 2 Ch 759 applied.

United Land Co v Great Eastern Rly Co (1875) LR 10 Ch App 586, *Taff Vale Rly Co v Gordon Canning* [1909] 2 Ch 48, *South Eastern Rly Co v Cooper* [1923] All ER Rep 111 and *British Rlys Board v Glass* [1964] 3 All ER 418 considered.

Note

For the obligation of a railway undertaker to make and maintain accommodation works, see 38 Halsbury's Laws (4th edn) para 871, and for cases on the subject, see 38 Digest (Reissue) 194–211, 1197–1365.

For the Railway Clauses Consolidation Act 1845, s 68, see 26 Halsbury's Statutes (3rd edn) 766.

Cases referred to in judgment

Bradburn v Morris, Morris v Bradburn (1876) 3 Ch D 812, CA, 19 Digest (Reissue) 10, 49.
British Rlys Board v Glass [1964] 3 All ER 418, [1965] Ch 538, [1964] 3 WLR 913, CA, 38 Digest (Reissue) 231, 1548.
Great Northern Rly Co v M'Alister [1897] 1 IR 587, 38 Digest (Reissue) 201, 1257.
Great Western Rly Co v Talbot [1902] 2 Ch 759, CA, 19 Digest (Reissue) 148, 1048.
R v Brown (1867) LR 2 QB 630, 38 Digest (Reissue) 212, 1377.
R v Fisher (1862) 3 B & S 191, 122 ER 72, 38 Digest (Reissue) 211, 1376.
Rhondda and Swansea Rly Co v Talbot [1897] 2 Ch 131, 38 Digest (Reissue) 195, 1209.
South Eastern Rly Co v Cooper (1923) 21 LGR 439; *rvsd* [1924] 1 Ch 211, [1923] All ER Rep 111, CA, 19 Digest (Reissue) 142, 1010.
Taff Vale Rly Co v Gordon Canning [1909] 2 Ch 48, 19 Digest (Reissue) 153, 1091.
United Land Co v Great Eastern Rly Co (1873) LR 17 Eq 158; *on appeal* (1875) LR 10 Ch App 586, 19 Digest (Reissue) 142, 1007.

Action

The plaintiffs, T R H Sampson Associates Ltd, brought an action against the defendants, the British Railways Board, seeking (i) a declaration that they were entitled to a right of way for all purposes and at all times over and along an approach road and bridge situated at West Street, Somerton, (ii) damages for the defendants' failure to maintain the bridge in good and sufficient repair, (iii) further or other relief. The facts are set out in the judgment.

Donald Hawkins for the plaintiffs.
Jules Sher QC and *Timothy Jennings* for the defendants.

Cur adv vult

18 June. The following judgment was delivered.

MICHAEL WHEELER QC. It may be convenient if I start by indicating the conclusions which I have reached. They are these. First, that the bridge with which I am concerned is accommodation work within s 68 of the Railway Clauses Consolidation Act 1845, so on that score the British Railways Board succeed. But, second, and particularly because this is a case of a bridge rather than a level crossing, while accepting that a change of user must not add to the burden on the Railways Board, and bearing in mind that the specifications laid down for the bridge are themselves restricting, I see no reason to hold that a mere change of user which does not increase the burden on the board or impede the proper operation of their railway, should be ruled out. So on that score the plaintiffs succeed.

An indenture dated 29 August 1903 made between three gentlemen then trading under the style or firm of Ord, Battiscombe & Elwes (who were called 'the Vendors') of the first part, various mortgagees and trustees of the second to the fifth parts, and the

Great Western Railway Co (which I shall call 'the company') of the sixth part recited, inter alia, that certain pieces of land set out on the plan annexed were required by the company for the purposes of their railway and the works connected therewith and that the company had under the Great Western Railway (New Works) Act 1898 and the Great Western Railway Act 1899 'and the Acts incorporated therewith or some or one of such Acts' power to take and use the same for those purposes; and that the vendors had agreed to sell those pieces of land for £1,385.

I must now go to the indenture, because having recited the price the indenture then continues:

> '. . . which price it has been agreed shall include compensation for all damage loss or inconvenience whether permanent temporary or recurring which shall be occasioned by severing the said pieces of land from the other lands of the Vendors or by otherwise injuriously affecting the Vendors or the said other lands by the construction of the Works of the Company or which they shall sustain by reason of the exercise as regards such other lands of the powers contained in the said Acts and for the right of pre-emption in the event of the said pieces of land or any part thereof becoming superfluous land and shall also be in full satisfaction for all accommodation and other works and things which might otherwise be required to be made or done under the said Acts or any of them for the benefit or accommodation of the adjoining property of the Vendors except the Works and things mentioned in the First Schedule hereunder written which are as soon as conveniently may be to be made and for ever maintained by the Company . . .'

The indenture then conveyed the pieces of land in question to the company and the company covenanted with the vendors as follows:

> '. . . that the Company shall as soon as conveniently may be make and for ever maintain the several works specified in the First Schedule hereto as Accommodation Works for the convenience of the adjoining lands of the Vendors and the owners and occupiers for the time being of the same . . .'

The first schedule to the indenture was headed 'Accommodation Works' and (save that I have numbered the various paragraphs for ease of reference) reads as follows:

'Accommodation Works

(1) A strong bridge capable of carrying a traction engine and trucks of a total weight of at least thirty five tons over the Railway twelve feet wide inside between parapets with strong side parapets and level with existing road and a properly stoned approach road having at least nine inches thick bed of cracked hard road metal thereon over the Vendor's [sic] adjoining land as shown on the said Plan such bridge to be maintained in good and sufficient repair by the Company

(2) The Company to be at liberty as far as affects the Vendors interest therein to close the present footpath in Numbers 69 and 70 and divert the same as shown on the said Plan

(3) The land under the Arches of the proposed viaduct through Number 42 to remain unfenced and open for the Vendors stock to depasture thereon

(4) The iron hurdles between Numbers 63 and 64 are reserved to the Vendors

(5) The Purchasers to erect a brick or stone wall properly coped and built on the boundary of Number 72 to a similar height to present garden wall so as to make garden wall of the same height and thickness as the garden wall now existing

(6) Temporary conveniences and a Bridge to be provided by the Company until these works are completed to the reasonable satisfaction of the Vendors

(7) The Company to dig and keep open a ditch on the North side of the land purchased in Number 14 East Lydford so as to drain the water from the adjoining land such ditch to be on the land hereinbefore conveyed but immediately adjoining the boundary line and to be of sufficient depth and capacity for the above named purpose as also to form a good fence against stock

(8) The Company upon entering into possession of the pieces or parcels of land hereinbefore conveyed are to erect a substantial ox and lamb proof fence on the boundary lines of the said pieces of land hereinbefore conveyed and are not by their Agents Servants Contractors or Workmen to trespass on the adjoining property of the Vendors

(9) The above Works to be performed to the reasonable satisfaction of the Vendors Surveyors.'

I should here mention that the expression 'accommodation works', though given capital initial letters in the covenant in the conveyance and in the heading to the first schedule, is not defined. But it is, I think, clear that it is, and was, a well-known expression in railway terminology which owed its origin to s 68 of the Railways Clauses Consolidation Act 1845. That Act was one of the Acts 'incorporated with' the Great Western Railway Acts 1898 and 1899 to which I have referred, and s 68, so far as material for present purposes, provides as follows. I propose to read the opening paragraph and the proviso:

'The company shall make and at all times thereafter maintain the following works for the accommodation of the owners and occupiers of lands adjoining the railway; (that is to say,) Such and so many convenient gates, bridges, arches, culverts, and passages over, under, or by the sides of or leading to or from the railway, as shall be necessary for the purpose of making good any interruptions caused by the railway to the use of the lands through which the railway shall be made; and such works shall be made forthwith after the part of the railway passing over such lands shall have been laid out or formed, or during the formation thereof . . . Provided always, that the company shall not be required to make such accommodation works in such a manner as would prevent or obstruct the working or using of the railway, nor to make any accommodation works with respect to which the owners and occupiers of the lands shall have agreed to receive and shall have been paid compensation instead of the making them.'

Here, too, 'accommodation works' is not expressly defined, but it is clear from the proviso that accommodation works are the works which the company is bound to make and maintain in accordance with the body of the section. It will be seen that in a case where s 68 applies it imposes a statutory obligation on the railway company and does not depend on agreement between the company and the owner of the land in question.

I should stress at the outset that s 68 is in terms designed for the purpose of making good any 'interruptions caused by the railway to the use of the lands through which the railway shall be made' which suggests, at first glance at least, that one has to start by considering the use to which the land was then being put in order to ascertain the user that was 'interrupted'. I should also mention that by s 73 of the 1845 Act the railway company cannot be compelled to make 'any further or additional accommodation works' for the use of owners and occupiers of adjoining land after five years from the completion of the works and the opening of the railway.

In the instant case, the bridge provided for in the indenture and referred to in the first schedule and the plan annexed was not, in the event, built precisely as originally intended but, by later agreement in 1905, at a point some sixty yards distant. It is common ground, however, that nothing turns on this and that the rights and obligations which attach to the bridge as built are the same as those which would have attached to the bridge as originally intended to be built.

The plaintiffs in the present case are the successors in title to the vendors under the 1903 indenture and the defendants are the successors to the Great Western Railway Co.

The present dispute concerns the nature and extent of the permitted user of the bridge in question, and although the proceedings as they came before me raised a number of questions, including questions of proof of title and a claim for damages, as a result of very sensible arrangements between counsel for the parties I am presently required to deal only with one main question of law and with what might be described as a

supplementary question, namely: is the bridge 'accommodation works' within the
meaning of, and governed by, s 68 of the Railway Clauses Consolidation Act 1845? If it
is, to what extent, if at all, is user by the plaintiffs permitted which differs materially
from the user to which the bridge was to be put in 1903?

Counsel for the plaintiffs claims that the indenture should be construed as operating
as an implied grant of user by the railway company at all times and for all purposes.

Counsel for the defendants claims that the defendants' obligation under the covenant
is at most limited to the obligation imposed by s 68 of the 1845 Act; and that as the land
now owned by the plaintiffs was shown in the plans deposited under the Great Western
Railway Act 1899 as being in the ownership of 'Somerton Brewery Company Limited'
and described as 'garden, orchard and field and occupation road' the construction of the
bridge conferred on the adjoining owners a right of way for the purposes for which it
would ordinarily have been used at the time of its construction: namely, in connection
with the Somerton Brewery. This, on one extreme view (since the brewery has long since
ceased to exist as such), would seem virtually to deprive the plaintiffs of any right of user
at all.

I start with counsel for the plaintiffs' contention that the grant under the 1903
indenture was for all time and for all purposes. Counsel for the plaintiffs accepts, of
course, that the purposes for which the bridge can properly be used are necessarily
conditioned by its size, construction and weight limit and, to some extent, by the
specification as to the approach road. He also accepts, I think, that it is implicit that the
indenture could not be construed in such a way as to obstruct the proper working of the
railway.

In support of a wide and general construction of the covenant, counsel for the plaintiffs
relies on the fact that the expression 'accommodation works' is not defined in the
indenture (any more, I might add, than in the 1845 Act) and that although the various
provisions in the first schedule are described as 'Accommodation Works' a number of
those provisions clearly relate to matters which, on any view, do not come within s 68
(see, for example, paras (2), (3) and (4)). Counsel for the plaintiffs contends that, leaving
out dependent clauses, the railway company's obligation under the covenant and para (1)
of the first schedule is to 'make and for ever maintain . . . a strong bridge . . . over the
Railway . . . and a properly stoned approach road . . . over the Vendor's adjoining land as
shown on the said Plan such bridge to be maintained in good and sufficient repair by the
Company'. And that, he says, by necessary implication gives the plaintiffs, as the vendors'
successors in title, the unrestricted right of user for which they contend.

Counsel for the plaintiffs and counsel for the defendants have between them referred
me to all the decided cases, I think, which bear on the question of what I might call a
general grant (such as the plaintiffs claim) as opposed to a s 68 easement (which is the
most that the defendants are prepared to concede). In three of those cases the court came
down in favour of a general grant.

The first in time was *United Land Co v Great Eastern Rly Co* (1873) LR 17 Eq 158; *on
appeal* (1875) LR 10 Ch App 586. But although the report at first instance, before Malins
V-C, appears to proceed on the broad proposition that a right of way over, under or across
a railway was prima facie general, it is clear that the decision in fact turned on the
construction of a very unusual section in a special Act which imposed on the railway
company an express obligation in the following terms:

'. . . to make and construct such convenient communications across, over, or
under the said railway [at that stage it is following closely s 68] . . . as shall, in the
judgment of the Commissioners for the time being of Her Majesty's Woods,
Forests, . . . be necessary for the convenient enjoyment and occupation of the lands
of Her Majesty; and such communications when so made shall at all times be kept
in good order and repair by and at the expense of [the railway].'

Bearing in mind the generality of the language of the section and the fact that it made
the commissioners for the time being the arbiters of what communications were

necessary and convenient, it is not surprising that the court construed the railway's
obligation in wide and general terms. The decision thus turned purely on the construction
of the special Act: and that this was the true ratio decidendi has since been recognised in
other cases where a general grant has been contended for (see for example the Court of
Appeal in *Great Western Rly Co v Talbot* [1902] 2 Ch 759 at 767). The decision does not
help me therefore in the instant case.   The second of the three cases is the Court of
Appeal decision in *South Eastern Rly Co v Cooper* [1924] 1 Ch 211, [1923] All ER Rep 111.
This was a level crossing case in which the defendants had been given an express grant in
very wide terms and although in the court below Romer J ((1923) 21 LGR 439) had come
to the conclusion that the railway company's grant was limited to what, under its own
general act, was the equivalent of s 68 of the 1845 Act, the Court of Appeal, taking into
account not only the language of the grant but also the circumstances in which it was
made, unanimously concluded that the grant should be construed as general. As Sargant
LJ put it ([1924] 1 Ch 211 at 234, [1923] All ER Rep 111 at 122):

> 'In this state of things, I see no reason for giving to the actual words of the grant
> of the easement in question any meaning short of their natural meaning—namely,
> a full and complete right of way for all purposes . . .'

In the result, therefore, this case too turned primarily on the question of construction of
the grant.

The last of the three cases, which is also the most recent, is the Court of Appeal decision
in *British Rlys Board v Glass* [1964] 3 All ER 418, [1965] Ch 538. This too was a level
crossing case in which the British Railways Board's predecessors in title had by agreement
made in 1847 purchased part of a field owned by the defendant's predecessors, the
purchase price being expressed to be in full compensation for, inter alia, rights to have
works done corresponding to those specified in s 68 of the 1845 Act, with the following
proviso:

> '. . . save and except that the [railway company] and their successors shall and will
> at all times hereafter allow unto me . . . my heirs and assigns at all times . . . a right
> of crossing the . . . railway to the extent of twelve feet in width on the level thereof
> with all manner of cattle to and from one part of the . . . land . . . to the other
> part . . . severed by the . . . railway.'

Like the two earlier cases, the decision of the Court of Appeal in *Glass* turned on the
construction of the wording of the grant. Lord Denning MR construed the proviso as a
saving exception to what would otherwise have been a complete waiver of rights under s
68; and accordingly he construed the proviso as itself being no more than an
accommodation right under s 68. But the majority (Harman and Davies LJJ) took the
point that the proviso (unlike s 68) did not impose on the railway company an obligation
to make or maintain anything. Moreover, as Davies LJ stressed ([1964] 3 All ER 418 at
430, [1965] Ch 538 at 564):

> 'It is . . . of the greatest importance to remember that, by the construction of the
> new branch railway line, the house and buildings of Bathampton farm, together
> with all the land to the north and east of the new line, were effectively cut off from
> all access to or approach from the only road leading to Bathampton village and the
> outside world at large by wheeled vehicles.'

Having regard to the terms of the covenant in the case before me it is only right to point
out that later in his judgment Davies LJ said ([1964] 3 All ER 418 at 430, [1965] Ch 538
at 565):

> 'Unless it was intended by the deed at present under consideration to grant a
> general right of crossing, it is difficult to see why, in contradistinction to the other
> parts of the document, this clause departs so markedly from the words and
> framework of s. 68. It would have been perfectly simple, had that been the intention
> of the parties, to have provided that the railway company should make, and that the
> railway company and its successors should maintain, a crossing or passage across the

line for the accommodation of the owner and occupiers of the land severed by the railway; but it looks as though the parties deliberately chose not to do this.'

In the result, therefore, the majority in *Glass* came down, as a matter of construction, in favour of a general grant.

With such guidance as I can obtain from these three cases, I, too, am left at the end of the day with a question of construction of the 1903 indenture in the light of the surrounding circumstances as they then existed. I should mention that some suggestion was made in the instant case that the construction of the railway would have cut off part of the land from access to a public highway but the evidence on this aspect was somewhat tenuous and was nothing like as compelling as the evidence on which Davies LJ commented in *Glass* in the first of the two passages which I have just quoted.

Be that as it may, the conclusion which I have reached is that the bridge in the instant case was (as the parties to the indenture themselves describe it) 'accommodation works' so that the implied right of user is not a general right but is a right which owes its origin to s 68 of the 1845 Act.

This, then, raises the subsidiary question of law as to the nature and extent of the s 68 right. Here, again, I have been helpfully referred to a number of reported decisions. In *R v Brown* (1867) LR 2 QB 630 the court contrasted the assessment of compensation by a jury with the power of magistrates to order compensation works under s 68 and they held that although compensation for damages by severance could properly take into account how far the prospective value of the land would be depreciated by severance, the magistrates had to determine what works were necessary on account of the interruption to the use of the land, that is to say the present and not the prospective use of it (see, for example, per Cockburn CJ and Shee J (at 632, 633).

Another helpful decision is the Irish case of *Great Northern Rly Co v M'Alister* [1897] 1 IR 587. This was a level crossing case but there was apparently no agreement between the parties so that their respective rights and obligations depended simply on the Railway Acts. But at the time when the railway was built, the land in question was agricultural land and the level crossing was little used. More recently, however, the owner of the land had opened a quarry and was transferring stone from the quarry over the level crossing by means of a traction engine and wagons. The railway company sought and obtained from the Vice-Chancellor an injunction to restrain this user, the basis of his decision being essentially that it was 'not one ever contemplated, or for which the level crossing was intended'.

The Court of Appeal upheld this decision but for somewhat differing reasons. The passage most commonly cited is from the judgment of FitzGibbon LJ (at 605–606) and is as follows:

'I base my judgment in favour of the plaintiffs [ie the railway company] upon two grounds—(1) that the user now claimed would impose a new burden upon the servient tenement which was not contemplated when the easement of the level crossing was granted; and (2) that the defendant cannot cross this particular piece of land (the railway) with an engine which will cause danger to the Company in the lawful use of their own land for its proper purpose. The dominant tenement, when the easement was created, was a farm of 100 acres, and the owner of such a tenement cannot materially increase the burden upon the servient tenement, nor materially alter the user originally authorised, so as to injuriously affect the servient tenement. The origin of the easement is clear; prescription is out of the case, and there is no express grant. The level crossing was an accommodation work erected under the Railway Clauses Act, 1845, s 68. The owner of the adjoining lands was entitled, when the railway was made, to a convenient passage over the railway sufficient to make good, so far as possible, any interruption which the construction of the railway caused by severance in the working of his farm, including, I should say, any alteration or extension of that working which could or ought to have been contemplated by the parties when the accommodation works were made and were accepted. Every physical circumstance may be taken into consideration in

determining now what was then in the minds of the parties as to the future user of
the crossing. The passage is only some 9 feet wide, and it is approached by a curved
road with a very steep gradient. The plaintiff got two accommodation works for his
farm; this level crossing, and a bridge. If he proceeded to use the bridge in 1895 for
a purpose for which it was not intended, and for which it was not fit—for example,
if he sent loads across it which it could not safely bear, he could certainly be
prevented from doing so. He seems to me to have no greater right to overtax the
level crossing by putting excessive weights or dangerous traffic upon it. But he fails
also upon the other ground, viz. that the easement now claimed is not the easement
which was originally granted. The furthest to which the original grant could be
carried was, that the defendant got a right to carry his agricultural traffic over this
level crossing, and it was, and is, suitable for all such traffic. But it is not suitable for
a traction engine drawing stones from a quarry: that is not agricultural traffic, and
upon that ground the case is within *Bradburn v. Morris* ((1876) 3 Ch D 812), the
authority as to minerals, referred to by [counsel for the railway company]. The user
which the defendant, as the owner of the dominant tenement, now seeks to make
of the railway would reduce the owners of the servient tenement to the alternative,
either of working their railway at an increased risk, or of incurring increased
expense in continuing to carry on their own lawful business in the same way as they
have hitherto done, and the defendant cannot impose either of these alternatives
upon them.'

M'Alister was expressly approved and adopted by the English Court of Appeal in *Great
Western Rly Co v Talbot* [1902] 2 Ch 759 to which I have already referred. There, Stirling
LJ who delivered the judgment of the court also referred with approval to a passage from
Rhondda and Swansea Rly Co v Talbot [1897] 2 Ch 131 at 137 where Lindley LJ had said:

'Now it has been decided, and very properly decided, in *Reg.* v. *Fisher* ((1862) 3 B
& S 191, 122 ER 72), and afterwards in *Reg.* v. *Brown* ((1867) LR 2 QB 630), that,
having regard to the enactment that the accommodation works shall be made
forthwith after the railway over such land shall have been laid out, the
accommodation works which the company may be required to make are such
accommodation works as are required at the time the land is taken, having regard
to its then use, and not accommodation works which may be required when the
character of the land, and perhaps the nature of the neighbourhood, is entirely
altered years afterwards.'

Great Western Rly Co v Talbot was of course another level crossing case, and the
defendant, who had originally had a tramway across the land in question to Port Talbot,
wanted to transport goods across the level crossing from places which were not served by
the tramway which existed when the level crossings were constructed. It was accepted
that the level crossings were accommodation works governed by s 68. But the defendant,
while accepting that he could not impose on the railway company a greater burden for
the maintenance of the level crossing, claimed that his increased user would not impose
any such additional burden. The covenant in question (see [1902] 2 Ch 759 at 760) was
in a deed dated 13 March 1868 under which the railway company covenanted that:

'they . . . their successors and assigns would from time to time and at all times
thereafter maintain respectively all the works specified in the schedule thereto "for
the accommodation of the owners and occupiers for the time being of the lands
adjoining the said railway".'

The Court of Appeal found in favour of the railway company and it is interesting to note
the form of the principal declaration which the court granted (see at 767–768):

'that the defendant is not entitled to use the level crossings for the purpose of
conveying goods and traffic so as substantially to increase the burden of the easement
by altering or enlarging its character, nature, or extent as enjoyed at or previous to
March 13, 1868 . . .'

The passage I read earlier explains the significance of that date.

a   Next comes the tennis club case of *Taff Vale Rly Co v Gordon Canning* [1909] 2 Ch 48. Again, this was a level crossing case. No trace could be found of any arrangement or agreement between the parties' predecessors in title, so that, as was common ground, the right of user depended simply on the statutory rights, powers and obligations under s 68. Since the level crossing had been built some sixty years previously, the character of the neighbourhood had entirely changed and the use of the level crossing by large numbers

b   of members of a new tennis club was of an entirely different character to the relatively small and occasional user when the adjoining land had been agricultural. Swinfen Eady J had no hesitation in holding that this increased user introduced a novel and serious element of danger into the safe working of the railway, enormously increased the risk of accident and imposed new and serious burdens on the railway company: accordingly, treating the law as laid down in *M'Alister* and *Great Western Rly Co v Talbot* as settled, he

c   said (at 57):

'User of this kind is, in my opinion, quite outside the purpose for which the land was used at the date when the plaintiffs [ie the railway company] acquired it, and does very substantially increase the burden upon the plaintiffs.'

I should add that the statement in the headnote to the *Taff Vale* case to the effect that a

d   landowner's future user of a level crossing is not restricted to the purposes (for example, agricultural purposes) for which it was used at the time the railway was constructed is not, I think, reflected in Swinfen Eady J's judgment.

In the *Taff Vale* case, too, the declaration which the judge made is of interest. It is in the following terms (at 58):

'... that the defendants are not entitled to use the level crossing as a means of

e   access to the ground for the tennis club and its members and friends, *or* otherwise so as substantially to increase the burden of the easement by altering or enlarging its character, nature, or extent as enjoyed at the time of the construction of the railway ...' (My emphasis.)

One can see at once that there are echoes in that declaration of the declaration which was

f   made in the earlier case to which I have referred.

It is interesting to note that the use of the disjunctive 'or' which I have emphasised in the above extract was taken by Harman LJ in *British Rlys Board v Glass* [1965] Ch 538 at 546 in the course of argument as indicating that the question to be considered was whether there had been an increase in the burden, not whether there had been a change of user. But he does not revert to this in his judgment. Indeed he appears to be

g   discounting the possibility of 'some totally different form of user', unless, perhaps, he was intending to limit this observation to cases of a prescriptive right or possibly a way of necessity (see [1964] 3 All ER 418 at 426, [1965] Ch 538 at 559).

The case before me is not concerned with any question of a prescriptive right (which was the landowner's second line of defence in *Glass*). It is obvious that a prescriptive right depends on, and indeed, stems from, user over a period, so that the actual extent of that

h   use governs the nature of the right acquired by prescription; and it may be that some of the judges, particularly in the older cases, have consciously or unconsciously drawn a parallel between a s 68 statutory right and a right acquired by prescription.

It will be observed that the cases regarding s 68 rights are almost all level crossing cases, and that (not surprisingly) emphasis is repeatedly put on the element of danger (and consequently on the increase in the burden) which a change of user (as in the *Taff Vale*

j   case) or an increase in the intensity of user (as in *Great Western Rly Co v Talbot*) almost inevitably brings. But what about a change of user which does not increase the burden? The reality, as I see it, is that none of the decided cases directly touches this point; because, at the end of the day the court has found on the facts that the burden had been increased, usually because the change of user in fact made the safe operation of the level crossing more difficult and therefore imposed added burdens on the railway company.

But is the same true of a bridge? The railway company's obligation in relation to a bridge is, as it seems to me, limited to its proper maintenance and of course a change of user or more intensive user might, on the facts of any particular case, increase that obligation. Nevertheless, leaving that aspect aside, is there any reason why, in a case such as the present, the use of the bridge should be limited by the use to which the adjoining lands were put in 1903 with (in the words of FitzGibbon LJ in *Great Northern Rly Co v M'Alister* [1897] 1 IR 587 at 605) 'any alteration or extension of that working which could or ought to have been contemplated by the parties when the accommodation works were made and were accepted'.

Common sense suggests that such a general limitation is both unrealistic and unreal in the case of a bridge. In the present case the railway company's obligations were (and are) limited by the specifications as to width, strength, construction and the like set out in para (1) of the first schedule to the indenture; but I see no reason why the use to which the bridge may properly be put should be further circumscribed provided that the use does not increase the railway company's burden of maintenance. Unlike the level crossing in the *Taff Vale* case, the bridge here has to be capable of carrying a traction engine and trucks of a total weight of at least 35 tons. It may well be that this obligation was imposed on the railway company because of the then requirements of the long-since defunct Somerton brewery. But I flatly decline to read into the schedule some implied term that the railway company's obligation to maintain the bridge 'in good and sufficient repair' and to do so 'for ever' was to terminate if the Somerton brewery ceased to carry on business.

My difficulty in the present case is that I am here concerned solely with the legal question of the nature and extent of the defendants' s 68 right of user; and that is a question which, in a sense, I have to answer in the abstract, because I have no facts against which to test it nor do I know the use which it might be desired to make of the bridge and the effect of that use on the railway company's maintenance obligation. But for the reasons which I have given, and notwithstanding the powerful references to the then state of user in some of the level crossing cases to which I have been referred, I have come to the following conclusions regarding the parties' rights and obligations in respect of the bridge:

(1) The plaintiffs have no general right of user, such as they have claimed; but the bridge was (and is) accommodation works governed by s 68 of the 1845 Act.

(2) The plaintiffs' basic right of user of the bridge is not limited to the use to which the adjoining land was put in 1903 or which was or ought to have been contemplated by the parties in 1903.

(3) If the plaintiffs desire to alter the user of the bridge, they are entitled to do so if, but only if, the change of user does not impose an added burden on the railway company: unlike the case of a level crossing that burden seems likely to be limited to the question of maintenance, but the onus of showing that the burden would not be increased will rest on the plaintiffs. The question will be one of fact.

As I explained at the outset of this judgment, I am not concerned with any question of damages and it would be quite wrong for me to express any views on it. But if my interpretation of the law is correct, and if it turns out as a matter of fact that the defendants are in default in their maintenance obligations and that the plaintiffs desire to make some modest change of user, possibly involving some minor alterations to the surface of the bridge and its approaches, there would seem to be, if I may say so, all the elements of a practical and sensible compromise. But on that aspect, I will say no more.

I am minded to make a declaration, the gist of which (and I shall leave it to counsel to agree the precise form with liberty to apply if they cannot do so) will be that the bridge is part of accommodation works within the meaning of s 68. The other arm of the declaration will in a sense be a truncated version of the *Great Western Rly Co v Talbot* [1902] 2 Ch 759 at 767–768 declaration which reads as follows:

'. . . that the defendant is not entitled to use the level crossings for the purpose of conveying goods and traffic so as substantially to increase the burden of the easement

a

by altering or enlarging its character, nature, or extent as enjoyed at or previous to March 13, 1868 . . .'

What I am minded to do is to declare that the plaintiffs are not restricted to the user which was actually in force or ought to have been contemplated in 1903 or 1905 so as to prohibit any change of user or intensification of user, provided that by so doing they do not increase the burden on the defendant board. I have not heard argument on the b detailed form of the proposed declaration so I will not say anything further about it but it seems to me that in the case of this bridge the British Railway Board's obligation is really only one of maintenance. I shall make no order as to costs.

Declaration accordingly.

c Solicitors: *Le Brasseur & Bury*, agents for *Woodforde & Drewett*, Castle Cary (for the plaintiffs); *M G Baker* (for the defendants).

Hazel Hartman   Barrister.

d # Millichamp and others v Jones

CHANCERY DIVISION
WARNER J
16, 17, 18 MARCH, 1 APRIL 1982

e *Option – Option to purchase – Exercise of option – Deposit – Provision for payment of deposit to purchaser on exercising option – Purchaser exercising option but inadvertently failing to pay deposit – Whether vendor entitled to cancel option agreement – Whether vendor required to give purchaser opportunity to pay deposit before cancelling agreement.*

By an agreement under seal, the defendant granted the plaintiffs an option to purchase a f plot of land. The agreement provided for the serving of a notice of intention to purchase and payment of a deposit within a prescribed time. The plaintiffs served the notice within the prescribed time but failed to pay the deposit. The defendant informed the plaintiffs that he did not intend to proceed with the agreement. The plaintiffs sought specific performance of the option agreement.

g **Held** – (1) A requirement in a contract for the sale of land that a deposit be paid by the purchaser was a fundamental term of the contract, breach of which entitled the vendor, if he so elected, to treat the contract as at an end and to sue for damages including the unpaid deposit (see p 274 d e); *Pollway Ltd v Abdullah* [1974] 2 All ER 381 applied; *Myton Ltd v Schwab-Morris* [1974] 1 All ER 326 not followed.

(2) However, where failure to pay the deposit was a mere oversight, it was incumbent h on the vendor, before he could treat the failure to pay the deposit as a repudiation of the contract, to tell the purchaser that he intended doing so and to give him the opportunity of complying with his obligation. Only if the purchaser then showed unwillingness or inability to comply was the vendor entitled to treat the contract as discharged. Since the plaintiffs had inadvertently and not deliberately omitted to pay the deposit they were entitled to specific performance of the option contract (see p 274 j to p 275 c and j); *Hare* j *v Nicoll* [1966] 1 All ER 285 distinguished.

Notes
For the payment of a deposit on making a contract for the sale of land, see 42 Halsbury's Laws (4th edn) para 92, and for cases on the subject, see 40 Digest (Repl) 241–242, 2026–2038.

Cases referred to in judgment

Beck v Box (1973) 231 EG 1295.

Dewar v Mintoft [1912] 2 KB 373, 40 Digest (Repl) 22, 92.

Edgewater Developments Co (a firm) v Bailey (1974) 118 SJ 312, CA, Digest (Cont Vol D) 116, 617a.

Hare v Nicoll [1966] 1 All ER 285, [1966] 2 QB 130, [1966] 2 WLR 441, CA, Digest (Cont Vol B) 665, 300a.

Johnson v Agnew [1979] 1 All ER 883, [1980] AC 367, [1979] 2 WLR, HL, Digest (Cont Vol E) 535, 2346b.

Lowe v Hope [1969] 3 All ER 605, [1970] Ch 94, [1969] 3 WLR 582, Digest (Cont Vol C) 866, 2051a.

Mersey Steel and Iron Co Ltd v Naylor Benson & Co (1884) 9 App Cas 434, [1881–5] All ER Rep 365, HL, 12 Digest (Reissue) 413, 3038.

Myton Ltd v Schwab-Morris [1974] 1 All ER 326, [1974] 1 WLR 331, Digest (Cont Vol D) 803, 2031a.

Pollway Ltd v Abdullah [1974] 2 All ER 381, [1974] 1 WLR 493, CA, 6 Digest (Reissue) 116, 863.

Walker v Ware, Hadlam and Buntingford Rly Co (1865) LR 1 Eq 195, 35 Beav 52, 55 ER 813, 11 Digest (Reissue) 260, 1074.

Cases also cited

Amalgamated Investment and Property Co Ltd v Texas Commerce International Bank Ltd [1981] 3 All ER 577, [1982] QB 84, CA.

Buckland v Farmer & Moody (a firm) [1978] 3 All ER 929, [1979] 1 WLR 221, CA.

Darnley (Earl) v London, Chatham and Dover Rly Co (1867) LR 2 HL 43.

Sudbrook Trading Estate Ltd v Eggleton [1981] 3 All ER 105, [1981] 3 WLR 361, CA.

Taylor Fashions Ltd v Liverpool Victoria Trustees Co Ltd [1981] 1 All ER 897, [1982] QB 133.

Action

By a writ issued on 3 October 1980, the plaintiffs, Francis William Millichamp, George Leonard Millichamp and Wilfred Henry Millichamp, sought as against the defendant, John Jones, specific performance of a contract dated 25 January 1970 whereby the defendant granted to the plaintiffs an option to purchase freehold land forming part of Manor House Farm, Silvington, Salop, and damages for breach of contract and/or rescission. The defendant counterclaimed, inter alia, for a declaration that he was entitled to a lien on the land in respect of sums payable under the contract. The facts are set out in the judgment.

Martin Buckley for the plaintiffs.

P M H Mottershead QC and R A Cooke for the defendant.

Cur adv vult

1 April. The following judgment was delivered.

WARNER J. This is an action for specific performance brought by three brothers, Mr Francis William Millichamp, Mr George Leonard Millichamp and Mr Wilfred Henry Millichamp, against their brother-in-law (their sister's husband), Mr John Jones. The parties are all farmers.

The story starts in 1969 when Mr William Millichamp, the plaintiffs' father, contracted to buy a farm at Silvington in Shropshire called Manor House Farm for a total price of £44,790. On 12 January 1970, he entered into a contract with the plaintiffs to sell the farm to them for £43,100. On the following day the plaintiffs contracted to sell some of the land forming part of the farm to the defendant for £14,575. That land which I will call the 'disputed land' comprised about 48½ acres. It seems that the defendant had agreed to help financially with the purchase of the farm and the arrangement was that the

plaintiffs should have an option to buy the disputed land back from the defendant at the
end of ten years. Manor House Farm and in particular the disputed land adjoins the
defendant's own farm which is called Lowe Farm. The contracts were completed together
on 28 January 1970 when the defendant took a conveyance of the disputed land direct
from Mr William Millichamp's vendor. On the same day an agreement under seal was
entered into between the defendant and the plaintiffs for the grant of the option. I must
read most of that agreement, in which the defendant was called the 'intending vendor'
and the plaintiffs were called the 'intending purchasers'. The material parts of the
agreement were as follows:

'1. In consideration of the sum of one Pound paid by the Intending Purchasers to
the Intending Vendor (receipt whereof the Intending Vendor hereby acknowledges)
the Intending Purchasers shall have the option of purchasing the property described
in the First Schedule hereto for an estate in fee simple in possession free from
incumbrances at the price (hereinafter called "the option price") of fourteen thousand
and five hundred and seventy five Pounds together with the sums mentioned in
clause (2) hereof.

2. In addition to the option price the Intending Purchasers shall pay to the
Intending Vendor sums equivalent to the following:—(a) Such sums as may become
payable by the Intending Vendor to the Inland Revenue or other Government
Department in respect of capital gains tax or any other form of tax duty or levy as a
result of the sale in pursuance of the exercise of the said option (b) Such sum as the
Intending Vendor shall have paid to the Tithe Redemption Commission in order to
redeem the tithe on the land following the Intending Vendor's acquisition of the
same.

3. The said option shall be exercisable by the Intending Purchasers giving to the
Intending Vendor notice in writing such notice to be served in accordance with the
provisions of clause 8 hereof and to be served not less than ten years and not more
than ten years and six months from the date hereof and if the same shall be exercised
then the Intending Vendor will sell the said property to the Intending Purchasers
for the said estate at the option price. If not so exercised by notice as given aforesaid
then the said option shall cease to be exercisable and shall expire ten years and six
months from the date hereof . . .

5. Upon the exercise of the said option the Intending Purchasers shall pay to the
Intending Vendor's Solicitors as stakeholders by way of deposit One thousand four
hundred and fifty seven Pounds ten shillings.

6. The date for completion shall unless otherwise agreed in writing be the first
day after the expiration of seven weeks from the date of the exercise of the said
option or if such day is a Sunday or public holiday the next following working
day . . .

8. The Contract for sale shall incorporate the Law Society's Conditions of Sale
1953 as extended varied or modified by the conditions hereof and so far as the same
are applicable to a sale by private treaty.

9. The Notice under this agreement shall be in writing and may be served on the
intending Vendor either personally or by leaving it for him at his last known place
of abode or by sending it by registered post or the recorded delivery service at such
premises or place.'

Then there is a schedule giving particulars of the disputed land.

It appears that since 1970 Manor House Farm, less the disputed land, has been farmed
by the plaintiffs in partnership while the disputed land has been farmed by the defendant
as part of Lowe Farm.

On 17 April 1980 the plaintiffs gave the defendant notice exercising the option. There
is no question but that that notice complied in every way with the option agreement.
The plaintiffs, however, did not pay the deposit envisaged by cl 5 of that agreement.

The solicitors that had acted for the plaintiffs in 1970 were Messrs Ivens & Morton of
Kidderminster. Those who had acted for the defendant were Messrs Marcy Hemingway

& Sons of Bewdley. It so happens that in the intervening ten years the two firms had amalgamated. At the time of and immediately following the service of the notice the *a* plaintiffs' interests were looked after by a Mr McConnell in the amalgamated firm's Kidderminster office where the firm continued to practice as Ivens & Morton, whilst those of the defendant were looked after by a Mr Hobson in the Bewdley office where the firm practised as 'Hemingways'.

After the plaintiffs' notice exercising the option had been served, there was an exchange of notes between Mr McConnell and Mr Hobson about a request that had been made by *b* the defendant for the date for completion of the sale to be deferred. Under cl 6 of the option agreement that date was to be seven weeks from the date of the exercise of the option unless otherwise agreed in writing. The defendant wanted an extension so as to enable him to harvest the grain that he had sown on the land in October 1979. That exchange of notes culminated in a written agreement signed by the plaintiffs and the defendant and dated 24 June 1980. That agreement, which I will call the 'variation *c* agreement', was in these terms:

'OPTION AGREEMENT dated 28th January 1970 between ourselves.
It is hereby agreed between us that the date for completion of the exercise of the option shall be the thirtieth day of September one thousand nine hundred and eighty or sooner by arrangement and It is also agreed that John Jones (named as *d* Vendor in the said Agreement) shall be entitled to retain and harvest the growing crops on the land comprised in the Agreement and to enter the land for such purposes.'

Mr McConnell, when he sent the variation agreement, signed by the plaintiffs, to Mr Hobson, sent with it a note in which, among other things, he said this:

'In order that there is no misunderstanding, may I please confirm that the *e* authority is solely for the purpose of extending the completion date contained in the Option Agreement. It does not in any way create any tenancy or give any other rights to Mr. Jones.'

The first plaintiff, who is the eldest of the three brothers and who told me that he mainly controlled the business side of their partnership affairs, and the defendant gave *f* evidence before me as to why the deposit was not paid. Neither Mr McConnell nor Mr Hobson gave evidence.

The first plaintiff told me that he and his brothers never saw the option agreement after they had executed it. The part executed by the defendant was kept by Messrs Ivens & Morton. In 1979 he sought advice from Messrs Ivens & Morton about exercising the option. Their advice was that notice would have to be given to the defendant. They *g* prepared the notice, which each of the plaintiffs signed, and sent it to the defendant. Nothing was said about payment of a deposit. The plaintiffs were unaware of the fact that the option agreement contained a provision for payment of a deposit. The first they heard of it was in September 1980 as a result of a conversation between the first plaintiff and the defendant.

The defendant's evidence was not quite as clear as the first plaintiff's, but the effect of *h* it to my mind was this. He knew that the option agreement contained a provision for payment of a deposit. He had a copy of the agreement, which he had looked at at some time though he could not remember when. When he received the notice exercising the option, he telephoned Mr Hobson and asked him to come and advise him about it. When Mr Hobson came their discussion centred on the need for the date for completion to be deferred so that the defendant could harvest his grain. To him that was the most *j* important thing. There was no mention of a deposit and the defendant did not think about it. He did not know that it had not been paid. Whether it had been paid or not was not important to him; he considered it to be a matter for the solicitors. That remained the position so far as he was concerned at the date of the variation agreement. The first person to raise the question of the deposit was the defendant's accountant who,

in late August 1980 asked the defendant whether it had been paid. The defendant told
a   him that he did not know, whereupon the accountant telephoned the solicitors and
found out that it had not been paid. It seems that the defendant then changed his
solicitors.

Shortly thereafter, early in September 1980, there was the conversation to which I
referred between the first plaintiff and the defendant, during the course of which the
defendant mentioned the non-payment of the deposit and said that he did not think he
b   would let the plaintiffs have the disputed land back. The first plaintiff consulted Messrs
Ivens & Morton who, in their turn, consulted counsel.

On 24 September 1980 the defendant's new solicitors, Messrs Norris & Miles, wrote
Messrs Ivens & Morton a letter in which, after referring to cl 5 of the option agreement
and to the fact that the deposit had never been paid, they said this:

'Mr. Jones has been advised that the effect of this clause is to make the payment
c   of the deposit immediately upon the exercise of the option a condition precedent to
the formation of an effective contract. That condition has not been performed and
it is now too late to perform it. Accordingly Mr. Jones is not bound by the agreement
and does not intend to proceed with it. For authority we would refer you to the
decision in *Myton v Schwab-Morris* ([1974] 1 All ER 326, [1974] 1 WLR 331).
d   Alternatively and in the same authority it has been held that failure to pay a deposit
is a breach of a fundamental term of a contract. Such a breach would entitle Mr.
Jones to treat the contract as discharged. He has decided to do this and accordingly
we as his agents give you notice that the contract is now discharged. In order that
the notice shall be given properly to your clients without wishing any professional
discourtesy to yourselves we have today written to your clients in similar terms and
e   enclose a copy of that letter.'

The letter to the plaintiffs was to the same effect.

On 25 September 1980 Messrs Ivens & Morton replied in these terms:

'We have received your letter of the 24th September 1980 and note the contents.
In anticipation of such a turn of events we have taken counsel's opinion and are
f   advised that our clients should commence proceedings for specific performance.
Arrangements to this end are in hand. We are advised to proffer the deposit of
£1457·50 and we therefore enclose our clients' cheque for this sum which is paid to
you as stakeholders.'

Messrs Norris & Miles refused, however, to accept the cheque and on 2 October 1980
g   they returned it to Messrs Ivens & Morton. On the following day the plaintiffs
commenced this action.

The defendant resists specific performance on two grounds. The first is the plaintiffs'
failure to pay the deposit. The second is that, so it is contended on the defendant's behalf,
the option agreement was void for uncertainty.

As regards the first ground, the defendant's case is put in three ways. First, it is said
h   that the payment of a deposit was a condition precedent to the formation of the contract,
so that no contract came into existence as a result of the purported exercise of the option.
Alternatively, it is said that the payment of a deposit was a condition subsequent, the
failure to perform which automatically discharged the contract. In the further alternative,
it is said that the requirement of a deposit was a fundamental term of the contract, the
breach of which entitled the defendant to treat it as discharged, and that his right so to
j   treat it was exercised by Messrs Norris & Miles in the letter of 24 September 1980.

Counsel for the defendant very properly referred me to a note 'Bouncing Deposits'
(1975) 39 Conv (NS) 313, in which it was pointed out that the authorities on the
consequences of the non-payment of a deposit required to be paid by a contract for the
sale of land were difficult to reconcile. He invited me to effect the judicial reconciliation
of those authorities for which the author of the note called. It seems to me that that is a

task that can only be carried out authoritatively by the Court of Appeal. I cannot do more
than express my own view in so far as that is necessary for the decision of this case.

The earliest authority on the point seems to be *Dewar v Mintoft* [1912] 2 KB 373. That
was a case of a sale by auction where the defendant, after the property had been knocked
down to him, refused to pay the deposit or to sign any memorandum. The plaintiff
vendor elected to treat the contract as discharged and sued for damages, including the
amount of the unpaid deposit. The main question was whether correspondence
subsequent to the sale constituted a sufficient memorandum to satisfy s 4 of the Statute
of Frauds. That question was resolved in favour of the plaintiff. Horridge J held that
there was a binding contract and that the plaintiff was entitled to the damages he had
claimed.

The next case is *Lowe v Hope* [1969] 3 All ER 605, [1970] Ch 94, a decision of
Pennycuick J on a motion for judgment in default of defence in a vendor's action for
specific performance or, alternatively, rescission. At the hearing of the motion the vendor
elected for rescission. The defendant appeared in person, but was not called on. The sale
there was by private treaty, but that was not the ground of Pennycuick J's decision. He
declined to follow *Dewar v Mintoft* because he thought that in such an action the plaintiff,
if he elected for rescission, was not entitled to recover the amount of an unpaid deposit.
That part of Pennycuick J's judgment seems to me to have been invalidated by the
decision of the House of Lords in *Johnson v Agnew* [1979] 1 All ER 883, [1980] AC 367,
which showed, to my mind, that *Dewar v Mintoft* was rightly decided. The important
feature of Pennycuick J's judgment, however, for present purposes, is that it proceeded
on the view that the vendor was entitled to bring his action for specific performance.
That would not, it seems to me, have been possible if the non-payment of the deposit
constituted a failure to perform a condition precedent which prevented the formation of
any contract at all, or a failure to perform a condition subsequent which automatically
discharged the contract.

So far as counsel's researches have shown, the suggestion that the requirement of a
deposit might constitute such a condition was made for the first time in *Beck v Box* (1973)
231 EG 1295. That was a motion for interlocutory relief before Goulding J. He said of
that suggestion that he was by no means persuaded that the stipulation in the contract
for the payment of a deposit did, on the true construction of the document, constitute a
condition precedent, though he expressed no final view on the point (see at 1297).

The case relied on by Messrs Norris & Miles in their letter of 24 September 1980,
Myton v Schwab-Morris [1974] 1 All ER 326, [1974] 1 WLR 331, was also a case before
Goulding J. In the course of his judgment Goulding J said ([1974] 1 All ER 326 at 330,
[1974] 1 WLR 331 at 336):

'Speaking in quite general terms for the moment of contracts to sell land or grant
a lease of land at a premium, without reference to the particular language of this
document, it is well established that a deposit is demanded and paid on the signing
of the contract as an earnest of the purchaser's ability and intention to complete the
purchase in due course. The vendor in the normal case never intends to be bound
by the contract without having the deposit in his own or his stakeholder's possession
as a protection against possible loss from default by the purchaser. No doubt it may
be thought that where building operations are in progress and still unfinished, the
vendor is even more concerned to have such a protection than in other cases. In any
ordinary case where a deposit on signing is demanded, if the purchaser says, "I am
sorry, I cannot find the deposit", the vendor would naturally reply, "I do not propose
to hand over the contract signed by me until I am paid". In the circumstances of the
present case, payment by cheque was made and received in the ordinary way as a
conditional payment. The cheque not having been met, the plaintiff company can
assert that its original rights remain. Accordingly, in my judgment, counsel for the
plaintiff company is right to say that cl 2 of the contract stated a condition precedent
to the contract taking effect as one of the lease or sale, and that the cheque having
been returned unpaid the plaintiff is not bound by the document. There is nothing,

in my view, in the language of the document or the special circumstances of the present case to produce a different result from that which I have reached by considering the general nature of the deposit on a contract of sale.'

Goulding J treated the point as one that was free from direct authority. *Lowe v Hope* had not been cited to him. Of *Dewar v Mintoft*, which had been cited, he said only that it showed that there was a possibility that if, in the correct analysis, the non-payment of the deposit constituted a breach of a fundamental term of the contract entitling the vendor to treat it as repudiated, the vendor might be able to claim payment of the amount of the deposit as a forfeited deposit even though it had never been received. Goulding J went on to say that in case he was wrong he would express his view on the merits of the alternative contention of counsel for the plaintiff company that the requirement of a deposit was a stipulation the breach of which could be treated as going to the root of the contract so that the vendor could elect to treat the contract as discharged. On that point Goulding J said ([1974] 1 All ER 326 at 331, [1974] 1 WLR 331 at 337):

> 'Once again, I have come to the conclusion that counsel for the plaintiff company's submission is to be preferred. If payment of a deposit was not a condition precedent to the obligation to grant the lease, it was at any rate, in my judgment, a term of so radical a nature that the defendant's failure to comply with it would entitle the plaintiff to renounce further performance. The same argument on the character and importance of a deposit, which persuaded me on the first point that the clause was a condition precedent, goes far to show that if it is not such a condition, then it is, at any rate, a fundamental term in the sense that I have indicated.'

Then, after a reference to *Mersey Steel and Iron Co Ltd v Naylor Benson & Co* (1884) 9 App Cas 434, [1881–5] All ER Rep 365, he went on ([1974] 1 All ER 326 at 332, [1974] 1 WLR 331 at 338):

> 'Now trying to construe the contract in the present case, it is to my mind quite clear that having a deposit paid and in hand as a protection against eventual default was to be the foundation of the obligation to complete the premises and grant a lease. It was not a mere instalment; it was to be an earnest for the ability and willingness of the defendant to complete. It is said that one cannot conclude from the inability of the defendant to find £7,000 on signing the contract that she will be unable to find £70,000 when the maisonette is ready and the completion date arises. In my judgment, the very nature of a deposit and the language of cl 2 of the contract make the payment of £7,000 on signing the agreed test of intention and ability to complete by payment of a further £63,000. I find counsel for the defendant's argument on that aspect of the matter unconvincing because it does not seem to me to agree with elementary notions, not perhaps precisely formulated, but quite clear to those who do business of this sort.'

Of the cases to which I was referred, the next chronologically is *Edgewater Developments Co (a firm) v Bailey* (1974) 118 SJ 312. It does not seem to me, however, that that case really assists on the present point.

The next case is *Pollway Ltd v Abdullah* [1974] 2 All ER 381, [1974] 1 WLR 493, a decision of the Court of Appeal consisting of Megaw, Buckley and Roskill LJJ. That, like *Dewar v Mintoft*, was a case of a sale by auction. The purchaser had given for the deposit a cheque which he subsequently stopped for reasons which were admitted to be wholly unjustifiable. The recital of the facts in the leading judgment of Roskill LJ continues as follows ([1974] 2 All ER 381 at 383, [1974] 1 WLR 493 at 495):

> 'The defendant was subsequently given time to comply with his obligations. He refused to do so. The vendors, as they were entitled to do, thereupon treated the defendant's conduct as a repudiation of the contract. They resold the property by subsequent auction, and we were told that the resale price was only £50 less than the price which the defendant agreed, but failed, to pay. The vendors' right to

rescind and to claim damages was not disputed. Both they and the auctioneers sued the defendant on the dishonoured cheque.'

Later in Roskill LJ's judgment there is this passage ([1974] 2 All ER 381 at 384, [1974] 1 WLR 493 at 496):

'The case appears to have been argued before the learned judge on the footing that the consideration for the cheque was the vendors' obligation to complete the sale. I will assume for the moment that this is correct. On this assumption, the contract of sale (the second of the three contracts already mentioned) still subsisted when the cheque was stopped. The vendors then still remained obliged to complete. True, the vendors became entitled to rescind immediately the cheque was stopped. But they did not immediately exercise that right. So long as they refrained from so doing, their obligation to perform the sale contract remained.'

Those passages are clearly inconsistent with the view that the defendant's refusal to pay the deposit prevented the contract from ever coming into existence, or automatically discharged it. *Myton Ltd v Schwab-Morris* was not, however, cited.

It is with the greatest diffidence and hesitation that I differ from a view taken by Goulding J, but it seems to me that unless a distinction is to be made between sales by auction and sales by private treaty, the weight of authority is in favour of the view that a requirement in a contract for the sale of land that a deposit should be paid by the purchaser does not constitute a condition precedent, failure to fulfil which prevents the contract from coming into existence, but is in general to be taken as a fundamental term of the contract, breach of which entitles the vendor, if he so elects, to treat the contract as at an end and to sue for damages including the amount of the unpaid deposit. Nor do I see that anything, either in the authorities or in principle, which calls for a distinction to be made in that respect between sales by auction and sales by private treaty.

In differing from Goulding J, I draw comfort from three considerations. The first is that *Lowe v Hope* [1969] 3 All ER 605, [1970] Ch 94 which, for the reasons I indicated earlier, seems to me inconsistent with the view he took, was not cited to him. The second is that Goulding J did not have, and, indeed, could not have had, before him the guidance afforded by the judgment of Roskill LJ in *Pollway Ltd v Abdullah*, a judgment with which Buckley and Megaw LJJ agreed. The third is that he did not have, and, again, could not have had, before him the guidance afforded by the speech of Lord Wilberforce in *Johnson v Agnew* [1979] 1 All ER 883, [1980] AC 367, which greatly clarified the law as to the remedies of a vendor under a contract for the sale of land where the purchaser is in breach and in the light of which, it seems to me, *Dewar v Mintoft* [1912] 2 KB 373 appears as a direct authority for the proposition I stated a moment ago.

The next question is whether cl 5 of the option agreement in the present case is, in accordance with the general rule, to be regarded as a fundamental term of that agreement or whether, on the contrary, there is something which, as a matter of construction of that agreement, in the light of the surrounding circumstances, takes it out of the general rule. At first sight, it seems repugnant to hold that a term of the agreement which neither the plaintiffs nor the defendant, nor, obviously, their solicitors, gave any thought to at the time when the option came to be exercised, was a fundamental term of it. I do not think, however, that the state of mind of the parties or their advisers at that time is the test. The question has to be answered, I think, by reference to the terms of the document itself, considered in the light of the circumstances as they were when it was executed. By that test, I see nothing to take this case out of the general rule.

What happened in 1980 suggests, however, another question, which is: what conduct on the part of the plaintiffs would constitute a breach of that fundamental term? In *Dewar v Mintoft* there was an actual refusal to pay the deposit, as there was also in *Pollway Ltd v Abdullah*. In *Myton Ltd v Schwab-Morris* the cheque for the deposit was dishonoured three times. Precisely what had happened in *Lowe v Hope* is not clear from the report. Here, there was mere oversight and the question is whether that, by itself, constituted a sufficient breach of the term to entitle the defendant to treat the contract as discharged. I do not think it did. There are no doubt cases of contracts where the mere failure to pay on time a sum due under the contract is sufficient to entitle the party to whom the payment should have been made to treat the contract as repudiated. But I think that it would be unnecessarily harsh to hold that that was so in a case of the present kind. The only authority cited to me suggesting that I should so hold was *Hare v Nicoll* [1966] 1 All ER 285, [1966] 2 QB 130, but that was a case of an option to buy back shares, not land, under a contract so framed that if payment were not made by the specified date, the option would lapse. That was quite a different situation in my view from the situation in the present case. In my judgment, in the present case it was incumbent on the defendant, before he could treat the plaintiffs' failure to pay the deposit as a repudiation of the contract, to tell them that he was minded so to do and to give them an opportunity of complying with their obligation. Only if they then showed in some way that they were unwilling or unable to comply with it, would he become entitled to consider their conduct a sufficiently clear breach of the contract to entitle him to treat it as discharged.

I observe, though I think of this only as reinforcing my view, that under cl 5 of the option agreement the deposit was to be paid to the defendant's solicitors. That, as it seems to me, necessarily envisaged some communication between the plaintiffs and the defendant about the deposit after the option had been exercised. It envisaged at least that the defendant would tell the plaintiffs who his solicitors were. Counsel for the defendant reminded me of the defendant's statement, in his oral evidence, that the plaintiffs knew in April 1980 who his solicitors were. But the defendant was not asked to explain what he meant by that bald statement. He may have meant only that the plaintiffs knew who his solicitors were in 1970 and that they had no reason to believe that he had changed them. Nor was the first plaintiff cross-examined on that point. Indeed, he was not cross-examined at all. In any event, I do not think that what matters is what the plaintiffs in fact knew or did not know in 1980. What matters is what cl 5 was intended to mean when the option agreement was signed in 1970. The parties cannot then have been certain that the plaintiffs would know, and know for sure, who the defendant's solicitors would be in ten years time. They must have envisaged that there would be some communication between the plaintiffs and the defendant about it.

Taking, as I do, that view of the case, I think it better to say nothing about the points as to waiver and as to estoppel which were taken on behalf of the plaintiffs by way of reply on the basis of the variation agreement.

I turn to the defendant's second line of defence: that the option agreement was void for uncertainty. The defendant's contention was that that was so because the sums payable by the plaintiffs under cl 2(a) of the agreement in respect of taxes and duties were payable on completion and yet could not be ascertained until after completion. Counsel for the plaintiffs conceded that those sums could not be ascertained until after completion, but he submitted that as a matter of construction of the agreement, they were payable, not on completion, but when ascertained. I think he is right. By virtue of condition 5 in the Law Society's 1953 Conditions of Sale (which were made applicable by cl 8 of the option agreement) what the plaintiffs have to pay on completion is what that condition calls the 'purchase money'. To see what the purchase money is one looks at cl 3 of the option agreement which says: '. . . the Intending Vendor will sell the said property to the Intending Purchasers . . . at the option price.' The option price is defined by cl 1 which is ambiguous, but that ambiguity is removed by cl 2 which refers to the sums payable thereunder as payable 'in addition to the option price'. Moreover, the contrast between the wording of cl 2(a) and that of cl 2(b) shows that the parties to the agreement envisaged that the sums payable under the former would not be ascertained at the time of completion, because cl 2(a) refers to 'Such sum as may become payable . . . as a result of the sale', whereas cl 2(b) refers to 'Such sum as the Intending Vendor shall have paid to the Tithe Redemption Commission . . .'

I, therefore, hold that that line of defence fails also and that the plaintiffs are entitled to the order for specific performance that they seek.

That is not quite the end of the case because there is a counterclaim which is, so far as material, in these terms:

'... if (but only if) it shall be held by the court that there is a binding contract for sale of the said land by the Defendant to the Plaintiffs.

THE DEFENDANT COUNTER-CLAIMS

(1) That it may be declared (a) how (in accordance with the judgment of the court) the sums payable under clause 2(a) of the 1970 agreement are to be computed and (b) when (in accordance with such judgment) the same are to be paid

(2) If and insofar as necessary an inquiry as to the sums so payable in accordance with the said declaration

(3) A declaration that the defendant is entitled to a lien on the said land in respect of the said sums with interest thereon at 15 per cent per annum until payment in full of the same (whether before or after conveyance of the said land to the plaintiffs).'

As to (1) and (2), it became common ground during the argument before me that the assessment or assessments, if any, made by the Inland Revenue on the defendant, once that assessment or those assessments had become final, would determine conclusively the amount or amounts payable by the plaintiffs to the defendant and that the plaintiffs would become liable to pay that amount, or those amounts, to the defendant on the same day, or days, as he became liable to pay the Revenue. That being common ground, counsel for the defendant conceded that it would not be appropriate for me to make the declarations or to order the enquiry sought by the counterclaim.

As to (3), counsel for the defendant conceded, rightly in my view, that he could not press the claim for interest, but he did press the defendant's claim to a lien. Counsel for the plaintiffs was at first inclined to resist that, but, subject to one point, his resistance vanished after counsel for the defendant had read a passage from *Snell's Principles of Equity* (27th edn, 1973) pp 445–446 and one of the authorities there cited, namely *Walker v Ware, Hadlam and Buntingford Rly Co* (1865) LR 1 Eq 195. The reservation by counsel for the plaintiffs was this, that the defendant's entitlement to a lien should not mean that he was entitled to possession of the land after completion. In my judgment, it does not. In those circumstances, I will hear counsel as to whether or not it would be appropriate for me to make a declaration as to the lien and, if so, as to the form that that declaration should take.

Order for specific performance. Counterclaim dismissed in part.

Solicitors: *Wedlake Bell*, agents for *Morgans*, Ludlow (for the plaintiffs); *Norris & Miles*, Tenbury Wells (for the defendants).

Azza M Abdallah   Barrister.

Verrall v Hackney London Borough Council

COURT OF APPEAL, CIVIL DIVISION
SIR JOHN DONALDSON MR, WATKINS AND MAY LJJ
1, 2, 18 NOVEMBER 1982

Magistrates – Jurisdiction – Warrant for distress for non-payment of rates – Unincorporated association and various different entities using premises – Assessment for rates made against member of association – Defence of non-occupation of premises – Whether magistrate having jurisdiction to entertain defence of non-occupation when defence not raised by way of appeal to Crown Court – General Rate Act 1967, s 7.

Rates – Rateable occupation – Occupation by unincorporated association – Rates demanded from member of association – Whether membership of association making member the 'occupier' of premises used by association.

Rates – Rateable occupation – Person liable for rates – Occupier – Premises described in valuation list as single hereditament – Premises used by different legal entities at different times – Whether any one user liable for rates on whole of premises.

NFP Ltd owned certain premises which were used for different purposes at different times by different legal entities, amongst which were a licensed club (whose members were also members of the National Front, an unincorporated association), two companies (whose purposes were almost identical to those of the National Front) and the publicity department of the National Front. The premises were shown as a single hereditament for rating purposes and were originally described as a 'warehouse and premises' but that was subsequently altered to 'stores, offices, clubroom and premises'. The defendant, who was a member of the National Front, an officer of the club and secretary to one of the companies, was responsible for the administration of the National Front and took part in arranging for it to occupy the premises. He was assessed for rates as the occupier of the hereditament. When the rates were not paid, the rating authority laid a complaint before a stipendiary magistrate for leave to issue a distress warrant against the defendant. The defendant contended that he was not the occupier of the premises and accordingly was not liable for payment of the rates. The magistrate found that the National Front was the paramount occupier of the premises and that all other uses were subordinate to the National Front's use. He held that, although he could not issue a distress warrant against the defendant on the ground merely that he was a member of the National Front, he could, however, do so on the ground that the defendant had expressly or impliedly authorised the occupation of the premises by the National Front or had ratified it. The defendant appealed by way of case stated seeking the determination of, inter alia, the questions (i) whether the National Front was in real and paramount occupation of the premises and (ii) whether the defendant was liable for the rates on the premises. The rating authority contended, inter alia, that since the defendant had not raised the defence of non-occupation by way of appeal to the Crown Court under s 7[a] of the General Rate Act 1967 it could not be raised by way of a defence to proceedings for a distress warrant. The judge held that he was bound by authority to accept the rating authority's contention and dismissed the appeal. The defendant appealed to the Court of Appeal.

Held – The appeal would be allowed for the following reasons—
    (1) On an application for a distress warrant for non-payment of rates, it was a good defence for the defendant to show that he was not in occupation of the hereditament. It followed that the magistrate had jurisdiction to investigate whether the defendant was

---

a   Section 7, so far as material, is set out at p 280 *e* to *h*, post

in occupation of the relevant hereditament (see p 282 e f, p 283 a and p 286 g h, post); dicta of Wills J in *Manchester Overseers v Headlam* (1888) 21 QBD at 98 and of Browne LJ in *Camden London Borough v Herwald* [1978] 2 All ER at 885 followed; *North Cornwall DC v Johnson* [1981] RVR 201, *Bird v Blakemore* [1982] RA 12 and *Newport BC v Williams* [1982] RVR 169 disapproved.

(2) Liability for rates depended on actual and exclusive occupation or possession of the rated premises. Applying that principle, the defendant was not liable for the rates on the premises used by the National Front, because (a) the mere fact that he was a member of an unincorporated association (which could not in law be the occupier of premises) could not make him the 'occupier' of the premises for rating purposes either as the sole occupier or jointly with the association, and (b) since the premises were rated under one entry in the valuation list and in the rate as one indivisible hereditament there could be only one occupier for rating purposes and there was no evidence that the defendant was the paramount occupier responsible for the rates. Accordingly, the magistrate was wrong in law to hold that the defendant was liable for the general rate on the premises for the period in question. The case would therefore be remitted to the magistrate with a direction to dismiss the summons against the defendant (see p 285 d e and p 286 d to h, post); *Re Briant Colour Printing Co Ltd* [1977] 3 All ER 968 and dictum of Lord Lane CJ in *R v Brighton Justices, ex p Howard* [1980] RA at 225 followed; *John Laing & Son Ltd v Kingswood Area Assessment Committee* [1949] 1 All ER 224 considered.

Notes

For rateable occupation, see 39 Halsbury's Laws (4th edn) paras 15–25, and for cases on the subject, see 38 Digest (Reissue) 288–293, 2048–2069.

For proceedings for the recovery of rates, see 39 Halsbury's Laws (4th edn) paras 236ff, and for cases on the subject, see 38 Digest (Reissue) 508–512, 3880–3920.

For the General Rate Act 1967, s 7, see 27 Halsbury's Statutes (3rd edn) 81.

Cases referred to in judgment

Bird v Blakemore [1982] RA 12.

Briant Colour Printing Co Ltd, Re [1977] 3 All ER 968, [1977] 1 WLR 942, CA, 38 Digest (Reissue) 288, 2051.

Bristol Governors of the Poor v Wait (1834) 1 Ad & El 264, 110 ER 1207, 18 Digest (Reissue) 417, 1409.

Camden London Borough v Herwald [1978] 2 All ER 880, [1978] QB 626, [1978] 3 WLR 47, CA, Digest (Reissue) 509, 3888.

Hampstead BC v Associated Cinema Properties Ltd [1944] 1 All ER 436, [1944] 1 KB 412, CA; affg [1943] 2 All ER 696, [1944] 1 KB 49, DC, 38 Digest (Reissue) 291, 2058.

Laing (John) & Son Ltd v Kingswood Area Assessment Committee [1949] 1 All ER 224, [1949] 1 KB 344, CA, 38 Digest (Reissue) 312, 2169.

London County Council v Wilkins [1956] 3 All ER 38, [1957] AC 362, HL, 38 Digest (Reissue) 292, 2068.

Manchester Overseer v Headlam (1888) 21 QBD 96, DC, 18 Digest (Reissue) 413, 1381.

Milward v Caffin (1779) 2 Wm Bl 1330, 96 ER 779, 18 Digest (Reissue) 422, 1459.

Newport BC v Williams [1982] RVR 169.

North Cornwall DC v Johnson [1981] RVR 201.

R v Brighton Justices, ex p Howard [1980] RA 222.

Westminster Corp v Southern Rly Co [1936] 2 All ER 322, [1936] AC 511, HL, 38 Digest (Reissue) 434, 3047.

Cases also cited

Case (Valuation Officer) v British Rlys Board [1972] RA 97.

Churchwardens and Overseers of the Poor of the Parish of Birmingham v Shaw (1849) 10 QB 868, 116 ER 329.

Debenhams Ltd v Ealing London Borough Council [1981] RA 194.

Harper v Carr (1797) 7 Term Rep 270, 101 ER 970.

Helman v Horsham and Worthing Assessment Committee [1949] 1 All ER 776, [1949] 2 KB
335, CA.
Pamplin v Preston BC [1980] RA 246.
Potts v Hickman [1940] 4 All ER 491, [1941] AC 212, HL.
Verrall v Great Yarmouth BC [1980] 1 All ER 839, [1981] QB 202, CA.
Whenman v Clark [1916] 1 KB 94, CA.

Appeal

On 15 January 1981 a complaint was laid before the metropolitan stipendiary magistrate
for the Petty Sessional Division of Thames by the respondents, Hackney London Borough
Council, that the appellant, Richard Verrall, was a person duly rated and assessed to the
general rate of the borough made on 22 March 1978, 28 March 1979 and 26 March 1980
in respect of premises at 73 Great Eastern Street, Shoreditch, London EC2 and that a
distress warrant be issued against him. On 23 June 1981 the magistrate issued a distress
warrant against the appellant on the grounds that a political party, namely the National
Front, which was an unincorporated association, was the paramount occupier of the
premises, that all other occupiers were subordinate to the National Front's use and that
the appellant expressly or impliedly authorised the occupation of the premises by the
National Front or ratified it. The appellant appealed by way of case stated to the Divisional
Court of the Queen's Bench Division. On 23 June 1982 Woolf J, hearing the Crown
Office List, dismissed the appeal on the ground that the magistrate had no jurisdiction to
entertain the defence that the appellant was not the occupier of the premises. The
appellant appealed to the Court of Appeal. The facts are set out in the judgment of the
court.

Cleveland Butterfield for the appellant.
Harry Sales for the respondents.

Cur adv vult

18 November. The following judgment of the court was delivered.

MAY LJ. This is an appeal from a judgment of Woolf J of 23 June 1982 dismissing an
appeal by the present appellant by way of case stated from the decision of a stipendiary
magistrate sitting at the Thames Magistrates' Court on 23 June 1981.

The magistrate had before him a summons issued on a complaint by the present
respondents, who are the rating authority for the borough of Hackney, pursuant to s 97
of the General Rate Act 1967. This summons alleged that the appellant was a person duly
rated and assessed to the general rate of the borough made respectively on 22 March
1978, 28 March 1979 and 26 March 1980 in the total sum of £10,076·41, but which he
had not paid. He was therefore summoned to appear at the Thames Magistrates' Court
to show cause why he had not done so. The relevant premises were Excalibur House, 73
Great Eastern Street, London EC2.

At the hearing before the magistrate, which in fact took place on three separate days
in January, April and June 1981, it immediately became apparent that the appellant's
defence was that he had not been the occupier of the relevant premises and was thus not
liable for the rates in respect of them on general principles.

The relevant statutory provisions are as follows. Section 1(2) of the General Rate Act
1967 provides:

'Every rating authority shall have power in accordance with this Act to make and
levy rates on the basis of an assessment in respect of the yearly value of property in
their rating area for the purpose of applying the proceeds thereof to local purposes
of a public nature.'

By s 3(1) a rate made by a rating authority is deemed to be made on the date on which it
is approved by the authority. In so far as is material, s 3(2) then provides that a resolution
of an authority specifying the amount per pound of rateable value at which the rate is to
be levied shall be taken to constitute approval of the rate.

Then there is s 16 of the 1967 Act which contains the fundamental provision that it is the occupier of property who is liable to be assessed to rates in respect of the hereditament which he occupies, according to its rateable value determined in accordance with the other provisions of the 1967 Act.

Part V of the 1967 Act provides for the preparation of a valuation list of the hereditaments within the area of the rating authority by the relevant valuation officer. The contents of such list are laid down by the Valuation Lists Rules 1972, SI 1972/1612. For present purposes it is sufficient to say that the list must contain a description of the material hereditament, its address, together with the name of the occupier if this is needed for the purposes of identification, and the rateable value of the premises. By virtue of s 108 of the 1967 Act, the valuation list is open to inspection by ratepayers.

Part V also contains provisions enabling persons aggrieved by the inclusion of any hereditament in the valuation list or by any value ascribed to it in that list, amongst other things, to make a proposal for an appropriate alteration to the list to the valuation officer. If such a proposal is agreed by the valuation officer, then he is required to alter the valuation list accordingly. If he does not agree the proposal, then the issue between the person aggrieved and the valuation officer is to be determined by a local valuation court constituted as set out in other provisions contained in Part V of the 1967 Act.

Section 18 contains general provisions for calculating the amount of the rate for which an occupier may be assessed, having regard to the rate made by the rating authority as applied to the rateable value of the relevant hereditament in the valuation list, all in accordance with the other sections of the 1967 Act to which we have already referred. The sum so calculated is levied on the person alleged to be liable to pay it by a demand note which has to contain information with respect to the matters set out in s 5(1) of the 1967 Act.

Section 7 provides for certain appeals in respect, inter alia, of the rate and the demand note. For the purposes of the present case only s 7(1) and (2) are material. These are in the following terms:

'(1) Subject to subsection (2) of this section, any person who—(a) is aggrieved by any rate; or (b) has any material objection to the inclusion or exclusion of any person in or from, or to the amount charged to any person in, any rate; or (c) is aggrieved by any neglect, act, or thing done or omitted by the rating authority, may appeal to the Crown Court and such appeal shall be commenced by giving notice to the appropriate officer of the Crown Court within twenty-one days of—(a) the date of publication of the rate under section 4 of this Act; or (b) the act or thing done by the rating authority; or (c) the giving of notice for the purposes of this section to the rating authority as to the neglect or omission concerned, whichever is the latest; and notice of any such appeal shall be given to the rating authority and to any person other than the appellant with respect to whom the rate may be required to be altered in consequence of the appeal; and any such person shall, if he so desires, be heard on the appeal.
(2) No appeal shall lie under this section in respect of any matter in respect of which relief might have been obtained under Part V of this Act by means of—(a) a proposal for the amendment of the current valuation list; or (b) an objection to such a proposal; or (c) an appeal against such an objection.'

Thus any disputed question relating to the valuation or description of the hereditament sought to be rated is a matter for the local valuation court and cannot be appealed to the Crown Court under s 7. On the other hand, a person to whom a rate demand has been addressed and on whom it has been served may appeal against it pursuant to the provisions of s 7 on the basis, for instance, that he was or is not the occupier of the relevant premises, at least where he has not been named as an occupier in the valuation list for identification purposes: whether or not in such a case an appeal would lie to the Crown Court on the ground of alleged non-occupation if the proposed appellant was so named in the valuation list is not a point which we need decide on this appeal. Our attention was drawn to the fact that similar appeal provisions to those in s 7, prior to

1972 to courts of quarter sessions, have been contained in all earlier rating legislation. We were, for instance, shown the similar provisions in the earliest Act in this field, namely s 6 of the Poor Relief Act 1601.

Reverting to the modern legislation, the 1967 Act then enacts that the payment of rates legally assessed on and duly demanded from a person may be enforced by distress and by the sale thereafter of that person's goods and chattels under Part VI of the Act. Ultimately, if there is insufficient distress and the non-payment of the rates is shown to have been due to the wilful refusal or culpable neglect of the person assessed, then he is liable to be committed to prison. The provisions of the 1967 Act relating to distress which are relevant to the present case are as follows:

'**96.**—(1) Subject to section 62 of this Act and to subsection (2) of this section, if any person fails to pay any sum legally assessed on and due from him in respect of a rate for seven days after it has been legally demanded of him, the payment of that sum may, subject to and in accordance with the provisions of this Part of this Act, be enforced by distress and sale of his goods and chattels under warrant issued by a magistrates' court; and, if there is insufficient distress, he may be liable to imprisonment under the provisions of this Part of this Act in that behalf . . .

97.—(1) The proceedings for the issue of a warrant of distress under this Part of this Act may be instituted by making complaint before a justice of the peace and applying for a summons requiring the person named in the complaint to appear before a magistrates' court to show why he has not paid the rate specified in the complaint . . .

98. The justices may state a case under the Magistrates' Courts Act 1980 when called upon to issue a warrant of distress under this Part of this Act.'

It was under these provisions that the appellant in the instant appeal was summoned before the Thames Magistrates' Court as we have already mentioned. As we have also said, he sought to show that he had not paid the rates assessed on him because he contended that he was not the occupier of the material hereditament at the relevant time. That such a defence to an alleged liability and demand for rates is so appealable to the Crown Court arguably provides a foundation for the contention that, if the defence of non-occupation is not raised by way of appeal under s 7, then it cannot be raised in answer to proceedings for a distress warrant in respect of the same sums under ss 96 and 97 of the 1967 Act. This contention has been advanced and has indeed succeeded in three recent decisions of the High Court in which it has been held that the question whether or not the person summoned had been the occupier of the hereditament is not a matter within the jurisdiction of the magistrates' court. The first of these, *North Cornwall DC v Johnson* [1981] RVR 201, decided by Forbes J on 3 February 1981, was drawn to the attention of the stipendiary magistrate in this case. However, as he had already started the hearing of the summons before the *North Cornwall* case was decided, and as the parties respectfully felt some doubt about the correctness of the decision in the light of earlier authorities, he continued to hear the summons before him and in the event stated the case on which the appellant appealed to Woolf J, and to the details of which we shall refer hereafter.

By the time that the instant appeal came before Woolf J the two further cases raising the same question as that raised by the *North Cornwall* case had been heard and each had been similarly decided. These were *Bird v Blakemore* [1982] RA 12, which was decided on 9 October 1981 by McNeill J, who expressly followed the earlier decision of Forbes J in the *North Cornwall* case; secondly, there was *Newport BC v Williams* [1982] RVR 169, decided on 5 May 1982 by Stephen Brown J, who expressly followed the decision of McNeill J in *Bird v Blakemore*. At the outset of the hearing of this appeal in the court below, counsel for the respondents drew the attention of the judge to these three decisions. Counsel did not refer to them in any detail but he told the judge of their effect. In these circumstances the judge decided that he should follow them and then leave them and the appeal before him for this court's consideration. He therefore dismissed

the appeal on the case stated by the stipendiary magistrate without going into the merits
at all.

Before this court, counsel for each of the parties made common cause on this issue.
They submitted that the three decisions in 1981 and 1982 were incorrect and that there
was binding authority to the contrary effect. It should be noted that no such authority
was cited to any of the judges who decided the three recent cases. We find this surprising
in the light of the clear statement to the contrary in *Ryde on Rating* (13th edn, 1976)
p 868 and the authorities which are there set out to support it. There is no need in this
judgment to consider in detail the cases of *Milward v Caffin* (1779) 2 Wm Bl 1330, 96 ER
779 or *Bristol Governors of the Poor v Wait* (1834) 1 Ad & El 264, 110 ER 1207. The specific
point arose again in *Manchester Overseers v Headlam* (1888) 21 QBD 96. We need only
quote a short passage from the judgment of Wills J where he said (at 98):

'It is undoubted law that a poor-rate made upon a person in respect of property
which he does not occupy, although unappealed against, will not support a distress
made upon that person in respect of the property which he does not occupy.'

In *Hampstead BC v Associated Cinema Properties Ltd* [1943] 2 All ER 696, [1944] 1 KB
49, DC; [1944] 1 All ER 436, [1944] 1 KB 412, CA, the issue was whether a limited
company had been in rateable occupation of premises in respect of which they had been
assessed for general rates. The facts had been investigated by the magistrates' court which
had held that the company had been in such occupation and that therefore a distress
warrant should issue. It was then held by both the Divisional Court and the Court of
Appeal that the magistrates had come to the wrong conclusion and that the facts found
by them did not establish rateable occupation. However, at no time was the point taken,
either by counsel or by either of the two courts, that the magistrates had had no
jurisdiction to investigate the question of occupation on the facts as they had done. Had
this point been raised and been a good one, it would have provided a simple and ready
answer to the appeal on the case stated. We think that the fact that it was not is clear
support for the proposition that the magistrates did in fact have the jurisdiction to
investigate the facts as they did.

Finally, in *Camden London Borough v Herwald* [1978] 2 All ER 880, [1978] 1 QB 626, a
decision of the Court of Appeal, the first issue was whether the application to the
magistrates under s 97 of the General Rate Act 1967 was a 'criminal cause or matter', in
which case the appeal from the Divisional Court which had heard an appeal by way of
case stated from the magistrates would only have lain to the House of Lords. It was held
that the investigation by a magistrates' court under this section of the 1967 Act was not
in a 'criminal cause or matter' but was a civil proceeding and that therefore the appeal
from the Divisional Court lay to the Court of Appeal. The second issue was whether the
defendant before the magistrates had been in occupation of a hereditament as described
in the valuation list. The Court of Appeal held that the true test in these matters was that
if the person rated was in occupation of premises which fulfilled the description in the
valuation list that was sufficient for the issue of a distress warrant. Nevertheless the court
went on to hold, differently from the Divisional Court, that on the facts the test was not
satisfied and that consequently no distress warrant could be issued. In the course of
giving the reserved judgment of the court, Browne LJ said ([1978] 2 All ER 880 at 885,
[1978] QB 626 at 639):

'It is well established that an application for a distress warrant to enforce payment
of rates can only be resisted on certain limited grounds. It is also well established
that one of such grounds is that the defendant is not in occupation of the
hereditament in respect of which it is sought to rate him.'

Later he said ([1978] 2 All ER 880 at 886–887, [1978] QB 626 at 641):

'As we have said, there is no doubt that on an application for a distress warrant it
is a defence for the defendant to show that he is not in occupation of the hereditament
at all (see, for example, *Hampstead Borough Council v Associated Cinema Properties Ltd*).'

In the light of these clear authorities we respectfully think that the three recent decisions at first instance to which we have referred were wrongly decided and should not be followed. In our opinion the stipendiary magistrate in the present case did have jurisdiction to investigate whether the appellant was in occupation of the relevant hereditament.

Once we had so decided on this appeal, and as Woolf J did not hear it on its merits, we considered whether it would be more appropriate to send it back to him for him to hear further or whether we should deal with the appeal on its merits ourselves. We were asked by both counsel, and decided, that we should take the latter course. There seemed to us to be no reason in law why we should not do so. Such a course of action would save the costs of a further hearing before Woolf J. If there were such a hearing, then there might still be an appeal from him to us on the merits which would also be obviated if we proceeded to hear the appeal on its merits at this stage.

We therefore turn to the facts of this case as they were found by the stipendiary magistrate. He first found that the rate had been properly made and demanded and all the necessary formalities had been complied with by the rating authority. The premises had been originally described in the valuation list as 'warehouse and premises' but this was subsequently altered by a proposal of the valuation officer himself dated 30 November 1979 to 'stores, offices, clubroom and premises (part under reconstruction)'. That alteration, as it was unopposed, was deemed to come into effect and did so on 1 April 1979. The demand for the rates due for the period was addressed to 'Mr Richard Verrall [the present appellant], National Front, 73 Great Eastern Street, London, E.C.2'. The amended amount due was £10,076·41, which included £3·25 for the costs of the summons. It is convenient to interpolate here that the magistrate found that the National Front is a political organisation, in law an unincorporated association whose members are governed by a constitution. We were not shown this constitution and nothing turns on it in this case.

These matters having been proved, in my opinion as a matter of law it was then for the appellant to show sufficient cause for not having paid the sum demanded. This we think is clear from the wording of s 97(1) of the 1967 Act and of the forms in Sch 12 which are referred to in s 97(2). In the event the appellant neither gave evidence himself nor called any witness to do so at the hearing before the magistrate. A number of agreed documents were put in during the opening of the case by counsel for the rating authority and a number of witnesses called on its behalf were cross-examined by counsel for the appellant. It was on this material that the appellant contended that he had been entitled not to pay the rates because he had not been the occupier of the relevant premises for the material period. Having regard, no doubt, to the way in which the demand for the rate had been addressed and to the well recognised concept of paramount occupancy in rating cases arising from the decision of the House of Lords in *Westminster Corp v Southern Rly Co* [1936] 2 All ER 322, [1936] AC 511, the appellant contended before the magistrate that the National Front had not been the paramount occupier of the premises, but that there had been a number of occupiers of different parts, including in particular a members' club known as the Excalibur Canteen and Refreshment Club which was an entirely separate entity which for part of the time occupied the third floor of Excalibur House. In any event, it was submitted that the appellant did not control the National Front and was not responsible for the occupation of the premises, by whomsoever this had occurred.

On behalf of the rating authority it was contended that the paramount occupier of the whole of the premises had been the National Front and that the magistrate could issue the distress warrant against the appellant, from whom the rates had been legally demanded as we have already mentioned, because he (the appellant) was and had throughout been a member of the National Front. Alternatively, it was argued that the magistrate could issue a distress warrant against the appellant on the ground that a member of an unincorporated association is liable for rates by analogy with the position in contract law, so it was said, where such a member is liable under a contract entered into by the association if he has expressly authorised the contract or ratified it.

On the evidence and arguments before him the magistrate first purported to find as a fact that the real, actual and paramount occupier had been the National Front. The premises were at all times owned by National Front Properties Ltd. This was a property company which, originally in any event, had had a substantial connection with the National Front. The magistrate then went on to find as a fact, as he recorded in the case stated, that differing parts of the premises had been used for various different purposes for varying periods by different legal entities and persons. He found himself unable to say for how long and for what purpose any particular legal entity had used any particular part of the premises but, asking himself the question referred to by Lord Russell in the *Westminster* case, he said that he had no difficulty in finding that the paramount and real occupier of the premises throughout the material time was the National Front. There had been at least four users of various parts of the premises at various times. Two were limited companies set up for the purposes of the National Front, controlled by it and whose activities were either wholly or almost wholly for its purposes. Another had been the publicity department of the National Front itself. Finally, there was the club to which we have already referred; this the magistrate said he also had no difficulty in finding was for the use of National Front members and that, although the actual membership fluctuated during the period and there was a dispute as to the steward of the club, it was virtually certain that the only members ever admitted to it were those accepted as being members of the National Front. The premises themselves were proclaimed in literature issued by the National Front as its headquarters.

In so far as the National Front itself was concerned, the magistrate recorded in the case that who amongst its members controlled it at any one time was a matter of continuous dispute. There were quarrels and factions amongst them and one High Court and one county court action during the period in question. In this connection he then found as facts that the present appellant was not only a member, but also a very prominent member of the National Front, having responsibility for its administration and thus of necessity taking part in the arrangements for its occupation of Excalibur House. He had an overseeing role; he signed some of the letters put in evidence before the magistrate on behalf of the National Front or its publicity department; he was an officer of the club and he was secretary of one of the two limited companies. He was also one of the parties to the High Court action.

In the result, having made the findings of fact as to paramount occupancy to which we have referred, the magistrate decided that he could not issue a distress warrant against the appellant on the ground merely that he was a member of the National Front, but that he could and did decide to issue such a warrant against him on the ground that he expressly or impliedly authorised the occupation of the relevant premises by the National Front or ratified it. It was in respect of those decisions that the present appellant asked for the case to be stated. In it the questions on which the opinion of the High Court was sought were: first, whether there was any or any sufficient evidence on which the magistrate, acting reasonably, could make his findings about the paramount occupancy that he did; second, whether the magistrate was wrong in law in holding that the appellant was liable for the general rate for the period in question in respect of the material premises as a person who expressly or impliedly authorised the occupation or ratified the occupation of those premises by the unincorporated body known as the National Front; third, whether as a matter of law there had been any or any sufficient evidence on which he could find that the appellant had indeed authorised the occupation of the building by the National Front either expressly or impliedly or by ratification.

Before this court, counsel for the rating authority expressly abandoned the contention on which he had succeeded in the magistrates' court, namely that on the findings of fact liability could be attached to the appellant on an analogy with what he had suggested was the position in contract and to which we have briefly referred. He submitted boldly that, where one can say that although a particular association is unincorporated, and thus not a legal entity, but both it and its members are clearly identifiable, then every such member is properly to be described as in beneficial occupation of premises used for the purposes of the association and thus liable for general rates if the necessary formalities are complied with.

Counsel for the appellant first argued that there had been no evidence to support the finding of the magistrate that the National Front had been in paramount occupation of the premises. Alternatively, if there had been such evidence, then mere membership of that or any other unincorporated organisation could not of itself attract liability for rates.

Counsel, however, did not seek to argue either before the magistrate or this court what we consider to be a fundamental point demonstrating an underlying fallacy in the argument on behalf of the rating authority and thus in the ultimate decision of the magistrate.

As we have said, and the magistrate found, the National Front was and is an unincorporated association and as such we do not think it could occupy anything. As Lord Lane CJ said in *R v Brighton Justices, ex p Howard* [1980] RA 222 at 225, about the unincorporated body involved there, '"Local Aid" could not occupy anything, because it was a nonentity'. Most unincorporated associations, such as clubs or charities, have trustees, or a committee, legal persons with funds available to pay the rates which it is recognised will have to be paid. It is these persons who, as a matter of law, usually occupy the relevant premises which are used for the purposes of their club or charity and are liable as such occupiers for the general rates. In our opinion, however, the unincorporated association which, speaking loosely, they run, can never be the occupier of those or any premises.

We think it follows that the mere fact that a person is a 'member' of an unincorporated association is insufficient material on which to base a finding that that person is the occupier of premises used for the purposes of the unincorporated association, either himself alone, still less jointly with the association.

The first and real question for the magistrate was who had been in rateable occupation of the material hereditament over the relevant period. When this question falls to be considered and answered in these cases we stress in the first place that any liability for rates depends on actual occupation or possession of premises. This is the first of the four well-established ingredients of the concept of rateable occupation approved by the Court of Appeal in *John Laing & Son Ltd v Kingswood Area Assessment Committee* [1949] 1 All ER 224, [1949] 1 KB 344 and recognised by the House of Lords in *London County Council v Wilkins* [1956] 3 All ER 38, [1957] AC 362. Legal title to or the right to possession of land is not by itself sufficient to render the person with that title or right to possession liable for rates in respect of that land. There must at the least be actual possession and some use of the hereditament rated.

Further, the second well-established ingredient of the concept of rateable occupation is that the actual occupation or possession must be exclusive for the purpose of the possession. Consideration of this ingredient is important in cases such as the present where there may have been more than one legal person using parts of the premises at times during the period for which rates are sought to be charged. In *Ryde on Rating* (13th edn, 1976) p 120 the editors give this warning:

'The occupation of land can be joint, and it is important to distinguish the case of a building in the hands of joint occupiers from that of a building of which the parts are let separately to several persons, each of whom is the occupier of the part let to him, and of that part only . . . If the whole building is rated, under one entry in the valuation list, and in the rate, as one indivisible rateable hereditament, no one tenant is liable for the rate on the whole, because he is not the occupier of the whole, nor can he be compelled to pay the rate on the part which he occupies, because there is nothing in the rate, or in the valuation list on which it is based, to show what is the value of that part.'

In *Re Briant Colour Printing Co Ltd* [1977] 3 All ER 968 at 977, [1977] 1 WLR 942 at 952–953 Buckley LJ summed up the position in this way:

'Both the fact of occupation and the identity of the occupier are questions of fact, to be answered on the evidence and the circumstances of the particular case. There cannot, I think, be two occupiers for rating purposes at one time of one hereditament. If a state of affairs arises in which two persons are in occupation of what is listed as one hereditament for rating purposes, each entitled to exclusive use for a particular purpose, the list must be amended to show two hereditaments in order to enable the rating authority to assess both occupiers. But if there are two persons each of whom makes some use of an immovable property concurrently, there may either be two co-existing hereditaments, the occupier of each one of which may be rateable; or there may be two concurrent uses of one hereditament, in which event it may be necessary to discover which of them has the paramount position so as to be rateable as the occupier.'

In the instant appeal the whole building, Excalibur House, was rated under one entry in the valuation list and in the rate as one indivisible hereditament. As we have said, the magistrate found as facts that the differing parts of the premises, the whole of which at all times was owned by National Front Properties Ltd, was used for various different purposes for varying periods by differing legal entities and persons. However, he was unable to say and was unable to make any finding of fact as to exactly how long and for what purpose or what legal entity used every particular part of the premises at any one time. In these circumstances, once one strikes down any question of any paramount occupancy of the whole building by the National Front as impossible in law, we do not think that there is anything in the case stated to entitle this court to hold, even on grounds different from those relied on by the magistrate, that the appellant was nevertheless as a question of fact the occupier of the whole premises. These may well have all been used for various purposes of the National Front; the appellant was found by the stipendiary magistrate to be a very prominent member of that organisation and responsible for its administration, indeed to have an overseeing role; he was an officer of the club and secretary of one of the two limited companies which had used the premises for part of the time. Nevertheless, even though it might be justifiable to hold on the material in the case stated that the present appellant played a very important part in all the activities which were taking place, for the same underlying purposes, throughout the premises over the relevant period, we do not think that it is possible to hold that he was throughout the occupier or one of a number of joint occupiers of the single hereditament comprised in the one entry in the valuation list and the rate. Further, we do not think that if we remitted this case to the magistrate for further hearing and argument in the light of our judgment there is any real possibility that the respondents would be able to satisfy him by any further evidence or argument that this appellant was the exclusive occupier of the whole hereditament for the relevant period so as to be entitled to the distress warrant against him which they seek.

We therefore answer both parts of the first of the questions posed in the case stated for the opinion of the court and the second part of the second question in the negative. In so far as the first part of the second question is concerned, we think that the magistrate was wrong in law in holding the appellant liable for the general rate on Excalibur House for the period in question on any ground. We would therefore allow this appeal and send the case back to the magistrate with a direction to dismiss the summons against the appellant for the distress warrant.

Appeal allowed. Application for leave to appeal to the House of Lords refused.

Solicitors: *J E Baring & Co* (for the appellant); *R A Benge* (for the respondents).

Diana Procter   Barrister.

Re Poh

HOUSE OF LORDS, APPEAL COMMITTEE
LORD DIPLOCK, LORD FRASER OF TULLYBELTON, LORD KEITH OF KINKEL, LORD SCARMAN AND
LORD ROSKILL
9 DECEMBER 1982

House of Lords – Appeal from Court of Appeal, Civil Division – Jurisdiction – Judicial review – Court of Appeal refusing leave to apply for judicial review – House of Lords having no jurisdiction to entertain petition against refusal – RSC Ord 53.

The House of Lords has no jurisdiction to entertain a petition to it for leave to appeal against the refusal of the Court of Appeal to grant leave to apply for judicial review under RSC Ord 53 (see p 288 *c d*, post).

Lane v Esdaile [1891] AC 210 and *Whitehouse v Board of Control* [1960] 3 All ER 182 followed.

Suthendran v Immigration Appeal Tribunal [1976] 3 All ER 611 considered.

Notes
For applications for leave to appeal to the House of Lords, see 10 Halsbury's Laws (4th edn) para 758.

Cases referred to
Housing of the Working Classes Act 1890, Re, ex p Stevenson [1892] 1 QB 609, CA, 11 Digest (Reissue) 326, 2102.

Lane v Esdaile [1891] AC 210, HL, 30 Digest (Reissue) 169, 34.

Suthendran v Immigration Appeal Tribunal [1976] 3 All ER 611, [1977] AC 359, [1976] 3 WLR 725, HL, 2 Digest (Reissue) 221, 1234.

Whitehouse v Board of Control [1960] 3 All ER 182, [1960] 1 WLR 1093, HL, 33 Digest (Repl) 714, 1693.

Petition for leave to appeal
Charles Poh (otherwise Francis Charles Anakwa), a citizen of Ghana, applied by petition to the House of Lords for leave to appeal to the House following the refusal of the Court of Appeal (Lord Lane CJ, Dunn and May LJJ) on 4 October 1982 and of Glidewell J hearing the Crown Office List on 29 July 1982 to grant the applicant leave to apply ex parte under RSC Ord 53 for judicial review by way of an order of certiorari to quash the decision of the Immigration Appeal Tribunal on 30 December 1981 refusing him leave to appeal against the determination of an adjudicator on 21 October 1981 dismissing his appeal against the decision of the Secretary of State for the Home Department on 20 October 1976 to make a deportation order against him under s 3(5)(a) of the Immigration Act 1971. The Court of Appeal additionally refused the applicant leave to appeal to the House of Lords. The applicant's petition to the House of Lords was, in the alternative, an original application to the House for leave to apply for judicial review. On the hearing of the petition the Treasury Solicitor took the preliminary objection that the House of Lords had no jurisdiction to hear the petition.

Peter Latham for the applicant.
Andrew Collins for the Treasury Solicitor.

LORD DIPLOCK. The history of this application for leave to appeal to their Lordships' House is that the applicant originally sought leave under RSC Ord 53, r 3 to apply for judicial review of a decision of the Immigration Appeal Tribunal. The application was heard ex parte by Glidewell J sitting as a Divisional Court and leave was refused. The applicant appealed ex parte by originating motion to the Court of Appeal, who also refused leave. From that refusal the applicant now seeks leave to appeal to their Lordships' House.

Their Lordships are not concerned with the procedure whereby this application moved from the Divisional Court to the Court of Appeal, because the question we have to consider is whether this House has jurisdiction to entertain the application. Counsel instructed by the Treasury Solicitor has taken the preliminary point that the House has no jurisdiction under the Appellate Jurisdiction Act 1876 to entertain an appeal from refusal of leave to apply for judicial review under RSC Ord 53. He relies on the construction of s 3 of the 1876 Act, which was approved by this House in *Lane v Esdaile* [1891] AC 210 and followed by the Court of Appeal in *Re Housing of the Working Classes Act 1890, ex p Stevenson* [1892] 1 QB 609, where the underlying common sense of the rule in *Lane v Esdaile* is stated clearly by Lord Esher MR, Fry and Lopes LJJ. The rule in *Lane v Esdaile* was again applied by the Appeal Committee of this House in *Whitehouse v Board of Control* [1960] 3 All ER 182, [1960] 1 WLR 1093.

In their Lordships' view this case is clearly covered by the rule in *Lane v Esdaile* and the House has no jurisdiction to entertain it. Our attention has been drawn to *Suthendran v Immigration Appeal Tribunal* [1976] 3 All ER 611, [1977] AC 359, in which it does appear that under the old RSC Ord 53, before its amendment in 1977, this House did entertain an appeal of a similar character to this which they dismissed; but the point of jurisdiction was never taken in the argument before this House and, in so far as the House did entertain the appeal, it must be regarded as having been entertained per incuriam. Their Lordships thus have no jurisdiction to grant leave in this case.

Petition dismissed.

Solicitors: *Kellner & Co*, Stratford (for the applicant); *Treasury Solicitor*.

Mary Rose Plummer   Barrister.

Joseph Rowntree Memorial Trust Housing Association Ltd and others v Attorney General

CHANCERY DIVISION
PETER GIBSON J
18, 19, 20 OCTOBER 1982

Charity – Benefit to community – Aged persons – Sale of dwellings to aged persons – Charity proposing to enter into schemes to provide dwellings for aged persons most in need of accommodation – Dwellings to be granted on long leases in consideration of capital payment – Whether schemes charitable.

The first plaintiff was an incorporated charitable association and the second to ninth plaintiffs were the trustees of a charitable trust. The charities wished to build small self-contained dwellings for sale to elderly people on long leases in consideration of a capital payment. By their objects clauses the association and the trust were to provide, inter alia, housing for elderly persons in need of such accommodation. They proposed to sell the dwellings by five different schemes. Under the first scheme long leases of dwellings consisting of flats or group bungalows designed for the needs of the elderly and with a warden and alarm system were to be sold to persons of retirement age in need of such accommodation for 70% of the cost of the premises, the balance being provided by a housing association grant. On the tenant's death the lease could be assigned to the tenant's spouse, or a family member living with the tenant who was eligible under the objects of the trust or association to acquire the lease. Failing such assignment or if the lease was terminated because the tenant had become incapable of managing his or her own affairs the lease was to revert to the association or trust and the outgoing tenant, or his estate, was to receive 70% of the then market value of the property. The second scheme was the same except that flats, not bungalows, were to be leased to eligible tenants on payment of the total cost of the flats and assignment to a spouse was only permitted if that did not infringe the objects of the association or trust. The third scheme was the same as the second except that in addition a prospective tenant's means had to be modest. The fourth scheme was identical to the first save that additional services such as a warden and an alarm system would not be provided. The fifth scheme was similar to the first except that additional services were omitted as with the fourth scheme, assignment could be made to any person over the age of 65, the tenant was to pay the full cost of the dwelling and the lease could only be determined by forfeiture. The Charity Commissioners doubted whether the schemes were in law charitable. They raised four objections, namely that the schemes operated by way of contractual bargain rather than by way of bounty, the benefits could not be withdrawn once provided, the schemes benefited private individuals rather than a charitable class, and the schemes were a commercial enterprise capable of producing a profit for the beneficiary. Before implementing any of the schemes the association and the trustees sought the determination by the court of the question whether all or any of the schemes were charitable in law.

Held – The implementing by the trust or the association of any of the five proposed schemes was charitable because such schemes were for the relief of the aged, notwithstanding that they operated by way of bargain rather than by way of bounty, the benefits could not be withdrawn once provided even if the beneficiary subsequently ceased to qualify, and even though it was possible for the beneficiary to make a profit on his or her capital contribution. Furthermore, the schemes were for the benefit of a charitable class and not for specific individuals. The trust and the association were therefore entitled to a declaration that all five schemes were charitable (see p 299 *d* to *j* and p 300 *a* to *c* and *e* to p 301 *a*, post).

Notes
For gifts for the relief of the aged, impotent and poor, see 5 Halsbury's Laws (4th edn) paras 514–521, and for cases on the subject, see 8(1) Digest (Reissue) 242–256, *20–111*.

Cases referred to in judgment
Abbey, Malvern Wells Ltd v Minister of Town and Country Planning [1951] 2 All ER 154, [1951] Ch 728, 45 Digest (Repl) 374, *189*.
Adams (decd), Re, Gee v Barnet Group Hospital Management Committee [1967] 3 All ER 285, [1968] Ch 80, [1967] 3 WLR 1088, CA, 8(1) Digest (Reissue) 357, *874*.
Bradbury, Re, Needham v Reekie [1950] 2 All ER 1150, 8(1) Digest (Reissue) 245, *43*.
Cottam's Will Trusts, Re, Midland Bank Exor Co v Huddersfield Corp [1955] 3 All ER 704, [1955] 1 WLR 1299, 8(1) Digest (Reissue) 244, *42*.
Estlin, Re, Prichard v Thomas (1903) 72 LJ Ch 687, 8(1) Digest (Reissue) 253, *97*.
Glyn's Will Trusts, Re, Public Trustee v A-G [1950] 2 All ER 1150n, 66 TLR (Pt 2) 512, 8(1) Digest (Reissue) 255, *106*.
Income Tax Special Purposes Comrs v Pemsel [1891] AC 531, [1891–4] All ER Rep 28, HL, 8(1) Digest (Reissue) 236, *1*.
IRC v Society for the Relief of Widows and Orphans of Medical Men (1926) 136 LT 60, 28(1) Digest (Reissue) 475, *1702*.
Le Cras v Perpetual Trustee Co Ltd, re Resch's Will Trusts [1967] 3 All ER 915, [1969] 1 AC 514, [1968] 3 WLR 1153, PC, 8(1) Digest (Reissue) 240, *10*.
Lewis (decd), Re, Public Trustee v Allen [1954] 3 All ER 257, [1955] Ch 104, [1954] 3 WLR 610, 8(1) Digest (Reissue) 245, *46*.
Lucas, Re, Rhys v A-G [1922] 2 Ch 52, [1922] All ER Rep 317, 8(1) Digest (Reissue) 245, *47*.

Monk, Re, Giffen v Wedd [1927] 2 Ch 197, [1927] All ER Rep 157, CA, 8(1) Digest (Reissue) 252, 79.

Neal, Re, Barclays Bank Ltd v Neal (1966) 110 SJ 549, 8(1) Digest (Reissue) 245, 48.

Robinson, Re, Davis v Robinson [1950] 2 All ER 1148, [1951] Ch 198, 8(1) Digest (Reissue) 244, 41.

Sanders' Will Trust, Re, Public Trustee v McLaren [1954] 1 All ER 667, [1954] Ch 265, [1954] 2 WLR 487, 8(1) Digest (Reissue) 247, 60.

Summons

By an amended originating summons dated 27 November 1981 the first plaintiff, Joseph Rowntree Memorial Trust Housing Association Ltd, and the second to ninth plaintiffs, Peter Maurice Barclay, Sir Donald James Barron, Charles Frederick Carter, Christopher John Rowntree, Frederick Seebohm, William Kaye Sessions, Herbert Cedric Shaw and Erica Frances Vere, who were the trustees of the Joseph Rowntree Memorial Housing Trust, applied for the determination, inter alia, of the question whether the plaintiffs might carry out any, and if so which, of five proposed schemes for the sale of dwellings to aged persons. The Attorney General was the defendant to the summons. The facts are set out in the judgment.

E G Nugee QC and *Charles Turnbull* for the plaintiffs.
C H McCall for the Attorney General.

Cur adv vult

20 October. The following judgment was delivered.

PETER GIBSON J. I have before me an originating summons raising questions as to the ability of two charities to enter into five schemes for the provision of housing for the aged. The first charity is the first plaintiff, the Joseph Rowntree Memorial Trust Housing Association Ltd (the association), a society registered on 11 November 1981 under the Industrial and Provident Societies Act 1965. The second charity is the Joseph Rowntree Memorial Housing Trust (the trust) of which the second to ninth plaintiffs are the present trustees. There is an overlap between those who run the two charities, seven of the trustees of the trust being members of the association.

This application is made because the Charity Commissioners have expressed the view that the schemes would not be charitable in law. Nevertheless, very properly, the commissioners have authorised the trustees of the trust to bring these proceedings and I have been told that the commissioners have been most helpful throughout. The only other party to these proceedings, the defendant, is Her Majesty's Attorney General. Counsel for the Attorney General has felt unable to support the reasoning of the commissioners for the views that they have expressed relating to the schemes and for the most part he has supported the plaintiffs, save for one qualification in relation to the trust implementing the third scheme and save for the fifth scheme. Nevertheless the matter has been presented to me fully and entirely fairly, as one might expect, by counsel for the plaintiffs and counsel for the Attorney General and I have all the material necessary, I think, on which to adjudicate on the matters put to the court.

I should say at the outset that the schemes in question have not yet been embarked on, still less implemented, so that to that extent the questions raised are future questions. The questions however are not hypothetical but relate to schemes which the plaintiffs would like to implement but which the commissioners are currently taking the view cannot properly be implemented by the plaintiffs. In the circumstances I accept the submission made by both counsel that it is proper for the court to answer the questions raised. It would be deplorable if the charities had to embark on schemes conscious that they were taking a risk of committing breaches of trust before the court could give any guidance on these matters.

Both charities bear in their title the name Joseph Rowntree, the Quaker philanthropist and cocoa manufacturer. He was the founder of a charitable trust from which the trust is derived by a deed dated 13 December 1904. In that deed he recited his desire both to alleviate the evils which arise from the insanitary and insufficient housing accommodation available for large numbers of the working classes and to secure to workers and persons of limited means in cities and towns some of the advantages of outdoor village life. The original object was expressed to be the improvement of the conditions of the working classes, defined to include persons having small incomes derived from invested capital, pensions or other sources in Great Britain and Ireland, by the provision of improved dwellings with open spaces and, where possible, gardens to be enjoyed therewith and the organisation of village communities with such facilities for the enjoyment of full and healthy lives as the trustees should consider desirable. It was expressly contemplated that houses might be let to the working classes as defined at a rent without placing them in the position of being recipients of a bounty. The trustees were given the widest powers to do any lawful acts which in their opinion should be conducive to carrying into effect the specified objects, including (subject to the consent of the Charity Commissioners) the power to sell, dispose of or let for any term of years any land subject to the trusts thereof on such terms and for such consideration as the trustees should think fit. Joseph Rowntree gave to that trust the name 'The Joseph Rowntree Village Trust'. That name was changed by private Act, the Joseph Rowntree Memorial Trust Act 1959, to 'The Joseph Rowntree Memorial Trust' and the objects of the trust were widened. It is unnecessary to rehearse the changes made to the objects as it is not those trusts which currently control the trust. The trustees' powers under the 1904 deed were retained but enlarged in certain respects.

The trust with which I am concerned and of which the second to ninth plaintiffs are the trustees was hived off from the original trust by a scheme made on 22 December 1967 by the Charity Commissioners and thereby it became a separate charity. The trustees were required to administer and manage the separate charity and its property in accordance with the 1904 deed, the 1959 Act and the scheme, but solely for objects set out (so far as material) as follows:

'The objects of the said separate charity shall be as follow so far only as concerned with the provision of houses for persons the majority of whom belong to the lower income group and other purposes incidental thereto and so far as in law charitable that is to say—(a) To provide, develop, construct and manage housing estates, houses or other residential accommodation or similar facilities for and for the families and dependants of persons who by reason of poverty, youth, age, infirmity or disablement are in need of such facilities or of care, attention, assistance or supervision and to provide or assist in the provision of educational facilities for, and for the dependants of, any such persons . . .'

I need not read para (b) of the objects clause. The trustees therefore of the trust, in so far as they would wish to provide housing for the aged, are subject to two limitations by that clause: (1) the majority of persons for whom they provide houses must belong to the lower income group; and (2) the persons for whom they provide housing must be by reason of poverty, youth, age, infirmity or disablement in need of such facilities or of care, attention, assistance or supervision.

The association's objects are—

'to carry on for the benefit of the community the business of (a) providing housing and any associated amenities for elderly persons in necessitous circumstances upon terms appropriate to their means; (b) providing for aged persons in need thereof housing and any associated amenities specially designed or adapted to meet the disabilities and requirements of such persons'

provided that the association shall not carry on or undertake any activity which is not in law charitable. Thus para (a) is limited to poor and elderly persons whereas para (b) is expressed in more general terms relating to the needs of the elderly. The rules of the association prohibit it from trading for profit and from paying or transferring any portion of its income or property to its members. Both the trust and the association have exclusively charitable objects.

I must now say something of the background to this application. Whilst almshouse charities have existed for centuries, housing associations had their origin about the middle of the last century. They were then concerned with improving conditions under which the poor lived in London and other cities, though rents were charged for accommodation which they provided as in the case of the Joseph Rowntree Trust. Local authority housing came after the voluntary housing movement commenced and never removed the need for the movement to continue its work. Housing associations have been given statutory recognition and financial encouragement by successive governments. The Housing Corp was set up under the Housing Act 1964 to foster the growth of cost-rent and co-ownership housing societies, and under the Housing Finance Act 1972 the Housing Corp's powers were extended to enable it to lend money to housing associations. Under the Housing Act 1974 the corporation's borrowing powers were substantially increased and it was required to set up a register of housing associations. Housing associations became eligible under that Act for a housing association grant. This is a single grant given at the commencement of a housing project to provide accommodation for letting. The amount of a grant is calculated by deducting from the total estimated cost of the project the amount that it is estimated can be serviced by the net income from the housing comprised in the project. The importance of housing association grants to housing associations can be seen from the fact that the National Federation of Housing Associations (the NFHA) gave a figure in 1979 of about 85% as a percentage of cost covered by such grants. The Housing Act 1980 expressly authorised housing association grants to be made available where a housing association lets accommodation at a premium calculated by reference to a percentage of the value of the dwelling or of the cost of providing it.

Housing associations have taken on themselves the task of catering for special housing needs not otherwise met and they are proud of their role as innovators in this field. It has been recognised that the elderly do have special housing needs and that it is desirable to have housing specially designed for the elderly. I cannot do better than read from a letter from the Charity Commissioners dated 2 August 1982 to the plaintiffs' solicitors, which sets out the current position:

'The problem of the elderly is a growing one in modern society. Longevity increases and the more traditional forms of family life and protection and care are no longer, for one reason or other, fashionable. But if elderly people by being helped to obtain suitable accommodation with an element of community or shared services or protection through the services of a warden can defer the time when they may fall on to State services or need a greater degree of shelter, such as a hospital or a geriatric ward, then this is in the long term to the benefit of the community as well as to the benefit of the individuals concerned.'

There is then a clear public benefit in the provision of such housing.

A particular need has emerged in relation to elderly owner-occupiers of dwellings. In 1978 there were some 2·1 million elderly owner-occupiers, a figure certain to rise as life expectancy increases. Such persons do not qualify at all or only with low priority for special housing for the elderly provided by local authorities, because such persons are considered to be adequately housed already or to have too much capital in comparison with other poorer applicants. There is evidence before me that the private sector has not yet adequately responded to the need for special housing for the elderly to be made available in the open market. Many elderly owner-occupiers while anxious to move from their present accommodation, which is often in excess of their needs, do not have adequate capital to invest in accommodation in the open market. Earlier schemes by housing associations were based on tenants purchasing loan stock which gave tenants no share in the equity of the premises which they occupied and hence no protection in an inflationary period for the money so invested. A need has been perceived for housing associations to provide special accommodation designed for the elderly in a form which allows interests in the property to be granted for a purchase price. The NFHA since the Housing Act 1980 has devised a standard scheme called 'the leasehold scheme for the elderly'. In addition to giving guidance on the selection of suitable sites (for example that they should be close to amenities) and on design requirements, the NFHA bases its scheme on a long-term lease for 60 years as the best means of safeguarding the interests of the landlords and the tenant and utilising the housing association grant. The NFHA handbook makes clear that the lease is intended to be a lease for life. The grant would contribute 30% of the estimated cost and the remaining 70% would be provided by the tenant. The lease would not be assignable, save to a surviving spouse or a relative or friend in each case living at the property at the tenant's death. Except when duly assigned, the lease reverts to the housing association when the tenant surrenders his lease or dies, or becomes a patient under the jurisdiction of the Court of Protection, or cannot manage his affairs, but the outgoing tenant or his estate is entitled to a capital sum equal to 70% of the then value of the property. The housing association's functions consist of finding and developing the property, setting up the arrangements and selecting the tenants, and then managing the property.

The association and the trustees of the trust want, if their respective constitutions permit them to do so, to build small self-contained dwellings for sale to elderly people on long leases in consideration of a capital payment. They have in mind five types of scheme, each of which is a variation in greater or lesser degree of the NFHA scheme.

The key factors of scheme 1 are set out in an affidavit of Sir Donald Barron, the third plaintiff, and follow closely the NFHA scheme. The site would be in an area where there is a considerable demand for special housing for persons who fulfil the following criteria, and I quote from Sir Donald Barron's affidavit:

'An applicant will not be offered a lease unless the following conditions are satisfied, namely that the applicant has attained the age of 65, if male, or the age of 60, if female, is able to pay the service charge under the lease, is able to lead an independent life, and is in need of the accommodation. An applicant will be considered to be in need of the accommodation if (i) the special features thereof will help to relieve him from some physical or psychological disability or infirmity and (ii) it is impossible or difficult for the applicant to find other accommodation or provide himself with facilities which would so relieve him to the same or substantially the same extent and (iii) his means are modest, that is to say are such that if permitted to participate in the Scheme his remaining financial resources (whether in terms of capital or income) may be expected not substantially, if at all, to exceed the amount required for the reasonable needs of himself and any dependant of his. Leases will be offered to those applicants considered to be in the most need of the accommodation.'

The dwellings would consist of flats or group bungalows and would be specifically designed to meet the disabilities and requirements of the elderly, and would conform with design and contract criteria laid down by the Housing Corp for sheltered accommodation, that is to say accommodation for the less active elderly with the provision of warden accommodation and a warden's office and an emergency alarm system, and probably a special laundry room. The tenant would pay a premium of 70% of the cost of the premises, the remaining 30% being met by the grant. The lease would contain provisions against the tenant parting with possession of the property and against assignment except to the tenant's spouse if living at the premises at the tenant's death, or a member of the tenant's family or household residing with the tenant at the tenant's death, provided that the grant of a lease to the latter person or persons would not infringe the objects of the landlords. It is thus expressly contemplated that there could be an assignment to the spouse of a tenant whether or not the grant of a lease to such a person would infringe the landlords' objects. The explanation for the inclusion of this provision is to be found in the Housing Act 1980. That Act allows certain tenancies not to be subject either to the provisions relating to secure tenancies giving tenants security of tenure beyond the contractual terms of the tenancy, or to the Leasehold Reform Act 1967, if certain conditions are satisfied. The most material condition is that laid down in s 140(4)(*b*) of the 1980 Act, that is to say that at the time when the lease is granted it complies with the requirements and regulations made by the Secretary of State for the purposes of the section. Unfortunately the regulations in question, which labour under the title of the Housing (Exclusion of Shared Ownership Tenancies from the Leasehold Reform Act 1967) Regulations 1982, SI 1982/62, state that the lease must be one which so far as material provides for an absolute covenant by the tenant against assignment of the property except to the tenant's spouse if residing at the property at the date of the tenant's death, and a provision similar to that which the plaintiffs propose to insert relating to members of the tenant's family and household. The risk, inherent in not complying with those regulations, of the tenancy being a secure tenancy and subject to the Leasehold Reform Act 1967 is one which the plaintiffs very naturally wish to avoid. Sir Donald Barron states that the omission of a restriction that the spouse of the tenant should qualify for the grant of a new lease is not in practice likely to be of much significance, since in the case of an applicant with a spouse both the existence of, and the circumstances of, the spouse would be taken into account in determining whether the proposed tenant was in need of the accommodation, and it is unlikely that a spouse to whom the lease is assigned would not at the date of assignment qualify for the grant of a new lease. I need not refer to any other special features of scheme 1.

Scheme 2 is the same as scheme 1 save that the housing would consist solely of flats and so would not be liable to the Leasehold Reform Act 1967. The scheme would not be subsidised by a housing association grant, and the tenant would therefore be required to pay a premium equal to 100% of the cost, and the right to assign to a spouse would be subject to a proviso that the grant to the spouse should not infringe the objects of the landlords. Thus the tenancy would probably be a secure tenancy. If the spouse was not a suitable assignee he or she would lose the right under the secure tenancy to remain in occupation if alternative accommodation were provided, and there is some evidence before me to indicate that local authorities in these circumstances would co-operate in providing such alternative accommodation.

Scheme 3 is identical with scheme 2 save that it would not be a condition of eligibility for a prospective tenant that his or her means were modest.

Scheme 4 is the same as scheme 1 except that the dwellings would be flats. There would be no warden's accommodation or office, no emergency alarm system or laundry room. This is because the premises would be let only to those elderly persons who are more active and so not in need of such special services. There would be provision for the payment of a rent where there is a non-eligible person in occupation of the premises, such rent to be 30% of the open market rental.

Scheme 5 is the same as scheme 1 save that the dwellings would be flats. There would again be no warden's accommodation or office, emergency alarm or laundry room, again because the premises would be let to the more active elderly. The covenant against assignment would be modified to permit assignment to a person over the age of 65 and there would be no option for the tenant to surrender the lease and no right for the landlords to determine it other than in the event of forfeiture. Also there would be no housing association grant, the tenant paying the full market value.

The views of the Charity Commissioners on schemes such as these were set out in para 102 to 108 of the Charity Commissioners' report for 1980 (HC Paper (1979–80) no 608). Paragraphs 104 and 105 are in the following form:

> '104. We had every sympathy with the motives behind the proposals and recognised that they were socially desirable and contained an element of benevolence. But were such schemes charitable in law? As the law stands, it is a charitable purpose to provide housing under the control of charity trustees for a charitable class of beneficiaries, usually either the poor, or the aged-poor, or the aged who are in need

of care and attention because of the disabilities of old age. It is the function of the charity trustees to appoint qualified beneficiaries, and it is inherent in the trusts that they must always have the power to remove beneficiaries for good reason. The beneficiaries receive the benefit provided by the charity by way of bounty; they have no right to it. But the provision of housing is not in itself a charitable purpose. Under these proposed schemes the housing associations would not be providing accommodation for a beneficiary class but parting with a legal interest in the property to a private individual. And the legal interest retained by the housing association would be administered not for the benefit of a charitable class but for the benefit of private individuals. In our view the provision of houses or flats on a contractual basis on the lines proposed could not be charitable. There are, of course, many instances where the beneficiaries of a charity contribute towards the cost of the benefits they receive, for example, in the case of almshouse residents, the payment of weekly contributions towards the maintenance of the almshouses, but in our view such payments are far removed from the type of payments made by lessees under the contractual arrangements of these schemes. The fact that on the surrender of a lease the lessee, or his estate, would receive 70% of the current value of the lease, which might well show a profit, seemed to us to underline the commercial aspect of the schemes.

105. A further objection stemmed from the fact that it is the relief, rather than the benefit, of the aged which is charitable. The need which has to be relieved is continuous and the charitable element disappears if that need disappears or the means of relieving it cease to be effective. Further, it would not be charitable to benefit an aged person beyond the point at which it was necessary to relieve his need. It seemed to us that to provide an aged person with a home for life, whatever his needs or circumstances, would be going too far. And if, for example, a lessee had to be moved permanently to a hospital geriatric ward, or somewhere similar, the continuance of the lease would provide no relief whatsoever. In our view there is a fundamental difference between the provision of a house or flat on a contractual basis and the provision of accommodation by way of bounty for so long as it may be required to relieve the beneficiary class.'

I hope I summarise the objections of the Charity Commissioners fairly as being the following: (1) the schemes provide for the aged only by way of bargain on a contractual basis rather than by way of bounty; (2) the benefits provided are not capable of being withdrawn at any time if the beneficiary subsequently ceases to qualify; (3) the schemes are for the benefit of private individuals, not for a charitable class; (4) the schemes are a commercial enterprise capable of producing profit for the beneficiary.

Before I deal with these objections it is appropriate to consider the scope of the charitable purpose which the plaintiffs claim the scheme carries out, that is to say in the words of the preamble to the Statute of Elizabeth (43 Eliz 1 c 4, the Charitable Uses Act 1601) 'the relief of aged persons'. That purpose is indeed part of the very first set of charitable purposes contained in the preamble: 'the relief of aged, impotent and poor people.' Looking at those words without going to authority and attempting to give them their natural meaning, I would have thought that two inferences therefrom were tolerably clear. First, the words 'aged, impotent and poor' must be read disjunctively. It would be as absurd to require that the aged must be impotent or poor as it would be to require the impotent to be aged or poor, or the poor to be aged or impotent. There will no doubt be many cases where the objects of charity prove to have two or more of the three qualities at the same time. Second, essential to the charitable purpose is that it should relieve aged, impotent and poor people. The word 'relief' implies that the persons in question have a need attributable to their condition as aged, impotent or poor persons which requires alleviating, and which those persons could not alleviate, or would find difficulty in alleviating, themselves from their own resources. The word 'relief' is not synonymous with 'benefit'.

Those inferences are in substance what both counsel submit are the true principles governing the charitable purpose of the relief of aged persons. Counsel for the plaintiffs stresses that any benefit provided must be related to the needs of the aged. Thus a gift of money to the aged millionaires of Mayfair would not relieve a need of theirs as aged persons. Counsel for the Attorney General similarly emphasises that to relieve a need of the aged attributable to their age would be charitable only if the means employed are appropriate to the need. He also points out that an element of public benefit must be found if the purpose is to be charitable. I turn then to authority to see if there is anything that compels a different conclusion.

In *Re Lucas, Rhys v A-G* [1922] 2 Ch 52 at 55, [1922] All ER Rep 317 at 318 Russell J was concerned with a bequest to the oldest respectable inhabitants of Gunville of the amount of 5s per week each. He held that the amount of the gift implied poverty. But he said:

> '. . . I am not satisfied that the requirement of old age would of itself be sufficient to constitute the gift a good charitable bequest, although there are several dicta to that effect in the books. I can find no case, and none has been cited to me, where the decision has been based upon age and nothing but age.'

In *Re Glyn's Will Trusts, Public Trustee v A-G* [1950] 2 All ER 1150n, 66 TLR (Pt 2) 510 Danckwerts J was faced with a bequest for building cottages for old women of the working classes of the age of 60 years or upwards. He said (66 TLR (Pt 2) 510 at 511):

> 'I have not the slightest doubt that this is a good charitable bequest. The preamble to the Statute of Elizabeth refers to the relief of aged, impotent and poor people. The words "aged, impotent and poor" should be read disjunctively. It has never been suggested that poor people must also be aged to be objects of charity, and there is no reason for holding that aged people must also be poor to come within the meaning of the preamble to the Statute. A trust for the relief of aged persons would be charitable unless it was qualified in some way which would clearly render it not charitable.'

He then went on to say that there was a sufficient context to show that the testatrix intended to benefit indigent persons.

In *Re Sanders's Will Trusts, Public Trustee v McLaren* [1954] 1 All ER 667 at 670, [1954] Ch 265 at 272 Harman J said that the ratio decidendi of *Re Glyn's Will Trusts* was that 'out of "old age" and "working class" you might argue that poverty was a necessary qualification'. But I share the views of the learned editor of *Tudor on the Law of Charities* (6th edn, 1967) p 61 that that is not what Danckwerts J said.

In *Re Bradbury, Needham v Reekie* [1950] 2 All ER 1150 Vaisey J followed *Re Glyn's Will Trust* in holding that a bequest to pay sums for the maintenance of an aged person in a nursing home was charitable.

In *Re Robinson, Davis v Robinson* [1950] 2 All ER 1148, [1951] Ch 198 a testator made a gift to the old people over 65 of a specified district to be given as his trustees thought best. Vaisey J held that the words 'aged, impotent and poor' in the preamble should be read disjunctively. He said it was sufficient that a gift should be to the aged, and commented on his decision in *Re Bradbury* that the aged person in a nursing home might be a person not at all in need of any sort of pecuniary assistance.

In *Re Cottam's Will Trusts, Midland Bank Exor Co v Huddersfield Corp* [1955] 3 All ER 704, [1955] 1 WLR 1299 a gift to provide flats for persons over 65 to be let at economic rents was said by Danckwerts J to be a trust for the benefit of aged persons and therefore prima facie charitable, though he went on to find it was a trust for the aged of small means.

In *Re Lewis (decd), Public Trustee v Allen* [1954] 3 All ER 257, [1955] Ch 106 there was a gift to ten blind girls, Tottenham residents if possible, of £100 each, and a similar gift to ten blind boys. Roxburgh J held that the words 'aged, impotent and poor' in the preamble must be read disjunctively and that the trust was therefore charitable.

In *Re Neal, Barclays Bank Ltd v Neal* (1966) 110 SJ 549 a testator provided a gift for the founding of a home for old persons. Further directions provided for fees to be charged a sufficient to maintain the home with sufficient staff to run it and cover the costs of the trustees. Goff J, in a very briefly reported judgment, said that in order to conclude whether a trust was charitable or not it was not necessary to find in it an element of relief against poverty, but it was sufficient to find an intention to relieve aged persons. The form of the gift and the directions were a provision for succouring and supplying such needs of old persons as they had because they were old persons. Therefore he held it was a charitable bequest.

b In *Re Adams (decd), Gee v Barnet Group Hospital Management Committee* [1967] 3 All ER 285 at 290, [1968] Ch 80 at 93, Danckwerts LJ again referred to the necessity of construing disjunctively the words 'impotent and poor' in the preamble. By parity of reasoning he must be taken to have been of the view that 'aged, impotent and poor' should be read disjunctively, too.

Lastly, in *Le Cras v Perpetual Trustee Co Ltd, re Resch's Will Trusts* [1967] 3 All ER 915,
c [1969] 1 AC 514 the Privy Council had to consider a gift of income to be applied for the general purposes of a named private hospital. The hospital charged substantial fees but was not run for the profit of individuals. Lord Wilberforce, delivering the judgment of the Board, referred to an objection that had been raised that the private hospital was not carried on for purposes beneficial to the community because it provided only for persons of means, capable of paying the fees required as a condition of admission. He said ([1967]
d 3 All ER 915 at 922, [1969] 1 AC 514 at 542).

'In dealing with this objection, it is necessary first to dispose of a misapprehension. It is not a condition of the validity of a trust for the relief of the sick that it should be limited to the poor sick. Whether one regards the charitable character of trusts for the relief of the sick as flowing from the word "impotent" ("aged, impotent and poor people") in the preamble to 43 Eliz. c. 4 or more broadly as derived from the
e conception of benefit to the community, there is no warrant for adding to the condition of sickness that of poverty. As early as *Income Tax Special Purposes Comrs. v. Pemsel* ([1891] AC 531 at 571, [1891–4] All ER Rep 28 at 49) LORD HERSCHELL was able to say: "I am unable to agree with the view that the sense in which 'charities' and 'charitable purpose' are popularly used is so restricted as this. I certainly cannot think that they are limited to the relief of wants occasioned by lack of pecuniary
f means. Many examples may, I think, be given of endowments for the relief of human necessities, which would be as generally termed charities as hospitals or almshouses, where, nevertheless, the necessities to be relieved do not result from poverty in its limited sense of the lack of money."'

He returned to the question of public benefit and need ([1967] 3 All ER 915 at 923,
g [1967] 1 AC 514 at 544):

'To provide, in response to public need, medical treatment otherwise inaccessible but in its nature expensive, without any profit motive, might well be charitable: on the other hand to limit admission to a nursing home to the rich would not be so. The test is essentially one of public benefit, and indirect as well as direct benefit
h enters into the account. In the present case, the element of public benefit is strongly present. It is not disputed that a need exists to provide accommodation and medical treatment in conditions of greater privacy and relaxation than would be possible in a general hospital and as a supplement to the facilities of a general hospital. This is what the private hospital does and it does so at, approximately, cost price. The service is needed by all, not only by the well-to-do. So far as its nature permits it is
j open to all: the charges are not low, but the evidence shows that it cannot be said that the poor are excluded . . .'

These authorities convincingly confirm the correctness of the proposition that the relief of the aged does not have to be relief for the aged poor. In other words the phrase 'aged, impotent and poor people' in the preamble must be read disjunctively. The decisions in *Re Glyn's Will Trusts, Re Bradbury, Re Robinson, Re Cottam's Will Trusts* and *Re*

Lewis give support to the view that it is a sufficient charitable purpose to benefit the aged, or the impotent, without more. But these are all decisions at first instance and with great respect to the judges who decided them they appear to me to pay no regard to the word 'relief'. I have no hesitation in preferring the approach adopted in *Re Neal* and *Le Cras v Perpetual Trustee Co Ltd* that there must be a need which is to be relieved by the charitable gift, such need being attributable to the aged or impotent condition of the person to be benefited. My attention was drawn to Picarda *The Law and Practice Relating to Charities* (1977) p 79, where a similar approach is adopted by the learned author.

In any event in the present case, as I have indicated, the plaintiffs do not submit that the proposed schemes are charitable simply because they are for the benefit of the aged. The plaintiffs have identified a particular need for special housing to be provided for the elderly in the ways proposed and it seems to me that on any view of the matter that is a charitable purpose, unless the fundamental objections of the charity commissioners to which I have referred are correct. To these I now turn.

The first objection is, as I have stated, that the scheme makes provision for the aged on a contractual basis as a bargain rather than by way of bounty. This objection is sometimes expressed in the form that relief is charitable only where it is given by way of bounty and not by way of bargain (see 5 Halsbury's Laws (4th edn) para 516). But as the learned editors recognise this does not mean that a gift cannot be charitable if it provides for the beneficiaries to contribute to the cost of the benefits they receive. There are numerous cases where beneficiaries only receive benefits from a charity by way of bargain. *Re Cottam* and *Le Cras v Perpetual Trustee Co Ltd* provide examples. Another class of cases relates to fee-paying schools (see for example *The Abbey, Malvern Wells Ltd v Minister of Town and Country Planning* [1951] 2 All ER 154, [1951] Ch 728). Another example relates to a gift for the provision of homes of rest for lady teachers at a rent (*Re Estlin, Prichard v Thomas* (1903) 72 LJ Ch 687). It is of course crucial in all these cases that the services provided by the gift are not provided for the private profit of the individuals providing the services.

The source of the statement that charity must be provided by way of bounty and not bargain is to be found in some remarks of Rowlatt J in *IRC v Society for the Relief of Widows and Orphans of Medical Men* (1926) 136 LT 60 at 65. This was a case relating to the statutory provisions allowing tax relief for income applicable to charitable purposes only of trusts or bodies established for charitable purposes only. Rowlatt J said:

> 'It seems to me that when it is said that the relief of poverty is a charity within the meaning of the rule which we are discussing that does mean the relief of poverty by way of bounty; it does not mean the relief of poverty by way of bargain. A purely mutual society among very poor people whose dependants would quite clearly always be very poor would not, I think, be a charity: it would be a business arrangement, as has been said in one of the cases, whereby contractual benefits accrued to people whose poverty makes them very much in need of them. That would not be a charity. I think, therefore, that the crux of this case is whether this is a case of that sort.'

He went on to hold that the case before him was not that of a mutual society: the beneficiaries had no right to anything.

In my judgment Rowlatt J's remarks must be understood in their limited context. They are entirely appropriate in determining whether a mutual society conferring rights on members is charitable. If a housing association were a co-operative under which the persons requiring the dwellings provided by the housing association had by that association's constitution contractual rights to the dwellings, that would no doubt not be charitable, but that is quite different from bodies set up like the trust and the association. The applicants for dwellings under the schemes which I am considering would have no right to any dwelling when they apply. The fact that the benefit given to them is in the form of a contract is immaterial to the charitable purpose in making the benefit available. I see nothing in this objection of the charity commissioners.

The second objection was that the schemes do not satisfy the requirement that the
a benefits they provide must be capable of being withdrawn at any time if the beneficiary
ceases to qualify. No doubt charities will, so far as practical and compatible with the
identified need which they seek to alleviate, try to secure that their housing stock
becomes available if the circumstances of the persons occupying the premises change.
But it does not seem to me to be an essential part of the charitable purpose to secure that
this should always be so. The nature of some benefits may be such that it will endure for
b some time, if benefits in that form are required to meet the particular need that has been
identified. Thus, in *Re Monk, Giffen v Wedd* [1927] 2 Ch 197, [1927] All ER Rep 157 a
testatrix set up a loan fund whereby loans for up to nine years were to be made available
to the poor. This was held to be charitable. No doubt the circumstances of the borrower
might change whilst the loan was outstanding. If the grant of a long-term leasehold
interest with the concomitant security of tenure that such an interest would give to the
c elderly is necessary to meet the identified needs of the elderly, then in my judgment that
is no objection to such a grant. The plaintiffs have put in evidence that they oppose the
inclusion in a lease of any provision entitling the plaintiffs to determine the lease in the
event of a change in financial circumstances of the tenant. Their main reason, which to
my mind is a cogent one, is the unsettling effect it could have on aged tenants. In any
event the distinction between what prima facie is a short-term letting and a long lease
d has been rendered somewhat illusory by statute. A charity may find it no less difficult to
recover possession from weekly tenants whose circumstances have changed than it would
to recover possession from a tenant under a long lease.

The third objection was that the schemes were for the benefit of private individuals
and not for a charitable class. I cannot accept that. The schemes are for the benefit of a
charitable class, that is to say the aged having certain needs requiring relief therefrom.
e The fact that, once the association and the trust have selected individuals to benefit from
the housing, those individuals are identified private individuals does not seem to me to
make the purpose in providing the housing a non-charitable one any more than a trust
for the relief of poverty ceases to be a charitable purpose when individual poor recipients
of bounty are selected.

The fourth objection was that the schemes were a commercial enterprise capable of
f producting a profit for the beneficiary. I have already discussed the cases which show
that the charging of an economic consideration for a charitable service that is provided
does not make the purpose in providing the service non-charitable, provided of course
that no profits accrue to the provider of the service. It is true that a tenant under the
schemes may recover more than he or she has put in, but that is at most incidental to the
charitable purpose. It is not a primary objective. The profit (if it be right to call the
g increased value of the equity a profit as distinct from a mere increase avoiding the effects
of inflation, as was intended) is not a profit at the expense of the charity, and indeed it
might be thought improper, if there be a profit, that it should accrue to the charity
which has provided no capital and not to the tenant which has provided most if not all
the capital. Again, I cannot see that this objection defeats the charitable character of the
schemes.
h I turn then to a consideration of the schemes themselves.

Subject only to one possible point scheme 1 seems to me to be plainly charitable as
designed to meet the special housing needs of the elderly. The one point is the somewhat
theoretical possibility that the lease may be assigned to a spouse who would not qualify
himself or herself for a new tenancy. Counsel for the Attorney General has not sought to
contend that this possibility removes the scheme from the realm of charity, and I agree
j with him and counsel for the plaintiffs that this incidental disadvantage is heavily
outweighed by the advantage to the plaintiffs of ensuring that the tenancies are not
secure tenancies or subject to the Leasehold Reform Act 1967.

Scheme 2 is, for similar reasons, a charitable scheme. The fact that it is not dependent
on a housing association grant seems to me to be immaterial to the charitable character
of the scheme. Further, the possibility that a spouse who would not qualify for the grant

to him or her of a new lease might remain in occupation under a secure tenancy and not
be found alternative accommodation is, again, merely an incidental effect and, I would *a*
add, an effect of statute, and in my judgment is not sufficient to make the scheme non-
charitable.

In respect to scheme 3 counsel for the Attorney General accepted, in my view rightly,
that the scheme was charitable, notwithstanding that the tenant's means did not have to
be modest. The other conditions of eligibility were, as I have stated, such as to ensure
that the applicant tenant is unable to meet his special needs by himself, but counsel for *b*
the Attorney General suggested that it would be inappropriate for the court to make a
declaration that the trustees of the trust were able to enter into this scheme because of
the trust's particular objects requiring it to provide housing for persons the majority of
whom belonged to the low income group. I agree that any declaration should be framed
such as to make clear that I have not made any decision in relation to the specific objects
of the trust or of the association. I shall return to the form of declaration shortly.   *c*

Scheme 4 providing as it does for rent to be payable by a non-qualified tenant seems to
me to be a fortiori a scheme to which no objection can be raised on charitable grounds.

I come lastly to scheme 5. Counsel for the Attorney General acknowledges that it
cannot be said that there could never be circumstances in which it would be appropriate
for the plaintiffs to enter into such a scheme, but he says that because of its manifest
disadvantages I should not declare that the plaintiffs can enter into such a scheme. To *d*
grant a lease for 60 years to a person aged at least 60 if female or 65 if male was, as he
rightly points out, to grant a lease likely to last well beyond the needs of the tenant.
There is a disadvantage to the tenant in not being able to surrender the lease and
disadvantages to the plaintiffs in not being able to have any say in selecting the assignee
of the tenant. Such assignee must be over 65 but may be a person who would not qualify
for the grant of a new lease. It is also a disadvantage to the plaintiffs not to be able to *e*
determine the lease save for forfeiture. On the other hand it does give greater security to
the tenant. Provided that a need to provide special housing with that advantage to the
elderly is identified, and ex hypothesi the original tenants will be in such need, I cannot
say that this scheme is not charitable. However, as a practical matter I would doubt if the
plaintiffs would find this scheme as attractive to carry out as the other schemes, because
of the disadvantages I have mentioned, and no doubt the association and the trustees of *f*
the trust will anxiously consider whether such a scheme provides the best means to carry
out its objects.

Implicit in the views which I have expressed are the answers to the specific matters
raised in the order authorising the trustees of the trust to bring these proceedings, but I
shall spell them out. In my judgment the trustees may provide accommodation in the
form of small self-contained dwellings for aged persons in need of such accommodation *g*
by granting it to them in consideration of the payment to the trustees of the whole or a
substantial part of the cost or market value of such dwellings in accordance with the
schemes. The presence or absence of the following provisions is not essential to the
charitable nature of the scheme, that is to say: (1) the housing association grant
contribution; (2) the provision of warden services, provided that the accommodation is
designed to meet the special needs of the elderly tenants; (3) the prohibition of any *h*
assignment except on the death of the tenant to his spouse or qualified member of the
family or household; (4) the right of the landlords to determine the lease on the death of
the tenant or on the tenant becoming incapable of managing his or her own affairs; (5)
the right of the tenant to surrender the lease.

Counsel for the plaintiffs has recognised that any declaration I make must not be taken
to authorise the association or the trustees of the trust to enter into any of the five schemes *j*
without regard to the specific objects of the association and the trust respectively, and the
discretions vested in them respectively.

Subject to the observations of counsel I would propose to grant a declaration in this
limited form, that is to say that it is in law charitable for the first plaintiff to carry out
each of the five schemes described in the affidavit affirmed in support hereof by Sir
Donald Barron on 29 September 1982 (the fourth and fifth schemes being limited to the

a provision of flats as dwellings) and to grant a like declaration in relation to the second to ninth plaintiffs.

Declaration accordingly.

Solicitors: *Asshetons* (for the plaintiffs); *Treasury Solicitor*.

b
Azza M Abdallah   Barrister.

c Scandinavian Trading Tanker Co AB v Flota Petrolera Ecuatoriana
The Scaptrade

COURT OF APPEAL, CIVIL DIVISION

d SIR JOHN DONALDSON MR, MAY AND ROBERT GOFF LJJ

16, 26 NOVEMBER 1982

Estoppel – Promissory estoppel – Reliance on conduct – Conduct required to be unequivocal – Previous acceptance by owner of ship of late payments by charterer of hire – Whether owner estopped from withdrawing ship for non-payment pursuant to contractual right.

e *Shipping – Charterparty – Time charter – Withdrawal – Default in payment of hire – Right of withdrawal exercised – Previous late payments accepted – Whether owner estopped from exercising contractual right to withdraw vessel.*

Shipping – Charterparty – Time charter – Withdrawal – Relief against forfeiture – Default in
f *payment of hire – Right of withdrawal exercised – Whether court having jurisdiction to grant relief against forfeiture.*

By a time charterparty dated 11 May 1977 in the Shelltime 3 form the owners chartered a vessel to the charterers for one year. The charter was renewed at the end of that period for a further two years. Payments of hire under the charter were to be made monthly in
g advance on the eighth day of each month. Clause 8 of the charter provided that if the charterers defaulted in paying the monthly hire instalment by the due date the owners could withdraw the vessel from hire. On some months, especially when the due date was a Saturday or a Sunday, payments were accepted up to three days late. The charterers failed to pay the instalment due on Sunday, 8 July 1979. On Thursday, 12 July, the instalment being still unpaid, the owners sent a telex to the charterers withdrawing the
h vessel. On 24 July the parties agreed that the vessel should continue in the service of the charterers while the question whether the owners were entitled to withdraw the vessel was litigated. It was further agreed that if the court found in favour of the owners the charterers would pay, from the date of recharter, hire at the increased market rate rather than the original contract rate. The owners sought and were granted a declaration that they were entitled to withdraw the vessel for non-payment of hire. The charterers appealed, contending (i) that the owners were prevented by equitable estoppel from relying on their strict legal right to withdraw the vessel for non-payment by the due date because of their previous acceptance of late payments and (ii) that the court had jurisdiction to extend, in appropriate cases, the equitable remedy of relief against forfeiture in order to relieve charterers from the consequences of withdrawal for non-payment of hire, and further that it in the circumstances it would be proper to grant them such discretionary relief.

Held – The appeal would be dismissed for the following reasons—

(1) In order successfully to raise a defence of equitable estoppel the charterers had to *a* establish, first, that the owners had represented unequivocally, or had acted in such a way that a reasonable man would infer that they had so represented, that they would not enforce their strict legal right under the contract between the parties to withdraw the vessel from the charterers' service in the event of a default in payment of a hire instalment by the due date and, second, that having regard to the dealings which had taken place between the parties it was inequitable to allow the owners to enforce their strict legal *b* right without having previously given the charterers notice that the right to withdraw the vessel for non-payment would be relied on in the future. On the facts, the owners could not be taken by their words or conduct to have made any such representation and in any event it was not inequitable to permit reliance on the clause since the owner's conduct had not in any way influenced the charterers' decision to fail to pay the relevant hire instalment on time (see p 304 *g* to p 305 *a* and *j* to p 306 *d*, post); *Hughes v* *c* *Metropolitan Rly Co* [1874–80] All ER Rep 187, *Woodhouse AC Israel Cocoa Ltd SA v Nigerian Marketing Co Ltd* [1972] 2 All ER 271 and *Bremer Handelsgesellschaft mbH v Vanden Avenne-Izegem PVBA* [1978] 2 Lloyd's Rep 109 applied.

(2) The court had no jurisdiction to apply the equitable remedy of relief against forfeiture to relieve a time charterer from the consequences of withdrawal of the chartered vessel by the owner following non-payment of hire instalments. The equitable *d* relief had no application to such commercial transactions when the parties had dealt with each other at arm's length and had been of equal bargaining strength. In charterparty transactions the need for certainty was of paramount importance and the existence of a jurisdiction to grant relief against forfeiture, however sparingly exercised, would be antipathetic to that primary consideration (see p 308 *b c* and *f* to p 309 *b* and *e* to *g*, post); dicta of Lord Simon in *Mardorf Peach & Co Ltd v Attica Sea Carriers Corp of Liberia, The* *e* *Laconia* [1977] 1 All ER 545 and of Lloyd J in *Afovos Shipping Co AS v R Pagnan & Flli, The Afovos* [1980] 2 Lloyd's Rep at 476–480 doubted.

Notes

For promissory estoppel, see 16 Halsbury's Laws (4th edn) para 1514, and for cases on the subject, see 21 Digest (Reissue) 8–16, 52–74.   *f*

For relief against forfeiture, see 16 Halsbury's Laws (4th edn) paras 1447–1451, and for cases on the subject, see 20 Digest (Reissue) 898–899, 6695–6703.

Cases referred to in judgment

Afovos Shipping Co AS v Pagnan, The Afovos [1982] 3 All ER 18, [1982] 1 WLR 848, CA; rvsg [1980] 2 Lloyd's Rep 469.   *g*

A/S Awilco v Fulvia SpA di Navigazione, The Chikuma [1981] 1 All ER 652, [1981] 1 WLR 314, HL.

Bremer Handelsgesellschaft mbH v Vanden Avenne-Izegem PVBA [1978] 2 Lloyd's Rep 109, HL.

China National Foreign Trade Transportation Corp v Evlogia Shipping Co SA of Panama, The Mihalios Xilas [1979] 2 All ER 1044, [1979] 1 WLR 1018, HL; rvsg [1979] 1 All ER *h* 657, [1978] 1 WLR 1257, CA, Digest (Cont Vol E) 549, 549e.

Hill v Barclay, (1811) 18 Ves 56, [1803–13] All ER Rep 379, 34 ER 238, 20 Digest (Reissue) 899, 6702.

Hughes v Metropolitan Rly Co (1877) 2 App Cas 439, [1874–80] All ER Rep 187, HL, 21 Digest (Reissue) 10, 55.

Mardorf Peach & Co Ltd v Attica Sea Carriers Corp of Liberia, The Laconia [1977] 1 All ER *j* 545, [1977] AC 850, [1977] 2 WLR 286, HL; rvsg [1976] 2 All ER 249, [1976] QB 835, [1976] 2 WLR 668, CA, Digest (Cont Vol E) 547, 539d..

Shiloh Spinners Ltd v Harding [1973] 1 All ER 90, [1973] AC 691, [1973] 2 WLR 28, HL, 31(2) Digest (Reissue) 794, 6574.

Stockloser v Johnson [1954] 1 All ER 630, [1954] 1 QB 476, [1954] 2 WLR 439, CA, 20 Digest (Reissue) 897, 6693.

Woodhouse AC Israel Cocoa Ltd SA v Nigerian Marketing Co Ltd [1972] 2 All ER 271, [1972]
AC 741, [1972] 2 WLR 1090, HL, 21 Digest (Reissue) 8, 52.

Cases also cited
Bird v Hildage [1947] 2 All ER 7, [1948] 1 KB 91, CA.
Maclaine v Gatty [1921] 1 AC 376, [1920] All ER Rep 70, HL.
National Carriers Ltd v Panalpina (Northern) Ltd [1981] 1 All ER 161, [1981] AC 675, HL.
Panoutsos v Raymond Hadley Corp of New York [1917] 2 KB 473, [1916–17] All ER Rep
448, CA.
Surrey Shipping Co Ltd v Campagnie Continental (France) SA, The Shackleford [1978] 1 WLR
1080, CA; *affg* [1978] 1 Lloyd's Rep 191.
Tankexpress (A/S) v Compagnie Financiere Belge des Petroles SA [1948] 2 All ER 939, [1949]
AC 76, HL.
Tradax Export SA v Dorada Compania Naviera SA, The Luterian [1982] 2 Lloyd's Rep 140.
Tyrer & Co v Hessler & Co (1902) 86 LT 697, CA.

Appeal
By notice of appeal dated 17 July 1981 the defendants, Flota Petrolera Ecuatoriana (the
charterers), appealed against the decision of Lloyd J given on 3 July 1981 whereby the
judge held that the plaintiffs were entitled to withdraw the vessel Scaptrade on 12 July
1979 from service under a charterparty dated 11 May 1977 made between the plaintiffs,
Scandinavian Trading Tanker Co AB (the owners), and the charterers and gave judgment
for the plaintiff in the sum of $1,375,761, being the balance plus interest between the
previous charterparty rate of $4·30 per ton and the current market rate of $8·50 per ton
agreed under a recharter of the vessel dated 24 July 1979. The facts are set out in the
judgment of the court.

Johan Steyn QC, P H Gross and *A G Bompas* for the charterers.
Kenneth Rokison QC and *Timothy Saloman* for the owners.

Cur adv vult

26 November. The following judgment of the court was delivered.

ROBERT GOFF LJ. There is before the court an appeal from a judgment of Lloyd J
under which he made a declaration that the respondents, Scandinavian Trading Tanker
Co AB, were entitled to withdraw a vessel named the Scaptrade from the service of the
appellants, Flota Petrolera Ecuatoriana, and also made certain consequential orders. We
shall in this judgment refer to the respondents as 'the owners', and to the appellants as
'the charterers'; and we shall refer to the Scaptrade as 'the vessel'.
    The matter arises as follows. The owners, who are a Swedish oil trading company,
chartered the vessel (as disponent owners) to the charterers, who are a state trading
corporation set up by the government of Ecuador. The charter, which was dated 11 May
1977, was a time charter in the Shelltime 3 form. The charter period was originally 12
months 30 days more or less in charterers' option; hire was payable monthly in advance
at the rate of $4·65 per ton of the vessel's deadweight per calendar month. By an
addendum dated 14 June 1978 the period of the charter was extended for a further 24
months, the rate of hire being $4·10 for the first 12 months and $4·30 for the second 12
months of the extended period, this second part of the extension being subject to the
approval of the charterers (and of certain head charterers) of the vessel's performance.
    The clause of the charter which dealt with the payment of hire was cl 8 of the printed
form. After making provision for the time and manner of payment, and allowing for
certain deductions to be made from the hire, the clause provided as follows: 'In default
of such payment Owners may withdraw the vessel from the service of the Charterers,
without prejudice to any claim Owners may otherwise have on Charterers under this
charter.' Since the vessel was delivered under the charter on 8 July 1977 it followed that

the monthly hire payments had to be paid on or before the eighth day of each month. We are concerned in this case primarily with the hire payment which fell due in July *a* 1979. The 8 July 1979 was in fact a Sunday. The charterers failed to pay the July hire instalment when due. We shall have to consider later in this judgment the circumstances in which this omission occurred. By that time the market had risen steeply, the market rate being almost double the charter rate. At 1546 hrs on Thursday, 12 July, the owners sent a telex to the sole brokers, Odin Marine Inc, withdrawing the vessel; that telex was passed on to the charterers at 1557 hrs on the same day. At that time the charterers had *b* paid no part of the relevant hire instalment to the owners.

Thereafter, on 24 July 1979, the parties entered into a without prejudice agreement under which the vessel resumed her service under the charter, the rate of hire being dependent on the answer to the question whether the owners were entitled to withdraw the vessel from the charterers' service. If they were so entitled, the difference between the old charter rate and the market rate payable under the without prejudice agreement *c* for the balance of the charter period has been estimated to be $1,200,000.

Before the judge four points were taken by the charterers. First, they submitted that, by leaving it until Tuesday, 12 July, before they purported to withdraw the vessel, the owners either failed to comply with an implied term of the charter that the right of withdrawal could only be exercised by them forthwith or promptly on the happening of any default in payment or within the shortest time reasonably necessary to enable the *d* owners to hear of the default and to give instructions or alternatively the owners must be taken to have elected to affirm the contract and so have lost their right of withdrawal. This submission was rejected by the judge, who held that there was no such implied term as alleged, and that no sufficient lapse of time had occurred from which it could be inferred that the owners had elected to affirm the contract. On this point there is no appeal. Second, the charterers submitted that, by reason of the owners having received *e* late payments of hire in the past without complaint, they could not exercise their right of withdrawal in July 1979 without prior notice to the charterers of their intention so to do. This submission the judge also rejected, on the basis that there had been no unequivocal representation by the owners, express or implied, that they would not insist on punctual payment. The charterers now appeal on this point. Third, the charterers asked for relief against forfeiture. The judge held that, assuming that he had jurisdiction *f* to grant such relief, he would not do so, primarily because the delay in payment was entirely the fault of the charterers. On this point also the charterers now appeal. The fourth point raised a question of construction of the without prejudice agreement. As to that, there is no appeal, and so we need not deal with it.

We turn therefore to the first of the two grounds of appeal, which relates to the effect of the owners having, before July 1979, accepted late payments of hire from the *g* charterers. There was no dispute that, in this connection, the applicable principle was that of equitable estoppel. There was also no dispute that, in order to bring themselves within that principle, the charterers had to establish that two criteria had been fulfilled. First, they had to establish that the owners had represented unequivocally that they would not enforce their strict legal right, under the contract between the parties, to withdraw the vessel from the charterers' service in the event of a default in payment of *h* an instalment of hire (see *Woodhouse AC Israel Cocoa Ltd SA v Nigerian Marketing Co Ltd* [1972] 2 All ER 271, [1972] AC 741). Second, they had to establish that in the circumstances it would be inequitable to allow the owners to enforce their strict legal right, having regard to the dealings which had taken place between the parties (see *Hughes v Metropolitan Rly Co* (1877) 2 App Cas 439 at 448, [1874–80] All ER Rep 187 at 191 per Lord Cairns LC). The first requirement may however be fulfilled if a reasonable man in *j* the shoes of the charterers would have inferred from the owners' conduct that they were making such a representation (see *Bremer Handelsgesellschaft mbH v Vanden Avenne-Izegem PVBA* [1978] 2 Lloyd's Rep 109 at 126 per Lord Salmon). As to the second requirement, since the equitable estoppel is founded on a representation, it can only be unconscionable for the representor (here the owners) to enforce his strict legal right if the conduct of the representee (here the charterers) has been so influenced by the representation as to call for the intervention of equity. Whether or not the representee's conduct has been so influenced must depend on the evidence; but the court is entitled to infer from the evidence that his conduct has been so influenced.

With these principles in mind, we turn to the question whether the owners did unequivocally represent that they would not exercise their strict legal right to withdraw the vessel from the charterers' service in the event of a default in payment of an instalment of hire. On this point we were provided (as was the judge) with a most helpful schedule setting out what had occurred in relation to the 24 instalments of hire paid before July 1979. From this it appears that several instalments were in fact paid late and were accepted without protest; but there was no consistent pattern. Taking (as the judge did) the date of receipt by the owners' bank of the telex transfers as being the date of payment, and ignoring both the first payment (which is often, as here, late, usually for administrative reasons) and the first payment at the commencement of the second year of the charter (the subject of a special agreement), the position was, as the judge found, that (1) six payments were made on time, (2) eight payments were one day late, (3) two payments were two days late and (4) six payments were three days late.

Now it is not at all easy to infer, from the mere fact that late payments had been accepted in the past by the owners without protest, an unequivocal representation by them not to exercise their strict legal right of withdrawal in the event of late payment by the charterers of a subsequent instalment of hire, if only because the circumstances prevailing at the time when the earlier late payments were accepted may not be the same as those prevailing in the future. Of course, if for example the charterers chose regularly to use a particular route for payment which involved the consequence that payments were always received by the owners, say, two days late, and the owners knowingly acquiesced in this course of conduct, the court might be able (depending on the circumstances) to infer a sufficient representation from the owners' conduct; but such a case is very far from the present. Even so, counsel for the charterers drew our attention to certain surrounding circumstances in the present case which, he submitted, should in conjunction with the acceptance by the owners of the late payments without protest entitle the court to infer the necessary representation. First, until the owners withdrew the ship, the charter was, as he put it, 'humming along'. The charterers were satisfied with the ship, indeed her performance was better than that warranted in the charter; and the owners regarded the charterers as first class charterers. Second, the owners were aware of the fact that payments had been made late. Third, at no time did the owners protest about late payments, or threaten withdrawal; this inaction had to be contrasted with vigilance on the part of the owners in enforcing their rights in other respects, for example, in complaining that hire statements contained insufficient particulars or were not supported by sufficient vouchers, or in pressing a claim in respect of the vessel's over-performance. Fourth, on at least one occasion the owners claimed interest in respect of the late payment of hire; and this conduct, submitted counsel for the charterers, was calculated to fortify an impression that the owners would not in future enforce their strict right of withdrawal. In our judgment, however, even taking all those factors into account, it is not possible to infer from the owners' conduct a sufficient representation to give rise to an equitable estoppel. In particular, the claim to interest on one occasion (which on the evidence was little more than a suggestion to the sole broker) indicates that the owners were recognising that, in the past, the charterers had been in breach and were suggesting that breaches of that kind called for compensation in the form of interest; such conduct involved no representation that they would not exercise their right of withdrawal in future. In truth, although the totality of the evidence may provide some explanation why the charterers, and especially the sole broker, were surprised when the owners decided to exercise their right of withdrawal when they did, it falls far short of an unequivocal representation by the owners that they would not exercise that right. On this point we find ourselves in agreement with the judge.

It is however also plain to us on the evidence that, in any event, the owners' conduct did not in any way influence the charterers' conduct in failing to pay the relevant hire instalment on time. In his judgment the judge stated that 'there was scant evidence of any reliance by the charterers'. We would go further, for, having been shown the relevant evidence, we are satisfied that the charterers' conduct in making the late payment in July 1979 was in no way influenced by the conduct of the owners. This is not even a case where the charterers were lulled into a state of false security by the owners' conduct, or where the owners' conduct, although not the sole cause, could be said to have contributed to the charterers' omission to pay in time. On the contrary, as appears from the evidence, the gentleman in the charterers' organisation immediately responsible for making the hire payment, a Mr Denoso, did not make the payment in time because he was instructed by his superior, Captain Fernandez, to hold his hand until it had become clearer whether the charter would continue for another year. As for Captain Fernandez, he suffered from the erroneous belief that, under this form of charter, the owners were not entitled to withdraw the vessel until after the expiry of ten days after giving notice to the charterers of their intention to do so, in other words that the charter contained an anti-technicality clause. In these circumstances, there can have been no causal connection at all between the owners' conduct and the charterers' omission to pay the July 1979 instalment of hire in time.

It follows that the charterers' appeal on this ground must fail.

We turn then to the second ground of appeal, which relates to relief against forfeiture. Now the question whether there is any equitable jurisdiction to intervene and relieve time charterers from the consequences of withdrawal for non-payment of hire has not, so far as we are aware, been the subject of any decision by the courts. The judge himself sought, as counsel, to raise the point in argument before the House of Lords in *Mardorf Peach & Co Ltd v Attica Sea Carriers Corp of Liberia, The Laconia* [1977] 1 All ER 545, [1977] AC 850. Their Lordships declined to permit him to do so, the point not having been argued below; but some of their Lordships nevertheless expressed tentative views on the subject without having had the benefit of argument. Lord Wilberforce was very dubious about extending the equitable doctrine of relief against forfeiture, applied in the past in the case of leases, to the very different context of a commercial contract such as a time charter (see [1977] 1 All ER 545 at 550, [1977] AC 850 at 869–870); Lord Salmon, Lord Fraser and Lord Russell all expressed opinions inimical to the grant of relief in such a case (see [1977] 1 All ER 545 at 557, 561–562, 565, [1977] AC 850 at 878, 883, 888). Lord Simon on the other hand was more favourably disposed towards extending the jurisdiction to grant relief to such cases, though even he recognised that it could only be invoked on extremely rare occasions (see [1977] 1 All ER 545 at 553–554, [1977] AC 850 at 873–874). In the same case, in the Court of Appeal, Lord Denning MR had expressed the opinion, on reflection, that equity would not have intervened in a commercial case of this kind (see [1976] 2 All ER 249 at 255–256, [1976] QB 835 at 847); later however, in *Afovos Shipping Co AS v Pagnan, The Afovos* [1982] 3 All ER 18, [1982] 1 WLR 848 he appears to have changed his mind on this point, though he was dissuaded by his brethren from dealing with the matter in his judgment. In *China National Foreign Trade Transportation Corp v Evlogia Shipping Co SA of Panama, The Mihalios Xilas* [1979] 1 All ER 657 at 672, [1978] 1 WLR 1257 at 1290 Geoffrey Lane LJ, in a dissenting judgment later upheld by the House of Lords, expressed in forceful terms the opinion that this 'was not an occasion on which the court should exercise a benevolent paternalism to mitigate the plainly expressed rigours of the agreement'. But the fullest discussion of the point is to be found in the judgment of Lloyd J himself in *The Afovos* [1980] 2 Lloyd's Rep 469 at 476–480 at first instance. He concluded that his own inclination would be 'to follow Lord Simon and to hold that there is a residual jurisdiction, in exceptional cases, to relieve against the effect of withdrawal clauses in time charter-parties'. However in that case, as in the present, he did not find it necessary to decide the point, because he held that he would not in any event have exercised the jurisdiction, if it existed, to grant relief. There were three reasons why he would not have been inclined to do so in *The Afovos*: (1) the charter provided its own machinery for relief in the form of an anti-technicality clause;

(2) the owner had not snatched at an opportunity to withdraw, but had gone further
a than they were bound in honour to go in pressing for payment before they withdrew;
and (3) the charterers were themselves to some extent to blame for what went wrong. In
the present case, the reason why the judge would not have been inclined to grant relief
(if he had the power to do so) was primarily the third of the reasons in *The Afovos*, viz
that the failure to pay the hire instalments on time arose from the charterers' own fault.

We have to confess that we feel some difficulty in approaching the matter in the same
b way as the judge, because, unless and until the nature and scope of the equitable
jurisdiction has been established in the present context, at least in broad terms, it may
not be possible to say whether or not the relevant criteria have been fulfilled in any
particular case. Our difficulty is perhaps best illustrated by the very matter relied on by
the judge in the present case (as before in *The Afovos*) as excluding relief, viz fault of the
charterers. We cannot help observe that default on the part of a tenant is not, unless
c wilful, likely to be of itself a bar to relief against forfeiture of a tenancy, either under the
old equitable jurisdiction as preserved by s 46 of the Supreme Court of Judicature
(Consolidation) Act 1925 (see *Hill v Barclay* (1811) 18 Ves 56 at 62–63, [1803–13] All ER
Rep 379 at 380 per Lord Eldon, *Shiloh Spinners Ltd v Harding* [1973] 1 All ER 90 at 102,
[1973] AC 691 at 723–4 per Lord Wilberforce) or under s 146 of the Law of Property Act
1925 (see *Woodfall on Landlord and Tenant* (28th edn) para 1-1940 and cases there cited).
d In any event, we have come to the conclusion (as indeed we were urged by counsel to do)
that the time has come when, in the interests of certainty, the courts must face up to the
question whether they have jurisdiction to grant relief in cases such as the present.

We proceed on the basis that the equitable jurisdiction which the charterers invoke
should not be regarded as rigidly confined to certain specific circumstances, or to be
incapable of development. Even so, we must have regard to the fact that, so far as is
e relevant to the present case, the principal areas in which courts of equity have been
prepared to grant relief in the past are (1) relief against the forfeiture of property, notably
in cases concerning mortgages and leases, and (2) relief against penalties. There has in
fact been a tendency in recent years (on which we do not feel called on to express any
opinion in the present case) to extend the latter form of relief in favour of a purchaser in
breach of a contract of sale where instalments of the purchase price already paid have
f been unconscionably retained by the vendor: see in particular *Stockloser v Johnson* [1954]
1 All ER 630 at 634ff, 637ff, [1954] 1 QB 476 at 483ff, 488ff per Somervell and Denning
LJJ; [1954] 1 All ER 630 at 640ff, [1954] 1 QB at 494ff) cf per Romer LJ. The equitable
relief may be available in the context of a transaction which can be described as
commercial, for example in the case of leases of commercial premises, and of penalties in
contracts which may be described as commercial (though foreign parties to English
g commercial contracts are sometimes startled to discover that this is so). However,
whatever may be the breadth of the application of these principles today, we need not be
surprised at the type of case in which equity has thought it right to intervene in the past.
No doubt at bottom the equitable jurisdiction 'rests upon the idea that it is not fair that a
person should use his legal rights to take advantage of another's misfortune, and still less
that he should scheme to get legal rights with this object in view': see *Holdsworth's History*
h *of English Law* vol 5 (3rd edn, 1945), p 330. However, the cases where equity has
intervened are cases where parties were frequently not at arm's length, and frequently
also where the relevant contract conferred an interest in land, the loss of which could
have serious personal consequences. Moreover, we doubt whether the term 'forfeiture' is
apt to describe the effect of a shipowner's act in withdrawing a ship from a time
charterer's service for non-payment of hire: see *The Laconia* [1977] 1 All ER 545 at 550,
j [1977] AC 850 at 869–870. It is trite law that, under a time charter, the ship remains in
the possession of the shipowner, who simply makes available to the time charterer the
services of his ship with master and crew over a period of time. In truth, in a case such as
the present, the charterers are asking the court to intervene to prevent the shipowners
from exercising their undoubted contractual right to determine a contract for services.
Of course, the question whether the court has any power so to intervene should not be

answered simply by inquiring whether the case is one to which the label 'forfeiture' can properly be applied. Even so, we cannot shut our eyes to the fact that we are being *a* invited to extend an equitable jurisdiction from areas in which its original application is easily explicable in historical and social terms to a very different area to which such considerations do not apply. The mere fact that its application in the case of leases has led to its being capable of application to some commercial transactions of the same kind provides, we consider, little or no justification for its extension to commercial contracts such as time charters. The question whether it should be so extended must be considered *b* on its merits, as a matter of policy, taking into account the relatively slight assistance available to us from the authorities, though the fact that the jurisdiction has never before been extended to purely commercial transactions must surely cause us to regard the extension, which we are now invited to make, with a considerable degree of caution.

Of course, it is well known that shipowners have on occasion snatched at opportunities to withdraw their ships for non-payment of hire, simply to take advantage of a rising *c* market; and that the exercise of such a right can lead to very substantial financial advantages being obtained by shipowners at the expense of time charterers, whose late payment of hire may have been the result of nothing more than error in their own offices or on the part of their bankers, leading to a delay in payment which may have been only of a very short duration. We can understand, even sympathise with, the expressed inclination of Lord Simon in *The Laconia*, and of Lloyd J in *The Afovos*, to hold that the *d* equitable jurisdiction should be extended to empower the court to grant relief in cases of this kind. Certainly the overt exercise of an equitable jurisdiction to grant relief on recognisable principles is, we think, a far more attractive proposition than the distortion of contractual terms by an over-benevolent construction or the illegitimate extension of the principles of election or equitable estoppel. When courts have in the past over-stretched established legal principles to achieve what they see to be justice in cases of this *e* kind, the House of Lords has expressed its disapproval in very clear terms: for the most recent example of this see the speech of Lord Bridge in *A/S Awilco v Fulvia SpA di Navigazione, The Chikuma* [1981] 1 All ER 652 at 658–659, [1981] 1 WLR 314 at 321– 322. Such expressions of opinion have not been concerned directly with the question whether equitable relief against 'forfeiture' should be available in those cases; but the stress they place on the need for certainty in commercial transactions is a matter which *f* we must take into account in considering the question in the present case.

Indeed, when we come to consider the nature of a contract such as a time charter, and the circumstances in which it is likely to be made, we see the most formidable arguments against the proposed extension of the equitable jurisdiction. In the first place, a time charter is a commercial transaction in the sense that it is generally entered into for the purposes of trade, between commercial organisations acting at arm's length. It is for the *g* parties to bargain about the terms of the contract. They can bargain not only about the form of charter to be used; they can also bargain about any amendments to the standard form, and about the rate of hire to be paid having regard to the other terms of the contract agreed between them. Parties to such contracts should be capable of looking after themselves; at the very least, they are capable of taking advice, and the services of brokers are available, and are frequently used, when negotiating terms. The possibility *h* that shipowners may snatch at the opportunity to withdraw ships from the service of time charterers for non-payment of hire must be very well known in the world of shipping; it must also be very well known that anti-technicality clauses are available which are effective to prevent any such occurrence. If a prospective time charterer wishes to have any such clause included in the charter, he can bargain for it; if he finds it necessary or desirable to agree to a charter which contains no such clause, he can warn *j* the relevant section of his office, and his bank, of the importance of securing timeous payment.

But the matter does not stop there. It is of the utmost importance in commercial transactions that, if any particular event occurs which may affect the parties' respective rights under a commercial contract, they should know where they stand. The courts

should so far as possible desist from placing obstacles in the way of either party
ascertaining his legal position, if necessary with the aid of advice from a qualified lawyer,
because it may be commercially desirable for action to be taken without delay, action
which may be irrevocable and which may have far-reaching consequences. It is for this
reason, of course, that the English courts have time and again asserted the need for
certainty in commercial transaction, for the simple reason that the parties to such
transactions are entitled to know where they stand and to act accordingly. In particular,
when a shipowner becomes entitled, under the terms of his contract, to withdraw a ship
from the service of a time charterer, he may well wish to act swiftly and irrevocably.
True, his problem may, in any particular case, prove to be capable of solution by entering
into a without prejudice agreement with the original time charterer, under which the
rate of hire payable in future will be made to depend on a decision, by arbitrators or by a
court, whether he was in law entitled to determine the charter. But this is not always
possible. He may wish to refix his ship elsewhere as soon as possible, to take advantage of
a favourable market. It is no answer to this difficulty that the ship may have cargo aboard
at the time, so that her services cannot immediately be made available to another
charterer (cf *The Afovos* [1980] 2 Lloyd's Rep 469 at 479 per Lloyd J); for one thing, the
ship may not have cargo on board, and for another she can be refixed immediately under
a charter to commence at the end of her laden voyage. Nor is it an answer that the parties
can immediately apply to arbitrators, or to a court, for a decision, and that both maritime
arbitrators and the Commercial Court in this country are prepared to act very quickly at
very short notice. For, quite apart from the fact that some delay is inherent in any legal
process, if the question to be decided is whether the tribunal is to grant equitable relief,
investigation of the relevant circumstances, and the collection of evidence for that
purpose, cannot ordinarily be carried out in a very short period of time.

For these reasons, tempting though it may be to follow the path which Lloyd J was
inclined to follow in *The Afovos*, we do not feel that it would be right to do so. The policy
which favours certainty in commercial transactions is so antipathetic to the form of
equitable intervention invoked by the charterers in the present case that we do not think
it would be right to extend that jurisdiction to relieve time charterers from the
consequences of withdrawal. We consider that the mere existence of such a jurisdiction
would constitute an undesirable fetter on the exercise by parties of their contractual
rights under a commercial transaction of this kind. It is not enough to say that it will
only be exercised in rare cases, for the mere possibility that it may be exercised can
produce uncertainty, disputes and litigation, and so prevent parties from knowing where
they stand, particularly as the jurisdiction, if available, would be discretionary and there
may be doubt whether it could successfully be invoked in any particular case.

For these reasons we hold that we have no jurisdiction to grant equitable relief of the
kind asked for by the charterers in the present case, and it follows that the second ground
of appeal must also be dismissed.

Appeal dismissed. Leave to appeal to the House of Lords refused.

20 January. The Appeal Committee of the House of Lords granted the charterers leave to appeal.

Solicitors: *Ince & Co* (for the charterers); *Sinclair Roche & Temperley* (for the owners).

Diana Procter   Barrister.

Evans Construction Co Ltd v Charrington & Co Ltd and another

COURT OF APPEAL, CIVIL DIVISION

WALLER, DONALDSON AND GRIFFITHS LJJ

5, 7, 8, 21 JULY 1982

Practice – Parties – Correction of name of party after expiry of limitation period – Leave – Application for leave to substitute name of new party – Whether leave to correct name of party should be given – RSC Ord 20, r 5 – CCR Ord 15, r 3(2).

In 1970 the landlords, Charrington & Co Ltd (Charringtons), a London based company in the Bass Charrington group, granted the tenants a seven-year lease of business premises to which the Landlord and Tenant Act 1954 applied. During the term of the lease Charringtons assigned the reversion to Bass Holdings Ltd (Bass), which was another company in the same group and based at Burton-upon-Trent. Charringtons continued to manage the property but as agents for Bass. In 1977 the tenants were granted a new lease of the premises for a term of three years. The lease was called a supplemental lease since it contained the same covenants as the original lease in 1970. Bass were correctly named in it as the landlords. When it expired the tenants held over under the 1954 Act. In September 1980 Charringtons, as managing agents for Bass, sent a notice under s 25 of the 1954 Act notifying them that the tenancy would be terminated on 15 April 1981 and that they would oppose any application to the court under s 24 for a new tenancy. The tenants' solicitor informed Charringtons that they were not prepared to give up possession. On 19 January 1981 he applied, on their behalf, to the county court for the grant of a new tenancy. Charringtons rather than Bass were inadvertently named as the landlords in the application and in consequence the application was served on Charringtons rather than Bass. Charringtons notified the tenants that they proposed to apply to have the application struck out on the ground that they were not the landlords. By then the tenants were out of time to make a fresh application correctly naming Bass as the landlords. Accordingly, in April 1981 they sought leave to correct the name of the landlords by substituting the name of Bass for that of Charringtons. Since the application for amendment had been made out of time the county court had jurisdiction under CCR Ord 15, r 3(2)[a] to allow an amendment out of time if it would be allowed by the High Court. The question therefore arose whether the amendment should be allowed under RSC Ord 20, r 5[b]. The tenants contended that the amendment should be allowed because RSC Ord 20, r 5(3) provided for an amendment to be made to correct the name of a party if there had been a genuine mistake notwithstanding 'that the effect of the amendment will be to substitute a new party'. Charrington and Bass contended that the amendment should not be allowed because it involved more than the mere alteration of the initials of a party or the spelling of a name. The county court judge allowed the amendment to be made. Charringtons appealed.

Held (Waller LJ dissenting) – On the true construction of RSC Ord 20, r 5, the court's power to allow the name of a party to be corrected was not confined to be the correction of misspellings in the name of a party or the addition of words which had been omitted from the name but extended to permitting a plaintiff who had intended to sue one person but who had named another as the defendant to substitute the name of the one

---

a Rule 3(2) provides: 'Where an application for an amendment is made after any relevant period of limitation has expired since the issue of the originating process, the court may nevertheless allow the amendment if it is such as the High Court would have power to allow in a like case.'

b Rule 5, so far as material, is set out at p 315 g to j, post

for that of the other if (a) the plaintiff had made a genuine mistake, (b) the mistake was not misleading or such as to cause any reasonable doubt as to the identity of the person intended to be sued, and (c) it would be just to make the amendment. Since it was clear from the evidence that the tenant's solicitor had intended to make their current landlords the respondents to the application for the new tenancy and that he had made a genuine mistake in naming Charringtons instead of Bass, since neither Charringtons nor Bass could have been misled by the mistake or have had any real doubt as to the identity of the person intended to be sued, and since it would not cause any injustice if the correction were made, the county court judge has been right to give leave for the name of Bass to be substituted for that of Charringtons. The appeal would accordingly be dismissed (see p 317 f to j, p 318 b c, and p 319 e to j and p 320 a to h, post).

Re Nos 55 and 57 Holmes Road, Kentish Town, [1958] 2 All ER 311, Rodriguez v Parker [1966] 2 All ER 349 and Mitchell v Harris Engineering Co Ltd [1967] 2 All ER 682 considered.

Notes

For amendments to correct the name of a party, see 28 Halsbury's Laws (4th edn) para 635 and 36 ibid para 69, and for cases on amendment of pleadings, see 37(1) Digest (Reissue) 251–272, 1679–1781.

For the Landlord and Tenant Act 1954, ss 24, 25, see 18 Halsbury's Statutes (3rd edn) 557, 559.

As from 1 September 1982 CCR 1936 Ord 15, r 3 was replaced by CCR 1981 Ord 15, r 1.

Cases referred to in judgments

Baxendale (Robert) Ltd v Davstone (Holdings) Ltd [1982] 3 All ER 496, [1982] 1 WLR 1385, CA.

Davies v Elsby Bros Ltd [1960] 3 All ER 672, [1961] 1 WLR 170, CA, 32 Digest (Reissue) 725, 5257.

Holmes Road, Kentish Town, Re Nos 55 and 57, Beardmore Motors Ltd v Birch Bros (Properties) Ltd [1958] 2 All ER 311, [1959] Ch 298, [1958] 2 WLR 975, 31(2) Digest (Reissue) 953, 7755.

Jones v Jones [1970] 3 All ER 47, [1970] 2 QB 576, [1970] 3 WLR 20, CA, Digest (Cont Vol C) 1080, 331a.

Lewis v Wolking Properties Ltd [1978] 1 All ER 427, [1978] 1 WLR 403, CA, Digest (Cont Vol E) 122, 3808a.

Liff v Peasley [1980] 1 All ER 623, [1980] 1 WLR 781, CA.

Mitchell v Harris Engineering Co Ltd [1967] 2 All ER 682, [1967] 2 QB 703, [1967] 3 WLR 447, CA, 37(1) Digest (Reissue) 264, 1733.

Rodriguez v Parker [1966] 2 All ER 349, [1967] 1 QB 116, [1966] 3 WLR 546, 32 Digest (Reissue) 726, 5267.

Cases also cited

Braniff v Holland & Hannen and Cubitts (Southern) Ltd [1969] 3 All ER 959, [1969] 1 WLR 1533, CA.

Dawson (Bradford) Ltd v Dove [1971] 1 All ER 554, [1971] 1 QB 330.

Eburne (S W) v Toome Investments [1977] CLY 445.

Garner v Heath Park Engineering Co [1975] CLY 1872.

Kammins Ballrooms Co Ltd v Zenith Investments (Torquay) Ltd [1970] 2 All ER 871, [1971] AC 850, HL.

Lucy v W T Henleys Telegraph Works Co Ltd [1969] 3 All ER 456, [1970] 1 QB 393, CA.

Piper v Muggleton [1956] 2 All ER 249, [1956] 2 QB 569, CA.

Seabridge v H Cox & Sons (Plant Hire) Ltd [1968] 1 All ER 570, [1968] 2 QB 46, CA.

Appeal

Charrington & Co Ltd (Charringtons), the first respondents to an originating application made by Evans Construction Co Ltd (the lessees) for a new tenancy, appealed against an order of his Honour Judge Baker sitting in Staines County Court, dated 28 April 1982, whereby the lessees were given leave to join Bass Holdings Ltd as second respondents to the application. The facts are set out in the judgment of Waller LJ.

Richard Salter for Charringtons.
Michael F Harris for the lessees.
Bass Holdings Ltd were not represented.

Cur adv vult

21 July. The following judgments were delivered.

WALLER LJ. This is an appeal from a decision of his Honour Judge Baker, sitting at Staines County Court, on 28 April 1982, when he ordered Bass Holdings Ltd, to be joined as second respondent to an originating application made by Evans Construction Co Ltd for a new lease. The facts were that by a lease dated 27 August 1970, between Evans Construction Co Ltd, hereinafter called 'the lessees', and Charrington and Co Ltd, hereinafter called 'Charrington', the lessees became tenants of a piece of land adjoining the Links Hotel at Ashford for seven years terminating 24 June 1976. There was a large plan with the lease identifying the land in question. The lessees held over and on 1 April 1977 entered into a new lease for three years from 25 June 1976, supplemental to the original lease but between Bass Ltd of High Street, Burton-upon-Trent and the lessees, reciting that Bass is now entitled to the reversion but adopting all the conditions of the original lease where appropriate. Charringtons' Estate Department continued to receive the rent. The lessees held over at the termination of the lease.

On 30 September 1981, a notice under s 25, terminating the tenancy, was served on the lessees. The notice was in the standard form, it identified the parcel of land by reference to the original lease and went on—

'We Charrington and Co Ltd of Anchor House, Mile End, LONDON E1 as agents for Bass Holdings Ltd High Street, BURTON ON TRENT, Staffordshire landlord of the above-mentioned premises, hereby give you notice terminating your tenancy on fifteenth day of April, 1982.'

It required notification of whether or not the tenant was willing to give possession, to be given within two months, and went on, saying that an application to the court for a new tenancy would be opposed, setting out the grounds. It was signed at the bottom with an illegible signature giving the address: Estate Department, Charrington and Co Ltd, Anchor House, London E1.

The lessees' solicitors acknowledged receipt on 12 October 1981, and gave notice that their clients were not prepared to give up possession. On 19 January 1982, an originating application headed: 'BETWEEN EVANS CONSTRUCTION COMPANY LIMITED APPLICANT and CHARRINGTON & CO. LIMITED RESPONDENT' was made to Staines County Court for the grant of a new tenancy. The application set out the particulars of the current tenancy so far as is relevant as follows:

'(b) (*Date of lease*) 27th August 1970; (c) (*Names of parties to lease or agreement*) (1) Charrington & Co. Limited; 2. Evans Construction Company Limited; (d) (*Term granted by lease*) 3 Years (now holding over); (e) (*Rent reserved by lease*) £1,500 ... 5. The name and address of the respondent on whom this application is intended to be served are:—"CHARRINGTON & COMPANY LIMITED, ANCHOR HOUSE, MILE END, LONDON E1."'

On 10 March 1982, Charringtons gave notice of intending to apply to have the originating application struck out, and on 30 March 1982 the application was struck out. It was struck out on the grounds that Charringtons were not the landlords.

The lessees appealed to the county court judge applying for leave to join Bass Holdings Ltd as second respondents and the judge granted that application on 28 April but gave leave to appeal.

The argument before us has not been just to reverse the order of the judge because it
a was submitted by the appellants, Charringtons, that the application before the judge was
on the wrong basis and should have been made (as the original notice of appeal had in
fact made it) for the substitution of Bass Holdings Ltd as the respondents in place of
Charrington. Counsel on behalf of Charringtons accepts that this is the true issue and we
have given leave to the respondents, the lessees, to file evidence relevant to this issue.

By virtue of the provisions of CCR 1936 Ord 40, r 8(1) and (1A) and Ord 8, r 35(1) an
b originating application must be served within two months of issue. This application was
issued on 19 January 1982, and therefore had to be served before 19 March 1982. It was
in fact served on Charringtons within that time, namely 2 February. The application to
amend was not made until 2 April, or alternatively 24 April, and is therefore out of time.
Nevertheless RSC Ord 20, r 5(2) would allow such an amendment if it is just to do so.

An application to correct the name of a party must be made under RSC Ord 20, r 5(3).
c The lessees seek to substitute Bass Holdings Ltd for Charringtons, and they submit this is
the correction of a name. We have been referred to a number of cases where corrections
have been made under this rule but in every case it is plainly a variation of the name, for
example R S Parker for R J Parker (see *Rodriguez v Parker* [1966] 2 All ER 349, [1967] 1
QB 116), Harris Ltd for Harris (Leeds) Ltd (see *Mitchell v Harris Engineering Co Ltd* [1967]
2 All ER 682, [1967] 2 QB 703). We were informed that no case could be found without
d this feature.

In the present case there was no mistake as to name. Mr Greenwood, the lessees'
solicitor, in his affidavit frankly states he thought Charringtons were the landlords. The
mistake here was not a mistake as to name; it was a mistake as to identity. Counsel for
Charringtons submits that the words 'notwithstanding that it is alleged that the effect of
the amendment will be to substitute a new party' is to cover the case where the alteration
e is small, for example an initial, or Leeds after Harris. It was clear who was intended but
it was alleged that it was a new party. If it was intended that it should be a new party the
words 'it is alleged that' would be unnecessary. In my opinion the words 'correct the
name of a party' do not cover a case such as the present when there was no mistake as to
name but the mistake was to identity. The words 'correct the name' are not apt to cover
the case of changing the party.

f That this conclusion is correct is in my opinion strengthened by considering the
consequences of allowing a change such as that which is sought in this case. No provision
is made under RSC Ord 20, r 5 for reservice. The rules about service under CCR 1936
Ord 8, r 35, are no doubt similar to the principles about service under RSC Ord 6, r 8. It
was held in *Jones v Jones* [1970] 3 All ER 47, [1970] 2 QB 576 that RSC Ord 6, r 8, was not
to be read as meaning that if a writ had been served on one defendant within the
g limitation period it was valid for service on another after the limitation period. If
therefore the new party was a different party from the one already served, that is to say
not where there was a mere name error, it would be necessary in a case such as the present
to make application for an extension of time and then the strict process under CCR 1936
Ord 8, r 35(2) would have to be considered.

The absence of provisions for reservice under RSC Ord 20, r 5, is I suggest because a
h mistake in the ordinary case was not misleading and did not cause any reason to doubt
the identity of the person it was intended to sue (see the words of RSC Ord 20, r 5(3), for
example R S Parker for R J Parker or Harris Engineering Ltd for Harris Engineering
(Leeds) Ltd). In the present case the application was properly served on Charringtons at
their registered office address, London E1, as set out in the notice. If Bass were substituted,
the application would have been served on Bass at their registered office in Burton-upon-
j Trent, also as set out in the notice. But the rules require service within two months and
CCR 1936 Ord 8, r 35(2) provides that time shall not be extended within the currency of
the period; it is only in exceptional circumstances that this provision will be overridden
(see *Lewis v Wolking Properties Ltd* [1978] 1 All ER 427, [1978] 1 WLR 403 and the
decision of this court in *Robert Baxendale Ltd v Davstone (Holdings) Ltd* [1982] 3 All ER
496).

It is said on behalf of the lessees that this is a case where the mistake has been induced by a combination of circumstances in that the original landlords were Charringtons and when the ownership was changed Charringtons continued to act as the agents for all *a* purposes; furthermore that the s 25 notice was signed on behalf of Charringtons Estate Department. There is no evidence in this case that Charringtons and/or Bass Holdings had deliberately conducted their affairs in order to mislead. These cases where mistakes are made as between landlord and tenant always cause some hardship but two commercial companies are concerned and in the circumstances there are no good reasons for straining the meaning of the rules. Accordingly, although the course of the argument before us *b* has proceeded on rather different grounds from the argument before the judge, I would have allowed this appeal and reversed the order of the judge adding Bass Holdings Ltd as a second respondent and not substitute Bass Holdings Ltd for Charringtons.

If I had felt able to take a different view of RSC Ord 20, r 5(3), namely that this was a change of names and that it was just to allow the change to be made, I would have agreed that time should be extended as proposed by Donaldson LJ. If it is just to allow the *c* amendment it would also be just to extend the time.

DONALDSON LJ. In 1970 Evans Construction Co Ltd (the lessees) took a lease from Charrington & Co Ltd of a piece of land fronting Fairholme Road, Ashford, Surrey, and of various buildings on it for use in connection with their business. The lease dated 27 August 1970 was for seven years from 24 June 1969; and accordingly was due to expire *d* on 24 June 1976. However, the Landlord and Tenant Act 1954 applied and the lease was renewable in accordance with the terms of that Act.

Some time during the currency of the 1970 lease or shortly thereafter, Charringtons assigned the reversion to Bass Ltd, another company in the Bass Charrington group. Bass Ltd subsequently changed their name to Bass Holdings Ltd, but nothing turns on that. Formal notice may or may not have been given of this assignment, but Charringtons *e* continued to act in the same way as theretofor, albeit now as managing agents for the new landlords.

On 1 April 1977 (a not inappropriate date in the light of later events) the lessees entered into a new lease. The landlords were Bass Ltd and the lease recited that it was supplemental to the original lease dated 27 August 1970. It was for a term of three years from 25 June 1976, and so was continuous with the term of the original lease. The term of this lease *f* expired on 24 June 1979, but again the 1954 Act applied and the lessees held over.

On 30 September 1981 Charringtons wrote to the lessees as follows:

> 'Dear Sirs
> *Land adjoining the Links Hotel Ashford.*
> We enclose Notice under the provisions of the Landlord and Tenant Act 1954 and would be pleased if you could sign the copy and return it in acknowledgement of *g* safe receipt.'

The notice itself was in the standard form. After identifying the land, it continued:

> '1. We Charrington & Co Ltd of Anchor House, Mile End, LONDON E1 as agents for Bass Holdings Ltd of High Street, BURTON ON TRENT, Staffordshire landlord (*Note* 7) of the above-mentioned premises, hereby give you notice terminating your *h* tenancy on the fifteenth day of April, 1982 (*Note* 1). 2. .... 3. We would oppose an application to the court (*Note* 3) under Part II of the Act for the grant of a new tenancy on the ground (*Note* 4) that we intend to carry out substantial works of demolition and reconstruction to provide additional car parking facilities at the Links Public House. 4. This notice is given under the provisions of section 25 of the Landlord and Tenant Act 1954. Your attention is called to the Notes overleaf.' *i*

The form was signed by an individual whose name is illegible and underneath the signature there appeared in print: '(*Landlord*)', and below that was typewritten: 'ESTATE DEPARTMENT CHARRINGTON & CO LTD ANCHOR HOUSE LONDON, E1'.

The lessees' solicitors wrote to Charringtons on 12 October 1981, acknowledging

receipt of the s 25 notice and informing them that the lessees were not prepared to give
up possession.

Under s 24(1) of the 1954 Act, the tenants thereupon became entitled to apply to the
county court for a new tenancy and, in accordance with s 29(3), any such application had
to be made not less than two or more than four months after the serving of the landlord's
notice. Accordingly, the application had to be entered with the county court on or before
30 January 1982.

In the event the lessees' solicitors entered the application with the Staines County
Court on 19 January 1982, but unfortunately it contained a number of errors. It named
Charrington & Co Ltd as respondents, it gave the date of the lease as 27 August 1970 (the
date of the original lease) instead of 1 April 1977 (the date of the supplemental lease), and
it named Charrington & Co Ltd as the other party to the lease, which was true of the
original lease but not of the supplemental lease. In para 5 of the application the name
and address of the respondent on whom the application was intended to be served was
given as 'CHARRINGTON & COMPANY LIMITED ANCHOR HOUSE, MILE END, LONDON E. 1'.

On 10 March 1982 Charringtons applied to the deputy registrar of the Staines County
Court for the application to be struck out on the grounds that they were not the lessees'
landlord. This application was successful. The lessees gave notice of appeal on the grounds
that instead of striking out the application, the learned deputy registrar should have
substituted Bass Ltd for Charringtons as respondents. Later they gave notice of intention
to apply to the judge to join Bass Holdings Ltd as additional respondents.

The matter came before his Honour Judge Baker, who on 28 April 1982 gave the
lessees leave to join Bass Holdings Ltd as additional respondents, and to make amendments
to the originating application correcting the errors to which I have referred. Charrington
now appeal, seeking an order that the originating application be struck out. Bass Holdings
Ltd have not appeared.

Bearing in mind that it is common ground that the statutory form of notice to quit on
which this application was founded was one rightly given on behalf of Bass Holdings Ltd
who were the landlords, that Charringtons are not the landlords and have no interest in
the property and that there are issues to be decided between the lessees and Bass Holdings
Ltd but no such issue between the lessees and Charringtons, I can see no sense in joining
Bass Holdings Ltd as additional respondents. In my judgment, the only question is
whether it is possible and right to substitute the name 'Bass Holdings Ltd' for 'Charrington
& Company Ltd'. A simpler solution would be to make a new application naming Bass
Holdings Ltd as respondents, but this cannot be done as any such application would be
out of time under s 29(3) of the 1954 Act.

The only possible basis for so amending the name of the respondents is under RSC Ord
20, r 5. This, so far as material, provides as follows:

> '(1) Subject to Order 15, rules 6, 7 and 8 and the following provisions of this rule,
> the Court may at any stage of the proceedings allow the plaintiff to amend his writ,
> or any party to amend his pleading, on such terms as to costs or otherwise as may be
> just and in such manner (if any) as it may direct.
>
> (2) Where an application to the Court for leave to make the amendment
> mentioned in paragraph (3), (4) or (5) is made after any relevant period of limitation
> current at the date of issue of the writ has expired, the Court may nevertheless grant
> such leave in the circumstances mentioned in that paragraph if it thinks it just to do
> so.
>
> (3) An amendment to correct the name of a party may be allowed under
> paragraph (2) notwithstanding that it is alleged that the effect of the amendment
> will be to substitute a new party if the Court is satisfied that the mistake sought to
> be corrected was a genuine mistake and was not misleading or such as to cause any
> reasonable doubt as to the identity of the person intending to sue or, as the case may
> be, intended to be sued . . .'

The lessees submit that this is a case in which they should be allowed to correct the

name of a party incorrectly named by mistake. This proposition has only to be stated for
it to be apparent that there should be evidence before the court that there had been a
mistake, but there was no such evidence before the county court. However, leave was
given to file an affidavit setting out the circumstances in which the name of Charrington
& Co Ltd came to be used to identify the respondent to the application and Mr
Greenwood, the lessees' solicitor, has sworn an affidavit which was filed in the course of
the appeal. So far as material, it is in the following terms:

'2. On or shortly before the 12th October 1981, I was handed by my Legal
Executive, a Mr. Dolman, a Section 25 Notice and covering letter dated the 30th
September 1981 addressed to the Applicants herein. Mr. Evans, the Managing
Director of the Applicants had brought them to my office and instructed Mr.
Dolman to take all necessary steps to protect his Company's interests, leaving the
entire matter for me to deal with. 3. I looked at the documents and concluded that
my Clients' landlord was Charrington & Company Limited. I appreciate now of
course that that was not a conclusion I should have reached. I have since wondered
how I managed to make that mistake. If Section 25 Notices are given by Agents
(and in my experience that is not at all un-common) that fact is invariably made
clear at the foot of the Section 25 Notice where there is provision for the Landlords'
signature. No such indication is given in this Notice. Secondly if Section 25 Notices
are given by Agents they will usually be given by Solicitors or Estate Agents. So far
as I know Charringtons are Brewers. I think I must have been influenced by those
factors. 4. That I did make this mistake is perfectly clear from a letter I wrote to the
Clients on the 12th October 1981 (a copy of which is now shown to me and marked
"K.G.1") and which I now produce, in which I describe Charringtons as "your
landlords". 5. I needed the lease to complete the details on the Originating
Application. The Lease was apparently with other Solicitors. Meanwhile as time was
running on, a draft Application was completed by one of my Assistants, adopting
my error as to the name of the Landlords and taking the other details from the
Section 25 Notice itself. The parts left uncompleted were the answers to paragraphs
2. (d) (e) (f) (g) (j) and paragraph 3. 6. According to the file the Leases were received
in my offices on the 11th January 1982. I do not remember seeing them. Certainly,
in the office draft of the Originating Application the uncompleted paragraphs were
filled in by me. They are in my handwriting, but whether those details were called
over to me by my Assistant, or whether I extracted them myself from the second
page of the Supplemental Lease, I really cannot remember, but whatever the
position, I failed to pick up the fact that Charrington & Company Limited were not
the Landlords. Whether I was misled by the description of the Second Lease as
"Supplemental" (which in my experience is a term usually used in Leases where the
identity of the Landlord remains the same) I really cannot now say. 7. So far as I am
concerned I thought Charrington & Co. Limited were my Clients' Landlords. I
would not have sent out the Originating Application to the County Court if I had
thought otherwise. I have been in General Practice as a Solicitor for 28 years. I know
that it is the Tenants' current Landlord against whom proceedings should be taken
under the 1954 Act. I run a very busy office. I ask the Court to accept that the
mistake I made was a genuine one and that I intended on behalf of my Clients to
sue the relevant landlords under the Act whom I mistakenly believed to be
Charrington & Co. Limited.'

A somewhat similar problem arose in *Re Nos 55 and 57, Holmes Road, Kentish Town,
Beardmore Motors Ltd v Birch Bros (Properties) Ltd* [1958] 2 All ER 311, [1959] Ch 298,
when the original landlord, Birch Bros Ltd, assigned their reversionary interest to Birch
Bros (Properties) Ltd and the lessees applied for a new tenancy under the 1954 Act
naming Birch Bros Ltd as respondents. By the time that the error was discovered it was
too late to issue a new summons against Birch Bros (Properties) Ltd. Harman J reluctantly
refused to allow any amendment in the name of the respondent. The basis of his decision

was that the difference in names reflected the different identities of two different parties, that the applicants had served Birch Bros Ltd and to allow the amendment would be to substitute a different legal entity as respondent and to deprive that entity of a vested right not to have to resist an application for a new lease after the expiration of the time limit prescribed in the 1954 Act. This was not, in his judgment, a case of misnomer or misdescription. Whether that decision was right or wrong is immaterial since RSC Ord 20, r 5, did not exist at the time. However, it may well have prompted the making of RSC Ord 20, r 5(3).

In *Rodriguez v Parker* [1966] 2 All ER 349, [1969] 1 QB 116 a frontal assault was made on RSC Ord 20, r 5(3) on the basis that it was ultra vires the Rule Committee. This failed. On the merits of the application, the claim was one for personal injuries suffered in a motor accident. The car was owned by R J Parker, but had been driven by his son, R S Parker. Accordingly the effect of amending the proceeding by substituting 'R S' Parker for 'R J' Parker was to substitute one actual person for another actual person as defendant. Nield J held ([1966] 2 All ER 349 at 365, [1967] 1 QB 116 at 139, that the court had to be satisfied that (1) the mistake sought to be corrected was a genuine mistake, (2) that the mistake was not misleading or such as to cause any reasonable doubt as to the identity of the person intended to be sued and (3) that it was just to make the amendment. He held that all three conditions were satisfied and gave the necessary leave.

A similar situation arose in *Mitchell v Harris Engineering Co Ltd* [1967] 2 All ER 682, [1967] 2 QB 703 where there were two companies, Harris Engineering Co Ltd and Harris Engineering Co (Leeds) Ltd. The plaintiff mistakenly sued 'Leeds' and then applied to strike this word out, thereby altering the name of the defendant to that of the other company. It was conceded that this would have the effect of substituting a different party as defendant and would deprive that party of the benefit of a defence under the Statute of Limitations. Nevertheless leave to amend was granted, Russell LJ holding that there had been a genuine mistake, that the writ was served on the secretary to both companies who could not have failed to observe that the writ was not intended for the Leeds company (see [1967] 2 All ER 682 at 688, [1967] 2 QB 703 at 721).

In applying RSC Ord 20, r 5(3), it is, in my judgment, important to bear in mind that there is a real distinction between suing A in the mistaken belief that A is the party who is responsible for the matters complained of and seeking to sue B, but mistakenly describing or naming him as A and thereby ending up suing A instead of B.

The rule is designed to correct the latter and not the former category of mistake. Which category is involved in any particular case depends on the intentions of the person making the mistake and they have to be determined on the evidence in the light of all the surrounding circumstances. In the instant case I have not the slightest difficulty in accepting Mr Greenwood's assertion that he intended to sue the relevant landlords under the 1954 Act. After all, he was responding on behalf of his lessee clients to a notice to quit given on behalf of the landlords and it would have been surprising, to say the least, if he had thought that it was appropriate to respond by claiming a new lease from the managing agents or any other stranger to the landlord and tenant relationship. Accordingly I would conclude that he made a genuine mistake of a character to which RSC Ord 20, r 5(3) can apply.

However, the matter does not stop there, because it is not every mistake of this character which can be corrected under the rules. The applicant for leave to amend has to satisfy the court that the mistake was not misleading or such as to cause any reasonable doubt as to the identity of the person intended to be sued. On the facts of the present case, I do not see how Charringtons or Bass Holdings Ltd, or anyone else familiar with the surrounding circumstances, could have been misled or could have had any real doubt as to the identity of the person intended to be sued. The notice to quit had been given by Charringtons as managing agents for Bass Holdings Ltd and the application in reply was intended for Bass Holdings Ltd albeit addressed to Charringtons.

Counsel for Charringtons then advances a somewhat subtle argument. He submits that whilst the rule may apply where the error in the name is such that there is or is

likely to be someone else of that name somewhere in the world, it has no application
where the name erroneously used is that of someone else who is connected with the *a*
transaction. This, he says, is why the rule uses the word 'alleged' in para (3). The rule is
contrasting a theoretical substitution of A for B with an actual substitution. I would
reject this submission as over subtle. I regard 'alleged' in this context as a short and
convenient way of saying 'notwithstanding that it is objected that . . .' and as reflecting
and overruling the objection which prevailed in *Re Nos 55 and 57, Holmes Road, Kentish
Town, Beardmore Motors Ltd v Birch Bros (Properties) Ltd* [1958] 2 All ER 311, [1959] Ch *b*
298 and in *Davies v Elsby Bros Ltd* [1960] 3 All ER 672, [1961] 1 WLR 170.

There remains a discretion whether to permit the amendment, for the court must be
satisfied that it is just to do so (see RSC Ord 20, r 5(2)). Suffice it to say that if the
amendment were allowed, Charringtons could have no complaint or regret. So far as
Bass Holdings is concerned, they would regret that they had been deprived of a wholly
adventitious chance of obtaining possession of the land without regard to the merits of *c*
their claim, but I do not regard this as a legitimate complaint in the circumstances of this
case.

There is, however, one further matter which goes to the exercise of the court's
discretion in deciding whether or not to allow this amendment. Counsel for Charringtons
submits that if the originating application is amended by deleting the name 'Charrington
& Co Ltd' and substituting 'Bass Holdings Ltd', Bass Holdings Ltd will be able to apply to *d*
have it struck out. If this is correct, it would clearly be wrong to allow the amendment.
It is therefore necessary to consider whether the application would be struck out.

The essence of the argument of counsel for Charringtons is that (a) an originating
application under the Landlord and Tenant Act 1954 must be served within two months
of the date on which it was filed or entered with the county court (CCR 1936 Ord 40, r 8,
and CCR 1936 Ord 8, r 35), ie not later than 19 March 1982, (b) in the absence of any *e*
agreement to the contrary, service on Bass Holdings Ltd has to be at its registered office
at Burton-upon-Trent (CCR 1936 Ord 8, r 26 and s 437 of the Companies Act 1948), (c)
no such service has been effected, (d) it is now too late to serve the application on Bass
Holdings Ltd because any order extending the two-month time limit must be made
before that period, or any extension of it, has expired and the overall power to extend
time limits under CCR 1936 Ord 13, r 5 has to be used very sparingly (see *Robert f
Baxendale Ltd v Davstone (Holdings) Ltd* [1982] 3 All ER 496.

The essence of the lessees' reply, as submitted by counsel for the lessees, is that (a) the
originating application was served on the only named respondent, Charringtons, within
the two months period, (b) this validates the application for the purposes of CCR 1936
Ord 8, r 35, whatever amendments may thereafter be made, (c) the amended application
will be served in the way in which all amended pleadings are served, namely on the other *g*
party or parties on the record, and (d) the fact that the amended application has to be
served differently from that appropriate to the unamended application is merely an
incident of the form which this particular amendment would take.

As I see it, the incorrect naming of a respondent will not necessarily affect service, but
may well do so. In the case of a natural person, the use of correct initials but a misspelt
surname coupled with the correct address for the intended respondent will probably lead *h*
to service on him. But an error in initials, other particulars being correct, may well lead
to the wrong member of the family being served and the greater the number of errors
the more likely it is that service will be on the wrong person. In the case of juridical
persons, the likelihood of the wrong person being served is even greater. I say that
because companies in a group often have similar names and the same address for their
respective registered offices. Service will be by post and process, if addressed to the wrong *j*
member of the juridical family, will inevitably lead to service on that member rather
than on the intended respondent.

Whilst at one stage I was attracted by the lessees' argument, I have come to the
conclusion that service on the wrong respondent can never constitute effective service for
the purposes of CCR 1936 Ord 8, r 35.

In *Jones v Jones* [1970] 3 All ER 47, [1970] 2 QB 576 this court held that service of a
writ on one defendant within the 12-month period of its validity did not prevent the
writ ceasing to be valid quoad a second defendant, who was not served within that period.
If, therefore, Charringtons are to be regarded as a separate entity from Bass Holdings Ltd,
service on Charringtons will not preserve the validity of the originating application
quoad Bass Holdings Ltd. If, on the other hand, the true view is that Charringtons by
amendment becomes Bass Holdings Ltd, a further question arises, namely when the
transformation occurred.

This problem was considered in *Liff v Peasley* [1980] 1 All ER 623, [1980] 1 WLR 781,
albeit in the context of adding a defendant. The competing theories of 'relation back' to
the date of the issue of the writ and of 'no useful purpose', ie no relation back (the joinder
being effective only from the date of the order giving leave for the additional defendant
to be joined) were studied in depth by Brandon LJ. Which is the true view is clearly one
of great difficulty but for present purposes, I do not think that it matters which is right.
If there is a 'relation back' and the effect of correcting 'Charringtons' to 'Bass Holdings
Ltd' is to amend the originating application retrospectively to the date of its entry in the
county court, there was quite clearly no proper service, because Charringtons' office is
not the place at which to serve Bass Holdings Ltd. If, on the other hand, there was no
relation back, as Charringtons have disappeared from the scene, no one has been served.

Is this an insuperable difficulty? If it is, RSC Ord 20, r 5(3) has an extremely limited
application in that it would always be necessary to prove that the 'right', ie the intended,
defendant had been served. So construed, it can only be used to rectify what amounts to
a clerical error. Furthermore, in this limited category of case, it would be most unlikely
that any issue could arise as to whether the process was misleading or whether there was
doubt about the intended defendant or whether it was just to allow the correction. These
qualifications would therefore be unnecessary. Accordingly, I do not think that it is so
limited. But if it is not so limited, and the rule can apply where there has been no service
on the intended respondent, what criteria should be applied in extending the time for
such service under CCR 1936 Ord 13, r 5? On the authorities, I must and do accept that
this is a power to be used sparingly, but RSC Ord 20, r 5(3) is itself hedged with every
sort of protection for the intended respondent: the mistake must be genuine, the error
in the name of the respondent must not be misleading or such as to cause any reasonable
doubt as to the identity of the intended respondent and, above all, it must be just to allow
the correction.

Those protections will of themselves make a successful application under RSC Ord 20,
r 5(3), something of a rarity, and in my judgment if leave to amend or correct would
otherwise be given under that rule, the court should not hesitate to make any necessary
extension of time under CCR 1936 Ord 13, r 5.

In the instant case all the criteria of RSC Ord 20, r 5(3) are met. The mistake was
genuine. Charringtons, as the managing agents of Bass Holdings Ltd, could not have
been misled and either they informed Bass Holdings Ltd of the originating application
or they should have done so. Bass Holdings Ltd could not have been misled. Neither
Charringtons nor Bass Holdings Ltd could have had any doubt that the lessees were
intending to name the landlord, ie Bass Holdings Ltd, as respondent. There can be no
injustice in requiring Bass Holdings Ltd to make good their claim to possession on its
merits.

I would order that Charringtons' name be deleted as a respondent, leaving only that of
Bass Holdings Ltd and I would extend the time for service on Bass Holdings Ltd until the
expiration of 14 days from today.

GRIFFITHS LJ. I will not repeat the facts which are fully set out in the judgments of
Waller and Donaldson LJJ. It is in my view clear beyond peradventure that the lessees'
solicitors at all times intended to apply for a new tenancy from the current landlord. Any
other intention would be absurd for the application was only made in response to the
current landlords' notice to quit.

The landlords who are one of the biggest brewery groups, had for their own purposes transferred the freehold of the premises from one company to another and then *a* apparently changed the name of that company, but at all times they corresponded with the lessees in the name of the company who originally granted the lease. In these circumstances the lessees' solicitors made a careless but understandable mistake when they named the current landlords as Charringtons Ltd and not Bass Holdings Ltd on the application for a new tenancy. That mistake cannot possibly have misled Bass Holdings Ltd who knew from 12 October that their lessees were not prepared to give up possession *b* and it can have come as no surprise to them that an application was made for a new tenancy within the permitted time limits.

It is not now possible to correct the mistake by adding Bass Holdings Ltd, as a party to the proceedings under CCR Ord 15, r 1, as the time for making the application for a new tenancy under s 29(3) of the 1954 Act has long since expired.

RSC Ord 20, r 5(2) however specifically empowers the court to allow an amendment *c* to correct the name of a party even though the relevent limitation period has expired, provided that it is just to do so. I have no doubt that it would be just to do so in this case, otherwise the Bass Holdings Ltd will be able to take advantage of a mistake by their lessees' solicitors the nature of which they must have been well aware and which cannot possibly have misled them.

But the question remains, does this case fall within the scope of RSC Ord 20, r 5(3)? Is *d* the rule to be limited to mere misspelling or some other slip such as leaving out one word in the long title of a company so that looking at the name on the proceedings the nature of the mistake can readily be seen; or is it to be more liberally construed so that it will cover the case when entirely the wrong name has been used? I see no reason why it should not include a case where entirely the wrong name has been used, provided it was not misleading, or such as to cause any reasonable doubt as to the identity of the person *e* intended to be sued.

The identity of the person intended to be sued is of course vital. But in this case I have no doubt that the identity of the person intended to be sued was the current landlord Bass Holdings Ltd. The wording of the rule makes it clear that it is not the identity of the person sued that it crucial, but the identity of the person *intended* to be sued, which is a very different matter. *f*

Test it this way, suppose after the solicitor had mistakenly completed the application for a new tenancy naming Charringtons Ltd as the landlord, his partner pointed out to him that the name of the landlord in the supplemental lease was Bass Ltd, now changed to Bass Holdings Ltd, and had asked the solicitor if he intended to proceed against Charringtons Ltd? The answer would have been 'Good heavens, No, I intend to proceed against the landlord; thank goodness you have pointed out my mistake. I must change *g* the name to Bass Holdings Ltd.' As the mistake in this case which led to using the wrong name for the current landlords did not mislead the Bass Holdings Ltd, and as in my view there can be no reasonable doubt as to the true identity of the person intended to be sued, this case falls within the scope of RSC Ord 20, r 5(3), and it would be just to correct the name of the respondent from Charringtons Ltd to Bass Holdings Ltd.

For these reasons and those given in the judgment of Donaldson LJ, with which I *h* agree, I would dismiss this appeal and agree with the order he proposes.

Appeal dismissed. Judge's order varied. Leave to appeal to the House of Lords refused.

Solicitors: *Loxleys* (for Charringtons); *Horne Engall & Freeman*, Egham (for the lessees).

Diana Brahams   Barrister.

R v Stipendiary Magistrate at Lambeth and another, ex parte McComb

QUEEN'S BENCH DIVISION
GRIFFITHS LJ AND MCCULLOUGH J
6, 7 OCTOBER 1982

COURT OF APPEAL, CIVIL DIVISION
SIR JOHN DONALDSON MR AND MAY LJ
12, 15 NOVEMBER 1982

Court of Appeal – Jurisdiction – Appeal from Divisional Court – Application for judicial review – Appeal not lying in any criminal cause or matter – Judicial review of decision relating to exhibits in criminal proceedings – Whether decision of Divisional Court a judgment in a 'criminal cause or matter' – Supreme Court Act 1981, s 18(1)(a).

Criminal evidence – Exhibits – Preservation and retention – Duty of court or prosecution – Exhibits needed for separate trials in different courts – Court in England and court abroad – Exhibits needed for committal proceedings in England and for appeal in Republic of Ireland – Exhibits released to English Director of Public Prosecutions by Irish court for use in committal proceedings in England – Director undertaking to return exhibits to Irish court on termination of committal proceedings – Whether Director required to seek consent of Crown Court or High Court before returning exhibits to Irish court in event of committal proceedings resulting in committal for trial.

Following a series of explosions in London in the winter of 1978–79 T was arrested and committed for trial at the Crown Court charged with offences in connection with those explosions. Whilst awaiting trial, however, T escaped from prison. At the beginning of 1982 the applicant was arrested and charged with substantially the same offences as T. In March 1982 T was arrested in the Republic of Ireland, where he was charged under reciprocal legislation with committing offences in England. In order to enable T's trial to proceed, the English Director of Public Prosecutions sent to the Irish court a large number of exhibits which had been produced in T's committal proceedings in England. In so acting the Director neither informed nor sought the consent of the Crown Court. T was convicted and sentenced. T gave notice of appeal to the Irish Court of Criminal Appeal, and the exhibits used in his trial accordingly came into the custody of the registrar of that court. In the mean time the English Director of Public Prosecutions was preparing the committal proceedings in respect of the applicant, and for that purpose he required some of the exhibits used in T's trial. He accordingly applied to the Irish Court of Criminal Appeal for their release. The Irish court granted the application on the Director's undertaking to return the exhibits to its registrar forthwith on the termination of the applicant's committal proceedings. After the commencement of the applicant's committal proceedings but before their conclusion, the applicant sought a declaration that the Director should not permit any of the exhibits produced in the applicant's committal proceedings to be removed from the jurisdiction of the Crown Court without order of that court or the High Court. If the Director were to be required to seek the consent of the Crown Court or the High Court before he could comply with his unqualified undertaking to the Irish court, he would, in the event of consent being refused, be placed in the position of being in contempt of either the Irish court or the English court. The Divisional Court refused to grant the declaration sought and the applicant appealed to the Court of Appeal. In addition to the consideration of the merits of the appeal, there also arose the question of the jurisdiction of the Civil Division of the Court of Appeal to hear it.

Held – (1) Since the order of the Divisional Court against which the applicant appealed was not itself one which could lead to a trial or punishment, it was not a judgment of the High Court in a 'criminal cause or matter' within s 31(1)(a)[a] of the Supreme Court Act 1981 and accordingly the Civil Division of the Court of Appeal had jurisdiction to hear the appeal (see p 329 g, p 330 a and p 332 f to h, post); *Amand v Secretary of State for Home Affairs* [1942] 2 All ER 381 considered; *R v Southampton Justices, ex p Green* [1975] 2 All ER 1073 and *R v Crown Court at Sheffield, ex p Brownlow* [1980] 2 All ER 444 doubted.

(2) Once an article had become an exhibit in a criminal case the court had a responsibility to preserve and retain it or to arrange for its preservation and retention for the purposes of justice, and the usual course was for the court to entrust the exhibits to the police or to the Director of Public Prosecutions subject to the same responsibility. Where the exhibits were so entrusted to the prosecution, the prosecution's duty was (a) to take all proper care to preserve the exhibits safe from loss or damage, (b) to co-operate with the defence in order to allow them reasonable access to the exhibits for the purpose of inspection and examination and (c) to produce the exhibits at the trial. Furthermore, in such cases the court could impose such restrictions on the prosecutor as it considered proper in all the circumstances; where it imposed no restrictions it was for the recipient of the exhibits to deal with them in whatever way appeared best for the purposes of justice, and if the recipient had doubts as to where his duty lay he could, but was not obliged to, apply to the court for directions, as could also the accused (see p 330 e to j and p 333 d e, post).

(3) Where there were exhibits which were common to separate criminal proceedings in two different courts, one in England and one abroad, both courts had the same or a similar responsibility in relation to the exhibits: each was primarily concerned with the accused or convicted person involved in its own proceedings, but each had also a wider responsibility for promoting the purposes of justice both in its own country and abroad. In order to avoid a clash of dates for the trials of the accused persons, mutual discussions had to and did take place, since to do otherwise would involve each court in a breach of its wider responsibility to promote the purposes of justice. Accordingly, since the exhibits which were produced in the applicant's committal proceedings had first been produced to the court which committed T for trial in England, it was wholly reasonable for the Director of Public Prosecutions to make them available to the Irish court when T fled to Ireland and was arrested and charged there, and there was no reason for him to seek the consent of either the English committing court or the English court to which T had been committed. Furthermore, since, in the ordinary course of events, a court in Ireland would not entrust exhibits produced to or retained by it to the English Director of Public Prosecutions, it had been necessary, in the applicant's case, for the Director to apply to the Irish court for custody of the exhibits, and that court had made an order which wholly met the Director's needs. If the applicant's committal proceedings resulted in his not being committed for trial, no problem would arise with respect to the exhibits. However, if the applicant were to be committed for trial in the Crown Court, the Director was required to return the exhibits to the Irish court in accordance with his undertaking, and the applicant could then apply to the Crown Court for an order that the Director be required to obtain the exhibits and make them available to the defence. Such a course was necessary because, although in the normal case of a committal responsibility for exhibits passed from the committing court to the Crown Court, in the peculiar circumstances of the applicant's case the Crown Court's responsibility for the exhibits was shared with, but subject to the overriding authority of, the Irish court. It followed that the applicant was not entitled to the declaration sought, and the appeal would accordingly be dismissed (see p 330 j to p 331 j, p 332 d e, p 333 e to h and p 334 a, post).

Notes

For the appellate jurisdiction of the Court of Appeal, Civil Division, see 10 Halsbury's

---

a   Section 18(1), so far as material, is set out at p 329 c, post

Laws (4th edn) para 900, and for cases on the subject, see 16 Digest (Reissue) 243, 2377–2382.

For matters which constitute a 'criminal cause or matter', see 11 Halsbury's Laws (4th edn) para 1505, and for cases on the subject, see 14(2) Digest (Reissue) 757–761, 6312–6346.

For retention of exhibits produced to justices in committal proceedings, see 11 Halsbury's Laws (4th edn) para 161.

For the Supreme Court Act 1981, s 18, see 51 Halsbury's Statutes (3rd edn) 608.

Cases referred to in judgments

Amand v Secretary of State for Home Affairs [1942] 2 All ER 381, [1943] AC 147, HL, 16 Digest (Reissue) 313, 3223.

Chic Fashions (West Wales) Ltd v Jones [1968] 1 All ER 229, [1968] 2 QB 299, [1968] 2 WLR 201, CA, 14(1) Digest (Reissue) 215, 1573.

Dillon v O'Brien and Davis (1887) 16 Cox CC 245, 14(1) Digest (Reissue) 193, *915.

Elias v Pasmore [1934] 2 KB 164, [1934] All ER Rep 380, 14(1) Digest (Reissue) 216, 1576.

Malone v Comr of Police of the Metropolis [1979] 1 All ER 256, [1980] QB 49, [1978] 3 WLR 936, CA, Digest (Cont Vol E) 133, 1573a.

Miliangos v George Frank (Textiles) Ltd [1975] 3 All ER 801, [1976] AC 443, [1975] 3 WLR 758, HL; *affg* [1975] 1 All ER 1076, [1975] QB 487, [1975] 2 WLR 555, CA, Digest (Cont Vol D) 571, 678b.

R v Crown Court at Sheffield, ex p Brownlow [1980] 2 All ER 444, [1980] QB 530, [1980] 2 WLR 892, DC and CA.

R v Lushington, ex p Otto [1894] 1 QB 420, DC, 22 Digest (Reissue) 469, 4698.

R v Southampton Justices, ex p Green [1975] 2 All ER 1073, [1976] QB 11, [1975] 3 WLR 277, CA, 30 Digest (Reissue) 176, 1370.

Cases also cited

Chief Constable of Kent v V [1982] 3 All ER 36, [1982] 3 WLR 462, CA.

Jennings v Quinn [1968] IR 305.

Lewis v Roe (1846) 10 JP 385n

R v Clifford (1824) 1 C & P 521, 171 ER 1300.

Truman (Frank) Export v Metropolitan Police Comr [1977] 3 All ER 431, [1977] QB 952.

Young v Bristol Aeroplane Co Ltd [1944] 2 All ER 293, [1944] KB 718, CA; *affd* [1946] 1 All ER 98, [1946] AC 163, HL.

Application for judicial review

John Gabriel McComb applied, with the leave of McCullough J granted on 14 September 1982, for (i) an order of prohibition prohibiting committal proceedings against him in the Lambeth Magistrates' Court, (ii) all necessary and consequential directions, and (iii) a declaration that the Director of Public Prosecutions should not cause or permit any of the exhibits produced to the Lambeth Magistrates' Court in the course of the said committal proceedings to be removed from the jurisdiction of the Crown Court without the order of the Crown Court or the High Court. The application was made in respect of a determination and decision of Brian Canham Esq, the stipendiary magistrate sitting at Lambeth Magistrates' Court on 13 September 1982. The respondents to the application were the stipendiary magistrate and Director of Public Prosecutions. The facts are set out in the judgment of Griffiths LJ.

Andrew Collins for the applicant.
Philip Vallance for the respondents.

GRIFFITHS LJ. In order to understand the nature of this application, it is necessary to recite some of the history that leads up to making the application before this court.

In this country, during the winter of 1978–79, a number of explosive devices were planted in various locations in London and elsewhere, some of which were detonated causing injury both to persons and to property. In the course of time a man by the name of Gerard Tuite was arrested in England and committed for trial to the Central Criminal Court in London on charges, inter alia, under s 3 of the Explosive Substances Act 1883 as substituted by s 7 of the Criminal Jurisdiction Act 1975 relating to those explosions.

Before he could be charged he escaped from Brixton prison. He went to Ireland and was eventually arrested there on 4 March 1982. It was decided not to seek his extradition to this country to face trial but the Director of Public Prosecutions instead invited the Director of Public Prosecutions in Dublin to consider instituting proceedings against him under s 3 of the Explosive Substances Act 1883 (Eire) as amended by s 4 of the Criminal Law Jurisdiction Act 1976 (Eire) for those offences.

I should explain that as a result of the amendment to the Explosive Substances Act 1883 in Eire it enabled Eire to try a man in respect of offences that he had committed in this country. This country, by the Criminal Jurisdiction Act 1975 enacted reciprocal provisions which enabled a person who had been causing explosions in Ireland, if caught here, to be tried here for those offences.

Gererd Tuite was charged with two counts on an indictment in respect of those offences and he appeared before the Special Criminal Court in Dublin. To enable that trial to proceed it was necessary to send to Dublin a large number of the exhibits which had been produced on his committal to the Central Criminal Court in this country. At the trial in Ireland, which was concluded on 13 July 1982, Tuite was found guilty and was sentenced to ten years' imprisonment. He has since lodged notice of appeal but as yet leave has not been granted.

At the beginning of 1982 the present applicant in these proceedings, John McComb, was arrested and he was charged with substantially the same offences as Tuite, namely being concerned with various explosions in London and elsewhere during the winter of 1978–79. Committal proceedings were then started against the applicant in the Lambeth Magistrates' Court on 13–14 September 1982. In order to commit the applicant it was necessary to produce a large number of the exhibits that were used in Tuite's trial. Those exhibits, subsequent to Tuite's trial in Dublin, were retained in the custody of the Court of Criminal Appeal in Dublin pending the possibility of Tuite appealing. In order to obtain their release, the Director of Public Prosecutions made application to the Court of Criminal Appeal in Dublin. The Court of Criminal Appeal in Dublin was prepared to release the exhibits on an undertaking being given by the Director of Public Prosecutions that the exhibits would be returned forthwith to the custody of the Court of Criminal Appeal in Dublin as soon as the applicant's committal had been completed.

That has given rise to the following problems. Those who are representing the applicant in this country are very anxious that the exhibits should be inspected and, if need be, forensically examined on behalf of the applicant. They say that if the exhibits are to be returned forthwith to Dublin they will have no opportunity of inspecting and examining them and it is wholly unreasonable to expect them to travel to Dublin for that purpose, particularly as the applicant is being defended on legal aid and the whole exercise would be at public expense. Therefore, the applicant's advisers are most anxious that these exhibits should remain in this country for a reasonable period so that, having obtained legal aid extended to the employment of a leader, a proper team can inspect and consider them.

Furthermore, they deposed to the fact that they are apprehensive that Tuite may not have his appeal heard for a very considerable time. The applicant has already been in custody since January 1982 and if there is no opportunity of getting at the exhibits until after Tuite's appeal is heard, when presumably the court in Ireland would release them and they would be returned here, it may be that the applicant would not be tried for many, many more months, during which he will have to remain in custody.

The immediate difficulty is that the sensible solution, which would be to keep the exhibits here for a period of time, perhaps eight weeks or so, and then return them to Ireland cannot be pursued without putting the Director in breach of the undertaking which he had given to the Court of Appeal in Ireland to return the exhibits forthwith.

The matter comes before this court against that background in the following manner. The committal proceedings were heard in the Lambeth Magistrates' Court and the exhibits which had come back from Ireland were all produced in that court, but before the applicant was formally committed application was made to this court for an order of prohibition prohibiting the committal proceedings continuing against the applicant in Lambeth Magistrates' Court and, further, for a declaration that the Director of Public Prosecutions should not permit any of the exhibits produced to the Lambeth Magistrates' Court in the course of the said committal proceedings to be removed from the jurisdiction of the Crown Court without order of the Crown Court or the High Court.

Counsel for the applicant has said to this court that he no longer wishes for an order of prohibition against the magistrate at Lambeth prohibiting him from committing the applicant because that was merely a procedural device to enable him to get his application for a declaration heard by this court before it was too late and the exhibits had gone back to Ireland out of the jurisdiction pursuant to the Director's undertaking. However, counsel does submit that in the circumstances of this case the Director would be in breach of his duty if, without leave of the Crown Court, he took the exhibits out of the jurisdiction and surrendered them to the custody of the Irish Court of Criminal Appeal because, says counsel, he would thereby put those exhibits out of his immediate control and this, he submits, would be a breach of his duty as the prosecutor in respect of those exhibits.

In support of this submission he has referred the court to a number of English and Irish authorities concerned with the power and the duty of the police to obtain and retain possession of evidence required for the purposes of a prosecution. I think it will be sufficient if I refer first to *R v Lushington, ex p Otto* [1894] 1 QB 420.

The facts of that case were that there was a hearing by a magistrate of an application for the extradition of a fugitive criminal on a charge of theft committed in France. Certain articles were produced under a subpoena duces tecum by a witness who had purchased them from the accused person in England and they were identified as part of the stolen property. The magistrate, having committed the accused to prison to await a warrant from the Secretary of State for his extradition, orally directed a constable in court to take charge of the property so produced and identified, in order that it might be produced at the French trial. The purchaser applied for an order directing the magistrate to order the property to be delivered up to him.

That case was concerned with the rights of the court and/or the police to retain property required for a trial, and in the course of his judgment Wright J said (at 423–424):

> 'In this country I take it that it is undoubted law that it is within the power of, and is the duty of, constables to retain for use in Court things which may be evidences of crime, and which have come into the possession of the constables without wrong on their part. I think it is also undoubted law that when articles have once been produced in court by witnesses it is right and necessary for the court, or the constable in whose charge they are placed (as is generally the case), to preserve and retain them, so that they may be always available for the purposes of justice until the trial is concluded.'

That case was referred to in more recent times with approval in *Elias v Pasmore* [1934] 2 KB 164, [1934] All ER Rep 380.

Founding himself on that passage in the judgment of Wright J, counsel for the applicant submitted that if the Director parts with possession to someone over whom he has no direct control, such as the Court of Criminal Appeal in Ireland, he cannot be said to have retained possession of the exhibits and is accordingly in breach of his duty. But that passage was in a judgment given before the unhappy development of organised international crime as we know it today, which is no respecter of national frontiers.

Today I would define the duty of the prosecution, which is as a general rule always entrusted by the courts with the exhibits pending trial and after committal, in the following terms: (1) to take all proper care to preserve the exhibits safe from loss or damage; (2) to co-operate with the defence in order to allow them reasonable access to the exhibits for the purpose of inspection and examination; and (3) to produce the exhibits at the trial.

At one stage in his submission counsel for the applicant suggested that this duty involved the prosecution at all times retaining the exhibits within their own possession and within the jurisdiction of the Crown Court, but I think a moment's consideration will show such a requirement would place a fetter on prosecuting authorities which would be very damaging to the public interest. Suppose you have a case of an international gang with one man caught in this country and committed for trial. The French police have good grounds for supposing that they have located another member of the gang and they are most anxious to look at certain of the exhibits which the English police have in order to confirm their suspicion. They have not yet arrested their man. If, in those circumstances, the prosecuting authorities are not to be at liberty to take those exhibits to the French police, show them to them and thus take them out of the jurisdiction, it may prevent the French police apprehending the other member of the gang. If, as at one stage in the argument counsel for the applicant submitted, it should only be done on application to the court and with the court's permission, the very fact of applying to the court and seeking the permission of the court will serve or may serve to alert the criminal in France that the French police are on his tail and give him the chance to absent himself.

In my view it is necessary that a degree of trust should be reposed in the prosecuting authorities in this country and they should be free, when the interests of justice require it, to take exhibits out of the jurisdiction. Of course, they must take the greatest care to ensure that they do not thereby breach their fundamental duty to take all reasonable care that they are not either lost or damaged and that they are available for production at the trial.

Counsel for the applicant next submitted that, if that was too extreme a position to take, at least the duty was such that the prosecuting authority must never part with the possession of the exhibits in such circumstances as even temporarily to put them beyond their immediate control. He submits that by taking these exhibits back to the Irish Court of Criminal Appeal and surrendering them to its custody they would temporarily put them beyond their control. So be it, they may be put temporarily beyond the immediate control of the Director, but it is, in my judgment, unthinkable that the Irish Court of Criminal Appeal will not take proper care of the exhibits and will not co-operate fully with this court in ensuring that those exhibits will, according to reasonable convenience, be available for the trial of the applicant in this country and, furthermore, be available in this country for any reasonable examination that the applicant's advisers may wish to make. I accordingly reject counsel's submission that there is a duty on the prosecuting authorities, whenever they are taking steps which may result in exhibits being temporarily out of their control, to obtain the permission of the court before doing so.

Of course situations will arise from time to time when it will undoubtedly be wise for the prosecution to make an application in respect of exhibits to the Crown Court. An obvious example would be if the exhibits are fast deteriorating and are a potential danger. Counsel for the applicant told us of a case in his own experience in which apparently a vast quantity of cannabis was deteriorating and it was necessary to destroy it. In such circumstances prudence dictates that an application should be made to the Crown Court and the court should be fully apprised of the course it is proposed to take and should approve it. Once exhibits have been produced to the court the court has jurisdiction over those exhibits and an interest in them pursuant to its duty to see that justice is done.

Another obvious example where it would be prudent to make an application to the court is if there was a dispute between the prosecution and the defence as to the nature of certain scientific tests that should be carried out on a certain exhibit. There may also be cases in which there may be doubts about the wisdom of temporarily parting with control over the exhibits because of the nature or character of the recipient into whose custody it is intended to entrust them and in such a case wisdom would dictate that the matter should be placed before the Crown Court.

Having said that, this cannot possibly be considered such a case. Here, the Director will be passing the exhibits back to the control of the Court of Criminal Appeal in Ireland, a recipient in whom he is entitled to have every confidence.

I should further state that we are quite satisfied by what we have heard from the Director that the utmost care has been taken of these exhibits. We are told that, when the time came to take them from this country after Tuite's abortive committal to the Central Criminal Court, a special officer was designated to be in charge of them. He took them over to Ireland, he remained with them throughout Tuite's trial as officer in charge of exhibits and, at the end of the trial, he personally saw to it that they were sealed and placed in the care of the Irish Court of Criminal Appeal. When the time came to bring them back here, that same officer was sent to bring them back and that same officer has been in charge of them here. If they are to go back it would be the same officer who will take them. We are quite satisfied that the Director in this case has been fully discharging his duties in respect of these exhibits.

During the course of the argument we were referred to the Magistrates' Courts Rules 1981, SI 1981/552, dealing with the procedure to be followed in respect of exhibits produced by witnesses who are conditionally bound (see r 11). We do not think any assistance is to be gained in the solution of this problem by considering those rules, which are purely procedural.

I would of course state that the problem we are considering is not a problem peculiar to Irish prosecutions arising out of explosions in this country. It is of general application and similar circumstances could well arise where one member of a drug conspiracy was being prosecuted in this country and another was caught whom it was wished to prosecute in Amsterdam.

For the reasons I have given, I would refuse the declaration sought by counsel for the applicant but I would add this. There must be a commonsense solution to the problem which the court faces. If Tuite is to have his appeal dealt with in the immediate future then, of course, the sensible thing is for these exhibits to go back to Ireland immediately after the committal and then be brought back here after Tuite's appeal has been dealt with. If, however, the fears of the applicant are well founded and Tuite will not have his appeal heard for a long time, then manifestly the sensible course is to leave the exhibits here for sufficient time for an examination to be made by the defence.

We are told that it is the intention of the Director to make an application to the Court of Criminal Appeal in Ireland in the immediate future and to place before them the problems that have arisen. I am quite satisfied that at the time the Director gave his undertaking no thought had been given to the problem that now arises. Nobody can be blamed for that because nobody can foresee every difficulty that is likely to arise in the course of a case. But now the difficulty has become apparent we respectfully ask the Irish Court of Criminal Appeal to give sympathetic consideration to releasing the Director from the stringent terms of his undertaking to enable examination of the exhibits prior to returning them to Ireland, if they are not going to deal with Tuite's appeal for some considerable time.

The sensible way to achieve this is for the Director not to move to complete the committal until he has made his application to the Irish court. I have no doubt whatever that a sensible solution will in fact be achieved. Accordingly, for these reasons, I would refuse the orders asked by the applicant.

McCULLOUGH J. I agree.

Application dismissed.

Dilys Tausz   Barrister.

Appeal

The applicant appealed to the Court of Appeal.

Andrew Collins and *Nigel Seed* for the applicant.
Simon D Brown and *Philip Vallance* for the respondents.

SIR JOHN DONALDSON MR. This is an appeal by John Gabriel McComb (the
applicant) against the refusal of the Divisional Court (Griffiths LJ and McCullough J) to
grant him a declaration concerning the duties of the Director of Public Prosecutions.

His claim arises in this way. In the winter of 1978–79 there were a series of explosions
in London. As a result of police investigations a man called Gerard Tuite was arrested
and committed for trial at the Central Criminal Court charged with offences in
connection with those explosions. Whilst awaiting trial he escaped from Brixton prison.

At the beginning of 1982 the applicant was arrested and charged with substantially
the same offences as Tuite, namely being concerned with various explosions in London
and elsewhere during the winter of 1978–79. In due course committal proceedings were
to be begun against the applicant, but before then the scene shifts to the Republic of
Ireland and back to Gerard Tuite.

On 4 March 1982 Tuite was arrested in Ireland. No application was made to extradite
him. Instead the Irish Director of Public Prosecutions charged Tuite with committing
offences in England, proceeding under the reciprocal legislation which has been enacted
by both countries. Tuite accordingly appeared before the Special Criminal Court in
Dublin. To enable his trial to proceed the English Director of Public Prosecutions sent to
Dublin a large number of exhibits which had been produced at the English proceedings
leading to the committal of Tuite for trial at the Central Criminal Court. The English
Director in so acting neither informed nor sought the consent of the Central Criminal
Court.

Tuite was convicted by the Dublin court and was sentenced to ten years' imprisonment.
He gave notice of appeal to the Court of Criminal Appeal of Ireland. Thereupon it no
doubt become the duty of the registrar of that court to obtain 'all documents, exhibits
and other things which appear necessary for the proper determination of the appeal or
application'. I quote from s 21(1)(*b*) of the English Criminal Appeal Act 1968, which I
feel sure has its Irish equivalent. At all events, the exhibits used at Tuite's trial came into
the custody of the registrar of the Irish Court of Criminal Appeal.

I must now return to England where the English Director of Public Prosecutions was
preparing for the committal proceedings in respect of the applicant. For this purpose he
needed to be able to produce some of the exhibits used in Tuite's trial. Accordingly he
applied to the Irish Court of Criminal Appeal for their release for this purpose. The Irish
court agreed provided that the Director undertook to return the exhibits to its registrar
forthwith on the termination of the committal proceedings in respect of the applicant.
It is difficult to see how the Irish court could have refrained from asking for this
undertaking in view of its duty to Tuite as an actual or potential appellant.

What seems to have escaped the attention of the English Director was that, if the
applicant was committed for trial, those defending him might need to examine the
exhibits and possibly undertake certain forensic examinations and tests on them during
the period between committal and trial.

The committal proceedings began on 13 or 14 September 1982 and have yet to be
concluded. The applicant applied for judicial review and, in the final form of the
proceedings, for a declaration that—

'the Director of Public Prosecutions shall not permit any of the exhibits produced
to the Lambeth Magistrates Court in the course of the . . . committal proceedings to
be removed from the jurisdiction of the Crown Court without order of the Crown
Court or the High Court.'

I should mention that the jurisdiction both of the Crown Court and of the High Court
a extends throughout England and Wales but not of course to any part of the Republic of
Ireland.

In a word the applicant was claiming that the English Director had to seek the consent
of the Crown Court or the High Court before he could comply with his unqualified
undertaking to the Irish Court of Criminal Appeal. Further the applicant would no
doubt seek to persuade the English courts of the need to refuse consent. If he did so, the
b English Director would be placed in the unenviable position of being in contempt of
either the Irish or the English court.

Before giving further consideration to this problem, it is necessary to advert to the
jurisdiction of this court, the Civil Division of the Court of Appeal. By s 18(1) of the
Supreme Court Act 1981, which re-enacts s 31(1) of the Supreme Court of Judicature
(Consolidation) Act 1925—

c
> 'No appeal shall lie to the Court of Appeal—(*a*) except as provided by the
> Administration of Justice Act 1960, from any judgment of the High Court in any
> criminal cause or matter . . .'

The exception is not material for present purposes and we have only to consider whether
the refusal of the Divisional Court was a judgment 'in any criminal cause or matter'. If it
d was, this court has no jurisdiction.

Until comparatively recently the leading authority on this topic was *Amand v Secretary
of State for Home Affairs* [1942] 2 All ER 381, [1943] AC 147. The relevant learning is to
be found in the speeches of Viscount Simon LC, Lord Wright and Lord Porter (see [1942]
2 All ER 381 at 385, 387–388, 389, [1943] AC 147 at 156, 160–162, 163–164). Those
speeches seemed to suggest that the words 'in any criminal cause or matter' should receive
e a wide construction and that a distinction had to be drawn between the proceedings in
which the order under appeal was made and the underlying proceedings to which the
relief sought by the applicant would apply if granted. It was the latter proceedings which
must not be a criminal cause or matter. If that was the correct view of that decision, this
court would have no jurisdiction, for the underlying proceedings here were clearly a
criminal cause or matter.

However *Amand's* case was considered by this court in *R v Southampton Justices, ex p
f Green* [1975] 2 All ER 1073, [1976] QB 11, in which application was made to quash an
order estreating a recognisance which had been entered into by a surety conditioned to
ensure the attendance of the accused at a criminal trial. It was also considered in *R v
Crown Court at Sheffield, ex p Brownlow* [1980] 2 All ER 444, [1980] QB 530, a case
concerning the right of a chief constable to 'vet' a jury. In both cases a more restricted
g view was taken of the ratio of *Amand's* case, the test being said to be whether the order
sought to be reviewed was itself criminal in the sense that it was one which could lead to
a trial or punishment.

Whatever my personal view of the ratio of *Amand's* case and however surprised I may
be at the view taken by this court in the later cases, I consider myself to be bound to
apply the law as stated in those cases. Whilst differing views have been expressed as to
h how courts should act when confronted with potentially inconsistent binding precedents
(see the speeches of Lord Simon and Lord Cross in *Miliangos v George Frank (Textiles) Ltd*
[1975] 3 All ER 801 at 823, 838, [1976] AC 443 at 479, 496), I consider that the better
view is that expressed by Lord Denning MR in the *Miliangos* case [1975] 1 All ER 1076
at 1084, [1975] QB 487 at 503 when that case was in the Court of Appeal:

j
> 'This court is bound to follow its own decisions—including majority decisions—
> except in closely defined circumstances. One of these is where a previous decision of
> this court, although not expressly overruled, cannot stand with a subsequent decision
> of the House of Lords. Note the word "subsequent".'

Where, however, a prior decision of the House of Lords has been considered by the court,
its decision must be accepted as being consistent with the earlier House of Lords decision

even if the basis of this consistency may not have been fully or satisfactorily explained. This approach is necessary in the interests of certainty.   *a*

Accordingly I consider that this court has jurisdiction. The duty of the Director of Public Prosecutions, which is the matter directly affected by the declaration sought by the applicant, is not a matter which can lead to his trial or punishment and so is not a criminal cause or matter.

I now turn to the substance of the matter. Counsel for the applicant submits to this court, as he submitted below, that the Director would be in breach of his duty if, without   *b* the leave of the Crown Court, or, before committal, of the magistrates' court, he took the exhibits out of the jurisdiction and surrendered them to the custody of the Irish Court of Criminal Appeal.

There is a long line of authority which is still developing and which is concerned with the right of the police to seize and detain chattels which are or may be material evidence in criminal proceedings. For present purposes it is sufficient to advert to *Dillon v O'Brien*   *c* *and Davis* (1887) 16 Cox CC 245, *R v Lushington, ex p Otto* [1894] 1 QB 420, *Elias v Pasmore* [1934] 2 KB 164, [1934] All ER Rep Rep 380, *Chic Fashions (West Wales) Ltd v Jones* [1968] 1 All ER 229, [1968] 2 QB 299 and *Malone v Comr of Police of the Metropolis* [1979] 1 All ER 256, [1980] QB 49. But none of these cases deals, as a matter of decision, with the relationship between the court and the prosecutor in relation to material which has been produced to a court as an exhibit. They are all concerned with the rights of the police   *d* against those who claim a proprietary or possessory interest in the chattel concerned.

However, in *R v Lushington* [1894] 1 QB 420 at 423–424 Wright J said:

> 'I think that it is also undoubted law that when articles have once been produced in Court by witnesses it is right and necessary for the Court, or the constable in whose charge they are placed (as is generally the case), to preserve and retain them, so that they may always be available for the purposes of justice until the trial is   *e* concluded.'

This suggests to me that, once an article has become an exhibit, the court has a responsibility in relation to it. That responsibility is to preserve and retain it, or to arrange for its preservation and retention, for the purposes of justice. The purposes of justice are to ensure that the accused is convicted if guilty and is acquitted if innocent. I would   *f* accept that this is the position and would further accept that the usual course is for the court to entrust the exhibits to the police or to the Director subject to the same responsibility. That responsibility was defined by Griffiths LJ in the instant case as being (1) to take all proper care to preserve the exhibits safe from loss or damage, (2) to co-operate with the defence in order to allow them reasonable access to the exhibits for the purpose of inspection and examination and (3) to produce the exhibits at the trial. That   *g* too I accept.

Counsel for the applicant submits that neither the police nor the Director can allow the exhibits to leave their custody or at least control if they are to discharge these duties. Alternatively, they cannot do so without first applying to the court seised of the criminal proceedings in which the exhibits were produced.

I disagree. Where a court entrusts exhibits to the police or the prosecutor, it can impose   *h* such restrictions as it considers proper in all the circumstances. In the case of a private prosecutor it would be more likely to impose such restrictions than in the case of a public prosecutor and indeed might well decide to retain the exhibits itself or to deliver them into the custody of the police. But, if the court imposes no restrictions, it is for the recipient of the exhibits to deal with them in whatever way appears best for the purposes of justice. If the recipient has doubts as to where his duty lies, he can apply to the court   *j* for directions, but he is under no obligation so to do. Equally, the accused can apply to the court for directions if he thinks it appropriate.

In the instant case we have exhibits which are common to two different sets of criminal proceedings, one in England and one in Ireland. We have two courts with the same or a similar responsibility in relation to the exhibits. Each is primarily concerned with the

accused or convicted person involved in its own proceedings, but each has a wider
a responsibility for promoting the purposes of justice both in its own country and abroad.
These overlapping responsibilities no more conflict than the duty of two English or two
Irish courts to bring accused persons to trial as soon as possible. The two courts, whether
English or Irish, may be minded to try the same person using different exhibits or to try
different people using the same exhibits, on the same date. Mutual discussions must and
do take place to avoid such a clash of dates. To do otherwise would involve each court in
b a breach of its wider responsibility to promote the purposes of justice. The position is
exactly the same where an Irish and an English court are involved.

The exhibits produced in the applicant's committal proceedings were first produced to
the court which committed Gerard Tuite for trial in England. Tuite having fled to
Ireland and being arrested and charged there, it was wholly reasonable that the Director
should make the exhibits available to the Irish court and there was no reason for him to
c seek the consent of the English committing court or of the Central Criminal Court to
which Tuite was committed. Tuite could have applied to the English courts for an order
prohibiting the adoption of this course, but he would undoubtedly have been told that
such an order would only be made if he returned to stand trial in England. He made no
such application.

Neither the Special Criminal Court in Dublin nor the Irish Court of Criminal Appeal
d would in the ordinary course of events entrust exhibits produced to or retained by them
to the English Director of Public Prosecutions. Why should they? Accordingly the
Director had to apply to the Irish court and did so. That court made an order which
wholly met the needs of the Director as he saw and explained them. The Irish Court of
Criminal Appeal not only needs the exhibits eventually but is under a statutory duty to
retain them. That this duty of retention does not prevent its allowing the Director to
e have temporary custody of them is fortunate, if not surprising. Clearly this duty of
retention will not prevent the Irish court again allowing the Director, or allowing
responsible persons concerned with the defence of the applicant, to have temporary
custody of them, provided that they apply to the Irish court and make out their case and
provided that they undertake to comply with such conditions as the Irish court may
impose.

f   Looking ahead, a situation could arise in which the applicant was convicted and
appealed to the English Court of Appeal, Criminal Division. That court would then have
a similar duty of retention to that of the Irish court, but no conflict would arise. One or
other court would have custody for the time being and each would co-operate with the
other to ensure that the exhibits were available to the court with the most immediate
need for them.

g   What happens next? The committal proceedings in the applicant's case are virtually
concluded. If he is not committed for trial, no problem arises. If he is committed for
trial, the Director should at once return the exhibits to the Irish court in accordance with
his undertaking unless he has previously been released from that undertaking.

What are the applicant's rights? If he is committed for trial, he can apply to the Crown
Court for an order that the Director be required to obtain the exhibits and make them
h available to the defence for inspection or testing. He has this right because the exhibits
have been produced to the committing court and on committal, in my judgment,
responsibility for those exhibits passes to the Crown Court by operation of law. However,
any such application would be bound to fail since, in the peculiar circumstances of this
case, the Crown Court would be sharing that responsibility with the Irish court and the
Irish court is that which first had actual custody and only released the exhibits subject to
j an unqualified undertaking by the Director to return them to it on the conclusion of the
committal proceedings. In other words, the Crown Court's responsibility is subject to
the overriding authority of the Irish court.

Where does this leave the applicant? He will have three courses open to him. First, he
can himself make application to the Irish court for the release of the exhibits. Second, he
can ask the Director to make such an application. Third, he can do nothing at this stage

and, if by the time of his trial, assuming that he is committed, he has not been allowed appropriate access to the exhibits, he can ask the court to refuse to permit them to be *a* given in evidence by the prosecution, that refusal being in exercise of its inherent power to make all such orders as are necessary to secure a fair trial.

Where does this leave the Director? He has already applied to the Irish court for facilities which will enable the applicant to have the same access to the exhibits as he would have had if Tuite's trial had not taken place in Dublin. That application has been adjourned pending the decision of this court, and the Director can pursue it. However, *b* unless that application is granted in the form of modifying his undertaking before the committal proceedings are concluded, the Director must return the exhibits to the Irish court forthwith on the conclusion of those proceedings.

Counsel for the applicant complains that this approach will or may lead to the exhibits commuting backwards and forwards across the Irish Sea and submits that this may well lead to the exhibits being damaged or to trace evidence disappearing. There may well be *c* some force in this and I do not doubt that this is a factor which the Irish court will take into account on the adjourned hearing of the Director's application. However, this problem is inherent in a situation in which at least four people have an interest in the exhibits, two of whom are in Ireland (the Irish Director and Tuite) and two of whom are in England (the English Director and the applicant). It is for the courts of the two countries to resolve the problem in the interests of the justice to which they are both *d* committed. If the English courts had had primary custody of the exhibits, it would have been for those courts to have taken the necessary decision. In fact it is the Irish courts which have primary custody. For my part I do not think that it matters which court is primarily seised of the problem. Both have the same object in view: the attainment of justice to the Irish Republic, to the Crown, to Tuite and to the applicant. In any given situation both can be expected to reach precisely similar decisions. *e*

The declaration sought by the applicant is not justified in law. I see no need to grant him any other declaration having very fully set out my own view of the law.

I would dismiss the appeal.

MAY LJ. On the question whether this court has jurisdiction to hear an appeal from *f* the order of the Divisional Court in the instant case, I agree that for the reasons stated by Sir John Donaldson MR we are bound to follow the previous decisions in *R v Southampton Justices, ex p Green* [1975] 2 All ER 1073, [1976] QB 11 and *R v Crown Court at Sheffield, ex p Brownlow* [1980] 2 All ER 444, [1980] QB 530, notwithstanding the provisions of what is now s 18 of the Supreme Court Act 1981. Very respectfully, however, I doubt whether the approach to the problem in the *Southampton Justices* case and thereafter is correct and, *g* were this court not so bound, as at present advised I would not adopt it myself. In my opinion, in this type of case, where there is an application for judicial review, the proper construction of s 18 requires the court to adopt the approach referred to in particular by Lord Wright in *Amand v Secretary of State for Home Affairs* [1942] 2 All ER 381 at 387, [1943] AC 147 at 160. In my view it is with reference to the nature of the underlying proceedings in respect of some aspect of which application for judicial review is made *h* that it must be determined whether there has been an order in a criminal cause or matter. I do not think it sensible or good law that had counsel for the applicant persisted in his application for an order of prohibition then, as he accepted, no appeal would lie to this court from the Divisional Court, but, because he has amended his prayer for relief and asks merely for the declaration in relation to the handling by the Director of Public Prosecutions of the exhibits in pending proceedings before magistrates and which will *j* be required hereafter for trial on indictment in the Crown Court, his application has by some invisible and illogical process been transmuted from one in a criminal cause or matter into one which is not such, and thus an appeal lies.

Were we not so bound by authority I would have dismissed this appeal in limine.

In so far as the merits are concerned, as Griffiths LJ said in his judgment in the

a   Divisional Court and as we all know is the position, in the great majority of cases exhibits prosecution pending the trial in the Crown Court. However, we have not been shown any case which shows precisely how they get into the hands of the prosecution in such circumstances, or relating to the duty of the prosecution with regard to them, or indeed to the court or courts which can make orders with respect to them, qua exhibits, at the various stages of the prosecution and trial process. We have heard no legal submission on

b   any of these points. There are two or three very limited statutory provisions relating to exhibits, but nothing which covers the situation in the present hearing. For my part I am reluctant and do not propose to lay down any precise rule which, however well intentioned, might in some other case prevent the smooth operation of a system which experience has shown works admirably in the vast majority of cases.

    I agree that the decision in *R v Lushington, ex p Otto* [1894] 1 QB 420 was not dealing

c   with any duty owed in respect of exhibits; indeed, I did not understand counsel for the applicant so to argue. In my judgment, *Lushington's* case was dealing with the power to retain and preserve articles, reasonably and properly needed, for purposes of criminal proceedings, as against someone having or alleging that he has a proprietary or at least a possessory title to those articles. Counsel argued that if there is that power then there must be some correlative duty. This may be; it normally is the position that where the

d   law gives someone a power it requires him to exercise it reasonably and for the purpose for which the power has been given. In the present case, as I think, this requires no more from whoever is exercising the power than to deal with the exhibits between committal and trial reasonably and so far as possible to achieve a fair trial in the event. For my part I would not particularise the duty on the prosecution any further, but I would respectfully not disagree with the three aspects of the duty set out in the judgment of Griffiths LJ to

e   which Sir John Donaldson MR has referred. It should be noted that if the same exhibits are needed for separate trials in different courts, perhaps in foreign countries, the same principles can still apply and in the latter case the question of comity will also arise.

    The next point to be considered is what court has what power to make orders with regard to exhibits if it is contended that the prosecution is not complying with the duty lying on it in relation to them. Clearly once the magistrate has committed for trial he is

f   functus and therefore has no further power in relation to the exhibits. Subject to further argument, I incline to the view that the Crown Court, by virtue of the provisions of s 45 of the Supreme Court Act 1981 and its inherent jurisdiction to secure a fair trial, has the power to make any orders which may be necessary to ensure that fair trial. The position and powers of the Divisional Court in these circumstances will have to be considered as and when occasion arises, having regard to the powers of the Crown Court and what is

g   now s 28(2) of the Supreme Court Act 1981.

    But in the instant case I am quite satisfied that the applicant is not entitled to the declaration sought. Accepting for the purposes of argument that the Director of Public Prosecutions is under the duty as I have stated it, or as particularised by Griffiths LJ, not only in my view do the terms of the declaration sought postulate a far wider duty but it is also my view that the applicant has entirely failed to show that the Director has acted

h   otherwise than in accordance with his obligations to the courts in both this country and Eire and to both Tuite and the present applicant. I would therefore refuse the application for the declaration and dismiss this appeal.

    Finally, as Griffiths LJ said, there must be a commonsense solution to the potential problem to which this court's attention has been drawn by the present application and one which I am sure is not insoluble in the context of the comity which must exist

j   between our courts and those of Eire. I can respectfully understand the decision of the Court of Criminal Appeal in Eire to adjourn the application by the Director of Public Prosecutions for England and Wales pending the final determination of the present appeal against the decision of the Divisional Court in this country. Now that this court has decided that that appeal is to be dismissed, the Director is in the position to restore his application to the court in Eire, when and where I have no doubt it will receive the

same sympathetic consideration as would a similar application to the courts of this
country were the situation and the players in it reversed.   *a*

For those reasons I agree that the appeal should be dismissed.

Appeal dismissed. Leave to appeal to the House of Lords refused.

Solicitors: *Gamlens,* agents for *George E Baker & Co,* Guildford (for the applicant); *Treasury
Solicitor.*   *b*

Frances Rustin   Barrister.

c

Merkur Island Shipping Corp v Laughton and others

COURT OF APPEAL, CIVIL DIVISION
SIR JOHN DONALDSON MR, O'CONNOR AND DILLON LJJ   *d*
19, 20, 21 OCTOBER, 4 NOVEMBER 1982

*Tort – Inducement to commit breach of contract – Indirect inducement – Interference with
performance of contract – Preconditions for cause of action.*

e

*Trade dispute – Acts done in contemplation or furtherance of trade dispute – In contemplation or
furtherance of – Secondary action in furtherance of dispute – Immunity of secondary action from
suit in tort – Contract for supply of services between employer who is party to dispute and
employer to whom secondary action relates – Vessel let on time charter by owners to charterers
and sub-let to sub-charterers – Sub-charterers contracting with tug company for towage services
to enable vessel to leave port – Vessel blacked while in port – Employees of tug company taking f
secondary action to prevent vessel leaving port – Whether contract for supply of services between
shipowners and tug company – Whether secondary action directly preventing supply of services
to shipowner – Whether secondary action preventing supply of services to any other person –
Whether secondary action by employees of tug company actionable in tort – Trade Union and
Labour Relations Act 1974, s 13(1) – Employment Act 1980, s 17(3)(6).*

g

*Statute – Amendment – Clarity of expression – Desirability for legislation not to be amended but
to be re-enacted in amended form.*

The shipowners were the registered owners of a cargo vessel sailing under a Liberian flag
of convenience which was time chartered to a Norwegian company and sub-chartered to   *h*
sub-charterers. On 6 July while the ship was at Tilbury a member of the crew complained
about low wages to an official of the International Transport Workers Union (the ITF).
The ITF investigated the complaint and requested the support of an affiliated union, the
Transport and General Workers Union (the TGWU), to black the ship. During
negotiations between the shipowners and the ITF the ship left Tilbury. On 14 July the
ITF learned that the vessel was due in Liverpool on the following day and accordingly   *j*
asked the TGWU to black the ship there. On 16 July, when the vessel was ready to sail
from Liverpool, a towage contract was made between the sub-charterers and a tug
company to take the vessel out of port. However the tug crew, who were members of
the TGWU, refused to operate the tugs and as a result the vessel was unable to leave port.
The refusal of the tug crew to take the vessel out was in breach of their contracts of

employment with the tug company. The shipowners sought and were granted
a interlocutory injunctions restraining the defendants from issuing instructions to or
encouraging workers concerned with the free passage and operation of vessels at Liverpool
to refuse to assist the free passage of their vessel and further requiring the defendants to
withdraw all such instructions and encouragement given. The shipowners also issued a
writ against the defendants, three officials of the ITF, seeking damages in tort for
unlawful interference with their charter contract with the charterers and for interference
b with their business generally. The defendants appealed, contending that the part of the
shipowners' writ relating to unlawful interference of the contract disclosed no cause of
action at common law since (i) they had no specific knowledge of the time charter, (ii)
the contract which they sought to disrupt was not the time charter but the towage
contract, and (iii) that any interference with the time charter was too remote to found
liability. They further contended that even if the writ did disclose a cause of action they
c were protected from an action in tort by the immunity provided by s 13(1)[a] of the Trade
Union and Labour Relations Act 1974 since their action had been in contemplation or
furtherance of a trade dispute and therefore was not actionable on the ground that 'it
induces another person to break a contract or interferes or induces any other person to
interfere with its performance'. The shipowners conceded that the defendants' actions
came within s 13(1) and would be protected if s 13(1) applied, but they contended that
d the immunity from action provided by s 13(1) had been removed by s 17[b] of the
Employment Act 1980 because the defendants' action did not fall within the category of
secondary action permitted by s 17(3) since there was no 'supply of . . . services . . . in
pursuance of a contract', within s 17(6), between 'an employer who is a party to the
dispute [ie the shipowners] and the employer . . . to [whom] the secondary action relates
[ie the tug company who employed the tug crew]', because the contract for the supply of
e towage services had been made not by the shipowners but by the sub-charterers, who
were not parties to the dispute. The defendants contended that since it was the vessel
which required the towage services the sub-charterers ought to be deemed to have been
the agents of the shipowners when entering into the towage contract.

Held – The appeal would be dismissed for the following reasons—
f   (1) An actionable interference with contractual relations was committed if a third
party, with knowledge of a contract between two other parties and with the intention of
causing its breach or of preventing its performance, induced or procured the employees
of one of those parties on whose services that party relied for the performance of his
contract to break their contracts of employment with him, and if the essential
preconditions for a cause of action based on interference with the performance of a
g contract were present. Those preconditions were (a) that the person charged with the
actionable interference knew of the existence of the contract and intended to procure its
breach, (b) that the person so charged definitely and unequivocally persuaded, induced
or procured the employees concerned to break their contracts of employment with such
intent, (c) that the employees so persuaded, induced or procured in fact broke their
contracts of employment, and (d) that the breach of contract forming the alleged subject
h of interference ensued as a necessary consequence of the breaches by the employees
concerned of their contracts of employment. Although there was a real distinction
between direct and indirect action designed to interfere with the performance of the
principal contract, there was no such distinction between different forms of indirect
action if the four preconditions were present. Since the defendants knew of the existence
of the time charter (and on the facts they did have such knowledge or were sufficiently
j familiar with the shipping industry to know that such a contract would in all the
circumstances have existed) and in the light of such knowledge used unlawful means
(namely calling out the tug crew) intending to prevent the due performance of the

a   Section 13(1) is set out at p 342 h j, post
b   Section 17, so far as material, is set out at p 343 a to g, post

contract in order to cause damage to the shipowners and since a necessary consequence
of calling out the tug crew was that the charterers were prevented from performing their *a*
contract thereby causing damage to the shipowners, the shipowners had a prima facie
cause of action against the defendants (see p 341 *g* to p 342 *a* and *c* to *g*, p 344 *d e*, p 345 *h*
to p 346 *h*, p 347 *d* to *g*, p 348 *g* to *j*, p 349 *b* to *g* and *j* to p 350 *c* and p 351 *b c*, post);
dictum of Jenkins LJ in *D C Thomson & Co Ltd v Deakin* [1952] 2 All ER at 379–380
applied; *GWK Ltd v Dunlop Rubber Co Ltd* (1926) 42 TLR 376 followed.

(2) Section 17 of the 1980 Act only preserved the immunity from actions in tort *b*
provided for by s 13(1) of the 1974 Act if the principal purpose of the secondary action
was to prevent the supply of services under a contract made between the employer
involved in the trade dispute and the employer affected by the secondary action.
Accordingly, if a contract for the supply of goods and services, within s 17(6) of the 1980
Act, was disrupted or prevented by secondary action and the contract was not one to
which the employer involved in the trade dispute or his agent was a party, but was *c*
instead made by someone else, the secondary action did not fall within the category of
secondary action permitted by s 17(3). Since the contract for the supply of the towage
services had been made not by the employer involved in the trade dispute (the
shipowners) but by someone (the sub-charterers) not involved in the dispute, and since
there was no indication that the sub-charterers had entered into the contract as agents for
the shipowners, the defendants' action was unlawful secondary action for which the *d*
shipowners had a cause of action. Furthermore (per O'Connor LJ), the means used by the
defendants was to prevent the supply of services to another person, namely the sub-
charterers, and therefore the defendants' secondary action did not have the purpose of
'directly' preventing or disrupting the supply of services 'otherwise than by means of
preventing . . . the supply of . . . services . . . to any other person' as required by s 17(6)(*b*)
in order to be lawful (see p 343 *h* to p 344 *d*, p 345 *b* to *g*, p 347 *g*, p 350 *e f h j* and p 351 *a* *e*
to *c*, post); *Marina Shipping Ltd v Laughton* [1982] 1 All ER 481 followed.

Per Sir John Donaldson MR. When legislating in respect of circumstances which
directly affect the man or woman in the street or on the shop floor, Parliament should
give as high a priority to clarity and simplicity of expression as to refinements of policy.
Where possible statutes, or complete parts of statutes, should not be amended but re-
enacted in amended form so that those concerned can read the provisions in a single *f*
document (see p 351 *g h*, post).

Notes

For the legal liability of trade unions, see Supplement to 38 Halsbury's Laws (3rd edn)
para 677B.3.

For the Trade Union and Labour Relations Act 1974, s 13(1) (as substituted by the *g*
Trade Union and Labour Relations (Amendment) Act 1976, s 3(2)), see 46 Halsbury's
Statutes (3rd edn) 1941.

For the Employment Act 1980, s 17, see 50(2) ibid 2635.

Cases referred to in judgments

GWK Ltd v Dunlop Rubber Co Ltd (1926) 42 TLR 376, 45 Digest (Repl) 307, *213*. *h*

Lumley v Gye (1853) 2 E & B 216, [1843–60] All ER Rep 208, 118 ER 749, 45 Digest
  (Repl) 304, *198*.

Marina Shipping Ltd v Laughton [1982] 1 All ER 481, [1982] QB 1127, [1982] 2 WLR 569,
  CA.

National Phonograph Co Ltd v Edison-Bell Consolidated Phonograph Co Ltd [1908] 1 Ch 335,
  [1904–7] All ER Rep 116, CA, 45 Digest (Reissue) 305, *206*.

NWL Ltd v Woods, NWL Ltd v Nelson [1979] 3 All ER 614, [1979] 1 WLR 1294, HL, *j*
  Digest (Cont Vol E) 612, *1457a*.

Porr v Shaw, The Marabu Porr [1979] 2 Lloyd's Rep 331, CA.

Quinn v Leatham [1901] AC 495, [1900–3] All ER Rep 1, HL, 45 Digest (Repl) 280, *33*.

Thomson (D C) & Co Ltd v Deakin [1952] 2 All ER 361, [1952] Ch 646, CA, 45 Digest (Repl)
  561, *1379*.

Torquay Hotel Co Ltd v Cousins [1969] 1 All ER 522, [1969] 2 Ch 106, [1969] 2 WLR 289, CA, Digest (Cont Vol C) 957, 224b.

Cases also cited

Acrow (Automation) Ltd v Rex Chainbelt Inc [1971] 3 All ER 1175, [1971] 1 WLR 1676, CA.
Allen v Flood [1898] AC 1, [1895–9] All ER Rep 52, HL.
Blandy Bros & Co Lda v Nello Simoni Ltd [1963] 2 Lloyd's Rep 393.
Bowles (F) & Sons Ltd v Lindley [1965] 1 Lloyd's Rep 207.
Branwhite v Worcester Works Finance Ltd [1968] 3 All ER 104, [1969] 1 AC 552, HL.
Duport Steels Ltd v Sirs [1980] 1 All ER 529, [1980] 1 WLR 142, HL.
Emerald Construction Co Ltd v Lowthian [1966] 1 All ER 1013, [1966] 1 WLR 691, CA.
Express Newspapers Ltd v MacShane [1980] 1 All ER 65, [1980] AC 672, HL.
Garnac Grain Co Inc v H M F Faure & Fairclough Ltd [1967] 2 All ER 353, [1968] AC 1130, HL.
Greig v Insole [1978] 3 All ER 449, [1978] 1 WLR 302.
Hadmor Productions Ltd v Hamilton [1982] 1 All ER 1042, [1982] 2 WLR 322, HL.
Mogul Steamship Co Ltd v McGregor, Gow & Co (1889) 23 QBD 598, [1891–4] All ER Rep 278, CA; affd [1892] AC 25, [1891–4] All ER Rep 263, HL.
Plessey Co plc v Wilson [1982] IRLR 198.
Rookes v Barnard [1964] 1 All ER 367, [1964] AC 1129, HL.
South Wales Miners' Federation v Glamorgan Coal Co Ltd [1905] AC 239, [1904–7] All ER Rep 211, HL.
Stratford (JT) & Son Ltd v Lindley [1964] 3 All ER 102, [1965] AC 269, HL.
Universe Tankships Inc of Monrovia v International Transport Workers Federation [1982] 2 All ER 67, [1982] 2 WLR 803, HL.

Interlocutory appeal

On 23 July 1982 Parker J granted to the plaintiffs, Merkur Island Shipping Corp (the shipowners), who were the owners of the vessel Hoegh Apapa which was chartered to Leif Hoegh & Co A/S and sub-chartered to Ned Lloyd, an interlocutory injunction restraining the defendants, Brian Laughton, Harry Shaw and Harold Lewis (who were officials of the International Transport Workers Federation), their servants, agents or otherwise from issuing instructions to and/or otherwise encouraging lockkeepers and/or tugmen and/or boatmen and/or pilots and/or linesmen and/or others concerned with the free passage and operation of vessels at Liverpool to refuse to assist the free passage or working of the vessel at Liverpool and ordering the defendants to withdraw all such instructions and/or encouragement already given. By a writ issued on 5 August 1982 the plaintiffs claimed against the defendants (i) damages for unlawful interference with the performance of a time charter made on 12 February 1982 between the plaintiffs and Leif Hoegh & Co A/S, (ii) damages for unlawful interference with the trade and business of the plaintiffs and (iii) an injunction in the terms of the interlocutory injunction granted. The defendants appealed against the order of Parker J. The facts are set out in the judgment of O'Connor LJ.

Cyril Newman QC, Nicholas Merriman and *Charles Macdonald* for the defendants.
Roger Buckley QC and *T R Charlton* for the shipowners.

Cur adv vult

4 November. The following judgments were delivered.

O'CONNOR LJ (giving the first judgment at the invitation of Sir John Donaldson MR). This is yet another case arising from the campaign of the International Transport Workers Federation (the ITF) to force shipowners, particularly those whose ships fly flags of convenience, to improve the pay and conditions of employment of their crews up to a standard set by the ITF. The pattern of events is well known: when a ship falls foul of the

ITF it declares her black, and calls on affiliated trade unions whose members man tugs, locks, cranes etc to deny those services to the ship. The ITF knows full well that to prevent a ship using a port for which she is bound, or impounding her in a port from which she is ready to sail, is bound to cause damage to the shipowner and this is the lever used to force a reluctant shipowner to agree terms acceptable to the ITF.

The plaintiffs own the Hoegh Apapa, a Liberian registered ship. The majority of the crew were Filipinos recruited in Manila. On 6 July 1982 the ship was in Tilbury when a crew member complained of low wages to an ITF representative. The usual drill went into action, but the ship escaped from Tilbury during negotiations for an agreement. On 14 July the ITF learnt that the ship was due in Liverpool on 15 July for loading. The ITF asked for help in particular from the Transport and General Workers Union (the TGWU) to black the ship. On 16 July the ship was ready to sail, but the tugmen in breach of their contract of employment refused to take her save to a lay berth. The lockkeepers also refused to work the gates to allow the ship out. Negotiations to settle the dispute failed so the shipowner applied for injunctions to lift the blacking and on 23 July 1982 Parker J granted injunctions to achieve that end. At about the time the judge was giving judgment tidal conditions forced the lockkeepers to open the gates and the ship took the opportunity to escape. In one sense this appeal by the ITF is academic, but it raises a matter of law of general importance on which the parties desire a ruling.

The ship was time chartered to Leif Hoegh & Co A/S under a charterparty dated 12 February 1982 and sub-chartered to Ned Lloyd by a fixture dated 14 July 1982. Clause 2 of the time charter provides:

'Whilst on hire the Charterers shall provide and pay for all the fuel except as otherwise agreed, Port Charges, normal Pilotages, Agencies, Commissions, Consular Charges (except those pertaining to the Crew), and all other usual expenses except those before stated, but when the vessel puts into a port for causes for which the vessel is responsible, then all such charges incurred shall be paid by the Owners . . .'

Other relevant clauses are cl 51, which provides:

'In the event of loss of time due to boycott of the vessel in any port or place by shore labour or others, or arising from Government restrictions by reason of the vessel's flag, or arising from the terms and conditions on which the members of the crew are employed, or by reason of the trading of this vessel, payment of hire shall cease for time thereby lost.'

And cl 60, which provides:

'Should the vessel be prevented from work for the reasons as outlined in Clauses 49/50/51 and 52 for more than ten days, Charterers shall have the option of cancelling this contract.'

Messrs Van Ommeren, agents for the sub-charterers, have a standing contract with Rea Towing for the provision of tugs to Ned Lloyd vessels. They ordered tugs for 5.00 pm on 16 July but, as I have said, the tugmen, members of the TGWU, refused to take the ship beyond a lay berth. The ITF was informed of the terms of the time charter by telex on 16 July.

By their writ the plaintiffs claimed damages from the defendants under two heads:

'(1) damages for deliberate interference with and/or threat to the performance of a time charter dated 12th February 1982 between the Plaintiffs and Leif Hoegh and Co. Aktieselskab, such interference and/or threat being brought about by unlawful means, namely wrongfully procuring and/or inducing and/or threatening to procure or induce lock keepers and/or tugmen and/or pilots and/or boatmen and/or linesmen and/or others concerned with the free passage and operation of vessels at Liverpool to refuse to assist the free passage or working of the "HOEGH APAPA" at Liverpool (2) Damages for deliberate interference with and/or threat to the trade and business of the Plaintiffs, such interference and/or threat being brought about by unlawful means namely wrongfully procuring and/or inducing and/or threatening to procure or induce lock keepers and/or tugmen and/or pilots and/or boatmen and/ or linesmen and/or others concerned with the free passage and operation of vessels at Liverpool to refuse to assist the free passage or working of the "HOEGH APAPA" at Liverpool.'

These claims are the basis for the injunctions claimed.

The plaintiffs' case for the grant of the injunctions was simple enough: they submit that the facts disclosed that they had unanswerable claims for damages at common law. They accept that the acts of the defendants giving rise to the common law claims would be protected by s 13 of the Trade Union and Labour Relations Act 1974 as amended in 1976 but for the provisions of s 17 of the Employment Act 1980.

The defendants contend that on the facts para (1) of the writ discloses no cause of action at common law, in the alternative that the immunity which they enjoy in respect of it and of that in para (2) of the writ is not removed by s 17 of the 1980 Act.

The issues in this case are identical with those which were before this court also on appeal from Parker J in *Marina Shipping Ltd v Laughton* [1982] 1 All ER 481, [1982] QB 1127. That was another case of the ITF blacking a ship on time charter, cl 2 of which was so far as material in identical terms to cl 2 of the charter in this case, and the contract for the port services was made by the charterers' agents. The writ claimed damages under the same two heads. Parker J and this court held that the defendants were not protected by s 13 of the 1974 Act because their immunity had been removed by s 17(1) of the 1980 Act, in that their acts amounted to secondary action within s 17(2) not legitimised by s 17(3) because there was no contract between the plaintiffs and the port authority as required by s 17(6).

Counsel for the defendants has submitted that we are not bound by the decision because as to the first ground alleged in the writ a concession was made that it disclosed a cause of action and that that concession was wrongly made, that as a result the court did not deal with the second ground and that, he submits, is not taken out of immunity by the 1980 Act.

In *Marina Shipping Ltd v Laughton* [1982] 1 All ER 481 at 485–486, [1982] QB 1127 at 1139 Lawton LJ said:

'The problem in this case is this. As I have already stated, had this blacking occurred before 1 August 1980 the plaintiff owners could not have come to the court asking for relief. That was so notwithstanding that, on the facts that I have recounted, they clearly had a cause of action for unlawful interference with their contract with the charterers and with such other persons with whom they had contracts for the transport of goods; and, secondly, they had a cause of action, prima facie, for interference with their business by the use of unlawful means. The blacking through the lockkeepers kept the vessel in dock and that necessarily meant, under cl 34 of the charterparty, that time was running against them. So that head of claim was as clear as any head of claim could be. It is also reasonably clear, on the facts of this case, that the blacking of the vessel necessarily meant that she could not be going about her ordinary work as a vessel. For the purposes of this appeal the existence of those causes of action has not been disputed.'

Brightman LJ said ([1982] 1 All ER 481 at 489, [1982] QB 1127 at 1143):

'The interlocutory relief sought by the plaintiffs is based on two alleged causes of action: (a) interference with the performance of the plaintiffs' contracts, namely the time charter and a contract of freight; and (b) interference with the plaintiffs' business by unlawful means. If either of these causes of action is soundly based interim relief must follow. I will deal first with cause of action (a). Having regard to the form which the relevant legislation takes, I think, as I indicated in argument, that one can best approach the problem in three stages. Stage 1: have the plaintiffs a cause of action at common law? If so, stage 2: is that cause of action removed by the 1974 Act? (When I refer to the 1974 Act I mean that Act as amended by the Trade Union and Labour Relations (Amendment) Act 1976.) If so, stage 3: is that cause of action restored by the 1980 Act? If so, the plaintiffs can sue, as also they can if a negative answer were given at stage 2. It is common ground that cause of action (a) is soundly based at common law. One can therefore pass to stage 2, where it is common ground, for the purposes of this motion, that such cause of action is removed by s 13(1)(a) of the 1974 Act. One therefore passes to stage 3 to consider whether that cause of action has been restored by the 1980 Act. That is where the controversy lies in the present case.'

Having resolved that controversy in favour of the plaintiffs, he said ([1982] 1 All ER 481 at 490, [1982] QB 1127 at 1145):

'It is unnecessary to express a view about cause of action (b), because the defendants' success in relation to that action would not detract from the plaintiffs' right to interim relief in connection with cause of action (a).'

Oliver LJ agreed with both judgments.

I will consider first the submission that the plaintiffs have no cause of action under the first ground of the writ. What is the tort alleged in that paragraph of the writ? The allegation is 'the deliberate interference with . . . the performance of [the] time charter by unlawful means'. The nature of this tort was considered by this court in *D C Thomson & Co Ltd v Deakin* [1952] 2 All ER 361, [1952] Ch 646. In that case the plaintiffs, a printing company, were in dispute with a union, NATSOPA, who had called their members employed by the plaintiffs out on strike. In order to bring pressure to bear on the plaintiffs the union asked for help from two other unions in order to stop the supply of paper by Bowaters to the plaintiffs under a running contract. In response loaders and drivers employed by Bowaters threatened to refuse to load paper for, or drive laden lorries to, the plaintiffs. In face of this threat Bowaters decided to stop delivering paper to the plaintiffs. Jenkins LJ considered the ingredients of the tort alleged. He began with *Lumley v Gye* (1853) 2 E & B 216, [1843–60] All ER Rep 208, a case of direct interference with a contract, Gye persuading a party to a contract to break it. He cited two passages from the speeches of Lord Macnaghten and Lord Lindley in *Quinn v Leathem* [1901] AC 495 at 510, 535, [1900–3] All ER Rep 1 at 9, 16. Lord Lindley, after declaring *Lumley v Gye* to be rightly decided, said:

'Further, the principle involved in it cannot be confined to inducements to break contracts of service, nor indeed to inducements to break any contracts. The principle which underlies the decision reaches all wrongful acts done intentionally to damage a particular individual, and actually damaging him.'

These passages have been applied in a wide variety of cases; for example, in *National Phonograph Co Ltd v Edison-Bell Consolidated Phonograph Co Ltd* [1908] 1 Ch 335, [1904–7] All ER Rep 116 the defendants, who were on the plaintiffs' stop list, by fraud obtained records from the plaintiffs' factor. This court held that the plaintiffs could recover on the ground that the defendants had by unlawful means interfered with their contract with their factor who was innocent.

Another example is *GWK Ltd v Dunlop Rubber Co Ltd* (1926) 42 TLR 376. GWK, manufacturers of motor cars, had an agreement with ARM, manufacturers of tyres (the second plaintiffs), to fit ARM tyres to all their new cars. They sent cars so fitted for exhibition by dealers at the Glasgow Motor Show. During the night before the show opened Dunlop men took off the ARM tyres and put on Dunlop tyres. Lord Heward CJ had no difficulty in holding that ARM were entitled to damages because Dunlop—

'had knowingly committed a violation of the A.R.M. Company's legal rights by interfering, without any justification whatever, with the contractual relations existing between them and the G.W.K. Company . . . with the intention of damaging the A.R.M. Company [which] had been thereby damnified.'

(See 42 TLR 376 at 377.)

Jenkins LJ in *D C Thomson & Co Ltd v Deakin* [1952] 2 All ER 361 at 378, [1952] Ch 646 at 695 regarded these cases as examples of what he called—

'direct invasion by the third party of the rights of one of the parties to the contract by prevailing on the other party to do, or doing in concert with him, or doing without reference to either party, that which is inconsistent with the contract, or by preventing, by means of actual physical restraint, one of the parties from being where he should be, or doing what he should do, under the contract.'

Jenkins LJ then went on to consider what can be called indirect invasion of the plaintiffs' rights under the contract between Thomson and Bowaters, and I think it necessary to quote a long passage from his judgment ([1952] 2 All ER 361 at 379–380, [1952] Ch 646 at 696–697):

'The plaintiffs' case does seem to me to involve an extension of the range of actionable interference with contractual rights beyond any actual instance of this type of wrong to be found in the decided cases. Here there is no direct invasion of the plaintiffs' rights under the contract. It was no part of their contract that these particular employees, or any particular employees, should be employed by Bowaters for the purposes of effecting deliveries of paper to them. Thus the breaches by these men of their contracts of service with Bowaters (if made out on the facts) did not in themselves involve any breach of Bowaters' contract with the plaintiffs. The breaches of the contracts of service (if made out) were, so to speak, at one remove from the breach of contract complained of. Nevertheless, I think that in principle an actionable interference with contractual relations may be committed by a third party who, with knowledge of a contract between two other persons and with the intention of causing its breach, or of preventing its performance, persuades, induces or procures the servants of one of those parties, on whose services he relies for the performance of his contract, to break their contracts of employment with him, either by leaving him without notice or by refusing to do what is necessary for the performance of his contract, provided that the breach of the contract between the two other persons intended to be brought about by the third party does in fact ensue as a necessary consequence of the third party's wrongful interference with the contracts of employment. I take this view because I see no distinction in principle for the present purpose between persuading a man to break his contract with another, preventing him by physical restraint from performing it, making his performance of it impossible by taking away or damaging his tools or machinery, and making his performance of it impossible by depriving him, in breach of their contracts, of the services of his employees. All these are wrongful acts, and, if done with knowledge and an intention to bring about a breach of a contract to which the person directly wronged is a party, and if in fact producing that result, I fail to see why they should not all alike fall within the sphere of actionable interference with contractual relations delimited by LORD MACNAGHTEN and LORD LINDLEY in Quinn v. Leathem ([1901] AC 495, [1900–3] All ER Rep 1). But, while admitting this form of actionable interference in principle, I would hold it strictly confined to cases where it is clearly shown, first, that the person charged with actionable interference knew of the existence of the contract and intended to procure its breach; secondly, that the person so charged did definitely and unequivocally persuade, induce or procure the employees concerned to break their contracts of employment with the intent I have mentioned; thirdly, that the employees so persuaded, induced or procured did in fact break their contracts of employment; and, fourthly, that breach of the contract forming the alleged subject of interference ensued as a necessary consequence of the breaches by the employees concerned of their contracts of employment.'

There is no doubt that Jenkins LJ was laying down the ingredients of what he regarded as an extension of actionable interference in the context of the facts in D C Thomson & Co Ltd v Deakin when Bowaters would have been the party directly wronged by the calling out of their employees. But when the four essential ingredients listed in the last paragraph that I have cited are considered, it will be seen that so long as the requirement that the interference with the contract is directly caused by the unlawful act (calling out employees) there is no reason to restrict the principle to cases where the employees are employees of one of the parties to the contract.

Morris LJ states the principle ([1952] 2 All ER 361 at 384, [1952] Ch 646 at 702):

'In this context the notion of interference involves something wrongful. The breach of contract must be brought about or procured or induced by some act which a man is not entitled to do, which may take the form of direct persuasion to break a contract or the intentional bringing about of a breach by indirect methods involving wrongdoing.'

In *Torquay Hotel Co Ltd v Cousins* [1969] 1 All ER 522 at 530, [1969] 2 Ch 106 at 138 Lord Denning MR said:

'. . . there must be interference in the execution of a contract. The interference is not confined to the procurement of a breach of contract. It extends to a case where a third person prevents or hinders one party from performing his contract, even though it be not a breach.'

In the present case I think it is clear that there is a good arguable case that the ITF with knowledge of the time charter used unlawful means (calling out the tugmen) intending to prevent the due performance of the contract in order to cause damage to the shipowners and that a necessary consequence of calling out the tugmen was that the charterers were prevented from performing their contract thereby causing damage to the shipowners.

In my judgment the concession made in *Marina Shipping Ltd v Laughton* [1982] 1 All ER 481, [1982] QB 1127 that these facts gave a cause of action in tort to the shipowners at common law was rightly made.

It was submitted that on the evidence it was not shown that the ITF had knowledge of the time charter when it asked the TGWU to call out the tugmen. In my judgment there are two answers to that submission. In the first place, the ITF is sufficiently familiar with the shipping industry to know that a ship such as this which has loaded cargo will have obligations under contract to leave port and head for her destination. In my judgment that is sufficient to satisfy the requirement. Second, the ITF had express knowledge of the time charter and the relevant term by 6.00 pm on 16 July from the telex sent to it by the shipowners' solicitors. It did not lift the blacking as it could have done, and it continued to prevent the charterers performing the contract by unlawful means and that is sufficient to give the cause of action, the other requirements being the same.

The defendants accept that para 2 of the writ discloses a good cause of action.

The shipowners accept that the acts of the defendants giving rise to the claims in paras (1) and (2) of the writ are protected by s 13 of the 1974 Act unless that protection is removed by s 17 of the Employment Act 1980.

For convenience I shall refer hereafter to the cause of action in para (1) of the writ as 'interference with contract' and that in para (2) as 'interference with trade or business'. I set out the provisions of s 13 of the 1974 Act (as amended by s 3 of the Trade Union and Labour Relations (Amendment) Act 1976) so far as relevant:

'*Acts in contemplation or furtherance of trade disputes.*—(1) An act done by a person in contemplation or furtherance of a trade dispute shall not be actionable in tort on the ground only—(*a*) that it induces another person to break a contract or interferes or induces any other person to interfere with its performance; or (*b*) that it consists in his threatening that a contract (whether one to which he is a party or not) will be broken or its performance interfered with, or that he will induce another person to break a contract or to interfere with its performance.

(2) For the avoidance of doubt it is hereby declared that an act done by a person in contemplation or furtherance of a trade dispute is not actionable in tort on the ground only that it is an interference with the trade, business or employment of another person, or with the right of another person to dispose of his capital or his labour as he wills . . .'

The act done was procuring the calling out of the tugmen. It was fairly and squarely within and so given immunity by s 13(1)(a) so far as interference with contract is concerned. Is that immunity removed by s 17 of the 1980 Act? Subsection (1) provides:

'Nothing in section 13 of the 1974 Act shall prevent an act from being actionable in tort on a ground specified in subsection (1)(a) or (b) of that section in any case where—(a) the contract concerned is not a contract of employment, and (b) one of the facts relied upon for the purpose of establishing liability is that there has been secondary action which is not action satisfying the requirements of subsection (3), (4) or (5) below.'

The contract concerned is the time charter so the requirement in s 17(1)(a) is fulfilled. One of the facts relied on for the purpose of establishing liability is the refusal of the tugmen to work the ship in breach of their contracts of employment. Is that secondary action within s 17(1)(b)? Subsection (2) provides:

'For the purposes of this section there is secondary action in relation to a trade dispute when, and only when, a person—(a) induces another to break a contract of employment or interferes or induces another to interfere with its performance, or (b) threatens that a contract of employment under which he or another is employed will be broken or its performance interfered with, or that he will induce another to break a contract of employment or to interfere with its performance, if the employer under the contract of employment is not a party to the trade dispute.'

The employers of the tugmen were not parties to the trade dispute so this was secondary action unless excluded by the provisions of sub-s (3), (4) or (5) of which only sub-s (3) is relevant:

'Secondary action satisfies the requirements of this subsection if—(a) the purpose or principal purpose of the secondary action was directly to prevent or disrupt the supply during the dispute of goods or services between an employer who is a party to the dispute and the employer under the contract of employment to which the secondary action relates; and (b) the secondary action (together with any corresponding action relating to other contracts of employment with the same employer) was likely to achieve that purpose.'

That subsection has to be construed together with sub-s (6):

'In subsections (3)(a) and (4)(a) above—(a) references to the supply of goods or services between two persons are references to the supply of goods or services by one to the other in pursuance of a contract between them substituting at the time of the secondary action, and (b) references to directly preventing or disrupting the supply are references to preventing or disrupting it otherwise than by means of preventing or disrupting the supply of goods or services by or to any other person.'

The purpose of the secondary action was to prevent the supply of services between the employer who was a party to the dispute, the shipowners, and the employer under the contract of employment to which the secondary action related, the tugowners, and the secondary action was likely to achieve that purpose. Nevertheless the secondary action was not within s 17(3)(a) for two reasons, (i) because there was no contract subsisting between the shipowners and the tugowners as required by s 17(6)(a), and (ii) because the purpose was not *directly* to prevent supply because the preventing was not 'otherwise than by means of preventing . . . the supply of . . . services . . . to any other person' as required by s 17(6)(b) in that the means used was to prevent supply of services by the tugowners to the charterers under the contract between them.

This last reason was not considered by the court in *Marina Shipping Ltd v Laughton* [1982] 1 All ER 481, [1982] QB 1127; but apart from that my reasons for holding that the defendants are not immune from suit for interference with contract are the same as those in the *Marina Shipping Ltd* case, which is binding on us in any event.

Counsel for the defendants submitted that it cannot have been the intention of Parliament to enable these shipowners, unquestionably a party to a trade dispute, to maintain an action for interference with contract. I do not agree with this submission. It seems to me that the intention of Parliament was to remove immunity from liability caused by secondary action as defined in the 1980 Act to anyone suffering damage who apart from the 1974 Act could maintain an action for it.

Counsel for the defendants submitted that as it was the ship that needed the services of the tug we should hold that on the facts of this case the agreement for the supply of the services of the tug was made on behalf of the shipowners at least for the purposes of s 17(6). Like the judge, I cannot accept that submission. A contract either subsists between two parties or it does not. There was no contract between the tugowners and the shipowners and it is not permissible to imply or invent one.

There remains the cause of action for interference with trade or business. It is said that this is within s 13(2) of the 1974 Act and that the immunity is not removed by s 17(1) of the 1980 Act. I do not think it possible to decide the limits of this immunity on the material at present available. It will be seen that the 'act done' is the same for both causes of action, and I do not think it follows from the wording of the sections that, in cases such as the present, the shipowner could not recover damages for interference with his trade or business beyond what might be called the special damage arising from the unlawful interference with contract. I would want to consider the effect of the words 'on the ground only' in both sub-s (1) and sub-s (2) of s 13 of the 1974 Act on the heads of damage claimed. For present purposes the judge was entitled to make the orders which he did on the basis of unlawful interference with contract. I would dismiss this appeal.

DILLON LJ. This is an appeal by the defendants, officials of the International Transport Workers Federation (the ITF), against an interlocutory injunction granted by Parker J restraining the defendants from 'blacking' the Liberian ship Hoegh Apapa in the port of Liverpool. In fact, owing to unusual tidal conditions, the ship was able to sail from Liverpool without the help of tugs or lockkeepers at about the time when the judge gave his judgment. That does not, however, to my mind diminish the importance of the issues raised in the action, although it does mean that there is no practical need for the continuation of the injunction.

The ITF has urged the court to give such assistance as it can, even on an interlocutory appeal, to clarify this fairly difficult area of law. The shipowners have not demurred, although they have stressed, correctly, that we are bound by the decision, on very similar facts, of the Court of Appeal in *Marina Shipping Ltd v Laughton* [1982] 1 All ER 481, [1982] QB 1127.

The ITF has been endeavouring for some time to induce, by 'blacking' if necessary, the owners of ships which sail under flags of convenience to pay wages to their crews and provide conditions of service in line with the scales of wages and conditions approved by the ITF. Since the ITF, being an international federation of trade unions, is a trade union in its own right, whether its blacking activities in England can be restrained by injunction tends to involve consideration of the trade union legislation for the time being in force in Britain.

Thus it is common ground that, in the years immediately before s 17 of the Employment Act 1980 came into force, no action could have been brought by shipowners in Britain, and no injunction could have been granted, to restrain blacking, such as the blacking of the Hoegh Apapa because of s 13 of the Trade Union and Labour Relations Act 1974 as amended by the Trade Union and Labour Relations (Amendment) Act 1976: see *NWL Ltd v Woods* [1979] 3 All ER 614, [1979] 1 WLR 1294. Section 17 of the 1980 Act provides that nothing in s 13 of the 1974 Act shall prevent an act from being actionable in tort on a ground specified in s 13(1)(a) or (b) in any case where certain rather complicated conditions are satisfied. Section 17 does not therefore confer a cause of action. It merely removes in certain circumstances the bar placed by s 13 of the 1974 Act on the bringing of certain actions which would have lain at common law.

The plaintiff shipowners have, therefore, to show, to the extent appropriate for the grant of interlocutory relief against defendants who were admittedly acting in contemplation or furtherance of a trade dispute, firstly, that what the defendants did in blacking the ship is actionable at the suit of the shipowners at common law and, secondly, that the conditions of s 17, for the removal of the bar of s 13, are satisfied.

In their writ, the shipowners formulate their claim under two alternative heads: under para (1) wrongful interference by unlawful means with a particular contract, namely the time charter between the shipowners and the Norwegian charterers Leif Hoegh & Co A/S, and under para (2) wrongful interference with the trade and business of the plaintiffs. The claim under para (2) is barred by s 13(2) of the 1974 Act, and that bar is unaffected by s 17 of the 1980 Act. That claim cannot therefore be sustained. The claim under para (1), however, if sustainable at common law, is based on a ground specified in s 13(1)(a) of the 1974 Act, and the bar on that claim previously imposed by s 13 is, if the conditions of s 17 of the 1980 Act are satisfied, lifted by s 17.

Section 17 was carefully analysed in the judgments of this court in *Marina Shipping Ltd v Laughton*. The section is concerned with secondary action in relation to a trade dispute and the court had in particular to consider the effect on s 17(3) of s 17(6)(a), which, as Lord Wedderburn puts it in *Clerk and Lindsell on the Law of Torts* (15th edn, 1982) p 795, 'appears to insert an objective test into the subjective formulation of the "purpose"' of the secondary action. The court held that if the contract, referred to in s 17(6)(a), for the goods or services the supply of which was prevented or disrupted by the secondary action was not a contract to which the employers party to the trade dispute, that is to say the shipowners, or their agents are parties, but was a contract made by someone else, namely the charterers or their agents, then the secondary action did not satisfy the requirements of s 17(3). Accordingly the shipowners could take advantage of the lifting by s 17 of the bar imposed by s 13 of the 1974 Act, and could pursue a common law claim for an injunction against the union's officials to restrain the blacking of the ship, as a wrongful interference with the charterparty.

Counsel for the defendants submits, firstly, that it is surprising if Parliament intended by s 17 to enable the employer who is a party to the trade dispute to bring proceedings to restrain officials of the union involved in the dispute, and, secondly, that it is odd that the legitimacy of secondary action by the disruption of the goods or services should, in a common commercial situation where several parties are working together on what may broadly be called the same venture, depend on the chance of how the contractual arrangements with the supplier of the goods or services have been made.

The function of the court is however merely to construe and apply s 17 which is drawn in general terms. That has been done for us in the *Marine Shipping Ltd* case on facts from which the facts of the present case cannot be distinguished in any way favourable to the defendants. We are bound by the *Marina Shipping Ltd* case and I say no more about s 17.

I turn then to the question whether what the defendants did is actionable at common law at the suit of the shipowners as a wrongful interference by unlawful means with the time charter. In the *Marina Shipping Ltd* case it was conceded that the shipowners would have an action at common law. Counsel for the defendants says that that concession need not have been made, and he submits that on a true appreciation the shipowners have no cause of action at common law against the defendants.

It has long been held that where C has a contract with D direct persuasion, procurement or inducement applied by X, a third party, to, for instance, C with knowledge of the contract and the intention of bringing about its breach is a wrongful act in itself. This is the primary form of the type of wrong commonly designated, in that form, 'procuring or inducing a breach of contract': see the judgment of Jenkins LJ in *D C Thomson & Co Ltd v Deakin* [1952] 2 All ER 361 at 377, [1952] Ch 646 at 692–693. This can be readily applied at common law to a situation where C is a charterer and D is a shipowner and the contract between them is a time charter.

In his judgment Jenkins LJ concluded that there was no difference in principle between persuading a man to break his contract with another, preventing him by physical restraint from performing it, making his performance of it impossible by taking away or damaging his tools or machinery, and making his performance of it impossible by depriving him, in breach of their contracts, of the services of his employees. Jenkins LJ continued ([1952] 2 All ER 361 at 379–380, [1952] Ch 646 at 696):

'All these are wrongful acts, and, if done with knowledge and an intention to bring about a breach of a contract to which the person directly wronged is a party, and if in fact producing that result, I fail to see why they should not all alike fall within the sphere of actionable interference with contractual relations . . . But, while admitting this form of actionable interference in principle, I would hold it strictly confined to cases where it is clearly shown, first, that the person charged with actionable interference knew of the existence of the contract and intended to procure its breach; secondly, that the person so charged did definitely and unequivocally persuade, induce or procure the employees concerned to break their contracts of employment with the intent I have mentioned; thirdly, that the employees so persuaded, induced or procured did in fact break their contracts of employment; and, fourthly, that breach of the contract forming the alleged subject of interference ensued as a necessary consequence of the breaches by the employees concerned of their contracts of employment. I should add that by the expression "necessary consequence" used here . . . I mean that it must be shown that, by reason of the withdrawal of the services of the employees concerned, the contract breaker was unable, as a matter of practical possibility, to perform his contract.'

Counsel for the defendants therefore accepts that, just as procuring or inducing a breach of contract is actionable at common law in its direct or primary form, so indirect interference at the first stage may be actionable if all four of Jenkins LJ's conditions are satisfied. That might be so in the instance given above if X, knowing of the charterparty and intending to bring about its breach, made performance impossible by depriving C, the charterer, in breach of his contract, of the services of his employees necessary for the performance of the contract. Counsel for the defendants submits, however, that indirect interference at a second or third stage is too remote to be actionable. Thus it is too remote for D to be able to sue if X makes performance of the charterparty impossible by depriving C of the services of B's tugs, even if they are the only tugs available to move the ship, by depriving B, in breach of their contracts of employment, of the services of B's employees.

A fortiori, it would be too remote for D to be able to sue if X deprived C of the services of B's tugs by persuading the employees of A, the fuel supplier, in breach of their contracts of employment with A, to refuse to supply B's tugs with fuel.

I cannot for my part see any distinction in principle between indirect interference at the first stage and indirect interference at a second or remoter stage. The logic which led Jenkins LJ to conclude that the tort, which had started in its primary form with direct interference, extended to indirect interference leads equally to the conclusion that an action lies for interference at a second or more remote stage provided that Jenkins LJ's four conditions are satisfied. The more indirect and remote the interference, the more difficult it may be to establish on the facts that these conditions are satisfied, in particular to establish that X, the alleged tortfeasor, did intend to interfere with the particular contract relied on by the plaintiff and that interference with that contract did ensue as a necessary consequence from the wrongful acts, remote though they were, that X brought about.

Jenkins LJ was only concerned with indirect interference with a contract which led to an actual breach of that contract. In *Torquay Hotel Co Ltd v Cousins* [1969] 1 All ER 522, [1969] 2 Ch 106 Lord Denning MR held that the tort extended to render actionable unlawful acts intended to interfere with and hinder the performance of the contract forming the alleged subject of the interference even though no actual breach of that contract occurred. In the *Torquay Hotel* case the relevant contract for the supply of fuel had contained a clause that neither party should be liable for any failure to fulfil any term of the contract if fulfilment was delayed, hindered or prevented by, among other things, labour disputes. The other members of the court, Russell and Winn LJJ, treated this exception clause as assuming a breach of contract but excluding liability in damages for

that breach in stated circumstances. Thus the acts of the union officials had caused a
breach of the contract and it was not necessary for Russell and Winn LJJ to follow Lord
Denning MR in extending the scope of the tort.

In the present case the charterparty includes provision in cl 51 that in the event of loss
of time due to boycott of the vessel in any port or place by shore labour or others, or
arising from the terms and conditions on which the members of the crew are employed,
payment of hire shall cease for time thereby lost. It also includes an option to the
charterers in cl 60 to cancel the contract if the ship is prevented from work for the reasons
as outlined in cl 51 and certain other clauses for more than ten days. It is said that these
clauses have the effect that the blacking could not result, however long continued, and
did not result, in any breach of the charterparty.

The present application is merely interlocutory, and in my judgment the shipowners
can say that they have at the least an arguable case for the trial, that Lord Denning MR
was right in the _Torquay Hotel_ case to extend the scope of the tort to interference by
unlawful means with the performance of a contract short of breach. Alternatively, they
have an arguable case that cll 51 and 60 of the charterparty are not significantly
distinguishable from the exception clause in the _Torquay Hotel_ case and are, like that
exception clause, only concerned with the consequences of an assumed breach. It is
unnecessary on this interlocutory appeal to express any final view on these points of law.

As to the facts, the defendants on their own evidence knew before the blacking in
Liverpool happened that the Hoegh Apapa was subject to a charterparty and the
defendants had, through an affiliate, been in touch with Leif Hoegh. They knew, before
the blacking took place, that the charterparty did not include any ITF clause guaranteeing
that the crew would be covered by terms and conditions of employment acceptable to
the ITF. They knew therefore that there was no opening for persuading the charterers to
put pressure on the shipowners to comply with the requirements of the ITF. They knew
also that the charterparty contained a clause to the effect that the ship would be off hire if
held up by government action or other problems. Against that background they intended
to stop the ship sailing from Liverpool. There is ample material to warrant the prima
facie conclusion for the purposes of this interlocutory application that the defendants
intended to bring the charterparty to an end by breach if they could not bring it to an
end without a breach. There is also ample material to warrant the conclusion that
conditions 2, 3 and 4 of Jenkins LJ's four conditions are satisfied.

I have set the foregoing out at length in deference to the importance of the issues and
to the thoroughness of the argument of counsel for the defendants. It would however be
sufficient to say that in my judgment Parker J was entirely right on a matter which was
within his discretion. His exercise of his discretion has not been faulted and I agree with
his judgment.

I would dismiss this appeal.

SIR JOHN DONALDSON MR. We were asked and agreed to expedite this appeal
and to do so notwithstanding that the ship had sailed. The justification was said to be
that the law was not clear and that this lack of clarity posed problems for a judge who is
asked, at short notice and as a matter of urgency, to grant an injunction. Having had the
benefit of the very clear arguments of counsel for the defendant trade union officials and
of counsel for the plaintiff shipowners, supported in the case of counsel for the defendants
by an invaluable written 'skeleton of argument', I have come to the conclusion that the
law is tolerably clear, but that the same cannot be said of the way in which it is expressed.

Marina Shipping Ltd v Laughton [1982] 1 All ER 481, [1982] QB 1127 involved two of
the three defendants in this appeal and is in many respects indistinguishable. In that case
Brightman LJ held that in cases such as this the court should adopt a three-stage approach
which involves asking and answering the following questions ([1982] 1 All ER 481 at
489, [1982] QB 1127 at 1143):

'Stage 1: have the plaintiffs a cause of action at common law? If so, stage 2: is that
cause of action removed by the 1974 Act [as amended]? . . . If so, stage 3: is that
cause of action restored by the 1980 Act? If so, the plaintiffs can sue, as also they can
if a negative answer were given at stage 2.'

I propose to adopt this approach.

Stage 1   *a*

Have the shipowners a cause of action at common law? As this is an appeal against an interlocutory order and the facts have still to be investigated, any answer must be tentative and without prejudice to how the question is to be answered if there is ever a full and final hearing. The shipowners have put forward two causes of action, conveniently set out in separate paragraphs of the writ. The first alleges deliberate interference with the performance of a time charter between the shipowners and Leif Hoegh & Co A/S, as *b* time charterers, brought about by unlawful means, namely wrongfully procuring tugmen and others to refuse to assist the free passage of the vessel at Liverpool. It is sufficient for present purposes to concentrate on the tugmen. The unlawful means alleged was the inducing of the tugmen to act in breach of their contracts of employment by refusing to tow the vessel to any place other than a lay berth. The second is similar to the first, save that the shipowners allege an intent to interfere with the shipowners' *c* business generally rather than with any particular contract to which the shipowners were a party.

In the *Marina Shipping Ltd* case it was conceded that the plaintiffs had a cause or causes of action at common law and accordingly counsel for the defendants submits that that decision is not binding on us so far as stage 1 is concerned. I think that this is right, although I cannot help thinking that the court would have itself raised the question if it *d* had not been satisfied that prima facie the concession was properly made.

Counsel for the defendants submits that the defendants induced the tug crews to break their contracts of employment with the intention of procuring a breach not of the time charter, but of the contract for towage services made by the tug owners with the sub-charterers. Indeed he submits that far from wanting to interfere with the performance of the time charter the defendants wished to see it enforced by the time charterers if, as *e* at one time they thought was the case, the time charter had contained a special ITF clause requiring the shipowners to pay ITF rates of wages. In the submission of counsel for the defendants, whilst the tug owners and the sub-charterers may well have had a cause of action based on these facts, the shipowners, being strangers to the contract for towage services, had none. Alternatively, if they had a cause of action, it was a cause of action based on an interference with the shipowners' trade or business generally rather than *f* interference with a specific contract to which the shipowners were parties. As such it is caught by s 13(2) of the Trade Union and Labour Relations Act 1974 as amended (to which I shall refer as 'the 1974 Act'), and is not restored by s 17 of the Employment Act 1980 as the only 'contract concerned' was one of employment.

The essential preconditions for the existence of a cause of action based on interference with the performance of a contract was stated by Jenkins LJ in *D C Thomson & Co Ltd v* *g* *Deakin* [1952] 2 All ER 361 at 379–380, [1952] 1 Ch 646 at 696–697 in the following terms:

'But, while admitting this form of actionable interference in principle, I would hold it strictly confined to cases where it is clearly shown, first, that the person charged with actionable interference knew of the existence of the contract and *h* intended to procure its breach; secondly, that the person so charged did definitely and unequivocally persuade, induce or procure the employees concerned to break their contracts of employment with the intent I have mentioned; thirdly, that the employees so persuaded, induced or procured did in fact break their contracts of employment; and, fourthly, that breach of the contract forming the alleged subject of interference ensued as a necessary consequence of the breaches by the employees *j* concerned of their contracts of employment. I should add that by the expression "necessary consequence" used here and elsewhere in this judgment I mean that it must be shown that, by reason of the withdrawal of the services of the employees concerned, the contract breaker was unable, as a matter of practical possibility, to perform his contract. In other words, I think the continuance of the services of the particular employees concerned must be so vital to the performance of the contract alleged to have been interfered with as to make the effect of their withdrawal comparable, for practical purposes, with a direct invasion of the contractual rights of the party aggrieved under the contract alleged to have been interfered with, as, for example (in the case of a contract for personal services), the physical restraint of the person by whom such services are to be performed.'

Are these conditions met?

1. Knowledge of and intention to breach the time charterparty

Whatever the precise degree of knowledge of the defendants at any particular time, faced with a laden ship which, as they well knew, was about to leave port, the defendants must in my judgment be deemed to have known of the almost certain existence of contracts of carriage to which the shipowners were parties. The wholly exceptional case would be that of a ship carrying the owner's own goods. Whether that contract or those contracts consisted of a time charter, a voyage charter or one or more bill of lading contracts or some or all of such contracts would have been immaterial to the defendants. Prima facie their intention was to immobilise the ship and in so doing to interfere with the performance by the owners of their contract or contracts of carriage; immobilising a laden ship which had no contractual obligation to move would have been a pointless exercise, since it would have brought no pressure to bear on the owners.

The argument that if the ITF clause had been included in the charterparty terms the defendants would have liked to have seen the time charterers enforcing that clause seems to me to be irrelevant. If the clause had existed and had been successfully enforced the trade dispute would have come to an end but, subject to that possibility, it is quite clear on the evidence that the defendants intended to interfere with the performance of the principal obligation under the time charter, namely an obligation to move the ship out of the port of Liverpool.

2. Inducement of breach of contract of employment with this intent

The inducement is admitted and the intent clear in the sense which I have already explained.

3. Actual breach of the tug owners' contracts of employment

This is not denied.

4. Breach of contract of carriage a necessary consequence of the tug crews' actions

On the evidence before the judge this was clear and it is his decision which we are called on to review. Subsequently the vessel left the port despite the inaction of the tug crews, but this only became possible when an adventurous master took advantage of the fact that an exceptional spring tide forced the lockkeepers to keep the dock gates open and made it possible to leave the dock without the assistance of tugs.

Accordingly the four conditions were met.

Counsel for the defendants submits that this is not enough and that there is a fifth condition. Before *D C Thomson & Co Ltd v Deakin* the authorities did not go beyond confirming the existence of a cause of action where there was a direct interference by the defendants with the performance of a contract to which the plaintiff was a party (the principal contract). *D C Thomson & Co Ltd v Deakin* extended this to a case where there was indirect interference with the principal contract by direct interference with the contracts of employment of those who were in fact intended to perform the principal contract. Accordingly Jenkins LJ said ([1952] 2 All ER 361 at 379, [1952] 1 Ch 646 at 696):

> '... in principle an actionable interference with contractual relations may be committed by a third party who, with knowledge of a contract between two other persons and with the intention of causing its breach, or of preventing its performance, persuades, induces or procures *the servants of one of those parties*, on whose services he relies for the performance of his contract, to break their contracts of employment with him ...' (My emphasis.)

Counsel for the defendants accordingly submits that we are being invited to make a further extension of the law.

I do not agree. It seems to me that there is a real distinction between direct and indirect

action designed to interfere with the performance of the principal contract, but that no
such distinction exists between different forms of indirect action provided that the four
conditions are fulfilled. All that can be said is that the more indirect the action of the
defendants the more difficult it may be to prove their knowledge of and intention to
interfere with the performance of the principal contract. In my judgment Jenkins LJ
spoke of interference with the contracts of employment of employees of one of the
parties of the principal contract only because that was the situation with which he was
confronted, but I do not think that he intended, or should have intended, to confine the
cause of action to that particular form of indirect interference.

Accordingly I would hold that prima facie the shipowners made out a cause of action
at common law.

Stage 2

This cause of action falls precisely within s 13(1)(a) of the 1974 Act and the defendants
are entitled to succeed, subject to the effect of s 17 of the 1980 Act.

Stage 3

In order to nullify the effects of s 13, a plaintiff must be able to pass through the
'gateways' of sub-s (1) of s 17. There are two such gateways, the first being simple to
recognise and the second exceedingly complex.

The first gateway is passed if the plaintiff can show that 'the contract concerned' is not
a contract of employment. In context this is a reference to the contract whose performance
is alleged to have been interfered with: in this appeal the time charter.

The second gateway is passed if the plaintiff can show that one of the facts relied on for
the purpose of establishing liability is that there has been secondary action which is not
action satisfying the requirements of sub-ss (3), (4) or (5), sub-ss (3)(a) and (4)(a) being
subject to interpretation pursuant to sub-s (6). In other words, the second gateway has
two sub-gateways. The first is passed if the action relied on meets the definition of
'secondary action' contained in sub-s (2). The second sub-gateway is open but will slam
in the face of the plaintiff if he relies on any of the types of secondary action specified in
sub-ss (3), (4) and (5).

In the present appeal there was secondary action: the defendants induced the tug crews
to break their contracts of employment and the shipowners, the employers in dispute,
were not parties to those contracts.

The next question is: what type of secondary action was this? Was it of a type specified
in one of the three subsections, in which case the second gateway will become shut and
locked? Counsel for the defendants submits that it was and that it falls squarely within
sub-s (3). Accordingly it is to that subsection that I must now turn.

Counsel for the defendants submits that the purpose, or principal purpose, of the
secondary action was directly to prevent or disrupt the supply of, inter alia, towage
services to the shipowners, the disputing employer, by the tug owners, the employers of
the tug's crews, if it was not merely the general purpose of disrupting the shipowners'
business.

I think that the purpose was specific and I accept the first limb of counsel's alternative
submissions. His difficulty is that it is not every prevention or disruption of supply
which causes sub-s (3) to shut the gateway. It is only a supply to (or by) the disputing
employer by (or to) a stranger to the dispute *in pursuance of a contract between those two
parties* (see sub-s (6)). In this case the towage services were no doubt being supplied to the
disputing employer (the shipowners), but they were not being supplied in pursuance of
a contract to which the shipowners were parties. The parties to the supply contract were
the tug owners and the sub-charterers. Accordingly this secondary action does not fit
sub-s (3), (4) or (5), and the second sub-gateway in sub-s (2) remains open leaving the
shipowners prima facie free to sue the defendants.

Counsel for the defendants takes two points in reply to this view. First, he submits
that the sub-charterer should be regarded as so closely connected with the shipowners as
to be their alter ego or agents and referred us to *Porr v Shaw, The Marabu Porr* [1979] 2
Lloyd's Rep 331, where the owners arranged for their crew to be employed by a separate
entity. This court held that this artificial separation of functions should be disregarded.

However the separation between an owner of a time-chartered vessel and a sub-charterer
is far from artificial and is in no way analogous.

The second point which counsel for the defendants takes is that the intention of
Parliament must have been to outlaw secondary action for the benefit of secondary
victims of that action rather than for the benefit of the primary parties to the dispute. I
do not think that this point is open to him in the light of the decision in *Marina Shipping
Ltd v Laughton*. But in any event Parliament could have adopted either a policy directed
at secondary action as such or one directed at the victims of such action. The only clue
which I have as to which policy was adopted is contained in the words of s 17 and they
seem to me to point to Parliament having adopted the first approach, namely one directed
at secondary action as such. This, on the facts of this case, enables the shipowners to
bypass the defences which would otherwise be open to the defendants under s 13 of the
1974 Act. Accordingly I would dismiss the appeal.

At the beginning of this judgment I said that whilst I had reached the conclusion that
the law was tolerably clear, the same could not be said of the way in which it was
expressed. The efficacy and maintenance of the rule of law, which is the foundation of
any parliamentary democracy, has at least two prerequisites. First, people must
understand that it is in their interests, as well as in that of the community as a whole,
that they should live their lives in accordance with the rules and all the rules. Second,
they must know what those rules are. Both are equally important, and it is the second
aspect of the rule of law which has caused me concern in the present case, the ITF having
disavowed any intention to break the law.

In industrial relations it is of vital importance that the worker on the shop floor, the
shop steward, the local union official, the district officer and the equivalent levels in
management should know what is and what is not 'offside'. And they must be able to
find this out for themselves by reading plain and simple words of guidance. The judges
of this court are all skilled lawyers of very considerable experience, yet it has taken us
hours to ascertain what is and what is not offside, even with the assistance of highly
experienced counsel. This cannot be right.

We have had to look at three Acts of Parliament, none intelligible without the other.
We have had to consider s 17 of the 1980 Act, which adopts the 'flow' method of
parliamentary draftsmanship, without the benefit of a flow diagram. We have
furthermore been faced with the additional complication that sub-s (6) of s 17 contains
definitions which distort the natural meaning of the words in the operative subsections.
It was not always like this. If you doubt me, look at the comparative simplicity and
clarity of Sir Mackenzie Chalmers's Sale of Goods Act 1893, his Bills of Exchange Act
1882 and his Marine Insurance Act 1906. But I do not criticise the draftsman. His
instructions may well have left him no option. My plea is that Parliament, when
legislating in respect of circumstances which directly affect the 'man or woman in the
street' or the 'man or woman on the shop floor', should give as high a priority to clarity
and simplicity of expression as to refinements of policy. Where possible statutes, or
complete parts of statutes, should not be amended but re-enacted in an amended form so
that those concerned can read the rules in a single document. When formulating policy,
ministers, of whatever political persuasion, should at all times be asking themselves and
asking parliamentary counsel: 'Is this concept too refined to be capable of expression in
basic English? If so, is there some way in which we can modify the policy so that it can
be so expressed?' Having to ask such questions would no doubt be frustrating for
ministers and the legislature generally, but in my judgment this is part of the price
which has to be paid if the rule of law is to be maintained.

Appeal dismissed. Leave to appeal to the House of Lords refused.

21 December. *The Appeal Committee of the House of Lords granted the defendants leave to appeal.*

Solicitors: *Clifford-Turner* (for the defendants); *Holman Fenwick & Willan* (for the
shipowners).

Diana Procter   Barrister.

Practice Direction

QUEEN'S BENCH DIVISION

Land registration – Production of register of title – Application for inspection of register etc – Procedure – Ex parte application in High Court – Affidavit that judgment debtor is proprietor of land or charge thereon – Procedure where sum not exceeding county court limit – Land Registration Act 1925, s 112(2)(3) – Charging Orders Act 1979, s 1(2).

1. Subject to the provisions of s 1(2) of the Charging Orders Act 1979, an application under s 112(2) of the Land Registration Act 1925 by a judgment creditor for inspection of a register or document in the custody of the registrar and relating to land or a charge without the authority of the judgment debtor may be made by an ex parte application in the proceedings in which judgment was obtained supported by affidavit showing prima facie evidence that the judgment debtor is the proprietor (whether solely or jointly with some other person or persons) of the land in question or of a charge thereon.

2. Where a judgment creditor wishes to take proceedings by way of a charging order on land for the enforcement of a High Court judgment for a sum not exceeding the current jurisdiction of a county court, application for inspection of the register should be made under s 112(3) of the Land Registration Act 1925 in the appropriate county court.

(This Practice Direction is made with the concurrence of the Chief Chancery Master in substitution for the Practice Direction of 23 June 1970 ([1970] 3 All ER 70, [1970] 1 WLR 1158), as amended by the Practice Direction of 10 October 1980 ([1980] 3 All ER 704, [1980] 1 WLR 1135), as set out as Masters' Practice Direction 16A in *The Supreme Court Practice 1982* vol 2, p 217, para 917.)

J B ELTON
17 January 1983   Senior Master of the Supreme Court.

Cooper v Motor Insurers' Bureau

QUEEN'S BENCH DIVISION

BARRY CHEDLOW QC SITTING AS A DEPUTY JUDGE OF THE HIGH COURT

18 JUNE, 12 JULY 1982

Motor insurance – Compulsory insurance against third party risks – Liabilities required to be covered – Permitted driver – Owner of vehicle permitting another person to drive it – Permitted driver injured because of defective brakes – Whether owner's liability to permitted driver required to be covered by third party insurance – Whether injury to permitted driver an injury to 'any person . . . arising out of' use of vehicle – Road Traffic Act 1972, ss 143(1), 145(3)(a).

Motor insurance – Rights of third parties against insurers – Motor Insurers' Bureau – Liability of bureau to satisfy judgment against uninsured driver – Liability required to be covered by insurance – Owner of vehicle permitting another person to drive it – Permitted driver injured because of defective brakes – Owner not insured – Whether bureau obliged to satisfy judgment against owner – Whether owner's liability to permitted driver required to be covered by insurance – Whether injury to permitted driver an injury to 'any person . . . arising out of' use of vehicle – Road Traffic Act 1972, ss 143(1), 145(3)(a) – Motor Insurers' Bureau (Compensation of Victims of Uninsured Drivers) Agreement.

K asked the plaintiff to road test K's motor cycle. During the road test the brakes on the motor cycle failed and the plaintiff collided with a car and was seriously injured. He brought an action against K claiming damages for negligence in respect of K's failure to warn him that the brakes were defective and obtained judgment for £214,207. K was unable to satisfy the judgment. Furthermore, he was not insured against third party risks as required by s 143(1)[a] of the Road Traffic Act 1972. The plaintiff brought an action against the Motor Insurers' Bureau seeking a declaration that by virtue of the bureau's undertaking given to the Secretary of State to compensate victims of uninsured drivers the bureau was liable to satisfy the judgment since it was a judgment in respect of a liability required to be covered by insurance, within the undertaking, because insurance against third party risks was required by s 145(3)(a)[b] of the 1972 Act to cover injury to 'any person . . . arising out of' the use of a vehicle on a road, which, it was contended, included a person who was permitted to use the vehicle and who was injured while using it. The plaintiff further contended that the third party risks required to be covered by s 143(1) were not confined to risks which were extraneous to the vehicle but included risks within the vehicle.

Held – On the true construction of s 143(1) of the 1972 Act, the third party liability required to be covered by insurance was confined to liability to persons other than the insured or a person permitted by him to use the vehicle who were injured by the use of the vehicle by the insured or the permitted driver; s 143(1) was not intended to require insurance against the policy holder's liability to the permitted driver himself for an injury sustained while he was using the vehicle. In regard to a permitted driver, all that the 1972 Act required was that he should be covered against liability to persons other than himself who were injured by his use of the vehicle. Furthermore, 'any person' in s 145(3)(a) of the 1972 Act was to be read in the context in which it was used, namely as referring to any person injured by the use of a vehicle by the insured or a permitted driver who was covered by insurance under s 143(1), and therefore did not enlarge the scope of liability beyond that required to be covered by s 143. It followed that K's liability to the plaintiff, being a liability to a permitted driver of the motor cycle, was not a

---

a   Section 143(1), so far as material, is set out at p 355 *a*, post

b   Section 145(3), so far as material, is set out at p 355 *b*, post

liability K would have been insured against if he had been insured in accordance with the 1972 Act. Accordingly, the judgment against K did not arise out of a liability required to be covered under the 1972 Act, and therefore the bureau was not required to satisfy the judgment (see p 357 c to j and p 359 b, post).

Dictum of Lord Porter in *Digby v General Accident Fire and Life Assurance Corp Ltd* [1942] 2 All ER at 331 applied.

Notes

For compulsory insurance in relation to motor vehicles, see 25 Halsbury's Laws (4th edn) paras 756, 759–760.

For the Motor Insurers' Bureau, see ibid paras 784, 785.

For the Road Traffic Act 1972, ss 143, 145, see 42 Halsbury's Statutes (3rd edn) 1786, 1790.

Cases referred to in judgment

Barnet Group Hospital Management Committee v Eagle Star Insurance Co Ltd [1959] 3 All ER 210, [1960] 1 QB 107, [1959] 3 WLR 610, 29 Digest (Reissue) 623, 5416.

Digby v General Accident Fire and Life Assurance Corp Ltd [1942] 2 All ER 319, [1943] AC 121, HL, 29 Digest (Reissue) 607, 5313.

Action

By a writ issued on 23 July 1981 the plaintiff, Clifford George Cooper, claimed against the Motor Insurers' Bureau, the defendant, a declaration or order that the bureau was liable to satisfy a judgment obtained by the plaintiff on 5 December 1980 in the High Court against Mr Brendon Killacky, for damages of £213,207·89 for personal injuries sustained by the plaintiff when testing Mr Killacky's motor cycle on a road, due to Mr Killacky's negligence in failing to warn the plaintiff that the brakes of the motor cycle were defective. Mr Killacky was not insured against third party risks as required by s 143(1) of the Road Traffic Act 1972, and was unable himself to satisfy the judgment. The plaintiff claimed that the judgment obtained against Mr Killacky was in respect of a 'relevant liability' within cl 2 of the Motor Insurers' Bureau (Compensation of Victims of Uninsured Drivers) Agreement, dated 22 November 1972, because Mr Killacky's liability to the plaintiff was one which would have been covered by compulsory insurance under s 143 of the 1972 Act by virtue of ss 143(1) and 145(3)(a) of that Act. The facts are set out in the judgment.

O B Popplewell QC and *Pamela Shaw* for the plaintiff.
Piers Ashworth QC and *Jonathan R Playford QC* for the Motor Insurers' Bureau.

Cur adv vult

12 July. The following judgment was delivered.

BARRY CHEDLOW QC. On 9 January 1973 a Mr Killacky asked the plaintiff, Mr Cooper, to road-test his, Mr Killacky's, motor cycle. During the course of this test, the brakes failed and the plaintiff collided with a motor car on the highway. The plaintiff was seriously injured and he sued Mr Killacky in negligence and on 5 December 1980 the plaintiff recovered judgment against Mr Killacky in the sum, including interest, of some £214,207·89. The magnitude of the sum is some indication of the severity of the injury which young Mr Cooper suffered and it is enough for me to say that, tragically, he is wheelchair-bound and suffers complete tetraplegia. Mr Killacky was quite unable to satisfy the judgment and the object of the litigation before me is to endeavour to cause the Motor Insurers' Bureau to satisfy this judgment.

The relevant insurance obligations under the Road Traffic Act 1972 are contained in ss 143 and 145 of that Act. The relevant part of s 143 is sub-s (1) which says:

'Subject to the provision of this Part of this Act, it shall not be lawful for a person to use, or to cause or to permit any other person to use, a motor vehicle on a road unless there is in force in relation to the use of the vehicle by that person or that other person, as the case may be, such policy of insurance or such a security in respect of third-party risks as complies, with the requirements of this Part of this Act . . .'

Section 145(3), as amended, reads:

'Subject to subsection (4) below, the policy—(a) must insure such person, persons or classes of persons as may be specified in the policy in respect of any liability which may be incurred by him or them in respect of the death of or bodily injury to any person caused by, or arising out of, the use of the vehicle on a road in Great Britain . . .'

Because of the hardship to persons injured by motor vehicles which should have been insured as required by the Road Traffic Act 1972 but were not, the Motor Insurers' Bureau agreed with the minister to satisfy judgments obtained by such injured persons if they fell within the category which should have been insured, subject to the Motor Insurers' Bureau being given notice.

The text of the agreement (the Motor Insurers' Bureau (Compensation of Victims of Uninsured Drivers) Agreement) dated 22 November 1972 between the Secretary of State for the Environment and the Motor Insurers' Bureau contains the two following material clauses for the purposes of this judgment. The first is headed 'Satisfaction of Claims by Motor Insurers' Bureau' and reads as follows:

'If judgment in respect of any relevant liability is obtained against any person or persons in any court in Great Britain whether or not such a person or persons be, in fact, covered by a contract of insurance, and any such judgment is not satisfied in full within seven days from the date upon which the person or persons in whose favour the judgment was given became entitled to enforce it, then M.I.B. will, subject to the provisions of Clauses 4, 5 and 6 hereof, pay, or satisfy, or cause to be paid or satisfied to or to the satisfaction of the person or persons in whose favour the judgment was given, any sum payable or remaining payable thereunder in respect of the relevant liability, including any sum awarded by the court in respect of interest on that sum and any taxed costs . . .'

The second relevant condition (cl 5(1)) is headed 'Conditions Precedent to M.I.B.'s Liability' and says:

'M.I.B. shall not incur any liability under Clause 2 of this agreement unless—(a) notice of the bringing of the proceedings is given before or within seven days after the commencement of the proceedings—(i) to M.I.B. in the case of proceedings in respect of a relevant liability which is either not covered by a contract of insurance or covered by a contract of insurance with an insurer whose identity cannot be ascertained . . .'

Now, on this state of the statutory liability under the Road Traffic Act 1972 and the text of the agreement with the Motor Insurers' Bureau, counsel for the plaintiff says that Mr Killacky's liability to the plaintiff was a liability which should have been covered under the Road Traffic Act 1972 and, second, although he concedes that no notice of the proceedings had been given to the Motor Insurers' Bureau as required by the last part of the text which I have read, he says that the Motor Insurers' Bureau cannot rely on that because they have waived that requirement. The defendants, the bureau, say, briefly, in answer to this that this was not a liability that fell to be covered at all and, certainly, there has been no waiver.

Hence, there are two questions for me to decide: first, are the Motor Insurers' Bureau liable to satisfy this judgment? and, second, if so, have the Motor Insurers' Bureau waived their right to be given notice?

Counsel for the plaintiff puts his arguments as follows: he says that the policy required in this case is one which insures against liability to any person, as set out in s 145(3)(a) of the 1972 Act, and those words must be given, he says, their ordinary meaning and include the plaintiff. The fact that he (the plaintiff) was driving is immaterial. He referred me to two cases where the words 'any person' had fallen to be considered. The first was *Digby v General Accident Fire and Life Assurance Corp Ltd* [1942] 2 All ER 319 at 326, [1943] AC 121 at 136 (the Merle Oberon case), where Lord Atkin dealing with the words 'any person' in the policy says:

'On examining the provisions of sect. 2 [of the insurance policy] it will be found that the first subsection deals with the policy-holder. Starting from the body of the policy "will indemnify the policyholder in respect of the [scheduled] automobile against . . . 2(1) all sums which the policyholder shall become legally liable to pay in respect of any claim by any person", including passengers, for loss of life or bodily injury or damage to property "caused by, through, or in connection with such automobile". "Any person" should surely receive its ordinary meaning of any member of the public. The policyholder himself cannot come within the terms not because he is not a person: but because the clause only relates to a claim by any person which the policyholder is legally liable to pay: and such a liability cannot exist on a supposed claim at the same time by and against himself.'

Counsel for the plaintiff also referred me to *Barnet Group Hospital Management Committee v Eagle Star Insurance Co Ltd* [1959] 3 All ER 210 at 213, [1960] 1 QB 107 at 115, where Salmon J said:

'The next question that arises is whether or not Mr. Groom was "any person" within the meaning of s. 36(2) [of the Road Traffic Act 1930]. Prima facie, Mr. Groom clearly is "any person". Counsel for the insurers argues, however, that "any person" means any person of the class required to be covered by the Act. Why should the court give such a limited construction to the meaning of the words "any person"? In my view, such a construction involves writing words into the statute which are not there. If the legislature had intended the payment mentioned in s. 36(2) to be confined to persons of the class required to be covered by the Act, it could have expressed that intention in plain language.'

Counsel for the plaintiff further says that the third party risks in s 143 of the 1972 Act are not confined to those extraneous to the vehicle; it can and does, he says, include those in or on it and he referred me to what Lord Porter said in *Digby's* case [1942] 2 All ER 319 at 331, [1943] AC 121 at 145, where these words were used:

'I doubt if the phrase "third party liability" when used in the policy has any such definite meaning as that ascribed to it by the respondents. In my view, in a policy such as this, indemnity against third-party liability is used in contradistinction to indemnity against "loss or damage" to the car and means only that the insurer will indemnify the insured against any proper claim made upon him by a person who is injured by the negligent driving of the car. I do not think that there is any question of first, second and third parties.'

Counsel for the plaintiff points to the words 'arising out of' in s 145(3)(a) as being likewise an indication that if the injury arises from the use of a motor car, the fact that the injury is to the invited driver is of no consequence. He also says that s 145(3) is wide enough to encompass his submissions.

Counsel for the Motor Insurers' Bureau says that s 143 is vital. He says that it is the user of the vehicle causing damage to others on the road which is the only liability that has to be covered. He says, looking at s 145(3)(a), that the plaintiff was using the vehicle and, therefore, it is the plaintiff's liability which must be covered. He says that Mr Killacky's liability to the plaintiff is not a liability which has to be covered, only the plaintiff's liability to others. He says that s 145, in any case, has to be construed in the context of s 143 and, therefore, the words 'any person' cannot be as wide as it is contended for by the plaintiff and that s 145 cannot increase the s 143 liability.

It is, I think, strange, and of some significance, it seems to me, that there is no case on all fours with the matter which is raised in this litigation and it is strange that the matter has not arisen in the past if the words are wide enough, indeed, to include the unsatisfied judgment by the user of the vehicle. I do not find that the authorities that have been cited in this matter are of great assistance. *Digby's* case, as it seems to me, turns very much on its own facts. The question in that case was whether the policyholder's own insurers were obliged to indemnify the insured's chauffeur, who had been successfully sued in negligence for the damages awarded to the policyholder as a passenger in her own car. The construction to be placed on the words which fell to be construed, namely 'any person including passengers', turns very much on the contract in the context in which they were to be found. I do not find that case helpful in construing the words 'any person' in the statute here. Similarly the *Barnet Hospital* case turned on whether the words 'any person' were to be construed as 'any person simpliciter' or as 'any person of the class required to be covered by the Act'.

I am unable to accept the construction of the statute which renders this a liability which falls to be covered under the Road Traffic Act 1972 and for which the Motor Insurers' Bureau are liable. Section 143 speaks, first, of the user and, second, of one who causes or permits user. These two situations must be covered against third party risks. I do not consider that s 143 is intended to insure against personal injury to the person actually using the vehicle. When s 145(3)(a) speaks of 'any person' it does so, in my view, in the limited context of the word 'use' in s 143 and is not enlarging the scope of the cover needed which is, in my judgment, that both the user or person permitted to use the vehicle should be covered against claims by persons injured by the use of the vehicle on the highway. I notice in passing that when Lord Porter, in the passage to which I referred in *Digby's* case [1942] 2 All ER 319 at 331, [1943] AC 121 at 145, was discussing third party liability he said:

'In my view, in a policy such as this, indemnity against third-party liability is used in contradistinction to indemnity against "loss or damage" to the car and means only that the insurer will indemnify the insured against any proper claim made upon him by a person who is injured by the negligent driving of the car.'

It seems to me that s 143 of the 1972 Act requires, on the facts of this case, that the plaintiff's user of the motor cycle should be covered against third party risks; the three parties here involved, in my view, are the insurers, the insured or his invitee, who is temporarily to be considered the insured, and third parties other than these two. It is the use, whether by the insured himself or his invitee, which has to be covered but the cover given to the invitee cannot give to the latter any greater right than the insured himself has and the insured has no such right himself. I consider that the only liability which falls to be covered under ss 143(1) and 145(3)(a) is the plaintiff's liability to others. Mr Killacky's liability to the plaintiff is not a liability which falls to be covered by the statute. If one supposes that the plaintiff had a policy covering him whilst riding Mr Killacky's motor cycle but Mr Killacky had none, if the plaintiff's arguments are correct, an offence would have been committed because Mr Killacky would have had no policy complying with s 143(1) to cover his liability to the plaintiff.

In these circumstances, I hold that the Motor Insurers' Bureau are under no obligation to satisfy this judgment since it did not arise out of a liability which fell to be covered under the Road Traffic Act 1972. In these circumstances, it becomes unnecessary for me to decide the question of waiver but, lest I should be wrong in the view I have formed and in deference to the arguments which have been addressed to me, it seems to me desirable that I should shortly deal with the estoppel issue.

This serious accident happened on 9 January 1973 and a writ was issued on the plaintiff's behalf against Mr Killacky on 3 December 1975. It is conceded by counsel for the plaintiff that no notice was given as required by cl 5 of the Motor Insurers' Bureau agreement with the minister before or within seven days after the commencement of the proceedings. Indeed, it was not, I think, until 9 May 1977, in a letter from the plaintiff's solicitors to the Motor Insurers' Bureau, that these proceedings were first brought to their attention. But counsel says that, notwithstanding that fact, the correspondence and the conduct of the Motor Insurers' Bureau and their advisers subsequently support his contention that the bureau waived their right to rely on that failure to give notice. He says the provisions as to notice were to protect the bureau against fraudulent claims where, for example, by some agreement, judgment was taken in default, or were to allow the bureau to investigate matters in the course of proceedings and before judgment was given. Counsel for the plaintiff says that the Motor Insurers' Bureau, by their conduct, had waived their right to rely on failure to give notice and that they are deemed to have waived the requirement. He says, moreover, that it would be unconscionable in all the circumstances here to allow the bureau to rely on this omission by the plaintiff.

If there is any waiver in this case it arises, it seems to me, from the correspondence between the parties. Shortly, the bureau say there is nothing in this correspondence to encourage the plaintiff to think that the 'notice point' would not be taken.

A study of the correspondence from the start shows that the Motor Insurers' Bureau were taking the view that this claim, if it resulted in a judgment, was not one which would fall within the provisions of the Motor Insurers' Bureau agreement with the minister: at an early stage they said: 'It would not be necessary for the Bureau to be informed of the issue of proceedings . . .' That, of course, is on the basis that they (the bureau) were not concerned. I do not understand that as saying, or implying, that, if they were, they would be waiving any right to rely on the absence or lateness of notice. Thereafter, this is the stance taken by the parties: on the plaintiff's side that the bureau should satisfy such a judgment; on the bureau's side that they were not concerned. Then the legal aid certificate was amended to allow the plaintiff to sue the bureau and the solicitors for the bureau come on the scene. Whether in the parting letter from the chief clerk to the Motor Insurers' Bureau there is a hint or suggestion that this action is a little late when he says, 'We see this accident occurred nearly four years ago and are wondering whether this action contemplated is in fact correct . . .' and that the question of delay is in someone's mind or not, one does not know.

Within seven days of the bureau's solicitors getting all the documents sent to them by the plaintiff's solicitors, the bureau's solicitors say two things: first, that there is no cause of action against the bureau and, in any case, no notice as required has been given. It is to be noticed that these two matters were raised within eight months of the first notification and the bureau point out that this compares with a delay of over four years after the accident before notice was given and that even that notice, in fact, is given one year and five months after the writ was issued. Counsel for the bureau points out that at no time prior to the defence did the plaintiff ever say in correspondence, 'You waived your entitlement to rely on this defence.'

The position adopted by the bureau was maintained in an affidavit sworn on 23 March 1978, when the bureau moved to strike out the plaintiff's claim against them. Letters were exchanged between counsel for the plaintiff, and counsel then appearing for the Motor Insurers' Bureau. One letter is an invitation by counsel for the plaintiff to counsel for the bureau to litigate the bureau's liability first so as to avoid extensive costs. Counsel for the plaintiff's letter having been passed to the solicitors for the bureau, those solicitors replied on 1 December 1978. Counsel for the plaintiff relied substantially on this letter since it is completely silent on his comment that the Motor Insurers' Bureau 'will not take the lateness of claim point'. He said in his letter:

'This encouraged the plaintiff to believe that this point would not be taken and the subsequent steps taken by the plaintiff were taken upon the faith of that waiver: that the defendants would not raise this defence.'

For my part, I feel quite unable to place that construction on the letter. The primary object of the letter to the Motor Insurer's Bureau was to invite them to litigate the question of their liability to satisfy the judgment. That they answer, as the correspondence shows. The fact that they did not specifically reply whether if and when they might be held liable they would raise the defence of late notification does not seem to me to give a ground to allege that the subsequent conduct by the plaintiff was induced by the implicit waiver by the bureau of their right to rely on the absence of notice. Certainly, the contents of the letter of 1 December 1978 do not seem to me such as expressly or implicitly to exclude the bureau from relying on the notice defence. I find it quite impossible to hold that the plaintiff's subsequent conduct was induced by any representation expressed or implied by the bureau or that there was any waiver as urged by the plaintiff on me on all the facts and correspondence here.

b   In the result, I should have found that there was no waiver here and that the bureau were not precluded from relying on this defence of absence of notice had the plaintiff succeeded in showing that this was a liability which had to be covered and for which unsatisfied judgment the Motor Insurers' Bureau were liable. In the result, and with very considerable sympathy for the young plaintiff, there must be judgment for the bureau.

c *Judgment for the Motor Insurers' Bureau.*

Solicitors: *Horwood & James*, Aylesbury (for the plaintiff); *L Bingham & Co* (for the Motor Insurers' Bureau).

K Mydeen Esq   Barrister.

d

Epping Forest District Council v Essex Rendering Ltd

e

HOUSE OF LORDS
LORD DIPLOCK, LORD ELWYN-JONES, LORD EDMUND-DAVIES, LORD ROSKILL AND LORD TEMPLEMAN
25 NOVEMBER 1982, 20 JANUARY 1983

f *Public health – Offensive trades – Consent of local authority to establishment of offensive trades – Requirement that consent be given in writing – Company carrying on offensive trades without written consent but with knowledge and approval of local authority for 23 years – Whether requirement that consent be in writing directory or mandatory – Whether local authority's course of conduct sufficient consent – Public Health Act 1936, ss 107(1), 283(1).*

g In 1958 W, the owner of a farm, commenced carrying on offensive trades there without first obtaining the consent of the local authority as required by s 107[a] of the Public Health Act 1936. W was unaware that the consent of the local authority was required. Between 1958 and 1981 the offensive trades were carried on first by W himself and then by the appellant company without concealment, to the knowledge of the local authority, and under the supervision of inspectors appointed by the local authority. Those inspectors h regularly visited the farm and when necessary made suggestions concerning the manner and scope of the offensive trades. There was no change in the manner in which the offensive trades were carried on over the relevant period. In May 1978 the local authority served notices on the appellants under s 107(2) of the 1936 Act to discontinue their trades forthwith. The appellants failed to comply with the notices and the local authority preferred informations against them and issued summonses alleging breaches of s 107 of j the 1936 Act. The appellants were convicted. Their appeal to the Divisional Court of the Queen's Bench Division against conviction was dismissed on the ground that the requirement in s 283(1)[b] of the 1936 Act that the consent of the local authority, including

---

a   Section 107, so far as material, is set out at p 361 *b c*, post
b   Section 283(1), so far as material, is set out at p 361 *d*, post

consent under s 107(1) to the establishment of an offensive trade, had to be given in writing was a mandatory requirement and accordingly consent could not be given by or implied from the local authority's course of conduct over a period of years. The appellants appealed to the House of Lords, contending that the requirement that the authority's consent be in writing was merely directory and not mandatory.

Held – The requirement that the consent of a local authority under s 107 of the 1936 Act to the establishment of an offensive trade was to be in writing in accordance with s 283(1) of that Act was mandatory and not directory, because the object of s 107 was to protect the public by making the establishment of an offensive trade without written consent a criminal offence. It was therefore important that the grant of consent should not be accidental, vague or informal. Since the appellants had not obtained the written consent of the authority they had been rightly convicted. The appeal would therefore be dismissed (see p 360 h j and p 362 j to p 363 c and g, post).

Notes
For the establishing and carrying on an offensive trade and consent to establishing an offensive trade, see 38 Halsbury's Laws (4th edn) paras 278–279.

For the Public Health Act 1936, ss 107, 283, see 26 Halsbury's Statutes (3rd edn) 276, 349.

Appeal
Essex Rendering Ltd (the company) appealed with leave of the House of Lords granted on 6 May 1982 against the decision of the Divisional Court of the Queen's Bench Division (Donaldson LJ and McCullough J) on 26 February 1982 dismissing an appeal by the company by way of case stated by justices for the county of Essex, acting in and for the petty sessional division of Epping and Ongar in respect of their adjudication as a magistrates' court sitting at Epping on 7 July 1981 whereby they convicted the company on informations preferred by Epping Forest District Council (the local authority) against the company of 12 offences of carrying on six offensive trades without the consent of the local authority in breach of s 107 of the Public Health Act 1936. The facts are set out in the opinion of Lord Templeman.

Harry Sales for the company.
R M K Gray for the local authority.

Their Lordships took time for consideration.

20 January. The following opinions were delivered.

LORD DIPLOCK. My Lords, I have had the advantage of reading in draft the speech of my noble and learned friend Lord Templeman. I agree with it and would dismiss the appeal.

LORD ELWYN-JONES. My Lords, I have had the advantage of reading in draft the speech prepared by my noble and learned friend Lord Templeman. I agree with it and for the reasons which he gives I would dismiss the appeal.

LORD EDMUND-DAVIES. My Lords, I have had the advantage of reading in draft the speech prepared by my noble and learned friend Lord Templeman. I agree with the reasons which have led him to answer the certified question of law as he has done, to dismiss the appeal, and to propose the order as to costs indicated by him.

LORD ROSKILL. My Lords, I have had the advantage of reading in draft the speech to be delivered by my noble and learned friend Lord Templeman. I agree with it and for the reasons he gives I would dismiss the appeal.

LORD TEMPLEMAN. My Lords, the question raised by this appeal is whether the statutory requirement of consent in writing from the local authority for the establishment of an offensive trade is mandatory or directory. The appellant company, Essex Rendering Ltd, claim and the respondent district council, Epping Forest District Council, dispute that the requirement is directory and therefore consent by conduct over a period of 23 years constitutes a defence to the criminal charge of carrying on an offensive trade established without consent.

Section 107 of the Public Health Act 1936 provided:

'(1) Any person who on any premises within a borough or urban district, or [certain rural districts or contibutory places] . . . establishes, without the consent of the local authority, any offensive trade as hereinafter defined shall be liable to a fine not exceeding fifty pounds . . .

(2) Any person who on any premises . . . as aforesaid, carries on an offensive trade established without such consent, if any, as at the date of the establishment of the trade was required by subsection (1) of this section . . . shall be liable to a fine not exceeding five pounds for every day on which he carries on the trade . . . after receiving notice from the local authority to discontinue the trade . . .'

By s 1 'local authority' means the council of a borough, urban district or rural council.

By s 283(1): 'All notices, orders, consents, demands and other documents authorised or required by or under this Act to be given, made or issued by a council . . . shall be in writing.'

Section 107 when first enacted did not normally apply to a rural district but in 1937 the Minister of Health, in exercise of powers conferred on him by s 13 of the Act, made an order whereby s 107 became applicable to Stapleford Abbotts, a contributory place whose local authority was the Ongar Rural District Council in Essex.

In 1958, Mr Watts, the owner of High House Farm in Stapleford Abbotts, there established six offensive trades defined by s 107, namely blood boiling, bone boiling, fat extracting, fat melting, tallow melting and tripe boiling. Mr Watts was unaware that the consent of the local authority was required for the establishment of these trades which he openly carried on from 1958 onwards.

The Local Government Act 1972 applied s 107 of the 1936 Act throughout the district of every local authority and extended the definition of offensive trades, but in this appeal nothing turns on the extensions and amendments effected in 1972 to the 1936 Act.

In 1973 the business at High House Farm and the operation of the six offensive trades passed from Mr Watts to the appellant company which is a family company established by Mr Watts. In 1974 the local authority in respect of High House Farm became the respondent district council.

Between 1958 and 1981 the six offensive trades established by Mr Watts were carried on first by Mr Watts himself and then by the company without concealment, to the knowledge of the local authority and under the supervision and discipline of inspectors appointed by the local authority. Those inspectors regularly visited High House Farm and, when necessary, made suggestions or gave directions concerning the manner and scope of the offensive trades carried on the premises. The evidence was that there was no material alteration in the manner in which the six offensive trades were carried on over the relevant period exceeding 20 years. No one told Mr Watts or the company that the establishment of the six offensive trades required consent in writing.

Nevertheless the district council thought fit to serve on the company on 18 May 1978 notices alleging that the six offensive trades were established without the consent of the district council and requiring the trades to be discontinued forthwith. The company, no doubt resentful at this surprising volte face on the part of the local authority and unwilling to accept the abrupt termination of its long established business failed to comply with the notices, relying on the indisputable fact that the local authority had in truth consented to the establishment and carrying on of the six offensive trades at High House Farm for the period and in the circumstances I have outlined.

The district council, unmoved, then laid informations and six summonses were issued against the company on 11 December 1978 alleging breaches of s 107 on 21 September

1978 by the carrying on of the six offensive trades on that date. Those summonses were adjourned and were ultimately restored to be heard with six further summonses issued on 30 June 1981 and alleging breaches of s 107 on 15 June 1981.

On 7 July 1981 the justices of the county of Essex convicted the company of the 12 offences of carrying on the six offensive trades without the consent of the local authority. The justices made an order of absolute discharge in respect of the six informations relating to the carrying on of the trade on 15 June 1981. In respect of each of the six informations relating to the carrying on of the offensive trades on 21 September 1978 the magistrates imposed a fine of £5 per day operative from 10 November 1981. The company was directed to apply to the district council before 10 November 1981 for consent and was ordered to pay £350 towards the district council's prosecution costs.

At the request of the company, the justices stated a case to the High Court. That case set out the relevant facts with clarity, admirably summarised the submissions and the relevant law and came to the conclusion that the company was in breach of s 107 because no consent in writing had been obtained for the establishment of the six offensive trades.

The company duly applied to the district council for consent in writing, so that the company could continue the offensive trades which the district council and their predecessors had accepted as inoffensive for 23 years. The district council which had consented by conduct refused to consent in writing. We were informed that an appeal against this refusal was dismissed by the magistrates but that a further appeal to the Crown Court is pending.

On 26 February 1982 the Divisional Court (Donaldson LJ and McCullough J) dismissed the company's appeal against conviction for breach of s 107. The Divisional Court set aside the fines imposed by the justices on the grounds that the justices had no power to fix a rate of fine to take effect in the future and remitted the matter to the justices to impose such penalty as they might feel appropriate. The Divisional Court refused leave to the company to appeal but such leave was subsequently granted by this House. The Divisional Court certified pursuant to s 1(2) of the Administration of Justice Act 1960 that a point of law of general public importance was involved, namely:

'Whether the consent of the local authority required by section 107(1) of the Public Health Act 1936 to the establishment of offensive trades as there defined must be given in writing in accordance with section 283(1) of that Act or whether for this purpose that provision is directory only and consent can be given or implied by a course of conduct over a period of years.'

When Parliament enacts that a consent shall be in writing any other form of consent is usually ineffective. But a consideration of the objects sought to be achieved by the legislation and of the consequences of denying the efficacy of any other form of consent may lead to the conclusion that Parliament was more concerned with the substance than with the form of consent.

Counsel for the company referred us to various sections in the Public Health Act 1936. They included ss 25, 34, 57, 73, 74, 85, 155, 159, 160, 242 and 263. In all these cases he contended it would be unfair or pedantic to give no effect to a consent which was oral or manifested by conduct. In so far as those sections required the consent of a local authority I was not persuaded by his argument. But it is unnecessary to consider the effect of s 283 which contains the stipulation that consent shall be in writing on different sections in the Public Health Act 1936, nor is it necessary to determine whether the requirements of s 283 are mandatory or directory for all purposes.

For present purposes it is sufficiently clear that the requirements of s 283 when applied to s 107 must be mandatory.

As a matter of legislative history, s 107 of the Public Health Act 1936 replaced s 112 of the Public Health Act 1875 which in turn replaced an earlier Act of 1848. In the 1875 Act the legislature did not rely on a general provision such as that which is to be found in s 283 of the Public Health Act 1936. Section 112 of the 1875 Act provided: 'Any person who ... establishes within the district of an urban authority, without their consent in writing, any offensive trade ...' shall be guilty of an offence.

a   The wording of the 1875 Act is so emphatic that it is impossible to reach the conclusion that the requirement of consent in writing was intended to be merely directory. As my noble and learned friend Lord Roskill pointed out in the course of argument, the 1936 Act was a consolidation measure and should not be construed, therefore, so as to change the relevant requirement from a mandatory to a directory nature.

b   But in any event consideration of the objects and effect of s 107 lead to the conclusion that no offensive trade can lawfully be established without the consent in writing made necessary by s 283. Section 107 is concerned with the establishment of an offensive trade which may cause injury or damage or discomfort to members of the public. Once consent has been given, the offensive trade may be continued indefinitely unless the local authority have, in exercise of their powers under s 107(3), only given consent for a limited period. From the point of view of the local authority and the public it is important that the grant of consent shall not be accidental or informal. Moreover, s 107

c   creates criminal offences. Prosecution, defence and magistracy must be able to determine whether an offence has been committed without recourse to vague or disputed recollections regarding events or conversations which might or might not constitute consent binding on the local authority.

Counsel for the company submitted that, if a strict application of s 283 is enforced, there will be hardship. Where an offensive trade is established and carried on, money is

d   expended and goodwill is acquired in reliance on the knowledge, consent and approval of the local authority and their qualified representatives. But hardship is a matter for the local authority. Where an offensive trade has been carried on for a long period with the knowledge, approval and consent of the local authority and no change has occurred or is threatened in the manner or extent of carrying on the trade in the future, the applicant for consent in writing will have strong grounds for urging and expecting a grant which

e   will legitimise his activities for the future.

In my opinion the mischief which would result from a restricted application of s 283 to s 107 outweighs the possibilities of individual hardship. The district council, however, have not given any reason why the palpable hardship in the present case has not been alleviated by the grant of a consent in writing on terms which will safeguard the company's business but will also protect the public. I can understand the anxiety of the

f   district council to defend a decision which establishes once and for all that the only consent which is relevant to s 107 is a formal consent in writing. But I see no reason why the company should pay more than is necessary for the failure of the local authority over a period of 23 years to enforce the provisions of s 107, or why the company should pay for the establishment of a binding precedent. Although the appeal must be dismissed, I propose that the order for costs made by the justices and by the Divisional Court should

g   be discharged and that no order should be made with regard to the costs of the appeal to this House. I would decide the point of law which has been raised by declaring that the consent of the local authority required by s 107(1) of the Public Health Act 1936 for the establishment of offensive trades as there defined must be given in writing in accordance with s 283(1) of that Act.

h   *Appeal dismissed.*

Solicitors: *Edwin Roast & Co* , Barking (for the company); *P J Cunliffe-Jones*, Epping (for the local authority).

Mary Rose Plummer   Barrister.

R v Abadom

COURT OF APPEAL, CRIMINAL DIVISION
KERR LJ, EWBANK AND LEONARD JJ
18, 25 JUNE 1982

Criminal evidence – Hearsay – Expert witness – Expert witness relying on unpublished work of other experts to arrive at his conclusion – Whether expert entitled to refer to work of others in his evidence – Whether reference to work of others in evidence infringing hearsay rule.

The appellant was charged with robbery. At his trial the Crown's case rested on evidence that the appellant had broken a window during the robbery and that fragments of glass found adhering to and imbedded in a pair of shoes taken from the appellant's home after his arrest had come from the window. An expert witness for the Crown gave forensic evidence that the glass from the window and the fragments found in the shoes had an identical refractive index. The witness gave evidence that he had consulted statistics compiled by the Home Office Central Research Establishment and had found that the refractive index referred to occurred in only 4% of all glass samples investigated by the establishment. He then gave his opinion that there was a very strong likelihood that the glass from the shoes originated from the window. The appellant was convicted. He appealed, contending that the evidence of the Home Office research establishment's statistics was hearsay and inadmissible because the expert witness had no personal knowledge of the analysis on which the statistics were based.

Held – When an expert witness was asked to express his opinion on a question, the primary facts on which that opinion was based had to be proved by admissible evidence given either by the expert himself or some other competent witness. However, once such facts were proved, the expert witness was then entitled to draw on the work (including unpublished work) of others in his field of expertise as part of the process of arriving at his conclusion, provided he referred to that material in his evidence so that the cogency and probative value of his conclusion could be tested by reference to that material. Reliance on the work of others and reference to it in evidence did not infringe the hearsay rule. Accordingly, the evidence of the Crown's expert witness in which he made reference to the Home Office research establishment's statistics was admissible. The appeal would therefore be dismissed (see p 365 *f*, p 366 *j* to p 367 *g* and p 368 *e* to p 369 *b*, post).

English Exporters (London) Ltd v Eldonwall Ltd [1973] 1 All ER 726 and *R v Turner* [1975] 1 All ER 70 applied.

Myers v DPP [1964] 2 All ER 881 distinguished.

Notes

For expert evidence, see 17 Halsbury's Laws (4th edn) para 83ff.

Cases referred to in judgment

English Exporters (London) Ltd v Eldonwall Ltd [1973] 1 All ER 726, [1973] Ch 415, [1973] 2 WLR 435, 22 Digest (Reissue) 566, 5509.
Myers v DPP [1964] 2 All ER 881, [1965] AC 1001, [1964] 3 WLR 145, HL, 22 Digest (Reissue) 63, 388.
R v Crayden [1978] 2 All ER 700, [1978] 1 WLR 604, CA, Digest (Cont Vol E) 141, 4906a
R v Patel [1981] 3 All ER 94, CA.
R v Shone (25 June 1982, unreported), CA.
R v Turner [1975] 1 All ER 70, [1975] QB 834, [1975] 2 WLR 56, CA, Digest (Cont Vol D) 328, 5771a.

Cases also cited
R v Halpin [1975] 2 All ER 1124, [1975] QB 907, CA.
R v Pettigrew (1980) 71 Cr App R 39, CA.

Appeal
Steven Abadom appealed against his conviction in the Crown Court at Newcastle upon Tyne on 14 March 1980 before Kenneth Jones J on a charge of robbery for which he was sentenced to six years' imprisonment. The appellant also appealed against sentence. The facts are set out in the judgment of the court.

Christopher Knox (assigned by the Registrar of Criminal Appeals) for the appellant.
David Robson QC for the Crown.

At the conclusion of argument Kerr LJ announced that the appeal would be dismissed for reasons to be given later.

25 June. The following judgment of the court was delivered.

KERR LJ. On 14 March 1980 the appellant was convicted of robbery at the Crown Court at Newcastle upon Tyne before Kenneth Jones J by a majority verdict of 11 to 1 and sentenced to six years' imprisonment. His application for leave to appeal against conviction and sentence was refused by the single judge, but on renewal of his application to the full court (Lawton LJ, Thompson and Jupp JJ) on 16 March 1982 he was given leave to appeal against conviction on one ground which was stated in the following terms by Lawton LJ:

'Leave to appeal is granted . . . on the point which seems to be that raised in this case, that is, the materials which can be used by expert witnesses when giving expert evidence.'

On 18 June we heard the appeal against conviction. We announced that the appeal would be dismissed and that we would give our reasons later. We also refused a renewed application for leave to appeal against the sentence of six years' imprisonment. We now give our reasons for these decisions.

The facts of the case can be shortly stated for present purposes. During the afternoon of Saturday, 25 August 1979 four masked and gloved men broke into the office of a family business run by a Mr and Mrs Williams who were working there together with other members of the family. The men were all wearing balaclava helmets with slits for the eyes, so that it was only possible for those present to form some general impression of their description, without being able to identify them thereafter. They were armed with cudgels and the leader broke an internal window in the office, no doubt in order to contribute to the fright which was naturally experienced by those present. They then demanded where the money was kept and, on this being indicated to them, made off with a sum of over £5,000 in cash from a drawer in the office.

The case for the prosecution was that the appellant was the leader who had broken the window. The main evidence against him was that a pair of his shoes removed by the police from his home after his arrest were found to have fragments of glass adhering and embedded in them, which, as the prosecution contended, had formed part of the broken window. There was evidence concerning the position of the fragments of glass which was consistent with the incident, in that some were found on the upper part and inside the shoes, while others were embedded in the sole, suggesting that some of the fragments had fallen from above and others had been trodden on by the appellant.

In order to seek to establish the likelihood of the fragments of glass having come from the broken window, the prosecution called two expert witnesses who were principal scientific officers at the Home Office forensic laboratories with considerable experience in the analysis of fragments of glass, a Mr R A Cooke and a Mr K W Smalldon. The defence also called an expert, a Mr J A Winterburn, an expert in glass technology who was employed by a glass manufacturer. Before considering the point argued on this appeal it is convenient briefly to summarise their evidence, of which we have seen a transcript. No criticism of the learned judge's summing up of their evidence to the jury was suggested on behalf of the appellant.

Mr Cooke explained that all glass has a refractive index, capable of being determined to five decimal places, which constitutes a measure as to how the light is bent when it passes into a particular piece of glass. He described the method of determining this index which he had used in this case. Using this method, he had compared several of the fragments of glass found in and on the shoes with each other and with the control sample, the glass of the broken window, and found that they all had the identical refractive index. Before expressing any opinion as to the likelihood or otherwise of the fragments of glass having come from the window, he was then asked about the frequency with which this particular refractive index is found to occur. In this connection he explained that it had been the practice of the Home Office Central Research Establishment to collate statistics of the refractive index of broken glass which had been analysed in forensic laboratories over a period of years, and that, having consulted these statistics, he found that this particular refractive index only occurred in 4% of all the analyses which had been made. If the analyses were limited to window glass, the frequency of occurrence was marginally lower. He was then asked whether, on the basis of his expert knowledge and the further analysis made by Mr Smalldon which he had seen and to which I turn in a moment, he was able to express any opinion as to the likely relationship of the glass fragments with the control sample. He answered this by saying:

'Well, considering that only 4% of controlled glass samples actually have this refractive index I consider there is very strong evidence that the glass from the shoes is in fact the same as the glass from the window, in fact it originated from the window.'

Mr Smalldon then gave evidence that he had carried out a chemical analysis of the fragments of glass and of the control sample, and that he had found that 'the two samples were similar on analysis and the analysis was typical of modern flat production glass', ie window glass.

Both experts were then fully cross-examined on their findings and conclusions. Thereafter Mr Winterburn was called for the defence. He did not challenge the evidence of these witnesses, but he pointed out that in relation to the total annual quantity of window glass which is manufactured, a quantity of 4% nevertheless represented something between 20,000 to 40,000 tons and that window glass having this refractive index was therefore not uncommon.

The point taken on this appeal was that the evidence of Mr Cooke, that the identical refractive index of the fragments of glass with that of the control sample occurred in only 4% of all controlled glass samples analysed and statistically collated in the Home Office Central Research Establishment, was inadmissible because it constituted hearsay evidence. It was said to be hearsay because Mr Cooke had no personal knowledge of the analyses whose results were collated in these statistics, save possibly a few for which he may have been personally responsible. This submission was challenged on behalf of the Crown, but no point was taken, in our view clearly rightly, on the ground that the admissibility of this evidence had not been challenged on behalf of the defence at the trial. In our view, the evidence was not inadmissible as hearsay. It is convenient to deal with this issue first on the basis of general principle and then to consider the authorities.

Mr Cooke was admittedly an expert, and was giving evidence as an expert, on the likelihood or otherwise of the fragments of glass having come from the control sample, the broken window. As an expert in this field he was entitled to express an opinion on this question, subject to laying the foundation for his opinion and subject, of course, to his evidence being tested by cross-examination for evaluation by the jury. In the context of evidence given by experts it is no more than a statement of the obvious that, in reaching their conclusion, they must be entitled to draw on material produced by others in the field in which their expertise lies. Indeed, it is part of their duty to consider any material which may be available in their field, and not to draw conclusions merely on the basis of their own experience, which is inevitably likely to be more limited than the general body of information which may be available to them. Further, when an expert has to consider the likelihood or unlikelihood of some occurrence or factual association in reaching his conclusion, as must often be necessary, the statistical results of the work of others in the same field must inevitably form an important ingredient in the cogency or probative value of his own conclusion in the particular case. Relative probabilities or improbabilities must frequently be an important factor in the evaluation of any expert opinion and, when any reliable statistical material is available which bears on this question, it must be part of the function and duty of the expert to take this into account.

However, it is also inherent in the nature of any statistical information that it will result from the work of others in the same field, whether or not the expert in question will himself have contributed to the bank of information available on the particular topic on which he is called on to express his opinion. Indeed, to exclude reliance on such information on the ground that it is inadmissible under the hearsay rule might inevitably lead to the distortion or unreliability of the opinion which the expert presents for evaluation by a judge or jury. Thus, in the present case, the probative value or otherwise of the identity of the refractive index as between the fragments and the control sample could not be assessed without some further information about the frequency of its occurrence. If all glass of the type in question had the same refractive index, this evidence would have virtually no probative value whatever. The extent to which this refractive index is common or uncommon must therefore be something which an expert must be entitled to take into account, and indeed must take into account, before he can properly express an opinion about the likelihood or unlikelihood of the fragments of glass having come from the window in question. The cogency or otherwise of the expert's conclusion on this point, in the light of, inter alia, the available statistical material against which this conclusion falls to be tested, must then be a matter for the jury.

We therefore consider that Mr Cooke's reliance on the statistical information collated by the Home Office Central Research Establishment, before arriving at his conclusion about the likely relationship between the fragments of glass and the control sample, was not only permissible in principle, but that it was an essential part of his function as an expert witness to take acount of this material.

However, we must then turn to the authorities on the basis of which it was submitted that this conclusion was wrong because it infringes the rule against hearsay.

It was common ground that the Home Office statistics did not form part of a record compiled in the course of a trade or business, so that s 1 of the Criminal Evidence Act 1965 has no application. We were therefore inevitably referred to the speeches of the majority of the House of Lords in *Myers v DPP* [1964] 2 All ER 881, [1965] AC 1001 which led to this enactment. However, *Myers v DPP* was not a case which had anything to do with expert evidence. It did not relate to the foundation for the opinion of an expert witness, but to proof of a fact: that engines of the cars in question bore a particular indelible block stamp which identified them with the allegedly stolen cars which were the subject matter of the indictment. This fact was sought to be proved by the production of a record of the block numbers of the cars compiled during their manufacture. The record in question had not been compiled by the witnesses who produced it in evidence, but they explained the system which resulted in its compilation. This evidence was held to infringe the rule against hearsay on the ground that the witnesses who produced the record had no personal knowledge of the accuracy of its contents. However, quite apart from the consideration that this decision had nothing do with expert evidence of opinion, but was concerned with evidence as to facts, the bounds of that decision appear to be still

unsettled in cases of systematically compiled records where evidence about the conclusions
to be drawn from such records is adduced from witnesses who were themselves concerned   *a*
in their compilation in the ordinary course of their duties. In this connection two
decisions of this court should be mentioned. *R v Shone* (25 June 1982, unreported), in
which we have also given judgment today, concerned the records which were kept by a
company of all articles sold in the course of its business. We held that it was open to a
witness, whose duty it was to keep the records, to testify that the inference to be drawn
from the absence of any entry concerning three articles which had disappeared from the   *b*
business was that they had not been sold, and that it was therefore open to the jury to
draw the inference that the articles were likely to have been stolen. In our view, this
inference of fact drawn by the witness in question was not inadmissible on the ground
that it was based on hearsay. Second, there is a dictum to the same effect in the decision
of this court in *R v Patel* [1981] 3 All ER 94 at 96 to which we have referred in our
judgment in *R v Shone*.   *c*

However, it was submitted that the present case was indistinguishable from the
decision in *Myers v DPP* since Mr Cooke had not been personally responsible for the
compilation of the Home Office statistics on which he relied, so that the inferences which
he drew from them must be inadmissible because they were based on hearsay. In our
view this conclusion does not follow, either as a matter of principle or on the basis of
authority. We are here concerned with the cogency or otherwise of an opinion expressed   *d*
by an expert in giving expert evidence. In that regard it seems to us that the process of
taking account of information stemming from the work of others in the same field is an
essential ingredient of the nature of expert evidence. So far as the question of principle is
concerned, we have already explained our reasons for this conclusion. So far as the
authorities are concerned, the position can be summarised as follows.

First, where an expert relies on the existence or non-existence of some fact which is   *e*
basic to the question on which he is asked to express his opinion, that fact must be proved
by admissible evidence: see *English Exporters (London) Ltd v Eldonwall Ltd* [1973] 1 All ER
726 at 731, [1973] Ch 415 at 421 per Megarry J and *R v Turner* [1975] 1 All ER 70 at 73,
[1975] QB 834 at 840. Thus, it would no doubt have been inadmissible if Mr Cooke had
said in the present case that he had been told by somebody else that the refractive index
of the fragments of glass and of the control sample was identical, and any opinion   *f*
expressed by him on this basis would then have been based on hearsay. If he had not
himself determined the refractive index, it would have been necessary to call the person
who had done so before Mr Cooke could have expressed any opinion based on this
determination. In this connection it is to be noted that Mr Smalldon was rightly called to
prove the chemical analysis made by him which Mr Cooke was asked to take into
account. Second, where the existence or non-existence of some fact is in issue, a report   *g*
made by an expert who is not called as a witness is not admissible as evidence of that fact
merely by the production of the report, even though it was made by an expert: see eg
R v Crayden [1978] 2 All ER 700 at 702, [1978] 1 WLR 604 at 606.

These, however, are in our judgment the limits of the hearsay rule in relation to
evidence of opinion given by experts, both in principle and on the authorities. In other
respects their evidence is not subject to the rule against hearsay in the same way as that   *h*
of witnesses of fact: see *English Exporters (London) Ltd v Eldonwall Ltd* [1973] 1 All ER 726
at 730, [1973] Ch 415 at 420 and *Phipson on Evidence* (12th edn, 1976) para 1207. Once
the primary facts on which their opinion is based have been proved by admissible
evidence, they are entitled to draw on the work of others as part of the process of arriving
at their conclusion. However, where they have done so, they should refer to this material
in their evidence so that the cogency and probative value of their conclusion can be tested   *j*
and evaluated by reference to it.

Thus, if in the present case the statistical tables of analyses made by the Home Office
forensic laboratories had appeared in a textbook or other publication, it could not be
doubted that Mr Cooke would have been entitled to rely on them for the purposes of his
evidence. Indeed, this was not challenged. But it does not seem to us, in relation to the

reliability of opinion evidence given by experts, that they must necessarily limit
a themselves to drawing on material which has been published in some form. Part of their
experience and expertise may well lie in their knowledge of unpublished material and in
their evaluation of it. The only rule in this regard, as it seems to us, is that they should
refer to such material in their evidence for the reasons stated above.

We accordingly conclude that Mr Cooke's reliance on the Home Office statistics did
not infringe the rule against hearsay and we dismiss the appeal against conviction.
b So far as concerns the application for leave to appeal against sentence, having regard to
the nature of this offence and the antecedents of the appellant we consider that the
sentence of six years was wholly appropriate, and we accordingly refuse this application.

[His Lordship then considered the possibility of an application being made by counsel
for the appellant for leave to appeal and stated that counsel, who was in the north of
England, could make such an application in writing by trying if possible to agree a
c question with counsel for the prosecution and then sending that to the court.]

Appeal dismissed.

18 October. *The court refused leave to appeal to the House of Lords but certified, under s 33(2) of
the Criminal Appeal Act 1968, that the following point of law of general public importance was
d involved in the decision: whether an expert witness, in giving evidence as to the likelihood or
unlikelihood of some occurrence, was entitled to refer to statistical material lying within the field
of his expertise of the accuracy of which he had no personal knowledge, but which he had no reason
to doubt.*

Solicitors: *Derek Brown,* Newcastle upon Tyne (for the Crown).
e

Jacqueline Charles   Barrister.

f
R v Britzman
R v Hall

COURT OF APPEAL, CRIMINAL DIVISION
LAWTON LJ, MICHAEL DAVIES AND BUSH JJ
g 12, 28 OCTOBER 1982

*Criminal evidence – Character of accused – Imputation on character of prosecutor or witness –
Discretion of court – Discretion to allow cross-examination of accused as to previous conviction –
Exercise of discretion – Prosecution witness alleging that accused had admitted guilt in course of
lengthy conversations – Accused denying that conversation took place – Accused not expressly
h alleging that prosecution witness had fabricated evidence against him – Whether imputation on
character of prosecution witness – Whether court should give prosecution leave to cross-examine
accused as to previous convictions – Criminal Evidence Act 1898, s 1(f)(ii).*

At the appellant's trial on a charge of burglary, the prosecution relied on the evidence of
three police officers, who stated that by implication he had admitted his guilt during
j certain lengthy conversations which they had recorded. When the appellant gave
evidence, he denied that the conversations had ever taken place. He did not, however, go
on to allege that the police officers had fabricated the evidence against him. The
prosecution applied for, and was granted, leave to cross-examine him as to his previous
convictions on the ground that the nature and conduct of the defence were such as to
involve imputations on the character of the witnesses for the prosecution within the

meaning of s 1(*f*)(ii)*ᵃ* of the Criminal Evidence Act 1898. The appellant was convicted.
He appealed, contending that cross-examination as to his previous convictions should not   *a*
have been allowed because in his defence he had not made any positive allegation of
impropriety on the part of the police.

Held – The nature and conduct of the appellant's defence did involve imputations on
the character of the police officers because, when the appellant denied that the alleged
conversations had taken place, he was not merely saying that one short incident had   *b*
never happened or that the police officers had made a mistake or had misunderstood
what he had said but was implying that they had fabricated a substantial and vital part of
their evidence. It was immaterial that he had not expressly alleged that they had
committed perjury. By putting the truth of their evidence in issue he had exposed
himself to the risk of being cross-examined as to his previous convictions. In the
circumstances the trial judge had rightly given the prosecution leave to cross-examine   *c*
him as to his past record, and the appeal would accordingly be dismissed (see p 372 *a* to *d*
and j to p 373 *b* and p 374 *g h*, post).

Guidelines on when, in a case where the defendant alleges that evidence against him
has been fabricated by witnesses for the prosecution, the court should exercise its
discretion by refusing to grant the prosecution leave to cross-examine the defendant as to
his previous convictions (see p 373 j to p 374 *c*, post).   *d*

Notes
For the cross-examination of a defendant as to character, see 11 Halsbury's Laws (4th edn)
para 388, and for cases on the subject, see 14(2) Digest (Reissue) 499–503, 4074–4125.

For the Criminal Evidence Act 1898, s 1, see 12 Halsbury's Statutes (3rd edn) 865.

e
Cases referred to in judgment
R v Clark [1955] 3 All ER 29, [1955] 2 QB 469, [1955] 3 WLR 313, CCA, 14(2) Digest
(Reissue) 641, 5193.
R v Jones (1923) 17 Cr App R 117, CCA, 14(2) Digest (Reissue) 641, 5192.
R v McGee and Cassidy (1979) 70 Cr App R 247, CA.
R v Nelson (Gerrard) (1978) 68 Cr App R 12, CA.
R v Tanner (1977) 66 Cr App R 56, CA.   *f*
Selvey v DPP [1968] 2 All ER 497, [1970] AC 304, [1968] 2 WLR 1494, HL, 14(2) Digest
642, 5203.

Case also cited
R v de Vere [1981] 3 All ER 473, [1982] QB 75, CA.   *g*

Appeal
On 6 November 1981 in the Crown Court at Croydon, before Mr Recorder Titheridge
QC and a jury, the appellants, Frederick John Britzman and Henry Hall, were each
convicted of burglary and sentenced to four years' imprisonment. They both appealed,
with leave, against conviction and sentence. The facts are set out in the judgment of the   *h*
court.

Nigel Ingram (assigned by the Registrar of Criminal Appeals) for the appellant Britzman.
Andrew Munday (assigned by the Registrar of Criminal Appeals) for the appellant Hall.
Tony Docking for the Crown.

Cur adv vult   *j*

──────────────────────────────

a   Section 1(*f*), so far as material provides: 'A person charged and called as a witness in pursuance of
     this Act shall not be asked, and if asked shall not be required to answer, any question tending to
     show that he has . . . been convicted of . . . any offence other than that wherewith he is then
     charged . . . unless . . . (ii) . . . the nature or conduct of the defence is such as to involve imputations
     on the character of . . . the witnesses for the prosecution . . .'

28 October. The following judgment of the court was delivered.

LAWTON LJ. On 6 November 1981 at the Crown Court at Croydon, after a trial before Mr Recorder Titheridge QC these appellants, Frederick John Britzman and Henry Hall, were convicted of burglary and each was sentenced to four years' imprisonment. The single judge gave them leave to appeal against their convictions and we have given them leave to appeal against their sentences.

On 29 May 1980 two men, posing as water board employees, persuaded a Mrs Mayell, then aged 88, to allow them to enter her house on a council estate at Putney in order to inspect her water system, giving as their excuse for doing so that there was reason to believe the supply to be contaminated. One of them, followed by Mrs Mayell, went into the kitchen and turned on the taps. The other went into another room and broke open and damaged a writing bureau which was locked. Mrs Mayell discovered this shortly after the two men had left. Nothing was missing. Mrs Mayell at once telephoned the police and gave them descriptions of both men. A police officer in a motor car was at once sent to search the area and about 15 minutes after the two men had left Mrs Mayell's house he stopped and arrested the two appellants within the limits of the council estate. Both fitted the descriptions given by Mrs Mayell. It was discovered later that Hall was wearing a wig. On 1 June 1980 they were both put on an identification parade but Mrs Mayell did not pick them out. At the trial it was accepted by the prosecution that without the evidence of what had happened after arrest there would have not have been enough to justify a conviction of either appellant.

The prosecution's case was that shortly after arrest on 29 May both appellants were interviewed separately by Det Con Self. Both denied guilt. Britzman said: 'If you think you can prove it, then I'll talk to you.' Hall said: 'You fucking prove something and I'll have it son.'

On 30 May they were both separately interviewed by Det Insp Whyte and Det Con Andrews. Britzman refused to answer any questions. Hall said: 'I won't admit anything until the time is right.' On 1 June Det Insp Whyte, accompanied this time by Det Con Boal, had a long interview with Britzman which both officers said they had recorded in their notebooks. The recorder reminded the jury of this interview in detail. If Britzman had said what he was alleged to have done, there was strong evidence from which the jury could infer guilt.

It is unnecessary to set out in this judgment all of what was alleged to have been said by Britzman. One part of it illustrates its tone:

> '*Det Insp Whyte.* Fred, we know you did the one at Putney Park Lane. There's no point in discussing it unless you want to put it on paper. *Britzman.* I might do that. Look, you've been fair with me so far. Let's stop pussy-footing about. We are probably fucked on that old woman, but it's still a bit iffy.
> *Det Insp Whyte.* Not as far as we are concerned. *Britzman.* It is if we get a jury.
> *Det Insp Whyte.* So. *Britzman.* It's a chance.'

Later that day, according to Det Con Boal, he heard the two appellants shouting to one another whilst in their cells. Once again, if his evidence was accepted by the jury, guilt could be inferred from what was said. One passage was as follows:

> '*Hall.* Look, we've only got to sweat this out. They can't keep us here for ever. That old bird won't pick us out. Just keep your mouth shut. We'll be OK. *Britzman.* We'll talk about it if they stick us together.
> *Hall.* I'll fucking do you if you say anything.'

Britzman's case was that he had not spoken at all to Det Con Self on 29 May or to Det Insp Whyte and Det Con Boal on 1 June nor had he had a shouting match with Hall in the cells as alleged by Det Con Boal. Counsel who appeared for Britzman and who is an experienced advocate in criminal cases, appreciated that putting his client's case to these police officers in cross-examination, as he had to do, was like walking through a legal minefield, because of the provisions of s 1(*f*)(ii) of the Criminal Evidence Act 1898. It is clear from the way Britzman gave his evidence that he too knew of the dangers, perhaps because his acquaintance with the criminal courts was longer than that of his counsel.   *a*

Any denial that the conversations had taken place at all necessarily meant by implication that the police officers had given false evidence which they had made up in order to get the appellants convicted. On the facts of this case there could be no question of mistake, misunderstanding or confusion. If Det Insp Whyte and Det Con Boal had made up this story, they had conspired together to commit perjury and had committed it. Det Con Self must have committed perjury when giving evidence about the alleged   *b*
conversation on 29 May and Det Con Boal must have done the same about the cell conversation. The conversation on 1 June about which two officers gave evidence was long and of a kind which could have appeared in a television film script for a crime series.

A defence to a criminal charge which suggests that prosecution witnesses have deliberately made up false evidence in order to secure a conviction must involve imputations on the characters of those witnesses with the consequence that the trial   *c*
judge may, in the exercise of his discretion, allow prosecuting counsel to cross-examine the defendant about offences of which he has been convicted. In our judgment this is what Parliament intended should happen in most cases. When allegations of the fabrication of evidence are made against prosecution witnesses, as they often are these days, juries are entitled to know about the characters of those making them.

The duty of the judge in such cases to exercise a discretion whether to allow prosecuting   *d*
counsel to cross-examine a defendant about previous convictions puts defending counsel in a difficulty because some judges, so counsel for Britzman told us and we accept from our own experience when we were at the Bar, will exercise their discretion in favour of the defendant if either he or his counsel avoids making specific allegations of misconduct. This practice has a long history and support for it can be found in *R v Clark* [1955] 3 All ER 29, [1955] 2 QB 469 and *R v Jones* (1923) 17 Cr App R 117. With such judges a   *e*
suggestion that a witness is mistaken or had misunderstood usually attracts a favourable exercise of discretion.

Britzman seems to have thought that Mr Recorder Titheridge might be such a judge, because he said in evidence that Det Insp Whyte had been mistaken in thinking that he had said what he was alleged to have done on 1 June. Counsel for Britzman in cross-examination contented himself with suggesting to the officers that the alleged   *f*
conversations had not taken place at all.

Mr Recorder Titheridge would have none of this delicate forensic language. When prosecuting counsel applied for leave to cross-examine Britzman about his previous convictions he ruled that he could do so. He gave a reasoned ruling, the essence of which is contained in the following passage:

'In my judgment, the delicacy with which cross-examination was conducted on   *g*
behalf of this defendant cannot hide the basic commonsense position, which is this; there is no room for error or mistake; it must be clear to the jury that the only real issue for their consideration, although, I repeat, it has never been so put to these police officers, that the only real issue for their consideration is whether the statements were made, or in the case of the conversation between the two defendants   *h*
whether the conversation took place, or whether those officers have made them up. There is simply no other possibility.'

Counsel for Britzman submitted that this ruling was wrong, because the defence amounted in reality to no more than a denial of the charge. In putting his case in that way he adopted what Viscount Dilhorne had said in *Selvey v DPP* [1968] 2 All ER 497 at 508, [1970] AC 304 at 339.   *j*

In our judgment the nature and conduct of the defence did involve imputations on the characters of the three officers, despite the delicacy of Britzman's language and the forensic skill of his counsel. The jury had to decide whether these officers had made up what they alleged had been said. If in any case that is the reality of the position and would be seen by a jury to be so, there is no room for drawing a distinction between a defence which is so conducted as to make specific allegations of fabrication and one in which the allegation arises by way of necessary and reasonable implication. Nor can any distinction be validly drawn between an allegation to commit perjury and one of conspiring to commit perjury; but, when the allegation is one of perjury only, discretion may have to be exercised in favour of the defendant more readily than with a conspiracy allegation, having regard to what was said by Viscount Dilhorne in *Selvey*.

This opinion is in accord with two decisions of this court, namely *R v Tanner* (1977) 66 Cr App R 56 and *R v McGee and Cassidy* (1979) 70 Cr App R 247. In *Tanner*, in a reserved judgment, Browne LJ said (at 64):

> 'In some cases the distinction may be a very narrow one, but that it exists in principle is clear. The decision whether a case is on one side of the line or the other must depend on the facts of each particular case. In our judgment, the nature and conduct of the defence in the present case did involve imputations on the character of the police officers. This was not a case of a denial of a single answer, nor was there any suggestion or possibility of mistake or misunderstanding. The appellant was denying not only his admission, but in the case of each interview a series of subsequent important answers attributed to him by the police. In spite of [defending counsel's] skilful handling of the cross-examination of the police officers; and of the defendant's evidence-in-chief, it necessarily followed in the circumstances of this case, that the appellant was saying impliedly that the police officers had made up a substantial and vital part of their evidence and that [the two] had conspired together to do so. He also said expressly that one of the police officers said that if he admitted the offence he would get bail. The judge's interventions were, in our judgment, merely bringing into the open what was already necessarily implicit.'

That passage applies aptly to this case.

In *R v Nelson* (1978) 68 Cr App R 12, which was decided about twelve months after *R v Tanner*, this court came to a different conclusion. Two grounds for this decision were given, both purporting to be based on the second of the propositions set out in Viscount Dilhorne's speech in *Selvey v DPP* [1968] 2 All ER 497 at 508, [1970] AC 304 at 339. The first was that the attempt to demonstrate a detective constable's unreliability as to a disputed interview was not based on any matter independent of his evidence. That ground will not apply in this case to the interview of 1 June, to which Det Insp Whyte and Det Con Boal spoke, since each gave evidence of what had happened. The second ground was, that the appellant's case was that the cross-examination was only directed at supporting his denials of the contents of the disputed interview; it was not directed at casting imputations to establish a defence.

We have found difficulty in following this reasoning. The challenge of the evidence was necessary to enable the appellant to establish his defence. Without the challenge he had no defence as he was alleged to have confessed. We prefer the decisions in *R v Tanner* and *R v McGee and Cassidy* to that in *R v Nelson*. In our judgment the learned recorder's ruling was right.

In deciding as we have, we have not overlooked the potentiality of unfairness to defendants with previous convictions which a rigid application of s 1(*f*)(ii) of the 1898 Act would cause and the difficulties in advising and deciding tactics which defending counsel have. No doubt it was appreciation of the potentiality of unfairness to defendants which led the House of Lords in *Selvey* to reject the Crown's submission in that case that judges had no discretion to refuse leave to cross-examine about previous convictions.

We hope that it will be helpful for both judges and counsel if we set out some guidelines for the exercise of discretion in favour of defendants. First, it should be used if there is nothing more than a denial, however emphatic or offensively made, of an act or even a short series of acts amounting to one incident or in what was said to have been a short interview. Examples are provided by the kind of evidence given in pickpocket cases and where the defendant is alleged to have said: 'Who grassed on me this time?' The position would be different however if there were a denial of evidence of a long period of detailed observation extending over hours and just as in this case and in *R v Tanner*, where there were denials of long conversations.

Second, cross-examination should only be allowed if the judge is sure that there is no possibility of mistake, misunderstanding or confusion and that the jury will inevitably have to decide whether the prosecution witnesses have fabricated evidence. Defendants sometimes make wild allegations when giving evidence. Allowance should be made for the strain of being in the witness box and the exaggerated use of language which sometimes results from such strain or lack of education or mental instability. Particular care should be used when a defendant is led into making allegations during cross-examination. The defendant who, during cross-examination, is driven to explaining away the evidence by saying it has been made up or planted on him usually convicts himself without having his previous convictions brought out. Finally, there is no need for the prosecution to rely on s 1(*f*)(ii) if the evidence against a defendant is overwhelming.

Having regard to our decision about the learned recorder's ruling, Hall has no separate cause to complain about the consequences of it. Having heard it, his counsel decided not to call him; so his previous convictions never were before the jury. Had the ruling been wrong a different problem would have arisen, but there is no need to consider it or what the solution would have been.

Counsel for Hall took a further point which, if well founded, which it was not, would have helped both appellants. At the beginning of the trial, after both appellants had been arraigned, prosecuting counsel told the recorder that Mrs Mayell, who was then 90, was seriously ill and would be unable to attend court. The trial was adjourned until the next day for a doctor to be called to prove this, defending counsel, somewhat surprisingly, being unwilling to accept a written report from the doctor which had been available the previous day. The doctor proved what she was expected to prove.

Counsel for Hall then submitted that although the evidence brought the case within s 13 of the Criminal Justice Act 1925 so as to allow Mrs Mayell's deposition to be read, the recorder should exercise his discretion against it being read. Why he should have done so defeats us. These was no dispute that Mrs Mayell had been a victim of a burglary. She had not picked out the appellants on the identification parade and the prosecution accepted that her evidence alone was not enough to convict the appellants. The recorder allowed Mrs Mayell's deposition to be read. He would have been wrong to do otherwise. To our surprise counsel for Hall persisted with this point in this court. It should not have been argued before us.

The recorder took a serious view of this case. It was a bad one of its kind. Women, particularly elderly ones, must be protected by the law from rogues such as these appellants. This, however, has to be said. Although they scared Mrs Mayell and damaged her bureau, they did not use or threaten her with violence and stole nothing from her. We consider that four years' imprisonment was over severe and that the sentence can be reduced to three years.

The appeal against conviction will be dismissed. The appeal against sentence will be allowed. The sentence of four years will be quashed and a sentence of three years substituted.

Appeal against conviction dismissed. Appeal against sentence allowed.

Solicitors: *D M O'Shea* (for the Crown).

Jacqueline Charles   Barrister.

Storey v National Coal Board

QUEEN'S BENCH DIVISION AT SHEFFIELD
MUSTILL J
8, 9, 10, 19 FEBRUARY 1982

Coal mining — Statutory duty — Breach — Breach by employee — Transport rules prohibiting employees riding on conveyors — Deliberate breach by employee — Duty of employer to secure that provisions of transport rules 'enforced' — Whether employer in breach of statutory duty — Mines and Quarries Act 1954, ss 37, 157.

Negligence — Duty to take care — Safety rules — Coal mine — Rules prohibiting employees riding on conveyors — Practice of employees to ride conveyors in breach of rules — Whether employer negligent in failing to prevent employees from doing what employees knew to be prohibited and unsafe — Mines and Quarries Act 1954, ss 37, 157.

The deceased, an experienced mineworker, was riding on a conveyor belt in the defendants' mine, when he was carried by the belt into a chute where he suffered fatal injuries. Under the defendants' transport rules made pursuant to s 37[a] of the Mines and Quarries Act 1954, riding on conveyors was prohibited and warning notices were installed throughout the mine to inform employees that riding on conveyors was prohibited and dangerous. The defendants also introduced a scheme whereby persons found guilty of riding on conveyors would suffer a fine by way of a deduction from pay. Nevertheless, after the notices were installed employees and on occasion colliery deputies and other officials continued to ride on conveyors. Fines for the offence were imposed very infrequently and were only of small sums. The deceased's widow brought an action against the defendants for damages for negligence and breach of statutory duty. The defendants, relying on s 157[b] of the 1954 Act, contended that 'it was impracticable to avoid or prevent the contravention' of s 37 by the employees and therefore they were not liable. The defendants further contended that in any event the deceased had been contributorily negligent.

Held – (1) The defendants were not negligent in their approach to the problem of employees riding on conveyors, since they had taken all reasonable steps to warn employees of the dangers involved in riding on conveyors and had succeeded in bringing home those dangers to the employees. The fact that officials also rode on conveyors did not amount to condonation of the practice by the management. Accordingly, the defendants were not negligent in failing to prevent their employees from doing what the employees recognised to be unsafe (see p 379 b to e, post); *Marshall v Hull Fishing Vessel Owners' Association Ltd* [1954] 2 Lloyd's Rep 495 applied.

(2) However, on the true construction of s 37 of the 1954 Act, the defendants were under a duty to 'enforce' their transport rules not merely by promulgating the rules and making them known to the employees as practices which were intended to be obeyed, but also by creating a mechanism designed to secure, and to be generally effective in securing, that the rules were actually obeyed. The defendants' system of enforcement of their rules was toothless and therefore ineffectual to prevent the deceased from riding on the conveyor and their failure to enforce the rules was therefore causative of his death. Accordingly, the defendants were in breach of their statutory duty under the 1954 Act. However, the deceased was himself at fault in that he must have known that riding conveyors was prohibited and yet, in spite of his experience, he proceeded to place himself in a position of danger. It followed that he bore a greater share of the responsibility

---

a   Section 37, so far as material, is set out at p 377 *j* to p 378 *a*, post
b   Section 157, so far as material, is set out at p 378 *b*, post

for what had happened and accordingly the damages when assessed would be reduced by
75% (see p 380 *a b j*, p 381 *e* to *g* and *j* and p 382 *a b*, post).   *a*

Notes
For defences to a civil action for breach of statutory duty, see 31 Halsbury's Laws (4th
edn) paras 429, 431, and for cases on the subject, see 36(1) Digest (Reissue) 256–257,
1002–1009.

For the Mines and Quarries Act 1954, ss 37, 157, see 22 Halsbury's Statutes (3rd edn)   *b*
315, 403.

Cases referred to in judgment
Imperial Chemical Industries Ltd v Shatwell [1964] 2 All ER 999, [1965] AC 656, [1964] 3
     WLR 329, HL, 36(1) Digest (Reissue) 257, 1008.
Marshall v Hull Fishing Vessel Owners' Association Ltd [1954] 2 Lloyd's Rep 495.
Yelland v Powell Duffryn Associated Collieries Ltd [1941] 1 All ER 278, [1941] 1 KB 154, CA,   *c*
     33 Digest (Repl) 891, 1281.

Cases also cited
Jayne v National Coal Board [1963] 2 All ER 220.
Qualcast (Wolverhampton) Ltd v Haynes [1959] 2 All ER 38, [1959] AC 743, HL.
                                                                                            d

Action
The plaintiff, Ada Storey, the widow and administratrix of the estate of George William
Storey, the deceased, brought an action under the Law Reform (Miscellaneous Provisions)
Act 1934 and the Fatal Accidents Act 1976 against the National Coal Board, the
defendants, for damages for negligence and/or breach of statutory duty in respect of a
fatal accident suffered by the deceased while employed by the defendants. The facts are   *e*
set out in the judgment.

J Barry Mortimer QC and *Simon Grenfell* for the plaintiff.
Humphrey Potts QC and *Michael Murphy* for the defendants.

                                                                            Cur adv vult *f*

19 February.   The following judgment was delivered.

MUSTILL J. This action stems from a fatal accident suffered by Mr George William
Storey on 20 September 1977. The circumstances of the accident were as follows. Along
the main intake of the Clowne seam at Kiveton Park colliery there ran a continuous belt   *g*
conveyor. This was fed with minerals by smaller conveyors discharging onto it at
intervals from the various districts. The main intake conveyor terminated at its outbye
end at a loader gate junction, where it fed through a chute onto another conveyor. The
present action is concerned with that part of the conveyor which lay between conveyor
transfer point C11 and the chute, a distance of about 1,100 yards. In this section, the roof
of the intake was about 8 feet above the floor. At the inbye end, the conveyor ran close   *h*
to the floor, but it climbed steadily along the length of its travel, until it reached a point
close to the chute, where it was less than 2 feet from the roof. Not long before the belt
reached the chute, the conveyor signal wire, which ran along the length of the belt for
most of its travel, changed direction so as to be out of reach of the belt. The conveyor was
some 3 feet wide and travelled at 5½ mph.

Some of the conveyors in the colliery were intended for conveying personnel. These   *j*
were provided with stages for mounting and dismounting and were subject to special
regulations as regards speed and clearances. They were also furnished with safety gates at
the alighting platforms. The other conveyors were intended for use only for carrying
materials and their use as a means of human transportation was forbidden. The main
intake conveyor was of the latter variety.

At the time of the accident, the deceased was working on the night shift as conveyor transfer point attendant, at the junction between a district conveyor and the main intake conveyor. He was 60 years of age and had long experience underground. He had in the past worked as a belt maintenance man.

In the ordinary way, the men would have left their place of work at the end of the shift at about 4.30 am, and would have been transported by paddy train to the pit bottom. On this occasion, however, the paddy train had been taken out of service for repair, and permission had been given (by whom and in precisely what manner did not appear from the evidence) for the men to leave their places of work early, so as to give them time to cover the considerable distance on foot which they would ordinarily have ridden. Undoubtedly, some of the men saved themselves the trouble by riding on the main intake conveyor. It is a fair inference that these men got off the conveyor at or not long after the junction where the belt was still at waist height. The deceased also got on the conveyor, but unfortunately he did not get off, either at this point or later. Instead, he was carried right to the end of the belt, where he was discharged into the chute. He fell head foremost, and received injuries from which he subsequently died.

These bare outlines of the accident are not in dispute. There are, however, two important questions, to which no definite answer can be given, in the light of the evidence adduced at the trial.

First, why did the deceased climb on to the belt? All the available information suggests that he was a sensible, thorough and experienced worker. He was described by his deputy, whose evidence in this and other respects I accept, as the very last person he would have thought would ride the conveyor. Moreover, another witness gave evidence that he had suggested on a previous occasion to the deceased that he should ride a proper man-carrying conveyor, and the deceased had refused. Why then did he choose on this particular night to act in a way which seems to have been completely out of character?

Second, why did the deceased not follow the example of the other men, and climb off the belt at a time when this was still comparatively easy? The further the ride continued, the more dangerous it became: a fact which must have been known to the younger men who alighted some hundreds of yards before the end of the belt.

It is probable that the answers to these questions are known, at least in part. The contemporary documents show that another man was travelling the belt in the company of the deceased and that he managed to escape by holding on to part of the conveyor support until the belt was stopped. He did not give evidence, so the reason for the deceased's actions must be a matter of speculation. It does, however, seem a reasonable inference that the deceased, who walked with some difficulty as a result of a previous accident, decided or was persuaded to save himself the long walk back to the pit bottom; that he was not familiar with this particular conveyor, and hence did not know that it approached dangerously close to the roof; that he was insufficiently agile to climb off when the belt has reached a substantial height above the ground; and that by the time he realised what was happening he was too late to save himself.

On the facts thus summarised, Mr Storey's widow brings an action under the Fatal Accidents Act 1976 and the Law Reform (Miscellaneous Provisions) Act 1954, alleging that the accident and the death of her husband were caused by the negligence and/or breach of statutory duty of the defendants, the National Coal Board.

The relevant statutory provision is to be found in s 37 of the Mines and Quarries Act 1954, the material parts of which read as follows:

'(1) The manager of every mine shall have power to make rules (hereafter in this Act referred to as "transport rules") with respect to the use of vehicles and conveyors in the mine and the conditions under which they may be so used and generally for securing the safe operation in the mine of vehicles and conveyors and the avoidance of bodily injury being caused to persons by reason of the running thereof, and in particular ... (d) prohibiting the conveyance in roads in the mine of persons in vehicles or on conveyors except in such circumstances and in accordance with such conditions, if any, as may be specified in the rules and specifying precautions to be observed when persons are so conveyed . . .

(6) It shall be the duty of the manager of every mine . . . (*b*) to secure that all other provisions of transport rules relating to the mine are executed and enforced . . .'

The defendants deny that on its true construction s 37(1)(*d*) is applicable to the present case, but in the alternative they rely on s 157 of the 1954 Act, which is in the following terms:

'It shall be a defence in any legal proceedings to recover damages and in any prosecution, in so far as the proceedings or prosecution are or is based on an allegation of a contravention, in relation to a mine or quarry, of—(*a*) a provision of this Act . . . to prove that it was impracticable to avoid or prevent the contravention.'

Further, the defendants say that the accident was entirely due to the voluntary act of the deceased in choosing to ride the conveyor rather than walk to the pit bottom or, alternatively, this conduct was at least a contributory cause of the loss.

Before discussing the issues thus raised, it is necessary to consider the position at Kiveton Park colliery, at the time of the accident, as regards the riding of conveyors which were not intended for that purpose. (For convenience, I will refer to these simply as conveyors. The practice relating to conveyors designed for man-riding has no bearing on the present case). Witnesses for both sides gave evidence on this topic. In the light of the evidence, I make the following findings.

(1) The riding of conveyors is dangerous. The main intake conveyor was especially dangerous, because of the low roof clearance at the outbye end, a feature which would not be obvious to someone unfamiliar with this particular conveyor who boarded at a place where the belt was closer to the floor. Nevertheless, the danger was of a type which is always liable to be present when a person rides a conveyor.

(2) The defendants made transport rules pursuant to s 37 of the 1954 Act. These provided that: 'Man-riding is prohibited except by means of specially designed man-riding conveyors. Man-riding on conveyors is prohibited.' A copy of these rules was displayed in a part of the pit-head baths where it could be seen by all underground workers.

(3) The defendants installed notices throughout the pit, both verbal and pictorial, which made it quite clear that man-riding on conveyors was prohibited. Such notices were installed at transfer points, where in most cases there was illumination. In particular, there was at least one such notice in full view of the deceased.

(4) As a result of the steps taken by the defendants all underground workers knew that man-riding on conveyors was prohibited.

(5) The defendants' safety officer did his best, by means of posters and personal contacts, to bring home to the workforce the dangers involved in man-riding.

(6) I am satisfied on the evidence, and would in any event have inferred as a matter of common sense, that every underground worker knew that man-riding was prohibited because the management believed it to be potentially dangerous.

(7) In co-operation with the trade unions, the defendants administered a scheme whereby persons shown to have been guilty of man-riding would suffer a deduction from pay, the proceeds being remitted to a charitable institution. Such deductions may have been made on more occasions than was shown in a fines book, inaugurated by the safety officer (which disclosed no 'fines' at all between July 1975 and January 1977), but the deductions were infrequent. The fines ranged in amount between 50p and £2 except in the case where an official was concerned. There the fine was increased to £4.

(8) Notwithstanding the prohibition, man-riding on conveyors did take place at Kiveton Park colliery, as indeed in other collieries throughout the land. It is impossible to state in quantitative terms how widespread this practice was at the time in question, beyond saying that it was by no means unusual.

(9) Those persons who rode the conveyors did so either because they underestimated

the risk of which they had been warned, or because they appreciated the risk but were
content to run it so as to save themselves trouble.

(10) The persons in charge of the management of the colliery knew that man-riding
took place and wished to stop it.

(11) On occasion, deputies or other officials rode on conveyors, and were seen doing
so by fellow-workmen.

In the light of these findings, I return to the issues of law. It is unnecessary to discuss
at length the claim based on an allegation that the defendants were in breach of their
duties of care at common law, for on the meaning which I give to the statutes the duty
thereunder is at least as wide as anything owed by the defendants at common law. For
completeness, however, I should state my conclusion that the defendants were not
negligent in their approach to the problem of man-riding. I find that they not only took
all reasonable steps towards warning their workforce of the dangers of man-riding, but
also succeeded in bringing these dangers home to them. I do not consider that the
instances of man-riding by officials amounted to any condonation of the practice by the
management, or any suggestion by the management that their warnings of the dangers
were not to be taken seriously. These instances were recognised by the workers for what
they were, namely as occasions on which important rules were broken by people who
ought to have known better. I would hesitate long before holding the defendants guilty
at common law for a failure to prevent their employees from doing what they knew to
be unsafe. The decision of Parker J in *Marshall v Hull Fishing Vessel Owners' Association Ltd*
[1954] 2 Lloyd's Rep 495 was concerned with stronger facts than the present, but it does
in my view indicate the right approach to a claim at common law, in circumstances
where employees steadfastly refuse to co-operate in measures taken for their own safety.

The claim for breach of statutory duty raises altogether more serious problems. The
first difficulty is to find the correct meaning of s 37(6)(*b*) of the 1954 Act. Two radically
opposed views were advanced in argument.

Counsel for the plaintiff laid stress on the word 'secure'. He pointed to instances in the
Act where language is used indicating that the employer is obliged only to use his best
efforts to produce a given result. Here, he has to 'secure' that the rules are 'enforced', ie
actually to produce the result that the rules which he has laid down are in all instances
obeyed.

Counsel for the defendants argued for an interpretation at the opposite extreme. A
rule was, he maintained, enforced once it was made known that the rule existed, and that
the maker expected it to be obeyed. The statute did not contemplate that the maker
would be required to do more than to bring the rule into effect, to promulgate the rule
and urge compliance with it.

I am unable to accept either of these interpretations. Where the section requires the
employer to secure that the rule is 'executed', it may be that an absolute standard of
performance is indeed required. In my view, however, even if this interpretation is
correct, it applies only to those acts which the employer is to do himself. The word
'enforce' is to my mind concerned with a different category of rule, namely those which
regulate the conduct of people other than the employer and his management. Here, the
legislature surely cannot have intended to create a duty to produce the result that the
rules are never broken, however ingenious or wilful the offender, and to produce the
further consequence that the manager is guilty of a criminal offence if this is what
happens. It is not an answer to say that the manager has a potential defence under s 157
of the 1954 Act, for the burden is placed on him, when making good a defence, and a
heavy burden too, for he has to show that it was impracticable to avoid or prevent the
infringement. Furthermore, the suggested meaning of the word 'enforced' is out of
accord with its ordinary usage. The criminal laws of a country may properly be regarded
as enforced, even though there are numerous persons who succeed in breaking them and
avoiding punishment: see per du Parcq LJ in *Yelland v Powell Duffryn Associated Collieries
Ltd* [1941] 1 All ER 278 at 285, [1941] 1 KB 154 at 165–166.

On the other hand, it seems to me that the defendants' interpretation puts their duty much too low. Making the rules applicable and making them known as practices which are intended to be obeyed are essential steps towards enforcement, but they are not sufficient steps. The concept also involves the creation of a mechanism designed to secure, and which is in general effective to secure, that the rules are actually obeyed. An injunction not to do something is not enforced if nothing happens when the order is disregarded.

This is not a complete solution to the problem, as is disclosed by the need to qualify the proposition by the words 'in general'. The point of enforcement is reached somewhere along the line between, at the one extreme, a hope that the rule will be complied with coupled with a passive acquiescence in breaches and, at the other, a zeal so far-reaching that not only are there no malefactors who escape detection and punishment, but there are no malefactors at all. I do not think it profitable to attempt a precise definition of the point at which the line is crossed. The question is one of degree, and must be approached according to the circumstances of each individual case.

Taking this as the starting point, one may examine the complaint of the plaintiff that the defendants did not go far enough beyond the mere publication of their rules to secure compliance with them. In my judgment, the matter must be approached in two different ways.

First, the allegations of breach must be put in the context of the characteristics of the deceased as an individual workman. Here, the plaintiff's case is as follows. The deceased was known to be (a) an elderly man, (b) a poor walker, (c) at work a long way from the pit bottom, (d) unable to avail himself of the ordinary means of transport, (e) therefore required to go by foot along a road partially uphill and somewhat watery. He was therefore a person exposed to the temptation of unlawful man-riding and the defendants ought to have taken steps to prevent him, as an individual, from falling into that temptation. In particular, they should either have posted officials by the belt to make sure that he did not try to ride it or closed down the belt as soon as the flow of minerals ceased.

I reject this argument. It is true that if persons responsible for the oversight of the mine had focused their attention on the situation of the deceased, they might very well have recognised that he was more exposed than most to the temptation of man-riding. But it is a non sequitur to assume that he was accordingly more likely than most to yield to the temptation. On the contrary, all that is known of him suggests that he was not someone who could have been expected to do any such thing. An observer, approaching the matter without hindsight, would very likely have concluded that it was the younger, more agile and more headstrong men who needed to be protected against themselves. In this respect I repeat the statement of the deputy that the deceased would be the last person he would have thought would ride the conveyor.

In many cases, this would be the end of the matter, for the extent of the employer's duty is related to the circumstances of the individual workman. In this particular instance, however, it would be wrong to conclude, just because the deceased was no more likely, and indeed rather less likely, than his workmates to break the rules, that the defendants could properly disregard altogether the possibility that he might nevertheless be tempted into breaking them. If the defendants ought to have done more to protect their workforce as a whole, then unless the deceased was someone whose characteristics put him in a class of his own, he should have been brought within the umbrella of the protection. Sound man as he was, I cannot see grounds for putting him in this special category.

The question therefore comes down to this. Given that the defendants did all that could be expected as regards bringing the rules, and the reasons for them, to the attention of their workers, did they go on to 'enforce' them? In my judgment they did not. If exhortation failed, as it did, sanctions would be required. These did not in any real sense exist. One example was given of a worker being transferred for a spell to the surface for conduct which involved man-riding. He was, however, also guilty of a breach of safety precautions which put his fellow-workers, as well as himself, at risk. Against simple man-riding, there was really no deterrent at all. If a worker was inclined to ride the conveyor, he could reflect that there was a good chance that he would not be caught by any official. If he were caught the official might well lack the moral courage to report him. This did quite often happen. If he did have the misfortune to be reported, it might well be that no action would be taken; and I am satisfied from the evidence of the safety officer that punishment by no means always followed on a report. And at the end of it all, he stood to be stopped a tiny fraction of his wage packet. This was the negation of discipline.

It might, if the evidence had taken a different course, have been necessary to consider whether it was impracticable to improve on this lenient attitude. In the event, however, there is no ground on which I could find that the defendants have satisfied the burden of proof under s 157 of the 1954 Act. One step which they might have taken was to bring together their officials, to impress on them their determination to stamp out this dangerous practice, and to make it clear to them and the workforce that they would be expected, as part of their jobs, to turn man-riders off the conveyor, and would receive the full backing of the management if they did so. In fact, nothing of the sort ever happened. More effective still would have been to impose real sanctions for breach; for example, fines that would really hurt, or transfer to a less well-paid job and, in the last resort, dismissal of persistent offenders. It is, of course, perfectly obvious that such a regime would have run into opposition. But that opposition might not have been insuperable, if the union could have been induced to lend its support. Whether the defendants ever thought of a more rigorous system, or tried to put one into effect, and what unpleasant consequences would have ensued for them if they had pressed ahead with it, are matters of complete speculation on the evidence as it stands.

So far as the evidence goes, the management was content to give full and explicit warning that man-riding was prohibited, and leave the rest to their workers. This would, in my view, be sufficient for the duty at common law, but nowhere near enough to found a defence under s 157 of the 1954 Act.

For those reasons, therefore, I conclude that the plaintiff has established a breach by the defendants of their statutory duty.

The next question is whether this breach was the cause of the deceased's death. If there had been a scheme which involved real sanctions and an atmosphere of real discipline in the enforcement of the rule, and if the deceased had nevertheless ridden the conveyor, it would have been possible to infer that the deceased was the sole author of his tragic accident. But I do not find it possible to hold that this was so in the present case. The purpose of the rules created by the management, and of their statutory requirement to enforce them, was to prevent people in the position of the deceased from exercising their freedom of choice in just such a way as the deceased exercised his. This being so, if the rules proved to be ineffectual, I find it impossible to regard the breach as wholly dissociated from the death of the deceased.

I do not find anything in *Imperial Chemical Industries Ltd v Shatwell* [1964] 2 All ER 999, [1965] AC 656 which requires a conclusion in favour of the defendants. Indeed, the general tenor of the discussion in the speeches delivered in that case appears to me to point the other way.

I should pause at this moment to mention two other ways in which the plaintiff advanced the case that there was here a breach of statutory duty.

First, it was said that the defendants should, in all the circumstances, have stopped the relevant section of the conveyor as soon as the last minerals went past. For my part, I doubt whether this is a realistic appreciation of what should and could have been done at the time. Furthermore, I am by no means satisfied that the removal of temptation to break the rules is the same as enforcing the rules.

Second, it was said that officials should have been posted at transfer points or at other places where boarding was likely to take place. Here again I doubt whether, on the evidence, it was practicable to police the rules in this way. The real fault of the system was that it was toothless.

There is one remaining issue, namely whether the recovery by the plaintiff should be reduced on account of the contributory negligence of the deceased. That the deceased was at fault here is undeniable. He must be taken to have known that man-riding was prohibited, and yet, in spite of his experience, he consented to place himself in a position of danger. It seems to me that he bears a heavy share of responsibility for the loss which so sadly happened. I believe this responsibility is greater than that of the defendants and I would assess it at 75%. Recovery will be reduced accordingly.

Judgment accordingly.

Solicitors: *Raley & Pratt*, Barnsley (for the plaintiff); *C T Peach,* Doncaster (for the defendants).

John M Collins Esq   Barrister.

Westfal-Larsen & Co A/S v Ikerigi Compania Naviera SA

The Messiniaki Bergen

QUEEN'S BENCH DIVISION (COMMERCIAL COURT)
BINGHAM J
14, 20 OCTOBER 1982

Arbitration – Agreement – Arbitration clause – Scope – Clause in charterparty – Clause providing for reference of disputes to arbitration – Clause providing for parties to elect to have dispute referred to arbitration – Charterers electing for arbitration – Whether arbitration clause an 'agreement' to arbitrate – Whether clause merely agreement to agree or giving option to arbitrate – Whether election only purporting to confer right to arbitrate on party to whom notice of the dispute given – Arbitration Act 1950, s 32.

Arbitration – Commencement – Charterparty – Notice – Notice of election to have dispute referred to arbitration – Clause in charterparty providing for reference of disputes to arbitration – Clause providing for parties to elect to have dispute referred to arbitration within 21 days of receiving notice of dispute – Dispute arising over damage to cargo – Consignees complaining of damage to owners – Owners informing charterers of complaint and holding charterers liable – Charterers disputing liability – Consignees commencing action against owners and charterers six months after complaint – Owners cross-claiming against charterers – Charterers electing to arbitrate eight months after dispute arose – Whether timely election – Whether time for election commencing to run when dispute arose or when notice of dispute given.

Arbitration – Res judicata – Arbitration in respect of issue decided by foreign court – Charterparty providing for contract to be governed by English law and for parties to elect to have disputes referred to arbitration by giving notice within stipulated time – Dispute arising over damage to cargo – Consignees suing owners and charterers for damages in New York court – Owners cross-claiming against charterers – Charterers seeking order to direct owners to arbitrate – New York court holding that charterers had made timely election to arbitrate – Whether ruling of New York court res judicata as to issue of election.

By a time charter dated 15 September 1969 in the Shelltime 3 form with additional clauses, the owners chartered a vessel to the charterers for a term of ten years. The charterparty provided under cl 40 that the charter was to be construed and the relations between the parties were to be determined in accordance with English law. Clause 40(b) further provided that any dispute arising under the charter was to be decided by the

English courts, provided that 'either party may elect to have the dispute referred to arbitration of a single arbitrator in London in accordance with the provisions of the Arbitration Act, 1950 . . . Such election [to] be made by written notice by one party to the other not later than 21 days after receipt of a notice given by one party to the other of a dispute having arisen under [the] charter'. In 1979 a cargo of toluene was carried on the vessel from the Virgin Islands to Japan. On arrival in Japan in October 1979 the cargo was found to be contaminated and the consignees complained to the owners. On 11 October the owners telexed the charterers informing them of the complaint and holding the charterers responsible for all consequences of the contamination. The following day the charterers replied by telex denying any liability and claiming the liability to be that of the owners. In May 1980 the various consignees of the cargo began four separate actions in New York against, inter alios, the owners and the charterers. On 10 July the owners filed and served in the lead action their answer to the consignees' complaint, in which they cross-claimed for an indemnity against the charterers. By a telex dated 31 July and by their answer to the complaint and cross-claim on the same date the charterers asserted their wish to arbitrate under cl 40(b) of the charterparty. On 26 September the charterers made the same election in terms covering the other three actions and cross-claimed against the owners. In September 1981 the charterers filed a motion in the New York court seeking dismissal of the owners' cross-claim against them and an order directing the owners to arbitrate under cl 40(b). At a hearing before the district court in New York the charterers contended that the question of whether there had been a timely election by them under cl 40(b) should be decided by the arbitrator or the English court. The district judge held that the arbitration provision was in the nature of an agreement to arbitrate which took effect when notice was given, at which point the notice became fixed and irrevocable. The district judge further held that the notice given by the charterers on 31 July 1980 was within 21 days of a claim being filed, which invoked the right to arbitrate under cl 40(b). The judge made an order to that effect. The owners filed a motion to reargue the matter in respect of the lead action on the ground, inter alia, that the court had failed to consider or had overlooked the plain meaning of cl 40(b) and the telexes of 11 and 12 October 1979. The motion was dismissed, but on similar motions in respect of the other three actions, the district judge stayed the claims. Subsequently the charterers settled the consignees' claims and the actions were dismissed, but no contribution to the settlement was made by the owners and accordingly the charterers' cross-claims against the owners remained outstanding. The charterers sought an order in the English court for the appointment of an arbitrator under s 10 of the 1950 Act. The owners contended (i) that the court had no jurisdiction to make an order under s 10 because there was no binding 'arbitration agreement' in existence within s 32[a] of the 1950 Act since instead of a 'written agreement to submit present and future differences to arbitration' there was only an agreement to agree to arbitrate or a contract giving the parties the option of arbitrating which was not in itself an arbitration agreement, and that in any event cl 40(b) only purported to confer a right to arbitrate on the party to whom notice of the dispute was given, so that the agreement lacked the mutuality necessary for a valid arbitration agreement, (ii) that the decision of the district judge was not res judicata since his decision was only procedural in nature and did not touch on the substantive rights and liabilities of the parties, and furthermore in three of the actions had only led to a stay of proceedings and not dismissal, and (iii) that the charterers' election to arbitrate under cl 40(b) had been out of time. The charterers contended that the issue of whether they had made a timely election to arbitrate had been fully argued in the district court in New York, that the district judge's ruling on the matter had been final and that accordingly the issue was res judicata. It was common ground that if, for the purposes of the election, time did not begin to run until after the owners had cross-claimed against the charterers the charterers' election on 31 July was timely.

---

a   Section 32, so far as material, provides: '. . . the expression "arbitration agreement" means a written
      agreement to submit present or future differences to arbitration, whether an arbitrator is named
      therein or not.'

Held – (1) Clause 40(b) of the charterparty was not merely an agreement to agree to arbitrate because (assuming the clause to be otherwise effective) when a valid election to arbitrate was made no further agreement was needed or contemplated for the arbitration to take place. Although there was no agreement to arbitrate until an election was made, once the election was duly made and the option to arbitrate exercised, a binding arbitration agreement came into existence. Since the agreement and the exercise of the option to arbitrate were both expressed in writing, the requirement of a written agreement under s 32 of the 1950 Act was satisfied. Furthermore, cl 40(b) stipulated that 'either party' could elect to have the dispute referred to arbitration and there was therefore no want of mutuality. It followed that the court had jurisdiction to make an appointment under s 10 of the 1950 Act (see p 385 *j* to p 386 *b* and *e* to *h*, post); *Baron v Sunderland Corp* [1966] 1 All ER 349 and *Union of India v Bharat Engineering Corp* (1977) 11 ILR (Delhi) 57 considered.

(2) Although the New York court had jurisdiction to determine whether the proceedings before it should be stayed or dismissed and had specifically addressed itself to the issue whether the charterers had given timely notice of election to arbitrate, it was not possible to conclude that the matter was res judicata even in the United States, because (a) under the rules of procedure applicable to the New York court the judge's decision was open to revision by the judge himself and could be appealed against and (b) there was room for doubt whether the judge's decision was a decision on the merits. It followed that the matter was not res judicata (see p 388 *h* to p 389 *e* and p 390 *b c*, post); dicta of Lord Reid and Lord Upjohn in *Carl-Zeiss-Stiftung v Rayner & Keeler Ltd (No 2)* [1966] 2 All ER at 555–556, 574 followed; *Lummus Co v Commonwealth Oil Refining Co* (1961) 297 F 2d 80 considered.

(3) On the true construction of cl 40(b) the making of a claim did not of itself give rise to a dispute. The question whether a dispute had arisen depended on the facts of the particular case. On the facts, a dispute had arisen between the parties when the charterers telexed the owners on 12 October 1979 asserting that the damage was the owners' liability and denying liability on their part. However, the time for electing to arbitrate ran not from the time when a dispute arose but from the time when notice was received that a dispute had arisen. Notice that a dispute had arisen was given by the owners by their pleading on 10 July 1980 and accordingly the charterers had made a timely election on 31 July. The notice was not required to comply with any technical form or to be expressed as a notice for the purposes of cl 40(b), but it did have to convey clearly, if not expressly, that a litigious or potentially litigious situation had arisen and that if the other party did not wish such litigation to proceed in the English courts he should exercise his election to arbitrate. It followed that the charterers were entitled to an order for the appointment of an arbitrator (see p 390 *e* to *j*, post).

Notes

For incorporation of an arbitration agreement in a contract, see 2 Halsbury's Laws (4th edn) para 522, and for cases on the subject, see 3 Digest (Reissue) 31–37, 160–185.

For the construction and scope of arbitration agreements, see 2 Halsbury's Laws (4th edn) paras 533–541, and for cases on the subject, see 3 Digest (Reissue) 43–52, 206–278.

For the doctrine of res judicata, see 16 Halsbury's Laws (4th edn) paras 1527–1529, and for cases on the subject generally, see 21 Digest (Reissue) 83–84, 551–554.

For the Arbitration Act 1950, ss 10, 32, see 2 Halsbury's Statutes (3rd edn) 442, 459.

Cases referred to in judgment

Baron v Sunderland Corp [1966] 1 All ER 349, [1966] 2 QB 56, [1966] 2 WLR 363, CA, 3 Digest (Reissue) 74, 386.

Carl-Zeiss-Stiftung v Rayner & Keeler Ltd (No 2) [1966] 2 All ER 536, [1967] 1 AC 853, [1966] 3 WLR 125, HL, 21 Digest (Reissue) 49, 316.

Lummus Co v Commonwealth Oil Refining Co (1961) 297 F 2d 80 (2d Cir).

Union of India v Bharat Engineering Corp (1977) 11 ILR (Delhi) 57.

Originating summons

The plaintiffs, Westfal-Larsen & Co A/S, issued an originating summons dated 10 July 1981 against the defendants, Ikerigi Compania Naviera SA, seeking an order that Mr Donald Davies or Mr John Potter or such person as the court considered fit be appointed as arbitrator to hear and determine disputes arising between the plaintiffs and the defendants under a charterparty dated 15 September 1969. The hearing was in chambers but judgment was given by Bingham J in open court. The facts are set out in the judgment.

Simon Crookenden for the plaintiffs.
Richard Aikens for the defendants.

Cur adv vult

20 October. The following judgment was delivered.

BINGHAM J. By this originating summons Westfal-Larsen & Co A/S, charterers of a vessel named Messiniaki Bergen, of which Ikerigi Compania Naviera SA are the owners, seek an order for the appointment of an arbitrator under s 10 of the Arbitration Act 1950. The application has given rise to some argument on the effect of a clause in a standard form of charterparty, for which reason I am giving judgment in open court.

By the charterparty, made on 15 September 1969, the vessel was chartered by the owners to the charterers for a term of ten years. The charter was on the Shelltime 3 form, with additional clauses. In the late summer and autumn of 1979 a cargo of toluene was carried from the Virgin Islands to Japan. The consignees of the cargo (of whom there were several) complained that it was contaminated. The only clause of the charterparty relevant for present purposes is cl 40 which is in these terms:

'(a) This charter shall be construed and the relations between the parties determined in accordance with the law of England.

(b) Any dispute arising under this charter shall be decided by the English courts to whose jurisdiction the parties agree whatever their domicile may be: Provided that either party may elect to have the dispute referred to the arbitration of a single arbitrator in London in accordance with the provisions of the Arbitration Act, 1950, or any statutory modification or re-enactment thereof for the time being in force. Such election shall be made by written notice by one party to the other not later than 21 days after receipt of a notice given by one party to the other of a dispute having arisen under this charter.'

The owners' first and most fundamental objection to the order sought rested on the submission that the court had no jurisdiction to make an order under s 10 of the 1950 Act in this case. Counsel for the owners pointed out (quite correctly) that before the court could make the order there must be an 'arbitration agreement', defined in s 32 of the 1950 Act to mean a written agreement to submit present or future differences to arbitration. Here, it was submitted, the parties' primary agreement was for determination of disputes by the English courts. There was no existing and binding agreement to arbitrate, as the 1950 Act required, but at best an agreement to agree (which was no agreement) or a contract of option (which was not a present agreement and so did not satisfy the 1950 Act). In any event, the clause only purported to confer a right to arbitrate on the party to whom notice was given, so that the agreement lacked the mutuality which was a necessary feature of a valid arbitration agreement. For his contention that a contract conferring an option is not itself an arbitration agreement counsel relied on *Union of India v Bharat Engineering Corp* (1977) 11 ILR (Delhi) 57. For his contention that an arbitration agreement must confer rights to arbitrate on both parties, counsel relied on that case and on *Baron v Sunderland Corp* [1966] 1 All ER 349, [1966] 2 QB 56.

I should be very sorry to conclude that these submissions are well founded for to do so would gravely disable a clause meaningful on its face and evidently accepted as effective by parties to agreements in this form. In the event I am satisfied that the objection is not well founded. The proviso is not an agreement to agree because on a valid election to arbitrate (and assuming the clause to be otherwise effective) no further agreement is needed or contemplated. It is, no doubt, true that by this clause the parties do not bind themselves to refer future disputes for determination by an arbitrator and in no other way. Instead, the clause confers an option, which may but need not be exercised. I see force in the contention that until an election is made there is no agreement to arbitrate, but once the election is duly made (and the option exercised) I share the opinion of the High Court of Delhi in the *Bharat* case that a binding arbitration agreement comes into existence. Where the option agreement and the exercise of the option are both, as here, expressed in writing, the statutory requirement of a written agreement is in my view satisfied.

Whether an arbitration agreement within the meaning of the 1950 Act must confer on both parties equally a right to insist on arbitration is a question which has aroused some controversy. In *Baron v Sunderland Corp* [1966] 1 All ER 349 at 351, [1966] 2 QB 56 at 64 Davies LJ said:

'It is necessary in an arbitration clause that each party shall agree to refer disputes to arbitration; and it is an essential ingredient in that that either party may in the event of a dispute arising refer it in the provided manner to arbitration. In other words, the clause must give bilateral rights of reference.'

This view was accepted and adopted by the High Court of Delhi in the *Bharat* case. On the other hand, the stay of proceedings sought in *Baron's* case was open to more fundamental objections than lack of mutuality in the arbitration clause relied on, and the editor of *Russell on Arbitration* (19th edn, 1979) pp 41–46 has expressed doubt whether, to be valid, an arbitration clause must afford equal rights to both parties. On my construction of the present clause, however, equal rights of recourse to arbitration are afforded to both parties and this question is one which I need not, and accordingly should not, decide. The proviso to cl 40(b) assumes that a dispute exists and stipulates that '*either* party' (my emphasis) may elect to have the dispute referred to arbitration. If one pauses there, it is plain that either the claimant or the respondent may insist on the reference and there would be no room for an argument by the owners to the contrary. That argument was founded on the second sentence of the proviso and was that the option to elect arbitration was conferred only on the party to whom notice of dispute was given. Whether that would, if true, be enough to render the clause unilateral and bad I need not consider because I do not read the clause in that way. The notice of election, like the notice of dispute, may be given 'by one party to the other'. No attempt is made, by any reference to 'such party' or 'that party' to identify the giver of the notice of election with the recipient of the notice of dispute, or to distinguish him. The matter is left at large by the use of language deliberately chosen as wide enough to mean either party in either situation. In the ordinary course of events it is no doubt likely that the prospective claimant gives notice of dispute and the prospective respondent elects arbitration, but I do not construe the language of the proviso as applying only to that sequence of events. I accordingly conclude that the objection taken to the jurisdiction of the court to make an appointment under s 10 must fail.

The next major question is whether the charterers have made a timely election of arbitration so as to take advantage of the proviso to cl 40(b). But the charterers (encouraged, I fear, by myself when the matter was before me on an earlier occasion) submit that this is an issue which cannot be argued before me since it has already been decided in their favour by a judge of the United States District Court for the Southern District of New York, and so is res judicata. The basis of this plea requires a little explanation.

Following the vessel's voyage to Japan, complaints of contamination were made by the consignees to the owners in about early October 1979. There was some exchange between the owners' and the charterers' P & I clubs and on 11 October 1979 the owners telexed to the charterers in these terms:

'Sumitomo, consignees of the alleged contaminated part cargo of 6,300 m/t toluene, are requesting l/guarantee for yen 200.000.000.—therefore please attend as necessary as you have already settle matters with the other consignees of same cargo because we ikerigi compania naviera, s.a., panama, owners of the "messiniaki bergen" which is on timecharter to you, westfal-larsen & co a/s bergen, under t/c party dated 15/9–69, hereby hold you fully responsible for the contamination of toluene loaded under your instructions and under your supervision and orders at st. croix about 24th august 1979 for discharging japan. We hereby also hold you responsible for all consequences arising out of the contamination of toluene including but not limited to expenses, costs, legal fees, delays and actions from cargo interests and/or others.'

It is apparent that the owners were both seeking a letter of guarantee in respect of Sumitomo's claims and holding the charterers responsible for all consequences of the contamination. The charterers replied on 12 October 1979:

'Rytex 11th "Messiniaki Bergen" voyage St. Croix/Japan August/Sept./Oct. 1979. We consider cargo damage to be owners liability and deny any charterers involvements Stop. Please take up question of l/guaranty with your P and I Club.'

Plainly the charterers were not accepting the owners' requests. Nothing very much happened then until, in about May 1980, four actions were begun in the United States District Court for the Southern District of New York by the consignees of the cargo. In the first, and lead, action the plaintiffs were Mitsui & Co Ltd and Mitsui & Co (USA) Inc, and the defendants were the owners, their managers, the charterers and two associated companies of the charterers. In the other three actions there were different consignees as plaintiffs (one of them being Sumitomo) but the same defendants. On 10 July 1980 the owners filed and served their answer to the consignees' complaint in the lead action, in which they cross-claimed an indemnity against the charterers and their associated companies. By a telex dated 31 July 1980, and by their answer to the complaint and cross-claim of the same date, the charterers asserted their wish to arbitrate under cl 40(b) of the charterparty. On 26 September 1980 the charterers made the same claim in terms clearly covering the other actions and not merely the lead action. Cross-claims were also made by the charterers against the owners. There matters stood until, in September 1981, a motion was filed on behalf of the charterers asking that the owners' cross-claims against them be dismissed and that the owners be directed to arbitrate. On behalf of the charterers' associated companies a stay of proceedings was sought. Affidavits, memoranda and briefs were submitted by the parties and an oral hearing took place before Judge Vincent L Broderick on 1 February 1982. At that hearing the charterers argued that the question whether there had been a timely election for arbitration was one for the arbitrator or the English court, not the district court, a view which the owners seem subsequently to have shared. The judge gave an oral ruling in these terms:

'I find that the provision here with respect to arbitration was in the nature of an agreement to arbitrate which came into full bloom when notice was given, at which point the right to arbitration became fixed and irrevocable. I find further that notice was given within 21 days of the time that a claim was filed in this action. I further find that that notice invoked the right to arbitrate which was provided for in the charter party. I, therefore, find that the charterers have an absolute right to arbitrate with respect to the disputes between the charterers and the owners. The action is dismissed with respect to the charterers. The other two third-party defendants do not have either an option agreement or a full-fledged arbitration agreement with the owners and thus are not entitled to invoke any right to arbitration, nor do I see that there is any provision in law for a tag-along. It does seem to me that the interests of justice will be served, however, if the action is stayed as between the defendants Ikerigi and Karageorgis, on the one hand, and the defendants Rederiet and Odfjell, on the other hand, pending a determination of the arbitration in England. The third-party defendant Westfal-Larsen will submit an order which will memorialize this ruling.'

He later made an order which included the following:

> 'Whereas, the Court finds that there was a provision in the nature of an agreement to arbitrate in Clause 40(b) of the charterparty between Ikerigi Cia. Naviera, S.A., Michail A. Karageorgis, S.A., and Westfal-Larsen & Co., A/S, under which the right to arbitrate would become final and irrevocable when notice was duly given, and Whereas, the Court finds that Westfal-Larsen & Co., A/S duly gave written notice of its election to arbitrate within 21 days of receipt of notice of a dispute under this charterparty, and said notice invoked Westfal-Larsen & Co. A/S's right to arbitrate, and Whereas, the Court finds that Westfal-Larsen & Co., A/S has an absolute right to arbitrate the disputes set forth in the cross-claims between Ikerigi Cia. Naviera, S.A., Michail A. Karageorgis, S.A., and Westfal-Larsen & Co., A/S, and, Whereas, the Court finds that co-defendants A/S Rederiet Odfjell, and Odfjell Westfal-Larsen Tankers, Inc., were not parties to the charterparty dated September 15, 1969, and are not entitled to invoke the arbitration clause set forth in Clause 40(b) of said charterparty, but that the interests of justice will be served by a stay of the cross-claim between them on the one hand and Ikerigi Cia. Naviera, S.A. and Michail A. Karageorgis, S.A. on the other, it is hereby Ordered, that the cross-claims filed between Ikerigi Cia. Naviera, S.A., Michail A. Karageorgis, S.A., and Westfal-Larsen & Co. A/S, are hereby dismissed, and the parties are directed to proceed to arbitration in London in accordance with the terms of the arbitration provision in the charterparty, and, it is further Ordered, that the cross-claims between Ikerigi Cia. Naviera, S.A., Michail A. Karageorgis, S.A., and A/S Rederiet Odfjell and Odfjell Westfal-Larsen Tankers, Inc., are hereby stayed pending the outcome of arbitration in London between Ikerigi Cia. Naviera, Michail A. Karageorgis, S.A. and Westfal-Larsen & Co. A/S.'

The owners then filed a motion to reargue the matter on the ground, among others, that the court had failed to consider or had overlooked the plain meaning of cl 40(b) of the charterparty and the telexes of 11 and 12 October 1979 already referred to. This motion the judge summarily denied. Encouraged, no doubt, by their success the owners sought similar orders in the other three actions, but the judge stayed the claims instead of dismissing them, expressing his decision in this way:

> 'In *Mitsui U.S.A.* [v *Ikerigi*] *supra*, I found that due notice was given of an election by defendant Westfal-Larsen & Co. A/S to arbitrate, and I found that said defendant had an absolute right to arbitrate. While I make no such finding here, I direct, in the interests of justice and in the exercise of control over my docket, a stay of the cross-claims between the Charterers and the Owners, pending the outcome of the arbitration in London between Ikerigi Cia. Naviera, Michail A. Karageorgis, S.A. and Westfal-Larsen & Co. A/S. which was ordered in *Mitsui U.S.A.* [v *Ikerigi*] *supra*.'

The most recent development is that the charterers have settled the consignees' claims, and the consignees' actions have been dismissed with prejudice, but no contribution to the settlement has been made by the owners and the charterers' cross-claims against the owners remain outstanding. That is what this litigation is now about.

With that by way of background, I turn to the issue of res judicata. It was common ground that the New York District Court had jurisdiction to determine whether proceedings before it should be dismissed or stayed and that both the present parties were before that court. The charterers contended that the question whether they had made a timely election to arbitrate had been fully argued before the district judge who had ruled on it. They further contended that his judgment on the point had been final, at least to the extent necessary to found a plea of res judicata. The owners challenged both those contentions.

In approaching the first of these issues I must bear in mind the need for caution in interpreting the meaning and effect of the decisions of a foreign court. Particularly apposite are the observations of Lord Reid and Lord Upjohn in *Carl-Zeiss-Stiftung v Rayner & Keeler Ltd (No 2)* [1966] 2 All ER 536 at 555–556, 574, [1967] 1 AC 853 at 918–919, 948–949. Two things persuade me that the district court did specifically address itself to the question whether the charterers gave timely notice of election to arbitrate within 21 days of notice of dispute. The first is the court's finding, already quoted, that the charterers duly gave written notice of election to arbitrate within 21 days of receipt of notice of a dispute under the charterparty. That finding, although in a form submitted by the charterers, was the subject of careful amendment and personal signature by the judge. The second is that, having received a motion to reargue, supported by a memorandum of law in which the effect of the October 1979 telexes was fully canvassed, the judge denied the motion. The most obvious reason for his doing so is, I think, that he had not (as was suggested) overlooked the effect of those telexes in the light of cl 40(b) but had taken them into account. I feel confident that the present issue was fairly and squarely before the district judge and was decided by him. I do not know why the judge made an order of suspension rather than dismissal in the later three cases, but I see no reason to suppose that this reflected uncertainty on his part concerning his earlier decision. I think he was probably waiting to see what happened here.

The second question, whether the decision of the district judge had (as a matter of United States law) the finality necessary to support a plea of res judicata, I find much more difficult. The charterers argued that it had, the owners that it had not. Both submitted affidavits by very well-qualified United States lawyers in support of their arguments. I have formed these conclusions.

1. By virtue of r 54(b) of the Federal Rules of Civil Procedure a judgment on a single claim where there are multiple claims or parties is not final, in the sense that it may thereafter be revised by the judge, unless he expressly determines that there is no just reason for delay and expressly directs the entry of judgment. The rule was applicable here and the judge made no such determination or direction. The result is that the order remained open to revision and was not appealable under that rule.

2. By 28 USC § 1292(a)(3) the Court of Appeals is specifically given jurisdiction over appeals from—

'Interlocutory decrees of . . . district courts or the judges thereof determining the rights and liability of the parties to admiralty cases in which appeals from final decrees are allowed.'

It is not disputed that the present was an Admiralty case, and appealability is relevant because (perhaps paradoxically) a decision of an inferior court is not generally regarded as finally determinative of the rights of the parties unless it is open to challenge on appeal. But the witnesses are in fundamental disagreement whether the decision of the district judge determined the rights and liability of the parties. The charterers submit that it did, because the arbitration clause was advanced as a defence and led in the lead case to dismissal of the owners' cross-claim. The owners submit that it did not, since the decision was of a procedural nature only, not touching on the substantive rights and liabilities of the parties, and in three of the four cases led to a stay of proceedings, not dismissal. Both sides were able to refer to authorities apparently supporting their arguments.

3. Judging the matter purely on the material before me and the argument I have heard, I incline to think that the charterers have had somewhat the better of the argument. I am impressed particularly by an opinion of Judge Friendly in *Lummus Co v Commonwealth Oil Refining Co* (1961) 297 F 2d 80 at 89, in the course of which he said:

'Whether a judgment, not "final" in the sense of 28 U.S.C. § 1291, ought nevertheless be considered "final" in the sense of precluding further litigation of the same issue, turns upon such factors as the nature of the decision (i.e., that it was not avowedly tentative), the adequacy of the hearing, and the opportunity for review. "Finality" in the context here relevant may mean little more than that the litigation of a particular issue has reached such a stage that a court sees no really good reason for permitting it to be litigated again.'

I am also impressed by the statement in 30A Corpus Juris Secundum § 624, p 720 to this effect:

'Some confusion in applying the rule has arisen from the difficulty of determining the precise line of demarcation between an interlocutory and a final decree, and the instances are not infrequent where decrees, although interlocutory in form and thus technically still under the control of the court until final decree, are yet considered as final in their determination of substantial rights, and thus are treated as final as far as modification or vacation is concerned, so that they will not be disturbed after the expiration of the term at which they are rendered.'

I am, however, conscious that I am dealing as an interlocutory matter with an issue of foreign law on which distinguished practitioners in that jurisdiction disagree. There must at the very least be room for doubt whether the judge's decision is to be regarded as a decision on the merits. I have not heard either witness cross-examined. I have not had the detailed oral assistance of an expert in interpreting the effect of the United States authorities. This being so, I feel unable to conclude, in the charterers' favour, that the district judge's decision would in the United States found a plea of res judicata. I am satisfied that it might, but I think it would be unsafe for me to go further than that. I do not reach the stage of considering how, as a matter of English law, the district court rulings should be regarded.

I must therefore determine whether the charterers made a timely election to arbitrate under cl 40(b) of the charterparty. The charterers accepted that if notice of dispute had been given in October 1979 they had not made any election in time. The owners accepted that if notice of dispute had been given by their cross-claim filed on 10 July 1980 (but not earlier) an election had been made in time. The argument accordingly centred on the meaning of 'dispute' and the requirements of a notice of dispute under the clause.

I am reluctant to attempt any legal definition of a term so well understood by owners and charterers as 'dispute'. It plainly indicates that a controversy, or contention, has arisen between the parties. It takes two to quarrel. The making of a claim or demand (as by the owners' telex of 11 October 1979) does not of itself give rise to a dispute, because the other party may accept it. Even the rejection of such claim or demand by such party need not give rise to a dispute, because the rejection may be expressly or impliedly accepted or may be put on grounds affording no arguable basis for rejection. Everything, I think, depends on the facts of the particular case and I do not think it is possible or desirable to generalise. It is, however, my opinion that the charterers' telex of 12 October, with its assertion that the cargo damage was the owners' liability and its flat rejection of any responsibility, did give rise to a dispute between the parties. But that is not the end of the matter, because under the clause time for electing arbitration runs not from the time when a dispute arises but from the time when notice is received that a dispute has arisen. Such a notice need not in my judgment comply with any technical form, and it need not be expressed to be a notice for the purposes of the clause, but it must be such a notice as would convey (clearly if not expressly) that a litigious or potentially litigious situation has arisen and that any party not wishing such litigation to proceed in the English courts should exercise the election to arbitrate. While the charterers' telex of 12 October gave rise to a dispute, it certainly did not give such a notice, and the owners gave no notice to the charterers at that point. This is not surprising: neither the owners nor the charterers then knew whether the consignees would sue; nor, if they did sue, whom they would sue; nor, if they sued the owners, whether there would be any claim for the owners to seek to pass on to the charterers. To issue proceedings or elect arbitration when it was unclear whether there was any effective claim to arbitrate could well have been thought premature. That, I suspect, is why no notice of dispute was given in October 1979, as I find it was not. When notice of dispute was given by the owners by the pleading in July 1980, the charterers made a timely election. The result is that in my judgment the charterers are entitled to the order which they seek.

Order for appointment of arbitrator. Leave to appeal to Court of Appeal.

Solicitors: *Ingledew Brown Bennison & Garrett* (for the charterers); *Ince & Co* (for the owners).

K Mydeen Esq   Barrister.

Robinson v Robinson

COURT OF APPEAL, CIVIL DIVISION
WALLER, KERR AND SLADE LJJ
14, 29 OCTOBER 1982

Husband and wife – Financial provision – Conduct of parties – Duty of magistrates' court to have regard to conduct – Circumstances in which regard should be had to conduct – Conduct obvious and gross – Wife deserting husband – Husband not committing any misconduct – Whether wife's conduct obvious and gross – Whether wife's conduct justifying reduction in financial provision – Domestic Proceedings and Magistrates' Courts Act 1978, ss 2, 3(1)(g).

The husband and wife were married in October 1976. The husband was a serving soldier and was posted overseas in 1978. The wife became homesick and generally disenchanted with army life. In 1980 they returned to England but when he was posted overseas again later that year she went to live with her parents. He returned to England in March 1981 but she did not rejoin him and in August 1981 she told him that she would never go back to him. She subsequently applied to the magistrates for an order for financial provision under s 2 of the Domestic Proceedings and Magistrates' Courts Act 1978. The magistrates found that she had formed the intention to desert the husband in March 1981, that his conduct prior to that date was not the reason for, and had not contributed to, her withdrawal of cohabitation, that the tension between the parties after April 1981 was caused primarily by her intention to withdraw from cohabitation, and that he had not committed any misconduct. They decided that her desertion was 'gross and obvious misconduct' and that under s 3(1)(g)[a] of the 1978 Act they should take it into account when making a financial provision order. They ordered the husband to pay the wife £15 per week for five years and indicated that, but for her conduct, they would have ordered him to pay substantially more. The wife appealed against the order, contending that her conduct had not been gross and obvious and that the magistrates were not justified in reducing the amount of the award.

Held – When considering an application under s 2 of the 1978 Act for financial provision, the past conduct of a wife was only to be taken into account, under s 3(1)(g) of that Act, in exceptional cases where it would offend a reasonable person's sense of justice to disregard such conduct. Since the husband was completely blameless and the marriage had broken down solely on account of the wife's decision to end cohabitation, the case was exceptional. The magistrates were therefore entitled to conclude that her conduct was gross and obvious and that it would be unjust to disregard it. Accordingly the appeal would be dismissed (see p 395 *a* to *g* and p 396 *j* to p 397 *c* and *f g*, post).

Wachtel v Wachtel [1973] 1 All ER 829 and *West v West* [1977] 2 All ER 705 followed.

Notes
For financial provision on divorce and matters to be considered by the court, see 13 Halsbury's Laws (4th edn) paras 1052, 1060.

For the Domestic Proceedings and Magistrates' Courts Act 1978, ss 2, 3, see 48 Halsbury's Statutes (3rd edn) 736, 738.

Cases referred to in judgment
Armstrong v Armstrong (1974) 118 SJ 579, CA.
Benmax v Austin Motor Co Ltd [1955] 1 All ER 326, [1955] AC 370, [1955] 2 WLR 418, HL, 36(2) Digest (Reissue) 883, 451.
Harnett v Harnett [1974] 1 All ER 764, [1974] 1 WLR 219, CA, Digest (Cont Vol D) 429, 6962Aj.

---

a   Section 3(1), so far as material, is set out at p 393 *d*, post

Kokosinski v Kokosinski [1980] 1 All ER 1106, [1980] Fam 72, [1980] 3 WLR 55.
Wachtel v Wachtel [1973] 1 All ER 113, [1973] Fam 72, [1973] 2 WLR 84; *on appeal*
    [1973] 1 All ER 829, [1973] Fam 72, [1973] 2 WLR 366, CA, Digest (Cont Vol D) 425,
    6962Aa.
West v West [1977] 2 All ER 705, [1978] Fam 1, [1977] 2 WLR 933, CA, Digest (Cont Vol
    E) 266, 6674a.

Appeal

By leave of the Divisional Court of the Family Division, the wife, Maureen Robinson,
appealed against an order of the Divisional Court (Sir John Arnold P and Butler-Sloss J),
dated 24 May 1982, dismissing her appeal against an order of East Penwith Magistrates'
Court, dated 20 January 1982, whereby, in response to an application by her for financial
provision under s 2 of the Domestic Proceedings and Magistrates' Courts Act 1978, they
directed that the husband, Tony Robinson, should pay her £15 per week for a period of
five years. The facts are set out in the judgment of Waller LJ.

Jonathan Barnes for the wife.
Anthony Myer for the husband.

Cur adv vult

29 October. The following judgments were delivered.

WALLER LJ. This is an appeal by leave from the Divisional Court of the Family
Division (Sir John Arnold P and Butler-Sloss J) dismissing an appeal from the East
Penwith Magistrates' Court. The magistrates' court had ordered the respondent husband
to pay under Part 1 of the Domestic Proceedings and Magistrates' Courts Act 1978, £15
per week to the appellant wife for five years. The wife appeals to this court submitting
that the order should have been for £45 per week with no limit of time. The court also
made an order of £15 per week for the child, but this does not arise before us.

The parties were married on 9 October 1976. The husband was a corporal in the army
and the wife ceased to work as a horse groom to marry him. For the first two years they
were in married quarters in Cambridgeshire. This was followed by 18 months in
Germany. In late 1980 the husband was to be posted to Belize. Before this the parties had
a married quarter in Kent and when the husband went to Belize the wife went to her
parents in Cornwall. By this time she knew she was pregnant and wrote to her husband
telling him so in January 1981. The husband returned from Belize in March 1981. The
wife decided then that she was not going back to her husband but she did not tell him
until August. She had been living with her parents since the previous September.

The magistrates found that for the first two years while they were in married quarters
in Cambridgeshire the marriage was happy but that during the period in Germany the
husband was away from his unit for varying periods of time and the wife 'became
homesick and generally disenchanted with army life'. She described her complaints in
detail in her evidence and the magistrates regarded her complaints about her husband's
conduct prior to March 1981, as trivial and found that 'they were not the reason for, nor
did they contribute to, [the wife's] withdrawal from cohabitation.' They went on: 'The
disputes/complaints after April, 1981, were caused by tension between the parties and
the prime reason for this tension was [the wife's] already formed intention to withdraw
from cohabitation.' Having found that the wife deserted the husband and that such
desertion was gross and obvious misconduct they said:

> '[The wife's] desertion of her husband, he not having committed any misconduct,
> was a matter of the gravest importance in relation to this marriage and was a matter
> to be taken into account together with all the other matters set out in Section 3 of

a
the Act when deciding what Financial Provision Order, if any, should be made in favour of the Applicant.'

On behalf of the wife it was submitted: (i) that the conduct found by the magistrates was not such as would justify the magistrates in making a substantial reduction in the amount paid to the wife on account of her conduct; (ii) that in considering an appeal from the magistrates the Divisional Court had wrongly regarded the whole case once the primary facts were found as a matter for the discretion of the magistrates with which

b they could not interfere.

Although the Matrimonial Proceedings and Property Act 1970 and the Matrimonial Causes Act 1973 altered the law in relation to maintenance in cases of divorce, it was not until 1978 that similar alterations were made for domestic proceedings in magistrates' courts. Section 25 of the 1973 Act, having set out the matters to be taken into consideration, concluded sub-s (1) by saying:

c
'. . . and so to exercise those powers as to place the parties, so far as it is practicable and, having regard to their conduct, just to do so, in the financial position in which they would have been if the marriage had not broken down and each had properly discharged his or her financial obligations and responsibilities towards the other.'

d Section 3(1)(g) of the Domestic Proceedings and Magistrates' Courts Act 1978 contains a provision which, although differently worded, it was not disputed before us was to the same effect. This provides as one of the matters to be taken into consideration:

'any other matter which in the circumstances of the case the court may consider relevant, including, so far as it is just to take it into account, the conduct of each of the parties in relation to the marriage.'

e In *Wachtel v Wachtel* [1973] 1 All ER 113 at 119, [1973] Fam 72 at 80 Ormrod J said:

'The court can only approach this issue in a broad way. It should bear in mind the new basis of divorce which recognises that, generally speaking, the causes of breakdown are complex and rarely to be found wholly or mainly on one side, and that the forensic process is not well-adapted to fine assessments or evaluations of

f behaviour, and that it is not only conduct in relation to the breakdown which may have to be considered. Conduct subsequent to the separation by either spouse may affect the discretion of the court in many ways, eg the appearance of signs of financial recklessness in the husband or of some form of socially unacceptable behaviour by the wife which would suggest to a reasonable person that in justice some modification to the order ought to be made. In my experience, however,

g conduct in these cases usually proves to be a marginal issue which exerts little effect on the ultimate result unless it is both obvious and gross.'

In delivering the judgment of the Court of Appeal in the same case Lord Denning MR, picking up the words of Ormrod J, said ([1973] 1 All ER 829 at 835–836, [1973] Fam 72 at 90):

h 'There will be many cases in which a wife (although once considered guilty or blameworthy) will have cared for the home and looked after the family for very many years. Is she to be deprived of the benefit otherwise to be accorded to her by s 5(1)(f) because she may share responsibility for the breakdown with her husband? There will no doubt be a residue of cases where the conduct of one of the parties is in the judge's words ([1973] 1 All ER 113 at 119, [1973] Fam 72 at 80) "both obvious

j and gross", so much so that to order one party to support another whose conduct falls into this category is repugnant to anyone's sense of justice. In such a case the court remains free to decline to afford financial support or to reduce the support which it would otherwise have ordered. But, short of cases falling into this category, the court should not reduce its order for financial provision merely because of what was formerly regarded as guilt or blame.'

In *Armstrong v Armstrong* (1974) 118 SJ 579, a decision of the Court of Appeal, which is cited by Wood J in *Kokosinski v Kokosinski* [1980] 1 All ER 1106 at 1116, [1980] Fam 72 at 84, Buckley LJ said:

> 'The expression "obvious and gross", as I ventured to say in the course of the argument, obviously is not a definitive expression. The Court of Appeal there, I think, indicated clearly what they had in mind by the use of those words, which they borrowed from the judgment of Ormrod J [in *Wachtel*] which was there under appeal. They said in the judgment of the court that it was not right for a court before whom an application came under s 4 of the Matrimonial Proceedings and Property Act 1970 to conduct a post-mortem into the matrimonial affairs of the parties: but that, if the conduct known to the court was such that it would be repugnant to anyone's sense of justice to say that it ought not to be taken into account in considering what financial provision should be made by one party for another, it was proper that it should be taken into account.'

Stephenson LJ in the course of his judgment said:

> 'On the first point as to the wife's conduct, bearing in mind what was said by Ormrod J and by Lord Denning MR in giving the judgment of this court in *Wachtel v Wachtel* [1973] 1 All ER 829, [1973] Fam 72, and what was said by Cairns and Roskill L JJ in *Harnett v Harnett* [1974] 1 All ER 764, [1974] 1 WLR 219, the question we have to ask ourselves seems to me to be: Would it offend a reasonable man's sense of justice that this wife's conduct should be left out of account in awarding her maintenance by a lump sum out of the proceeds of this sale and that it should have no effect on the financial provision which the husband ought to be ordered to pay her? Would it be inequitable or unjust to disregard her conduct?'

Finally in *West v West* [1977] 2 All ER 705, [1978] Fam 1 the Court of Appeal considered whether or not a case, where the parties, although the wife had had two children, had never lived together for more than a few days at a time, was one where a substantial reduction could be made. The trial judge had found that by far the greater burden of responsibility for the failure to start the marriage was on the wife, but decided that the conduct did not quite reach the pitch which would render it within the description in *Wachtel v Wachtel*. On appeal Sir John Pennycuick said ([1978] Fam 1 at 8; cf [1977] 2 All ER 705 at 711):

> 'I do not think the judge was right when he held that the wife's conduct in this matter, as he found it as a fact, was not obvious and gross misconduct in relation to this marriage. I find it difficult to think of any conduct more gross than totally to fail to set up any married life at all where it is no fault of anyone else, but for the reasons which the judge held to be predominantly her own fault. It seems to me that that was a gross and obvious misconduct and once that is accepted then the whole attack on the judge's conclusion goes, though he may not have reached that conclusion by quite the right route. I suspect that the word "gross" has given rise to some misunderstanding in this connection, and that the word "gross" has been given an imputation of moral blame. In fact, I do not think the word "gross" really carries any sort of moral judgment. It means I think no more than "of the greatest importance".'

Counsel on behalf of the wife, submitted that *West v West* [1977] 2 All ER 705, [1978] Fam 1 was a worse case than the present in that (a) there was no period when the parties were living together, and (b) there was no explanation for the wife's final desertion, whereas in the present case the parties did live together for 4½ years and an explanation for the wife's desertion was her dislike of army life. There is, however, an important point of difference in that in *West v West* the judge found that the husband had to accept a share of the responsibility for the breakdown or failure to start the marriage, although by far and away the greater burden was on the wife. In the present case the husband was

said to be blameless. In my opinion there is very little to choose between them. For the
a husband to be blameless is an unusual feature and the fact that the marriage broke down
in just over four years does not make the case so different when this feature is taken into
account. This is not the kind of case Ormrod J refers to when he says: 'Generally speaking
the causes of breakdown are complex and rarely to be found wholly or mainly on one
side.'

The magistrates held that this was 'gross and obvious misconduct' and in so doing were
b referring to the test applied by Lord Denning MR and Ormrod J. The words 'gross and
obvious misconduct' can be somewhat misleading, but as I understand it they were
referring to the fact that this was an unusual case far removed from those where much
blame could be put on both sides and it was a case where it would have been unjust to
give the financial support which would normally be given. In answer to the question
would it offend a reasonable man's sense of justice that this wife's conduct should be left
c out of account in deciding the financial provision which the husband should make, the
magistrates were answering 'Yes it would' when they said: '[Her desertion] he not having
committed any misconduct was a matter of gravest importance in relation to this
marriage.' On the facts found, the behaviour of the wife was quite capable of being
within the terms I have outlined above. In my opinion it is quite impossible to interfere
with the decision of the magistrates.

d Counsel for the wife also sought to argue that the Divisional Court had misdirected
itself in relation to discretion. Having regard to the conclusion I have just expressed this
question does not arise. Section 3 of the 1978 Act is concerned with the exercise of
discretion, and once it is established that the facts are such that the case is capable of
coming within the test set out in the cases I have cited above, the appellate court should
not interfere with the discretion of the magistrates unless it is clearly satisfied that they
e were wrong. I am not so satisfied. Accordingly I would dismiss this appeal.

KERR LJ. I agree with the judgment delivered by Waller LJ. I have also had the
advantage of reading the judgment to be delivered by Slade LJ, with which I also agree. I
would only point out, by way of emphasis, that in the present case the magistrates have
not only drastically reduced the amount of weekly maintenance but have also limited it
f in point of time to five years, no doubt because the child will then reach school age. I
agree that this appeal should be dismissed.

SLADE LJ. I agree, but will add some observations of my own, albeit with diffidence
in a field which is not very familiar to me.

In the past there has been some conflict of judicial opinion as to the extent to which an
g appellate court is entitled to interfere with the exercise of a discretion by a court of first
instance in cases relating to the custody of children or applications for maintenance by
one spouse against another. None of the authorities containing statements of principle in
this context have been cited to the court in the present case. However, I approach the
case on the following footing, which I think is supported by the authorities. While it
was, I think, the duty of the Divisional Court to review the manner in which the
h magistrates exercised their discretion in the light of the facts found by them, it would
not have been entitled to reverse any primary finding of fact by the magistrates unless
clearly satisfied that it was wrong and would not have been entitled to interfere with the
exercise of their discretion unless satisfied that they had misdirected themselves on a
point of principle or that the exercise of their discretion was clearly wrong for other
reasons. I do not think that the submissions on either side have been inconsistent with
j this approach to the case.

Indeed counsel on behalf of the wife expressly accepted that, in order to disturb the
magistrates' primary findings of fact, he would have to show that they were plainly
wrong, and he said that he did not seek to do so. Nevertheless he sought to draw a
distinction between the finding of a specific fact and a finding of fact which is really no
more than an inference drawn from facts specifically found. He cited the decision of the

House of Lords in *Benmax v Austin Motor Co Ltd* [1955] 1 All ER 326, [1955] AC 370 as
authority for the proposition that in the latter instance an appellate tribunal may be more
willing to differ from a finding of fact made by the inferior court than in the former
instance.

In the present case, if I understood him correctly, counsel for the wife submitted that
the conclusion of the magistrates that the wife's desertion of the husband was 'gross and
obvious' conduct, within the meaning of that phrase as used by Ormrod J and by the
Court of Appeal in *Wachtel v Wachtel* [1973] 1 All ER 113 at 119, [1973] Fam 72 at 80;
[1973] 1 All ER 829 at 835, [1973] Fam 72 at 90, was no more than an inference drawn
from the primary facts found by them. Such inference in his submission was manifestly
a wrong one and vitiated all the conclusions reached on its basis.

Section 3(1)(g) of the Domestic Proceedings and Magistrates' Courts Act 1978 by its
terms expressly empowers and indeed obliges the court on an application for maintenance,
such as that of the wife in the present case, to have regard to the conduct of each of the
parties in relation to the marriage 'so far as it is just to take it into account'. Section 25 of
the Matrimonial Causes Act 1973 similarly by its terms expressly empowers and obliges
the court, in exercising its powers under the subsection, to have regard to the party's
conduct, so far as it is just to do so.

If one were to disregard the line of authority beginning with *Wachtel v Wachtel*, I
would have thought it difficult even to argue that the magistrates in the present case
were clearly wrong in regarding it as 'just' to take into account the wife's conduct, and,
having done so, substantially to reduce the amount of maintenance which they would
otherwise have awarded to her. Among their primary findings of fact were findings that
(i) the wife formed an intention to desert the husband in March 1981, (ii) her complaints
about his conduct prior to that date were trivial and they were not the reason for, nor did
they contribute to, her withdrawal from cohabitation, (iii) the disputes after April 1981
were caused by tension between the parties for which the prime reason was the wife's
already formed intention to withdraw from cohabitation, (iv) the husband had not
committed any misconduct.

Since the passing of the 1978 Act, it is plain that even a wife who has deserted her
husband without just cause is still entitled to apply for maintenance under that Act.
Nevertheless, on the basis of these facts as found by the magistrates, it was obviously a
tenable view, which they in fact held, that justice required that the husband who had
been compelled to start a new life on his own, through no fault or wish of his, should not
have to pay as much maintenance to the wife as he would have had to pay her if
misconduct on his part had been responsible for the break-up of the marriage.

As Buckley LJ pointed out in *Armstrong v Armstrong* (1974) 118 SJ 579, in a passage to
which Waller LJ has referred, the expression 'obvious and gross', which appears in none
of the relevant statutes, is not a definitive expression. The statement of principle by Lord
Denning MR in *Wachtel v Wachtel* [1973] 1 All ER 829 at 835–836, [1973] Fam 72 at 90
was made in response to an invitation by counsel to give guidelines as to the proper
manner for the exercise of the statutory discretion to award maintenance (see [1973] 1
All ER 829 at 833, [1973] Fam 72 at 87). Nevertheless it is said in effect on behalf of the
wife that the discretion conferred on the magistrates in the present case by the wording
of s 3(1)(g) of the 1978 Act was fettered by these guidelines. And indeed it was accepted
by the magistrates and has been common ground before this court, that *Wachtel v Wachtel*
is a binding authority and that the guidelines must be observed according to their proper
meaning when s 3(1)(g) of that Act falls to be applied, no less than in the case of s 25 of
the Matrimonial Causes Act 1973.

The proper meaning to be attached to the guidelines themselves is in my opinion to
be found in the passages of the judgments of Buckley and Stephenson LJJ in *Armstrong v
Armstrong* which Waller LJ has quoted and with which I respectfully agree. The
guidelines, if I have understood them correctly, essentially amount to this. The past
conduct of a wife should cause the court in the exercise of its statutory discretion to
reduce or eliminate the amount of maintenance which it would otherwise have awarded

to her only if it has been shown to be such that it would offend a reasonable person's
sense of justice to disregard such conduct. Save in such an exceptional case, the court
should not take past conduct into account: to do so would be repugnant to the principles
of the relevant legislation, which does not contemplate that there will ordinarily be a
minute investigation into the shares of responsibility for the breakdown of a marriage.

Though of course they did not expressly formulate them in these terms, I see no reason
to suppose that the magistrates did not understand and apply the *Wachtel v Wachtel*
guidelines substantially in this sense. I think it is clear from the reasons given by them
for their decision that they regarded this as an exceptional case where the sole reason for
the break-up of the marriage had been shown to be the decision of the wife to end
cohabitation and leave a blameless husband and that accordingly they considered it
would not be just to disregard her conduct by awarding her the full amount which they
would otherwise have awarded her. In my judgment they were entitled to reach this
conclusion on the facts found by them and I can see no sufficient ground for holding that
such exercise of their discretion was wrong, or that they misdirected themselves in
principle.

Counsel for the wife forcefully submitted that the present case was what he described
as a 'run-of-the-mill desertion' and suggested that, if the magistrates' decision were to be
upheld, this would in many future cases open the floodgates to the type of inquiry into
the history of a marriage which the decision in *Wachtel v Wachtel* was intended to avoid.
I do not agree. The finding by the magistrates to the effect that the blame lay wholly on
one side make this an exceptional case.

The magistrates in their reasons indicated that, but for the wife's conduct, they would
have applied the 'one-third formula' in assessing her maintenance, but that, having
regard to her conduct, they thought it just that she should for a term of five years receive
£15 per week, this being a figure which they regarded as representing approximately
one-tenth of the joint gross incomes. The reduction was therefore a substantial one, even
though, as was pointed out in the judgments of the Divisional Court, £15 per week in
fact represented more nearly one-eighth than one-tenth of the relevant incomes, if the
normal method of calculating fractions was applied.

Nevertheless I do not think it can be said that the magistrates, in making this rather
modest award, limited in time as it was, misdirected themselves on any point of principle.
Nor, after considering all the facts of the case as found by them, am I satisfied that the
exercise of their discretion was for any other reason clearly wrong.

In all the circumstances, I agree that the Divisional Court was right not to disturb the
magistrates' decision. I too would dismiss this appeal.

Appeal dismissed.

Solicitors: *Dudley-Cooke Wilberforce Allen,* agents for *Walters & Barbary,* Camborne (for
the wife); *Denton Hall & Burgin,* agents for *Stewart & Knight,* Camborne (for the husband).

Sophie Craven   Barrister.

Gill and another v El Vino Co Ltd   a

COURT OF APPEAL, CIVIL DIVISION
EVELEIGH, GRIFFITHS LJJ AND SIR ROGER ORMROD
8 NOVEMBER 1982

Discrimination – Men and women – Provision of goods, facilities or services – Serving drinks at b
wine bar – Men permitted to stand and drink in bar area – Women served only while seated
away from bar area – Women complaining of less favourable treatment – Whether unlawful
discrimination against women on ground of sex – Sex Discrimination Act 1975, ss 1(1)(a), 29(1).

The defendants were the owners of a popular wine bar in the City of London. Although
a man could buy a drink at the bar and consume it in that area or at one of the tables
away from the bar area, it was the defendants' practice not to allow women to drink   c
while standing in the bar area and to insist on not serving them with drinks unless they
were away from the bar area and seated at one of the tables. The plaintiffs were two
women who went to the bar and ordered drinks. The barman refused to serve them at
the bar and told them that the drinks would be brought to them if they sat at a table.
The plaintiffs claimed that they had been unlawfully discriminated against on the ground
of their sex in that the defendants had treated them less favourably than a man within   d
the meaning of s 1(1)(a)[a] of the Sex Discrimination Act 1975 by refusing to serve them
drinks at the bar. They sought a declaration that the defendants, being 'concerned with
the provision . . . of goods, facilities or services to the public' had refused or deliberately
omitted to provide the plaintiffs with facilities or services offered to male customers
within s 29[b] of the 1975 Act. The judge held that there had been no discrimination since
being refused the facilities or services afforded in the bar area could not be described as   e
being detrimental to female customers. The plaintiffs appealed.

Held – The 1975 Act was a non-technical Act which dealt with ordinary everyday
behaviour and the relative positions of men and women and accordingly was to be
construed by looking at the words of the statute and no further. In construing s 29(1) of   f
the 1975 Act the test to be applied was whether the plaintiffs were refused, or the
defendants had deliberately omitted to provide them with, goods, facilities or services.
Where that happened, a comparison was to be made between the treatment of a man and
a woman to see whether they had been treated less favourably than a man within s 1(1)(a)
of the 1975 Act. By refusing to serve women at the bar, the defendants denied women
the opportunity to drink where others (men) drank and to mix with other people who
were drinking in the wine bar, and, since there was greater manoeuvrability and   g
flexibility for conversation and for social intercourse in the bar area, they denied women
a choice of companions and also, to a degree, more ready access to the barman.
Accordingly, women were being treated less favourably than men in that they could not
drink at the bar where men could. Furthermore, the maxim de minimis non curat lex
was not appropriate where that which had been denied to the plaintiffs was the very   h
thing that Parliament sought to provide, namely facilities and services on an equal basis.
The special attractiveness of the bar area was clearly greatly appreciated and was in great
demand by men, and therefore it could not be assumed that there was no true demand
by women. It followed that the defendants had acted in breach of s 29 of the 1975 Act in
that they had allowed male customers to stand and drink at the bar if they so wished but
had not allowed female customers to do likewise. The appeal would therefore be allowed
and a declaration would be granted accordingly (see p 401 d to p 402 g and j to p 403 e   j
and g, post).
Ministry of Defence v Jeremiah [1979] 3 All ER 833 distinguished.

---

a   Section 1(1), so far as material, is set out at p 400 g, post
b   Section 29, so far as material, is set out at p 400 h to p 401 a, post

Notes
a For sex discrimination generally, see 16 Halsbury's Laws (4th edn) para 771:2.
   For the Sex Discrimination Act 1975, ss 1, 29, see 45 Halsbury's Statutes (3rd edn) 227,
248.

Case referred to in judgments
Ministry of Defence v Jeremiah [1979] 3 All ER 833, [1980] QB 87, [1979] 3 WLR 857, CA,
b 20 Digest (Reissue) 589, 4500.

Cases also cited
c *Peake v Automotive Products Ltd* [1978] 1 All ER 106, [1978] QB 233, CA.
Quinn v Williams Furniture Ltd [1981] ICR 328, CA.
Schmidt v Austicks Bookshops Ltd [1978] ICR 85, EAT.

Appeal
The plaintiffs, Mrs Tess Gill and Miss Anna Coote, appealed from the decision of his
Honour Judge Ranking in the Mayor's and City of London Court on 15 July 1981 giving
judgment for the defendants, El Vino Co Ltd, on the plaintiffs' claim for a declaration
that the defendants had acted in breach of s 29(1) of the Sex Discrimination Act 1975 and
d an injunction restraining the defendants, their servants and agents, from continuing to
breach the Act. In his judgment Judge Ranking found the following facts. On 2 February
1981 the two plaintiffs, Mrs Gill, who was a solicitor, and Miss Coote, who was a
journalist, went into the bar at El Vino's Wine Bar, 47 Fleet Street, London EC4, and
asked to be served with two glasses of dry white wine. The barman politely refused to
serve them at the bar and said that if they sat down at a table the drinks would be brought
e to them. There was a house rule at El Vino's that women, unlike men, would not be
served with drinks at the bar but would be served if they sat at one of the tables, in which
case the drinks would be brought to them. As a result of that episode the plaintiffs
brought an action, alleging in the particulars of claim that El Vino breached s 29(1) of
the Sex Discrimination Act 1975 and asking for an injunction to restrain further breaches
by the defendants. El Vino's of Fleet Street was one of the best known and most popular
f wine bars in the City of London. It was just over one hundred years old and opened at its
present premises in Fleet Street in 1923. In the same year it was formed into a limited
company. The premises consisted of a bar space entered through the main door in Fleet
Street. Beyond was a smoking room with chairs and tables. To the right of the main
entrance were two more tables with chairs. Downstairs was a restaurant where lunch was
served. On the left of the main entrance was a small area for off-licence sales. The actual
g bar space was 16 ft 8 in long and 8 ft wide, so it was rather long and narrow. There were
nine tables in the smoking room with chairs, with four people at each table. The smoking
room was partitioned off from the bar area, with an open entrance from the bar to the
smoking room. The two tables by the main entrance each had four chairs. Along the
wall opposite the bar was a long wine rack with sliding doors containing over one
hundred different wines. The furnishing and decor of El Vino's were deliberately old
h fashioned. Only wines and spirits were served there, no beers. Standards were high. Male
customers were required to wear jackets and ties and all were to refrain from bad
language. In spite of its perhaps unusual features El Vino's was immensely popular. Its
everyday customers were largely lawyers and journalists and those connected with those
professions. It was open from 11.30 am to 3 pm and from 5 pm to 8 pm. From about
12.30 pm onwards in the afternoon and from 5.45 pm onwards in the evening the bar
j was often extremely crowded; so much so that on occasions it had been described to be
like the inside of a tube train at the rush hour. That overcrowding was aggravated by the
need for the bar staff to fetch wines from time to time from the wine rack opposite the
bar. At peak hours there was therefore in the bar a fair amount of pushing and jostling.
The rule that ladies were required to take their drinks at tables was introduced in about
1943 or 1944. Before the 1939–45 war very few ladies worked in Fleet Street, but during
the war their numbers increased enormously. They began to go to El Vino's. At first El

Vino's provided a few stools at the bar. Then more stools were needed. Then the stools
got in the way and the ladies' handbags tended to clutter up the bar itself. So the rule was   *a*
introduced. Its purpose was to relieve the congestion at the bar and to spare the ladies the
discomfort of standing at the bar where they might be pushed about and jostled. At the
time of the plaintiffs' action some 15% of El Vino's bar customers were ladies. They were
treated as follows. A lady might go up to the bar and order a drink or drinks and pay,
but she could not drink at the bar or in the bar area. She was required to go to one of the
tables in the smoking room or by the main entrance and take a chair, where she would   *b*
be served with the drinks she had ordered. If she sat at a table by the door she would be
served by a person from behind the bar. If she went to the smoking room a waitress
would serve her at the table. A special waitress was provided in the smoking room. She
could take orders from the customers at the tables, and there was a special hatch in the
smoking room communicating directly with the bar where she would place her orders
with the barman or barmaid. He or she would give the waitress's orders priority over the   *c*
orders of customers at the bar. If when a lady went to the smoking room there were no
empty chairs she could stand in the smoking room until a chair became vacant and
could, while she was waiting, be served with her drink. If no chairs were free the waitress
would do what she could to find her a seat and could fetch a chair from the restaurant
downstairs for her. Standing by the tables at the main entrance or the provision of extra
chairs there was not practicable because of the traffic through the doors. Since the chairs   *d*
and tables were not for the exclusive use of lady customers but were available on exactly
the same terms to male customers, one of the main points made by the plaintiffs in
relation to sex discrimination was that male customers had a choice of standing at the bar
or in the bar area, or of sitting at a table, but that the ladies had no such choice and were
required to sit at a table.

e

John Melville Williams QC and *Sadie Robarts* for the plaintiffs.
Eldred Tabachnik QC and *Elisabeth Laing* for the defendants.

EVELEIGH LJ. The facts of this case have been very carefully set out in the judgment
of his Honour Judge Ranking. He describes the layout at El Vino's and the fact that two
ladies were not permitted to buy drinks at the bar and consume them in the front area   *f*
where men do stand and drink at the bar and over the whole of that area.
    The plaintiffs claimed that they were the victims of unlawful discrimination contrary
to the Sex Discrimination Act 1975, and the relevant paragraph of the particulars of
claim state: 'It is the practice of the Defendant to allow male customers to be served at
the bar if they wish to be served but not to allow female customers to be served at the
bar.' Section 1(1) of the 1975 Act reads: *g*

    'A person discriminates against a women in any circumstances relevant to the
    purposes of any provision of this Act if—(a) on the ground of her sex he treats her
    less favourably than he treats, or would treat, a man . . .'

Section 29(1) of the Act reads:

    'It is unlawful for any person concerned with the provision (for payment or not)   *h*
    of goods, facilities or services to the public or a section of the public to discriminate
    against a woman who seeks to obtain or use those goods, facilities or services—(a) by
    refusing or deliberately omitting to provide her with any of them, or (b) by refusing
    or deliberately omitting to provide her with goods, facilities or services of the like
    quality, in the like manner and on the like terms as are normal in his case in relation
    to male members of the public, or (where she belongs to a section of the public) to   *j*
    male members of that section.'

Then, so far as relevant, s 29(2) reads:

    'The following are examples of the facilities and services mentioned in subsection
    (1)—(a) access to and use of any place which members of the public or a section of

the public are permitted to enter . . . (e) facilities for entertainment, recreation or refreshment.'

The judge came to the conclusion, on the facts of this case, that there was no discrimination, in that he found that the ladies were not treated less favourably by the defendants than they treated a man or men. In coming to that conclusion the judge was, in my opinion, influenced by reference to other cases, and in particular by reference to *Ministry of Defence v Jeremiah* [1979] 3 All ER 833, [1980] QB 87, and he quoted the words of Brightman LJ where he said ([1979] 3 All ER 833 at 840, [1980] QB 87 at 103):

'I do not say that the mere deprivation of choice for one sex, or some other differentiation in their treatment, is necessarily unlawful discrimination. The deprivation of choice, or differentiation, in the sort of case we are considering, must be associated with a detriment.'

It seems to me that the judge in this case took the view that he could not call it a detriment for women to be refused the facilities afforded in the particular area in El Vino's which we have to consider and therefore there was no discrimination.

In my judgment, the correct way to approach this case is to take the simple words of the statute and try to apply them. It sometimes is helpful in judgments to substitute some other phraseology which the judge thinks is more apposite in the particular case under consideration, but that is by no means always necessary and if it can be avoided it is desirable to do so. It is also, in my view, desirable to avoid looking at cases where substituted phraseology has been invoked, because the next step is that one goes on to rephrase the substituted phraseology, and on and on one goes and departs further and further from the approach which the statute indicates. Now this is not a technical statute and, therefore, is not of a kind where one should or need go for the meaning of words to other decided cases. It is a simple statute seeking to deal with ordinary everyday behaviour and the relative positions of men and women.

The reference to 'detriment' in Brightman LJ's passage was necessary because that was a case under s 6(2) of the Act, and s 6(2)(b) reads:

'It is unlawful for a person, in the case of a woman employed by him at an establishment in Great Britain, to discriminate against her . . . (b) by dismissing her or subjecting her to any other detriment.'

So the words 'subjecting her to any other detriment' refer to the manner or the means used in discriminating. Compare in the present case the words of s 29(1)(a) 'by refusing or deliberately omitting to provide her with [goods, facilities or services]' or the corresponding words in s 29(1)(b). One has to ask in the present case: was she refused, or was there deliberate omission to provide her with, goods, facilities or services? In *Ministry of Defence v Jeremiah* [1979] 3 All ER 833, [1980] QB 87 there had to be asked: was she subjected to a detriment? But once those questions have been answered, it is then necessary to go simply to s 1(1)(a) and ask the question: when that happened, was she treated less favourably than a man would have been treated? In other words, to apply s 1 of the Act, one has to make a comparison between the treatment of a man and a woman.

What is the comparison in this case? A woman is denied certain things that a man can have. As a matter of fact in this case, what are they? She was denied the opportunity to drink where others drank, to mix with other people who were drinking in El Vino's. She was denied in fact a choice of companions. There may be only one or two seats vacant at a table. The person who takes the one or two seats may have to wait a considerable time in order to be joined by companions with whom she wishes to converse. If there is only one seat available or two seats available and you happen to be in a group of four you may prefer to stand together and talk together, but you cannot talk together if it is obligatory to go and sit at a table where there is not room for all four at once. Furthermore, you can talk with more ease, some people may find, when you are closer together and not separated by the width of a table. You can converse with a greater number of people. One has only to use one's imagination and think of a group of people standing at a bar of a public house; they may number two or three, they may number seven, eight or nine, all forming part of the one group. So that it seems to me that in the standing area (which was the male preserve) there was great manoeuvrability and flexibility for conversation and for social intercourse with others. There was, to a degree, more ready access to the barman. If a lady met a man or saw a man at the bar with whom she would like to converse and have a drink she would have to go to a table and find a place there, and the man might not wish to sit at a table. There is not, therefore, the same ability to join other people if you have to go to a table as there is if you are allowed to be among the men who are standing.

It seems to me, and I do not apologise for going no further into the matter than saying 'it seems to me', that that is treating a woman less favourably than a man. It is as stark as all that, and I find myself incapable of explaining further the reasons for that conclusion. I pose the question in the statute and in that way I answer it.

It is said here that this is de minimis. In coming to the conclusion that it was de minimis the judge again was influenced by the emphasis on 'detriment'. In the present case, as I have said, we are not enjoined to ask if there was detriment, although, in passing, I myself, on the usual understanding of that word, would say there was, but we are not enjoined to ask that. We are enjoined to ask: was there a refusal of a facility? There clearly was. Can it be said that the refusal of that facility was a matter that could be classified as de minimis? In other words, it seems to me that involves saying, 'Well, she was less favourably treated but only very slightly'. I find it very difficult to invoke the maxim de minimis non curat lex in a situation where that which has been denied to the plaintiff is the very thing that Parliament seeks to provide, namely facilities and services on an equal basis. But on the facts of this particular case the whole rather special attractiveness of the particular area of the premises in question is denied to the woman. Its popularity is undoubted. It affords a somewhat unique atmosphere which is clearly greatly appreciated and is in great demand by men, and I cannot, therefore, assume that there is no true demand for it by women.

The judge was influenced in his judgment by being told that the system had operated for some thirty years and there had been very few complaints, and very few complaints even after the Sex Discrimination Act 1975 came into force. That may be a matter to have some regard to, but it cannot, in my view, outweigh the obvious fact, namely that there is a deprivation of a facility that is greatly prized by men and was sought by the plaintiffs. I cannot believe that, from the point of view of women generally speaking, it is right to say that this was de minimis.

For those reasons I would allow this appeal.

GRIFFITHS LJ. I agree.

El Vino's is no ordinary wine bar. It has become a unique institution in Fleet Street. Every day it is thronged with journalists, solicitors, barristers exchanging the gossip of the day. No doubt it is the source of many false rumours which have dashed the hopes of many an aspirant to a High Court appointment. Now if a man wishes to take a drink in El Vino's he can drink, if he wishes, by joining the throng which crowds round the bar and there he can join his friends and pick up, no doubt, many an interesting piece of gossip, particularly if he is a journalist. Or, alternatively, if he wishes, he can go and sit down at one of the two tables that are on the right immediately behind the main door of the premises. Thirdly, he has the alternative, if he wishes, to pass through the partition and enter the little smoking room at the back, which is equipped with a number of tables and chairs. But there is no doubt that very many men choose to stand among the throng drinking at the bar.

But if a woman wishes to go to El Vino's, she is not allowed to join the throng before the bar. She must drink either at one of the two tables on the right of the entrance, or she must pass through the throng and drink in the smoking room at the back. There is no doubt whatever that she is refused facilities that are accorded to men, and the only question that remains is: is she being treated less favourably than men? I think that

permits of only one answer: of course she is. She is not being allowed to drink where she
may wish to drink, namely standing up among the many people gathered in front of the
bar. There are many reasons why she may want to do so. Her friends may be there. She
may not want to break them up and force them to move to some other part of the
premises where she is permitted to drink. Or she may wish, if she is a journalist, to join
a group in the hope of picking up the gossip of the day. If male journalists are permitted
to do it, why shouldn't she? If she is denied it she is being treated less favourably than
her male colleagues.

For the reasons given by Eveleigh LJ, I think the county court judge was distracted by
the authorities which were cited to him dealing with the meaning of 'detriment' in
s 6(2)(*b*). Furthermore, I cannot regard this as de minimis; women are denied a facility
which may be of particular importance to a journalist.

Accordingly, for these reasons and those given by Eveleigh LJ, I agree that this appeal
must be allowed.

SIR ROGER ORMROD. I too agree.

The question posed by s 29(1) of the 1975 Act is unusually simple compared with most
questions posed by statutes. We are enjoined simply to ask whether on this evidence the
plaintiffs in this case were 'treated less favourably' than a man or men would have been.
To my mind, the fact that men have the two options which Eveleigh LJ has mentioned
makes only one answer to that question possible. Men have these options and the options
are valuable to them, and I find it impossible to say, where one sex has an option and the
other has not, that there is not a differentiation between them and, prima facie, a
differentiation which results in less favourable treatment.

The passage which was relied on from Brightman LJ's judgment in *Ministry of Defence
v Jeremiah* [1979] 3 All ER 833 at 840, [1980] QB 87 at 104 clearly refers to a different
situation altogether. It is important to note that in the passage quoted he said: 'In such a
case [that is referring to the "ladies only" requirement] a court would conclude that there
was no sensible detriment to the men flowing from the absence of choice', but if he had
been asking himself the question whether the ladies were being treated more favourably
than the men in that situation he could only have given one answer. If men were
standing in the corridor of a train when there were no seats in the rest of the train and
women were sitting in half-empty compartments, the men would obviously be treated
less favourably than the women.

On the de minimis point I do not wish to add anything, although one can well
understand that El Vino's may feel that they have been 'stood up', if one may use a
colloquial expression, and that they are being attacked in circumstances which
presumably Parliament did not envisage when the Act was passed, but we have only to
answer the question posed by the statute, and for the reasons which I have given and
those which Eveleigh and Griffiths LJJ have given there can be, in my judgment, only
one answer, namely, to put the case formalistically, that there is no evidence on which
the judge could find that there was no discrimination. I too would allow the appeal.

*Appeal allowed. Declaration that the defendants acted in breach of s 29 of the Sex Discrimination
Act 1975. Leave to appeal to the House of Lords refused.*

Solicitors: *Seifert Sedley & Co* (for the plaintiffs); *Waterhouse & Co* (for the defendants).

Henrietta Steinberg   Barrister.

Tracomin SA v Sudan Oil Seeds Co Ltd

QUEEN'S BENCH DIVISION (COMMERCIAL COURT)
STAUGHTON J
17, 22, 23, 24 JUNE, 15 SEPTEMBER, 6 OCTOBER 1982

Conflict of laws – Foreign judgment – Enforcement or recognition – Jurisdiction of foreign court – Submission to jurisdiction by defendant – Sudanese company contracting to sell goods to Swiss company – Contract evidenced by sold note – Sold note referring to conditions of contract 'as per' standard form – Standard form stating that disputes to be referred to arbitration in London – Buyers bringing action in Swiss court for damages for breach of contract – Sellers entering plea in Swiss court requesting stay of proceedings on ground that dispute should be settled under arbitration clause incorporated into contract – Swiss court dismissing plea – Sellers asking arbitrators to proceed with arbitration in London – Buyers claiming that sellers estopped by Swiss judgment from asserting that arbitration clause incorporated into contract – Whether Swiss judgment should be recognised or enforced by English court – Civil Jurisdiction and Judgments Act 1982, ss 32, 33, Sch 13, para 8.

A dispute arose between the Swiss buyers and the Sudanese sellers of a consignment of peanuts. The contract of sale was evidenced by a sold note which stated that the conditions of the contract were to be 'as per' contract form 20 of the Federation of Oils, Seeds and Fats Associations Ltd. Form 20 stated that a contract to which it referred was to be governed by English law, that any dispute was to be submitted to arbitration in London, and that neither party was to take legal proceedings until the dispute had been determined by arbitration. The sellers had no assets in England but they did have assets in Switzerland. The buyers accordingly obtained a sequestration order in Switzerland against those assets and commenced an action in a Swiss court claiming damages from the sellers. At the same time they nominated an arbitrator in London in case the Swiss court held that they were bound under the arbitration clause in form 20 to settle the dispute by arbitration. The sellers, who also nominated an arbitrator, entered a plea in the Swiss court requesting a stay of the action on the ground that the dispute should be decided under the arbitration clause. The Swiss court dismissed the sellers' plea on the ground that under Swiss law an arbitration clause had to be specifically referred to if it was to form part of a contract by incorporation. After an unsuccessful appeal the sellers invited the arbitrators in London to proceed with the arbitration. The buyers thereupon applied to the High Court in England for a declaration that the arbitrators had no jurisdiction to determine the dispute. The buyers contended that, although the arbitration clause would have been incorporated into the contract under English law, the sellers, by their voluntary submission to the jurisdiction of the Swiss court, which had ruled against the incorporation of the arbitration clause, were estopped under the doctrine of estoppel per rem judicatem from asserting that the arbitration clause had been incorporated in the contract. During the course of the hearing ss 32[a] and 33[b] of the Civil Jurisdiction and Judgments Act 1982 came into force and the question arose what effect, if any, that Act had on the case. Section 32(1) provided that a judgment of a court of an overseas country was not to be recognised or enforced in the United Kingdom if the bringing of proceedings in the overseas court was contrary to an agreement for the settlement of the dispute, the other party did not agree to the proceedings being brought in the overseas court and the other party did not submit to that court's jurisdiction. Section 32(3) provided that the court was not bound by any decision of the overseas court relating to any matter referred to in s 32(1). Section 33(1) provided that the person against whom the judgment was given was not to be regarded as 'having submitted to the jurisdiction

---

a   Section 32, so far as material, is set out at p 411 *e* to *h*, post
b   Section 33, so far as material, is set out at p 411 *j* to p 412 *a*, post

a of the court' by reason only of the fact that he appeared in the proceedings for the purpose of requesting a stay of proceedings on the ground that the dispute should be submitted to arbitration. Under transitional provisions contained in para 8ᶜ of Sch 13 to the 1982 Act the provisions of s 32 relating to non-recognition were not to apply where 'proceedings at common law for [the] enforcement' of a foreign judgment had been finally determined before the coming into force of s 32.

b **Held** – The buyers' application for a declaration would be refused for the following reasons—
(1) Paragraph 8 of Sch 13 to the 1982 Act did not have the effect that the provisions of s 32 relating to non-recognition were not to apply to the judgment obtained in the Swiss court by the buyers, because, if the buyers were seeking enforcement of the Swiss judgment, proceedings at common law for its enforcement had not been finally
c determined before the coming into force of s 32, and if the buyers were merely seeking recognition rather than enforcement then they had to do so within the terms of s 32, since s 32 was in force at the date of judgment (see p 412 d to f and p 416 b c, post).
(2) Applying the provisions of s 33(1) of the 1982 Act, the sellers were to be deemed not to have submitted to the jurisdiction of the Swiss court merely because they had entered a plea requesting a stay of proceedings on the ground that the dispute should be
d decided under the arbitration agreement. Accordingly, applying the provisions of s 32, the court could not recognise or enforce the judgment of the Swiss court, because under English law there was a valid arbitration agreement and the bringing of proceedings in the Swiss court by the buyers was contrary to that agreement (see p 411 g, p 412 a j and p 416 b c, post); Henry v Geopresco International Ltd [1975] 2 All ER 702 considered.

e **Notes**
For recognition of foreign judgments, see 8 Halsbury's Laws (4th edn) para 767, and for cases on the subject, see 11 Digest (Reissue) 606–617, 1505–1599.
For estoppel per rem judicatam, see 16 Halsbury's Laws (4th edn) paras 1528–1533, and for cases on the subject, see 21 Digest (Reissue) 18–37, 85–231.

f **Cases referred to in judgment**
Atlantic Star, The, Atlantic Star (owners) v Bona Spes (owners) [1973] 2 All ER 175, [1974] AC 436, [1973] 2 WLR 795, HL; rvsg [1972] 3 All ER 705, [1973] 2 QB 364, [1973] 2 WLR 746, CA; affg [1972] 1 Lloyd's Rep 534, 11 Digest (Reissue) 645, 1777.
Black-Clawson International Ltd v Papierwerke Waldhof-Aschaffenburg AG [1975] 1 All ER 810, [1975] AC 591, [1975] 2 WLR 513, HL, Digest (Cont Vol D) 108, 1591a.
g Carl-Zeiss-Stiftung v Rayner and Keeler Ltd (No 2) [1966] 2 All ER 536, [1967] 1 AC 853, [1966] 3 WLR 125, HL, 21 Digest (Reissue) 49, 316.
Castrique v Imrie (1870) LR 4 HL 414, [1861–73] All ER Rep 508, HL, 21 Digest (Reissue) 79, 527.
Craxfords (Ramsgate) Ltd v Williams and Steer Manufacturing Co Ltd [1954] 3 All ER 17, [1954] 1 WLR 1130, 44 Digest (Repl) 300, 1298.
h Godard v Gray (1870) LR 6 QB 139, 11 Digest (Reissue) 608, 1535.
Henderson v Henderson (1843) 3 Hare 100, [1843–60] All ER Rep 378, 67 ER 313, 21 Digest (Reissue) 56, 374.
Henry v Geopresco International Ltd [1975] 2 All ER 702, [1976] QB 726, [1975] 3 WLR 620, CA, Digest (Cont Vol D) 108, 1413a.
Huntly (Marchioness) v Gaskell [1905] 2 Ch 656, [1904–7] All ER Rep 625, CA, 21 Digest
j (Reissue) 28, 166.
Panchaud Frères SA v Etablissements General Grain Co [1970] 1 Lloyd's Rep 53, CA, Digest (Cont Vol C) 856, 1046a.

---

c   Paragraph 8, so far as material, is set out at p 412 c, post

Rousillon v Rousillon (1880) 14 ChD 351, 11 Digest (Reissue) 486, 898.
Simpson v Fogo (1863) 1 Hem & M 195, 71 ER 85, 11 Digest (Reissue) 407, 443.
Spurling (J) Ltd v Bradshaw [1956] 2 All ER 121, [1956] 1 WLR 461, CA, 3 Digest (Reissue) 447, 3007.
Unterweser Reederei GmbH v Zapata Off-Shore Co, The Chaparral [1968] 2 Lloyd's Rep 158, CA.
Vervaeke v Smith (Messina and A-G intervening) [1982] 2 All ER 144, [1982] 2 WLR 855, HL.

Action

The plaintiff buyers, Tracomin SA, brought an action against the defendant sellers, Sudan Oil Seeds Co Ltd, seeking (i) a declaration that A P Beaton and G Bridge had no jurisdiction as arbitrators to determine any dispute between the plaintiffs and the defendants arising out of two contracts, dated respectively 30 November 1980 and 6 December 1980, because the parties had never agreed, in those contracts or elsewhere, to refer such disputes to arbitration, and (ii) an order restraining the defendants, by themselves, their servants or agents, from proceeding with or taking any step in a reference (or purported reference) to the arbitration of A P Beaton and G Bridge made under the Rules of Arbitration and Appeal of the Federation of Oils, Seeds and Fats Associations Ltd of disputes arising under the two contracts made between the plaintiffs and the defendants. The facts are set out in the judgment.

David Grace for the buyers.
Nicholas Merriman for the sellers.

Cur adv vult

6 October. The following judgment was delivered.

STAUGHTON J. The trial of this action, which was estimated to last half a day, began on 17 June 1982. It continued on 22, 23 and 24 June. There was then little apparently left in the action; but the arrangements of the court did not enable the hearing to be concluded forthwith. Efforts were made by the court to resume the case in July, but without success; and by agreement between the parties or their counsel it was refixed for 15 September. The hearing was then concluded.

In the ordinary way that would be just another tale of an action that lasts longer than anticipated, as must inevitably happen from time to time. But here there was a most important consequence. Sections 32 and 33 of the Civil Jurisdiction and Judgments Act 1982 came into force on 24 August 1982. When the hearing was resumed in September, counsel were not aware of the provisions of the 1982 Act. It only came to the attention of the court by means of *Court Business*, a useful but internal publication of the Lord Chancellor's Department. It has a most material bearing on this action.

The case is not itself a case about peanuts. It is about who shall decide a case about peanuts. The rival candidates are, on the one hand, arbitrators appointed under the rules of the Federation of Oils, Seeds and Fats Associations Ltd (FOSFA), and on the other the cantonal court for the canton of Vaud in the Confederation of Switzerland.

The dispute brings to light a problem which has recently been called to the attention of the Commercial Court Committee, that is to say, the different treatment in common law and some civil law countries of attempts to incorporate an arbitration clause into a contract.

In English law, wording which would suffice to incorporate any other term will suffice equally to incorporate an arbitration clause. That is the general rule, but it is subject to two exceptions. First, by ss 1 and 32 of the Arbitration Act 1950, if the arbitration agreement is not in writing the authority of an arbitrator or umpire may be revoked. This is not directly concerned with the point about incorporation, but is allied to it.

Second, where it is sought to incorporate in a bill of lading the arbitration clause in a charterparty, rather special rules apply. This case is not affected by either of those exceptions.

By Swiss law, on the other hand, or at any rate that prevailing in the canton of Vaud, it seems that an arbitration clause must be specially mentioned in the contract which the parties have signed, if it is to be incorporated. In addition, if the party who is to be compelled to arbitrate was not a person of business experience, his attention must have been drawn to the arbitration clause: see *J Spurling Ltd v Bradshaw* [1956] 2 All ER 121 at 125, [1956] 1 WLR 461 at 466 per Denning LJ:

> 'Some clauses which I have seen would need to be printed in red ink on the face of the document with a red hand pointing to it before the notice could be held to be sufficient.'

It is not necessary, for the purposes of this judgment, to state the Swiss law with precision, and I do not profess to have done so. I believe that Italian law likewise requires more positive identification of an arbitration clause for it to be incorporated, compared with English law.

Sudan Oil Seeds Ltd (the sellers) made two contracts to sell hand-picked selected peanuts to Tracomin SA (the buyers). The sellers are said to be connected in some way with the government of the Sudan and to have no assets in England and Wales. The buyers carry on business at Lausanne in the canton of Vaud. The first contract, dated 30 November 1980, was for 2,000 tons of HPS peanuts at $US1,750 per ton c & f Hamburg/Rotterdam, shipment as to 650 tons January/February 1981, 650 tons February/March 1981 and 700 tons March/April 1981. The second contract, dated 6 December 1980, was for 2,000 tons of the same commodity shipped to the same ports at $US1,800 per ton, shipment in four instalments of 500 tons each starting February/March and ending May/June. I was told that the price of HPS peanuts is $US700 per ton in normal times; but that it rose as high as $US2,500 in the period with which the dispute is concerned (and fell again), owing to a failure of the United States crop for 1980.

Three shipments were made under the contracts. One was the first portion of the first contract, 650 tons, January/February. This is said to have been contaminated with Caphra beetles, and therefore unfit for human consumption. It had been shipped on by the buyers to Norfolk, Virginia, where it would have fetched a colossal price; but it had to be returned to Europe and sold for cattle food.

Then there was the second parcel under the first contract, 650 tons February/March. All or part of that shipment is said to have suffered the same fate. Third, there was the first shipment of 500 tons under the second contract. The shipment date was extended by agreement up to 15 April 1981. The parcel is said to have been contaminated by aflatoxin, which is poisonous, so that it too was unfit for human consumption.

The other four shipments were not made. In one instance the sellers asked for an extension of the shipment period. When the buyers refused an extension, the sellers refused to ship. Thereafter the buyers regarded themselves as entitled to determine the entire unperformed obligations under the two contracts and did so. The sellers maintain that this was repudiation by the buyers.

So there are a number of disputes between the parties, involving both claims and counterclaims, and substantial sums of money.

Both contracts were made on a document which is called a 'sold note'. It appears to be specially typed for the transaction in question, is signed on behalf of both the buyers and the sellers, and contains the term: 'OTHER CONDITIONS: As per F.O.S.F.A. Contract No. 20.'

There is no express reference to any arbitration clause. But contract form no 20 of FOSFA provides:

> '18. DOMICILE: This contract shall be deemed to have been made in England and the construction, validity and performance thereof shall be governed in all respects by English law. Any dispute arising out of or in connection therewith shall be

submitted to arbitration in accordance with the Rules of the Federation. The serving of proceedings upon any party by sending same to their last known address together with leaving a copy of such proceedings at the offices of the Federation shall be deemed good service, rule of law or equity to the contrary notwithstanding...

20. ARBITRATION: Any dispute arising out of this contract, including any question of law arising in connection therewith, shall be referred to arbitration in London (or elsewhere if so agreed) in accordance with the Rules of Arbitration and Appeal of the Federation of Oils, Seeds and Fats Associations Limited, in force at the date of this contract and of which both parties hereto shall be deemed to be cognizant. Neither party hereto, nor any persons claiming under either of them shall bring any action or other legal proceedings against the other of them in respect of any such dispute until such dispute shall first have been heard and determined by the arbitrators, umpire or Board of Appeal (as the case may be), in accordance with the Rules of Arbitration and Appeal of the Federation, and it is hereby expressly agreed and declared that the obtaining of an Award from the arbitrators, umpire or Board of Appeal (as the case may be), shall be a condition precedent to the right of either party hereto or of any person claiming under either of them to bring any action or other legal proceedings against the other of them in respect of any such dispute.'

There is conflicting evidence as to how common it is for merchants in this trade to use only a sold note, and not either the actual printed FOSFA form or an abbreviated version of it. In English law the point is of no conceivable importance, so I need not decide it. In commodity trading generally it is in my experience very common to use only a bought or sold note, but I cannot say from recollection whether the same is true for the particular commodities traded under the auspices of FOSFA.

The buyers aver that they became concerned how their claims against the sellers could be enforced, as the sellers had no assets in this jurisdiction. They did, however, know that the sellers had two sets of shipping documents lodged with banks in Switzerland, those being, as I understand the position, documents which the buyers had themselves rejected.

On 12 May 1981 a judge of the peace in Lausanne on the application of the buyers ordered both sets of documents to be sequestrated. What happened thereafter is set out in the affidavit of Mr Robinson, the buyers' solicitor:

'20. The Buyers immediately commenced an action against the Sellers in the Cantonal Court of Vaud claiming damages. They also sent a telex to the Sellers nominating Mr A.P. Beaton as their arbitrator in FOSFA arbitration. They took this step because it was necessary for them to preserve their position with regard to the validation of the sequestration order if the Swiss Court should decide (contrary to what they had been advised would probably be the case) that there was a valid agreement to arbitrate and should stay their action pursuant to the arbitration clause. Apart from appointing Mr Beaton the Buyers have taken no step whatever in the arbitration.'

I should add that the buyers' telex was dated 14 May 1981. The sellers, by a telex in reply dated 18 May 1981, appointed Mr G Bridge as their arbitrator. Both appointments referred only to the two shipments that had been made under the first contract. Mr Robinson continues:

'21. On 11th August 1981 the Buyers applied to the Cantonal Court to validate the sequestration. On 29th September 1981 the Sellers lodged a "requête en déclinatoire" in the Cantonal Court. This has been variously translated as "an objection" or a "plea in bar". It is the Swiss equivalent of an English stay under the Arbitration Act. It is the normal method of ensuring that where there is a valid arbitration agreement and one party brings an action in the Court the action is stayed and the parties left to their remedy in arbitration.

a 22. The Sellers plea in bar in which they were the Plaintiffs and the Buyers Defendants was heard as a preliminary matter on 7th December 1981. Both sides were represented by Swiss Avocats.

23. By a written judgment given on 12th January 1982 the learned Judge (Judge Reymond) dismissed the plea in bar. Copies of his judgment in French and in translation are now produced and shown to me in a bundle marked "M.L.B.R.2" together with all the other Swiss Court documents in the Buyers' possession.

b 24. The Sellers appealed from this decision to the Cantonal Court of Appeal. The three Judges of the Court of Appeal met to consider the case on 27th April 1982. Both sides had lodged with the Court written submissions. The parties and their Avocats were not entitled to make further oral submissions but were permitted to attend the hearing and listen to the deliberations of the Court. I have been informed by Maître Rusconi and verily believe that at the conclusion of the hearing the

c President announced that the Judges were unanimously of the view that the appeal should be dismissed and that they would give their reasons in writing at a later date.

25. Since then the formal order dismissing the appeal has been issued but the reasoned judgment is not yet available.

26. It is still open to the Sellers to seek to appeal to the Federal Supreme Court of Switzerland, the highest Court in Switzerland.'

d Mr Charles Deans, in an affidavit sworn on behalf of the sellers, says: 'I am instructed that [the sellers] are intending to appeal against the decision.'

The reasons of the cantonal Court of Appeal have since been obtained and put before me. It would seem that the Swiss proceedings in point of form relate only to the first of the two contracts. I say that because the judgment at first instance began as follows (in

e translation):

'By application . . . of sequestration of 11 August 1981, Tracomin SA, of Lausanne, plaintiff as to the merits and respondent in interim objection, applies with costs for the defendant Sudan Oil Seeds Co Ltd of Khartoum, Sudan, to be found to be indebted to it in the sum of Fr 2,571,732 with interest at 5% pa to run from 11 May 1981. The plaintiff company's claim is based on alleged wrong performance of a

f contract entered into between the parties on 30 November 1980 whereby Tracomin SA purchased of Sudan Oil Seeds Co Ltd for resale 2,000 tonnes of shelled peanuts HPS Sudan, the plaintiff company relying in substance on the goods delivered having been infested with Caphra insects rendering them unmarketable and thus involving it in a loss of Fr 2,571,732.'

g There are other indications to the same effect. But it must be emphasised that this is only a formal point; no different issues arose on the two contracts so far as the plea in bar was concerned.

Meanwhile in St Mary Axe, as counsel for the buyers put it, the sellers are inviting the arbitrators to proceed with an arbitration or arbitrations encompassing all the sellers' claims, and the arbitrators intend to do so, unless restrained by this court. Hence these

h proceedings.

During the argument counsel for the buyers said that his clients' concern in this action was to preserve the security which they had obtained in Switzerland. I then asked whether they would agree to a FOSFA arbitration, if the sellers agreed that the security in Switzerland would be available to meet any award in the buyers' favour. After a short adjournment counsel on behalf of the sellers did offer to agree that the security should be

j so available. Counsel for the buyers did not feel able to accept the offer, as it might not be possible to carry it into effect in Switzerland.

I mention that interlude because, if there is any discretion to be exercised in this case, I should take into account that an apparently reasonable offer was refused without any very convincing reason. However, I do not myself think that this case does turn on any discretion. The buyers claim both a declaration and an injunction. Of course an

injunction is a discretionary remedy. But in any event I ought to decide and declare the
rights of the parties; and the claim for an injunction, if necessary at all, is of secondary
importance. In one sense a declaration too is a discretionary remedy. However, there
would in this case be no point in my deciding the issue and then refusing to make a
declaration as to the result.

Counsel for the buyers frankly concedes that, by English law, the arbitration clause is
incorporated into and forms part of the contract in this case. He also concedes that an
English court must apply English law in determining whether the arbitration clause
from FOSFA form no 20 is incorporated in the contract, because FOSFA form no 20
provides for English law.

The case for the buyers is that the question whether the arbitration clause is
incorporated in the contract has already been decided, between these parties, by and on
appeal from the cantonal court of Vaud. Therefore, it is said, the doctrine of estoppel per
rem judicatam enables the buyers to assert, and prevents the sellers from denying, that
the clause is not incorporated.

Aside from questions of form, to which I will return later, it is clear beyond doubt that
the sellers were asking the Swiss courts to decide that the arbitration clause was
incorporated; and that the Swiss courts, accepting the buyers' argument to the contrary,
have held that the clause was not incorporated. It is also tolerably clear that, at any rate in
the appellate court, one of the arguments relied on by the sellers was the fact that the
buyers had already appointed a FOSFA arbitrator. So one may assume until the contrary
is shown, that the court did not overlook that point.

What is also clear, however, is that the Swiss courts applied Swiss law. So far as one can
tell, nobody asked them to do anything else. The Court of Appeal in Switzerland
apparently considered of its own motion whether English law was applicable, and,
likewise apparently, would have applied English law if there had been any evidence of it.
But neither party relied on English law in the Swiss courts. That is evidently the reason
why they arrived at a conclusion which, as counsel for the buyers concedes, an English
court would not have reached. But, he now submits, the sellers in this court are bound
by that conclusion. I must bear in mind what Lord Upjohn said in *Carl-Zeiss-Stiftung v
Rayner & Keeler Ltd (No 2)* [1966] 2 All ER 536 at 573, [1967] 1 AC 853 at 947: 'All
estoppels are not odious but must be applied so as to work justice and not injustice . . .'
On the other hand it is inherent in the nature of issue estoppel that the court is prevented
from inquiring into the truth, and sometimes even from acting on what it knows to be
the truth: see, for example, *Henry v Geopresco International Ltd* [1975] 2 All ER 702 at
704–706, [1976] QB 726 at 731–732 per Roskill LJ, where the judgment of a foreign
court was described, on one issue, as 'plainly incorrect'; nevertheless it was enforced.

There are six grounds on which counsel for the sellers argues that the doctrine of res
judicata does not apply in this case, as follows. (1) The decision relied on was not reached
by a court of competent jurisdiction. (2) The only matter decided by it was that the Swiss
courts had jurisdiction. (3) The Swiss judgment is not final and conclusive on the merits.
(4) The issue decided was one of Swiss law and not English law. (5) The judgment should
not be enforced by reason of the rule in *Simpson v Fogo* (1863) 1 Hem & M 195, 71 ER 85.
(6) The buyers are precluded from relying on the Swiss decision by reason of their
conduct in appointing an arbitrator. I shall consider each of these grounds in turn; and
thereafter certain other arguments relating to the remedies claimed.

(1) *Competent court*

The doctrine does not apply unless the Swiss courts had jurisdiction to determine the
issue, both by their own law and in the eyes of English law. The two aspects of this
question are not, of course, coextensive. Many foreign courts exercise exorbitant
jurisdiction, as do the English courts under RSC Ord 11. But English law does not always
recognise such jurisdiction exercised by others.

In the present case there has been no challenge before me to the jurisdiction of the

Swiss courts by their own law. The only evidence on the point, so far as I can see, is the
a two Swiss judgments themselves. But in the absence of any challenge I accept these as
proof that the Swiss courts had jurisdiction by Swiss law.

The circumstances in which an English court accords jurisdiction to a foreign court
were set out by Fry J in *Rousillon v Rousillon* (1880) 14 Ch D 351 at 371:

> 'The Courts of this country consider the defendant bound where he is a subject of
> the foreign country in which the judgment has been obtained; where he was
b > resident in the foreign country when the action began; where the defendant in the
> character of plaintiff has selected the forum in which he is afterwards sued; where
> he has voluntarily appeared; where he has contracted to submit himself to the
> forum in which the judgment was obtained, and, possibly if *Becquet* v. *MacCarthy*
> ((1831) 2 B & Ad 951, 109 ER 1396) be right, where the defendant has real estate
> within the foreign jurisdiction, in respect of which the cause of action arose whilst
c > he was within that jurisdiction.'

That passage has since been followed on many occasions, although counsel for the
buyers accepts that there may perhaps now be some argument that jurisdiction cannot
be based on nationality alone. What is relied on here is the fourth case, where the
defendant voluntarily appeared in the foreign proceedings. There is no doubt that the
d sellers appeared in the Swiss courts. They were represented by a Swiss avocat, they lodged
their objection or plea in bar, and they appealed to the cantonal Court of Appeal. The
question is, whether their appearance was voluntary. Until 24 August 1982 that was
governed by the decision in *Henry v Geopresco International Ltd*. Being bound by that
decision, I would have held that the sellers' appearance was voluntary, and that the Swiss
court therefore had jurisdiction in the eyes of English law. But now I must apply the
e Civil Jurisdiction and Judgments Act 1982. Section 32(1) of the Act provides:

> 'Subject to the following provisions of this section, a judgment given by a court
> of an overseas country in any proceedings shall not be recognised or enforced in the
> United Kingdom if—(a) the bringing of those proceedings in that court was contrary
> to an agreement under which the dispute in question was to be settled otherwise
> than by proceedings in the courts of that country; and (b) those proceedings were
f > not brought in that court by, or with the agreement of, the person against whom
> the judgment was given; and (c) that person did not counterclaim in the proceedings
> or otherwise submit to the jurisdiction of that court.'

Subject to one point, it follows that the Swiss judgment will neither be enforced nor
recognised here, because in the eyes of English law there was an arbitration agreement.
g The decision of the Swiss court that there was no arbitration agreement is immaterial:
see s 32(3):

> 'In determining whether a judgment given by a court of an overseas country
> should be recognised or enforced in the United Kingdom, a court in the United
> Kingdom shall not be bound by any decision of the overseas court relating to any of
h > the matters mentioned in subsection (1) or (2).'

But the effect of s 32(1) is subject to the proviso that the sellers did not 'otherwise
submit to the jurisdiction' of the Swiss court. If *Henry*'s case still prevailed, I would have
held that they had done so. The point is now dealt with in s 33(1):

> 'For the purposes of determining whether a judgment given by a court of an
> overseas country should be recognised or enforced in England and Wales or
j > Northern Ireland, the person against whom the judgment was given shall not be
> regarded as having submitted to the jurisdiction of the court by reason only of the
> fact that he appeared (conditionally or otherwise) in the proceedings for all or any
> one or more of the following purposes, namely—(a) to contest the jurisdiction of
> the court; (b) to ask the court to dismiss or stay the proceedings on the ground that

the dispute in question should be submitted to arbitration or to the determination of the courts of another country; (c) to protect, or obtain the release of, property seized or threatened with seizure in the proceedings.'

That subsection might have been tailor-made for this case. The sellers must accordingly not be regarded as having submitted to the jurisdiction of the Swiss court.

However, counsel for the buyers submits that the transitional provisions of the 1982 Act do not have the result that it applies in the present case. Part I of Sch 13 deals with commencement; it provides that ss 32 and 33 come into force at the end of a period of six weeks beginning with the day on which the Act was passed, ie 13 July 1982. Part II deals with transitional provisions. Paragraph 8(1) of that part reads:

'Section 32 shall not apply to any judgment—(a) which has been registered under Part II of the Administration of Justice Act 1920, Part I of the Foreign Judgments (Reciprocal Enforcement) Act 1933 or Part I of the Maintenance Orders (Reciprocal Enforcement) Act 1972 before the time when that section comes into force; or (b) in respect of which proceedings at common law for its enforcement have been finally determined before that time.

Similar provision is made in relation to s 33.

It will be noted that para 8(1) refers only to enforcement, and not recognition, in contrast with s 32 itself, which reads 'shall not be recognised or enforced'. There is an important distinction between the recognition and the enforcement of foreign judgments: see *Dicey and Morris on the Conflict of Laws* (10th edn, 1980) pp 1035–1037. Paragraph 8(1)(b) was in my judgment using the word 'enforcement' in its correct technical sense. That is shown by the context, since para 8(1)(a) refers to enforcement by statute, and para 8(1)(b) to 'proceedings at common law for its enforcement'. It is plain, to my mind, that recognition has been deliberately omitted.

Counsel for the buyers submits that in the present action the court is not being asked to enforce the Swiss judgment, but merely to recognise it. He may be right; but I need not decide the point. If the present action seeks enforcement, then ss 32 and 33 apply, since in terms of para 8(1) proceedings had not been finally determined when they came into force. If on the other hand it seeks recognition, the position is that today, when I deliver judgment, ss 32 and 33 are in force as part of the law of the United Kingdom (except that s 33 apparently does not apply in Scotland); and there is no transitional provision which excludes the present case from their effect.

That conclusion is reinforced, and any alarm one might have felt at the prospect of a party being deprived of the fruits of his pending action is diminished, by the fact that the doctrine of res judicata is adjectival, evidentiary or procedural rather than substantive (see the speech of Lord Simon in *Vervaeke v Smith* [1982] 2 All ER 144 at 156, [1982] 2 WLR 855 at 870). Furthermore:

'The presumption against retrospective construction has no application to enactments which affect only the procedure and practice of the courts. No person has a vested interest in any course of procedure.'

(See *Maxwell on the Interpretation of Statutes* (12th edn, 1969), p 222.)

That principle was applied to a defence under the Statute of Frauds in *Craxfords (Ramsgate) Ltd v Williams and Steer Manufacturing Co Ltd* [1954] 3 All ER 17, [1954] 1 WLR 1130. I see no reason why it should not also apply to estoppel per rem judicatam.

Accordingly I hold that the Swiss court did not, in the eyes of English law, have jurisdiction to pronounce the judgment relied on.

In the light of my decision on this first point, the remaining issues do not arise. But I shall express my views on them briefly, for two reasons: first, they were fully argued and may become relevant if this case goes further; second, I understand that there may be argument as to costs on the basis that the buyers would have succeeded but for a recent change in the law.

(2) *What was decided by the Swiss courts?*

Aside from questions of form it is clear beyond doubt that the Swiss courts were asked to decide that the arbitration clause was incorporated in the contract; and they decided that it was not. It is in my judgment immaterial that, in point of form, the application was based on the assertion that the cantonal court 'lacks competence to take cognisance of the pleadings of [the buyers]'. Issue estoppel is not concerned with the form of order, but with (1) what necessarily had to be decided and (2) what was in fact decided. The question whether there was a valid agreement to arbitrate was an issue which qualified under both (1) and (2) so as to be capable of giving rise to issue estoppel.

(3) *Final and conclusive on the merits*

This issue comprised two separate points, although they are closely allied to each other. First, is the Swiss judgment shown to be final and conclusive? Second, was it a judgment on the merits?

Had the present case been concluded in June, I would have decided the first point against the buyers. In *Carl-Zeiss-Stiftung v Rayner and Keeler Ltd (No 2)* at least four members of the House of Lords held that it was for the party relying on a foreign judgment to prove that it was final and conclusive. And at least three held that the burden had not been discharged in that case. Here there was no word in the affidavit sworn on the buyers' behalf to show that the Swiss judgment was final and conclusive. However, that defect has been remedied by para 4 of a further affidavit sworn by their solicitor on 14 September 1982. So the delay in completing the trial of this action has saved them from failure on one ground, although it has caused their failure on another.

The sellers argue that estoppel per rem judicatam can only arise from a decision on the merits, and not from a procedural decision of an interlocutory nature. For that submission they have the authority of *Marchioness Huntly v Gaskell* [1905] 2 Ch 656, [1904–7] All ER Rep 625 and the speech of Lord Hodson in the *Carl-Zeiss* case [1966] 2 All ER 536 at 561, [1967] 1 AC 853 at 927.

There is, I think, no doubt that such a principle exists. But I confess to some difficulty in ascertaining the precise boundaries of the expression 'on the merits'. As was observed by Roskill LJ in *Henry v Geopresco International Ltd* [1975] 2 All ER 702 at 720, [1976] QB 726 at 749, after considering *Black-Clawson International Ltd v Papierwerke Waldhof-Aschaffenburg AG* [1975] 1 All ER 810, [1975] AC 591, the expression has a slightly different meaning in the context of a case about submission to a foreign jurisdiction (where an action is brought to enforce the foreign judgment here), from that which it bears in the context of a foreign judgment as res judicata. In the former case, the contrast is between protesting against the jurisdiction and arguing the merits: all which is not jurisdiction is merits, subject now, of course, to the Civil Jurisdiction and Judgments Act 1982.

Why the phrase should be used differently in the latter context, when a foreign judgment is relied on as res judicata, is not altogether clear. But a distinction appears to exist. In *Black-Clawson International Ltd v Papierwerke Waldhof-Aschaffenburg AG* [1975] 1 All ER 810 at 825, [1975] AC 591 at 626 Viscount Dilhorne said:

'It was not a judgment "on the merits", an expression used not infrequently by lawyers . . . and one to which I must confess I have no difficulty in attaching a meaning. It was a decision that the German period of limitation applied and that the appellant's claim was consequently time-barred.'

In *Carl-Zeiss-Stiftung v Rayner & Keeler Ltd (No 2)* [1966] 2 All ER 536 at 555, [1967] 1 AC 853 at 918–919 Lord Reid said:

'It is clear that there can be no estoppel of this character unless the former judgment was a final judgment on the merits. But what does that mean in connexion with issue estoppel? When we are dealing with cause of action estoppel it means that the merits of the cause of action must be finally disposed of so that the matter cannot be raised again in the foreign country . . . When we come to issue estoppel, I think that by parity of reasoning we should have to be satisfied that the issues in question cannot be relitigated in the foreign country.'

It appears to me that at least a majority of the House of Lords in the *Carl-Zeiss* case held that a judgment on the issue of capacity to sue was either a judgment on the merits of the case, or at any rate a judgment on the merits of an issue. I cannot see any ground for treating differently a judgment on the issue whether an arbitration clause was incorporated in the contract. So I would regard the Swiss judgment in this case as likewise a judgment on the merits.

(4) *The decision was based on Swiss law*

It is manifest, as I have already said, that the decision in Switzerland was based on Swiss law; and counsel for the buyers concedes that this court must decide the case by English law. Could the estoppel nevertheless prevail? There appear to be two strands of authority bearing on the question. The first starts with the judgment of Wigram V-C in *Henderson v Henderson* (1843) 3 Hare 100 at 115, [1843–60] All ER Rep 378 at 381:

'. . . where a given matter becomes the subject of litigation in, and of adjudication by, a Court of competent jurisdiction, the Court requires the parties . . . to bring forward their whole case, and will not (except under special circumstances) permit the same parties to open the same subject of litigation in respect of matter which might have been brought forward as part of the subject in contest, but which was not brought forward, only because they have, from negligence, inadvertence, or even accident, omitted part of their case. The plea of *res judicata* applies . . .'

That was a case of cause of action estoppel. The question whether the same doctrine applied to issue estoppel was considered in the *Carl-Zeiss* case. All of their Lordships were, I think, to a greater or lesser degree against the application of the doctrine in *Henderson v Henderson* to issue estoppel based on the decision of a foreign court.

However, it is argued for the buyers that, whatever the general rule may be, at least the decision of a foreign court in accordance with its own law is binding, notwithstanding that an English court would have applied English law. The cases cited in support of that proposition were *Castrique v Imrie* (1870) LR 4 HL 414, [1861–73] All ER Rep 508 and *Godard v Gray* (1870) LR 6 QB 139. In *Castrique's* case a French court had either acted on a wrong view of English law, or else applied French law when English law should have been applied. Nevertheless its judgment was held to be binding. In *Godard's* case it was argued that the judgment of a French court had proceeded on a mistaken notion of English law. But it appears from the judgment of Hannen J (at 154) that the French court was never informed of what the English law was. The French judgment was enforced.

If those two cases are in point, it would follow that the decision of the Swiss courts is binding here, notwithstanding that it proceeded on Swiss law, whereas the issue here has to be determined by English law. However, counsel for the sellers submits that both those cases were based on cause of action estoppel, where the rule in *Henderson v Henderson* would unquestionably apply. He says that in the present case of issue estoppel it does not.

He also relies on the *Black-Clawson* case [1975] 1 All ER 810 at 825, [1975] AC 591 at 625, whereby Viscount Dilhorne said:

'What then was the question adjudicated on by the District Court of Munich on 30th November 1972? . . . It was a decision that the German period of limitation applied and that the appellant's claim was consequently time-barred.'

Viscount Dilhorne held, as one of the majority in that decision, that the foreign judgment was no bar to an action in England.

Counsel for the buyers seeks to distinguish that decision. He observes that it was not a case where a point that could have been raised was not raised; the German courts had to apply the German limitation period. He also relies on *Vervaeke v Smith* [1982] 2 All ER

144, [1982] 2 WLR 855, which was apparently a case of issue estoppel, at any rate in part,

a where the doctrine in *Henderson v Henderson* was applied. After considerable hesitation, I conclude that the buyers are right on this point. It is no obstacle to the plea of res judicata in this case that the Swiss courts applied Swiss law.

(5) *The rule in Simpson v Fogo*

I can deal with this point shortly. The authority of *Simpson v Fogo* (1863) 1 Hem & M

b 195, 71 ER 85 is very much open to question: see the *Carl-Zeiss* case [1966] 2 All ER 536 at 557, 592, [1967] 1 AC 853 at 922, 978 per Lord Reid and Lord Wilberforce. At its highest, it applies only—

'in the case of a Court wilfully determining that it will not, according to the usual comity, recognise the law of other nations when clearly and plainly put before it . . .'

c (See *Castrique v Imrie* (1870) LR 4 HL 414 at 445, [1861–73] All ER Rep 508 at 512 per Lord Hatherley LC.)

Nothing remotely like that happened in this case.

(6) *The buyers' appointment of an arbitrator*

As already mentioned, the buyers did appoint Mr Beaton as arbitrator on 14 May 1981,

d two days after they had obtained the sequestration order in Switzerland. They did so to preserve their position, in case it should be held in Switzerland that there was a valid agreement to arbitrate. They have taken no other step in the arbitration.

Counsel for the sellers submits that this conduct on the part of the buyers amounted to an assertion that there was a valid arbitration clause; and that the sellers acted on it by appointing their own arbitrator and incurring a liability to pay his fee. Alternatively he

e submits that the buyers are bound by that assertion, whether the sellers acted on it or not, by reason of the doctrine in *Panchaud Frères SA v Etablissements General Grain Co* [1970] 1 Lloyd's Rep 53 at 59: see per Winn LJ:

'. . . an inchoate doctrine stemming from the manifest convenience of consistency in pragmatic affairs, negativing any liberty to blow hot and cold in commercial conduct.'

f

I readily accept that the buyers were blowing hot and cold. Counsel for the buyers submitted that a party who is plaintiff in one jurisdiction, and whose proceedings there are being challenged, can protect himself by commencing proceedings elsewhere, without prejudicing his position. I do not hold any such proposition of law to be established by the cases which counsel for the buyers cited to support it: *Unterweser*

g *Reederei GmbH v Zapata Off-shore Co, The Chaparral* [1968] 2 Lloyd's Rep 158 and *The Atlantic Star* [1973] 2 All ER 175, [1974] AC 436 at first instance and on appeal. But that result may occur, on the facts, in a particular case.

I am not convinced that the sellers acted on any assertion by the buyers that there was a valid arbitration clause. They do not say so in their affidavit, and it seems quite likely that they would have appointed an arbitrator even if the buyers had not done so.

h I have already held that the plea of res judicata fails on another ground, quite apart from the buyers' conduct in appointing an arbitrator. If the plea had otherwise succeeded, I consider that the buyers' claim in this action would not have failed on this point, because that conduct was itself part of the issue decided by the Swiss court. A supplementary brief to the cantonal Court of Appeal, contained in a letter dated 27 April 1982, expressly raised the point. There is no need for the doctrine of *Henderson v*

j *Henderson*, or any argument as to what might have been argued but was not; the point was in issue before, and must have been decided by, the court of appeal.

(7) *Remedies*

Counsel for the sellers argued that I should not, in any event, grant an injunction, since the buyers' conduct in starting proceedings in Switzerland was, at the time, a deliberate and calculated breach of the arbitration clause. That is as it may be. But if the plea of res judicata had prevailed, I should be precluded from acting on the view that there was a binding arbitration clause, in determining liability in this action. I do not see *a* how I could be any the less precluded from acting on it in deciding what remedies are available to the buyers.

Counsel for the sellers also argued that, since the Swiss proceedings were in point of form concerned with one only of the two contracts, any declaration or injunction would likewise relate only to that contract. This argument appears to me to be well founded. If I had been otherwise in favour of the buyers' contention, I should have limited any *b* declaration or injunction granted to the contract dated 30 November 1980. The result would have been somewhat absurd; but I suppose that there is always a risk of absurdity in the application of the doctrine of issue estoppel.

In the result I give judgment for the sellers (the defendants) in this action. And it has been agreed, I believe, that any consequential applications shall be made at a later date?

c

Judgment for the sellers.

Solicitors: *Richards Butler & Co* (for the buyers); *William A Crump & Son* (for the sellers).

K Mydeen Esq   Barrister.

d

Clark v MacLennan and another

QUEEN'S BENCH DIVISION
PETER PAIN J
e
8–11, 14–17, 21–25, 28–30 JUNE, 2 JULY 1982

*Medical practitioner – Negligence – Test of liability – Conformity with practices accepted as proper by responsible members of profession – Unsuccessful operation – Operation departing from orthodox course of treatment – Plaintiff left disabled – Onus of proof on defendant to show departure from established practice not a breach of duty – Onus of proof on defendant to show *f* plaintiff's injuries not caused by breach of duty.*

The plaintiff, who was about to give birth to her first child, was admitted to a hospital administered by the second defendants, a health authority. The baby was delivered on 11 June 1975. Soon after the birth the plaintiff began to suffer from stress incontinence, a not uncommon post-natal condition whereby normal bladder control was lost when *g* the sufferer was subjected to mild physical stress. The defendant's disability was particularly acute and after conventional treatment failed to bring about an improvement the first defendant, a gynaecologist, performed an anterior colporrhaphy operation on 10 July 1975. It was normal practice among gynaecologists not to perform such an operation until at least three months after birth so as to ensure its success and to prevent the risk of haemorrhage. The operation was not successful and after it was performed haemorrhage *h* occurred causing the repair to break down. Two further anterior colporrhaphy operations were necessary, and they were carried out on 16 January 1976 and in October 1979. Neither was successful with the result that the stress incontinence from which the plaintiff suffered became a permanent disability. She brought an action for damages claiming that the defendants had been negligent in the care and treatment administered to her. *j*

Held – Although in an action in negligence the onus of proof normally rested on the plaintiff, in a case where a general duty of care arose and there was a failure to take a recognised precaution and that failure was followed by the very damage which that precaution was designed to prevent, the burden of proof lay on the defendant to show, first, that he was not in breach of any duty and, second, if he failed to prove that he had

not been in breach of duty, that the damage suffered by the plaintiff did not result from
a the breach. Accordingly, a doctor owed a duty to his patient to observe the precautions
which were normal in the course of the treatment that he gave. Where a patient suffered
damage after there had been a departure from the orthodox course of treatment the court
had to inquire whether the doctor had taken all proper factors into account prior to
taking action in order to determine whether that departure was justified. If it was not,
that departure was a breach of the duty owed to the patient. On the facts, it was a general
b precautionary practice amongst gynaecologists that an anterior colporrhaphy should not
normally be performed on a patient until at least three months after the birth of a child.
The departure from that general practice by the first defendant and the second defendants'
staff was not justified and accordingly there had been a breach of the duty of care owed
to the plaintiff. Moreover, the defendants had failed to establish that the damage suffered
by the plaintiff had not flowed from their breach of the duty of care. The defendants had
c therefore been negligent and the plaintiff was entitled to judgment against the second
defendants, who in the circumstances were vicariously responsible for the first defendant
and their staff (see p 424 *j* to p 425 *c*, p 427 *g* to *j*, p 432 *e* to *g* and p 433 *e f*, post).

Hunter v Hanley 1955 SLT 213, Bolam v Friern Hospital Management Committee [1957] 2
All ER 118, Davies v Taylor [1972] 3 All ER 836, McGhee v National Coal Board [1972] 3
All ER 1008 and Whitehouse v Jordan [1981] 1 All ER 267 applied.

d **Notes**
For the standard of care required of doctors, see 34 Halsbury's Laws (4th edn) para 12,
and for cases on the subject, see 33 Digest (Reissue) 262–288, 2162–2330.

Cases referred to in judgment
e Bolam v Friern Hospital Management Committee [1957] 2 All ER 118, [1957] 1 WLR 582,
    DC, 33 Digest (Reissue) 273, 2245.
Davies v Taylor [1972] 3 All ER 836, [1974] AC 207, [1972] 3 WLR 801, HL, 36(1) Digest
    (Reissue) 348, 1400.
Hunter v Hanley 1955 SLT 213.
McGhee v National Coal Board [1972] 3 All ER 1008, [1973] 1 WLR 1, HL, 36(1) Digest
f   (Reissue) 62, 219.
Whitehouse v Jordan [1981] 1 All ER 267, [1981] 1 WLR 246, HL; affg [1980] 1 All ER
    650, CA, 33 Digest (Reissue) 265, 2182.

Action
By a writ issued on 6 June 1978 the plaintiff, Jacqueline Mary Clark, claimed against the
g first defendant, Alistair G MacLennan, and the second defendants, the Oxfordshire Area
Health Authority, damages in negligence for personal injuries sustained during the
course of post-natal surgery and treatment received after the birth of her child on 11 June
1975. The facts are set out in the judgment.

E A Machin QC, Michael Spencer and Michael Powers for the plaintiff.
h Ian Kennedy QC and Adrian Whitfield for the first and second defendants.

Cur adv vult
2 July. The following judgment was delivered.

PETER PAIN J. On 31 May 1975 the plaintiff went into the John Radcliffe Hospital at
j Oxford, managed by the second defendants, to have her first baby. She was admitted for
rest and assessment before the baby was actually due because some difficulty was expected
in delivery. However, no more difficulty was encountered than could be overcome by
the use of forceps and her baby daughter was delivered on 11 June.

Within a couple of days she was found to be suffering from stress incontinence. Stress
incontinence is a condition in which spurts of urine are emitted from the bladder when
it is subjected to some external physical stress, for example by sneezing or coughing. In

severe cases, quite small stresses may cause incontinence. It is to be distinguished from frank incontinence, which is common in old age, when the muscular control of the neck of the bladder breaks down; it is also different from urge incontinence, which occurs when the bladder becomes overfull and the person is not in a position to satisfy the urge to relieve himself.

Stress incontinence is a condition not infrequently found in women shortly after they have given birth. In the course of pregnancy, the uterus becomes greatly enlarged and much heavier. It exerts a pressure on the bladder which lies beneath the uterus. This may displace the bladder in a downward direction.

With the strains which are associated with childbirth, the muscles at the neck of the bladder which control the emission of urine into the urethra may be weakened. As a result of that weakness, normal control may be lost when some external stress is placed on the bladder.

The urethra is divided from the vagina by a narrow wall. Where the bladder has descended it is often possible to see a bulging of the vaginal wall. By 13 June the plaintiff was found to be suffering from severe stress incontinence. This was a great misfortune for her. It was not a condition for which there was a certain cure. Even if it were cured, it was likely to reoccur if she added to her family. She faced a handicap for the future which was in no way the fault of the defendants but which she associated with the birth.

On 16 June the plaintiff was seen by the first defendant and Professor Turnbull. Professor Turnbull was in charge of the unit in the care of which the plaintiff was, and the first defendant was his senior registrar. The leakage of urine was so considerable that Professor Turnbull at first feared a fistula. A fistula is a puncture between the bladder and the vagina through which urine may leak. The urine will thus bypass the normal control at the bladder neck and leak uncontrollably down the vagina. The professor examined the vagina by speculum and could find no fistula.

A fistula might have been caused by forceps at delivery, the professor feared. His examination may have caused the plaintiff to have had the false impression, which she undoubtedly retained for some time, that her stress incontinence was due to mishandling at the delivery of her child. The professor and the first defendant examined the plaintiff and recommended conservative treatment. This was to consist of (1) the passage of time which would allow the affected organs to return to their prepregnant condition, (2) pelvic floor exercises which are the exercises normally taught by physiotherapists to women after childbirth, (3) faradism, a form of electrical treatment designed to restore muscle tone to the bladder neck, and (4) an antibiotic called septrin. I accept the first defendant's evidence that at this stage he and Professor Turnbull were optimistic as to improvement.

The intention was that the plaintiff was to remain an in-patient at the John Radcliffe Hospital and to be taken to the Churchill Hospital nearby for faradism and physiotherapy. The first defendant made a short note of the examination which contained two mistakes. Instead of 'faradism' he noted 'short wave diathermy'; he also noted: 'Review, Wednesday the 18th. If better, home; if not, see the Professor.' Professor Turnbull says he could not possibly have agreed to have seen her on Wednesday as he was fully committed elsewhere. After this, the first defendant went on leave and did not see the plaintiff again until 27 June.

Professor Turnbull spoke to the physiotherapist at the Churchill Hospital and told her about the plaintiff and asked that Dr Scott, the specialist there in physiotherapy, should give her such treatment as he should advise. Professor Turnbull mentioned that he had suggested two to three weeks of faradism. The request for physiotherapy sent by Dr Howes, Professor Turnbull's houseman, to the Churchill Hospital asked for pelvic floor faradism. I have not heard evidence from Dr Scott but it would appear from the record produced by the Churchill Hospital that Dr Scott saw the plaintiff on 19 June and advised a course of faradism daily for two to three weeks but with the provision that the plaintiff should be reassessed on 27 June.

There then ensued a chapter of accidents for which the second defendants are responsible in law. On 19 June the plaintiff was discharged home without having seen Professor Turnbull again. According to the second defendants' practice, she should have seen a doctor on discharge and a note should have been made. No such note exists. A

formal note should have been sent to her general practitioner, Dr Hussain. A note was
sent but it was not properly completed. It omitted the vital information that the plaintiff
was suffering from stress incontinence and it was not signed by a doctor.

This was a sad omission as the counsel and encouragement which a general practitioner
may give can play some considerable part in persuading a patient to continue with
conservative treatment. On Thursday, 19 June Professor Turnbull telephoned the ward
to ask about the plaintiff. He was told that she had been discharged to her home. He felt
that a comment which he had made when he saw her on 16 June to the effect that he was
sure that she would be happier at home, if appropriate arrangements could be made, had
been misinterpreted. He was told by the ward sister that the plaintiff's general
practitioner had been informed and that appropriate transport arrangements had been
made. He understood that this meant that an ambulance had been arranged to take the
plaintiff from her parents' home at Garsington, about 12 miles from Oxford, each day to
the Churchill Hospital. It was not until the subsequent September that he learned that
the staff had merely arranged transport to take the plaintiff to her parents' home.

Thinking that the plaintiff would be making her daily visits to the Churchill Hospital
and would be in the care of her general practitioner, he decided not to recall her to the
John Radcliffe Hospital. The plaintiff was left in an impossible position as she could
hardly use public transport while leaking urine. She visited the Churchill Hospital twice
in the next week when she was able to get a lift. I am satisfied that she did not go daily
despite the Churchill Hospital notes. She found faradism, which involved electrical
treatment per anum, painful and distasteful. She did her exercises. She was visited by the
health visitor and by Dr Hussain on 26 June. His note records: 'Had paralysed bladder
after delivery now 15 days ago. Feels very distressed. Dribbling all the time.' It is not
clear from the note 'paralysed bladder' whether Dr Hussain appreciated, without having
been told by the hospital, that her trouble was stress incontinence.

She felt that she was getting no better and on 27 June she returned, by appointment,
to the John Radcliffe Hospital. On examination a small cystocele, that is a bulge, was
observed in the vaginal wall and stress incontinence was demonstrated. It was decided
then to keep her in hospital and to try the use of a pessary over the weekend. A pessary
can loosely be described as a squashy ring which can be pushed to the top of the vagina
so as to provide some support for the bladder and possibly relieve the condition while
natural healing tales place. Pessaries come in a number of different shapes and sizes.

There was no improvement as a result of the use of this pessary and on 30 June the
first defendant discussed with Professor Turnbull the desirability of an anterior
colporrhaphy operation. A provisional booking was made for 9 July. A further opinion
was sought from Mr Williamson.

On 1 July the decision to undertake the operation on 10 July was confirmed, subject to
there being no improvement in the mean time and the plaintiff was discharged home. I
will return to the way in which this decision was made later in the judgment.

Anterior colporrhaphy is a specialist operation performed frequently by gynaecologists.
The purpose of the operation is to restore the bladder to its natural position if it has
descended and then to support the bladder neck by stitches which are inserted on either
side of the urethra and then drawn tight so that they pull the connective tissue in
underneath the bladder and bladder neck. Entry is made through the vagina. The
surgeon opens the vaginal wall by incision. He then turns the vaginal skin back on either
side of the incision by dissecting the skin off the underlying tissue. This exposes the
bladder neck and urethra which he frees from their attachments to the deeper structures.

For this purpose he need not use a knife. Dissection may be possible by the fingers
after an injection of saline. Having freed the bladder neck and the urethra the surgeon
then restores them to their proper position. The bladder neck is normally supported by
connective tissue which consists largely of muscle and contains a number of blood vessels.
He inserts stitches so that one end is in the connective tissue which underlies the vaginal
wall and the other end is in the connective tissue which lies on the further side of the
urethra. He draws each stitch together so pulling in the connective tissue beneath the
bladder neck.

He will often, as was the first defendant's practice, insert two rows of stitches. These stitches are called the buttress sutures. He then closes the incision in the vaginal wall and stitches that. It will be apparent that an important requirement of this operation is that the connective tissue should provide a good anchor for the buttress sutures. If the stitches pull out on either side, the operation will be a failure.

The nature of the plaintiff's complaint is twofold and it can be summarised in this way: (1) the operation was performed too soon; and (2) the haemorrhage which followed the operation was not properly treated. I do not think it is necessary to go in further detail into the allegations made in the statement of claim. The defences which have been filed deny negligence but do not contain any additional material. There has been an exchange of letters with regard to the pleadings. On 30 March 1982 the plaintiff's advisers wrote to ask what the position would be if the first defendant were to adopt at the trial the attitude that, even if the decision to operate when he did was an error of judgment, he was not negligent in that he relied on the judgment of others and, in particular, his consultant, Professor Turnbull. To that the defendants' solicitors replied:

'The position is that Professor Turnbull was the consultant in charge and as such in a sense could be said to have "supervised" Mr MacLennan. But their decision as to the time to operate was a joint one. If however for some reason Professor Turnbull and not Mr MacLennan was found negligent, your client would not be prejudiced because the second Defendant would accept liability on behalf of Professor Turnbull. And in any event, both practitioners are members of the same defence organisation; you need have no fears about indemnity here. Thus, we can foresee no circumstances in which your client's interests require the implication of Professor Turnbull in the action.'

On 10 July the first defendant performed an operation for anterior colporrhaphy. At the conclusion of the evidence counsel for the plaintiff indicated that the allegations of negligence as to the post-operational treatment were abandoned. Clearly, counsel was right in this decision. The one point in the case which had seemed fairly simple to me as the evidence proceeded was that these allegations could not succeed.

But as this part of the case involved an attack on the first defendant, because he alone was responsible for this treatment, it is only fair to him that I should say a few words about it. The case against him was built up on a careful study of the hospital notes. But of course these do not tell the whole story. The evidence made it clear that the first defendant was closely in touch with the plaintiff until 8 am on the day following the operation, so that no question of neglect arises. It was asserted that the first defendant was slow to recognise that there was internal bleeding and that he should have taken the plaintiff back to the operating theatre and reinvestigated her to establish and tie off the source of the haemorrhage.

The medical evidence showed clearly that there are two schools of thought: (1) those who feel it so important to deal with the haemorrhage that they are prepared to sacrifice the repair; and (2) those who wish to deal with the haemorrhage by conservative treatment if possible and so leave the repair intact in the hope that it will not be prejudiced by the effects of the haemorrhage. The first defendant followed the latter school. The measures he took were effective in restoring blood pressure and, although the plaintiff had a few bad hours, there was no anxiety about her by the time that the first defendant went off duty the next morning.

I am satisfied by the evidence of Sir John Dewhurst, one of the defendants' expert witnesses, that at the beginning of an investigation the surgeon has no idea of the source of the bleeding and that it is purposeless to begin the search for the source unless one is prepared, if necessary, to penetrate beyond the buttress sutures which must involve undoing them. No half measures are possible. No possible criticism can be made of the first defendant's decision to treat the plaintiff in the way that he did. But it is necessary to make one or two findings about the operation for the purpose of considering the validity of the decision to operate. It is common ground that if substantial haemorrhage occurred the tissues would be softened and the repair would be endangered. Although the first defendant reported in his notes of the operation 'average or less blood loss' and wrote immediately after the operation to the plaintiff's general practitioner to say that

there were no complications, it is now accepted that there was substantial internal
a haemorrhage.

There was a good deal of debate as to the amount of internal bleeding. The plaintiff
sought to assess her blood loss by pointing to the fall in her haemoglobin following the
operation at the time when she had been transfused with five units (approximately 4 pt)
of blood. A calculation was put forward that she had lost 4 to 5 pt of blood through
internal bleeding. It is not suggested that this was an accurate measurement and the first
b defendant criticised the method of calculation suggesting that internal bleeding accounted
for only 1½ to 2 pt.

The evidence is too vague to justify any finding further than that there was substantial
internal bleeding of a quantity somewhere between these two figures. The method of
buttress stitching employed by the first defendant was first to insert the catgut of all the
stitches and then to draw them tight and tie them. When inserting the catgut his needle
c penetrated an area which he could not see. I shall consider the source of the bleeding
later.

On 19 July the plaintiff was discharged home from hospital. The notes on that date
show: 'Occasional incontinence yesterday.' She attended for a post-operation examination
on 18 August and the notes for that date show: 'Still had occasional stress. Review in 3
months if still has stress. See Professor. A difficult one.' The plaintiff was however very
d dissatisfied about her condition and treatment. Accordingly, she consulted solicitors,
who wrote on 9 September 1975 asking the hospital to keep her fully informed of the
position. As a result, there was a meeting on 29 September at the out-patients' department
which was attended by the plaintiff, Mrs Robinson, chairman of the Patients' Association,
the first defendant and Professor Turnbull. It was clear by then that the repair had broken
down and on examination a small moderate cystocele was found to be present in the
e vagina. One of the complaints was that there was a leaking of urine during sexual
intercourse which the plaintiff naturally found extremely distressing and which was
causing marital problems.

The plaintiff was sympathetically received and arrangements were made for her to be
admitted once more on 6 October for investigation and possibly for a further operation
known as the Oxford sling. However, the plaintiff and her husband were not satisfied
f and she was then referred by her panel doctor to Professor Huntingford at the London
Hospital. He examined her on 3 October and found that the repair carried out in July
appeared to have completely broken down. Her condition did not improve and on 16
January 1976 she underwent a second anterior colporrhaphy performed by Professor
Huntingford. This appeared at first to be successful. But by June 1976 further leakage
was occurring.

g She became pregnant again in December 1976 and the leakage then became much
worse and continued during pregnancy. She was delivered of her second child by
Caesarian operation in September 1977. She made a good recovery and appeared to have
regained bladder control. But unhappily matters got worse in the subsequent months
and she saw Professor Huntingford again in March 1979, when he concurred in the view
that control had again broken down. In October 1979 Professor Huntingford carried out
h a third anterior colporrhaphy and his report of January 1980 shows that he regarded her
as finally cured.

Unhappily, this proved to be a somewhat over-optimistic assessment as she still has
considerable trouble. The account she gave me of her present condition, which I accept,
is that although she is a lot better after the last repair she is still incontinent if she sneezes
or coughs on a full bladder. Whenever she goes out socially she has to wear a pad and she
i is very conscious of the smell. If she hears the bell ring at home she gets tense and leaks.
The trouble is worse in cold weather. Shivering induces leaking. She cannot run without
leaking or play tennis, although she has tried jogging recently when wearing a towel.
She is embarrassed when she dances. She had to give up her part-time job which involved
lifting basketware. She would like to work in an office as a shorthand typist, which she
did before marriage. But she would not have the confidence to do that because of her
incontinence.

She normally wears a skirt rather than jeans so that it does not show if she leaks. Before her first child was born she had a good social life, physically active, playing tennis, going dancing and so on. I accept the plaintiff's complaints as to her present condition. I *a* thought that she was a truthful witness, although allowances have to be made for the lapse of time since much of this history occurred. As to her condition at any particular time, I have relied more on medical notes and reports than on her recollection. I have no doubt that she feels some sense of grievance and it is plain that she does not understand much medicine; but I do not think that she has allowed that to colour her account of the facts.

The plaintiff called three witnesses in support of her case in addition to her husband. *b* The first and main witness was Professor Huntingford, who gave evidence as to the treatment he had given her and also evidence based on the hospital notes why he considered the defendants to be negligent. He was supported by Dr Smallwood, who is a general practitioner specialising in obstetrics and who is very familiar with this operation, and Mr Rickford, a gynaecological surgeon of many years standing.   *c*

I found the three witnesses who represented the orthodox view of the medical profession were absolutely reliable. It seemed to me they were strictly objective, singularly lacking in dogmatism and quite prepared to give an answer favourable to the defendants when the question demanded it.

The first defendant gave evidence on his own behalf. I do not doubt that he is a brilliant surgeon and that he was compassionate and caring in the way in which he dealt *d* with the plaintiff. I thought that he was very fair in the way that he gave his evidence although he plainly felt aggrieved at the way a case had been built up against him. Naturally enough, he was anxious to justify himself and was somewhat defensive.

Professor Turnbull also gave lengthy evidence. He is clearly an outstanding gynaecologist and a most impressive individual. I have no doubt that he shows the greatest care with his patients. But occasionally there crept into his evidence a certain *e* recklessness in seeking to establish a point. His references to Dr Scott were a particular example. This apart, he too was a completely reliable witness. The defendants were supported by Dr Hytten, a physiologist of high repute whom I regard as a completely reliable scientist. Mr Williamson, who was one of Professor Turnbull's registrars at the time of the operation, also gave evidence. But, as he was called in to give an opinion whether the plaintiff's condition was due to irritation of the bladder, a trouble of which *f* he had specialist knowledge, and as he negatived this possibility, his evidence was not of any great moment. Finally, there was Sir John Dewhurst. He too is a gynaecologist of great distinction and a former president of the Royal College of Gynaecologists. I felt complete confidence in his objectivity as an expert witness.

Very often one finds in medical disputes that there is little difference between the medical witnesses once they go into the box. This case was the exception. There was a *g* wide range of differences and I found it very difficult to choose between them. The case was made even more difficult by the fact that the defendants were developing new theories as the case went on. On two occasions Professor Huntingford had to be recalled to deal with substantial points which had not been put to him when he was first cross-examined.

The plaintiff's action sounds in negligence. This is an unfortunate name for the cause *h* of action in this case because her complaint is not that the surgeons did something careless, such as leaving a swab in at an operation site, but rather that their considered decision showed a want of proper professional skill and care.

The John Radcliffe Hospital and Professor Turnbull are of the highest standing in their profession but I must not let that deter me from an examination of whether they proceeded with due professional care in the present case. Counsel for the defendants *j* referred to Professor Turnbull's status as 'Olympian'. My recollection of classical mythology is that the gods on Olympus were no strangers to error.

I turn therefore to the authorities. I begin with the classic statement of McNair J in *Bolam v Friern Hospital Management Committee* [1957] 2 All ER 118 at 121–122, [1957] 1 WLR 582 at 586–587. This was a case with a jury and McNair J was giving the charge to the jury, explaining the law to them. The judge said:

'Before I turn to that, I must explain what in law we mean by "negligence". In the ordinary case which does not involve any special skill, negligence in law means this: Some failure to do some act which a reasonable man in the circumstances would do, or doing some act which a reasonable man in the circumstances would not do; and if that failure or doing of that act results in injury, then there is a cause of action. How do you test whether this act or failure is negligent? In an ordinary case it is generally said, that you judge that by the action of the man in the street. He is the ordinary man. In one case it has been said that you judge it by the conduct of the man on the top of a Clapham omnibus. He is the ordinary man. But where you get a situation which involves the use of some special skill or competence, then the test whether there has been negligence or not is not the test of the man on the top of a Clapham omnibus, because he has not got this special skill. The test is the standard of the ordinary skilled man exercising and professing to have that special skill. A man need not possess the highest expert skill at the risk of being found negligent. It is well-established law that it is sufficient if he exercises the ordinary skill of an ordinary competent man exercising that particular art. I do not think that I quarrel much with any of the submissions in law which have been put before you by counsel. Counsel for the plaintiff put it in this way, that in the case of a medical man negligence means failure to act in accordance with the standards of reasonably competent medical men at the time. That is a perfectly accurate statement, as long as it is remembered that there may be one or more perfectly proper standards; and if a medical man conforms with one of those proper standards then he is not negligent. Counsel for the plaintiff was also right, in my judgment, in saying that a mere personal belief that a particular technique is best is no defence unless that belief is based on reasonable grounds. That again is unexceptionable. But the emphasis which is laid by counsel for the defendants is on this aspect of negligence: He submitted to you that the real question on which you have to make up your mind on each of the three major points to be considered is whether the defendants, in acting in the way in which they did, were acting in accordance with a practice of competent respected professional opinion. Counsel for the defendants submitted that if you are satisfied that they were acting in accordance with a practice of a competent body of professional opinion, then it would be wrong for you to hold that negligence was established. I referred, before I started these observations, to a statement which is contained in a recent Scottish case, *Hunter* v. *Hanley* (1955 SLT 213 at 217), which dealt with medical matters, where the Lord President (LORD CLYDE) said this: "In the realm of diagnosis and treatment there is ample scope for genuine difference of opinion, and one man clearly is not negligent merely because his conclusion differs from that of other professional men, nor because he has displayed less skill or knowledge than others would have shown. The true test for establishing negligence in diagnosis or treatment on the part of a doctor is whether he has been proved to be guilty of such failure as no doctor of ordinary skill would be guilty of if acting with ordinary care." If that statement of the true test is qualified by the words "in all the circumstances", counsel for the plaintiff would not seek to say that that expression of opinion does not accord with English law. It is just a question of expression. I myself would prefer to put it this way: A doctor is not guilty of negligence if he has acted in accordance with a practice accepted as proper by a responsible body of medical men skilled in that particular art. I do not think there is much difference in sense. It is just a different way of expressing the same thought. Putting it the other way round, a doctor is not negligent, if he is acting in accordance with such a practice, merely because there is a body of opinion that takes a contrary view. At the same time, that does not mean that a medical man can obstinately and pig-headedly carry on with some old technique if it has been proved to be contrary to what is really substantially the whole of informed medical opinion. Otherwise you might get men today saying: "I don't believe in anaesthetics. I don't believe in antiseptics. I am going to continue to do my surgery in the way it was done in the eighteenth century". That clearly would be wrong.'

That passage has been specifically approved by the House of Lords in *Whitehouse v Jordan* [1981] 1 All ER 267, [1981] 1 WLR 246. I desire to refer not only to that but also to one or two further passages in the speeches of their Lordships in that case which are of assistance to me in solving the present problem. Lord Edmund-Davies in the course of his speech said ([1981] 1 All ER 267 at 276–277, [1981] 1 WLR 246 at 257–258):

> 'The principal questions calling for decision are: (a) in what manner did Mr Jordan use the forceps? and (b) was that manner consistent with the degree of skill which a member of his profession is required by law to exercise? Surprising though it is at this late stage in the development of the law of negligence, counsel for Mr Jordan persisted in submitting that his client should be completely exculpated were the answer to question (b), "Well, at the worst he was guilty of an error of clinical judgment". My Lords, it is high time that the unacceptability of such an answer be finally exposed. To say that a surgeon committed an error of clinical judgment is wholly ambiguous, for, while some such errors may be completely consistent with the due exercise of professional skill, other acts or omissions in the course of exercising "clinical judgment" may be so glaringly below proper standards as to make a finding of negligence inevitable. Indeed, I should have regarded this as a truism were it not that, despite the exposure of the "false antithesis" by Donaldson LJ in his dissenting judgment in the Court of Appeal, counsel for the defendants adhered to it before your Lordships. But doctors and surgeons fall into no special category, and, to avoid any future disputation of a similar kind, I would have it accepted that the true doctrine was enunciated, and by no means for the first time, by McNair J in *Bolam v Friern Hospital Management Committee* [1957] 2 All ER 118 at 121, [1957] 1 WLR 582 at 586 ... If a surgeon fails to measure up to that standard in *any* respect ("clinical judgment" or otherwise), he has been negligent and should be so adjudged.' (Lord Edmund-Davies's emphasis.)

Lord Fraser, in the course of his speech (see [1981] 1 All ER 267 at 281, [1981] 1 WLR 246 at 263), referred to a passage in the judgment of Lord Denning MR (see [1980] 1 All ER 650 at 658) and said that Lord Denning MR went on to say:

> ' "We must say, and say firmly, that, in a professional man an error of judgment is not negligent." Having regard to the context, I think that Lord Denning MR must have meant to say that an error of judgment "is not *necessarily* negligent". But in my respectful opinion, the statement as it stands is not an accurate statement of the law. Merely to describe something as an error of judgment tells us nothing about whether it is negligent or not. The true position is that an error of judgment may, or may not, be negligent; it depends on the nature of the error. If it is one that would not have been made by a reasonably competent professional man professing to have the standard and type of skill that the defendant held himself out as having, and acting with ordinary care, then it is negligent. If, on the other hand, it is an error that a man, acting with ordinary care, might have made, then it is not negligence.' (Lord Fraser's emphasis.)

Again, I refer to Lord Russell who said ([1981] 1 All ER 267 at 284, [1981] 1 WLR 246 at 268):

> 'Some passages in the Court of Appeal might suggest that if a doctor makes an error of judgment he cannot be found guilty of negligence. This must be wrong. An error of judgment is not per se incompatible with negligence, as Donaldson LJ pointed out. I would accept the phrase "a mere error of judgment" if the impact of the word "mere" is to indicate that not all errors of judgment show a lapse from the standard of skill and care required to be exercised to avoid a charge of negligence.'

It follows from these authorities that a doctor owes a duty to his patient to observe the precautions which are normal in the course of the treatment that he gives. But, where there are two schools of thought as to the right course to be followed, he may not be charged with negligence simply because he chooses one course rather than the other.

a   Where however there is but one orthodox course of treatment and he chooses to depart from that, his position is different. It is not enough for him to say as to his decision simply that it was based on his clinical judgment. One has to inquire whether he took all proper factors into account which he knew or should have known, and whether his departure from the orthodox course can be justified on the basis of these factors.

The burden of proof lies on the plaintiff. To succeed she must show, first, that there was a breach of duty and, second, that her damage flowed from that breach. It is against
b   the second defendants that her attack is principally directed. They are liable for all the mistakes that were made, whether by Professor Turnbull or the staff.

In his final speech, counsel for the plaintiff very fairly did not press the case against the first defendant. The evidence made it apparent that he was acting under the direction of Professor Turnbull. I accept, as he said, that he would not have made the decision to operate on his own.

c   But an important question arises as to the burden of proof. It may seem that to base one's judgment on the burden of proof is the last resort of a judge who cannot make up his mind. But, when one is faced by medical evidence made more difficult by the fact that medical experts disagree on a number of matters of medical fact, it seems to me to be a legitimate resort.

Counsel for the plaintiff relied heavily on *McGhee v National Coal Board* [1972] 3 All ER
d   1008, [1973] 1 WLR 1 for this purpose. That was a case where a workman established that his employers were in breach of their common law duty because they had failed to provide adequate washing facilities for him while working in the brick kiln. In consequence, he had cycled home caked in brick dust and shortly after he developed dermatitis. The Court of Session rejected his claim on the ground that he had failed to show on the balance of probabilities that a breach of duty caused or materially contributed
e   to his dermatitis.

The matter went to the House of Lords and in the course of his speech, Lord Reid said ([1972] 3 All ER 1008 at 1010–1011, [1973] 1 WLR 1 at 4):

'It was held in the Court of Session that the appellant had to prove that his additional exposure to injury caused by his having to bicycle home unwashed caused the disease in the sense that it was more probable than not that this additional
f   exposure to injury was the cause of it. I do not think that that is the proper approach ... But I think that in cases like this we must take a broader view of causation. The medical evidence is to the effect that the fact that the man had to cycle home caked with grime and sweat added materially to the risk that this disease might develop. It does not and could not explain just why that is so. But experience shews that it is so. Plainly that must be because what happens while the man remains unwashed
g   can have a causative effect, though just how the cause operates is uncertain. I cannot accept the view expressed in the Inner House that once the man left the brick kiln he left behind the causes which made him liable to develop dermatitis. That seems to me quite inconsistent with a proper interpretation of the medical evidence. Nor can I accept the distinction drawn by the Lord Ordinary between materially increasing the risk that the disease will occur and making a material contribution to
h   its occurrence. There may be some logical ground for such a distinction where our knowledge of all the material factors is complete. But it has often been said that the legal concept of causation is not based on logic or philosophy. It is based on the practical way in which the ordinary man's mind works in the every-day affairs of life. From a broad and practical viewpoint I can see no substantial difference between saying that what the respondents did materially increased the risk of injury to the
j   appellant and saying that what the respondents did made a material contribution to his injury.'

Lord Wilberforce put the matter in this way ([1972] 3 All ER 1008 at 1012, [1973] 1 WLR 1 at 6):

'But the question remains whether a pursuer must necessarily fail if, after he has shown a breach of duty, involving an increase of risk of disease, he cannot positively

prove that this increase of risk caused or materially contributed to the disease while
his employers cannot positively prove the contrary. In this intermediate case there
is an appearance of logic in the view that the pursuer, on whom the onus lies, should
fail—a logic which dictated the judgments below. The question is whether we
should be satisfied, in factual situations like the present, with this logical approach.
In my opinion, there are further considerations of importance. First, it is a sound
principle that where a person has, by breach of duty of care, created a risk, and
injury occurs within the area of that risk, the loss should be borne by him unless he
shows that it had some other cause. Secondly, from the evidential point of view, one
may ask, why should a man who is able to show that his employer should have
taken certain precautions, because without them there is a risk, or an added risk, of
injury or disease, and who in fact sustains exactly that injury or disease, have to
assume the burden of proving more: namely, that it was the addition to the risk,
caused by the breach of duty, which caused or materially contributed to the injury?
In many cases, of which the present is typical, this is impossible to prove, just
because honest medical opinion cannot segregate the causes of an illness between
compound causes. And if one asks which of the parties, the workman or the
employers, should suffer from this inherent evidential difficulty, the answer as a
matter of policy or justice should be that it is the creator of that risk who, ex
hypothesi, must be taken to have foreseen the possibility of damage, who should
bear its consequences.'

Lord Simon said ([1972] 3 All ER 1008 at 1014, [1973] 1 WLR 1 at 8):

'In my view, a failure to take steps which would bring about a material reduction
of the risk involves, in this type of case, a substantial contribution to the injury. In
this type of case a stark distinction between breach of duty and causation is unreal.
If the provision of shower baths was (as the evidence showed) a precaution which
any reasonable employer in the respondents' position would take, it means that such
employer should have foreseen that failure to take the precaution would, more
probably than not, substantially contribute towards injury; this is sufficient prima
facie evidence.'

Then I refer to Lord Kilbrandon's speech ([1972] 3 All ER 1008 at 1015–1016, [1973]
1 WLR 1 at 9–10):

'As it was put to, and accepted by, the consultant physician giving evidence for
the respondents, assuming that a workman had to work in a hot atmosphere and
exposed to the risk of ash and dust over his working day, if he was given the
opportunity to have a shower, and in fact took the shower that would materially
reduce the risk to that man's skin of injury from those working conditions. It was
for this reason that the Court of Session has held that it was the duty of the
respondents, which they failed to carry out, to supply the appellant with facilities
for taking a shower after he had finished work. That can only be because knowledge
must be imputed to the respondents that if the appellant's body were to continue to
be exposed to the dirt and sweat, inevitably attendant on his conditions of work,
which were operating on him *after* he had finished work—being the only dirt and
sweat that a shower could have removed—it was more probable that he would
contract the disease than if no shower had been taken. It is, in the present state of
medical knowledge, impossible to say that if the appellant had taken a shower he
would certainly not have got the disease, and it is equally impossible to say that
another man, in exactly the same case as the appellant, would on the contrary
certainly have got it. In that state of facts, what the appellant had to establish, as a
condition of his substantiating a claim against the respondents, is that their admitted
breach of the duty which they owed to him caused or materially contributed to the
damage which he has suffered. He has proved that there was a precaution, neglected
by the respondents, which, if adopted by them, as their duty in law demanded,
would have made it less likely that he would have suffered that damage. The
argument against him, as I follow it, is that that only shows that the provision of a

shower bath would have reduced the risk of injury: it does not show that in his case
he would more probably not have contracted the disease had the bath been provided.
It would have been possible to state the argument in this way: "The appellant cannot
show that it is more probable than not that, if a shower had been provided, he as an
individual would not have contracted dermatitis. Therefore it is impossible to say
that the respondents were under a duty to him as an individual to supply a shower;
A cannot have owed to B a duty to take a precaution the absence of which B fails to
show probably caused him injury." The duty can only be examined in relation to
the individual who complains of the breach of it; it is not owed to him as a mere
potential victim of dermatitis; and this is unaffected by the fact that other men, for
reasons we do not understand, would not have required the benefit of the precaution.
But once the breach of duty to the appellant has been accepted, this argument seems
to me to become untenable. It depends on drawing a distinction between the
possibility and the probability of the efficacy of the precautions. I do not find it easy
to say in the abstract where one shades into the other; it seems to me to depend very
much on the nature of the case. This is a case in which the actual chain of events in
the man's body leading up to the injury is not clearly known. But there are effective
precautions which ought to be taken in order to prevent it. When you find it proved
(a) that the defenders knew that to take the precaution reduces the risk, chance,
possibility or probability of the contracting of a disease, (b) that the precaution has
not been taken, and (c) that the disease has supervened, it is difficult to see how those
defenders can demand more by way of proof of the probability that the failure
caused or contributed to the physical breakdown.'

On the basis of this authority, counsel for the plaintiff contended that, if the plaintiff
could show (1) that there was a general practice not to perform an anterior colporrhaphy
until at least three months after birth, (2) that one of the reasons for this practice was to
protect the patient from the risk of haemorrhage and a breakdown of the repair, (3) that
an operation was performed within four weeks and (4) that haemorrhage occurred and
the repair broke down, then the burden of showing that he was not in breach of duty
shifted to the defendants.

It must be correct on the basis of *McGhee* to say that the burden shifts so far as damages
are concerned. But does the burden shift so far as the duty is concerned? Must the
medical practitioner justify his departure from the usual practice?

It is very difficult to draw a distinction between the damage and the duty where the
duty arises only because of a need to guard against the damage. In *McGhee's* case it was
accepted there there was a breach of duty. In the present case the question of whether
there was a breach remains in issue.

It seems to me that it follows from *McGhee* that where there is a situation in which a
general duty of care arises and there is a failure to take a precaution, and that very damage
occurs against which the precaution is designed to be a protection, then the burden lies
on the defendant to show that he was not in breach of duty as well as to show that the
damage did not result from his breach of duty. I shall therefore apply this approach to
the evidence in this case. I first have to ask myself whether the plaintiff has established
that it is a general practice among gynaecologists that an anterior colporrhaphy should
not ordinarily be performed until at least three months after birth. That this is the
general practice was accepted by Professor Huntingford, Mr Smallwood, Mr Rickford,
the first defendant and Sir John Dewhurst. Professor Turnbull suggested late in the case
that this will apply only where there was prolapse of the bladder or uterus without stress
incontinence.

I am satisfied that this is the general practice. It is not an absolute rule: Mr Rickford
made passing reference to considering the operation at six weeks in a particular case.
Professor Huntingford, in one of his reports, refers to waiting 8 to 12 weeks. Exceptions
can be considered, but they require justification. I am satisfied that this is not a case
where there are two schools of thought. This is the general practice among gynaecologists
and any departure from it requires justification.

No witness, despite the vast experience that they combined, was able to point to any instance where this operation had been performed at less than three months let alone four weeks.

I come next to the reasons for this general practice. The first reason is that time is the great healer. In a great many cases stress incontinence will disappear without operation. Secondly, if an operation is necessary, the chances of success are much better after three months.

In the course of pregnancy the uterus increases greatly in size and consequently the blood supply to the uterus increases and the organs in the area of the uterus increase greatly in content. The tissues become engorged with blood. Following birth a process known as involution takes place which involves the disposal by the system of the surplus material as it returns to normal. The surplus material is carried away by the bloodstream in the veins which return the blood to the heart. While the tissues remain engorged, and the veins remain enlarged, they are softer and more liable to damage at operation. If they are so damaged they bleed; where the blood supply is abundant, they bleed profusely. Bleeding at the site of the buttress sutures softens the tissues in which the stitches are anchored so that they are likely to give way. If they do so, the repair is likely to break down. The bleeding, if substantial, is likely to lead to haemorrhage, which is always a serious complication. Therefore it is better to wait until three months, by which time one can be reasonably sure that involution will be complete. By that time the muscular tissue which may have been strained in the course of birth, especially where there has been a forceps delivery, will have had time to recover and the blood supply and the tissues will have returned to normal.

The return to normal may be assisted by pelvic floor exercises. As is a matter of routine women are instructed in these by a physiotherapist shortly after birth. An electrical treatment known as faradism may assist. So may the use of a pessary which may hold the bladder in the proper position while involution takes place.

An additional reason for delay is that it is better for a woman to complete her family before undergoing this operation as a subsequent birth may cause the repair to break down.

For these reasons, an operation may well be delayed for far longer than three months. But it is conceded that severe stress incontinence which is not yielding to time or treatment will be a reason for doing the operation sooner rather than later. So I am satisfied that the position can be summarised thus: it is better to wait for at least three months because recovery may be so good that an operation is not necessary, and, if it is not, it is better to wait until the body has so far recovered as to reduce the risk of haemorrhage and of breakdown of the operation as far as possible.

Some risk of haemorrhage always remains, but it is slight as anterior colporrhaphy is not normally a very bloody operation. This type of operation evolved in the 1880s. The general practice has developed as a result of the clinical experience of gynaecologists since then. It may be that gynaecologists err on the side of caution when estimating the time for involution to be completed, but the practice is hardly to be criticised on that account.

It is common ground that the operation did take place at four weeks, that haemorrhage occurred and that the operation did break down. In my view, counsel for the plaintiff has therefore succeeded in establishing the four matters which shift the burden of proof to the defendants. Counsel for the defendants points out that it is only a rule of thumb that one should wait for three months and not an absolute rule. Initially he conducted his cross-examination on a basis that an operation at four weeks would be justified (a) where the stress incontinence is very severe (it is common ground that the plaintiff's incontinence was very severe), (b) where no improvement has been achieved by conservative methods, and (c) where the plaintiff finds her condition quite intolerable.

Now I come to look in more detail at the treatment to see whether all factors were taken into account in arriving at the decision to operate. I start at the point of 27 June when the plaintiff returned to hospital. At that stage Professor Turnbull delegated to the first defendant the day-to-day care of the plaintiff and in particular her counselling. He felt that he had got off on the wrong foot when he saw the plaintiff on 16 June. She appeared to resent the suggestion that the incontinence might be due to some physical a defect in her. His memory is not clear whether he saw the plaintiff on 27 June but there is no doubt that he was in close touch with her case.

Neither the first defendant nor Professor Turnbull were then aware of the blunders that had been made when the plaintiff was discharged. No inquiry was made of Dr Scott at the Churchill Hospital as to the plaintiff's treatment and progress, nor was there any consultation with the plaintiff's general practitioner. The plaintiff came back to hospital complaining that she was no better, in a very miserable condition. On examination no

b sign of improvement was found. The first defendant then decided to keep her in hospital over the weekend and to try the use of a pessary. This was not successful.

The evidence of the plaintiff's three experts and of Sir John Dewhurst was that, if one pessary did not give the results, another shape or size should be tried with the patient's consent. The first defendant tells me that the plaintiff found the use of a pessary distasteful, and this I accept, although the plaintiff could not remember its use. But it

c was plain to me from the first defendant's evidence that he made no real attempt to persuade the plaintiff to try an alternative type or to explain to her why a further attempt was necessary.

The first defendant and Professor Turnbull arrived at the conclusion that the conservative treatment had failed. This conclusion was not in my opinion justified by the facts. It had been ordered on 16 June and it cannot be said that it had been given a

d fair trial by 27 June.

It is not simply a matter of the plaintiff's failure to attend the Churchill Hospital: there is no consideration of what Dr Scott had advised, no consideration of whether she had been doing the exercises properly and no appreciation that the general practitioner had not been able to help her because he was not properly informed. I think Professor Turnbull arrived at his conclusion all too hastily, partly because he was not well informed

e and partly because he had little confidence in the conservative treatment. His view was that by and large this condition was cured either by the lapse of time or by operation and that where no improvement showed during the early weeks surgery was indicated. He held this view despite the fact that he alone of all the witnesses had had experience of a case as severe as the case of the plaintiff's. He remembered two cases of such severity many years ago when he was a registrar and said that so far as his memory went they

f were both cured by conservative treatment.

Nor am I satisfied that the plaintiff found her condition intolerable. I accept that she was deeply distressed and rather desperate by 27 June, but this was a condition which was partly due to the way in which her discharge on 19 June had been bungled. One of her main complaints was that she was not kept informed as to her condition. I refer to the first letter which was sent to the hospital by her solicitors. This was sent on 9

g September and it says:

'We have advised Mrs Clark about her legal situation at her request. But at this stage we are concerned with another matter: namely, that Mrs Clark is not satisfied that she is being kept fully informed of what is being done for her by her hospital. We should be obliged if you will ensure that the fullest possible information is passed on to Mrs Clark and shall be glad to hear from you that this will be done.'

h Professor Turnbull accepted that, although the plaintiff was very upset, she was co-operative. He had no doubt that she would act on his advice and that her husband would support her in doing so. He agreed that it would have been perfectly reasonable for apology to have been made and for assurance given that things would be put right, and that she could then have been urged to pursue her conservative treatment. At first I

j thought he agreed that he would have done this if he had known the true facts. But later it appeared he was saying that while this would have been a reasonable course, he would not have followed it. He took the view that it was safe to operate at one month and that she should be spared further suffering.

One cannot but sympathise with the plaintiff. There is no doubt that she suffered greatly but I do not think that it was established that her suffering was intolerable. She had an attentive husband; she had gone to live with her parents; she was in the care of

her general practitioner and the health visitor, both of whom were helpful. A defect such
as incontinence can more easily be borne if it is talked through. This is illustrated by the
way in which the marital trouble caused by the incontinence has now been overcome
and the plaintiff is now very close to her husband. Given proper counselling as to her
condition and intelligent deployment of those available to help, a great deal could have
been done to alleviate her position for the next two months. So I find that conservative
treatment had not failed because it had never been properly tried and that the plaintiff's
condition, though grievous, was not intolerable. Therefore the defence as initially put
fails.

Now I come to consider the defence as it developed after initial cross-examination. The
first defendant began it when he asserted that this case was unique and that therefore the
rule of thumb about not operating before three months did not apply.

This did not impress me. The operation is just the same whether the condition is
severe or moderate. The reasons for the practice appear to be just the same. The first
defendant agreed that it would not be right for the surgeon to perform the operation too
soon and thereby risk failure simply because the patient was distressed. Professor
Turnbull went a good deal further. He boldly asserted that at four weeks involution was
virtually complete and that an operation stood as good a chance of success as at three
months. He pointed to the hospital notes on 27 June '6/52 AV Uterus' to show that the
plaintiff was involuting rapidly. The significance of this note was that it showed the
plaintiff's uterus had reduced by 27 June to the size it would have been when she was six
weeks pregnant. Mr Rickford said he would have expected it to have been at the ten
weeks size.

It was common ground that involution is rapid immediately after birth and was in
large part complete by four weeks but no other witness than Dr Hytten and possibly
Professor Turnbull took the view that it was wholly complete. Sir John Dewhurst said
that in any case he would want to be sure that involution was complete or well nigh
complete before he would operate. It would seem to me to be right that an operation
on a patient who was suspected of having a natural weakness, as was the case of the plaintiff,
should be delayed until it was reasonably certain that involution was complete.

The defendants relied on the evidence of Dr Hytten to support Professor Turnbull's
views. Dr Hytten was a physiologist who was medically qualified as well as being a PhD
but had not had any clinical experience for many years. He had made a search of learned
articles to establish how fast involution took place after childbirth. We examined several
articles but I did not find them very satisfying as a basis for justifying operative treatment.
The material on which findings were based was very slender. I attach more importance
to Dr Hytten's own view. He said that there were no studies as to involution of the
bladder neck, but a study of other organs of generation showed that involution was
complete in four weeks. There was no reason in his view why the bladder neck should
be different. Indeed, he doubted whether that part became engorged with blood during
pregnancy to the extent that gynaecologists supposed.

Dr Hytten agreed that no gynaecologist had ever asked his views on this. It would
appear that contact between the physiologist and gynaecologist is lacking, at least in this
field. This is strange, as the reason for the practice I have described is largely physiological.
It may arise because there is so little opportunity of conducting studies of the behaviour
of the bladder neck.

Sir John Dewhurst, with his great experience, said that he did not know of the views
expressed by Dr Hytten before this case. He was ready to accept that the orthodox view
might require to be altered if Dr Hytten were right. But it is quite clear that Dr Hytten's
views, be they right or wrong, have not yet affected the practice on which the plaintiff
relies. I do not think that these views could possibly justify a departure from the general
practice. A deal more inquiry is needed. I have it very much in mind that future research
may show that gynaecologists have been unduly cautious and Professor Turnbull is right.
Practice may be varied in the light of experience so that it sanctions this operation even
at four weeks at some future time. These are matters on which I cannot possibly judge.

a   As of today I am satisfied that there is a general practice from which Professor Turnbull departed when he asked the first defendant to undertake this operation. He was misled by a misunderstanding about the plaintiff's first discharge, he was sceptical about the reasons for the general practice and he was mistrustful of conservative measures; the only conservative measure which he really valued was to allow time to pass, but in this case only a very short period had elapsed without improvement.

I find the second defendants vicariously responsible both for him and for his staff who
b   had misled him. They were in breach of duty.

I now come to consider whether the defendants can show that the damage suffered did not flow from that breach of duty. The defendants rely heavily on the note made by the first defendant at the operation, 'Average or less blood loss', and also on the letter that he wrote to the plaintiff's general practitioner immediately after the operation reporting an uncomplicated and successful operation. Yet the first defendant agreed in cross-
c   examination that bleeding was severe and that it was greater than you would expect with an anterior colporrhaphy. The plaintiff relies on the note, 'Friable vaginal skin'. 'Friable' means thin and liable to tear. If involution were complete the vaginal skin of a woman of the plaintiff's age should not be in this condition.

The first defendant, as was his usual practice, used adrenalin at the operation to reduce bleeding. There is a dispute as to how far adrenalin reduced bleeding: Professor
d   Huntingford said it reduced it to virtually nothing in all blood vessels whether engorged or not; Sir John Dewhurst said that he thought it reduced it proportionately so that engorged veins still had a greater flow but he declined any expert knowledge of this. I cannot resolve such a clash. The first defendant said there was no engorgement. But after this lapse of time I doubt whether he has any recollection, apart from his notes.

Counsel for the defendants pointed out that the reduction in the size of the uterus was
e   also consistent with rapid involution. Despite this, there was no dispute that the haemorrhage had taken place. I think the first defendant was a little slow to recognise it and the evidence is plain that he was unable to find haematoma. There can be no doubt that there was substantial haemorrhage. Where then did the blood come from? The first defendant agreed that internal bleeding must arise from one of two sources: either vascularity or the fact that he had punctured a blood vessel which he could not see when
f   inserting his stitches. It was odd that this latter explanation emerged first when the first defendant was under cross-examination. He said that he had thought of it on the afternoon of the operation and if it was thought to be important it should have played a larger part in counsel for the defendants' very thorough cross-examination of the plaintiff's witnesses. At first I viewed it with some suspicion as a rather desperate afterthought. I asked the first defendant some questions about it. He explained that
g   when he inserted his stitches by needle he would be going into an area in which he could not see. If a loss of blood were immediately apparent he would tie off the blood vessels, but as he was penetrating an area beyond the operation site bleeding might not be apparent before the operation site was closed. The whole operation only took about half an hour. Once the site was closed bleeding would not be visible unless the bleeding took place per vaginam. It would only become apparent from such signs as raised pulse rate
h   and fall in blood pressure.

The first defendant's theory acquired support in a curious way. On the eleventh day of the trial, Professor Turnbull produced a new theory as to the location of the haematoma. As this had never been put to the plaintiff's witnesses I allowed Professor Huntingford to be recalled yet again. In the course of dealing with this point, counsel for the defendants asked him fresh questions about engorgement. Professor Huntingford said that the blood
j   which the plaintiff lost was in his view predominantly venous. The venous blood is returned to the heart by the veins at a comparatively sedate pace. The arterial blood is pumped out by the heart to the various parts of the body through the arteries much faster.

Professor Huntingford's view was that if the plaintiff's loss of blood had been arterial she would have show signs of severe shock which are not indicated by the hospital notes.

The incision in the vaginal wall at operation was bound to cut both veins and arteries. But there are no arteries around the bladder neck. In that area there are one or more venous plexuses, that is to say webs of vein, and it was Professor Huntingford's view that the internal bleeding probably originated here.

This was the area that the first defendant's needle would penetrate when making his stitches. His answer therefore gave support to the first defendant's explanation. Professor Huntingford still adhered to his view that bleeding was severe because the venous plexuses were engorged. He agreed that there was nothing in the hospital notes to support this point of view. One might expect similar notes in the case of a patient who had not recently been pregnant and who haemorrhaged.

It is at this point that the burden of proof becomes so important. If the first defendant is right as to the source of bleeding, it came from the venous plexus which he could not see, so he could not tell whether it was engorged or not. It is really impossible for me to make a finding whether the veins were engorged or not. In order to show that there was no damage, the defendants would have to show that they were not engorged and that on the balance of probabilities the breakdown of the operation was due to one of those haemorrhages which may occur without negligence. This in my view the defendants failed to do.

The theory that Professor Turnbull propounded on the eleventh day was that the abdominal pain suffered by the plaintiff was caused by a haematoma which had formed as a result of the haemorrhage and which was compressing the ureters, that is to say, in effect, the pipes which lead from the kidneys to the bladder. I found this theory so difficult to understand that at the time I failed to examine its relevance to the case. I still am unable to follow it. It may be that it related to the criticism of the post-operational treatment which was then still a live issue. In any case, I felt that the evidence given in reply by Professor Huntingford reduced this theory to the category of the distinctly improbable. I was confirmed in this view by the evidence of Sir John Dewhurst. I do not think that this theory would assist the defendants. There were times in the course of the trial when I felt an attempt was being made to blind me with science.

Having considered all the points raised by the defendants, I hold that the defendants have failed to establish that it was justifiable to perform the operation of anterior colporrhaphy on the plaintiff only four weeks after birth. Consequently, there was a breach of the duty of care owed to the plaintiff. I do not need to seek to divide that responsibility against individuals since the second defendants are vicariously liable for all those concerned in treating the plaintiff. Further I hold that the defendants have failed to show that on the balance of probabilities the injury which the plaintiff sustained, namely the haemorrhage and the breakdown of the operational repair, did not result from the breach of duty.

The plaintiff therefore succeeds in her action and I have to consider quantum of damage. It is clear that the plaintiff could not have been certain that the operation would have been successful. She would have undergone an unpleasant period waiting for the operation and then, through nobody's fault, might have found that it did her little or no good. Her subsequent history shows that she did have a weakness in the region of the bladder neck, however hurt she may have felt when Professor Turnbull told her so. I have been referred to *Davies v Taylor* [1972] 3 All ER 836, [1974] AC 207. This shows that when one is dealing with a hypothetical event one values the chance the plaintiff has of a successful outcome. One does not have to decide on the balance of probabilities what the outcome will be.

It seems to me therefore, and I think counsel agreed with this, that the correct approach is first to value the plaintiff's disability. Then I should make a small deduction to allow for the pain and suffering she would have undergone while awaiting an operation. Then I should discount this figure to allow for the fact that the plaintiff's chances of a successful outcome were a good deal less than 100%.

I know of no authority which has any bearing on the damages appropriate to stress incontinence, nor have I been referred to any. Professor Turnbull's evidence was that the plaintiff was a rather fastidious young woman who felt herself demeaned by this

condition. I have already described her condition today. An alternative repair operation
a is available but neither Professor Huntingford nor Sir John Dewhurst recommended it. I
therefore treat her as someone whose condition will continue until the menopause when
according to Professor Huntingford it is likely to get worse.

I regard this as a very serious interference in the enjoyment of life. No doubt the
plaintiff has learnt to live with it to some extent but it is something which will never be
long absent in her mind. On the other hand, it is not a seriously disabling injury, so I
b must not allow myself to overstress the disgust that it engenders. I think an appropriate
figure is £10,000. To this there falls to be added a figure of £600 for special damage.
There is a continuing loss in respect of pads, extra pants, washing and dry cleaning. The
figure for this has been agreed at £108·50 per annum. She is now 28 and this loss will be
lifelong. I think 15 years' purchase will be appropriate. This then totals £1,627·50.

There is also a figure for loss of earnings. She would have wished to go back to office
c work and feels, I think rightly, that this will not be possible in her condition. She will
therefore take a part-time driving job. It is agreed that there will be a net loss of £520
per annum. There is no reason to suppose that she will not carry on with this job for
many years. But she is not the main wage earner of the family as her husband has a
regular job with the Post Office.

I think it would therefore be right to take a rather low number of years' purchase and
d it seems to me that ten is the correct multiplier. The figure under this head will therefore
be £5,200. This gives me a total of £17,427·50.

I must deduct from this a figure for pain and suffering while awaiting the operation if
it had been done at the right time and I put this at £300. The general chance of obtaining
a reasonable result from this operation has been put at 70% to 80%. The figure that the
first defendant put to the plaintiff was two in three. This is slightly lower. I think it
e accurately reflects the fact that the plaintiff was a problem case and the chances of success
were therefore a little lower. I therefore take two-thirds of £17,127·50, which is
£11,418·33.

I have already given my reasons why the plaintiff should not succeed against the first
defendant. Accordingly, the case against the first defendant will be dismissed. She will
have judgment against the second defendants for £11,418·33.

f I cannot leave this case without expressing my regret that I have had to spend so long
examining the decision of so distinguished a gynaecologist as Professor Turnbull. I trust
that what I have had to say in no way tarnishes a great reputation, and I would echo the
words that were used by Donaldson LJ when *Whitehouse v Jordan* [1980] 1 All ER 650 at
666 was in the Court of Appeal. He said:

g 'There are very few professional men who will assert that they have never fallen
below the high standards rightly expected of them. That they have never been
negligent. If they do, it is unlikely that they should be believed. And this is as true
of lawyers as of medical men. If the judge's conclusion is right, what distinguishes
Mr Jordan from his professional colleagues is not that on one isolated occasion his
acknowledged skill partially deserted him, but that damage resulted. Whether or
not damage results from a negligent act is almost always a matter of chance and it
h ill becomes anyone to adopt an attitude of superiority.'

Counsel for the defendants has referred to Professor Turnbull's Olympian reputation.
I hope Professor Turnbull will take comfort in the thought that even Apollo, the god of
healing, and the father of Aesculapius, had his moments of weakness.

j *Judgment for the plaintiff accordingly.*

Solicitors: *Ferguson Bricknell & Co*, Oxford (for the plaintiff); *Hempsons* (for the first
defendant); *Cole & Cole*, Oxford (for the second defendant).

K Mydeen Esq   Barrister.

R v Goldstein

    a

HOUSE OF LORDS

LORD DIPLOCK, LORD EDMUND-DAVIES, LORD KEITH OF KINKEL, LORD ROSKILL AND LORD BRIGHTMAN

18 DECEMBER 1982, 20 JANUARY 1983

Criminal law – Trial – Evidence in absence of jury – Question of law – Interpretation of EEC *b*
Treaty – Question whether prohibition on importation contrary to terms of treaty – Whether
question of law to be determined by judge in absence of jury – European Communities Act 1972, s
3(1) – EEC Treaty, arts 30, 36.

The issue whether a prohibition on importation imposed by United Kingdom legislation
is ineffective by virtue of art 30[a] of the EEC Treaty, which prohibits quantitative *c*
restrictions on imports between member states of the EEC, or is 'justified on grounds
of . . . public policy or public security [or] the protection of . . . life', within art 36[b] of the
treaty, is a question regarding the meaning or effect of the EEC Treaty which, by virtue
of s 3(1)[c] of the European Communities Act 1972, is to be treated as a question of law for
the purposes of all legal proceedings. Accordingly, if that issue arises in a criminal trial it
is an issue for the judge and not the jury to decide and may be heard by the judge in the *d*
absence of the jury (see p 435 *a*, p 437 *g* to *j* and p 438 *c* to *h*, post).

Where a party seeks to propound to the House of Lords a series of propositions of law
on which his case is based, he should include them in, or with, his printed case or (in
default) hand them in as a typed statement at the hearing (see p 438 *d* to *j*, post).

Decision of the Court of Appeal [1982] 3 All ER 53 affirmed.

 e

Notes

For prohibitions on imports to the United Kingdom from member states of the European
Community, see 12 Halsbury's Laws (4th edn) paras 1054–1063.

For evidence in the absence of the jury, see 11 ibid para 302, and for cases on the
subject, see 14(2) Digest (Reissue) 827–828, 7097–7098.

For the European Communities Act 1972, s 3, see 42 Halsbury's Statutes (3rd edn) 84. *f*

For the EEC Treaty, arts 30, 36, see 42A ibid 525, 528.

Case referred to in opinions

Imports of Poultry Meat, Re, EC Commission v UK Case 40/82 [1982] 3 CMLR 497, CJEC.

Appeal

 g

Alexander Joseph Goldstein appealed with leave of the Court of Appeal granted on 2
April 1982 against the decision of the Court of Appeal, Criminal Division (Lord Lane CJ,
Lloyd and Eastham JJ) ([1982] 3 All ER 53, [1982] 1 WLR 804) on 1 April 1982
dismissing the appellant's appeal against his conviction under s 170(2) of the Customs
and Excise Management Act 1979 of being knowingly concerned in the fraudulent
evasion of the prohibition on importation of certain radiotelephonic apparatus imposed *h*
by reg 3 of the Radio Telephonic Transmitters (Control of Manufacture and Importation)
Order 1968, SI 1968/61, made under s 7(1) of the Wireless Telegraphy Act 1967, in the
Crown Court at Ipswich on 2 December 1980 before his Honour Judge Binns and a jury.
The facts are set out in the opinion of Lord Diplock.

Louis Blom-Cooper QC and *Gordon Bennett* for the appellant.
Peter Archer QC and *John Devaux* for the Crown.   *j*

Their Lordships took time for consideration.

---

a   Article 30 is set out at p 435 *e*, post
b   Article 36, so far as material, is set out at p 435 *g*, post
c   Section 3(1) is set out at p 437 *d*, post

20 January. The following opinions were delivered.

LORD DIPLOCK. My Lords, this appeal turns on a short question of statutory construction: do the words of s 3(1) of the European Communities Act 1972 mean what they say? Despite the ingenuity of the arguments to the contrary that have been addressed to us, my answer to that question is Yes.

The only facts that it is necessary to recount are that the appellant was caught in the act of clandestinely importing into the United Kingdom from Belgium at the port of Felixstowe 50 'citizens' band' radio sets capable of transmitting on a frequency between 26·1 and 29·7 MHz (the apparatus).

The manufacture, whether or not for sale, and the importation into the United Kingdom of apparatus of this class has, since 1968, been prohibited by the Radiotelephonic Transmitters (Control of Manufacture and Importation) Order 1968, SI 1968/61, made under s 7(1) of the Wireless Telegraphy Act 1967.

The appellant was charged on indictment with an offence under s 170(2) of the Customs and Excise Management Act 1979 of being knowingly concerned in a fraudulent evasion of such prohibition with respect to the apparatus. On arraignment he pleaded not guilty to the offence; and the facts relating to the clandestine importation were proved and not disputed at the trial which was held in the Crown Court at Ipswich before his Honour Judge Binns and a jury. At the conclusion of the prosecution's case a submission made on his behalf that the 1968 order, in so far as it prohibited the importation of the apparatus from member states of the European Communities, was contrary to art 30 of the EEC Treaty, and was pro tanto rendered ultra vires and of no effect in law by s 2(1) of the European Communities Act 1972.

Article 30 provides:

'Quantitative restrictions on imports and all measures having equivalent effect shall, without prejudice to the following provisions, be prohibited between Member States.'

This article, it is well settled, is one to which, in accordance with the treaty, legal effect is to be given in the United Kingdom without further enactment and is therefore one to which s 2(1) of the European Communities Act 1972 applies. It is to be recognised in law and enforced accordingly. It is also well established, not surprisingly, by the jurisprudence (ie case law) of the Court of Justice of the European Communities that a total prohibition on imports is a quantitative restriction within the meaning of art 30.

This ban on quantitative restrictions, however, is not absolute: it is qualified by art 36 of the EEC Treaty which, so far as is relevant to the present appeal, reads:

'The provisions of Articles 30 to 34 shall not preclude prohibitions or restrictions on imports . . . justified on grounds of . . . public policy or public security; the protection of health and life of humans . . . Such prohibitions or restrictions shall not, however, constitute a means of arbitrary discrimination or a disguised restriction on trade between Member States.'

At the trial of the appellant the prosecution, while conceding that prima facie the prohibition on importation of the apparatus from member states imposed by the 1968 order fell within art 30, contended that it was nevertheless saved by art 36 as being justified on grounds of public policy, public security and the protection of health and life of humans. It was, rightly, conceded by the prosecution that the onus of proving that the prohibition was justified under art 36 lay on the Crown and that for this purpose it would be necessary to call evidence directed to showing what adverse effects the abolition of the prohibition of importation of the apparatus into the United Kingdom from member states would have on public policy, public security and the protection of health and life of humans. Accordingly, after uncontested evidence of the facts of the clandestine importation had been given, oral evidence directed to this purpose was called before the judge in the absence of the jury, a course to which counsel for the appellant agreed. The judge expressed himself as being satisfied beyond reasonable doubt by that evidence that the prohibition was justified on all three grounds mentioned above. He accordingly

ruled that the existence of the offence with which the accused was charged was made out
and, again with the acquiescence of counsel for the appellant, he directed the jury that
on the uncontested facts as to the importation of the apparatus by the appellant they were
bound to convict him of the offence with which he was charged.

The jurisprudence of the European Court on the scope of art 36 in creating exceptions
to the prohibition on quantitative restrictions of imports imposed by art 30 is to be found
in a series of decisions of the European Court that are referred to and conveniently
summarised in the opinion of Mr Advocate-General Capotorti in one of the latest cases,
Re Imports of Poultry Meat, EC Commission v UK Case 40/82 [1982] 3 CMLR 497 at 516, in
a passage from which I have omitted any reference to arbitrary discrimination or
disguised restriction on trade between member states, since it is conceded that the 1968
order which prohibits manufacture in the United Kingdom as well as importation does
not fall within the last sentence of art 36. The passage reads:

> '. . . a State which relies upon Article 36 and upon which it is incumbent to prove
> that the restrictive measures introduced satisfy the conditions laid down in that
> provision may not confine itself to stating that the measures are in fact based on one
> of the grounds indicated—for example, protection of the health and life of animals—
> but must demonstrate that those measures are necessary in order to attain the
> desired objective; and that it was impossible to take an alternative course of action
> which was equally effective and yet less liable to restrict trade.'

To demonstrate what it is required to demonstrate in order to enable a state to avail
itself of the derogation from art 30 for which art 36 provides, it is necessary to adduce
factual evidence (1) to identify the various mischiefs which the challenged restrictive
measures were intended to prevent, (2) to show that those mischiefs could not have
equally effectively been cured by other measures less restrictive of trade and (3) to show
that the measures were not disproportionately severe having regard to the gravity of the
mischiefs against which they were directed. This last-mentioned consideration involves
the concept in Community law (derived principally from German law) called
'proportionality'. In plain English it means 'You must not use a steam hammer to crack
a nut, if a nutcracker would do'.

It was for these purposes alone that oral expert evidence was adduced before Judge
Binns. The effect of it was summarised by the Court of Appeal as follows ([1982] 3 All
ER 53 at 56–57, [1982] 1 WLR 804 at 808):

> 'The effect of their [sc the expert witnesses] evidence, if believed, was to show that
> the use of the citizens' band radio on the 27 MHz waveband was to adversely affect
> a whole variety of electronic devices which are in use up and down the length and
> breadth of this country. But suffice it to mention but a few. First of all, aircraft
> instrument landing systems, which operate either on this wavelength or a harmonic
> of it; hospital bleep paging systems, whereby doctors and officials in hospitals can
> be summoned by a centrally operated radio signal; fire services and police wave-
> lengths and communication systems; alarm systems which are available to some old
> people living on their own to communicate to a central point if they are in need of
> assistance and so on. There was one particular witness, a Major A, doing service in
> Northern Ireland. He gave specific evidence that citizens' band radios are a method
> popular among terrorists in Northern Ireland, both for detonating by remote control
> explosive devices and for alerting fellow terrorists to police movements and so on,
> and are therefore, in that part of the United Kingdom, a valuable adjunct to murder
> and violence.'

The appellant's submission in the Court of Appeal, raised by an eleventh-hour
amendment to his notice of appeal despite the consent of his counsel in the Crown Court
to the course there followed by the judge, was that the evidence thus summarised by the
Court of Appeal and called exclusively for the purpose of demonstrating that the
prohibition of import of the apparatus into the United Kingdom from member states

was justified by art 36 ought to have been given in the presence of the jury, and that it
was the function of the jury alone on a proper direction from the judge as to the meaning
and effect of Community law to determine whether that evidence established beyond
reasonable doubt the validity under art 36 of the 1968 order in so far as it imposed a
prohibition on the importation of the apparatus into the United Kingdom from Belgium
by the appellant.

This submission, which was rejected by the Court of Appeal, is reflected in the
questions of law which it certified as being involved, viz:

'(1) Is the issue whether the prohibition on importation contained in the
Radiotelephonic Transmitters (Control of Manufacture and Importation) Order
1968, Statutory Instrument No. 61 of 1968, is ineffective by virtue of Articles 30
and 36 of the Treaty establishing the European Economic Community to be decided
by the Judge alone, whether or not evidence has to be called? (2) Does the answer
to question (1) differ depending on whether such issue is raised before or after
arraignment?'

My Lords, to answer these questions it is in my view unnecessary to go further than to
look at s 3(1) of the European Communities Act 1972, which is in the following terms:

'For the purposes of all legal proceedings any question as to the meaning or effect
of any of the Treaties, or as to the validity, meaning or effect of any Community
instrument, shall be treated as a question of law (and, if not referred to the European
Court, be for determination as such in accordance with the principles laid down by
and any relevant decision of the European Court).'

The 1968 order and the 1967 Act under which it was made pre-dated the European
Communities Act 1972 and the entry of the United Kingdom as a member state of the
European Economic Community, so the determination of the question whether the
importation into the United Kingdom of apparatus of the class described in the order
after the United Kingdom had become a member state of the EEC still constituted an
offence, notwithstanding that such importation was from another member state,
depended on whether in English law arts 30 and 36 of the EEC Treaty, on their true
construction, had the effect of repealing the 1968 order or rendering it ultra vires to the
extent, at any rate, that it purported to apply to the importation of the apparatus from
other member states.

This question is in my view incontestably a question as to the meaning and effect of
one of the treaties. It thus falls fairly and squarely within s 3(1) of the European
Communities Act 1972, and by virtue of that subsection is for the purposes of all legal
proceedings to be treated as a question of law, and thus, in a criminal trial, as a question
for the judge and not a question for the jury. Nothing could in my view be plainer.

So I would answer the first certified question Yes.

The second certified question I would answer No. In view of the express provisions of
s 3(1) of the European Communities Act 1972, it cannot make any difference at what
stage of the legal proceedings a question arises as to the effect or meaning of any
Community instrument. The question is always to be treated as a question of law.

It is not possible to foresee all the circumstances in which such a question of law may
arise in the course of legal proceedings and on this matter it would, in my view, be
unwise for this House to assume the role of auspices. So far as criminal trials, whether
summary or on indictment, are concerned, it would in my view be appropriate for your
Lordships to leave it to the Criminal Division of the Court of Appeal to lay down such
guidelines for trial courts as its experience may suggest are desirable as to the most
convenient procedure for dealing with s 3(1) questions if they should arise. I see no
reason, however, for differing from the view expressed by the Court of Appeal in its
judgment in the instant case that, where it is apparent from the outset (as it may not
always be) that a s 3(1) question will arise, the most appropriate time to take it is by a
motion to quash the indictment before arraignment.

My Lords, it was also submitted on behalf of the appellant that Judge Binns had misdirected himself as to the meaning of art 36 of the EEC Treaty in that he had failed to consider whether the prosecution had shown that the mischief proved by the expert evidence summarised by the Court of Appeal could not have equally effectively been cured by other measures less drastic than the total prohibition of importation. For my part, I have been unable to discern in his judgment any such misdirection. No practical alternative to complete prohibition was suggested or put to the expert witnesses in cross-examination, except that all the important services referred to in the evidence should change to some frequency different from that which had been hitherto reserved for them and on which the apparatus was designed to operate. This would indeed be using a steam hammer to crack a nut, and the judge was, in my view, quite right to pay no attention to it. Even assuming that he did misdirect himself, however, the question was one of law and accordingly it was one on which the Court of Appeal itself was bound to correct him if he were wrong. The Court of Appeal was referred to the relevant case law of the European Court and did not misdirect itself. So there is nothing in this submission either.

I would accordingly dismiss the appeal and answer the certified questions in the manner I have indicated above.

In the course of his sustained argument, counsel for the appellant propounded a series of propositions which I have not found it necessary to set out for the purpose of answering the certified questions and disposing of the appeal. These propositions were read out at dictation speed so that your Lordships could transcribe them into your notebooks. It would be of great convenience where this method of exposition is adopted if each of their Lordships could be provided at the hearing with a typed statement of the propositions to be relied on, if these propositions have not already been set out in the party's written case, which is the proper place for them.

LORD EDMUND-DAVIES. My Lords, I have had the advantage of reading in draft the speech prepared by my noble and learned friend Lord Diplock. I agree with it, and for the reasons he gives I would answer the certified questions in the manner indicated by him and dismiss the appeal.

LORD KEITH OF KINKEL. My Lords, for the reasons given in the speech of my noble and learned friend Lord Diplock, which I have had the benefit of reading in draft and with which I agree, I too would dismiss the appeal.

LORD ROSKILL. My Lords, I have had the advantage of reading in draft the speech delivered by my noble and learned friend Lord Diplock. I agree with it and for the reasons he gives I would dismiss the appeal.

LORD BRIGHTMAN. My Lords, I also would dismiss this appeal for the reasons given by my noble and learned friend Lord Diplock, and I would answer the certified questions in the manner indicated by him.

I respectfully and whole-heartedly agree with the concluding observations of my noble and learned friend Lord Diplock. I find it invaluable to be presented by counsel with a series of carefully formulated propositions on which his case is based. But I find it both irksome and time-comsuming to have to take down such propositions in long-hand, when they could so readily be incuded in, or with, the printed case or (in default) handed in at the hearing. I have ventured to repeat what your Lordship has said, because this plea has been made so frequently without effect during my brief experience in your Lordships' House, and I thought that if it was said twice it might perhaps be heard.

Appeal dismissed.

Solicitors: *Harold Weston & Co* (for the appellant); *Solicitor for the Customs and Excise.*

Mary Rose Plummer   Barrister.

Griffiths and another v Secretary of State for the Environment and another

HOUSE OF LORDS

LORD FRASER OF TULLYBELTON, LORD ELWYN-JONES, LORD SCARMAN, LORD BRIDGE OF HARWICH AND LORD BRANDON OF OAKBROOK

16, 17 NOVEMBER 1982, 20 JANUARY 1983

Town and country planning – Appeal to minister against refusal of planning permission – Notification of decision – Notification by letter – Challenge to minister's decision – Time limit for making application to High Court to quash decision – Time limit of six weeks from date on which 'action' is taken – Whether time limit running from date letter signed and dated or from when notification received by applicant – Town and Country Planning Act 1971, s 245(1).

The appellant sought planning permission under the Town and Country Planning Act 1971 for the erection of a farmhouse on his land. The local authority refused his application and he appealed under s 36 of the 1971 Act to the Secretary of State for the Environment, who dismissed his appeal. The appellant was notified of the Secretary of State's decision by a letter dated and posted on 8 December 1980 which he received on 13 December 1980. Under s 245(1)ᵃ the appellant, as a person aggrieved by the Secretary of State's action, was entitled to apply to the High Court to quash the Secretary of State's decision provided he applied 'within six weeks from the date on which . . . [the Secretary of State's] action is taken'. The appellant applied to the High Court on 22 January 1981 for an order quashing the Secretary of State's decision. The Secretary of State applied to strike out the application on the ground that the six-week time limit ran from the date on which the Secretary of State's letter was signed or posted and therefore expired on 19 January, ie before the appellant made his application to the High Court. The appellant contended that the six-week time limit did not begin to run until he received notification of the Secretary of State's decision and that therefore the time limit did not expire until 24 January 1981. The judge upheld the Secretary of State's contentions and struck out the appellant's application. The appellant's appeal to the Court of Appeal was dismissed. The appellant appealed to the House of Lords.

Held (Lord Scarman dissenting) – When deciding an appeal under s 36 of the 1971 Act the process of decision making by the Secretary of State was completed for the purposes of s 245 of that Act when the letter recording the Secretary of State's decision was typed, signed and date-stamped. Accordingly, the date on which 'action' was taken by the Secretary of State in respect of the appellant's planning application was 8 December 1980 and the time limit for applying to the High Court ran from that date. The appellant's High Court application was therefore time-barred and properly struck out. The appeal would accordingly be dismissed (see p 440 *d g* and p 446 *j* to p 447 *a* and *f* to *j*, post).

Notes

For appeals against decisions of the Secretary of State in town and country planning matters, see 37 Halsbury's Laws (3rd edn) 329–331, paras 434–437.

For the Town and Country Planning Act 1971, ss 36, 242, 245, see 41 Halsbury's Statutes (3rd edn) 1628, 1854, 1859.

Case referred to in opinions

Carltona Ltd v Comrs of Works [1943] 2 All ER 560, CA, 17 Digest (Reissue) 490, *131*.

Appeal

P Eldridge Griffiths and his wife Hilma A Griffiths appealed by leave of the Appeal

---

a   Section 245(1), is set out at p 444 *g h*, post

Committee of the House of Lords granted on 29 March 1982 against the decision of the Court of Appeal (Cumming-Bruce, Templeman and Dunn LJJ) on 26 January 1982 *a* dismissing the appellants' appeal from an order dated 10 March 1982 of Sir Douglas Frank QC sitting as a deputy judge of the High Court in chambers affirming the decision of Master Thompson on 4 March 1981 striking out an application by the appellants to quash a decision of the first respondent, the Secretary of State for the Environment, whereby, by a letter signed by a duly authorised officer dated 8 December 1980, he dismissed the appellants' appeal from the decision of the second respondents, Bromley *b* London Borough Council, as local planning authority, refusing an application by the appellants for planning permission to develop their land. The facts are set out in the opinion of Lord Bridge.

The appellant P Eldridge Griffiths appeared in person.
Simon D Brown for the respondents.   *c*

Their Lordships took time for consideration.

20 January. The following opinions were delivered.

LORD FRASER OF TULLYBELTON. My Lords, I have had the advantage of *d* reading in draft the speech prepared by my noble and learned friend Lord Bridge. I agree with it, and for the reasons which he gives I would dismiss this appeal.

LORD ELWYN-JONES. My Lords, the Town and Country Planning Act 1971 makes a specific provision in s 245 that persons aggrieved by any relevant 'action' of the Secretary of State should be able to make an application to the High Court. However, it imposes a *e* time limit on the making of such applications of six weeks from the date on which the 'action' is taken. Whereas numerous provisions of the 1971 Act impose an express obligation on the Secretary of State to give notice, no such obligation is imposed by s 242.

This could have the regrettable result in a given case of an aggrieved person being denied, by reason of late or delayed delivery to him of the Secretary of State's decision or for reasons of administrative convenience, any reasonable opportunity to seek advice and *f* to make an application in time to the court. The fact that in the instant case the appellant received the Secretary of State's decision more than five weeks before he became time-barred and thus had a reasonable opportunity to apply to the High Court in good time is too fortuitous to be reassuring.

It is with reluctance that I have nevertheless come to the same conclusion as that arrived at by my noble and learned friend Lord Bridge, whose speech I have had the *g* advantage of reading, on the construction of the relevant provisions of the 1971 Act. I, too, would dismiss this appeal.

LORD SCARMAN. My Lords, when the Secretary of State in the exercise of the appellate power conferred on him by s 36(3) of the Town and Country Planning Act 1971 decides to dismiss an appeal from, or reverse or vary, the decision of a local planning *h* authority on an application for planning permission to develop land, what is the date of the action taken by him? This is the critical question in this appeal.

The Secretary of State submits that it is the date evidenced by the date-stamp, in the absence of any evidence to the contrary on which the letter declaring his decision is signed, in this case 8 December 1980. Alternatively, he submits that it is the date of posting, by which is meant the date on which it is confided either to the posting process *j* of his department or to the Post Office, also, according to the only information available, 8 December 1980 in this case.

The appellant, Mr Eldridge Griffiths, is the owner of land, which he sought planning permission to develop. He is aggrieved by the refusal of the Secretary of State on appeal to permit the development. He applied to the High Court to quash the action of the Secretary of State. The Secretary of State took the preliminary point that his application

was out of time. Mr Griffiths lost before the judge, and in the Court of Appeal. He now
appeals to your Lordships' House. He has argued his appeal in person with skill, brevity
and clarity. He submits that the action taken by the Secretary of State (always assuming,
which he challenges, that there is satisfactory evidence in the affidavits that he himself
took any action) was not complete until 13 December 1980, the date on which Mr
Griffiths (as also, presumably, the other appellant, his wife, who has taken no part in the
appeal) received the letter of decision which was the first notice either of them received
of the Secretary of State's decision.

The Court of Appeal rejected the first submission of the Secretary of State, but accepted
the second. Templeman LJ delivered the first judgment, from which I quote two
passages. First:

> 'It seems to me that he took that action when he made up his mind *and* when he
> gave effect to the decision which he had reached by dispatching notice of his
> decision.' (My emphasis.)

And the second:

> 'It seems to me that it cannot be said that the minister has taken action until he
> has committed some irrevocable step.'

The learned Lord Justice found that confiding a letter to the post was an irrevocable step
(on which Mr Griffiths's dry comment was, 'So it may be; but it does not follow that it
arrives'). Dunn and Cumming-Bruce LJJ agreed with Templeman LJ.

The reason why it is necessary to determine the date on which action was taken by the
Secretary of State is that s 245(1) of the 1971 Act prescribes six weeks from the date on
which the action was taken as the period within which an aggrieved person may apply
to the High Court to quash his action. If the date was 8 December 1980, Mr Griffiths was
out of time when he made his application to the High Court on 22 January 1981. If the
date was, as he submits, 13 December 1980, he was within the time prescribed by law.

In the Court of Appeal Cumming-Bruce LJ offered a concise summary (which I
gratefully borrow) of Mr Griffiths's argument, only to reject it as having to yield to the
specific words of the subsection. The learned Lord Justice noted that Mr Griffiths began,
as he did in your Lordships' House, by asking the question: how can anyone be 'aggrieved'
by action on the part of the Secretary of State until he is told what it is? Therefore, in
construing the subsection it can only be feasible to place on it a construction that time
begins to run from the date on which the owner or occupier of the land affected by the
decision had his first opportunity of knowing that he was aggrieved, ie the date on which
he learns, or has a proper opportunity of learning, what is the action taken by the
Secretary of State.

This is a powerful and attractive submission. It is difficult in terms of justice to justify
a conclusion that Parliament, when conferring a right of access to the courts, has used
language which can result in the right being lost before the aggrieved landowner even
knows or has a proper opportunity of knowing he has a grievance in respect of which he
might wish to avail himself of the right. At the very least, Parliament could be expected
to have enacted some safeguard against so unjust an eventuality.

The question, therefore, to be asked before imputing to Parliament any such disturbing
intention is whether the language of s 245(1) in its context is so specific that no other
conclusion is possible. The basic case of the respondents is that it must be in the public
interest that in some circumstances an applicant's right of access to the court has to yield
to the need for a swift finality of decision. This is, of course, a possible conclusion, for we
are in the realm of public law where, on occasions, private right must yield to public
interest. But even in public law justice remains as one of the true interests of the law, not
to be cut down or immobilised further than Parliament by express enactment or
necessary implication plainly requires. And it is unjust that one who is given a right of
access to the High Court should be at risk of losing it before he knows, or can know, of
the existence of a decision which entitles him to exercise it.

Does then the language of the section command this anomalous result? It all depends, as the Court of Appeal recognised, on the meaning to be given to that very ordinary, imprecise word 'action' in its statutory context. The Court of Appeal refused to accept *a* that the arcane moment of decision taken either by the Secretary of State in his closet or by some responsible official at his desk (the decision may, of course, be taken by an official: see *Carltona Ltd v Comrs of Works* [1943] 2 All ER 560) should be sufficient to determine the date from which time is to run against a person aggrieved by the decision. Action must, they thought, mean more than that. Their solution was to look for an easily ascertainable 'irrevocable step', ie the moment after which the Secretary of State could *b* not recall his decision. I agree with them that 'action' need not, as a matter of ordinary English usage, be confined to a single act but may embrace a course of action. I also agree with them that in public law, where the rights of the public as well as of the person directly affected by the decision have to be considered, an easily ascertained date is necessary in order that there may be no doubt as to the time when a decision becomes final, ie one which 'shall not be questioned in any legal proceedings whatsoever' (see *c* s 242(1) of the 1971 Act).

I accept, therefore, that Parliament must have intended an easily ascertained final date from which time is to run. I also accept that 'action' can refer to a course of action which includes but is not completed by the act of decision. Since no decision can be challenged unless its existence be known, a challengeable decision must be one for which the law provides a proper opportunity to challenge. If the words 'action is taken' in s 245 be *d* construed as including both the decision and the giving of notice to the owner or occupier of the affected land, certainty is achieved and a reasonable opportunity, even if not always the full period of six weeks, is provided to challenge the decision in the High Court. This is because s 283 of the 1971 Act provides a code for the giving of notice when required or authorised under the Act. The section permits notice to be given in a variety of ways, eg delivering it personally, leaving it at the last known place of abode of the person *e* concerned, dispatch by prepaid registered letter or by recorded delivery service, or, in the last resort, affixing it on the land. If, therefore, for one reason or another, it cannot be proved that the aggrieved person actually received the notice, there are ways of proving notice by reference to an ascertainable date and with due safeguards for the aggrieved person.

It is, however, urged that the context negatives any such construction of the words *f* 'action is taken'. Two points are made. First, s 245(3) provides that the 'action' to which the section applies is that which is mentioned in s 242(3). The latter subsection lists eleven 'descriptions' of action. Ten of them are 'decisions' and one of them is a 'direction', all of them being acts of the Secretary of State. The action in the present case is included as 'any decision of the Secretary of State on an appeal under section 36 of this Act': see s 242(3)(b). It is submitted, therefore, that the word 'action', where it appears in s 245, *g* refers only to the decision or the direction of the Secretary of State and not to the notification of it to the aggrieved landowner (or occupier). I draw no such inference. It is common enough to describe something by a word which picks out its essential feature. 'Decision' is a perfectly apt description of a course of action taken under s 36 of the 1971 Act, for the essence of the action is the decision to allow or dismiss the appeal. The purpose of description being to describe (not to define), I find nothing in the language of *h* s 242 or s 245 which compels a construction of 'action' as a single act. I therefore reject the argument based on the 'descriptions' of action listed in s 242(3).

The second point arises from the fact that s 245 applies not only to the action mentioned in that subsection but also the orders mentioned in sub-s (2) of the same section and provides that time shall run 'from the date on which the order is confirmed'. Confirmation is a formal act by the Secretary of State, and, unlike the word 'action', is not *j* capable of being construed as a course of action. It is, therefore, submitted that, as Parliament has provided for time to run from confirmation of an order irrespective of whether the persons aggrieved have notice of it or not, there is no reason to suppose that Parliament intended otherwise in respect of the other matter to which s 245 applies, namely any action taken by the Secretary of State which falls within one of the descriptions listed in s 242(3).

This facile equation is no guide to the interpretation of s 245. Orders confirmed by the
a Secretary of State are the subject of express provision as to notice; 'action on the part of
the Secretary of State to which this section applies' is not. I take two illustrations. The
section applies to 'any order under section 51 of this Act' (see s 242(2)(b)). A s 51 order
requires discontinuance of the use of land or, as the case may be, removal (or alteration)
of a building. The order does not take effect unless it is confirmed by the Secretary of
State. Where an order is confirmed, the local planning authority shall serve a copy of it
b on the owner and occupier of the land (see s 51(7)). If, as it is submitted, time under s
245 runs from the date of confirmation of the order, the aggrieved person has the
safeguard of the duty to give the notice imposed by the section. It is true that inevitably
he will have less than six weeks; but, if the statutory duty of notice is performed, he will
have a reasonable opportunity to make his challenge. If the true construction of 'action'
is, as I think, a course of action completed by notice to the owner or occupier of the land
c affected, the same position will arise if notice is served by registered post or recorded
delivery or in any of the ways envisaged by s 283. In both cases, therefore, ie that of a s
51 order of which notice has to be given by the local planning authority and that of
'action' interpreted as referring to a course of action completed by the giving of notice to
the owner or occupier, a reasonable opportunity to challenge within the prescribed
period will be given, even though the full six weeks will not invariably be available.
d   My second illustration is that of a tree preservation order. This also is an order which,
when confirmed, can be challenged by application to the High Court made under, and
within the time limit set by, s 245(1). The 1971 Act again envisages the giving of notice
after confirmation, but leaves the detailed provision to regulations (see s 60(5) of the Act).
     It is, therefore, substantially true that, save where the public interest clearly requires
the contrary, the 1971 Act and the regulations made thereunder contain provision for
e the giving of notice or orders and decisions made by the Secretary of State so as to ensure
that within the time prescribed by law the person, be he the owner or occupier, whose
land is the subject of the order or decision has a reasonable opportunity to consider his
position and, if so advised, to challenge the order or decision. (It is assumed, reasonably
in my opinion, that if notice is given to the owner or occupier, it is sufficient.) If the
words 'action taken' in s 245 be construed as a reference to a course of action beginning
f with the Secretary of State's decision and completed by the giving of such notice, the
same just result would ensue. A construction which limited the words to the act of
decision would not have the same result, for it would then be possible for the right of
challenge to be lost without the owner or occupier of the land knowing of the decision
or having the protection of the procedures established by s 283 as acceptable methods of
giving notice. If this means that the Department of the Environment must go to a little
g extra expense and trouble in instituting s 283 procedures in respect of the decisions and
directions listed in s 242(3) of the 1971 Act, it is a small price to pay for doing justice;
and it would promote that certainty which is needed in matters of public law.
     It is true that on the facts of this case Mr Griffiths had five weeks plus a day or so in
which to make his application. It is also true that this was a reasonable opportunity, even
though it was not the full period of six weeks which Mr Griffiths (and others) might
h reasonably think was their statutory right. But the issue is not one of fact, but is as to the
construction to be placed on the statute. If the Secretary of State's submission is correct,
the statute, because it is silent as to the giving of notice in respect of the action taken by
him, imposes no legal duty on him to give notice to anyone. It follows that an owner or
occupier of the land, who is aggrieved by the decision, is deprived of the right to notice
under s 283. He has no right to be informed; nor has he the protection of the statutory
j safeguards for the giving of notice. I would not hold that Parliament intended anything
so arbitrary unless the language of the enactment revealed that such was its intention.
But the language of the section is wide enough to obviate the need to attribute any such
intention to Parliament.
     For these reasons I would allow the appeal.

LORD BRIDGE OF HARWICH. My Lords, there are nominally two appellants who are husband and wife. Your Lordships were given to understand that they have parted and that the husband alone, Mr Eldridge Griffiths, is now interested in the subject matter of the appeal. It will be convenient to refer to him as the appellant and to recount the history as though he had throughout been the sole party concerned in the relevant transaction. The appellant argued his case in person, if I may say so, with a degree of skill, courtesy and restraint rarely displayed by a litigant in person. The fact that he was not professionally represented, he can be assured, in no way operated to his disadvantage.

The appellant applied for outline planning permission under the Town and Country Planning Act 1971 for the erection of a farmhouse on land at Orpington, Kent. This was refused by the second respondents, as local planning authority. The appellant appealed to the first respondent, to whom I shall refer as the Secretary of State, under s 36 of the 1971 Act. A letter from the Department of the Environment bearing the reference APP/5007/A/80/02871 and the date-stamp 8 December 1980 was sent to the appellant. It concluded with the words: '. . . the Secretary of State hereby dismisses your appeal.' This letter was received by the appellant on 13 December 1980.

By a notice of motion entered and served on 22 January 1981 the appellant applied to the High Court 'for an order that a decision made by the Secretary of State for the Environment on planning appeal 5007/A/80/02871 be quashed'. By summons dated 4 February 1981 the Secretary of State applied to strike out the appellant's application on the ground that it was not made within the time limited by s 245 of the 1971 Act. An order to strike out the application was made by Master Thompson on 4 March 1981, affirmed by Sir Douglas Frank QC, sitting as a deputy High Court judge, on 10 March 1981, and further affirmed by the Court of Appeal on different grounds on 26 January 1982. The appellant appeals from the decision of the Court of Appeal by leave of your Lordships' House.

It will be convenient to set out the provisions of ss 242 and 245 of the 1971 Act on which this appeal primarily depends:

'242.—(1) Except as provided by the following provisions of this Part of this Act, the validity of . . . (d) any such order as is mentioned in subsection (2) of this section, whether before or after it has been confirmed; or (e) any such action on the part of the Secretary of State as is mentioned in subsection (3) of this section, shall not be questioned in any legal proceedings whatsoever . . .

(3) The action referred to in subsection (1)(e) of this section is action on the part of the Secretary of State of any of the following descriptions, that is to say . . . (b) any decision of the Secretary of State on an appeal under section 36 of this Act . . .

245.—(1) If any person—(a) is aggrieved by any order to which this section applies and desires to question the validity of that order, on the grounds that the order is not within the powers of this Act, or that any of the relevant requirements have not been complied with in relation to that order; or (b) is aggrieved by any action on the part of the Secretary of State to which this section applies and desires to question the validity of that action, on the grounds that the action is not within the powers of this Act, or that any of the relevant requirements have not been complied with in relation to that action, he may, within six weeks from the date on which the order is confirmed or the action is taken, as the case may be, make an application to the High Court under this section.

(2) Without prejudice to subsection (1) of this section, if the authority directly concerned with any order to which this section applies, or with any action on the part of the Secretary of State to which this section applies, desire to question the validity of that order or action on any of the grounds mentioned in subsection (1) of this section, the authority may, within six weeks from the date on which the order is confirmed or the action is taken, as the case may be, make an application to the High Court under this section.

(3) This section applies to any such order as is mentioned in subsection (2) of section 242 of this Act and to any such action on the part of the Secretary of State as is mentioned in subsection (3) of that section . . .'

For brevity I have not included in these citations from the 1971 Act s 242(2), which lists
a five types of order, nor the provisions of s 242(3), except para (*b*), which lists another ten
types of action, to all of which the provisions of s 245 apply. In considering when time
begins to run for the purpose of calculating the six weeks' time limit set by s 245 it will,
however, be necessary to refer later to some of these other cases.

At the outset the appellant sought to argue that the Secretary of State had never decided
his planning appeal at all. This point is not open to him on the hearing of the present
b appeal. What he sought to question by his notice of motion was certainly a purported
decision of the Secretary of State on an appeal under s 36 of the 1971 Act. The validity of
that purported decision can only be questioned if the application was made in due time.

The important point raised by the appeal is what, on the true construction of s 245, is
the meaning of the words 'the date on which . . . the action is taken' both generally in
relation to action of the several kinds enumerated in s 243(3) and specifically in relation
c to a decision of the Secretary of State on an appeal under s 36 of the 1971 Act.

The appellant forcibly argued that no one can be 'aggrieved' under s 245 by something
of which he is unaware. It follows from this, he submitted, that the action to which
s 245(1)(*b*) refers cannot have been taken on any date earlier than the date when the
notification of it was received by the aggrieved person. If this is right, since the appellant
did not receive notice of the Secretary of State's decision until 13 December 1980, his
d notice of motion on 22 January 1981 was in time.

Counsel for the Secretary of State contends that the effective date when action of the
kind in question is taken, sc making a decision on a planning appeal, is when, in
accordance with the practice of the Department of the Environment, the decision is
recorded in a formal document, ie a decision letter concluding with the words 'the
Secretary of State hereby dismisses (or, as the case may be, allows) the appeal', which is
e both signed on behalf of the Secretary of State and date-stamped. In this case that action
was taken on 8 December 1980, from which it follows that, if counsel is right, the
appellant's notice of motion was out of time.

The Court of Appeal rejected both these arguments and held that the Secretary of State
cannot be said to have made any decision until he has taken an irrevocable step which
puts it out of his power to change his mind and that, since a decision letter can be recalled
f and the decision varied at any moment until it is posted, it is the date of posting which is
the date of the relevant action from which time runs under s 245(1). They inferred,
however, from facts put before them by counsel in argument and verified by affidavit
sworn and filed on the same date as the hearing and decision of the appeal that the
decision letter in this case had in fact been posted on 8 December 1980 and accordingly
that the appellant's application to quash the decision had rightly been struck out on the
g ground that it was not made in time.

A fourth possible view has emerged in the course of the discussion of this appeal. This
is that there is an implied statutory obligation on the Secretary of State to give notice of
his decision on a planning appeal, presumably to all interested parties, that the giving of
such notice is an integral part of the process of making the decision and that the obligation
can only be complied with in accordance with the terms of s 283(1) of the 1971 Act,
h which provides:

'Subject to the provisions of this section, any notice or other document required
or authorised to be served or given under this Act may be served or given either—
(*a*) by delivering it to the person on whom it is to be served or to whom it is to be
given; or (*b*) by leaving it at the usual or last known place of abode of that person, or
j in a case where an address for service has been given by that person, at that address;
or (*c*) by sending it in a prepaid registered letter, or by the recorded delivery service,
addressed to that person at his usual or last known place of abode, or, in a case where
an address for service has been given by that person, at that address; or (*d*) in the
case of an incorporated company or body, by delivering it to the secretary or clerk
of the company or body at their registered or principal office, or sending it in a

prepaid registered letter, or by the recorded delivery service, addressed to the secretary or clerk of the company or body at that office.'

In the instant case there was no evidence that the decision letter was sent to the appellant by registered post or recorded delivery service. Hence, on this view, the appellant would be entitled to succeed on the ground that the Secretary of State had failed to prove that the notice of motion was out of time.

My Lords, it seems to me, first, that one would expect the provisions of s 245(1) and (2) to operate to give a clear, certain and consistent answer to the question when the date occurs from which time runs both in relation to the orders to which s 242(2) applies and in relation to action of the several kinds indicated by s 242(3), second, that when one finds in the 1971 Act numerous provisions imposing an express obligation to give notice it is impossible to imply a statutory obligation (as opposed to a duty in the course of good administration) to give notice, where no express obligation is imposed, third, that the possibility that maladministration by failure to notify a decision promptly might work an injustice, even to the extent of depriving an interested party of his opportunity to institute proceedings under s 245, is not a sufficient ground to distort the natural meaning of the language of the statute.

Two instances demonstrate conclusively, to my mind, that the 1971 Act itself draws a distinction between the confirmation of an order to which s 242(2) applies and the taking of action to which s 242(3) applies on the one hand and the notification to interested parties of that order or action on the other.

Section 51 of the 1971 Act empowers the local planning authority to make orders requiring an existing use of land to be discontinued or a building to be altered or removed. Section 242(2) applies to such orders. Such an order does not take effect unless confirmed by the Secretary of State: see s 51(4). Section 51(7) provides:

'Where an order under this section has been confirmed by the Secretary of State, the local planning authority shall serve a copy of the order on the owner and occupier of the land to which the order relates.'

Hence the confirmation of an order to which s 242(2) relates is an event distinct from the notification of the confirmed order to the interested parties. The two events may, and almost invariably will, occur on different dates. It is from the date of the first event, not the second, that time runs under s 245.

When, under Part VII of the Act, parties have become entitled to, and have claimed, compensation arising from an unfavourable planning decision, s 38 empowers the Secretary of State to give directions which, put shortly, have the effect of reducing or extinguishing liability to pay compensation by deeming a more favourable planning decision to have been given. The 'giving by the Secretary of State of any direction under section 38' is action to which s 242(3)(c) applies. Section 39(3) provides:

'Where the Secretary of State gives a direction under section 38 of this Act, he shall give notice of the direction to the local planning authority to whose decision the direction relates, and to every person (if any) who made, and has not since withdrawn, a claim for compensation in respect of that decision.'

Hence, here again, the giving of the direction, which is the relevant action taken, is distinct from the notification of the direction to interested parties.

Like s 242(3)(b) all the other kinds of action listed under the subsection, except that in para (c), consist in 'a decision by the Secretary of State' under various provisions of the 1971 Act. As a matter of language, when the generic term 'action' is used to refer to various categories of decision, it seems to me that it can only refer to the making of the decision, not to its notification to third parties. Coupled with the instances cited from ss 51 and 39 this makes it impossible, in my opinion, even if one could imply a statutory obligation to give notice of the decision, to hold that compliance with that obligation is part of the taking of the relevant action or can affect the date on which the action is taken within the meaning of s 245. If this is right, this appeal cannot succeed on the ground that the decision letter was not proved to have been sent by registered post or recorded delivery, nor, a fortiori, on the ground argued by the appellant.

It is appropriate, nevertheless, to test the validity of this conclusion by considering the consequences to which a contrary construction of the 1971 Act would lead. The vital factor to bear in mind is that, when the Secretary of State makes a decision on a planning appeal, as with most, if not all, of the other categories of action to which s 242(3) applies, a multiplicity of parties may be affected. In all planning appeals under s 36 there will at least be the appellant and the local planning authority. But in many cases there will also be the owner or owners of the land affected, who may be different persons from the applicant for planning permission, and the tenants of any agricultural holdings any part of which is comprised in the land affected. These parties are entitled to make representations and when they have done so are expressly entitled to notice of the decision: see s 29(3) as applied by s 36(5). The local planning authority have their own express right under s 245(2) to take proceedings questioning the decision. All the others are potentially aggrieved persons under s 245(1). This seems to me to point to the extreme improbability of Parliament having intended that the date when the action is taken for the purposes of s 245 should be determined by the date on which notice is given to a multiplicity of parties, which would presumably mean the date when the last necessary notice was given.

It must be remembered that, where, as has been held in the instant case, a decision to refuse planning permission on appeal becomes immune to challenge by lapse of time, the appellant can always make a fresh application; though I must certainly not be understood as encouraging the present appellant to take that course. The six weeks' time limit is of much greater importance in a case where the decision was to grant planning permission. Six weeks after the Secretary of State has granted permission for development on appeal, the applicant for that permission should be in a position to proceed with confidence to carry out the development or to buy or sell the land with the benefit of the permission. But if time does not start to run until all interested parties have been given notice of the decision, and if, by some administrative oversight, the decision was never communicated either to the local planning authority or to a tenant farmer, the permission would be liable to be invalidated after the development had been carried out or the land had changed hands at a price reflecting the value of the planning permission. I do not believe such a bizarre result can have been intended.

My Lords, I appreciate the force of the Court of Appeal's view that the Secretary of State does not make his decision until it becomes irrevocable by posting the decision letter but, with respect, I cannot agree with it. When a letter recording a decision of the Secretary of State made 'hereby' has been typed, signed on behalf of the Secretary of State and date-stamped, it seems to me that the process of decision making is complete and that the letter itself is not the less a decision of the Secretary of State because it is still in his power to revoke it. I would accordingly accept the submission of counsel for the Secretary of State that the relevant action is taken on the date stamped on the decision letter. The same principle would operate, mutatis mutandis, to determine the date on which any other action is taken of a kind to which s 242(3) applies or on which any order to which s 242(2) applies is confirmed.

For these reasons I would dismiss the appeal.

LORD BRANDON OF OAKBROOK. My Lords, I have had the advantage of reading in advance the speech prepared by my noble and learned friend Lord Bridge. I agree with it, and for the reasons which he gives I would dismiss the appeal.

Appeal dismissed.

Solicitors: *Treasury Solicitor.*

Mary Rose Plummer   Barrister.

Practice Direction

COURT OF APPEAL, CIVIL DIVISION

Court of Appeal – Appeal – Dismissal – Consent – Practice – Request for dismissal of civil appeals – Initialling request – Initialling by judge of court or by Registrar of Civil Appeals.

Consequent on the creation of the office of Registrar of Civil Appeals, the Practice Direction of 21 February 1938 ([1938] WN 89 and set out in amended form in *The Supreme Court Practice 1982* vol 1, para 59/5/3, p 933) is being further amended to enable the registrar and any judge of the court to initial requests for the dismissal of civil appeals. In its amended form it reads:

'Where an appellant is sui juris and does not desire to prosecute an appeal he may present a request signed by his solicitor stating that he is sui juris and asking to have the appeal dismissed, in which case (subject to the request being initialled by a judge of the court or by the Registrar of Civil Appeals) the appeal will be dismissed and struck out of the list and an order will if necessary be drawn up directing payment of the costs by the appellant, such costs to be taxed in case the parties differ.

Where the parties are sui juris and a settlement has been reached disposing of the appeal they may present a request signed by the solicitors for all parties to the appeal stating that they are sui juris including the terms of settlement and asking that the appeal be dismissed by consent, in which case (subject to the request being initialled by a judge of the court or by the Registrar of Civil Appeals) the appeal will be dismissed and struck out of the list and an order will if necessary be drawn up.

If the appellant desires to have the appeal dismissed without costs his request must be accompanied by a consent signed by the respondents' solicitors stating that the respondents are sui juris and consent to the dismissal of the appeal without costs, in which case (subject to the request being initialled by a judge of the court or by the Registrar of Civil Appeals) the appeal will be dismissed and struck out of the list.

Where any party has no solicitor on the record any such request or consent must be signed by him personally.

All other applications as to the dismissal of an appeal and all applications for an order by consent reversing or varying the order under appeal will be placed in the list and dealt with in court.'

11 January 1983   JOHN DONALDSON MR

Afovos Shipping Co SA v Pagnan and another

The Afovos

HOUSE OF LORDS

LORD HAILSHAM OF ST MARYLEBONE LC, LORD DIPLOCK, LORD KEITH OF KINKEL, LORD ROSKILL
AND LORD BRIGHTMAN

6, 7 DECEMBER 1982, 27 JANUARY 1983

Shipping – Time charterparty – Withdrawal of vessel for non-payment of hire – Punctual payment – Anti-technicality clause – Owners to give 48 hours' notice of withdrawal of ship – Payment not made on due date – Owners giving notice of withdrawal of ship if payment not received – Notice of withdrawal given at end of banking hours on due date of payment – Whether default occurring at end of banking hours or at midnight on due date – Whether owners' notice to rectify valid.

By a time charterparty dated 8 February 1978 in the New York Produce Exchange form, the owners chartered a vessel to the charterers for a period of two years. Under the terms of the charterparty hire was payable semi-monthly in advance at a designated bank in London. In the event of the charterers failing to pay the hire punctually and regularly, the owners were to be at liberty to withdraw the vessel from hire. The charterparty further provided by cl 31, an 'anti-technicality' clause, that if the hire was not received 'When . . . due' the owners were to give the charterers 48 hours' notice to rectify the default before exercising the right of withdrawal. The charterers paid hire punctually until the end of May 1979 but the credit transfer from the charterers' bank of the next instalment, due on 14 June, did not reach the owners' bank on that date because of an error by both banks. At 1640 hrs on 14 June the owners' agents sent a telex to the charterers stating that they had been instructed 'in case we do not receive the hire which is due today' to give notice to the charterers under cl 31 of the charterparty of withdrawal of the vessel. The instalment due was not received by the owners within 48 hours of the telex and the owners accordingly claimed to be entitled to withdraw the vessel. The charterers, relying on the general rule that payment was not due until midnight on the due date for payment, contended, inter alia, that the telex sent by the owners' agents was premature and therefore was not an effective notice under cl 31. The owners contended that, where payment was to be made to a specified bank, the time at which hire became overdue was the time at which normal banking hours closed. The judge held that the hire was due on the last day for payment and that a notice given at any time on that day constituted a proper notice to rectify. The judge accordingly held that the owners were entitled to withdraw the vessel. The charterers appealed to the Court of Appeal, which held that the charterers were not in default until midnight on the due date, that the notice was premature and ineffective and that therefore the owners were not entitled to withdraw the vessel. The owners appealed to the House of Lords.

Held – On the true construction of the charterparty the time for giving 48 hours' notice under cl 31 did not arise until the charterers were in default and, applying the principle that where a person was obliged to do a particular act on or before a particular day he was not in default until the end of that day, the charterers were not in default until midnight on 14 June 1979. The owners' notice under cl 31 was therefore premature and ineffective and they were not entitled to withdraw the vessel from the charterers. The owners were not entitled to rely on the procedure of the recipient bank to foreshorten the time allowed for punctual payment, nor were they entitled to rely on the doctrine of anticipatory breach because that doctrine related only to repudiation arising out of fundamental breach and delay in paying one instalment of hire did not amount to a fundamental breach. The appeal would accordingly be dismissed (see p 452 *d e*, p 453 *g h*, p 454 *a* to *d f h* to p 455 *c e* to p 456 *a d*, post).

Decision of the Court of Appeal [1982] 3 All ER 18 affirmed.

Notes

For withdrawal of a ship for non-payment of hire, see 35 Halsbury's Laws (3rd edn) 281, para 423, and for cases on the subject, see 41 Digest (Repl) 229, 532–539.

Cases referred to in opinions

Brimnes, The, Tenax Steamship Co Ltd v The Brimnes (owners) [1973] 1 All ER 769, [1973] 1 WLR 386; affd [1974] 3 All ER 88, [1975] QB 929, [1974] 3 WLR 613, CA, Digest (Cont Vol D) 819, 482b.

Photo Production Ltd v Securicor Transport Ltd [1980] 1 All ER 556, [1980] AC 827, [1980] 2 WLR 283, HL.

Startup v Macdonald (1843) 6 Man & G 593, 134 ER 1029, Ex Ch, 12 Digest (Reissue) 396, 2886.

Appeal

Afovos Shipping Co SA, the owners of the motor vessel Afovos, appealed with leave of the Appeal Committee of the House of Lords granted on 6 May 1982 against the decision of the Court of Appeal (Lord Denning MR, Griffiths and Kerr LJJ) ([1982] 3 All ER 18, [1982] 1 WLR 848) on 2 March 1982 allowing an appeal by Romano Pagnan and Pietro Pagnan, trading as R Pagnan & Flli, the charterers, against the judgment of Lloyd J given on 19 June 1980 whereby he declared (i) that the owners were entitled under the terms of a charterparty dated 8 February 1978 to withdraw the vessel from service, (ii) that the owners had given valid notice of withdrawal under the terms of the charterparty and (iii) that they had effectively withdrawn the vessel. The Court of Appeal held that the owners were not entitled to withdraw the vessel because although payment of hire was overdue they had not given a contractual 48 hours' notice as required by cl 31 of the charterparty. The facts are set out in the opinion of Lord Hailsham LC.

Colin Ross-Munro QC and Martin Moore-Bick for the owners.
Kenneth Rokison QC and Richard Wood for the charterers.

Their Lordships took time for consideration.

27 January. The following opinions were delivered.

LORD HAILSHAM OF ST MARYLEBONE LC. My Lords, on 18 June 1979, in circumstances hereafter to be described, the appellants as shipowners purported to withdraw the ship Afovos from a time charter dated 8 February 1978 on the New York Produce Exchange form by which she was let to the respondents as charterers for two years three months more or less at charterer's option from delivery date on 14 February 1978. The purported ground was a right of withdrawal conferred by a clause in the charter. The formal question in this appeal is whether the owners were entitled so to act, and whether their action was effective to achieve its purpose.

The commercial reality is, as happens not seldom, somewhat different. By a without prejudice agreement the ship remained on charter to the respondents for the rest of the charter period. The real question in dispute is whether the hire is to be at the original rate of $US1·97½ per ton or an enhanced rate reflecting the market at the time of the purported withdrawal. The difference is about $US2½m.

The result of the appeal depends on the construction of two clauses in the charter and the effect to be given to the purported notice of withdrawal. It will be convenient to deal first with the terms of the two clauses to be construed, and then to recite the facts, of which the purported notice of withdrawal was one.

The arrangements for payment and the right of withdrawal were contained in cl 5 of the charter which provided as follows:

'Payment of said hire to be made in London, to the FIRST NATIONAL BANK OF CHICAGO . . . London EC3P 3DR, for the credit of ANGELICOUSSIS SHIPHOLDING GROUP, LIMITED . . . in cash in United States Currency, semi-monthly in advance . . . otherwise failing the punctual and regular payment of the hire . . . the Owners shall be at liberty to withdraw the vessel from the service of the Charterers . . .'

This is the first of the two clauses which falls to be construed. The severity of the right of the withdrawal contained in the last phrase was mitigated by an 'anti-technicality clause' contained in cl 31 of the charter. This anti-technicality clause was in the following terms:

'When hire is due and not received the Owners, before exercising the option of withdrawing the vessel from the Charter-Party, will give Charterers fortyeight hours notice, Saturdays, Sundays and Holidays excluded and will not withdraw the vessel if the hire is paid within these fortyeight hours.'

This is the second clause to be construed.

In the events which happened, the hire was punctually paid up to and including 11 June 1979 when there occurred a chapter of accidents, for so only can it be described, which gave rise to the present dispute. On that date the charterers gave instructions in good time to their bankers, the Padua branch of the Credito Italiano, to pay the instalment then currently due for payment on or before 14 June 1979 in accordance with the charter to the London branch of the First National Bank of Chicago for the credit of Angelicoussis Shipholding Group Ltd. This the Padua bank purported to do by telex on 13 June. Both banks were in funds and were in account with one another. But for one unfortuante circumstance there was no reason why the transaction should not have been completed in due time.

The London branch of the Chicago bank had originally possessed three telex call numbers, the last two digits of which were respectively 16, 17 and 18. But that numbered 18 had been abandoned in 1975 and by 1979 had been allotted to a third party. Nevertheless, in the relevant directories for 1976, 1977 and 1978 the old call number had continued to be recorded under the name of the Chicago bank, and as at 14 June 1979 the Padua bank was using the 1978 edition. By a singular mischance the Padua branch tried first to connect with 16 and 17 and found, in the first case, that there was no reply and, in the second, that the number was engaged. The third time the Padua bank connected with the number 18 and there was a reply from the third party; and though the answering call was wrong the Padua bank transmitted the telex to the third party and the error was not discovered and corrected until 19 June, when the payment of the instalment was admittedly overdue.

In the mean time, on 14 June 1979, which was the last day for paying the instalment, the owners had purported to exercise their rights under cl 31. At 1640 hrs (London time) on that day, which was a Thursday, they sent to the charterers through their London agents the following telex:

'Owners have instructed us that in case we do not receive the hire which is due today, to give charterers notice as per cl 31 of the charter-party for withdrawal of the vessel from their service.'

The telex, we were told, was received five minutes later. Allowing for the intervening Saturday and Sunday, 48 hours from the receipt of this telex would have expired at 1645 hrs on Monday, 18 June. At 1920 hrs on that day the owners sent to the charterers a telex purporting to withdraw the vessel from their service.

This resulted in a dispute giving rise to the present proceedings commenced by writ by the owners as plaintiffs claiming on a specially indorsed statement of claim a declaration that they were entitled to withdraw the vessel. At first instance Lloyd J decided in their favour, but his judgment was reversed by the Court of Appeal ([1982] 3 All ER 18, [1982] 1 WLR 848), and so the matter comes before your Lordships' House for final disposal by leave of the Appeal Committee.

A number of questions arose for debate at one time or another. Only a small number of these were still alive by the time of the appeal before your Lordships, and, in my view, the case can be disposed of by considering only two, viz: (1) at what point of time on 14 June 1979, apart from the mitigation of cl 31, would the right of withdrawal have arisen under cl 5 of the charter? and (2) on the assumption that, at 1640 or 1645 hrs on 14 June 1979, the point of time indicated by the answer to the first question had not been reached, were the owners entitled to send a notice exercising their option under cl 31 in advance of that point of time? In addition to these questions the Court of Appeal decided that the purported notice under cl 31 was deficient in point of form, not being in a sufficiently unqualified form. In the event, their Lordships did not find it necessary to hear argument on this last point, since, if the first two questions were decided in a sense adverse to the owners, it was not necessary to decide it nor did it raise any question of general application, depending as it did on the precise wording which the owners chose to use. For myself I am far from saying that I am satisfied the Court of Appeal was wrong on this last point, but in the absence of argument and since it is unnecessary to decide the question, I prefer not to express a concluded opinion.

Of the two questions which must be decided, the second appears to me to be plain beyond argument. Both the grammatical meaning of cl 31 and the policy considerations underlying the contract require that the moment of time at which the 48 hours' notice must be given did not arise until after the moment of time at which, apart from the clause, the right of withdrawal would have accrued. I agree with the judgments of the Court of Appeal that both the expression 'due and received', and the reference to the right as an 'option', really only admit of this sense. The argument which appealed to the judge that notice could be given at any time during the last day available for payment of the instalment (ie at any time after midnight on 13–14 June or alternatively at some point of time when it was unlikely that the instalment would be paid timeously) failed to make any impression on me at all. The notice can only be given 'when hire is due and not received', which cannot arise before the time postulated by the answer given to the first question (whatever that answer may be), and the notice can only be given when there is (or apart from cl 31 would be) already in existence, an 'option' capable of exercise of 'withdrawing the vessel from the Charter-Party', and that option can only be exercised after the arrival of the same point of time.

Even if the point of cl 31 were ambiguous, which in my judgment it is not, I would be greatly impressed by the view of the Court of Appeal. Quite obviously the clause was inserted in order to save the charterer, who may (as in this case) be quite innocent even of the knowledge that his payment had not been received, from the extremely onerous effects (in this case a cost of $2½m) of cl 5, and equally obviously if the owners' arguments be accepted a premature notice would have the effect of allowing the shipowner to reduce the effective period of 48 hrs notice by anything up to 24 hours. I found particularly convincing two passages in the judgment of Griffiths LJ ([1982] 3 All ER 18 at 24, 25, [1982] 1 WLR 848 at 856, 857). The first is when he said:

'The owners purported to give notice under cl 31 at 1640 hrs on 14 June. Assuming for the moment that the form of the notice was good, the charterers say it was premature because the owners cannot give notice until the charterers are in breach of their obligation to pay. The purpose of the notice, say the charterers, is firstly to inform the charterer that he has failed to make a payment by the due date and then to give him a period of 48 hours' grace in which to pay. At first blush it might appear rather naive to say that the charterers need to be told that they have not paid the owners. But this is not the case; payments of this kind are normally made by telex through a number of banks, and it may well be that through some slip-up the money does not arrive in the owner's account as quickly as the charterer has the right to expect. Once the charterer has instructed his bank to pay, he has no further direct control over the payment which is now in the banking chain. The charterer in this case gave his bank in Italy instructions to pay on 11 June which should have been ample time for payment to be made by 14 June but, as we know, payment was not made by 18 June. I therefore accept the charterers do require to be told by the owners that payment has not been received. There is little point in telling the charterer that payment has not been received until the time for payment has expired; if the charterer is told that payment has not been received before the time for payment has expired, he may not realise the urgency of the matter and continue to expect that the payment will be credited in time. On the other hand, if he is told after the time for payment has expired, he will realise he is in breach and has only 48 hours in which to save himself.'

The second passage is when he said:

'Then I ask myself: which result are commercial men likely to have intended? A construction that results in a simple situation expressed thus: "You haven't paid up when you should have done; pay in 48 hours or lose the ship." Or a construction that gives this result: "I warn you that, although the final time for payment has not yet arrived, I have not yet received payment, and if I do not receive payment when I should, then you will lose the ship if you don't pay me what you owe me in the extra time this notice gives you which is calculated by adding to your deadline for payment so many hours of this 48-hour notice as have not expired by the final time for payment? I suppose they would prefer the first construction. Finally, if notice can be given before the charterer is in default, it does little more than add some unspecified period of less than 48 hours to the time for payment. It does not give the charterer notice that he is in default, nor does it give him a period of grace.'

I have only to add that the option given by cl 31 is not one which the owner is bound to exercise. On the contrary, if the market charge for hire had moved the other way, it seems to me extremely unlikely that he would have wished to do so.

In the result, I conclude that the crux of this case depends on the answer given to the first of the two questions I have posed. This was: at what point of time apart from the mitigation of cl 31 would the right of withdrawal under cl 5 of the charter have arisen? To put the question in the terms of cl 5: at what point of time can the charterers be said to have been 'failing the punctual and regular payment of the hire'? Since the punctual payment of only one instalment is in question, for the purpose of the present appeal one need only ask the question in the simpler form: what is the latest point of time on 14 June 1979 which would have constituted punctual payment of the instalment? To this question I believe that, in principle, only one answer is possible, namely at midnight on the last day available to them for the due and punctual payment of the hire, ie 14 June. I take it to be a general principle of law not requiring authority that where a person under an obligation to do a particular act has to do it on or before a particular date he has the whole of that day to peform his duty. No doubt as the hours pass it becomes less and less probable that he will be able to do it. That is the risk he runs. But he is not actually in default until the time arrives. The only point on which I would differ from the Court of Appeal is its apparent reliance on the decision in *Startup v Macdonald* (1843) 6 Man & G 593, 134 ER 1029 as authority for this proposition. No doubt the general proposition is to be found in several of the judgments in that case (eg 6 Man & G 593 at 612, 616, 619, 622, 624, 134 ER 1029 at 1037, 1040, 1041, 1042 per Rolfe B, Williams and Patteson JJ, Alderson and Parke BB), as it is in the dicta of Donaldson J and Lord Russell also cited in the Court of Appeal. But the actual facts in *Startup v Macdonald,* and the particular decision founded on them, arising as they do out of the special verdict of the jury in that case, were too individual themselves to constitute a ratio decidendi for that decision. In my view, in his judgment at first instance Lloyd J allowed himself to be deflected from his application of the present rule to the construction of cl 5 of the charter by an analysis of the actual probability of the charterer being in default if his telex were received after counter hours in the bank, after 1640 hrs in the afternoon, or even later before midnight. But that, to my mind, is a false analysis probably based on a false analogy which, indeed, in the course of discussion, counsel for the owners invited us to draw. The question is not when the charterer would cease to be likely to pay in time but when, to quote cl 5, 'punctual payment' would have failed. In my opinion this moment must relate to a particular hour, and is not dependent on the modalities of the recipient bank. It is the hour of midnight to which the general rule applies.

To escape from this meaning, counsel for the owners sought to rely on the doctrine of anticipatory breach. But this is not the basis on which cl 31 stood to be invoked, or on which an actual breach of cl 5 can be said to have occurred. No doubt if there had been a total repudiation of the whole contract the owners could have elected to treat the contract as at end. But then they would not have been required to invoke cl 31 to do so or to give 48 hours' notice of their election. A breach of cl 5 occurred, and could only occur, at a particular moment of time, and it was only on the occurrence of that breach that, on the true construction of the charter, notice could be given under cl 31. There is no reason, in my judgment, to place the moment of time at which 'punctual payment' ceased to be possible at any moment earlier than midnight on 14 June 1979, in accordance with the general rule to which I have referred. Lest I should be misunderstood on this point, I would add that, since writing the above, I have read in draft and agree with, the additional remarks of my noble and learned friend Lord Diplock on this aspect of the present appeal.

There is only one other brief note that I would add. Our attention was rightly drawn in the course of argument to the remarks of Brandon J in *The Brimnes, Tenax Steamship Co Ltd v The Brimnes (owners)* [1973] 1 All ER 769, [1973] 1 WLR 386 and of the Court of Appeal in the same case ([1974] 3 All ER 88, [1975] QB 929) regarding what is to be regarded as the time of payment when effected by telex transfers. I do not feel that the present case is a suitable occasion to decide this question in your Lordships' House, and, in view of my opinion on the two issues I have endeavoured to answer, I do not feel it is necessary to do so.

In the result I consider that the appeal should be dismissed with costs.

LORD DIPLOCK. My Lords, I agree entirely with the speech of my noble and learned friend Lord Hailsham LC, and am content to limit my own remarks to a brief comment on the shipowners' tabula in naufragio: 'anticipatory breach'.

The clause of the charterparty of which it was submitted that the charterers were in breach by anticipation as early as 1640 hrs on Thursday, 14 June 1979 was cl 5; and the event relied on as constituting an anticipatory breach of that clause was that by that time, as a result of the failure by the charterers' agents, their bankers Credito Italiano in Padua, to send a timeous telex correctly addressed to First National Bank of Chicago in London, the charterers had disabled themselves from making payment on 14 June 1979, in the manner specified in that clause, of the instalment of hire due on that date.

Although the findings of fact by Lloyd J do not go quite as far as this, I will assume in the owners' favour that it would have been impossible to transfer money which would be credited on 14 June 1979 to the account specified in cl 5, after 1640 hrs on that date; so that, as respects the semi-monthly instalment of hire due on 14 June, breach by the charterers of cl 5 was inevitable by the time the shipowners' telex of the 14 June 1979 was sent. Nevertheless the doctrine of anticipatory breach by conduct which disables a party to a contract from performing one of his primary obligations under the contract has in my view no application to a breach of such a clause.

The relevant portions of cl 5 have been set out by Lord Hailsham LC. The first part of the clause imposes on the respondents as charterers a primary obligation to pay the 'said hire' (which by cl 4 had been fixed at a monthly rate and pro rata for any part of a month) punctually and regularly in advance by semi-monthly instalments in the manner specified, which would involve the payment of a minimum of 42 and a maximum of 54 instalments, during the period of the charter. Failure to comply with this primary obligation by delay in payment of one instalment is incapable in law of amounting to a 'fundamental breach' of contract by the charterers in the sense to which I suggested in *Photo Production Ltd v Securicor Transport Ltd* [1980] 1 All ER 556 at 566, [1980] AC 827 at 849 this expression, if used as a term of legal art, ought to be confined. The reason is that such delay in payment of one half-monthly instalment would not have the effect of depriving the owners of substantially the whole benefit which it was the intention of the parties that the owners should obtain from the unexpired period of the time charter extending over a period of between 21 and 27 months.

The second part of cl 5, however, starting with the word 'otherwise' goes on to provide expressly what the rights of the owners are to be in the event of any such breach by the charterers of their primary obligation to make punctual payment of an instalment. The owners are to be at liberty to withdraw the vessel from the service of the charterers; in other words they are entitled to treat the breach when it occurs as a breach of condition and so giving them the right to elect to treat it as putting an end to all their own primary obligations under the charterparty then remaining unperformed. But although failure by the charterers in punctual payment of any instalment, however brief the delay involved may be, is made a breach of condition it is not also thereby converted into a fundamental breach; and it is to fundamental breaches alone that the doctrine of anticipatory breach is applicable.

The general rule is that a primary obligation is converted into a secondary obligation (whether a 'general secondary obligation' or an 'anticipatory secondary obligation' in the nomenclature of the analysis used in my speech in *Photo Production Ltd v Securicor Transport Ltd*) when and only when the breach of the primary obligation actually occurs. Up until then the primary obligations of both parties which have not yet been performed remain intact. The exception is where one party has manifested to the other party his intention no longer to perform the contract and the result of the non-performance would be to deprive the other party of substantially the whole benefit which it was the intention of the parties that that other party should obtain from the primary obligations of both parties remaining to be performed. In such a case, to which the term 'repudiation' is applicable, the party not in default need not wait until the actual breach: he may elect to treat the secondary obligations of the other party as arising forthwith.

The doctrine of anticipatory breach is but a species of the genus repudiation and applies only to fundamental breach. If one party to a contract states expressly or by implication to the other party in advance that he will not be able to perform a particular primary obligation on his part under the contract when the time for performance arrives, the question whether the other party may elect to treat the statement as a repudiation depends on whether the threatened non-performance would have the effect of depriving that other party of substantially the whole benefit which it was the intention of the parties that he should obtain from the primary obligations of the parties under the contract then remaining unperformed. If it would not have that effect there is no repudiation, and the other party cannot elect to put an end to such primary obligations remaining to be performed. The non-performance threatened must itself satisfy the criteria of a fundamental breach.

Similarly, where a party to a contract, whether by failure to take timeous action or by any other default, has put it out of his power to perform a particular primary obligation, the right of the other party to elect to treat this as a repudiation of the contract by conduct depends on whether the resulting non-performance would amount to a fundamental breach. Clearly, in the instant case delay in payment of one semi-monthly instalment of hire would not.

LORD KEITH OF KINKEL. My Lords, I have had the benefit of reading in draft the speeches delivered by my noble and learned friends Lord Hailsham LC and Lord Diplock. I agree with both of them, and for the reasons they give I too would dismiss the appeal.

LORD ROSKILL. My Lords, I have had the advantage of reading in draft the speeches of my learned and noble friends Lord Hailsham LC and Lord Diplock. I agree with

them, and for the reasons they give I too would dismiss this appeal. I wish to add some
observations on one matter only, that adverted to in the penultimate paragraph in the
former speech. In that paragraph my noble and learned friend Lord Hailsham LC refers
to certain passages in the judgments of Brandon J and of the Court of Appeal in *The
Brimnes, Tenex Steamship Co Ltd v The Brimnes (owners)* [1973] 1 All ER 769, [1973] 1 WLR
386; [1974] 3 All ER 88, [1975] QB 929, in connection with the time of payment where
payment is required to be made by telex transfer. In the instant case Lloyd J ([1980] 2
Lloyd's Rep 469 at 473) referred to these and other observations on this topic and stated
that he would hold that payment is complete 'when the telex is received and tested by
the receiving bank'. My Lords, I agree that the correctness or otherwise of these several
observations does not have to be determined in this appeal. But, as at present advised, I
think that the correct answer, whatever it may be, is likely to depend, at least in most
cases, on proof of the practice of bankers current when the question arises rather than on
any determination of it as a matter of law. No doubt, if and when the question does
hereafter arise, the requisite evidence will be forthcoming as indeed similar evidence was
adduced in the present case before Lloyd J.

LORD BRIGHTMAN. My Lords, I too would dismiss this appeal for the reasons
given by my noble and learned friends Lord Hailsham LC and Lord Diplock.

Appeal dismissed.

Solicitors: *Constant & Constant* (for the owners); *Middleton Potts & Co* (for the charterers).

Mary Rose Plummer Barrister.

Bond v Chief Constable of Kent

QUEEN'S BENCH DIVISION
GRIFFITHS LJ AND MCCULLOUGH J
6 OCTOBER 1982

*Sentence – Compensation order – Compensation for personal injury, loss or damage resulting
from offence – Anxiety and distress directly caused by offence – Defendant throwing stone through
window of house – Magistrates awarding compensation to occupier for his distress and anxiety –
Whether distress and anxiety amounting to 'personal injury . . . or damage' resulting from offence
– Powers of Criminal Courts Act 1973, s 35(1).*

In the early hours of the morning the occupier of a house became aware that a man, the
defendant, was behaving strangely in· the occupier's front garden and accordingly he
telephoned the police. Before the police arrived the defendant threw a stone through a
window of the house. The occupier was terrified, feared that there would be a sustained
attack on the house and felt compelled to gather his wife and children together into one
room for safety. The defendant was charged with unlawful damage to the window,
contrary to s 1(1) of the Criminal Damage Act 1971, and he pleaded guilty to the charge
before the magistrates. The magistrates, acting under s 35(1)[a] of the Powers of Criminal
Courts Act 1973, made awards to the occupier of £25 at the prosecutor's request to
compensate for replacing the window and £25 of their own motion to compensate for
the distress and anxiety suffered by the occupier, on the ground that the distress and
anxiety was a 'personal injury . . . resulting from [the defendant's] offence'. The defendant
appealed against the award for distress and anxiety.

---

a   Section 35(1), so far as material, is set out at p 458 e, post

Held – Anxiety and distress which was directly caused by a defendant's offence could be
a either 'personal injury' or 'damage' resulting from the offence within s 35(1) of the 1973
Act. Further, the rule that compensation for criminal damage should not be awarded
unless the amount in question was agreed or proved did not apply to the award of a small
sum for anxiety or distress. It followed that, since the occupier's terror was directly
occasioned by the defendant's attack on his house, the magistrates were entitled under
s 35(1) to award the sum of £25 of their own motion as compensation for the occupier's
b distress and anxiety (see p 458 h j and p 459 e f, post).
    R v Thomson Holidays Ltd [1974] 1 All ER 823 applied.
    R v Vivian [1979] 1 All ER 48 distinguished.
    Per McCullough J. In determining whether compensation should be awarded under s
35(1) of the 1973 Act, the court should approach the matter broadly, in a commonsense
way, by asking itself whether the loss or damage can fairly be said to have resulted from
c the offence, and should not become enmeshed in questions of causation appropriate to
the assessment of damages under the law of contract and tort (see p 459 g h, post).
    Dictum of Lawton LJ in *R v Thomson Holidays Ltd* [1974] 1 All ER at 829 applied.

Notes
For the power of a magistrates' court to make compensation orders for personal injury,
d loss or damage resulting from an offence, see 29 Halsbury's Laws (4th edn) para 423 and
11 ibid para 804, and for cases on the subject, see 14(2) Digest (Reissue) 861–864, 7455–
7491.
    For the Powers of Criminal Courts Act 1973, s 35, see 43 Halsbury's Statutes (3rd edn)
331.

e **Cases referred to in judgments**
Berkeley v Orchard [1975] Crim LR 225, DC.
R v Thomson Holidays Ltd [1974] 1 All ER 823, [1974] QB 592, [1974] 2 WLR 371, CA,
    Digest (Cont Vol D) 985, 1100d.
R v Vivian [1979] 1 All ER 48, [1979] 1 WLR 291, CA, Digest (Cont Vol E) 148, 7475(1).

f **Case also cited**
R v Howell (Anthony) (1978) 66 Cr App R 179, CA.

Case stated
Kenneth John Bond appealed by way of a case stated by the justices for the County of
g Kent acting in and for the petty sessional division of Gravesham, sitting at Gravesend, in
respect of their adjudication on 15 January 1982 on an information preferred against the
appellant by the Chief Constable of Kent alleging that on 30 August 1981 at Gravesend
the appellant damaged a window valued at £25 without lawful excuse, being the
property of Ivor Tony Mancini, intending to damage it or being reckless whether it
would be damaged, contrary to s 1(1) of the Criminal Damage Act 1971. The appellant
h pleaded guilty to the charge. The magistrates, having found the facts, were of the opinion
that Mr Mancini had been considerably frightened by the events surrounding the
commission of the offence and decided that, in addition to making at the prosecutor's
request an award of compensation of £25 to compensate Mr Mancini for the cost of
replacing the window, they would also award Mr Mancini a further £25 by way of
compensation for the distress and anxiety occasioned to him by the appellant's behaviour.
j Accordingly, in addition to fining the appellant £50, the magistrates made a compensation
order in the sum of £50, pursuant to s 35 of the Powers of Criminal Courts Act 1973.
The appellant appealed against the compensation order. The questions for the opinion of
the court were (1) whether distress and anxiety could constitute an injury for the purposes
of an award of compensation under s 35 of the 1973 Act, and (2) whether the magistrates
were correct in awarding Mr Mancini £25 compensation for his distress and anxiety

occasioned by the appellant's behaviour when committing the offence of criminal damage. The facts are set out in the judgment of Griffiths LJ.

a

Benjamin Conlon for the appellant.
The chief constable did not appear.

GRIFFITHS LJ. This is an appeal by way of case stated from an order of the magistrates sitting in the petty sessional division of Gravesham who, on 15 January 1982, after the *b* appellant had pleaded guilty to a charge of causing damage to property contrary to s 1(1) of the Criminal Damage Act 1971, made an order that he pay the sum of £25 as compensation to the occupier of the house that he had damaged because of the distress and anxiety suffered by the occupier as a result of the appellant's behaviour.

The facts of the case are briefly these. In the early hours of 30 August 1981 the occupiers of the house were aroused by noises coming from their front garden, and *c* became aware of the presence of a man behaving strangely and stumbling about. They telephoned the police but before the police arrived a stone was thrown through the window of the house. The occupier of the house was terrified, fearing that there would be a sustained attack and felt compelled to gather his wife and children into one room for safety. The police, on arrival, found the appellant to be in a drunken state. He was then arrested and taken to Gravesend police station.

d

The magistrates were asked by the prosecutor to consider awarding £25 compensation which was the cost of replacing the damaged window, but of their own motion they also considered whether or not they should not award some modest sum to compensate the occupier of the house for what must undoubtedly have been a most terrifying and frightening experience.

They considered the terms of s 35(1) of the Powers of Criminal Courts Act 1973, which *e* provides that 'on application or otherwise' they may make 'an order . . . requiring [the appellant] to pay compensation for any personal injury, loss or damage resulting from that offence . . .' The magistrates rightly considered that there was a sufficient nexus between the behaviour and the terror caused to the occupier. Indeed, it was the only cause of the occupier's terror.

In those circumstances it appears to me that the only question for consideration by this *f* court is whether the fright and distress suffered can be fairly covered by either the words 'personal injury' or 'damage' contained in s 35.

We have been referred to three authorities by counsel for the appellant but the first two, in my view, carry the matter that we have to decide nowhere. He referred us to the decision of this court in *Berkeley v Orchard* [1975] Crim LR 225. In that case a man was charged with the unlawful possession of a drug, contrary to the Misuse of Drugs Act *g* 1971 and it so happened that another man had apparently taken some of the drug that was in this man's possession. The magistrates accordingly ordered him to pay compensation to the man who had taken the drug. That appeal was allowed because this court held that there was not a sufficient causal connection between the offence of simple possession, for which the defendant had been convicted, and the fact that some other man took the drug. In this case there is a manifest direct causal connection. *h*

The next case cited was *R v Vivian* [1979] 1 All ER 48, [1979] 1 WLR 291. In that case the defendant had been convicted of taking and driving away a motor car, and driving it recklessly. In the course of that he collided with and damaged another car, the estimate of repairs being £209. The judge in that case ordered him to pay compensation in the sum of £100. However, the estimate was fiercely contested by the defendant as being grossly excessive, and this court held that a compensation order should not be made *j* unless the sum claimed by the victim as compensation for damage resulting from the offence was either agreed or had been proved. That case is clearly limited to what I will call 'quantifiable physical damage'. It has no application to small sums of money awarded for personal injury or for the results of assaults or behaviour with which we are concerned in this case.

The final case was *R v Thomson Holidays Ltd* [1974] 1 All ER 823, [1974] QB 592. In
a that case, Thomson Holidays Ltd had sold a package holiday and they were convicted of
an offence under the Trade Descriptions Act 1968, the nature of which was that they had
recklessly made a false representation in the course of their trade or business as to the
amenity or accommodation provided by their hotel, contrary to s 14(1)(b) of that Act.
The facts revealed that the hotel fell very, very far short of the legitimate expectations of
anyone reading the brochure and, as a result, the customers had been very gravely
b disappointed in their holiday. They were awarded the modest sum of £50 by way of
compensation for that disappointment.

In giving the judgment of the court Lawton LJ said ([1974] 1 All ER 823 at 829, [1974]
QB 592 at 599):

'Section 1(1) of this Act is intended to be applied by both magistrates and judges
sitting in the Crown Court and the reference to offences taken into consideration
c shows that the court making a compensation order may not be apprised of the
detailed facts of such offences. It must do what it can to make a just order on such
information as it has. Whenever the making of an order for compensation is
appropriate the court must ask itself whether loss or damage can fairly be said to
have resulted to anyone from the offence for which the accused has been convicted
or has been taken into consideration. We have no hesitation in saying that on the
d facts of this case the failure to provide Mr and Mrs Brown with the amenities which
they expected to find available did result from the offences for which the appellants
were convicted.'

If the disappointment and inconvenience of a ruined holiday falls within the word
'damage' in s 35 of the Powers of Criminal Courts Act 1973, I for my part have no doubt
e that the terror directly occasioned by this attack on the occupier's house falls either
within 'personal injury' or alternatively within the word 'damage' in s 35 of the 1973
Act, and the magistrates were fully entitled to award the modest sum of £25. I would
dismiss this appeal.

McCULLOUGH J. I agree. In *R v Thomson Holidays Ltd* [1974] 1 All ER 823 at 829,
f [1974] QB 592 at 599 Lawton LJ said:

'Parliament, we are sure, never intended to introduce into the criminal law the
concepts of causation which apply to the assessment of damages under the law of
contract and tort.'

In my judgment, the sense of that observation is this: that in assessing whether
g compensation should be awarded under s 35 of the Powers of Criminal Courts Act 1973
the court should approach the matter in a broad commonsense way and should not allow
itself to become enmeshed in the refined questions of causation which can sometimes
arise in claims for damages under the law of contract or tort. The court simply has to ask
itself whether the loss or damage can fairly be said to have resulted from the offence.
This court plainly did that.

h
Appeal dismissed.

Solicitors: *Hatten Wyatt & Co*, Gravesend (for the appellant).

Sepala Munasinghe Esq   Barrister.

R v Leeds Justices, ex parte Sykes

QUEEN'S BENCH DIVISION
GRIFFITHS LJ AND MCCULLOUGH J
26 OCTOBER 1982

Criminal law – Committal – Preliminary hearing before justices – Order lifting reporting restrictions – More than one accused – Objections by one accused to lifting of reporting restrictions – Factors to be considered by examining magistrates in deciding whether to order reporting restrictions to be lifted – Whether 'in the interests of justice' to order lifting of restrictions – Magistrates' Courts Act 1980, s 8(2A).

In committal proceedings brought against the applicant and his four co-accused for conspiracy to rob, one of the co-accused, P, applied to the examining magistrates to have the restrictions on reporting the committal proceedings imposed by s 8(1) of the Magistrates' Court Act 1980 lifted, because he wanted to make a public protest against alleged conduct of the police in first indicating to him that they would not proceed with all the charges against him and then deciding to proceed with all the charges. P's application was supported by another of the co-accused for the same reason, but the applicant opposed the lifting of reporting restrictions because he believed that his trial would be prejudiced if the evidence at the committal proceedings was given wide publicity. The magistrates made an order pursuant to s 8(2A)[a] of the 1980 Act that reporting restrictions on the committal proceedings should be lifted because it was 'in the interests of justice to do so'. The applicant applied for certiorari to quash the order.

Held – (1) Where there was a division of opinion among co-accused whether committal proceedings should be reported, s 8(2A) of the 1980 Act placed on the accused who wished to have the proceedings reported the burden of satisfying the magistrates that it was 'in the interests of justice' that they should make an order lifting reporting restrictions. In deciding whether it was in the interests of justice to do so, the magistrates had to balance the conflicting views of the co-accused and to have regard to the rule contained in s 8(1) of the 1980 Act that, prima facie, committal proceedings should not be reported and to the fact that 'the interests of justice' referred to in s 8(2A) required, as a paramount consideration, that all the accused should have a fair trial. Accordingly, where a co-accused objected to the lifting of reporting restrictions on the grounds that wide reporting of the committal proceedings might colour the view of the jury ultimately trying the case, the magistrates should make an order lifting reporting restrictions only where a powerful case for reporting the proceedings was made out by the other co-accused (see p 462 a b d to f and p 464 h, post); dictum of Shaw LJ in *R v Horsham Justices, ex p Farquharson* [1982] 2 All ER at 289 applied.

(2) Since giving publicity to P's grievance against the police was not likely to have any effect on the ultimate fairness of his trial and was merely a peripheral factor in deciding whether it was in the interests of justice that reporting restrictions in respect of the committal proceedings should be lifted, it was a factor of little or no weight when balanced against the applicant's objection that his trial would be prejudiced if the committal proceedings were reported. It followed that in ordering the lifting of reporting restrictions the magistrates had not weighed the balance fairly between the interests of the applicant and his co-accused. Accordingly certiorari would be granted to quash the magistrates' order (see p 464 d to h, post).

Notes

For restrictions on reporting committal proceedings, see 11 Halsbury's Laws (4th edn) para 139.

---

a Section 8(2A) is set out at p 461 j, post

For the Magistrates' Courts Act 1980, s 8, see 50(2) Halsbury's Statutes (3rd edn) 1448,
a and for s 8(2A) of the 1980 Act (as inserted by the Criminal Justice (Amendment) Act
1981), see 51 ibid 1081.

Case referred to in judgments
R v Horsham Justices, ex p Farquharson [1982] 2 All ER 269, [1982] QB 762, [1982] 2 WLR
430, DC and CA.

b

Application for judicial review
Harry Sykes applied, with the leave of the Divisional Court granted on 29 June 1982, for
an order of certiorari to quash an order made by the Leeds justices on 23 March 1982
lifting reporting restrictions on committal proceedings in respect of the applicant and his
four co-accused. The application to the justices to have reporting restrictions lifted had
c been made by one of the applicant's co-accused, Ronald William Priestley, and supported
by another co-accused, but had been opposed by the applicant. The grounds of the
application for certiorari were, inter alia, that in committal proceedings under s 6(1) of
the Magistrates' Courts Act 1980 where there was more than one defendant, it was
contrary to 'the interest of justice', within s 8(2A) of the 1980 Act, to lift reporting
restrictions on committal proceedings unless all the defendants agreed that the restrictions
d be lifted. The facts are set out in the judgment of Griffiths LJ.

Robert McCall Thoresby for the applicant.
Paul F Worsley for the co-accused Priestley.

The justices did not appear.

e

GRIFFITHS LJ. In these proceedings the applicant, Harry Sykes, seeks an order of
certiorari directed to the Leeds Magistrates' Court to quash an order made by the
magistrates sitting at Leeds on 23 March 1982 that reporting restrictions be raised in
respect of committal proceedings of Sykes and his co-accused, in respect of a prosecution
under s 1 of the Criminal Law Act 1977 for conspiracy to rob. This is, so far as counsel's
f researches have revealed, the first occasion on which this court has had to consider an
order made by magistrates for the lifting of reporting restrictions on committal
proceedings pursuant to the provisions of s 8(2A) of the Magistrates' Courts Act 1980.
  I will introduce the matter with a very short recital of the historical events that led up
to the enactment of s 8(2A). Prior to 1967 there was no general restriction on the press
reporting of committal proceedings but there was such publicity given to the press
g reporting of the committal proceedings in the case of the trial of Dr Bodkin Adams that
Parliament enacted, in 1967, that henceforward the only reporting of committal
proceedings would be of purely formal matter, unless the accused (or if there were more
than one accused, one of the accused) had specifically requested that the reporting
restrictions be lifted. If such a request was made, then the magistrates had no discretion,
they had to allow the committal proceedings to be reported.
h There then followed the committal proceedings in a recent trial where there was a
division of opinion among the co-accused on whether or not there should be reporting
of the committal proceedings. As the law then stood, the fact that one of the accused
requested that the proceedings be reported compelled the magistrates to make an order
to that effect and there was very wide publicity of those committal proceedings.
  It was in consequence of that, that Parliament enacted s 8(2A) of the Magistrates' Courts
i Act 1980, which provides as follows:

> 'Where in the case of two or more accused one of them objects to the making of
> an order under subsection (2) above [that is to say, an order that reporting of the
> committal proceedings be permitted], the court shall make the order if, and only if,
> it is satisfied, after hearing the representations of the accused, that it is in the interests
> of justice to do so.'

The position is that, prima facie, there is to be no reporting of committal proceedings; reporting restrictions are to be lifted in the case of a single accused if he wishes; in the *a* case of a number of accused, the reporting restrictions are to be lifted if they all wish it, but if there is a division of opinion among the accused whether or not the committal proceedings should be reported, then it is for the magistrates to make the decision. It is quite clear from the wording of s 8(2A) that there is a burden on him who wishes the proceedings to be reported to satisfy the magistrates that it is in the interests of justice to do so. Colloquial, but easily understandable, and emphatic words are used. I repeat, 'the *b* court shall make the order if and only if it is satisfied . . .'

It is not desirable for this court, on the first occasion that the matter comes before it, to make any attempt to give a definition of the phrase 'it is in the interests of justice to do so'. The phrase has been considered obiter by the Court of Appeal in *R v Horsham Justices, ex p Farquharson* [1982] 2 All ER 269, [1982] QB 762. I for my part would certainly adopt that part of Shaw LJ's judgment where he says ([1982] 2 All ER 269 at 289, [1982] QB *c* 762 at 797):

> 'Although that section introduces "the interests of justice" as a factor which must be considered by the justices in determining whether to lift the prohibition on publication, it would seem that it is the interests of justice as affecting the defendants that the court must consider, for only they are entitled to make representations to the court in this regard.' *d*

Without attempting any comprehensive definition, the interests of justice incorporate as a paramount consideration that the accused should have a fair trial. When the magistrates have to balance the request for the committal proceedings to be reported, they must bear in mind that the prima facie rule is that committal proceedings should not be reported, and only if a powerful case is made out for their reporting should they *e* be prepared to make an order when one of the accused objects, particularly if the ground of objection is that very reason that led Parliament to provide that, as a general rule, proceedings should not be reported, namely that there is a risk that if the proceedings are widely reported, the reports may colour the views of the jury which ultimately has to try the case.

Against that background of the legislation, I turn to consider the actual facts of the *f* present case that led up to the making of this order. Harry Sykes, the applicant, is charged with conspiracy to rob, together with some other men called Hinchcliffe, Keith, Aldridge and Priestley. Initially, he, Sykes, appeared on 14 December 1981 and was admitted to bail. He has then appeared before the court on a large number of occasions on remand. His co-accused, Priestley, is represented by a different solicitor, a Mr Sugare, and Priestley was in custody until the remand hearing on 2 March 1982, when he was allowed bail. *g*

At the hearing on 23 March 1982 Mr Sugare, Priestley's solicitor, applied to raise reporting restrictions. The basis of his application was that at the hearing on 2 March a police officer had indicated to him that certain charges against his client, Priestley, would be dropped and that was why bail was not opposed on 2 March. On 23 March, that is the date of the application, Mr Sugare said that he was told that the charges were not to be dropped after all and he wanted to protest about it. *h*

The affidavit of Mr Barrington Black, who is Sykes's solicitor, deposed to a second reason advanced by Mr Sugare, which is not clearly expressed and which neither this court nor counsel has been able to elucidate. I will do no more than read it. It stated:

> 'It is right to say that he did mention that although that was the main aspect of the application he was concerned in view of the publicity given at the time of the *j* arrest that this should be publicly aired.'

In Mr Sugare's own affidavit, he deposed to the fact that the basis of his application was correctly stated in the affidavit of Mr Barrington Black, so that carries us no further. But this much is absolutely plain, the principal reason for lifting the reporting restrictions put forward by Mr Sugare was to enable him to make a public protest at what he

obviously considered to be unfair, or at least unkind, conduct on the part of the police,
a namely indicating to Priestley's legal advisers that they might not or would not be going
on with some of the charges and then about three weeks later saying: 'No, the decision
has been taken to go on with all of them.'

Mr Barrington Black, before the magistrates, opposed the application to raise the
reporting restrictions. He submitted that the reason put forward by Mr Sugare, as his
principal reason, could not be considered by the magistrates as a reason falling within the
b phrase 'in the interests of justice' and made the point that, if after the committal
proceedings Mr Sugare's client was cleared, there would be ample opportunity for him
then to make a statement to the press about this matter, which could be fully reported.

The magistrates were obviously unfamiliar with this new procedure and that is not
surprising as it had only been very recently introduced. They made a preliminary
decision, saying that the reporting restrictions would be lifted in so far as the case against
c Priestley alone was concerned. That is not permitted under the 1980 Act. If the reporting
restrictions are to be lifted, then they are to be lifted in respect of the committal
proceedings in their entirety. They cannot be lifted piecemeal.

Then a Mr Stowe, who was acting as the solicitor on behalf of another of the accused (a
man called Aldridge), indicated that he supported the application to raise the restrictions
made by Mr Sugare in so far as Aldridge was concerned. Mr Barrington Black pointed
d out to the magistrates that they in fact had no power to raise reporting restrictions
relating to individual accused, but nevertheless the magistrates did purport to raise the
restrictions in respect of Aldridge. However, their error was then pointed out to them,
presumably by the clerk of the court, and they then decided that they would raise the
restrictions in respect of all the defendants.

Mr Sugare's affidavit, in so far as it is relevant, I have already referred to. Mr Stowe has
e sworn an affidavit in which he deposed that his client, Aldridge, initially instructed him
towards the middle of December 1981 to make an application to raise restrictions, but at
that stage, because Mr Barrington Black told him that he would be objecting to the
raising of restrictions, he decided not to proceed with his application. However, when
Mr Sugare again applied to raise the restrictions on 23 March, Mr Stowe then supported
the application. There is no suggestion by Mr Stowe that he relied on any grounds other
f than those put forward by Mr Sugare and, indeed, in the final paragraph of his affidavit,
he said:

> 'I have no reasons as a solicitor in charge of Ralph Ernest Aldridge's case to require
> press restrictions to be raised for any subsequent proceedings as the purpose for my
> application was satisfied on the 23rd March 1982.'

g I have read that to draw attention to the fact that there is no suggestion by Mr Stowe
that he ever put forward as an independent ground that he wished the reporting
restrictions to be raised so that there might be an opportunity of missing witnesses, vital
to the defence case, identifying themselves and putting themselves forward.

I turn now to the affidavit of Mr Eric Buller, who was chairman of the magistrates at
the time of this adjudication. He deposes as follows:

h > 'Initially the accused Keith, Priestley and Sykes were before the court with their
> respective solicitors Mr. Sugare and Mr. Black, when Mr. Sugare made application
> that reporting restrictions be raised as the police had indicated earlier that they
> would not proceed with certain charges against his client, whereas on the 23rd
> March 1982 the police indicated that those charges would not be dropped. Mr. Black
> for Sykes opposed the application. After consideration my fellow magistrate and I
> felt that it would be in the interests of justice to raise reporting restrictions in respect
> of the accused Priestley and I announced our decision. Immediately our mistake
> was brought to my notice by the clerk, I rectified the error and with all the accused
> present, heard Mr. Stowe for the accused Aldridge make an application for reporting
> restrictions to be raised on the ground that the subsequent publicity would bring

the case to the notice of potential witnesses. Again, Mr. Black opposed the applications.'

There we have a very clear conflict of recollection between the three legal advisers appearing to make or oppose the application as the case may be on the one side, and that of the chairman of the magistrates on the other. But very fairly, in the last paragraph of his affidavit, Mr Buller said:

'I make this affidavit, without the benefit of contemporary notes, from my recollection of proceedings heard four months ago.'

This court is not satisfied that in fact any ground was put forward by Mr Stowe to the effect that the subsequent publicity would bring the case to the notice of potential witnesses. We find it inconceivable, if that really was the object of Mr Stowe's application, that he should not recollect it and would not have set it out quite clearly in his affidavit because it is freely conceded by the applicant that such an application would merit really serious consideration by the magistrates when deciding whether or not it was in the interests of justice that the proceedings should be reported.

Accordingly, I approach this case on the basis that the only substantial ground put forward was that Mr Sugare had at one stage been told by the police that his client would not have to face all the charges and that at a later stage the police told him they were going on with all those charges.

I have no doubt that that engendered a sense of disappointment in the breast of Mr Sugare and his client. They may have felt aggrieved about it, but for my part I am quite unable to see how giving publicity to that state of affairs is likely to have any effect whatever on the ultimate fairness of the trial of the accused. Looked at strictly, it is difficult to see that it would be a relevant matter to be canvassed at the trial. It might possibly be introduced by way of cross-examination of one of the police officers to sow a little prejudice but I can well envisage a robust judge telling counsel fairly sharply that the jury were there to weigh the evidence and decide the guilt of the men on the material placed before them and not to speculate what may or may not have been the police's view of the strength of the case at an earlier stage of the proceedings.

If it has any significance at all, it can only be of the most peripheral significance when deciding whether or not it is in the interests of justice that there should be reporting of these proceedings. It can really be of no weight when weighed against the objection of one accused who believes that his trial will be prejudiced if there is wide publicity of the evidence on which the prosecution will ultimately ask the jury to try the case.

Accordingly, I have come to the conclusion that the magistrates in this case cannot have appreciated the nature of the inquiry that they were required to make under s 8(2A) of the 1980 Act and that they did not weigh the balance fairly between the accused.

I would quash this decision. That will not mean, of course, that when these proceedings come to be heard, which I believe is on 15 November 1982, a fresh application cannot be made on behalf of one or other of the accused for reporting of the proceedings if they wish to do so. That will then have to be considered on its merits. I therefore would allow this appeal and order certiorari to go.

McCULLOUGH J. So would I, for the same reasons.

Application allowed. Certiorari granted.

Solicitors: *Sidney Torrance & Co*, agents for *Barrington Black Austin & Co*, Leeds (for the applicant); *Anthony Sugare & Co*, Leeds (for the co-accused Priestley).

April Weiss   Barrister.

a # Project Development Co Ltd SA v KMK Securities Ltd and others (Syndicate Bank intervening)

b # Fidelity International Bank v International Finance and Exchange Corp (Syndicate Bank intervening)

QUEEN'S BENCH DIVISION (COMMERCIAL COURT)

PARKER J

c 6 JULY 1982

Injunction – Interlocutory – Danger that defendant may transfer assets out of jurisdiction – Costs of innocent third party – Variation of injunction – Innocent third party successfully seeking variation of injunction – Third party entitled to reasonable costs of application – Costs to be taxed on solicitor and own client basis – Burden of establishing reasonableness of costs on third party –
d *RSC Ord 62, r 29(1).*

Where an innocent third party who is affected by a Mareva injunction successfully applies to the court for a variation of the order he ought to have all his costs incurred in respect of the application so long as they are not unreasonable in amount or unreasonably incurred. Such costs should be taxed on the solicitor and own client basis, but with a *e* special direction that, notwithstanding the terms of RSC Ord 62, r 29[a], the burden of establishing the reasonableness of incurring the costs and of their amount should be on the third party to whom the costs have been awarded. A plaintiff who resorts to the Mareva jurisdiction must expect to pay, and should in justice pay, all reasonable expenses and all reasonable costs to which innocent third parties may be put by his actions (see p 466 *j* to p 467 *b* and *f* to *j* and p 468 *a b*, post).
f *EMI Records Ltd v Ian Cameron Wallace Ltd* [1982] 2 All ER 980 considered.

Notes
For the assessment of costs generally, see 37 Halsbury's Laws (4th edn) para 744, and for costs as between a solicitor and his own client, see ibid para 747.

Case referred to in judgment
g *EMI Records Ltd v Ian Cameron Wallace Ltd* [1982] 2 All ER 980, [1982] 3 WLR 245.

Summonses
By a writ issued on 12 February 1982 the plaintiffs, Project Development Co Ltd SA, brought an action against several defendants, including the first defendant, KMK

---

h a   Rule 29, so far as material, provides:
'(1) On the taxation of a solicitor's bill to his own client (except a bill to be paid out of the legal aid fund under the Legal Aid Act 1974 or a bill with respect to non-contentious business) all costs shall be allowed except in so far as they are of an unreasonable amount or have been unreasonably incurred.
(2) For the purposes of paragraph (1), all costs incurred with the express or implied approval of *j* the client shall, subject to paragraph (3), be conclusively presumed to have been reasonably incurred and, where the amount thereof has been expressly or impliedly approved by the client, to have been reasonable in amount.
(3) For the purpose of paragraph (1), any costs which in the circumstances of the case are of an unusual nature and such that they would not be allowed on a taxation of costs in a case to which rule 28(2) applies shall, unless the solicitor expressly informed his client before they were incurred that they might not be so allowed, be presumed, until the contrary is shown, to have been unreasonably incurred . . .'

Securities Ltd, and the third defendant, International Finance and Exchange Corp. On ex parte applications in chambers on 15 February and 3 March 1982 Webster J granted the plaintiffs certain interlocutory relief including, inter alia, Mareva injunctions restraining the defendants from removing out of the jurisdiction or in any way disposing of their assets within the jurisdiction until futher order. On an ex parte application in chambers on 29 April 1982 Mustill J granted Fidelity Bank a Mareva injunction restraining International Finance and Exchange Corp from removing or otherwise disposing of their assets within the jurisdiction until further order. The interveners, Syndicate Bank, applied to the court by two summonses dated 24 May 1982 to have the Mareva injunctions varied so as to permit them to set off a specified sum standing to the credit of International Finance and Exchange Corp at a branch of the interveners in London in reduction of its indebtedness to the interveners. The judge allowed the variation. The summonses were heard in chambers but judgment on the issue of the taxation of costs (to which this report is confined) was given by Parker J in open court.

Mark Potter QC for the plaintiffs.
Roger Toulson for the interveners.

PARKER J. This judgment in open court deals only with the costs of successful applications by intervening third parties to vary Mareva injunctions so that they should not affect assets in the hands of those third parties. The judgment is given in open court since it is an essential aspect of the jurisdiction to grant Mareva types of injunction that the position of innocent third parties should be fully protected, and since there is as yet no decision as to the basis on which a successful third party should have his costs after argument on the matter. I have been referred to a case where a special order was made and to a case where a special order was not made, but in neither case does there appear to have been any argument as to the principle on which the court should proceed. In *The Supreme Court Practice 1982* vol 1, p 521, para 29/1/11E there appears the following:

'It should perhaps be further emphasised that, if any person or body who is notified of a Mareva injunction which of course he must recognise at the risk of being guilty of contempt of court is put to any expense in regard to it, that expense must be paid by the plaintiff... Presumably, such a person or body could be allowed to intervene in the action under O. 15, r 6... in order, if necessary, to obtain an order for his costs to be taxed and paid by the plaintiff, and he may be entitled to have his costs taxed on a solicitor and own client basis or at least on the common fund basis. In his turn, the plaintiff may be entitled to recover such costs owed as against the defendant.'

That paragraph, whilst citing authority for the proposition that the third party is entitled to have his expenses, cites no authority for the second observation that costs might be awarded on a solicitor and own client basis or, at least, on the common fund basis.

In the present cases the interveners, having succeeded in their applications, applied for their costs on a solicitor and own client basis. The plaintiffs contended that costs on a party and party basis was all that should be awarded, and that the special orders should be preserved for using in a penal fashion. In my judgment neither of these submissions is right. The solicitor and own client basis applied in full under RSC Ord 62, r 29(1) would, or might, expose the plaintiffs to the payment of extravagant costs. I see no reason for making an order on such a basis. The party and party basis, however, requires that only such costs as were necessary and proper for the attainment of justice or enforcing or defending the rights of the party whose costs are being taxed shall be allowed. That provision results, or may result, in costs which are both reasonably incurred and reasonable in amount being disallowed on the ground that they were unnecessary. In my judgment an innocent third party affected by a Mareva injunction ought, if he has to apply to the court for variation of the order and is successful in so doing, to have all costs incurred, so long as they are not unreasonable in amount or unreasonably incurred; and a plaintiff who resorts to the draconian remedy of a Mareva injunction should expect to

pay such costs. If in pursuit of his rights against a defendant he initiates an order of the
court affecting assets in the hands of third parties, and that order is later varied at the
instance of third parties so as to exclude assets in their hands, justice appears to me to
require that all the innocent third parties' costs should be paid by the plaintiff unless they
are unreasonable. Hence I reject the party and party basis.

There appears to me no logic and no justification for saying that the innocent third
party shall have his expenses in complying with the order so long as reasonable, but shall
not be entitled to have his costs of setting aside the order so long as reasonable. The
choice, in my view, lies between a common fund basis and the indemnity basis as
explained by Sir Robert Megarry V-C in the very recent case of *EMI Records Ltd v Ian
Cameron Wallace Ltd* [1982] 2 All ER 980, [1982] 3 WLR 245, or possibly by a special
variation of one or other basis of taxation, the possibility of making which was expressly
recognised by the Vice-Chancellor. The common fund basis is more generous than the
party and party basis, and covers, on the wording, a reasonable amount in respect of all
costs reasonably incurred. On the face of it, that would appear to give the innocent third
party everything to which he is entitled, but a taxation on a common fund basis, if no
special direction is made, leaves the taxing master fettered by the provisions of RSC Ord
62, App 2 and results in a comparatively small uplift over the party and party basis.

The indemnity basis, as explained by Sir Robert Megarry V-C, results in the application
of RSC Ord 62, r 29(1), but without the presumptions included in Ord 62, r 29(2) and
(3). Rule 29(1) provides that on the taxation of a solicitor's bill to his own client, except a
bill to be paid out of the legal aid fund under the Legal Aid Act 1974 or a bill with respect
to non-contentious business, all costs shall be allowed, except in so far as they are of an
unreasonable amount or have been unreasonably incurred. On the wording of the two
provisions, it would appear that the only difference between the common fund basis and
the solicitor and own client basis is that in a common fund taxation it is for the successful
party to establish the reasonableness, whereas on the solicitor and client basis the reverse
applies and the costs will be taken to be reasonable, unless they are shown to be of an
unreasonable amount or to have been unreasonably incurred. But in practice the position
is different, in that on a common fund basis the taxation is done under the constraint of
App 2.

It appears to me that, whilst the successful third party intervener should be allowed all
his reasonable costs, it is right that he should have to establish, as he does on the common
fund basis, the reasonableness of the costs for which he is contending. There appear to be
two substantially similar ways of achieving that result, one of which is to direct that the
costs should be taxed on the solicitor and own client basis, with a special direction that,
notwithstanding the terms of Ord 62, r 29(1), the burden of establishing the
reasonableness of the incurring of the costs and the reasonableness of the amount should
be on the third party to whom the costs have been awarded. The other is to order costs to
be paid on a common fund basis, with a direction to the taxing master to exercise his
discretion under Ord 62, r 32(2), a method which was expressly referred to by Sir Robert
Megarry V-C in his judgment. The effect of such a direction is to remove the restriction
which would otherwise apply under App 2.

It appears to me that the only satisfactory course is the former, inasmuch as if the
taxation is directed to be made on a common fund basis, coupled with a direction to the
taxing master to exercise his discretion under r 32(2), the decision as to the extent to
which that discretion will be applied will be left to the taxing master, whereas if the
special provision is attached to an indemnity basis order then the result which appears to
me to be desirable will certainly be achieved. That will result in the plaintiffs having to
pay to the intervener all costs which would be allowed under Ord 62, r 29(1) with the
exception or with the qualification only that despite the wording of Ord 62, r 29(1) it
will be for the interveners to establish that the costs are not unreasonable in amount and
have not been unreasonably incurred. Such a special direction, counsel for the plaintiffs
submits, will cause great difficulty or may cause great difficulty to the taxing masters. It
may be that it will, in so far as it is something different from anything which has
previously been ordered. But I can see no reason why such a simple variation should

cause any serious difficulty, the more particularly when taxing masters have already to
deal with taxations on a common fund basis, where the burden of proof is as I have stated
it shall be in the present case. I am concerned only to see that the result of the taxation is
that the intervening third party has those costs which I have indicated it appears to me in
Mareva cases, save in exceptional circumstances, he ought to have.

It should, I think, be stressed that a plaintiff who resorts to the Mareva jurisdiction
must expect to pay, and should in justice pay, all reasonable expenses and all reasonable
costs to which innocent third parties may be put by his actions; and it is on that basis that
I make the order which I do.

Order accordingly.

Solicitors: *Berwin Leighton* (for the plaintiffs); *Simmons & Simmons* (for the interveners).

K Mydeen Esq   Barrister.

Banque de l'Indochine et de Suez SA v J H Rayner (Mincing Lane) Ltd

QUEEN'S BENCH DIVISION (COMMERCIAL COURT)
PARKER J
21, 22, 23 JUNE, 21 JULY 1982

*Bank – Documentary credit – Irrevocable credit – Payment under reserve – Payment under
reserve by confirming bank to beneficiary – Effect – Confirming bank alleging documents tendered
not complying with terms of credit – Beneficiary disputing alleged discrepancies in documents –
Confirming bank making payment under reserve – Issuing bank rejecting documents on account of
discrepancies – Whether confirming bank immediately entitled to be reimbursed by beneficiary –
Whether necessary for confirming bank to show that tender of documents defective.*

The defendants agreed to sell certain goods to the buyers. Payment was to be made by an
irrevocable letter of credit to be issued by a bank in Djibouti and confirmed by the
plaintiff bank. The defendants tendered to the plaintiffs the documents specified in the
letter of credit and requested payment. The plaintiffs considered that the documents did
not comply with the terms of the letter of credit but, when the defendants disputed the
alleged discrepancies in the documents, they offered to make the payment 'under reserve'.
The defendants accepted the offer and the plaintiffs duly paid the amount stated in the
letter of credit. The documents were forwarded to the issuing bank in Djibouti, which
refused to accept them because of the discrepancies specified by the plaintiffs. The
plaintiffs immediately claimed reimbursement from the defendants. When the
defendants refused to repay the money, on the ground that they were under no obligation
to repay unless one or more of the specified discrepancies was established as being a valid
ground for refusing payment in the first place, the plaintiffs brought an action against
them to recover the money, claiming that, once the documents had been rejected because
of the specified discrepancies, they immediately became entitled to repayment of the
amount paid under reserve (with interest from the date of payment) irrespective of
whether any of the discrepancies would in law have been a sufficient ground for refusing
to make the payment originally.

Held – The fact that the payment had been made 'under reserve' did not mean that, as
soon as the issuing bank rejected the documents, the plaintiffs were entitled to demand
their money back irrespective of whether in law they were obliged to pay the defendants
when they did. By making payment 'under reserve' they had merely reserved the right

to get the money back if it was subsequently shown that it was not contractually payable
a at the date of payment, ie because the documents tendered called for inquiry. On the
facts, the discrepancies in the documents tendered by the defendants clearly called for
inquiry and it followed that, because the money had not been contractually payable at
the date of payment, the plaintiffs were entitled to have it refunded with interest from
that date (see p 471 *j* to p 472 *c e j*, p 474 *h* to p 475 *c*, post).

Dictum of Donaldson J in M *Golodetz & Co Inc v Czarnikow-Rionda Co Inc, The Galatea*
b [1979] 2 All ER at 739 applied.

Notes

For commercial letters of credit, see 3 Halsbury's Laws (4th edn) paras 131–137, for the
stipulation for and tender of documents, see ibid paras 140–141, and for cases on the
subjects, see 3 Digest (Reissue) 665–670, 4121–4137.
c
Cases referred to in judgment

Bank Melli Iran v Barclays Bank (Dominion Colonial and Overseas) [1951] 2 Lloyd's Rep 367,
3 Digest (Reissue) 669, 4136.
Commercial Banking Co of Sydney Ltd v Jalsard Pty Ltd [1973] AC 279, [1972] 3 WLR 566,
PC, Digest (Cont Vol D) 789, 2124a.
d *Equitable Trust Co of New York v Dawson Partners Ltd* (1926) 27 Ll L Rep 49, HL.
Golodetz (M) *& Co Inc v Czarnikow-Rionda Co Inc, The Galatea* [1979] 2 All ER 726; *affd*
[1980] 1 All ER 501, [1980] 1 WLR 495, CA.
Hansson v Hamel & Horley Ltd [1922] 2 AC 36, [1922] All ER Rep 237, HL, 39 Digest
(Repl) 706, 1956.
Midland Bank Ltd v Seymour [1955] 2 Lloyd's Rep 147.

e
Action

The plaintiffs, Banque de l'Indochine et de Suez SA, brought an action against the
defendants, J H Rayner (Mincing Lane) Ltd, claiming, inter alia, the return of
$US1,010,000 which they had paid to the defendants under an agreement made on 26
August 1981, and interest on that sum from the date on which it had been paid. The
f facts are set out in the judgment.

Mark Saville QC and *Michael G Collins* for the plaintiffs.
Maurice Megrah QC and *Roger Ter Haar* for the defendants.

Cur adv vult

g
21 July. The following judgment was delivered.

PARKER J. By a letter dated 8 July 1981 the plaintiff bank notified the defendants of,
and themselves confirmed, an irrevocable letter of credit opened by a Djibouti bank in
favour of the defendants by order of buyers under a contract of sale with the defendants
h dated 25 June 1981.

Under cover of a letter dated 24 August 1981 the defendants tendered documents
under the credit and requested payment of the sum of $US1,010,000 which, subject to a
5% margin, was the full amount of the credit.

Having examined the documents in accordance with their ordinary system the
plaintiffs considered that the tender was defective for a number of reasons. On 26 August,
j however, after a telephone conversation between Mr Rowe for the plaintiffs and Mr
Grimsey for the defendants, they remitted the amount requested to the defendants' bank.
They notified the defendants that they had done so by letter of the same date. That letter,
after notification of the remittance, continued:

'Kindly note that as arranged with Mr. Grimsey payment is effected under reserve due to the discrepancies listed below:

1. Absence SS Co Certificate certifying vessel belongs to Shipping Co. that is a member of International Shipping Conference.

2. Bill of Lading clause "not portmarked, vessel not responsible for incorrect delivery. Any extra expense incurred in consequence to be borne by consignees".

3. Letter of Credit states: "Insurance payable in excess of Credit against documentary evidence" implying that evidence of insurance should be presented (although no insurance documents called for). Our ref. DJ 11132.

4. Certificates of Weight, Quality, Packing and Certificates of Origin and EUR 1 Certificate cannot be related to remaining documents or to Letter of Credit.

We return the above credit duly endorsed.'

It is to be noted that there is no indication whatever as to the consequences of the payment being made under reserve.

In their points of claim the plaintiffs allege that, in the prior telephone conversation, it was agreed between Mr Rowe and Mr Grimsey that payment should be effected under reserve. This is denied in the defence. Having heard evidence from both participants I find (i) that in that conversation Mr Rowe specified the four discrepancies mentioned in the subsequent letter, (ii) that Mr Grimsey expressed the view that none of them was a material discrepancy and that the tender was a good tender under the credit, (iii) that Mr Rowe adhered to the view that the discrepancies were material and rendered the tender bad but offered to make the payment requested under reserve, (iv) that Mr Grimsey, albeit reluctantly, accepted the offer, recognising that prompt payment would not otherwise be secured, and (v) that, as in the letter, the consequences of the payment being made under reserve were not stated or discussed. Accordingly I find that it was agreed between the parties that, due to the alleged and specified but contested discrepancies, payment should be made and accepted under reserve.

By their points of defence the defendants allege that there was no consideration for such an agreement but it was accepted in argument, quite rightly, that this allegation was unsustainable. There plainly was consideration. The plaintiffs genuinely believed that by reason of the alleged discrepancies they were entitled to refuse payment and, had the defendants not been prepared to accept the payment under reserve, they would not then have been paid. They might have established later that none of the alleged discrepancies entitled the plaintiffs to withhold payment, but that is another matter.

The plaintiffs informed the issuing bank in Djibouti that they had made payment under reserve for the first three of the four discrepancies mentioned in their letter to the defendants and on 27 August received the reply that the buyers objected to the negotiation, but they did not say on what ground. On being pressed, however, they stated that the buyers refused categorically to lift the reserve, more especially for discrepancy no 2.

The plaintiffs contend that the documents having been rejected for the specified discrepancies they became at once entitled to repayment of the amount paid under reserve, together with interest from the date of original payment until repayment, whether or not the discrepancies or any of them were in law sufficient to entitle them to have refused payment in the first place. As to this they accept that the third of the discrepancies mentioned in the letter is unsustainable but they seek to maintain the other three.

The principal matter for determination is the extent of the obligations of a beneficiary under a letter of credit who accepts a payment under reserve.

Counsel for the plaintiffs submitted that the payment was a provisional one and that a beneficiary was obliged, having accepted payment under reserve, to repay on demand with interest from the date of original payment if the documents were rejected by the issuing bank for any of the specified reasons, or if any of the specified reasons, albeit not relied on by the issuing bank, was in law a valid objection to payment. He accepted that if the documents were rejected by the issuing bank solely for some reason not specified, whether such reason was good or bad, the beneficiary was entitled to retain the payment.

He also accepted that if, in the end, the beneficiary established that none of the specified discrepancies was a valid ground for refusing payment he would be entitled in substance to be repaid if he had himself previously repaid, or, if he had not done so, to retain the original payment.

Counsel for the defendants contended that there was no obligation to repay unless one or more of the specified discrepancies was established or agreed to have been a valid ground for refusing payment, but accepted that, if it was so established, there was an obligation to repay with interest.

There is thus little between the parties in the end result, but the determination of the precise position is said to be a matter of great importance commercially.

There is no authority as to the consequences of a payment under a letter of credit being made under reserve in respect of iregularities although such payments are frequently made and this is recognised both in the textbooks and in the Uniform Customs and Practice for Documentary Credits (1974 revision, International Chamber of Commerce Publication no 290), art 8(g) of which provides:

> 'If the remitting bank draws the attention of the issuing bank to any irregularities in the documents or advises such bank that it has paid accepted or negotiated under reserve or against a guarantee in respect of such irregularities, the issuing bank shall not thereby be relieved of any of its obligations under this article. Such guarante' or reserve concerns only the relations between the remitting bank and the beneficiary.'

This article does not mention a third method of dealing with irregularities, real or supposed, which is also commonly used, namely a letter of indemnity by which the beneficiary, in consideration of the payment being made notwithstanding the irregularities, promises to indemnify the confirming bank against any loss it may suffer by reason of so paying.

It is clear from the evidence that no uniform banking practice exists either as to the form of the indemnity or guarantee which is used in the case of payment notwithstanding irregularities, or as to the consequences of a payment being made under reserve. There was evidence that payment was normally made under reserve only when the beneficiary was a reputable and valued customer of the remitting bank but no one appears really to have considered what the consequences would be.

If there is no dispute but that there are irregularities justifying non-payment, there appears to be no difficulty. The natural import of paying under reserve is that if the remitting bank does not, by reason of the irregularities, recover payment, the beneficiary will pay back. It is where, however, as here, there is dispute as to the validity of the alleged irregularities that the problem arises.

In the absence of any established custom the question I have to determine is what is the meaning of the expression 'in the light of surrounding circumstances', or, as it is now called, 'the factual matrix'.

The circumstances in which such payments, and in particular the present payment, are made are (i) that the remitting bank genuinely believes that there are one or more discrepancies justifying non-payment, (ii) that the beneficiary believes that the bank is wrong and that he is entitled to payment, and (iii) that both parties hope that, notwithstanding the alleged irregularities, the issuing bank will take up the documents and reimburse the remitting bank.

The question which arises appears to me to be: did the parties, in such circumstances, by paying and accepting under reserve intend that the bank should be entitled to repayment notwithstanding that it was in law obliged to pay when it did? Or was it merely intended that the position of the bank should be protected to the extent that the customer should not thereafter be entitled to resist a demand for repayment on the ground that the payment was unqualified and that he was therefore entitled to retain the payment even if one or more of the iregularities was in law valid?

The first of these two possibilities appears to me to import into the expression 'under reserve' more than the words can fairly bear. It would do more than reserve something.

It would create a right, albeit perhaps temporary, to have money repaid notwithstanding that at the time of original payment that money was contractually payable. A more natural and, as I think, commercially sensible meaning to give to the words is that the bank reserves the right to have the money back if it was not at the date of payment contractually payable.

Such a meaning is, moreover, one which accords with the realities of the situation. At the time of the payment under reserve the beneficiary either is or is not entitled to payment. If he is entitled to payment the bank should have paid him without reserve and he should in justice be entitled to retain that which was from the start due to him. I find it impossible to suppose that either he or the bank intended by the use of the words to put him under an obligation to repay and then claim against the bank. On the other hand there is every reason to protect the bank from being unable to reclaim even if at least one of the discrepancies was valid. It is this protection only which in my judgment the bank obtains when a payment is made and accepted under reserve.

The matter may be tested by reference to the circumstances of this case. One of the alleged discrepancies, no 3, advanced by the plaintiffs is now accepted by them as being invalid. Had that been the only discrepancy and payment had been made under reserve in respect of that alone the issuing bank might have been prepared to accept the documents, in which case the reserve would have been lifted and the beneficiary will have retained payment. Suppose, however, the issuing bank had refused on the particular ground and the confirming bank had then demanded repayment. Suppose, further, that the beneficiary had refused repayment on the ground that the objection was invalid. Could such a defence be struck out and judgment given for the bank with no stay of execution, leaving the beneficiary to a counterclaim, the trial of which might keep him out of money which was rightly his for years? I do not consider that it could. His case vis-à-vis the bank is that the bank have reserved the right to have the money back if they were right, not to have it back even if they were wrong. This is what in my judgment the reserve gives the bank. To achieve the results for which the bank contend, clearer words would be required.

It should be noted, furthermore, that counsel for the plaintiffs' contention produces within itself difficulties. He says that repayment is to be made if either (a) the issuing bank rejects for one of the specified reasons or (b) if any of the specified reasons was in law valid albeit not relied on by the issuing bank.

Alternative (b) will not arise if alternative (a) applies. Alternative (b) therefore presupposes that the issuing bank has rejected for a reason other than one of the specified reasons. But it is accepted that in such a case the reserve will not avail the confirming bank. The two are therefore inconsistent. If, however, the issuing bank reject for a reason other than one of the specified reasons, so that the confirming bank does not get paid, there appears to be no reason why it should not recover from the beneficiary if, but only if, it can show that one of the specified reasons was in law valid. Counsel for the defendants accepts that it can. Alternative (b) therefore marries with the defendants' contention but not with that of the plaintiffs. Even if it could be reconciled with such contention it produces the result that in certain cases the confirming bank would have to establish that a specified reason was in law valid and that in others it need not do so, and neither from the evidence nor on principle can I see any basis on which such a distinction could be made.

It is now necessary to consider the validity of the discrepancies on which the bank will rely. I consider each in turn.

1. *Absence steamship company certificate certifying vessel belongs to shipping company that is member of International Shipping Conference*

[His Lordship reviewed the evidence and concluded:] The requirement for a certificate was, in my view, a reasonable requirement and accordingly the plaintiffs were entitled to regard its absence as a valid ground for refusing payment even if, as was in fact the case, the vessel was a Conference Line vessel.

a   The matter is, however, of relatively little importance since prior to the expiry of the credit a certificate was supplied and the alleged defect was cured.

2. *Bill of lading clause 'not portmarked, vessel not responsible for incorrect delivery. Any extra expense incurred in consequence to be borne by consignee'.*

[His Lordship set out the grounds of the plaintiffs' objection, and, after reviewing the evidence, concluded:] There was no requirement that the goods should be portmarked and the clause was not in any way unusual. The second objection was in my judgment
b invalid.

4. *Certificates of weight, quality, packing and certificates of origin and EUR 1 certificate cannot be related to remaining documents or to the letter of credit*

The credit called for the following documents: signed commercial invoices in five copies; full set clean on board bills of lading; certificate of origin; EUR 1 certificate; and
c certificate of weight, quality and packing evidencing shipment from EEC port not later than 31 August 1981 for transportation to Djibouti in transit Yemen.

No complaint is made concerning the commercial invoice or, save as to the point with which I have already dealt, concerning the bills of lading. The complaint is simply that the three certificates called for could not be related to the remaining documents or to the letter of credit.

d There were tendered two certificates of origin, three EUR 1 certificates and two certificates of weight, quality and packing. I consider each type in turn.

Certificates of origin

One covered 20,000 bags, 1,009 gross 1,000 metric tons net of sugar of the correct description. It stated the consignor to be IPI Trade International of Paris, the consignee to be the defendants 'pour compte Coweltants' and the consignment to be by 'transports
e mixtes' to Djibouti port in transit Yemen. It did not mention a carrying vessel at all. The other covered 1,009·6 gross 1,000 metric tons net of sugar of a like description. It stated the consignor to be Lanvin of Dijon, the consignee to be 'to order', the destination to be Djibouti port in transit Yemen and the consignment to be by sea by 'MV Markhor or substitute'.

f Both certificates were dated 14 August 1981, some six days prior to the bill of lading.

EUR 1 certificates

One stated the exporter to be Lanvin of Dijon, the consignee to be Tate & Lyle London 'pour le compte de ses coweltants à Djibouti'. It covered 20,000 bags 1,009·6 kg gross of sugar of the correct description. It is signed at Dijon. It does not state 'in transit Yemen' after Djibouti. It mentions Tate & Lyle for the first time. No *net* weight is given albeit
g the number of bags and the net weight per bag appears, so that the net weight could be calculated.

One stated the exporter to be IPI Trade International of Paris and the consignee to be defendants, 'pour le Yemen', the destination to be Yemen du Nord and the transport to be by rail. It covered 504 kg gross 500 kg net and added to the description of the sugar an extra phrase. It is dated Lille, 17 August 1981.
h The third was in the same terms as that last mentioned, save that it stated 505 tonnes gross no net weight being given, and that it was dated 18 August 1981. The number of bags was not stated.

In neither of the last two documents was there any mention of Djibouti.

Certificates of weight, quality and packing

j One relates to the Lanvin consignment, is dated 14 August 1981 and states the name of the vessel to be MV Markhor or substitute and the shipment to be from Antwerp to Djibouti port in transit Yemen. The other relates to 1,000 metric tons of sugar of the correct description. It states that the sugar is produced by the sugar manufacturers Baghia-Say and is to travel from Anvers to Djibouti port in transit Yemen. Baghia-Say has not previously figured.

It is conceded by the defendants that these documents do not each bear on their face a
plain link with others which were presented, but it is contended (1) that under art 7 of
the Uniform Customs and Practice it is sufficient if the documents appear on their face
to be consistent with one another, and these documents did so appear, (2) that under art
32(c) none of the documents was required to do more than describe the goods in general
terms not inconsistent with the description of the goods in the credit, and they did so, (3)
that the documents fall within art 33 of the Uniform Customs and Practice and should
therefore have been accepted as tendered, and (4) that, as a set, the documents complied
with the credit and this was sufficient on the authority of *Midland Bank Ltd v Seymour*
[1955] 2 Lloyd's Rep 147.

For the plaintiffs it is contended that neither individually nor as a set were the
documents in order. Not only was there no link on the face of each with others in the
entire set but, taken as a whole, there were inconsistences or inadequacies. They relied
principally on *Bank Melli Iran v Barclays Bank (Dominion Colonial and Overseas)* [1951] 2
Lloyd's Rep 367 and on Lord Sumner's well-known statement in *Equitable Trust Co of
New York v Dawson Partners Ltd* (1926) 27 Ll L Rep 49 at 52: 'There is no room for
documents which are almost the same, or which will do just as well,' which has been
frequently referred to since.

I have no doubt that, so long as the documents can be plainly seen to be linked with
each other, are not inconsistent with each other or with the terms of the credit, do not
call for inquiry and between them state all that is required in the credit, the beneficiary
is entitled to be paid. I also accept, as did counsel for the plaintiffs, that Lord Sumner's
statement cannot be taken as requiring rigid meticulous fulfilment of precise wording
in all cases. Some margin must and can be allowed, but it is slight, and banks will be at
risk in most cases where there is less than strict compliance. They may pay on a reasonable
interpretation where instructions are ambiguous (see *Commercial Banking Co of Sydney Ltd
v Jalsard Pty Ltd* [1973] AC 279 at 285–286), but where the instructions from the issuing
bank are clear they are obliged to see to it that the instructions are complied with and
entitled to refuse payment to the beneficiary unless they are.

In the *Jalsard* case Lord Diplock said (at 286):

> 'The banker is not concerned as to whether the documents for which the buyer
> has stipulated serve any useful commercial purpose or as to why the customer called
> for tender of a document of a particular description. Both the issuing banker and
> his correspondent bank have to make quick decisions as to whether a document
> which has been tendered by the seller complies with the requirements of a credit . . .'

This restates and re-emphasises what Lord Sumner said in *Hansson v Hamel & Horley Ltd*
[1922] 2 AC 36 at 46, [1922] All ER Rep 237 at 241, which was recently applied by
Donaldson J in *Golodetz & Co v Czarnikow Rionda Co Inc, The Galatea* [1979] 2 All ER 726,
a case cited in argument before me. There Lord Sumner said: 'These documents have to
be handled by banks, they have to be taken up or rejected promptly and without any
opportunity for prolonged inquiry . . .' Having quoted from Lord Sumner, Donaldson J
said (at 739):

> 'I need hardly say I accept this proposition unreservedly. A tender of documents
> which, properly read and understood, calls for further enquiry or are such as to
> invite litigation is clearly a bad tender.'

In the present case the tender was, in my judgment, bad, both as to individual
documents and as a set. The document clearly called for inquiry. It may well be that the
use of the words 'sucre blanc de betterave à l'état solide non denature' to the description
of the goods in the credit, which appear in two of the three EUR 1 certificates, made no
difference, but those words do not appear in the credit nor do they appear in the certificate
of origin which is said to relate to the same parcel. The three EUR 1 certificates cannot
be seen on their face to cover 2,000 metric tons net. The third one gives the gross weight
only and does not state what number of bags is covered. The two quality certificates refer
to two apparently different voyages and one of them introduces an entirely new company
on the scene. The only thing to connect it with the certificate of origin to which it is

supposed to relate is the destination. There are other matters in addition. I do not
a consider that the documents are on their face consistent with each other. It is accepted
that they are in any event not on their face linked with each other and they do not show
EUR 1 certificates as to the required quantity.

The defendants are not saved by art 32(c) or art 33 of the Uniform Customs and
Practice. Article 32(2) cannot save a description which adds words to the description in
the credit. Such words can make the documents inconsistent and it is in documents that the
b bank deals. Article 33 cannot be understood to mean that banks must accept any
document tendered, even if inconsistent. It will, however, enable the bank to accept, for
example, a certificate of quality even if not by an independent person. To go further is to
create absurdity. A certificate of origin which on its face did not apparently cover the
quantity of goods would clearly not be sufficient, and would not be saved by the article.

In the result the tender was in my judgment bad and the plaintiffs are entitled to the
c return of their money with interest from date of payment.

Judgment for the plaintiffs.

Solicitors: *Durrant Piesse* (for the plaintiffs); *Clyde & Co* (for the defendants).

d   K Mydeen Esq   Barrister.

R v Dover Magistrates' Court, ex parte Kidner

e QUEEN'S BENCH DIVISION (CROWN OFFICE LIST)
WOOLF J
18 NOVEMBER 1982

Husband and wife – Maintenance – Arrears – Remission – Notice of intention to remit arrears –
Magistrates failing to notify wife of husband's application for remission of arrears – Magistrates
f *remitting arrears – No provision for appeal against remission of arrears – Whether wife entitled*
to judicial review of magistrates' decision – Guardianship of Infants Act 1971, s 13(3) –
Magistrates' Courts Act 1980, s 95 – Magistrates' Courts Rules 1981, r 44.

Judicial review – Practice – Matrimonial and family matters – Applications for leave to seek
judicial review – Applications to contain request that matter be dealt with by judge of Family
g *Division.*

At the hearing of proceedings in a magistrates' court under s 13(3)[a] of the Guardianship
of Minors Act 1971 to enforce arrears of maintenance which a husband had been ordered
to pay to the wife in respect of the three children of the marriage pursuant to an order
made under the 1971 Act, the husband applied to the magistrates for the remission of
h certain of the arrears. In the exercise of their powers under s 95[b] of the Magistrates'
Courts Act 1980 the magistrates made an order remitting the arrears but without giving
the wife notice of their intention to do so, as they were required to by r 44(1)[c] of the

a   Section 13(3), so far as material, provides: 'An order of a magistrates' court for the payment of
money under this Act may be enforced in like manner as an affiliation order . . .'
j b   Section 95, so far as material, provides: 'On the hearing of a complaint for the enforcement,
revocation, revival, variation or discharge of . . . an order enforceable as an affiliation order, the
court may remit the whole or any part of the sum due under the order.'
c   Rule 44(1), so far as material, provides: 'Before remitting the whole or any part of a sum due
under . . . an order enforceable as an affiliation order under section 95 of the [Magistrates' Court
Act 1980], the court shall, except save where it appears to it to be unnecessary or impracticable to
do so, cause the person in whose favour the order is made or, if that person is a child, the child or
the person with whom the child has his home to be notified of its intention and shall afford to

(Continued on p 476)

Magistrates' Courts Rules 1981. There being no power to appeal against an order remitting arrears under an order under the 1971 Act, the wife applied in the Queen's *a* Bench Division for judicial review of the magistrates' decision.

Held – By failing to give the wife notice under r 44 of the 1981 rules before remitting the arrears of maintenance, the magistrates had denied the wife an opportunity to make representations to the court in a matter in respect of which she had a real interest, for a remission of arrears would result in her receiving less money under the maintenance *b* order. Since there was no power to appeal against a remission of arrears under an order made under the 1971 Act, it was appropriate to make an order of certiorari quashing the magistrates' order and remitting the matter to the magistrates so that they could reconsider the husband's application after giving the wife notice of it. The wife's application would accordingly be granted (see p 477 *a b d* to *f j*, post).

Per curiam. It is desirable that applications for leave to seek judicial review of *c* matrimonial and family orders should include a request that, if leave is granted, the matter may be dealt with by a judge of the Family Division (see p 477 *g h*, post).

Notes
For the remission of arrears due under orders enforceable as affiliation orders, see 29 Halsbury's Laws (4th edn) para 427.

For the Guardianship of Infants Act 1971, s 13, see 41 Halsbury's Statutes (3rd edn) *d* 770.

For the Magistrates' Courts Act 1980, s 95, see 50(2) ibid 1525.

Application for judicial review
The wife applied, with the leave of Stephen Brown J granted on 27 May 1982, for an order of certiorari to quash an order made by the Dover Magistrates' Court on 19 August *e* 1981 remitting arrears of maintenance amounting to £300 due from the husband under an order of the Maidstone Magistrates' Court dated 17 November 1980. The facts are set out in the judgment.

Thomas Coningsby for the applicant.
The magistrates and the husband did not appear. *f*

WOOLF J. This is an application for judicial review in respect of an order made on 19 August 1981 by the Dover Magistrates' Court. The application is unopposed either by the magistrates or by the husband of the applicant. However, I have been greatly assisted by the very clear submissions which have been made by counsel for the applicant, who has warned me of all the possible pitfalls in the way of making the order that seems to *g* me to be clearly appropriate in this case.

The applicant was married to the respondent on 12 March 1960 and there were three children in the family. Unhappily, that marriage broke down and on 1 October 1981 an order was made for the custody and maintenance of the three children of the family, under the Guardianship of Minors Act 1971. In so far as it is relevant for the purposes of this application, the sum of £10 per week was to be paid in respect of each child. There *h* was unfortunately a mistake made by the Maidstone Magistrates' Court as to the terms of the order, but it is not necessary for my purposes to go into that mistake.

Arrears developed in relation to the order because the respondent did not pay the sums which he should have done. As the respondent was living in the area of the Dover Magistrates' Court, it fell to them to take steps for enforcement. They did so and, at the hearing of the enforcement proceedings, the respondent very properly made an *j* application for remission of certain of the arrears. If the proper procedure had been followed, in respect of the present applicant, no complaint should have been made as to what the magistrates did because they have got jurisdiction to remit arrears.

(Continued from p 475)
such person a reasonable opportunity to make representations to the court . . . and such representations shall be considered by the court.'

However, they failed to give any notice to the applicant of the fact that the respondent
a was seeking to have the arrears remitted. Even if there were no statutory provisions, it is
obvious that this was a matter in respect of which the applicant had a real interest and on
which she might wish to make representations, because if the arrears were remitted the
money which she could receive would be reduced. I am not surprised, therefore, to learn
under the instruction of counsel that there is a provision contained in the Magistrates'
Courts Rules 1981, SI 1981/552, which expressly requires notice to be given. Although
b it is not necessary for me to read it, that is to be found in r 44.

The rule was not applied in this case, the applicant never heard of the application to
remit, and the order to remit was made without giving the applicant any opportunity of
dealing with the matter. She naturally feels aggrieved.

The remedy which was adopted in this case gave rise to some concern. This was an
order made under the Guardianship of Minors Act 1971. So far as counsel's research goes,
c there is no power to appeal against an order remitting the arrears under an order made
under that Act. A possible candidate for giving such right of appeal is s 29 of the
Domestic Proceedings and Magistrates' Courts Act 1978, but an examination of the terms
of that section makes it clear to me that counsel is right in saying that it does not apply
because this is not one of the categories of cases specifically provided for in that section. I
do not need to go into the other statutory provisions to which counsel referred. He did
d so to make it clear to me that this particular case fell within the provisions of r 44, to
which I have made reference, and I am satisfied that they do.

It seems to me that although there was delay in this case that delay was excusable in
the circumstances indicated in the evidence which is before me. I am satisfied that,
whereas the local magistrates could well come to the same decision which they did when
they decided that the arrears should be remitted on 19 August 1981, there is at least a
e prospect that if the applicant had an opportunity to make representations she could
persuade the magistrates to come to a different conclusion. That being so, she is obviously
in a position where she should be entitled to make representations. She should not be
deprived of the chance of achieving a different decision. Accordingly, it seems to me that
this is a case where an order of certiorari should be made and that the decision to remit
should be quashed and the matter should be remitted to the Dover magistrates so that
f they can reconsider the application of the respondent to have the arrears remitted, after
the applicant has been given notice of that application.

Before I leave the case, I would like to make a comment of a general nature. There are
a number of matrimonial and family type orders from time to time on which judicial
review is sought under RSC Ord 53. It seems to me that, where an application of that
sort is being made, it would be in the interests of all concerned if the applicant could
g include a request in his application that, if leave is granted, the matter should be dealt
with by a Family Division judge rather than a Queen's Bench Division judge in the
normal way. The question could then be considered by the Crown Office and if the
President agrees the case can be heard by a judge of the Family Division. Quite apart
from the benefit which would be achieved by the matter coming before a Family
Division judge by way of speedier disposal, because of such a judge's familiarity with the
h legislation, it would have the advantage that decisions in these matters are in line with
decisions taken by the Divisional Court of the Family Division in relation to appeals from
magistrates' courts. This is especially desirable where, as here, the only reason why it has
not gone before such a Family Division court is because there is no express power of
appeal.

Accordingly, I grant the application in the way I have indicated.

j

Order of certiorari granted.

Solicitors: *Bower Cotton & Bower*, agents for *E A Morling & Sons*, Maidstone (for the
applicant).

N P Metcalfe Esq   Barrister.

Carson v Carson

COURT OF APPEAL, CIVIL DIVISION
ORMROD, O'CONNOR LJJ AND SHELDON J
25 JUNE 1981

*Divorce – Property – Adjustment order – Variation – Settlement order – Matrimonial home –
Matrimonial home settled on trustees on trust for sale for husband and wife jointly – Order
postponing sale until youngest child attaining 18 or completing full-time education or until wife
requesting or consenting to sale – Subsequent to settlement order wife becoming unemployed and
husband remarrying – Wife wishing to secure matrimonial home for herself – Wife applying for
second property adjustment order transferring home to her absolutely – Wife also applying for
leave to appeal against original order six years out of time – Whether court having jurisdiction to
entertain second application – Whether wife should be granted leave to appeal against original
order – Matrimonial Causes Act 1973, ss 24(1)(a)(b), 31.*

After the husband and wife's divorce the wife applied in ancillary proceedings for an
order under s 24(1)(a)[a] of the Matrimonial Causes Act 1973 transferring the husband's
interest in the matrimonial home to her or an order under s 24(1)(b) settling the property
on such terms as the court thought proper. The wife and the two children of the marriage
were living in the matrimonial home. On 20 May 1975 a settlement order was made by
a judge under s 24(1)(b) transferring the home to trustees on trust for sale for the husband
and wife jointly and ordering that the sale of the property be postponed until the
youngest child attained 18 or completed full-time education or until the wife requested
or consented to a sale, whichever was the earliest, or until further order of the court. An
order was also made for periodical payments by the husband in favour of the wife and
children. Both parties were given leave to appeal against the orders. For some two years
the husband substantially complied with the periodical payments order. In October 1978
the wife, who believed that the husband had not fully disclosed his means when the 1975
order was made, applied to a registrar for an increase in her periodical payments. The
registrar concluded that the husband's means were greater than he had disclosed and
substantially increased the wife's periodical payments. Thereafter the husband, who had
remarried, deliberately failed to comply fully with the varied order despite the wife's
efforts to enforce it, and large arrears accumulated in consequence. Furthermore, there
was evidence that after the order was varied the husband divested himself of most of his
assets. The wife's position then changed because she lost her employment and had to
draw unemployment benefit. The wife feared that when the time came to sell the
matrimonial home under the trust for sale her half share in the proceeds of sale would
not be adequate to purchase another home for herself and that she had little prospect of
enforcing the order for periodical payments. The wife accordingly applied to another
judge for, in effect, a second property adjustment order transferring the matrimonial
home to her absolutely under s 24(1)(a), in order to give her security in the matrimonial
home. If such an order were made the wife intended to forego her claim to periodical
payments. The judge held that he had no jurisdiction to entertain the application because
a property adjustment order had already been made in respect of the home. The wife
appealed against the judge's refusal to entertain her application for a property adjustment
order and also applied for an extension of the time for appealing from the property

---

[a] Section 24(1), so far as material, provides: 'On granting a decree of divorce . . . or at any time
thereafter . . . the court may make any one or more of the following orders, that is to say—(a) an
order that a party to the marriage shall transfer to the other party . . . such property as may be so
specified, being property to which the first-mentioned party is entitled . . . (b) an order that a
settlement of such property as may be so specified, being property to which a party to the marriage
is so entitled, be made to the satisfaction of the court for the benefit of the other party to the
marriage and of the children of the family or either or any of them . . .'

a adjustment order made in 1975 on the ground that it should be reviewed because of the
events that had occurred since it was made.

Held – (1) Since the wife's application in 1981 for a property adjustment order was
made in relation to the same capital asset as that to which the 1975 property adjustment
order related, and since the 1975 order was intended to be a final order, the court was
precluded by s 31[b] of the 1973 Act from entertaining the 1981 application. Accordingly,
b the wife's appeal from the judge's refusal to entertain her application would be dismissed
(see p 481 g h, p 483 e f and p 484 g j, post).

(2) It was only in very exceptional circumstances that the court would grant leave to
appeal against a property adjustment order when the appeal was long out of time. Having
regard to all the circumstances, including the facts that the parties' position had changed
radically since the 1975 order, that it would be difficult to investigate the parties' financial
c position in 1975 all over again, that there ought to be finality to the litigation and that
the effect of giving leave to appeal would be to outflank s 31 of the 1973 Act, the wife's
application for leave to appeal from the 1975 order would be refused, despite the justice
of her case (see p 482 g, p 483 a b d to g, p 484 e to g and p 485 e to g, post); *Re Berkeley,
Borrer v Berkeley* [1944] 2 All ER 395 applied.

d **Notes**
For the principles of assessment of ancillary relief after divorce, see 13 Halsbury's Laws
(4th edn) paras 1060–1068.

For the Matrimonial Causes Act 1973, ss 24, 31, see 43 Halsbury's Statutes (3rd edn)
566, 576.

e **Cases referred to in judgments**
Baker v Market Harborough Industrial Co-op Society Ltd [1953] 1 WLR 1472, CA, 36(1)
Digest (Reissue) 241, 932.
Berkeley, Re, Borrer v Berkeley [1944] 2 All ER 395, [1945] Ch 1, CA, 51 Digest (Repl) 807,
3635.
Chaterjee v Chaterjee [1976] 1 All ER 719, [1976] Fam 199, [1976] 2 WLR 397, CA, Digest
f (Cont Vol E) 274, 6962Aq(iii).
Gatti v Shoosmith [1939] 3 All ER 916, [1939] Ch 841, CA, 51 Digest (Repl) 806, 3631.
Jenkins v Richard Thomas & Baldwins Ltd [1966] 2 All ER 15, [1966] 1 WLR 476, CA, 17
Digest (Reissue) 223, 963.
Mesher v Mesher and Hall (1973) [1980] 1 All ER 126, CA.
Mulholland v Mitchell [1971] 1 All ER 307, [1971] AC 666, [1971] 2 WLR 93, HL, Digest
g (Cont Vol D) 1062, 3829a.
Murphy v Stone Wallwork (Charlton) Ltd [1969] 2 All ER 949, [1969] 1 WLR 1023, HL,
Digest (Cont Vol C) 1098, 3808b.
Property and Reversionary Investment Corp Ltd v Templar [1978] 2 All ER 433, [1977] 1
WLR 1223, CA, Digest (Cont Vol E) 668, 3636a.
Wigfull (J) & Sons' Trade Marks, Re [1919] 1 Ch 52, CA, 51 Digest (Repl) 807, 3636.
h

---

b   Section 31, so far as material, provides:
'(1) Where the court has made an order to which this section applies, then, subject to the
provisions of this section, the court shall have power to vary or discharge the order or to suspend
any provision thereof temporarily and to revive the operation of any provision so suspended.
j   (2) This section applies to the following orders, that is to say . . . (e) any order for a settlement of
property under section 24(1)(b) . . . being an order made on or after the grant of a decree of judicial
separation . . .
(4) The court shall not exercise the powers conferred by this section in relation to an order for a
settlement under section 24(1)(b) . . . except on an application made in proceedings—(a) for the
rescission of the decree of judicial separation by reference to which the order was made, or (b) for
the dissolution of the marriage in question . . .'

Appeal and application

The wife, Tina Angela Carson, appealed, with the leave of Ewbank J, from his order, *a*
made in chambers on 10 February 1981 on a preliminary issue, that he had no jurisdiction
to entertain an application by the wife for a transfer of property order under s 24(1)(a) of
the Matrimonial Causes Act 1973 transferring to her absolutely the former matrimonial
home in Stanmore, Middlesex, because on 20 May 1975 Payne J had made a property
adjustment order in regard to the same property under s 24(1)(b) of the 1973 Act settling
the property on trustees on trust for sale and ordering that the proceeds of sale be held on *b*
trust for the husband, David Carson, and the wife in equal shares, that the sale be
postponed until the children of the marriage attained 18 or completed their full-time
education, or until the wife's request or consent to a sale, or until further order of the
court. The wife further applied for an extension of the time for appealing from Payne J's
order of 20 May 1975. The facts are set out in the judgment of Ormrod LJ.

c
J C J Tatham for the wife.
Michael Irvine for the husband.

ORMROD LJ. In this case we have before us two separate matters. The first is an appeal
from a judgment of Ewbank J given on 10 February 1981, by which he held that he had
no jurisdiction to entertain an application by the wife for what amounts to a second *d*
property adjustment order under s 24 of the Matrimonial Causes Act 1973. The second
matter is an application for an extension of time for appealing from a much earlier order
made by Payne J in 1975, dealing with the property problems of these spouses.

The wife is the appellant and applicant in each case. It is a sad and difficult case which
we have listened to very sympathetically indeed. Briefly the facts are these. The parties
were married in 1967. The parties have two girls who are now aged 12 and 10. They *e*
lived in the matrimonial home, in Stanmore. That was accommodation which was
provided by the husband's parents and the property is on a 99-year lease running from
1961 and there is no mortgage on it. The marriage broke down. The wife petitioned for
divorce in 1972, asking for the usual forms of ancillary relief. That marriage was duly
dissolved on 17 October 1973 and a decree absolute was made on 20 November 1974. At
the time of the divorce the parties had come to an agreement about their property *f*
matters, which need only be mentioned shortly because it never became effective. The
agreement was that the wife would forego any claim to the matrimonial home and the
husband would provide the deposit which was required for her to purchase a new house
and he would pay the mortgage. They were never able to agree on a new house, or he
was never able to meet that obligation and so the agreement was never implemented.

On 21 January 1975 the wife gave notice of her intention to bring her application for *g*
ancillary relief before the court. She applied at that stage for a transfer of the maisonette
in Stanmore to her or, alternatively, a settlement of that property on such terms as the
court thought right.

The matter was fully heard by Payne J and he made the order, in respect of which
application is now made for leave to appeal out of time, on 20 May 1975. It was a difficult
case. It is quite clear that the judge thought that the husband, who until shortly before *h*
the hearing had been a market trader, had not made a full or satisfactory disclosure of his
means, and the judge said that, in the circumstances, he had had to act to some extent on
speculation to make good the defects of the disclosure. At the end of the day he made an
order which provided for the house to be transferred to trustees on trust for sale, to be
held by the parties jointly, the sale to be postponed on the usual terms of the *Mesher v
Mesher* type order ((1973) [1980] 1 All ER 126) (that is until the youngest child was 18 *j*
years of age or had ceased full-time education) and it contained provisions for the trust
coming to an end at an earlier date if the wife remarried, and so on. The precise terms of
the order are—

'the Respondent do convey the matrimonial home at . . . Stanmore, Middlesex, to
trustees on trust for sale, the proceeds of sale to be held on trust for the Petitioner

and Respondent in equal shares, the sale to be postponed until the death or remarriage of the Petitioner or until the said children and each of them attain the age of 18 years or complete full time education or until the request or consent of the Petitioner whichever is the earliest [and these words were added] or until further order of the court.'

It was common ground that the wife should live in the house thereafter and that the husband should vacate it.

The judge also made an order for periodical payments in favour of the wife in the sum of £1,250 per annum less tax, payable weekly, and at the rate of £6 a week for each of the two children. There the matter rested.

At first it seems clear that the husband kept up the payments under the order more or less. There were some arrears and there was a certain amount of dissatisfaction up to that stage. Certainly there were endless difficulties between them. The matter then came back, on the wife's application to increase the amount of the order, before Mr Registrar Guest on 10 October 1978. Once again the registrar had great difficulty with the husband in ascertaining what his financial position really was. It was again an unsatisfactory investigation, and it resulted in the registrar concluding that the husband was to be regarded as having an income of around £12,000 a year. The registrar substantially increased the order for periodical payments and under that order very large arrears accumulated. It does look as though the husband was determinedly not complying with that order. By the time the matter came before Ewbank J in 1981 the arrears were agreed at something in excess of £4,000.

The wife's position was very difficult. She had had employment but she has now lost it and is drawing unemployment benefit. But the matter which really worries her is the threat that in eight or nine years time she will be obliged to sell her home and with half of the proceeds she is going to be in a very unfavourable position for rehousing herself. With this large amount of arrears which has accumulated, and with every prospect from her point of view of the arrears increasing as time goes by, she wanted to obtain an order which would give her security in the maisonette in Stanmore. So in the first place, in February 1981, she applied to Ewbank J for what is, in effect, a second transfer of property order, transferring the maisonette to her absolutely, on the basis that she would forego thereafter her claim to periodical payments.

The argument before Ewbank J on that matter proceeded on the basis that, under s 24 of the Matrimonial Causes Act 1973, she was entitled, in the words of sub-s (1), 'On granting a decree of divorce . . . or at any time thereafter . . .' to make application for one or other of the orders set out in that subsection. The difficulty for her was that an order had already been made by Payne J in 1975, and counsel for the wife argued that, although an order had been made under s 24(1)(b) ordering a settlement of the property, that did not preclude the judge later from making another property adjustment order, this time under para (a), for a transfer of property to the wife. The judge held that he had no such power and, in my judgment, he was plainly right. This is a case where an attempt was being made to obtain a second property adjustment order in relation to the same capital asset and it is not necessary in this judgment to consider what the position might have been if some other capital asset was involved. In my judgment the judge in the court below was completely right in rejecting that application by the wife. If he had entertained it, he would clearly have been running counter to the provisions of s 31 of the 1973 Act, which make it clear that the court has no power to vary a property adjustment order in any circumstances.

It is necessary to mention the words, to which I drew attention, at the conclusion of Payne J's order in relation to the house, 'until further order of the court.' At first sight it might have seemed possible that the wife would have been able to take advantage of that and invite the court to postpone the sale beyond the period when the youngest child reaches 18 or ceases full-time education, but, looking at the judge's judgment, it is perfectly clear that that provision was put in the order to deal with the possibility of an earlier sale becoming necessary, for some unforeseeable reason, and it was certainly not included with a view to a further postponement of the sale after one or other of the events which I have mentioned has taken place. As counsel for the wife readily agreed, he could not take advantage of those words in the order.

Counsel for the wife falls back on his application for leave to appeal long out of time. He starts with this advantage, that the judge gave both parties leave to appeal at the conclusion of his order, and so what counsel requires is an extension of time for appealing from that order.

In the course of his judgment, Ewbank J made it quite clear that he thought it was highly desirable in the interests of all parties in this case that there should be what he called a 'clean break', and he thought the sensible arrangement would be now for the husband to transfer his interest in the former matrimonial home to the wife and that she, as she was prepared to do, should forego her periodical payments. But he recognised that he had no power to do it and the husband was not prepared to consent.

It is in those circumstances that we have to consider this unusual application for leave to appeal six years after the event.

Counsel for the husband has referred us to all the relevant authorities and it is only necessary briefly to state the principles which govern this type of situation. It can be found very conveniently in a judgment of Lord Greene MR in *Re Berkeley, Borrer v Berkeley* [1944] 2 All ER 395 at 397, [1945] Ch 1 at 4. The facts of that case are entirely different from this case and need not be recited. It is only necessary to read Lord Greene MR's statement of the principle. He said:

'It seems to me that the principle to be extracted is this. It is not sufficient for a party to come to the court and say: "A subsequent decision of a superior court has said that the principle of law on which my case was decided was wrong." The court will immediately say to him: "That bald statement is not enough for you. What are the circumstances? What are the facts? What is the nature of the judgment? Who are the parties affected? What, if anything, has been done under it?" In other words, the whole of the circumstances must be looked at. If the court, in the light of those circumstances, considers it just to extend the time, then it will do so. That seems to me to be the proper principle, and it is entirely in accordance with the view taken by this court in *Gatti v. Shoosmith* ([1939] 3 All ER 916, [1939] Ch 841), the most recent case under this rule.'

That appears to be the principle on which the courts have acted, both before and since that case was decided.

We were referred to a number of cases in which that principle has been applied, always, of course, with reluctance, because it is extremely dangerous to allow appeals long out of time when everybody concerned has acted on the assumption that the decision was right. It is only, therefore, in very exceptional circumstances that the court will give leave so long out of time.

The problem in this case (and it makes it unnecessary to examine the personal injury cases at all) is, as counsel for the husband very clearly submitted in the course of his able and helpful argument, the fact that this order has been acted on. It has been acted on because the husband has, for the first two years at any rate, complied reasonably well with the orders for periodical payments and that, even after Mr Registrar Guest's very substantial increase of those orders, he has paid quite substantial sums under the varied order. As counsel for the husband submits, it makes it almost impossible to go back to the original order made in May 1975 and start again.

Ewbank J dealt with the arrears, in part by remitting some of them and in part by providing that they should be payable only out of the husband's share of the matrimonial home when it came to be sold. That has been provided for as far as it can be.

This is a case in which there is no doubt that the wife has suffered a great deal, and it is also a case in which she will suffer considerably. It is a very good example of the chickens coming home to roost with the *Mesher v Mesher* type of order which became so fashionable in and around 1975 and afterwards. It was not for some little time that the

dangers of the Mesher v Mesher type of order came to be appreciated. In this case the
a danger is staring us in the face. In eight or nine years' time the wife in this case will
inevitably be homeless and in a very weak position to rehouse herself out of her share of
the proceeds of sale of this property. That, coupled with the deliberate conduct on the
part of the husband in not complying with the periodical payments order (and we are
entitled to assume that it was deliberate since he has been sent to prison at least once on
judgment summonses, and there have been endless judgment summonses, so we are
b told), does create a situation which enables counsel for the wife at least to argue that the
justice of the case would be served by our giving leave to appeal so far out of time.

I am sympathetic to that submission, but counsel for the husband has convinced me
that it is not a course which we can properly take. We cannot, in the circumstances of
this case, go back to square one and start again. In the personal injury cases it was
comparatively easy for this court, having given leave to appeal long out of time, to raise
c the sum awarded in damages in each of these cases because it was quite clear that the
original order had been made on the assumption, in one case, that the defendants would
continue to employ the plaintiff at a wage which was comparable to that which he had
been earning before the accident; in another case an order had been made on the
assumption that the widow was not going to be married, whereas she married very
shortly after the order was made. In all those circumstances it was comparatively easy for
d this court on the appeal to adjust the amount of damages, either up or down as the case
may be. But the situation is much more complicated in this case. Both sides have changed
their positions radically since the order was made. The husband has remarried and is in
the process of his second divorce. The wife's position has also changed. In those
circumstances, although the argument of counsel for the wife is attractive, and although
I feel that the justice of the case would justify our interfering with the 1975 order if we
e properly could, I am reluctantly driven to the conclusion by the argument of counsel for
the husband that we should not accede to counsel for the wife's submission. I say that
with regret, but without feeling that there is any alternative.

I would dismiss the appeal from Ewbank J's judgment and refuse leave to appeal out
of time.

f **O'CONNOR LJ.** I agree that the appeal from Ewbank J should be dismissed for the
reasons given by Ormrod LJ.

As to the application for leave to appeal out of time against the order Payne J made in
1975, like Ormrod LJ I have great sympathy for the wife's position, and had I thought it
right to do so I would not have hesitated to have given leave, but an examination of the
authorities makes it clear that this really is impossible. If one looks at the personal injury
g cases to which we were referred (Murphy v Stone Wallwork (Charlton) Ltd [1969] 2 All ER
949, [1969] 1 WLR 1023, Mulholland v Mitchell [1971] 1 All ER 307, [1971] AC 666 and
Jenkins v Richard Thomas & Baldwins Ltd [1966] 2 All ER 15, [1966] 1 WLR 476) it would
be seen in each of those cases that the real issue before the Court of Appeal, and in
Mulholland v Mitchell before the House of Lords, was whether it was right to admit fresh
evidence of events happening after the judgment at first instance. In all save one of the
h cases the appeals were all brought within time and the question of extending time was
only hinted at in one case, and the references to it in the other cases all concerned whether
it was right to admit fresh evidence. The reason that those cases are relevant here is
because the only ground for the wife's application for leave to appeal out of time is that
events have occurred subsequent to the order of Payne J which make it just and right to
review the order.

I do not regard it as useful to examine a number of authorities where time has been
j extended. I will give only one example. In Baker v Market Harborough Industrial Co-op
Society Ltd [1953] 1 WLR 1472 the same facts had given rise to two conflicting decisions
at first instance, and after the second decision, which was six months after the first one, it
was clear that the Court of Appeal should rule which was right and time was extended in
respect of the first decision so that both appeals could be dealt with together.

Re Berkeley, Borrer v Berkeley [1944] 2 All ER 395, [1945] Ch 1, to which Ormrod LJ has referred, citing a passage from the judgment of Lord Greene MR, was an example of a case where there had been a change in the law. One will find in the books other cases where there has been a decision in the House of Lords reversing a previous decision, and it is against that background that the passage from Lord Greene MR's judgment is to be read.

But in the present case one has to look at what it is that has happened since the order which, it is submitted, makes it right and just to reopen the matter. The answer to that is that, for the first two years from 1975 to 1977, there was no possible ground for interfering with the order of Payne J. By and large the husband had made the periodical payments. He was in arrears to some small extent, but during those two years nobody could say that there were any grounds whatever for reopening the matter by considering fresh evidence of supervening events. It is only from October 1978, when a variation was made under the Matrimonial Causes Act 1973 of the amount of the periodical payments and backdated to April 1978, that trouble really arose. It is submitted that thereafter the husband turned sour and effectively refused to make the periodical payments. It is not right on the evidence to say that he paid none, but there is evidence that he divested himself of some of his business assets which he had got at that stage, and it could be said that he frustrated the order. Even if that be right, the remedy which the law gives in those circumstances is to enforce the order, and that the wife sought to do by all the means which were open to her: taking out judgment summonses, committing the husband to prison for contempt for not obeying the order of the court. Those are remedies which are open to her and, if they are exercised together with the performance of the agreement for a period of two years, it seems to me to make it quite impossible to turn round now and say that those events are themselves good grounds for enlarging the time for appeal (and it is enlarging it for something like six years) and starting afresh.

Like Ormrod J, I regard it as quite impossible, if leave were given, for this court to reach a conclusion on the evidence before it. It simply would not be possible, even if I thought it would be right. There are a large number of factors which would have to be reinvestigated and it simply would not be just and right in this case to do that. There has got to be an end to litigation. Parliament has expressly excluded a variation of this kind of order from s 31 of the 1973 Act and, for my part, I think it is only in exceptional circumstances that one can go behind that section and reopen the matter as it is sought to do here. Like Ormrod J, I would refuse the application for an extension of time for leave to appeal.

SHELDON J. I agree that the appeal against the judgment of Ewbank J should be dismissed and that leave to appeal out of time against the order of Payne J should be refused.

There are four questions this court may have to answer. The first two are the two preliminary points raised in Ewbank J's first judgment of 10 February 1981, the third is whether to give the wife leave to appeal out of time against Payne J's order of 20 May 1975 and, if we do, the fourth is whether to allow that appeal.

As to the first of the preliminary points, I agree with Ewbank J and for the same reasons that he gave, that, in general terms, the fact that an order has been made under one subsection of s 23 or s 24 of the Matrimonial Causes Act 1973 does not itself preclude a later application for an order under another such subsection.

As to the second of the preliminary points, whether the terms of Payne J's order themselves preclude any such further application, I also agree with his conclusions for two reasons. The first is that it is clear from the judgment of Payne J that he intended to dispose of all the wife's outstanding claims for financial relief, and to effect a comprehensive settlement of all the financial and property issues between the parties, from which it follows, in my opinion, that save as provided by s 31 of the 1973 Act no further order could be made. Second, as the only asset with which we are concerned, the wife's home, has been dealt with by an order under s 24(1)(*b*), it would be impossible, so long as Payne J's order stands, to make some further order in regard to it.

I also agree with Ewbank J that, in the circumstances of this case, it is immaterial in
this context that the order of Payne J did not in terms dismiss the wife's applications for
any other form of relief. That was clearly intended by Payne J.

Thus, the wife, in order to protect her future and to obtain what she regards as proper
provision for her children and herself, has been driven at this late stage, some six years
after the order, to seek to set Payne J's order aside. In general terms her reasons for so
doing, as they have been put on her behalf, are that events have shown that her husband
not only has successfully divested himself of all his assets other than his half share of the
equity in the house in question, but also has accumulated arrears of maintenance of over
£4,000 which she has no means of recovering until years ahead when the house is sold.
It is clear, moreover, from the judgments of all those who from time to time have had
dealings with the husband in this connection (Payne J in 1975, Mr Registrar Guest in
1978 and now Ewbank J) that he is to be regarded as unreliable and devious in his
evidence and financial transactions.

I agree with counsel for the wife that the court has a very wide discretion in deciding
whether or not to grant a party leave to appeal out of time. As put succinctly by Swinfen
Eady MR in Re J Wigfull & Sons' Trade Marks [1919] 1 Ch 52 at 59: '. . . the Court has
power to enlarge the time for appealing if it is just that, under the circumstances, an
order enlarging the time should be made.' Some of the relevant considerations, moreover,
are referred to in the judgments of Lord Greene MR in Re Berkeley, Borrer v Berkeley
[1944] 2 All ER 395, [1945] Ch 1, in Property and Reversionary Investment Corp Ltd v
Templar [1978] 2 All ER 433, [1977] 1 WLR 1223 and in the speech of Lord Wilberforce
in Mulholland v Mitchell [1971] 1 All ER 307 at 312, [1971] AC 666 at 679.

Taking all those matters into account, and in spite of the delay, I have been very
tempted to say that the wife in this case should be given leave to appeal out of time and
that the appeal against Payne J's order should be allowed so that the whole matter could
be remitted to Ewbank J, or some other judge, to be reheard. On further reflection,
however, I have been driven to the conclusion that, however the husband may have
behaved, particularly after the order of Mr Registrar Guest, it would not be in the
interests of justice to take such a course. It would raise extremely complex problems as
to what should be done now if the husband's present financial position is as he claims. It
might result in an order less favourable to the wife than she already has. Nor should it be
forgotten, as O'Connor LJ has pointed out, that, whatever his later shortcomings, the
husband for some two years did comply substantially with the order made by Payne J. A
further objection is that, if we allowed the wife's appeal, we would be outflanking s 31 of
the 1973 Act by permitting a variation of a property adjustment order made some six
years ago. That is not, in my view, by itself an overriding objection: see per Ormrod LJ
in Chaterjee v Chaterjee [1976] 1 All ER 719 at 724, [1976] Fam 199 at 207. In the event,
however, added to all the other factors in this case, including the husband's present
liabilities to his second wife and other parties, it leaves me with the inescapable conclusion
that it would not be in the interests of justice to extend the time for appealing the order
of Payne J.

Appeal and application dismissed. Leave to appeal to the House of Lords refused.

Solicitors: *Whitelock & Storr* (for the wife); *Malkin Cullis & Sumption* (for the husband).

Bebe Chua   Barrister.

Norman v Norman

FAMILY DIVISION
WOOD J
9 JULY, 26 AUGUST 1982

Divorce – Property – Adjustment order – Variation – Settlement order – Matrimonial home – Matrimonial home settled on husband and wife on trust for sale – Order postponing sale until youngest child of family ceasing to receive full-time education – Husband wishing to buy home for himself out of his share of proceeds of sale of matrimonial home – Husband applying for immediate sale of home – Whether jurisdiction to vary property adjustment order by ordering earlier sale – Whether order creating trust for sale a 'further order for the sale of . . . property' which could be varied – Whether order a final order which could not be varied – Matrimonial Causes Act 1973, ss 24(1)(b), 24A(1), 31(2)(f).

The parties' marriage was dissolved by decree absolute in October 1978. The wife and the five children of the marriage, the two youngest of whom were aged 14 and 16, lived in the former matrimonial home. The father was living with friends. On 9 July 1979 in ancillary proceedings the registrar made a property adjustment order under s 24(1)(b)[a] of the Matrimonial Causes Act 1973 settling the matrimonial home on trust for sale on the husband and wife equally, the sale to be postponed until the youngest child ceased to receive full-time education or training. The registrar further ordered that the property should then be sold and the proceeds divided equally between the husband and wife. In 1982 the husband wished to buy a home for himself out of the proceeds of sale of the matrimonial home and applied to the registrar for an order under s 24A(1)[b] of the 1973 Act for the immediate sale of the home. The registrar refused the application on the ground that he had no jurisdiction under s 24A(1) to vary the 1979 property adjustment order by ordering an earlier sale because the 1979 order was a final order which, by virtue of s 31[c] of the 1973 Act, could not be varied after the dissolution of the marriage. The husband appealed.

Held – An order for sale under s 24A(1) of the 1973 Act, being in terms a 'further order' to, inter alia, an order made under s 24 of that Act, was a separate order from, and ancillary to, an order made under s 24, and therefore an order could not be made under s 24A(1) to vary an existing property adjustment order made under s 24(1). Furthermore, an order for the settlement of property on trust for sale made under s 24(1)(b) was not 'an

---

a   Section 24(1), so far as material, provides: 'On granting a decree of divorce . . . or at any time thereafter . . . the court may make any one or more of the following orders, that is to say . . . (b) an order that a settlement of such property as may be so specified, being property to which a party to the marriage is so entitled, be made to the satisfaction of the court for the benefit of the other party to the marriage and of the children of the family or either or any of them . . .'

b   Section 24A(1), so far as material, provides: 'Where the court makes under section . . . 24 of this Act . . . a property adjustment order, then, on making that order or at any time thereafter, the court may make a further order for the sale of such property as may be specified in the order, being property in which or in the proceeds of sale of which either or both of the parties to the marriage has or have a beneficial interest, either in possession or reversion.'

c   Section 31, so far as material, provides:
'(1) Where the court has made an order to which this section applies, then, subject to the provisions of this section, the court shall have power to vary . . . the order . . .
(2) This section applies to the following orders, that is to say . . . (e) any order for a settlement of property under section 24(1)(b) . . . being an order made on or after the grant of a decree of judicial separation; (f) any order made under section 24A(1) above for the sale of property.
(4) The court shall not exercise the powers conferred by this section in relation to an order for a settlement under section 24(1)(b) . . . except on an application made in proceedings—(a) for the rescission of the decree of judicial separation by reference to which the order was made, or (b) for the dissolution of the marriage in question.'

order for the sale of [the] property' within s 24A(1) even though the settlement order
a contained a provision for the sale of the property at a later date. Accordingly, the
provisions of s 31(2)(*f*) of the 1973 Act applicable to the variation of orders made under
s 24A(1) did not apply to a settlement order made under s 24(1)(*b*). Instead, an order
under s 24(1)(*b*) remained a final order which, by virtue of s 31(4), could not be varied
after the dissolution of the marriage. It followed that the 1979 order, being a property
adjustment order under s 24(1)(*b*) and not an order for sale under s 24A(1), could not be
b varied under either s 24A(1) or s 31(2)(*f*). The proper procedure for the husband to
follow if there was disagreement between him and the wife concerning the date for the
sale of the property was for the husband to apply to the court by summons for an order
for sale under s 30^d of the Law of Property Act 1925. The application would accordingly
be adjourned to allow the husband to issue such a summons (see p 489 *d* to p 490 *c*, post).
        Carson v Carson [1983] 1 All ER 478 applied.
c   *Ward v Ward and Greene* [1980] 1 All ER 176n considered.
        Per curiam. It is important when drawing up a property adjustment order which
includes an ancillary order for sale under s 24A(1) of the 1973 Act to make it clear that
the order under s 24A(1) is a separate order from the property adjustment order (see
p 489 *g*, post).

d **Notes**
For property adjustment orders, see 13 Halsbury's Laws (4th edn) paras 1052, 1116, and
for the variation of such orders, see ibid paras 1133, 1150, 1168.
        For the Law of Property Act 1925, s 30 see 27 Halsbury's Statutes (3rd edn) 385.
        For the Matrimonial Causes Act 1973, ss 24, 31, see 43 ibid 566, 576, and for ss 24A
and 32(1)(*f*) of the 1973 Act (as inserted by the Matrimonial Homes and Property Act
e 1981, ss 7 and 8), see 51 ibid 1035, 1036.

Cases referred to in judgment
Carson v Carson [1983] 1 All ER 478, CA.
Mesher v Mesher and Hall (1973) [1980] 1 All ER 126, CA.
Ward v Ward and Greene [1980] 1 All ER 176n, [1980] 1 WLR 4, CA.

f
Appeal
On 9 July 1979 Mr Registrar Bayne-Powell, in ancillary proceedings following the
husband and wife's divorce, made a property adjustment order whereby the former
matrimonial home was settled on trust for sale on the husband and wife equally, the wife
was given liberty to remain in the property until the last child of the family ceased full-
g time education or training and the property was then to be sold under the trust for sale
and the net proceeds divided equally between the husband and wife. On 11 February
1982 the husband applied under s 24A of the Matrimonial Causes Act 1973 for an
immediate sale of the property to enable him to buy a home for himself with his share
of the proceeds of sale. On 11 May 1982 the registrar refused the husband's application
on the ground that he had no jurisdiction under s 24A to order a sale of the property
h earlier than under the property adjustment order made on 9 July 1979 because that order
was a final order which could not be varied under s 31 of the 1973 Act. The husband
appealed. The appeal was heard in chambers but judgment was given by Wood J in open
court. The facts are set out in the judgment.

Howard Shaw for the husband.
Augustus Ullstein for the wife.

j   *Cur adv vult*

---

d Section 30, so far as material, provides: 'If the trustees for sale refuse to sell . . . any person interested
   may apply to the court for . . . [an] order for giving effect to the proposed transaction or for any
   order directing the trustees for sale to give effect thereto, and the court may make such order as it
   thinks fit.'

26 August. The following judgment was delivered.

WOOD J. This marriage took place on 1 April 1954. It was dissolved by decree absolute on 25 October 1978. On 9 July 1979 Mr Registrar Bayne-Powell made a final order in financial ancillary proceedings which reads as follows:

'It is ordered that the property known as . . . be settled on the parties equally. The petitioner to be at liberty to remain in the said property until the last child of the family to do so ceases to receive full-time education or training, and then the said property be sold and the net proceeds of sale divided equally between the parties, but the petitioner to have credit for any moneys paid for structural or external repairs (but not redecoration) carried out by her.'

On 11 May 1982 Mr Registrar Bayne-Powell refused an application by the husband for an earlier sale of the property on the grounds that he had no jurisdiction to make the order. The husband now appeals.

There are five children of the family: Julia now aged nearly 30, Norman aged 26, Anne born on 21 January 1962, Alison born on 20 May 1966 and Lorraine born on 15 June 1968. All live at the matrimonial home. The wife works, and the four eldest children are financially self-supporting. Alison has started work recently. From 1971 the husband showed signs of mental illness and has now been diagnosed as suffering from chronic paranoid schizophrenia. His sole source of income is sickness benefit of £36 per week. For the past two years he has been cared for by a friend. This cannot continue.

The matrimonial home is now worth £30,000, or rather more. There is no mortgage. The husband would like to buy a mobile house and the site for himself. It would cost him about £10,000. With the remaining money the wife would be able to buy a house for herself, Lorraine and possibly some, if not all, of the remaining children.

Against that outline of facts, the husband now applies for an order that the sale of the matrimonial home take place forthwith and that £10,000 be paid to him. He would be content to leave the remainder of his share in the new house.

As I have said, his application came before the registrar on 11 May 1982. Counsel for the wife submitted that the court had no jurisdiction to make the order, and Mr Registrar Bayne-Powell so found. The facts have not been argued, and I have only set them out in skeletal form in order to understand the background to the issue. At present, it is solely one of jurisdiction.

On 1 October 1981, ss 7 and 8 of the Matrimonial Homes and Property Act 1981 were brought into force, and at the request of the parties and of the registrar I have been asked to consider the general effect of the amendments to the Matrimonial Causes Act 1973 made by the 1981 Act and to give my reasons in open court.

The law prior to the changes effected by the 1981 Act was as follows. On 1 May 1979 the Court of Appeal in *Ward v Ward and Greene* [1980] 1 All ER 176, [1980] 1 WLR 4 decided that a court had power to order the sale of property in proceedings brought under ss 23 and 24 of the 1973 Act without the necessity of issuing proceedings under s 17 of the Married Women's Property Act 1882, or s 30 of the Law of Property Act 1925, provided that the circumstances were such as to bring the case within one or other of those Acts, which gave the necessary power to the court to order a sale. This case was drawn to the notice of the profession by a Practice Note dated 4 December 1979 ([1980] 1 WLR 4).

By the provisions of ss 21, 23 and 24 of the 1973 Act, in financial relief proceedings following a decree of divorce there are two types of orders: 'financial provision orders' under s 23, and 'property adjustment orders' under s 24. The variation of certain orders for financial relief is dealt with by s 31. Without reciting the provisions in detail, it is quite clear from s 31(2)(e), and sub-s (4) or sub-s (5) of s 31, that after decree of divorce there can be no variation of any order made under s 24, a property adjustment order. They are final orders. This is made clear in *Carson v Carson* [1983] 1 All ER 478. The order made at first instance in that case was not dissimilar to the one made in the present

case, but it ended with the words '. . . or until further order of the court'. Of that phrase
a Ormrod LJ, giving the leading judgment, said (at 481):

> 'It is necessary to mention the words, to which I drew attention, at the conclusion
> of Payne J's order in relation to the house, "until further order of the court." At first
> sight it might have seemed possible that the wife would have been able to take
> advantage of that and invite the court to postpone the sale beyond the period when
> the youngest child reaches 18 or ceases full-time education, but looking at the,
b judge's judgment, it is perfectly clear that that provision was put in the order to deal
> with the possibility of an earlier sale becoming necessary, for some unforeseeable
> reason, and it was certainly not included with a view to a further postponement of
> the sale after one or other of the events which I have mentioned has taken place. As
> counsel for the wife readily agreed, he could not take advantage of those words in
> the order.'

c That particular phrase is not included in the present order. As I understand the reasoning
of the Court of Appeal, its view was that such an application was a working out of a
property adjustment order and not a variation of it.

Mr Registrar Bayne-Powell's order of 9 July 1979 created a trust for sale, a settlement,
and in the event of disagreement between the trustees, in this case former husband and
d former wife, either can apply under s 30 of the Law of Property Act 1925, and the court
in its wide discretion can either order a sale and, if thought right, impose terms; or it can
decline to make an order, leaving the property unsold, unless and until the trustees reach
agreement or the court makes an order at some future date.

No summons under s 30 of the Law of Property Act 1925 is before me. I must bear in
mind the general approach suggested by the Court of Appeal in *Ward v Ward and Greene*
e [1980] 1 All ER 176, [1980] 1 WLR 4, but in that case the court was dealing with the
making of an original order at first instance and not with the variation of a property
adjustment order. Such a variation is not permitted by s 31 of the 1973 Act.

On the law as it was before the amendments in the 1981 Act, I take the view that this
husband would need to issue a summons under s 30 of the 1925 Act, and that the
registrar was right in his judgment.

f By s 7, the 1981 Act introduces a new section into the 1973 Act, namely s 24A. It does
not amend s 23 or s 24. The provisions of s 24A are to apply, as it states, to an order for
secured periodical payments and to an order for a lump sum, each under s 23, and to a
property adjustment order under s 24. It is also clear, in my judgment, that the order for
sale under s 24A is a 'further order', and therefore a separate order from those under ss 23
and 24 mentioned earlier in s 24A. It is ancillary to the orders envisaged by paras (a) to
g (d) of s 24(1), and it will be important to ensure clarity when drawing up orders which
include such an order for sale.

Thus, for example, when making an order under s 24(1)(a) or (b) it may be necessary
to make a s 24A order to take effect before the order creating a settlement or the payment
of a lump sum. In other circumstances it may be necessary to return to a court for an
order under s 24A if a lump sum has not been paid by a given date. However, neither the
h lump sum order itself nor the settlement is an order made under s 24A. They are each
property adjustment orders under s 24. Thus, a trust for sale is not an order made under
s 24A, although it contains provisions for the sale of trust property at a later date.

In my judgment, this understanding of the effect of s 24A is supported by the
provisions of s 8(2) of the 1981 Act, which reads:

> 'In section 31 of the said Act of 1973 (which provides for the variation and
j discharge of certain orders for financial relief)—(a) at the end of subsection (2) there
> shall be inserted the following paragraph—"(f) Any order made under section
> 24A(1) above for the sale of property". . . .'

It is to be noted that this amendment has two effects. First, it adds to s 31(2) a type of
order which can be varied; and, second, it leaves untouched the direction that property

adjustment orders under s 24 shall not be varied save in the special circumstances
mentioned.

    The order made on 9 July 1979 is an order establishing a trust for sale, and the power
to order a sale is not affected by the new s 24A and the amended s 31. The question
whether the words 'until further order' or 'liberty to apply' should be read into the order
of July 1979 has not been argued before me. If such wording can properly be read into
the order, then on the authority of *Carson v Carson* a court would have the power to
shorten but not to extend the time within which to order a sale under the trust for sale.

    Comments have been made recently in the Court of Appeal about the problems raised
by *Mesher* orders (see *Mesher v Mesher and Hall* [1980] 1 All ER 126), and the background
to the present case illustrates yet again further problems. I will not at present make the
orders sought, and I propose to adjourn the present summons and to give the husband
an opportunity, if so advised, to issue a summons under s 30 of the Law of Property Act
1925. Both matters can then return to the court to be heard together. My reason for
adjourning the present summons and not dismissing it is to leave open the argument
that further words should be read into the order of July 1979.

*Summons adjourned. Leave to husband to issue summons under s 30 of Law of Property Act 1925
within 14 days. Leave to appeal.*

Solicitors: *Hooper Holt & Co*, Redhill (for the husband); *Maybury & Co*, Crawley (for the
wife).

                                       Bebe Chua   Barrister.

R v Liverpool City Justices, ex parte Topping

QUEEN'S BENCH DIVISION

ACKNER LJ AND WEBSTER J

8, 12 NOVEMBER 1982

*Magistrates – Bias – Knowledge of other charges against defendants – Discretion not to continue
hearing charge where possible bias arising from knowing of other charges – Test of bias – Proper
test whether appearance of bias and not whether actual bias – Appearance of bias where fair-
minded person sitting in court with knowledge of relevant facts would think fair trial impossible.*

*Magistrates – Procedure – Court register – Computer used to produce sheets forming register –
Sheets containing all outstanding charges against defendant and convictions on which he is awaiting
sentence – Whether practice of putting such court sheets before magistrates wrong in law –
Magistrates' Courts Rules 1981, r 66. .*

Where magistrates who are about to try a charge against a defendant become aware of
other unrelated charges against him they have a discretion whether to continue to hear
the charge they are about to try. In exercising that discretion, the test to be applied by
the magistrates is whether in the circumstances there would be the appearance of bias on
their part, rather than actual bias, if they proceeded to hear the charge. Whether there
would be the appearance of bias depends on whether a reasonable and fair-minded person
sitting in court with knowledge of all the relevant facts would reasonably think that it
would be impossible for the defendant to have a fair trial of the charge by the bench as it
is then constituted (see p 493 h j and p 494 e h j, post); dictum of Lord Denning MR in
Metropolitan Properties Co (FGC) Ltd v Lannon [1968] 3 All ER at 310 and *R v Uxbridge
Justices, ex p Burbridge* (1972) Times, 21 June, applied; *R v Sandwich Justices, ex p Berry*
(1981) 74 Cr App R 132 explained.

Since r 66ᵃ of the Magistrates' Courts Rules 1981, which gives authority to keep a court
a register, does not provide for the entry in the register of any offence or matter of
complaint other than that on which the court is about to adjudicate (or offences associated
with or to be heard therewith) and since the court sheets produced by a magistrates'
court's computer are part of that court's register, it follows that the practice of putting
before the magistrates computerised court sheets containing all outstanding charges
against a defendant and convictions on which he awaits sentence is wrong in law (see
b p 496 c d, post); dictum of Frankfurter J in *Public Utilities Commission of the District of
Columbia v Pollak* (1952) 343 US at 466–467 applied.

Notes
For test of disqualification of justices by bias, see 29 Halsbury's Laws (4th edn) para 257,
and for cases on the subject, see 33 Digest (Reissue) 73–75, 259–271.

c
Cases referred to in judgment
Allinson v General Council of Medical Education and Registration [1894] 1 QB 750, [1891–4]
    All ER Rep 768, CA, 33 Digest (Reissue) 296, 2364.
Hannam v Bradford City Council [1970] 2 All ER 690, [1970] 1 WLR 937, CA, 19 Digest
    (Reissue) 550, 4133.
d *Metropolitan Properties Co (FGC) Ltd v Lannon* [1968] 3 All ER 304, [1969] 1 QB 577,
    [1968] 3 WLR 694, CA, 31(2) Digest (Reissue) 1071, 8400.
Public Utilities Commission of the District of Columbia v Pollak (1952) 343 US 451.
R v McLean, ex p Aikens (1974) 139 JP 261, DC.
R v Sandwich Justices, ex p Berry (1981) 74 Cr App R 132, DC.
R v Uxbridge Justices, ex p Burbridge (1972) Times, 21 June, DC.

e
Cases also cited
B (T A) (an infant), Re [1970] 3 All ER 705, [1971] Ch 270.
Huziak v Andrychuk (1977) 1 CRNS 132, Sask QB.
Mason v Chief of Police (1965) 10 WIR 249.
Police v Pereira [1977] 1 NZLR 547.
f *R v Altrincham Justices, ex p Pennington* [1975] 2 All ER 78, [1975] QB 549, DC.
R v Box [1963] 3 All ER 240, [1964] 1 QB 430, CCA.
R v Colchester Magistrate, ex p Beck [1979] 2 All ER 1035, [1979] QB 674, DC.
R v Governor of Brixton Prison, ex p Thompson (1970) 114 SJ 187, DC.
R v Hood [1968] 2 All ER 56, [1968] 1 WLR 773, CA.
R v McElligott, ex p Gallagher and Seal [1972] Crim LR 332, DC.
g *R v Rashbrook* [1969] Crim LR 602, CA.
Steeples v Derbyshire CC [1981] JPL 582.

Application for judicial review
Rodney Topping applied, with the leave of the Divisional Court granted on 8 November
1982, for (1) an order of certiorari to quash the decisions of the Liverpool City justices (a)
h refusing to entertain an application that they should not continue to hear a charge of
criminal damage against the applicant having been made aware from the court sheets
placed in front of them of seven other charges against him, (b) ordering the trial of the
charge of criminal damage to continue and (c) convicting the applicant on that charge,
(2) an order of mandamus directing the justices to exercise their discretion by entertaining

j   a   Rule 66, so far as material, provides:
        '(1) The clerk of every magistrates' court shall keep a register in which there shall be entered—
        (a) a minute or memorandum of every adjudication of the court; (b) a minute or memorandum of
        every other proceeding or thing required by these rules or any other enactment to be so entered.
        (2) The register shall be in the prescribed form, and entries in the register shall include, where
        relevant, such particulars as are provided for in the said form . . .'

the application that they should not continue to hear the trial of the charge of criminal damage, (3) a declaration that the practice of producing for a bench of justices *a* computerised court sheets showing, in addition to the charge the bench was about to try, all other outstanding charges against the defendant and all outstanding convictions on which he was awaiting sentence, was wrong in law, (4) an injunction directing the justices to reprogramme their computer or otherwise arrange the court sheets so that when about to try a defendant on a charge they were not made aware of any other charges outstanding against him. The respondent to the application was the prosecutor, *b* the chief constable of Liverpool. The facts are set out in the judgment of the court.

Louis Blom-Cooper QC and *Andrew Moran* for the applicant.
Ian Campbell for the chief constable.

Cur adv vult *c*

12 November. The following judgment of the court was delivered.

ACKNER LJ. On 23 December 1981 the applicant, Rodney Topping, appeared before the Liverpool City justices to stand trial on an allegation of criminal damage to a door. On his appearance it was apparent to the applicant's solicitor that court sheets prepared *d* and produced by a recently installed computer disclosed the fact that Mr Topping was also charged with seven other offences. These offences included six of failing to answer to bail and one of being found drunk in a public place. Mr Topping's solicitor submitted that the bench, as constituted, should not continue to hear the allegation as they would, or might be, prejudiced by their knowledge from the court sheets of these outstanding charges (to which he had not yet pleaded). What happened next is of considerable *e* importance.

Mr Broudie, Mr Topping's solicitor, has confirmed on affidavit that the following took place. Before the magistrates considered the submission, their clerk stated in open court that since the new computer had been installed, the question, which was the subject of the submission, had been considered by the clerk to the justices, who had decided that in the circumstances such as those pertaining in this case it was not prejudicial for the *f* justices to be informed of other charges laid against the defendant. Mr Broudie then submitted that the decision was one which only the justices could make and it was not a proper decision for the clerk to the justices. In answer to this, the chairman of the magistrates stated that he sympathised with the solicitor's argument, but that the trial should continue.

These are clear, positive allegations and if we are to accept them, it must follow that *g* the justices neither considered nor adjudicated on the submission.

Mr Pearson is the clerk to the justices for the city of Liverpool and he has sworn an affidavit which contains this paragraph:

'Applications similar to the one said to have been made before the Court on the 23rd December 1981 have previously been made in Liverpool. I have instructed my court clerks that they should advise Magistrates that there is no good reason in law *h* why they should not proceed to deal with cases where they know that there are a number of charges against a single defendant, if they are so minded.'

He adds that when he gave these instructions he was mindful of the decision of *R v Sandwich Justices, ex p Berry* (1981) 74 Cr App R 132.

Mr Bankes, who is the principal assistant employed at the Liverpool City Magistrates' *j* Court, was the court clerk on the day in question. He was unable to remember the application being made, but stated in his affidavit that he had been instructed in the past by Mr Pearson that in such cases he was to advise the justices that there was nothing wrong in law in their proceeding with cases where there were a number of charges on the register sheets before them which related to separate matters, if they saw fit to do so.

Mr Shields was the chairman of the bench which dealt with Mr Topping's case. He could not remember the details of any application. All he could say was that he could not recall having a case in which he or his fellow magistrates 'felt prejudiced by seeing sheets showing a number of offences alleged against the defendant. I am sure that had I felt any such prejudice I would have sought the advice of the Court clerk as to the proper course of action'.

If Mr Broudie's submission had in fact been considered and ruled on by the magistrates, we would have expected that there would have been some note, let alone some residual recollection of the event. No such note has been produced. Moreover, to our mind, considering the full terms of Mr Pearson's affidavit, to further parts of which we shall refer later, and that of Mr Bankes to which we have already made reference, it seems to us inherently probable that what is described by Mr Broudie took place.

We are accordingly satisfied that the magistrates never exercised their discretion whether to continue with the hearing and accordingly we grant an order of certiorari quashing the conviction.

However, this application raises questions of fundamental importance, and we would not wish to avoid dealing with them by deciding this case on the narrow question whether the justices ever embarked on the exercise of their discretion. There are two important and fundamental questions which this application raises.

1. *What should be the proper approach of the magistrates, having learned of previous convictions and/or outstanding charges, to an application made to them not to try the case?*

Mr Pearson in his affidavit, purporting to rely on *R v Sandwich Justices, ex p Berry* (1982) 74 Cr App R 132, stated that where the magistrates become aware that the defendant has pleaded guilty to offences for which he has not yet been sentenced, or that there are outstanding charges against him, the advice he would give to the justices is that they can properly deal with the charge before them, 'unless they felt prejudiced by the information appearing before them'. With respect, we think Mr Pearson is wrong: firstly, because he has misunderstood the breadth of the *Sandwich* decision and, secondly, because the test is not the subjective one which he suggests.

The *Sandwich* case was, as the facts disclose and as Donaldson LJ who gave the leading judgment of the Divisional Court made clear, a very unusual case. The applicant had the misfortune to attract the attention of the police in the context of his driving on no less than six different occasions between August and October 1980. There were six sets of charges, each set of charges relating to one particular day. His solicitor made an application that each set should be tried by a fresh bench of magistrates in order, as he said, that there should be no prejudice. The magistrates considered the applications and decided that they should hear the informations seriatim. This they proceeded to do and they found the applicant guilty on some and not guilty on others. The Divisional Court held that the magistrates had a discretion, which discretion was of course reviewable if it had been exercised on wrong principles. However, on the facts of that particular case it could not be said that there had been any wrongful exercise of that discretion. As Donaldson LJ pointed out, the case had the unusual feature that the defence which was being put forward in relation to the breathalyser offences was that the police were out to get this man for one offence or another as a result of some disagreement between him and them in the more or less distant past. There had been an alleged campaign of police harassment and, if that defence was to be made good, it was essential that the same bench should be appraised of the full extent of this harassment. We do not take the view that this case is an authority for any broad principle other than that the magistrates have a discretion, which discretion they must exercise judicially. This is of course common ground. It certainly does not decide what test the justices should apply when a question of bias or prejudice is raised, and it certainly is not a charter for the Liverpool computer system, which raises the second important question in this case.

As regards the appropriate test, as far back as *Allinson v General Council of Medical Education and Registration* [1894] 1 QB 750 at 758, [1891–4] All ER Rep 768 at 771 per

Lord Esher MR, there was authority that the test of actual bias, as distinct from the
appearance of bias, is inappropriate:

> 'The question is not, whether in fact he was or was not biased. The Court cannot
> inquire into that . . . In the administration of justice, whether by a recognised legal
> Court or by persons who, although not a legal public Court, are acting in a similar
> capacity, public policy requires that, in order that there should be no doubt about
> the purity of the administration, any person who is to take part in it should not be
> in such a position that he might be suspected of being biased.'

More recently Lord Denning MR has preferred the test of the appearance of bias to
that of actual bias. In *Metropolitan Properties Co (FGC) Ltd v Lannon* [1968] 3 All ER 304 at
310, [1969] 1 QB 577 at 599 he said:

> '. . . in considering whether there was a real likelihood of bias, the court does not
> look at the mind of the justice himself or at the mind of the chairman of the
> tribunal, or whoever it may be, who sits in a judicial capacity. It does not look to see
> if there was a real likelihood that he would, or did, in fact favour one side at the
> expense of the other. The court looks at the impression which would be given to
> other people. Even if he was as impartial as could be, nevertheless if right-minded
> persons would think that, in the circumstances, there was a real likelihood of bias
> on his part, then he should not sit . . . There must be circumstances from which a
> reasonable man would think it likely or probable that the justice, or chairman, as
> the case may be, would, or did, favour one side unfairly at the expense of the other.
> The court will not enquire whether he did, in fact, favour one side unfairly. Suffice
> it that reasonable people might think he did. The reason is plain enough. Justice
> must be rooted in confidence; and confidence is destroyed when right-minded
> people go away thinking: "The judge was biased."'

In our view, therefore, the correct test to apply is whether there is the appearance of
bias, rather than whether there is actual bias.

In the past there has also been a conflict of view as to the way in which that test should
be applied. Must there appear to be a real likelihood of bias? Or is it enough if there
appears to be a reasonable suspicion of bias? (For a discussion on the cases, see *de Smith's
Judicial Review of Administrative Action* (4th edn, 1980) pp 262–264 and H W R Wade,
Administrative Law (5th edn, 1982) pp 430–432.) We accept the view of Cross LJ,
expressed in *Hannam v Bradford City Council* [1970] 2 All ER 690 at 700, [1970] 1 WLR
937 at 949, that there is really little, if any, difference between the two tests:

> 'If a reasonable person who has no knowledge of the matter beyond knowledge
> of the relationship which subsists between some members of the tribunal and one
> of the parties would think that there might well be bias, then there is in his opinion
> a real likelihood of bias. Of course, someone else with inside knowledge of the
> character of the members in question might say: "Although things don't look very
> well, in fact there is no real likelihood of bias." But that would be beside the point,
> because the question is not whether the tribunal will in fact be biased, but whether
> a reasonable man with no inside knowledge might well think that it might be
> biased.'

We conclude that the test to be applied can conveniently be expressed by slightly
adapting the words of Lord Widgery CJ in a test which he laid down in *R v Uxbridge
Justices, ex p Burbridge* (1972) Times, 21 June and referred to by him in *R v McLean, ex p
Aikens* (1974) 139 JP 261 at 266: would a reasonable and fair-minded person sitting in
court and knowing all the relevant facts have a reasonable suspicion that a fair trial for
the applicant was not possible?

Assuming, therefore, that the magistrates had applied the test advised by Mr Pearson:
'Do I feel prejudiced?' then they would have applied the wrong test, exercised their
discretion on the wrong principle and the same result, namely the quashing of the
conviction, would follow.

2. The computer system

a   We are asked to make a declaration that the practice of producing for a bench of magistrates computerised court sheets, showing all charges and convictions (in respect of which convictions the defendant is awaiting sentence by the court) then outstanding and including the charge which the bench is about to try, is wrong in law.

We have had the advantage of an affidavit from Mr Cobley, a practising solicitor, who before joining his present firm was employed as a senior clerk at the Liverpool City
b   Magistrates' Court. He was originally engaged in November 1973 as a court clerk and was later promoted to senior court clerk and was so engaged from the period November 1973 until 31 March 1980. He states that during the period he was employed as a court clerk, he became very familiar with the register system used at that court and made many entries in the register himself. During the whole period he was engaged as a court clerk at Liverpool City Magistrates' Court, it was the practice that, when a defendant was
c   to stand trial, the only matters which the magistrates had in front of them on the court register sheet was the offence or offences, if they were connected, to be tried. If by some error an *unrelated* offence, for example, one which was to be dealt with by way of sentence after trial, was typed on the same register sheet, new register sheets would be prepared showing the offence to be tried on a register sheet on its own. The clerk to the court would return the other register sheets and would not show them to the magistrates until
d   after the conclusion of the trial. He further states that it was the generally accepted view that to do otherwise would be to prejudice the magistrates. He recalls occasions when magistrates had inadvertently seen sheets bearing the offences which were for sentence or plea after trial, then the trial was moved to either another court or had been adjourned to be heard by a fresh bench of magistrates.

All this is now changed thanks to the use made of the computer. It is apparently
e   programmed in such a way that it produces in relation to each defendant one list which shows not only the charge which is to be heard, but all other charges, related or unrelated, which are outstanding and all convictions, whether the result of a plea of guilty or a conviction, which are awaiting sentence. This is no doubt very convenient for the administration and may be of great advantage for the office staff. In our judgment it is most undesirable that such a document should be put before the magistrates and for
f   these reasons. (1) Defendants in person will now know what other charges or convictions have thus been drawn to the magistrates' attention, and will therefore be deprived of any opportunity to make the appropriate application. (2) Even those who are represented may be unaware of the material which has been put before the magistrates. (3) Having arrived at court prepared for the trial, the expense of witnesses being incurred, a defendant or his advocate may well be very averse to making an application which will
g   result in an adjournment, and thereby obliged to run the risk of prejudice, to which risk he should not be subjected. (4) While on occasions it may be necessary to make an application for the trial by another bench of magistrates, the system should be such that such occasions are as rare as possible. A system which is calculated to make this a regular event must be a bad system.

Counsel for the applicant very aptly cites the following from the statement of
h   Frankfurter J in *Public Utilities Commission of the District of Columbia v Pollak* (1952) 343 US 451 at 466–467:

'The judicial process demands that a judge move within the framework of relevant legal rules and the covenanted modes of thought for ascertaining them. He must think dispassionately and submerge private feeling on every aspect of a case.
j   There is a good deal of shallow talk that the judicial robe does not change the man within it. It does. The fact is that on the whole judges do lay aside private views in discharging their judicial functions. This is achieved through training, professional habits, self-discipline and that fortunate alchemy by which men are loyal to the obligation with which they are entrusted. But it is also true that reason cannot control the subconscious influence of feelings of which it is unaware. When there is ground for believing that such unconscious feelings may operate in the ultimate

judgment, or may not unfairly lead others to believe they are operating, judges recuse themselves. They do not sit in judgment. They do this for a variety of *a* reasons. The guiding consideration is that the administration of justice should reasonably appear to be disinterested as well as be so in fact.'

In the affidavits put in on behalf of the justices, there is no suggestion that they are incapable of controlling their computer. The chief constable, who was represented on this application, provided us with no information to suggest that there cannot be put before the justices the limited material as occurred in the pre-computer era. To our mind *b* there is a real danger that administrative convenience is being given greater priority than the requirements of justice. We therefore repeat that in our judgment the practice of putting before the justices' court sheets expressed in this fashion is most undesirable. Can it also be said to be wrong in law?

It was common ground between counsel who appeared on this application that the 'court sheets' referred to in it are in fact the court register; this we were able to confirm *c* by our own inspection. The authority for the keeping of the court register is contained in r 66 of the Magistrates' Courts Rules 1981, SI 1981/552. It is sufficient for present purposes to note that neither that rule, nor the form prescribed in it (Form 148 in *Stone's Justices' Manual* 1982, vol 3, p 7625) contains provision for the entry in the register, or in any particular sheet of it, of any offence or matter of complaint other than that (or, where associated offences or complaints are heard together, those) in respect of which the court *d* is to adjudicate. For this reason, therefore, we grant the declaration sought, that the practice complained of by the applicant is wrong in law.

Certiorari and declaration granted.

Solicitors: *Seifert Sedley & Co*, agents for *R M Broudie & Co*, Liverpool (for the applicant); *Brian H Crebbin*, Liverpool (for the chief constable).

N P Metcalfe Esq   Barrister.

_a City of Birmingham District Council v O and another

HOUSE OF LORDS
LORD DIPLOCK, LORD WILBERFORCE, LORD KEITH OF KINKEL, LORD ROSKILL AND LORD BRIGHTMAN
b 29, 30 NOVEMBER 1982, 27 JANUARY 1983

Local government – Documents – Inspection – Inspection by councillor – Application for adoption order – Social services committee report on suitability of prospective adoptive parents – Councillor of housing sub-committee requesting disclosure of social services report – Councillor claiming disclosure necessary to enable her to perform duties as councillor – Social services committee
c *withholding report – Whether councillor entitled to see report.*

The applicants were the foster parents of a child who was in the care of a city council. The applicants wished to adopt the child and applied for approval to do so to the council, which was a recognised adoption agency and which had, as required by s 2(1) of the Local Authority Social Services Act 1970, delegated its social services functions to a social *d* services committee. That committee had in turn set up a sub-committee to deal with adoption matters and the applicants' request for approval was referred to the sub-committee. While the application was being considered, the applicants fell into arrears with the rent of their council house and were called before a sub-committee of the housing committee in connection with the arrears. During the course of the interview with the foster mother, a councillor on the sub-committee learnt that the husband had *e* served a prison sentence. Later the councillor also discovered that the applicants had a long history of rent arrears. The councillor became alarmed at the suitability of the applicants as foster parents and referred the matter to the social services department. Both the department and the social services committee reviewed the case and ultimately gave approval to the applicants being prospective adoptive parents. However, the councillor was not satisfied with the result and asked to see the relevant files of the social *f* services department. The council's solicitor advised the department that the councillor should be allowed to see the files in order that she could properly carry out her duties as a councillor. The council by resolution approved that advice. The applicants applied for an order prohibiting the council from disclosing to the councillor any information about the foster parents obtained or recorded in confidence by the social services department, contending that, since the councillor was not a member of the social services committee, *g* she had no duties as a councillor which required her to be acquainted with the contents of the social services department's files on the applicants. The Divisional Court refused the application on the grounds that since the adoption agency was the council itself, and the councillor was a member of the council with a genuine interest in the matter, she was entitled to see the files even though she was not a member of the social services committee. On appeal by the applicants the Court of Appeal held that because of the *h* confidentiality of the files and the fact that the councillor was not a member of the social services committee and had no particular duty or responsibility in adoption matters the council should be prohibited from disclosing the files to the councillor. The council appealed to the House of Lords.

Held – It followed from the general principle that a councillor was entitled by virtue of *j* his office to have access to all written material in the possession of the council provided he had good reason for such access, first, that a councillor ex hypothesi normally had good reason for such access to all written material in the possession of a committee of which he was a member and, second, that he had no automatic right of access to material in the possession of a committee of which he was not a member. In the case of information in the possession of a committee of which he was not a member, a councillor had to demonstrate a need to know such information in order to be able to carry out his duties as a councillor properly, the decision whether the councillor should have access to such information being ultimately a decision for the council itself, although the council *a* was entitled expressly or impliedly to delegate the function of deciding whether he should have access to such information. Applying those principles, there were undoubtedly grounds for questioning the wisdom of the proposed adoption, and the council itself would ultimately be responsible if the adoption should prove unsuccessful. It was therefore not unreasonable for the council to permit the councillor to have access, in confidence, to the files of the council's social services department relating to the child *b* and the applicants. The position was not altered by the fact that the council had delegated its functions in relation to adoption to the social services committee, because it retained a residual responsibility for the committee's actions and an obligation, in appropriate circumstances, to exercise some degree of control over the committee. The appeal would accordingly be allowed (see p 499 *a* to *d*, p 501 *e* to *g*, p 504 *g h*, p 505 *c* to p 506 *a* and p 507 *a* to *g*, post).   *c*

R v Barnes BC, ex p Conlan [1938] 3 All ER 226 applied.

Per curiam. Where information in the possession of a council relates to matters as delicate and confidential as child care and adoption, access to the information should be strictly screened to prevent unnecessary dissemination of details relating to the child, its natural parents, any foster parents or applicants for adoption, and the sources of the information (see p 499 *a* to *d* and p 505 *e f*, post).   *d*

Decision of the Court of Appeal sub nom R v City of Birmingham DC, ex p O [1982] 2 All ER 356 reversed.

Notes

For a local councillor's right to inspect documents in the council's possession, see 28 Halsbury's Laws (4th edn) para 1349, and for cases on inspection of a corporation's books *e* and documents, see 13 Digest (Reissue) 234–236, 2044–2062.

For the Local Authority Social Services Act 1970, s 2, see 40 Halsbury's Statutes (3rd edn) 992.

Cases referred to in opinions

Associated Provincial Picture Houses Ltd v Wednesbury Corp [1947] 2 All ER 680, [1948] 1 *f* KB 223, CA, 45 Digest (Repl) 215, 189.

Manton v Brighton Corp [1951] 2 All ER 101, [1951] 2 KB 393, 33 Digest (Reissue) 23, 71.

R v Barnes BC, ex p Conlan [1938] 3 All ER 226, 16 Digest (Reissue) 362, 3839.

R v Southwold Corp, ex p Wrightson (1907) 97 LT 431, DC, 16 Digest (Reissue) 362, 3838.

Appeal

The City of Birmingham District Council appealed with leave of the Court of Appeal *g* against the decision of the Court of Appeal (Lord Denning MR and Sir Sebag Shaw, Donaldson LJ dissenting) ([1982] 2 All ER 356, [1982] 1 WLR 679) on 19 February 1982 allowing an appeal by the applicants, Mr and Mrs O, against the decision of the Divisional Court of the Queen's Bench Division (Eveleigh LJ and Watkins J) on 25 March 1980 whereby the court refused an application for judicial review by way of an order of prohibition to prevent the council by its officers, servants or agents from disclosing to *h* Councillor Mrs Alice Willetts any information about the applicants, or either of them, obtained or recorded about them in confidence by the social services department of the council. The facts are set out in the opinion of Lord Brightman.

Raymond Sears QC and Ian Croxford for the council.
Stephen Sedley and Elizabeth Lawson for the applicants.   *j*

Their Lordships took time for consideration.

27 January. The following opinions were delivered.

LORD DIPLOCK. My Lords, I have had the advantage of reading in draft the speech

of my noble and learned friend Lord Brightman. I agree with it and for the reasons he
a gives I would allow the appeal.

LORD WILBERFORCE. My Lords, I have had the benefit of reading in advance the
speech to be delivered by my noble and learned friend Lord Brightman. This leaves me
in no doubt that the judgment of Donaldson LJ in the Court of Appeal was correct. For
the reasons there given and for those expounded by my noble and learned friend I would
b allow the appeal. I associate myself with those who have commented with regret on the
unfortunate delay which has taken place as regards the adoption of the child concerned.

LORD KEITH OF KINKEL. My Lords, I agree that for the reasons set out in the
speech of my noble and learned friend Lord Brightman, which I have had the benefit of
reading in draft, this appeal should be allowed.

c
LORD ROSKILL. My Lords, I have had the advantage of reading in draft the speech
of my noble and learned friend Lord Brightman. I agree with it and for the reasons he
gives I would allow the appeal.

LORD BRIGHTMAN. My Lords, this appeal raises an important question as to the
d circumstances in which a member of a district council, in intended performance of such
member's responsibilities as a councillor, is entitled to inquire into the transactions of a
committee of which the councillor is not a member. A difference of view has arisen in
the highly delicate and confidential area of a proposed adoption, where the welfare of the
child proposed to be adopted transcends most other considerations.

My Lords, there is one consideration which I wish to place in the forefront of my
e speech. It is an inevitable feature of local government today that there must be delegation
of the multifarious functions of a local authority among numerous committees, sub-
committees and individual officers. No local authority could function efficiently
otherwise. Section 101 of the Local Government Act 1972 provides for this delegation in
general terms, as did previous enactments. Section 3(3) of the Local Authority Social
Services Act 1970, as I shall mention later, particularly so provides in relation to the
f delegation by a local authority of its social services functions to its social services
committee. Nevertheless, I would deprecate any suggestion that the committee system,
in the absence of clear statutory provision to the contrary, in any way fragments the
responsibility of the council of the local authority as a whole.

Before I turn to the particular facts of this dispute, it will be convenient to summarise
the legislative position. The activities of a local authority in relation to adoptions are
g governed by the Adoption Act 1958 and regulations made thereunder and by the Local
Authority Social Services Act 1970.

Section 28 of the Adoption Act 1958 empowers a local authority, if it so wishes, to
make and participate in arrangements for the adoption of children. Section 32(3) of the
Act empowers the Secretary of State to make regulations with respect to the exercise by
local authorities of these functions, and such regulations may make provision for purposes
h corresponding with the purposes for which the Secretary of State has power to make
regulations under s 32(1) in relation to registered adoption societies. Those purposes are
specified in Sch 3. They are described as purposes—

'1. For regulating the conduct of negotiations entered into by or on behalf of
registered adoption societies with persons who, having the care and possession of
infants, are desirous of causing the infants to be adopted, and in particular for
j securing . . .'

The only purpose specified in Sch 3 which need be set out is:

'2. For requiring that the case of every infant proposed to be delivered by or on
behalf of a registered adoption society into the care and possession of a person
proposing to adopt him shall be considered by a committee (to be called a "case

committee") appointed by the society for the purpose and consisting of not less than three persons.'

a

Combined regulations have been made under sub-ss (1) and (3) relating to both registered adoption societies and local authorities. They are now contained in the Adoption Agencies Regulations 1976, SI 1976/1796. In these regulations the expression 'adoption agency' is used to mean both a registered adoption society and a local authority (exercising adoption functions). The regulations cover five topics, as shown by the b crossheadings, namely: (i) the registration of adoption societies, (ii) the composition of case committees, (iii) the duties of adoption agencies in making arrangments for adoption, (iv) supervision and medical reports on placement for adoption and (v) disclosure of information in relation to the adoption.

Except under heading (i), which is concerned only with adoption societies, the regulations apply to 'adoption agencies', that is to say to both an adoption society and a c local authority, without drawing any distinction between their respective duties and responsibilities (subject to immaterial exceptions in regs 8(g), 11(a) and 12).

My Lords, I must pause in my consideration of the regulations to say a word about 'case committees'. The function of a case committee is described in para 2 of Sch 3 to the 1958 Act, which I have already read. It is apparent from reg 2 ('Interpretation') of the 1976 regulations that the case committees of a local authority are to be set up by the d authority's social services committee, of which more later. Regulation 6 governs the composition of a case committee: it shall consist of 'not less than three persons each of whom shall be competent to judge whether the proposed placing is likely to promote the welfare of the child', and is to include if practicable at least one man and one woman. Paragraph 2 of Sch 3 to the 1958 Act envisages to my mind that an adoption agency will have a number of case committees, to one of which every proposed adoption will be e assigned, although this is not obligatory and an adoption agency could lawfully operate with a single case committee if such committee could competently handle all the agency's adoptions.

I continue with my consideration of the 1976 regulations. I fear that this survey of the statutory provisions is somewhat protracted, but in my opinion a close study of Sch 3 to the 1958 Act and of the regulations made under s 32 is needed to enable one to view the f case in its proper context.

Regulation 8 defines the steps which are to be taken before a child is placed by or on behalf of an adoption agency in the actual custody of a proposed adopter. A placement prior to adoption is a prerequisite of an adoption order under s 3 of the Adoption Act 1958. Some of these steps are the responsibility of the case committee, but most are expressed to be the responsibility of the adoption agency, that is to say the adoption g society or the local authority. It is the responsibility of the *adoption agency* to ascertain the particulars set out in Sch 4; these cover numerous factual matters concerning the child, its natural parents and the proposed adopters. It is also the responsibility of the *adoption agency* to obtain a detailed medical report on the child as required by Sch 5, to assess the personality of the proposed adopter and, if the proposed adopters are a married couple, to assess if possible the stability of the marriage, to have an inspection made of the h proposed adoptive home, and to make inquiries to satisfy itself that it would not be detrimental to the child to be kept by the adopter at such home. On the other hand it is the responsibility of the *case committee* to interview, or cause to be interviewed, the proposed adopter, and it is a prerequisite of the placing that the *case committee* shall have approved of it, after ascertaining if practicable the wishes and feelings of the child, and after considering all the information obtained pursuant to reg 8. j

After the child has been placed in the custody of the proposed adopter, it is the responsibility of the *adoption agency* under reg 9 to make adequate arrangements for supervision, and to arrange for the child to be visited by a representative of the *adoption agency* as often as the *case committee* considers it necessary. It is also the responsibility of the *adoption agency* to obtain certain additional medical reports. Regulation 10 imposes a duty of confidentiality to which I will refer later. Regulation 11 imposes on the *adoption*

agency the duty of protecting the confidentiality of, and of preserving, records and
a documents relating to the negotiations between itself and the proposed adopter.
   The Local Authority Social Services Act 1970 is a statute which covers a wider field
than adoption. It imposes on every local authority the duty of establishing a social
services committee. Under s 2 of that Act 'there shall stand referred' to that committee
all matters relating to the discharge by the authority of its functions under some twenty
statutes concerned with social welfare, including its functions (if assumed) under the
b Adoption Act 1958 in relation to the making, and participating in, arrangements for the
adoption of children, and the care, possession and supervision of children awaiting
adoption. Under s 3(3) the local authority is entitled, but not bound, to delegate to its
social services committee any matters which stand referred; but, if there is no such
delegation, the local authority before exercising such a function itself must consider a
report of the social services committee with respect thereto. The social services committee
c may, under s 4, establish sub-committees and may sub-delegate. Under s 5 the majority
of the members of a social services committee must be members of the local authority,
and a sub-committee must include at least one member of the local authority.
   Finally, I must refer briefly to the part played by the adoption agency when the
adoption application comes before the court. In the High Court, notice of the application
has to be given to the adoption agency, which has a right of audience by its officer or
d servant: see the Adoption (High Court) Rules 1976, SI 1976/1645, rr 18(3), 19(2). In the
county court, the adoption agency is a respondent to the application: see the Adoption
(County Court) Rules 1976, SI 1976/1644, r 4(2)(g). The effect of para 6 of Sch 2 to the
High Court rules, and of the same paragraph and schedule to the county court rules, is
that the guardian ad litem of the child is required to obtain from the adoption agency
such information concerning the child as the agency has in its possession and which the
e agency considers might assist the court in deciding whether or not the child should be
adopted by the applicant.
   My Lords, I have referred at some length to the statutory provisions in order to
demonstrate, I hope beyond argument, that it is the members of the adoption society, or
the members of the local authority, together with the guardian ad litem, who must bear
the ultimate responsibility for recommending a proposed adoption to the court, and not
f the case committee or any other committee of the adoption society or local authority,
and that in the case of a local authority acting as an adoption agency the case committee
is clearly accountable to the social services committee, and the social services committee
is clearly accountable to the local authority, and the local authority is clearly accountable
to the court, for the due performance of their respective duties in relation to an adoption.
   I turn next to the position within the City of Birmingham District Council at the
g relevant time. The council acts as an adoption agency. It has established a social services
committee as required by the 1970 Act. In 1975 the council delegated to its social services
committee the powers and duties of the council under the 1970 Act, which had the
effect, I will assume, of authorising the social services committee in the name of the
council to make, and participate in, arrangements for the adoption of children. Such
delegation, which was revocable, had no effect on the accountability of the case committee
h or other limbs of the social services department to the social services committee, or of the
social services committee to the council, or of the council to the court.
   The council has a staff of some 600 social workers. It did not, at the relevant time, have
any case committee so called. It did however have a so-called central adoption panel
which presumably discharged the duties of a case committee.
   I turn at last to the particular facts of this case. The child concerned, named Emma,
j was born in March 1975. In August Emma was placed by her parents, informally, in the
care of the respondents to this appeal, whom I will call the applicants because it is they
who are seeking judicial review. The applicants are a husband and wife with four
children of their own. In September 1975 the applicants were evicted by the council
from their home for non-payment of rent, and were accommodated in a hostel
until, in January 1976, they were provided with a council tenancy at their present
address. In August 1976 the social services department of the council inquired from the

housing department whether the latter had any information about the suitability of
boarding a child with the applicants. The housing department declined to recommend   *a*
such a placement. However, at some time during 1976, the social services department
'fostered out' Emma with the applicants, which I apprehend amounted to an approval of
the existing informal arrangement. In the summer of 1977 the applicants sought
approval from the social services department to their adoption of Emma. Approval was
provisionally given by the council's central adoption panel in March 1978. The applicants
again fell into arrear with their rent. Mrs Willetts is a member of the council and also of   *b*
the council's housing committee. The applicants were asked to attend a meeting of a sub-
committee of the housing committee on 26 July 1978 in connection with their rent
arrears. During the course of this interview Mrs Willetts, who was a member of the sub-
committee, learnt that the husband had served a prison sentence for some undisclosed
offence. She also discovered a little later that the applicants had a long history of rent
arrears. In the result Mrs Willetts became alarmed about the suitability of the applicants   *c*
as foster parents. She approached Mr Williamson, the deputy director of social services,
and asked for the matter to be looked into. Various inquiries were instituted and reports
produced within the social services department, which ultimately led to a letter on 5
January 1979 from Mrs Cooke, a councillor and the chairman of one of the social services
sub-committees, assuring Mrs Willetts that the writer was satisfied that the applicants
were properly caring for Emma, and offering an opportunity for discussion.   *d*
     Mrs Willetts replied to Mrs Cooke on 4 February 1979 explaining why she did not feel
sufficiently reassured. She agreed that it was by then much too late to remove Emma
from the care of the applicants, but said she was disturbed to learn that the applicants
might in the very near future be allowed to adopt Emma. Mrs Cooke replied on 21
February, but Mrs Willetts still was not satisfied. She approached Mr Williamson and
asked to see the relevant files. Thereupon Mr Williamson sought the advice of Mr Wilson,   *e*
the solicitor to the council, 'as to whether or not he was bound to disclose the files'. Mr
Wilson deposes that he—

     'advised Mr. Williamson that it had been, and was reasonably necessary, for [her]
     to see the files in order that she could properly carry out her duties as a City
     Councillor. It appeared to me that the request had arisen out of the discharge by   *f*
     Councillor Mrs. Willetts of her duties as a member of the Housing Committee, and
     seemed to be a natural progression from problems thereby disclosed. Of course I
     further advised that the Councillor be reminded of the confidential nature of the
     contents of the files.'

It was arranged that the files should be shown to Mrs Willetts on 8 June.
     To anticipate events for a moment, the action proposed to be taken by Mr Williamson   *g*
was approved by the social services committee on 11 July 1979, and was also approved at
some stage by a resolution of the council (see [1982] 2 All ER 356 at 368, [1982] 1 WLR
679 at 695).
     Before Mr Williamson could act, an application was made to the court in the name of
the applicants for leave to apply for judicial review, and seeking an order prohibiting the
council from disclosing to Mrs Willetts any information about the applicants obtained or   *h*
recorded in confidence by the council's social services department. The grounds for the
application were stated to be that Mrs Willetts, not being a member of the social services
committee, had no duties as a councillor which required her to be acquainted with the
contents of the social services department's file on the applicants. The application was
supported by an affidavit of Mr Skemp, a solicitor in the employment of Small Heath
Community Law Centre, who described himself as instructed as agent for the Saltley   *j*
Action Centre.
     In the course of her affidavit in reply, Mrs Willetts deposed:

     'I felt that the matters which I had raised could and ought to have been cleared up
     from information already held by [the social services department] in its files . . . In

my view this was a matter of public interest about which as a City Councillor I had a duty to apprise myself of the available information and make an informed decision about what, if anything, I should do. As a matter of course I expected to receive and treat information as confidential . . . It is true that I do not serve on the Social Services Committee, nor do I represent the area of the City in which the applicants live. Nevertheless it is my belief that the information gathered by officers and employees of the Council is gathered for the purposes of the City Council. Thus as a Councillor having become concerned in this matter I believe it to be my duty to come to an informed opinion upon the policy of the Council on the child Emma. Further, it is not my stated intention to interfere with the adoption of Emma. However I am concerned that any steps which the Council should take in respect of the child should be in her best interests.'

This was followed by an affidavit of Mrs Dolan. She is a social worker employed by the council in its social services department. She is described as a team leader in Area 7, and she stated that she supervised a team of seven social workers and ancillary specialist workers. She says that the social worker assigned to Emma's case was a member of her team until he was posted elsewhere in September 1978, since when she herself had assumed the social work responsibility for Emma and the applicants.

Mrs Dolan's affidavit clearly reveals the difference of view which has arisen between the members of the council and those employed by the council. After referring to the functions of the central adoption panel, which she described as having the 'duty of deciding whether persons in the position of the Applicants shall be approved as prospective adopters', she added:

'No councillors sit on the Panel, and it is my understanding that the Panel is not accountable to the local authority for its decisions . . . the information [on the files] is solicited and communicated upon the express understanding that it is confidential: that is to say, that it is for the eyes only of those concerned with preparing and subsequently appraising reports on the suitability of the Applicants to be initially foster parents and subsequently adoptive parents.'

This affidavit concluded the evidence. No affidavit was sworn by either of the applicants, and their views are not even reflected in the evidence sworn on their behalf, save for four lines in Mr Skemp's affidavit stating that they 'fear that [Mrs Willetts] will attempt to make use of the contents of the file to assist her in her stated intention of interfering with the proposed adoption'. This is denied by Mrs Willetts.

My Lords, I have no doubt at all that this dispute is basically one between social workers employed by the council and the council itself as to the right of the social workers to independence in this sensitive area. I venture to doubt whether the applicants themselves are much concerned with the question whether, as a matter of principle, their files can be disclosed in confidence to a member of the council, although no doubt they would be deeply concerned at the prospect of disclosure to any person who might be represented to them as a trouble-maker. In making these observations I do not wish to minimise the importance of the issue which is raised, or to cast the smallest doubt on the integrity and dedication of those who work in the council's social services department.

Leave to issue a notice of motion for judicial review was granted on 8 June 1979, together with an order on the council against disclosing the files. The motion, notice of which was issued on 11 June, for some reason did not reach the Divisional Court until March of the following year. The Divisional Court held that as the adoption agency was the council itself, and that as Mrs Willetts was a member of the council with a genuine concern in the matter, she was entitled to see the files although she was not a member of the social services committee. Eveleigh LJ said:

'A councillor's right rests on membership of the agency itself, in which lies the primary responsibility, and which exercises and has responsibility for exercising the function under the Adoption Act 1958.'

This logical approach did not commend itself to the majority of the Court of Appeal. Lord Denning MR said ([1982] 2 All ER 356 at 360, [1982] 1 WLR 679 at 685):   *a*

'... I think this case stands on its own. It is because of the confidentiality of the documents and because they concerned the welfare of a child. This brings into play the consideration of the public interests involved. It requires us to hold the balance between them ... On the one hand there is the public interest in maintaining the confidence in the files, so as to ensure that the contents are not communicated any more widely than is necessary. On the other hand, there is the public interest in the *b* members of the council being sufficiently well informed to carry out their duties. Holding the balance between these two public interests, I am quite clear that the files should be available only to the members of the social services committee and the officers of the social services department. The duties and the responsibilities of the council have been specially delegated to them. There is no need whatever for the files to be shown to other members, like Mrs Willetts, who are not members of *c* the committee and have no particular duty or responsibility in the matter.'

Sir Sebag Shaw agreed. His view is summarised in a sentence towards the end of his judgment ([1982] 2 All ER 356 at 368, [1982] 1 WLR 679 at 695):

'As a member of the council she could raise in council whatever matters appeared to her to call for inquiry or investigation; it is quite a different matter to make *d* peremptory inroads into the functioning of committees with which she had no direct concern.'

Donaldson LJ dissented. His view was much the same as that of the Divisional Court. He said ([1982] 2 All ER 356 at 364, [1982] 1 WLR 679 at 689):

'Bearing in mind that it is the local authority and not the individual social worker *e* which is performing the statutory duty (the social worker is, as it were, the instrument used by the authority) confidential information given to the social worker is given to the authority. However, those who give it are entitled to expect, and social workers can reasonably assure them, that, save as may be necessary for the performance of the authority's statutory duties, the information will never be *f* divulged to anyone outside the authority or to anyone within the authority who has no need to know.'

He then asked himself the question: who decides whether an elected member of the local authority can see particular documents? and answered that it was the local authority, acting by its authorised officer or, in the last resort, acting in council. He added that in the instant case the council approved the decision of the deputy director of social services, *g* and that decision could not be disturbed unless on the facts it was one that no reasonable authority could have taken.

My Lords, I entertain no doubt as to the correctness of the decision of the Divisional Court and of Donaldson LJ. The general principle must be that a councillor is entitled by virtue of his office to have access to all written material in the possession of the local authority of which he is a member, provided that he has good reason for such access. I *h* apprehend that there can be no challenge to that general principle, which was undisputed half a century ago (see *R v Barnes BC, ex p Conlan* [1938] 3 All ER 226). At the risk of being repetitive, I would like to read an extract from the judgment of the Divisional Court in that case (at 230) which was quoted by Donaldson LJ in his written judgment:

'As to the right of a councillor to inspect all documents in possession of the *j* council, there was no dispute at the bar that such a right exists, so far as his access to the documents is reasonably necessary to enable the councillor properly to perform his duties as a member of the council. The common law right of a councillor to inspect documents in the possession of the council arises from his common law duty to keep himself informed of all matters necessary to enable him properly to

discharge his duty as a councillor. There must be some limit to this duty. To hold
that each councillor of such a body as, for instance, the London County Council, is
charged with the duty of making himself familiar with every document in the
possession of that body would be to impose an impossible burden upon individual
councillors. The duties are therefore divided amongst various committees and sub-
committees. In our judgment, it is plain that, as was decided in *R. v. Southwold
Corpn., Ex p. Wrightson* ((1907) 97 LT 431 at 431–432): "a councillor has no right to
a roving commission to go and examine books or documents of a corporation
because he is a councillor. Mere curiosity or desire to see and inspect documents in
not sufficient".'

In the case of a committee of which he is a member, a councillor as a general rule will
ex hypothesi have good reason for access to all written material of such committee. So I
do not doubt that each member of the social services committee is entitled by virtue of
his office to see all the papers which have come into the possession of a social worker in
the course of his duties as an employee of the council. There is no room for any secrecy
as between a social worker and a member of the social services committee.

In the case of a committee of which the councillor is not a member, different
considerations must apply. The outside councillor, as I will call him, has no automatic
right of access to documentary material. Of him, it cannot be said that he necessarily has
good reason, and is necessarily entitled, to inspect all written material in the possession
of the council and every committee and the officers thereof. What Donaldson LJ
described as a 'need to know' must be demonstrated. As he put it ([1982] 2 All ER 356 at
364, [1982] 1 WLR 679 at 690):

'No official has any right to acquire any part of the authority's stock of information,
whether or not confidential, save in so far as it is needed by him in order that he
should be able to do his job. In a word, he has to have a "need to know".'

The 'need to know' test involves the application of a screening process, and this in turn
raises the question of the nature of the screen and who is to apply it. To my mind, in the
case of an area as delicate and confidential as that of child care and adoption, the screening
process should be administered with great strictness. The utmost care must be taken to
prevent the unnecessary dissemination within the council of details relating to the child,
to its natural parents, to any foster or adoptive parents, and of sources of information.
More than that need not be said, because the subject matter sufficiently speaks for itself.

The decision whether the outside councillor has a good reason for access to the
information is ultimately one to be taken by the councillors themselves sitting in council.
But the council may expressly, or by implication, delegate to others the right to decide
whether an application for access to material is to be acceded to, subject to resort to a
meeting of the council if the decision of the delegate is challenged. Although the point
does not arise directly for decision, in the instant case I would think that, in the absence
of express directions from the council, the deputy director and the director of social
services would have an implied right to accede to, or to refuse, such a request as that
made by Mrs Willetts, by virtue of their respective offices. In the event of a continued
difference of opinion, the decision would ultimately lie with the councillors meeting in
council. There the matter would rest. The court has no jurisdiction to substitute its own
opinion. The decision of the council is the final word, subject only to an application for
judicial review under s 31 of the Supreme Court Act 1981 on *Wednesbury* principles (see
Associated Provincial Picture Houses Ltd v Wednesbury Corp [1947] 2 All ER 680, [1948] 1
KB 223).

The position is not altered by the fact that in the instant case the council delegated its
adoption functions to its social services committee. As was pointed out by Slade J in
Manton v Brighton Corp [1951] 2 All ER 101, [1951] 2 KB 393, and as was emphasised by
Donaldson LJ in his judgment, delegation by a principal to an agent does not deprive the
principal (in the words of the Lord Justice) of 'a residual responsibility for the activities

of the delegate and an obligation, in appropriate circumstances, to exercise some degree of control' (see [1982] 2 All ER 356 at 365, [1982] 1 WLR 679 at 691).

This leads to the final question arising on this appeal, namely whether the decision to permit access to relevant files was one which could have been taken by a reasonable local authority. Unless this question is decided in the negative, this appeal must inevitably succeed.

At this stage it is perhaps relevant to look at reg 10 of the Adoption Agencies Regulations 1976. It reads as follows:

'Any information obtained by any person, in the course of negotiations entered into by or on behalf of the agency with a person proposing to place a child with an agency for adoption, or with a person proposing to adopt him, shall be treated as confidential and shall not be disclosed except so far as may be necessary for the purpose of proceedings under [the Adoption Act 1958 or the Children Act 1975]; or for the purposes of regulations 13 or 14 [which are not material]; or for the proper excution of his duty; or to a person who is authorised in writing by or on behalf of the Secretary of State to obtain the information for the purposes of research.'

This regulation was placed at the forefront of the submissions made on behalf of the applicants when the matter was heard by the Divisional Court, where it was argued that the regulation prohibited divulgement outside the membership of the social services committee. The answer given by Eveleigh LJ was that the regulation must at least have envisaged that the person obtaining the information would pass it on to the adoption agency, in this case the council of which Mrs Willetts was a member. The regulation was not discussed in the judgments in the Court of Appeal. The majority judgments rest on the more general ground of the public interest in maintaining the confidence of the files, which outweighs the public interest in councillors being sufficiently well informed to carry out their duties (see [1982] 2 All ER 356 at 360, [1982] 1 WLR 679 at 685 per Lord Denning MR), and the fact that 'the intensely personal functions of the social services committee as set out in Sch 1 are isolated from other functions of the local authority', and that—

'Information which is gleaned and gathered for the purpose of discharging the duties of the committee must generally be of a kind which demands that it be regarded as confidential and that it be used in no other way than for the due discharge of the obligations and responsibilities of the social services committee.'

(See [1982] 2 All ER 356 at 367, [1982] 1 WLR 679 at 693 per Sir Sebag Shaw.)

The applicants, in their printed case, after describing the duty of confidentiality as a duty set out in reg 10 and also as a duty which exists in the public interest and as a matter of public policy, submit that 'Whether the test is the "need to know" or a balance of conflicting interests, access to the material files in the present case cannot as a matter of law go beyond members of the Social Services Committee, and may not even extend so far'.

My Lords, no one doubts the confidentiality of the files in this case. In my opinion reg 10 adds nothing to the degree of that confidentiality, and I doubt whether it is even relevant as between a councillor and a social worker. The power of the Secretary of State to make regulations with respect to the exercise by local authorities of their function of making or participating in arrangements for the adoption of children was conferred by s 32(3) of the Adoption Act 1958 by reference to sub-s (1). The power is confined to the purposes set out (in relation to adoption societies) in Sch 3 to that Act and for prescribing anything which by Pt II of the Act is authorised or required to be prescribed.

Only para 1 of Sch 3 is material to the point under discussion. The purpose there described is 'regulating the conduct of negotiations entered into by or on behalf of registered adoption societies with persons who, having the care and possession of infants,

are desirous of causing the infants to be adopted . . .' Against this background, it seems
a to me that reg 10 is not concerned with *access* to information within the adoption society
or local authority but with *disclosure* outside the society or authority.

Once the conclusion is reached that access to the relevant files outside the membership
of the social services committee is not precluded as a matter of law, this case falls into a
very small compass, namely whether a reasonable body of councillors could form the
view that Mrs Willetts had made out a case for being allowed access to the files. I do not
b think that it can successfully be maintained that no reasonable council could take that
view.

There were undoubtedly grounds for questioning the wisdom of the proposed
adoption. If the adoption had taken place and come to grief, the persons ultimately
responsible would have been the members of the council and not the members of the
central adoption panel or the members of the social services committee. The councillors
c could not have washed their hands of a disaster, and said that it was nothing to do with
them, that it was all the fault of the central adoption panel. In the case of a councillor
with a bona fide and reasonably based concern for a problem of this sort, who is not a
mere busybody, it seems to me that the bias, if any, should be in favour of allowing
access to information rather than concealing information. The names of people, if not
relevant, can readily be hidden; for example, in the present case the names of the natural
d parents. Probably Mrs Willetts would have conceded that information about the natural
parents was irrelevant to her purpose. In this case what is complained of is that
information was about to be made too freely available. Usually the complaint is the other
way round, and non-disclosure is under attack. I would urge your Lordships to hesitate
before deciding that access to information is being unreasonably allowed, particularly
when such access is approved by the immediate possessor of the information, namely the
e social services committee, as well as by the council's solicitor, the council's general
purposes committee and the council itself. Viewing the matter broadly, I do not think
that there is anything unreasonable in the council's forming the view that the interests
of Emma and the legitimate interests of the applicants will be in no way prejudiced by
the fact that Mrs Willetts is permitted to have access in confidence to files about her and
about those who desire to adopt her.

f It was urged on your Lordships that the real decision to grant access in this case was
made by the council's solicitor, that he so advised because he believed that access could
not lawfully be refused, and that on the evidence the director of social services, the social
services committee and the council never appreciated the discretion which was vested in
them. I do not accept this interpretation of the evidence, and in any event the onus is on
the applicants to establish that the local authority reached a decision that no reasonable
g authority could have approved. That burden of proof is not in my opinion discharged.

So I would allow this appeal, and restore the order of the Divisional Court dismissing
the motion.

There is one disturbing aspect of this case. Usually proceedings concerning the welfare
of an infant are given top priority. The order of the Divisional Court was made on 25
March 1980. This was followed by an understandable delay, because a legal aid certificate
h was not forthcoming for the applicants and a fund-raising exercise had to be mounted.
This was concluded by February 1981, and thereafter nothing stood in the way of the
hearing of the appeal. But the appeal was not heard until almost a year later. Your
Lordships were told that this extraordinary delay had not affected the proposed adoption,
which was deferred for other reasons. The consequence of such a delay might, however,
have been serious.

j I should perhaps also mention that in the order made by the Court of Appeal a
restriction on reporting was imposed pursuant to s 39 of the Children and Young Persons
Act 1933, and a direction was also made that only initials be used in any reporting
publications in relation to the names of the applicants. No doubt similar reticence will
be observed in relation to the appeal to your Lordships' House.

The order of the Court of Appeal also records an undertaking by the council to pay all the costs incurred and occasioned by the appeal to your Lordships' House.

a

Appeal allowed.

Solicitors: *Sharpe Pritchard & Co*, agents for F H Wilson, Birmingham (for the council); *Fisher Meredith*, agents for Roberta McDonald, Birmingham (for the applicants).

b

Mary Rose Plummer   Barrister.

Brooks Associates Inc and another v Basu and another (Department for National Savings, garnishee)

c

QUEEN'S BENCH DIVISION

WOOLF J

14, 20 JULY 1982

Execution – Attachment of money payable by Crown to judgment debtor – Jurisdiction – National *d* Savings Bank investment deposit account – Attachment of money in judgment debtor's account – Account held at bank's head office in Scotland – Bank having branches in England where money could be repaid – Whether court having jurisdiction to attach money in investment deposit account – Crown Proceedings Act 1947, s 27(1) – RSC Ord 49, r 1.

The judgment debtor failed to satisfy a judgment debt of $US67,500. The judgment *e* creditors discovered that he had £10,000 in an investment deposit account with the National Savings Bank and wished to attach that sum. As the National Savings Bank was part of the Crown, they applied to the High Court under RSC Ord 77, r 16(2) for an order under s 27(1)[a] of the Crown Proceedings Act 1947, as amended by s 139(1)[b] of the Supreme Court Act 1981, directing that the £10,000 be paid to them. At the hearing of *f* the application the bank contended that since under RSC Ord 49, r 1(1)[c] the court could only attach a debt payable to a judgment debtor by a person 'within the jurisdiction' and since all investment deposit accounts with the National Savings Bank were held at the bank's head office in Glasgow, which was outside the jurisdiction, the court had no power to make an order in respect of money held in the judgment debtor's investment deposit account. Repayment of money in an investment deposit account could only be made at a branch of the National Savings Bank in England if a warrant issued by the bank's head *g* office was presented at the branch.

Held – Although in the case of a commercial bank a promise to pay to a customer money due under an account was a promise to pay at the branch of the bank where the account was kept and therefore if the branch was outside the jurisdiction the account could not *h* be attached, the same principle did not apply to the Crown because the Crown in right of the United Kingdom was, in respect of banking activities carried on in England, always

---

a Section 27(1), so far as material, is set out at p 510 *a* to *c*, post

b Section 139(1), so far as material, is set out at p 510 *c*, post

c Rule 1(1) provides: 'Where a person (in this Order referred to as "the judgment creditor") has *j* obtained a judgment or order for the payment by some other person (in this Order referred to as "the judgment debtor") of a sum of money amounting in value to at least £50, not being a judgment or order for the payment of money into court, and any other person within the jurisdiction (in this Order referred to as "the garnishee") is indebted to the judgment debtor, the Court may, subject to the provisions of this Order and of any enactment, order the garnishee to pay the judgment creditor the amount of any debt due or accruing due to the judgment debtor from the garnishee, or so much thereof as is sufficient to satisfy that judgment or order and the costs of the garnishee proceedings.'

a within the jurisdiction of the English courts. Accordingly, the fact that the head office of the National Savings Bank was located in Glasgow for administrative reasons did not affect the power of the court to make an order under s 27 of the 1947 Act ordering payment to the judgment creditors of the funds held in the judgment debtor's account with the National Savings Bank (see p 510 h j and p 512 b c e f, post).

Richardson v Richardson (National Bank of India Ltd, garnishees) [1927] All ER Rep 92 distinguished.

b **Notes**
For attachment of debts in respect of money due from the Crown, see 17 Halsbury's Laws (4th edn) para 545.
    For the National Savings Bank, see 3 ibid para 31.
    For the Crown Proceedings Act 1947, s 27, see 8 Halsbury's Statutes (3rd edn) 864.
c   For the Supreme Court Act 1981, s 139, see 51 ibid 665.

Case referred to in judgment
Richardson v Richardson (National Bank of India Ltd, garnishees) [1927] P 228, [1927] All ER Rep 92, 3 Digest (Reissue) 554, 3592.

d **Appeal**
Brooks Associates Inc and Douglas Nathaniel Brooks (the judgment creditors) appealed against a decision of Master Waldman, given on 5 July 1982, whereby he dismissed an application, under RSC Ord 77, r 16, by the judgment creditors for an order under s 27(1) of the Crown Proceedings Act 1947 restraining Kalyan Basu, the first judgment debtor, from receiving money payable to him from his investment deposit account with the
e National Savings Bank and directing payment of the money to the judgment creditors to satisfy a debt due to them under a judgment given in their favour on 5 March 1982 in an action which they had brought against the first and second judgment debtors. The appeal was heard in chambers but judgment was given by Woolf J in open court. The facts are set out in the judgment.

f *William Blair* for the judgment creditors.
Mr J G Ward, solicitor, for the Department for National Savings.
The judgment debtors did not appear.

Cur adv vult

g 20 July. The following judgment was delivered.

WOOLF J. This appeal is against a decision of Master Waldman, given on 5 July 1982. The issue is whether or not the court has jurisdiction to attach, on the application of a judgment creditor, moneys standing to the credit of the judgment debtor with the National Savings Bank. Master Waldman decided that the court had no jurisdiction to
h make such an order and the judgment creditors have appealed against this decision.
    The judgment creditors obtained judgment in their favour from Jupp J on 5 March 1982 for $US67,500. The judgment was in connection with a deception practised by the first judgment debtor who had been convicted on 6 May 1982. The first judgment debtor has an investment deposit account with the National Savings Bank, which is in credit in the sum of approximately £10,000. Accordingly, the judgment creditors wish
j to attach this sum. Because the National Savings Bank is part of the Crown, the application did not take the form of the ordinary garnishee proceedings, but instead was an application under RSC Ord 77, r 16(2), for an order under s 27(1) of the Crown Proceedings Act 1947 to restrain the first judgment debtor from receiving the money payable to him and directing payment of the money to the judgment creditors.
    Prior to the coming into force of the Supreme Court Act 1981 an application for an order under s 27(1) of the Crown Proceedings Act 1947 in respect of money deposited in

the National Savings Bank was expressly excluded. The relevant parts of the section then provided:

'Where any money is payable by the Crown to some person who, under any order of any court, is liable to pay any money to any other person, and that other person would, if the money so payable by the Crown were money payable by a subject, be entitled under rules of court to obtain an order for the attachment thereof as a debt due or accruing due, or an order for the appointment of a sequestrator or receiver to receive the money on his behalf, the High Court may, subject to the provisions of this Act and in accordance with rules of court, make an order restraining the first-mentioned person from receiving that money and directing payment thereof to that other person, or to the sequestrator or receiver: Provided that no such order shall be made in respect of . . . (c) any money payable by the Crown to any person on account of a deposit in the National Savings Bank.'

Section 139(1) of the Supreme Court Act 1981 provided that proviso (c) to s 27(1) of the 1947 Act shall 'cease to have effect'. In addition, it gave the Lord Chancellor power to direct that the section should not apply in relation to, inter alia, any money payable by the Crown to any person on account of any deposit in the National Savings Bank. The wording of s 27, prior to its amendment, would imply that at the time of the Crown Proceedings Act 1947 it was thought that, but for the proviso (c), s 27 would have applied to money deposited in the National Savings Bank. Similarly, Parliament must have intended by the changes made by s 139 of the Supreme Court Act 1981 to enable at least certain deposits to be attached unless the Lord Chancellor directed otherwise. Accordingly, as this is a case where an order should be made if it is possible to do so, it is at first sight surprising that the master should have come to the conclusion that there was no power to make an order. The explanation for the decision of the master is to be found in the arguments advanced before him based on the fact that the principal office of the National Savings Bank is in Glasgow, outside the jurisdiction of this court.

It was, and is, contended on behalf of the bank that s 27 of the 1947 Act only applies where the body against whom an order is sought would be liable to have an order for attachment made against it were it not part of the Crown. Assuming that the bank was not part of the Crown, RSC Ord 49(1) required that it should be a person within the jurisdiction before an order to garnishee could be made and as, according to the argument, the bank is not within the jurisdiction, so it is contended that an order cannot be made under s 27, at least in respect of the debt which it is to be sought to be attached in this case. Counsel for the judgment creditors argues that the National Savings Bank can, for the purposes of Ord 49(1), be a person within the jurisdiction, since it operates through savings bank offices within the jurisdiction and repayment can be obtained from such offices.

Not surprisingly, bearing in mind that the amendment to the Crown Proceedings Act 1947 was only made by the Supreme Court Act 1981, there has been no previous authority on this point. However, both parties seek to rely on the authorities dealing with the position of ordinary banks. Counsel on behalf of the judgment creditors relied in particular on *Richardson v Richardson (National Bank of India, garnishees)* [1927] P 228, [1927] All ER Rep 92. In that case Hill J decided that, before a deposit with a bank could be attached, it must be properly recoverable within the jurisdiction and that, in the case of a bank, the promise of the bank is to pay at the branch of the bank where the account is kept, and the bank is not to be called on to pay until payment is demanded at the branch at which the account is kept. Accordingly, then the judgment debtor's balance with a foreign branch of an English bank did not constitute a debt recoverable within the jurisdiction, and so it could not be attached by garnishee proceedings.

I was also referred to *Dicey and Morris on Conflict of Laws* (10th edn, 1980). The comment to r 84 states:

'In England it has been held that garnishment proceedings will be allowed, although the principal debtor is out of the jurisdiction, if the debt is properly

recoverable, that is, situated in England, but not otherwise. Thus a debt due from
an English bank to a foreign debtor can be garnished, but a debt due from the
foreign branch of an English or foreign bank to a foreign debtor cannot be
garnished.'

Rule 76 of *Dicey and Morris* states:

'The *situs* of things is determined as follows: (1) Choses in action generally are
situate in the country where they are properly recoverable or can be enforced . . .'

The difficulty of applying by analogy the approach in relation to an ordinary bank to
the National Savings Bank is that the National Savings Bank does not have the same sort
of branches as an ordinary bank, and it cannot be said that any particular creditor of the
National Savings Bank has an account at a particular office. Both parties, therefore, sought
to rely on the place of repayment of deposits. On behalf of the judgment creditor, it is
argued that if repayment can be demanded in England, there must be jurisdiction. On
behalf of the National Savings Bank, on the other hand, it was argued that in relation to
investment accounts, as they were normally payable by a warrant which was drawn at
the head office in Glasgow and sent from there to the depositor, payment should be
treated as being made in Scotland, thus, so it was argued, depriving the English courts of
jurisdiction.

The rights of depositors as to withdrawals from the National Savings Bank are laid
down in the National Savings Bank Act 1971 and the National Savings Bank Regulations
1972, SI 1972/764. Section 7 of the 1971 Act provides:

'(1) Subject to subsection (2) below, where a depositor, or a person legally
authorised to claim on behalf of a depositor, makes in the prescribed form a demand
for repayment of a deposit, or part of a deposit, authority for payment shall be
transmitted to the depositor forthwith, and the depositor shall be absolutely entitled
within ten days after his demand is made to repayment, at any place at which
deposits can be withdrawn, of any sum due to him.
(2) The terms as to notice of withdrawal of investment deposits shall be such as
may from time to time be prescribed; and accordingly so much of subsection (1)
above as entitles a depositor to repayment within ten days of his demand and
requires the immediate transmission to him of authority therefor shall not apply in
relation to investment deposits . . .'

It is not necessary for me to read sub-s (3).

The regulations distinguish between ordinary and investment deposits. A limited
sum, now £100, may be withdrawn from any savings bank or bank office without
previous notice in the case of ordinary deposits (reg 22). There is also the right to
withdraw an increased amount from an ordinary deposit by telegraph at savings bank
offices (reg 23). Both ordinary deposits and investment deposits can be withdrawn either
by an uncrossed warrant payable in cash or by a crossed warrant payable only through a
bank. An uncrossed warrant is payable on presentation of the relative deposit book at the
place named in the warrant or otherwise in accordance with the directions contained
therein. Although a crossed warrant is not negotiable, it is in many respects similar to a
cheque (reg 21). The difference between withdrawal by warrant in the case of an ordinary
and an investment account is that in the case of an investment account a month's notice
must be given of the intention to withdraw.

In the course of argument, Mr Ward for the National Savings Bank conceded that in
the case of ordinary deposits, because they were payable in part at savings bank offices on
demand, there would be jurisdiction to make an order. However, with regard to
investment deposits he maintained (I consider with a considerable degree of justification)
that the payment took place when the warrant was sent by the National Savings Bank
and not when the warrant was received or presented for payment. However, I find great
difficulty in answering the problem by reference to the approach adopted in relation to
other banks. I have already referred to the fact that a customer of the National Savings

Bank does not have an account at an individual branch. It seems to me that it cannot have been the intention of Parliament that different principles shall apply to ordinary *a* deposits than those that apply to investment deposits. This difficulty is emphasised by the fact that it is possible to convert ordinary deposits into investment deposits and vice versa. It is also unreal to have regard to the method of repayment of deposits by the person entitled to them in the ordinary way when considering the entitlement of the judgment creditor who is not proposing to exercise the ordinary rights of a depositor.

I would therefore adopt a much more general approach. It seems to me that the short *b* answer to the problem is that the Crown in the right of the United Kingdom is at least in respect of banking activities carried on in England always within the jurisdiction of the English courts, and while in the case of a commercial bank it is possible, although the bank conducts business within the jurisdiction, to say that the particular account is not within the jurisdiction, the same principle cannot be applied to the Crown. The administrative reasons which explain why the head office of the National Savings Bank *c* is in Glasgow cannot affect the obvious intent of s 139 of the Supreme Court Act 1981. After all, the ultimate liability to repay ordinary or investment deposits is that of the Treasury which, by s 25 of the National Savings Bank Act 1971, is under a duty to provide the Director of Savings with such sums out of consolidated funds as is necessary to meet any claims in respect of ordinary or investment deposits which cannot be met.

It may be true that this result would produce a different position in Scotland than in *d* England because the Scottish legislation has not been amended in the same way as the English legislation has been amended by the Supreme Court Act 1981. However, this cannot be an argument in favour of the bank's contention, since clearly by enacting s 139, Parliament intended to make a change which only applied to England. It may also be true, as was contended on behalf of the National Savings Bank, that s 10 of the 1981 Act provides an alternative method which has hitherto been used by the bank to assist *e* judgment creditors by using the settlement of disputes procedure which that section lays down. However, again this cannot, in my view, affect the conclusion which I have come to as the proper approach to the change in the law made by s 139 of the 1981 Act.

Accordingly, I am prepared in this case to make an order in favour of the judgment creditors to the extent to which the judgment debtor is in credit with the National Savings Bank. *f*

I should say, before I conclude, that I was particularly grateful in this case to the very able arguments advanced on both sides.

Order accordingly.

Solicitors: *Taylor Tyrrell Lewis & Craig* (for the judgment creditors); *Treasury Solicitor*.

K Mydeen Esq   Barrister.

Fellowes v Rother District Council

QUEEN'S BENCH DIVISION

ROBERT GOFF J

9, 10, 11 JUNE, 29 JULY 1982

Negligence – Duty to take care – Statutory powers – Act performed in exercise of power – Local authority – Coast protection authority – Authority lowering groyne in purported exercise of statutory power – Landowner's property adjoining groyne subsequently washed away – Landowner claiming loss of land due to authority's negligence – Whether authority owing duty of care to landowner at common law – Whether authority could be liable for loss of land.

The Coast Protection Act 1949 conferred on coast protection authorities power to carry out such coast protection works as appeared to them necessary or expedient. In the purported exercise of that power a coast protection authority carried out certain repairs to a groyne on a beach adjoining the plaintiff's property. In the course of the work the height of the groyne was lowered. Some time later part of the plaintiff's land adjoining the groyne was washed away by the sea. He brought an action against the authority claiming damages for negligence, alleging that the authority owed him a duty at common law to take reasonable care when carrying out the repair work, and that lowering the height of the groyne was a breach of that duty because that had created a scouring effect causing the sea to wash away part of his land. The authority denied liability, contending that the plaintiff could not rely on the common law duty of care because it had acted bona fide in pursuance of the discretionary power conferred on it by the 1949 Act, which provided a statutory remedy for complaints about work undertaken in the exercise of such power. The question whether the authority could be held responsible for the damage to the plaintiff's property if the alleged facts were proved was tried as a preliminary issue.

Held – (1) A plaintiff who brought an action for damages for negligence at common law against a public body which purported to act in pursuance of a statutory power could succeed only if he could show (a) that the act complained of was not within the limits of a discretion bona fide exercised under the relevant power, (b) that, having regard to all the circumstances (including the legislation creating the relevant power), there was sufficient proximity between the plaintiff and the defendant to create a duty of care on the part of the defendant to avoid damage to the plaintiff of the type complained of, (c) that there was no ground for negativing, reducing or limiting the duty of care and (d) that it was reasonably foreseeable that the act of the defendant, or those for whom he was vicariously responsible, was likely to cause damage of the type in fact suffered by the plaintiff by reason of such act. In considering those matters, there was no rule that, merely because the defendant was acting under a statutory power as opposed to a statutory duty, liability was contingent on the defendant causing the plaintiff fresh or additional damage (see p 520 *g* and p 522 *a* to *d* and *h* to p 523 *a*, post); *Anns v Merton London Borough* [1977] 2 All ER 492 applied; *Geddis v Proprietors of Bann Reservoir* (1878) 3 App Cas 430, *Sheppard v Glossop Corp* [1921] All ER Rep 61, *East Suffolk Rivers Catchment Board v Kent* [1940] 4 All ER 527 and *Home Office v Dorset Yacht Co Ltd* [1970] 2 All ER 294 considered.

(2) Assuming the plaintiff could establish that the lowering of the groyne was not within the area of the discretionary power conferred on the defendants by the 1949 Act, the facts as pleaded disclosed (a) that there was a sufficient relationship of proximity between the parties to create a duty of care by the authority to avoid the type of damage of which the plaintiff complained and (b) that there were no grounds for negativing or limiting that duty of care. The fact that the 1949 Act provided a remedy in relation to works undertaken by a coast protection authority did not affect the existence of the duty of care, because that remedy applied only to acts within the area of the authority's

discretionary power. However, to succeed in the action the plaintiff would still have to establish that it was reasonably foreseeable that the act of the authority, or those for whom it was vicariously responsible, in lowering the groyne was likely to cause part of the plaintiff's land to be washed away by the sea and had in fact caused such damage (see p 523 d to p 524 b, post).

Notes

For the duty to take care, see 34 Halsbury's Laws (4th edn) para 5, and for cases on the subject, see 36(1) Digest (Reissue) 17–55, 34–177.

For the Coast Protection Act 1949, see 39 Halsbury's Statutes (3rd edn) 571.

Cases referred to in judgment

Anns v Merton London Borough [1977] 2 All ER 492, [1978] AC 728, [1977] 2 WLR 1024, HL, Digest (Cont Vol E) 449, 99b.

Ayr Harbour Trustees v Oswald (1883) 8 App Cas 623, HL, 11 Digest (Reissue) 103, 5.

Donoghue (or M'Alister) v Stevenson [1932] AC 562, [1932] All ER Rep 1, HL, 36(1) Digest (Reissue) 144, 562.

Dutton v Bognor Regis United Building Co Ltd [1972] 1 All ER 462, [1972] 1 QB 373, [1972] 2 WLR 299, CA, 36(1) Digest (Reissue) 30, 98.

East Suffolk Rivers Catchment Board v Kent [1940] 4 All ER 527, [1941] AC 74, HL, 41 Digest (Repl) 57, 370.

Geddis v Proprietors of Bann Reservoir (1878) 3 App Cas 430, HL, 1(1) Digest (Reissue) 107, 618.

Home Office v Dorset Yacht Co Ltd [1970] 2 All ER 294, [1970] AC 1004, [1970] 2 WLR 1140, HL, 26(1) Digest (Reissue) 27, 93.

Sheppard v Glossop Corp [1921] 3 KB 132, [1921] All ER Rep 61, CA, 1(1) Digest (Reissue) 120, 691.

Preliminary issue

The plaintiff, James Henry Fellowes, the owner of a property known as Talbots, 41 Hartfield Road, Cooden, Bexhill-on-Sea, East Sussex, brought an action against the defendants, the Rother District Council, the coast protection authority for the Bexhill-on-Sea area, claiming damages for negligence. In his statement of claim he alleged, inter alia, that in carrying out works of sea defence, the defendants were under a duty of care at common law to carry out such works with reasonable care and in reasonable time and that in breach of such duty they had failed to do so, with the result that he had suffered loss and damage by the erosion of his land and the loss of property. In their defence the defendants denied that they were under any such duty of care. At their request, Master Elton ordered, with the consent of the plaintiff, that the following questions of law should be tried as a preliminary issue: (1) whether the defendants, if they carried out works of sea defence, were under such a duty of care; (2) if they were under any such duty, whether (a) such duty was owed to, and/or whether a breach of such duty was ever actionable by, any owner of land fronting the sea within the area for which the defendants were the coastal protection authority and/or the plaintiff at all or on proof of the facts pleaded in his statement of claim. The facts are set out in the judgment.

William Macpherson QC for the plaintiff.
Patrick Phillips QC and Jeremy Stuart-Smith for the defendants.

Cur adv vult

29 July. The following judgment was delivered.

ROBERT GOFF J. There is before the court a preliminary issue of law which has been ordered to be tried in this action.

The plaintiff, Mr Fellowes, is claiming damages from the defendants, the Rother

District Council. The plaintiff owns a property called Talbots on the coast near Bexhill-on-Sea in East Sussex. The defendants are the coast protection authority for the coast in that part of England. In November 1977, following storms in that part of the world, the coast in the area of the plaintiff's property suffered erosion, as the result of which he claims that he lost three metres of his garden across its full width, together with certain other items of property: fencing, gates, a garden shed, concrete paths and steps, and so on. For this damage to his property he claims that the defendants are liable in law.

In his statement of claim he had put his case in three alternative ways. First, he had claimed that the defendants were in breach of their statutory duty, as the coast protection authority, to protect the coast and prevent erosion. Second, he has claimed that they were in breach of a duty, independently of statute, as local authority for the relevant part of the coast to maintain the integrity of the coastline and prevent erosion. Third, he had claimed that they carried out works of sea defence in the area, and were under a duty of care at common law to carry out such works with reasonable care and in a reasonable time; and that, in breach of such duty, they failed to do so, and thereby caused the damage which occurred.

However, at the commencement of the hearing before me, the plaintiff abandoned his first two grounds of claim, recognising that the defendants were under no such duty as alleged and that the relevant statute created only a power which enabled them to take certain steps for the protection of the coastline. It followed that, before me, the only relevant head of claim was based on negligence at common law, the duty of care being alleged in para 3 of the statement of claim; the plaintiff's title to his property being alleged in para 4; the breach of duty in para 5; and the alleged damage in para 6. It also followed that, before me, the only issue which I had to determine was the third of the three preliminary issues ordered to be tried, which reads as follows:

'(1) Whether or not the Defendants, if they carried out works of sea defence, were under the duties or any of them alleged in Paragraph 3 of the Statement of Claim.

(2) If the Defendant Council were under any such duty alleged in Paragraph 3 of the Statement of Claim, whether or not (a) Such duty was owed to and/or (b) a breach of such duty was ever actionable by (A) any owner of land fronting the sea within the area for which the Defendant Council was the Coast Protection Authority and/or (B) the plaintiff at all or upon the proof of the facts pleaded in Paragraphs 4, 5 and 6 of the Statement of Claim.'

As I have said, the alleged breach of duty is set out in para 5 of the statement of claim, under which are set out particulars of negligence. These particulars were substantially amended during the hearing before me. Originally there were eight paragraphs of particulars; of these, all were abandoned except paras (iii) and (viii) (which were renumbered (i) and (ii)), to which was appended a summary. The surviving particulars and the new summary read as follows:

'(i) [The defendants] failed to appreciate that by the provision and extent of Groyne 64 the inadequacy of Groyne 63 would be aggravated causing excessive littoral drift with consequent damage to the plaintiff's property.

(ii) The Defendants lowered the Northern end of Groyne 64 thereby causing heavy seas to be channelled round the Northern end of the said Groyne.

The nature of the Plaintiff's case hereunder is that the Defendants in lowering the height of the Groyne 64 created a scouring effect and thereby caused the sea to wash away the Plaintiff's land. This damage would not have occurred had the Defendants not lowered the height of Groyne 64. The damage as caused and referred to above was made worse because Groyne 63 was constructed too short.'

For the sake of clarity, I should record (as is not disputed) that the beach opposite the plaintiff's property and the adjoining properties consisted of shingle, and that at intervals along this beach there were groynes running out to sea. These groynes, which had been installed very many years ago by some predecessor in title of the defendants, consisted of substantial stakes driven into the foreshore, which had lateral beams fixed to them, and boarding fixed to the framework so created, some of which over the passage of time had become missing.

The plaintiff's case was that the defendants, as the coast protection authority for the district, in carrying out repairs to groyne 64 (which extended out to sea to one side of the plaintiff's property), negligently lowered the height of that groyne, and, in so doing, they created a scouring effect, which was aggravated by the fact that groyne 63 (which extended out to sea to the other side of the plaintiff's property) was too short, and that this scouring effect caused the sea to wash away part of the land, including the end of the plaintiff's garden, as alleged in para 6 of the statement of claim. The question I have to decide is whether these alleged facts, if proved, would result in any liability on the part of the defendants for the damage to the plaintiff's property.

It will be convenient if I begin by setting out in summary the defendant's position as coast protection authority. This is governed by the Coast Protection Act 1949. For present purposes, the most relevant sections of the Act are, it appears, ss 4, 5, 12 and 29.

Section 1 of the 1949 Act provides that the council of each maritime district shall (unless a coast protection board is established under s 2) be the coast protection authority for the district. Section 4 provides for the general powers of coast protection authorities, and provides in particular, in sub-s (1), that the coast protection authority shall—

> 'have power to carry out such coast protection work, whether within or outside their area, as may appear to them to be necessary or expedient for the protection of any land in their area'.

Section 4(2) and (3) confer power on such authorities to enter into certain agreements and to acquire land. Section 4(4) provides as follows:

> 'Without prejudice to the powers hereinafter conferred on coast protection authorities, the foregoing provisions of this section shall have effect only for the purpose of removing any limitation imposed by law on the capacity of such an authority by virtue of its constitution; and the said provisions shall not authorise any act or omission on the part of such an authority which apart from this section is actionable at the suit of any person on any ground other than such a limitation.'

Section 5 of the 1949 Act makes elaborate provision for the procedure to be followed when a coast protection authority proposes to carry out coast protection work (other than work of maintenance or repair). The procedure includes publishing notice of the proposal, following which any person may serve notice of objection to the proposal. If the ground of objection is, inter alia, that the proposed work will be detrimental to the protection of any land specified in the notice, the minister shall either cause a local inquiry to be heard, or shall give the objector and other persons affected an opportunity of being heard; and the minister shall, after considering a report, determine the objection. He shall then either approve the proposal, or direct the coast protection authority not to carry it out, or impose modifications or conditions as he thinks fit. Where the proposed work requires the exercise of compulsory powers, or it is considered that persons interested in land benefited by the proposed works ought to pay charges in respect of the work, then there are special provisions in the 1949 Act (in ss 6 to 11) concerning such work, requiring confirmation by the minister, and again (under s 8) publication of notice of the proposed work scheme, and the opportunity for objection, including objection on the ground that the proposed work will be detrimental to the protection of land specified in the notice of objection.

Section 12 provides for general powers of maintenance and repair of works. Subsections (1) and (2) provide as follows:

> '(1) Where it appears to a coast protection authority that for the protection of land in their area any works are in need of maintenance or repair, the authority may serve on the owner and occupier of the land on which the works are situated a notice specifying the work of maintenance or repair which the authority consider to be

necessary and a period after the expiration of which the authority will carry out that work if it has not been previously completed.

(2) If at the expiration of the period specified in a notice under the last foregoing subsection the work so specified has not been completed, the authority may take all necessary steps for carrying out the work.'

Section 13(1) provides as follows:

'Where under the last foregoing section a coast protection authority have carried out any work of maintenance or repair on works not being works constructed, altered or improved under a works scheme and not being works in respect of which a scheme under this section has come into operation, the authority may, subject to the provisions of this section, on the completion of the work recover the reasonable cost of the carrying out of the work from the owner or occupier of the land on which the works are situated.'

Section 19 makes provision for compensation in certain circumstances. Subsection (1) provides as follows:

'Where on a claim being made under this section it is shown—(a) that the value of an interest of any person in land has been depreciated, or that any person has suffered damage by being disturbed in his enjoyment of land, in consequence of the carrying out of coast protection work by a coast protection authority in the exercise of the powers conferred by this Part of this Act, or (b) that the value of such an interest as aforesaid has been depreciated in consequence of the refusal of consent for which application has been made under section sixteen of this Act, or in consequence of the granting of such consent subject to conditions, the coast protection authority shall pay to that person compensation equal to the amount of the depreciation or damage: Provided that a person shall not be entitled to compensation under paragraph (a) of this subsection unless the act or omission causing the depreciation or disturbance would have been actionable at his suit if it had been done or omitted otherwise than in the exercise of statutory powers.'

Finally, I must refer to s 29, which provides as follows:

'(1) If complaint is made to the Minister that a coast protection authority have failed to take sufficient measures for the protection of any land in their area, or he is of the opinion that an investigation should be made into the need for any such measures or the sufficiency of any measures so taken, he may cause a local inquiry to be held into the matter.

(2) If after a local inquiry has been held under this section the Minister is satisfied that there has been such a failure on the part of a coast protection authority, he may make an order declaring them to be in default and directing them to exercise such of their powers under this Act as may be specified in the order in such manner and within such time as may be so specified.'

Such are the provisions of the relevant statute. I turn then to the issue which I have to decide. In considering the problem in this case I have the benefit of guidance from a number of decisions of the superior courts, including certain leading cases decided in the House of Lords. I have particularly in mind *Geddis v Proprietors of Bann Reservoir* (1878) 3 App Cas 430, *Sheppard v Glossop Corp* [1921] 3 KB 132, [1921] All ER Rep 61, *East Suffolk Rivers Catchment Board v Kent* [1940] 4 All ER 527, [1941] AC 74, *Home Office v Dorset Yacht Co Ltd* [1970] 2 All ER 294, [1970] AC 1004 and *Anns v Merton London Borough* [1977] 2 All ER 492, [1978] AC 728. A reading of these cases shows the law to have been in a continuous state of development, which is scarcely surprising as the cases themselves span a century.

Geddis v Proprietors of Bann Reservoir, although primarily concerned with the construction of a private Act of Parliament, is perhaps most noteworthy today as containing a statement of law by Lord Blackburn (a statement which was itself the culmination of earlier authorities) recognising that an action may lie for doing that which the legislature has authorised if done negligently. He said (3 App Cas 430 at 455–456):

> 'For I take it, without citing cases, that it is now thoroughly established that no action will lie for doing that which the legislature has authorized, if it be done without negligence, although it does occasion damage to anyone; but an action does lie for doing that which the legislature has authorized, if it be done negligently. And I think that if by a reasonable exercise of the powers, either given by statute to the promoters, or which they have at common law, the damage could be prevented it is, within this rule, "negligence" not to make such reasonable exercise of their powers.'

It is, however, clear from the later authorities that this statement of principle must be read in its context as referring to private Acts of Parliament, such as those which confer on statutory undertakers a power to do a certain act which would otherwise be unlawful, in particular a power of interfering with the property rights of others. By conferring such a power, Parliament cannot have intended that it should be exercised in such a manner as to injure another person or his property, when by the reasonable exercise of the power such injury could have been prevented. It follows that any such exercise of power is outside the authority conferred by Parliament. No question arises, in such circumstances, of the defendant undertakers having acted intra vires. Such a question does, however, arise in the case of a public Act of Parliament or delegated legislation, or acts done pursuant to any such statute or delegated legislation, conferring a power on some public body or official. In such a case, it cannot simply be said that 'an action does lie for doing that which the legislature has authorised, if it be done negligently'. For in such a case, if the act or omission falls properly within the area of what has variously been called policy, or discretion, no action will lie; the act or omission will be intra vires, and any criticism as to the exercise of the power is a matter for bodies other than the courts.

The next two cases, *Sheppard v Glossop Corp* and *East Suffolk Rivers Catchment Board v Kent*, are concerned with a different aspect of this branch of the law. In each case it was established, apparently without qualification, that where a statute confers on a body a power to do a certain act, then (since no liability can attach to that body for omitting to do that act) even if the body does exercise its power, no liability can attach to it for damage which would have been suffered by the plaintiff in any event if the body had not exercised the power. It is no accident that both cases were concerned with statutes conferring powers on public bodies, and that the powers so conferred were capable, if exercised, of preventing damage from being suffered by others. *Sheppard* was concerned with a statute conferring on an authority a power to supply street lighting. An action was brought by a private individual against the authority for damages for personal injuries suffered by him when, in a street in which lighting had been installed by the authority, he fell over a retaining wall and suffered serious personal injuries, his fall taking place after 9 pm, which was the hour at which the authority had decided, for reasons of economy, to turn off the lights. The action failed. Scrutton LJ said ([1921] 3 KB 132 at 145; cf [1921] All ER Rep 61 at 68):

> 'It is left to their discretion to light or not to light; therefore they need not light at all; if for a time they light they may discontinue either wholly or partially in point of time or point of space, and the mere discontinuance is no breach of duty. That is, of course, subject to this; that if they place an obstruction in the highway they must by lighting or warning, or by watchmen or fences or other reasonable means, guard against the danger they have themselves created.'

That decision was approved by the House of Lords in the *East Suffolk* case. The defendants were a catchment board, constituted under the Land Drainage Act 1930, for the main rivers of East Suffolk, among them the River Deben. The board's powers under

the Act included the power to repair the walls or banks of rivers, where broken through.
The River Deben's walls or banks were seriously breached by a combination of high tides
and a northerly gale, with the consequence that the plaintiff's land was flooded. It was
held that the method adopted and the staff employed by the board to repair the breach
were so inefficient that, whereas the breach could reasonably have been closed in 14 days,
this was not achieved until after the lapse of 164 days. The plaintiff's claim for damages
resulting from the prolonged inundation of his land failed. The board had no duty to
intervene; if it had not intervened, the damage would have been suffered in any event;
the board could not therefore be liable in negligence unless, in the course of exercising
its statutory powers, it had inflicted fresh injury on the plaintiff through lack of care and
skill. Viscount Simon LC said of Lord Blackburn's statement of principle in *Geddis*
([1940] 4 All ER 527 at 532–533, [1941] AC 74 at 87):

> '... it would be misapplied if it were supposed to support the proposition that a
> public body, which owes no duty to render any service, may become liable at the
> suit of an individual, if once it takes it upon itself to render some service, for failing
> to render reasonably adequate and efficient service. On the other hand, if the public
> body by its unskilful intervention created new dangers or traps, it would be liable
> for its negligence to those who suffered thereby.'

That statement of the law has, however, to be read in the light of the later decision of
the House of Lords in *Anns v Merton London Borough.*
The next case, *Dorset Yacht Co,* is of particular assistance in the present context because
it contains an illuminating explanation by Lord Diplock of the circumstances in which a
public body, or officer, may be liable in negligence. The case was concerned with a claim
for damages by the Dorset Yacht Co against the Home Office in respect of damage alleged
to have been caused to a yacht by borstal boys who had escaped from the control and
supervision of borstal officers responsible for their care. The preliminary issue before the
House of Lords was (in summary) whether, on the facts pleaded, the Home Office as
servants or agents owed a duty of care to the yacht company in the circumstances of the
case. It was held that, in principle, such a duty of care was owed to the plaintiff, albeit in
limited circumstances. Lord Diplock expressed his conclusion as follows ([1970] 2 All
ER 294 at 335, [1970] AC 1004 at 1071):

> 'If ... it can be established at the trial of this action: (1) that the borstal officers in
> failing to take precautions to prevent the trainees from escaping were acting in
> breach of their instructions and not in bona fide exercise of a discretion delegated to
> them by the Home Office as to the degree of control to be adopted: and (2) that it
> was reasonably foreseeable by the officers that if these particular trainees did escape
> they would be likely to appropriate a boat moored in the vicinity of Brownsea Island
> for the purpose of eluding immediate pursuit and to cause damage to it, the borstal
> officers would be in breach of a duty of care owed to the respondents and the
> respondents would, in my view, have a cause of action against the Home Office as
> vicariously liable for the "negligence" of the borstal officers.'

The case was, of course, concerned with the question whether, as a matter of policy, a
duty of care existed in the circumstances pleaded, and also in particular with the question
of liability of one person to another for damage caused by a third party within his control.
However, in the course of his speech Lord Diplock discussed the scope of the principle
formulated by Lord Blackburn in *Geddis*, pointing out that that principle was stated with
reference to private Acts under which powers were conferred on statutory undertakers
to carry out works which interfered with the common law proprietary rights of others.
In the *Dorset Yacht* case, however, the general public interest was involved. Lord Diplock
said ([1970] 2 All ER 294 at 331–332, [1970] AC 1004 at 1067–1068):

> 'These interests, unlike those of a person who sustains damage to his property or
> person by the tortious act or omission of another, do not fall within any category of
> property or rights recognised in English law as entitled to protection by a civil action

for damages. The conflicting interests of the various categories of persons likely to be affected by an act or omission of the custodian of a borstal trainee which has as its consequence his release or his escape are thus of different kinds for which in law there is no common basis for comparison. If the reasonable man when directing his mind to the act or omission which has this consequence ought to have in contemplation persons in all the categories directly affected and also the general public interest in the reformation of young offenders, there is no criterion by which a court can assess where the balance lies between the weight to be given to one interest and that to be given to another. . . . It is, I apprehend, for practical reasons of this kind that over the past century the public law concept of ultra vires has replaced the civil law concept of negligence as the test of the legality, and consequently of the actionability, of acts or omissions of government departments or public authorities done in the exercise of a discretion conferred on them by Parliament as to the means by which they are to achieve a particular public purpose. According to this concept Parliament has entrusted to the department or authority charged with the administration of the statute the exclusive right to determine the particular means within the limits laid down by the statute by which its purpose can best be fulfilled. It is not the function of the court, for which it would be ill-suited, to substitute its own view of the appropriate·means for that of the department or authority by granting a remedy by way of a civil action at law to a private citizen adversely affected by the way in which the discretion has been exercised. Its function is confined in the first instance to deciding whether the act or omission complained of fell within the statutory limits imposed on the department's or authority's discretion. Only if it did not would the court have jurisdiction to determine whether or not the act or omission, not being justified by the statute, constituted an actionable infringement of the plaintiff's rights in civil law. These considerations lead me to the conclusion that neither the intentional release of a borstal trainee under supervision, nor the unintended escape of a borstal trainee still under detention which was the consequence of the application of a system of relaxed control intentionally adopted by the Home Office as conducive to the reformation of trainees, can have been intended by Parliament to give rise to any cause of action on the part of any private citizen unless the system adopted was so unrelated to any purpose of reformation that no reasonable person could have reached a bona fide conclusion that it was conducive to that purpose. Only then would the decision to adopt it be ultra vires in public law.'

It follows that if, in a case in which powers are conferred on some public body or official, the plaintiff is unable to show that an act or omission of that body or official was not within the limits of a discretion bona fide exercised, any claim for damages for negligence based on that act or omission must fail; the discharge of this burden is a prerequisite of success in an action of negligence in such a case.

I come finally to the decision in *Anns v Merton London Borough*. In that case the House of Lords held (again on a preliminary issue), affirming on slightly different grounds the decision of the Court of Appeal in *Dutton v Bognor Regis United Building Co Ltd* [1972] 1 All ER 462, [1972] 1 QB 373, that an action might lie at the suit of the occupier of a house or flat against a local authority for negligence in permitting (through inadequate or, alternatively, no inspection) the builder of the relevant building to build it with insufficiently deep foundations as a result of which structural movement occurred causing damage to the occupier's dwelling. The leading speech was delivered by Lord Wilberforce. After considering the relevant provisions of the Public Health Act 1936, which conferred on specified authorities the powers to make byelaws for regulating, inter alia, the construction of buildings, and also considering the relevant byelaws made by the predecessors of the defendant council, he concluded that a situation of 'proximity' existed between the council and owners or occupiers of houses, because it must be within the reasonable contemplation of the local authority that failure to comply with the

byelaws' requirements as to foundations might give rise to a hidden defect which in the
future might cause damage to the buildings affecting the safety and health of owners and
occupiers. However, in defining the circumstances in which the law should impose on
the local authority a duty in private law, he recognised that most, if not all, statutes
relating to public authorities, and indeed their implementation, contained within them
a large area of policy, or discretion; and he held that before a plaintiff could begin to rely
on a common law duty of care he must prove that the action taken was not within the
limits of a discretion bona fide exercised; though, if he could prove this, in principle he
should be able to sue.

He then went on to consider a submission, advanced by the defendant council, founded
on the *East Suffolk* case, that inspection by local authorities of buildings under construction
was made pursuant not to a statutory duty but to a statutory power, and that since the
local authority was under no duty to inspect, it need not inspect at all, and so could not
be liable for negligent inspection. This argument Lord Wilberforce rejected. He said
([1977] 2 All ER 492 at 501, [1978] AC 728 at 755):

> 'I think that this is too crude an argument. It overlooks the fact that local
> authorities are public bodies operating under statute with a clear responsibility for
> public health in their area. They must, and in fact do, make their discretionary
> decisions responsibly and for reasons which accord with the statutory purposes; cf
> *Ayr Harbour Trustees v Oswald* (1883) 8 App Cas 623 at 639 per Lord Watson: "...
> the powers which [s 10] confers are discretionary ... But it is the plain import of
> the clause that the harbour trustees ... shall be vested with, and shall avail
> themselves of, these discretionary powers whenever and as often as they may be of
> opinion that the public interest will be promoted by their exercise."·If they do not
> exercise their discretion in this way they can be challenged in the courts. Thus, to
> say that councils are under no duty to inspect, is not a sufficient statement of the
> position. They are under a duty to give proper consideration to the question whether
> they should inspect or not. Their immunity from attack, in the event of failure to
> inspect, in other words, though great is not absolute. And because it is not absolute,
> the necessary premise for the proposition "if no duty to inspect, then no duty to take
> care in inspection" vanishes.'

He likewise later rejected a related argument that—

> 'there is an absolute distinction in the law between statutory duty and statutory
> power—the former giving rise to possible liability, the latter not; or at least not
> doing so unless the exercise of the power involves some positive act creating some
> fresh or additional damage.'

(See [1977] 2 All ER 492 at 501, [1978] AC 728 at 755.)

The *East Suffolk* case he interpreted as being a good example of a case where—

> 'operational activity, at the breach in the wall, was still well within a discretionary
> area, so that the plaintiff's task in contending for a duty of care was a difficult one.'

(See [1977] 2 All ER 492 at 502, [1978] AC 728 at 757.)

Sheppard's case was likewise interpreted as being a case where the action taken to
extinguish the street lighting was within the local authority's discretion and so not
actionable. But, more fundamentally, he stated that the law at the present time requires
to be—

> 'understood and applied with the recognition that, quite apart from such
> consequences as may flow from an examination of the duties laid down by the
> particular statute, there may be room, once one is outside the area of legitimate
> discretion or policy, for a duty of care at common law. It is irrelevant to the existence
> of this duty of care whether what is created by the statute is a duty or a power: the
> duty of care may exist in either case. The difference between the two lies in this,

that, in the case of a power, liability cannot exist unless the act complained of lies
outside the ambit of the power.'

a

(See [1977] 2 All ER 492 at 503, [1978] AC 728 at 758.)

From these authorities the following principles can, as I understand it, be derived.
Where a plaintiff claims damages for negligence at common law against a public body or
official purporting to act in pursuance of a power conferred by statute or other legislation,
he can only succeed if he can show (1) that the act complained of was not within the
limits of a discretion bona fide exercised under the relevant power, (2) that having regard
to all the circumstances, including the legislation creating the relevant power, there was
sufficient proximity to create a duty of care on the defendant to avoid damage to the
plaintiff of the type complained of, and no ground for negativing (or reducing or
limiting) such duty of care, (3) that it was reasonably foreseeable by the defendant, or by
those for whom he was vicariously responsible, that the act complained of was likely to
cause damage of the type in fact suffered by the plaintiff by reason of such act.

b

c

In considering these questions, there is no rule that, merely because the defendant was
acting under a statutory power as opposed to a statutory duty, liability is contingent on
the defendant causing the plaintiff fresh or additional damage.

Of these principles, it is perhaps the proviso at their conclusion which, in the light of
the earlier cases, creates the greatest difficulty. Running through the speech of Lord
Wilberforce in the *Anns* case there is the implication that, if in the *East Suffolk* case it
could have been shown by the plaintiff that the choice of method of closing the breach
in the river wall was not within the limits of a discretion bona fide exercised, he should
have been entitled to succeed, even though the damage suffered by him was not fresh or
additional damage. It is possible that Lord Atkin, who dissented in the *East Suffolk* case,
did so on the basis that if the catchment board had not taken on itself the task of closing
the breach in the wall, the plaintiff himself could have done so (see [1940] 4 All ER 527
at 536, [1941] AC 74 at 92), which could be a sufficient basis for holding that the
prolongation of the inundation beyond the time which the plaintiff himself would have
taken to close the breach constituted fresh or additional damage. As I read Lord
Wilberforce's speech, however, he would go beyond this. Provided that the conditions I
have listed above are fulfilled, the plaintiff is entitled to succeed. In a case such as the *East
Suffolk* case it would not matter that, if the defendants had not intervened at all, the
inundation would have continued for as long as it in fact continued; once they have
intervened then, provided in particular that the choice of method was not within any
bona fide exercise of the relevant discretion but there was, for example, simply bad
workmanship by a workman in negligently carrying out his instructions, the authority
may be liable for any prolonged or renewed inundation consequent on such negligence.
The underlying basis appears to be that citizens are entitled to expect that powers
conferred on public authorities will be exercised, and entitled therefore to expect that
such powers will be exercised with due care, subject to being unable to found a cause of
action on an act done within the limit of a discretion bona fide exercised and to the
ordinary criteria of an action in negligence being fulfilled. Such powers cannot be
regarded as mere liberties, or as mere authority to invade the proprietary interests of
another, as under private Acts of Parliament. So, although a mere omission by a public
authority to exercise a statutory power will not ordinarily be actionable by a private
citizen as such (being within the area of discretion), nevertheless the local authority may
be responsible for the consequences of a negligent act done in a purported exercise of the
power (but not in fact within the limits of a discretion bona fide exercised) even though
no fresh or additional damage is caused.

d

e

f

g

h

j

In considering the concluding part of the second principle (viz whether there is any
ground for negativing any duty of care which would otherwise arise), it may be necessary
to consider whether a duty of care is excluded by the terms of the relevant legislation. In
most cases, however, this is likely to be irrelevant, because of the effect of the first
principle. This is because, generally speaking, where, for example, the terms of a statute
conferring a power establish procedures for challenging a proposed exercise of the power,

the plaintiff may be unable to succeed in an action of negligence at common law founded
a on such exercise of the power, not so much because the statute provides another exclusive
remedy, but because any such exercise of the power will fall within the limits of a
discretion bona fide exercised.

In the light of these principles, I turn to consider the problem in the present case. In
doing so, I cannot help regretting that the master who ordered a preliminary issue in this
case did not heed the warning of Lord Diplock in *Home Office v Dorset Yacht Co Ltd* [1970]
b 2 All ER 294 at 323, [1970] AC 1004 at 1057 that in a case such as this preliminary issues
are not always desirable. Certainly, in the present case, although the preliminary issue
has had the effect of confining the plaintiff's case within more reasonable bounds, it
would have been far simpler, and more sensible, for the whole case to be heard, rather
than that this court should decide a disembodied question of law. However, that is the
task now presented to me.

c It is not, I think, possible for me to provide a specific answer to the question of law as
posed, for everything must depend, in the first instance, on the plaintiff establishing the
first of the three matters which he has to prove, viz that the act complained of was not
within the limits of the discretion bona fide exercised under the relevant powers. The act
complained of is now, in the light of the revised particulars of negligence, the lowering
of the height of groyne 64. There is no sufficient pleading addressed to this particular
d matter, which has to be decided in the light of the evidence called before the trial judge.
On the assumption, however, that the plaintiff establishes that the act complained of was
not within the limits of a discretion bona fide exercised under the relevant power, then
the question arises whether there was sufficient proximity to create a duty of care on the
defendants to avoid damage of the type complained of. On the facts as pleaded, I am
satisfied that on that assumption there was sufficient proximity to give rise to such a duty
e of care. This is not a case which gives rise to any particular extension of the duty of care
into a new field. It is concerned simply with physical damage to the plaintiff's property,
arising from the alleged negligent alteration to the height of a certain groyne creating a
state of affairs which is alleged to have resulted in the occurrence of such physical damage.
To adopt the language of Lord Wilberforce in *Anns v Merton London Borough* [1977] 2 All
ER 492 at 498–499, [1978] AC 728 at 751–752, there was a sufficient relationship of
f proximity or neighbourhood between the defendants and the plaintiff such that, in the
reasonable contemplation of the former, carelessness on their part might be likely to
cause damage to the latter of the type complained of, so that a prima facie duty of care
arose; and I am unaware of any considerations which ought to negative, or reduce or
limit, the scope of the duty or the damages to which a breach of it might give rise. It is
true that no case has been cited to me similar to the present in which it has been held
g that a duty of care exists in such circumstances. But it is consistent with the principle in
Donoghue v Stevenson [1932] AC 562, [1932] All ER Rep 1 that such a duty of care should
exist; and I can see no reason of policy for not here adopting the general principle, given,
of course, that this is not a case where a discretion has been bona fide exercised, and I
know of no authority which would inhibit the application of the general principle in the
present case. Furthermore, in considering whether there is any ground for negativing
h any such duty of care, I have taken into account the provisions of the Coast Protection
Act 1949, which conferred the relevant powers on the defendants, the more important
of which provisions I have summarised earlier in this judgment. These provisions
include, in ss 5 and 29, procedure for objecting to, or complaining about, certain works
undertaken or proposed to be undertaken by coastal protection authorities. However, in
so far as such provisions provide for exclusive remedies, this cannot, in my judgment,
j affect the existence of any duty of care, because the statutory remedies only apply in
relation to the exercise of the authority's discretion, where in any event no duty of care is
imposed on the authority.

I therefore hold that, assuming that the plaintiff can establish that this is not a case
where a discretion has been bona fide exercised by the defendants, there was, on the facts
pleaded, a duty of care on the defendants to avoid damage to the plaintiff of the type

complained of. Of course, even assuming that the plaintiff surmounts the hurdle of discretion, this will leave to be decided at the trial the further question whether, on the evidence, it was reasonably foreseeable by the defendants, or those for whom they were vicariously responsible, that the relevant act was likely to cause damage of the type alleged to have been suffered by the plaintiff, and, further, that it did in fact cause such damage.

In these circumstances, I would welcome the assistance of counsel in answering the question of law posed to me. It seems possible that the question of law is not appropriately framed. It ignores the question whether the act complained of was within the limits of a discretion bona fide exercised; furthermore, the obligation alleged in para 3 of the statement of claim (which is the most material paragraph for present purposes) that the defendants were 'under a duty to carry out the said or other required works within a reasonable time of the said works becoming necessary' appears to me to be an immaterial averment. It may be that the question of law itself requires some amendment. In any event, however, counsel should have the opportunity to address the court on the appropriate order now to be made in the light of the principles set out in this judgment.

[After hearing submissions from counsel, Robert Goff J decided that the pleadings should be reformulated and that he should order an adjournment, to a date to be fixed, so that he could then decide, with the help of the amended pleadings, how the matter should proceed.]

Order accordingly.

24 January 1983. Following the trial of the action, Michael Davies J dismissed the action and ordered judgment to be entered for the defendants.

Solicitors: *R J Fellowes & Son*, Walthamstow (for the plaintiff); *Barlow Lyde & Gilbert* (for the defendants).

K Mydeen Esq   Barrister.

Procedure Direction

HOUSE OF LORDS

House of Lords – Leave to appeal – Petition for leave to appeal – Competency – Court of Appeal or Divisional Court refusing ex parte application for leave to apply for judicial review – Petition for leave to appeal to House of Lords against refusal incompetent – RSC Ord 53.

The Appeal Committee of the House of Lords have made the following amendments to Direction no 6 as to Procedure applicable to Civil Appeals (Form of Appeal, Directions as to Procedure and Standing Orders (the Blue Book, 1981) p 9):

Direction 6(1)(a) is amended by leaving out in the last line the words 'except in cases of Judicial Review'.

Direction 6(1) is amended by inserting after sub-para (a) a new sub-paragraph:

'(aa) Petitions for leave to appeal to the House of Lords against a refusal by the Court of Appeal or a Divisional Court of the Queen's Bench Division to grant an ex parte application for leave to apply for judicial review under Order 53 of the Rules of the Supreme Court.'

PETER HENDERSON
Clerk of the Parliaments.

26 January 1983

Kelly v Purvis

QUEEN'S BENCH DIVISION
ACKNER LJ AND WEBSTER J
11, 12 NOVEMBER, 2 DECEMBER 1982

Criminal law – Brothel – Keeping a brothel – Meaning of brothel – Massage parlour offering sexual services not including full sexual intercourse – Whether essential that normal sexual intercourse be provided to establish that premises used as brothel – Whether sufficient that acts amounting to prostitution by more than one woman took place on premises – Sexual Offences Act 1956, s 33.

Between October 1981 and January 1982 the respondent assisted in the management of a licensed massage parlour. On payment of the appropriate fee on entry, massage or massage and sauna were provided. During the massage extra services were offered by the masseuse concerned for an additional fee, such services involving masturbation. Those fees were usually paid direct to the masseuse. There was no evidence that the additional fees were treated as part of the takings of the establishment, nor was there any evidence that full sexual intercourse was offered at the establishment. The respondent was fully aware of the sexual services provided by the masseuses, and she herself also acted as a masseuse and had offered the same services. An information was laid by the prosecutor alleging that the respondent assisted in the management of a brothel, contrary to s 33[a] of the Sexual Offences Act 1956. The magistrate dismissed the information, holding that, although the women concerned were common prostitutes, the premises were not a brothel because there was not sufficient evidence that sexual intercourse within the 1956 Act was provided. On an appeal by the prosecutor by way of case stated the question for the opinion of the court was whether on a charge of assisting in the management of a brothel contrary to s 33 of the 1956 Act it was essential that there was evidence that normal sexual intercourse was provided there or whether it was sufficient to prove that acts amounting to prostitution by more than one woman took place on the premises. The respondent contended that a 'brothel' was generally recognised as meaning an establishment to which male persons resorted for the purpose of having full sexual intercourse with prostitutes.

Held – On a charge of assisting in the management of a brothel, contrary to s 33 of the 1956 Act, it was not essential that there was evidence that normal sexual intercourse was provided in the premises. It was sufficient to prove that more than one woman offered herself as a participant in physical acts of indecency for the sexual gratification of men. Accordingly, the appeal would be allowed and the case would be remitted to the magistrate for reconsideration (see p 529 e to g, post).

Dicta of Grove and Lopes JJ in *R v Holland, Lincolnshire Justices* (1882) 46 JP at 312, 313, *Caldwell v Leech* [1911–13] All ER Rep 703, *Winter v Woolfe* [1930] All ER Rep 623, *R v Webb* [1963] 3 All ER 177 and *Gorman v Standen* [1963] 3 All ER 627 considered.

Per curiam. In order for premises to constitute a brothel, it is not essential to show that they are in fact used for the purpose of prostitution (which involves payment for services rendered), since a brothel also exists where women offer sexual intercourse without charging (see p 528 g h, post).

Winter v Woolfe [1930] All ER Rep 623 followed.

Notes

For the use of premises as a brothel, see 11 Halsbury's Laws (4th edn) para 1059, and for cases on the subject, see 15 Digest (Reissue) 1058–1059, 9103–9106.

For the Sexual Offences Act 1956, s 33, see 8 Halsbury's Statutes (3rd edn) 434.

---

a   Section 33 is set out at p 527 *f*, post.

Cases referred to in judgment
Caldwell v Leech (1913) 109 LT 188, [1911–13] All ER Rep 703, DC, 15 Digest (Reissue)   *a*
1057, 9094.
Durose v Wilson (1907) 96 LT 645, DC, 15 Digest (Reissue) 1057, 9095.
Gorman v Standen, Palace-Clark v Standen [1963] 3 All ER 627, [1964] 1 QB 294, [1963] 3
WLR 917, DC, 15 Digest (Reissue) 1058, 9103.
R v de Munck [1918] 1 KB 635, [1918–19] All ER Rep 499, CCA, 15 Digest (Reissue)
1226, 10485.   *b*
R v Holland, Lincolnshire Justices (1882) 46 JP 312, 15 Digest (Reissue) 1056, 9084.
R v Webb [1963] 3 All ER 177, [1964] 1 QB 357, [1963] 3 WLR 638, CCA, 15 Digest
(Reissue) 1226, 10486.
Singleton v Ellison [1895] 1 QB 607, DC, 15 Digest (Reissue) 1057, 9091.
Winter v Woolfe [1931] 1 KB 549, [1930] All ER Rep 623, CCA, 15 Digest (Reissue) 1058,
9097.   *c*

Cases also cited
Abbot v Smith [1964] 3 All ER 762, [1965] 2 QB 662n.
Dickinson v Fletcher (1873) LR 9 CP 1.
R v Chapman [1931] 2 KB 606, CCA.
R v Corrie [1973] Crim LR 381.   *d*
Woodhouse v Hall (1980) 72 Cr App R 39, DC.

Case stated
Robert Kelly (the prosecutor), a sergeant in the Metropolitan Police, appealed by way of
case stated against the decision of W E C Robins Esq, a metropolitan stipendiary
magistrate in and for the petty sessional division of South Westminster in the Inner   *e*
London Commission Area, by which the magistrate dismissed an information preferred
by the prosecutor against the respondent, Christine Purvis, alleging that between 20
October 1981 and 20 January 1982 the respondent assisted in the management of
premises known as Celebrity Sauna, 85 Charlotte Street, London W1, contrary to s 33 of
the Sexual Offences Act 1956. The facts are set out in the judgment of the court.
                                                                                 f
Victor Temple for the prosecutor.
R Alun Jones for the respondent.

                                                                    Cur adv vult

2 December. The following judgment of the court was delivered.   *g*

ACKNER LJ. This appeal by the prosecution by way of case stated from the
adjudication on 6 April 1982 by the stipendiary magistrate, Mr Robins, sitting at the
Bow Street Magistrates' Court raises the question: what constitutes a brothel?
   Only the prosecution evidence was heard, because the magistrate accepted the defence
submission that the prosecution had failed to establish the offence alleged, namely that   *h*
between 20 October 1981 and 20 January 1982 the respondent, assisted in the
management of a brothel at premises known as Celebrity Sauna, 85 Charlotte Street,
London W1, contrary to s 33 of the Sexual Offences Act 1956.
   The prosecution evidence established, prima facie, the following facts. Between 20
October 1981 and 20 January 1982 the respondent was assisting in the management of a
massage parlour licensed by the appropriate local authority. The premises consisted of a   *j*
lounge/reception area, two changing rooms, three massage rooms, a solarium, a sauna
and two shower cubicles. On payment of the appropriate fee on entry, massage or sauna
and massage were provided. During the massage extra services were offered by the
masseuse concerned for additional fees, such services involving the masturbation of the
client by the masseuse. These fees were usually paid direct to the masseuse. There is no

evidence that the additional fees were treated as part of the takings of the establishment.
The respondent was fully aware of the sexual services provided by the masseuses, and she
herself also acted as a masseuse and performed masturbation. There was no evidence that
full sexual intercourse was offered at the establishment, although when asked by the
appellant: 'Do any of the girls do full sex?', the respondent replied: 'Only with regulars,
sir. We do not know you, sir. You will have to discuss it with the girls.'

The magistrate was satisfied that the women concerned were common prostitutes. He
was not, however, satisfied that a prima facie case had been made out that the premises
were a brothel, by reason of the absence of evidence that sexual intercourse within the
meaning of the Sexual Offences Act 1956 was provided.

The magistrate's finding that the women concerned were common prostitutes was not
challenged. Whereas under American law prostitution is the 'practice of the female
offering her body to an indiscriminate intercourse with men, usually for hire', it is well
established that in English law prostitution is proved if it be shown 'that a woman offers
her body commonly for lewdness for payment in return' (see *R v de Munck* [1918] 1 KB
635 at 637–638, [1918–19] All ER Rep 499 at 500 per Darling J applied in *R v Webb*
[1963] 3 All ER 177, [1964] 1 QB 357). *R v Webb* was also a case of a massage parlour
where the masseuses masturbated their clients. In that case, the point was taken by the
defendant that the definition given by Darling J should be read as confined to cases where
the woman offers her body for lewdness in what one might call a passive way, or where
she submits to something being done to her. Lord Parker CJ, giving the judgment of the
court, observed that the words used by Darling J are not words of the Sexual Offences Act
1956, but merely the judge's definition, for the purposes of that case, of circumstances in
which prostitution may be said to have been proved. In the judgment of that court, the
expression 'a woman offers her body commonly for lewdness' includes a case where a
woman offers herself as a participant in physical acts of indecency for the sexual
gratification of men.

It is thus common ground that these premises were used for the purpose of prostitution.
Is that sufficient for it to qualify as a brothel, or does the prosecution have to establish
that sexual intercourse takes place with the women who use the premises?

There is no definition in s 33 of the Sexual Offences Act 1956 as to what constitutes a
brothel. The section merely provides: 'It is an offence for a person to keep a brothel, or to
manage, or act or assist in the management of, a brothel.' That offence derives from the
Criminal Law Amendment Act 1885, where in s 13 it is provided that: 'Any person
who—(1.) keeps or manages or acts or assists in the management of a brothel . . .' shall
commit an offence. That Act, too, gives no definition of a brothel. In such circumstances,
as Lord Parker CJ pointed out in *Gorman v Standen, Palace-Clark v Standen* [1963] 3 All ER
627 at 630, [1964] 1 QB 294 at 301, one is driven back to the meaning of 'brothel' at
common law.

In *Stephen's Digest of the Criminal Law* (9th edn, 1950) p 142 the definition of a 'common
bawdy-house' is given as 'a house or room or set of rooms in any house kept for the
purpose of prostitution'. In *Gorman's* case Lord Parker CJ stated that, at common law, a
brothel was the same thing as a bawdy-house. He pointed out that the definition of what
is involved in a bawdy-house or a brothel had been variously stated in the cases ([1963] 3
All ER 627 at 630, [1964] 1 QB 294 at 301):

> 'Sometimes it is stated as a place to which persons of both sexes resort for the
> purpose of prostitution; sometimes it is referred to as a place used by persons of both
> sexes for the purposes of prostitution.'

The form of indictment for keeping a bawdy-house was referred to by Avory J in *Caldwell
v Leech* (1913) 109 LT 188 at 191, [1911–13] All ER Rep 703 at 707:

> 'Did keep and maintain a certain house and in the said house for filthy lucre and
> gain divers evil-disposed persons, women as well as men, upon the times and days
> aforesaid as well in the night as in the day unlawfully and wickedly did receive and
> entertain . . .'

In general the cases have been concerned, not so much with the activities which went
on in the premises, as with the number of women who have to be involved, the extent   *a*
of the control or management and whether the women must be professionals or only
amateurs. In *Singleton v Ellison* [1895] 1 QB 607 it was held that where a woman occupied
a house and had men in for the purpose of fornication with her she had not committed
the offence of keeping a brothel within the meaning of the Criminal Law Amendment
Act 1885. Wills J said ([1895] 1 QB 607 at 608):

> 'A brothel is the same thing as "a bawdy house"—a term which has a well-known   *b*
> meaning as used by lawyers and in Acts of Parliament. In its legal acceptation it
> applies to a place resorted to by persons of both sexes for the purpose of prostitution.
> It is certainly not applicable to the state of things described by the magistrates in this
> case, where one woman receives a number of men.'

In *Durose v Wilson* (1907) 96 LT 645, a case involving a block of flats where a number   *c*
of the tenants were in the habit of bringing different men nightly to the premises for the
purpose of prostitution, *Singleton v Ellison* was differentiated. A T Lawrence J, however,
stated (at 646): '. . . a brothel is such a place as that described in that case—that is, premises
used by more than one woman for prostitution.' Avory J in *Caldwell v Leech* 109 LT 188
at 191, [1911–13] All ER Rep 703 at 707 expressed his entire agreement with the
judgment of A T Lawrence J and stated: 'In my opinion the whole fundamental idea of a   *d*
bawdy-house is that it is a house to which persons of both sexes indiscriminately make
resort for the purposes of prostitution.'

The case on which the respondent strongly relies, and which persuaded the magistrate
to dismiss the information, is *Winter v Woolfe* [1931] 1 KB 549, [1930] All ER Rep 623.
That case concerned a cottage about two miles from Cambridge, frequented in the main
by undergraduates, where sexual intercourse took place with a number of women. The   *e*
women were not, however, proved to be prostitutes, and therefore, at the close of the
case for the prosecution, it was successfully submitted that there was no case to answer.
Accordingly, they held that, although the occupier of the cottage knew what was going
on, the premises were not being used as a brothel. Avory J held that the justices had
'given too restricted a meaning to the word "brothel" as it is used at common law, and as
it is used in s 13 of the Criminal Law Amendment Act, 1885' (see [1931] 1 KB 549 at   *f*
554, [1930] All ER Rep 623 at 625). It was not necessary to prove that the women
resorting to the premises were prostitutes, known as such to the police, or that they
received payment for acts of fornication committed by them with men. It was sufficient
to prove that with the knowledge of the occupier persons of opposite sexes were permitted
there to have illicit sexual intercourse. That case, in our judgment, merely demonstrates
that to constitute premises as a brothel it is not essential to show that they are in fact used   *g*
for the purpose of prostitution, which involves payment for services rendered. A brothel
is also constituted where the women (for there must be more than one woman) do not
charge for sexual intercourse.

In the course of his judgment (see [1931] 1 KB 549 at 555, [1930] All ER Rep 623 at
625) and this is essentially what is relied on by the respondent, Avory J expressed his
willingness to accept the definition of a brothel given by Grove and Lopes JJ in *R v*   *h*
Holland, Lincolnshire Justices (1882) 46 JP 312. Grove J, said (at 312):

> 'The sole question is, whether there was any evidence to support this conviction
> before the justices for permitting these licensed premises to be a brothel . . . I don't
> think that the matter of nuisance is of any importance, for it is too well known that
> these places are often kept in such a way as to be no nuisance at all, but kept perfectly
> private. But what needs only to be proved is this, namely, that the premises were   *j*
> kept knowingly for the purpose of people having illicit sexual connection there.'

Lopes J said (at 313):

> 'Now the sole question before the justices was, whether the applicant permitted
> his premises to be a brothel. What is the meaning of permitting the premises to be

a brothel? I think my brother *Grove* has given a very apt definition, namely, that it
a is permitting people of opposite sexes to come there and have illicit sexual
intercourse. That is a very complete and satisfactory definition of the whole matter.'

The *Lincolnshire* case was concerned with whether there was any evidence to support
the conviction by the justices for permitting licensed premises to be a brothel. There was
evidence that two prostitutes accompanied by two men went into the house, that the
police had watched the house, that they observed soon afterwards, by shadows on the
b blinds, these four people undressing in a double-bedded room. When the police, at a
later hour, knocked at the door, considerable delay occurred in opening it. Then they
found that the two prostitutes had been transferred to the bed of the landlord's wife,
three women in one bed, while in the double-bedded room were the two men by
themselves. It was argued that the conviction could not be supported by the evidence of
one isolated act. The court, however, held that, although only one instance was proved,
c still it supplied strong evidence of the mode of conducting the house, and it was
reasonably to be inferred that this had not been a solitary instance of such conduct, but
one of many such instances. There was the concealment of the two prostitutes by the
wife of the landlord showing that this had been no extraordinary case but a frequent
occurrence. The wife gave no evidence. The justices were thus held not to be bound to
state a case, there being no point of law raised before them. That case merely decided
d that there was evidence before the magistrates from which they could infer either that
the premises were being used for the purposes of prostitution or that persons of opposite
sexes were permitted there to have illicit sexual intercourse. It was not a case which called
for an exhaustive definition of a brothel. Avory J, in expressing his willingness to accept
the definitions given by Grove and Lopes JJ, was doing no more than justifying his view
that the justices in *Winter v Woolfe* [1931] 1 KB 549, [1930] All ER Rep 623 were giving
e too restricted a meaning to the word 'brothel'.

We therefore answer the question raised by the case stated in these terms. On a charge
of assisting in the management of a brothel in contravention of s 33 of the Sexual
Offences Act 1956, it is not essential that there be evidence that normal sexual intercourse
is provided in the premises. It is sufficient to prove that more than one women offers
herself as a participant in physical acts of indecency for the sexual gratification of men.
f We should perhaps add, although this has not featured in our reasoning, that the view
which we have expressed above does give content to s 6 of the Sexual Offences Act 1967,
which provides that premises shall be treated for the purposes of ss 33 to 35 of the 1956
Act as a brothel if people resort to it for the purpose of lewd homosexual practices in
circumstances in which resort thereto for lewd heterosexual practices would have led to
it being treated as a brothel for the purposes of those sections.
g The appeal will be allowed and the case remitted to the magistrate to hear and
determine according to the law as it has been laid down by this court.

Appeal allowed. Case remitted to the magistrate.

Solicitors: *D M O'Shea* (for the appellant); *Peters & Peters* (for the respondent).

Sophie Craven   Barrister.

R v Uxbridge Justices, ex parte Heward-Mills *a*

QUEEN'S BENCH DIVISION (CROWN OFFICE LIST)
MCCULLOUGH J
13 OCTOBER 1982

Criminal law – Bail – Recognisance – Forfeiture – Magistrates' court – Surety's means –
Magistrates refusing to hear evidence of means – Whether surety's means relevant in determining *b*
amount of recognisance to be forfeited – Magistrates' Courts Act 1980, s 120(3).

The applicant entered into a recognisance in the sum of £7,000 to secure the defendant's
appearance in court. The defendant failed to surrender to his bail and the applicant was
summoned to show cause why the recognisance of £7,000 should not be forfeited. At
the hearing of the summons the magistrates heard evidence regarding the applicant's *c*
culpability for the defendant's non-appearance in court, but declined to hear evidence or
submissions regarding the applicant's means because they took the view that a surety's
means were not a matter to be taken into consideration when considering forfeiture of a
bail recognisance under s 120*d* of the Magistrates' Courts Act 1980. The magistrates
ordered the applicant to forfeit £5,000 of his recognisance and stated that the applicant's
means would be considered when the mode of payment was determined. The applicant *d*
applied for certiorari to quash the forfeiture order on the ground (i) that the magistrates
lacked jurisdiction to make the order because they failed to inquire into, or admit
evidence of, the applicant's means before making the order or (ii) that in exercising their
discretion under s 120(3) to remit part of the recognisance they failed to exercise that
discretion judicially because they failed to take into account the applicant's means.

 e

Held – A surety under a bail recognisance, in discharging the burden of satisfying the
magistrates that the full amount of a recognisance should not be forfeited, was entitled
to put before the magistrates evidence of his means, as well as evidence that he was not
culpable for the defendant's non-appearance. It followed that the magistrates were
mistaken in refusing to hear the surety's evidence regarding his means before making
the forfeiture order and certiorari would be issued to quash the order (see p 535 *a b* and *f*
p 536 *c d* and *h*, post).

R v Southampton Justices, ex p Green [1975] 2 All ER 1073 and *R v Horseferry Road*
Magistrates' Court, ex p Pearson [1976] 2 All ER 264 applied.

Notes
For forfeiture of a recognisance, see 29 Halsbury's Laws (4th edn) para 445, and for cases *g*
on the subject, see 14(1) Digest (Reissue) 237–238, 1709–1714.

For the Magistrates' Courts Act 1980, s 120, see 50(2) Halsbury's Statutes (3rd edn)
1546.

Cases referred to in judgment
R v Crown Court at Ipswich, ex p Reddington [1981] Crim LR 618. *h*
R v Crown Court at Oxford, ex p Jones and Jacobs (29 June 1982, unreported).
R v Horseferry Road Magistrates' Court, ex p Pearson [1976] 2 All ER 264, [1976] 1 WLR
   511, DC, 14(1) Digest (Reissue) 317, 2449.
R v Knightsbridge Crown Court, ex p Newton [1980] Crim LR 715, DC.
R v Southampton Justices, ex p Corker (1976) 120 SJ 214, DC.
R v Southampton Justices, ex p Green [1975] 2 All ER 1073, [1976] QB 11, [1975] 3 WLR *j*
   277, CA, 33 Digest (Reissue) 176, 1370.
R v Tottenham Magistrates' Court, ex p Riccardi (1977) 66 Cr App R 150, DC.
R v Waltham Forest Justices, ex p Parfrey [1980] Crim LR 571, DC.

---

a   Section 120, so far as material, is set out at p 531 *e* to *h*, post

Application for judicial review

a The applicant, Ivor Heward-Mills, applied, with the leave of McNeill J granted on 7 April
1982, for judicial review by way of certiorari to quash an order made by the Uxbridge
justices on 1 February 1982, that the sum of £5,000 be estreated to the court by way of
forfeiture of the applicant's bail recognisance of £7,000, and that all proceedings on the
order be stayed until after the hearing of the application or further order. The grounds
of the application were that (1) the court lacked jurisdiction to make the order by reason
b of its failure to inquire into the applicant's means and/or by reason of its refusal to admit
evidence of means before making the order, (2) the court failed to exercise its discretion
judicially in deciding that the applicant's means should not be taken into account in
assessing the sum, if any, to be forfeited and (3) the record of the court disclosed errors of
law, namely the matters referred to in (1) and (2) above. The facts are set out in the
judgment.

c
David Christie for the applicant.
The justices did not appear.

McCULLOUGH J. This is an application for judicial review of a decision of the
Uxbridge justices made on 1 February 1982, to the effect that the sum of £5,000 be
d estreated from the applicant who had stood bail for a defendant who had failed to appear
at that court on 12 January 1982.
    It has been suggested that there is some difficulty in understanding the principles to
be applied when questions of this kind fall for consideration. Therefore, it may be helpful
if, as briefly as possible, I take the relevant cases in chronological order, and extract from
them the material paragraphs of principle.
e   The relevant statutory provisions which govern the forfeiture of recognisances are
presently to be found in s 120 of the Magistrates' Courts Act 1980. Subsection (1) reads:

    'Where . . . any recognizance is conditioned for the appearance of a person before
    a magistrates' court or for his doing any other thing connected with a proceeding
    before a magistrates' court, and the recognizance appears to the court to be forfeited,
f   the court may, subject to subsection (2) below, declare the recognizance to be
    forfeited and adjudge the persons bound thereby, whether as a principal or sureties,
    or any of them, to pay the sum in which they are respectively bound.'

For the purposes of this case, sub-s (2) does not matter.

    '(3) The court which declares the recognizance to be forfeited may, instead of
g   adjudging any person to pay the whole sum in which he is bound, adjudge him to
    pay part only of the sum or remit the sum.
    (4) Payment of any sum adjudged to be paid under this section . . . may be
    enforced, and any such sum shall be applied, as if it were a fine and as if the
    adjudication were a summary conviction of an offence not punishable with
    imprisonment . . . but at any time before the issue of a warrant of commitment to
h   enforce payment of the sum, or before the sale of goods under a warrant of distress
    to satisfy the sum, the court may remit the whole or any part of the sum either
    absolutely or on such conditions as the court thinks just.'

Nor do I think that sub-s (5) matters for present purposes.
    Formerly, these provisions were contained in s 96 of the Magistrates' Courts Act 1952,
in effectively the same words. Some of the relevant cases are reported and some are not.
j All, with one exception, are decisions of this court, that exception being the first. That is
R v Southampton Justices, ex p Green [1975] 2 All ER 1073 at 1077–1078, [1976] QB 11 at
19, where Lord Denning MR said:

    'By what principles are the justices to be guided? They ought, I think, to consider
    to what extent the surety was at fault. If he or she connived at the disappearance of

the accused man, or aided it or abetted it, it would be proper to forfeit the whole of the sum. If he or she was wanting in due diligence to secure his appearance, it might be proper to forfeit the whole or a substantial part of it, depending on the degree of fault. If he or she was guilty of no want of diligence and used every effort to secure the appearance of the accused man, it might be proper to remit it entirely.'

The second case is *R v Southampton Justices, ex p Corker* (1976) 120 SJ 214; I have not seen that report but I have a transcript of the judgment. It was decided in this court, on 10 February 1976, the court comprising Lord Widgery CJ, Kilner Brown and Watkins JJ. The material passage in the transcript is as follows:

'The other two points, I think, are points on which justices must have further guidance than that which the decision in *ex p Green* presently affords to them. It is said, and no doubt absolutely correctly, that the degree of culpability of the surety is a factor which must be taken into account when deciding whether to forfeit the whole or part of his recognisance. One first of all has to ask oneself on whom is the onus in these matters, and it seems to me that the onus is clearly on the surety. The surety has undertaken a recognisance for a certain sum of money, and prima facie he can and intends to pay it. If he wants to say he cannot afford it, or that it is not fair he should pay it, he ought to make the running. It is he who should set the scene. When it comes to culpability one has to remember, I think, that the great majority of sureties have very little opportunity to control the movements of the accused person. If surety and accused live in the same family that is one thing, but if they live apart it may be that the surety will have very little opportunity of seeing whether or not the accused attends court. It cannot be right in my judgment that a surety who has entered into an obligation for several hundreds of pounds is able to excuse himself when the time comes by simply saying, "Well, of course I had very little chance to observe him and therefore it really was not my fault." These are all things that ought to be taken into account when the decision to give the recognisance is taken, and the same with means. It would defeat the whole system of bail, I think, if it became generally known that the amount payable was strictly limited according to the surety's means and that anybody who had no means would not have to pay. Imagine the relish and speed with which persons would accept the obligation of surety if they were penniless and knew that that was a total answer to any kind of obligation on the recognisance. The real pull of bail, the real effective force that it exerts, is that it may cause the offender to attend his trial rather than subject his nearest and dearest who has gone surety for him to undue pain and discomfort. But be that as it may, it cannot be the law, I venture to think, that a surety can escape entirely by saying that he was not culpable and was penniless. These are matters which he should have some regard to before he enters into his recognisance, and it must in turn be the subject of regard when any question of forfeiture arises.'

The third case is *R v Horseferry Road Magistrates' Court, ex p Pearson* [1976] 2 All ER 264, [1976] 1 WLR 511. This was a decision of Lord Widgery CJ sitting with Thompson and Kenneth Jones JJ. The material passage relates to that part of Lord Denning MR's judgment in *Ex p Green* to which I have referred. It reads as follows ([1976] 2 All ER 264 at 266–267, [1976] 1 WLR 511 at 514):

'I find it difficult, with all respect to Lord Denning MR, entirely to follow this passage that I have read because the forfeiture of recognisance is in no sense a penalty imposed on the surety for misconduct. I do not doubt that the magistrate, before forfeiting the recognisance, must consider amongst other things the conduct of the surety and see whether it was open to criticism or not. But one must, I think, start all these problems on the footing that the surety has seriously entered into a serious obligation and ought to pay the amount which he or she has promised unless there are circumstances in the case, relating either to her means or her culpability, which make it fair and just to pay a smaller sum. Looked at from that point of view, *R v*

Southampton Justices [and by that, of course, he meant *Ex p Green*] is a helpful authority in the present instance and I would apply it accordingly. For the reasons I have already given I do not propose to say any more about the applicant's means. There is no reason why the magistrate should go any further, and I would like to reject totally the proposition which, as I understand it, is put before us by counsel for the applicant that there is an obligation on the magistrate in these cases to indulge in an enquiry of his own, to send for the police and make them ring up the police station where the accused person lives, and so on. That seems to me to be totally wrong and quite unworkable. The magistrate must proceed on the basis of the evidence before him. True, where the applicant is not represented he must help her as the court will always help an unrepresented person, ask questions on her behalf and do things of that kind, but that there is any obligation to investigate the situation beyond that I reject straightaway.'

The next case is *R v Tottenham Magistrates' Court, ex p Riccardi* (1977) 66 Cr App R 150. It is a decision of Lord Widgery CJ, sitting with Eveleigh and Forbes JJ. The only passage to which I wish to refer is from the judgment of Eveleigh J, when he said (at 155):

'I would, however, wish to emphasise that the question under section 96(3) of the Magistrates' Courts Act 1952 is in no way to be regarded as a case of justices determining a fine as it has been put forward in this case. The recognisance is not a fine and it is not a punishment either.'

The next is another unreported case, *R v Waltham Forest Justices, ex p Parfrey* [1980] Crim LR 571, decided on 10 June 1980, by Donaldson LJ and Woolf J. In the transcript of Donaldson LJ's judgment appears this passage:

'The obligation entered into by someone who enters into a recognisance as a surety is a very serious obligation indeed. I hope that nothing I say today will suggest the contrary. There is an obligation on a surety to be fully satisfied that he or she can meet the liability which will arise if the accused person does not surrender to his bail. This failure to surrender is not a theoretical possibility, though a surety may think it is. The unhappy event of arrested persons not surrendering happens frequently. There is a real risk. Indeed it is difficult to conceive of a set of circumstances in which a surety can be absolutely sure that the accused will surrender to his bail. So let no one think that this is an obligation which can be entered into lightly. Furthermore, the burden of satisfying a court that the full sum should not be forfeit is a very heavy one, so again let no one think that they can simply appear before the magistrates and tell some hard luck story, whereupon the magistrates will say, "Well, be more careful in future." We are not dealing with that character of obligation at all.'

Then, having referred to *Ex p Green*, Donaldson LJ continued:

'Lest this passage be misunderstood by justices, as I think it might well be misunderstood, let me stress the fact that Lord Denning MR said that, if there was no want of due diligence and every effort had been made to secure the appearance of the accused man, it *might* (not that it would necessarily, but it *might*) be proper to remit it entirely. For my part, I think that Lord Denning MR was contemplating a wholly extreme and exceptional case when he said that. I do not, for my part, believe that he ever intended to suggest that the mere fact that every effort to secure the appearance of the accused man had been made and that there was no want of due diligence involved the proposition that the amount of the obligation should be remitted entirely.'

I turn to what was said by Woolf J:

'I agree. In relation to any applications of this sort which might be considered in the future I draw attention to the fact that in s 96 of the Magistrates' Courts Act

1952, which deals with the forfeiture of recognisances, there is in sub-s (4) a proviso in these terms: "Provided that, at any time before the issue of a warrant of commitment to enforce payment of the sum . . . the court may remit the whole or any part of the sum either absolutely or on such conditions as the court thinks just." If, therefore, the only matter of complaint is that there was not a proper consideration of the means of the applicant, the appropriate course is to apply again to the magistrates' court under that provision and ask the court then to take account of the means.'

The next case is R v Knightsbridge Crown Court, ex p Newton [1980] Crim LR 715. Certainly, in one respect, this report is inaccurate when compared with the transcript of the judgment as approved by the judge who gave it, Donaldson LJ. The report says:

'The judge probably had tried to apply his mind to the question of culpability, but unfortunately he had failed to ask the applicant what steps he had taken when he discovered that the woman had absconded.'

The relevant passage in the transcript of the judgment reads:

'For my part, I think the judge probably did try to apply his mind to the question of culpability, but unfortunately he failed to ask one question, which I think was or may in the circumstances of this case have been of vital importance. He failed to ask Mr Newton what he had done when he found that there was a likelihood that Mrs Garcia would not surrender to her bail.'

In the transcript one finds this statement of principle from Donaldson LJ, who was sitting on this occasion with Mustill J:

'It has been said by this court, and by other courts time and again, that entering into suretyship (going bail for someone, to use the common phrase) is an extremely serious matter not to be lightly undertaken, and those who go bail must understand that, if the accused fails to surrender to his bail, it is only in the most exceptional cases that the court will be prepared to modify the prima facie position, which is that the amount for which the person concerned has stood surety will be forfeit in full.'

The next case is also unreported. It is R v Crown Court at Ipswich, ex p Reddington [1981] Crim LR 618, decided on 2 February 1981, by Forbes J. The relevant passage in the judgment reads:

'Of course, anyone who stands surety for someone's attendance must have solemnly undertaken that they are good for the amount of the surety, that they have sufficient resources available. So that when considering the question of means it is a little difficult for a surety to say that he has not got the money which, when entering the recognisance, he must have indicated that he had at that time. But it clearly would be right, and that case [Ex p Green] is authoritative, that courts considering the estreatment of recognisance must consider not only the extent of the surety's resources and the ability to meet what is in effect a financial penalty in those circumstances.'

Lastly, simply for the sake of completeness, I mention R v Crown Court at Oxford, ex p Jones and Jacobs (29 June 1982, unreported), which was decided by me.
In the transcript one finds the following:

'One has to arrive at a decision which is fair and just in all the circumstances. In doing so one must assess the surety's culpability. One must also consider his means. One must remember that one is not fixing a penalty for misconduct. One is deciding whether to mitigate the ordinary principle which is that if somebody says: "I promise to pay £20,000 if X does not turn up at court", and X does not turn up at court, then £20,000 is forfeited.'

Having summarised all the passages in the cases where this topic falls to be considered
a as a matter of principle, so far as I know and as far as the research done by counsel has
shown, I would draw together the more important principles to be derived from the
authorities, as follows. (1) When a defendant for whose attendance a person has stood
surety fails to appear, the full recognisance should be forfeited, unless it appears fair and
just that a lesser sum should be forfeited or none at all. (2) The burden of satisfying the
court that the full sum should not be forfeited rests on the surety and is a heavy one. It is
b for him to lay before the court the evidence of want of culpability and of means on which
he relies. (3) Where a surety is unrepresented the court should assist him by explaining
these principles in ordinary language, and giving him the opportunity to call evidence
and advance argument in relation to them.

What happened in this case was a little unusual. The applicant was represented by a
solicitor before the Uxbridge magistrates' court, on 1 February 1982. He was answering
c a summons to show cause why he should not forfeit the sum of £7,000, which was the
sum in which he had stood surety for the defendant, who had failed to surrender to his
bail.

The affidavit of the solicitor who appeared for him says:

> 'Before the hearing there was some discussion between myself and the clerk to
> the justices as to the way in which the proceedings should be conducted which
d centred around the decision of the Court of Appeal in *R v Southampton Justices, ex p*
> *Green* and *R v Southampton Justices, ex p Corker* . . . I then called the applicant herein
> to give evidence of his culpability but no evidence whatsoever as to his means was
> given. Having done this I submitted to the justices that on the above authorities
> they should arrive at a figure based solely on the issue of culpability and then make
> further enquiries of the applicant herein's means and in the light of that means
e enquiry to exercise their discretion in much the same way as they would when
> considering the imposition of a fine in arriving at the sum to be forfeit.'

The deponent says that he realises that was not the way he should have been submitting
that the magistrates should have approached the matter. His narrative continues:

> 'To my surprise the justices having retired returned and announced that they
f were ordering the applicant herein to forfeit the sum of £5,000 and stated that his
> means were not something they should even take into consideration or hear evidence
> of but that they would hold a means enquiry on the 3rd March 1982 in order to
> determine the mode of payment, i e, as to whether the sum forfeit should be paid
> by instalments or otherwise. At this hearing [and by that he means the hearing of 3
> March] I sought clarification of the record from the clerk and he stated that the
g applicant herein's means had not been taken into consideration in any way
> whatsoever in arriving at the sum to be forfeit under the terms of the recognizance.'

By that he means in arriving at the sum to be forfeit as determined on 1 February.

There is an affidavit from the chairman of the justices, who was sitting on 1 February.
She says:

h
> 'The clerk of the court outlined the history of the case and drew our attention to
> the principles laid down in the case of *R v Southampton Justices, ex p Green* for our
> guidance when dealing with the forfeiture of a recognizance. We then proceeded to
> enquire into the culpability of the applicant for the non-appearance of the defendant
> Mr Sowah. Mr Millman on behalf of the applicant then stated that we were obliged
> to enquire into the applicant's means before reaching a decision as to forfeiture. We
j were surprised by this statement as the applicant had been accepted as a suitable
> surety by an earlier court and he had agreed to stand in the sum of £7,000. To be
> bound to reconsider his means at this stage appeared to defeat the object of bail with
> sureties. In support of his argument Mr Millman referred to the case of *R v*
> *Southampton Justices, ex p Corker* in 1976. We took the view that a means enquiry
> was not mandatory and that in order not to defeat the object of bail with sureties it

was for the applicant to show that his means had changed through some circumstance
beyond his control. Mr Millman did not draw our attention to any such *a*
circumstance. We were faced with a further complication in that the applicant
asserted that he had given false information about his means on the 18th December
1981 when he stated that he had £7,000 in a bank account. We did not have the
note taken by the clerk on the 18th December but accepted that the applicant had
stated that he was worth £7,000. We were unable to determine the truth and it
appeared contrary to the interests of justice to allow the applicant to escape his *b*
liability by changing his means to suit the occasion. On the basis of culpability alone
we ordered that he should forfeit £5,000 of his recognizance. We granted him time
to pay until the 3rd March 1982.'

It is thus clear that, in fixing the sum of £5,000, the justices did not hear any evidence
from the applicant as to his means, or any argument from his solicitor on the question of
means. It is clear from the authorities that, although the justices were not obliged to *c*
initiate an inquiry into this topic, they were obliged to hear such evidence as the applicant
wanted them to hear on the question of his means, and such argument on this topic as
his solicitor wished to advance.

Accordingly, in my judgment, they proceeded under a mistaken view of the law. For
that reason the decision should be quashed.

Before deciding that the discretionary remedy of certiorari should be granted to quash *d*
this decision, I considered whether or not the justices managed to put the matter right
on 3 March 1982, at the second hearing.

What happened, according to the lady magistrate's affidavit, was this. She says:

'On the 3rd March 1982 I was again chairman of the bench sitting with two
different colleagues when the applicant appeared represented by Mr Millman. We
were asked to remit the whole or part of the forfeited recognizance, but in the *e*
absence of good reason for so doing refused the application.'

The justices' clerk, who was sitting that day, has exhibited the notes of evidence that
were taken. It is clear that the applicant gave sworn evidence in which he dealt with his
means.

My first impression, on reading these papers, was that the magistrates had put right *f*
on the second occasion what had gone wrong on the first, and that they were reconsidering
de novo whether the sum of £5,000 ought to be forfeit, as indeed they had the power to
do under s 120(4) of the 1980 Act, as was adverted to by Woolf J in *Ex p Parfrey*.

I think, looking at the affidavit as a whole and having regard to the fact that the lady
justice continued, in relation to the hearing on 3 March, by saying, 'We then proceeded
to conduct a means enquiry with a view to enforcement of the forfeited recognizance,' it
is clear that the court sitting on 3 March was taking the same view of the law as it had *g*
taken on 1 February, namely that means were irrelevant, save as to the time, if any,
which should be allowed for the payment of the sum which was to be forfeit, that sum
having been decided on the basis of culpability.

Accordingly, I do not think that the matter was put right on 3 March in the way
adumbrated by Woolf J. Had I thought so, I would have refused the application for an *h*
order of certiorari. This matter must be considered de novo by a fresh bench of
magistrates, in accordance with the principles to which I have endeavoured to draw
attention.

In saying what I have, I do not want it to be thought that I am suggesting that £5,000
was the right sum, or too much, or too little. Nothing that I have said today must fetter
the justices when the position is reconsidered in the light of the principles to which I *j*
have drawn attention.

Application granted.

Solicitors: *Arnold Fooks Chadwick & Co* (for the applicant).

Sepala Munasinghe Barrister.

Bland v Chief Supplementary Benefit Officer

COURT OF APPEAL, CIVIL DIVISION
SIR JOHN DONALDSON MR, KERR LJ AND SIR SEBAG SHAW
1 DECEMBER 1982

Supplementary benefit – Social security commissioner – Appeal from decision of commissioner on question of law – Appeal from commissioner's refusal of leave to appeal from decision of supplementary benefit appeal tribunal – Whether refusal of leave a 'decision' by commissioner – Whether Court of Appeal having jurisdiction to entertain appeal from commissioner's refusal of leave – Social Security Act 1980, s 14(2).

The applicant, who was physically disabled and in receipt of a supplementary allowance, made a claim under the appropriate benefit regulations for a single payment for bedding. Part of his claim was refused. He appealed to a supplementary benefit appeal tribunal, which upheld the refusal of his claim. He then applied to a social security commissioner pursuant to r 8(1)[a] of the Supplementary Benefit and Family Income Supplements (Appeals) Rules 1980, for leave to appeal from the tribunal's decision on the ground that the decision was erroneous in law. The commissioner refused leave to appeal to her from the tribunal's decision and also refused an application under s 14(2)(a)[b] of the Social Security Act 1980 for leave to appeal against her refusal to the Court of Appeal, on the ground that a commissioner's refusal of leave to appeal to him from a tribunal was not a 'decision' by the commissioner in respect of which there was a right of appeal under s 14(1) and (2) of the 1980 Act. The applicant applied to the Court of Appeal for leave to appeal to that court against the commissioner's refusal under s 14(2)(b), contending that, since an appeal to a commissioner from a tribunal's decision could only be on a point of law, the commissioner's refusal of leave to appeal to her was a 'decision' within s 14(2) and was not merely the exercise of a discretion from which, it was conceded, no appeal could lie.

Held – A decision of a social security commissioner under r 8(1) of the 1980 rules to grant or refuse leave to appeal to the commissioner from a decision of a tribunal was not a 'decision' from which s 14 of the 1980 Act contemplated there should be an appeal with leave, since it was not a decision which was determinative of the matters in dispute. If a commissioner's refusal of leave to appeal to him caused a wrong decision of a tribunal to stand, the proper remedy was to seek judicial review of the tribunal's decision. It followed that the Court of Appeal had no jurisdiction to grant the applicant leave to appeal from the commissioner's refusal of leave to appeal. The application would therefore be dismissed (see p 541 c to p 542 a, post).

Re Housing of the Working Classes Act 1890, ex p Stevenson [1892] 1 QB 609 applied.

Notes
For appeals to the Court of Appeal from Social Security Commissioners, see 33 Halsbury's Laws (4th edn) para 641.

For the Social Security Act 1980, s 14, see 50(2) Halsbury's Statutes (4th edn) 1711.

Cases referred to in judgments
Housing of the Working Classes Act 1890, Re, ex p Stevenson [1892] 1 QB 609, CA, 11 Digest (Reissue) 326, 2102.

Lane v Esdaile [1891] AC 210, HL, 30 Digest (Reissue) 169, 34.

Cases also cited
Podbery v Peak [1981] 1 All ER 699, [1981] Ch 344, CA.

---

a   Rule 8(1) is set out at p 514 f, post
b   Section 14, so far as material, is set out at p 539 f g, post

R v Preston Supplementary Benefits Appeals Tribunal, ex p Moore [1975] 2 All ER 807, [1975]
1 WLR 624, CA.

Whitehouse v Board of Control [1960] 3 All ER 182, [1960] 1 WLR 1093, HL.

Application for leave to appeal

This was an application by Simon Peter Bland for leave to appeal from the decision of a
social security commissioner, Mrs R F M Heggs, dated 30 March 1982, notified to Mr
Bland on 27 April 1982, refusing him leave to appeal to the commissioner from a
decision of the Coventry Supplementary Benefit Appeal Tribunal given on 27 August
1981 that Mr Bland was not entitled to a single payment for a new mattress. The Chief
Supplementary Benefit Officer was the respondent to the proceedings. The facts are set
out in the judgment of Sir John Donaldson MR.

Mark Rowland for Mr Bland.
Simon D Brown for the respondent.

SIR JOHN DONALDSON MR. On this occasion the court is concerned with an
application by Mr Simon Peter Bland. The application raises an interesting and important
point. It is this: has the Court of Appeal any jurisdiction to give leave to appeal from the
refusal of a social security commissioner to give leave to appeal *to her* from a decision of
the supplementary benefit appeal tribunal?

The dispute itself arose in June 1981. In the previous month Mr Bland, who was
physically disabled and in receipt of a supplementary allowance, claimed a single payment
under the Supplementary Benefit (Single Payments) Regulations 1980, SI 1980/985, the
basis of the claim being that he was entitled to money with which to buy a bed, a mattress
and blankets and possibly also sheets. He was given £23.33 for sheets and two blankets,
but was refused any payment in respect of the bed and a mattress.

He was aggrieved with that decision, and appealed on 22 June 1981 to the Coventry
Supplementary Benefit Appeal Tribunal. Two months later that tribunal rejected his
appeal. He was again aggrieved, and he applied to the social security commissioner for
leave to appeal to her. The basis of his application for leave to appeal was a submission
that the supplementary benefit appeal tribunal had misconstrued the relevant regulations
and, further or alternatively, had failed to give sufficient reasons and had failed to make
sufficient findings to enable him and his advisers to know whether or not it had
misconstrued the regulations. For my part, although it is not material to this appeal, I
think that there is a great deal to be said for that submission. Unfortunately Mrs Heggs,
the commissioner, took a different view, and refused leave to appeal *to her*.

At that stage the Child Poverty Action Group entered on the scene, and made a request
on behalf of Mr Bland to Mrs Heggs for leave to appeal to the Court of Appeal from her
refusal of leave to appeal *to her*. Mrs Heggs considered that application, and rejected it on
the ground that she had no jurisdiction to grant leave to appeal to the Court of Appeal
from a decision by her that there should be no leave to appeal *to her*. I stress in each case
the words 'to her' not to emphasise the fact that she is a lady commissioner rather than a
male commissioner, but to point the difference between the case where the commissioner
is concerned with leave to appeal to the Court of Appeal and where the commissioner is
concerned with leave to appeal to the commissioner from the supplementary benefit
appeal tribunal.

At that stage an application was made to this court for leave to appeal from Mrs Heggs's
refusal. The matter came before Slade LJ, who referred the application to the full court,
and ordered that it was to follow the hearing of an appeal by a Mr Morrell and that, if
leave was granted, the appeal should be heard immediately after the grant of leave. He
also gave liberty to apply to vary his order.

The chief supplementary benefit officer, who was the respondent in these proceedings,
now applies to this court pursuant to the leave granted by Slade LJ asking us to vary the
order determining here and now whether there is jurisdiction to grant leave to appeal to
this court (because, if there is jurisdiction, there is no doubt that leave would be granted)

and also to vary the order that this matter shall await the hearing of Mr Morrell's appeal.
a There is no problem about that.
    Accordingly what we have to consider is the question of jurisdiction. It is tacitly
admitted that the decision of the supplementary benefit tribunal is not really satisfactory.
It is further said by counsel on behalf of the respondent that once the question of
jurisdiction can be got out of the way, then what is from Mr Bland's point of view the
important question, namely his entitlement to a grant for a bed and mattress, can possibly
b be dealt with to his satisfaction without resort to courts of law. I have certainly been a
little struck, listening to the appeal, by the fact that, important though this question of
jurisdiction undoubtedly is, it is far removed from what these proceedings are really
about, namely Mr Bland's bed and mattress. However that may be, it is an interesting
and important point that we now have to decide, and I would only say that I sincerely
hope that Mr Bland's application will be resolved to his satisfaction and that of the chief
c supplementary benefit officer in the near future.
    What counsel for the respondent submits is this. He says that there is no jurisdiction
in the Court of Appeal to grant leave to appeal in these circumstances, but that is not to
say that Mr Bland is without a remedy. Mr Bland should have applied to the Divisional
Court of the Queen's Bench Division claiming a judicial review of the decision of the
supplementary benefit appeal tribunal with which he was aggrieved. From the way in
d which the submission was made, I infer that had Mr Bland done that there would not
have been any very spirited opposition on the part of the chief supplementary benefit
officer on the facts of this case. Nevertheless counsel for the respondent points out that
the review jurisdiction of the Divisional Court is different in kind, in some respects more
limited and in other respects less limited, than is the appellate jurisdiction of the High
Court. That is right, and it is quite inappropriate in my judgment that this court should
e seek to define what are the limits of the review jurisdiction of the Divisional Court. That
will be developed case by case, and the principles are already well established.
    So I return to the question whether there is a right of appeal to this court. This court is
the creature of statute, and it is necessary to point to some statutory right of appeal before
it can have jurisdiction. On the facts of this case counsel who has appeared for Mr Bland,
points to s 14(1) of the Social Security Act 1980. That is in these terms:

f   'Subject to subsections (2) and (3) of this section, an appeal on a question of law
    shall lie to the appropriate court from any decision of a Commissioner.'

'A Commissioner' is of course a social security commissioner. 'The appropriate court' is
the Court of Appeal, as is clear from sub-s (4) of s 14. Subsection (3) is immaterial for
present purposes since it merely defines the categories of persons entitled to appeal. The
g important subsection is sub-s (2), which reads as follows:

       'No appeal under this section shall lie from a decision except—(a) with the leave
    of the Commissioner who gave the decision or, in a case prescribed by regulations,
    with the leave of a Commissioner selected in accordance with regulations; or (b) if
    he refuses leave, with the leave of the appropriate court.'

h Reconstructing that subsection to make it slightly more intelligible, it reads: 'No appeal
under this section shall lie from a decision except with the leave of the Commissioner or,
if he refuses leave, of the Court of Appeal.'
    What counsel for Mr Bland says is that here there was quite clearly a decision by Mrs
Heggs, namely a decision that there should be no leave to appeal to her. It follows, he
j submits, that s 14(2) gives this court jurisdiction to give leave to appeal against that
decision.
    What is said by counsel for the respondent is that 'decision' in s 14 means an order
determinative of the matter in dispute, or possibly an order determining how the matter
shall be determined, the ordinary interlocutory procedural order which is made in any
form of legal proceedings. But, in his submission, the grant or refusal of leave to appeal
is not such a decision at all. It is by contrast merely the grant or refusal of a permission

which determines nothing at all except whether the applicant is or is not permitted to appeal.

Now that argument might at first sight seem somewhat refined, but it is well-founded in authority. The two cases on which counsel for the respondent relies are a decision of the House of Lords in *Lane v Esdaile* [1891] AC 210 and *Re Housing of the Working Classes Act 1890, ex p Stevenson* [1892] 1 QB 609. For my purposes I think it necessary only to refer to the decision of the Court of Appeal in *Ex p Stevenson* which follows *Lane v Esdaile* and possibly has a wider ratio than that of *Lane v Esdaile* and is, of course, equally binding on us.

Stevenson's case concerned the Housing of the Working Classes Act 1890 whereby it was provided that where a party was dissatisfied with the amount of compensation which he had been awarded under Part I of the Act, he—

'may, upon obtaining the leave of the High Court, which leave may be granted by such Court, or any judge thereof at chambers, in a summary manner, and upon being satisfied that a failure of justice will take place if the leave is not granted, submit the question of the proper amount of compensation to a jury.'

In *Stevenson's* case a judge in chambers refused to grant that leave, and the Divisional Court held that there was no appeal to them from his decision. There was then an appeal from the decision of the Divisional Court to the Court of Appeal, that court being composed of Lord Esher MR, Fry and Lopes LJJ. Lord Esher MR said ([1892] 1 QB 609 at 610–611):

'It is clear that, in effect, the provision is that the party dissatisfied may apply for the leave of the High Court to appeal from the decision of the arbitrator to a jury. The High Court may grant such leave, either sitting as a Divisional Court, or through a judge thereof sitting in chambers, on being satisfied that justice requires it. If anything further were needed to shew that the proceeding is an appeal, it is to be found in the subsequent provisions of the schedule as to costs, which distinctly speak of it as such. I am, on principle and on consideration of the authorities that have been cited, prepared to lay down the proposition that, wherever power is given to a legal authority to grant or refuse leave to appeal, the decision of that authority is, from the very nature of the thing, final and conclusive and without appeal, unless an appeal from it is expressly given [then he refers to *Lane v Esdaile*].'

Fry LJ said (at 612):

'The legislature has thought fit to impose a condition in respect of this right of appeal, viz., that the leave of the High Court must be obtained, which leave is to be granted in the manner pointed out, viz., either by the Divisional Court or by a judge at chambers. Then is the order—for such I will assume it to be—of the High Court, granting or refusing leave to appeal, subject to appeal? In my opinion it is not. I do not come to that conclusion on the ground that the word "order" is not properly applicable to it; but from the nature of the thing and the object of the legislature in imposing this fetter on appeals. The object clearly was to prevent frivolous and needless appeals. If, from an order refusing leave to appeal, there may be an appeal, the result will be that, in attempting to prevent needless and frivolous appeals, the legislature will have introduced a new series of appeals with regard to the leave to appeal.'

Then Lopes LJ said (at 613):

'If an appeal were allowed from the granting or refusal of leave to appeal, the result would be that, instead of checking appeals, they might be multiplied to a most mischievous extent; for an appeal from the granting or refusal of leave might be carried from the Divisional Court to this Court, and from this Court to the House of Lords. For these reasons I think that the preliminary objection must prevail.'

Counsel for Mr Bland, faced with this authority, seeks to distinguish it on the grounds

that both in *Stevenson's* case [1892] 1 QB 609 and in *Lane v Esdaile* [1891] AC 210, and it
a may be in other cases which have followed *Lane v Esdaile*, what was under consideration
was a refusal of leave to appeal in the exercise of discretion; and he says that it is possible
to distinguish the present case on the basis that Mrs Heggs was not, as he submits,
exercising a discretion but had been led into a manifest error of law. He says that where
leave to appeal is refused and that refusal constitutes an error of law, then these cases do
not apply.

b   For my part I commend his ingenuity, but I am bound to say that I cannot find any
trace in the authorities of any justification for that submission. The reasoning of the
Court of Appeal in *Stevenson's* case is not based on a refusal to interfere with a discretion.
The court held that the grant or refusal of leave to appeal is a very special kind of decision
from which prima facie there can be no appeal, and, as Lord Esher MR said for the
reasons set out in the judgments, it would require express words to enable any appeal to
c be brought.

      Section 14 does contemplate an appeal from decisions of the commissioner, and I
would accept that, in a sense, the grant or refusal of leave to appeal to the commissioner
is a decision, just as in *Stevenson's* case it was accepted that the grant or refusal of leave to
appeal was an order of the High Court, but it is not the kind of decision which in my
judgment s 14 contemplates. That section relates to a decision which determines the
d matters in dispute.

      Accordingly, following *Stevenson's* case, I would hold that there is no jurisdiction in
this court to grant leave, and for that reason the application should be dismissed. If
necessary, Mr Bland should seek judicial review but, as I apprehend, it will probably not
be necessary for him to do so.

e **KERR LJ.** I entirely agree. I would only add that when counsel for Mr Bland was asked
on which provision he relies in order to seek to distinguish the decision in this case,
whether to refuse or, as the case may be, to grant leave to appeal by the commissioner to
her, from the authorities to which Sir John Donaldson MR has referred, he relied on r 8
of the Supplementary Benefit and Family Income Supplements (Appeals) Rules 1980, SI
1980/1605. This provides in para (1):

f   'Subject to paragraph (3) [which is irrelevant] any person who is a party to
      proceedings before a tribunal may appeal to a Commissioner, with the leave of a
      Commissioner, against any decision of the tribunal given in those proceedings on
      the ground that the decision is erroneous in point of law.'

His submission was accordingly that an appeal to the commissioner would only lie on a
g point of law. With that I obviously agree. But I do not agree that the decision of the
commissioner whether to grant or refuse leave under that rule places it in a different
category from the decisions whether to grant or refuse leave which were under
consideration in the authorities to which Sir John Donaldson MR has referred.

      It is clearly a sine qua non requirement of this rule that an appeal will only lie on a
point of law. However, superimposed on that, it is still a matter for the decision of the
h commissioner whether, given the fact that appeals can only be brought on a point of law,
the commissioner is willing to grant or refuse leave.

      I therefore cannot see that the fact that appeals to the commissioner can only lie on
points of law raises any ground of distinction. If, by refusing leave to appeal on a point
of law, the commissioner causes a decision of the tribunal to stand when that decision is
wrong in law, then it seems to me that any remedy can only be sought by means of
j judicial review and not by appeal to this court. I therefore agree that this appeal must be
dismissed.

SIR SEBAG SHAW. I also agree. An appeal from a decision under s 14(1) of the 1980
Act must mean an appeal from a decision on some matter of law which is the basis of the
commissioner's finding. If one included in that the refusal of leave, one would remove a
valuable and important practical barrier to the pursuit of frivolous appeals. Accordingly,

although I accept that a refusal may in certain circumstances be termed a decision, it is not the kind of decision which is contemplated by sub-s (2)(a) of s 14. Otherwise the *a* brake which the statute puts on the proliferation of appeals from the commissioner would be made abortive.

I too would refuse this application.

Application dismissed.

Solicitors: *Roger J Smith* (for Mr Bland); *Solicitor to the Department of Health and Social Security* (for the respondent).

Diana Procter   Barrister.

Glantre Engineering Ltd v Goodhand (Inspector of Taxes)

CHANCERY DIVISION
WARNER J
2, 17 NOVEMBER 1982

Income tax – Emoluments from office or employment – Receipt 'from' employment – Purpose of employer in making payment – Inducement to give up professional status and to become and continue as employee – Company making lump sum payment to chartered accountant on taking up employment with company – Whether payment 'emolument' from employment – Income and Corporation Taxes Act 1970, ss 181(1), 183(1).

In 1977 the taxpayer company required a financial director for its rapidly expanding engineering business. It made an offer to W, a chartered accountant who worked for an international firm of accountants. The offer included a lump sum payment of £10,000 'as an inducement' to him to leave the firm. W accepted the offer and, on taking up his employment, was paid the £10,000. The Crown claimed that the payment was an emolument from W's employment with the taxpayer company within s 183(1)[a] of the Income and Corporation Taxes Act 1970 and made a determination of income tax payable by the taxpayer company under reg 29 of the Income Tax (Employments) Regulations 1973 in respect of the £10,000. The taxpayer company appealed, contending that the payment was not something in the nature of a reward for services past, present or future, but was something to compensate W for his loss attendant on the occurrence, and as a necessary and ancillary aspect, of his leaving the firm in order to put himself in a position to take up employment with the taxpayer company and that accordingly it was not an emolument from W's employment chargeable to tax under Sch E pursuant to s 181(1)[b] of the 1970 Act. The Special Commissioners held that the payment was an inducement held out to W to enter into the company's employment and formed part of his contract of service and was therefore chargeable to tax under Sch E in s 181(1) of the 1970 Act. The taxpayer company appealed.

Held – The quality of a payment made to an employee at the inception of his *j* employment, i e whether or not it constituted an emolument from his employment, was essentially a question of fact to be decided by the commissioners on a consideration of all the evidence before them and their determination could not be set aside by the court

---

a Section 183(1), so far as material, is set out at p 554 *h*, post
b Section 181(1), so far as material, is set out at p 554 *g*, post

a unless it was inconsistent with the only reasonable conclusion to be drawn from the evidence. On the facts, it could not be said that the only reasonable conclusion to be drawn from the evidence before the commissioners was that the payment of the £10,000 to W was severable from the other benefits to which W became entitled under the agreement between himself and the taxpayer company, and was other than an added inducement to him to change his job and enter the full-time employment of the company. It followed, therefore, that the payment of £10,000 was chargeable to tax as

b an emolument from W's employment under Sch E in s 181(1) of the 1970 Act. The appeal would therefore be dismissed (see p 551 b c and p 556 d to f, post).

Edwards (Inspector of Taxes) v Bairstow [1955] 3 All ER 48 applied.

Hose v Warwick (Inspector of Taxes) (1946) 27 TC 459, Jarrold (Inspector of Taxes) v Boustead [1964] 3 All ER 76 and Pritchard (Inspector of Taxes) v Arundale [1971] 3 All ER

c 1011 distinguished.

Notes

For voluntary payments to a holder of an office or employment, see 23 Halsbury's Laws (4th edn) para 644, and for cases on the subject, see 28(1) Digest (Reissue) 323–331, 1148–1193.

For the Income and Corporation Taxes Act 1970, ss 181, 183, see 33 Halsbury's Statutes

d (3rd edn) 255, 260.

For the Income Tax (Employments) Regulations 1973, reg 29, see 11 Halsbury's Statutory Instruments (3rd reissue) 64.

Cases referred to in judgment

Edwards (Inspector of Taxes) v Bairstow [1955] 3 All ER 48, [1956] AC 14, [1955] 3 WLR

e 410, HL, 28(1) Digest (Reissue) 566, 2089.

Hochstrasser (Inspector of Taxes) v Mayes [1959] 3 All ER 817, [1960] AC 376, [1960] 2 WLR 63, HL; affg [1958] 3 All ER 285, [1959] Ch 22, [1958] 3 WLR 215, CA; affg [1958] 1 All ER 369, [1959] Ch 22, [1958] 2 WLR 982, 28(1) Digest (Reissue) 326, 1164.

Hose v Warwick (Inspector of Taxes) (1946) 27 TC 459, 28(1) Digest (Reissue) 330, 1183.

f Jarrold (Inspector of Taxes) v Boustead [1964] 3 All ER 76, [1964] 1 WLR 1357, CA, 28(1) Digest (Reissue) 331, 1189.

Laidler v Perry (Inspector of Taxes) [1965] 2 All ER 121, [1966] AC 16, [1965] 2 WLR 1171, HL, 28(1) Digest (Reissue) 338, 1226.

Pritchard (Inspector of Taxes) v Arundale [1971] 3 All ER 1011, [1972] Ch 229, [1971] 3 WLR 877, Digest (Cont Vol D) 464, 1226b.

g **Cases also cited**

Brumby (Inspector of Taxes) v Milner [1976] 3 All ER 636, [1976] 1 WLR 1096, HL.

Holland (Inspector of Taxes) v Geoghegan [1972] 3 All ER 333, [1972] 1 WLR 1473.

Moorhouse (Inspector of Taxes) v Dolland [1955] 1 All ER 93, [1955] Ch 284, CA.

Cameron v Prendergast (Inspector of Taxes) [1940] 2 All ER 35, [1940] AC 549, HL.

h **Case stated**

1. On 5, 6 and 7 October 1981 the Commissioners for the Special Purposes of the Income Tax Acts heard the appeal of Glantre Engineering Ltd (the company) against a determination made under reg 29 of the Income Tax (Employments) Regulations 1973, SI 1973/334, whereby it was determined that a sum of tax amounting to £5,738 was

j payable by the company in respect of the year of assessment 1977–78.

2. Shortly stated the questions for the commissioners' decision were whether a sum of £10,000 paid by the company in January 1978 to Mr Francis W Wells was income of Mr Wells chargeable to income tax in the year 1977–78 under Sch E as an emolument falling within the terms of Case I of that schedule (Income and Corporation Taxes Act 1970, s 181(1)), or, if the said sum was not income so chargeable, whether it was a payment chargeable to tax under Sch E by virtue of the provisions of s 187 of that Act.

3. Mr Derek A Gilbert (a director of the company) and Mr Francis W Wells gave evidence before the commissioners.

4. The only documents proved or admitted before the commissioners were three letters dated respectively 12 August, 9 September and 26 October 1977, the terms of which were set out in full in their decision.

5. The facts which the commissioners found proved or admitted and the contentions of the parties were set out in their decision.

6. The commissioners who heard the appeal took time to consider their decision and gave it in writing on 4 November 1981.

7. By way of amplification of their decision the commissioners recorded that the oral evidence of Mr Wells confirmed, and they accepted, that the factors referred to by Mr Wells in his letter of 9 September 1977 constituted Mr Wells's motives for securing 'some financial inducement to leave Whinney Murray Ernst and Ernst' as stated in that letter, and that Mr Wells genuinely believed that the disadvantages referred to would flow from his changing the course of his career. The commissioners found both on the terms of his letter and on his oral evidence that he sought the additional money more as a protection against the risks involved in the move than as compensation for the loss of advantages. While, therefore, the commissioners accepted the first proposition contained in the second sentence of Mr Richards's contention (iv) (see para 4, pp 547–548, post), they did not accept the second so far as it represented a gloss or extension of what was said in Mr Wells's letter of 9 September 1977. The commissioners also accepted that, as stated in Mr Gilbert's letter of 26 October 1977, the company offered (and subsequently paid) the sum of £10,000 in order to meet Mr Wells's feelings in the matter as put by Mr Wells in his letter.

8. As appears from the decision, the commissioners found in favour of the Crown on the question arising under s 181(1) of the Income and Corporation Taxes Act 1970 and accordingly did not have to reach a concluded view on the alternative question arising under s 187 of that Act. As further appears from their decision they adjourned the hearing for agreement of the figures to be determined.

9. Agreement was in due course reached between the parties in the figure of £4,426 and on 5 February 1982 the commissioners adjusted the determination accordingly.

10. The company immediately after the determination of the appeal declared to the commissioners its dissatisfaction therewith as being erroneous in point of law and on 4 March 1982 required them to state a case for the opinion of the High Court pursuant to the Taxes Management Act 1970, s 56.

11. The questions of law for the opinion of the Court were: (a) (i) whether on the facts found by the commissioners as set out in their decision there was evidence on which they could properly arrive at their decision and (ii) whether on the facts so found their determination of the appeal was correct in law; alternatively, (b) whether on the facts so found and on the true construction of s 187(1) and (2) of the Income and Corporation Taxes Act 1970 tax was chargeable under Sch E in respect of the payment of the sum of £10,000 to Mr Wells in January 1978, in accordance with s 187.

DECISION

1. This is an appeal by Glantre Engineering Ltd (the company) against a determination made under reg 29 of the Income Tax (Employments) Regulations 1973, SI 1973/334. The questions for our decision are whether a sum of £10,000 paid by the company in January 1978 to Mr Francis W Wells was income of Mr Wells chargeable to tax in the year 1977–78 under Sch E as an emolument falling within the terms of Case I of that schedule (s 181(1) of the Income and Corporation Taxes Act 1970); alternatively, if the sum was not income so chargeable, whether it was a payment chargeable to tax under Sch E by virtue of the provisions of s 187 of that Act.

2. The evidence before us consisted of copies of three letters which passed between directors of the company and Mr Wells during the period August to October 1977 and

the oral evidence of Mr Derek Gilbert, a joint managing director of the company and Mr
a Wells. The primary facts are as follows.
  (a) The company was incorporated in 1970 with the name Glantre Farms Ltd and (as
its name suggests) its principal asset was a farm in Wales. Its 100 issued shares were held
by members of Mr Wells's family and the land was farmed by Mr Wells's brother. In
1972 that brother took up farming in Australia; the company's farm was sold, and the
company became (for a short time) a shell. Mr Wells acquired the two shares in the
b company previously held by his brother.
  (b) Mr Wells is a chartered accountant. He qualified in 1971 and having joined Peat
Marwick Mitchell & Co spent a year in Australia. He returned in 1973, and joined
Whinney Murray & Co in London.
  (c) Mr Wells and Mr Gilbert have been friends since they were small children. Mr
Gilbert is an electrical engineer. After graduating, he worked successively for two large
c electrical engineering firms and was employed by them in their overseas sales
departments. While so engaged he made a number of contacts in the Middle East, among
whom were a Mr Damar and a Mrs Sikafi.
  (d) In 1973 Mr Gilbert, Mr Damar and Mrs Sikafi decided to set up in business on
their own account, exporting electrical and mechanical engineering equipment to the
Middle East. Mr Gilbert discussed their plans with Mr Wells (who had just returned
d from Australia). Mr Wells suggested that they take over the company which was no
longer of use to the Wells family. In the event the company's name was changed to
Glantre Engineering Ltd and its issued share capital was increased in 1974 to 6,002 shares
of which Mr Gilbert and each of his associates acquired 2,000. Mr Wells retained the two
shares which he already held. Mr Wells was appointed a director of the company in order
to provide some expertise in company administration which Mr Gilbert and his associates
e lacked. The company started trading in its new guise at the beginning of 1974.
  (e) During the four years 1974 to 1977 Mr Wells's participation in the running of the
business was of a limited nature. The books were sent or brought to him from time to
time and he prepared the company's annual accounts for audit. This was a spare-time
activity and he received fees for it amounting to some £2,000 a year depending on the
work entailed. Mr Wells remained a full-time employee of Whinney Murray & Co in
f London until the end of 1975; he then moved to Whinney Murray Ernst & Ernst, an
associated (but distinct) firm of chartered accountants practising internationally. He went
to the Paris office of that firm as a specialist in computer auditing. Mr Wells possessed an
additional qualification not commonly found among those able to use computers for
audit purposes: he had mastered the technique of programming computers. Mr Wells
was promoted in the Paris office in 1977 (when he was aged about 30) and he told us that
g he had hoped to be offered a partnership four or five years later.
  (f) The business of the company expanded rapidly. Its turnover figures for its first
three years were (approximately) £50,000, £280,000 and £550,000. An important part
of its trade consisted in dealing in electric cables. In January 1977 the company recruited,
as a senior employee, a Mr Parry, who had immediately previously been the export
manager of a large company, Delta Enfield Cables Ltd, for which the company acted as
h sales agent in Saudi Arabia. In pursuance of arrangements made before Mr Parry joined
the company, the company paid Mr Parry two sums totalling £13,500. The quality of
that payment was not before the commissioners in this appeal.
  (g) By the summer of 1977 it had become apparent to Mr Gilbert and Mr Damar that
the company required a full time accountant and they decided to approach Mr Wells.
Mr Gilbert visited Mr Wells and the matter was discussed between them. On 12 August
j 1977 a letter, signed by Mr Damar, but drafted by Mr Gilbert, was sent to Mr Wells as
follows:

  'Further to your discussions with Derek [Mr Gilbert] in Paris on 6th and 7th
  August 1977, we are pleased to offer you full time employment with Glantre
  Engineering as Financial Director from 1st January 1978. In outline the applicable

terms and conditions would be as follows: a) Salary: £9000 per annum. Reviewable annually. b) A company car of nominal value £2750–£3000 would be provided for your use. c) Usual travel and entertainment expenses incurred would be reimbursed. d) Additional bonus payments could be made at the board's discretion based on improved profitability or efficiency that can be directly attributable to your efforts. e) Your principal duties would be to take over, operate and improve as necessary, the accounting and finance systems of GE and associate companies. The areas in which we are particularly looking for improvement in 1978 are credit control, cash flow forecasting, regular reporting and production of accounting figures on a divisional basis. f) We imagine that it would be at least six months before all the above were under control, allowing you time to look further afield. However, once you were in this position, say by July 1978, we would look to you to produce feasibility studies on the introduction of computing of the order processing systems. If as we expect, the early studies show that computerisation would be beneficial, then we would expect you to conduct all aspects in introducing and operating computer systems. g) Another development area which we feel would prove both profitable for the company and complementary to our existing activities would be provision of financial and investment consultancy and management services for our Arab clients. We are in touch with a number of individuals in both Saudi and Iraq who would like to place funds on the investment market, or directly in property or in industry in the UK. h) We also understand that should you have any time to spare you could be in a position to offer computer auditing consultancy to existing contacts of yours in the UK or France on a fee basis, and with a rate of say £15·00/ FF125 per hour plus expenses. We shall certainly be interested in the possibility of offering this to those clients through the company. i) While we are not in a position to offer any increase in your shareholding in the company, we would be prepared to consider at a future date, the formation of a separate company in which you were to have a substantial shareholding. Such a company could both, firstly, service the Glantre group accounting/financial requirements and secondly, provide external services of the kind suggested in (g) and (h) above. However, until such a company is formed, we would offer you additional incentive payments amounting to 20% of the net fees earned by yourself for the company in respect of (g) and (h) above. We look forward to receiving your early response to this proposal.'

(h) Mr Wells replied on 9 September:

'Thank you for your letter of 12 August 1977, which I found awaiting me last week on my return to Paris. Whilst I appreciate entirely that the proposed salary is more than generous for the duties involved, I do feel that in accepting any full-time employment with Glantre Engineering Ltd and of course leaving Whinney Murray Ernst and Ernst, I am sacrificing certain benefits with them—professional status as a Chartered Accountant in a leading International accountancy firm, the possibility of partnership status within several years and also the certainty of security in the future. On joining Glantre Engineering Ltd, I surrender the professional status of an independent Chartered Accountant, I lose forever the chance of partnership in London or Paris, and I am joining a company which is albeit highly successful at the moment, but it has only been running three years under its present management, and can offer no long-term security whatsoever, and in the event of its ceasing trading would have no assets at all to compensate those employees made redundant. In view of these factors, I do feel that it would not be unreasonable to be offered some financial inducement to leave Whinney Murray Ernst and Ernst. Before considering further your offer, I will be glad to hear your views on these thoughts.'

At the time of writing that letter Mr Wells knew that Mr Parry had joined the company and was aware of the £13,500 which had recently been paid to him; but as Mr Wells was not yet engaged in preparing the company's accounts for the year to March 1978 he did not then know the circumstances in any detail.

(i) Mr Wells's suggestion that he should receive some financial inducement was the subject of a telephone discussion between him and Mr Gilbert and a sum of £10,000 was arrived at. That amount was influenced by the amount paid to Mr Parry, but otherwise was (as Mr Wells put it) just 'a round figure'. Shortly afterwards, on 26 October 1977, Mr Gilbert wrote to Mr Wells as follows:

'Thank you for your letter of 9th September 1977 in reply to Amjad's [Mr Damar's] letter offering you full-time employment with Glantre Engineering Ltd. We understand your concern about giving up the security of working with an international firm of Chartered Accountants, and consequently we are prepared to make a revised offer being: 1. A lump sum of £10,000 as an inducement to leave Whinney Murray Ernst and Ernst. 2. A salary of £9,000 a year consisting of £8,000 p.a. paid monthly and a bonus of £1,000 after 12 months. All other conditions of employment to remain as per our offer of 12th August 1977. I look forward to receiving your further comments on our proposals.'

Mr Wells accepted the company's revised offer by telephone on the day following his receipt of that letter.

(j) Mr Wells left Whinney Murray Ernst & Ernst at the end of 1977 and took up his new post with the company on 1 January 1978. The agreed sum of £10,000 was paid to him by the company during the same month.

(k) The change in the place of Mr Wells's employment from Paris to Wembley (where the company's offices were situated) naturally involved a domestic move. Mr Wells had however retained the house in London in which he had lived before moving to Paris and no problem arose over rehousing himself and his family.

(l) Mr Wells hoped that the company would continue to prosper and that his full time appointment with it would be of a permanent nature. Unfortunately, the company failed to obtain certain contracts in 1979–80 and its results for that year were very poor. The staff was reduced and Mr Wells's post was abolished at the end of August 1980. It was not suggested to him that the £10,000 (or any part thereof) should be repaid to the company; indeed, he was permitted to take with him a computer which the company had acquired. Mr Wells is now a self-employed consultant in the field of computer accountancy. He has retained his directorship of the company.

3. We will deal first with the Crown's claim that the sum of £10,000 paid to Mr Wells was chargeable to tax under Sch E on the ground that it was an emolument of his employment with the company falling within s 181 of the Income and Corporation Taxes Act 1970 (Case I).

4. On that issue Mr Richards, who appeared for the company, contended: (i) that it was for the Crown to satisfy us that the payment was an emolument falling within Case I of Sch E; (ii) that the payment was not an emolument of Mr Wells's employment with the company, because it was not 'something in the nature of a reward for services past, present or future' (to use the words of Upjohn J in *Hochstrasser (Inspector of Taxes) v Mayes* [1958] 1 All ER 369 at 375, [1959] Ch 22 at 33, approved by Viscount Simonds in the same case (see [1959] 3 All ER 817 at 821, [1960] AC 376 at 388)); on the contrary, (iii) that the payment was shown on the evidence to have been made to Mr Wells to compensate him for private losses attendant on the occurrence, and as a necessary and ancillary aspect, of his leaving his employment with Whinney Murray Ernst & Ernst in order to put himself in a position to take up employment with the company (in referring to 'private losses' counsel for the company was referring in substance to the various disadvantages which Mr Wells saw in accepting the company's offer as first made and which he set out in his letter of 9 September 1977. To that list was added before us the loss of the agreeable life-style that Mr and Mrs Wells had been able to adopt in Paris); (iv) that the character of a payment such as that in the present case falls to be ascertained from the recipient's point of view and that that is a subjective matter; Mr Wells's evidence should satisfy us both that Mr Wells genuinely believed that the disadvantages which he set out in his letter of 9 September 1977 would flow from his changing the course of his

career and also that in suggesting that the company might make him an additional
payment he was specifically seeking compensation for the loss of the advantage which he   *a*
actually or prospectively enjoyed in his existing job; (v) that, although Mr Gilbert's letter
of 26 October 1977 (together with Mr Damar's earlier letter and Mr Wells's telephoned
acceptance) constituted Mr Wells's service contract, the inclusion of a reference to the
lump sum of £10,000 in that letter did not conclusively stamp the payment with the
character of an emolument of his employment; such a payment can be severed from the
'service' element in the contract and should be so severed in this case as being a payment   *b*
made for a consideration other than Mr Wells's services.

5. The Crown contended: (i) that the real purpose (or, if there were more than one,
the primary purpose) of the £10,000 payment was to obtain Mr Wells's services in the
future on the terms agreed; (ii) that payments for future services fall within the charge
to tax under s 181; and (iii) further, and in particular, that payments made under agreed
terms of appointment are, on authority, chargeable to tax under s 181.   *c*

6. As has often been said, the difficulties in this field lie not so much in the principles
of law to be applied as in their application to the facts. But the arguments addressed to us
on this occasion did disclose a difference of approach to the problem which made it
necessary for us to decide whether, as a matter of law, the circumstances surrounding the
lump sum payment made to Mr Wells should be judged objectively or whether, as
counsel for the company contended, it should be judged subjectively and exclusively   *d*
from Mr Wells's point of view.

7. On that point we say at once that we considered that an objective approach is the
correct one. The cases in which the payer's motive has been regarded as a material factor
are legion. Furthermore, in cases of the same class as the present, namely cases where the
payment in question has been made in accordance with a contractual stipulation, the
solution of the problem has lain in discovering the real nature of the transaction on the   *e*
true construction of the contract; and questions of construction are resolved objectively.
Indeed, if the real nature of the payment is remuneration, the parties to a contract of
service cannot keep the payment out of the ambit of Sch E simply by attaching a different
label to the payment (see *Dale (Inspector of Taxes) v de Soissons* [1950] 2 All ER 460); and if
that is so it cannot be that the character of the payment can effectively be determined by
the ipse dixit of one party.   *f*

8. It does not however follow from that that a payment made in accordance with a
term contained in the document constituting a contract of service partakes inevitably of
the nature of remuneration. It is likely to do so, and in most cases it does. But an
examination of the facts may disclose that the employer will obtain under the contract as
a whole benefits distinct from the employee's services. A good example is provided by
Hose v Warwick (Inspector of Taxes) (1946) 27 TC 459. Under the contract in that case the   *g*
employer obtained not only Mr Hose's services but also the full benefit during the term
of the contract of Mr Hose's existing and valuable business connections, and a covenant
restricting competition thereafter. In such a case it may well be held that a sum payable
under the contract in addition to obvious remuneration is genuinely attributable to the
factors other than the services. On that footing the employment is not the true source of
the additional payment and the case is outside the scope of s 181.   *h*

9. The decided cases nearest to the present seemed to us to be *Jarrold (Inspector of
Taxes) v Boustead* [1964] 3 All ER 76, [1964] 1 WLR 1357 and the two others heard with
it (the Rugby footballers' cases). As here, the lump sum payments were made on the
occasion of the players taking up their employments. As here, the employers had only
one visible motive in making the payments, namely to obtain the employees' services.
The clubs obtained no additional benefits. The Court of Appeal held, in agreement with   *j*
the Special Commissioners but differing from Pennycuick J, that the contracts were
capable of being construed in such a way as to attribute the payment of the lump sums
not to the anticipated services of the players but to the permanent loss of amateur status
which automatically resulted from their entering into the contracts.

10. Not surprisingly, the formulation of Mr Richards's contentions in the present case

owes a good deal to the way in which the Special Commissioners expressed their findings
a in the Rugby footballers' cases; and he was naturally at some pains to emphasise the
aspects of the present case which are equally to be found in them. In particular, he
fastened on the 'compensation' element.

11. However, in our view *Jarrold v Boustead*, properly understood, is not authority for
the simple proposition that a payment made at the commencement of an employment
is outside s 181 if, in entering on the employment, the employee can show that he has
b suffered some sort of 'loss' to which the payment is capable of being attributed. The core
of the decision of the Court of Appeal is contained, we believe, in the words of Lord
Denning MR ([1964] 3 All ER 76 at 80, [1964] 1 WLR 1357 at 1365):

> 'When read with the by-laws, I think that [the agreements] should be interpreted
> as saying that the £3,000 was paid as a consideration for Mr. Boustead's relinquishing
> his amateur status, which meant relinquishing it for the whole of his life. The other
c > payments were payments per match and were only for the next playing season.
> They might last only for seven months. The relinquishment of his amateur status
> was for life.'

These words are followed by an example the significance of which seems to us to lie in
the fact that the deprivation there suffered by the employee is out of all proportion to the
d benefits which he derives from the employment. *Jarrold v Boustead* shows that the natural
presumption that the prospective employment is the real source of any payment made
by an employer at the commencement of an employment may be rebutted if the
employment involves for the employee a loss of a substantial personal right. That
decision may represent something of an extension of the principle found in cases like
Hose v Warwick in that the right need not be of a commercial nature and its loss need not
e enure to the benefit of the employer. The losses suffered by the taxpayers in the
footballers' cases differed somewhat in quantitative terms (the loss of amateur status
clearly had more far-reaching effects for Mr Boustead than for the others) but the quality
of the loss was the same for all: it was a loss of status and of the personal rights flowing
therefrom.

12. In our view, *Jarrold v Boustead* is only of limited assistance to us in deciding the
f present case, and that in a negative sense. In our judgment, the situation here is very
different in its essentials. As may happen in the course of anyone's career (especially
perhaps during the early years) Mr Wells was faced with a choice: in his case, between
private practice and an accountancy career in commerce. Each path had its attractions,
but the choice of one would probably mean that the opportunities which would or might
arise under the other would be missed. (We say 'probably' because we have some
g difficulty in accepting that Mr Wells's leaving private practice when he did was quite as
irrevocable a step as he seemed to think it was.) The company's initial offer as set out in
Mr Damar's letter of 12 August 1977 was a tempting one because the salary compared
very favourably with his existing salary, and a car was added. The latter was a 'perk' not
at that time generally offered to employees in accountancy private practice. It also
appeared that employment with the company would give him considerable scope in his
h chosen specialism, work with computers. But Mr Wells was already in private practice,
so acceptance of the offer would involve change and it gives us no surprise that he should
seek some extra inducement to make that change. Furthermore, Mr Wells told us that
his wife received the company's offer with a certain lack of enthusiasm; that we think
provided an additional reason for looking for something more.

13. The most natural construction of Mr Gilbert's letter of 26 October 1977 which
j contained the company's revised offer is that the sum of £10,000 constituted a
straightforward inducement to Mr Wells to change his job. In our view, Mr Wells's letter
of 9 September 1977 (which may be regarded as explaining the reference to 'inducement'
in Mr Gilbert's letter) is entirely consistent with that construction, which we hold to be
the correct one. This is not a case in which any substantial rights have been given up,
such as might encourage the view that there was some consideration distinct from the

employment with the company for the £10,000 payment. We appreciate that, in the abstract, the word 'inducement' may (as Pennycuick J indicated in *Jarrold v Boustead*) be somewhat ambiguous but it is generally understood in a sense which results in the payment falling on the s 181 side of the line. Speaking of the payments with which *Hochstrasser v Mayes* [1958] 1 All ER 369 at 377, [1959] Ch 22 at 37 was concerned Upjohn J said: '[The housing agreement] formed no part of his contract of service, nor was it an inducement held out to him to enter into the company's employment . . .' In our view, the present, by contrast, *is* such a case. We find that the £10,000 payment was properly chargeable to tax under s 181.

14. Having arrived at a decision adverse to the company on s 181 we are not called on to express a concluded view on the alternative charge under s 187, and we do not propose to do so. The arguments which Mr Richards addressed to us on that section were entirely directed to the construction of the section: we understood him to accept that, if literally construed, the section applied on the facts of the case to the lump sum payment made to Mr Wells. Shortly stated, Mr Richards argued that the terms of s 187 were so wide that they were, if read literally, liable to bring into charge payments which were so remote from what might be described as 'mainstream Sch E' that Parliament cannot have intended them to be within the section. He accordingly contended that, as a matter of necessity, either (a) the words in sub-s (2) 'directly or indirectly in consideration or in consequence of, or otherwise in connection with, the termination of the . . . employment' do not include payments which are not in any way rewards for past services but are merely payments made on the occasion of the employee's departure or (b) the words in sub-s (1) 'or by any other person' should be limited to include only persons connected in some way with the employer (eg, in the case of a company employer, its holding company).

15. As at present advised we are not persuaded by the argument. The charge under s 187 is entirely distinct from that under s 181; it was plainly designed to cover cases not falling within s 181 and it would not seem right to import into it a 'remuneration' flavour which could tend to render it otiose. While we suspect that the section was not designed (at any rate primarily) for cases such as the present, Mr Richards's second contention would seem to involve a substantial addition of words to sub-s (1) and such emendation of the statute, however well intentioned, is not permissible (cf *Vestey v IRC (Nos 1 and 2)* [1979] 3 All ER 976 at 982–983, [1980] AC 1148 at 1169–1170 per Lord Wilberforce). Finally, it seems to us that the force of any argument of necessity is not a little reduced by the exemptions and reliefs provided by s 188. We note in particular sub-s (3) of the latter section, which must in practice remove from the charge to tax most of the cases which would fall within the words but not perhaps the real aim of s 187. We might go further and observe that if s 187 should be read as to ally it closely to s 181 it is not very easy to see the justification for that particular relief.

16. We understand that the sum of tax claimed in the determination under appeal may require adjustment and we therefore uphold the determination in principle, on the footing that the £10,000 paid by the company to Mr Wells in January 1977 was properly chargeable to income tax under Case I of Sch E. We adjourn the hearing for the parties to reach agreement, if possible, on the appropriate figure.

Ian Richards for the company.
Robert Carnwath for the Crown.

Cur adv vult

17 November. The following judgment was delivered.

WARNER J. This is an appeal by a company called Glantre Engineering Ltd (the company) against a decision of the Special Commissioners upholding in principle a determination made by the inspector of taxes under reg 29 of the Income Tax (Employments) Regulations 1973, SI 1973/334.

Shortly stated, the questions for the decision of the commissioners were (1) whether a
a sum of £10,000 paid by the company in January 1978 to Mr F W Wells was income of
his, chargeable to income tax under Case I of Sch E and (2) if that sum was not income so
chargeable, whether it was a payment chargeable to tax under Sch E by virtue of s 187 of
the Income and Corporation Taxes Act 1970.

The commissioners decided that the payment was chargeable to tax under Case I of
Sch E. They were accordingly not called on to express a concluded view on the alternative
b charge under s 187, and they did not do so, though they did comment on some of the
arguments that had been presented to them on that section.

Having heard argument on the first question, I formed the view that it was open to
the commissioners, on the facts found by them, to reach the conclusion that they did on
that question and that it was not, therefore, necessary for me to hear argument on the
second question. I took time, however, to formulate my reasons for taking that view.

c I need not, I think, rehearse the facts about the history of the company, about Mr
Wells's career down to August 1977 and about the relationship between Mr Wells and
the company down to that time, which are set out in the written decision of the
commissioners annexed to the case stated. That is not to say, of course, that I do not have
those facts well in mind.

The crucial facts about the making of the agreement under which the sum of £10,000
d was paid to Mr Wells are these. After Mr Gilbert's visit to Mr Wells in early August 1977,
a letter dated 12 August 1977 was sent to Mr Wells on behalf of the company offering
him full-time employment with the company as financial director from 1 January 1978.
The letter went on: 'In outline the applicable terms and conditions would be as follows:
a) Salary: £9000 per annum. Reviewable annually. b) A company car of nominal value
£2750–£3000 would be provided for your use. c) Usual travel and entertainment
e expenses incurred would be reimbursed.' There followed further paragraphs lettered (d)
to (i) setting out proposed terms as to what Mr Wells's duties would be and as to other
benefits that he might earn. The letter concluded: 'We look forward to receiving your
early response to this proposal.'

Mr Wells replied on 9 September:

f 'Thank you for your letter of 12 August 1977, which I found awaiting me last
week on my return to Paris. Whilst I appreciate entirely that the proposed salary is
more than generous for the duties involved, I do feel that in accepting any full-time
employment with [the company] and of course leaving Whinney Murray Ernst and
Ernst, I am sacrificing certain benefits with them—professional status as a Chartered
Accountant in a leading International accountancy firm, the possibility of partnership
status within several years and also the certainty of security in the future. On joining
g [the company], I surrender the professional status of an independent Chartered
Accountant, I lose forever the chance of partnership in London or Paris, and I am
joining a company which is albeit highly successful at the moment, but it has only
been running three years under its present management, and can offer no long-term
security whatsoever, and in the event of its ceasing trading would have no assets at
h all to compensate those employees made redundant. In view of these factors, I do
feel that it would not be unreasonable to be offered some financial inducement to
leave Whinney Murray Ernst and Ernst. Before considering further your offer, I
will be glad to hear your views on these thoughts.'

Mr Wells's suggestion that he should receive some financial inducement to leave
Whinney Murray Ernst & Ernst was the subject of a subsequent telephone discussion
j between him and Mr Gilbert, during the course of which a sum of £10,000 was arrived
at. Shortly afterwards, on 26 October 1977, Mr Gilbert wrote to Mr Wells as follows:

'Thank you for your letter of 9th September 1977 in reply to Amjad's letter
offering you full-time employment with [the company]. We understand your
concern about giving up the security of working with an international firm of
Chartered Accountants, and consequently we are prepared to make a revised offer

being: 1. A lump sum of £10,000 as an inducement to leave Whinney Murray Ernst and Ernst. 2. A salary of £9,000 a year consisting of £8,000 p.a. paid monthly and a bonus of £1,000 after 12 months. All other conditions of employment to remain as per our offer of 12th August 1977. I look forward to receiving your further comments on our proposals.'

Mr Wells accepted the company's revised offer by telephone on the day following his receipt of that letter.

The Special Commissioners found that the factors referred to by Mr Wells in his letter of 9 September 1977 constituted his motives for securing what he described as 'some financial inducement to leave Whinney Murray Ernst and Ernst', and that Mr Wells genuinely believed that the disadvantages he referred to would flow from his changing the course of his career. They also found that, as had been stated in Mr Gilbert's letter, the company offered, and subsequently paid, the sum of £10,000 in order to meet Mr Wells's feelings in the matter as expressed by Mr Wells in his letter. They included in para 7 of the case stated this somewhat cryptic sentence: 'We found both on the terms of his letter and on his oral evidence that he sought the additional money more as a protection against the risks involved in the move than as compensation for the loss of advantages.' That seems to mean that they thought that the loss of security was a more important factor in Mr Wells's mind than the loss of status as a chartered accountant in private practice or the loss of the prospect of a partnership. That would seem to be borne out by Mr Gilbert's letter, which, of the three factors, mentions only 'your concern about giving up the security of working with an international firm of Chartered Accountants'.

At all events, Mr Wells left Whinney Murray Ernst & Ernst at the end of 1977 and took up his new post with the company on 1 January 1978. The agreed sum of £10,000 was paid to him by the company during the same month. The change in the place of Mr Wells's employment from Paris to Wembley, where the company's offices were, naturally involved a domestic move. Mr Wells had, however, kept the house in London in which he had lived before moving to Paris, and no problem arose over rehousing himself and his family. Mr Wells hoped that the company would continue to prosper and that his full-time appointment with it would be of a permanent nature. Unfortunately, the company failed to obtain certain contracts in 1979–80, and its results for that year were very poor. The staff was reduced and Mr Wells's post was abolished at the end of August 1980. It was not suggested to him that the £10,000, or any part of it, should be repaid to the company. Mr Wells is now a self-employed consultant in the field of computer accountancy. He has retained his directorship of the company.

In setting out their reasons for their decision, the Special Commissioners acknowledged that a payment made in accordance with a term in a contract of service does not inevitably partake of the nature of remuneration. They cited *Hose v Warwick (Inspector of Taxes)* (1946) 27 TC 459 as affording an illustration of that. They considered that *Jarrold (Inspector of Taxes) v Boustead* [1964] 3 All ER 76, [1964] 1 WLR 1357 was, of the decided cases, the nearest to the present case. Counsel for the taxpayer company submitted that *Pritchard (Inspector of Taxes) v Arundale* [1971] 3 All ER 1011, [1972] Ch 229, which he told me had been cited to the Special Commissioners but which they did not refer to in their decision, was nearer. Counsel for the Crown suggested that the reason why the Special Commissioners did not think so was that, in *Pritchard v Arundale*, the payment, or more precisely the transfer of shares, had been made not by the employer but by a third party. At all events, the Special Commissioners distinguished *Jarrold v Boustead*.

They expressed their conclusion in para 12 of their decision in these terms:

'As may happen in the course of anyone's career (especially perhaps during the early years) Mr Wells was faced with a choice: in his case, between private practice and an accountancy career in commerce. Each path had its attractions, but the choice of one would probably mean that the opportunities which would or might arise under the other would be missed. (We say "probably" because we have some difficulty in accepting that Mr Wells's leaving private practice when he did was quite as irrevocable a step as he seemed to think it was.)'

Pausing there, counsel for the company criticised the Special Commissioners for
a having, in that parenthesis, substituted what he called their own 'value judgment' for the
uncontradicted evidence of Mr Wells. I think, however, for my part, that the Special
Commissioners were entitled to use their own judgment in assessing the weight of Mr
Wells's evidence. In any case, I doubt if what they said in that parenthesis played a crucial
part in their decision.

The Special Commissioners continued:

b   'The company's initial offer as set out in Mr Damar's letter of 12 August 1977 was
a tempting one because the salary compared very favourably with his existing salary,
and a car was added. The latter was a "perk" not at that time generally offered to
employees in accountancy private practice. It also appeared that employment with
the company would give him considerable scope in his chosen specialism, work
with computers. But Mr Wells was already in private practice, so acceptance of the
c offer would involve change and it gives us no surprise that he should seek some
extra inducement to make that change. Furthermore, Mr Wells told us that his wife
received the company's offer with a certain lack of enthusiasm; that we think
provided an additional reason for looking for something more. The most natural
construction of Mr Gilbert's letter of 26 October 1977 which contained the
company's revised offer is that the sum of £10,000 constituted a straightforward
d inducement to Mr Wells to change his job. In our view, Mr Wells's letter of 9
September 1977 (which may be regarded as explaining the reference to "inducement"
in Mr Gilbert's letter) is entirely consistent, with that construction which we hold to
be the correct one. This is not a case in which any substantial rights have been given
up, such as might encourage the view that there was some consideration distinct
from the employment with the company for the £10,000 payment. We appreciate
e that, in the abstract, the word "inducement" may (as Pennycuick J indicated in
Jarrold v Boustead) be somewhat ambiguous but it is generally understood in a sense
which results in the payment falling on the s 181 side of the line [s 181 being, of
course, the section of the 1970 Act that contains Sch E]. Speaking of the payments
with which *Hochstrasser v Mayes* [1958] 1 All ER 369 at 377, [1959] Ch 22 at 37 was
concerned Upjohn J said: "[The housing agreement] formed no part of his contract
f of service, nor was it an inducement held out to him to enter into the company's
employment . . .." In our view, the present, by contrast, *is* such a case.'

The essence of the attack on that by counsel for the taxpayer company was that the
Special Commissioners' view that the sum of £10,000 constituted a straightforward
inducement to Mr Wells to change his job was inconsistent with the primary facts that
they had found. The true conclusion from those primary facts, counsel submitted, was
g that that sum was paid pursuant to an agreement to compensate Mr Wells for the losses
he would suffer in putting himself in a position to enter the full-time employment of
the company, those losses being the loss of his professional status as a chartered accountant
in a leading international accountancy firm, the loss of the prospect of a partnership in
that firm and the loss of the certainty of security in the future. That agreement, counsel
for the company submitted, was severable from the agreement under which Mr Wells
h was to render services to the company, for which the £9,000 a year, and the other
benefits that had originally been offered to him, were, as Mr Wells himself had
acknowledged, already ample reward.

In support of those submissions counsel for the company put forward an argument
which had, if I may so express it, a warp and a weft. The warp was derived from the well-
known passage in the judgment of Upjohn J in *Hochstrasser (Inspector of Taxes) v Mayes*
j [1958] 1 All ER 369 at 374–375, [1959] Ch 22 at 33, which was approved, with an
immaterial reservation, by Viscount Simonds in the same case (see [1959] 3 All ER 817
at 821, [1960] AC 376 at 388), and which has been cited many times since. That passage
is as follows:

    'In my judgment, the authorities show this, that it is a question to be answered in
the light of the particular facts of every case whether or not a particular payment is

or is not a profit arising from the employment. Disregarding entirely contracts for
full consideration in money or money's worth and personal presents, in my *a*
judgment not every payment made to an employee is necessarily made to him as a
profit arising from his employment. Indeed, in my judgment, the authorities show
that, to be a profit arising from the employment, the payment must be made in
reference to the service the employee renders by virtue of his office, and it must be
something in the nature of a reward for services past, present or future.'

Counsel for the company relied on that passage as meaning that a payment made to an *b*
employee, in order to be a profit arising from his employment, must be in the nature of
a reward for services rendered or to be rendered by him by virtue of his employment.

One must, however, in my opinion, always bear in mind that, in tax cases, it is the
words of the relevant statutes that have to be interpreted and applied, not the words of
passages in judgments, which, however eminent may have been those who delivered
them, are inevitably related to the facts of the cases in which they were delivered and to *c*
the arguments presented to the court in those cases. As Lord Reid said in *Laidler v Perry*
(Inspector of Taxes) [1965] 2 All ER 121 at 124, [1966] AC 16 at 30:

'There is a wealth of authority on this matter and various glosses on or paraphrases
of the words in the Act of 1952 appear in judicial opinions, including speeches in
this House. No doubt they were helpful in the circumstances of the cases in which *d*
they were used, but in the end we must always return to the words in the statute . . .'

Later in the same speech Lord Reid said of the passage in the judgment of Upjohn J in
Hochstrasser v Mayes on which counsel for the taxpayer company relies ([1965] 2 All ER
121 at 125, [1966] AC 16 at 31):

'. . . I think that, although the word "reward" has been used in many of the cases, *e*
it is not apt to include all the cases which can fall within the statutory words. To
give only one instance, it is clear that a sum given to an employee in the hope or
expectation that the gift will produce good service by him in future is taxable; but
one can hardly be said to reward a man for something which he has not yet done
and may never do.'

Lord Reid said that because, on the facts of the case before him, the phrase 'reward for *f*
services' was an inappropriate paraphrase of the relevant words of the statute.

The relevant statutory provisions here are, first, those of Sch E itself contained in
s 181(1) of the 1970 Act and, second, those of s 183(1) of that Act in so far as they define
the expression 'emoluments' in Sch E. The relevant words of Sch E are:

'1. Tax under this Schedule shall be charged in respect of any office or employment *g*
on emoluments therefrom . . .'

The emoluments, in order to be chargeable, have to fall under one or more of the Cases
of Sch E, but it is not in dispute here that the sum of £10,000, if it constituted
emoluments from Mr Wells's office or employment with the company, fell under Case
I. The definition of 'emoluments' in s 183(1) is: *h*

'. . . the expression "emoluments" shall include all salaries, fees, wages, perquisites
and profits whatsoever.'

Thus the question in this case is not, strictly speaking, whether the sum of £10,000
was paid to Mr Wells as a reward for services to be rendered by him to the company but
whether that sum constituted an emolument, in the wide sense indicated by s 183(1), *j*
from his full-time employment by the company.

The weft of counsel's argument was derived from the three authorities that I referred
to earlier, namely *Hose v Warwick, Jarrold v Boustead* and *Pritchard v Arundale*. Counsel
submitted that those authorities established that, where at the inception of a person's
employment a payment was made to him to compensate him for an identifiable loss that

he would incur as a result of taking up the employment, that payment was not an
a emolument from the employment. Counsel for the company went so far as to say that
that proposition would apply if a lump sum were paid to the person in question in order
to induce him to move his residence from an attractive area to a less attractive one so as
to enable him to take up the employment, though the proposition would not apply if
the inducement to him to do that took the form of a larger salary. In my judgment, the
authorities do not support so general a proposition.

b In *Hose v Warwick* the payment of £30,000 was made to Mr Hose as compensation for
his relinquishing his personal business connection which had been professionally valued
at that sum. In fairness to counsel for the company, he conceded that the facts of that
case were significantly different from those of this case.

Jarrold v Boustead is, I think, best understood if one contrasts the judgment of
Pennycuick J at first instance with the judgments in the Court of Appeal, particularly
c that of Lord Denning MR. Pennycuick J held that it was not permissible, in ascertaining
the consideration for which the signing-on fee of £3,000 that was in question there had
been paid, to look outside the terms of the agreement under which it was paid. On that
footing there was no escape from the conclusion that the consideration for the signing-
on fee was the obligation undertaken by Mr Boustead to play Rugby football for the Hull
Football Club. The Court of Appeal, however, held that, to ascertain the nature of the
d signing-on fee, it was necessary to look also at the byelaws of the Rugby League. When
that was done, it became clear that the signing-on fee was compensation to Mr Boustead
for relinquishing for ever his amateur status and the advantages that flowed from that.
Byelaw 24 of the Rugby League provided:

'A player who relinquishes his amateur status is permitted to receive a signing-on
fee from the club with which he first registers as a professional player. No club shall
e pay, or offer to pay a signing-on fee to a player who has previously been registered
as a professional player with the League.'

Thus it was open to the commissioners who heard that case to hold, as they did hold, that
the £3,000 was not an emolument of Mr Boustead from his employment by the Hull
Football Club. It was a once-for-all inducement to him to give up a status that precluded
f him from being employed by any club in the league.

In his judgment, Lord Denning MR mentioned a hypothetical case that had been
discussed during the argument. He said ([1964] 3 All ER 76 at 80, [1964] 1 WLR 1357
at 1365):

'Suppose there was a man who was an expert organist but was very fond of
playing golf on Sundays. He is asked to become the organist of the parish church
g for the ensuing seven months at a salary of £10 a month. It is expressly stipulated
by this strange parish council that, if he takes up the post, he is to give up Sunday
golf for the rest of his life. Thereupon he says that, if he is to give up golf, he wants
an extra £500; and they agree to pay it. In such a case the £500 is not a payment for
his services as an organist for seven months. It is a payment for relinquishing what
he considered to be an advantage to him.'

h That is why, of course, counsel for the company placed so much emphasis on the fact
that, in the present case, Mr Wells was giving up irrevocably, or so at all events he
thought, the status of a chartered accountant in private practice. But, as I have already
indicated, the Special Commissioners appear to have taken the view that that was a less
important factor than the loss of security that Mr Wells would suffer as a result of leaving
j the employment of Whinney Murray Ernst & Ernst.

So I come to *Pritchard v Arundale*, with which counsel for the company submitted that
the present case was 'on all fours'. That, certainly, is not so. In the first place, as I have
already mentioned, *Pritchard v Arundale* was a case not of a payment by the employer but
of a transfer of shares by a third party. Second, Mr Arundale was not merely changing
from one employment to another. He was exchanging the status of a partner, indeed a

senior partner, in a firm of chartered accountants for that of joint managing director of, and shareholder in, a company. Third, as Megarry J pointed out, the tripartite agreement *a* under which Mr Arundale entered the service of the company and received the shares was so framed that he was entitled to the transfer of the shares 'forthwith' after the execution of the agreement but was not to enter into the service of the company until some months later. He might therefore have died after receiving the shares but before entering on his office or employment with the company. That fact explains, I think, a passage towards the end of judgment of Megarry J, by which I was at one time troubled, *b* in which he drew a distinction between a payment made for undertaking an office or employment and a payment flowing from the office or employment, the latter being within Sch E but the former not.

Indeed, perceiving that feature of *Pritchard v Arundale*, counsel for the company boldly submitted that in the present case Mr Wells would have been entitled, under the agreement between him and the taxpayer company, to receive the £10,000 even though *c* he never entered the service of the company, provided that he left the employment of Whinney Murray Ernst & Ernst. That, it seems to me, cannot be right. If Mr Wells had left the employment of Whinney Murray Ernst & Ernst, taken the £10,000 and then gone to work, say, for another firm of chartered accountants, I do not doubt that any court before which subsequent litigation between him and the company came would have held him to be in breach of the agreement. *d*

It seems to me that the ratio decidendi of *Jarrold v Boustead* and of *Pritchard v Arundale* is that the quality of a payment made to an employee at the inception of his employment, that is to say whether or not it constitutes an emolument from his employment, is essentially a question of fact to be decided by the appellate commissioners on a consideration of all the evidence before them, and that, on the familiar principles laid down in *Edwards (Inspector of Taxes) v Bairstow* [1955] 3 All ER 48, [1956] AC 14, their *e* determination is not to be set aside by the court unless it is inconsistent with the only reasonable conclusion to be drawn from that evidence. I cannot hold that, in the present case, the only reasonable conclusion to be drawn from the evidence before the Special Commissioners was, as contended by counsel for the company, that the payment of £10,000 to Mr Wells was severable from the other benefits to which he became entitled under the agreement between himself and the company, and was other than an added *f* inducement to him to change his job and enter the full-time employment of the company. If it was the latter, it was, so it seems to me, an emolument from that employment within the meaning of Sch E.

Appeal dismissed.

g

Solicitors: *Crossman Block & Keith* (for the company); *Solicitor of Inland Revenue.*

Nirmala Harlow   Barrister.

American Express Co and another v British Airways Board

QUEEN'S BENCH DIVISION

LLOYD J

9, 10, 11, 24 NOVEMBER 1982

Post Office – Carriage of mail – Exclusion of liability – Extent of exclusion – Liability in bailment – Carriage of postal packet overseas by agent of Post Office – Packet stolen while in custody of agent – Statutory immunity of Post Office and persons engaged in carriage of mail from 'proceedings in tort' for loss or damage to post – Whether 'proceedings in tort' including action in bailment – Post Office Act 1969, s 29.

Post Office – Registered postal packet – Carriage overseas – Carriage by air – Carriage of postal packet by agent of Post Office – Statutory immunity of Post Office and persons engaged in carriage of mail from 'proceedings in tort' for loss or damage to post – International convention imposing liability on international carriers of goods by air for loss of registered baggage – Whether liability of carriers of goods by air prevailing over immunity of Post Office and persons engaged in carriage of mail – Whether 'proceedings in tort' including proceedings in respect of liability as carrier of goods by air – Carriage by Air Act 1961, Sch 1, art 18 – Post Office Act 1969, s 29.

In February 1978 the plaintiffs handed over a postal packet containing travellers cheques worth $US40,000 to the Post Office in Brighton for transmission to Swaziland. The Post Office tendered the packet in a sealed airmail bag to the defendants, an air carrier, at Heathrow Airport for carriage by air to Swaziland. In the course of loading at the airport, an employee of the defendants stole the packet and it was never recovered. The plaintiffs sued the defendants for loss of the packet. The defendants admitted the loss but claimed that they were immune from liability by virtue of s 29(3)[a] of the Post Office Act 1969, which provided that 'No person engaged in or about the carriage of mail ... shall be subject ... to any civil liability for any loss or damage in the case of which liability of the Post Office therefor is excluded ...' Section 29(1) of the 1969 Act provided that 'no proceedings in tort shall lie against the Post Office in respect of any loss or damage suffered by any person'. A preliminary point arose whether if the Post Office had been sued the proceedings would have been 'proceedings in tort' within s 29(1) and, if so, whether the defendants could take advantage of the vicarious immunity provided by s 29(3). The plaintiffs contended (i) that they were suing not in tort but for breach of bailment, and that nothing in s 29(1) excluded liability for breach of bailment as distinct from liability in tort, (ii) that the defendants were subject to a statutory liability as an air carrier for 'damage sustained in the event of the ... loss of ... any registered baggage or any cargo, if the occurrence which caused the damage so sustained took place during the carriage by air', by virtue of art 18[b] of the Warsaw Convention, as amended at The Hague in 1955 and as set out in Sch 1 to the Carriage by Air Act 1961 and applied to the carriage of mail and postal packets by the Carriage by Air Acts (Application of Provisions) Order 1967, and (iii) that s 29(3) did not exclude the defendant's statutory liability under art 18 which existed independently of any liability which might exist in tort or contract.

Held – The defendants were entitled to take advantage of the vicarious immunity provided by s 29(3) of the 1969 Act, for the following reasons—

(1) On the true construction of the 1969 Act the Post Office was entitled to immunity under s 29(1) because to hold otherwise would mean that the Post Office could not be liable in tort for conversion or negligence but could be liable for those same torts in bailment and would also mean that the Post Office's liability for loss or damage to

---

a　Section 29, so far as material, is set out at p 559 *b c*, post

b　Article 18, so far as material is set out at p 562 *f*, post

registered inland post was limited under s 30 of the 1969 Act whereas its liability for loss
or damage to all other post was unlimited. It was to be presumed that Parliament did not   *a*
intend such absurd results when enacting s 29 (see p 560 *h j*, p 561 *a* and *f* and p 564 *c*,
post); *Triefus & Co Ltd v Post Office* [1957] 2 All ER 387 and dictum of Geoffrey Lane LJ
in *Harold Stephen & Co Ltd v Post Office* [1978] 1 All ER at 944 followed.

(2) Assuming that art 18 of the Warsaw Convention created a statutory cause of action,
it did not follow that the cause of action was outside the protection conferred by s 29 of
the 1969 Act. The statutory cause of action against the carrier was one which, if   *b*
proceedings were brought against the Post Office, could properly be described as
'proceedings in tort', within s 29(1), since breach of statutory duty was normally treated
as part of the general law of tort and the fact that the breach of statutory duty could not
be equated with any particular tort, such as negligence, did not prevent it coming under
same general heading of tort. Accordingly, the phrase 'proceedings in tort' in s 29(1) was
used in the general sense, and included breach of statutory duty if the remedy could   *c*
properly be described as being tortious in character. It therefore included breaches of the
statutory duty imposed on the defendants under art 18 (see p 563 *d e* and *j* to p 564 *c*,
post).

Notes

For exclusion of liability in relation to postal services, see 36 Halsbury's Laws (4th edn)   *d*
para 686.

For the duty of care and diligence of a bailee for valuable consideration, see 2 ibid para
1539, and for cases on the subject, see 3 Digest (Reissue) 436–440, 2953–2978.

For the Carriage by Air Act 1961, Sch 1, art 18, see 2 Halsbury's Statutes (3rd edn) 616.

For the Post Office Act 1969, ss 29, 30, see 25 ibid 502, 503.

For the Carriage by Air Acts (Application of Provisions) Order 1967, see 3 Halsbury's   *e*
Statutory Instruments (4th reissue) 40.

Cases referred to in judgment

Benjamins v British European Airways (1978) 572 F 2d 913.

Building and Civil Engineering Holidays Scheme Management Ltd v Post Office [1965] 1 All ER
163, [1966] 1 QB 247, [1965] 2 WLR 72, CA, 37(1) Digest (Reissue) 350, 2218.   *f*

Komlos v Compagnie Nationale Air France (1953) 209 F 2d 436.

Morris v C W Martin & Sons Ltd [1965] 2 All ER 725, [1966] 1 QB 716, [1965] 3 WLR
276, 3 Digest (Reissue) 436, 2958.

Noel v Linea Aeropostal Venezolana (1957) 247 F 2d 677.

Stephen (Harold) & Co Ltd v Post Office [1978] 1 All ER 939, [1977] 1 WLR 1172, CA, 37(1)
Digest (Reissue) 353, 2229.

Triefus & Co Ltd v Post Office [1957] 2 All ER 387, [1957] 2 QB 352, [1957] 3 WLR 1, CA.   *g*

Whitfield v Lord le Despencer (1778) 2 Cowp 754, 98 ER 1344, 37(1) Digest (Reissue) 350,
2216.

Winkfield, The [1902] P 42, [1900–3] All ER Rep 346, CA, 37(1) Digest (Reissue) 360,
2275.

Preliminary issue   *h*

By a writ issued on 21 February 1980 the plaintiffs, American Express Co, American
Express International Corp and Standard Bank of Swaziland, claimed against the
defendants, the British Airways Board, inter alia, damages for the loss of a postal packet
of travellers cheques having a total face value of $US40,000. On 8 July 1981 the
defendants served a defence claiming immunity from proceedings by virtue of s 29 of
the Post Office Act 1969. On 21 May 1982 Parker J ordered that the question or issue of   *j*
the liability of the defendants be tried as a preliminary issue. The facts are set out in the
judgment.

Geoffrey Kinley for the plaintiffs.
John Wilmers QC and *Robert S Webb* for the defendants.

Cur adv vult

24 November. The following judgment was delivered.

a

LLOYD J. In this case the plaintiffs, American Express Co and American Express International Banking Corp, sue the defendants, British Airways Board, for loss of a postal packet containing travellers cheques. The face value of the travellers cheques was $US40,000. The defendants admit the loss, but say that they are protected by s 29(3) of the Post Office Act 1969. Section 29(3) provides:

b

'No person engaged in or about the carriage of mail and no officer, servant, agent or sub-contractor of such person shall be subject except at the suit of the Post Office to any civil liability for any loss or damage in the case of which liability of the Post Office therefor is excluded by subsection (1) of this section.'

Section 29(1) provides:

c

'Save as provided by the next following section, no proceedings in tort shall lie against the Post Office in respect of any loss or damage suffered by any person by reason of—(a) anything done or omitted to be done in relation to anything in the post or omission to carry out arrangements for the collection of anything to be conveyed by post . . .'

d

The 'next following section' referred to in s 29(1) is s 30. Section 30 imposes a limited liability on the Post Office in respect of registered inland packets, and is of no relevance on the facts of this case.

Thus the sole question is whether if the Post Office had been sued in this case the proceedings would have been proceedings in tort, within the meaning of s 29(1), and, if so, whether the defendants can take advantage of the vicarious immunity provided by s 29(3).

e

The facts are set out in an agreed statement of facts. They are briefly as follows. On 22 February 1978 the plaintiffs handed over a postal packet containing the travellers cheques to the Post Office in Brighton. I need not distinguish between the first and second named plaintiffs. The packet was addressed to the Standard Bank in Swaziland. On 22 or 23 February the Post Office tendered the packet in a sealed airmail bag to the defendants at

f

Heathrow for carriage to Johannesburg and onward carriage to Swaziland. The defendants employed a man called Osborne as a loader at Heathrow. In the course of loading the aircraft, Osborne stole the packet. It was never recovered. Two years later, in February 1980, Osborne pleaded guilty at the Old Bailey to theft contrary to s 1 of the Theft Act 1968. Two other men employed with Osborne as loaders at Heathrow pleaded guilty to charges of handling.

g

The facts are thus extremely simple. As to the law, I was told that the case raised questions of great importance and would undoubtedly be taken all the way to the House of Lords if necessary. A large number of authorities, English and American, were cited. At the end of it all, it seems to me that the law on the point is almost as simple as the facts.

The first point taken by counsel on behalf of the plaintiffs is that though the plaintiffs

h

could undoubtedly have sued in tort for conversion, and been met by a defence under s 29(3), they are in fact suing for breach of bailment. Nothing in s 29(1) excludes liability for breach of bailment, as distinct from liability in tort. Accordingly, the defendants are not entitled to vicarious immunity under s 29(3).

Counsel for the plaintiffs referred to a number of famous cases, including The Winkfield [1902] P 42, [1900–3] All ER Rep 346, in order to establish the proposition that

j

the Post Office were bailees of the package and the defendants sub-bailees. But that proposition was conceded by counsel for the defendants at the outset. Counsel for the defendants further conceded that the defendants owed the same duty to the plaintiffs as if they were bailees for reward.

Next, counsel for the plaintiffs referred me to Professor Sir Percy Winfield's book on The Province of the Law of Tort (1931) and the judgment of Lord Denning MR in Building and Civil Engineering Holidays Scheme Management Ltd v Post Office [1965] 1 All ER 163,

[1966] 1 QB 247, in order to establish that an action in bailment is something separate
and distinct from an action in tort or contract.

In the *Building and Civil Engineering* case [1965] 1 All ER 163 at 167, [1966] 1 QB 247
at 261 Lord Denning MR said:

> 'An action against a bailee can often be put, not as an action in contract, nor in
> tort, but as an action on its own, sui generis, arising out of the possession had by the
> bailee of the goods,'

and then Lord Denning MR refered to *Winfield on the Province of the Law of Tort* p 100 and
Fifoot's History of the Common Law (1949) p 24.

Again, there was not much dispute about that proposition.

The real dispute in the case is whether, granted that an action in bailment is sui
generis, proceedings in bailment against the Post Office are nevertheless excluded by
s 29(1) of the 1969 Act. Counsel for the plaintiffs submitted that this is still an open
question and should be answered in favour of the plaintiffs. I cannot agree.

In *Triefus & Co Ltd v Post Office* [1957] 2 All ER 387, [1957] 2 QB 352 two postal packets
containing diamonds were stolen by an employee of the Post Office. The plaintiffs, who
were the owners of the two packets, claimed against the Post Office, inter alia, for breach
of contract of carriage and breach of bailment. According to the statement of facts (see
[1957] 2 QB 352 at 353), the plaintiffs alleged in their pleading that on two dates—

> 'they had handed to the Post Office at Hatton Garden two postal packets containing
> diamonds valued at £3,380 and £17,998 respectively, for carriage and transmission
> to New Zealand, the packets being properly packed, secured, registered, declared,
> and in all respects in accordance with the appropriate Post Office regulations, all
> proper dues, charges and duties thereon being paid; that the Post Office had accepted
> the packets and thereby entered into contracts of carriage, or alternatively of
> bailment, with the company, the terms of which included, inter alia, that they
> would act reasonably in connection with the carriage and transmission, use care and
> diligence, employ only adequate post officers, carry and transmit the packets by an
> efficient and appropriate system, and not lose the packets. They alleged that the Post
> Office were in breach of each of those terms, whereby the packets had been mislaid
> or stolen, and that they had thereby suffered loss or damage.'

The Court of Appeal held on a preliminary question of law that the action must fail
on the ground stated by Lord Mansfield in *Whitfield v Lord le Despencer* (1778) 2 Cowp
754, 98 ER 1344. Both Hodson and Parker LJJ referred to s 9 of the Crown Proceedings
Act 1947, which is the lineal predecessor of s 29 and which, like s 29, excluded liability
in tort. Parker LJ said ([1957] 2 All ER 387 at 394, [1957] 2 QB 352 at 368):

> 'It is true that that section is clearly dealing with tort; but, for myself, I find it
> inconceivable that if Parliament thought that there was any doubt as to the
> contractual position (or, rather, the absence of a contract) it would not clearly have
> been dealt with in the Act.'

Adopting the same language, it seems to me inconceivable that if Parliament thought
there was any doubt as to the possible liability of the Post Office in bailment, as distinct
from tort, it would not have been dealt with in the 1969 Act.

To my mind it would make nonsense of s 29 of the 1969 Act to hold that the Post
Office can be liable for breach of bailment. As explained by Diplock LJ in *Morris v C W
Martin & Sons Ltd* [1965] 2 All ER 725, [1966] 1 QB 716, the two most obvious duties
arising out of the relationship of bailor and bailee are the duties on the part of the bailee
(1) to take reasonable care of the goods and (2) not to convert them. Both negligence and
conversion are, of course, typical torts. The advantage to the plaintiff in laying his action
in bailment is that it shifts the burden of proof. It is for the bailee to explain how the loss
occurred. In that sense the plaintiff's task is easier in bailment, the defendant's more
difficult. It would be a curious result if Parliament had, by s 29(1), given the Post Office
full protection in negligence and conversion where, as defendants, their task is easier, but

not in bailment where, for the reasons I have just mentioned, their task is more difficult.
a Furthermore, by s 30 Parliament has imposed on the Post Office, as I have already mentioned, a limited liability in respect of loss or damage of registered inland packets. It would be an even more curious result if it had left the Post Office subject to unlimited liability in the case of all other post, by allowing the plaintiff to adopt the simple expedient of suing in bailment.

In *Harold Stephen & Co Ltd v Post Office* [1978] 1 All ER 939, [1977] 1 WLR 1172 the
b plaintiff brought an action in detinue or bailment claiming delivery up of their mail, which had been detained by Post Office workers in pursuance of an industrial dispute. They asked the court to grant a mandatory injunction. The court refused the mandatory injunction as a matter of discretion. In the course of his judgment Lord Denning MR referred to s 9 of the Post Office Act as well as s 29, and continued ([1978] 1 All ER 939 at 942, [1977] 1 WLR 1172 at 1177):

c
> 'Counsel for the plaintiffs suggested that those exceptions were so unreasonable and so wide that it would be well if the courts could find a way round it. He hoped that we might do it by reason of an action in detinue or an action in bailment whereby these companies here could say, "You have my letters, they are addressed to me, they are mine, you are holding them up, deliver them to me". He said that
d the sections did not exclude an action of detinue such as that. I would like to think that that may be so, but I would not like to pronounce on it finally today. It is too difficult a subject-matter.'

However, at the very end of his judgment in the same case Lord Denning MR said ([1978] 1 All ER 939 at 943, [1977] 1 WLR 1172 at 1179):

e
> 'Although one has the greatest sympathy with the plaintiffs (the companies) in the most injurious situation in which they have been placed, and although one would like to help them if one possibly could, it seems to me that the courts probably have no jurisdiction in view of the statute.'

Geoffrey Lane LJ started his judgment as follows ([1978] 1 All ER 939 at 944, [1977] 1
f WLR 1172 at 1179–1180):

> 'I agree. I do not propose to consider the liability in bailment (as opposed to contract or tort) of the Post Office to any particular member of the public who may have suffered damage due to the actions of the Post Office employees, save to say that liability in bailment, if it were to exist, would seem to render largely meaningless s 29 of the Post Office Act 1969.'

g
I respectfully adopt what was said by Geoffrey Lane LJ in that case.

I need not explore the first submission of counsel for the plaintiffs any further, because in the end he decided not to develop the argument to its full extent, preferring to reserve the matter for a higher court.

I now turn to counsel's second submission. It is necessary to start by describing the
h legislative background. By the Carriage by Air Act 1932, now repealed, Parliament gave statutory effect to the Warsaw Convention, signed on 12 October 1929. The convention is set out in the Sch 1 to the 1932 Act. It is described as 'A Convention for the Unification of Certain Rules Relating to International Carriage by Air'. By art 1 it applies to all international carriage by air. By art 2(2) it does not apply to carriage performed under the terms of any international postal convention. Chapter III of the convention, comprising arts 17 to 30, deals with the liability of the carrier. Article 18 provides:
j

> '(1) The carrier is liable for damage sustained in the event of the destruction or loss of, or of damage to, any registered luggage or any goods, if the occurrence which caused the damage so sustained took place during the carriage by air . . .'

The Carriage by Air Act 1961, which repealed the 1932 Act, was enacted to give effect to the modifications to the convention agreed at The Hague in 1955. The amended

Warsaw Convention is set out in Sch 1 to the 1961 Act. Article 18 is, so far as relevant, in identical terms. By s 10(1) of the 1961 Act it was provided:

'Her Majesty may by Order in Council apply the First Schedule to this Act, together with any other provisions of this Act, to carriage by air, not being carriage by air to which the Convention applies, of such descriptions as may be specified in the Order, subject to such exceptions, adaptations and modifications, if any, as may be so specified.'

The 1961 Act was brought into force by the Carriage by Air Convention Order 1967, SI 1967/479. The same day there came into operation the Carriage by Air Acts (Application of Provisions) Order 1967, SI 1967/480 (I shall refer to that order as the 1967 order). That order was made under s 10 of the 1961 Act and applied the Warsaw-Hague Convention to non-international carriage, and the carriage of mail and postal packets, with certain modifications and adaptations as set out in Part I of Sch 1 to the order. The order also provides for the application of the Guadalahara Convention to non-international carriage and carriage of mail and postal packets, with certain modifications and adaptations as set out in Part 2 of Sch 1. The Guadalahara Convention was signed on 18 September 1961, too late to be incorporated in the 1961 Act. It is set out in the schedule to the Carriage by Air (Supplementary Provisions) Act 1962. The object of the Guadalahara Convention was, broadly, to give the actual carrier the same protection as the contracting carrier.

Returning to the 1967 order, para 9 of Part II of Sch 1 provides:

'The following Article shall be added:—"Nothing herein shall impose any liability on the Postmaster General or any other authority for the time being established by or under any Act of Parliament to provide postal services".'

Part IIIA of the schedule sets out the Warsaw-Hague Convention as modified by the order. Part IIIB sets out the Guadalahara Convention as modified by the order, and with the addition of the provision relating to the Postmaster General to which I have just referred.

For convenience, and since this part of the argument turns on the language of the article, I will read art 18 (this time of the amended Warsaw convertion set out in Sch 1 to the 1961 Act) again:

'(1) The carrier is liable for damage sustained in the event of the destruction or loss of, or of damage to, any registered baggage or any cargo, if the occurrence which caused the damage so sustained took place during the carriage by air . . .'

The second submission of counsel for the plaintiffs is that art 18 creates a statutory liability, independent of any liability which might exist in tort or contract. Section 29(3) of the Post Office Act 1969 excludes the liability of the defendants in respect of tort. But it does not refer in terms to the liability specifically imposed on carriers by air of mail or postal packages under the 1967 order. If there is a conflict between the 1967 order and s 29(3) of the 1969 Act then, according to counsel, the 1967 order should prevail.

The question whether art 18 of the Warsaw-Hague Convention creates an independent cause of action has been the subject of much discussion in the United States over a number of years. In *Komlos v Compagnie Nationale Air France* (1953) 209 F 2d 436 the Second Circuit Court of Appeals held that the convention does not create a cause of action. It creates a presumption which throws on the carrier the burden of establishing a defence under art 20, not unlike the position in bailment. *Komlos* was followed in 1957 by the same Circuit Court of Appeals in *Noel v Linea Aeropostal Venezolana* (1957) 247 F 2d 677. But then, in a case called *Benjamins v British European Airways* (1978) 572 F 2d 913, an action which arose out of the Trident air disaster at Staines in 1972, the Second Circuit Court of Appeals overruled its earlier decisions, holding that the convention does create a cause of action.

It may be wondered why it matters. The answer is that in the United States it determines whether the federal courts have jurisdiction or not. If the convention does

not create a cause of action, the federal courts have no jurisdiction to hear claims in the
a absence of diversity of citizenship. Such claims could only be brought in the state courts.
If, on the other hand, the convention creates a cause of action, the federal courts would
have jurisdiction in all cases.

In the United States the legal effect of arts 17 and 18 is thus a question of great practical
importance. It has no such practical importance in England; and there is little English
authority on the point, though it is discussed at some length in *Shawcross and Beaumont*
b *on Air Law* (4th edn, 1977). Counsel for the defendants tried to persuade me that I ought
to take sides on the issue which has divided the American courts. He submitted that the
reasoning of the minority judgment in *Benjamins* is much more compelling than the
reasoning of the majority, which he described (and it was his language) as 'lamentable'.
In particular, the majority seemed to have been influenced by the construction which
they put on s 1(4) of the 1932 Act, ignoring the fact that the 1932 Act has been repealed,
c and replaced by s 3 of the 1961 Act, which, if anything, supports the opposite view.

For myself, I am quite unwilling to enter the lists in this dispute. So far as English law
is concerned, I am prepared to assume, without deciding, that art 18 does create a
statutory cause of action similar to the cause of action created by the Fatal Accidents Act
1846 or, nearer home, the cause of action created by s 30 of the Post Office Act 1969. In
the *Building and Civil Engineering* case [1965] 1 All ER 163 at 167, [1966] 1 QB 247 at 260
d Lord Denning MR described the action under s 30 as being 'entirely statutory'. Similar
language was used by Pearson LJ (see [1965] 1 All ER 163 at 170, [1966] 1 QB 247 at
265).

Assuming, then, that art 18 creates a statutory cause of action, does it follow, as counsel
for the plaintiffs submitted, that the cause of action is outside the protection conferred
by s 29(1) of the 1969 Act? In my opinion, it clearly does not. In the judgment of Pearson
e LJ, to which I have just referred, he described the statutory cause of action as being of a
'tortious character'. The question in that case turned on the proper measure of damages.
Pearson LJ said ([1965] 1 All ER 163 at 171, [1966] 1 QB 247 at 266):

'In the absence of any special provision or clear implication from the section, we
naturally resort to the ordinary rules for the assessment of damages in tort.'

f In the present case the question is whether the statutory cause of action against the
carrier is one in respect of which, if proceedings were brought against the Post Office,
they would properly be described as proceedings in tort within the meaning of s 29(1) of
the 1969 Act. The answer, in my view, is clearly Yes.

Breach of statutory duty is normally treated as being part of the general law of tort.
Thus in *Salmond on the Law of Torts* (18th edn, 1981) p 231 it is said:

g 'When a duty is created by a statute the breach of which is an actionable tort, it is
a question of construction whether the liability is absolute, or depends on wrongful
intent or negligence on the part of the defendant.'

Many other textbooks which were cited are to the same effect. Thus in *Clarke and
Lindsell on Tort* (15th edn, 1982) p 59, under the heading 'Breach of Statutory Duty', there
h is this passage:

'Apart from changes made in subsidiary rules of specific torts, statute has given
rise to two main lines of development which are of increasing daily importance.
First, a breach of a statute may give rise to an action commonly spoken of as an
action for breach of statutory duty which is for most practical purposes the creation
of a tort or of a group of torts which is, or are, *sui generis*.'

j The fact that the breach of statutory duty cannot be equated with any particular tort,
for example negligence, does not prevent it coming under the same general heading.
Thus the question in the present case comes to this: when Parliament used the phrase
'proceedings in tort' in s 29(1) of the 1969 Act, was it referring to particular torts such as
negligence or conversion, or was it using the word in a more general sense, so as to

include breach of statutory duty if the remedy for the breach of that statutory duty could be properly described as being 'tortious in character'? I have no doubt at all that the *a* phrase 'proceedings in tort' was used in the more general sense, and therefore includes breaches of the statutory duty imposed on the defendants under art 18. If I am right about that, then that is an end of the case. The liability of the Post Office would have been excluded under s 29(1), and the defendants are entitled to their vicarious immunity by virtue of s 29(3).

Counsel for the defendants had an alternative argument based on art 11 of the *b* Guadalahara Convention as amended by the 1967 order. But, as I am in the defendants' favour on what I regard as the main point, I need not deal with the alternative argument. Nor need I consider what purpose Parliament may have had in applying the Warsaw-Hague Convention and the Guadalahara Convention to the carriage of mail and postal packets in the first place. It is sufficient to say that the meaning of s 29(1) of the 1969 Act is clear in its terms, and that it overrides the 1967 order to the extent that their provisions *c* are in conflict.

In my judgment, counsel for the plaintiffs fails on both his arguments, and the preliminary issue must, therefore, be decided in favour of the defendants.

Preliminary issue decided in favour of defendants and action dismissed.

d

Solicitors: *Clyde & Co* (for the plaintiffs); *Beaumont & Son* (for the defendants).

K Mydeen Esq   Barrister.

Roberts Petroleum Ltd v Bernard Kenny Ltd (in liquidation)

e

HOUSE OF LORDS

LORD DIPLOCK, LORD EDMUND-DAVIES, LORD KEITH OF KINKEL, LORD ROSKILL AND LORD BRIGHTMAN

15, 16, 20 DECEMBER 1982, 10 FEBRUARY 1983

f

Execution – Charging order – Discretion – Discretion to make absolute charging order nisi – Sufficient cause to refuse to make order absolute – Resolution to wind up debtor company on ground of insolvency – Tentative scheme of arrangement agreed to by main body of creditors – Inevitable that debtor company would go into liquidation – Creditor obtaining charging order nisi – Whether sufficient cause to refuse to make absolute order nisi – Whether debtor's insolvency and inevitability of liquidation 'sufficient cause' for refusing to make order absolute – Whether *g* *necessary to prove scheme of arrangement agreed to by main body of creditors was likely to succeed – Administration of Justice Act 1956, s 35(1) – RSC Ord 50, r 1(6).*

House of Lords – Procedure – Citation of authorities – Unreported decisions – Unreported decisions of Court of Appeal not to be cited without leave of House of Lords.

h

The plaintiff supplied petroleum products to the defendant company, which owned two petrol filling stations. By November 1978 the defendant company was in financial difficulties and owed substantial sums to its suppliers, including the plaintiff. On 8 March 1979 the plaintiff issued a writ against the defendant company claiming £74,000. Shortly afterwards, another of the defendant company's trade creditors obtained judgment in default of appearance against it for the sum of £22,500. On 16 March *j* insolvency accountants who had been asked to prepare a statement of the defendant company's affairs gave notice to the company's creditors of an informal meeting of creditors to be held on 26 March. On 23 March the plaintiff entered judgment in default of appearance against the defendant company for its claim for £74,000 and on the same day the district registrar, in exercise of the power conferred on the High Court by s 35(1)[a]

a   Section 35(1), so far as material, is set out at p 569 *b*, post

of the Administration of Justice Act 1956, imposed a charging order nisi charging the
a land on which the defendant's two filling stations stood with payment of the judgment
debt. The registrar's order fixed 4 April as the date on which, unless the defendant
company showed 'sufficient cause' to the contrary, the charging order would be made
absolute, pursuant to RSC Ord 50, r 1(6)[b]. On 2 April at an extraordinary meeting of the
defendant company resolutions were passed that the company be wound up and a
liquidator appointed. On 4 April the district registrar, having considered all the
b circumstances, concluded that the plaintiff's charging order nisi should be made absolute
and he so ordered. The defendant company appealed to the judge in chambers, who
allowed the appeal and discharged the charging order, on the grounds that by 4 April the
defendant company was insolvent and irretrievably on the way to liquidation and that
therefore, in considering whether to make the charging order absolute, paramount
consideration ought to be given to obtaining equal treatment for all the defendant
c company's unsecured creditors, and the plaintiff ought not to be allowed to keep the
advantage it had obtained under the charging order nisi, even though the plaintiff had
not obtained the charging order nisi by any sharp practice. The plaintiff appealed to the
Court of Appeal, which allowed the appeal and exercised its discretion to make the order
absolute on the ground that insolvency of a company followed by liquidation was not of
itself sufficient to justify the court in refusing to make absolute a charging order nisi and
d that there had to be some other factor present, such as a scheme of arrangement set up
by the main body of creditors which had a reasonable prospect of success, before there
was 'sufficient cause' not to make the charging order absolute. The defendant company
appealed to the House of Lords.

Held – If the court made a charging order nisi over land owned by a company in favour
e of a judgment creditor pursuant to s 35(1) of the 1956 Act and if, before the court
considered, pursuant to RSC Ord 50, r 1(6), whether to make the order absolute, a
statutory scheme for dealing with its assets was irrevocably imposed on the company by
resolution or a winding-up order, the court should, when it came to make that
consideration, exercise its discretion by refusing to make the order absolute. By so
exercising its discretion the land would fall into the statutory scheme for dealing with
f the assets for the benefit of all creditors, and a judgment creditor who had, at the time
the statutory scheme came into being, no more than a defeasible right to retain the asset
would be prevented from gaining an advantage over the general body of unsecured
creditors. It followed that the resolution of 2 April 1979 placing the defendant company
in liquidation and appointing a liquidator was a 'sufficient cause' within Ord 50, r 1(6)
for not making absolute the charging order obtained by the plaintiff on 23 March (see
g p 566 h j, p 568 b to e, p 572 j to p 573 e and p 576 f to h, post).

    Hudson's Concrete Products Ltd v D B Evans (Bilston) Ltd (1961) 105 SJ 281, *D Wilson
(Birmingham) Ltd v Metropolitan Property Developments Ltd* [1975] 2 All ER 814 and *Rainbow
v Moorgate Properties Ltd* [1975] 2 All ER 821 considered.
    Burston Finance Ltd (in liq) v Godfrey [1976] 2 All ER 976 doubted.
    Per curiam. The House of Lords will decline to allow transcripts of unreported
h judgments of the Court of Appeal, Civil Division, to be cited at the hearing of appeals by
the House unless leave is given to do so. Leave will only be granted if counsel is able to
assure the House that the unreported transcript contains a statement of a relevant
principle of law which is binding on the Court of Appeal and which is not to be found in
a case appearing in a recognised law report (see p 567 j to p 568 e and p 576 h, post).
    Decision of the Court of Appeal [1982] 1 All ER 685 reversed.

j

Notes
For the procedure for making absolute a charging order nisi, see 17 Halsbury's Laws (4th
edn) para 566, and for cases on charging orders on land, see 21 Digest (Reissue) 492–493,
4004–4006.

---

b   Rule 1(6) is set out at p 569 d e, post

For the Administration of Justice Act 1956, s 35, see 18 Halsbury's Statutes (3rd edn) 21.

As from 3 June 1980 s 35(1) of the 1956 Act was replaced by s 1(1) of the Charging Orders Act 1979, and RSC Ord 50, r 1(6) was replaced by RSC Ord 50, r 3 (as substituted by RSC (Amendment) 1980, SI 1980/629).

Cases referred to in opinions

Ayerst (Inspector of Taxes) v C & K (Construction) Ltd [1975] 2 All ER 537, [1976] AC 167, [1975] 3 WLR 16, HL, Digest (Cont Vol D) 492, 1664a.

Burston Finance Ltd (in liq) v Godfrey [1976] 2 All ER 976, [1976] 1 WLR 719, CA, 21 Digest (Reissue) 492, 4006.

Caribbean Products (Yam Importers) Ltd, Re, Tickler v Swains Packaging Ltd [1966] 1 All ER 181, [1966] Ch 331, [1966] 2 WLR 153, CA, 10 Digest (Reissue) 1171, 7291.

Centrebind Ltd, Re [1966] 3 All ER 889, [1967] 1 WLR 377, 10 Digest (Reissue) 1133, 7034.

Haly v Barry (1868) LR 3 Ch App 452, LJJ, 21 Digest (Reissue) 501, 4070.

Hudson's Concrete Products Ltd v D B Evans (Bilston) Ltd [1961] CA Transcript 110, 105 SJ 281.

Rainbow v Moorgate Properties Ltd [1975] 2 All ER 821, [1975] 1 WLR 788, CA, 21 Digest (Reissue) 500, 4067.

Westbury v Twigg & Co [1892] 1 QB 77, PC, 10 Digest (Reissue) 1170, 7285.

Wilson (D) (Birmingham) Ltd v Metropolitan Property Developments Ltd [1975] 2 All ER 814, CA, 21 Digest (Reissue) 483, 3912.

Appeal

The defendant, Bernard Kenny Ltd (in liq) (Kenny), appealed by leave of the Appeal Committee of the House of Lords granted on 11 March 1982 against the decision of the Court of Appeal (Lord Brandon of Oakbrook, Cumming-Bruce LJ and Dame Elizabeth Lane) ([1982] 1 All ER 685, [1982] 1 WLR 301) on 11 December 1981 which allowed an appeal by the plaintiff, Roberts Petroleum Ltd (Roberts), from the judgment in chambers of Bristow J on 13 October 1980 and restored the order made by Mr District Registrar Scott on 4 April 1979 in the Scunthorpe District Registry whereby he adjudged that a charging order nisi obtained on 23 March 1979 by Roberts on two petrol stations owned by Kenny should be made absolute and the receivership imposed on that date should be continued. The facts are set out in the opinion of Lord Brightman.

Andrew Morritt QC and Michael Crystal for Kenny.
Anthony Hidden QC and Paul W Miller for Roberts.

Their Lordships took time for consideration.

10 February. The following opinions were delivered.

LORD DIPLOCK. My Lords, my noble and learned friend Lord Brightman in his speech says all that need to be said about the facts that give rise to this appeal and the law applicable to them. I agree with the conclusion that he reaches and the reasoning by which he supports it and I, too, would allow the appeal and restore the judgment of Bristow J.

I do desire, however, to comment on the use sought to be made both in this House and in the Court of Appeal of previous judgments of that court which do not appear in any series of published law reports. This is a growing practice and one which, in my view, ought to be discouraged.

Transcripts of the shorthand notes of oral judgments delivered since April 1951 by members of the Court of Appeal, nearly all extempore, have been preserved at the Royal Courts of Justice, formerly in the Bar Library but since 1978 in the Supreme Court Library. For much of this period this course has been followed as respects all judgments

of the Civil Division of the Court of Appeal, though recently some degree of selectivity
a has been adopted as to judgments to be indexed and incorporated in the bound volumes.
(Unreported judgments which have been delivered since the beginning of 1980 are now
also included in the computerised data base known as LEXIS and this has facilitated
reference to them.) Two such transcripts are referred to in the judgment of the Court of
Appeal in the instant case. One of these was a case, *Hudson's Concrete Products Ltd v D B
Evans (Bilston) Ltd* [1961] CA Transcript 110, to which my noble and learned friend refers,
b which had been the subject of a note in the Solicitors' Journal (see 105 SJ 281). The other
had not been noted in any professional journal, nor had either of the two additional
transcripts to which your Lordships were referred at the hearing in this House. For my
part, I gained no assistance from perusal of any of these transcripts. None of them laid
down a relevant principle of law that was not to be found in reported cases; the only
result of referring to the transcripts was that the length of the hearing was extended
c unnecessarily.

This is not surprising. In a judgment, particularly one that has not been reduced into
writing before delivery, a judge, whether at first instance or on appeal, has his mind
concentrated on the particular facts of the case before him and the course which the oral
argument has taken. This may have involved agreement or concessions, tacit or explicit,
as to the applicable law, made by counsel for the litigating parties in what they conceived
d to be the interests of their respective clients in obtaining a favourable outcome of the
particular case.

The primary duty of the Court of Appeal on an appeal in any case is to determine the
matter actually in dispute between the parties. Such propositions of law as members of
the court find necessary to state and previous authorities to which they find it convenient
to refer in order to justify the disposition of the actual proceedings before them will be
e tailored to the facts of the particular case. Accordingly, propositions of law may well be
stated in terms either more general or more specific than would have been used if he
who gave the judgment had had in mind somewhat different facts, or had heard a legal
argument more expansive than had been necessary in order to determine the particular
appeal. Even when making successive revisions of drafts of my own written speeches for
delivery on appeals to this House, which usually involve principles of law of wider
f application than the particular case under appeal, I often find it necessary to continue to
introduce subordinate clauses supplementing or qualifying the simpler, and stylistically
preferable, wording in which statements of law have been expressed in earlier drafts.

There are two classes of printed law reports: the two weekly series of general law
reports, (a) the Weekly Law Reports of the Incorporated Council of Law Reporting, of
which the more important, contained in volumes 2 and 3, are later reproduced in the
g Law Reports proper, together with a summary of the arguments of counsel, and (b) the
All England Law Reports, which report much the same cases as the former series; these
do not err on the side of over-selectivity. Then there are the various series of specialised
law reports which seem to have proliferated in the course of the last few decades; these
may be useful in helping lawyers practising in specialised fields to predict the likely
outcome of the particular case in which they are advising or instituting proceedings, by
h seeing how previous cases in which the facts were in various respects analogous were
actually decided; but these specialised reports contain only a small minority of leading
judgments in which some new principle of law of general application in the specialised
field of law is authoritatively propounded, as distinct from some previously accepted
principle being applied to the facts of a particular case. If a civil judgment of the Court
of Appeal (which has a heavy case load and sits concurrently in several civil divisions) has
j not found its way into the generalised series of law reports or even into one of the
specialised series, it is most unlikely to be of any assistance to your Lordships on an appeal
which is sufficiently important to reach this House.

My Lords, in my opinion, the time has come when your Lordships should adopt the
practice of declining to allow transcripts of unreported judgments of the Civil Division
of the Court of Appeal to be cited on the hearing of appeals to this House unless leave is
given to do so, and that such leave should only be granted on counsel's giving an assurance

that the transcript contains a statement of some principle of law, relevant to an issue in the appeal to this House, that is binding on the Court of Appeal and of which the *a* substance, as distinct from the mere choice, of phraseology, is not to be found in any judgment of that court that has appeared in one of the generalised or specialised series of reports.

LORD EDMUND-DAVIES. My Lords, I have had the advantage of reading in draft the speech prepared by my noble and learned friend Lord Brightman. For the reasons he *b* has developed, with which I am in respectful agreement, I would make the orders indicated by him and allow the appeal.

I likewise concur in the views expressed by my noble and learned friend Lord Diplock regarding the desirability of curbing in the manner he suggests the modern practice of citing in your Lordships' House an inordinate number of transcripts of unreported decisions of the Court of Appeal.   *c*

LORD KEITH OF KINKEL. My Lords, I have had the benefit of reading in draft the speech to be delivered by my noble and learned friend Lord Brightman. I agree with it, and for the reasons he gives I too would allow the appeal.

I have also to record my respectful agreement with the observations of my noble and learned friend Lord Diplock on the use of unreported decisions of the Court of Appeal.   *d*

LORD ROSKILL. My Lords, I have had the advantage of reading in draft the speeches of my noble and learned friends Lord Diplock and Lord Brightman. As regards this appeal I agree with all that my noble and learned friend Lord Brightman has said and with the conclusion which he reaches that this appeal should be allowed and the judgment of Bristow J restored.   *e*

As regards the use of unreported decisions of the Court of Appeal, I entirely agree with the speech of my noble and learned friend Lord Diplock and I respectfully indorse in particular that which he has said in the last paragraph of that speech.

LORD BRIGHTMAN. My Lords, the question which arises on this appeal can be shortly stated. A judgment creditor of a company obtains a charging order nisi over the *f* land of the debtor company and the appointment of a receiver. The company thereafter convenes a meeting of its shareholders on short notice and resolves on voluntary liquidation. In these circumstances, can the court in the proper exercise of its discretion make the order absolute? The High Court judge thought not. The Court of Appeal thought Yes, reaching the same conclusion as the district registrar before whom the matter had first come.   *g*

The question, as I have stated it, has not been before the court for decision in any reported case. Indeed, there is little reported authority on problems which can arise in this area of the law. The question is of importance to the commercial community. If the respondent is right, and an intervening voluntary liquidation does not inhibit the making absolute of a prior order nisi, there is every incentive for judgment creditors to issue execution at the last moment of an insolvent company's life in order to secure their *h* position and gain a last minute advantage over less agile or more patient creditors. If the appellant is right, then the interval between the order nisi and the consideration of an order absolute allows time for a voluntary winding-up resolution or the presentation of a winding-up petition, with the consequent possibility of preserving the position of the unsecured creditors as a whole.

The power of the High Court to grant a judgment creditor a charging order over the *j* land of the judgment debtor was at the relevant time contained in s 35 of the Administration of Justice Act 1956, and was regulated by RSC Ord 50. Prior to 1 January 1957, and indeed dating back to the Judgments Act 1838, a different system prevailed to which it is unnecessary to refer. Section 35 has now been replaced by the Charging Orders Act 1979 and there is also a new version of Ord 50. This appeal is concerned only

with the previous legislation and order, but the principle involved in the appeal no doubt
a   applies to the new jurisdiction although that is not a matter for present decision. .
Section 35 of the 1956 Act (as amended by the deletion of references to the county
court) provided as follows:

'(1) The High Court may, for the purpose of enforcing a judgment or order . . .
for the payment of money to a person, by order impose on any such land or interest
in land of the debtor as may be specified in the order a charge for securing the
b   payment of any moneys due or to become due under the judgment or order.
(2) An order under subsection (1) of this section may be made either absolutely
or subject to conditions as to notifying the debtor or as to the time when the charge
is to become enforceable or as to other matters . . .'

Section 36 of the 1956 Act extended the power of the court to appoint a receiver for
the purpose of enforcing the charge mentioned in s 35(1).
c   Order 50, rr 1 and 9 were in the following terms:

'1.—(1) The power to make an order under section 35 of the Administration of
Justice Act, 1956 imposing a charge on land or interest in land of a judgment debtor
shall be exercisable by the Court.
(2) Any such order shall in the first instance be an order to show cause, specifying
d   the time and place for further consideration of the matter and imposing the charge
until that time in any event.
(3) An application for an order under the said section 35 may be made ex parte . . .
(6) On the further consideration of the matter the Court shall, unless it appears
(whether on the representation of the judgment debtor or otherwise) that there is
sufficient cause to the contrary, make the order absolute with or without
e   modifications.
(7) Where on the further consideration of the matter it appears to the Court that
the order should not be made absolute, it shall discharge the order.'

'9 . . . a master . . . shall have power—(a) to appoint a receiver to enforce a charge
imposed by an order under rule 1 . . .'

f   It will be seen that, although the 1956 Act authorised the order to be made 'either
absolutely or subject to conditions as to notifying the debtor', the Supreme Court Rules
made a two-stage approach obligatory. There is an initial application, which will
invariably be ex parte, on which the court may make an order nisi. The matter then
comes up for further consideration, which will invariably be inter partes, when the court
may make the existing order absolute, with or without modification. Otherwise the
g   court discharges the order.
The question involved in this case is the propriety of the decision of the High Court
judge not to make the order absolute. This he was bound to do unless on the application
for further consideration 'it appears . . . that there is sufficient cause to the contrary'. So
the question for decision by your Lordships' House is whether the judge could in the
instant case properly take the view that there was sufficient cause not to make the order
h   absolute.
I turn to the facts of this case. On 24 January 1979 Cawoods Fuel Oils Ltd (Cawoods)
issued proceedings against the appellant company, Bernard Kenny Ltd (Kenny), for
£22,500 for goods supplied. On 8 March 1979 the respondent company, Roberts
Petroleum Ltd (Roberts), sued Kenny for the sum of £74,001 for goods supplied. Four
days later Cawoods signed judgment in default of appearance. On 16 March a firm of
j   liquidation accountants acting on behalf of Kenny wrote to Roberts, Cawoods and other
creditors stating that they had advised Kenny to call an informal meeting of creditors for
26 March, and requesting the addressee 'if you have taken proceedings or are
contemplating taking proceedings would you please hold these over pending the outcome
of the Meeting'. It is apparent from an affidavit sworn on 23 March 1979 by a
representative of the solicitors acting for Roberts that the insolvency of Kenny was fully

appreciated by Roberts and those acting on its behalf. On 23 March Roberts signed
judgment against Kenny in default of appearance for the amount of the debt and costs. *a*
On the same day Roberts applied for and obtained from the Scunthorpe District Registry
of the Queen's Bench Division a charging order nisi over two pieces of land belonging to
Roberts, and also an order appointing Mr D C Panter to be the receiver to enforce the
charging order.

The order nisi made by the registrar on 23 March was in the following form:

'IT IS ORDERED . . . that, unless sufficient cause to the contrary be shown . . . on the *b*
4th day of April 1979 . . . the said land or interest in land of the Defendant shall,
and it is ordered that in the meantime it do, stand charged that the payment of
£74,055·57 due on the said Judgment together with the costs of this application and
the Plaintiff by their Solicitors undertaking to abide by any order the Court may
make as to damages, costs, expenses etc., in case the Court should hereafter be of
opinion that the said Defendant shall have sustained any loss or damage by reason *c*
of this order which the Plaintiff ought to pay should the appointment of the
Receiver be not continued at the Hearing . . . IT IS FURTHER ordered that David
Crosby Panter be appointed without security . . . to be the Receiver to enforce the
Charging Order imposed on the Defendant's interest in the properties, namely . . .
and to receive any moneys receivable in consequence of enforcing the said Charging
Order . . . AND that all questions as to the passing of his accounts and payment *d*
thereunder and all further questions be reserved until further order AND it is further
ordered that the Plaintiff's costs of this application be taxed or agreed and paid by
the Defendant.'

I have recited the order fully in order to show its breadth. It created an immediate
charge. It made an immediate appointment of a receiver. Roberts was converted *e*
immediately into a secured creditor. By implication the order empowered the receiver
to act immediately, though at the risk of Roberts in case the order were not made
absolute. It even made an award of costs against the (as yet unheard) judgment debtor.
But all this was subject to sufficient cause not being shown to the contrary on 4 April. In
other words, the order was defeasible, without prejudice to the validity of any interim
acts of the receiver, but subject to the judgment creditor's cross-undertaking in damages *f*
in case the order was discharged.

On 26 March 1979 the informal meeting of creditors was held. The majority of the
creditors (including Roberts) were present or represented. The trade debts amounted to
£173,634, and the estimated deficiency as regards creditors was estimated at £106,954.
There is a lengthy minute of the meeting in evidence, and it includes the following
passages: *g*

'One Creditor present asked why an informal meeting of Creditors had been
convened and he was told that it was originally the intention of the Company to
request a 56 day moratorium in order that attempts could be made to dispose of the
freehold properties on a going concern basis. The possibility of a moratorium is
now in doubt in view of the action being taken by several creditors and if the *h*
moratorium is to proceed it will necessitate all such actions being withdrawn and
no further actions being commenced by Creditors.'

And a little later:

'Any scheme of moratorium would require the necessary safeguards to protect
the interests of all Creditors and would require supervision. It was suggested that at
the conclusion of any moratorium the Company should in any event be liquidated. *j*
It was agreed that those Creditors who have commenced action against the Company,
in particular Roberts Petroleum Limited, should consider their position and the
representative of Roberts Petroleum Limited was asked to advise Mr. C. Ward
[Kenny's solicitor] of his clients decision within 48 hours of the meeting concluding.'

On 2 April the four shareholders of Kenny voted to accept short notice of a general

meeting of the company and it was thereupon resolved that the company be placed in
a voluntary liquidation and that a member of the firm of accountants advising Kenny
should be appointed liquidator. The meeting of creditors required by s 293 of the
Companies Act 1948 was not convened until a later date, but this does not affect the
validity of the resolution to wind up or the appointment of the liquidator; so held by
Plowman J in Re Centrebind Ltd [1966] 3 All ER 889, [1967] 1 WLR 377, with which
decision I agree.

b   On 4 April the charging order was made absolute by the registrar. It was in the
following terms:

'IT IS ORDERED that the following land or interest in land of [Kenny] namely . . .
Stand charged with the payment of £74,055·57 . . . and interest thereon . . . and
that the Plaintiff's costs to be taxed and the said costs to be added to the judgment
debt AND it is further ordered that the Receivership be continued.'

c

My Lords, it is clear from the evidence, and indeed it is common ground, that Roberts
applied to the district registrar for a charging order in the hope of obtaining an advantage
over other unsecured creditors, and that the shareholders of Kenny, on professional
advice, put the company into voluntary liquidation at short notice in the hope of
depriving Roberts of that advantage. Neither step nor counterstep casts any discredit on
d those involved. There was nothing in the nature of sharp practice on either side, nor has
this been suggested in your Lordships' House. A person who has the misfortune to have
given credit to a company which runs into financial difficulties has every right to seek to
secure himself. Any such company or its other creditors have every right to hasten
liquidation in order to thwart such a purpose.
     After a delay caused by a procedural misunderstanding (the time for appeal being
e extended in consequence) Kenny appealed against the registrar's order. On 13 October
1980 the matter came before Bristow J in chambers; so there is no transcript of his
judgment. All that we have in front of us is a note agreed by counsel, and not, as we
should have, a note approved by the judge himself. The note records the judge as having
directed himself as follows:

f   'If, at the time when the court has to decide whether or not to make the order
absolute, the company is irretrievably on the road to dissolution, then the
consideration of obtaining equal treatment for all the unsecured creditors in order
to do equity becomes paramount and the creditor who, even without any degree of
foul play or trickery, has obtained an advantage (which is still provisional) is not to
be allowed to keep that advantage. That seems to follow from consideration of the
g   cases.'

'Irretrievably on the road to dissolution' may or may not have been the actual words
by the judge to formulate the test which he applied to the exercise of his discretion. A
company is irretrievably on the road to dissolution (dissolution is provided for by ss 274
and 290 of the Companies Act 1948) as soon as a winding-up order has been made or a
winding-up resolution has been passed, subject only to the power of the court to stay the
h winding up. It was suggested in argument that the judge said, or meant, not dissolution
but liquidation, i e that if a company were irretrievably bankrupt, though not necessarily
in liquidation, the order nisi would not be made absolute. It matters not which expression
he used. Kenny had gone into liquidation between order nisi and order absolute, and on
either formulation that fact was decisive in the view of the judge.
     Kenny appealed. The appeal came before the Court of Appeal in October 1981, with
j Lord Brandon presiding. He delivered a judgment on 11 December, with which
Cumming-Bruce LJ and Dame Elizabeth Lane concurred. He pointed out (see [1982] 1
All ER 685 at 690, [1982] 1 WLR 301 at 307), in my respectful view correctly, that cases
like the present involve a conflict between two well-established principles of law, which
were, first, that—

'a judgment creditor is in general entitled to enforce a money judgment which he has lawfully obtained against a judgment debtor by all or any of the means of execution prescribed by the relevant rules of court'

and, second, that—

'when a judgment debtor, whether he be a natural person or a corporate body, has become insolvent, all the unsecured creditors should be treated equally, each receiving the same proportionate share of the inadequate fund available as all the others.'

Lord Brandon then set out certain principles deduced from the authorities which had been cited to the court, the important ones for present purposes being:

'(6) The following combination of circumstances, if proved to the satisfaction of the court, will generally justify the court in exercising its discretion by refusing to make the order absolute: (i) the fact that the judgment debtor is insolvent; and (ii) the fact that a scheme of arrangement has been set on foot by the main body of creditors and has a reasonable prospect of succeeding. (7) In the absence of the combination of circumstance referred to in (6) above, the court will generally be justified in exercising its discretion by making the order absolute.'

Lord Brandon (see [1982] 1 All ER 685 at 691, [1982] 1 WLR 301 at 308) rejected the submission on behalf of Kenny that—

'the insolvency of a company, followed or to be followed inevitably, later, by a liquidation, is enough of itself to justify the court in exercising its discretion by refusing to make an order nisi absolute. There must . . . be some further factor in the situation, the most common such factor being that a scheme of arrangement has been set on foot by the main body of creditors and has a reasonable prospect of succeeding.'

He then concluded that it was not possible to say—

'that there was in existence at the material time a well advanced scheme of arrangement set up by the main body of creditors which had a reasonable chance of success.'

On that ground the court allowed the appeal. This conclusion followed the majority decision in *Burston Finance Ltd (in liq) v Godfrey* [1976] 2 All ER 976, [1976] 1 WLR 719, which was binding on the court, and to which I shall refer later.

The matter now comes before your Lordships by leave of your Lordships' House.

An order for the compulsory winding up of a company, or a resolution of the company in general meeting for voluntary winding up, in each case brings into operation a statutory scheme for dealing with the assets of the company (see *Ayerst (Inspector of Taxes) v C & K (Contruction) Ltd* [1975] 2 All ER 537, [1976] AC 167). Save for some procedural details, there is no difference in this respect between a compulsory and a voluntary winding up. The statutory duty of the liquidator in each case is to collect the assets of the company and to apply them in discharge of its liabilities. For this purpose unsecured creditors, unless preferred or deferred, rank equally and share pari passu (see s 317 of the Companies Act 1948). The assets which the liquidator is able to collect and distribute are however necessarily those which are free from a charge.

The basic question, therefore, which confronts the court when it is faced with an application by an execution creditor to convert an order nisi into an order absolute in a case such as the present is whether the asset in question should fall outside the statutory scheme which, by virtue of the liquidation, is then in existence or should be subject to that scheme. In the absence of persuasive authority to the contrary, and it will of course be necessary to consider the authorities, I would myself have thought that the court should exercise its discretion so that the asset falls within the statutory scheme. The purpose of the further consideration of the order nisi is to enable the court to review the position inter partes. At the date of the order nisi the court has made no irrevocable decision. If therefore the statutory scheme for dealing with the assets of the company has been irrevocably imposed on the company, by resolution or winding-up order, before the court has irrevocably determined to give the creditor the benefit of a charging order, I would have thought that the statutory scheme should prevail. Unquestionably that would be the position if the winding-up order or resolution had preceded the order nisi: see s 228 of the Companies Act 1948 (compulsory liquidation) and *Westbury v Twigg & Co Ltd* [1892] 1 QB 77 (voluntary liquidation). To my mind the position should be the same if liquidation commences after the order nisi but before the court has committed itself to a final order. I do not see why a creditor should gain an advantage merely because he has a revocable order for security at the time when the statutory scheme comes into existence.

The main thrust of Roberts's argument is that the order nisi imposes an immediate charge, which is correct, and that therefore at the date of the commencement of the liquidation the assets were already outside the statutory scheme. That proposition, by reference to that date, is also correct. The liquidator was unable, at that date, to collect those assets by going into possession, because the receiver was already in possession. But the weakness of the argument to my mind is that Roberts had no more than a defeasible charge at the date of the commencement of the liquidation, so that the right of the receiver to retain the asset as against the liquidator was only a defeasible right. Neither the precarious existence of the charge nor the precarious possession of the receiver seems to me to afford a convincing reason for consolidating the position of the judgment creditor vis-à-vis the general body of unsecured creditors and thereby defeat quoad that asset the statutory scheme which was already in full force and effect. So, unless there is convincing authority pointing to a different conclusion, I would regard the intervention of the statutory scheme as a sufficient and indeed decisive 'cause to the contrary'. I can see no logic in an additional requirement 'such as a scheme of arrangement, formal or informal, agreed or being negotiated amongst creditors'; I have taken these words from *Burston Finance Ltd (in liq) v Godfrey* [1976] 2 All ER 976 at 990, [1976] 1 WLR 719 at 734, to which I refer later.

I think that this tentative conclusion accords with the general sense of those sections of the Companies Act 1948 which preclude inroads into the assets of a company once liquidation has begun. Under s 226, in the interval between the presentation of a winding-up petition and a winding-up order, an application may be made to the court in which any action or proceeding is pending to stay the proceedings. Under s 228, where a company is being wound up by the court, any execution put in force against the estate of the company after the commencement of the winding up is void. Under s 231, when a winding-up order has been made, no action or proceeding may be proceeded with or commenced against the company except by leave of the court. Under s 307, where a company is in voluntary liquidation, the liquidator may apply to the court to stay proceedings against the company. Under s 325, to which it will be necessary to return, an execution creditor cannot retain the benefit of his execution against the liquidator if the execution is incomplete at the date of the commencement of the winding up.

I turn now to the reported authorities. There is a brief report of a case heard in the Court of Appeal in 1961, *Hudson's Concrete Products Ltd v D B Evans (Bilston) Ltd* 105 SJ 281, which appears to be consistent with the view that I have provisionally formed. In that case a garnishee order nisi was made on 20 December 1960. On 16 January 1961 the debtor company issued a summons under s 206 of the Companies Act 1948 to obtain the sanction of the court to a scheme of arrangement between the company and its creditors. On the same day a creditor presented a winding-up petition. On 17 January the registrar made the order nisi absolute. The position therefore was that between the date of the order nisi and the date of the order absolute the assets of the company became prospectively subject to a scheme consisting either of a scheme of arrangement sanctioned by the court or of the statutory scheme applicable to a liquidation. The Court of Appeal discharged the order nisi. The difference between the facts of that case and the facts of the instant case is that in *Hudson*, in the interval between the order nisi and the further consideration, the assets had only become prospectively subject to a court scheme or the statutory scheme, while in the instant case they had become actually subject to the statutory scheme. If, therefore, *Hudson* was correctly decided, the instant case is a fortiori. *a*

D Wilson (Birmingham) Ltd v Metropolitan Property Developments Ltd [1975] 2 All ER 814 is to the same effect. In that case garnishee orders nisi were made on 12 September 1974, at which time a scheme of arrangement under s 206 was in course of preparation relating to the affairs of the group to which the debtor company belonged. On 22 October the debtor company presented its own petition for a compulsory winding-up order. On 1 November the garnishee orders were made absolute. The Court of Appeal discharged the *b* orders holding that the case was not distinguishable from *Hudson*, which should be followed.

Rainbow v Moorgate Properties Ltd [1975] 2 All ER 821, [1975] 1 WLR 788 is to the same effect, and concerned another company of the same group. On 11 November 1974 the judgment creditor obtained a charging order nisi against land of the judgment debtor. On 3 December the judgment debtor presented its own petition to wind up. On *c* 4 December the registrar made the order absolute. On appeal, the Court of Appeal discharged the order, following its previous decisions in *Hudson* and *Wilson*.

Burston Finance Ltd (in liq) v Godfrey [1976] 2 All ER 976, [1976] 1 WLR 719 requires fuller consideration. It arose in the bankruptcy of two individual debtors. On 5 February 1975 the judgment creditor obtained a charging order nisi against the debtors, further consideration being fixed for 20 February. On 19 February the debtors presented their *d* own petitions in bankruptcy. Receiving orders were made, and both debtors were adjudged bankrupt, on the same day. On 20 February the orders nisi were made absolute. The official receiver had had no notice of the adjourned application, and the two bankrupts to all practical intents consented to the order nisi being made absolute. A month later a trustee in bankruptcy was appointed to act in place of the official receiver, and he successfully applied to be added as a defendant to the judgment creditor's action. *e* He then appealed to the Court of Appeal. The contention of the judgment creditor was that both on principle and authority the receiving order and adjudication, being matters subsequent to the order nisi, should be excluded from consideration. That submission was based on *Haly v Barry* (1868) LR 3 Ch App 452, to which in *Hudson*, *Wilson* and *Rainbow* the court had not been referred. However, this submission was rejected by Megaw and Scarman LJJ, although accepted by Shaw LJ. On the question whether, *f* admitting evidence of the receivership and adjudication, the order absolute ought to stand, Megaw LJ said ([1976] 2 All ER 976 at 988, [1976] 1 WLR 719 at 732):

> 'In the end, after hesitation, I have reached the conclusion that the trustee in bankruptcy has failed to show that it would be inequitable in the circumstances that the order should be made absolute. So sufficient cause is not shown and the charging order should stand. I reach that conclusion mainly because there was here, so far as *g* the evidence goes, no understanding nor any indication of any attempt to reach an understanding among the creditors of the bankrupts, or among any of them, as to common forbearance from pressing individual remedies, in the interests of all. Nor is there any evidence that the plaintiffs exercised undue haste to obtain a preferred position for themselves as compared with the general body of creditors; nor that they took, or sought to take, unfair advantage of any knowledge which they had *h* acquired of any other matter or circumstance which was unknown to the other creditors.'

Scarman LJ adopted a similar approach. He said ([1976] 2 All ER 976 at 990, [1976] 1 WLR 719 at 734):

> '... the mere fact of a receiving order, or even an adjudication of bankruptcy, *j* subsequent to the order nisi, would not necessarily suffice [as sufficient cause for refusing to make the order absolute]: if, however, there were other circumstances, such as a scheme of arrangement, formal or informal, agreed or being negotiated amongst creditors, the court might well think it equitable to refuse to make the order absolute.'

Burston therefore is a decision of the Court of Appeal that a bankruptcy adjudication,
a and by parity of reasoning the liquidation of an insolvent company, between order nisi
and further consideration is not sufficient cause by itself for refusing to make the order
absolute. The decisions in *Hudson, Wilson* and *Rainbow* were interpreted as being based
on the fact that there were in each case significant circumstances in addition to the
presentation of a winding-up petition, notably the preparation of a scheme of arrangement
or moratorium, from which it could be inferred that an understanding existed between
b creditors as to common forbearance from pressing ahead with individual remedies, in
the interests of all, 'a holding back of action for the common benefit' (see [1976] 2 All ER
976 at 986, [1976] 1 WLR 719 at 731).

In the instant case it is plain that there was no understanding for forbearance but at
most a hope among many of the creditors that there would be. Roberts agreed neither at
the meeting of 26 March nor later to exercise any forbearance. In none of the reported
c cases which your Lordships have been asked to consider has actual liquidation, and
therefore the actual imposition of the statutory scheme for regulating the affairs of an
insolvent, intervened between order nisi and the further consideration, except in *Burston*.
In the other relevant cases liquidation, or a scheme of arrangement, was in imminent
prospect but was not a fact.

No doubt there are differences between winding-up procedures and bankruptcy
d procedures, but I doubt whether it is possible to decide this case in favour of Kenny
without disapproving *Burston*. Admittedly each case is a matter for individual judgment
in the circumstances of that particular case, for the question is whether it appears to the
court or to the judge that sufficient cause is shown against making the order absolute.
There are no facts relied on by Kenny in the instant case except its insolvency plus
intervening liquidation, and, if they are 'sufficient cause' in the instant case, similar
e circumstances ought to have been 'sufficient cause' in *Burston*.

My Lords, if a company goes into liquidation in the interval between order nisi and
the application for order absolute, so that its assets have become subject to the statutory
scheme, I do not see the importance of inquiring whether its assets were prospectively
subject to a s 206 scheme. I can well understand the relevance of a prospective s 206
scheme in the absence of a winding up but not once liquidation has intervened.

f In addition to the submission that the intervention of a winding-up resolution was not
enough, by itself, to constitute sufficient cause for discharging the order nisi, Roberts
relied on s 325 of the Companies Act 1948. This section enables the liquidator of a
company to deny the judgment creditor the benefit of his execution in certain
circumstances. It is in the following terms (as amended by s 36 of the Administration of
Justice Act 1956):

g   '(1) Where a creditor has issued execution against the goods or lands of a company
      or has attached any debt due to the company, and the company is subsequently
      wound up, he shall not be entitled to retain the benefit of the execution or
      attachment against the liquidator in the winding up of the company unless he has
      completed the execution or attachment before the commencement of the winding
      up: Provided that—(a) where any creditor has had notice of a meeting having been
h   called at which a resolution for voluntary winding up is to be proposed, the date on
      which the creditor so had notice shall, for the purposes of the foregoing provision,
      be substituted for the date of the commencement of the winding up . . . (c) the
      rights conferred by this subsection on the liquidator may be set aside by the court
      in favour of the creditor to such extent and subject to such terms as the court may
      think fit.
      (2) For the purposes of this section, an execution against goods shall be taken to
i   be completed by seizure and sale, and an attachment of a debt shall be deemed to be
      completed by receipt of the debt, and an execution against land shall be deemed to
      be completed by seizure or by the appointment of a receiver . . .'

I doubt whether s 325 has any direct application to the present case, because it is
dealing with the right of a creditor to retain the benefit of a completed execution as

against the liquidator, and I think that it only comes into play after an order has been made absolute. It was not referred to in the judgments below. Nevertheless I think that *a* the section has an important bearing on the case, for it would be odd if the court seised of the action took the view that it would be wrong to make an order absolute in circumstances in which, if an order absolute were made, the liquidator would under the terms of s 325 be unable to deny the execution creditor the benefit of the execution. So I think it is necessary to look at s 325 and see what, in the instant case, the legal position would have been if the order had been made absolute and the liquidator had invoked *b* s 325. The argument of the respondent Roberts is that, on the plain wording of the section, the liquidator would have no right to deny Roberts the benefit of its execution. Roberts had issued execution against Kenny when it applied for and obtained an order nisi. At the date of the order nisi Roberts had received no notice of a meeting having been called at which a resolution for voluntary winding up would be proposed. Roberts had obtained an order for the appointment of a receiver. Therefore in the terms of the *c* section execution was deemed to be completed before the date of the winding up.

The argument is formidable but I do not think it is correct. When the section speaks of an execution against land being 'deemed to be completed . . . by the appointment of a receiver' I think that it is looking at a final order of the court effecting such appointment, and not at an order which is made provisionally, ex parte, pending further consideration by the court when the application is heard inter partes. I would expect to find clear words *d* if I am to construe 'completion', even 'deemed completion', as comprehending a mere interim appointment of a receiver which is made ex parte and is not a final appointment. 'Completion' of execution infers an element of finality. In the case of execution against goods, there must be both seizure and sale. In the case of an attachment of a debt there must be receipt of the debt. A debt due to the judgment debtor would not be paid to the judgment creditor under a garnishee order which was merely nisi. The argument based *e* on s 325 is at best an argument by analogy to what the position would be if the order were made absolute and the liquidator invoked this section. I think the argument founders because it is based on a misconstruction of the section.

We have been referred to only one case where s 325 was directly in point, namely *Re Caribbean Products (Yam Importers) Ltd* [1966] 1 All ER 181, [1966] 1 Ch 331. Although this case was much discussed during the course of the argument, I do not gain much *f* assistance from it as pointing to a solution of the present case.

My Lords, I return to the point at issue, whether Bristow J correctly held that the liquidation of Kenny, that is to say the imposition on the assets of an insolvent company of the statutory scheme for the distribution of those assets among the unsecured creditors, was a 'sufficient cause' for not converting the order nisi into an order absolute. I think that he was correct, for the reasons which I have stated. I reach this conclusion without *g* any regret. First, it may help to avert an unseemly scramble by creditors to achieve priority at the last moment. Second, it establishes a clear working rule, and avoids the uncertainties of an inquiry whether a scheme of arrangement 'has been set on foot and has a reasonable prospect of succeeding'. I would allow this appeal, discharge the order absolute which was made by the registrar and restored by the Court of Appeal, and also discharge the order nisi. *h*

In conclusion, I wish to express my complete agreement with the observations of my noble and learned friend Lord Diplock on the use in your Lordships' House of transcripts of shorthand notes of unreported judgments of the Court of Appeal.

Appeal allowed. Orders nisi and absolute discharged. Order of Bristow J of 13 October 1980 restored. *j*

Solicitors: *William F Prior & Co*, agents for *R C Moorhouse & Co*, Leeds (for Kenny); *Collyer-Bristow*, agents for *Sergeant & Collins*, Scunthorpe (for Roberts).

Mary Rose Plummer   Barrister.

R v Sullivan

COURT OF APPEAL, CRIMINAL DIVISION
LAWTON LJ, MICHAEL DAVIES AND BUSH JJ
19 OCTOBER, 9 DECEMBER 1982

Criminal law – Automatism – Insanity distinguished – Epileptic seizure – Seizure causing total deprivation of understanding and memory – Epileptic inflicting grievous bodily harm during seizure – Whether accused entitled to rely on automatism as a defence – Whether accused's condition during seizure amounting to insanity – Whether proper verdict not guilty by reason of insanity – Trial of Lunatics Act 1883, s 2(1) – Criminal Procedure (Insanity) Act 1964, s 5(1).

The defendant was charged with inflicting grievous bodily harm on P. At his trial he admitted inflicting grievous bodily harm on P, who was a friend, but asserted by way of a defence that he had done so while in the final stage of recovering from a minor epileptic seizure. The undisputed medical evidence at the trial was that the effect on the functioning of the brain of such a seizure was that the epileptic could have no memory of, and would not be conscious of, what he had done during the seizure. The trial judge ruled that the defence amounted to one of insanity, rather than a defence of automatism, and that if the jury accepted the defence they would be required to return the special verdict of not guilty by reason of insanity provided for in s 2(1)[a] of the Trial of Lunatics Act 1883, and that in consequence the judge would be required, by virtue of s 5(1)[b] of the Criminal Procedure (Insanity) Act 1964, to order the defendant to be detained in a special hospital. To avoid those consequences the defendant changed his plea to guilty of the lesser offence of assault occasioning actual bodily harm and was convicted of that offence. He was sentenced to probation under medical supervision. He appealed against the conviction on the ground that the judge's ruling was erroneous in law and had deprived him of the opportunity of pleading the defence of automatism to the charge of inflicting grievous bodily harm which would have been likely to result in an acquittal.

Held – Although the M'Naghten Rules, which stated what constituted insanity, were more apt to apply to a person whose mental faculties were malfunctioning, rather than to a person whose mental faculties were completely absent, when he committed an offence, the common law concept of insanity still applied in the absence of any statutory definition of insanity. Although extended in 1800 to include delusions while committing an offence, the common law concept of insanity still embraced acts carried out when there was a total lack of understanding and memory due to a morbid inherent condition of the brain. Accordingly, if epilepsy brought about a total lack of understanding and memory during the course of which an offence was committed, the special verdict provided for in s 2(1) of the 1883 Act was appropriate. It followed that the judge's ruling had been correct, and the appeal would accordingly be dismissed (see p 578 *h*, p 581 *e* to *h* and p 582 *a* to *f*, post).

Arnold's Case (1724) 16 St Tr 695 applied.

Hadfield's Case (1800) 27 St Tr 1281 and *M'Naghten's Case* [1843–60] All ER Rep 229 explained.

Notes

For the defence of insanity, see 11 Halsbury's Laws (4th edn) para 30, and for cases on the subject, see 14(1) Digest (Reissue) 37–47, 143–218.

For the Trial of Lunatics Act 1883, s 2, see 8 Halsbury's Statutes (3rd edn) 225.

For the Criminal Procedure (Insanity) Act 1964, s 5, see ibid 528.

---

a Section 2(1) is set out at p 581 *j*, post
b Section 5(1), so far as material, provides: 'Where—(*a*) a special verdict is returned . . . the court shall make an order that the accused be admitted to such hospital as may be specified by the Secretary of State.'

Cases referred to in judgment

Arnold's Case (1724) 16 St Tr 695, 14(1) Digest (Reissue) 38, *150*.

Hadfield's Case (1800) 27 St Tr 1281, 14(1) Digest (Reissue) 38, *151*.

M'Naghten's Case (1843) 10 Cl & Fin 200, [1843–60] All ER 229, 8 ER 718, 4 St Tr NS 847, HL, 14(1) Digest (Reissue) 38, *156*.

R v Quick, R v Paddison [1973] 3 All ER 347, [1973] QB 910, [1973] 3 WLR 26, CA, Digest (Cont Vol D) 145, *269b*.

Cases also cited

Bratty v A-G for Northern Ireland [1961] 3 All ER 523, [1963] AC 386, HL.

Hill v Baxter [1958] 1 All ER 193, [1958] 1 QB 277, DC.

R v Burns (Dafydd John) (1973) 58 Cr App R 364, CA.

R v Charlson [1955] 1 All ER 859, [1955] 1 WLR 317, CCA.

R v Isitt (1977) 67 Cr App R 44, CA.

R v Kemp [1956] 3 All ER 249, [1957] 1 QB 399.

Appeal

The appellant, Patrick Joseph Sullivan, was charged on an indictment with causing grievous bodily harm with intent to do so (count 1) and with inflicting grievous bodily harm (count 2). At his trial at the Central Criminal Court before his Honour Judge Lymbery QC and a jury he pleaded not guilty to those counts. He conceded that he inflicted bodily harm on a man named Payne but put forward the defence that he did so while recovering from a seizure due to epilepsy and did not know what he was doing. At the close of the appellant's case the trial judge ruled that that defence constituted one of automatism by reason of insanity, and not of automatism simpliciter and consequently if the jury accepted the defence the verdict would, under s 2(1) of the Trial by Lunatics Act 1883, have to be not guilty by reason of insanity and the judge would have to make an order detaining the appellant in a special hospital, under s 5 of the Criminal Procedure (Insanity) Act 1964. To avoid the consequences of being found insane the appellant changed his plea to guilty under count 2 of the lesser offence of assault occasioning actual bodily harm and on 15 January 1982 he was convicted of that offence. He was sentenced to probation under medical supervision. He appealed against the conviction on the ground that the trial judge had erred in law in ruling that the defence was not one of automatism but amounted to a defence of insanity, and had thereby deprived the appellant, on the basis of a defence of automatism, of a likely verdict of not guilty on those counts. The facts are set out in the judgment of the court.

Bruce Speller (assigned by the Registrar of Criminal Appeals) for the appellant.
Stephen Mitchell for the Crown.

Cur adv vult

9 December. The following judgment of the court was delivered.

LAWTON LJ. Both Michael Davies J and Bush J are out of London today. It is for me to read the judgment of the court. Its text has been seen and approved by both my brethren. We have also had an opportunity to consider what should be done if an application is made for leave to appeal to the House of Lords and we have agreed what should be done.

On 14 January 1982 at the Central Criminal Court this appellant pleaded not guilty to causing grievous bodily harm with intent to do grievous bodily harm (count 1) and to inflicting grievous bodily harm (count 2). He did not challenge the Crown's evidence that he had inflicted grievous bodily harm on an elderly man named Payne, aged 80. His defence was that he had done so while in the final stage of recovering from a minor seizure due to epilepsy. According to the medical evidence which was called on his

behalf, the onset of this kind of seizure is marked by the discharge of electrical impulses
into the brain which react on centres controlling its functions, one of which is memory.
During the recovery stage, known to doctors as the post-ictal stage, the sufferer does not
know what bodily movements he may be making.

At the close of the defendant's case, the trial judge, his Honour Judge Lymbery QC,
ruled that the defence put forward was one of 'automatism by reason of insanity rather
than automatism simpliciter'. If the jury accepted the defence evidence, as they were
likely to do, there being no challenge by the Crown either to the factual evidence given
by the appellant or to the opinions on medical matters given by the two experienced
consultant physicians who were called, the verdict would have been not guilty by reason
of insanity and the judge would have had to order that the appellant should be committed
to such hospital as might be specified by the Secretary of State: see the Criminal Procedure
(Insanity) Act 1964, s 5.

Understandably, this prospect did not attract the appellant. On the advice of his
counsel, he asked for leave to change his plea on count 2 to one of guilty to assault
occasioning actual bodily harm. The judge agreed and the Crown accepted it. The jury,
by direction, returned a verdict of guilty to assault occasioning actual bodily harm. The
trial ended with the appellant being put on probation for three years.

The appellant now appeals against his conviction on the ground that the judge was
wrong in ruling that on the evidence a defence of 'automatism simpliciter' was not
available to him, thereby depriving him of the likely verdict of not guilty.

The appeal brings out starkly, untainted by the possibly bogus element of most
defences of automatism, two problems which from time to time have to be considered
by the courts. They are these. First, whether persons who have no understanding of what
they are doing because of an inherent morbid condition of their brain, should be regarded
as insane in law. Second, whether persons suffering from minor epileptic seizures (often
referred to as petit mal but more accurately as a temporal lobe epilepsy or psychomotor
epilepsy), and many do, can be said to be insane in law when they are having such a
seizure. Dr Fenwick, who is in charge of the neuropsychiatric epilepsy unit at the
Maudsley Hospital, said it is 'extremely rare' for a sufferer from petit mal to act violently
during an epileptic seizure but it can occur and it is unpredictable whether and when it
will.

The appellant has suffered from epilepsy since childhood and before 1979 he had had
grand mal fits. He had had the misfortune to suffer brain damage on two occasions; once
as the result of an accident, the second time as the consequence of an assault. The brain
damage on this occasion had been serious. His brain damage tended to retard his recovery
from fits. He had had fits while working at the Tate Gallery, and on occasions there he
had shown aggressiveness towards anyone trying to help him when he was having a fit.
According to the medical evidence, this does occur. It is more in the nature of pushing
helpers away than doing violence to them.

He had been under Dr Fenwick's care at the Maudsley Hospital since 1977. He was
given drugs to control his fits. They reduced their frequency but did not stop them
altogether. In May 1981 there were medical reasons to believe he had not been taking
the full dosage which had been prescribed for him, but this may have been due to a
misunderstanding between him and the hospital.

On 8 May 1981 the appellant and Mr Payne, who were on good terms with one
another, were sitting chatting in a flat of a neighbour, Mrs Killett. According to the
appellant, whose evidence was not challenged, he next remembered standing by a
window and seeing Mr Payne, who had sustained injuries to his face, on the floor. The
appellant said that he remembered asking Mr Payne what he had done to his face. He
then saw a cigarette on the floor, which he knew must have been his as he was the only
smoker present. He suspected that something had happened to him. He left the flat but
returned almost at once and asked Mrs Killett whether anything had in fact happened to
him. She told him that he had kicked Mr Payne, adding, 'You [are] not well, Pat.' He
said that he had no memory of what had happened.

The two physicians, to whom we have already referred, gave evidence about the nature of petit mal and its effect on the functions of the brain. Dr Fenwick gave a detailed account of what happens during a seizure. He said that sufferers from this kind of epilepsy would not have any memory of what they had done and would not be conscious of doing what they did. When re-examined, he was asked what was the medical definition of disease of the mind. He answered as follows:

'It is a disorder of the highest level of brain function which we normally think of as mind, involving consciousness, attention, perception, feelings, co-ordinating motor activity and thinking and reasoning in some proportion. This disorder must be prolonged for a period of time, usually more than a day. These disorders of brain function fall into classes with specific signs and symptoms and are known as mental illnesses.'

Dr Pamela Taylor agreed with this definition with the qualification that, in her opinion, the disturbance should last for a minimum of one month. The Crown called no medical evidence.

The starting point for consideration of the issues which arise in this case is to consider what at common law, before 1800, had to be shown to rebut an inference that an unlawful act had been done maliciously. A vivid illustration is provided by the trial of Edward Arnold for maliciously and wilfully shooting at Lord Onslow.

It is reported verbatim in the State Trials series (see (1724) 16 St Tr 695). The evidence established that the defendant had bought powder and shot, he went up to Lord Onslow with a cocked gun, took aim and fired. Evidence was called on the defendant's behalf to prove that he was mad. What was established was that for a long time he had behaved eccentrically, and looked and talked in a wild way, often to himself. There was some evidence that he suffered from delusions, as, for example, that imps danced in his room all night. He was clearly suffering from what would now be called a mental disorder within the meaning of the Mental Health Act 1959, but his brain was functioning so as to give him understanding and memory of what he was doing when he aimed a shot at Lord Onslow. Counsel for the Crown submitted that the evidence did not entitle the defendant to be acquitted. Tracy J directed the jury as follows (at 764–765):

'This is the evidence on both sides. Now I have laid it before you; and you must consider it: and the shooting my lord Onslow, which is the fact for which this prisoner is indicted, is proved beyond all manner of contradiction; but whether this shooting was malicious, that depends upon the sanity of the man. That he shot, and that wilfully [is proved]: but whether maliciously, that is the thing: that is the question; whether this man hath the use of his reason and sense? If he was under the visitation of God, and could not distinguish between good and evil, and did not know what he did, though he committed the greatest offence, yet he could not be guilty of any offence against any law whatsoever; for guilt arises from the mind, and the wicked will and intention of the man. If a man be deprived of his reason, and consequently of his intention, he cannot be guilty; and if that be the case, though he had actually killed my lord Onslow, he is exempted from punishment: punishment is intended for example, and to deter other persons from wicked designs; but the punishment of a madman, a person that hath no design, can have no example. This is on one side. On the other side, we must be very cautious; it is not every frantic and idle humour of a man, that will exempt him from justice, and the punishment of the law. When a man is guilty of a great offence, it must be very plain and clear, before a man is allowed such an exemption; therefore it is not every kind of frantic humour or something unaccountable in a man's actions, that points him out to be such a madman as to be exempted from punishment: it must be a man that is totally deprived of his understanding and memory, and doth not know what he is doing no more than an infant, than a brute, or a wild beast, such a one is never the subject of punishment.'

Arnold was found guilty and sentenced to death. Execution was respited. He died in gaol 30 years later.

a   At common law, so it seems to us, this appellant could have asked for a verdict of not guilty by reason of the fact that his epilepsy, which would have been regarded as a visitation of God, had totally deprived him of his understanding and memory. The injustice of such a restricted conception of insanity was clear. The law developed at the end of the eighteenth century in order to ensure that justice could be done to those who, although not wholly deprived of their understanding and memory, suffered from delusions of a kind which took control of their reasoning and intellectual faculties.

b   In *Hadfield's Case* (1800) 27 St Tr 1281 the defendant having been charged with high treason in attempting to assassinate George III, a defence of insanity was raised. The Attorney General, when opening the case for the Crown, stated what he submitted was the common law on insanity and gave examples of those who were deemed not responsible, including 'a person who is suffering the severity, for instance, of a violent fever'. Such a person 'may do an act of which he is perfectly unconscious, and for which, *c* therefore, he cannot be deemed to be responsible' (at 1286).

   Erskine, who appeared for the defendant, accepted that in the past there had had to be a total deprivation of understanding and memory to support such a plea but he went on to submit that the concept of legal insanity should be extended to include delusions. The presiding judge, Lord Kenyon CJ, having heard the evidence called by Erskine and with the concurrence of his brethren and the Attorney General, virtually directed the jury to *d* acquit, which they did, their verdict being as follows: 'We find the prisoner Not Guilty; he being under the influence of Insanity at the time the act was committed.' It was accepted that Hadfield ought not to be discharged but remanded to the confinement from which he came. The Criminal Lunatics Act 1800 made his continued confinement lawful.

   Hadfield's Case was an extension to the common law concept of insanity as a defence *e* and nothing more. *M'Naghten's Case* (1843) 10 Cl & Fin 200, [1843–60] All ER Rep 229 called for consideration of a defence of insane delusion. It was said on the defendant's behalf that he was not capable of exercising any control over acts which had a connection with his delusion. M'Naghten was acquitted on the ground of insanity. The discussion in the House of Lords which followed this acquittal brought about the well-known answers which all the judges (Maule J dissenting) gave to the questions which their *f* Lordships put to them. The questions themselves show that what was being considered was the law relating to criminal acts done by a person alleged to be suffering from insane delusions. The well-known words 'the accused was labouring under such a defect of reason, from disease of the mind, as not to know the nature and quality of the act he was doing, or, if he did know it, that he did not know that what he was doing was wrong' (see 4 St Tr NS 847) aptly refer to someone whose mental faculties such as consciousness, *g* attention, perception, feeling, co-ordination and thinking are working but not as they should do. They are not so apt to apply to an accused's mental state when his brain, because of epilepsy, cannot function at all in a way which is relevant to criminal liability. If a man does not know what he is doing, in no legal sense can the physical movements of his limbs which cause injury or damage to others be said to be his acts. The higher levels of brain function have not been working at all. His mind, in the ordinary sense of *h* that word, has not gone with his physical movements. Absence of relevant brain function rather than malfunctioning of mind led to Mr Payne being injured. The pre-1800 common law concept of insanity took in acts brought about through the absence of relevant brain function.

   The Trial of Lunatics Act 1883, s 2(1), as amended by s 1 of the Criminal Procedure (Insanity) Act 1964, provides as follows:

j   'Where in any indictment or information any act or omission is charged against any person as an offence, and it is given in evidence on the trial of such person for that offence that he was insane, so as not to be responsible, according to law, for his actions at the time when the act was done or omission made, then, if it appears to the jury before whom such person is tried that he did the act or made the omission charged, but was insane as aforesaid at the time when he did or made the same, the jury shall return a special verdict that the accused is not guilty by reason of insanity.'

If the evidence at a trial goes to prove insanity, the issue is raised even though the defendant does not want it raised.

There is no statutory definition of insanity and there never has been one for the purposes of the criminal law. The answers given by the judges to the House of Lords following M'Naghten's Case were not given in the course of any judicial proceedings. It follows that the special verdict has to be returned whenever there is evidence of a total lack of understanding and memory due to a morbid inherent condition of the brain. Epilepsy brings about such total lack of understanding and memory as can other morbid inherent conditions of the brain.

We appreciate that this approach to the effects of insanity on responsibility for acts which, prima facie, are criminal, differs from that which has been made by other judges of great experience. We have been led to it by consideration of some of the old cases and have been unable to find any reason why the restricted concepts of the common law should not still apply to those cases to which those concepts would have been applied before the law took a humane step forward so as to excuse from criminal liability those who suffered from insane delusions.

We do not consider it necessary to review the cases which have dealt with insanity by way of the concept of 'disease of the mind' in so far as that concept differs from the pre-1800 concept. They were all considered in R v Quick [1973] 3 All ER 347, [1973] QB 910, which stressed that such a malfunctioning of transitory effect caused to the body by some external factor such as violence, drugs, including anaesthetics, alcohol and hypnotic influences, could not fairly be said to be due to disease. The Crown in this appeal did not seek to argue that R v Quick was wrongly decided.

It follows that this appeal must be dismissed. To some, this may seem a harsh decision; but it should be remembered that persons who, through disease, cause injury to others and may do so again, are a potential danger to all who may come into contact with them. It is in the public interest that they should be put under medical care for as long as is reasonably necessary for the protection of others, but no longer. The modern form of order for confinement following a special verdict gives the Secretary of State a wide discretion as to the kind of hospital to which a defendant should be sent and how long he should stay there.

As we have already said, this appellant could have sought a verdict of not guilty by reason of insanity. Indeed, on the undisputed evidence and on the ruling of the trial judge, which we have held to be correct, perhaps such would strictly have been the right verdict. The acceptance by the judge and the Crown of a plea of guilty to count 2 might accordingly be said to have been illogical but merciful. However, in the particular circumstances of this case, it was entirely proper and, in our opinion, as in that of the trial judge, enabled justice to be done.

Appeal dismissed.

The court refused leave to appeal to the House of Lords but certified, under s 33(2) of the Criminal Appeal Act 1968, that the following point of law of general public importance was involved in the decision: whether a person who was proved to have occasioned, contrary to s 47 of the Offences against the Person Act 1861, actual bodily harm to another whilst recovering from a seizure due to psychomotor epilepsy and who did not know what he was doing when he caused such harm and had no memory of what he did should be found not guilty by reason of insanity.

10 February 1983. The Appeal Committee of the House of Lords granted the appellant leave to appeal.

Solicitors: D M O'Shea (for the Crown).

Jacqueline Charles   Barrister.

JEB Fasteners Ltd v Marks Bloom & Co (a firm)

COURT OF APPEAL, CIVIL DIVISION

STEPHENSON, DONALDSON LJJ AND SIR SEBAG SHAW

28, 29 JUNE, 22 JULY 1982

Negligence – Information or advice – Knowledge third party might rely on information – Auditor – Preparation of company's accounts – Duty to prospective investor – Auditor negligent in preparing accounts – Auditor aware when preparing accounts that company requiring outside financial support – Accounts made available to plaintiffs – Plaintiffs taking over company – Whether plaintiffs incurring loss because of reliance on accounts.

In 1975 the plaintiffs entered into negotiations to take over a manufacturing company which had recently started trading in the same products as the plaintiffs. During the negotiations the defendants, who were the company's accountants and who knew that the plaintiffs were negotiating to take over the company, produced audited accounts for the company's first trading year, being the year ended 31 October 1974, and having certified them as being accurate made the accounts available to the plaintiffs. The figures in the accounts were in certain respects substantially inaccurate. In particular, they showed that the company had done reasonably well in its first year and put an inflated value on its stock. The plaintiffs decided to take over the company, their primary motive for doing so being to acquire the services of the company's two directors, who had considerable experience in the trade. Accordingly, in June 1975 the plaintiffs completed the take-over of the company. At the time of the take-over the plaintiffs knew that the company had experienced financial difficulties in its first year and that its stock was worth less than the figure put on it in the accounts. The plaintiffs therefore knew that the accounts were inaccurate but did not appreciate the full extent of the inaccuracy. The take-over was unsuccessful and the plaintiffs suffered considerable loss as a result. They brought an action against the defendants claiming damages for breach of the defendants' duty of care to the plaintiffs, as prospective buyers of the company, to take care in preparing the company's accounts, alleging that the defendants were negligent in the preparation of the accounts and that the plaintiffs had relied on the accuracy of the accounts in deciding to take over the company. The judge held that the defendants had been negligent in the preparation of the accounts and that the plaintiffs did 'rely on' the accounts in the sense that they had studied the accounts before the take-over and the picture of the company presented by the accounts had encouraged them to proceed with the take-over. However, the judge went on to hold that, because the plaintiffs' motive for the take-over was to obtain the services of the company's two directors and because the plaintiffs had formed their own view as to the value of the company's stock, the plaintiffs would have proceeded with the take-over in any event and therefore the defendants' negligence had not been a cause of the plaintiffs' loss. The judge accordingly dismissed the plaintiffs' action. The plaintiffs appealed, contending that as a matter of law and logic the judge could not on the one hand find that the plaintiffs had relied on the accounts and yet on the other hand dismiss their claim on the ground that the defendants' negligence was not a cause of their loss.

Held – The terms 'reliance' and 'relied on' were capable of bearing either a narrow and precise meaning of 'induced' or 'wholly dependent on' or a wider meaning of 'being encouraged or supported in' taking a decision by subsidiary factors which if untrue would be a matter of disappointment but would not effect the taking of the decision. Furthermore (per Stephenson LJ), in the context of negligent misrepresentation the false misrepresentation had to play a real and substantial, although not necessarily decisive,

part in inducing the plaintiff to act if it was to be a cause of the loss because the plaintiff
'relied on' it (in the narrow sense of that term). The judge had been ambiguous in using   a
the term 'rely on' to mean 'encouraged' rather than 'induced' and he had been wrong to
separate out as different issues the question whether the plaintiffs relied on the accounts
and the question whether the plaintiffs had suffered loss by relying on the accounts: both
were merely different ways of stating the issue of causation. Nevertheless, it was clear
that the judge's underlying reasoning had been that although the plaintiffs had been
aware of and had considered the accounts they had not to any material degree affected   b
the plaintiffs' judgment in deciding to take over the company, and, on the facts, there
was ample evidence to support that conclusion. The appeal would therefore be dismissed
(see p 585 j to p 586 b and p 587 e f and j to p 589 h, post).

Decision of Woolf J [1981] 3 All ER 289 affirmed.

Notes
For damages for negligent statements in precontractual negotiations, see 31 Halsbury's
Laws (4th edn) paras 1099–1102.

Cases referred to in judgment
Hedley Byrne & Co Ltd v Heller & Partners Ltd [1963] 2 All ER 575, [1964] AC 465, [1963]
    3 WLR 101, HL, 36(1) Digest (Reissue) 24, 84.
Ross v Caunters (a firm) [1979] 3 All ER 580, [1980] Ch 297, [1979] 3 WLR 605, Digest
    (Cont Vol E) 451, 158b.

Cases also cited
Smith v Chadwick (1882) 20 Ch D 27, CA; affd (1884) 9 App Cas 187, HL.
Edgington v Fitzmaurice (1885) 29 Ch D 459, [1881–5] All ER Rep 856, CA.

Appeal
The plaintiffs, JEB Fasteners Ltd, appealed against the decision of Woolf J ([1981] 3 All
ER 289) given on 19 December 1980 dismissing the plaintiffs' claim against the
defendants, Marks Bloom & Co, a firm of accountants, for damages for negligence in
preparing the audited accounts of a company called BG Fasteners Ltd which the plaintiffs   f
were negotiating to take over and did take over thereby suffering loss. The facts are set
out in the judgment of Sir Sebag Shaw.

Murray Pickering for the plaintiffs.
Quintin J Iwi for the defendants.

Cur adv vult

22 July. The following judgments were delivered.

SIR SEBAG SHAW (giving the first judgment at the invitation of Stephenson LJ). This
is an appeal from a judgment of Woolf J given on 19 December 1980 ([1981] 3 All ER   h
289), when he dismissed the plaintiffs' claim for damages for professional negligence
against a firm of chartered accountants who practise as Marks, Bloom & Co.

The plaintiffs, JEB Fasteners Ltd, are a family company whose business was concerned
with different types of screws and other fastenings. Two brothers, John and Eric Bufton,
conducted its affairs at times material to the history of this matter, but Eric had
unfortunately died before the action was tried. In 1974 JEB Fasteners came into a   j
windfall in the form of £25,000 compensation for the compulsory acquisition of their
old premises. The Buftons thought to use this for the expansion of their company's
business. At about that time a small company, also concerned with the sale of screws and
the like, had come into existence and was having to cope with its teething troubles. Its
name was BG Fasteners Ltd and its two directors were a Mr Godridge and a Mr Wigg.

a The former was known to the Buftons as a keen, able and energetic salesman. His experience and knowledge of the trade was exceptional. The auditors of BG Fasteners were the defendants Marks Bloom & Co, of which firm Mr Marks was the partner concerned with the affairs of that company.

In June 1975 there was a take-over by JEB Fasteners of BG Fasteners, after a period of negotiation and investigation. In the course of those negotiations there were produced the audited accounts of BG Fasteners for the year ended 31 October 1974. They were

b certified in the usual way by Marks Bloom & Co as giving a true and fair view of the state of the company's (ie BG Fasteners') affairs as at 31 October 1974 and of its profit at that date. Mr John Bufton asserted that he placed great, indeed absolute, reliance on the certification by a firm of chartered accountants. As it turned out, the figures in the accounts were in certain respects substantially inaccurate. The take-over took place towards the end of June 1975. Mr John Bufton claimed that at that time he was not

c aware that the accounts did not present an accurate picture of BG Fasteners' affairs. JEB Fasteners acquired the share capital of BG Fasteners consisting of 500 shares at £1 each in exchange for 100 £1 shares in JEB Fasteners. Mr Godridge and Mr Wigg each had 50 of those shares and they were appointed directors of JEB Fasteners. That company soon discovered that the take-over was an expensive mistake. They lost a good deal of money as a result of that venture. They brought this action against the defendants alleging that

d the defendants owed to JEB Fasteners, as potential buyers of the assets and undertakings of BG Fasteners, a duty to take care in the presentation and compilation of the accounts of that company for the year ended 31 October 1974; and furthermore that they had been negligent in the performance of that duty.

Woolf J began his very careful judgment by considering the law as it had developed since *Hedley Byrne & Co Ltd v Heller & Partners Ltd* [1963] 2 All ER 575, [1964] AC 465.

e After a compendious review of all the relevant authorities, he concluded that the defendants came within the ambit of potential liability to the plaintiffs for negligence in the certification of BG Fasteners' accounts.

Having arrived at, and stated, that conclusion which opened the door to liability (and which was not in issue in the appeal, for no respondent's notice in that regard had been served), the judge went on to summarise the issues between the parties. I reproduce his

f analysis for it demonstrates the origin of the seemingly fallacious character of his ultimate decision. The summary appears thus (see [1981] 3 All ER 289 at 297–298):

'1. The foreseeability issue: [This is expanded in the judgment, but is immaterial now]. 2. The reliance issue: in coming to their decision to take over BG Fasteners Ltd, did the plaintiffs rely on the accounts audited by the defendants? 3. The negligence issue: were the defendants negligent in the preparation of those accounts?

g 4. The causation issue: that is, did the plaintiffs suffer any loss in consequence of the alleged negligence? 5. The contributory negligence issue: that is, did the plaintiffs contribute to their alleged loss by their own negligence? 6. The quantum issue: the assessment of the plaintiffs' alleged loss.'

Having considered these issues seriatim, and in detailed relation to the evidence which

h had occupied seven days of the hearing, the judge found in favour of the plaintiffs on issues 2 and 3, but in favour of the defendants on issue 4, and he proceeded to give judgment for the defendants.

The plaintiffs and those who advised them may be forgiven for regarding this outcome as a startling paradox. Counsel for the plaintiffs developed the theme of inconsistency with earnest and justifiable insistence. He contended that once the judge had found that

j the plaintiffs relied on the audited accounts he was logically precluded from negativing causation. In a general and superficial sense this argument rested on an apparently sound foundation; but it does not in my view, survive a close inspection of Woolf J's elaborate review of the evidence and his assessment of its total effect; and this is so despite the fact that 'to rely on' and 'to be influenced by' are, in general, correlative terms.

It seems to me, with all respect to the judge, that he fell into a metaphysical trap of his own devising when he separated issues 2 and 4 and treated them as distinct from each other. Issue 4 as defined in the judgment can be translated thus: 'Did the plaintiffs suffer a any loss because of the defendants' certification of the inaccurate accounts?' This is merely another way of stating issue 2. It is this analytical over-refinement which has led to the doubts which have arisen as to the true effect of the judgment. It is, therefore, necessary to look with care at the whole of the relevant text in order to ascertain which finding of the judge must prevail. What he *intended* to be his dominant finding is clear from his declared judgment. Is such an outcome not supportable having regard to his findings of b fact in relation to the whole case?

It is necessary to go back to the early history. I have already mentioned that Mr John Bufton and his late brother were looking for a means of expanding JEB Fasteners' business when in 1974 they had £25,000 of capital to utilise. They were much attracted by the idea of taking over BG Fasterners for the good commercial prospects such an arrangement would offer, quite apart from that company's immediate financial situation. It was a c business not long in operation which could be fostered; it operated in a different area from JEB Fasteners whose territory would thus be enlarged. Lastly, and very importantly, as Mr Bufton put it in his testimony at the time:

> 'Perhaps with our money and our purchasing power of JEB Fasteners and maybe
> with the ability of the salesman Bill Godridge, who had been an expert Guest, Keen
> salesman and managing director of other fastener companies, we thought we could d
> really make a go of it.'

This represented the primary impulse leading to the take-over; but it might be diminished or extinguished if BG Fasteners could not be made a viable business. It was known to be in financial difficulty after only a year or so of existence when the approach to JEB Fasteners was made. When its accounts for what was effectively the first year of its e trading were produced, Mr Bufton and his brother found matters to query. The value of the stock shown was grossly inflated; so before the take-over JEB Fasteners sent its own 'team' to examine the stock and assess its value. The figure shown in the accounts was £23,080·36. Mr Bufton's team valued it at £12,000. This was not the only respect in which the accounts might have been patently misleading: expenses were said to have been understated; a sum of £2,606 for purchases had been omitted, probably by f inadvertence, but it made the accounts inaccurate; and there were items of interest on relatively small amounts. Mr Bufton said in his evidence:

> 'I had to make a decision on those accounts which were in front of me which
> virtually said nothing. It was a small company who owned little assets apart from
> debtors and stock and the company was not making a profit nor making a loss, so it g
> was quite immaterial to me.'

This again reflects what I have described as the primary and impelling motive for the take-over. There is no doubt that Mr John Bufton and his brother and other colleagues were aware of certain aspects of the accounts which were unsatisfactory. They were not further examined because in a broad commercial sense they were not of the first importance. It is true that at one stage of his evidence Mr John Bufton said that he relied h on the stock valuation of £23,000 and did not know that it was exaggerated until after the take-over. This was, however, in direct opposition to what he later conceded, namely that he had been shown a copy of the draft accounts in which a number of items, notably the stock figure, had been altered by him or his colleagues. He said at one stage:

> '... despite the peculiarity of the stock figure, Eric and I, we said okay, it looks a j
> bit odd but we'll accept the audited balance sheet figure.'

Elsewhere he stated:

> '... we merely saw monthly sales of 6,000–4,000, so we largely bought I suppose
> without detailed knowledge.'

It is possible that by the date of the trial Mr Bufton, who attributed his brother's
a premature demise to the troubles and anxieties which developed from the take-over, had
no clear or certain recollection of what were the matters that affected his judgment back
in the spring and early summer of 1975.

The judge concluded ([1981] 3 All ER 289 at 301) that he did not—

b
'think that the accounts up to October 1974 were of critical importance to the
plaintiffs, but this does not mean they did not rely on them . . . Such a picture
would certainly encourage him [Mr Bufton] to take over the company, and in that
sense I think the plaintiffs relied on the accounts, although . . . I think that before
the take-over Mr Bufton had reservations as to the accuracy of the accounts and their
limited influence would be the importance he attached to the auditors' certificate.'

When dealing with the causation issue, Woolf J expressed his view more emphatically.
c He said (at 305):

'I have therefore come to the conclusion that before the acquisition, Mr Bufton
knew there was something seriously wrong with the stock valuation.'

This is wholly incompatible with any reliance by Mr Bufton on the auditors' certificate
which was belied by his own direct information.
d When the judge summed up his views as to the issue of causation, he said (at 305):

'At first sight my conclusion on causation may seem inconsistent with my finding
that the plaintiffs relied on the accounts.'

One can hardly dissent from that observation; but the judgment continues:

e
'The distinction as I see it is that you can be influenced by something even though
if you had not been influenced you would have acted in the same way.'

What the judge is really stating as his underlying meaning is that, while the content
of the accounts was observed and considered by Messrs John and Eric Bufton, it did not
in any material degree affect their judgment in deciding whether or not to take over BG
Fasteners Ltd.
f For these reasons it appears to me that the appeal should be dismissed.

DONALDSON LJ (read by Stephenson LJ). I add a word only in deference to the
exhaustive argument of counsel for the plaintiffs. In essence he complains that the judge
could not, as a matter of law and logic, both find that the plaintiffs relied on the audited
g accounts in deciding whether to take over BG Fasteners Ltd and yet dismiss their claim
on the ground that the defendants' negligence in the auditing of those accounts was not
a cause of the plaintiffs' loss.

The plaintiffs did not take the usual precaution of requiring the directors of BG
Fasteners Ltd to warrant the accuracy of the audited accounts and the fact that there had
been no material change in the profitability of the company since the end of the period
h covered by those accounts. Accordingly, they cannot sue the directors for breach of
warranty but must rely on a claim against the defendant auditors for negligent mis-
statement. Furthermore, the measure of damage is different. It is not the difference
between the value of the company if the facts had been as stated in the accounts and its
actual value, but the loss which the plaintiffs have sustained as a result of acting in
reliance on the accuracy of the accounts.
j It is the plaintiffs' case that they took over BG Fasteners Ltd in reliance on the accuracy
of those accounts and that they would not have done so if they had known the true facts.
If they had been able to make this good, they would indeed have been entitled to recover
the losses which they have incurred and which, ex hypothesi, they would not have
incurred if they had not taken over the company. The judge has held that the plaintiffs
did indeed rely on the accuracy of the accounts, but that there was no, or no sufficient,

causal connection between this reliance and the decision to take over BG Fasteners Ltd to justify an award of damages.

Counsel for the plaintiffs attacks the judge's conclusion on two fronts. First, he submits that the evidence does not support the findings of fact. Sir Sebag Shaw has adverted fully to this aspect and I need only say that in my judgment this was supremely a case in which the trial judge is in a better position to find the primary facts and to draw inferences from those facts than is an appellate court. There was ample evidence to support the judge's conclusions of fact. Second, he submits that if the plaintiffs relied on the accuracy of the accounts when deciding to take over BG Fasteners Ltd, it follows inevitably that there was a sufficient causal connection to establish the plaintiffs' claim.

The fallacy of this latter submission lies in regarding the concept of 'reliance' as being both narrow and precise. Counsel for the plaintiffs interprets or defines 'reliance' as if it meant 'wholly dependent on'. In reality, while 'reliance' can bear this meaning, it does not necessarily do so. In real life decisions are made on the basis of a complex of assumptions of fact. Some of these may be fundamental to the validity of the decision. 'But for' that assumption, the decision would not be made. Others may be important factors in reaching the decision and collectively, but not individually, fundamental to its validity. Yet others may be subsidiary factors which support or encourage the taking of the decision. If these latter assumptions are falsified in the event, whether individually or collectively, this will be a cause for disappointment to the decision-taker, but will not affect the essential validity of his decision in the sense that if the truth had been known or suspected before the decision was taken, the same decision would still have been made.

In holding that the plaintiffs relied on the accuracy of the accounts, the judge expressly and rightly defined his terms. He said ([1981] 3 All ER 289 at 301):

'I have no doubt that [the accounts] were studied by Mr Bufton with care and they would indicate to him, as he said in evidence, that if they were correct the company, during its first year, had done reasonably well and was in a position of balance where it was making neither profits nor losses. Such a picture would certainly encourage him to take over the company, and *in that sense* I think the plaintiffs relied on the accounts . . .' (My emphasis.)

However, he also held that the plaintiffs would not have acted differently if they had known the true position as to the accounts. In reaching this latter conclusion he was no doubt influenced by the fact that, as he found, the plaintiffs had checked the stock before deciding to take over the company and knew, or ought to have known, that the value of stock shown in the accounts was at least suspect, if not demonstrably wrong.

I can see no contradiction in the judge's findings of fact and on the basis of those findings it is an inevitable conclusion that the errors in the accounts had no causal connection with the losses which the plaintiffs incurred as a result of taking over BG Fasteners Ltd.

STEPHENSON LJ. I agree with the judgment of Sir Sebag Shaw, and that this appeal should be dismissed, because I have no doubt that the judge was justified in finding on the evidence that the defendants' negligent misrepresentation of the financial position of BG Fasteners Ltd did not cause the plaintiffs to take over that company and consequently suffer the financial loss they claimed. But I am of opinion that that finding was inconsistent with the finding that the plaintiffs relied on the accounts in the sense, and the only sense, in which those words can properly be used in a *Hedley Byrne* case (see *Hedley Byrne & Co Ltd v Heller & Partners Ltd* [1963] 2 All ER 575, [1964] AC 465), namely that the plaintiffs were induced by the misrepresentation contained in the accounts to take over the company.

In such a case the cause of action is the same as in all claims for damages for misrepresentation. The representation must be false, and it must induce the plaintiff to act on it to his detriment. If it does, he relies on it; if it does not, he does not. He may, of course, rely on other things as well. What operates on his mind, or motivates him, or influences him to act as he does, may be a number of things, some operating more or less

strongly, one perhaps predominating, as the judge found here was the fact that the
a plaintiffs 'thought that Mr Godridge and Mr Wigg, in the form of BG Fasteners Ltd,
would be the ideal vehicle to complement their existing business (see [1981] 3 All ER
289 at 301); another, not 'of critical importance' as the judge found (at 301), was the false
accounts in this case. But, as long as a misrepresentation plays a real and substantial part,
though not by itself a decisive part, in inducing a plaintiff to act, it is a cause of his loss
and he relies on it, no matter how strong or how many are the other matters which play
b their part in inducing him to act. In the words of Sir Robert Megarry V-C which the
judge quoted from his judgment in *Ross v Caunters (a firm)* [1979] 3 All ER 580 at 592,
[1980] Ch 297 at 313: 'In this type of case, reliance forms part of the test of liability, as
well as part of the chain of causation . . .' To say, as the judge did (see [1981] 3 All ER 289
at 301), that the false picture represented by the defendants' accounts 'would certainly
encourage him [the plaintiffs' director, Mr Bufton] to take over the company, and in that
c sense I think the plaintiffs relied on the accounts', with a reference to Mr Bufton's
reservations about their accuracy and 'their limited influence' is not to deny them any
influence, but only to accord them less influence than the high regard for Mr Godridge
and Mr Wigg which the judge said 'influenced' Mr Bufton and his brother to take over
the company (at 299). This is, to my mind, confirmed by the judge's attempted
reconciliation (at 305) of his apparently inconsistent findings on the reliance and causation
d issues, 'that you can be influenced by something even though if you had not been
influenced you would have acted in the same way'.

I appreciate and accept the judge's finding that Mr Bufton was wrong in saying that he
would not have purchased the company if the accounts had shown its true financial
position and that in fact the plaintiffs would still have acted in exactly the same way and
taken over the company. But that was because Mr Bufton and his brother were motivated
e by 'the two men, Mr Godridge and Mr Wigg' (at 305), not by the accounts to any
substantial extent.

If that is not what the judge meant, if the plaintiffs' directors were motivated or
influenced by the accounts to any substantial extent, there would be the necessary
reliance on the misrepresentation they contained to make a case of the kind which the
law takes into account, and sometimes describes in Latin as a causa causans, and the judge
f should have found for the plaintiffs. Nor would it necessarily follow from his finding
that the plaintiffs would have taken over the company without having false accounts to
consider, that the judge's conclusion was right: he had to decide what in fact caused the
plaintiffs to take over the company when they did have the false accounts before them.
If however, and only if, the false accounts had no real or substantial effect in inducing the
plaintiffs' directors to take over the company would the misrepresentation they contained
g not be that sort of cause, but what the law puts out of account as a mere causa sine qua
non, and it would be wrong, in my judgment, to regard the plaintiffs' directors as relying
on it and acting as they did.

'I relied on his figure of [£23,000 for the value of the stock]. It is as simple as that,' said
Mr Bufton. I agree with him that it is as simple as that. If he did, the plaintiffs should
have had judgment. Only if he did not was the judge right. And it is only because the
h judge complicated the matter by introducing what would have encouraged for what did
induce, and so finding reliance where no true reliance was, that he has given counsel for
the plaintiffs any real ground for appealing his judgment that the defendants did not
cause the plaintiffs' loss.

Appeal dismissed.

j Solicitors: *Taylor Garrett* (for the plaintiffs); *Hewitt Woollacott & Chown* (for the
defendants).

Sophie Craven   Barrister.

Athens Maritime Enterprises Corp v Hellenic Mutual War Risks Association (Bermuda) Ltd

The Andreas Lemos

QUEEN'S BENCH DIVISION (COMMERCIAL COURT)
STAUGHTON J
8, 9, 24 JUNE 1982

Marine insurance – Perils insured against – Piracy – Riot – Ship's equipment stolen when ship anchored within port limits – Thieves using or threatening to use force to make good escape after theft – Whether theft arising from act of piracy or a riot.

Under the terms of a contract of insurance the defendants, a mutual war risks association, in effect provided insurance cover for loss of materials, machinery and equipment from the shipowners' vessel occurring as the result of piracy and riots. On 22 June 1977 the vessel was anchored within port limits and within the territorial waters of the Republic of Bangladesh. Thieves armed with knives boarded the vessel and began to steal equipment. They were discovered by the crew and although the thieves at first offered resistance by brandishing their knives they fled from the ship when confronted by the ship's crew, some of whom were armed. The total value of the lost equipment was $US5,754. The owners maintained that the association was bound to indemnify them for the loss. The association denied liability. By an originating summons the owners sought the court's determination of the issue whether the loss had arisen from either an act of piracy or a riot.

Held – The association was not required to indemnify the owners for the loss, for the following reasons—

(1) For the purposes of the construction of a marine insurance policy a vessel did not have to be outside territorial waters for an act committed against it to constitute piracy. It was enough that the vessel was at sea at the time of the act, or that the act could be described as a maritime offence. However, 'piracy' in the context of a policy of marine insurance meant theft at sea involving force, or threat of force, to commit the theft and, since the incident involving the shipowners' vessel had been a clandestine theft in which force, or the threat of force, had only been used by the thieves when discovered in order to make good their escape, it did not amount to piracy (see p 598 *b* to *d*, p 599 *b* e to *g*, p 600 *b* to *d* and p 601 *f*, post); *Republic of Bolivia v Indemnity Mutual Marine Assurance Co Ltd* [1908–10] All ER Rep 260 and *Shell International Petroleum Co Ltd v Gibbs* [1982] 1 All ER 1057 applied.

(2) Furthermore, for the purposes of the construction of an insurance policy, a 'riot' occurred when three or more people carried out a common purpose using force or violence, not merely in or about the common purpose but displayed in such a manner as to alarm a reasonable person, against persons who opposed them in the execution of that common purpose. Applying that test, it was clear that the loss had not resulted from a riot since the thieves had only used, or threatened to use, force to flee from the ship when discovered after the theft had taken place (see p 600 *j* to p 601 *d* and *f*, post); *Field v Receiver of Metropolitan Police* [1904–7] All ER Rep 435 and dictum of Kerr LJ in *Shell International Petroleum Co Ltd v Gibbs* [1982] 1 All ER at 1066 applied.

Notes

For loss caused by acts of piracy or riots, see 25 Halsbury's Laws (4th edn) para 162, and for cases on the subject, see 29 Digest (Repl) 282–284, 2447–2455.

Cases referred to in judgment

a *Allen v Flood* [1898] AC 1, [1895–9] All ER Rep 52, HL, 1(1) Digest (Reissue) 33, 232.

Bolivia, Republic of v Indemnity Mutual Marine Assurance Co Ltd [1909] 1 KB 785; affd [1909] 1 KB 785, [1908–10] All ER Rep 260, CA, 29 Digest (Reissue) 282, 2447.

Field v Receiver of Metropolitan Police [1907] 2 KB 853, [1904–7] All ER Rep 435, 15 Digest (Reissue) 917, 7857.

London and Lancashire Fire Insurance Co Ltd v Bolands Ltd [1924] AC 836, [1924] All ER
b Rep 642, HL, 29 Digest (Reissue) 561, 5008.

Magellan Pirates, The (1853) 1 Ecc & Ad 81, 164 ER 47, 15 Digest (Reissue) 1008, 8741.

Nishina Trading Co Ltd v Chiyoda Fire and Marine Insurance Co Ltd [1969] 2 All ER 776, [1969] 2 QB 449, [1969] 2 WLR 1094, CA, 29 Digest (Reissue) 284, 2455.

Pan American World Airways Inc v Aetna Casualty and Surety Co [1974] 1 Lloyd's Rep 207, US District Ct; affd [1975] 1 Lloyd's Rep 77, US Ct of Appeals.

c *People v Lol-lo* (1922) 1 Ann Digest 164.

Piracy Jure Gentium, Re [1934] AC 586, [1934] All ER Rep 506, PC, 15 Digest (Reissue) 1009, 8749.

R v Anderson (1868) LR 1 CCR 161, [1861–73] All ER Rep 999, CCR, 14(1) Digest (Reissue) 158, 1103.

R v Hale (Robert) (1978) 68 Cr App R 415, CA.

d *Sarah, The* (1862) Lush 549, 167 ER 248, 1(1) Digest (Reissue) 224, 1258.

Shell International Petroleum Co Ltd v Gibbs [1982] 1 All ER 225, [1982] QB 946, [1982] 2 WLR 745; on appeal [1982] 1 All ER 1057, [1982] QB 946, [1982] 2 WLR 745, CA.

United Africa Co Ltd v mv Tolten (owners), The Tolten [1946] 2 All ER 372, [1946] P 135, CA, 11 Digest (Reissue) 398, 387.

US v Furlong (1820) 5 Wheat 184.

e *US v Smith* (1820) 5 Wheat 153.

Zeta, The, Mersey Docks and Harbour Board v Turner [1893] AC 468, HL, 1(1) Digest (Reissue) 264, 1566.

Originating summons

f By an originating summons dated 23 August 1981 the plaintiffs, Athens Maritime Enterprises Corp, sought the determination of the question whether the plaintiffs were entitled to be indemnified by the defendants, Hellenic Mutual War Risks Association (Bermuda) Ltd, for loss of ship's materials and equipment from the plaintiffs' vessel Andreas Lemos while the vessel was anchored in the Chittagong roads, Bangladesh, on 22 June 1977. The facts are set out in the judgment.

g *Anthony Hallgarten QC* and *Elizabeth Birch* for the plaintiffs.
Mark Saville QC and *Sarah Miller* for the defendants.

Cur adv vult

h 24 June. The following judgment was delivered.

STAUGHTON J. The plaintiffs, who are the owners of the vessel Andreas Lemos, insured her hull and machinery on the terms of the standard form of English marine
j policy with the F C & S clause attached, or so I must assume for the purpose of this action. They also entered the vessel in the defendants' association, which is a mutual association providing insurance against war risks, as its name shows. Then misfortune occurred in the shape of a loss of ship's material and equipment. It was taken in the night by a gang of men armed with knives, while the vessel was anchored in the Chittagong roads on 22 June 1977. The loss amounted to $US5,754·40.

The dispute is about whether the loss comes within the cover provided by the marine policy, or whether it should be borne by the war risks association. I was told that in fact such a small claim might not be payable at all if it is within the cover provided by the marine policy, as it might not exceed a deductible item provided by that policy. But with that I am not concerned. I was also told that a number of other similar disputes have occurred. That may not be as unlikely as it seems, since The Bay of Bengal Pilot (10th edn, 1978) p 83 now states of the port of Chittagong: 'Thieving, especially of mooring ropes, was reported (1978) to be very prevalent both at outer anchorages and alongside.' This action was tried on an agreed statement of facts, and the defendant association has agreed to bear the costs of both parties.

The rules of the association, so far as material, provide that the vessel was insured against:

'Loss, where partial or total of (i) the entered Ship's Hull, Materials, Machinery and all other parts and equipment thereof (ii) Freight (including time charter hire and anticipated freight), Premiums, disbursements, commissions and profits when caused by the risks set out in paragraphs (A) and (B) of Part A of this Rule:—

(A) The risks excluded from the Standard Form of English Marine Policy by:—(i) The following clause (hereinafter called "the F.C. and S. clause"):—Warranted free of capture, seizure, arrest, restraint or detainment and the consequences thereof or of any attempt thereat; also from the consequences of hostilities or warlike operations, whether there be a declaration of war or not; but this warranty shall not exclude collision, contact with any fixed or floating object (other than a mine or torpedo), stranding, heavy weather or fire unless caused directly (and independently of the nature of the voyage or service which the vessel concerned or in the case of collision, any other vessel involved therein is performing) by a hostile act by or against a belligerent power; and for the purpose of this warranty "power" includes any authority maintaining naval, military or air forces in association with a power. Further warranted free from the consequences of civil war, revolution, rebellion, insurrection, or civil strife arising therefrom or piracy . . .

(B) (iii) strikes, locked out workmen or persons taking part in labour disturbances, riots or civil commotions: (iv) persons acting maliciously . . .'

The facts giving rise to the claim are as set out in the report of the master of the vessel, Captain M Dakoronias, dated 22 June 1977 which reads as follows:

'16.40: Vessel anchored Chittagong roads 3·5 miles east of light beacon PATENGA. 21.20: Sailor on watch Oliver Alfredo on his usual round for checking ship's safety came in a hurry to officers and crew messroom and shouted that there are many armed people on the forecastle throwing into the sea ship's lines, mooring and other equipment. Officers and crew we run forward, having armed ourselves with whatever we could lay our hands on such as jacks, knives and I holding vessel's pistol, also the two 2nd Officers, vessel's rockets we proceeded towards forecastle on which about 6–7 natives holding long knives threatened first to stop us. When they saw my pistol and 2nd Officer fired rockets very near them they frightened and jumped into the sea. After investigation we found out that 4 ship's mooring lines were missing completely and the 5th line was cut by knife as thieves had not time to pull it out from the forecastle. Also missing other equipment per separate list attached. 21.40: Tried to contact with shore harbour master or other shore authority unsuccessfully by V.H.F. Sailor Oliver Alfredo said that when he first went forward he saw that the pirates had long knives and were threatening him as he was running away to the accommodation asking for assistance. Before arrival we had secured all storerooms and forecastle doors and openings by padlocks from outside and chain with ducklets from the inside. The pirates must have climbed on to the vessel by using grapnels as the anchor chain hole was completely secured. They then entered into the forecastle by way of the anchor chain in the chain locker. The pirates in

a
their hurry to leave the vessel left behind a native long knife like a sickle or parang. I would like to make it clear that all manholes, doors, etc. leading to lockers which are not going to be used are secured by welding, and the remaining lockers in use are secured by padlocks and chains.'

I should add that the rules of the association provide by r 3(A):

b
'The association shall not be liable for:—(1) Any loss damage or expense covered by the Standard Form of English Marine Policy with the Institute Time Clauses Hulls (Edition of 1.10.1970) attached with the F.C. & S. Clause . . . inserted therein or which would have been covered thereby if the ship had been insured under such a Policy.'

Rule 47(B) states:

c
'These Rules and all contracts of insurance made by the Association shall be subject to and incorporate the provisions of the Marine Insurance Act 1906 of the United Kingdom and any statutory modifications thereof except in so far as such Act or modification thereof may have been excluded by these Rules or by any term of such contracts.'

d
It is agreed that the court may draw all reasonable inferences of fact from the report. Counsel for the owners invited me to draw the following inferences: (1) the six or seven men were acting in concert as a gang or band or company; (2) they were not lawfully on board the vessel; (3) they came by one or more craft, since otherwise there would be no point in throwing the ship's ropes overboard; (4) they were for a time in effective control of the forepart of the vessel; (5) they were seriously armed, viz with knives. Counsel for
e
the association did not controvert any of those suggested inferences. I find that they can reasonably, and should, be drawn.

Counsel for the association put before me, without objection on the part of the owners, further material which established the following: (1) the place where the vessel was anchored in Chittagong roads was 2·8 miles from the land, and within the port limits; (2) it was also within the 12-mile breadth of territorial sea claimed by the Republic of
f
Bangladesh.

Counsel for the owners submitted that the loss was within the association's war risks cover, on three grounds. He said that it was a loss by (i) piracy or (ii) riots or (iii) persons acting maliciously.

However, before me he did not seek to succeed on the third ground, but merely to reserve it in case the dispute goes to a higher court. He observed that the phrase 'persons
g
acting maliciously' was considered by the Court of Appeal in *Nishina Trading Co Ltd v Chiyoda Fire and Marine Insurance Co Ltd* [1969] 2 All ER 776, [1969] 2 QB 449. There also it was associated by its context with 'riots' and 'civil commotions'. Lord Denning MR said ([1969] 2 All ER 776 at 779, [1969] 2 QB 449 at 462): 'I think "maliciously" here means spite, or ill will, or the like.' Edmund Davies LJ agreed. Phillimore LJ said that the clause was 'obviously intended to deal with damage effected in the course of some
h
civil disturbance' (see [1969] 2 All ER 776 at 783, [1969] 2 QB 449 at 467). Counsel for the owners also observed that in *Shell International Petroleum Co Ltd v Gibbs* [1982] 1 All ER 225 at 239, [1982] 2 QB 946 at 965–966 the *Nishina* case was followed by Mustill J on this point, as on others, and in the Court of Appeal counsel for the owners in the *Shell* case accepted that he could not rely on the peril of 'persons acting maliciously' (see [1982] 1 All ER 1057 at 1062, [1982] QB 946 at 986). Those are the authorities which persuaded
j
counsel for the owners not to rely on it before me. However, as a trailer for what his argument might be in a higher court, he referred me to *Allen v Flood* [1898] AC 1 at 93–94, [1895–9] All ER Rep 52 at 68. There Lord Watson said, quoting from an earlier judgment of Bowen LJ: '"Maliciously" . . . means and implies an intention to do an act which is wrongful to the detriment of another.' There, for the present at any rate, the point rests.

So I turn to piracy and riots. At the start I must mention again what has been described as 'the convoluted process by which war risks insurance is put together'. There are two *a* sections in Part A of r (ii) in the present case. Both provide cover. But for convenience I shall call section (A) 'the negative cover' (for want of a better phrase), and section (B) 'the positive cover'.

Section (A) provides cover against the risks excluded from the standard form of marine policy by the F C & S clause. One therefore has to inquire, first, whether a particular casualty would have been covered by the standard form of marine policy; and, second, *b* whether it has been excluded by the F C & S clause from that policy. If the answer to both questions is affirmative, then the negative cover of the war risks association comes into force: see Arnould *Law of Marine Insurance and Average* (16th edn, 1981) para 880. One can see the sense of such an arrangement for an insured, who does not want to fall between two stools; but it is something of a burden for everbody else.

Section (B), the positive cover, provides insurance against a number of perils, including *c* riots. At first sight one does not need to inquire whether a loss caused by riots is also covered by the marine policy, and double insurance may occur. But then one turns to r 3(A)(1), which provides that the association shall not be liable for any loss, damage or expense covered by the standard form of marine policy with the F C & S clause inserted therein. So that question does have to be asked after all.

The relevant perils in the standard form of marine policy are 'pirates, rovers, thieves'. *d* I am by no means clear what are rovers, and no attention was directed to them in argument. So I consider only pirates and thieves. The shape of the inquiry is then as follows:

Section (A): the negative cover

(1) Was the loss caused by pirates and/or thieves? (2) If so, is it excluded from the *e* marine cover by the word 'piracy' in the F C & S clause?

If both questions are answered Yes, section (A) of the war risks cover operates. Theoretically one should go on to ask, in terms of r 3(A)(1), whether the loss is nevertheless covered by the standard form of policy. But I do not see how, in the premises, it could be.

f

Section (B): the positive cover

(1) Was the loss caused by riots? (2) If so, is it nevertheless covered by the standard form of marine policy, and therefore excluded from the association's cover by r 3(A)(1)?

Counsel for the association submitted that the second question would be relevant here if I were to decide that the casualty came within the term 'riots', but also within the term *g* 'thieves'. In that event, he argued, the loss would not be covered by the war risks association. Counsel for the owners countered that with the argument that the words 'covered by' in r 3(A)(1) mean covered by the same peril. No authority was advanced for that proposition, and I can see no rhyme or reason for it. What the parties were interested in was excluding double insurance, in meal or in malt. They were not in the least concerned whether the double insurance arose because the same peril was insured, eo *h* nomine, by both sets of insurers, or because different wording in the two contracts was equally applicable to the facts of a particular casualty.

So I accept the submission of counsel for the association that a loss by riots is excluded from the positive cover of the association, if it is also a loss by thieves. No similar argument arises on the negative cover. Most, if not all, pirates are also thieves, but the exclusion of 'piracy' from the marine cover by the F C & S clause refers to pirates who are *j* thieves as well as any other pirates. The association's cover therefore insures against loss by piracy, even if it is also a loss by thieves.

Piracy

After that lengthy introduction, I turn to consider piracy. Counsel for the association took two points. First, he argued that the casualty was not caused by piracy because it

occurred within the territorial waters of Bangladesh, and, second, that force or the threat
a of force is an essential element of piracy, and on the facts it could not be shown that any
had occurred at such a time as to cause the loss.

As to the first point, there is compelling authority for the view that in public
international law piracy can only occur outside the jurisdiction of any state: see
Oppenheim's International Law (8th edn, 1955) vol 1, para 272 ('the open sea' is defined in
para 252 so as to exclude the maritime belt); Colombos *International Law of the Sea* (6th
b edn, 1967) para 457 ('Piracy consists of acts of violence done on the high seas without
recognised authority and outside the jurisdiction of any civilised State. The zone of
operations is the high seas. When such acts are committed within territorial waters,
jurisdiction belongs to the littoral State'); art 15 of the Convention on the High Seas
(1958), (Geneva, 29 April 1958; TS 5 (1963); Cmnd 1929) to be found in Singh
International Conventions of Merchant Shipping (2nd edn, 1973) pp 1460–1466. A contrary
c view is, however, tentatively suggested in Greig *International Law* (2nd edn, 1976) p 332.

Both the need for a definition of piracy in public international law and the reason why
that definition is, in general, confined to acts committed on the high seas appear from art
19 of the convention:

'On the high seas, or in any other place outside the jurisdiction of any State, every
State may seize a pirate ship or aircraft, or a ship taken by piracy and under the
d control of pirates, and arrest the persons and seize the property on board. The courts
of the State which carried out the seizure may decide upon the penalties to be
imposed, and may also determine the action to be taken with regard to the ships,
aircraft or property, subject to the rights of third parties acting in good faith.'

When robbery with violence is committed within the jurisdiction of a state, it is not
e thought necessary to give every state the right to seize, prosecute and punish the
offenders.

It is by no means self-evident that similar considerations point to the same definition
of piracy for domestic purposes, and in particular for the interpretation of a contract of
insurance. Counsel for the association submitted that, if I held that there was a loss by
piracy in the present case, then every robber on board a houseboat on the Thames will be
f liable to prosecution in every country in the world. I do not accept that submission. It is
not my intention to derogate from the existing rules of public international law on the
topic of piracy, even if I have power to do so. But a different rule, for the purpose of
interpreting contracts of insurance, will not give rise to the disastrous consequence
envisaged by the submission of counsel for the association. A shipowner whose property
is taken by robbers is not much concerned whether that takes place in or outside
g territorial waters. Nor should I have thought that the precise location was of much
concern to insurers, save to the extent that robbery is a good deal more likely on board a
ship in a port or estuary, than it is 12 miles out or more.

So I turn to the authorities on piracy in a domestic context. Counsel for the owners
referred me to the *Oxford English Dictionary*:

'Piracy. The action or practice of a pirate. 1. The practice or crime of robbery
h and depredation on the sea or navigable rivers etc., or by descent from the sea upon
the coast, by persons not holding a commission from an established civilised
state . . .'

Next, *Re Piracy Jure Gentium* [1934] AC 586, [1934] All ER Rep 506. This decided,
according to a headnote whose brevity might form a model for today ([1934] AC 586):

j 'Actual robbery is not an essential element of the crime of piracy jure gentium. A
frustrated attempt to commit a piratical robbery is equally piracy jure gentium.'

The case was not directly concerned with public international law, but with the offence
of piracy at common law as opposed to statute. However, the Judicial Committee
evidently considered that it ought to be decided by reference to international law. The
question was referred to the Judicial Committee by Order in Council, following the

acquittal of some unsuccessful pirates in Hong Kong. Viscount Sankey LC, delivering
the advice of the Board, cited a large number of definitions by various writers and judges. *a*
As the case was not concerned with the location of the alleged piracy, no great importance
can be attached to his citation of them for the present purpose. But one notices Sir Charles
Hedges, 'within the jurisdiction of the Admiralty'; *Dana's Wheaton,* 'the high seas';
Blackstone and *East,* 'the high seas'; *Oxford English Dictionary* already cited; Story J, 'upon
the sea'; Dr Lushington and Sir Robert Phillimore, 'the high seas'; and *Kenny,* 'at sea' (see
[1934] AC 586 at 591, 592, 593, 595, 596, 598, [1934] All ER Rep 506 at 509, 509, 510, *b*
511, 512, 512–513, 513).

Russell on Crime (12th edn, 1964), p 1533 also cites Sir Charles Hedges, 'within the
jurisdiction of the Admiralty'. That phrase is, I think, counsel for the owners' preferred
candidate as providing a geographical limit to what is piracy. The jurisdiction of the
Admiralty court today is, and has for some time been, based on statute. But as Scott LJ
pointed out in *United Africa Co v mv Tolten (owners), The Tolten* [1946] 2 All ER 372 at 381, *c*
[1946] P 135 at 154:

> 'The limiting rules of the common law about venue were unknown in the Court
> of Admiralty; and the universality of the world area over which it administered
> justice both civil and criminal affords a striking contrast to the locally restrictive
> rules of common law jurisdiction.'

d

He explained the extent of that jurisdiction ([1946] 2 All ER 372 at 382, [1946] P 135 at
156):

> 'Different phrases have been used, by both Admiralty and common law judges
> and in Admiralty documents, to describe the world wide ambit of Admiralty
> jurisdiction, but none is more all-embracing than the one used most often—"the
> high seas". Dr. LUSHINGTON used it repeatedly. In *The Sarah* ((1862) Lush 549 at 550, *e*
> 167 ER 248 at 249) he said: "The court has original jurisdiction, because the matter
> complained of is a tort committed on the high seas". LORD HERSCHELL cited that
> observation with approval in *The Zeta* ([1893] AC 468 at 480). But, as so used, the
> descriptive phrase "high seas" had no reference to territorial waters or any other
> concept of public international law: on the contrary, it included as far as the tide *f*
> reached up rivers. It was for this reason that it became convenient to find a practical
> boundary. That was afforded by stopping at the first bridge; and in the early days
> when the law of the sea took shape there were few bridges across the tidal reaches of
> rivers. Other descriptions emphasizing the extensive signification of the phrase
> "high seas" are "in places where great ships go", a geographical term which would
> reach a long way up most navigable rivers in those days when probably a ship of
> 300 tons was accounted "great". Another descriptive form of words used by *g*
> BLACKBURN, J., in *R. v. Anderson* ((1868) LR 1 CCR 161 at 169) was ". . . at a place
> where the tide flows and below all bridges . . ." These expressions all mean the same
> thing, although the word "place" imports something visually identifiable and no
> doubt had reference to places where land and sea meet.'

The view that this test should provide the geographical limit to piracy is supported by *h*
The Magellan Pirates (1853) 1 Ecc & Ad 81, 164 ER 47. Dr Lushington did there refer to
the high seas, no doubt in the sense mentioned by Scott LJ. But he also cited, with
apparent approval, this passage from *Russell on Crime*:

> 'If a robbery be committed in creeks, harbours, ports, &c., in foreign countries,
> the Court of Admiralty indisputably has jurisdiction of it, and such offence is
> consequently piracy.'

j

(See (1853) 1 Ecc & Ad 81 at 84, 164 ER 47 at 49.)

If it is still good law, that authority is directly in point. Dr Lushington did later
indicate a possible restriction', so as to exclude acts committed in the ports of a foreign
state; but he did not himself support that restriction.

The point arose directly in *Republic of Bolivia v Indemnity Mutual Marine Assurance Co Ltd* [1909] 1 KB 785. That case was concerned with a marine policy providing cover against loss by piracy. Goods intended for the Bolivian government were seized by Brazilian malcontents who wished to resist Bolivian authority. It was ultimately held in the Court of Appeal that they were not pirates, because they were acting for public and political motives.

However, it was also argued that this was not piracy because the vessel was at the time in the River Acre, a tributary of a tributary of the Amazon. Pickford J said this about the point (at 789–790):

'One definition which was relied on was that given in Russell on Crimes, 6th ed., vol. i. p. 260, and which is as follows: "The offence of piracy at common law consists in committing those acts of robbery and depredation upon the high seas which if committed on land would have amounted to felony there." It was said that these goods were forcibly stolen, that there was a felony, and that the offence came within that definition, because "the high seas" there mentioned must be extended to all waters over which there was Admiralty jurisdiction. In *Reg. v. Anderson* ((1868) LR 1 CCR 161, [1861–73] All ER Rep 999) the jurisdiction of the Admiralty was held to extend to a ship some distance up the river Garonne, and therefore it is argued that this place was within the jurisdiction of the Admiralty. As to that, all I will say at the moment is that I am not satisfied that an illegal act by Brazilians in a place situated upon a tributary of a tributary of the Amazon, that act consisting in taking from a Brazilian ship goods belonging to the Bolivian Government, comes within the jurisdiction of the British Admiralty, but, in the view I take of the case, it is not necessary to decide that point. I was also referred to the definitions of piracy given in Hall's International Law and Oppenheim's International Law. The definition given by the latter writer does not seem to be of much assistance to the plaintiffs, as he says that the offence must be committed on the high seas. The definition given by Hall is, no doubt, very wide, but as I have already said, I am not at all sure that what might be piracy in international law is necessarily piracy within the meaning of the term in a policy of insurance.'

In the Court of Appeal Vaughan Williams LJ took a firmer view. He said ([1909] 1 KB 785 at 798, [1908–10] All ER Rep 260 at 266):

'Pickford J. has decided this case, expressly leaving out of determination all definitions of piracy for purposes of either international or English municipal law. He has decided the case merely on the meaning of the word "piracy" in this particular policy. I wish, however, to say for myself, though we have not got to decide that question, in case of any difficulty hereafter as to the meaning of the judgment of Pickford J. or of that of the Court of Appeal, that in my opinion there is no pretence for calling what in this case had happened on the borders of Brazil and Bolivia piracy. In the first place, I do not think that the place where these events happened, which was not on the Amazon where it ran into the sea, but on a branch river running into another branch river of the Amazon, was a place where a piracy could be committed. After all, this was a policy of marine insurance, and the loss sought to be covered was alleged to be loss by piracy, or something ejusdem generis. Whatever the definition of piracy may be, in my opinion piracy is a maritime offence, and what took place on this river, running partly in Brazil and partly in Bolivia, far up country, did not take place on the ocean at all. That distant place was not the theatre on which piracy could be committed. It is a region which cannot be said to be, like the ocean, under the jurisdiction of no particular power. It was under the jurisdiction of either Brazil or Bolivia. That part of the river is not the highway of the world, where ships of all nations can go protected only by the law of nations. It is a place where, if any ships go, they go, not on the sea, but on a river running in occupied territory which is under the government of a specific nation which has jurisdiction there. I wish to add one word in relation to the distinction between piracy jure gentium and piracy by municipal law. Whatever other limitation there might be in this policy, it could, in my opinion, only extend to piracy jure gentium, and not to robbery on a river which at that point had been running through land for a long distance and had to run for a further distance, and both banks of which there belonged to Bolivia.'

Farwell LJ said that he would express no opinion on this point. Kennedy LJ was disposed to accept that in general, piracy was robbery 'at sea' (see [1909] 1 KB 785 at 802, [1908–10] All ER Rep 260 at 268). But he concluded that a different meaning must have been intended in this policy, since it covered only a river transit.

In the face of that authority, I cannot accept counsel for the owners' submission that piracy may be committed anywhere within the common law jurisdiction of the Court of Admiralty, 'in places where great ships go', or 'at a place where the tide flows and below all bridges'. But I see no reason to limit piracy to acts outside territorial waters. In the context of an insurance policy, if a ship is, in the ordinary meaning of the phrase, 'at sea' (per Kennedy LJ), or if the attack on her can be described as 'a maritime offence' (per Vaughan Williams LJ), then for the business purposes of a policy of insurance she is, in my judgment, in a place where piracy can be committed.

That view is supported to some extent by the Marine Insurance Act 1906, Sch 1, r 8:

'The term "pirates" includes passengers who mutiny and rioters who attack the ship from the shore.'

It is not easy to envisage a ship being attacked by rioters from the shore when she is outside territorial waters; but it could happen, I suppose, when she is 'at sea'.

Three American cases were cited. US v Smith (1820) 5 Wheat 153 is of interest as containing a scholarly collection by Story J of ancient authorities. US v Furlong (1820) 5 Wheat 184 provides direct support for the conclusion I have reached. There Johnson J, delivering the opinion of the United States Supreme Court, said (at 199–200):

'It was also moved in two of the cases of piracy that as the offences charged were committed on vessels then lying at anchor near the shore of the islands of Mayo and Bonavista, in a road and within a marine league of the shore, the prisoners could not be convicted: 1. Because the words "out of the jurisdiction of any particular State" in the 8th section of the act of 1790 includes foreign as well as domestic States; 2. Because the vessel at anchor in a road is not a vessel on the high seas, as charged in the indictment. On the first point, we think it obvious that *out of any particular State*, must be construed to mean *"out of any one of the United States."* By examining the context, it will be seen, that *particular State* is uniformly used in contradistinction to *United States*. For what reason it is not easy to imagine; but it is obvious that the only piracies omitted to be punished by that act, are land piracies, and piracies committed within our waters. On the second point, we are of opinion, that a vessel in an open road may well be found by juries to be on the seas. It is historically known, that in prosecuting trade with many places, vessels lie at anchor in open situations, (and especially where the trade winds blow) under the lee of the land. Such vessels are neither in a river, haven, basin or bay, and are nowhere unless it be on the seas. Being at anchor is immaterial, for this might happen in a thousand places in the open ocean, as on the Banks of Newfoundland. Nor can it be objected that it was within the jurisdictional limits of a foreign State; for, those limits, though neutral to war, are not neutral to crimes.'

The same conclusion about territorial waters was reached in People v Lol-lo (1922) 1 Ann Dig 164.

Next, I have to consider whether force or a threat of force is an essential element of piracy. Rule 8 in Sch 1 of the 1906 Act is not of much assistance, although it is consistent with the proposition that force or a threat of force is required. Counsel for the owners a observes that while many, if not all, definitions refer to robbery, some also include 'depredation' and 'plunder'. Those activities, he suggests, do not necessarily include force or a threat of force.

The only case to which I was referred that bears directly on the point was *Re Piracy Jure Gentium* [1934] AC 586, [1934] All ER Rep 506, and that went no further than holding that an attempt at robbery would amount to piracy, even if the substantive offence were not achieved. But the general tenor of the authorities supports the conclusion b that theft without force or a threat of force cannot be piracy. Thus *Carver's Carriage by Sea* (12th edn) para 183 has the definition:

'Piracy is forcible robbery at sea, whether committed by marauders from outside the ship, or by mariners or passengers within it.'

The same statement, in the fourth edition of *Carver,* was generally approved by Kennedy c LJ in *Republic of Bolivia v Indemnity Mutual Assurance Co Ltd* [1909] 1 KB 785 at 802, [1908–10] All ER Rep 260 at 268. (Others, including Dr Lushington, would include murder; but that is immaterial for present purposes.) Lord Denning MR in *Shell International Petroleum Co Ltd v Gibbs* [1982] 1 All ER 1057 at 1062, [1982] QB 946 at 986 said:

d '"Pirates" and "thieves" These perils have been very narrowly construed. There were no "pirates" here because there was no forcible robbery. There were no "thieves" here because there were no violent means. This was accepted by Shell and no claim was made in this regard before the judge.'

I hold that theft without force or a threat of force is not piracy under a policy of marine insurance.
e How then stands a case of piracy on the facts? I draw the inference that the armed men who came on board the Andreas Lemos intended, and expected, to steal without violence. However, I infer also that they anticipated the possibility of some resistance or interference by a night-watchman, and intended to use force or a threat of force if that possibility materialised. I doubt that they expected to be able to defeat the master and crew if it came to a pitched battle.
f So much for their intentions. What in fact happened was that the theft was complete before they were discovered, or at any rate before any force or threat of force occurred. The contrary is not established by the agreed statement of facts. Counsel for the owners invites me to infer that the fifth mooring line, which was 'cut by knife as thieves had not time to pull it out from the forecastle', must have been stolen during or after the first use of force or threat of force. This argument itself has some force, but I do not feel able to g draw that inference. The case is, in my judgment, one of clandestine theft which was discovered; force or a threat of force was used by the men to make good their escape.

Section 8(1) of the Theft Act 1968 provides:

'A person is guilty of robbery if he steals, and immediately before or at the time of doing so, and in order to do so, he uses force on any person or puts or seeks to put h any person in fear of being then and there subjected to force.'

Archbold's Criminal Pleading, Evidence and Practice (40th edn, 1979) para 1482 states:

'Force used only to get away after committing a theft does not seem naturally to be regarded as robbery.'

j This is followed by a discussion as to when theft is first complete, by appropriation. I would, with respect, deprecate any over-elaborate analysis of the sequence of events, either for the purpose of the criminal law or in the context of the present case. That view may perhaps have the support of the Court of Appeal, for counsel for the owners found in the Supplement to *Archbold* the case of *R v Hale* [1978] 68 Cr App R 415. There the court said (at 418):

'. . . the act of appropriation does not suddenly cease. It is a continuous act and it is a matter for the jury to decide whether or not the act of appropriation has *a* finished.'

I gladly follow that test. But I conclude that the act of appropriation had finished in this case when the force or a threat of force was first used, or at any rate the contrary is not proved. The act of appropriation finished when the goods were thrown into the sea, presumably into or near a boat or boats which had brought the armed men. There was *b* no loss by piracy.

That conclusion seems to me to accord with the commercial sense of the matter. The association, by the word piracy, insures the loss caused to shipowners because their employees are overpowered by force, or terrified into submission. It does not insure the loss caused to shipowners when their night-watchman is asleep (as might occur, although it did not in this case) and thieves steal clandestinely. The very notion of piracy is *c* inconsistent with clandestine theft. Counsel for the owners described this as a prosaic form of piracy; a recent judge might have preferred the word 'anaemic'. It is not necessary that the thieves must raise the pirate flag and fire a shot across the victim's bows before they can be called pirates. But piracy is not committed by stealth. This case is very near to the borderline; but it must not on that account be allowed to make bad law. *d*

Riots

If one takes the word in its current and popular meaning, nobody but a Sloane Ranger would say of this casualty, 'It was a riot.' The word today means the sort of civil disturbance which has recently occurred in Brixton, Bristol or Wormwood Scrubs. *e* Counsel for the association referred me, in this connection, to *Pan American World Airways Inc v Aetna Casualty and Surety Co* [1974] 1 Lloyd's Rep 207, decided in the United States District Court for the Southern District of New York. There an aircraft had been hijacked and blown up by members of the Popular Front for the Liberation of Palestine. The insurers denied liability on the ground that this was a loss by 'riots', and therefore excluded. Frankel DJ expressed some forthright criticism of English jurisprudence on *f* this point, and declined to depart from the current and ordinary meaning of the word.

That approach attracts considerable sympathy, at any rate from me, and at any rate in theory. But on further examination it cannot be adopted for an English policy of marine insurance. Take, for example, the word 'rovers'. Its only current and popular meaning is, I suppose, a species of motorcar, such as Ford or Vauxhall. The expression 'letters of mart', although it occurs in the United States Constitution, is meaningless in popular *g* speech, and was regarded by the *Oxford English Dictionary* as obsolete in 1908. But the dictionary tells us that 'so far as European nations are concerned the issue of letters of mart was abolished by the Congress of Paris in 1856'. Kerr LJ said in *Shell International Petroleum Co Ltd v Gibbs* [1982] 1 All ER 1057 at 1065, [1982] QB 946 at 990:

'As it has been said many times in many authorities, in construing the various archaic expressions which are still to be found in this form of policy, one cannot go *h* by their ordinary meaning in our language today, but one must treat them as terms of art and interpret them in accordance with their original meaning.'

I therefore adopt, for this purpose, the definition of a riot provided in *Field v Receiver of Metropolitan Police* [1907] 2 KB 853 at 860, [1904–7] All ER Rep 435 at 437 by Phillimore J, and set out in the headnote ([1907] 2 KB 853): *j*

'In order to constitute a riot five elements are necessary—(1) a number of persons not less than three; (2) a common purpose; (3) execution or inception of the common purpose; (4) an intent on the part of the number of persons to help one another, by force if necessary, against any person who may oppose them in the execution of the

a
common purpose; (5) force or violence, not merely used in and about the common purpose, but displayed in such a manner as to alarm at least one person of reasonable firmness and courage.'

That definition was, I think, applied by the House of Lords to a policy of insurance in *London and Lancashire Fire Insurance Co Ltd v Bolands Ltd* [1924] AC 836, [1924] All ER Rep 642. I apply it in this case. In *Republic of Bolivia v Indemnity Mutual Assurance Co Ltd*
b
[1909] 1 KB 785 at 804; cf [1908–10] All ER Rep 260 at 269 Kennedy LJ said:

'I do not think that any business man would say that those acts constituted "piracy" in the sense in which that term is used in this policy. They are more like the matters mentioned in the warranted free clause, such as riot or civil commotion.'

But even by that test the claim based on riots fails, for the same reason that it failed
c
when based on 'piracy'. A riot did occur. But it was not complete until after the loss; the loss was not caused by the riot. Or at any rate the contrary is not established by the agreed statement of facts. Clandestine thieves who use or threaten violence in order to escape, after the theft has been committed, do not give rise to a loss by riots any more than a loss by piracy.

That conclusion makes it unnecessary to decide whether the loss was also a loss by
d
thieves, so that it could not be recovered under the association's rules even if caused by riots for the reasons given earlier in this judgment. I do not feel that I should decide that point, as it was not fully argued. Rule 9 in Sch 1 of the Marine Insurance Act 1906 provides:

'The term "thieves" does not cover clandestine theft, or a theft committed by any one of the ship's company, whether crew or passengers.'

e
Lord Denning MR, in the passage I have already cited from the *Shell Petroleum* case, associated thieves with 'violent means'. Kerr LJ in the same case said ([1982] 1 All ER 1057 at 1066, [1982] QB 946 at 990): '"Thieves" can only apply to what have become known as "assailing thieves".'

I say no more about the point, particularly as it might affect the insurers on the marine
f
policy, who are not parties to this action.

The question in the originating summons is answered No.

Order acordingly; defendant association not liable to indemnify plaintiffs' loss.

Solicitors: *Clyde & Co* (for the plaintiffs); *Richards Butler & Co* (for the defendants).

K Mydeen Esq Barrister.

Pickwell v Camden London Borough Council   *a*

QUEEN'S BENCH DIVISION

ORMROD LJ AND FORBES J

29, 30, 31 MARCH, 1, 29 APRIL 1982

Public authority – Statutory powers – Misuse of power – Power to fix wage rates for employees   *b*
– Strike by employees causing crisis in local authority's administration – Local authority agreeing
to substantial increase in wage rates for striking employees – District auditor considering wage
rates excessive and seeking declaration that authority's decision unlawful – Jurisdiction of court –
Exercise of court's jurisdiction – Test to be applied by court – No evidence that authority's decision
unreasonable – Whether authority's decision unlawful – Local Government Act 1972, s 161.

In November 1978 formal wage-fixing talks took place at a national level between trade   *c*
unions representing local authority manual workers and local authority representatives.
By January 1979 the national negotiations had become so protracted that manual workers
employed by the respondent local authority embarked on a series of strikes in support of
their national claim for conditions which included a 35-hour week and a £60 minimum
weekly wage. The strikes disrupted the provision of vital services to such an extent that
real hardship was caused and the authority's administrative machinery was placed in a   *d*
position of near-collapse. On 13 February the Labour group of councillors, which was
the controlling party on the authority, met and agreed that the striking workers should
be offered a 35-hour week and a £60 minimum weekly wage. The Labour group put
that offer to the employees, who accepted it and returned to work on 26 February. On 7
March at a full council meeting of the authority a resolution to adopt that agreement was
passed by 31 votes to 24. On 8 March the national claim was settled when manual   *e*
workers agreed nationally to accept much less favourable terms than those accepted by
the authority's employees. A year later, on 5 March 1980, the authority's council met
and voted to implement a further cost-of-living increase which had been negotiated at the
national level rather than absorb it within the extra pay margin enjoyed by the
authority's manual workers over and above that paid to other local authorities' manual
workers. The district auditor considered that the payments were excessive and applied to   *f*
the court under s 161[a] of the Local Government Act 1972 for, inter alia, a declaration
that the authority's settlement reached with its manual workers and the later decision to
pay the full cost-of-living increase were unlawful.

Held – The application for a declaration would be refused for the following reasons—
    (1) (Per Ormrod LJ) The court would only exercise its supervisory jurisdiction under   *g*
s 161 of the 1972 Act if it was shown that a local authority had exceeded or abused its
statutory powers or the discretion given to it by statute. Furthermore, excessive
expenditure on a lawful object or the failure to consider relevant matters or the
considering of irrelevant matters was no more than evidence that a local authority had
acted ultra vires and did not in itself amount to illegality. Instead, the court had to be   *h*
concerned with the quality of the decision itself rather than the methods by which it was
reached. In order to establish that the authority had exceeded its statutory powers it had
to be shown either that the decision to agree to the demands of its manual workers was
made for some purpose other than to fix wage rates or that it was, in all the circumstances,
one which no reasonable authority could have made. It had not been contended, nor
could it be said, that the decision had been made for extraneous reasons and on the
evidence available the authority could not be said to have acted unreasonably (see p 624   *j*
d to *f*, p 625 *b* to *e*, p 627 *d* and p 628 *b c* and *f* to p 629 *c* and *e*, post); *Re Decision of Walker*
[1944] 1 All ER 614, *Re Decision of Hurle-Hobbs* [1944] 2 All ER 261, *Associated Provincial*

Picture Houses Ltd v Wednesbury Corp [1947] 2 All ER 680 and dictum of Diplock LJ in
a *Luby v Newcastle-under-Lyme Corp* [1964] 1 All ER at 89 applied; *Roberts v Hopwood* [1925]
All ER Rep 24, *Prescott v Birmingham Corp* [1954] 3 All ER 698 and *Bromley London Borough
Council v Greater London Council* [1982] 1 All ER 129 distinguished.

(2) (Per Forbes J) In exercising its supervisory jurisdiction under s 161 of the 1972 Act
the court was to apply the well-established test applicable to decisions made by local
authorities pursuant to a discretion conferred by Parliament, namely whether in reaching
b its decision the authority had been affected by immaterial considerations or, conversely,
had ignored material considerations, or had acted in a way that no reasonable authority
properly directing itself to what was material could have concluded that it was entitled
so to act. Further, the court would be less inclined to hold that an authority had acted
ultra vires when its decision had been made in an emergency to provide a solution to an
urgent and pressing problem. Accordingly, having regard to the conditions which
c prevailed at the time when the controlling Labour group of councillors decided to agree
that the demands of the authority's manual workers should be met, it was not a necessary
inference that the group had taken account of irrelevant considerations, or had ignored
relevant factors, or had acted unreasonably. Furthermore, applying the same test, the
authority had not acted ultra vires when it decided to confirm the settlement reached
with the manual workers by the Labour group or when it decided not to absorb the later
d cost-of-living increase within the extra pay margin enjoyed by its manual workers (see
p 612 d b, p 614 b to e and j to p 615 a f g, p 616 a b, p 619 h j, p 620 c d, p 621 a to d and
p 622 d to p 623 a and j to p 624 d, post); *Re Decision of Hurle-Hobbs* [1944] 2 All ER 261,
Associated Provincial Picture Houses Ltd v Wednesbury Corp [1947] 2 All ER 680 and
Mixnam's Properties Ltd v Chertsey UDC [1964] 2 All ER 627 applied; *Roberts v Hopwood*
[1925] All ER Rep 24 and *Prescott v Birmingham Corp* [1954] 3 All ER 698 distinguished.

e **Notes**
For district auditors duties in local government, see 28 Halsbury's Laws (4th edn) paras
1306–1307, and for cases on accounts and audit, see 33 Digest (Reissue) 35–42, 107–129.

For limits of local authorities powers, see 28 Halsbury's Laws (4th edn) para 1314.

For the Local Government Act 1972, s 161, see 42 Halsbury's Statutes (3rd edn) 984.

f As from a day to be appointed, s 19 of the Local Government Finance Act 1982 makes
new provision with respect to applications to the court for a declaration that an item of
account is unlawful, and from that date s 161 of the 1972 Act is to be repealed by s 38 of,
and Pt IV of Sch 6 to, the 1982 Act.

Cases referred to in judgments
g *Associated Provincial Picture Houses Ltd v Wednesbury Corp* [1947] 2 All ER 680, [1948] KB
223, CA, 45 Digest (Repl) 215, *189*.

Bracegirdle v Oxley, Bracegirdle v Cobley [1947] 1 All ER 126, [1947] KB 349, DC, 33 Digest
(Reissue) 178, *1378*.

Bromley London Borough Council v Greater London Council [1982] 1 All ER 129, [1982] 2
WLR 62, CA and HL.

h *Hurle-Hobbs, Re Decision of* [1944] 2 All ER 261, CA.

Kruse v Johnson [1898] 2 QB 1, [1895–9] All ER Rep 105, DC, 13 Digest (Reissue) 259,
2316.

Luby v Newcastle-under-Lyme Corp [1964] 3 All ER 169, [1965] 1 QB 214, [1964] 3 WLR
500, CA; *affg* [1964] 1 All ER 84, [1964] 2 QB 64, [1964] 2 WLR 475, 26 Digest
(Reissue) 803, *5346*.

j *Mixnam's Properties Ltd v Chertsey UDC* [1964] 2 All ER 627, [1965] AC 735, [1964] 2
WLR 1210, HL; *affg* [1963] 2 All ER 787, [1964] 1 QB 214, [1963] 3 WLR 38, CA, 45
Digest (Repl) 359, *126*.

Prescott v Birmingham Corp [1954] 3 All ER 698, [1955] Ch 210, [1954] 3 WLR 990, CA,
33 Digest (Reissue) 44, *135*.

Roberts v Cunningham (1925) 134 LT 421, HL, 33 Digest (Reissue) 25, *76*.

Roberts v Hopwood [1925] AC 578, [1925] All ER Rep 24, HL; *rvsg* sub nom *R v Roberts*
[1924] 2 KB 695, CA, 33 Digest (Reissue) 24, 74.

Secretary of State for Employment v Associated Society of Locomotive Engineers and Firemen (No
2) [1972] 2 All ER 949, [1972] 2 QB 455, [1972] 2 WLR 1370, CA.

Short v Poole Corp [1926] Ch 66, [1925] All ER Rep 74, CA, 19 Digest (Reissue) 548, 4125.

Tiller v Atlantic Coast Line Railroad Co (1948) 318 US 54.

Walker, Re Decision of [1944] 1 All ER 614, [1944] 1 KB 644, CA, 33 Digest (Reissue) 24,
75.

Woolwich BC v Roberts (1927) 96 LJKB 757, HL, 33 Digest (Reissue) 25, 77.

Motion
Ian Maclean Pickwell, the metropolitan district auditor, applied to the court under
s 161(1) of the Local Government Act 1972 for a declaration that wages paid to certain
manual workers employed by the first respondent, Camden London Borough Council,
during the financial years 1978–79, 1979–80 and 1980–81 were contrary to law and for
consequential orders under s 161(2) that the second to thirty-second respondents, being
councillors of Camden London Borough Council who had on 7 March 1979 voted to
confirm a pay settlement reached with the workers, were personally liable for excessive
expenditure by the council during that period. The facts are set out in the judgment of
Forbes J.

David Widdicombe QC and *Guy Roots* for the district auditor.
Roger Henderson QC and *Charles George* for Camden London Borough Council.
Anthony Scrivener QC and *Robert Carnwath* for 28 of the councillors.
Ronald Bernstein QC and *Julian Gibson-Watt* for one of the councillors.
Two of the councillors did not appear.

Cur adv vult

29 April. The following judgments were delivered.

FORBES J (giving the first judgment at the invitation of Ormrod LJ). In this case the
district auditor for the metropolitan district, Mr Ian Pickwell, moves the court for a
declaration under s 161 of the Local Government Act 1972 that certain items of account
in the accounts of the London Borough of Camden are contrary to law and for other
consequential orders affecting the 31 councillors of that borough who he says were
responsible for authorising the illegal payments. The items of account are for wages paid
to certain manual workers employed by the borough in the three years 1978–79 to 1980–
81. The amounts are these: for the year 1978–79: £250,000; for the year 1979–80:
£530,000; and for the year 1980–81: £370,000. The payments of these wages arose as a
result of a decision by Camden council to settle locally a national strike of manual
workers employed by local authorities. I propose to deal first with the history of that
strike and in what follows it must be remembered that the local history was being played
out against a background of national negotiations which were going on simultaneously.
Before starting that history I should say a brief word about the negotiation machinery
which was involved. I can take this from a helpful explanation set out in the affidavit of
Mr Pickwell, the metropolitan district auditor:

'6. Local government pay negotiations for manual workers are based on a system
involving joint negotiating councils, at both national and provincial level, for the
various groups of employees.
7. The main concern of the national bodies is to secure the largest possible
measure of agreement in producing nationally recognised terms and conditions of
employment. The national councils consist of an employees' side which is
representative of the trade unions and, on the employers' side, elected members of

a   local authorities nominated by the local authority associations, the GLC and the
employers' side of the provincial councils.

8. Manual workers in local government can be classified into two main groups,
and this is reflected in both the national joint council organisation and in the pattern
of trade union representation. Some trades and occupations, and the related trade
unions, are found in local government but operate mainly outside. An example of
such a trade union is the Amalgamated Union of Engineering Workers, and the
b   corresponding national body is the Joint Negotiating Committee for Local Authority
Services (Engineering Craftsmen). Other trades and occupations, and some unions,
operate exclusively in the public sector, including local government. In this group,
the largest trade union is the National Union of Public Employees ("NUPE") and the
corresponding national body is the National Joint Council for Local Authorities'
Services (Manual Workers) ("the NJC").

c   9. The national conditions of service for manual workers are set out in the
National Joint Council for Local Authority Services (Manual Workers) Handbook
(revised 1979) (the "Handbook").

10. The provincial joint negotiating councils referred to in paragraph 6 above
consist of representatives of the trade unions on the employees' side and
representatives of each local authority in the area on the employers' side. The
d   functions of a provincial council are to consider matters which, although not
necessarily of national importance, require agreement in an area rather than in
relation to a single local authority. For example a London Allowance applies within
the boundaries of authorities in the area of the Greater London Council.

11. The provincial council for London is The Greater London Joint Council (the
"GLJC"). The national conditions of service for manual workers, with London
e   variations, are also published in the Greater London Joint Council for Local
Authorities' Services (Manual Workers) Schedule of Wages and Working Conditions
(October 1977) ("the Schedule").

12. Thus there is a national system of negotiation concerning terms and
conditions of employment. Agreements reached by the national bodies are not
automatically binding upon authorities and their employees but they are widely
f   accepted, although there may be local variations.

13. Both the Handbook and the Schedule contain the following statement: "The
maintenance of a uniform rate of pay for each occupation is inherent in the Joint
Council system of wage regulation. Thus, no variation from the schedule rates shall
be introduced by any local authority without first obtaining the sanction of the
National Council or the Provincial Council as appropriate. The rates of Wages . . .
g   are standard wage rates fixed by the National Council for occupations nationally
graded." The uniform rates of pay referred to in the Handbook and the Schedule
are fixed by reference to the various jobs done by manual workers. There is, for
most jobs, a single rate for any particular job. There are seven main wage groups
designated A to G in which most manual occupations are listed. In addition, special
rates are fixed for those occupations not listed in groups A to G.

h   14. Both the Handbook and the Schedule also contain the following statement:
"A normal working week shall consist of forty hours exclusive of meal times . . ."
The working week for Camden manual workers was reduced to 37½ hours in
January 1975.

On 21 September 1978 the trade union side of the NJC lodged a national claim. The
i   claim was in these terms, as set out in Mr Pickwell's affidavit:

'16. The Trade Union Side Secretary of the NJC sent to the Employers' Side
Secretary a letter dated 21st September 1978 and headed "Wage Claim—1978",
"I.M.P.I." (Document 1) pages 1–2. The claim contained the following main
elements: 1. A fully-consolidated basic rate of £60·00 per week. 2. A reduced
working week of 35 hours, without loss of pay. 3. Annual holidays to be based upon

a minimum entitlement of four weeks after one year's service. 4. Improved shift
allowances, differentials and other plus payments. 5. Improved productivity lead-in *a*
or other in lieu payments. 6. Cost of living protection of the settlement.
7. Improved sick pay entitlements.'

Although there were important negotiations at a later date in relation to items 3 to 7 of
that claim, the main issues which arise in this case revolve around items 1 and 2. On 17
October 1978 the NJC employers met but made no offer to the trade union side. There *b*
were of course behind-the-scenes talks and negotiations going on for most of the time.
On 30 October 1978 the NJC employers met again but still made no offer. On 4
November 1978 the claim became formally effective. On 24 November 1978 the
employers made an offer of a 5% increase and on 12 December of that year this offer was
rejected by the union side. On 3 January, unconnected with the local government
manual workers but nevertheless having some effect in Camden, there was a national *c*
strike of tanker drivers. This affected heating supplies for council buildings and
establishments nationally. On 22 January 1979 there was a national one-day strike of
local authority manual workers. In Camden selective strike action by manual workers
started on 29 January. Refuse collectors took part in a one-day strike on that day;
plumbers and plumbers' mates were called out on indefinite strike and so were two
petrol pump attendants, and NALGO instructed their members not to carry out the *d*
duties of the two petrol pump attendants who were on strike. On 1 February 1979 the
majority of Camden's depots employing manual workers were picketed by the union.
On 5 February the GLJC reported to its members that there had been an agreement
between the three main unions, the GMWU, NUPE and the TGWU, on co-ordinating
industrial action in support of the manual workers' pay claim. On 30 January 1979 the
NJC employers met again. It should be appreciated that one of the difficulties facing the *e*
employers' side was that to some extent the generosity of their offer would be affected by
the attitude of the government. This was a period in which the government of the day,
a Labour government, was attempting to influence the level of wage settlements by
establishing a guideline of 5% within which they wished settlements to fall. The offer of
5% made by the employers in November had been in accordance with that guideline.
On 30 January the NJC employers were told that the government would agree a *f*
settlement of 8·8% with a comparability study. The meeting was told however that the
current norm for settlements was running at between 13 and 14% and it was doubted
whether an offer of 8·8% would prove at all attractive to the trade unions. Eventually the
meeting decided to make no offer pending further discussions with the government. On
3 and 6 February, the Prime Minister confirmed that the government would support
8·8% with a comparability study. On 6 February the Camden branch of NUPE resolved *g*
on indefinite strike action in pursuit of their claim for a £60 per week minimum wage
and a 35-hour week. On 7 February the employers' side of the NJC met and considered
among other things the suggestion from the GLJC that an increase of 10% should be
offered together with a comparability review and discussions on self-financing
productivity arrangements. The NJC employers however decided to make an offer of
8·8% without the comparability study. That decision was communicated by the *h*
Association of Metropolitan Authorities to members, including Camden, by a letter of 8
February which contained this sentence: 'The matter was discussed at today's meeting of
the AMA Policy Committee [a different body from the NJC employers] when it was
agreed to ask metropolitan authorities to stand firm and not to reach local settlements.'
On 9 February the GLJC proposed to the NJC that there should be an immediate
employer/trade union approach to government to secure a settlement. *j*
   On 13 February there occurred a meeting of the Labour group of the Camden council.
The Labour Party was the controlling party on that council and meetings of party groups
of this kind are common if not universal in local authority practice, the purpose of the
meetings being to settle in advance policy questions before council meetings take place.
It will be necessary to return in some detail to this meeting at a later stage, but it is

sufficient to say at this moment that, although Councillor Shaw, the leader of the Labour
a   group, and a very respected, experienced and influential figure in local authority circles
in London, was in favour of waiting to see whether anything useful came out of the
national negotiations, after considerable discussion the group, by 14 votes to 13, decided
not to accept Councillor Shaw's proposals but to make a local settlement with the trade
union side. It was then resolved by 15 votes to 9 that local negotiations should be opened
on the basis of the £60 per week and 35-hour week claim but with a number of other
b   matters, including in particular the position about bonuses, to be the subject of those
further negotiations. The resolution adopted was in these terms:

> 'This Group agrees the NUPE claims for a basic wage of £60 for a 35 hour week
> and resolves to open local negotiations to implement this decision. This new basic
> wage to include the consolidation of awards under earlier phases of the Government's
> pay policy and also the existing guaranteed bonus schemes. We accept that this
c   > policy will reduce differentials and resolve that the reduction in basic hours should
> lead to an increase in employment rather than overtime.'

Negotiations then continued with the local branch of NUPE on this basis. These
negotiations were led on the council side by Councillor Bethell as Councillor Shaw, the
leader of the council, and Councillor Jewell, the chairman of the staff and management
d   services committee, were both ill. Councillor Bethell was chairman of the community
planning and resources committee. The union side was led by the branch secretary of
Camden NUPE, a Mr John Suddaby. As a result of these negotiations the leader of the
council wrote on 21 February to Mr Suddaby putting forward a formal offer to end the
current dispute; the offer was on the mistaken basis that there had then been reached a
national agreement and that the Camden settlement should take account of that
e   agreement and in addition pay a special Camden supplement to guarantee £60 gross per
full-time employee per week: a 35-hour week was also offered compared to the existing
37½-hour week. In fact the employers' side of the NJC had made an offer on 21 February.
The offer was broadly this: £3·50 addition to the basic rates of pay backdated to 4
November 1978 and a comparability study for local government manual workers and a
supplement of £1 per week to be paid to all employees working more than 35 hours a
f   week in advance of the first stage of the comparability study. This offer was accepted by
the union side but when it was put to the NUPE executive it was rejected.

On 21 February there was a meeting of the full Camden council. Councillor Shaw
reported to the council the course of the national and local negotiations. In the course of
that report Councillor Shaw described the offer as a very generous one. The meeting was
open to the public and one of the objects of this statement was to encourage the strikers
g   to go back to work. On 22 February there was a long meeting between council
representatives led by Councillor Bethell and NUPE representatives including Mr
Suddaby, the branch secretary. One of the main questions discussed was whether bonus
payments should be taken into account for the purpose of calculating whether a worker
qualified for the £60 per week minimum. In the end the councillors were successful in
resisting the NUPE claim that bonus payments should be disregarded. The NUPE
h   representatives took away with them the councillors' proposals as explained and clarified
at that meeting. On the morning of 23 February the local NUPE branch accepted the
councillors' offer, and on that day Councillor Shaw wrote to Mr Suddaby explaining the
procedure for ratification of the offer by the council and confirming the agreement that
there should be no victimisation by either side. On Monday, 26 February the strikers
went back to work.

j   The committees of the council had been kept in touch with negotiations as they
proceeded, the staff and management services committee on 5 February, the policy
advisory sub-committee of the community planning and resources committee on 15
February. In addition it is clear that members had asked to be kept informed of what was
going on and themselves knew at first hand what effect the strike was having on the
services provided by the borough. On 28 February, that is two days after the Camden

workers had returned to work, the settlement was reported to the community planning
and resources committee, who, by 6 votes to 5, approved the settlement and
recommended to the council that it should be approved and adopted and applied to all
Camden's manual workers. On 7 March the full council met. The report and
recommendation of the community planning and resources committee of 28 February
was put to the council, who resolved by 31 votes to 24 to receive and adopt the report.
Of the 31 councillors who voted for the adoption 29 are now before the court, 28 of them
represented by Mr Scrivener, and one, Mr Sofer, represented by Mr Bernstein.

During this period national negotiations had been going on but no details, so far as we
know, were given to individual local authorities until, on 8 March, the employers'
secretary of the NJC wrote to member authorities informing them that the claim was
settled. Details were given in a joint circular letter of 9 March. The agreed national
settlement can be described as follows: (1) an agreed flat rate increase of £3·50 per week
to each manual worker irrespective of grade payable from 4 November 1978; (2) an
agreement that (a) there should be a comparability study comparing terms and conditions
in other sections of the economy, (b) that any award made as a result of the comparability
study should be paid in two halves, the first from the pay week which included 1 August
1979, the second from the pay week beginning 1 April 1980 (it was accepted that
between those dates would fall the annual settlement due in November 1979), (c) that
pending the comparability study award a flat rate increase of £1 per week should be paid
from 22 February 1979.

On 7 March 1979, that is the day before that letter, the Prime Minister had made an
announcement in Parliament of his intention to set up a standing commission on pay
comparability. The chairman of this commission was to be Professor Hugh Clegg. The
commission duly reported and its recommendations in relation to manual workers were
accepted and paid.

The comparison of the rates of pay of comparable workers in Camden and in other
London boroughs as a result of the national settlement, the Camden settlement, the
Clegg Commission award and subsequent NJC awards is complicated. The various awards
affected different groups of workers differently. It is of course the district auditor's case
that such a comparison must be done, and that, when done, it shows so great an excess
payment in Camden as to be ipso facto unreasonable and ultra vires. To make this point
the district auditor necessarily produced a number of tables of figures. I do not think it is
necessary myself to do more than trace the broad outline of what happened to the worst
paid and best paid groups in the manual workers' table. The lowest paid group was group
A. Before 4 November 1978 the NJC weekly rate was £42·85. As a result of the national
settlement announced on 8 March 1979, the NJC weekly rate from 4 November 1978
became £46·35 by the addition of the £3·50 flat rate increase. On 22 February 1979,
again as a result of the national settlement reached on 8 March, the weekly rate was raised
to £47·35, the £1 addition being the flat increase agreed to take effect from that date.
From 26 February 1979 Camden manual workers in this Group were paid not £47·35
but £60, an increase, referred to throughout this case as the 'Camden supplement', of
£12·65. When compared with workers in this group elsewhere this meant that Camden
were paying their workers 26·7% more than were other boroughs.

Turning to the best paid workers, group G, before 4 November 1978 their NJC weekly
rate was £48·70. From 4 November 1978 the flat rate increase gave them £52·20 and
from 22 February 1979 the further £1 flat rate increase gave them £53·20. Because the
Camden local agreement involved not upsetting the differentials between the grades the
Camden supplement paid to this group of workers was the same as that paid to the lowest
group, namely £12·65. This brought up group G workers to £65·85 from 26 February,
23·8% more than in other boroughs.

So matters rested until the Clegg report in August 1979. This, somewhat surprisingly,
favoured the better paid workers at the expense of the lower paid. The effect of
implementing the first instalment from 1 August 1979 was to bring the NJC weekly
rates for group A workers up from £47·35 to £47·73 and the group G workers from

£53·20 to £57·12. The Clegg increases were deducted from the Camden supplement
a thus leaving none of the manual workers in Camden any better off. Group A workers
continued to receive £60 (Camden supplement now £12·27) and group G £65·85
(Camden supplement £8·73). The percentage differences between Camden workers and
those in other boroughs thus dropped to 25·7% and 15·3% for these groups.

The next round of wage claims for manual workers had an effective date of 4
November 1979. On 10 October the Camden branch of NUPE made a claim for a
b minimum basic wage of £75. On 17 January 1980 the NJC agreed new rates of pay to
take effect from 4 November 1979. These raised weekly rates for group A workers to
£53·52 and for group G to £64·45. These increases have been described as, and there is
no doubt were intended as, 'cost-of-living' increases. The question arose whether they
should be paid by Camden in addition to the Camden supplement or whether they
should be deducted from it. The matter was put to a special joint meeting of the policy
c and resources committee and the staff and management service committee of the
Camden council on 28 February 1980. This meeting had the benefit of a joint detailed
report by the chief executive and the director of finance on the financial and legal
implications of the choices open to the council. That joint meeting resolved to
recommend to the council—

d   'That the 1979 National Wage Award be paid to all manual workers without
         further adjustment to the Camden Supplement with the exception of the reduction
         due to payment of Stage 2 of the Clegg Comparability Award; and that as soon as
         possible a review be undertaken of the wage structure of non-bonus earners with a
         view to replacing the Camden Supplement by a system of bonus payment linked to
         increased productivity.'

e This recommendation was approved at the full council meeting on 5 March 1980 by 27
votes to 21.

The result of this was, if one returns to consider manual workers in groups A and G
again, that from 4 November 1979 the NJC rates were for group A workers £53·52, but
in Camden the supplement of £12·27 continued to be paid bringing this group up to
£65·79 or 22·9% over other boroughs, and for group G workers £64·45, while in
f Camden the Camden supplement of £8·73 continued to be paid bringing them up to
£73·18 or 13·5% in excess of other boroughs.

On 1 April 1980 the second stage of Clegg came in. This served to reduce pro rata the
Camden supplement so that once again the Camden workers did not benefit. The NJC
rate for group A was £54·90 brought up in Camden to the previous wage of £65·79, the
supplement being then at a reduced rate of £10·89 or 19·8% in excess of other boroughs,
g while group G workers with an NJC rate of £69·36 still received £73·18 in Camden
representing a supplement of £3·82 or an excess of 5·5%.

A further NJC award was made taking effect from 3 November 1980. By the time
Camden came to consider it the district auditor had informed Camden of his intention
to seek the present declaration. The matter went before the policy and resources
committee on 5 February 1981. That committee resolved to recommend to the council
h as follows:

         '(a) That the maximum proportion of the Camden Supplement be merged into
         the November 1980 National Pay Award. (b) That the balance of the Camden
         Supplement be replaced with effect from 1 April 1981 by a satisfactory system of
         payments related to increased productivity and flexibility in the method of work,
         covering for employees' absence through sickness, reduced supervision, good
j   attendance, etc., in line with the council's decision on 5 March 1980.'

This recommendation was adopted by the council on 18 February 1981.

With effect from 3 November 1980 therefore the position was as follows: group A
workers were entitled to an NJC rate of £59·50. In Camden they remained on £65·79.
The effect was to reduce the supplement for these workers to £6·29 or an excess of 10·6%.

Workers in groups B to F inclusive received no additional increase as a result of the
November 1980 award but the effect was progressively to reduce the Camden supplement. *a*
For workers in group G the new NJC rate was £73·95, which brought them above the
previous rate which they had enjoyed as a result of the supplement. Their pay thus went
to the new NJC rate of £73·95 and no supplement was paid to them.

I have set out these figures at some length because much of the district auditor's
argument that the wage payments were unlawful stems from his contention that the
rates paid in Camden were so much in excess of that paid in other boroughs that they are *b*
wholly unreasonable.

But the district auditor has another shot in his locker. These comparisons he says are
not the right comparisons because the NJC rates were based on a 40-hour and not a 35-
hour week. If allowance is made for this and the comparison made on an hourly basis,
the percentage excess is increased. To take an example, the excess from 26 February 1979
in the case of group A workers (the worst case) as a percentage goes up from 26·7% to *c*
44·8%. Although this increased percentage reduces, as successive stages of the Clegg
awards were taken into account in calculating the wage on which the Camden supplement
was based, after 3 November 1980 the excess paid in Camden, calculated as a percentage
over the rates paid in other London boroughs, and working of course on an hourly rate,
was still 26·3% for group A workers and 14·3% for group G.

Having reached this point the district auditor begins to calculate the amounts of what *d*
he regards as unlawful expenditure. To do this he first allows the combined increases
afforded by the NJC and Clegg awards; these, he says, give the level of 'reasonable' wages.
Accepting that the Camden council was entitled to be generous to its workers, but not
without regard to commercial considerations, he allows a 15% margin over the Clegg
rate. To this margin he adds a further 2½% because of the variation, over the periods of
the respective annual accounts, in the numbers of employees in each of the groups. *e*
Anything in excess of this he regards as contrary to law. The result of performing these
mathematical exercises in relation to the items of account for wages for manual employees
affected by the supplement for each of the three years under scrutiny was to produce the
following as excess payments:

1978–79	£50,000	
1979–80	£530,000	*f*
1980–81	£370,000	
Total	£950,000	

It is this total figure which he suggests should be surcharged on the 31 councillors who
voted on 7 March 1979 to approve the settlement reached with NUPE in February 1979. *g*
The approach adopted by the district auditor was one which he felt himself constrained
to adopt on his reading of *Roberts v Hopwood* [1925] AC 578, [1925] All ER Rep 24, a case
much relied on by counsel for the district auditor and one to which I shall have to return
later. But before looking at the relevant law, I think I should say that the district auditor's
mathematical comparisons are not accepted as correct by the borough. They have filed
an affidavit by Professor Metcalfe, an expert in the field of economics of pay and *h*
employment, who challenges the conclusions of the district auditor. He first points out
that in Camden manual workers were already on a 37½-hour week without anyone
suggesting that this was contrary to law; a comparison with a 40-hour week therefore
produces the wrong figure for hourly rates. Second, he suggests that the district auditor
is in error in taking together instead of separately the effect of paying the Camden
supplement and of introducing a 35-hour instead of a 37½-hour week. But I think that *j*
his main criticism is that the district auditor is wrong in basing his calculations of the
unlawful 'excess' on a comparison of the wages paid only to those who in fact received
the supplement. The claim by NUPE was for all manual workers; only some benefited
from the supplement. Professor Metcalfe points out that it is commonplace in wage
bargaining for an employer to consider the rise in his total labour costs and be prepared

in consequence to see, within that rise, some workers receive larger increases than others.
a He has reminded us that in the immediately past negotiations this year the Civil Service
Department is offering an increase which it states is 4% although, across the grades, the
increases vary from 0% to 6%. If the cost of the Camden supplement is taken across the
wage bill for the whole of the workers for whom NUPE made their original claim then
it is equivalent to an increase of 10·2% at February 1979 rates and 5·3% at rates current
in April 1980. These figures he points out are well within the 15% margin allowed by
b the district auditor.

I have no desire to enter into the argument, more appropriate to economists than
lawyers, about the correct method of making these comparisons. On the face of it there
seems to me much to be said for Professor Metcalfe's general approach based on the total
additional wages bill for all the workers included in the claim. Similarly I think it might
be demonstrated that the district auditor's approach in comparing hourly rates based on
c a 40-hour week is erroneous by simply looking at his calculation for group G workers
after 3 November 1980. He accepts that by then the Camden supplement had been
phased out for these workers but he still claims that, on an hourly basis, these workers
were being paid hourly wages at an excess rate of 14·3%, an excess saved from illegality
only by his allowance for discretion of 15%. But in fact, as these workers were already on
a 37½-hour week, which of itself had never been regarded as unlawful, the comparison
d must surely be with the 37½-hour and not the 40-hour week, the latter simply being
irrelevant in Camden.

If Professor Metcalfe is right in his approach there would, on the figures, be no excess
payment which, adopting the district auditor's addition for discretion and other factors,
could possibly be regarded as unlawful. But, whether the district auditor or Professor
Metcalfe be right, the existence of so fundamental a divergence of opinion on a matter so
e important must cast some doubt on whether it can properly be said that no reasonable
authority could possibly have acted as did Camden in this instance.

I should now look at the provisions of the Local Government Act 1972 which govern
these proceedings before this court, but before doing so I propose to glance briefly at the
statutory provisions which preceded them. In doing this I am not seeking to derive
assistance in the interpretation of the 1972 Act but to contrast the past and present
f position of the court and the district auditor and to indicate the statutory background
against which some of the authorities were decided.

The first situation to look at is that obtaining before 1933 under the Public Health Act
1875. I do not propose to read the statute in extenso. It is sufficient to say that it provided
for the annual audit of local authority accounts by district auditors and contained these
provisions:

g   '**247.** . . (6) Any ratepayer or owner of property in the district may be present at
the audit, and may make any objection to such account before the auditor; and such
ratepayers and owners shall have the same right of appeal against allowances by an
auditor as they have by law against disallowances.

(7) Any auditor acting in pursuance of this section shall disallow every item of
account contrary to law, and surcharge the same on the person making or authorising
h the making of the illegal payments and shall charge against any person accounting
the amount of any deficiency or loss incurred by the negligence or misconduct of
that person, or on any sum which ought to have been but is not brought into
account by that person, and shall in every case certify the amount due from such
person, and on application by any party aggrieved shall state in writing the reasons
for his decision . . .'

i and so on.

The section also provided so far as is relevant that any person so surcharged, or any
ratepayer or owner aggrieved by a refusal to disallow, may apply to the Divisional Court
for certiorari or alternatively appeal to the Local Government Board. The duties of that
board were subsequently taken over by the Minister of Health.

The features of this procedure were thus that the district auditor himself made the
surcharge, and he was under a mandatory duty to do so, wherever the item of account   *a*
was contrary to law. The challenge to that decision before the courts was by certiorari.
This inevitably meant that the court was exercising a supervisory and not an appellate
jurisdiction. It also meant that the onus was on the applicant to show that the district
auditor was wrong. Where the court is exercising a supervisory jurisdiction its approach
to the matter in hand is necessarily different from its approach when acting as a court of
appeal. The approach is often referred to as the *Wednesbury* doctrine because the elements   *b*
are conveniently summarised in the judgment of Lord Greene MR in *Associated Provincial
Picture Houses Ltd v Wednesbury Corp* [1947] 2 All ER 680, [1948] 1 KB 223. Since there
has been considerable argument in this case on the extent of the *Wednesbury* principle
and its application to the matter before us I should read two passages from that judgment
([1947] 2 All ER 680 at 682–683, [1948] 1 KB 223 at 228–229):

                                                                 c

    'What, then, is the power of the courts? The courts can only interfere with an act
of an executive authority if it be shown that the authority have contravened the law.
It is for those who assert that the local authority have contravened the law to
establish that proposition. On the face of it, a condition of this kind is perfectly
lawful. It is not to be assumed *prima facie* that responsible bodies like local authorities
will exceed their powers, and the court, whenever it is alleged that the local authority   *d*
have contravened the law, must not substitute itself for the local authority. It is only
concerned with seeing whether or not the proposition is made good. When an
executive discretion is entrusted by Parliament to a local authority, what purports
to be an exercise of that discretion can only be challenged in the courts in a very
limited class of case. It must always be remembered that the court is not a court of
appeal. The law recognises certain principles on which the discretion must be   *e*
exercised, but within the four corners of those principles the discretion is an absolute
one and cannot be questioned in any court of law. What, then, are those principles?
They are perfectly well understood. The exercise of such a discretion must be a real
exercise of the discretion. If, in the statute conferring the discretion, there is to be
found, expressly or by implication, matters to which the authority exercising the
discretion ought to have regard, then, in exercising the discretion, they must have   *f*
regard to those matters. Conversely, if the nature of the subject-matter and the
general interpretation of the Act make it clear that certain matters would not be
germane to the matter in question, they must disregard those matters. Expressions
have been used in cases where the powers of local authorities came to be considered
relating to the sort of thing that may give rise to interference by the court. Bad
faith, dishonesty—those, of course, stand by themselves—unreasonableness,   *g*
attention given to extraneous circumstances, disregard of public policy, and things
like that have all been referred to as being matters which are relevant for
consideration. In the present case we have heard a great deal about the meaning of
the word "unreasonable". It is true the discretion must be exercised reasonably.
What does that mean? Lawyers familiar with the phraseology commonly used in
relation to the exercise of statutory discretions often use the word "unreasonable" in   *h*
a rather comprehensive sense. It is frequently used as a general description of the
things that must not be done. For instance, a person entrusted with a discretion
must direct himself properly in law. He must call his own attention to the matters
which he is bound to consider. He must exclude from his consideration matters
which are irrelevant to the matter that he has to consider. If he does not obey those
rules, he may truly be said, and often is said, to be acting "unreasonably". Similarly,   *j*
you may have something so absurd that no sensible person could ever dream that it
lay within the powers of the authority. WARRINGTON, L.J., I think it was, gave the
example of the red-haired teacher, dismissed because she had red hair. That is
unreasonable in one sense. In another sense it is taking into consideration extraneous
matters. It is so unreasonable that it might almost be described as being done in bad
faith. In fact, all these things largely fall under one head.'

Lord Greene MR then gave a useful summary ([1947] 2 All ER 680 at 685, [1948] 1
a KB 223 at 233):

> 'I do not wish to repeat what I have said, but it might be useful to summarise
> once again the principle, which seems to me to be that the court is entitled to
> investigate the action of the local authority with a view to seeing whether it has
> taken into account matters which it ought not to take account, or, conversely, has
> refused to take into account or neglected to take into account matters which it ought
b
> to take into account. Once that question is answered in favour of the local authority,
> it may still be possible to say that the local authority, nevertheless, have come to a
> conclusion so unreasonable that no reasonable authority could ever have come to it.
> In such a case, again, I think the court can interfere. The power of the court to
> interfere in each case is not that of an appellate authority to override a decision of
> the local authority, but is that of a judicial authority which is concerned, and
c
> concerned only, to see whether the local authority have contravened the law by
> acting in excess of the powers which Parliament has confided in it.'

I might add a very short passage from another authority which I think is very helpful.
In *Mixnam's Properties Ltd v Chertsey UDC* [1963] 2 All ER 787 at 799, [1964] 1 QB 214 at
237 Diplock LJ said:
d
> 'Thus, the kind of unreasonableness which invalidates a bye-law is not the
> antonym of "reasonableness" in the sense in which that expression is used in the
> common law, but such manifest arbitrariness, injustice or partiality that a court
> would say: "Parliament never intended to give authority to make such rules; they
> are unreasonable and ultra vires". . . '

e The last sentence in that passage is a quotation from the judgment of Lord Russell CJ in
Kruse v Johnson [1898] 2 QB 91 at 99, [1895–99] All ER Rep 105 at 110.
I have indicated that the principles enshrined in the *Wednesbury* case are only another
way of looking at the approach which the court adopts when exercising a supervisory
rather than an appellate jurisdiction. Precisely the same approach is to be found when
the Divisional Court is exercising the same kind of jurisdiction in criminal matters. The
f authority for that is *Bracegirdle v Oxley* [1947] 1 All ER 126, [1947] 1 KB 349 and I take a
short passage from the judgment of Lord Goddard CJ ([1947] 1 All ER 126 at 127, [1947]
1 KB 349 at 353):

> 'It is, of course, said that we are bound by the findings of fact set out in the Case
> by the justices, and it is perfectly true that this court does not sit as a general court
> of appeal against justices' decisions in the same way as quarter sessions, for instance,
g
> sit as a court of appeal against the decisions of courts of summary jurisdiction. In
> this court we only sit to review the justices' decisions on points of law, being bound
> by the facts which they find, provided always that there is evidence on which the
> justices can come to the conclusions of fact at which they arrive. I should state that
> the court has had the advantage of argument from Mr. Parker, on the instructions
h of the Treasury Solicitor, who has intervened as *amicus curiae* to enable the court to
> have the benefit of a full argument on one side and the other, and Mr. Parker
> concedes that, if justices come to a decision to which no reasonable bench of justices,
> applying their minds to proper considerations and giving themselves proper
> directions, can come, then this court can interfere, because the position then is
> exactly the same as though the justices have come to a decision of fact which there
j   was no evidence to support.'

And an even shorter passage from Humphreys J ([1947] 1 All ER 126 at 129, [1947] 1 KB
349 at 356):

> 'I desire to say no more than this as to the action which the court has thought
> right to take. For a very great number of years, whenever justices have found facts
> from which only one conclusion can be drawn by reasonable persons honestly

applying their minds to the question before them, and have refused to draw that only conclusion, then this court has invariably upset the decision of the justices in *a* the appropriate manner.'

Thus, only a year before the *Wednesbury* decision, the Divisional Court was describing its approach in words which, allowing for the difference between the criminal and civil jurisdictions of this court, are strikingly similar to those used in *Wednesbury*. The principles of *Wednesbury* can therefore be seen as the corollary of the assertion of a supervisory rather than an appellate jurisdiction and involve, so far as is material here, *b* the three brief propositions: (1) an authority must not be affected by immaterial or ignore material considerations; (2) an authority must not act in such a way that it can be said of it that no reasonable authority, properly directing itself to what was material, could have concluded that it was entitled so to act; and (3) in reviewing the acts of an authority the court will not substitute its own view of how a discretion should be exercised for that of the authority entrusted by Parliament with the discretion. *c*

The principles enshrined in the *Wednesbury* case of course long pre-date that decision. It is possible to argue that there is only one principle, that of 'unreasonableness' as that term is used in this context. Indeed that is the argument here of Mr Scrivener, who appears for 28 of the councillors. It is possible also to argue, as counsel does, that the question to which *Wednesbury* is addressed is simply whether or not the act under *d* scrutiny is ultra vires. There is much to be said for these arguments. But I think *Wednesbury* is dealing largely with the question of the exercise of a statutory discretion. It is true that the abuse of a statutory discretion can, if not always then nearly always, be put as an ultra vires act, on the basis that the discretion given was not intended to cover the action taken. But, while the abuse of a discretionary power can almost always be regarded as ultra vires, an action which is ultra vires is not always the abuse of a discretionary power. There are acts which may not be covered by a statutory power at all *e* and others where some want of form produces an illegality. But the majority of cases which come before the courts are concerned with the abuse of discretionary powers and here it is not helpful to pursue too far a philosophical argument whether a disregard of a material consideration is to be regarded as subsumed in the concept of unreasonableness or as a separate ground of challenge. Counsel for the district auditor puts the case on the basis of the relevant/irrelevant argument; counsel for the 28 councillors says it is merely *f* a question of unreasonableness and therefore of vires. I think the matter has to be looked at from both points of view, accepting that they may well overlap. The one thing which is beyond question is that the court in the exercise of its supervisory jurisdiction never allows itself to substitute its own discretion for that of the body to whom discretion has been given.

The Local Government Act 1933 repealed the provisions of the Public Health Act *g* 1875. The provisions relating to district auditors are to be found in Part X. There is again a provision for a right of objection to the accounts which the district auditor is engaged in auditing. The right was given, not to a ratepayer or property owner, as in the 1875 Act, but, curiously, to any local government elector for the local authority area. The duties of the district auditor however remained the same, and in the same mandatory form. The arrangements for challenging the district auditors' decisions were markedly *h* different. Any person aggrieved by any decision of the district auditor, whether to disallow or to refuse to do so, could appeal either to the High Court or the minister. The powers of the court or the minister are given in s 229(2), which, so far as is relevant, is in these terms:

'The Court or Minister on such an appeal shall have power to confirm, vary or *j* quash the decision of the auditor, and to remit the case to the auditor with such directions as the Court or Minister thinks fit for giving effect to the decision on appeal . . .'

I think that it has never been doubted that these words effectively mean that the court's jurisdiction was still intended to be a supervisory one and that therefore the principles

which, merely as a convenient shorthand, one refers to as the *Wednesbury* principles
apply. Subject to that explanation the position remained precisely as it was under the
1875 Act, ie the mandatory duty lay on the district auditor, the onus lay on the party
aggrieved to show that he had been wrong and the question still remained: was the item
of account contrary to law?

The modern position is to be found in s 161 of the Local Government Act 1972. I need
not look at the provisions governing the audit itself. A local government elector for the
area still has his right of objection to the accounts. Section 161, so far as relevant,
provides:

> '(1) Where the audit of any accounts under this Part of this Act is carried out by a
> district auditor and it appears to him that any item of account is contrary to law he
> may apply to the court for a declaration that the item is contrary to law except
> where it is sanctioned by the Secretary of State.
>
> (2) On an application under subsection (1) above the court may make or refuse
> to make the declaration asked for, and where the court makes that declaration then,
> subject to subsection (3) below, it may also—(a) order that any person responsible
> for incurring or authorising any expenditure declared unlawful shall repay it in
> whole or in part to the body in question and, where two or more persons are found
> to be responsible, that they shall be jointly and severally liable to repay it as aforesaid;
> and (b) if any such expenditure exceeds £2,000 and the person responsible for
> incurring or authorising it is a member of a local authority, order him to be
> disqualified for being a member of a local authority, order him to be disqualified
> for being a member of a local authority for a specified period; and (c) order
> rectification of the accounts.
>
> (3) The court shall not make an order under subsection (2)(a) or (b) above if the
> court is satisfied that the person responsible for incurring or authorising any such
> expenditure acted reasonably or in the belief that the expenditure was authorised by
> law, and in any other case shall have regard to all the circumstances, including that
> person's means and ability to repay that expenditure or any part of it . . .'

It is clear that there has been a fundamental change in the position of the district
auditor in relation to items in the account which may be contrary to law. The district
auditor is no longer under a duty to disallow such items or to surcharge the amounts on
the persons responsible. He has a discretionary power to make an application to the court
for a declaration. The court too is in a fundamentally different situation. It is not to
embark on the process of seeing whether the district auditor was right. It must itself
decide all questions which arise, both of fact and law. The onus is also altered: the onus
of satisfying the court that the item of account is contrary to law is now on the district
auditor.

These fundamental differences are underlined by the provisions made for occasions
where sums have not been brought properly into account or where there has been a loss
or deficiency caused by misconduct. In such cases both the 1875 and the 1933 Acts
provided procedures for the district auditor to follow similar to those for items contrary
to law including his mandatory duty to surcharge. The provisions for challenging all
those decisions were precisely the same. But now, without reading the subsection,
sub-s (4) provides for a mandatory duty to certify the sum not brought into account or
lost by misconduct and provides that either the district auditor or the body whose
accounts are being audited may recover the sum so certified for the benefit of the body.
Subsection (6) gives the disappointed objector to the accounts, where the district auditor
has refused to apply for a declaration, a right to appeal to the court and the court then has
the same power as it has when the district auditor does apply. There is a right given to
the appropriate person to appeal to the court against a decision either to certify or not to
certify and there again the court is given the power to confirm, vary or quash the
decision. The procedure for cases of failure properly to account or loss by misconduct
remains therefore almost as it was under the older Acts. It is only in cases concerned with
items contrary to law that a fundamental change has been made.

Although counsel for the 28 councillors suggested that the court was, under the provisions of s 161(1), acting as a court of first instance, and while this is partially true, I a cannot think that Parliament intended to make so fundamental a change in the approach of this court to the discharge of its duties as to make it necessary to abandon its traditional supervisory jurisdiction. No counsel has suggested otherwise and all, though with differing emphasis on different elements, accept that the proper approach is that of *Wednesbury*. I think that in considering whether items are contrary to law that is the approach which should be adopted.

Before leaving the appropriate statutory provisions I should refer to the power given to local authorities to pay wages. Section 112 of the Local Government Act 1972 is in these terms:

'(1) . . . a local authority shall appoint such officers as they think necessary for the proper discharge by the authority of such of their . . . functions as fall to be discharged by them . . .
(2) An officer appointed under subsection (1) above shall hold office on such reasonable terms and conditions, including conditions as to remuneration, as the authority appointing him think fit . . .'

It is accepted that the term 'officer' covers all employees including manual workers.

I turn now to the authorities. The industry of counsel has provided us with many, and speaking for myself I am very grateful to all counsel not only for referring us to these authorities but also for their most helpful observations on them. If I do not myself refer to them all it is only because I do not wish to lengthen further what is inevitably a lengthy judgment.

The authority much relied on by counsel for the district auditor is *Roberts v Hopwood* [1925] AC 578, [1925] All ER Rep 24. I do not think it is necessary to read this case in detail: we have been taken through the opinions of their Lordships in extenso. The question to be decided was whether an order of certiorari should go to bring up and quash a decision of the district auditor that certain items of account in the accounts of the Metropolitan Borough of Poplar were unlawful. A power existed to pay such wages 'as [the council] may think fit.' The first task confronting their Lordships was to decide whether those words gave the council an unfettered and unchallengeable discretion. They decided that they did not and that in each and every case the salary and wages paid must be reasonable, but at least some of their Lordships accepted that an element of discretion existed in deciding what was reasonable and that 'the court ought to show great reluctance before they attempt to determine how, in their opinion, the discretion ought to be exercised' (see [1925] AC 578 at 588, [1925] All ER Rep 24 at 30 per Lord Buckmaster).

Following the decision on this preliminary step in the reasoning their Lordships then went on to approve the district auditor's method, which was to decide what was a reasonable wage and then examine the justification put forward by the council for paying wages in excess of that. Their Lordships found that the wages in fact paid bore no relation to the shift in the value of money (for the wages to be paid went up when the cost of living increased but were not to come down when it decreased), the general market level of wages or the extent of the work done in return for the wage; no justification could be found in relation to any of these factors. The only justification put forward was one which Lord Atkinson characterised as guided 'by some eccentric principles of socialistic philanthropy, or by a feminist ambition to secure the equality of the sexes in the matter of wages in the world of labour' (see [1925] AC 578 at 594, [1925] All ER Rep 24 at 33). So regarded the payments in excess of what was reasonable could not be thought of as wages at all but as gifts or gratuities; such payments were not covered by a power to pay wages and were unlawful. I propose to read two passages, one from the opinion of Lord Sumner and one from that of Lord Wrenbury. First Lord Sumner, dealing with the justification put forward by the council, said ([1925] AC 578 at 609–610, [1925] All ER Rep 24 at 40–41):

'Their reason the respondents give as follows: "The council did not and does not take the view that wages paid should be exclusively related to the cost of living. They have from time to time carefully considered the question of the wages and are of the opinion as a matter of policy that a public authority should be a model employer and that a minimum rate of 4*l.* is the least wage which ought to be paid to an adult having regard to the efficiency of their workpeople, the duty of a public authority both to the ratepayers and to its employees, the purchasing power of the wages and other considerations which are relevant to their decision as to wages." From this carefully considered answer I think it is plain that the respondents have deliberately decided not to be guided by ordinary economic (and economical) considerations. The first sentence above quoted means that, when the cost of living passes 4*l.* a week, the rate of wages paid will follow it upwards, but, however it may fall, the 4*l.* rate will be stabilised and will stand. There is nothing definite about the statement that a public authority should be a model employer. To whom is it to be a model? If to other public authorities, the council's resolution is vox clamantis in deserto, for other authorities, with rare exceptions, turn a deaf ear to it. If to other private employers, the example of the council is necessarily thrown away on concerns, which must make both ends meet and have not the ratepayers' purse to draw on. Whatever "having regard to the efficiency of their workpeople" may mean, it is not proved or suggested that the workpeople employed in Poplar are in any way exceptional in their powers of work, or that the cost of maintaining a workman's efficiency is higher in Poplar than elsewhere. The one definite thing is that the respondents contend that no adult employee should in any circumstances have less than 4*l.* a week, whether young or old, male or female, married or single, skilled or unskilled. It is not shown that the women's work is the same as, or is comparable with, the men's, or that the women inter se or the men inter se are engaged in equivalent tasks. I express no opinion as to the merits of this view, that the dignity of adult labour requires at least a 4*l.* wage, nor has the honesty of those who entertain it been questioned, but I think it is plain that such a course, whether it be ideal or social or political or all three, forms no part of the conduct, as ordinarily understood, of such practical enterprises as borough councils are by statute authorized to engage in. No authority and no statutory provision was cited to your Lordships, which enables a borough council to give practical effect, at the ratepayers' expense, to such an abstract resolution, nor am I for my own part aware of any. I am, therefore, of opinion that on their own showing the respondents have exercised such discretion as the Metropolis Management Act [1855] gives to the council in the matter of wages upon principles which are not open to the council, and for objects which are beyond their powers.'

Lord Wrenbury said ([1925] AC 578 at 612, [1925] All ER Rep 24 at 42):

'Wages in a particular service are such sum as a reasonable person, guiding himself by an investigation of the current rate in fact found to be paid in the particular industry, and acting upon the principle that efficient service is better commanded by paying an efficient wage, would find to be the proper sum. The figure to be sought is not the lowest figure at which the service could be obtained, nor is it the highest figure which a generous employer might, upon grounds of philanthropy or generosity, pay out of his own pocket. It is a figure which is not to be based upon or increased by motives of philanthropy nor even of generosity stripped of commercial considerations. It is such figure as is the reasonable pecuniary equivalent of the service rendered. Anything beyond this is not wages. It is an addition to wages, and is a gratuity. The authority is to pay not such sum but such wages as they think fit.'

It is plain that the district auditor in this case considered that he was following the guidance given by their Lordships in *Roberts v Hopwood*. It should be noted however that, although traces may be found in that case of a consideration by their Lordships of failure to take into account relevant matters, the fact is that the case of the Poplar councillors was that in reality their decision was based on the concept that £4 a week was *a* the minimum wage which they thought, without regard to current wage rates but having regard to the dignity of labour, ought to be paid to an adult worker. Looking at the wage itself and the reasons advanced for paying it the inference was irresistible that no question of whether the remuneration was appropriate for the work required or whether it compared in any way with wage rates paid elsewhere could possibly have been taken into account. The case seems to me to decide no more than this, that where *b* the inevitable inference which must be drawn is that an obviously excessive wage payment was agreed to be paid without any regard to any commercial consideration and solely on some extraneous principle, as, for instance, philanthropy, such a payment can only be regarded as a gift and is not covered by a statutory power to pay reasonable wages. Looking back, as we do, over sixty years of progress in the field of social reform and industrial relations some of their Lordships' observations may, with the benefit of this *c* hindsight, appear unsympathetic. But what has changed over those years is our attitudes to what should be regarded as pure philanthropy; the basic legal principle, that a payment is illegal which cannot be justified by reference to the objects for which a statutory power is granted, still remains. We have been referred to two further cases from the same era: *Roberts v Cunningham* (1926) 134 LT 421 and *Woolwich BC v Roberts* (1927) 96 LJKB 757, but I do not think that either of these cases serves to modify what I conceive to be the *d* principle of *Roberts v Hopwood*.

In *Prescott v Birmingham Corp* [1954] 3 All ER 698 at 706, [1955] 1 Ch 210 at 235 Jenkins LJ underlines this principle:

'Local authorities are not, of course, trustees for their ratepayers, but they do, we think, owe an analogous fiduciary duty to their ratepayers in relation to the application of funds contributed by the latter. Thus local authorities running an *e* omnibus undertaking at the risk of their ratepayers, in the sense that any deficiencies must be met by an addition to the rates, are not, in our view, entitled, merely on the strength of a general power, to charge different fares to different passengers or classes of passengers, to make a gift to a particular class of persons of rights of free travel on their vehicles, simply because the local authority concerned are of opinion that the favoured class of persons ought, on benevolent or philanthropic grounds, to *f* be accorded that benefit. In other words they are not, in our view, entitled to use their discriminatory power as proprietors of the transport undertaking in order to confer out of rates a special benefit on some particular class of inhabitants whom they, as the local authority for the town or district in question, may think deserving of such assistance. In the absence of clear statutory authority for such a proceeding (which to our mind a mere general power to charge differential fares certainly is *g* not), we would for our part regard it as illegal on the ground that, to put the matter bluntly, it would amount simply to the making of a gift or present in money's worth to a particular section of the local community at the expense of the general body of ratepayers.'

Of course it is plain that a local authority owes a fiduciary duty to its ratepayers; it also *h* owes a duty, laid on it specifically by Parliament, to provide a wide range of services for its inhabitants, be they ratepayers, electors or neither. It is entitled as an employer to have regard to the interests and welfare of its workforce, as any good employer should. It must therefore often be involved in balancing fairly these interests, which may frequently conflict. As it is the ratepayers, ignoring for this purpose grants from central government, who largely find the money which the local authority spends, and as it is the account of *j* that money which the district auditor is engaged in checking, it is right to regard the district auditor as the ratepayers' watchdog. It may be interesting to speculate on what was Parliament's intention when in 1933 it took away the right of a ratepayer or property owner to challenge items of account and transferred that right to local government electors, but I suppose one possible result is to underscore the importance of the district

auditor's role in looking after the ratepayers' interests. But I think despite this the district
a auditor in considering the accounts, and certainly the court in considering any application
for a declaration under s 161, must have due regard to the other duties which the local
authority has to discharge. If it can be shown, and the onus is now on the district auditor
to show it, that a local authority has deliberately tipped the balance in favour of one
interest over others then, whether this be put as taking into account irrelevant material
or as that brand of unreasonableness to which *Wednesbury* refers, it is plainly something
b beyond the power which was entrusted to it.

I do not think there is anything useful to be gained from *Re Decision of Walker* [1944]
1 All ER 614, [1944] 1 KB 644. That case merely demonstrates that if the amount of
wages is reasonable in itself the motives for paying them can be disregarded. But support
for the way of looking at these things which I have just sought to outline may be gathered
from *Re Decision of Hurle-Hobbs* [1944] 2 All ER 261. That was a case in which a local
c authority, despite the existence of a contract for the collection of refuse at a fixed sum,
agreed to make payments to the contractor in excess of the fixed amount because of the
contractor's increased costs due to the war. The Court of Appeal refused to hold that such
payments were illegal. A short passage from the judgment of Lord Greene MR will
suffice ([1944] 2 All ER 261 at 263–264):

d   '. . . it was a case where it seems to me that reasonable people acting with full
      consciousness of their duty to the ratepayers might start the investigation with the
      view that "this is probably a case where something has got to be done." Of course, if
      a local authority confronted with such a demand did not address its mind to what
      was in the interests of the ratepayers, but merely considered the interests of the
      contractor, and acted with a view to enabling him to keep his profits up to the
      standard that he had expected, they would not be acting in a proper way having
e   regard to the fiduciary position they occupy. But this council did, on the evidence,
      and there is not the slightest reason for doubting its genuineness, apply their minds
      to the real governing matter which should determine their action, namely, the
      interests of the ratepayers of the borough in having an efficient standard of refuse
      collection and disposal maintained. I can see no warrant for the suggestion that they
      were endeavouring to secure by the action they took some result other than that. It
f   is not a proper inference, in my opinion, to draw from the facts that they were
      concerning themselves merely with the interests of the contractor, securing for him
      a standard of profit on which his original contract was based, or something of that
      kind. What they were anxious to do was to keep up the high standard of efficiency
      which this contractor, on the evidence, had given them in the past, a standard which
      I cannot help thinking was probably substantially higher than could have been
g   exacted under the precise legal obligations created by the contract. Anyhow, the
      standard was one which impressed the council, and one which they were anxious to
      have maintained.'

Before leaving the authorities I should advert to one other matter. In deciding whether
or not a local authority has acted unreasonably as that term is understood in this
h jurisdiction it is the court which has to decide on the matter before it whether the action
can properly be so regarded. But not infrequently the facts on which the decision was
based can be shown at that stage, sometimes with hindsight, to have been other than
they appeared to those making the decision. There may be circumstances in which this
makes no difference; if a local authority receives legal advice, even from its chief
executive, to the effect that a course of action may properly in law be taken, and it
j subsequently transpires that such advice was wrong, this will not render the act legal.
But there are frequently circumstances in which, if an authority honestly and properly
(in the sense that there has been no failure to take reasonable steps to discover the truth)
believes that the facts are such-and-such and subsequently this turns out to be wrong, it
would not be proper to consider that the question of unreasonableness falls to be
determined by regarding solely the facts as they turn out to have been. If authority for

this proposition is needed I would rely on a short passage from the judgment of Lord Denning MR in *Secretary of State for Employment v Associated Society of Locomotive Engineers* a *and Firemen (No 2)* [1972] 2 All ER 949 at 967–968, [1972] 2 QB 455 at 492:

'. . . what is the effect of the words "If it appears to the Secretary of State"? This, in my opinion, does not mean that the Minister's decision is put beyond challenge. The scope available to the challenger depends very much on the subject-matter with which the Minister is dealing. In this case I would think that, if the Minister does not act in good faith, or if he acts on extraneous considerations which ought not to *b* influence him, or if he plainly misdirects himself in fact or in law, it may well be that a court would interfere; but when he honestly takes a view of the facts or the law which could reasonably be entertained, then his decision is not to be set aside simply because thereafter someone thinks that his view was wrong. After all, this is an emergency procedure. It has to be set in motion quickly, when there is no time for minute analysis of facts or of law. The whole process would be made of no effect *c* if the Minister's decision was afterwards to be conned over word by word, letter by letter, to see if he has in any way misdirected himself. That cannot be right.'

That dictum also shows that a decision taken in an emergency must not be scrutinised as closely as one taken not under such pressure.

I turn now to submissions made by counsel for the district auditor in this case. These *d* are, as I understand them, as follows. (1) That the councillors conceded the basic £60 per week wage and the 35-hour week without any negotiation on the principle. The only negotiations were on whether bonus payments should or should not be taken into account.

(2) That, having regard to this concession of the principle, there are three ways of looking at the question whether it was lawful or unlawful: (a) was it a case where relevant *e* or irrelevant factors invalidated the decision? (b) was it invalid because it was so unreasonable that no reasonable council could have taken it? (c) if the proper way of looking at the council's task is that it was engaged in balancing the various interests which it had a duty to consider, did it get the balance wrong?

(3) So far as (2)(a) is concerned, the council failed to take into account the following relevant matters: (a) the existence of and progress in the national negotiations, (b) the *f* rate of inflation, (c) the general market level of wages, (d) the interests of the ratepayers, and (e) any legal advice. In addition they took into account an irrelevant matter, namely (f) philanthropic enthusiasm.

(4) Turning to (2)(b), the district auditor founds himself on his calculations which show percentage increases over other London boroughs of the sizes to which previous attention has been drawn. *g*

(5) So far as (2)(c) is concerned, again the figures speak for themselves, says the district auditor. The magnitude of the excess shows that the balancing exercise cannot properly have been carried out.

It is not disputed that that council conceded the principle of £60 a week and a 35-hour week. It is hotly denied that this was to concede the principle of the union claim. It is pointed out by Camden that the union was claiming a £60 per week basic minimum *h* wage, with all that meant for the calculation of overtime rates and bonus payments. What was conceded was a £60 per week guaranteed minimum earnings level, not at all the same thing. But, subject to that, there is, as I understand it, no challenge to the district auditor's claim that there were no formal negotiations locally before the decision of the Labour group on 13 February.

When one looks at the matters which counsel for the district auditor says are relevant *j* and which he maintains were not taken into account, there is acceptance by the borough that no legal advice was taken before the decision of 13 February, though it is pointed out that the chief executive has deposed in his affidavit to the fact that he did not regard the settlement as unlawful, so that presumably, if he had been asked for an opinion, he would so have advised. The other matters, however, counsel is constrained to accept,

cannot be regarded as covered by any evidence that they were not taken into account;
a the warrant for saying that they were ignored is that this is the inevitable inference from
the excessive payment. Similarly there is no evidence that the councillors were swayed,
improperly, or at all, by philanthropic enthusiasm other than an inference from the size
of the payments. And when one looks at the evidence to support the charge of
unreasonableness or failure to balance fairly, again the only matter which can be argued
is that the excessive nature of the payments must lead to those conclusions.

b   I desire to make two general observations about these submissions. The first is that
when applying the principles of *Wednesbury*, which is to say, when exercising its
supervisory jurisdiction, the court is not concerned with whether due or proper weight
is given to a material consideration: the weight to be given to such a matter is for the
body exercising the discretion to determine; the court will no more substitute its own
view of the importance of any relevant matter than it will do so for any other matter of
c statutory discretion. In considering whether it is right to conclude that ineluctably the
only inference is that a relevant matter has been ignored the court should I think be very
wary of coming to that conclusion: to weigh up a relevant matter and to conclude that
the weight to be accorded to it is nil lies within the scope of discretion and is not
necessarily to be equated with ignoring it. And the second is that, while such a conclusion
might sometimes be justified, despite the reluctance of the court to interfere in the
d exercise by a statutory authority of discretionary powers, where the decision is taken
freely, voluntarily and under no pressure, the position may be very different where an
emergency dictates a rapid solution to an urgent and pressing problem.

    Counsel for the district auditor's questions really resolve themselves into one: would it
be right, and the onus is on him to show that it is, for this court to conclude that the only
reasonable inference from the fact that these excessive payments were made is that
e Camden ignored relevant material, was motivated by philanthropic enthusiasm, was
wholly unreasonable in the *Wednesbury* sense, or failed fairly to hold the balance between
conflicting interests? Before making any judgment on this question one must look at a
matter, so far only referred to briefly, namely the effect of the NUPE strike on the
discharge by Camden of its duty to provide the statutory range of services for its
inhabitants.

f   [His Lordship then considered an affidavit sworn by the controller of personnel services
of Camden in which the events which occurred from 7 February to 21 February 1979
and the effects of the strike on the operation of Camden's services were described in
detail. His Lordship continued:] The damaging effect which the strike was having on
the council's services was known to the councillors who took the decision on 13 February.
In addition they considered that the strike was having a worse effect in Camden than in
g other London boroughs. This, it was thought, was largely due to the fact, and I quote
from the affidavit of Mr Rutter, the controller of personnel services for Camden, that 'in
Camden the employee leadership was unusually single-minded and effective; moreover
the union officials approached the clash with the council from a position that was in part
ideological'. He also said 'the Council was faced by a challenge which was determined
and ideologically committed'. In support of this he exhibits to his affidavit an article
h contributed to the *New Left Review* (No 16, July–August 1979) by that selfsame Mr John
Suddaby who was the Camden branch secretary of NUPE. It is a brilliantly written and
fascinating account of the local union campaign from one of its main directing minds.
Having described how he and some like-minded members succeeded in supplanting the
old local leadership ('the branch was led by a right-wing Labour branch secretary and a
branch chairman who was a member of the Tory Party') he goes on to detail the new
j leadership's concentration on raising the pay of the lowest paid member by equating this
aim with the fight for a £60 minimum basic wage. The difficulties of mobilising the
members for all-out strike action suggested that a temporary concentration on selective
action might act as a stimulus, hence the decision to call out the plumbers and the petrol
pump attendants. He shows how gradually these tactics led to the indefinite strike action
of the dustmen and the transport drivers. The stage was then set for the resolution for an

indefinite all-out strike of all members on 6 February. He shows how there was a difference in the strike committee whether 'to consider the strike from a political point *a* of view or from a simple "no compromise" stance'. The writer favoured the former. He shows that his hopes that other boroughs would follow Camden 'in a mounting strike wave' were not fulfilled and he mourns the absence 'within the Labour group [ie on the Camden council] of a strong and well-organised left caucus'. It seems to me that Mr Rutter's view of the ideologically committed nature of the local NUPE leadership is amply demonstrated by this article. Although Mr Suddaby asserts later in the article that *b* the borough's acceptance 'was very near the full claim', this is undoubtedly a self-congratulatory remark and is wholly unjustifed on the facts (although the district auditor sought to rely on it), which show that bonus earners were almost entirely excluded from the supplement.

Mr Rutter has also deposed to the position in other London boroughs as at 7 February according to the information in the council's possession at that date. This supports *c* entirely his view that nearly all other boroughs were in a very much more favourable position than Camden. Although the district auditor has sought to show that in fact the position was not as bad as it might have appeared I detect no challenge to the reasonableness of the council's view in early February of that position.

The position is thus that on 13 February the Labour group's decision to agree to a £60 minimum earnings level and a 35-hour week was not taken freely and voluntarily and *d* without pressure. The council was faced with a position where vital services had been so disrupted that real hardship was being caused, not only to the elderly and handicapped, but to the commercial concerns who pay rates but have no elective voice, and where the whole administrative machine of the borough was in imminent danger of having to close down. To this should be added a belief, not unreasonable in the circumstances, that negotiations at national level were not being pursued as effectively or speedily as was *e* required. It seems to me that in this climate we are worlds away from Poplar in the 1920s where a calm and deliberate decision to indulge in what then passed for philanthropy was being taken. Nor do I regard it as the inevitable inference to be drawn from the payment in those circumstances of what might in others be regarded as excessive wages that the group ignored the interests of the ratepayers or any other relevant consideration or in any way can be regarded as unreasonable as that term is *f* understood in the *Wednesbury* case. I remain wholly unsatisfied that the district auditor has made out a case for declaring the decision to concede the £60 minimum and the 35-hour week unlawful.

But that does not end the difficulties facing the district auditor. It is not the decision of the group on 13 February which is challenged. That decision cannot itself be challenged by the district auditor because the item of account he wishes to have declared *g* unlawful is an item in the accounts of the borough, for which the council is responsible and not the Labour group. The only decision which can properly be challenged is the council's decision of 7 March. The more counsel for the district auditor insisted that the decision of 13 February had 'sold the pass' the more it became apparent that the decision on 7 March must be looked at in a different light from the earlier one. The 31 councillors who voted to ratify the final settlement were not the 14 who voted to settle on 13 *h* February though they probably included them. By the time the council came to consider the matter another highly relevant consideration had to be taken into account, namely, if counsel for the district auditor is right, that the pass had been sold and the strikers were back at work. The possible repercussions on the future for industrial relations in Camden and the almost inevitable reaction of the workforce to a refusal to ratify an agreement, on the faith of which a return to work had been secured, would be only too plain. It *j* should not be thought of course, when virtually all local authorities operate on the principle that the councillors owing allegiance to one political party or another meet in advance of council meetings to discuss policy questions, that a decision by a controlling party group can always be followed in council without considering afresh whatever matters are relevant; the fact that a decision has been taken by a party group to do

something which is unlawful does not alter its illegality. But in the present instance the
a decision of 13 February fell to be looked at on 7 March in the light of the further
considerations which I have mentioned, and these only serve to make less likely the
inference that the decision was improperly made.

The district auditor also challenges the decision by the council on 5 March 1980 not to
reduce the Camden supplement by the amount of the NJC award which took effect from
4 November 1979. On 5 March the council had before it the recommendation of a joint
b meeting of the staff and management services committee and the community planning
and resources committee. I have already dealt with that joint meeting and its sequel
when setting out the history. It will be remembered that the meeting had before it a
joint report by the council's chief executive and their director of finance. It is necessary,
in order to see how the committees were being advised, to read a short section of the
advice on the legal position by the chief executive given in that report:

c   'The Council now has the opportunity to reduce the Camden Supplement even
       further and to bring the Camden wage structure more into line with the national
       structure by absorbing the most recent national award. In my opinion this course
       of action must be given serious consideration and a decision not to adopt it, i.e. to
       pay the national award in addition to the Camden Supplement, must carry a risk of
       being declared illegal if nothing further is done to reduce or replace the supplement.
d   However, it is known that there are other local variations to the national wage
       structure and it is therefore probable that the reasonableness of the Council's decision
       will be assessed in part by reference to the earnings levels for similar work in other
       local authorities. I consider that it is also relevant for the Council to take into account
       the possible consequences of reducing the Camden Supplement, the likely reaction
       of the workforce to this and the reasonableness of withdrawing further the benefits
e   which the workforce have enjoyed during the past twelve months. Furthermore
       the reduction of the Camden Supplement would cause the greatest hardship to those
       manual workers who are unable to supplement their wages by earning bonus
       payments. A policy of assisting these non-bonus earners can be justified provided it
       is kept within reasonable limits and it would therefore be open to the Council to
       consider a review of the wage structure of this class of employee with a view to
f   replacing the Camden Supplement by a system of bonus payments linked to
       increased productivity. These are matters for the judgment of the Council to be
       exercised in the light of all information contained in this report. If after due
       consideration the Council is satisfied that it would be reasonable to pay the recent
       national award then I consider that it is important that an examination of the
       position of the different groups of non-bonus earners be commenced without delay
g   so that the Council can then consider alternative ways of attracting bonus to them.'

It should also be remembered that the NJC award was regarded as, and intended as, a
cost-of-living increase, that is one justified not by any increase in productivity but solely
to keep the wages at the same purchasing power as they had enjoyed at the last wage
round. To take away what the unions would undoubtedly regard as an increase justified
h solely on these grounds would in all probability have led in Camden to local industrial
action or at best a worsening in the relations between management and workers; the
possibility of these consequences must, however one looks at it, have been a proper and
relevant matter for the councillors to bear in mind, as indeed the chief executive had
pointed out. In fact the recommendation from the committees adopted the advice of the
chief executive contained in the penultimate paragraph from his report which I have just
j read.

In considering the attitudes and actions of the council in accepting this recommendation
I reiterate what I have earlier said about the importance of not assuming that, because a
relevant matter has apparently been ignored, one must leap to the conclusion that it has
not been taken into account. It is impossible to conclude that the members of the two
committees or of the council took no account of the matters set out at considerable length

in this joint report. The proper inference it seems to me is that they did take them into account and that the weight they gave to those matters lay squarely within the discretion *a* in matters of policy which is entrusted to councillors of local authorities. I do not consider that it is shown that there was anything improper or unlawful about the councillors' decision of 5 March 1980.

The district auditor was of course right to make this application. The power to do so falls just as much within his discretion as did the power to pay the wages he seeks to challenge, and, although different factors affect the two discretions, I do not wish to give *b* any impression that the district auditor exercised his discretion wrongly in this matter. Much publicity, and much of it hostile, was attracted to the Camden decision. It is clear that the district auditor thought that Camden had given in too easily, and without a fight, to the strikers' demands. But there is nothing here to suggest that there was any collusion or collaboration between councillors and the strikers. If there had been, this would of course have been wholly improper and would have struck directly at the good *c* faith of the council's decision to pay these wages. But as it is I can only reiterate that in my view it is not possible in the circumstances of this case to draw the inference that the council here ignored relevant material, was guided by improper motives, or acted in such a way as no reasonable council could properly act. I would refuse the declaration asked.

ORMROD LJ. Section 161 of the Local Government Act 1972, under which these proceedings are brought, has radically changed the role of the district auditor, and of the court. He has ceased to be the adjudicator with power to disallow and surcharge, and has become the applicant: the court is no longer an appellate court, reviewing the decision of the district auditor; it is now a tribunal of first instance, adjudicating directly on the actions of the local authority, and making the initial decision itself. The district auditor *e* is now in the invidious position of a quasi-prosecutor with responsibility for deciding to launch, and for conducting, the proceedings in this court. The court must now find the primary facts for itself and make the effective decision, on material submitted, in the first place, by the district auditor, on affidavit in a form more like a report than a statement of evidence, and on affidavits filed by the respondents. In the present case there has been no direct conflict of evidence on a critical issue, but there might have *f* been. The district auditor's calculations are challenged by expert evidence filed on behalf of the respondents. Fortunately, it is not necessary, in the event, to resolve this dispute, though it might have had the most important effect on the individual respondents. There is a partially unresolved issue which, as will appear, is relevant to my conclusion, namely the severity of the effects of the crisis in February and March 1979 on Camden, and its response, as compared with that of similar local authorities, but the evidence filed *g* by the district auditor is insufficient to rebut the detailed evidence of the respondents on this point.

It is against this background that we have to approach this case, fully conscious of the difficulties of the district auditor, and his embarrassing role as a litigant with the burden of proof. Nothing in this judgment is intended as a criticism of Mr Pickwell personally.

To succeed in this application he has to establish that the items of account in question, *h* that is the payment of wages to manual workers at rates pursuant to the resolution of 7 March 1979, was 'contrary to law', in so far as it exceeded the proper amount. The district auditor has quantified the excess payments as follows: in the years 1978–79, £50,000; 1979–80, £530,000; 1980–81, £370,000.

The case is put in alternative ways. In his affidavit the district auditor relies primarily on the headnote to *Roberts v Hopwood* [1925] AC 578, which he quotes in full, and *j* submits, in substance, that payments by Camden in excess of the national rate, as fixed either by the National Joint Council (NJC) or in the Clegg report, increased by 15% to allow for local conditions, were excessive and so contrary to law. Counsel for the district auditor, in argument on his behalf, relied chiefly on *Associated Provincial Picture Houses Ltd v Wednesbury Corp* [1947] 2 All ER 680, [1948] 1 KB 223 on the basis that the

respondents must have taken into account matters which they ought not to have taken
a into account or must have failed to take into account matters which they ought to have
taken into account, with the consequence that their decision to pay wages at the rates
fixed by the resolution of 7 March 1979 was contrary to law. Alternatively, he submitted
that the decision was one to which no reasonable authority could ever have come, and so
was contrary to law.

Counsel for Camden and for the individual councillors, who are respondents to this
b application, while challenging the district auditor's assessment of the facts of the case, go
further and submit that neither *Roberts v Hopwood* nor the *Wednesbury* case, when
analysed, support the propositions of law on which the district auditor's case is based.
They contend that a decision of a local authority can only be said to be 'contrary to law',
in a case of this kind, if it can be established that the local authority has in some way
exceeded or abused its statutory powers, or the discretion given to it by statute; in other
c words, that it has acted ultra vires. They argue that excessive expenditure on a lawful
object, or a failure to take relevant matters into account, or the taking into account of
irrelevant matters is, in effect, evidence that the local authority has, or may have, acted
ultra vires and, therefore, contrary to law, but does not amount in itself to illegality. In
other words, there may be a failure to comply with Lord Greene MR's formula, or
undoubtedly extravagant expenditure, without rendering the decision or the action of
d the local authority's 'contrary to law'. However, some actions or decisions may be so far
out of line with the 'norm', or so self-evidently erroneous, that the court may be justified
in drawing the inference that the local authority has purported to use the discretion,
given to it for one purpose, in reality to achieve an ulterior or collateral objective which
is ultra vires. This argument directs attention to the quality or character of the decision
itself, rather than to the methods by which it is reached.

e   In my judgment, this is the proper way to approach the question of whether an item
of expenditure is 'contrary to law'. But there is a growing tendency to treat particular
expressions used by judges in their judgments, taken out of context, as if they were
propositions of law in themselves. This is especially true of the concluding passage in
Lord Greene MR's judgment in the *Wednesbury* case [1949] 2 All ER 680 at 685, [1948] 1
KB 223 at 233–234, which is frequently cited without reference to the body of the
f judgment, and is coming to be regarded as a proposition of law in itself. This is a process
which Frankfurter J once described in these words: 'A phrase begins life as a literary
expression; its felicity leads to its easy repetition; and repetition soon establishes it as a
legal formula, indiscriminately used to express different and sometimes contradictory
ideas' (see *Tiller v Atlantic Coast Line Railroad Co* (1943) 318 US 54 at 68).

With that warning in mind, I turn to the authorities, and in particular to *Roberts v
g Hopwood* [1925] AC 578, [1925] All ER Rep 24, which is the foundation of the district
auditor's case, as he sees it, in order to sift out, so far as I can, the ratio decidendi from the
literary expressions, often of great felicity, used by the judges in explaining the reasons
for their decision.

The decision in *Roberts v Hopwood*, in my judgment, turned on the conclusion that the
resolution of the Poplar Borough Council to pay a minimum wage of £4 per week to all
h adult employees, regardless of the work they did, their sex and the fall in the cost of
living, was not passed in the exercise of the council's statutory power to pay such
reasonable wages as it saw fit, but that it was purporting to use this power not to pay
wages but, for social, political, idealogical or other reasons, to make gifts or gratuities to
the staff, which it had no power to do. The payments were, therefore, ultra vires and,
therefore, contrary to law. This, as is clear from the report of the judgments in the Court
j of Appeal (see [1924] 2 KB 695), was the main point relied on by the district auditor in
disallowing the extra expenditure and surcharging the councillors.

Lord Buckmaster said ([1925] AC 578 at 590, [1925] All ER Rep 24 at 30):

'It appears to me, for the reasons I have given, that they cannot be brought into
account the considerations which they say influenced them, and that they did not

base their decision upon the ground that the reward for work is the value of the
work reasonably and even generously measured, but that they took an arbitrary *a*
principle and fixed an arbitrary sum, which was not a *real* exercise of the discretion
imposed upon them by the statute.' (My emphasis.)

Lord Atkinson said ([1925] AC 578 at 600, [1925] All ER Rep 24 at 35): 'I concur with
the auditor in thinking that what has been given to the women as wages is really to a
great extent gifts and gratuities disguised as wages, and is therefore illegal.' He had earlier
dismissed the suggestion that the councillors could rely on a mandate from their *b*
constituents to put this scale of wages into force.

Lord Sumner said ([1925] AC 578 at 610, [1925] All ER Rep 24 at 41):

'I am, therefore, of opinion that on their own showing the respondents have
exercised such discretion as the Metropolis Management Act [1855] gives to the
council in the matter of wages upon *principles* which are not open to the council, *c*
and for objects which are beyond their powers.' (My emphasis.)

Lord Wrenbury and Lord Carson expressed similar views (see [1925] AC 578 at 612,
618, [1925] All ER Rep 24 at 42, 44–45).

The headnote to the report ([1925] AC 578) is misleading because it suggests that the
decision depended on the unreasonableness of the exercise of the discretion and the
excessiveness of the expenditure, that is a quantitative rather than a qualitative test. The *d*
speeches certainly contain numerous expressions which could be used to support the
headnote but, in my judgment, it does not accurately reflect the ratio decidendi.

This view is in accordance with the later cases. In *Re Decision of Walker* [1944] 1 All ER
614, the Court of Appeal had to consider a decision by the Birmingham corporation to
pay its non-manual employees a 'children's allowance' at the rate of 2s 6d per week for
each child. This was disallowed by the district auditor, but allowed by the Divisional *e*
Court and affirmed by the Court of Appeal. Once Goddard LJ had convinced himself
(though not seemingly without difficulty) that the payments could properly be described
as 'wages', he was satisfied that the corporation had power to make them. He also applied
the quantitative test of reasonableness. Du Parcq LJ said (at 616):

'That case [ie *Roberts v Hopwood*] made it clear that a local authority cannot be said *f*
to be acting in the lawful exercise of its discretion to fix wages when it grants to its
employees, nominally as wages, amounts arrived at arbitrarily, without consideration
of any of those matters which an employer, acting reasonably, would normally take
into account ... As I understand the decision, however, it does not follow that
expenditure may properly be disallowed, or a surcharge levied, whenever the local
authority's reasons for the expenditure are ill-advised, stupid or even (it may be) *g*
dishonest.'

The same approach was adopted by the Court of Appeal in *Re Decision of Hurle-Hobbs*
[1944] 2 All ER 261, a case in which the district auditor disallowed certain extra payments
to a contractor for the removal of refuse in the borough of Lambeth. This case is
analogous in many ways to the present case, and Lord Greene MR's judgment is very
helpful. The council was criticised for numerous omissions in arriving at its decision to *h*
pay the contractor sums over and above those which were provided for in his contract,
and it made what proved later to be a very bad bargain. Similar criticisms are made by
the district auditor in this case. Lord Greene MR said (at 264):

'Of course, if a local authority confronted with such a demand did not address its
mind to what was in the interests of the ratepayers, but merely considered the *j*
interests of the contractor, and acted with a view to enabling him to keep his profits
up to the standard that he had expected, they would not be acting in a proper way
having regard to the fiduciary position they occupy ... It is not a proper inference,
in my opinion, to draw from the facts that they were concerning themselves merely
with the interests of the contractor ...'

The reasoning in that case, to my mind, applies, mutatis mutandis, to the present case. It
a is not suggested, and if it was there is no evidence before the court to support such a
suggestion, that in deciding to concede a minimum wage of £60 per week for a 35-hour
week Camden was concerning itself merely with the interests of NUPE, or colluding
with the strikers.

The next case is the *Wednesbury* case [1947] 2 All ER 680 at 685, [1948] 1 KB 223 at
233, the cornerstone of counsel for the district auditor's argument, which is based on the
b language used by Lord Greene MR, in summarising his judgment, when he said:

> '. . . the court is entitled to investigate the action of the local authority with a view
> to seeing whether it has taken into account matters which it ought not to take into
> account, or, conversely, has refused to take into account or neglected to take into
> account matters which it ought to take into account. Once that question is answered
> in favour of the local authority, it may still be possible to say that the local authority,
c nevertheless, have come to a conclusion so unreasonable that no reasonable authority
> could ever have come to it. In such a case, again, I think the court can interfere.'

This is the passage which has given rise to the so-called *Wednesbury* principles, the
classic formula for defining the limitation on the powers of the court to interfere with
the exercise of the discretion of administrative bodies. But it is not, and was not intended
d to be, a definition of illegality. Failure by a local authority to conform to these principles
exposes its decision to review by the court, but it does not necessarily make it illegal or
contrary to law. Lord Greene MR makes this point in the next sentence of his judgment,
which is often overlooked. He said:

> 'The power of the court to interfere in each case is not that of an appellate
> authority to override a decision of the local authority, but is that of a judicial
e authority which is concerned, and concerned only, to see whether the local authority
> have contravened the law by *acting in excess of the powers* which Parliament has
> confided in it.' (My emphasis.)

Earlier in his judgment Lord Greene MR was at pains to explain the meaning of the
word 'unreasonable' in this context: he used it as equivalent to saying that no reasonable
f authority could have exercised its discretion in such a way, and added that this could
almost be described as 'being done in bad faith' (see [1947] 2 All ER 680 at 683, [1948] 1
KB 223 at 230). He confirmed that the ratio decidendi in *Roberts* v *Hopwood* was that the
payments in question were not wages at all, and said that that case was no authority for
the proposition that the court had an overriding power to decide what is reasonable, and
what is unreasonable: 'The court has nothing of the kind' (see [1948] 1 KB 223 at 232).
g Frankfurter J's process of evolution of a legal formula has gone a long way in this
instance. The great felicity with which the *Wednesbury* principles are expressed has led to
much repetition, and there is a danger of their being 'indiscriminately used to express
different . . . ideas'.

Prescott v *Birmingham Corp* [1954] 3 All ER 698 at 706, [1955] 1 Ch 210 at 235 is
another ultra vires case which follows *Roberts* v *Hopwood*. Jenkins LJ said:

h
> 'In other words, they are not, in our view, entitled to use their discriminatory
> power as proprietors of the transport undertaking in order to confer out of rates a
> special benefit on some particular class of inhabitants whom they, as the local
> authority for the town or district in question, may think deserving of such assistance.
> In the absence of clear statutory authority for such a proceeding (which to our mind
> a mere general power to charge differential fares certainly is not) we would, for our
j part, regard it as illegal, on the ground that, to put the matter bluntly, it would
> amount simply to the making of a gift or present in money's worth to a particular
> section of the local community at the expense of the general body of ratepayers.'

The reason why a general power to charge different fares to different classes of passengers
was insufficient to justify free travel for old age pensioners was that the local authority

owed a fiduciary duty to its ratepayers and so could not make a gift of free travel to them
without breaching this duty.

In *Luby v Newcastle-under-Lyme Corp* [1964] 1 All ER 84 at 89, [1964] 2 QB 64 at 72
Diplock LJ defined the powers of the court in these cases as follows:

'The court's control over the exercise by a local authority of a discretion conferred
on the authority by Parliament is limited to ensuring that a local authority have
acted within the powers conferred. It is not for the court to substitute its own view
of what is a desirable policy in relation to the subject-matter of the discretion so
conferred. It is only if it is exercised in a manner which no reasonable man could
consider justifiable that the court is entitled to interfere.'

In my judgment, this passage should be regarded as definitive of the court's powers,
and should be adhered to in all cases in which it is claimed that an authority has misused
its discretionary power.

The latest case is *Bromley London Borough Council v Greater London Council* [1982] 1 All
ER 129, [1982] 2 WLR 62. This again was an ultra vires case which involved difficult
questions of construction of some obscurely worded statutory provisions. It turned,
primarily, on statutory interpretation. The lengthy judgments are a mine of felicitous
'literary expressions', but the ratio decidendi was that the statutory powers of the Greater
London Council did not extend far enough to enable it to institute, at the cost of the
ratepayers, a very heavily subsidised fare structure for London Transport. In so far as the
speeches in the House of Lords dealt with the question of discretion, they affirmed
Jenkins LJ's opinion in *Prescott v Birmingham Corp* [1954] 1 All ER 698, [1955] 1 Ch 210
that local authorities owe a fiduciary duty to their ratepayers. As in *Prescott's* case, the
existence of this duty was a relevant factor to be taken into account in determining the
ambit of the statutory powers. However, it would not be right to regard this case as
authority for the general proposition that this fiduciary duty opens up a route by which
the courts can investigate and, if thought appropriate, interfere with any exercise of their
discretionary powers by local authorities. This would completely undermine the
principles of the *Wednesbury* case, and make nonsense of Diplocks LJ's definition of the
court's powers in *Luby's* case.

In my judgment, therefore, if the district auditor is to succeed in his application for a
declaration that Camden's expenditure, arising from its decision to pay its manual
workers a minimum wage of £60 per week for a 35-hour week, was 'contrary to law', he
must establish that Camden was acting in excess of its statutory powers. There are only
two ways by which this could be done in this case. The first is by showing that the
decision was not, in reality, a decision made in the exercise of its statutory power to fix
wage rates, but for some other extraneous, irrelevant or collateral purpose, for example
to undermine the incomes policy, or to sabotage, for political purposes, the national
negotiations which were proceeding simultaneously, or to achieve some other social or
political objective. The second is by satisfying the court that no reasonable local authority
would have made such a decision in the circumstances prevailing in Camden in February
and March 1979.

The first of these alternatives has never been put forward by, or on behalf of, the
district auditor, and it is right to say in the clearest terms that there is no evidence at all
that Camden, or the respondent councillors, had any extraneous objective in mind. All
the evidence shows that its sole purpose was to settle as quickly as possible a strike which
was having a very serious effect on the inhabitants of the borough.

The second requires rather more consideration because the wage settlement
undoubtedly involved a very large and immediate increase in the wages to be paid to the
manual workers. The district auditor has expressed the opinion that the settlement was
unreasonably high. His figures are challenged by Camden in various ways, but, on any
view, the increase was large and, from NUPE's point of view, the outcome of the strike
was probably more favourable than they expected. But the question for this court is not
whether Camden made a bad bargain for the ratepayers' or was precipitate in making

the offer to the strikers, or could have achieved a cheaper settlement by waiting, or made
a   a better bargain by different tactics. These are matters for the electorate at the next
election. The question for the court is whether the evidence establishes that no reasonable
local authority could have made a settlement on such terms. So to hold would require a
detailed appraisal of the state of affairs in Camden in February and March 1979,
comparisons with the experiences of other boroughs, and of prevailing wage rates in
comparable jobs in other sectors, all of which would have to be related to the crisis which
b   plainly existed, and in the midst of which the decision was made. The evidence before
the court is, in my judgment, quite insufficient to permit the court to make any such
finding of fact, which would require clear and compelling evidence, that is assuming
that the court could properly make such a finding on purely quantitative as opposed to
qualitative grounds. Such a conclusion, as Lord Greene MR recognised in the *Wednesbury*
case [1947] 2 All ER 680 at 683, [1948] 1 KB 223 at 230, would have to amount almost
c   to a finding that Camden and the councillors must have acted in bad faith.

Some reliance was also placed on the fiduciary duty owed by Camden to its ratepayers,
but this line of attack must have a very limited application, if any, in a case in which the
local authority had ample authority to determine wage rates and was genuinely acting
on that authority and on its appreciation of the problems and conditions with which it
was confronted. The fiduciary duty, as I understand it, arises because councillors are
d   entrusted with ratepayers' money to use it for duly, that is legally, authorised purposes
and not otherwise, much as trustees hold the trust fund, to apply it for the purposes
authorised by the trust instrument, or by statute, as the case may be.

My conclusion, therefore, is that these items of expenditure were not contrary to law,
and it is not for this court to pass judgment on the wisdom or unwisdom of the wage
settlement of March 1979. The application, therefore, fails.

e
Application refused.

Solicitors: *Clifford-Turner* (for the district auditor); *F Nickson* (for Camden London
Borough Council); *Bernard Sheridan & Co* (for 28 of the councillors); *Marian Cohen,*
Shepherd's Bush (for one of the councillors).

f
N P Metcalfe Esq   Barrister.

Official Solicitor v Stype Investments
g   # (Jersey) Ltd

CHANCERY DIVISION
WHITFORD J
13, 14, 18 OCTOBER 1982

h   *Practice – Service out of the jurisdiction – Land within the jurisdiction – Action founded on
contract and on trust – Settlor conveying land in England to Jersey company – Company
undertaking under declaration of trust to hold land as bare nominee and to account to settlor for
proceeds of sale if land sold – Company contracting to sell land – Settlor dying before completion
of sale – Bulk of proceeds of sale paid at company's request into its bank account in Jersey –
Remainder of proceeds held in England – Official Solicitor appointed administrator ad colligenda*
j   *bona – Action in England by Official Solicitor against company – Official Solicitor seeking
declaration that proceeds of sale held in trust for settlor's estate – Whether Official Solicitor should
be granted leave to serve proceedings on company out of jurisdiction – RSC Ord 11, r 1(1)(b)(e)(f).*

On 23 May 1979 C conveyed certain land situated in England to S Ltd, a Jersey company.
Under a declaration of trust made on the same day between C and the company, S Ltd

undertook (i) to hold the land as a bare nominee for C, (ii) to convey it at any time, at C's request, either to him personally or to any purchaser from him, and (iii) to account to C for the net proceeds of sale and the net rents and profits until sale. On 25 May, at C's request, S Ltd agreed to sell the land to P Ltd, an English company, for just over £20m. C died on 26 July and the sale was completed on 28 September. On S Ltd's instructions P Ltd paid £20m of the purchase price into S Ltd's bank account in Jersey. The remainder, some £60,000 to £75,000, was left in England. The Crown claimed that the proceeds of the sale were property of C situated in England, and at the Crown's request a grant of letters of administration ad colligenda bona was issued to the Official Solicitor. Pursuant to his duties under the grant, the Official Solicitor sought and was granted leave under RSC Ord 11, r 1(1)ᵃ to issue and serve a writ on S Ltd in Jersey seeking (i) a declaration that from 23 May 1979 until his death the proceeds of sale were held in trust for C, and after his death for his estate, (ii) an account of the proceeds of sale, (iii) an inquiry as to the whereabouts of the proceeds, (iv) an order for the payment of the proceeds to the Official Solicitor, (v) an injunction restraining dealings in the proceeds, (vi) damages, and (vii) an order for administration and other consequential relief. S Ltd applied to have the order giving leave to serve the writ out of the jurisdiction set aside, on the ground, inter alia, that the Official Solicitor's claim did not fall within Ord 11, r 1(1).

Held – S Ltd's motion would be dismissed for the following reasons—

(1) Even though the land had been sold at the time the Official Solicitor applied for leave, the Official Solicitor was none the less seeking to enforce a 'deed [or] contract . . . affecting land situate within the jurisdiction', within RSC Ord 11, r 1(1)(b), since he was attempting to enforce the obligations which the declaration of trust had imposed on S Ltd regarding the land, which obligations continued not only after the death of C but also after the sale of the land. Leave to serve the writ out of the jurisdiction was therefore permissible under r 1(1)(b) (see p 635 d h j and p 640 d e, post).

(2) The action was also an action 'for the execution, as to property situate within the jurisdiction, of the trusts of a written instrument, being trusts that ought to be executed according to English law', within RSC Ord 11, r 1(1)(e), because part of the property (the £60,000 to £75,000) was situated within the jurisdiction and that part and the £20m were both part of a single fund. Justice could only be done if the two parts of the fund were dealt with together in one single suit. Furthermore, all the 'property' could be said to be 'within the jurisdiction' at the date of the issue of the writ, since the relevant property included not only the £60,000 to £75,000 in England but also the Official Solicitor's right to an account and right to payment of the money received by S Ltd as being a debt due to C's estate. Leave to serve the writ out of the jurisdiction was therefore permissible under r 1(1)(e) (see p 637 d to g and p 640 d e, post); A-G v Drapers Co (1894) 1 IR 185 and IRC v Stype Investments (Jersey) Ltd [1981] 2 All ER 394 followed.

(3) Since the Official Solicitor was alleging that S Ltd was in breach not only of its obligations as trustee but also of its contractual obligations under the declaration of trust,

---

a   Rule 1(1), so far as material, provides: '. . . service of a writ, out of the jurisdiction is permissible with the leave of the Court in the following cases, that is to say . . . (b) if an act, deed, will, contract, obligation or liability affecting land situate within the jurisdiction is sought to be construed, rectified, set aside or enforced in the action begun by the writ . . . (e) if the action begun by the writ is for the execution, as to property situate within the jurisdiction, of the trusts of a written instrument, being trusts that ought to be executed according to English law and of which the person to be served with the writ is a trustee or if the action begun by the writ is for any relief or remedy which might be obtained in any such action as aforesaid; (f) if the action begun by the writ is brought against a defendant . . . to enforce, rescind, dissolve, annul or otherwise affect a contract, or to recover damages or obtain other relief in respect of the breach of a contract, being (in either case) a contract which—(i) was made within the jurisdiction, or (ii) was made by or through an agent trading or residing within the jurisdiction on behalf of a principal trading or residing out of the jurisdiction, or (iii) is by its terms, or by implication, governed by English law . . .'

the action was also an action to 'obtain . . . relief in respect of the breach of a contract',
a within RSC Ord 11, r 1(1)(*f*), since r 1(1)(*f*) was not confined to applications for leave to
serve out of the jurisdiction founded exclusively on breach of contract but extended to
applications founded on both trustee and contractual obligations. Leave to serve the writ
out of the jurisdiction was therefore permissible under r 1(1)(*f*) (see p 639 *b c f g* and
p 640 *d e*, post); *Hughes v Oxenham* [1913] 1 Ch 254 explained.

b **Notes**
For leave to serve a writ out of the jurisdiction, see 37 Halsbury's Laws (4th edn) paras
171, 172, and for cases on the subject, see 50 Digest (Repl) 336–365, 646–852.

Cases referred to in judgment
A-G v Drapers Co (1894) 1 IR 185, CA, 50 Digest (Repl) 338, 670.
c *Agnew v Usher* (1884) 14 QBD 78; *affd* 51 LT 752, CA, 50 Digest (Repl) 338, 667.
Creswell v Parker (1879) 11 Ch D 601, CA, 50 Digest (Repl) 369, 874.
Hughes v Oxenham [1913] 1 Ch 254, CA, 50 Digest (Repl) 344, 700.
IRC v Stype Investments (Jersey) Ltd [1981] 2 All ER 394, [1981] Ch 367, [1981] 3 WLR
    426; *rvsd* [1982] 3 All ER 419, [1982] Ch 456, [1982] 3 WLR 228, CA.
Kaye v Sutherland (1888) 20 QBD 147, 50 Digest (Repl) 338, 668.
d *New York Breweries Co v A-G* [1899] AC 62, HL, 23 Digest (Reissue) 78, 967.
Tassell v Hallen [1892] 1 QB 321, DC, 50 Digest (Repl) 336, 651.
Winter v Winter [1894] 1 Ch 421, 50 Digest (Repl) 340, 680.

Cases also cited
Hagen, The [1908] P 189, [1908–10] All ER Rep 21, CA.
e *Siskina (cargo owners) v Distos Compania Naviera SA, The Siskina* [1977] 3 All ER 803, [1979]
    AC 210, HL.
Total Oil GB Ltd v Marbonanza Compania Naviera SA [1975] CA Transcript 298.
Waterhouse v Reid [1938] 1 All ER 235, [1938] 1 KB 743, CA.

Motions
f On 28 June 1982 the plaintiff, the Official Solicitor, was given leave to serve a writ out of
the jurisdiction on the defendants, Stype Investments (Jersey) Ltd, and leave to serve a
notice of motion returnable on 26 July 1982, and was granted, ex parte, a Mareva
injunction freezing assets of the defendants within the jurisdiction. On 26 July 1982 a
similar order was made in another action which the plaintiff had brought against the
defendants. By two notices of motion, dated respectively 31 August 1982 and 2 September
g 1982, the defendants applied in each action to set aside the orders giving the plaintiff
leave to effect service out of the jurisdiction. At the same time the plaintiff moved for an
order continuing the Mareva injunction in both actions. The facts are set out in the
judgment.

Donald Nicholls QC and *R G B McCombe* for the plaintiff.
h *John Knox QC* and *John Weeks* for the defendants.

Cur adv vult

18 October. The following judgment was delivered.

j **WHITFORD J.** I have before me four motions, two in action 1982 C No 5277 and two
in action 1982 O No 2689. In both actions the Official Solicitor, as administrator of the
estate of the late Sir Charles Clore, is the plaintiff; Stype Investments (Jersey) Ltd are the
defendants. In the first action Dillon J gave leave to serve the proceedings out of the
jurisdiction on 28 June 1982. He also gave leave to serve a notice of motion returnable
on 26 July 1982 and granted ex parte Mareva relief, freezing assets of the defendants

within the jurisdiction, these assets amounting to a not inconsiderable sum. A similar
order was made in the second action on 26 July 1982. The defendants move in both
actions to set aside the orders giving leave to serve out of the jurisdiction. The plaintiff
moves in both actions for a continuance of the Mareva relief.

Counsel for the defendants and counsel for the plaintiff being agreed that the outcome
so far as the Mareva relief is concerned must depend on the outcome of the defendants'
applications to set aside, I will deal first with the defendants' motion in the first action.
The grounds of their application are set out in their notice of motion. They say that the
order should be set aside because the claim does not fall within any relevant paragraph of
RSC Ord 11, r 1, because this court is not the forum conveniens, because similar
proceedings have been started in Jersey and it is undesirable that there should be a
duplication of proceedings, and because there has not been a good arguable case made
out by the plaintiff for service.

Before me the case was argued on RSC Ord 11, r 1(1)(b), (e), (f) and (g), counsel for the
plaintiff expressly reserving his position under sub-para (h), or any other sub-paragraph,
in the event that he is unsuccessful under sub-paras (b), (e), (f) and (g). This, counsel for
the defendants accepted, as he is perfectly entitled to do. Indeed, one point made by
counsel for the defendants was that failure on this occasion would not necessarily preclude
success on some other occasion so far as the plaintiff is concerned.

The litigation arises out of the state in which the affairs of Sir Charles stood at the date
of his death. It is not the only litigation which has been started following his death, as is
apparent from the terms of the notice of motion. The Inland Revenue Commissioners in
this country have served an originating summons on the defendants claiming, inter alia,
an account for the purpose of ascertaining the tax alleged to be due to them. The Inland
Revenue Commissioners, having secured leave to serve the originating summons out of
the jurisdiction, these defendants applied successfully, before Goulding J for an order
setting aside service (see IRC v Stype Investments (Jersey) Ltd [1981] 2 All ER 394, [1981]
Ch 367). Goulding J's decision was reversed in the Court of Appeal ([1982] 3 All ER 419,
[1982] Ch 456). Much of the background relevant to be considered on the defendants'
application before me is dealt with in detail in the judgment of the Court of Appeal, to
which I was taken by both counsel for the plaintiff and counsel for the defendants. It
will, however, be convenient if I summarise the relevant facts, as I understand them,
from the affidavits before me.

Sir Charles had a domicile of origin in this country. His domicile at the date of his
death on 26 July 1979 is a matter of dispute. In April 1979 he made two wills. The first,
dealing with his property in Monaco, is of no relevance. The second, of which the
executors were a Mr Meyohas, a Mr Kasierer and a Mr Karlweis, gave all his property,
other than the Monaco property, to the trustees of a settlement created by Sir Charles in
February 1979. This settlement, exhibited to the affidavit of Mr Venables, the Official
Solicitor, names the same three gentlemen as trustees. It is expressed to be governed by
the law of the island of Jersey. The trust fund is held on trust to pay the income to Sir
Charles during his lifetime. Subject to this it is held on trust in favour of certain
charitable foundations established by Sir Charles. Mr Karlweis has apparently renounced
his executorship and resigned as trustee, but nothing turns on this.

On 23 May 1979 Sir Charles conveyed the property and land, the subject of the first
action, referred to as the Hereford estate, to the defendants. On the same day there was
executed the declaration of trust. It is between the defendants and Sir Charles. It is short
and it is important, so I will read it:

'WHEREAS by a Conveyance to be made between the said Sir Charles Clore ("the
Owner") of the one part and the Company of the other part the freehold property
briefly described in the Schedule hereto is to be conveyed to the Company in fee
simple and notwithstanding anything therein contained it is intended that no
beneficial interest in the property should pass to the Company but that the Company
should hold the said property as a bare nominee for the Owner

NOW THIS DEED WITNESSES and it is hereby agreed and declared as follows:—

(1) THE Company acknowledges that the said property will continue to remain in the beneficial ownership of the Owner and that the Company will hold the same as his nominee and to his order and that it will at any time at his request convey the said property either to the Owner personally or to any other person or persons company or companies nominated by him or to any purchaser from him in the event of the property being sold.

(2) THE Company undertakes to account to the Owner for the net proceeds of sale of the said property and for the net rents and profits arising therefrom until sale but shall be entitled out of such proceeds or net rents and profits to pay any outgoings or charges arising in respect of the property so far as the same shall not have been paid and discharged by the Owner personally.'

On a direction given by Sir Charles the defendants, in anticipation, no doubt, of what they hoped was going to happen, had agreed, on 25 May, to sell the Hereford estate to the Prudential Assurance Co Ltd, completion to take place on 28 September. Sir Charles died in July. Completion took place on 28 September. But before this, following the death of Sir Charles, consideration was obviously given to the way in which the proceeds of the sale, amounting to something over £20m, should be dealt with. Eminent counsel advised in August 1976 that these moneys should not pass through the hands of the defendants' solicitors, because if the defendants' solicitors were then to pass them on to anyone other than an English personal representative they might then find themselves liable for capital transfer tax as executors de son tort. At some time on or shortly prior to 11 September 1979 advice was given in consultation by another eminent counsel to the effect that the proceeds of sale of the Hereford estate should be remitted to an account of the defendants in Jersey. Instructions, which appear subsequently to have been ratified by a resolution of the directors, were forthwith given that this should be done, and in the result the proceeds of sale were removed from the jurisdiction.

Following this event the Commissioners of Inland Revenue issued their originating summons, with the results I have indicated so far as the question of service out of the jurisdiction in the originating summons is concerned. There was also an application, at the request of the Inland Revenue, that letters of administration ad colligenda bona be granted to the Official Solicitor. This was granted. This grant also came before the Court of Appeal in *IRC v Stype Investments (Jersey) Ltd* [1982] 3 All ER 419 at 430–431, [1982] Ch 456 at 476–477. On this aspect of the matter the Court of Appeal said:

'On 3 August 1981 the senior registrar of the Family Division, at the request of the Inland Revenue, authorised a grant ad colligenda bona to the estate of Sir Charles to be issued to the Official Solicitor, under s 162(1) proviso (b) of the Supreme Court of Judicature (Consolidation) Act 1925. The executors named in the will of Sir Charles appealed to Ewbank J, who dismissed the appeal on 4 December 1981 ... The executors appeal to this court. The grant should have been issued to the executors in the absence of special circumstances. We agree with the judge that there were special circumstances. There are no grounds for interfering with his decision. The executors contend that the administration of the estate will be cheaper and more expeditious if they are given a grant. They do not intend to make provision or offer security for the payment of any capital transfer tax which may be found to be due and payable by the executors. Nor do they intend to pay or offer security for the capital transfer tax which may be found to be due and payable by them as trustees of the personal settlement of Sir Charles. The executors as directors of Stype Investments share responsibility for the fact that £20m of the English assets are now locked up in Jersey. The executors as directors of Stype Investments share responsibility for opposing strenuously the efforts of the Inland Revenue to obtain payment by Stype Investments at least to the extent of its assets now in England of any capital transfer tax which may be found to be payable in respect of the English estate of Sir Charles. The executors, for reasons which are paltry and disingenuous,

have opposed a grant to the Official Solicitor and have thus delayed investigation
into the affairs of the estate of Sir Charles. The appointment of the Official Solicitor *a*
will render academic the dispute as to whether Stype Investments constituted itself
executor de son tort. If the £20m now in Jersey represents property of Sir Charles
situated in the United Kingdom at his death, the Official Solicitor, as personal
representative of Sir Charles constituted in this country, will be able to sue Stype
Investments in this country for failing to collect the debt owed by the Prudential in
this country and for failing to retain the £20m in this country available to be paid *b*
over to the Official Solicitor as personal representative of Sir Charles constituted in
England. At the request of the Inland Revenue the English court would grant an
injunction restraining Stype Investments from transferring any of its assets out of
the jurisdiction until the Official Solicitor has taken a grant, instituted proceedings
against Stype Investments and obtained an interlocutory injunction in those
proceedings. In the circumstances, the appointment of the executors as personal *c*
representatives duly constituted in this country would be bizarre. The appeal of the
executors against the decision of Ewbank J is a sinister and time-wasting exercise
and must be dismissed.'

There are, in fact, considerable assets held by the defendants in this country, approaching
I think something in the order of £20m. On an application for leave to appeal against *d*
the decision of the Court of Appeal to the House of Lords the defendants were
unsuccessful.

The question is: should the leave granted to the plaintiff to serve out of the jurisdiction
have been given; should the defendants' request that the order be set aside be acceded to?

Although the Commissioners of Inland Revenue were responsible for securing the
grant of letters of administration to the plaintiff, the plaintiff is not, of course, in any *e*
sense to be considered as being a creature of the Inland Revenue. The letters of
administration were granted for the sole purpose of enabling the plaintiff—

'(i) to collect get in and realise the estate of the deceased (ii) to discharge the debts
of the deceased (iii) to pay all . . . expenses and all taxes and duties payable by reason
of the death (iv) to take legal proceedings in England or elsewhere to get in the estate
(v) to sell any chattels securities or other property belonging to the deceased to *f*
provide for duty or tax (vi) to preserve the property of the deceased (vii) to store the
property of the deceased (viii) to give discharges for debts due to the estate (ix) to
receive notices of assessment and pursue any tax appeals (x) to do all acts in
connection with or necessary or desirable for the preservation and collection of the
said deceased's estate and until further representation be granted.'

In pursuance of his obligation the plaintiff has started this action. He claims in his writ a *g*
declaration that the proceeds of sale of the Hereford estate were, as from 23 May 1979,
held in trust for the deceased and, since his death, for his estate. He claims an account of
the proceeds of sale and an inquiry as to their whereabouts. These are all matters which
ought, I should have thought, on the face of it, to be capable of relatively speedy
resolution. He asks for an order for payment of the proceeds of sale. He seeks injunctions *h*
restraining dealings in such proceeds. He seeks damages, an order for administration and
other consequential relief.

It is, of course, for the plaintiff to satisfy the court that his case is one in which service
out of the jurisdiction is permissible. He has to satisfy the court that his case falls within
one or more of the sub-paras (a) to (p) of RSC Ord 11, r 1(1). The plaintiff accepts that
each cause of action asserted must so fall, and that impermissible claims cannot be added *j*
to permissible claims.

Of the sub-paragraphs relied on I can take first sub-para (b). Omitting the words of
lesser relevance the question is: is this a case in which a deed or contract affecting land
situate within the jurisdiction is sought to be enforced?

Counsel for the defendants says it is not because at the date of application for leave there was no relevant land within the jurisdiction. The Hereford estate had been sold. Counsel for the plaintiff says: 'Look at the declaration of trust. The plaintiff seeks to enforce the defendants' obligations hereunder. They have covenanted to account for the proceeds of sale. The deed is a deed affecting land.' RSC Ord 11 has never been buried full fathom five, but it has suffered many changes over the years. It has become rich in the opportunities it provides for argument and, to my mind, exceedingly strange in some of the results which have flowed therefrom. It is not always easy to be absolutely certain what the form of the order was, so frequent have been the changes, at the date when any relevant authority has to be considered, but I think, with the assistance of both counsel, those difficulties have been overcome at all times during the citation of authority before me. Its foundations were laid in a period when international trade was relatively minuscule. Communications by the standards of today when, by the touch of a computer you can do in seconds what 150 years ago would have taken days if not weeks or months, have altered out of all recognition. A point may perhaps have been reached when a reconsideration of the terms of this order would be timely, but I must take it as I find it with such assistance as I can derive from the authorities, some of which are related to circumstances bearing little relationship to contemporary conditions.

If there had been no sale I did not understand counsel for defendants to suggest that the plaintiff could not have sought relief by way of a declaration. His case was that once the sale had taken place, wherever the proceeds might then be lodged, even, as I understand it, if they were still in this country, sub-para (b), at least, could be of no avail to the plaintiff.

The meaning of the word 'affect' in the context of RSC Ord 11 has been considered in a number of cases. In *Agnew v Usher* (1884) 14 QBD 78 it was held that an action to recover rent was not an action to enforce a contract 'affecting' land. Three years later a tenant's action for compensation for tenant-right, according to the custom of the country, was held to be an action to enforce a contract affecting land: see *Kaye v Sutherland* (1888) 20 QBD 147. In that case it was argued by the defendant, seeking to set aside an order for service out of the jurisdiction, that the obligation was no more than a personal obligation binding on the landlord, and in no sense an obligation affecting the land. On the appeal Stephen J held that the contract was one affecting land because it was made subject to the custom of the country: it affected a certain definite portion of land. Not, said Stephen J, so strong a case as the custom of gavelkind or borough English, but strong enough. His view was that the land was affected in that it was held subject to the custom forming part of the contract under which land was usually dealt with in Yorkshire. Charles J agreed.

In *Tassell v Hallen* [1892] 1 QB 321 an action against the assignee of a lease for breach of a repairing covenant was held to be an action on a contract affecting land. Here it was argued that the action was no more than an action for damages for breach of contract. The court, following *Kaye v Sutherland*, held that although the claim in damages was based on a personal agreement to pay compensation it was brought on a covenant to repair, which was necessarily a covenant running with the land, and so the contract could be said to be a contract affecting land.

In my view it is only necessary to read the declaration of trust, and I have already stated its terms, to see that it is a deed, and, indeed, a contract affecting land, for it ascertains the obligations of the defendants touching the Hereford estate, obligations which continued after the death of Sir Charles and after the sale of the property. I find support for this view in a case to which I shall be referring in greater detail when I come, as I now do, to sub-para (e).

I am also of the opinion that counsel for the plaintiff is right when he says that the subject of the action falls within sub-para (e). Here the first question is: is this an action for the execution as to property situate within the jurisdiction of the trusts of a written instrument being trusts that ought to be executed according to English law? There is no doubt as to the status of the defendants. The second part of sub-para (e) raises the alternative question: is this an action for any relief or remedy which might be obtained in any such action?

It is convenient, at this stage, to refer to one fact I have not so far mentioned, which apparently only came to light at a relatively late stage. At one time it was thought that *a* the entirety of the proceeds of sale of the Hereford estate had been transmitted to Jersey. It was subsequently ascertained that there is still in this country a sum of between possibly £60,000 and £75,000, and counsel for the defendants concedes that the plaintiff is entitled to leave under sub-para (e), but confined to this £60,000 to £75,000, that being property situate within the jurisdiction. Counsel for the plaintiff was not tempted by this concession to abandon his stance that his claim falls under sub-para (e) in respect of *b* the totality of the monies.

Both counsel referred me to a case heard before the Court of Appeal in Ireland, A-G v *Drapers Co* (1894) 1 IR 185, which centred round a dispute arising out of a sale by the Drapers Company of property which had come to them from the Irish Society. The Drapers Company, at the relevant date, still held some of the property in Ireland, but the proceeds of sale of the bulk which they had originally held had been transmitted to *c* England. What was sought was first of all a declaration that the remaining lands were held by the Drapers Company as trustees, secondly a declaration that the sale of the lands which had been sold was a breach of trust, and thirdly an inquiry. This is a case which is of considerable relevance to the decision I have already given under sub-para (b). It is also of considerable relevance to sub-para (e), which in its then existing form in Ireland was sub-para (d). I shall follow counsel, when referring to the case, in substituting sub-para *d* (e) for sub-para (d).

Palles CB found that the case fell within sub-para (b) but expressed no opinion as to the application of sub-para (e). It is convenient to read from his judgment where he said (at 196–197):

'The argument for the defendants is twofold:—1, that upon the true construction *e* of clause (b), a suit, to be within it, must be one in which the "contract, obligation, or liability", which is its subject-matter, is sought to be enforced *so far only* as relates to the land or hereditaments within the jurisdiction; 2, that a trust of land is not an "obligation or liability" within the order. As to the first argument, the construction suggested imports by implication into clause (b) a limitation similar to that contained in clauses (a) and [(e)], in each of which it rests, not upon implication, but upon *f* express words. To be within (a), the *whole* subject-matter of the action must be land within the jurisdiction. Under [(e)] the object of the suit is expressly limited to the execution (as to property situate within the jurisdiction) of the trusts of the instrument. Such a limitation is not expressed in, nor can it be implied from, the words of clause (b). To be within the clause, the only condition is that the "obligation or liability" shall affect land or hereditaments within the jurisdiction, but it will not *g* the less affect them because it also affects other property. But further, suits to construe, set aside, or rectify deeds relating to lands within the jurisdiction are also within the clause. The argument relied on would therefore involve this, that in such a suit a deed which included property other than land could not be set aside or rectified as a whole, and that the construction adopted by the Court would be binding only as regards the realty in Ireland. There can be no implication which *h* would involve such consequences.'

FitzGibbon LJ said at the beginning of his judgment (at 203):

'While concurring with all that the Chief Baron has said, I should regard this case as falling within both subsections (b) and [(e)]; and I think that a decision in favour *j* of the appellants would result in splitting up suits, and making two actions necessary, where under the former practice one would have been enough. It is to be borne in mind that, in dealing with this question here, we are not asked to say whether the Court below has rightly exercised its discretion, but only whether the jurisdiction exists to entertain the action in Ireland.'

He continued (see at 204–205) to deal with the liabilities, but I can go to the conclusion
a of his judgment where he came back to the broad ground and said (at 207):

> 'This is an action for the execution of a trust, and we are bound to assume at
> present that the alleged trust is to be found in a written instrument; part of the trust
> property still forthcoming is land within the jurisdiction, and all of it would still be
> so, but for acts of the defendants alleged to be unlawful. I guard myself against
b > saying that a trustee of property situate within the jurisdiction can escape being
> sued here because he has conveyed the property away, but so long as part of it
> remains here, though these rules were intended to limit the exercise of jurisdiction
> in some respects, I hold that it was never intended that a suit for the execution of
> one trust should be split into two; and where the trust is to be executed with respect
> to some property within the jurisdiction, the liability of the trustee, upon his single
> obligation, is all within the same jurisdiction, and the same Court can give plenary
c > relief, and is not to be limited by the mode in which the trustee has disposed of part
> of the trust property.'

Barry LJ was of the view that the case fell within sub-para (*b*). As to sub-para (*e*) he said: 'I
d do not say that it does not fall within sub-section [(*e*)]. It might be within both.'
Here was a case in which it was considered that justice could only be done if the
remaining land and the money proceeds were dealt with in one action. Equally in the
present case, in my view, justice can only be done if you deal with this £60,000 to
£75,000 which is within the jurisdiction and the interest of the plaintiff in the £20m,
which I believe now has grown to something in the order of £30m, together. Nothing
could be less likely to do justice than a fragmentation of suits. The plaintiff is, in my
e view, entitled to seek relief in respect of the entirety of the proceeds of sale and the case
for service out of the jurisdiction was good under sub-para (*e*).
In coming to a conclusion on sub-para (*e*) I have proceeded on the basis that it stands
admitted that part of the property was within the jurisdiction at the date of the issue of
the writ, but a part of what was and must, in my view, be dealt with as a single fund. On
f the reasoning of Palles CB, and on the reasoning and finding of FitzGibbon LJ, as well, in
my own view, on the plain meaning to be attached to sub-para (*e*), which at the time of
the Irish decision would appear not to have had the second limb, the plaintiff succeeds
under this head.
Let me assume, however, that the whole of the 'property' must, to meet the
requirement of sub-para (*e*), have been within the jurisdiction at the date of the writ.
What, then, is the relevant property? This, in my view, is not to be confined to cash, the
g proceeds of sale, but must include the right to an account and the right to payment of
monies received, which existed at the date of the death of Sir Charles and continued in
existence thereafter.
In *IRC v Stype Investments (Jersey) Ltd* [1982] 3 All ER 419 at 428, [1982] Ch 456 at 473
the Court of Appeal said:

h
> 'The executors named in the will of Sir Charles could have obtained the same
> relief even if they had not proved the will of Sir Charles in England. Any creditor
> of the estate of Sir Charles in England and any beneficiary terested in the estate of
> Sir Charles could have obtained the same relief. The only difference would have
> been that the order of the court would have required the balance of the purchase
> price paid into court by the Prudential, after payment out of the costs and charges
j > of Stype Investments, to remain in court to the account of the personal representatives
> of Sir Charles when constituted in England. An order by any interested party
> ensuring that £20m remained in England would have been made because the
> interests of Sir Charles in the purchase price was property situate in England at the
> date of his death.'

I can go over to the passage which includes part of a passage on which counsel for the defendants laid considerable emphasis, where the court said ([1982] 3 All ER 419 at 429, [1982] Ch 456 at 474):

'After the death of Sir Charles, Stype Investments was entitled and bound to complete the contract with the Prudential and to receive the purchase price of £20m. But the right in equity to the purchase price was property situate in England at the death of Sir Charles and the £20m therefore belonged to the personal representatives of Sir Charles when constituted in England and to nobody else for the purpose of carrying out and completing administration of the English estate. By procuring payment of the £20m in Jersey, Stype Investments transferred the right to the £20m from the personal representatives constituted in England to the personal representatives constituted in Jersey. If this were not the case, Stype Investments would have no difficulty now in transferring the £20m from Jersey to England where it belongs. The act of transferring title from English personal representatives to Jersey personal representatives constituted an inter-meddling with the English estate and constituted Stype Investments executor de son tort. In New York Breweries Co v A-G [1899] AC 62 an English company transferred shares in the company from the name of a deceased domiciled American into the names of his executors who had proved his will in New York, but, to the knowledge of the company, had not obtained, and did not intend to obtain, probate in England. The company also paid dividends and interest to the executors. It was held that the company had "taken possession of and administered" part of the testator's estate, that the company was executor de son tort and that the company was personally liable to deliver an account and pay such duty as would have been payable if probate had been obtained in England.'

These passages, taken with the passage I have already read (see [1982] 3 All ER 419 at 430–431, [1982] Ch 456 at 476–477), draw the distinction which I have sought to draw between the property in the form of cash and the proprietorial interest of the plaintiff in the right to collect the debt due to the estate of the late Sir Charles.

I will add one brief word about the relevant date. To come within sub-para (e), or, indeed, sub-para (b), must the land or property in question have been situate within the jurisdiction at the date of the application for leave? On the finding I have reached the question is academic. I would just add this. Counsel for the defendants relied on Winter v Winter [1894] 1 Ch 421 in support of the proposition that the relevant date for this purpose is the date of the application for leave to serve out of the jurisdiction. Winter v Winter was a case where the plaintiff was seeking the execution of a trust. There was no property the subject of the trust within the jurisdiction. Stirling J in his judgment said (at 423):

'The rule does not in terms define the period at which the property is to be situate within the jurisdiction; but, seeing that the rule relates to service, and that the language with which I am dealing imposes a condition on the fulfilment of which the propriety of the service depends, I think the period to be regarded must be when leave to effect service is given, though if property were found within the jurisdiction when service was actually effected, or, at the latest, when such an application as the present is made, the Court may possibly take that circumstance into consideration. For the present purpose it is not necessary to inquire further: there was not at the time when leave to serve out of the jurisdiction was obtained, nor has there been since, any property situate within the jurisdiction subject to the trusts of the settlement mentioned in the writ and statement of claim. The motion, therefore, succeeds. It may be right to add, that although for the purpose of obtaining leave to serve out of the jurisdiction the existence of some property within the jurisdiction must be shewn, I do not think that it follows that other property which subsequently comes within the jurisdiction cannot be dealt with in the course of the same action a   if once properly commenced, or that it would be necessary to issue a fresh writ for the purpose of executing the trusts as to such property.'

I confess that, but for this judgment, which must be binding on me, I would have taken the date on which the cause of action accrued as the relevant date rather than the date of application for leave to serve.

That brings me to sub-para (f), for although sub-para (g) was relied on, both counsel b were agreed that sub-paras (f) and (g) stand or fall together. Here the question is a simple one: is this an action to enforce or recover damages in respect of a breach of a contract made within the jurisdiction? By the deed forming the declaration of trust the defendants, the plaintiff says, undertook, under the second covenant, to do certain things. They must either fulfil their obligation, an obligation in contract as much as it is in trust, or pay damages. I am not prepared to accept the submission of counsel for the defendants that the action is a trust action and nothing more. There are trustee obligations, there are c   contractual obligations. These are not mutually exclusive.

Creswell v Parker (1879) 11 Ch D 601, which I understood counsel for the defendants to be relying on, appears to me to have turned on discretion. *Hughes v Oxenham* [1913] 1 Ch 254, which at least brings us into this century, was a case where it was held that the action (which was an action to enforce security and not an action on any contract to pay a d   mortgage debt) was not an action founded on breach of contract. There Cozens-Hardy MR said (at 257):

'The words "founded on any breach or alleged breach of the contract" [and I pause to observe that the words 'founded on' no longer appear; they appear to have been somewhat emasculated by the substitution of the words 'otherwise affect'] are words which are not found anywhere else in the Rules; but I think they must mean this:
e   an action in which you cannot get any relief unless you proceed upon and are dependent upon a contract. In the present case the relief granted would be identical if there had been no covenant by anybody to pay, for mortgages without any covenant to pay are quite well known, not so frequent as others, but perfectly lawful; and there are many instances of them in the books. But the form of relief is exactly the same, whether there is or is not a covenant to pay.'

f   This passage does not, in my view, decide, as counsel for the defendants suggested it did, that you can only rely on sub-para (f) if you have no other string to your bow. It decides only that to succeed on sub-para (f) you must be able to succeed in contract. Cozens-Hardy MR did not insert between the words 'are' and 'dependent' the word 'exclusively', which is what counsel for the defendants notionally asks me to do.

g   There remain certain other matters, though perhaps these were not put forward by counsel for the defendants with quite the same enthusiasm. It has been held that if leave to serve is to be given the plaintiff must have a good arguable case, meaning thereby, apparently, something better than a prima facie case. Counsel for the defendants submitted that in the light of the decision of the Court of Appeal in *IRC v Stype Investments (Jersey) Ltd* there is no case. He relied on a passage which I have already read h   (see [1982] 3 All ER 419 at 429, [1982] Ch 456 at 474), but this takes no account of the concluding passages in the judgment of the Court of Appeal which I have also read. The moneys may have left England, but that is not the whole of the story.

Under the Mareva injunction granted in this action the assets of the defendants in this country are frozen. They are not inconsiderable; as I have said, I think they are something of the order of £30m. Counsel for the defendants points out that they are already frozen i   at the suit of the Commissioners of Inland Revenue. I must take account, I think, of the fact that there are many claims on the estate of Sir Charles. His son is contesting the validity of the settlement created by Sir Charles in February 1978 to which I have earlier referred. If Mr Alan Clore succeeds in his contest the ensuing intestacy may no doubt be to his advantage. This is a suit brought in Jersey. The Official Solicitor seeks to obtain a grant of representation to the deceased's estate in Jersey. Counsel for the defendants

suggested this must involve a duplication of proceedings, which is to be avoided. Counsel
for the defendants urges that Jersey is the forum conveniens; the balance of convenience, *a*
he suggests, tips in favour of the Royal Court of Jersey.

The Official Solicitor is understandably anxious to protect such assets as may be within
the jurisdiction of the Jersey court, for the assets which are available in this country may
not, at the end of the day, be sufficient to meet the obligations. Whether he will get a
grant in Jersey must be doubtful. His application is opposed by Mr Alan Clore and is
opposed by the defendants. In Jersey the Attorney General is entering the lists. Nothing *b*
is less likely than that the Royal Court of Jersey will feel itself moved to any considerable
extent to do anything in aid of a Revenue obligation in this country.

It seems plain that the United Kingdom assets, as I have said, may be insufficient to
meet the United Kingdom creditors. If Sir Charles was in fact domiciled in England at
the date of his death it seems highly probable that they certainly will not be.

In my view the Official Solicitor ought to be allowed to proceed to get in the assets of *c*
Sir Charles's English estate. As I have already said, the proceedings would appear to me
to be relatively straightforward and simple and should not take long. It cannot be
oppressive on the defendants. The proceedings in Jersey are plainly going to be complex
in the extreme and of indefinite duration. In my view this court is the forum conveniens
and the balance falls in favour of this court.

In the second action no question arises under RSC Ord 11 and counsel for the *d*
defendants was content that the result on arguable case, forum conveniens and general
balance should follow the result in the first action.

Both the defendants' motions fail and, counsel for the defendants having indicated
that in this event he would not be opposing the plaintiff's motions for a continuance of
the relevant Mareva injunction, the plaintiff's motions in both actions succeed.

e

Order accordingly.

Solicitors: *Freshfields* (for the plaintiff); *Cameron Markby* (for the defendants).

Evelyn M C Budd   Barrister.

a

Broxtowe Borough Council v Birch and others

COURT OF APPEAL, CIVIL DIVISION

STEPHENSON, OLIVER AND SLADE LJJ

15, 16, 17 NOVEMBER, 6 DECEMBER 1982

b

Rates – Exemption – Place of public religious worship – Public – Proper test of public religious worship – Private premises used by Christian sect for meetings for religious worship – Sect not advertising their activities – No notice board outside premises to advertise meetings – Sect prepared to admit properly disposed members of public who presented themselves for worship – Whether proper test that public at large invited by some outward indication to worship – General **c** *Rate Act 1967, s 39(2).*

A Christian sect (the brethren) used private premises, consisting of two halls, as meeting places for religious worship. The owners and occupiers of the halls were trustees on the brethren's behalf. The halls were registered as meeting places for religious worship under the Places of Worship Registration Act 1855, and were licensed for the solemnisation of
d marriages. The brethren were not a proselytising sect and did not believe in advertising their activities. The external appearance of each hall gave no indication that it was used for religious worship and there were no notice-boards outside the halls to advertise meetings held in the halls. Some 250 to 300 brethren regularly attended meetings held in one hall and some 50 brethren attended meetings held in the other hall. Each Saturday the brethren held open-air meetings in the streets at which they preached about the sect
e to arouse interest in it, but they did not use banners to advertise their presence in the streets and did not distribute leaflets advertising meetings in the halls or invite members of the public who showed interest in the sect to their meetings. There was evidence that the brethren would admit to meetings in the halls any properly disposed member of the public who presented himself there, but in recent years only two members of the public had joined meetings in the halls. The rating authority proposed that the halls should be
f entered in the rating list with specified rateable values on the ground that they were not 'places of public religious worship' and so exempt from rating under s 39(2)[a] of the General Rate Act 1967. The trustees and the valuation officer objected to the rating authority's proposals. Those objections were upheld by the local valuation court. On appeal by the rating authority the Lands Tribunal held that the mere fact that properly disposed members of the public would be admitted to worship in the halls was not
g sufficient to constitute them places of public religious worship within s 39, and that the proper test was whether members of the public were invited to worship there. The tribunal allowed the rating authority's appeal. The trustees appealed to the Court of Appeal, contending that the proper test was whether those who controlled the halls objected to properly disposed members of the public attending the halls to worship there.

h **Held** – Private premises used for religious worship by a community could only be a place of 'public religious worship' within s 39(2) of the 1967 Act if either the public at large were invited to worship there by some outward and visible indication that the premises were used for religious worship and members of the public were not regarded as trespassers if they came to worship there, or there was evidence that the public at large in fact attended the premises to worship. Accordingly, it was not sufficient that the
j subjective attitude of the community worshipping there was that they would admit any properly disposed member of the public who presented himself to worship there. An outward and visible indication that the public were invited to worship there might consist of the style of architecture of the premises indicating that the premises were used for religious worship, or a notice-board outside the premises advertising services held there, or the advertising of the services in leaflets distributed to the public or in

---

a   Section 39(2), so far as material, is set out at p 643 j, post

newspapers, or public appeals by the worshipping community to attend the services. Since there was no evidence that the brethren invited the public at large to worship in *a* the halls and since in fact the brethren's method of conducting their affairs tended to exclude the public and render worship in the halls private worship by a particular sect, the halls were not places of public religious worship within s 39(2). The halls were therefore rateable. The trustee's appeal would accordingly be dismissed (see p 649 *j* to p 650 *a*, p 651 *c* to *j*, p 652 *c* to *h*, p 653 *b*, p 654 *h* to p 655 *d* and *j* to p 656 *b* and p 657 *c* to *j*, post).

Dicta of Lord Morris and of Lord Pearce in *Church of Jesus Christ of Latter-Day Saints v* *b* *Henning (Valuation Officer)* [1963] 2 All ER at 738, 739 and of Lowe J in *Association of the Franciscan Order of Friars Minor v City of Kew* [1944] VLR at 202 considered.

Notes

For exemption from rates of places of public religious worship, see 39 Halsbury's Laws (4th edn) para 60, and for cases on the subject, see 38 Digest (Reissue) 358, 2428–2431. *c*

For the Places of Worship Registration Act 1855, see Halsbury's Statutes (3rd edn) 1504.

For the General Rate Act 1967, s 39, see 27 ibid 130.

Cases referred to in judgments

Association of the Franciscan Order of Friars Minor v City of Kew [1944] VLR 199. *d*
Church of Jesus Christ of Latter-Day Saints v Henning (Valuation Officer) [1963] 2 All ER 733, [1964] AC 420, [1963] 3 WLR 88, HL; *affg* [1962] 3 All ER 364, [1962] 1 WLR 1091, CA, 38 Digest (Reissue) 358, 2431.
Stradling v Higgins [1932] 1 Ch 143, [1931] All ER Rep 772, 19 Digest (Reissue) 381, 2986.

Case stated *e*

On 28 March 1979 Broxtowe Borough Council (the rating authority) made two proposals for the alteration of the valuation list by entering on the list, at specified values, two meeting halls situated at Cyprus Avenue and 60 Hillside Road, Beeston, owned and occupied by the Trustees of the Arnesby Trust (the trustees) on behalf of members of a company of Christians known as the Exclusive Brethren, on the ground that the halls were not exempt from rating under s 39(1) of the General Rate Act 1967 because they *f* did not constitute places of public religious worship within s 39(2)(a) of the 1967 Act. The local valuation officer and the trustees objected to the proposals. On 29 February 1980 the local valuation court upheld their objections and held that the two halls were places of public religious worship and were therefore exempt from rating under s 39. The rating authority appealed to the Lands Tribunal (J H Emlyn Jones Esq), who allowed the appeals on the ground that the two halls were not places of public religious worship *g* within s 39. The trustees appealed from that decision by way of a case stated for the Court of Appeal, on the ground that the decision was erroneous in law, contending that, as the meeting halls were open to any properly disposed member of the public who wished to be present, they were places of public religious worship to which s 39 of the 1967 Act applied. The valuation officer supported the rating authority in asking the court to uphold the Lands Tribunal's decision. The facts are set out in the judgment of *h* Stephenson LJ.

F M Ferris QC and *Guy Seward QC* for the trustees.
Alan Fletcher for the valuation officer.
David Micklethwait for the rating authority.

Cur adv vult *j*

6 December. The following judgments were delivered.

STEPHENSON LJ. This is an appeal by the trustees of the Arnesby Trust acting on behalf of members of a company of Christians known as the Exclusive Brethren by case

a
stated from a decision of the Lands Tribunal (J H Emlyn Jones Esq FRICS) dated 18 June
1981, by which he reversed two decisions of a local valuation court for Nottinghamshire
and directed entries in the valuation list of two hereditaments occupied by the trustees.

The two hereditaments were meeting halls in Beeston. They are shown in the valuation
list for Broxtowe Borough as places of public religious worship exempt under s 39 of the
General Rate Act 1967. The rating authority proposed on 28 March 1979 that one
meeting hall, in Cyprus Avenue, should be entered on the list at a gross value of £200
b
and a rateable value of £140 and that the other, in Hillside Road, should be entered at a
gross value of £1,474 and a rateable value of £1,200. Both the trustees and the valuation
officer objected to those proposals. On 29 February 1980 the valuation court upheld their
objections, held that the two halls were exempt and dismissed the appeals of the rating
authority. The Lands Tribunal upheld the appeals of the rating authority from that
decision, held that the two halls were not exempt and so directed the entries already
c
mentioned. The trustees are aggrieved by that decision and counsel on their behalf asks
this court to hold that it was erroneous in law and should be replaced by the decision of
the valuation court. Counsel for the respondent valuation officer supports counsel for the
rating authority in asking us to uphold the tribunal's decision.

The questions on which our decision is desired by the case stated by the member of
the Lands Tribunal on 9 March 1982 are:
d

'(1) whether upon the findings of fact I came to a correct decision in law in
deciding that the two meeting halls in question are not places of public religious
worship and accordingly are not hereditaments to which section 39 of the General
Rate Act 1967 applies;
e
(2) whether in so deciding I misdirected myself in law by having regard not only
to the question whether the said meeting halls were open to any properly disposed
member of the public who wished to be present but also to a consideration of the
extent to which members of the public were invited to attend or were aware of the
fact that religious worship was observed on the premises;
(3) whether there was evidence upon which I was entitled to find:—(a) that
members of the public were not invited to attend meetings at the meeting halls; (b)
f
that the Brethren worship privately behind closed doors; (c) that the Brethren by
the removal of the notice board at Hillside Road have taken positive action to keep
their meetings secret; (d) that the passages from "The Recovery and Maintenance of
the Truth" at pages 82 and 316 which are set out in my decision at page 8 represent
a fair summary which illustrates in a general way the doctrine accepted by the
Brethren.'
g

The long delay in signing the case was the result of efforts, not altogether successful, to
persuade the member of the Lands Tribunal to state further facts regarded as favourable
to the trustees, a matter to which I shall have to refer later.

There is no doubt that these two halls are used as places of meeting for religious
worship; they have been certified and registered as such under s 2 of the Places of
h
Worship Registration Act 1855. But that is not enough to exempt them from rating.
Section 39 of the General Rate Act 1967, re-enacting s 7 of the Rating and Valuation
(Miscellaneous Provisions) Act 1955, provided:

'(1) Subject to the provisions of this section, and without prejudice to any
j
exemption from, or privilege in respect of, rates under any enactment other than
this section, no hereditament to which this section applies shall, in the case of any
rating area, be liable to be rated for any rate period.
(2) This section applies to the following hereditaments, that is to say—(a) places
of public religious worship which belong to the Church of England or to the Church
in Wales (within the meaning of the Welsh Church Act 1914), or which are for the
time being certified as required by law as places of religious worship . . .'

To be exempt therefore, the halls must be 'places of *public* religious worship'. The
valuation court concluded that they were, the Lands Tribunal 'not without reluctance'   *a*
that they were not. The member found the problem presented by this case to be one of
great difficulty, and the able argument of counsel for the trustees that his conclusion was
wrong, and wrong in law mainly because he applied the wrong test, has been most
impressive. But I have come to the conclusion that his decision was right and will give
my reasons.

The decision is important not only to the brethren in Beeston and this rating authority.   *b*
For we are told that there may be 300 other halls where the brethren of the same
persuasion as those the trustees represent meet for worship, which may lose the statutory
exemption which they now enjoy. We are told also that, if the decision stands, the
Registrar-General may have to reconsider the registration of many of these halls as
buildings for the solemnisation of marriages under s 41 of the Marriage Act 1949, as
amended.   *c*

The material facts are, in my opinion, these. The brethren are a branch of a fellowship
of Christians, often known as Plymouth Brethren because, though they were founded in
Dublin in 1829, J N Darby established their first main centre in England at Plymouth in
1830. About 1849 they divided into 'open brethren' and 'exclusive brethren'. About
1960 and again in 1970 the exclusive brethren were further divided into those who
followed and those who did not follow the leadership of James Taylor junior, principally   *d*
in his teaching about separation from evil. It is the exclusive brethren who still follow
James Taylor junior, who are the brethren represented by the trustees of the Arnesby
Trust in this case. This historical background the member took from a judgment of Fox J
in other proceedings by the exclusive brethren, and though counsel for the trustees has
questioned the member's statement that it was all 'non-contentious', I do not think my
selection from it is in serious dispute.   *e*

The two halls were acquired by the trustees under a trust deed of 9 July 1965. Clauses
3(b) and 4 provide:

'(3) ... (b) The Trustees desire (though without thereby creating any trust) that
the primary charitable purpose to which the Trust property shall be devoted shall
be to employ the same for providing a meeting place or meeting places in England
for the preaching of the Word of God and such other religious purposes for   *f*
Christians as the Trustees shall in their absolute discretion permit.

(4) The Trustees may use the Trust property or any part thereof or permit the
same to be used for the purposes of religious meetings of Christians or for any other
charitable purpose or purposes which the Trustees may from time to time in their
absolute discretion select but for no other purposes ...'

  g

The Hillside Road building is a single-storey brick-built building in a residential area
entered through double gates with car parking space for 80 cars. It was designed by the
trustees and first used in 1967. The main meeting hall seats 450 to 500 people. The
Cyprus Avenue building is more like a scout hut or classroom; a prefabricated hut first
occupied in 1971 and accommodating 70 to 80 people. There is nothing about either
building to indicate that it is a place of worship, either in its architectural design or by   *h*
way of a notice-board. There had been a notice-board outside the Hillside Road building
stating that the Word of God would be preached at certain times on Sunday; but that was
removed years ago, according to the member of the Lands Tribunal to comply with the
teaching of James Taylor junior, and no notice-board was ever put up outside the Cyprus
Avenue hut.

The use made of these two halls is explained in the passage which I now quote from   *j*
the tribunal's decision:

'The brethren have no constitution and there is no formal ministry. They give
the appearance of being modelled on the early Christian Church. The unit is the
household and several households are related to one meeting room. Meeting rooms
are collected into a "city". The two Beeston meetings form part of the Nottingham

city which over the past few years has comprised three or four meeting rooms in Nottingham and one in Derby. The adjoining city is the Leicester city, comprising three meetings in Leicester and one in Loughborough. There is a considerable interchange between the two cities. In a typical period of 14 days the meeting halls are used for meetings of religious worship the times and general nature of which and the approximate number of persons attending are set out as follows:—

Day and Time		Hillside Road Type of Meeting	Number Attending	Cyprus Avenue Type of Meeting	Number Attending
Sunday	6 am	Breaking of bread	36	Breaking of bread	46
	9 am	Scripture reading	300		
	11.30 am	Preaching	300		
	3 pm			Preaching	50–60
Monday	7 pm	Prayer meeting	36	Prayer meeting	46
Tuesday	7.45 pm	Ministry meeting	160		
Thursday	7.45 pm	Scripture reading	250		
Friday	7.45 pm			Scripture reading	50–60
Saturday	6 am	Care meeting (monthly)	160–170		
	9 am	Scripture reading (except when care meeting is held)	300		
Sunday	6 am	Breaking of bread	36	Breaking of bread	46
	5 pm	Preaching	300		
Monday	7 pm	Prayer meeting	36	Prayer meeting	46
Tuesday	7.45 pm	Ministry meeting	160		
Thursday	7.45 pm	Scripture reading	250		
Friday	7.45 pm			Scripture reading	50–60

The meetings at Hillside Road where the numbers attending are 250 or 300 represent the full attendance of the brethren in the two cities—not all brethren being able to attend the scripture reading on the week day evening. On alternate Sundays, the 9.30 am scripture reading and the 11.30 am preaching meetings are held in the Leicester city. The meetings attended by 160–170 people would seem to represent the Nottingham city and the meetings attended by 36 of the brethren represent those local to the Hillside Road meeting. Those attending the Cyprus Avenue meetings are local to that assembly and they also attend at Hillside Road for the larger meetings. It is accepted on all sides that attendance at the Sunday morning breaking of bread and at the monthly care meeting (where matters of administration and spiritual concern are raised and discussed) is restricted to those who are "in fellowship" and those who are not recognised in this way would be barred from attending. The appellant rating authority, however, do not suggest that that exclusion in itself is sufficient to establish that the hereditaments do not qualify as places of public worship and concede that if the use of the meeting halls on other *a* occasions is properly to be described as public religious worship then the hereditaments qualify for exemption.'

It is apparent from this table that there is a noteworthy stability in the numbers attending these meetings, indicating that they consisted mainly, if not entirely, of the households of the brethren. There was, however, some evidence of attendance by members of the public from outside those households: (1) evidence, which the member *b* accepted from four members of the brethren, from which he 'formed the opinion that they were a sincere and devout group of men who arranged their lives strictly by reference to the scriptures as the only source of truth'; and (2) evidence from two officers of the rating authority. Most important was the evidence of Mr Birch, one of the trustees: I give the member's summary of it in his decision in full:

'First of all Mr Birch, who is one of the trustees, referred to the open-air street meetings which the brethren hold on Saturday mornings in Nottingham and Beeston. He said that the purpose of the brethren was to bring people to Christ: if they showed interest they would normally be invited to the home of one of the brethren or given a home telephone number. The brethren do not regard themselves as a recruiting agency and their object was not to get as many members as possible *d* to join them. "We do not advertise but if it is God's will that someone is to come he will come. We do not tell an enquirer where our meetings are or when unless he asks." Any properly disposed person was welcome to attend any of the meetings except the breaking of bread and the care meeting, but they would not want people who came to mock or cause trouble. During the past 12 months three people had approached the speakers at the open-air meetings, two of whom had asked for *e* information about the meetings of the brethren and one of them, after a fortnight, made contact with one of the brethren and subsequently came to a preaching meeting. On another occasion "a man turned up at a meeting and said he had been to many other churches in Beeston and that he would give us a try. I turned him away. I regret it now and I would not do it again but the occasion has not arisen." The notice-board was taken down following the teaching of James Taylor Junior: *f* the only acceptable form of advertising was by personal example. Mr Birch stated that over a period of years about thirty newcomers had joined the brethren in the Nottingham city, that is, the three or four meeting halls in Nottingham and the one in Derby.'

Mr McCroft confirmed that the brethren would be glad if anyone wished to attend any of their meetings other than the breaking of the bread or the care meeting. A brother *g* who persisted in any action incompatible with piety would be 'withdrawn' from the fellowship and barred from attending meetings of the brethren anywhere in the world. 'He would not encourage anyone to come into the fellowship—though hope was that people would be led by God's will and that is why the notice-boards were removed.' He it was who, according to Mr Taylor of the rating authority, spoke to him and his colleague when they attended a meeting at Hillside Road one evening in October 1979, and gave *h* them a hymn book and a bible. Mr Taylor did not feel he was made welcome and no one else approached them, though Mr McCroft said he called out 'Good night' as they got to the gates on leaving.

Mr Oates had joined the brethren by attending a meeting in about 1955, and said that to his knowledge the only newcomer who had come to Cyprus Avenue was the one man to whom he had given his telephone number after an open-air street meeting, apparently *j* the same man as Mr Birch referred to.

Mr Emerson had attended meetings over the years and was eventually admitted to fellowship, and said that if anyone today wished to attend meetings as he had in the 1950's, he would be glad to see them.

Mr Edge had gone with another colleague from the rating authority to a Hillside Road
meeting in February or March 1979 after obtaining a list of meetings from Mr Birch.
His account of it was:

> 'They met no one in the foyer so went into the meeting room and sat down at the
> back. "A gentleman came up and asked us if we believed in the word of the Lord.
> We said we did and asked if we could stay. He said he would have to consult one of
> the other brethren. We followed him to the foyer where he spoke to another
> gentleman who had just arrived who seemed to be an elder. He said we would be
> allowed to stay but we then left."'

The only other evidence was about meetings generally and came from the words of
James Taylor junior:

> '. . . in the course of a meeting held in New Zealand in 1962. He had this to say:
> "Our gospel meetings are not private: we do not shut people out, but we certainly
> would not want people coming in to give us trouble. Our meetings are open in that
> sense for anybody to hear the gospel"; and in 1964 in London in a reference to the
> injunction given to St Paul in Acts ix 6, "But rise up and enter into the city", he said:
> "Anybody following you would see where you went. If they wanted to be interested
> in where you went, they would see you go into some room. Would they not say,
> 'What is he going in there for?' and if they were interested enough they might come
> and knock on the door. 'What is inside here?' You would not deny that, if somebody
> wanted to find out what you were in there for, you can show that you are a man
> with a pitcher of water. You have gone into the city; you are going into the place of
> testimony, and there you are going to meet with Christ. That is what you want all
> men to do."'

Two additional findings of fact were made at the request of the parties:

> '(1) The doors of the meetings halls are not locked while meetings are in progress.
> (2) The Hillside Road meeting hall is a place licensed for the conduct of marriage
> ceremonies although no one who was not of the brethren would in fact be married
> there.'

The member concluded his decision in this way:

> 'It remains a fact, however, that the members of the brethren remain a closely
> knit esoteric circle or "family"; and in practice the only newcomers that are admitted
> are the children who grow up within the family. Counsel for the trustees invites
> me to answer the question, "Who is turned away?" The answer may well be that no
> one is turned away but one of the reasons at any rate why this is so is that no one is
> invited. Similarly, it is not enough in my judgment to say that properly disposed
> persons who come in reverence and behave themselves are welcomed. The reality
> of the situation is that there are no such properly disposed persons, because the
> brethren, by their application of the doctrine of separation from evil, worship
> privately behind closed doors, and by the removal of the notice board at Hillside
> Road have taken positive action to keep their meetings secret.'

Hence arise the three questions formulated for our decision which I have read. The
first two are plain enough; but how can the third be answered without having all the
evidence which was before the tribunal but is not before us?

The trustees have decided on the advice of their counsel not to apply for judicial review
to order the tribunal to include further facts in the case or to annex a transcript of the
evidence to it, and not to apply for the case to be remitted to the tribunal. We must
therefore take the case as it is and decide whether, on the evidence and the findings of
fact contained in it, the member came to a correct decision in law or misdirected himself
by applying what has been called the 'invitation' test.

Plainly religious worship may be, and indeed must be, either public or private, and it is often easy to say which. As the member put the matter, at one end of the spectrum is   *a* the religious worship practised in the parish churches of the Church of England and in the chapels of Roman Catholics and nonconformists, at the other the private devotions of individuals in the bedroom or in the domestic setting of family prayers. The churches and chapels are places of public religious worship, the rooms in houses where men and women worship alone or with their households are not, though all are buildings in private ownership. The meeting halls of these brethren lie somewhere between those   *b* two examples and near the borderline which divides the private from the public.

The trustees' principal contention is that they are on the public side of the line if the right test is applied, which has been called the 'properly disposed persons' test. It is derived from the speech of Lord Morris in the Mormon Temple case, *Church of Jesus Christ of Latter-Day Saints v Henning (Valuation Officer)* [1963] 2 All ER 733 at 738, [1964] AC 420 at 435, where he said: *c*

> 'I consider that there is a distinction between private or domestic or family worship on the one hand and public religious worship on the other. In my view the conception of public religious worship involves the coming together for corporate worship of a congregation or meeting or assembly of people, but I think that it further involves that the worship is in a place which is open to all properly disposed persons who wish to be present.'   *d*

Lord Pearce, with whose speech the whole House agreed in deciding that the Mormon Temple was not a place of public religious worship exempted by s 7(2) of the Rating and Valuation (Miscellaneous Provisions) Act 1955, said much the same thing when considering what admitting the public to religious worship involved and the effect of the Church of England's power to exclude notorious evil livers. He observed ([1963] 2 All   *e* ER 733 at 739, [1964] AC 420 at 437):

> 'For this purpose the admission of the public means, I think, the admission of those members of the public who are reasonably suitable, who come in reverence not mockery, and who are prepared to behave in reasonable conformity to the requirements of the religion which they are visiting e.g., by covering their heads   *f* where that is required or by removing their shoes on entering a mosque.'

The same approach is indicated in a passage quoted by Lord Pearce (see [1963] 2 All ER 733 at 741, [1964] AC 420 at 440) from the judgment of Lowe J in the Supreme Court of Victoria in *Association of the Franciscan Order of Friars Minor v City of Kew* [1944] VLR 199 at 202, stating his opinion that—

> 'worship to be public must not only be open without discrimination to the   *g* relevant public, but also be performed in public.'

And it is conceded that the last six words do not add, or should not be allowed to add, anything.

It is submitted accordingly that where members of the public are admitted to a place of worship and the only members of the public who are not admitted but excluded are   *h* those who are not properly disposed or well behaved, there is a place of public religious worship, exempt from rating. It does not cease to be such a place because in fact no well-disposed member of the public comes to worship there: it is enough that it is open to such members of the public. It was also suggested that the congregation of regular worshippers from the religious body owning the place of worship might itself constitute the necessary public element, and that suggestion could be supported by ss 41 and 42 of   *j* the Marriage Act 1949, to which I have already referred, in the provisions it contains for registering and cancelling the registration on behalf of a congregation of a building for the solemnisation of marriages on the application of at least 20 householders who state that it is used by them as their usual place of public religious worship. There is, however, more force, in my judgment, in the submission that no user or actual attendance by the general public is necessary, otherwise a remote village parish church, never visited by

strangers to add to its constant congregation of local residents, would not qualify for
exemption for rating.

a These halls, says counsel for the trustees, satisfy the 'properly disposed persons' test.

On the other side the rating authority's submission is that to be open to the public for
religious worship a place must invite the public to come and worship. A church by its
architectural features or its position in a churchyard usually tells the public that it is a
place of religious worship and, if it has a notice-board outside giving the times of services
b or advertises them in a newspaper, it makes them public and invites the attendance of all
those made aware of them.

This 'invitation' test comes from the judgment of Maugham J in the Salvation Army
Hall case, *Stradling v Higgins* [1932] 1 Ch 143 at 150–151, [1931] All ER Rep 772 at 775.
In deciding that two halls were used for the purposes of a place of public religious
worship under ss 1 and 5 of the Places of Worship (Enfranchisement) Act 1920, he said—

c   '... I am perfectly satisfied that the Salvation Army Hall is used for the purpose
        of holding, among other things, religious services which are open to all, and that it
        has never been the practice of the Salvation Army to possess or own places of worship
        which are not places of public worship in the sense that the public are not admitted.
        It is true, as will appear in one moment, that sometimes there are buildings used for
        the purposes of children, but to my mind a place is none the less a place of public
d   worship because the public who are invited to that place are a particular section of
        the public, such as either children or men or women. That seems to me to be clear
        as a matter of common sense. It has been rightly said that "public" is a word of very
        elastic meaning, and I cannot conceive that within the true meaning of the definition
        as contained in this Act worship is any the less public worship because on a particular
        occasion a section only of the public is invited to attend.'

e The judge there seems to treat a place of public worship as a place to which the public
are invited and public worship as worship which the public are invited to attend.

This approach was followed by Lowe J in another passage of his judgment in the
Victoria case where he said of the chapel of a missionary college of priests, lay brothers
and students ([1944] VLR 199 at 204):

f   'But the ceremonies were private. The outside public were not encouraged to
        attend services in the chapel and apart from the residents of the college, the only
        persons, with the rarest exception, to attend from the outside public were the lay
        members of a committee to further the missionary work of the college. In so far as
        the application of the exception requires a finding of fact I find that the chapel of
        the college was not used for public worship.'

g There was, submits counsel for the rating authority, no invitation to the public or
encouragement of them to attend the meetings of the brethren in these halls, and
therefore the 'invitation' test is not satisfied and the claim to exemption not made good.
When in *Henning's* case [1962] 3 All ER 364 at 368, [1962] 1 WLR 1091 at 1099 Donovan
LJ asked the question, 'Why should places of public worship be exempt at all from rates?'
h he said:

        'The only rational answer seems to be that they cater for, and are used by, and for
        the benefit of, a section of the public sufficiently large to be significant in this
        context [of fiscal legislation].'

The small section of Mormons to whom the temple was open was clearly not large
enough to be significant, nor, I think, is the small section of brethren to whom these
j halls are open. Worship would not be public because conducted in the presence of a
congregation of 20 persons or households. Whether a place is used for public or private
worship does not, in my judgment, depend simply on numbers, whether of those who
decide what the worship is to be or of those who come from outside the worshipping
community to join in that worship. Though there may be congregations of particular
religious bodies so large as to be significant sections of the public, Mr Birch and the other

witnesses were, in my judgment, right to claim publicity for their worship on the ground
that persons outside their fellowship were welcome to attend their meetings and counsel
for the trustees was right to treat the 'properly disposed persons' test as requiring the   *a*
attendance, or at least the possibility of attendance, of such newcomers from outside.

None of the authorities cited to us is directly helpful in deciding which is the right test
to apply. Maugham J was considering a statute which had nothing to do with rateability.
Lowe J had to consider the rateability of three pieces of land occupied by three different
orders of the Roman Catholic Church, a monastery with a church and retreat house   *b*
occupied by the Franciscan Order of Friars Minor, a convent with a chapel occupied by
nuns of an enclosed Carmelite Order, and the Pallottine Missionary College with a chapel.
Section 249 of the Local Government Act 1928 as amended required land to be used
exclusively for public worship if it were to qualify for exemption and he held that none
of the land occupied by the religious orders qualified, because there were large areas
beyond the buildings used for worship which were used for other purposes than worship,   *c*
whether public or private. He did, however, contradict the submission that a retreat
could be a form of public worship and it was with reference to the friars' retreat house,
and not as might be thought from Lord Pearce's allusion to it in the Mormon Temple
case with reference to the nuns' chapel, that he made the statement, which Lord Pearce
partly quoted and I have already quoted, that public worship must be open to the relevant
public and be performed in public. And in the other passage which I have quoted from   *d*
his judgment he did decide that the missionary college did not qualify for exemption on
the second ground that it was not used for public worship but for private ceremonies, a
reason which would appear to apply a fortiori to the convent chapel services. (Lord
Denning MR agreed with the way in which Lowe J regarded public worship: see [1962]
3 All ER 364 at 367, [1962] 1 WLR 1091 at 1098.) The House of Lords ([1963] 2 All ER
733, [1964] AC 420) decided that the Mormon Temple was not a place of public religious   *e*
worship because, unlike Mormon chapels, it was not open to the public at large but only
to a select class of 'Mormons of good standing' who qualified for one year for a
'recommend' from a local 'bishop' endorsed by a 'president'. Lord Pearce, however,
reached his conclusion after taking into account the long history of the exemption of
churches of the Established Church since the Poor Relief Act 1601, and the extension of
the exemption to similar places of worship belonging to other denominations by the   *f*
Poor Rate Exemption Act 1833. I read a passage from his opinion which contains
material on which both the brethren and the rating authority rely, as did the tribunal
([1963] 2 All ER 733 at 741, [1964] AC 420 at 440–441):

'By the Act of 1833 the legislature was intending to extend the privileges of
exemption enjoyed by the Anglican churches to similar places of worship belonging
to other denominations. Since the Church of England worshipped with open doors   *g*
and its worship was in that sense public, it is unlikely that the legislators intended
by the word "public" some more subjective meaning which would embrace in the
phrase "public religious worship" any congregational worship observed behind
doors closed to the public. I find it impossible, therefore, to hold that the words
"places of public religious worship" include places which, though from the
worshippers' point of view they were public as opposed to domestic, yet in the more   *h*
ordinary sense were not public since the public was excluded. This view accords
with that of LOWE, J., in the *Association of the Franciscan Order of Friars Minor v. City
of Kew* ([1944] VLR 199), where in considering a statutory exemption for "land used
exclusively for public worship" he held inter alia that the chapel of an Enclosed
Order of Carmelite Nuns was not exempted. He said (at 202): "In my opinion
worship to be public must . . . be open without discrimination to the relevant   *j*
public". By the word "relevant" he left open the question of how universal and
indiscriminating must be the admission of the public. The question is one of fact
and there might clearly be difficult questions whether some discrimination might
be insufficient to deprive the worship of its public character. Furthermore it is less
likely on general grounds that Parliament intended to give exemption to religious

services that exclude the public since exemptions from rating, though not necessarily
consistent, show a general pattern of intention to benefit those activities which are
for the good of the general public. All religious services that open their doors to the
public may, in an age of religious tolerance, claim to perform some spiritual service
to the general public.'

There is nothing, in my judgment, to help solve the problem raised by this appeal in
the exemption of public parks, highways and bridges or in the rating of public car parks,
public libraries, public houses and public conveniences. For the appeal is concerned not
with the question whether these halls are public places but whether they are places of
public worship. They are in fact private places and in that fact lies, in my judgment, the
key to the right answer and the correct test to apply.

A building on private property must somehow declare itself open to the public if
activities which are carried on inside it are to be public, and the nature of those activities
must be brought to the notice of the outside world if they are not to be private activities.
As it was variously put from the Bench: the worship must be made public; the doors of
the place of worship must be open not merely subjectively in the minds and hearts of the
worshipping community but objectively in some manifestation of their intention that it
should be open; there must be signs to indicate at least that the place is a place of religious
worship, perhaps also that acts of such worship are performed there at particular times,
and that the public would not be trespassers if they entered but have permission, express
or implied, to go there and to attend worship there.

Such signs may be given by the building itself. That the doors are really open to the
public in fact and not only in theory may be indicated by numbers of people entering
the building or of motor cars and cycles parking outside it. Many, if not most, churches
and chapels indicate their nature and the nature of what goes on inside them by their
style of architecture or religious symbols or the ringing of a bell, as well as by notices of
services on a notice-board, or in leaflets or newspapers, or by speakers preaching and
appealing to the public in the open air or by house to house calls. There may be places of
religious worship which without any of these attractions are in fact used for worship by
members of the public at large. If there are such, they would qualify by the fact that
their services were 'performed in public'. On the other hand there may be places of
religious worship advertised as such by some or all of the means I have enumerated,
where nevertheless no member of the general public ever attends the services or
meetings. Such a church or meeting hall also would qualify by being open to the public.
But I agree with counsel for the valuation officer that one or other mark must be present
to make a place of worship public, and here there is neither any outward and visible sign
that these halls are used for meetings for religious worship, nor any evidence of
attendance at them by members of the public, except rarely by one or two. The
'invitation' test is the right one and there is no evidence of invitation.

The picture presented by the evidence is very different from the picture of a place of
public religious worship, as the ordinary person would, I think, derive it from such
obvious places of public worship as churches and chapels. But the courts of a country
with an established church must be careful not to assume that all meeting places of other
faiths are readily identifiable or even that all places of Christian worship still bear the
recognised, and recognisable, style and features of earlier ecclesiastical buildings. Nor
must our courts deny to other religions an element of spiritual benefit to the general
public, to which Lord Pearce referred in a passage I have already quoted, or restrict
unfairly the extension which Parliament has granted of the privilege originally reserved
to Anglican church buildings. On the other hand, that extension must not go beyond
the limits defined by Parliament in the statutory exemption which is the subject of this
appeal. The question is whether in all the circumstances disclosed by the evidence before
the tribunal the exemption extends not necessarily to this sect but to these buildings of
theirs.

The evidence of the beliefs and practices of the brethren is, of course, relevant, but it is
the nature and use of these two halls which is of decisive importance. Other meeting

halls of other branches of the brethren may have notice-boards or attendance figures which might make them places of public religious worship. But in considering whether their worship in these halls is public the brethren must be judged, like all others who have to prove facts in our courts, not by what they believe or intend but by what they do. According to Mr James Taylor junior, their gospel meetings are not private but open for anybody, and the brethren want all men to come into the place of testimony. And in this connection counsel for the trustees called our attention to two passages in St Paul's Epistles in Mr Darby's translation (1 Cor 14: 23–25 and 1 Tim 2: 1–4) supporting the Christian belief that God desires that all men, including unbelievers, should come to the truth. But it is for the courts, not for Mr Taylor, to say whether the meetings held in these halls are private or public, and his ipse dixit cannot conclude the matter in favour of their publicity if on the evidence they are private, and made or kept private by his own teachings. For that on the evidence is the position. Men and women must come to these meetings by the example of the brethren or by the will of God, not by any form of advertising. Hence the notice-board was removed from outside the Hillside Road hall. Persons of different faiths, or of no faith, can understand and admire such a belief, but its effect is to deny publicity to the prayer meetings, ministry meetings, scripture readings and preachings which take place in these halls. The practice of not advertising or issuing invitations to the public may not be calculated to keep them out in the sense that it may not be designed or intended to do so, but it has that effect and that is what matters. I agree with the submission by counsel on behalf of the rating authority that it does not matter why the brethren act as they do but what matters is how they act; and their practice, explained by the beliefs on which it is based, has resulted in the meagre attendance of outsiders attested by the evidence.

The subsidiary submission of counsel for the trustees was that if his main submission failed and the member was right to apply the 'invitation' test, he was wrong to hold that it had not been satisified because there was evidence of invitation to these meetings.

In the end he relied on the evidence of open-air meetings held in the streets on Saturdays. There was no evidence that the brethren who spoke at them identified their sect by banners or distributed leaflets advertising their meetings in the halls: if a listener asked for information he would be given it and he might be invited to the home of a brother and thence to a meeting. Even if there were instances of such inquirers being informed of the time and place of meetings, and even if some sort of testing or vetting was not an object of inviting them to a member's household, these invitations to individuals, as it were man to man, are not in my opinion, the sort of invitation to the public at large which is required to satisfy the test and make these halls places of public worship.

I come, therefore, to the conclusion that the effect of what was done and not done by the brethren in respect of these halls and the meetings and worship in them was to exclude the public and to make and keep the meetings and worship private. The case is not so plain as the Mormon Temple case, where the excluding conduct was direct and positive. Here the policy was equally deliberate even if its results were not intended, but the facts of the case are nearer to the Victorian case and the religious worship of the religious orders which was there considered. I would dismiss the appeal simply on the ground that the religious worship in these two hereditaments was private.

I do not altogether agree with the way in which the case was put before the tribunal and the way in which the member expressed the tribunal's decision. The tribunal heard and accepted a submission that these meetings were secret behind closed doors, and that this secrecy and the removal of the notice-board advertising these meetings came from the desire of the brethren to be separated from evil.

I would accept that, exclusive though the brethren are, perhaps particularly the branch of them with which we are concerned, the notice-board was removed because they wished people to come to God and his worship in their meetings by other means. I would accept also that the language used, derived as it is from Lord Pearce's description of one extreme in the Mormon Temple case, goes too far in its suggestion of a secret society meeting behind locked doors with overtones of conspiracy, or fear of persecution, which a do not apply to places near the middle of the spectrum, are insulting to the trustees and the brethren for whom they act and are unjustified by the evidence of their beliefs and practice. Counsel for the valuation officer pointed out that it would be an offence under s 11 of the Places of Worship Act 1812 to meet behind locked doors, and the first additional finding of fact acquitted the trustees of that illegality.

I am indebted to the clear and careful decision of the member and I respectfully agree with his assessment of the reality of the situation, but not with his final statement of the b reason for it.

In my judgment the meetings in these halls were not secret, but they were not public. The hereditaments are accordingly rateable and the appeal should be dismissed.

OLIVER LJ (read by Slade LJ). The point raised by this appeal is a short one and turns entirely on the correct interpretation of the words 'places of public religious worship' in c s 39 of the General Rate Act 1967. In order to qualify for exemption under the provisions of the section the tenement in question must fulfil two conditions. It must, first, be registered as a place of worship under the Places of Worship Registration Act 1855 and, second, it must be used (although not, as the authorities show, necessarily exclusively used) as a place of public religious worship. There is no question that both the halls with which the appeal is concerned are registered under the 1855 Act. The only question is d whether the religious worship for which they are undoubtedly used is 'public' worship.

Now it is clearly not enough to satisfy the condition that a place is in fact used for the purpose of religious worship by a member of the public or two or more members of the public. Every citizen in the country is a member of the public but it would be a misuse of language to describe his devotions in the privacy of his own home or at the home of some like-minded friends or relations as 'public religious worship'. Counsel for the e trustees does not so contend and the difference which separates the parties is really simply a difference as to the degree of 'publicity' which is necessary before a place can be said to become a place of public worship.

Both sides agree that the test cannot simply be one of the numbers of people resorting to the place. For instance, a small rural parish church at which a small congregation of two or three people gather on, perhaps, alternate Sundays, will still be a place of public f worship even though on each occasion that congregation is composed of the same persons. Such a test is, in any event, precluded by the decision of the House of Lords in *Church of Jesus Christ of Latter-Day Saints v Henning (Valuation Officer)* [1963] 2 All ER 733, [1964] AC 420, which is conveniently referred to as the Mormon Temple case. There are numbers of persons capable of attending the temple were potentially substantial, but it failed to satisfy the condition because the qualifying conditions for admission showed g that it was not in fact open to 'the public'. It is equally deducible from that decision that the mere fact that those who attend do so publicly, in the sense of openly and without concealment, does not convert what is essentially a private occasion into a public one.

The test propounded by Lord Morris in that case is as follows ([1963] 2 All ER 733 at 738, [1964] AC 420 at 435):

h   '. . . the conception of public religious worship involves the coming together for corporate worship of a congregation or meeting or assembly of people, but I think that it further involves that the worship is in a place which is open to all properly disposed persons who wish to be present.'

A similar, though perhaps not quite identical, opinion is to be found in the speech of Lord Pearce, with which the majority of their Lordships agreed. He observed ([1963] 2 j All ER 733 at 739, [1964] AC 420 at 437):

    'For this purpose the admission of the public means, I think, the admission of those members of the public who are reasonably suitable, who come in reverence not mockery, and who are prepared to behave in reasonable conformity to the requirements of the religion which they are visiting . . .'

Thus far this seems to be an echo of Lord Morris's view, but it is qualified to some degree

later in Lord Pearce's speech where he cites ([1963] 2 All ER 733 at 741, [1964] AC 420
at 440), apparently with approval, the following sentence from the judgment of Lowe J　　*a*
in the Australian case *Association of the Franciscan Order of Friars Minor v City of Kew*
[1944] VLR 199 at 202:

> 'In my opinion worship to be public must . . . be open without discrimination to
> the relevant public . . .'

Lord Pearce continued:　　　　　　　　　　　　　　　　　　　　　　　　　　*b*

> 'By the word "relevant" he left open the question of how universal and
> indiscriminating must be the admission of the public. The question is one of fact,
> and there may clearly be difficult questions whether some discrimination may be
> insufficient to deprive the worship of its public character.'

The ratio of Lowe J's decision is not altogether easy to isolate, but this qualification or　*c*
refinement accords with the decision of Maugham J in *Stradling v Higgins* [1932] 1 Ch
143 at 151, [1931] All ER Rep 772 at 775, who observed:

> 'It has been rightly said that "public" is a word of very elastic meaning, and I
> cannot conceive that within the true meaning of the definition as contained in this
> Act worship is any the less public worship because on a particular occasion a section
> only of the public is invited to attend.'　　　　　　　　　　　　　　　　*d*

It should perhaps be added that the Act to which he referred was the Places of Worship
(Enfranchisement) Act 1920 and not a rating statute.

However, the refinement, if it is one, is really immaterial for present purposes, and the
contest has turned essentially on what is meant by Lord Morris's phrase 'open to all
properly disposed persons who wish to be present'.　　　　　　　　　　　　*e*

Counsel for the trustees, contends, and this is his primary submission, that this means
merely that those who have control of the place in question do not, subjectively, have
any objection to a properly disposed person attending, in the sense that if such a person
did present himself and seek admission, he would not be turned away. If this is the test,
then he submits that it is clearly satisfied in the instant case because the member of the
Lands Tribunal accepted both the trustees' evidence as to their subjective intentions and　*f*
the evidence of the two officers of the rating authority who had actually sought and
obtained admission. Counsel for the rating authority on the other hand argues that an
activity carried on cannot be said to be an activity publicly carried on in the absence of
some outward indication that the public are either invited or permitted to participate in
it. Such an indication may take a variety of forms; for instance, carrying on the activity
in a place which is habitually frequented by the public. The example which immediately
springs to mind is the Salvation Army band. In the absence of some such outward　　*g*
indication, he suggests, the activity partakes of an essentially private and inward-looking
nature and cannot be treated as public merely because the activity is carried on by
members, perhaps even a substantial number of members, of the public who, in the
privacy of their own thoughts, would not object to others being present.

For my part, I find myself unable to accept the submissions of counsel for the trustees,　*h*
persuasive though they were. One starts, as it seems to me, from the proposition that the
premises with which the appeal is concerned are private premises to which members of
the general public, whether well- or ill-disposed, have no possible right of access in the
absence of a licence or invitation from the owners. An activity, that is to say the religious
worship of a number of individuals who are clearly invitees of the trustees, takes place
there. One then asks, is that activity one which is 'open to all properly disposed persons'　*j*
or, to put it another way, do the trustees extend an invitation, or grant a licence, to
members of the public who may be thought to be properly disposed to take part in it? In
my judgment the answer to that, on the facts found by the member, must plainly be in
the negative. It is, to my mind, quite insufficient to say, 'Well, if properly disposed
members of the public knew about our activities we should not turn them away.' I do
not wish to be thought to be doubting the truth of that, but it simply does not seem to
me to turn an essentially private gathering into a public one. One has to look at the

matter using one's common sense as a normally law-abiding member of the public. Such a person does not (or one certainly hopes that he does not) intrude on an activity conducted on private property unless he is either expressly invited to do so or unless the circumstances are such as to lead him to believe that he has either an invitation or at least a licence to participate. One cannot start from the presumption that the public is composed of gatecrashers, or even of amiable, interested and well-disposed gatecrashers. In my judgment some open invitation or notification of permission is essential before it can be said that such an activity is a 'public' activity or is 'open to all'. I entirely appreciate the criticism of counsel for the trustees that this results in the formulation of a test which may be blurred at the edges. How, he asks forensically, is one to say that the invitation is to be transmitted? For instance, does it consist, or can it consist, simply of a particular type of architectural design? Is a notice-board essential? Supposing a building of quite unobtrusive design (bearing in mind that a good many Sikh temples up and down the country consist of private houses adapted for religious purposes) what sort of outward manifestation of invitation is required? The fact that the test suggested above may give rise to questions such as these in individual cases does not seem to me, however, to detract at all from its validity. Whether an invitation is issued is a jury question, it is a question of fact and degree in each case and none the worse for that.

I find myself, therefore, unable to accept the primary submission of counsel for the trustees and I go on to consider his secondary and alternative submission that, if an invitation to the public be necessary, such an invitation is to be found in the facts found by the member. Now it is not suggested that the buildings with which this appeal is concerned are in any way remarkable or that their purpose as places of worship would be obvious to anyone seeing them. There was a faint suggestion that since they are registered under the 1855 Act, and since the register is public, a member of the public could ascertain by searching the register that they were registered as places of worship. But counsel for the trustees was unable to suggest any convincing reason why members of the public should wish to search the register nor why, if they did, they should conclude that they were invited to attend and participate, for the register is not a register of places of *public* worship.

Nor is it suggested that there is any visible sign to indicate that the buildings concerned are so used. Indeed, the evidence was that the only visible sign that ever did exist, a notice-board, was deliberately taken down in deference to the teaching of James Taylor junior precisely because it might lead to the brethren being brought into contact with unsuitable persons. What is relied on is the evidence, which the member accepted, of public preachings. It was accepted that the brethren are not a proselytising sect. Indeed it is one of the tenets of their faith that those who are led to join them do so, not as a result of missionary recruitment, but by the will of God, activated by the example of the lives of the brethren. Thus the public preachings serve and are intended to serve only the purpose of arousing interest. If they do result in interested members of the public making inquiries, then whilst the inquirer would not be positively discouraged from attending worship at one or other of the meeting houses if he expressed the desire and inquired how, when and where he could do so, the normal routine (if that is not too strong a word for what appears to have been a relatively rare occurrence) would be for him first to be invited to the home of one of the brethren and then to be invited to attend meetings for worship only if he continued to express genuine interest. This, in my judgment, is altogether too tenuous and too indirect to constitute an invitation to the public. I think, with Stephenson LJ, that the member was going beyond what the evidence warranted when he described the brethren as worshipping 'behind closed doors' and as taking positive action 'to keep their meetings secret'. To that extent I accept the submissions of counsel for the trustees. The findings of fact in the member's reasons do not, I think, warrant the suggestion of clandestine activity or deliberate concealment. Nevertheless, their method of conducting their affairs does, as it seems to me, have the practical effect that their meetings are in fact private and secret in the sense that there is no readily discernible way in which anyone not already a member of the brethren would be likely to find out about them. Nobody questions for a moment the devoutness or sincerity of the brethren and it is no doubt a misfortune if they are precluded from

taking advantage of an exemption accorded to more publicity-seeking, and, for aught I
know, less deserving, religious bodies. But the fact is that their faith is, of its very nature,   a
a faith which, although it emphasises in full the importance of public example, involves
the very antithesis of public religious worship.

For these reasons and those given more fully in the judgment of Stephenson LJ, I agree
that the member came to the correct conclusion and that the appeal must be dismissed.

SLADE LJ. I agree with both judgments that have been delivered.   b

It is perhaps worth emphasising the limited nature of this court's powers to interfere
with a decision of the Lands Tribunal such as this. The general rule stated by s 3(4) of the
Lands Tribunal Act 1949 is that a decision of the tribunal shall be final. This rule is
subject to a proviso contained in the subsection which enables a person aggrieved by such
a decision to appeal to the court on a point of law, by way of case stated. The present
appeal is brought under this proviso, which does not permit appeals on questions of fact.   c

If the two places of religious worship with which it is concerned are to attract the
relevant exemption under s 39 of the General Rate Act 1967, the nature of such religious
worship must be 'public', within the meaning of that section. In substance the principal
question of law arising on this appeal is whether they fulfil this qualification.

Another question (the third) raised by the case stated refers to certain findings by the
member which appear to be findings of fact to which the brethren object. The case stated   d
elevates this question to one of law by asking whether there was evidence on which the
member was entitled to make these findings. The four findings in question are the
following:

> '(a) that members of the public were not invited to attend meetings at the
> meeting halls; (b) that the brethren worship privately behind closed doors; (c) that
> the brethren by the removal of the notice board at Hillside Road have taken positive   e
> action to keep their meetings secret; (d) that the passages from "The Recovery and
> Maintenance of the Truth" at pages 82 and 316 which are set out in my decision at
> page 8 represent a fair summary which illustrates in a general way the doctrine
> accepted by the Brethren.'

The case stated neither annexes a transcript of the evidence, nor contains even a   f
summary of the evidence on which the member relied in making the findings to which
objection is taken. I therefore agree with Stephenson LJ that it is impossible for this court
to answer the third question raised by the case stated.

Nevertheless, with respect to the member's careful decision, I think that the four
findings in issue are not perhaps very happily expressed. It is not clear to me whether the
first, which is to be found in one sentence of the decision, is intended as a finding of   g
primary fact in itself, or is merely intended as a summary of the other facts referred to in
the decision. The fourth is of somewhat vague and uncertain import. The second and
third could be read as having a somewhat sinister flavour, which I do not think the
member intended. He himself paid personal tribute to the four members of the brethren
who gave evidence before him as 'a sincere and devout group of men who arranged their
lives strictly by reference to the scriptures as the only source of truth'.

For my own part, therefore, I am content to approach this appeal on the footing that   h
the particular sentences in the decision to which objection is taken are wholly disregarded.
Even disregarding them, however, the following crucial facts seem to me to emerge
indisputably from the decision. (1) The brethren do not think it right to exert any
positive encouragement to other persons to come to their meetings. They do not advertise
either themselves or their meetings. Their belief is that those attending their meetings
should be inspired by the example of the way of life of the brethren and brought to the   j
meetings by the hand of God. (2) They do not tell an inquirer the place or time of their
meetings unless he specifically asks. (3) There is nothing in the external appearance of
either meeting hall to indicate the use to which the building is put. (4) No notice-board
is in position outside either meeting hall indicating the use of the building. When the
Hillside Road premises were erected in about 1967, there was a board which stated that
the Word of God would be preached at certain times on Sunday, or words to that effect,

a but this notice was removed many years ago. No notice-board has at any time been in position informing the passer-by of the use to which the Cyprus Avenue premises is put. (5) Apart from the attendance at the Hillside Road premises of representatives of the rating authority, there has been no more than one newcomer at either hall in recent years.

b Despite all these facts, counsel for the trustees in his attractive argument has submitted that the nature of the religious worship at both halls can still be properly described as 'public' within the relevant definition, on the grounds that the meetings of the brethren with certain exceptions (the breaking of bread meetings and the care meetings) are open to all properly disposed persons who wish to be present.

c Lord Morris in his speech in *Church of Jesus Christ of Latter-Day Saints v Henning (Valuation Officer)* [1963] 2 All ER 733 at 738, [1964] AC 420 at 435 certainly made it clear that in his view religious worship cannot properly be described as 'public' within the relevant definition, *unless* it occurs in a place which is 'open to all properly disposed persons who wish to be present'. Lord Pearce said much the same thing ([1963] 2 All ER 733 at 739, [1964] AC 420 at 437). But I do not for one moment think that either of them would have intended to suggest that a group of persons who meet together for corporate religious worship outside their homes can render the nature of such worship 'public' for rating purposes, merely by establishing an unannounced convention that

d properly disposed persons who turn up and seek to attend their meetings shall not be refused admission. The 'openness' or otherwise of the meeting cannot, in my view, be tested simply by reference to what is passing through the minds of the persons present.

What more then is required? In no case to which we have been referred has the court attempted to lay down any comprehensive and exhaustive definition of the phrase 'public religious worship' and I would not attempt one. With Stephenson and Oliver LJJ,

e however, I am of the opinion that it does necessarily involve at least the element of some invitation, express or implied, to members of the public to attend the meeting in question. This conclusion is supported by the judgments of Maugham J in *Stradling v Higgins* [1932] 1 Ch 143 at 151, [1931] All ER Rep 772 at 775 and of Lowe J in *Association of the Franciscan Order of Friars Minor v City of Kew* [1944] VLR 199 at 204, which was referred to with apparent approval by Lord Pearce in the *Henning* case. Furthermore, it

f seems to me to accord with common sense and the ordinary use of language.

In my judgment a meeting of a group of persons which takes place on private premises cannot be said to be 'public' within the ordinary meaning of words, unless members of the public, or of the particular section of the public who are most concerned, are given some notice that they will not be treated as trespassers or intruders, if they seek to enter the premises and attend the meeting. The forms which such notice may take are many

g and various. In some cases the external appearance of the relevant building might perhaps even by itself be said to give members of the public sufficient notice that they will be welcome. That some such notice is necessary, however, I feel no doubt.

Reverting to the five crucial facts to which I have referred earlier in this judgment, I do not say that any one of them in isolation would inevitably have disqualified the brethren from obtaining the relief from rates which they seek in respect of these two

h meeting halls. Cumulatively, however, in my opinion they make it impossible to say that the member erred in law in his conclusion that the two halls are not 'places of public religious worship' within the relevant exemption.

For these reasons and the other reasons given by Stephenson and Oliver LJJ, I agree that this appeal should be dismissed.

j *Appeal dismissed. Leave to appeal to the House of Lords refused.*

20 January 1983. The Appeal Committee of the House of Lords (Lord Diplock, Lord Roskill and Lord Brandon of Oakbrook) dismissed a petition by the trustees for leave to appeal.

Solicitors: *George Carter & Co* (for the trustees); *Solicitor of Inland Revenue*; *P D C Brown*, Beeston (for the rating authority).

Diana Brahams   Barrister.

Intpro Properties (UK) Ltd v Sauvel and others

QUEEN'S BENCH DIVISION
BRISTOW J
25, 26 NOVEMBER 1982

Constitutional law – Diplomatic privilege – Immunity from legal process – Private residence of diplomatic agent – Lease of residence – Action to enforce obligations under lease – Landlord letting house to French government for use as residence of diplomatic agent – French government undertaking to allow landlord to enter premises for inspection and repairs – Landlord refused access in breach of undertaking – Whether diplomatic agent protected from suit by diplomatic immunity – Whether action a 'real action' exempting diplomat from immunity – Diplomatic Privileges Act 1964, Sch 1, arts 1, 31, 37.

Constitutional law – Foreign sovereign state – Immunity from suit – Exceptions – Proceedings relating to interest or possession of immovable property – Action to enforce obligation under lease – Landlord letting house to French government – House used as residence of diplomatic agent – Whether court having jurisdiction to entertain action by landlord to enter and repair premises – Whether proceedings relating to an interest in or possession of property – Whether property used for purposes of diplomatic mission – Whether French government immune from proceedings – State Immunity Act 1978, ss 6, 16(1)(b).

In August 1971 the plaintiff let to the French government (represented by the French Consul General in London) certain premises for a term of four years. By a clause in the lease the French government agreed not to use the premises for any purpose other than that of a private dwelling house in the occupation of a named diplomat with the French embassy in London. The French government further agreed to permit the plaintiff or its agents, with or without workmen, at reasonable times during the lease to enter into and on the premises for the purpose of inspecting and examining the premises and carrying out repairs. The diplomat occupied the premises as a home for him and his family and for use in carrying out his social obligations as a diplomat. In January 1982 dry rot appeared in the house and the plaintiff instructed contractors to carry out remedial work. However, access to the premises was denied to the workmen by the diplomat. The plaintiff issued a writ against the diplomat seeking an injunction to restrain him from preventing access to the premises or interfering with the repair work, and damages. The diplomat applied to set aside the writ on the ground that, as a member of the diplomatic staff of the French mission, he was a 'diplomatic agent' within art 1ª of the Vienna Convention on Diplomatic Relations, as set out in Sch 1 to the Diplomatic Privileges Act 1964, and accordingly enjoyed diplomatic immunity. The judge in chambers granted leave to amend the writ to join the French government as a party to the action and adjourned the proceedings for service to be effected on the Consul General. The French government gave notice under RSC Ord 12, r 8 of its intention to contest the proceedings with a view to setting aside the writ on the ground that it could not be impleaded in the English courts. On the hearing of the diplomat's application to strike out the writ the questions arose (i) whether the diplomat was a proper party to the proceedings and (ii) if he was, whether he was entitled to immunity from the proceedings by virtue of his diplomatic status. By virtue of arts 1(e) and 37(1)ᵇ of the Vienna convention a diplomatic

---

a   Article 1, so far as material, provides: '... (e) a "diplomatic agent" is the head of the mission or a member of the diplomatic staff of the mission ...'

b   Article 37(1), so far as material, provides: 'The members of the family of a diplomatic agent forming part of his household shall, if they are not nationals of the receiving State, enjoy the privileges and immunities specified ...'

agent and his family enjoyed the privileges and immunities conferred by the convention.
a By virtue of art 31(1)(*a*)[c] a diplomatic agent enjoyed immunity from civil proceedings 'except in the case of . . . a real action relating to private immovable property . . . unless he holds it on behalf of [his own] State for the purposes of the mission'. In regard to the plaintiff's claim against the French government the question arose whether the court had jurisdiction to entertain the action. By virtue of s 6(1)[d] of the State Immunity Act 1978 a foreign state was not immune from proceedings relating to 'any interest of the
b State in, or its possession or use of, immovable property in the United Kingdom' or 'any obligation of the State arising out of its interest in, or possession or use of, any such property'. However, by virtue of s 16(1)(*b*)[e] that exception from immunity did not extend to proceedings concerning 'property used for the purposes of a diplomatic mission'.

Held – The diplomat's application would be granted and the plaintiff's action dismissed,
c for the following reasons—
(1) A 'real action' as described in art 31(1)(*a*) of the 1961 Vienna convention was a concept unknown to English law (except in the Admiralty jurisdiction), but, however it was defined, the plaintiff's action, being a normal action in personam to enforce the obligations arising from the lease together with damages, could not be described as a 'real action' within art 31(1)(*a*) of the convention. Since the plaintiff's action was not a real
d action the diplomat would be protected from suit by the general immunity conferred by art 31 if he was properly joined as a defendant, but in any event, although the diplomat occupied the premises, it was the French government and not the diplomat who 'held' the premises for the purposes of art 31. In so far as the diplomat had done anything material he had done it on behalf of the French government and he was merely the licensee in occupation and the servant of the French government. Since he did not 'hold'
e the property on behalf of the French government he was not a proper party to the action (see p 661 *h* to p 662 *a* and *g*, post).
(2) The plaintiff's action related not just to the French government's use of the premises but also to the rights and obligations arising from its possession of the premises and was therefore an action falling within the exception from diplomatic immunity set out in s 6(1) of the 1978 Act. However, since the premises were used by the French
f government as a residence for one of its officials they were 'used for the purposes of a diplomatic mission' within s 16(1)(*b*) of the 1978 Act, and the French government was therefore immune from proceedings in respect of the premises (see p 662 *d* to *g*, post).

Notes
For sovereign immunity from suit, see 8 Halsbury's Laws (4th edn) para 410 and 18 ibid
g para 1548, and for cases on the subject, see 1(1) Digest (Reissue) 54–59, 358–382.
For the Diplomatic Privileges Act 1964, Sch 1, arts 1, 31, 37, see 6 Halsbury's Statutes (3rd edn) 1017, 1019, 1022.
For the State Immunity Act 1978, ss 6, 16, see 48 ibid 92, 99.

Application
h The plaintiff, Intpro Properties (UK) Ltd, issued a writ dated 4 November 1982 against the defendants, M Dominique Sauvel, a minister at the French Embassy in London, and

---

c Article 31(1), so far as material, provides: 'A diplomatic agent . . . shall also enjoy immunity from [the receiving state's] civil and administrative jurisdiction, except in the case of: (*a*) a real action relating to private immovable property situated in the territory of the receiving State, unless he holds it on behalf of the sending State for the purposes of the mission . . .'
j *d* Section 6(1) provides: 'A State is not immune as respects proceedings relating to—(*a*) any interest of the State in, or its possesion or use of, immovable property in the United Kingdom; or (*b*) any obligation of the State arising out of its interest in, or its possession or use of, any such property.'
e Section 16(1), so far as material, provides: '. . . (*b*) section 6(1) above does not apply to proceedings concerning a State's title to or its possession of property used for the purposes of a diplomatic mission.'

his wife, Mme Danielle Sauvel, seeking an injunction restraining the defendants or their
servants or agents from preventing access to the plaintiff's property at 19 Pelham   a
Crescent, London SW7, which was occupied by the defendants under a lease, or in any
way interfering with repair works to be carried out by the plaintiff, and damages. An ex
parte injunction was granted by a judge in chambers. On 5 November the defendants
again denied access to the plaintiff and the ex parte injunction was stayed. On 10
November the defendants applied to set aside the writ on the ground that they were
entitled to diplomatic immunity. On 11 November Comyn J granted leave to the   b
plaintiff to amend the writ to join the government of the Republic of France and to serve
the writ on the French Consul General in London. On 18 November the French
government gave notice of intention to contest the proceedings in order to have the writ
set aside. The defendants' application was heard and judgment was given in chambers.
The case is reported by permission of Bristow J. The facts are set out in the judgment.

Eugene Cotran for the plaintiff.   c
Christopher Thomas as amicus curiae.

BRISTOW J. On 8 August 1979 Intpro Properties (UK) Ltd (Intpro) let to the French
government, represented by the French Consul General in London, premises at 19
Pelham Crescent, London SW7, for a term of four years from that date at a rent rising   d
from £23,400 p a to £31,145. The French government covenanted by cl 2(xv) not to use
the premises for any other purposes than that of a private dwelling house in the
occupation of M Dominique Sauvel and his family. It covenanted by cl 2(ix) to permit
Intpro or its agents with or without workmen at all reasonable times during the lease to
enter into and on the premises for the purpose of inspecting and examining the premises
and carrying out any repairs.   e
     M Sauvel is a minister of the French diplomatic staff, financial counsellor to the
embassy in London, and occupies 19 Pelham Crescent with his wife and children as his
private residence and for use in carrying out his social obligations as a senior diplomatic
agent. That is why the French government took the house for him to live in.
     In January 1982 dry rot made its appearance above the dining room window. Miss
Katharine Myres of JEM International Management Ltd, Intpro's managing agents,   f
instructed contractors to deal with it, and started negotiations with the Sauvels to get the
work done with the minimum of inconvenience. As the year progressed so did the dry
rot, and it became apparent that the remedial works would be so extensive that the
family would be unable to live a normal family life in the house while they were
performed. Dry rot specialists were called in. Difficulties multiplied. Finally on 2
November access to the house was denied to the builders who intended to start the   g
remedial works.
     Intpro regard themselves as liable for the cost of works to remedy the dry rot which
involves the structure of the house. It is accordingly a serious matter for them that they
should be prevented from getting on with the job. I am told that the Sauvels have
another house in view and hope to move out of 19 Pelham Crescent during January
1983.   h
     On 4 November 1982 a writ was issued by Intpro against M and Mme Sauvel claiming
injunctions to restrain them from preventing access to 19 Pelham Crescent or interfering
with repair work. Damages are also claimed. An ex parte application was made to the
judge in chambers for an interim injunction, and this was granted. But on 5 November,
when access was again denied, the ex parte injunction was stayed. On 10 November
there was an application on behalf of the Sauvels to set aside the writ on the basis that   j
they enjoy diplomatic immunity. On 11 November this, together with the inter partes
summons to renew the injunction, came on before Comyn J in chambers. He gave leave
to amend to join the French government, being the tenants under the lease, and to effect
service on the Consul General. He adjourned the proceedings for this to be done. On 18
November service was acknowledged on behalf of the French government, which gave

notice of intention to contest the proceedings, so taking the first step now available under
a   RSC Ord 12, r 8, in place of a conditional appearance, with a view to setting aside the
writ on the ground that it cannot be impleaded in the English courts.

When the summons came on before me I was told (1) that counsel, who had
represented the Sauvels before Comyn J, no longer had instructions from the Sauvels, (2)
that they were not present in person, (3) that no one was instructed before me on behalf
of the French government.

b   Since the summons involves an important question of diplomatic immunity and of
the jurisdiction of the court to entertain this action or grant the relief sought by way of
injunction, it is necessary for the court to examine the jurisdiction point of its own
motion. It seemed to me to be wrong to rely wholly on the help that counsel appearing
on behalf of the plaintiffs could give me, and that to do so would place him in an
invidious position. Mr Thomas, who had very properly appeared to tell me about the
c   situation in respect of the defendants, kindly accepted my invitation to act on the spot as
amicus curiae. Both counsel have been a great help to me by guiding me through the
relevant statutory provisions.

The Diplomatic Privileges Act 1964 replaced the previous law on diplomatic immunity
which was part statute, part common law. By s 2 it incorporated certain articles of the
Vienna Convention on Diplomatic Relations (Vienna, 18 April 1961; TS 19 (1965);
d   Cmnd 2565) into the domestic law of the United Kingdom, setting them out in the
English translation of the treaty in Sch 1.

Articles 1(e) and 37 have the effect that M and Mme Sauvel enjoy the privileges and
immunities conferred on 'diplomatic agents'. By art 30 the private residence of a
diplomatic agent shall enjoy the same inviolability and protection as the premises of the
mission. By art 22 the premises of the mission are inviolable, and immune from search,
e   requisition, attachment or execution. By art 31(1)(a) a diplomatic agent enjoys immunity
from the civil jurisdiction of the receiving state except in the case of a real action relating
to private immovable property situated in the territory of the receiving state, unless he
holds it on behalf of the sending state for the purposes of the mission. By art 31(3) no
measures of execution may be taken against a diplomatic agent in connection with a real
action relating to immovable property not held on behalf of the sending state for the
f   purposes of the mission unless they can be taken without infringing the inviolability of
his person or his residence.

A 'real action' is a creature unknown to English law since the Middle Ages. The term
in the 1964 Act is a literal translation of 'une action réelle' in the French master text of
the treaty. There is no evidence before me from an expert in French law on the nature of
an action réelle. If Intpro wishes to rely on this action being a 'real action' it is for it to
g   show me what action réelle means in the terms of the concepts known to English law.
Commentators, of whose value I have no expert evidence, suggest that it means an action
where the ownership or possession of immovable property is in question (Satow's Guide
to Diplomatic Practice (5th edn, 1979) p 125), procedure regarding rights in rem over real
estate (Szaszy International Civil Procedure (1967) p 408), actions where the relief sought is
a declaration of title, an order for sale or an order for possession (Denza Diplomatic Law).
h   'Droit réel' in the European Glossary of Legal and Administrative Terminology is translated as
'right in rem' as distinct from 'right in personam'. Except in the case of Admiralty
jurisdiction in relation to ships that is a concept unknown to English law.

In my judgment, Intpro's action does not in any way fit the concept of 'action réelle' as
reflected in the commentaries. It is a normal action in personam to enforce by injunction
the obligations arising from a lease, and for damages. If the Sauvels are properly joined
j   as defendants, they are in my judgment protected from suit by art 31 because the action
against them is not a real action.

Are they proper parties? They are not the tenants, although they occupy 19 Pelham
Crescent. They do so as their home, and for the social obligations appropriate to their
status. If it were necessary to decide the point, I would hold that they do not 'hold' 19
Pelham Crescent within the meaning of art 31(1)(a) at all. It is the French government

itself which is the 'holder' of the private immovable property which is 19 Pelham
Crescent. In so far as the Sauvels have done anything material they have done it on behalf   *a*
of the French government whose licensees in occupation of the property and whose
servants they are, and they are immune from action in this court.

What is the position of the Republic of France in relation to this action?

The State Immunity Act 1978 provides by s 1 that a state is immune from the
jurisdiction of the courts of the United Kingdom except as provided in the 1978 Act, and
a court shall give effect to the immunity even though the state does not appear in the   *b*
proceedings. It is not (as I understand) seriously contested by Intpro that the Republic of
France has submitted to the jurisdiction. of the English court in this action. The
acknowledgment of service, something necessary to the claiming of immunity, cannot
of itself in my judgment amount to a submission, even though the state has not gone
further and made the actual claim.

By s 6(1) a state is not immune as respects proceedings relating to any interest of the   *c*
state in, or its possession or use of, immovable property in the United Kingdom or any
obligation of the state arising out of its interest in or its possession or use of such property.
By s 6(4) a court may entertain proceedings against a person other than the state
notwithstanding that the proceedings relate to property which is in possession of the
state, if the state would not have been immune had the proceedings been brought against
it. Here the state is now a party, the Sauvels are no more than agents of the state, and   *d*
they enjoy the protection of art 31(1)(a) of Sch 1 to the 1964 Act. In my judgment it is
the state which is the proper party, and the court should not entertain proceedings against
the Sauvels.

By s 16(1)(b), s 6(1) does not apply to proceedings concerning a state's title to or its
possession of property used for the purposes of a diplomatic mission.

Note that what is here in play is simply title or possession, and not use, as in s 6(1). In   *e*
my judgment this action is an action relating to rights and obligations which arise from
the state's possession of 19 Pelham Crescent under its contract of tenancy, and so is not
simply an action relating to its use of the premises. In my judgment, however, the
property, in relation to the state's possession of which this action is brought, is property
used by the state for the purposes of a diplomatic mission. It is used to house the financial
counsellor of the embassy of London in his capacity as such, plus his family, in   *f*
circumstances appropriate to his official situation.

Accordingly, in my judgment the court has no jurisdiction to entertain this action
against the Republic of France. Even if it had, s 13(2)(a) of the 1978 Act would have
excluded the remedy of injunction. If Intpro suffers injustice in the circumstances which
have led to this action being brought, its only remedy is to enlist the aid of the executive.
The judiciary can in my judgment do nothing for it, and this action must be dismissed.   *g*

Application allowed and action dismissed. Leave to appeal.

Solicitors: *Philip Conway Thomas & Co* (for the plaintiff); *Thompson Quarrell* (for the
amicus curiae).

K Mydeen Esq   Barrister.

Moore v Green

QUEEN'S BENCH DIVISION
GRIFFITHS LJ AND McCULLOUGH J
6 OCTOBER 1982

Criminal law – Obstructing constable in execution of duty – Wilful obstruction – Acts amounting to wilful obstruction – Constable warning licensee of public house of possible police raid on premises – Warning given to ensure licensee not caught by police while breaking licensing laws – Whether warning amounting to 'wilful obstruction' of police in execution of their duty – Police Act 1964, s 51(3).

A constable who regularly drank at a public house and knew that the licensee allowed drinking after licensing hours learnt from a colleague in his police force that a group from the force might investigate the conduct of the licensee's premises that night. The constable warned the licensee about the possible investigation and consequently that night the licensee strictly observed the licensing hours. The constable was charged with wilfully obstructing officers of his force in the execution of their duty, contrary to s 51(3)[a] of the Police Act 1964. The magistrates convicted him. The constable appealed against the conviction to the Crown Court, which found that the constable did not know for certain that the police group were going to investigate the premises, that he told the licensee about the possible investigation to ensure that the licensee would not be caught breaking the licensing laws, and that he did not intend to obstruct the police group. The Crown Court held that although the constable had obstructed the police in the execution of their duty he had not done so wilfully and intentionally and therefore had not committed the offence charged. The prosecutor appealed to the Divisional Court.

Held – Since the logical conclusion from the finding that the constable warned the licensee to ensure that the licensee would not be caught breaking the law was that the constable also intended that the police should not catch the licensee breaking the law, it followed that he intended to and did obstruct the police when giving the warning to the licensee. It was immaterial that he did not appreciate that his warning amounted to obstruction. The prosecutor's appeal would be allowed and the case remitted to the Crown Court with a direction to convict (see p 666 f to j, post).

Willmott v Atack [1976] 3 All ER 794 applied.

Per curiam. Hostility towards the police is not a separate element of the offence of obstructing the police in the execution of their duty, contrary to s 51(3) of the 1964 Act. What is required to be shown is that the accused did an act with the intention of thereby obstructing the police (see p 665 j and p 666 h j, post).

Dictum of Croom-Johnson J in Willmott v Atack [1976] 3 All ER at 800 explained.

Notes

For obstructing a constable in the execution of his duty, see 11 Halsbury's Laws (4th edn) para 962, and for cases on the subject see 15 Digest (Reissue) 985–991, 8546–8590.

For the Police Act 1964, s 51, see 25 Halsbury's Statutes (3rd edn) 364.

Cases referred to in judgments

Green v Moore [1982] 1 All ER 428, [1982] QB 1044, [1982] 2 WLR 671, DC.

Willmott v Atack [1976] 3 All ER 794, [1977] QB 498, [1976] 3 WLR 753, DC, 15 Digest (Reissue) 990, 8581.

---

a   Section 51(3), so far as material, provides: 'Any person who . . . wilfully obstructs a constable in the execution of his duty . . . shall be guilty of an offence . . .'

Case stated

The prosecutor, Police Sgt Moore, appealed by way of a case stated by the Crown Court   *a*
at Newport (his Honour Judge Hopkin Morgan QC and justices) in respect of its decision
given on 18 or 19 February 1982 allowing the appeal of the defendant, Nigel Anthony
Green, to the Crown Court from his conviction in Cwmbran Magistrates' Court of
wilfully obstructing Sgt Moore and other officers of Gwent Constabulary acting in the
execution of their duty, contrary to s 51(3) of the Police Act 1964. The questions raised
in the case stated for the consideration of the High Court were (1) whether on the facts   *b*
found by the Crown Court its conclusion that the defendant's obstruction of the police
was not wilful and intentional, and therefore he was not guilty of the offence charged,
was one that a reasonable court could come to, and (2) whether when a licensee is warned
of the presence of police officers in the vicinity so as to ensure that he does not contravene
the licensing laws, the person warning the licensee commits an offence under s 51(3) of
the 1964 Act only if he knows that the licensee's premises are definitely going to be   *c*
checked by the police. The facts are set out in the judgment of McCullough J.

Gerard Elias for the prosecutor.
Tom Crowther QC for Mr Green.

McCULLOUGH J (delivering the first judgment at the invitation of Griffiths LJ). This   *d*
is an appeal by way of case stated from the Crown Court at Newport which on either 18
or 19 February 1982 (the date is not clear) allowed the appeal of the defendant, Mr Green,
against his conviction by the Cwmbran Magistrates' Court on 28 July 1980 of a charge of
wilfully obstructing Police Sgt Moore and other officers of the Gwent Constabulary
support group, constables of the Gwent Constabulary, acting in the execution of their
duty. The defendant was then a probationary constable in the force.   *e*

The hearing before the Crown Court began on 22 October 1980. At the close of the
case for the prosecution a submission that there was no case to answer was upheld. The
prosecutor appealed successfully by way of case stated and on 4 November 1981, the case
was remitted to the Crown Court with a direction that the hearing be continued. The
reserved judgment of this court is now reported (see [1982] 1 All ER 428, [1982] QB
1044). The background to the case is fully set out in the report and only a brief summary   *f*
of the facts is necessary.

A police support group, under Sgt Moore, visited Chepstow one night in June 1980
with the aim of discovering whether the landlord of the Castle Hotel was permitting
drinking to take place after hours. A police constable, who was not himself a member of
the group but was a member of the force, learnt of this and told Probationary Pc Green
to tell the landlord the support group were in Chepstow. So at about 10.30 pm that   *g*
evening Pc Green did just that. As a result, licensing hours were strictly observed and it
became obvious to the support group that there was no point in paying any further
attention to the hotel that night.

Pc Green was interviewed very soon afterwards and admitted having forewarned the
landlord. Asked why he had done this, he said: 'I wasn't sure it was to be raided, but I
guessed so, as I saw the support group van in the area and I thought I would warn him as   *h*
I am a regular there and I get information from the licensee. I know they drink late but
I don't.' A little later he said: 'I saw the support group van in the town. As I drink in the
Castle and know they drink late, I went down to warn the licensee.'

At the resumed hearing, Mr Green gave evidence. The court found the following
further facts. (1) Mr Green knew that the support group were in Chepstow on the night
in question. (2) Mr Green knew that the support group regularly visited Chepstow to   *j*
check on street disorders and the conduct of licensed premises after hours. (3) Mr Green
did not know that the support group were specifically intending to raid the Castle Hotel.
(4) Mr Green knew that after-hours drinking sometimes occurred at the Castle Hotel. (5)
Mr Green told the landlord of the Castle Hotel that the support group were in town and
intended thereby to ensure that there would be no after-hours drinking and that the

landlord did not run the risk of being caught by the support group officers. (6) Mr Green
told us that he had no intention to obstruct the support group and did not realise that his
conduct might interfere with officers in the course of their duty. In this, as in every
aspect of his evidence, we found him to be utterly truthful.

I shall come back to findings (5) and (6). The case continues:

'Having heard the evidence and submissions we determined the appeal by posing
and answering three questions: (1) Was there any obstruction of a constable? On the
facts we found that there was. (2) Were the constable and the support group acting
in the execution of their duty? On the facts we found that they were. [No question
arises as to either of those two findings. The next is the material one:] (3) Was the
obstruction intended to obstruct the constable and the support group in the
execution of their duty? We found that his obstruction of the police was not wilful
and intentional and that he was therefore not guilty of the offence.'

The question for this court is:

'Whether on all the facts found our conclusion in relation to the third question
was one that a reasonable court could have come to.'

All the relevant cases on this branch of the law were referred to in *Green v Moore* [1982]
1 All ER 428, [1982] QB 1044, when it was before this court on 4 November 1981. That
appeal was not concerned with the question which we have to consider today, but
towards the end of the judgment of the court Donaldson LJ said ([1982] 1 All ER 428 at
433, [1982] QB 1044 at 1052):

'The distinction between action which is and action which is not intended to
obstruct a constable in the execution of his duty is well illustrated by the facts in
Willmott v Atack [1976] 3 All ER 794, [1977] QB 498. Mr Willmott got in the way
of police officers trying to force an arrested man to get into a police car and thereby
quite clearly obstructed them. His purpose was, however, to assist the police by
persuading the man to go quietly. He was acquitted. However, on the facts of the
present case, it is quite clear that the respondent's intention was to assist the landlord
and not the police.'

The last four words 'and not the police' were, of course, added because Donaldson LJ
was contrasting the facts of the case he was considering with the very unusual facts in
Willmott v Atack, where the defendant was asserting that his interference was to assist the
police.

In *Willmott v Atack* the first judgment was given by Croom-Johnson J who said [1976]
3 All ER 794 at 800, [1977] QB 498 at 504–505:

'When one looks at the whole context of s 51 [of the Police Act 1964], dealing as
it does with assaults on constables in sub-s (1) and concluding in sub-s (3) with
resistance and wilful obstruction in the execution of the duty, I am of the view that
the interpretation of this subsection for which the appellant contends is the right
one. It fits the words "wilfully obstructs" in the context of the subsection, and in my
view there must be something in the nature of a criminal intent of the kind which
means that it is done with the idea of some form of hostility to the police with the
intention of seeing that what is done is to obstruct, and that it is not enough merely
to show that he intended to do what he did and that it did in fact have the result of
the police being obstructed.'

May J and Lord Widgery CJ agreed.

I do not understand the reference to 'hostility' to indicate a separate element of the
offence. I understand the word to bear the same meaning as the phrase which Croom-
Johnson J used immediately afterwards, namely 'The intention of seeing that what is
done is to obstruct . . .'

Counsel for the prosecutor submits that, on any sensible view of the facts found by the Crown Court, Mr Green must have had that intention. Counsel for Mr Green submits *a* that the Crown Court found in terms that he did not; he relies in particular on finding (6).

All the findings of fact to which I have referred are taken from a document which was put in this morning by agreement between counsel. Although this sets out the facts which the parties agree were found by the Crown Court, the document has not been approved by that court. A somewhat different list of the findings of fact is contained in the case stated. This was signed by the court in the erroneous belief that it had been *b* approved by those representing Mr Green. This morning it emerged that this was not so and the new version was agreed on the basis of notes which were made of the reserved judgment given by the Crown Court. We have treated the case as amended by this document.

Counsel for Mr Green submits that finding (6) is in effect a finding that Mr Green was a silly young man who did not appreciate the consequences of what he was doing; he was *c* a young probationary constable who was doing no more than obeying the instruction of his superior, a fully fledged police constable.

In my judgment, the crucial finding of fact is not (6) but (5). Finding (6) is that when Mr Green was giving evidence before the Crown Court he honestly believed that on the night in question he had no intention to obstruct and no realisation that his conduct might interfere with officers in the course of their duty. Finding (5) is concerned with *d* what he actually did. He knew that after-hours drinking went on; he must have realised that it might very well take place that night; he had been told that the support group were in town; he knew that they might very well visit the Castle Hotel; he realised that if they did do that and if the landlord were not warned, then after-hours drinking might very well take place and the landlord would be caught. He told the landlord so that there would be no after-hours drinking that night, not because he had a concern that the law *e* should be obeyed but, as the finding shows, because he had a concern that the landlord would not be caught disobeying it, which of course means caught by the support group that night.

It is a matter of simple logic that if a man intends that X will not be caught by the police breaking the law, he intends that the police shall not catch X breaking the law. In my judgment the inevitable conclusion from finding (5) is that Mr Green intended to *f* prevent the support group from discovering that the landlord was permitting the after-hours drinking which he realised might well take place, and be discovered, if he did not give the warning. Whether he appreciated that this would amount in law to an obstruction is immaterial. If there is a conflict between findings (5) and (6) I have no doubt that finding (5) should prevail. It makes no difference that he was persuaded or told to give the warning by somebody else. At best that is a matter of mitigation. Nor *g* does it make any difference that he did not know for certain that the support group intended to pay attention to the Castle Hotel that night.

In my judgment, no tribunal of fact could reasonably have found other than that Mr Green intended to obstruct in the way described by Croom-Johnson J in *Willmott v Atack*, and no reasonable tribunal could have done other than convict. I therefore would allow this appeal. *h*

GRIFFITHS LJ. I agree. This young police officer, Mr Green, tipped off the landlord of the pub at which he was a regular drinker to ensure that the landlord would not be caught by the police support group, who had come to Chepstow that night for the purpose of investigating drinking after hours. It appears to me that that is the clearest *j* possible case of obstructing police officers in the execution of their duty. In my view, the only conclusion which a court reasonably directing itself could have come to is that this young policeman was guilty of this offence. Accordingly, for these reasons and those given by McCullough J, this case will be remitted to the Crown Court with a direction that they enter a conviction and then consider the sentence they should pass.

a   *Appeal allowed ; case remitted to Crown Court with direction to enter a conviction and consider sentence to be passed.*

Solicitors: *Director of Public Prosecutions ; Derek James & Vaux*, Newport (for the defendant).

Sepala Munasinghe Esq   Barrister.

b

Hills v Ellis

QUEEN'S BENCH DIVISION

c   GRIFFITHS LJ AND McCULLOUGH J

28 OCTOBER 1982

Criminal law – Obstructing constable in execution of duty – Wilful obstruction – Acts amounting to wilful obstruction – Defendant interfering with arrest because he thought police officer was arresting innocent person – Whether bystander can ever lawfully interfere with a lawful arrest –

d   *Whether defendant's act amounting to 'wilful obstruction' of police – Police Act 1964, s 51(3).*

While leaving a football match the appellant saw two men fighting and formed the view that one of them was the innocent party in the fight. The appellant then saw a police officer arresting the man he thought was innocent. The appellant approached them with the intention of intervening on the part of the arrested man and, being unable to make

e   his voice heard above the noise of the crowd, he grabbed the police officer's elbow to draw the officer's attention to the fact that he was arresting the wrong man. Another police officer warned the appellant that if he did not desist he might himself be arrested for obstructing the police. The appellant persisted in trying to stop the arrest and was charged with wilful obstruction of a police officer in the execution of his duty, contrary to s 51(3)*ᵃ* of the Police Act 1964. The magistrates convicted the appellant on the ground

f   that even though the appellant genuinely wished to prevent the arrest of a person he thought to be innocent his behaviour, in the circumstances prevailing at the time of the arrest, was unreasonable and constituted an obstacle to the police officer in carrying out the arrest. The appellant appealed, contending that he had not 'wilfully obstructed' a police officer within s 51(3) because (i) he had acted with lawful excuse, since he had a moral duty to draw the officer's attention to the fact that he was arresting the wrong

g   man, and (ii) since his motive was to correct the police officer's error in arresting the wrong person, he had not acted with hostility towards the police officer. It was conceded that the officer was lawfully arresting the man.

Held – A private citizen could never have a lawful excuse for interfering with an arrest by a police officer which was lawful. A person 'wilfully obstructed' a police officer in the

h   execution of his duty, within s 51(3) of the 1964 Act, whenever he deliberately did an act with the intention of bringing about a state of affairs which, viewed objectively, amounted to obstruction of the police, i e which made it more difficult for them to carry out their duty. A person's motives for wanting to prevent an arrest or the fact that he did not appreciate that interfering with the arrest would be obstruction were irrelevant. Since the appellant had deliberately grabbed the officer with the intention of intervening

j   on behalf of the person whom the officer was arresting and of causing the officer to revise his decision to arrest him, it followed that, viewed objectively, the appellant intended to obstruct the officer. Accordingly, he had wilfully obstructed the police officer within

---

a   Section 51(3), so far as material, provides: 'Any person who . . . wilfully obstructs a constable in the execution of his duty . . . shall be guilty of an offence . . .'

s 51(3). It followed that the appeal would be dismissed (see p 669 j, p 670 b c h j and p 671 b to e and j to p 672 b, post).

Willmott v Atack [1976] 3 All ER 794 distinguished.

Dictum of Lord Parker CJ in Rice v Connolly [1966] 2 All ER at 651–652 explained.

Per curiam. Acting with 'hostility' towards the police means no more than that the defendant's actions were aimed at the police, and not that the defendant must have had a hostile motive in obstructing the police (see p 670 g to j, post).

Dictum of Croom-Johnson J in Willmott v Atack [1976] 3 All ER at 800 explained.

Notes

For obstructing a constable in the execution of his duty, see 11 Halsbury's Laws (4th edn) para 962, and for cases on the subject, see 15 Digest (Reissue) 985–991, 8546–8590.

For the Police Act 1964, s 51, see 25 Halsbury's Statutes (3rd edn) 364.

Cases referred to in judgments

Green v Moore [1982] 1 All ER 428, [1982] QB 1044, [1982] 2 WLR 671, DC.

Rice v Connolly [1966] 2 All ER 649, [1966] 2 QB 414, [1966] 3 WLR 17, DC, 15 Digest (Reissue) 989, 8578.

Willmott v Atack [1976] 3 All ER 794, [1977] QB 498, [1976] 3 WLR 753, DC, 15 Digest (Reissue) 990, 8581.

Case stated

Stephen Mark Hills appealed by way of a case stated by the justices for the Middlesex Area of Greater London acting in and for the petty sessional division of Edmonton in respect of their adjudication as a magistrates' court sitting at Tottenham on 1 April 1982. On 19 January 1982 an information was preferred by the respondent, Barry Ellis, against the appellant that on 2 January 1982 he wilfully obstructed Robert Grey, a police officer, in the execution of his duty, contrary to s 51(3) of the Police Act 1964. The justices, having found the facts and heard the parties' contentions, were of the opinion that although the appellant's intervention in the arrest of a man by Pc Grey had been activated by the genuine motive that he thought Pc Grey was arresting an innocent person, the manner in which the appellant had acted was in all the circumstances unreasonable and a positive obstacle to the arrest, and for those reasons the justices decided to convict the appellant. Having regard to the circumstances of the offence and the appellant's character, the justices were of opinion that it was inexpedient to inflict any punishment on him and that a probation order was inappropriate. They therefore made an order discharging him absolutely. The question for the opinion of the High Court was whether on the facts found and the law to be applied to those facts the justices were correct in arriving at a decision to convict the appellant. The facts found are set out in the judgment of Griffiths LJ.

Paul Morgan for the appellant.
J S Wiggs for the respondent.

GRIFFITHS LJ. This is an appeal by way of case stated from a decision of the justices sitting for the petty sessional division of Edmonton, who convicted this appellant of the offence of wilfully obstructing a police officer in the execution of his duty contrary to s 51(3) of the Police Act 1964.

The facts found by the justices were as follows. On Saturday, 2 January 1982 the appellant and a friend of his were in Park Lane, Tottenham, having just left a football match which had taken place at the Tottenham Hotspur football ground. The appellant saw a fight between two men and he formed the view that one of the men was the innocent party in the fight. He then saw Pc Robert Grey go up and arrest the man whom this appellant thought to be the innocent party. The appellant approached with the intention of intervening on the part of the arrested man. In order to attract the attention

a
of the arresting officer, and in an effort to overcome the noise of the crowd leaving the
match, the appellant addressed the officer in a raised voice, but due to the noise, the
officer failed to hear what the appellant said. The appellant then grabbed the officer by
the elbow in order to draw the officer's attention to the fact that, in the appellant's
opinion, he was arresting the wrong man, and that he was in a position to provide cogent
evidence, if they wished to have it, which might make the officer revise his decision to
arrest the person he was trying to apprehend. The respondent, who is also a police officer,

b
saw the appellant addressing Pc Grey in a raised voice and also saw the appellant grab Pc
Grey by the elbow. The respondent warned the appellant that he should stop and that
failure to do so might lead to his arrest for obstructing Pc Grey. However, the appellant
persisted in his behaviour, and thereupon he was arrested by the respondent and charged.

Those are the salient facts found by the justices, and on those facts they expressed the
following opinion:

c
'We were of opinion that the appellant in intervening in the processes of arrest
had conducted himself in an excited and agitated fashion. That the manner in
which the appellant interfered in the process of arrest failed to take into account the
problems of the police officer in making an arrest against the background of many
people leaving the football ground when violence amongst football supporters is a
prevalent phenomenon. Seen in this light the appellant's actions were intrusive and

d
a considerable impediment of the police officer in making his arrest.'

I interject here to say that it has never been suggested, either before the justices or in
this court, that the officer was not making a lawful arrest. It was never suggested, despite
the opinion of this appellant, that the officer did not have reasonable grounds for arresting
the man he was trying to apprehend. The justices continued:

e
'We decided that it was not for us to prognosticate on the lawfulness of the arrest
of the man regarded by the appellant to be the innocent party ... We considered
that the respective predicaments of both the appellant and respondent dictated a
necessity for the appellant, in making his views known to the authorities to act with
prudence and either follow or make his way to the police station to which the
arrested man was to be taken. There the appellant would have been able to make

f
his representations on the issues in an atmosphere of relative quietude. We
considered that although his interference in the arrest was based in genuine motives,
the manner in which the appellant had acted was unreasonable in the prevailing
circumstances and was a positive obstacle to the police officer in his arrest. For these
reasons we determined to convict the appellant ... The question for the opinion of
the High Court is whether on the facts as found by us and the law applied to those

g
facts we were correct in arriving at a decision to convict the appellant of the offence
with which he was charged.'

In presenting his submissions on behalf of this appellant, counsel has referred the court
first to the decision of the Divisional Court in *Rice v Connolly* [1966] 2 All ER 694 at 651–
652, [1966] 2 QB 414 at 419 in which Lord Parker CJ considered the ingredient of this

h
offence. He said:

'What the prosecution have to prove is that there was an obstructing of a constable,
that the constable was at the time acting in the execution of his duty, and that the
person obstructing did so wilfully. To carry the matter a little further, it is in my
view clear that to "obstruct" in s. 51(3) [of the Police Act 1964] is to do any act which
makes it more difficult for the police to carry out their duty.'

j
I pause there. There can be no doubt in this case that there was an obstruction within
the meaning of that definition. The appellant was actually grabbing hold of the officer
when in very difficult conditions, at the end of a football match, he was trying to arrest a
man. Lord Parker LJ then continued to consider the element of wilfulness in the offence,
and he said:

'The only remaining element of the alleged offence, and the one on which in my judgment this case depends, is whether the obstructing of which the appellant was *a* guilty was a wilful obstruction. "Wilful" in this context in my judgment means not only "intentional" but also connotes something which is done without lawful excuse, and that indeed is conceded by counsel . . .'

What is submitted in this case on behalf of the appellant is that his action was not wilful in the sense of being done without lawful excuse, because he had a moral duty to draw to the attention of the officer that he was arresting the wrong man. I cannot accept *b* that submission. Here was an officer, acting in the course of his duty, arresting a man. It would be quite intolerable if citizens, who may genuinely believe the wrong man was arrested, were entitled to lay hands on the police and obstruct them in that arrest because they thought that some other person should be arrested. One has only got to state the proposition to see the enormous abuse to which any such power on the part of the citizen might be put. A private citizen has no lawful excuse to interfere with a lawful arrest by *c* a police officer. Accordingly, he was acting without lawful excuse within the definition as stated by Lord Parker CJ in *Rice v Connolly*.

The only other authority cited in support of the appellant's submission is *Willmott v Atack* [1976] 3 All ER 794, [1977] QB 498. The facts in that case were very different. A police officer was attempting to restrain a man under arrest and to get him into a police car. The defendant intervened, not with the intention of making it more difficult for the *d* police officer to get the man into the police car, but with the intention of helping the officer. But due to the clumsiness of his intervention, the man in fact escaped. There is no doubt that in those circumstances the first part of the definition of 'wilfully obstructing' has been fulfilled. The officer had, in fact, been obstructed, but the court held that it had not been a wilful obstruction. Croom-Johnson J expressed the view of the court in the following way ([1976] 3 All ER 794 at 800, [1977] QB 498 at 504–505): *e*

'When one looks at the whole context of s 51, dealing as it does with assaults on constables in sub-s (1) and concluding in sub-s (3) with resistance and wilful obstruction in the execution of the duty, I am of the view that the interpretation of this subsection for which the appellant contends is the right one. It fits the words "wilfully obstructs" in the context of the subsection, and in my view there must be *f* something in the nature of a criminal intent of the kind which means that it is done with the idea of some form of hostility to the police with the intention of seeing that what is done is to obstruct, and that it is not enough merely to show that he intended to do what he did and that it did, in fact, have the result of the police being obstructed.'

The appellant's counsel argues from that passage that, as the motive here was merely *g* to correct a policeman's error, it cannot be said that he, the appellant, was acting with any hostility towards the police. But in my view, the phrase 'hostility towards the police' in that passage means no more than that the actions of the defendant are aimed at the police. There can be no doubt here that his action in grabbing the policeman's arm was aimed at that policeman. It was an attempt to get that policeman to desist from the arrest that he was making. In my view, this is as clear a case as we can have of obstructing a *h* police officer in the course of his duty, and the justices came to the right decision. But as always, one finds the justices took a very sensible view of the overall circumstances, and being satisfied of the appellant's overall motive, they gave him an absolute discharge.

For the reasons I have given, I would dismiss this appeal.

McCULLOUGH J. I agree. The submissions on behalf of the appellant, both here and *j* below, are based on what it was submitted were his motives and lack of hostility towards the policeman. Those references to motives and hostility were clearly based on *Willmott v Atack* [1976] 3 All ER 794, [1977] QB 498, which I regard as a difficult case. Willmott had been convicted by the Crown Court, which had been of the opinion that the prosecution need only prove that Willmott interfered deliberately with the action of a

police officer and in so doing, in fact, obstructed the officer (see [1976] 3 All ER 794 at
a 796, [1977] QB 498 at 500). In this the Crown Court clearly misdirected itself, and
accordingly Willmott's conviction was quashed.

I am uncertain what Croom-Johnson J had in mind when he used the word 'hostility'
in the passage cited by Griffiths LJ. Hostility suggests emotion and motive, but motive
and emotion are alike irrelevant in criminal law. What matters is intention, that is what
state of affairs the defendant intended to bring about. What motive he had while so
b intending is irrelevant.

What is meant by an 'intention to obstruct'? I would construe 'wilfully obstructs' as
doing deliberate actions with the intention of bringing about a state of affairs which,
objectively regarded, amount to an obstruction as that phrase was explained by Lord
Parker CJ in *Rice v Connolly* [1966] 2 All ER 649 at 651, [1966] 2 QB 414 at 419, ie
making it more difficult for the police to carry out their duty. The fact that the defendant
c might not himself have called that state of affairs an obstruction is, to my mind,
immaterial. This is not to say that it is enough to do deliberate actions which, in fact,
obstruct; there must be an intention that those actions should result in the further state
of affairs to which I have been referring.

If I may give an example. D interferes while a police officer, P, is arresting X, and
delays the arrest. It is not enough that his deliberate actions in fact delay the arrest. If D
d intends to prevent P from arresting X, then D is guilty because it is his intention to do
that which, objectively regarded, amounts to an obstruction, that is to say, to prevent the
arrest. D's motives for wanting to prevent the arrest are immaterial. He is guilty even
though he feels no hostility to the officer. He is guilty even though he believes the officer
is arresting the wrong man. He is guilty even though he does not appreciate that
interfering with the arrest amounts to what would be regarded objectively as an
e obstruction.

It may very well be that what I have been endeavouring to express would accord with
Croom-Johnson J's opinion. I am not certain that May J in his three paragraph judgment
was adopting what Croom-Johnson J had said about hostility. But even if he was, I think
that what I have said can stand with his judgment. Lord Widgery CJ's judgment is in
two sentences. He did not adopt the reasoning of the other two judges. He merely said
f that the question posed should be answered in the negative. The question is in the form:

> '. . . whether . . . it is sufficient for the Prosecution to prove that the Defendant
> wilfully did an act which obstructed the police officer in the execution of his duty,
> or must the prosecution further prove that . . .'

(See [1976] 3 All ER 794 at 798, [1977] QB 498 at 502.)
g It is quite plain that, in saying that the question must be answered in the negative,
Lord Widgery CJ was referring only to the first part of the question.

The facts found by the Crown Court in *Willmott v Atack* are not easy to reconcile with
one another. Although it is said (see [1976] 3 All ER 794 at 796, [1977] QB 498 at 499)
that Willmott attempted to interfere and in doing so pushed the officer in the throat
while he was holding and restraining the other man, Howe, who was under arrest, the
h court did not see that as an assault (see [1976] 3 All ER 794 at 796, [1977] QB 498 at 500);
and although Willmott's actions were to be found to be deliberate, the court did not
anywhere say in terms that he was trying to prevent the arrest or secure the man's release.
For these reasons it is, in my judgment, impossible to derive much assistance from the
facts of that case.

It is to be noted that in *Green v Moore* [1982] 1 All ER 428 at 433, [1982] QB 1044 at
j 1052 Donaldson LJ in speaking of *Willmott v Atack*, and when comparing the facts of the
case he was considering with *Willmott v Atack*, did not speak in terms of hostility.

When one comes to the facts of this case, all the essentials are present. The appellant
deliberately grabbed the officer. In so doing he intended to intervene on behalf of the
person whom the officer was arresting. He intended to cause the officer to revise his
decision to arrest that man. It is therefore clear that he intended to do that which in fact

amounted to an obstruction of the officer, namely to interfere with his actions in arresting and detaining the man. His motive for intending to interfere in this way is irrelevant. *a* The fact that he may have harboured no feeling of hostility towards the officer is likewise irrelevant. So too, it is irrelevant whether or not he realised that interfering with an arrest was an obstruction as that word is generally understood.

In my judgment this appeal fails.

Appeal dismissed.   *b*

25 *November. The court refused leave to appeal to the House of Lords but certified, under s 1(2) of the Administration of Justice Act 1960, that the following point of law of general public importance was involved in the decision: whether the mens rea required for the offence of obstructing a police officer in the execution of his duty under s 51(3) of the Police Act 1964 to be committed was merely the intent to do a deliberate act with the intent of bringing about a state of* *c* *affairs which viewed objectively amounted to an obstruction of the police.*

Solicitors: *Crossman & Co*, Cambridge (for the appellant); *D M O'Shea* (for the respondent).

Sepala Munasinghe Esq   Barrister.
d

Seven Seas Transportation Ltd v Pacifico Union Marina Corp
The Oceanic Amity
e

QUEEN'S BENCH DIVISION (COMMERCIAL COURT)
STAUGHTON J
10, 11 JUNE 1982

Shipping – Time charter party – Exceptions – Loss or damage arising from negligent navigation *f* *– Vessel chartered for lightening operations – Charterparty purporting to incorporate US Carriage of Goods by Sea Act – US Act exempting owners of chartered vessel from liability for 'loss or damage arising or resulting from . . . neglect . . . in navigation' – Chartered vessel causing damage to charterers' vessel because of negligent navigation – Whether owners of chartered vessel liable for damage – Whether US Act applying to charterparties – Whether US Act only applying in respect of carriage to or from US ports – Whether US Act applying to exempt owners from* *g* *liability for damage – Carriage of Goods by Sea Act 1936 (US), s 4 (2)(a).*

Shipping – Time charterparty – Exceptions – Negligent navigation – Errors of navigation – Charterparty exempting shipowners from liability for 'errors of navigation' – Whether 'errors of navigation' including negligent navigation.

The claimants, who were the owners of a vessel in which they had carried a cargo of grain *h* to a port in India, chartered another vessel owned by the respondents for the purpose of lightening their own vessel, which was too deeply laden to enter port. On three separate occasions during the lightening operations damage was caused to the claimants' vessel as a result of negligent navigation by the crew of the respondents' vessel. Clause 24 of the charterparty under which the respondents' vessel was chartered incorporated the Carriage *j* of Goods by Sea Act 1936 of the United States of America, which by s 4(2)(a)[a] exempted the carrier (the respondents) from liability for 'loss or damage arising or resulting from [the] Act, neglect, or default of . . . the servants of the carrier in the navigation or in the

---

a   Section 4(2), so far as material, is set out at p 677 *a*, post

management of the ship'. Clause 16 of the charterparty further exempted the owners
a from liability for 'errors of Navigation'. Clause 39 imposed an obligation on the
respondents to ensure that the vessel was seaworthy. The claimants contended that they
were entitled to damages arising out of the negligent navigation of the respondents'
vessel. The dispute was referred to a sole arbitrator, who found that, although the
respondents had been negligent, they were exempted from liability by cl 24, which, he
held, validly incorporated s 4(2)(a) of the US Act in the charterparty. He further found
b that cl 39 imposed an absolute obligation of seaworthiness. At the request of both parties
the arbitrator stated a special case seeking the determination of the court on the question
whether the respondents were exempted from liability by cl 24 of the charterparty. The
claimants contended that cl 24 did not exempt the respondents because (i) the US Act
was intended to apply only to bills of lading and not to charterparties, (ii) the US Act was
in conflict with the express terms of the charterparty since it only imposed an obligation
c on the respondents to use due diligence to ensure the vessel was seaworthy whereas cl 39
imposed an absolute obligation as to seaworthiness, (iii) on the true construction of cl 24
the US Act only applied to voyages either to or from the United States under the
charterparty, and (iv) s 4(2)(a) of the US Act did not apply to damage caused to the
claimants' vessel since it only exempted liability for loss of, or damage to, goods conveyed
pursuant to the charterparty.

d

Held – The respondents were not liable for the damage to the claimants' vessel, for the
following reasons—
    (1) Clause 24 of the charterparty was effective in incorporating into the charterparty
the United States Carriage of Goods by Sea Act, which applied notwithstanding that the
Act had not been intended to apply to charterparties. Because of the way the charterparty
e was put together from various different printed forms available, the inconsistency
between cl 39 and the Act did not prevent incorporation, since it was a perfectly proper
and legitimate approach for the court to construe the contract as a whole and to conclude
that some portions were modified or even superseded by others. Furthermore, on its true
construction the US Act as incorporated into the charterparty applied to all voyages under
the charterparty and not just those going to or from the United States (see p 677 *f* to *h*, p
f 678 *b* to *j* and p 686 *a b*, post); *Adamastos Shipping Co Ltd v Anglo-Saxon Petroleum Co Ltd*
[1958] 1 All ER 725 followed.
    (2) On a broad construction of s 4(2)(a) of the US Act as incorporated into the
charterparty the damage to the claimants' vessel had occurred in relation to the loading
of the chartered vessel, and since the loading had been a major part of the contemplated
adventure for which the respondents' vessel had been chartered it was 'loss or damage
g arising or resulting from' the negligent navigation of that vessel. Accordingly s 4(2)(a) of
the US Act applied to exempt the respondents from liability for the physical damage
caused to the claimants' vessel (see p 683 *c* to *g* and p 686 *a b*, post); *Adamastos Shipping Co
Ltd v Anglo-Saxon Petroleum Co Ltd* [1958] 1 All ER 725 and *Australian Oil Refining Pty Ltd
v R W Miller & Co Pty Ltd* [1968] 1 Lloyd's Rep 448 followed.
    Per curiam. A clause in a charterparty exempting a shipowner from liability for loss
h or damage arising out of 'errors of navigation' does not provide exemption in respect of
negligent navigation (see p 685 *h j*, post).

Notes
For exemption of a shipowner from liability for loss or damage, see 43 Halsbury's Laws
j (4th edn) para 760, for immunity of a shipowner in respect of the navigation or
management of a ship, see ibid para 779, and for cases on exemption of a shipowner for
negligence, see 41 Digest (Repl) 303–316, 1137–1206.
    The US Carriage of Goods by Sea Act 1936, s 4(2)(a) corresponds to the Carriage of
Goods by Sea Act 1971, Sch, art IV(2)(a). For art IV(2)(a) of the schedule to the Act, see 41
Halsbury's Statutes (3rd edn) 1323.

Cases referred to in judgment

Adamastos Shipping Co Ltd v Anglo-Saxon Petroleum Co Ltd [1958] 1 All ER 725, [1959] AC 133, [1958] 2 WLR 688, HL; rvsg [1957] 2 All ER 311, [1957] 2 QB 233, [1957] 2 WLR 968, CA; rvsg [1957] 1 All ER 673, [1957] 2 QB 233, [1957] 2 WLR 509, 41 Digest (Repl) 315, 1198.

Australian Oil Refining Pty Ltd v R W Miller & Co Pty Ltd [1968] 1 Lloyd's Rep 448, Aust HC.

Bremer Handelsgesellschaft mbH v Vanden Avenne-Izegem PVBA [1978] 2 Lloyd's Rep 109.

Canada Steamship Lines Ltd v R [1952] 1 All ER 305, [1952] AC 192, PC, 11 Digest (Reissue) 697, * 213

Goulandris Bros Ltd v B Goldman & Sons Ltd [1957] 3 All ER 100, [1958] 1 QB 74, [1957] 2 WLR 596, 41 Digest (Repl) 520, 2946.

Lamport & Holt Lines Ltd v Coubro & Scrutton (M & I) Ltd, The Raphael [1982] 2 Lloyd's Rep 42, CA.

Photo Production Ltd v Securicor Transport Ltd [1980] 1 All ER 556, [1980] AC 827, [1980] 2 WLR 283, HL; rvsg [1978] 3 All ER 146, [1978] 1 WLR 856, CA, Digest (Cont Vol E) 111, 3407a.

Polemis and Furness Withy & Co Ltd, Re [1921] 3 KB 560, [1921] All ER Rep 40, CA, 17 Digest (Reissue) 135, 313.

Renton (G H) & Co Ltd v Palmyra Trading Corp of Panama [1956] 3 All ER 957, [1957] AC 149, [1957] 2 WLR 45, HL, 41 Digest (Repl) 419, 2045.

Smith v South Wales Switchgear Ltd [1978] 1 All ER 18, [1978] 1 WLR 165, HL, 26 Digest (Reissue) 303, 2273.

Special case stated

The claimants, Seven Seas Transportation Ltd, by a time charter dated 26 June 1975 chartered the vessel Oceanic Amity owned by the respondents, Pacifico Union Morina Corp, for the purpose of lightening the claimant's own vessel, the Satya Kailash, which was too deeply laden to enter port at Tuticorin, India. On 7, 12 and 14 July 1975 the vessels were damaged when they came into contact with each other during the lightening operations. Pursuant to an agreement dated 9 March 1977 the parties agreed to refer the dispute over liability to John Franklin Willmer QC as sole arbitrator. The arbitrator held that the respondents were exempted from liability by cl 24, but not by cl 16, of the time charter. At the request of the parties the arbitrator stated a special case for the decision of the High Court pursuant to s 21(1)(a) of the Arbitration Act 1950 for the determination of the question whether on the true construction of the time charterparty the respondents were exempt by reason of the provisions of either cl 16 or cl 24 thereof from liability for physical damage to the claimants' vessel Satya Kailash and consequential loss caused by the negligence of their master in the navigation or management of the Oceanic Amity while coming alongside or departing from the Satya Kailash. The facts are set out in the judgment.

Michael Thomas QC and Belinda Bucknall for the claimants.
Nicholas Phillips QC and Jonathan Sumption for the respondents.

STAUGHTON J. This case arises from an arbitration in which the claimants were Seven Seas Transportation Ltd who were owners of a vessel called Satya Kailash, which had brought a cargo of grain from the United States ports to India. But here they feature as charterers of another vessel, the Oceanic Amity.

The respondents were the owners of that vessel, the Oceanic Amity. The facts, in brief outline, are that the Satya Kailash had loaded this grain in US ports and contracted to carry it to India, but when she arrived off Tuticorin she was too deeply laden to enter the

port. So, on 26 June 1975, the claimants chartered the Oceanic Amity for the express
a purposes of lightening her so that she could enter the port. The charter was for a period
of 20 to 40 days. On 4 July 1975 the Oceanic Amity berthed alongside the Sataya Kailash
(if that is the right expression). Tuticorin, as I was told, is a relatively sheltered anchorage
but there is some swell from time to time and there were occasions when the lightening
operation had necessarily to be interrupted.

On three occasions, which are those with which I am primarily concerned, damage
b occurred to the Satya Kailash by the negligent navigation of those on board the Oceanic
Amity. Those were on 7, 12 and 14 July.

The charterparty had contained provision for arbitration, but that was superseded by
an agreement between the parties which provided that the disputes should be referred to
the sole arbitrament of Mr John Franklin Willmer QC. The arbitration agreement also
provided that there could be an appeal from his decision to an appeal arbitrator appointed
by the senior Lloyd's salvage arbitrator. It also provided, as I understand it, that that right
c of appeal could not be exercised if the arbitrator had stated his award in the form of a
special case. Hence, this matter comes before me in the form of a consultative case. The
arbitrator has stated proposed decisions in the form of a consultative case under s 21(1)(a)
of the Arbitration Act 1950. He does not formally express his own view, but merely
indicates what it would be. Thus, when I have concluded my consideration of this
d matter, subject to any appeal that there may be from my decision, it can go back to the
arbitrator, who, as I understand it, has still to calculate any damages involved; and then,
if either party thinks fit, an appeal lies as to matters of fact and law to an appeal arbitrator.
Whether this is the most economical and swift way of disposing of the matter is a point
which will no doubt emerge one day.

I was given a summary of the arbitrator's provisional conclusions by counsel for the
e claimants, which was as follows. Firstly, he found that there was some damage on 11
July (that is not one of the three incidents I am concerned with). That was caused by
unseaworthiness of the Oceanic Amity. The arbitrator held that there was an absolute
obligation of seaworthiness on the part of the respondents and so the claimants could
recover in respect of that damage. Even if he had not held that there was an absolute
obligation of seaworthiness, he would have held that the respondents had failed to prove
f due diligence to make the Oceanic Amity seaworthy. With that aspect to the dispute I
am not concerned. Secondly, he held that on 7, 12 and 14 July there was damage to the
Satya Kailash caused by the negligent navigation of the master of the Oceanic Amity.
Thirdly, he held that an exception of errors of navigation in the charterparty did not
exempt the respondents from liability for that damage, because in the context the
exemption was not of negligent navigation. Fourthly, he held that the respondents were
g exempt from liability in respect of the incidents of 7, 12 and 14 July, by reason of the
United States Carriage of Goods by Sea Act 1936 incorporated in the charterparty. He
held that that Act applied to the lightening operation and that s 4(2) of the Act excused
the carrier from liability for loss and damage, such as occurred in those three incidents.
Fifthly, he held that the Oceanic Amity was seaworthy in respect of the competence of
her master, notwithstanding these three acts of negligence. Sixthly, he held that in
h respect of another incident on 16 July, when the Oceanic Amity was damaged, and in
respect of which the respondents counterclaimed on the grounds that the place of
discharging was unsafe, the respondents failed. Seventhly, he made findings as to the
damage which occurred on each occasion.

The question in the case which the court is asked to answer is in para 9 of the award:

'Whether, upon the true construction of the time charterparty dated the 26th
j   June, 1975, the Respondents are exempt by reason of the provisions of either clause
16 or clause 24 thereof from liability for physical damage to the Claimants' vessel
"Satya Kailash" and consequential loss caused by the negligence of their master in
the navigation or management of the "Oceanic Amity" while coming alongside or
departing from the "Satya Kailash".'

It is evident that the arbitrator's provisional decision in answer to that question would
be: 'Not exempt by virtue of cl 16 but exempt by virtue of cl 24.'
The charterparty provided, so far as is material:

'That the said Owners agree to let, and the said Charterers agree to hire the said
vessel, from the time of delivery, for about 20/40 days lightening operation in
Charterers' option . . . to be placed at the disposal of the Charterers [by means of]
delivery safe port West Coast India. It is understood Charterers intend to use vessel
to lighten grain from mother ship to Indian ports.'

Clause 16 provided:

'That should the Vessel be lost, money paid in advance and not earned (reckoning
from the date of loss or being last heard of) shall be returned to the Charterers at
once. The act of God, enemies, fire, restraint of Princes, Rulers and People, and all
dangers and accidents of the Seas, Rivers, Machinery, Boilers and Steam Navigation,
and errors of Navigation throughout this Charter Party, always mutually excepted.'

Clause 19 contained the 'New Jason clause', which provided:

'In the event of accident, danger, damage, or disaster, before or after
commencement of the voyage resulting from any cause whatsoever, whether due
to negligence or not, for which, or for the consequences of which, the carrier is not
responsible, by statute, contract, or otherwise, the goods, the shipper and the
consignee, jointly and severally, shall contribute with the carrier in general average
to the payment of any sacrifices, losses, or expenses of a general average nature that
may be made or incurred, and shall pay salvage and special charges incurred in
respect of the goods.'

Clause 24 provided:

'It is also mutually agreed that this Charter is subject to all the terms and
provisions of and all the exemptions from liability contained in the Act of Congress
of the United States approved on the 13th day of February, 1893 and entitled "An
Act relating to Navigation of Vessels, etc," in respect of all cargo shipped under this
charter to or from the United States of America. It is further subject to the following
clauses, both of which are to be included in all bills of lading issued hereunder:

U.S.A Clause Paramount.
This bill of lading shall have effect subject to the provisions of the Carriage of Goods
by Sea Act of the United States, approved April 16, 1936 which shall be deemed to
be incorporated herein, and nothing herein contained shall be deemed a surrender
by the carrier of any of its rights or immunities or an increase of any of its
responsibilities or liabilities under said Act. If any term of this bill of lading be
repugnant to said Act to any extent, such term shall be void to that extent but no
further.'

There is then, in the printed form, a 'Both-to-Blame Collision Clause', which is deleted in
ink and replaced by a 'New Both-to-Blame Collision Clause' elsewhere in the charter, that
is to say in cl 40. Finally, I should read cl 39:

'The vessel on delivery and during Charter Party is classed B.V., fully seaworthy,
ready, clean and suitable to receive and carry food grains. The ship's holds/tweendeck
shall also be free from loose scale.'

Now, the issues before me are four. Firstly, is the Carriage of Goods by Sea Act 1936 of
the United States effectively incorporated in this charterparty? Secondly, is its effect
confined to voyages to or from the United States ports? If so, then it has no effect because
the Oceanic Amity made no voyage to or from a United States port so far as this affair is
concerned, nor was it ever contemplated that she would do so. Thirdly, was the damage
to the Satya Kailash loss or damage within s 4(2) of the United States Carriage of Goods
by Sea Act? That section provides:

'Neither the carrier nor the ship shall be responsible for loss or damage arising or
resulting from—(a) Act, neglect, or default of the master, mariner, pilot, or the
servants of the carrier in the navigation or in the management of the ship . . .'

Fourthly, are the respondents exempted from liability for the damage to the Satya Kailash
by reason of the exception of errors of navigation in cl 16? I deal with those issues in
turn.

1 Incorporation

The United States Carriage of Goods by Sea Act 1936 is designed for bills of lading. By
s 5 it provides, as does the English Act, that it shall not be applicable to charterparties.
Nevertheless, here it is provided of the charterparty: 'It is further subject to the following
clauses both of which are to be included in all bills of lading issued hereunder.'

I have been referred to *Adamastos Shipping Co Ltd v Anglo-Saxon Petroleum Co Ltd* [1958]
1 All ER 725, [1959] AC 133. There the facts were that cl 52 of the charterparty provided:

'It is agreed that the Chamber of Shipping War Risks Clauses, dated April, 1937,
New Jason Clause, Paramount Clause, and Both to Blame Collision Clause, as
attached, are to be incorporated in this charterparty.'

The paramount clause on a typed slip was, like the other clauses named, physically
attached to the charterparty and was in these terms:

'Paramount clause. This bill of lading shall have effect subject to the provisions of
the Carriage of Goods by Sea Act of the United States, approved April 16, 1936,
which shall be deemed to be incorporated herein, and nothing herein contained
shall be deemed a surrender by the carrier of any of its rights or immunities or an
increase of any of its responsibilities or liabilities under said Act. If any term of this
bill of lading be repugnant to said Act to any extent, such term shall be void to that
extent, but no further.'

That is the same as the clause set out in the charterparty in this case.

The House of Lords held unanimously that the Carriage of Goods by Sea Act of the
United States was incorporated in the charterparty in that case. It is right to say that the
incorporation clause in that case was a typed clause; and therefore had received the special
attention of the parties. Here, it is printed in the form of charterparty. That does not
seem to me to be a material distinction in this case. The arbitrator here regarded this as a
stronger case for incorporation than the *Adamastos* case. I agree that, in some degree, it is.
The words in cl 24 'It is further subject to the following clauses, both of which are to be
included in all bills of lading issued hereunder' did not feature in the *Adamastos* case. 'It'
means the charterparty; and, as it seems to me, here the clause says clearly that the
charterparty is to be subject to the United States Carriage of Goods by Sea Act. 'Which',
and that means 'and they, the clauses', are to be also incorporated in bills of lading.
Furthermore, the parties did direct their attention specifically to cl 24 when they struck
out the both-to-blame collision clause. It is difficult to conceive that they can have
overlooked that there was a United States clause paramount or failed to strike that out if
they also wished to do so.

Counsel for the claimants submits that, whatever conclusion one would otherwise
have reached, one must bear in mind cl 39, which, as the arbitrator has held, imposes an
absolute obligation of seaworthiness. I say nothing whatever about whether I agree with
the arbitrator's conclusion on that point because it has not been argued before me; I just
assume it to be correct. Now, counsel for the claimants points out that the United States
Act has only an obligation to exercise due diligence to make the ship seaworthy. He says
that that is the principal feature of the United States Act and that it is evident that the
parties cannot have intended to incorporate the Hague Rules if they reversed the principal
feature of those rules by cl 39. I do not agree that the more limited obligation to use due
diligence to make the ship seaworthy is the principal feature of the Hague Rules. It seems
to me that there are perhaps five principal features: the due diligence obligation; the

obligation properly and carefully to load, stow, carry, keep and care for the goods; the
exemption of act, neglect or default in the navigation or management of the ship; the *a*
one year time limit in art III, r 6; and the package limit in art IV, r 5. I would say that
those would be generally considered to be the principal features of the Hague Rules and
to be of equal importance, although perhaps the package limit features less often in
practice than the other four. But, even if counsel is right, one has to bear in mind the
way these commercial contracts are made. They are not drafted by a single hand as a
coherent whole. The actual contract signed by the parties is, so far as my experience goes, *b*
not considered at the time by a lawyer at all. It is put together from the printed forms
that are available, both the charterparty form and other clauses, together with the parties'
own variations or additions. In those circumstances it is not surprising if one comes on
first a clause such as cl 24, incorporating the United States Carriage of Goods by Sea Act,
and then a clause such as cl 39, modifying either one of the principal provisions of that
Act or the principal provision of that Act. That is a fairly common feature of these *c*
commercial contracts, not only in shipping but in marine insurance also. There, the
parties proceed successively to put in some provisions and then to modify them or take
them out later. As Viscount Simonds said in the *Adamastos* case [1958] 1 All ER 725 at
732, [1959] AC 133 at 155: 'It is obvious that there is much in the Act which in relation
to this charterparty is insensible, or, as I would rather say, inapplicable, and must be
disregarded.' *d*
    It is a perfectly proper and legitimate approach to construe the contract as a whole and
to accept that some portions of it may be modified or even superseded by others. So I
conclude that the United States Carriage of Goods by Sea Act is incorporated.

2 *Does it apply to voyages other than those to or from United States ports?*
    In the *Adamastos* case, by a majority of three to two, the House of Lords held that the *e*
incorporation of the Act there applied to voyages to and from other ports than those in
the United States, or, rather more accurately, to and from all ports including those in the
United States and those elsewhere. Viscount Simonds dealt with the point when he said
([1958] 1 All ER 725 at 732, [1959] AC 133 at 155):

> 'The contract between the parties is of world-wide scope; the area of state
> jurisdiction is necessarily limited, and, because it is limited, the Act is given a *f*
> restricted operation. No reason has been suggested, nor, as far as I am aware, could
> be suggested, why a similar restriction should be imported into the contract. On the
> contrary, to do so would, from the commercial point of view, make nonsense of it.
> I find it easy, therefore, as did the learned judge, to construe this contract as making
> the substituted standard of obligation coterminous with the enterprise.'

It is true that the *Adamastos* case was about a consecutive voyage charter, whereas this is *g*
concerned with a time charter; but I cannot see any relevant distinction there.
    Counsel for the claimants points out that in cl 24 it is expressly mentioned that the
Harter Act (which is the Act of Congress of 13 February 1893) shall apply 'in respect of
all cargo shipped under this charter to or from the United States of America'. He submits
that one carries on that express limitation of the incorporation of the Harter Act into the *h*
next sentence, which incorporates the Carriage of Goods by Sea Act. I am afraid that I
reach the opposite conclusion. I consider that the parties expressly limited the application
of the Harter Act in contrast to the application of the United States Carriage of Goods by
Sea Act.

3 *Loss or damage* *j*
    These words occur on their own in s 4(1) and (2) of the Act without any express
qualification. So, too, do they occur without qualification in s 3(6), which deals with the
time limit. In s 3(8), which, in effect, prevents contracting out of the Act to a limited
extent, the words are 'loss or damage to or in connection with the goods'. In s 4(5), which
deals with package limitation, the words again are 'loss or damage to or in connection

with the goods'. There have been a number of cases considering these words. The first
a was *G H Renton & Co Ltd v Palmyra Trading Corp of Panama* [1956] 3 All ER 957, [1957]
AC 149. That was concerned with the English art III, r 8. The House of Lords there held
that the words 'loss or damage to or in connection with the goods' were not limited to
physical loss and damage, but were wide enough to include financial harm by reason of
the goods being delivered at the wrong destination. Turning to the words 'loss or damage'
on their own, one can say that they will certainly not be narrower than 'loss or damage to
b or in connection with the goods'.

There is some authority for the view that they are not much wider. That is *Goulandris
Bros Ltd v B Goldman & Sons Ltd* [1957] 3 All ER 100, [1958] 1 QB 74, which was
concerned with the English art III, r 6. It was there held that that article was not wide
enough to cover financial loss by reason of the cargo owners having to pay a general
average contribution towards the shipowners' expenditure. Pearson J reached that
c conclusion notwithstanding two factors at least which connected the loss with the goods,
that is to say, firstly, that the shipowners had a lien for it and, secondly, that the amount
of their claim for contribution would be based on the sound arrived value of the goods.
That case was decided before the decision in the *Adamastos* case in the House of Lords.
Counsel for the respondents submits that it cannot stand with it. I do not have to decide
whether he is right about that and I do not do so. What I am concerned with, as was the
d *Adamastos* case, is the meaning of 'loss or damage' in s 4(1) and (2).

Now the 'loss and damage' claimed in the *Adamastos* case seems to have been, at any
rate for the most part, the loss of the right to perform more voyages in the period of the
consecutive voyage charter by reason of the dilatory and negligent manner in which such
voyages as there were came to be performed.

The question for the court, as agreed before Devlin J, at first instance, is set out in
e *Anglo-Saxon Petroleum Co Ltd v Adamastos Shipping Co* Ltd [1957] 1 All ER 673 at 676,
[1957] 2 QB 233 at 247: '(3) Do the words "loss or damage" in s. 4(1) and/or s. (2) of the
Act relate only to physical loss of or damage to goods?' Apparently the view was taken at
that stage that no more definitive question could be answered. Devlin J dealt with the
matter as follows ([1957] 1 All ER 673 at 680, [1957] 2 QB 233 at 253):

> f 'The last question asks whether the words "loss or damage" in s. 4(1) and (2) of the
> Act relate only to physical loss of or damage to goods. The words themselves are not
> qualified or limited by anything in the section. The Act is dealing with
> responsibilities and liabilities under contracts of carriage of goods by sea, and clearly
> such contractual liabilities are not limited to physical damage. A carrier may be
> liable for loss caused to the shipper by delay or misdelivery, even though the goods
> themselves are intact. I can see no reason why the general words "loss or damage"
> g should be limited to physical loss or damage. The only limitation which is, I think,
> to be put on them is that which is to be derived from s. 2 which is headed: "Risks".
> The "loss or damage" must, in my opinion, arise in relation to the "loading,
> handling, stowage, carriage, custody, care, and discharge of such goods", but is
> subject to no other limitation. In *G. H. Renton & Co., Ltd. v. Palmyra Trading Corpn.
> of Panama* the House of Lords held that the words "loss or damage to or in connection
> h with goods" in art. III, r. 8 [of the Hague Rules], were not limited to actual loss of or
> physical damage to the goods; and I should give the same meaning to "in relation
> to" as to "in connection with".'

Then, right at the end of his judgment, the judge went on to consider whether the loss
of voyages claimed would be loss or damage within that test. He said that he was doing
j so as both parties had asked him to express a view on it, although it appears from a
footnote to the report that that may not have been correct (see [1957] 2 QB 233 at 254–
255). What the judge said was that the loss or damage in that case was very remote. He
went on ([1957] 2 QB 233 at 255): 'From what I understand at present of the nature of
the loss or damage claimed, it seems to me to be unlikely that section 4 would apply to
it.'

When the matter came before the House of Lords, three members of the House dealt with the point. In the headnote to the case there it is said [1959] AC 133 at 134–135):   *a*

> 'The words "loss or damage" in section 4 of the Act, relating to the immunity of the carrier, refer not only to physical loss or damage to goods but also covered the charterers' loss in only being able to complete fewer voyages than they would otherwise have done.'

Counsel for the claimants submitted in opening that the headnote there was inaccurate   *b* and that the House reached no decision whether loss of voyages was comprehended within loss or damage in s 4. After having the benefit of hearing counsel for the respondents' submission, he was, I think, prepared to resile from that position and to acknowledge that the House had decided that point; at any rate, I conclude that the House did.

The reason for reaching that conclusion is that a revised question of law appears to   *c* have been prepared for the House of Lords (see [1959] AC 133 at 139–140). At the conclusion of the speech of Viscount Simonds one sees the order proposed in answer to that question of law (see [1958] 1 All ER 725 at 734, [1959] AC 133 at 159). The two other members of the House who dealt with the matter agreed with the question of law proposed from the Woolsack. When one analyses the question of law and the way it was answered, one sees that it comes to this, that the House declared that the shipowners   *d* were exempted from liability for loss or damage of the kind claimed. It is apparent that the kind of loss or damage claimed was loss of voyages.

Now, so much for the decision of the House. I must also pay some attention to their Lordships' reasons.   ·

Viscount Simonds had this to say, dealing with the topic of whether the Hague Rules applied to non-cargo carrying voyages ([1958] 1 All ER 725 at 732, [1959] AC 133 at   *e* 155–156):

> 'I do not want to anticipate what will presently be said about the nature of the loss or damage in respect of which obligations and immunities are created by the Act. I will merely assume that it is not confined to loss or damage to goods but extends also to the loss suffered by the charterers owing to the delay caused by   *f* unseaworthiness, the loss in fact alleged to have been suffered by the charterers in the present case.'

Then he said ([1958] 1 All ER 725 at 733, [1959] AC 133 at 157):

> 'I come now to the question of loss or damage. Owing to the delay caused by the unseaworthiness of the vessel, she was able to complete fewer voyages than she   *g* otherwise would have done within the period of the charter. The charterers, therefore, claimed damages in a very large sum, the claim being for the difference between the charter and market rates of freight on cargo-carrying voyages which might have been performed within the eighteen months if she had been continuously fit for service. I have stated the claim in the words of the learned judge. The question is whether the words "loss or damage" in s. 4(1) or s. 4(2) of the   *h* Act relate only to physical loss of, or damage to, goods. This is a short point on which I can only adopt the reasoning and conclusion of the learned judge. It is perhaps sufficient to say that there is nothing in s. 4(1) or s. 4(2) which expressly limits loss or damage to physical loss or damage to the goods, and that s. 2 does not constrain me to put a narrower meaning on the words.'

At first sight, Viscount Simonds there appears to be confining himself to the question   *j* of whether the words were limited to physical loss and damage. In saying this he accepts the reasoning and conclusion of Devlin J. He evidently accepts that they were not so confined. He also accepts, I think, the importance attached by Devlin J, to s 2 of the United States Act, which provides:

a
'Subject to the provisions of section 6, under every contract of carriage of goods by sea, the carrier in relation to the loading, handling, stowage, carriage, custody, care, and discharge of such goods, shall be subject to the responsibilities and liabilities and entitled to the rights and immunities hereinafter set forth.'

However, I do not think that he can be accepting the conclusion of Devlin J, if conclusion it was, that the loss and damage alleged were not covered by s 4. Indeed, it is evident that he was not accepting that conclusion because of the form of order which was made, as I
b have already observed.

It may well be that counsel for the respondents is right in his submission that the only issue in the Adamastos case in the House of Lords was whether loss or damage was confined to physical loss or damage. It may well be that once it was decided that there was no such restriction then no other point was argued. Lord Keith is more explicit
c ([1958] 1 All ER 725 at 749, [1959] AC 133 at 181):

'As to the nature of the loss or damage for which immunity may be claimed, I see no reason for limiting this to physical loss of or damage to goods. Here, again, the force of the argument for such a limitation stems from the fact that the United States Act applied only to goods carried under bills of lading. Even in such a case it does not follow that loss or damage is limited to physical loss of or damage to goods.
d Section 3(8) shows that the loss or damage contemplated is "loss or damage to or in connexion with the goods", and it has been held in this House that such loss or damage is not limited to physical loss or damage: G. H. Renton & Co., Ltd. v. Palmyra Trading Corpn. of Panama. I proceed, however, on the view that the subject-matter of the contract here was voyages, and loss of voyages naturally falls under the words "loss or damage".'

e
Lord Keith certainly disagrees with the provisional view of Devlin J that art IV did not apply to loss of voyages. He does not expressly apply the s 2 test. He looks to the subject matter of the contract.

Finally, Lord Somervell said ([1958] 1 All ER 725 at 752–753, [1959] AC 133 at 186):

'I agree with the learned judge that "loss or damage" in the Act is not limited to
f physical damage to the goods. I also agree that the loss or damage must arise in relation to the "loading, handling, stowage, carriage, custody, care, and discharge of such goods." The form of the claim here depends, of course, on the fact that the provisions of the Act have been incorporated into a charterparty for successive voyages. Under a contract with a particular shipper later to be evidenced by a bill of lading issued to him or under a "received for shipment" bill of lading, the shipper,
g or prospective shipper, might have a similar kind of claim; if, for example, the shipowner failed to ship the goods and freights had risen. The claim is, in my opinion, in relation to loading and carriage of goods and this point, therefore, also fails.'

Lord Somervell, like Viscount Simonds, expressly agrees with the test of Devlin J based
h on s 2, but, like Lord Keith, expressly finds the loss or damage claimed to be within art IV, rr 1 and 2.

I accept what appears to have been the common view of Devlin J, Viscount Simonds and Lord Somervell, that the loss or damage must, in some way, be in relation to the matters specified in s 2 of the United States Act.

Counsel for the respondents submitted that in some cases that section would be
j entirely displaced in the process of incorporation. But he accepted that it had not been displaced here, or, at any rate, he initially accepted that, although he was later minded to qualify that acceptance.

Before I apply that test to the present case, I must go on to consider the Australian case of Australian Oil Refining Pty Ltd v R W Miller & Co Pty Ltd [1968] 1 Lloyd's Rep 448. On the facts it was much the closest to the present case of any of the authorities cited. The

vessel in that case was chartered to load at a wharf belonging to the charterers. The
charterparty provided by cl 15:

a

'The Owners shall not be responsible for loss or damage arising or resulting from
... Act, Neglect or Default of the Master, mariner, pilot or the servants of the
Owners in the navigation or in the management of the vessel.'

Clause 30 provided:

'Whenever the vessel is about to proceed to a berth at the Charterer's wharf or   b
submarine terminal in Botany Bay and notwithstanding anything to the contrary
contained in this Charter Party the Owners shall instruct the Master of the ship to
engage a pilot ... for the purpose of directing or advising the Master as to such
berthing and the Charterers shall pay the charges of such pilot.'

Then cl 33 incorporated the Hague Rules.

c

It will be observed that cl 15 is word for word lifted from art IV(2)(a) of the Hague
Rules. It will also be observed that it was plainly contemplated by the charterparty that
the vessel would load at the charterer's wharf. She did that and, in the process of doing
so, collided with it and caused damage to it; and the action was brought to recover
compensation in respect of that damage.

Macfarlan J, at first instance, held, or else it was conceded, that art IV(2)(a) would not   d
cover loss or damage to the charterer's wharf. He held that cl 15 (which used the same
words) likewise did not cover damage to the charterer's wharf. So, the owners were not
protected by it. His decision was reversed by a majority of three to two in the High Court
of Australia. The reasoning there was that, whilst art IV(2)(a) would not cover damage to
the charterer's wharf, cl 15 did, in the particular context of this charterparty.

One can see from the judgment of Owen J that there was no issue as to the meaning of   e
art IV(2)(a). He says (at 456):

'It is conceded that the "loss or damage" of which r. 2 speaks is limited to loss or
damage "in relation to the loading, handling, stowage, carriage, custody, care and
discharge" of the goods the subject of the contract of carriage contained in the
charter-party: *Adamastos Shipping Company, Ltd. v. Anglo-Saxon Petroleum Company
Ltd.*, and no suggestion has been made that in the present case any of the provisions   f
of Art. IV afford an answer to the plaintiff's claim.'

Barwick CJ says this (at 452):

'In this case, in my opinion, the limitation of the generality of the expression "loss
or damage" in Clause 15 must similarly be found in the relationship of the parties
and the nature and extent of the rights and obligations exacted and given by each to   g
the other rather than in the attribution to them of an intention to use the expression
in their contract regulating their mutual rights and obligations in a sense which is
traditionally appropriate to the more limited relationship and to the more limited
contractual obligation.'

Kitto J says (at 453):

h

'If it were not for the presence of Clause 10 and Clause 30 in the charter-party and
the fact that under Clause 10 the respondent as charterer had indicated its wharf in
Botany Bay as the place where the cargo was to be loaded, I should have held that
the application of Clause 15 was limited to loss or damage to the cargo. But this
would have been because the stipulation in Clause 15 that the owners should not be   j
responsible for loss or damage, though not explicitly limited to loss or damage
suffered by the charterers in respect of any particular property, must have been
construed as referring only to loss or damage in respect of property of the charterers
which the contract envisaged as involved in the performance of the contract on the
part of the shipowners, and the only such property would have been the cargo of
oil.'

However, as the contract envisaged the use of the charterer's wharf, then cl 15, likewise,
he held, included damage to the charterer's wharf in matters which it covered.
Windeyer J dissented, and his judgment is interesting because of some observations he
makes on the general position (at 455):

> 'Do the words "loss or damage" in Clause 15 mean that the appellant was to be
> absolved from all liability for damages of any kind, and howsoever arising, which
> its vessel, or its servants or agents, should cause to the respondent when carrying out
> or attempting to carry out the contract? If the words "loss or damage" be quite
> unconfined, then presumably they would extend to a case in which the shipowner's
> vessel collided on the high seas with another ship or boat belonging to the charterer
> or carrying cargo for the charterer, thereby causing the charterer pecuniary loss or
> damage.'

And then he gives other examples.

Now, I entirely accept that, in the ordinary way, art IV(2)(a) is not intended to deal
with casual encounters between the shipowner's ship and property of the charterers
wherever it may be found in the world; but I also respectfully accept and adopt the
majority decision in that case, which is that, in construing the words of cl 15, it was
legitimate and proper to take into account the nature of the adventure contemplated as
disclosed by the charterparty.

It seems to me that these two cases, the *Adamastos* case and the *Australian Oil Co* case,
provide two slightly different routes to the same conclusion.

The route taken by the House of Lords in the *Adamastos* case must have been to give a
broad construction to the limiting words in s 2, 'in relation to the loading, handling,
stowage, carriage, custody, care, and discharge of goods', in the light of the contemplated
adventure.

The route taken by the High Court of Australia in the *Australian Oil Co* case (where it
was conceded that a narrow construction should be placed on art IV(2)(a), and, in any
event, it did not matter) was to give a broad construction to cl 15, the words specially
incorporated in that charter, again in the light of the contemplated adventure.

By those two tests I conclude that the loss or damage in this case was within art IV(2)(a).
It was, on a broad construction, in relation to the loading of the vessel. It all occurred
while the loading was in process, or very nearly so, when the vessel was either arriving to
load or departing from loading. It was all a major part of the contemplated adventure. I
therefore hold, in agreement with the arbitrator, that the words 'loss or damage' in art
IV(2)(a) cover the damage to the claimants' vessel in this case.

4 Errors in navigation

Strictly speaking, this point does not arise as I have already found one provision in the
charterparty which exempts the shipowners. However, I ought to deal with it as it was
fully argued before me and the case may go elsewhere. It must be dealt with on the
assumption, because only then does it arise, that the respondents are not protected by art
IV(2)(a). On that hypothesis there is a certain irony in the fact that the point has to be
considered at all. Most bills of lading and many charterparties contain, as this one does,
an old-fashioned list of exemptions which, in the ordinary way, one does not even bother
to read in the small print as soon as one has found that the Hague Rules are incorporated.
The reason for that is that in the ordinary way the Hague Rules, by art III, r 8, will render
invalid any attempt to rely on wider exceptions than those which they provide. Article
III, r 8 only invalidates any clause, covenant or agreement relieving the carrier or the ship
from liability for loss or damage to or in connection with the goods. On the hypothesis
in which I consider this question, that is to say that art IV(2)(a) is *not* a defence because
the loss or damage which it refers to did not relate to the goods, then equally art III, r 8
would not render the other exceptions immaterial.

Counsel for the respondents has observed, and established, that an exemption of
negligent navigation was in common use, both by private contract and by the Harter
Act, in the year 1913, when this form of charter was first brought into use. However,

what it refers to is not negligent navigation but errors in navigation. Counsel for the claimants submits that that does not apply to negligent errors because it does not say so. *a* Counsel for the respondents concedes that an error in navigation *may* be either negligent or without negligence, although he says that the former occur far more commonly than the latter, at any rate with today's navigational aids.

So the basis of counsel for the claimants' argument is made out that these words are capable of referring both to negligent and non-negligent errors, and do not necessarily, of themselves, point only to negligent errors.   *b*

Next, counsel for the claimants referred to Re Polemis and Furness Withy & Co Ltd [1921] 3 KB 560, [1921] All ER Rep 40. That was a case of an exemption of fire. The word 'fire' is likewise capable of covering both an innocent fire and a negligent fire. A strong Court of Appeal consisting of Bankes, Warrington and Scrutton LJJ, held unanimously and in plain terms that as the clause did not refer to negligent fire it was no protection where a fire had been occasioned by negligence. If that is still the law, then *c* the answer would be plain and simple in the present case. But the law on exemption clauses has not stood still. Until recently it was set out in Smith v South Wales Switchgear Co Ltd [1978] 1 All ER 18 at 30, [1978] 1 WLR 165 at 178, in particular where Lord Keith quotes three propositions set out by the Privy Council in Canada Steamship Lines Ltd v R [1952] 1 All ER 305 at 310, [1952] AC 192 at 208:

> '(i) If the clause contains language which expressly exempts the person in whose *d* favour it is made (hereafter called "the proferens") from the consequence of the negligence of his own servants, effect must be given to that provision . . . (ii) If there is no express reference to negligence, the court must consider whether the words are wide enough, in their ordinary meaning, to cover negligence on the part of the servants of the proferens. If a doubt arises at this point, it must be resolved against the proferens . . . (iii) If the words used are wide enough for the above purpose, the *e* court must then consider whether "the head of damage may be based on some ground other than that of negligence" . . . The "other ground" must not be so fanciful or remote that the proferens cannot be supposed to have desired protection against it . . .'

Am I then to inquire whether a shipowner, under this form of charter, would be liable *f* for an error of navigation in the absence of negligence? If I have to do so, the answer is, I am told, by no means clear, although the extent of the argument is indicated only by counsel for the respondents saying that it is dealt with in Scrutton on Charterparties (18th edn, 1974) pp 199–207.

I do not consider that I do have to ask that question in the present case. Counsel for the respondents referred me to a recent decision of the Court of Appeal, Lamport & Holt Lines *g* Ltd v Coubro & Scrutton (M & I) Ltd, The Raphael [1982] 2 Lloyd's Rep 42. In that case all three members of the court said that the passage I have quoted from Smith v South Wales Switchgear Co Ltd and, before that, from Canada Steamship Lines Ltd v R lays down only guidelines and is not a statute. Thus, Donaldson LJ said (at 45): 'On the other hand, it would be a fatal error to regard them as if they were the words of a codifying and, still worse an amending, statute.' May LJ said (at 48):   *h*

> 'They are and were only intended to be guidelines, not words in a statute, and at the end of the day the duty of the court is just to construe the relevant clause. With Lord Justice Donaldson, I agree with this approach.'

And (at 49):   *j*

> 'Such an approach indeed underlines the fact that the exercise upon which the Court is engaged in these cases is one of construction, that it is one of deciding what the parties meant or must be deemed to have meant by the words they used; the guidelines or tests which are referred to in the many authorities are only to be used by the courts as aids to the successful and correct solution of such exercise.'

Stephenson LJ said (at 51):

> '. . . they are not provisions in a statute but aids to interpretation, and the Court's duty is always to construe the clause in question to see what it means, what it plainly means to any ordinarily literate and sensible person . . . There is no artificial rule to compel the Court either to construe a clause as covering negligence because it has no other subject matter or as not covering negligence because it might have a subject matter too improbable and far-fetched to have been contemplated and covered.'

Directing myself in accordance with those statements of the law I turn again to cl 16 in the charterparty. The exemptions to which it refers are:

> 'The act of God, enemies, fire, restraint of Princes, Rulers and People, and all dangers and accidents of the Seas, Rivers, Machinery, Boilers and Steam Navigation, and errors of Navigation throughout this Charter Party.'

The first thing that strikes one is that many, if not all, of the listed perils assume that the shipowner would be liable, without negligence. That seems to be the theory of the clause. It may be that when this clause was first drafted, the draftsman decided against perusing the appropriate equivalent of *Scrutton on Charterparties* (18th edn, 1974) pp 199–207, but instead did assume that a shipowner would be liable without negligence. At any rate, it seems to me that the clause is based on the assumption that there could be such liability and sets out to deal with it. If I am wrong about that, it is, at any rate, a possible construction and it is for the party who seeks to rely on an exemption clause to produce clear wording to protect himself: see *Photo Production Ltd v Securicor Transport Ltd* [1980] 1 All ER 556 at 567, [1980] AC 827 at 850 per Lord Diplock.

So I conclude that cl 16 would not, by itself, be protection to the respondents. In doing so, I agree with the reasoning of the arbitrator in para 10 of his award on what he describes as 'the narrower context of the clause'. He says:

> 'Its narrower context is that of a clause containing a whole list of matters (which I have not thought it necessary fully to set out) all of which are matters arising without fault on the part of the Owners. Reading the clause as a whole, it is not one concerned to deal with fault.'

I should mention three other points made by counsel for the claimants. If sound, they would have bolstered the conclusion which I have reached on the construction of the clause, and there is a temptation to use them for that purpose; but in my judgment they do not have that effect. The first is cl 19 of the charterparty, which expressly uses the words 'whether due to negligence or not'. That, he says, shows that the draftsman knew how to exempt negligence when he wanted to. The trouble with that argument is that, as everybody knows, the new Jason clause was lifted from elsewhere when it was put into this charterparty. It is absurd to suppose that this charterparty had one draftsman, when everybody knows that it did not. The situation is similar to that described by Lord Wilberforce in *Bremer Handelsgesellschaft mbH v Vanden Avenne-Izegem PVBA* [1978] 2 Lloyd's Rep 109 at 113 when he referred to the GAFTA Form 100 as having 'the appearance of a collage of clauses separately drafted'.

Next, counsel for the claimants says that error of navigation is similar to error of judgment, and therefore necessarily means non-negligent error. I do not consider that that conclusion is correct. The phrase 'error of judgment' has come to be a term of art in the law, especially reserved for non-negligent mistakes. Merely because the errors of navigators are described as 'errors of navigation' it does not seem to me to follow that one should give that phrase too a similar meaning.

Thirdly, counsel for the claimants observes that the Harter Act (which is set out in *Carver's Carriage by Sea* (12th edn, 1971) vol 1, para 240, pp 209–210) refers to 'faults or errors in navigation'. Therefore, he submits, one of the United States statutes, expressly referred to in this charterparty itself, distinguishes between fault on the one hand, and error on the other, in navigation. I must say that one has to dredge rather far down in

the bucket to find much weight in that point. Maybe it is of some slight help in the
construction of cl 16 of this charterparty, but I would say very slight indeed. However,
for the reasons I have already given, I agree with the arbitrator's conclusion that cl 16 by
itself would not be a defence for the respondents in this case.

I therefore answer the question of law in para 9 of the award as follows: Yes, by reason
of cl 24, although not by reason of cl 16.

Question asked in case stated answered in the affirmative. Leave to appeal granted.

Solicitors: *Richards Butler & Co* (for the claimants); *Ince & Co* (for the respondents).

K Mydeen Esq   Barrister.

Industrie Chimiche Italia Centrale SpA v Nea Ninemia Shipping Co SA

The Emmanuel C

QUEEN'S BENCH DIVISION (COMMERCIAL COURT)
BINGHAM J
8, 11 NOVEMBER 1982

*Shipping – Time charterparty – Exceptions – Negligent navigation – Errors of navigation –
Charterparty exempting shipowners from liability for 'errors of navigation' – Whether 'errors of
navigation' including negligent navigation.*

By a time charter dated 1 December 1977 in the New York Produce Exchange form with
additions and deletions, the owners chartered a vessel to the charterers for one transatlantic
round trip via the St Lawrence. Under the terms of the charterparty the vessel was not
demised to the charterers and the owners remained responsible for its navigation. The
charterparty further provided, by cl 16, that if the vessel was lost, hire already paid in
advance by the charterers was to be returned to them, 'all dangers and accidents of the
Seas . . . and errors of Navigation . . . always mutually excepted'. On 20 December the
vessel grounded in the St Lawrence River and thereafter became a constructive loss. The
charterers claimed damages (agreed to amount to $US120,000) from the owners but the
owners refused to meet the claim. The dispute was referred to arbitration in London as
provided by the charterparty. The arbitrator found that the grounding was caused by the
negligence, ie the negligent navigation, of those on board the vessel and held that cl 16
did not exempt the owners from the consequences of the negligent navigation. On
appeal by way of a special case stated by the arbitrator for the decision of the High Court,
the owners contended (i) that the expression 'errors of navigation' in cl 16 included
negligent errors of navigation, (ii) that it was normally assumed in shipping circles that a
clause such as cl 16 exempted shipowners from liability for negligent navigation, and
(iii) that non-negligent errors of navigation fell within 'dangers and accidents of the Seas'
and therefore if 'errors of navigation' did not include negligent navigation the expression
was otiose.

Held – The owners were liable for the consequences of the negligent navigation and the
arbitrator's award to that effect would be upheld, for the following reasons—
(1) Clause 16 of the charterparty was to be construed by applying the principle that it
was inherently improbable that one party to a contract should intend to absolve the other
party from the consequences of the latter's own negligence. Accordingly, cl 16 was

presumed not to exempt the owners from the consequences of their negligent navigation
a unless the contrary was expressed or implied. Furthermore, cl 16 was to be construed
according to what a reasonably informed member of shipping circles would understand
or intend it to mean (see p 689 *f* to *j* and p 692 *c*, post); dictum of May LJ in *Lamport &*
Holt Lines Ltd v Coubro & Scrutton (M *& I*) *Ltd, The Raphael* [1982] 2 Lloyd's Rep at 49–50
applied.

(2) On the true construction of cl 16 of the charterparty 'errors of navigation' did not
b include negligent errors of navigation, because (a) the clause contained no express
reference to negligence, nor any synonym for it, whereas it was not unusual for
exemption clauses in the shipping commercial world to expressly exclude liability for
negligence, (b) the term 'error' was not primarily suggestive of negligence, and (c) none
of the events specified in cl 16 was clearly indicative of negligence whereas some were
clearly inconsistent with negligence. Accordingly, cl 16 did not operate to exempt the
c owners from liability (see p 690 *j* to p 691 *d* and *h* to p 692 *c*, post); *Re Polemis and Furness*
Withy & Co Ltd [1921] All ER Rep 40, *Canada Steamship Lines Ltd v R* [1952] 1 All ER 305,
Lamport & Holt Lines Ltd v Coubro & Scrutton (M *& I*) *Ltd, The Raphael* [1982] 2 Lloyd's
Rep 42 and *Seven Seas Transportation Ltd v Pacifico Union Marina Corp, The Oceanic Amity*
[1983] 1 All ER 672 considered.

d **Notes**
For immunity of a shipowner in respect of the navigation or management of a ship, see
42 Halsbury's Laws (4th edn) para 779, and for cases on exemption of a shipowner for
negligence, see 41 Digest (Repl) 303–316, 1137–1206.

Cases referred to in judgment
e *Alderslade v Hendon Laundry Ltd* [1945] 1 All ER 244, [1945] KB 189, 3 Digest (Reissue)
    469, 3116.
Burma, The (1911) 187 F 94.
Canada Steamship Lines Ltd v R [1952] 1 All ER 305, [1952] AC 192, PC, 11 Digest (Reissue)
    697, *213.
Dobell (G E) *& Co v Steamship Rossmore Co Ltd* [1895] 2 QB 408, [1895–9] All ER Rep 885,
f   CA, 41 Digest (Repl) 307, 1159.
Hollier v Rambler Motors (AMC) *Ltd* [1972] 1 All ER 399, [1972] 2 QB 71, [1972] 2 WLR
    401, CA, 3 Digest (Reissue) 439, 2971.
Lamport & Holt Lines Ltd v Coubro & Scrutton (M *& I*) *Ltd, The Raphael* [1982] 2 Lloyd's
    Rep 42, CA.
Polemis and Furness Withy & Co Ltd, Re [1921] 3 KB 560, [1921] All ER Rep 40, CA, 36(1)
g   Digest (Reissue) 64, 232.
Price & Co v Union Lighterage Co [1904] 1 KB 412, [1904–7] All ER Rep 227, 8(1) Digest
    (Reissue) 51, 292.
Rutter v Palmer [1922] 2 KB 87, [1922] All ER Rep 367, 3 Digest (Reissue) 438, 2968.
Seven Seas Transportation Ltd v Pacifico Union Marina Corp, The Oceanic Amity [1983] 1 All
    ER 672.
h *Smith v South Wales Switchgear Co Ltd* [1978] 1 All ER 18, [1978] 1 WLR 165, HL, Digest
    (Cont Vol E) 240, 1871b.

Special case stated
Nea Ninemia Shipping Co SA (the owners) by a time charter dated 1 December 1977
j chartered the vessel the Emmanuel C to Industrie Chimiche Italia Centrale SpA (the
charterers) for one transatlantic round trip via the St Lawrence. On 20 December the
vessel grounded in the St Lawrence River and thereafter became a constructive loss. The
charterers claimed damages in respect of overpaid hire and bunkers and in respect of
additional expenses incurred in chartering a substitute vessel. The owners counterclaimed
for damages for loss of the vessel. At the hearing of the arbitration, the sole arbitrator,
Mr Donald Davies, made an interim order on 27 November 1981 in favour of the
charterers. By a final award dated 26 May 1982 in the form of a special case for the

decision of the High Court the arbitrator awarded, subject to the court's decision, that the grounding of the vessel was caused by the negligence of those on board the vessel and   *a* that in consequence the owners were liable to the charterers for damages agreed at $US120,000. The question of law raised in the special case was whether on the facts found and on the true construction of the charterparty the owners were liable to the charterers in damages for breach of the charterparty and, if not, whether the charterers were entitled to recover from the owners any and if so what sum consequent on the frustration of the charterparty. The facts are set out in the judgment.   *b*

Stewart Boyd QC for the owners.
Martin Moore-Bick for the charterers.

                                                     Cur adv vult

  c

11 November. The following judgment was delivered.

BINGHAM J. This is an award in the form of a special case stated for the opinion of the court by Mr Donald Davies as sole arbitrator in an arbitration between Industrie Chimiche Italia Centrale SpA as charterers and Nea Ninemia Shipping Co SA as owners of a vessel named the Emmanuel C. The case raises one short but important point   *d* concerning the effect of an exemption clause: does it protect the owners against liability for negligent errors of navigation or only where the errors occur without negligence on the part of the owners, their servants or agents?

The vessel grounded in the St Lawrence River at 1140 hrs on 20 December 1977 and thereafter became a constructive total loss. The arbitrator has found that the grounding was caused by the negligence (meaning the negligent navigation) of those on the vessel.   *e* The effect of the clause is thus crucial. If, as the arbitrator thought, the clause does not protect the owners against liability for negligent errors of navigation, it is agreed that the charterers are entitled to damages of $US120,000. If, contrary to his view, the owners are protected, the charterparty is to be treated as frustrated, and the charterers are then entitled to the reduced sum of $US26,632·69.

The charterparty was dated 1 December 1977 and was on the New York Produce   *f* Exchange form with additions and deletions. It was for one transatlantic round trip via the St Lawrence. The clauses of importance for present purposes are these:

> '16. That should the Vessel be lost, money paid in advance and not earned (reckoning from the date of loss or being last heard of) shall be returned to the Charterers at once. The act of God, enemies, fire, restraint of Princes, Rulers and People, and all dangers and accidents of the Seas, Rivers, Machinery, Boilers and   *g* Steam Navigation, and errors of Navigation throughout this Charter Party, always mutually excepted . . .
>
> 24. It is also mutually agreed that this Charter is subject to all the terms and provisions of and all the exemptions from liability contained in the Act of Congress of the United States approved on the 13th day of February, 1893, and entitled "An Act relating to Navigation of Vessels, etc.," in respect of all cargo shipped under this   *h* charter to or from the United States of America . . .
>
> 26. Nothing herein stated is to be construed as a demise of the vessel to the Time Charterers. The owners to remain responsible for the navigation of the vessel, acts of pilots and tugboats, insurance, crew, and all other matters, same as when trading for their own account.'

As printed, the charter contained a USA Clause Paramount incorporating the United   *j* States Carriage of Goods by Sea Act 1936, but this was deleted and replaced by the provision: 'All Bills of Lading are further subject to United States Clause Paramount.'

The correct approach of the court to exemption clauses such as cl 16 has been the subject of authoritative guidance in a series of cases which includes *Price & Co v Union*

Lighterage Co [1904] 1 KB 412, [1904–7] All ER Rep 227, *Rutter v Palmer* [1922] 2 KB 87,
a [1922] All ER Rep 367, *Alderslade v Hendon Laundry Ltd* [1945] 1 All ER 244, [1945] KB
189, *Canada Steamship Lines Ltd v R* [1952] 1 All ER 305, [1952] AC 192, *Hollier v Rambler
Motors (AMC) Ltd* [1972] 1 All ER 399, [1972] 2 QB 71, *Smith v South Wales Switchgear Co
Ltd* [1978] 1 All ER 18, [1978] 1 WLR 165 and *Lamport & Holt Lines Ltd v Coubro &
Scrutton (M & I) Ltd, The Raphael* [1982] 2 Lloyd's Rep 42. I need not make lengthy
citations from these authorities because the last of them contains a most helpful
b distillation of the relevant principles (at 44–45, 47–49, 50–51 per Donaldson, May and
Stephenson LJJ). I would simply cite one paragraph from the judgment of May LJ, which
provides a very succinct summary of certain important points (at 49–50):

'Thus, if an exemption clause of the kind we are considering excludes liability for
negligence expressly, then the Courts will give effect to the exemption. If it does
not do so expressly, but its wording is clear and wide enough to do so by implication,
c then the question becomes whether the contracting parties so intended. If the only
head of liability upon which the clause can bite in the circumstances of a given case
is negligence, and the parties did or must be deemed to have applied their minds to
this eventuality, then clearly it is not difficult for a Court to hold that this was what
the parties intended—that this is its proper construction. Indeed, to hold otherwise
would be contrary to commonsense. On the other hand if there is a head of liability
d upon which the clause could bite in addition to negligence then, because it is more
unlikely than not that a party will be ready to excuse his other contracting party
from the consequences of the latter's negligence, the clause will generally be
construed as not covering negligence. If the parties did or must be deemed to have
applied their minds to the potential alternative head of liability at the time the
contract was made then, in the absence of any express reference to negligence, the
e Courts can sensibly only conclude that the relevant clause was not intended to cover
negligence and will refuse so to construe it. In other words, the Court asks itself
what in all the relevant circumstances the parties intended the alleged exemption
clause to mean.'

From the cases the following general conclusions in my opinion emerge.
f   1. Since it is inherently improbable that one party to a contract should intend to
absolve the other party from the consequences of the latter's own negligence, the court
will presume a clause not to have that effect unless the contrary is plainly shown by clear
words or by implication.
2. Statements made in one case may assist in deciding another but cannot literally
determine the decision, since in each case the task is one of construction to ascertain the
g actual or imputed intention of the parties to the contract in question.
3. In carrying out that task of construction the court should not treat commercial
parties as if they were law students (see *The Raphael* [1982] 2 Lloyd's Rep 42 at 46 per
Donaldson LJ). Often the test of what would be understood or intended by the ordinarily
literate and sensible person will be appropriate (see *Hollier's* case [1972] 1 All ER 399 at
404, [1972] 2 QB 71 at 78 per Salmon LJ and *The Raphael* [1982] 2 Lloyd's Rep 42 at 51
h per Stephenson LJ). Picking up these references counsel for the owners suggested that
the court should adopt the standard of the intelligent layman. I accept that this will in
many cases be an appropriate standard. But where a contract is made in a specialised
business by two practitioners in that business I think a somewhat different standard is
indicated, approximating to that of the reasonably informed practitioner in the field in
question.
j   4. Where the words used are wide enough to cover negligent as well as non-negligent
acts or omissions but practically speaking the clause lacks substance if it is not construed
as covering negligent acts or omissions, the court may in the circumstances of a given
case infer that the parties intended the clause to cover negligence (as in *The Raphael*) but
it need not do so (see *Hollier's* case). All depends on the proper inference to be drawn in
the instant case.

Counsel for the owners contended that cl 16 was effective to protect the owners against liability for negligence on a number of grounds of which the most important were these. a

(1) The expression 'errors of navigation' is plainly wide enough to include negligent errors. The intelligent layman would think of 'errors' primarily as negligent errors. The flavour of negligence was reflected in the *Shorter Oxford English Dictionary* definition: 'Something incorrectly done through ignorance or inadvertence; a mistake.' It was a legal refinement to divide errors into those which were negligent and those which were not, and even lawyers tended to classify the latter as errors of judgment (although even b those could be negligent).

(2) It was the normal working assumption in shipping circles that liability for negligent navigation would be excepted. The exception was contained in the Harter Act, s 3 (*G E Dobell & Co v Steamship Rossmore Co Ltd* [1895] 2 QB 408 at 410, [1895–9] All ER Rep 885 at 886), which was incorporated in this charterparty, and also in the Hague Rules which, via the USA Clause Paramount and the United States Carriage of Goods by c Sea Act 1936, were incorporated in the charterparty form as printed. Although the Harter Act did not apply to the voyage here in question, which was to Canada, and the charterparty form was amended so as to apply the USA Clause Paramount to the bills of lading but not the charterparty, it could not be supposed that by that amendment the parties intended to give 'errors of navigation' a more extended meaning than would have been sensible where the Harter Act applied or when the incorporation of the USA Clause d Paramount remained unamended.

(3) Unless 'errors of navigation' were construed to include negligent errors the reference lacked substance because it was very hard to conceive of an error of navigation which was not negligent and which would not be covered by 'dangers and accidents of the Seas'. There was, it was true, an abstruse and academic legal argument whether the liability of a carrier by sea was not analogous to that of a common carrier by land, making e him liable for all non- or misperformance nót attributable to act of God, act of the Queen's enemies or inherent vice (see *Scrutton on Charterparties* (18th edn, 1974) p 198; *Carver's Carriage by Sea* (12th edn, 1971) vol 1, para 4) but that was not something which the intelligent layman could credibly be thought to have had in mind. Counsel for the owners reserved the right to argue hereafter that the position of a carrier by sea was not in any event analogous to that of a common carrier. f

(4) The provenance and content of cl 16 made it inappropriate to embark on detailed legal analysis of it. There was no common theme to be discerned in the clause and no internal consistency. It contained exceptions for the act of God and enemies, which were unnecessary even if the common carrier analogy were valid; it would be odd if there were no exception for negligent errors of navigation, the more so since this was the one item (as compared, for example, with fire or accident) which specified not merely a result g but carried one into the state of mind of the owner in pursuit of the cause.

(5) When the United State Court of Appeals for the Second Circuit had considered the clause, it had been held that, although 'dangers and accidents' could not in the absence of express provision to the contrary be held to include the results of negligence, the conclusion might have been different if the expression 'errors of steam navigation' had been used: see *The Burma* (1911) 187 F 94 at 97. h

(6) Although Staughton J in *Seven Seas Transportation Ltd v Pacifico Union Marina Corp, The Oceanic Amity* [1983] 1 All ER 672 had held that cl 16 did not confer exemption in respect of negligent errors of navigation, he showed excessive subtlety in assuming that there could be liability without negligence and moreover failed to follow the three-stage process of reasoning recommended by the Privy Council in *Canada Steamship Lines Ltd v R* [1952] 1 All ER 305 at 310, [1952] AC 192 at 208. In any event, a number of the j arguments addressed to me had not been addressed to Staughton J.

It is plain from this summary that counsel for the owners mounted an extremely formidable argument. I embark on my consideration of it from common ground. Clause 16 contains no express reference to negligence, and no synonym for negligence. This is not, of course, fatal to the owners' argument; if it were, there would have been no need a for the *Canada Steamship* formulation, and *The Raphael* could not have been decided as it was. But it does mean that the owners' task thereafter is a heavy one. This is the more so where there is not, as there is in some fields, a reluctance to describe negligence as such, and I bear in mind the arbitrator's observation in his award:

b 'In the shipping commercial world it is not unusual to see exemption clauses which clearly expressly exclude liability for negligence so that, in general, there is, and never has been, any reluctance to use appropriate language to make it abundantly clear that negligence is being excepted.'

I agree, and counsel for the charterers did not argue to the contrary, that 'error' in its ordinary connotation may mean a negligent as well as a non-negligent error. I do not, however, think that the word 'error' is primarily suggestive of negligence. The arbitrator thought it to be neutral, and so do I. The *Oxford English Dictionary* adds to the definition
c quoted above, after 'mistake', the additional words 'e.g. in calculation, judgement, speech, writing, action, etc.', and this reflects what I take to be the common belief, that errors in different spheres may but need not be negligent. If anything I think the intelligent layman is less ready than the lawyer to regard an error as likely to be negligent because he tends to regard negligence as something more heinous and unforgivable than the lawyer, who knows how easily it can on occasions occur and (if he is honest) how
d universally.

It is, of course, true that in the printed form of this charterparty the Harter Act (where applicable) and the Hague Rules were incorporated, both providing protection against negligent errors of navigation. I do not, however, think that one can infer from this that cl 16 was intended to have the same effect, nor can one ignore the fact that the form was amended to make the Hague Rules inapplicable to this charterparty. The Harter Act did
e not apply anyway. It may of course be that in making the amendment the parties had some other point in mind altogether, but I think more importance is to be attached to the fact of the amendment than to speculation concerning the reason for it.

Counsel for the charterers did not suggest examples of errors of navigation which would not be covered by 'dangers and accidents of the Seas', but instead rested his case that the reference did not lack substance if it were read as excluding negligent errors of
f navigation on the unresolved issue as to the extent of the sea carrier's common law liability. If the intelligent layman had never heard of that controversy, he submitted, the reasonably informed shipping man probably had, at least sufficiently to entertain doubt as to a carrier's liability, since those engaged in shipping tended to have a greater knowledge of legal niceties than members of most other professions. I accept this submission. It matters not that a carrier might, if the issue were fully investigated, be
g held to have no liability for errors of navigation unless they were negligent; the important question is whether protection against the possibility of such liability could reasonably have been sought, and I conclude that it could.

It would undoubtedly be wrong to approach this charterparty form on the assumption that it represents the work of a single all-seeing creator. It is notorious that such forms contain clauses drawn from different sources, and inserted at different times, sometimes
h to meet special problems. Users of the form, moreover, do not take it as it stands but vary, delete and add to its contents freely. Counsel for the owners is accordingly right to warn against close textual analysis of cl 16, and indeed the clause raises problems for each of the parties. There are, I think, only two points to be made, and both help the charterers. First, while none of the events specified in the clause is clearly indicative of negligence, some of them (such as act of God or restraint of princes) are plainly
j inconsistent with it. Second, on the only occasion known to me when an English court has had to consider the meaning of a peril included in this clause which might be the result of negligence or might not, the expression was interpreted as not including the peril when it was the result of negligence: see *Re Polemis and Furness Withy & Co Ltd* [1921] 3 KB 560, [1921] All ER Rep 40, where the meaning of 'fire' in a clause somewhat similar to this was ruled on. It is quite true that fire is a result, whereas 'errors of

navigation' carry one into the mind of the owners' servants, but that does not seem to me to advance the argument very much, save perhaps in making the lack of any express **a** reference to negligence the more striking. The obiter, and very tentative, expression opinion of the United States Court of Appeals in *The Burma* (1911) 187 F 94 does not dissuade me from the conclusion to which the foregoing arguments, as it seems to me, lead.

I am naturally reassured to find that Staughton J arrived at the same conclusion. It may be that the effect of the clause has been more fully argued in this case than it was **b** before him, since it is the only point in this case whereas it was one of several in the other, but I find no fault in his reasoning and I do not think the additional arguments presented to me are of decisive significance.

I accordingly conclude, in agreement with the arbitrator, that on the facts found and on the true construction of the charterparty the owners are liable to the charterers in damages for breach of the charterparty in the agreed sum of $US120,000. I uphold the **c** arbitrator's award. That conclusion makes it unnecessary to answer the alternative question posed for the opinion of the court.

Arbitrator's award upheld.

Solicitors: *Holman Fenwick & Willan* (for the owners); *Middleton Potts & Co* (for the **d** charterers).

K Mydeen Esq   Barrister.

Worldwide Carriers Ltd and another v   e
Ardtran International Ltd and others

QUEEN'S BENCH DIVISION (COMMERCIAL COURT)
PARKER J
1, 21 JULY 1982   **f**

Carriers – Contract – Carriage of goods – Action arising out of carriage – Limitation period – Loss or damage to goods – Failure to deliver goods – Owner claiming damages – Whether claim for damage to goods or for total loss – Date from which limitation period runs – Carriage of Goods by Road Act 1965, Sch, art 32(1).

g

Carriers – Contract – Carriage of goods – Action arising out of carriage – Limitation period – Successive carriage – Owner of goods claiming against first carrier – First carrier notifying second carrier of receipt of claim – Whether submission of claim to first carrier suspending limitation period in respect of owner's claim against second carrier – Carriage of Goods by Road Act 1965, Sch, art 32(2).

h

In June 1979 the first defendants agreed to transport under a contract of carriage a quantity of brass plated steelcord from France to England. The contract was subject to the Convention on the Contract for the International Carriage of Goods by Road 1965 (CMR), as set out in the schedule to the Carriage of Goods by Road Act 1965. The first part of the journey was sub-contracted to the second defendants and on 26 June while in their care the consignment was so damaged that its only value was as scrap. The **j** consignment was returned to the French consignor. By a letter dated 2 July the plaintiffs claimed compensation from the first defendants. That claim was passed on to the second defendants between 5 and 7 July together with a statement that the second defendants were being held 'entirely responsible for all losses'. On 6 January 1981 the plaintiffs submitted a formal written claim to the second defendants and on 12 March they issued

a writ against, inter alios, the second defendants claiming damages representing the
a difference between the value of the goods as consigned and their scrap value. The second
defendants sought an order that the claim against them be struck out on the ground that
the plaintiffs had not made any claim against them within one year of the loss or damage
as required by art 32(1)[a] of CMR and therefore the claim against them was time-barred.
The plaintiffs contended (i) that the limitation period contained in art 32(1) did not apply
because their claim was for 'damage' rather than loss and although their claim would
b otherwise fall within art 32(1)(a) the limitation period in art 32(1)(a) ran 'from the date
of delivery' and there had been no delivery of the goods, (ii) that, even if art 32(1) applied,
they had made a written claim to the first defendants which had the effect under art
32(2)[b], so it was contended, of suspending the limitation period in respect of all other
carriers, including the second defendants, and (iii) that the second defendants' knowledge
that a claim was being made and that it would be passed on to them was sufficient under
c art 32(2) to suspend the limitation period. The second defendants contended, inter alia,
that the plaintiffs' claim was for a 'total loss' within art 32(1)(b) and therefore the
limitation period ran from the date on which the goods were taken over by them or that
the claim fell within the category of 'all other cases' and therefore under art 32(1)(c) the
limitation period ran from the making of the contract of carriage.

d **Held** – The plaintiffs' claim against the second defendants was time-barred and would
be struck out for the following reasons—
   (1) Where damage occurred but there was no delivery of goods, there was a 'total loss'
of the goods within art 32(1)(b) of CMR because under art 20(1)[c] of that convention non-
delivery of the goods was to be treated as 'conclusive evidence of the loss of the goods'. In
any event, since art 32 was plainly intended to be comprehensive and to cover all claims
e arising under CMR, it was to be presumed that, if a claim did not fall within either art
32(1)(a) or art 32(1)(b) so that the limitation period there prescribed applied, it necessarily
fell within the category of 'all other cases' for which art 32(1)(c) prescribed a limitation
period (see p 697 h to p 698 b and d, post); *William Tatton & Co Ltd v Ferrymasters Ltd*
[1974] 1 Lloyd's Rep 203 and *Moto Vespa v MAT (Britannia Express) Ltd* [1979] 1 Lloyd's
Rep 175 distinguished.
f   (2) Where there was carriage by successive carriers and damage occurred to the goods
being carried, a written claim submitted by the owner of the goods to the first or to just
one carrier did not have the effect of suspending the limitation period from running
against all the carriers under art 32(2) of CMR. Furthermore, although art 32(2) did not
require any particular formality, it did require that a written claim be addressed to the
carrier against whom the owner of the goods was claiming if the limitation period was
to be suspended under art 32(2) in respect of that carrier. Mere knowledge on the part of
g one carrier that the owner of the goods was suing another carrier who intended to sue
him was not sufficient to suspend the limitation period in respect of any claim that
might be made against him by the owner (see p 698 j and p 699 a to d, post).
   (3) Since the plaintiffs had not submitted a written claim to the second defendants
until 6 January 1981, which was outside the limitation period prescribed by art 32(1)(b)
h or (c), and since the claim submitted to the first defendants on 2 July 1979 did not have
the effect of suspending the limitation period under art 32(2) in respect of the plaintiffs'
claim against the second defendants, that claim was time-barred (see p 699 d to f, post).

Notes
For the limitation period in respect of action arising from a contract of international
j carriage by road governed by the CMR, see 5 Halsbury's Laws (4th edn) para 437.
   For the Carriage of Goods by Road Act 1965, Sch, arts 20, 32, see 28 Halsbury's Statutes
(3rd edn) 450, 455.

---

a   Article 32(1), so far as material, is set out at p 694 j to p 695 a, post
b   Article 32(2), so far as material, is set out at p 695 c d, post
c   Article 20(1) is set out at p 696 g h, post

Cases referred to in judgment
Anon (1973) 8 ETL 620, Oberlandesgericht, Dusseldorf.
Anon (1978) 13 ETL 742, Tribunal de Commerce, Paris.
Moto Vespa v MAT (Britannia Express) Ltd [1979] 1 Lloyd's Rep 175.
Tatton (William) & Co Ltd v Ferrymasters Ltd [1974] 1 Lloyd's Rep 203.
Verdier v Nazionale di Trasporti Flli Gondrand (1968) 4 ETL 918, Cour d'Appel d'Aix-en-
Provence.

Summons
By a summons dated 4 May 1982 the second defendants, VGN Les Transport Associes,
applied for an order that the claim against them in the writ dated 12 March 1981 and
points of claim dated 2 April 1982 issued and served by the first plaintiffs, Worldwide
Carriers Ltd, and the second plaintiffs, Firestone Tyre and Rubber Co Ltd, against the
first defendants, Ardtran International Ltd, the second defendants, and the third
defendants, Inter Vervoer Gheeraert PVBA, be struck out on the grounds that the claim
disclosed no reasonable cause of action, or was frivolous and/or vexatious and/or an abuse
of the process of the court, or was time-barred under art 32 of the Convention on the
Contract for the International Carriage of Goods by Road 1965. The summons was heard
in chambers but judgment was given in open court. The facts are set out in the judgment.

Julian Malins for the second defendants.
Peter Gross for the first and second plaintiffs.
The first and third defendants were not represented.

Cur adv vult

21 July. The following judgment was delivered.

PARKER J. In June 1979 the first plaintiffs on their own behalf or on behalf of the
second plaintiffs entered into a contract with the first defendants for the carriage of 12
cardboard boxes of brass plated steelcord from Lens in France to Wrexham in England.
It is common ground that that contract was subject to the terms of the Schedule to the
Carriage of Goods by Road Act 1965, generally known by its French abbreviation CMR.
The first defendants sub-contracted the first leg of the journey from Lens to Zeebrugge
to the third defendants, who in turn sub-contracted to the second defendants. On 26
June while the consignment was in the possession of the second defendants en route
from Lens to Zeebrugge, there was an accident. As a result the goods were exposed to the
weather and became useless for the purpose for which they were required by the
consignee, the second plaintiffs. They were returned to the consignor in Lens on 29 June.
They were subsequently examined by a surveyor appointed by a Belgian court who, in a
preliminary report dated 3 January 1980 and a final report dated 5 February 1980,
concluded that the extent of the damages was such that the entire consignment must be
regarded as a total loss as steelcord, and had no value other than as scrap.
    In this action, which was commenced by writ dated 12 March 1981, the plaintiffs seek
to recover from the defendants the difference between the value of the goods as consigned
and the scrap value. The points of claim were served on 2 April 1982, and on 4 May 1982
the second defendants issued the summons presently before the court seeking an order
that the writ and points of claim as against them be struck out on the ground that the
plaintiffs' claim against them is time-barred under the provision of art 32 of CMR.
    Article 32(1), so far as immediately material, provides:

'1. The period of limitation for an action arising out of carriage under this
Convention shall be one year . . . The period of limitation shall begin to run: (*a*) in
the case of partial loss, damage or delay in delivery, from the date of delivery; (*b*) in
the case of total loss, from the thirtieth day after the expiry of the agreed time-limit
or where there is no agreed time-limit from the sixtieth day from the date on which

a the goods were taken over by the carrier; (c) in all other cases, on the expiry of three
months after the making of the contract of carriage.'

The second defendants contend that the plaintiffs' claim falls within either (b) or (c), (a)
being inapplicable since there was no delivery.

If this is correct the plaintiffs accept that, subject to the provisions of art 32(2), which I
shall mention shortly, their claim is time-barred.

b They contend however that the claim does not fall within art 32(1) at all. It is, they
say, a claim for damage and not loss. It is therefore within sub-para (a) but that sub-
paragraph cannot apply because there was no delivery. Since the claim falls within sub-
para (a) it cannot be within sub-para (c) which applies to 'other cases'. Hence there is no
point of time at which the limitation period begins to run and thus no effective period of
limitation provided by CMR.

They contend further that, if their first contention is wrong, the claim is saved by art
c 32(2), which provides so far as directly material:

'A written claim shall suspend the period of limitation until such date as the
carrier rejects the claim by notification in writing and returns the documents
attached thereto . . . The burden of proof of receipt of the claim, or of the reply and
of the return of the documents, shall rest with the party relying upon these facts . . .'

d No written claim was made by or on behalf of the plaintiffs until 6 January 1981, by
which time the claim, if within art 32, had already become time-barred, but by letter
dated 2 July 1979 the first plaintiffs claimed against the first defendants. This claim led
to a telex on 5 July from the first defendants' insurers to the third defendants expressly
stated to be sent on behalf of the first defendants. So far as material it read:

e '3) World-Wide carriers damage to steelcord collected Firestone Lens France
26.6.79 . . . re 3) above customers tell us that the whole of the consignment is
unusable and that the loss is estimated at 20,000 sterling. Please advise your insurers
urgently and confirm by telex that they have the matter in hand.'

f The third defendants on receipt of this telex wrote immediately to the second
defendants enclosing a copy of the telex and saying: 'We hereby hold you entirely
responsible for all losses.'

There is thus no doubt that by about 6 or 7 July 1979 the second defendants had
received a written claim from the third defendants and were aware that the plaintiffs
were claiming against the first defendants who were in turn claiming against the third
g defendants. The second defendants also attended the survey by the surveyor appointed
by the Belgian court.

The evidence before me at this stage does not reveal what, if any, reply was sent by the
first defendants to the plaintiffs' written claim of 2 July, or by the third defendants in
response to the telex of 5 July, or by the second defendants to the third defendants'
written claim of 5 July. The exhibited correspondence contains nothing from 5 July
h 1979 to 29 May 1980, on which day the first plaintiffs wrote to the first defendants asking
for a six months' extension of the limitation period. No reply having been received to
this request by 25 June 1980, the goods insurers telexed the first defendants pressing for
a reply and saying: 'No doubt you have pursued extension of time bar with your
subcontractor haulier and we would like confirmation of the time limit extension.'

This request was, it appears, repeated on or about 30 June to the third defendants, who
j replied that they had passed it to the second defendants and this information was given
on 3 July 1980 by the first defendants to the plaintiffs. It was not suggested that the
second defendants or indeed the first or third defendants ever granted any extension of
the limitation period.

The plaintiffs contend that if, contrary to their primary contention, art 32(1) applies at
all, then the claim against the second defendants is not time-barred on one of two

grounds. The first of these grounds is that on its true construction art 32(2) requires for suspension of the period of limitation against all carriers a written claim to the first carrier only, that such a claim having been made on 6 July 1979 the period of limitation was then suspended, and that no rejection of the claim having been proved it remained thereafter in suspense.

The second ground is that so long as a carrier under CMR knows that a claim is being made against some carrier and that that carrier will seek to pass it on to him, that is sufficient to suspend the limitation period. On the evidence, the second defendants knew from a few days after the accident that a claim was being made and that the first and third defendants intended to pass it on; they were involved in the survey in early 1980, and in May/June 1980 they were also involved in the question of an extension of the time limit. Hence the limitation period was suspended.

The three issues raised on the construction of CMR are all of considerable importance and for this reason this judgment is given in open court. I shall consider them in the order in which I have already mentioned them.

Does art 3 2(1) apply at all?

The first question which arises under this head is whether the plaintiffs' claim is for damage and thus prima facie within art 32(1)(a) or for total loss and thus within art 32(1)(b).

A similar question arose in *William Tatton & Co Ltd v Ferrymasters Ltd* [1974] 1 Lloyd's Rep 203 in connection with the carriage of a machine with an invoice value of £32,000. The machine was severely damaged in an accident and was returned to the makers who certified that they had been able to use certain parts of the machine to the maximum value of £9,000. No question of limitation arose but it was material to the assessment of damages to decide whether the claim was for damage or for total or partial loss, the compensation recoverable being different in the two cases. The plaintiffs contended that the machine was so badly damaged that it retained only scrap value and there was therefore a constructive total loss. Browne J held that the case was one of damage not loss. He dealt with this argument very briefly, saying only (at 206):

> 'It seems to me that in the ordinary sense in which the words "loss" and "damage" are used in connection with carriage of goods, this was plainly a case of damage, it is true very serious damage, and not of loss.'

I respectfully agree. Had the goods in fact been reloaded and delivered instead of being returned it would in my judgment be doing violence to the language to say that the case was one of loss and not damage. Article 20(1) of CMR, however, provides:

> 'The fact that the goods have not been delivered within thirty days following the expiry of the agreed time-limit, or, if there is no agreed time-limit, within sixty days from the time when the carrier took over the goods, shall be conclusive evidence of the loss of the goods, and the person entitled to make a claim may thereupon treat them as lost.'

The second defendants contend that that article necessarily makes the claim one for total loss and thus within art 32(1)(b), the wording of which follows exactly that of art 20(1). The plaintiffs cannot, it is said, advance at one and the same time the case that there was no delivery and therefore no application of art 32(1)(a) and the case that there was damage and not loss. If there was no delivery then under CMR the case is to or can be treated as one of total loss.

In *Tatton v Ferrymasters*, art 20(1) was, it appears, not mentioned at all although in that case also the goods were returned to sender without completion of the contracted journey. It was not mentioned either in *Moto Vespa v MAT (Britannia Express) Ltd* [1979] 1 Lloyd's Rep 175 which is the decision on which the plaintiffs principally rely. In that case the contract was for the carriage of two lathes from Birmingham to Madrid. The lathes were very badly damaged in an accident when nearing Madrid but were reloaded onto another

vehicle and taken to Madrid. They were there rejected by the plaintiffs, who were
consignees, without being offloaded and were taken back to Birmingham.

The defendants there relied on limitation to defeat the claim but the plaintiffs
contended, as do the plaintiffs here, that the case was one of damage and thus within art
32(1)(a), that that article did not apply because there had been no delivery, that since the
case was one of damage there was no room for the application of art 32(1)(c) and,
accordingly, that there was no period of limitation under CMR. Mocatta J upheld this
contention. He said (at 180):

> 'The first question arising is whether art. 32, par. 1(a) applies. The lathes were
> undoubtedly damaged, but were they delivered? Mr. Clarke [counsel for the third
> party and second defendants] argued that they were and Mr. Longmore [counsel for
> the plaintiffs] that they were not. The accident happened on Dec 15. The goods
> were then transferred to another vehicle and taken to Madrid where they were
> rejected by the plaintiffs and were sent back to Barcelona without being unloaded.
> It would seem a fair conclusion that their rejection in Madrid took place before Dec.
> 20. Article 15 of the Convention envisages the possibility of circumstances
> preventing delivery after the arrival of the goods at their destination and I take the
> view that the circumstances here were an example of a situation to which art. 15
> applied. I do not, therefore, think there was a delivery as in art. 32, par. 1(a). Mr.
> Longmore argued from this that there was no relevant period of limitation provided
> for by the Convention, which does of course sometimes turn out to be the case; on
> this I think he was right. I did at one time wonder whether if par. 1(a) did not apply,
> then par. 1(c) would be applicable as applying "in all other cases". On consideration,
> however, I do not think this can be the right view, since the introductory words to
> par. 1(c) deal with all cases other than partial loss, damage, or total loss and here
> there was undoubtedly damage.'

This is, accordingly, a direct decision in favour of the plaintiffs and they argue that it
should be followed at all events on an application to strike out such as is presently before
the court.

Although in that case the contractual journey was completed, the decision that there
was no delivery renders the case for present purposes the same as that presently before
me.

There can be no doubt that on an application such as the present no relief should be
granted unless the case is a clear one and that in almost all cases the existence of an
authority in favour of the opposing party, albeit not binding, would be sufficient to
require refusal of relief. Where, however, the facts are not in dispute, the point at issue is
a narrow one on which no further light could be thrown if there were a trial, or possibly
a trial of the particular issue as a preliminary point, the authorities relied on have not
taken into account a clearly material point and the court reaches a clear conclusion, it
would in my judgment be a denial of justice not to dispose of the matter at once. It is not
suggested that any further light is likely to be thrown on the matter by fuller argument
and I therefore propose to decide the point presently under consideration and also the
other two points which are in like case.

The opening words in art 32 plainly show that it was intended to be comprehensive
and to cover all claims arising under CMR. It will, as it seems to me, do so if either (i)
cases of damage but non-delivery necessarily fall within art 32(1)(b) as a result of the
provisions of art 20(1), or (ii) if the words 'in all other cases' in sub-para (c) of art 32(1)
apply to all cases where neither sub-para (a) nor sub-para (b) provide, in the particular
case, a point from which the one year period which is prescribed for *all* actions under
CMR can run.

Mocatta J rejected the second alternative but did not consider the first. Browne J did
not consider either because in his case the point did not arise at all.

Having regard to the wording used in arts 20(1) and 32(1)(b) it appears to me that in
cases such as the present art 32(1)(b) applies, and it appears that it has been so held in
France in the Tribunal de Commerce, Paris ((1978) 13 ETL 742) (see Malcolm A Clarke

International Carriage of Goods by Road (1982): CMR para 59). If, however, I were wrong about this, I would have no hesitation in holding that art 32(1)(c) does apply to all cases where a starting point for the period of limitation cannot be found under art 32(1)(a) or (b) and thus that the present case falls within it if, contrary to my conclusion, it is a claim for damage rather than loss.

There is moreover an alternative basis which might apply in some cases when goods are returned to sender. Under art 12(1) the sender has the right to dispose of the goods, in particular by asking the carrier to stop the goods in transit, to change the place at which delivery is to take place or to deliver the goods to a consignee other than the consignee indicated in the consignment note. Under art 12(2) this right subsists until the second copy of the consignment note is handed to the consignee or the consignee exercises his right under art 13(1). If, therefore, on hearing of damage the sender requires the goods to be returned to him he is doing no more than stopping the goods in transit, changing the place of delivery and changing the consignee. When these instructions are carried out it appears to me that, at least in some cases, there will have been a delivery under the contract and thus that art 32(1)(a) applies. It may be that this was so in the present case. There is in the documents some evidence to this effect. It is, however, unnecessary to reach a conclusion on the point or to cause it to be considered further in the light of the conclusion I have reached that the claim is within art 32(1)(b) and that, if that is wrong, it is within art 32(1)(c).

Suspension of period by virtue of written claim to first defendants

Under art 34 of CMR, if the carriage is governed by a single contract but is performed by successive carriers, each is responsible for the performance of the whole operation. But under art 36, except in certain cases, legal proceedings may only be brought against the first and last carriers and the carrier who was performing that portion of the carriage during which the event causing the loss, damage or delay occurred. All carriers against whom action lies may be sued in one action. The plaintiffs in the present case had therefore a choice as to whom they should sue. They could, had they so wished, have sued, for example, the first defendants alone or the second defendants alone.

A carrier who has paid compensation under CMR is entitled under art 37 to recover such compensation, together with interest, costs and expenses, from the other carriers who have taken part in the carriage, subject to the following provisions:

'(a) the carrier responsible for the loss or damage shall be solely liable for the compensation whether paid by himself or by another carrier; (b) when the loss or damage has been caused by the action of two or more carriers, each of them shall pay an amount proportionate to his share of liability; should it be impossible to apportion the liability, each carrier shall be liable in proportion to the share of the payment for the carriage which is due to him; (c) if it cannot be ascertained to which carriers liability is attributable for the loss or damage, the amount of the compensation shall be apportioned between all the carriers as laid down in (b) above.'

The second defendants might therefore, if not sued by the plaintiffs, have been later sued by the first or third defendants.

Under art 39(4), the provisions of art 32 apply to claims between carriers but the period of limitation does not run until either the date of the judicial decision resulting in the payment which gives rise to the contribution claim or, if there is no judicial decision, from the date of payment.

It is plain from the above that one carrier's claim against another is entirely separate from the claim by the goods owner. It does not arise unless and until he has paid, and, when it does arise, the limitation period, or rather the date from which the period begins to run, is different from that which applies to claims by goods interests. The provisions of art 32 with regard to suspension of the period do, however, apply equally.

On the plain wording of art 32(2) a plaintiff who, when met by a limitation plea, wishes to set up suspension must show that the party relying on the time-bar has received a written claim from him, or at all events from what I call goods interests. This is in a accordance with the decision in the Court of Appeal in Aix-en-Provence dated 8 November 1968 in *Verdier v Nazionale di Transporti Flli Gondrand* (1968) 4 ETL 918, a copy of which was supplied to me and to the decision of the Dusseldorf State Court of Appeal on 13 January 1973 ((1973) 8 ETL 620), a copy of which was also supplied. This is essential for art 32(2) plainly gives the right to the carrier to stop the suspension by rejecting the claim and he clearly cannot do so unless the claim is made against him. Furthermore, to stop the suspension not only must the claim be rejected but the b documents, if any, must be returned.

To hold that a written claim to the first carrier or indeed to any one carrier creates a suspension of the period against all is in my judgment not possible. The sender or consignee may have no intention of suing any of them save one. The one sued may know there is no real defence and not trouble to reject a written claim against him. On what basis could it be contended that by presenting a written claim to the only one of several c against whom he wished to proceed he had suspended the period of limitation from running in favour of those whom he had at any rate at the time no wish to sue? I can think of no such basis. If it were right it would mean that a carrier who had heard nothing of a claim until long after the limitation period could be met with the answer to the time bar: 'Oh, but although we made no written claim against you, time was suspended almost at once by our claim against "X" and it is still in suspense.' This is not, d in my judgment, what art 32 says or means. I reject the submission that a written claim to the first or one carrier suspends the period running in respect of all carriers.

Suspension of period by reason of second defendants' knowledge of claim

I can dispose of this point very shortly. No doubt art 32(2) does not require any particular formality but it does require a written claim of some sort and it must be clear e that the claim is a claim by the goods owners rather than the separate and different claim over by one carrier against another. I can see no basis on which information from one carrier that a claim is being made by goods owners against him and that he intends to claim against another carrier can, even if in writing, constitute a written claim under art 32 suspending limitation in respect of a claim which goods owners are not making against that other carrier. I therefore reject the third submission made on behalf of the f plaintiffs and hold that the plaintiffs' claim against the second defendants is statute barred. In these circumstances they are, in my judgment, entitled to be removed from the action. The writ and points of claim as against them must be struck out.

I am far from clear what good this will do them for it would appear that under art 39(1) they will be bound by the result of the action, but that is a matter for them.

g *Writ and points of claim against the second defendants struck out.*

Solicitors: *Ince & Co* (for the first and second plaintiffs); *Hedleys* (for the second defendants).

K Mydeen Esq   Barrister.

h

C M Van Stillevoldt BV v El Carriers Inc

COURT OF APPEAL, CIVIL DIVISION
GRIFFITHS LJ
j 8, 9 DECEMBER 1982

Court of Appeal – Jurisdiction – Appeal from registrar – Jurisdiction of single judge – Appeal to single judge from registrar's determination in proceedings incidental to pending cause or matter – Jurisdiction of single judge – Whether judge entitled to consider matter afresh unfettered by registrar's decision – Whether judge limited to reviewing exercise of registrar's discretion – Supreme Court Act 1981, s 58(1) – RSC Ord 59, r 14(11).

The jurisdiction conferred on a single judge of the Court of Appeal, Civil Division, by
the Supreme Court Act 1981, s 58(1)[a] and RSC Ord 59, r 14(11)[b] to hear appeals from the
determination of the registrar of civil appeals in proceedings incidental to a cause or
matter pending before the Court of Appeal entitles the single judge to consider the
matter in question afresh unfettered by the registrar's decision and thus to exercise his
own discretion in the matter. It follows that the single judge is not limited to reviewing
the manner in which the registrar exercised his discretion (see p 701 j to p 702 a and d to
f and p 704 c, post).

Evans v Bartlam [1937] 2 All ER 646 applied.

Adherence to the timetable provided by the rules of court is essential to the orderly
conduct of business in the Court of Appeal. In particular the setting down of an appeal
in time is a vital step in proceedings because it informs the registrar's office that an appeal
is in fact effective. The Court of Appeal will therefore ensure, for the benefit of all
litigants, that the timetable provided by rules of court is adhered to by litigants and that
the business of the court is conducted in an expeditious and orderly manner (see p 703 h
j, post).

Notes

For applications to a single judge of the Court of Appeal, see 37 Halsbury's Laws (4th
edn) para 695.

For the Supreme Court Act 1981, s 58, see 51 Halsbury's Statutes (3rd edn) 1254.

Cases referred to in judgment

Cooper v Cooper [1936] 2 All ER 542, CA, 27(2) Digest (Reissue) 720, 5589.

Evans v Bartlam [1937] 2 All ER 646, [1937] AC 473, HL, 37(1) Digest (Reissue) 246,
1646.

Revici v Prentice Hall Inc [1969] 1 All ER 772, [1969] 1 WLR 157, CA, Digest (Cont Vol C)
1097, 3621a.

Interlocutory appeal

The plaintiffs, C M Van Stillevoldt BV, the receivers of cargo shipped on a vessel owned
by the defendants, El Carriers Inc, appealed to a single judge of the Court of Appeal from
the refusal of the Registrar of Civil Appeals to extend the time for setting down the
plaintiffs' appeal from a decision of Staughton J given on 6 July 1982 dismissing the
plaintiffs' application for an extension of time for commencing arbitration proceedings
between the parties on the ground that in the circumstances the judge had no power to
extend the time. A point of general importance arose on the appeal to the judge, as to the
nature of the jurisdiction of a single judge of the Court of Appeal when hearing an appeal
from the registrar under RSC Ord 59, r 14, and accordingly, although the appeal was
heard in chambers, at the invitation of the parties judgment was given by Griffiths LJ in
open court. The facts are set out in the judgment.

Iain Milligan for the plaintiffs.
Edmund Broadbent for the defendants.

GRIFFITHS LJ. This is an appeal to a single judge of the Court of Appeal from the
refusal of the registrar of the Court of Appeal to extend the time for setting down an
appeal. I am giving judgment in open court at the invitation of the parties because a
point of general importance has been argued concerning the nature of the jurisdiction of
a single judge of the Court of Appeal when hearing an appeal from the registrar under
the new provisions of RSC Ord 59, r 14.

The plaintiffs submit that my jurisdiction is the same as that of a judge in chambers
when hearing an appeal from a master or registrar. It is well settled that in such cases the
judge is in no way fettered by the master's or the registrar's decision. It is the duty of the

---

a Section 58(1) is set out at p 701 c d, post
b Rule 14(11) is set out at p 701 e, post

judge to consider the matter afresh and to exercise his own discretion, of course having due regard to the decision below but being in no way inhibited by it in the exercise of his discretion. By contrast, if the judge's decision is then appealed to the Court of Appeal, the Court of Appeal will only interfere if it is satisfied that the judge has exercised his discretion wrongly, applying principles to that determination which are now too well established to require repeating.

The defendants, however, submit that my function is limited to a review of the manner in which the registrar exercised his discretion, and only if satisfied that it has been wrongly exercised am I free to consider the case anew. In short, the respondents submit that my jurisdiction is that of the Court of Appeal reviewing the discretion of the judge.

This appeal, as will shortly appear, is nicely balanced, and the nature of my jurisdiction is of crucial, not academic, importance.

Section 58 of the Supreme Court Act 1981 provides:

'(1) Any jurisdiction exercisable in any proceedings incidental to any cause or matter pending before the civil division of the Court of Appeal and not involving the determination of an appeal may, if and so far as rules of court so provide, be exercised (with or without a hearing) by a single judge of that court, whether in court or in chambers, or by the registrar of civil appeals.

(2) Rules of court may provide for decisions of a single judge or the registrar of civil appeals acting by virtue of subsection (1) to be called in question in such manner as may be prescribed; but, except as may be provided by rules of court, no appeal shall lie from a decision of a single judge or that registrar so acting.'

I turn now to consider the new provisions of Ord 59, r 14. The relevant ones are to be found in paras (11) and (12). Paragraph (11) reads:

'An appeal shall lie to a single judge from any determination made by the registrar and shall be brought by way of fresh application made within 10 days of the determination appealed against.'

Paragraph (12) reads:

'An appeal shall lie to the Court of Appeal from any determination by a single judge under this Order and shall be brought by way of fresh application made within 10 days of the determination appealed against. Provided that an appeal shall not lie to the Court of Appeal without the leave of that Court in respect of a determination of the registrar which has been reviewed by a single judge.'

The plaintiffs point to the words in para (11) which indicate that the appeal to the single judge is to be by way of fresh application, and they rely on those words as a clear indication that the judge is intended to hear the matter afresh and to decide it by applying his own judgment and discretion to the issues before him.

In answer to that the defendants point out that in para (12) precisely the same wording is used in respect of the appeal to the full Court of Appeal from the decisions of the single judge. Furthermore, they draw attention to the concluding words of para (12):

'Provided that an appeal shall not lie to the Court of Appeal without the leave of that Court in respect of a determination of the registrar which has been reviewed by a single judge.'

And they submit that the use of the word 'reviewed' indicates that it is the intention of the rule that the decision of the registrar should be approached in the same way as the Court of Appeal will ordinarily review the decision of a judge of the High Court, namely that it will recognise that the discretion is that of the judge and not of the Court of Appeal and only interfere if the discretion has in their judgment been wrongly exercised, albeit that, if they had been considering the matter afresh themselves, they might not have exercised the discretion in the same manner as the judge. I see the weight of that

argument but it is, in my view, to read too much into the use of the word 'reviewed' in
the proviso. I believe that to be no more than a shorthand way of referring to the fact a
that there has been an appeal from the registrar.

I remind myself of the words of Lord Atkin in *Evans v Bartlam* [1937] 2 All ER 646 at
648–649, [1937] AC 473 at 478. It will be remembered that that was the authority which
finally settled the nature of the jurisdiction exercised by a judge when hearing an appeal
from a master. Lord Atkin said:

> 'I only stay to mention a contention of the respondent that, the master having b
> exercised his discretion, the judge in chambers should not reverse him unless it was
> made evident that the master had exercised his discretion on wrong principles. I
> wish to state my conviction that, where there is a discretionary jurisdiction given to
> the court or a judge, the judge in chambers is in no way fettered by the previous
> exercise of the master's discretion. His own discretion is intended by the rules to
> determine the parties' rights, and he is entitled to exercise it as though the matter c
> came before him for the first time. He will, of course, give the weight it deserves to
> the previous decision of the master, but he is in no way bound by it. This, in my
> experience, has always been the practice in chambers, and I am glad to find it
> confirmed by the recent decision of the Court of Appeal in *Cooper* v. *Cooper* ([1936]
> 2 All ER 542) with which I entirely agree.'
>
> d

I can for myself see no reason why there should be any difference in approach in the
case of a single judge of the Court of Appeal hearing an appeal from the registrar of the
Civil Division of the Court of Appeal than when a judge of first instance is hearing an
appeal from a master or a district registrar. It seems to me that, if anything, the indication
is that there is a stronger case to be made for a judge of the Court of Appeal exercising his
own discretion than a judge of first instance. I am quite satisfied from the wording of the e
rules and the general background of the law against which they were framed that it
cannot be the intention that there should be a different approach to appeals from the
registrar of the Court of Appeal than that which pertains in respect of appeals from a
master or district registrar. Accordingly I conclude that it is my duty to consider the facts
raised by this appeal afresh and to use my own discretion.

I turn therefore to the facts of this appeal. I take them gratefully from the admirably f
clear and succinct statement to be found in the reserved judgment of the registrar:

> 'The facts relating to the substantive proceedings are in brief as follows. The
> plaintiffs were receivers of a cargo of rice which had been shipped from Louisiana
> to Holland. The rice was carried in the vessel Pantazis L, of which the defendants
> were the owners. The vessel arrived at the port of discharge on 24 April 1980.
> Discharge of the cargo of rice began on 1 May 1980 and was completed on the g
> following day. The contractual terms under which the cargo was carried included
> provisions requiring disputes to be referred to arbitration. By virtue of provisions
> incorporated in that contract the time limit for the appointment of an arbitrator
> was that laid down by s 3(6) of the United States Carriage of Goods by Sea Act 1936,
> namely 12 months from the date on which the discharge of the cargo was completed.
> Failure to appoint an arbitrator within that time limit caused the claim to become h
> barred. By 6 April 1981 no arbitrator had been appointed. On that date the Dutch
> lawyers acting for the plaintiffs instructed Sinclair Roche & Temperley, who have
> since then been the plaintiffs' English solicitors. The time limit for appointment of
> the arbitrator ran out on 2 May 1981 and still no arbitrator had been appointed.
> Three days later, on 5 May 1981, Sinclair Roche & Temperley gave notice of the
> appointment of Dr Kingsley as arbitrator. On 7 May 1981 the other side replied to j
> Sinclair Roche & Temperley that the claim had been barred since 2 May 1981. On
> 11 May 1981 an originating summons was issued on behalf of the plaintiffs whereby
> they applied under s 27 of the Arbitration Act 1950 for an extension of time for the
> appointment of an arbitrator. That originating summons came before Staughton J
> on 6 July 1982. The defendants argued on two grounds that the relief sought should

be refused. First, they argued that there was no jurisdiction to grant an extension under s 27 unless the contract was governed by English law, and that the proper law of the contract for the carriage of the cargo in this case was other than English law. Second, that, even if there were jurisdiction under s 27, an extension should not be granted. Staughton J held: (1) That this was a question of substance and not of procedure and therefore s 27 of the 1950 Act did not apply unless the proper law of the contract was English law. (2) That the proper law of the contract in this case was not English law. (3) That, if there had been jurisdiction to entertain the application under s 27, he would have excused the three-day delay in giving notice of appointment of an arbitrator. The order giving effect to Staughton J's judgment was perfected on 3 August 1982.'

By agreement between the parties, the time for serving notice of appeal was extended to 12 October 1982. This was sensible co-operation between the solicitors because it enabled a transcript of the judgment to be obtained so that the notice of appeal could be properly framed. Furthermore, of course, there was the intervention of the long vacation. The notice of appeal was served on behalf of the plaintiffs on 12 October 1982. In consequence, the last day for the setting down of the appeal was 21 October 1982, that is seven days plus a weekend: see Ord 3, r 2(5), and Ord 52, r 5(1). In fact, no attempt was made to set the appeal down until 8 November. It was not until 29 October that the plaintiffs' solicitors appreciated that they were out of time for setting down the appeal. On that date there was a conversation between Mr Hughes of the plaintiffs' solicitors and Mr Taylor of the defendants' solicitors. During the conversation Mr Hughes appreciated for the first time that he was out of time in setting down the appeal, but he formed the impression that it was not the intention of the defendants' solicitors to take any point on this and accordingly he should have no difficulty in obtaining an extension of time for setting down from the registrar. However, that expectation was short-lived because on 2 November he received a telex from the defendants' solicitors which made it quite plain that there was at least a very real risk that they would be objecting to his setting the case down out of time.

Several more days then passed before he did attempt to set the case down; it was on 8 November that he first applied to do so. Because the defendants were objecting, the matter came on for hearing before the registrar on 17 November 1982.

Mr Hughes put in an affidavit before the registrar giving an explanation for his failure to set the case down within the time limited by the rules, summarised accurately by the registrar, as falling under four heads. First, he was extremely busy during the weeks in question; second, his wife had been in hospital during the three weeks prior to 30 October; third, he was trying to prepare a proper bundle of documents for the court; and, fourth, he believed and expected that some degree of latitude would be allowed in a case such as this since these are City firms of commercial solicitors who deal with each other frequently, and certainly in the period between 29 October and 2 November he had been under the impression that the defendants were not taking any point on his failure to set down.

At this stage I wish to make an observation on the fourth ground set out in his affidavit, namely a belief that there is no real need for commercial solicitors in circumstances such as this to adhere to the timetables provided by the rules of court. It cannot be over-stressed that adherence to the timetable provided by the rules is essential to the orderly conduct of business in the Court of Appeal. The setting down of an appeal is a vital step because it is this step that informs the registrar's office that an appeal is in fact effective. The decision of the Court of Appeal in *Revici v Prentice Hall Inc* [1969] 1 All ER 772, [1969] 1 WLR 157 has already drawn attention to the importance of solicitors adhering to the timetable provided by the rules of court; and I take this opportunity now to warn the profession that the attitude of the court to the previous lax practices is hardening in order to ensure for the benefit of all litigants that the business of the Court of Appeal is conducted in an expeditious and orderly manner.

The registrar, in my judgment, took into account all the relevant matters when approaching the determination of the application before him. He stated them in the following words:

'In my judgment, all the relevant factors must be taken into account in deciding how to exercise the discretion to extend time. Those factors include the length of the delay, the reasons for the delay, whether there is an arguable case on the appeal, and the degree of prejudice to the defendant if time is extended.'

If I had to approach this matter by considering whether or not the registrar had erred in his approach to the exercise of his discretion because he had applied the wrong principles of law or had given a wholly erroneous weight to some matter or failed to take into account some other matter, I should unhesitatingly come to the conclusion that I could not interfere with his discretion; it appears to me that he has taken all the relevant matters into consideration. However, I have to exercise my own discretion in this case; and I have after some hesitation, in a case which I, like the registrar, found to be a difficult case, come to the conclusion that the balance comes down on the other side to that chosen by the registrar. Looking at the factors in this case as set out by the registrar, first, the length of delay is short: we are dealing with a matter of days, not weeks or months. The reasons for delay are set out in Mr Hughes's affidavit. I have already criticised his fourth reason; but there were other reasons, namely pressure of work and the very unfortunate extra burden cast on him by the illness of his wife, and to some extent being lulled into a false sense of security for a very short period of the delay. There is certainly an arguable case on appeal; that is placed beyond doubt by the fact that Staughton J gave leave to appeal. Finally, there is no question in this case of the defendants being in any way prejudiced if the time is extended save for this fact of course, that they will now have to face the appeal rather than the plaintiffs having the door slammed in their faces at this stage.

The registrar was persuaded that time should not be extended because this was the second occasion on which it would appear that these solicitors had allowed an important time limit to pass. Counsel for the plaintiffs argued that the registrar should not have taken into account the fact that these solicitors failed to appoint an arbitrator in due time and were compelled to apply to Staughton J for an extension. He submitted that that was a matter of contractual obligation between the solicitors and their own clients and should be disregarded for the purposes of the exercise of the registrar's discretion. I emphatically reject that submission. If a party through their solicitors show that they are consistently ignoring important time limits, it becomes progressively more difficult for the court to show further indulgence; and the registrar was quite right to take that factor into account. However, for my part I think that it was too draconian an approach to refuse these plaintiffs the opportunity of continuing this litigation because at an earlier stage their solicitors were as little as three days out of time. I appreciate that those three days may in the end turn out to be absolutely crucial; but, if it had lain within Staughton J's power to extend the time limit, he indicated that he did not consider that degree of delay as a serious matter; he regarded it, he said, as a peccadillo.

Of course the fact that the defendants do not suffer prejudice is not a determinative matter, but it is undoubtedly a very important factor to weigh in the balance; and, as the defendants in this case will suffer no true prejudice by the extension of the time limit, I propose to allow this appeal and give a short extension of 48 hours during which this appeal is to be set down.

Appeal allowed.

Solicitors: *Sinclair Roche & Temperley* (for the plaintiffs); *Richards Butler & Co* (for the defendants).

Frances Rustin   Barrister.

A M & S Europe Ltd v Commission of the European Communities
(Case 155/79)

COURT OF JUSTICE OF THE EUROPEAN COMMUNITIES

JUDGES MERTENS DE WILMARS (PRESIDENT), BOSCO, TOUFFAIT, DUE (PRESIDENTS OF CHAMBERS), PESCATORE, LORD MACKENZIE STUART, O'KEEFFE, KOOPMANS, EVERLING, CHLOROS AND GRÉVISSE

18 MAY 1982

ADVOCATE-GENERAL J-P WARNER

19 NOVEMBER 1980, 28 JANUARY 1981

ADVOCATE-GENERAL SIR GORDON SLYNN

27 OCTOBER 1981, 26 JANUARY 1982

European Economic Community – Restrictive trade practices – Investigation of undertakings – Requirement that undertaking produce documents in connection with investigation – Documents containing communications between lawyer and client – Legal privilege claimed in respect of documents – Existence in Community law of principle of legal protection for written communications between lawyer and client applicable to documents required to be produced in course of investigation into infringements of Community rules on competition – Application of principle of protection of confidentiality in Community law – Procedures applicable in applying principle – EEC Treaty, arts 85, 86, 185 – EEC Council Regulation 17, art 14(3).

In February 1979 officials of the Commission of the European Communities carried out an investigation at the applicant company's premises pursuant to art 14[a] of EEC Council Regulation 17 of 6 February 1962 in order to verify that there was no infringement of the rules on competition contained in arts 85 and 86 of the EEC Treaty. At the conclusion of the investigation the officials required the applicant to make available certain specified documents which they wished to see in connection with the investigation. The applicant refused to make available certain documents on the ground that they were protected by legal confidentiality. The documents consisted of solicitor's instructions to counsel, communications between an outside solicitor and the applicant or one of its parent companies containing legal advice or requests for legal advice, documents containing legal advice or requests for legal advice from an in-house lawyer employed by the applicant or one of its parent companies and communications between executives of the applicant and one of its parent companies recording legal advice or requests for legal advice. Almost all the documents included communications made or connected with legal opinions given in 1972–73 during the period preceding, and immediately following, the accession of the United Kingdom to the EEC and were principally concerned with how far it might be possible to avoid conflict between the applicant and the Community authorities on the applicant's position with regard to, in particular, the EEC provisions on competition. The Commission, by art 1(b) of its decision of 6 July 1979 taken under art 14(3) of Regulation 17, required the applicant to produce the contested documents. The applicant agreed to show parts of each document to the Commission inspectors so that they might reasonably satisfy themselves that the documents were indeed privileged as claimed but the Commission refused to accept that proposal, insisting that an inspector must have the right to read the whole of a document in order to determine whether it

---

a Article 14, so far as material, provides:
   '1. In carrying out the duties assigned to it [to investigate suspected infringements of the rules on competition in the EEC Treaty], the Commission may undertake all necessary investigations into undertakings and associations of undertakings. To this end the officials authorised by the Commission are empowered: (a) to examine the books and other business records; (b) to take copies of or extracts from the books and business records . . .
   3. Undertakings and associations of undertakings shall submit to investigations ordered by decision of the Commission . . .'

was privileged. The applicant applied to the Court of Justice of the European
Communities for (i) a review of art 1(b) of the Commission's decision and (ii) a declaration   a
that it was void or, alternatively, a declaration that it was void in so far as it required the
applicant to produce for examination by the Commission the whole of each of the
documents for which the applicant claimed privilege. The applicant contended that in
all member states of the EEC the principle of legal protection of written communications
between lawyer and client was recognised, although the scope of the protection and the
means of securing it varied from state to state, and that therefore the Commission could   b
not when undertaking an investigation pursuant to art 14(3) of Regulation 17 insist on
the production, at least in their entirety, of written communications between lawyer and
client if the undertaking under investigation claimed protection and took reasonable
steps to satisfy the Commission that the protection was properly claimed on the ground
that the documents in question were in fact covered by legal privilege. The Commission
contended that the principle did not apply to documents when their production was   c
required in the course of an investigation under art 14 of Regulation 17.

Held – (1) Written communications between lawyer and client, in so far as they had a
bearing on the market activities of an undertaking as regards compliance with the EEC
Treaty rules on competition, fell within the category of documents referred to in arts 11   d
and 14 of Regulation 17 which the EC Commission might require to be produced in the
course of an investigation into infringements of arts 85 and 86 of the treaty if the
Commission considered that disclosure of those documents was necessary for the purpose
of the investigation. In principle it was for the Commission itself and not the undertaking
concerned or a third party, whether an expert or arbitrator, to decide whether or not a
document must be produced to it (see p 741 h j, post).   e
   (2) However, the Commission's power under Regulation 17 to require production of
such documents was subject to the restriction imposed by the need to protect the
confidentiality of business records common to all the member states of the EEC.
Accordingly, the confidentiality of written communications between lawyer and client,
provided that such communications were made for the purpose and in the interests of
the client's rights of defence and provided that they emanated from independent lawyers,   f
ie lawyers who were not bound to the client by a relationship of employment, were
protected against disclosure under the regulation. With respect to rights of defence, the
protection covered all written communications exchanged after the initiation of the
administrative procedure under Regulation 17 which might lead to a decision on the
application of arts 85 and 86 of the EEC Treaty or to a decision imposing a pecuniary
sanction on the undertaking. Moreover, the protection extended to earlier written   g
communications which had a relationship to the subject matter of that procedure. In so
far as the confidentiality applied to written communications between an independent
lawyer and his client, it applied without distinction to any lawyer entitled to practice in
a member state, regardless of the member state in which the client lived, subject to the
limits laid down in EEC Council Directive 77/249, which facilitated the effective exercise
by lawyers of freedom to provide services (see p 742 a to p 743 d, post).   h
   (3) Where an undertaking under investigation under art 14 of Regulation 17 refused
to produce business records consisting of communications between itself and its lawyer
on the ground that the documents were protected by legal professional privilege, it was
nevertheless required to provide the Commission's authorised agents with relevant
material which demonstrated that the communications fulfilled the conditions for being
granted legal protection, although it was not bound to reveal the contents of the   j
communications in question. If the Commission was not satisfied that the communications were protected in law, it might make a decision, pursuant to art 14(3) of Regulation
17, ordering production of the communications in question and, if necessary, impose on
the undertaking pecuniary penalties for non-production; where that was done it was
open to the undertaking to bring an action to have the Court of Justice decide whether
the documents were protected and the court could in such a case and if it considered that

the circumstances so required order, under art 185 of the EEC Treaty, that the operation
a   of the decision be suspended (see p 743 e, to p 744 a, post).

(4) The written communications in issue, to the extent that they were made or
connected with legal opinions given during the period preceding and immediately
following, and in connection with, the accession of the United Kingdom to the EEC, fell
within the context of the rights of defence and the lawyer's specific duties in that
connection and, in so far as they emanated from an independent lawyer entitled to
b   practice in a member state, were to be considered as confidential and beyond the
Commission's power of investigation under art 14 of Regulation 17 despite the lapse of
time between the communications and the initiation of the procedure under Regulation
17. It followed therefore that, to the extent that art 1(b) of the contested decision required
the applicant to produce those documents, the decision was void but the application
would be dismissed in respect of the other documents for which protection had been
c   claimed (see p 744 b to h, post).

Per Advocate-General Warner. The right to confidential communication between
lawyer and client is not a fundamental human right; it is a right that the laws of civilised
countries generally recognise, a right not lightly to be denied, but not one so entrenched
that, in the Community, the Council could never legislate to override or modify it (see
p 744 d to f, post).

d   Per Advocate-General Slynn. The rule protecting the confidentiality of written
communications between lawyer and client covers communications between lawyer and
client made for the purpose of obtaining or giving legal advice in whoever's hands they
are and whether legal proceedings have begun or not. It covers also the contents of that
advice (given orally or in writing), in whatever form it is recorded, whether in a letter, a
summary, a note or minutes (see p 733 e, post).

e   **Notes**
For investigation and hearings of suspected infringements of EEC competition rules, see
Supplement to 38 Halsbury's Laws (3rd edn) para 185G.6.

For privileged documents generally, see 17 Halsbury's Laws (4th edn) para 237.

For the EEC Treaty, arts 85, 86, 185, see 42A Halsbury's Statutes (3rd edn) 1178, 1183,
f   440.

For the EEC Council Regulation 17 of 6 February 1962, arts 11, 14, see ibid 1195,
1196.

Cases cited
ACF Chemiefarma NV v EC Commission Case 41/69 [1970] ECR 661, CJEC.
Aktien-Zuckerfabrik Schöppenstadt v EC Council Case 5/71 [1971] ECR 975, CJEC.
g   *Amministrazione delle Finanze dello Stato v Sas Mediterranea Importazione Rappresentanze
Esportazione Commercio (MIRECO)* Case 826/79 [1980] ECR 2559, CJEC.
Appraillé [1952] Recueil des Arrêts du Conseil d'État (Lebon) 512, France.
Associazione Industrie Siderurgiche Italiane (ASSIDER) v ECSC High Authority Case 3/54
[1954–1956] ECR 63, CJEC.
Delhauter v Caisse Général d'Épargne et de Retraite [1962] JT 171, Belgium Conseil d'État.
h   *Director of Investigation and Research and Shell Canada Ltd, Re* (1975) 55 DLR (3d) 713, Fed
CA.
EC Commission v Italian Republic Case 267/78 [1980] ECR 31, CJEC.
Hoffmann-La Roche & Co AG v EC Commission Case 85/76 [1979] ECR 461, CJEC, 21 Digest
(Reissue) 281, 1800.
Imperial Chemical Industries Ltd v EC Commission Case 48/69 [1972] ECR 619, CJEC.
j   *Internationale Handelsgesellschaft mbH v Einfuhr- und Vorratsstelle für Getreide und Futtermittel*
Case 11/70 [1970] ECR 1125, CJEC.
IRC v West-Walker [1954] NZLR 191, NZ CA.
Koninklijke Nederlandsche Hoogovensen Staallfabrieken NV v ECSC High Authority Case 14/61
[1962] ECR 253, CJEC.
LTU Lufttransportunternehmen GmbH & Co KG v Eurocontrol Case 29/76 [1976] ECR 1541,
CJEC.

National Panasonic (UK) Ltd v EC Commission Case 136/79 [1981] 2 All ER 1, [1980] ECR 2033, CJEC, 21 Digest (Reissue) 283, *1807*.

Netherlands State v Rüffer Case 814/79 [1980] ECR 3807, CJEC.

Nold (J) Kohlen- und Baustoffgrosshandlung v EC Commission 4/73 [1974] ECR 491, CJEC.

Nold (I) KG v ECSC High Authority Case 18/57 [1959] ECR 41, CJEC.

NTN Toyo Bearing Co Ltd v EC Council Case 113/77 [1979] ECR 1185, CJEC.

Prais v EC Council Case 130/75 [1976] ECR 1589, CJEC, 21 Digest (Reissue) 296, *1862*.

Präsident Ruhrkohlen-Verkaufsgesellschaft mbH v ECSC High Authority Joined Cases 36–38 and 40/59 [1960] ECR 423, EJEC.

SA Métallurgique d'Ésperance-Longdoz v ECSC High Authority Case 3/65 [1965] ECR 1065, EJEC.

Transocean Marine Paint Association v EC Commission Case 17/74 [1974] ECR 1063, CJEC, 21 Digest (Reissue) 284, *1817*.

Truman (Frank) Export Ltd v Metropolitan Police Comr [1977] 3 All ER 431, [1977] 1 QB 952, [1977] 3 WLR 257, Digest (Cont Vol E) 132, *1570a*.

Waugh v British Rlys Board [1979] 2 All ER 1169, [1980] AC 521, [1979] 3 WLR 150, HL, Digest (Cont Vol E) 183, *943(1)*.

Werhahn (Wilhelm) Hansamühle v EC Council Joined Cases 63 to 69/72 [1973] ECR 1229, EJEC.

Application

By application dated 4 October 1979 A M & S Europe Ltd, a company incorporated in England, applied to the Court of Justice of the European Communities for (1) a review by the court under art 173 of the EEC Treaty of the legality of art 1(b) of the decision of the Commission of the European Communities of 6 July 1979 which required the applicant to submit to an investigation at its premises at Bristol and Avonmouth pursuant to art 14(3) of EEC Council Regulation 17 of 6 February 1962 and to produce certain business records in respect of some of which the applicant claimed legal privilege, and (2) a declaration under art 174 of the EEC Treaty that art 1(b) of the decision of 6 July 1979 was void; or, alternatively, a declaration that it was void in so far as it required the applicant to produce for examination by the Commission the whole of those documents. The United Kingdom, the French Republic and the Consultative Committee of the Bars and Law Societies of the European Community were granted leave to intervene in the proceedings. The language of the case was English. The facts are set out in the opinions of the Advocates-General.

Jeremy Lever QC and *Christopher Bellamy* (both of the Bar of England and Wales) for the applicant.

Samuel Silkin QC and *David Vaughan QC* (both of the Bar of England and Wales) for the United Kingdom, supporting the application.

D A O Edward QC (of the Scottish Bar) and *J-R Thys* (of the Brussels Bar) for the Consultative Committee of the Bars and Law Societies of the European Community, supporting the application.

John Temple Lang, of the Commission's Legal Service, for the Commission.

A Carnelutti for the French Republic, supporting the Commission.

28 January. **The Advocate-General (J-P Warner)** delivered the following opinion: My Lords,

I. Introductory

In this action, which is brought against the Commission under art 173 of the EEC Treaty, the applicant is an English company called A M & S Europe Ltd. It is a subsidiary of an Australian company, Australian Mining and Smelting Ltd. Both companies belong to the well-known Rio Tinto Zinc group. A subsidiary of the applicant owns and operates a zinc smelter at Avonmouth, near Bristol.

On 10 February 1978 the member of the Commission responsible for competition

policy ordered investigations to be carried out under art 14 of EEC Council Regulation
a   17 into a number of undertakings in the zinc industry, which were suspected of having
jointly fixed prices and conditions of sale, controlled production and shared out markets,
in breach of art 85 of the EEC Treaty. The applicant was one of those undertakings.

Article 14 of Regulation 17 is so familiar to your Lordships that I do not think it
necessary to read it. The court was recently concerned with it in *National Panasonic (UK)*
Ltd v EC Commission Case 136/79 [1981] 2 All ER 1. The questions at issue in this case are,
b   however, different from those that were at issue there.

The questions here at issue relate to the extent to which, and the manner in which,
communications between a lawyer and his client may be protected from disclosure in an
investigation under art 14. Before I state the facts of the case and the precise nature of the
questions to which they give rise, it may be helpful if I say something about the
background.

c   *II. The background*

Article 20 of Regulation 17, which is headed 'Professional secrecy', imposes on the
Commission and the competent authorities of the member states, their officials and other
servants an obligation not to disclose information acquired by them as a result of the
application of the regulation and 'of the kind covered by the obligation of professional
secrecy'. The reference there to 'professional secrecy' is obviously a reference to the
d   concept known in French law for instance as 'le secret professionnel', which is a wide
concept in the sense that it applies not only to lawyers but to anyone whose occupation
leads him to be entrusted with confidential information, eg members of the medical
profession and government officials.

It might be suggested, though no one did so in argument before us in this case, that
the express reference in art 20 to 'professional secrecy' and the absence of any express
e   reference to any such concept elsewhere in the regulation must be taken to mean that
the authors of the regulation intended to exclude the application of any such concept
otherwise than in the circumstances described in art 20. That would however be, so it
seems to me, a somewhat rash application of that unreliable maxim expressio unius est
exclusio alterius.

The Commission and the French government suggested on the other hand that the
f   'legislative history' of art 14 showed that the Council, when enacting Regulation 17, had
deliberately rejected the idea that any concept of 'professional secrecy' should apply in
the context of that article. They relied, in so doing, on the rejection by the Council of
amendments urged by the European Parliament to the Commission's proposal for what
became Regulation 17. As your Lordships know, I entertain grave doubt whether it is
permissible to interpret a Council regulation by reference to its 'legislative history'. Be
g   that as it may, I do not think that, in this instance, an examination of the 'legislative
history' of art 14 leads to the conclusion suggested by the Commission and the French
government.

The Parliament's amendments had their origin in a report made by its Internal Market
Committee on the Commission's proposal (the 'Deringer Report', European Parliament
Document 57/1961). In para 121 of that report the committee voiced a number of
h   criticisms of arts 9 and 11 of the proposal, which became respectively arts 11 and 14 of
the regulation. Article 11 of the regulation, your Lordships remember, empowers the
Commission to request and, where necessary, to require information from, among
others, 'undertakings and associations of undertakings'. Most of the committee's criticisms
had nothing to do with the present problem. Paragraph 121 contained, however, a
sentence in these terms:

j   'En tout cas, toute personne tenue de fournir des renseignements doit avoir le
droit de refuser le témoignage tout comme le secret professionnel, par exemple des
avocats et des experts-comptables, doit être garanti'.

When one turns to the amendments proposed by the committee (at pp 44 to 46 of its
report) one finds that in fact it proposed none to what is now art 14. It proposed a series
of amendments to what is now art 11 designed to give effect to the criticisms it had

expressed in para 121, and in particular to the view that owners or representatives of undertakings called on to supply information should not be required to answer *a* incriminating questions. There was no mention in the proposed amendments of 'le secret professionnel'. The formal opinion of the Parliament, embodied in a resolution dated 19 October 1961, did not differ in any material respect from what had been proposed by the committee.

It seems that, of the laws of the original member states, only German law recognises the general principle that a person may refuse to answer incriminating questions. That *b* principle is of course recognised in English law also. It is however distinct from the principle that safeguards the confidentiality of communications between a lawyer and his client. One can understand that the Council should have wished to exclude from what is now art 11 of the regulation a rule that a person should not be required to answer incriminating questions, for that might have defeated the very purpose of the article or at least rendered it largely ineffective. But one cannot, in my opinion, draw from the fact *c* that the Council rejected the Parliament's suggestion in that respect the conclusion that the Council deliberately decided against the application of any principle protecting the confidentiality of communications between lawyer and client in the context either of art 11 or of art 14.

Regulation 17 was adopted by the Council on 6 February 1962. We were told by the Commission that the absence from art 14 of any reference to communications between *d* lawyer and client did not seem to have given rise to any difficulty in the early years of its application. The Commission did not, however, enlarge on that, so that we do not know how often art 14 was invoked in those years, or to what extent cases then occurred in which Commission officials carrying out investigations came across communications of the kind in question. The Commission went on to tell us that, after the accession of the new member states, the subject was raised more frequently in discussion in professional *e* circles and short articles were published on it.

In 1976 the Consultative Committee of the Bars and Law Societies of the European Community (the CCBE) published a report by D A O Edward QC, of the Scottish Bar, entitled 'The Professional Secret, Confidentiality and Legal Professional Privilege in the Nine Member States of the European Community' (the Edward Report). Mr Edward, who was subsequently president of the CCBE, represented that body in the present *f* proceedings before us. In the preparation of his report he was advised and assisted by distinguished members of the Bars of all the countries of the Community.

The title of the Edward Report is significant. 'The Professional Secret' is of course a literal translation into English of 'le secret professionnel'. 'Confidentiality' is the name given to the relevant concept in Scottish law, whilst 'legal professional privilege' is the name given to it in English and Irish law, an inaccurate name as Lord Wilberforce *g* pointed out in *Waugh v British Rlys Board* [1979] 2 All ER 1169 at 1172, [1980] AC 521 at 531.

The Edward Report dealt with a host of problems of common interest to the Bars of the member states ranging far beyond the particular questions with which your Lordships are concerned in the present case. I do not propose to embark on an analysis of it, or even to attempt a summary of it. Beyond saying that it was, and still is, a remarkable feat of *h* comparative law, I will confine myself to one comment on it, which is this. The report rests on the premise that there is a fundamental difference between the laws of the original six member states on the one hand and the laws of Ireland and of the United Kingdom on the other hand, whilst the law of Denmark should be considered separately. But, and this thought struck me when I first read the report in 1976, the report itself unconsciously demonstrates that that is a mistaken approach, first, because of differences *j* between the laws of 'the original six' that the report brings out and, second, because of differences between the laws of England and of Scotland that the report overlooks. The report was however, in my opinion, right in concluding that the differences between the laws of the different countries in the Community 'are differences of approach or method (made necessary by their fundamentally different legal systems) rather than differences of result'. That is not to say, of course, that the result is everywhere uniform.

In 1977 two members of the Legal Service of the Commission, Dr C D Ehlermann, its
a Director-General, and Dr D Oldekop, wrote a paper for the following year's congress of
the FIDE in Copenhagen. The views they expressed in that paper were of course their
personal views. They could not commit the Commission. Having regard, however, to
the standing of Dr Ehlermann and Dr Oldekop, and also to the fact that the relevant
passage in their paper is comparatively short, I propose to cite it almost in full. They said
(FIDE, Copenhagen 1978, vol 3, pp 11.5–11.6):

b   'The question whether and if so, to what extent, communications between a
         lawyer and his client are or should be protected under Community law against
         discovery by the Commission . . . constitutes a question of due process that should
         be mentioned in the context of a discussion dealing with the rights of defence with
         regard to the investigation powers of the Commission. In all of the Member States
         the secrecy of the relationship between a lawyer and his client enjoys legal protection
c   against discovery by administrative authorities and even the judiciary, although
         within varying limits and by different methods. These limits and methods cannot
         be described in this paper.'

The authors refer the reader instead to the Edward Report, and go on:

d   'In the area of Community law, the problem had been discussed during the
         deliberations of the European Parliament concerning the adoption of Regulation
         17/62; on the basis of the "Deringer Report", the European Parliament made a
         recommendation in favour of the protection of professional privilege. However,
         this recommendation was not adopted by the Council.'

Your Lordships know that, in that respect, my interpretation of what happened differs
e from the authors', who continue:

         'After the enlargement of the Communities the discussion has been revived on
         the background of the particularly extensive protection of professional privilege in
         the UK and Ireland (which extends not only to independent lawyers but also to
         lawyers who are full-time employees of the client). Community law contains no
         specific and express rules relating to the protection of legal professional privilege in
f   administrative procedures (Art. 20 Reg. 17/62 prohibits only disclosure of secrets *by*
         the Commission, but not *to* the Commission)'.

Then, after a reference to art 32(2) of the Rules of Procedure of this court, the authors
conclude:

         'Considering the legal situation in the Member States it seems justified to assume
g   that there exists a general principle of law, applicable in Community law as part of
         "the law" in the sense of Art. 164 EEC Treaty (Arts. 31 ECSC Treaty, 136 EAEC
         Treaty), which, within certain limits, assures the professional privilege, also in
         administrative proceedings. Until now, the protection of professional privilege has
         not proved to be a particularly sensitive issue in the practice of the Commission and
         the extent of the appropriate protection is open to discussion. It is clear, though,
h   that this protection ends where the lawyer himself assists or participates in illegal
         activities of his client. In the context of a future comprehensive and balanced
         solution of all the issues involved, there seems to be no reason to treat salaried
         lawyers employed by their client differently from independent lawyers in
         professional practice, provided that they are effectively subject to similar rules of
         professional ethics and discipline.'

j On 22 June 1978 the Commission gave its official view in answer to a question put
down by M Cousté in the Parliament (Written Question 63/78). The Commission's
answer to that question was as follows:

         'Article 14 of Council Regulation No. 17/62 empowers the Commission to check
         and copy all correspondence and other business papers of a firm or association of
         firms, including papers prepared for it by outside lawyers and legal consultants.

Community competition legislation does not provide for any protection for legal
papers. But the Commission, wishing to act fairly, follow the rules in the *a*
competition law of certain Member States and is willing not to use as evidence of
infringements of the Community competition rules any strictly legal papers written
with a view to seeking or giving opinions on points of law to be observed or relating
to the preparation or planning of the defence of the firm or association of firms
concerned. When the Commission comes across such papers it does not copy them.
Subject to review by the Court of Justice, it is for the Commission to determine the *b*
nature of a given paper. Lastly, the Commission would remind the Honourable
Member that, by virtue of Article 20 of Regulation No. 17/62 of the Council,
Commission staff are bound by an obligation of professional secrecy in all matters
relating to the enforcement of Articles 85 and 86 of the EEC Treaty.'

I turn back to the facts of this case.

III. The facts of the case

It seems that, at all events so far as the applicant was concerned, the original decision
of the member of the Commission responsible for competition policy to intitate an
investigation was not a formal decision under para 3 of art 14, but one that led only to
officials of the Commission being authorised to carry out an investigation under paras 1
and 2 of that article.

On 20 February 1979 three officials of the Commission (whom I will call 'the
inspectors') appeared at the applicant's premises at Bristol, accompanied by an official of
the Office of Fair Trading, which is the 'competent authority' in the United Kingdom for
the purposes of art 14. The inspectors were armed with 'authorisations to investigate'
issued under art 14(2). Those were served on the applicant's managing director, A T
Thomson, and the investigation proceeded on that and the following day, in the presence *e*
of two representatives of the applicant's solicitors. At the end of it the inspectors left
taking with them copies of about 35 documents. They also left with Mr Thomson a
written request for further documents relating to certain specified matters.

Mr Thomson responded to that request by a letter dated 26 March 1979, with which
he sent to the Commission seven files of documents. He told the Commission however,
in that letter, that the applicant's solicitors, during their review of the documents, had *f*
indicated that they felt that some of them were 'covered by the doctrine of legal privilege'.
For that reason those documents were not produced. Descriptions of them were set out,
in 17 numbered paragraphs, in an appendix to the letter.

From those descriptions it seems that the documents withheld fell broadly into four
categories: (i) solicitors' instructions to counsel, (ii) communications between an outside
solicitor and the applicant or one of its parent companies containing legal advice or *g*
requests for legal advice, (iii) documents containing legal advice or requests for legal
advice from an 'in-house' lawyer employed by the applicant or by one of its parent
companies and (iv) communications between executives of the applicant or one of its
parent companies recording legal advice or requests for legal advice.

Mr Thomson also said in his letter that the applicant's solicitors had indicated that
certain passages of documents included in the files to be sent to the Commission were of *h*
no relevance to the investigation it was conducting. Those passages had been deleted and
the solicitors would shortly be sending to the Commission a statutory declaration
describing the deleted passages so that it might be 'satisfied' on that point.

Mr Thomson suggested that, should the Commission 'need further confirmation
regarding the privileged documents or the deleted passages', it should contact the
applicant's solicitors to discuss the matter. *j*

On 5 April 1979 the solicitors wrote to the Commission enclosing the promised
statutory declaration.

The commission did not follow up Mr Thomson's suggestion of discussions with the
applicant's solicitors. Without, so it seems, any further communication with the applicant
or its solicitors, it adopted, on 6 July 1979, a decision under art 14(3) addressed to the
applicant (EEC Commission Decision 79/670).

The preamble to that decision, after reciting the facts, continued as follows as regards the documents for which 'legal privilege' was claimed:

'Community competition legislation does not provide for any protection for legal papers. However, as the Commission made clear in its reply to Written Question No. 63/78 in the European Parliament, asked by Mr. Cousté, the Commission "follows the rules in the competition law of certain Member States and is willing not to use as evidence of infringement of Community competition rules any strictly legal papers written with a view to seeking or giving opinions on points of law to be observed or relating to the preparation or planning of the defence of the firm or association of firms concerned. When the Commission comes across such papers it does not copy them". Clearly neither the undertaking concerned nor its legal advisers can be the ultimate or only arbiter either as to questions of fact or of law, as to whether any given document is one of these kinds of documents and was written in circumstances which would justify its not being used. Under existing Community law, and subject to review by the Court of Justice, it is for the Commission to determine whether a given document should be used or not. Therefore it is necessary for A M & S Europe Ltd. to allow the Commission's inspector to look at the documents, and to ask questions in connection with them, as far as is necessary for the purpose of establishing whether they should be used or not. If the inspector considers that they should not be used, he will not take any copies and the documents will not be used subsequently by the Commission as evidence of any infringement.'

The preamble then dealt with the applicant's claim to be allowed to delete from documents that were admittedly relevant to the investigation passages that its solicitors considered irrelevant. I need not read the recitals about that, because that claim was subsequently dropped by the applicant and is not an issue in the present action.

Article 1 of the decision required the applicant to submit to an investigation at its premises at Bristol and Avonmouth and in particular to produce for examination the business records required by the Commission officials responsible for the investigation 'which are in whole or in part connected with the subject of the inquiry'. The article then set out in paragraphs lettered (a), (b) and (c) three categories of business records which were 'in particular' to be produced. Paragraph (a) specified the documents that were the subject of the written request made to Mr Thomson on 21 February and some others. Paragraph (b) specified 'all documents for which legal privilege is claimed, as listed in the appendix to A M & S Europe Limited's letter of 26 March 1979 to the Commission'. Paragraph (c) specified the complete texts of the documents from which passages had been deleted. Article 2 provided that the investigation should begin on or after 9 July 1979.

On 25 July 1979 two of the Commission's inspectors who had carried out the earlier investigation in February attended at the applicant's premises at Bristol and served the decision. They then carried out a further investigation at those premises, which lasted until 27 July. During the investigation it was made clear on behalf of the applicant that it was willing to produce all the documents within art 1(a) of the decision, with the exception of some for which 'legal privilege' was claimed, and also to produce complete copies of the documents mentioned in art 1(c). The inspectors took copies of some documents and asked for copies of others.

The applicant declined to show the inspectors the entirety of the documents referred to in art 1(b) of the decision. Its solicitors told the inspectors that, in their view, Community law did not require the applicant to disclose to them the contents of those documents, but that they were willing to let the inspectors see parts of the documents in question so that they could satisfy themselves that they were indeed privileged. The inspectors indicated that they were unwilling to proceed on the basis of seeing parts only of the documents. The applicant's solicitors proposed that the matter be discussed at a meeting to be arranged between the applicant's legal advisers and representatives of the Commission in Brussels. The investigation was then halted as respects the documents for which privilege was claimed, pending such a meeting.

On 2 August 1979 the applicant's solicitors wrote to the Commission enclosing copies of the remaining documents specified in art 1(a) but listing some 13 which they were *a* withholding on the ground that they too were covered by 'legal privilege'. All those documents except one were eventually disclosed to the Commission.

The meeting was held at Brussels on 18 September 1979 between officials of the Commission's Directorate-General of Competition (DG IV) and of its Legal Service, on the one hand, and the applicant's counsel and solicitors on the other. It was largely abortive.   *b*

The applicant's counsel (Jeremy Lever QC), relying to some extent on the passage in the preamble to the decision stating that it was necessary for the inspector 'to look at the documents, and to ask questions in connection with them, as far as is necessary for the purpose of establishing whether they should be used or not', proposed a procedure under which enough of each document would be shown to the inspectors to satisfy them of its privileged status. He emphasised that, if the inspectors were allowed to see the whole of *c* a document, its confidentiality would be lost, particularly as the Commission, whilst stating that it would not use as evidence a document that had been written with a view to seeking or giving legal advice, had never said that its inspectors were debarred from using knowledge acquired by them from the perusal of such a document. Mr Lever added that, if, on being shown what the applicant's advisers considered was enough of a document to enable 'any reasonable inspector' to judge whether it was privileged, the *d* inspector should still feel unsatisfied, there would be a clear issue for submission to this court whether the applicant had adequately complied with the decision.

The Commission's representative considered however that the Commission's decision required the production of the whole of the withheld documents to the inspectors. They conceded that, in practice, the inspectors might well need to see only part of a document to determine that it should not be used as evidence by the Commission, but they *e* considered it essential that the inspectors should have access to the entire document and that the inspectors alone should decide which parts of the document they would read in order to satisfy themselves that it should not be used.

In the upshot, all that was agreed between the parties at the meeting was that the dispute between them would have to be brought before this court by means of proceedings taken by the applicant under art 173 of the EEC Treaty to challenge the *f* Commission's decision, and that, if such proceedings were taken, the Commission would, until the court had given judgment, refrain from imposing any fine or penalty on the applicant for failure to comply with the decision.

Accordingly, on 4 October 1979, the applicant commenced the present action, in which it claims a declaration that art 1(b) of the decision is void or, alternatively, void 'in so far as it necessarily requires the disclosure to the Commission's inspector of the whole *g* of each of the documents for which the applicant claims protection on grounds of legal confidence'.

IV. The issues in the case

The application was framed on the footing that there was no dispute between the parties as to the existence of a principle of Community law protecting communications *h* between lawyer and client from disclosure, and that the issue between them was only as to procedure, the question being to what extent, if at all, the Commission was entitled to look at a document in order to determine whether a claim that it was privileged from disclosure in accordance with that principle was valid.

From the outset the Commission seemed to indorse that view of the case. It began by asking for an extension of time for lodging its defence while the applicant considered a *j* letter that it (the Commission) wrote to the applicant's solicitors on 31 October 1979. In that letter the Commission said:

'On reconsideration, the services of the Commission consider that the proposal put forward on behalf of A M & S at the meeting on 18 September 1979 and the practice thought appropriate by the Commission may not be as different as had previously appeared to be the case. Accordingly this letter is written to suggest that the documents now in question should be shown to the representative of D.G. IV on a basis similar to that outlined by Mr. Lever. This is of course without prejudice to the legal arguments of either party in the proceedings before the Court or in any difference of opinion which may arise over whether particular documents are protected, and without prejudice to further clarification by the Commission of its intended practice. The services of the commission have always considered that, depending on the circumstances, documents for which protection is claimed need not be read in full by the Commission's inspector for the purpose of establishing whether they should be regarded as protected or not. The services of the Commission consider that the question of the extent to which the inspector must be able to examine the contents of documents for which protection is claimed must be governed by the following principles:

— the public interest in ensuring that all relevant evidence be submitted to the Commission and the Court requires that a claim that a document is protected must be clearly established.

— For that purpose the inspector responsible must be put in a position in which he can be satisfied objectively and with reasonable certainty that the document is one which is protected under Community law.

— The document is to be inspected only as far as is necessary for the purpose of establishing with the appropriate degree of certainty whether it is protected or not.

— The extent to which it may be necessary for the inspector to see the text of the document will depend on all the circumstances. In practice it would normally be sufficient for him to see the first and last pages of the document and the headings, if any, provided that these clearly show the nature of the entire document. In cases where for any reason such a disclosure does not permit the question of protection to be determined with the appropriate degree of certainty, the inspector must have a right to see other substantial parts of the document (in addition of course to obtaining evidence outside the text of the document itself if necessary).

I hope that this letter may be a sufficient basis to enable you to meet with Commission officials again. If so, it would be useful if you had with you copies of all the documents in question . . .'

The offer contained in that letter was declined on behalf of the applicant, mainly because the Commission did not thereby resile from its view that its inspectors were, in the last resort, entitled to see as much of a document as they thought fit before deciding whether it was privileged.

On 17 December 1979 the Commission lodged its defence, whereby it made two further concessions. The first was that its decision was to be interpreted as meaning that—

'the inspector is authorised to look at documents for which protection is claimed only "as far as is necessary for the purpose of establishing whether they should be used or not", i.e. used as evidence.'

The second was that—

'the Commission is prepared to give an assurance that its inspectors will be instructed that they are not to use any knowledge which they may gain as a result of inspecting documents for the purpose of deciding whether they are protected.'

Reliance was placed on behalf of the Commission, in subsequent argument before us, on the fact that it had made those concessions.

The Commission's defence, apart from announcing those concessions, fell into two parts. The first part consisted of a general discussion of the question of the protection of 'legal confidence' in Community law. It was there that the Commission put forward its contention, with which I have already dealt, about the 'legislative history' of art 14. In that part also the Commission referred to the Edward Report, to the paper written for a the FIDE Congress by Dr Ehlermann and Dr Oldekop, and to the answer given by the Commission to M Cousté's Parliamentary Question 63/78. The Commission then went on to discuss two sources of authority on English law, which, in my opinion, it has misunderstood: the Law Reform Committee's 16th Report on 'Privilege in Civil Proceedings' (Cmnd 3472) and the decision of the House of Lords in *Waugh v British Rlys Board* [1979] 2 All ER 1169, [1980] AC 521. (I shall discuss those authorities in a b moment.) The Commission concluded that—

'the question whether protection should be given for legal confidence, and if so how far it should be given and by what mechanism it should be controlled, are questions of policy to be decided pragmatically according to circumstances'

and not questions of principle. The Commission expressed its agreement with the c applicant that 'the issues in this case are entirely questions of procedure'. In the second part of the defence it argued in favour of a procedure 'on the lines set out in' its letter of 31 October 1979.

The applicant in its reply stated 'the very narrow issue that divides the parties' to be:

'In order to verify claims for protection of documents under the principle of legal confidence, is the Commission entitled, as it claims, to inspect the documents for d which the claim is made? Or, as the Applicants claim, must the Commission take advantage of other means of verification that do not involve the Commission itself gaining knowledge of the legal confidences that are to be protected?'

The view that the issue in the case was a narrow one, relating only to the procedure whereby the question whether a document was protected from disclosure should be e decided, was reiterated by the Commission in its rejoinder.

Of the interveners, the British and French governments both stated their views on the question of substantive law, the British government contending that the concept of 'legal professional privilege' or 'confidentiality' or 'secret professionnel' formed part of 'the law' of the Community in the sense borne by that expression in art 164 of the EEC Treaty, and the French government contending the contrary. Neither government, however, f developed the point at all fully in its written observations. The CCBE, on the other hand, pointed out that 'questions of procedure do not arise in vacuo' and that it would be necessary for the court, before it could decide the procedural question, to decide whether there was a principle of Community law affording, as of right, protection against disclosure of confidential communications between lawyer and client, and, if so, what its scope was. The CCBE accordingly made very full written submissions on those questions. g The court agreed with the CCBE and invited the parties and the intervening governments to make submissions at the hearing on those questions of principle.

The applicant and the British and French governments did so. Counsel for the Commission, on the other hand, told us that his instructions were to remain neutral on that issue and to leave it to 'the wisdom of the court'. He was to stand by the answer given by the Commission to M Cousté and neither to accept nor to dispute that there was h a principle of Community law such as was contended for by the applicant, the British government and the CCBE. He pointed out that, if there were no such principle, the Commission must necessarily win this case, whilst, if there were such a principle, the Commission's arguments on the procedural question would be relevant.

There are thus in my opinion two major issues in this case. The first is whether the exercise by the Commission of its powers under art 14 of Regulation 17 is subject to a j principle affording, as of right, protection against the disclosure of communications passing between a lawyer and his client for the purpose of seeking or giving legal advice. The court is not, I think, called on, if it holds in favour of the existence of such a principle, to define in this case its precise scope, for instance to say to what extent it may apply where the communications are between an undertaking and a lawyer employed on its own staff (an 'in-house' lawyer), or may not apply where, in the words of Dr Ehlermann

and Dr Oldekop, 'the lawyer himself assists or participates in illegal activities of his client'.
a The second issue is, if such a principle exists, as to the correct procedure for giving effect
to it.

V. *The issue of principle*

As respects the first issue I propose to begin by dealing with a suggestion that was
tentatively put forward on behalf of the British government, to the effect that, if the
b court should hold that there was no principle of Community law of the kind for which
it primarily contended, the solution might lie in holding that, in the absence of any
relevant Community law, the provisions of the national law of each member state should
be applied in relation to documents found in that member state. That solution, the
British government said, would at least secure that the expectations of those who obtained
legal advice in each member state were not disappointed: the same rights could be
c invoked against the Community authority as against national authorities. Moreover, the
adoption of that solution would act as a spur to the enactment of Community legislation
on the subject. The British government cited, as affording some support for such an
approach, *EC Commission v Italian Republic* Case 267/78 [1980] ECR 31.

In my opinion that solution will not do. As the British government itself acknowledged,
the preamble to Regulation 17 repeatedly refers to the need for arts 85 and 86 of the EEC
d Treaty to be applied in a uniform manner in the member states, and it does so specifically
in relation to the Commission's powers to undertake investigations. *EC Commission v
Italian Republic* is in my opinion distinguishable because the Community legislation there
in question did not confer powers of investigation directly on the Commission itself; it
merely enabled the Commission to be 'associated with' inspection measures carried out
by the national authorities.

e Having regard to the attitudes adopted by the parties and by the other interveners, the
French government bore alone the burden of arguing that there was no principle of
Community law restricting the powers of the Commission under art 14 of Regulation
17. In so doing the French government relied mainly on two propositions: (i) that there
was no express provision of Community law imposing such a restriction and (ii) that the
relevant laws of the member states were too disparate for there to be derived from them
f any general principle that might apply. The French government went so far as to suggest
that the present case represented an attempt to foist on the Community what was no
more than a domestic rule of English law.

The French government's first proposition is unquestionably correct. This court,
however, has never regarded the absence of an express provision as precluding it from
holding that a general principle of law could affect the application of Community
g legislation. Were it otherwise, Community law would admit, for example, of no
principle of proportionality, of no protection for legitimate expectations, of no right to
be heard (except where expressly provided for) and of no guarantee of fundamental
human rights. The French government referred to *ACF Chemiefarma NV v EC Commission*
Case 41/69 [1970] ECR 661, where the court held that it could not write into Regulation
17 a period of limitation within which the Commission must initiate proceedings against
h an undertaking. That case is not, however, in my opinion, in point, because there can be
no general principle about the length of a limitation period, if any. The imposition of it
necessarily involves a choice that can be made only by a legislative act.

So the real question here is whether or not the laws of the member states evince the
existence of a general principle of the kind in question. I agree with the CCBE that, if
such a principle can be distilled from them, it matters not if its conceptual origin, the
j methods whereby it has been developed or even the scope of its application in detail
differ from member state to member state.

I have already said that I did not propose to analyse or even to summarise the contents
of the Edward Report. Nor do I propose to attempt an analysis of all the further
authorities that have been placed before the court as a result of the researches undertaken
by the CCBE and by counsel for the applicant since the Edward Report was written.
From an examination of that wealth of material, which covers the laws of all the member

states except Greece (because the case was argued before the accession of Greece to the Community) and also the laws of some non-member states, certain obvious conclusions a can be drawn. (i) As the French government conceded, some protection for the confidentiality of communications between lawyer and client is given by the laws of all the member states. In every member state the hard core of the relevant law is that a lawyer cannot be called on to give evidence of what he has been told by his client. But everywhere the protection extends beyond that. (ii) In all member states the protection is afforded primarily by imposing on the lawyer an obligation not to disclose the contents b of those communications. In some countries (eg France) a breach of that obligation by the lawyer is a criminal offence. In others (eg England) it is only a civil wrong. In some countries (eg England) the obligation is owed only to the client, so that it is extinguished if the client waives his right to performance of it. In other countries (eg France) the obligation is considered to be 'd'ordre publique', so that waiver by the client is not enough: the lawyer retains a discretion whether or not to disclose the contents of the c communication. Incidental differences such as those do not, however, in my opinion, go to the heart of the matter. (iii) In each country the development of the law has been largely conditioned by procedural rules characteristic of the legal system of that country. In England, for instance, much of the law has been developed in the context of 'general discovery' in civil proceedings. That is a procedure under which, at an interlocutory stage in a civil action, each party is required to disclose to the other all the documents in his d possession, custody or power relating to matters in question in the action, whether or not such documents would be admissible in evidence. Documents covered by 'legal professional privilege' are exempt from such discovery. The procedure has, I believe, no exact equivalent in the legal system of any non-common law country, not even in the Scottish system. In Belgium and France on the other hand many of the authorities are concerned with the powers and obligations of the 'juge d'instruction', particularly when e carrying out a search at the professional chambers of an 'avocat'. The 'juge d'instruction' has, as we learned in EC Commission v Italian Republic, no direct equivalent in many other member states. There again, however, such incidental differences do not, in my opinion, go to the heart of the matter. (iv) To some extent also the development of the law in each country has been conditioned by the organisation of the legal profession in that country, for instance, in England by the existence of the distinctive roles of barristers and solicitors, f and in France by the distinctions between 'avocats plaidants', 'avocats consultants', 'avoués' and 'notaires'. Once again, such differences do not, in my opinion, go to the heart of the matter.

Here we are concerned with documents found at the premises of the client which are claimed to be, or to reproduce, communications passing between the client and his lawyer for the purpose of requesting or giving legal advice. The question is whether such g documents are protected from disclosure to a public authority exercising a statutory power of search.

As to that I must begin, I think, by saying a word about English law, partly because of the widespread impression that English law is, in this field, the most developed, and partly because, as I indicated earlier, the Commission has in my opinion misinterpreted some of the authorities relating to that law. h

In English law the doctrine misnamed 'legal professional privilege' (misnamed because that label suggests a privilege accorded to the legal profession) protects two distinct categories of documents. The first category is communications between a person and his lawyer for the purpose of obtaining or giving legal advice, whether or not in connection with pending or contemplated legal proceedings. The second category is communications between a person or his lawyer and third parties for the purpose of preparing for pending j or contemplated legal proceedings. That distinction is clearly brought out in the authorities to which the Commission referred, the 16th Report of the Law Reform Committee on 'Privilege in Civil Proceedings' (Cmnd 3472) and the opinions in the House of Lords in Waugh v British Rlys Board [1979] 2 All ER 1169 esp at 1181, [1980] AC 521 esp at 541–542 per Lord Edmund-Davies.

Waugh v British Rlys Board was about a document in the second category, namely a

railway accident report which had been prepared for two distinct purposes, one of which
a was to enable the board's solicitor to advise it on, and to conduct on its behalf, any
litigation that might arise from the accident. It was held that the report was not
privileged because, in the case of a document in the second category, the purpose of
preparing for legal proceedings must be the sole or dominant purpose. That requirement
is however irrelevant in the case of documents in the first category, with which alone we
are concerned in the present case. *Waugh v British Rlys Board* is not therefore, in my
b opinion, in point in this case.

From the Law Reform Committee report the Commission deduced two propositions,
neither of which, in my opinion, it supports. The first was that 'privilege' in English law
is essentially a right to withhold evidence from a tribunal. This proposition the
Commission deduced from the first sentence of the report, which reads as follows:

c   'Privilege in the law of evidence is the right of a person to insist on there being
       withheld from a judicial tribunal information which might assist it to ascertain facts
       relevant to an issue upon which it is adjudicating.'

The point here is that the terms of reference of the committee did not require it to
examine the law of privilege generally, but only to examine its operation in civil
litigation. Hence the committee's definition of its scope in that sentence. The committee
d did not thereby mean, and could not have meant, that 'privilege' was no more than part
of the law of evidence in civil proceedings. From the remainder of the first paragraph of
the report the Commission deduced that the approach of English law to 'privilege' was
pragmatic and that the extent of the protection it gave in any case depended on the
particular circumstances of that case. In a general sense that is true. But the point that
the committee was making, so far as here relevant, was that in some cases the law gives a
e person an absolute right to claim privilege, whilst in others it accords the judge a
discretion. As subsequent paragraphs of the report make clear (see in particular paras 17
to 23), where 'legal professional privilege' applies, it confers an absolute right; the judge
has no discretion. Nor did the committee recommend any change in the law in that
respect.

Thus, in my opinion, the English authorities relied on by the Commission do not
f support the propositions for which it cited them.

As regards statutory powers of search, the starting point of English law, as we were
reminded by the CCBE and by the British government, is that the confidential character
of a communication between a lawyer and his client comes into existence at the time
when the communication is made. The right to have that confidentiality protected arises
at the same time and continues thereafter for evermore. The right may however be
g overridden or modified by a statute.

Some United Kingdom statutes conferring powers of investigation expressly preserve
the right. Such is in particular the case of s 85 of the Fair Trading Act 1973 and ss 3 and
7 of the Competition Act 1980. Thus, in the very field of competition law with which
we are here concerned, the relevant United Kingdom statutes preserve the right as against
the United Kingdom authorities.

h Some United Kingdom statutes preserve the right, but subject to modification. An
example of that is to be found in para 5 of Sch 4 to the Finance Act 1975.

Lastly, some United Kingdom statutes are, like Regulation 17, silent on the point.
Counsel for the British government hesitated to say that, in such a case, the presumption
was that the right was preserved. There is a surprising dearth of United Kingdom judicial
authority directly on that question. The only case that comes anywhere near dealing
with it seems to be *Frank Truman Export Ltd v Metropolitan Police Comr* [1977] 3 All ER
431, [1977] 1 QB 952, but it does not really do so. We were however referred on behalf
of the applicant to the well-established principle of English law that a statute is not to be
interpreted as altering the common law to a greater extent than its terms provide, either
expressly or by necessary implication: see *Maxwell on the Interpretation of Statutes* (12th
edn, 1969) pp 116ff. We were also referred on behalf of the applicant to cases in Canada
and in New Zealand where that principle has been applied to statutes conferring powers

of investigation on public authorities without saying anything about the privilege of communications between lawyer and client, and where, accordingly, it has been held *a* that such statutes did not override that privilege: see in particular *Re Director of Investigation and Research and Shell Canada Ltd* (1975) 55 DLR (3d) 713, where the Federal Court of Appeal of Canada so held in relation to s 10 of the Canadian Combines Investigation Act (a competition law provision), and *IRC v West-Walker* [1954] NZLR 191, where the Court of Appeal of New Zealand so held in relation to s 163 of the Land and Income Tax Act of New Zealand (a fiscal law provision). Decisions of the superior *b* courts of Canada and of New Zealand are of persuasive authority in the English courts and I can, for my part, see no good reason why an English court should not follow those particular decisions. I conclude that, if a provision like art 14 of Regulation 17 were to be found in an English statute, it would almost certainly be held not to override the confidentiality of communications between lawyer and client.

I must next say a word about the laws of Belgium and of France, because particular *c* reliance was placed on them, on the one hand by the applicant and the CCBE and on the other hand by the French government.

It seems clear from the authorities to which we have been referred that, in those two countries, the law protecting the confidentiality of communications between lawyer and client has developed not only on the basis of the concept of the 'secret professionnel' but on the basis also of the concepts of 'les droits de la défense' and of 'le secret des lettres'. *d* The latter, sometimes called 'le secret des lettres missives' or 'le secret des lettres confidentielles', appears to be particularly important.

A helpful summary of the resultant law is to be found in a report and an opinion presented to the Belgian Conseil d'État by its auditeur, M C Huberlant, in *Delhauter v Caisse Générale d'Épargne et de Retraite* [1962] JT 171. The Conseil d'État followed his opinion and held that the defendant could not be called on to disclose an opinion *e* (consultation) that it had received from its 'avocat' even though it had expressly relied on it in the decision that was under challenge before the Conseil d'État.

Most of the Belgian and French authorities concerning statutory powers of search are about the obligations of the juge d'instruction when carrying out a criminal investigation. It is clear that he must respect the confidentiality of communications between a lawyer and his client. The French 'Code de Procédure Pénale', by arts 56, 76 and 96, expressly *f* requires him to take beforehand effective measures to ensure that the 'secret professionnel' and the 'droits de la défense' shall be respected, wherever he may search. When the juge d'instruction searches the professional chambers of an avocat, he is accompanied by the bâtonnier or his representative, whose role it is to make sure that the confidentiality of communications between the avocat and his clients is respected.

The French government drew our attention, however, to an important exception to *g* the general rule. The French Ordonnance 45–1484 of 30 June 1945, which is described in its title as relating to 'la constatation, la poursuite et la répression des infractions à la législation économique', provides, by art 15:

> 'Les agents visés à l'article 6 (paragraphes 1 et 2) peuvent exiger la communication, en quelque main qu'ils se trouvent, et procéder à la saisie des documents de toute nature (comptabilité, copies de lettres, carnets de chèques, traites, comptes en *h* banque, etc.), propres à faciliter l'accomplissement de leur mission. Ils ont le droit de prélever des échantillons.
>
> Les agents de la direction générale du contrôle économique, des régies financières, de la répression des fraudes et des poids et mesures peuvent également, sans se voir opposer le secret professionnel, consulter tous documents dans les administrations ou offices de l'État, des départments, des communes et des colonies, les établissements *j* publics et assimilés, les établissements et organismes placés sous le contrôle de l'État, ainsi que les entreprises et services concédés par l'État, les départements, les communes et les colonies.'

It was held by the French Conseil d'État in the *Appraillé* case [1952] Recueil des Arrêts du Conseil d'État (Lebon) 512 that, although only the second paragraph of art 15 expressly

excluded the application of 'le secret professionnel', it was also excluded by the first
a paragraph, so that M Appraillé, an 'avoué', had properly been fined for refusing to disclose
confidential documents.

That decision shows of course that in France, as in England, an aptly worded statutory
provision can override the confidentiality of communications between a lawyer and his
client. It also shows how the Conseil d'État interpreted the particular statutory provision
there in question. But it does not, so it seems to me, establish the existence of a general
b rule of French law that, if a statutory provision conferring a power of investigation is
silent as to such communications, it automatically overrides their confidentiality.

The laws of the other countries of the Community were not discussed in anything like
the same detail in the argument before us. I hope that I shall not be thought to minimise
their importance if I confine myself, as regards them, to referring your Lordships to the
written observations of the CCBE, and in particular to the appendices thereto, and to
c saying that the authorities there cited seem to me, on the whole, to lend support to the
CCBE's submissions. It seems at all events clear that, in no country other than France,
does legislation confer on the authorities responsible for the administration of competition
law powers of investigation enabling them to disregard the confidentiality of
communications between lawyer and client. Indeed, had it been otherwise, it is difficult
to see how Dr Ehlermann and Dr Oldekop could have reached the conclusions they did.
d There is however one point on which I think that the submissions of the applicant and
of the CCBE went too far. They submitted that the right to confidential communication
between lawyer and client was a fundamental human right. I do not think it is. There is
no mention of it, as such, in the European Convention for the Protection of Human
Rights and Fundamental Freedoms (Rome, 4 November 1950; TS 71 (1953); Cmd 8969),
or, seemingly, in the constitution of any member state; and your Lordships have already
e seen that, in England and in France at least, it is acknowledged to be a right that can be
overridden or modified by an appropriately worded statute. The material placed before
the court by the CCBE shows that that is so also in Belgium. In my opinion it is a right
that the laws of civilised countries generally recognise, a right not lightly to be denied,
but not one so entrenched that, in the Community, the Council could never legislate to
override or modify it. I agree, however, that the Council cannot be held to have
f overridden it simply by dint of saying nothing about it.

My conclusion, therefore, on this part of the case, is that the powers of the Commission
under art 14 of Regulation 17 are exercisable subject to the right of the undertaking
under investigation to claim confidentiality for communications passing between itself
and its lawyers for the purpose of seeking or giving legal advice.

The next question is as to the procedure that is appropriate to secure that right whilst
g avoiding its abuse.

VI. The procedural issue

The fundamental basis of the Commission's position on that issue is that the only
satisfactory way of deciding whether a document is entitled to protection is by allowing
someone to look at it. With that I agree.

h The Commission goes on to say that, under present arrangements, that someone can
only be its own inspector. As your Lordships have seen, the Commission concedes that
in many cases the inspector need not look at the whole of the document in order to be
satisfied. But, the Commission submits, the forms that communications between a
lawyer and his client may take are so diverse that the inspector must be allowed to look
at as much of the document as he thinks fit and, if necessary, at the whole of it. The
j Commission stresses the concessions that it has made that not only will a protected
document not be copied but the inspector will not be allowed to use knowledge that he
has gained from it. In that connection the Commission says that, under the organisation
of its Directorate-General of Competition, the role of the inspector is only to gather
evidence. The evidence so collected is handed over to an official in another directorate of
the Directorate-General, who becomes the 'rapporteur' in the case. The inspector who
sees the document is not the person who later decides whether there is sufficient evidence

that the undertaking concerned has infringed the EEC Treaty. That is the responsibility of other officials, including members of the Legal Service, and ultimately of the *a* Commission itself.

The Commission considers that, under those arrangements, the only opportunity that this court can have to review an inspector's decision whether a document is entitled to protection or not is in an action brought by the undertaking concerned under art 173 of the EEC Treaty to challenge any eventual decision of the Commission that the undertaking has been guilty of an infringement of the treaty. If then the court found *b* that the decision had been based in a sufficiently important respect on information contained in a document that should have been treated as protected but was not, the court could declare the decision void. There was, the Commission submitted, in the present state of the legislation, no earlier stage at which the court could be called on to intervene.

To be fair to the Commission, it does not claim that the procedure it contends for is *c* perfect. It states its readiness to alter the procedure by regulation and says that it 'will of course be guided by anything the court may say in its judgment in this case'. The Commission submits, however, that 'with the safeguards outlined its procedure is a reasonably satisfactory procedure and the only procedure available under existing Community law', and that 'until it is changed, it must be used'.

I will say at once that I do not share the Commission's view that that is the only *d* procedure available under existing Community law. Nor am I sure that the Commission is itself empowered to alter the relevant legislation. Article 87 of the EEC Treaty confers legislative powers only on the Council and, whilst the Council has delegated some legislative powers to the Commission by art 24 of Regulation 17, it is by no means clear that they extend to the present subject matter.

I am also impressed by some of the criticisms made by the applicant and others of the *e* procedure favoured by the Commission.

In the first place, that procedure, in my opinion, confers too much power on the inspector, who need not be a lawyer and who, even if he is a lawyer, may make mistakes, not least because we are in an area of Community law that is still largely uncharted. If the inspector erroneously decides, in the case of a document which in truth is entitled to protection, that it is not entitled to protection, there is nothing to stop him taking copies *f* of it, or to stop it thereafter being freely used by the Commission. In such a case the suggested remedy in an eventual action before this court will be illusory. The dissemination of a document that should have remained confidential will have taken place long before any such action can be brought. Moreover, the availability of that remedy will depend on the Commission reaching a decision adverse to the undertaking concerned and on its basing that decision to a material extent on the contents of that *g* document.

Alternatively, the inspector may, having seen the confidential contents of a document, decide that it is protected. In that case he is required by the Commission's instructions to put what he has seen out of his mind. We all know how difficult it is, even for a judge, to perform that feat. But, even if the inspector does conscientiously and successfully perform it, those affected will not be able to be sure that he has done so. We were *h* reminded by the applicant, in this connection, of the maxim that justice should not only be done, but should manifestly and undoubtedly be seen to be done. We were also told by counsel for the applicant that, despite the division of functions between the inspector and other officials within the Commission's Directorate-General of Competition, it is none the less the practice for the inspector to attend the oral hearing held by the Commission, and for him to participate in it by putting questions to representatives of *j* the undertaking or undertakings concerned. It would be impossible, in my opinion, for anyone to be sure that a question put by the inspector, the answer to which would be recorded and could be used in evidence, had not been inspired, albeit unconsciously perhaps, by something that he had read in the protected document.

The fundamental flaw in the procedure advocated by the Commission, or perhaps rather in the thinking that underlies it, seems to me to be that it misapprehends the real

basis of the principle protecting the confidentiality of communications between a lawyer
a and his client, which, in a nutshell, is that, in a civilised society, a man is entitled to feel
that what passes between him and his lawyer is secure from disclosure. That principle is
accordingly breached as soon as there is disclosure of the contents of such a communication,
and not merely by its being used in evidence. That is not to say, of course, that, where a
genuine dispute arises whether a document is entitled to protection, someone should not
look at it to resolve the dispute. But that someone should, in general, be independent of
b the parties to the dispute, and be himself secure, which is another way of saying that the
determination of such a dispute is essentially a judicial function.

The applicant's main submission was that, until on the initiative of the Commission
the Council made a regulation for the verification of claims for protection of documents
on grounds of 'legal confidence', it was incumbent both on the undertaking claiming
such protection and on the Commission to take reasonable steps to agree on a means of
c verification that did not involve the Commission itself being entitled to see the contents
of the documents, since that would be 'a clear denial' of the principle of the protection of
'legal confidence'. In the event of ultimate disagreement between the parties, it would,
the applicant submitted, be for this court to inspect the documents and adjudicate on the
dispute.

The applicant envisaged that, if the Commission and the undertaking concerned in a
d particular case disagreed on the question whether each of them had taken such 'reasonable
steps', the Commission could proceed to take a decision imposing on the undertaking a
fine under art 15(1)(c) of Regulation 17 or periodic penalty payments under art 16(1)(d)
of that regulation. The dispute could then be brought before this court by way of an
action by the undertaking under art 173 of the EEC Treaty challenging that decision.

The applicant made various suggestions as to the sort of 'reasonable steps' that the
e parties might take, whilst emphasising that those steps might vary from case to case and
might be for discussion between the undertaking and the Commission. The applicant
instanced an attempt by the undertaking concerned, such as it had itself made in the
appendix to Mr Thomson's letter of 26 March 1979, to give a careful description of the
nature of the documents, and an attempt, again such as it had itself made, to show
Commission officials enough of each document to persuade them of its nature. As a last
f resort the applicant envisaged the possibility for the parties to agree on 'a reputable
experienced and wholly independent lawyer' who could inspect the documents and
verify their description. If the undertaking refused a request by the Commission that the
documents should be submitted to such an independent lawyer, it should, the applicant
said, be held to have acted unreasonably and therefore disentitled to succeed in any action
it might bring before this court to challenge a decision of the Commission imposing a
g fine or penalties on it.

The applicant conceded that that was an 'improvised' procedure but submitted that
improvisation was inevitable in the absence of legislation prescribing a proper procedure.
The blame lay with the Commission for not having exercised its power to propose such
legislation.

There are to my mind two objections to the course thus proposed by the applicant.
h The first is that the task of this court in this case is to lay down what is the correct
procedure in the present state of Community law, not to give its approval to suggestions
for improvisation pending the enactment of further Community legislation, if any. The
second is that the adoption of that course would involve departing in two ways from the
institutional structure of the Community as laid down in the EEC Treaty. First, it would
involve delegating a power of decision to a person, 'the independent lawyer', not
j recognised by the treaty. Second, it would involve requiring the Commission to adopt a
decision in ignorance of the full facts on which the decision was based, leaving those facts
to be ascertained by this court. The latter objection applies also, in my opinion, to
somewhat analogous procedures that were suggested to us on behalf of the British
government and of the CCBE.

I have come to the conclusion that it is impossible, and it is indeed logically impossible,
to envisage a procedure which, on the one hand, ensures that the contents of a document

for which protection is claimed are not disclosed to anyone in the Commission so long as
there has been no authoritative decision that that claim is ill-founded whilst, on the other   *a*
hand, leaving it to the Commission to decide in the first instance on the validity of that
claim, so as to pave the way for proceedings about it in this court.

One might envisage a procedure under which the existing internal arrangements of
the Commission were improved, so that, for instance, where an undertaking claimed
protection for a particular document and was unable to persuade the Commission's
inspector, on the spot, of its protected nature, the document could be sent in a sealed   *b*
envelope for perusal by, say, someone in the Commission's Legal Service, who would be
required to impart its contents only to the members of the Commission responsible for
taking the actual decision on the claim, and who would be required, also, to take no
further personal part in the case. But I can find no provision in the present legislation on
the basis of which such a procedure could be prescribed, and it would still be open to the
objection that it necessitated disclosure of the contents of the document to persons within   *c*
the Commission.

In the result I am of the opinion that the solution lies in a submission that was made
on behalf of the CCBE, and also by counsel for the applicant at the hearing, as an
alternative to his main submission. It is that resort should be had to the national courts.
That solution differs, of course, from the solution put forward by the British government
as its alternative submission on the issue of principle, in that it involves, not the   *d*
application of national law, but the application by the national courts of Community
law, those courts being able, when in doubt, to refer to this court under art 177 of the
EEC Treaty.

There is, in my opinion, a sound legislative basis for that solution in para 6 of art 14 of
Regulation 17, which requires a member state, where an undertaking 'opposes' an
investigation ordered pursuant to that article, to 'afford the necessary assistance to the   *e*
officials authorised by the Commission'. The organs of the member state there referred
to must include its courts. Moreover, resort to them appears all the more logical when
one bears in mind that, by virtue of art 13 of the regulation, an investigation ordered by
the Commission under art 14, including one ordered by decision of the Commission
under art 14(3), may be undertaken by officials of the competent authorities of the
member states instead of by officials of the Commission. Where a dispute of the present   *f*
kind arose between an undertaking in a member state and the competent authority of
that member state, the natural forum for resolving it would be the courts of that state.
Indeed, it is difficult to envisage any other. It would, I think, be odd if the appropriate
forum differed according to whether the investigation was being carried out by officials
of the national authority, assisted or not by officials of the Commission under art 13(2),
or by officials of the Commission, assisted or not by officials of the national authority   *g*
under art 14(5). It is to be observed that the ultimate sanctions provided for by arts
15(1)(c) and 16(1)(d) apply in either case. There is of course no difficulty in the way of
the Commission appearing as a party to proceedings in the courts of a member state: see
art 211 of the EEC Treaty.

Counsel for the Commission, at the hearing, questioned whether that solution would
be appropriate. He did so, as I understand him, on three grounds.   *h*

The first was that an appropriate procedure might not exist in all member states. He
himself, however, rather destroyed that ground when he conceded, on the basis of para
13 of the judgment of this court in *Amministrazione delle Finanze dello Stato v Sas
Mediterranea Importazione Rappresentanze Esportazione Commercio (MIRECO)* Case 826/79
[1980] ECR 2559, which had been cited by counsel for the applicant, that resort to the
national courts would be appropriate where the dispute arose between an undertaking   *j*
and a national authority enforcing Community competition law. At all events, art 14(6)
of Regulation 17 seems to me, particularly in the light of art 5 of the EEC Treaty, amply
adequate to require member states to introduce the necessary procedures if and in so far
as they do not already exist.

Counsel's second ground was that, if the matter were left to national courts, there
would be a risk that in practice they would apply their national rules of law. That, in my

opinion, is not a tenable ground. National courts are used to distinguishing between
a cases where they must apply their national law and cases where they must apply
Community law. Indeed, it is their duty so to do.

Counsel's third ground was at first sight more impressive. It was that resort to the
national courts would cause delay. One answer to that is of course that the risk of delay is
no reason for denying a person justice. But in any case I think that the risk can be
exaggerated. The paucity of reported cases about disputes of the present kind shows that
b they are in fact rare. That is so even in England, where, so it seems from what we have
learnt in the present case, the legal profession is particularly alert to the need to protect
confidential documents, and where both the substantive and the procedural law afford
ample opportunities for litigation about it. I think it probable that, in practice, provided
that the Commission's inspectors exercise common sense, such a dispute will arise only
where either the undertaking concerned is using delaying tactics, in which case the
c competent national courts should make short shrift of it, or where a genuine question of
principle is at stake, in which case it will be right that that question should be properly
considered.

VII. Conclusions

It follows, in my opinion, that art 1(*b*) of the Commission's decision of 9 July 1979
d should be declared void and that the applicant is entitled to its costs as against the
Commission.

If your Lordships share my view, the British government and the CCBE, as successful
interveners, who asked for costs, will also be entitled to them as against the Commission:
see art 69(2) of the Rules of Procedure of the court (the English text of which is, as I
ventured to point out in *Prais v EC Council* Case 130/75 [1976] ECR 1589 at 1609–1610,
e defective). The CCBE did not in fact ask for costs until the hearing, but that has been
held to be sufficient: see *NTN Toyo Bearing Co Ltd v EC Council* Case 113/77 [1979] ECR
1185 at 1192, 1210–1211, 1274. As regards the French government, I think that justice
will be done if it is simply left to bear its own costs.

f   On 4 February 1981 the court made an order that the oral procedure should be
reopened and by letter dated 17 July the parties were invited to present oral argument on
a series of new points.

26 January. **The Advocate-General (Sir Gordon Slynn)** delivered the following
opinion: My Lords, in February 1979 officials of the Commission required the applicant
g to make available documents which they wished to see in connection with an investigation
being conducted pursuant to art 14(1) of EEC Council Regulation 17 of 6 February 1962.
This was said to be an investigation of competitive conditions concerning the production
and distribution of zinc metal and its alloys and zinc concentrates in order to verify that
there is no infringement of arts 85 and 86 of the EEC Treaty. The applicant produced
copies of most of the documents. Some, however, were not produced, so far as relevant,
h on the basis that they were covered by legal confidentiality, which entitled the applicant
to withhold them. Following discussion and correspondence, the Commission, by art
1(*b*) of a decision dated 6 July 1979, taken pursuant to art 14(3) of the regulation, required
the applicant to produce those documents. The applicant thereupon applied to the court
pursuant to art 173 of the EEC Treaty for a declaration that art 1(*b*) of the decision was
void, or alternatively was void in so far as it necessarily required the applicant to disclose
j to the Commission's inspector the whole of each of the documents for which the
applicant claimed protection on grounds of legal confidence. After the applicant, the
Commission, the Consultative Committee of the Bars and Law Societies of the European
Community (the CCBE) and the governments of the United Kingdom and France had
made written and oral submissions, Mr Advocate-General Warner gave his opinion on
28 January 1981 that art 1(*b*) of the decision should be declared void. The factual
background of the dispute in the issues as they then appeared are fully set out in his

opinion, and I do not consider that it is of any assistance to the court for me to repeat
them.

On 4 February 1981 the court, being of the opinion that certain details (such as the
date on which, and the place where, the documents were drawn up, the exact occupation
and status of the author and the addressee, and sufficient information as to the nature of
the contents of the documents) were not available, made an order that the oral procedure
should be reopened and that the documents should be sent to the court in a sealed
envelope, in order that a report might be made on them.

These documents were sent and the judge-rapporteur and I examined them. A record
of the nature of the documents was made, which was communicated to the parties.
Although the documents produced fall broadly into the categories summarised by Mr
Advocate-General Warner in his opinion (see p 712 g, ante), I think that in view of the
importance of the case it is proper to identify more particularly the nature of the
documents in issue.

The documents in issue can be divided into three categories. First, those asking for
advice, ie (i) requests for legal advice made by a solicitor employed by a company
providing, inter alia, legal advice to the applicant (the service company) destined for two
barristers in private practice (document 1); (ii) requests for legal advice made by
executives of the applicant and sent to a solicitor in private practice in England (document
5); and (iii) a telex suggesting that legal advice should be sought from solicitors in private
practice in a third country relating to the law of that country, sent by an executive of the
applicant to an executive of the applicant's immediate parent (document 13).

Second, those giving advice, ie (i) a memorandum containing legal advice concerning
the law of a third country sent by a solicitor qualified in that country and employed by a
member of the group of which the applicant is a part to the employees of another
member of the group other than the applicant (document 2); (ii) a letter containing legal
advice concerning the law of a third country sent by a firm of solicitors in private practice
in that country to a person employed by the applicant's immediate parent in the group
(document 3); (iii) a letter containing legal advice sent from a solicitor in private practice
in England to an executive of a member of the group other than the applicant (document
7); (iv) letters containing legal advice sent by a solicitor in private practice in England to
various executives of the applicant (document 4); and (v) a memorandum containing
legal advice sent by a solicitor employed by the service company to an executive of the
applicant (document 10).

Third, those summarising advice, ie (i) a memorandum summarising legal advice
given by a solicitor employed by the service company and sent by one executive of the
applicant to another (document 11); (ii) a memorandum summarising legal advice given
by a solicitor employed by the service company and sent by an executive of the applicant
to an executive of its immediate parent (document 16); (iii) a memorandum summarising
legal advice given by a solicitor in private practice in England sent by one executive of
the applicant to another (document 12); (iv) telexes summarising legal advice received
from barristers and solicitors in private practice in a third country concerning the law of
that country and passing between an executive of the applicant and an executive of its
immediate parent (document 17).

The parties were invited to state at the reopened oral hearing their views on the law as
to, and legal opinions relating to, the existence and extent of the protection granted in
investigative proceedings instituted by public authorities for the purpose of detecting
offences of an economic nature, especially in the field of competition, to correspondence
passing between (a) two lawyers, (b) an independent lawyer and his client, (c) an
undertaking and a lawyer in a permanent contractual relationship, or who is an employee
of the undertaking, (d) a legal adviser to and an employee of an undertaking or an
employee of an associated undertaking, and (e) employees of an undertaking, or different
but associated undertakings, where the correspondence mentions legal advice given by
an independent lawyer or a legal adviser serving one of the undertakings or other
undertakings in the same group.

At the reopened oral hearing, further submissions were made on behalf of all those

who participated in the first hearing, in the course of which counsel dealt not only with
a the specific matters referred to in the court's order, but, as they were invited to do, with
the questions of principle to be decided.

It seems necessary, first, to decide what really are the issues to be considered in this
application at this stage. As Mr Advocate-General Warner shows in detail, the Commission
has been prepared to accept that, whatever the strict legal position, it would not *use*
certain documents. In the decision itself, reference is made to the answer, given in reply
b to Written Question 63/78 in the European Parliament asked by M Cousté, to the effect
that the Commission—

> 'wishing to act fairly, follows the rules in the competition law of certain member
> states and is willing not to use as evidence of infringements of the Community
> competition rules any strictly legal papers written with a view to seeking or giving
> opinions on points of law to be observed or relating to the preparation or planning
c > of the defence of the firm or association of firms concerned. When the Commission
> comes across such papers it does not copy them.'

The Commission asserted, however, that the Commission's inspector could look at the
documents and ask questions 'as far as is necessary for the purpose of establishing whether
they should be used or not'. By a letter to the applicant's solicitors dated 31 October 1979
d the Commission stressed that it had always accepted that the inspector need not read the
letters in full. He was to be put in such a position that he would be satisfied 'objectively
and with reasonable certainty that the document is one which is protected under
Community law'. By its defence the Commission stated that it is 'prepared to give an
assurance that inspectors will be instructed not to use any knowledge which they may
gain as a result of inspecting documents' for the purpose of deciding whether they are
e protected, and, second, that the inspector was authorised to look at documents only so far
as was necessary to establish whether or not they should be used as evidence.

By its rejoinder the Commission accepted that—

> 'there is a broad general principle or policy that there is a right to obtain legal
> advice in confidence, and that this implies some protection from disclosure for the
> documents seeking or giving that advice.'
f

It took the position that the sole issue was whether there was a procedure by which the
question of protection should be decided and that the only procedure which existed was
that the inspector should be left to decide the question for himself. If the document was
used and, at the end of the day, a decision was taken that there had been an infringement,
the company concerned could apply to the court to annul the decision under art 173 of
g the EEC Treaty.

At the first oral hearing the Commission felt it right not to make submissions whether
a principle of protection from disclosure existed as a matter of Community law. At the
second hearing, counsel for the Commission submitted that four principles were relevant
to the case, in the present state of Community competition law, as facets of a general
'principle of protection of legal confidence'. These were as follows. (i) Documents written
h to or by a lawyer which deals with the defence of a client in a procedure which has begun
may not be used as evidence and may not be disclosed to anyone except the person
responsible for deciding whether the document is protected by the principle or not. This
principle applies whether the documents are found in the hands of the lawyer or his
client and applies only where the lawyer is being consulted qua lawyer. (ii) Documents
written to a lawyer or by a lawyer requesting or giving legal advice (even if they are not
j protected by the first principle) may not be used as evidence if they are found in the
hands of the lawyer. Such documents need not be disclosed to anyone except the person
responsible for deciding whether the document is protected or not. Such a principle
applies only where the lawyer is being consulted qua lawyer and ceases to apply if the
lawyer is himself assisting or participating in the unlawful activities of his client. (iii)
There must be some person other than the lawyer and his client who is responsible for
deciding whether a document is entitled to protection and in the present state of

Community law that person is the Commission's inspector. (iv) Where an authority, such as the Commission, has formally stated that it will not use certain documents as *a* evidence (even when it is not prevented by law from using them in that way) enterprises are entitled to rely on that statement (unless it has been amended). If the Commission were in a particular case to use evidence of a kind which it said it would not use, that fact would be a ground for annulling the decision based on the evidence in question, if the evidence was important enough to make annulment of the decision appropriate.

'Lawyer' is accepted by the Commission to cover both a lawyer in private practice and *b* a salaried lawyer, employed by a company, so long as he is effectively subject to a comparable regime of professional ethics and discipline as is the lawyer in private practice in the member state in which he practises.

As I understand the Commission's position, the fourth principle is accepted to be a principle of law as well as the other three, but on the basis of legal certainty or perhaps what in the common law would be called an estoppel.   *c*

The applicant, whilst no doubt accepting that the first and fourth principles are better than nothing, certainly does not accept the second and third principles as framed. It contends for a wider statement of principle. In this it is supported by the United Kingdom government and the CCBE. The French government, whilst accepting the third principle if there is any rule of protection, rejects the others as formulated by the Commission as not being part of Community law.   *d*

It is plain that the initial position taken by the applicant and the Commission that this case was solely about procedure, and that issues about the limits of protection could be worked out later, cannot be accepted. Indeed, it seems to me that the CCBE and counsel for the French government were right at the outset when they contended that it was necessary to decide whether there existed any right to be protected before any question of procedure arose. The issue broadly is not how what appeared originally to be put *e* forward by the Commission as an administrative concession should be implemented but whether any principle of protection of legal confidence exists, and if so (a) its scope in relation to the documents in issue here and (b) how a dispute about the right to claim the benefit of that principle should be resolved.

During the second oral hearing, counsel for the Commission stated that the Commission did not any longer wish to *use* documents numbered 1 to 10 in the list of *f* documents which until then were in dispute. No doubt whatever the outcome of the case it will in fact adhere to that statement. At first glance it may seem tempting to take a short cut and to ignore those documents for the purpose of this opinion and for the court's decision. In my view it would be wrong to do so. The parties are still at issue about the real question. The Commission asserts the right to see them, even though it is prepared to waive that right; the applicant denies that right. Moreover, they belong to a *g* category of documents which is central to the questions which remain to be decided. In view of the time and attention given by the court and the parties to this issue, it is in my view right, and perhaps inevitable, that the documents should be considered as a whole.

The Commission's investigative powers for the purpose of carrying out the duties assigned to it by art 89 of the EEC Treaty, and provisions adopted under art 87 of the treaty, are so far as relevant conferred by art 14 of Regulation 17. It may 'undertake all *h* necessary investigations into undertakings and associations of undertakings' and, to that end, its authorised officials are empowered to examine books and business records, to take copies of them and to ask for oral explanations. There is no reference to any exemption or protection which may be claimed on the basis of legal confidence. Is that silence conclusive that no such protection is capable of applying in any form and in any situation? In my view it is not. The essential inquiry is, first, whether there is a principle *j* of Community law existing independently of the regulation, and, second, whether the regulation does on a proper construction restrict the application of that principle. The question is not whether a principle of Community law derogates from art 14 but whether art 14 excludes the application of a principle of Community law.

Accordingly, as I see it, in order to decide whether art 1(*b*) of the Commission's decision should stand it is necessary to resolve the following questions: (a) whether there exists a

general principle of Community law which, subject to the third question, protects
a documents containing what have been called legal confidences, and the contents of those
documents, from production and use in judicial, quasi-judicial or administrative
proceedings; (b) if so, whether the documents in issue in the present case are covered by
that principle; (c) whether, properly construed, Regulation 17 (and in particular art 14)
prevents the principle from applying in the course of an investigation by the Commission;
(d) how any question whether documents are covered by the principle is to be resolved
b in the absence of agreement between the Commission and the enterprise concerned.

That general principles which have not been expressly stated in the EEC Treaty or in
subordinate legislation may exist as part of Community law, the observance of which the
court is required to ensure, needs no emphasis. This was made clear in an article by Judge
Pescatore, 'Les droits de l'homme et l'intégration européenne' [1968] Les Cahiers de Droit
Européen 629. It does not seem to me that the principle is limited to 'fundamental rights'
c which are more particularly dealt with in the article. It has a broader base. Such indeed
appears to be accepted by both parties to this application. The Commission argues that
there has to be a consensus among the laws of all the member states, and that the court
cannot establish a principle which goes beyond that accepted by any one of the member
states. It cited no specific authority for that proposition, nor did it indicate what is the
necessary level or degree of consensus required to establish the existence of a general
d principle. The CCBE, whose views broadly on the point were adopted by the applicant,
submits that the aim of Community law is to find the best solution in qualitative terms,
having regard to the spirit, orientation and general tendency of the national laws. In
support it cites: P Reuter in Mélanges Rolin (1964) p 273; the article by Judge Pescatore
pp 654–655; Ipsen Europäisches Gemeinschaftsrecht (1972) p 114; W Ganshof van der
Meersch l'Ordre Juridique des Communautés Européennes (1975) pp 150, 163; Louis l'Ordre
e Juridique Communautaire (1979) p 164; and Zweigert Novelles (1969) para 1203.

Mr Advocate-General Lagrange adopted a comparable approach in Koninklijke
Nederlandsche Hoogovensen Staalfabrieken NV v ECSC High Authority Case 14/61 [1962] ECR
253 at 283–284, and it is reflected elsewhere (see e g Aktien-Zuckerfabrik Schöppenstedt v EC
Council Case 5/71, [1971] ECR 975 at 989 and Wilhelm Werhahn Hansamühle v EC Council
Joined Cases 63 to 69/72, [1973] ECR 1229 at 1259–1260). I do not set out these passages,
f but it seems to be valuable to remind the court of the views of Judge Kutscher concerning
the deduction of general principles of law from a study of the laws of the member states:

> 'There is complete agreement that when the Court interprets or supplements
> Community law on a comparative law basis it is not obliged to take the minimum
> which the national solutions have in common, or their arithmetic mean or the
> solution produced by a majority of the legal systems as the basis of its decision. The
g Court has to weigh up and evaluate the particular problem and search for the "best"
> and "most appropriate" solution.'

(See 'Methods of Interpretation as seen by a Judge at the Court of Justice', Judicial and
Academic Conference 1976, p 29.)

That national law may be looked at on a comparative basis as an aid to consideration of
h what is Community law is shown in many cases of which Associazone Industrie Siderurgiche
Italiane (ASSIDER) v ECSC High Authority Case 3/54 [1954–1956] ECR 63, LTU
Lufttransportunternehmen GmbH & Co KG v Eurocontrol Case 29/76 [1976] ECR 1541 at
1550, para 3, Netherlands State v Rüffer Case 814/79 [1980] ECR 3807, Nold v EC
Commission Case 4/73 [1974] ECR 491 at 507, para 13, SA Métallurgique Espérance-Longdoz
v ECSC High Authority Case 3/65 [1965] ECR 1065 at 1090 may be taken as examples.
i Such a course is followed not to import national laws as such into Community law but to
use it as a means of discovering an unwritten principle of Community law (see e g I Nold
KG v ECSC High Authority Case 18/57 [1959] ECR 41 at 73–74, Präsident Ruhrkohlen-
Verkaufsgesellschaft mbH v ECSC High Authority Joined Cases 36–38 and 40/59 [1960] ECR
423 at 438 and at 450 per Mr Advocate-General Lagrange Internationale Handelgesellschaft
mbH v Einfuhr-und Vorratsstelle für Getreide und Futtermittel Case 11/70 [1970] ECR 1125
at 1134, paras 3, 4 and at 1146–1147 per Mr Advocate-General Dutheillet de Lamothe).

The suggestions made at times in this case, implicitly if not explicitly, that the applicant was trying to force into an unreceptive mould a purely local rule of the common law a seems to me unfair to the argument of the applicant, who was seeking, like the CCBE and the United Kingdom government, to distil a principle which is part of Community law by reference to national laws and which, in its detailed application, required adaptation to Community procedures.

In looking at national laws it does not seem to me that it can be a precondition of the existence of a rule of Community law that the principle should be expressed identically, b or should be applied in identical form, in all of the member states. Unanimity, as to a subject which is relevant to a Community law problem, may well be a strong indication of the existence of a rule of Community law. Total unanimity of expression and application is not, however, necessary. It is at best unlikely, not least as the Community grows in size. It seems to me highly probable that there are differences in the various member states in the application of the principles of 'la bonne administration de la c justice', rejection of 'un deni de justice' and in the 'principe de proportionalité' referred to in the article by Judge Pescatore [1968] Les Cahiers de Droit Européen 629 at 643. Yet such differences do not prevent such principles from being part of Community law. Indeed, in *Transocean Marine Paint Association v EC Commission* Case 17/74 [1974] ECR 1063 it was accepted that a right to be heard existed even though Mr Advocate-General Warner found, in the relevant context, that the rule audi alteram partem existed only in d some of the member states. The fact that proceedings in one member state may be criminal, in others civil, that judicial procedures differ, that for historical reasons different practices are adopted, different conditions apply, makes divergence inevitable. In my opinion, what has to be looked for is a general principle, even if broadly expressed. If that is widely accepted then it may, if relevant, be found to be part of Community law. It is then for the court to declare how that principle is worked out in the best and most e appropriate way, to use Judge Kutscher's words, in the context of Community proceedings. Nor is the fact that in some member states the general principle may have been modified or excluded, in certain contexts covered by legislation, fatal to the existence of the principle. It is for the member states and (within their various powers) those who make the Community legislation to decide whether the general principle which exists should be modified or excluded. f

Because of these divergencies in procedure and practice, it is, in my view, important not to fasten too closely on a detailed comparison of particular labels or rules. What matters is the overall picture. Thus the question is not whether 'legal professional privilege' (a misnomer and the right of the client) is identical with 'le secret professionnel' (the duty, inter alia, of the lawyer), which plainly it is not, but whether from various sources a concept of the protection of legal confidence emerges, e g in England from the g 'privilege' and any rules as to the protection of confidentiality in France from an amalgam of 'le secret professionnel', 'les droits de la défense' and rules applicable to 'le secret des lettres confidentielles'.

The court has received from the parties much detail as to the law and practice in the various member states. I refer to it with some trepidation, partly because each member of the court has infinitely more knowledge of the position in his own member state than h a lawyer from another jurisdiction, partly because disagreement as to what is the law of a particular member state arose even during the oral hearing. Counsel for the French government, apparently, does not accept that the CCBE has correctly appreciated or stated the law of France and other member states, even though representatives of French Bars and the Bars of other member states are associated with the CCBE, and even though lawyers from those member states are quoted directly. He says they have got it wrong. j For my own part I do not accept his submission that United Kingdom counsel have not correctly stated the effect of the law of the United Kingdom or his analysis of it. I am quite satisfied that in this particular area he, in his turn, got it wrong by only looking at one part of the subject. I do not say this in any sense by way of criticism. On the contrary the efforts which he (as well as other counsel) made to deal with the issues before the court deserve tribute. I refer to these divergences only to illustrate the difficulties which a the court and the parties encounter if they seek to contrast too minutely the detailed ways in which confidentiality and the right to a fair trial are protected in the member states, ways which are determined by the factors to which I have referred. This however is in no way fatal to the existence of some right of protection for legal documents. It merely emphasises, to use Mr Advocate-General Warner's phrase, that one must go to the heart of the matter.

b The court has been provided with extracts from legislation, case decisions and the opinions of academic authors and a welter of case references. Rather than set these out in extenso, I propose to summarise what seem to me to be the relevant features for present purposes, fully conscious of the risks that a summary may oversimplify and is incomplete. I deal first with the general position as to the protection of legal confidence and then consider the position in relation to competition law.

c In Belgium it seems that confidential communications between lawyer and client are protected and cannot be seized or used as evidence. Although the basis of the rule may have been that information confided to the lawyer must be protected, it seems from the opinion of Monsieur l'Auditeur Huberlant and the decision of the Conseil d'État of 8 June 1961 in *Delhauter's* case [1962] JT 171 that it also covers confidential advice given to the client. There exists also a more general principle which protects the privacy of correspondence (see arts 10 and 22 of the Constitution).

d In Denmark the rule of the professional secret prevents lawyers from giving evidence of confidential information confided to them in their professional capacity and a lawyer can refuse to produce documents covered by professional secrecy. Communications between an accused person and his lawyer are protected in the hands of the accused under art 786 of the Code of Procedure. This rule seems to apply also in civil proceedings.

e In Germany confidential communications to a lawyer are protected in his hands, and breach of the professional confidentiality by a lawyer is a criminal offence. Thus such documents in the hands of the lawyer cannot be seized (see art 97 of the code of Criminal Procedure). Documents in the hands of the client can, it appears, be seized unless they come into existence after the commencement of criminal proceedings (decision of the Bundesgerichtshof of 13 August 1973, [1973] NJW 2035).

f In France breach of the rule of professional secrecy is a criminal offence and, although it seems that documents may be seized in some circumstances even in the hands of the lawyer, the importance of the rule is stressed in Lemaire *Les règles de la profession de l'avocat* which has been provided for the court. This rule appears to be closely linked with the right to a fair trial (les droits de la défense).

g The principle of the 'droits de la défense' appears to cover confidential documents passing in both directions between lawyer and client (see eg the decision of the Cour d'Appel de Paris of 13 November 1979, [1980] Gazette du Palais nos 90 to 92) and includes protection from seizure of legal advice given to the client before commencement of proceedings and found in his possession or in the possession of a person associated with him (Tribunal correctionnel de Nanterre, Décision of 18 December 1980, [1981] Gazette du Palais 68, a decision, it should be stated, which is under appeal). There is also it seems a wider protection for confidential letters than exists under the common law systems.

h In view of the attention which has been paid in particular to the law of France during the argument, it is of interest to observe that what I have summarised above is put, perhaps even more strongly, in para 357 of Plaisant, Franceschelli and Lassier *Droit Européen de la Concurrence*:

j 'Sans aucun doute, l'application de la loi française, par exemple, aurait pour effet de rendre inaccessible le dossier détenu par un avocat régulièrement inscrit à un barreau, en raison de ses règles déontologiques et notamment par le respect du secret professionnel prévu par l'article 378 du Code pénal. De même, les documents adressés par un avocat à ses clients demeurent couverts par le secret professionnel, surtout si la correspondance lui est adressée de manière confidentielle.'

In Greece it seems that confidential communications in the hands of lawyers are protected in investigative proceedings instituted by judicial or administrative authorities.

Documents in the hands of the client are covered by the general principle of privacy
defined in art 9 of the Constitution. The power to search the client's premises is *a*
circumscribed by art 253ff. of the Code of Criminal Procedure.

In Ireland and the United Kingdom, although there may be differences in detail,
broadly the law of the two member states is the same and it is set out more fully in the
opinion of Mr Advocate-General Warner. It should be repeated, however, that it covers
both (a) communications between a person and his lawyer for the purpose of obtaining
or giving legal advice whether or not in connection with pending or contemplated legal *b*
proceedings and (b) communications between a person and his lawyer and other persons
for the dominant purpose of preparing for pending or contemplated legal proceedings.

In Italy, as in most of the member states, the law forbids lawyers from giving evidence
of the information confided in them by their clients and entitles them to withhold
documents covered by the doctrine of professional secrecy. On the other hand, it seems
that, in the case of criminal investigations, documents held by a lawyer may be seized *c*
unless they have been entrusted to him for the preparation of his client's defence.
Protection is wider in civil proceedings but it does not, in any case, appear to extend to
documents in the hands of the client. It seems that, in the case of lawyers, professional
secrecy is a reflection of the right to a fair trial guaranteed by art 24 of the Constitution
(see de Leone 'Il segreto professionale: limiti e guaranzie' [1978] Rivista Italiana di Diritto
e Procedura Penale 675). *d*

In Luxembourg rules of professional secrecy and 'les droits de la défense', it would
seem, protect legal confidences in the hands of the lawyer, and of the client after
proceedings have begun, but little case law has been produced showing the application
of these rules in practice.

Dutch law forbids the revelation of confidences by persons exercising a profession,
such as lawyers. Coupled with this there is a right to refuse to give evidence on matters *e*
covered by professional secrecy. These matters include not only the information revealed
by the client but also, in the case of lawyers, the legal advice they have given (see, for
example, the decisions of the Gerechtshof of the Province of Drenthe, 17 November
1869, W p 3161, and the Arrondissementsrechtbank of Rotterdam, 18 October 1954,
[1955] NJ no 368). Article 98 of the Code of Criminal Procedure provides that, when the
premises of someone bound by professional secrecy are searched, the doctrine of *f*
professional secrecy must be observed and documents covered by it cannot be seized.
There appears to be no authority holding or denying that legal correspondence found in
the hands of the client is protected.

This summary is substantially, if not entirely, accepted by the Commission, the
applicant and the body representing the Bars of all the member states as being a fair and
acceptable statement of the laws of the member states. *g*

It seems to me significant that they were able to reach agreement as to the existence of
the principles which are set out in the document which they prepared to read to the
court.

From this it is plain, as indeed seems inevitable, that the position in all the member
states is not identical. It is to my mind equally plain that there exists in all the member
states a recognition that the public interest and the proper administration of justice *h*
demand as a general rule that a client should be able to speak freely, frankly and fully to
his lawyer. As it is put in *Les règles de la profession d'avocat*:

'Il faut que le client "puisse avoir, en son avocat, une confiance sans limite", qu'il
puisse "négliger avec lui les précautions qu'on prend dans les affaires ordinaires";
qu'il ne craigne pas "d'ouvrir son âme tout entière à son défenseur et s'abandonner à
sa foi".' *j*

Whether it is described as the right of the client or the duty of the lawyer, this principle
has nothing to do with the protection or privilege of the lawyer. It springs essentially
from the basic need of a man in a civilised society to be able to turn to his lawyer for
advice and help, and, if proceedings begin, for representation; it springs no less from the
advantages to a society which evolves complex law reaching into all the business affairs

of persons, real and legal, that they should be able to know what they can do under the
a law, what is forbidden, where they must tread circumspectly, where they run risks.
The fact that this principle of confidentiality between lawyer and client may be given
effect to in different ways, and that it is not coextensive in its application at any point in
time, in all the member states, does not mean that the principle does not exist. In my
opinion it should be declared to be a rule of Community law. The way in which and the
extent to which it applies in Community law and in relation to Community transactions
b and procedures needs to be worked out to achieve the best and most appropriate solution
in the light not only of considerations of the practices of the various member states, but
of the interests of the Community and its institutions, member states and individuals
which are subject to its laws.
It is universally accepted that confidential documents of the kind to which I have
referred in the hands of the lawyer are protected. If one considers the real purpose of the
c protection and gets away from labels and procedures, like legal professional privilege and
'secret professionnel' which may not give the whole picture, I can for my part see no
justifiable distinction between such documents in the hands of the lawyer and in the
hands of the client. If the lawyer has one copy and the client another, both should be
protected. The request and the reply, if relating to legal advice, are of the same nature.
To tell the client that if he leaves his documents at his lawyer's office they will be
d protected but that, if he keeps them himself, they are not seems to me indefensible and
likely to encourage, for example, the giving or oral advice if it is unfavourable advice,
and the destruction or transfer to the lawyer's office of documents. It would be quite
extraordinary that if the lawyer's documents were, by chance, left at the client's premises,
the day the inspector called, they must be produced, but that if the lawyer took his file
away with him they would not. In my opinion the rule covers communications between
e lawyer and client made for the purpose of obtaining or giving legal advice in whoever's
hands they are and whether legal proceedings have begun or not. It covers also the
contents of that advice (given orally or in writing), in whatever form it is recorded,
whether in a letter or in a summary or in a note or in minutes.
The position of the lawyer who is employed as such by an undertaking has been much
canvassed. As I understand it, in some member states full-time employment is
f incompatible with the full professional status of a lawyer (apparently in Belgium, France,
Italy and Luxembourg); in others, the employed lawyer remains subject to professional
discipline and ethics. Where the lawyer who is employed remains a member of the
profession and subject to its discipline and ethics, in my opinion he is to be treated for
present purposes in the same way as lawyers in private practice, so long as he is acting as
a lawyer. Cases can arise where the lawyer exercises other functions (such as in England
g those of a company secretary) and of course, any communication in such other capacity
would not be covered. A lawyer in private practice who is a member or associate of a
large firm may act for long periods for only one client. If his communications are
protected, so it seems to me, should be those of the lawyer who is a member of the legal
department of a company. I would reject any suggestion that lawyers (professionally
qualified and subject to professional discipline) who are employed full time by the
h Community institutions, by government departments or in the legal departments of
private undertakings are not to be regarded as having such professional independence as
to prevent them from being within the rule. Accordingly, I consider that counsel for the
Commission is right to accept that, provided he is subject to rules of professional
discipline and ethics, the salaried lawyer should for present purposes be treated in the
same way as the lawyer in private practice. The same position, it seems to me, ought to
j apply to confidential communications between a lawyer qualified in one jurisdiction and
a lawyer qualified in a different jurisdiction about the affairs of their mutual or respective
clients.
The proper administration of the law and the rights of the individual are not of course
the only aspects of the public interest. These may have to be balanced against other
aspects of the public interest with which they may, or may appear to, conflict. A
legislature may decide that one of these which would otherwise apply should be cut

down or removed in areas where other aspects of the public interest should prevail. The
elimination of restrictive practices, or fetters on free competition, is such an interest and, *a*
obviously, at the present time an important one. Can it be said that there is a rule widely
accepted in the member states that the protection of legal confidence should yield to the
powers needed to investiate alleged infringement of competition law?

I am not aware of any provision of national law which expressly excludes all right of
legal confidence from competition inquiries or proceedings.

As I understand it, the Belgian Law of 27 May 1960 makes no mention of le secret *b*
professionnel. Nor, however, does the statute dealing with criminal investigations.
Silence does not remove the right of professional secrecy in the latter context, so that it
may be doubted whether it does in the former, although there is, semble, no decided case
on the subject.

In Denmark the relevant legislation gives no right to seize documents and a court
order must first be sought in order to obtain their disclosure. So far this has not apparently *c*
been necessary because the persons investigated have complied with requests to produce
documents. However, since confidentiality in Danish law does not apparently extend to
documents in the hands of the client, the limiting or overriding of a principle of
confidentiality does not seem to arise.

According to a letter from the Bundeskartellamt, the German Federal Cartel Office,
submitted at the hearing, searches and seizures made in the context of 'administrative *d*
fines' proceedings pursuant to the Gesetz gegen Wettbewerbsbeschränkungen (GWB),
the Restraint of Competition Act, in Germany are expressly subject to the rules set out in
the Code of Criminal Procedure. As a result, confidentiality, in so far as it is respected in
German law, is upheld and documents found in the hands of the client may not be seized
if they came into existence after the commencement of proceedings. On the other hand,
investigations under arts 46 and 51ff of the GWB, which are similar to proceedings under *e*
art 14 of Regulation 17, are not subject to any express limitations. It is nevertheless
accepted by the Bundeskartellamt and by commentators that confidentiality is protected
to the same extent and documents may not in any event be seized without an order of a
judge.

In France it seems to be accepted that the silence of the law (ie art 15 of Ordonnance
45/1484) does override professional secrecy (see the decision of the Conseil d'État in the *f*
Appraillé case [1952] Recueil des Arrêts du Conseil d'État (Lebon) 512) unless the
correspondence in question is 'liée d'une défense'. The liberal interpretation given to this
expression by the Tribunal Correctionnel de Nanterre in its decision of 18 December
1980, if upheld on appeal, would bring the position in France broadly into line with that
in Germany and, it seems, Belgium. This decision has been criticised however.

Articles 25 and 26 of the Greek Law 703/1977, which empower the Service for the *g*
Protection of Competition to obtain any necessary information and to search premises,
expressly preserve confidentiality, by referring to art 9 of the Constitution and arts 212
and 253ff of the Code of Criminal Procedure.

Paragraph 7(2) of Sch 1 to the Restrictive Practices Act 1972 of Ireland expressly
subjects the powers of the Restrictive Practices Commission to examine witnesses on
oath and require them to produce documents to the doctrine of legal professional *h*
privilege. The Examiner of Restrictive Practices has extensive powers similar to those in
art 14 of Regulation 17, but s 15 of the Restrictive Practices Act 1972 allows a person
under investigation to apply to a court for a declaration that the exercise of the examiner's
powers are not warranted by 'the exigencies of the common good'. The Irish concept of
legal professional privilege, like the English, is justified as being in the public interest
(and may therefore be held to be for the common good) but the Restrictive Practices Act *j*
1972 seems to require the Irish courts to assess the public interest for and against the
exercise of the examiner's powers.

There is it seems no relevant legislation in Italy so the situation does not arise. It
appears, however, that in the case of investigations in the context of administrative
proceedings, where legislation often does not contain detailed provisions relating to
powers of inspection, it has been speculated that the rules relating to criminal and civil

investigations (which do preserve confidentiality) would apply, depending on the nature of the proceedings (see *Giannini Diritto Amministrativo* (1970) vol 2, pp 970 ff). This view again is challenged.

Article 5 of the Law of 17 June 1970 of Luxembourg gives the Commission des Pratiques Commerciales Restrictives wide powers of investigation. Under art 6 it may also request the Ministre de l'Economie Nationale to undertake an inquiry, the minister designating the officials responsible for the investigation. Their powers are defined by reference to art 8 of the Law of 30 June 1961, which concerns price controls. That article gives the Office des Prix 'Le droit d'investigation le plus large'. Neither art 5 of the Law of 17 June 1970 nor art 8 of the Law of 30 June 1961 contains any express limitations on the powers of investigation given by them and there is, it seems, no relevant case law whether any rule of legal confidence would apply in competition matters. It is, however, relevant to observe, as I undertand it, that the Commission des Pratiques Commerciales Restrictives is purely a fact-finding body with no decision-making power (art 3 of the Law of 17 June). Its function is to carry out investigations at the request of the minister and to draw up a report (which may contain the dissenting opinions of the members of the commission). Enforcement of the law is a matter for the minister and, from his decisions, an appeal lies to the Conseil d'État. The minister cannot directly impose a fine; at most he can prohibit a particular practice and penal sanctions may be imposed if his decision is not complied with (arts 7 and 8). As a result, the position in Luxembourg is different from that obtaining under Regulation 17. The commission is both investigator and judge and can impose fines.

In the Netherlands art 25 of the Wet Economische Delicten, the Economic Crimes Act, provides that, unless stated otherwise, economic offences are subject to the rules in the Code of Criminal Procedure (which, as has been seen, appears to uphold confidentiality). Article 19 of the Wet deals with powers of inspection but expressly preserves confidentiality. Article 18 of the Wet Economische Mededinging, the Economic Competition Act, is to the same effect.

Legislation in the United Kingdom expressly preserves confidentiality (see s 85 of the Fair Trading Act 1973, s 37 of the Restrictive Trade Practices Act 1976 and s 3 of the Competition Act 1980). It seems likely that, in England, an express provision would be required in order to restrict or override legal professional privilege.

It thus seems clear that there is no universal, or even widely accepted, rule that such protection of legal confidence as exists is excluded in competition matters. At most, there is doubt in some cases; the general rule is that the protection continues.

On behalf of the French government it has been said that art 14 of Regulation 17, properly construed, gives the Commission powers of investigation that are completely unlimited, and unfettered by any principle of confidentiality.

It is said that silence regarding the principle of confidentiality indicates that it is overridden entirely. Reliance has been placed on the legislative history of Regulation 17 to show that the Council considered the question of limiting the Commission's powers in this way and then rejected it. While entertaining doubts whether it is permissible to interpret a regulation by reference to its legislative history, Mr Advocate-General Warner took the view that the Council had not deliberately decided against the application of any principle of confidentiality. At the second hearing, his conclusion was attacked by counsel for the French government and the Commission.

Whilst I share those doubts, in view of the second hearing it is necessary to consider again whether the legislative history of Regulation 17 in any event clearly expresses the intention of the draftsmen. The preamble states that the Commission must have the power to require production of the information and carry out the investigations necessary to bring to light the restrictive practices prohibited by the EEC Treaty. The regulation contains four provisions giving effect to this, arts 11 to 14. As can be seen from a comparison of the original draft, the amendments proposed by the Parliament's Internal Market Committee (both to be found in the 'Deringer Report', European Parliament Document 57/1961), the Parliament's amendments (JOCE 73 of 15 November 1961, p 1409) and the final version, extensive changes were made to what is now art 11 but,

apart from a redrafting of art 14(6), only minor textual amendments were made to art
14(2), (3) and (5).

As far as these articles were concerned, the committee raised several points concerning
the general principle observed by states founded on the rule of law. In this context, it
said (para 121):

'... toute personne tenue de fournir des renseignements doit avoir le droit de
refuser le témoignage tout comme le secret professionnel, par exemple des avocats
et des experts-comptables, doit être garantie. En cas de perquisition, il faut prévoir
l'intervention du tribunal du fait que d'après la loi fondamentale allemande, par
exemple, des perquisitions ne peuvent être faites que sur mandat du juge. La
possibilité pour l'intéressé d'introduire un recours devant la Cour de justice contre
la décision de la Commission ne remplace pas le mandat de perquisition du juge, car
le renversement de la charge de la demande restreint d'une façon inadmissible la
défense de l'intéressé.'

The only proposed change, however, was to the draft art 11, to which the following
paragraph was added:

'Sont tenus de fournir les renseignements demandés les propriétaires d'une
entreprise ou leurs représentants et, dans le cas de personnes morales, de sociétés ou
d'associations n'ayant pas la personnalité juridique, les personnes chargées de les
représenter selon la loi ou les statuts. Les personnes tenues de fournir les
renseignements peuvent refuser de répondre aux questions lorsque ladite réponse
risque de les exposer elles-mêmes ou d'exposer une des personnes pouvant refuser
de témoigner en vertu du code national de procédure, ou les entreprises ou les
associations d'enterprises qu'ils (sic) représentent, à des sanctions pénales.'

When Regulation 17 was adopted, the second sentence was omitted. It is quite clear that
this sentence corresponds to no known doctrine of professional secrecy in any of the
member states. Its closest resemblance is to the rule, recognised in German law (and also
English law for that matter), that a person may refuse to answer incriminating questions.
Paragraph 121 of the Deringer Report shows the close attention being paid to German
law.

Not all the report's recommendations were proposed as amendments to the draft and
it is possible that the wish that professional secrecy be protected had the same fate as the
suggestion that searches should be subject to the issue of a judicial warrant. Nevertheless,
if the Parliament's proposed amendment to art 11 could be construed as a reference to
professional secrecy, the question arises why no similar amendment was proposed in
relation to art 14. There is no clear answer.

Such information as to the legislative history as is available is far from giving a clear
indication of the intentions of the draftsmen. The most that I think can be said is that a
limitation on the Commission's powers of investigation relevant to this case occurred to
the Parliament's Internal Market Committee but that it proposed no amendment to give
effect to such a limitation. There is no indication that either the Commission or the
Council thought of it or, if they did, what they thought. The legislative history does not,
therefore, in my view, offer any useful guidance to the interpretation of art 14.

It is impossible to accept the argument put forward that disclosure of documents to an
authorised official pursuant to art 14 does not in any way breach the confidence widely
protected in member states, as has been shown from the summary already given. Nor do
I accept the argument that proceedings under art 14 are purely administrative and fact-
finding so that the rule cannot apply in any event. There is no clear-cut division in the
procedure under Regulation 17 between a fact finding and a quasi-judicial stage in the
investigation. The same Directorate-General is involved throughout. I refer in any event
to what was said by the court in *Hoffman-La Roche & Co AG v EC Commission* Case 85/76
[1979] ECR 461 at 511, para 9:

'Observance of the [right to a fair trial] is in all proceedings in which sanctions, in
particular fines or penalty payments, may be imposed a fundamental principle of

Community law which must be respected even if the proceedings in question are administrative proceedings.'

In my opinion, therefore, the rule of protection is not excluded by the nature of the process.

In his paper on methods of interpretation in 1976 (p 38), Judge Kutscher said that a measure adopted by a Community institution—

'is to be interpreted—if at all possible—so that it is compatible with the superior law of the Treaties and the general principles of law which, too, are attributed a status superior to that of subordinate law. Other interpretations which would lead to incompatibility with the superior law, and thus to the inapplicability or to the invalidity of the measure adopted by the institution, are to be disregarded.'

I am fully alive to the importance of enforcing arts 85 and 86 of the EEC Treaty, to the need to obtain all information as to what has been done by those concerned and to the difficulties of obtaining evidence to establish the truth. None the less on its proper construction, art 14 does not, in my opinion, empower the Commission to examine documents covered by the general principle of confidentiality as I consider that it is to be found in Community law.

I am accordingly of the opinion that the view taken by the Commission that as a matter of law it cannot be said that there is no rule for the protection of legal confidence in Community law was correct. That rule, however, is wider, as I have described earlier, and, in my view, more logical than the limited rule proposed by the Commission. It is a general rule of Community law to be derived from a consideration of the general principle applied, albeit in different ways, in the member states. It does not depend on an administrative concession, nor is it derived from any concept of estoppel flowing from an answer given to a parliamentary question, and which, in theory at any rate, it might one day be said could be abrogated for the future. It is not excluded in the area of competition investigations; nor does art 14 prevent it from applying.

It follows that in my opinion the views expressed by Dr Ehlermann and Dr Oldekop (which are set out in Mr Advocate-General Warner's opinion (see p 711 b to j, ante) and to which, albeit they were writing in a personal capacity, I would attach considerable weight) were substantially correct. Those views in essence are shared by J Sedemund *Due process in Community law* and in other articles to which the court has been referred.

One particular problem in this case relates to the documents prepared by or for members of the Rio Tinto Zinc Group other than the applicant. As the court indicated in *Imperial Chemical Industries Ltd v EC Commission* Case 48/69 [1972] ECR 619 at 662, the reality of the relationship between the members of a group of companies forming one economic unit may mean that their separate legal personality has to be treated as a formal rather than a substantial distinction, particularly in the field of competition. Moreover, legal advice prepared by either lawyers employed or those in private practice retained by one member of the group may in fact be requested on behalf of all the members of the group. This is certainly the case where there exists, as here, one member of the group whose function it is to supply legal advice to the group as a whole. In this situation it seems right that the common interest of all the members of the group should be regarded as justifying the retention of confidentiality in respect of documents drawn up by or for one member of the group and found in the possession of another.

Some of the documents, eg document 13, contain matter not falling within the categories of (a) communications between lawyer and client (or lawyer and lawyer) and of (b) records of such communications to which I have referred. Those parts must be produced. There is not in practice any real difficulty in covering up the parts which are protected. This apart, I consider that all the documents which remain in issue are protected from production to the Commission.

Although the procedural question ceased to be the primary question, it remained an important part of the Commission's case that (a) whether documents are protected cannot depend on the ipse dixit of the undertaking and (b) that in the present state of

Community law the inspector himself must decide the question, subject to his right to
consult with his colleagues in general terms, if he is in doubt. I agree with the first part a
of the contention. I find the second wholly unacceptable. It seems to me that in a number
of member states the decision whether a document is protected is not left to be decided
by the enforcing and investigating authority, and such a course would be unacceptable. I
do not repeat the views expressed by Mr Advocate-General Warner on this aspect of the
matter but I adopt them. I agree with him that an independent tribunal must decide the
question. It is too simplistic a view to say that the inspector can put out of his mind, b
wholly, any protected material which he may read in the course of making his decision.
Judges sometimes have to do it, but their training is different and even for them it is not
always an easy task. The English position has been overstated in the arguments on behalf
of the French government since not infrequently a decision whether documents are
protected is taken as a separate process and by a different judge from the trial judge.
Moreover, in this area it seems to me that it is important to have regard to the sense of c
injustice which may be felt by those who are subject to investigation. The enterprise
concerned will no doubt often be left uncertain whether the inspector really has put the
matter aside or whether consciously or not he has gone on to ask questions or pursue
inquiries which can only have been derived from protected information. This is in no
sense a reflection on the good faith or intention of the inspector. It derives simply from
the difficulty of knowing whether he has been influenced unconsciously by what he has d
read and which ex hypothesi he should not have seen.

In this context I find the answer to M Cousté unsatisfactory; the Commission's
undertaking is only not to *use* the document. It seems to me that if the protection has
come into existence the Commission should not *see* the document. The public interest
which gives rise to the principle of confidentiality comes into existence at the moment
when advice is required and given, and it continues thereafter irrespective of when the e
question of production for inspection arises.

I cannot share the equanimity with which the Commission suggests that all can be put
right in the end. It is said that, if protected information is used to lead to a decision that
there has been an infringement, that decision may be set aside by the court. Such an
approach to my mind leaves out of account important considerations. The protected
information (ex hypothesi wrongly used) may be the cornerstone of the Commission's f
case; it may appear at an early stage in the inquiry; the inquiry may be, and often is,
lengthy, demanding great time and effort on the part of the Commission's staff. The cost
to the Community, and therefore eventually to the taxpayer, and to the private enterprise
concerned, may be huge. It is to my mind more satisfactory, more fair and more efficient
if this kind of point can be resolved at an earlier stage. Unless Community legislation
establishes that it is not possible to resolve such issues at an earlier stage, I consider the g
arguments in favour of obtaining a ruling, before the documents are seen and used, to be
overwhelming. It is in any event wrong that such protected information should continue
to be used if means of deciding whether it is protected are available. I do not consider
that for such a ruling to be given at an early stage involves a conflict between the
functions of the Commission and whatever is the appropriate judicial tribunal. The
functions of the two in achieving the true aims of the EEC Treaty and Community law h
are complementary and not conflicting.

Mr Advocate-General Warner has put forward a number of considerations in favour of
the matter being resolved by national courts as a matter of Community law, although he
rejects, as I would reject, the suggestion put forward that protection should depend on
the national law of the member state in which the documents are found. The course he
has suggested is obviously one possible course, although some difficulty may arise from j
the fact that in some jurisdictions it appears that it is the bâtonnier, rather than a court,
who decides whether the documents are privileged.

There seems to me an alternative course which I do not consider to be subject to all the
disadvantages which have been attributed to it. It seems to me that, once the question of
principle has been decided by the court, the issues in most future cases are likely to be
short. In the majority of cases the parties are likely to be able to reach agreement whether

a document in fact is within the principle, the undertaking's lawyer being able to satisfy the inspector as to the nature of the document, without disclosing the contents. If disputes arise, the Commission, if not satisfied, can take a decision which can be referred to the court, as was done in this case, and perhaps be dealt with by a chamber. In the light of experience in comparable matters, I do not accept that the floodgates would be open as is contended. Nor should any weight be attached to the references made to delays and tactics which it is said occur in American proceedings. American lawyers are the first to point out that such delays do not form part of the United Kingdom system. The court has methods available to it to curb unmeritorious applications. Even if costs against the undertaking do not deter, few lawyers acting in this kind of work are likely to risk serious criticism by the court in its judgment by bringing hopeless disputes as to the documents before it.

Accordingly, it seems to me that the better course is that when a dispute does arise the matter should be referred to this court as has been done in the present proceedings.

It is, then, my opinion that, subject to what I have said about parts of the documents in dispute, art 1(b) of the Commission's decision of 6 July 1979 should be declared void and the Commission should be ordered to pay the applicant's costs. There is no reason derived from the subsequent proceedings, in my view, to depart from Mr Advocate-General Warner's recommendation that the Commission should also pay the costs of the successful interveners, the United Kingdom government and the CCBE, and that the French government should bear its own costs.

18 May. **THE COURT OF JUSTICE** delivered its judgment which, having summarised the facts, procedure and submissions of the parties, dealt with the law as follows:

1. By application lodged at the court registry on 4 October 1979 A M & S Europe Ltd, which is based in the United Kingdom, instituted proceedings pursuant to the second paragraph of art 173 of the EEC Treaty to have art 1(b) of an individual decision notified to it, namely EEC Commission Decision 79/760 of 6 July 1979, declared void. That provision required the applicant to produce for examination by officers of the Commission charged with carrying out an investigation all the documents for which legal privilege was claimed, as listed in the appendix to A M & S Europe's letter of 26 March 1979 to the Commission.

2. The application is based on the submission that in all the member states written communications between lawyer and client are protected by virtue of a principle common to all those states, although the scope of that protection and the means of securing it vary from one country to another. According to the applicant, it follows from that principle, which in its view also applies 'within possible limits' in Community law, that the Commission may not, when undertaking an investigation pursuant to art 14(3) of EEC Council Regulation 17 of 6 February 1962, claim production, at least in their entirety, of written communications between lawyer and client if the undertaking claims protection and takes 'reasonable steps to satisfy the Commission that the protection is properly claimed' on the ground that the documents in question are in fact covered by legal privilege.

3. On the basis of that premise the applicant contends that it is a denial of the principle of confidentiality to permit an authority seeking information or undertaking an investigation, such as the Commission in this instance, against which the principle of protection is relied on, to inspect protected documents in breach of their confidential nature. However, it concedes that 'the Commission has a prima facie right to see the documents . . . in the possession of an undertaking' by virtue of art 14 of Regulation 17, and that by virtue of that right 'it is still the Commission that takes the decision whether the documents are protected or not, but on the basis of a description of the documents' and not on the basis of an examination of the whole of each document by its inspectors.

4. In that respect the applicant accepts that initially the undertaking claiming protection must provide the Commission with sufficient material on which to base an

assessment; for example, the undertaking may provide a description of the documents and show the Commission's inspectors 'parts of the documents', without disclosing the *a* contents for which protection is claimed, in order to satisfy the Commission that the documents are in fact protected. Should the Commission remain unsatisfied as to the confidential nature of the documents in question the undertaking would be obliged to permit 'inspection by an independent third party who will verify the description of the contents of the documents'.

5. The contested decision, based on the principle that it is for the Commission to *b* determine whether a given document should be used or not, requires A M & S Europe Ltd to allow the Commission's authorised inspectors to examine the documents in question in their entirety. Claiming that those documents satisfy the conditions for legal protection as described above, the applicant has requested the court to declare art 1(*b*) of the above-mentioned decision void or, alternatively, to declare it void in so far as it requires the disclosure to the Commission's inspector of the whole of each of the *c* documents for which the applicant claims protection on the grounds of legal confidence.

6. The United Kingdom, intervening, essentially supports the argument put forward by the applicant, and maintains that the principle of legal protection of written communications between lawyer and client is recognised as such in the various countries of the Community, even though there is no single, harmonised concept the boundaries of which do not vary. It accepts that the concept may be the subject of differing *d* approaches in the various member states.

7. As to the most suitable procedure for resolving disputes which might arise between the undertaking and the Commission whether certain documents are of a confidential nature or not, the United Kingdom proposes that if the Commission's inspector is not satisfied by the evidence supplied by the undertaking, an independent expert should be consulted, and, should the dispute not be resolved, the matter should be brought before *e* the Court of Justice by the party concerned following the adoption by the Commission of a decision under Regulation 17.

8. The view taken by the Consultative Committee of the Bars and Law Societies of the European Community (hereinafter referred to as 'the Consultative Committee'), which has also intervened in support of the applicant's conclusions, is that a right of confidential communication between lawyer and client (in both directions) is recognised as a *f* fundamental, constitutional or human right, accessory or complementary to other such rights which are expressly recognised, and that as such that right should be recognised and applied as part of Community law. After pointing out that the concept is not a static one, but is continually evolving, the Consultative Committee concludes that, if the undertaking and the Commission cannot agree whether a document is of a confidential nature or not, the most appropriate procedure would be to have recourse to an expert's *g* report, or to arbitrarion. Assuming, moreover, that the court is the sole tribunal with jurisdiction to settle such a dispute it ought in that case to be necessary for it only to determine whether or not the contested documents are of a confidential nature on the basis of an expert's report obtained pursuant to an order under art 49 of the Rules of Procedure.

9. To all those arguments the Commission replies that, even if there exists in *h* Community law a general principle protecting confidential communications between lawyer and client, the extent of such protection is not to be defined in general and abstract terms, but must be established in the light of the special features of the relevant Community rules, having regard to their wording and structure, and to the needs which they are designed to serve.

10. The Commission concludes that, on a correct construction of art 14 of Regulation *j* 17, the principle on which the applicant relies cannot apply to documents the production of which is required in the course of an investigation which has been ordered under that article, including written communications between the undertaking concerned and its lawyers.

11. The applicant's argument is, the Commission maintains, all the more unacceptable inasmuch as in practical terms it offers no effective means whereby the inspectors may

be assured of the true content and nature of the contested documents. On the contrary,
a the solutions which the applicant proposes would have the effect, particularly in view of
the protracted nature of any arbitration procedure (even assuming that such a procedure
were permissible in law) of delaying considerably, or even of nullifying, the Commission's
efforts to bring to light infringements of arts 85 and 86 of the EEC Treaty, thereby
frustrating the essential aims of Regulation 17.

12. The government of the French Republic, intervening in support of the conclusions
b of the Commission, observes that as yet Community law does not contain any provision
for the protection of documents exchanged between a legal adviser and his client.
Therefore, it concludes, the Commission must be allowed to exercise its powers under
art 14 of Regulation 17 without having to encounter the objection that the documents
whose disclosure it considers necessary in order to carry out the duties assigned to it by
that regulation are confidential. To permit the legal adviser and the undertaking subject
c to a proceeding in a matter concerning competition to be the arbiters of the question
whether or not a document is protected would, in the opinion of the French government,
not be compatible with Community law and would inevitably create grave inconsistencies
in the application of the rules governing competition.

13. It is apparent from the application, as well as from the legal basis of the contested
decision, that the dispute in this case is essentially concerned with the interpretation of
d art 14 of EEC Council Regulation 17 of 6 February 1962 for the purpose of determining
what limits, if any, are imposed on the Commission's exercise of its powers of
investigation under that provision by virtue of the protection afforded by the law to the
confidentiality of written communications between lawyer and client.

14. Once the existence of such protection under Community law has been confirmed,
and the conditions governing its application have been defined, it must be determined
e which of the documents referred to in art 1(b) of the contested decision may possibly be
considered as confidential and therefore beyond the Commission's powers of investigation.
Since some of those documents have in the mean time been produced to the Commission
by the applicant of its own volition, the documents to be considered now are those which
were lodged in a sealed envelope at the court registry on 9 March 1981 pursuant to the
court's order of 4 February 1981 reopening the oral procedure in this case.

f
(a) The interpretation of art 14 of EEC Council Regulation 17

15. The purpose of Regulation 17, which was adopted pursuant to the first paragraph
of art 87(1) of the EEC Treaty, is, according to para (2)(a) and (b) of that article, 'to ensure
compliance with the prohibitions laid down in Article 85(1) and in Article 86' of the
treaty and 'to lay down detailed rules for the application of Article 85(3)'. The regulation
g is thus intended to ensure that the aim stated in art 3(f) of the treaty is achieved. To that
end it confers on the Commission wide powers of investigation and of obtaining
information by providing in the eighth recital in its preamble that the Commission must
be empowered, throughout the Common Market, to require such information to be
supplied and to undertake such investigations 'as are necessary' to bring to light
infringements of arts 85 and 86 of the treaty.

h 16. In arts 11 and 14 of the regulation, therefore, it is provided that the Commission
may obtain 'information' and undertake the 'necessary' investigations, for the purpose of
proceedings in respect of infringements of the rules governing competition. Article 14(1)
in particular empowers the Commission to require production of business records, that
is to say documents concerning the market activities of the undertaking, in particular as
regards compliance with those rules. Written communications between lawyer and
j client fall, in so far as they have a bearing on such activities, within the category of
documents referred to in arts 11 and 14.

17. Furthermore, since the documents which the Commission may demand are, as
art 14(1) confirms, those whose disclosure it considers 'necessary' in order that it may
bring to light an infringement of the treaty rules on competition, it is in principle for
the Commission itself, and not the undertaking concerned or a third party, whether an
expert or an arbitrator, to decide whether or not a document must be produced to it.

(b) Applicability of the protection of confidentiality in Community law

18. However, the above rules do not exclude the possibility of recognising, subject to *a*
certain conditions, that certain business records are of a confidential nature. Community
law, which derives from not only the economic but also the legal interpenetration of the
member states, must take into account the principles and concepts common to the laws
of those states concerning the observance of confidentiality, in particular, as regards
certain communications between lawyer and client. That confidentiality serves the
requirement, the importance of which is recognised in all of the member states, that any *b*
person must be able, without constraint, to consult a lawyer whose profession entails the
giving of independent legal advice to all those in need of it.

19. As far as the protection of written communications between lawyer and client is
concerned, it is apparent from the legal systems of the member states that, although the
principle of such protection is generally recognised, its scope and the criteria for applying
it vary, as has, indeed, been conceded both by the applicant and by the parties who have· *c*
intervened in support of its conclusions.

20. Whilst in some of the member states the protection against disclosure afforded to
written communications between lawyer and client is based principally on a recognition
of the very nature of the legal profession, inasmuch as it contributes towards the
maintenance of the rule of law, in other member states the same protection is justified
by the more specific requirement (which, moreover, is also recognised in the first- *d*
mentioned states) that the rights of the defence must be respected.

21. Apart from these differences, however, there are to be found in the national laws
of the member states common criteria inasmuch as those laws protect, in similar
circumstances, the confidentiality of written communications between lawyer and client
provided that, on the one hand, such communications are made for the purposes and in
the interests of the client's rights of defence and, on the other hand, they emanate from *e*
independent lawyers, that is to say lawyers who are not bound to the client by a
relationship of employment.

22. Viewed in that context Regulation 17 must be interpreted as protecting, in its
turn, the confidentiality of written communications between lawyer and client subject
to those two conditions, and thus incorporating such elements of that protection as are
common to the laws of the member states. *f*

23. As far as the first of those two conditions is concerned, in Regulation 17 itself, in
particular in the eleventh recital in its preamble and in the provisions contained in art
19, care is taken to ensure that the rights of the defence may be exercised to the full, and
the protection of the confidentiality of written communications between lawyer and
client is an essential corollary to those rights. In those circumstances, such protection
must, if it is to be effective, be recognised as covering all written communications *g*
exchanged after the initiation of the administration procedure under Regulation 17
which may lead to a decision on the application of arts 85 and 86 of the EEC Treaty or to
a decision imposing a pecuniary sanction on the undertaking. It must also be possible to
extend it to earlier written communications which have a relationship to the subject
matter of that procedure.

24. As regards the second condition, it should be stated that the requirement as to the *h*
position and status as an independent lawyer, which must be fulfilled by the legal adviser
from whom the written communications which may be protected emanate, is based on
a conception of the lawyer's role as collaborating in the administration of justice by the
courts and as being required to provide, in full independence, and in the overriding
interests of that cause, such legal assistance as the client needs. The counterpart of that
protection lies in the rules of professional ethics and discipline which are laid down and *j*
enforced in the general interest by institutions endowed with the requisite powers for
that purpose. Such a conception reflects the legal traditions common to the member
states and is also to be found in legal order of the Community, as is demonstrated by art
17 of the Protocols on the Statutes of the Court of Justice of the EEC and the EAEC, and
also by art 20 of the Protocol on the Statute of the Court of Justice of the ECSC.

25. Having regard to the principles of the EEC Treaty concerning freedom of

establishment and the freedom to provide services the protection thus afforded by
a Community law, in particular in the context of Regulation 17, to written communications
between lawyer and client must apply without distinction to any lawyer entitled to
practise his profession in one of the member states, regardless of the member state in
which the client lives.

26. Such protection may not be extended beyond those limits, which are determined
by the scope of the common rules on the exercise of the legal profession as laid down in
b EEC Council Directive 77/249 of 22 March 1977, which is based in its turn on the
mutual recognition by all the member states of the national legal concepts of each of
them on this subject.

27. In view of all these factors it must therefore be concluded that although Regulation
17, and in particular art 14 thereof, interpreted in the light of its wording, structure and
aims, and having regard to the laws of the member states, empowers the Commission to
c require, in the course of an investigation within the meaning of that article, production
of the business documents the disclosure of which it considers necessary, including
written communications between lawyer and client, for proceedings in respect of any
infringements of arts 85 and 86 of the EEC Treaty, that power is, however, subject to a
restriction imposed by the need to protect confidentiality, on the conditions defined
above, and provided that the communications in question are exchanged between an
d independent lawyer, that is to say one who is not bound to his client by a relationship of
employment, and his client.

28. Finally, it should be remarked that the principle of confidentiality does not
prevent a lawyer's client from disclosing the written communications between them if
he considers that it is in his interests to do so.

e
(c) The procedures relating to the application of the principle of confidentiality

29. If an undertaking which is the subject of an investigation under art 14 of
Regulation 17 refuses, on the ground that it is entitled to protection of the confidentiality
of information, to produce, among the business records demanded by the Commission,
written communications between itself and its lawyer, it must nevertheless provide the
f Commission's authorised agents with relevant material of such a nature as to demonstrate
that the communications fulfil the conditions for being granted legal protection as
defined above, although it is not bound to reveal the contents of the communications in
question.

30. Where the Commission is not satisfied that such evidence has been supplied, the
appraisal of those conditions is not a matter which may be left to an arbitrator or to a
g national authority. Since this is a matter involving an appraisal and a decision which
affect the conditions under which the Commission may act in a field as vital to the
functioning of the Common Market as that of compliance with the rules on competition,
the solution of disputes as to the application of the protection of the confidentiality of
written communications between lawyer and client may be sought only at Community
level.

h   31. In that case it is for the Commission to order, pursuant to art 14(3) of Regulation
17, production of the communications in question and, if necessary, to impose on the
undertaking fines or periodic penalty payments under that regulation as a penalty for the
undertaking's refusal either to supply such additional evidence as the Commission
considers necessary or to produce the communications in question whose confidentiality,
in the Commission's view, is not protected in law.

j   32. The fact that by virtue of art 185 of the EEC Treaty any action brought by the
undertaking concerned against such decisions does not have suspensory effect provides
an answer to the Commission's concern as to the effect of the time taken by the procedure
before the court on the efficacy of the supervision which the Commission is called on to
exercise in regard to compliance with the EEC Treaty rules on competition, whilst on
the other hand the interests of the undertaking concerned are safeguarded by the
possibility which exists under arts 185 and 186 of the treaty, as well as under art 83 of

the Rules of Procedure of the court, of obtaining an order suspending the application of the decision which has been taken, or any other interim measure.

(d) The confidential nature of the documents at issue

33. It is apparent from the documents which the applicant lodged at the court on 9 March 1981 that almost all the communications which they include were made or are connected with legal opinions which were given towards the end of 1972 and during the first half of 1973.

34. It appears that the communications in question were drawn up during the period preceding, and immediately following, the accession of the United Kingdom to the Community, and that they are principally concerned with how far it might be possible to avoid conflict between the applicant and the Community authorities on the applicant's position, in particular with regard to the Community provisions on competition. In spite of the time which elapsed between the said communications and the initiation of a procedure, those circumstances are sufficient to justify considering the communications as falling within the context of the rights of the defence and the lawyer's specific duties in that connection. They must therefore be protected from disclosure.

35. In view of that relationship and in the light of the foregoing considerations the written communications at issue must accordingly be considered, in so far as they emanate from an independent lawyer entitled to practise his profession in a member state, as confidential and on that ground beyond the Commission's power of investigation under art 14 of Regulation 17.

36. Having regard to the particular nature of those communications art 1(b) of the contested decision must be declared void in so far as it requires the applicant to produce the documents mentioned in the appendix to its letter to the Commission of 26 March 1979 and listed in the schedule of documents lodged at the court on 9 March 1981 under nos 1(a) and (b), 4(a) to (f), 5 and 7.

37. Nevertheless, the application must be dismissed inasmuch as it is directed against the provisions in the above-mentioned art 1(b) relating to documents other than those referred to above, which are likewise listed in the above-mentioned appendix and schedule and which have not yet been produced to the Commission.

Costs

38. Under art 69(2) of the Rules of Procedure the unsuccessful party is to be ordered to pay the costs. Under art 69(3) the court may order that the parties bear their own costs in whole or in part where each party succeeds on some and fails on other heads or where the circumstances are exceptional.

39. Since the parties to the action and the interveners have failed on some heads they must bear their own costs.

On those grounds, the court hereby: (1) declares art 1(b) of EEC Commission Decision 79/760 of 6 July 1979 void inasmuch as it requires the applicant to produce the documents which are mentioned in the appendix to the letter from the applicant to the Commission of 26 March 1979 and listed in the schedule of documents lodged at the court on 9 March 1981 under nos 1(a) and (b), 4(a) to (f), 5 and 7; (2) for the rest, dismisses the application; (3) orders the parties to the action and the interveners to bear their own costs.

Agents: *Graham Child* of Slaughter & May (for the applicant); *W H Godwin*, Treasury Solicitor's Department (for the United Kingdom); *John Temple Lang*, Legal Service of the EC Commission (for the Commission); *N Museux* and *A Carnelutti* (for the French Republic).

Mary Rose Plummer   Barrister.

Shell International Petroleum Co Ltd v Gibbs
The Salem

HOUSE OF LORDS

LORD DIPLOCK, LORD SCARMAN, LORD ROSKILL, LORD BRANDON OF OAKBROOK AND LORD BRIGHTMAN

11, 12 JANUARY, 17 FEBRUARY 1983

Marine insurance – Perils insured against – Taking at sea – Loss of cargo – Lloyd's SG policy – Shipowner and captain diverting ship to unauthorised port and off-loading most of cargo – Off-loaded cargo fraudulently sold to third party – Ship taken out to sea and scuttled with remainder of cargo – Whether diversion of ship to unauthorised port a 'taking at sea' – Whether off-loading in port a 'taking at sea' – Whether diversion of ship and off-loading of cargo a deemed barratry – Whether loss of remainder of cargo when ship scuttled caused by 'perils' of the sea.

The owners of a ship conspired with others to steal and then sell a cargo of oil. In accordance with their plan they obtained a purchase contract from a South African consortium, which provided for the delivery of a cargo of oil to Durban, and using that contract obtained finance from a bank, which they then used to purchase a tanker to carry the cargo. They chartered the tanker to innocent charterers who wanted a cargo of oil transported from Kuwait to Europe and then manned the ship with a master and crew who were parties to the conspiracy. The cargo of 195,000 tons of oil was loaded on board at a Kuwaiti port and the ship then followed the normal course from Kuwait to Europe until it was off Durban. The ship then put into Durban and most of the cargo (some 180,000 tons) was discharged and delivered to the South African consortium. The ship then left Durban and, together with the remainder of the cargo (some 15,000 tons), was scuttled at sea. During the voyage from Kuwait to Durban the charterers sold the cargo cif to the plaintiffs. Following the scuttling, the plaintiffs claimed against the insurers of the cargo under the Lloyd's SG policy of marine insurance under which the cargo was insured, claiming, inter alia, that the loss of the cargo fell within the perils 'takings at sea . . . and . . . all other perils, losses, and misfortunes' against which the policy insured the cargo owners. The insurers rejected the claim and the plaintiffs brought proceedings to recover the sum insured under the policy. The judge held that there had been a 'taking at sea' at the moment when the ship turned aside from the direct course for Europe and made for Durban, and accordingly gave judgment for the plaintiffs. The insurers appealed to the Court of Appeal, which allowed the appeal in respect of the cargo off-loaded at Durban. The court held that the off-loading was not a 'taking at sea' within the policy and further held that the loss did not fall within 'all other perils, losses, and misfortunes' because those further insured risks only applied when the ship was at sea and not when it was in port. The Court of Appeal dismissed the appeal in respect of the balance of the cargo lost when the ship was scuttled, on the ground that the sinking was a loss caused by perils of the sea and was within the policy. The plaintiffs appealed to the House of Lords, contending that the loss of the cargo was within the policy either because it had arisen from a 'taking at sea' or because the policy stated that the insured party's right of recovery was not to be prejudiced by the fact that the loss was attributable to the wrongful act of the shipowners and therefore, on the true construction of the policy and by analogy with a loss by scuttling which was deemed to be a loss by perils of the sea vis-à-vis an innocent cargo owner, the misappropriation of the cargo by the shipowners was deemed to be barratry vis-à-vis the innocent cargo owners, notwithstanding that the barratry was committed by, rather than against, the shipowners. The insurers cross-appealed, contending that the balance of the cargo had been lost as a result of fraud or fraudulent conspiracy and not due to perils of the sea.

Held – (1) The peril 'taking at sea' in a Lloyd's SG policy was confined to capture or seizure of a cargo at sea and did not extend to wrongful misappropriation of the cargo by the shipowner. The plaintiffs, as owners of the cargo, were therefore not entitled to recover the value of the cargo from the insurers on the basis that it had been subject to a 'taking at sea' (see p 747 *b c*, p 749 *j*, p 751 *d e* and p 753 *d e*, post); *Nishina Trading Co Ltd v Chiyoda Fire and Marine Insurance Co Ltd, The Mandarin Star* [1969] 2 All ER 776 overruled.

(2) The plaintiffs were not entitled to rely on the clause in the policy stating that their right of recovery was not to be prejudiced by the fact that the loss was attributable to the wrongful act of the shipowners in order to treat the misappropriation of the cargo by the shipowners as a deemed barratry since by definition that peril could only be committed against a shipowner. The plaintiffs' appeal would therefore be dismissed (see p 747 *b c*, p 752 *d e* and p 753 *c* to *e*, post).

(3) It was clear that the proximate cause of the loss of the balance of the cargo was that it was a loss by perils of the sea within the policy and not loss by fraud or fraudulent conspiracy, since (a) there was a distinction between fraud or fraudulent conspiracy and overt acts done in furtherance of that fraud or fraudulent conspiracy and (b) it could not be said that the conspiracy was bound to succeed or that the loss was inevitable once the cargo was first taken on board. It followed that the plaintiffs were entitled to recover that loss under the policy. The insurers' cross-appeal would therefore be dismissed (see p 747 *b c* and p 752 *j* to p 753 *a* and *c* to *e*, post).

Decision of the Court of Appeal [1982] 1 All ER 1057 affirmed.

Notes

For loss caused by taking at sea, see 25 Halsbury's Laws (4th edn) para 157, and for cases on the subject, see 29 Digest (Reissue) 276–284, 2411–2455.

Cases referred to in opinions

Cory (John) & Sons v Burr (1883) 8 App Cas 393, [1881–5] All ER Rep 414, HL, 29 Digest (Reissue) 277, 2424.

Johanna Oldendorff, The, E L Oldendorff & Co GmbH v Tradax Export SA [1973] 3 All ER 148, [1974] AC 479, [1973] 3 WLR 382, HL, Digest (Cont Vol D) 828, 2543a.

Nishina Trading Co Ltd v Chiyoda Fire and Marine Insurance Co Ltd, The Mandarin Star [1969] 2 All ER 776, [1969] 2 QB 449, [1969] 2 WLR 1094, CA; affg [1968] 3 All ER 712, [1968] 1 WLR 1325, 29 Digest (Reissue) 284, 2455.

Rickards v Forestal Land, Timber and Rlys Co Ltd, Robertson v Middows Ltd, Kann v W W Howard Bros & Co Ltd [1941] 3 All ER 62, [1942] AC 50, HL, 29 Digest (Reissue) 352, 2934.

Samuel (P) & Co Ltd v Dumas [1924] AC 431, [1924] All ER Rep 66, HL, 29 Digest (Reissue) 151, 1364.

Sociedad Financiera de Bienes Raices SA v Agrimpex Hungarian Trading Co for Agricultural Products, The Aello [1960] 2 All ER 578, [1961] AC 135, [1960] 3 WLR 145, HL, 41 Digest (Repl) 333, 1304.

Appeal

The plaintiffs, Shell International Petroleum Co Ltd (Shell), appealed with leave of the Court of Appeal against the decision of the Court of Appeal (Lord Denning MR, Kerr and May LJJ) ([1982] 1 All ER 1057, [1982] 2 WLR 745) given on 12 February 1982 allowing in part an appeal by the defendant, Caryl Antony Vaughan Gibbs, sued as a representative for other underwriters, against the judgment of Mustill J ([1982] 1 All ER 225, [1982] 2 WLR 745) given on 9 April 1981 granting Shell a declaration that it was entitled to recover the amount of its loss under a policy of marine insurance dated 19 January 1980 insuring a cargo of 196,231 metric tons of Kuwaiti crude oil loaded on board the tanker Salem at Mena al Ahmadi, Kuwait, on or about 10 December 1979. The Court of Appeal held that Shell was entitled to recover only in respect of 15,840 metric tons of the cargo of crude oil under the policy. The underwriters cross-appealed against the decision. The facts are set out in the opinion of Lord Roskill.

Gordon Pollock QC and *Bernard Eder* for Shell.
a *Robert Alexander QC* and *Michael Dean QC* for the underwriters.

Their Lordships took time for consideration.

17 February. The following opinions were delivered.

b **LORD DIPLOCK.** My Lords, I have had the advantage of reading in draft the speech of my noble and learned friend Lord Roskill. I agree with it and for the reasons he gives I would dismiss the appeal and cross-appeal.

LORD SCARMAN. My Lords, I have had the advantage of reading in draft the speech to be delivered by my noble and learned friend Lord Roskill. For the reasons he gives I
c would dismiss the appeal and cross-appeal.

LORD ROSKILL. My Lords, this appeal by Shell International Petroleum Co Ltd (Shell) arises in an action brought by them against a representative underwriter to recover no less than $US56,318,517·42 from the London insurance market in respect of the total
d loss of a cargo of nearly 200,000 tons of crude oil which Shell had bought on c i f terms and of which Shell were undoubtedly wholly deprived as a result of a gigantic fraud perpetrated for the express purpose of sending this cargo of crude oil to South Africa in defiance of the ban on the export of oil from the Arabian Gulf to that country, instead of to Italy, as the contractual documents on the basis of which Shell had bought this cargo enjoined.

e   This cargo was insured on the terms and conditions of a standard Lloyd's marine insurance policy (SG form) to which were appended, inter alia, the 'Institute cargo clauses (FPA)', the 'Institute war clauses' and the 'Institute strikes riots and civil commotions clauses'. It should be emphasised that the cargo might have been, but was not, insured against all risks.
      Though the terms of the standard policy are well known I set out in full that part
f which recites the list of perils insured against:

      'Touching the adventures and perils which we the assurers are contented to bear and do take upon us in this voyage: they are of the seas, men of war, fire, enemies, pirates, rovers, thieves, jettisons, letters of mart and countermart, surprisals, takings at sea, arrests, restraints, and detainments of all kings, princes, and people, of what nation, condition, or quality soever, barratry of the master and mariners, and of all
g   other perils, losses and misfortunes, that have or shall come to the hurt, detriment or damage of the said goods and merchandises, and ship, etc., or any part thereof . . .'

      So far as the various Institute clauses are concerned, only one sentence of one clause, namely the second sentence of cl 8 of the Institute cargo clauses (FPA) is now relevant.
h Against the rubric 'Seaworthiness Admitted Clause', cl 8 reads thus:

      'The seaworthiness of the vessel as between the Assured and Underwriters is hereby admitted. In the event of loss the Assured's right of recovery hereunder shall not be prejudiced by the fact that the loss may have been attributable to the wrongful act or misconduct of the shipowners or their servants, committed without the privity of the Assured . . .'

j   It was common ground that this second sentence was first added, although not entirely in its present form, for the benefit of innocent mortgagees of ships and cargo owners to surmount the decision of the majority of this House in *P Samuel & Co Ltd v Dumas* [1924] AC 431, [1924] All ER Rep 66 that a loss by deliberate scuttling of a vessel is not a loss by perils of the seas.
      My Lords, fraud on the scale of that perpetrated in the instant case requires elaborate

devising, preparation and execution if it is to succeed as this fraud ultimately did. The
astonishing story of this fraud is contained in full detail in an agreed statement of facts   a
containing no less than 48 paragraphs on the basis of which this case was tried at first
instance by Mustill J. The judge prefaced his judgment by quoting para 2 of that agreed
statement which he said sufficiently stated those facts by reference to which the many
issues of law raised before him fell to be determined. Most of those issues no longer arise
and your Lordships are only concerned with three. I propose to adopt the same course as
did the judge. Those concerned to learn the whole story must read the agreed statement,   b
including the remarkable story of the purchase and financing of the purchase of the
Salem itself.

Paragraph 2 of the agreed statement reads thus:

'The conspirators were planning and preparing the fraud from at least as early as
October 1979. In the result the conspirators achieved their object as follows:—(i)
They obtained a purchase contract from the South African Strategic Fuel Fund   c
Association (SFF) providing for the delivery of a cargo of Saudi Arabian crude-oil to
Durban; (ii) They used that contract to obtain an advance payment from a South
African bank (Mercabank Ltd) sufficient to finance the purchase of a suitable tanker
to carry such a cargo from the Arabian Gulf; (iii) They purchased such a tanker (the
"Salem"); (iv) They manned that tanker with a Master and principal officers (these
included Captain Georgoulis and Chief Officer Annivas) who were parties to the   d
conspiracy and with a crew which was likely to be amenable to the conspirators'
instructions; (v) They chartered out the tanker to an innocent charterer (Pontoil SA)
for a laden voyage (in the event) from Kuwait to Europe; (vi) They deceived the
charterer (Pontoil SA) and the shipper (Kuwait Oil Co) of this cargo and the Kuwait
Authorities none of whom would have permitted the loading of the cargo nor the
departure of the vessel had they known the conspirators' actual intentions; (vii)   e
Either before or after loading they procured the agreement of SFF to accept a cargo
of Kuwaiti oil in place of a Saudi Arabian oil and at a slightly reduced price; (viii)
They carried the cargo to and discharged as much as possible of it at Durban; (ix)
They collected the price from SFF; (x) They scuttled the tanker in the Atlantic so as
to attempt to conceal what had occurred. The final event in this sequence—the
scuttling of the vessel—was completed on 17th January 1980.'   f

To these facts I would add the following. The quantity actually discharged at Durban
was 180,392 metric tons. The balance, about 15,840 metric tons, remained on board
when the Salem left Durban and was physically lost when the Salem was scuttled off
Dakar on 17 January 1980. The conspirators ultimately received directly or indirectly
some $US45m from the South African Strategic Fuel Fund Association.   g

My Lords, the three questions with which alone your Lordships' House is now
concerned are these. First, was the cargo totally lost by 'takings at sea'? Second, was the
cargo totally lost by what was called in argument 'deemed barratry', the suggested
'deeming' arising by reason of cl 8 of the Institute cargo clauses (FPA)? Third, was the
balance of the cargo left on board at Durban and physically lost when the Salem was
scuttled lost by peril of the sea, one of the insured perils, or by the fraud or fraudulent   h
conspiracy of the conspirators, which were not? Mustill J answered the first question,
Yes. The Court of Appeal (Lord Denning MR, Kerr and May LJJ) answered that question,
No. Mustill J and the Court of Appeal both answered the second question, No. Mustill J
did not have to answer the third question. The Court of Appeal unanimously held that
loss to be by peril of the sea.

Mustill J therefore gave judgment for Shell for the amount claimed on the basis that   j
the entire cargo was totally lost by 'takings at sea' (see [1982] 1 All ER 225 at 244, [1982]
2 WLR 745 at 770). The Court of Appeal reversed that decision, but in the light of their
answers to the third question held that Shell could recover in respect of the destruction
of the balance of the cargo when the Salem was scuttled, as for a loss by peril of the sea
(see [1982] 1 All ER 1057, [1982] 2 WLR 745 at 771–791). This last conclusion is the
subject of the underwriters' cross-appeal.

My Lords, I propose to consider each of these three questions in turn.

a

'Takings at sea'

In approaching this, now the most important question in this appeal, the trial judge was faced with a previous decision of the Court of Appeal (Lord Denning MR, Edmund-Davies and Phillimore LJJ) in *Nishina Trading Co Ltd v Chiyoda Fire and Marine Insurance Co Ltd, The Mandarin Star* [1969] 2 All ER 776, [1969] 2 QB 449. The Court of Appeal,

b reversing Donaldson J (see [1968] 3 All ER 712, [1968] 1 WLR 1325), there held that on the unusual facts of that case that peril not being confined to such peril as capture or seizure. The facts briefly stated were that a dispute had arisen between the owners and the charterers, the latter of whom were entitled to have the goods taken to Kobe. The ship with the goods on board was anchored off Kobe to which she was contractually bound to go when her owners ordered her to proceed to Hong

c Kong. She went there with the goods still on board and there discharged the goods. It was held by the Court of Appeal that there was a 'taking at sea' when the master changed course and instead of continuing as bailees from the cargo owners he and the shipowners assumed dominion over the goods inconsistent with the cargo owners' rights, thus converting the goods to their own use.

My Lords, the conclusion reached by the Court of Appeal is tantamount to holding

d that the peril of 'takings at sea' includes the risk of a shipowner wrongfully misappropriating the goods even though the standard form of SG policy does not otherwise cover 'theft' or 'misappropriation' and even though the peril of 'thieves' does not, by reason of r 9 of the rules for the construction of a marine policy in Sch 1 to the Marine Insurance Act 1906 cover 'clandestine theft or theft committed by crew or passengers'. The conclusion reached by the Court of Appeal was said to be founded on a

e paragraph in the speech of Lord Wright in this House in *Rickards v Forestal Land, Timber and Rlys Co Ltd* [1941] 3 All ER 62 at 76–77, [1942] AC 50 at 79–80.

My Lords, it cannot be gainsaid that, if this decision of the Court of Appeal was correct, it changed the meaning attributed to the phrase 'takings at sea' for the preceding 300 or 400 years. As I have already stated, Mustill J was bound by that decision. But in his judgment (see [1982] 1 All ER 225 at 240, [1982] 2 WLR 745 at 764) he referred to a

f large number of well-known textbooks on the law of marine insurance which clearly showed that the established view was that this peril forms 'part of the group of perils which also includes arrests, restraints and detainments of all kings, princes and peoples . . .' The judge added that in none of these books, to three of which I shall shortly refer, 'is there any hint that the peril extends to a dishonest taking by a shipowner'. Nevertheless he felt himself bound to hold that the decision in *The Mandarin Star* extended the

g meaning of this peril to cover a 'wrongful misappropriation by a bailee, just as much as by anyone else'. This was the foundation of the judge's judgment in favour of Shell on the entirety of their claim.

When the present case reached the Court of Appeal Lord Denning MR recanted and said that his earlier decision had been wrong, had been based on a misunderstanding of what Lord Wright said and should not be followed as having been a decision reached 'per

h incuriam': (see [1982] 1 All ER 1057 at 1063, [1982] 2 WLR 745 at 775–776). Kerr LJ, while agreeing that *The Mandarin Star* had been wrongly decided, said that the Court of Appeal was bound by the decision. The Lord Justice none the less felt able to distinguish it (see [1982] 1 All ER 1057 at 1068, [1982] 2 WLR 745 at 781). May LJ, while agreeing that the Court of Appeal was bound by the decision and unpersuaded that it was wrong, held, assuming it to be right, that on the facts there was no 'taking *at sea*' (my emphasis).

j The taking had been at the single buoy mooring at Durban and that was not 'at sea' (see [1982] 1 All ER 1057 at 1072–1074, [1982] 2 WLR 745 at 787–789).

My Lords, in common with all your Lordships I entertain no doubt that *The Mandarin Star* was wrongly decided. Indeed, counsel for Shell found it virtually impossible to support the decision. I suspect that had Mustill J, when writing his scholarly and careful judgment, been free to disregard it, he would have declined to follow it. I have already mentioned his reference to the textbooks which supported what had always been believed to be the relevant law. I need only to refer to three. First, there is the statement of the law by the late Mr Arthur Cohen PC, KC in an article in 17 Halsbury's Laws (1st edn) *a* paras 870–871. This article has long been regarded as of the highest authority on this branch of the law. Under the cross-heading, which includes the phrase 'Seizure or takings at sea', the learned author stated: "Seizures and takings at sea include deprivation of possession, whether the seizure or taking was lawful or unlawful, and whether by enemies or pirates.' Gow *Marine Insurance* (1st edn, 1896) p 114 stated: '"Taking at sea" is commonly expressed in modern commercial language as "seizure".' Templeman *Marine* *b* *Insurance* (1st edn, 1903) p 34 stated: '"Surprisals and Takings at Sea". These words require no explanation, being merely another way of expressing "Capture".' It is tempting but in present circumstances superfluous to explore the history of this phrase as illustrated by the extracts from the many learned works and documents of authority as profound as they are ancient, the material for which has been most helpfully collected and provided for your Lordships by the parties.   *c*

Indeed, I would venture the view that one has only to look at the phrase in its context in the list of perils insured against and then to construe it in that context to see that the construction adopted in these three works and indeed others is plainly correct. It is in truth only in *The Mandarin Star* that one finds this single departure from historic orthodoxy. Yet it is that heresy which counsel for Shell has eloquently invited your Lordships to declare henceforth to be or at least to be deemed to be orthodox doctrine on *d* the ground of stare decisis and the need for certainty in the field of common law.

My Lords, this House has on many recent occasions stressed the need for certainty in the law and especially in the field of commercial law. Counsel's plea on this ground in no way falls on deaf ears. He contended that, wrong as the decision in *The Mandarin Star* might be, yet nevertheless it stood from 28 February 1969 when it was given until 12 February 1982 when Lord Denning MR recanted. He pointed out that the cover now *e* sought to be enforced by Shell had been concluded between those dates. The present cover must, he said, be taken to have been so concluded on the basis that *The Mandarin Star* was correctly decided since there was no sign of the London and other insurance markets having meanwhile taken any steps to alter the standard form of policy or any of the Institute clauses to circumvent that decision. He claimed that because of the small sum involved *The Mandarin Star* must have been a test case, a claim emphatically *f* challenged by counsel for the underwriters. No attempt had been made in that or in any other case to test the matter in this House.

My Lords, when a decision has stood for many years and can be clearly shown to have been acted on repeatedly, your Lordships have often said that the decision should not be lightly overruled, if at all. But I know of no case and counsel for Shell referred your Lordships to none, where a decision only a few years old and now almost by concession *g* agreed to be wrong has been held none the less to require to be deemed to be right because of the principle of stare decisis, especially where as already stated, the decision is but a single deviation from several centuries of orthodox doctrine. Moreover, adherence to the heresy would, I think, cause great practical difficulty. Were this decision now to be declared to be the law, not only would the law as it has stood for several centuries and on the basis of which it cannot be doubted that the Marine Insurance Act 1906 was *h* drafted and enacted be substantially changed by judicial decision, but your Lordships would be holding that wrongful misappropriation by a shipowner of goods on board is capable of being a 'taking at sea'. Endless disputes would then be likely to arise whether, and if so, when any such 'taking' was a 'taking at sea'. The debate in the present appeal whether any such 'taking', if there were a 'taking' at all, took place at the loading port or on deviation to Durban or on coupling at the single buoy mooring at Durban or on *j* completion of discharge at the single buoy mooring or at some other place or point of time was a 'taking at sea' is eloquent of the possibility of future disputes, were the submission of counsel for Shell to be accepted. In truth its acceptance would create not the certainty which he emphasised was so desirable but uncertainty in an area where hitherto certainty has prevailed.

My Lords, two other matters may perhaps be usefully mentioned in this connection.
a First, the policy sued on in *The Mandarin Star* does not appear to have been issued on the
London market but in Japan and there is nothing to show that the decision has caused
difficulties on the London market. Moreover, even where a decision of the Court of
Appeal has in the past caused difficulties in London and for what may well be good
reasons it has not been practicable to bring that particular decision to this House for
consideration, it may often happen that some considerable time elapses before another
b case arises which raises substantially the same point and which is of sufficient importance
either in principle or in amount to justify the trouble and expense of a voyage to your
Lordships' House to have the law considered and, if proper, brought back on course.

It is for this among other reasons that I am not impressed by the emphasis of counsel
for Shell on the fact that no step had been taken between 1969 and the conclusion of the
present cover to secure a contractual variation of the decision in *The Mandarin Star*.
c Second, your Lordships' House has recently shown itself ready to review a previous
decision where that decision has produced uncertainty and difficulty in application. The
reversal of *Sociedad Financiera de Bienes Raices SA v Agrimpex Hungarian Trading Co for
Agricultural Products, The Aello* [1960] 2 All ER 578, [1961] AC 135 in *The Johanna
Oldendorff, E L Oldendorff & Co GmbH v Tradax Export SA* [1973] 3 All ER 148, [1974] AC
479 illustrates this. But the present situation is the reverse. Here your Lordships' House
d is being asked to perpetuate a wrong decision which will cause uncertainty when the
correct decision as well as the reaffirmation of well-established law will secure certainty.
I invite your Lordships unhesitatingly to hold that *The Mandarin Star* was wrongly
decided and should be cast into what Lord Macmillan in this House once called that
special limbo reserved for wrongly decided cases. Your Lordships may think that this
House should take this opportunity of firmly declaring that the standard Lloyd's SG
e policy does not cover wrongful misappropriation of cargo by a shipowner. If cargo
interests require that cover, they must seek either an all risks policy or some other
appropriate form of cover.

My Lords I can deal more briefly with the two other issues.

'Deemed barratry'
f   As an alternative to his main submission, counsel for Shell advanced an ingenious
argument based on cl 8 of the Institute cargo clauses (FPA). He did not seek to revive the
original submission rejected by Mustill J that there was a loss of barratry. But he
contended that by reason of cl 8 there was a loss by what he called 'deemed barratry'. The
argument ran thus. In *P Samuel & Co v Dumas* [1924] AC 431, [1924] All ER Rep 66 this
House, notwithstanding Lord Sumner's vigorous dissent, held that a loss by scuttling was
g not a loss by perils of the sea. The innocent mortgagee and by parity of reasoning the
innocent cargo owner who lost in the one case his security and in the other his cargo
could therefore not recover as for a loss by perils of the sea when the ship was deliberately
cast away with the privity of her owners. It was common ground that the second sentence
of cl 8 both in its original and present forms was designed to remedy this obvious
injustice. It may be that the wording of this sentence in the Institute cargo clauses (FPA)
h incorporated in the policy in the instant case is not the most apt that might have been
chosen to express that undoubted intention; but that it and its predecessor have been
effective to do so has been the common understanding in the London insurance market
ever since the second sentence of cl 8 was introduced shortly after the decision of this
House in *P Samuel & Co v Dumas*. In the instant case, the underwriters concede that it was
the common intention of the parties that cl 8 should entitle Shell to have a loss caused by
the scuttling of the ship treated as a loss proximately caused by a peril of the sea. On their
true construction, it may be that the actual words of cl 8 would not have this effect. If
they did not, then Shell would be entitled to rectification of the policy to give effect to
the common intention of the parties. The assured under every Lloyd's SG policy on cargo
incorporating the Institute cargo clauses (FPA) and issued on the London market since
1925 would similarly have been entitled to have their policies rectified.

The present argument proceeded on the basis that the clause achieved its objective by
treating the loss by scuttling as a loss by perils of the sea by excluding from consideration **a**
that element of privity of the shipowner to the scuttling which alone prevented the loss
from being treated as a loss by that insured peril. Counsel for Shell called this a 'deemed
loss' by perils of the sea. He then sought to apply that reasoning to a loss by barratry.

'Barratry', as r 11 of the rules of construction and indeed the common law made plain,
involves a wrongful act being committed by the master or crew to the prejudice of the
shipowners. In the present case there was a wrongful act, indeed there were several **b**
wrongful acts, wilfully committed by the master and crew. But what prevented that act
or those acts giving rise to a loss by barratry was that so far from being wilfully committed
to the prejudice of the shipowners the master and crew were acting in conspiracy with
the shipowners. But, it was argued, cl 8, in the interest of the innocent assured, enjoined
that the assured's right of recovery should not be prejudiced by the fact that the loss
might be, and in this case was, attributable to the wrongful act of the shipowners without **c**
which there would be a loss by barratry. Therefore it was argued there is a loss by
'deemed barratry'.

My Lords, one cannot fail to admire the ingenuity which devised this submission to
which I hope my summary does not do injustice. But Kerr LJ disposed of the submission
in a single sentence of his judgment with a succinctness on which I cannot hope to
improve and which I gratefully adopt (see [1982] 1 All ER 1057 at 1071, [1982] 2 WLR **d**
745 at 785): 'The one peril to which this sentence [ie the second sentence of cl 8] clearly
cannot apply is barratry, since this is by definition one which can only be committed
against the shipowners . . .' The emphasis is that of the Lord Justice. This submission
therefore fails for that reason. It follows that Shell's appeal also fails and must be
dismissed.

e

Causation

The third and final question is raised by the underwriters in their cross-appeal. It is as
to the causation of the loss of the cargo on board when the Salem was scuttled. It was
argued that the Court of Appeal was wrong in holding that the balance of the cargo
which was then lost was lost by perils of the sea. Counsel for the underwriters submitted
that it was lost by fraud or fraudulent conspiracy and not by perils of the sea. The former **f**
were not perils insured against. This is simply a question of causation. It was accepted by
counsel for the underwriters that if the submission were wrong, Shell could recover for
this loss because of cl 8, this being one of the situations with which cl 8 was intended to
deal.

My Lords, questions of causation are mixed questions of fact and law and opinions
may and often do differ on them. But I do not detect any difference of opinion between **g**
any of your Lordships and the Court of Appeal in the instant case. Section 55 of the
Marine Insurance Act 1906 prescribes that insurers are liable for 'any loss proximately
caused by a peril insured against'. This is the statutory application of the long-established
principle of marine insurance law expressed in the Latin phrase causa proxima non
remota spectatur: see the note in *Chalmers on Marine Insurance* (8th edn, 1976) p 79. No
doubt the balance of the cargo would not have been lost but for the fraud or fraudulent **h**
conspiracy. But that alone does not make either of those causes the proximate cause of
that loss any more than the fact that the seizure of the ship in *John Cory & Sons v Burr*
(1883) 8 App Cas 393, [1881–5] All ER Rep 414 would not have happened without the
prior barratrous acts of smuggling by those on board the ship made the loss of the ship a
loss by barratry and not by seizure. To accept the submission of counsel for the
underwriters in principle would, in my view, come perilously near ignoring what had **j**
been laid down by this House in that case in passages which it is not necessary to repeat.
But principle apart, I think the facts of the present case in any event preclude the
acceptance of the submission. First, the concept of fraud or fraudulent conspiracy as
distinct from overt acts done in furtherance of that fraud or fraudulent conspiracy as the
proximate cause of a loss is one which I find difficult to accept. Second, I am very far
from satisfied that when the Salem sailed from Mina the fraud or fraudulent conspiracy

a was bound to succeed, or, to use the phrase used in argument, that the cargo was 'doomed'. In connection with another part of his argument counsel for Shell drew your Lordships' attention to the details of a remarkable document, evidencing an agreement concluded between the conspirators and the South African authorities as late as 19 December 1979, by which date the Salem was proceeding slowly down the east coast of Africa awaiting final instructions. He also referred your Lordships to the agreed statement of facts. In short, the conspirators at that date had still to persuade the South African
b authorities to accept Kuwaiti oil and not Saudi Arabian oil and documentation which bore no relationship to that which ought to have been tendered to them. It is perhaps eloquent of the determination of the South African authorities to get this oil to Durban under any circumstances that they were willing at that late date to accept what was proffered against an indemnity in circumstances which even the most credulous buyer in the open market would not have considered for one moment, thus enabling the
c conspirators to succeed in their objective.

My Lords, in complete agreement with the Court of Appeal on this issue I do not think it can be doubted that having regard to cl 8 or at least by reason of the concession made on behalf of underwriters with regard to that clause, this final loss was by perils of the seas. That being so, it follows that to that limited extent Shell can recover.

In the result I would dismiss both appeal and cross-appeal, each with costs.

d
LORD BRANDON OF OAKBROOK. My Lords, I have had the advantage of reading in draft the speech prepared by my noble and learned friend Lord Roskill. I agree with it, and for the reasons which he gives I would dismiss both the appeal and the cross-appeal.

e **LORD BRIGHTMAN.** My Lords, I would dismiss this appeal and the cross-appeal for the reasons given by my noble and learned friend Lord Roskill.

Appeal and cross-appeal dismissed.

Solicitors: *Elborne Mitchell & Co* (for Shell); *Clyde & Co* (for the underwriters).

f
Mary Rose Plummer   Barrister.

Ford v Warwickshire County Council
g
HOUSE OF LORDS

LORD DIPLOCK, LORD KEITH OF KINKEL, LORD ROSKILL, LORD BRANDON OF OAKBROOK AND LORD BRIGHTMAN

18, 19 JANUARY, 17 FEBRUARY 1983

h *Employment – Continuity – Period of continuous employment – Temporary cessation of work – Teacher employed part-time under eight successive fixed-term contracts covering academic year – No contract of employment during summer vacation – Resumption of employment at beginning of each academic year – Employee's contract not renewed at end of one academic year for next – Whether employee 'absent from work on account of temporary cessation of work' – Whether employee entitled to claim redundancy payment – Employment Protection (Consolidation) Act*
j *1978, Sch 13, para 9(1)(b).*

The appellant was employed as a part-time lecturer at one of the respondent council's colleges of further education under eight successive fixed-term contracts which started at the beginning and terminated automatically without notice at the end of a single academic year. During the summer vacation between the expiry of one fixed-term contract and the commencement of the next the appellant did no work for the council and had no contract of employment with it. When the appellant's current fixed-term contract expired in July 1979 the appellant was not re-engaged by the council for the *a* academic year beginning in September 1979. The appellant complained that she had been unfairly dismissed and claimed a redundancy payment. The industrial tribunal held that they had no jurisdiction to entertain her claim, on the ground that she was not qualified by a long enough period of continuous employment because the continuity of her employment was broken by the summer vacation, when she could not be treated as having been 'absent from work' on account of a 'temporary cessation of work' for the *b* purposes of para 9(1)(b)*ᵃ* of Sch 13 to the Employment Protection (Consolidation) Act 1978. The appellant appealed to the Employment Appeal Tribunal, which dismissed her appeal. The Court of Appeal affirmed that decision and the appellant appealed to the House of Lords. The council conceded that each of the intervals between the appellant's successive fixed-term contracts could properly be characterised as 'temporary'.

c

Held – (1) The expression 'absent from work' in para 9(1)(b) of Sch 13 to the 1978 Act meant not only that the employee was not doing any actual work for his employer but that there was no contract of employment subsisting between him and his employer which would entitle the latter to require him to do any work. It followed that the phrase 'the employee is absent from work on account of a temporary cessation of work', as a description of a period of time referred to the interval between (a) the date on which the *d* employee who would otherwise be continuing to work under an existing contract of employment was dismissed, because for the time being his employer had no work for him to do, and (b) the date on which he was re-engaged under a fresh contract of employment to do work which had become available. It further followed that the phrase 'on account of a temporary cessation of work' referred to the reason why the employer dismissed the employee, thus making it necessary for the tribunal to inquire what the *e* reason for the dismissal was. Accordingly, the fact that the employer had foreseen the unavailability of work far enough in advance to anticipate it by giving notice to the employee terminating his contract of employment did not prevent the absence from work following the expiry of the notice from being caused 'on account of a temporary cessation for work' (see p 758 *b* to *f*, p 760 *h* to p 761 *a*, p 762 *g h*, p 763 *c* to *e* and p 764 *g h*, post).

f
(2) Since the meaning of the word 'dismissal' in s 55(2)(b) of the 1978 Act in relation to unfair dismissal and in s 83(2)(b)*ᵇ* of that Act in relation to redundancy payments had been assimilated by making the expression applicable to contracts of employment for a fixed term, to which it would not otherwise be appropriate in its ordinary meaning, para 9(1) applied to cases where a contract of employment for a fixed term had expired and on expiry had not been renewed by the employer, in exactly the same way as it was *g* applicable to contracts of employment of indefinite duration which were terminated by the employer by notice. It followed therefore that para 9 was not concerned with the means for bringing the employment to an end temporarily but with the reasons for bringing it to an end, ie whether it was on account of a temporary cessation of work. Accordingly in 1979 the appellant was in a position to say that she had been dismissed (see p 758 *f* to *h*, p 759 *f g* and p 760 *h* to p 761 *a* and *e* to *h*, post); *Rashid v Inner London* *h* *Education Authority* [1977] ICR 157 overruled.
(3) The scheme of the 1978 Act as a whole showed that the word 'temporary' in para 9(1)(b) of Sch 13 was used in the sense of 'transient', ie lasting only for a relatively short time. Accordingly, the continuity of employment for the purposes of the 1978 Act in relation to unfair dismissal and redundancy payments was not broken unless and until, looking retrospectively from the date of the expiry of the fixed-term contract on which *j* the employee's claim was based, there was to be found between one fixed-term contract and its immediate predecessor an interval that could be characterised as short relative to the combined duration of the two fixed-term contracts. Whether it could be so

---

a   Paragraph 9(1) is set out at p 757 *f g*, post
b   Section 83(2), so far as material, is set out at p 756 *h j*, post

characterised was a question of fact and degree and so was to be decided by an industrial
a   tribunal. It followed therefore that in view of the concession made by the council that
each of the intervals between the appellant's successive fixed-term contracts could
properly be characterised as 'temporary', the appeal would be allowed since the appellant
had satisfied the requirements of five years' continuous employment and the case would
be remitted to the industrial tribunal to determine the matter accordingly (see p 759 g to
p 760 b e f and h to p 761 a, p 762 h j and p 764 h j, post)

b   Per curiam. Successive periods of seasonal employment under fixed-term contracts,
such as employment in agriculture during harvest-time or in hotel work during the
summer season, will qualify only as continuous employment if the length of the period
between two successive seasonal contracts is so short in comparison with the length of
the season during which the employee is employed as properly to be regarded by the
industrial tribunal as no more than a 'temporary' cessation of work (see p 760 g to p 761
c   a, post).

Notes

For computation of period of continuous employment and continuity of employment
for the purpose of defining the right to a redundancy payment, see 16 Halsbury's Laws
(4th edn) paras 605, 656, 658, and for cases on the subject, see 20 Digest (Reissue) 354–
d   360, 3131–3150.

For the Employment Protection (Consolidation) Act 1978, ss 55, 83, Sch 13, para 9, see
48 Halsbury's Statutes (3rd edn) 503, 539, 651.

As from 1 December 1982 s 151 of the 1978 Act was substituted by s 20 of, and para
7(1) of Sch 2 to, of the Employment Act 1982.

Cases referred to in opinions

e   *Fitzgerald v Hall Russell & Co Ltd* [1969] 3 All ER 1140, [1970] AC 984, [1969] 3 WLR
868, HL, 20 Digest (Reissue) 355, 3134.
Hunter v Smith's Dock Co Ltd [1968] 2 All ER 81, [1968] 1 WLR 1865, DC, 20 Digest
(Reissue) 357, 3142.
Moncrieff v Tayside Regional Council (18 November 1982, unreported), Court of Session.
Rashid v Inner London Education Authority [1977] ICR 157, EAT, 20 Digest (Reissue) 356,
f   3136.

Appeal

The applicant, Georgina Ann Ford (Mrs Ford), appealed against the decision of the Court
of Appeal (Stephenson, O'Connor LJJ and Sir Stanley Rees) on 5 April 1982 dismissing
her appeal against a decision of the Employment Appeal Tribunal (Waterhouse J, Mrs D
g   Ewing and Mrs D Lancaster) on 14 October 1980 which affirmed a decision of an
industrial tribunal (chairman G E Foster) sitting at Birmingham on 15 January 1980,
whereby the tribunal decided that it did not have jurisdiction under s 151 of, and para
9(1)(b) of Sch 13 to, the Employment Protection (Consolidation) Act 1978 to entertain
Mrs Ford's complaint of unfair dismissal and application for a redundancy payment in
respect of her employment by the respondent, Warwickshire County Council, as a part-
h   time lecturer. The facts are set out in the opinion of Lord Diplock.

Alexander Irvine QC and *Andrew Hillier* for Mrs Ford.
Leonard Caplan QC and *Jonathan Sofer* for the council.

Their Lordships took time for consideration.

j   17 February. The following opinions were delivered.

LORD DIPLOCK. My Lords, in eight successive academic years, starting at some date
in September each year and ending at some date in July in the following year, the
appellant, Mrs Ford, was employed by the Mid-Warwickshire College of Further
Education. She was not re-engaged for the academic year beginning in September 1979.
The staff at the college consists of a number of full-time lecturers, who are paid an

annual salary for a working year of 38 weeks, of which 36 weeks are in term time; and
nearly twice as many part-time lecturers are engaged to take particular courses. These are **a**
employed on fixed-term contracts for the duration of the particular course, which may
be less than one academic year. In Mrs Ford's case, however, she had successive contracts
of employment, each of which started at the beginning and terminated automatically,
without notice, at the end of a single academic year. There was also provision (which, in
the event, was never exercised) for earlier termination by either side on one week's notice.
Part-time lecturers are paid at an hourly rate for the actual number of hours worked. The **b**
weekly number of hours varies considerably from lecturer to lecturer. In Mrs Ford's case,
the number of hours worked in each week of the academic year under her successive
fixed-term contracts hovered around 16 hours. In some periods of weeks it was more, in
others somewhat less than 16; but it is unnecessary to go into details for it is not disputed
that she had been employed for a long enough continuous period of employment, and
for a sufficient number of hours in each week, to qualify for remedies against unfair **c**
dismissal and for redundancy pay if, but only if, the weeks which constituted the
summer vacation between the expiry of one fixed-term contract and the commencement
of the next are to be treated as periods of employment notwithstanding that during these
Mrs Ford did no work for the council and had no contract of employment with it.

So the only question for your Lordships is whether such weeks are to be so treated or
not. The answer to the question depends on the meaning to be given to para 9 of Sch 13 **d**
to the Employment Protection (Consolidation) Act 1978 which appears under the cross-
heading 'Periods in which there is no contract of employment'. It will be necessary to
quote this paragraph in extenso, but first it may be helpful to say something about the
context of the Act both general and immediate in which the paragraph appears.

My Lords, the 1978 Act consolidated a number of provisions in comparatively recent
antecedent statutes which had done much to bring the relationship between employee **e**
and employer out of the field of contract and into that of status. By s 140 contracting out
of rights conferred on employees by the Act, apart from certain exceptions that are not
relevant for present purposes, is prohibited. The scheme of the Act, in general, is that
status to benefit from particular rights conferred by the Act on employees against their
employer is acquired by an employee by having been continuously employed by the
same employer (or a predecessor or transferee treated for the purposes of the Act as the **f**
same employer) for a specified minimum period immediately preceding his exercise of
the right in question. As respects some rights, for example guarantee payments, the
specified minimum qualifying period of continuous employment is short; as respects
others, for example maternity payment and the right to return to work after pregnancy
or confinement, it is longer. In particular, as respects those two rights with which your
Lordships are directly concerned in the instant case, (1) for the right under Part V of the **g**
Act not to be unfairly dismissed, the specified minimum qualifying period of continuous
employment prior to dismissal is 52 weeks, and (2) for the right under Part VI of the Act
to a redundancy payment on dismissal, it is 104 weeks.

'Dismissal', for the purposes both of rights in respect of unfair dismissal and of rights
to redundancy payments, is given by the Act an extended meaning expressed in identical
terms in s 55(2) in relation to unfair dismissal and s 83(2) in relation to redundancy **h**
payments. I take them from s 83(2):

> 'An employee shall be treated as dismissed by his employer if, but only if,—(a)
> the contract under which he is employed by the employer is terminated by the
> employer, whether it is so terminated by notice or without notice, or (b) where
> under that contract he is employed for a fixed term, that term expires without being
> renewed under the same contract, or (c) the employee terminates that contract, with **j**
> or without notice, in circumstances . . . such that he is entitled to terminate it
> without notice by reason of the employer's conduct.'

The words at the end of para (b), 'renewed under the same contract', may not be the most
elegant way of expressing what the draftsman obviously meant, viz under a new contract

for a further term (whether fixed or indefinite) of which the provisions, except as respects
a   the term, do not differ from those of the contract that has expired. Strong support for
this view as to the intended meaning of the words can, in my view, be found in the
interpretation section, s 153, which says that 'renewal' *includes* extension and references
to renewing a contract for a fixed term shall be construed accordingly and the provisions
to be found in s 82(3) and (5)(*a*). So, for the purposes of the case which your Lordships
have to consider, non-renewal by the employer of a contract of employment for a fixed
b   term which has expired is assimilated to the termination by the employer of a contract
of employment of indefinite duration which is terminable by notice.

Schedule 13 is stated by s 151 to contain provisions 'for ascertaining [for the purposes
of the Act] the length of an employee's period of employment and whether that
employment has been continuous'. In the instant case we are concerned primarily not
with length but with continuity. Paragraph 2 of Sch 13 provides:

c   'Except so far as otherwise provided by the following provisions of this Schedule,
any week which does not count under paragraphs 3 to 13 breaks the continuity of
the period of employment.'

The computation is in weeks, and by para 3 any week in which the employee is employed
for 16 hours or more is to count. Paragraphs 4 to 7 appear under the rubric 'Employment
d   governed by contract'. Paragraph 4 provides that all weeks that are governed by a contract
of employment which 'normally involves employment for sixteen hours or more weekly'
shall count even though in the particular week the employee works less hours or none at
all. Paragraphs 5 to 7 contain various provisions dealing with circumstances in which
weeks during which the employee is required by his contract of employment to work
less than sixteen hours are to count in the computation of the length of his continuous
e   employment.

All periods during which there is a subsisting contract of employment between the
employee and the employer are thus catered for by paras 4 to 7. That is why (pace Lord
Upjohn in *Fitzgerald v Hall Russell & Co Ltd* [1969] 3 All ER 1140 at 1149–1150, [1970]
AC 984 at 1000) the rubric 'Periods in which there is no contract of employment' which
appears above para 9 is appropriate. Paragraph 9 is in the following terms:

f   '(1) If in any week the employee is, for the whole or part of the week—(*a*)
incapable of work in consequence of sickness or injury, or (*b*) absent from work on
account of a temporary cessation of work, or (*c*) absent from work in circumstances
such that, by arrangement or custom, he is regarded as continuing in the
employment of his employer for all or any purposes, or (*d*) absent from work wholly
or partly because of pregnancy or confinement, that week shall, notwithstanding
g   that it does not fall under paragraph 3, 4 or 5, count as a period of employment.
(2) Not more than twenty-six weeks shall count under paragraph (*a*) or, subject
to paragraph 10, under paragraph (*d*) of sub-paragraph (1) between any periods
falling under paragraph 3, 4 or 5.'

It never comes into operation where a contract of employment with the same employer
h   (or an employer who for the purposes of the Act is to be treated as the same employer)
has been in force for an uninterrupted period up to the time of its termination; it is
dealing only with periods which are not to be treated as interrupting a continuing period
of employment under a contract of employment, notwithstanding that during the period
of interruption there is in law no subsisting contract of employment.

In *Fitzgerald v Hall Russell & Co Ltd* this House so held in a case falling under para
j   9(1)(*b*). There the employee had been engaged under a contract of indefinite duration
which had already lasted some four years. This contract the employer had determined
by notice because for the time being there was no work available for the employee, a
riveter in a ship-repairer's yard, to do. When the work became available again, some
eight weeks later, he was re-engaged under a fresh contract of employment of indefinite
duration on the same terms as previously. After re-engagement his fresh contract of

employment continued for another five years when he was again dismissed, this time
admittedly on grounds of redundancy. The question before this House was whether the *a*
interval of eight weeks between the two contracts of employment broke the continuity
of his period of employment, so as to prevent his four years' employment before that gap
of eight weeks to be taken into account for the purpose of calculating his redundancy
payment. This House determined that provided the cessation could properly be regarded
as being 'temporary', which was a matter to be determined by the industrial tribunal
looking at all the facts and circumstances from the time of the first dismissal to the time *b*
of the dismissal on which the claim to redundancy payment was based, the eight weeks
during which no contract of employment between the employee and the employer was
in existence could properly be regarded as a cessation of work that was temporary only.

My Lords, since para 9 only applies to an interval of time between the coming to an
end of one contract of employment and the beginning of a fresh contract of employment,
the expression 'absent from work', where it appears in para 9(1)(b), (c) and (d), must mean *c*
not only that the employee is not doing any actual work for his employer but that there
is no contract of employment subsisting between him and his employer that would
entitle the latter to require him to do any work. So in this context the phrase 'the
employee is absent from work on account of a temporary cessation of work' as descriptive
of a period of time, as it would seem to me, must refer to the interval between (1) the
date on which the employee who would otherwise be continuing to work under an *d*
existing contract of employment is dismissed because for the time being his employer
has no work for him to do, and (2) the date on which work for him to do having become
again available he is re-engaged under a fresh contract of employment to do it; and the
words 'on account of a temporary cessation of work' refer to the reason why the employer
dismissed the employee, and make it necessary to inquire what the reason for the
dismissal was. The fact that the unavailability of work had been foreseen by the employer *e*
sufficiently far in advance to enable him to anticipate it by giving to the employee a
notice to terminate his contract of employment that is of sufficient length to satisfy the
requirements of s 49 of the Act (which may be as long as 12 weeks) cannot alter the
reason for the dismissal or prevent the absence from work following on the expiry of the
notice from being 'on account of a temporary cessation of work'.

I turn from 'dismissal' in the ordinary sense of the term, which requires action on the *f*
part of the employer to terminate the contract of employment between him and his
employee, to 'dismissal' in the extended sense given to it by ss 55(2)(b) and 83(2)(b), by
making the expression applicable to contracts of employment for a fixed term, to which
it would not be appropriate in its ordinary sense. Mere inaction by the employer, ie
failure to renew the contract on the expiry of the fixed term, is for the purposes of
remedies for unfair dismissal and entitlement to redundancy payment assimilated to *g*
'dismissal' in its ordinary sense which was the subject of the decision of this House in
Fitzgerald v Hall Russell & Co Ltd.

My Lords, I am quite unable to be persuaded that para 9(1) is *not* applicable to cases
where a contract of employment for a fixed term has expired and on expiry has not been
renewed by the employer, in exactly the same way as it is applicable to contracts of
employment of indefinite duration which are terminated by the employer by notice. *h*
One looks to see what was the reason for the employer's failure to renew the contract on
the expiry of its fixed term and asks oneself the question: was that reason 'a temporary
cessation of work', within the meaning of that phrase in para 9(1)(b)?

There are many employments, of which teaching is one of the largest and most
obvious, in which it is perfectly possible to predict with accuracy the periods in which
the educational institution at which a teacher who is employed to conduct courses in *j*
particular subjects will have no work available for that teacher to do, ie during the three
annual school holidays or during vacations at universities and other institutions of further
education. As the evidence in the instant case discloses, it is a common practice to employ
part-time teachers of courses at institutions of further education under successive fixed-
term contracts the length of which is fixed according to the duration of the particular

course and expires at the end of it. In the interval between successive courses which may
a coincide with the end of one academic year at an institution of further education and the
beginning of the next but may be considerably longer, there is no work available at the
institution for the teacher to do, and he remains without any contract of employment
until the course is resumed, when he again becomes employed under a fresh fixed-term
contract.

A somewhat similar practice is followed in relation to what are known as 'supply
b teachers' in schools, although in their case each fixed-term contract is for a single term
only. During each of the three annual school holidays between school terms the supply
teacher has no contract of employment.

The case of a supply teacher who had been employed under fixed-term contracts for
each successive school term over a period which extended to ten years in all, at the end of
which he was told that, owing to a decline in the numbers of schoolchildren, his services
c would not be required in the next school term, came before the Employment Appeal
Tribunal in *Rashid v Inner London Education Authority* [1977] ICR 157. His claim for a
redundancy payment calculated on the basis of a ten-year length of continuous service
was rejected by the tribunal, though I have not been able to discover anywhere in the
judgment what were the steps in any reasoning that led them to that conclusion. The
decision, however, appears to have been treated, as it was by the Court of Appeal in the
d instant case, as authority for the proposition that where a fixed-term contract expires and
there is an interval before another fixed-term contract comes into effect what, for the
purposes of para 9(1)(b), is to be regarded as the 'real reason' for the employee's absence
from work during that interval is the fact that he has no contract of employment and is
not the temporary cessation of work available for that teacher to do, notwithstanding
that the non-availability of work continues throughout that interval and is why the
e education authority did not find it necessary to employ the teacher during it.

My Lords, neither in the judgment in *Rashid's* case nor in the judgments of the
Employment Appeal Tribunal or the Court of Appeal in the instant case is there any
reference to either s 55(2) or s 83(2), which assimilate non-renewal of a fixed-term
contract of employment on the expiry of the fixed term to the termination of a contract
of employment of indefinite duration by notice given to the employee by the employer.
f It must in my view follow from this assimilation that, just as in the latter case one must
look at the reason why the employer terminated the contract of employment, so in the
former one must look at the reason why the employer did not renew the contract on the
expiry of its fixed term, and decide whether that reason was 'a temporary cessation of
work' within para 9(1)(b) as that expression was interpreted by this House in *Fitzgerald v
Hall Russell & Co Ltd*. In so far as *Rashid's* case is to be regarded as deciding otherwise, for
g the reasons given earlier in this speech it is, in my view wrong, and ought to be overruled
by this House.

From the fact that there is no work available for the employee to do for the employer
during the whole of the interval between the end of one fixed-term contract of
employment and the beginning of the next, and that this was the reason for his non-
employment during that interval, it does not necessarily follow that the interval
h constitutes a '*temporary* cessation of work'. In harmony with what this House held in
Fitzgerald's case, para 9(1)(b), in cases of employment under a succession of fixed-term
contracts of employment with intervals in between, requires one to look back from the
date of the expiry of the fixed-term contract in respect of the non-renewal of which the
employee's claim is made over the whole period during which the employee has been
intermittently employed by the same employer, in order to see whether the interval
j between one fixed-term contract and the fixed-term contract that next preceded it was
short in duration relative to the combined duration of those two fixed-term contracts
during which work had continued, for the whole scheme of the Act appears to me to
show that it is in the sense of 'transient', ie lasting only for a relatively short time, that
the word 'temporary' is used in para 9(1)(b). So, the continuity of employment for the
purposes of the Act in relation to unfair dismissal and redundancy payments is not

broken unless and until, looking backwards from the date of the expiry of the fixed-term contract on which the employee's claim is based, there is to be found between one fixed- *a* term contract and its immediate predecessor an interval that cannot be characterised as short relatively to the combined duration of the two fixed-term contracts. Whether it can be so characterised is a question of fact and degree and so is for decision by an industrial tribunal rather than by the Employment Appeal Tribunal or an appellate court of law.

In the instant case this was not a question to which the industrial tribunal ever *b* addressed their minds. They took the view that *Rashid's* case had decided that they had no 'jurisdiction' (as they put it) to entertain Mrs Ford's claim. The use of the expression 'jurisdiction' was mistaken and its continued use may be misleading in cases where an employee claims that he has been continuously employed within the meaning of the Act for a period long enough to qualify him for a remedy for unfair dismissal or to receive a redundancy payment, and the employer contests this. Whether an employee is so *c* qualified or not is an issue which, in respect of a disputed claim for a remedy for unfair dismissal, s 67 and, in respect of a claim for redundancy payment, s 91 of the Act give to an industrial tribunal exclusive jurisdiction to determine in the first instance, subject to an appeal to the Employment Appeal Tribunal but only on a question of law. It was in the exercise of that jurisdiction that the industrial tribunal decided that Mrs Ford's history of employment prior to her dismissal in July 1979 was not such as would qualify *d* her for any remedy for unfair dismissal or any redundancy payment; and the reason why they so decided and did not address their minds to the relevant question whether the cessations of work between her various successive fixed-term contracts of employment were 'temporary' in the sense that I have described was wrong in law. So, in the ordinary way on allowing the appeal the appropriate course would be for your Lordships to include that question among those remitted to the industrial tribunal for their decision, *e* as the House did in *Fitzgerald's* case.

In the instant case, however, it is conceded by the council that each of the intervals between Mrs Ford's successive fixed-term contracts could properly be characterised as 'temporary'. I would therefore allow the appeal and remit Mrs Ford's claims to the industrial tribunal to decide such other matters, if any, as may remain in dispute between her and the council. *f*

My Lords, as I indicated at the outset, the length of successive fixed-term contracts on which part-time lecturers are employed and the intervals between them vary considerably with the particular course that the part-time lecturer is engaged to teach; so it by no means follows that a similar concession would be made or would be appropriate in each of their cases. It also follows from what I have said that successive periods of seasonal employment of other kinds under fixed-term contracts, such as employment in *g* agriculture during harvest-time or in hotel work during the summer season, will only qualify as continuous employment if the length of the period between two successive seasonal contracts is so short in comparison with the length of the season during which the employee is employed as properly to be regarded by the industrial tribunal as no more than a *temporary* cessation of work in the sense that I have indicated.

LORD KEITH OF KINKEL. My Lords, for the reasons given in the speeches of my *h* noble and learned friends Lord Diplock and Lord Brightman, which I have had the benefit of reading in draft and with which I agree, I too would allow the appeal.

LORD ROSKILL. My Lords, in the course of his judgment in the Court of Appeal Stephenson LJ said that it was only 'after some vacillation' that he had concluded that the submissions on behalf of the council were correct. I confess that during the hearing of this appeal I likewise found those submissions most persuasive and at its conclusion was *j* disposed to accept them. But further consideration and the advantage of reading in draft the speeches of my noble and learned friends Lord Diplock and Lord Brightman finally persuaded me that my initial conclusion was wrong. For the reasons given in those speeches I therefore agree that this appeal succeeds.

LORD BRANDON OF OAKBROOK. My Lords, I have had the advantage of

reading in draft the speeches prepared by my noble and learned friends Lord Diplock
a and Lord Brightman. I agree with both speeches, and for the reasons given in them
would allow the appeal.

LORD BRIGHTMAN. My Lords, I entirely agree with the views expressed by my
noble and learned friend Diplock. As, however, we are differing from the unanimous
decision of the members of the industrial tribunal, the Employment Appeal Tribunal
b and the Court of Appeal, as well as departing from *Rashid v Inner London Education
Authority* [1977] ICR 157, to which my noble and learned friend has referred, I would
like, out of respect for this weight of contrary authority to add my own observations.

The question for decision for this House is whether the appellant, employed by the
Warwickshire County Council from 1971 to 1979 under a succession of ten month
contracts in each academic year at the Mid-Warwickshire College of Further Education,
c was 'continuously employed' for the purposes of Part V (unfair dismissal) and Part VI
(redundancy payments) of the Employment Protection (Consolidation) Act 1978. The
two-months' break which occurred during the summer vacation between successive
contracts of employment precluded continuous employment in fact. But the Act contains
a number of deeming provisions, and the problem is whether, by reason of one such
deeming provision, each of the two months' breaks nevertheless counts as a period of
d employment so as to produce continuous employment over the years in question.

Part V of the Act, as I have indicated, deals with unfair dismissal. Section 54 confers a
general right on an employee not to be unfairly dismissed, save where his case is excluded
by, inter alia, s 64(1)(a). This is the relevant exclusion for present purposes. In its
amended form it requires, as a general rule, that an employee complaining of unfair
dismissal shall have been 'continuously employed' for 52 weeks. The appellant's
e continuous employment, apart from the deeming provisions of the Act, never exceeded
44 weeks or thereabouts.

It is a prerequisite to a claim of unfair dismissal that the complainant should have been
dismissed. Section 55(2) enlarges the meaning of 'dismissal'. It is to include not only the
case where the contract of employment is determined by the employer, but also the case
where 'under that contract [the employee] is employed for a fixed term', and 'that term
f expires without being renewed under the same contract'. 'Renewal' is defined by s 153
to include 'extension, and any reference to renewing a contract for a fixed term shall be
construed accordingly'. The section says 'renewing a contract or a fixed term', but I take
this to be a misprint for 'for a fixed term', although the wording is the same in s 56 of the
Redundancy Payments Act 1965.

Each of the appellant's contracts of employment was a fixed-term contract, and none
g was extended or otherwise renewed. It follows that in 1979 the appellant was in a
position to say that she had been dismissed and she could have said the same in any
previous year after the expiry of the fixed term of her last contract. Her claim of unfair
dismissal would however fail in limine under s 64 unless she could establish that she had
been 'continuously employed' for the requisite period.

Part VI of the Act deals with redundancy payments. The right to a payment arises as a
h general rule where the employee has been 'continuously employed' for the requisite
period and is, inter alia, dismissed by reason of redundancy. The requisite period is, as a
general rule, the period of two years. 'Dismiss' has, for present purposes, the same
meaning in this part as under Part V, and so includes the expiry of a fixed-term contract
without being extended or otherwise renewed.

Continuous employment for a qualifying period is therefore a necessary ingredient of
j a claim of unfair dismissal and a claim for a redundancy payment. Section 151(1) directs
one to Sch 13 for the dual purpose of ascertaining the length of an employee's period of
employment and whether that employment has been continuous.

Schedule 13 is headed 'Computation of Period of Employment'. It prescribes the rules
for ascertaining whether the employment has been continuous and how many weeks the
employee is to be credited with. Paragraph 1(1) of the schedule establishes the week as
the unit of account. Paragraph 2 provides:

'Except so far as otherwise provided by the following provisions of this Schedule, any week that does not count under paragraphs 3 to 13 breaks the continuity of the period of employment.'

Paragraphs 3 to 13 then state, expressly or by implication, what weeks are to 'count' and what weeks are not to 'count'. Paragraph 3 is introduced by the cross-heading 'Normal working weeks'. It provides that any week in which the employee is employed for 16 hours or more is to count. However, paras 4, 5 and 6, which are cross-headed 'Employment governed by contract', provide that a week is to count in certain circumstances although the weekly employment falls below the 16 hours required by para 3. This relaxation is allowed (very shortly stated) if during the week the employment is governed by a contract which 'normally involves' at least 16 hours employment per week (para 4); or if the employment ceases to be governed by a 16-hour contract (as I will call it) and becomes governed by an 8-hour contract for a period of up to 26 weeks (para 5), or if the employment is governed by an 8-hour contract for at least five years (para 6). I can pass over paras 7 and 8. Paragraph 9, which is the important one, is cross-headed 'Periods in which there is no contract of employment'. It further relaxes the para 3 rule. It only comes into play where the employee's contract of employment has ceased. This relaxation of the rule applies if the employee is incapable of work, or absent from work, brought about in consequence of, or on account of, or because of, or in the circumstances of, the event described, the events being sickness or injury, temporary cessation of work, an arrangement or custom which deems continuity of employment, and pregnancy or confinement. The wording of para 9, so far as relevant for present purposes, is:

'(1) If in any week the employee is, for the whole or part of the week . . . (b) absent from work on account of a temporary cessation of work . . . that week shall notwithstanding that it does not fall under paragraph 3, 4 or 5, count as a period of employment . . .'

I need not refer to the remaining paragraphs of Sch 13, which contain intricate regulations concerning those weeks which are 'to count' or not 'to count' in computing periods of employment.

The appellant was not working 16 hours a week, or at all, during the 11 or so vacation weeks between early July and late September in each year. Therefore the vacation weeks do not 'count' under para 3. Nor can they 'count' under paras 4, 5 or 6, which relax the strict rule in para 3, because during the vacation weeks 'the employee's relations with the employer were not governed by a contract of employment', to use the phraseology of these paragraphs. In the result the appellant's continuity of employment was disrupted by the vacation weeks, and the qualifying period prescribed by s 64 (as amended) and s 81 were not achieved, unless the vacation weeks can be made to count under para 9(1)(b).

I have two preliminary observations on para 9(1)(b). First, the 'work' to which para 9 is directed is the employee's work, that is to say the work available for the employee personally: see the decision of this House in *Fitzgerald v Hall Russell & Co Ltd* [1969] 3 All ER 1140 at 1151, [1970] AC 984 at 1002. Lord Parker CJ called it 'his job': see *Hunter v Smith's Dock Co Ltd* [1968] 2 All ER 81 at 84 [1968] 1 WLR 1865 at 1869. Second, it is fundamental to the construction and application of para 9(1)(b) that one looks backward over the period of employment the continuity of which is in question and views the events which have happened, and then asks oneself whether the proper interpretation of those events is that, with hindsight, the employee has been 'absent from work on account of a temporary cessation of work'. That was the approach of Lord Parker CJ in *Hunter's* case and it was approved by this House in *Fitzgerald's* case [1969] 3 All ER 1140 at 1152, [1970] AC 984 at 1003.

In the instant case it is in my opinion correct to say, as a matter of analysis, that the appellant was not at her work at the college during the vacation weeks 'on account of' the expiry of the fixed term of the contract under which she had, during the preceding weeks of the academic year, been performing this work, and that the duration of that term was fixed by the contract in anticipation of the fact that her work would not be

required to be done during the vacation weeks. Does it follow that she was, during the
a   vacation weeks, 'absent from [her] work' and, if so, was such 'absence' 'on account of' 'a
cessation' of her work? 'Temporary' need not be considered. If the other conditions of
para 9(1)(b) are satisfied there is no dispute that each cessation during the vacation weeks
until July 1979 was temporary.

I take first the requirement of being 'absent from [her] work'. I felt initially some
difficulty in applying this description to the appellant with reference to the vacation
b   weeks. An employee who has ceased to be in contractual employment because the fixed
term of her contract has expired would not ordinarily be described as 'absent' from her
work. Nor would an employee who has been dismissed and whose notice of dismissal (if
any) has expired. Admittedly she is not at her (former) work, but to describe her as
'absent' from her former work would be an unusual use of that word. But the word does
not really cause any difficulty. Paragraph 9(1)(b) is looking at a situation where the
c   employee's contract of employment has terminated but cessation of work is, in the events
which happen, of a temporary character. It is therefore not inappropriate to describe the
employee during the interval as 'absent from work' because ex hypothesi the employee
returns shortly to the work. Furthermore, para 9(1)(b) is clearly intended to apply to a
case where the employee is dismissed owing to non-availability of work; any argument
that an employee whose fixed term of employment has expired is not 'absent' from work
d   would be equally applicable to the case of the dismissed employee. Finally, in *Fitzgerald's*
case this House held that a welder dismissed on 28 November 1962 owing to unavailability
of work and re-engaged on 21 January 1963 was 'absent from work' during the
intervening period. So there can be no doubt that the appellant is properly described as
having been 'absent from work' during each of the summer vacations between September
1971 and July 1979.

e   I turn finally to consider the requirement that the absence from work shall have been
'on account of a temporary cessation of work'. The argument against the appellant
seemed to me at first sight formidable. As a matter of strict analysis, as I have already
indicated, the appellant was not at work after the expiry of the fixed term of each contract
because, thereafter, the contract does not entitle or require her to be at work. She would
have had no right to work after the start of the summer vacation even if her work had
f   unexpectedly become available in the summer vacation. Unless the contract is extended,
the appellant would not be at work after July for the simple reason that the contractual
term has ended by effluxion of time. The expected cessation of work on (say) 8 July is
the reason why the term of the contract of employment was fixed in (say) the previous
August so as to end on 8 July. When 8 July comes the employee ceases to be at work
because that is the expiry date of the contract and not because the work then ceases,
g   which may or may not be the case. To put the matter shortly, the appellant is absent
from work during the summer vacation on account of the expiry of the fixed term of
the contract, such term having been fixed in anticipation of the cessation of her work.
The cause of her absence from her work is therefore the expiry of the fixed term and not
the cessation of her work.

However, I have come to the conclusion that this argument is not correct on the true
h   construction of the 1978 Act. I will seek to illustrate the reason in stages. Suppose that in
August 1977 the appellant was engaged under a contract of employment of indefinite
duration, starting in September 1977, subject to one week's notice on either side. Suppose
that on 1 July 1978 the council gave the appellant one week's notice because her pottery
class would not extend beyond 8 July 1978. Suppose that in August 1978 she was engaged
under a similar but new contract of employment for an indefinite term starting in
j   September 1978. It could not, I apprehend, be doubted that she would have been absent
from work within the meaning of the Act during the 1978 summer vacation on account
of a temporary cessation of her work.

Suppose that her contract was determinable by one month's notice on either side, and
that such notice was therefore given on 8 June 1978. Again, I apprehend that there is no
doubt that the vacation period would 'count' on the true construction of the Act.

Both these cases are susceptible to the same analysis as the fixed term contract, that is to say the appellant's work comes to an end on 8 July because that is the date of expiry of the notice; the notice is served on 8 June, or 1 July, in anticipation of the fact that her *a* work will cease on 8 July, which in the event may or may not prove to be the case. The argument that a fixed term contract ceases on account of the effluxion of time can equally be applied to these two hypothetical cases; the work ceases because the term of the notice has expired. In the cases supposed the immediate cause of cessation of work is, in a sense, the expiry of the notices of dismissal; the effective cause is the anticipated cessation of work. *b*

There is no essential difference in my view where the contract of employment is for a fixed term, the term being fixed by reference to the anticipated availability of work. In the fixed-term contract of the kind which features in this case the employer, in effect, gives notice when the contract is signed of the date when the employment is to cease, instead of reserving to himself the right to give such notice at a later date. If para 9(1)(*b*) is intended to apply to a case where notice of dismissal is served during the currency of *c* the contract on account of an anticipated cessation of work, I can see no logical reason why it should be supposed not to apply where the contract itself indicates when the employment is to cease, if that is on account of the anticipated cessation of work. In my view para 9(1)(*b*) is not concerned with the means employed for bringing the employment to an end temporarily but with the reason for bringing it to an end.

I think that this approach to para 9(1)(*b*) is consistent with ss 55(2) and 83(2). For the *d* purposes of a claim of unfair dismissal and a claim for a redundancy payment, no distinction is to be drawn between a contract for an indefinite period which is terminated by a dismissal notice and a contract for a fixed period which expires without being extended or otherwise renewed. In each case the employee is to be treated as dismissed by the employer. If it is irrelevant to the employee's right to claim on the ground of unfair dismissal, or to claim a redundancy payment, whether the employee's work has *e* ended owing to the expiry of the fixed term of the contract or owing to the expiry of the term of the notice of dismissal, it seems to me entirely consistent that the 'counting' process under para 9(1)(*b*) should likewise have no regard to the question whether the 'absence from work' was the immediate result of the dismissal notice, or the immediate result of the expiry of a fixed term specified in the contract. The absence must be 'on account of a temporary cessation of work', but that requirement can be satisfied equally *f* by a cessation which exists or is anticipated when the employee is dismissed with notice or by a cessation which exists when he is dismissed without notice, or by a cessation which is anticipated when the fixed term is introduced into the contract.

I therefore reach the conclusion that the appellant can properly be described as 'absent from work' during each of the vacation periods which spanned her successive contracts of employment and that such absence can properly be described as 'on account of a *g* temporary cessation of work' notwithstanding that the contract was brought to an end by the expiry of its fixed term, instead of by the expiry of the term of the dismissal notice, and that an expected cessation of work which governs the length of the fixed term satisfies the words 'on account of a temporary cessation of work', just as an expected cessation of work which leads to a dismissal notice would have satisfied those words.

In the result I respectfully differ from the conclusion reached in this case by the courts *h* below. It must also follow that I find myself unable to agree with the conclusion reached by the Court of Session in the somewhat similar case of *Moncrieff v Tayside Regional Council* (18 November 1982, unreported).

I would allow the appeal.

Appeal allowed. Cause remitted to industrial tribunal with a direction to entertain appellant's *j* *complaint of unfair dismissal and her application for a redundancy payment accordingly.*

Solicitors: *Hugh Pierce* (for Mrs Ford); *Sharpe Pritchard & Co*, agents for *John W Hayes*, Warwick (for the council).

Mary Rose Plummer   Barrister.

a # Khawaja v Secretary of State for the Home Department
and another appeal

HOUSE OF LORDS

b LORD FRASER OF TULLYBELTON, LORD WILBERFORCE, LORD SCARMAN, LORD BRIDGE OF HARWICH
AND LORD TEMPLEMAN
25, 26, 27, 28 OCTOBER, 1, 2 NOVEMBER 1982, 10 FEBRUARY 1983

Immigration – Illegal entry and other offences – Illegal entry – Illegal entrant – Whether 'illegal entrant' confined to persons entering clandestinely and avoiding immigration control or including
c *persons obtaining leave to enter by fraud or deception – Immigration Act 1971, s 33(1).*

Immigration – Leave to enter – Non-patrial – Right of entry – Change of circumstances removing basis on which entry certificate granted – Applicant eligible for entry as unmarried dependant at time application made – Applicant married after application made but before entry certificate granted – Whether applicant under obligation when entering to disclose change of circumstances
d *– Whether non-disclosure amounting to fraud or deception – Whether applicant obtaining leave to enter by fraud or deception an 'illegal entrant' – Whether court entitled to examine evidence relied on by immigration officer – Whether court limited to inquiring whether immigration officer had reasonable grounds to conclude that applicant was illegal entrant – Immigration Act 1971, s 33(1).*

e *Judicial review – Evidence – Cross-examination – Court's discretion to allow cross-examination of deponents to affidavits – Exercise of discretion – RSC Ord 53.*

The appellant in the first case was a Pakistani national living in Belgium, where in December 1979 he went through a bigamous form of marriage ceremony with B, who was settled in England. In March 1980 he arrived at Manchester airport and told the
f immigration officer that he had come for a visit of one week, but he made no mention of his marriage. The immigration officer granted him leave to enter as a visitor for one month. In April he married B in England, B's previous marriage having by then been dissolved. The appellant then applied to the Home Office for an extension of his leave to enter, stating that he desired to visit members of his family in the United Kingdom but without mentioning his marriage. Subsequently he informed the Home Office that he
g had married B and applied for indefinite leave to remain. The Home Office rejected his application and decided that his leave to enter had been vitiated by deception so that he was to be treated as an illegal entrant who had no right of appeal while in the United Kingdom. The Home Office accordingly authorised the detention of the applicant pending deportation. In the notification given to the appellant an immigration officer stated that there were 'reasonable grounds to conclude' that he was an illegal entrant. The
h appellant applied for judicial review of the decision to detain him. His application was dismissed by the judge, whose decision was upheld by the Court of Appeal. The appellant appealed to the House of Lords.

The appellant in the second case was born in India in 1956. In June 1972 his father entered the United Kingdom for settlement, having before that date applied for an entry certificate for the appellant as his dependant. In January 1973 the appellant married in
j India. In January 1975 the appellant, then aged 18, was given indefinite leave to enter the United Kingdom to join his father and he did so. The immigration rules then in force required a child aged 18 or over to qualify for admission in his own right unless he was 'an unmarried and fully dependent son under 21 . . . who formed part of the family unit overseas' and whose whole family was settled in the United Kingdom. The

immigration authorities learned of the appellant's marriage and in November 1978 he
was detained as an illegal entrant pending deportation. When notifying the appellant of   a
his decision the immigration officer stated that he was satisfied that there were 'reasonable
grounds to conclude' that the appellant was an illegal entrant. The appellant applied for
judicial review of the decision to detain him. His application was dismissed by the
Divisional Court, and its decision was upheld by the Court of Appeal. The appellant
appealed to the House of Lords.

In both appeals the issues arose (i) whether the expression 'illegal entrant' in s 33(1)^a of   b
the Immigration Act 1971 was confined to persons who entered the United Kingdom by
clandestine means and had never passed through immigration control and (ii) whether,
on an application for judicial review of an immigration officer's decision to order the
detention and removal of an illegal entrant, the court was limited to deciding whether
there were reasonable grounds for the immigration officer's decision or whether the
court was required to decide itself whether the person was an illegal entrant.   c

Held – (1) On the true construction of s 33(1) of the 1971 Act the term 'illegal entrant'
was not confined to a person who entered the United Kingdom by clandestine means
thereby avoiding immigration controls but included a person who obtained leave to
enter from an immigration officer by use of deception or fraud. However, although in
some instances silence as to a material fact coupled with conduct could amount to   d
deception or fraud, the 1971 Act did not impose a positive duty of candour on an
applicant seeking leave to enter, so that non-disclosure of relevant facts did not in itself
constitute fraud or deception (see p 771 j, p 772 a, p 773 d, p 779 c to e and h, p 787 h j,
p 788 a b and p 793 f g, post); R v Secretary of State for the Home Dept, ex p Hussain [1978]
2 All ER 423, R v Secretary of State for the Home Dept, ex p Choudhary [1978] 3 All ER 790
and Zamir v Secretary of State for the Home Dept [1980] 2 All ER 768 applied; dictum of   e
Lord Wilberforce in Zamir v Secretary of State for the Home Dept [1980] 2 All ER at 773
disapproved.

(2) Where an executive officer's power to make a decision which would restrict or take
away a subject's liberty was dependent on the existence of certain facts the court was not
limited merely to inquiring whether the executive officer had reasonable grounds for
believing that those precedent facts existed when he acted. Instead the court had to be   f
satisfied on the civil standard of proof to a high degree of probability that those facts did
in fact exist at the time the power was exercised. Accordingly a statement by an
immigration officer that he had reasonable grounds to conclude that a person was an
illegal entrant did not preclude the court from examining the evidence relied on by the
officer and determining whether it satisfied the requisite standard of proof. That principle
applied both to applications for habeas corpus and to applications for judicial review (see   g
p 772 c to f h j, p 777 g to p 778 a, p 781 a, p 783 b c, p 784 c to f, p 791 b and j to p 792 d,
p 793 a b f g and p 794 j, post); dicta of Lord Atkin in Eshugbayi Eleko v Government of
Nigeria (Officer Administering) [1931] All ER Rep at 49, of Lord Atkin in Liversidge v
Anderson [1941] 3 All ER at 362, Bater v Bater [1950] 2 All ER 458, Hornal v Neuberger
Products Ltd [1956] 3 All ER 970, Re Dellow's Will Trusts, Lloyds Bank Ltd v Institute of
Cancer Research [1964] 1 All ER 771, Blyth v Blyth [1966] 1 All ER 524, R v Brixton Prison   h
Governor, ex p Ahson [1969] 2 All ER 347, dictum of Lord Denning MR in R v Governor
of Pentonville Prison, ex p Azam [1973] 2 All ER at 750–751 and IRC v Rossminster Ltd
[1980] 1 All ER 93 applied; R v Secretary of State for the Home Dept, ex p Hussain [1978] 2
All ER 423, R v Secretary of State for the Home Dept, ex p Choudhary [1978] 3 All ER 790
and Zamir v Secretary of State for the Home Dept [1980] 2 All ER 768 overruled.

(3) Applying those principles, the appeal in the first case would be dismissed since the   j
evidence proved overwhelmingly that the appellant in that case had deceived the
immigration authority in order to obtain leave to enter which would not have been
given were it not for the deception, and the appeal in the second case would be allowed
since the evidence failed to prove that the appellant in that case was guilty of deception

a   Section 33(1), so far as material, is set out at p 785 d, post

so as to render him an illegal entrant (see p 772 *j* to p 773 *a*, p 778 *b* to *d*, p 784 *g h*, p 793
a *b* to *g* and p 795 *f g*, post).

Per curiam. The court's discretion under RSC Ord 53 to allow cross-examination of
deponents to affidavits in applications for judicial review should only be exercised when
justice so demands; the cases will be rare when it will be essential, in the interests of
justice, to require the attendance for cross-examination of a deponent from overseas (see
p 772 *h j*, p 774 *h*, p 777 *j*, p 784 *e*, p 792 *d* to *f* and p 795 *a* to *c*, post).

b   Decision of the Court of Appeal sub nom *R v Secretary of State for the Home Dept, ex p
Khawaja* [1982] 2 All ER 523 affirmed.

Notes

For illegal entry into the United Kingdom, see 4 Halsbury's Laws (4th edn) paras 976,
1027.

c   For the Immigration Act 1971, s 33, see 41 Halsbury's Statutes (3rd edn) 52.

Cases referred to in opinions

Associated Provincial Picture Houses Ltd v Wednesbury Corp [1947] 2 All ER 680, [1948] 1
    KB 223, CA, 45 Digest (Repl) 215, 189.
Azam v Secretary of State for the Home Dept [1973] 2 All ER 765, [1974] AC 18, [1973] 2
d   WLR 1058, HL; *affg* [1973] 2 All ER 741, [1974] AC 18, [1973] 2 WLR 949, CA, 2
    Digest (Reissue) 199, 1153.
Bater v Bater [1950] 2 All ER 458, [1951] P 35, CA, 27(1) Digest (Reissue) 364, 2653.
Blyth v Blyth [1966] 1 All ER 524, [1966] AC 643, [1966] 2 WLR 634, HL, 27(1) Digest
    (Reissue) 534, 3838.
Bushel's Case (1670) Vaugh 135, T Jo 13, 124 ER 1006, 84 ER 1123, 16 Digest (Reissue)
e   300, 3009.
Dellow's Will Trusts, Re, Lloyds Bank Ltd v Institute of Cancer Research [1964] 1 All ER 771,
    [1964] 1 WLR 451, 22 Digest (Reissue) 47, 267.
Eshugbayi Eleko v Government of Nigeria (Officer Administering) [1931] AC 662, [1931] All
    ER Rep 44, PC, 8(2) Digest (Reissue) 767, 417.
Greene v Secretary of State for Home Affairs [1941] 3 All ER 388, [1942] AC 284, HL, 17
f   Digest (Reissue) 467, 29.
Hornal v Neuberger Products Ltd [1956] 3 All ER 970, [1957] 1 QB 247, [1956] 3 WLR
    1034, CA, 22 Digest (Reissue) 47, 268.
IRC v Rossminster Ltd [1980] 1 All ER 93, [1980] AC 952, [1980] 2 WLR 1, HL, Digest
    (Cont Vol E) 316, 2153f.
Jones v Secretary of State for Social Services, Hudson v Secretary of State for Social Services
g   [1972] 1 All ER 145, [1972] AC 944, [1972] 2 WLR 210, HL, Digest (Cont Vol D) 683,
    4585b.
Khan v Secretary of State for the Home Dept [1977] 3 All ER 538, [1977] 1 WLR 1466, CA,
    2 Digest (Reissue) 199, 1154.
Liversidge v Anderson [1941] 3 All ER 338, [1942] AC 206, HL, 17 Digest (Reissue) 467,
    28.
h *Pirelli General Cable Works Ltd v Oscar Faber & Partners (a firm)* [1983] 1 All ER 65, [1983]
    2 WLR 6, HL.
R v Brixton Prison Governor, ex p Ahson [1969] 2 All ER 347, [1969] 2 QB 222, [1969] 2
    WLR 618, DC, 2 Digest (Reissue) 206, 1173.
R v Home Secretary, ex p Budd [1942] 1 All ER 373, [1942] 2 KB 14, CA, 17 Digest
    (Reissue) 468, 30.
j *R v Immigration Appeal Tribunal, ex p Abdul Malik Hussain* (18 June 1982, unreported), DC.
R v Risley Remand Centre (Governor), ex p Maqboul Hussain (4 May 1976, unreported), DC.
R v Secretary of State for the Home Dept, ex p Akhtar [1980] 2 All ER 735, [1981] QB 46,
    [1980] 3 WLR 302, CA.
R v Secretary of State for the Home Dept, ex p Badwal (Pinky) (29 April 1980, unreported),
    DC.
R v Secretary of State for the Home Dept, ex p Choudhary [1978] 3 All ER 790, [1978] 1 WLR
    1177, CA, Digest (Cont Vol E) 8, 1154b.

R v Secretary of State for the Home Dept, ex p Hussain [1978] 2 All ER 423, [1978] 1 WLR 700, DC and CA, Digest (Cont Vol E) 8, *1154a*.

R v Secretary of State for the Home Dept, ex p Iqbal [1979] 1 All ER 675, [1979] QB 264, [1978] 3 WLR 884, DC; *on appeal* [1979] 1 All ER 685, [1979] QB 276, [1979] 1 WLR 425, CA, Digest (Cont Vol E) 167, *743a*.

R v Secretary of State for the Home Dept, ex p Jayakody [1982] 1 All ER 461, [1982] 1 WLR 405, CA.

R v Secretary of State for the Home Dept, ex p Yasmeen (11 February 1982, unreported), DC.

Singh (Tirath) v Secretary of State for the Home Dept [1980] CA Transcript 686.

Sommersett's Case (1772) 20 State Tr 1, 11 Digest (Reissue) 486, 901.

Wright v Wright (1948) 77 CLR 191.

Zamir v Secretary of State for the Home Dept [1980] 2 All ER 768, [1980] AC 930, [1980] 3 WLR 249, HL.

Appeals

Khera v Secretary of State for the Home Department

Bohar Singh Khera appealed by leave of the Appeal Committee of the House of Lords granted on 9 July 1982 against the decision of the Court of Appeal (Ormrod, Dunn LJJ and Sir Sebag Shaw) on 12 February 1982 dismissing the appellant's appeal against the decision of the Divisional Court of the Queen's Bench Division (Donaldson LJ and Hodgson J) on 11 November 1980 dismissing an application for judicial review by way of an order of certiorari to quash the determination of the Secretary of State dated 22 November 1978 declaring the appellant to be an illegal entrant under the Immigration Act 1971 and authorising the detention and removal of the appellant under para 16(2) of Sch 2 to the 1971 Act and/or the determination to admit him temporarily on terms dated 7 December 1978. The facts are set out in the opinion of Lord Fraser.

Khawaja v Secretary of State for the Home Department

Salamatullah Khawaja appealed by leave of the Appeal Committee of the House of Lords granted on 17 June 1982 against the decision of the Court of Appeal (Lord Denning MR, Eveleigh and Donaldson LJJ) ([1982] 2 All ER 523, [1982] 1 WLR 625) on 26 February 1982 dismissing the appellant's appeal against the decision of Forbes J, hearing the Crown Office list, on 11 November 1981 dismissing an application for judicial review by way of (i) an order of certiorari to quash the decision of the Secretary of State that the appellant was an illegal entrant under the Immigration Act 1971 and authorising the detention of the appellant under para 16(2) of Sch 2 to the 1971 Act and (ii) an order of mandamus directing the Secretary of State to redetermine the application for variation of leave made by the appellant on 11 April 1980. The facts are set out in the opinion of Lord Fraser.

Louis Blom-Cooper QC and *Michael Beloff QC* for the appellant Khera.
Michael Kershaw QC and *Ian W McIvor* for the appellant Khawaja.
Simon D Brown and *Andrew Collins* for the Secretary of State.

Their Lordships took time for consideration.

10 February. The following opinions were delivered.

LORD FRASER OF TULLYBELTON. My Lords, these two appeals were heard together. The appellants are immigrants into the United Kingdom. After they had obtained leave to enter, and had entered the United Kingdom, further information about them came to the knowledge of the Home Office, in consequence of which immigration officers decided that both appellants had obtained leave to enter by practising fraud or deception on the immigration officers at their respective ports of entry, and that they were therefore 'illegal entrants' within the meaning of the Immigration Act 1971. The officers who considered the further information ordered, in each case, that the appellant should be detained pending his summary removal as an illegal entrant. The appellants

both applied to the courts for judicial review of these decisions, and for orders of certiorari
a   to quash the detention orders. The practical question now before your Lordships' House
is whether either, or both, of the applications for judicial review should be granted, with
the result that certiorari would be issued to quash the detention order or orders.

Khera: the facts
The cases differ widely in their facts, which I must now summarise. The appellant
b   Khera was born in India on 21 August 1956. He is a citizen of India and is subject to
immigration control under the Immigration Act 1971. His father was employed by the
(British) Ministry of Defence as a police officer in Singapore from 1951 to 1971, and he
was registered in Singapore as a citizen of the United Kingdom and Colonies in February
1961. In May 1972 the appellant's father applied for an entry certificate to the United
Kingdom for the appellant's mother and the appellant as his dependants, and in June
c   1972 the father himself entered the United Kingdom for settlement. In January 1973
the appellant, then aged 16½ years, married in India. The fact of his marriage became of
importance as will appear later. Thereafter, the appellant and his mother were at first
refused entry certificates to the United Kingdom, on the ground that they were not
related to his father. But on 4 October 1974 their appeal to an adjudicator was allowed,
and on 12 January 1975 they were given indefinite leave to enter the United Kingdom,
d   and they entered. In November 1978, in consequence of an application from the
appellant's wife to enter the United Kingdom with the children of her marriage to the
appellant, the marriage came to light and, after inquiries had been made, an immigration
officer ordered that the appellant be detained as an illegal entrant, pending summary
removal under para 16(2) of Sch 2 to the 1971 Act. The detention order against the
appellant Khera was made on 22 November 1978. He was only actually detained for
e   about a fortnight, and on 8 December 1978 he was temporarily admitted to the United
Kingdom under para 21 of Sch 2 to the 1971 Act, subject to certain restrictions as to his
place of residence and other matters. But the appeal has been dealt with all along as if the
appellant were still detained, and I think that is right because his personal liberty is
undoubtedly restricted.

The appellant applied for judicial review of the decision of 22 November 1978. The
f   history of the application is a little unusual. It was dismissed by the Divisional Court, and
then by the Court of Appeal. On 6 May 1982 his petition for leave to appeal to this House
was dismissed by the Appeal Committee of this House, but on 9 July 1982 the Appeal
Committee (which had by that time granted leave to the appellant Khawaja to appeal)
discharged its order of 6 May applicable to the case of the appellant Khera, and granted
leave to him also to appeal.

g   It was at one time contended on behalf of the Secretary of State that there had been
four separate occasions between the refusal of the clearance certificate to the appellant
and the eventual grant of leave to enter on which the appellant, or his father, ought to
have disclosed to the immigration authorities that the appellant had been married, but
on which one or other of them had failed to do so. But at the hearing in this House
counsel for the Secretary of State conceded that, for reasons which I need not particularise,
h   failure to disclose the marriage on the first three of these occasions could not be founded
on as amounting to deception. Counsel relied eventually only on the fourth occasion,
which was on 16 December 1974, when the applicant underwent a medical examination
in India after the successful appeal to the adjudicator. The Home Office, in correspondence,
asserted that on that occasion the appellant had falsely told the medical officer that he
was not married, and that this lie had been a material factor in the grant of a clearance
i   certificate to him. If the lie were established, it undoubtedly would be material because
the appellant was by then (15 December 1974) aged more than 18, and under the
immigration rules then in force (Statement of Immigration Rules for Control on Entry:
Commonwealth Citizens: HC Paper (1972–73) no 79, r 44) children aged 18 or more had
to qualify for admission in their own right, with the exception that 'an *unmarried* and
fully dependent son under 21 . . . who formed part of the family unit overseas may be
admitted if the whole family are settled in the United Kingdom or are being admitted

for settlement' (emphasis added). (The rules have now been changed: see Statement of
Changes in Immigration Rules (HC Paper (1979–80) no 394). The relevant rules are rr 46   a
and 47, which do not contain the same exception in favour of unmarried sons over 18
and under 21.)

The lie alleged to have been told by the appellant to the medical officer was referred to
by the Home Office in letters to a member of your Lordships' House who had taken up
the appellant's case, the letters being dated 14 February and 4 April 1979. Thereafter, the
appellant's father swore an affidavit on 27 June 1979 in which he said that the appellant   b
denied having made any statement to the medical officer to the effect that he was
unmarried. The father added, by way of explanation, that the appellant spoke Punjabi
and had not been able to communicate satisfactorily with the medical officer, who did
not appear to speak that language. There is no evidence, on affidavit or otherwise, on
behalf of the respondent setting out the respondent's account of the interview with the
medical officer. The only affidavit on behalf of the respondent is dated 30 October 1980,   c
and was sworn by a Mr Chalmers, who appears to be the immigration officer who made
the decision of 22 November 1978 that the appellant was an illegal entrant. In that
affidavit he referred to the three occasions, now no longer relied on, on which the
appellant or his father had not disclosed that he had been married, but he made no
reference to the medical examination. It must, therefore, be taken that in reaching his
decision he did not rely on what happened at the medical examination. If the alleged lie   d
was to be part of the basis for his decision it should have been mentioned in Mr Chalmer's
affidavit; that was all the more necessary as it had been denied by the appellant's father
on his behalf. As it is now conceded that the failure to disclose on the three earlier
occasions did not amount to deception, and as they are apparently the only occasions on
which Mr Chalmers relied in coming to his decision, the inevitable consequence is, in
my opinion, that Mr Chalmers was not entitled, on the evidence that was before him, to   e
decide that the appellant had been guilty of deception.

I note in passing that the notice of the immigration officer's decision of 22 November
1978 begins with the following statement (with emphasis added):

> 'Having considered all the information available to me, I am satisfied that there
> are *reasonable grounds to conclude* that you are an illegal entrant in accordance with
> the provisions of the Immigration Act 1971 . . .'   f

The notice does not state that the officer was satisfied that 'you *are* an illegal entrant'. I
shall consider later whether the wording indicates that the immigration officer applied
the wrong test.

I should mention one ground on which counsel for Khera sought to distinguish his
case from that of *Zamir v Secretary of State for the Home Dept* [1980] 2 All ER 768, [1980]   g
AC 930, to which I shall refer in what follows. In *Zamir* the appellant had married *after*
he had been given entry clearance and the deception which this House held he had
practised consisted of failing to disclose a material change of circumstances occurring
since entry clearance had been obtained. In the present case, the appellant's marriage
took place *before* he had obtained entry clearance and, if there had been any deception, it
would have consisted of failing to disclose a material fact when his application was under   h
consideration. In my opinion, there is no relevant difference between the two cases in
this respect. What matters is that the alleged failure to disclose, whether it took place
before or after entry clearance had been obtained, would have been a material factor in
enabling the appellant to enter the United Kingdom.

Khawaja: the facts   j

I come now to the case of the appellant Khawaja. His application for judicial review
was refused by Forbes J and by the Court of Appeal (see [1982] 2 All ER 523, [1982] 1
WLR 625). Leave to appeal to your Lordships' House was given by the Appeal Committee
on 17 June 1982.

This appellant is a national of Pakistan and is not a patrial, that is to say he does not
have a right of abode in the United Kingdom: see s 2(6) of the 1971 Act. In October 1978

the appellant enrolled as a student at the University of Brussels, and in August 1979 he
a applied to the British Embassy in Brussels for a visa to enter the United Kingdom as a
visitor for two weeks. The Home Office made investigations and instructed the embassy
to refuse the application. But before the appellant had been served with the notice of
refusal he travelled by air to Manchester, where he arrived on 17 March 1980, and was
granted leave to enter as a visitor for one month. He told the immigration officer at
Manchester that he was visiting the United Kingdom for one week to see his cousin, and
b that he would be returning to Brussels to continue his studies. He had a return ticket
valid for 23 March 1980. On 11 April 1980, that is during the month for which his leave
was valid, solicitors on his behalf wrote to the Home Office stating that he wished to
obtain an extension of his visa. On 29 April 1980 the same solicitors wrote saying that
the appellant had visited their office since 11 April and had informed them that he had
been married on 10 April 1980 to a lady named Mrs Butt and that he wished to obtain
c indefinite leave to remain with her, as she was settled in the United Kingdom.
Investigations were then made by the Home Office which established that the appellant
had gone through a civil ceremony of marriage with Mrs Butt in Brussels on 21
December 1979, followed by a Muslim ceremony on 26 December 1979. They further
established that Mrs Butt had travelled with the appellant to Manchester on 17 March
1980 but had presented herself to a different immigration officer from the one who dealt
d with the appellant, and that Mrs Butt had applied for and been granted entry for an
indefinite period as a returning resident.

On 4 May 1981 an immigration officer named Mr Osborne decided that there were
'reasonable grounds to conclude' that the appellant was an illegal immigrant and
authorised his detention under para 16(2) of Sch 2 to the 1971 Act, pending summary
removal under that Act. When Mr Osborne made his decision he had before him an
e affidavit from the immigration officer who had granted the appellant's limited leave to
enter on 17 March 1980. That affidavit, and also Mr Osborne's affidavit, are now before
us. Mr Osborne states that if the officer who granted leave had been aware on 17 March
1980 that the appellant had previously made an unsuccessful application for a visa and
that he had, before his arrival, undergone marriage ceremonies in Brussels with a woman
settled in the United Kingdom, and that that lady was travelling with him and seeking
f entry as a returning resident, the immigration officer could not have been satisfied that
the appellant intended to leave the country after a visit of a month but must have
concluded that he was entering with the intention of settling here. It is, therefore,
apparent that the non-disclosure of the appellant's marriage was a material factor in his
obtaining leave. The appellant was not, in fact, entitled to enter with Mrs Butt, either as
her husband or as her fiancé, without a visa, although he may have believed otherwise.
g It remains to consider whether the non-disclosure amounted to deception or fraud and,
if so, whether the appellant thereby became an illegal entrant.

Issues of general importance
Three issues of general importance arise. The first of these issues relates to the true
meaning of the expression 'illegal entrant' in the 1971 Act; does it mean, as the appellants
h submitted, only persons who have entered the United Kingdom clandestinely without
presenting themselves to an immigration officer at a port of entry and seeking leave to
enter, or does it include also persons who have entered the country having obtained leave
to do so by practising some form of deceit or fraud on an immigration officer? On that
question I am in complete agreement with my noble and learned friend Lord Bridge that
the expression 'illegal entrant' is not limited to persons who have entered the country
j clandestinely, but that it includes also any person who has obtained leave to enter by
practising fraud or deception in contravention of s 26(1)(c) of the 1971 Act. I agree also
with Lord Bridge's observations on the passage in the speech of Lord Wilberforce in
Zamir [1980] 2 All ER 768 at 773, [1980] AC 930 at 950, where Lord Wilberforce
expressed the opinion that an alien seeking entry to the United Kingdom owes 'a positive
duty of candour on all material facts which denote a change of circumstances since the
issue of the entry clearance'. The opinion was not a necessary part of the reasoning

leading to Lord Wilberforce's conclusion, but was obiter. At the time when his speech was delivered I agreed with all of it including that passage, but further reflection, in the *a* light of the arguments in the present appeals, has convinced me that it would be wrong to construe the 1971 Act as if it imposed on persons applying for leave to enter a duty of candour approximating to uberrima fides. But, of course, deception may arise from silence as to a material fact in some circumstances; for example, the silence of the appellant Khawaja about the fact of his marriage to Mrs Butt and the fact that she had accompanied him on the flight to Manchester were, in my view, capable of constituting *b* deception, even if he had not told any direct lies to the immigration officer.

The second general issue relates to the function of the courts and of this House in its judicial capacity when dealing with applications for judicial review in cases of this sort: is their function limited to deciding whether there was evidence on which the immigration officer or other appropriate official in the Home Office could reasonably come to his decision (provided he acted fairly and not in breach of the rules of natural *c* justice), or does it extend to deciding whether the decision was justified and in accordance with the evidence? On this question I agree with my noble and learned friends Lord Scarman and Lord Bridge that an immigration officer is only entitled to order the detention and removal of a person who has entered the country by virtue of an ex facie valid permission if the person *is* an illegal entrant. That is a 'precedent fact' which has to be established. It is not enough that the immigration officer reasonably believes him to *d* be an illegal entrant if the evidence does not justify his belief. Accordingly, the duty of the court must be beyond inquiring only whether he had reasonable grounds for his belief. In both the present cases the immigration officers stated, in what appears to be a standard formula, that there were 'reasonable grounds to conclude etc'. That formula indicates, in my opinion, that they applied the wrong test, but, as it happens, the facts in the present cases are so clear that I do not think the point is of practical importance.

With regard to the standard of proof, I agree with my noble and learned friend Lord *e* Scarman that, for the reasons explained by him, the appropriate standard is that which applies generally in civil proceedings, namely proof on a balance of probabilities, the degree of probability being proportionate to the nature and gravity of the issue. As cases such as those in the present appeals involve grave issues of personal liberty, the degree of probability required will be high. *f*

It must be remembered that, in spite of the court's decision, affirming that of the immigration officer that the illegal immigrant be removed from this country, it will still be open to him to appeal under s 16 of the 1971 Act to an adjudicator against the decision to remove him. The fact that he is not entitled to appeal so long as he is in this country (see s 16(2)) puts him at a serious disadvantage, but I do not think it is proper to regard the right of appeal as worthless. At least the possibility remains that there may be cases, *g* rare perhaps, where an appeal to the adjudicator might still succeed.

The third general issue is whether, if your Lordships accept the view that the duty of the courts is not limited to inquiring whether there was evidence on which the immigration officer was entitled to decide as he did, the House should now depart from the train of decisions culminating in *Zamir* to the contrary effect. Any such departure from precedent requires careful consideration because of the undesirability of disturbing *h* settled rules. But in the present case I am clearly of opinion that the decision in *Zamir*, to which I was a party, was erroneous in stating that the function of the court was only to see whether there were reasonable grounds for the decision of the immigration officer. None of the special reasons mentioned in the practice direction of 1966 (see *Note* [1966] 3 All ER 77, [1966] 1 WLR 1234) against departure from precedent apply here, and I consider that in the circumstances the House ought to do so. *j*

On the facts which I narrated at the beginning of this speech I am of opinion that in the case of Khera the immigration officer erred in deciding that the appellant had obtained permission to enter by deception; indeed, there was no evidence of the particular deception (the alleged lie to the medical officer) on which his decision was based. In the case of Khawaja, the appellant was plainly guilty of deception in the respects which I have already mentioned.

I would allow the appeal of Khera and dismiss the appeal of Khawaja.

LORD WILBERFORCE. My Lords, my noble and learned friend Lord Fraser has fully stated the facts relevant to these two appeals. In itself, neither presents any great difficulty, but an extensive argument has been developed on points of principle concerning 'illegal entrants', particularly those who obtain entry to the United Kingdom by fraud or deception, and as to the disposal of those points directly or indirectly in *Zamir v Secretary of State for the Home Dept* [1980] 2 All ER 768, [1980] AC 930.

Two of these may be disposed of fairly shortly.

The first is the fundamental question whether those who obtain entry by fraud or deception may, as a matter of law, viz the construction of the Immigration Act 1971, be dealt with as illegal entrants at all or whether, as the appellants contend, the Act only treated as illegal entrants persons who entered clandestinely, for example by small boats on the beaches. This point, which had never before been suggested in any of the many deception cases until it was raised in the oral argument of the appellant in *Zamir*, was, nevertheless, there fully considered. This House, indorsing the law on which the courts had consistently acted at least since 1976, decided against the appellant's argument, and held that fraud or deception vitiated permission to enter so that the person concerned could be treated as an illegal entrant. I adhere to the opinion I expressed in *Zamir* and, without disrespect to careful argument of counsel for the appellant Khera, do not propose to repeat or extend argument on the point.

The second concerns a passage in the opinion I delivered in *Zamir* as to the positive duty of candour which, I suggested, rested on those seeking entry to the United Kingdom. It was not necessary for the decision, since the view taken was that *Zamir* was a case of clear deception. The passage combines two lines of thought which ought to have been more clearly separated. The first relates to conduct which might vitiate the leave to enter and should indicate that vitiation may result not only from positive acts of deception but also from concealment of or silence as to facts material to the granting or withholding of leave to enter, including those indicating a change of circumstances since entry clearance was granted. The passage was dealing, and I deal here, with the case of deception or concealment by the intending entrant him/herself, leaving for separate consideration in an appropriate case that of deception or concealment by another person.

The second line of thought was prompted by the great number and variety of cases of deception, often organised for money, which have come before the courts. I ventured the opinion that a system of consideration of individual cases for the privilege of admission to this country can only work humanely and efficiently on a basis of candour and good faith on the part of those seeking entry. If here I trespassed onto the ground of moral judgment, I am unrepentant.

The third point on which the appellants sought reconsideration of *Zamir's* case related to the scope of judicial review by the courts of decisions by the Secretary of State to remove 'illegal entrants' and to the power and duty of the courts on habeas corpus challenges to the detention of such persons. These remedies of judicial review and habeas corpus are, of course, historically quite distinct and procedurally are governed by different statutory rules, but I do not think that in the present context it is necessary to give them distinct consideration. In practice, many applicants seek both remedies. The court considers both any detention which may be in force and the order for removal: the one is normally ancillary to the other. I do not think that it would be appropriate unless unavoidable to make a distinction between the two remedies and I propose to deal with both under a common principle. Each of the present cases appears, in fact, to be of judicial review.

In *Zamir* the main argument on this part of the case was that cases where it was sought to remove an 'illegal entrant' were part of a category of 'precedent fact' cases, where an administrative discretion exists if, but only if, some precedent fact is established to exist, and the existence of which is independently triable by a court. The best known example of this is *Eshugbayi Eleko v Government of Nigeria (Officer Administering)* [1931] AC 662, [1931] All ER Rep 44, where the discretionary power was exercisable only if the person

affected was a native chief, so that whether he was such a chief or not was what is
sometimes called a jurisdictional or collateral fact. The argument in this form was *a*
rejected in *Zamir*, I venture to think correctly. This rejection however in no way involves
rejection of a right of judicial review of the factual element in an administrative decision.
The present, as other illegal entrant cases, does involve the making of a finding of fact by
the administration as can be seen by an examination of the administrative process. In
fact, this falls into two parts: first, a determination by the authorities that a person is an
illegal entrant; second, a discretionary decision by the Secretary of State to remove him *b*
from the country and meanwhile to detain him. Separate principles in my opinion
govern these two stages. As regards the latter, review may take place on those principles,
now well familiar, which govern the review of discretionary decisions, a relevant question
being whether a reasonable person, or body, could have come to that decision and the
decision being upheld if the answer is positive. Review of the former stage depends on a
different formulation, namely one appropriate as regards a determination of fact by an *c*
administrative body. If error has crept into the decisions of the courts, which I do not
think is, in fact, suggested, or into the formulation of their reasons, it had lain in the
application to the first stage of language appropriate to the second, viz in asking whether
a reasonable immigration officer could have made the determination that he did. That is
not, in my opinion, the correct question.

It is, I think, helpful to test the above analysis by considering what actually happens in *d*
'illegal entrant' cases. A person is found in this country in circumstances which give rise
to doubt whether he is entitled to be here or not; often suspicions are provoked by an
application made by him to bring in his family. So investigations are made by the Home
Office, under powers which it undoubtedly has under the 1971 Act (s 4 and Sch 2, paras
2 and 3). Inquiry is made, of him and other witnesses, when and how he came to the
United Kingdom, what documents he had, what leave, if any, to enter was given. Further *e*
inquiry may have to be made in his country of origin; often this is done through the
High Commission there and through the entry clearance officer from whom he may
have obtained an initial clearance. Sometimes very extensive inquiries have to be made.
In *R v Secretary of State for the Home Dept, ex p Yasmeen* (11 February 1982, unreported)
the officer made a visit to the village where it was said that the applicant had married,
taking photographs of her and her alleged husband or fiancé. These he showed to a group *f*
of four or five women, he spoke to other women and then to a group of eight to ten
people. He interviewed the fiancé. He sent a report to the Home Office. On this an
immigration officer interviewed the applicant and put to her the report of the entry
clearance officer. That officer concluded that in spite of her denials, the applicant was
married. The whole case was then reviewed by an officer of the Home Office, who took
the view that she was an illegal entrant, for reasons which he stated. The point is, and I *g*
tried to make this in *Zamir*, that the conclusion that a person is an illegal entrant is a
conclusion of fact reached by immigration authorities on the basis of investigations and
interviews which they have power to conduct, including interviews of the person
concerned, of an extensive character, often abroad, and of documents whose authenticity
has to be verified by inquiries.

Now there is no doubt that the courts have jurisdiction to review the facts on which *h*
the Home Office's conclusion was reached; there is no doubt that procedural means exist,
whether under the head of habeas corpus or of judicial review, for findings of fact to be
made, by the use of affidavit evidence or cross-examination on them or oral evidence.
There is no doubt that, questions of liberty and allegations of deception being involved,
the court both can and should review the facts with care. The sole question is as to the
nature of this review. How far can, or should, the court find the facts for itself, how far *j*
should it accept, or consider itself bound to accept, or entitled to accept, the findings of
the administrative authorities? On principle one would expect that, on the one hand, the
court, exercising powers of review, would not act as a court of appeal or attempt to try or
retry the issue. On the other hand, since the critical conclusion of fact is one reached by
an administrative authority (as opposed to a judicial body) the court would think it
proper to review it in order to see whether it was properly reached, not only as a matter

of procedure but also in substance and in law. But let us test this principle on actual cases
a in order to see what rules have emerged; the material is considerable and has been
worked on by judges of eminence and experience particularly in the field of habeas
corpus. We are able now to see at what points weaknesses may have developed.

I take first *R v Brixton Prison Governor, ex p Ahson* [1969] 2 All ER 347, [1969] 2 QB
222, decided under the Commonwealth Immigrants Act 1962. Under that Act the
jurisdiction to detain in custody could only be exercised if the person concerned was
b examined within 24 hours of landing. It was held that it was for the detaining authority
to prove compliance with this condition. This was a simple case of 'jurisdictional fact'.
Lord Parker CJ put it thus ([1969] 2 All ER 347 at 352, [1969] 2 QB 222 at 231):

'... if the applicant ... challenges that return ... claiming that there was no
jurisdiction ... to make the order ... it would ... be for the executive to negative
that challenge by proving that jurisdiction in fact existed.'
c

The applicant not having proved the absence of this fact, and the respondent not having
proved its existence beyond doubt, the court decided the case on the burden of proof.
There can be no doubt as to the correctness of this case, but the area to which it relates is
different from that which concerns us.

In *Azam v Secretary of State for the Home Dept* [1973] 2 All ER 765, [1974] AC 18 the
d courts were concerned with illegal entrants and with their position under the 1971 Act.
Counsel for the appellant Khera relied strongly on this case, claimed that *Zamir* had
disregarded it and invited the House to 'reinstate' it.

The applicants had entered the United Kingdom clandestinely and orders were made
against them under Sch 2 to the 1971 Act. They applied for habeas corpus. In the Court
of Appeal Lord Denning MR referred to the fact that under s 16 of the 1971 Act an
e applicant has a right of appeal on the ground 'that on the facts of the case he is not an
illegal entrant', and he held that the existence of this right does not take away the right
to apply for the writ: '... if he make a prima facie case that he is not an illegal entrant, he
is entitled to have a writ of habeas corpus to have the matter determined' (see [1973] 2
All ER 741 at 750–751, [1974] AC 18 at 31–32). In this House the decision of the Court
of Appeal was affirmed and their Lordships proceeded to review the issue of fact.

f I have no doubt that the proposition of Lord Denning MR referred to was correct; if it
was not referred to in this House or in the later cases, including *Zamir*, it is because it is
almost axiomatic. Nothing said in *Zamir* was intended to cut it down. But it does not
decide anything as to the scope of the review of facts which may be carried out on habeas
corpus and it certainly does not suggest that such review is the same or as extensive as a
review carried out under the procedure of appeal. The case itself merely illustrates a kind
g of review which is evidently possible and which was carried out.

The governing authority as to the practice of the courts as regards persons who enter
by fraud or deception is *R v Secretary of State for the Home Dept, ex p Hussain* [1978] 2 All
ER 423, [1978] 1 WLR 700. This contains some important pronouncements. Lord
Widgery CJ, sitting in the Divisional Court, said that questions of fact are ultimately for
the Secretary of State and that there are limits to the extent to which the court can go:
h '... our obligation ... is to be satisfied that the Home Office approach to the problem is
one taken in good faith. Further we have to decide whether there is or is not adequate
evidence' (see [1978] 2 All ER 423 at 426, [1978] 1 WLR 700 at 703). This statement was
approved by Geoffrey Lane LJ in the Court of Appeal, but the Lord Justice did, after so
approving it, say in his own words ([1978] 2 All ER 423 at 429, [1978] 1 WLR 700 at
707): 'If, on the evidence taken as a whole, the Secretary of State has grounds, and
j reasonable grounds, for coming to the conclusion that the applicant is here illegally ...
this court will not interfere.' The Court of Appeal, however, in fact carefully considered
the evidence, and indeed admitted and considered fresh evidence. On the basis of the
whole of it, it found that the permission to enter was obtained by fraud. That the court
was prepared to make its own finding is particularly clear in the judgment of Megaw LJ.
In *Zamir* this House considered *Hussain* to be correct; I continue so to consider it, if
properly understood. It should not be understood, as in some later cases it may have

been, as authority that the reviewing court has nothing more to do than to consider
whether the Secretary of State, or his responsible officer, *could reasonably have come* to the   **a**
conclusion that the applicant was an illegal entrant, nor that the task of either person is
to decide whether the applicant could *reasonably be so regarded*.

R v Secretary of State for the Home Dept, ex p Choudhary [1978] 3 All ER 790, [1978] 1
WLR 1177, decided shortly after *Hussain*, marks a difference of approach. It was a habeas
corpus case and Lord Denning MR said that where on the evidence the Secretary of State
had reasonable grounds the court could not inquire further into the truth of the factual   **b**
basis on which the Home Office had exercised its discretion. The immigration officer
must decide the facts; if the applicant was dissatisfied, the remedy was by appeal: there
was no remedy by habeas corpus. Geoffrey Lane LJ similarly accepted the 'reasonable
grounds' basis for upholding the decision of the Secretary of State (see [1978] 3 All ER
790 at 794, [1978] 1 WLR 1177 at 1183). It is true that *Choudhary* was a case where, on
any view, the applicant was an illegal entrant, so that it need not be applied to other cases   **c**
where that fact may be in doubt. Nevertheless, *Choudhary* is a case which appears to apply
a test more appropriate to a case of review of an administrative discretion and to restrict
the duty of the court on habeas corpus applications to examine the factual basis for
detention of the applicant.

In *R v Secretary of State for the Home Dept, ex p Iqbal* [1979] 1 All ER 685, [1979] 1 QB
264 the Divisional Court again followed *Hussain* and applied the judgment of Geoffrey   **d**
Lane LJ. The judgment used the words: 'It was for the Secretary of State to weigh the
evidence', words sufficiently correct in themselves but liable to convey the impression
that the court cannot itself do so (see [1979] 1 All ER 675 at 678, [1979] QB 264 at 267).

In *Tirath Singh v Secretary of State for the Home Dept* [1980] CA Transcript 686 the Court
of Appeal went further along the same road. The question being whether the applicant
entered as an illegal entrant before 1 January 1973, Megaw LJ said that it was not for the   **e**
court of review to investigate evidence. The court may look at the evidence in order to
see whether it is such that the Secretary of State or other authority could as a reasonable
person have arrived at his decision on that material and in order to see whether there was
any substantial unfairness. I do not think that the learned Lord Justice was in this first
respect quite consistent with his previous judgment in *Hussain*.

In *R v Secretary of State for the Home Dept, ex p Pinky Badwal* (29 April 1980, unreported)   **f**
the question was whether the applicant was a patrial, an issue which in turn depended
on some conflicting and unreliable evidence concerning her marriage or marriages. The
judgment quotes from a previous decision of Templemen LJ in *R v Secretary of State for
the Home Dept, ex p Akhtar* [1980] 2 All ER 735, [1981] QB 46 where expressions are
reported to the effect that the immigration officer had 'reasonable ground' for finding
that the applicant had entered in contravention of the immigration laws, and had   **g**
reasonable grounds for believing the applicant to be an illegal entrant. To the extent that
Pinky Badwal took this approach, it was not, in my opinion, applying the right principle
or correctly following *Hussain*. But I think that the case makes the valid point that, since
by para 2 of Sch 2 to the 1971 Act an immigration officer has power to determine
whether a person is a patrial and whether, if he is not, he may or may not enter the
United Kingdom without leave, he must have power to determine whether a person is   **h**
an illegal entrant. The existence of such a power does not, of course, mean that his
determination is not subject to review by the court, but an argument that his
determination is ultra vires, though suggested at one time (see, for example, *Choudhary*),
has not survived.

Ex p Yasmeen (11 February 1982, unreported) has already been referred to as to its facts
for the purpose of showing the nature of the determination which in many cases has to   **j**
be made by the immigration authorities, and the inherent limits which exist on the
court's power of review. In carrying out the review the court, in that case, again, in my
respectful opinion, deviated to some extend from *Hussain*. When the result of the
inquiries in India was first reviewed by Mr Osborne of the Home Office, he (correctly)
viewed his task as being to decide whether, on this material, the applicant was an illegal
entrant. He found that she was, for reasons assigned. Woolf J, having doubts as to the

effect of the evidence (which doubts, if I am right, he was entitled to have), asked the
a Home Office to reconsider the position, and further inquiries were made. On this Mr
Osborne stated that he 'had reasonable grounds' for forming the opinion he had formed,
a statement which was (justly) criticised by the court, he should simply have made a
decision. But in the end the court seems to have concluded that Mr Osborne had
reasonable grounds for his opinion, the judge stating that it was irrelevant whether he
would have come to the same conclusion. While the decision was almost certainly
b correct, the phraseology was perhaps unfortunate in so far as it limited the power and
duty of the reviewing court.

This tendency seems to have become accepted in *R v Immigration Appeal Tribunal, ex p
Abdul Malik Hussain* (18 July 1982, unreported), where on a judicial review of an
adjudicator's decision under s 16 of the Act it was said that it is well established that the
court cannot interfere so long as there were reasonable grounds for the Secretary of State
c to reach his conclusion.

My Lords, I have ventured on this review of some of the cases (there are many more
which might have been examined) in order to show two things. First, that, whatever the
theory may be, the courts have in general been willing and able to review for themselves
the factual basis, on which decisions by immigration officers that persons are illegal
entrants and analogous decisions are made, within the limits open to them. And the cases
d vividly illustrate what those limits are. They are dictated, on the one hand, by the fact
that of necessity extensive fact-finding operations have to be carried out by the
immigration authorities which cannot be repeated by the reviewing court; on the other
hand, by the fact that these operations are carried out by administrative, not judicial,
officers inevitably not wholly qualified in the process of assessing and applying evidence.
Second, that they have not always consistently or correctly stated the basis on which such
e review should be made. In some instances, and this seems to be more marked in recent
cases, there has been a tendency to limit the courts' power to that of ascertaining whether
there was evidence on which a reasonable Secretary of State or an officer of his could have
reached the decision. While there are cases where the facts are so clear that it would not
make any practical difference whether this was the test or whether the court ought to
appraise the evidence for itself, there may be other cases, and indeed the case of Khera
f may be one, where a different result would follow and where the 'reasonable grounds'
formula (in fact used in Khera's case) would understate the court's duty. While the case
of *Zamir* fell into the former class, there were expressions used which support the
'reasonable grounds' approach which, in the light of the argument we have heard and
after a further consideration of the case, require some correction.

I would therefore restate the respective functions of the immigration authorities and
g of the courts as follows. (1) The immigration authorities have the power and the duty to
determine and to act on the facts material for the detention as illegal entrants of persons
prior to removal from the United Kingdom. (2) Any person whom the Secretary of State
proposes to remove as an illegal entrant, and who is detained, may apply for a writ of
habeas corpus or for judicial review. On such an application the Secretary of State or the
immigration authorities if they seek to support the detention or removal (the burden
h being on them) should depose to the grounds on which the decision to detain or remove
was made, setting out essential factual evidence taken into account and exhibiting
documents sufficiently fully to enable the courts to carry out their function of review.
(3) The court's investigation of the facts is of a supervisory character and not by way of
appeal (it should not be forgotten that a right of appeal as to the facts exists under s 16 of
the 1971 Act even though Parliament has thought fit to impose conditions on its
j exercise). It should appraise the quality of the evidence and decide whether that justifies
the conclusion reached, e g whether it justifies a conclusion that the applicant obtained
permission to enter by fraud or deceit. An allegation that he has done so being of a
serious character and involving issues of personal liberty requires a corresponding degree
of satisfaction as to the evidence. If the court is not satisfied with any part of the evidence
it may remit the matter for reconsideration or itself receive further evidence. It should
quash the detention order where the evidence was not such as the authorities should have

relied on or where the evidence received does not justify the decision reached or, of
course, for any serious procedural irregularity.   *a*

As regards the present appeals, in Khera's case there was a good deal of discussion in
both the Divisional Court and in the Court of Appeal of the 'candour' passage in *Zamir*. I
have dealt with this and regret that it should have caused some difficulty to the judges.
As regards the evidence, Ormrod LJ thought that the applicant had 'demonstrably failed
to disclose a material fact'. Dunn LJ found that it was open to the immigration officer to
come to his conclusion and there was ample evidence to justify him in doing so. He   *b*
followed the passage in *Zamir* dealing with the powers of the court. I am not convinced
that either of the Lords Justices really misdirected himself in law; I think that both may
in fact have appraised the evidence for himself. But I am satisfied, for reasons given by
my noble and learned friend Lord Fraser, and which I need not state in my own words,
that the evidence placed before the court by Mr Chalmers on behalf of the Home Office,
though raising a case of suspicion and doubt, was not sufficient to make good a case of *c*
deception or concealment of a material fact and that the reviewing court should have so
found. Mr Khera's appeal must be allowed.

In Khawaja's case Lord Denning MR stated the facts as deposed to and reached the
conclusion that the case was one of 'gross deception'. It is true that he added the words
'the Home Secretary was quite entitled to treat him as an illegal entrant', but I do not
read this as taking a 'reasonable grounds' approach, rather as saying that on the facts   *d*
before the Court of Appeal the Secretary of State was right. I have no doubt that on the
proper standard of review the decision was correct and would dismiss the appeal.

LORD SCARMAN. My Lords, the facts of these two cases have been fully set out and
analysed by my noble and learned friend Lord Fraser. I will proceed, therefore, at once
to a consideration of the law.   *e*

Two questions of law fall to be considered in the two appeals. Both arise under the
Immigration Act 1971. One is as to the construction to be put on the definition of 'illegal
entrant' which is contained in s 33(1) of that Act. The other is as to the proper scope of
judicial review where the immigration authority has decided to exercise its statutory
power to remove an illegal entrant from the United Kingdom and detains him, or
permits his temporary admission into the country subject to restrictions pending   *f*
removal.

Both questions were considered and answered by the House in the recent case of *Zamir
v Secretary of State for the Home Dept* [1980] 2 All ER 768, [1980] AC 930. The House in
these two appeals is being invited to reconsider that decision and to depart from it, using
the power to depart from precedent which the House declared by its practice statement
of 1966 it was prepared to use in certain circumstances (see *Note* [1966] 3 All ER 77,   *g*
[1966] 1 WLR 1234).

The practice statement is an affirmation of the importance of precedent 'as an
indispensable foundation upon which to decide what is the law and its application to
individual cases'. However, it recognises that 'too rigid adherence to precedent may lead
to injustice in a particular case and also unduly restrict the proper development of the
law'. The House will depart in the exceptional case from the precedent of a previous   *h*
decision 'when it appears right to do so'. This formula indicates that the House must be
satisfied not only that adherence to the precedent would involve the risk of injustice and
obstruct the proper development of the law, but also that a judicial departure by the
House from the precedent is the safe and appropriate way of remedying the injustice and
developing the law. The possibility that legislation may be the better course is one which,
though not mentioned in the statement, the House will not overlook (a recent illustration *j*
is its decision in *Pirelli General Cable Works Ltd v Oscar Faber & Partners (a firm)* [1983] 1
All ER 65, [1983] 2 WLR 6). Provided, however, due attention is paid to the dangers of
uncertainty in certain branches of the law (especially the criminal law) the House, as it
has already in a number of cases made clear, will, if it thinks it right, depart from a
previous decision whether the decision be ancient or modern and whether the point of
law arises on the construction of a statute or in the judge-made common law or equity.

Three propositions of law were enunciated in *Zamir* by a unanimous House: (1) that a
a person who has succeeded in entering the United Kingdom by committing an offence
under the Act is an illegal entrant as defined by s 33(1) of that Act: he has entered 'in
breach of the immigration laws'; (2) that a person who has to seek leave to enter the
United Kingdom owes to the immigration authority a positive duty of candour, i e a duty
to disclose material facts even though he be asked no questions and has neither expressly
nor by his conduct implicitly made any false representation as to them; (3) that, if the
b immigration authority has reasonable grounds for believing that a person is an illegal
entrant, the decision to remove him and to detain him until he is removed is for the
authority. It is not subject to review by the courts, save to the limited extent recognised
by what has come to be called the *Wednesbury* principle (see *Associated Provincial Picture
Houses Ltd v Wednesbury Corp* [1947] 2 All ER 680, [1948] 1 KB 223).

For the reasons developed by my noble and learned friend Lord Bridge, I entertain no
c doubt that in *Zamir* the House correctly construed the definition of 'illegal entrant' in
s 33(1) of the 1971 Act as covering one who has obtained leave to enter by deception. It
is an offence for a person who is being examined by an immigration officer to make a
statement or representation which he knows to be false or does not believe to be true (see
s 26(1)(c) of the Act). Silence can, of course, constitute a representation of fact; it depends
on conduct and circumstances. If the offence is committed, it is a breach of the
d immigration laws. The definition therefore covers a person who by committing the
offence obtains leave to enter the United Kingdom.

It was strenuously argued that the definition must be limited to persons who enter the
country by evading immigration control, e g clandestinely over the beach. Even if I were
disposed to accept this submission, I would not do so in the face of the unanimous
decision in *Zamir*. I see nothing unjust in the construction the House then put on the
e statutory definition, nor any threat to the proper development of the law.

In *Zamir* deception was proved. Lord Wilberforce observed that the case was, in his
opinion, disposable under any test. It was not necessary, therefore, for the House to
consider whether even where there is not deliberate deception a person seeking leave to
enter the United Kingdon owes a positive duty of candour to the immigration authority.
The House's expression of opinion that he does was obiter. It is certainly an entrant's
f duty to answer truthfully the questions put to him and to provide such information as is
required of him (see Sch 2, para 4). But the Act goes no further. He may, or may not,
know what facts are material. The immigration officer does, or ought to, know the
matters relevant to the decision he has to make. Immigration control is, no doubt, an
important safeguard for our society. Parliament has entrusted the control to immigration
officers and the Secretary of State (see s 4). To allow officers to rely on an entrant
g honouring a duty of positive candour, by which is meant a duty to volunteer relevant
information, would seem perhaps a disingenuous approach to the administration of
control: some might think it conducive to slack rather than to 'sensitive' administration
(see *Zamir* [1980] 2 All ER 768 at 773, [1980] AC 930 at 950). The 1971 Act does impose
a duty not to deceive the immigration officer. It makes no express provision for any
higher or more comprehensive duty; nor is it possible, in my view, to imply any such
h duty. Accordingly, I reject the view that there is a duty of positive candour imposed by
the immigration laws and that mere non-disclosure by an entrant of material facts in the
absence of fraud is a breach of the immigration laws.

Real difficulties, however, arise in respect of the third proposition of law in *Zamir*.
This was part of the ratio decidendi. The House approved a line of authority (beginning
with *R v Secretary of State for the Home Dept, ex p Hussain* [1978] 2 All ER 423, [1978] 1
j WLR 700) which put a gloss on the words of the critical provision in the 1971 Act, i e Sch
2, para 9.

The paragraph declares an illegal entrant to be liable to removal. It provides that where
an illegal entrant is not given leave to enter or remain in the United Kingdom an
immigration officer may give directions for his removal. Unless he (or the Secretary of
State: see para 10) gives such directions, no power to detain him arises; for para 16(2)
provides a power to detain only in respect of a person who may be so removed. Similarly,

para 21 of the schedule empowers the release of a person from detention and his temporary admission into the United Kingdom subject to restrictions as to residence and reporting to the police only if that person may be lawfully removed from the country. The gloss which the House in *Zamir* put on the words of para 9 was to read them as meaning not 'where a person *is* an illegal entrant' but 'where the immigration officer *has reasonable grounds for believing a person to be* an illegal entrant' he may be removed if not given leave to enter.

If it be sought to justify the gloss as a proper construction of the statutory language, there is a difficulty. The gloss requires the introduction into the paragraph of words that are not there. Must they, then, be implied? This question lies at the heart of the problem.

In *Zamir* the House was impressed with the difficulties arising if the implication were not to be made. The House attached importance to three considerations: (1) the line of cases beginning with *Hussain*, in which the Court of Appeal had held it necessary to make the implication; (2) the scheme of the 1971 Act; and, especially, (3) the nature and process of the power of decision conferred by the 1971 Act on immigration officers.

These considerations, in the view of the House, made it necessary to reject the appellant's argument based on the well-established principle that, where the exercise of an executive power depends on the precedent establishment of an objective fact, it is for the court, if there be a challenge by way of judicial review, to decide whether the precedent requirement has been satisfied. In *Azam v Secretary of State for the Home Dept* [1973] 2 All ER 741 at 753, [1974] AC 18 at 34 Lord Denning MR (in the Court of Appeal) considered the principle applicable in the case of removal of an illegal entrant. The House recognised the existence of the principle, but, following and approving *Hussain*, opted for a construction of the legislation which would oust it (see [1973] 2 All ER 765, [1974] AC 18).

In rejecting the appellant's argument based on the 'precedent fact' principle of review Lord Wilberforce said ([1980] 2 All ER 768 at 772, [1980] AC 930 at 948):

'My Lords, for the reasons I have given I am of opinion that the whole scheme of the Act is against this argument. It is true that it does not, in relation to the decisions in question, use such words as "in the opinion of the Secretary of State" or "the Secretary of State must be satisfied", but it is not necessary for such a formula to be used in order to take the case out of the "precedent fact" category. The nature and process of decision conferred on immigration officers by existing legislation is incompatible with any requirement for the establishment of precedent objective facts whose existence the court may verify.'

He therefore implied into para 9 the words needed to bring it outside the 'precedent fact' category of provision.

My Lords, in most cases I would defer to a recent decision of your Lordships' House on a question of construction, even if I thought it wrong. I do not do so in this context because for reasons which I shall develop I am convinced that the *Zamir* reasoning gave insufficient weight to the important (I would say fundamental) consideration that we are here concerned with, the scope of judicial review of a power which inevitably infringes the liberty of those subjected to it. This consideration, if it be good, outweighs, in my judgment, any difficulties in the administration of immigration control to which the application of the principle might give rise.

The *Zamir* construction of para 9 deprives those subjected to the power of that degree of judicial protection which I think can be shown to have been the policy of our law to afford to persons with whose liberty the executive is seeking to interfere. It does therefore, in my view, tend to obstruct the proper development and application of the safeguards our law provides for the liberty of those within its jurisdiction. If I can make good this view of the law, it must be right to depart from the precedent of *Zamir*. I, therefore, now turn to the reasons why I conclude that it is correct.

The *Zamir* decision would limit judicial review where the executive has decided to remove someone from the country as being an illegal entrant to the *Wednesbury* principle.

This principle is undoubtedly correct in cases where it is appropriate. But, as I understand
a the law, it cannot extend to interference with liberty unless Parliament had unequivocally
enacted that it should. The principle was formulated by Lord Greene MR in *Associated
Provincial Picture Houses Ltd v Wednesbury Corp* [1947] 2 All ER 680, [1948] 1 KB 223.
The case concerned the conditions imposed on the issue of a licence. The principle
formulated was that the courts will not intervene to quash the decision of a statutory
authority unless it can be shown that the authority erred in law, was guilty of a breach of
b natural justice or acted 'unreasonably'. If the authority has considered the matters which
it is its duty to consider and has excluded irrelevant matters, its decision is not reviewable
unless so absurd that no reasonable authority could have reached it. The principle
excludes the court from substituting its own view of the facts for that of the authority.
   Such exclusion of the power and duty of the courts runs counter to the development
of the safeguards which our law provides for the liberty of the subject. The law has
c largely developed through the process of habeas corpus. But in the common law habeas
corpus was itself of limited scope, though a rapid and effective remedy where it applied.
It brought the gaoler and his prisoner into court; but, if the respondent's return to the
writ was valid on its face, that was the end of the matter. The court could not take the
case further. The great statute of 1816, the Habeas Corpus Act 1816, 'An Act for more
effectually securing the Liberty of the Subject', substantially extended the scope of the
d process. It conferred on the judges the power in non-criminal cases to inquire into the
truth of the facts contained in the return. Section 3 is the beginning of the modern
jurisprudence, the effect of which is to displace, unless Parliament by plain words
otherwise provides, the *Wednesbury* principle in cases where liberty is infringed by an act
of the executive. The section deserves quotation:

e   'In all cases provided for by this Act, although the return to any writ of habeas
      corpus shall be good and sufficient in law, it shall be lawful for the justice or baron,
      before whom such writ may be returnable, to proceed to examine into the truth of
      the facts set forth in such return . . . and to do therein as to justice shall appertain
      . . .'

The court's duty is to examine into the truth of the facts set forth in the return; the
f section thereby contemplates the possibility of an investigation by the court so that it
may satisfy itself where the truth lies. There is here a principle which the judges, faced
with decisions by statutory authorities which restrict or take away liberty, have accepted
as being justly met by the rule, the existence of which was recognised in *Zamir*, though
not applied, that, where the exercise of executive power depends on the precedent
establishment of an objective fact, the courts will decide whether the requirement has
g been satisfied.
   The classic dissent of Lord Atkin in *Liversidge v Anderson* [1941] 3 All ER 338, [1942]
AC 206 is now accepted as correct not only on the point of construction of reg 18B of the
Defence (General) Regulations 1939, SR & O 1939/927, but in its declaration of English
legal principle (see *IRC v Rossminster Ltd* [1980] 1 All ER 80 at 93, 104, [1980] AC 952 at
1011, 1025). Lord Atkin put it thus ([1941] 3 All ER 338 at 362, [1942] AC 206 at 245):

h   '. . . that in English law every imprisonment is *prima facie* unlawful, and that it is
      for a person directing imprisonment to justify his act.'

   In an earlier Privy Council decision Lord Atkin had made the same point in the specific
case of an executive decision. In *Eshugbayi Eleko v Government of Nigeria (Officer
Administering)* [1931] AC 662 at 670, [1931] All ER Rep 44 at 49 Lord Atkin said:

j   'In accordance with British jurisprudence no member of the executive can
      interfere with the liberty or property of a British subject except on the condition
      that he can support the legality of his action before a court of justice. And it is the
      tradition of British justice that judges should not shrink from deciding such issues
      in the face of the executive.'

For, as Blackstone said of habeas corpus, describing it as a high prerogative writ (3 Bl Com (12th edn, 1794) 131):   a

'the King is at all times entitled to have an account why the liberty of any kind of his subjects is restrained, wherever that restraint may be inflicted.'

There are, of course, procedural differences between habeas corpus and the modern statutory judicial review. *Zamir* was a case of habeas corpus; in the instant cases the effective relief sought is certiorari to quash the immigration officer's decision. But the   b nature of the remedy sought cannot affect the principle of the law. In both cases liberty is in issue. 'Judicial review' under RSC Ord 53 and the modern statute is available only by leave of the court. The writ of habeas corpus issues as of right. But the difference arises not in the law's substance but from the nature of the remedy appropriate to the case. The writ issues as of right summoning into court the person in whose custody the subject is. It gets the custodian into court; but discharge from custody is not possible   c unless 'the party hath a probable cause to be delivered', as Vaughan CJ put it (see *Bushel's Case* (1670) T Jo 13, 84 ER 1123) in words quoted by Blackstone (3 Bl Com (12th edn, 1794) 132). This remains the law today and effectually puts habeas corpus in like case with the other form of judicial review. Whatever the process, the party seeking relief carries the initial burden of showing he has a case fit to be considered by the court.

Accordingly, faced with the jealous care our law traditionally devotes to the protection   d of the liberty of those who are subject to its jurisdiction, I find it impossible to imply into the statute words the effect of which would be to take the provision, para 9 of Sch 2 of the 1971 Act, 'out of the "precedent fact" category' (see *Zamir* [1980] 2 All ER 768 at 772, [1980] AC 930 at 948 per Lord Wilberforce). If Parliament intends to exclude effective judicial review of the exercise of a power in restraint of liberty, it must make its meaning crystal clear.   e

Two points remain. First, does our law's protection extend to aliens and non-patrials? There is a suggestion that, because an alien is liable to expulsion under the royal prerogative and a non-patrial has no right of abode, it is less difficult to infer a Parliamentary intention to deprive them of effective judicial review and a decision to infringe their liberty. And, second, the problem of proof.

Habeas corpus protection is often expressed as limited to 'British subjects'. Is it really   f limited to British nationals? Suffice it to say that the case law has given an emphatic No to the question. Every person within the jurisdiction enjoys the equal protection of our laws. There is no distinction between British nationals and others. He who is subject to English law is entitled to its protection. This principle has been in the law at least since Lord Mansfield freed 'the black' in *Sommersett's Case* (1772) 1 State Tr 1 at 20. There is nothing here to encourage in the case of aliens or non-patrials the implication of words   g excluding the judicial review our law normally accords to those whose liberty is infringed.

Second, there is the problem of proof. The initial burden is on the applicant. At what stage, if at all, is it transferred to the respondent? And, if it is transferred, what is the standard of proof he has to meet? It is clear from the passages cited from Lord Atkin's opinions in *Liversidge v Anderson* and *Eshugbayi's* case that in cases where the exercise of   h executive discretion interferes with liberty or property rights he saw the burden of justifying the legality of the decision as being on the executive. Once the applicant has shown a prima facie case, this is the law. It was so recognised by Lord Parker CJ in *R v Brixton Prison Governor, ex p Ahson* [1969] 2 All ER 347, [1969] 2 QB 222 and by Lord Denning MR in the Court of Appeal in *Azam v Secretary of State for the Home Dept* [1973] 2 All ER 741 at 751, [1974] AC 18 at 32. And, I would add, it is not possible to construe   j s 3 of the Habeas Corpus Act 1816 as meaning anything different.

The law is less certain as to the standard of proof. The choice is commonly thought to be between proof beyond reasonable doubt, as in criminal cases, and the civil standard of the balance of probabilities; and there is distinguished authority for the view that in habeas corpus proceedings the standard is beyond reasonable doubt, since liberty is at

stake. This appears to have been the view of Lord Atkin (see *Eshugbayi's* case [1931] AC
a 662 at 670, [1931] All ER Rep 44 at 49), and certainly was the view of Lord Parker CJ
(see *Ahson's* case).

But there is a line of authority which casts doubt on their view. The Court of Appeal
has held that the standard of proof of criminal offences in civil proceedings is that of the
balance of probabilities: see *Hornal v Neuberger Products Ltd* [1956] 3 All ER 970, [1957]
1 QB 247. As judicial review whether under the modern statutory procedure or s 3 of
b the Habeas Corpus Act 1816 is a civil proceeding, it would appear to be right, if *Hornal's*
case was correctly decided, to apply the civil standard of proof.

My Lords, I have come to the conclusion that the choice between the two standards is
not one of any great moment. It is largely a matter of words. There is no need to import
into this branch of the civil law the formula used for the guidance of juries in criminal
cases. The civil standard as interpreted and applied by the civil courts will meet the ends
c of justice.

The issue has been discussed in a number of cases. In *Bater v Bater* [1950] 2 All ER 458,
[1951] P 35 the trial judge had said that the petitioner, who alleged cruelty by her
husband, must prove her case beyond reasonable doubt. This was held by the Court of
Appeal not to be a misdirection. But Denning LJ observed that, had the judge said the
case required to be proved with the same strictness as a crime in a criminal court, that
d would have been a misdirection. He put it thus ([1950] 2 All ER 458 at 459, [1951] P 35
at 36–37):

'The difference of opinion which has been evoked about the standard of proof in
these cases may well turn out to be more a matter of words than anything else. It is
true that by our law a higher standard of proof is required in criminal cases than in
civil cases, but this is subject to the qualification that there is no absolute standard in
e either case.'

And a little later he added:

'So also in civil cases. The case may be proved by a preponderance of probability,
but there may be degrees of probability within that standard. The degree depends
f on the subject-matter. A civil court, when considering a charge of fraud, will
naturally require for itself a higher degree of probability than that which it would
require when asking if negligence were established. It does not adopt so high a
degree as a criminal court, even when it is considering a charge of a criminal nature,
but still it does require a degree of probability which is commensurate with the
occasion.'

g It is clear that all three members of the court (Bucknill, Somervell and Denning LJJ)
found difficulty in distinguishing between the two standards. If a court has to be satisfied,
how can it at the same time entertain a reasonable doubt (see [1950] 2 All ER 458, [1951]
P 35 at 36 per Bucknill LJ)?

In *Hornal v Neuberger Products Ltd* the Court of Appeal had to consider the standard of
proof where fraud is alleged in civil proceedings. The court held that the standard was
h the balance of probabilities. But, since the degree of probability required to tip the
balance will vary according to the nature and gravity of the issue—

'no real mischief results from an acceptance of the fact that there is some difference
of approach in civil actions . . . the very elements of gravity become a part of the
whole range of circumstances which have to be weighed in the scale when deciding
j as to the balance of probabilities.'

(See [1956] 3 All ER 970 at 978, [1957] 1 QB 247 at 266 per Morris LJ.)

A notable application of the principle that civil courts apply the balance of probabilities
is to be found in the will case in which Ungoed-Thomas J had to decide whether the wife
had feloniously killed her husband (see *Re Dellow's Will Trusts, Lloyds Bank Ltd v Institute*

of Cancer Research [1964] 1 All ER 771, [1964] 1 WLR 451). He held the crime proved
on the balance of probabilities.

Hornal's case was approved by this House in the divorce case, *Blyth v Blyth* [1966] 1 All
ER 524, [1966] AC 643. Lord Denning picked up what he had said in *Bater* and *Hornal*
and concluded that—

> 'so far as the *grounds* for divorce are concerned, the case, like any civil case, may
> be proved by a preponderance of probability, but the degree of probability depends
> on the subject-matter. In proportion as the offence is grave, so ought the proof to be
> clear.'

(See [1966] 1 All ER 524 at 536, [1966] AC 643 at 669.)

My Lords, I would adopt as appropriate to cases of restraint put by the executive on
the liberty of the individual the civil standard flexibility applied in the way set forth in
the cases cited; and I would direct particular attention to the words of Morris LJ already
quoted. It is not necessary to import into the civil proceedings of judicial review the
formula devised by judges for the guidance of juries in criminal cases. Liberty is at stake;
that is, as the court recognised in *Bater* and in *Hornal*, a grave matter. The reviewing
court will therefore require to be satisfied that the facts which are required for the
justification of the restraint put on liberty do exist. The flexibility of the civil standard of
proof suffices to ensure that the court will require the high degree of probability which
is appropriate to what is at stake. 'The nature and gravity of an issue necessarily
determines the manner of attaining reasonable satisfaction of the truth of the issue' (see
Dixon J in *Wright v Wright* (1948) 77 CLR 191 at 210). I would, therefore, adopt the civil
standard flexibly applied in the way described in the case law to which I have referred.
And I completely agree with the observation made by my noble and learned friend Lord
Bridge that the difficulties of proof in many immigration cases afford no valid ground
for lowering the standard of proof required.

Accordingly, it is enough to say that, where the burden lies on the executive to justify
the exercise of a power of detention, the facts relied on as justification must be proved to
the satisfaction of the court. A preponderance of probability suffices; but the degree of
probability must be such that the court is satisfied. The strictness of the criminal formula
is unnecessary to enable justice to be done; and its lack of flexibility in a jurisdiction
where the technicalities of the law of evidence must not be allowed to become the master
of the court could be a positive disadvantage inhibiting the efficacy of the developing
safeguard of judicial review in the field of public law.

For these reasons I conclude that in these two appeals, once the applicant had shown,
as each did, that he had entered the United Kingdom with the leave of the immigration
officer, the burden of proving that he had obtained leave by deception was on the
executive and the standard of proof was the balance of probabilities. In Khera's case, the
executive failed to prove that he was guilty of deception. In Khawaja's case the evidence
that he deceived the immigration authority was overwhelming. Accordingly, I would
allow the appeal of Khera and dismiss that of Khawaja.

LORD BRIDGE OF HARWICH. My Lords, these two appeals come before your
Lordships' House in unusual circumstances. On 17 July 1980 the House delivered
judgment in *Zamir v Secretary of State for the Home Dept* [1980] 2 All ER 768, [1980] AC
930. Both the decisions now appealed from were given by the Court of Appeal on the
ground that they were bound by *Zamir* to decide as they did. In the case of Khera, leave
to appeal, having been refused by the Court of Appeal, was also initially refused by the
House. But a petition to the House for leave to appeal in the case of Khawaja was later
granted on the grounds not only that it raised a question as to the scope of the decision in
Zamir, but also that it might be appropriate that the questions of law which *Zamir* has
decided should be re-examined. In the light of this decision, the petition for leave to
appeal by Khera was reconsidered, the original order refusing leave discharged and leave
granted.

a   Against this background, as was to be expected, your Lordships have heard exceptionally full and comprehensive argument directed to three main questions. (1) Who can be treated as an illegal entrant under the Immigration Act 1971? (2) When a person has been detained as an illegal entrant under the authority of an immigration officer pursuant to paras 9 and 16(2) of Sch 2 to the 1971 Act pending the giving and implementation of directions for his removal under that schedule, what is the scope of the court's power to review the legality of the detention and proposed removal and how

b   should it be exercised? (3) In so far as the answers your Lordships are minded to give to either of the two previous questions differ from the answers given to the same questions in *Zamir*, would it be appropriate to depart from *Zamir* pursuant to the practice statement on judicial precedent made by the House on 26 July 1966 (see *Note* [1966] 3 All ER 77, [1966] 1 WLR 1234) to the extent necessary to assert that those answers represent the present law?

c   Before turning to the facts of the two cases under appeal, I propose to consider these three clearly defined questions of law.

Who is an illegal entrant?

       Section 33(1) of the 1971 Act provides:

d   '... "entrant" means a person entering or seeking to enter the United Kingdom, and "illegal entrant" means a person unlawfully entering or seeking to enter in breach of a deportation order or of the immigration laws, and includes also a person who has so entered ... "immigration laws" means this Act and any law for purposes similar to this Act which is for the time being or has (before or after the passing of this Act) been in force in any part of the United Kingdom and Islands ...'

e   Before examining these definitions it is necessary to consider their significance in the scheme of the Act. The Act provides machinery for the control of entry into and residence in the United Kingdom of non-patrials. Non-patrials may or may not be British subjects. Whenever a non-patrial enters the United Kingdom he requires leave to do so; leave may be given for an indefinite or for a limited period, and, if given for a limited period, may be subject to certain specified conditions (see s 3(1)). Once a non-patrial has

f   entered and is resident in the United Kingdom he may be liable to expulsion by one or other of two distinct procedures, viz (i) by deportation under s 5 and Sch 3, (ii) by summary removal under s 4 and Sch 2. Subject to the preservation of the royal prerogative in relation to aliens by s 33(5), which is not presently relevant, there is no other procedure for expulsion.

       The grounds for deportation of a non-patrial, so far as relevant are: (i) that 'having only
g   a limited leave to enter or remain, he does not observe a condition attached to the leave or remains beyond the time limited by the leave' (see s 3(5)(a)); (ii) that 'the Secretary of State deems his deportation to be conducive to the public good' (see s 3(5)(b)); (iii) that he has been recommended for deportation by a court on conviction of an offence punishable with imprisonment (see s 3(6)).

       The procedure for deportation ensures that, before the deportation order is made, ie
h   while the person proposed to be deported is still in the United Kingdom, certain rights of appeal are exercisable. These are in case (i) appeal to an adjudicator and a limited right of further appeal from the adjudicator to the Immigration Appeal Tribunal, in case (ii) a limited right of appeal direct to the Immigration Appeal Tribunal (see s 15). There is no appeal to the statutory appellate authorities in case (iii).

       The only ground for summary removal by directions given pursuant to para 8 or 10
j   of Sch 2 of a resident non-patrial is that he is an illegal entrant, which, in this context, must mean that he comes within the relevant words of the definition as 'a person who has entered the United Kingdom in breach of a deportation order or of the immigration laws'. A deportation order invalidates any leave to enter granted before or after the order was made and remains in force until it is revoked or the person to whom the order applies becomes patrial (see s 5). Hence, entry in breach of a deportation order presents

no problem. The relevant problem of illegal entry is that of entry 'in breach of the immigration laws', which in turn, more shortly, means entry 'in breach of the Act'.

A right of appeal against directions for removal lies to an adjudicator with a limited further right of appeal to the Immigration Appeal Tribunal but these rights are not exercisable while the appellant is still in the United Kingdom, ie in effect until the directions for removal have been implemented (see s 16).

There is a clear and unbroken line of authority that where permission to enter has been obtained by the fraud of the entrant he is an illegal entrant and can be removed by the summary procedure. The principle was first stated in the unreported decision of the Divisional Court in *R v Risley Remand Centre (Governor), ex p Maqbool Hussain* on 4 May 1976, when it does not seem to have been contested. Having quoted the s 33 definition, Lord Widgery CJ said:

> 'There was no doubt whatever, and it is not disputed, that when the applicant came through Heathrow on 2 November 1974 he was an illegal entrant. The fraud which he practised in regard to the passport would clearly entitle the Home Office to describe him as a person who entered in breach of the immigration laws.'

The principle was applied by the Court of Appeal in *R v Secretary of State for the Home Dept, ex p Hussain* [1978] 2 All ER 423, [1978] WLR 700 and *R v Secretary of State for the Home Dept, ex p Choudhary* [1978] 3 All ER 790, [1978] 1 WLR 1177, which have been followed in numerous subsequent cases. The whole line of authority received the imprimatur of this House in a single sentence in the speech of Lord Wilberforce in *Zamir* [1980] 2 All ER 768 at 771, [1980] AC 930 at 947 (concurred in by all the other noble Lords) when he said:

> 'The basis on which the Secretary of State seeks to justify the detention and removal of the applicant is that the leave to enter the United Kingdom was vitiated by deception and there is ample authority that an apparent leave to enter which has been obtained by deception is vitiated, as not being "leave [given] in accordance with this Act" (s 3(1)): see *R v Secretary of State for the Home Department, ex parte Hussain* [1978] 2 All ER 423, [1978] 1 WLR 700 and numerous cases following.'

Counsel for the appellant Khera challenges this principle. He submits that the only resident non-patrial who can be removed summarily as an illegal entrant is one who, having entered clandestinely, has never passed through immigration control and has thus succeeded in entering without the grant of any leave whatever. When leave to enter has been obtained by fraud, that leave, he contends, is not void but voidable.

If it is desired to expel one who has obtained leave to enter by fraud, this, says counsel for the appellant Khera, can be achieved in one of two ways, viz (i) by securing a conviction coupled with a recommendation for deportation under s 26(1)(c) by which a person is guilty of an offence punishable with a fine or imprisonment if 'he makes or causes to be made to an immigration officer or other person lawfully acting in the execution of this Act a return, statement or representation which he knows to be false or does not believe to be true' or (ii) by deportation under s 3(5)(b) on the ground that the Secretary of State deems his deportation to be conducive to the public good. Both these procedures, counsel points out, incorporate suitable safeguards for the person alleged to have entered by fraud. In the one case he has his full rights, including appellate rights, as a defendant in criminal proceedings. In the other he has his rights of appeal to the appellate authorities under the 1971 Act. These are contrasted with the right of appeal given by s 16, which, being exercisable only after the appellant has left the country, is virtually valueless. We were indeed told by counsel for the Secretary of State in the course of argument that only one s 16 appeal has ever succeeded. I should perhaps add here in parenthesis, for the avoidance of misunderstanding, that very different considerations apply to appeals under s 13. If a person seeking entry to the United Kingdom chooses to present himself at a port of entry without either an entry clearance or a work permit, there are obvious and important reasons why his right of appeal against refusal of leave

to enter should not carry with it any right of entry for the purpose of presenting that
a appeal.

I see great force in the contention that the illegal entrant proposed to be removed by
the summary procedure requires the protection of some effective judicial process before
removal. But I shall return to this when considering the second main question raised by
these appeals, to which, in my view, it is primarily relevant. I do not find it persuasive in
considering who is an illegal entrant. On the contrary, if the only procedures available to
b secure the expulsion of a non-patrial who has obtained leave to enter by fraud are those
suggested by counsel for the appellant Khera, it seems to me that there is a startling
lacuna in the Act. A conviction under s 26(1)(c) would not necessarily lead to a
recommendation for deportation; moreover, being a summary offence, it must normally
be prosecuted within six months of commission, though, exceptionally, this time limit
may be extended to a maximum of three years (see s 28). Those who have obtained leave
c to enter by fraud are frequently not exposed until after three years from their arrival. On
the other hand, the power given to the Secretary of State to deem deportation to be ·
conducive to the public good seems to me to be intended for cases where the continued
presence of the deportee would be objectionable on some positive and specific ground.
The examples given in s 15(3), 'that his deportation is conducive to the public good as
being in the interests of national security or of the relations between the United Kingdom
d and any other country or for other reasons of a political nature', although clearly not
exhaustive, nevertheless illustrate the kind of objection contemplated. I cannot suppose
that this power was ever intended to be invoked as a means of deporting a perfectly
respectable established resident on grounds arising from the circumstances of his original
entry. On the other hand, no one has suggested in argument that a non-patrial who has
obtained leave to enter by fraud should not be liable to expulsion when the fraud is
e exposed, nor doubted that one would expect the Act to provide for such a case. That
provision, I conclude, has to be found, if anywhere, in the statutory machinery for the
removal of an illegal entrant.

Despite the wealth of authority on the subject, there is nowhere to be found in the
relevant judgments (perhaps because none was thought necessary) a definitive exposition
of the reasons why a person who has obtained leave to enter by fraud is an illegal entrant.
f To say that the fraud 'vitiates' the leave or that the leave is not 'in accordance with the
Act' is, with respect, to state a conclusion without explaining the steps by which it is
reached. Since we are here concerned with purely statutory law, I think there are dangers
in introducing maxims of the common law as to the effect of fraud on common law
transactions and still greater dangers in seeking to apply the concepts of 'void' and
'voidable'. In a number of recent cases in your Lordships' House it has been pointed out
g that these transplants from the field of contract do not readily take root in the field of
public law. This is well illustrated in the judgment of the Court of Appeal in the instant
case of Khawaja [1982] 1 WLR 625 at 630; cf [1982] 2 All ER 523, at 527, where
Donaldson LJ spoke of the appellant's leave to enter as being 'voidable ab initio', which I
find, with respect, an impossibly difficult legal category to comprehend.

My Lords, in my opinion, the question whether a person who has obtained leave to
h enter by fraud 'has entered in breach of the Act' is purely one of construction. If the fraud
was a contravention of s 26(1)(c) of the Act, the provisions of which I have already quoted,
and if that fraud was the effective means of obtaining leave to enter, in other words if,
but for the fraud, leave to enter would not have been granted, then the contravention of
the Act and the obtaining of leave to enter were the two inseparable elements of the
single process of entry and it must inevitably follow that the entry itself was 'in breach of
j the Act'. It is on this simple ground and subject to the limitations that it implies that I
would rest my conclusion that those who obtain leave to enter fraudulently have rightly
been treated as illegal entrants. I would add, however, that if I had reached an opposite
conclusion, the issue turning at the very least on an arguable point of construction, I
should not have thought it appropriate, on this point, to depart from Zamir.

It remains to consider some of the implications of the principle stated in the foregoing paragraph. First, it is clear that a *mere* non-disclosure to the immigration officer by the person seeking permission to enter of a fact known to him cannot, by itself, amount to a contravention of s 26(1)(c). In so far as the passage in the speech of Lord Wilberforce in *Zamir* [1980] 2 All ER 768 at 773, [1980] AC 930 at 950 may be understood as imposing on an applicant for leave to enter a duty of candour approximating to uberrima fides the breach of which would have the same effect as fraud, it cannot, I think, be accepted. If intended in that sense, it was obiter, was not supported in the present case by counsel for the Secretary of State and, as I understand, does not now find favour with my noble and learned friend Lord Wilberforce himself. On the other hand, as Lord Wilberforce said in *Zamir*: 'It is clear on general principles of law that deception may arise from conduct, or from conduct accompanied by silence as to a material fact.' The relevant words of s 26(1)(c), 'a statement or representation which he knows to be false or does not believe to be true', embodying as they do the classic definition of a fraudulent deception, are amply wide enough to allow for the operation of this salutary principle.

Next, I would point out that the process of reasoning which I have suggested as justifying the conclusion that a person who obtains leave to enter by fraud is an illegal entrant avoids the necessity to characterise the leave to enter itself as a nullity. It is for the immigration authorities to decide whether or not to seek to secure the summary removal of an illegal entrant by invoking their powers under Sch 2. If they do not do so, the leave to enter stands. On this view, there is no illogicality or inconsistency in the indication given in para 88 of the Statement of Changes in Immigration Rules (HC Paper (1979–80) no 394) that, on an application for an extension of leave to enter granted for a limited period—

> 'refusal will be the normal course if the applicant has made false representations in obtaining leave to enter (including the giving of undertakings, express or implied, which he has not honoured, as to the duration and purpose of his stay)...'

Similarly, the Gilbertian situation which arose in *R v Secretary of State for the Home Dept, ex p Jayakody* [1982] 1 All ER 461, [1982] 1 WLR 405, where an adjudicator, on an appeal against the refusal by the Secretary of State to extend the appellant's limited leave to remain in the United Kingdom, held that the leave to enter had been obtained by fraud and therefore that there was no leave capable of being varied, on the analysis I have suggested, simply could not arise.

Finally, I would wish to leave for consideration on a future occasion the difficult questions that may arise when leave to enter has been obtained by the fraud of a third party, but the person entering had no knowledge of the fraud. I am not convinced that *Khan v Secretary of State for the Home Dept* [1977] 3 All ER 538, [1977] 1 WLR 1466, where it was held that the innocent wife who obtained leave to enter on a false passport procured for her by her husband was an illegal entrant, was rightly decided. In such cases the proper conclusion may depend on a variety of circumstances and I think it safer to express no present view but to leave such cases to be decided as they arise.

The court's power to review a decision to detain and remove an illegal entrant

The 1971 Act provides by s 4(2):

> 'The provisions of Schedule 2 to this Act shall have effect with respect to ... (c) the exercise by immigration officers of their powers in relation to entry into the United Kingdom, and the removal from the United Kingdom of persons refused leave to enter or entering or remaining unlawfully ...'

Paragraphs 2 to 6 of Sch 2 are concerned with the procedure governing the exercise of the power to grant or refuse leave to enter. The cross-heading to paras 8 to 11 is: 'Removal of persons refused leave to enter and illegal entrants.' Detailed provisions as to the giving of directions for removal are to be found primarily in para 8, which empowers the immigration officer to give such directions 'where a person arriving in the United Kingdom 'is refused leave to enter'. The vital provisions for present purposes are the following:

'9. Where an illegal entrant is not given leave to enter or remain in the United
Kingdom, an immigration officer may give any such directions in respect of him as
in a case within paragraph 8 above are authorised by para 8(1) . . .

16 . . . (2) A person in respect of whom directions may be given under any of
paragraphs 8 to 14 above may be detained under the authority of an immigration
officer pending the giving of directions and pending his removal in pursuance of
any directions given . . .'

Here again the authorities from *R v Secretary of State for the Home Dept, ex p Hussain* to
Zamir have consistently affirmed the principle that the decision of an immigration officer
to detain and remove a person as an illegal entrant under these provisions can only be
attacked successfully on the ground that there was no evidence on which the immigration
officer could reasonably conclude that he was an illegal entrant.

It will be seen at once that this principle gives to an executive officer, subject, no doubt,
in reaching his conclusions of fact to a duty to act fairly, a draconian power of arrest and
expulsion based on his own decision of fact which, if there was any evidence to support
it, cannot be examined by any judicial process until after it has been acted on and then in
circumstances where the person removed, being unable to attend the hearing of his
appeal, has no realistic prospect of prosecuting it with success.

It will be further observed that to justify the principle important words have to be
read into para 9 of Sch 2 by implication. That paragraph, on the face of the language
used, authorises the removal of a person who is an illegal entrant. The courts have applied
it as if it authorised the removal of a person whom an immigration officer on reasonable
grounds believes to be an illegal entrant. The all-important question is whether such an
implication can be justified.

The presently prevailing doctrine was first enunciated in *R v Secretary of State for the
Home Dept, ex p Hussain* by Geoffrey Lane LJ. He explained the suggested basis of the
doctrine rather more fully in *R v Secretary of State for the Home Dept, ex p Choudhary* [1978]
3 All ER 790 at 794, [1978] 1 WLR 1177 at 1183, where he said:

'The whole object of this part of the 1971 Act, read as a whole, is to ensure that
there is a procedure, and a readily available and easy procedure, whereby the
Secretary of State can detain pending removal any person such as the appellant in
this case. The Secretary of State obviously, from the nature of things, has no desire
to detain a man longer than is necessary to get him out of this country and back to
Pakistan, or wherever it was he came from. It is conceded by counsel for Mr
Choudhary, and, if I may say so, rightly conceded, that a reasonable belief held by
the Secretary of State is sufficient to justify the initial detention of the man; but it is
said that, once the Secretary of State's enquiries are at an end, then one has to
examine the basis of fact and, if that shows that the Secretary of State had got the
factual basis wrong, then the whole of the detention from the moment the enquiries
have come to an end and onwards is unlawful. With that submission I cannot agree.
It seems to me that the detention in circumstances such as these is throughout a
matter for the discretion of the Secretary of State; and, if he was acting on reasonable
grounds and acting bona fide on those reasonable grounds, then he is protected.'

In *Zamir* [1980] 2 All ER 768 at 772, [1980] AC 930 at 948–949 Lord Wilberforce said:

'The nature and process of decision conferred on immigration officers by existing
legislation is incompatible with any requirement for the establishment of precedent
objective facts whose existence the court may verify. The immigration officer,
whether at the stage of entry or at that of removal, has to consider a complex of
statutory rules and non-statutory guidelines. He has to act on documentary evidence
and such other evidence as inquiries may provide. Often there will be documents
whose genuineness is doubtful, statements which cannot be verified, misunderstand-
ings as to what was said, practices and attitudes in a foreign state which have to be
estimated. There is room for appreciation, even for discretion.'

He proceeds to contrast the disadvantageous position of the Divisional Court as a fact-finding tribunal in the relevant field.

But perhaps the most colourful expression of the argument which can be advanced in support of the prevailing doctrine is to be found in the judgment of Lord Lane CJ in the Divisional Court in the unreported decision of *R v Secretary of State for the Home Dept, ex p Pinky Badwal* given on 29 April 1980, where he said:

> 'No distinction can properly be drawn between a person who is discovered at the airport trying to enter illegally and a person who by skill, fraud and deceit manages to get past the immigration officer at the airport and is then interviewed that night by the immigration officer in his hotel, the immigration officer by that time having gathered the necessary information of the fraud or deceit. There can be no possible distinction in principle between those two situations.'

It appears to me, with every respect, that all these approaches rely on the statutory juxtaposition of the immigration officer's power to refuse leave to enter and thereupon to order removal of the unsuccessful aspiring entrant with his power to order removal of an illegal entrant after entry as a ground for assimilating the principles by which the two powers are governed. The somewhat improbable illustration chosen in the last passage cited to justify the assimilation is, I say with all due deference, calculated to obscure and minimise the real and important difference between the two powers. Whenever a non-patrial comes from abroad he needs leave to enter the United Kingdom and the decision whether or not such leave should be granted is fairly and squarely committed to the immigration officer by the statute. This necessarily entrusts all relevant decisions of fact, as well as the application to the facts of the relevant rules and any necessary exercise of discretion, to the immigration officer. If leave to enter is refused, that decision can plainly only be challenged on the now familiar grounds on which the court has jurisdiction to review a public law decision committed by statute to an administrative authority. Following a refusal of leave to enter there can be no successful challenge to a consequential order for detention and directions for removal unless the refusal of leave to enter can itself be successfully impugned. But the detention and removal of a non-patrial resident in this country, who may or may not be a British subject, who may have been here for many years and who, on the face of it, enjoys the benefit of an express grant of leave to be here, on the ground that he is an illegal entrant, seems to me to be dependent on fundamentally different considerations. A person seeking leave to enter requires a decision in his favour which the immigration officer alone is empowered to give. The established resident who entered with express permission enjoys an existing status of which, so far as the express language of the statute goes, the immigration officer has no power whatsoever to deprive him.

My Lords, we should, I submit, regard with extreme jealousy any claim by the executive to imprison a citizen without trial and allow it only if it is clearly justified by the statutory language relied on. The fact that, in the case we are considering, detention is preliminary and incidental to expulsion from the country in my view strengthens rather than weakens the case for a robust exercise of the judicial function in safeguarding the citizen's rights.

So far as I know, no case before the decisions under the Act which we are presently considering has held imprisonment without trial by executive order to be justified by anything less than the plainest statutory language, with the sole exception of the majority decision of your Lordships' House in *Liversidge v Anderson* [1941] 3 All ER 338, [1942] AC 206. No one needs to be reminded of the now celebrated dissenting speech of Lord Atkin in that case, or of his withering condemnation of the process of writing into the statutory language there under consideration the words which were necessary to sustain the decision of the majority. Lord Atkin's dissent now has the approval of your Lordships' House in *IRC v Rossminster Ltd* [1980] 1 All ER 80, [1980] AC 952.

A person who has entered the United Kingdom with leave and who is detained under Sch 2, para 16(2) pending removal as an illegal entrant on the ground that he obtained

leave to enter by fraud is entitled to challenge the action taken and proposed to be taken
a against him both by application for habeas corpus and by application for judicial review.
On the view I take, para 9 of Sch 2 must be construed as meaning no more and no less
than it says. There is no room for any implication qualifying the words 'illegal entrant'.
From this it would follow that, while, prima facie, the order for detention under para
16(2) would be a sufficient return to the writ of habeas corpus, proof by the applicant
that he had been granted leave to enter would shift the onus back to the immigration
b officer to prove that the leave had been obtained in contravention of s 26(1)(*c*) of the Act,
in other words by fraud.

I find indirect support for this view in *R v Brixton Prison Governor, ex p Ahson* [1969] 2
All ER 347, [1969] 2 QB 222, where many of the earlier authorities on habeas corpus are
reviewed. *Ahson* was a case arising under the predecessor of the 1971 Act, the
Commonwealth Immigrants Act 1962. The issue was whether immigrants who had
c entered the United Kingdom clandestinely were lawfully detained. This depended on
whether they had been arrested within 24 hours of their entry. The majority of the
Divisional Court (Lord Parker CJ and Blain J) held that the onus lay on the executive to
prove beyond reasonable doubt the fulfilment of the condition precedent to the right to
arrest.

More directly in point is a passage from the judgment of Lord Denning MR in *R v
d Pentonville Prison Governor, ex p Azam* [1973] 2 All ER 741 at 750–751, [1974] AC 18 at
31–32, as follows:

'Once the Secretary of State gives directions that a man is to be removed on the
ground that he is an illegal entrant, the man is given a right of appeal to an
adjudicator on the ground that, on the facts of the case, he was not in law an illegal
entrant: see s 16(1) of the 1971 Act. He has no right of appeal on any other ground:
e cf s 13(4). But there is a very significant provision in the Act. He cannot appeal so
long as he is in the United Kingdom: see s 16(2). He can only appeal after he has
been removed, that is, presumably when he has got back to his homeland. Such an
appeal would not seem to be a very beneficial remedy if a mistake has been made.
These provisions as to appeal give rise to a question of the first importance. Do they
take away a person's right to come to the High Court and seek a writ of habeas
f corpus? I do not think so. If Parliament is to suspend habeas corpus, it must do so
expressly or by clear implication. Even in the days of the war, when the enemy
were at the gate, habeas corpus was not suspended or taken away. When a man was
detained under reg 18B [of the Defence (General) Regulations 1939, SR & O 1939/
927], he was entitled to apply for a writ of habeas corpus if he could show a prima
facie case that he was unlawfully detained. During the war, a man called Budd made
g an application which was successful, because the prerequisites of a lawful detention
had not been complied with. But, in his next application he failed, because the
Home Secretary had made a return which could not be faulted: see *R v Home
Secretary, ex parte Budd* [1942] 1 All ER 373 at 376, [1942] 2 KB 14 at 22–23. Lord
Greene MR put an illustration which is appropriate here: ". . . if, for example, a
regulation empowered the Home Secretary to detain any person who was in fact an
h alien, the court could inquire into the nationality of the applicant, since, if it
transpired that he was not in fact an alien, his detention would be *ultra vires*." Under
Sch 2 the power to detain and remove applies in respect to a person who is in truth
an illegal entrant. If a man can make a prima facie case that he is not an illegal
entrant, he is entitled to a writ of habeas corpus as of right: see *Greene v Secretary of
State for Home Affairs* [1941] 3 All ER 388 at 400, [1942] AC 284 at 302 per Lord
j Wright. The court has no discretion to refuse it. Unlike certiorari or mandamus, a
writ of habeas corpus is of right to every man who is unlawfully detained. If a prima
facie case is shown that a man is unlawfully detained, it is for the one who detains
him to make a return justifying it.'

Accordingly, I have no doubt that when a person detained and proposed to be removed as an illegal entrant enjoys the right to be in this country in pursuance of leave to enter and remain here which is valid on its face the onus lies on the immigration officer to *a* prove the fact that the leave was obtained by fraud in contravention of s 26(1)(c) of the 1971 Act. The question about which I have felt most difficulty concerns the standard of proof required to discharge that onus. I was at first inclined to regard the judgment of Lord Parker CJ in *Ahson's* case as sufficient authority for the proposition that proof is required beyond reasonable doubt. But I have been persuaded by the reasoning on this point in the speech of my noble and learned friend Lord Scarman and by the authorities *b* which he cites that that proposition cannot be sustained. These have led me to the conclusion that the civil standard of proof by a preponderance of probability will suffice, always provided that, in view of the gravity of the charge of fraud which has to be made out and of the consequences which will follow if it is, the court should not be satisfied with anything less than probability of a high degree. I would add that the inherent difficulties of discovering and proving the true facts in many immigration cases can *c* afford no valid ground for lowering or relaxing the standard of proof required. If unlimited leave to enter was granted perhaps years before and the essential facts relied on to establish the fraud alleged can only be proved by documentary and affidavit evidence of past events which occurred in some remote part of the Indian subcontinent, the courts should be less, rather than more, ready to accept anything short of convincing proof. On the other hand it must be accepted that proof to the appropriate standard can, and in the *d* vast majority of cases will, be provided, in accordance with the established practice of the Divisional Court, by affidavit evidence alone. I understand all your Lordships to be agreed that nothing said in the present case should be construed as a charter to alleged illegal entrants who challenge their detention and proposed removal to demand the attendance of deponents to affidavits for cross-examination. Whether to permit cross-examination will remain a matter for the court in its discretion to decide. It may be that *e* the express discretion conferred on the court to permit cross-examination by the new procedure for judicial review under RSC Ord 53 has been too sparingly exercised when deponents could readily attend court. But, however that may be, the discretion to allow cross-examination should only be exercised when justice so demands. The cases will be rare when it will be essential, in the interests of justice, to require the attendance for cross-examination of a deponent from overseas. If the alleged illegal entrant applying for *f* habeas corpus, certiorari or both files an affidavit putting in issue the primary facts alleged against him he will himself be readily available for cross-examination, which should enable the court in the great majority of cases to decide whether or not he is a witness of truth. If he is believed, he will succeed in his application. If he is disbelieved, there will be nothing to stop the court relying on affidavit evidence, provided it is inherently credible and convincing, to prove the fraud alleged against him, even though *g* it has not been tested by cross-examination.

Should the House depart from Zamir in relation to the court's power to review the detention and removal of an alleged illegal entrant under Sch 2 to the Act?

The point in question does not fall into any of the categories in which the practice direction of 1966 indicated the need for special caution. By departing from *Zamir* your *h* Lordships would not be altering the criminal law or 'disturbing retrospectively the basis on which contracts, settlements of property and fiscal arrangements have been entered into'. The consideration that the decision in *Zamir* is relatively recent is, in relation to the use of the practice direction, one which has evoked conflicting expressions of opinion in your Lordships' House and it seems to me safest to regard it as a neutral factor. The question, however, concerns a matter of high constitutional principle affecting the liberty *j* of the subject and the delineation of the respective functions of the executive and the judiciary. In *Jones v Secretary of State for Social Services* [1972] 1 All ER 145, [1972] AC 944 Lord Reid thought it inappropriate to depart from an earlier decision in a case where 'no broad issue of justice or public policy is involved nor is any question of legal principle'. The present question does, in my opinion, involve a broad issue of justice and public

policy and an important question of legal principle. But what weighs most heavily with
a me in reaching the conclusion that the House should depart from the view expressed in
Zamir on this point is that my noble and learned friends Lord Wilberforce, who delivered
the leading speech in Zamir, and Lord Fraser, who agreed with it, are, as I understand,
after the fuller argument we have heard in these appeals, persuaded in principle that the
power of the court to review the detention and summary removal of an alleged illegal
entrant under Sch 2 was too narrowly stated in Zamir and must include power to decide
b whether the applicant for relief is or is not in fact an illegal entrant.

The instant appeals
    The facts of both appeals are summarised in the speech of my noble and learned friend
Lord Fraser and I need only refer to them briefly. In the case of Khera it is sufficient to
say that the evidence fails to prove that the appellant's leave to enter was obtained by any
c kind of fraud or deception. The appellant Khawaja, on arrival at Manchester Airport on
17 March 1980, told the immigration officer that he was visiting the United Kingdom
for one week to see a cousin, that he would then return to Brussels, and he showed the
officer a return ticket dated 23 March 1980. He was given leave to enter for one month.
The surrounding circumstances, fully disclosed in the evidence, lead to the irresistible
inference that what he told the officer was a deliberate lie. The appellant had travelled
d from Brussels to Manchester with a lady who had the right to reside in the United
Kingdom with whom he had already gone through a bigamous ceremony of marriage.
They entered through different desks at immigration control to conceal the connection
between them. The lady's previous marriage was dissolved on 3 April. The appellant
married her on 10 April. Having applied on 11 April for an extension of his temporary
leave to remain, without disclosing the marriage, he made a further application on 29
e April for indefinite leave to remain as the husband of the lady entitled to reside here. It
is perfectly clear that the appellant's intention from the outset was to settle in the United
Kingdom with his wife. He may or may not have believed, erroneously, that the
marriage would entitle him to leave to settle here, but that is immaterial. His blatant lie
to the immigration officer as to his intention was a contravention of s 26(1)(c) of the 1971
Act. If he had disclosed his true intention, he would not have been granted leave to enter.
f In this case the evidence clearly proves that the appellant was an illegal entrant.
    My Lords, I would allow the appeal of Khera and dismiss the appeal of Khawaja.

LORD TEMPLEMAN. My Lords, for the reasons given by my noble and learned
friend Lord Bridge, I too would allow the appeal of Khera and dismiss the appeal of
Khawaja.
g   In an ideal world there would be no restrictions on immigration. In the actual world
accidents of history, geography and climate create pressures to emigrate which are not
matched by facilities for reception. Hence the imposition of immigration controls
designed to produce a logical and just system for admitting those numbers and categories
of long-term and short-term applicants for entry who can be absorbed without disastrous
economic, administrative or social consequences. If immigration controls are, or are
h thought to be, necessary there must be machinery for the qualification and selection of
entrants and for the enforcement of the controls.
    Section 3 of the Immigration Act 1971 provides that a person who has no right of
abode in the United Kingdom shall not enter the United Kingdom unless given leave to
do so in accordance with the Act. By the same section the Secretary of State must lay
before Parliament rules as to the practice to be followed in the administration of the Act
j for regulating the entry into and stay in the United Kingdom of persons requiring leave
to do so. The 1971 Act and the immigration rules constitute the machinery for the
enforcement of immigration control.
    By s 4 the power of granting or refusing leave to enter the United Kingdom is
conferred on immigration officers. An appeal lies from an immigration officer to an
adjudicator, and from the adjudicator to the Immigration Appeal Tribunal. By s 13(3)

no appeal can be brought against a refusal of leave to enter so long as the applicant is in the United Kingdom unless he was refused leave at a port of entry and at a time when he held a current entry clearance or was a person named in a current work permit. The system of issuing entry certificates and work permits enables the task of checking qualifications and entitlement to selection to be carried out in the country of origin of the immigrant, although the final power of deciding whether the immigrant shall be given leave to enter rests with the immigration officer, subject to the appeal procedure provided by the Act.

The Act does not permit (save in the case of holders of current entry clearances or work permits) any right of appeal against refusal of leave to enter to be pursued while the applicant remains in the United Kingdom. In the absence of such a provision, any applicant refused leave to enter would have to be detained, or permitted to enter, for the purpose of arguing before the adjudicator and the tribunal that he ought to have been permitted to enter. In those circumstances, immigration control would become inefficient and unworkable. In many cases material facts relevant to an appeal can only be ascertained from the country of origin of the applicant to which he is removed. The adjudicator and the tribunal are not bound by strict rules of evidence but may receive on behalf of the applicant, and on behalf of the immigration authorities, written representations and reports of investigations which may take some time and involve inquiries as to identity, births, marriages, deaths and other circumstances in remote countrysides.

If an immigration officer in the exercise of his powers refuses leave to enter, the officer and the Secretary of State have powers under paras 8 and 10 of Sch 2 to the Act to procure the removal of the applicant from the United Kingdom, and under para 16 to order his detention pending removal. These powers of detention and removal are also essential in order to ensure that immigration controls are effective.

In addition to the statutory rights of appeal given to an applicant who seeks leave to enter the United Kingdom, the court retains power in habeas corpus and judicial review proceedings to protect any applicant who complains that he has not been fairly treated. The court, if satisfied of unfair treatment, may order the applicant to be released from detention and may forbid his removal from the United Kingdom.

An applicant who requires leave from an immigration officer to enter the United Kingdom is entitled to proper consideration by the immigration officer, but he has no right to enter or remain in the United Kingdom. It is for the immigration officer and not the court to decide whether leave to enter shall be given.

Once, however, an applicant has obtained from the immigration officer leave to enter the United Kingdom, he becomes an entrant entitled as of right to remain in the United Kingdom during the currency and on the terms of the leave granted to him. The rights of such an entrant are forfeited if he is found to have obtained leave to enter by fraud. An entrant who has obtained leave to enter by fraud is an illegal entrant and is liable to be detained and removed from the United Kingdom at the behest of the immigration officer or the Secretary of State pursuant to paras 9, 10 and 16 of Sch 2 to the Act. But these powers of detention and removal only apply to an illegal entrant. An entrant threatened with forfeiture of his rights may seek the protection of the court in habeas corpus and judicial review proceedings, asserting that he did not obtain leave to enter by fraud, that he is not an illegal entrant and that therefore the immigration authorities have no power to detain him or to remove him from the United Kingdom. If the court is not satisfied that the entrant obtained leave to enter by fraud, the court will protect the entrant against detention and removal.

I agree with my noble and learned friend Lord Scarman that the burden of proving that leave to enter was obtained by fraud and that consequently the entrant is an illegal entrant liable to arrest and expulsion can only be discharged by the immigration authorities manifesting to the satisfaction of the court a high degree of probability.

It does not follow that the court must disregard written statements by witnesses who are not available for cross-examination or documents which are not supported by direct written or oral evidence as to the circumstances in which they came into existence.

In habeas corpus and judicial review proceedings evidence will be by affidavit, subject
a to cross-examination at the discretion of the court. It may be necessary for the court to
reach a conclusion on the available information and without the benefit of oral evidence
or of a prolonged investigation in the country of origin of the entrant. If fraud has been
concealed for a number of years, witnesses of recorded statements may not be available
to provide affidavits as to the circumstances in which those statements were prepared,
composed and signed. Those statements may appear before the court as exhibits to
b affidavits from persons in whose custody the statements have been preserved. It will be
for the court to determine what weight to attach to any of the information provided. It
will be for the court to consider any explanations furnished by the entrant and his
witnesses and to judge the reliability of the entrant under cross-examination.

In Khera's case, for example, it is said that there was available a record of Khera's
medical examination bearing the thumb-print or signature of Khera himself and the
c signature of the medical officer. The record is said to have contained the statement that
Khera was unmarried. The medical officer might or might not have been available, and
might or might not have recollected the interview. Faced with any such record Khera
himself could have given evidence and been cross-examined as to the recorded statement
that he was unmarried. It would have been open to the court on consideration of the
record and other circumstances, and on consideration of the cross-examination of Khera,
d to have decided that fraud was not made out. But it would also have been open to the
court to conclude that Khera had lied to the medical officer, and to disbelieve any
proffered explanation that the record had been prepared previously to Khera's marriage,
or that Khera from Amritsar had failed to make himself understood to anyone present at
the interview in Delhi. It would also have been open to the court to infer that Khera had
told a lie to the medical officer and subsequently kept silent to the immigration officer
e about his marriage because he must have appreciated that his marriage had defeated or
prejudiced his chances of obtaining admission to the United Kingdom. But in the event
the immigration authorities failed to produce any record of the medical examination
which in correspondence they claimed to exist.

If the court decides that on the available information fraud on the part of the entrant
in obtaining leave to enter the United Kingdom has been made out, the entrant will be
f liable to be removed from the United Kingdom pursuant to directions by the immigration
authorities.

Both Khera and Khawaja obtained leave to enter the United Kingdom. Fraud has been
made out against Khawaja and his appeal must be dismissed. Fraud has not been made
out against Khera and his appeal must be allowed.

g *Appeal of Khera allowed; declaration that the appellant is lawfully in the United Kingdom and
has indefinite leave to enter and/or remain; case remitted to Queen's Bench Division to grant
certiorari quashing determination of Home Office on 22 November 1978.*

Appeal of Khawaja dismissed.

Solicitors: *Daniel P Debidin & Co,* Hanwell (for Khera); *Barry Lewis,* agents for *Elders,* Sale
(for Khawaja); *Treasury Solicitor.*

Mary Rose Plummer   Barrister.

Carrington and others v Therm-A-Stor Ltd   *a*

COURT OF APPEAL, CIVIL DIVISION
SIR JOHN DONALDSON MR, WATKINS AND MAY LJJ
11, 12, 18 NOVEMBER 1982

Unfair dismissal – Determination whether dismissal fair or unfair – Dismissal for an inadmissible *b*
reason – Dismissal for trade union membership – Union applying to employer for recognition –
Employer reacting by instructing chargehands to dismiss 20 employees – Dismissed employees
claiming their dismissal due to union membership or activities – Whether employees dismissed for
trade union activities – Whether necessary for each employee to show that his dismissal was due to
his particular union membership or activity – Employment Protection (Consolidation) Act 1978,
s 58.

 c

A number of employees at the employer's factory decided to attempt to introduce
unionisation into the factory. They had a recruiting drive on behalf of a particular union
and, after 90% of the workforce had joined or applied to join the union, the union's
district secretary wrote to the employer asking him to recognise the union. Two days
after receiving the request, the employer instructed the factory chargehands to select 20 *d*
employees for dismissal. It was left to the chargehands to decide who should be chosen.
Four of the dismissed employees applied to an industrial tribunal for compensation
under the Employment Protection (Consolidation) Act 1978 on the ground that they had
been unfairly dismissed, within the meaning of s 58(1)(a) of that Act, because the reason
for their dismissal was their actual or proposed union membership and activities. The
industrial tribunal found that the employer was strongly against unions and that the
dismissals were his reaction to the union's request for recognition. However, the tribunal *e*
rejected the employees' claims for compensation on the ground that there was no
evidence that the chargehands had taken into account any individual's union membership
or activities when making their selection and therefore none of the employees could
show that the 'reason' for his particular dismissal came within s 58. The employees
appealed to the Employment Appeal Tribunal, which allowed the appeal on the ground *f*
that it was to be presumed that s 58 was intended to protect an employee against dismissal
by his employer as a reaction to a union request for recognition. On appeal by the
employer to the court of appeal,

Held – The intervention of the chargehands was to be disregarded for the purposes of
the claims under s 58 of the 1978 Act because that intervention was concerned solely *g*
with the selection of the employees for dismissal and not with the reason for their
dismissal. However, on the true construction of s 58, the dismissal of an employee was
to be regarded as unfair only if he could show that it was due to his own actual or
proposed trade union membership or activities. Since the reason why each of the
employees was dismissed had nothing to do with anything which he personally had done
or proposed to do, it followed that none of them were entitled to compensation under *h*
the 1978 Act by virtue of s 58. The employer's appeal would accordingly be allowed (see
p 799 *a b e* and *j* to p 800 *b*, post).

Notes
For the Employment Protection (Consolidation) Act 1978, s 58, see 48 Halsburys Statutes *j*
(3rd edn) 509.
   As from 1 December 1982, s 58 of the 1978 Act was replaced by s 3 of the Employment
Act 1982.

---

a   Section 58(1), so far as material, is set out at p 797 g, post

Case cited

a *Rath v Cruden Construction Ltd* [1982] ICR 60, EAT.

Appeal

Therm-A-Stor Ltd (the employers) appealed against a decision of the Employment Appeal Tribunal (Phillips J, Mr J D Hughes and Mrs M E Sutherland), given on 2 July 1981, whereby it allowed an appeal by Paul Benjamin Carrington, John Atkins, Peter Stephen

b Hall and Raymond Frank Crutchley (the employees) against a decision of an industrial tribunal (chairman Mr James Freeman) sitting at Cambridge, which was registered on 31 December 1980 and which dismissed a claim by each of the employees for compensation under the Employment Protection (Consolidation) Act 1978 for unfair dismissal. The facts are set out in the judgment of Sir John Donaldson MR.

c *Bruce Reynolds* for the employers.
Eldred Tabachnik QC and *Richard Field* for the employees.

Cur adv vult

d 18 November. The following judgments were delivered.

SIR JOHN DONALDSON MR. This appeal will be allowed for the reasons set out in my judgment and in the judgment of May LJ, both of which have been handed to counsel, and in addition Watkins LJ authorises me to say that he agrees with both judgments.

e   All four respondents, employees, were most unfairly dismissed. Of that there can be no real doubt. But the industrial tribunal and the Employment Appeal Tribunal have disagreed on whether, in the particular circumstances of their dismissal, they are entitled to compensation. The industrial tribunal thought not. The appeal tribunal thought so. We have to decide which was right.

All four had started work for Therm-A-Stor, the employers, at Peterborough less than

f 52 weeks before they were dismissed. Accordingly they were ineligible for compensation under the usual provisions governing unfair dismissals. However, an employee can surmount this obstacle if he can show not only that he was unfairly dismissed, but that he was dismissed for what is quaintly called 'an inadmissible reason' (see the Employment Protection (Consolidation) Act 1978, s 64(3)). Accordingly this is what the four employees set out to do.

g   Section 58(1) of the Act provides that a dismissal shall be unfair:

'if the reason for it (or, if more than one, the principal reason) was that the employee—(a) was, or proposed to become, a member of an independent trade union; (b) had taken, or proposed to take, part at any appropriate time in the activities of an independent trade union; or (c) had refused, or proposed to refuse, to become or remain a member of a trade union which was not an independent trade

h union.'

Section 58(5) brands such a reason as an 'inadmissible reason'.

It was the right and the duty of the industrial tribunal to find the facts and they have done so. The concern of the appeal tribunal, and our concern on any appeal, is only with the law. Accordingly I take the facts from the reasons of the industrial tribunal. The employers' Peterborough factory opened for the first time in the autumn of 1979. Come

j the spring and a number of the employees, including one of the four employees decided to try to introduce a trade union into the factory. They recruited on behalf of the Transport and General Workers' Union and by late April between 60 and 65 of the 70 employees had joined or applied to join. On 27 April they met the union's district secretary and asked him to apply to the company for recognition of the union. Next day,

28 April, the district secretary wrote to Mr Morris, the managing director, setting out the union's case for recognition.

Two days later, on 30 April, there was a meeting of the employers' management committee at their headquarters at Perivale. Mr Morris, who had received the union's letter, took the chair. The committee decided to dismiss 20 of the Peterborough employees immediately. Next day Mr Morris went to Peterborough and instructed the eight chargehands to select 20 employees for dismissal, it being left entirely to them to decide who should be chosen. The four respondents were among the group who were dismissed.

The employers claimed that the reason for the dismissals was a redundancy situation. Whilst it is true that all was not well with the employers' business and that the possibility of redundancies at Peterborough was already under consideration, the industrial tribunal had no difficulty in concluding that there was a quite different reason for the sudden dismissals. This was that Mr Morris was strongly anti-union and the dismissals were his reaction to the union's letter seeking recognition.

The industrial tribunal rejected the four employees' claims because, although the reason for all four dismissals was reaction to the attempt by the union to obtain recognition, each of the four was selected for dismissal by chargehands who did not take any account of actual or proposed union membership or actual or proposed participation in union activities by those employees concerned. Accordingly the industrial tribunal considered that none of the four could show that the reason for his dismissal was *his* union membership or activities.

The appeal tribunal took a different view. Their reasoning is set out at the end of the judgment delivered by Phillips J in the following terms ([1982] ICR 8 at 13–14):

'Where we part company with the industrial tribunal, and where in a sense maybe it can be said they have misdirected themselves, can be seen from what they say about the employee, Mr. Crutchley, in paragraph 18: "To put the point in concrete terms, if one takes the case of Mr. Crutchley . . . it is quite clear to us on the evidence . . . he would have been dismissed even if he had not been a member of the trade union. Indeed, we accept the evidence given to us by his chargehand that he did not know that Mr. Crutchley was a member of the trade union." The importance they attach to that example is shown by the next word, "Therefore," and so to some extent they based themselves on it: "Therefore, it seems to us that . . ." They then state the conclusion which they reach, which we have already read. But it is worth examining the example. Assume Mr. Crutchley was not a member of the union. One asks oneself, "Why was he dismissed?" The answer is that he was dismissed because the district secretary wrote the letter of April 28, the general purport and tenor of which was have already sought to summarise. One can translate that and say that the reason for Mr. Crutchley's dismissal was the involvement of the trade union; and so he would be being dismissed, albeit he was not a member of the union, because of the involvement by way of reprisal for the involvement of the trade union. Well, obviously he cannot complain in the terms of section 58 that he was dismissed for the reason that he was, or proposed to become, a member of the union or that he had taken, or proposed to take, part in the activities of an independent trade union: because he neither had nor did. However, if one contrasts his position with that of one of the other employees (or, indeed, with his own position as it would be if he was a member of the trade union) surely, it can be said of him that the reason for his dismissal was that he was, or proposed to become, a member of a trade union or had taken, or proposed to take, part in the activities of a trade union? Any other conclusion, it seems to us, would put an extraordinarily narrow construction upon section 58 and render it wholly inoperative in many instances where it must have been intended to apply.'

As I see it, the first question for consideration is whether the fact that the chargehands undertook the selection for dismissal means that the chargehands' reason (probably last

in, first out) was the reason for the men's dismissal. Counsel for the employees submits
that so to conclude is to confuse the reason for dismissal with the basis for selection. As
he rightly points out they are two quite different things and are so treated in s 59 of the
Act in relation to redundancy. Where redundancy is the reason for the dismissal, the
dismissal is not necessarily unfair. However the method of selection for dismissal can
make the dismissal unfair. For my part I think that this is right and that the intervention
of the chargehands can be disregarded as being concerned solely with selection and not
with the reason for dismissal.

So far so good, but the four employees still have obstacles in their way. The industrial
tribunal did not find that the employers or Mr Morris decided to dismiss the group of 20
men because any or all of them had joined the union or proposed to do so or had taken
part in union activities or proposed to do so. He decided to dismiss them by way of
reaction to the union's letter seeking recognition. The reason for the dismissals was the
union's plea for recognition.

Counsel for the employees seeks to overcome this obstacle by submitting that s 58
should be construed in such a way as to recognise what he called its 'collective dimension'.
In his submission membership of a trade union is not a solo activity; it assumes other
members. Similarly it is difficult, if not impossible, to take part in the activities of a trade
union unless others do so. The whole concept of union activities has an essentially plural
basis. Accordingly if the four employees were members of a wider group, they were all
in fact members of the Transport and General Workers' Union, and the reason for the
dismissals was the activities of that group, it follows, as he submits, that the reason for
their dismissal was their union membership or activities, albeit with others.

I regard this as a valiant attempt at purposive construction of the statute, but in my
judgment it goes beyond permissible limits. As I read the section it is concerned solely
with the dismissal of an employee and provides that it shall be regarded as unfair if the
reason was that the (ie that) employee had done or proposed to do one or more specified
things. The reason why each of the four employees was dismissed had nothing to do
with anything which the employee concerned had personally done or proposed to do.
The section therefore has no application.

The appeal tribunal describe this as a narrow construction and said that the section, so
construed, would be rendered wholly inoperative in many instances where it must have
been intended to apply. If by this they meant that some protection should be given to
new employees if their jobs may be put at risk merely because a trade union has applied
for recognition, I would not dissent. Indeed I would go further and agree that in such
circumstances the union has a justifiable grievance. It is at risk of suffering considerable
damage. If an employer can act in this way with impunity, employees in other factories
might well hesitate before joining a union. I also agree with the appeal tribunal that it is
the duty of the courts to give effect to the intentions of Parliament. However the concept
that Parliament 'must have intended' a particular result is not without its dangers. If
regard is had solely to the apparent mischief and the need for a remedy, it is only too easy
for a judge to persuade himself that Parliament must have intended to provide the
remedy which he would himself have decreed if he had had legislative power. In fact
Parliament may not have taken the same view of what is a mischief, may have decided
as a matter of policy not to legislate for a legal remedy or may simply have failed to
realise that the situation could ever arise. This is not to say that statutes are to be construed
in blinkers or with a narrow and legalistic literalness, but only that effect should be given
to the intentions of Parliament as expressed in the statute, applying the normal canons of
construction for resolving ambiguities or any lack of clarity.

Tempted as I am to provide the four employees with a remedy for what was an
indefensible reaction to a simple request for union recognition, which could have been
granted or politely refused, I cannot construe s 58 as being intended to deal with such a
situation. The section is not concerned with an employer's reactions to a trade union's
activities, but with his reactions to an individual employee's activities in a trade union
context.

With regret, I would allow the appeal and restore the decision of the industrial tribunal.

MAY LJ. I agree that this appeal must be allowed for the reasons set out by Sir John Donaldson MR in his judgment. I share his regret at the result because on the findings of the industrial tribunal Mr Morris's reaction to his receipt of Mr Nolan's letter was ill-advised and a clear failure to observe good industrial practice within his company. Nevertheless I do not think that the dismissals of any of the four employees to this appeal can be brought within the wording of s 58 of the 1978 Act even though that section was clearly aimed at a mischief very similar to that which befell the four employees.

Appeal allowed. Application for leave to appeal to the House of Lords refused.

20 January 1983. The Appeal Committee of the House of Lords (Lord Diplock, Lord Roskill and Lord Brandon of Oakbrook) dismissed a petition by the employees for leave to appeal.

Solicitors: *Rochman Landau & Co* (for the employers); *Pattinson & Brewer* (for the employees).

Frances Rustin Barrister.

Practice Direction

QUEEN'S BENCH DIVISION

Practice — Funds in court — Transfer to High Court from county court — Minors' funds — Procedure — County Courts Act 1959, s 174A — Supreme Court Funds Rules 1975, r 22(4).

Pursuant to s 174A of the County Courts Act 1959 many county courts are now transferring the funds held by them to the High Court.

By r 22(4) of the Supreme Court Funds Rules 1975 (as substituted by the Supreme Court Funds (Amendment) Rules 1981, SI 1981/1589, r 10), 'Where money is lodged at a District Registry it shall be forwarded forthwith to the Court Funds Office . . .'

Hitherto in cases in which it was desirable that there should be local control over investment or disposal of the funds of minors it was the practice to order payment into the appropriate county court, unless those funds were substantial.

For the future in the London county courts areas the appropriate local control will be exercised by the master making the order. Outside the London county courts areas it will normally be the appropriate district registrar.

Accordingly, the following order should be applied for in appropriate cases where the next friend resides outside the London county courts areas (unless the next friend wishes that the minor's money should remain under the control of the master):

> 'The defendant within   days do pay the sum of £   into the Court Funds Office to be invested and accumulated in Short Term Investment Account for the benefit of the minor   pending further order, and that all further proceedings relating to the investment and application of the said fund be transferred to the District Registry.'

Masters' Practice Forms 165 to 172 will be amended accordingly in due course.

J B ELTON
7 February 1983   Senior Master, Queen's Bench Division.

Mallalieu v Drummond (Inspector of Taxes)

COURT OF APPEAL, CIVIL DIVISION

SIR JOHN DONALDSON MR, KERR LJ AND SIR SEBAG SHAW

13, 14 DECEMBER 1982

Income tax – Deduction in computing profits – Expenditure wholly and exclusively laid out or expended for purposes of trade – Purpose of expenditure – Barrister's clothing – Woman barrister's court clothes – Whether expenditure incurred in replacing, cleaning and laundering clothes deductible – Income and Corporation Taxes Act 1970, s 130(a).

The taxpayer was a practising barrister. During the year 1976–77 she spent some £564 on the replacement, cleaning and laundering of certain items of clothing which she wore in court, and she sought to deduct that sum when computing the profits of her profession as being 'wholly and exclusively . . . expended for the purposes of [her] profession' within s 130(a)ᵈ of the Income and Corporation Taxes Act 1970. The inspector of taxes disallowed the deduction and the taxpayer appealed to the General Commissioners. The commissioners found, as facts, that the taxpayer had ample other clothing for the purposes of warmth and decency, that she would not have purchased any of the disputed items had it not been for the requirement of her profession that she should be so clothed, that when she wore court clothes travelling to chambers on a day when she was not booked to go to court it was only because she had always to be ready to go to court at short notice, that she bought the disputed items only because she would not have been permitted to appear in court if she did not, when in court, wear them or similar clothes, and that the preservation of warmth and decency was not a consideration in her mind when she bought them. The commissioners considered that, notwithstanding that the taxpayer's sole motive in choosing the particular clothes was to satisfy the requirements of her profession and that had she been free to do so she would have worn different clothes, the expenditure had a dual purpose, the professional one of enabling her to earn profits in her profession and the non-professional one of enabling her to be properly clothed while on her way to chambers or to court and while she was thereafter engaged on her professional activity. They therefore held that, because of that dual purpose, the taxpayer was not entitled to the deduction claimed. On an appeal by the taxpayer, the judge held that there was no evidence to support the commissioners' conclusion that the taxpayer had a dual purpose in mind, but only evidence to conclude that the expenditure on the disputed items was incurred by the taxpayer solely for the purpose of carrying on her profession, and that the benefits of warmth and decency which she would enjoy while wearing the clothes were purely incidental to the carrying on of her profession. Accordingly, he held that the expenditure was deductable and allowed the appeal. The Crown appealed.

Held – Since, by their findings, the commissioners had themselves determined that the taxpayer's sole and entire purpose in incurring the expenditure on the disputed items was a professional purpose, and that any other benefit to the taxpayer was purely incidental, their conclusion that the taxpayer had a dual purpose was wholly inconsistent with their findings of fact and therefore an error of law which the judge was right to correct. It followed that the appeal would be dismissed (see p 806 *d* to *f* and *j*, p 807 *c* and p 808 *f* to p 809 *a*, post).

Edwards (Inspector of Taxes) v Bairstow [1955] 3 All ER 48, dictum of Oliver J in *Sargent (Inspector of Taxes) v Barnes* [1978] 2 All ER at 744 and *Robinson (Inspector of Taxes) v Scott Bader Co Ltd* [1981] 2 All ER 1116 applied.

---

a   Section 130, so far as material, provides: 'Subject to the provisions of the Tax Acts, in computing the amount of the profits or gains to be charged under Case I or Case II of Schedule D, no sum shall be deducted in respect of—(a) any disbursements or expenses, not being money wholly and exclusively laid out or expended for the purposes of the trade, profession or vocation . . .'

Hillyer v Leeke (Inspector of Taxes) [1976] STC 490, *Woodcock v IRC* [1977] STC 405 and *Ward (Inspector of Taxes) v Dunn* [1979] STC 178 distinguished.

Notes

For deduction of expenditure laid out wholly and exclusively for the purposes of a trade or profession, see 23 Halsbury's Laws (4th edn) paras 295, 305–306, and for cases on the subject, see 28(1) Digest (Reissue) 141–158, 421–505.

For the Income and Corporation Taxes Act 1970, s 130, see 33 Halsbury's Statutes (3rd edn) 182.

Cases referred to in judgments

Bentleys Stokes & Lowless v Beeson (Inspector of Taxes) [1952] 2 All ER 82, CA, 28(1) Digest (Reissue) 150, 465.

Cooper (Inspector of Taxes) v Stubbs [1925] 2 KB 753, [1925] All ER Rep 643, CA, 28(1) Digest (Reissue) 25, 95.

Edwards (Inspector of Taxes) v Bairstow [1955] 3 All ER 48, [1956] AC 14, [1955] 3 WLR 410, HL, 28(1) Digest (Reissue) 566, 2089.

Hillyer v Leeke (Inspector of Taxes) [1976] STC 490, Digest (Cont Vol E) 287, 505c.

Robinson (Inspector of Taxes) v Scott Bader Co Ltd [1981] 2 All ER 1116, [1981] 1 WLR 1135, CA; *affg* [1980] 2 All ER 780, [1980] 1 WLR 755.

Sargent (Inspector of Taxes) v Barnes [1978] 2 All ER 737, [1978] 1 WLR 823, Digest (Cont Vol E) 288, 760a.

Ward (Inspector of Taxes) v Dunn [1979] STC 178.

Woodcock v IRC [1977] STC 405, Digest (Cont Vol E) 287, 505d.

Appeal

The Crown appealed against the judgment of Slade J ([1981] STC 391) given on 12 March 1981 whereby he allowed an appeal by way of case stated (set out at [1981] STC 392–397) by Ann Mallalieu (the taxpayer) against the determination of the Commissioners for the General Purposes of the Income Tax for the Division of the Middle Temple in the City of London dismissing the taxpayer's appeal against an assessment made on her under Case II of Sch D for the year of assessment 1977–78 in respect of her claim to be entitled to deduct in computing the profits of her profession as a barrister the sum of £564·38 expended on the replacement, cleaning and laundering of certain items of clothing used by her for the purposes of her profession. The facts are set out in the judgment of Sir John Donaldson MR.

Andrew Park QC and *David C Milne* for the taxpayer.
Peter Millett QC and *Michael Hart* for the Crown.

SIR JOHN DONALDSON MR. Miss Ann Mallalieu (the taxpayer) is a practising barrister. During her accounting year 1976–77 she expended £564·38 on the replacement, cleaning and laundering of certain items of clothing and she sought to deduct this sum when computing the profits of her profession for the year of assessment. The inspector of taxes disallowed this deduction and the taxpayer appealed. Subject to the minor item of the cost of collars, the General Commissioners upheld the inspector's decision. The taxpayer again appealed, this time to Slade J, and this time she succeeded. His judgment sets the scene and contains most of the relevant material (see [1981] STC 391). The Crown now appeals. It is now agreed that all costs relating to collars are deductible and that we need not pursue any possible distinction between shoes and any other form of clothing. It is also agreed that all the expenditure was of a revenue nature. Accordingly, the issue is whether the cost of purchasing and cleaning or laundering black tights, black shoes, black suits, black dresses and white shirts is deductible.

It is common ground that if the taxpayer is to succeed she must show that the relevant expenditure was 'wholly and exclusively laid out or expended for the purposes of the

trade, profession or vocation' (see s 130(a) of the Income and Corporation Taxes Act
a 1970).
    The essence of the General Commissioners' decision is contained in the second part of
para 9 of their reasons, which is in the following terms ([1981] STC 391 at 396):

> 'We consider, in the present case, that when [the taxpayer] laid out money on
> clothes for wearing in court her purpose in making that expenditure was to enable
> her to earn profits in her profession and also to enable her to be properly clothed
b > during the time she was on her way to chambers or to court and while she was
> thereafter engaged in her professional activity, and in the other circumstances
> indicated in para 2. We do not consider that the fact that her sole motive in choosing
> the particular clothes was to satisfy the requirements of her profession or that if she
> had been free to do so she would have worn clothes of a different style on such
> occasions altered the purpose of the expenditure which remained the purpose of
c > purchasing clothes that would keep her warm and clad during the part of the day
> when she was pursuing her career as well as the purpose of helping her to earn profits
> in that career. We think, therefore, that the expenditure had a dual purpose, one
> professional and one non-professional, and we, therefore, hold that, subject to one
> matter which we mention hereafter, she is not entitled to deduct the sums claimed.'

d (Might I parenthetically make a small plea that if General Commissioners are stating a case
which includes the written reasons which they have previously given to the parties the
paragraphs in the case may be so numbered, or those of the written reasons so renumbered,
that there is no confusion between the paragraphs of the case and those of the written
reasons.)
    The essence of Slade J's decision is to be found in the following passage from his
e judgment ([1981] STC 391 at 406):

> 'On the facts as found by the commissioners, the taxpayer, as a human being,
> neither needed nor wanted the clothes in question. In incurring the expenditure on
> them she had no thought of warmth and decency. As the commissioners found, she
> bought them "only because she would not have been permitted to appear in court if
> she did not wear, when in court, them or other clothes like them". In the
f > circumstances, I think that, with all respect to the commissioners, there was no
> evidence to support the inference which they finally drew to the effect that she had a
> dual purpose in mind. On the evidence, I am driven to the conclusion that the
> relevant expenditure in the present case was incurred by her solely for the purpose of
> carrying on her profession, and that the benefits of warmth and decency, which she
> would enjoy while wearing the clothes during the various times referred to by the
g > commissioners in para 9 of their decision, were purely incidental to the carrying on
> of her profession. In these circumstances the expenses are, in my judgment,
> deductible.'

    The starting point of the Crown's argument is that the General Commissioners'
conclusion was one of fact and degree which it is impossible to characterise as being
h 'erroneous in point of law'. Accordingly, it is unappealable under s 56(1) of the Taxes
Management Act 1970. This submission led, inevitably, to Edwards (Inspector of Taxes) v
Bairstow [1955] 3 All ER 48, [1956] AC 14. That case establishes that where the facts
warrant a determination either way, the issue is one of degree and is therefore a question
of fact (see [1955] 3 All ER 48 at 56, [1956] AC 14 at 33 per Lord Radcliffe), but that, if the
facts found are such that no person acting judicially, and properly instructed as to the
j relevant law, could have come to the determination under appeal, the court must intervene
and that it does so on the basis that there is no evidence to support the determination or
that the evidence is inconsistent with and contradictory of the determination or that the
true and only reasonable conclusion contradicts the determination (see [1955] 3 All ER 48
at 57, [1956] AC 14 at 36, per Lord Radcliffe). Lord Simonds dealt with the matter in
somewhat more specific terms when he said ([1955] 3 All ER 48 at 53, [1956] AC 14 at 29):

'The primary facts as they are sometimes called do not, in my opinion, justify the inference or conclusion which the commissioners have drawn; not only do they not justify it but they lead irresistibly to the opposite inference or conclusion. It is, therefore, a case in which, whether it be said of the commissioners that their finding is perverse or that they have misdirected themselves in law by a misunderstanding of the statutory language or otherwise, their determination cannot stand.'

Without apology, I make one further reference to Lord Radcliffe's speech because, as it seems to me, it epitomises the relationship between the General Commissioners and the courts. He said ([1955] 3 All ER 48 at 59, [1956] AC 14 at 38–39):

'I think it possible that the English courts have been led to be rather over-ready to treat these questions as "pure questions of fact" by some observations of WARRINGTON and ATKIN L.JJ., in *Cooper* v. *Stubbs* ([1925] 2 KB 753, [1925] All ER Rep 643). If so, I would say, with very great respect, that I think it a pity that such a tendency should persist. As I see it, the reason why the courts do not interfere with commissioners' findings or determinations when they really do involve nothing but questions of fact is not any supposed advantage in the commissioners of greater experience in matters of business, or any other matters. The reason is simply that, by the system that has been set up, the commissioners are the first tribunal to try an appeal and, in the interests of the efficient administration of justice, their decisions can only be upset on appeal if they have been positively wrong in law. The court is not a second opinion, where there is reasonable ground for the first. But there is no reason to make a mystery about the subjects that commissioners deal with, or to invite the courts to impose any exceptional restraints on themselves because they are dealing with cases that arise out of facts found by commissioners. Their duty is no more than to examine those facts with a decent respect for the tribunal appealed from and, if they think that the only reasonable conclusion on the facts found is inconsistent with the determination come to, to say so without more ado.'

It follows that the judgment of Slade J should only be upheld if on the primary facts found by the General Commissioners they could not properly have concluded that the expenditure was dual-purpose expenditure incurred partly for professional and partly for non-professional purposes, i e being warm and decently clad. If they could properly so find, it is nothing to the point that other commissioners or Slade J, or indeed this court, would have reached a different conclusion.

Counsel for the Crown accepted that the purpose referred to in the section is the purpose of the taxpayer. In other words, the test is subjective. But he submitted that purpose, 'the end in view', must not be confused with motive, 'the reason why'. But this distinction does not appear to have been present in the mind of Romer LJ when giving the judgment of the Court of Appeal in *Bentleys Stokes & Lowless v Beeson (Inspector of Taxes)* [1952] 2 All ER 82, as indeed was pointed out by Walton J in *Robinson (Inspector of Taxes) v Scott Bader Co Ltd* [1980] 2 All ER 780 at 788, [1980] 1 WLR 755 at 760, but in deference to argument of counsel for the Crown I will eschew any other word or concept than 'purpose' which is, after all, the word used by the legislature.

What was the end in view? The General Commissioners had to look into the taxpayer's mind at the moment when the expenditure was incurred and not at the moment when the clothes were being donned. When the clothes were being donned, the taxpayer had to make two decisions. First, whether to wear clothes at all. In that decision, she would undoubtedly be influenced by considerations of warmth and decency. Second, having decided to wear clothes, she had to decide which clothes to wear. In that decision, questions of warmth and decency were quite irrelevant. The commissioners' primary findings of fact on this are as follows. I quote from para 4 of their case ([1981] STC 391 at 393):

'... (f) At all material times the taxpayer had a private wardrobe of clothes and shoes which was amply sufficient to keep her clothed and shod in comfort and decency, without having to resort to any of the disputed items. She would not have

purchased any of the disputed items had it not been for the requirement of her
profession that she should comply with the notes for guidance when appearing in
court. (g) The taxpayer normally drove when going to and from court or her
chambers. On such journeys she wore her court clothes even on those occasions when
she was going to her chambers and was not already booked to go to court on that day,
as she had always to be ready to go to court at short notice. On the relatively rare
occasions when she wished to spend the day in chambers reading papers and had
asked her clerk not to arrange for her to go to court she would normally wear clothes
such as she wore at the hearing before the commissioners, i e: smart clothes from her
non-court wardrobe not suitable for wearing in court . . . (j) Though it must have
been the case, and she agreed, that by wearing her court clothes for a large part of her
working lifetime she saved the clothes of her private wardrobe from wear and tear, it
was accepted that this fact was not a consideration in her mind when she bought the
disputed items. She bought such items only because she would not have been
permitted to appear in court if she did not wear, when in court, them or other clothes
like them. Similarly the preservation of warmth and decency was not a consideration
which crossed her mind when she bought the disputed items . . .'

Faced with these primary findings, counsel for the Crown becomes remarkably less
subjective in his approach. He submits that, whatever a taxpayer may identify as the
primary purpose of expenditure on clothes of a type which can be worn in everyday life,
his or her secondary purpose must be to keep warm and to be decently clothed or, to put it
at its lowest, this is a possible conclusion of fact.

In pursuit of this argument he referred us to *Hillyer v Leeke (Inspector of Taxes)* [1976]
STC 490, which was, he submitted, quite indistinguishable. There the taxpayer bought
ordinary suits which he used solely whilst at work, yet it was held that his purchases had a
dual purpose. The Crown argued, and Goulding J accepted—

'that where the clothing worn is not of a special character dictated by the occupation
as a matter of physical necessity but is ordinary civilian clothing of a standard required
for the occupation, you cannot say that the one purpose is merely incidental to the
other.'

(See [1976] STC 490 at 492–493.)

This decision was followed in *Woodcock v IRC* [1977] STC 405 and in *Ward (Inspector of
Taxes) v Dunn* [1979] STC 178.

In my judgment the present appeal is distinguishable from those cases in that it is here
found as a primary fact that the taxpayer had an ample supply of other clothes and shoes to
keep her clothed in comfort and decency. Those decisions are all consistent with a state of
fact in which the taxpayers had indeed sufficient clothes for this purpose but only if those
used at work were included. Accordingly, on this supposition, they had to buy the work-
clothes for warmth and decency and, whilst their purpose was to acquire clothes suitable
for work, this was not the sole purpose.

Counsel for the Crown at one time was driven to submit that if expenditure is such as to
meet the primary needs of a human being as such, which includes keeping warm and
being decently attired, the taxpayer must be deemed to have incurred the relevant
expenditure for this purpose. However, as counsel for the taxpayer pointed out, there are
other needs which superficially at least would appear to be in the same category, e g external
warmth and shelter. Yet no one has ever suggested that the cost of providing an office or
chambers as shelter and expenditure on heating is incurred for a dual purpose. It is true to
say that counsel for the Crown in reply said that this was different because you had shelter
at home and you had heating at home, and what you were supplying was heat and shelter
in duplicate elsewhere. Beyond recalling the argument, I do not think it is necessary to
take the matter further since either it would involve embarking on an entirely different
case or, still worse, it might inspire the Revenue to start disallowing the cost of renting and
heating chambers.

I approach the matter on the same basis as did Oliver J in *Sargent (Inspector of Taxes) v Barnes* [1978] 2 All ER 737 at 744, [1978] 1 WLR 823 at 830. He said:

'This is an area in which it is difficult and, I think, positively dangerous to seek to lay down any general proposition designed to serve as a touchstone for all cases. The statute, by its very terms, directs the court to look at the purpose for which the expense was incurred in an individual case, and that necessarily involves a consideration of the intention governing or the reason behind a particular expenditure, which must depend in every case on its own individual facts. The stone which kills two birds may be aimed at one and kill another as a fortuitous or fortunate consequence; or it may be aimed at both. But it is only in the former case that the statute permits the taxpayer to deduct its cost.'

Accordingly, I ask myself whether the taxpayer in incurring the expenditure was aiming at one bird or two, accepting fully that she hit two, professional propriety and her needs as a human being. If she aimed at two, the expenditure was not deductible. If she aimed at the professional bird and fortuitously, fortunately, accidentally or incidentally hit the non-professional bird, the expenditure was deductible.

In answering that question I must and do accept the General Commissioners' primary findings of fact. (a) The taxpayer had ample other clothing for purposes of warmth and decency. (b) She would not have purchased any of the disputed items had it not been for the requirement of her profession that she should be so clothed. (c) When she wore court clothes travelling to chambers on a day when she was not booked to go to court, it was only because she had always to be ready to go to court at short notice. (d) She bought this clothing only because she would not have been permitted to appear in court if she did not, when in court, wear them or other clothes like them. (e) The preservation of warmth and decency was not a consideration which crossed her mind when she bought the disputed items.

These statements by the General Commissioners do not record evidence or submissions by the taxpayer. They are findings of fact. From those findings of fact there is in my judgment only one reasonable conclusion to be drawn, namely that the taxpayer's sole purpose in incurring the expenditure was a professional purpose, any other benefit being purely incidental. If that is right, then the determination of the General Commissioners cannot stand since it is wholly inconsistent with it. In such circumstances Lord Radcliffe bids me to say so without more ado. I would be quite willing to do so, but in deference to the unique experience and expertise of these particular General Commissioners I would only add that I think they must have been overpersuaded by the advocacy of Miss Wyman of the office of the Solicitor of Inland Revenue, who according to para 6 of the case submitted (see [1981] STC 391 at 394):

'... (b) that expenditure incurred in satisfying ordinary basic human needs can never be incurred "wholly and exclusively" for professional purposes even though the particular way in which those needs were met might be dictated by the requirements of the profession; (c) that expenditure on ordinary clothing such as was freely worn by persons not engaged in the profession could not be laid out "wholly and exclusively" for the purposes of the profession and a main and not merely incidental object of that expenditure was the advantage to the taxpayer as a living human being in meeting the needs of warmth and decency . . .'

If the General Commissioners did accept these submissions, and they really must have done in order to reach their conclusion, they erred in law. It may be rare for expenditure on ordinary clothing to be 'wholly and exclusively' incurred for the purposes of a profession, but it can happen and it did happen in this case.

Accordingly I would dismiss the appeal.

KERR LJ. Counsel for the Crown has argued two points on this appeal. First, that the conclusion of the commissioners was right because, in effect, it was an inevitable conclusion,

given the fact that the subject matter of the expenditure was clothing, and that the taxpayer
a inevitably had to be clothed in public, for comfort, warmth and decency, whatever she
might be doing. Second, he submitted that, even if this went too far, the commissioners'
conclusion that this was a case of a 'dual-purpose' expenditure was one which it was open
to them to reach, that it could not be shown to be 'erroneous in point of law' and that the
judge was therefore not entitled to substitute his conclusion for that of the commissioners.

The first of these submissions is very clearly stated in para 6 (b) and (c) of the case, setting
b out the contentions of the inspector, which Sir John Donaldson MR has already quoted in
full. In the same way as he, I would emphasise the words 'can never' in (b) and 'could not'
in (c).

In effect, this amounts to a submission that any disbursement or expense which serves
the purpose of meeting 'ordinary basic human needs' can by its nature never have been
laid out wholly and exclusively for the purposes of anyone's trade, profession or vocation,
c because it must inevitably also have been laid out in order to meet such human need. I
cannot accept this, and one can think of many examples which demonstrate the contrary.
Thus, food and drink was not disqualified as such in *Bentleys Stokes & Lowless v Beeson
(Inspector of Taxes)* [1952] 2 All ER 82. The cost of heating a taxpayer's place of work would
not be disqualified on the ground that warmth is a basic human need. And a requirement
to wear something in the nature of a uniform, such as dress trousers and a tailcoat with all
d the trimmings, bought or hired by a freelance waiter, which he would never consider
acquiring otherwise than as his professional apparel, could not possibly be disqualified
solely on the ground that one of his purposes in acquiring them was the avoidance of
having to perform his duties in his underclothes.

However, when some expenditure is incurred which is required for professional purposes
and which also meets an ordinary need, such as the need to be clothed in public, then the
e expenditure may, from the taxpayer's point of view, 'kill two birds with one stone'. He or
she may be fortunate, subject to the views of the inspector or thereafter the commissioners,
in being able to acquire something for more than one purpose. Whether or not this is so,
or to what extent, is a question of fact and degree. This, I think, applies particularly to
clothing, because everyone has to be clothed in public, apart from wholly exceptional
circumstances, such as a theatrical performance in the nude. Accordingly, a taxpayer's
f expense of acquiring, hiring or replacing clothing of a particular kind, which is required
for some professional purpose, may at the same time fulfil the ordinary purpose of enabling
the taxpayer to be clothed as opposed to being unclothed or insufficiently clothed. This
will be so, in particular, where the clothing in question is relatively ordinary; the more
ordinary it is, the easier it must be to infer that the purpose of the taxpayer's expenditure
was not exclusively for professional purposes but also in part for the everyday purposes for
g which people need clothes.

This brings me to the second submission of counsel for the Crown. He points out that
the clothes which are the subject matter of the present case are ordinary, in the sense that
they can be worn to fulfil the dual purpose of meeting the requirements of a member of
the Bar appearing in court and that at the same time they are also clothes of a kind which
are not outré in the sense of something which is clearly only in the nature of a professional
h uniform. Therefore, he submits, they are clothes which fulfil a dual purpose, professional
and non-professional, with the result that the expenditure necessary to acquire or replace
them (as to which no distinction has been suggested for present purposes) is expenditure
incurred for a dual purpose, which is therefore fatal to the taxpayer under s 130 of the
Income and Corporation Taxes Act 1970.

Viewed in the abstract and in the great majority of cases, a conclusion to this effect
j would clearly be unassailable if it were found as a fact by the commissioners in any given
case. It was so found, or at any rate the taxpayer did not succeed in establishing the
contrary, in *Hillyer v Leeke (Inspector of Taxes)* [1976] STC 490 and *Woodcock v IRC* [1977]
STC 405; and Walton J reached the same conclusion in *Ward (Inspector of Taxes) v Dunn*
[1979] STC 178. The issue in the present case, however, is whether the commissioners'
findings entitled them to arrive at the same conclusion on their own findings of primary
fact.

The second submission of counsel for the Crown, that the commissioners' conclusion to the same effect in the present case cannot be shown to have been erroneous in point of law, is the one on which my mind has wavered a great deal during the argument. However, two fundamental principles must be borne in mind in this connection. First, the decisive question is the taxpayer's subjective purpose at the time when the expenditure was incurred: see most recently the decision of this court in *Robinson (Inspector of Taxes) v Scott Bader Co Ltd* [1981] 2 All ER 1116, [1981] 1 WLR 1135. If that is found to have been for a single purpose which qualifies for tax relief, then this is conclusive, and it does not then matter if the effect of the expenditure is also, even perhaps inevitably, something which does not so qualify. Thus, once it was found in that case that the purpose of the taxpayer company was to further its trade in France by investing expenditure in a French subsidiary company, it was open to the commissioners to disregard the inevitable effect that the expenditure would also constitute a benefit for the subsidiary.

The second principle is that, once the commissioners have made their primary findings of fact, it is open to the courts to review as a matter of law the inferences which they have drawn from them, although the courts will only do so if, on the evidence or as a matter of law, the true or only reasonable conclusion contradicts the determination of the commissioners: see *Edwards (Inspector of Taxes) v Bairstow* [1955] 3 All ER 48 at 57, [1956] AC 14 at 36, in one of the tests propounded by Lord Radcliffe.

In the present case, as it seems to me, the primary findings of fact are wholly exceptional in the sense that they are conclusive in the taxpayer's favour. In particular, para 4(f) and (j) of the case and para 8 of the decision (see [1981] STC 391 at 393, 395) contain unqualified findings to the effect that the taxpayer's sole purpose in incurring the expenditure for the clothes in question was that she had to have them in order to exercise her profession and that she had no need for them, nor any other purpose, when she acquired them. True, they were clothes of a kind which also fulfilled the taxpayer's ordinary purposes while she was wearing them. In the result, therefore, the expenditure in question 'killed two birds with one stone', to repeat the illustration given by Oliver J in *Sargent (Inspector of Taxes) v Barnes* [1978] 2 All ER 737 at 744, [1978] 1 WLR 823 at 830 on which counsel for the Crown relied. Sir John Donaldson MR has already quoted the passage which I also have in mind in this connection.

In the present case I agree that the stone killed what may be described as a second non-professional bird by way of a fortuitous or fortunate consequence; but on the commissioners' own findings the expenditure was aimed only at the professional bird. This may well be an exceptional conclusion of fact, but it is so found. The judge said several times that the commissioners' conclusion involved a confusion between purpose and incidental effect. The distinction between these must usually be entirely a matter for the commissioners on which their decision would be unassailable, and this was the main consideration which has troubled me in the present case. But in this case they have, by their findings, themselves determined the taxpayer's sole and entire purpose as being professional. By these findings they have, in effect, stated themselves out of court so far as any ultimate conclusion to the contrary is concerned. All that remains can only be incidental effect; there is no room for a conclusion that there was a dual purpose. In my view the commissioners' ultimate conclusion can only have been based, as Sir John Donaldson MR said, on their acceptance of the Crown's contentions in para 6(b) and (c) of the case, viz that a dual purpose must inevitably follow in this case. However, for the reasons already stated, I consider that the acceptance of this as an inevitable consequence involves a fallacy, and I would accordingly dismiss this appeal.

SIR SEBAG SHAW. I agree. I have little to add to the judgments which have already been given. The commissioners fell into the error of stating their findings of fact as to the purpose for which the taxpayer bought the clothes, and then incongruously came to the conclusion that there was a dual purpose at the time of the purchase when of course there was not. There was a single purpose, as indeed the commissioners said. There was a fortuitous and incidental benefit which arose from it which was inescapable so far as the taxpayer was concerned; it was not that she adopted it but that she could not avoid it.

a   In those circumstances, it was certainly open to Slade J to review the findings of fact, and he was right in the conclusion he came to which was that, properly viewed, the fact that there was more than one purpose did not in any way preclude the taxpayer from being entitled to claim the relief which she sought in respect of her professional clothing. I would dismiss the appeal.

Appeal dismissed. Leave to appeal to the House of Lords refused.

b   *10 February 1983. The Appeal Committee of the House of Lords granted the Crown leave to appeal.*

Solicitors: *Solicitor of Inland Revenue*; *Penningtons* (for the taxpayer).

Nirmala Harlow Barrister.

c

d   # Catlin v Cyprus Finance Corp (London) Ltd (Catlin, third party)

QUEEN'S BENCH DIVISION
BINGHAM J
e   18, 19, 20, 26 OCTOBER 1982

Bank – Account – Joint account – Mandate to honour only instructions signed by husband and wife – Bank transferring solely on husband's instructions, funds from account to him for his own use – Wife bringing action against bank claiming damages for breach of mandate – Wife not joining husband as party – Whether bank owing duty to account holders jointly or severally –
f   *Whether failure of wife to join husband as party fatal to her claim.*

The plaintiff and her husband deposited funds in a joint account which they opened with the defendant bank. The deposit was made according to the terms of an express mandate which required that the bank would only make payments out of the account on the joint signatures of both account holders. Subsequently the bank, acting solely on the husband's
g   instructions, negligently transferred funds from the account to him for his own use without the plaintiff's knowledge or authority, causing her to suffer a loss. She brought an action against the bank claiming damages for breach of its mandate. The husband was not joined as a party to the proceedings. The bank contended that in the absence of the husband as a party the plaintiff's claim must fail because the bank owed a single obligation to the joint account holders jointly and the obligation could only be enforced
h   in an action to which both account holders were parties.

Held – The bank's agreement to honour only those instructions signed by both account holders carried with it a duty not to honour instructions which were not signed in that manner. That duty was owed to the account holders severally, and accordingly, where a breach of the mandate occurred, it could be enforced at the suit of the innocent account
j   holder alone. It followed that the plaintiff was entitled to the relief which she sought (see p 816 j to p 817 e, post).

Jackson v White and Midland Bank Ltd [1967] 2 Lloyd's Rep 68 followed.
Brandon v Scott (1857) 7 E & B 234, *Twibell v London Suburban Bank* [1869] WN 127, *Macdonald v Tacquah Gold Mines Co* (1884) 13 QBD 535 and *Ardern v Bank of New South Wales* [1956] VLR 569 considered.
Brewer v Westminster Bank Ltd [1952] 2 All ER 650 not followed.

Notes

For joint bank accounts, see 3 Halsburys Laws (4th edn) para 44, and for cases on the *a*
subject, see 3 Digest (Reissue) 580–585, 3713–3730.

For parties to proceedings, see 37 Halsbury's Laws (4th edn) paras 215–219, and for
cases on the subject, see 50 Digest (Repl) 436–465, 1366–1596.

Cases referred to in judgment

Ardern v Bank of New South Wales [1956] VLR 569, 3 Digest (Reissue) 581, *2847.   *b*
Baker v Barclays Bank Ltd [1955] 2 All ER 571, [1955] 1 WLR 822, 3 Digest (Reissue) 649,
4051.
Brandon v Scott (1857) 7 E & B 234, 119 ER 1234, 3 Digest (Reissue) 501, 3299.
Brewer v Westminster Bank Ltd [1952] 2 All ER 650, 3 Digest (Reissue) 580, 3712.
Hirschhorn v Evans [1938] 3 All ER 491, [1938] 2 KB 801, CA, 3 Digest (Reissue) 566,
3654.   *c*
Husband v Davis (1851) 10 CB 645, 138 ER 256, 3 Digest (Reissue) 580, 3713.
Innes (assignee of R & C Hingeston, bankrupts) v Stephenson (1831) 1 Mood & R 145, 174 ER
50, 3 Digest (Reissue) 580, 3714.
Jackson v White and Midland Bank Ltd [1967] 2 Lloyd's Rep 68, 3 Digest (Reissue) 581,
3715.
Macdonald v Tacquah Gold Mines Co (1884) 13 QBD 535, CA, 21 Digest (Reissue) 469,   *d*
3756.
Stone v Marsh Stracey and Graham (1827) 6 B & C 551, 108 ER 554, 3 Digest (Reissue) 507,
3321.
Twibell v London Suburban Bank [1869] WN 127, 3 Digest (Reissue) 581, 3719.
Welch v Bank of England [1955] 1 All ER 811, [1955] Ch 508, [1955] 2 WLR 757, 3 Digest
(Reissue) 506, 3317.   *e*

Action

The plaintiff, Beryl Catlin, brought an action against the defendants, Cyprus Finance
Corp (London) Ltd, seeking (i) a declaration that the defendants had wrongly debited a
joint account which was in the name of the plaintiff and her former husband, Gordon
Frederick Catlin, with certain sums, (ii) damages, amounting to half the sum so debited, *f*
for breach of a mandate which she and Mr Catlin had given to the defendants, (iii)
interest on that sum at such rate and for such period as the court thought just and proper.
The defendants issued a third party notice against Mr Catlin claiming an indemnity, but
he was subsequently debarred from defending the claim because he failed to comply
with an interlocutory order. The facts are set out in the judgment.

Michael Gettleson for the plaintiff.   *g*
Austin Allison for the bank.

Cur adv vult

h

26 October. The following judgment was delivered.

BINGHAM J. Mrs Beryl Catlin, the plaintiff in this action, claims as the former holder
of a joint account in respect of money debited to that account in alleged breach of
mandate. The defendant bank, Cyprus Finance Corp (London) Ltd, is a subsidiary of
Bank of Cyprus (London) Ltd (BOCL) which is itself a subsidiary of Bank of Cyprus Ltd *j*
(BOC). There are third party proceedings between the defendant bank and Mr Catlin,
the plaintiff's former husband, which he has been debarred from defending because of
an interlocutory default earlier this year.

The general background to the case can be briefly summarised. In 1972 Mrs Catlin
and her husband sold a hotel which they owned and ran in Liverpool and retired with
their two children to Cyprus where they already owned a flat. There they bought two

more flats. Towards the end of that year, for reasons which I need not go into, Mr and
a Mrs Catlin separated. They have not lived together since. In the summer of 1974 the
Turkish invasion of Cyprus took place. The consequences for Mrs Catlin and her children
were catastrophic. All their property was in the area of Famagusta, which was sealed off
by Turkish troops; the flat they were living in was bombed and their furniture badly
damaged. After six months under canvas in a refugee camp on one of the British
sovereign bases, she and the children were able to return to Famagusta by courtesy of the
b Turkish occupying forces and they have since then been living in the flat of a German
lady dispossessed by the troubles. Their own flats remain inaccessible and may in any
event be uninhabitable.

The immediate facts giving rise to this case are a little more involved. At about the
time that they went to Cyprus Mr and Mrs Catlin opened with the defendant bank a
joint external deposit account, no 289, into which they paid some of the proceeds of sale
c of the hotel. The money was on nine months' call. It seems that there may have been
some delay in completing the formal mandate to the bank but at some time, not later
than 2 February 1973, and probably earlier, Mr and Mrs Catlin instructed the bank in
writing that all orders for payment or transfer from the account were to be signed by
both of them. The mandate which they signed on 2 February 1973 was on BOCL's
standard form of application to open a joint account adapted for use by the bank. It listed
d their names at the top and they both signed it. All the directions to the bank were
expressed in the first person plural. Any overdraft on the account was to be their joint
and several responsibility. The mandate was contained in one document and was
expressed as a request by Mr and Mrs Catlin jointly to the bank. It is noteworthy that
Mrs Catlin had a special reason for insisting that the bank should only honour orders for
payment and transfer on the signature of both joint account holders: she and her husband
e had previously had a joint account operable on one signature only, and Mr Catlin had
taken advantage of this to make drawings for his own use and for purposes of which she
did not approve.

On 2 November 1972 a letter was sent to the bank in London in these terms:

'Re: Our nine months' notice account with you. No. 289.
Notice is hereby given to the effect that nine months from this date we will
f withdraw the balance of our above account with you, plus accrued interest. Unless
otherwise instructed please transfer above amount to Bank of Cyprus Ltd.,
Famagusta, in my favour.'

The letter was signed by Mr Catlin alone. At the top of the letter the name and address
of the sender were given as follows:—

g 'Mr. Gordon and Mrs. Barye Catlin,
c/o Riviera Court Hotel,
Kennedy Ave., Flat 25,
Famagusta.'

That was the address at which the family had lived but which Mr Catlin had just left.
The obvious misspelling of Mrs Catlin's name, left uncorrected, supports her evidence
h that she did not draft or type the letter. I accept that she knew nothing of it. The
probability is that the letter was typed at the BOC branch in Famagusta. The defendant
bank, perhaps mindful of their mandate, did not accept the instruction of Mr Catlin
alone. An approach was made to Mrs Catlin and resulted in a letter to the bank signed by
both joint account holders dated 2 January 1973. It read:

j 'Re: Our nine months' notice account with you. No. 289.
Further to our letter dated 2.11.72 requesting you to transfer the balance of our
above account with you to Bank of Cyprus Ltd., Famagusta, Cyprus, in our favour,
we hereby authorise you and request you to consider our instructions mentioned
therein final and irrevocable.'

Mr and Mrs Catlin signed the letter at BOC's local branch. It bore the same misspelling
of Mrs Catlin's name as the earlier letter.

At the expiry of the nine months' notice the sum standing to the credit of the joint
account, no 289, was transferred to a joint account with the BOC branch at Famagusta
and converted into Cyprus pounds. The Catlins could not complain of the transfer,
which was in accordance with their instructions, but they could and did complain of the
currency conversion which they had never required. On 28 August 1973 Mrs Catlin
typed a letter which both she and her husband signed, which included the following
paragraphs:

'At no time were you instructed to send this money for conversion into Cyprus
pounds. We gave instructions last November on advice from our then local bank
manager at Famagusta to request you to send the balance of the money to Famagusta
at the end of the nine months call. It was then on deposit with the above co. This
cash should have been left in sterling for us to decide what we wished to do with the
same. Furthermore we expected you to notify us of your intentions in sending this
cash prior to doing so. These instructions have reduced our account by over £317
and we do not agree that this should be our loss. As we have stated you had no
authority whatsoever to convert the same.'

There followed some little correspondence which culminated in the payment by the
bank of £234·94 in settlement of this exchange loss. Although an addressee of at least
three letters from the defendants, Mrs Catlin never saw them because her husband had
arranged for the post to go to him. She did not know the outcome of this incident until
she learned of it in the course of these proceedings.

Well before the exchange matter was settled, the funds transferred to Cyprus on the
Catlins' instructions had been transferred back to the bank in London. On 30 August
1973 these funds, amounting to £21,325·65, were placed in a nine months' notice joint
account in the name of Mr and Mrs Catlin. There was no new mandate, and no different
instructions were given to the defendants, but they gave this joint account a new number,
0316. No notice of this number, or of the fact that a new account had been opened, was
given to either account holder. Thus it was that the old account number was given when,
on 18 March 1974, Mr and Mrs Catlin met at the BOC branch in Famagusta to sign a
further instruction to the defendants:

'Re: Our nine months notice account. No. 289–739 external.
We hereby give you notice that we will withdraw balance of our account with
you in 9 months from today subject to confirmation by Bank of Cyprus Ltd.,
Famagusta, two weeks prior the 9 months.'

The object of this instruction plainly was to free the funds at the end of nine months
but to prevent their transfer to Cyprus. This letter was forwarded by BOC, and the
defendant bank confirmed the instructions received in a letter seen only by Mr Catlin. It
gave the first indication of the new account number, 0316.

By the autumn of 1974 the BOC branch in Famagusta was inaccessible because of the
invasions. Mrs Catlin and her children were in the refugee camp. So also was Mr Catlin,
but in a different part of a large camp. Relations between them were distant and formal.
On 18 November 1974 the Larnaca branch of the BOC forwarded to the defendant bank
a letter 'addressed to you by the above customers'. It was a letter showing the sender as
'Mr. Gordon and Mrs. Beryl Catlin, Anzio Camp, Dhekelia, Cyprus' and containing the
following:

'Re: our joint nine months notice account with you.
Regarding our above-mentioned account we hereby give you notice that no
amount should be transferred to Cyprus . . . After hearing from you we shall give
you instructions regarding the time of notice for which our above account should
be kept.'

It was signed by Mr Catlin alone. The defendant bank addressed its answer to Mr and
Mrs Catlin, care of BOC in Larnaca, but Mrs Catlin never saw it.

On 22 January 1975 BOC at Larnaca forwarded to the defendant bank a further letter
a 'addressed to you by your customer Mr. Gordon Catlin for action'. The letter showed the
sender as 'Mr. and Mrs. G. Catlin, now of Anzio Camp, BFPO 53, Dhekelia, Cyprus.' That
was an address at which the Catlins had never lived together and which Mrs Catlin, if she
had not already left it, was on the immediate point of leaving. The letter was signed by
Mr Catlin alone and read:

b   'Re: Joint nine months notice account. No. 45003164.
        Referring to the above account I hereby request you to make the following
arrangements.
        1. Transfer the sum of sterling £1,000 to the credit of the account of Mr. George
Giorgallides with Barclays Bank International Ltd., Piccadilly Branch, London.
        2. Transfer the sum of £1,000 sterling to a demand current account external
with Bank of Cyprus, London, Ltd., 27–31, Charlotte St., London, W.1. in my
c   name, i.e. in the name of Mr. Gordon Catlin, address as on head of this letter. Due
notice has already been given to you which expired in December, 1974.
        3. Transfer all remaining balance plus accrued interest into a three months'
notice external account in the joint names of Mr. and Mrs. G. Catlin with you which
will continue until you receive instructions. Kindly confirm that all above
        arrangements have been done and thank you for your kind services.
d   Yours faithfully, Gordon Catlin.'

In the left hand corner appeared the words: 'The signature of Mr. Gordon Catlin is
confirmed. Bank of Cyprus Ltd, Larnaca Branch', and the signature of the manager.
Some difficulty was caused by these instructions because the account of Mr Giorgallides
could not be traced. But on 25 or 26 February 1975 three transfers were made: £1,000
e was transferred into a current account in the name of Mr Giorgallides; £1,000 into a
current account no 4825 in the name of Mr Catlin; and the balance of £23,164·39 into a
joint three months' notice external account in the name of Mr and Mrs Catlin. This was
given the number 0284. These transfers were plainly in breach of mandate. There was
only one signature on the instruction. The defendant bank was, no doubt, ignorant of
the Catlins' circumstances, but BOC (acting as agents) were not, because when meetings
f at the branch had to be arranged for letters to be signed BOC had had to communicate
with Mr and Mrs Catlin at quite different addresses. From this new account further
transfers were made: on 17 June 1975, of £20,000 to a seven days' notice account in the
name of Mr Catlin alone; and on 23 September, of £3,893·13 to the same account. A
further transfer of the £20,000 sum was later made. In the course of these transactions a
number of letters were written by Mr Catlin in the format already noted, with the
g senders shown as himself and his wife 'now of Anzio Camp'. Three of the defendant
bank's acknowledgments were signed by Mr Andreas Constantinou, an employee of
BOCL seconded to act as the bank's deputy manager. Before acting on Mr Catlin's sole
instructions he asked to see the customer's mandate. It could not be found, possibly
because the bank and BOCL were in the course of moving, possibly because the account
number had changed, possibly because the document was in storage or mislaid. But Mr
h Constantinou concluded that he could safely act on Mr Catlin's instructions. A number
of things led him to this conclusion: they included what he was told by his manager and
the girls in the office; the form of Mr Catlin's instructions, assuming authority to give
instructions and showing that he and Mrs Catlin were living together; and the verification
of Mr Catlin's signature by the BOC manager in Larnaca. These things explain, but
cannot excuse, the defendant bank's failure to comply with a very clear mandate. In
j about March 1976 Mr Constantinou learned the truth; he saw the original joint mandate
signed in February 1973 and satisfied himself that there had been no other mandate. He
realised that an irregularity had occurred and tried to rectify it, but the only opportunity
to do so was in respect of the current account no 4825 in Mr Catlin's name into which
£1,000 had been transferred on 25 February 1975. On 31 March 1976 he wrote a letter
to BOCL, where that account was:

'Re: Mr. G.F. Catlin. Current Account No. 11048253.

Please note that as a result of an error on our behalf we advised you in March, *a* 1975 to proceed with the opening of the above current account in spite of the fact that our original mandate was in the joint names of Mr. G.F. Catlin and Mrs. B. Catlin and that both signatures were necessary for the operation of the account. You are therefore requested to close current account No. 11048253 and establish a new account in the above mentioned joint names, bearing in mind that both signatures are required for any movement on this account.'   *b*

The result of his letter was that account no 4825 was closed, with a note that there was to be no further movement on the account without reference to head office. The funds in the account, amounting to £897·26, were transferred to a new joint current account in the names of Mr and Mrs Catlin, Anzio Camp. There the funds remain.

The position of Mrs Catlin meanwhile had been unenviable. She had received no correspondence. She had received no bank statements since before, probably well before, *c* July 1974 (and it is not suggested that any had been sent to her). She had lived on money sent from her building society account in Liverpool, with additional gifts from her brother. She had lost her home and most of her possessions and had two children to support. Her only major asset remaining was (as she thought) her interest in joint account no 289. But she began to hear whispers that all was not well with this account, and wisely decided to make inquiries of the defendant bank and BOCL. Between August 1975 and *d* November 1976 she wrote six letters. All of them reached the bank or BOCL but all were ignored except the last, to which she received only a very unsatisfactory answer and this was after the British High Commission had become involved. Some attempt was made to arrange a meeting between her and the bank's legal adviser in Cyprus in the summer of 1976, but she did not receive notice of the appointment until two months after it should have taken place (by which time the legal adviser was safely home in London). *e* That was no fault of the bank but it took two further letters from Mrs Catlin before, for the first time, she received any account of what had happened. She then learned that £897·26 in a current account was all that remained of her asset.

The factual contest between Mrs Catlin and the defendant bank before me was very limited. It was contended by the bank that Mrs Catlin had given her husband actual authority to conduct the original joint account on her behalf as well as his own. Reliance *f* was placed on the letters of 2 November 1972 and 2 January 1973, and 18 March and 18 November 1974 (to which I have referred) as showing such authority. It was said to be contrary to the inherent probabilities that Mrs Catlin should not have discussed these matters with her husband and authorised him to act as he did. Having heard Mrs Catlin (although not Mr Catlin) give evidence, and having studied the documents, I am quite satisfied that this suggestion is entirely wrong. Mrs Catlin was ready to accept her *g* husband's (and the bank manager's) advice on where the joint account moneys could most advantageously be deposited, but she had originally insisted on joint signatures to prevent depredations on the joint account by her husband and nothing which had happened since could have had any other effect than to strengthen her reliance on that safeguard. Although in the witness box Mrs Catlin showed a surprising lack of bitterness, I feel quite sure that she was at all times determined that her husband should not have *h* unimpeded access to the account.

The factual position can therefore be put very shortly. Mrs Catlin and her husband deposited funds in a joint deposit account with the bank on terms of an express mandate that no payment out of the account should be made save on the joint signatures of both account holders. In breach of that mandate, and without the knowledge or authority of Mrs Catlin, the bank negligently transferred all the funds out of the account on the *j* instructions of Mr Catlin and to his use. Mrs Catlin has, as a result, suffered a loss to the extent of her half-share interest in the funds in the account, reduced only by her half-share interest in the sum of £897·26 which remains. One might suppose that there could be no answer to her claim. But the bank submits, in reliance on authority and legal

principle, that it must fail. I should be sorry to conclude that it is right. Mrs Catlin has
a suffered serious loss through no fault of her own. A rule that denies her any remedy in
such circumstances is not one that could be viewed with complacency.

The linchpin of the bank's argument was the decision of McNair J in *Brewer v
Westminster Bank Ltd* [1952] 2 All ER 650, and I need hardly say that any decision of that
learned and experienced judge, particularly in a field such as this, commands the utmost
respect. The facts were that two executors opened a joint account with the defendant
b bank, to be operated on both their signatures. One of the executors, forging the signature
of his co-executor and fellow joint account holder, drew cheques on the account and
applied the proceeds to his own use. The innocent executor sued the bank and her co-
executor for a declaration that the bank had wrongly debited the joint account with the
sum of the forged cheques. The judge dismissed the plaintiff's claim. His reasoning
which led to this conclusion involved four steps. (1) The obligation undertaken by the
c bank towards the joint account holders was a single obligation owed to them jointly to
honour drawings signed by them both. (2) The single joint right of the account holders
against the bank could be enforced only if both joint contractors were parties, the guilty
joint contractor being joined as a defendant if he was unwilling to be joined as a plaintiff.
(3) It made no difference whether the guilty co-contractor were joined as plaintiff or
defendant, since in either event the issue fell to be determined as if he were a plaintiff.
d (4) If the guilty co-contractor had been joined as a plaintiff the claim would have been
bound to fail, since a party may not found an action on his own misconduct.

In support of step (1) the judge relied on the Court of Appeal decision in *Hirschhorn v
Evans* [1938] 3 All ER 491, [1938] 2 KB 801, which, following the earlier Court of Appeal
decision in *Macdonald v Tacquah Gold Mines Co* (1884) 13 QBD 535, undoubtedly
establishes that a debt owed to one of two joint account holders cannot be garnisheed in
e respect of a debt owed by one of the joint account holders only since the former debt is
owed to the joint account holders jointly and not to either of them severally. Step (2)
reflected the principle, never to my knowledge doubted, that joint obligations must be
jointly enforced, with procedural consequences which are familiar. Steps (3) and (4)
depended on a general principle stated by Crompton J in *Brandon v Scott* (1857) 7 E & B
234 at 237, 119 ER 1234 at 1235 in this way:

f
> 'The principle is, that several cannot sue at law jointly, unless each one is in a
> position to sue. The decisions cited establish that, where a person is disabled from
> suing alone, he cannot enable himself to sue by joining others as coplaintiffs.'

In that case goods jointly deposited by three depositors had been wrongly delivered to
one of the three, who subsequently sued with the other two depositors in respect of the
g wrongful delivery of the goods. It was held that since he was disabled from complaining
of the defendants' conduct in giving the goods to him, so also were his co-plaintiffs who
depended on the same joint title to bring suit.

In *Brewer's* case the judge acquitted the bank of any negligence, so skilful were the
forgeries, with the result that both bank and plaintiff were equally the victim of the
forger's fraud. The present case is different, since the bank acted in clear breach of an
h express mandate with no plausible excuse for doing so. None the less, the ratio of that
decision clearly covers this case and on the judge's premise of a single obligation owed by
the bank to the account holders jointly his reasoning cannot be faulted. But the decision
is not free from difficulty, even if the merits are put on one side. It takes no account of
Twibell v London Suburban Bank [1869] WN 127, which was not cited to him, a decision
which, although inadequately reported, shows that on facts indistinguishable from the
j present a joint contractor recovered damages in the Court of Common Pleas in respect of
a wrongly honoured cheque for a moiety of the sum for which the cheque was drawn.
Furthermore, at the end of his judgment McNair J said ([1952] 2 All ER 650 at 656):

> 'The final point with which I need deal is that raised in para. 3A of the defence,
> namely, that by paying the amount of the forged cheques to the second defendant,

the bank obtained a good discharge against both executors. It was frankly and
necessarily admitted by counsel on behalf of the bank that the logical consequence
of this submission was that the bank could have obtained a good discharge against   *a*
the plaintiff if they had—contrary to the express terms of the mandate—paid the
second defendant against cheques bearing his signature alone. It is sufficient for me
to say that as at present advised the defendant bank's contention on this plea seems
to me to be inconsistent with the decisions in *Stone* v. *Marsh* ((1827) 6 B & C 551,
108 ER 554); *Innes (assignee of R. & C. Hingeston, Bankrupts)* v. *Stephenson* ((1831) 1   *b*
Mood & R 145, 174 ER 50); and *Husband* v. *Davis* ((1851) 10 CB 645, 138 ER 256).'

Having studied those cases I respectfully agree with the judge's tentative conclusion
concerning them; but if payment to one joint contractor in breach of mandate does not
give the debtor a good discharge, so that his obligation remains, it is anomalous that such
obligation should be unenforceable by either or both of the joint contractors.

The decision in *Brewer's* case has not been allowed to sleep in peace. An appeal by the   *c*
unsuccessful plaintiff to the Court of Appeal was settled by the bank at the end of
counsel's opening, apparently on terms that she recovered damages and was indemnified
against her costs. Professor Glanville Williams criticised the decision, suggesting that
since payment to one joint contractor was not a performance of the bank's duty to pay
both jointly, being something outside of and irrelevant to the contractual obligation, the
proper solution was for both contractors to join in an action against the bank, which   *d*
could counterclaim against the contractor who had received payment (see (1953) 16 MLR
232). The late Sir Arthur Goodhart suggested a different solution: the bank made an
agreement with the executors jointly that it would honour any drawings signed by them
jointly and it also made a separate agreement with each of the executors severally that it
would not honour any drawings unless he or she had signed them (see (1953) 68 LQR
446). In *Welch v Bank of England* [1955] 1 All ER 811 at 821, [1955] Ch 508 at 532,   *e*
Harman J professed not to understand the decision in *Brewer's* case, observing that the
joint interest point, if a good defence in law, was none in equity, but that was a case based
on a right of property, on which ground Devlin J in *Baker v Barclays Bank Ltd* [1955] 2 All
ER 571 at 579, [1955] 1 WLR 822 at 831 distinguished both it and that case from *Brewer*;
he pointed out, without questioning the decision in *Brewer*, that it was concerned with a
contractual obligation only. In *Ardern v Bank of New South Wales* [1956] VLR 569 the   *f*
Supreme Court of Victoria was confronted with a case indistinguishable from *Brewer*:
after detailed argument Martin J adopted what may be called the Goodhart solution,
following *Twibell's* case and declining to follow *Brewer*. In *Jackson v White and Midland
Bank Ltd* [1967] 2 Lloyd's Rep 68, where a similar point arose yet again, Park J adopted
the same course, having fully reviewed the authorities. The editors of *Paget's Law of
Banking* (8th edn 1972) pp 76–79 criticise *Brewer* and clearly approve the decision of Park   *g*
J. It is highly undesirable that this question should continue to be litigated.

It is clear that the ordinary relationship of banker and customer is that of debtor and
creditor, the debt owed by one to the other being a legal chose in action. It is equally
clear that a sum standing to the credit of a joint account is a debt owed to the creditors
jointly, not enforceable by either on his own. But was McNair J correct in his premise of
a single obligation owed by the bank to the account holders or was Sir Arthur Goodhart   *h*
right to postulate a separate agreement with each of the executors severally that the bank
would not honour drawings unless he or she had signed them? It was pointed out on
behalf of these defendants that the mandate was a single document, signed by each joint
account holder and containing no hint of anything other than a joint obligation save
where a joint and several responsibility for any overdraft was expressly provided for. But
it is still necessary to consider whether a single obligation owed jointly exhausts what   *j*
may be taken to be the undoubted contractual intention of the parties so far as the duty
of the bank is concerned. The defendants agreed to honour instructions signed by both
account holders. This no doubt imported a negative duty not to honour instructions not
signed by both account holders. This duty also could, in theory, have been owed jointly,
but it must (to make sense) have been owed to the account holders severally, because the
only purpose of requiring two signatures was to obviate the possibility of independent

action by one account holder to the detriment of the other. A duty on the defendants
a which could only be enforced jointly with the party against the possibility of whose
misconduct a safeguard was sought, and where the occurrence of such misconduct
through the negligent breach of mandate by the defendants would deprive the innocent
party of any remedy, would in practical terms be worthless. Indeed, it would be worse
than worthless, because a customer would reasonably rely on the two-signature safeguard
and refrain from active supervision of the account, only to find when loss (allegedly
b irreparable) has resulted that the reliance was misplaced. The reality of this transaction
was otherwise. Mrs Catlin wanted, and thought she had obtained, an undertaking from
the bank that orders for payment would not be honoured without her signature. I cannot
conceive that the bank for its part did not intend to incur such an obligation to her (and
also, mutatis mutandis, to Mr Catlin). Had she raised the question at the outset I feel sure
that they would have assured her of the personal protection which she obtained from the
c mandate. The duty of complying with a simple mandate on pain of indemnifying the
customer is not, after all, something which is to a banker either unfamiliar or onerous.
In my opinion the Goodhart solution reflects the substance of the bargain which the
parties made. I conclude that Mrs Catlin is entitled in principle to the relief which she
seeks. I will hear counsel as to the precise sum for which judgment should be given, and
on interest.
d   I should mention briefly one procedural matter canvassed before me. Counsel for the
bank objected that in this case, unlike almost all the others except *Ardern*, the fellow
joint contractor was not a party, either as plaintiff or defendant. That was said to
invalidate the proceedings. Counsel for Mrs Catlin defended the non-joinder of Mr Catlin
as a defendant on the ground that the plaintiff's case rested on a several, not a joint,
obligation, and in omitting to join Mr Catlin the plaintiff had had the procedural courage
e of her substantive convictions. Whether, had I taken a different view, I could and would
have ordered the joinder of Mr Catlin under RSC Ord 15, r 6, I need not pause to consider,
since it follows from my conclusion on the legal issue that I consider the non-joinder of
Mr Catlin to have been justified.
    I turn lastly to the bank's claim for an indemnity against Mr Catlin as third party. He
served points of defence in December 1978 and gave further and better particulars in
f March 1982 but was debarred from defending for want of discovery later in that month.
He played no part in the hearing before me. The effective claim by the bank against Mr
Catlin was that in 1974 and 1975 he falsely represented that he (a) had the authority of
Mrs Catlin to give instructions in relation to the moneys held on account by the bank
and (b) was at all material times living with Mrs Catlin at Anzio Camp, Dhekelia, Cyprus.
Thus the claim was laid in deceit, the essence of it being that Mr Catlin had misled the
g bank into believing that he had authority to give instructions on Mrs Catlin's behalf. The
representations were made in the letters from which I have quoted the most material
passages. Mr Catlin must have known that he did not have authority to act for Mrs Catlin
but quite deliberately framed his letters to suggest that he had. Evidence of the bank's
reliance on these representations as a significant, although not sole, cause of their conduct,
was given by Mr Constantinou and I accept it. I hold the bank's claim to be made out.
h They are entitled to judgment against Mr Catlin for the sum which they are ordered to
pay Mrs Catlin.
    I should like in conclusion to compliment counsel for the bank, on his conduct of this
case. It was not an easy, still less an attractive, case to present but in his conduct of it he
showed skill, tact and good judgment of a high order.

i *Judgment for the plaintiff against the defendant bank in the sum of £12,497, with interest.*
Judgment for the bank against the third party, Mr Catlin, in the third party proceedings for the
sum which they must pay to the plaintiff.

Solicitors: *Davis Campbell & Co*, Liverpool (for the plaintiff); *Payne Hicks Beach & Co* (for
the bank).

K Mydeen Esq   Barrister.

Windsor and Maidenhead Royal Borough Council v Brandrose Investments Ltd

COURT OF APPEAL, CIVIL DIVISION
LAWTON, GRIFFITHS AND DILLON LJJ
16, 17 DECEMBER 1982, 27 JANUARY 1983

Town and country planning – Conservation area – Control of demolition – Agreement between planning authority and developer allowing development of land in conservation area – Agreement not specifically prohibiting demolition of buildings on land – Development not capable of being carried out without demolition of buildings – Developer demolishing buildings without consent of planning authority – Whether consent of authority necessary for demolition of buildings – Whether agreement containing implied consent of authority to demolition – Whether authority able to prohibit demolition in spite of implied consent in agreement – Town and Country Planning Act 1971, ss 52(3), 277A(2).

The defendants owned land and buildings adjoining land owned by the local planning authority. In January 1976 the defendants and the local authority entered into two agreements, namely a land exchange agreement and an agreement under s 52ᵃ of the Town and Country Planning Act 1971, to enable both parties to develop their sites. As the local authority well knew the development of the defendants' site could not be carried out without demolishing certain buildings which stood on the site. Section 52(1) provided that a local planning authority could enter into an agreement with any person interested in land in its area for the purpose of restricting or regulating the development or use of that land. Section 52(3)(a) further provided that nothing in s 52 or in any agreement made thereunder was to be construed as restricting 'any powers exercisable by [a local planning authority] so long as those powers were exercised in accordance with . . . a development plan, or . . . directions . . . given by the Secretary of State'. There was no development plan or direction of the Secretary of State affecting the defendants' site. In October 1976 the local authority granted the defendants outline planning permission to develop their property along the lines contemplated by the two agreements but in March 1978 the local authority designated a conservation area, pursuant to s 277ᵇ of the 1971 Act, which included the defendants' site. Under s 277A(2)ᶜ of the 1971 Act a building in a conservation area could not be demolished without the specific consent of

---

a Section 52, so far as material, provides:
   '(1) A local planning authority may enter into an agreement with any person interested in land in their area for the purpose of restricting or regulating the development or use of the land, either permanently or during such period as may be prescribed by the agreement; and any such agreement may contain such incidental or consequential provisions (including provisions of a financial character) as appear to the local planning authority to be necessary or expedient for the purposes of the agreement.
   (2) An agreement made under this section with any person interested in land may be enforced by the local planning authority against persons deriving title under that person in respect of that land, as if the local planning authority were possessed of adjacent land and as if the agreement had been expressed to be made for the benefit of such land.
   (3) Nothing in this section or in any agreement made thereunder shall be construed—(a) as restricting the exercise, in relation to land which is the subject of any such agreement, of any powers exercisable by any Minister or authority under this Act so long as those powers are exercised in accordance with the provisions of the development plan, or in accordance with any directions which may have been given by the Secretary of State as to the provisions to be included in such a plan; or (b) as requiring the exercise of any such powers otherwise than as mentioned in paragraph (a) of this subsection . . .'
b Section 277, so far as material, is set out at p 823 a b, post
c Section 277A(2) is set out at p 821 a, post

the local authority. In June 1979 the defendants started to demolish the buildings on
a their site without the local authority's consent. The local authority issued a writ seeking
an injunction to restrain the defendants from demolishing the buildings and a declaration
that they were not entitled to demolish them. At the trial the defendants contended that
the effect of s 52(3)(a) was that the local authority was only prohibited from restricting
its powers by agreement if there was a development plan or a direction given by the
Secretary of State affecting the property, and in the absence of such a plan or direction
b the local authority had effectively bound itself by the s 52 agreement not to use its powers
to designate the defendants' site as a conservation area. The issues arose (i) whether the
local authority could lawfully enter into an agreement having the effect of disentitling it
from requiring consent under s 277A to the demolition of the buildings, and (ii) if so,
whether the agreement it had entered into with the defendants under s 52 had that
effect. The judge held that in the absence of a development plan or a direction of the
c Secretary of State the s 52 agreement had the effect in law of limiting the local authority's
power to take steps to prevent the demolition of the buildings and further held that the
local authority could not use its statutory powers under s 277A to prevent such demolition.
The plaintiffs appealed.

Held – On the true construction of s 52(3) of the 1971 Act a local planning authority was
d not empowered by s 52(3) to bind itself by an agreement not to exercise the powers
conferred on it by s 277 of the 1971 Act to designate areas as conservation areas which it
had a public duty to exercise. Since neither s 52 itself nor the s 52 agreement could
inhibit the local authority from including the defendants' land in the conservation area,
the buildings on the defendants' land were subject to the prohibition against demolition
imposed by s 277A(2) of the 1971 Act at the time the defendants started to demolish
e them, and in the absence of the local authority's consent they were not entitled to
demolish the buildings even though the land exchange agreement, the s 52 agreement
and the grant of planning permission by the local authority had all proceeded on the
basis that the buildings would have to be demolished. The appeal would accordingly be
allowed (see p 822 *e* and *j* to p 823 *a* and *d* to *f* post).

f **Notes**
For demolition of buildings in conservation areas, see 34 Halsbury's Laws (4th edn) para
686.
For agreements with a local planning authority regulating development or use of land,
see 37 Halsbury's Laws (3rd edn) 276, para 374, and for cases on the subject, see 45 Digest
g Repl) 334–335, 31–32.
For the Town and Country Planning Act 1971, s 52, see 41 Halsbury's Statutes (3rd
edn) 1648, and for ss 277, 277A of that Act (as inserted by the Town and Country
Amenities Act 1974, s 1), see 44 ibid 1744, 1745.

Cases cited
h *Birkdale District Electric Supply Co v Southport Corp* [1926] AC 355, HL.
Ransom & Luck Ltd v Surbiton BC [1949] 1 All ER 185, [1949] Ch 180, CA.
Reardon Smith Line Ltd v Hansen-Tangen [1976] 3 All ER 570, [1976] 1 WLR 989, HL.
Shindler v Northern Raincoat Co Ltd [1960] 2 All ER 239, [1960] 1 WLR 1038, Assizes.

j **Appeal**
The plaintiffs, Windsor and Maidenhead Royal Borough Council, appealed against the
judgment of Fox J ([1981] 3 All ER 38, [1981] 1 WLR 1083) on 6 February 1981 whereby
he dismissed the plaintiffs' claim against the defendants, Brandrose Investments Ltd, for
a declaration that the defendants were not entitled to demolish the buildings known as
107–111 Peascod Street without obtaining the consent of the plaintiffs, the local planning

authority, pursuant to s 277A of the Town and Country Planning Act 1971. The facts are set out in the judgment of Lawton LJ.

Lionel Read QC and *Timothy Stow* for the plaintiffs.
Kenneth Bagnall QC and *Kirk Reynolds* for the defendants.

Cur adv vult

27 January. The following judgment of the court was delivered.

LAWTON LJ. This is an appeal by the plaintiffs against an order made by Fox J on 6 February 1981, whereby he dismissed the plaintiffs' claim against the defendants for a declaration that the defendants had not been entitled in law to demolish, as they had done, certain buildings known as 107–111 Peascod Street, Windsor (see [1981] 3 All ER 38, [1981] 1 WLR 1083).

The plaintiffs in this court have accepted that their claim has no merit and that it could have been dismissed by the judge on the ground that it was not a proper case for the making of the declaration claimed. They have appealed, so their counsel told us, because the judge, when dismissing their claim, gave as his reason for doing so his construction of s 52 of the Town and Country Planning Act 1971, which they submitted was wrong and which, if not corrected by this court, was likely to have serious consequences in the application and administration of planning legislation.

In or about 1973 the defendants, who are property developers, had, or expected to get, proprietary rights over 107–111 Peascod Street, which is part of the main shopping area of Windsor and near the castle. The plaintiffs owned land to the rear of 107–111 Peascod Street. Both parties wanted to develop what they had got. Between 1973 and 1975 they negotiated to see whether they could develop their holdings together. These negotiations came to nothing. The plaintiffs then started compulsory purchase proceedings to acquire the defendants' holdings. These proceedings were compromised. Two agreements, both dated 22 January 1976, gave effect to the compromise. Their general purport, so far as relevant to this appeal, was as follows. A building line was agreed. The defendants were to develop the Peascod Street side of it, the plaintiffs the other. Pieces of land on the wrong side of the building line from each party's standpoint were to be exchanged. The declared object of the exchange was to enable each party 'successfully to complete its own development' (see the third recital of the land exchange agreement). The other agreement was declared to be made by the plaintiffs as 'local planning authority' and its third recital was in these terms:

'IT IS INTENDED that the development of the land of the Developer [that is the defendants] and the incidental development of the Corporation's land shall be regulated in accordance with the provisions of Section 52 of the Town and Country Planning Act 1971.'

Clause 2(a) provided as follows:

'THE CORPORATION hereby covenants and agrees with the Developer that the Developer may build up to the said line "X" "Y" "Z" and along its length at levels "B" "D" and "E" on the said plan No. 2.'

There followed detailed provisions about building heights. In this court it was accepted by the plaintiffs that the defendants could not start the development contemplated by these two agreements without demolishing the buildings which then stood in Peascod Street. These buildings had no architectural or historic interest in themselves but whilst standing they formed part of an attractive town vista towards the castle.

On 5 October 1976 the plaintiffs granted the defendants outline planning permission to develop their Peascod Street site along the lines contemplated by the two agreements; but the parties had difficulty in agreeing the details of the design and external appearance of the buildings to be erected. These were not settled until the beginning of 1982.

a On 29 March 1978 the plaintiffs designated an area, which included the part of Peascod Street which the defendants intended to develop, as a conservation area pursuant to s 277 of the Town and Country Planning Act 1971, as amended by the Town and Country Amenities Act 1974. Section 277A(2) of the 1971 Act, as amended, provided: 'A building to which this section applies shall not be demolished without the consent of the appropriate authority.' The section did apply to Peascod Street. Subsection (3) made it clear that consent to demolition had to be given specifically and was not to be inferred b from the grant of planning permission. It followed, prima facie, that once the conservation order had been made the defendants could not lawfully demolish the buildings standing on their land in Peascod Street which had to be demolished, as the plaintiffs well knew, before they could start the development which the plaintiffs had given them planning permission to carry out and which the plaintiffs had intended to be part of a large-scale development of an important part of Windsor's main shopping area. In these c circumstances, by any standard other than those which sometimes are applied in town halls, the problem of consent to demolish could, indeed should, have been settled without recourse to litigation. The plaintiffs had acquired benefits under the two agreements by reason of the exchange of land and the arrangements for building up to an agreed line without regard to ancient lights and certain rights of way. Provided they were satisfied that the defendants did not intend, after demolishing the existing buildings, to leave an d ugly gap in Peascod Street for a long time they could not properly have refused consent to demolish.

Unfortunately, on or about 29 June 1979, whether through ignorance or wilfully and without the plaintiffs' consent, the defendants started to demolish their buildings. Even if the defendants had behaved wilfully the plaintiffs should have been able to deal with the problem without recourse to law. They preferred to call the law in aid.

e On 2 July 1979 they applied for and obtained ex parte an injunction restraining the defendants for a short time from demolishing or continuing to demolish their buildings in Peascod Street. The next day they issued a writ claiming an injunction to restrain the defendants from demolishing the buildings and a declaration that they were not entitled to demolish them. In addition they served the defendants with two enforcement notices. They next applied to Walton J for their ex parte injunction to be continued until trial. f On 11 July 1979 he refused to make such an order, giving as a reason that the agreement which the plaintiffs, as local planning authority, had made with the defendants pursuant to s 52 of the Town and Country Planning Act 1971 may have entitled the defendants to demolish the buildings. The defendants went on doing so.

Despite this lack of initial success the plaintiffs pursued their claim, but without marked diligence. A statement of claim was delivered on 27 February 1980 claiming g only a declaration. By this date the buildings had been demolished so there was no point in asking for an injunction. The defendants delivered a defence on 16 May 1980. For the purposes of this appeal, the important paragraph in their defence was in these terms:

h '... upon a true construction of Section 52 of the said Act and of the agreement made thereunder dated 22nd January 1976, and by reason of the other matters hereinbefore referred to, the Plaintiffs' power to include the Defendants' said land and buildings in a Conservation Area could be exercised only in accordance with the terms of any statutorily authorised development plan. The Plaintiffs' purported exercise of their said powers was not in accordance with any such plan, and was for that reason also void and of no effect.'

j They then applied by sumons to strike out the plaintiffs' statement of claim as disclosing no cause of action. That summons was adjourned into court before Fox J and heard by him on 6 February 1981. By this time the enforcement notices had been withdrawn. On learning what was involved in the case and that all the facts were agreed the judge suggested that the hearing should be treated as the trial of the action. Both parties agreed. After argument he dismissed the plaintiffs' claim. He stated his conclusion in these terms ([1981] 3 All ER 38 at 45, [1981] 1 WLR 1083 at 1091):

'My conclusion, therefore, is the same as that of Walton J, namely that in view of s 52(3) the plaintiffs cannot use any of their statutory powers against the defendants to prevent the demolition of the buildings, unless what the plaintiffs are proposing is in accordance with the development plan. There was not and is not any development plan. The result, in my view, is that the plaintiffs could not enforce their powers under s 277A in relation to the extension of the conservation area, so as to prevent the demolition of these Peascod Street buildings.'

It is that conclusion which has led to this appeal, the determination of which, in our judgment, turns on the construction of s 52 when considered in its context in the 1971 Act as amended. We regard the context as a most important aid to the construction of s 52. Both in and out of context, however, s 52 is a most difficult section to construe. Counsel for the plaintiffs, with all his experience of this planning legislation, was driven to concentrate on what sub-s (3) did not mean rather than on what it did.

We start with its position in the Act. Section 52 comes in Part III, which is headed 'General Planning Control'. Planning control applies to development as defined in s 22 and planning permission is required, subject to exceptions, for the carrying out of any development of land. There are to be local planning authorities to whom applications for planning permission shall be made. Specific classes of person likely to be affected by the grant of planning permission are to be given notice of applications (see ss 26, 27 and 28). Under s 29 local planning authorities are to determine applications for planning permission but when doing so they 'shall have regard to the provisions of the development plan, so far as material to the application, and to any other material considerations' and may grant planning permission, unconditionally or subject to such conditions as they think fit, or refuse. Section 29 is the linchpin of this part of the Act. When exercising their powers under it a local planning authority are performing a public duty. They cannot bind themselves in advance how they will perform it, nor can they do more than what the Act says they can do. They can impose conditions on the grant of planning permission but they have no power under s 29, nor any other section, to make an applicant comply with their conditions; but if he fails to do so his planning permission will lapse. An applicant, however, may be willing to undertake to comply with the conditions. He may indicate his willingness in negotiations with the local planning authority before making an application, as may happen when a large-scale development is being planned; or he may do so when he learns what conditions the local planning authority intend to impose. Section 52(1) empowers a local planning authority to make agreements to achieve ends which they could not achieve without the consent of an applicant for planning permission. It does not empower a local planning authority to grant planning permission otherwise than as provided by ss 26 to 29 of the Act. It follows that an agreement made pursuant to s 52 before planning permission has been granted, as the relevant agreement in this case was, may become irrelevant if planning permission is not granted or ineffective if conditions are imposed inconsistent with the agreement because circumstances may change between the time when a s 52 agreement is made and when the local planning authority comes to perform their public duty of determining a planning application. Were the law otherwise, s 52 agreements would be the equivalents of planning permissions to the prejudice of those entitled under ss 26 to 28 to object to grants. Section 52(2) enables a local planning authority to enforce an agreement made under sub-s (1) against persons deriving title from the other party to the agreement. Counsel for the defendants did not suggest that the relevant agreement in this case operated to give the defendants planning permission. They did not think it had done so when they made it because they applied for planning permission in October 1976; and, even if it had operated to grant planning permission, it would not have got rid of the need for consent to demolish under the conservation order unless s 52 conferred such a power. As we have already pointed out, sub-s (1) confers powers which are merely incidental to the granting of planning permission. We can see no other purpose behind that subsection. Nor can we construe the difficult sub-s (3) as restricting the exercise by a

local planning authority of any of their statutory powers which they have a public duty
a   to exercise. It is trite law that a statutory body which has public duties to perform (and a
local planning authority are such a body) cannot lawfully agree not to exercise its powers.
Under s 277(1) of the 1971 Act, as amended:

> 'Every local planning authority shall from time to time determine which parts of
> their area are areas of special architectural or historic interest the character or
> appearance of which it is desirable to preserve or enhance, and shall designate such
b   > areas as conservation areas.'

The plaintiffs performed this statutory duty and decided to include part of Peascod Street
in a new conservation area. There is no suggestion, and certainly no evidence, that they
acted in bad faith. The Act provides no means for persons claiming to be adversely
affected by a conservation order to get it set aside. Once such an order has been made,
c   s 277A(2) applies. Local planning authorities were given no dispensing powers but the
Secretary of State was (see sub-s (4)). He has given directions under that subsection. One
of them is that s 277A shall not apply to '. . . (d) any building required to be demolished
by virtue of any provisions of an agreement made under section 52 of the Act' (see
Department of the Environment circular 23/77). It was accepted by counsel for the
defendants in this court that the s 52 agreement in this case did not require the defendants
d   to demolish any buildings. In these circumstances we find it impossible to say that there
is anything either in s 52 itself or in the s 52 agreement which should have inhibited the
plaintiffs from including 107–111 Peascod Street in the conservation area.

Whatever s 52(3) means, and we share the bemusement of counsel for the plaintiffs, it
cannot in our judgment be construed as empowering a local planning authority to bind
themselves not to exercise the powers given to them by s 277 of the Act which they have
e   a public duty to exercise.

It follows that the defendants were not entitled to demolish their buildings without
the plaintiffs' consent and that they have suffered no damage as a result of the plaintiffs
obtaining an ex parte injunction on 2 July 1979. In the exercise of discretion we would
not, however, grant the plaintiffs the declaration which they claimed. In our opinion this
litigation should never have started. To the limited extent indicated we would allow the
f   appeal.

*Appeal allowed but in exercise of court's discretion no declaration granted. Leave to appeal to
House of Lords refused.*

Solicitors: *B P Smith*, Maidenhead (for the plaintiffs); *Lovegrove & Durant*, Windsor (for
the defendants).

Mary Rose Plummer   Barrister.

Selvanayagam v University of the West Indies

a

PRIVY COUNCIL

LORD FRASER OF TULLYBELTON, LORD SCARMAN, LORD BRIDGE OF HARWICH, LORD BRANDON OF OAKBROOK AND LORD TEMPLEMAN

13 DECEMBER 1982, 14 FEBRUARY 1983

b

Damages – Mitigation of loss – Reasonable steps to mitigate damage – Standard of reasonableness – Personal injury – Plaintiff rejecting medical recommendation of surgery for injury – Reasonableness of refusal of surgery – Burden of proof – Whether reasonableness to be judged in light of all the circumstances including the medical advice or only in light of the medical advice.

c

Privy Council – Damages – Appeal – Erroneous assessment by trial judge – Substitution of Board's own assessment – Board's practice.

A plaintiff in an action for damages for personal injuries who rejects a medical recommendation in favour of surgery must, in order to discharge the burden on him of proving that he acted reasonably in regard to his duty to mitigate his damage, prove not d just that, in view of the medical advice taken alone, his refusal to have surgery was reasonable, but that in all the circumstances, including in particular the medical advice, he acted reasonably in refusing surgery (see p 827 *c* to *g*, post); dictum of Lord Merriman P in *The Guildford* [1956] 2 All ER at 919 and *Fazlic v Milingimbi Community Inc* (1981) 38 ALR 424 applied; dictum of Viscount Simon LC in *Richardson v Redpath Brown & Co Ltd* [1944] 1 All ER at 112 considered. e

Although on an appeal to it the Judicial Committee of the Privy Council has the power to substitute its own assessment of damages for an erroneous award made by the trial judge, it is not the Board's practice to do so, because it lacks knowledge of the relevant local conditions and circumstances; instead the Board will remit the question of damages to the local court for assessment on the basis of the rulings given by the Board on the appeal (see p 828 *e* to *g*, post); dicta of Lord Diplock in *Paul v Rendell* (1981) 34 ALR at f 579, 581 applied.

Notes

For a plaintiff's duty to mitigate his loss and the standard of conduct required of him in that respect, see 12 Halsbury's Laws (4th edn) paras 1193–1194, and for cases on the subject, see 17 Digest (Reissue) 124–133, 242–302. g

For interference by the Judicial Committee of the Privy Council with the trial judge's assessment of local matters, see 10 Halsbury's Laws (4th edn) para 821.

Cases referred to in judgment

Fazlic v Milingimbi Community Inc (1981) 38 ALR 424, Aust HC.

Guildford, The, ss Temple Bar (owners) v mv Guildford (owners) [1956] 2 All ER 915, [1956] h P 364, [1956] 3 WLR 474, 42 Digest (Reissue) 915, 7095.

Paul v Rendell (1981) 34 ALR 569, PC.

Richardson v Redpath Brown & Co Ltd [1944] 1 All ER 110, [1944] AC 62, HL, 34 Digest (Repl) 600, 4112.

Appeal

j

Ponnampalam Selvanayagam appealed with the leave of the Court of Appeal of Trinidad and Tobago granted on 9 March 1981 against a judgment of that court (Corbin, Kelsick and Hassanali JJA) given on 31 July 1980 whereby the court allowed the appeal of the respondent, the University of the West Indies, against the judgment of the High Court of Trinidad and Tobago (Scott J) awarding the appellant damages for personal injury of a $77,527·92 with costs and interest against the respondent and substituted an award of $31,001·95 with interest and dismissed the appellant's cross-appeal on the quantum of damages. The facts are set out in the judgment of the Board.

Fenton Ramsahoye SC (of the Trinidad and Tobago Bar) and *Stephen Sedley* for the appellant. *Stuart McKinnon QC* and *Patrick Twigg* for the respondent.

b   14 February. The following judgment of the Board was delivered.

LORD SCARMAN. The appellant is the plaintiff in an action for damages for personal injuries brought in the High Court of Trinidad and Tobago against the respondent, the University of the West Indies. He established liability, rebutted a defence of contributory negligence and recovered judgment for $77,527·92 damages; interest was awarded from

c   date of writ at the rate of 6% pa on the sum of $1,534·67, which was the agreed amount of special damage accrued at the date of the statement of claim. The respondent appealed on the issues of contributory negligence and quantum of damages; the appellant cross-appealed on the issue of damages. The Court of Appeal allowed the appeal and dismissed the cross-appeal. The court found that there was contributory negligence and apportioned the appellant's share of the blame for the accident at one-third. The court further held

d   that the appellant had unreasonably refused to undergo an operation which, if successful, would have probably regained for him within a few months some 80% of his mobility, thereby enabling him to resume his working life as a highly qualified professional engineer. Accordingly the court reassessed the damages on the basis that, had he acted reasonably, he was likely to have completely recovered his earning capacity within six months of his accident. They then reduced the total of their assessment by one-third to

e   give effect to their finding on contributory negligence and gave judgment for $31,001·95 with appropriate interest.

Pursuant to his right under s 109 of the Constitution of the Republic of Trinidad and Tobago the appellant appeals to the Judicial Committee of the Privy Council. He takes three points: (1) that the Court of Appeal erred in law in substituting its view for that of the trial judge on the issue of contributory negligence; (2) that the judge's finding that

f   he acted reasonably, alternatively that the respondent has not shown him to have acted unreasonably, in refusing the operation should not be disturbed; (3) that the Court of Appeal was wrong to dismiss his cross-appeal on damages: for the trial judge made so great an error in estimating his loss of future earnings that on accepted principles an appellate court should have intervened and made its own assessment. If he should succeed on his third point, he asks this Board to make the assessment on the basis of the

g   facts found by the trial judge.

In 1975 the appellant was the professor of civil engineering appointed and employed by the respondent. On 5 August of that year he was walking along a passageway in a building on the campus of the university when he fell into a trench which extended across the width of the passage. The time was 11.15 in the morning. But the light in the passage was not good because of the nature of the structures then surrounding it.

h   Building work, the detail of which it is unnecessary to describe, was then in progress. Conflicting evidence as to the degree of light was given by the appellant and his witness, a Mr Suite, on one side and by Mr Bruce, the university's assistant dean of the faculty of engineering, on the other. The trial judge accepted the evidence of Mr Suite that the hole was unguarded, that the light in the passage was bad ('very dark' was the judge's description) and that artificial light (of which there was none) was needed to see the works associated with the hole, a sight of which could have alerted the appellant to his danger.

Counsel for the university at the conclusion of the evidence conceded negligence. Thereafter the issue on liability was as to contributory negligence on the part of the appellant. The case against him was that he failed to keep a proper look-out. The trial judge delivered a very long judgment, notable for an extended recital of the evidence;

nevertheless he stated his conclusion pithily enough: 'I find in all the circumstances of
the present case that the hole constituted an unusual danger and that mere inattention   a
on the part of the plaintiff would not render him contributorily negligent.' This was a
finding of fact which, in the opinion of their Lordships, was on the evidence open to the
trial judge to make. The Court of Appeal, however, after directing itself correctly as to
the role of an appellate tribunal when reviewing findings of fact and degree reached at
first instance, criticised the judge for omitting to make specific findings fundamental to
the issues in the case. The criticism is, in their Lordships' view, misplaced. There was a   b
very substantial conflict of evidence as to the appellant's knowledge of the state of the
passageway and as to the degree of light available. It is understandable that the Court of
Appeal may have felt disposed to criticise the judgment at first instance as unstructured
and prolix. But it is abundantly clear that the judge had the evidence, all of it, very much
in mind. It is, of course, not necessary for a trial judge to make explicit findings on every
disputed piece of evidence. If it is clear that he has the evidence in mind, it suffices for   c
him to state his final conclusion, as the trial judge did in the passage already quoted.
Only the appellant could give evidence as to the accident: for he alone was there. There
were conflicts of evidence, which the judge had well in mind, between the appellant and
Mr Bruce as to the appellant's previous knowledge of the state of the passageway; and
between Mr Bruce and Mr Suite as well as the appellant as to the degree of light in it.
After referring to these critical questions, he stated his finding that the circumstances   d
were such that 'mere inattention' would not render the appellant contributorily negligent.
Had he reached a different conclusion, he could not have been challenged, as the Court
of Appeal has demonstrated. But that is not the issue. The question is: was there evidence
on which the trial judge could properly reach the conclusion which he did? And the
answer must be: abundant evidence, if he chose to accept it. And it is plain from his
finding that he did accept it.   e
   Their Lordships now turn to the second point in the appeal. Was the Court of Appeal
right to reverse the judge's finding that the appellant acted reasonably in refusing an
operation to his neck?
   The appellant suffered severe and painful injuries to his left foot and ankle, his neck
and his left shoulder, elbow and hip. He called two doctors. Mr Lalla, a consultant
orthopaedic surgeon, treated him for his injuries both in hospital and later as an out-   f
patient. In a report of 11 October 1975 he found the movements of the ankle joint
limited in all directions and expressed the opinion that the ankle injury would lead to
osteo-arthritis of the sub-talar joint which might become progressive. A year later he
reported that the arthritis was becoming progressive. At trial he expressed doubt as to
the value of surgery on the ankle, and commented that, as the appellant was a diabetic,
there might be complications of infection. In his opinion surgery on the ankle would be   g
ill-advised. There is, however, no indication in the evidence that Mr Lalla gave any such
advice to the appellant. He certainly gave no advice whether surgery was to be
recommended for the neck injury.
   Mr Lalla referred the neck injury to Dr Ghouralal, a consultant neuro-surgeon. He
found a serious condition: two herniated (in layman's language 'slipped') discs and
diabetes (a random blood sugar count of 240 mg%). The diagnosis of the neck condition,   h
which was confirmed in later reports, was cervical spondylosis giving rise to pain and
stiffness of movement. Dr Ghouralal believed that surgical therapy to the neck would
help. If there were no operation, the neck would get worse, in his opinion. It would be a
major operation but 'not very risky' (the judge so noted his evidence). Chances of success
would be 'quite good', movement increasing after about six months to 80% of normal.
He, therefore, did recommend in 1975 an operation, and was of the opinion that some   j
six months later the appellant would have been fit to resume his professional work.
   At the very end of his evidence, in re-examination, Dr Ghouralal added that the
appellant knew of the risks of infection which a diabetic would run and that 'It is for the
patient to decide on whether he should have the operation or not' (judge's note of his
evidence). At a later stage counsel for the appellant applied for leave to lead new evidence

in respect of the refusal to have an operation in 1975 and, in particular, to recall Dr
a Ghouralal so that he might ask him whether he had informed the appellant of the risks
involved. Counsel for the respondent objected. The judge refused leave, saying that Dr
Ghouralal's evidence was clear on the point.

In dealing with Mr Lalla's evidence the judge made a mistake. He spoke of Mr Lalla's
positive advice against an operation. But Mr Lalla gave no such advice, though it was his
opinion that an operation to the ankle was not to be recommended and that diabetes
b presented a complication if surgery should be carried out. The mistake was unfortunate
but is, in their Lordships' opinion, of no consequence: for the judge fully understood Dr
Ghouralal's evidence and appreciated its significance. The judge's refusal to allow the
doctor to be recalled indicates two things. First, he had formed a view that Dr Ghouralal's
opinion in the light of the diabetes complication was that the decision whether to operate
or not was best left to the patient. This, their Lordships think, was a very fair appreciation
c of what the doctor was saying. Second, the judge could not in the circumstances have
refused leave, unless he had concluded, the medical evidence being then complete, that
the appellant had established the reasonableness of his decision not to have the operation.

Their Lordships do not doubt that the burden of proving reasonableness was on the
appellant. It always is, in a case in which it is suggested that, had a plaintiff made a
different decision, his loss would have been less than it actually was. The point was
d succinctly made in an admiralty case of collision at sea by Lord Merriman P: The
Guildford, ss Temple Bar (owners) v mv Guildford (owners) [1956] 2 All ER 915 at 919, [1956]
P 364 at 370. Their Lordships would add a further comment on the law, well established
though it is. The rule that a plaintiff who rejects a medical recommendation in favour of
surgery must show that he acted reasonably is based on the principle that a plaintiff is
under a duty to act reasonably so as to mitigate his damage. Their Lordships respectfully
e agree with the opinion expressed on the point by the High Court of Australia in Fazlic v
Milingimbi Community Inc (1981) 38 ALR 424 at 430, to which they were helpfully referred
by counsel for the appellant. The question is one of fact and, as already mentioned, the
burden of proof is on the plaintiff. In Richardson v Redpath Brown & Co Ltd, [1944] 1 All
ER 110 at 112, [1944] AC 62 at 68 Viscount Simon LC said that the material question is
'whether the workman [ie the plaintiff] who refuses to be operated upon is acting
f reasonably in view of the advice he has received'. Their Lordships would, with respect,
put the question in more general terms. Though the advice received will almost always
be a major factor for consideration, the true question is whether in all the circumstances,
including particularly the medical advice received, the plaintiff acted reasonably in
refusing surgery. Their Lordships note that in Fazlic's case (at 428) the High Court of
Australia took the same view.

g For these reasons, their Lordships are of the opinion that the Court of Appeal was
wrong to reverse the judge. He was right to treat the question as one of fact and to put
the burden of proof on the appellant. And there was evidence on which he could properly
conclude that the appellant had discharged it.

Their Lordships now approach the third question in the appeal on the basis that the
appellant has established liability, has rebutted the defence of contributory negligence
h and has shown that he acted reasonably in refusing operative treatment for his neck. The
appellant's submission is that by failing to itemise the various heads of general damages
the trial judge was led into a gross underestimate of his loss of future earnings (or earning
capacity). The appellant was 55 at the date of trial (54 when he suffered the accident), of
high standing in his profession and of considerable international experience. He was
earning at the time of the accident $46,605 pa; but his employment was due to end on
i 31 December 1975. It had been his intention to return to his native country, Sri Lanka,
where he believed he could earn as a consultant something between $60,000 and $75,000
pa. He had a genuine prospect of obtaining an appointment in an agency of the United
Nations Organisation, in which event he would be able to earn a salary of $60,000 pa
free of tax. The judge expressed himself as sanguine in his belief that the appellant, but
for his accident, would have established a consultancy practice in Sri Lanka, and was not

prepared to disregard the possibility of a United Nations appointment. The accident left
the appellant virtually unemployable; certainly not capable of establishing a consultancy   a
practice or obtaining a United Nations post. In these circumstances, although the judge
made no express finding, it would be reasonable to infer that at the time of the accident
the appellant could have looked forward to some five to six years of remunerative
employment or practice. This prospect he has totally lost.

The judge awarded $75,000 to take care of all the general damage: pain and suffering,
loss of amenities and loss of the pecuniary prospects outlined above. He recognised the   b
appellant's pain and suffering as 'intense', he accepted that the taking of analgesics would
be necessary for the rest of his life and that the pleasures of gardening, dancing,
swimming and social activities would be denied him. On any view of the case, a
substantial sum should have been awarded the appellant under this head. A sum of
$25,000 would not have been unreasonable. If so, can the balance of the general damages
awarded, ie $50,000, be a proper compensation for the loss of the earning prospects of   c
this well qualified and experienced professional man aged 54? Or perhaps more
accurately, can an award of $75,000 properly compensate him for his pain and suffering,
his loss of amenities and the loss of his earning prospects?

It is obvious that the award represents a gross underassessment of the true loss. On the
judge's findings the loss of future earnings alone cannot be less than a figure of $150,000,
and it could be much higher. Counsel asked the Board to assess a figure and suggested a   d
sum of $288,000 for loss of earnings to which would have to be added a substantial sum
for the other items of general damage.

Their Lordships clearly have the power to substitute their assessment of damages for
the erroneous award made by the trial judge: see s 109(7) of the Constitution of the
Republic of Trinidad and Tobago. But they think it would be very unwise to do so. They
lack the knowledge that a judge of the High Court would have of social and economic   e
conditions in Trinidad and Tobago and the scale of awards in other comparable cases;
they lack the knowledge which a trial judge has of the character, personality and attitude
of the claimant; and it would be contrary, as their Lordships understand it, to the practice
of the Judicial Committee to make an assessment. Their Lordships have in mind what
was said by Lord Diplock delivering the judgment of the Board in the Australian appeal,
Paul v Rendell (1981) 34 ALR 569 at 579, 581, as to the risks inherent in the Board's lack   f
of knowledge of local circumstances. Their Lordships, therefore, have decided that the
question of general damages must be remitted for assessment by a High Court judge on
the basis of the rulings given by the Board in this appeal. Nothing, however, that their
Lordships have said on matters of fact relevant to the issue of damages is to bind the
judge on the rehearing other than that he must proceed on the basis that liability has
been established, contributory negligence negatived and that the appellant acted   g
reasonably in refusing operative treatment.

Their Lordships are concerned at the delay imposed by the protracted period over
which this simple case has been allowed to run. The accident was on 5 August 1975, and
finality has not yet been achieved. On 17 December 1976 the trial judge in giving
judgment stayed execution on payment within 28 days of the special damages $2,527·92,
and of $25,000 on account of general damages. Under RSC Ord 29, r 12 if a plaintiff has   h
obtained judgment for damages to be assessed the court may, if it thinks fit and subject
to certain specified conditions, order an interim payment not exceeding a reasonable
proportion of the damages which in the opinion of the court are likely to be recovered.

It was not suggested that the Judicial Committee does not have the power to order an
interim payment. Indeed, it plainly has under the Constitution: see s 109(7). Their
Lordships' decision on the appeal is in effect a judgment for damages to be assessed. They   j
are of the opinion that the sum of $77,527·92, which was the total of the judge's award
less interest, would be a reasonable sum to order by way of interim payment and that, as
$27,527·92 has already been paid, a further sum of $50,000 ought to be paid to the
appellant.

Accordingly, their Lordships allow the appeal, quash the judgment of the Court of
Appeal and direct (a) that judgment be entered for the appellant for damages to be

a assessed and (b) that the university pay to the appellant $50,000 within 14 days of their Lordships' order being filed in the Court of Appeal. The appellant is to have his costs here and below to date. The costs of the assessment of damages will be in the discretion of the judge who takes the case.

Appeal allowed.

b Solicitors: *Ingledew Brown Bennison & Garrett* (for the appellant); *Barlow Lyde & Gilbert* (for the respondent).

Mary Rose Plummer   Barrister.

c

R v Gilmartin

COURT OF APPEAL, CRIMINAL DIVISION
ROBERT GOFF LJ, KILNER BROWN AND LEONARD JJ
2 DECEMBER 1982

d *Criminal law – Obtaining property by deception – Deception – Cheque – Postdated cheque – Representation by drawer – Extent of representation – Postdated cheque dishonoured on presentation – Whether drawer merely representing that he was a customer of bank on which it was drawn – Whether drawer impliedly representing that there would be sufficient funds in account to meet cheque on presentation – Theft Act 1968, s 15.*

e *Criminal law – Obtaining pecuniary advantage by deception – Deception – Implied representation – Cheque – Representation by drawer – Extent of representation – Drawer giving postdated cheque – Drawer having insufficient funds in account to meet cheque – Cheque dishonoured on presentation – Whether drawer impliedly representing that cheque was a valid order for payment of sum specified – Theft Act 1968, s 16.*

f The appellant ran a stationery business which he carried on through a company which owed money to a creditor. The company's bank account was heavily overdrawn and there was no prospect of the bank extending the company's overdraft facilities or of any money being paid into the account in the immediate future. The appellant gave the creditor a postdated cheque which he signed on behalf of the company. He also obtained stationery from suppliers by giving them cheques which were similarly postdated and signed on behalf of the company. No money was paid into the account thereafter and the cheques were dishonoured on presentation. The appellant was charged with (i) dishonestly obtaining goods from the suppliers by deception, contrary to s 15[a] of the Theft Act 1968, and (ii) dishonestly obtaining the deferment of a debt due to the creditor by deception, contrary to s 16[b] of the 1968 Act. The charge in each case alleged that the relevant 'deception' by the appellant consisted of a false 'representation' that the cheque in question was a good and valid order for the payment of the sum specified in the cheque. The appellant submitted that no such representation could be inferred from the mere act of giving a postdated cheque, and that the only representation about the present

---

a Section 15, so far as material, is set out at p 832 *d e*, post
b Section 16, so far as material, provides:
  '(1) A person who by any deception dishonestly obtains for himself or another any pecuniary advantage shall on conviction on indictment be liable to imprisonment for a term not exceeding five years.
  (2) The cases in which a pecuniary advantage within the meaning of this section is to be regarded as obtained for a person are cases where—(*a*) any debt . . . for which he . . . is . . . liable . . . is deferred . . .
  (3) For purposes of this section "deception" has the same meaning as in section 15 of this Act.'

state of affairs which could properly be implied from such an act was that the drawer of
the cheque (or the company on whose behalf it was drawn) was a customer of the bank   a
on which it was drawn. The trial judge rejected the submission, and the appellant was
convicted. He appealed.

Held – By simply giving a cheque, whether postdated or not, the drawer impliedly
represented that the state of facts existing at the date of delivery was such that in the
ordinary course of events it would, on presentation for payment on or after the date   b
specified in the cheque, be met. It followed that the judge had rightly rejected the
appellant's submission and the appeal would accordingly be dismissed (see p 835 c to j,
post).
   R v Hazelton (1874) LR 2 CCR 134 and dictum of Lord Diplock in Metropolitan Police
Comr v Charles [1976] 3 All ER at 113–114 followed.
   R v Page [1971] 2 All ER 870 considered.   c

Notes
For obtaining property by deception, see 11 Halsbury's Laws (4th edn) paras 1278, 1284,
and for cases on the subject, see 15 Digest (Reissue) 1386–1387, 1423–1424, 12131–
12137, 12479–12502.
   For obtaining a pecuniary advantage by deception, see 11 Halsbury's Laws (4th edn)   d
para 1279, and for cases on the subject, see 15 Digest (Reissue) 1387–1390, 12138–12152.
   For the Theft Act 1968, ss 15, 16, see 8 Halsbury's Statutes (3rd edn) 792, 793.
   As from 20 October 1978 s 16(2)(a) of the 1968 Act was replaced by the Theft Act
1978, which made other provision against fraudulent conduct.

Cases referred to in judgment   e
Metropolitan Police Comr v Charles [1976] 3 All ER 112, [1977] AC 177, [1976] 3 WLR
   431, HL, 15 Digest (Reissue) 1390, 12150.
R v Hazelton (1874) LR 2 CCR 134, CCR, 15 Digest (Reissue) 1424, 12499.
R v Maytum-White (1957) 42 Cr App R 165, CCA, 15 Digest (Reissue) 1424, 12502.
R v Page [1971] 2 All ER 870, [1971] 2 QB 330n, [1971] 2 WLR 1308n, CA, 15 Digest
   (Reissue) 1388, 12140.   f

Appeal
On 18 February 1982 in the Crown Court at St Albans, before his Honour Judge Watling
QC and a jury, Anthony Gilmartin was convicted on three counts (counts 1 to 3) of
obtaining property by deception, contrary to s 15 of the Theft Act 1968, and on one
count (count 4) of obtaining a pecuniary advantage by deception, contrary to s 16 of the g
Act. He was sentenced to 18 months' imprisonment on each count concurrent but
suspended for two years. He appealed against conviction. The facts are set out in the
judgment of the court.

Nicholas Yell (assigned by the Registrar of Criminal Appeals) for the appellant.
Stephen Waine for the Crown.   h

ROBERT GOFF LJ delivered the following judgment of the court. There is before the
court an appeal by Anthony Gilmartin against his conviction at St Albans Crown Court
on 18 February 1982, on three counts of obtaining property by deception, and one count
of obtaining a pecuniary advantage by deception, contrary to ss 15 and 16 of the Theft
Act 1968 respectively. The trial on the fourth count took place under s 16 of the Act   j
before it was amended by the Theft Act 1978. The appellant was sentenced to 18 months'
imprisonment on each count concurrent, but suspended for 2 years.
   The appeal raises a question of law and for that reason the facts of the case can be
briefly stated. Until September 1978, the appellant ran a business in Luton buying and
selling stationery, greeting cards, wrapping paper and other similar goods. He had

formed a private company called Friendship Card Co Ltd which carried on the business,
a but it was to all intents and purposes a one man business. The company had a bank
account at a branch of Barclays Bank in Luton and there was an overdraft on the account.
However, up to July 1978 the account was operated in a regular manner and at the
beginning of July the debit balance stood at only about £380. Then suddenly large sums
were drawn on the account which resulted in a very substantial increase in the overdraft.
By 13 July the overdraft stood at £3,877 and by 23 July it had increased to £5,488.
b Payments into the account seem to have ceased after 4 August and there was practically
no movement in the account at all except for some small debits on a standing order. By
the middle of August the overdraft stood at over £5,700 and by 1 September it stood at
over £6,000, the precise total being £6,067·66. It was against this background that the
appellant engaged in the transactions which led to his conviction.

I take first counts 1 to 3 inclusive which were concerned with obtaining property by
c deception. On three occasions the appellant obtained goods, giving cheques signed by
him on behalf of Friendship Card Co Ltd in payment for the goods. On the first occasion,
he gave a cheque dated 27 August 1978, in the sum of £1,166·40; on the second he gave
a cheque which was dated 14 September 1978, in the sum of £1,403·57, and on the third
he gave a cheque dated 25 August 1978, in the sum of £6,264. The first two of those
cheques were made payable to a company called Angel Cards Ltd and were handed over
d to a Mr Brown of that company. It seems that these cheques were handed over in blank
and the date was actually inserted by Mr Brown, in the first cheque six days later and in
the second a month later. These two transactions were the subject matter of counts 1 and
2 of the indictment, but they were in fact specimen counts taken from some seven
transactions involving £7,602 in all.

The cheque which was the subject matter of count 3 was made payable to a company
e called Croft Greetings Ltd. This was handed over to a Mr York of that company and
postdated by one day. All these cheques, the subject matter of counts 1 to 3, were
dishonoured on presentation.

Count 4 was concerned with obtaining a pecuniary advantage by deception. The
appellant had a running account with a company called County Lithographics Ltd and
subsequently gave to a Mr Murray of that company a cheque made payable to County
f Lithographics Ltd postdated to 27 August 1978, signed by the appellant on behalf of
Friendship Card Co Ltd in the sum of £1,600. That cheque too was dishonoured on
presentation and the case for the prosecution was that the appellant thereby obtained a
pecuniary advantage in the form of deferment of the debt.

To complete the picture, there was evidence before the jury that between 11 and 30
August, the appellant through his company sold the stock he had obtained in this way,
g about £14,000 worth of cards, paper and other goods, and that although in the past he
had received payment from this purchaser in the form of cheques payable to Friendship
Card Co Ltd, on this occasion he requested and obtained cheques made payable to cash.
Three of the four cheques he received in this way, dated respectively 11, 24 and 30
August 1978, amounting in all to just under £11,000, were cashed, but none of that cash
found its way into the account of Friendship Card Co Ltd with Barclays Bank.

h The appellant then disappeared and was not seen for a considerable time, but in
September 1980, the police caught up with him and he was interviewed. In due course
he was prosecuted on the four counts I have already referred to and was convicted. At the
trial he maintained that the postdated cheques were not intended to be presented, the
intention being that the three cheques, the subject matter of the first three counts, should
be bought back for cash and that the cheque which was the subject matter of count 4
should be handed over simply for what were called bookkeeping purposes. But this
defence must have been disbelieved by the jury when they convicted him on the four
counts on the indictment.

The point of law which arises on the appeal and which was the subject matter of a
submission by counsel to the judge, his Honour Judge Watling QC, who presided over
the trial, and of a ruling by him, is as follows. Each of the four counts in the indictment

alleges that the relevant deception by the appellant consisted of a false representation that
the cheque in question was a good and valid order for the payment of the sum specified   a
in the cheque. All the cheques in question were postdated cheques, it being accepted by
both prosecution and defence that the cheques given to Mr Brown, even if completed by
him, must be regarded as postdated cheques, having regard to the dates entered in those
cheques. The submission for the defence before the judge, which was repeated before
this court, was that by giving a postdated cheque the drawer impliedly represents no
more than that he (or any company on whose behalf he draws the cheque) is a customer   b
of the bank on which the cheque is drawn, and makes no implied representation
concerning the honouring of the cheque. On this basis, since Friendship Card Co Ltd did
indeed have an account with Barclays Bank at all relevant times, counsel for the appellant
submitted to the judge below that there was no case to answer. However, the submission
was rejected by the judge and, as I have said, the jury duly convicted the appellant on all
four counts.   c
     In considering this submission, we must first refer to the relevant statutory provisions.
Section 15(1) of the Theft Act 1968 provides:

> 'A person who by any deception dishonestly obtains property belonging to
> another, with the intention of permanently depriving the other of it, shall on
> conviction on indictment be liable to imprisonment for a term not exceeding ten   d
> years.'

I can ignore sub-ss (2) and (3) which are not material to present purposes, but I must set
out sub-s (4) which reads:

> 'For purposes of this section "deception" means any deception (whether deliberate
> or reckless) by words or conduct as to fact or as to law, including a deception as to   e
> the present intentions of the person using the deception or any other person.'

I need not set out s 16, which is concerned with dishonestly obtaining a pecuniary
advantage by deception, because by sub-s (3) of that section, deception in s 16 has the
same meaning as in s 15 of the 1968 Act. It is plain that the deception in these
circumstances must involve a representation by the accused whether by words or
conduct. The question which arises in this case relates to the nature of the representation   f
which is implied by the simple fact of giving a cheque and, in the present case in
particular, the nature of the representation implied by the giving of a postdated cheque.
     This matter has been the subject of some discussion in the authorities and there is also
a most useful discussion in *Archbold's Criminal Pleading, Evidence and Practice* (41st edn,
1982) pp 1087–1090, paras 18-91–18-95 which has been of considerable assistance to us.
The leading authority on the subject is now the decision of the House of Lords in   g
Metropolitan Police Comr v Charles [1976] 3 All ER 112, [1977] AC 177. That case was
concerned with obtaining a pecuniary advantage by deception contrary to s 16 of the
1968 Act. But the deception in that case involved the use, or rather abuse, of a credit card
together with cheques to obtain the benefit of facilities from the defendant's bank far
beyond those authorised by his bank manager. The speeches of their Lordships in that
case were to a considerable extent concerned with the nature of the representation to be   h
implied by the use of a credit card, but they also touched on the representation to be
implied in the giving of a cheque without the use of a credit card. Of their Lordships,
Lord Diplock, Viscount Dilhorne and Lord Edmund-Davies all delivered speeches,
although Lord Diplock and Viscount Dilhorne expressly agreed with the other two
speeches so delivered. The other two of their Lordships, Lord Salmon and Lord Fraser,
simply agreed with the three speeches delivered. Before quoting the relevant passages   j
from those speeches so delivered, it would be helpful if I were to set out a passage from
Kenny's Outlines of Criminal Law (19th edn, 1966) p 359, para 346, which was cited by
both Viscount Dilhorne and Lord Edmund-Davies and was referred to in the speech of
Lord Diplock. The passage reads:

> 'Similarly, the familiar act of drawing a cheque (a document which on the face of

it is only a command of a future act) has been held to imply at least three statements about the present (1) that the drawer has an account with that bank; (2) that he has authority to draw on it for that amount; (3) that the cheque, as drawn, is a valid order for the payment of that amount (i.e. that the present state of affairs is such that, in the ordinary course of events, the cheque will on its future presentment be duly honoured). It may be well to point out, however, that it does not imply any representation that the drawer now has money in this bank to the amount drawn for, inasmuch as he may well have authority to overdraw, or may intend to pay in (before the cheque can be presented) sufficient money to meet it.'

That passage was cited with approval by Phillimore LJ in R v Page [1971] 2 All ER 870 at 874, [1971] 2 QB 330 at 333, a decision of this court concerned with an offence under s 16 of the 1968 Act.

I turn now to the relevant passages in their Lordships' speeches in *Metropolitan Police Comr v Charles*. Lord Diplock said ([1976] 3 All ER 112 at 113–114, [1977] AC 177 at 182):

'To take first the case in which no cheque card is involved, it is no doubt true to say that all the payee is concerned with is that the cheque should be honoured by the bank, and that to induce the payee to take the cheque all that the drawer is concerned to do is to assure him that as far as can reasonably be foreseen this is what will happen. But payment by the bank cannot reasonably be foreseen as likely unless the fact be that the cheque is one which the bank on which it is drawn is bound, by an existing contract with the drawer, to pay on presentment or, if not strictly bound to do so, could reasonably be expected to pay in the normal course of dealing. This, I think to be a simpler way of expressing the statement of existing facts which is to be implied from the familiar act of drawing a cheque than that cited by my noble and learned friend, Lord Edmund-Davies, from Kenny which was adopted by the Court of Appeal in *R v Page* [1971] 2 All ER 870, [1971] 2 QB 330. It combines representations (1) and (3) from Kenny, but it omits representation (2). A customer needs no authority from his banker to draw a cheque on him; it is the banker who needs authority from the customer to pay it on presentment.'

Viscount Dilhorne, having quoted the passage from *Kenny*, said ([1976] 3 All ER 112 at 116–117, [1977] AC 177 at 185–186):

'Until the enactment of the Theft Act 1968 it was necessary in order to obtain a conviction for false pretences to establish that there had been a false pretence of an existing fact. This, I suspect, was the reason for considering whether the representation made on the giving of a cheque included representations as to existing facts. Ordinarily the recipient of a cheque accepts it in the belief that it will be honoured on presentment. It will not be honoured if it is drawn on a bank at which the drawer has not an account and I see no difficulty in holding that the first of the representations stated by Kenny can be implied. But I doubt if the second is correct. On one view it is only expressing the third representation in different words. If one is entitled or authorised to draw a cheque for the amount stated on it, then the cheque is a valid order for the payment of that amount and will in the ordinary course of events be honoured on presentment. If one has funds in one's current account at a bank, then one is entitled to draw on them. The bank does not give authority for a cheque to be drawn. Similarly, if one has been allowed an overdraft, the bank undertakes to honour cheques up to the amount of the overdraft but the bank does not authorise the drawing of a particular cheque. Kenny recognises that the giving of a cheque does not imply that there is money in the bank to meet it. If a man draws a cheque knowing that there are no funds to meet it or that it is drawn for an amount which will lead to his overdraft limit being exceeded but honestly intending to pay in the money required to meet the cheque before it is presented, he would not in the old days have been convicted of false pretences for there would not have been an intent to defraud, and now, if he had that honest belief, he is unlikely to have been found to have been acting dishonestly. Can it nevertheless be said that when drawing such a cheque with that intent, a man represents that he has the authority of the bank to draw it? I do not think so. The reality is in my view that a man who gives a cheque represents that it will be met on presentment, and if a cheque is accepted by the payee, it is in the belief that it will be met.'

Finally, Lord Edmund-Davies, having likewise quoted the passage from *Kenny*, said ([1976] 3 All ER 112 at 120–121, [1977] AC 177 at 190–191):

'My noble and learned friend, Lord Fraser of Tullybelton, rightly pointed out that representations (1) and (2) were supererogatory in the light of representation (3), which embraced both of them. My noble and learned friend, Lord Diplock, also criticised representation (2) on the ground that the representation made by the simple act of drawing a cheque does not relate to or rest on "authority" but is rather a representation that the drawer has contracted with his bank to honour his cheques. Notwithstanding the antiquity of the quoted passage, it accordingly appears right to restrict the representation made by the act of drawing and handing over a cheque to that which has been conveniently labelled "Page (3)". The legal position created by such an act was even more laconically described by Pollock B in *R v Hazelton* (1874) LR 2 CCR 134 at 140 in this way: "I think the real representation made is that the cheque will be paid. It may be said that that is a representation as to a future event. But that is not really so. It means that the existing state of facts is such that in ordinary course the cheque will be met." '

It might perhaps be thought from the manner in which Viscount Dilhorne expressed himself that he considered that in the case of offences under ss 15 and 16 of the 1968 Act the relevant representation need not be a representation of existing facts, but can extend to include a representation as to the future. However, both Lord Diplock and Lord Edmund-Davies made it plain that the relevant representation must be a representation as to existing facts. This was certainly so under the old law relating to obtaining by false pretences before the coming into effect of the 1968 Act, and that this is still so is (putting on one side the immaterial reference to a representation of law) plain from the definition of deception in s 15(4) of the Act, referring as it does to deception by words or conduct as to fact, and also confining a representation as to intentions to the present intentions of the accused. For these reasons we do not consider that it would be right to read Viscount Dilhorne's speech as permitting the relevant representation to be not merely one of existing facts or law, but also one as to the future.

It appears from the speeches of their Lordships, however, that the often quoted passage from *Kenny* can no longer be regarded as providing an accurate guide to the relevant representation in that the second element, viz that the drawer has authority to draw on his account at the relevant bank for the amount specified on the cheque, must be rejected for the reasons stated by Lord Diplock. Moreover, the first of *Kenny's* three elements is, as Lord Edmund-Davies pointed out in agreement with Lord Fraser, logically covered by the third. The third element specified by *Kenny* was expressed by him in two different ways, that is to say (1) a statement that the cheque as drawn is a valid order for the payment of the amount of the cheque and (2), as an explanation of the first, a statement that the present state of affairs is such that in the ordinary course of events the cheque will on its future presentment be duly honoured. These two are, if the first is read literally, not identical, since the first statement can be read as referring to the future. It is, however, for the reasons we have already given only relevant to have regard to a representation as to existing facts and therefore the first of these two statements must be read as limited by the second. The second is, moreover, plainly derived from the words of Pollock B in *R v Hazelton* (1874) LR 2 CCR 134 at 140, quoted with approval by Lord Edmund-Davies in *Metropolitan Police Comr v Charles* [1976] 3 All ER 112 at 121, [1977] AC 177 at 191, viz that the representation implied in the giving of a cheque is that 'the existing state of facts is such that in ordinary course the cheque will be met.' This terse but neat epitome of the representation is in our judgment entirely consistent with the

view expressed in rather different words by Lord Diplock in *Metropolitan Police Comr v*
a *Charles* [1976] 3 All ER 112 at 113–114, [1977] AC 177 at 182, and should properly be
regarded as an authoritative statement of the law.

Is the position any different in the case of a postdated cheque? Counsel for the
appellant, relying in particular on a passage from *Archbold* p 1090, submits that it is. The
relevant passage from *Archbold* reads (I quote only the conclusion of the relevant
paragraph):

b
'... the only representation about the present that can properly be said to be
implied in the mere act of drawing a post-dated cheque is that the drawer is a
customer of the bank concerned.'

That the drawing of a postdated cheque does generally imply a representation to that
effect is plain, since the cheque itself consists of a request to the drawer's bank to pay the
c money. Authority for this proposition is to be found in the decision of this court in *R v*
Maytum-White (1957) 42 Cr App R 165. But that case, which was concerned with a
situation where the drawer had no such account, provides no authority that the implied
representation is to be limited to that fact and no more. We can see no reason why in the
case of a postdated cheque the drawer does not impliedly represent that the existing facts
at the date when he delivers the cheque to the payee or to his agent are such that in the
d ordinary course the cheque will, on presentation on or after the date specified in the
cheque, be met.

Take the case where, as in this instance, a postdated cheque is issued when the account
is heavily overdrawn and there is, as the drawer well knows, no prospect of any future
funds being paid into the account before the date when the cheque matures, or of the
bank providing further overdraft facilities before that date. In such a case it appears to us
e that the drawer is as much guilty of deception as he would be in the case of a cheque
which is not postdated. Indeed, where the drawer gives a cheque which is not postdated
his account may be overdrawn and he may have no arrangement with his bank for
further overdraft facilities, but he may have in his pocket another cheque payable to him
which he intends to pay into his account immediately and which when paid in will
enable the cheque which he himself has drawn to be paid on presentation; if so it is
f difficult to see that he has made any misrepresentation. In these circumstances, we can
see no relevant distinction between the case of a cheque which has not been postdated
and one which has.

For the sake of clarity, we consider that in the generality of cases under ss 15 and 16 of
the 1968 Act the courts should proceed on the basis that by the simple giving of a cheque,
whether postdated or not, the drawer impliedly represents that the state of facts existing
g at the date of delivery of the cheque is such that in the ordinary course the cheque will
on presentation for payment on or after the date specified in the cheque, be met.

It follows that we are unable to accept the argument advanced by counsel on behalf of
the appellant in the present case. It is right that we should observe that the expression
used by the judge in directing the jury in the present case did not precisely accord with
the law as we have stated it to be, in that the expression there used by him could be read
h as referring not simply to existing facts, but as to the future. However, at the end of the
summing up, counsel for the prosecution very properly intervened in the presence of the
jury to suggest that it was appropriate to emphasise that the representation was such that
the existing state of affairs in connections with his bank account was such that in the
ordinary course the cheques would be met, a proposition that the judge then accepted as
correct. In these circumstances, we are satisfied that there was no misdirection to the
j jury. The appeal against conviction is therefore dismissed.

Appeal dismissed.

Solicitors: *Knowles Cave & Co*, Luton (for the Crown).

Jacqueline Charles   Barrister.

Thames Water Authority v Elmbridge Borough Council

COURT OF APPEAL, CIVIL DIVISION
STEPHENSON, DUNN AND DILLON LJJ
6, 7, 8, 10 DECEMBER 1982

Public authority – Statutory powers – Excessive exercise of statutory powers – Local authority resolution appropriating land – Local authority having no power to appropriate part of land – Whether resolution valid to appropriate balance of land – Whether whole resolution invalid.

Local authority – Land – Power to appropriate land – Exercise of power – Local authority appropriating land by resolution under power to acquire land immediately for planning purposes – Whether planning purpose required to be implemented immediately – Whether resolution invalid if planning purpose not implemented immediately – Town and Country Planning Act 1971, s 112(1)(d).

The predecessor of the respondent council was the owner of two parcels of land which were used for sewage disposal purposes. One of those parcels of land was edged pink and the other blue on a plan. Section 163 of the Local Government Act 1933 provided for appropriation of land by a local authority for authorised purposes when the land was no longer required for its original purpose and s 112(1)(d)[a] of the Town and Country Planning Act 1971 permitted a local authority '... to acquire land immediately for a purpose which it is necessary to achieve in the interests of the proper planning of an area in which the land is situated'. On 7 November 1972 the council passed a resolution pursuant to s 163 of the 1933 Act appropriating the pink land from sewerage to planning purposes within the meaning of s 112(1) of the 1971 Act and on 17 July 1973 it passed a further resolution appropriating the blue land for planning purposes. However, a pumping station which was designated green on the plan and which was within the area edged in blue was still in use for sewerage purposes. On 1 April 1974, on local government reorganisation, the claimant water authority assumed responsibility from the council for sewage treatment and occupied the green land for that purpose. The water authority claimed that on its true construction s 112(1) required the purpose for which the land was appropriated to be implemented 'immediately' and since the council had not done that the resolutions appropriating the land were invalid, with the result that both parcels of land had been transferred to it on local government reorganisation in 1974. The water authority also contended that the correct method of construing the second resolution was to see whether the green land could be severed from the blue land referred to in the resolution by applying a 'blue pencil' test and that since it could not, because the green land could not be identified and segregated on the face of the resolution, the whole resolution was invalid. The council contended that the second resolution was a valid appropriation of the blue land except for the green land, which could be identified by reference to the plan and could be severed. The dispute was referred to arbitration. The sole arbitrator found in favour of the council. The water authority appealed by way of a special case stated for the High Court. The judge rejected the water authority's argument as to the construction of s 112(1) but held that the green land could not be severed to make the second resolution valid in regard to the remaining blue land since that approach did not give effect to the council's intention. The council appealed to the Court of Appeal and the water authority cross-appealed on the issue of the true construction of s 112.

Held – The appeal would be allowed and the cross-appeal would be dismissed for the following reasons—

---

a Section 112(1), so far as material, is set out at p 845 c d, post

a (1) The so-called 'blue pencil test', which developed in the private law field where the
court was concerned with rights and obligations of the parties, had no application to
public law, where the court was concerned not so much with rights and obligations or
intentions of a public authority as with whether it had the power to act as it had and
where the court adopted a wider approach to the question of severance. Instead, when a
public authority which acted by resolution or other document exceeded its powers, and
the extent of the illegality was capable of being isolated and identified with precision by
b reference to the surrounding circumstances, the court could enforce the valid part that
remained even though there was nothing in the document itself to isolate and identify
the part where the power had been exceeded. Since the land marked green on the plan
was easily identifiable, by reference to the plan and other circumstances, as land which
the council had no power to appropriate, it was easily separable from the rest of the land
which the council did have power to appropriate. The second resolution was therefore
c invalid in respect of the green land but valid as regards the rest (see p 840 j to p 841 d,
p 842 b, p 844 c to e h j, p 846 b c e to h, p 847 b g j to p 848 h, post); Alexander v Alexander
(1755) 2 Ves Sen 640, Re Turner, Hudson v Turner [1931] All ER Rep 782, Potato Marketing
Board v Merricks [1958] 2 All ER 538, Kent CC v Kingsway Investments (Kent) Ltd [1970] 1
All ER 70, Dunkley v Evans [1981] 3 All ER 285 and United City Merchants (Investments) Ltd
v Royal Bank of Canada [1982] 2 All ER 720 applied.
d (2) On its true construction the word 'immediately' in s 112(1)(d) of the 1971 Act
referred merely to the acquisition of land and did not require the purpose for which the
land was acquired to be put into effect immediately (see p 845 j to p 846 b and p 848 g h,
post).
Per curiam. It is misleading to apply the term 'severance', as used in relation to the
construction of private documents, to the process whereby the court considers extrinsic
e factors to determine the extent to which a document purporting to be an exercise of a
power vested in a public authority is an excessive exercise of that power since that term
is used in private law to describe the quite separate process of construction of a document
to determine whether a provision can stand and be enforced despite the invalidity, for
extrinsic reasons, of some other provisions of the document (see p 844 f g, p 847 c d and
p 848 g h, post).

f **Notes**
For severance of partly invalid orders, instruments or actions, see 1 Halsbury's Laws (4th
edn) para 26.
For the Local Government Act 1933, s 163, see 19 Halsbury's Statutes (3rd edn) 492.
For the Town and Country Planning Act 1971, s 112, see 41 ibid 1718.
g As from 1 April 1974 (in respect of non-county boroughs) s 163 of the 1933 Act was
replaced by s 122 of the Local Government Act 1972.
As from 13 November 1980 s 112(1) of the 1971 Act was substituted by the Local
Government, Planning and Land Act 1980, s 91(1).

Cases referred to in judgments
h Alexander v Alexander (1755) 2 Ves Sen 640, 28 ER 408, 37 Digest (Repl) 261, 204.
Associated Provincial Picture Houses Ltd v Wednesbury Corp [1947] 2 All ER 680, [1948] KB
223, CA, 45 Digest (Repl) 215, 189.
Dennis & Co Ltd v Munn [1949] 1 All ER 616, [1949] 2 KB 327, CA, 17 Digest (Reissue)
503, 179.
Dunkley v Evans [1981] 3 All ER 285, [1981] 1 WLR 1522.
j Jackson Stansfield & Sons v Butterworth [1948] 2 All ER 558, CA, 17 Digest (Reissue) 503,
178.
Kent CC v Kingsway Investments (Kent) Ltd [1970] 1 All ER 70, [1971] AC 72, [1970] 2
WLR 397, HL; rvsg [1969] 1 All ER 601, [1969] 2 QB 333, [1969] 2 WLR 249, Digest
(Cont Vol C) 970, 61a.
Olsen v City of Camberwell Corp [1926] VLR 58.
Potato Marketing Board v Merricks [1958] 2 All ER 538, [1958] 2 QB 316, [1958] 3 WLR
135, 2 Digest (Reissue) 159, 976.

Ralli Bros v Compañia Naviera Sota y Aznar [1920] 2 KB 287, [1920] All ER Rep 427, CA,
    11 Digest (Reissue) 476, 843.
Strickland v Hayes [1896] 1 QB 290, DC.
Turner, Re, Hudson v Turner [1932] 1 Ch 31, [1931] All ER Rep 782, 37 Digest (Repl) 286,
    411.
United City Merchants (Investments) Ltd v Royal Bank of Canada [1982] 2 All ER 720, [1982]
    2 WLR 1039, HL; *rvsg* [1981] 3 All ER 142, [1982] QB 208, [1981] 3 WLR 242, CA.
Wilson Smithett & Cope Ltd v Terruzzi [1976] 1 All ER 817, [1976] QB 683, [1976] 2 WLR
    418, CA, Digest (Cont Vol E) 178, 213a.

Appeal and cross-appeal
Elmbridge Borough Council appealed against the decision of Sir Douglas Frank QC
sitting as deputy judge of the High Court on 20 May 1981 on an appeal from the
arbitrator, Mr Peter Boydell QC, in a dispute between the Thames Water Authority as
claimant and the council as respondent concerning the vesting of three parcels of land
(the 'pink land', the 'blue land' and the 'green land' delineated on plan 611/OS/4) situated
at Oyster Lane, Byfleet and known as the New Haw sewage treatment works. The
arbitrator decided that the pink land and the blue land were validly vested in the council
by resolutions of the council on 7 November 1972 and 7 July 1973 but that those
resolutions were not effective to vest the green land, which was therefore vested in the
water authority. On appeal by the water authority by way of special case stated the
deputy judge held that the council's resolutions were only valid to vest the pink land in
the council and that therefore the blue and green land was vested in the water authority.
The council appealed, claiming that the pink land and the blue land were vested in it.
The water authority cross-appealed claiming that all three parcels were vested in it. The
facts are set out in the judgment of Dunn LJ.

Konrad Schiemann QC and *Alan Fletcher* for the borough council.
Peter Mottershead QC and *Guy Seward QC* for the water authority.

                                                                        Cur adv vult

10 December. The following judgments were delivered.

DUNN LJ (giving the first judgment at the invitation of Stephenson LJ). The principal
question raised by this appeal is as to the effect of two resolutions, dated respectively 7
November 1972 and 17 July 1973, passed by the former Walton and Weybridge Urban
District Council, who were the predecessors of the Elmbridge Borough Council, the
appellants.
    The facts are agreed; I take them from the agreed statement. Down to 1 April 1974,
when the local government reorganisation took place, the Walton and Weybridge Urban
District Council (which I shall call 'the urban district council') was the owner of land at
Byfleet consisting of 1·87 hectares, edged pink on the plan (which I shall call 'the pink
land') and land 2·785 hectares in extent, edged blue on the plan (which I shall call 'the
blue land'). That land was used for sewage disposal purposes.
    In about April 1971 the urban district council started to construct a new sewage
treatment works at Weybridge, with the intention that the previous works should cease
to operate when the new works came into operation. On 7 November 1972 the urban
district council adopted a recommendation of its policy committee and approved by its
finance committee, in the following terms:

    '. . . in respect of the land known as New Haw Sewage Works, Oyster Lane,
    Byfleet, and in accordance with the provisions of Section 163 of the Local
    Government Act 1933, as amended by Section 23 of the Town and Country Planning
    Act, 1959, (i) the Council do now appropriate the area of land not currently used in
    connection with the Sewage Works, as shown edged pink on plan no. 611/OS/4,

a
from sewerage to planning purposes within the meaning of Section 112(1) of the Town and Country Planning Act, 1971, and, (ii) on cessation of its current use, the remaining area of land, shown edged blue on plan no. 611/OS/4, be similarly appropriated for planning purposes . . .'

On 7 November 1972 none of the pink land was in fact used for sewage or sewerage disposal purposes. On 17 July 1973 the urban district council adopted a recommendation of their finance committee in these terms:

b

'. . . it be formally recorded that the use for sewerage purposes of the area of land at New Haw Sewage Works, Oyster Lane, Byfleet, shown edged blue on plan no. 611/OS/4, has now ceased and, in accordance with the Council's previous decision, is appropriated by resolution for planning purposes.'

c
On 17 July 1973 the New Haw sewage treatment works had ceased to operate and no part of the blue land was used for sewage or sewerage disposal purposes, save that a pumping station had been constructed on the land, 0·0298 hectares in extent, shown edged green on the plan (which I shall call 'the green land') as part of the Seven Arches sewage treatment works scheme at Weyhill, and that pumping station had been in operation since 29 June 1973. The access to the pumping station from Oyster Lane was along a roadway edged with a broken green line on the plan.

d
Since 1 April 1974 and following the local government reorganisation, the green land, including the pumping station, has been occupied by the Thames Water Authority, the respondent to the appeal (whom I shall call 'the water authority'); and the Elmbridge Borough Council (whom I shall call 'the borough council') formally admitted that that land was transferred to the water authority by reason of art 8 of the Local Authorities (England) (Property etc) Order 1973, SI 1973/1861, and that the water authority has a right of access, with or without vehicles, over the roadway edged with broken green lines.

e

A dispute arose between the water authority and the borough council as to the effect of the two resolutions of 7 November 1972 and 17 July 1973, which was referred to arbitration pursuant to art 39 of the 1973 order. At the arbitration the rival contentions, so far as they are material to this appeal, were as follows: the water authority contended that the land the subject of the two resolutions should be transferred to the authority under the provisions of the 1973 order, as those resolutions did not validly appropriate the land for planning purposes in that, in relation to the blue land, the resolution of 17 July 1973 was passed at a time when part of the land, namely the green land, was still used for sewerage purposes. The borough council contended that, except for the green land, the land which was the subject of the resolutions was transferred to them under the order, because the green land was severable from the rest of the land and the resolution was effective to appropriate all the land used, except the green land.

f

g
The arbitrator, Mr Peter Boydell QC, held in favour of the borough council that the resolution of 17 July 1973 could be severed, so that it constituted a valid appropriation of the blue land, excluding the green land. A case was stated for the opinion of the High Court, which was heard by Sir Douglas Frank QC sitting as a deputy High Court judge, and he gave his decision on 20 May 1980. He disagreed with the arbitrator; he held that the resolution could not be severed so as to exclude the green land, and that consequently the whole resolution was invalid and all the blue land passed to the authority on 1 April 1974. The borough council now appeals against that decision.

h

The power of appropriation is contained in s 163 of the Local Government Act 1933 and, so far as is material, sub-s (1) of that section provides: 'Any land belonging to a local authority and not required for the purposes for which it was acquired or has since been appropriated may be appropriated for any other purpose approved by the Minister for which the local authority are authorised to acquire land . . .'. That section was amended by s 23 of the Town and Country Planning Act 1959 to provide that the approval of the minister was not necessary, but otherwise the section remains in the terms which I have read.

j

It follows from that section that on 17 July 1973 the urban district council had no power to appropriate the green land because it was still required for the purposes for *a* which it was acquired, namely use for sewage disposal. Equally, the urban district council would have had power to appropriate the remainder of the blue land, since that land was not required for such purposes. The question on this appeal is whether the whole resolution of 17 July 1973 is bad, or only that part of it which related to the green land, leaving the remainder of the resolution effective.

On 1 April 1974 and pursuant to arts 8 and 9 of the 1973 order all sewage disposal *b* works vested in local authorities and all their functions exercisable for the purposes of sewerage and sewage disposal were transferred to, and vested in, the local water authorities. If, therefore, the water authority is right in its contention that the appropriation on 17 July 1973 was invalid, on 1 April 1974 the whole of the blue land vested by operation of law in the water authority.

The reasons for the judge's decision are in the following terms: *c*

'Of course the difficulty I am in is that nearly all cases on severance relate to restraint of trade. The planning cases do not help at all. There is no authority, I think, which assists me save that one must apply some test of reasonableness and common sense. I think I would stop short in practice of saying that an appropriation fails because a council have accidentally included a bit of land which they should not, when that can simply be deleted by taking a tracing and drawing on the *d* boundary. I think that if the matter stopped there then I would agree with [counsel for the borough council]. However the matter is more complex than that. It is complex in two ways, albeit related. The first is that in severing one can only sever if at the same time one is implementing the intention of the party responsible for the document, implementing it as far as it validly can be implemented. But in this case the intention of the council was, as [counsel for the borough council] says, *e* expressed in the resolution of 1972, that is to say that the blue land should not be appropriated until the cessation of its current use. Then I find, as I have said, that it was formally recorded that that use had ceased in July 1973, whereas it had not, and so the appropriation went ahead on a false basis of fact. Therefore it cannot be said that by severing one is then implementing the declared intention of the council. There is a further difficulty and it is this: the access to the disposal works, to the blue *f* land, was from a private right of way. The pumping station was situated on the other side of the site. Therefore, in order to reach the pumping station a means of access would have to be provided across land appropriated for another purpose. It is not an access which is defined on the land, because all the land was used for sewage disposal and there was no roadway as such across it, at least none of which there is any evidence. It is possible that following this appropriation the council might have *g* let the appropriated land on a long lease to a company of developers for developing with factories for reletting to nominated tenants. That is not an uncommon practice. Therefore, if that happened, what would be the access to the pumping station? It seems to follow from that that there could not be a severance unless at the same time land was also severed for the purpose of providing an access. I appreciate these are in a way highly technical points, but they are there. I think that both matters I *h* have mentioned stand in the way of severance and are fatal to it.'

Counsel for the borough council in this court pointed out that, had it not been for the two matters which he referred to as difficulties, the judge would have found for the borough council. So far as the first difficulty is concerned, counsel submitted that the judge must be taken as saying that the urban district council intended to transfer the *j* whole of the blue land, and that if the resolution were severed in the way suggested that would not be giving effect to the intention of the urban district council. Counsel for the borough council said that, if the resolution of 17 July 1973 is read by reference to the resolution of 7 November 1972, it is plain that the urban district council did not intend to appropriate the blue land until use for sewage disposal had ceased, and that that had not occurred by 17 July 1973. In any event, said counsel for the borough council, public

law is not concerned with the intentions of authorities so much as with their powers, and
a the plain fact was that on 17 July 1973 the urban district council had no power to
appropriate the green land.

As to the second difficulty of the judge, relating to access to the green land over the
blue land, counsel for the borough council submitted that the judge must have
overlooked the agreed fact that there was access to the green land over the roadway
hatched green on the plan. Moreover, the judge was not referred to art 8 of the Local
b Authorities etc (England) (Property etc: Further Provision) Order 1974, SI 1974/406,
which provides machinery whereby one authority is required to grant easements to
another authority where, as a result of art 8 of the 1973 order, parts of any land are vested
in two different authorities and any easement is required over one part to enable the
other part to be used.

I can well understand that the judge was worried, notwithstanding the agreed fact to
c which I have referred, if he thought that the effect of the severance of the resolution
might be that the water authority would not be able to use the green land because it
would not have the right of access to it; and if he had been referred to the 1974 order his
view might have been different. In my judgment the submissions of counsel for the
borough council are well founded, and I think it was unnecessary for the judge to have
been troubled by the two difficulties to which he referred.

d That, however, is not the end of the matter. Counsel for the water authority submitted
that the court can only sever when the authors of the document have themselves so
framed the document that the part to be discarded is already segregated on the face of
the document. The question of severance only arises if there is something which, on a
perusal of the document itself, is capable of severance; and the court is not entitled to
look at the factual situation on the ground, but is confined to the four corners of the
e document. He submitted that there was no case, whether concerned with contracts in
restraint of trade, statutory orders, byelaws or planning permission subject to conditions,
in which the court has severed the bad provisions from the good unless the bad provisions
appear in the documents themselves. He said that the court would not consider severance
until the severable or excisable part had been identified in the document itself. This is
known as the 'blue pencil test'.

f In my view this is a very narrow point. Council for the water authority conceded that,
if the green land had, on 17 July 1973, not been in the ownership of the urban district
council, then an appropriation of the blue land, excluding the green land, would have
been valid, notwithstanding that the green land was not mentioned in the resolution.
But he submitted that as the green land was in the ownership of the urban district
council, and it had the power to appropriate it by closing down the pumping station, the
g whole appropriation of the blue land was invalid. This, he said, is because the green land
was not identified in the resolution and therefore, applying the blue pencil test, there
was nothing to sever.

It is true that in restraint of trade cases covenants have apparently been severed only
when they contain a narrower as well as a wider limitation. But this is in the context that
prima facie all covenants in restraint of trade are unlawful and void, and the doctrine of
h severance has been kept within strict limits. I agree with the judge that the planning
cases are of little help to us in our problem. *Kent CC v Kingsway Investments (Kent) Ltd*
[1969] 1 All ER 601, [1969] 2 QB 333, CA; [1970] 1 All ER 70, [1971] AC 72 is a good
example of a case in which the question was whether an ultra vires condition vitiated the
whole planning permission, or whether it could be severed so as to preserve the planning
permission itself, shorn of the ultra vires condition. I am, however, helped by a passage
j in the speech of Lord Reid where he said ([1970] 1 All ER 70 at 75, [1971] AC 72 at 90):

'There is a surprising dearth of authority on this matter for it may affect many
classes of case besides those relating to town and country planning—cases where an
authority has granted a licence or permission coupled with an ultra vires condition
or limitation. The question of severance has often arisen with regard to contracts.
But there the position is quite different. It is a general rule that the court will not

remake a contract and to strike out one term and leave the rest in operation is
remaking the contract. So it is not surprising that there can only be severance of a a
contract in exceptional circumstances. But that is not so with regard to a unilateral
licence or permission.'

It is important to remember that we are here concerned not with private law but with
public law. Public law is not concerned with rights and obligations so much as powers,
and the cases show that the courts have adopted a wider approach to the question of
severance in public law than they have in private law. *Potato Marketing Board v Merricks* b
[1958] 2 All ER 538 at 547, [1958] 2 QB 316 at 333, was a public law case. Devlin J said:

'There does not appear to be any authority on the point whether a demand is, in
such circumstances, invalidated. I must, therefore, find the right answer as a matter
of principle, and I think that the principle to be applied is that which is applied to
all classes of documents which are partly good and partly bad because, for example, c
they are in part illegal or ultra vires. In all these cases, the question to be asked is
whether the bad part can be effectively severed from the good.'

It was said by counsel for the water authority that in that case the bad part appeared in
the document itself, but that was not the ratio of the decision, and the statement of
Devlin J is quite general in its terms and was approved expressly by Lord Reid in the
Kingsway Investments case [1970] 1 All ER 70 at 76, [1971] AC 72 at 91. I adopt it as an d
accurate statement, certainly so far as public law is concerned.

Dunkley v Evans [1981] 3 All ER 285, [1981] 1 WLR 1522 is an important decision of
the Divisional Court which was not cited to the judge because at the time of his judgment
it had not been decided. The case arose out of a prosecution in relation to herring fishing
in a prohibited area within British fishing limits, contrary to a statutory order. The
defendants admitted that they had fished in an area over which the minister had power e
to make an order under the relevant Act, but contended that the order itself was invalid
because the prohibited area included certain waters off Northern Ireland over which the
ministerial power to make orders was excluded by a section of the principal Act. The
justices accepted this submission and dismissed the informations, and on appeal to the
Divisional Court the appeal was allowed. In the course of his judgment Ormrod LJ said
([1981] 3 All ER 285 at 287, [1981] 1 WLR 1522 at 1524): f

'The general principle is stated in 1 Halsbury's Laws (4th edn) para 26 thus:
"Unless the invalid part is inextricably interconnected with the valid, a court is
entitled to set aside or disregard the invalid part, leaving the rest intact." The
principle is more fully formulated in the judgment of Cussen J in the Supreme
Court of Victoria in *Olsen v City of Camberwell Corpn* [1926] VLR 58 at 68, where he g
said: "If the enactment with the invalid portion omitted is so radically or substantially
different a law as to the subject matter dealt with by what remains from what it
would be with the omitted portions forming part of it as to warrant the belief that
the legislative body intended it as a whole only, or in other words, to warrant belief
that if all could not be carried into effect, the legislative body would not have enacted
the remainder independently, then the whole must fail." We respectfully agree h
with and adopt this statement of the law. It would be difficult to imagine a clearer
example than the present case of a law which the legislative body would have
enacted independently of the offending portion and which is so little affected by
eliminating the invalid portion. This is clearly, therefore, an order which the court
should not strive officiously to kill to any greater extent than it is compelled to do.'

Then, having summarised one of the points of counsel for the defendants, Ormrod LJ j
continued ([1981] 3 All ER 285 at 288, [1981] 1 WLR 1522 at 1525):

'His main point, however, was that the court could not sever the invalid portion
of this order from the remainder because it was not possible to excise from the text
of the order the words which rendered part of it invalid. This is the so-called "blue
pencil test". This test has been elaborated mainly in connection with covenants in

restraint of trade. No doubt the court will not and cannot rewrite contracts, and so
a   confines itself to deleting part of the text when it is able to do so. The same policy
has been followed in relation to byelaws where the text permitted (see *Strickland v
Hayes* [1896] 1 QB 290) and to a demand for a return, part of which could be struck
out from a form (see *Potato Marketing Board v Merricks* [1958] 2 All ER 538, [1958]
2 QB 316). We can see no reason why the powers of the court to sever the invalid
portion of a piece of subordinate legislation from the valid should be restricted to
b   cases where the text of the legislation lends itself to judicial surgery or textual
emendation by excision.'

Counsel for the water authority pointed out in this court: (1) that *Olsen v City of
Camberwell Corp*, the Australian case relied on by the Divisional Court, was a byelaw case
in which the invalid byelaws appeared on the face of the document and were therefore
severable from the remainder under the blue pencil test; (2) that in *Dunkley v Evans* itself
c   the illegality was apparent from the principal Act, which the court was entitled to look
at in construing the order. I do not think it is possible to distinguish *Dunkley v Evans*
from the instant case in this way. In *Dunkley v Evans*, in order to find the invalidity, the
court had to look outside the order at the principal Act. So here; in order to find the
invalidity, the court has to look outside the resolution at the factual situation on the
ground, namely that the green land is still being used for sewage disposal.
d   That approach was followed by Ackner LJ in *United City Merchants (Investments) Ltd v
Royal Bank of Canada* [1981] 3 All ER 142 at 166, [1982] QB 208 at 242. Ackner LJ said:

'The agreement, not being "illegal", we do not have to consider whether the
whole contract can be said to be "tainted" because that part which is a monetary
transaction in disguise was contrary to the exchange control regulations of Peru.
e   The monetary transactions in disguise being clearly identifiable, I can see no problem
in the court refusing to enforce the merchandise contract to the extent that it was
an exchange contract. Accordingly, if the plaintiffs had sued on the merchandise
contract, they would have been entitled to recover so much of the true and genuine
price of the goods as was then due and owing.'

f   Griffiths LJ said ([1981] 3 All ER 142 at 173–174, [1982] QB 208 at 251):

'I do not however see why the court should not give judgment on the letter of
credit for that sum which is in payment for the machinery and freight. These sums
are easily identifiable, and nothing in the Order in Council renders them
unenforceable. In refusing to give judgment for so much of the claim that relates to
the unenforceable exchange contract the court would be following the precedents
g   set in *Ralli Brothers v Compañia Naviera Sota y Aznar* [1920] 2 KB 287, [1920] All ER
Rep 427, in which judgment was given for freight up to 875 pesetas per tonne but
refused as to the excess which was illegal under Spanish law, and the building
contract cases in which judgment was given for that part of the work for which a
licence had been obtained but refused for the unlicensed excess: see *Jackson Stansfield
& Sons v Butterworth* [1948] 2 All ER 558 and *Dennis & Co Ltd v Munn* [1949] 1 All
h   ER 616, [1949] 2 KB 327. The object of the Order in Council will be achieved by
refusing judgment for so much of the claim as will frustrate the performance of the
exchange contract. I see no reason why the court should go further and prevent the
plaintiff from recovering payment for the machinery which has been lying in a
warehouse in Peru for the last five years.'

j   The same thought was expressed by Lord Diplock in the House of Lords ([1982] 2 All
ER 720 at 730, [1982] 2 WLR 1039 at 1051):

'I avoid speaking of "severability", for this expression is appropriate where the
task on which the court is engaged is construing the language that the parties have
used in a written contract. The question whether and to what extent a contract is
unenforceable under the Bretton Woods Agreements Order in Council 1946 because
it is a monetary transaction in disguise is *not* a question of construction of the

contract but a question of the substance of the transaction to which enforcement of the contract will give effect. If the matter were to be determined simply as a question *a* of construction, the contract between the sellers and the confirming bank constituted by the documentary credit fell altogether outside the Bretton Woods Agreements: it was not a contract to exchange one currency for another currency but a contract to pay currency for documents which included documents of title to goods. On the contrary, the task on which the court is engaged is to penetrate any disguise presented by the actual words the parties have used, to identify any monetary *b* transaction (in the narrow sense of that expression as used in [*Wilson Smithett & Cope Ltd v Terruzzi* [1976] 1 All ER 817, [1976] QB 683]) which those words were intended to conceal and to refuse to enforce the contract to the extent that to do so would give effect to the monetary transaction.'

That was admittedly a contract case but the principle seems to me to apply a fortiori to public law. The question in the instant case is not as to the true construction of the *c* resolution but whether, and to what extent, the urban district council had power to give effect to it. For that purpose the court is entitled, and indeed bound, to look outside the document itself to see whether the urban district council, in fact and in law, had power to do what the resolution on the face of it purports to authorise. In this case it finds an easily identifiable part, namely the green land, which the urban district council had no power to appropriate. There is no more difficulty in deciding whether the resolution was *d* invalid in respect of that part and valid in respect of the remainder than if the green land had been identified in the resolution itself, and no difficulty in the court declaring that the resolution is invalid in respect of the green land and valid in respect of the remainder.

It does not seem to me to matter whether one calls that process severance or whether one calls it modification of the resolution, or whether one uses some other word, or expression, to describe it. In the realm of judicial review it could be dealt with by *e* declarations that the purported appropriation of the green land was ultra vires and of the remainder intra vires.

Much of the difficulty in the case seems to me to have been caused by the very use of the word 'severance', which, in relation to the construction of documents and in particular of covenants in restraint of trade, has acquired a special and technical meaning. Its use in this case demonstrates the danger of using such words in their general or ordinary *f* meaning to describe a process in which the court is in fact considering the validity of the purported exercise of power by a local authority. The label given to the process tends to confuse the reality of the process itself by imposing rules of law designed to deal with quite different situations. I would echo the words of Ormrod LJ in *Dunkley v Evans*, that the court should not strive officiously to kill to any extent greater than it is compelled to do. If, as here, it is perfectly plain that the urban district council had no power to do what *g* it purported to do in respect of an easily identifiable parcel of land, it would not be conducive to good public administration for the court officiously to hold that the whole document, including that part which was within the power of the council, was invalid.

Finally, counsel for the water authority submitted that *Dunkley v Evans* was wrongly decided. For the above reasons, I do not agree. The case affords a welcome breath of fresh air into a branch of the law which was in danger of becoming stifled by technicalities. In *h* my judgment the judge was right in his preliminary view on this point; I would allow the appeal and answer question C in the special case as follows: that the bad part of the resolution can be severed from the remainder.

I turn now to deal with the cross-appeal, which relates only to the pink land, although if right it would also apply to the blue land. It is desirable to restate the precise terms of the resolution of 7 November 1972, because the cross-appeal is concerned with that *j* resolution. The material part reads:

'. . . (i) the Council do now appropriate the area of land not currently used in connection with the Sewage Works, as shown edged pink (on [the] plan . . . from sewerage to planning purposes within the meaning of Section 112(1) of the Town and Country Planning Act, 1971 . . .'

As I have said, s 163 gives the council power to appropriate land for any purpose for
a which it is authorised to acquire land, and in order to discover what land the local
authority is authorised to acquire one has to look at s 112 of the Town and Country
Planning Act 1971. That section empowers the Secretary of State to authorise a local
authority to acquire compulsorily any land within its area if he is satisfied of one of four
matters set out in separate paragraphs. Those matters are described disjunctively and, as
counsel for the water authority submitted, are mutually exclusive. Counsel's first point
b on the cross-appeal was that the resolution was bad on its face because it did not specify
under which of the four paragraphs of s 112(1) the urban district council was purporting
to act. It was never suggested, either before the arbitrator or the deputy judge, that the
resolution was ineffective on that ground, which does not appear in the notice of appeal;
there was no application to amend the notice of appeal, so the point is not open in this
court and counsel for the water authority did not seek to press it.
c   His second point, which is the main point of the cross-appeal, depends on the precise
wording of s 112(1)(d), which it was common ground was the paragraph which was
applicable. That is in the following terms:

'that it is expedient to acquire the land immediately for a purpose which it is
necessary to achieve in the interests of the proper planning of an area in which the
land is situated.'
d
Counsel submitted that the word 'immediately' relates to the purpose which it is
necessary to achieve in the interests of proper planning; he submitted that the provision
was an emergency provision and that there must be evidence of a specific purpose which
was intended to be implemented immediately.
Even if counsel for the water authority is right about that, I cannot see how, on the
e principles set out in *Associated Provincial Picture Houses Ltd v Wednesbury Corp* [1947] 2
All ER 680, [1948] KB 223, the court could interfere with the actions of the council
having regard to the limitations on the word 'immediately' imposed by planning
procedure. In his judgment, having referred to counsel for the water authority's
contention, the judge said:

'The learned arbitrator was unable to accept that contention and neither am I. It
f   seems to me that, looking at the documents from 1969 onwards, the council were
taking active steps. These included discussions with developers, potential occupiers
of the land, and with the county council, as the local planning authority, all with a
view to relocating non-conforming industrial users within that part of the county.
It does not seem to me that it is necessary to define an area with boundaries; the area
is the one in which the removal of the non-conforming users is sought.'
g
That last sentence relates to part of counsel's submission, which was that not only was
there no evidence of an emergency situation, but the evidence did not demonstrate what
the area was, and the whole thing was in a state of flux.
In the particulars of the agreed statement of facts it was stated that the intention of the
urban district council was to use both parcels of land to relocate non-conforming
h industrial users from elsewhere in this district, though it was envisaged that in the
interim part of the site might continue to be used by a Mr Russell as a market garden. If
one looks at s 112(1)(d), it seems to me that the area to which reference is made relates to
the area of the local authority, and the 'proper planning' relates to proper planning in
that area.
In the course of the argument I put it to counsel for the water authority that, if a local
j authority was of the opinion that proper planning required the development of an
industrial estate in its area in order to attract traders from outside the area, that would
fall within the paragraph, and he agreed. I only mention that because it does not seem to
me necessary for the judge to have defined the area in the way in which he did in the last
sentence to which I have referred; indeed, I do not think that the definition is the one
which is provided by the subsection. But in any event I do not accept counsel's
construction of the paragraph. He sought to support that construction by reference to

other sections of the 1971 Act, but, properly understood, those sections do not support his construction. In any event, there is no ambiguity in the plain words in s 112(1)(d); the adverb 'immediately' in the context refers, as a matter of grammar, and can only refer, to the acquisition of the land, and does not require that the purpose for which the land is to be acquired should immediately be put into effect. Counsel for the water authority conceded that, if that was the true construction, then no criticism could be made of the steps taken by the urban district council to acquire it.

For those reasons I would dismiss the cross-appeal.

DILLON LJ. I agree that the appeal should be allowed and that the cross-appeal should be dismissed. I only add a little on the question of severance, as it has been called, which was the main point argued by counsel for the water authority on the appeal relating to the blue land.

The resolution of the old Walton and Weybridge Uurban District Council of 17 July 1973 to appropriate the blue land for planning purposes raises no difficulty on its face. To realise that there is anything wrong with it, it is necessary to look outside the terms of the resolution and to consider the terms of the council's powers of appropriation and the underlying facts. It is then apparent, firstly, that the council's power of appropriation, conferred on it by s 163 of the Local Government Act 1933, is only exercisable in respect of land which is no longer required for the purpose for which it was originally acquired, or has since been appropriated, and, secondly, that part of the blue land, namely the green land, was at the time of the resolution, and still is, required by the council for the sewage disposal purposes for which it was originally acquired. It is apparent, therefore, that the council's resolution represents an excessive exercise of the council's power of appropriation. But examination of the underlying facts shows also that there is no difficulty at all in identifying the extent of the excess. The green land is shown by green boundary lines on the agreed plan B, and its precise area is given to four points of decimals of a hectare in the agreed statement of facts.

In private law the effect of excessive exercise of a power is not in doubt. As Maugham J said in Re Turner, Hudson v Turner [1932] 1 Ch 31 at 37, [1931] All ER Rep 782 at 785:

'When the donee of a power of appointment has purported to exercise the power for an amount greater than that over which it was given, the appointment is good with regard to the correct amount.'

Nearly two hundred years before, Clarke MR had adopted much the same approach when he said in Alexander v Alexander (1755) 2 Ves Sen 640 at 644, 28 ER 408 at 411: 'If the court can see the boundaries it will be good for the execution of the power, and void as to the excess.' This is the sensible approach and I see no reason why there should not be a similar approach in public law.

None the less, counsel for the water authority submits that there is in public law, though not in private law, an overriding requirement that an excessive exercise of a power will be wholly void, and not merely void as to the excess, unless the document exercising the power is so worded as to include words describing the permitted exercise of the power as well as further words describing the excess in such a way that the excess can be excised by the use of a blue pencil, leaving unaltered the wording in the document expressly covering the permitted exercise of the power. I fail to see the sense or logic of such a requirement.

Any excessive exercise of a power, whether in public or private law, is likely to be the result of a mistake on the part of the person exercising the power, ie an erroneous belief that the power extends further than it in truth does. But it is in the highest degree unlikely that that person will realise that he is making such a mistake and yet will not correct it. Therefore it is unlikely to happen, and if it does happen it will be purely fortuitous, that the wording of the exercise of the power will describe in express terms the extent of the permitted exercise of the power as part of the wording used to achieve a wider, and in truth excessive, execution of it. Therefore, if counsel for the water

authority's overriding blue pencil requirement is in truth a requirement of public law, it
a would depend on chance, and not on any actual or presumed intention of the person
exercising the power, or on any rational process of construction of the relevant document,
whether the purported exercise of the power is wholly void or pro tanto valid.

In the next place, the blue pencil test is sought to be introduced into public law from
that field of private law which is concerned with the enforcement of contracts, in
particular of contracts in restraint of trade. Rather special considerations in the field of
b public policy apply, however, to the enforcement of contracts in restraint of trade, and it
is these considerations which are the justification of the blue pencil test; they have no
relevance to the exercise, or excessive exercise, of powers by local authorities or other
public authorities. The only link between these two fields of law is that the word
'severance' may in practice be used, whether correctly or not, in both. But it is not used
to describe the same process. In the field of contract it is used to describe the process of
c construction of the contract to determine whether one provision of the contract can stand
and be enforced despite the invalidity for extrinsic reasons of some other provision of the
contract. But in the context with which we are concerned the term 'severance' is used
merely to determine the extent to which the extrinsic reasons invalidate a provision of
the document. The two processes are by no means necessarily the same.

Quite apart from the lack of logic or sense to support it, counsel for the water
d authority's supposed overriding requirement is inconsistent, in my judgment, with the
approach adopted by the Divisional Court in *Dunkley v Evans* [1981] 3 All ER 285 at 288,
[1981] 1 WLR 1522 at 1525. That was a case of excessive exercise of a power. Ministers
had by a statutory instrument purported to impose fishery restrictions over a large area
of sea, described only by reference to its overall boundary lines which in truth exceeded
the area over which they were, by the relevant statute, empowered to impose restrictions.
e There Ormrod LJ said:

> 'We can see no reason why the powers of the court to sever the invalid portion of
> a piece of subordinate legislation from the valid should be restricted to cases where
> the text of the legislation lends itself to judicial surgery or textual emendation by
> excision.'

f Counsel for the water authority has submitted that the approach of the court in
Dunkley v Evans was wrong, and indeed that the case was wrongly decided. In my
judgment *Dunkley v Evans* was, if I may respectfully say so, a sensible and correct decision,
and it is indistinguishable from the present case.

In *Dunkley v Evans* the court applied, in the field of public law, the general principle
stated in 1 Halsbury's Laws (4th edn) para 26, which Dunn LJ has already read. That, as I
g see it, is substantially the same test as Clarke MR laid down, in the language of his time,
in the passage in *Alexander v Alexander* which I have read. In the present case there is no
difficulty in holding that the appropriation of the blue land to planning purposes in July
1973 was valid save as to the green land, and I would so hold.

STEPHENSON LJ. For some centuries our courts have been applying to the benevolent
h interpretation of written instruments of all kinds, including statutes, the commonsense
principle preserved in latin as ut res magis valeat quam pereat: Co Litt 36A; Broom's Select
Legal Maxims (10th edn, 1939) p 361.

By applying that principle they have been able not only to make sense of near nonsense
but also to give effect to what is good and enforce what is valid, while refusing to enforce
what is bad and giving no effect to what is invalid. This latter exercise can be carried out,
j and can, of course, be carried out only, where the good and bad parts are clearly
identifiable and the bad part can be separated from the good and rejected without
affecting the validity of the remaining part. But this ought to be done whenever the
good and bad parts can be so identified and separated and what remains is clearly valid in
the sense that there is nothing inherently unenforceable about it and all the surrounding
circumstances indicate that common sense and the intention of the maker of any
document which includes both good and bad parts would give effect to it.

There will be cases where no such identification and separation of good from bad is possible and the invalidity of one part will taint and invalidate the whole. (The curate's *a* egg was such a tainted whole, whatever its deferential consumer may have intended to hint to the contrary.) But I cannot see why this should be so in every case where the document which confronts the court does not itself identify the invalid part. To treat every such document as the egg of the curate would disable the court, by a matter of form only, from dividing what is clearly divisible into its component parts, as I tried to point out in *United City Merchants (Investments) Ltd v Royal Bank of Canada* [1981] 3 All ER *b* 142 at 157–158, [1982] QB 208 at 229, where a number of authorities were cited to the court, and others were referred to, on the application of what was there called (apparently in error) severance in the field of private contracts.

But, where what is alleged to be invalid and unenforceable can be isolated and identified with precision, the court should not refuse to enforce the rest, as Ackner LJ pointed out in *United City Merchants (Investments) Ltd v Royal Bank of Canada* [1981] 3 All *c* ER 142 at 166, [1982] QB 208 at 242 in the passage which Dunn LJ has read. That is so when there is nothing in the document to isolate and identify the unenforceable, but outside circumstances supply the identification and reveal the true nature of the transaction, as the House of Lords held in that case: see the speech of Lord Diplock in the passage quoted by Dunn LJ ([1982] 2 All ER 720 at 730, [1982] 2 WLR 1039 at 1050– 1051).

This principle of enforcing the enforceable as far as possible, of making the thing work *d* and not be lost, applies alike in private and public law. In private law it will generally be applied where what is agreed is partly illegal, in public law where what is ordered is partly ultra vires, as Devlin J indicated in the passage cited by Dunn LJ from *Potato Marketing Board v Merricks* [1958] 2 All ER 538 at 547, [1958] 2 QB 316 at 333. Though it may be easier to apply the principle where the contract or resolution intrinsically *e* identifies the illegal or ultra vires matter, it is in my judgment equally applicable where, as here, the thing is extrinsic and identifiable by looking outside. There may also be cases where the court cannot be certain what the author of a written contract, for example, would have intended if he had known the facts which made part performance impossible, or the law which made part performance unlawful or beyond his powers. Then the court cannot enforce what remains. But counsel for the water authority has failed to persuade *f* me that there can be any such doubt about the urban district council's intention in resolving on this appropriation not to exceed its powers.

I accordingly reject counsel for the water authority's submission that the appropriating resolution is invalid in toto because it does not itself separate the green land from the rest of the blue, and I hold that the identification of the green land and its 0·0298 hectares by inspection of the site gives the court the same power, by whatever name it is called, to *g* validate the appropriation of the rest of the blue land.

I therefore agree that the borough council's appeal should be allowed for the reasons given by Dunn and Dillon LJJ.

I also agree that the water authority's cross-appeal should be dismissed for the reasons given by Dunn LJ.

h

Appeal allowed. Cross-appeal dismissed. Leave to appeal to House of Lords refused.

Solicitors: *D W Jenkins*, Walton-on-Thames (for the borough council); *R A R Gray* (for the water authority).

Diana Brahams   Barrister.

H and another v Schering Chemicals Ltd and another

QUEEN'S BENCH DIVISION

BINGHAM J

29 JUNE 1981

Document – Admissibility in evidence – Record as evidence of facts stated therein – Record – Articles and letters published in learned journals – Plaintiffs claiming damages against pharmaceutical companies for personal injuries caused by drug – Plaintiffs seeking to adduce as evidence documents consisting of summaries of research into drug and articles and letters published in medical journals – Whether documents admissible as 'records' – Whether documents admissible under court's discretion to order that evidence of any fact 'shall be given . . . in such manner as may be specified' – Whether documents could form part of plaintiffs' evidence by incorporation into evidence of expert witness – Civil Evidence Act 1968, s 4(1) – RSC Ord 38, r 3(1).

Evidence – Expert witness – Reference to publications of other experts – Probative value of documents referred to.

The plaintiffs brought actions against the defendants, who were pharmaceutical companies, claiming damages for personal injuries alleged to be caused by the defendants' negligence in manufacturing and marketing a drug used by the plaintiffs. The major issues in the actions were whether the drug in fact caused the injuries complained of and whether in manufacturing and marketing the drug the defendants were negligent. The plaintiffs applied for an order allowing them to adduce as evidence in the actions copies of documents consisting of summaries of the results of research into the drug, and articles and letters about the drug published in medical journals. The plaintiffs contended they were entitled to adduce the documents as evidence on the grounds (i) that the documents constituted 'records' within s 4(1)[a] of the Civil Evidence Act 1968 and thus were admissible evidence of the facts stated therein, or (ii) even if they were not, they could be admitted under RSC Ord 38, r 3(1)[b], which enabled the court to 'order that evidence of any . . . fact shall be given at the trial in such manner as may be specified'. It was contended that r 3 gave the court discretion to admit as evidence any material that was not otherwise admissible. It was common ground that expert witnesses who gave evidence at the trial would be entitled to refer to the articles in question as part of the body of medical knowledge within their field of expertise.

Held – (1) For the purposes of s 4(1) of the 1968 Act a 'record' meant any document which could be regarded as an original or primary source of information in the sense that it either gave effect to a transaction or contained a contemporaneous register of information supplied by those with direct knowledge of the facts. Judged by that standard the documents in question, being merely a digest or analysis of primary or original sources of information, were not 'records' since they were not primary or original sources of information. Accordingly they were not admissible under s 4(1) of the 1968 Act (see p 852 *d e g h*, post).

(2) The documents could not be admitted as evidence under RSC Ord 38, r 3 because the object of r 3 was merely to facilitate proof of largely formal matters which, although in issue, were peripheral to the major issues in the action, rather than to permit the admission of material relating to crucial issues in an action which would not rank as evidence under the rules of evidence. Accordingly, the court could not order the admission under r 3 of material which was not otherwise admissible even under s 4 of the 1968 Act (see p 853 *e f*, post).

---

a   Section 4(1) is set out at p 851 *j* to p 852 *a*, post

b   Rule 3(1) is set out at p 852 *h*, post

(3) However, since the expert witnesses at the trial would be able to refer to the articles in question as part of the body of their expertise, and if they did so the court would have *a* to admit the articles in evidence in the sense of reading them and giving the factual assertions in them such weight as was thought fit, it followed that the plaintiffs would be able to incorporate the articles as part of their evidence by means of having the expert witnesses at the trial refer to them. In all the circumstances, the court would make no order on the application (see p 853 g to j and p 854 b c g to j, post); dictum of Cooke J in *Seyfang v G D Searle & Co* [1973] 1 All ER at 292–293 applied. *b*

Per curiam. If an expert refers to the results of research published by a reputable authority in a reputable journal the court will ordinarily regard those results as supporting any inferences fairly to be drawn from them, unless or until a different approach is shown to be correct (see p 853 j, post).

Notes *c*

For the admissibility of records as evidence, see 17 Halsbury's Laws (4th edn) para 58, and for cases on the subject, see 22 Digest (Reissue) 83–84, 519–520.

For expert evidence, see 17 Halsbury's Laws (4th edn) para 83.

For the Civil Evidence Act 1968, s 4, see 12 Halsbury's Statutes (3rd edn) 913.

Cases referred to in judgment *d*

Edmonds v Edmonds [1947] P 67, CA, 22 Digest (Reissue) 272, 2485.

Knight (decd) v David (decd) [1971] 3 All ER 1066, [1971] 1 WLR 1671, 22 Digest (Reissue) 83, 519.

Koscot Interplanetary (UK) Ltd, Re [1972] 3 All ER 829, 22 Digest (Reissue) 275, 2492.

R v Jones, R v Sullivan [1978] 2 All ER 718, [1978] 1 WLR 195, CA, Digest (Cont Vol E) 141, 4906b. *e*

R v Tirado (1974) 59 Cr App R 80, CA.

Seyfang v G D Searle & Co [1973] 1 All ER 290, [1973] QB 148, [1973] 2 WLR 17, 22 Digest (Reissue) 667, 7123.

Taylor v Taylor (Taylor intervening, Holmes cited) [1970] 2 All ER 609, [1970] 1 WLR 1148, CA, 22 Digest (Reissue) 307, 2872.

Thrasyvoulous Ioannou v Papa Christoforos Demetriou [1952] 1 All ER 179, [1952] AC 84, *f* PC, 22 Digest (Reissue) 342, 3284.

Application and preliminary issue

By writ issued on 19 September 1977 the plaintiffs, D W, an infant suing by his father and next friend, his father and his mother, brought an action against the defendants, *g* Schering Chemicals Ltd, and Schering AG (whose principal place of business was in the Federal Republic of Germany) claiming damages for personal injuries, pain, suffering and loss sustained by the infant and for loss and damage sustained by his parents, caused by his mother taking the drug Primodos whilst she was pregnant with the infant, on the ground that the defendants negligently manufactured the drug and/or supplied it and/or caused or permitted it to be used as a pregnancy testing drug. By a writ issued on 19 *h* December 1978 R H, an infant suing by his mother and next friend, and his mother brought an action against the same defendants making a similar claim against them. By applications dated 16 June 1982 the plaintiffs in each action applied under RSC Ord 38, r 3 for an order that evidence be given at the trial of the actions by the production of copies of certain specified documents consisting of summaries of the results of research into the drug and articles and letters published in medical journals concerning the drug, *j* as evidence of the facts stated in the documents. Further, at the hearing of the applications, the judge, Bingham J, directed that there be tried as a preliminary issue whether the documents in question were 'records' within s 4 of the Civil Evidence Act 1968. The application was heard in chambers. The case is reported by permission of Bingham J. The facts are set out in the judgment.

Peter Weitzman QC and *Andrew Bano* for the plaintiffs.

a   *Roy Beldam QC, Gavin Lightman QC* and *Michael Spencer* for the defendants.

BINGHAM J. In these actions the plaintiffs sue for damages for personal injuries caused, as it is alleged, by the negligence of the defendants in the marketing and manufacturing of Primodos.

Two major issues arise in the action, as I understand it, first, an issue whether the
b   defendants were negligent as alleged in that respect, and, second, a fundamental issue whether the drug, of which complaint is made, did in fact cause the injuries of which the plaintiffs complain.

The application before me is an application issued on behalf of all the plaintiffs in the action under RSC Ord 38, r 3 for an order that evidence shall be given at the trial of these actions by the production of copies of the documents listed in the schedule annexed
c   thereto of (1) all the facts set out in the documents or in the alternative (2) the facts in each of the documents set out in the notice to admit facts served on the defendants on 18 May 1981. That notice refers to a substantial bundle which is before me and which is divided into effectively 20 sections. In each section there is a notice to admit facts and a list of the facts of which admission is sought. There are a notice and particulars relating to statements which it is sought to adduce in evidence under s 4 of the Civil Evidence
d   Act 1968, and there is in each case a document. The nature of that document varies. Sometimes it is a document summarising the results of research, sometimes an article in a medical journal and sometimes a letter published in a medical journal, such as, for example, the Lancet, there being several of these documents which are in fact letters to the Lancet.

It is common ground, as I understand it, that these articles can be referred to for the
e   purpose of showing the state of general professional knowledge, which is of course relevant to the issue as to what the defendants knew or ought to have known at any given time. It is further common ground that the articles can be referred to by experts as part of the corpus of medical knowledge within the expertise of a medical expert.

But the plaintiffs want to prove the facts and the results of the research as summarised in the articles for the purpose of showing, on the strength of those facts and results, that
f   the administering of the drug did cause the injuries complained of, and for that purpose the plaintiffs want the articles to be admitted in evidence for the purpose of proving those facts. The defendants, for obvious and understandable reasons, contend that that cannot be done.

The plaintiffs' argument in a nutshell is that these articles are admissible in evidence as records under s 4 of the Civil Evidence Act 1968. In any event, the plaintiffs continue,
g   the court has discretion to admit the articles in evidence under RSC Ord 38, r 3, even if the articles are not strictly admissible under the 1968 Act, and the plaintiffs contend that the court should exercise its discretion in this case in favour of admitting the documents.

I should make it clear that the 1968 Act process of notice and counter-notice has not been completed at this stage. Notices under the Act have been given; counter-notices have not yet been given and therefore it is, strictly speaking, premature to consider the
h   position under the 1968 Act in detail. But the question has been argued whether these documents are records under the Act, and it may very well be that the answer to that question is relevant to the exercise of the discretion under Ord 38, r 3.

Accordingly it seems both proper and helpful to express a view on the 1968 Act question at this stage, and I think it is convenient to do so first of all.

Section 4(1) of the 1968 Act says:

j
'Without prejudice to section 5 of this Act, in any civil proceedings a statement contained in a document shall, subject to this section and to rules of court, be admissible as evidence of any fact stated therein of which direct oral evidence would be admissible, if the document is, or forms part of, a record compiled by a person acting under a duty from information which was supplied by a person (whether

acting under a duty or not) who had, or may reasonably be supposed to have had, personal knowledge of the matters dealt with in that information and which, if not supplied by that person to the compiler of the record directly, was supplied by him to the compiler of the record indirectly through one or more intermediaries each acting under a duty.'

The first question in this case is whether these documents are records. Counsel for the plaintiffs submits that the tendency which the 1968 Act was intended to advance is towards admitting hearsay evidence, subject always to the questions of weight which are left for the determination of the trial court. He further points out that the word 'record' is given a wide meaning, and he is certainly right in submitting that in *R v Jones* [1978] 2 All ER 718, [1978] 1 WLR 195 a very wide meaning is given to that expression, significantly wider than was indicated in *R v Tirado* (1974) 59 Cr App R 80 at 90.

Counsel for the defendants submits that, be that as it may, these documents, in issue in this case, are simply not records. They are, he says, an analysis of records or a digest of records but not themselves a record. He further says that there is a danger in admitting material, sometimes said in the course of the material itself to be tentative, and that there is too much unknown about the research underlying these documents to make it safe to admit them as evidence.

Having considered the matter as best I can in the light of the arguments and the authorities, I have come to the conclusion that the documents which form part of the large bundle before me are not records within the meaning of s 4 of the 1968 Act. The intention of that section was, I believe, to admit in evidence records which a historian would regard as original or primary sources, that is documents which either give effect to a transaction itself or which contain a contemporaneous register of information supplied by those with direct knowledge of the facts.

Judged by this standard, the commercial documents in *R v Jones* [1978] 2 All ER 718, [1978] 1 WLR 195, the tithe map in *Knight (decd) v David (decd)* [1971] 3 All ER 1066, [1971] 1 WLR 1671, the record in *Edmonds v Edmonds* [1947] P 67 and the transcript in *Taylor v Taylor* [1970] 2 All ER 609, [1970] 1 WLR 1148 would rank as records as in those cases they were held to be.

On the other hand, the documents in *Thrasyvoulous Ioannou v Papa Christoforos Demetriou* [1952] 1 All ER 179, [1952] AC 84, the file of letters in *R v Tirado* (1974) 59 Cr App R 80 and the summary of cases in *Re Koscot Interplanetary (UK) Ltd* [1972] 3 All ER 829 would fail to be admitted as records, as in the first two cases they did.

Judged by the same standard the documents in the present case, I think, are not records and are not primary or original sources. They are a digest or analysis of records which must exist or have existed, but they are not themselves those records. If the plaintiffs' submission were right it would, I think, mean that anyone who wrote a letter to The Times, having done research and summarising the result of that research in his letter, would find his letter admissible as evidence of the facts under s 4. That is not, I think, the intent of the section, and accordingly, whatever counter-notice was served in response to the plaintiffs' notice the effect would not, in my judgment, be to make the evidence admissible under s 4.

I accordingly turn to consider the position under RSC Ord 38, r 3 which provides:

'(1) Without prejudice to rule 2, the Court may, at or before the trial of any action, order that evidence of any particular fact shall be given at the trial in such manner as may be specified by the order.

(2) The power conferred by paragraph (1) extends in particular to ordering that evidence of any particular fact may be given at the trial—(a) by statement on oath of information or belief, or (b) by the production of documents or entries in books, or (c) by copies of documents or entries in books, or (d) in the case of a fact which is or was a matter of common knowledge either generally or in a particular district, by the production of a specified newspaper which contains a statement of that fact.'

a   Counsel for the plaintiffs submits that on its face that rule gives the court a discretion to
    admit evidence not otherwise admissible. He points out that the rule is made under
    s 99(1)(i) of the Supreme Court of Judicature (Consolidation) Act 1925, which authorises
    rules to be made—

>   'For regulating the means by which particular facts may be proved, and the mode
>   in which evidence thereof may be given, in any proceedings or on any application
b >   in connection with or at any stage of the proceedings.'

    The language of the rule clearly, as he submits, picks up the language of the subsection.
    Moreover, he says that s 101 of the same Act makes it clear that the effect of such a rule
    if properly made may be to vary, alter or derogate from the rules of evidence as generally
    understood. Section 101 provides:

c >   'Nothing in this Act and, subject as hereinafter in this section expressly provided,
>   nothing in rules of court made under this Act, shall affect the mode of giving
>   evidence by the oral examination of witnesses in trials with a jury, or the rules of
>   evidence, or the law relating to jurymen or juries: Provided that nothing in this
>   section shall—(a) prejudice the operation of any rules of court made in pursuance of
>   the express power conferred by this Act to make rules of court for regulating the
d >   means by which particular facts may be proved and the mode in which evidence
>   thereof may be given; or (b) affect the power of the court for special reasons to allow
>   depositions or affidavits to be read.'

    Counsel for the plaintiffs submits that the express purpose of the proviso is to permit
    the admission of evidence not otherwise admissible. I am not myself persuaded that that
    is so. I think it may very well be that the purpose of ss 99(1)(i) and 101 and the rule itself
e   may be to permit the giving of secondary evidence instead of what would ordinarily be
    regarded as the best evidence, rather than to permit the adducing in evidence at all. As I
    say, I believe that to be the position, although I have some doubts about the effect of Ord
    38, r 3(2)(a) and (d). But even if I am wrong, I think that the object of the rule is to
    permit the proof of matters, or to facilitate the proof of matters, which, although in issue,
    are largely peripheral to the major issue in the action, that is to facilitate the proof of
f   matters which are largely, although not completely, formal. It is not, I think, the purpose
    of this rule to permit the adducing on an issue crucial to the outcome, as here, of material
    which does not rank as evidence, even for purposes of the 1968 Act and the rules of court.

    Accordingly I feel unable in the exercise of my discretion, if the evidence is not
    admissible under the 1968 Act, to order that it be admitted under Ord 38, r 3. I would,
    however, add, and it is an important part of my conclusion on the matter, the following.
g   It is, as I have said, common ground that these articles can be referred to by experts as
    part of the general corpus of medical knowledge falling within the expertise of an expert
    in this field. That of course means that an expert who says (and I am looking at it from
    the plaintiffs' point of view for the purposes of my example), 'I consider that there is a
    causal connection between the taking of the drug and the resulting deformity,' can
    fortify his opinion by referring to learned articles, publications, letters as reinforcing the
h   view to which he has come. In doing do, he can make reference to papers in which a
    contrary opinion may be expressed but in which figures are set out which he regards as
    supporting his contention. In such a situation one asks: are the figures and statistics set
    out in such an article strictly proved? And I think the answer is No. I think that they are
    none the less of probative value when referred to and relied on by an expert in the
    manner in which I have indicated. If an expert refers to the results of research published
j   by a reputable authority in a reputable journal the court would, I think, ordinarily regard
    those results as supporting inferences fairly to be drawn from them, unless or until a
    different approach was shown to be proper.

    Let me apply that to this case. Counsel for the defendants submits that there are great
    dangers in relying on these results contained in this material. For example, he says that
    certain of them refer to pills having been prescribed but leave it uncertain whether the

pills were taken. If the pills were taken the results as published often leave it unclear at what stage of a pregnancy they were taken. Were they, for example, taken at a stage *a* when it was too late for the fetus to be affected by the pills, even if they were capable of having an injurious effect in other circumstances? How were the control cases matched? How were the histories taken? How were the cases identified, and so on? All of these are valid points which will fall to be considered and assessed when they are made and when they are put to and discussed with any expert who relies on the articles. It may be that some of the answers will be found in the papers themselves. It may be that other matters *b* will be left in doubt. It may very well be that grounds will emerge for viewing the results of the research with caution or scepticism. But in my judgment the proper approach of this court is to admit the articles, in the sense of reading them, and to give the factual assertions in those articles such weight as appears to the court, having heard any cross-examination or other evidence, to be proper.

That is the proper approach I think derives support from the judgment of Cooke J in *c* *Seyfang v G D Searle & Co* [1973] 1 All ER 290, [1973] QB 148. That was a case in which there was litigation in the United States on a somewhat similar issue to the present issue, the issue in that case being whether there was a causative link between the taking of the contraceptive pill and thrombo-embolic disorder. One of the parties to the United States litigation sought to subpoena certain British experts who had published the results of their research on this subject, for the purpose of establishing the causative link on which *d* they relied. In the course of giving his judgment, Cooke J said ([1973] 1 All ER 290 at 292–293, [1973] QB 148 at 151):

'Mr Baggott says in his affidavit that taking the testimony of the two doctors is the only way in which he can get the contents of the four articles into evidence in the action. While I accept that as a correct statement of Ohio law, in the absence of *e* evidence to the contrary, I must confess that I find it surprising. The four articles now form part of the corpus of medical expertise on this particular subject. I apprehend that in England a medical expert witness with the proper qualifications would be allowed to refer to the articles as part of that corpus of expertise, even though he was not the author of the articles himself. It does appear to me with the greatest respect that a system which does not permit experts to refer in their expert *f* evidence to the publications of other experts in the same field is a system which puts peculiar difficulties in the way of proof of matters which depend on expert opinion.'

That seems to me with respect to be the right approach to the matter, and I say so with the greater diffidence, having regard to the fact that I think the judge's observations reflect a submission made to him by counsel for the doctors in that case. *g*

Accordingly the plaintiffs are, in my judgment, entitled by means of expert evidence to incorporate the contents of the articles in their evidence in this case, and it will be given such weight as in the light of any other evidence and of any cross-examination appears to be proper.

Now this is, I am conscious, a matter of considerable importance in the present case, and I am anxious that both parties should have the opportunity to test my conclusions if *h* they wish to do so. In the ordinary way my inclination would be to make no order on this application which would unquestionably entitle counsel for the plaintiffs to appeal against it, if he considers that my rejection either of his argument on the 1968 Act or on Ord 38, r 3 should be challenged, but I think that if I make no order on the application it makes it very hard for counsel for the defendants to challenged the order, and therefore, subject to the wishes of the defendants, I would be willing to make an order under Ord *j* 38, r 3, that the articles can be incorporated by reference in the evidence of expert witnesses called by the plaintiffs in order to give Counsel for the defendants an order that he can appeal against. But I should add that I consider the making of such an order under Ord 38, r 3 to be strictly unnecessary, and therefore it will be something of a procedural device in order to enable him to take the matter to the Court of Appeal if he wishes.

Determination on preliminary issue that documents not records within s 4 of the Civil Evidence
a *Act 1968. No order on the application. Leave to appeal.*

Solicitors: Mildred & Beaumont, Battersea (for the plaintiffs); McKenna & Co (for the
defendants).

K Mydeen Esq   Barrister.

b

Kirkup v British Rail Engineering Ltd
c # and other appeals

QUEEN'S BENCH DIVISION
CROOM-JOHNSON J
29 JULY, 4 OCTOBER 1982

d *Practice – Evidence – Expert evidence – Disclosure to other parties – Time for disclosure –*
Personal injuries action – Non-medical experts' reports – Court ordering disclosure of reports –
Whether disclosure should be mutual – Whether court may order one party to disclose his expert's
report first – RSC Ord 38, r 37.

The plaintiff brought an action against the defendants, who operated 12 railway
e engineering works in various places throughout the country, alleging that over a long
period of time he had worked for the defendants in conditions in which he became deaf
because of the defendants' negligence or breach of statutory duty. On the summons for
directions the master ordered that the plaintiff disclose his non-medical expert's reports
not later than 28 days after setting down and that the defendants disclose their report
within 42 days thereafter. The plaintiff appealed against the master's order, contending
f that, in exercising his discretion under RSC Ord 38, r 37[a] to order disclosure of the
reports, the master should have ordered mutual disclosure.

Held – (1) Although mutuality and fairness was one of the reasons for disclosure of
experts' reports in personal injuries actions, it was not the only one, nor was it of such
overriding importance that it governed the situation in every case. Other important
g considerations were the saving of costs, the avoidance of surprise and the need to avoid
amendments at the trial. In a proper case it was permissible to order one party to disclose
his report first, so that the expert consulted by the other party could address his mind
specifically to the points made in it, since, although it might appear to give the later party
an advantage, it could do much towards crystallising the issues and might lead to an
earlier and fairer settlement of the action (see p 858 g h, post); Ollett v Bristol Aerojet Ltd
h [1979] 3 All ER 544n applied.

(2) Since the defendants' works throughout the country had given rise to some 3,000
claims for damages for alleged industrially-caused deafness, since it was hardly feasible
that only one expert engineer was advising all the plaintiffs, since the circumstances of
each claim differed as to the degree and length of exposure to noise and since it was
unreasonable to expect the defendants to have one ready-made standard engineer's report
j available for use every time a claim was made against them, it was not in the circumstances
unreasonable to require the plaintiff to disclose his expert's report so that the defendants
might consider the issue raised by it and ask their own expert to deal with it. The appeal
would accordingly be dismissed (see p 858 j to p 859 b, post).

_____

a   Rule 37, so far as material, is set out at p 858 a, post

Notes

For disclosure of expert evidence in the form of a report in actions for personal injuries, *a*
see 37 Halsbury's Laws (4th edn) para 463.

Cases referred to in judgment

Ollett v Bristol Aerojet Ltd [1979] 3 All ER 544n, [1979] 1 WLR 1197n.

Worrall v Reich [1955] 1 All ER 363, [1955] 1 QB 296, [1955] 2 WLR 338, CA, 51 Digest
(Repl) 607, 2283.   *b*

Interlocutory appeal and references

Kirkup v British Rail Engineering Ltd

By writ dated 27 July 1979 the plaintiff, Arthur Kirkup, brought an action against the
defendants, British Rail Engineering Ltd, for damages for personal injuries and
consequential loss as a result of contracting a hearing condition as a result of exposure to *c*
excessive noise in the course of his employment with the defendants at their premises at
Shildon, Co Durham, owing to the negligence and/or breach of statutory duty of the
defendants, their servants or agents. On 28 January 1982 Master Creightmore ordered,
inter alia, that the plaintiff disclose his engineer's report not later than 28 days after
setting down and that the defendants disclose their engineer's report within 42 days
thereafter. The plaintiff appealed against that part of the master's order and applied for *d*
the parties' engineers' reports to be mutually disclosed within 28 days after setting down.

Priestley v British Rail Engineering Ltd

By writ dated 1 July 1980 the plaintiff, John Priestley, brought an action against the
defendants, British Rail Engineering Ltd, for damages for personal injuries and
consequential loss as a result of contracting a hearing condition as a result of exposure to *e*
excessive noise in the course of his employment with the defendants at their premises at
Shildon, Co Durham, since 1965 owing to the negligence and/or breach of statutory duty
of the defendants, their servants or agents. On 29 January 1982 Master Elton adjourned
an application by the defendants for an order that the plaintiff disclose his engineer's
report first and that the defendants disclose their engineer's report after that to give the
defendants an opportunity to file an affidavit in support of their application. By consent *f*
the question of disclosures was argued before the judge.

Painter v British Rail Engineering Ltd

By writ dated 13 May 1981 the plaintiff, Ronald Walter Painter, brought an action
against the defendants, British Rail Engineering Ltd, for damages for physical harm,
noise-induced hearing loss and tinnitus, loss and damage sustained by reason of the *g*
negligence and/or breach of statutory duty on the part of the defendants, their servants
or agents at their premises at Ruckholt Road, Leyton, London E10, since about 1964. On
9 July 1982 Master Creightmore referred the question of disclosure of engineers' reports
to the judge in chambers under RSC Ord 32, r 12.

The three cases were heard in chambers but judgment was given by Croom-Johnson J
in open court.   *h*

K L May for the plaintiffs Kirkup and Priestley.
Diana Cotton for the plaintiff Painter.
William Gage QC for the defendants.

Cur adv vult
j

4 October. The following judgment was delivered.

CROOM-JOHNSON J. Each of these matters covers a simple point on the disclosure
of the reports of non-medical expert witnesses in personal injuries actions. Each plaintiff
sues the defendants alleging that over a long period of time he worked for them in

conditions in which he became deaf because the defendants failed in a legal duty owed to
him. Each case will eventually involve hearing evidence about the levels of noise to
which the plaintiff was subjected at different times and places in the course of his
employment.

The position in each action, on the summons for directions, is at present as follows.
Kirkup's case: the master ordered that the plaintiff disclose his experts' reports not later
than 28 days after setting down and that the defendants disclose their reports within 42
days thereafter. The plaintiff appeals against that order. *Priestley's* case: a request for
interrogatories was referred to me by the master, and this has already been dealt with.
The question of disclosure of experts' reports is still with the master, who adjourned the
plaintiff's application so that the defendants might file an affidavit. By consent I have
heard argument on that subject, since the same counsel are involved as in *Kirkup's* case.
Painter's case: the question of disclosure of experts' reports was referred to me under RSC
Ord 32, r 12.

The basic rule is that experts' reports, whether medical or non-medical, made on the
advice of legal advisers and for the purpose of litigation, are privileged: see *Worrall v
Reich* [1955] 1 All ER 363, [1955] 1 QB 296. In personal injury actions, for a number of
reasons, special provisions have been made within the Rules of the Supreme Court.
Needless to say, the present are all personal injury actions. The reasons are many and
include the saving of time and costs at the interlocutory stage, to bring the action on for
trial more quickly, to try and reach agreement on the experts' reports so as to save costs
at trial, and to cut down the inevitable shadow-boxing associated with litigation. A party
who does not want to disclose his expert evidence may still sit tight on *Worrall v Reich*,
but, if he does, his right to call any expert evidence at all is limited and may be prohibited.

The first short cut is found in Ord 25, r 8(1)(b). This provides that without the need
for any application to the court the parties shall disclose to each other, normally within
ten weeks after close of pleadings, the reports of those experts on which they intend to
rely. This is with a view to the reports being agreed. If there is no agreement, those
experts (and only those) may be called. That disclosure means mutual exchange: see Ord
25, r 8(2). But either party has the right to apply to the court for different directions, if
he wishes to proceed differently: see Ord 25, r 8(3).

All applications relating to the calling of expert evidence are made under Ord 38,
r 36(1). Unless such an application is made, then, with some exceptions, no expert
evidence may be called if (in personal injury actions) the short cut provided by Ord 25, r
8(1) has not been used. When there is such an application, any direction made under it
must be complied with.

In ordinary actions for personal injuries there is an obligation on the court to order
disclosure 'unless the Court considers that there is sufficient reason for not doing so': see
Ord 38, r 37(2). This applies whether the evidence relates to medical or non-medical
matters, and the burden of proof is on whoever it is who is urging non-disclosure. This
explains the master's adjournment in *Priestley's* case.

But two questions have to be decided on the construction of Ord 38, r 37(2). (i) What
is the extent of the court's discretion whether or not to order disclosure? (ii) What is the
extent of the court's discretion as to the time or times by which disclosure (if ordered) is
to be made?

The extent of the court's discretion in personal injuries cases
Order 38, r 37(3) deals with medical matters. It reads as follows (where relevant):

> 'Where the expert evidence relates to medical matters the Court may, if it thinks
> fit, treat the following circumstances as sufficient reason for not giving a direction
> . . . namely, that the expert evidence may contain an expression of opinion—(i) as
> to the manner in which the personal injuries were sustained; or (ii) as to the
> genuineness of the symptoms of which complaint is made.'

The question here is whether the two instances given are exclusive (ie the only two reasons which may be regarded as sufficient) or are simply examples. Non-medical matters are dealt with by Ord 38, r 37(4); it reads:

'Where the expert evidence does not relate to medical matters, the Court may, if it thinks fit, treat as a sufficient reason for not giving a direction . . . any of the circumstances set out in sub-paragraphs (a) or (b) of rule 38(2).'

It is therefore necessary to look at r 38. This deals with expert evidence in actions other than personal injuries. Rule 38(2) reads:

'In deciding whether to give a direction under paragraph (1) [of r 38] the Court shall have regard to all the circumstances and may, to such extent as it thinks fit, treat any of the following circumstances as affording a sufficient reason for not giving such a direction:—(a) that the expert evidence is or will be based to any material extent upon a version of the facts in dispute between the parties; or (b) that the expert evidence is or will be based to any material extent upon facts which are neither—(i) ascertainable by the expert by the exercise of his own powers of observation, nor (ii) within his general professional knowledge and experience.'

It is noticeable that r 37(4), in incorporating r 38(2)(a) and (b), does not incorporate those words in r 38(2) which allow the court to have regard to 'all the circumstances', which could be regarded as a pointer in favour, to some extent, of the exclusive interpretation.

On the other hand, r 37(2), although it directs prima facie disclosure, reserves to the court a judicial discretion not to do so. In both para (3) and para (4) of r 37, if the instances there given were meant to be the only circumstances in which that discretion might be exercised, one would have expected to find some express words of limitation, which are not there.

The conclusion to which I have come is that paras (3) and (4) of r 37 contain guidelines for everyday use but are not the only circumstances in which a direction for disclosure may be withheld.

Once the extent of the judicial discretion is solved in this way, then the same discretion applies to the time or times by which disclosure shall be made. The notes to *The Supreme Court Practice 1982* vol 1, paras 38/35/5, 38/37–39/2, pp 675, 678 lay emphasis on having an 'exchange date' for the reports, so that neither side gets the report of the other side first and thereby a presumed advantage. The object, it is said, is 'fairness and mutuality'. It is noticeable that where there is an automatic disclosure, as provided by Ord 25, r 8(2), there is express provision for mutual exchange. This is not repeated in Ord 38, r 37. Must this therefore apply to every disclosure, even disclosure under Ord 38, r 37? In a simple case, such as *Ollett v Bristol Aerojet Ltd* [1979] 3 All ER 544n, [1979] 1 WLR 1197n, this would be an obvious course to be taken. The question in the present case is whether the order made by the master in *Kirkup* for sequential disclosure is allowable or proper.

Mutuality and fairness is one of the reasons for disclosure of experts' reports in personal injury actions, but it is not the only one, nor of such overriding importance that it governs the situation in every case. Other important considerations are the saving of costs and the reasons given by Ackner J in *Ollett's* case, ie the avoidance of surprise and the need to avoid amendments at trial. In a proper case it may well be permissible to order one party to disclose his report first, so that the expert consulted by the other party may address his mind specifically to the points made in it. Although to do this may be said, in one sense, to give the latter party an advantage, it may do much towards crystallising the issues and may even lead to an earlier and fairer settlement of the action.

What then is the position in the instant cases? They are not run-of-the-mill cases, although there are a lot of them. I am told that the defendants have 12 works in various places in this country which have given rise to 3,000 claims for damages arising from alleged industrially-caused deafness. The solicitors acting for the various plaintiffs are not all the same firm. It is hardly feasible that only one expert engineer is advising all the plaintiffs. The circumstances of each claim must differ as to the degrees and lengths of exposure to noise. It would be unreasonable to expect the defendants to have one ready-made standard engineer's report available to be trotted out every time a claim is made *a* against them. The pleadings in the three actions which I have seen are not in the least informative as to particularity. It would not be unreasonable, in appropriate circumstances, to require the plaintiff to show his hand by sending his expert's report so that the defendants may consider the issues raised by it and ask their own expert to deal with it.

Accordingly, I would dismiss the appeal from the master's order in *Kirkup's* case. In *Priestley's* case, I would leave the matter where it is, with the master, who will no doubt *b* consider the defendants' affidavit when he gets it and make his decision under Ord 38, r 37. In *Painter's* case, the matter should be dealt with as in *Priestley's* case or as the parties are otherwise advised or may agree.

Appeal in Kirkup v British Rail Engineering Ltd dismissed. Leave to appeal to the Court of Appeal.

c *Summons for directions in Priestley v British Rail Engineering Ltd to be decided by master on receipt of defendants' affidavit.*

Summons for directions in Painter v British Rail Engineering Ltd returned to master to complete his findings. Leave to appeal to the Court of Appeal.

d Solicitors: *Evill & Coleman*, Putney (for the plaintiffs Kirkup and Priestley); *Rowleys & Blewitts*, Wimbledon (for the plaintiff Painter); *Michael G Baker* (for the defendants).

K Mydeen Esq   Barrister.

Peart v Stewart

e
HOUSE OF LORDS
LORD DIPLOCK, LORD KEITH OF KINKEL, LORD ROSKILL, LORD BRIDGE OF HARWICH AND LORD
BRANDON OF OAKBROOK
9 FEBRUARY, 10 MARCH 1983

f *Contempt of court – County court – Jurisdiction – Breach of injunction – Whether county court an 'inferior court' – Whether court's power to commit person to prison for civil contempt restricted to committal for fixed term not exceeding one month – Contempt of Court Act 1981, s 14(1).*

A county court is an 'inferior court' for the purposes of s 14(1)*a* of the Contempt of Court *g* Act 1981 and accordingly the power of a county court to commit a person to prison for civil contempt is restricted to committal for a fixed term not exceeding one month (see p 861 *b c*, p 862 *d*, p 863 *f g* and p 864 *c* to *f*, post).

Martin v Bannister (1879) 4 QBD 491 considered.
Decision of the Court of Appeal [1982] 2 All ER 369 reversed.

h **Notes**
For the jurisdiction of the county court to commit for civil contempt, see 10 Halsbury's Laws (4th edn) para 59.
For the Contempt of Court Act 1981, s 14, see 51 Halsbury's Statutes (3rd edn) 507.

Case referred to in opinions
i *Martin v Bannister* (1879) 4 QBD 212, 491, DC and CA, 13 Digest (Reissue) 407, *3397*.

Appeal
Desmond Anthony Stewart appealed by leave of the Appeal Committee of the House of Lords granted on 29 March 1982 against the decision of the Court of Appeal (Ormrod LJ

a Section 14(1) is set out at p 860 *g*, post

and Booth J) ([1982] 2 All ER 369, [1982] 1 WLR 389) on 21 December 1981 dismissing
the appellant's appeal from an order of his Honour Judge McDonnell sitting in the   *a*
Lambeth County Court on 7 October 1981 whereby it was ordered that the appellant be
committed to prison for a period of six months for breach of an order dated 2 July 1981
made under s 1 of the Domestic Violence and Matrimonial Proceedings Act 1976
restraining the appellant from assaulting the respondent, Marcia Patricia Peart, and
ordering him to leave the property where he was living with the respondent as man and
wife. The facts are set out in the opinion of Lord Diplock.   *b*

John Byrt QC and *Nasreen Pearce* for the appellant.
Simon D Brown as amicus curiae.
The respondent did not appear.

Their Lordships took time for consideration.   *c*

10 March. The following opinions were delivered.

LORD DIPLOCK. My Lords, this appeal raises a question as to the true construction
of s 14(1) of the Contempt of Court Act 1981. The facts that give rise to it can be stated
in two sentences. An injunction was granted by the Lambeth County Court under s 1 of   *d*
the Domestic Violence and Matrimonial Proceedings Act 1976 excluding the appellant,
Stewart, from the flat where he was living with the respondent as man and wife. He
disobeyed the injunction and, for this contempt of court, he was committed to prison for
six months by the county court judge.

Stewart appealed to the Court of Appeal for the committal order to be varied by
reducing the period of imprisonment to one month. The ground of his appeal was that   *e*
the county court's power to commit a person to prison for a civil contempt of court is
restricted by s 14(1) of the Contempt of Court Act 1981 to committal for a fixed term
not exceeding one month. Whether the county court's power is so restricted depends on
whether it is an 'inferior court' within the meaning of that expression as used in s 14 or
whether, as the Court of Appeal held it to be, it is a 'superior court' as defined in s 19,
with the consequence that its power under s 14(1) to commit a person to prison for civil *f*
contempt of court is subject to the higher maximum period of two years (see [1982] 2
All ER 369, [1982] 1 WLR 389).

Although it will be necessary to refer to some other provisions of the 1981 Act it is
helpful to set out s 14 in extenso (except for sub-s (3)) and also the definitions of 'court'
and 'superior court' in s 19:   *g*

> '**14.**—(1) In any case where a court has power to commit a person to prison for
> contempt of court and (apart from this provision) no limitation applies to the period
> of committal, the committal shall (without prejudice to the power of the court to
> order his earlier discharge) be for a fixed term, and that term shall not on any
> occasion exceed two years in the case of committal by a superior court, or one month
> in the case of committal by an inferior court.   *h*
>
> (2) In any case where an inferior court has power to fine a person for contempt of
> court and (apart from this provision) no limit applies to the amount of the fine, the
> fine shall not on any occasion exceed £500 ...
>
> (4) Each of the superior courts shall have the like power to make a hospital order
> or guardianship order under section 60 of the Mental Health Act 1959 in the case of
> a person suffering from mental illness or severe subnormality who could otherwise   *j*
> be committed to prison for contempt of court as the Crown Court has under that
> section in the case of a person convicted of an offence.
>
> (5) The enactments specified in Part III of Schedule 2 shall have effect subject to
> the amendments set out in that Part, being amendments relating to the penalties
> and procedure in respect of certain offences of contempt in coroners' courts, county
> courts and magistrates' courts ...

19. In this Act—"court" includes any tribunal or body exercising the judicial power of the State, and "legal proceedings" shall be construed accordingly ... "superior court" means the Court of Appeal, the High Court, the Crown Court, the Courts-Martial Appeal Court, the Restrictive Practices Court, the Employment Appeal Tribunal and any other court exercising in relation to its proceedings powers equivalent to those of the High Court, and includes the House of Lords in the exercise of its appellate jurisdiction.'

There is no definition of 'inferior court', so prima facie this expression was intended to bear its ordinary meaning.

My Lords, it is in my view too plain for argument that the county court is and always has been since its statutory inception by the County Courts Act 1846 an 'inferior court' within the ordinary meaning of that term. It bears all the indicia of an inferior court of record. Its jurisdiction is limited. It is subject to the supervisory jurisdiction of the High Court exercised by orders of certiorari, prohibition and mandamus: ss 115 to 119 of the County Courts Act 1959 so provide. In view of the argument that prevailed in the Court of Appeal there is a certain irony in the fact that it was precisely because a county court was an 'inferior court' that it was held in *Martin v Bannister* (1879) 4 QBD 212 (DC), 491 (CA) that it was invested with the power to grant injunctions and enforce them by attachment under s 89 of the Supreme Court of Judicature Act 1873. That section, so far as is relevant provided:

'Every inferior Court ... shall, as regards all causes of action within its jurisdiction ... have power to grant, and shall grant in any proceedings before such Court, such relief, redress, or remedy, or combination of remedies, either absolute or conditional ... in as full and ample a manner as might and ought to be done in the like case by the High Court of Justice.'

The definition section of the 1873 Act did not contain any reference to the expression 'inferior court', so the courts in *Martin v Bannister* in treating the county court as an inferior court were holding it to be such in the ordinary meaning of that term.

Section 89 of the 1873 Act and the corresponding section (s 202) of the Supreme Court of Judicature (Consolidation) Act 1925, in which it was stated in the definition section (s 225) that '"Inferior court" includes a county court as well as any *other* inferior court', remained the only statutory source of the power of the county court to grant and to enforce injunctions until the passing of the County Courts Act 1934. With the substitution of 'Every county court' for 'Every inferior Court', s 71 of that Act (now replaced by s 74 of the County Courts Act 1959) was in substantially identical terms to those of s 202 of the 1925 Act; and consequential amendments were made to s 202; but the definition of 'inferior court' in the 1925 Act was left unchanged and the Act continued to refer, in s 208, to county courts and 'any *other* inferior court of record'. It is likewise referred to as an 'inferior court' in s 13(2) of the Administration of Justice Act 1960, which gives a right of appeal from any order of a county court in the exercise of its jurisdiction to punish for contempt of court.

Section 74 of the County Courts Act 1959, in the amended form in which it is now in force, reads as follows:

'(1) Every county court, as regards any cause of action for the time being within its jurisdiction, shall—(a) grant such relief, redress or remedy or combination of remedies, either absolute or conditional; and (b) give such and the like effect to every ground of defence or counterclaim equitable or legal; as ought to be granted or given in the like case by the High Court and in as full and ample a manner.

(2) For the purposes of this section it shall be assumed (notwithstanding any enactment to the contrary) that any proceedings which can be commenced in a county court could be commenced in the High Court.'

My Lords, the argument which prevailed in the Court of Appeal was based on the definition of 'superior court' in s 19 of the Contempt of Court Act 1981. A county court, it was contended, when exercising its power to commit persons to prison for breach of an injunction, fell within the description 'any other court exercising in relation to its proceedings powers equivalent to those of the High Court'.

The county court has statutory powers to commit for criminal contempt of court specifically conferred on it by s 157 of the 1959 Act. There are also powers conferred on it by ss 30 and 127 which are analogous to committal for criminal contempt and are so treated by s 13(5)(b) of the Administration of Justice Act 1960, but committal under any of these powers is subject to a statutory maximum of one month and the right to impose a fine is restricted to a maximum of £20, a sum which in each case was increased to £500 by s 14(5) of and Sch 2, Pt III, paras 2, 3 and 5 to the Contempt of Court Act 1981. So s 14(1) of the Contempt of Court Act 1981 in the case of a county court was dealing only with its power to commit for a civil contempt of court, since this was the only kind of contempt for which at the time of the Act no limitation applied to the period of committal. It follows from *Martin v Bannister* that its powers of committal for disobedience of an injunction are derived from s 74 and are to be exercised in the like case and in as full and ample a manner as the High Court. So, the argument goes, a county court when exercising this power falls within the description of 'any other court exercising in relation to its proceedings powers equivalent to those of the High Court', and is for the purposes of s 14(1) a superior and not an inferior court, even though when exercising others of its powers it remains an inferior court.

I find myself unable to accept this argument. The Contempt of Court Act 1981 is drafted on the assumption that there is a dichotomy (in the accurate sense of the term) between superior and inferior courts. All courts within the definition of 'court' in s 19 fall into one or other of those two mutually exclusive classes. None falls into both classes. The intention to create this dichotomy is nowhere made clearer than in s 14 itself. By sub-s (1) a superior court may commit a contemnor to prison for a maximum of two years; an inferior court may only commit him for a maximum of one month, a period which coincides with the maximum period for which a county court may make a committal order for a criminal contempt of court. By sub-s (2) an inferior court may not fine a person guilty of a civil contempt of court more than £500, a figure which coincides with the maximum amount a county court may fine a contemnor for a criminal contempt, as increased by the amendments to the relevant sections of the County Courts Act 1959 effected by Sch 2, Pt III to the Contempt of Court Act 1981; a superior court is subject to no limitation as to the amount that it may fine a contemnor for civil or criminal contempt. By sub-s (4) a superior court may make a hospital or guardianship order in appropriate cases instead of a committal order; an inferior court has no such power.

The definition of 'superior court' in s 19 appears to consist of a list of courts that fall within that class. The list starts with six courts identified by their names. The county court, to which there are references by its name in ss 13 and 14(5), is not among them although it grants far more injunctions than any other court in England and Wales. The three courts named in the definition of 'superior court' which do not form part of the Supreme Court itself are constituted and described as 'superior courts of record' by the statutes that created them. The words that follow the list of named courts, sandwiched as they are between the list and a reference to the House of Lords in the exercise of its appellate jurisdiction, are in my view, words to which the principle of construction noscitur a sociis applies. Like what precedes them and what follows them, they too are intended to identify courts, whether already existing or which may thereafter be created, and to do so by reference to the general powers (the word is in the plural) that the court exercises in relation to its proceedings. Appearing where they do, and without the insertion of the conjunction 'when' between 'any other court' and 'exercising', the words on which the argument that found favour with the Court of Appeal is founded ought not, in my view, to be construed as referring not to a court as such but to the exercise by

any court, even though it be an inferior court, of a particular power which is equivalent
a to a power exercisable by the High Court. Any such construction of 'superior court' so as
to embrace an inferior court when it was exercising particular powers but not otherwise
would need to be complemented by a special definition of 'inferior court' departing from
its ordinary meaning (in which it had been used in statutes from 1873 to 1960) so as to
exclude such court from being an 'inferior court' within the meaning of this particular
Act when, but only when, the county court was exercising particular powers. There is
b no such special definition.

My Lords, by the conclusion of the hearing, counsel had not found themselves able to
point to any existing court which fell within the words of description which I have been
discussing. Since starting to write this speech I have found one example of an existing
court that would appear to fit the description, viz an election court constituted under
s 110 of the Representation of the People Act 1949. Though constituted by two judges
c of the High Court it is a court quite separate from the High Court; and s 110(2), so far as
it relates to an election court sitting in England and Wales, provides: 'The election court
shall, subject to the provisions of this Act, have the same powers, jurisdiction and
authority as a judge of the High Court . . .' A judge of the High Court was empowered
by the Supreme Court of Judicature (Consolidation) Act 1925, and is now empowered by
the Supreme Court Act 1981, to exercise the powers of the High Court itself. So an
d election court is one which exercises in relation to its proceedings powers (in the plural)
equivalent to those of the High Court.

I should, however, have reached the same conclusion on the construction of the
definition of 'superior court' in s 19, even if it were impossible to point to any existing
court which complied with the description and one were driven to the conclusion that
the draftsman was making anticipatory provision for possible new courts that might be
e subsequently created with the status of superior courts of record. In these circumstances
I do not think that it is incumbent on this House to hold a further hearing at which
counsel would be given an opportunity to make submissions about the status of an
election court. The matter is too peripheral to the decision of this appeal.

Reverting then to s 14(1) itself, a county court for the purposes of that subsection must
be either a superior court or an inferior court; it cannot be both. It falls fairly and
f squarely within the well-established meaning of the expression 'inferior court'. If there
are two possible constructions of the definition of 'superior court' in s 19, one of which
would include and the other exclude a county court, the ambiguity ought to be resolved
in favour of exclusion for three reasons. To do so (1) avoids altering the well-established
meaning of inferior court as including county court, (2) is in favour of the liberty of the
subject, (3) is consistent with the corresponding limit of one month on the period for
g which a county court can commit a person to prison for a criminal contempt of court.
When pressed, counsel who, in the absence of representation of the respondent, helpfully
addressed us as amicus curiae felt compelled to concede that, if a county court was not an
inferior court for the purpose of sub-s (1) of s 14, it could not be an inferior court for the
purposes of sub-s (2). If this were so, its power to fine contemnors for civil contempt of
court would be subject to no limit at all, whereas if it is an inferior court it would be
h subject to the limit of £500, which is consistent with the raising to the same figure by
the Contempt of Court Act 1981 itself of the maximum fine a county court can impose
for a criminal contempt of court.

My Lords, s 14 operates on the powers of the county court to grant injunctions in the
exercise of its jurisdiction generally; it is not confined to its matrimonial jurisdiction or
its jurisdiction under ss 1 and 2 of the Domestic Violence and Matrimonial Proceedings
i Act 1976. In support of the argument that succeeded in the Court of Appeal it was
suggested that any other construction would lead to anomalous results in matrimonial
proceedings, since in such proceedings it was often a matter of chance whether a
particular cause was dealt with by a High Court judge or by a county court judge.
Parliament, it was suggested, could hardly have intended that the severity of the

punishment whether by imprisonment or fine that could be inflicted on a person who was in breach of an injunction should depend on the status of the judge by whom the contempt was dealt with.

My Lords, that Parliament did regard the status of the judge by whom the contempt was dealt with as relevant to the maximum penalty that he could inflict is apparent from the provisions of s 15 which deal with Scottish proceedings. The parallel with England and Wales is close. The Court of Session's powers of imprisonment for contempt of court are for a fixed term not exceeding two years, but its powers to fine are unlimited in amount. The powers of the sheriff court (whose civil jurisdiction is wider than that of a county court in England and Wales) to deal with contempt of court by imprisonment is limited to a maximum of three months and the maximum fine he may impose is £500; while in the case of a district court the corresponding maxima are 60 days and £200.

If for Scotland Parliament thought it right to treat the status of the judge by whom the contempt of court is dealt with as relevant to the maximum punishment he is empowered to inflict, any argument that it cannot have intended to do likewise for England and Wales, and that therefore 'inferior court' in s 14(1) cannot have been intended to bear its ordinary meaning, falls to the ground.

My Lords, for all these reasons I would allow this appeal and reduce from six months to one month the period for which the appellant was ordered to be imprisoned.

LORD KEITH OF KINKEL. My Lords, for the reasons set out in the speech of my noble and learned friend Lord Diplock, which I have had the benefit of reading in draft and with which I agree, I too would allow the appeal.

LORD ROSKILL. My Lords, I have had the advantage of reading in draft the speech of my noble and learned friend Lord Diplock. I agree with it and for the reasons he gives I too would allow this appeal.

LORD BRIDGE OF HARWICH. My Lords, for the reasons given by my noble and learned friend Lord Diplock I too would allow this appeal.

LORD BRANDON OF OAKBROOK. My Lords, I have had the advantage of reading in draft the speech prepared by my noble and learned friend Lord Diplock. I agree with it, and for the reasons which he gives I would allow the appeal.

Appeal allowed. Sentence reduced from six months to one month.

Solicitors: *Ronald Fletcher Baker & Co* (for the appellant); *Treasury Solicitor.*

Mary Rose Plummer   Barrister.

R v Amey
R v James and another

COURT OF APPEAL, CRIMINAL DIVISION
KERR LJ AND KILNER BROWN J
6 NOVEMBER, 20 DECEMBER 1982

Sentence – Compensation – Order – Principles applicable in making order – Compensation order not to be made unless sum claimed by victim is agreed or proved – Degree of proof required – Necessity for amount of loss to be proved by evidence.

Sentence – Compensation – Order – Inability of convicted person to meet all claims in full – How assets should be apportioned.

Sentence – Compensation – Order – Persons jointly convicted – Principles applicable in making order.

A court before which a person is convicted of theft or obtaining property by deception or dishonest handling should only make an order requiring him to pay compensation for any loss or damage resulting from the offence if the sum claimed in respect of the loss or damage is either agreed or 'proved', ie established by evidence and not by inference or guesswork (see p 866 *g h*, post); *R v Vivian* [1979] 1 All ER 48 applied.

Where several claimants for compensation establish claims against a convicted person and he has insufficient funds to meet each claim in full, the court should normally make orders which apportion the compensation on a pro rata basis, but it may depart from that basis where there are strong grounds for doing so (eg where there are several small claims and one large claim and a pro rata apportionment would lead to the small claimants being compensated to a wholly inadequate degree). In such cases the court may select some of the claimants and order that compensation be paid to them to the exclusion of the others (see p 866 *h* to p 867 *b*, post).

Where two or more persons are jointly convicted and one claimant for compensation establishes a claim against them with regard to one item, the court should generally make an order requiring each of them to pay the amount awarded in equal proportions. The court should not draw a distinction between the two convicted persons unless it is shown that one of them was more responsible than the other or that their ability to pay is markedly different (see p 867 *b c*, post).

Notes
For compensation orders in criminal proceedings, see 11 Halsbury's Laws (4th edn) para 804, and for cases on the subject, see 14(2) Digest (Reissue) 861–864, 7455–7491.

Case referred to in judgment
R v Vivian [1979] 1 All ER 48, [1979] 1 WLR 291, CA, Digest (Cont Vol E) 148, 7475.

Appeals
R v Amey
On 5 February 1982 in the Crown Court at Bournemouth before Mr Recorder Alan Rawley QC the appellant Amey pleaded guilty to the following offences: theft (counts 1 and 3), forging a valuable security (counts 3 and 5), obtaining property on a forged instrument (count 4), evasion of a liability by deception (count 6), obtaining property by deception (counts 7 and 8); and asked for 14 other offences to be taken into consideration. He was placed on probation for two years with a condition of treatment and ordered to pay £5,289·93 compensation at the rate of £125 per month. He appealed against the compensation order. The facts are set out in the judgment of the court.

R v James and another

On 19 February 1982 in the Crown Court at Cardiff before Mr Recorder G H M Daniel **a**
and a jury the appellants James and Meah were convicted and sentenced as follows: the
appellant James was (i) convicted of dishonestly handling stolen goods by assisting, for
which he was sentenced to six months' imprisonment, suspended for two years, and
ordered to pay £140 compensation; (ii) convicted of obtaining property by deception,
for which he was sentenced to a concurrent term of one month's imprisonment,
suspended for two years. In addition, as he was in breach of a community service order **b**
of 240 hours, he was sentenced to a consecutive term of six months' imprisonment and
to concurrent terms of one month's imprisonment, all suspended for two years for the
offences for which he was ordered to carry out the community service order. The
appellant Meah was (i) convicted of dishonestly handling stolen goods by receiving, for
which he was sentenced to nine months' imprisonment, suspended for two years, and
ordered to pay £280 compensation, and (ii) convicted of obtaining property by deception, **c**
for which he was sentenced to one month's imprisonment concurrent, which was also
suspended for two years. Both appellants appealed against the compensation order. The
facts are set out in the judgment of the court.

Nicolas Morrow Brown (assigned by the Registrar of Criminal Appeals) for the appellant
  Amey.   **d**
Richard A Jones (assigned by the Registrar of Criminal Appeals) for the appellants James
  and Meah.

Cur adv vult

20 December. The following judgment of the court was delivered.   **e**

KILNER BROWN J. These two separate appeals raise the same questions with regard
to orders of compensation made in the Crown Court in cases of theft, obtaining property
by deception and dishonest handling. Recent experience in the Court of Appeal, Criminal
Division, indicates that orders for compensation are still being made without proper
consideration of the principles involved. These have been laid down in a number of **f**
authorities which are conveniently summarised both in *Archbold's* Pleading, Evidence
and Practice in Criminal Cases (41st edn, 1982) and in *Morrish and McLean on the Crown
Court* (10th edn, 1980). In the instant cases under appeal two aspects have had to be
considered. The first is what is involved in the requirement of proof before an order can
be made; the second, which is a new point, is whether it is proper, where there are a
number of claimants, to select one or more to the exclusion of others if there is an **g**
inability to pay the whole amount of compensation.

   In *R v Vivian* [1979] 1 All ER 48 at 50, [1979] 1 WLR 291 at 293 it was said that—

   'no order for compensation should be made unless the sum claimed . . . is either
   agreed or has been proved . . . in the absence of agreement or evidence as to the
   correct amount which could be claimed . . . no order for compensation should have
   been made . . .'.   **h**

As orders for compensation, although a quick way of dealing with what is in essence a
civil claim, are nevertheless part of a criminal process and may be supported by a term of
imprisonment in default, care must be taken to ensure that the evidence is sufficient
before making an order. Proof means proof by evidence and not by inference or
guesswork. If the obligation is established, an inability to pay the whole amount can **j**
easily be dealt with where there are not a number of claimants, by scaling down the
apportioning to a degree commensurate with the total liability. Where however there
are several claimants and one of them has a large claim which is much greater than those
of others who have small claims, then difficulty may arise. An apportionment on a pro
rata basis may lead to one or more small claimants being compensated to a wholly
inadequate degree.

In theory the civil remedy is still there, but in reality this may be either impossible or
a futile. Moreover it may be that a loss of a small sum or an article of relatively small
intrinsic value may be a very serious matter to some individuals. We consider that in the
inherent discretionary power of the court to see that justice is done it would be open to a
judge, if there were strong grounds for doing so, to depart from the normal pro rata basis
to make such adjustment as is reasonable. But this discretion should only be exercised
rarely. It may create more problems than it solves, and what is justice for one may be an
b injustice for another. As a general rule apportionment, and not selection, should be the
adopted course where there are insufficient means to meet every established claim.

One further aspect of the proper method of dealing with compensation arose in the
second case, although the point was not taken or argued. Nevertheless, as it has arisen in
other cases in the Court of Appeal recently, it is appropriate to deal with it. Where there
are two or more jointly convicted persons against whom orders for compensation may
c be made on behalf of one claimant with regard to one item, the amount should in general
be awarded in equal proportions. Distinction should only be made where it can be shown
that one of the convicted persons was more responsible than the other or where the
ability or inability to pay is markedly different.

We now turn to consider the actual cases before us.

d R v Amey

On 5 February 1982 in the Crown Court at Bournemouth this appellant pleaded guilty
to an indictment which contained eight counts. There were two charges of theft, two of
forging a valuable security, one of obtaining property on a forged instrument, one of
evading a liability by deception and two of obtaining property by deception. In addition
he asked for other offences, similar in nature, to be taken into consideration. He was
e placed on probation for a period of two years with a condition of treatment and he was
ordered to pay the sum of £5,289·93 by way of compensation. He appeals against that
part of the sentence which ordered compensation by leave of the single judge.

The only count which calls for any examination of the facts was the first. The appellant
agreed to garage a 50-year old three wheeler Morgan sports car for a friend of his named
Rooke. When Mr Rooke went abroad the appellant sold the car to a London dealer for
f £600. That man dismantled the thing and sold all the bits and pieces for a total amount
of £900. No doubt this ancient jalopy was Mr Rooke's pride and joy and in his eyes was
worth £3,000 to him.

The police in charge of the prosecution made a full schedule of all the claims for
compensation put in by the various persons who had lost money or an article and
included the claim by Mr Rooke at his figure of £3,000. This was the only item which
g was challenged in the whole schedule, which indicated a total of £7,289·83 claimed by
eight individuals and the National Westminster Bank, whose claim of £2,867·75 was by
far the largest single claim apart from that put in by Mr Rooke.

The recorder's attention was directed very properly and fairly by counsel for the
prosecution to the principle in R v Vivian [1979] 1 All ER 48, [1979] 1 WLR 291 and
suggested that the evidence as to Mr Rooke's car was that its value was either £600 or at
h the most £900. Notwithstanding this helpful warning, the recorder acted only in part
and substituted for the claim of £3,000 his own figure of £1,000. For this there was no
justification whatever and the figure which was proved in our judgment was the sum of
£600. The reduction from £7,289·83 to £5,289·83 was explained by the recorder's
substitution of £3,000 by the figure of £1,000. He should have reduced the total to
£4,889·83. That is the first error and we substitute that total and the figure of £600 for
j Mr Rooke as being the amounts which were agreed or proved.

The recorder then went on to consider the appellant's ability to pay. In our judgment
he then fell into further error. The appellant, aged 21, was unemployed and in receipt of
social security benefits. His only financial assets were an actual sum of £360 in a bank
account and the notional one of a loan of £2,000 in favour of a friend who might or
might not be able to pay it off at the rate of £50 a month. This was speculative. His
father was prepared to provide him with free board and lodging and to employ him as a

garage hand at a net wage of £40 a week. Somewhat to our surprise the appellant, through counsel, offered to pay as much as £100 per month; we cannot go behind that, but we àre of the opinion that the order of payment at the rate of £125 a month was harsh and unrealistic. The recorder was wrong to say, as he did, that the appellant had to make sure that his friend paid him back the money he was owed and, if necessary, to take legal action to obtain it. Furthermore an order to pay £5,000 at £125 a month would extend the order for a period in excess of three years, which offends against yet another of the well-established principles that orders should not be made if payment by instalments extends over too long a period.

Taking into account the £360 which was immediately available, a realistic assessment of ability to pay was about £2,000, that is two-fifths of the total claim. If this process had been properly carried out and some figure like £2,000 was arrived at, it would have become at once apparent that the eight individuals were entitled in all to £2,022·08 and the bank to £2,867·75.

If ever there was an instance of the rare occasion when the claimants should have been selected, and no order on a pro rata basis have been made, this was it. It would be a great hardship on the eight individuals to receive only two-fifths of their proved claim and to be forced to resort to civil process for the balance. On the other hand the bank would be far better placed to seek and obtain judgment in the county court for the amount they were entitled to. It would not be a futile exercise and the judgment debt could probably be met in full over a period of years. By excluding the bank from the order for compensation, it does not mean they are excluded from a proper claim; they are being denied the quick opportunity of getting their money, and that is all.

This appeal is allowed. The order for compensation in favour of the eight individuals remains, as amended in the case of Rooke, to the total of £2,022·08. These claims to be dealt with at the rate of £100 per month to be paid to the collecting officer at the local magistrates' court office. The order in favour of the National Westminster Bank is quashed.

Before parting with this case we would wish to express the hope that never again will the Court of Appeal be required to go through the process of any similar analysis, which is the duty of the tribunal at first instance.

R v James and another

On 19 February 1982 in the Crown Court at Cardiff, these two appellants, James and Meah, were convicted and sentenced as follows: James was convicted of an offence of dishonest handling of stolen goods by assisting, for which he was sentenced to six months' imprisonment suspended for two years and a compensation order in the sum of £140 was made. He was also convicted of obtaining property by deception for which he was sentenced to a concurrent term of one month's imprisonment again suspended for two years. In addition, as he was in breach of a community service order of 240 hours, he was sentenced to a consecutive term of six months and concurrent sentences of one month, all suspended for two years, for the offences for which he was ordered to carry out the community service order. Thus in all he was sentenced to a suspended term of 12 months' imprisonment and ordered to pay compensation of £140.

Meah was convicted of an offence of dishonest handling by receiving, for which he was sentenced to nine months' imprisonment suspended for two years and a compensation order in the sum of £280 was made. He was also convicted of obtaining property by deception for which he was sentenced to one month's imprisonment concurrent also suspended for two years. A restitution order with reference to a Dynachord Echo Chamber was made against both appellants but no complaint is made about that.

Both appellants appeal against sentence by leave of the single judge. He granted leave with reference to the compensation orders only, but having done so, we are obliged to consider the sentence as a whole. We can deal with the suspended sentences by saying that there is no substance in the criticisms made and we reject them.

The facts of the case are simple. On 27 April 1981 a quantity of hi-fi equipment was stolen from a parked car. On the following day the two appellants jointly sold some of

a the stolen items to a secondhand dealer and when interviewed Meah admitted that it was
he who received the items but maintained that he had honestly bought them for £7, a
ridiculous proposition which the jury rejected.

The compensation order was made in the proportion of two to one, Meah being
ordered to pay twice as much as James, as he was the more responsible. No point is taken
about that. The submission is that there was no proof of loss as required by the authority
of R v Vivian [1979] 1 All ER 48, [1979] 1 WLR 291 and it was also submitted that
b further clarification should be given of the term proof. As to that we repeat what we said
at the beginning of this judgment. We apply that test to this case. Was there sufficient
evidence to enable the recorder to find proof of loss? The matter was fully and properly
investigated by counsel and by the recorder, and evidence of replacement value was
given by the owner whose evidence was thoroughly tested in cross-examination.
Compared with some cases which have recently come before the Court of Appeal, this
c case is a model of how investigation of value should properly be carried out. We can see
no reason to criticise or differ from the recorder's order as to compensation and the
appeals of James and Meah are dismissed.

Appeal of the appellant Amey allowed.
Appeal of the appellants James and Meah dismissed.

d

Sophie Craven   Barrister.

e # Gibson v Wales

QUEEN'S BENCH DIVISION
GRIFFITHS LJ AND McCULLOUGH J
28, 29 OCTOBER 1982

f *Criminal law – Offensive weapons – Article made or adapted for use for causing injury – Flick
knife – Whether an offensive weapon per se – Prevention of Crime Act 1953, s 1(1)(4).*

A flick knife is an offensive weapon per se for the purposes of s 1(1)[a] of the Prevention of
Crime Act 1953 because it is to be regarded as an 'article made . . . for use for causing
injury to the person' within the definition of an 'offensive weapon' in s 1(4) of that Act,
g and, being an offensive weapon per se, the burden is on the person found in a public
place in possession of a flick knife to prove that he was in possession of it for an innocent
purpose (see p 871 f g and p 872 f to h, post).
Dictum of Salmon J in *R v Petrie* [1961] 1 All ER at 468 applied.

Notes
h For possession of offensive weapons, see 11 Halsbury's Laws (4th edn) para 852, and for
cases on the subject, see 15 Digest (Reissue) 900–903, 7758–7777.
For the Prevention of Crime Act 1953, s 1, see 8 Halsbury's Statutes (3rd edn) 407.

Cases referred to in judgment
R v Petrie [1961] 1 All ER 466, [1961] 1 WLR 358, CCA, 15 Digest (Reissue) 901, 7770.
j R v Williamson (1977) 67 Cr App R 35, CA.

a   Section 1, so far as material, provides:
'(1) Any person who without lawful authority or reasonable excuse, the proof whereof shall lie
on him, has with him in any public place any offensive weapon shall be guilty of an offence . . .
(4) In this section . . . "offensive weapon" means any article made or adapted for use for causing
injury to the person, or intended by the person having it with him for such use by him.'

Case also cited
Bryan v Mott (1975) 62 Cr App R 71, DC.   *a*

Case stated
Bernard William Gibson applied by way of a case stated by the justices for the County of
Lancaster in respect of their adjudication as a magistrates' court sitting at Burnley on 12
February 1982. On 7 December 1981 an information was preferred by the appellant, an
inspector of police in the Lancashire Constabulary, against the respondent, Adrian   *b*
Michael Wales, that on 14 October 1981 at Burnley he had with him without lawful
authority or reasonable excuse in a public place, namely Curzon Street, a flick knife,
being an offensive weapon, contrary to s 1 of the Prevention of Crime Act 1953. The
magistrates found that the knife was not an offensive weapon per se within the 1953 Act
and that the appellant had not proved that it was the respondent's intention to use the
knife to cause injury to person. Accordingly, they found that there was no case to answer   *c*
and dismissed the information. The question for the opinion of the High Court was
whether a flick knife, as defined in the Restriction of Offensive Weapons Act 1959, was
an offensive weapon made or adapted for use for causing injury to the person and
therefore an offensive weapon per se contrary to s 1(1) of the Prevention of Crime Act
1953. The facts are set out in the judgment of Griffiths LJ.

                                                                                        d
Harold Singer for the appellant.
Charles Mahon for the respondent.

GRIFFITHS LJ. This is an appeal by a prosecutor by way of case stated from a decision
of the justices for the County of Lancashire who on 12 February 1982, sitting at Burnley, *e*
acquitted the respondent of being in possession of an offensive weapon contrary to s 1 of
the Prevention of Crime Act 1953 on their finding that a flick knife was not an offensive
weapon per se within the meaning of the 1953 Act.
    The question before this court is posed as follows: whether a flick knife as defined in
the Restriction of Offensive Weapons Act 1959 is an offensive weapon made or adapted
for use for causing injury to the person, and therefore an offensive weapon per se contrary *f*
to s 1(1) of the Prevention of Crime Act 1953.
    The facts of this case, very shortly, are as follows. At 12.10 am on 14 October 1981
two police officers were on duty when they saw the respondent, who was in Curzon
Street, a public place, take a knife from the back pocket of his trousers and operate it,
showing it to two youths. He handed the knife to one of the youths who himself operated
it, and then he put it back in his pocket. He was approached by the two policemen who   *g*
asked him what he was doing there, and he answered that he was waiting for a girlfriend
in order to give her a coat to keep her warm on the way home. He said that his only
worry was that she would come out linked with some other bloke and there would be a
riot. When asked what he meant, he said he would not start any trouble there but would
wait until he got her back to Brierfield. He was questioned about the knife and he
produced it. It was seen to be a flick knife. He was asked for an explanation. He replied   *h*
by saying he had no explanation. He was not sure if he was allowed to have it. He was
then arrested for having with him in a public place an offensive weapon.
    The magistrates, having heard argument, came to the conclusion that this flick knife
was not what is commonly referred to as an offensive weapon per se, ie that within the
meaning of s 1(4) of the Prevention of Crime Act 1953 it was not an article made or
adapted for use for causing injury to the person. Having arrived at that conclusion they   *j*
then went on to consider whether the prosecution had satisfied them that this young
man had it on his person with the intention of using it for an offensive purpose, and they
concluded that the prosecution had not discharged that burden of proof. Accordingly,
they acquitted the young man of the offence.
    We have been told by this court that if we do answer the question in the affirmative
and say that the magistrates should have found the flick knife to be an offensive weapon

per se, nevertheless, the prosecution do not invite us to return the case to the magistrates.
a   What the prosecution seek is guidance from this court on the very important question as
to the category of offensive weapon into which the flick knife falls. Does it fall to be
considered as an offensive weapon per se in that it is an article made or adapted for
causing injury, or does it fall into the second category, namely a weapon which the
prosecution have to prove in every case is being carried for an offensive purpose before a
conviction can be secured?

b   Anybody who has had the experience of travelling around the country trying serious
crime, as Her Majesty's judges have, will readily appreciate the dangerous nature of such
a weapon and how frequently it is used to inflict fearful injuries. A flick knife is a
singularly dangerous weapon because it can be held concealed in the hand in the course
of a quarrel which may start with fisticuffs and suddenly be released and used before the
other party engaged in the fight has any chance whatever to appreciate that he is to be
c   attacked by a man with a knife.

The attitude of Parliament to flick knives is revealed by the terms of a special statute
designed to deal with flick knives. The Act is the Restriction of Offensive Weapons Act
1959. It is headed: 'An Act to amend the law in relation to the making and disposing and
importation of flick knives and other dangerous weapons.' Section 1 reads as follows:

d   '(1) Any person who manufactures, sells or hires or offers for sale or hire, . . . or
lends or gives to any other person—(a) any knife which has a blade which opens
automatically by hand pressure applied to a button, spring or other device in or
attached to the handle of the knife, sometimes known as a "flick knife" or "flick
gun" . . . shall be guilty of an offence and shall be liable on summary conviction in
the case of a first offence to imprisonment for a term not exceeding three months or
to a fine not exceeding fifty pounds . . .'

e   It is interesting to observe that, stringent though that protection was, it was then
further extended by Parliament by the Restriction of Offensive Weapons Act 1961. That
Act provided that in addition to anybody who sold or offered for sale a flick knife,
anybody who exposed or had in his possession for the purposes of sale or hire a flick knife
was guilty of an offence.

f   The effect of those two statutes was to absolutely outlaw flick knives, but it is
interesting to note a significant omission. There is nothing in the statutes which makes
it an offence to possess a flick knife. The only intelligible explanation for that is that
Parliament must have considered that that position was adequately catered for by the
provisions of the 1953 Act on the assumption that nobody could realistically consider
that a flick knife was other than a dangerous weapon made for an offensive purpose.
g   Accordingly, anybody who carried one on his person in a public place could be prosecuted
under the 1953 Act. But the submission that attracted the magistrates in this case was
founded on a decision of this court in R v Williamson (1977) 67 Cr App R 35. That was a
case in which a judge had directed a jury that they should convict a man who had been
found in possession of a sheath knife in a public place on the ground that a sheath knife
was an offensive weapon per se. The court held that it was a question of fact for the jury
h   in every case to decide into which class the weapon found on the accused fell. Was it to
be considered an offensive weapon per se because it was made or adapted for this purpose,
or did it fall into the latter category, namely a weapon that they were able to show was in
his possession for an offensive purpose?

The distinction is a very important one because, if the weapon is considered an
offensive weapon per se, the burden falls on the accused to show that he has a lawful
excuse for having it on him. But, if it is not an offensive weapon per se, then the burden
j   is on the prosecution to prove that he had this particular weapon for an offensive purpose.
The court there held that in the case of a sheath knife the matter must be left to the jury.
This is, of course, readily understandable because almost every boy scout has a sheath
knife, and indeed, many cubs and girl guides and one can readily appreciate that sheath
knives are not made specifically for the purpose of being used as offensive weapons. In
giving the judgment of the court Geoffrey Lane LJ said (at 38–39):

'It was for the jury to decide whether a weapon held by the defendant was an offensive weapon, bearing in mind the definition in the section which I have just *a* read [s 1(4) of the Prevention of Crime Act 1953]. Consequently, whether the object in the possession of the defendant in any case can properly be described as an offensive weapon is a matter not for the judge but for the jury to decide. The jury must determine whether they feel sure that the object was made or adapted for use in causing injury to the person or was intended by the person having it with him for such use by him. There may be circumstances in which it is possible to say there *b* is no evidence to the contrary in a particular case, but that is not the case here. If there is such a case, then in those circumstances the judge might, unobjectionably, direct the jury in those terms, but those cases must be rare. In normal cases of this sort, it remains a question for the jury, although the judge, after proper warnings to the jury, may add his own view on the subject.'

It is also interesting to note that the views of Salmon J in an earlier case set out a *c* number of objects which that judge clearly considered would obviously fall into the category of weapons that were offensive per se. In *R v Petrie* [1961] 1 All ER 466 at 468, [1961] 1 WLR 358 at 361 Salmon J said:

.   'It is clear that the definition section of the Act [s 1(4) of the Prevention of Crime Act 1953] contemplates offensive weapons of, at any rate, two classes, namely, (a) an *d* article which per se is an offensive weapon, that is to say, an article made or adapted for use for causing injury to the person; and (b) an article which, though it is not . made or adapted for such use, is carried with the intent so to use it. A cosh, a knuckleduster, and a revolver are examples of articles in the first class. A sandbag and a razor are examples of articles in the second class.

If a cosh or a knuckleduster is an offensive weapon per se, then so too should a flick knife *e* be considered.

In my view, taking into account the views of the community as expressed by Parliament in the 1959 Act as amended by the 1961 Act, the time has now come when it must be appreciated that there is no reasonable alternative to the view that a flick knife is a dangerous weapon per se. It is made for the purpose of causing injury to the person. It *f* may sometimes be used for wholly innocent purposes, even possessed for innocent purposes, but there will be a very heavy burden on any person in possession of a flick knife to satisfy any court that he had it for such an innocent purpose. I would say that the magistrates here on the facts of this case fell into error and that a flick knife is now to be regarded as an offensive weapon per se for the purposes of s 1(1) of the Prevention of Crime Act 1953.

g .

McCULLOUGH J. Whether a flick knife is an article made for use for causing injury to the person is a question of fact, but in my judgment it is a question which admits of only one answer: it is.

For the reasons given by Griffiths LJ I take this to have been the view held by Parliament in 1953 and 1961 and to be beyond argument. I too would allow this appeal. *h*

Appeal allowed.

Solicitors: *Sharpe Pritchard & Co*, agents for *J V Bates*, Preston (for the appellant); *Steele Ford & Newton*, Nelson (for the respondent).

Sepala Munasinghe Esq   Barrister.

a

Amin Rasheed Shipping Corp v Kuwait Insurance Co
The Al Wahab

b

COURT OF APPEAL, CIVIL DIVISION

SIR JOHN DONALDSON MR, MAY AND ROBERT GOFF LJJ

22, 23, 24, 25 NOVEMBER, 15 DECEMBER 1982

c

Conflict of laws – Contract – Proper law of contract – Insurance policy – Marine insurance – Lloyd's SG form – Kuwaiti insurance company insuring vessel owned by Liberian company resident in Dubai – Policy based on Lloyd's standard marine insurance policy – Policy not specifying proper law of contract – Policy issued and to be performed in Kuwait – Liberian owners seeking to bring proceedings in England against Kuwaiti insurers – Owners seeking leave to serve writ on insurers out of jurisdiction – Whether English law to be inferred as proper law from use of Lloyd's policy – Whether court should grant leave to serve writ out of jurisdiction – RSC Ord 11, r 1(f)(iii).

d

The plaintiffs, a Liberian company resident in Dubai, owned a vessel which they insured with the defendants, a Kuwaiti insurance company. The policy, which was based on the Lloyd's SG form as set out in Sch 1 to the Marine Insurance Act 1906, insured the vessel against war and marine risk for a period of 12 months from April 1977. The cover was renewed for 1978–79 and 1979–80. The policy was issued in Kuwait and provided for claims to be paid in Kuwait although the currency specified was expressed in sterling. In

e

1980 the vessel was seized by the Saudi Arabian authorities and the plaintiffs claimed under the policy for constructive loss of the vessel. The defendants rejected the claim and the plaintiffs sought leave in the English courts to serve proceedings against the defendants under RSC Ord 11, r 1(f)(iii)[a], which empowered the court to give leave to serve proceedings out of the jurisdiction if the action was brought to recover damages for breach of a contract which was 'by its terms, or by implication, governed by English law'.

f

The judge refused leave on the ground that the proper law of the contract was Kuwaiti law, not English law. The judge further held that, even if English law was the proper law of the contract, he would nevertheless have exercised his discretion by refusing to give leave to serve the proceedings outside the jurisdiction. The plaintiffs appealed, contending (i) that, by entering into a policy based on Lloyd's standard form, the parties intended English law to apply to the contract, unless there were other potent indications

g

to show a contrary intention, (ii) that at the date of the issue of the policy in 1979 there was no marine insurance law in Kuwait, and when taken in conjunction with the use of a policy based on Lloyd's standard form that showed that there was an overwhelming connection with English law, and (iii) that, subsequent to the date of the 1979 policy, a further policy was issued in 1980 in respect of the vessel which, it was contended, was clearly governed by English law, and, since the two policies were identical, it must have

h

been intended that the 1979 policy was to be governed by English law. In 1980, after the 1979 policy had been issued, a marine insurance code was introduced into Kuwaiti law.

Held (Sir John Donaldson MR dissenting) – The appeal would be dismissed for the following reasons—

(1) In ascertaining the proper law of the contract the court could only look to the

j

---

a   Rule 1, so far as material, provides: '... service of a writ out of the jurisdiction is permissible with the leave of the Court ... (*f*) if the action begun by the writ is brought against a defendant not domiciled or ordinarily resident in Scotland ... to recover damages or obtain other relief in respect of the breach of a contract, being ... a contract which ... (iii) is by its terms, or by implication, governed by English law ...'

relevant contract and any relevant facts and circumstances occurring or existing prior to
the making of the contract. The court could not look at the conduct of the parties after *a*
the relevant contract was made to construe that contract in general or to decide its proper
law in particular. The relevant contract was the 1979 policy and accordingly the court
was not entitled to look to the 1980 policy, to its terms or to the provisions of the Kuwaiti
marine insurance law which came into force after the 1979 policy was issued in order to
determine the proper law of the contract (see p 882 *f* to *j*, p 885 *h*, p 890 *g* to *j* and p 891
b to *e*, post); *James Miller & Partners Ltd v Whitworth Street Estates (Manchester) Ltd* [1970] *b*
1 All ER 796, *Compagnie d'Armement Maritime SA v Compagnie Tunisienne de Navigation SA*
[1970] 3 All ER 71 and *L Schuler AG v Wickman Machine Tool Sales Ltd* [1973] 2 All ER 39
followed.

(2) (Per May LJ) The proper law of the contract was to be determined by considering
the system of law with which the contract had its closest and most real connection, which
in turn was to be determined by considering all the relevant facts, such as the place where *c*
the contract was made, the nationalities of the parties, where performance was to take
place, the currency stipulated for payment under the contract and the form of the
contract. Although the facts that the parties were a Kuwaiti company and a Liberian
company resident in Dubai and that the contract was made in and was to be performed
in Kuwait were all relevant, the decisive factor was the form of the contract. The
terminology of the Lloyd's SG policy could not be properly construed or applied without *d*
reference to, or the application of, English law and since in the absence of Kuwaiti marine
insurance law at the time of the 1979 policy the Kuwaiti courts would have to refer to
English law it followed that the system of law with which the 1979 policy had its closest
and most real connection was English law, which was accordingly the proper law of the
contract. However, it had not been shown that the judge had erred in the exercise of his
discretion on the ground that the dispute was better litigated in Kuwait, since the judge *e*
had taken into account the juridical advantages and disadvantages to both sides of a trial
in Kuwait or a trial in London before coming down in favour of Kuwait, and had rightly
declined to enter into any examination of the fairness or fitness of the Kuwaiti courts to
investigate the dispute between the parties. Accordingly the judge's exercise of his
discretion should not be interfered with (see p 883 *f* to p 884 *a d e* and p 885 *c* to *h*, post);
James Miller & Partners Ltd v Whitworth Street Estates (Manchester) Ltd [1970] 1 All ER 796 *f*
and *MacShannon v Rockware Glass Ltd* [1978] 1 All ER 625 and *Hadmor Productions Ltd v
Hamilton* [1982] 1 All ER 1042 followed; *Re United Rlys of Havana and Regla Warehouses
Ltd* [1960] 2 All ER 332 considered.

(3) (Per Robert Goff LJ) The proper law of the contract was Kuwaiti law, because—
(a) although there was no marine insurance law in Kuwait at the time of the 1979
policy, there was a comprehensible basis on which the Kuwaiti courts could and *g*
apparently did adjudicate on marine insurance disputes, and the fact that the Kuwaiti
courts could, and no doubt would, have recourse to English law and practice when
analysing the terminology used in policies based on Lloyd's SG form and might even
adopt principles of English marine insurance law in doing so did not render the decisions
of the Kuwaiti courts any the less decisions on Kuwaiti law (see p 888 *c* to *g* and p 891 *c*
to *e*, post);   *h*
(b) although each case depended on its own circumstances, the fact that in the field of
insurance certain English forms of contract, particularly the Lloyd's SG form of marine
insurance, had become part of the currency of international commerce and were very
widely used throughout the world meant that the absence of express provisions for the
governing law and jurisdiction did not mean that there was a strong indication that
English law should apply. Accordingly, the judge had been right to refuse leave to serve *j*
proceedings out of the jurisdiction (see p 889 *a* to *h* and p 891 *c* to *e*, post).

Per May LJ. Where the material available to the Court of Appeal is precisely the same
as was available to the judge below there is no logical reason why the Court of Appeal
may not examine the exercise of a discretion afresh and in fact the Court of Appeal is
bound to exercise its own discretion (see p 885 *a*, post); dictum of Lord Wright in *Evans
v Bartlam* [1937] 2 All ER at 654 followed.

Notes

a For the determination of the proper law of a contract, see 8 Halsbury's Laws (4th edn) paras 583–591, and for cases on the subject, see 11 Digest (Reissue) 458–459, 760–776.
For the Marine Insurance Act 1906, Sch 1, see 17 Halsbury's Statutes (3rd edn) 882.

Cases referred to in judgments

Aratra Potato Co Ltd v Egyptian Navigation Co, The El Amria [1981] 2 Lloyd's Rep 119, CA.

b *Atlantic Star, The, Atlantic Star (owners) v Bona Spes (owners)* [1973] 2 All ER 175, [1974] AC 436, [1973] 2 WLR 795, 11 Digest (Reissue) 645, *1777.*

Bonython v Commonwealth of Australia [1951] AC 201, PC, 35 Digest (Repl) 189, 32.

Citadel Insurance Co v Atlantic Union Insurance Co SA [1982] 2 Lloyd's Rep 543, CA.

Compagnie d'Armement Maritime SA v Compagnie Tunisienne de Navigation SA [1970] 3 All ER 71, [1971] AC 572, [1970] 3 WLR 389, HL, 11 Digest (Reissue) 457, *759.*

c *Evans v Bartlam* [1937] 2 All ER 646, [1937] AC 473, HL, 37(1) Digest (Reissue) 246, *1646.*

Hadmor Productions Ltd v Hamilton [1982] 1 All ER 1042, [1982] 2 WLR 322, HL.

Industrie, The [1894] P 58, CA, 11 Digest (Reissue) 473, *832.*

MacShannon v Rockware Glass Ltd [1978] 1 All ER 625, [1978] AC 795, [1978] 2 WLR 362, HL, 37(1) Digest (Reissue) 293, *1875.*

d *Miller (James) & Partners Ltd v Whitworth Street Estates (Manchester) Ltd* [1970] 1 All ER 796, [1970] AC 583, [1970] 2 WLR 728, HL; rvsg [1969] 2 All ER 210, [1969] 1 WLR 377, CA, 11 Digest (Reissue) 462, *776.*

Schuler (L) AG v Wickman Machine Tool Sales Ltd [1973] 2 All ER 39, [1974] AC 235, [1973] 2 WLR 683, HL, Digest (Cont Vol D) 123, *3613a.*

United Rlys of Havana and Regla Warehouses Ltd, Re [1960] 2 All ER 332, [1961] AC 1007,
e [1960] 2 WLR 969, HL, 11 Digest (Reissue) 489, *919.*

Cases also cited

A/S August Freuchen v Steen Hansen (1919) 1 Ll L Rep 393.

Evans Marshall & Co Ltd v Bertola SA [1973] 1 All ER 992, [1973] 1 WLR 349, CA.

Mackender v Feldia AG [1966] 3 All ER 847, [1967] 2 QB 590, CA.

f *Rossano v Manufacturers Life Assurance Co Ltd* [1962] 2 All ER 214, [1963] 2 QB 352.

Spurrier v La Cloche [1902] AC 446, [1900–3] All ER Rep 277, PC.

Trendtex Trading Corp v Crédit Suisse [1980] 3 All ER 721, [1980] QB 629, CA.

Vita Food Products Inc v Unus Shipping Co Ltd [1939] 1 All ER 513, [1939] AC 277, PC.

Appeal

g By an order of Robert Goff J dated 22 May 1981, the plaintiffs, Amin Rasheed Shipping Corp, were granted leave to issue a writ of summons out of the jurisdiction and to serve notice of the writ on the defendants, Kuwait Insurance Co. On the application of the defendants, Bingham J, by an order dated 30 March 1982, ordered that the order of Robert Goff J, the writ of summons issued pursuant thereto, the service of notice and all subsequent proceedings be set aside on the grounds that the court had no jurisdiction to
h grant leave under RSC Ord 11, r 1(*f*)(iii) to serve proceedings out of the jurisdiction. The plaintiffs appealed. The facts are set out in the judgment of Sir John Donaldson MR.

Colin Ross-Munro QC and *Barbara Dohmann* for the plaintiffs.
Adrian Hamilton QC and *R J Thomas* for the defendants.

j   *Cur adv vult*

15 December. The following judgments were delivered.

SIR JOHN DONALDSON MR. This is an appeal from an order of Bingham J setting aside service of proceedings on the defendants, Kuwait Insurance Co. The basis of the judge's order was that neither sub-para (ii) nor sub-para (iii) of RSC Ord 11, r 1(*f*) applied and that in consequence there was no jurisdiction to uphold the ex parte grant of leave to serve the proceedings out of the jurisdiction. That leave had necessarily been granted on   *a* a prima facie view of the situation, and by the time that the matter came before Bingham J the material available was far more extensive. The judge further held that if, contrary to his view, the plaintiffs' claim fell within Ord 11 he would still, in the exercise of his discretion, have set the service aside.

Paragraph (*f*)(ii) is no longer relied on and we have been concerned solely with para (*f*)(iii). This authorises, but does not require, the court to give leave to serve proceedings *b* out of the jurisdiction if the action is brought to recover damages in respect of the breach of a contract which 'is by its terms, or by implication, governed by English law':

> 'Parties are entitled to agree what is to be the proper law of their contract, and if they do not make any such agreement then the law will determine what is the proper law . . . [The agreement] need not be in express words. Like any other *c* agreement it may be inferred from reading their contract as a whole in light of relevant circumstances known to both parties when they made their contract.'

(Per Lord Reid in *James Miller & Partners Ltd v Whitworth Street Estates Ltd* [1970] 1 All ER 796 at 798, [1970] AC 583 at 603.)

In the instant appeal it is not suggested that there was any agreement between the *d* parties in express terms or that any such agreement can be inferred. Accordingly the choice of proper law has to be determined on accepted principles governing the conflict of laws and, this being an English court, we have to apply English principles. The test to be derived from the authorities can be simply stated: the proper law of any contract is that system of law with which the transaction has its closest and most real connection (see *Dicey and Morris on the Conflict of Laws* (10th edn, 1980) r 145 and *Re United Rlys of Havana and Regla Warehouses Ltd* [1960] 2 All ER 332, [1961] AC 1007). But stating the *e* test is one thing; applying it is quite another. By its nature the test involves an exercise in judgment, a weighing of a multitude of different factors. Indeed there is no limit to the number of factors which can be taken into account, provided only that they have some bearing on 'the transaction'. The word is important because it directs the court's attention to the contractual matrix and excludes consideration of matters which, although important to one of the parties, are extraneous to the transaction itself and may be *f* unknown to the other party. In the instant appeal, the defendants' reinsurance arrangements were in this category.

The insurance effected by the plaintiffs was on a small cargo vessel of landing craft type, the Al Wahab. The plaintiffs themselves are a Liberian company, but their business was carried on from Dubai and it was their Dubai address which was rightly given on the writ. The defendants are a Kuwaiti insurance company. The vessel was first insured *g* against war and marine risks for 12 months from 29 April 1977 and the cover was renewed for 1978–9 and 1979–80. The claim is on the 1979–80 policy, under which the trading limits were Arabian Gulf. The basis of the claim is irrelevant to a determination of the proper law of the contract, although relevant to an exercise of discretion, and it is sufficient for immediate purposes to record that the plaintiffs allege that the vessel became a constructive total loss consequent on her seizure in Saudi Arabia by the *h* authorities of that country.

The factors which we were invited to weigh were as follows: (a) the insurance was placed by Rasheed Shipping (London) Ltd, an English associated company of the plaintiffs, through J H Minet Ltd, London brokers; (b) premiums were paid in sterling to Minet in London; (c) the negotiation of claims and settlements on the defendants' policies issued to the plaintiffs was undertaken in London; (d) claims had been paid in *j* London through Minet, often by credit note; (e) Minet acted as the defendants' reinsurance brokers, both generally and in respect of this policy; (f) Minet maintained a running account with the defendants in London; (g) Minet maintained a running account with the plaintiffs in London; (h) from the policy being issued in Kuwait it was

sent by the defendants to Minet in London who sent it on to the plaintiffs; (i) the form
a   of the policy and the terms and language in which it was expressed; (j) the fact that the
money of account was English sterling; (k) the fact that claims were payable in Kuwait;
(l) the fact that the defendants were a Kuwait company and the plaintiffs a Liberian
company resident in Dubai in the United Arab Emirates.

In my judgment, factors (a) to (h) inclusive are either irrelevant or weightless. I
appreciate that at first sight this is a somewhat startling conclusion, but I have no doubt
b   that it is right. The essential nature of the transaction, the 1979–80 contract of insurance,
was that it was a direct renewal of the 1978–9 policy which was itself a direct renewal of
the 1977–8 policy. The first policy was negotiated and issued in Kuwait without any
London intervention. Minet originally came into the picture as the defendants'
reinsurance brokers, the plaintiffs being asked to send various documents to them as
such. This occurred after the 1977–8 policy had been issued. Later the plaintiffs' London
c   company was formed or acquired and Minet began to act for the plaintiffs as well as
continuing to act for the defendants as reinsurance brokers. The financial administration
of the insurances came to be routed through London as a matter of administrative
convenience, but the essential nature of the insurance of the vessel, which is the
transaction with which we are concerned, was quite unchanged between 1977 and 1980
and so too was the system of law with which that transaction had the closest and most
d   real connection.

It is common ground that there are only two starters in the proper law race. They are
Kuwaiti law and English law. Pointing towards Kuwaiti law are the facts that the
defendants are a Kuwaiti company, the plaintiffs are not an English company and,
although not Kuwaiti, carry on business in the Arabian Gulf, the policy was issued in
Kuwait and it provides for claims to be paid in Kuwait where, prima facie, the premium
e   would also be payable. Against this is to be set the form of the policy and the fact that it
is written in English sterling. In my judgment the use of sterling as the money of
account and payment is of very little, if any, significance as whatever the proper law I
would have expected a policy on a vessel which traded outside Kuwaiti waters to be
written in an internationally accepted currency and probably in English sterling or US
dollars.

f   Accordingly I am left with the form and terms of the policy itself. It is a single factor,
but of very considerable weight. The policy is based on the Lloyd's SG form of policy set
out in Sch 1 to the Marine Insurance Act 1906. The modifications consist of slight
adaptations to take account of the fact that the underwriter is a single company, rather
than a congeries of individuals or syndicates, the omission of all words appropriate solely
to the insurance of goods, a minor further amendment of the memorandum with regard
g   to particular average, the words 'sunk or burnt' being added, the omission of the warranty
that the policy is as good as 'the surest writing or policy of assurance heretofore made in
Lombard Street, or in the Royal Exchange, or elsewhere in London' and the addition of
the traditional f c and s clause in the body of the policy. That said, the provenance of the
policy is clear at the most casual glance.

The marine risks covered are those set out in the traditional words of the SG policy and
h   such of the Institute Time Clauses, Hulls 1.10.70 as are incorporated by cl 3 of the
Institute War and Strikes Clauses, Hulls, Time 1.10.70, which latter clauses provided the
war and strike risk cover. There was neither adaptation nor even reprinting of the latter
clauses, which were attached to the policy in the form of a print made in England and
sold by Witherby & Co Ltd of London. The primary war risk cover is in the following
terms:

j   '1. Subject always to the exclusions hereinafter referred to, this insurance covers
only
        (1)(a) the risks excluded from the Standard Form of English Marine Policy by the
clause;' [and the f c and s clause is set out verbatim] (b) the cover excluded from the
Standard Form of English Marine Policy with the Institute Time Clauses—Hulls

1.10.70 (including 4/4ths Collision Clause) attached, by the clause:—"Warranted free from loss damage liability or expense arising from:—(a) the detonation of an *a* explosive (b) any weapon of war and caused by any person acting maliciously or from a political motive";

(2) loss of or damage to the property hereby insured caused by:—(a) hostilities, warlike operations, civil war, revolution, rebellion, insurrection, or civil strife arising therefrom; (b) mines, torpedoes, bombs or other engines of war . . .'

The judge in deciding that the proper law of the contract was the law of Kuwait *b* seemed to take the view that the English law of marine insurance had now reached a point of international or transnational acceptance where it had become internationalised or denationalised. He said:

'The use of an English standard form may be a powerful, even a conclusive, indication that the parties intended to contract with reference to English law: see, *c* for example, *The Industrie* [1894] P 58. But there is, in my judgment, a factor here which cannot be ignored in assessing whether and, if so, how strongly that inference should be drawn. The evidence in this case plainly establishes that this form of marine policy, produced and developed in the London insurance market, has achieved a worldwide currency. Partly this is due to the long history, the great experience, the professional expertise and the high standing of that market, *d* combined with the traditional dominance of London as a commercial centre. Partly it is due to the process of imperial fertilisation which has led to reproduction of the Marine Insurance Act 1906 in far corners of the globe. The result is that in Western Europe, Australia and New Zealand, South Africa, Singapore, North Yemen, Israel, various parts of black Africa, Indonesia, China and elsewhere, the standard form of English marine policy is in regular use. In Kuwait itself the form has been used *e* since insurance companies were first set up 20 years ago. Similar use is made in other parts of the Gulf and the Middle East. Sometimes there is an express choice of jurisdiction. Often the reference to Lombard Street, the Royal Exchange or elsewhere in London is deleted. But frequently there is no express choice of jurisdiction and subject to that deletion the policy wording substantially remains as in the schedule to the 1906 Act, often with the Institute clauses added. Sometimes *f* the text is translated (as it is into Chinese); sometimes, as here, it is not. But it seems fair to conclude on the evidence that this form is part of the lingua franca of international marine insurance. [Counsel for the plaintiffs] accepts that for the purposes of this part of the argument the proper law would be the same if this policy had been issued by [the defendants] to [the plaintiffs] locally in Dubai without any interposition of a London agent, and the same would seem to follow if the same *g* form of policy were used between insurer and assured elsewhere in the world. Does this mean that, in the absence of express choice of law or jurisdiction clauses, they all subject themselves to English law with its potential consequences under our law on jurisdiction? In the absence of other and potent indications I should myself be slow to draw the inference that by using (to change the metaphor) the common currency of international marine insurance parties should be taken to intend to *h* subject their contract to English law or to establish a close and real connection with England. A similar point may be made concerning the Institute War and Strikes Clauses. Reference to these may conveniently be made as reference to a well-known and established norm, but the more international and generally used the reference is the less specifically English it becomes.'

He then went on to consider the state of the law of Kuwait, which is a civil law *j* country. At the relevant time it had no code specifically relating to marine or non-marine insurance. That came in August 1980 after the casualty. The judge said:

'Now it is of course well known that with the exploitation of its oil resources over the last 30 years the wealth and standing of Kuwait have been greatly enhanced. It

has within a relatively very short period been called on to provide itself with laws
appropriate to its role as an important financial and commercial centre. Thus it
appears that no enacted law of marine insurance came into effect until August 1980,
after this casualty, and this law was not retrospective, save in one respect which
seems to me on the evidence to be irrelevant for present purposes. But this does not
mean that there was no law before. The Kuwait Commercial Code, drafted by a
very distinguished Egyptian jurist, the late Professor Sanhoory, has been in force
since 1961 and covers in a general way the whole field of contract. It provides that
in the absence of a specific law the judge may decide according to custom, whether
local or general. Even without this provision I have no doubt that a Kuwaiti judge,
like any other, faced with a question of construction on which domestic authority
was lacking, would seek assistance from any jurisdiction in which there was helpful
authority. Polonius's strictures on borrowing and lending have never been regarded
by judges or jurisists as applying to them. A Kuwaiti judge might go first to
Egyptian and French authorities and thence to the English, or he might go straight
to the English, but he could by either route inform himself of the interpretation
with which some phrases in the policy have become encrusted. It would, however,
be very doubtful if such resort would be necessary since much of the language of
the policy, even in translation, would be quite as readily intelligible to a denizen of
the Arabian Gulf as to residents of older established commercial centres. Other
phrases are to be found in the Hague Rules which Kuwait adopted into its law some
time ago. I see no reason why the Kuwaiti courts would encounter difficulty in
giving the policy its correct commercial interpretation.'

With the greatest respect to the judge, this last sentence seems to me to reveal an error
of approach. First, the Kuwaiti courts would not be concerned only with interpretation.
They would also be concerned with the special concepts of the law of marine insurance,
such as ademption of loss, the difference between abandonment and notice of
abandonment, the concept of warranty in marine insurance and so on. Second, it is
nothing to the point that in relation to a particular claim these concepts may be irrelevant,
because the proper law of the contract falls to be determined when the contract is made
and before any question of a claim arises. Once the possible issues to be decided by a
court are at large and not confined by the nature of any particular claim, no court,
whether English or Kuwaiti, could have any confidence that the dispute could be
determined without difficulty. Third, in the context of proper law as contrasted with
discretion, the possible judicial difficulties are immaterial. The sole question is with what
system of law the transaction has the closest and most real connection.

It was perhaps for some such reason that, before us, the argument changed or at least
was approached from a slightly different direction. Counsel for the defendants submitted
that the body of law which would normally be described as 'the English law of marine
insurance' could equally well be described, and in the present context should be described,
as 'the Kuwaiti law of marine insurance'. The starting point for this somewhat startling
submission is the judge's view that this body of law has lost its nationality of origin, at
least to the extent that it has left these shores. Counsel for the defendants then submitted
that it settled throughout the world and, in the case of Kuwait at least, has been
naturalised.

I find the concept of a supernational or transnational body of law difficult to accept. It
seems to me that all private law has a nationality, although I fully accept that laws of
different nationalities may be identical, whether by design, by common social pressures
leading to common solutions or by common origin. But, however that may be, my task
is to decide what is the proper law of this contract and that proper law must be a national
law: either English or Kuwaiti. English law is something which I am supposed to know.
Kuwaiti law is a matter of fact to be determined on the evidence.

The evidence is that there have been very few marine insurance cases in the courts of
Kuwait and that the codified law of Kuwait makes no special provision for marine or
indeed non-marine insurance. A Kuwaiti judge faced with this policy and a problem of

interpretation would, as the judge put it, 'seek assistance from any jurisdiction in which
there was helpful authority'. If he was faced with a problem of substantive law, such as   *a*
the nature of the constructive total loss and the rights which thereby accrue to an assured,
he would be bound to have resort, directly or indirectly, to the English statute and to
English authorities. If, however, he was faced with a problem concerning the formation
of the contract, he would no doubt have regard exclusively to Kuwaiti law. The crucial
question is whether, when a Kuwaiti judge informs himself of the law of marine
insurance, he is informing himself of Kuwaiti or of English law. For my part, bearing in   *b*
mind the fact that the law of Kuwait is largely codified, that the codes make no reference
to marine insurance and that marine insurance is a new 'industry' in Kuwait, I have no
doubt that he is informing himself of English law. It might be difficult if he was
informing himself on English law for the light which that might shed on the Kuwaiti
law of marine insurance but there is no such law. If that is right, the policy has a close
connection both with Kuwaiti law as the law of the place of the formation of the contract   *c*
and the law of the place of performance and with English law as the law governing the
substantive rights and obligations of the parties. Since a choice has to be made, it seems
to me that quantitatively and qualitatively the law with which the transaction has the
closest and most real connection is that of England.

It follows that I take a different view from that of the judge and consider that the
English courts are authorised by RSC Ord 11 to permit service of the proceedings outside   *d*
the jurisdiction.

I now turn to the exercise of discretion. Here the nature of the plaintiffs' claim is
relevant. They based their claim on an allegation that on 28 February 1980 the Saudi
Arabian authorities detained the vessel at the port of Ras Al Khafji, that they were thereby
deprived of the possession of the vessel which deprivation continued until the issue of
the writ on 8 June 1981, that notices of abandonment were given on 31 October 1980   *e*
and on 28 April 1981 which were rejected, the defendants at the same time undertaking
to put the plaintiffs in the same position as if a writ had been issued on the days on which
the respective notices were received, that at the times when the respective notices were
given it was unlikely that the plaintiffs would recover possession within a reasonable
time or at all and that the plaintiffs were insured against perils of the sea, arrests, restraints
and detainment of all kings, princes and people of what nature, condition or quality   *f*
soever. They also based their claim, in the alternative, on deterioration of the vessel
during detention leading to a constructive total loss on figures.

The defendants will raise a defence based on an allegation that the vessel was engaged
in smuggling.

The judge said:

'I must briefly indicate how I would exercise my discretion in case my decision   *g*
on the application of the rules is held to be wrong. In urging that I should, in the
exercise of my discretion, uphold the order by which this court assumed jurisdiction,
[counsel for the plaintiffs] relied on a number of matters. Prominent among these
were the facts that the master and crew speak English but not Arabic, that those
who fixed the oral charter to Ras Al Khafji are now resident here, that the policy
documents are in English and would have to be translated for trial in Kuwait, that   *h*
English expressions would be less familiar to a Kuwaiti judge, that the costs of
litigating there would be greater and irrecoverable even in the event of success, that
the progress of the litigation including appeals would be slow, that there are in
Kuwait relatively restricted rights of cross-examination and discovery, and, lastly,
that there are in Kuwait no specialised commercial judges and no specialised series
of commercial law reports. [Counsel for the defendants] replied that the witnesses,   *j*
particularly any witnesses from Saudi Arabia, could very much more easily and
cheaply travel to Kuwait than here, that a Kuwaiti judge would be very much more
familiar than this court with trading practices in the Gulf and much better able to
analyse and assess evidence of what happened in Saudi Arabia, and that it is in any
event entirely impermissible to review the legal institutions of friendly foreign

a

states with a view to accepting jurisdiction if, on what is bound to appear a somewhat chauvinistic comparison, defects can be found in their procedures as compared with our own. If, contrary to my view, the contract in issue was made here or through Minet as agent of [the defendants], although I am right in holding that the proper law of the contract was Kuwaiti, I would have no hesitation in exercising my discretion against upholding service. The English links would in that event be so fortuitous, so mechanical and so minor that I would not regard them as sufficient

b

justification for taking the very serious step of subjecting a Kuwaiti company to the jurisdiction of this court in an essentially Kuwaiti cause. The matters relied on by [counsel for the plaintiffs] would not, singly or cumulatively, alter that view. If, contrary to my view, the proper law of the contract is English and not Kuwaiti, [the plaintiffs'] position is much stronger since there is always an advantage in any court applying its own law rather than a foreign law. One must, however, look at this

c

action. There are two main questions to be determined, one factual, the other legal. The factual question is: what were the vessel (or the master and crew) engaged in on the visit to Ras Al Khafji and what exactly happened thereafter? The legal question is: do those facts entitle [the plaintiffs] to recover or do they fall within an exception in the policy? The factual question can, I think, be determined as well in Kuwait as here, possibly better, and with no clear overall balance of convenience. The legal

d

question would appear to raise little difficulty once the facts are determined. I accept [counsel for the defendants'] submission that I should not embark on a critique of Kuwait's legal institutions and therefore I shall not do so, save to remark, first, that in certain obvious respects they resemble our own until relatively recent times, second, that in any civil law system there will be differences when comparison is made with our own common law procedures, mostly springing from the different and much more active role of the judge in a civil law system and, third, that I have

e

been given no reason to doubt that a Kuwaiti judge would set himself throughly and justly to determine the truth in this case. Balancing all these factors, I would still exercise my discretion against upholding service, although on this hypothesis I would regard the balance as being much less heavily in [the defendants'] favour. It follows that in my judgment [the defendants] are entitled to the order which they

f

seek.'

For my part I do not share the judge's belief that once the facts are determined the legal question appears to raise little difficulty. I would not wish to put ideas into anyone's head, but I can see some very interesting arguments on whether deterioration due to inaction during detention constitutes 'damage to a ship ... by a peril insured against'. The concept of unlikelihood of regaining possession is also not without its possibilities

g

from the point of view of an enthusiastic maritime lawyer. It is only if smuggling is established and the exception of 'arrest, restraint or detainment ... by reason of infringement of any customs regulations' becomes applicable that I would be reasonably confident that there would be no legal problems.

However I do share the judge's reluctance to embark on a comparative critique of the machinery of justice as it exists in the Commercial Court in London and in the courts in

h

Kuwait. Whether, and to what extent, I am entitled to do so was discussed in argument, but I think that I can confine myself to matters which have, on any view, to be taken into account. In favour of Kuwait is the fact that the defendants are there and that the policy is a Kuwaiti policy, albeit one whose proper law is English. Furthermore I fully accept that a Kuwaiti judge would have a much better appreciation of the Gulf environment in which the events took place. I also accept that it would be cheaper for Saudi Arabian

j

witnesses to attend a Kuwaiti court than one in London, but, on the evidence, I am left wondering whether they could be persuaded to attend court in either place. In favour of London is the fact that the master and crew speak English, but not Arabic, that those who fix the oral charter and know what adventure the vessel was, or should have been, engaged on are now in this country and that no translation of documents would be necessary. To my mind these factors are self-balancing or marginally favour London.

This leaves out of account the special position of the Commercial Court. The judge described the policy as part of the lingua franca of international marine insurance. He *a* could also have said that the Commercial Court in London was the curia franca of international commerce, in so far as that commerce is based on the rules and concepts of English law. It may be situated in London, but, unlike the courts of Kuwait, those of Scotland or other English courts (other perhaps than the Admiralty Court), it is far more than a national or domestic court; it is an international commercial court the overwhelming majority of whose judgments are concerned with the rights and *b* obligations of foreign nationals. It is a court which has an unrivalled expertise in marine insurance where that insurance is governed by English law. This is the result of the sheer volume of work of this nature which comes to the court and to the practitioners from whom the judges of the court are appointed.

I have reminded myself that the function of this court in relation to the exercise of discretion is initially one of review only (see *Hadmor Productions Ltd v Hamilton* [1982] 1 *c* All ER 1042 at 1046, [1982] 2 WLR 322 at 325 per Lord Diplock). However, with respect, I think that the judge misappreciated the problems which would confront a Kuwaiti judge when he concentrated on the task of interpreting the words of the policy from English into Arabic and I also think that he erred in treating, or appearing to treat, the Commercial Court as being merely an alternative national court. I also take account of the fact that the judge was faced with the difficult exercise of indicating how he would *d* have exercised his discretion in a hypothetical situation, namely if, contrary to his view, the proper law of the contract had been Kuwaiti. In the circumstances I feel able to substitute my own view of how the discretion should be exercised and I would exercise it in favour of refusing the application to set aside the service of the proceedings and by allowing the appeal.

e

MAY LJ. The first question which has to be answered in this appeal is whether the insurance policy issued by the defendants on 29 April 1979 was by its terms, or by implication, governed by English law. In other words, was the proper law of that contract English law? If it was, then by virtue of RSC Ord 11, r 1(1)(*f*)(iii) the English courts can assume jurisdiction in the present dispute between the parties, provided that in their discretion they think it right to do so. Given such potential jurisdiction, the question of *f* how the court should exercise that discretion in all the circumstances is the second issue which arises on this appeal.

In my opinion it is to the circumstances of the 1979 policy that we must look. It is under that policy that the plaintiffs' claim is laid. To ascertain its proper law I think that we can only look to it and to any relevant facts and circumstances occurring or existing prior to its making. In my opinion the speeches in the House of Lords in *Compagnie* *g* *d'Armement Maritime SA v Compagnie Tunisienne de Navigation SA* [1970] 3 All ER 71, [1971] AC 572 and *L Schuler AG v Wickman Machine Tool Sales Ltd* [1973] 2 All ER 39, [1974] AC 235 make it quite clear that we cannot look at the conduct of the parties after the relevant contract was made to help us construe that contract in general or to decide its proper law in particular. In the present appeal, therefore, we must exclude the 1980 policy, its terms, the provisions of Kuwaiti marine insurance law which came into force *h* on 1 August 1980, as well as the defendants' reinsurance arrangements which were made after the date of the 1979 policy, from the material at which this court may look to decide the proper law of that earlier policy.

Where the parties to a contract have not expressly stated the law which they agree is to apply to it, by which, amongst other matters, its interpretation, its validity and the mode of its performance is to be governed, and where their intention cannot be inferred from *j* the circumstances, the familiar test by which then to ascertain its proper law is to decide with which system of law the transaction to which the contract gives rise has its closest and most real connection: per Lord Simonds in *Bonython v Commonwealth of Australia* [1951] AC 201 at 219. In his speech in *Re United Railways of Havana and Regla Warehouses Ltd* [1960] 2 All ER 332 at 356, [1961] AC 1007 at 1068 Lord Denning used the phrase

'with what country . . .' rather than 'with which system of law . . .', but later said that the
a latter phrase was the correct one: see his judgment in the Court of Appeal in *Whitworth
Street Estates Ltd v James Miller & Partners Ltd* [1969] 2 All ER 210 at 212, [1969] 1 WLR
377 at 380. The facts of that latter case were such that, had the correct question been as
he had suggested earlier, he would have answered it differently from the way in which
he answered it when directing his mind to the closest system of law. This was because a
test based on the concept of the closest country tends to emphasise the place where the
b contract is made and the place where it is to be performed, particularly if the two are the
same, as important factors; whereas a test based on the closest system of law arguably
looks more to the form of the contract and whether or not this reflects decisions
previously made in the particular system of law which is contended for as the proper
law.

When the *Whitworth Street Estates* case [1970] 1 All ER 796, [1970] AC 583 was decided
c in the House of Lords, three of their Lordships upheld the Court of Appeal's decision that
the proper law of the contract in that case, an English RIBA form relating to building
works in Scotland, was English, whilst Lord Reid and Lord Wilberforce took the view
that the proper law was that of Scotland. Both Lord Reid and Lord Hodson, the latter one
of the majority, expressed the view, however, that the two versions of the test came to
very much the same thing or, if not, that they should be combined, the one prevailing
d where performance was a decisive factor, the other gaining the ground when it was not.

Although the point might be thought to be one of mere semantics, I think that the
present case also shows that it is not. If I am to look for the closest country to the actual
transaction between the only two possible competitors, Kuwait and England, then I
think that I am driven to choose Kuwait. If, on the other hand, I am to look at the closest
system of law, then subject to the argument that that part of English marine insurance
e law which relates particularly to the Lloyd's SG policy and the Institute Clauses has by
now become naturalised in and must be considered part of the law of Kuwait, and indeed
of many other countries throughout the world, I am satisfied that I must choose England.

In my opinion the correct approach in law to this and similar cases is to pose the
particular question in the form 'with what system of law etc?' and then to consider as
matters of fact all the relevant factors, such as the place where the contract was made, the
f nationalities of the parties, where performance was to take place, the currency stipulated
for any payment under the contract, the form of the contract itself and so on, giving to
each relevant factor such respective weight as the facts and circumstances of the particular
case require.

In the present one, as I have said, the only two contenders are the law of Kuwait and
that of England. That in the field of marine insurance law the former, for obvious and
g understandable reasons, was in 1979–80 not as developed or as encrusted with precedent
as the latter, is in my view irrelevant. The nature of the contract was such that in my
opinion where it was to be performed, however, namely Kuwait, is a relevant but by no
means a decisive factor. The same can be said about the fact that it provided for payment
in sterling, which is an international currency. That the parties to the contract were a
Kuwaiti company on the one hand and a Liberian company resident in Dubai, and that
h the contract was made in Kuwait, are both relevant and more important factors. In my
opinion the factors said to point to English law, which are in truth founded on the fact
that the brokers, J H Minet Ltd, carried on business in London, are either irrelevant in
the present context or, if relevant, of very little weight. I take the same view of the mere
fact that the contract was in the English language.

I think that the fundamental question in this case on this issue is the importance to be
j attached to the form of the contract. That it is expressed in English is, as I have said, of
little importance on its own. That the English words used, however, clearly reflect the
Lloyd's SG policy, even though there are omissions and variations, and the Institute
Clauses, and in reality cannot be properly construed or applied without at least reference
to, if not the application of, the vast body of English legal learning and decisions on each,
is in my opinion of crucial importance. Without I hope begging the question, the effect

of the whole of the evidence before the judge below and this court is that the rights inter
se of the two parties to the 1979 policy cannot be determined, once the facts of the fate of   *a*
the material vessel have been found, without at least reference to, if not the application
of, English law.

For my part, it is the argument which is based on the suggested naturalisation of
English marine insurance law in Kuwait, or on its adoption as a Kuwaiti child, which in
truth begs the question or is at least circular. It is clear that when the 1979 policy was
made there was no indigenous Kuwaiti law specifically referable to marine insurance by   *b*
which disputes on the policy could be decided. The argument therefore proceeds that, if
one were to postulate such a dispute before a Kuwaiti court in 1979, that court would in
all probability look to English marine insurance law to assist on the meaning and effect
of the policy; if it did so, it would reach the answer which the parties intended, by the
use of the particular forms, that it should reach in the postulated circumstances. Thus
the Kuwaiti court and the law which it would apply would properly and competently   *c*
achieve the intended result, and the mere fact that it would have to go to English law in
order to do so is insufficient to invalidate the original postulate of a proper Kuwaiti law.
With respect I do not find this a logical argument, and I think that it does beg the very
question it sets out to answer. The case where a foreign country has expressly adopted a
large part of English marine insurance law by legislation is in my opinion entirely
distinguishable. So also may be other cases with different facts involving other countries,   *d*
but where an English form of policy is used.

I think that, in relation to a contract such as the 1979 policy, dealing with the matters
with which it did deal, determining principally the financial rights of the parties in the
various situations which it contemplated, the form in which it was expressed and the fact
that clearly this reflected so many English decisions and concepts is the decisive factor on
the particular facts of this case. On this point, therefore, I would differ respectfully from   *e*
the judge below and hold that the proper law of the 1979 policy was English law.

The second issue which arises in this appeal, namely that of discretion, comprises two
points. The first is based on the fact that the judge below expressed the view that even if
he were wrong on the question of proper law, and that the correct opinion was that this
was English, he would still exercise his discretion against upholding service in the
circumstances of this case. It was submitted that consequently it was not open to this   *f*
court to take a different view on the question of discretion, exercising an original one of
our own, unless we were satisfied that the judge had erred within the scope of the
principles restated by Lord Diplock in *Hadmor Productions Ltd v Hamilton* [1982] 1 All ER
1042, [1982] 2 WLR 322.

The plaintiffs replied, first, that, once the judge had decided in favour of a Kuwaiti
proper law, the views he thereafter expressed about the way in which he would in other   *g*
circumstances have exercised his discretion were not essential to his decision to set aside
the original order obtained ex parte and were thus obiter. If on appeal this court were to
take a different view on the proper law issue, then the principles adverted to in the
Hadmor Productions case would not apply and we would be entitled to exercise an original
discretion of our own. I do not agree. So to hold would be unrealistic. I do not think that
the views of the judge below on how he would or would not exercise his discretion were   *h*
obiter. Even if, strictly, they were neither essential to his decision nor an alternative
route by which to reach it, they were not merely a tentative expression of his views
without full argument, but a considered statement after hearing extended submissions
on both sides. As such this court cannot be entitled to approach them in any different
way.

I add, very respectfully, that I think that the question whether, and if so in what   *j*
circumstances, an appellate court is entitled to review the exercise of a discretion by a
lower court in a case where the material available to the former is precisely the same as
was available to the latter is one to which the courts have not given consistent answers.
Where the court below has, for instance, seen witnesses and exercised its discretion in
whole or in part on its assessment of them and their evidence, then clearly any appellate

tribunal must and does operate under self-imposed restrictions. Where, however, this is
a not the situation, then although the views of the judge below are of course entitled to the
fullest respect, I see no logical, still less legal, reason why the Court of Appeal may not,
indeed is not bound to, 'examine anew the relevant facts and circumstances in order to
exercise a discretion by way of review which may reverse or vary the order' (see per Lord
Wright in *Evans v Bartlam* [1937] 2 All ER 646 at 654, [1937] AC 473 at 486).

In the present case, however, both sides agreed that the principles set out in the *Hadmor*
b *Productions* case were applicable to the instant appeal, and as the latest expression of the
highest opinion on the point I am clearly bound to follow them. In this context, counsel
for the plaintiffs secondly submitted that even if the judge's expressed views on the
exercise of his discretion could not be said to be obiter, thus entitling this court to exercise
its own discretion on the point, he nevertheless erred in accepting the submission that he
should not embark on a critique of Kuwait's legal institutions and in failing to take into
c account the evidence on the various points set out in para 8(ii) of the plaintiffs' notice of
appeal.

In my opinion, however, the judge was correct in declining to enter on any
examination of the legal institutions in Kuwait in so far as the fairness or fitness of any
investigation there of the dispute between the parties was concerned: see per Brandon LJ
in *Aratra Potato Co Ltd v Egyptian Navigation Co, The El Amria* [1981] 2 Lloyd's Rep 119 at
d 126–127. A number of passages in the speeches delivered in *MacShannon v Rockware Glass
Ltd* [1978] 1 All ER 625, [1978] AC 795 make it clear nevertheless that the judge was
entitled to take into account the juridical advantages and disadvantages to both sides of
trials in Kuwait and London respectively in considering how to exercise his discretion.
The relevant juridical considerations were indeed those set out in para 8(ii) of the notice
of appeal but these, contrary to the plaintiffs' submission, I think that it is apparent from
e the part of the judge's judgment quoted by Sir John Donaldson MR the judge below did
have in mind and did take into account.

In my opinion, therefore, it was not shown that the judge erred in principle in reaching
the conclusion that had English law been the proper law of the 1979 policy he would
have exercised his discretion in favour of the defendants, or that it was clearly wrong. In
these circumstances, therefore, for the reasons I have given, I do not think that this court
f should seek to exercise any original discretion in this matter in its turn.

However, were it open to me to exercise my own discretion in this case, I should do so
in the same way as did the judge. I should do so, first, remembering that the onus is on
the plaintiffs, second, by applying the modern test, appropriately rewritten to take
account that this is not a case in which a stay is sought by a defendant but effectively
leave to proceed by a plaintiff, stated by Lord Diplock in the *Rockware Glass* case [1978] 1
g All ER 625 at 630, [1978] AC 795 at 811–812 and, third, by what I respectfully agree is
almost an instinctive process (per Lord Wilberforce in *The Atlantic Star, Atlantic Star
(owners) v Bona Spes (owners)* [1973] 2 All ER 175 at 193–194, [1974] AC 436 at 468) to
decide what justice demands: per Lord Salmon in *Rockware Glass* [1978] 1 All ER 625 at
635, [1978] AC 795 at 819.

In the result, though for a reason different from that principally relied on by the judge
h below, I would dismiss this appeal.

ROBERT GOFF LJ. There is before the court an appeal by the plaintiffs, Amin
Rasheed Shipping Corp, against a judgment of Bingham J in which he set aside an order,
made on an ex parte application by the plaintiffs, granting them leave to serve proceedings
on the defendants, Kuwait Insurance Co, out of the jurisdiction, in Kuwait.

j   The plaintiffs are a Liberian corporation. They are one of a group of shipping
companies, which include a management company in Dubai and a London company.
They owned a small vessel (formerly a landing craft) called the Al Wahab (which I shall
call 'the vessel'). They insured the vessel with the defendants; the dispute in the present
case relates to a claim by them against the defendants under their war risks cover. The
defendants are an insurance company which, as their name implies, is based in Kuwait.

Their head office is in Kuwait; they have branches elsewhere in the Arabian Gulf, but no
branch in London. The cover originally granted by the defendants for the vessel was for   *a*
a period of 12 months, starting from 29 April 1977. Cover was renewed for further
periods of 12 months from 29 April 1978 and again from 29 April 1979. It is under the
policy issued in respect of the period commencing 29 April 1979 that the events occurred
which have given rise to the plaintiffs' claim against the defendants. These events were
summarised by the judge as follows:

'On 28 February 1980 the vessel entered Ras Al Khafji, a small port in Saudi   *b*
Arabia, just south of Kuwait. The master and crew were seized by the Saudi Arabian
authorities and imprisoned. The crew were released in August 1980 and the master
in April 1981. The vessel remained where it was with no crew on board, apparently
confiscated. It appears, although the evidence is scant and the Saudi Arabian decision
as translated in evidence before me is somewhat opaque, that the master was thought
to be using the vessel to try and smuggle diesel oil from Saudi Arabia to the United   *c*
Arab Emirates. This accusation is strongly denied by the plaintiffs and the truth of
it is likely to be a central issue in the action. Neither the plaintiffs nor, it would
seem, the defendants feel it prudent to visit Saudi Arabia to inspect the vessel or
investigate the matter.'

These events gave rise to a claim by the plaintiffs for the total loss of the vessel, under the   *d*
Institute War and Strikes Clauses appended to and forming part of the cover under their
policy with the defendants. In answer to that claim, the defendants are relying on the
exception in cl 4(1)(e) of the Institute Clauses, viz 'This insurance excludes (1) loss,
damage or expense arising from . . . (e) arrest, restraint or detainment . . . by reason of
infringement of any customs regulations'.

Before Bingham J the plaintiffs sought to justify the grant of leave to serve proceedings   *e*
out of the jurisdiction on three grounds: first, that the contract was made in England (in
London); second, that the contract was made by or through an agent (J H Minet & Co
Ltd, whom I shall refer to as 'Minet') trading within the jurisdiction on behalf of the
defendants; and, third, that the contract was governed by English law. The judge found
little difficulty in rejecting the first two of these submissions; he held in particular that,
so far as was relevant, Minet acted as the agents of the plaintiffs, not of the defendants.   *f*
On these two points there is no appeal, though I shall have to consider the position of
Minet later in this judgment. On the plaintiffs' third submission the judge held that the
proper law of the relevant policy was not English law but the law of Kuwait. He therefore
held that the court had no power to grant leave to serve proceedings out of the
jurisdiction. He also indicated that, if he was held to have erred in so holding, he would
even so have exercised his discretion against upholding service. The two questions   *g*
canvassed in argument before this court were, first, whether the judge was right in his
conclusion on the proper law of the contract and, second, if he was wrong, how the
discretion should be exercised.

I turn therefore to the proper law of the contract. This consisted of a policy which,
although obviously in the defendants' standard form, equally obviously was derived
from the Lloyd's standard SG form of policy (set out in Sch 1 to the Marine Insurance Act   *h*
1906), or possibly from a companies' form based on the Lloyd's form. It is headed with
the defendants' name (in English and Arabic), together with the address of the defendants'
head office, and its cable address and telex and telephone numbers, in Kuwait. It is a
valued policy: both the sum insured (£400,000) and the premium (£1,200) are expressed
in sterling, though since sterling is an international currency this is of little or no
materiality. The period of the cover is specified (29 April 1979 to 29 April 1980). The   *j*
cover is expressed to be 'subject to Institute War and Strikes Clauses Hulls dated 1.10.70
as attached'; the familiar Institute Clauses are appended to the policy, unamended. There
follow two warranties typewritten in the policy, the latter being 'Warranted trading in
Arabian Gulf Waters only', a provision which I do not regard as relevant for present
purposes. The risks expressed to be covered on the face of the policy are in the hallowed

form set out in the standard Lloyd's form; they are followed by an f c and s clause. Indeed
a the only discernible differences (omitting trivia) between the policy and the standard
Lloyd's form are: (1) the standard Lloyd's form is on ship and goods, whereas this policy
is on hull only; (2) the standard Lloyd's form includes the words:

> 'And it is agreed by us, the insurers, that this writing or policy of assurance shall
> be of as much force and effect as the surest writing or policy of assurance heretofore
> made in Lombard Street, or in the Royal Exchange, or elsewhere in London'

b whereas those words are omitted from the present policy; (3) this policy contains an f c
and s clause. None of these distinctions was regarded by the judge as being of any
significance. The first is plainly not, nor is the last, since the f c and s clause is a familiar
addition to Lloyd's policies; and the second the judge attributed to understandable
feelings of national pride, a conclusion from which I see no reason to differ. Much more
c material are certain express additions to the policy, recording that the defendants had
issued the policy in Kuwait, and providing 'claims (if any) payable at Kuwait'.

Such was the policy. There was no dispute between the parties that, since there was no
express choice of proper law, and there was no material from which an inference could
be drawn as to the parties' intention with regard to its proper law, the contract must be
governed by the system of law with which it had its closest and most real connection. As
d to that, the defendants founded their argument in favour of Kuwaiti law primarily on
the simple facts that the policy was issued in Kuwait, by a Kuwaiti insurance company
carrying on business in Kuwait, and that, since it provided that claims (if any) were
payable in Kuwait, it provided for performance in Kuwait. In answer, counsel on behalf
of the plaintiffs advanced the following submissions.

(1) By entering into a policy based on Lloyd's standard form, the parties thereto
e intended English law to apply, unless there were other potent indications to show a
contrary intention.

(2) An analysis of how business was conducted between the plaintiffs, the defendants
and Minet showed that the 'centre of gravity' of the relevant business was based in
London; this was an important factor in deciding what was the proper law of the policy.

(3) At the date of the issue of the policy, there was no marine insurance law in Kuwait.
f This factor pointed strongly towards English law; when taken in conjunction with the
use of a policy based on Lloyd's standard form, there was an overwhelming connection
with English law.

(4) Subsequent to the date of the policy, on 22 November 1980 a further policy was
issued by the defendants to the plaintiffs in respect of the vessel. It was plain that this
subsequent policy was governed by English law. As the two policies were identical, it
g followed that the policy now in question (that dated April 1979) must also have been
intended to have been governed by English law.

I find it convenient first to consider the third of these submissions, which was based
on the statement that, at the date of the issue of the policy, there was no marine insurance
law in Kuwait. The effect of the evidence before the court on this point was as follows.
On 15 August 1980 there came into effect in Kuwait Law No 28/1980, title V of which
h is entitled Marine Insurance. This is a comprehensive law of marine insurance which,
not being based on English law, differs from it in certain significant respects (for example,
in its definition of a constructive total loss). Before that law came into effect, there was
no marine insurance law as such in Kuwait. Even so the courts in Kuwait, which has
over the past 30 years developed into an important commercial and financial centre, have
dealt with cases concerning marine insurance; no doubt, lawyers practising in Kuwait
j must have considered many more of such cases, which did not trouble the courts. Since
1961 there has been in force in Kuwait a Commercial Code which, while not dealing
with marine insurance as such, made provision in general terms for the law of contract,
and in particular provided (in art 4) that, in the absence of any particular applicable law,
the judge will decide according to custom and that, in the absence of custom, the
principles of natural law and equity are to be applied. On the affidavit evidence of a Mr

Al Saleh, if Kuwaiti law in fact provided no assistance—

'the Judge would rely upon any knowledge or experience that he had of the clause *a* in question. Failing this he would resort to the jurisprudence from which the terminology emerged or developed. The Egyptian Courts have resorted to English authorities when analysing certain terminology which is used in Lloyd's Insurance Policies which have been used verbatim by Egyptian Insurance Companies. In these cases the matters were nevertheless dealt with by the Egyptian rather than the English Courts. Thus Kuwaiti Courts in considering marine policies would probably *b* follow Egyptian interpretations. They would nevertheless construe the contract as a whole in accordance with Kuwaiti legal principles.'

I know of no evidence which contradicts that statement, which indeed accords with what I would expect any responsible court to do in such circumstances.

In the light of this evidence, I am unable to accept the submission of counsel for the *c* plaintiffs that there was, at the time of the issue of the relevant policy, no marine insurance law in Kuwait. It is true that there was no marine insurance law as such; but there was a perfectly comprehensible basis on which the Kuwaiti courts, applying Kuwaiti law, could and apparently did adjudicate on disputes in cases of marine insurance. True, Kuwaiti lawyers and courts could, and no doubt would, have recourse to English law and practice when analysing the terminology used in policies based on *d* Lloyd's form, and might even adopt principles of English marine insurance law; but the mere fact that they did so would not render their decisions any the less decisions on Kuwaiti law, just as an English court, when relying (though perhaps less heavily) on decisions of courts of independent common law jurisdictions as persuasive authority, is nevertheless making a decision in accordance with English law. When these points were put to him in argument, counsel for the plaintiffs roundly asserted that, since Kuwaiti *e* law is codified, there was no room for recourse to English cases as persuasive authority as there would be in an uncodified system; therefore, when the Kuwaiti courts had recourse to English law in cases of marine insurance, this could only have been on the basis that they were applying English law as such. However, quite apart from the fact that this submission is inconsistent with the evidence of Mr Al Saleh, it leads to the conclusion that, in the case of a policy governed by Kuwaiti law entered into before 15 August 1980, *f* no Kuwaiti lawyer advising on the policy or Kuwaiti court adjudicating on it would have been entitled to look for guidance elsewhere in construing the policy, a conclusion which I find offensive to common sense. It follows that I, like the judge, am unable to accept this submission.

I turn next to the first submission of counsel for the plaintiffs, which was to the effect that the use of a form of policy based on Lloyd's standard form indicated an intention *g* that English law was to apply to the policy. In this connection, counsel relied not only on the use of the form of policy itself, and the use of the Institute Clauses, but also on certain express references in the Institute Clauses (1) to the standard form of *English* marine policy in relation to the risks covered and to exception 4(2)(a), and (2) to *English* law in exception 4(3), which excludes from the cover 'any claim for expenses arising from delay except such expenses as would be recoverable in principle in English law and practice *h* under the York-Antwerp Rules 1950'.

It is of course obvious that the policy in question was based almost literally on the standard Lloyd's policy, and literally on the Institute Clauses. Even so, it is necessary to exercise care when considering whether, in any particular case, the use of an English form should give rise to an inference that the proper law of the contract is English law. Much water flowed under the bridge between *The Industrie* [1894] P 58, a case in which *j* the Court of Appeal was prepared to pay particular regard to the fact that the parties had used an English printed form of charterparty, and *Compagnie d'Armement Maritime SA v Compagnie Tunisienne de Navigation SA* [1970] 3 All ER 71, [1971] AC 572, when counsel's disinclination to rely on the fact that an English form of charterparty was used met with the evident approval of the House of Lords (see, eg, [1970] 3 All ER 71 at 73–74, [1971]

AC 572 at 583 per Lord Reid). Of course, each case depends in any event on its own
a particular circumstances; but the fact remains that, in the field of insurance, certain
English forms of contract have become part of the currency of international commerce.
On the evidence before this court, it is plain that of no form of contract is this statement
more true than Lloyd's SG form of marine insurance policy, which is very widely used
throughout the world. This is particularly so in the case of countries which at one time
or another have been subject to British influence; but it is by no means confined to such
b countries. Thus in such countries as China and Indonesia insurance policies based on
Lloyd's form are in regular use. Such policies are also in regular use, not only in Kuwait,
but also elsewhere in the Arabian Gulf and in the Middle East. There was evidence that,
when policies in such form are used in such countries, particularly in Europe, there will
often be express provision for the governing law and for jurisdiction, e g that the policy
shall be governed by English law but that the courts of the relevant European country
c shall have jurisdiction. But, like the judge, I find it very difficult to believe that, in the
absence of any express provision for the governing law or exclusive jurisdiction clause,
the use of a form of policy which has become so much a part of the currency of
international commerce provides of itself any very strong indication that English law
should apply. For myself, I do not derive any particular guidance from the references to
the standard form of English marine policy, or (in cl 4(3)) to English law, in the Institute
d Clauses. These speak to the origin of the form, and have the effect of defining the scope
of the cover with reference to the English form and (in one respect) to English law, but,
enshrined as they are in a form which has to all intents and purposes become an
international form, are of little probative effect as to the proper law of the policy.
Obviously many expressions used in the policy are highly technical, and in construing
them the courts of any country may have recourse to the English decided cases and to
e English practice. On the evidence before the court, the courts of Kuwait would be likely
to take this course; though it appears that they might do so via Egyptian law, and it by
no means follows that they would adopt the English law of marine insurance in all
respects. Counsel for the defendants pointed out, with force, that this submission of the
plaintiffs would be equally applicable to any policy issued in Lloyd's form, or based on
Lloyd's form, in any part of the world, where the policy made no express provision for
f its governing law and contained no exclusive jurisdiction clause. This extravagant result
serves to underline, in my judgment, the basic fallacy of the argument of counsel for the
plaintiffs, which is that, although the historical origin of the policy may be English, and
although English law and practice may provide a useful source of persuasive authority
on the construction of the policy wherever it may be used, nevertheless the use of a form
which has become an international form of contract provides of itself little connection
g with English law for the purpose of ascertaining the proper law of the contract. Certainly,
when I set the use of the form in the present case against the factors relied on by the
defendants, the issue of the policy in Kuwait, by a Kuwaiti insurance company carrying
on business in Kuwait, and provision in the policy for performance in Kuwait, I consider
that these factors heavily outweigh the point arising from the form of the policy. On this
point, too, therefore, I find myself in agreement with the reasoning and conclusion of
h the judge.
   The other two submissions of counsel for the plaintiffs I can deal with comparatively
briefly. His second submission was that the 'centre of gravity' of the relevant business
was based in London. The phrase 'centre of gravity' had been culled from the judgment
of Kerr LJ in the decision of this court in Citadel Insurance Co v Atlantic Union Insurance Co
SA [1982] 2 Lloyd's Rep 543. But this elegant phrase is certainly not a term of art; and,
j to be frank, it was really being used in an attempt to breathe fresh life into the defunct
argument of counsel for the plaintiffs, which had failed before the judge and on which
there was no appeal, that the contract was made through the agency of Minet. Once it
had been established, as it was, that for the purposes of making the contract Minet acted
not as agents of the defendants but as agents of the plaintiffs, then their role in the
transaction ceased to be of assistance to the argument of counsel for the plaintiffs. Counsel

for the plaintiffs listed no less than eight ways in which Minet played a part in relation to
the policy. I need not list them here: they related either to Minet's role as agents of the   a
plaintiffs; or to a ministerial role, dealing with policy documents, premiums and
settlement of claims; or to their role in handling the defendants' reinsurance (which
interestingly, though this is of no relevance to the present issue, provided in one case for
Kuwaiti jurisdiction, and in the other for Kuwaiti law and jurisdiction). I can see no force
in this point.

Finally, in his fourth submission, counsel for the plaintiffs sought to rely on the later   b
policy dated 22 November 1980. His argument ran as follows. That policy was issued
after the coming into effect of the new Kuwaiti marine insurance law on 15 August
1980. Nevertheless, it infringed certain requirements of the new law. In particular, it
was not written in the Arabic language, as required by art 269(1); certain printed terms
were not 'given prominence by being written in bold characters or a larger size than the
others', as required by art 269(2); it did not contain particulars of the hour (as well as the   c
day) of the policy, or of the domicile (address) of the assured, as required by art 271(1)(i)
and (iii) respectively. These omissions indicated strongly, submitted counsel for the
plaintiffs, that the parties could not have intended the policy to be governed by Kuwaiti
law, but rather that it should be governed by English law.

In point of fact the policy, which was in identical terms to the policy dated April 1979
except that the premium had been increased from £1,200 to £2,000, was expressed to   d
provide cover as from 29 April 1980, the date of expiry of the cover under the previous
policy. I can only assume that it was intended to protect the position having regard to
the possibility that the constructive total loss of the vessel had not been established as at
the date of expiry of the old policy. However, I will assume for the purposes of this point
that the policy was caught by the provisions of the new marine insurance law. Even so,
there are in my judgment insuperable objections to this argument. First, it is right to   e
observe that, although the effect of the failure to comply with art 269(2) would be, on
the express words of that article, to render the relevant terms null and void, there is no
evidence of what would be the effect of non-compliance with art 269(1) or art 271(1). I
do not know whether such non-compliance would be something which the Kuwaiti
court could overlook at its discretion, or whether there would be some mandatory
consequence, and if so what. It is obvious that the translation of the defendants' form of   f
policy, and of the Institute Clauses, into the Arabic language could have been no easy
matter; and it would perhaps not be surprising if, for a short time after the introduction
of substantial new legislation, business was carried on as before and the requirements of
the legislation were not in all respects strictly complied with. In my judgment, any
evidence to be derived from the making of this new policy (if admissible) is equivocal:
on such evidence as is available to the court, it is just as likely that the new policy was a   g
Kuwaiti policy which in certain respects infringed the new Kuwaiti law as it was that the
policy was an English policy; and entering into the new policy in such circumstances
provides no indication in point of fact as to the parties' intention concerning the law of
the earlier policy. But second, in any event, the new policy is in my judgment
inadmissible as evidence of the proper law of the earlier contract. In my judgment, the
proper law of any contract has to be ascertained from the terms of that contract, and   h
from the relevant surrounding circumstances as existing at the date of the contract. Of
course, the parties can subsequently agree, expressly or impliedly, to a change in the
proper law: or circumstances may subsequently occur by virtue of which one or both are
subsequently estopped, by representation or convention, from asserting that the proper
law has not been so changed. There is however, not surprisingly, no allegation of any
such variation of the contract, or of any such estoppel. But it is simply not permissible to   j
pray in aid the later policy as evidence to be taken into account for the purposes of
ascertaining the proper law of the earlier policy. It is, in my judgment, plain from the
decision of the House of Lords in *James Miller & Partners Ltd v Whitworth Street Estates
(Manchester) Ltd* [1970] 1 All ER 796, [1970] AC 583 that such evidence is inadmissible
for that purpose. That case was concerned, inter alia, with the question whether a

construction contract was governed by English law or by Scottish law; and it was held
a that it was not permissible to have regard to the conduct of the parties subsequent to the
making of the contract for the purposes of ascertaining the proper law where no variation
or estoppel was alleged. I refer in particular to the analysis of the case by Lord Simon in
the later case of *L Schuler AG v Wickman Machine Tool Sales Ltd* [1973] 2 All ER 39 at
57–61, [1974] AC 235 at 265–270.

Some reliance was also placed by counsel for the plaintiffs on the fact that, after the
b seizure of the vessel in Saudi Arabia, the parties had followed the English practice in
relation to notices of abandonment, the defendants rejecting the plaintiffs' notice but
treating them as being in the same position as if a writ had been issued. However, quite
apart from the fact that their subsequent course of dealing was inadmissible as evidence
of the proper law of the policy, it is to be observed that there was evidence that this was
the common practice in Kuwait, under policies issued by Kuwaiti insurance companies;
c and it is consistent with the evidence that the English law and practice as to abandonment
and ademption of loss had been adopted, at least in practice, as part of Kuwaiti law. I can
see no force in this point.

It follows that I am unable to accept any of the submissions advanced by counsel on
behalf of the plaintiffs. I find myself in agreement with the judge that the contract was
governed by the law of Kuwait.

d   It follows that, in my judgment, the judge was right to set aside the order granting
leave to serve proceedings out of the jurisdiction, there being no jurisdiction under RSC
Ord 11 to make such an order. I would therefore dismiss the appeal. I express no opinion
on the view expressed by the judge as to how he would have exercised his discretion if
he was wrong on the question of jurisdiction, because, on my view of the case, that
question does not arise.

e

Appeal dismissed. Leave to appeal to the House of Lords granted.

Solicitors: *Constant & Constant* (for the plaintiffs); *Ince & Co* (for the defendants).

Frances Rustin   Barrister.

Department of Transport v North West Water Authority

QUEEN'S BENCH DIVISION

WEBSTER J

15, 16 NOVEMBER, 3 DECEMBER 1982

Nuisance – Defence – Statutory authority – Action for damages for nuisance arising from escape of water from burst water main under street – Water main laid by water authority under statutory duty to supply water – Street authority claiming cost of repairs to street from water authority – Whether water authority liable for nuisance caused without negligence – Public Utilities Street Works Act 1950, s 18(2).

The defendants, a water authority who were under a statutory duty to supply water within their area, were responsible for a water main (which was a 'code-regulated work' within s 1(5)[a] of the Public Utilities Street Works Act 1950) running underneath a street which was under the control of the plaintiffs, a street authority. In 1978 the main burst and as a result damage was caused to part of the street. There had been no negligence on the part of the defendants or their predecessors in the laying or maintenance of the water main and the defendants used all reasonable diligence to prevent the main becoming a nuisance. Section 18(2)(b)[b] of the 1950 Act provided that if a nuisance was caused by the discharge of water from apparatus the placing or maintenance of which was a code-regulated work which a water authority had power to undertake without the consent of a street authority then 'nothing in the enactment which confers the relevant power [to execute works in a street] shall exonerate the [water authority] from any action or other proceeding at the suit . . . of the street authority'. The plaintiffs carried out the necessary repairs to the street and claimed reimbursement of the cost of the repairs from the defendants, who accepted that they were liable for the amount which represented the cost of gaining access through the street to repair the broken main but disputed liability for damage to the street caused by the escape of the water. The defendants conceded that the escape of water constituted a nuisance which would have been actionable at common law at the suit of the plaintiffs but they contended that s 18(2)(b) absolved them from liability because (i) s 18(2)(b) did not, in contrast to other provisions of the 1950 Act, impose in clear terms a strict or absolute liability, and in the absence of negligence they were not liable for a nuisance attributable to the exercise of a duty to supply water imposed by statute, or (ii) even if s 18(2)(b) did create strict or absolute liability it did so in terms only where the nuisance was attributable to the exercise of a statutory 'power' and not where it was attributable to the exercise of a statutory duty such as that imposed on the defendants.

Held – Section 18(2)(b) of the 1950 Act was not be construed literally because such a construction would conflict with other provisions of that Act. Therefore, construing s 18(2)(b) in the context of the 1950 Act as a whole and other similar provisions within that Act, s 18(2)(b) provided that nothing in the enactment which conferred the relevant power on the water authority to execute works in the street, nor the fact that the nuisance was attributable to the exercise of such power, exonerated the water authority from action at the suit of the street authority. So construed the effect of s 18(2)(b) was to create a liability by removing any exoneration from liability which the defendants might have received from the 1950 Act, so that the defendants were liable for the nuisance in the same way as they would have been if the nuisance had not been attributable to the exercise of a statutory power or duty. Accordingly, although s 18(2)(b) used the term 'power', it was irrelevant that the defendants were acting under a statutory duty since

---

a   Section 1(5), so far as material, is set out at p 896 j, post

b   Section 18(2), so far as material, is set out at p 894 j to p 895 b, post

every statutory duty subsumed a relevant power. Furthermore, although s 18(2)(b)
a imposed a strict or absolute duty on the defendants in that it deprived them of the
defence that the nuisance was not attributable to their negligence, it did not deprive
them of other defences such as that the nuisance was caused by an act of the plaintiff or
an independent third party or by an act of God. It followed that on the true construction
of s 18(2)(b) the defendants were liable for the nuisance attributable to the exercise by
them of their statutory duty notwithstanding that they were not negligent. The
b defendants were therefore liable for the costs of repairing the damage to the street and
for reimbursing the plaintiffs for the cost of the repairs (see p 898 b to g, p 899 b to j and
p 900 d to j, post).

Dictum of Willes J in *Abel v Lee* (1871) LR 6 CP at 371 considered.

Notes
For the defence of statutory immunity in actions for nuisance, see 34 Halsbury's Laws
c (4th edn) para 375.

For the liability of public bodies for nuisance, see ibid para 368, and for cases on
nuisance caused in the exercise of a statutory power, see 36(1) Digest (Reissue) 416,
86–87.

For the Public Utilities Street Works Act 1950, ss 1, 18, 19, see 15 Halsbury's Statutes
(3rd edn) 64, 89, 90.
d

Cases referred to in judgment
Abel v Lee (1871) LR 6 CP 365, 44 Digest (Repl) 199, *115*.
Allen v Gulf Oil Refining Ltd [1981] 1 All ER 353, [1981] AC 1001, [1981] 2 WLR 188, HL.
Charing Cross Electricity Supply Co v Hydraulic Power Co [1914] 3 KB 772, [1914–15] All
    ER Rep 85, CA, 36(1) Digest (Reissue) 448, *354*.
e *Dunne v North Western Gas Board* [1963] 3 All ER 916, [1964] 2 QB 806, [1964] 2 WLR
    164, CA, 47 Digest (Repl) 595, *124*.
Green v Chelsea Waterworks Co (1894) 70 LT 547, [1891–4] All ER Rep 543, CA, 1(1)
    Digest (Reissue) 105, *609*.
Hammond v St Pancras Vestry (1874) LR 9 CP 316, 44 Digest (Repl) 313, *1446*.
Longhurst v Metropolitan Water Board [1948] 2 All ER 834, HL, 47 Digest (Repl) 595, *125*.
f *Midwood & Co Ltd v Manchester Corp* [1905] 2 KB 597, CA, 20 Digest (Reissue) 222, *2259*.
Rylands v Fletcher (1868) LR 3 HL 330, [1861–73] All ER Rep 1, HL, 36(1) Digest
    (Reissue) 446, *349*.
Smeaton v Ilford Corp [1954] 1 All ER 923, [1954] Ch 450, [1954] 2 WLR 668, 36(1)
    Digest (Reissue) 456, *383*.
Stretton's Derby Brewery Co v Derby Corp [1894] 1 Ch 431, [1891–4] All ER Rep 731, 38
g   Digest (Reissue) 77, *431*.

Action
The plaintiffs, the Department of Transport, brought an action in the Warrington County
Court against the defendants, the North West Water Authority, claiming damages of
£1,014·87 representing the cost of repairs a street which were necessary following the
escape of water from a burst water main under the control of the defendants. By an order
h made on 22 February 1982 his Honour Judge Seys Llewellyn transferred the action to
the High Court pursuant to s 44 of the County Courts Act 1959. On 20 March 1982
Master Waldman ordered, with the consent of the parties, that the action be set down to
be tried on an agreed statement of facts. The facts are set out in the judgment.

John Davies QC and *Simon D Brown* for the plaintiffs.
i *John Roch QC* and *G W Wingate-Saul* for the defendants.

Cur adv vult

3 December. The following judgment was delivered.

WEBSTER J. All the facts which give rise to this action are agreed and I recite them in
the terms in which they are agreed (but not in the same order as that in which they are

set out in the agreed statement of facts), without distinguishing between agreed facts and
facts agreed 'for the purpose of this action' and without omitting any matter   *a*
notwithstanding that nothing may seem to have turned on it at the trial.

The plaintiffs were at all material times the highway authority for the A57 trunk road
and in particular the stretch of that road outside 746 Warrington Road, Rainhill. That
section is no longer a trunk road. The plaintiffs are a 'street authority', and that stretch of
road is a 'street', within the meaning assigned to those expressions by s 39(1) of the Public
Utilities Street Works Act 1950. Since, later in this judgment, I shall have to make   *b*
references both to highway authorities and to street authorities, I add (in an attempt to
avert confusion) that s 39(1) defines 'street authority' as having the meaning assigned to
it by s 2, and that by s 2(4) 'street authority' means, where the street is a maintainable
highway, the highway authority.

The defendants are a water authority and are, and at all material times have been, the
authority responsible for the 4-in water main running approximately 2 ft 6 in underneath   *c*
that stretch of trunk road. At all material times they have acted in pursuance of the
Water Act 1973.

The main was laid under the Rainhill Gas and Water Act 1870. The water supply was
administered by the Rainhill Gas and Water Co under that Act. An agreement of 10
December 1926 transferred the water undertaking to Whiston Rural District Council,
the transfer date being 1 November 1927.   *d*

Under s 119(2) of the Liverpool Corporation Act 1927 the undertaking so transferred
formed part of the water works undertaking of the Liverpool Corporation. Section 53 of
the Liverpool Corporation Act 1921 empowered the Liverpool Corporation to supply
water; and s 54 of that Act defined the limits within which that power might be
exercised, which were extended to include Rainhill under the 1927 Act. (I was not
referred at the trial of this action to the Gas and Water Act 1870, the Liverpool   *e*
Corporation Act 1921 or the Liverpool Corporation Act 1927.)

On or about 7 September 1978 the water main burst, as a result of which damage was
caused to the stretch of the trunk road. There was no negligence on the part of the
defendants or their servants or agents or on the part of the defendants' predecessors, for
whom the defendants are liable, or their servants or agents, in respect of the laying or
maintenance (including discovery and repair of the burst) of the main which burst; and   *f*
the defendants used all reasonable diligence to prevent the main becoming a nuisance.

The water which was discharged from the main when it burst on or about 7 September
1978 was water required for the purposes of a supply or service afforded by the
defendants, which at the time of, or immediately before, the discharge was an apparatus
of the defendants the placing or maintenance of which was a code-regulated work within
the meaning of s 18(2)(*b*) of the 1950 Act.   *g*

The damage to the road was an appreciable obstruction of the public right of highway.
The total cost to the plaintiffs of the work carried out in making good the damage to
their highway was £1,014·87. Of that total, the sum of £459·66 is accepted by the
defendants to represent the cost which would have been incurred in any event in
obtaining access through the highway to repair the broken water main. The defendants
on 17 September 1981 acknowledged, and have since discharged, liability in this sum   *h*
but they have at all times disputed any liability in respect of the remainder of the total
cost, namely that part representing the cost of repairing the damage due to the escape of
water from the broken water main.

Expressed shortly, therefore, the issue between the parties is whether or not the
defendants are liable to pay damages to the plaintiffs to compensate them for the cost of
repairing the damage to the highway caused by the escape of water from the main; and   *j*
that issue in turn depends on the construction of s 18(2) of the 1950 Act, which, so far as
material, provides:

'If any nuisance is caused—(*a*) by the execution of code-regulated works, or (*b*) by
explosion, ignition or discharge of, or any other event occurring to, gas, electricity,

a
water or any other thing required for the purposes of a supply or service afforded by any undertakers which at the time of or immediately before the event in question was in apparatus of those undertakers the placing or maintenance of which was or is a code-regulated work . . . nothing in the enactment which confers the relevant power to which section one of this Act applies . . . shall exonerate the undertakers from any action or other proceeding at the suit . . . (i) of the street authority . . .'

b
Powers to which s 1 of the Act applies are 'any statutory power to execute undertakers' works in a street . . .'

It was also accepted at the trial by counsel on behalf of the defendants that the escape of water constituted a nuisance at common law actionable at the suit of the plaintiffs; and it was accepted by counsel on behalf of the plaintiffs that he could not seek to establish liability for the escape, on the part of the defendants, without relying on s 18(2).

c
In order to consider the issue as I have expressed it, it is necessary, as both counsel agreed, to set that issue against the background of the common law rules which govern the liability for nuisance of bodies exercising statutory authority. In my view, it is not necessary to analyse those rules in any detail: it is sufficient for this purpose to express them in the following broad terms.

1. In the absence of negligence, a body is not liable for a nuisance which is attributable to the exercise by it of a duty imposed on it by statute: see *Hammond v St Pancras Corp* (1874) LR 9 CP 316.

d
2. It is not liable in those circumstances even if by statute it is expressly made liable, or not exempted from liability, for nuisance: see *Stretton's Derby Brewery Co v Derby Corp* [1894] 1 Ch 431, [1891–4] All ER Rep 731 and *Smeaton v Ilford Corp* [1954] 1 All ER 923, [1954] Ch 450.

3. In the absence of negligence, a body is not liable for a nuisance which is attributable to the exercise by it of a power conferred by statute if, by statute, it is not expressly either made liable, or not exempted from liability, for nuisance: see *Midwood & Co Ltd v Manchester Corp* [1905] 2 KB 597, *Longhurst v Metropolitan Water Board* [1948] 2 All ER 834 and *Dunne v North Western Gas Board* [1963] 3 All ER 916, [1964] 2 QB 806.

4. A body is liable for a nuisance by it attributable to the exercise of a power conferred by statute, even without negligence, if by statute it is expressly either made liable, or not exempted from liability, for nuisance: see *Charing Cross Electricity Supply Co v Hydraulic Power Co* [1914] 3 KB 772, [1914–15] All ER Rep 85.

In these rules, references to absence of negligence are references to—

g
'the qualification, or condition, that the statutory powers are exercised without "negligence", that word here being used in a special sense so as to require the undertaker, as a condition of obtaining immunity from action, to carry out the work and conduct the operation with all reasonable regard and care for the interests of other persons . . .'

(See *Allen v Gulf Oil Refining Ltd* [1981] 1 All ER 353 at 356, [1981] AC 1001 at 1011 per Lord Wilberforce.)

h
References to nuisance are to be taken as references either to liability in nuisance simpliciter, or to liability under the rule in *Rylands v Fletcher* (1868) LR 3 HL 330, [1861–73] All ER Rep 1.

The agreed fact that there was no negligence on the part of the defendants or their servants or agents, or on the part of the defendants' predecessors, in respect of the laying or maintenance of the main (including discovery and repair of the burst), and, in particular, that the defendants used all reasonable diligence to prevent the main becoming

j
a nuisance, constitutes an agreement that the exercise of statutory duty to which the burst was attributable was a duty exercised without 'negligence' within the meaning of that word given to it by Lord Wilberforce in *Allen v Gulf Oil Refining Ltd*.

Before considering the rival contentions of the parties as to the proper construction of s 18(2), there is one other matter which it may be necessary for me to decide, namely

whether the escape of water was attributable to the exercise by the defendants of a
statutory duty or whether it was attributable to the exercise of a statutory power. Counsel *a*
on behalf of the plaintiffs submitted that, whereas the defendants may have been under
a duty to make water supplies available under s 11 of the Water Act 1973, none the less
neither they nor their predecessors were under any duty to lay the water pipe in the
highway: they had no more than a power to do that, so that the escape of water from the
main was attributable not to the exercise of a statutory duty but of a statutory power.
But in my view the burst and the consequent nuisance occurred not because of the laying *b*
of the main but because of the pressure of water in the main; and, in my judgment, if
the question be material, the burst and escape of water was attributable to the exercise by
the defendants of a statutory duty, not of a statutory power.

I turn now to the rival contentions as to the meaning and effect of s 18(2). In short,
counsel on behalf of the plaintiffs contends that that subsection creates either an absolute
or a strict liability, such that the defendants are liable for the nuisance attributable to the *c*
exercise by them of their statutory duty notwithstanding that they were not negligent.
Counsel on behalf of the defendants contends that the effect of the subsection is to do no
more than to deprive them of the right to rely on any statutory provision which would
otherwise relieve them of liability, and that, since the nuisance was attributable to the
exercise by the defendants of a statutory duty, they could not be made liable for this
nuisance in accordance with the rules I have stated even if some statute had expressly *d*
imposed liability on them for nuisance, and a fortiori where, as here, the effect of the
subsection is merely to deprive them of any right which they might have to rely on a
statutory immunity.

The detailed submissions made by counsel on behalf of the plaintiffs in support of his
contention refer to, and rely on much of the scheme of, the 1950 Act as a whole; and it is
in any event necessary to have regard to that Act as a whole, and to certain of its *e*
provisions, in order to place s 18(2) in its context, which must be done in order to
construe it properly. Accordingly, I will set out the terms, or the substance, of various
provisions of the Act which appear to me to be relevant to the construction of s 18(2).

The long title, so far as is material, is in the following terms:

> 'An Act to enact uniform provisions for regulating relations as to apparatus in *f*
> streets between authorities, bodies and persons having statutory powers to place and
> deal with apparatus therein, and those having the control or management of streets
> and others concerned in the exercise of such powers . . . and for purposes connected
> with the matters aforesaid.'

Section 1 provides, so far as material, as follows:

g

> '(1) Sections three to fourteen of this Act and the First, Second and Third
> Schedules thereto (in this Act referred to as "the street works code") shall have effect
> in relation to powers to which this section applies, that is to say, any statutory power
> to execute undertakers' works in a street . . . with a view to—(a) providing a uniform
> set of provisions for the protection of authorities, bodies and persons concerned in
> the mode of exercise of such powers as having the control or management of *h*
> streets . . .
> (2) In this Act the expression "undertakers' works" means works . . . for any
> purposes other than road purposes, being works of any of the following kinds, that
> is to say—(a) Placing apparatus. Inspecting, maintaining, adjusting, repairing,
> altering or renewing apparatus. Changing the position of apparatus or removing it.
> (b) Breaking up or opening a street . . . for the purposes of works mentioned in *j*
> paragraph (a) of this subsection . . .
> (5) In this Act the expression "code-regulated works" means undertakers' works
> executed or proposed to be executed—(a) in exercise of a power to which this section
> applies, being a power in relation to which the street works code has effect . . .'

Sections 3 to 14 make various provisions for the submission of plans and sections of
a proposed street works, for the settlement by arbitration of any dispute as to the place
where or the mode in which the works are to be carried out, as to the reinstatement of
streets after the execution of works, and as to other related matters.

Section 17 has the effect of enabling an undertaker to execute code-regulated works in
a highway without the consent of the highway authority. Its provisions, so far as material,
are as follows:

b   '(1) Undertakers may, without obtaining any consent to which this subsection
       applies, execute in a maintainable highway any code-regulated works which they
       would be entitled to execute therein with that consent . . . This subsection applies
       to any consent of any of the following authorities, bodies and persons which apart
       from this subsection they or he would have been entitled in the following capacity
       to require the undertakers to obtain, that is to say any consent—(i) of the highway
c   authority as such, or (ii) of any transport authority . . .
       (2) All enactments passed or made before the passing of this Act which require
       the obtaining of consents which the preceding subsection renders not requisite,
       whether being public general enactments or special enactments, shall cease to have
       effect in so far as they so required, and no enactment passed after the passing of this
       Act shall be construed as requiring the obtaining of any such consent unless the
d   contrary intention appears therein . . .'

So much for the wider context of s 18(2). Its narrower context consists of the other
subsections of s 18, and s 19. Section 18(1), so far as material, provides:

e   'If by the execution lawfully of code-regulated works in a street damage is caused
       to property of the street authority . . . the undertakers shall pay compensation to the
       street authority . . . equal to the expense reasonably incurred by them of making
       good the damage to that property . . . Provided that undertakers shall not be liable
       by virtue of this subsection in respect of any damage if it would not have been
       sustained but for misconduct or negligence on the part of the authority or managers
       or their contractors or any person in the employ of the authority or managers or
f   their contractors . . .'

I have already set out the relevant provisions of sub-s (2). Subsections (3) and (4)
provide:

       '(3) The preceding provisions of this section shall not confer any rights on a
       transport authority . . .
g   (4) . . . the preceding provisions of this section shall not exonerate undertakers
       from any liability to which they are subject apart from the preceding provisions of
       this section, whether to a street authority . . . or to any other person.'

Section 19, so far as material, provides:

       '(1) If either—(a) by the execution of code-regulated works in a street which is
h   carried by or goes under a bridge vested in a transport authority or which crosses or
       is crossed by other property held or used for the purposes of a transport
       undertaking . . . damage is caused to the bridge or other property, or flooding or
       other obstruction thereof is caused, the undertakers shall indemnify the transport
       authority against expense reasonably incurred by them of making good the damage
       or removing the obstruction, and against any loss sustained by them in respect of
j   interference with traffic resulting directly from the damage or obstruction: Provided
       that undertakers shall not be liable by virtue of this subsection in respect of any
       damage or obstruction if it would not have been sustained or have occurred but for
       misconduct or negligence on the part of the authority or their contractors or any
       person in the employ of the authority or their contractors . . .'

The expression 'transport authority' is defined by s 39(1), but the definition is of no relevance to the argument.

I now turn to the detailed submissions as to the construction and effect of s 18(2). a

Counsel on behalf of the plaintiffs submits, in effect: that a nuisance can be committed without negligence (using the word in its ordinary sense); that ordinarily a statutory undertaker which commits a nuisance is liable for it, whether or not the nuisance was attributable to its negligence (in whatever sense that word is used); that it is only exonerated from that liability, according to the rules which I have set out above, where b the nuisance is attributable to the exercise of a statutory power or duty; that it is therefore the enactment which confers the power or imposes the duty which 'exonerates' it from liability; and that the clear effect of the words of s 18(2) following the end of para (b) is to remove that exoneration so that, once again, the undertaker is liable for the nuisance as it would otherwise be had the nuisance not been attributable to the exercise of a statutory power or duty. His principal submission, in argument, was that the construction for c which he contends is consistent with the scheme of the 1950 Act as a whole, and in particular that part of it which regulates and unifies the relationship between the four main public utilities on the one hand and street and transport authorities on the other, and that that construction would have the sensible effect of providing an expeditious apportionment of damage, as between two public bodies (a street authority and a public utility), where damage is caused which is in one way or another attributable to code- d regulated works, without the necessity of investigating the many other questions which otherwise might arise, such as whether the damage was attributable to the exercise of a statutory power or duty, whether there had been any negligence in the execution of the original works or in their subsequent maintenance and what, precisely, caused the damage in question. He submits that the use of the word 'power' rather than 'duty' in the subsection is of no relevance since every statutory duty subsumes a relevant power. e

The effect of the construction for which he contends is that the subsection, while depriving the undertaker of the defence that the nuisance or event was not attributable to his 'negligence', does not deprive him of any other defences which might be available, such as that the nuisance was caused by the act of the plaintiff, or by act of God, or by the act of an independent third party. He submits that the application of his construction to the facts of this case has the result that the escape of water following the burst did f constitute a nuisance caused by an event such as is defined by s 18(2)(b), that the defendants are unable, because of the effect of the subsection, to rely on the fact that the explosion was attributable to the exercise of a statutory power or duty without negligence and that, since they seek to rely on no other defence, they are therefore liable for the nuisance.

The arguments of counsel on behalf of the defendants, if I have correctly summarised g them, are: that, if a statutory provision is to have the effect of imposing a strict or absolute liability, it must use words which clearly have that effect; that the words of the subsection do not have that clear effect, and are to be contrasted with other statutory provisions which do have that effect; that, if the subsection is to have the effect for which the plaintiffs contend, then it is necessary to add words to it in order to give it that effect, which should not lightly be done; and that, even if, contrary to his contention, the h subsection creates an absolute or strict liability where otherwise there would be no such liability, it does so only where the nuisance is attributable to the exercise by the undertaker of a statutory power.

The other statutory provisions to which counsel on behalf of the defendants refers, and which he seeks to contrast with s 18(2), are s 8 of the Telegraph Act 1878, s 14 of the Gas Act 1965, s 6 of the Water Act 1981 and ss 18(1) and 19(1) of the 1950 Act itself. But in j my view none of those provisions asssists him. Those of the Telegraph Act 1878, the Gas Act 1965 and the Water Act 1981 are all concerned with the liability of the undertaker in question to the public generally rather than with liability to a particular authority and for that reason alone are not strictly comparable; s 8 of the Telegraph Act and s 6 of the

Water Act deal with damage rather than nuisance and are, therefore, the equivalent
a of ss 18(1) and s 19(1) of the 1950 Act rather than with s 18(2); and s 14(1) of the Gas
Act imposes an absolute liability, again for damage rather than for nuisance, in
respect of what is obviously a potentially highly dangerous activity. The differences
between the wording of ss 18(1) and 19(1) of the 1950 Act on the one hand and of s 18(2)
on the other are, in my view, attributable to the fact that the first two of those subsections
impose an absolute or a strict liability for damage whereas, in my view and for reasons
b which will appear, the third makes strict a liability for nuisance which would otherwise
not be so.

For reasons which I am about to express, I conclude that the subsection has the effect
for which the plaintiffs contend. It cannot, in my view, be said clearly to have that effect
if regard is had only to the words of the subsection itself, since the words 'nothing in the
enactment . . . shall exonerate the undertakers' would, if literally construed, only affect
c an undertaker whose enabling Act contains a provision to the effect that the undertaker
is not to be liable for a nuisance. If, therefore, the subsection were clearly to have the
effect for which the plaintiffs contend, it would, in my view, be necessary to add after the
word 'power' where it secondly appears words such as 'nor the fact that the nuisance is
attributable to the exercise of such a power'. But in my judgment it is to be given that
effect, as a matter of construction, if regard is had not merely to the words of the
d subsection itself but to the other sections of the Act to which I have referred, and
particularly to the provisions of ss 18(1) and 19(1). For it seems to me that to give to
s 18(2) its literal construction would be to give it a construction inconsistent with the
effect of those provisions, whereas to give it the construction for which the plaintiffs
contend would be to give it a construction consistent with those provisions. For in my
view the effect of ss 18(1) and 19(1) is, as it were in consideration for the power given to
e undertakers to carry out code-regulated works without the consent of the highway or
transport authority, to impose on those undertakers liability to those authorities for
damage caused by code-regulated works whether or not that damage is caused by
negligence; and, as it seems to me, sub-s (2) appears as a separate provision because it is
possible that a wrong, properly described as a nuisance, could be caused by the execution
of code-regulated works or a specified event without necessarily causing damage to
f property of the street authority in question and because the street authority may have an
interest in preventing or recovering damages for a nuisance even though no damage has
been caused to its property. The construction of sub-s (2) as being one which creates a
liability rather than as being one which deprives an undertaker of a defence is, though
perhaps not to any great extent, confirmed by the terms of sub-s (3) ('The preceding
provisions of this section shall not confer any rights . . .').

g In order to justify any construction of ss 18 and 19 as a whole, that construction must,
or at least should, be consistent with a reasonable explanation for the fact that ss 18(1)
and 19(1) each contain a proviso in identical terms, whereas s 18(2) contains no such
proviso. In my view, that explanation, given the construction which I put on s 18(2), is
that the proviso is a necessary proviso to s 18(1) and 19(1) but is not needed in s 18(2)
because, whereas it is clearly appropriate to provide the defence of contributory
h negligence on the part of the plaintiff where the cause of action is one of strict liability
for damage caused, no such provision is necessary in s 18(2) because the act of the plaintiff
would be a defence to an action brought in reliance on that subsection in any event.
Conversely, it can be seen to be necessary to add to sub-s (2) words which have the effect
that the undertaker is to be liable even where the nuisance is not attributable to its
negligence because, at common law, that defence would be available to it in an action for
j nuisance; whereas the very wording of ss 18(1) and 19(1) is sufficient to create strict
liability without negligence.

In support of his submission that words should not lightly be added to the subsection,
counsel on behalf of the defendants relied on the dictum of Willes J in *Abel v Lee* (1871)
LR 6 CP 365 at 371, where he said:

'No doubt the general rule.is that the language of an Act of Parliament is to be read according to its ordinary grammatical construction, unless so reading it would *a* entail some absurdity, repugnancy, or injustice . . . But I utterly repudiate the notion that it is competent to a judge to modify the language of an Act of Parliament in order to bring it in accordance with his views as to what is right or reasonable.'

I do not take the view, however, that I have notionally added the words, to which I have already referred, in order to bring the subsection in accordance with my views of *b* what is right or reasonable; I have notionally added them so as to give to the subsection the construction which, in my view, in its context, is properly to be given to it.

There is another reason which I would add for construing s 18(2) as I do. Counsel on behalf of the defendants submits that the only effect of the subsection is to remove an immunity from action or other process where a plaintiff authority has established that a nuisance has been caused by one of the prescribed matters. He referred me to no *c* particular provision of any particular enactment which would have that effect, if that be the true effect of the subsection, so that I have not been provided with any illustration, in any particular instance, of the way in which that effect is achieved. On the contrary, each of the authorities (which I have already cited) to which he referred when making submissions about the ordinary rules, save three, retained the liability of the undertakers in question for nuisance; those three are *Green v Chelsea Water Works* (1894) 70 LT 547, *d* [1891–4] All ER Rep 543, *Longhurst v Metropolitan Water Board* [1948] All ER 834 and *Allen v Gulf Oil Refining Ltd* [1981] 1 All ER 353, [1981] AC 1001. Moreover, it seems inherently improbable that any enactment conferring a relevant power would exonerate the undertaker entirely from any action or other proceeding at the suit of a relevant authority; it seems much more likely that if such an enactment were to contain some such provision, it would be a provision which exonerated the undertaker from liability *e* for nuisance in the absence of negligence, so as to conform with the general law which I have already described. Were that to be the only practical effect of the subsection, if it is to be given the meaning for which the defendants contend, it would be precisely the same as its effect if it is given the meaning for which the plaintiffs contend. It seems to me, therefore, if the subsection were to have the effect for which the defendants contend rather than that for which the plaintiffs contend, either that it would have no practical *f* effect or that at best its practical effect would be uncertain. I would, if necessary, justify the addition of the words to which I have already referred for the purpose of avoiding that uncertainty.

As to the final argument of counsel on behalf of the defendants that if the subsection, contrary to his contention, creates a strict liability where otherwise there would not be one, it only does so in relation to a nuisance attributable to the exercise of a statutory *g* duty and does not do so in relation to a nuisance attributable to the exercise of a statutory power, it seems to me that, with respect, he misreads the significance of the word 'power' in the subsection. In my view, it does not have any effect so as to qualify the nature of the nuisance caused. Its grammatical effect on the literal wording of the subsection is merely to identify the enactment referred to; but its substantive effect on the subsection, given the meaning of that subsection which I have ascribed to it, is in my view that the *h* subsection only creates a strict liability for nuisance caused by (see para (*a*)), or in a defined connection with (see para (*b*)), the execution of code-regulated works where those works have been executed by the undertaker in question pursuant to statutory powers. It may be said that this effect is unnecessary and tautologous, because by virtue of s 1(1), as it seems, no code-regulated works can be executed other than pursuant to a statutory power; but, as the draftsman has not in any event adopted wording which has the precise *j* effect of achieving the meaning which in my view the subsection bears when properly construed, it is perhaps less surprising that its wording should contain such a tautology.

For all these reasons in my judgment the plaintiffs are entitled to judgment against the defendants in the sum of £555·21, being the balance of the total cost to the plaintiffs of making good the damage, namely £1,014·87, after giving credit to the defendants for £459·66 already paid by them.

Judgment for the plaintiffs. Certificate granted to the defendants, under s 12 of the Administration
a *of Justice Act 1969, to apply to the House of Lords for leave to appeal direct to the House.*

Solicitors: *Treasury Solicitor ; Keogh Ritson & Co*, Bolton (for the defendants).

K Mydeen Esq   Barrister.

b

R v Lincolnshire (Kesteven) Justices, ex parte O'Connor

c
QUEEN'S BENCH DIVISION
LORD LANE CJ AND ACKNER LJ
20, 28 JANUARY 1983

Sentence – Hospital order – Power of court to make hospital order – Magistrates' court –
d *Defendant charged with offence and asked whether he elected for summary trial – Defendant not*
understanding what was meant – Defendant making no reply – Evidence clearly showing
defendant had committed offence – Whether justices bound to act as examining magistrates because
defendant had not consented to summary trial – Whether justices entitled to make hospital order
without trying defendant – Mental Health Act 1959, s 60(2) – Magistrates' Courts Act 1980,
ss 18, 20(3)(b).

e

The defendant, a voluntary patient at a mental hospital, was charged with assault
occasioning actual bodily harm to an occupational therapist at the hospital. Before
appearing before the magistrates he was examined by two medical practitioners, who
reported that he was suffering from a mental disorder which warranted his detention in
hospital for medical treatment. Their report was placed before the magistrates when he
f appeared before them. After the charge had been read out to the defendant in court, and
after considering, in accordance with s 19 of the Magistrates' Courts Act 1980, whether
summary trial or trial on indictment was more suitable, the magistrates stated that it
appeared to them that the offence was suitable for summary trial. The clerk of the court,
in accordance with s 20(3)[a] of the 1980 Act, then asked the defendant whether he
consented to being tried summarily or whether he wished to be tried by a jury. He did
g not reply but it was clear that he had not understood what had been said and that he was
incapable of making a decision. Since there was no dispute as to the facts on which the
charge was based and since the court knew from the medical report that the defendant
was suffering from a mental disorder requiring treatment, his solicitor asked the
magistrates to make an order under s 60(2)[b] of the Mental Health Act 1959, detaining
him in hospital without conviction. However, the magistrates stated that since the
h defendant had not consented to a summary trial they were bound by the terms of ss 18[c]
and 20(3)(b) of the 1980 Act to act merely as examining justices, and that consequently,
since they could not try the case, they could not consider making an order under s 60(2)
of the 1959 Act. An application was made on behalf of the defendant for an order of
mandamus requiring them to exercise their jurisdiction under s 60(2) and make a
hospital order.

j
---
a   Section 20(3), so far as material, provides: '. . . the court shall ask [the accused] whether he consents
    to be tried summarily or wishes to be tried by a jury, and—(a) if he consents to be tried summarily,
    shall proceed to the summary trial of the information; (b) if he does not . . . consent [to be tried
    summarily], shall proceed to inquire into the information as examining justices.'
b   Section 60(2) is set out at p 903 e, post
c   Section 18, so far as material, is set out at p 903 h, post

Held – On the true construction of s 60(2) of the 1959 Act, magistrates had jurisdiction to make a hospital order in an appropriate case without embarking on a trial in accordance *a* with the provisions of the 1980 Act. That power should, however, be exercised only rarely and usually only if those acting for the defendant consented to such an order being made. In all the circumstances, therefore, it was an appropriate case for the magistrates to consider whether to make a hospital order, and the case would accordingly be remitted to them to reconsider the matter (see p 904 *c* to *f*, post).

b

Notes

For magistrates' courts' powers and hospital orders, see 29 Halsbury's Laws (4th edn) para 421; for the powers of courts to order hospital admission under the Mental Health Act 1959, see 30 ibid para 1169, and for cases on mentally disordered offenders, see 14(2) Digest (Reissue) 725–727, 6074–6085.

For the Mental Health Act 1959, s 60, see 25 Halsbury's Statutes (3rd edn) 97.   *c*

For the Magistrates' Courts Act 1980, ss 18, 19, 20, see 50(2) ibid 1459, 1460, 1461.

Application for judicial review

Patrick Francis O'Connor applied by his next friend, Yvonne Sandra Wells, with the leave of Leonard J granted on 31 December 1982, for an order of mandamus, directed to the justices of the peace in and for the petty sessional division of Kesteven in the County of *d* Lincoln, requiring them to exercise the jurisdiction conferred on them by s 60(2) of the Mental Health Act 1959 and to consider making an order under s 60(1) of that Act authorising his admission to, and detention in, Harmston Hall Hospital, although they had not convicted him of an offence. The facts are set out in the judgment of the court.

John Snell for the applicant.   *e*
Simeon Maskrey for the prosecutor.

Cur adv vult

28 January. The following judgment of the court was delivered.   *f*

LORD LANE CJ. This is an application for judicial review by way of mandamus directed to the justices sitting for the petty sessional division of Kesteven in the county of Lincoln.

The applicant is Patrick Francis O'Connor, who acts through his next friend, Yvonne Sandra Wells. The applicant suffers from severe mental abnormality. It is very difficult *g* for anyone to communicate with him. He was at all material times resident as a voluntary patient at Harmston Hall Hospital near Lincoln, which caters for people suffering from this sort of disability.

On 6 May 1982 the applicant assaulted one of the occupational therapists employed at the hospital. As a result he appeared before the justices on 15 October 1982 charged with assault occasioning actual bodily harm. The court heard reports from two medical *h* practitioners, both approved for the purpose of s 28 of the Mental Health Act 1959. They had examined the applicant and their opinion was that he was suffering from subnormality and mental illness, and that the mental disorder warranted his detention in hospital for medical treatment. Arrangements had been made for admission to Harmston Hall Hospital in the event of a hospital order being made.

The applicant was represented by a solicitor. The clerk to the justices read the charge *j* to the applicant. The prosecution and the accused were each given an opportunity to make representations as to which mode of trial would be more suitable. The chairman announced that it appeared to the court that the offence was suitable for summary trial. The clerk, acting under the provisions of s 20(3) of the Magistrates' Courts Act 1980, then asked the applicant whether he consented to summary trial (see s 20(3)(g)) or whether he wished to be tried by a jury. It was clear that the applicant neither understood what was

a meant nor was capable of making such a decision. He in fact said nothing.

The justices were asked by the applicant's solicitor to exercise their powers under s 60(2) of the Mental Health Act 1959 (a course specifically recommended by one of the medical practitioners), namely to make a hospital order without convicting the applicant. The justices declined to consider the possibility of taking such action.

Section 60 of the Mental Health Act 1959 provides:

b
'(1) Where a person is convicted before the Crown Court of an offence other than an offence the sentence for which is fixed by law, or is convicted by a magistrates' court of an offence punishable on summary conviction with imprisonment, and the following conditions are satisfied, that is to say—(a) the court is satisfied, on the written or oral evidence of two medical practitioners (complying with the provisions of section sixty-two of this Act),—(i) that the offender is suffering from mental

c illness, psychopathic disorder, subnormality or severe subnormality; and (ii) that the mental disorder is of a nature or degree which warrants the detention of the patient in a hospital for medical treatment, or the reception of the patient into guardianship under this Act; and (b) the court is of opinion, having regard to all the circumstances including the nature of the offence and the character and antecedents of the offender, and to the other available methods of dealing with him, that the

d most suitable method of disposing of the case is by means of an order under this section, the court may by order authorise his admission to and detention in such hospital as may be specified in the order or, as the case may be, place him under the guardianship of a local social services authority or of such other person approved by a local social services authority as may be so specified.

(2) Where a person is charged before a magistrates' court with any act or omission

e as an offence and the court would have power, on convicting him of that offence, to make an order under subsection (1) of this section in his case as being a person suffering from mental illness or severe subnormality, then, if the court is satisfied that the accused did the act or made the omission charged, the court may, if it thinks fit, make such an order without convicting him . . .'

f   The argument on behalf of the applicant is simple. Looking at s 60(2), every condition for the making of the order is satisfied. The applicant was charged before the magistrates with an act as an offence. The court would have power on convicting him of that offence to make an order under sub-s (1) as being a person suffering from mental illness or severe subnormality. (The necessary medical evidence was before the court.) The court could be satisfied that the applicant did assault the therapist occasioning her actual bodily harm.

g There were reasonable grounds for that belief. Indeed no one disputed the facts.

Counsel for the prosecution, to whom we are indebted for his arguments, puts the matter thus: the justices are governed by the provisions of the Magistrates' Courts Act 1980, s 18 which, so far as material, provides:

'(1) Sections 19 to 23 below shall have effect where a person who has attained the age of 17 appears or is brought before a magistrates' court on an information

h charging him with an offence triable either way.

(2) . . . everything that the court is required to do under sections 19 to 22 below must be done before any evidence is called . . .'

Therefore there must be a *trial* before the powers under s 60(2) of the 1959 Act can be exercised, although it need not proceed as far as a conviction.

j As already stated it was not possible to comply with s 20(3)(a) of the 1980 Act. Accordingly the justices came to the conclusion, on advice, that they had no option but to inquire into the information as examining justices (see s 20(3)(b)). In short, since they could not hear any evidence until the provisions of s 20 had been satisfied, they could not be satisfied that the applicant did the act, as they are required to do, before taking steps under s 60(2) of the 1959 Act.

The point is not a simple one. If the justices' view is correct, the scope for acting under s 60(2) is remarkably limited. Whereas if the contentions advanced on behalf of the *a* applicant are correct, the justices are given a power which can save much cumbersome, time-consuming and unnecessary procedure.

If there is a committal for trial, the matter goes before the Crown Court and a jury is empanelled to try the issue of unfitness. If, as was to be expected in this case, the jury were to decide that the applicant was under a disability so that he could not be tried, then the Crown Court would have been obliged to make an order admitting him to such *b* hospital as might be specified by the Secretary of State, no doubt Harmston Hall Hospital. However, on being so admitted the applicant would have to be treated for the purpose of the Mental Health Act 1959 as if he had been so admitted in pursuance of a hospital order made under s 60, together with an order restricting discharge under s 65 without limitation as to time (see the Criminal Procedure (Insanity) Act 1964, s 5 (as amended by the Courts Act 1971, s 56(4), Sch 11, Part IV) and Sch 1, para 2(1)). Such an *c* order would have been wholly disproportionate, both to the offence charged and to the applicant's mental condition.

Moreover, once the justices have embarked on summary proceedings (which in their view they would have to do before acting under s 60(2)), there seems to be no reason to break off the trial in order to apply s 60(2). On the other hand, as counsel for the prosecutor points out, it may seem strange if the justices are in effect given powers to *d* decide matters which in the Crown Court would have to be determined by a jury specially empanelled for the purpose.

In our judgment the words of s 60(2) are clear. It gives the justices power in an appropriate case to make a hospital order without convicting the defendant. No trial is therefore called for. The circumstances in which it will be appropriate to exercise this unusual power are bound to be very rare and will usually require, as in this case, the *e* consent of those acting for the defendant if he is under a disability so that he cannot be tried. In our judgment this is just the sort of rare case which Parliament must have contemplated as justifying the justices having such a power. Whether they see fit to exercise it is a matter for them. Of course in the unlikely event of the justices exceeding the proper limits of their powers, their actions would be subject to review.

This application accordingly succeeds. We do not feel it necessary to make a formal *f* order of mandamus. No doubt the justices will read this judgment and act accordingly.

Application granted

Solicitors: *Robbins Olivey & Blake Lapthorn*, agents for *Andrew & Co*, Lincoln (for the applicant); *Sharpe Pritchard & Co*, agents for *B G Coase*, Lincoln (for the prosecutor).

N P Metcalfe Esq   Barrister.

Bergin v Bergin

FAMILY DIVISION

SIR JOHN ARNOLD P AND HEILBRON J

28 JUNE 1982

Husband and wife – Summary proceedings – Financial provision – Magistrates' court –
Application for financial provision order – Grounds of application – Respondent's behaviour such
that applicant cannot reasonably be expected to live with respondent – Test to be applied in
determining whether applicant entitled to order – Domestic Proceedings and Magistrates' Courts
Act 1978, ss 1(c), 2(1).

Where a spouse applies under s 1(c)[a] of the Domestic Proceedings and Magistrates' Courts
Act 1978 to a magistrates' court for an order for financial provision under s 2(1)[b] of that
Act, ie on the ground that the respondent has behaved in such a way that the applicant
cannot reasonably be expected to live with the respondent, the magistrates in deciding
whether to make the order should apply the same test as that applied by the High Court
on a petition for divorce under s 1(2)(b)[c] of the Matrimonial Causes Act 1973, namely
whether any right-thinking person would conclude that the respondent has behaved in
such a way that the applicant could not reasonably be expected to live with the
respondent, taking into account the whole of the circumstances and the characters and
personalities of the parties (see p 908 e to p 909 a, post).

Livingstone-Stallard v Livingstone-Stallard [1974] 2 All ER 766 and *O'Neill v O'Neill* [1975]
3 All ER 289 applied.

Notes

For applications for financial provision in magistrates' courts, see Supplement to 13
Halsbury's Laws (4th edn) para 1261.

For the Domestic Proceedings and Magistrates' Courts Act 1978, ss 1, 2, see 48
Halsbury's Statutes (3rd edn) 734, 736.

For the Matrimonial Causes Act 1973, s 1, see 43 ibid 541.

Cases referred to in judgments

Livingstone-Stallard v Livingstone-Stallard [1974] 2 All ER 766, [1974] Fam 47, [1974] 3
WLR 302, Digest (Cont Vol D) 403, *263 1d.*

O'Neill v O'Neill [1975] 3 All ER 289, [1975] 1 WLR 1118, CA, Digest (Cont Vol D) 404,
263 1f.

Case also cited

Ash v Ash [1972] 1 All ER 582, [1972] Fam 135.

Appeal

The wife, Olive Florence Bergin, appealed against an order made by the justices of the
petty sessional division of Teesdale and Wear Valley sitting at Bishop Auckland

---

a   Section 1, so far as material, provides: 'Either party to a marriage may apply to a magistrates' court
    for an order under section 2 of this Act on the ground that the other party to the marriage . . . (c)
    has behaved in such a way that the applicant cannot reasonably be expected to live with the
    respondent . . .'

b   Section 2(1), so far as material, provides: 'Where on an application for an order under this section
    the applicant satisfies the court of any ground mentioned in section 1 of this Act, the court may
    . . . make [an order for financial provision].'

c   Section 1(2), so far as material, provides: 'The court hearing a petition for divorce shall not hold the
    marriage to have broken down irretrievably unless the petitioner satisfies the court of any one or
    more of the following facts, that is to say . . . (b) that the respondent has behaved in such a way that
    the petitioner cannot reasonably be expected to live with the respondent . . .'

Magistrates' Court in the County of Durham on 21 August 1981 whereby they dismissed
her application under s 1(c) of the Domestic Proceedings and Magistrates' Court Act 1978 　*a*
for an order under s 2 of that Act requiring the husband, Barry Bergin, to pay her such
weekly sums as the justices thought reasonable. The appeal first came before Anthony
Lincoln J in the High Court at Newcastle-upon-Tyne. He found that the justices'
statement of their reasons for their decision was inadequate and unsatisfactory. He
ordered the appeal to be stayed and directed the justices to answer the following
questions: 1. did they accept that the wife sustained the injuries she alleged or lesser 　*b*
injuries than she alleged or no injuries at all? 2. if she sustained the injuries alleged or
lesser injuries, and in particular in relation to the throwing of furniture on the very last
occasion, did they find that she was frightened and left the house because of her fear or
did they reject the evidence? 3. if they accepted the evidence and having indicated the
level of violence, if any, which they have found, did they find that she could not
reasonably be expected to live with a man who was guilty of such acts or not? The 　*c*
justices submitted their answers and the wife was given leave to amend her notice of
appeal in the light of them. The appeal then came before the Divisional Court. The facts
and the justices' answers are set out in the judgment of Heilbron J.

Jack Maurice for the wife.
Christine Harmer for the husband.　　　　　　　　　　　　　　　　　　　　　　　　*d*

HEILBRON J (delivering the first judgment at the invitation of Sir John Arnold P).
This appeal was first heard in the High Court at Newcastle by Anthony Lincoln J on 28
January 1982. The first notice of appeal was dated 25 September 1981; an amended
notice was put in by leave of the judge.

At the conclusion of his judgment, in which the judge dealt with the history of the 　*e*
marriage, Anthony Lincoln J, finding a statement of the justices' reasons inadequate and
unsatisfactory, formulated certain questions to be answered by the justices in order to
clarify those reasons which had been given after the original hearing on 21 August 1981,
and the matter was adjourned.

Olive Florence Bergin, the wife, continues that appeal to this court. It is from an order
made by the Teesdale and Wear Valley justices sitting at the Woodhouse Close, Bishop 　*f*
Auckland Magistrates' Court, when they dismissed her application for an order for
financial provision under s 2 of the Domestic Proceedings and Magistrates' Courts Act
1978, on the ground that the respondent, her husband, had behaved in such a way that
she could not reasonably be expected to live with him.

The magistrates have provided answers, to which I will refer presently, to the
questionnaire sent to them on behalf of Anthony Lincoln J. As a result, there is a 　*g*
supplemental notice of appeal before this court, which deals with the answers which
enlarge on and, hopefully in certain instances, clarify the original reasons for the
magistrates' decision.

The case in a sense is quite a simple one. The wife was married on 29 March 1980 in
St Mary's Church, Barnard Castle. There were no children of the marriage, but she gave
evidence at the magistrates' court that there was a child born prematurely. The couple 　*h*
lived in a flat in Galgate and later moved to a place called Woodside Cottage. She
complained that her husband was 'knocking her about', and referred to a number of
instances of assaults on her by her husband during the year of the marriage. She had in
fact lived with her husband some months before the marriage and she alleged that she
had been hit on one occasion during that association. She also complained that there was
a certain amount of drinking, but basically she made allegations, which if true cannot be 　*j*
other than serious, namely that she received black eyes and a cut face on three separate
occasions during 1980. It was not clear to Anthony Lincoln J whether, in the magistrates'
reasons, they accepted that the alleged acts of violence occurred or whether, if they did
occur, they were trivial.

In answer to the judges first question it is now quite plain what the magistrates had in
a   mind. They said:

>   'We accept that the alleged acts of violence did occur, namely, (a) in June 1980
>   when the wife received a black eye and facial injuries; (b) in the autumn of 1980
>   when the husband hit his wife in the face; and (c) between Christmas and New Year
>   1980 when the wife received a black eye.'

b   Those were the acts alleged by the wife, and they cannot be other than deliberate. It was
suggested by the husband that one of them was accidental but the magistrates did not
accept that explanation and they found that those assaults took place. They said further
that they believed her account of these events was exaggerated, and reiterated what they
said in their earlier reasons (and this may be why they thought the events were
exaggerated) that on none of these occasions did she consider herself in need of medical
c   attention or protection from the police: 'In our opinion she accepted the situation as part
of their married life.'

Certain matters may have given the magistrates the idea that this lady was exaggerating,
because although they clearly found that she received these injuries, she did not seek
medical attention (no doubt she thought that she could look after a black eye equally
well herself) and she did not go to the police. It is not for every assault that a wife would
d   wish to go to the police to get her husband into trouble, but in this case the black eyes
were undoubtedly seen by her mother and one or more of them were seen by a lady
called Mrs Hindmarsh, whose credibility does not seem to have been challenged. The
wife appears to have covered up for her husband, and to have invented a reason for their
having occurred which was not due to her husband's violence. It is noteworthy that on
one occasion she mentioned to Mrs Hindmarsh that one of these injuries had been caused
e   by walking into the garage door, and Mrs Hindmarsh pointed out that this lady did not
have a garage. It is now quite clear that she was merely trying to make life tolerable; she
was trying to make the marriage work and for about twelve months she put up with this
violence from her husband.

There came a time in June 1981 when about three days after both she and her husband
learned that she was pregnant (we understand, and there does not appear to be any
f   dispute, that she was then about two months pregnant) late one night, it was after 11
o'clock, her husband came back home after drinking and started throwing the furniture
about. There seems to have been some misunderstanding or confusion, no doubt due to
a reading of the notes, which appear to compress two instances into one, and we accept
that, as counsel submitted, the magistrates seem to have been under the misapprehension
that two incidents took place on the same night. Having had our attention directed to
g   the notes of evidence, it seems reasonably clear that when the husband started to throw
the furniture about on the night that the wife eventually left the matrimonial home, he
had already sustained an injury to his wrist on an earlier occasion and the fact that on
that night he had his wrist in plaster was not challenged. But be that as it may, the most
reasonable explanation of a somewhat confused piece of evidence is that there were two
incidents.

h   The last incident is important because whatever happened on that night, this wife,
some ten years older than her husband, decided that enough was enough. It seems that
this unruly incident by the husband, which did not in fact cause her any personal injury,
caused her (and I will leave the reasons for the moment) at 1·30 in the morning, when
she was in the somewhat precarious condition of a two months' pregnancy, to leave the
matrimonial home. What she did was to go to her friend's house, Mrs Hindmarsh. She
j   banged on the window and asked to be let in. Mrs Hindmarsh's evidence (and this was
unchallenged) was that she was petrified, and it is not unreasonable to suppose that Mrs
Hindmarsh was telling the truth, because one has only to visualise the picture of a woman
in that condition running away from the house in the early hours of the morning and
begging to be let in by her friend.

The magistrates did not appear to take that view. It seems that they overlooked the evidence of Mrs Hindmarsh in coming to a decision on this particular aspect of the case, *a* because having been asked to deal with whether the wife was frightened when she left the house, whether she left that house because of her fear or whether they rejected the evidence, they answered:

> 'We do not find that the wife was in fear, and taking into account the whole of the circumstances and the character and personalities of the parties, we do not consider that the husband behaved in such a way that his wife could not reasonably *b* be expected to live with him.'

I will return to the finding that the wife was not in fear; I merely mention that thereafter the magistrates also dealt with their finding for their reasons for the breakdown of the marriage and why she left. What I think they were doing was to try to discover some reason why, if she was not in fear, she left her husband. They thought the reason (this *c* appears in their last answer) was that she was bored, that she took a dislike to the area, that she was worried and unhappy, and that her pregnancy added to her anxiety, and she did not have the use of a car. If she was not in fear, and the cumulative effect of these black eyes and facial injuries did not have any bearing on her actions, then perhaps the magistrates were right to look for other reasons.

It is, however, very difficult to understand, in the light of the evidence of these *d* injuries, which were not trivial and which it is indeed agreed were serious, how she would not in the end be in fear, which Mrs Hindmarsh said she was. It is difficult to see how the magistrates came to the conclusion in answer to question 2, 'We do not find that the wife was in fear'.

We have been most helpfully referred to a number of authorities by the counsel. None of them is on all fours with the facts of this case, but in *Livingstone-Stallard v Livingstone-* *e* *Stallard* [1974] 2 All ER 766 at 771, [1974] Fam 47 at 54 (approved and applied by the Court of Appeal in *O'Neill v O'Neill* [1975] 3 All ER 289 at 295, [1975] 1 WLR 1118 at 1125) Dunn J said:

> '... I ask myself the question: would any right-thinking person come to the conclusion that this husband has behaved in such a way that this wife cannot reasonably be expected to live with him, taking into account the whole of the *f* circumstances and the characters and personalities of the parties?'

indicating the approach which the court must use as the test in assessing what is reasonable.

It should be pointed out, and it is important to note, that the approach of the magistrates to the Domestic Proceedings and Magistrates' Courts Act 1978, ss 1 and 2, *g* should be similar to that of the High Court. The words of s 1(c) of the 1978 Act, are almost identical to those of s 1(2)(b) of the Matrimonial Causes Act 1973, and the test to be applied by both the magistrates' court and the High Court should be the same.

Unfortunately, the magistrates erred in their approach to the evidence and they took the view, contrary to the unchallenged evidence, that although the wife tolerated the three incidents, she was not in fear even when she left on the fourth occasion. It is very *h* difficult to see how they could have come to that conclusion. The fact that a wife puts up with violence from her husband for over a period of a year is no reason to justify a finding that on the last occasion when she decided that she could tolerate it no longer, she was not entitled to pray in aid this section to indicate that her husband's behaviour was such that she should not reasonably be expected to live with him. It seems to me that that particular finding of the justices 'We do not find that the wife was in fear' is a perverse *j* one and, for my part, I would allow this appeal.

SIR JOHN ARNOLD P. I agree. I will add a word only because we differ from the magistrates.

In the first place, I would like to emphasise what Heilbron J has said that the question

for magistrates in a case which is alleged to arise under s 1(c) of the Domestic Proceedings
a and Magistrates' Courts Act 1978 must be the same question as arises in the Family
Division under s 1(2)(b) of the Matrimonial Causes Act 1973.

Secondly, it seems to me to be plain that what was said by Roskill LJ and agreed to by
Browne LJ in *O'Neill v O'Neill* [1975] 3 All ER 289 at 295–296, [1975] 1 WLR 1118 at
1125–1126 by way of commentary on *Livingstone-Stallard v Livingstone-Stallard* [1974] 2
All ER 766, [1974] Fam 47 was part of the ratio decidendi of the Court of Appeal in
b *O'Neill v O'Neill* and that any departure from that principle would necessarily therefore
be per incuriam. What Roskill LJ said, after citing the passage from the judgment of
Dunn J in *Livingstone-Stallard v Livingstone-Stallard,* was this:

'That sentence is quoted in the current edition of Rayden on Divorce (12th Edn
(1974), p 217, para 25, note (e)) which correctly states the law which has to be
applied. Accordingly, I ask myself the same question that Dunn J asked himself in
c the *Livingstone-Stallard* case.'

And what Browne LJ said was: 'For the reasons given by Cairns and Roskill LJJ this appeal
should be allowed.' So there is the plainest adoption by the Court of Appeal in part of the
ratio decidendi of the proposition of Dunn J in *Livingstone-Stallard v Livingstone-Stallard.*

This wife tolerated the first three incidents, all of them incidents of violence, and on
d that matter so far the magistrates were, in my judgment, entitled if they so desired to
take the view that this particular wife was debarred from saying as regards those
particular incidents that this particular husband had been guilty of behaviour such as to
make it unreasonable to require her to live further with him.

But then there came a fourth incident. It was the incident of throwing the furniture
about soon after the wife learned of her pregnancy. In relation to that the finding that
e the magistrates offer, that the wife was not in fear, seems to me to be plainly perverse
because the undisputed evidence of Mrs Hindmarsh was that she was petrified. The
magistrates record in the notes of evidence at one point in relation to the matter of
throwing furniture about that that did not cause the wife to decide to leave the husband,
but it is possible only to contemplate that particular statement as relating to an earlier
incident and not the final incident which caused the breach.

f In my judgment, for the reasons Heilbron J has given, this appeal must be allowed.

Appeal allowed.

Solicitors: *Cameron Markby*, agents for *Darling Heslop & Forster*, Barnard Castle (for the
wife); *Pritchard Englefield & Tobin*, agents for *Dawson Arnott & Pickering*, Barnard Castle
(for the husband).

Bebe Chua   Barrister.

Air Canada and others v Secretary of State for Trade and another (No 2)

HOUSE OF LORDS

LORD FRASER OF TULLYBELTON, LORD WILBERFORCE, LORD EDMUND-DAVIES, LORD SCARMAN AND LORD TEMPLEMAN

17, 18, 19 JANUARY, 10 MARCH 1983

Discovery – Privilege – Production contrary to public interest – Class of documents – Documents relating to government policy – Communications between government ministers – Documents prepared for use of ministers in formulating government policy – Certificate on behalf of Crown claiming privilege from disclosure on ground of public interest – Production sought by plaintiffs in action seeking declaration that minister abused his powers – Requirements for establishing that disclosure or inspection necessary for due administration of justice – When court can override certificate – Whether disclosure necessary in public interest for due administration of justice – Whether person seeking production must prove that documents likely to assist his case – Whether sufficient to prove that documents likely to affect decision in case.

Landing charges at Heathrow Airport, London, were fixed by the British Airports Authority (the BAA), a statutory body which owned and managed the airport and which was itself statutorily subject to the financial supervision of the Secretary of State for Trade. In 1979 and 1980 the BAA imposed substantial increases in landing charges at Heathrow. The plaintiffs, a group of 18 international airlines which used the airport, objected to the increases, claiming that they were excessive and discriminatory. They brought an action against the Secretary of State and the BAA alleging, as against the Secretary of State, that he had directed the BAA to increase the landing charges, that he had done so for the dominant purpose of implementing general government policy and in particular to give effect to the government's desire to reduce public sector borrowing, and that in doing so he had acted ultra vires and unlawfully because his power to give directions to the BAA was confined to giving directions for the purposes of the Airports Authority Act 1975 under which the BAA operated. At the discovery stage in the action the Secretary of State produced to the plaintiffs the documents which had passed between the Department of Trade and the BAA regarding the increased charges but refused the plaintiffs' request to produce another class of documents (the ministerial documents) which comprised communications which had passed between government ministers and briefs, minutes and memoranda prepared for the use of ministers at their meetings, all of which related to the formulation of government policy regarding the BAA and the limitation of public sector borrowing, and in particular the exercise by the Secretary of State of his power to control the BAA's borrowing. It was claimed on behalf of the Secretary of State that the ministerial documents were privileged from disclosure by virtue of public interest immunity. The Secretary of State tendered certificates on behalf of the Crown which gave relevant grounds for claiming public interest immunity from disclosure in the interests of the proper functioning of government. The plaintiffs nevertheless claimed that the documents were necessary for the fair disposal of the case, within RSC Ord 24, r 13[a], and submitted that the court, acting under r 13(2), should itself inspect the documents to determine whether that was so. The judge ordered that the documents be produced for his inspection and then, subject to his inspection, to the

a Rule 13 provides:
    '(1) No order for the production of any documents for inspection or to the Court shall be made under any of the foregoing rules unless the Court is of opinion that the order is necessary either for disposing fairly of the cause or matter or for saving costs.
    (2) Where on an application under this Order for production of any document for inspection or to the Court privilege from such production is claimed or objection is made to such production on any other ground, the Court may inspect the document for the purpose of deciding whether the claim or objection is valid.'

plaintiffs, on the ground that, even if they were not likely to assist the plaintiffs' case and
a might even harm it, they would substantially assist the court in eliciting the true facts of
the case and would thereby affect the court's decision, and that demonstrated a sufficient
public interest in the production of the documents (subject to the judge's inspection) on
the ground of the due administration of justice outweighing the public interest in their
non-disclosure. The Secretary of State appealed, contending that a party seeking
production of documents had to show that the documents were likely to assist his case
b and that the plaintiffs had failed to do so. The Court of Appeal upheld that contention
and allowed the Secretary of State's appeal. The plaintiffs appealed to the House of Lords.

Held – The appeal would be dismissed for the following reasons—
(1) (Per Lord Fraser, Lord Wilberforce and Lord Edmund-Davies) Given the nature of
the adversarial system of deciding cases, the task of the court was to decide a case fairly
between the parties on the evidence available, and not to ascertain some independent
c truth by seeking out evidence of its own accord. Thus a party was free, if he so wished,
to withhold information that would help his case. It followed that a party seeking to
compel the other party or an independent person to disclose information was required to
show that the information was likely to help his own case or damage his adversary's case,
in the sense that there was a reasonable probability and not just a mere speculative belief
that it would do so. Furthermore, that principle applied both at the stage of a private
d inspection of documents by the judge and at the later stage of ordering production of the
documents to the other party, since the purpose of a private inspection was to determine
whether production should be ordered. Since any information contained in the
ministerial documents would almost certainly tend merely to repeat published
information already known to and relied on by the plaintiffs and would be unlikely to
assist the plaintiffs further, the plaintiffs had not made out a case for inspection of the
e documents (see p 916 e to g, p 917 d to p 918 f, p 919 g to j, p 920 c to e and g to p 921 d
and g to p 922 a c to e and j to p 923 g, post); Conway v Rimmer [1968] 1 All ER 874 and
Burmah Oil Co Ltd v Bank of England (A-G intervening) [1979] 3 All ER 700 considered.
(2) (Per Lord Scarman and Lord Templeman) Although the court should inspect
documents when it considered that their disclosure might materially assist either of the
f parties or the court in determining the issues, and not merely when the party seeking
production established that the documents were likely to assist his own case, it was
nevertheless for the party seeking production to establish that the documents were likely
to be necessary for fairly disposing of the issues. On the facts, however, the plaintiffs had
failed to do that in respect of the ministerial documents (see p 924 e to p 925 b and h and
p 927 d to j, post); dicta of Lord Reid and Lord Pearce in Conway v Rimmer [1968] 1 All
ER at 888, 911 applied.
g Per Lord Fraser. Cabinet minutes, although entitled to a high degree of protection
against disclosure, are not automatically immune from disclosure (see p 915 c d, post);
Nixon v US (1974) 418 US 683 and Sankey v Whitlam (1978) 21 ALR 505 considered;
dictum of Lord Reid in Conway v Rimmer [1968] 1 All ER at 888 doubted.
Decision of the Court of Appeal [1983] 1 All ER 161 affirmed.

h **Notes**
For withholding documents on the ground of public interest and Crown privilege, see
13 Halsbury's Laws (4th edn) paras 86–91, and for cases on the subject, see 18 Digest
(Reissue) 154–160, 1265–1301.
For the Airports Authority Act 1975, see 45 Halsbury's Statutes (3rd edn) 48.

j **Cases referred to in opinions**
Burmah Oil Co Ltd v Bank of England (A-G intervening) [1979] 3 All ER 700, [1980] AC 1090,
[1979] 3 WLR 722, HL, Digest (Cont Vol E) 184, 1277a.
Compagnie Financière et Commerciale du Pacifique v Peruvian Guano Co (1882) 11 QBD 55,
CA, 18 Digest (Reissue) 48, 338.
Conway v Rimmer [1968] 1 All ER 874, [1968] AC 910, [1968] 2 WLR 998, HL, 18 Digest
(Reissue) 155, 1273.

Crompton (Alfred) Amusement Machines Ltd v Customs and Excise Comrs (No 2) [1973] 2 All
ER 1169, [1974] AC 405, [1973] 3 WLR 268, HL, 18 Digest (Reissue) 103, 756.   *a*
D v National Society for the Prevention of Cruelty to Children [1977] 1 All ER 589, [1978] AC
171, [1977] 2 WLR 201, HL, Digest (Cont Vol E) 102, 756.
Environmental Defence Society Inc v South Pacific Aluminium Ltd (No 2) [1981] 1 NZLR 153.
Glasgow Corp v Central Land Board 1956 SC (HL) 1.
Nixon v US (1974) 418 US 683.
Rogers v Secretary of State for the Home Dept, Gaming Board for GB v Rogers [1972] 2 All ER   *b*
1057, [1973] AC 388, [1972] 3 WLR 279, HL, 16 Digest (Reissue) 406, 4466.
Sankey v Whitlam (1978) 21 ALR 505.
Science Research Council v Nassé, BL Cars Ltd v Vyas [1979] 3 All ER 673, [1980] AC 1028,
[1979] 3 WLR 762, HL, Digest (Cont Vol E) 186, 1301d.
Williams v Home Office [1981] 1 All ER 1151.
Woodworth v Conroy [1976] 1 All ER 107, [1976] QB 884, [1976] 2 WLR 338, CA, 32   *c*
Digest (Reissue) 400, 3249.

Interlocutory appeal
The plaintiffs, a group of 18 international airlines headed by Air Canada, appealed with
the leave of the Court of Appeal against the decision of the Court of Appeal (Lord
Denning MR, Watkins and Fox LJJ) ([1983] 1 All ER 161) on 24 September 1982   *d*
allowing an appeal by the first defendant, the Secretary of State for Trade, and dismissing
the plaintiffs' cross-appeal against the judgment of Bingham J ([1983] 1 All ER 161) on 6
May 1982 and order dated 16 May 1982 whereby, in proceedings brought by the
plaintiffs against the Secretary of State and the second defendant, the British Airports
Authority (the BAA), he ordered the Secretary of State to produce for inspection by him
certain documents set out in category A of a certificate dated 26 June 1981, but not those   *e*
contained in category B of the certificate, for which the Crown claimed immunity from
production on the ground that both categories of documents belonged to a class the
production of which would be injurious to the public interest. The Court of Appeal held
that both categories of documents were immune from production. The facts are set out
in the opinion of Lord Fraser.

Samuel Stamler QC and *Michael Crystal* for the appellants.   *f*
The Lord Advocate (Lord Mackay of Clashfern QC), Simon D Brown and *Christopher Clarke* for
the Secretary of State.
The BAA was not represented.

At the conclusion of the argument Lord Fraser announced that in view of the imminence
of the trial of the action their Lordships would indicate their decision in the matter and   *g*
give their reasons later. His Lordship then announced that the appeal would be dismissed.

10 March. The following opinions were delivered.

LORD FRASER OF TULLYBELTON. My Lords, this appeal is concerned with
the question of when and in what circumstances the court should exercise its power to
inspect documents which are relevant to an action, with a view to ordering their   *h*
production, when their production has been objected to on behalf of the Crown on the
ground that they fall within a class of documents the production of which would be
injurious to the public interest.
The appellants are a group of 18 international airlines, headed by Air Canada, all of
which operate into and out of Heathrow Airport. They are the plaintiffs in the action.
There are two respondents. One is the British Airports Authority (the BAA), a statutory   *j*
body whose main function is to own and manage several airports in the United Kingdom,
including Heathrow. Its functions are now regulated by the Airports Authority Act
1975. It is the second defendant and the second respondent. The first defendant and first
respondent is the Secretary of State for Trade, who has under the 1975 Act certain
supervisory powers over the BAA, particularly in financial matters. He is the only
respondent who was represented before your Lordships' House.

The appellants object to the charges made by the BAA for the use of Heathrow Airport,
a and particularly to increases in the charges made in November 1979 and April 1980,
which they allege are excessive in amount and discriminatory in character. All parties
accept that, although the BAA has no express statutory power to charge airlines for the
use of Heathrow, it has an implied power to do so. On several occasions since 1976 the
BAA has increased its charges at Heathrow in ways to which the appellants object, but, so
far as the present appeal is concerned, the only relevant increases are those which applied
b from 1 November 1979 and 1 April 1980. The case made by the appellants falls under
four main heads. The first head, with which alone this appeal is concerned, has been
called 'the constitutional case'. It is summarised in para 22 of the reeamended points of
claim, which includes an averment that the increases from 1 November 1979 and/or 1
April 1980—

c   'were ultra vires the BAA and unlawful and not imposed in the proper exercise of
        its discretion under the 1975 Act but were substantially caused or contributed to by
        the ultra vires and unlawful directions, requirements or interference of the Secretary
        of State whose dominant purpose was the implementation of non-aviation related
        government policy (and particularly to achieve any reduction, whether temporary
        or otherwise, in the public sector borrowing requirement) and who at no time paid
        any or any sufficient regard to his own powers and duties, the powers and duties of
d   the BAA or the international obligations of the United Kingdom . . .'

These are partly averments of fact, viz that the Secretary of State 'imposed' the increases
by directions and requirements, and partly averments of law, viz that his directions were
ultra vires and unlawful. In relation to the factual averments a large number of
documents have been produced without objection on behalf of the Secretary of State,
e including virtually all the relevant communications between the Department of Trade
and the BAA. These communications may well tend to show whether the Secretary of
State imposed charges or agreed them with the BAA. The averments relating to ultra
vires depend partly on construction of the 1975 Act, which will not be assisted by the
production of documents, but they also raise the question of what was 'the dominant
purpose' of the Secretary of State in acting as he did. The appellants' case on that briefly
f is that the Secretary of State had power to give financial directions to the BAA, but only
for the purposes of the 1975 Act, and not for other purposes such as reducing the public
sector borrowing requirement. They say that, because the Secretary of State's dominant
purpose was to reduce the public sector borrowing requirement, his directions were ultra
vires and unlawful. In order to investigate what was the Secretary of State's dominant
purpose, they wish to refer to the documents the production of which is objected to on
g behalf of the Crown.
I need not refer to the heads of the action other than the constitutional head. The relief
sought under that head, as against the Secretary of State, is a declaration that certain
specified acts of his were ultra vires and unlawful. The reliefs sought under the first head,
as against the BAA, include declarations that its user charges since 1 November 1979
and/or 1 April 1980 were ultra vires and unlawful, injunctions restraining the BAA from
h imposing those charges on the appellants and a declaration that the appellants are entitled
to repayment of the charges in whole or in part. Relief is sought as against both
respondents in this action, and the judge (Bingham J) held that, in the circumstances,
procedure by way of action was more appropriate than the procedure under RSC Ord 53
which would have been available against the first respondent. His view on that point has
not been challenged.
j The Treasury Solicitor on behalf of the Secretary of State served on the appellants a list
of documents, but he objected to production of certain of the documents in the list. The
objection was supported by a certificate dated 26 June 1981 by Sir Kenneth Clucas KCB,
the then Permanent Secretary to the Department of Trade, claiming immunity for two
categories of documents in the list. Category A consist of approximately 100 documents
being communications between, to and from ministers (including ministers' personal
secretaries acting on behalf of ministers) and minutes and briefs for ministers, other

documents considered by ministers, drafts for consideration by ministers and memoranda of meetings attended by ministers. The certificate explained that all these documents *a* relate to:

'(a) The formulation of the policy of the previous Government in relation to the early consideration of the policy of the British Airports Authority ("BAA") commencing in 1977 . . . (b) In relation to formulation of the policy of the present Government regarding the limitation of borrowing by the Public Sector with particular regard to the exercise of the Secretary of State's powers to control the *b* BAA's borrowing and the effect of BAA's plans for substantial capital expenditure. (c) In relation to formulation of the policy to be adopted by the present Government towards the BAA's proposals for landing fees for 1980–81 . . . (d) In relation to formulation of the policy to be adopted by the present Government in view of representations by Members of Parliament and the varous airlines using London Heathrow Airport and their representatives.   *c*

CATEGORY B   These consist of communications between, to and from senior officials of the Department of Trade, of the Treasury, of the Foreign & Commonwealth Office and of the Departments of Energy, Industry and Transport . . . relating to the formulation of one or more aspects of the policy described in Category A.'

d

The certificate further provided, inter alia:

'5. It is, in my opinion, necessary for the proper functioning of the public service that the documents in Category A and Category B should be withheld from production. They are all documents falling within the class of documents relating to the formulation of Government policy. Such policy was decided at a high level, involving as it did matters of major economic importance to the United Kingdom. *e* The documents in question cannot properly be described as routine documents . . .'

The certificate explains further the reasons for objection on lines very similar to the certificate referred to in *Burmah Oil Co Ltd v Bank of England* [1979] 3 All ER 700, [1980] AC 1090. It was accepted on behalf of the appellants that the objections were valid, that is to say that the certificate stated grounds which were relevant and persuasive, and that *f* it was in proper form. The reason why it was granted by the permanent secretary and not by a minister was that some of the documents related to formulation of the policy of the previous government which, by constitutional practice, are not disclosed to their successors in another government. A supplemental certificate was made on 10 September 1981 by Sir Kenneth Clucas in respect of a further document but nothing turns on it. There were further supplemental certificates by Sir Kenneth Clucas's successor as *g* Permanent Secretary of the Department of Trade and by the Secretary of the Cabinet. These were made after the decision by Bingham J and no special point arises on them.

By order dated 16 May 1982 Bingham J ordered the Secretary of State to produce for inspection by himself (the judge) the documents in category A, but not those in category B. He further directed that the order for production should be stayed pending an appeal by the Secretary of State for which he gave leave. The order for a stay was in accordance *h* with usual and proper practice in cases where documents are ordered to be produced in spite of a claim to public interest immunity.

The Court of Appeal (Lord Denning MR, Watkins and Fox LJJ) ([1983] 1 All ER 161) unanimously allowed the Secretary of State's appeal from the decision of Bingham J, so far as it ordered production of the documents, and gave leave to appeal to your Lordships' House.   *j*

In considering the present law of England on what has come to be called public interest immunity, in relation to the production of documents, it is not necessary to go further back than *Conway v Rimmer* [1968] 1 All ER 874, [1968] AC 910, where this House decided that a certificate by a minister stating that production of documents of a certain class would be contrary to the public interest was not conclusive. Lord Reid said ([1968] 1 All ER 874 at 888, [1968] AC 910 at 952):

a
'I would therefore propose that the House ought now to decide that courts have and are entitled to exercise a power and duty to hold a balance between the public interest, as expressed by a Minister, to withhold certain documents or other evidence, and the public interest in ensuring the proper administration of justice.'

A little further on Lord Reid went on to say:

b
'I do not doubt that there are certain classes of documents which ought not to be disclosed whatever their contents may be. Virtually everyone agrees that cabinet minutes and the like ought not to be disclosed until such time as they are only of historical interest.'

The latter observation was strictly speaking obiter in *Conway v Rimmer*, where the documents in question were reports on a probationer police constable by his superiors.

c
I do not think that even Cabinet minutes are completely immune from disclosure in a case where, for example, the issue in a litigation involves serious misconduct by a Cabinet minister. Such cases have occurred in Australia (see *Sankey v Whitlam* (1978) 21 ALR 505) and in the United States (see *Nixon v US* (1974) 418 US 683) but fortunately not in the United Kingdom: see also the New Zealand case of *Environmental Defence Society Inc v South Pacific Aluminium Ltd (No 2)* [1981] 1 NZLR 153. But, while Cabinet documents do not have complete immunity, they are entitled to a high degree of protection against

d
disclosure. In the present case the documents in category A do not enjoy quite the status of Cabinet minutes, but they approach that level in that they may disclose the reasons for Cabinet decisions and the process by which the decisions were reached. The reasons why such documents should not normally be disclosed until they have become of purely historical interest were considered in the *Burmah Oil* case [1979] 3 All ER 700 at 707, [1980] AC 1090 at 1112, where Lord Wilberforce said:

e
'One such ground is the need for candour in communication between those concerned with policy making. It seems now rather fashionable to decry this, but if as a ground it may at one time have been exaggerated, it has now, in my opinion, received an excessive dose of cold water. I am certainly not prepared, against the view of the Minister, to discount the need, in the formation of such very controversial policy as that with which we are here involved, for frank and

f
uninhibited advice from the bank to the government, from and between civil servants and between Ministers ... Another such ground is to protect from inspection by possible critics the inner working of government while forming important governmental policy. I do not believe that scepticism has invaded this, or that it is for the courts to assume the role of advocates for open government. If, as I believe, this is a valid ground for protection, it must continue to operate beyond the

g
time span of a particular episode. Concretely, to reveal what advice which was *then* sought and given and the mechanism for seeking and considering such advice might well make the process of government more difficult *now*. On this point too I am certainly not prepared to be wiser than the Minister.'

Although Lord Wilberforce dissented from the majority as to the result in that case, I

h
do not think that his statement of the reasons for supporting public interest immunity were in any way in conflict with the views of the majority.

In the present case, then, we have documents which are admittedly relevant to the matters in issue, in the sense explained in *Compagnie Financière et Commerciale du Pacifique v Peruvian Guano Co* (1882) 11 QBD 55 at 63 by Brett LJ. I am willing to assume that they are, in the words of RSC Ord 24, r 13, 'necessary ... for disposing fairly of the cause' on

j
the (perhaps not very rigorous) standard which would apply if this were an ordinary case in which public interest immunity had not been claimed. But it has been claimed, and the onus therefore is on the appellants, as the parties seeking disclosure, to show why the documents ought to be produced for inspection by the court privately. The question of whether the court, having inspected them privately, should order them to be produced publicly is a separate question which does not arise at this stage, although as I shall seek to show in a moment it is in my opinion relevant.

Counsel for for the appellants submitted a persuasive argument to the effect that no harm could be done by a judge inspecting the documents in private, and that, as they *a* might be of determinative importance in the decision of the action, the judge should 'take a peep', as Lord Edmund-Davies put it in the *Burmah Oil* case [1979] 3 All ER 700 at 721, [1980] AC 1090 at 1129. Counsel for the appellants submitted that when the question was whether the court should inspect the documents in private the parties seeking disclosure only had to show that the documents were likely to be 'very significant' for decision of the case without regard to whether they were likely to assist him or his *b* opponent. But he accepted that when the judge, having inspected the documents, came to the later question of whether to order them to be produced the question was different and it then became relevant to consider whether disclosure would assist the party seeking it.

We were referred to some observations in reported cases to the effect that the court should have all relevant information before it whichever party it might help: see for *c* example *Alfred Crompton Amusement Machines Ltd v Customs and Excise Comrs (No 2)* [1973] 2 All ER 1169 at 1185, [1974] AC 405 at 434 per Lord Cross. As a general rule that is, of course, true, but it is subject to some qualification. The very existence of legal professional privilege and of public interest immunity constitutes qualification. The importance of the general rule was emphasised by all the noble and learned Lords who delivered reasoned speeches in *D v National Society for the Prevention of Cruelty to Children* [1977] 1 *d* All ER 589, [1978] AC 171 but none of them was considering the present question, nor the difference between the inspection stage and the production stage. Nor was any of them contemplating the possibility of a person being compelled to disclose information in his own favour which he preferred to keep private. In an adversarial system such as exists in the United Kingdom a party is free to withhold information that would help his case if he wishes, perhaps for reasons of delicacy or personal privacy. He cannot be *e* compelled to disclose it against his will. It follows in my opinion that a party who seeks to compel his opponent, or an independent person, to disclose information must show that the information is likely to help his own case. It would be illogical to apply a different rule at the stage of inspection from that which applies at the stage of production. After all, the purpose of inspection by the court in many cases, including the present, would be to let the court see whether there is material in favour of disclosure which *f* should be put in the scales to weigh against the material in favour of immunity. Inspection is with a view to the possibility of ordering production, and in my opinion inspection ought not to be ordered unless the court is persuaded that inspection is likely to satisfy it that it ought to take the further step of ordering production.

A great variety of expressions have been used in the reported cases to explain the considerations that ought to influence judges in deciding whether to order inspection. In *g* *Conway v Rimmer* [1968] 1 All ER 874 at 888, [1968] AC 910 at 953 Lord Reid said:

'If [the judge] decides that on balance the documents ought probably to be produced, I think that it would generally be best that he should see them before ordering production, and if he thinks that the Minister's reasons are not clearly expressed, he will have to see the documents before ordering production.'

(The latter point does not arise in this appeal, because the reasons why the documents *h* ought not to be produced are clearly and fully expressed in Sir Kenneth Clucas's certificate.) In the same case Lord Morris said that there was no reason why there should not be a private examination of a document by a court 'if such an examination becomes really necessary' and later he said that the power to examine documents privately was one which should be 'sparingly exercised' (see [1968] 1 All ER 874 at 896, 900, [1968] AC 910 at 964, 971). In the *Burmah Oil* case [1979] 3 All ER 700 at 711, [1980] AC 1090 *j* at 1117 Lord Wilberforce said that it was not desirable for the court to assume the task of inspection—

'except in rare instances where a strong positive case is made out, certainly not on a bare unsupported assertion by the party seeking production that something to help him may be found, or on some unsupported, viz speculative, hunch of its own'.

Of all the formulations I have seen, that is, I think, the one least favourable to inspection.

a Lord Edmund-Davies in the *Burmah Oil* case [1979] 3 All ER 700 at 721, [1980] AC 1090 at 1129 quoted with approval the passage I have just quoted from Lord Reid's speech in *Conway v Rimmer*. A little lower down Lord Edmund-Davies, as I understand him, expressed the view that a judge should not hesitate to call for production of documents for his private inspection if they are '"likely" to contain material substantially useful to the party seeking discovery'. Lord Keith ([1979] 3 All ER 700 at 725–726, [1980] AC

b 1090 at 1135) referred to—

> 'situations where grave doubt arises, and the court feels that it cannot properly decide on which side the balance falls without privately inspecting the documents'

And Lord Scarman said ([1979] 3 All ER 700 at 734, [1980] AC 1090 at 1145):

c   'Inspection by the court is, I accept, a power to be exercised only if the court is in doubt, after considering the certificate, the issues in the case and the relevance of the documents whose disclosure is sought.'

My Lords, I do not think it would be possible to state a test in a form which could be applied in all cases. Circumstances vary greatly. The weight of the public interest against

d disclosure will vary according to the nature of the particular documents in question; for example, it will in general be stronger where the documents are Cabinet papers than when they are at a lower level. The weight of the public interest in favour of disclosure will vary even more widely, because it depends on the probable evidential value to the party seeking disclosure of the particular documents, in almost infinitely variable circumstances of individual cases. The most that can usefully be said is that, in order to persuade the court even to inspect documents for which public interest immunity is

e claimed, the party seeking disclosure ought at least to satisfy the court that the documents are very likely to contain material which would give substantial support to his contention on an issue which arises in the case, and that without them he might be 'deprived of the means of . . . proper presentation' of his case: see *Glasgow Corp v Central Land Board* 1956 SC (HL) 1 at 18 per Lord Radcliffe. It will be plain that that formulation has been mainly derived from the speech of Lord Edmund-Davies in the *Burmah Oil* case [1979] 3 All ER

f 700 at 721, [1980] AC 1090 at 1129 and from the opinion of McNeill J in *Williams v Home Office* [1981] 1 All ER 1151 at 1154. It assumes, of course, that the party seeking disclosure has already shown in his pleadings that he has a cause of action, and that he has some material to support it. Otherwise he would merely be 'fishing'.

The test is intended to be fairly strict. It ought to be so in any case where a valid claim for public interest immunity has been made. Public interest immunity is not a privilege

g which may be waived by the Crown or by any party. In *Rogers v Secretary of State for the Home Dept, Gaming Board for GB v Rogers* [1972] 2 All ER 1057 at 1060, [1973] AC 388 at 400 Lord Reid said:

> 'There is no question of any privilege in the ordinary sense of the word. The real question is whether the public interest requires that the letter shall not be produced

h   and whether that public interest is so strong as to override the ordinary right and interest of a litigant that he shall be able to lay before a court of justice all relevant evidence.'

When the claim is a 'class' claim judges will often not be well qualified to estimate its strength, because they may not be fully aware of the importance of the class of documents to the public administration as a whole. Moreover, whether the claim is a 'class' claim or

j a 'contents' claim, the court will have to make its decision on whether to order production, after having inspected the documents privately, without having the assistance of argument from counsel. It should therefore, in my opinion, not be encouraged to 'take a peep' just on the off chance of finding something useful. It should inspect documents only where it has definite grounds for expecting to find material of real importance to the party seeking disclosure.

Applying these considerations to the present appeal, I am of opinion that the case for inspection of the category A documents by the court has not been made out. The appeal *a* proceeds on the basis, expressly accepted for the purpose of the present argument by the Lord Advocate, on behalf of the Secretary of State, that the appellants have a cause of action under the constitutional head of the case. It is abundantly clear that they already have documents to support their case, viz the White Paper on *The Nationalised Industries* (Cmnd 7131) published March 1978 and a statement by the Secretary of State to the House of Commons on 26 February 1980 in which he announced that he had set a target *b* of 6% per annum on net assets revalued at current cost as a reasonable target for the BAA, and referred to the White Paper. An extract from the statement is quoted in the appellants' pleadings and it is not necessary for me to repeat it here[1]. The respondents admit the extract although they deny that the 6% target was 'imposed'. The appellants do not make any case that the Secretary of State's true reasons were different from those which he had publicly announced. In these circumstances it seems to me that any *c* information contained in the category A documents would almost certainly tend merely to repeat the information already known to and relied on by the appellants, and published to the world. It is unlikely to add anything material. It is therefore unlikely that access to category A documents would assist the appellants in proving their case. I agree with the way the matter was put by Watkins LJ in the Court of Appeal when he said ([1983] 1 All ER 161 at 185): *d*

> 'It seems to me that whether there has been an abuse of power by the Secretary of State will either emerge directly or by inference from those documents [sc the documents already produced] or not at all.'

The case for inspection has therefore not been made out.

When Bingham J decided to inspect the documents in category A, he did so on the *e* view that he was not concerned with the question whether they were likely to help the appellants, but that the relevant question for him was whether they were likely to affect the outcome of the case 'one way or the other'. For the reasons I have endeavoured to explain, I consider that that is a erroneous view, and that his exercise of discretion is accordingly vitiated.

I would dismiss the appeal with costs. *f*

LORD WILBERFORCE. My Lords, my noble and learned friend Lord Fraser has described the background against which this appeal must be decided; I shall not duplicate his narrative. We are concerned with a claim for discovery of documents in which the parties' respective positions are familiar and one could say ritualised. The relevant pleas in the action (and they are only some of many) challenge the validity of certain actions *g* said to have been taken by the Secretary of State for Trade in relation to the fixing by the British Airports Authority (the BAA) of charges for the use by the appellant airlines of Heathrow Airport. The Secretary of State, it is said, has acted beyond his powers, and/or has exercised his powers and discretion for purposes other than those for which they were conferred, viz (briefly) for the purpose of reducing the government's public sector borrowing requirement. In support of these allegations, discovery is sought of a number *h* of documents which, it is claimed, might throw light on the manner in which, and the purpose for which, the Secretary of State exercised his power or his discretion; such documents appear to satisfy the threshold test of relevancy. The Secretary of State's answer is to claim public interest immunity; certificates are put in and signed by top-ranking civil servants (this is because the actions of successive governments are involved and a powerful convention prevents ministers having access to papers of their *j* predecessors). I need not set these out: they are similar in form and content to those presented in *Burmah Oil Co Ltd v Bank of England* [1979] 3 All ER 700, [1980] AC 1090, and they make what I there called a well-fortified case. The documents now in issue, in

---

1 The extract is set out in the opinion of Lord Templeman at p 926 *c d*, post

fact, can claim to bear a higher degree of confidentiality than those involved in the
a *Burmah Oil* case: they relate directly to the making of decisions as to government policy
in a sensitive area, viz the economic and financial policy of the government, particularly
in relation to nationalised industries, by ministers and civil servants prior to consideration
in Cabinet, and familiar contentions are put forward as to the need to protect them
against disclosure in the interest of the confidentiality of the inner working of government
and of the free and candid expression of views. It is relevant to add that it is shown that
b there are in existence Cabinet papers bearing on these same matters. These are not asked
for, but their existence underlines the high level status and confidentiality of those whose
production is sought. It is not, at this stage, disputed that the documents in question fall
within the class for which protection is claimed, nor that the claim for protection is put
on what is accepted to be the highest grade.

The appellants' claim for discovery and production rests, as it must, on their assertion
c that they are necessary for the disposal fairly of the case (see RSC Ord 24, r 13). There is a
public interest, they say, in justice being done to their case and this public interest has to
be weighed against the contrary public interest for immunity which the Secretary of
State puts forward. As it is not known what the documents may contain, it is not possible
for this weighing process to be carried out unless they are inspected. Consequently, and
their counsel prudently confined himself to this contention, they ask that the court
d should privately inspect the documents, as, under the rule (Ord 24, r 13(2)), it has power
to do. The judge accepted this submission, but the Court of Appeal reversed his decision.

What then are the criteria on which a decision should be made to inspect, or not to do
so? This matter was discussed at length in the opinions of the House of Lords in the
Burmah Oil case. The main difference of opinion between the majority and the minority
opinions related to the likelihood, on the facts of that case, that the documents, inspection
e of which was claimed, would be supportive of the plaintiffs' case, the minority regarding
this likelihood as purely speculative, the majority as amounting to a degree (differently
expressed) of probability. Leaving this difference aside as not relevant here, there are
three questions which now to be answered. (1) What is it that the documents must
be likely (in whatever degree) to support? (2) What is the degree of likelihood that must
be shown? (3) Is that degree of likelihood attained?

f   (1) On this point there was a difference in opinion between Bingham J and the Court
of Appeal. The judge held that documents would be necessary for fairly disposing of a
case or (his gloss) for the due administration of justice if they give substantial assistance
to the court in determining the facts on which the decision in the case would depend.
He considered that they were very likely to affect the outcome 'one way or the other'.
The Court of Appeal, on the other hand, held that there must be a likelihood that the
g documents would support the case of the party seeking discovery.

On this point I agree with the Court of Appeal. In a contest purely between one
litigant and another, such as the present, the task of the court is to do, and be seen to be
doing, justice between the parties, a duty reflected by the word 'fairly' in the rule. There
is no higher or additional duty to ascertain some independent truth. It often happens,
from the imperfection of evidence, or the withholding of it, sometimes by the party in
h whose favour it would tell if presented, that an adjudication has to be made which is not,
and is known not to be, the whole truth of the matter; yet, if the decision has been in
accordance with the available evidence and with the law, justice will have been fairly
done. It is in aid of justice in this sense that discovery may be ordered, and it is so ordered
on the application of one of the parties who must make out his case for it. If he is not
able to do so, that is an end of the matter. There is no independent power in the court to
j say that, nevertheless, it would like to inspect the documents, with a view to possible
production, for its own assistance.

So far as authority is concerned, I do not find that the cases prior to the *Burmah Oil* case
support a contrary view. Counsel for the appellants was certainly able to find a number
of sentences which appeared to do so: see *Conway v Rimmer* [1968] 1 All ER 874 at 878,
[1968] AC 910 at 937 et al, *Rogers v Secretary of State for the Home Dept, Gaming Board for
GB v Rogers* [1972] 2 All ER 1057, [1973] AC 388 ('all relevant evidence'), *Alfred Crompton*

Amusement Machines Ltd v Customs and Excise Comrs (No 2) [1973] 2 All ER 1169, [1974] AC 405 ('all the relevant material'), *D v National Society for the Prevention of Cruelty to* **a** *Children* [1977] 1 All ER 589 at 600, [1978] AC 171 at 225 ('the truth, the whole truth and nothing but the truth') et al. Statements the other way may be found in *Glasgow Corp v Central Land Board* 1956 SC (HL) 1. None of these cases was concerned with any possible distinction between what might assist both parties or either party and what might assist the party seeking discovery, nor was there any discussion as to such distinction. In *Conway v Rimmer* the documents asked for were sought by both sides, a **b** fact which easily explains, and indeed called for, references to assisting either side. So I do not find the observations of assistance here. In the *Burmah Oil* case [1979] 3 All ER 700 at 721, 726, [1980] AC 1090 at 1129, 1135–1136 the opinions referred both to the interest in the administration of justice and to the likelihood of supporting the case of the plaintiff: see per Lord Edmund-Davies, 'likely to contain material substantially useful to the party seeking discovery'; per Lord Keith, 'a reasonable probability exists of **c** finding . . . substantial support to the contention [of the appellants].' In that case, too, the present distinction sought to be made was not relevant or argued. We are therefore free to decide this case on a commonsense interpretation of the rules and on principle. This leads, in my opinion, to the view adopted by the Court of Appeal.

(2) The degree of likelihood (of providing support for the plaintiff's case) may be variously expressed: 'likely' was the word used by Lord Edmund-Davies in the *Burmah* **d** *Oil* case; a 'reasonable probability' by Lord Keith. Both expressions must mean something beyond speculation, some concrete ground for belief which takes the case beyond a mere 'fishing' expedition. One cannot attain greater precision in stating what must be a matter of estimation. I would accept either formula.

(3) This must be considered in relation to the separate limbs of what has been called 'the constitutional case'. **e**

(a) There is, first, an allegation that the Secretary of State imposed a financial target on the BAA and that he had no power to do so. This is in part a contention of law; factually it depends on what was done by the Secretary of State vis-à-vis the BAA. All documents passing between the Secretary of State and the BAA, or recording any exchanges between them, have been disclosed and no claim for immunity made for them; so the discovery requested of internal documents is unlikely to assist. The judge so held and I agree. **f**

(b) There is, second, the allegation that the Secretary of State took 'irrelevant' considerations into account in that his dominant purpose was to contain the public sector borrowing requirement and to implement government policy in accordance with a White Paper. As to this allegation, there is available the White Paper on *The Nationalised Industries* (Cmnd 7131), there is also available the text of the statement made by the Secretary of State in the House of Commons on 26 February 1980, and a letter dated 13 **g** December 1979 from the Department of Trade to the managing director of the BAA. These documents are direct and primary evidence as to the policy in fact followed by the Secretary of State in relation to the matters complained of and the appellants' case (this aspect of it), for good or ill, must primarily depend on them. By contrast, the documents of which inspection is sought relate to the formation of this policy, as to category A by ministers and as to category B by officials of the various interested government **h** departments. As compared with the pronouncements I have referred to, they are of a wholly secondary character. I am unable to see that any case, still less any convincing case, can be made for saying that, even assuming that they are admissible at all, they would add, in any material way, to the first hand evidence which has been provided.

(c) There is, third, the allegation that the Secretary of State failed to take into account certain relevant considerations, viz his own obligations under the Civil Aviation Act **j** 1949, the duties of the BAA under statute and common law and international obligations of the United Kingdom. But here, too, the actions of the Secretary of State speak for themselves. On these facts, the appellants' case, such as it is, can be argued. I am unable to understand how documents relating to the formation of policy can assist in proving (though it might disprove) negative allegations such as these. I regard it, moreover, as most undesirable that a party merely by alleging that his ministerial opponent failed to

take some legal consideration into account should be able, thereby, to call for inspection,
a with a view to production, of confidential documents possibly bearing on the matters
which he did take into account. In the present case, any foundation, other than, I repeat,
the decision itself, is wholly lacking.

As to points (b) and (c), the judgment of Bingham J contains this important passage
([1983] 1 All ER 161 at 170):

b   'If it were necessary for the plaintiffs . . . to show a likelihood that the documents,
if produced, would help them I could not on the material put before me conclude
that they had done so. There are indications both ways. It would be wrong to guess.'

I respectfully agree. It was only because the judge applied a different test (that they
would be 'helpful') that he concluded for inspection of category A. On the correct test he
would have reached the same conclusion as the Court of Appeal and that which I have
c been compelled to reach.

I would dismiss the appeal.

LORD EDMUND-DAVIES. My Lords, I respectfully concur in the views expressed
in the speech of my noble and learned friend Lord Fraser, which I have had the advantage
of reading in draft form. He has set out all matters relevant to this appeal and I shall not
d repeat them. I desire to do no more than to add some short observations.

The narrow issues presently calling for decision are thus set out in the appellants'
printed case:

'(i) The circumstances in which the court should examine documents privately
before deciding whether to order their production; and in particular (ii) whether
the party seeking such examination discharges the burden of showing that
e documents are necessary for disposing fairly of the cause by showing that they are
likely to give the court substantial assistance in determining the issues; or whether
he must go further and show that they are likely to assist his own case.'

My Lords, I proceed to state the obvious. Under our Supreme Court practice, discovery
of documents between parties to an action with pleadings (as in the present case) is
f restricted to documents 'relating to matters in question in the action' (RSC Ord 24, r
1(1)), and no order for their inspection by the other party or to the court may be made
'unless the Court is of opinion that the order is necessary either for disposing fairly of the
cause or matter or for saving costs' (Ord 24, r 13(1)). It is common sense that the litigant
seeking an order for discovery is interested, not in abstract justice, but in gaining support
for the case he is presenting, and the sole task of the court is to decide whether he should
g get it. Applying that test, any document which, it is reasonable to suppose, contains
information which *may* enable the party applying for discovery either to advance his
own case or to damage that of his adversary, if it is a document which may fairly lead
him to a train of inquiry which may have either of those two consequences, must be
disclosed (see *Compagnie Financière et Commerciale du Pacifique v Peruvian Guano Co* (1882)
11 QBD 55 at 63 per Brett LJ). So it was that in *Glasgow Corp v Central Land Board* 1956
h SC (HL) 1 at 18, 20 Lord Radcliffe spoke of the need that 'a litigant who has *a case to
maintain* should not be deprived of the means of *its* proper presentation by anything less
than a weighty public reason,' and concluded, 'Nor . . . do I feel any clear conviction that
the production of the documents sought for is in any real sense *essential to the appellants'
case*' (emphasis added). It follows that, at every stage of interlocutory proceedings for
discovery, the test to be applied is: will the material sought be such as is likely to advance
j the seeker's case, either affirmatively or indirectly by weakening the case of his opponent?
To take but one more example out of many, such was again the test applied by the Court
of Appeal in *Woodworth v Conroy* [1976] 1 All ER 107, [1976] 1 QB 884.

It is accordingly insufficient for a litigant to urge that the documents he seeks to
inspect are *relevant* to the proceedings. For, although relevant, they may be of merely
vestigial importance, or they may be of importance (great or small) only to his opponent's
case. And to urge that, on principle, justice is most likely to be done if free access is had

to all relevant documents is pointless, for it carries no weight in our adversarial system of law.

So far, I have been speaking of legal practice and procedure in general. But this is no run-of-the-mill case. It falls into the special category where a party resists disclosing admittedly relevant material on the ground that the documents are of a class the production of which would be injurious to the public interest. It is common ground in this appeal that a valid claim for public interest immunity has been made by the respondents in proper form. Applicable to this case, therefore, is the provision in r 15 of Ord 24 that:

'The foregoing provisions of this Order shall be without prejudice to any rule of law which authorises or requires the withholding of any document on the ground that the disclosure of it would be injurious to the public interest.'

And, as the defendant resisting discovery is Her Majesty's Secretary of State for Trade, a similar provision in s 28(2) of the Crown Proceedings Act 1947 is equally applicable.

The principles governing discovery in such special cases as the present were exhaustively considered by your Lordships' House in *Burmah Oil Co Ltd v Bank of England* [1979] 3 All ER 700, [1980] AC 1090, and I shall not restate them. Suffice it to say that, provided that certain conditions have been satisfied, the stage may be reached when the court will be obliged to conduct a 'balancing' exercise, consisting in weighing (a) the public interest in the due administration of justice against (b) the public interest established by the claim for immunity. And it is for the party seeking discovery to establish clearly that the scale falls decisively in favour of (a) if he is to succeed in his quest. If he fails, even material clearly 'necessary . . . for disposing fairly of the cause or matter' must be withheld.

In the light of the foregoing observations, I turn to consider some passages in the clear and helpful judgment of the trial judge ([1983] 1 All ER 161 at 167, 170; the emphasis is mine):

'In my judgment, documents are necessary for fairly disposing of a cause or for the due administration of justice if they give substantial assistance to the court *in determining the facts on which the decision in the cause will depend* . . . I conclude that some of the documents covered by this certificate are necessary in *this* sense . . . I therefore proceed on the assumption that there is a public interest both in production and in non-disclosure . . . Nothing that I have said indicates that there should be a different rule where public interest immunity is claimed and challenged than in any other case.'

'If it were necessary for the plaintiffs . . . to show a likelihood that the documents, if produced, would help *them* I could not on the material put before me conclude that they had done so. There are indications both ways. It would be wrong to guess.'

'But I do not regard the chance that these documents will be helpful as at all speculative. The strong probability is, in my judgment, that they will be of great assistance in resolving these [second and third] issues one way or the other, possibly even determinative.'

In the light of those observations, the judge made an order—

'That the Secretary of State do produce for inspection by the Judge the documents listed in Category A of the Certificate of the Permanent Secretary to the Department of Trade . . . such order to be stayed pending an appeal by the Secretary of State. Leave to appeal by the Secretary of State . . .'

Did the judge adopt the right approach to the preliminary question of whether he should make such an order? At that stage he was treating the case exactly as though no claim to immunity had been made; in other words, it was being regarded simply as one governed by Ord 24, r 13(1) and (2). But, as I have sought to demonstrate, this required him first to be satisfied that production to the plaintiffs of the withheld documents was necessary to afford them a fair opportunity of establishing the case *they* were presenting against the

defendants. Yet, save on the assumption that unfettered disclosure of all relevant material
a is always best calculated to make for justice and should therefore be fostered, had the
judge any grounds on which he could properly conclude that he should privately
examine the documents?

My Lords, I think his own language demonstrated that no such ground existed. The
first and second passages cited expressly revealed that his decision to take what in the
Burmah Oil case I described as a 'peep' was based solely on the belief that this would assist
b him 'in determining the facts on which the decision in the case will depend', even though
(as the judge said in the third passage cited) those facts could operate 'one way or the
other', ie for the plaintiffs, or against them, or possibly related exclusively to the
defendant's case.

In these circumstances I do not consider that the conditions implicit in Ord 24, r 13(1)
itself were complied with. And, if I am right, that in itself involves the dismissal of this
c appeal. But, when one further adverts to the immunity claim, the position becomes, if
anything, even clearer. It was urged for the appellants that, when only a private inspection
by the court is under consideration, the test is different from that appropriate to ordering
production to the other side. The appellants distinguished between the two stages by
saying:

d
'At the earlier stage it is sufficient that [the judge] should be satisfied that the
documents . . . are likely to be of substantial assistance to the Court in determining
the issues. It is at the second stage, when the Judge is examining the documents,
that it becomes relevant to consider which side they help.'

For the reasons I have earlier stated, in my judgment this is incorrect. The difference
between the two stages is not one of nature, but simply of degree, expressed by Lord
e Reid in *Conway v Rimmer* [1968] 1 All ER 874 at 888–889, [1968] AC 910 at 953 by
saying:

'If [the judge] decides that on balance the documents *probably* ought to be
produced, I think it would generally be best that he should see them before ordering
production . . . If on reading the document he . . . thinks that it *ought* to be produced,
he will order its production.' (Emphasis added.)

f
It would be unbecoming of me to advert to the test I myself propounded in the *Burmah
Oil* case [1979] 3 All ER 700 at 721, [1980] AC 1090 at 1129, save to say that I adhere to
it and that it was clearly not complied with here.

My Lords, for these reasons I concur in dismissing the appeal with costs.

g **LORD SCARMAN.** My Lords, others of your Lordships have analysed the issues, and
narrated the facts, of this complex litigation. I shall, therefore, confine my speech to the
narrow issue which we have to decide. The appeal raises an issue, not previously explored
by the House, arising on the discovery of documents which belong to a class in respect of
which the Crown has made a powerful claim in proper form for immunity from
production in the public interest. The appeal illustrates, if illustration be needed, that the
h House's decision in *Conway v Rimmer* [1968] 1 All ER 874, [1968] AC 910 was the
beginning, but not the end, of a chapter in the law's development in this branch of the
law.

The issue is specific and within a small compass. The Crown having made its objection
to production in proper form, in what circumstances should the court inspect privately
the documents before determining whether they, or any of them, should be produced?

j   The court, of course, has a discretion; but the discretion must be exercised in
accordance with principle. The principle governing the production of disclosed
documents is embodied in RSC Ord 24, r 13. No order for the production of any
documents for inspection or to the court shall be made unless the court is of the opinion
that the order is necessary either for disposing fairly of the cause or matter or for saving
costs: see r 13(1). And the court may inspect the document for the purpose of deciding
whether the objection to production is valid: see r 13(2). The rule provides a measure of

protection for a party's documents irrespective of their class or contents and independently
of any privilege or immunity. While the existence of all documents in a party's possession *a*
or control relating to matters in question in the action must be 'discovered', that is to say
disclosed, to the other party (or parties), he is not obliged to produce them unless the
court is of the opinion that production is necessary.

It may well be that, where there is no claim of confidentiality or public interest
immunity or any objection on the ground of privilege, the courts follow a relaxed
practice, allowing production on the basis of relevance. This is sensible, bearing in mind *b*
the extended meaning given to relevance in *Compagnie Financière et Commerciale du
Pacifique v Peruvian Guano Co* (1882) 11 QBD 55. But very different considerations arise if
a reasoned objection to production is put forward. In *Science Research Council v Nassè*
[1979] 3 All ER 673, [1980] AC 1028 your Lordships' House ruled that, even where there
is no question of public interest immunity but the documents are confidential in
character, the court should not order production unless it thought it necessary. An *c*
objection based on public interest immunity, if properly formulated, must carry at least
as much weight as an objection on the ground of confidentiality.

Faced with a properly formulated certificate claiming public interest immunity, the
court must first examine the grounds put forward. If it is a 'class' objection and the
documents (as in *Conway v Rimmer*) are routine in character, the court may inspect so as
to ascertain the strength of the public interest in immunity and the needs of justice *d*
before deciding whether to order production. If it is a 'contents' claim, eg a specific
national security matter, the court will ordinarily accept the judgment of the minister.
But if it is a class claim in which the objection on the face of the certificate is a strong one,
as in this case where the documents are minutes and memoranda passing at a high level
between ministers and their advisers and concerned with the formulation of policy, the
court will pay great regard to the minister's view (or that of the senior official who has *e*
signed the certificate). It will not inspect unless there is a likelihood that the documents
will be necessary for disposing fairly of the case or saving costs. Certainly, if, like
Bingham J in this case, the court should think that the documents might be
'determinative' of the issues in the action to which they relate, the court should inspect,
for in such a case there may be grave doubt which way the balance of public interest falls
(see *Burmah Oil Co Ltd v Bank of England* [1979] 3 All ER 700 at 725–726, 734, [1980] AC *f*
1090 at 1134–1135, 1145). But, unless the court is satisfied on the material presented to
it that the documents are likely to be necessary for fairly disposing of the case, it will not
inspect for the simple reason that unless the likelihood exists there is nothing to set
against the public interest in immunity from production.

The judge, Bingham J, correctly appreciated the principle of the matter. He decided
to inspect because he believed that the documents in question were very likely to be *g*
'necessary for the just determination of the second and third issues in the plaintiffs'
constitutional case' (see [1983] 1 All ER 161 at 170). Here I consider he fell into error.
For the reasons given in the speech of my noble and learned friend Lord Templeman, I
do not think that the appellants have been able to show that the documents whose
production they are seeking are likely to be necessary for fairly disposing of the issues in
their 'constitutional' case. Indeed, my noble and learned friend has demonstrated that *h*
they are unnecessary. Accordingly, for this reason, but for no other, I would hold that
the judge was wrong to decide to inspect the documents.

On all other questions I find myself in agreement with the judge. In particular, I am
persuaded by his reasoning that the public interest in the administration of justice, which
the court has to put into the balance against the public interest immunity, is as he put it
([1983] 1 All ER 161 at 167): *j*

> 'In my judgment documents are necessary for fairly disposing of a cause or for
> the due administration of justice if they give substantial assistance to the court in
> determining the facts on which the decision in the cause will depend.'

The judge rejected, in my view rightly, the view which has commended itself to the
Court of Appeal and to some of your Lordships that the criterion for determining

whether to inspect or not is whether the party seeking production can establish the
likelihood that the documents will assist his case or damage that of his opponent. No
doubt that is what he is seeking; no doubt also, it is a very relevant consideration for the
court. But it would be dangerous to elevate it into a principle of the law of discovery.
Discovery is one of the few exceptions to the adversarial character of our legal process. It
assists parties and the court to discover the truth. By so doing, it not only helps towards a
just determination: it also saves costs. A party who discovers timeously a document fatal
to his case is assisted as effectively, although less to his liking, as one who discovers the
winning card; for he can save himself and others the heavy costs of litigation. There is
another important aspect of the matter. The Crown, when it puts forward a public
interest immunity objection, is not claiming a privilege but discharging a duty. The
duty arises whether the document assists or damages the Crown's case or if, as in a case to
which the Crown is not a party, it neither helps nor injures the Crown. It is not for the
Crown but for the court to determine whether the document should be produced.
Usually, but not always, the critical factor will be whether the party seeking production
has shown the document will help him. But it may be necessary for a fair determination
or for saving costs even if it does not. Therefore, although it is likely to make little
difference in practice, I would think it better in principle to retain the formulation of the
interests to be balanced which Lord Reid gave us in *Conway v Rimmer* [1968] 1 All ER
874 at 888, [1968] AC 910 at 940:

> 'It is universally recognised that here there are two kinds of public interest which
> may clash. There is the public interest that harm shall not be done to the nation or
> the public service by disclosure of certain documents, and there is the public interest
> that the administration of justice shall not be frustrated by the withholding of
> documents which must be produced if justice is to be done.'

And I do so for the reasons given by Lord Pearce in the same case (see [1968] 1 All ER
874 at 911, [1968] AC 910 at 987). Describing the two conflicting interests, he said of the
administration of justice that the judge—

> 'can consider whether the documents in question are of much or little weight in
> the litigation, whether their absence will result in a complete or partial denial of
> justice to one or other of the parties or perhaps to both, and what is the importance
> of the particular litigation to the parties and the public.'

Basically, the reason for selecting the criterion of justice, irrespective of whether it
assists the party seeking production, is that the Crown may not have regard to party
advantage in deciding whether or not to object to production on the ground of public
interest immunity. It is its duty to bring the objection, if it believes it to be sound, to the
attention of the court. It is for the court, not the Crown, to balance the two public
interests, that of the functioning and security of the public service, which is the sphere
within which the executive has the duty to make an assessment, and that of justice, on
which the executive is not competent to pass judgment.

For these reasons I would dismiss the appeal.

LORD TEMPLEMAN. My Lords, the appellant airlines ask the court to inspect
documents for which public interest immunity from disclosure has been asserted by the
Secretary of State. The airlines submit that inspection by the court is necessary to enable
the court to determine whether the public interest immunity from disclosure should
prevail over the public interest in the attainment of justice.

By s 1(1) of the Airports Authority Act 1975 the British Airports Authority (the BAA)
owns and manages Heathrow and other airports. The BAA's revenue consists largely of
landing and other charges imposed on airlines which make use of the airport facilities.
By s 2(7) the Secretary of State may, after consultation with the BAA, give to the BAA
directions of a general character as to the exercise and performance by the BAA of its
functions in relation to matters which appear to him to affect the national interest, and it
shall be the duty of the BAA to give effect to any such directions. Section 4 recorded the

fact that the BAA was indebted to the government in the sum of £52·91m. Section 5
authorised the Secretary of State to control the amount of any borrowing by the BAA, *a*
whether temporary or permanent, and forbade the BAA in any event to incur debts
which, including the initial debt of £52·91m, exceeded in the aggregate £125m.

In a White Paper entitled *The Nationalised Industries* (Cmnd 7131) presented to
Parliament in March 1978 the government announced that financial targets would be set
for the nationalised industries. In general each nationalised industry would be expected
to cover its costs and a reasonable rate of profit and to contain or reduce its need to *b*
borrow. Paragraph 73 was in these terms:

'The level of each financial target will be decided industry by industry. It will
take account of a wide range of factors. These will include the expected return from
effective, cost conscious management of existing and new assets; market prospects;
the scope for improved productivity and efficiency; the opportunity cost of capital;
the implications for the Public Sector Borrowing Requirement; counter-inflation *c*
policy; and social or sectoral objectives for, e.g. the energy and transport industries.
When the target has been settled for the industry, the Secretary of State will
announce it to Parliament. He will indicate the main assumptions on which it is
based: for example, any particular social or sectoral objectives which the Government
has set the industry, and which may have affected the level of the target; the broad
implications for the industry's pricing; and any other important factors of which *d*
Parliament and the public should know when they subsequently judge the industry's
performance against the target.'

On 26 February 1980 the Secretary of State announced in the House of Commons that
(979 HC Official Report (5th series) written answers cols 499–500:

'I have decided that a reasonable financial duty for the British Airports Authority *e*
would be to achieve on average a rate of return of 6 per cent. per annum on net
assets revalued at current cost over the three financial years 1980–81 to 1982–83.
The target is related to current cost operating profit after taking account of
depreciation but before interest and tax. This target is set in accordance with the
principles given in Command 7131 and will be adjusted if necessary after the
introduction of the proposed new current cost accounting standard. It is designed to *f*
be consistent with the BAA's progressing towards a rate of return on their airports
operations of 5 per cent. in real terms on its new investment . . .'

By 1980 the debt of the BAA to the government had increased from £52·91m to
£62m. The BAA was minded to spend a further £200m in the near future and ultimately
£700m to provide for a new terminal at Heathrow and other airport developments. *g*
Applying or influenced by the White Paper policy, the Secretary of State and the Treasury
instructed the BAA that the BAA would not be allowed to borrow and that the BAA
should budget to attain its financial target and to find money for the proposed
developments by increased airport charges and by postponing or curtailing the speed of
development. The BAA reluctantly accepted the instructions of the Secretary of State and
with the approval of the Secretary of State increased landing charges to the extent thought *h*
necessary to meet its financial target and otherwise to comply with the instructions
received from the Secretary of State.

The airlines argue that the BAA owed the airlines a duty, based on and enforceable
under domestic law, European Community law or international law, to limit landing
charges to sums which were 'fair, just and reasonable', that the BAA is in breach of that
duty and that it is the function of the court to determine on a quantum meruit basis how *j*
much should be paid when an aeroplane lands at Heathrow. The airlines also assert that
the government, responsible for the national economy and armed with the powers
contained in the Airports Authority Act 1975, cannot lawfully inform the BAA that the
country cannot afford to lend any more money to the BAA and that the BAA must pay
its way and earn a commercial profit and not subsidise present air travellers at the expense
of future air travellers or at the expense of the taxpayers.

The nature and extent of the powers and duties of the Secretary of State and the BAA

raise issues of law. The facts relevant to those legal issues are fully documented. The
a   correspondence and records of discussions between representatives of the Secretary of
State and representatives of the BAA disclose the reasoned views expressed by the
Secretary of State with regard to the finances and charges of the BAA, and the actions
which the Secretary of State wished the BAA to take. The correspondence and records of
the BAA disclose the negotiations between the Secretary of State and the BAA, the actions
which the BAA wished to take and the extent to which the actions eventually taken by
b   the BAA were influenced by the Secretary of State. All the relevant documents have been
disclosed and some of them are incorporated in the pleadings. The airlines do not suggest
that the Secretary of State and the BAA have concealed any of their actions or motives.
There is no doubt that the policy of the government set forth in the White Paper
exercised some influence over the views of the Secretary of State and over the actions of
the BAA, although the extent of such influence is disputed. The airlines assert that the
c   conduct and motives of the Secretary of State and the BAA were dictated by government
policy and result in breaches of duty by both the Secretary of State and the BAA. The
airlines have inspected all the documents which show the influence of government policy
on the Secretary of State and the BAA.

The airlines now wish to go further. They wish to inspect privileged documents which
relate to the evolution of the policy which was accepted by the government and set forth
d   in the White Paper. The airlines seek to discover the views expressed by individual
ministers and civil servants when they were evolving and agreeing the policy which was
ultimately expressed in the White Paper and which was implemented in relation to the
BAA. It may be that in the evolution of policy a minister or civil servant changed his
mind or opposed the adoption of the policy or put forward views similar to those
subsequently urged by the BAA or the airlines in opposition to increased charges. But
e   the disclosure of privileged documents relating to evolution of government policy is not
necessary to enable the airlines to prove the extent which that policy after it had been
expressly adopted by the government became responsible for the conduct of the Secretary
of State and the actions of the BAA. The airlines did not suggest or illustrate any fact or
motive which might be hidden in the privileged documents, which might be important
or significant in the present proceedings but which were not subsequently revealed in
f   the correspondence between the government and the BAA which has been now disclosed.

For these reasons and for the reasons given by my noble and learned friend Lord
Fraser, I would dismiss the appeal.

I agree with my noble and learned friend Lord Scarman for the reasons he has deployed
that the court should inspect the documents if the court considers the disclosure of the
documents may materially assist any of the parties to the proceedings. If the plaintiff
g   seeks discovery against the assertion which the defendant feels under a duty to put
forward of public interest immunity, the judge may find the documents are wholly or
partly favourable to the plaintiff's case or wholly or partly fatal to the plaintiff's case. In
either event the judge must decide whether the public interest in maintaining the
confidential nature of the document prevails over the public interest in ensuring that
justice is achieved. If the public interest in confidentiality prevails the judge will decline
h   to allow the plaintiff to see the documents. If the judge decides in all the circumstances
that the claim for public interest immunity is not strong enough to prevail over the
public interest in justice, the judge will allow the plaintiff to inspect the documents. In
that case either party is free to use the documents for the purposes of the proceedings but
is not bound to do so. If both parties in their discretion for the same or different reasons
decide not to rely on the documents, the documents will not be revealed to the public.
j   The plaintiff who will only have inspected the documents in order to determine whether
or not to make use of them in the proceedings will not be allowed to make use of the
documents for any other purpose.

Appeal dismissed.

Solicitors: *Freshfields* (for the appellants); *Treasury Solicitor.*

Mary Rose Plummer   Barrister.

Practice Direction

a

LORD CHANCELLOR'S DEPARTMENT

Practice – Funds in court – Investment of funds in court – Payments to be placed to deposit account and not short-term investment account – Deposit rate – Payment of deposit interest – Short-term investment account only available for money held in court for benefit of successful plaintiffs under disability – Payments to which new rules apply – Supreme Court Funds (Amendment) Rules 1983 – County Court Funds (Amendment) Rules 1983.

b

The Lord Chancellor's Department has issued the following notice:

On 1 April 1983 the Supreme Court Funds (Amendment) Rules 1983 and the County Court Funds (Amendment) Rules 1983, SI 1983/290 and 291 respectively, come into force. The main purpose of these two instruments is to alter the way in which satisfaction payments and payments into court under order to abide the event will be treated with regard to earning interest.

c

At present such payments may be placed, at the appropriate time, to a short-term investment account on the application of one of the parties to the proceedings. The new rules will change the present system in the following respects: (a) such payments will in future be placed to a deposit account and not to a short-term investment account; (b) the deposit rate is to be raised from its present level (5%) to 9½% per annum; (c) deposit interest will be paid on a day-to-day basis instead of in respect of whole months only; (d) money eligible for interest will be placed automatically to deposit after the appropriate interval so that there will be no need for an application for this purpose by any party.

d

In future the short-term investment account will be available only to 'funds' in the narrower sense, ie money held in court for the benefit of successful plaintiffs under disability.

e

The new rules apply generally to all payments into court made after 1 April 1983, with the following exceptions: (a) money which the court had ordered to be placed to a short-term investment account before 1 April 1983 will be so placed even if it is not lodged in court until after 1 April 1983; (b) money which has started to earn short-term investment interest before 1 April 1983 will continue to do so in accordance with the previous rules.

f

Money lodged in court before 1 April 1983 but which does not fall within categories (a) or (b) above will not be eligible for short-term investment interest and may be placed to a deposit account only on an application by a party.

g

11 March 1983

R v King

COURT OF APPEAL, CRIMINAL DIVISION
DUNN LJ, LAWSON AND HIRST JJ
9 NOVEMBER 1982, 11 JANUARY 1983

Criminal evidence – Expert evidence – Legal professional privilege – Communications between solicitor and expert witness – Handwriting expert consulted by accused's solicitor – Documents made available to expert by solicitor for examination – Whether Crown entitled to call expert as witness – Whether Crown entitled to require production of documents made available to expert by accused's solicitor – Whether documents protected by legal professional privilege.

The rule of evidence that legal professional privilege attaches to confidential communications between a solicitor and an expert but not to the expert's opinion or the chattels or documents on which he has based his opinion applies to criminal as well as civil proceedings. Accordingly, in a criminal trial the Crown is entitled to call on subpoena as a witness a handwriting expert whom the defence has consulted but does not wish to call as a witness, and is further entitled to production of documents sent to the expert by the defence for examination and on which the expert has based his opinion, provided the documents are not protected by legal professional privilege (see p 931 c to f and j to p 932 a and e, post).

Harmony Shipping Co SA v Davis [1979] 3 All ER 177 applied.

Dictum of Swanwick J in *Frank Truman Export Ltd v Metropolitan Police Comr* [1977] 3 All ER at 439, 440–441 doubted.

Notes

For expert opinion as evidence in criminal trials, see 11 Halsbury's Laws (4th edn) para 445.

For compellability of witnesses and privilege, see ibid para 464, and for cases on the subject, see 14(2) Digest (Reissue) 625–628, 5079–5098.

Cases referred to in judgment

Harmony Shipping Co SA v Davis [1979] 3 All ER 177, sub nom *Harmony Shipping Co SA v Saudi Europe Line Ltd* [1979] 1 WLR 1380, CA, Digest (Cont Vol E) 220, 1887a.

R v Beck [1982] 1 All ER 807, [1982] 1 WLR 461, CA.

R v Justice of the Peace for Peterborough, ex p Hicks [1978] 1 All ER 225, [1977] 1 WLR 1371, DC, Digest (Cont Vol E) 142, 5091.

R v Stainton (1982) Times, 9 November.

Truman (Frank) Export Ltd v Metropolitan Police Comr [1977] 3 All ER 431, [1977] QB 952, [1977] 3 WLR 257, Digest (Cont Vol E) 132, 1570a.

Appeal

David Andrew King appealed against his conviction on 21 May 1982 in the Crown Court at Leeds before his Honour Judge Herrod QC and a jury on a charge of conspiracy to defraud for which he was sentenced to 12 months' imprisonment and made subject to a criminal bankruptcy order for the sum of £42,361·51 and an order under s 188(1) of the Companies Act 1948 barring him from managing a company for five years. The appellant also appealed against sentence. The facts are set out in the judgment of the court.

Robert S Smith for the appellant.
Brian Walsh QC and *Paul Hoffman* for the Crown.

At the conclusion of the argument the court announced that the appeal against conviction would be dismissed but that the sentence of imprisonment would be varied by ordering to be suspended the part remaining unserved, and that it would give its reasons later.

11 January. The following judgment of the court was delivered.

DUNN LJ. The question of law which falls for decision in this appeal is whether legal professional privilege attaches to a document in the possession of a handwriting expert,

which emanated from the appellant and was sent by him to his solicitors for examination
by the expert, so as to render the document inadmissible in evidence when the expert
was called on subpoena by the Crown as a witness at the trial of the appellant.

The question arises in this way. The appellant was charged with a man named Bush
on an indictment which included a count of conspiracy to defraud the suppliers of Bush's
insolvent jewellery company, Ford Bush Diamonds Ltd of 11 York Place, Leeds, between
May and August 1980, by false representations that the company was solvent, that the
business was being conducted honestly, that King was named Stevens (who did not exist)
and that the company intended to pay for goods supplied or to return goods sent on
approbation.

In the course of preparation for the trial, the Crown had reason to believe that certain
documents were being manufactured by the appellant for the purpose of his defence.
The appellant's solicitors requested the Crown to send a number of company documents
in the possession of the Crown to a Mr Radley, the handwriting expert. It therefore
occurred to some bright person in the prosecution team that it would be interesting to
discover what other documents had been sent to Mr Radley as control documents to
compare with the documents produced by the Crown. Accordingly subpoenas ad
testificandum and duces tecum were served on Mr Radley.

At the trial objection was taken, in the absence of the jury, to Mr Radley being called
to produce any documents in his possession emanating from the defence, on the ground
that such documents constituted a communication for the purpose of enabling the
appellant's solicitors to advise or act in the proceedings, and were consequently privileged.
After hearing submissions on both sides the judge ruled that such documents were not
privileged. The Crown did not seek to adduce evidence from Mr Radley as to the
instructions given by the solicitors to him. They simply wished to ascertain what
documents he had received from the solicitors and his findings on examination of those
documents.

In fact the Crown struck gold. Mr Radley produced a document, which became
exhibit 257, purporting to be an invoice dated 26 February 1981, printed with the
address 'F & M Jewellery, Queen's Arcade, Leeds' for the sum of £5,000 for diamond
jewellery. The signature purported to be that of A Josephs. Mr Radley said the signature
had been taken by a tracing from another exhibit, exhibit 138, which could only have
come into the appellant's hands after the committal proceedings. If the signature had
been genuine, it would have supported a possible defence that Josephs, who shared an
office at 11 York Place, was party to the conspiracy and was calling himself Stevens.
Moreover, F & M Jewellery was the name of a business set up by Bush at the end of June
1980. The evidence of Flockton, an employee of Bush who was called by the Crown, was
that at the time of the move to Queen's Arcade Bush was on holiday in Corfu, and the
appellant had assisted in the move and visited Queen's Arcade to receive messages from
an answering machine and to deliver advertising material.

Although the appellant did not give evidence, his case was that he took no part in
running the business and had no access to the books of F & M Jewellery. The Crown said
exhibit 257 gave the lie to that and further that the appellant must have been responsible
for the forgery of Josephs's signature in order to throw blame on Josephs and exculpate
himself. This, said the Crown, was the hallmark of a guilty man.

At the conclusion of the trial, the jury convicted the appellant, who now appeals
against conviction. The first ground of appeal was that the judge was wrong in law in
ruling that no legal privilege attached to exhibit 257, and that to permit the Crown to
call Mr Radley to produce the document was a material irregularity.

Counsel on behalf of the appellant submitted in this court that any communication
passing between a solicitor and a third party for the purpose of taking advice was
privileged. He relied on a passage in *Cross on Evidence* (5th edn, 1979) p 286 in the
following terms:

'The rationale of the head of legal professional privilege under consideration was
succinctly stated by the Law Reform Committee to be "to facilitate the obtaining
and preparation of evidence by a party to an action in support of his case". The

a   privilege is essential to the adversary system of procedure which would be
     unworkable if parties were obliged to disclose communications with prospective
     witnesses.'

     While accepting that there is no property in a witness, counsel for the appellant submitted
     that at common law an expert who had been consulted by solicitors for one party should
     not be called as a witness by the other party to give evidence as to any communication
b   sent to him by the solicitors. Counsel submitted that exhibit 257 formed part of the
     communication from the defendant's solicitors to the expert.
         Alternatively, counsel submitted that, if that was not the general rule, there is a
     difference between civil actions and criminal trials, and that in criminal trials privilege
     extends not only to communications requesting advice, but also to the article which the
     client submits as the subject matter on which the advice is to be given. He relied in
c   support of that proposition on a dictum of Swanwick J in *Frank Truman Export Ltd v
     Metropolitan Police Comr* [1977] 3 All ER 431 at 439, 440–441, [1977] QB 952 at 961, 963.
         Dealing first with the general position, the rule is that in the case of expert witnesses
     legal professional privilege attaches to confidential communications between the solicitor
     and the expert, but it does not attach to the chattels or documents on which the expert
     based his opinion, or to the independent opinion of the expert himself: see *Harmony
d   Shipping Co v Davis* [1979] 3 All ER 177 at 181, [1979] 1 WLR 1380 at 1385 per Lord
     Denning MR. The reasons for that are that there is no property in an expert witness any
     more than in any other witness and the court is entitled, in order to ascertain the truth,
     to have the actual facts which the expert has observed adduced before it in considering
     his opinion.
         In general then no privilege will attach to exhibit 257. It was one of the documents
e   examined by Mr Radley, on which he based his opinion, and the court was entitled to
     have it adduced in evidence. Is there any difference because the document was examined
     in criminal proceedings rather than in civil proceedings? On principle we can see no
     reason why that should be so. It would be strange if a forger could hide behind a claim
     of legal professional privilege by the simple device of sending all the incriminating
     documents in his possession to his solicitors to be examined by an expert. The only hint
f   of authority to the contrary is the dictum of Swanwick J in *Frank Truman Export Ltd v
     Metropolitan Police Comr*. That case was cited, though not referred to, in the judgments in
     R v Justice of the Peace for Peterborough, ex p Hicks [1978] 1 All ER 225, [1977] 1 WLR
     1371. In that case a search warrant was ordered under s 16 of the Forgery Act 1913,
     empowering police officers to search a solicitor's premises and seize a forged document.
     On an application for certiorari to quash the order for the warrant the Divisional Court
g   held that any privilege which the solicitors may have had in respect of the document was
     the privilege of the client, and since the client had no lawful excuse for possessing the
     document, the application was dismissed. Eveleigh J said ([1978] 1 All ER 225 at 228,
     [1977] 1 WLR 1371 at 1374):

         'The claim of privilege, it is true, applies to documents in the hands of solicitors
h   in a great variety of circumstances, but it is the privilege of the client. When one
         looks at s 16 [of the Forgery Act 1913] there is nothing to indicate that an exception
         shall be made in the case of documents in the hands of solicitors, which could have
         been done had Parliament so intended. Right to the forefront of one's consideration
         of this point is that the solicitor holds the document in the right of his client and
         can assert in respect of its seizure no greater authority than the client himself or
         herself possesses. The client in this case would have possessed no lawful authority or
j   excuse that would prevent the document's seizure. In my view the solicitor himself
         can be in no better position. The solicitor's authority or excuse in a case like this is
         the authority or excuse of the client.'

     In this case it is conceded that, if exhibit 257 had been in the possession of the appellant,
     no privilege would have attached, and, accordingly, no greater privilege can attach to the
     document because it has passed through the hands of his solicitor. The Divisional Court

in *R v Justice of the Peace for Peterborough* did not consider that any special rule applied because the privilege was claimed in criminal proceedings.

We do not regard *Frank Truman Export Ltd v Metropolitan Police Comr* as authority for the proposition that any such rule does exist. The observations of Swanwick J to that effect were not necessary for his decision, which related to the validity of searches and seizures under warrant rather than to questions of privilege. We agree with the observations on that case which appear in *Cross on Evidence* (5th edn, 1979) p 287:

> 'In civil cases documents which have come into existence before advice was sought or litigation contemplated have to be disclosed on discovery, but the judgment of SWANWICK, J., in *Frank Truman Export, Ltd. v. Metropolitan Police Commissioner* suggests that documents and other property left by a client with his solicitor in good faith in order that he may be advised thereon are privileged in criminal proceedings. The fact that there is no pre-trial discovery in a criminal case and the prosecution's inability to oblige the accused to produce documents at the trial render the conception of legal professional privilege somewhat out of place in this context. In the *Truman* case documents were taken from the office of the accused's solicitor by the police pursuant to a search warrant. It was held that the police were entitled to retain a number of them because, although they were privileged, some were covered by the terms of the warrant and others were relevant to a charge of conspiracy pending against the accused. The same result might have been reached on the basis that the documents could, in the circumstances, have been retained if they had been procured by a search of the accused's premises. The problem before the court related to the validity of searches and seizures rather than privilege.'

For those reasons the judge was right to allow Mr Radley to be called and to produce exhibit 257.

The second ground of appeal is that the judge should have directed the jury that there was evidence on which they could find that Flockton was an accomplice, and the judge should accordingly have given the appropriate warning as to accomplices, coupled with a direction as to corroboration. Flockton was employed by Bush, who, having pleaded guilty and been sentenced, gave evidence for the Crown. The judge gave a full accomplice warning and direction in respect of Bush. Bush and Flockton gave the only direct evidence of the appellant's involvement in the business of the company. As Bush was on holiday from 23 June for three weeks, when the fraudulent trading was at its height, the evidence of Flockton, who was working at the premises at the time, was plainly of great importance to the case of the Crown. Although it was conceded by the defence that Flockton was not a party to the actual agreement to defraud suppliers, it was submitted that on his own evidence he had assisted in the fraudulent trading of the company by using the fictitious name 'Stevens' himself while Bush was in Corfu, and had assisted Bush in a number of other ways to defraud creditors of the company. It was also submitted that Flockton had lied to the police on a number of occasions in order to protect Bush.

The judge gave the following warning in respect of Flockton's evidence in the summing up. He said:

> 'Well, the first evidence we must look at in support is the evidence of Mr Flockton. If you think that his evidence is true, if you think that his evidence can be accepted standing alone, if you think that his evidence is truthful and reliable then it can amount to corroboration of the evidence of Mr Bush. You will bear in mind of course that, although he was not an accomplice in the sense that he is alleged to have been tied up in this dishonest scheme of things, he has a long existing friendship with Mr Bush and the defence did not withdraw from making swingeing criticisms of Mr Flockton. They even imputed dishonesty to Mr Flockton, and you must look at Mr Flockton's evidence very carefully and not only at his evidence but his demeanour in the witness box, and he was in the witness box for long enough.'

The judge recited the various criticisms which had been made by the defence of Flockton's

a evidence and then said:

'Well, there it is. It is a matter for you. You saw him and you must judge him.
Did he strike you as being yet another of these "flash Harrys" we've seen and heard
so much about in this case, or did he strike you as being a very simple, straightforward
young man who came as something of a breath of fresh air into this otherwise
tainted, dishonest case? Entirely a matter for you. You must make up your own
b minds about Mr Flockton.'

The law on this question is now clear since R v Beck [1982] 1 All ER 807, [1982] 1 WLR
461 and R v Stainton (1982) Times, 9 November. Unless there is evidence that the witness
might have been a potential participant in the actual offence charged, then the appropriate
warning to the jury is matter for the judge; it is not necessary for him to give the full
c accomplice warning and direction as to corroboration. As was said in the judgment of
the court in R v Beck [1982] 1 All ER 807 at 813, [1982] 1 WLR 461 at 469:

'While we in no way wish to detract from the obligation on a judge to advise a
jury to proceed with caution where there is material to suggest that a witness's
evidence may be tainted by an improper motive, and the strength of that advice
must vary according to the facts of the case, we cannot accept that there is any
d obligation to give the accomplice warning with all that entails, when it is common
ground that there is no basis for suggesting that the witness is a participant or in any
way involved in the crime the subject matter of the trial.'

It was never suggested in the course of the trial that Flockton was a party to the
agreement to defraud creditors. The question of his being an accomplice was only raised
e by counsel for the defence in the absence of the jury while the judge was summing up.
The judge rejected a submission that the accomplice warning should have been given,
saying that there was no evidence which justified that. We agree, although the judge was
plainly right, in view of the various matters put to Flockton, to give them the warning
which he did as to their approach to Flockton's evidence.

We would only add this. In addition to the evidence of Bush and Flockton, there was
f independent evidence which linked the appellant to the management of the company,
and thus tended to show that he was a party to the fraudulent trading. For example, four
pairs of ear-rings, which were part of two large consignments from suppliers of the
company, were found in the boot of the appellant's car. A Mr Pathak, a supplier, left a
message on the answer phone for Mr Stevens to ring him. A note was found concerning
this message, written by the appellant, and later Pathak received a call from 'Mr Stevens'
g in response to his message on the answer phone. Engelhard Industries had a discussion
with 'Mr Stevens' regarding the debt owed to them. On the suppliers card kept by the
company, the amount of this debt had been written in the appellant's handwriting.
Birmingham Gem Co arranged with 'Mr Stevens' by telephone for the payment of
£4,600 direct into their account at the bank. Details of the account were given to 'Mr
Stevens' only. The same day this amount was paid into that account by the appellant. In
h the view of this court the evidence that the appellant was a party to the conspiracy was
overwhelming, and we have no doubt about this conviction. We therefore dismiss the
appeal against conviction.

As to sentence, on 17 June 1982 the appellant's sentence was amended to one of 12
months' imprisonment, and a criminal bankruptcy order for £42,361·51 was made as
well as an order under s 88(1) of the Companies Act 1948 preventing him from managing
j a company for five years. Bush had been sentenced on 4 May before the trial started
(having pleaded guilty to the same count) to 12 months' imprisonment, 6 months of
which was suspended. No financial penalty was imposed on Bush. Neither Bush nor the
appellant had any previous convictions. The appellant was younger than Bush, being 33,
and married with two children. He had been a company director since 1976 and at the
time of the trial was earning £14,500 per year. Although there was evidence before us
that the appellant's wife suffered as a result of his absence in prison, the substantial

ground of appeal was the disparity between the sentence passed on Bush and that passed on the appellant. While it was accepted that Bush was entitled to a discount for his plea of guilty and giving evidence for the Crown, it was said on the appellant's behalf that the discount was too great bearing in mind (1) that Bush had lied in the witness box, (2) that the appellant had effectively received double the prison sentence of Bush, (3) that Bush had received no financial penalty and the appellant would be left liable for the whole deficiency of £42,000 through the criminal bankruptcy order, and (4) that the appellant is debarred from managing a company for five years while Bush is free to start up again in business now that he is released from prison.

We think that there is force in those submissions. We do not propose to interfere with the criminal bankruptcy order, or the disqualification as a director. The judge would have had power to make a criminal bankruptcy order against both defendants for the full amount of the deficiency, and we see no reason why the appellant should not have to bear the whole of that, especially as a large part of the deficiency arose when Bush was in Corfu at a time when the appellant was effectively running the company. Also the judge was right to disqualify the appellant from managing a company for five years. He is a very dishonest man indeed and quite unfitted to manage any trading company. But, because the appellant may have a justifiable sense of grievance that Bush was dealt with so comparatively leniently, we will vary the sentence of imprisonment by ordering the remainder of it from the date when we made our order on the appeal to be suspended. To that extent and for those reasons we allow the appeal against sentence.

Appeal against conviction dismissed. Appeal against sentence varied. Leave to appeal refused. Application for certificate, under s 33(2) of the Criminal Appeal Act 1968, that a point of law of general public importance was involved in the decision refused.

· Solicitors: *J Levi & Co*, Leeds (for the appellant); *Director of Public Prosecutions.*

Sepala Munasinghe Esq   Barrister.

Practice Direction

QUEEN'S BENCH DIVISION

Practice – Interest – Pleading – Claim – Debt or liquidated sum – Indorsements for interest – Contractual interest – Bills of Exchange Act 1882 – Supreme Court Act 1981, s 35A – RSC Ord 6, r 2(1)(b), Ord 13, r 1(2), Ord 18, r 8, Ord 22, r 1(8).

On 1 April 1983 the Law Reform (Miscellaneous Provisions) Act 1934, s 3 ceases to have effect, and s 35A of the Supreme Court Act 1981 and the consequential amendments to RSC Ord 13, r 1(2), Ord 18, r 8 and Ord 22, r 1(8) come into operation (see s 15 of and Sch 1 to the Administration of Justice Act 1982 and RSC (Amendment No 3) 1982, SI 1982/1786).

This direction replaces the Practice Direction of 28 October 1982 ([1982] 3 All ER 1151, [1982] 1 WLR 1448) accordingly.

1. *Interest under s 35A of the Supreme Court Act 1981*

(A) *Indorsements complying with RSC Ord 13, r 1(2)*
   The procedure, including procedure under RSC Ord 6, r 2(1)(b), will be as for claims for contractual interest. See para 2 below.
   (a) The statement of claim must plead (i) the cause of action, with particulars, the sum

a claimed and the date when payment was due, (ii) the claim for interest under s 35A of the Supreme Court Act 1981, the rate of interest claimed and the amount of interest claimed from the date when payment was due to the date of issue of the writ (the rate of interest claimed must not exceed the rate of interest on judgment debts current at the date of issue of the writ; the current rate is 12% (see the Judgment Debts (Rate of Interest) (No 2) Order 1982, SI 1982/1427)).

b (b) The statement of claim should also include a claim for further interest at the aforesaid rate under the 1981 Act from the date of issue of writ to judgment or sooner payment. This should be shown as a daily rate to assist calculation when judgment is entered.

(c) See para 2(b) below for the 14-day costs indorsement.

(B) *Indorsements for interest to be assessed*

c If the plaintiff seeks interest at a higher rate than current judgment debts interest, or for any other reason requires interest on a debt to be assessed, he must plead a claim for interest under s 35A of the Supreme Court Act 1981 and enter judgment for interest to be assessed.

2. *Contractual interest*

d (a) The statement of claim must give sufficient particulars of the contract relied on and, in particular, must show (i) the date from which interest is payable, (ii) the rate of interest fixed by the contract, (iii) the amount of interest due at the issue of the writ.

(b) The interest up to the issue of the writ should be claimed in the prayer and included in the sum entered in the indorsement for 14-day costs. This indorsement must be made; if the defendant pays the principal sum, the interest to the date of the writ and the 14-day costs within the 14 days, the action is stayed and no further interest is payable.

e (c) The statement of claim should also contain a prayer for further interest at the contract rate from the issue of the writ to judgment or sooner payment. It is often helpful to work out and show this interest also as a daily rate.

(d) If the defendant makes default in giving notice of intention to defend or in serving a defence, the plaintiff may sign judgment for the principal sum, interest to the date of the writ, further interest calculated to the date of judgment and scale costs. This last

f calculation is checked by the court when judgment is entered, and it is for this reason that the statement of claim must give sufficient information to enable this to be done quickly.

3. *Interest under the Bills of Exchange Act 1882*

g (a) By s 57 of the Bills of Exchange Act 1882 the holder of a cheque (or other bill of exchange) which is dishonoured when duly presented is entitled to recover, in addition to the amount of the cheque, interest as liquidated damages from the date of dishonour until the date of judgment or sooner payment.

(b) There is no prescribed rate of interest; the plaintiff may properly ask for a reasonable rate around or somewhat above base rate. If a high rate is asked, there may be difficulty in entering a default judgment while the matter is referred to the Practice

h Master (see s 57(3) of the 1882 Act). Short-term investment account rate is a safe guide.

(c) The statement of claim should set out the date of dishonour, the rate of interest claimed, a calculation of the interest due at the date of the issue of the writ, and prayers for this interest and further interest until judgment or sooner payment. The procedure is as explained for contractual interest in para 2(b) to (d) above.

j   *Note*: The expression 'judgment or sooner payment' is used in this direction because the right to interest after judgment is almost always under the Judgments Act 1838 *only*.

JOHN ELTON
24 February 1983   Senior Master, Queen's Bench Division.

R v Criminal Injuries Compensation Board, ex parte Thompstone
R v Criminal Injuries Compensation Board, ex parte Crowe

QUEEN'S BENCH DIVISION (CROWN OFFICE LIST)

STEPHEN BROWN J

14, 17 JANUARY 1983

Compensation – Criminal injuries – Reduction of award or rejection of claim – Character and way of life of victim – Victim having criminal record of violence and dishonesty – Victim injured in unprovoked assault – No connection between assault and victim's character and way of life – Whether Criminal Injuries Compensation Board entitled to withhold award – Criminal Injuries Compensation Scheme (1979 revision), para 6(c).

Between 1950 and 1979 the applicant was convicted on numerous occasions of crimes involving violence and dishonesty. In 1980 he was the victim of an unprovoked assault. He applied to the Criminal Injuries Compensation Board for compensation, under the Criminal Injuries Compensation Scheme, for the injuries inflicted on him by his assailant. A list of his previous convictions was placed before the board. The board found that there was no connection between the assault and his previous criminal propensity and activities but, under para 6(c)*ᵃ* of the scheme, it rejected his application on the ground that it would not be appropriate, in view of 'his character and way of life' as disclosed by his previous convictions, to award him compensation from public funds. He applied for an order of certiorari to bring up and quash the board's decision on the ground that it had no jurisdiction under para 6(c) to withhold compensation where there was no connection between the injury complained of and the victim's character and way of life.

Held – The Criminal Injuries Compensation Scheme was intended to afford the widest possible discretion to the board in its administration of the scheme, and, on the true construction of para 6(c) of the scheme, the board's discretion to withhold or reduce compensation on the ground of the victim's 'character and way of life' was not limited by any requirement that there should be a connection between his character and way of life and the incident in respect of which he claimed compensation. In the circumstances, the board's rejection of the applicant's claim was wholly and properly within its discretion. Accordingly the application for certiorari would be dismissed (see p 943 *g* and p 944 *a*, post).

Notes

For compensation for victims of crimes of violence, see 11 Halsbury's Laws (4th edn) para 805, and for cases on the subject, see 14(2) Digest (Reissue) 865–867, 7493–7499.

Cases referred to in judgment

Associated Provincial Picture Houses Ltd v Wednesbury Corp [1947] 2 All ER 680, [1948] 1 KB 223, CA, 45 Digest (Repl) 215, 189.

R v Criminal Injuries Compensation Board, ex p Ince [1973] 3 All ER 808, [1973] 1 WLR 1334, CA, 14(2) Digest (Reissue) 866, 7496.

R v Criminal Injuries Compensation Board, ex p Lain [1967] 2 All ER 770, [1967] 2 QB 864, [1967] 3 WLR 348, DC, 14(2) Digest (Reissue) 866, 7499.

---

a Paragraph 6, so far as material, is set out at p 939 *h j*, post

Applications for judicial review

a

R v Criminal Injuries Compensation Board, ex p Thompstone

Thomas Thompstone applied, with the leave of Glidewell J granted on 20 August 1982, (i) for an order of certiorari to bring up and quash a decision of the Criminal Injuries Compensation Board, given on 10 December 1981, rejecting his claim for compensation for injuries sustained on 19 March 1980, (ii) for a declaration that he was entitled to compensation under the Criminal Injuries Compensation Scheme and (iii) for an order

b of mandamus requiring the board to hear and determine his claim according to the scheme. The facts are set out in the judgment.

R v Criminal Injuries Compensation Board, ex p Crowe

George Norman Crowe applied, with the leave of McNeill J granted on 21 December

c 1982, (i) for an order of certiorari to bring up and quash a decision of the Criminal Injuries Compensation Board, given on 8 September 1982, rejecting his claim for compensation for injuries sustained on 2 December 1980 and (ii) for an order remitting his claim to the board for reconsideration. The facts are set out in the judgment.

Stephen Sedley for the applicant Thompstone.

d *Robert S Smith* for the applicant Crowe.
Simon D Brown for the board.

Cur adv vult

17 January. The following judgment was delivered.

e

STEPHEN BROWN J. These are two applications for judicial review of decisions of the Criminal Injuries Compensation Board dated 10 December 1981 and 8 September 1982. In each case the board, after an oral hearing before three of its members, refused the applicant's application for compensation for injuries and loss sustained as a result of an unprovoked assault, 'having regard to his character and way of life' as disclosed by his

f previous convictions. In each case the board arrived at its decision in the light of the provisions of para 6(c) of the Criminal Injuries Compensation Scheme, as revised in October 1979. Since both applications before the court raise the same point with regard to the true construction and application of para 6(c) of the scheme, the parties have invited the court to hear the applications together and the court has agreed to do so.

In relation to the application of Thomas Thompstone, the facts are that Mr Thompstone

g was assaulted by a man named Taylor whilst at his home in Eccles, Manchester on 19 March 1980. He suffered a stab wound which necessitated a laparatomy being performed on him when it was discovered that his liver had been injured. However, he has made a full recovery.

He applied to the Criminal Injuries Compensation Board for an ex gratia payment of compensation on 1 June 1980. The application was first considered by a single member

h of the board, Sir William Carter, who, on 3 March 1981, disallowed the application, stating: 'The applicant leads a life of serious crime including dishonesty and violence. It is inappropriate to award compensation from public funds.'

The applicant did not accept this decision and exercised his right to apply for a hearing before three members of the board, excluding the single member in question. This hearing took place at Manchester on 10 December 1981 before Sir Alun Davies QC, Mr

j Esyr Lewis QC and Miss B P Cooper QC. The applicant was represented by a solicitor at this hearing. The applicant agreed that the list of previous convictions produced to him was correct. This showed that he had been convicted of numerous crimes of violence and dishonesty extending over a period of 28 years. However, he had not been convicted or in trouble since his last conviction in September 1979, some two years beforehand, and on that occasion he was made the subject of a community service order. His solicitor produced letters from members of the probation service in support of the applicant's recent good behaviour. The solicitor submitted that the applicant's criminal record must be balanced with the fact that the applicant was the victim of an unprovoked attack and that following the community service order the applicant had not been in any trouble.

In giving its decision, the board stated that it—

'gave full weight to the reformed character of the applicant during the previous two years. The applicant's list of previous convictions was, however, long and included crimes of dishonesty and violence and therefore the application was rejected. The board also stated that if the applicant were to be assaulted in the future and in the mean time the applicant had maintained his reformed character, the board might well take another view, but at this stage it was too soon after the last conviction to make an award.'

In the case of the applicant George Norman Crowe, the facts are that he was the victim of an assault by a man named Carl Russell, a drinking companion, at his home in Leeds on 2 December 1980. He sustained a fracture of the right leg. Russell was subsequently convicted of the offence of unlawful wounding and sentenced to a term of three months' imprisonment.

Mr Crowe applied to the Criminal Injuries Compensation Board for an award of compensation on 26 February 1981. The single member, Sir William Carter, disallowed the application on 26 May 1982, stating:

'The applicant and his assailant were drunk and ended up quarrelling. Moreover, the applicant's record of convictions for dishonesty before and since the injury is a bad one. The application is rejected under para 6(c) of the scheme.'

The applicant would not accept this decision and asked for a hearing before three board members. This was held at Leeds on 8 September 1982 before Miss Beryl Cooper QC, Miss Shirley Ritchie QC and Mr Stuart Shields QC. The applicant was represented by a solicitor. The board expressed itself as being—

'satisfied that a crime of violence had been the cause of the injury to the applicant, that the circumstances of the injury came within the scheme and that the injuries were directly attributable to the incident.'

The applicant's list of convictions was placed before the board, from which it appeared that the applicant, aged 41, had appeared before the court on some 29 separate occasions between 1957 and 1982 for offences of dishonesty, but not for any offences of violence. He had been released from a sentence of imprisonment some months before the incident giving rise to his application for compensation, but he again appeared before the Crown Court at Leeds on 2 September 1981 for offences of burglary and dishonesty (handling stolen goods). The sentence was then deferred until 2 March 1982, but in the mean time he acquired two further convictions for burglary and theft. He was sentenced to a term of 11 months' imprisonment at the Crown Court at Leeds on 16 February 1982.

The board gave its reasons in writing for its determination on 7 January 1983. It said that it had—

'to decide the amount of any reduction in respect of convictions, character and way of life, and any attempt of the applicant to rehabilitate himself. Whilst it is true that the board will be slow to reject an application on this ground it was felt in this case that the applicant had numerous convictions for dishonesty of a serious nature, and that as shown by his convictions in 1982 had made no attempt to rehabilitate himself.'

The board considered the application of para 6(c) of the scheme to the case and after retiring to consider their decision decided that 'having regard to the applicant's character and way of life as disclosed by his convictions, it was not appropriate that he should receive any award at all from public funds'. It did not apparently take into account the earlier suggestion of drunkenness.

A copy of this scheme, applicable to both these cases, is to be found in the bundle of
a documents in the case of Thomas Thompstone. This document states:

'The Scheme for compensating victims of crimes of violence was announced in
both Houses of Parliament on 24th June 1964, and in its original form came into
operation on 1st August 1964. The Scheme has since been modified in a number of
respects. The revised 1979 Scheme which applies to all incidents occurring on and
after 1 October is set out below.'

b
There then follow, first of all, details of the administration of the scheme. Paragraph 1
states:

'The Compensation Scheme will be administered by the Criminal Injuries
Compensation Board, which will be assisted by appropriate staff. Appointments to
the Board will be made by the Secretary of State, after consultation with the Lord
c Chancellor and, where appropriate, the Lord Advocate.'

It also states that the chairman and members of the board will be legally qualified.
Paragraph 2 states:

'The Board will be provided with money through a Grant-in-Aid out of which
payments for compensation awarded in accordance with the principles set out below
d will be made. Their net expenditure will fall on the Votes of the Home Office and
the Scottish Home and Health Department.'

Paragraph 3 states:

'The Board will be entirely responsible for deciding what compensation should
be paid in individual cases and their decisions will not be subject to appeal or to
e Ministerial review. The general working of the Scheme will, however, be kept
under review by the Government and the Board will submit annually to the Home
Secretary and the Secretary of State for Scotland a full report on the operation of the
Scheme, together with their accounts. The report and accounts will be open to
debate in Parliament.'

f The second section of the scheme is entitled: 'Scope of the Scheme.' Paragraph 4, under
this heading, states:

'The Board will entertain applications for *ex gratia* payments of compensation in
any case where the applicant or, in the case of an application by a spouse or
dependant . . . sustained in Great Britain . . . personal injury directly attributable (a)
to a crime of violence (including arson or poisoning) . . .'

g
Paragraph 5 provides:

'Compensation will not be payable unless the Board are satisfied that the injury
was one for which the total amount of compensation payable after deduction of
social security benefits [shall not be less than £250].'

h Paragraph 6 states as follows:

'The Board may withhold or reduce compensation if they consider that—(a) the
applicant has not taken, without delay, all reasonable steps to inform the police, or
any other authority considered by the Board to be appropriate for the purpose, of
the circumstances of the injury and to co-operate with the police or other authority
in bringing the offender to justice; or (b) the applicant has failed to give all reasonable
j assistance to the Board or other authority in connection with the application; or (c)
having regard to the conduct of the applicant before, during or after the events
giving rise to the claim or to his character and way of life—and, in applications
under paragraphs 15 and 16 below, to the character, conduct and way of life of the
deceased and of the applicant—it is inappropriate that a full award, or any award at
all, be granted . . .'

In each of the cases before the court, the board arrived at its determination having regard to, and by applying, the provisions of para 6(c) to the circumstances of the applicant. It decided in each case that having regard to the character and way of life of the applicant no award at all should be made. Each applicant now seeks judicial review of the relevant decision of the board, contending that the board erred in law in denying to the applicant any award of compensation for criminal assault, notwithstanding that the admitted character and criminal way of life of the applicant was wholly unconnected with and had no bearing on the circumstances of the assault on him. Each alleges that on the true construction of para 6(c) of the scheme the board had no power to disallow his application.

Counsel for the applicant Thompstone, whose submissions have also been adopted by counsel for the applicant Crowe, contended that para 6(c) required that there should be a nexus between the character and conduct and way of life of the applicant and the injury suffered before it could be considered inappropriate to make an award, and that since the board had specifically found in each case that there was no such nexus its decision to make no award was bad in law.

Citing *R v Criminal Injuries Compensation Board, ex p Lain* [1967] 2 All ER 770, [1967] 2 QB 864, counsel for the applicant Thompstone submitted that the board's functions were an exercise of prerogative power by proclamation and that in making an award the board was acting quasi-judicially and was subject to the supervisory jurisdiction of the courts. He submitted that, read as a whole, para 6(c) meant the question to be asked was: 'Has the applicant, by his conduct or way of life and character, assumed some responsibility for what has happened?' He sought support from a comparison with the wording of the predecessor of para 6(c), which in the previous scheme which obtained prior to 1 October 1969 was para 17. That paragraph stated:

'The Board will reduce the amount of compensation or reject the application altogether if, having regard to the conduct of the victim, including his conduct before and after the events giving rise to the claim, and to his character and way of life it is inappropriate that he should be granted a full award or any award at all.'

Counsel for the applicant Thompstone relied on the word 'including' in that paragraph, which does not in fact appear in para 6(c) of the present scheme, and he also submitted that the interpretation of para 6(c) for which he contended was consistent with para 7 of the present scheme, although this paragraph, he conceded, dealt with a separate matter. In particular, however, he relied on a written parliamentary answer given by the Secretary of State for the Home Department on 20 July 1972 and recorded in Hansard (841 HC Official Report (5th series) written answers cols 148–149). It was also referred to in 11 Halsbury's Laws (4th edn) para 805, n 17. Mr Alfred Morris MP had asked the Secretary of State the following questions:

'(1) What criteria are applied by the Criminal Injuries Compensation Board in interpreting the meaning of the word "conduct" in paragraph 17 of the Criminal Injuries Compensation Scheme; to what extent it applies the standards of negligence at civil law in laying down such criteria; and what guidance has been given by his Department on this subject; (2) What estimate he has made of the effect on crime prevention of the interpretation of the word "conduct" as set out in paragraph 17 of the Criminal Injuries Compensation Scheme as meaning negligence at civil law; and what action he proposes to take.'

Mr Mark Carlisle MP, giving the answer on behalf of the Secretary of State, is recorded as having said:

'The interpretation of the scheme is a matter for the board, and I would refer the hon. Member to the comments on paragraph 17 in the board's Seventh Report (Cmnd. 4812). The Home Office has given the board no guidance on the paragraph, except to inform it that it is not intended to exclude from compensation a person of criminal habits who is the victim of criminal injuries wholly unconnected with his

a criminal character and background. I am not aware that the board has indicated that it interprets "conduct" as including negligence at civil law.'

Counsel for the applicant Thompstone told the court that the Home Office had been asked to disclose the information referred to by Mr Carlisle but that the Home Office had replied that they now had no record of the matter. Counsel for the applicant Thompstone also submitted that, whilst the parliamentary answer itself was not a directive, nevertheless it was evidence that directions or guidance had been given by the Secretary of State to the b board which constituted an explanation by the Crown as to the meaning of the proclamation of the scheme and must be regarded as being part of the scheme. This, he submitted, showed that it was implicit in the scheme that not only conduct but also character and way of life must have some bearing on the relevant incident before being taken into account. It would be fundamentally inconsistent, he said, with quasi-judicial proceedings to cause public funds to be disbursed on a capricious basis.

c Counsel for the applicant Thompstone accepted that para 6(c) did not contemplate that any specific connected act would have to be established in order for an award to be considered inappropriate, but it would, for example, include an applicant who had habitually associated with violent people or who lived the style of life in which violence was habitual. However, it would not have the effect of excluding a terrorist whose crimes or way of life were not connected with the relevant incident.

d Counsel for the applicant Crowe made similar submissions saying that the board administered the scheme but did not devise it.

Counsel for the board submitted that the question for the court was a pure question of the construction of para 6(c) unembellished and unaffected by parliamentary answers or explanatory statements. He contended that it was clear that the scheme conferred the widest possible discretion on the board and that this was illustrated by a number of e explanatory statements, in particular by para 3 of the scheme as published, that the relevant phrase in para 6(c) was disjunctive from that relating to conduct at the commencement of the paragraph, and that the point made by counsel for the applicant Thompstone as to the wording of para 17 of the preceding scheme was a false one as the word 'including' had been omitted from para 6(c) because the word 'during' had now been added, but this had no relevance to the point in issue.

f In so far as it might be appropriate to consider the constitutional status of the published scheme as a proclamation under the prerogative of the Secretary of State, he agreed that it was but he did not accept that Mr Carlisle's parliamentary answer in 1972 could be regarded as adding to or amending the scheme, or as directing the board in the exercise of its discretion. He referred to the ninth report of the board for 1973 and to the later parliamentary answers of Mr Don Concannon MP in 1976 and of Mr Patrick Mayhew g MP in 1982, all of which, he submitted, indicated that the applicant's interpretation of Mr Carlisle's answer of 1972 was erroneous.

The ninth report for the year ended 31 March 1973 (Cmnd 5468) contained a paragraph headed 'The Working of the Scheme' and in the course of that paragraph it stated:

h '... the statement which is to be found in Appendix F represents the Board's present interpretation of the Scheme and will be followed when single member awards are made and at hearings.'

Appendix F includes a reference to what was then para 17 of the scheme, and para J of that appendix (at p 37) is headed 'Character and Way of Life' and it states:

j '1. The general rule is that the victim must satisfy the Board that his injuries are not directly attributable to his previous bad character and way of life.
2. But a victim whose record shows that he is a man of violence and has himself been guilty of serious crimes of violence, will not receive an award and a victim who has persistently obtained his living by committing offences of dishonesty and has not made a serious attempt to earn an honest living will not receive an award.

3. If a man has given up his criminal ways and has for a substantial period of time tried to earn an honest living his previous bad character will be disregarded.'

The answer of Mr Concannon of 1976 was given in answer to a question asked by Mr Airey Neave MP. The question (and again this is recorded in Hansard) was:

'Is the Minister of State aware that the Chairman of the Criminal Injuries Compensation Board in Britain, Mr. Ogden, has stated that in future he will make no awards to persons convicted of terrorist activities? Is not this the legislation which should be amended to bring Northern Ireland into line with that principle? Does the Minister agree that compensation awards should be made on the same basis throughout the United Kingdom?'

Mr Concannon, for the Secretary of State, said:

'Again, I can go no further. I am aware of Mr. Ogden's statement, with which I, personally, concur, but I still ask the hon. Gentleman to wait a little longer, until the proposals have been prepared.'

The answer of Mr Mayhew, given in January 1982, was given in answer to a question put by Mr David Marshall MP. This was a written answer and again recorded in Hansard. It is reported that—

'Mr. David Marshall asked the Secretary of State for the Home Department if he will take steps to revise the criminal injuries compensation scheme so as to ensure that victims of crimes are not penalised, when assessing compensation, by having committed an offence of a minor kind, or when the offence has been expunged from the victim's record, and in particular when the offence in either case is one of an unconnected nature.'

Mr Mayhew replied:

'We have no plans to limit the Criminal Injuries Compensation Board's general discretion under the scheme to take account of an applicant's character and way of life in considering eligibility for compensation from public funds. The board's approach to the exercise of this discretion is explained in its seventeenth report— Cmnd. 8401, page 62, paragraph K. An applicant who is dissatisfied with a decision on the amount of compensation by a single member of the board—for example, because of the way in which his discretion has been exercised—is entitled to a hearing of his or her case before three other members.'

The reference to para K of the seventeenth report of the board is a reference to a policy statement issued by the board, first of all, in its annual report to Parliament and thereafter made available to all applicants, from September 1981, for awards of compensation. That has been produced and it has been acknowledged that each of the applicants in the present cases had received a copy of this statement when making their applications for compensation.

The document is headed:

'The Board are required to examine each application on its merits and in making their decision will exercise their discretion subject to a proper interpretation of the Scheme. This statement is issued for the benefit of applicants and their advisers as a guide as to how the Board are likely to determine applications in respect of incidents occurring on and after 1 October 1979. However, it is emphasised that each application will be decided on its merits and what is said herein does not fetter the discretion of individual Board Members or Board Members at a hearing. This statement supersedes all previous decisions made at Board Meetings and statements made in previous annual reports which touch upon the interpretation of the 1979 Revised "New" Scheme.'

The statement then sets out a number of matters which are not relevant to the present applications. Paragraph 6 includes a sub-para (c), which is headed 'Conduct'. It reads:

'1. Conduct in this Paragraph means something which is reprehensible or provocative, something which can fairly be described as bad conduct or misconduct. 2. There is no limitation upon the sort of conduct that may be taken into consideration but the Board will not think in terms of contributory negligence when acting under this clause. *R. v. Criminal Injuries Compensation Board ex parte Ince* ([1973] 3 All ER 808, [1973] 1 WLR 1334).'

Paragraph F, being the same as para 6 of the new 1979 scheme, is headed 'Gangs and Terrorists'. It states:

'A terrorist or a member of a violent gang is rarely awarded compensation, notwithstanding that his injuries may have been unconnected with his membership of the gang or his terrorist activities, but each case will be considered on its merits.'

Paragraph G, is headed 'Immoral Conduct' and states:

'Immoral conduct is not by itself a reason for reducing an award. Immoral conduct may be provocative or reprehensible in which case the rule relating to provocation or reprehensible conduct will apply.'

Then para K is headed 'Character and Way of Life' and states:

'Whether or not an application should be rejected completely or, if not rejected the amount of any reduction because of character and way of life, will be decided upon according to the applicant's record of convictions and any attempt he may have made to reform himself. The Board will not reject an application completely on the ground of character and way of life unless the applicant has a conviction for a very serious crime of violence or some other very serious crime, more than one recent conviction for less serious crimes of violence or other serious crimes or numerous convictions for dishonesty of a serious nature. A person with numerous convictions for petty offences which have not caused serious trouble to anyone else, for example, offences of drunkenness, minor breaches of the peace or trivial thefts will not have his application rejected completely but he may have his award reduced. A past conviction even for a serious crime will not permanently bar an applicant from an award. The Board would be unlikely to reject the application of an applicant with convictions who has been injured in a genuine attempt to uphold the law or when giving assistance to someone who was being attacked. It is again emphasised that each case will be decided on the basis of its own particular facts.'

In my judgment, the issue raised by these applications is one of pure construction. I am satisfied that the scheme, as published, is intended to afford the widest possible discretion to the board in its administration of the scheme. Paragraph 6(c) gives the board discretion to withhold or reduce compensation, both having regard to the conduct of the applicant in relation to the incident and, furthermore, having regard to his character and way of life. In my judgment, this latter consideration is not limited to matters relevant in some way to the particular incident.

It has been said that the policy of the board is not to disburse public money to those who prey on the public. This policy clearly has the specific approval of the Secretary of State, having regard to the evidence of the parliamentary answer of Mr Mayhew and his reference to the board's policy, and in particular to para K referred to above. Furthermore, since the board's annual reports to Parliament are subject to debate, it must be taken that the policy set out in the statement has the approval of Parliament. It must be appreciated that the scheme is one which provides for the making for ex gratia payments; it is not a statutory provision providing enforceable rights. The fair and proper administration of the scheme is safeguarded by the constitution of the board which is appointed to administer it, and by the fact that the supervisory jurisdiction of the High Court extends to the board.

In the present cases the issue is solely one relating to the legal powers of the board. In particular the decisions are not challenged on what might be referred to as the *Wednesbury* principle: see *Associated Provincial Picture Houses Ltd v Wednesbury Corp* [1947] 2 All ER

680, [1948] 1 KB 223. I am satisfied that the decisions arrived at were wholly and properly within the discretion of the board.
Accordingly, the applications are refused in each case.

Applications dismissed.

Solicitors: *Sharpe Pritchard & Co*, agents for *Casson & Co*, Salford (for the applicant Thompstone); *Sidney Torrance & Co*, agents for *Barrington Black Austin & Co*, Leeds (for the applicant Crowe); *Treasury Solicitor*.

Sepala Munasinghe Esq   Barrister.

Alec Lobb (Garages) Ltd and others v Total Oil GB Ltd

CHANCERY DIVISION
PETER MILLETT QC SITTING AS A DEPUTY JUDGE OF THE HIGH COURT
1–5, 8–12, 17–19 MARCH, 6, 7, 10–14 MAY, 24 JUNE 1982

Restraint of trade by agreement – Petrol filling station – Solus agreement – Mortgage – Agreement between owner of garage and petrol supplier for exclusive purchase and resale of supplier's products – Company owning filling station becoming insolvent – Company agreeing to solus agreement in lease and lease-back transaction designed to raise finance from supplier to prevent company's insolvency – Company leasing garage to supplier for 51 years in return for premium – Supplier immediately leasing-back garage to proprietor of company – Whether tie in lease-back void as being in unreasonable restraint of trade.

Contract – Duress – Economic duress – Commercial pressure – What constitutes duress in commercial contract – Transaction between tied dealer and petrol supplier – Transaction to raise finance from supplier – Whether supplier's refusal to release dealer from pre-existing contractual tie with supplier economic duress.

Equity – Unconscionable bargain – Contract – Matters to be established to render contract harsh and unconscionable bargain – Contract between insolvent garage company and petrol supplier to raise further finance for company – Contract consisting of lease of garage for 51 years to supplier and lease-back for 21 years to proprietor of company – Transaction amounting to acquisition by supplier of interest in equity of redemption – Whether harsh and unconscionable bargain – Whether supplier taking unfair advantage of company's financial situation – Whether terms of contract unfair – Whether acquisition by mortgagee of equity of redemption inherently objectionable.

The plaintiffs were a company and a mother and her son, who were the shareholders and directors of the company. The mother and son wished to develop freehold premises owned by the company as a garage and petrol filling station but lacked the finance to do so. Accordingly, they arranged in 1964 for the plaintiff company to borrow £15,000 from the defendants, a petrol company, on the security of a legal charge on the premises created by the plaintiff company in favour of the defendants. The charge contained a covenant (a tie covenant) by the plaintiff company to purchase the defendants' petrol exclusively during the continuance of the loan (which was repayable by instalments over 18 years) and for a further period thereafter, and made the charge irredeemable during the period of the loan. In 1965 and 1968 the plaintiff company created similar charges in favour of the defendants in order to borrow more money. As a result of a legal decision in 1967 that a tie covenant for 21 years was an unreasonable restraint of trade, in 1968

the plaintiffs and the defendants treated the current tie covenant under the charges as
a having only a further four years to run. By November 1968 the plaintiff company,
though trading profitably, was unable to meet its debts under the charges or under a
bank overdraft, and the bank (but not the defendants) exerted pressure on the company
to repay its debt. The mother and son stood to lose their livelihood and face personal
bankruptcy if the plaintiff company was wound up due to insolvency. In November
1968 the son felt unable to resort to any other petrol company for finance because of the
b tie with the defendants and wrote to the defendants seeking their advice on the financial
measures which could be taken to rescue the plaintiff company from insolvency.
Negotiations took place between the parties in which the plaintiffs were separately and
independently advised by solicitors and accountants. The defendants, although reluctant
to enter into any further transaction with the plaintiffs, wished to preserve the garage as
an outlet for sales of their petrol. Accordingly, they agreed to put further capital into the
c plaintiff company by means of a lease and lease-back transaction, comprising a lease of
the garage premises to the defendants for 51 years in return for the payment to the
plaintiff company of a premium of £35,000 (based on a fair valuation of the premises as
a tied site) and the immediate lease-back of the premises, by an underlease in the
defendants' standard form of lease, to the son personally for a term of 21 years at a rent
of £2,250, which represented an adequate return on the premium paid by the defendants.
d In accordance with the defendants' standard lease, the underlease contained a tie covenant
by the son to purchase the defendants' petrol exclusively for the 21-year term of the
underlease, provisions for a mutual break of the underlease at the end of the seventh and
fourteenth years and an absolute prohibition on assignment of the underlease. The
transaction extinguished the existing charges. Completion of the transaction took place
in July 1969, by which time the current tie covenant under the charges was treated as
e having 3½ years to run. Payment of the plaintiff company's debts and costs absorbed most
of the premium received from the defendants, leaving little of the premium left over for
use as working capital. The transaction thus failed in its object of rescuing the company
from the constraints of inadequate working capital. However, the plaintiffs took no steps
to have the transaction set aside but instead spent the next few years seeking to renegotiate
it, and in 1977 obtained the defendants' consent to add the son's adult children as tenants
f under the underlease and the defendants' confirmation that they would not break the
underlease at the end of the fourteenth year to obtain the premises for themselves. It was
not until 1976 that the plaintiffs intimated that they might challenge the validity of the
transaction, and not until June 1979 that they issued a writ against the defendants
claiming to have the transaction set aside. The plaintiffs contended that the transaction
(i) was procured by economic duress, (ii) was a harsh and unconscionable bargain, (iii)
g resulted from the defendants' abuse of a fiduciary or confidential relationship or (iv) was
a transaction between mortgagor and mortgagee improperly entered into. In the
alternative, the plaintiffs contended that the tie covenant in the underlease was void as
being an unreasonable restraint of trade, thereby rendering the whole lease and lease-
back transaction invalid. At the hearing the parties were agreed that a garage owner who
agreed to a substantial extension of an existing short-term tie with petrol suppliers, eg an
h extension from 3½ years to 21 years, would be giving up his freedom to trade and that
such an arrangement would be in breach of the doctrine against unreasonable restraint
of trade. Further, the defendants conceded that the doctrine of restraint of trade applied
to a lease and lease-back transaction between the original covenantor and the supplier
where the lease-back to the covenantor was for virtually the whole term of the lease and
the reversion to the supplier was purely nominal, since in such circumstances the
j transaction would be merely a facade for the tie covenant. The defendants contended,
however, that the doctrine did not apply (i) where there was a substantial reversion on
the lease-back to the supplier, or (ii) where the tie was part of the terms of a rescue
operation by the supplier of an insolvent garage owner, or (iii) where the lease-back was
to a third party (viz the son) who had no previous right to trade from the premises and
was not to the original covenantor (viz the company).

Held – (1) There were no grounds for setting aside the whole of the lease and lease-back transaction, because—

(a) it had not been obtained by economic duress on the part of the defendants, ie by commercial pressure which had coerced the plaintiffs' will and vitiated their consent to the transaction, since the plaintiffs had not established (i) that they entered into the transaction unwillingly with no real alternative but to submit to the defendants' demand, or (ii) that their apparent consent to the transaction was exacted by the defendants' coercive acts, or (iii) that they repudiated the transaction as soon as the pressure on them was relaxed. A party's refusal to waive performance by the other party of that party's existing contractual obligations under a previous transaction which had been freely entered into could not constitute economic pressure on the other party to enter into a fresh transaction. Accordingly, the existence of the tie covenant in the charges at the date of the lease and lease-back transaction did not constitute economic duress on the part of the defendants (see p 960 *e* to p 961 *a* and *c*, post); *Pao On v Lau Yiu* [1979] 3 All ER 65 considered;

(b) the transaction was not a harsh and unconscionable bargain which a court of equity would set aside, since the plaintiffs had not established that either the defendants' conduct in relation to the plaintiffs' position or the terms of the transaction were improper. The plaintiffs had been separately advised and the defendants, far from pressuring the plaintiffs, had been reluctant to enter into the transaction. Furthermore, although the effect of the transaction was that the defendants acquired, under the legal charges, a substantial interest in the plaintiff company's equity of redemption, that was not inherently objectionable, since a mortgagee was not prohibited from purchasing the mortgagor's equity of redemption by a transaction which was subsequent to and separate and independent from the mortgage. On the contrary, the court would only set aside such a transaction if circumstances existed which would enable the court to set it aside if the parties had not been mortgagor and mortgagee. Nor were the defendants when acquiring the lease required to pay the full value of the premises free from the tie on the basis that they were acting as mortgagees, since the transaction was independent of the mortgage and the defendants were entitled to acquire the lease on the negotiated basis of a fair valuation of the premises as tied premises. It followed that the defendants had not acquired the lease at an undervalue. Furthermore, the mutual break provisions and the prohibition against assignment in the underlease were not unfair terms since they were terms in the defendants' standard form of lease which were generally accepted within the trade (see p 961 *h*, p 962 *a* to *c e*, p 963 *a* to *f* and p 964 *h* to p 965 *j*, post); *Knight v Marjoribanks* (1849) 2 Mac & G 10 and *Multiservice Bookbinding Ltd v Marden* [1978] 2 All ER 489 applied;

(c) there had not been an abuse by the defendants of a fiduciary or confidential relationship, because, even though the parties, as tied dealer and sole supplier, might be partners in a common enterprise in which each reposed confidence in the other, the lease and lease-back transaction was not related to that enterprise and the parties had conflicting interests in regard to it. Moreover, even if it could be said that the plaintiffs had relied on the defendants' advice in entering into the transaction so that there was a fiduciary or confidential relationship between them, the defendants had not abused that relationship (see p 963 *j* to p 964 *a* and *e f*, post); *Tufton v Sperni* [1952] 2 TLR 516 and *Lloyds Bank Ltd v Bundy* [1974] 3 All ER 757 distinguished.

(2) However, the tie covenant in the underlease was void as being an unreasonable restraint of trade, because—

(a) it was a precondition of the application of the doctrine of restraint of trade to a tie covenant that the covenantor was required to give up some freedom to trade which he enjoyed previously and which but for the covenant he would continue to enjoy. That precondition was fulfilled if freedom to trade was given up by a landowner when he extended for a further 21 years an existing tie covenant with a supplier which was shortly due to expire (see p 967 *j*, p 968 *a g* and p 972 *g h*, post); *Esso Petroleum Co Ltd v Harper's Garage (Stourport) Ltd* [1967] 1 All ER 699 applied;

(b) the lease and underlease were to be regarded as a single transaction an incident of

which was the tie covenant in the underlease, and therefore, although the plaintiff
a company was entitled in law to deprive itself altogether of the right to trade from the
premises forever or for the limited period of the 51-year lease by parting with the land,
it was not entitled to retain the land or its existing interest in it and at the same time
unduly restrict the right to trade from the premises during the period of the lease-back,
notwithstanding the reversion on the lease-back (see p 968 *g h* and p 969 *c* to *e*, post);
dictum of Lord Morris in *Esso Petroleum Co Ltd v Harper's Garage (Stourport) Ltd* [1967] 1
b All ER at 717 applied;

   (c) the fact that the transaction was a genuine commercial transaction to raise finance
from a supplier (the defendants) to rescue the plaintiff company from insolvency and the
fact that there was a public interest in the rescue of ailing but viable businesses, so that
the transaction was not merely a vehicle for the tie covenant, could not prevent the
doctrine of restraint of trade applying to the tie covenant (see p 969 *h j*, p 970 *a b* and
c p 972 *b c*, post); dictum of Lord Macmillan in *Vancouver Malt and Sake Brewing Co Ltd v
Vancouver Breweries Ltd* [1934] All ER Rep at 42 applied;

   (d) since the doctrine of restraint of trade would have applied if the underlease had
been granted to the plaintiff company as the original covenantor, its application, being a
matter of public policy, could not be circumvented by the device of granting the
underlease to a third party (the son) who had no previous personal right to trade from
d the premises (see p 971 *e* to *h*, post); *Esso Petroleum Co Ltd v Harper's Garage (Stourport) Ltd*
[1967] 1 All ER 699 applied.

   (3) It followed that, since the tie covenant was clearly severable from those terms of
the underlease which did not form part of the tie, those terms of the underlease remained
valid and enforceable, as did the lease (see p 971 *h j* and p 972 *a* and *d* to *h*, post); *Wallis v
Day* (1837) 2 M & W 273 applied; *Vancouver Malt and Sake Brewing Co Ltd v Vancouver
e Breweries Ltd* [1934] All ER Rep 38 and *Amoco Australia Pty Ltd v Rocca Bros Motor
Engineering Co Pty Ltd* [1975] 1 All ER 968 distinguished; *Cleveland Petroleum Co Ltd v
Dartstone Ltd* [1969] 1 All ER 201 considered.

Notes

For contracts entered into under duress, see 9 Halsbury's Laws (4th edn) para 297, and
for cases on the subject, see 12 Digest (Reissue) 118–120, 640–651.
f   For setting aside unconscionable bargains, see 16 Halsbury's Laws (4th edn) para 1233.
   For equitable relief in cases of fiduciary relationship, see ibid para 1454.
   For agreements in restraint of trade, see 38 Halsbury's Laws (3rd edn) 20, para 13, and
for cases on the subject, see 45 Digest (Repl) 443–449, 271–297.

Cases referred to in judgment

g *Amoco Australia Pty Ltd v Rocca Bros Motor Engineering Co Pty Ltd* [1975] 1 All ER 968,
   [1975] AC 561, [1975] 2 WLR 779, PC, 45 Digest (Cont Vol D) 941, *132ab*.
Blomley v Ryan (1954) 99 CLR 362.
Clark v Malpas (1862) 4 De GF & J 401, 45 ER 1238, LJJ, 25 Digest (Reissue) 174, *1384.*
Clegg v Hands (1890) 44 Ch D 503, CA, 31(1) Digest (Reissue) 331, *2622.*
Cleveland Petroleum Co Ltd v Dartstone Ltd [1969] 1 All ER 201, [1969] 1 WLR 116, CA,
h   Digest (Cont Vol C) 984, *130aa.*
Cooper v Twibill (1812) 3 Camp 286n, 170 ER 1384n, NP, 18 Digest (Reissue) 269, *10.*
Esso Petroleum Co Ltd v Harper's Garage (Stourport) Ltd [1967] 1 All ER 699, [1968] AC
   269, [1967] 2 WLR 871, HL, Digest (Cont Vol C) 985, *132a.*
Gubbins v Creed (1804) 2 Sch & Lef 214, 35 Digest (Repl) 582, **1006.*
Hickes v Cooke (1816) 4 Dow 16, 3 ER 1074, HL, 35 Digest (Repl) 358, *619.*
j *Knight v Marjoribanks* (1849) 2 Mac & G 10, 42 ER 10, LC, 35 Digest (Repl) 428, *1218.*
Lloyds Bank Ltd v Bundy [1974] 3 All ER 757, [1975] QB 326, [1974] 3 WLR 501, CA,
   Digest (Cont Vol D) 118, *764a.*
Multiservice Bookbinding Ltd v Marden [1978] 2 All ER 489, [1979] Ch 84, [1978] 2 WLR
   535, Digest (Cont Vol E) 428, *22a.*
Pao On v Lau Yiu [1979] 3 All ER 65, [1980] AC 614, [1979] 3 WLR 435, PC, Digest (Cont
   Vol E) 107, *1899a.*

Samuel v Jarrah Timber and Wood Paving Corp [1904] AC 323, HL, 35 Digest (Repl) 404, 1006.

Tate v Williamson (1866) LR 2 Ch App 55, LC, 12 Digest (Reissue) 141, 800.

Tufton v Sperni [1952] 2 TLR 516, CA, 25 Digest (Reissue) 189, 1550.

Vancouver Malt and Sake Brewing Co Ltd v Vancouver Breweries Ltd [1934] AC 181, [1934] All ER Rep 38, PC, 45 Digest (Repl) 489, 766.

Vernon v Bethell (1762) 2 Eden 110, 28 ER 838, LC, 35 Digest (Repl) 409, 1054.

Wallis v Day (1837) 2 M & W 273, 150 ER 759, 45 Digest (Repl) 490, 774.

Webb v Rorke (1806) 2 Sch & Lef 661, 35 Digest (Repl) 410, *410.

Cases also cited

Amalgamated Investment & Property Co Ltd (in liq) v Texas Commerce International Bank Ltd [1981] 3 All ER 577, [1982] QB 84, CA.

Aylesford (Earl) v Morris (1873) 8 Ch App 484, [1861–73] All ER Rep 300, LC & LJ.

Barrett v Hartley (1866) LR 2 EQ 789.

Barton v Armstrong [1975] 2 All ER 465, [1976] AC 104, PC.

Bowen v Edwards (1661) 1 Rep Ch 221, 21 ER 555.

Burmah Oil Co Ltd v Bank of England [1979] 3 All ER 700, [1980] AC 1090, HL.

Clifford Davis Management Ltd v WEA Records Ltd [1975] 1 All ER 237, [1975] 1 WLR 61, CA.

Cresswell v Potter [1978] 1 WLR 255.

Davies v London and Provincial Marine Insurance Co (1878) 8 Ch D 469.

Esso Petroleum Co Ltd v Mardon [1975] 1 All ER 203, [1975] QB 819.

Farrar v Farrars Ltd (1888) 40 Ch D 395, CA.

Ford v Olden (1867) LR 3 Eq 461.

Fry v Lane (1888) 40 Ch D 312.

Grangeside Properties Ltd v Collingwoods Securities Ltd [1964] 1 All ER 143, [1964] 1 WLR 139, CA.

Hedley Byrne & Co Ltd v Heller & Partners Ltd [1963] 2 All ER 575, [1964] AC 465, HL.

Inche Noriah v Shaik Allie Bin Omar [1929] AC 127, PC.

Jones v Lipman [1962] 1 All ER 442, [1962] 1 WLR 832.

Morony v O'Dea (1809) 1 Ball & B 109.

Nutt v Easton [1899] 1 Ch 873; *affd on other grounds* [1900] 1 Ch 29, CA.

Petrofina (Gt Britain) Ltd v Martin [1966] 1 All ER 126, [1966] Ch 146, CA.

Prees v Coke (1871) LR 6 Ch App 645.

Regent Oil Co Ltd v Strick (Inspector of Taxes) [1965] 3 All ER 174, [1966] AC 295, HL.

Schroeder (A) Music Publishing Co Ltd v Macaulay [1974] 3 All ER 616, [1974] 1 WLR 1308, HL.

Shell UK Ltd v Lostock Garage Ltd [1977] 1 All ER 481, [1976] 1 WLR 1187, CA.

Wyatt v Kreglinger and Fernau [1933] 1 KB 793, CA.

Action

By a writ dated 11 June 1979 the plaintiffs, Alec Lobb Garages Ltd, Alec Thomas Lobb and Bertha Alexandra Lobb, claimed against the defendants, Total Oil GB Ltd, the appropriate declarations in answer to the following questions: (1) whether a transaction contained in an agreement and a lease and underlease both dated 25 July 1979, was an agreement in unreasonable restraint of trade and unenforceable; (2) whether the transaction was the purchase by the defendants as mortgagees of an interest in the mortgaged property during the currency of the mortgage and in all the circumstances of the case ought to be set aside; (3) whether the transaction ought to be treated as a mortgage although in form a lease and underlease and accordingly was redeemable and if so (a) an order for redemption and (b) all necessary accounts and inquiries on the footing of redemption; and (4) whether the plaintiff company was bound to repay any part of a sum of £35,000 in the event of the answer to questions (1), (2) or (3) or any of them being in the affirmative. The facts are set out in the judgment.

E W H Christie for the plaintiffs.

a *John Peppitt QC* and *Peter Cresswell* for the defendants.

Cur adv vult

24 June. The following judgment was delivered.

PETER MILLETT QC. The original plaintiffs in this action were Mr Alec Lobb, his
b mother Mrs Bertha Lobb, and Alec Lobb (Garages) Ltd, a small private company of
which Mr and Mrs Lobb were the sole proprietors, being the only directors and
shareholders. Shortly after the issue of the writ, however, Mr Lobb died, and the action
has been carried on by his executors. Mr Lobb's elder son Geoffrey has since become a
director and shareholder of the company. He is now its managing director.

Despite its name, the plaintiff company is the proprietor of a single garage and petrol
c filling station in South Street, Braintree, Essex. At all material times the freehold interest
in the premises has belonged to and remained vested in the company. The present action
is concerned with a transaction which took place in July 1969 when the plaintiff company
granted a lease of the site to the defendants for a term of 51 years at a peppercorn rent in
return for a premium of £35,000, and the defendants granted an underlease of the site
to Mr and Mrs Lobb for 21 years, on terms which I shall describe in more detail hereafter,
d and subject to an exclusive petrol tie in favour of the defendants.

The plaintiffs claim, first, that the transaction in truth and in law constituted a
mortgage and not a lease and lease-back; and they seek to redeem it on repayment of the
so-called premium of £35,000. Second, and in the alternative, they claim to have the
transaction set aside on appropriate terms, contending (i) that it was procured by
economic duress, or (ii) that it was a harsh and unconscionable bargain, or (iii) that it
e resulted from the abuse by the defendants of a fiduciary or confidential relationship
between the parties, or (iv) that it was a transaction improperly entered into between
mortgagor and mortgagee. Third, and in the further alternative, they contend that the
petrol tie contained in the underlease is an unreasonable restraint of trade and so void,
and they claim that its invalidity so infects the whole transaction that neither the lease
nor the underlease can stand.

f Mr Lobb was a former racing driver, and was well known in the locality. He and his
father ran a small road haulage business. In 1960 Mr Lobb's father died, and the business
declined. Unhappily, Mr Lobb suffered from multiple sclerosis. He and his mother
decided to give up the transport business and to develop part of the site as a garage and
petrol filling station. They formed the plaintiff company for this purpose, and in 1964
they sold off the assets of the former business together with part of the site, and after
g paying off the debts of the business put what remained of the proceeds into the new
venture.

Despite this, Mr and Mrs Lobb lacked the necessary finance to develop the site
themselves. They approached a number of petrol companies for financial assistance.
Apparently the defendants offered the best terms, and accordingly Mr and Mrs Lobb
entered into arrangements with the defendants to borrow up to £15,000 on the security
h of a legal mortgage, in return for an exclusive petrol tie for 20 years.

On 19 February 1964 the plaintiff company charged the premises to the defendants to
secure repayment of a principal sum of £7,500 with interest at 4% pa and further
advances not exceeding an additional £7,500 to be advanced against architects' certificates
and to be interest-free. The two sums were to be repaid by quarterly instalments over 18
years. The defendants were not to call in their money in the mean time, provided that
j the instalments were duly paid, and the plaintiff company was not free to redeem the
charge during the same period. The legal charge contained an exclusive petrol tie in
favour of the defendants to last during the continuance of the security and for a further
minimum period of two years thereafter. The plaintiff company was not, without the
defendants' consent, to sell the premises subject to the charge unless it procured the
purchaser to enter into a like tie agreement with the defendants. Mr and Mrs Lobb
joined in the legal charge as guarantors.

During 1964 the plaintiff company entered into a number of agreements with the defendants to acquire equipment on hire or hire purchase. One such agreement was for the hire of three 2,000-gallon underground petrol tanks, valued at £1,179, for a period of 20 years at an annual rent of £1. The costs of installation were borne by the defendants, who retained the property in the equipment. The value of the tanks was to be written off over 20 years, at the end of which time they were to belong to the plaintiff company without further payment.

As early as February 1965 the plaintiff company found itself in financial difficulties. It fell into arrear with its payments under the legal charge, and had to borrow from the bank to pay for petrol. On 7 July 1965 Mrs Lobb advanced a sum of £3,500 to the plaintiff company out of her own resources, and took a floating charge over the company's assets.

Later charges were created as follows. (1) On 25 December 1965 the plaintiff company granted a further charge to the defendants to secure repayment of a further sum of £2,500 advanced to enable the building works to be completed. The advance carried interest at 6% pa and was repayable over 18 years. The defendants were not to call for repayment in the mean time, provided that the instalments were duly paid, but the plaintiff company was free to redeem at any time on six months' notice. The charge contained a petrol tie to last during the continuance of the security. Mr and Mrs Lobb joined as guarantors. (2) On 29 April 1966 the plaintiff company granted a second charge to the Midland Bank to secure present and future indebtedness. (3) On 2 January 1968 the plaintiff company granted a further charge to the defendants to secure repayment of a further advance of £3,000 with interest at 5% repayable over 20 years. The defendants were not to call for repayment in the mean time, provided that the instalments were duly paid, but the plaintiff company was free to redeem by 12 months' notice expiring at any time more than five years after the date of the charge. The charge contained a petrol tie during the continuance of the security. Mr and Mrs Lobb joined as guarantors, and the Midland Bank entered into a deed of postponement to enable the further charge to be created in priority to its own second charge.

The plaintiff company was seriously undercapitalised, and throughout the period from 1964 to 1969 suffered severe cash flow problems. It found it impossible to meet the instalments due to the defendants on time, and ran up substantial indebtedness on product account. In April 1965 it had been allowed to pay for deliveries of petrol by the system known as load over load, by which each delivery is paid for in arrear at the time of the next delivery. This was a concession; the normal terms then offered by the defendants to their dealers required payment of cash on delivery. In September 1967, however, as part of the arrangements for the advance of £3,000, which was intended to fund the plaintiff company over a longer period by providing additional working capital, this facility was withdrawn, and thenceforth the defendants insisted on all supplies being paid for by cash on delivery.

1968 was a particularly difficult year. By April 1968 the plaintiff company's outstanding debt to the defendants on product account had reached £1,759 8s 9d, and the defendants required the plaintiff company to pay this off by monthly payments of £200 each. The plaintiff company was exceeding its overdraft limit at the bank, and Mr Coles, the bank manager, became convinced that ultimately the company would fail. Its financial difficulties were aggravated by overmanning on the forecourt, and the theft of green shield stamps to an estimated value of £1,000. The trading account for the year ended 31 May 1968 showed a trading loss of £363 4s 10d. After directors' remuneration of £2,000, bank charges and loan interest of £1,466 9s 3d, depreciation and sundry other expenses, the net loss for the year was £9,715 11s 2d. At Mr Coles's insistence, Mr Lobb arranged for a six-month audit, and he also took other remedial measures which proved successful; an employee, suspected of dishonesty, was dismissed. The trading account for the six months ended 30 November 1968 showed a gross profit of £5,734 1s 0d, and after directors' remuneration for the half year of £1,000, bank charges and loan interest of £1,028 4s 0d, depreciation and other expenses, the net profit for the period was

£1,046 10s 2d. Corresponding figures for the full year to 31 May 1969 were £12,168 4s 8d
a and £2,727 17s 9d respectively.

During 1968 Mr Coles was unsuccessfully attempting to enforce the company's
overdraft limit, which was £4,500; and he was compelled from time to time to dishonour
cheques on presentation. Mr Lobb sold his house, but was able to put only some £300 or
so of the proceeds into the company's bank account; and he negotiated a new stocking
arrangement with United Dominions Trust Ltd which gave him a little more cash.
b Despite this the company repeatedly exceeded its overdraft limit, and Mr Coles repeatedly
dishonoured cheques. In November 1968, two cheques drawn in favour of the defendants
for a total of £1,200 were re-presented after having been dishonoured once already. Mr
Coles agreed to meet one of them, putting the company some £500 over its limit, but he
refused to meet the other unless further moneys were paid into the account before it was
presented for the third time.

c Although, by the end of 1968, the company was trading profitably, it was a constant
struggle to find the cash with which to meet commitments. There was a total lack of
liquidity. Although it never reached the position where the company had to stop trading,
it was unable to meet its debts as they fell due. An injection of further capital was
urgently required.

On 28 November 1968 Mr Lobb wrote to the defendants in the following terms:

d   'As you appreciate we are having a very difficult time financially, and we have
now had a brief report from our accountants as to our last financial year, this shows
a loss due to over staffing in an effort to improve forecourt service and consequently
increased gallonage and the misappropriation of green shield stamps to the extent
of £1,000. Steps have been taken to rectify these matters by the cutting down of
staff and installation of a stamp dispensing machine, our accountants forecast that
e   with these measures we will now show a profit, to prove this we are having a six-
month audit. With these facts in mind, I can foresee a period of 12 to 18 months of
very tough going financially and for us to continue trading we would have to ask
your help to tide us over this period. We finish in December the £200 monthly
payments we have been making to clear back debts. The only other alternative
solution that I can offer is to lease the forecourt to Total for a set number of years
f   and then rent it back, this should then solve our financial difficulties, the rent for
the lease being paid by the saving in Bank charges and taking advantage of cash
discount and larger petrol deliveries, etc. I would appreciate your advice on the
alternatives as soon as possible so that the embarrassing state we are in at the moment
can be stopped.'

On 2 December 1968 Mr Lomas, the defendants' branch retail manager, replied
g saying, inter alia:

'We are copying your letter to Mr. A. C. Ennis with a request that he discusses the
various alternative measures with you as soon as possible. On receipt of Mr. Ennis's
report we will either let you have our observations or arrange a meeting with the
undersigned or our Mr. I. P. Kirkwood.'

h This exchange of letters was followed by two meetings between Mr Lobb and
representatives of the defendants. The first meeting took place during December and
was attended by Mr Lobb, Mr Ennis, the defendants' local representative, and Mr Nevill,
a more senior employee of the defendants described to me as a negotiator. There was a
general discussion of the various alternatives open, including a possible lease of the
forecourt; but nothing was decided. Mr Nevill and Mr Ennis were perfectly frank with
j Mr Lobb, telling him that, once the current petrol tie with the defendants expired in two
or three years' time, he would be completely free to negotiate a new deal with another
oil company. This may seem strange at first sight, for it will be remembered that, under
the 1964 charge, the petrol tie was to last for 22 years. But *Esso Petroleum Co Ltd v Harper's
Garage (Stourport) Ltd* [1967] 1 All ER 699, [1968] AC 269 had been decided by the House
of Lords in February 1967 and the news that 21-year ties could be successfully challenged

must, I think, have reached Mr Lobb's ears well before December 1968. Indeed, prior to negotiating the further advance of £3,000 from the defendants in July 1967 Mr Lobb *a* had let it be known that he had been thinking of breaking the tie and had approached Esso. This may have been bluff, for Mr Lobb was very happy with the defendants; but it indicates that Mr Lobb was well aware that, if time and his own financial difficulties permitted, he might have a reasonable bargaining position. Indeed, one of the first steps Mr Lobb took when he instructed solicitors later was to ask to see a copy of the further charge dated 2 January 1968 and to be advised as to the duration of the tie. He learned *b* that it had almost four years to run. In those circumstances, as the defendants' witnesses frankly admitted, he had little or no bargaining position.

The second, and more important, meeting took place shortly before 13 January 1969 and was attended by Mr Lobb, Mr Story, who had taken over as real estate assistant of the defendants' newly-formed eastern region from the beginning of the year, Mr Nevill, and Mr Ennis. The meeting lasted some three hours. Mr Story was the senior representative *c* of the defendants present; Mr Nevill and Mr Ennis made little contribution to the discussion.

Before I describe what occurred at that meeting, I should say something about those who took part. Mr Story was a senior and responsible employee of the defendants; Mr Ennis was a humbler employee of more limited intellectual ability, but simple, frank and honest. They both gave evidence before me. I found them careful and impressive *d* witnesses. I have no hesitation in accepting their evidence. Mr Nevill left the defendants' employment shortly after the meeting, and has not given evidence before me.

Unhappily, I have not had the advantage of seeing Mr or Mrs Lobb in the witness box. Mr Lobb made a statement in June 1979 shortly before his death, and this was admitted in evidence under the Civil Evidence Act 1968. Mrs Lobb, who is now aged 81, swore an affidavit in November 1980 after she had suffered a stroke; and she was subsequently *e* examined and cross-examined before an examiner in December 1981.

Several of the witnesses have described Mr Lobb to me as he appeared to them in 1969. Their accounts tally. He was an extrovert, jolly and friendly, with an outgoing personality. He was intensely loyal to the defendants; he was a Total dealer, and was always to be found at the defendants' annual gatherings. He was over-confident in his own abilities. He thought of himself as a clever businessman, and kept his advisers at a distance. He *f* did not take his solicitors into his confidence, or ask them for comprehensive advice on his affairs. He would listen courteously to what they had to say, make a humorous remark, and ignore their advice. They found him exasperating. He was inaccurate on matters of detail: Mr Coles told me, for example, that when reporting on car deals he would get the prices wrong. He was a confused and muddled man. Mr Lobb's shortcomings as a witness are easily demonstrated. In his statement, for example, he *g* records the fact the plaintiff company's overdraft limit at the bank in 1969 was £1,000. In fact, it was £4,500. It is not, of course, surprising that Mr Lobb's recollection should be at fault after the passage of ten years; but I am not encouraged to rely on the accuracy of Mr Lobb's statement by his evident failure to verify easily verifiable facts before he made it. This is not intended to be a criticism of Mr Lobb or his advisers; they may simply not have had time. *h*

Mrs Lobb kept the plaintiff company's books and, according to Mr Collins, the company's accountant, did not keep them very well. She had no understanding of financial affairs, and left the negotiations to her son. Her evidence was derived almost entirely from what Mr Lobb had told her. I find her evidence no more reliable than his. I am not prepared to accept the evidence of either of them except where it is corroborated by other evidence or is inherently probable. *j*

Before attending the meeting, Mr Story had read the files, and knew the extent of the plaintiff company's indebtedness to the defendants. He was also aware in general terms of the company's financial difficulties, and considered that the Lobbs were on the verge of bankruptcy. He had consulted his superiors. The decision had been taken to mount a rescue if possible, by recapitalising the business in an endeavour to keep it afloat. Before the meeeting, Mr Story had also telephoned Mr Lobb and asked him to arrange for his

accountant to be present, so that the overall financial position of the plaintiff company
a could be established. Mr Lobb apparently agreed, and shortly after the meeting began it
was joined by another man who was introduced by Mr Lobb. Mr Story told me that he
had the appearance of a professional man; but he took little if any part in the proceedings,
and it has not been possible to identify him. It was not Mr Collins; nor was it any of the
other witnesses who have given evidence before me.

Mr Story gained the impression that the business was overstaffed and that there was
b too little supervision of the staff. He was unable to obtain sight of any accounts, or to
establish the amounts owed to other creditors apart from the defendants.

Mr Story discussed the possibility of the defendants buying the freehold of the site and
leasing it back to the plaintiff company. Although Mr Lobb asked him to consider
making an offer for the freehold, Mr Story gained the clear impression that Mr Lobb
would not part with it.

c Mr Story then suggested a lease and lease-back arrangement. He must, I think, have .
made it clear that the defendants would not be prepared to confine the transaction to the
forecourt alone. He indicated that there might be tax advantages if the lease to the
defendants were for at least 51 years, and he suggested that Mr Lobb take advice on this.

The terms of the lease-back were also discussed. Mr Story told Mr Lobb that this would
have to be on the defendants' standard terms and conditions, which included mutual
d break clauses and periodic rent reviews. He told Mr Lobb that the maximum term for
which the defendants would grant a lease-back was 21 years. Mr Story had not brought a
copy of the defendants' standard form of underlease to the meeting, but he undertook to
send one to Mr Lobb.

Mr Lobb must have been concerned about his security of tenure, and Mr Story
reassured him, telling him that there would be no question of his being thrown out,
e provided that he was a good tenant. Mr Story told me that this was discussed in relation
to the break clauses, but I think it is likely to have been said in relation to the expiry of
the 21-year term as well; and this is confirmed by an internal memorandum made by
Mr Story in 1971.

Money was also discussed. Mr Story had considered the value of the property. He had
arrived at a figure of £45,000 for the freehold, and rather less for a long lease; but this
f was the result of a rough and ready calculation based purely on the gallonage, and taking
no account of the particular characteristics of the property. In fact, Mr Story did not find
the site attractive; if the defendants were not already involved, he would not have
recommended a purchase at all, and certainly not at that figure. But the calculation
provided him with a useful yardstick; and he told Mr Lobb that he thought that the
defendants would pay between £35,000 and £40,000 for a 51-year lease, but that it
g would be necessary to have the property professionally valued.

At the end of the meeting, Mr Story undertook to have the property valued, and to try
to obtain for Mr Lobb the best offer on the best terms he could. He said in evidence: 'I
told him that I would offer as good a deal as I could get him. To some extent he placed
himself in my hands.'

However, Mr Story was also fairly brutal. He warned Mr Lobb that this was his last
h chance. He told him that, by realising the value of the site, he was exhausting his interest
in the property, and would have no more collateral to offer. And if he became a tenant,
he would have to adhere strictly to the terms of the lease. The business would have to
receive his undivided attention.

Mr Lobb gained the firm impression from the meeting that, once the 21-year term of
the lease-back had expired, the plaintiff company would be allowed to remain in
j occupation rent-free or at only a nominal rent. He reported as much to Mr Coles on 15
January. It is possible that Mr Lobb assumed that, since the choice of 51 years was
dictated solely by tax considerations, the 30-year reversion was purely cosmetic; or it may
be that he assumed that, no rent having been agreed on for the 30-year period, none was
payable; but it is profitless to speculate. Mr Story could not recall any discussion of the
position after the expiry of the lease-back; but he was adamant that he did not tell Mr
Lobb that the plaintiff company could stay on without paying an economic rent, as this

would have been totally unreasonable; and I accept this. It was put to Mr Story that this was not the case, as the defendants entered into just such an arrangement with another dealer in 1971. That transaction, however, was essentially different. The parties negotiated a 21-year lease and lease-back, and agreed a premium on that basis. For tax reasons, both terms were then extended to 51 years, with no rent and no covenants during the last 30 years; but the premium was unchanged. In the present case, the defendants were being asked to pay a premium for a 51-year lease, not for a 21-year lease; and an arrangement for the plaintiff company to pay no rent during the last 30 years would not have made commercial sense without an appropriate reduction in the premium.

From 9 January 1969 the defendants insisted, not merely on cash on delivery for supplies of petrol, but on bankers' orders on delivery. This was not at Mr Story's instigation, but that of the defendants' credit control department. Mr Story told me that he was unaware of it at the time. It was embarrassing for Mr Lobb, and may have increased the pressure on him to negotiate satisfactory terms with the defendants. It was not suggested to Mr Story by counsel who appeared for the plaintiffs, that the defendants were prompted by an improper desire to bring unfair pressure on Mr Lobb to meet their terms; and I am not prepared to find that it was. It was a reasonable commercial precaution on the part of the defendants, who had already received a number of cheques from the plaintiff company which had been dishonoured on presentation, and who had only recently learned from Mr Lobb of the extent of the company's financial difficulties. At no stage in the negotiations did Mr Lobb seek any change in the procedure for paying for deliveries of petrol; and even when the transaction was completed in July, the defendants did not relax their insistence on bankers' orders on delivery. I find that the change in the payment requirements was commercially justified and was unconnected with the negotiations.

After the second meeting, Mr Lobb consulted solicitors, Messrs M W Young of Braintree, and saw Mr Rishworth. This was a small, local firm with a general and varied practice, typical of a small country town. Mr Young was the sole proprietor; he was clerk to the local justices, and handled criminal and matrimonial work. Mr Rishworth was the only employed solicitor. He had been admitted in 1966 and joined the firm in 1968. He handled conveyancing and commercial work. He was particularly interested in tax.

On 14 January 1969 Mr Rishworth wrote to the defendants' solicitors, recording: 'I am in the course of advising my client generally in relation to their business.' In fact, Mr Rishworth's instructions were not as general as this. Mr Lobb had not taken Mr Rishworth into his confidence, nor had he asked him to do more than advise on and, if so instructed, carry out on his behalf the proposed transaction. Mr Rishworth knew little of the company's financial affairs, though he knew that it was having a difficult time, and that it was under pressure from the bank to reduce its overdraft.

Mr Lobb supplied Mr Rishworth with the copy of the defendants' standard form of underlease which Mr Story had forwarded to him following the meeting. At this stage, many of the clauses had blanks in them, to be completed after negotiation. On 20 January 1969 Mr Rishworth wrote to Mr Lobb drawing attention to certain of the clauses in the form of underlease which gave cause for concern, including the break clauses and the provisions for periodic rent review, and advising him of the tax consequences of the proposed transaction. He confirmed that 51 years was the shortest period for which the lease could be granted if a charge to income tax on the premium was to be avoided. He also pointed out, at some length, that even with a 51 years' lease capital gains tax would be payable. Mr Rishworth reported that he had sent a copy of the letter to Mr Collins, and expressed the hope that, once the amount of the premium had been agreed, Mr Collins would be able to compute the amount of capital gains tax that would eventually be payable.

No further meeting took place between the parties, but Mr Ennis called frequently at the garage, and was no doubt asked about progress and urged to speed things up. He saw Mrs Lobb from time to time during these visits and discussed matters with her. On one occasion, for example, she asked him what a peppercorn rent was, and he told her that it

was just a nominal rent. He was sure, however, that this was in the context of the rent
a payable by the defendants under their head lease; not of the rent payable by the plaintiff
company on the expiry of the underlease. This was confirmed by Mrs Lobb's own
evidence; she said that she had asked the meaning of a peppercorn rent because she had
seen a reference to it in the legal documents. This can only have been the lease.

Following the second meeting, Mr Story instructed Henry Berney & Co, estate agents
and valuers in London with a specialist knowledge of garage properties, to value the
b premises, and in due course received a report dated 10 February. This put a value of
£45,000 on the freehold interest subject to the existing tie, and stated that, in the opinion
of the valuers, a premium of £35,000 to £40,000 would be a reasonable premium to pay
for a 51-year lease of the entire premises at a peppercorn rent, subject to a lease-back for a
term of 21 years at a rent of £2,250 per annum. The defendants did not disclose this
report to Mr and Mrs Lobb, nor were they asked to do so. Mr Berney told me, and I
c accept, that although the report did not mention the rent review clauses, he was aware
that they were included in the defendants' standard form of lease, and he assumed that
the stated rent was for the initial period only. He also told me, and I accept, that by
'reasonable' he meant reasonable from the point of view of both parties. If the figure
which the defendants proposed to pay had been below the market value, he would have
said so.

d Shortly thereafter, Mr and Mrs Lobb were told, possibly by Mr Ennis, that the
defendants would be prepared to offer £35,000. On 17 February 1969 Mrs Lobb is
recorded as informing Mr Coles that the defendants had 'offered a leasing arrangement
at the figure of £35,000, and the Lobbs are now trying to push it up towards £40,000'.
Mr Coles told me: 'The Lobbs understood that it was in their interest to push for as high
a figure as they could. I certainly told them so several times. It is doubtful if they could
e have been so muddled as to think that it was in their interest to obtain a lower figure,
though it would have been in character if they were.'

In fact, Mr Lobb made no attempt to negotiate a higher figure than £35,000, at least
with Mr Story, and, in the light of Mr Story's misgivings about the value of the property,
and the unenthusiastic reception of his proposal by his superiors, it is doubtful if Mr
Lobb would have succeeded if he had tried.

f Mr Story had told Mr Lobb at the second meeting that the initial rent under the
underlease would depend on the size of the premium; the defendants would expect a 6%
return. This may have led to some confusion of thought on the part of Mr and Mrs Lobb.
According to Mr Lobb's statement, he was told that 'the amount of money we had to pay
would depend on the amount of money that we wished to borrow. The smaller the
amount we wished to borrow, the smaller the repayments on the lease would be'.
g According to Mrs Lobb's affidavit: 'Mr Ennis said that he favoured the smaller amount,
and asked if we could get along with £35,000, because the smaller the amount the less
we would have to pay on the lease.' In her evidence before the examiner, she said that
Mr Ennis told her: 'If you had £35,000 it would be better because you wouldn't have so
much to pay back, and so I said £35,000 would be sufficient.'

I accept this evidence; it was most effectively corroborated by Mr Ennis himself. He
h knew that the higher the premium the higher the rent would be, and that Mr Lobb
would want to pay as little rent as possible; 'so', he told me in evidence, 'he would have
wanted to borrow the minimum amount of money'. Mr Ennis thought that this was a
statement of the obvious. He told me that he did say to Mrs Lobb that it would be better
to go for the lower premium; but that he did not say that to Mr Lobb. I find as a fact that
he did not say anything to this effect in Mr Story's presence at the all-important second
j meeting in January; but that he did say something to this effect to Mrs Lobb on one or
more of his later visits to the garage. This suggests that Mr or Mrs Lobb may have tried
to discuss the amount of the premium with Mr Ennis in an attempt to push it up.

As I have said, Mr Lobb was a confused and muddled man. According to Mr Young,
Mr Lobb told him that he was proposing to borrow £35,000 from the defendants, and
to repay it over 21 years. Mr Young told him that this was not the transaction into which

he was proposing to enter, and explained its true nature to him. So did Mr Rishworth. I
am satisfied that the defendants were offering a lease and lease-back and not a loan, and
that there was no question of the premium being repaid, that Mr Young and Mr
Rishworth both made this clear to Mr Lobb, and that he understood the general effect of
the proposed transaction. Nor do I consider that Mr Lobb was led by the defendants to
believe, or at the time did believe, that it would be against his interest to negotiate a
higher premium. If he failed to do so, it was, in my judgment, because he trusted Mr
Story to obtain for him the best deal he could, and perhaps because he had a shrewd idea
himself that the property was not worth more. I am also satisfied that the amount of the
premium was arrived at solely by reference to the value of the property, and not by
reference to the financial needs of the plaintiff company, although these were naturally
discussed and were of course relevant in establishing the viability of the business if the
proposed transaction was undertaken.

My Story's recommendation was put before his superiors. It did not receive an
enthusiastic reception. The defendants' legal department advised its rejection; but Mr
Backhouse, who was a marketing man in a head office appointment, regarded this as a
'non-marketing attitude'. He noted Mr Lobb's impressive sales performance, and took
the view that, if there were a way of keeping him in business, it should be tried. He
minuted his opinion that the deal should go ahead, *provided* that the underlease to the
plaintiff company should be on the usual terms with break clauses and rent reviews.

The proposal was eventually recommended by the defendants' retail manager on 16
April 1969 on the basis that the price payable was realistic in the light of the valuation,
and that the transaction was the best method of resolving the problem and at the same
time securing the outlet. It was subsequently approved by both the chairman and the
managing director. The chairman, however, stipulated that no credit should be given to
the dealer; and that vigorous attempts should be made to obtain the freehold interest at
no extra cost. On the same day, Mr Story telephoned Mr Lobb and told him that the deal
had received management approval.

Mr Lobb meanwhile was under continuing pressure from the bank, and he urged Mr
Story to let him have a letter of confirmation of the deal as soon as possible so that he
could show it to Mr Coles. Accordingly, on 23 April 1969 Mr Story wrote a letter to the
plaintiff company, expressed to be 'subject to contract', outlining the main terms and
reporting that management approval had been given to them. On 5 May Mr Story
recorded in an internal memorandum that he had been unsuccessful in negotiating the
acquisition of the freehold. Mr Lobb, he reported, was adamant, and would not consider
relinquishing the freehold of the site. There was then further delay while the defendants
instructed their solicitors, and it was not until 6 June that Mr Rishworth received
telephone confirmation of the transaction from the defendants' solicitors. This was
confirmed by letter dated 9 June 1969 in the following terms:

'We understand that it has been agreed subject to Contract that our Clients will
take a lease for a term of 51 years from Alec Lobb (Garages) Limited for a premium
of £35,000 and at a peppercorn rental and that our Clients will then lease-back the
premises for a term of 21 years at a basic rent of £2,250 per annum to your Client
Mr Alec Lobb, in his personal capacity. The transaction is to be conditional upon
the repayment to our Clients of all sums owing by your Client Alec Lobb (Garages)
Limited. We will prepare and submit a draft underlease for approval. If you would
also like us to prepare and submit a draft of the proposed Head Lease, please let us
know.'

Mr Rishworth accepted the invitation extended to him by that letter, and in due
course received drafts of both lease and underlease. The underlease was to be (i) in favour
of Mr Lobb personally, (ii) for a term of 21 years with mutual break provisions at the end
of the seventh and fourteenth years of the term, (iii) at an initial rent of £2,250 per
annum with upward only rent reviews at the end of the eighth and fifteenth years of the
term, (iv) with an exclusive petrol tie in favour of the defendants, and (v) with an absolute
prohibition on assignment. As part of the tie, the defendants were to have the right, at

any time, by six months' notice to determine the underlease if less than 170,000 gallons
a of petrol supplied by the defendants were sold in any year. In 1969 the actual gallonage
(achieved by the use of green shield stamps) was 230,000 gallons.

Mr Rishworth was concerned at the discrepancy between the term of the head lease
and that of the underlease. He foresaw problems over the 30-year gap. He understood
the reasons for the choice of 51 years for the lease term, but not for the choice of 21 years
for the underlease. It did not, however, occur to him to ask for a longer term, or for an
b option to renew. Instead, he asked the defendants' solicitors for confirmation that the
head lease would be surrendered on the expiry of the underlease. This was refused. Mr
Rishworth considered the effect of the Landlord and Tenant Act 1954 and concluded that
his clients were reasonably protected.

Mr Rishworth was also concerned about three other matters. (i) The break clauses.
Right from the start, Mr Rishworth asked for these to be deleted. The defendants refused.
c (ii) The absolute prohibition on assignment. Mr Rishworth attempted to negotiate a
modification, but this too was refused. (iii) The insistence on the underlease being
granted, not to the plaintiff company, but to Mr Lobb personally. This, coupled with the
absolute prohibition on assignment, was a matter of serious concern to Mr Rishworth.
Mr Lobb suffered from multiple sclerosis, and his life expectancy was poor. Mrs Lobb
was aged 68. Neither was likely to be alive throughout the whole term of the underlease.
d Mr Lobb had two sons, the elder, Geoffrey, being then 15; it was likely that one or both
would wish to take over the business in a few years' time.

Mr Rishworth asked for the underlease to be in the name of the plaintiff company.
The defendants' solicitors refused this request, explaining:

'It has been suggested that in a transaction of this nature the supply provisions
could be held by the Court to be invalid if the premises are leased to the person or
e company already in possession. We have therefore advised our clients that the lease-
back should be to a different person or company. We would be perfectly happy to
advise our clients to agree to the premises being leased to another limited company
which is a wholly owned subsidiary of Alec Lobb (Garages) Limited so long as Mr
Lobb acts as guarantor. We look forward to hearing further from you in due course.'

f
For some reason which he was unable to explain, Mr Rishworth did not take up this
suggestion. Instead, he asked for the underlease to be granted to Mr and Mrs Lobb
jointly, and this was agreed.

Mr Rishworth was frustrated by his failure to obtain any amendments to the draft
underlease, and he discussed his concern with Mr Young. At a long meeting with Mr
and Mrs Lobb at the garage on 10 July, Mr Rishworth reported on his lack of progress,
g and advised them not to proceed. He drew particular attention to the break clauses, and
to the absolute prohibition on assignment. Mr Lobb instructed him to proceed. Mr
Rishworth said in evidence that Mr Lobb understood very clearly that he was giving up
possession for 51 years and getting back (at best) possession for only 21 years. He had also
drawn Mr Lobb's attention to the rent review clause, and said that Mr Lobb understood
h the implications of this. But, he said, Mr Lobb took the view that he had no alternative.

Mr Young had supported his colleague. During this period he had spoken with Mr
Coles, and with Mr Lobb. He had told Mr Lobb forcefully that the transaction was a
foolish one, and that he should not go ahead with it. But, as Mr Young told me, Mr Lobb
was under pressure from the bank; he saw the transaction as the only way of getting the
bank off his back.

j Completion took place on 25 July 1969. At that date, a total of £24,334 14s 9d was
owing to the defendants. In addition, there was a sum of £406 16s 11d due in respect of
rent for the remainder of the current quarter under the underlease. This left a balance of
only £10,258 8s 4d due from the defendants on completion.

In order to allow the transaction to proceed, Mrs Lobb released her floating charge
without payment; but the bank required payment in full before releasing its second
mortgage; and this cost £7,000 or thereabouts. With its security discharged, the bank

withdrew the plaintiff company's overdraft facility, and insisted on the account being
maintained in credit for the future.

In rejecting Mr Rishworth's reasons for not proceeding with the transaction, Mr Lobb's
judgment was almost certainly sound. As a lawyer, Mr Rishworth was properly concerned
at the detailed provisions of the underlease, and the apparent precariousness of Mr Lobb's
position. But the defendants had no retail operation of their own; and Mr Lobb rightly
recognised that, provided he was a good tenant, he had nothing to fear from the break
clauses, or from the absolute prohibition on assignment. When the time came, there was
unlikely to be any objection to his sons taking over the business.

As a rescue operation, however, the transaction was not well designed. It was intended
to reduce the plaintiff company's outgoings by eliminating the need to repay instalments
of borrowed capital. But against this must be set the fact that the plaintiff company was
incurring a liability to pay an annual rent of £2,250 pa, representing a return of
approximately 6¼% on the premium of £35,000, and was using the premium to discharge
debts due to the defendants at lower rates of interest. Of the moneys owing to the
defendants on 25 July 1969 £5,849 4s 6d was interest-free, £5,729 3s 4d carried interest
at 4%, and £2,962 10s 0d carried interest at 5%. In addition the defendants required
payment of the balance of the moneys due for the hire of the underground pumps,
which cost only £1 a year. It is not at all clear why the defendants insisted on the
payment of this sum, which seems most unreasonable; it is probable that the question
was never considered by any employee of the defendants sufficiently senior to be able to
distinguish between payment of this sum and repayment of the other debts owing to the
defendants. If so, this was largely Mr Lobb's fault; he never consulted Mr Rishworth
about the matter or asked him to take it up with the defendants.

However that may be, it was plainly not in the interests of the plaintiff company to
repay these sums at a cost of 6¼% pa. I do not even know whether the company's
outgoings were reduced as a result of the transaction, or, if so, by how much, for no one
did the necessary calculations at the time.

The transaction also failed in its object of providing the plaintiff company with
adequate working capital. The bank required the overdraft to be repaid, and United
Dominions Trust Ltd insisted on repayment of £1,800 or so to bring the stocking loan
within its agreed limit. After these payments, the plaintiff company was probably left
with no more than £1,000. Three days after completion, Mr Lobb reported to Mr Story:
'Like all things they never work out as you plan and everyone has jumped in and
demanded their pound of flesh.' By December 1969 the plaintiff company was once
again short of money and its cheques were again being dishonoured.

Moreover, the transaction was extremely expensive: legal fees and disbursements came
to over £460, and there was still a liability to capital gains tax to come. The chargeable
gain was duly assessed in 1975; the tax payable was £6,674.

If Mr Lobb had sought and obtained comprehensive financial advice, it is most
unlikely that he would ever have agreed to the transaction. This is not because it was in
any way unfair or unreasonable, but because it did not offer an appropriate solution to
the plaintiff company's problems. It is difficult to believe that, had a full financial
appraisal been undertaken, some other means of relieving the company's chronic shortage
of working capital (as, for example, by a temporary moratorium on the repayments of
principal to the defendants) could not have been devised.

In 1971 Mr and Mrs Lobb found it necessary to apply for the defendants' consent
(which was granted) for the use of the underlease as security for a bank overdraft. On Mr
Lobb's instructions, Mr Rishworth took the opportunity to seek confirmation from the
defendants' solicitors that when the underlease expired the rent charged by the defendants
would be a peppercorn and not a commercial rent. Mr Rishworth added (as he had
indeed made very clear to Mr Lobb) that this was not his own understanding of the
matter. When pressed for details, Mr Rishworth wrote that his clients were adamant
that, at a meeting attended by Mr Story and Mr Ennis, a clear representation to this effect
had been made to them. Mr Story was consulted, and denied that any such representation

had been made. The defendants' solicitors reported this to Mr Rishworth, and reminded
a him that in the correspondence during July 1969 they had made it abundantly clear that
their clients would not agree to surrender the residue of their 51-year lease on the expiry
of the underlease. They pointed out that this attitude was inconsistent with any
understanding that the underlessees would be allowed to remain in occupation after the
end of the underlease without paying a full rack rent. Mr Lobb did not pursue the matter
further for the time being, and it has not formed the basis for any relief claimed in the
b present action.

In 1973, with the consent of the plaintiff company as head lessor, the defendants
converted the premises to a self-service station at a cost of £19,009. The rent under the
underlease was increased to £3,500. The defendants' object, clearly recorded in their
internal memoranda, was to 'obtain maximum sales from the increased potential and
have a competitive site for years to come'.

c The defendants, of course, would never have contemplated the expenditure of over
£19,000 on the site if they had realised that their lease would be challenged, and on their
behalf it was argued that in these circumstances it would now be unjust and inequitable
to set the lease aside. The plaintiffs sought to counter this argument by offering not only
to repay the premium of £35,000 but also to reimburse the defendants for their
expenditure on the site, with interest if necessary.

d In 1975 the plaintiff company duly received an assessment to capital gains tax on the
part disposal constituted by the granting of the lease, and Mr Lobb, reporting this to the
defendants, complained that he had been misled by them into thinking that, if a 51-year
term were granted, no tax at all would be payable. This was not, of course, correct.

On 22 July 1976 the plaintiffs' solicitors wrote to the defendants' solicitors, stating that
counsel's opinion had been taken, and that he had advised that the lease could be set aside
e on repayment of the premium. This was the first intimation to the defendants that the
plaintiffs might seek to challenge the validity of the lease and lease-back transaction.

The first rent review date fell due in July 1977 and shortly before this Mr Lobb wrote
to the defendants, claiming that the only reason for the grant of a 51-year lease was to
avoid paying tax, and that this had not proved successful. He repeated that he had been
told that only a peppercorn rent would be charged during the last 30 years, and he asked
f for the 30-year period to be deleted.

Counsel who appeared for the defendants denounced this as a 'try-on', prompted by
the imminence of the rent review date; but I do not accept this. I have no doubt that Mr
Lobb, whether from confusion of thought or from the defect of a selective memory,
sincerely though mistakenly believed that he had been misled, and that he suffered from
a genuine though unjustified sense of grievance as a result.

g In due course, Mr Poole, the defendants' regional retail manager of their eastern
region, saw Mr Lobb and reported on the situation to his superiors. Mr Lobb, he reported,
wanted to vary the underlease to include his two sons, who were both working in the
business; and he was concerned at the break clause in the fourteenth year, fearing that
the defendants might want to turn him out in order to obtain possession for their own
use. He was also extremely unhappy about the position when the underlease came to an
h end. On 20 July 1977, following a further meeting with Mr Lobb, the defendants agreed
(i) to add Mr Lobb's two sons as tenants under the underlease, and (ii) to confirm that the
defendants did not intend to exercise the break clause at the end of the fourteenth year
of the term in order to obtain possession of the site for their own use. In addition, the
defendants offered either (i) that the existing underlease should continue unchanged, but
with the rent increased to take account of the current rent review; the underlease would
i then expire on 24 July 1990, or (ii) that the existing underlease be surrendered and a new
underlease be granted for a term of 21 years commencing on the date on which the
existing underlease was surrendered, with small automatic yearly increases in rent, or
alternatively with periodic rent reviews every seven years. Such an underlease would
thus continue until 1998.

Unfortunately, this attempt to meet Mr Lobb's grievances was not accepted, and the

writ in the present action was issued on 11 June 1979. The relief claimed did not reflect
or relate, directly or indirectly, to any of the matters of which Mr Lobb had been   a
complaining. He had become progressively more disenchanted with the deal he had
made nearly ten years before. Hitherto, he had sought to improve its terms; now he
sought to set it aside altogether.

The plaintiffs' first contention was that the transaction, in form a lease and lease-back,
was in reality a mortgage, the lease having been granted to the defendants by way of
security only and in order to secure the repayment of the so-called premium of £35,000;   b
and they claimed the right to redeem. In his opening speech, however, counsel for the
plaintiffs conceded that the documents were not a sham, and that they recorded the
whole bargain between the parties. In the light of this concession, which in my judgment
was rightly made, the claim is hopeless. There was no understanding or arrangement
that the £35,000 should be repayable, whether as a matter of obligation or of right; the
defendants (as both Mr Story and Mr Backhouse told me) were unwilling to advance any   c
further money to the plaintiff company, and would not have been prepared to enter into
the transaction on this basis. Counsel for the plaintiffs pointed out that both Mr Lobb
and Mr Ennis used the language of borrowing and repayment, and that the whole object
of the transaction (from the point of view of the plaintiff company) was to raise money.
But loose and inaccurate talk cannot prevail over the true intentions of the parties,
objectively ascertained; while the defendants' object was not only to assist the plaintiff   d
company, but also to secure the outlet by acquiring a substantial proprietary interest in
the site. As counsel for the defendants pointed out, money can be raised in many different
ways, of which borrowing is only one. It was not the method adopted in this case.

The plaintiffs next contended that the transaction of lease and lease-back was obtained
by economic duress and should be set aside accordingly. This is a branch of the law which
is still developing in this country, but I accept that commercial pressure may constitute   e
duress and render a transaction voidable, provided that the pressure amounts to a coercion
of the will which vitiates consent: see Pao On v Lau Yiu [1979] 3 All ER 65, [1980] AC
614. Economic duress, however, is still a form of duress. A plaintiff who seeks to set
aside a transaction on the grounds of economic duress must therefore establish that he
entered into it unwillingly (not necessarily under protest, though the absence of protest
will be highly relevant), that he had no realistic alternative but to submit to the   f
defendant's demands, that his apparent consent was exacted from him by improper
pressure exerted by or on behalf of the defendant, and that he repudiated the transaction
as soon as the pressure was relaxed.

In my judgment, the plaintiffs have completely failed to establish such a case. It is
possible that Mr Lobb had no realistic alternative (though even this is doubtful); but he
certainly did not enter into the transaction under any compulsion on the part of the   g
defendants. He was under no pressure from them to accept their terms. The plaintiff
company was in great financial difficulties, but these were of its own making. It was
under considerable financial pressure, but this came from the bank and, to a lesser extent,
from United Dominions Trust Ltd, not from the defendants. The defendants drove a
hard bargain; their terms were offered virtually on a take-it-or-leave-it basis. But this
proceeded from their reluctance to enter into the transaction, which they did not consider   h
particularly attractive. Had Mr Lobb found some other means of solving his problems,
and broken off the discussions, Mr Story at least would have been delighted. If there was
any pressure to conclude the deal, it came from Mr Lobb and, indirectly, from his bank.
Nor was Mr Lobb under such compelling necessity that he was forced to submit to
whatever demands the defendants might choose to make; on the contrary, he was able to
and did, refuse their attempts to obtain the freehold.

Counsel for the plaintiffs insisted that pressure was exercised by the defendants; it was,   j
he said, the existence of the petrol tie, with its four years to run, which made it impossible
for Mr Lobb to seek help elsewhere, and put the plaintiff company at the mercy of the
defendants. But the defendants could not be required to release the plaintiff company
from its pre-existing contractual obligations, freely entered into without duress of any

kind, before entering into fresh dealings with the plaintiff company, on pain of having
a those fresh dealings vitiated by duress if they did not. It is not necessary to consider to
what extent, in order to constitute economic duress the pressure must be improper, but
it must, in my judgment, consist of something more than a refusal to waive performance
of an existing contractual obligation.

But even if (contrary to my view) the existence of the tie in the 1968 charge constituted
coercive pressure on the part of the defendants, the plaintiff company neither protested
b at the time nor took prompt action to repudiate the transaction of lease and lease-back
once the pressure was removed. The pre-existing tie disappeared, together with the 1968
charge, on completion; yet the plaintiff company, far from repudiating the transaction,
affirmed it. It spent the balance of the proceeds, over £10,000, on discharging debts due
to other creditors; and made no attempt to raise finance from other sources, such as
another oil company, to enable it to repay the premium and have the transaction set
c aside. Instead, it spent the next few years in attempting to renegotiate the deal; and
allowed seven years to pass before giving notice of, and ten years before bringing, its
claim to set the transaction aside. In my judgment, to set the transaction aside in those
circumstances on the ground of economic duress is out of the question.

The plaintiffs next submitted that the transaction of lease and lease-back was a harsh
and unconscionable bargain of a kind which a court of equity will not allow to stand. In
d such a case the court is concerned, not with the reality of the weaker party's consent, but
with the conduct of the stronger; for the word 'unconscionable' seems to relate both to
the terms of the bargain and to the behaviour of the stronger party. It is not enough to
show that the bargain was a hard or unreasonable one; it must be shown that 'one of the
parties to it has imposed the objectionable terms in a morally reprehensible manner, that
is to say, in a way which affects his conscience': see *Multiservice Bookbinding Ltd v Marden*
e [1978] 2 All ER 489 at 502, [1979] Ch 84 at 110 per Browne-Wilkinson J.

It is probably not possible to reconcile all the authorities, some of which are of great
antiquity, on this head of equitable relief, which came into greater prominence with the
repeal of the usury laws in the nineteenth century. But if the cases are examined, it will
be seen that three elements have almost invariably been present before the court has
interfered. First, one party has been at a serious disadvantage to the other, whether
f through poverty, or ignorance, or lack of advice, or otherwise, so that circumstances
existed of which unfair advantage could be taken: see, for example, *Blomley v Ryan* (1954)
99 CLR 362, where, to the knowledge of one party, the other was by reason of his
intoxication in no condition to negotiate intelligently. Second, this weakness of the one
party has been exploited by the other in some morally culpable manner: see, for example,
Clark v Malpas (1862) 4 De GF & J 401, 45 ER 1238, where a poor and illiterate man was
g induced to enter into a transaction of an unusual nature, without proper independent
advice, and in great haste. And third, the resulting transaction has been, not merely hard
or improvident, but overreaching and oppressive. Where there has been a sale at an
undervalue, the undervalue has almost always been substantial, so that it calls for an
explanation, and is in itself indicative of the presence of some fraud, undue influence, or
other such feature. In short, there must, in my judgment, be some impropriety, both in
h the conduct of the stronger party and in the terms of the transaction itself (though the
former may often be inferred from the latter in the absence of an innocent explanation)
which in the traditional phrase 'shocks the conscience of the court', and makes it against
equity and good conscience of the stronger party to retain the benefit of a transaction he
has unfairly obtained.

Counsel for the defendants frankly accepted that the first of these elements was
j present. The desperate financial position of the plaintiff company and of Mr and Mrs
Lobb, who faced not only the loss of their livelihood but personal bankruptcy if the
company failed, the pressure from the bank, and the existence of the petrol tie which
precluded recourse to other sources of finance, together resulted in a situation of which
unfair advantage could be taken by the defendants. But, he submitted, no such advantage
was taken.

I can find nothing whatever for criticism in the defendants' conduct. The plaintiff
company was advised throughout by its own solicitors and accountants, who were   a
completely independent of the defendants. The defendants were not to know that Mr
Lobb had not taken his advisers into his confidence, and had neither asked for nor
received comprehensive legal and financial advice. Mr Rishworth had written that he
was advising his clients 'generally in relation to their business', and there was no reason
for the defendants to disbelieve him. They did not press Mr Lobb for a quick decision;
there was no undue haste. On the contrary, it was Mr Lobb and his solicitors who urged   b
speed; the defendants were somewhat dilatory, though the delay was due in part to their
own internal administrative procedures. They were unenthusiastic; they did not regard
the deal as particularly favourable to them. They recognised the advantage of securing
the outlet; but they had had the site professionally valued, and were advised that they
were paying a realistic price. From first to last, there is not a trace, in any of their internal
memoranda, of any appreciation of the fact that they were getting a bargain. They had   c
no reason to believe, and I am satisfied that they did not believe, that they were acquiring
the site at an undervalue.

Nor were they. Garage premises are not difficult to value, and not surprisingly there
was a substantial measure of agreement between the two experienced valuers called as
expert witnesses by the parties. A Mr Baker gave evidence for the plaintiffs; Mr Berney,
who had carried out the original valuation in 1969, gave evidence for the defendants.   d
They agreed that since the site was subject to a tie with nearly four years to run, it was
the value of the tied site which was material. Mr Baker valued the freehold subject to the
tie at £50,000; Mr Berney supported his original valuation of £45,000. Both agreed that
the initial rent of £2,250 reserved by the underlease was significantly below the market
rent, and that this factor gave the underlease a capital value and reduced the value of the
lease. Mr Berney confirmed his original valuation; he put the value of the 51-year lease,   e
subject to the underlease, at between £35,000 and £40,000. Mr Baker valued it at
£35,000. On the plaintiffs' own expert's evidence, there was no undervalue.

Counsel for the plaintiffs, however, insisted that all this was irrelevant. As a matter of
law, he argued, the defendants were obliged to pay, not the value of the tied site, but the
full value of the site without the tie; and they had thus acquired it at a gross undervalue.
Mr Baker valued the freehold free of tie at £60,000, and the lease subject to the underlease   f
at £52,000. Mr Berney, who was the more careful witness and whose evidence I prefer,
thought these figures too high. He put the freehold value of the untied site at £50,000,
with a corresponding reduction in the value of the lease.

Counsel for the plaintiffs pointed out that if the defendants had chosen to enforce their
security by exercising their power of sale, they would have been obliged to account to
the plaintiff company for the price they would have received if they had sold the property   g
free from the tie; accordingly, he argued, if they were to pay a fair price for the equity of
redemption, they must offer to pay the untied value. The premise is correct; but I cannot
see why the conclusion follows. The two situations are completely different.

A mortgagee in possession is required to account, both in respect of the rents and
profits and in respect of the proceeds of sale, not only for what he has in fact received but
also for what he might by proper diligence have received. His right to sell the mortgaged   h
property, like his right to enter into possession, is given to him only for the purpose of
enabling him to recover the money secured thereon; and it is part of his contract with
the mortgagor that he should be diligent in doing so. He cannot depreciate the property
by maintaining against the purchaser the existence of a tie which he himself imposed as
part of the security; for he is selling the mortgaged property, not merely the mortgagor's
interest therein.   j

Moreover, such a tie will normally be co-extensive with the security; it cannot survive
redemption, or it may be open to challenge as a clog on the equity. In order to support a
tie, therefore, the mortgagor's right to redeem will usually be suspended during the
subsistence of the tie. A mortgagee who takes steps to enforce his security, however,
cannot at the same time refuse to accept an offer of redemption. By putting the property

up for sale, he thus voluntarily puts himself in a position where he is bound to accept
a redemption, and, with it, the ending of the tie.

None of this has any application where, as part of a separate and independent
transaction, the mortgagee acquires the mortgagor's equity of redemption. In such a
situation, the mortgagee is not enforcing his security, nor is he exercising a power
conferred on him by the mortgage. The subject matter of his purchase is not the
mortgaged property but the mortgagor's interest therein. The price payable is a matter
b for negotiation, not account; and there is no basis on which the mortgagee can be
required to pay more than the value of that interest, or more than the price which the
mortgagor could obtain from a sale of his interest to a third party. That price will
naturally reflect the existence of the tie. It will also, of course, take account of the amount
secured on the property, liability for which is undertaken by the purchaser; but the
transaction is not the equivalent of redemption, whether the purchaser is a third party or
c the mortgagee himself. Where the purchaser is the mortgagee, the mortgage debt and
the security come to an end by merger, not redemption.

Accordingly, on the evidence before me I find that there was no element of undervalue
in the present case. The defendants paid a fair price for what they bought.

The terms of the underlease, and in particular the mutual break clause and the absolute
prohibition on assignment, were strongly criticised by counsel for the plaintiffs, but I
d cannot find that they were unreasonable, let alone unconscionable. They were in the
standard form of lease which the defendants offered to prospective tenants, and I have no
reason to think that they were not generally acceptable to dealers. The defendants' refusal
to accept any amendment proceeded largely from their doubts, based on past experience,
that Mr and Mrs Lobb would prove to be good tenants; though I have no doubt that they
were also influenced by a natural reluctance to make a concession in one case lest it be
e taken as a precedent for others.

I have already described the defendants' insistence on being repaid a capital sum in
respect of the underground tanks as unreasonable; but this was inadvertent. It resulted
from a faulty analysis on the part of the defendants, and the sum involved was relatively
small. I cannot regard the defendants' insistence on being paid the sum in question as
oppressive; nor in any case would it justify setting aside the entire transaction of lease
f and lease-back (as distinct from the payment itself, as to which I have heard no argument).

Accordingly, I reject the plaintiffs' claim to set the lease and underlease aside as a harsh
and unconscionable bargain.

The plaintiffs next submitted that there was a fiduciary or confidential relationship
between the parties which was abused by the defendants. Counsel for the plaintiffs put
his case in two ways. First, he stressed the close relationship which naturally existed
g between the defendants and one of their own dealers, and pointed to the frequency of
the visits made by the local representative. The parties, he claimed, were partners in a
common enterprise. They shared a common interest in increasing the sales of petrol and
exploiting the maximum potential of the site. He relied on *Tufton v Sperni* [1952] 2 TLR
516 where the parties were co-operating in a charitable object, and it was said by Evershed
MR that in regard to matters related to their common objective, each necessarily reposed
h confidence in the other and each accordingly possessed that influence which naturally
grew out of the confidence (at 523).

That, however, was a very different case. As Jenkins LJ said of the defendant (at 531–
532):

> '... if he advised or proposed any course of action as calculated to further the
> [common] object, that advice or proposal should be given or made with a genuine
j >   and disinterested intention of furthering the [common] object and not, while
> ostensibly given or made with such intention, designed in reality to secure some
> personal advantage to himself.'

In the present case, the defendants' offer to acquire a proprietary interest in the site was
not related to any aspect of the parties' common enterprise, and was not put forward as

intended to further their common objectives. Mr Lobb was under no illusion whatever that in relation to the transaction of lease and lease-back he and the defendants had conflicting interests.

Second, counsel for the plaintiffs relied on *Lloyds Bank Ltd v Bundy* [1974] 3 All ER 757, [1975] QB 326. Mr Lobb had, he submitted, sought the defendants' help, and to the knowledge of the defendants, he relied on their advice. The defendants, he claimed, accepted a duty of fiduciary care towards him, and they did not discharge it.

In making this submission, counsel for the plaintiffs relied on a number of different matters. There were the terms of Mr Lobb's letter of 28 November 1968 and in particular the concluding sentence which began with the words: 'I would appreciate your advice on the alternatives as soon as possible.' It is, however, clear from the context that Mr Lobb was not asking for the defendants' advice as to what *he* should do, but for advice (in the sense of information) as to what they might be prepared to do. Then there was Mr Story's advice to Mr Lobb that, if he became a tenant, he would have to adhere strictly to the terms of his lease. But this was in the nature of a warning rather than advice; Mr Lobb went ahead in spite of it, not in reliance on it. Then there was Mr Story's promise to Mr Lobb to obtain from his employers the best deal he could get for him. But this did not constitute Mr Story an agent for Mr Lobb. At the most, it was a promise, faithfully discharged, that he would recommend the deal to his superiors, and that they would offer what they considered to be a fair price, coupled perhaps with a suggestion that there would be no point in Mr Lobb trying to improve the terms that he was offered. Finally, there was Mr Ennis's advice to Mrs Lobb that 'it would be better' to go for £35,000 as this would keep the rent down. But this was quite insufficient to impose a fiduciary duty on the defendants. Mr Ennis was a lowly employee, not authorised to conduct negotiations, and Mr Lobb cannot sensibly have relied on his advice as given on behalf of the defendants. Moreover, his remark was made informally to Mrs Lobb; there is no evidence that it was acted on by Mr Lobb; or that even Mr Ennis, let alone his superiors, realised that Mr Lobb was relying on his advice. I do not underestimate the degree of trust and confidence which Mr Lobb, as a loyal Total dealer, must have reposed in the defendants. I have no doubt that he trusted them to deal fairly with him, if only because their reputation and goodwill with other dealers would suffer if they did not. But this is very far from finding that he relied on their advice, or that they accepted a fiduciary duty of care towards him.

Even if a relationship of confidentiality existed, however, I am not prepared to find that it was abused. In *Lloyds Bank Ltd v Bundy* [1974] 3 All ER 757, [1975] QB 326 the duty would have been fully discharged if the bank had sent Mr Bundy to obtain independent advice. In the present case, Mr Lobb had independent advice from the outset. True, the defendants did not disclose the valuation they had received from Henry Berney & Co, and if this had shown their offer to be grossly inadequate, their failure to disclose it would no doubt have constituted a breach of any duty of fiduciary care which existed. The fact that Mr Lobb was in receipt of independent advice would in those circumstances have been 'of no consequence, once it is established that there was a concealment of a material fact, which the defendant was bound to disclose': see *Tate v Williamson* (1866) LR 2 Ch App 55 at 65 per Lord Chelmsford LC. There can, however, be no breach of duty in failing to disclose a valuation which supports the offer made.

The main way in which the plaintiffs put their case, however, was to contend that this was a transaction between a mortgagor and a mortgagee during the subsistence of the mortgage, and that as such it could not be allowed to stand unless positively shown to be in all respects fair and reasonable and beneficial to the mortgagor. Counsel for the plaintiffs submitted that a mortgagee cannot acquire the mortgaged property or any substantial interest therein from the mortgagor during the currency of the mortgage or by any agreement between them while the relationship of mortgagor and mortgagee subsists (otherwise than by foreclosure or by purchase at auction with the mortgagee bidding with the leave of the court) except at full market price and as a result of an arm's length bargain with the mortgagor being free from pressure of any kind. Counsel for

the plaintiffs submitted that the case was a fortiori where the mortgage contained a tie,
a so that the relationship was not only that of mortgagor and mortgagee but dealer and
sole supplier.

I cannot accept any of this. Counsel for the plaintiffs cited a large number of authorities,
but none of them supported his proposition, and I do not recognise the principle on
which it rests. Certainly the equity of redemption cannot be extinguished by any
covenant or agreement made *at the time of the mortgage and as part of the mortgage*
b *transaction* (see *Vernon v Bethell* (1762) 2 Eden 110 at 113, 28 ER 838 at 839; *Samuel v*
Jarrah Timber and Wood Paving Corp [1904] AC 323); but this does not prohibit the
mortgagee from purchasing the mortgagor's equity of redemption by a subsequent
transaction, separate from and independent of the mortgage. There was a conflict of
judicial opinion at the beginning of the nineteenth century, never finally resolved,
whether a dealing between mortgagor and mortgagee which left the mortgage on foot,
c such as the grant of a long lease to the mortgagee, should if impeached within a reasonable
time be set aside without proof of undervalue as a clog on the equity of redemption, or
whether it should be set aside only on evidence of oppression and undervalue (see *Gubbins*
v Creed (1804) 2 Sch & Lef 214; *Webb v Rorke* (1806) 2 Sch & Lef 661; and *Hickes v Cooke*
(1816) 4 Dow 16, 3 ER 1074, where the opposing views were expressed by Lord Redesdale
and Lord Eldon LC respectively). I do not have to resolve this ancient dispute: Lord
d Redesdale was careful in *Webb v Rorke* to distinguish the case where the mortgage was
discharged by the transaction, as on the sale and purchase of the equity of redemption;
the two cases, he pointed out, were totally different.

It has been repeatedly stated that the purchase of the equity of redemption by a
mortgagee will be jealously scrutinised by the court; but it is clear that there is no
inherent objection to it. The circumstance that the two parties are trustee and beneficiary
e does not affect any dealing with property which is not the subject of the trust.
Accordingly, in *Knight v Marjoribanks* (1849) 2 Mac & G 10, 42 ER 10, Lord Cottenham
LC held that the rule that a trustee cannot purchase from his cestui que trust does not
apply to the purchase of the equity of redemption by a mortgagee. Such a transaction, he
said, could be impeached only on grounds which would have been sufficient if it had
taken place in the ordinary manner between parties who were strangers to each other.

f In the development of the equitable jurisdiction to relieve against fraud and oppression,
there was a natural tendency to categorise cases by reference to the relationship between
the parties or the special situation of the weaker party. Thus equity frequently intervened
to protect the expectant heir, the reversioner, and the mortgagor. As the law has
progressed, however, it has become possible to analyse the basis of the court's jurisdiction
and the criteria for its exercise. It can now be seen that all those cases are merely particular
g examples of situations in which one party may be unfairly exploited by the other.

In my judgment there are no special rules applicable to the purchase of the equity of
redemption by a mortgagee. The only significance of the relationship of mortgagor and
mortgagee (or of tied dealer and sole supplier) is that it affords to the unscrupulous
mortgagee the opportunity to take an unfair advantage of the mortgagor. It is for this
reason that the court will scrutinise the transaction with care; but if it is to be set aside,
h whether for fraud or duress or as a harsh and unconscionable bargain, it can be set aside
only if circumstances exist which would enable a transaction to be impeached between
parties who were not mortgagor and mortgagee. The only relationship which requires
different and higher standards is a fiduciary or confidential relationship.

Accordingly, although counsel for the plaintiffs has properly urged on me every
consideration which could possibly be put forward on the plaintiffs' behalf, I conclude
j that no grounds exist for setting aside the lease and underlease; and it is unnecessary for
me to consider whether, if such grounds existed, the plaintiffs' claim (save in so far as it
is based on economic duress) would be barred by laches.

Lastly, the plaintiffs contended that the petrol tie in the underlease, which was to
continue for the whole duration of the underlease, was an unreasonable restraint of trade
and so void. In *Esso Petroleum Co Ltd v Harper's Garage (Stourport) Ltd* [1967] 1 All ER

699, [1968] AC 269 the House of Lords held that, in the absence of evidence to justify it, a tie of 21 years in a mortgage went beyond what was reasonable and was void. In the a present case, the defendants have not attempted to call evidence to justify the length of the tie; nor have they relied on the existence of the mutual break clause to argue that the tie was only for a period of seven years. Mr and Mrs Lobb could of course have freed themselves from the tie after the expiry of that period, but only by ridding themselves of the underlease and losing the right to trade altogether from the site.

Instead, the defendants have argued (i) that the doctrine of restraint of trade has no b application to a sale and lease-back, even where the lease-back is to the original owner, (ii) that it has no application, or alternatively that a tie (however long) is justifiable, where the restraint is imposed as a term of the rescue of an insolvent trader, and (iii) that in any event the doctrine has no application where the lease-back is not to the original owner but to a third party, however closely connected, having no previous right to trade from the site.

Before dealing with these contentions, I should observe that, following the Report of c the Monopolies Commission on the Supply of Petrol to Retailers in the United Kingdom published in July 1965 (HC Paper (1964–65) no 264) the Board of Trade made the Solus Petrol Order 1966, SI 1966/894, which laid down a maximum period for which solus petrol ties could be imposed. Subsequently, I have been told, the Board of Trade exacted undertakings from the oil companies in substantially similar terms. From the definitions d of 'company premises' in the order and undertakings, it seems that neither applies to land or premises owned or leased by the supplier. No argument however, was addressed to me on the scope of the order or undertakings; nor was it suggested by either counsel that, in considering the requirements of public policy, I should be guided by what the Board of Trade considered to be appropriate. I therefore approach the questions I have to decide, as I was invited by both counsel to do, uninfluenced by the scope or contents of e the 1966 order or undertakings.

In order that the defendants' submissions can be understood, it is necessary to refer at greater length to the decision of the House of Lords in the Harper case [1967] 1 All ER 699, [1968] AC 269. The House held (i) that the ordinary negative covenants preventing the use of a particular site for trading were not within the doctrine of restraint of trade, because a person buying or leasing a particular piece of land had no previous right to f trade there and, when he took possession subject to a negative covenant, he gave up no freedom which he had previously possessed, but (ii) that the agreements in that case (where the tie was contained in a mortgage) were within the scope of the doctrine of restraint of trade since the appellants were giving up their previous right to sell other petrol. Lord Reid said ([1967] 1 All ER 699 at 707–708, [1968] AC 269 at 298):

> 'It is true that it would be an innovation to hold that ordinary negative covenants g preventing the use of a particular site for trading of all kinds or of a particular kind are within the scope of the doctrine of restraint of trade. I do not think they are. Restraint of trade appears to me to imply that a man contracts to give up some freedom which otherwise he would have had. A person buying or leasing land had no previous right to be there at all, let alone to trade there, and, when he takes possession of that land subject to a negative restrictive covenant, he gives up no right h or freedom which he previously had ... In the present case the respondents, before they made this agreement, were entitled to use this land in any lawful way that they chose, and by making this agreement they agreed to restrict their right by giving up their right to sell there petrol not supplied by the appellants.'

Lord Morris said ([1967] 1 All ER 699 at 714, [1968] AC 269 at 309): j

> 'There is a considerable difference between the covenants in the present case and covenants of the kind which might be entered into by a purchaser or by a lessee. If one who seeks to take a lease of land knows that the only lease which is available to him is a lease with a restriction, then he must either take what is offered (on the appropriate financial terms) or he must seek a lease elsewhere. No feature of public

policy requires that, if he freely contracted, he should be excused from honouring
his contract. In no rational sense could it be said that, if he took a lease with a
restriction as to trading, he was entering into a contract that interfered with the free
exercise of his trade or his business or with his "individual liberty of action in
trading". His freedom to pursue his trade or earn his living is not impaired merely
because there is some land belonging to someone else on which he cannot enter for
the purposes of his trade or business. In such a situation (ie, that of voluntarily
taking a lease of land with a restrictive covenant) it would not seem sensible to
regard the doctrine of restraint of trade as having application. There would be
nothing which could be described as interference with individual liberty of action
in trading. There is a clear difference between the case where someone fetters his
future by parting with a freedom which he possesses, and the case where someone
seeks to claim a greater freedom than that which he possesses or has arranged to
acquire. So, also, if someone seeks to buy a part of the land of a vendor and can only
buy on the terms that he will covenant with the vendor not to put the land to some
particular use, there would seem in principle to be no reason why the contract
should not be honoured.'

Lord Hodson said ([1967] 1 All ER 699 at 719, [1968] AC 269 at 316–317):

'My lords, I do not think that it is possible to accept this general proposition. All
dealings with land are not in the same category; the purchaser of land who promises
not to deal with the land he buys in a particular way is not derogating from any
right he has, but is acquiring a new right by virtue of his purchase. The same
consideration may apply to a lessee who accepts restraints on his use of land; on the
other hand, if you subject yourself to restrictions as to the use to be made of your
own land so that you can no longer do what you were doing before, you are
restraining trade and there is no reason why the doctrine should not apply.'

I should add he went on to say: 'It is difficult to devise a formula relating to land which
covers all cases in which the doctrine should be excluded.'

Lord Pearce said ([1967] 1 All ER 699 at 724–725, [1968] AC 269 at 325):

'It seems clear that covenants restraining the use of the land imposed as a condition
of any sale or lease to the covenantor (or his successors) should not be unenforceable.
It would be intolerable if, when a man chooses of his own free will to buy, or take a
tenancy of, land which is made subject to a tie (doing so on terms more favourable
to himself owing to the existence of the tie) he can then repudiate the tie while
retaining the benefit. I do not accept the argument of counsel for the respondents
that such transactions are subject to the doctrine, but will never as a matter of fact
be held unreasonable. In my view, they are not subject to the doctrine at all.
Certainly public policy gives little justification for their subjection to it. This view
would accord with the brewers' cases in which (after an earlier unfavourable protest
by Lord Ellenborough, C. J., in Cooper v. Twibill ((1812) 3 Comp 286n, 170 ER
1384n) the law has, for many years past, been firmly settled in allowing covenants
tying the publican (as lessee or purchaser) to a particular brewer (e.g. Clegg v. Hands
((1890) 44 Ch D 503)). In one case, however, in 1869 . . . a perpetual tie on a sale of
land was subjected to scrutiny and was held to be reasonable; but to allow a
permanent tie is not very different from holding it exempt from scrutiny. It may
be, however, that when a man fetters with a restraint land which he already owns
or occupies, the fetter comes within the scrutiny of the court.'

It is thus a precondition of the application of the doctrine of restraint of trade that the
covenantor should be giving up some freedom to trade which he previously enjoyed and
which, but for the covenant, he would continue to enjoy. More than one of their
Lordships, however, warned that it was difficult to devise a satisfactory formula which
would cover all cases where the doctrine should be extended, or to define its limits on
any satisfactory basis.

The plaintiff company was not, of course, free to trade as it liked from the site in July
1969; it was subject to an existing tie with 3½ years to run. The underlease, however, *a*
extended the tie to 21 years, and it was common ground between counsel that for present
purposes an owner subject to an existing tie of relatively short duration gives up a
freedom to trade if he agrees to a substantial extension of the period of the tie.

Counsel for the defendants conceded that the doctrine applies to a lease and lease-back
to the original covenantor where the lease-back is for the whole term of the lease less the
last few days, so that the covenantee's reversion is purely nominal. He felt constrained to *b*
make this concession by the decisions of the Court of Appeal in *Cleveland Petroleum Co
Ltd v Dartstone Ltd* [1969] 1 All ER 201, [1969] 1 WLR 116 and the Privy Council in
Amoco Australia Pty Ltd v Rocca Bros Motor Engineering Co Pty Ltd [1975] 1 All ER 968,
[1975] AC 561. In such cases, counsel for the defendants claimed, the lease and lease-back
are merely a facade to support the tie. Where, however, the covenantee acquires a
substantial reversion, the situation is entirely different. In the present case, he pointed *c*
out, the plaintiff company lost all right to trade from the site for 51 years, together with
the right to possession, when it granted the lease; and this the law allowed. In the scintilla
temporis between the execution of the lease by the plaintiff company and the execution
of the underlease by the defendants, the plaintiff company enjoyed no freedom to trade
from the site. By entering into the underlease immediately thereafter, the covenantors
gave up no existing freedom, but acquired a new, though limited, right to trade. It *d*
would, counsel for the defendants forcefully submitted, be absurd to suppose that public
policy, which viewed with equanimity the right of the covenantor to enter into the lease
and thereby deprive the covenantor of all right to trade from the site for 51 years, should
cavil at the underlease, which restored to the covenantor a limited right to trade from
the site for 21 years.

I have found these arguments attractive, but I cannot accept them. Where there is a *e*
substantial reversion on the lease-back, it may well be impossible to describe the lease
and lease-back as merely a facade to support a tie; but it does not follow that, where the
reversion is purely nominal, the transaction is a mere facade. A lease at a premium and a
lease-back for the same period less only a few days at a rack rent, without any tie, is a
recognisable commercial transaction serving a recognisable commercial purpose; it is a
means of raising money. Even where a tie is incorporated, the purpose of the transaction *f*
may not be the same for both parties; the object of one party may be to obtain the tie,
while the object of the other may be to raise finance. To ask which object is predominant
is meaningless. So the distinction which counsel for the defendants seeks to draw is
hardly a satisfactory one. Moreover, it does not cure the alleged absurdity of which he
complains, but merely replaces it with another. Given that, on the authorities and by
concession, it is contrary to public policy for a landowner to include a tie in a lease and *g*
lease-back for 21 years, it is not easy to understand on what principle of public policy he
should be allowed to do so provided only that he goes further and also parts with a
substantial interest in the land thereafter.

But there is, I think, a more fundamental objection. In my judgment it cannot be
right for present purposes to separate the lease and underlease in this way; they were
merely the component elements of a single transaction. I observe that Lord Morris *h*
refused to separate such elements in the *Harper* case [1967] 1 All ER 699 at 717, [1968]
AC 269 at 314, where he stated that 'the solus agreement, the loan agreement and the
mortgage can be linked together as incidents of one transaction'.

Arguments based on the scintilla temporis between the execution of the lease and the
execution of the underlease may be appropriate where what is in issue is the priority of
competing proprietary interests, for in such cases the chronological order in which they *j*
were created or clothed with the legal estate is often decisive. But in my view such
arguments are out of place where what is in issue is the application of a doctrine of public
policy to contractual obligations. Had the transaction of lease and underlease been
preceded by a binding contract between the parties, counsel for the defendants' argument
could not have been advanced. It cannot make any difference, for present purposes, that

the transaction was preceded, not by a binding contract, but by an agreement subject to
a contract.

I have considered whether, treating a lease and lease-back as a single transaction, a
slightly different distinction may be drawn, applying the doctrine of restraint of trade to
a transaction of lease and lease-back which is merely a vehicle for the inclusion of the tie,
but not to one which can be regarded as a sensible commercial transaction apart from the
tie. I have come to the conclusion that the approach is not open to me. As I shall explain
b later, the *Amoco* case [1975] 1 All ER 968, [1975] AC 561 was of the former kind, and
may be distinguished from the present on this ground; but the *Cleveland* case [1969] 1
All ER 201, [1969] 1 WLR 116 was of the latter kind and cannot be so distinguished.
Furthermore, where the tie is included in a mortgage to secure the repayment of a
substantial advance of capital, as in the *Harper* case [1967] 1 All ER 699, [1968] AC 269
itself, the transaction is almost inevitably a sensible commercial transaction and not a
c mere vehicle for the inclusion of the tie; yet the doctrine applies. It cannot be right to
adopt one test where the money is raised by way of mortgage and another where it is
raised by way of lease and lease-back.

Accordingly, in my judgment, a lease for 51 years subject to a lease-back for 21 years
to the covenantor coupled with a tie for the duration of the lease-back must be treated as
a single transaction whereby the covenantor gives up his existing freedom to trade,
d partially for the first 21 years and wholly for the last 30; and the doctrine of restraint of
trade is applicable to the tie. I cannot accept counsel for the defendants' argument that
the result is absurd, for what he calls an absurdity seems to me to be inherent in the
approach of the House of Lords in the *Harper* case. Granted the premise, by which I am
bound, I am compelled to conclude that an estate owner is free to deprive himself
altogether of the right to trade from his land, forever or for a limited period, by parting
e with the land; but he is not free to retain his land or present interest in it and at the same
time unduly restrict his right to trade from it.

Counsel for the defendants next submitted that, on the very special facts of the present
case, either the doctrine of restraint of trade did not apply or the imposition of the tie
was not contrary to public policy. As I have pointed out, it is a precondition of the
application of the doctrine that the covenantor should give up some freedom to trade
f which he previously enjoyed and which, but for the covenant, he would continue to
enjoy. In the present case, the plaintiff company was insolvent. Without the financial
assistance provided by the defendants, there was no realistic prospect, in July 1969, that
the plaintiff company would continue in business for any length of time, and certainly
not for the 3½ years until the existing tie expired. If public policy required that the
plaintiff company be permitted to trade from the site freely and without restriction, that
g option was not available. The freedom of trade which was given up by the plaintiff
company and the Lobbs (who faced bankruptcy if the company failed) was illusory; the
limited right to trade which they acquired under the underlease was real. So, it was said,
the relevant precondition for the application of the doctrine was not present. More
attractively, counsel for the defendants argued that this was a case in which there were
competing public interests; and that the transaction was for the benefit of Mr and Mrs
h Lobb, and for the public benefit as well, since it enabled them to avoid the loss of their
livelihood and eventual bankruptcy.

There is certainly an important public interest in the rescue and rehabilitation of ailing
but viable businesses, and the law should be slow to place obstacles in the way of those
who attempt such rescues. But the price exacted must be one which the law permits.
The defendants' arguments were decisively rejected by Lord Macmillan in *Vancouver*
j *Malt and Sake Brewing Co Ltd v Vancouver Breweries Ltd* [1934] AC 181 at 191–192, [1934]
All ER Rep 38 at 42:

'Nor did it help the respondents . . . to argue that the contract was to their benefit
and even to the public benefit by enabling them to avoid closing down or insolvency.
The receipt of a sum of money can generally be shown to be advantageous to a

business man, but his liberty to trade is not an asset which the law will permit him
to barter for money except in special circumstances and within well recognized   a
limitations.'

I cannot accept the suggestion that insolvency is a 'special circumstance' for this purpose.
Quite apart from the fact that Lord Macmillan evidently had it in mind, if a man's liberty
to trade is not an asset which the law will permit him to barter for money, it cannot
become so merely because he is in debt and has nothing else to sell.   b

Accordingly, I conclude that if the underlease had been granted to the plaintiff
company, it would have been subject to the doctrine of restraint of trade and the tie,
being for 21 years, would have been unreasonable. Does it make any difference that the
underlease was granted, not to the plaintiff company, but to Mr and Mrs Lobb?

The facts are that this was done at the insistence of the defendants, and for the sole
purpose of avoiding the application of the doctrine of restraint of trade to the underlease. c
Mr and Mrs Lobb did not want the underlease to be in their names; on their behalf Mr
Rishworth expressly asked for it to be granted to the plaintiff company. The defendants
refused this request, but they made it clear that they did not care who should take the
underlease provided that (i) it was not the plaintiff company, (ii) if it was a subsidiary of
the plaintiff company, Mr Lobb should guarantee the rent and covenants, (iii) there
should be continuity in the management of the business. From first to last, it was   d
understood by all concerned that Mr and Mrs Lobb would continue to carry on the
management of the business: to enable them to do so was an important object of the
transaction, and for them the whole object. After 1969 the plaintiff company continued
to carry on the business much as before, though now as a licensee of Mr and Mrs Lobb,
and in the name of 'Alec Lobb Garages' (without the 'Ltd') so that the defendants were
unaware that the business was still owned by the company.   e

In these circumstances, counsel for the defendants conceded that the change of
ownership was a stratagem to validate the tie; but, he submitted, I am bound by the
decision of the Court of Appeal in *Cleveland Petroleum Co Ltd v Dartstone Ltd* [1969] 1 All
ER 201, [1969] 1 WLR 116 to hold that the stratagem was effective. In that case, a Mr
Sainsbury, who owned the freehold of garage premises, granted a lease to an oil company
of the entire site for 25 years in return for a premium, and the oil company granted an   f
underlease of the premises for 25 years less three days at a rack rent to a company called
County Oak Service Station Ltd, in which Mr Sainsbury was the predominant shareholder.
The underlease contained a petrol tie. The transaction took place in 1960, eight years
before the decision of the House of Lords in the *Harper* case [1967] 1 All ER 699, [1968]
AC 269. The underlease was subsequently assigned, and was ultimately assigned to
Dartstone Ltd, which entered into a direct covenant with the oil company to observe the   g
covenants (including the tie) in the underlease. The question was whether the tie could
be challenged as an unreasonable restraint of trade. There was, of course, an easy answer
to this; for, whatever may have been the position before the assignment, Dartstone Ltd
was plainly bound by the tie. It was acquiring leasehold premises from which it had no
previous right to trade; it was giving up no freedom to trade which it previously enjoyed;
and the doctrine of restraint of trade could have no application to the covenants into   h
which it freely entered.

But all three members of the court went further. They held that County Oak Service
Station Ltd had also been bound originally by the covenants in the underlease. They
drew a distinction between Mr Sainsbury and his company. Lord Denning MR and
Salmon LJ decided the case on the ground that there was no evidence that the company
had been running the business before the underlease was granted; Russell LJ on the   j
ground that, even if it was, it had no sufficient interest in the premises to entitle it to a
claim that it had a right to do so.

The appeal was an interlocutory one, and the arguments of counsel are not recorded.
Nevertheless, it seems most unlikely that the present point was considered. It seems to
have been assumed that Mr Sainsbury could not be identified with his company. The
report of the case does not contain any explanation for the fact that the underlease was

granted to the company and not to Mr Sainsbury; for all I know, this may have been
a done at Mr Sainsbury's request. But, as Salmon LJ pointed out, in view of the dates it
cannot have been a mere device for validating the tie; and the Lord Justice expressly kept
open for further consideration the question whether such a device would be effective.

Curiously, a close examination of the facts in the *Harper* case discloses that the opposite
assumption was made in that case. The premises were originally owned by Mr and Mrs
Harper. In 1959 they formed the company Harper's Garage (Stourport) Ltd. In July 1962
b Esso granted the company a loan to buy the premises from Mr and Mrs Harper and
improve them. The company acquired the premises, mortgaged them to Esso to secure
repayment of the loan, and entered into a petrol tie. Mr and Mrs Harper may thus have
been fettering an existing right to trade, but their company was not; it had no previous
right to trade from the land. So either Mr and Mrs Harper and their company were
assumed without argument to be one and the same, or the decision must have gone the
c other way.

In this state of the authorities, I consider that I am free to reach my own conclusion.
Counsel for the defendants insisted that a company is a legal person, separate and distinct
from its shareholders and that the corporate veil should not be pierced unless it was a
sham, or the interests of justice required it. I do not find such arguments helpful. In the
first place, it is not really a question of piercing the corporate veil: the same problem
d would arise where the original owner was a married man and the lease-back was made to
his wife. In the second place, counsel for the defendants was compelled to acknowledge
that the corporate veil might be pierced not only where the interests of justice, but also
where the interests of the public required it. But this is merely to state the problem, not
solve it; the whole question is whether the public interest requires the original owner
and the covenantor to be identified in a situation like the present.

e I have not found this an easy question. I have difficulty in discerning the particular
feature of public policy which allows a 21-year tie to be included in a lease to anyone else,
but not in a lease-back to the original estate owner; or which allows an estate owner to
part with all right to trade from his land by disposing of his land, but not to part with
the one while retaining the other. As a result, I have a similar difficulty in understanding
why the public interest should require the plaintiff company to part altogether with its
f land and business and deny Mr and Mrs Lobb the harmless subterfuge by which they
were able to retain their livelihood. But it seems to me all these consequences are inherent
in the approach of the majority of their Lordships in the *Harper* case. Given that the
doctrine of restraint of trade applies to a sale and lease-back to the original estate owner,
its application cannot in my judgment be circumvented by a transparent device adopted
for the purpose. Public policy is concerned with matters of substance and reality; and the
g substance and reality of the present transaction was that the plaintiff company raised
finance on its land, but by a lease and lease-back rather than by a mortgage; and that the
business continued to be carried on by and for the benefit of the same persons as before.
The ownership of the site passed from the company to Mr and Mrs Lobb; but the tie was
not imposed in the course of the change of ownership; the change of ownership was
effected in order to bolster the tie. In these circumstances, I conclude that the doctrine of
h restraint of trade applies to this underlease, with the result that the tie is invalid.

Counsel for the plaintiffs contended that the invalidity of the tie infected the whole
transaction, so that neither the lease nor the underlease could stand. This is a startling
proposition which I have no hesitation in rejecting. The invalidity of one contractual
obligation which is contrary to public policy does not nullify the whole contract, for the
valid obligations may be severed and enforced: see *Wallis v Day* (1837) 2 M & W 273,
j 150 ER 759. It is otherwise where the invalid obligation forms the whole of the
consideration, as in *Vancouver Malt and Sake Brewing Co Ltd v Vancouver Breweries Ltd*
[1934] AC 181, [1934] All ER Rep 38, or where the deletion of the invalid obligation
'alters entirely the scope and intention of the agreement' so that what is left is no longer
'a reasonable arrangement between the parties' or an 'intelligible economic transaction in
itself': see the various formulations referred to by Lord Cross in *Amoco Australia Pty Ltd v
Rocca Bros Motor Engineering Co Pty Ltd* [1975] 1 All ER 968 at 977, [1975] AC 561 at 578.

In my judgment, the tie is clearly severable from the underlease. Counsel for the plaintiffs pressed me strongly with the decision in the *Amoco* case, where the opposite **a** conclusion was reached, but that was concerned with a very different transaction. There the oil company spent a substantial sum in installing pumps and other equipment; and thereupon the dealer leased the site to the oil company for 15 years at a yearly rent of £1 plus (in effect) a petrol rebate, and took a lease-back of the site for 15 years less one day at a yearly rent of £1. The lease and lease-back were merely a facade for the inclusion of the tie, which was the true consideration for the expenditure by the oil company. Shorn of **b** the tie, the lease and lease-back were unintelligible and the transaction as a whole made no commercial sense.

That is not the case here. The securing of the outlet was a major object of the defendants in entering into the transaction, but it was not their only object; while even without the tie the lease at a premium and lease-back at a rack rent still constitute a recognisable and commercially intelligible transaction. **c**

On this footing it was common ground that the following provisions of the underlease must be struck out: cl 2 (15) (bunkering); cl 3 and the second schedule (the petrol tie); cl 5(4) (the defendants' right to break if insufficient of their petrol sold); cl 6 (records and accounts).

This, however, did not satisfy counsel for the plaintiffs. He submitted that, in addition, the following clauses in the underlease formed part of the tie and should be struck out: **d** cl 2(9) (the absolute prohibition on assignment); cl 2(10) (the covenant against change of user); cl 2(16) (the defendants' right to enter and effect improvements); cl 2(17) (the covenant against change of name); cl 5(3) (the mutual break clause).

I do not agree that any of these is invalid. In my view, the court should strike out no more than is strictly necessary to satisfy the requirements of public policy and to leave what remains intelligible. An absolute prohibition on assignment, such as is found in **e** cl 2(9), is a feature of many a lease which contains no tie and has no connection with the tie. It is plainly valid. The covenant against change of user in cl 2(10) is in itself a restraint of trade, but a normal and reasonable one. It is purely negative and has no necessary connection with the tie. The site was adapted for use as a garage and service station and possessed inherent goodwill as such. The defendants, as reversioners, were legitimately entitled to insist that the user be retained and that the goodwill be preserved for their **f** own benefit on the expiry of the term. The clause is valid. The same applies to cl 2(16), which is not in terms related to improvements considered desirable by the defendants as suppliers of petrol and must in the absence of a tie be treated as referring to improvements bona fide considered desirable by them as reversioners. Clause 2(17) is of negligible importance, and neither party addressed me on it. I think it must remain. The mutual break clause in cl 5(3) is of major importance, but it has no connection with the tie. In **g** this respect it is to be contrasted with the break clause in cl 5(4). Indeed counsel for the plaintiffs did not seek to argue that the whole of cl 5(3) should be struck out, but only that the words 'Total or' should be deleted. This cannot be right.

Accordingly, I propose to declare that cll 2(15), 3, 5(4), 6 and the whole of the second schedule of the underlease are void as an unreasonable restraint of trade. Subject thereto, I shall declare that the lease and the remainder of the underlease are valid and enforceable **h** and take effect according to their tenor.

Declaration accordingly.

Solicitors: *Kenwright & Cox*, agents for *Young & Co*, Braintree (for the plaintiffs); *Denton Hall & Burgin* (for the defendants).

Hazel Hartman   Barrister.

Kealey v Heard

a

QUEEN'S BENCH DIVISION

MANN J

7, 8, 9 DECEMBER 1982

b Building – Working places – Contractor – Regulations imposing duty on contractors to ensure safety of working places – Whether owner of property employing specialist tradesmen to work on his property a 'contractor' – Construction (Working Places) Regulations 1966, reg 3.

Negligence – Duty to take care – Extent of duty to contractor – Equipment provided for contractor – Duty to exercise care and control over equipment – Property owner providing scaffolding for contractor – Property owner not superintending scaffolding – Property owner relying on responsible tradesmen to erect scaffolding – Scaffolding having hazard created by unknown person – Planks on scaffolding collapsing under contractor's weight – Contractor injured in subsequent fall – Res ipsa loquitur – Whether property owner discharging duty of care owed to contractor.

c

d In 1978 the defendant purchased two adjoining properties for the purpose of converting them into flats. Rather than engage a building contractor to effect the conversions he employed specialist tradesmen individually and employed the plaintiff, a self-employed plasterer, under that arrangement. On 6 March 1979 the plaintiff arrived at the properties to find that scaffolding had been erected by another specialist tradesman for the plaintiff's use. Planks which had been placed on the scaffolding by an unknown workman collapsed e when the plaintiff walked on them, causing him to fall to the ground and suffer injuries. The plaintiff brought an action for damages, contending (i) that the defendant had been in breach of the statutory duties imposed on contractors in relation to the safety of working places by reg 3[a] of the Construction (Working Places) Regulations 1966, and (ii) that although the plaintiff could not prove who had positioned the planks on the scaffolding, thereby creating the hazard, the defendant was nevertheless liable in f negligence under the principle of res ipsa loquitur. The defendant denied liability, contending (i) that he was not a 'contractor' within the meaning of reg 3 so that the regulations did not apply to him, (ii) that, although he had not provided any superintendence of the scaffolding, he had employed responsible tradesmen to erect it and had not himself been negligent, and (iii) that in any event the plaintiff had been contributorily negligent.

g **Held** – (1) The defendant was not a 'contractor' within the meaning of reg 3(1) of the 1966 regulations since that term referred to a person who himself undertook building operations whereas the defendant had merely hired independent contractors who had undertaken the building operations. It followed that the plaintiff could not succeed with a claim based on a breach by the defendant of the statutory duties imposed on contractors by the 1966 regulations (see p 976 a to d, post).

h (2) The defendant was liable in negligence under the principle of res ipsa loquitur since by not providing superintendence of the scaffolding he had failed to discharge the duty he owed to the plaintiff to exercise proper care and control over the building appliances on his property and therefore he could not rebut the inference that the plaintiff's injuries resulted from a breach of that duty (see p 976 g to j, post); dictum of Bigham J in Marney v Scott [1899] 1 QB at 989–990 applied.

j (3) The plaintiff had not been contributorily negligent since on the facts there was nothing in the appearance of the scaffolding to put him on inquiry as to its dangers. There would accordingly be judgment for the plaintiff (see p 976 j to p 977 b and e, post).

---

a   Regulation 3, so far as material, is set out at p 975 j, post

Notes

For the duty of an occupier, see 34 Halsbury's Laws (4th edn) para 21, and for cases on   *a*
the subject, see 36(1) Digest (Reissue) 75–79, 299–309.

For the Construction (Working Places) Regulations 1966, reg 3, see 8 Halsbury's
Statutory Instruments (3rd reissue) 306.

Cases referred to in judgment

Marney v Scott [1899] 1 QB 986, 36(1) Digest (Reissue) 82, 324.   *b*
Wheeler v Copas [1981] 3 All ER 405.

Action

By a writ issued on 7 August 1979 the plaintiff, Augustus William Kealey, claimed
damages in negligence and for breach of statutory duty against the defendant, Anthony
R Heard, for personal injury and loss of earnings resulting from a fall from scaffolding   *c*
suffered by the plaintiff while employed by the defendant at the defendant's premises.
The facts are set out in the judgment.

Ivan Krolick for the plaintiff.
H John Leslie for the defendant.

d

Cur adv vult

9 December. The following judgment was delivered.

MANN J. In this action the plaintiff claims damages for personal injuries sustained on 6   *e*
March 1979. The plaintiff's date of birth was 2 October 1927. He was, and is, a self-
employed plastering contractor.

There is no dispute that on 6 March 1979 the plaintiff sustained an injury. It is
described in the agreed medical reports. The latest and agreed medical opinion is dated 6
November 1979 and is:

> 'This man sustained a fracture of the glenoid bone of the scapula with minimal   *f*
> displacement of the surface of the joint, bruising of the right lower ribs and bruising
> of his thigh as a result of the accident. He has made an excellent recovery from the
> effect of these injuries and has no disability relating to the thigh or lower ribs. The
> right shoulder is similarly comfortable apart from a mild aching pain after a lot of
> overhead work. I would not expect him to have any significant disability in the
> future. There is a slight irregularity in the joint surface of the glenoid but as the   *g*
> shoulder is a dependent joint arthritic changes of any significance may not be
> anticipated.'

It appears that the injury was not serious and recovery has been excellent.

The background to the case is as follows. In 1978 the defendant purchased a pair of
semi-derelict houses known as 5–7 Lansdowne Place, Hove. He desired to rehabilitate   *h*
them. The original intention was that the rehabilitated premises should be used as a
nursing home. The subsequent intention was that the rehabilitation should take the
form of a conversion into flat units. This intention was effected and the flats were
demised on a leasehold basis. This small piece of property development was not effected
by using a building contractor in the ordinary sense. For sensible reasons of economy the
defendant employed specialist tradesmen individually. One such was the plaintiff,   *j*
another such was Scaffolding GB Ltd (SGB), which erected the requisite scaffolding.
Boards were moved about on that scaffolding in order to accommodate the needs of the
moment. The defendant told his specialist tradesmen what he wanted done to the
premises but he did not tell them how to do it. The roles of the employer and the
architect under a conventional building contract were, in him, combined..

The plaintiff first worked for the defendant at 5–7 Lansdowne Place in December

1978. Thereafter there was an interval before he returned to work at the premises at a
date in early 1979 which I cannot determine. At all events, by 6 March 1979 he had
returned to the site. Of that day the plaintiff told me four things. (1) There was a labourer
working on the site who was not employed by him but who was experienced as a
bricklayer's labourer. (2) He was told by the defendant to work on the rendering at the
rear outside of nos 5–7 and was told 'his [ie the defendant's] labourer would knock-up
the sand and cement and get the scaffold ready'. (3) He worked first on no 5 and then
went on to no 7. Here I should explain that at the rear of each house there is a sunken
courtyard into which basement french windows give access. The plaintiff says he was
concerned to work around the windows on the ground floor, above the courtyard. This
he could not do without use of the scaffold which had been erected by SGB. (4) He went
to no 7 and found the scaffold fully sheeted (ie with planks already in position) at ground
floor level. Who actually sheeted it is not known and the name and status of the labourer
are likewise unknown. The plaintiff further told me that he worked first on the ground
floor right, at no 7, then stepped across to the ground floor left. When he so stepped onto
the boards they caved in and he fell to the floor of the courtyard.

The plaintiff suggests that the circumstances of the caving in of the boards were as
follows. Adjacent to the ground floor left wall were six planks, in pairs of three, parallel
to the wall. The pair of three nearest to the french windows were supported on two
transoms. The pair of three furthest from the french windows was supported at one end
by the edge of the courtyard and at the other they rested on their three companions.
One, or perhaps two, of the three was additionally supported by a putlock. The
arrangement effected a trap which the plaintiff suggested he sprang when he stepped on
the one or two boards supported only by two of the other three boards, that is the three
boards nearest the french windows. Having sprung the trap he fell through it.

If the plaintiff is to be believed there was a trap and whoever laid it was guilty of an act
of great folly.

The defendant on the other hand denies any such conversation or instruction such as
the plaintiff alleges occurred on 6 March and said he cannot recollect the presence of any
labourer at that time. The defendant plainly had no direct knowledge of the state of the
scaffold boards either before or after the accident. The movement of the boards about the
scaffolding he regarded as the responsibility of the tradesmen concerned.

Where there is a conflict of evidence I unhesitatingly prefer the plaintiff's version of
events. He appeared to me to have a direct and positive recollection of those events. The
defendant was quite unquestionably honest but he was constantly searching his
recollection, a word used many times, and more than once pleaded that we were going
back three years. I do not believe that the defendant attached any importance to the
incident at the time. Indeed, he told me that he did not look at the scaffolding until
maybe two or three days after the accident. In my judgment he was seeking to put
matters together at a very late stage when his recollection of what occurred had become
unreliable.

I thus accept the plaintiff's version of events except in one particular. I do not feel able
to attach any weight or importance to the possessive pronoun 'his' which the plaintiff
said the defendant employed when he referred to the labourer. As I have said, the identity
and status of the labourer are quite unknown.

What then, having accepted the plaintiff's account as I have indicated, is the position
in law? His case was pleaded as breach of statutory duty and negligence. The breach of
statutory duty asserts breaches of the Construction (Working Places) Regulations 1966,
SI 1966/94. Under r 2 of those regulations they apply, so far as material, to building
operations undertaken by way of trade or business. That is the application. Those who
are obliged to comply with the regulations are described in r 3 as being as follows:

> 'It shall be the duty of every contractor, and every employer of workmen, who is
> undertaking any of the operations or works to which these Regulations apply . . . to
> comply with . . .'

and there are then specified certain regulations.

It is conceded that if there was on the defendant an obligation under the regulations then there was a breach of at least regs 11 and 25(2) and (4). The critical question *a* therefore is: was there an obligation under the regulations? The defendant was not an employer of workmen. He employed the people he did as independent contractors. That was of the essence of his modus operandi. The question therefore is: is he obliged as a contractor? No, said the defendant, 'contractor' means building contractor. It must be so, he said, otherwise a mere houseowner who engaged a builder to improve his premises would be subjected to obligations under the regulations. *b*

There is, so far as the researches of counsel go, no authority on the meaning of the word 'contractor'. The matter may be of some importance because I believe the defendant's method of operation is now an increasingly common practice. It may at once be observed that the word 'contractor' is not in fact prefaced by the word 'building'. Taking the word 'contractor' alone and applying to it its ordinary meaning, the defendant was a contractor: he had contracts with his tradesmen. I see no reason to avoid the *c* ordinary meaning of the word 'contractor' and hence the question is: was he a contractor undertaking any of the operations to which the regulations apply? That is to say, so far as material, building operations. In my judgment he was not. He was not undertaking building operations; he was hiring independent contractors to undertake building operations. I therefore conclude that the obligations under the regulations do not apply to a person who is operating in the way in which the defendant was in this case. If I be *d* wrong in my construction I have already indicated that a breach of regulation was conceded. So far as fault or contributory negligence is concerned, I shall deal with that later.

The alternative head of claim is in negligence, and reliance is placed on the judgment of Bigham J in *Marney v Scott* [1899] 1 QB 986 at 989–990, where he said:

'I think that a man who intends that others shall come upon property of which *e* he is the occupier for purposes of work or business in which he is interested, owes a duty to those who do so come to use reasonable care to see that the property and the appliances upon it which it is intended shall be used in the work are fit for the purpose to which they are to be put, and he does not discharge this duty by merely contracting with competent people to do the work for him.' *f*

The greater part of that passage was quoted with approval by Chapman J in *Wheeler v Copas* [1981] 3 All ER 405 at 408.

The duty of care is not, as I understood the defendant's case, disputed. The question is: was it broken? If I had been satisfied that the labourer was an employee of the defendant and that he had sheeted the scaffold prior to the plaintiff's appearance on it there would, of course, be no difficulty; there would be a plain case of vicarious liability. That is not *g* the case. The plaintiff relies on the proposition encapsulated in the phrase res ipsa loquitur. He says, and I agree, that traps on scaffolding do not happen if those who have the control of it exercise proper care. He further says, and I agree, the defendant has given no explanation how the accident came to occur. It remains therefore to consider whether the defendant has shown that there was no lack of care on his part. Of course the attention which a person such as the defendant has to show must depend on the *h* circumstances of each case, but here the defendant frankly admitted that he did nothing. His attitude was that he employed a responsible contractor to put up the scaffolding and thereafter the changing of the boards from lift to lift, or place to place, was the concern of his tradespeople and not him. In my judgment that attitude is not good enough. If a person chooses to build by the method selected by the defendant then ought he to provide at least some form of superintendence either by himself or by another in order *j* that his common law duty may be discharged. I conclude that there is a breach of duty owed at common law.

The next question is: was the plaintiff at fault? In my judgment he was not. He says when he arrived at no 7 the boards were laid out in an orderly fashion and he told me in terms that there was nothing which was apparent which would have put him on inquiry as to the existence of a trap. He is an experienced man and I accept what he said. I

a therefore find neither fault nor contributory negligence. I should add that such allegations as were made as to fault or contributory negligence in the pleadings bore little if any resemblance to the suggestions which were put before me.

There remains the question of damages. The accident was a shock no doubt, but the plaintiff was able to drive home shortly thereafter. The actual injury made it not possible for him to work for four months. There was initially some aching pain, but by 21 May

b 1979 the orthopaedic surgeon was able to say: 'The aching pain is becoming less marked with his everyday activities. Initially he got a lot of pain at night but this is also beginning to improve.' He has made an excellent recovery although his arm did ache for about one month after returning to work. He told me his home life was not affected to any real degree by the accident although for a while he could not play with his young grandchildren. His hospital attendances were as an out-patient.

c In the circumstances, for the pain, initial shock and temporary disability I think an award of £550 is appropriate for general damages. The plaintiff was off work for a period which can, I think, reasonably be rounded to four months. Had the accident not occurred then I think it most likely that he would have continued to work for the defendant, who thought him a good workman and who praised his work. I cannot be confident that there would have been employment for him throughout the four months at the premises

d of the defendant and I cannot be confident that he would have found other employment for the balance of the period. Plasterers, I am told, sometimes pass a week or two without work. Making allowance for my lack of confidence in these two regards I think a period of 15 weeks would be appropriate. So far as earnings are concerned I take the plaintiff's figure of £90 per week as what he was getting from the defendant. Multiplied by 15 we get £1,350, less tax at 30%, gives us £945, less half of the statutory benefits, gives us

e £595. There will therefore be judgment for the plaintiff for £550 general damages and £595 special damages.

Judgment for the plaintiff accordingly.

Solicitors: *Turner Peacock*, agents for *Edward Harte & Co,* Brighton (for the plaintiff); *Neale Godfree*, Brighton (for the defendant).

K Mydeen Esq   Barrister.

R v Miller

HOUSE OF LORDS
LORD DIPLOCK, LORD KEITH OF KINKEL, LORD BRIDGE OF HARWICH, LORD BRANDON OF
OAKBROOK AND LORD BRIGHTMAN
16 FEBRUARY, 17 MARCH 1983

*Criminal law – Damage to property – Arson – Actus reus – Coincidence of actus reus and mens
rea – Accused accidentally starting fire – Accused later having opportunity to put out fire –
Accused failing to do so – Property damaged as a result – Whether omission of accused to act
sufficient actus reus – Whether coincidence of actus reus and mens rea – Criminal Damage Act
1971, s 1(1)(3).*

The actus reus of the offence of arson, contrary to s 1(1) and (3)^aof the Criminal Damage
Act 1971, is present if the defendant accidentally starts a fire and thereafter, intending to
destroy or damage property belonging to another or being reckless whether any such
property would be destroyed or damaged, fails to take any steps to extinguish the fire or
prevent damage to such property by that fire (see p 981 *d* to *f*, p 982 *f* to *j*, and p 983 *j* to
p 984 *b*, post).

Dictum of Stephen J in *R v Tolson* [1886–90] All ER Rep at 36–37 applied.

R v Caldwell [1981] 1 All ER 961 distinguished.

Observations on the direction to the jury in cases alleging arson, contrary to s 1(1) of
the 1971 Act, where the accused was initially unaware that he had done an act that in
fact set in train events which, by the time he became aware of them, would make it
obvious to anyone who gave his mind to them that they presented a risk that property
belonging to another would be damaged (see p 983 *g* to p 984 *b*, post).

Observations on the desirability of avoiding the use of the phrases 'actus reus' and
'mens rea' to refer to the conduct of an accused and his state of mind at the time of that
conduct (see p 979 *h* to p 980 *b*, p 981 *d* and p 983 *j* to p 984 *b*, post).

Decision of the Court of Appeal [1982] 2 All ER 386 affirmed.

Notes

For the offence of destroying or damaging property, see 11 Halsbury's Laws (4th edn)
para 1306, and for cases on the subject, see 15 Digest (Reissue) 1439–1440, 12,690–
12,693.

For the Criminal Damage Act 1971, s 1, see 41 Halsbury's Statutes (3rd edn) 409.

Cases referred to in opinions

Fagan v Metropolitan Police Comr [1968] 3 All ER 442, [1969] 1 QB 439, [1968] 3 WLR
1120, DC, 15 Digest (Reissue) 1175, 9992.

R v Caldwell [1981] 1 All ER 961, [1982] AC 341, [1981] 2 WLR 509, HL.

R v Lawrence [1981] 1 All ER 974, [1982] AC 510, [1982] 1 WLR 524, HL.

R v Tolson (1889) 23 QBD 168, [1886–90] All ER Rep 26, CCR, 15 Digest (Reissue) 1028,
8922.

Sweet v Parsley [1969] 1 All ER 347, [1970] AC 132, [1969] 2 WLR 470, HL, 15 Digest
(Reissue) 1084, 9179.

Appeal

On 26 June 1981 in the Crown Court at Leicester before Mr Recorder Matthewman QC
and a jury the appellant, James Miller, was convicted of arson, contrary to s 1(1) and (3)
of the Criminal Damage Act 1971, and sentenced to six months' imprisonment. He
appealed to the Court of Appeal, Criminal Division (Ackner, May LJJ and Stocker J)
([1982] 2 All ER 386, [1982] QB 532), which dismissed his appeal on 3 March 1982 but
granted leave to appeal to the House of Lords and certified, under s 33(2) of the Criminal

---

a   Section 1, so far as material, is set out at p 980 *d e*, post

Appeal Act 1968, that the following point of law of general public importance was
a involved in its decision: whether the actus reus of the offence of arson was present when
a defendant accidentally started a fire and thereafter, intending to destroy or damage
property belonging to another or being reckless whether any such property would be
destroyed or damaged, failed to take any steps to extinguish the fire or prevent damage
to such property by that fire. The facts are set out in the opinion of Lord Diplock.

b *John Gorman QC* and *Patrick Thomas* for the appellant.
Anthony Palmer QC and *David McCarthy* for the Crown.

Their Lordships took time for consideration.

17th March. The following opinions were delivered.

c **LORD DIPLOCK.** My Lords, the facts which give rise to this appeal are sufficiently
narrated in the written statement made to the police by the appellant Miller. That
statement, subject to two minor orthographical corrections, reads:

'Last night I went out for a few drinks and at closing time I went back to the
house where I have been kipping for a couple of weeks. I went upstairs into the
back bedroom where I've been sleeping. I lay on my mattress and lit a cigarette. I
d must have fell to sleep because I woke up to find the mattress on fire. I just got up
and went into the next room and went back to sleep. Then the next thing I
remember was the police and fire people arriving. I hadn't got anything to put the
fire out with so I just left it.'

He was charged on indictment with the offence of 'arson contrary to section 1(1) and
e (3) of the Criminal Damage Act, 1971'; the particulars of offence were that he—

'on a date unknown between the 13th and 16th days of August 1980, without
lawful excuse damaged by fire a house known as No. 9 Grantham Road, Sparkbrook,
intending to do damage to such property or recklessly as to whether such property
would be damaged.'

f He was tried in the Crown Court at Leicester before a recorder and a jury. He did not
give evidence, and the facts as set out in his statement were not disputed. He was found
guilty and sentenced to six months' imprisonment.
From his conviction he appealed to the Court of Appeal on the ground, which is one
of law alone, that the undisputed facts did not disclose any offence under s 1 of the
Criminal Damage Act 1971. The appeal was dismissed (see [1982] 2 All ER 386, [1982]
g QB 532), but leave to appeal to your Lordships' House was granted by the Court of
Appeal, which certified that the following question of law of general public importance
was involved:

'Whether the actus reus of the offence of arson is present when a Defendant
accidentally starts a fire and thereafter, intending to destroy or damage property
belonging to another or being reckless as to whether any such property would be
h destroyed or damaged, fails to take any steps to extinguish the fire or prevent
damage to such property by that fire?'

The question speaks of 'actus reus'. This expression is derived from Coke's brocard (3
Co Inst ch 1, fo 10), 'Actus non facit reum, nisi mens sit rea,' by converting incorrectly
into an adjective the word reus which was there used correctly in the accusative case as a
j noun. As long ago as 1889 in *R v Tolson* 23 QBD 168 at 185–187, [1886–90] All ER Rep
26 at 36–37 Stephen J when dealing with a statutory offence, as are your Lordships in the
instant case, condemned the phrase as likely to mislead, though his criticism in that case
was primarily directed to the use of the expression 'mens rea'. In the instant case, as the
argument before this House has in my view demonstrated, it is the use of the expression
'actus reus' that is liable to mislead, since it suggests that some positive act on the part of

the accused is needed to make him guilty of a crime and that a failure or omission to act is insufficient to give rise to criminal liability unless some express provision in the statute that creates the offence so provides.

My Lords, it would I think be conducive to clarity of analysis of the ingredients of a crime that is created by statute, as are the great majority of criminal offences today, if we were to avoid bad Latin and instead to think and speak (as did Stephen J in those parts of his judgment in *R v Tolson* to which I referred at greater length in *Sweet v Parsley* [1969] 1 All ER 347 at 361, [1970] AC 132 at 162–163) about the conduct of the accused and his state of mind at the time of that conduct, instead of speaking of actus reus and mens rea.

The question before your Lordships in this appeal is one that is confined to the true construction of the words used in particular provisions in a particular statute, viz s 1(1) and (3) of the Criminal Damage Act 1971. Those particular provisions will fall to be construed in the light of general principles of English criminal law so well established that it is the practice of parliamentary draftsmen to leave them unexpressed in criminal statutes, on the confident assumption that a court of law will treat those principles as intended by Parliament to be applicable to the particular offence unless expressly modified or excluded. But this does not mean that your Lordships are doing any more than construing the particular statutory provisions. These I now set out:

'(1) A person who without lawful excuse destroys or damages any property belonging to another intending to destroy or damage any such property or being reckless as to whether any such property would be destroyed or damaged shall be guilty of an offence . . .
(3) An offence committed under this section by destroying or damaging property by fire shall be charged as arson.'

This definition of arson makes it a 'result-crime' in the classification adopted by Professor Gordon in his work *The Criminal Law of Scotland* (2nd edn, 1978). The crime is not complete unless and until the conduct of the accused has caused property belonging to another to be destroyed or damaged.

In the instant case property belonging to another, the house, was damaged; it was not destroyed. So in the interest of brevity it will be convenient to refer to damage to property and omit reference to destruction. I should also mention, in parenthesis, that in this appeal your Lordships are concerned only with the completed crime of arson, not with related inchoate offences such as attempt or conspiracy to destroy or damage property belonging to another, to which somewhat different considerations will apply. Nor does this appeal raise any question of 'lawful excuse'. None was suggested.

The first question to be answered where a completed crime of arson is charged is: did a physical act of the accused start the fire which spread and damaged property belonging to another (or did his act cause an existing fire, which he had not started but which would otherwise have burnt itself out harmlessly, to spread and damage property belonging to another)? I have added the words in brackets for completeness. They do not arise in the instant case; in cases where they do, the accused, for the purposes of the analysis which follows, may be regarded as having started a fresh fire.

The first question is a pure question of causation; it is one of fact to be decided by the jury in a trial on indictment. It should be answered No if, in relation to the fire during the period starting immediately before its ignition and ending with its extinction, the role of the accused was at no time more than that of a passive bystander. In such a case the subsequent questions to which I shall be turning would not arise. The conduct of the parabolical priest and Levite on the road to Jericho may have been indeed deplorable, but English law has not so far developed to the stage of treating it as criminal; and if it ever were to do so there would be difficulties in defining what should be the limits of the offence.

If, on the other hand the question, which I now confine to: 'Did a physical act of the accused start the fire which spread and damaged property belonging to another?', is answered 'Yes', as it was by the jury in the instant case, then for the purpose of the further

questions the answers to which are determinative of his guilt of the offence of arson, the
a conduct of the accused, throughout the period from immediately before the moment of
ignition to the completion of the damage to the property by the fire, is relevant; so is his
state of mind throughout that period.

Since arson is a result-crime the period may be considerable, and during it the conduct
of the accused that is causative of the result may consist not only of his doing physical
acts which cause the fire to start or spread but also of his failing to take measures that lie
b within his power to counteract the danger that he has himself created. And if his conduct,
active or passive, varies in the course of the period, so may his state of mind at the time
of each piece of conduct. If, at the time of any particular piece of conduct by the accused
that is causative of the result, the state of mind that actuates his conduct falls within the
description of one or other of the states of mind that are made a necessary ingredient of
the offence of arson by s 1(1) of the Criminal Damage Act 1971 (ie intending to damage
c property belonging to another or being reckless whether such property would be
damaged), I know of no principle of English criminal law that would prevent his being
guilty of the offence created by that subsection. Likewise I see no rational ground for
excluding from conduct capable of giving rise to criminal liability conduct which consists
of failing to take measures that lie within one's power to counteract a danger that one has
oneself created, if at the time of such conduct one's state of mind is such as constitutes a
d necessary ingredient of the offence. I venture to think that the habit of lawyers to talk of
'actus reus', suggestive as it is of action rather than inaction, is responsible for any
erroneous notion that failure to act cannot give rise to criminal liability in English law.

No one has been bold enough to suggest that if, in the instant case, the accused had
been aware at the time that he dropped the cigarette that it would probably set fire to his
mattress and yet had taken no steps to extinguish it he would not have been guilty of the
e offence of arson, since he would have damaged property of another being reckless
whether any such property would be damaged.

I cannot see any good reason why, so far as liability under criminal law is concerned, it
should matter at what point of time after the resultant damage is complete a person
becomes aware that he has done a physical act which, whether or not he appreciated that
it would at the time when he did it, does in fact create a risk that property of another will
f be damaged, provided that, at the moment of awareness, it lies within his power to take
steps, either himself or by calling for the assistance of the fire brigade if this be necessary,
to prevent or minimise the damage to the property at risk.

Let me take first the case of the person who has thrown away a lighted cigarette
expecting it to go out harmlessly, but later becomes aware that, although he did not
intend it to do so, it has, in the event, caused some inflammable material to smoulder
g and that unless the smouldering is extinguished promptly, an act that the person who
dropped the cigarette could perform without danger to himself or difficulty, the
inflammable material will be likely to burst into flames and damage some other person's
property. The person who dropped the cigarette deliberately refrains from doing
anything to extinguish the smouldering. His reason for so refraining is that he intends
that the risk which his own act had originally created, though it was only subsequently
h that he became aware of this, should fructify in actual damage to that other person's
property; and what he so intends in fact occurs. There can be no sensible reason why he
should not be guilty of arson. If he would be guilty of arson, having appreciated the risk
of damage at the very moment of dropping the lighted cigarette, it would be quite
irrational that he should not be guilty if he first appreciated the risk at some later point in
time but when it was still possible for him to take steps to prevent or minimise the
j damage.

In that example the state of mind involved was that described in the definition of the
statutory offence as 'intending' to damage property belonging to another. This state of
mind necessarily connotes an appreciation by the accused that the situation that he has
by his own act created involves the risk that property belonging to another will be
damaged. This is not necessarily so with the other state of mind, described in the

definition of the statutory offence as 'being reckless as to whether any such property would be damaged'. To this other state of mind I now turn; it is the state of mind which is directly involved in the instant case. Where the state of mind relied on by the prosecution is that of 'intending', the risk of damage to property belonging to another created by the physical act of the accused need not be such as would be obvious to anyone who took the trouble to give his mind to it; but the accused himself cannot form the intention that it should fructify in actual damage unless he himself recognises the existence of some risk of this happening. In contrast to this, where the state of mind relied on is 'being reckless', the risk created by the physical act of the accused that property belonging to another would be damaged must be one that would be obvious to anyone who had given his mind to it at whatever is the relevant time for determining whether the state of mind of the accused fitted the description 'being reckless whether such property would be damaged': see *R v Caldwell* [1981] 1 All ER 961 at 965, [1982] AC 341 at 352; see also *R v Lawrence* [1981] 1 All ER 974 at 982, [1982] AC 510 at 526 for a similar requirement in the mental element in the statutory offence of reckless driving.

In *R v Caldwell* this House was concerned with what was treated throughout as being a single act of the accused, viz starting a fire in the ground floor room of a residential hotel which caused some damage to it; although, if closer analysis of his conduct, as distinct from his state of mind, had been relevant, what he did must have been recognised as consisting of a series of successive acts. Throughout that sequence of acts, however, the state of mind of Caldwell remained unchanged, his acknowledged intention was to damage the hotel and to revenge himself on its owner, and he pleaded guilty to an offence under s 1(1) of the 1971 Act; the question at issue in the appeal was whether in carrying out this avowed intention he was reckless whether the life of another would be thereby endangered, so as to make him guilty also of the more serious offence under s 1(2). This House did not have to consider the case of an accused who, although he becomes aware that, as the result of an initial act of his own, events have occurred that present an obvious risk that property belonging to another will be damaged, only becomes aware of this at some time after he has done the initial act. So the precise language suggested in *R v Caldwell* as appropriate in summing up to a jury in the ordinary run of cases under s 1(1) of the 1971 Act requires some slight adaptation to make it applicable to the particular and unusual facts of the instant case.

My Lords, just as in the first example that I took the fact that the accused's intent to damage the property of another was not formed until, as a result of his initial act in dropping the cigarette, events had occurred which presented a risk that another person's property would be damaged ought not under any sensible system of law to absolve him from criminal liability, so too in a case where the relevant state of mind is not intent but recklessness I see no reason in common sense and justice why mutatis mutandis a similar principle should not apply to impose criminal liability on him. If in the former case he is criminally liable because he refrains from taking steps that are open to him to try to prevent or minimise the damage caused by the risk he has himself created and he so refrains because he intends such damage to occur, so in the latter case, when as a result of his own initial act in dropping the cigarette events have occurred which would have made it obvious to anyone who troubled to give his mind to them that they presented a risk that another person's property would be damaged, he should likewise be criminally liable if he refrains from taking steps that lie within his power to try and prevent the damage caused by the risk that he himself has created, and so refrains either because he has not given any thought to the possibility of there being any such risk or because, although he has recognised that there was some risk involved, he has none the less decided to take that risk.

My Lords, in the instant case the prosecution did not rely on the state of mind of the accused as being reckless during that part of his conduct that consisted of his lighting and smoking a cigarette while lying on his mattress and falling asleep without extinguishing it. So the jury were not invited to make any finding as to this. What the prosecution did rely on as being reckless was his state of mind during that part of his conduct after he awoke to find that he had set his mattress on fire and that it was smouldering, but did a   not then take any steps either to try to extinguish it himself or to send for the fire brigade, but simply went into the other room to resume his slumbers, leaving the fire from the already smouldering mattress to spread and to damage that part of the house in which the mattress was.

The recorder, in his lucid summing up to the jury (they took 22 minutes only to reach their verdict), told them that the accused, having by his own act started a fire in the mattress which, when he became aware of its existence, presented an obvious risk of

b   damaging the house, became under a duty to take some action to put it out. The Court of Appeal upheld the conviction, but its ratio decidendi appears to be somewhat different from that of the recorder. As I understand the judgment, in effect it treats the whole course of conduct of the accused, from the moment at which he fell asleep and dropped the cigarette onto the mattress until the time the damage to the house by fire was complete, as a continuous act of the accused, and holds that it is sufficient to constitute

c   the statutory offence of arson if at any stage in that course of conduct the state of mind of the accused, when he fails to try to prevent or minimise the damage which will result from his initial act, although it lies within his power to do so, is that of being reckless whether property belonging to another would be damaged.

My Lords, these alternative ways of analysing the legal theory that justifies a decision which has received nothing but commendation for its accord with common sense and

d   justice have, since the publication of the judgment of the Court of Appeal in the instant case, provoked academic controversy. Each theory has distinguished support. Professor J C Smith espouses the 'duty theory' (see [1982] Crim LR 526 at 528); Professor Glanville Williams who, after the decision of the Divisional Court in *Fagan v Metropolitan Police Comr* [1968] 3 All ER 442, [1969] 1 QB 439 appears to have been attracted by the duty theory, now prefers that of the continuous act (see [1982] Crim LR 773). When applied

e   to cases where a person has unknowingly done an act which sets in train events that, when he becomes aware of them, present an obvious risk that property belonging to another will be damaged, both theories lead to an identical result; and, since what your Lordships are concerned with is to give guidance to trial judges in their task of summing up to juries, I would for this purpose adopt the duty theory as being the easier to explain to a jury; though I would commend the use of the word 'responsibility', rather than

f   'duty' which is more appropriate to civil than to criminal law since it suggests an obligation owed to another person, ie the person to whom the endangered property belongs, whereas a criminal statute defines combinations of conduct and state of mind which render a person liable to punishment by the state itself.

While, in the general run of cases of destruction or damage to property belonging to another by fire (or other means) where the prosecution relies on the recklessness of the

g   accused, the direction recommended by this House in *R v Caldwell* is appropriate, in the exceptional case (which is most likely to be one of arson and of which the instant appeal affords a striking example), where the accused is initially unaware that he has done an act that in fact sets in train events which, by the time the accused becomes aware of them, would make it obvious to anyone who troubled to give his mind to them that they present a risk that property belonging to another would be damaged, a suitable direction

h   to the jury would be that the accused is guilty of the offence under s 1(1) of the 1971 Act if, when he does become aware that the events in question have happened as a result of his own act, he does not try to prevent or reduce the risk of damage by his own efforts or if necessary by sending for help from the fire brigade and the reason why he does not is either because he has not given any thought to the possibility of there being any such risk or because having recognised that there was some risk involved he has decided not

j   to try to prevent or reduce it.

So, while deprecating the use of the expression 'actus reus' in the certified question, I would answer that question Yes and would dismiss the appeal.

LORD KEITH OF KINKEL. My Lords, for the reasons given in the speech of my noble and learned friend Lord Diplock which I have had the benefit of reading in draft and with which I agree, I too would dismiss this appeal.

LORD BRIDGE OF HARWICH. My Lords, for the reasons given by my noble and learned friend Lord Diplock I would dismiss this appeal.

LORD BRANDON OF OAKBROOK. My Lords, I have had the advantage of reading in draft the speech prepared by my noble and learned friend Lord Diplock. I agree with it, and for the reasons which he gives I would answer the certified question Yes and dismiss the appeal.

LORD BRIGHTMAN. My Lords, I would dismiss this appeal for the reasons given by my noble and learned friend Lord Diplock.

Appeal dismissed. Certified question answered in the affirmative.

Solicitors: *Lee Bolton & Lee*, agents for *Michael T Purcell & Co*, Birmingham (for the appellant): *Sharpe Pritchard & Co*, agents for *Ian S Manson*, Birmingham (for the Crown).

Mary Rose Plummer　Barrister.

Clayton v Chief Constable of Norfolk
and another appeal

HOUSE OF LORDS

LORD FRASER OF TULLYBELTON, LORD EDMUND-DAVIES, LORD SCARMAN, LORD ROSKILL AND LORD TEMPLEMAN

16 FEBRUARY, 17 MARCH 1983

Magistrates – Information – Hearing two or more together – Consent of defendant – Separate informations against one or more defendants – Connected facts – Whether court having power to hear informations together without consent of defendants.

Where a defendant is charged on several informations or where two or more defendants are charged on separate informations and in each case the facts are connected the informations may, if the magistrates think fit, be heard and determined together. However, before allowing a joint trial the magistrates should seek the consent of both the prosecution and the defence to the adoption of such a course. If consent from either side is not forthcoming the magistrates should then consider the rival submissions and any necessary advice from their clerk before ruling as they think fit in the overall interests of justice. In particular, the absence of the defendant's consent should not be treated as an automatic bar to a joint trial, and if the defendant's consent is not forthcoming, either by reason of an express refusal or because the defendant is absent or not represented, the magistrates should seek the views of the prosecution and if necessary the advice of their clerk before ruling as they think fit in the overall interests of justice, provided, however, that a joint trial should not be ordered if it would not be fair and just to the defendant (see p 985 e to g, p 989 e g h, p 990 h and p 992 a to j, post).

R v Assim [1966] 2 All ER 881 applied.

Notes

For the scope of informations, see 29 Halsbury's Laws (4th edn) para 318, and for cases on the subject, see 33 Digest (Reissue) 165, 1281–1285.

Cases referred to in opinions

Aldus v Watson [1973] 2 All ER 1018, [1973] QB 902, [1973] 2 WLR 1007, DC, 33 Digest (Reissue) 165, 1283.

Brangwynne v Evans [1962] 1 All ER 446, [1962] 1 WLR 267, DC, 33 Digest (Reissue) 165, 1284.

Edwards v Jones [1947] 1 All ER 830, [1947] KB 659, DC, 33 Digest (Reissue) 116, 743.
Lawrence v Same [1968] 1 All ER 1191, [1968] 2 QB 93, [1968] 2 WLR 1062, DC.
R v Ashbourne Justices, ex p Naden (1950) 48 LGR 268, DC.
R v Assim [1966] 2 All ER 881, [1966] 2 QB 249, [1966] 3 WLR 55, CCA, 14(1) Digest (Reissue) 292, 2232.
R v Camberwell Green Justices, ex p Christie [1978] 2 All ER 377, [1978] 2 QB 602, [1978] 2 WLR 794, DC, Digest (Cont Vol E) 134, 1581a.

Consolidated appeals

The Chief Constable of Norfolk appealed with leave of the Appeal Committee of the House of Lords granted on 9 December 1982 against the decision of the Divisional Court of the Queen's Bench Division (Griffiths LJ and Forbes J) on 25 June 1982 allowing applications by the respondents, Terence Edward Clayton and Eileen Annie Clayton, his wife, for judicial review by way of orders of certiorari to quash the convictions of the respondents and quashing their convictions by the justices for the petty sessional division of Hunstanton in the county of Norfolk on 24 August 1981 of offences against s 78 of the Post Office Act 1969. The Divisional Court certified, under s 1(2) of the Administration of Justice Act 1960, that two points of law of general public importance were involved in its decision but refused leave to appeal to the House of Lords. The facts are set out in the opinion of Lord Roskill.

Roger Titheridge QC and *John Farmer* for the appellant.
Barry Green QC and *Andrew Don* for the respondents.

Their Lordships took time for consideration.

17 March. The following opinions were delivered.

LORD FRASER OF TULLYBELTON. My Lords, I have had the advantage of reading in draft the speech prepared by my noble and learned friend Lord Roskill. I agree with it, and, for the reasons stated in it, I would allow these appeals and answer the two certified questions in the negative.

LORD EDMUND-DAVIES. My Lords, I, too, have had the advantage of reading in draft form the speech prepared by my noble and learned friend Lord Roskill. I accept the reasons which have led him to answer in the negative the two certified questions, and I accordingly concur in allowing these appeals.

LORD SCARMAN. My Lords, for the reasons developed by my noble and learned friend Lord Roskill in his speech, a draft of which I have had the opportunity of seeing, I would allow the appeals and answer the two certified questions in the negative.

LORD ROSKILL. My Lords, these consolidated appeals by the Chief Constable of Norfolk raise an important question of practice and procedure in magistrates' courts in England and Wales. The respondents are husband and wife. On 24 June 1981 a single summons was issued against the first respondent, whom I shall call 'the husband', in respect of three informations which had been laid against him on the same day alleging offences against s 78 of the Post Office Act 1969. Of these three informations, the first two alleged offences against the husband alone. The third information alleged a similar offence jointly with the second respondent, 'the wife'. A separate summons was then also issued against the wife in respect of two informations laid against her. The first alleged a single offence by her against the same section. The second alleged the same joint offence with which the husband had been charged in the third information against him which I have just mentioned.

On 29 June 1981 the cases were in the warned list at Hunstanton Magistrates' Court in Norfolk. The husband appeared in person. The wife was represented by her solicitor. Pleas of not guilty were intimated though not formally taken, whereupon the cases were

adjourned until 24 August 1981. Some deplorably abusive letters were then written to
the clerk to the Hunstanton justices, the upshot of which was that the husband said that   *a*
neither he nor his wife would appear at the adjourned hearing on 24 August. He asked
for an adjournment until October, a request with which the clerk was unable to comply.
On 24 August both cases were in the list and were called. Neither the husband nor the
wife appeared and the wife was no longer represented. Both cases involving all five
informations were heard by the justices at the same time. No consents were given by or
on behalf of either the husband or the wife to this course. Convictions and fines followed   *b*
on all five informations. The husband gave notice of appeal to the Crown Court sitting
at King's Lynn. On the hearing of this appeal on 29 January 1982 the point was taken for
the first time that all the convictions were bad because all five informations had been
tried together without consent. The Crown Court judge, his Honour Judge Binns,
adjourned the appeal to enable an application for judicial review to be made. Leave was
granted to both the husband and wife by McCullough J on 11 March 1982. The   *c*
Divisional Court (Griffiths LJ and Forbes J) heard the applications on 25 June 1982 and
quashed the convictions for the reasons given in a judgment delivered by Griffiths LJ.
There can be no doubt that the Divisional Court was bound by authority to quash the
convictions and to make the orders sought.

Griffiths LJ clearly arrived at this conclusion with marked reluctance since he said at
the end of his judgment: '. . . although for my part I see absolutely no merit in the   *d*
applicants' case at all, they are entitled on this technicality to have their convictions
quashed.' The Divisional Court certified two questions of law as of general public
importance:

> '(1) Whether the consent of the defendant is necessary to the trial together of two
> or more informations; and (2) whether the consent of the defendants is necessary to
> the trial together of two or more defendants who are charged on separate   *e*
> informations.'

Leave to appeal to your Lordships' House was refused by the Divisional Court but
subsequently was given by this House in order that the opportunity might be taken to
consider this important question.

There were before the Divisional Court affidavits by the clerk to the Hunstanton   *f*
justices, one in each case, stating in effect that the practice followed on this occasion was
one which was widespread in magistrates' courts and was 'accepted as normal practice in
the vast majority of cases'. Counsel for the respondents challenged the correctness of this
statement but no evidence was adduced to contradict it. I would only observe that the
practice deposed to, however sensible it may seem, is not easy to reconcile with the
successive decisions of the Divisional Court to which I am about to refer and which were   *g*
binding on all magistrates' courts as they were on the Divisional Court itself in the
present cases.

My Lords, though your Lordships had the benefit of massive citation by counsel of
nineteenth century cases claimed to be relevant to the present problem, I think that its
consideration is best approached by reference to the most recent authorities since it is
they which obliged the Divisional Court to quash the present convictions.   *h*

In *Edwards v Jones* [1947] 1 All ER 830, [1947] KB 659 the appellant had been charged
in a single information with both dangerous and careless driving. Before the justices a
submission had been made that the information was bad for duplicity in that it charged
two offences in a single information contrary to s 10 of the Summary Jurisdiction Act
1848 and that the prosecution should elect on which charge to proceed. The prosecutor
declined so to elect and the justices heard the information as it stood and convicted of   *j*
careless driving only. The appellant appealed by way of case stated. The appeal succeeded
and the conviction was quashed on the ground that the information was bad for duplicity
contrary to s 10, as indeed it plainly was. But in giving judgment Lord Goddard CJ went
on to say ([1947] KB 659 at 662; cf [1947] 1 All ER 830 at 832):

> 'If there are two informations or summonses against a defendant, in which the
> facts are very much the same, of course it is quite open to the defendant to say that

he will agree to their being heard at once. That is constantly done and there is no reason why it should not be done. In this case the defendant did not agree to anything of the sort. He took the objection that the information was bad, and so it was. No agreement by the defendant would put that right.'

Lord Goddard CJ, after referring to certain provisions in the then Road Traffic Act, said ([1947] 1 All ER 830 at 832, [1947] KB 659 at 664):

'That emphasises the point which I have been making that the defendant is never to be called on to answer two charges at the same time unless there are two separate informations and he consents to their being heard together.'

Though, as I have pointed out already, the issue in that case was whether the information was bad for duplicity, it seems clear that Lord Goddard LJ was stating categorically, albeit obiter, that where there were two or more informations they could not be tried together unless the defendant consented. If this be correct the practice followed in the instant cases must be wrong.

Three years later however, in *R v Ashbourne Justices, ex p Naden* (1950) 48 LGR 268, a somewhat similar point arose, again before a Divisional Court with Lord Goddard CJ presiding. The applicant had been charged on two separate informations, one alleging dangerous and the other careless driving. The two informations were heard together without the applicant's express consent. The applicant was convicted on the second. Lord Goddard CJ said (at 269):

'The chairman of the justices in his affidavit says that, where two summonses of this kind are issued, it is the practice of the court to hear them together. That is a perfectly sensible practice, but it is desirable, indeed right and regular, that in such cases the question should be put to the defendant in terms: "do you consent to these two summonses being heard together?"; and he or she should answer in clear terms yes or no. In this case, we think, the court was well justified in assuming that the solicitor for the applicant did consent to the charges being heard together; but even if there was an irregularity in the proceedings, it does not follow that this court will grant *certiorari* to quash the conviction. *Certiorari* will be granted *ex debito justitiae*, no doubt, where a court acts without jurisdiction: consent cannot give a court jurisdiction and a court cannot confer jurisdiction upon itself ... Where, however, it is a mere matter of some irregularity, this Court has a discretion whether it will grant *certiorari* or not and will look to see whether any injustice has been done by the so-called irregularity.'

I stress the words 'a mere matter of some irregularity', that is to say 'irregularity' in a matter of practice and procedure. The report does not show whether the earlier decision in *Edwards v Jones* was drawn to the attention of the court but the observations just quoted are inconsistent with the obiter observations in that case.

I turn to *Brangwynne v Evans* [1962] 1 All ER 446, [1962] 1 WLR 267. The appellant was charged with three separate offences of shoplifting. He objected to the three charges being heard together but the justices held that they had a discretion whether to try the charges separately or together and decided to try them together. The resulting convictions were quashed. In giving the leading judgment Lord Parker CJ, who referred to both the cases above cited, said ([1962] 1 All ER 446 at 446–447, [1962] 1 WLR 267 at 268):

'I have sympathy with these justices because one would feel that, today at any rate, it would be right that they should have jurisdiction in a case such as this to hear the three informations together, the discretion being exercised in such a way as would not create prejudice for the defendant. I am quite satisfied, however, that it has always been a principle of our law that a defendant can only be called on to answer one charge at a time in a magistrates' court. An illustration of that is to be found in s. 10 of the Summary Jurisdiction Act, 1848, and in r. 14 of the Magistrates Courts' Rules, 1952, whereby it is expressly provided that no information shall contain more than one charge. That is a good illustration of the principle to which I have referred, and, although there is no statutory provision on the point, it would seem to follow that, if that principle is to be adhered to, two informations, albeit each containing one charge, ought not to be tried at the same time, unless, of course, the defendant consents.'

Lord Parker CJ concluded his judgment by saying ([1962] 1 All ER 446 at 447–448, [1962] 1 WLR 267 at 269–270):

'. . . in my judgment the principle is one of perfectly general application and, accordingly, justices should never proceed to hear two informations at the same time without expressly asking the defendant whether he consents to that course. If he does so consent, then, as the cases show, there is no objection. The next question is: what, in those circumstances, should be done? It seems to me that the conviction on these three informations was reached contrary to law in the sense that the procedure which the justices adopted ought never to have been adopted and, as it was contrary to law, the only course which this court can take is to quash those convictions.'

It is plain from these passages that Lord Parker CJ thought that there was no 'jurisdiction' and that what the justices did was 'contrary to law', thus going considerably further than Lord Goddard CJ had done in the two previous cases. Lord Parker CJ repeated this opinion in *Lawrence v Same* [1968] 1 All ER 1191 at 1193, [1968] 2 QB 93 at 97, where he said:

'It has always been, or at any rate since s. 10 of the Summary Jurisdiction Act, 1848, was passed, impossible for magistrates to try more than one information alleging one offence at the same time; that of course is apart from the defendant consenting to the trial of more than one offence. That is now to be found in r. 14 of the Magistrates' Courts Rules, 1952, and is supported by abundant authority, of which a recent one is *Brangwynne v. Evans*.'

Finally there is the decision of the Divisional Court in *Aldus v Watson* [1973] 2 All ER 1018, [1973] QB 902. Four separate informations against four defendants were tried together without the consent of those defendants and each was convicted. Two appealed. Lord Widgery CJ accepted that there was no direct authority on the point but by analogy applied the reasoning in *Brangwynne v Evans* and the Divisional Court held that just as one defendant could not be tried on two informations without his consent so two defendants could not be tried together on separate informations without their consent even though the facts were as closely related as it is possible to imagine.

My Lords, these cases collectively constitute a formidable body of authority, supported by no less than three successive Lord Chief Justices, against the appellant's submissions. But it will have been observed that Lord Parker CJ in particular rested his decision on absence of 'jurisdiction' to try two informations together without consent, saying the practice was 'contrary to law' and founding much on s 10 of the 1848 Act. If this view can be shown to be wrong and the matter shown not to be one of jurisdiction or of substantive law but only of practice and procedure, then the great weight which I would otherwise attach to Lord Parker CJ's views, which in their turn were the foundation of Lord Widgery CJ's subsequent view, must necessarily be lessened, especially in view of Lord Goddard CJ's observations in the *Ashbourne* case about 'a mere matter of some irregularity'. In this connection it is relevant to observe that if Lord Parker CJ were correct in his emphasis on want of 'jurisdiction' it is difficult to see how consent can give jurisdiction which would otherwise be lacking because in principle, if there is no jurisdiction in a court which is the creature of statute and whose powers are delimited by statute, jurisdiction cannot be conferred by consent, as Lord Goddard CJ himself pointed out in his judgment in the *Ashbourne* case 48 LGR 268 at 269.

I therefore turn to s 10 of the 1848 Act. This statute (11 & 12 Vict c 43) was one of three statutes passed in that year with consecutive chapter numbers 42, 43 and 44, commonly known as Jervis's Acts. These created magistrates' courts in something akin to their modern form and defined their powers, functions and jurisdiction. I set out the whole of s 10 although it is only the last few lines which are presently relevant:

'... every such complaint upon which a justice or justices of the peace is or are or
shall be authorized by law to make an order, and every information for any offence
or act punishable upon summary conviction, unless some particular Act of
Parliament shall otherwise require, may respectively be made or laid without any
oath or affirmation being made of the truth thereof; except in cases of informations
where the justice or justices receiving the same shall thereupon issue his or their
warrant in the first instance to apprehend the defendant as aforesaid, and in every
such case where the justice or justices shall issue his or their warrant in the first
instance the matter of such information shall be substantiated by the oath of
affirmation of the informant, or by some witness or witnesses on his behalf, before
any such warrant shall be issued; and every such complaint shall be for one matter
of complaint only, and not for two or more matters of complaint; and every such
information shall be for one offence only, and not for two or more offences; and
every such complaint or information may be laid or made by the complainant or
informant in person, or by his counsel or attorney or other person authorized in
that behalf.'

Much time was spent before your Lordships' House in debating what the position was
before 1848 and your Lordships' attention was drawn to various learned works such as
Stone's Justices Manual (5th edn, 1844, and 7th edn, 1877). I hope I shall not appear
unappreciative of the research which enabled these and other works to be placed before
your Lordships if I say that I do not find it helpful to attempt to discover the position
before 1848 even if it were now possible to do so with the requisite degree of certainty
required for an expression of opinion by this House. Jervis's Acts were a group of statutes
which can fairly be described as a complete code defining what courts of summary
jurisdiction might and might not thenceforth do. It seems to me clear that the relevant
words of s 10 are directed to preventing duplicity in informations. They are not directed
to preventing as a matter of statutory prohibition either the trial of two or more
informations at the same time or the trial of two or more offenders together where the
relevant facts are sufficiently clearly related. The object of the rule against duplicity has
always been that there should be no uncertainty as to the offence charged. But there is no
such uncertainty where two or more informations are properly laid against an alleged
offender. He knows that he is charged as stated in each information. Section 10 has of
course long since been repealed. Its modern counterpart is r 12(1) of the Magistrates'
Courts Rules 1981, SI 1981/552, which reads:

'*Information to be for one offence only*
Subject to any Act passed after 2nd October 1848, a magistrates' court shall not
proceed to the trial of an information that charges more than one offence.'

This rule is plainly designed to prevent informations being duplicitous.

Counsel for the respondents did not seek to support the view that there was no
jurisdiction in a magistrates' court to try more than one information at the same time or
that to do so was contrary to law. I think he was right to make this concession for it is
impossible to extract the necessary prohibition from the language of s 10 or from r 12(1).
He was therefore unable to support the reasoning underlying Lord Parker CJ's two
judgments and therefore Lord Widgery CJ's later judgment which followed the first of
Lord Parker CJ's. He contented himself with submitting that, as a result of the practice
or convention which had evolved, it was an irregularity to try more than one information
at the same time and similarly to try more than one offender charged on separate
informations at the same time however closely related the facts might be.

Both counsel for the appellant and counsel for the respondents invited your Lordships
to examine many nineteenth century and some early twentieth century authorities. I do
not propose to follow the trail which they have laid for two reasons. First, I have found it
difficult to deduce any consistent pattern from these cases, some most inadequately
reported and others mutually inconsistent. Second, unless restricted by statute,
magistrates' courts, guided where necessary by higher courts, are entitled to develop their
own practice and procedure and to adapt it to contemporary needs. Practice and

procedure must never be allowed to become inflexible. They are the servants not the masters of the judicial process. I doubt whether any consistent practice in the last century can be deduced from these cases for some undoubtedly demonstrate a clear refusal on the part of some courts to interfere where two or more informations or indeed offenders have plainly been tried together.

What I think is clear is that by 1947 a rule of practice and procedure had evolved, whether or not it was correctly based on s 10 of the 1848 Act, which made it irregular for any magistrates' court to try more than one information at the same time in the absence of consent. But the *Ashbourne* case shows that even in 1950 the rule had not become an absolute one and that certiorari would not issue to cure 'a mere matter of some irregularity', for example a failure clearly to obtain the necessary consent from the defendant. It can further be said that this rule developed during the ensuing 25 years so that by 1973 it had similarly become an irregularity to try together several defendants charged on informations in the absence of consent, even though the relevant facts were closely related.

It is plain that in some of these cases the Divisional Court reached its conclusion with reluctance since effect was having to be given to most unmeritorious technicalities, as in the instant cases. It is also plain that a rule designed to avoid any risk of injustice to defendants had become in danger of being an obstacle to the simple and sensible administration of justice in magistrates' courts, where it is of particular importance that that administration should be both simple and sensible. Magistrates' courts today try the vast majority of criminal cases that arise for hearing in this country as well as many civil cases. Any rule of practice or procedure which make their task more difficult or demands subservience to technicalities is to be deprecated and your Lordships may think that this House should now encourage the adoption of rules of procedure and practice which encourage the better attainment of justice, which includes the interests of the prosecution as well as of defendants, so long as the necessary safeguards are maintained to prevent any risk of injustice to defendants.

My Lords, in the last two decades much additional work has been entrusted to magistrates' courts and magistrates receive training to enable them to learn their business and to bear this extra workload. Many cases are now tried summarily which 20 or 30 years ago would have been tried at quarter sessions or even assizes. The policy of Parliament has been to legislate so as to lighten the ever increasing burden now borne by the Crown Court by transferring a part of that burden to magistrates' courts. The evolution of the offence triable 'either way' is an example of this policy. It is not entirely easy to see why in principle, when, subject to certain well-established safeguards and to the discretion of the trial judge to sever counts in an indictment and to order separate trials of those severed counts, indictments can today contain many counts and charge more than one offender where the facts alleged show the necessary connection, magistrates' courts should invariably be compelled in the absence of express consent to try separately each information and each offender who is separately charged, however closely the facts are connected. No statute enjoins that magistrates' courts should follow this procedure or prohibits them from adopting that practice and procedure best suited to contemporary needs.

My Lords, in *R v Assim* [1966] 2 All ER 881, [1966] 2 QB 249 a five-judge Court of Criminal Appeal presided over by Lord Parker CJ considered at length the circumstances in which it was proper to join separate offenders charged on separate counts in the same indictment. The court understandably shrank from laying down exhaustive rules dealing specifically with every type of case. But in its judgment, delivered by Sachs J, the court laid down this general rule of practice in relation to indictments ([1966] 2 All ER 881 at 887–888, [1966] 2 QB 249 at 261):

'As a general rule it is, of course, no more proper to have tried by the same jury several offenders on charges of committing individual offences that have nothing to do with each other, than it is to try before the same jury offences committed by the same person that have nothing to do with each other. Where, however, the matters which constitute the individual offences of the several offenders are on the available

evidence so related, whether in time or by other factors, that the interests of justice
are best served by their being tried together, then they can properly be the subject
of counts in one indictment and can, subject always to the discretion of the court,
be tried together. Such a rule, of course, includes cases where there is evidence that
several offenders acted in concert but is not limited to such cases. Again, while the
court has in mind the classes of case that have been particularly the subject of
discussion before it, such as incidents which, irrespective of there appearing a joint
charge in the indictment, are contemporaneous (as where there has been something
in the nature of an affray), or successive (as in protection racket cases), or linked in a
similar manner as where two persons individually in the course of the same trial
commit perjury as regards the same or a closely connected fact, the court does not
intend the operation of the rule to be restricted so as to apply only to such cases as
have been discussed before it.'

This principle was applied to committal proceedings in magistrates' courts by the
Divisional Court in R v Camberwell Green Justices, ex p Christie [1978] 2 All ER 377, [1978]
QB 602. One information had been laid against a father charging him with murder of
his child. A second information was laid against a woman charging her with an offence
against the Children and Young Persons Act 1933. The father objected to the joinder of
the committal proceedings against him and the woman on the ground that the magistrate
had no power to hear them together since there were two informations against separate
defendants charging each with a different offence. The stipendiary magistrate decided to
hear the committal proceedings together and the father then sought to stop him from so
doing. Reliance was naturally placed by counsel for the father on the decision in Aldus v
Watson, which he asserted decided that a concurrent summary trial was 'unlawful'. But
the Divisional Court applied the reasoning in Assim's case in the passage I have just quoted
and held that, where the offenders and the offences for whom and for which committal
was sought could be joined in one indictment, joint committal proceedings could
properly take place. It may be that Lord Widgery CJ in giving judgment in Christie's case
[1978] 2 All ER 377 at 380, [1978] QB 602 at 607 had second thoughts about what he
had said in Aldus v Watson, for he said:

'. . . indeed I think it is probably wise not to be too far reaching in dicta which are
concerned with matters of practice. Practice should vary from time to time, and the
variation and correction of practice should not be restricted by excessively wide
judgments already appearing in the law reports.'

In an earlier part of his judgment he had plainly recognised the problem to which that
decision could give rise in a case where, under s 18(3) of the Magistrates' Courts Act 1952,
magistrates began to inquire into an information as examining justices with a view to
committal for trial and then in pursuance of the powers conferred by that subsection
decided to try the cases summarily. As examining justices they could, as the decision in
Christie's case shows, hear concurrently the committal proceedings against two defendants
charged on separate informations. Yet what was to happen once those proceedings had
become summary proceedings? This difficulty becomes even more apparent when one
looks at the present legislation, namely s 25(2) and (3) of the Magistrates' Courts Act
1980, the effect of which is correctly summarised in the sidenote as 'Power to change
from summary trial to committal proceedings, and vice versa'. Can magistrates continue
to hear without consent the several informations together in the summary proceedings
or do they have to start again hearing them separately?

My Lords, the practical difficulties which arise from rigid adherence to the rule of
practice enunciated in Edwards v Jones and in the later cases to which I have referred are
indeed manifest. Common sense today dictates that in the interests of justice as a whole
magistrates should have a discretion in what manner they deal with these problems.
Suppose a defendant has ten or twelve motoring offences charged in separate informations
laid against him. He does not appear. If the present rule of practice is allowed to prevail,
each of those ten or twelve informations must be heard separately, often with the same
witness or witnesses called and recalled ten or twelve times to repeat themselves.

Obstruction by a defendant is put at a premium. Today I see no compelling reason why your Lordships should not say that the practice in magistrates' courts in these matters *a* should henceforth be analogous to the practice prescribed in *Assim*'s case in relation to trials on indictment. Where a defendant is charged on several informations and the facts are connected, for example motoring offences or several charges of shoplifting, I can see no reason why those informations should not, if the justices think fit, be heard together. Similarly, if two or more defendants are charged on separate informations but the facts are connected, I can see no reason why they should not, if the justices think fit, be heard *b* together. In the present cases there were separate informations against the husband and the wife and a joint information against them both. I can see no rational objection to all those informations being heard and determined together. Of course, when this question arises, as from time to time it will arise, justices will be well advised to inquire both of the prosecution and of the defence whether either side has any objection to all the informations being heard together. If consent is forthcoming on both sides there is no *c* problem. If such consent is not forthcoming, the justices should then consider the rival submissions and, under any necessary advice from their clerk, rule as they think right in the overall interest of justice. If the defendant is absent or not represented, the justices, of course, should seek the views of the prosecution and again if necessary the advice of their clerk and then rule as they think fit in the overall interests of justice. Absence of consent, either express where the defendant is present or represented and objects or *d* necessarily brought about by his absence or the absence of representation, should no longer in practice be regarded as a complete and automatic bar to hearing more than one information at the same time or informations against more than one defendant charged on separate informations at the same time when in the justices' view the facts are sufficiently closely connected to justify this course and there is no risk of injustice to the defendants by its adoption. Accordingly, the justices should always ask themselves *e* whether it would be fair and just to the defendant or defendants to allow a joint trial. Only if the answer is clearly in the affirmative should they order joint trial in the absence of consent by or on behalf of the defendant.

To give magistrates' courts this discretion and to change the practice and procedure which has seemingly prevailed in recent years is not to invite magistrates' courts to embark on long and complicated summary trials with many charges being heard and *f* many offenders being tried all at the same time. As Sachs J said in *Assim*'s case, it is impossible to lay down general rules applicable to every case which may arise, but if justices ask themselves, before finally ruling, the single question, what is the fairest thing to do in all the circumstances in the interests of everyone concerned, they are unlikely to err in their conclusion, for the aim of the judicial process is to secure a fair trial and rules of practice and procedure are designed to that end and not otherwise. *g*

My Lords, in the result I would allow these two appeals and refuse the applications for judicial review. I would answer both the certified questions in the negative. Since the appeals to the Crown Court at King's Lynn were adjourned pending the applications for judicial review which have now failed, these cases must be remitted to that court to continue with the hearing of the appeals. Your Lordships may think it right in all the circumstances of these appeals to order that the costs of both the appellant and the *h* respondents should be paid out of central funds.

LORD TEMPLEMAN. My Lords, for the reasons advanced by my noble and learned friend Lord Roskill, I would allow these appeals and answer both certified questions in the negative.

Appeals allowed. Certified questions answered in the negative. Causes remitted to Crown Court *j* *at King's Lynn to continue hearing of appeals against determination of Hunstanton Magistrates' Court.*

Solicitors: *Sharpe Pritchard & Co*, agents for *D I Tomlinson*, Norwich (for the appellant); *Metcalfe Copeman & Pettefar*, King's Lynn (for the respondents).

Mary Rose Plummer   Barrister.

R v Wilson (Clarence)

COURT OF APPEAL, CRIMINAL DIVISION
WATKINS LJ, CANTLEY AND HIRST JJ
28 JANUARY 1983

Indictment – Conviction of lesser offence – Inflicting grievous bodily harm – Particulars of way grievous bodily harm caused not specified – Whether open to jury to convict of lesser offence of assault occasioning actual bodily harm – Offences against the Person Act 1861, s 20 – Criminal Law Act 1967, s 6(3).

The appellant, a motorist, misunderstood a pedestrian's signals and nearly ran him down. The appellant got out of his car and punched the pedestrian in the face, injuring him quite seriously. The appellant was charged in an indictment containing one count only, namely that he inflicted grievous bodily harm on the pedestrian (those being the particulars of the offence), contrary to s 20[a] of the Offences against the Person Act 1861. At the trial the judge refused an application by the Crown to amend the indictment either by adding a count charging the lesser offence of assault occasioning actual bodily harm contrary to s 47 of the 1861 Act or by amending the existing count by giving particulars of the way the grievous bodily harm had been caused by adding the words 'by assaulting' the pedestrian, so that the existing count would then include the essential element of the lesser offence. However, the judge ruled that under s 6(3)[b] of the Criminal Law Act 1967 it was open to the jury to find the appellant guilty, on the existing count, of the alternative offence of assault occasioning actual bodily harm. The jury returned a verdict of not guilty of inflicting grievous bodily harm but guilty of assault occasioning actual bodily harm. The appellant was thereupon convicted of the latter offence. He appealed against the conviction on the ground that the judge's ruling was erroneous in law.

Held – Assault occasioning actual bodily harm was not an essential ingredient of the offence of inflicting grievous bodily harm contrary to s 20 of the 1861 Act because grievous bodily harm could be inflicted where the accused intentionally did an act which although not a direct application of force to the victim nevertheless directly resulted in force being applied to him so that he suffered grievous bodily harm. Furthermore, the infliction of grievous bodily harm did not necessarily involve assault and battery on the victim, since the term 'inflict' did not necessarily connote an assault. Since the only offence charged in the indictment was inflicting grievous bodily harm contrary to s 20 of the 1861 Act, the allegations in the indictment did not include, either expressly or by implication, an allegation of assault occasioning actual bodily harm and accordingly it had not been open to the jury to find the appellant guilty of the latter offence by virtue of s 6(3) of the 1967 Act. It followed that the judge's ruling had been erroneous and, since it had resulted in the appellant's conviction, the conviction would be quashed (see p 996 e f h and p 998 j to p 999 a and f, post).

R v Springfield (1969) 53 Cr App R 608 and *R v Salisbury* [1976] VR 452 applied.
R v Snewing [1972] Crim LR 267 explained.

Notes

For the power to convict of an offence other than that charged, see 11 Halsbury's Laws (4th edn) para 311, and for cases on the subject see 14(1) Digest (Reissue) 416–422, 3522–3609.

For grievous bodily harm, see 11 Halsbury's Laws (4th edn) para 1199, and for cases on the subject, see 15 Digest (Reissue) 1180–1181, 10068–10076.

---

a Section 20, so far as material, provides: 'Whosoever shall unlawfully and maliciously . . . inflict any grievous bodily harm upon any other person, either with or without any weapon or instrument, shall be guilty of a misdemeanor . . .'
b Section 6(3) is set out at p 996 c d, post

For the Offences against the Person Act 1861, ss 20, 47, see 8 Halsbury's Statutes (3rd edn) 154, 165.

For the Criminal Law Act 1967, s 6, see ibid 557.

Cases referred to in judgment

Cartledge v Allen [1973] Crim LR 530, DC.

R v Austin (1973) 58 Cr App R 163, CA.

R v Clarence (1888) 22 QBD 23, [1886–90] All ER Rep 133, CCR, 15 Digest (Reissue) 1180, 10071.

R v Halliday (1889) 61 LT 701, [1886–90] All ER Rep 1028, CCR, 15 Digest (Reissue) 1181, 10073.

R v Lambert (1976) 65 Cr App R 12, CA.

R v Lillis [1972] 2 All ER 1209, [1972] 2 QB 236, [1972] 2 WLR 1409, CA, 14(1) Digest (Reissue) 420, 3583.

R v Martin (1881) 8 QBD 54, [1881–5] All ER Rep 699, CCR, 14(2) Digest (Reissue) 484, 3991.

R v McCready [1978] 3 All ER 967, [1978] 1 WLR 1376, CA, Digest (Cont Vol E) 137, 3554b.

R v Salisbury [1976] VR 452.

R v Snewing [1972] Crim LR 267, CA.

R v Springfield (1969) 53 Cr App R 608, CA, 14(1) Digest (Reissue) 419, 3563.

R v Taylor (1869) LR 1 CCR 194, 14(1) Digest (Reissue) 418, 3558.

Cases also cited

Dodwell v Burford (1669) 1 Mod 24, 86 ER 703.

R v Roberts (1971) 56 Cr App R 95, CA.

Scott v Shepherd (1773) 3 Wils 403, [1558–1774] All ER Rep 295, 95 ER 1124, CP.

Application for leave to appeal against conviction

On 4 November 1981 in the Crown Court at Kingston-upon-Thames before his Honour Judge Rubin and a jury the appellant, Clarence George Wilson, on an indictment containing a single count of inflicting grievous bodily harm contrary to s 20 of the Offences against the Person Act 1861, was acquitted of inflicting grievous bodily harm but convicted of the lesser offence of assault occasioning actual bodily harm. He was sentenced to one month's imprisonment suspended for two years. He applied to the full court for leave to appeal against the conviction on the grounds that the trial judge (1) misdirected the jury in telling them that a verdict of assault occasioning actual bodily harm was available as an alternative verdict on the indictment, (2) misdirected himself in holding that an assault occasioning actual bodily harm was synonymous with inflicting actual bodily harm and (3) in following *R v Snewing* [1972] Crim LR 267, he followed a case which either was wrongly decided or, being decided on its own special facts, he ought not to have followed. The full court granted leave to appeal and proceeded to hear the appeal. The facts are set out in the judgment of the court.

David Guy (assigned by the Registrar of Criminal Appeals) for the appellant.
Derek Zeitlin for the Crown.

CANTLEY J delivered the following judgment of the court. On 4 November 1981, in the Crown Court at Kingston, the appellant was acquitted of a charge of inflicting grievous bodily harm, contrary to s 20 of the Offences against the Person Act 1861. He was convicted, however, as an alternative, of an offence of assault occasioning actual bodily harm. The indictment contained merely a single count, alleging in the particulars simply that 'on the 7th day of November, 1980, Clarence George Wilson maliciously inflicted grievous bodily harm on Maxim James Latham'.

In relating what happened it is important not to lose sight of the facts of this case,
a because everything that has been said and argued should be considered in relation to the
facts and the actual indictment. The victim was a Mr Latham, who was intending, on 7
November at about 11 o'clock at night, to cross a road in south London. As he was about
to leave the footpath, he noticed a previously stationary motor car move away from the
curb. He waved the car on, but it stopped. When he proceeded to cross, the car started
and nearly ran him down. It was a case of misunderstanding between the pedestrian and
b the driver (the appellant) such as does happen from time to time. Obviously, one
supposes, the driver (the appellant) thought that the pedestrian's signals were still
operative, so he started the car, and the pedestrian thought that the driver had not
accepted his invitation to proceed, so he went onto the roadway.

The car stopped. The appellant got out and possibly, although this remained a matter
of uncertainty at the trial, another male passenger also got out. There was then what is
c sometimes called a 'punch-up'. According to the evidence of the victim, Mr Latham,
which must have been accepted by the jury, the appellant came up to him and punched
him in the face. He, that is Mr Latham, retaliated or defended himself by reasonable
• violence, but was overwhelmed by the continued attack on him by the appellant, helped
possibly by this mysterious third man whose existence was never conclusively established.

Mr Latham was quite seriously injured, so that the appellant may consider himself
d fortunate that the jury did not take the view that he had inflicted grievous bodily harm
on Mr Latham. There was, therefore, evidence, as the jury accepted, that there was an
assault occasioning actual bodily harm, even if it did not qualify as a case of maliciously
inflicting grievous bodily harm.

Realising the understandable disposition of juries to incline towards the soft option,
counsel who appeared for the Crown sought at the outset to amend the indictment by
e adding a count of assault occasioning actual bodily harm. The judge refused to allow that
amendment. He was quite right to do so, because there was nothing in the committal
evidence which supported the additional suggested charge against the appellant. The
judge's hands were tied completely by s 2(2) of the Administration of Justice
(Miscellaneous Provisions) Act 1933 and the proviso to that subsection.

Counsel for the Crown then applied, as an alternative remedy, for leave to amend the
f existing count under s 20 of the Offences against the Person Act 1861, by adding to the
particulars the words 'by assaulting him'. This is a practice which has been approved by
this court in R v McCready [1978] 3 All ER 967 at 971, [1978] 1 WLR 1376 at 1382,
where Lawton LJ, who presided over the court which consisted of himself, Mars-Jones
and Gibson JJ, said:

g　　'We were told by counsel that because of the decisions in R v Austin (1973) 58 Cr
App R 163 and R v Lambert (1976) 65 Cr App R 12 some draftsmen of indictments
now give particulars of the way in which the grievous bodily harm was caused as,
for example, by such words as "by assaulting him". We approve of this practice.'

Those observations were obiter. Therefore, although they have the weighty authority
of that distinguished Lord Justice, supported by the other members of the court, they are
h not yet binding as decided law. The editors of Archbold's Criminal Pleading, Evidence and
Practice (41st edn, 1982) p 464, para 4–462 do not, however, approve of that suggested
practice, even though it is now, from time to time, followed. Whether their objections
are correct or not is a matter which may sometime have to be decided, but the practice at
least seems to be sensible and harmless if confined to the example given. Particulars, so
long as they are particulars of the offence alleged, are not normally embarrassing by
j condescending to detail. Section 3(1) of the Indictments Act 1915 requires 'such
particulars as may be necessary for giving reasonable information as to the nature of the
charge.'

The judge declined to allow this amendment. He did so in these terms:

'It is said that one could avoid the difficulty by amending the existing count. For
my part, I think it would be wrong to try to avoid that difficulty, which was of the

prosecution's own making by the way that this matter was committed for trial, and it is quite clear from the notice of additional evidence that the job could have been done properly ab initio.'

It may be, if the editors of *Archbold* are right, that the judge's decision was correct but it was not founded on the right reasons. The primary function of the courts is to administer justice as between the parties rather than to discipline practitioners. However, the judge then ruled that, following *R v Snewing* [1972] Crim LR 267 of which this court has a transcript, it was open to the jury, on the count as it stood, to convict the appellant on the charge of assault occasioning actual bodily harm, and he directed the jury accordingly. The sole question in this appeal is whether he was entitled to give that direction to the jury or whether it was erroneous. I will refer to *R v Snewing* in due course.

It is necessary to begin with the statutory provisions which govern this matter. Those are contained in s 6(3) of the Criminal Law Act 1967. That subsection provides:

> 'Where, on a person's trial on indictment for any offence except treason or murder, the jury find him not guilty of the offence specifically charged in the indictment, but the allegations in the indictment amount to or include (expressly or by implication) an allegation of another offence falling within the jurisdiction of the court of trial, the jury may find him guilty of that other offence or of an offence of which he could be found guilty on an indictment specifically charging that other offence.'

The question in this case is whether 'expressly or by implication' an allegation of assault occasioning actual bodily harm is included in the allegations in the indictment.

Counsel for the Crown, in his attractive and erudite argument, has submitted, among other things, that the allegation is 'expressly' one of the allegations in the indictment, because the word 'inflicted' means by assault and battery. In the view of this court, that is not necessarily the meaning to be attached to the word 'inflicted': the precise meaning to be attached to that word must depend, ultimately, on its context.

In the *Shorter Oxford Dictionary* the word 'inflict' is said to mean 'to lay on as a stroke, blow, or wound', or 'to impose', or 'to cause to be borne'. Among the literary examples given of the use of that word, there is a quotation which reads: 'We should be inflicted with less . . . twaddle.' It is easy to give other examples of the use of the word. It is a perfectly correct use of the word to say that hardship has been inflicted; even, in appropriate cases, that poverty has been inflicted. In neither of those phrases is it expressed or even implied that there was violence involved.

It should also be noted that in s 23 of the Offences against the Person Act 1861 it is provided:

> 'Whosoever shall unlawfully and maliciously administer to or cause to be administered to or taken by any other person any poison or other destructive or noxious thing . . . so as thereby to *inflict* upon such person any grievous bodily harm, shall be guilty of [an offence punishable by ten years' imprisonment].'

This statement does not in our view include or connote an allegation of assault. That does not, of course, conclude the necessary investigation; one has to inquire: do the allegations in this indictment impliedly include the allegation of assault occasioning actual bodily harm? I have already recited in full the words in the particulars of offence in the indictment.

In *R v Springfield* (1969) 53 Cr App R 608 at 610–611 Sachs LJ put the matter in this way:

> 'Where an indictment thus charges a major offence without setting out any particulars of the matters relied upon, what is the correct test for ascertaining whether it contains allegations which expressly or impliedly include an allegation

of a lesser offence? The test is to see whether it is a necessary step towards establishing
the major offence to prove the commission of the lesser offence: in other words, is
the lesser offence an essential ingredient of the major one?'

We respectfully adopt that test, which already has the approval of a full court consisting
of five judges in R v Lillis [1972] 2 All ER 1209 at 1213, [1972] 2 QB 236 at 241.

The Offences against the Person Act was passed as long ago as 1861 and, therefore,
there is a whole body of authority arising from prosecutions under s 20. In 1881 there
was the case of R v Martin (1881) 8 QBD 54, [1881–5] All ER Rep 699. The facts of that
case are these (8 QBD 54):

> 'Shortly before the conclusion of a performance at a theatre, M. [the accused],
> with the intention and with the result of causing terror in the minds of persons
> leaving the theatre, put out the gaslights on a staircase which a large number of such
> persons had to descend in order to leave the theatre, and he also, with the intention
> and with the result of obstructing the exit, placed an iron bar across a doorway
> through which they had in leaving to pass.'

He succeeded in causing panic in those leaving the theatre. They rushed down the
staircase and, by reason of the pressure and struggling of the crowd, certain of the
audience were severely injured. It was held that on those facts an offence under s 20 of
the Offences against the Person Act 1861 was established. Lord Coleridge CJ said of the
defendant (8 QBD 54 at 58; cf [1881–5] All ER Rep 699 at 701):

> 'He acted "unlawfully and maliciously," not that he had any personal malice
> against the particular individuals injured, but in the sense of doing an unlawful act
> calculated to injure, and by which others were in fact injured. Just as in the case of a
> man who unlawfully fires a gun among a crowd, it is murder if one of the crowd is
> thereby killed.'

Stephen J agreed. He said (8 QBD 54 at 58; cf [1881–5] All ER Rep 699 at 701):

> 'Now, it seems to me, that if the prisoner did that which he did as a mere piece of
> foolish mischief unlawfully and without excuse, he did it "wilfully," that is
> "maliciously", within the meaning of the statute.'

In R v Halliday (1889) 61 LT 701 the facts were these:

> 'In order to escape from the violence of her husband, who had used threats to his
> wife amounting to threats against her life, the wife got out of a window, and in so
> doing fell to the ground and broke her leg.'

She injured herself falling from the window and the husband, Halliday, was convicted of
an offence under s 20. Lord Coleridge CJ said (at 702):

> 'If a man creates in another man's mind an immediate sense of danger which
> causes such person to try to escape, and in so doing he injures himself, the person
> who creates such a state of mind is responsible for the injuries which result. I think
> that in this case there was abundant evidence that there was a sense of immediate
> danger in the mind of the woman caused by the acts of the prisoner, and that her
> injuries resulted from what such sense of danger caused her to do. I am therefore of
> opinion that the prisoner was rightly convicted . . .'

Mathew J said (at 702):

> 'I am of the same opinion. The jury must be taken to have inferred that the act of
> escaping from the window and the act of the daughter [who was helping the victim]
> were the consequences of the prisoner's acts . . .'

Much more recently, in Cartledge v Allen [1973] Crim LR 530, the same principle was
followed in the Divisional Court. There, the facts were these:

'The defendant while in the company of about ten other youths threatened N [the victim] and as a result of those threats N panicked, ran off pursued by some of the youths but not by the defendant and sought refuge in a nearby public-house. As he entered the public-house he put his hand through the glass panel of the door and injured it.'

The defendant, who was not near the public house at the time, was charged with inflicting grievous bodily harm, contrary to s 20, and was convicted. The Divisional Court upheld the conviction, on the ground that—

'there was a *nexus* between the acts of the defendant and the injury [of the victim] which entitled the justices to say that the injury was the natural consequence of the defendant's action. Therefore the defendant's acts amounted to an infliction of grievous bodily harm.' (My emphasis.)

This topic has been very carefully and usefully considered in the Supreme Court of Victoria in *R v Salisbury* [1976] VR 452 in a judgment of the full court. The judgment reviewed all the relevant authorities going back to the 1861 Act, including *R v Clarence* (1888) 22 QBD 23, [1886–90] All ER Rep 133, with particular reference to the judgment of Wills J (see [1976] VR 452 at 457). Young CJ said (at 460–461):

'From the examination of the cases on s. 20 of the English Act [and I should interpolate that the court was considering a practically identical provision in the Australian legislation], it appears that the English Courts, from at least 1881 (when *R. v. Martin* (8 QBD 54, [1881–5] All ER Rep 699) was decided) to 1973 (when *Cartledge v. Allen* ([1973] Crim LR 530) was decided), in one line of cases have held facts to disclose the offence of inflicting grievous bodily harm without being concerned to make any inquiry whether those facts also constituted an assault. In these cases, the Courts have held that grievous bodily harm has been "inflicted", where they were satisfied that an intentional act of the accused had resulted in serious physical harm to the victim, by force being violently applied to his body, even though the accused had not applied such force directly to the body of the victim by an assault, but had done something which directly resulted in the application of that force. At the same time, during this period, the English Courts have continued to maintain the proposition enunciated in *R. v. Taylor* (LR 1 CCR 194) that assault is an alternative verdict to inflicting grievous bodily harm. [He then referred to *R v Snewing* [1972] Crim LR 267.] None of the cases in the two lines of English authorities are binding on us, though all are of considerable persuasive power. Having examined the cases for the purpose of obtaining assistance with the construction of s. 19A, we have found the reasoning in the line of authority which includes *R. v. Martin* ... the judgment of Wills, J., in *R. v. Clarence* ... and *R. v. Halliday* ... more persuasive and of more assistance in construing s. 19A than the line which has continued to maintain that assault is an alternative verdict on a charge of inflicting grievous bodily harm. [Later he continued:] In our opinion, grievous bodily harm may be inflicted, contrary to s. 19A, either where the accused has directly and violently "inflicted" it by assaulting the victim, or where the accused has "inflicted" it by doing something, intentionally, which, though it is not itself a direct application of force to the body of the victim, does directly, result in force being applied violently to the body of the victim, so that he suffers grievous bodily harm. Hence, the lesser misdemeanours of assault occasioning actual bodily harm and common assault, contrary to s. 37, are not necessarily included in the misdemeanour of inflicting grievous bodily harm, contrary to s. 19A.'

This court takes the same view on the authorities so neatly summarised in that extract from the judgment of the Supreme Court of Victoria. Applying the test suggested by Sachs LJ in *R v Springfield* (1969) 53 Cr App R 608 at 610–611, we consider that assault occasioning actual bodily harm is not an essential ingredient of the offence of unlawfully

and maliciously inflicting grievous bodily harm. However, it is still necessary to refer to
a *R v Snewing* [1972] Crim LR 267, because the trial judge founded his direction on it.

We have had the advantage of reading a transcript of the judgment of Orr LJ, who
gave the judgment of the court in that case, from which it appears that the question
which was argued and considered by the court was whether the presiding chairman had
given the right answer to a question which the jury asked at the end of the trial. Orr LJ
said:

b   'Now, in this case the only ground of appeal against conviction is that the learned
        chairman, having correctly directed the jury [when] summing up that as respects
        the two charges of grievous bodily harm, it was open to them to find verdicts of not
        guilty to that offence but guilty of occasioning actual bodily harm, the complaint is
        that at the end of the summing up, after the jury had retired and come back with a
        question, he gave a wrong answer to that question. There is agreement that the
c   terms of the question sent to the chairman by the jury were: "We believe that
        Snewing is guilty of actual bodily harm, not grievous bodily harm: is this legally",
        and then it reads either "possible" or "permissible" . . . the chairman replied . . . "No.
        The only alternative that you can make would be just of common assault." I do not
        need to read further.'

d   The Court of Appeal decided that the chairman was wrong and he should have
answered Yes, that they could have found the appellant guilty of assault occasioning
actual bodily harm. Reading the transcript of the judgment, it seems to us that
throughout counsel and the court proceeded on the assumption that on a charge under
s 20, of inflicting grievous bodily harm, it was open to the jury to convict of the offence
of assault occasioning actual bodily harm. The contrary does not appear to have been
e argued or considered.

In those circumstances, we do not regard *R v Snewing* as being decisive on the question
which is directly before this court. We do not deem it appropriate that we should regard
it as an authority contrary to the other line of authorities which we have already
considered and approved. It follows that, in our view, the judge's direction was founded
on an erroneous conception of the interpretation applicable to this indictment under s 20
f of the Offences against the Person Act 1861. As the appellant's conviction directly
resulted from that direction, it must be quashed.

Appeal allowed.

g *10 February. The court refused leave to appeal to the House of Lords but certified, under s 33(2)
of the Criminal Appeal Act 1968, that the following point of law of general public importance
was involved in the decision: whether on a charge of inflicting grievous bodily harm contrary to
s 20 of the Offences against the Person Act 1861, it is open to a jury to return a verdict of not
guilty as charged but guilty of assault occasioning actual bodily harm.*

17 March. The Appeal Committee of the House of Lords granted the Crown leave to appeal.

Solicitors: *D M O'Shea* (for the Crown).

                                                        Raina Levy   Barrister.

R v Jenkins (Edward John)
R v Jenkins (Ronald Patrick)

COURT OF APPEAL, CRIMINAL DIVISION

PURCHAS LJ, TALBOT AND STAUGHTON JJ

11, 18 FEBRUARY 1983

Indictment – Conviction of lesser offence – Inflicting grievous bodily harm – Charge of burglary by entering a building as a trespasser and inflicting grievous bodily harm – Whether open to jury to convict of lesser offence of assault occasioning actual bodily harm – Criminal Law Act 1967, s 6(3) – Theft Act 1968, s 9(1)(b).

The offence of burglary by entering a building as a trespasser and inflicting grievous bodily harm on a person therein, contrary to s 9(1)(b)[a] of the Theft Act 1968, does not necessarily involve an assault occasioning actual bodily harm on the victim, within s 47 of the Offences against the Person Act 1861, because, applying the construction of the similar phrase in s 20[b] of the 1861 Act, the phrase 'inflict . . . grievous bodily harm' in s 9(1)(b) of the 1968 Act is to be construed widely and not in the restricted sense of necessarily involving an assault occasioning actual bodily harm. It follows that where the charge against the accused is solely one of burglary contrary to s 9(1)(b) of the 1968 Act the allegations in the charge do not amount to or include for the purposes of s 6(3)[c] of the Criminal Law Act 1967 an allegation of the lesser offence of assault occasioning actual bodily harm, and in consequence the jury are not entitled to return a verdict of not guilty of the burglary but guilty of the lesser offence of assault occasioning actual bodily harm (see p 1005 e to g, post).

R v Springfield (1969) 53 Cr App R 608, *R v Salisbury* [1976] VR 452 and *R v Wilson (Clarence)* [1983] 1 All ER 993 applied.

R v Clarence [1886–90] All ER Rep 133 considered.

Notes

For the power to convict of an offence other than that charged, see 11 Halsbury's Laws (4th edn) para 311, and for cases on the subject, see 14(1) Digest (Reissue) 416–422, 3522–3609.

For burglary, see 11 Halsbury's Laws (4th edn) para 1274, and for cases on the subject, see 15 Digest (Reissue) 1346, 11676–11677.

For the Offences against the Person Act 1861, s 20, see 8 Halsbury's Statutes (3rd edn) 154.

For the Criminal Law Act 1967, s 6, see ibid 557.

For the Theft Act 1968, s 9, see ibid 788.

Cases referred to in judgment

DPP v Merriman [1972] 3 All ER 42, [1973] AC 584, [1972] 3 WLR 545, 14(2) Digest (Reissue) 814, 7016.

R v Austin (1973) 58 Cr App R 163, CA.

R v Carpenter (30 July 1979, unreported), CA.

R v Clarence (1888) 22 QBD 23, [1886–90] All ER Rep 133, CCR, 15 Digest (Reissue) 1180, 10071.

---

a　Section 9(1), so far as material, provides: 'A person is guilty of burglary if. . . (b) having entered any building or part of a building as a trespasser he steals or attempts to steal anything in the building or that part of it or inflicts or attempts to inflict on any person therein any grievous bodily harm.'

b　Section 20 provides: 'Whosoever shall unlawfully and maliciously wound or inflict any grievous bodily harm upon any other person, either with or without any weapon or instrument, shall be guilty of a misdemeanor, and being convicted thereof shall be liable to be kept in penal servitude.'

c　Section 6(3), so far as material, is set out at p 1003 j, post

R v Hodgson [1973] 2 All ER 552, [1973] QB 565, [1973] 2 WLR 570, Digest (Cont Vol
D) 171, 3511*aa*.
R v Lambert (1976) 65 Cr App R 12, CA.
R v Lillis [1972] 2 All ER 1209, [1972] 2 QB 236, [1972] 2 WLR 1409, CA, 14(1) Digest
(Reissue) 420, 3583.
R v McCready [1978] 3 All ER 967, [1978] 1 WLR 1376, CA, Digest (Cont Vol E) 137,
3554*b*.
R v Salisbury [1976] VR 452.
R v Snewing [1972] Crim LR 267, CA.
R v Springfield (1969) 53 Cr App R 608, CA, 14(1) Digest (Reissue) 419, 3563.
R v Wilson (Clarence) [1983] 1 All ER 993, [1983] 1 WLR 356, CA.

Applications for leave to appeal against conviction

The applicants, Edward John Jenkins and Ronald Patrick Jenkins, were jointly charged
in an indictment containing one count of burglary contrary to s 9(1)(b) of the Theft Act
1968. On 4 December 1981 in the Crown Court at Canterbury before Mr Recorder
Michael Lewis QC and a jury they were found not guilty of burglary but guilty of assault
occasioning actual bodily harm contrary to s 47 of the Offences against the Person Act
1861. Edward John Jenkins was sentenced to seven days' imprisonment and Ronald
Patrick Jenkins to 21 days' imprisonment. The applicants applied to the full court for
leave to appeal against conviction on the ground, inter alia, that the recorder erred in law
in ruling and directing the jury that it was open to a jury on the charge laid in the
indictment, ie burglary contrary to s 9(1)(b) of the 1968 Act, to return a verdict of assault
occasioning actual bodily harm. The court granted leave to appeal and treated the
applications as the substantive appeals. The facts are set out in the judgment of the court.

Gregory Stone (assigned by the Registrar of Criminal Appeals) for the applicants.
Anthony Webb for the Crown.

At the conclusion of the argument the court announced that, for reasons to be given
later, the appeals would be allowed and the convictions quashed, leave to appeal to the
House of Lords would be refused but the court would be prepared to certify the
involvement of a point of law of general public importance.

18 February. The following judgment of the court was delivered.

PURCHAS LJ. The judgment that I am about to read has been seen by Staughton J,
who is not now present, and he agrees with it. On 4 December 1981 in the Crown Court
at Canterbury the applicants, who were jointly charged with burglary, were each found
not guilty of burglary, but guilty of assault occasioning actual bodily harm. They now
apply for leave to appeal against conviction, the applications having been referred directly
to the full court by the registrar.

The history leading to the appearance before the court of the applicants, who are father
(Edward John Jenkins) and son (Ronald Patrick Jenkins), involves two families called
Wilson and Jenkins. The members of the Jenkins family involved are the two applicants
and Richard Leslie Jenkins, brother of Ronald Jenkins. Richard Jenkins was a member of
the local police force and was called as a witness for the prosecution. The Wilson family
consisted of Mr and Mrs Wilson, their 10-year-old daughter, Andrea, and their 17-year-
old son.

At the material time Mrs Wilson was living with Ronald Jenkins at 1 Brook Avenue,
Garlings, Margate, Kent. She had left Mr Wilson and her children at 47 St James Road,
Margate, in June 1981. Mr Wilson and their children had remained living at the family
home at St James Park Road.

On 3 July 1981 Mr Wilson found himself outside the Jenkins's home. The reason he
gave was that he wished to see Mrs Wilson, as did Andrea, who was in the back of his car.

Whatever may have been the real circumstances surrounding this visit, it is clear that a serious altercation arose when a number of male members of the Jenkins family issued *a* from the house, causing Mr Wilson to drive away in a hurry. It was said that he nearly drove over one or more of the Jenkins family in making his escape. Amongst those present were the two applicants and Richard Jenkins. Mr Wilson drove home to 47 St James Road, with three members of the Jenkins family in hot pursuit. He tried to bar himself inside the house, but the applicants burst in and a fight ensued, in the course of which Mr Wilson received serious injury necessitating his admission to hospital for *b* treatment, and Andrea, who was a witness, fled in terror to summon assistance from neighbours. We have been told by counsel that the facts disclosed on the statements served under s 2 of the Criminal Justice Act 1967 would permit the addition of a count alleging assault occasioning actual bodily harm within s 47 of the Offences against the Person Act 1861, under the provisions of proviso (i) to s 2(2) of the Administration of Justice (Miscellaneous Provisions) Act 1933 (as amended).   *c*

On these facts the applicants were arraigned on an indictment containing one count, reading:

'STATEMENT OF OFFENCE
Burglary, contrary to section 9 (1) (*b*) of the Theft Act 1968.

d

PARTICULARS OF OFFENCE
Edward John Jenkins and Ronald Patrick Jenkins on the 3rd day of July 1981 at Westgate in the County of Kent having entered a building situate at 47 St. James Park Road as trespassers inflicted grievous bodily harm upon Jeffrey Brian Wilson therein.'

At the beginning of the trial the recorder discussed with counsel both for the Crown and *e* for the two applicants the possibility of amending the indictment under his powers in s 5 of the Indictments Act 1915 so as to permit the jury, by s 6(3) of the Criminal Law Act 1967, to return an alternative verdict of assault occasioning actual bodily harm.

The recorder clearly had in mind a course which had grown up of adding the words 'by assaulting him' to the particulars in counts alleging offences under s 18 of the Offences against the Person Act 1861. This practice was recognised and approved in the judgment *f* of this court in *R v McCready* [1978] 3 All ER 967 at 971, [1978] 1 WLR 1376 at 1382:

'For the reasons already set out in this judgment, if the particulars of offence do not specify the way in which grievous bodily harm was caused, there can be no plea to or verdict of unlawful wounding or assault occasioning actual bodily harm or common assault. We were told by counsel that because of the decisions in *R v Austin* *g* (1973) 58 Cr App R 163 and *R v Lambert* (1976) 65 Cr App R 12, some draftsmen of indictments now give particulars of the way in which the grievous bodily harm was caused as, for example, by such words as "by assaulting him". We approve of this practice.

Finally we would remind trial judges of their powers of amending indictments. All too often indictments charge offences under s 18 when there is little prospect of *h* a verdict of guilty but every likelihood of a jury returning a verdict of guilty to a lesser offence. Whenever there is this possibility the judge of his own motion can always amend the indictment so as to enable an accused to plead to, or a jury to return a verdict of, a lesser offence, provided always of course that no prejudice is likely to arise to the accused.'

The second paragraph cited above was clearly an indication by Lawton LJ that, in the *j* particular facts of that case, the court ought really to have acted of its own motion and added a count charging the lesser offence of assault. If this had been done there would have been no problem. Unfortunately, in the instant case the recorder's attention was focussed exclusively on the first of the two paragraphs cited above. In this case likewise, had an alternative count of assault occasioning actual bodily harm been added, no problems would have arisen.

There was lengthy argument during which the recorder was referred to *R v Snewing*
[1972] Crim 267, *R v Clarence* (1888) 22 QBD 23, [1886–90] All ER Rep 133 and *R v Hodgson* [1973] 2 All ER 552, [1973] QB 565 as well as, of course, *R v McCready* [1978] 3 All ER 967, [1978] 1 WLR 1376. In his ruling the recorder compared the wording of s 9(1)(b) of the Theft Act 1968 with part of the definition of the offence created by s 20 of the Offences against the Person Act 1861 relating specifically to 'the infliction of grievous bodily harm'. We quote an extract from his ruling:

'I raised the matter without having read *R v McCready* (recently, at all events), and having only a vague recollection of the reasoning behind the decision. But it is distinguishable from the situation before me because here I am dealing with "the infliction of grievous bodily harm", whereas it was "causing" in *R v McCready*, a s 18 offence. I am further fortified by the reference I have seen to *R v Clarence* (although it has not been possible for counsel to bring me that authority) . . . On the basis of the reference to it (which I think is clear authority of very long standing), the word "inflict" within s 20 necessarily involves an assault. Accordingly, in my judgment, by virtue of the provisions of s 6 (3) of the Criminal Law Act 1967, the indictment as presently laid is capable of permitting the jury to find, if they think it appropriate, assault occasioning actual bodily harm. In other words, that lesser offence is, in my view, by necessary implication at the very least, contained in the particulars of the offence here charged. I shall, in due course, so direct the jury.'

In fairness to the recorder, we mention that during the course of the lengthy argument counsel who appeared for Edward Jenkins but does not appear before us opposed counsel for the Crown's application to add the words 'by assault', on the basis that the authorities showed that the word 'inflict' did imply an assault, and that to add that to the particular count would be to add nothing. Counsel for the applicants before us did not adopt this argument.

By their proposed grounds of appeal each applicant relies on two main grounds: (1) that the recorder was wrong to leave the alternative verdict to the jury, and (2) that the recorder was wrong in refusing an application made to quash the indictment because the words 'unlawfully' or 'maliciously' were not included in the particulars. The basis of this submission would have been that s 9 of the Theft Act 1968 relates to 'offences' (see the words of s 9(1)(a) and (2) of that Act). Although s 9(1)(b) does not contain the word 'offence', that word must be implied by reason of its association with the subsections immediately preceding and following it. Therefore, it being possible that 'to inflict grievous bodily harm' might not be an offence in extreme circumstances such as self-defence or some other lawful excuse, the particulars relating to 'inflicting grievous bodily harm' simpliciter disclosed no offence. Rightly, if we may say so, counsel who now appears for both applicants abandoned this ground as part of his application for leave to appeal.

Edward Jenkins had a third ground of appeal, which related to the conduct of the recorder during the hearing of evidence. It was apparent to us that this ground had no substance, and very properly, before the appeal was listed, counsel for the applicants communicated with the court, indicating that he did not intend to rely on this third ground. The applications therefore are now neatly within the ambit of the first ground.

As cited above, the count charged two elements: (1) entering as a trespasser, and (2) inflicting grievous bodily harm. As will be indicated subsequently, we are not confident, that additional words such as 'by assaulting him' can be effective either to vary the nature of the offence with which the accused is charged or to extend the area of his criminal liability in terms of s 6(3) of the Criminal Law Act 1967, the relevant part of which reads:

'Where, on a person's trial on indictment for any offence except treason or murder, the jury find him not guilty of the offence specifically charged in the indictment, but the allegations in the indictment amount to or include (expressly or by implication) an allegation of another offence . . . the jury may find him guilty of that other offence or of an offence of which he could be found guilty on an indictment specifically charging that other offence.'

If the offence of unlawfully inflicting grievous bodily harm does not necessarily involve proving an assault, and if the depositions or statements do not disclose evidence justifying *a* the addition of a count alleging an offence under s 47 of the 1861 Act, the addition of words in the particulars should not, in our view, be used to achieve what could not be done under the 1933 Act. However, the point does not arise here and has not been fully argued. Moreover, in both *R v McCready* [1978] 3 All ER 967, [1978] 1 WLR 1376 and *R v Wilson (Clarence)* [1983] 1 All ER 993, [1983] 1 WLR 356 the situation was the same.

The possibility of a wide interpretation of the words 'or of an offence of which he *b* could be found guilty on an indictment specifically charging that other offence', to embrace an offence of assault occasioning actual bodily harm where a count alleging that offence could have been added, is not open to us for consideration, in view of *R v Springfield* (1969) 53 Cr App R 608, as specifically referred to and approved in *R v Lillis* [1972] 2 All ER 1209 at 1211–1212, [1972] 2 QB 236 at 240, where reference is made to part of the judgment of Sachs LJ in *R v Springfield*, viz: *c*

> 'The test is to see whether it is a *necessary* step towards establishing the major offence to prove the commission of the lesser offence: in other words, is the lesser offence an essential ingredient of the major one?' (My emphasis).

It is to be noted that the words of s 6(3) make no reference to greater or lesser offences, but merely refer to the proving of another offence being expressly or by implication an *d* ingredient of the offence charged.

In the instant appeal two specific questions arise. (1) Is the meaning of the phrase 'inflict ... grievous bodily harm' in s 9(1)(*b*), and presumably s 9(2), the same as its meaning in s 20 of the Offences against the Person Act 1861? (2) Does the expression 'inflict grievous bodily harm' necessarily involve an assault by the accused on the victim?

If the judgments of the majority of the judges in *R v Clarence* (1888) 22 QBD 23, *e* [1886–90] All ER Rep 133 are correct, as was accepted by the Court of Appeal, Criminal Division in *R v Snewing* [1972] Crim LR 267 and *R v Carpenter* (30 July 1979, unreported), to give a proper interpretation of s 9(1)(*b*) of the Theft Act 1968 the answer to the first question may have to be in the negative; but if the judgments of the minority, including Wills J in *R v Clarence*, are right, the meaning of the expression in the two Acts will be the same. *f*

The intention of Parliament in enacting s 9 of the Theft Act 1968, as appears from a consideration of the section as a whole within the context of s 1 (ordinary theft) with a maximum term of imprisonment of 10 years, s 9 (burglary) with a maximum sentence of 14 years, and s 10 (aggravated burglary) and s 8 (robbery), both offences carrying a maximum sentence of imprisonment for life, would indicate that, where a person enters a building as a trespasser, either with an intent to commit any of a number of specified *g* offences, or, having entered as a trespasser, steals or attempts to steal (itself an offence, but one of lesser gravity), then that person should be liable to the greater penalty provided by s 9. Where he inflicts or attempts to inflict on any person grievous bodily harm then this of itself, in conjunction with the trespass which is the essential ingredient of an offence under s 9 would, if committed unlawfully and maliciously, be of itself an offence under s 20 of the Offences against the Person Act 1861. If, however, it is committed by a *h* trespasser in a dwelling, then again under s 9 of the 1968 Act the extra penalty is incurred.

It seems unlikely that in this context Parliament intended to restrict the expression 'inflict grievous bodily harm' to the narrow area of assault. To test this proposition it may be helpful to consider a set of circumstance that could not be described as fanciful. An intruder gains access to the house without breaking in (where there is an open window, for instance). He is on the premises as a trespasser, and his intrusion is observed by *j* someone in the house of whom he may not even be aware, and as a result that person suffers severe shock, with a resulting stroke. In such a case it is difficult to see how an assault could be alleged; but nevertheless his presence would have been a direct cause of the stroke, which must amount to grievous bodily harm. Should such an event fall outside the provisions of s 9, when causing some damage to the property falls fairly within it? We cite this as merely one example. For other examples, all of which would

be relevant, we refer to the judgments in cases where the meaning of the words 'inflict
a grievous bodily harm' are considered in relation to s 20 of the 1861 Act.

If the decision in *R v Salisbury* [1976] VR 452, as approved and adopted in *R v Wilson*
(Clarence) [1983] 1 All ER 993, [1983] 1 WLR 356, is correct, no problem arises, since the
wide meaning of the expression 'inflict grievous bodily harm' in s 20 held in *R v Wilson*
would equally cover the meaning of those words which we consider must be the true
interpretation of s 9(1)(*b*) if that section is to be given its proper force. It is to be noticed
b that *R v Salisbury* [1976] VR 452 was not cited to the court in *R v Carpenter* (30 July 1979,
unreported), nor was *R v Carpenter* cited to the court in *R v Wilson*. But in both *R v
Carpenter* and *R v Wilson* it appears that there was full argument during which the court
was referred to the leading case of *R v Clarence* (1888) 22 QBD 23, [1886–90] All ER Rep
133.

We have therefore to consider the present case, albeit relating to a different offence,
c but raising in practice almost equivalent questions of law, in the context of two
conflicting judgments of this court. The position is however easily resolved by part of
the speech of Lord Diplock in *DPP v Merriman* [1972] 3 All ER 42 at 58, [1973] AC 584
at 605:

d   'These decisions it [the Criminal Division of the Court of Appeal] rightly treated
     as binding, for although the Criminal Division of the Court of Appeal is not so
     strictly bound by its own previous decisions as is the Civil Division, its liberty to
     depart from a precedent which it is convinced was erroneous is restricted to cases
     where the departure is in favour of the accused.'

In this case we may depart from the decision in *R v Carpenter*, as to do so would be in
favour of the applicants. But we may not depart from the decision in *R v Wilson*, for the
e contrary reason. We are therefore bound by the decision in *R v Wilson* to hold that the
meaning to be given to 'inflict grievous bodily harm' in s 20 of the 1861 Act is not
exclusively restricted to assaults within the meaning of 'assault' in s 47. This precedent
strongly supports our own approach to the meaning of the same words in s 9(1)(*b*) of the
Theft Act 1968. In enacting s 9(1)(*b*) Parliament clearly had in mind the commission of
an offence under s 20 of the 1861 Act. Although the strict wording of s 9(1)(*b*) would not
f necessarily confine the court to an exactly equivalent interpretation, it is clearly
convenient that this should be so. On the other hand, we would not feel ourselves bound
by the decision in *R v Carpenter* if that were the only precedent and *R v Wilson* had not
been decided. For the reasons already given in this judgment, regardless of the
interpretation given to the words in s 20 of the 1861 Act, we would be of the opinion
that they have the wider meaning in s 9(1)(*b*) of the 1968 Act, and that therefore in any
g event, for the reasons set out in *R v Wilson*, it was not open to the jury under the
provisions of s 6(3) of the 1967 Act to consider an alternative verdict of assault occasioning
actual bodily harm. It is to be noticed that in *R v Wilson* there was no evidence disclosed
on the depositions or statements which would have enabled the court to add a count to
the indictment under s 47, as would have been the case in *R v McCready* [1978] 3 All ER
967, [1978] 1 WLR 1376 or the instant case.

h   For these reasons we hold that the recorder erred in leaving to the jury the alternative
verdict of assault occasioning actual bodily harm. We therefore grant leave to appeal
against conviction to both applicants. Counsel for the applicants has told us that he has
instructions to consent to our treating the applications as the substantive appeals. We
therefore allow the appeals by both applicants and quash both convictions.

Before parting with the case we wish to express our sympathy with the recorder, who
j clearly took great pains in considering a difficult legal problem; but we cannot avoid
expressing regret that he did not take the course open to him under s 6 of the Indictments
Act 1915 of adding a count to the indictment; a course which was open to him under the
1967 Act in the particular circumstances of this case, and which towards the end of his
ruling he acknowledged was desirable.

Appeals allowed. Convictions quashed.

The court refused leave to appeal to the House of Lords but certified, under s 33(2) of the Criminal Appeal Act 1968, that the following point of law of general public importance was involved in its decision: whether on a charge of burglary contrary to s 9(1)(b) of the Theft Act 1968, the particulars of the offence being that the accused having entered a building as trespassers inflicted grievous bodily harm on a person therein, it was open to a jury to return a verdict of not guilty as charged but guilty of assault occasioning actual bodily harm.

Solicitors: *Richard A Crabb*, Maidstone (for the Crown).

Raina Levy   Barrister.

R v Agritraders Ltd

COURT OF APPEAL, CRIMINAL DIVISION
WATKINS LJ, KILNER BROWN AND RUSSELL JJ
22 OCTOBER 1982, 25 JANUARY 1983

Criminal law – Costs – Award out of central funds – Court of Appeal – Defendant's conviction by Crown Court quashed on appeal to Court of Appeal – Order made for payment of defence costs 'here and below' out of central funds – Scope of order – Whether order including costs of committal proceedings – Costs in Criminal Cases Act 1973, s 7(1)(3).

Criminal law – Costs – Award out of central funds – Court of Appeal – Defendant's conviction by Crown Court quashed on appeal by Court of Appeal – Order made for payment of defence costs 'here and below' out of central funds – Need for bills regarding proceedings below to be submitted to Registrar of Criminal Appeals – Costs in Criminal Cases Act 1973, s 7(4).

The defendants were charged with certain offences. The magistrates' court committed them for trial at the Crown Court, where they were subsequently convicted. They appealed to the Court of Appeal, which allowed the appeal and quashed the convictions. Counsel for the defendants then applied for an order, under s 7(1)[a] of the Costs in Criminal Cases Act 1973, that the defence costs be paid out of central funds. The Court of Appeal ordered that the costs 'here and below' be so paid. The defendants' solicitors then sent out three bills of costs, one to the Registrar of Criminal Appeals in respect of the appeal, one to the Crown Court in respect of the trial, and one to the magistrates' court in respect of the committal proceedings. The Registrar of Criminal Appeals knew nothing about the bills sent to the two lower courts until after they had been taxed and paid. As soon as he heard about them, he informed the solicitors that all the bills should have been submitted to him. He agreed to allow the Crown Court payment to stand but informed the solicitors that they had to return the money paid out by the magistrates' court because the Court of Appeal order only covered the costs incurred in the Court of Appeal and the Crown Court. The solicitors contended that under the order the defendants were entitled, by virtue of s 7(3) of the 1973 Act, not only to their costs in the Court of Appeal and the Crown Court but also to those 'in any court below' where the proceedings which were the subject of the appeal had been heard. They submitted that s 7(3) defined the costs referred to in s 7(1) and that consequently an order for costs under s 7(1) included costs incurred in the Court of Appeal and any court below unless a specific order to the contrary was made.

Held – (1) The Registrar of Criminal Appeals was, by virtue of s 7(4) of the 1973 Act, the relevant taxing authority in respect of orders for costs made under s 7(1) of that Act, and accordingly the Crown Court and the magistrates' court had erred in agreeing to receive, tax and pay the bills submitted to them (see p 1008 *e f*, post).

---

a Section 7 is set out at p 1008 f to j, post

a (2) When the Court of Appeal made an order for 'costs here and below' the order referred to the costs in the Court of Appeal and in the court immediately below, ie the court from which the appeal emanated. On the true construction of s 7 of the 1973 Act the provisions of s 7(1) were quite distinct from those of s 7(3), which did not come into play until an order had been made under s 7(1) specifying the courts to which it applied. Accordingly, under s 7(3), it was only the costs properly incurred by an appellant 'in any court' specified in the order which had to be paid out of central funds. It followed that,
b since the Court of Appeal order covered only the defendants' costs in that court and the court immediately below it, the solicitors would be required to refund the money paid out by the magistrates' court (see p 1010 a to e and j to p 1011 a, post).

Notes

For the award of costs out of central funds by the Court of Appeal, Criminal Division, see
c 11 Halsbury's Laws (4th edn) para 790, and for cases on the subject see 14(2) Digest (Reissue) 859–860, 7435–7439 and 50 Digest (Repl) 533, 1998, 536, 2029.

For the Costs in Criminal Cases Act 1973, s 7, see 43 Halsbury's Statutes (3rd edn) 273.

Cases referred to in judgment

Inchcape, Re, Craigmyle v Inchcape [1942] 2 All ER 157, [1942] Ch 394, 50 Digest (Repl)
d 533, 1998.

Lawrie v Lees (1881) 7 App Cas 19, HL, 50 Digest (Repl) 536, 2029.

R v Michael [1976] 1 All ER 629, [1976] QB 414, [1975] 3 WLR 1227, 14(2) Digest (Reissue) 859, 7437.

Case also cited

e *R v Lytham Justices, ex p Carter* [1975] Crim LR 225, DC.

Application

On 23 January 1981 in the Crown Court at Exeter before his Honour Judge Best and a jury, the applicants, Agritraders Ltd, were convicted of offences under the Medicines Act 1968 and sentenced. They appealed against the convictions. On 17 November 1981 the
f Court of Appeal, Criminal Division (Watkins LJ, Kilner Brown and Russell JJ) allowed the appeal, quashed the convictions and directed that the applicants were to have their 'costs out of central funds here and below'. The Criminal Appeal Office interpreted that as meaning the costs incurred in the proceedings in the Court of Appeal and in the Crown Court. The applicants contended that they were also entitled to their costs in respect of the committal proceedings before the magistrates. The Registrar of Criminal Appeals consulted the Court of Appeal about the matter. It informed the applicants that
g the Criminal Appeal Office's construction of the order was correct. The applicants asked for the application to be relisted in order that the matter might be fully argued and that they might, if necessary, apply to have the order as to costs amended so as to include their costs in the magistrates' court. The facts are set out in the judgment of the court.

h *John M Bowyer* for the applicants.

Cur adv vult

25 January. The following judgment of the court was delivered.

WATKINS LJ. This is an unusual application. It arises out of the following circumstances. On 23 January 1981 in the Crown Court at Exeter before his Honour
j Judge Best and a jury the appellants, Agritraders Ltd, were convicted of (1) possessing a medicinal product labelled in such a way that it was likely to mislead and (2) possessing a medicinal product labelled in such a way as to falsely describe the product, contrary to ss 85(5) and 91(1) of the Medicines Act 1968. They were fined £250 on each count and ordered to pay £1,250 towards the costs of the prosecution. The jury found them not guilty of four similar offences, three of those verdicts being by the direction of the judge.

They appealed against their convictions. This court, constituted as it is now, allowed their appeal and quashed their convictions. Our judgment was delivered on 17 November 1981, wherein it was made clear that the appeal was allowed principally because crucial *a* evidence of the scientific analysis of veterinary medicines taken from the appellants' premises was, as presented during the trial, inadmissible. This point was unfortunately not raised at any time during the trial. It was taken here at the instigation of this court.

Counsel applied for the appellants' costs to be paid out of central funds. In granting the application we said that they should have 'costs out of central funds here and below'. The order was drawn up subsequently in those precise terms. A copy of it was sent to the *b* appellants' solicitors in April 1982. They had already (being aware, we are sure, of the terms of the order we made, if only because it was indorsed on counsel's brief) prepared three bills of the appellants' costs, one in respect of the appeal which was sent to the registrar of the Court of Appeal, Criminal Division, one in respect of the trial, which was sent to the Crown Court at Exeter and one in respect of the committal proceedings, which was sent to the magistrates' court. The bills sent to the Crown Court and to the *c* magistrates' court were taxed and paid at those courts without the knowledge or authority of the registrar. The sum obtained from central funds relating to the magistrates' court was in the region of £2,300.

There was a delay in taxing the costs of the appeal, which prompted the solicitors to write letters, some of them in intemperate terms, to the registrar, whose office is responsible for taxing thousands of bills in a year. From this correspondence the taxing *d* officer here learnt of the payments already made by the Crown and magistrates' courts respectively and wrote to the solicitors to the effect that (1) the registrar is the taxing authority following an appeal, to whom all bills and fee notes should have been submitted, (2) the sums already paid out were not authorised by him, (3) the registrar would allow the Crown Court payment to stand, and (4) seeing that the phrase 'the court below' which was contained in the order did not include the magistrates' court, the sum *e* obtained from there should be returned to the clerk to the justices forthwith.

In our view the registrar is unquestionably the taxing authority. Therefore, all bills should have been sent to him. It was wrong of both the Crown Court and the magistrates' court to agree to receive, to tax and to pay the bills. The registrar's authority is derived from s 7 of the Costs in Criminal Cases Act 1973, which provides:

'(1) When the Court of Appeal allow an appeal under Part I of the Criminal *f* Appeal Act 1968 against—(a) conviction, or (b) a verdict of not guilty by reason of insanity, or (c) a finding under section 4 of the Criminal Procedure (Insanity) Act 1964 that the appellant is under disability, the court may order the payment out of central funds of the costs of the appellant.

(2) On determining an appeal or application for leave to appeal under Part I of the Criminal Appeal Act 1968, the Court of Appeal may order the payment out of *g* central funds of the costs of the prosecutor.

(3) The costs payable out of central funds under subsection (1) or (2) above shall be such sums as appear to the Court of Appeal reasonably sufficient to compensate the party concerned for any expenses properly incurred by him in the appeal or application (including any proceedings preliminary or incidental thereto) or in any court below. *h*

(4) The amount of costs ordered to be paid under this section shall (except where it is a specific amount ordered to be paid towards a person's expenses as a whole) be ascertained as soon as practicable by the registrar of criminal appeals.'

The taxing officer was, so the solicitors contended, in error in demanding the return of the whole sum paid out of the magistrates' court, because a part of it was in respect of *j* the hearing of charges against the appellants which the magistrates dismissed, the remainder being attributable to the committal of the appellants in the present case. This contention may well be valid, but it is of no consequence to what we are called on to decide. He was challenged too about the construction he put on the phrase 'the court below'. The registrar was consulted and so was this court about this matter, with the result that the solicitors were informed that the taxing officer's construction was correct.

The solicitors asked that counsel be heard on their behalf to argue to the contrary, despite
a   their being informed that, as is the fact, he had not made an application to us for the costs
incurred at the magistrates' court to be paid out of central funds.

In view of their persistence in pursuing this request, and so that they should be given
the opportunity in court of ventilating their obvious grievance about the full effect of
the order for costs we made, we agreed to hear counsel on their behalf. He, it should be
said, represented the appellants in their successful appeal.

b   It is necessary in examining his submissions first of all to recite from the transcript
what took place at the conclusion of the appeal when the application on behalf of the
appellants for costs was made:

'Mr Bowyer. There remains the matter of costs, my Lord. As your Lordships
know, costs below were dealt with by an order that the defendants pay the specified
c   sum of £1,250. There is also the matter of the costs here. I would ask your Lordships
to make an order in their favour in respect of both sets of costs. That would seem to
meet the justice of the case.

Watkins LJ. The question of costs below does not arise. You have had your
conviction set aside, so all the penalties go with it.

Mr Bowyer. We incurred costs there.
d   Watkins LJ. You are asking for an order for costs now in your favour below?

Mr Bowyer. That is right, my Lord, because the outcome of your Lordships'
decision is that there was never really a complete case. There was never the analyst's
evidence which was an indispensable element.

Watkins LJ. What do you say, Mr De Freitas?

Mr De Freitas. It may be a case where your Lordships feel it appropriate that the
e   costs should be awarded out of central funds. If I may say this, my Lord, at the stage
when the case reached the Crown Court Mr Scuffam had given a written statement,
which obviously on reflection, in view of the evidence that he gave——

Kilner Brown J. Mr De Freitas, forgive me, I do not think it is necessary to elaborate.
There is a recent reiteration of the Practice Direction which says that where there is
a complete acquittal, normally costs should be awarded out of central funds. It is
f   only where the prosecution have been shown to have misbehaved that an order is
made against them.

Mr De Freitas. I am obliged to your Lordship. In this case no question of that
arises. It then becomes a question of whether your Lordships order that both sets of
costs be out of central funds.

Watkins LJ. There will be costs out of central funds here and below.'
g
Kilner Brown J's abbreviated reference to misbehaviour was, to quote the Practice
Direction of 5 November 1981 ([1981] 3 All ER 703, [1981] 1 WLR 1383), a reference to
acting spitefully, or instituting or continuing the proceedings without reasonable cause.

We desire to say at this juncture that we were not in doubt at the hearing of the appeal,
and do not doubt now, that counsel for the applicants made an application to us for the
h   appellants' costs in the Court of Appeal and in the Crown Court ('the court below') only,
and that we granted his application to that extent and no more. This is also, in our view,
clear beyond peradventure from reading the portion of the transcript already recited.

None the less, and undaunted by what we say, counsel submits, although agreeing that
in making his application for costs he referred only to those incurred in the Court of
Appeal and in the Crown Court, that if this court makes an order for costs 'here and
j   below' from central funds, an appellant is entitled, by virtue of the provisions of s 7(3) of
the 1973 Act, to costs in any and every court below where the proceedings the subject of
appeal have been heard. The purpose of s 7(3), he says, is to define the costs referred to in
s 7(1), so that an order for costs made under sub-s (1) includes costs incurred in this court
and all courts below, unless a specific contrary order is made. He points to a similarity in
the provisions of ss 5 and 6 of the 1973 Act, which relate to appeals in the Divisional
Court and the House of Lords, which he maintains have the like effect.

We find this submission almost incomprehensible. By s 7(1) this court *may*, in its discretion obviously, order the payment out of central funds of the costs of the appellant. *a* In the exercise of that discretion the court is entitled to award an appellant his costs in this court and refuse him his costs in the Crown Court. It may award him his costs in the Crown Court too; likewise the magistrates' court. It will exercise its discretion, if invited to do so, in respect of each court in turn, having regard to the circumstances in which an appeal against conviction has been allowed in this court, the circumstances obtaining in the Crown Court, bearing in mind the practice direction of 5 November 1981 and the *b* circumstances of the committal proceedings. The considerations involved in each of this variety of circumstances will inevitably be different and demand, therefore, a separate exercise of the discretion.

It is only when an order for costs is made under s 7(1) of the 1973 Act, and in respect of a court specified in the order, that s 7(3) comes into play. It bites on the order for costs only so far as that goes and provides that the costs thereby payable *shall* be such as to the *c* Court of Appeal appear reasonably sufficient to compensate the appellant for any expenses properly incurred by him in any court in respect of which an order for costs has been made. This mandatory provision, providing for the extent of the compensation, empowers this court in making its award to make an order for costs simpliciter (they will then be taxed) or to make an order in a fixed sum or sums in deciding what is reasonably sufficient to compensate an appellant. The discretionary power in sub-s (1) is entirely *d* distinct from the mandatory provision in sub-s (3) as we have construed it. They do not react on one another, as counsel seems to think they do, so as to lead to the conclusion that an order for costs in the terms 'here and below' means any and every court below.

To put a different construction from this on these two subsections would, we think, amount to a complete misunderstanding of their plainly stated provisions, which, as we have explained them, have been, in our experience, regularly applied in this court ever *e* since the enactment of the 1973 Act. Moreover similar provisions appeared in s 24 of the Criminal Appeal Act 1968 and were similarly applied here.

Support for the construction we make of s 7 of the 1973 Act is, we think, also to be found, contrary to another of counsel's submissions, in s 3 of the 1973 Act ('Awards by Crown Courts'). This makes no reference to 'any court below' as do ss 5, 6 and 7. This is because there is only one court below a Crown Court, namely a magistrates' court, for *f* which reason it was obviously thought necessary (see s 3(9)) to provide the Crown Court with the power, in its discretion, to award costs in that court by specifically and separately providing for it in s 3(9). An order made by the Crown Court for 'the costs of the defence' will not include costs incurred in the magistrates' court if there is no reference to the magistrates' court in the order: see *R v Michael* [1976] 1 All ER 629, [1976] QB 414 with the decision in which on this point we entirely agree. *g*

Counsel referred us to the provisions for awards of costs in the Costs in Criminal Cases Act 1952, which he claimed, unavailingly so far as we are concerned, assisted him in the construction he sought to put on s 7 of the 1973 Act. This was an unimpressive argument to which we see no need to make more than a passing and dismissive reference.

This brings us to the use, frequently made, of the phrase 'costs here and below' and the meaning attributed to it. In the notes to RSC Ord 62, r 4 in *The Supreme Court Practice* *h* *1982*, vol 1, p 1014, para 62/4/6, it is stated:

'Where on an appeal from the Divisional Court to the Court of Appeal an order is made dismissing the appeal with costs "here and below", the reference is to costs in the Divisional Court. Costs incurred at quarter sessions (now Crown Court) from which the appeal was brought to the High Court are not included.'

We agree, but counsel, when faced with this note, had no hesitation in asserting that it *j* was referable only to civil proceedings. He provided us with no foundation for this assertion. We are satisfied there is none. In our opinion whenever the phrase 'costs here and below' is used in the Court of Appeal in civil and criminal matters the reference is to the Court of Appeal and the court immediately below, ie the court from which the

a
appeal emanated. Before this application was made we had never heard any other meaning attributed to it. This, we believe, is because prior to this application no one has sought to argue that it can be otherwise construed.

The next submission was to the effect that the combination of Kilner Brown J's intervention when Mr De Freitas was addressing the court, allied to the contents of the 1981 practice direction already mentioned, led him to understand, albeit mistakenly, that our intention was to award the appellants their costs in the magistrates' court. It is
b
with regret that we feel obliged to say that we found this to be a surprising and in the circumstances extraordinary contention. We hope that counsel on reflection has already concluded that it would have been wise of him to have omitted it from his otherwise responsible, though unacceptable, submissions to this court.

Finally, if, as we do, we reject his submissions, we are invited to consider counsel's invitation to us to reconsider our award of costs so as to include those incurred in the
c
magistrates' court.

In *R v Michael* his Honour Judge Rubin cogently and very helpfully reviewed the inherent jurisdiction of the court to vary its own orders. In that case he varied an order for costs as drawn up, which he had made in the Crown Court, so as to give effect to his intention, which was to include in the order costs incurred in the magistrates' court. In his judgment he referred ([1976] 1 All ER 629 at 632, [1976] QB 414 at 418) to what
d
Lord Penzance said in *Lawrie v Lees* (1881) 7 App Cas 19 at 34–35:

> 'I cannot doubt that under the original powers of the Court, quite independent of any order that is made under the Judicature Act, every Court has the power to vary its own orders which are drawn up mechanically in the registry or in the office of the court—to vary them in such a way as to carry out its own meaning, and where language has been used which is doubtful, to make it plain. I think that power is
e
> inherent in every Court.'

Seeing that the order as drawn up in the present case expresses our intention precisely we, whilst recognising our power in appropriate circumstances to do so, decline to vary the order. We see no reason why we should.

The ingenuity of counsel was seemingly inexhaustible, for he went on to ask us to
f
regard his omission to make an application for costs in the magistrates' court as an oversight which was the product of forgetfulness. He referred us to the quotation in *R v Michael* [1976] 1 All ER 629 at 633, [1976] QB 414 at 419 from Morton J's judgment in *Re Inchcape* [1942] 2 All ER 157 at 160, [1942] Ch 394 at 399:

> 'It is true that, when the case was before me, I made the order which I intended to make in regard to the costs for which I was asked to make provision. There was,
g
> however, an accidental omission on the part of counsel, and I did not make the order which I would have made if that accidental omission had not occurred.'

Morton J made this order under the then existing slip rule, but we have no reason to doubt that the inherent jurisdiction of this court would enable us to reconsider an order for costs, so as to enlarge it in some particular way, if we were satisfied that the omission
h
to make the material application was due to a genuine accidental omission on the part of counsel. We regret to have to say that we do not accept that there was an accidental omission to ask for costs in the present case.

Finally, we think it right to say that regardless of whether we have the jurisdiction, which we are inclined to doubt, to entertain a fresh application for costs, which has arisen as a result of an afterthought, we should, in the circumstances of the present case, refuse
j
it out of hand.

Order not varied.

Solicitors: *Pethybridges & Best*, Great Torrington (for the applicants).

Raina Levy   Barrister.

Lidster and another v Owen

a

COURT OF APPEAL, CIVIL DIVISION
WALLER, DUNN AND SLADE LJJ
22, 23 FEBRUARY 1983

Entertainment – Music and dancing licence – Renewal of licence – Application for renewal –
Jurisdiction of licensing justices – Restriction of permitted hours on renewal – Justices refusing   b
renewal of licence on ground that refusal necessary for maintenance of public order – Whether
justices entitled to consider matters external to premises when premises themselves well-conducted
– Public Health Acts Amendment Act 1890, s 51.

On the true construction of s 51[a] of the Public Health Acts Amendment Act 1890
magistrates have a wide discretion in the 'regulation' of premises used for public dancing,   c
music or other entertainment and are entitled to take into account considerations which
are both internal and external to the premises when deciding whether to grant or renew
a music and dancing licence for particular premises. Thus in exercising their discretion
magistrates are entitled to have regard to the character and location of the premises and
to refuse a licence for premises, even though they are well-conducted, if persons leaving
the premises create an unacceptable degree of public disorder when they leave (see p 1014   d
e f, p 1015 d to h and p 1016 f g,post).
Sharpe v Wakefield [1886–90] All ER Rep 651 applied.

Notes
For renewal of justices' licences, see 26 Halsbury's Laws (4th edn) para 85, and for cases   e
on the subject, see 30 Digest (Reissue) 41, 301–309.
For the Public Health Acts Amendment Act 1890, s 51, see 26 Halsbury's Statutes (3rd
edn) 98.

Case referred to in judgments
Sharp v Wakefield [1891] AC 173, [1886–90] All ER Rep 651, HL, 30 Digest (Reissue) 12,   f
51.

Case also cited
Marsden v Birmingham Licensing Justices [1975] 3 All ER 517, Crown Court.

Appeal   g
John Douglas Lidster and John Maynard appealed from the order of Hodgson J hearing
the Crown Office list on 11 January 1982 whereby he dismissed their appeal by way of
case stated against an adjudication of Her Majesty's justices of the peace for the County of
Dorset acting in and for the petty sessional division of Bournemouth on 20 March 1981
whereby the justices refused the application to renew the public music, singing and
dancing licence held by the appellants in respect of premises known as the Stateside   h
Center, Bournemouth on the grounds of the objection of the respondent, David Owen,
Chief Constable of Dorset Police, that the continued existence of the licence was

---

a   Section 51, so far as material, provides: 'For the regulation of places ordinarily used for public
    dancing or music, or other public entertainment of the like kind, the following provisions shall
    have effect (namely):—1 ... a house, room, garden, or other place ... shall not be kept or used for   j
    public dancing, singing, music or other public entertainment of the like kind without a licence
    for the purpose or purposes for which the same respectively is to be used first obtained from the
    licensing justices ... 2. Such justices may ... grant licences to such persons as they think fit to
    keep or use houses ... or places for all or any of the purposes aforesaid upon such terms and
    conditions, and subject to such restrictions as they by the respective licences determine ...'

prejudicial to the maintenance of public order and the peace. The facts are set out in the
a judgment of Waller LJ.

Jarlath Finney for the appellants.
John Bull for the respondent.

b WALLER LJ. After a hearing lasting five days, the Bournemouth justices, at their
adjourned general licensing meeting on 20 March 1981, refused to renew the public
dancing, singing and music licence of the appellants in respect of the Stateside Center.
On appeal by way of case stated, Hodgson J hearing the Crown Office list dismissed the
appeal, and upheld the decision of the justices.

The Stateside Center was situated adjacent to Glen Fern Road, in the central area of
c Bournemouth. Also situated in that road, in close proximity (although under an entirely
separate management), were two other premises, namely the Outlook and the Maison
Royale.

The Stateside Center comprised a discotheque and a concert theatre; the discotheque
had the benefit of a liquor licence, and a music, singing and dancing licence, with a
special hours' certificate. The permitted hours were, therefore, from 6.30 pm each
d weekday, until 1 am.

Up to 1978 the licence had run until 2 am, but at the beginning of 1978 the justices
had cut back the time from 2 am to 1 am, so that until the hearing of this case the
closing time was 1 am.

On 15 January 1981 the respondent, who is the Chief Constable of Bournemouth,
served notice on the appellants that he would object to the renewal of the licence, on the
e ground that its continuation was prejudicial to the maintenance of public order and
peace.

At the hearing before the licensing justices, the evidence called by the police showed
that there was a very considerable amount of violence and crime in the immediate
neighbourhood of these discotheques and that it was at its worst immediately after the
discotheque had closed. This required a considerable number of extra police to be drafted
f to the area to deal with that problem.

There are two paragraphs in the case stated, which summarise the position.

'(k) Vandalism, violence, excessive noise, disorder and indecent behaviour had
been rife at night and in the early hours of the morning in central Bournemouth
during 1980 and particularly so in the Glen Fern Road and Old Christchurch Road
areas.

g   (l) In order to preserve the peace and maintain law and order the police had
found it necessary to re-deploy their resources with a concentration of personnel in
the Glen Fern Road area. This re-deployment had resulted in officers being drafted
into central Bournemouth from other districts.'

The judge, in the course of his judgment, having cited those two paragraphs, said:

h   'An appalling picture emerges. [The second appellant] called it unique in his
experience and said that he had never before heard of excess such as this. It is clear
that, when excited by drink, bright lights and loud music, the customers of these
discos spilled onto the roads, many of them behaved in a manner which was wholly
unacceptable. He [the second appellant] had to accept that some of those so behaving
came from the Stateside premises; indeed, on one occasion 300 people from Stateside
i went in a body towards the beach causing damage as they went.'

Although the evidence was that the appellants' premises were properly managed and
administered, the incidence of crime strongly suggested that it was caused by the extra
drinking hours after public houses closed at 11 pm.

The appellants were informed that an application, with a closing time of midnight, would be granted; but, although the other two discos accepted this alternative, the appellants did not. They appealed to the Divisional Court and now, that appeal having been dismissed, they appeal to this court.

The background of the appellants' appeal is that, having regard to the fact that no suggestion was made that their premises were other than perfectly well run, it was not open to the justices to refuse to renew their licence.

The provisions governing music and dancing licences are contained in s 51 of the Public Health Acts Amendment Act 1890, which reads (so far as is relevant): 'For the *regulation* of places ordinarily used for public dancing or music, or other public entertainment of the like kind, the following provisions shall have effect . . .' Subsection 1 deals with the necessity for a licence, and then sub-s 2 (which is the important one) reads:

> 'Such justices may, under the hands of a majority of them assembled at their general annual licensing meeting or at any adjournment thereof or at any special session convened with fourteen days previous notice, grant licences to such persons as they think fit to keep or use houses, rooms, gardens or places for all or any of the purposes aforesaid upon such terms and conditions, and subject to such restrictions as they by the respective licences determine . . .'

Then the subsection provides that the licence shall run for a year.

By sub-s 10 it is provided that: 'No notice need be given under sub-section four of this section when the application is for a renewal of any existing licence held by the applicant for the same premises.'

It was argued on behalf of the appellants that the word 'regulation' at the beginning of s 51 does not cover the sort of decision which was made in this case, and is intended to deal with the internal affairs of the licensee, and, secondly, that it was not within the powers of the justices to determine a licence on grounds relating solely to the benefit of the community. In my opinion, the word 'regulate' is apt to cover both internal and external considerations. The *Shorter Oxford English Dictionary* gives, as one of the meanings of 'regulate', 'subject to . . . restrictions' and that, in my view, is exactly what the justices were seeking to do in this case, namely to subject the appellants to the restriction of hours from 1 am to 12 midnight.

The judge, in reaching his decision, relied on *Sharp v Wakefield* [1891] AC 173, [1886–90] All ER Rep 651. This was a case under a different statute, namely the Alehouse Act 1828. Section 1 provided that:

> '. . . it shall be lawful for the justices . . . assembled at such meeting . . . to grant licences for the purposes aforesaid, to such persons as the said justices shall, in the execution of the powers herein contained and in the exercise of their discretion, deem fit and proper.'

By s 13, the licence was to remain in force for one year. The renewal provisions were contained in s 42 of the Licensing Act 1872.

In that case, on an application for a renewal of a licence, it was refused. On an appeal to quarter sessions, reasons were given, namely:

> 'On the hearing of an application for the renewal of a licence for the sale of intoxicating liquors under the Licensing Acts, 1828 and 1874, the licensing justices have a discretion to refuse the renewal on the ground of the remoteness from police supervision and the character and necessities of the neighbourhood.'

The appellant in that case, having appealed, first of all, to quarter sessions, then appealed to the Divisional Court and then to the Court of Appeal and ultimately to the House of Lords.

Counsel for the appellants has sought to distinguish that case on the ground that it was concerned with the police, and with a different statute, but the words of that statute (namely the 1828 Act) are similar though not identical with the present case. The House *a* of Lords, when dealing with that case, thought it was a plain case, and each of their Lordships said words to that effect in the course of their speeches. The argument there was that it was not open to the justices to refuse to renew a licence on considerations that had nothing to do with the licensee, and counsel for the appellants sought to distinguish that case because of the great emphasis which was placed in the statute relating to the licence on police supervision.

b But, as I have already indicated, the justices had refused to renew the licence, not only on the ground of remoteness of police supervision, but on the ground of the character and the necessities and locality of the neighbourhood in which the inn was situated.

Lord Macnaghten, in a very short judgment, said ([1891] AC 173 at 187, [1886–90] All ER Rep 651 at 657):

c '. . . for the reasons which have been stated by my noble and learned friends, and which it is unnecessary for me to repeat, I also am of opinion that it is clear beyond the possibility of doubt or question that the Act of 1828 conferred upon the licensing justices the same discretion in the case of an application for what is now termed a renewal, as in the case of a person applying for a licence for the first time, and that there is nothing in the subsequent legislation to do away with or impair or fetter that discretion, although there has been an alteration in procedure in favour of applicants for renewed licences.'

d So he regarded that as being clear beyond peradventure.

Lord Hannen said ([1891] AC 173 at 187–188, [1886–90] All ER Rep 651 at 657):

e 'It was long ago decided, and I think rightly decided, that the justices were under that Act entitled and bound to consider the needs of the neighbourhood on an application for a licence to a person seeking to keep a house for the sale of exciseable liquors, and that their discretion was equally wide in the case of a person already keeping such a house, as in one where the application was by a person not before licensed.'

Whether or not this court is technically bound by the decision of the House of Lords in that case need not be determined, this being a different statute from that which was *f* there considered. But every word of the reasoning of their Lordships in that case would apply when considering the present case.

Furthermore, as I have already said, the words of the section of the 1828 Act are similar, though not identical, with the words of this Act.

I have no doubt that the judge was right in his conclusion that the appeal should be dismissed and that the justices were perfectly entitled, in the circumstances of the case, *g* to reject the application for renewal, and accordingly, I would dismiss this appeal.

DUNN LJ. I agree. The words of s 51 of the Public Health Acts Amendment Act 1890 give the justices a wide discretion whether to grant or renew a licence, and in my view, in exercising that discretion, they were quite entitled to take into account considerations of public order, even though the premises themselves were well-conducted.

h For the reasons given by Waller LJ, I too would dismiss this appeal.

SLADE LJ. I agree. I would, for my part, accept that *Sharp v Wakefield* [1891] AC 173, [1886–90] All ER Rep 651, which was concerned with the Licensing Acts 1828, 1872 and 1874, does not bind this court in considering the construction of s 51 of the Public Health Acts Amendment Act 1890. Though the judge said that that decision was *j* 'conclusive' of the present matter, I would not, with respect to him, go so far as that.

Nevertheless, I agree that it does lend strong support by analogy to his decision and to the construction of s 51 which Waller LJ has propounded.

First, it was common ground in that case that the discretion and power given to justices by s 1 of the Licensing Act 1828, to grant licences for the sale of intoxicating liquors to such persons as they should, in the exercise of their discretion, 'deem fit and proper' conferred on them a power, and even a duty, 'to consider the wants of the neighbourhood with reference both to its population, means of inspection by the proper authorities, and so forth' (see [1891] AC 173 at 178, [1886–90] All ER Rep 651 at 653 per Lord Halsbury LC).

Second, the reasoning which led the House of Lords in that case to decide that no greater fetter was placed on the justices' discretion, in considering whether or not to renew a licence, than was imposed in considering whether or not to grant it in the first place seems to me to apply, mutatis mutandis, in the construction of s 51 of the 1890 Act. As Lord Halsbury LC said ([1891] AC 173 at 178, [1886–90] All ER Rep 651 at 653): 'If this is the original jurisdiction, what sense or reason could there be in making these topics irrelevant in any future grant?'

I would accept that the legislature, in enacting s 51, certainly contemplated that the licences of persons who were conducting their business on premises in a proper manner would, ordinarily, have their licences renewed. Subsections 9 and 10 of s 51 seem to me to point clearly in that direction. The legislature had similarly contemplated in enacting the legislation considered by the House of Lords in *Sharpe v Wakefield* [1891] AC 173 at 184, [1886–90] All ER Rep 651 at 655–656 per Lord Bramwell. Earlier in his speech Lord Bramwell had pointed out that the hardship of stopping the trade of a man who was getting an honest living from a lawful trade (and had done so, perhaps, for years, with probably an expense at the outset) might well be taken into consideration on a renewal under the Liquor Licensing Acts (see [1891] AC 173 at 183, [1886–90] All ER Rep 651 at 655).

Nevertheless, as he observed (see [1891] AC 173 at 184, [1886–90] All ER Rep 651 at 656), the mere fact that the legislature contemplated that ordinarily licences would be renewed, did not help counsel for the appellants in that case to show that a renewal might not be refused for the reasons given there.

While similar considerations apply in the present instance, it does seem to me that the appellants have been rather unlucky, bearing in mind that theirs was the first of three relevant discotheques on the scene, and their running of the premises has not been criticised in any way. I have, for my part, some sympathy with them.

Nevertheless, the evidence before the justices showed that, throughout 1980, what the justices described in the case stated as a 'quite unacceptable degree of public disorder' existed in the Glen Fern Road and Old Christchurch Road areas of Bournemouth, and that the principal factor creating this disorder was the number of persons leaving the appellants' premises and the other discotheque premises in Glen Fern Road at one o'clock in the morning.

I have no doubt that the justices were entitled to take these factors into account when considering whether or not to renew the appellants' licence.

In my opinion Hodgson J was clearly right in giving an affirmative answer to the question put to him, namely whether there was sufficient or any evidence to justify the ruling by the justices that the licence should not be renewed.

For these and the further reasons given by Waller and Dunn LJJ, I, too, would dismiss this appeal.

Appeal dismissed.

Solicitors: *Rooks Rider & Co*, agents for *Marshall Harvey & Keats*, Bournemouth (for the appellants); *Michael J Davies*, Dorchester (for the respondent).

Sophie Craven   Barrister.

Richards v Richards

COURT OF APPEAL, CIVIL DIVISION
CUMMING-BRUCE AND DILLON LJJ
29, 30 NOVEMBER, 6 DECEMBER 1982

Injunction – Exclusion of party from matrimonial home – Divorce proceedings pending – Wife having moved out of matrimonial home with children of marriage and living in unsuitable accommodation – Wife applying for order excluding husband from matrimonial home – Wife not having reasonable grounds for refusing to live in matrimonial home with husband but refusing to return while husband living there – Whether grounds for court to exclude husband from matrimonial home – Whether needs of children rather than justice between husband and wife proper test of whether husband should be excluded.

The husband and wife were married in 1974 and had two young children. In January 1982 the wife filed a petition for divorce on the ground that the marriage had irretrievably broken down because of the husband's unreasonable behaviour. The allegations in the petition about the husband's behaviour were extremely flimsy and amounted to little more than that the wife had become disenchanted with the husband. The husband wished the marriage to continue and filed an answer denying the wife's allegations and asking that the petition be dismissed. After filing the petition the wife remained in the matrimonial home for several months performing her duties as a wife and mother, but she moved out of the matrimonial bedroom. In June 1982 she left the matrimonial home with the children and went to live temporarily with a woman friend. Each weekend and during the husband's holidays she brought the children back to the matrimonial home and the husband looked after them. The wife intended to set up a permanent establishment with another man but those plans came to nothing and her woman friend asked her to leave by November. The wife made strenuous efforts to find other accommodation for herself and the children but she could only find temporary accommodation in a council caravan which was unsuitable for the children, particularly in winter. The wife therefore applied to a judge, in October 1982, for an order excluding the husband from the matrimonial home so that she and the children could return to live there, on the grounds that there was no other suitable accommodation for the children and the wife would not live with the husband. The judge found that there was nothing in the husband's behaviour to give the wife any reasonable ground for refusing to return to live with him in the matrimonial home; nevertheless, because the wife, who was strong-willed and did not want a reconciliation with the husband, would not return to the matrimonial home while the husband was living there, and because it was in the children's interests that they should live in the matrimonial home with the mother, the judge made an order excluding the husband from the matrimonial home, even though he thought it unjust to the husband to do so. The husband appealed against the exclusion order.

Held – Where a wife who had commenced divorce proceedings and who had moved out of the matrimonial home with the children of the marriage into unsuitable accommodation applied for an order to exclude the husband from the matrimonial home in order to enable her to return to the home with the children, then, provided the court was satisfied that her application was a genuine attempt to secure adequate accommodation for the children and not merely a tactical device to give her an advantage in the divorce proceedings, the court would look to find a just result for the family as a whole, rather than as between the husband and wife only, since the needs of the children were the paramount consideration. Accordingly, if the wife could establish that the children's needs required that they should return with their mother to the matrimonial home, then, even if the wife could not show that she had any reasonable grounds for

refusing to return to live with the husband in the matrimonial home, the court could
make an order excluding him from the home. Since, on the facts, the wife's application   *a*
was genuinely made to secure adequate accommodation for the children whose needs
required that they return to live in the matrimonial home, the judge had been right to
make an order excluding the husband from the home, even though the wife had no
reasonable grounds for refusing to live with him and even though she might not
subsequently be granted a divorce. The husband's appeal would therefore be dismissed
(see p 1023 *j*, p 1024 *c* to *f*, p 1025 *d* to p 1026 *f*, p 1027 *e*, p 1029 *d* to *g* and p 1030 *a* to *f*,   *b*
post).

    Bassett v Bassett [1975] 1 All ER 513, *Walker v Walker* [1978] 3 All ER 141 and *Samson
v Samson* [1982] 1 All ER 780 followed.

    Elsworth v Elsworth (1979) 1 FLR 245 and *Myers v Myers* [1982] 1 All ER 776
disapproved.

Notes   *c*

For the grant of an injunction excluding a spouse from the matrimonial home, see 13
Halsbury's Laws (4th edn) para 1228, and for cases on the subject, see 27(2) Digest
(Reissue) 936, 7549–7559.

Cases referred to in judgment

Bassett v Bassett [1975] 1 All ER 513, [1975] Fam 76, [1975] 2 WLR 270, CA, Digest (Cont   *d*
    Vol D) 434, 7555c.
Dockers' Labour Club and Institute Ltd v Race Relations Board [1974] 3 All ER 592, [1976]
    AC 285, [1974] 3 WLR 533, HL, 2 Digest (Reissue) 317, 1785.
Elsworth v Elsworth (1979) 1 FLR 245, CA.
Hall v Hall [1971] 1 All ER 762, [1971] 1 WLR 404, CA, 27(1) Digest (Reissue) 299, 2242.
Myers v Myers [1982] 1 All ER 776, [1982] 1 WLR 247, CA.   *e*
Samson v Samson [1982] 1 All ER 780, [1982] 1 WLR 252, CA.
Walker v Walker [1978] 3 All ER 141, [1978] 1 WLR 533, CA, Digest (Cont Vol E) 277,
    7555d.

Cases also cited

Hooper v Hooper [1981] CA Bound Transcript 192.   *f*
Phillips v Phillips [1973] 2 All ER 423, [1973] 1 WLR 615, CA.
Rennick v Rennick [1978] 1 All ER 817, [1977] 1 WLR 1455, CA.

Interlocutory appeal

By an application dated 15 October 1982 Christine Norma Richards (the wife) applied (1)
for an order restraining Gordon William Richards (the husband) from molesting her and   *g*
(2) for an order that he should quit and deliver up possession to her of the matrimonial
home at 13 Stoborough Green, Wareham, in the County of Dorset. On 8 November
1982 his Honour Judge Pennant sitting as a judge of the High Court in Weymouth
ordered the husband to leave the matrimonial home on or before 22 November 1982.
The husband appealed. The grounds of the appeal were that the judge misdirected
himself in making the order in that (1) he made the order despite his express declaration   *h*
that it was unjust to make it, (2) he found that it was in the interests of the two young
children of the marriage to make the order despite evidence that the wife's refusal to
return to live with the husband was distressing the children, (3) he made the order
despite the unlikelihood of the wife being granted a decree of divorce on her petition for
divorce dated 8 January 1982, (4) he made the order in the absence of any allegation of
any physical or mental distress caused to the wife by the husband, and (5) he made the   *j*
order in the absence of any reason why the wife should not return to live with the
husband. The facts are set out in the judgment of Cumming-Bruce LJ.

Simon Levene for the husband.
Patrick Back QC and *Timothy Coombes* for the wife.

                                                 Cur adv vult

6 December. The following judgments were delivered.

a

CUMMING-BRUCE LJ. The husband married the wife in November 1974. Their daughter was born in April 1977, their son in March 1979, so they are 5½ and 3½ years old.

On 8 January 1982 the family was living together in a council house in Stoborough, Dorset. The husband worked in a steady job as a bricklayer, being away from home at

b his work during the daytime five days a week. According to his evidence, as far as he was aware their marriage was relatively settled, though in the early days of the marriage she had twice left him because she was having an affair with another man, but that he regarded as forgotten and past history.

On 8 January the wife filed a petition for divorce on the ground that the marriage had irretrievably broken down and that her husband had behaved in such a way that she

c could not reasonably be expected to live with him. The pleaded particulars of this allegation are as follows:

'a) Throughout the marriage the Respondent has paid little regard to the Petitioner's feelings. He never remembers the Petitioner's Birthday or Wedding Anniversary and even when the Petitioner reminds him of these events the Respondent takes no action with regard thereto. Similarly at Christmas time the

d Respondent does not buy presents save that in 1979 and 1980 he bought the Petitioner a box of chocolates for Christmas.

b) Prior to the birth of the children the Respondent frequently indicated that he wished to have children but when the Petitioner became pregnant he took no interest whatever in her welfare and well being.

c) At the time of the birth of [the daughter] the Petitioner was in Hospital and as

e soon as the child was born the Respondent left the Petitioner at the Hospital and went to visit his parents and then went out socially with friends. He did not notify the Petitioner's parents of the birth of their Grandchild thereby causing worry and distress to the Petitioner.

d) During the time that the Petitioner was pregnant with [the son] on the one occasion she felt the child kicking and asked the Respondent to put his hand on her

f stomach to feel the child's movements. The Respondent refused and threw a hard backed book at the Petitioner's stomach. This caused an argument and the Petitioner spent that night sleeping on the settee.

e) At the time of the birth of [the son] the Petitioner was neglected by the Respondent and received no card, flowers or any other gift or sign of affection from the Respondent, thereby causing the Petitioner distress and embarrassment.

g f) The Respondent pays no regard to the Petitioner in respect of informing her of his arrangements. He does not inform the Petitioner as to when he is having holiday from work and frequently the Petitioner only becomes aware that he has holiday when he does not go to work.

g) The Respondent refuses to take the Petitioner out socially. On one occasion at a Company Dance the Respondent at first refused to dance with the Petitioner and

h when eventually he was forced to he immediately left the room afterwards. He refuses to take the Petitioner to the Cinema.

h) The Respondent owns a dog which causes considerable damage in the Matrimonial Home. The Petitioner has frequently asked that the Respondent disposes of the dog but he refuses, thereby causing the Petitioner additional work and expense and distress.

j i) Throughout the marriage the Respondent has shown a selfish attitude and as an example of this whenever the Petitioner has bought him a present or item of clothing he does not even acknowledge the gift nor thank the Petitioner thereby causing her distress.

j) Over the past year as a result of the Respondent's behaviour the Petitioner has suffered severe nervous depression and at one stage threatened suicide. She is receiving treatment for her nerves and takes Valium tablets.'

The husband was taken by surprise by the petition. In his affidavit he described how, after the petition was served, he asked her whether she still wanted to cook for him, and so forth, and she said that she did. She moved out of their bedroom into one of the children's rooms and the children thereafter shared a room. She went out a good deal in the evenings and on one occasion told him that she had been seeing a man called David, with whom the children got on very well and with whom she was going to live. Nothing came of that and she continued living at home.

In March the husband filed an answer to her petition, denying her allegations in apparently impressive detail and saying that if, which was not admitted, she suffered from severe nervous depression his behaviour did not cause it. He did not seek care and control of the children, but asked for joint custody and asked that the petition should be dismissed.

The older child began school in Stoborough. On 1 June 1982 the wife left home, taking the children with her. She went to stay in the house of a friend, Mrs Moore, in Swanage, eight miles from Stoborough, driving their daughter to and from school at Swanage during the week, and taking both children to stay with their father at home at weekends from Friday teatime to Sunday evening. She also took the children to stay with their father during two periods when he was on holiday.

Soon after establishing herself in Swanage, she went with the children to stay with a man called Alan in Hanworthy, but she did not stay long. This explains three letters from her solicitors to his solicitors dated 12, 19 and 22 July 1982. I quote from the letter dated 12 July:

'We write to advise you that our client will be moving from her present address in the near future to establish a new home. In the circumstances we feel it appropriate to deal with the contents of the Matrimonial Home at this stage.'

On 19 July they wrote:

'Thank you for your letters of the 14th July together with enclosed Affidavit [an affidavit of means]. We write to confirm that our client will not be seeking Maintenance in respect of herself.'

On 22 July they wrote again:

'Further to our letter of the 19th July we are now instructed that our client will not be moving in the near future and will remain at her Swanage address. She intends to remain there for the immediate future.'

In evidence before the judge the wife described her move to stay with Alan as a business arrangement. The judge said that he had more than a suspicion that she had been committing adultery. After the collapse of the project to move from Swanage to set up home with Alan at Hanworthy, she came back with the children to live again at Mrs Moore's house at Swanage which, according to her evidence, had only been a temporary arrangement.

On 2 August the welfare officer reported on reconciliation and joint custody. The welfare officer reported that she had been to the home in Stoborough before the wife and the children had left, and had spoken to the children. The little girl was able to express that she did not want her parents to part. She said that it was evident that the husband was distressed by the divorce proceedings and unable to accept that his marriage could be terminated for the grounds stated. As she was leaving, the wife followed her from the house and told her in confidence that she would be moving to Swanage during the first week of June. Later she visited the wife at the address in Swanage where she and the children were sharing one bedroom with Mrs Moore, but she again made it clear that she did not wish to try and work towards a reconciliation, though her only grounds for discontent were those stated in her petition. She said she would have been content with a legal separation. She told the welfare officer that, since leaving her husband, she had no one to turn to as her family had cut her off. Apparently they disapproved of her goings-

on. She had been prescribed tranquillisers, confirmed by her doctor, and she had recently
a had to start taking them again.

Then the welfare officer, seeing the husband again, found that he still could not accept
the idea of divorce and said he would welcome his wife back. She had gone on other
occasions but she had always forgiven her and had never referred to these episodes. She
reported that he was a man whose interests centred on his family and home and he was
still working on improvements to the central heating system and seemed determined to
b think only in terms of continuing to live there though, said the welfare officer, it is
hardly likely that the council will fail to evict him. Doubtless when reporting in those
terms, the welfare officer had in mind that, if the parents had to live apart from each
other and did live apart from each other, the council would appropriate the house to
whichever parent had care and control of the children.

She reported that access had been taking place at weekends, the wife bringing the
c children over and leaving them with the husband until Sunday night, and when she
asked the husband whether he could manage the children on his own he was amused.
He said he had been in the habit of looking after them. As he did not drive he depended
on his wife bringing the children over in the car.

The welfare officer's conclusion was: 'Although [the husband] would gladly be
reconciled, [the wife] maintained the attitude expressed in her petition.' That meant that
d she maintained the attitude that the marriage had irretrievably broken down.

In the final paragraph of the report, the welfare officer said:

> 'In view of the children's need of their father, of the couple's proven ability to co-
> operate and of concern for the children's security, the court may feel that joint
> custody is desirable and workable.'

e That advice is explained by the fact that the welfare officer was asked to report on two
things: the prospect of reconciliation and the husband's prayer in his answer in which he
did not seek care and control of the children but asked for joint custody.

This was the background of the wife's application dated 15 October 1982 seeking (1)
an injunction that her husband be restrained from molesting her and (2) an order that he
quit and deliver up possession of the matrimonial home and not return thereto. This was
f supported by an affidavit of the wife dated the same day which, with the summons, was
not served on the husband until Wednesday, 3 November. The husband could not
consult his solicitors about it until 5 November, but managed to file an affidavit in reply
on 8 November, the very date of the hearing. Obviously the wife could not file an
affidavit in reply to that. There was no application for an adjournment and both parties
gave brief evidence before the judge.

g The wife then said that she had to leave Mrs Moore's house on 22 November, that she
had been to the council and had tried to get accommodation from them. But all they had
been able to provide was a caravan. She said she would not return to the matrimonial
home while her husband was there.

We have an approved note of the judge's judgment. The parties agreed that it should
be supplemented by one addition which the judge had not had an opportunity to
h approve. The origin of that addition is a note taken by the wife's solicitors, which the
husband's solicitors accept as accurate and which I will read. In his judgment the judge
found that the wife was strong-willed and did not wish to be in the same house as her
husband and said she could not bear to be with him. The addition reads: 'But it isn't true
that she can't bear to live with him.'

The significant findings of the judge were as follows. (1) The practical probability in
j the case was that the children would continue to live with their mother, but that their
father would look after them when he was not working, which usually meant at
weekends. (2) The allegations in the petition struck the judge as 'rubbishy' and 'very
flimsy indeed'. (Leading counsel for the wife in the appeal before us accepted that the
particulars of behaviour on which the wife relied were flimsy.) (3) The elder child of $5\frac{1}{2}$
did not want her parents to separate. (4) The wife was living in overcrowded

accommodation not fit as a home for the children. (It is easy to appreciate that a caravan provided by the council is far from ideal and indeed unsuitable as a home for the children, at any rate during the winter.) (5) The wife had no reasonable grounds for refusing to return to live in the same house as her husband. (6) He contrasted the instant case with *Samson v Samson* [1982] 1 All ER 780, [1982] 1 WLR 252 in which the judge had found that the wife was relentless and unforgiving to her husband's faults and failings and could not bear to be in the same house as him. The judge found that that was not the case before him because it was not true that the wife could not bear to live with him. But the judge found that the wife is strong-willed and does not wish to be in the same house as her husband. (The wife had given the following evidence before the judge: 'I have nowhere to go. I have no friends or relatives. I will not return to the matrimonial home while my husband is there. If he leaves I and the two children would return'.) (7) The matrimonial home was a house provided by the public for the four people, the grown-ups and the two children. (8) That being so, the public interest is best met by installing the children in that home, which in practice means installing their mother too. (9) It was by no means certain that there would be a divorce, but, though it was unjust for the husband, it seemed right to grant the order sought by the wife, turning her husband out, in the interests of the children.

It appears sufficiently clearly from the judgment, in spite of the finding of the judge that it was not true that the wife could not bear to be with her husband, that the reality of the situation which he, the judge, had to face and accept was that she would refuse to return with the children, whom she had to look after, at any rate during the week, to the matrimonial home as long as her husband was living there.

As the judge stated at the beginning of his judgment, he was confronted with two apparently conflicting lines of authority which culminated in two cases in this court. The first case is *Myers v Myers* [1982] 1 All ER 776, [1982] 1 WLR 247. The division of the court hearing that appeal was presided over by Sir John Arnold P sitting with O'Connor LJ and Stephen Brown J. In that case, in a judgment delivered by the President, with which the other members of the court agreed, the ratio was that it was wrong to make the injunction sought by a wife seeking to turn her husband out of the matrimonial home unless the court found that her grounds for refusing to live in the home with her husband were reasonable. Even though the wife might state that she was not prepared to return to the matrimonial home because she did not want to live there with her husband, if she could show no reasonable grounds for her reluctance to return home, then, although the effect might be that the children would be left living with the mother in unsatisfactory accommodation, it would be wrong to grant an injunction against the husband which, on ordinary principles, could only be granted if it was just and reasonable to make the order sought. In that case the Court of Appeal held that the wife had failed to show that it was reasonable for her to refuse to return to live with her husband.

Having read that case the judge proceeded to read the next reported case in this court, *Samson v Samson* [1982] 1 All ER 780, [1982] 1 WLR 252, in which Ormrod LJ presided sitting with Dunn LJ and Heilbron J. There again the husband and wife had been living with their two children in the matrimonial home and the wife had left, taking with her the children aged one year and five years. She went to live in grossly overcrowded conditions in her mother's house and then asked the court for an order excluding the husband from the matrimonial home so that she could return to it with the children. The headnote accurately recites ([1982] 1 All ER 780):

> 'The reasons which she gave for leaving were vague. The judge found that the parties could not get on together and that the wife would not return to the matrimonial home while the husband was living there. He thought that her attitude towards the husband was relentless and uncompromising and he expressed sympathy for him, but he felt that, because the existing living arrangements for the children were so unsatisfactory, he ought in their interests to make the order sought.'

The decision of the court was summarised in the headnote as follows ([1982] 1 All ER 780):

a
'The court had to deal in a strictly practical way with applications to exclude a spouse from the matrimonial home and make the best possible order in the circumstances, having regard to the interests of all concerned. In doing so, the court had to consider first the welfare of any children involved and then be guided largely by that, and since the judge had adopted that approach there were no grounds for interfering with his decision.'

b
In his judgment Ormrod LJ considered Myers v Myers which had been decided in this court on 4 December 1981 when Sir John Arnold P was presiding; Samson v Samson was decided by this court on the following 12 January. In his judgment Ormrod LJ referred to the line of cases which had formed the basis of the decision of the court in Myers v Myers and considered also the judgment in that case. There was a mistake in Ormrod LJ's judgment (see [1982] 1 All ER 780 at 782, [1982] 1 WLR 252 at 255): he said that in Myers v Myers the Court of Appeal had not been referred to Walker v Walker [1978] 3 All ER 141, [1978] 1 WLR 533 or Bassett v Bassett [1975] 1 All ER 513, [1975] Fam 76. Bassett v Bassett was decided in 1975 and Walker v Walker was decided in 1978 and in both of those cases the court had stated that the ruling principle should be to consider the interests of the children as the paramount consideration and that where there was a conflict between the interests of the parents against whom no reasonable objection was raised, if the only way to establish children who had to be in their mother's care in a proper and appropriate home was to install them with her as their custodian in the matrimonial home, then she must be installed there. And if the inevitable price of installing the wife with the children in the matrimonial home was that the husband, against whom no reasonable grounds had been shown, had to go, then he, as the father, must recognise the paramount needs of the children. Justice in that context meant not justice as between the two grown-ups but justice in relation to the family, recognising that the interests of the children were paramount where they conflicted with the interests of one of the grown-ups. But, as appears from the report of Myers v Myers [1982] 1 All ER 776, [1982] 1 WLR 247, Bassett v Bassett and Walker v Walker were cited. This court in Samson v Samson three weeks later did not realise that. The reason why it was not realised is that in the judgment delivered by Sir John Arnold P, with whom the other members of the court agreed, there is no reference to either of those cases, although both had been cited. That was the reason why the court in Samson v Samson fell into error in thinking that Bassett v Bassett and Walker v Walker had not been cited to this court. But, though Walker v Walker and Bassett v Bassett had been cited in Myers v Myers, the citation evidently had little impact on the reasoning of the court, because there was no examination in the judgments of the way in which the law had been stated between the earlier cases referred to and relied on by Sir John Arnold P in Myers v Myers and December 1981 when Myers v Myers was heard. When this court had to consider the problem in Samson v Samson it examined the decision in Myers v Myers critically, considering the cases referred to by the President in his judgment and in the light of Walker v Walker and Bassett v Bassett.

As Ormrod LJ stated at the end of his judgment ([1982] 1 All ER 780 at 783, [1982] 1 WLR 252 at 256–257), what is required in these situations, as was held in Walker v Walker and Bassett v Bassett, 'is to approach this matter on a strictly practical basis, looking first to the welfare of the children and being very largely guided by it' (as had been done at first instance in Samson v Samson).

The ratio of Samson v Samson, following Walker v Walker, and in particular following exactly the principles enunciated by Geoffrey Lane LJ in Walker v Walker, is that the court has to do justice on the wife's application in an injunction against the husband, but that the justice in question is not concerned only with justice between the two grown-ups: it is the justice of the practical situation facing the family and, where the needs of the children make it virtually imperative that they be returned to the matrimonial home because their mother, who has to look after them, has no other appropriate accommodation for them, the father has to accept that the personal interests of his children are such that his personal interests must be subordinated to the children. That was the principle

enunciated in *Walker v Walker*, following *Bassett v Bassett*, which was not critically
examined by Sir John Arnold P in *Myers v Myers* when he followed a line of authority to
the effect that what the court should look at is justice between the parents, such that an
injunction against the husband and father, turning him out of his home, should only be
granted if there were reasonable grounds for the wife refusing to go back to live with
him.

That was the background to the decision of the judge in the present case when he
decided to follow the decision of this court in *Samson v Samson* rather than the decision of
this court in *Myers v Myers*, Those two decisions clearly being based on conflicting
rationes decidendi.

How does the matter fall to be dealt with by this court, on the facts of this particular
case?

In *Bassett v Bassett* and *Walker v Walker* the court referred to an earlier case of *Hall v
Hall* [1971] 1 All ER 762, [1971] 1 WLR 404, in which Sachs LJ had emphasised that the
court must be wary against granting injunctions in this context, whether under the
Domestic Violence and Matrimonial Proceedings Act 1976 or in matrimonial proceedings
after a petition for dissolution, in case the whole proceedings are merely a device to try
to turn the husband out of the matrimonial home. Secondly, the court must be wary of
allowing the application for an injunction to be used simply for tactical purposes in order
to give one party to a matrimonial dispute an advantage over the other.

The importance of caution in those two regards has been recognised, both in *Bassett v
Bassett* and *Walker v Walker*, and it is clear that in any such case the court must be on its
guard. Being on our guard, we looked at the petition for divorce in this case. As the
judge said, the allegations against the husband are flimsy and rubbishy and he thought it
unlikely that there would be a decree of dissolution. But, as Ormrod LJ stated in earlier
cases, on interlocutory proceedings for an injunction, the court has not got the material
to form a considered evaluation of the prospects of success when the day comes for the
court to consider whether to grant a decree on the petition, and it is dangerous to try to
form a final view on the validity of allegations in the petition when they fall to be
scrutinised merely in interlocutory proceedings for an injunction at an early stage in
matrimonial proceedings. 'Flimsy' and 'rubbishy' as the judge found the petitioner's
allegations in her petition, it would clearly be wrong to hold that the filing of the petition
itself was a device founding an application to turn the husband out of the matrimonial
home, because the history is quite inconsistent with that. That history was this. She filed
her petition. For a short time she continued to stay in the matrimonial home and agreed
to perform her wifely and motherly duties in the matrimonial home. She did not suggest
for a moment at that stage that what she was up to was turning her husband out. What
she was up to was leaving the matrimonial home herself with her children in pursuit of
an affair which she thought was going to provide her with a home. But that affair was
very brief and burnt itself out remarkably quickly. When that happened, the wife
returned with the children to the matrimonial home and lived there for months cooking
for her husband and looking after the children.

In June one reaches the next stage. She told her husband that she was going to other
accommodation with the children and, indeed, on the evidence before the judge, when
she left on 1 June, the husband did not even know where she had gone. It turned out
that she went to her friend in Swanage, Mrs Moore, some eight miles away from
Stoborough. She installed herself and the children there. On Fridays she drove the
children over to Stoborough and left them with the husband until she picked them up
again on Sunday evening. Their little girl continued to go to school in Stoborough, the
wife driving the child over from Swanage to Stoborough, and picking her up after school.
When the husband had a fortnight's holiday in the summer and was able to look after
the children, the wife brought the children to him and they lived with him. That
happened again in October, when he had another holiday. Then in June she appears to
have moved, although the findings of the judge are not explicit, but it seems clear that
she moved with a view to establishing herself permanently with a gentleman called Alan

a which, it was stated in this court, she contemplated as a business arrangement that broke down because the gentleman, Alan, had other ideas which were not her ideas and so it was very brief. When it ended she did not then institute proceedings to turn her husband out, she went back to her friend, Mrs Moore, in Swanage. It was that Alan episode which explains the solicitors' letters from which I have quoted certain paragraphs, that on 12 July she was proposing to establish a new home and wanted some of the furniture from the matrimonial home because she was apparently going to move the furniture to Alan's

b house, which was sparsely furnished.

A week later she confirmed that she was not asking for money in respect of herself, but three days later a letter came saying that she had changed her mind and intended staying with Mrs Moore at Swanage.

On the evidence, what instigated her application by summons for the two injunctions which she sought was the fact that she had gone to Mrs Moore originally on a temporary

c basis and when the plan to go to Alan had broken down she had found herself back with Mrs Moore, but Mrs Moore had said that she had got to be out by 22 November. She (the wife) then went to the council. She had looked at and answered advertisements. The council could not give her a home adequate for the children but installed her in a caravan. That was the accommodation situation for herself and the children which formed the background of her application to turn her husband out of the matrimonial home because

d the children needed it, the children needed her, and she was not prepared to return to the matrimonial home unless her husband went.

Having warned myself of the importance of caution, I would find on these facts, first, that the petition itself, though the judge (and myself) do not think much of the allegations, does not appear in any sense to have been a device with the objective of turning the husband out of the home. It is quite obvious that, over a period of months,

e she was making strenuous efforts to establish herself in a home with the children, away from the matrimonial home, and that when those efforts broke down she did her best to obtain accommodation through the council but ended up with the prospect of installing the children through the winter in a caravan, which was the only accommodation which the council could provide. In that situation her application to turn the husband out of the matrimonial home was not a device as part of a planned campaign, with its foundation

f in a bogus petition, culminating in an application to turn him out; it was a situation where she had instituted genuine though flimsy matrimonial proceedings of dissolution, tried to find other accommodation, reconciled herself for many months to staying at home cooking for her husband and children, then again trying to find other suitable accommodation, first Mrs Moore's rather restricted accommodation but suitable certainly for the summer and probably in the autumn, and genuine efforts thereafter first to

g establish herself and the children with Alan in his home and then to get the council to give her independent accommodation. When all that failed she came to the court and said, 'Look at me: here are the children in a caravan; I am not going to live in the matrimonial home with my husband but the children ought to have a proper home.'

In my view, having warned myself of the importance of caution, which as I have said in, at any rate, one earlier case is of the utmost importance, I do not find that there is

h ground on this history of fact for a finding that this application to turn the husband out of the matrimonial home can fairly be described as a device or as a tactical weapon in the matrimonial conflict. I think the judge was right, if I may with respect say so, in holding that, at the end of the day, this was a genuine attempt by a mother who, for reasons best known to herself, got herself into a fix for accommodation, in which in the circumstances that had arisen she could not find any way of looking after the children, as she had to do

j during the week, save by installing them in the matrimonial home, which she simply could not bring herself to do while her husband was there, though no court would or could hold that she had any reasonable grounds for her refusal. I would hold that the judge was right in this situation to follow the approach of the court stated in *Walker v Walker* [1978] 3 All ER 141, [1978] 1 WLR 533 and affirmed in *Samson v Samson* [1982] 1 All ER 780, [1982] 1 WLR 252, and I would hold that in this situation, where matrimonial proceedings are not a device, though they may not have much prospect of success, and where on the facts the court can safely say that the application to oust the husband from the matrimonial home is not a mere tactical weapon in the matrimonial dispute, the decision on the application for an interlocutory injunction should be taken on the principles stated and affirmed by this court in *Samson v Samson*. The justice in question is justice in relation to the needs of the grown-ups and the needs of the children. If it is established that the needs of the children, who have to be looked after by the mother, point totally to the importance of establishing them back in the matrimonial home with the mother to look after them, as the needs of the children are paramount, the relevant justice for which the court has to look is the justice as it affects the whole family, with the needs of the children being paramount. In this case, the judge having to exercise his discretion in a difficult and painful situation in which he found no ground for reproaching the husband in respect of his behaviour and no grounds for holding that the wife was reasonable in her settled determination to refuse to return with the children to the matrimonial home, the conflict of interest had to be solved by determining the needs of the children, and where those needs conflicted, as they did on the facts, with the needs of the husband the needs of the children were paramount.

In this situation, although there is no reasonable ground for preferring the interests of the wife against the interests of the husband, when the needs of the family as a whole are considered, the wife has to look after the children, at any rate during the week, the children have no appropriate home except in the matrimonial home and the wife will not take them there while the husband is there, and so the children must be installed in the matrimonial home with the wife having their care and control and the husband has to leave.

Those are the correct principles. For the future I would hold that judges follow the principles within *Walker v Walker, Samson v Samson* and in this appeal, in interlocutory applications in which the needs of children conflict with the needs of a parent against whom no reasonable grounds for living apart have been shown. For these reasons I would dismiss this appeal.

I have had the advantage of reading the judgment about to be delivered by Dillon LJ. I agree with it and have decided that it is unnecessary for me to deal in greater analytical detail than I have with the cases referred to in Dillon LJ's judgment. But I would add this. In the answer filed by the husband in the matrimonial proceedings, he seeks joint custody. He has never sought sole care and control of the children and, given his work situation, he is not in a position to care personally for the children during the five days of the working week. He is in a position to care for the children during the weekends and during his holidays, and indeed, since his wife left on 1 June, that is just what he has been doing. She has had the common sense to bring the children to him on Friday evenings so that the husband has been looking after both children during the weekends until she picks them up again on Sunday evenings, and also during his two holiday periods. He has practised the maternal role. He laughed when the welfare officer asked if he could look after the children. He said, and the evidence before the judge confirms, that he is adept at looking after the children. He can do a great many of the maternal jobs (as we still call them), as well as the paternal jobs; so where does that leave him?

By our order the wife is to be installed in the matrimonial home and the husband must leave when he can make other arrangements. I have not yet referred to those arrangements. They are explained in evidence. He may be able to live with his father, which he does not think would be very satisfactory but it is possible, and that is not far from Stoborough. The husband does not drive the car; the wife does. On the evidence, ever since January, she has been eager to lead an independent life, free from her obligations to her husband and, on two occasions referred to in evidence, she has been pursuing a life with different men. I can see no reason to think that those hopes and expectations of the wife are likely to be changed as the result of the order that we make. Ever since she left she has been content to drop the children at home to be looked after by the husband at weekends and holidays. It has the advantage for her that it enabled her a to continue to pursue her independent life, whatever that may mean. What is going to happen now? I was tempted at one stage to think that perhaps in this court the form of the order might be to establish the wife in the matrimonial home from Monday to Friday, or Sunday night to Friday, and the husband, on finishing work on Friday evening, to go back there and stay until Sunday evening. If his wife likes to stay while he is there, so much the better. If she prefers to go, well let her go somewhere else. She could fix herself up with a bedsit, leaving the children at home. But on reflection I take the view

b that that would not be right in this court. There has been no such suggestion from the bar and it was never canvassed before the judge. The practical details have not been worked out as to how easy or difficult it might be for the wife to fix herself up with a bedsit or, if there is enough money, with a bed and breakfast room or cheap hotel room. We know not. Nor do we know what the husband might think about that idea. I would content myself with this observation. The parties may well think it sensible to think

c about it and, if they can, to agree something. If they cannot agree anything the husband, after taking advice, may decide, in the situation in which the wife has been installed in his place in the matrimonial home, to apply for staying access to the children at weekends and during holidays. In default of agreement it may be that he will seek staying access in the matrimonial home on terms that his wife could stay if she wanted, or could go away if she did not want to stay. That is something else which may have to be worked out.

d If there has to be an application for staying access, the appropriate course is for the application to be heard as a matter of urgency and expedition by the judge, his Honour Judge Pennant, sitting as a High Court judge, because the matter is so closely tied up with the ouster proceedings that it is right that that judge should continue to handle the situation. I would not make any order about access. I would leave that to the parties in the first place and, if necessary, to the judge with the greatest urgency and, in any event,

e to be heard and disposed of by the judge before the end of this term.

For the reasons I have stated and the reasons about to be stated by Dillon LJ, I would dismiss the appeal.

DILLON LJ. This is an appeal against an ouster order made by his Honour Judge Pennant sitting as a judge of the High Court on 8 November 1982, whereby he required

f the husband, who is the respondent to a divorce petition, to vacate the matrimonial home, a council house in Stoborough, Dorset, in order that the petitioner may return to live there with the two children of the marriage now aged $5\frac{1}{2}$ and $3\frac{1}{2}$.

The judge was faced with the difficulty that there are conflicting decisions of the Court of Appeal as to the main questions which the court should ask itself when faced with an application by one spouse, who is a party to divorce proceedings, to exclude the other

g from the matrimonial home in a case where there are young children of the family.

In *Hall v Hall* [1971] 1 All ER 762 at 765, [1971] 1 WLR 404 at 407, which was the earliest of the cases to which we were referred, Sachs LJ stated that it is impossible to lay down general rules as to when orders evicting a spouse from the home should be made. That is, of course, correct, but experience has shown that it is necessary that there should be guidelines to assist the court and it is highly embarrassing if, as up to now, the

h guidelines laid down by different decisions of the Court of Appeal are in conflict. It is a far from happy situation, if in every case of an application for an order excluding a spouse from the matrimonial home the court has to sift through seven or eight previous decisions of this court in an endeavour to discern what the correct approach should be.

In *Hall v Hall* the facts were unusual, in that the house was large enough to provide accommodation for both spouses and their children pending the hearing of the petition.

j Both spouses showed a degree of self-restraint or sophistication and accordingly, though there were strains, a continued sharing of the house was not impossible or intolerable. Therefore an ouster order made at first instance was discharged. There was no question there of the wife having to find other accommodation for herself and the children; only the accommodation of the husband was in question.

In *Bassett v Bassett* [1975] 1 All ER 513 at 517–518, [1975] Fam 76 at 82–83 consideration of the state of the marriage relationship featured very strongly in the court's decision. Ormrod LJ stated:

'It is also necessary, I think, particularly in these days, to have regard to the state of the marriage relationship. If, as in this case, the relationship has completely broken down—as I have already said, the wife is petitioning on the ground that the husband's behaviour is so unreasonable that she could not reasonably be expected to live with him, and the husband is proposing to file an answer in the same terms— the hardship may be considerably less on the spouse who is required to leave, because sooner or later the question of the occupancy of the matrimonial home will have to be decided and one or other of the spouses will be leaving in any event. Counsel for the husband admitted in the course of her submissions to us that after the decree nisi in this case there was a strong probability, on the present facts, that the wife would in fact obtain the use of this flat as a house for herself and the child. So the effects of an order made on this application will still be drastic but they will only be felt by this husband sooner rather than later. This does not, of course, mean, and I should be very sorry if anything that I say was interpreted to mean, that a wife can expect to be able to turn the husband out of the matrimonial home merely by filing a petition and applying to the court.'

In *Walker v Walker* [1978] 3 All ER 141 at 144, [1978] 1 WLR 533 at 538, to which I shall refer later, this approach was taken further, and Ormrod LJ deplored the use of such words as 'impossible' and 'intolerable' in the context of ouster applications. These were, of course, the words which had been used in *Hall v Hall* [1971] 1 All ER 762, [1971] 1 WLR 404.

In *Elsworth v Elsworth* (1979) 1 FLR 245, decided six months after *Walker v Walker*, Orr LJ, in giving the leading judgment and after referring to *Walker v Walker*, said that there was an initial problem, before considering who was to go from the matrimonial home. The first question the court should ask was whether there was any prima facie good reason why the wife, who had left the home taking the children with her, should not go back to the house to live with the husband and the children there. In the present case the judge has expressly found that the wife has no reasonable ground for refusing to return to live in the same house as her husband. If *Elsworth v Elsworth* correctly sets out the first question it would follow in the present case that no ouster order ought to be made.

The allegations of behaviour on the husband's part made by the wife in her divorce petition in the present case are described by the judge as rubbishy. Counsel for the wife has described the petition as flimsy in the extreme. He summed it up as amounting to no more than that the wife was disenchanted with the husband. The judge has said that a few years ago it would on no account have been allowed to give a decree of divorce in such a case. But it has not been averred that the presentation of such a petition by the wife was an abuse of the process of the court, and we are told that in the present climate of opinion orders for dissolution of the marriage are often made on such weak petitions, if in the event not contested.

In *Myers v Myers* [1982] 1 All ER 776, [1982] 1 WLR 247, decided on 4 December 1981, this court applied *Elsworth v Elsworth* (1979) 1 FLR 245. The facts were similar to those of *Elsworth v Elsworth*. The court discharged an ouster order made against a husband by the county court judge on the ground that the wife had failed to show that it was reasonable for her to refuse to go back to join the husband in the matrimonial home. There was a child of the family living in cramped and overcrowded quarters because the wife had taken the child with her away from the matrimonial home. But the court disregarded that factor because the only reason for the child remaining in overcrowded conditions was the mother's unreasonable unwillingness to return to the matrimonial home if the husband was still there.

In *Samson v Samson* [1982] 1 All ER 780, [1982] 1 WLR 252, however, decided on 12 January 1982, this court reverted to the approach adopted in *Bassett v Bassett* [1975] 1 All

ER 513, [1975] Fam 76 and *Walker v Walker* [1978] 3 All ER 141, [1978] 1 WLR 533 in
a preference to the approach adopted in *Elsworth v Elsworth* and *Myers v Myers*.
Unfortunately *Myers v Myers* had not been reported when *Samson v Samson* was decided,
and in *Samson v Samson* both Ormrod and Dunn LJJ concluded, erroneously as now
appears from the reports of *Myers v Myers*, that *Bassett v Bassett* and *Walker v Walker* had
not been cited in *Myers v Myers*. As to *Elsworth v Elsworth*, Ormrod LJ said that it appeared
to reintroduce the old issue whether the wife was justified in leaving, while Dunn LJ said
b that *Elsworth v Elsworth* was inconsistent with both *Bassett v Bassett* and with *Walker v
Walker* and that it was unfortunate that it had been reported (see [1982] 1 All ER 780 at
782, 784, [1982] 1 WLR 252 at 255, 257). Plainly the court in *Elsworth v Elsworth* had
seen no inconsistency.

It seems to me that as one division of the Court of Appeal has, in *Samson v Samson*,
preferred the decisions in *Bassett v Bassett* and *Walker v Walker* to the decisions in *Elsworth
v Elsworth* and *Myers v Myers* (albeit in part through a misapprehension that *Myers v
Myers* may have been decided without adequate citation of authority) it would be quite
wrong for this division of the court to throw the matter back into the melting pot by
preferring *Myers v Myers* to *Samson v Samson* as counsel for the husband has asked us to.
Elsworth v Elsworth and *Myers v Myers* ought henceforth not to be followed unless and
until the House of Lords rules otherwise.

d Quite apart from any question of binding authority, it seems to me that the approach
in *Bassett v Bassett* and *Walker v Walker* is to be preferred. In his judgment in *Walker v
Walker* [1978] 3 All ER 141 at 143, [1978] 1 WLR 533 at 536, which for my part I regard
as of the utmost assistance in this field of law, Geoffrey Lane LJ expressed the view that
authority is of little value in cases such as these. What the court has to decide is what is
in all the circumstances of the case fair, just and reasonable, and if it is fair, just and
reasonable that the husband should be excluded from the matrimonial home then that
e is what must happen. He went on to say ([1978] 3 All ER 141 at 144, [1978] 1 WLR 533
at 538):

'But the real problem is who is to go and the solution to that is to be found in the
children: who keeps the children?, because the person who keeps the children has
to stay there, there can be no question about that. Quite apart from the custody
f order, there can be no alternative to the fact that the wife is the person who must
look after the children. That being so, the answer is plain: the husband must go and
the order must be made excluding him from the matrimonial home.'

Subject to the overriding warning given by Sachs LJ in *Hall v Hall* [1971] 1 All ER 762
at 765, [1971] 1 WLR 404 at 407 that it is impossible to lay down general rules, I take the
g law to be as laid down in *Walker v Walker* by Geoffrey Lane LJ and in *Bassett v Bassett*.
The grounds on which a marriage can be dissolved are, of course, laid down by
Parliament. None the less, in so far as family law is a matter for the courts, it is important
that family law keeps abreast with the practicalities of the times and is not bound by
rules which by common thinking might be regarded as anachronistic or unrealistic.
Marriage is an institution which I personally regard as fundamental to the civilisation of
h our society, and of inestimable benefit to those who have the good fortune to be happily
married. But it is an institution which depends on the continued co-operation of the
spouses, and the mutual confidence and trust which is its greatest strength can be speedily
destroyed by one spouse who becomes disenchanted with the other.

Lord Diplock is on record as stating, in a somewhat different context, that the legal
process is not adequate to analyse the multifarious and inscrutable reasons why a Dr Fell
j remained unloved (see *Dockers' Labour Club and Institute Ltd v Race Relations Board* [1974]
3 All ER 592 at 598, [1976] AC 285 at 296). I doubt if it is necessarily much better
equipped to analyse satisfactorily why Dr Fell's wife has become disenchanted with him
and unwilling to continue living in the same home with him.

The wife in the present case was described by the judge as strong-willed and it may
well be that she must bear the major responsibility, in so far as it is a question of

responsibility, for the breakdown of the marriage. But it is unrealistic, when litigation has reached this stage, to suppose that there is any live prospect of reconciliation, despite *a* the husband's hopes, and it would be unrealistic to order the wife to live with her husband. The judge found that it was not true that the wife could not bear to live with the husband, but he accepted, as I read his judgment, that she would not live with him.

So far as the children are concerned, the undisputed facts are simple. They are aged 5½ and 3½. The husband looks after them at weekends and when he has holidays. But on ordinary working days he is at work from 7.30 am to 4.30 pm. He cannot conceivably *b* look after them then. The children must live with their mother, despite her shortcomings. There is no alternative. At the moment they do indeed live with her, but in a caravan provided by the local authority on a temporary basis which cannot be adequate or proper accommodation for the children in midwinter. The wife has nowhere to go. There is no money. On the judge's findings she would for the purposes of the Housing (Homeless Persons) Act 1977 be regarded as intentionally homeless, and she has parted brass rags *c* with her own mother since her own mother takes the view that she had no good reason for leaving the husband. One can well feel little sympathy for the wife, but it is not just that the children should suffer through the wife's shortcomings, or through her unreasonable refusal to return to live with her husband.

The judge was very troubled by the justice of the case. He said, in the course of his judgment, that he thought it thoroughly unjust to turn out this husband, but justice no *d* longer seemed to play any part in this branch of the law. That wry comment is no doubt correct if the justice looked for is justice solely as between the husband and the wife, the protagonists in the litigation. But in family law where there are children of the family there has to be a broader approach, as indeed the judge appreciated. When in *Walker v Walker* [1978] 3 All ER 141 at 143, [1978] 1 WLR 533 at 536, Geoffrey Lane LJ said that the court had to decide what was fair, just and reasonable, he did not simply mean fair, *e* just and reasonable as between the husband and the wife without regard to the interests of the children. In view of the interests and needs of the children, what is fair, just and reasonable in the present case is that the children should go back to the matrimonial home with their mother to look after them, and as, in view of the mother's attitude, that requires that the husband must go then go he must.

The conclusion reached, however reluctantly, by the judge was, in my judgment, *f* correct, and I would dismiss this appeal.

I regard it as important that the husband should continue to have the maximum possible access during the weekends and during his holidays. The details, however, are not before us and that is a matter which, if the parties are unable to reach agreement, must be referred back to the judge.

Appeal dismissed.

10 February 1983. The Appeal Committee of the House of Lords granted the husband leave to appeal.

Solicitors: *Edmund Buck & Co*, Swanage (for the husband); *Neville-Jones & Howie*, Wareham (for the wife).

                                                                                 Bebe Chua   Barrister.

Bellerby v Carle and another

HOUSE OF LORDS
LORD DIPLOCK, LORD KEITH OF KINKEL, LORD ROSKILL, LORD BRIDGE OF HARWICH AND LORD BRANDON OF OAKBROOK
15 FEBRUARY, 17 MARCH 1983

Weights and measures – Weighing and measuring equipment for use for trade – Offences – Having possession for use for trade any false or unjust measuring equipment – Measuring equipment used for sale of intoxicating liquor – Measuring equipment not under control of licensee and supplied and maintained by another – Licensee forbidden to interfere with or adjust measuring equipment – Measuring equipment defective – Licensee not knowing or suspecting that measuring equipment defective – Whether licensee having 'in his possession' defective measuring equipment – Weights and Measures Act 1963, s 16(1).

The two respondents were joint licensees of licensed premises under a justices' on-licence to cover all intoxicating liquor which they held on behalf of a company which owned the premises. The first respondent was the general manager of the premises and spent all his time there; the second respondent was a regional director and manager of the company and a multiple licence holder for it and he visited the premises frequently to ensure that they were properly run. The premises had three bars, each of which had 12 pumps each supplied with a line from a keg. Two lines linked to a pump ran from each keg. The quantity of beer dispensed from each pump/line was governed by a measuring instrument owned, supplied, maintained and serviced by a brewery company under a contract between it and the owner of the premises. The brewery company had inspected and overhauled all the beer measuring instruments on 23 January 1981 and they had been stamped and sealed by it in accordance with normal practice by the weights and measures inspectorate. The respondents were both expressly forbidden to interfere with or adjust the measuring equipment. On 12 February, during a routine inspection of the premises, an inspector of weights and measures discovered that of the five beer measuring instruments then being used three of them used to dispense lager were dispensing smaller quantities than permitted by law. He accordingly broke the seals on all three defective instruments which until then had been intact and obliterated the stamps. The respondents, who had relied entirely on the brewery company for the accuracy of the beer measuring instruments, neither knew nor suspected that the three instruments found to be defective were faulty. The appellant, a consumer protection officer of the local authority, preferred informations against the respondents charging each with having in his possession for use for trade an unjust measuring instrument, contrary to s 16(1)[a] of the Weights and Measures Act 1963. The magistrates dismissed the informations on the ground that it had not been proved to them beyond reasonable doubt that the three unjust beer measuring instruments had been in the possession of the respondents or either of them. The appellant appealed to the Divisional Court, contending that since under the 1963 Act the two respondents were the only persons who could lawfully sell intoxicating liquor at the premises they were necessarily to be regarded as having in their possession the equipment used in selling, including the beer measuring instruments, even though those instruments were not under their control. The Divisional Court dismissed the appeal and the appellant appealed to the House of Lords.

Held – A person could not 'have in his possession' weighing or measuring equipment, within s 16(1) of the 1963 Act, unless he had some degree of control over it, and the mere fact that, as licensee, he was the only person lawfully entitled, whether by himself or his

---

a Section 16, so far as material, is set out at p 1034·*d e*, post

agents, to use the equipment concerned for selling intoxicating liquor to customers did
not necessarily or of itself create a situation in which he 'has possession of' that equipment a
within s 16(1). It followed therefore that since the instruments were not in fact under
the control of the respondents and were supplied and maintained by another the
respondents were not guilty of the offence charged. The appeal would accordingly be
dismissed (see p 1032 j to p 1033 b and p 1036 b to f, post).

Goodfellow v Johnson [1965] 1 All ER 941 and Sopp v Long [1969] 1 All ER 855
considered.

Per curiam. The offence of having possession for use for trade any weighing or b
measuring equipment which is false or unjust, contrary to s 16(1) of the 1963 Act, being
an offence to which the defence in s 16(2) does not apply, is an offence of strict liability
(see p 1032 j to p 1033 b and p 1034 h j, post).

Notes   c
For use for trade or having in one's possession for such use false or unjust measuring
equipment, see 39 Halsbury's Laws (3rd edn) para 1207.

For the Weights and Measures Act 1963, s 16, see 39 Halsbury's Statutes (3rd edn) 742.

Cases referred to in opinions
Goodfellow v Johnson [1965] 1 All ER 941, [1966] 1 QB 83, [1965] 2 WLR 1235, DC, 25 d
    Digest (Reissue) 93, 823.
Sopp v Long [1969] 1 All ER 855, [1970] 1 QB 518, [1969] 2 WLR 587, DC, 30 Digest
    (Reissue) 126, 888.

Appeal
Ian Gilbert Bellerby, deputy borough consumer protection officer for Haringey London e
Borough Council, appealed with leave of the Appeal Committee of the House of Lords
granted on 14 October 1982 against the decision of the Divisional Court of the Queen's
Bench Division (Griffiths LJ and Forbes J) on 7 July 1982 dismissing the appellant's
appeals by way of case stated by the justices for the Middlesex area of Greater London
acting in and for the petty sessional division of Edmonton in respect of their adjudication
as a magistrates' court sitting at Tottenham on 3 July 1981 whereby they dismissed three f
informations preferred by the appellant against each of the two respondents, John Carle
and James Dove Cameron, that each on 12 February 1981 at the Mayfair, 415 High Road,
Tottenham, London N17, had in his possession for use for trade a Distillers Mark 6 beer
measuring instrument which was unjust, contrary to s 16(1) of the Weights and Measures
Act 1963. The Divisional Court certified, under s 1(2) of the Administration of Justice
Act 1960, that a point of law of general public importance was involved in its decision g
but refused leave to appeal to the House of Lords. The facts are set out in the opinion of
Lord Brandon.

James Goudie for the appellant.
Mark Cran for the respondents.

Their Lordships took time for consideration.   h

17 March. The following opinions were delivered.

LORD DIPLOCK. My Lords, I have had the advantage of reading in draft the speech
of my noble and learned friend Lord Brandon. I agree with it and for the reasons he gives j
I would dismiss the appeal.

LORD KEITH OF KINKEL. My Lords, for the reasons given in the speech to be
delivered by my noble and learned friend Lord Brandon, with which I agree, I too would
dismiss the appeal.

LORD ROSKILL. My Lords, I have had the advantage of reading in draft the speech
a of my noble and learned friend Lord Brandon. For the reasons he gives I would answer
the certified question as he proposes and dismiss this appeal.

LORD BRIDGE OF HARWICH. My Lords, for the reasons given by my noble and
learned friend Lord Brandon I too would dismiss the appeal.

b **LORD BRANDON OF OAKBROOK.** My Lords, on 12 April 1981 the appellant,
Ian Gilbert Bellerby, deputy borough consumer protection officer for the Haringey
London Borough Council, preferred in the Tottenham Magistrates' Court, in the petty
sessional division of Edmonton, in the Middlesex area of Greater London, three separate
informations against each of the two respondents, John Carle and James Dove Cameron.
Each information charged, against Mr Carle in the one case and against Mr Cameron in
c the other, that on 12 February 1981 at the Mayfair, 415 High Road, Tottenham, London
N17 he did have in his possession for use for trade a Distillers Mark 6 beer measuring
instrument which was unjust, contrary to s 16(1) of the Weights and Measures Act 1963.

On 3 July 1981 the magistrates, with the respondents' consent, heard all the six
informations together, and dismissed them all. The appellant then appealed against such
dismissals, by way of case stated, to the Divisional Court of the Queen's Bench Division.
d That court, by an order dated 2 August 1982, dismissed all the appeals, certified that they
raised a point of law of general public importance, but refused the appellant leave to
appeal to your Lordships' House. Leave to the appellant to do so was later given by the
Appeal Committee.

The point of law certified by the Divisional Court is in these terms:

e 'Whether an employee of a company who is the holder of a Justices On-Licence
on behalf of that company is thereby necessarily "in possession" of a measuring
instrument within the meaning of Section 16(1) of the Weights and Measures Act
1963 where— a) the instrument was used for that part of the company's trade
consisting of the sale by retail of intoxicating liquor but b) the instrument is not in
fact under his control and was supplied and maintained by another.'

f My Lords, the facts found by the magistrates and set out in the case stated can be
summarised as follows. The Mayfair at 415 High Road, Tottenham was licensed premises,
owned by Mecca Ltd. The two respondents were joint licensees under an on-licence to
cover intoxicating liquor of all kinds issued by the licensing committee for the petty
sessional division of Edmonton. The first respondent, Mr Carle, was the general manager
of the premises and spent all his time there. The second respondent, Mr Cameron, was a
regional director and manager of Mecca, and a multiple licence holder for that company.
g He visited the Mayfair frequently in order to ensure that it was run properly. Also acting
in a supervisory capacity at the premises was a Mrs Greenland, who was the catering
manageress responsible to the second respondent.

The premises had three bars, each of which had 12 pumps each supplied with a line
from a keg. Two lines linked to a pump ran from each keg. The quantity of beer
h dispensed by each pump/line was governed by a measuring instrument owned, supplied,
maintained and serviced by Watneys (London) Ltd under a contract between that
company and Mecca. Mrs Greenland had immediate responsibility for the bars and their
associated equipment. Watneys had inspected and overhauled all the beer measuring
instruments on 23 January 1981, and in view of that Mrs Greenland regarded all such
instruments as being accurate. The instruments had been stamped by Watneys, and had
been sealed, in accordance with normal practice, by the weights and measures
j inspectorate. Mrs Greenland and both the respondents were expressly forbidden to
interfere with or adjust the measuring equipment.

At 9.45 pm on Thursday, 12 February 1981 John McCrohan, an inspector of weights
and measures, made a routine inspection of the Mayfair. He found that only one of the
three bars and only five of the 12 beer lines in it were being used. He tested each of the

five beer measuring instruments in the beer lines being used. He found that three of
them used for dispensing lager were dispensing quantities smaller, by appreciably more
than the permitted margin of 0·10 fl oz, than the quantities of 10 fl oz which they should
have been dispensing. He broke the weights and measures seals, which had until then
been intact, on all three defective instruments.

Mr McCrohan subsequently interviewed the first respondent on 12 February and the
second respondent on 16 February 1981. Both told him that they had relied entirely on
Watneys for the accuracy of the beer measuring instruments, and neither knew nor
suspected that the three instruments found to be defective were in that condition.

The magistrates dismissed the informations on the ground that it had not been proved
to them beyond reasonable doubt that the three unjust beer measuring instruments were
in the possession of the respondents or either of them.

The relevant provisions of the Weights and Measures Act 1963 are contained in ss 9,
16, 17 and 58, which provide, so far as material, as follows:

'**9.**—(1) For the purposes of this Act, the expression "use for trade" means . . . use
in Great Britain in connection with, or with a view to, a transaction for—(a) the
transferring or rendering of money or money's worth . . . where—(i) the transaction
is by reference to quantity or is a transaction for the purposes of which there is made
or implied a statement of the quantity of goods to which the transaction relates; and
(ii) the use is for the purpose of the determination or statement of that quantity . . .

16.—(1) If any person uses for trade, or has in his possession for use for trade, any
weighing or measuring equipment which is false or unjust, he shall be guilty of an
offence and the equipment shall be liable to be forfeited.

(2) Without prejudice to the liability of any equipment to be forfeited, it shall be
a defence for any person charged with an offence under subsection (1) of this section
in respect of the use for trade of any equipment to show—(a) that he used the
equipment only in the course of his employment by some other person; and (b) that
he neither knew, nor might reasonably have been expected to know, nor had any
reason to suspect, the equipment to be false or unjust . . .

17. Where any weighing or measuring equipment is found in the possession of
any person carrying on trade or on any premises which are used for trade, that
person or, as the case may be, the occupier of those premises shall be deemed for the
purposes of this Act, unless the contrary is proved, to have that equipment in his
possession for use for trade . . .

58.—(1) Save where the context otherwise requires, in this Act the following
expressions have the following meanings respectively, that is to say . . . "occupier"
. . . in relation to the use of any place for any purpose, means . . . the person for the
time being using that place for that purpose . . .'

It is to be observed that s 16(1) creates two distinct offences. The first offence is using
for trade any weighing or measuring equipment which is false or unjust. The second
offence is having in one's possession for use for trade any such weighing or measuring
equipment. So far as the first offence, using for trade, is concerned, s 16(2) affords a
statutory defence to any person charged with it. So far, however, as the second offence,
having in one's possession, is concerned, no such statutory defence is afforded. It follows
that, while the first offence is one in respect of which the state of mind of the person
charged, in relation to his knowledge, means of knowledge and reason for suspicion of
falsity or unjustness of the weighing or measuring equipment concerned, is an essential
ingredient, the second offence is one in respect of which the state of mind of the person
charged, in relation to the same or any other matters, is not an ingredient of the offence
at all. In other words the second offence is one of strict liability.

In the present case it would have been possible for the two respondents to be charged
with the first offence created by s 16(1), in which case they would have had the
opportunity of relying on the statutory defence afforded by s 16(2). In the event, however,

a both respondents were charged only with the second offence created by s 16(2), with the result that they were denied the opportunity of relying on that or any other statutory defence.

I set out earlier the terms of the point of law certified by the Divisional Court as being of general public importance. That point, when related to the facts of the present case, postulates a situation with two elements in it. The first element is that the measuring instrument concerned was used for that part of Mecca's trade which consisted of the sale

b by retail of intoxicating liquor. The second element is that such instrument was not in fact under the control of either of the two respondents and was supplied to Mecca, and maintained for them, by Watneys. The point of law certified is whether, in a situation with those two elements in it, either of the two respondents, being the joint holders of a justices on-licence for Mecca, necessarily 'had in his possession' the measuring instrument concerned within the meaning of s 16(1) of the 1963 Act.

c The main contention for the appellant was that, because each of the respondents was a licensee, each must necessarily be regarded as having 'had in his possession' the beer measuring instruments with which the Mayfair was equipped, and that the further circumstances, that the instruments were not under the control of either of the respondents and that they were supplied and maintained by Watneys, made no difference.

In support of that contention it was argued that, since under the Licensing Acts the

d two respondents were the only persons who could lawfully sell intoxicating liquor at the Mayfair, they were necessarily to be regarded as having in their possession all the equipment used in such selling, including the beer measuring instruments, even though such instruments were not under their control.

Two authorities were cited as supporting, by analogy at least, that argument. The first such authority is *Goodfellow v Johnson* [1965] 1 All ER 941, [1966] 1 QB 83. In that case

e the defendant was the manager and licensee of a licensed house owned by a brewery company. On a certain day a sampling officer visited the premises and bought three double measures of gin. He was served by a barmaid, who was employed by the brewery company, and not by the defendant. The latter was at the time in another part of the building. On analysis the gin so served was found to consist of 82 parts of gin and 18 parts of excess water. At the hearing before a stipendiary magistrate of an information

f charging the defendant with selling to the prejudice of the purchaser food which was not of the quality demanded, contrary to s 2 of the Food and Drugs Act 1955, the defendant contended that he was not responsible in law for the sale made by the barmaid. The stipendiary magistrate dismissed the information on the ground that the barmaid was the servant of the brewery company and not that of the defendant. On appeal by the prosecutor by way of case stated to the Divisional Court of the Queen's Bench Division,

g it was held that, under the relevant provisions of the Licensing Acts, the brewery company could not lawfully perform the acts of handling and handing over the gin to the sampling officer, that the defendant was the only person who could lawfully, by himself or through others, perform those acts, that the barmaid had, therefore, to be regarded as the agent of the defendant, not that of the brewery company, in respect of such performance, and that the defendant was responsible for what she did in that

h capacity.

The second authority relied on for the appellant is *Sopp v Long* [1969] 1 All ER 855, [1970] 1 QB 518. In that case the defendant was the licensee of a number of railway station refreshment rooms at one of which a barmaid, in selling whisky by measurement to a customer, delivered a short measure. The defendant had never met the barmaid, or visited the refreshment room, and had delegated his authority to supervise such

j establishments to a general manager, then to a district manager and finally to the manageress of the refreshment room. He had drafted instructions to managers and manageresses of all refreshment rooms in respect of which he was the licensee with the object of ensuring strict compliance with the law. The defendant was convicted by a magistrates' court of 'causing' to be delivered to the customer a lesser quantity than that purported to be sold contrary to s 24(1) of the Weights and Measures Act 1963. He appealed to quarter sessions, where the recorder, holding that the defendant could not *a* 'cause' a short measure to be delivered when there was no evidence that he actively caused or counselled the lesser quantity to be delivered, allowed the appeal. On a further appeal by the prosecutor by way of case stated to the Divisional Court of the Queen's Bench Division it was held that, under s 24(1) of the 1963 Act, knowledge or prior authorisation was not an essential ingredient of the offence of causing a short measure to be delivered, that it was the defendant, as licensee, who sold the short measure, and by the sale, *b* conducted through the barmaid as his agent, he had 'caused' it to be delivered, and that, accordingly, the original conviction should be restored.

I do not, as at present advised, see any reason to doubt the correctness of these two decisions. They establish the proposition that, where a licensee of licensed premises, who is alone permitted under the Licensing Acts to handle and hand over intoxicating liquor to a customer at such premises, chooses to perform those acts through the agency of *c* another person, such as a barmaid employed by the same company or other organisation as he is employed by, he is under the same criminal liability for such other person's acts as he would be if he had performed them himself.

It seems to me, however, to be a very large step from the proposition that a licensee is responsible for the acts of his agent in handling intoxicating liquor and handing it over to a customer to the further proposition that he must necessarily be regarded as 'having *d* in his possession' the measuring equipment used in the course of performing those acts, even though such equipment is not under his control, and is supplied and maintained by someone else. Indeed, I find it hard to see how there can be any logical connection between the two propositions at all.

It is not, in my view, necessary for the purposes of this appeal (even if it were possible, which I doubt) to lay down an exhaustive definition of the expression 'has in his *e* possession' as used in s 16(1) of the 1963 Act. It is sufficient to say two things: first, that a person cannot 'have in his possession' weighing or measuring equipment, within the meaning of s 16(1), unless he has at least some degree of control over it; and, second, that the mere fact that, as licensee, he is the only person lawfully entitled, by himself or his agents, to use the equipment concerned for selling intoxicating liquor to customers does not necessarily or of itself create a situation in which he 'has possession of' such equipment *f* within the meaning of that subsection. I would, therefore, reject the main contention for the appellant.

An alternative contention put forward for the appellant was that, even if a licensee of licensed premises does not, by virtue alone of his holding that position, have actual possession of any measuring equipment which he uses, he is nevertheless deemed to have it under s 17.

There are, as it seems to me, two unanswerable objections to this alternative contention. *g* The first objection is that the certified question does not postulate, either expressly or by necessary implication, that the licensee to whom it refers is the occupier of any licensed premises concerned. This is no doubt because the case stated by the magistrates does not contain any finding that either of the respondents was the occupier of the Mayfair. The second objection is that the deeming provision contained in s 17 only operates 'unless the *h* contrary' is proved, that is to say unless it is proved that the occupier of licensed premises does not actually 'have possession' of the weighing and measuring equipment found at them. On the facts postulated in the certified question the contrary would, in my opinion, be clearly proved.

I would add one more observation. The second offence created by s 16(1) is, as I indicated earlier, an offence of strict liability. If, therefore, contrary to my opinion, there *j* is any ambiguity in the meaning of the expression 'has possession of' as used in that subsection, such ambiguity should be resolved in favour of the respondents and not of the appellant.

For the reasons which I have given I would answer the certified question in the negative, and dismiss the appeal with costs.

a *Appeal dismissed. Certified question answered in the negative.*

Solicitors: *T R B Tiernay*, Wood Green (for the appellant); *M J Kusel & Co* (for the respondents).

Mary Rose Plummer   Barrister.

b

Jones v Jones

QUEEN'S BENCH DIVISION
STOCKER J
c 5 NOVEMBER 1982

Damages – Personal injury – Divorce – Divorce caused by injury – Loss of future earnings – Maintenance of family – Loss arising from liability to spouse in divorce proceedings – Plaintiff severely injured because of defendant's negligence – Plaintiff's marriage breaking up because of his injuries – Plaintiff's wife claiming maintenance and lump sum provision for herself and *d* *children – Whether loss caused to plaintiff arising out of break-up of marriage recoverable – Whether loss included in amount allowed for maintenance already included in award of damages for loss of future earnings.*

As a result of an accident caused by the defendant's admitted negligence the plaintiff, a young married man with two children, sustained serious injuries which left him unable *e* to work or manage his own affairs. His marriage broke down as a result of his injuries and his wife divorced him. In ancillary matrimonial proceedings which were pending in the Family Division the wife claimed from the plaintiff secured maintenance and lump sum provision for herself and the children. At the trial of the plaintiff's action against the defendant for damages for personal injury, in which the quantum of damages was the only issue, the plaintiff was awarded, inter alia, an agreed sum of damages for his loss *f* of future earnings based on a multiplier of 12. That sum included a substantial amount for the capitalised equivalent of the money he would have expended over the 12 years on maintaining his family if the accident had not occurred and the marriage had subsisted. The plaintiff claimed that he was also entitled to recover, as a separate head of damage, damages in respect of the probable award that would be made to the wife and children in the matrimonial proceedings, because (i) the break-up of the marriage and the *g* consequent liability to pay the wife maintenance or a lump sum were caused by the defendant's negligence and were therefore in principle a recoverable loss in the personal injury action in respect of the sums likely to be payable to the wife in the matrimonial proceedings, and (ii) the loss was sufficiently proved as a separate head of damage, even though the award for loss of future earnings included a sum for the cost of maintaining the plaintiff's family, because it was well known that it cost a husband more to maintain *h* his family after a divorce than it did to maintain them in his own home under a subsisting marriage and, furthermore, the plaintiff would have to pay more tax because he would lose the married man's tax allowance after the divorce.

Held – In an action for damages for personal injury, loss to the plaintiff arising out of the break-up of his marriage was in principle a recoverable head of damage, and was not *j* too remote from the defendant's tort, if it was established that the break-up of the marriage had been caused by the defendant's negligence and if the loss was proved and quantified with the degree of certainty necessary to support an award of damages in a personal injury action. Since, however, the plaintiff had failed to prove that the cost of maintaining his family following the dissolution of his marriage would exceed the amount for maintenance already included in the award of damages for loss of future

earnings, his claim would be rejected on the ground that it had not been sufficiently
proved or quantified (see p 1040 c d and p 1041 c d, post).

a

Notes
For the general principles of damages for personal injury, for damages for pecuniary loss
and for damages for future loss of earnings, see 12 Halsbury's Laws (4th edn) paras 1146,
1151, 1155–1156.

b

Case referred to in judgment
Daubney v Daubney (1976) 6 Fam Law 113.

Action
By a writ issued on 12 December 1977 the plaintiff, Eric Ernest Jones, suing by the
Official Solicitor as his next friend, claimed against the defendant, Michael Andrew Jones,
damages for personal injuries and consequential loss resulting from a motor accident on
9 August 1975 caused by the defendant's negligence. The defendant admitted liability
and the only issue was the quantum of the damages. The facts are set out in the judgment.

c

Michael Kennedy QC and *Thomas Corrie* for the plaintiff.
L S Shields QC and *J E Fletcher* for the defendant.

d

STOCKER J. I think there would be no advantage in my reserving this judgment. It is
really a matter of impression rather than consideration of authorities.
   This is a claim for damages arising out of an accident which occurred on 9 August
1975. The plaintiff was a pillion passenger on a motorcycle ridden by the defendant
which for some reason left the road, and the plaintiff suffered injuries. He was then 29
years of age. The claim is brought by the Official Solicitor as his next friend, the plaintiff's
affairs being administered by the Court of Protection. The injuries included severe head
injury, so that the plaintiff is no longer capable of gainful employment or of handling
his own affairs. There is no issue on liability, so that the matter comes before me solely
on the question of damages. As a matter of history, the plaintiff is now looked after by
his mother, who is a lady now aged 61. The plaintiff was a married man; he had a wife
and two small children. That marriage has been dissolved by a decree absolute of divorce
on 6 January 1982, and it is agreed between the parties that the cause of the break-up of
the marriage was this accident, and accordingly was caused by the negligence of the
defendant.
   The matter comes before me to decide two disputed issues between the parties and to
approve those parts of the award of damages which have already been agreed. It might
therefore be convenient to state what the agreed heads of damage are.

e

f

g

   Firstly, general damages for pain and suffering and loss of memory: £27,000 plus the
appropriate interest. That sum includes the loss of amenity and the emotional pain
resultant from the break-up of the marriage. It does not include any financial loss
resultant on that break-up.
   Secondly, special damages, including loss of earnings to date: £25,000, again plus the
appropriate amount of interest. That sum includes £4,000 which has been the expenses
of the mother in the medical care of the plaintiff.
   Thirdly, future loss of earnings: £69,000, which I am told has been based on a
multiplier of 12.
   Fourthly, the plaintiff will be looked after, as he is at present, by his mother. It is
agreed that the annual cost of the medical attentions which will be provided by his
mother are £1,500 a year, and it has been agreed, though of course it is a matter of
speculation, that at her age of 61 the plaintiff might expect to be in his mother's care for
a further 9 years. Of course, it may prove to be longer or the vagaries of life may curtail
that period. One simply does not know. But the agreed figure for that part of the matter
is that there should be a multiplier of 6, resulting in an award of £9,000.

h

j

a   It is further agreed that after the services of the mother are no longer available the plaintiff will have to be accommodated in some form of institution, such as a nursing home, and that the annual cost of that will be £5,000 per annum. It is in issue whether, from that £5,000 per annum, there should be deducted so much of it as might represent his ordinary food and accommodation which he would have had to have expended on himself in any event.

b   The issues, therefore, that I have to decide are, first, the appropriate multiplier to apply to the proper sum for future nursing costs. The second issue is: is there to be a deduction from the agreed figure of £5,000 per annum in respect of the plaintiff's own living expenses which are saved, ex hypothesi, by his residence in a nursing home? And, third, can the plaintiff recover as a loss the sums which are likely to be awarded to the wife and children in the Family Division in proceedings in ancillary claims to the matrimonial proceedings, the wife having claimed all the appropriate relief, such as secured

c   maintenance and a lump sum?

The plaintiff submits that the court, when considering the wife's application for those ancillary reliefs, will have regard to the lump sum which is awarded in these proceedings, even though the whole of the plaintiff's resources relate to damages for personal injuries or consequential loss. The court has been referred in that respect to the case of *Daubney v Daubney* (1976) 6 Fam Law 113. The plaintiff has also argued that the Court of Protection

d   has power to pay moneys out to the wife and children of a patient even though the sum in the hands of the Court of Protection is related specifically to the plaintiff's claim for injuries and consequential loss, the power being derived from s 102 of the Mental Health Act 1959, and the plaintiff submits that such sum as may be awarded to the wife, or, of course, of the capitalised value of any regular payments, is a loss consequent on the accident and is thus recoverable.

e   The proposition is put in the form (as indeed it must be) that the loss derives from the fact that more will have to be expended, either by court order or by agreement, than would have been expended on the wife and children in any event had there been no accident. Counsel for the plaintiff, for whose lucid and clear argument I am very much indebted, initially submitted that the way that I should reflect, in the award of damages, that proposition is by increasing the multiplier appropriate to the award in respect of

f   future nursing home costs on the basis that the Family Division or the Court of Protection will necessarily have to have regard to the totality of the sum available without considering the various heads under which that total is derived. Without at this moment in any way expressing any view on the general principle for which counsel for the plaintiff contends, namely that there has been a recoverable loss by reason of the break-up of the plaintiff's marriage and the consequent liability to pay maintenance or a lump

g   sum to his wife, it seems to me that that basis on which he puts it is really not a tenable one. The task that I have to do is to try and assess a sum paid now which will represent agreed costs of a nursing home arising in the future, probably in about nine years' time, and it would seem to me to be quite contrary to principle that I should seek to assess a loss for an ascertained purpose in the future by reference other than to the appropriate criteria for the assessment of that loss. To seek to increase that sum by reference to losses

h   which derive from a wholly different basis appears to me to be manifestly wrong in principle. Accordingly, I propose to derive and decide the multiplier appropriate to the future costs of nursing home attendance by reference to the ordinary criteria and not by reference to any potential loss that the plaintiff may otherwise suffer in respect of the break-up of his marriage, viz his potential liability to the wife in respect of the ancillary relief referred to. That, however, does not decide the principle. It simply decides that

j   that particular application of the principle for which counsel contends is not, in my view, the correct one.

It is submitted that when the Family Division consider this matter, or I suppose those who consider it in an attempt to agree figures, they will apply the principle of inquiring what are the reasonable needs of the wife having regard to the reasonable needs of the husband. I accept that as the appropriate principle on which the decision will be made;

indeed it is not in dispute. It does, however, seem to me that there would be serious breach of comity between divisions of the High Court if the Family Division, in having *a* regard to that problem, were to regard as available means of the husband a sum specifically awarded to him and held by the Court of Protection in respect of future costs arising solely for his own future maintenance. In other words, the costs of a nursing home to which he will have to go, it would seem to me, would not fall as part of the sum for which the Family Division would have regard. I cannot, of course, in any way influence the decisions of the Family Division, but it would surprise me if such future *b* costs specifically awarded in the Queen's Bench Division for that particular purpose were to be taken into account in assessing the resources of the husband so far as they are available for the benefit of the wife in maintenance proceedings. And in maintenance proceedings the same applies to those costs which have already, or will in the future, be expended by the mother performing the similar functions.

It is said that there is a loss in principle due to the wife's potential claim and, although *c* I have never myself in my experience either on the Bench or at the Bar encountered a claim of this nature nor, I think, have either leading or junior counsel who appear before me today, it seems to me that, as a matter of principle, if it can be established that the break-up of this marriage is (as it is admitted to have been) due to the negligence of the defendant, that is to say admittedly was caused by the accident, there is no reason in principle why it should not be a recoverable head of damage. The problems in assessing *d* such a loss are obvious. There are imponderable factors. The former wife is 28 years of age, and one does not know what her future is likely to be or even what her position will be by the time the matter comes before the Family Division.

There are imponderable and difficult problems over tax. The plaintiff, had there been no accident, would no doubt have enjoyed (if that is ever the right word in the context of income tax) the benefits of marriage allowance, whereas presumably the income from *e* the investment of the damages will attract tax at a higher rate. So that there are many imponderables, and I do not think I would assist this judgment by enumerating them, even if indeed I could at this moment foresee them. But I must make this observation, that the agreement with regard to the plaintiff's future earnings, based on a 12-year multiplier, of £69,600 has been calculated, I am told, by reference to his agreed annual loss net of tax. It thus includes that sum which the plaintiff, had there been no accident, *f* would have expended on his wife and family. It is not a sum which represents his own personal loss of future earnings disregarding the expenses that he would have had, as every married person has, arising from his wife and family. Indeed, in most walks of life the maintenance of a wife and family is by far the greatest source of expenditure of total income. Therefore to that extent the plaintiff in this award has already received the capitalised equivalent of the sum which he would have expended on his wife and family *g* out of his earnings. It is not suggested that he had, or would have had, any other fund out of which he could have maintained his family other than his earnings, and once those are capitalised, as they have been here by agreement, by reference to the net sum after tax but without further deduction for the objects that he would have expended his earnings on, namely his wife and children, there has already been awarded to the plaintiff in that agreed figure a substantial sum representing his costs of maintaining his family. *h*

Counsel for the plaintiff says Yes, that may be so, and indeed he agrees it is so, but it does not go far enough to cover the potential liability in question. He says the proposition that a man is not sustaining a loss when he has to make payments, either of capital or by way of maintenance, to a wife who is not resident under the same roof as himself and to children who are not resident under the same roof as himself, is sufficiently obvious that any married man would know that it is more expensive to maintain a wife and children *j* in a separate establishment than it is in your own, and that accordingly although the sum for future loss of earnings already embraces a capitalisation of the sums that would be spent on the wife, there must be a further loss beyond that. He also points out that there is likely to be a tax loss directly relevant to the separation of the husband and wife since whereas he would have received marriage allowance he will not in the future, and therefore will be paying more in tax than he would have done had his marriage survived.

a   Now there is great force in those arguments. Unhappily, they appear to me to raise problems so imponderable as to be incapable of quantification. I simply do not know whether, in addition to the capital already awarded to the husband for future loss of earnings, ie the source out of which he would have maintained his family, there now arises further losses. I have considerable sympathy with the argument of counsel when he suggests that that must be so, and indeed he may be right, but I do not think it would

b   be correct for me to make such speculation what the appropriate sum would be in the absence of established or agreed specific heads under which such an award can be made.

Therefore on that issue, which I confess I found not only novel but extremely difficult, I have come to the conclusion and adjudge that counsel for the plaintiff is right in principle that, if these losses can be proved on the balance of probability and quantified

c   with such a degree of certainty as would be appropriate to support an award, such losses would be a recoverable head of damage in an action of this kind and not too remote from the standpoint of the tortfeasor, but for the reasons I have endeavoured to give I do not think that he has sufficiently proved that there are losses, that is to say that the cost of maintenance of his wife and children already embraced in the future loss of earnings figure can be increased by a recoverable loss of something over and above it, though one

d   has suspicions that that may well be. I reject the claim on the grounds that such further loss is incapable of being proved or quantified.

Now turning to the other two issues, it is agreed that the costs of nursing home attendance, which on actuarial tables might well be expected to arise in nine years' time, will be £5,000 per annum. The plaintiff, as I have said, was 29 years of age when the accident occurred and will be 46 years of age when notionally the need for nursing home

e   attendance arises. His expectations of life, again actuarially derived, are 34½ years today, at the date of trial, and 26 years in 9 years' time when he is notionally 46. Were I assessing the matter as to the quantification of capitalisation of future losses, by way of medical attention and so on today, I would take a multiplier of 15. In fact 6 of those 15 years have already been embraced in the agreed figure of £9,000, that part of the cost which will exist during the period taken as the multiplier over which his mother will be looking

f   after him. In my view the proper multiplier, therefore, for the capitalisation of the nursing home attendance and residence is the balance, the figure of 9. It seems to me that by taking that figure, whether it be regarded in isolation as the 9 or the totality as 15, represents already the discount that is needed for the factor of the receipt of capital in advance. Clearly, on the hypothesis put forward, the plaintiff will be receiving now as damages the lump sum which notionally will not start to arise as an annual cost for a

g   further 9 years. None the less, his expectation of life in 9 years' time will still be 26, and in my view, therefore, the adoption of a multiplier of 15, or the balance of 9 to that part of this head of damage, reflects and embraces in it the factor of capital in advance. I therefore answer the question which has been put before me by counsel for decision as to the appropriate multiplier for the nursing home attendance as the figure of 9.

The final question, therefore, is: should that figure be applied to £5,000, the agreed

h   costs or likely costs of nursing home attendance, or should it be some smaller figure to reflect the fact that when he is living as a resident in a nursing home he will be saving those parts of his living expenses which he would have incurred had he been living at home? It seems to me that the answer to that question must be Yes. He will be saving the cost of meals at home because it is included in the £5,000 per annum in the nursing home, and in so far as it is a factor capable of quantification I suppose other expenses, such as heating, lighting and possibly the annual cost of accommodation as well. I have

j   not been given any evidence, and as far as I know it is not the subject of evidence, as to how the £5,000 is broken down. The figure I propose to adopt is the figure £1,000. I would reduce £5,000 to £4,000 to take into account that factor that he will, when living in such a nursing home, be thereby saved expenses which he would otherwise have incurred; and accordingly applying the multiplier of 9 to the resultant multiplicand of

£4,000, I would award £36,000 under that head of damage. The total award will accordingly be £167,100.

a

Judgment for the plaintiff accordingly.

Solicitors: *Wedlake Bell*, agents for *Gabb & Co*, Hereford (for the plaintiff); *Philip Baker King & Co*, Birmingham (for the defendant).

b

K Mydeen Esq   Barrister.

c

Customs and Excise Commissioners v ApS Samex (Hanil Synthetic Fiber Industrial Co Ltd, third party)

d

QUEEN'S BENCH DIVISION (COMMERCIAL COURT)
BINGHAM J
13, 14 DECEMBER 1982

European Economic Community – Reference to European Court – Request for preliminary ruling concerning interpretation of Community law – Power of national court to refer question deemed necessary to enable court to give judgment – Discretion of national court to refer question – Guidelines for court considering reference – Community regulation concerning quantitative limits in respect of textile goods imported from third countries – Implementation of regulation by member states – Importation of textile goods from third country into United Kingdom – Goods not complying with conditions of import licence – Goods forfeited by customs authorities – Whether action of customs authorities contrary to Community legislation – Whether reference to European Court appropriate – EEC Treaty, art 177 – EEC Council Regulation 3059/78.

e

f

By EEC Council Regulation 3059/78, a special management procedure was established allocating quantitative limits in respect of the importation of textile goods from certain supplying countries outside the European Community. The detailed implementation of the importation scheme was left to individual member states, who were to issue the import authorisation of textiles up to the allocation of their quota for each year. The defendant, a Danish import company, contracted to buy 199 bales of yarn from a company in South Korea, which was a 'supplying country' under the regulation. The contract was c i f Southampton and provided for shipment at the end of January 1980. In December 1979 the Korean company issued an invoice which showed the port of loading as Busan in Korea, the final destination as Southampton, and that the named vessel in which the yarn was to be shipped would sail on or about 31 December 1979. A certificate of origin was issued by the Korean authorities which gave similar details. The defendant obtained an import licence from the Department of Trade in respect of the yarn which was valid until 31 March 1980 but only for goods shipped on or before 31 December 1979. However, when the bill of lading was issued by the carrier in England, it showed that the bales of yarn had been laden on board the vessel on 15 January 1980. On arrival in England, the goods were seized by the customs authorities on the ground that the defendant did not have a valid import licence because the goods had been shipped after 31 December 1979. On the defendant's failure to pay a fine or to give an undertaking to re-export the goods outside the Community, the Customs and Excise Commissioners applied to the court for an order for the condemnation of the goods. The defendant

g

h

j

a sought a reference to the Court of Justice of the European Communities under art 177^{*a*} of the EEC Treaty, on the ground that it had a defence to the commissioners' action under Community law and in particular under Regulation 3059/78. It contended (i) that on the true construction of the regulation the United Kingdom authorities had no power to impose conditions in the import licence and accordingly the licence should not have contained the time limit of 31 December 1979, (ii) that the goods had been 'shipped' within the meaning of Regulation 3059/78 in that they had cleared customs in South

b Korea and all the relevant documents had been issued by 31 December 1979, (iii) that the United Kingdom authorities were not entitled to impose any sanction other than the refusal of entry when faced with goods which were imported in breach of an import licence, and (iv) that if the commissioners had power to seize the goods that power was a power subject to Community law principles, in particular the principle of proportionality, and the seizure of the goods was out of proportion to the necessary need to enforce the

c regulation.

Held – (1) On the true construction of art 177 of the EEC Treaty it was clear that, so far as the court of first instance was concerned, there were two questions to be answered, namely (a) whether a decision on the question of Community law was necessary to enable it to give judgment, and (b) if so, whether the court should in the exercise of its discretion

d order that a reference be made. In deciding the first question, the court should have regard to the advantages enjoyed by the Court of Justice in having an overall view of the Community and its institutions, a detailed knowledge of the treaties and of much of the subordinate legislation made under them, and an intimate familiarity with the functioning of the Community which a national judge denied the collective experience of the Court of Justice could not hope to achieve. However, it did not follow that a

e reference should be made by a national court of first instance whenever a litigant raised a serious point of Community law and sought a reference, or whenever he indicated an intention to appeal against a refusal to order a reference to the Court of Justice (see p 1054 *f* to *h* and p 1055 *g* to p 1056 *c*, post).

(2) In deciding whether a decision of the Court of Justice was necessary, the court should consider whether the point was conclusive and determinative of the litigation,

f whether the same or substantially the same point had already been decided by the Court of Justice in a previous case, whether the point was reasonably clear and free from doubt, and what the relevant facts of the case were. If the same or substantially the same point had already been decided by the Court of Justice in a previous case the English court ought to follow that previous decision without making a further reference, and if the point was reasonably clear and free from doubt there was no need to interpret the treaty

g but merely to apply it. On the facts, the answer given by the Court of Justice would be substantially, if not totally, determinative of the litigation, it was not suggested that there was any previous ruling by the Court of Justice either on the regulation in question or on any analogous regulation which gave a clear answer to the questions on which the defendant sought a reference, none of those questions were so free from doubt as to render those points acte claire, and the essential facts of the case were already agreed.

h Accordingly, the prerequisites for a reference to the Court of Justice being necessary had been fulfilled (see p 1051 *a b*, p 1052 *e* to *g*, p 1054 *h j* and p 1055 *b c*, post); dictum of Lord Denning MR in *H P Bulmer Ltd v J Bollinger SA* [1974] 2 All ER at 1234–1235 followed.

(3) In exercising its discretion to make or refuse a reference to the Court of Justice the court would consider (a) the length of time which might elapse before a ruling could be

j obtained from the Court of Justice, (b) the undesirability of overloading the Court of Justice, (c) the need to formulate the question clearly so that the question was one of interpretation of the treaty only and not of the facts, (d) the difficulty and importance of the point at issue, (e) the expense, (f) the wishes of both parties, and (g) whether the

---

a Article 177 is set out at p 1054 *d e*, post

question was one raised bona fide or merely to obstruct or delay an almost inevitable
judgment thus denying the other party his remedy meanwhile. Although it seemed *a*
unlikely that the defendant would succeed, its arguments were not hopeless and they
were of potential importance. Moreover, if the defendant appealed to the Court of Appeal
and that court held a reference to be necessary, the delay and expense would be increased.
Accordingly, the court would exercise its discretion by granting an order for reference
(see p 1055 *d* and p 1056 *c* to *h*, post); dictum of Lord Denning MR in *HP Bulmer Ltd v J
Bollinger SA* [1974] 2 All ER at 1235–1236 followed.   *b*

Notes
For references to the Court of Justice of the European Communities, see 37 Halsbury's
Laws (4th edn) paras 642–648.
    For the EEC Treaty, art 177, see 42A Halsbury's Statutes (3rd edn) 436.

c

Cases referred to in judgment
Balkan-Import-Export GmbH v Hauptzollamt Berlin-Packhof Case 5/73 [1973] ECR 1091,
    CJEC.
Bulmer (H P) Ltd v J Bollinger SA [1974] 2 All ER 1226, [1974] Ch 401, [1974] 3 WLR 202,
    CA, 21 Digest (Reissue) 240, *1630*.
Criel (Suzanne), née Donckerwolcke and Henri Schou v Procureur de la République au Tribunal *d*
    de Grande Instance, Lille and Director-General of Customs Case 41/76 [1976] ECR 1921,
    CJEC.
Hauptzollamt Hamburg-Oberelbe v Firma Paul G Bollman Case 40/69 [1970] ECR 69, CJEC.
Internationale Handelsgesellschaft mbH v Einfuhr- und Vorratsstelle für Getreide und Futtermittel
    Case 11/70 [1970] ECR 1125, [1972] CMLR 155, CJEC.
Werhahn (Wilhelm) Hansamühle v EC Council Joined Cases 63 to 69/72 [1973] ECR 1229, *e*
    CJEC.

Preliminary issue
By a writ issued on 16 October 1980 in the Commercial Court of the Queen's Bench
Division, the plaintiffs, the Customs and Excise Commissioners, sought against the
defendant, ApS Samex, an order for the condemnation of 199 bales of acrylic yarn *f*
pursuant to para 6 of Sch 3 to the Customs and Excise Management Act 1979 on the
grounds that the condition of the import licence in respect of the date of shipment was
not complied with and that the goods were accordingly deemed to be prohibited goods.
By its defence the defendant raised the issue of whether the seizure of the goods by the
commissioners was lawful under the law of the EEC Community. Pursuant to an order
of Parker J dated 14 January 1982 the defendant served a third party notice on the third *g*
party, Hanil Synthetic Fiber Industrial Co Ltd, claiming that the third party was in
breach of contract in supplying the yarn but failing to provide the defendant with valid
documents to enable the yarn to be imported into the United Kingdom. The facts are set
out in the judgment.

John Laws for the commissioners.   *h*
Christopher Bellamy for the defendant.
The third party was not represented.

BINGHAM J. In this case the plaintiffs, the Commissioners of Customs and Excise,
seek an order for condemnation of 199 bales of acrylic yarn under para 6 of Sch 3 to the
Customs and Excise Management Act 1979. The defendant, ApS Samex, a Danish *j*
company, resists that order. It contends that it has a defence to the commissioners' action
under Community law, in particular, under EEC Council Regulation 3059/78 and under
general principles of Community law. It accordingly seeks a reference to the Court of
Justice of the European Communities at Luxembourg in order that those questions may
be determined.

a   It is common ground that unless the points of community law are decided in the defendant's favour, or unless there is a reference, the commissioners must succeed in obtaining the order that they seek.

I should add that there is a third party in this proceeding, Hanil Synthetic Fiber Industrial Co Ltd, which has been joined by Samex as a third party. It is a South Korean company, which has not served an acknowledgement of service or entered an appearance and has played no part in these proceedings whatever.

b   Before turning to the facts which give rise to the action and the application to refer to the Court of Justice, I should briefly refer to the relevant Community legislation, without which the story itself is largely unintelligible. I go first to Council Regulation 3059/78, which was made on 21 December 1978. It has a long preamble in which reference is made in some detail to the previous background concerning imports of textiles to the Community from third countries and, in particular, reference is made to an earlier

c   Commission regulation, Regulation 3019/77, which governed the import of such textiles effectively during the year 1978. One recital to the present regulation reads:

'Whereas it is necessary to replace these provisional arrangements with a definitive system incorporating all the measures necessary to ensure the application of the negotiated arrangements.'

d   And a further recital to which I should refer provides:

'Whereas, in order to apply Community quantitative limits in conformity with the Agreements negotiated with the supplying countries, it is necessary to establish a special management procedure; whereas it is desirable that such common management system be decentralized by allocating the quantitative limits among the Member States, and that the import authorizations be issued by the Member

e   States' authorities in accordance with the double-checking system defined in the Agreements.'

All of the preamble is of relevance in understanding the regulation, but I shall confine myself to those extracts and go straight to the substance of the regulation in art 1. Article 1(1) reads:

f   'This Regulation shall apply to imports into the Community of the textile products listed in Annex I and originating in the countries listed in Annex II (hereinafter called "supplying countries").'

Article 1(3):

g   'Subject to the provisions of this Regulation the importation into the Community of the textile products referred to in paragraph 1 shall not be subject to quantitative restrictions or measures having equivalent effect to such restriction.'

Article 3:

h   '1. The importation into the Community of the textile products listed in Annex IV originating in one of the supplying countries listed in that Annex and shipped between 1 January 1978 and 31 December 1982 shall be subject to the annual Community quantitative limits laid down in that Annex.

2. The release for free circulation in the Community of imports subject to the Community quantitative limits referred to in paragraph 1 shall be subject to the presentation of an import authorization or equivalent document issued by the Member States' authorities in accordance with Article 10.

j   3. The authorized imports shall be charged against the Community quantitative limits laid down for the year in which the products are shipped in the supplying country concerned . . .'

I should refer also to art 10:

'1. The authorities of the Member States shall issue the import authorizations or equivalent documents provided for in Article 3(2) up to the amount of their shares, taking into account the measures taken pursuant to Articles 7, 8 and 9.

2. The import authorizations or equivalent documents shall be issued in accordance with Annexes V and VI.

3. The quantities of products covered by the import authorizations or equivalent documents provided for in Article 3 shall be charged against the share of the Member State which issued those authorizations or documents.'

Article 17:

'The Member States shall inform the Commission forthwith of all measures taken pursuant to this Regulation and of all laws, regulations or administrative provisions concerning arrangements for importation of the products covered by this Regulation.'

In Annex I there is a list of textile products which includes the acrylic yarn with which this case is concerned. Annex II contains a list of supplying countries, which list includes South Korea, the relevant supplying country for present purposes. Annex III relates to certificates of origin and has been referred to because of certain provisions contained in this annex relating to verification by national authorities. I should refer to art 3 of this annex:

'1. Subsequent verification of certificates of origin shall be carried out at random, or whenever the competent Community authorities have reasonable doubt as to the authenticity of the certificate or as to the accuracy of the information regarding the true origin of the product in question. In such cases the competent authorities in the Community shall return the certificate of origin or a copy thereof to the competent governmental authority in the supplying country concerned, giving, where appropriate, the reasons of form or substance for an enquiry. If the invoice has been submitted, such invoice or a copy thereof shall be attached to the certificate or its copy. The authorities shall also forward any information that has been obtained suggesting that the particulars given on the said certificate are inaccurate . . .

4. Should such verifications reveal abuse or major irregularities in the use of declarations of origin, the Member State concerned shall inform the Commission of this fact. The Commission shall pass the information on to the other Member States . . .

6. Random recourse to the procedures specified in this Article must not constitute an obstacle to the release for home use of the products in question.'

Annex IV sets out by category of textile product and by supplying country the annual quantity for the years 1978 to 1982 inclusive which the regulation permits to be imported into each member state of the Community. Thus, if one takes as an example the United Kingdom and this particular product, one finds a quota rising from 1,000 metric tons in 1978 to 1,401 metric tons in 1982. In Annex V is contained the double-checking system on which the regulation system depends. Article 1 of that annex reads:

'The competent government authorities of the supplying countries shall issue an export licence in respect of all consignments of textile products subject to the quantitative limits established in Annex IV, up to the level of the said limits and the corresponding shares.'

Article 2:

'The export licence shall conform to the specimen appended to Annex VI and may also contain a translation into another language. It must certify, *inter alia*, that the quantity of goods in question has been set off against the quantitative limit and the share established for the category of the product concerned . . .'

So far as South Korea is concerned, the regulation is to be treated as coming into force on
19 February 1978. Article 3 of this annex reads:

'The validity of import authorizations granted by the authorities of the Member
States shall be subject to the validity of and the quantities indicated in the export
licences issued by the competent authorities of the supplier countries on the basis of
which the import authorizations were granted.'

Article 4:

'Exports shall be set off against the quantitative limits and shares established for
the year for which the export licence has been issued.'

Article 5:

'1. The authorities of the Member State designated on the export licence as the
country of destination shall issue an import licence automatically within a maximum
of five working days of the presentation by the importer of the original of the
corresponding export licence or, in the case of [and I omit immaterial territories]
South Korea . . . of a certified true copy of such licence.
2. The import authorizations shall be valid for six months . . .
4. The importer's declaration or request shall only mention or contain
. . . (f) possibly dates of payment and delivery and a copy of the bill of lading and of
. the purchase contract . . .'

Article 7:

'1. Should the authorities of a Member State find that the total volume covered
by the export licences issued by a supplying country for a given category exceeds
the share established for that category, the said authorities shall suspend the issue of
import authorisations or equivalent documents and immediately inform both the
authorities of the supplying country and the Commission.
2. The Commission shall immediately initiate consultations with the authorities
of the supplying country . . .'

Annex VI provides in art 2:

'The export licence and the certificate of origin may be issued after the shipment
of the products to which they relate. In such cases they must bear the endorsement
"délivré è posteriori" or "issued retrospectively" or "expedido con posterioridad".'

Next, before we part with Annex VI, is the specimen export licence, which contains in
box 3, 'Quota year', in box 4, 'Category, number', in box 8, 'Place and date of shipment—
Means of transport', and in box 13:

'CERTIFICATION BY THE COMPETENT AUTHORITY . . . I, the undersigned, certify that
the goods described above have been charged against the quantitative limit
established for the year shown in box No 3 in respect of the category shown in box
No 4 by the provisions regulating trade in textile products with the European
Economic Community . . .'

Since the date of that regulation there has been a further regulation made on 30
October 1979, Council Regulation 2559/79, which sets out an agreement between the
European Community and the Republic of Korea. That agreement provides in art 18(2):
'This Agreement shall apply with effect from 1 January 1978', and one of its annexes is a
protocol entitled 'Double checking system', which provides in art 4:

'Exports shall be set off against the quantitative limits established for the year in
which shipment of the goods has been effected, even if the export licence is issued
after such shipment.'

In this case the third party, Hanil Synthetic Fiber Industrial Co Ltd, contracted to sell the 199 bales of yarn with which I am concerned by a sale contract dated 30 November 1979. The contract was cif Southampton and provided for shipment at the end of *a* January 1980. A few days later, on 4 December 1979, the defendant, Samex, sold the goods on to the Willow Dye Works Ltd at Leicester, in England, their contract providing for delivery January shipment from Korea 'Expected arrival UK March 1980 . . . Seller will undertake the custom clearance into EEC'.

On 28 December 1979 Hanil issued to the defendant its commercial invoice. That showed the port of loading as Busan, in Korea, the final destination as Southampton, and *b* the carrier as the vessel 'Ever Vital', sailing on or about 31 December 1979.

On 31 December 1979 the Republic of Korea apparently indorsed or issued its certificate of origin under the generalised system of preferences. The exporter was shown as Hanil, the consignee as the defendant, Samex, the means of transport and route described as 'From Busan, Korea To Southampton Sailing on or about: Dec. 31, 1979 Name: "Ever Vital"'. That document bears the stamp of the Ministry of Commerce and *c* Industry of Korea and a date stamp and also a typed date of 31 December 1979.

I then come to the export licence, which is in precisely the form prescribed by Regulation 3059/78. It shows the quota year for these goods as 1979, the category being no 22, in which this acrylic yarn falls; the box showing the exporter contains a reference to Hanil and the consignee is the defendant, Samex; the box headed 'Place and date of shipment—Means of transport' is left blank, but the certification by the competent *d* authority required on the form is duly given. The document bears the date 31 December 1979, and the document bears the stamp, 'Certificate of export licence of textile of the Ministry of Commerce and Industry of the Republic of Korea'.

Pan Korea Express Co Ltd issued a document entitled 'Combined Transport Bill of Lading', which bears a stamp 'On board' and a date apparently 31 December 1979, the shipper again Hanil, the consignee 'To order', the notified party is the defendant, the *e* place of receipt is shown as Busan, Korea, port of loading Busan, Korea, the ocean vessel 'Ever Vital', and the port of discharge Felixstowe, place of delivery Southampton.

Some time later, as it would appear 1 February 1980, Evergreen Line issued its combined transport bill of lading. It was apparently the carrier which was to transport the goods to this country. The important difference between this combined transport bill of lading and that issued by Pan Korea is that on this bill of lading the goods are *f* shown as laden on board the vessel on 15 January 1980, the vessel still being the 'Ever Vital', which was the vessel previously mentioned.

On 31 January 1980 the defendant applied to the Department of Trade in this country for an import licence in respect of this yarn. With its application its enclosed a copy of the export licence issued by the Republic of Korea. On, I think, 5 February 1980 the Department of Trade duly issued the import licence. The licence provided (and these are *g* the material points for present purposes): 'This licence will cease to be valid after 31 March 1980', and bore a further indorsement: 'Only valid for goods shipped on or before 31 Dec 1979.'

The goods were duly transported to this country and arrived at Felixstowe on some date in March.

On 21 March 1980 the commissioners issued a notice of seizure of the yarn. On 15 *h* April 1980, in response to a letter and telephone call from the defendant's solicitors, the commissioners wrote a letter, in which they outlined the reasons for taking the action which they had taken. The letter reads:

'The goods in question were seized in the presence of Mr Franks of Harcourt Shipping Agency Ltd. of Felixstowe who acted as the importers' authorised agent in this matter. Notice of seizure under para 1(1) of schedule 3 to the Customs and *j* Excise Management Act 1979 was not therefore required. The reason for seizure of the goods was that they did not have a valid Import Licence as that submitted with the import entry was valid only for goods shipped on or before 31st December, 1979. A Bill of Lading was submitted by the agent which showed the date of shipment as the 31st December 1979, but further enquiries showed that the vessel a Ever Vital was passing Suez en route for Singapore on that date and that the Bill of Lading issued by the shippers Evergreen Line shows the date laden on board as the 15th January, 1980. I enclose a copy of the Bill of Lading as requested.'

I should further make reference to a letter written by the commissioners on 11 August 1980, in which they write as follows:

b 'In reply to your various letters culminating in that of 6 August 1980 I am now able to advise you that after full consideration of the reports of their officers, the Commissioners are prepared to exercise their mitigating powers under Section 152 of the Customs and Excise Management Act 1979 and to restore the seized goods to your clients on the following conditions: (a) the claim against seizure is withdrawn in writing. (b) the sum of £7,500 is paid to the Chief Cashier, HM Customs and Excise, King's Beam House, Mark Lane, London EC3 7HE. The remittance should

c be made payable to the Commissioners of Customs and Excise and the above reference should be quoted, and (c) the goods are re-exported outside the EEC under Customs and Excise control within 3 months of the date of this letter unless a current valid import licence is produced covering the quantity imported. In this connection your clients should contact Mr Bergonzi at Haven House . . . Will you please advise this office whether your clients wish to accept the above offer. If they

d do not and the claim against seizure is not withdrawn the Commissioners will have no option but to take proceedings for the condemnation of the goods in accordance with the provisions of paragraph 6 of schedule 3 to the above Act.'

In the event the importer, the defendant, did not take advantage of that offer, and it is I think clear, as was accepted by counsel for the commissioners in argument, that had it sought to take advantage of the opportunity to import the goods under a new and valid

e import licence the full duty and VAT would have been payable, so that in effect it would have lost the sum of £7,500. It is not, I think, necessary to refer in detail to the Customs and Excise Management Act 1979, since it is not argued that under the provisions of that Act and subject to the questions of Community law which are said to be raised the commissioners did not have power to act as they did. I should perhaps simply make reference to s 49(1)(b), which provides:

f 'Where . . . (b) any goods are imported, landed or unloaded contrary to any prohibition or restriction for the time being in force with respect thereto under or by virtue of any enactment . . . those goods shall, subject to subsection (2) below, be liable to forfeiture.'

g That, by reason of a statutory background which I need not go into, is the section under which the commissioners acted, and their powers of detention, forfeiture and seizure are set out in s 139 of the 1979 Act.

The detailed provisions governing seizure and forfeiture are set out in Sch 3 of the 1979 Act, and I should draw attention to para 16, which provides:

h 'Where any thing has been seized as liable to forfeiture the Commissioners may at any time if they see fit and notwithstanding that the thing has not yet been condemned, or is not yet deemed to have been condemned, as forfeited—(a) deliver it up to any claimant upon his paying to the Commissioners such sum as they think proper, being a sum not exceeding that which in their opinion represents the value of the thing, including any duty or tax chargeable thereon which has not been paid . . .'

j A somewhat similar power is conferred on the commissioners by s 152 of the 1979 Act, which gives the commissioners authority to mitigate penalties, compound breaches and, putting the matter generally, relieve those in default under the 1979 Act of the full consequences to which they might otherwise be subjected. It is only, I think, necessary for me to add to that brief recital two things: first, that the approximate value of the goods at the time of import and now is of the order of £30,000, a little more or a little less, and, second, that this is not a case in which the commissioners accuse the importer, the defendant, of any fraud on its part.   *a*

I come then to the four contentions of Community law in respect of which counsel for the defendant sought a reference to the Court of Justice. His first submission was that on the true construction of Regulation 3059/78 the United Kingdom authorities had no power to impose any condition in the licence. His attack therefore was concentrated on the inclusion in the Department of Trade's import licence of the words, 'Only valid for goods shipped on or before 31 Dec. 79'. Putting his argument very briefly, I summarise   *b* counsel's argument as follows. The regulation, he submitted, provided a complete code or system for regulating imports into the Community. Article 1(3) provided that there should be no quantitative restrictions other than those laid down in the regulation. The procedure prescribed by the regulation was that the supplying country should issue an export licence and the importing country should automatically issue an import licence. The member state was not, he submitted, entitled to take any additional measures which   *c* would impede or restrict the flow of imports duly supported by an export licence and an import licence, and, in particular, it was not open to the national authority to go behind what was shown on the face of the export licence in giving its import authorisation. It was not, he submitted, proper for the commissioners to inquire into the fact, which might or might not be known to the importer, concerning the precise date on which the goods had been shipped from the supplying country. In support of those submissions   *d* counsel for the defendant relied on two cases in particular, *Hauptzollamt Hamburg-Oberelbe v Firma Paul G Bollman* [1970] ECR 69 and *Suzanne Criel, née Donckerwolcke and Henri Schou v Procureur de la République* [1976] ECR 1921. Those authorities he relied on as showing that member states were precluded from taking steps to alter the scope or supplement the provisions of a Community regulation.

In the course of an extremely well argued and forceful reply counsel took direct issue   *e* with that approach on behalf of the commissioners. The whole object and scheme of the regulation, he submitted, was to impose quantitative control on the imports to the Community of textiles from supplying countries. The mechanism provided by the Community for exercising that control was an annual quota per supplying country per member state. That annual quota governed the quantity which supplying country A could export to member state B. It was, counsel for the commissioners submitted,   *f* inherent in and essential to the effective functioning of the Community regime that the member states should be in a position to monitor and regulate imports to ensure that the imports which were presented for entry into the country complied with the export licence and, in particular, complied with the provision of the licence as to the quota year and thus the year of shipment. More specifically, counsel for the commissioners submitted that having regard to the scheme of the regulation an import licence can never   *g* be an authorisation to import goods simpliciter but must always be a permission to import goods charged against a specific annual quota. Secondly, he submitted that, since the charging of imports against an annual quota is fixed by reference to the year in which the goods are shipped, the licence must be circumscribed in some way; if not, it would potentially authorise imports not charged against any annual quota at all. Thirdly, he submitted that this condition contained in the import licence did not infringe the   *h* regulation as it was a necessary implementation of the regulation.

For my part, I accept that where the Community has legislated within a field and assumed responsibility for it a member state is not permitted to take national measures which vary or in any way distort the Community measures and their effect. It is not, for example, open to any member state to impose requirements which are a disguised quantitative restriction or a hidden barrier to the entry of imports. But that does not, as   *j* it would seem to me, mean that a member state cannot take any measures, even if genuinely necessary, in a loyal attempt to make Community legislation effective. It does appear to me that the scheme of the regulation is to leave the detailed implementation of the regulation to the member states, and my own impression is that what the United Kingdom authorities have done here is not to frustrate or derogate from the Community

regulation but to give it effect. I do not, however, regard that conclusion as so obviously
a right as to preclude the possibility of any other tribunal taking another view. It has
emerged in some past cases that, even where questions have been considered by national
courts to be clearly answerable in one sense, they have ultimately been answered by the
Court of Justice in another. While, therefore, my view on this question is clearly in
favour of the commissioners, I would not go to the length of describing this question as
being so clear and obvious as to be properly describable as acte claire.

b   The second question which counsel for the defendant argued was to this effect. He
submitted that on the true construction of Regulation 3059/78 the goods had been
shipped within the meaning of the regulation in 1979, by 'shipped' meaning that they
had cleared customs in South Korea and that all relevant documentation had been issued.
It does appear from the documents before me that the goods had been loaded inland into
a container at the manufacturer's factory at Kimhae. They had then been transported to
c the docks in their container and only their loading onto the vessel was awaited. Counsel
referred me to a number of different references to 'shipped' and 'shipment' in this and
other regulations. He referred me to definitions of the expression in English and he also
referred me to other language versions of the regulation and to dictionary definitions of
the words there used in French, German, Italian, Danish and Dutch.

      Counsel for the commissioners submitted that there were theoretically four possible
d meanings which can be given to the word 'shipped': first, dispatched from the territory
of the supplying country, and that would be the meaning for which counsel primarily
contended; second, dispatched on the journey which would take the goods out of the
supplying territory; third, placed on board the ship or conveyance which would take
them out of the supplying territory; and, fourth, dispatched from the premises of the
shipper or consignor and cleared through customs. While, as I say, counsel for the
e commissioners contended for the first meaning, he pointed out that for purposes of this
case any of the first three meanings would be good enough to enable him to succeed, and
he submitted that meaning 4, on which basis alone the defendant could succeed, was
unacceptable. For my part, I would be inclined to define the transitive verb 'to ship' as
Dr Johnson did, 'to put into a ship', adding only to 'ship' 'or other final conveyance',
because I would think it plain that to load a train which was to carry the goods out of the
f territory or a lorry which was to carry the goods out of the territory or an aeroplane
which would carry the goods out of the territory would amount to the same thing, so
that the moment of shipment was the moment of loading. It may be that where goods
are consigned inland in a container, where there will be no transhipment, no unpacking
and no breaking of bulk, goods may be shipped at that earlier moment but that, as I
understand the facts, is not this case since in any event the goods were unloaded from
g lorries at the docks and awaited loading in the vessel. On this point I consider that the
legal question raised on the Community instrument comes very close to being acte claire.
The references in the other instruments to which I have been referred suggest that
putting goods on board the final conveyance is the meaning which the Community
legislators intended. It may possibly be that there is a different intention in the other
foreign language versions of the regulation, but I see nothing in any of the foreign
h language versions, so far as I am able to understand them, which points at all clearly
towards any different meaning. There may be a different meaning intended by those
who drafted the instrument but I regard it as unlikely.

      The third question which arises was put by counsel for the defendant in this way. He
submitted that the United Kingdom authorities are not entitled to impose any sanction
other than to refuse entry when faced with goods which an importer seeks to import in
j breach of an import licence. His submission effectively was that, under the regulation, if
goods did not comply with an export licence and a valid import licence it was open to
the commissioners to refuse entry, which would of course involve permitting the
importer to take the goods away, but it was not open to the commissioners to forfeit or
condemn the goods or to impose on an innocent importer a very substantial monetary
penalty, at any rate if he was willing to take the goods elsewhere. Counsel for the

defendant pointed out that there was no provision for any sanction in the parent
regulation and the introduction of such a sanction amounted to a variation or a a
supplementation of the regulation.

Counsel for the commissioners submitted bluntly that there was nothing in the
regulation or in any Community legal principle to say that member states may not
impose sanctions for breach of Community law. The general position, he submitted, was
that sanctions and penalties are for the member state; there was no provision for
harmonisation of sanctions among the member states and it certainly did not mean that b
no sanctions were permissible because none were specified in the regulations. He,
moreover, submitted that the sanction in this case, far from derogating from any purpose
evident in the Community legislation, was clearly intended to promote and advance it,
and he relied on art 5 of the EEC Treaty:

> 'Member States shall take all appropriate measures, whether general or particular,
> to ensure fulfilment of the obligations arising out of this Treaty or resulting from c
> action taken by the institutions of the Community. They shall facilitate the
> achievement of the Community's tasks. They shall abstain from any measure which
> could jeopardise the attainment of the objectives of this Treaty.'

Counsel for the commissioners accordingly submitted that the United Kingdom were
acting clearly and solely in support of Regulation 3059/78 and in no way undermining d
or frustrating it. He also pointed out that, if the argument of counsel for the defendant
were right, a very substantial inroad would be made into the powers recently conferred
on the commissioners by the 1979 Act. To that extent the question raised by the
submission of counsel for the defendant is one of obvious importance. For my part I
would conclude that the argument presented for the commissioners is correct. The
Community itself has no customs officers to man the ports, any more than it has patrol e
boats to guard the fishing grounds. The enforcement of Community legislation is very
largely a matter for the member states in accordance with Community law, and it would
seem to me that it is open to member states to impose sanctions genuinely intended to
make Community provisions effective. This is, however, a question on which, so far as I
know, there is no Community authority which is at all close, let alone direct. The
problem is not one on which, so far as I know, the Court of Justice has ruled in any f
context at all analogous to the present. While I would, having regard to my own view,
clearly expect the answer to be that which commends itself to me, I do not feel that it
would be right to regard the answer as so clear and obvious as to make the matter acte
claire.

The fourth submission of counsel for the defendant was that, if the commissioners had
power to seize, that was a power subject to Community law principles and, in particular, g
the principle of proportionality, and he submitted that the seizure would here be out of
proportion to the necessary need to enforce the regulation. In support of that submission
he referred me to *Internationale Handelsgesellschaft mbH v Einfuhr- und Vorratsstelle für
Getriede und Futtermittel* [1970] ECR 1125 and, in particular, to a short extract from the
Advocate-General's address (at 1147):

> 'In fact, the fundamental right invoked here—that the individual should not have h
> his freedom of action limited beyond the degree necessary for the general interest—
> is already guaranteed both by the general principles of Community law, the
> compliance with which is ensured by the Court and by an express provision of the
> Treaty.'

He also referred to the *Donckerwolcke* case [1976] ECR 1921 at 1938–1939, to which I j
have already made reference, and in particular to two paragraphs of the court's judgment:

> '38 In general terms any administrative or penal measure which goes beyond
> what is strictly necessary for the purposes of enabling the importing Member State
> to obtain reasonably complete and accurate information on the movement of goods

falling within specific measures of commercial policy must be regarded as a measure
a   having an effect equivalent to a quantitative restriction prohibited by the Treaty . . .
    42   Such a requirement would, however, fall under the prohibition contained
in Article 30 of the Treaty if the importer were required to declare, with regard to
origin, something other than what he knows or may reasonably be expected to
know, or if the omission or inaccuracy of that declaration were to attract penalties
disproportionate to the nature of a contravention of a purely administrative
b   character.'

That was a case dealing with a suggested restriction on free circulation, and the facts were
quite different from the present case, but it was relied on because of its reference to the
principle of proportionality.
    Counsel for the commissioners in answer to this submission advanced a number of
arguments. First, he submitted that the only possible question for the Court of Justice
c   was whether member states were fixed with the principle of proportionality in framing
any sanction powers which were relevant to the implementation of the United Kingdom
treaty obligations under Regulation 3059/78. Counsel did not accept that the member
states were subject to the principle of proportionality in implementing that legislation.
He went on to submit, second, that even if, as a matter of Community law, the
d   commissioners were fixed with the principle of proportionality it was quite impossible
to say that the commissioners had transgressed that principle on the facts of this case, and
it would be impossible to say that the 1979 Act gave powers which systematically
transgressed the principle of proportionality. In respect of the latter submission (that it
would be impossible to say that the 1979 Act systematically transgressed the principle of
proportionality), counsel drew attention to the fact (a) that the power of forfeiture was an
aid to the implementation of the treaty, (b) that it was a necessary aid in order that
e   importers should know that they brought in goods without a valid import licence at
their own commercial risk, (c) that the power to seize was not an unchallengeable
administrative power, since the seizure had to be vindicated by court proceedings, and
(d) that the power to forfeit was not, as it were, an unrestrainable juggernaut but was a
discriminating power which permitted the commissioners to mitigate and reduce any
f   penalty where they judged it right. In respect of his first submission under that head,
that it was impossible to say that the commissioners had transgressed the principle here,
he drew attention to the offer to accept £7,500, although he acknowledged that that was
subject to the withdrawal of the claim and the re-export within three months or
alternatively the loss of £7,500 if the goods were imported to this country under a valid
licence. Third, in respect of this question, he pointed out that proportionality had in
some cases been treated as something to be judged in the first instance by the body bound
g   to apply the principle rather than by any Community organ or by the court. Thus, he
said, the penalties to be imposed on an importer in default were a matter falling within
the margin of appreciation proper to be accorded to the commissioners as the
administrative authority responsible for controlling entry of goods into this country. He
referred to *Wilhelm Werhahn Hansamühle v EC Council* [1973] ECR 1229, and submitted
h   that the measures here did not go beyond what might be considered necessary. He also
referred to *Balkan-Import-Export GmbH v Hauptzollamt Berlin-Packhof* [1975] ECR 1091.
Fourth, he submitted that in some of the cases a link was suggested between
disproportionality and breach of Community law, and he naturally relied strongly on
the fact that in this case, if his earlier submissions were right, the commissioners' action
had been taken in support of Community law and not in derogation from it. Fifth, he
j   urged again that the penalty imposed by the commissioners in this case in no way
represented an attack on the Community's aim, which was only to allow complying
goods to enter member states and was in no way intended to permit the wholesale
introduction of goods which did not comply with the quota.
    This is a question to which, as it seems to me, any English judge comes with a measure
of unfamiliarity. It is not, certainly by this name, a principle familiar in the common

law, and it seems to me that questions do arise here as to, first, whether the principle is one that binds the commissioners in their exercise of powers pursuant to Regulation *a* 3059/78, and if it does apply there is, I think, a further question what principles should govern the approach of the court in reviewing any challenge to those powers or, putting it another way, what considerations should the court have regard in any review which it is proper for it to undertake. In his answer to this submission counsel for the commissioners did not submit that the answer to the submission was acte claire. He rather answered by way of saying that even if the commissioners were bound by the *b* principle of proportionality no court properly directed could hold that they had in any way breached that principle on the facts of this case. That submission may very well turn out to be well founded, but before one can judge whether it is well founded or not it seems to me essential that this court should be quite clear what it is legitimate to take into account in reviewing the question to the extent to which the court may properly review it.   *c*

That, therefore, being the background, so far as the law, the facts and the submissions of the parties are concerned, I turn to consider whether in all the circumstances it is proper for the questions which counsel for the defendant has raised to be referred to the Court of Justice under art 177 of the treaty. Article 177 reads:

> 'The Court of Justice shall have jurisdiction to give preliminary rulings concerning: (*a*) the interpretation of this Treaty; (*b*) the validity and interpretation *d* of acts of the institutions of the Community; (*c*) the interpretation of the statutes of bodies established by an act of the Council, where those statutes so provide.
>
> Where such a question is raised before any court or tribunal of a Member State, that court or tribunal may, if it considers that a decision on the question is necessary to enable it to give judgment, request the Court of Justice to give a ruling thereon.
>
> Where any such question is raised in a case pending before a court or tribunal of *e* a Member State, against whose decisions there is no judicial remedy under national law, that court or tribunal shall bring the matter before the Court of Justice.'

From the language of the article it is, I think, clear that, so far as the court of first instance is concerned, there are two questions to be answered: first, whether a decision on the question of Community law is necessary to enable it to give judgment, and, if it is so *f* necessary, whether the court should in the exercise of its discretion order that a reference be made.

The guidelines as to the proper approach on both those questions were given by the Court of Appeal in *H P Bulmer Ltd v J Bollinger SA* [1974] 2 All ER 1226 at 1234ff, [1974] Ch 401 at 422ff. Lord Denning MR draws attention to four points relevant to the question whether a decision is necessary. The first of those is that the point must be *g* conclusive. On the facts of this case, as I understand it, the answer to be given by the Court of Justice will be conclusive in this sense, that if the answers are adverse to the defendant that will admittedly be the end of its case. If the answers are given favourably to the defendant, then depending on what those answers are and which of them are favourable, there may be some short issues or a short issue to be tried, but there is, I think, no doubt that the answer which the Court of Justice will give will be substantially, *h* if not quite totally, determinative of this litigation.

The second point raised with reference to the necessity of a decision is previous ruling. Lord Denning MR says ([1974] 2 All ER 1226 at 1235, [1974] Ch 401 at 422):

> 'In some cases, however, it may be found that the same point—or substantially the same point—has already been decided by the European Court in a previous case. In that event it is not necessary for the English court to decide it. It can follow the *j* previous decision without troubling the European Court.'

That, no doubt true in some cases, does not, I think, apply in this case, since it is not suggested that there is any previous ruling either on this regulation or on any analogous regulation which yields a clear answer to the present litigation.

Third, Lord Denning MR lists acte claire and says ([1974] 2 All ER 1226 at 1235,
a [1974] Ch 401 at 423):

> 'In other cases the English court may consider the point is reasonably clear and
> free from doubt. In that event there is no need to interpret the treaty but only to
> apply it, and that is the task of the English court.'

It certainly is of course the task of the English court to apply it, but it must apply the
b treaty properly interpreted. As I have indicated, I myself feel that the first three questions
raised should certainly, if it rested with me, be answered in favour of the commissioners,
but I do not regard the matter as so free from doubt as to render those points acte claire,
and I certainly do not regard the fourth point on the principle of proportionality as either
reasonably clear or reasonably free from doubt.

Point four: Lord Denning MR says, 'Decide the facts first.' That, with respect, is an
c injunction of obvious merit. The present case is one in which the essential facts are
agreed and on the very minor areas of disagreement or non-agreement the facts can
without doubt be settled in a form which will enable the relevant question to be
answered.

I therefore turn to the guidelines which Lord Denning MR has indicated governing
the exercise of discretion. He mentions, first, the time to get a ruling, second, the
d undesirability of overloading the Court of Justice, third, the need to formulate the
question clearly, fourth, the difficulty and importance of the point. Under that head he
says ([1974] 2 All ER 1226 at 1236, [1974] Ch 401 at 424):

> '*Difficulty and importance.* Unless the point is really difficult and important, it
> would seem better for the English judge to decide it himself. For in so doing, much
> delay and expense will be saved. So far the English judges have not shirked their
e > responsibilities. They have decided several points of interpretation on the treaty to
> the satisfaction, I hope, of the parties.'

He refers, fifth, to expense, and, sixth, to the wishes of the parties. Under that head he
says ([1974] 2 All ER 1226 at 1236, [1974] Ch 401 at 425):

> 'If both parties want the point to be referred to the European Court, the English
f > court should have regard to their wishes, but it should not give them undue weight.
> The English court should hesitate before making a reference against the wishes of
> one of the parties, seeing the expense and delay which it involves.'

Lord Denning MR then goes on to discuss the principles of interpretation and draws
attention to the different approach which is required in interpreting Community
g legislation as compared with our own domestic legislation.

In endeavouring to follow and respect these guidelines I find myself in some difficulty,
because it was submitted by counsel on behalf of the defendant that the issues raised by
his client should be resolved by the Court of Justice as the court best fitted to do so, and I
find this a consideration which does give me some pause for thought. Sitting as a judge
in a national court, asked to decide questions of Community law, I am very conscious of
h the advantages enjoyed by the Court of Justice. It has a panoramic view of the Community
and its institutions, a detailed knowledge of the treaties and of much subordinate
legislation made under them, and an intimate familiarity with the functioning of the
Community market which no national judge denied the collective experience of the
Court of Justice could hope to achieve. Where questions of administrative intention and
practice arise the Court of Justice can receive submissions from the Community
j institutions, as also where relations between the Community and non-member states are
in issue. Where the interests of member states are affected they can intervene to make
their views known. That is a material consideration in this case since there is some slight
evidence that the practice of different member states is divergent. Where comparison
falls to be made between Community texts in different languages, all texts being equally
authentic, the multinational Court of Justice is equipped to carry out the task in a way

which no national judge, whatever his linguistic skills, could rival. The interpretation of Community instruments involves very often not the process familiar to common lawyers **a** of laboriously extracting the meaning from words used but the more creative process of supplying flesh to a spare and loosely constructed skeleton. The choice between alternative submissions may turn not on purely legal considerations, but on a broader view of what the orderly development of the Community requires. These are matters which the Court of Justice is very much better placed to assess and determine than a national court. **b**

It does not follow from this that a reference should be made by a national court of first instance wherever a litigant raises a serious point of Community law and seeks a reference, or wherever he indicates an intention to appeal, even if he announces an intention to appeal, if necessary, to the highest court which is effectively bound to refer the question to the Court of Justice. For example, as *H P Bulmer Ltd v J Bollinger SA* points out, it can rarely be necessary to make a reference until the relevant facts have been **c** found, and unless the points raised are substantially determinative of the action. Or the question raised may admit of only one possible answer, or it may be covered by Community authority precisely in point, although even here some slight caution is necessary since the Court of Justice is not strictly bound by its own decisions. These considerations relate to whether a decision is necessary. Other considerations may affect the exercise of discretion. Sometimes no doubt it may appear that the question is raised **d** mischievously, not in the bona fide hope of success but in order to obstruct or delay an almost inevitable adverse judgment, denying the other party his remedy meanwhile. In my judgment none of these contra-indications obtains here. While I think the defendant unlikely to succeed, I do not regard its arguments as hopeless and they are of potential importance. I have been referred to no authority precisely in point and, so far as I know, Regulation 3059/78 has never been considered by the Court of Justice. The defendant is **e** at present denied the possession or use of the yarn but is paying and will continue to pay for its storage, at least unless some other arrangement is made for disposal of the goods. It has already given security for the commissioners' costs under para 10(2) of Sch 3 to the Customs and Excise Management Act 1979, and has expressed willingness to increase that security. If a reference produces a ruling unfavourable to it, it will almost certainly be ordered to pay the costs incurred by the commissioners as a result of it. It has nothing **f** to hope from delay, save the hope of success. The reference to the Court of Justice would be unlikely to take longer than appeals have normally taken to reach the Court of Appeal, at least until recently, and unlikely to cost much more. If, at the Court of Appeal stage, a reference were held to be necessary, the delay and expense would be roughly doubled. I discount the indication of counsel for the defendant that if denied a reference in this court his client would probably, according to his present instructions, appeal to the Court **g** of Appeal and seek a reference there, but in all the circumstances this does appear to me to be an appropriate case in which questions of potentially great importance in the operation of the Community's system for regulating imports to member states should be reviewed.

I shall accordingly order a reference under art 177 of the EEC Treaty. The precise form of that reference is something that I think will have to be the subject of discussion **h** hereafter.

Order that questions of Community law settled by the parties and approved by the judge be referred to the Court of Justice of the European Communities for a preliminary ruling in accordance with art 177 of the EEC Treaty. Costs reserved.

Solicitors: *Solicitor for the Customs and Excise; Durrant Piesse* (for the defendant).

K Mydeen Esq   Barrister.

Chiltern District Council v Hodgetts and another

a

HOUSE OF LORDS

LORD DIPLOCK, LORD KEITH OF KINKEL, LORD ROSKILL, LORD BRIDGE OF HARWICH AND LORD BRANDON OF OAKBROOK

b 14 FEBRUARY, 17 MARCH 1983

Town and country planning – Enforcement notice – Contravention – Information – Information alleging contravention 'on and since' certain date – Whether a continuing offence – Whether information bad for duplicity – Town and Country Planning Act 1971, s 89(5).

c Magistrates – Information – Duplicity – Contravention of enforcement notice – Information alleging initial failure to comply with notice 'on and since' certain date – Whether continuing offence – Whether information bad for duplicity – Town and Country Planning Act 1971, s 89(5).

In September 1980 the appellants, a local planning authority, laid informations against *d* each of the respondents pursuant to s 89[a] of the Town and Country Planning Act 1971 alleging that each respondent had 'on and since' 27 May 1980 permitted certain land and buildings to be used in contravention of an enforcement notice served by the appellants on the respondents. The magistrates convicted the respondents, who then appealed to the Crown Court, contending, inter alia, that the informations were bad for duplicity because s 89(5) created a single continuing offence which occurred and repeated itself *e* each day during the period of default, whereas the informations, by alleging such default 'on and since' 27 May 1980, contained more than one offence. The Crown Court held that it was bound by previous authority to uphold that contention and allow the appeal. The appellants appealed to the Divisional Court, which dismissed the appeal on the ground that it also was bound by the same authority to hold that the informations were bad for duplicity. The appellants appealed to the House of Lords.

f

Held – It was not an essential characteristic of a single criminal offence that the prohibited act or omission took place once and for all on a single day, since it could take place continuously or intermittently over a period of time and still remain a single offence. Section 89 of the 1971 Act created two types of offence arising out of non-compliance with an enforcement notice requiring either that the owner of the land do something on *g* it (a 'do notice') or that the user of the land desist from doing something on it (a 'desist notice'). Those two offences were the initial offence of not complying with the notice within the period allowed, contrary to s 89(1) and the first part of s 89(5), and the further offence of continuing to refuse to comply with the notice, contrary to s 89(4) and the second part of s 89(5). Both offences were single offences. In particular, the initial and further offences arising out of a 'desist notice' and the further offence arising out of a 'do *h* notice' were all single offences and not a series of separate offences even though they might take place over a period of time. It followed that an information which alleged that the respondent had failed to comply with an enforcement notice 'on and since' a certain date was not bad for duplicity, since it only alleged a single offence. The appeal would accordingly be allowed (see p 1058 *h*, p 1059 *e f*, p 1060 *f* to *j* and p 1061 *d* to *g*, post).

j   *Parry v Forest of Dean DC* (1976) 34 P & CR 209 overruled.

Per curiam. Although there is nothing wrong with an information alleging a failure to comply with an enforcement notice 'on and since' a specified date, the better practice is for an offence under the first part of s 89(5) of the 1971 Act to be charged as having been committed between two specified dates, namely the date when compliance with

---

a Section 89, so far as material, is set out at p 1060 *a* to *d*, post

the notice was first required and the date when the information was laid or the notice complied with, whichever was the earlier (see p 1058 *h* and p 1061 *a* to *c* and *f g*, post).   *a*

Notes
For use of land or operations in contravention of enforcement notice, see 37 Halsbury's Laws (3rd edn) 351, para 453.

For requirement that an information must not charge more than one offence, see 29 Halsbury's Laws (4th edn) para 318, and for cases on the subject, see 33 Digest (Reissue)   *b*
116–117, 739–750.

For the Town and Country Planning Act 1971, s 89, see 41 Halsbury's Statutes (3rd edn) 1695.

Case referred to in opinions
Parry v Forest of Dean DC (1976) 34 P & CR 209, DC, Digest (Cont Vol E) 601, 116(*i*).   *c*

Appeal
Chiltern District Council appealed pursuant to leave granted by the Divisional Court of the Queen's Bench Division on 1 June 1982 against the decision of the Divisional Court (Donaldson LJ and Webster J) on 14 May 1982 dismissing an appeal by the appellants by way of case stated against the decision of his Honour Judge Verney and justices in the   *d*
Crown Court at Aylesbury on 22 May 1981 allowing an appeal by the respondents, George Henry Hodgetts and Helena Hodgetts, his wife, against their convictions on 27 November 1980 by the justices of the peace for the county of Buckingham acting for and in the petty sessional division of Amersham sitting as a magistrates' court on the hearing of informations against each of the respondents preferred by the appellants pursuant to s 89(5) of the Town and Country Planning Act 1971 alleging that each respondent had   *e*
on and since 27 May 1980 permitted certain buildings situate at and known as Tanit, Broomfield Hill, Great Missenden, Bucks to be used for the purpose of an office and for the storage of builders' materials in contravention of an enforcement notice served pursuant to s 87 of the 1971 Act. The Divisional Court certified that a point of law of general public importance was involved in its decision. The facts are set out in the opinion of Lord Roskill.   *f*

Raymond Sears QC and *Jonathan Milner* for the appellants.
Harry Sales and *Edward Denehan* for the respondents.

Their Lordships took time for consideration.

17 March. The following opinions were delivered.   *g*

LORD DIPLOCK. My Lords, I have had the advantage of reading in draft the speech of my noble and learned friend Lord Roskill. I agree with it and for the reasons he gives I would allow the appeal.

LORD KEITH OF KINKEL. My Lords, I agree that the appeal should be allowed for   *h*
the reasons set out in the speech of my noble and learned friend Lord Roskill.

LORD ROSKILL. My Lords, on 8 September 1980 the appellants laid informations against each of the respondents and on the same day summonses were issued. Each information alleged, as was the fact, that each respondent had on 23 January 1980 been   *j*
served with an enforcement notice under s 87 of the Town and Country Planning Act 1971 requiring steps to be taken to discontinue the use of certain lands and buildings at Great Missenden in Buckinghamshire for certain stated purposes within three months from 27 February 1980 and that that respondent had 'on and since 27th May, 1980'

permitted that use contrary to s 89(5) of the 1971 Act in contravention of that notice. On
a 27 November 1980 the first respondent was convicted by the Amersham justices and so
far as presently relevant fined £100 and ordered to pay £50 costs. The second respondent,
who did not appear, was similarly convicted and the same penalty was imposed. On
1 December 1980 notices of appeal to the Crown Court were given. Five grounds of
appeal were ultimately advanced of which the second alone is presently relevant. This
alleged that 'The information in this case was bad for duplicity and the conviction
b thereon by the magistrates was therefore wrong and cannot be upheld'.

This submission was advanced for the first time in the Crown Court and was founded
on the decision of the Divisional Court in *Parry v Forest of Dean DC* (1976) 34 P & CR
209. The Crown Court at Aylesbury (his Honour Judge Verney and justices) heard the
appeal on 22 May 1981. By agreement, only the submission just referred to was advanced.
The Crown Court, in my view rightly, decided that it was bound by *Parry's* case to hold
c that the information was bad for duplicity and accordingly allowed the appeal. A case
was stated for the opinion of the High Court 'whether we correctly decided in point of
law that the said information was bad for duplicity'.

On 14 May 1982 the case stated came before the Divisional Court (Donaldson LJ and
Webster J). The Divisional Court, also rightly as I think, felt that it was bound by *Parry's*
case to reach the same conclusion. No argument was heard and the appeal was formally
d dismissed. But the Divisional Court certified this question as one of general public

> 'Whether an information · which alleges initial failure to comply with the
> provisions of an enforcement notice under section 89(5) of the Town and Country
> Planning Act, 1971 "on and since a certain date" is bad for duplicity.'

Clearly the Divisional Court was doubtful of the correctness of the decision in *Parry's*
e case and therefore properly gave leave to appeal to your Lordships' House.

My Lords, whether or not *Parry's* case was rightly decided depends on the true
construction of s 89(5) of the 1971 Act. The question is a short one and, in common with
all your Lordships, I am of clear opinion that *Parry's* case was wrongly decided. Your
Lordships were told that the decision had caused considerable practical difficulty to
planning authorities when carrying out their statutory duty of securing compliance with
f enforcement notices. As is not uncommon with decisions which cause practical difficulty,
attempts, often unsatisfactory, are subsequently made to distinguish them. As a result
fine distinctions are drawn and the law becomes uncertain and even obscure. Your
Lordships' House now has the opportunity of removing the obscurities and simplifying
the administration of this branch of the law.

In *Parry's* case the Divisional Court (Lord Widgery CJ, Forbes and Slynn JJ) undoubtedly
g held that the information there in question was bad for duplicity because it charged
more than one offence. The relevant enforcement notice had been dated 8 November
1971 and the information complained that Parry had used the land in contravention of
the notice 'since January 8th 1972'. It was argued that s 89(5) of the 1971 Act created
what Lord Widgery CJ called 'a continuing offence', by which he meant one which
'repeats itself every day. In other words, a new offence is created every day'. Accordingly,
h it was successfully urged on Parry's behalf that not only did the information go back
beyond the six months' period permitted by s 104 of the Magistrates' Courts Act 1952
but 'also charged a very large number of offences in one information'.

My Lords, since it is *Parry's* case which is the source of the present difficulties, I'do not
find it necessary to consider either earlier or later cases, reported or unreported.

For ease of reference I set out the relevant parts of s 89(1), (4) and (5) for it seems clear
j that sub-s (5) cannot be construed in isolation from the rest of the section (in passing I
would mention that the former six months' time limit under the Magistrates' Courts Act
1952 for laying informations which was applicable at the time of *Parry's* case is no longer
relevant since the Criminal Law Act 1977, by ss 16 and 18, made the relevant offences
'triable either way' and therefore not subject to any relevant time limit):

'(1) Subject to the provisions of this section, where an enforcement notice has been served on the person who, at the time when the notice was served on him, was *a* the owner of the land to which it relates, then, if any steps required by the notice to be taken (other than the discontinuance of a use of land) have not been taken within the period allowed for compliance with the notice, that person shall be liable on summary conviction to a fine not exceeding £400 or on conviction on indictment to a fine . . .

(4) If, after a person has been convicted under the preceding provisions of this *b* section, he does not as soon as practicable do everything in his power to secure compliance with the enforcement notice, he shall be guilty of a further offence and liable—(a) on summary conviction to a fine not exceeding £50 for each day following his first conviction on which any of the requirements of the enforcement notice (other than the discontinuance of the use of land) remain unfulfilled; or (b) on conviction on indictment to a fine.   *c*

(5) Where, by virtue of an enforcement notice, a use of land is required to be discontinued, or any conditions or limitations are required to be complied with in respect of a use of land or in respect of the carrying out of operations thereon, then if any person used the land or causes or permits it to be used, or carries out those operations or causes or permits them to be carried out, in contravention of the notice, he shall be guilty of an offence, and shall be liable on summary conviction to *d* a fine not exceeding £400, or on conviction on indictment to a fine; and if the use is continued after the conviction he shall be guilty of a further offence and liable on summary conviction to a fine not exceeding £50 for each day on which the use is so continued, or on conviction on indictment to a fine . . .'

My Lords, much of the difficulty which has arisen in connection with these subsections *e* is due to the use of the words 'continuous' or 'continuing' offence as descriptive of the offences chargeable without regard to the fact that neither adjective is to be found in the subsections creating the offences and also without consideration of the precise meaning to be given to those adjectives in the context in which they have been used.

Section 89 deals with penalties for non-compliance with two classes of enforcement notices: (a) those, dealt with in sub-ss (1) to (4), which require the owner of land to do *f* something on it (do notices), and (b) those, dealt with in sub-s (5), which require the user of land to stop doing something on it (desist notices). As respects each of these classes of notice the section creates two types of offences: (i) an initial offence created by sub-s (1) and by the first limb of sub-s (5) down to the semi-colon, respectively; and (ii) what is described as a 'further offence' which is created by sub-s (4) and by the second limb of sub-s (5) after the semi-colon, respectively, and can only be committed by a person who *g* has already been convicted of the corresponding initial offence.

It is not an essential characteristic of a criminal offence that any prohibited act or omission, in order to constitute a single offence, should take place once and for all on a single day. It may take place, whether continuously or intermittently, over a period of time. The initial offence created by sub-s (1) in the case of non-compliance with a 'do notice' is complete once and for all when the period for compliance with the notice *h* expires; but it is plainly contemplated that the further offence of non-compliance with a 'do notice' created by sub-s (4), though it too is a single offence, may take place over a period of time, since the penalty for it is made dependent on the number of days on which it takes place.

Similarly, as respects non-compliance with a 'desist notice', it is in my view clear that the initial offence (as well as the further offence), though it too may take place over a *j* period, whether continuously or intermittently (e g holding a Sunday market), is a single offence and not a series of separate offences committed each day that the non-compliance prior to the first conviction for non-compliance continues. If it were otherwise it would have the bizarre consequence that on summary conviction a fine of £400 per diem could be imposed for each such separate offence committed before the offender received his

first conviction, whereas for any further offence committed after the offender against a
a 'desist notice' had been convicted a daily fine of only £50 could be inflicted. Uniquely a
previous conviction would be a positive advantage to the offender. This can hardly have
been Parliament's intention.

My Lords, in the instant case each information, as already stated, charged the offence
'on and since' a specified date. Your Lordships were told that this was the practice now
often adopted by prosecuting authorities in these cases. I see no objection to that practice,
b but it might be preferable if hereafter offences under the first limb of s 89(5) were
charged as having been committed between two specified dates, the termini usually
being on the one hand the date when compliance with the enforcement notice first
became due and on the other hand a date not later than the date when the information
was laid, or of course some earlier date if meanwhile the enforcement notice had been
complied with. Indictments frequently charge offences as having been committed
c between certain dates. I see no reason in principle why the same practice should not be
followed with these informations.

My Lords, I have not found it necessary to review individually all the cases, reported
or unreported, mentioned in argument or to criticise or to support this phrase or that in
the several judgments. I have endeavoured in this speech to state the correct principles to
be applied as I believe them to be and, to the extent that there are passages in some of
d these judgments to a different effect, they should no longer be regarded as good law.

Since only one point was argued in the Crown Court the other grounds specified in
the notice of appeal have yet to be heard and determined. I would, therefore, allow the
appeal, answer the certified question in the negative and remit this case to the Crown
Court at Aylesbury to hear and determine the remaining grounds of appeal.

This appeal has been brought by a local authority for the purpose of clarifying the law,
e so your Lordships may think it unjust that the costs in this House should fall on the
respondents. If your Lordships agree I would propose that the order for costs made in the
Divisional Court be not disturbed and that your Lordships should further order that the
costs of both the appellants and the respondents in this House be paid out of central
funds.

f **LORD BRIDGE OF HARWICH.** My Lords, for the reasons given by my noble and
learned friend Lord Roskill I agree that this appeal should be allowed and the further
orders made as he proposes.

LORD BRANDON OF OAKBROOK. My Lords, I have had the advantage of
reading in draft the speech prepared by my noble and learned friend Lord Roskill. I
g agree with it and for the reasons which he gives I would allow the appeal.

*Appeal allowed. Certified question answered in the negative and cause remitted to the Crown
Court at Aylesbury to hear and determine the remaining grounds of appeal against the orders of
the Amersham Magistrates' Court of 27 November 1980.*

Solicitors: *Sharpe Pritchard & Co* (for the appellants); *Kingsford Dorman*, agents for *Masons*,
Milton Keynes (for the respondents).

Mary Rose Plummer   Barrister.

Mandla and another v Dowell Lee and another

HOUSE OF LORDS

LORD FRASER OF TULLYBELTON, LORD EDMUND-DAVIES, LORD ROSKILL, LORD BRANDON OF OAKBROOK AND LORD TEMPLEMAN

28 FEBRUARY, I, 2, 24 MARCH 1983

Race relations – Discrimination – Discrimination against racial group – Sikhs – Racial group defined by reference to colour, race, nationality or ethnic or national origins – Ethnic or national origins – Ethnic – Headmaster refusing to admit Sikh boy to school unless he removed his turban and cut his hair – Headmaster desiring to minimise religious distinctions in school which wearing of turbans would accentuate – Whether unlawful discrimination – Whether Sikhs a 'racial group' – Whether Sikhs a group defined by reference to 'ethnic or national origins' – Whether discrimination justifiable – Race Relations Act 1976, ss 1(1)(b), 3(1).

The headmaster of a private school refused to admit as a pupil to the school a boy who was an orthodox Sikh, and who therefore wore long hair under a turban, unless he removed the turban and cut his hair. The headmaster's reasons for his refusal were that the wearing of a turban, being a manifestation of the boy's ethnic origins, would accentuate religious and social distinctions in the school which, being a multiracial school based on the Christian faith, the headmaster desired to minimise. The boy, suing by his father, sought a declaration in the county court that the refusal to admit him unless he removed his turban and cut his hair was unlawful discrimination under s 1(1)(b)[a] of the Race Relations Act 1976 against a member of a 'racial group' as defined in s 3(1)[b] of that Act. The boy contended that the headmaster's 'no turban' rule amounted to discrimination within s 1(1)(b)(i) and (ii) because the boy was not a member of a 'racial group . . . who can comply' with the rule and the headmaster could not show the rule to be 'justifiable irrespective of [the boy's] ethnic . . . origins'. The evidence before the court was that the Sikhs were originally a religious community founded at about the end of the fifteenth century in the Punjab area of India, and that the Sikhs were no longer a purely religious group but were a separate community with distinctive customs such as the wearing of long hair and a turban although racially they were indistinguishable from other Punjabis, with whom they shared a common language. The judge dismissed the boy's claim on the ground that Sikhs were not a 'racial group' within the definition of that term in s 3(1) of the 1976 Act since Sikhs could not be 'defined by reference to . . . ethnic or national origins'. The boy appealed, contending that the term 'ethnic' embraced more than merely a racial concept and meant a cultural, linguistic or religious community. It was common ground that Sikhism was primarily a religion, that the adherents of a religion were not as such a 'racial group' within the 1976 Act and that discrimination in regard to religious practices was not unlawful. The Court of Appeal dismissed the boy's appeal on the grounds that a group could be defined by reference to its ethnic origins within s 3(1) of the 1976 Act only if the group could be distinguished from other groups by definable racial characteristics with which members of the group were born and that Sikhs had no such characteristics peculiar to Sikhs. The boy appealed to the House of Lords.

Held – The appeal would be allowed for the following reasons—

(1) The term 'ethnic' in s 3 of the 1976 Act was to be construed relatively widely in a broad cultural and historic sense. For a group to constitute an 'ethnic group' for the purposes of the 1976 Act it had to regard itself, and be regarded by others, as a distinct community by virtue of certain characteristics, two of which were essential. First it had

---

a Section 1(1) is set out at p 1065 a b, post
b Section 3(1), so far as material, is set out at p 1065 g, post

to have a long shared history, of which the group was conscious as distinguishing it from
a other groups, and the memory of which it kept alive, and second it had to have a cultural
tradition of its own, including family and social customs and manners, often but not
necessarily associated with religious observance. In addition, the following characteristics
could also be relevant, namely (a) either a common geographical origin or descent from
a small number of common ancestors, (b) a common language, which did not necessarily
have to be peculiar to the group, (c) a common literature peculiar to the group, (d) a
b common religion different from that of neighbouring groups or from the general
community surrounding it, and (e) the characteristic of being a minority or being an
oppressed or a dominant group within a larger community. Applying those characteristics,
the Sikhs were a group defined by reference to 'ethnic origins' for the purpose of the
1976 Act even though they were not racially distinguishable from other people living in
the Punjab (see p 1066 *b c* and *g* to p 1067 *g*, p 1068 *f*, p 1069 *a* to *e*, p 1071 *b* to *e* and
c p 1072 *d* to *j*, post); *King-Ansell v Police* [1979] 2 NZLR 531 adopted.
     (2) The words 'can comply' in s 1(1)(*b*)(i) of the 1976 Act were not to be read literally,
ie as meaning 'can physically' so as to indicate a theoretical possibility, but were to be
construed as meaning 'can in practice' or 'can, consistently with the cultural conditions
of the racial group' to which the person belonged. The 'no turban' rule was not a
requirement with which the applicant boy could, consistently with the customs of being
d a Sikh, comply and therefore the application of that rule to him by the headmaster was
unlawful discrimination (see p 1069 *f* to *h*, p 1071 *b* to *e* and p 1072 *h j*, post); *Price v Civil
Service Commission* [1978] 1 All ER 1228 applied.
     (3) The 'no turban' rule was not 'justifiable' within the meaning of s (1)(*b*)(ii) of the
1976 Act merely because the headmaster had a genuine belief that the school would
provide a better system of education if it were allowed to discriminate against those who
e wore turbans (see p 1069 *h j*, p 1070 *a* to *d* and *f*, p 1071 *b* to *e* and p 1072 *h j*, post).
     Decision of the Court of Appeal [1982] 3 All ER 1108 reversed.

Notes

For the general meaning of unlawful discrimination on ground of ethnic or national
f origins, see 4 Halsbury's Laws (4th edn) para 1035.
     For the Race Relations Act 1976, ss 1, 3, see 46 Halsbury's Statutes (3rd edn) 395, 397.

Cases referred to in opinions

Ealing London Borough v Race Relations Board [1972] 1 All ER 105, [1972] AC 342, [1972]
     2 WLR 71, HL, 2 Digest (Reissue) 316, 1783.
g *King-Ansell v Police* [1979] 2 NZLR 531, NZ CA.
Panesar v Nestlé Co Ltd [1980] ICR 144, CA.
Price v Civil Service Commission [1978] 1 All ER 1228, [1977] 1 WLR 1417, EAT, Digest
     (Cont Vol E) 407, 72Ab.

h **Appeal**

The plaintiffs, Sewa Singh Mandla and his son, Gurinder Singh Mandla, an infant suing
by his father and next friend, who were both Sikhs, appealed by leave of the Appeal
Committee of the House of Lords granted on 18 November 1982 against the decision of
the Court of Appeal (Lord Denning MR, Oliver and Kerr LJJ) ([1982] 3 All ER 1108,
[1983] QB 1) on 29 July 1982 dismissing their appeal against the judgment of his Honour
j Judge Gosling sitting in the Birmingham County Court on 10 December 1980 whereby
he dismissed the plaintiffs' claim against the defendants, Mr A G Dowell Lee and Park
Grove Private School Ltd, the headmaster and owner respectively of Park Grove School,
Birmingham, for, inter alia, a declaration that the defendants had committed an act of
unlawful discrimination against the plaintiffs within the Race Relations Act 1976 by
refusing to admit the second plaintiff to the school as a pupil unless he removed his

turban and cut his hair to conform with the school rules. The facts are set out in the opinion of Lord Fraser.

a

Alexander Irvine QC and *Harjit Singh* for the appellants.
The first respondent appeared in person.
The second respondent was not represented.

Their Lordships took time for consideration.

b

24 March. The following opinions were delivered.

LORD FRASER OF TULLYBELTON. My Lords, the main question in this appeal is whether Sikhs are a 'racial group' for the purposes of the Race Relations Act 1976. For *c* reasons that will appear, the answer to this question depends on whether they are a group defined by reference to 'ethnic origins'.

The appellants (plaintiffs) are Sikhs. The first appellant is a solicitor in Birmingham and he is the father of the second appellant. The second appellant was, at the material date, a boy of school age. The first respondent (first defendant) is the headmaster of an independent school in Birmingham called Park Grove School. The second respondent is *d* a company which owns the school, and in which the first respondent and his wife are principal shareholders. In what follows I shall refer to the first respondent as 'the respondent'. In July 1978 the first appellant wished to enter his son as a pupil at Park Grove School, and he brought the boy to an interview with the respondent. The first appellant explained that he wished his son to grow up as an orthodox Sikh, and that one of the rules which he had to observe was to wear a turban. That is because the turban is *e* regarded by Sikhs as a sign of their communal identity. At the interview, the respondent said that wearing a turban would be against the school rules which required all pupils to wear school uniform, and he did not think he could allow it, but he promised to think the matter over. A few days later he wrote to the first appellant saying that he had decided he could not relax the school rules and thus, in effect, saying that he would not accept the boy if he insisted on wearing a turban. The second appellant was then sent to *f* another school, where he was allowed to wear a turban, and, so far as the appellants as individuals are concerned, that is the end of the story.

But the first appellant complained to the Commission for Racial Equality that the respondent had discriminated against him and his son on racial grounds. The commission took up the case and they are the real appellants before your Lordships' House. The case clearly raises an important question of construction of the 1976 Act, on which the *g* commission wishes to have a decision, and they have undertaken, very properly, to pay the costs of the respondent in this House, whichever party succeeds in the appeal. In the county court Judge Gosling held that Sikhs were not a racial group, and therefore that there had been no discrimination contrary to the 1976 Act. The Court of Appeal (Lord Denning MR, Oliver and Kerr LJJ) ([1982] 3 All ER 1108, [1983] QB 1) agreed with that view. The commission, using the name of the appellants, now appeals to this House. *h*

The main purpose of the 1976 Act is to prohibit discrimination against people on racial grounds, and more generally, to make provision with respect to relations between people of different racial groups. So much appears from the long title. The scheme of the Act, so far as is relevant to this appeal, is to define in Part I what is meant by racial discrimination and then in later parts to prohibit such discrimination in various fields including employment, provision of goods, services and other things, and by s 17 in the *j* field of education. There can be no doubt that, if there has been racial discrimination against the appellants in the present case, it was in the field of education, and was contrary to s 17(a) which makes it unlawful for the proprietor of an independent school to discriminate against a person in the terms on which the school offers to admit him as a pupil. The only question is whether any racial discrimination has occurred.

Racial discrimination is defined in s 1(1), which provides as follows:

> 'A person discriminates against another in any circumstances relevant for the purposes of any provision of this Act if—(a) on racial grounds he treats that other less favourably than he treats or would treat other persons; or (b) he applies to that other a requirement or condition which he applies or would apply equally to persons not of the same racial group as that other but—(i) which is such that the proportion of persons of the same racial group as that other who can comply with it is considerably smaller than the proportion of persons not of that racial group who can comply with it; and (ii) which he cannot show to be justifiable irrespective of the colour, race, nationality or ethnic or national origins of the person to whom it is applied; and (iii) which is to the detriment of that other because he cannot comply with it.'

The type of discrimination referred to in para (a) of that subsection is generally called 'direct' discrimination. When the present proceedings began in the county court, direct discrimination was alleged, but the judge held that there had been no direct discrimination, and his judgment on that point was not challenged in the Court of Appeal or before your Lordships' House. The appellants' case in this House was based entirely on 'indirect' discrimination, that is discrimination contrary to s 1(1)(b). When the proceedings began the appellants claimed damages, but that claim was not pursued before this House. Having regard to s 57(3) of the 1976 Act, it would have been unlikely to succeed. They now seek only a declaration that there has been unlawful discrimination against them contrary to the Act.

The case against the respondent under s 1(1)(b) is that he discriminated against the second appellant because he applied to him a requirement or condition (namely the 'no turban' rule) which he applied equally to pupils not of the same racial group as the second respondent (ie to pupils who were not Sikhs) but (i) which is such that the proportion of Sikhs who can comply with it is considerably smaller than the proportion of non-Sikhs who can comply with it and (ii) which the respondent cannot show to be justifiable irrespective of the colour, etc of the second appellant, and (iii) which is to the detriment of the second appellant because he cannot comply with it. As I have already said, the first main question is whether the Sikhs are a racial group. If they are, then two further questions arise. Question two is what is the meaning of 'can' in s 1(1)(b)(i), and question three is, what is the meaning of 'justifiable' in para (b)(ii) of that subsection?

'Ethnic origins'

Racial group is defined in s 3(1) of that Act, which provides:

> '..."racial group" means a group of persons defined by reference to colour, race, nationality or ethnic or national origins, and references to a person's racial group refer to any racial group into which he falls.'

It is suggested that Sikhs are a group defined by reference to colour, race, nationality or national origins. In none of these respects are they distinguishable from many other groups, especially those living, like most Sikhs, in the Punjab. The argument turns entirely on whether they are a group defined by 'ethnic' origins'. It is therefore necessary to ascertain the sense in which the words 'ethnic' is used in the 1976 Act. We were referred to various dictionary definitions. The *Oxford English Dictionary* (1897 edn) gives two meanings of 'ethnic'. The first is 'pertaining to nations not Christian or Jewish; gentile, heathen, pagan'. That clearly cannot be its meaning in the 1976 Act, because it is inconceivable that Parliament would have legislated against racial discrimination intending that the protection should not apply either to Christians or (above all) to Jews. Neither party contended that that was the relevant meaning for the present purpose. The second meaning given in the *Oxford English Dictionary* (1897 edn) was 'pertaining to race; peculiar to a race or nation; ethnological'. A slightly shorter form of that meaning (omitting 'peculiar to a race or nation') was given by the *Concise Oxford Dictionary* in 1934 and was expressly accepted by Lord Denning MR as the correct meaning for the present purpose. Oliver and Kerr LJJ also accepted that meaning as being substantially correct, *a* and Oliver LJ said that the word 'ethnic' in its popular meaning involved 'essentially a racial concept: the concept of something with which the members of the group are born; some fixed or inherited characteristic' (see [1982] 3 All ER 1108 at 1116–1117, [1983] QB 1 at 15). The respondent, who appeared on his own behalf, submitted that that was the relevant meaning of 'ethnic' in the 1976 Act, and that it did not apply to Sikhs because they were essentially a religious group, and they shared their racial characteristics *b* with other religious groups, including Hindus and Muslims, living in the Punjab.

My Lords, I recognise that 'ethnic' conveys a flavour of race but it cannot, in my opinion, have been used in the 1976 Act in a strict racial or biological sense. For one things it would be absurd to suppose that Parliament can have intended that membership of a particular racial group should depend on scientific proof that a person possessed the relevant distinctive biological characteristics (assuming that such characteristics exist). *c* The practical difficulties of such proof would be prohibitive, and it is clear that Parliament must have used the word in some more popular sense. For another thing, the briefest glance at the evidence in this case is enough to show that, within the human race, there are very few, if any, distinctions which are scientifically recognised as racial. I respectfully agree with the view of Lord Simon in *Ealing London Borough v Race Relations Board* [1972] *d* 1 All ER 105 at 115, [1972] AC 342 at 362, referring to the long title of the Race Relations Act 1968 (which was in terms identical with part of the long title of the 1976 Act), when he said:

'Moreover, "racial" is not a term of art, either legal or, I surmise, scientific. I apprehend that anthropologists would dispute how far the word "race" is biologically at all relevant to the species amusingly called homo sapiens.' *e*

A few lines lower down, after quoting part of s 1(1) of the 1968 Act, Lord Simon said:

'This is rubbery and elusive language—understandably when the draftsman is dealing with so unprecise a concept as "race" in its popular sense and endeavouring to leave no loophole for evasion.' *f*

I turn, therefore, to the third and wider meaning which is given in the *Supplement to the Oxford English Dictionary* vol 1 (A–G) (1972). It is as follows: 'pertaining to or having common racial, cultural, religious, or linguistic characteristics, esp. designating a racial or other group within a larger system . . .' Counsel for the appellants, while not accepting the third (1972) meaning as directly applicable for the present purpose, relied on it to this extent, that it introduces a reference to cultural and other characteristics, and is not *g* limited to racial characteristics. The 1972 meaning is, in my opinion, too loose and vague to be accepted as it stands. It is capable of being read as implying that any one of the adjectives, 'racial, cultural, religious *or* linguistic', would be enough to constitute an ethnic group. That cannot be the sense in which 'ethnic' is used in the 1976 Act, as that Act is not concerned at all with discrimination on religious grounds. Similarly, it cannot have been used to mean simply any 'racial *or other* group'. If that were the meaning of *h* 'ethnic', it would add nothing to the word group, and would lead to a result which would be unacceptably wide. But in seeking for the true meaning of 'ethnic' in the statute, we are not tied to the precise definition in any dictionary. The value of the 1972 definition is, in my view, that it shows that ethnic has come to be commonly used in a sense appreciably wider than the strictly racial or biological. That appears to me to be consistent with the ordinary experience of those who read newspapers at the present day. In my *j* opinion, the word 'ethnic' still retains a racial flavour but it is used nowadays in an extended sense to include other characteristics which may be commonly thought of as being associated with common racial origin.

For a group to constitute an ethnic group in the sense of the 1976 Act, it must, in my opinion, regard itself, and be regarded by others, as a distinct community by virtue of a certain characteristics. Some of these characteristics are essential; others are not essential but one or more of them will commonly be found and will help to distinguish the group from the surrounding community. The conditions which appear to me to be essential are these: (1) a long shared history, of which the group is conscious as distinguishing it from other groups, and the memory of which it keeps alive; (2) a cultural tradition of its own, including family and social customs and manners, often but not necessarily associated with religious observance. In addition to those two essential characteristics the

b following characteristics are, in my opinion, relevant: (3) either a common geographical origin, or descent from a small number of common ancestors; (4) a common language, not necessarily peculiar to the group; (5) a common literature peculiar to the group; (6) a common religion different from that of neighbouring groups or from the general community surrounding it; (7) being a minority or being an oppressed or a dominant group within a larger community, for example a conquered people (say, the inhabitants

c of England shortly after the Norman conquest) and their conquerors might both be ethnic groups.

A group defined by reference to enough of these characteristics would be capable of including converts, for example, persons who marry into the group, and of excluding apostates. Provided a person who joins the group feels himself or herself to be a member of it, and is accepted by other members, then he is, for the purpose of the 1976 Act, a

d member. That appears to be consistent with the words at the end of sub-s (1) of s 3: 'references to a person's racial group refer to any racial group into which he falls.' In my opinion, it is possible for a person to fall into a particular racial group either by birth or by adherence, and it makes no difference, so far as the 1976 Act is concerned, by which route he finds his way into the group. This view does not involve creating any inconsistency between direct discrimination under para (a) and indirect discrimination

e under para (b). A person may treat another relatively unfavourably 'on racial grounds' because he regards that other as being of a particular race, or belonging to a particular racial group, even if his belief is, from a scientific point of view, completely erroneous.

Finally, on this part of the argument, I think it is proper to mention that the word 'ethnic' is of Greek origin, being derived from the Greek word 'ethnos' the basic meaning of which appears to have been simply 'a group' not limited by reference to racial or any

f other distinguishing characteristics: see Liddell and Scott's Greek–English Lexicon (8th edn (Oxford), 1897). I do not suggest that the meaning of the English word in a modern statute ought to be governed by the meaning of the Greek word from which it is derived, but the fact that the meaning of the latter was wide avoids one possible limitation on the meaning of the English word.

My Lords, I have attempted so far to explain the reasons why, in my opinion, the word

g 'ethnic' in the 1976 Act should be construed relatively widely, in what was referred to by counsel for the appellants as a broad, cultural/historic sense. The conclusion at which I have arrived by construction of the 1976 Act itself is greatly strengthened by consideration of the decision of the Court of Appeal in New Zealand (Richmond P, Woodhouse and Richardson JJ) in King-Ansell v Police [1979] 2 NZLR 531. That case was discovered by the industry of the appellants' counsel, but unfortunately not until after the Court of Appeal

h in England had decided the case now under appeal. If it had been before the Court of Appeal it might well have affected their decision. In that case the appellant had been convicted by a magistrate of an offence under the New Zealand Race Relations Act 1971, the offence consisting of publishing a pamphlet with intent to incite ill-will against Jews, 'on the ground of their ethnic origins'. The question of law arising on the appeal concerned the meaning to be given to the words 'ethnic ... origins of that group of

j persons' in s 25(1) of the Act. The decision of the Court of Appeal was that Jews in New Zealand did form a group with common ethnic origins within the meaning of the Act. The structure of the New Zealand Act differs considerably from that of the 1976 Act, but the offence created by s 25 of the New Zealand Act (viz inciting ill-will against any group of persons on the ground of their 'colour, race, or ethnic or national origins') raises the same question of construction as the present appeal, in a context which is identical, except that the New Zealand Act does not mention 'nationality', and the 1976 Act does. The reasoning of all members of the New Zealand court was substantially similar, and it *a* can, I think, be sufficiently indicated by quoting the following short passages. The first is from the judgment of Woodhouse J where, after referring to the meaning given by the *Supplement to the Oxford English Dictionary* vol 1 (A–G) (1972), which I have already quoted, he says (at 538):

> 'The distinguishing features of an ethnic group or of the ethnic origins of a group would usually depend upon a combination, present together, of characteristics of *b* the kind indicated in the Supplement. In any case it would be a mistake to regard this or any other dictionary meaning as though it had to be imported word for word into a statutory definition and construed accordingly. However, subject to those qualifications, I think that for the purposes of construing the expression "ethnic origins" the 1972 Supplement is a helpful guide and I accept it.'

Richardson J said (at 542):   *c*

> 'The real test is whether the individuals or the group regard themselves and are regarded by others in the community as having a particular historical identity in terms of their colour or their racial, national or ethnic origins. That must be based on a belief shared by members of the group.'

And the same judge said (at 543):   *d*

> '. . . a group is identifiable in terms of its ethnic origins if it is a segment of the population distinguished from others by a sufficient combination of shared customs, beliefs, traditions and characteristics derived from a common or presumed common past, even if not drawn from what in biological terms is a common racial stock. It is that combination which gives them an historically determined social identity in their own eyes and in the eyes of those outside the group, they have a distinct social *e* identity based not simply on group cohesion and solidarity but also on their belief as to their historical antecedents.'

My Lords, that last passage sums up in a way on which I could not hope to improve the views which I have been endeavouring to express. It is important that courts in English-speaking countries should, if possible, construe the words which we are *f* considering in the same way where they occur in the same context, and I am happy to say that I find no difficulty at all in agreeing with the construction favoured by the New Zealand Court of Appeal.

There is only one respect in which that decision rests on a basis that is not fully applicable to the instant appeal. That appears from the long title of the New Zealand Act which is as follows: *g*

> 'An Act to affirm and promote racial equality in New Zealand and to implement the International Convention on the Elimination of All Forms of Racial Discrimination.'

Neither the 1976 Act nor its predecessors in the United Kingdom, the Race Relations Acts 1965 and 1968, refer to the International Convention on the Elimination of All *h* Forms of Racial Discrimination. The convention was adopted on 7 March 1966, and was signed by the United Kingdom on 11 October 1966, subject to reservations which are not now material. It was not ratified by the United Kingdom until 7 March 1969 (see Cmnd 4108, August 1969). Under the convention the states parties undertook, inter alia, to prohibit racial discrimination in all its forms, and to guarantee the rights of everyone 'without distinction as to race, colour, or national or ethnic origin' of equality before the *j* law, notably in certain rights which were specified including education (art 5(e)(v)). The words which I have quoted are very close to the words found in the 1976 Act and in its predecessors in this country, and they are certainly quite consistent with these United Kingdom Acts having been passed in implementation of the obligation imposed by the convention. But it is unnecessary to rely in this case on any special rules of construction applicable to legislation which gives effect to international conventions because, for the a reasons already explained, a strict or legalistic construction of the words would not, in any event, be appropriate.

The respondent admitted, rightly in my opinion, that, if the proper construction of the word 'ethnic' in s 3 of the 1976 Act is a wide one, on lines such as I have suggested, the Sikhs would qualify as a group defined by ethnic orgins for the purposes of the Act. It is, therefore, unnecessary to consider in any detail the relevant characteristics of the Sikhs. They were originally a religious community founded about the end of the

b fifteenth century in the Punjab by Guru Nanak, who was born in 1469. But the community is no longer purely religious in character. Their present position is summarised sufficiently for present purposes in the opinion of the county court judge in the following passage:

> 'The evidence in my judgment shows that Sikhs are a distinctive and self-conscious community. They have a history going back to the fifteenth century. They have a
c written language which a small proportion of Sikhs can read but which can be read by a much higher proportion of Sikhs than of Hindus. They were at one time politically supreme in the Punjab.'

The result is, in my opinion, that Sikhs are a group defined by a reference to ethnic origins for the purpose of the 1976 Act, although they are not biologically distinguishable from the other peoples living in the Punjab. That is true whether one is considering the

d position before the partition of 1947, when the Sikhs lived mainly in that part of the Punjab which is now Pakistan, or after 1947, since when most of them have moved into India. It is, therefore, necessary to consider whether the respondent has indirectly discriminated against the appellants in the sense of s 1(1)(b) of the 1976 Act. That raises the two subsidiary questions I have already mentioned.

e *'Can comply'*

It is obvious that Sikhs, like anyone else, 'can' refrain from wearing a turban, if 'can' is construed literally. But if the broad cultural/historic meaning of ethnic is the appropriate meaning of the word in the 1976 Act, then a literal reading of the word 'can' would deprive Sikhs and members of other groups defined by reference to their ethnic origins of much of the protection which Parliament evidently intended the 1976 Act to afford

f to them. They 'can' comply with almost any requirement or condition if they are willing to give up their distinctive customs and cultural rules. On the other hand, if ethnic means inherited or unalterable, as the Court of Appeal thought it did, then 'can' ought logically to be read literally. The word 'can' is used with many shades of meaning. In the context of s 1(1)(b)(i) of the 1976 Act it must, in my opinion, have been intended by Parliament to be read not as meaning 'can physically', so as to indicate a theoretical

g possibility, but as meaning 'can in practice' or 'can consistently with the customs and cultural conditions of the racial group'. The latter meaning was attributed to the word by the Employment Appeal Tribunal in *Price v Civil Service Commission* [1978] 1 All ER 1228, [1977] 1 WLR 1417, on a construction of the parallel provision in the Sex Discrimination Act 1975. I agree with their construction of the word in that context. Accordingly I am of opinion that the 'no turban' rule was not one with which the second

h appellant could, in the relevant sense, comply.

'Justifiable'

The word 'justifiable' occurs in s 1(1)(b)(ii). It raises a problem which is, in my opinion, more difficult than the problem of the word 'can'. But in the end I have reached a firm opinion that the respondent has not been able to show that the 'no turban' rule was

j justifiable in the relevant sense. Regarded purely from the point of view of the respondent, it was no doubt perfectly justifiable. He explained that he had no intention of discriminating against Sikhs. In 1978 the school had about 300 pupils (about 75% boys and 25% girls) of whom over 200 were English, five were Sikhs, 34 Hindus, 16 Persians, six negroes, seven Chinese and 15 from European countries. The reasons for having a school uniform were largely reasons of practical convenience, to minimise external differences between races and social classes, to discourage the 'competitive fashions' which

he said tend to exist in a teenage community, and to present a Christian image of the
school to outsiders, including prospective parents. The respondent explained the difficulty   *a*
for a headmaster of explaining to a non-Sikh pupil why the rules about wearing correct
school uniform were enforced against him if they were relaxed in favour of a Sikh. In
my view these reasons could not, either individually or collectively, provide a sufficient
justification for the respondent to apply a condition that is prima facie discriminatory
under the 1976 Act.

An attempted justification of the 'no turban' rule, which requires more serious   *b*
consideration, was that the respondent sought to run a Christian school, accepting pupils
of all religions and races, and that he objected to the turban on the ground that it was an
outward manifestation of a non-Christian faith. Indeed, he regarded it as amounting to a
challenge to that faith. I have much sympathy with the respondent on this part of the
case and I would have been glad to find that the rule was justifiable within the meaning
of the statute, if I could have done so. But in my opinion that is impossible. The onus   *c*
under para (*b*)(ii) is on the respondent to show that the condition which he seeks to apply
is not indeed a necessary condition, but that it is in all circumstances justifiable
'irrespective of the colour, race, nationality or ethnic or national origins of the person to
whom it is applied', that is to say that it is justifiable without regard to the ethnic origins
of that person. But in this case the principal justification on which the respondent relies
is that the turban is objectionable just because it is a manifestation of the second   *d*
appellant's ethnic origins. That is not, in my view, a justification which is admissible
under para (*b*)(ii). The kind of justification that might fall within that provision would
be one based on public health, as in *Panesar v Nestlé Co Ltd* [1980] ICR 144, where the
Court of Appeal held that a rule forbidding the wearing of beards in the respondent's
chocolate factory was justifiable within the meaning of s 1(1)(*b*)(ii) on hygienic grounds,
notwithstanding that the proportion of Sikhs who could [sc conscientiously] comply   *e*
with it was considerably smaller than the proportion of non-Sikhs who could comply
with it. Again, it might be possible for the school to show that a rule insisting on a fixed
diet, which included some dish (for example, pork) which some racial groups could not
conscientiously eat was justifiable if the school proved that the cost of providing special
meals for the particular group would be prohibitive. Questions of that sort would be
questions of fact for the tribunal of fact, and if there was evidence on which it could find   *f*
the condition to be justifiable its finding would not be liable to be disturbed on appeal.

But in the present case I am of opinion that the respondent has not been able to show
that the 'no turban' rule was justifiable.

Final considerations

Before parting with the case I must refer to some observations by the Court of Appeal   *g*
which suggest that the conduct of the Commission for Racial Equality in this case has
been in some way unreasonable or oppressive. Lord Denning MR ([1982] 3 All ER 1108
at 1114, [1983] QB 1 at 13) merely expressed regret that the commission had taken up
the case. But Oliver LJ ([1982] 3 All ER 1108 at 1118, [1983] QB 1 at 18) used stronger
language and suggested that the machinery of the 1976 Act had been operated against
the respondent as 'an engine of oppression'. Kerr LJ ([1982] 3 All ER 1108 at 1123,   *h*
[1983] QB 1 at 25) referred to notes of an interview between the respondent and an
official of the commission which he said read in part 'more like an inquisition than an
interview' and which he regarded as harassment of the respondent.

My Lords, I must say that I regard these strictures on the commission and its officials
as entirely unjustified. The commission has a difficult task, and no doubt its inquiries
will be resented by some and are liable to be regarded as objectionable and inquisitive.   *j*
But the respondent in this case, who conducted his appeal with restraint and skill, made
no complaint of his treatment at the hands of the commission. He was specifically asked
by some of my noble and learned friends to point out any part of the notes of his
interview with the commission's official to which he objected, and he said there were
none and that an objection of that sort formed no part of his case. The lady who
conducted the interview on behalf of the commission gave evidence in the county court,

and no suggestion was put to her in cross-examination that she had not conducted it
a properly. Opinions may legitimately differ as to the usefulness of the commission's
activities, but its functions have been laid down by Parliament and, in my view, the
actions of the commission itself in this case and of its official who interviewed the
respondent on 3 November 1978 were perfectly proper and in accordance with its
statutory duty.

I would allow this appeal. The appellants have agreed to pay the costs of the respondent
b in this House and they do not seek to disturb the order for costs in the lower courts in
favour of the present respondent made by the Court of Appeal.

LORD EDMUND-DAVIES. My Lords, I have found this case unfortunate in several
ways and by no means free from difficulty. But I have had the advantage of reading in
draft form the speeches prepared by my noble and learned friends Lord Fraser and Lord
c Templeman. They are in conformity with the conclusion at which I had ultimately
arrived, and I do not find it necessary or desirable to add any observations of my own. I
therefore restrict myself to concurring that the appeal should be allowed.

LORD ROSKILL. My Lords, I have had the advantage of reading in draft the speeches
prepared by my noble and learned friends Lord Fraser and Lord Templeman. For the
reasons given in those speeches I too would allow this appeal.
d

LORD BRANDON OF OAKBROOK. My Lords, I have had the advantage of
reading in draft the speeches prepared by my noble and learned friends Lord Fraser and
Lord Templeman. I agree with both speeches, and for the reasons which they give I
would allow the appeal.

e **LORD TEMPLEMAN.** My Lords, the Race Relations Act 1976 outlaws discrimination
in specified fields of activities against defined racial groups. The fields of activity in which
discrimination is made a criminal offence are employment, education and the provision
of goods, facilities, services and premises. Presumably Parliament considered that
discrimination in these fields was most widespread and harmful. By s 3 of the 1976 Act
the racial groups against which discrimination may not be practised are groups 'defined
f by reference to colour, race, nationality or ethnic or national origins'. Presumably
Parliament considered that the protection of these groups against discrimination was the
most necessary. The 1976 Act does not outlaw discrimination against a group of persons
defined by reference to religion. Presumably Parliament considered that the amount of
discrimination on religious grounds does not constitute a severe burden on members of
religious groups. The 1976 Act does not apply and has no reference to the situation in
g Northern Ireland. The Court of Appeal thought that the Sikhs were only members of a
religion or at best members of a religion and culture. But the evidence of the origins and
history of the Sikhs which was adduced by the parties to the present litigation disclosed
that the Sikhs are more than a religion and a culture. And in view of the history of this
country since the 1939–45 war I find it impossible to believe that Parliament intended to
exclude the Sikhs from the benefit of the Race Relations Act 1976 and to allow
h discrimination to be practised against the Sikhs in those fields of activity where, as the
present case illustrates, discrimination is likely to occur.

Section 17 of the 1976 Act makes it unlawful for the proprietor of a school to
discriminate against a person in the terms on which the school offers to admit him to the
school as a pupil. By s 1(1):

j 'A person discriminates against another . . . if . . . (b) he applies to that other a
requirement or condition which he applies or would apply equally to persons not of
the same racial group as that other but—(i) which is such that the proportion of
persons of the same racial group as that other who can comply with it is considerably
smaller than the proportion of persons not of that racial group who can comply
with it; and (ii) which he cannot show to be justifiable irrespective of the colour,
race, nationality or ethnic or national origins of the person to whom it is applied . . .'

The respondents are only willing to admit the appellant Gurinder Singh to Park Grove School if he complies with the school rules. Rule 22 stipulates that 'Boys' hair must be *a* cut so as not to touch the collar . . .' As an orthodox Sikh Gurinder Singh must allow his hair to grow unshorn. Rule 20 requires boys to wear the school uniform. The method adopted by orthodox Sikhs for containing unshorn hair is the wearing of a turban; a school cap is useless for that purpose. Gurinder Singh says he cannot comply with rr 22 or 20 because he is a Sikh and on his behalf it is argued that Sikhs constitute a racial group, being a group of persons defined within the 1976 Act and cannot comply with rr *b* 22 or 20, whereas all non-Sikhs can comply with those rules, then the school is guilty of discrimination against the Sikh Gurinder Singh unless the respondents can show that rr 22 and 20 are justifiable irrespective of the ethnic origin of Gurinder Singh.

In the course of the argument attention was directed to the dictionary definitions of the adjective 'ethnic'. But it is common ground that some definitions constitute the Sikhs a relevant group of ethnic origin whereas other definitions would exclude them. The *c* true construction of the expression 'ethnic origins' must be deducted from the 1976 Act. A racial group means a group of persons defined by reference to colour, race, nationality or ethnic or national origins. I agree with the Court of Appeal that in this context ethnic origins have a good deal in common with the concept of race just as national origins have a good deal in common with the concept of nationality. But the statutory definition of a racial group envisages that a group defined by reference to ethnic origin may be different *d* from a group defined by reference to race, just as a group defined by reference to national origins may be different from a group defined by reference to nationality. In my opinion, for the purposes of the 1976 Act a group of persons defined by reference to ethnic origins must possess some of the characteristics of a race, namely group descent, a group of geographical origin and a group history. The evidence shows that the Sikhs satisfy these tests. They are more than a religious sect, they are almost a race and almost a nation. As *e* a race, the Sikhs share a common colour, and a common physique based on common ancestors from that part of the Punjab which is centred on Amritsar. They fail to qualify as a separate race because in racial origin prior to the inception of Sikhism they cannot be distinguished from other inhabitants of the Punjab. As a nation the Sikhs defeated the Moghuls, and established a kingdom in the Punjab which they lost as a result of the first and second Sikh wars; they fail to qualify as a separate nation or as a separate nationality *f* because their kingdom never achieved a sufficient degree of recognition or permanence. The Sikhs qualify as a group defined by ethnic origins because they consitute a separate and distinct community derived from the racial characteristics I have mentioned. They also justify the conditions enumerated by my noble and learned friend Lord Fraser. The Sikh community has accepted converts who do not comply with those conditions. Some persons who have the same ethnic origins as the Sikhs have ceased to be members of the *g* Sikh community. But the Sikhs remain a group of persons forming a community recognisable by ethnic origins within the meaning of the 1976 Act. Gurinder Singh is a member of the Sikh community which qualifies as a racial group for the purposes of the 1976 Act.

I agree with my noble and learned friend that Gurinder Singh cannot comply with the school rules without becoming a victim of discrimination. The discrimination cannot be *h* justified by a genuine belief that the school would provide a better system of education if it were allowed to discriminate. I also agree that the Commission for Racial Equality were under a duty properly to investigate the present complaint of discrimination and that their conduct was not oppressive.

I agree that the appeal should be allowed.

j

Appeal allowed.

Solicitors: *Bindman & Partners* (for the appellants).

Mary Rose Plummer   Barrister.

a

Avon County Council v Howlett

COURT OF APPEAL, CIVIL DIVISION

CUMMING-BRUCE, EVELEIGH AND SLADE LJJ

20, 21, 22 JULY, 21 DECEMBER 1982

b   *Estoppel – Representation – Mistake – Payment of money – Employer overpaying employee by mistake – Employer representing that employee entitled to treat money as his own – Employee spending part of money in reliance on representation – Whether employer estopped from recovering whole of money or only the part spent.*

c   *Mistake – Recovery of money paid – Nature of mistake – Mistake of law or of fact – Burden of proof – Overpayment of salary by mistake – Action by employer to recover money overpaid – Overpayment recoverable only if paid under mistake of fact – Burden of proof that money paid under mistake of fact lying on employer.*

d The defendant was injured in the course of his employment with the plaintiffs and as a result was absent from work for nearly two years. The plaintiffs subsequently discovered that during that period, under their computerised system for the payment of wages, they had overpaid him to the extent of £1,007. They brought an action against him claiming repayment of that sum on the ground that it had been paid by mistake. In his defence the defendant claimed (i) that the money was irrecoverable because it had been paid under a mistake of law and not of fact, and (ii) that in any event the plaintiffs were *e* estopped from pursuing any part of their claim because (a) they had represented to him that he was entitled to treat the money as his own, (b) in reliance on that representation he had spent money which he would not otherwise have done and (c) the overpayment was not due to any fault on his part. The judge held that the mistake which had led to the overpayment was one of fact since the plaintiffs' employees had not fed the correct information into the computer, that the plaintiffs were estopped from reclaiming that part of the money which the defendant claimed he had spent in reliance on their *f* representation, but that they were not estopped from reclaiming the balance because it would not be inequitable for them to require the defendant to repay it. He accordingly gave judgment for the plaintiffs for the balance. The defendant appealed.

g **Held** – (1) Since the plaintiffs had discharged the onus of proving that the overpayment had occurred due to a mistake of fact and not of law they were prima facie entitled to recover the full amount of the overpayment (see p 1076 *h j*, p 1077 *a b* and p 1084 *e* to p 1085 *b*, post).

(2) However, estoppel by representation, being a rule of evidence which precluded a representor from averring facts which were contrary to his own representations, could not operate pro tanto and therefore since, on the facts, all the conditions for the application *h* of that estoppel had been satisfied it followed that the plaintiffs were prevented from recovering any part of the overpayment. Accordingly, the appeal would be allowed and the judgment of the trial judge set aside (see p 1076 *h j*, p 1078 *a b*, p 1087 *a b*, p 1088 *g* to *j* and p 1089 *e f*, post); *Skyring v Greenwood* [1824–34] All ER Rep 104, *Ogilvie v West Australian Mortgage and Agency Corp Ltd* [1896] AC 257, *Holt v Markham* [1922] All ER Rep 134, *R E Jones Ltd v Waring & Gillow Ltd* [1926] All ER Rep 36, *Greenwood v Martins* *j* *Bank Ltd* [1932] All ER Rep 318 and *Amalgamated Investment and Property Co Ltd (in liq) v Texas Commerce International Bank Ltd* [1981] 3 All ER 577 considered.

Per Cumming-Bruce LJ. A plaintiff who is faced with a defence of estoppel and wishes to argue that it would be inequitable for the defendant to retain money paid to him under a mistake of fact should plead, by way of reply, the facts on which he relies (see p 1076 *f* and *j*, post).

Notes

For estoppel by representation, see 16 Halsbury's Laws (4th edn) paras 1591–1602, and ⓐ
for cases on the subject, see 21 Digest (Reissue) 156–166, 1130–1171.

For recovery of money paid under mistake, see 32 Halsbury's Laws (4th edn) paras 63–
74, and for cases on the subject, see 35 Digest (Repl) 158–166, 475–527.

Cases referred to in judgments

Adams v Naylor [1946] 2 All ER 241, [1946] AC 543, HL, 17 Digest (Reissue) 546, 543.   ⓑ
Allcard v Walker [1896] 2 Ch 369, 35 Digest (Repl) 96, 16.
Amalgamated Investment and Property Co Ltd (in liq) v Texas Commerce International Bank Ltd
[1981] 1 All ER 923, [1981] 2 WLR 554; *affd on other grounds* [1981] 3 All ER 577,
[1982] QB 84, [1981] 3 WLR 565, CA.
Bilbie v Lumley (1802) 2 East 469, [1775–1802] All ER Rep 425, 102 ER 448, 35 Digest
(Repl) 172, 570.   ⓒ
Cooper v Phibbs (1867) LR 2 HL 149, 35 Digest (Repl) 98, 28.
Fung Kai Sun v Chan Fui Hing [1951] AC 489, PC, 21 Digest (Reissue) 208, 1489.
Greenwood v Martins Bank Ltd [1933] AC 51, [1932] All ER Rep 318, HL; *affg* [1932] 1 KB
371, CA, 21 Digest (Reissue) 207, 1484.
Holt v Markham [1923] 1 KB 504, [1922] All ER Rep 134, CA, 21 Digest (Reissue) 178,
1245.   ⓓ
Jones (RE) Ltd v Waring & Gillow Ltd [1926] AC 670, [1926] All ER Rep 36, HL, 35 Digest
(Repl) 161, 492.
Kelly v Solari (1841) 9 M & W 54, [1835–42] All ER Rep 320, 152 ER 24, 35 Digest (Repl)
164, 512.
Larner v London CC [1949] 1 All ER 964, [1949] 2 KB 683, CA, 35 Digest (Repl) 170, 558.
Lloyds Bank Ltd v Brooks (1950) 6 Legal Decisions Affecting Bankers 161.   ⓔ
Ministry of Health v Simpson [1950] 2 All ER 1137, [1951] AC 251, 32 Digest (Reissue)
575, 4343.
Ogilvie v West Australian Mortgage and Agency Corp Ltd [1896] AC 257, PC, 21 Digest
(Reissue) 208, 1488.
Skyring v Greenwood (1825) 4 B & C 281, [1824–34] All ER Rep 104, 107 ER 1064, 21
Digest (Reissue) 208, 1490.   ⓕ

Appeal

The defendant, Harold Ellis Howlett, appealed against a judgment of Sheldon J, dated 20
July 1981, whereby it was ordered that the plaintiffs, Avon County Council, were entitled
to recover from the defendant the sum of £460·39 (subject to their undertaking not to
enforce the judgment without the leave of the court) and that the defendant's   ⓖ
counterclaim be dismissed. The facts are set out in the judgment of Slade LJ.

John M Bowyer for the defendant.
David H Fletcher for the plaintiffs.

Cur adv vult   ⓗ

21 December. The following judgments were delivered.

CUMMING-BRUCE LJ. The course which the case took at the hearing gives rise to
difficulty in determining how far the decision of this court can be relied on as establishing
how the law of estoppel will be applied to other cases. The difficulty is the result of the   ⓙ
fact that the judge admitted evidence which satisfied him that the defendant had spent
all moneys overpaid but then decided the case on an artificial case pleaded in the defence.
The defendant's counsel, on instructions, deliberately refused to apply to amend the
defence in order to reconcile the detriment pleaded in para 12 of the reamended defence
with the evidence of the defendant. So the judge found as a fact that the defendant had

spent all the £1,007 which he had received as an overpayment due to the plaintiffs'
a mistake but decided the case on the basis of the pleaded case which alleged that he had
only spent £546·61 and that there was no evidence about what had happened to the
balance of £460·39. This was untrue. The judge solved the practical problem by making
an order in the following terms:

> 'IT IS ORDERED that the Plaintiff is entitled to recover from the Defendant the sum
> of £460·39 the Plaintiff having undertaken not to execute this judgement without
b > leave of the court and that the Defendant's Counterclaim is dismissed AND there is
> no order as to costs.'

The judgment was, in my view, based on a hypothetical state of facts, without
substance or reality, because the judge in the course of his judgment had found that the
defendant had spent all the £1,007. I quote:

c > 'At an early stage of the hearing, however, it also became clear that all the money
> so overpaid had long since been spent by the recipient, and indeed, that [the
> defendant] neither had nor would be likely in the future to have sufficient funds
> with which to meet any judgment that might be given against him. On my
> inquiring of the parties, however, whether there was any purpose in incurring
> further costs in this connection I was told that the local government reorganisation
d > in question had resulted in a number of similar overpayments having been made to
> other individuals and that, accordingly, both the council and the union concerned
> (the Confederation of Health Service Employees) wished to use this as a test case, so
> far as possible, to establish the various rights and liabilities. I was also told that the
> [plaintiff] council, if they succeeded in their claim against [the defendants], were
> prepared to undertake not, without leave of the court, to seek to enforce any such
e > judgment against him.'

In *Adams v Naylor* [1946] 2 All ER 241, [1946] AC 543 the House of Lords disapproved
a practice whereby the Crown authorities nominated a defendant in order to bring into
court for judgment issues which were really issues between the plaintiff and the Crown,
but for convenience disguised in the pleadings as issues between the plaintiff and the
f personal defendant. As Lord Uthwatt stated ([1946] 2 All ER 241 at 247, [1946] AC 543
at 555):

> 'It was not open to the parties to this suit by agreement to have the matter dealt
> with on the footing, proved to be false, that the defendant was in occupation of the
> land in question. The matter could not be dealt with on the basis wished by the
> Crown.'

g
In the instant case the appellant/defendant has no practical reason for objecting to the
order against which he appeals. There is on the judge's finding quoted above no reason
for thinking that he will ever have to pay anything back to the plaintiffs. The appeal is
brought in order to obtain the decision of the court on a purely hypothetical question of
detriment in its relevance to the law of estoppel. The hypothetical question is of general
h importance, and is said to be of importance in other cases in which the local authority
and the defendant's union are concerned. I have found the resolution of the hypothetical
question difficult; it is not easy to determine whether and when the court will restrict
the effect of an estoppel if to apply it with the full rigour will clearly produce injustice.
Viscount Cave LC in *R E Jones Ltd v Waring & Gillow Ltd* [1926] AC 670 at 685, [1926]
All ER Rep 36 at 42 evidently thought that the court should find a way of preventing a
j party so using estoppel as to make a profit, and Lord Denning MR thought that estoppel
was a flexible doctrine: see *Amalgamated Investment and Property Co Ltd (in liq) v Texas
Commerce International Bank Ltd* [1981] 3 All ER 577 at 584, [1982] QB 84 at 122. These
cases afford strong reasons for refusing to give a judgment founded on estoppel on facts
which exist only in the mind of the pleader. The law does not and should not develop by
such a device, and the ratio of such a decision is liable to be seriously misleading. I do not

consider that the decision of this court in the instant appeal is authority for the proposition that, where on the facts it would be clearly inequitable to allow a party to make a profit *a* by pleading estoppel, the court will necessarily be powerless to prevent it.

In argument before us on this hypothetical question, it was contended on behalf of the defendant that where the defendant successfully proved that he had acted to his detriment on a representation by the plaintiff which was inconsistent with the true facts, and that his detriment was proved to be substantial in the sense that it was not de minimis, he was entitled to keep all the money paid through the mistake which the plaintiff was *b* estopped from alleging, even though the result was to leave him with a windfall profit. Alternatively it was contended that if he was liable to repay any sum on the ground that it was inequitable for him to retain it (a) the onus lay on the plaintiff to prove the facts that made such retention inequitable and (b) on the pleadings the plaintiffs had alleged no such facts or resulting inequity.

Having regard to the facts actually found by the judge, the whole of this argument *c* was fanciful. The money had never been paid as a single sum to the defendant. £1,007 represented the total arrived at by adding together a large number of small sums received over a period of many months and paid as the remuneration on which he relied for discharge of his ordinary living expenses. By the date of trial nothing was left, and the judge found that it would be inequitable to require the defendant to repay anything. It would, in my view, be quite wrong in those circumstances for the court to indulge in *d* speculation about where the onus might lie having regard to pleadings that were accepted by both parties to be a fiction. In other cases it may be a nice question whether on the pleaded facts the plaintiffs have established prima facie that it would be inequitable to retain some of the money had and received by a mistake which the plaintiffs are estopped from denying. If the defendant by his defence has raised estoppel, the plaintiff may by reply contend that it is inequitable to allow the defendant to retain part or all of the *e* benefit of the mistake; the defendant may plead by rebuttal facts repelling the charge that retention is inequitable. At trial the evidential burden may shift. But none of this arises in this case because the facts found by the judge demonstrate that the case raised in certain of the grounds of appeal is a fiction.

My conclusion is that, once the judge had held that it would be inequitable to require the defendant to repay any part of the moneys overpaid, he should have refused to decide *f* the case on a basis which was neither pleaded nor supported by evidence. If the plaintiffs wished to argue that it was inequitable that the defendant should retain some part of the £1,007, they should have pleaded the facts relied on in support of that plea. It was submitted by counsel for the plaintiffs that only the defendant could know what had happened to the money, so to require the plaintiffs to plead facts giving rise to an equity in their favour is to place on them a burden impossible to discharge. I disagree. The *g* solution of their procedural problem may in the appropriate case lie in an application for discovery of documents and answers to interrogatories. But before the judge there was no reply by the plaintiffs alleging that it was inequitable for the defendant to retain any part of the money, and the evidence which the judge admitted proved that it was not inequitable. So on the case as pleaded, and on the evidence before him, there was no material on which he could hold that the defendant was liable to pay back any part of the *h* money paid to him by the proved mistake of fact.

For these reasons I would allow the appeal.

I have had the advantage of reading the judgment that Slade LJ is about to deliver. I agree with it, though I go further than he does in my view that there is a fundamental objection to the approach of the judge in that he yielded to the persuasions of the parties, or perhaps more realistically to the persuasions of the union supporting the defendant *j* and of the council to try a question which had become hypothetical once more of the facts had emerged in evidence before him. I have however myself been enticed into expressing my views obiter on the necessity for a pleading by way of reply in any case in which the plaintiff, faced by a defence raising estoppel, seeks to raise a plea that it is inequitable for the defendant to retain a windfall. It might have been wiser to restrict a myself to the issues which actually arose on the facts found by the judge. But whether on any given state of facts the law recognises any such equity as that propounded by the plaintiffs must await a case in which it is necessary to decide the question.

EVELEIGH LJ. The plaintiffs overpaid the defendant because of a mistake. For the reasons set out in the judgment of Slade LJ, with which I respectfully agree, the mistake was one of fact. The terms of the defendant's contract of employment and the manner in

b which the plaintiffs controlled the assessment of the defendant's pay show that they were under a duty to him to determine his entitlement and not to misrepresent it. They represented to him that his entitlement was those sums which they paid to him from time to time. Those sums in truth over a period from January 1974 to October 1976 amounted to an overpayment of £1,007. It is admitted that in respect of that overpayment the plaintiffs are to be taken as having represented to the defendant that he was entitled

c to treat the whole of the money as his own. The defendant positively relied on this representation. The overpayment was spread over the period. The amount depending as it did on the complicated regulations relating to sick pay was not easy to determine. The defendant spent it in ordinary living expenses and in the purchase of a suit for £53·50 and for the hire purchase of a motor car involving the total outlay of £486 less £65 received in part exchange for his own car. He did not claim £86·11 social security benefit

d to which he would have been entitled had his income been less. He and his wife were careful people. They spent reasonably according to their position and the income which they were receiving. As the judge found, they put aside each week in different envelopes sufficient money to be able to meet the current household bills when they were received and they used the balance to meet their day-to-day expenses. They might, as he found, occasionally be able to put some aside for a rainy day but in general the more they had

e left in their pockets the more they were able to spend and they found it possible for the defendant to buy his new suit and to exchange his old car for another secondhand one. Had it been known that the defendant's true wage entitlement was less than that which he was receiving they would have governed their expenditure accordingly. They were a careful couple and no one has suggested the contrary.

On those facts, as the judge indicated, the plaintiffs' claim would fail completely.

f However, in para 12 of his defence the defendant pleaded only limited expenditure in relying on the plaintiffs' representation; he made no claim for additional social security benefits and he incurred expenditure which he would not have incurred had his income been as the plaintiffs now asserted, namely (1) the purchase of clothes and (2) the hire purchase of a motor car. Paragraph 13 read: 'In the premises the Plaintiffs are estopped by their said representations from pursuing any part of their claim herein.' Earlier in the

g defence, namely para 10 thereof, it was pleaded that the defendant had telephoned the education department because he and his wife were anxious about their financial situation with mounting medicine bills, travelling to and from hospital, the increased cost of living and an ageing motor car becoming difficult for the defendant to drive because of his injuries and queried his salary cheque only to be assured that it was in order. It might be thought that the pleadings as a whole did indicate that the defendant

h was spending all that he was receiving but there is no doubt that only the three items amounting to £546·61 were specifically pleaded as having been the subject of expenditure incurred in reliance on the plaintiffs' representations. Quite clearly the judge was asked to determine the case on the basis that those three items were the only ones being put forward as additional expenditure so incurred. The defendant's counsel declined an invitation to amend his pleadings to put the defence on a broader basis.

j The judge was therefore asked to decide the case on the basis that there had been an overpayment of £1,007 caused by a mistake of fact and that the defendant, relying on a representation that he was entitled to the £1,007, spent £546·61 of it. The problem as thus posed contained no information whether or not it would be unconscionable for the defendant to retain the balance of the sum. It contained no information on which the court could determine whether or not it would be unfair to make him repay. Having, in

effect, been asked to ignore his finding of fact which was so favourable to the defendant I
can readily understand the judge coming to the conclusion which he did. However, not *a*
without some hesitation, I have reached the same conclusion as Slade LJ, namely that,
once the defendant had shown detriment which prevented the plaintiffs from asserting
the truth behind the payment, that obstacle barred the whole of their claim, for, pleaded
simply as a case of mistake, evidence of the defendant's true entitlement was essential if
the plaintiffs were to succeed. I think that this must follow from the speech of Lord
Watson in *Ogilvie v West Australian Mortgage and Agency Corp Ltd* [1896] AC 257 and *b*
Fung Kai Sun v Chan Fui Hing [1951] AC 489, in which the former case was considered.
Strictly speaking the words of Lord Watson were obiter, but as Slade LJ has pointed out,
the decision of the Court of Appeal in *Greenwood v Martins Bank Ltd* [1932] 1 KB 371 was
to the same effect. In that case Scrutton LJ said (at 383–384):

> 'If the claim of the Bank were for damages for failure to disclose, it might be that
> the improbabilities of recovering anything in the action might be taken into *c*
> account; but the authorities show that in a question of estoppel, where the question
> is whether the customer is estopped from alleging that certain bills are forgeries, if
> the bank has lost something, the value of that something is not the measure of its
> claim, but, the customer being estopped from proving the bills forgeries, the bank
> gains by the amount of the bills.'

d

I would not for myself regard *Skyring v Greenwood* (1825) 4 B & C 281, [1824–34] All
ER Rep 104 and *Holt v Markham* [1923] 1 KB 504, [1922] All ER Rep 134 as determining
the same question. Those cases may be explained on the basis that the defendant's manner
of living generally had been influenced by the payments made to them so that although
they had not been able to point to specific items of expenditure amounting to the whole
sum in question the money had none the less been spent. Alternatively such cases may *e*
be said to rest on the basis that to compel the defendant to make any repayment would
be to impose on him an overall financial strain brought about only by his being misled
as to his financial position by the representations of the plaintiffs.

However, I am far from saying that, whenever the recipient of money paid under a
mistake has been led to think that it is his, then he will be entitled to retain the whole by
demonstrating that he has spent part of it. The payment may involve no representation, *f*
as where a debtor presents an account to a creditor. Then while there might have been a
representation there may be circumstances which would render it unconscionable for
the defendant to retain a balance in his hands. There may also be circumstances which
would make·it unfair to allow the plaintiff to recover. It may be that it is important to
determine whether or not the plaintiff making the representation owes a duty to the
defendant as was the case in *Ogilvie v West Australian Mortgage and Agency Corp Ltd*. I too *g*
am unhappy in being asked to decide a case in an unreal situation and I am content to say
that the question we have been asked to determine is that already decided in *Greenwood v
Martins Bank Ltd* by Scrutton LJ.

SLADE LJ. Where an employer has a large payroll, there must always exist the risk
that, due to error or inadvertence, an employee may be paid either greater or lesser sums *h*
than those to which he is strictly entitled under his contract of service. There are many
potential sources of such error and the advent of computerisation has introduced yet
another one. The present is such a case. Mr Harold Ellis Howlett, the defendant in the
action, has been overpaid in a sum of £1,007 by his former employers, the County
Council of Avon, who are the plaintiffs in the action. Sheldon J, in a judgment of 20 July
1981 gave judgment for the plaintiffs in the sum of £460·39 subject to an undertaking *j*
by the plaintiffs not to enforce the judgment without the leave of the court and dismissed
a counterclaim by the defendant. The defendant now appeals from this judgment,
seeking an order that the plaintiffs' claim be wholly dismissed.

The case raises difficult and important questions of law concerning the principles
governing the recovery of money paid under a mistake and the relevance of the doctrine
of estoppel in this context. The essential facts of the cases are quite simple.

The facts

a   Before 1 April 1974 the defendant had been employed by the Bristol City Council as a
teacher in charge of sports and physical education at the New Fosseway School, Bristol.
On 1 April 1974, as a result of local government reorganisation which came into effect
on that date, the plaintiff council succeeded to the rights and liabilities of the Bristol City
Council in the field of education. Thus, on that date the defendant entered the
employment of the plaintiffs.

b   The defendant, however, was not then able to undertake any duties for the plaintiffs,
because he had unfortunately been injured in an accident in one of the class-rooms,
which had occurred on 8 January 1974. In the event, he returned to work only for about
six weeks between 5 April and 18 May 1976. Ill-health then once again prevented him
from working until he reached the retirement age of 65 on 6 October 1976. A claim by
him against the plaintiffs for damages for injury and loss arising from the accident was
c   pursued to trial and dismissed.

It is common ground that, following his accident on 8 January 1974 and consequent
absence from work, the defendant, under his conditions of service, was entitled to be
paid at full rates of pay for the first six months, at half rates for the next six months and
to no pay thereafter, so long as he was not working.

In fact the plaintiffs continued to pay him at full rates for several months beyond the
d   expiration of the first six months' period, that is to say until September 1974. They then
continued to pay him at half rates long beyond the expiration of the second six months'
period, that is to say until August 1975. There is in evidence an agreed schedule which
shows the net amounts which the defendant actually received from the plaintiffs or their
predecessors for each of the months January 1974 to August 1975 inclusive. This schedule
shows the component parts of each net payment, that is to say 'basic pay', an addition for
e   'threshold' and deductions for 'sick benefit', 'superannuation', 'tax', 'national insurance'
and 'graduated pension'. The net amounts thus received by the defendant over the period
January 1974 until August 1975 totalled £1,900·66.

Some time after August 1975 the plaintiffs discovered that, up to and including
January 1975, the defendant had been regularly overpaid and that after January 1975 he
had been paid for seven months when he should not have been paid anything at all.
f   There is an agreed schedule which shows the net amounts which he should have received
for each of the months January 1974 to January 1975, inclusive, if the payments had
been correctly calculated. It contains a breakdown of the figures similar to that in the
other schedule I have referred to and indicates that the aggregate of the net amounts
which were in fact due to be paid to the defendant over the period January 1974 to
January 1975 inclusive was only £950·65, resulting in an overpayment of £950·01. It is
g   also common ground that he was overpaid by an additional small sum of £56·99. These
two sums of £950·01 and £56·99 produced the sum of £1,007 on which the present
claim is based.

On 23 December 1976 the plaintiffs issued a writ against the defendant indorsed with
a very short statement of claim, which claimed repayment of the sum of £1,007, thereby
alleged to represent 'an overpayment of salary and sickness benefit paid to the defendant
h   by mistake'. The pleading gave no further indication at all as to the nature of the mistake
alleged.

On 19 April 1978 an order was made in Bristol District Registry that the plaintiffs
should serve on the defendant, inter alia, the following further and better particulars of
the statement of claim:

j   '(1) Specify the mistake alleged to have occasioned the payment, indicating upon
what basis the plaintiffs took the view that the Defendant was entitled to the
payments they made to him . . .'

Further and better particulars under this head were served by the plaintiffs on 18 May
1978 pursuant to this order. They read as follows:

'The mistake made was in assuming that the Defendant was entitled to the sums
which were paid to him whereas his total entitlement was a lesser sum by the

amount claimed in this action. It was a mistaken view. The mistaken basis upon which the mistaken view was formed is irrelevant to these proceedings.'

On 5 March 1980 the defendant's solicitors, apparently unaware or forgetful of the particulars that had already been delivered, served a similar request on the plaintiffs' solicitors. The plaintiffs' solicitors on 16 June 1980 replied stating that the request had been answered by particulars served on 18 May 1978. The defendant's legal advisers thereafter apparently pursued this request no further, so that, by the time the action came to trial, the only particulars of the allegations of mistake were those rather unenlightening particulars which had been served on 18 May 1978.

Meantime the defendant had served a defence and counterclaim. This pleading was in due course amended and reamended. The counterclaim is not relevant on this appeal. I need only refer to a few of the contents of the defence. Paragraph 15 pleaded that, if, which was denied, any of the payments were made by a mistake, such mistake was a mistake of law and the plaintiffs were for that reason not entitled to recover any of them. The defence, however, also asserted, as a quite separate plea, that the plaintiffs are in any event estopped from pursuing any part of their claim by reason of various representations made by them to the defendant. The representations relied on are to be found set out in detail in paras 9, 10 and 10B of the defence. In para 11 it is asserted that by the documents, conversation and conduct referred to in paras 9, 10 and 10A the plaintiffs and/or their predecessors represented to the defendant that he was entitled to each of the relevant sums paid to him. Paragraph 12 of the defence reads as follows:

> 'The Defendant relying as he was entitled and instructed by the Plaintiffs and their said predecessors to do, upon the said representations: (a) Made no claim to and was not paid additional social security benefits by way of increase of Industrial Disablement Benefit because of special hardship or to Supplementary Benefit and/or rent rebate and/or rates rebate to which he would or might have been entitled had his income during the said period been as the Plaintiffs now seek to assert it should have been and which in the case of the said benefits, he cannot now claim or obtain or which, in case of the said rebates (and alternatively to the above, in the case of the said benefits), he will only be able to obtain at cost and expense to himself and after considerable delay. (b) Incurred expenditure which he would not have incurred had his income been as the Plaintiffs now assert it should have been namely: (i) purchase of clothes to the amount of £53·50 from Montague Burton Ltd. on the 21st June 1975 (instalment payment for which was completed in February 1976). (ii) hire purchase through United Dominion Trust of a motor car from Wrington Service Station. Bishopsworth Road, Bristol in August 1975. Its cash price was £395. The Defendant paid £130 in cash and was allowed £65 credit against his old car the balance of £200 plus £91 interest being payable at £12 per month.'

Paragraph 13 alleged that 'in the premises the plaintiffs are estopped by their said representations from pursuing any part of their claim herein'.

Further and better particulars were in due course delivered of the loss alleged in para 12(a) of the defence, which limited it to £86·11. The expenditure referred to in para 12(b) of the defence was quantified at the trial in an agreed sum of £460·50. It followed that the defence as pleaded did not allege specific detriment to have been suffered by the defendant in reliance on the representations beyond a sum of £546·61.

However, at an early stage of the trial it became clear that, notwithstanding the form of para 12 of the defence, all the money so overpaid had long since been spent by him and indeed that the defendant neither had, nor was likely to obtain, sufficient funds with which to meet any judgment that might be given against him. The judge therefore inquired of the parties whether there was any purpose in incurring further costs in this connection. He was told that the local government reorganisation in question had resulted in a number of similar overpayments having been made to other individuals and that accordingly both the plaintiff council and the union which supported the

defendant (the Confederation of Health Service Employees) wished to use this as a test
a case, so far as possible to establish the various rights and liabilities. He was also told that
the plaintiff council, if they succeeded in their claim, were prepared to undertake not to
seek to enforce any such judgment against the defendant without the leave of the court.
He therefore proceeded to hear the case to its conclusion.

It appears that the contentious issues of fact at the trial fell within a narrow compass.
It was not disputed by or on behalf of the defendant that overpayments totalling £1,007
b had been made to him. Counsel for the plaintiffs conceded that representations of fact
had been made by or on behalf of the plaintiffs to the defendant which had led him to
believe that he was entitled to treat all the relevant payments as his own, and that these
representations were capable of giving rise to an estoppel if the other conditions necessary
for the application of the doctrine were satisfied. It was not asserted that the defendant
had received any of the relevant sums in the knowledge that he was not entitled to them.
c In these circumstances it appears that the contentious issues of fact principally concerned
the circumstances in which the overpayments had come to be made in the first place.

The judgment of Sheldon J

The plaintiff council called as their only witness on this aspect of the case, Mr D J
Hewlett, a group leader in the staffing and pay division of that part of their organisation
d which deals with the payment of teachers. He had been employed in a similar capacity
by the Bristol council before the takeover on 1 April 1974.

The judge at an early stage in his judgment referred to an argument advanced by
counsel for the defendant to the effect that the mistakes leading to the relevant
overpayments were mistakes not of fact but of law, or at least that, as the plaintiff council
could not identify the clerk who made the error or errors, or who fed the information
into the computer, they could not establish that the mistake was one of fact rather than
e one of law derived from some misinterpretation of the relevant regulations and salary
scales. Sheldon J, however, clearly felt no difficulty in rejecting this particular argument,
in just six lines of his judgment as follows:

> 'In all the circumstances however, and having heard the evidence of Mr D J
> Hewlett, head of the county council's staffing and payroll division, I have no doubt
f > whatever that the overpayments were an oversight and due entirely to a mistake or
> mistakes of fact on the part of the council staff.'

The judge obviously found the question of estoppel a more difficult one. Having
observed that there had been a representation of fact sufficient to give rise to an estoppel,
he stated the principle which guided him:

g > 'In such a case, in my opinion, the payer will be estopped from claiming
> restitution if and to the extent that the payee, bona fide, in reliance on the
> representation and without notice of the plaintiff's claim, has so changed his position
> that it would be inequitable to require him to repay the money, provided that the
> payment or overpayment in question was not due substantially to the payee's own
> fault: *Larner v London CC* [1949] 1 All ER 964, [1949] 2 KB 683. With that proviso
h > too, however, this case is not concerned.'

In the course of a further investigation of the authorities Sheldon J again referred to
the consideration 'whether and to what extent it would be inequitable for him [the
recipient] to be compelled to repay the money or any part of it'. He said that he was
satisfied that, on the real facts of the case, the defendant did bona fide, in reliance on the
j plaintiffs' representations that he was entitled to treat the money as his own, and without
notice of their claim, spend the whole of the sums overpaid in ordinary living expenses
or otherwise for his own purposes, and that it *would* be inequitable to require him to
repay them. He said that, on these facts as found by him, and if those had been the issues
raised by the pleadings, he would have had no hesitation in dismissing the plaintiffs'
claim in toto and giving judgment for the defendant. However he went on to say:

'The issues raised by the pleadings, however, in my opinion, are not so wide. For whatever reason, moreover, whether to preserve its value as a test case or for any other reason, [counsel] instructed by the union on [the defendant's] behalf made it clear that he did not intend to apply to reamend the defence and counterclaim. [Counsel], too on behalf of the council, was anxious that the case should be decided strictly on the pleadings as they stand. In all the circumstances, moreover, and having regard to their undertaking, I am satisfied that there is no risk of [the defendant] being prejudiced by such a course.'

He pointed out that the form of the defence limited the detriment alleged to have been suffered by the defendant in reliance on the representations to the loss of a claim for £86·11 social security benefit and expenditure of some £460·50. He observed that there was no allegation that the balance of some £460·39 had been spent in reliance on the plaintiffs' representations and that the mere fact that the money had been spent beyond recall was no defence to the claim. He rejected a submission that the doctrine of estoppel would have prevented the plaintiffs from recovering any part of the £1,007 even if the balance of £460·39 had still been sitting untouched in some deposit account. In his opinion—

'the payer will be estopped from claiming restitution only if and to the extent that the payee, if he has satisfied the other requirements in this connection, has so changed his position that it would be inequitable to require him to repay the sum of money in question.'

Strictly on the case as pleaded in the statement of claim, the judge concluded that the plaintiffs, though estopped from reclaiming the £546·61 lost or expended by the defendant in reliance on their representations, were nevertheless entitled to claim repayment of the outstanding balance of £460·39, because it would not be inequitable to require him to repay it.

The plaintiffs have not sought to challenge the judge's conclusion that the £546·61 is irrecoverable. As to this point there is no appeal. The issue on this appeal by the defendant solely concerns the £460·39.

It may be that there were good reasons (for example, relating to costs) why the defendant's counsel did not avail himself of the opportunity to apply to reamend his defence so as to plead all the true material facts. From the point of view of the court, the present situation is not wholly satisfactory, since the case is perilously near to being one of a hypothetical nature. Nevertheless, at the request of both parties, who regard it as a test case, this court has been willing to deal with it on the same basis as the trial judge, that is to say on the footing that both sides must be confined to the limits of the facts as both pleaded and proved in evidence.

Mistake

I now turn to consider whether the excessive payments totalling £1,007 made by the plaintiffs to the defendant were made under a mistake and if so what was the nature of that mistake. It is common ground that the onus of proving that there was a mistake lies on the plaintiffs: see, for example *Holt v Markham* [1923] 1 KB 504 at 511, [1922] All ER Rep 134 at 140 per Warrington LJ. Furthermore it is common ground that the mistake in question must be one which can be properly categorised as being a mistake of fact rather than a mistake of law, since payments made under what is properly categorised as a mistake of law are not generally recoverable.

Parke B authoritatively stated the principles governing the recovery of money paid under a mistake of fact in *Kelly v Solari* (1841) 9 M & W 54 at 58–59, [1835–42] All ER Rep 320 at 322 as follows:

'I think that where money is paid to another under the influence of a mistake, that is, upon the supposition that a specific fact is true, which would entitle the other to the money, but which fact is untrue, and the money would not have been paid if it had been known to the payer that the fact was untrue an action will lie to recover it back, and it is against conscience to retain it; though a demand may be necessary in those cases in which the party receiving may have been ignorant of the mistake ... If indeed, the money is intentionally paid, without reference to the truth or falsehood of the fact, the plaintiff meaning to waive all inquiry into it, and that the person receiving shall have the money at all events, whether the fact be true or false, the latter is certainly entitled to retain it; but if it is paid under the impression of the truth of a fact which is untrue, it may, generally speaking, be recovered back, however careless the party paying may have been, in omitting to use due diligence to inquire into the fact. In such a case the receiver was not entitled to it, nor intended to have it.'

This statement of the relevant principles were cited with approval by Lord Shaw and Lord Carson in *R E Jones Ltd v Waring & Gillow Ltd* [1926] AC 670 at 688, 698, [1926] All ER 36 at 42, 48. Its correctness has not been challenged in the present case. In this instance the evidence of Mr Hewlett in my opinion clearly establishes on the balance of probabilities that the extra moneys were paid to the defendant under a mistake of some kind on the part of the plaintiffs or their servants or agents. This is not a case where, to quote the words of Parke B—

'the money is intentionally paid, without reference to the truth or falsehood of the fact, the plaintiff meaning to waive all inquiry into it, and that the person receiving shall have the money at all events, whether the fact be true or false ...'

And counsel for the defendant, as I understood his argument, did not seek so to contend.

On this aspect of the case, his argument has been substantially founded on the propositions (i) that the plaintiffs have not proved by their evidence that the relevant mistakes were mistakes of fact rather than of law and (ii) that, if these were mistakes of law, the plaintiffs would not be entitled to recover the money.

The only evidence called at the trial on behalf of the plaintiffs to explain and identify the relevant mistakes was that of Mr Hewlett. Through no fault of his own, his evidence was somewhat sparse. He explained in chief that problems in converting the data taken from the computer records of the Bristol council gave rise to mistakes affecting a number of employees. Save in one respect relating to the defendant, he did not particularise as to the nature of these mistakes, and indeed, with this one exception, he was not invited by counsel on either side to do so. His examination, cross-examination and re-examination were all conducted on the footing that only one mistake occurred in relation to the defendant, such mistake being that the pay clerk concerned did not instruct the computer at the plaintiffs' office to reduce the defendant's pay to half pay until too late, with the result that for a period of time he was paid at the full rate when he should have been paid at only half rate. Counsel for the defendant in cross-examination understandably sought to extract an admission from Mr Hewlett which might tend to show that the relevant mistake had been one of law. In the course of his cross-examination, in answer to the question: 'A pay clerk incorrectly interpreted his conditions?' Mr Hewlett replied: 'Obviously. Yes, sir.' I take the reference to 'conditions' in this context as being a reference to the defendant's conditions of service. However, later in cross-examination, Mr Hewlett made it clear that he could not say from his own knowledge how the mistake occurred, because, after a large turnover of staff in the plaintiffs' office, he was not in a position to identify the pay clerk who had failed to give the computer the correct instructions. Furthermore in re-examination he made it clear that he did not regard the defendant's conditions of service as containing any relevant ambiguity. He was asked: 'Is there any room for a different interpretation?' He replied:

'There could have been only one interpretation in my view, but if that interpretation is not actioned correctly it does not alter the interpretation. There is only one set of conditions which can apply. The employer has laid down an entitlement to so many months full pay and so many months half pay.'

The first of the grounds of appeal set out in the defendant's notice of appeal asserts that
the judge misdirected himself in law and in fact in holding that the sums claimed by the *a*
plaintiffs were paid by them to the defendant under a mistake of fact when—

'the evidence before him showed that the Plaintiffs were unable to identify the
person who made the mistake or to establish what specific fact, if any, thought to be
true but in fact untrue which was the basis of the payment of any of the said sums
or to exclude on the balance of probabilities the possibility that the payments were *b*
made under a mistake of law or by mere misadvertance and the tenor of the
evidence of their witness Mr D J Hewlett ... was that upon the Plaintiffs taking
over from the 1st April 1974 certain functions of the City and County of Bristol ...
errors had been made as a result of misinterpretation of that other authority's records
and/or of the Defendant's conditions of employment, but he could give no evidence
as to how or why this had occurred in the Plaintiffs' case.'

c

Estoppel apart, these were substantially the grounds argued by counsel for the
defendant before this court. I think there is some force in them. I also think there is
some force in his submission that the further and better particulars of the statement of
claim, which I have already quoted, were not an adequate plea of a mistake of fact,
because the pleaded assumption that 'the Defendant was entitled to the sums which were
paid to him' *could* have been based on a mistaken view of the law. However, so far as I *d*
am aware, no objection was taken to the sufficiency of the pleading, as a plea of a mistake
of fact, either before or at the trial, and I do not think it would be right to decide this
appeal on this pleading point.

On the substantial issues, I have come to the conclusion that there was sufficient
evidence before the judge to support the inference that, on the balance of probabilities,
the mistakes which led to the relevant overpayments were mistakes of fact and not *e*
mistakes of law. Though there is no precise evidence to this effect, I think it a reasonable
inference from the evidence as a whole that any pay clerk employed by the plaintiffs
would have been likely to know the simple fact that an employee of the plaintiff council,
such as the defendant, while absent from work following an accident, was under his
conditions of service entitled to be paid at full rates of pay for the first six months of his
absence, at half rates for the next six months of absence and to no pay thereafter. *f*
Accordingly, on the evidence, I think it a fair inference on the balance of probabilities
that the reason why the plaintiffs continued to pay the defendant at full rates after the
end of the first six months of his absence from work was that the pay clerks concerned
were unaware or had forgotten that more than six months had elapsed since the
defendant's accident and for this reason failed to give the appropriate instructions to the
computer, which would have led to the appropriate reduction in the defendant's pay at *g*
the appropriate time. This was in my view plainly a mistake of fact rather than one of
law.

Other errors clearly occurred, which were not explored by either side in evidence at
the trial. In particular the defendant continued to be paid half pay for seven months after
January 1975 when he should have been paid nothing at all. A comparison of the two
schedules referred to earlier in the judgment reveals a number of further discrepancies *h*
(for example, relating to deductions for sick benefit) between the amounts which he
actually received and those which he should have received. Counsel for the defendant
urged that they might have been caused by a misinterpretation of documents, such as
the relevant regulations setting out the entitlement of the plaintiffs' employees while
absent from work. He submitted that such misinterpretation would have constituted a
mistake of law: see, for example, *Holt v Markham* [1923] 1 KB 504, [1922] All ER Rep *j*
134 and *Ministry of Health v Simpson* [1950] 2 All ER 1137 at 1142–1145, [1951] AC 251
at 269–273. However, nothing appearing from the evidence or submitted in argument
leads me to think there is any real likelihood that these errors were caused by mistakes of
law rather than of fact. On the evidence, I think it a fair inference that the reason why
the plaintiffs continued to pay the defendant after the end of the first 12 months of his

a absence from work was that the pay clerks concerned were unaware or had forgotten that this 12-month period had expired. The other errors in my opinion are similarly likely to have occurred simply through incorrect factual data having been fed into the plaintiffs' computers. Thus in my opinion, albeit by a fairly narrow margin, the plaintiffs have discharged the onus which falls on them of showing that the overpayments were made under mistakes of fact.

b However, since this is a test case, I would like to add the following observations before leaving this aspect of it. Though in the present instance the incorrect final figures were produced by computers, it has not been suggested that the fault was that of the computers themselves. It was human error that gave rise to the mistakes, by feeding the computers with the wrong data. In the present instance it has not been possible for the plaintiffs to identify the individual person or persons who were responsible for the errors. However, in other similar cases the court might well expect the responsible individuals to be *c* identified and called as witnesses. Employers who pay their employees under a computerised system should not in my opinion assume from the decision of this court in the present case that, if they overpay their employees through some kind of mistake, they are entitled to recover it simply for the asking, provided only that they are not barred by estoppel or some other special defence. The borderline between mistakes of law and mistakes of fact is not clearly defined in the cases. Decisions such as *Cooper v* *d* *Phibbs* (1867) LR 2 HL 149 and *Allcard v Walker* [1896] 2 Ch 369 suggest that the courts are not quick to extend the former category. The distinction has been the subject of some criticism. The learned authors of Goff and Jones's *Law of Restitution* (2nd edn, 1978) p 91 express the view that the principle in *Bilbie v Lumley* (1802) 2 East 469, [1775–1802] All ER Rep 425 should only preclude recovery of money which was paid in settlement of an honest claim and that any other payment made under a mistake of law should be *e* recoverable, if it would have been recoverable had the mistake been one of fact. Nevertheless the distinction still exists in English law. I think the burden will still fall on an employer who seeks to recover an overpayment from an overpaid employee to satisfy the court that, on the balance of probabilities in all the circumstances of the case, it was a mistake of fact which gave rise to the overpayment. The plaintiffs in the present instance in my opinion succeed in relation to this issue only because they have discharged this *f* burden on the particular facts of the case.

Estoppel

I now turn to the defence of estoppel. The following general propositions of law are to be found set out in Goff and Jones's *Law of Restitution* (2nd edn, 1978) pp 554–555 (though *g* I do not quote them verbatim). A plaintiff will be estopped from asserting his claim to restitution if the following conditions are satisfied: (a) the plaintiff must generally have made a representation of fact which led the defendant to believe that he was entitled to treat the money as his own; (b) the defendant must have, bona fide and without notice of the plaintiff's claim, consequently changed his position; (c) the payment must not have been primarily caused by the fault of the defendant.

h In my opinion these propositions are entirely consistent both with the general principles which govern the doctrine of estoppel and with the authorities which have been cited to this court, illustrating the relevance of estoppel as a defence to claims to restitution. Examples of the more important of such authorities are *Skyring v Greenwood* (1825) 4 B & C 281, [1824–34] All ER Rep 104, *Holt v Markham* [1923] 1 KB 504, [1922] All ER Rep 134 and *Lloyds Bank Ltd v Brooks* (1950) 6 Legal Decisions Affecting Bankers *j* 161.

In the present case it is common ground that the plaintiffs made representations to the defendant which led him to believe that he was entitled to treat the entirety of the overpaid moneys as his own. This was conceded by the plaintiffs' at the trial, so that the judge did not find it necessary in his judgment to give any particulars at all of the relevant representations. Certain authorities suggest that a plea of estoppel can afford a good

defence to a claim for restitution only if the plaintiff owed a duty to the defendant to
speak or act in a particular way: see, for example, *R E Jones v Waring & Gillow Ltd* [1926]　**a**
AC 670 at 693, [1926] All ER Rep 36 at 46 per Lord Sumner and *Lloyds Bank Ltd v Brooks*
(at 168 ff). However, this point causes no difficulty for the defendant in the present case
since the plaintiffs, as the defendant's employers, in my opinion clearly owed him a duty
not to misrepresent the amount of the pay to which he was entitled from time to time,
unless the misrepresentations were caused by incorrect information given to them by
the defendant. It has not been suggested that the misrepresentations were so caused or　**b**
that the overpayments were brought about by the defendant's own fault.

The judge found as a fact that the defendant had, bona fide and without notice of the
plaintiffs' claim, changed his position in reliance on the representations, by losing the
claim for £86·11 social security benefit and expending the sum of £460·50 which I have
already mentioned. In the circumstances and in accordance with the principles already
stated, he was in my opinion clearly right to hold that the plaintiffs' claim was barred by　**c**
estoppel to the extent of at least £546·61 and there is no challenge to this part of his
decision. However, according to the defendant's case as specifically pleaded, the change
of position which he has undergone in reliance on the plaintiffs' representations has only
deprived him of the opportunity to return £546·61 of the overpayment; it has not
deprived him of the opportunity to return the outstanding balance of £460·39 which, so
far as the pleading reveals, may be still in his possession.　**d**

The judge considered that the defence of estoppel was in effect capable of being applied
pro tanto, in the sense that a payer who has overpaid a payee, even in circumstances
where all of conditions (a), (b) and (c) above are satisfied, will be precluded from claiming
restitution only to the extent that it would be inequitable to require the payee to repay
the relevant sums or part of the relevant sums in question. The judge clearly regarded
the doctrine of estoppel as being a flexible doctrine, as indeed Lord Denning MR so　**e**
described it in *Amalgamated Investment and Property Co Ltd (in liq) v Texas Commerce
International Bank Ltd* [1981] 3 All ER 577 at 584, [1982] QB 84 at 122.

If I may respectfully say so, I feel some sympathy with the judge's point of view. I also
initially found unattractive the submission, placed before and rejected by him, that, if
the defendant be treated as having spent in reliance on the plaintiffs' representations
some £546·61 of the £1,007 received, the plaintiffs could not recover the balance of　**f**
£460·39, even if it were still sitting untouched in some deposit account. At first sight
such a conclusion would seem to leave the defendant unjustly enriched.

On further reflection, however, I think that references to broad concepts of justice or
equity in a context such as the present may be somewhat misleading, as well as uncertain
in their application. The conclusion of the judge in the present case really involves the
proposition that, if the defendant is successfully to resist a claim for repayment of the　**g**
entire sum of £1,007, the onus falls on him to prove specifically that the pecuniary
amount of the prejudice suffered by him as a result of relying on the relevant
representations made by the plaintiffs equals or exceeds that sum. For present purposes,
however, one has to postulate a situation in which the defendant was perfectly entitled
to conduct his business affairs on the assumption that the relevant representations were
true, until he was told otherwise. Meantime, a defendant in the situation of the defendant　**h**
in the present case may, in reliance on the representations, have either altered his general
mode of living or undertaken commitments or incurred expenditure or entered into
other transactions which it may be very difficult for him subsequently to recall and
identify retrospectively in complete detail; he may even have done so, while leaving
some of the particular moneys paid to him by the plaintiff untouched. If the pecuniary
amount of his prejudice has to be precisely quantified by a defendant in such　**j**
circumstances, he may be faced with obvious difficulties of proof. Thus, though extreme
hypothetical cases can be envisaged, and indeed were canvassed in argument, in which
broad considerations of equity and justice might appear to require the barring of a
plaintiff's claim only pro tanto, if this were legally possible, I would not expect many
such cases to arise in practice. In any event I do not consider the present case to be one of

them, even on the basis of the facts as pleaded. I prefer to approach it simply by what I
a regard as the established legal principles governing the doctrine of estoppel.

Estoppel by representation is a rule of evidence, the consequence of which is simply to
preclude the representor from averring facts contrary to his own representation: see
Spencer Bower and Turner on Estoppel by Representation (3rd edn, 1977) p 112. It follows
that a party who, as a result of being able to rely on an estoppel, succeeds on a cause of
action on which, without being able to rely on it, he would necessarily have failed may
b be able to recover more than the actual damage suffered by him as a result of the
representation which gave rise to it. Thus if a bank's customer is estopped from asserting
that a cheque with which he has been debited is a forgery, because of his failure to inform
the bank in due time, so that it could have had recourse to the forger, the debit will stand
for the whole amount and not merely that which could have been recovered from the
forger: see *Ogilvie v West Australian Mortgage and Agency Corp Ltd* [1896] AC 257 at 270.
c In this case Lord Watson said:

> 'There are some obiter dicta favouring the suggestion that, in a case like the
> present, where the amount of the forged cheques is about 1500l., the estoppel
> against the customer ought to be restricted to the actual sum which the bank could
> have recovered from the forger. But these dicta seem to refer, not to the law as it
> was, but as it ought to be; and, in any view of them, they are contrary to all authority
d and practice.'

The decision of the Court of Appeal in *Greenwood v Martins Bank Ltd* [1932] 1 KB 371;
affd [1933] AC 51, [1932] All ER Rep 318 is to the same effect.

So far as they go, the authorities suggest that, in cases where estoppel by representation
is available as a defence to a claim for money had and received, the courts similarly do
e not treat the operation of the estoppel as being restricted to the precise amount of the
detriment which the representee proves he has suffered in reliance on the representation.
In *Skyring v Greenwood* (1825) 4 B & C 281, [1824–34] All ER Rep 104 the paymasters of
a military corps had given credit in account to an officer for a period from January 1817
to November 1820 for certain increased pay. They had mistakenly supposed that this
had been granted by a general order of 1806 to an officer of his situation. But in fact the
f paymasters had been informed in 1816 that the Board of Ordnance would not allow the
increased payments to persons in the officer's situation. A statement of that account was
delivered to the officer early in 1821, giving him credit for the increased pay to which
they supposed him to be entitled. After the officer's death in 1822, his personal
representatives sought to recover the whole of the pay which had been credited to him.
The defendants claimed the right to retain the overpaid sums. The Court of King's Bench
g rejected this claim, apparently without any inquiry as to the amount of the expenditure
or financial commitments which the officer had incurred in reliance on the erroneous
credit. The basis of the court's decision is to be found in the following passage from the
judgment of Abbot CJ (4 B & C 281 at 289, [1824–34] All ER Rep 104 at 106–107):

> 'I think it was their duty to communicate to the deceased the information which
> they had received from the Board of Ordnance; but they forbore to do so, and they
h suffered him to suppose during all the intervening time that he was entitled to the
> increased allowances. It is of great importance to any man, and certainly not less to
> military men than others, that they should not be led to suppose that their annual
> income is greater than it really is. Every prudent man accommodates his mode of
> living to what he supposes to be his income; it therefore works a great prejudice to
> any man, if after having had credit given him in account for certain sums, and
j having been allowed to draw on his agent on the faith that those sums belonged to
> him, he may be called upon to pay them back.'

In *Holt v Markham* [1923] 1 KB 504, [1922] All ER Rep 134 the defendant was a
demobilised officer of the Royal Air Force. His name was on a list called the Emergency
List. This meant that, under a certain military regulation, he was entitled to a gratuity at

a lower rate than if he was not on that list. The plaintiffs acted as the government's agents
for the payment of gratuities to demobilised officers. In ignorance of the fact that the   *a*
defendant was on the Emergency List, but also in forgetfulness of the regulation, and not
appreciating the materiality of an officer being on that list, they paid the defendant his
gratuity at the higher rate to which he would have been entitled if he had not been on it.
Subsequently they sought to recover this sum. But by then the defendant, thinking this
matter was concluded, had sold his holding of War Savings Certificates and invested a
substantial sum in a company which subsequently went into liquidation (see [1923] 1   *b*
KB 504 at 507). The Court of Appeal held that the plaintiffs' action failed on two grounds,
first that the plaintiffs' mistake was one of law rather than of fact and second that, as their
conduct had led the defendant to believe that he might treat the money as his own and
he had altered his position in that belief, the plaintiffs were estopped from alleging that
the money had been paid under a mistake. Scrutton LJ put the matter very simply
([1923] 1 KB 504 at 514, [1922] All ER Rep 134 at 141–142):   *c*

> 'I think this is a simple case of estoppel. The plaintiffs represented to the defendant
> that he was entitled to a certain sum of money and paid it and after a lapse of time
> sufficient to enable any mistake to be rectified he acted upon that representation
> and spent the money.'

However, the facts as set out in the report of the case do not indicate that the defendant   *d*
had necessarily spent the whole of his gratuity and Bankes and Warrington LJJ were
careful not to suggest that they did. They clearly regarded it as immaterial whether or
not he had. Thus Bankes LJ said ([1923] 1 KB 504 at 511, [1922] All ER Rep 134 at 139):

> '. . . it appears that for a considerable time he was left under the impression that,
> although there had been at one time a doubt about his title to the money, that doubt
> had been removed, and in consequence he parted with his War Savings Certificates.   *e*
> Having done that it seems to me that he altered his position for the worse, and
> consequently the plaintiffs are estopped from alleging that the payment was made
> under a mistake of fact.'

Warrington LJ referred to the defendant as having spent 'the whole or a large part of
the gratuity which had been paid to him . . .' (see [1923] 1 KB 504 at 512, [1922] All ER   *f*
Rep 134 at 140).

If it were in every case possible for the doctrine of estoppel by representation to operate
merely pro tanto in cases where it is being involved as a defence to an action for money
had and received, I think that the Court of King's Bench in *Skyring v Greenwood* and the
Court of Appeal in *Holt v Markham*, and indeed Lynskey J in *Lloyds Bank Ltd v Brooks*,
would have been bound to conduct a much more exact process of quantification of the   *g*
alteration of the financial position of the recipients which had occurred by reason of the
representations. The courts, however, in those cases, manifestly regarded any such process
as irrelevant and inappropriate. All the relevant conditions for the operation of an
estoppel being satisfied in those cases, the plea operated as a rule of evidence which
precluded the payers from recovering any part of the money mistakenly overpaid or
from retaining any part of the moneys mistakenly overcredited.   *h*

I think that no authority has been cited, other than the judgment of the judge, which
directly supports the proposition that estoppel is capable of operating merely pro tanto
in a case such as the present, where it is otherwise capable of being invoked as a complete
defence to an action for money had and received. For the reasons which I have given, I
conclude that such a proposition is contrary to principle and authority. Goff and Jones in
The Law of Restitution (2nd edn, 1978) p 556 do not assert any such proposition, but they   *j*
do say this:

> 'The effect of such an estoppel will generally be to defeat the claim altogether.
> But where the defendant's change of position has deprived him of the opportunity
> to return only part of the money he has received, to dismiss the plaintiff's claim in

a its entirety would enable the defendant to make a profit out of the transaction. This should not be allowed. In such circumstances the court may only give effect to the estoppel, subject to the defendant's undertaking to repay to the plaintiff any part of the sum received which he ought not to be entitled to keep.'

b The suggestion of an undertaking stems from the speech of Viscount Cave LC in *R E Jones Ltd v Waring & Gillow Ltd* [1926] AC 670, [1926] All ER Rep 36. In that case the majority of the House of Lords held that the plaintiffs were entitled to recover certain moneys on the principle of *Kelly v Solari* (1841) 9 M & W 54, [1835–42] All ER Rep 320. Viscount Cave LC, who dissented and with whom Lord Atkinson agreed, considered that the plaintiffs were estopped from recovering the money. On the particular facts, however, the operation of an estoppel in this manner would have left the defendants with a profit. The defendants disclaimed any desire to make such a profit and offered an undertaking (in effect) to return it to the plaintiffs. Viscount Cave LC expressed the view that such *c* undertaking should be recited in the order to be made on the appeal, but said that, subject to the undertaking, he would dismiss it (see [1926] AC 670 at 685, [1926] All ER Rep 36 at 42).

d I recognise that in some circumstances the doctrine of estoppel could be said to give rise to injustice if it operated so as to defeat in its entirety an action which would otherwise lie for money had and received. This might be the case for example where the sums sought to be recovered were so large as to bear no relation to any detriment which the recipient could possibly have suffered. I would for my part prefer to leave open the question whether in such a case the court would have jurisdiction, in the exercise of its discretion, to exact an undertaking of the nature referred to by Viscount Cave LC, if it was not voluntarily proffered by the defendant.

e On the particular facts of the present case as pleaded and proved, however, I could in any event see no sufficient ground for exacting any such undertaking from the defendant in the exercise of the court's discretion, even assuming that such discretion existed. The conditions for the operation of an estoppel have in my opinion all been satisfied. For the reasons which I have given, both on principle and in accordance with authority, I conclude that such estoppel bars the whole of the plaintiffs' claim.

f I would accordingly allow this appeal. I would set aside the judgment of the judge and in lieu thereof dismiss the plaintiffs' claim with costs. I am reassured by the knowledge that, as appears from his judgment, this is the decision which the judge himself would have thought the proper one, if he had not regarded the form of the defendant's pleading as compelling a different conclusion.

Appeal allowed. Leave to appeal to the House of Lords refused.

Solicitors: *Gillhams*, Harlesden (for the defendant); *N J L Pearce*, Bristol (for the plaintiffs).

Henrietta Steinberg   Barrister.

National House-Building Council v Fraser and another

QUEEN'S BENCH DIVISION

SIR DOUGLAS FRANK QC SITTING AS A DEPUTY JUDGE OF THE HIGH COURT

1, 21 DECEMBER 1982

Guarantee – Construction – Guarantee by housebuilding company's directors to National House-Building Council – Directors guaranteeing that company would comply with council's rules – Directors guaranteeing that if company failed to do so they would indemnify council 'against all losses incurred by the council by reason thereof' – Guarantee of three years' duration – Company building house within three-year period which did not comply with council's rules – Purchaser of house claiming cost of remedying defects – After expiry of three-year guarantee period purchaser awarded costs of remedying defects – Council honouring award and claiming indemnity from directors – Whether 'loss incurred by council' within period of guarantee – Whether directors liable to indemnify council.

In 1973 a newly formed housebuilding company asked the National House-Building Council if it would place the company on its national register of housebuilders. The council agreed to do so on condition that the directors of the company gave the council a guarantee that they would indemnify the council against any claim made in respect of houses sold by the company during the next three years. On 27 February 1974 the directors gave the council a guarantee which stated that they guaranteed that the company would perform the obligations imposed on it by the council's rules and that, if it failed to do so, the directors would indemnify the council 'against all losses . . . incurred by the Council by reason thereof'. The guarantee further stated that it was to expire 'three years from the date hereof'. In 1974 the company built some houses which did not comply with the council's rules as to design and construction. The houses were subsequently sold. One of the purchasers started arbitration proceedings, claiming the cost of remedying defects which had resulted from the company's breach of the council's rules. On 2 August 1978 the arbitrator awarded the purchaser £14,635·07. The company failed to honour the award, so the council, in accordance with its rules, satisfied it and then claimed reimbursement from the company. The company failed to pay, so the council claimed the £14,635·07 from the directors of the company under the guarantee. The directors contended that they were not liable because the guarantee had expired on 27 February 1977 and the council had not 'incurred a loss' within the meaning of the guarantee until August 1978, when the company failed to pay the £14,635·07 and the council was required to honour the arbitrator's award.

Held – On the true construction of the guarantee the directors' obligation to indemnify the council arose not at the date when the loss was quantified but at the date when the company failed to carry out its obligations under the council's rules. It followed that because the company had failed to discharge its duties to the council within the three-year period, ie by building houses which did not comply with the council's rules, the directors were liable under the guarantee to indemnify the council in respect of the £14,635·07 (see p 1092 g to j and p 1093 h, post).

Forster v Outred & Co [1982] 2 All ER 753 applied.

Thomas v Nottingham Inc Football Club [1972] 1 All ER 1176 considered.

Holland v Teed (1848) 7 Hare 50 not followed.

Notes

For the duration of a surety's liability, see 20 Halsbury's Laws (4th edn) para 162, and for cases on the subject generally, see 26 Digest (Reissue) 147–149, 914–927.

For the determination of a guarantee, see 3 Halsbury's Laws (4th edn) para 179.

Cases referred to in judgment

a
Forster v Outred & Co [1982] 2 All ER 753, [1982] 1 WLR 86, CA.
Holland v Teed (1848) 7 Hare 50, 68 ER 20, 26 Digest (Reissue) 285, 2148.
Thomas v Nottingham Inc Football Club [1972] 1 All ER 1176, [1972] Ch 596, [1972] 2 WLR 1025, 26 Digest (Reissue) 189, 1226.
Westminster Bank Ltd v Sassoon (1926) Times, 27 November.

b **Preliminary issue**

The plaintiffs, the National House-Building Council (formerly the National House-Builders Registration Council), brought an action against the defendants, Malcolm A H Fraser and Graham T A Bateson, seeking (i) a declaration that, by virtue of a guarantee dated 27 February 1974, the defendants were liable to indemnify the plaintiffs against a loss of £14,635·07 incurred by them as a result of an arbitration award dated 2 August
c 1978, (ii) an order that the defendants pay them the £14,635·07, and (iii) interest pursuant to statute. The defendants denied liability, contending that the loss had been incurred by the plaintiffs outside the period of the guarantee. The question of whether the defendants were liable to indemnify the plaintiffs was tried as a preliminary issue. The facts are set out in the judgment.

d *Gabriel Moss* for the plaintiffs.
Barry Green QC and *Dingle Clark* for the defendants.

Cur adv vult

e 21 December. The following judgment was delivered.

SIR DOUGLAS FRANK QC. The plaintiffs' claim in this action is for £14,635·07, said to be due to them by the defendants under a guarantee. In 1973 a new housebuilding company called Otterbourne Court Ltd, which I shall refer to as 'the company', was formed with the defendants as its directors. On 24 September the company applied to
f the plaintiffs to be placed on the National Register of House Builders. On 23 January 1974 the plaintiffs' secretary told the company that they would be recommended for acceptance on the National Register as a probationer, subject to certain conditions, one of which was in these terms:

'That the Directors of your Company give a joint and several guarantee to the
g Council that they will indemnify the Council against any claim made in respect of dwellings sold by your Company during the first three years. The form of guarantee required by the Council is enclosed.'

By an agreement dated 27 February 1974, the defendants guaranteed the performance by the company of the obligations on the company as a probationer or as a registered housebuilder. The guarantee was in these terms:

h 'If the Probationer whether as a Probationer or as a Registered House Builder shall in any respect fail to carry out the obligations or shall commit any breach of the regulations then the Guarantors will indemnify the Council against all losses damages costs expense or otherwise which may be incurred by the Council by reason thereof. This guarantee shall expire three years from the date hereof.'

j In 1974 the company built houses at Budleigh Salterton. Subsequently, one of the purchasers commenced arbitration proceedings and on 2 August 1978 was awarded the amount claimed in these proceedings. The company failed to honour the award and so accordingly, under the NHBC scheme, which is well known and does not need to be described, the award was honoured by the plaintiffs.

The NHBC rules, which it is common ground bind the company, provide that, where the plaintiffs have made any payment to a purchaser in discharge of the liability of the housebuilders whose name is on the register, any sum so paid shall be recoverable on demand by the plaintiffs from the housebuilders. As the company have failed to reimburse the plaintiffs, the plaintiffs contend that the defendants are liable under their guarantee.

It is the defendants' case that the guarantee expired on 27 February 1977, ie three years from the date on which it was given, that the plaintiffs had not then incurred any loss, and that the loss was incurred after that date.

Those are the matters now before me to be tried as a preliminary issue. Counsel for the defendants made two submissions: (i) that the losses were incurred after the expiry of the guarantee, and (ii) that the guarantee did not expire before where the loss was merely a potential loss before its expiry.

As to (i), counsel for the defendants said that the plaintiffs could be called on to pay only when the award was made, and so the plaintiffs incurred their loss when the company failed to pay the award. When the company failed to carry out its obligations or committed breaches of the regulations, the loss had not yet occurred. At the date of the breach, the loss is potential only, thus if the breach is remedied or the buyer does not notify it in the specified time, no loss results. The construction of the guarantee is not affected by the events after the date when executed and the court should adopt a constrained construction of the words 'all losses incurred'.

As to (ii), counsel for the defendants said that the guarantee could only apply to a house built before the guarantee expired and therefore the fact that the house was sold before then was irrelevant.

The plaintiffs' case involves adding to the end of cl 4 of the guarantee the words 'save in respect of breaches of regulations which took place before expiry'.

Such rewriting goes beyond the natural construction of the words and no implied term was pleaded. If the clause is ambiguous it must be construed contra proferentem. The choice of three years is arbitrary and suggests a sharp cut-off point for liability under the guarantee or where the plaintiffs' liability may last for ten years. The three-year period was taken, although the plaintiffs could have put no finite period or could have made the guarantee renewable. The word 'expiry' has the flavour of extinguishment of rights. So much for the summary of counsel for the defendants' submissions.

It is admitted in the defence that the company, in the words of the regulations, failed to carry out its obligations to the plaintiffs in that the dwellings were not designed and constructed in a manner at least sufficient to satisfy in all respects the plaintiffs' requirements and that the company had undertaken in its agreement with the plaintiffs to honour any award made by an arbitrator as a consequence of such failure and the whole of the award related to the costs of remedying such defects and damage. Hence it is not disputed that, had the award been made within a three-year period, the defendants would have been liable.

In the absence of authority I should have little hesitation in deciding that the defendants' obligation to indemnify the plaintiffs arose at the time of the company's failure to carry out its obligations. The fact that the costs to be incurred by the plaintiffs had not then been quantified seems to me nothing to the point. What was being guaranteed was the company's duty to fulfil its obligation and the failure to discharge that duty occurred within the three-year period. It is inherently absurd that a guarantor's obligation should depend on the date of the quantification of a loss. If that were the effect of the three-year limitation, then the guarantor's liability could depend on whether or not the dispute went to arbitration and the time elapsing before the arbitrator gave his award.

Counsel for the defendants, referring to 3 Halsbury's Laws (4th edn) para 179, quoted the following passage:

'... It appears that a continuing guarantee cannot be revoked so as to exclude outstanding liabilities properly undertaken by the banker on the faith of it, such as

a
bills accepted by him current at the time of notice of revocation; if, however, the guarantee is for a specified period, it does not cover obligations undertaken, but not dischargeable, within that period unless it is so worded as to do so . . .'

The case relied on in the footnotes is *Holland v Teed* (1848) 7 Hare 50, 68 ER 20. However, in my judgment, the later cases do not support the second part of the passage I have quoted. Thus in *Westminster Bank Ltd v Sassoon* (1926) Times, 27 November, a

b
guarantee to a bank was given and at the end of the form were added the words 'This guarantee will expire on 30th June 1925'. The defendant received no letters from the bank until October 1925, but it was held that the guarantee was a continuing one and that the defendant was liable.

In *Thomas v Nottingham Inc Football Club* [1972] 1 All ER 1176, [1972] 1 Ch 596, the plaintiff guarantor exercised his right to determine his guarantee. In the course of his judgment Goff J said ([1972] 1 All ER 1176 at 1177, [1972] 1 Ch 596 at 600):

c
'Having so retired, the guarantor then exercised his undoubted right under cl 2, to which I have referred, to determine his guarantee. That, of course, did not exonerate him from liability on it in respect of the position as it then stood, but it made it cease to be operative for the future.'

d
Forster v Outred & Co [1982] 2 All ER 753, [1982] 1 WLR 86 concerned the date the cause of action for negligence against solicitors arose. The plaintiff had charged her property as security for a loss. The plaintiff claimed damage for negligence and/or breach of contract by the defendants in failing properly to advise her when the mortgage was executed. The question for the Court of Appeal was when did the cause of action arise. It was held that it was complete at the time the negligent advice was given. In the course

e
of his judgment Stephenson LJ said ([1982] 2 All ER 753 at 764, [1982] 1 WLR 86 at 98):

'Although there is no more direct authority than those cases among those which have been cited to us, I would accept counsel for the defendants' statement of the law and would conclude that, on the facts of this case, the plaintiff has suffered actual damage through the negligence of her solicitors by entering into the mortgage deed, the effect of which has been to incumber her interest in her freehold estate

f
with this legal charge and subject her to a liability which may, according to matters completely outside her control, mature into financial loss, as indeed it did. It seems to me that the plaintiff did suffer actual damage in those ways; and subject to that liability and with that incumbrance on the mortgage property was then entitled to claim damages (not, I would think, an indemnity and probably not a declaration) for the alleged negligence of the solicitor which she alleges caused her that damage.

g
In those circumstances her cause of action was complete on 8 February 1973 and the writ which she issued on 25 March 1980 was issued too late to come within the six years' period of limitation.'

It seems to me that the facts in that case are sufficiently analagous to those in the instant case to support the preliminary conclusion I have described above. The cause of

h
action in the case just cited can be equated with the breach of regulation in the instant case. If the wide words used in Halsbury's Laws of England are supported in *Holland v Teed* then it seems that they cannot stand against recent and more persuasive authorities.

It follows from the foregoing that I hold that by the date of the expiry of the guarantee the plaintiffs had incurred the loss the subject of this action and that the defendants are liable to indemnify them against that loss.

j
Judgment accordingly.

Solicitors: *Samuel Tonkin & Co* (for the plaintiffs); *Dale & Newbery*, Shepperton (for the defendants).

K Mydeen Esq   Barrister.

Burton v British Railways Board

EMPLOYMENT APPEAL TRIBUNAL
BROWNE-WILKINSON J, MRS M E SUTHERLAND AND MR R THOMAS
25 OCTOBER 1982

Costs – Employment Appeal Tribunal – Reference to Court of Justice of the European Communities – European Court reserving costs of reference to Employment Appeal Tribunal – Whether appeal tribunal having jurisdiction to make order for costs of reference – Employment Appeal Tribunal Rules 1980, r 27.

The employee brought proceedings against his employers under the Sex Discrimination Act 1975. His application was dismissed by the industrial tribunal, which treated the case as falling entirely under the 1975 Act although arguments relating to a possible claim under the EEC Treaty and other Community law had been ventilated. The employee appealed to the Employment Appeal Tribunal. The appeal tribunal formed the view, which was not challenged, that important questions of Community law did arise and, without opposition from the employers, the case was referred to the Court of Justice of the European Communities. In the result the European Court decided the reference in favour of the employers, and reserved to the appeal tribunal the costs of the reference. The employers invited the employee to withdraw proceedings subject to him paying their costs. There followed some correspondence between the parties in which the employee made it clear that he was not prepared to pay the costs and pointing out that there was no power to order him to pay them. The employers persisted in their application, and were told that, if they went ahead with their application for the costs of the reference, the employee would seek his costs incurred in that application. On the application,

Held – (1) Since it could not be said that the reference to the Court of Justice of the European Communities was unnecessary, improper or vexatious, or that there had been unreasonable delay or other unreasonable conduct in relation to them, the Employment Appeal Tribunal (which had no jurisdiction to award costs except as authorised by r 27[a] of the Employment Appeal Tribunal Rules 1980) could not make any order for the payment of the employers' costs of the reference to the European Court, any hardship to the employers not being a matter which the appeal tribunal could take into account (see p 1096 *a* to *c f g* and *j* to p 1097 *a*, post).

(2) The application by the employers in the Employment Appeal Tribunal for their costs of the reference to the European Court had, however, been made by them with notice that they had no case, and in persisting with their application they had effectively forced the employee to incur the costs of the application. In so doing the employers had been guilty of unreasonable conduct and in the circumstances it was appropriate to order the employers to pay the costs of the application (see p 1097 *a*, post).

Per curiam. Until such time as the Employment Appeal Tribunal's powers to award costs are modified to allow it to order an unsuccessful party on a reference to the Court of Justice of the European Communities to pay all or any of the costs of the reference, it may be that the appeal tribunal should consider making it a term of such a reference that the parties should agree how the costs of the reference are to be dealt with (see p 1096 *d e*, post).

---

a   Rule 27, so far as material, is set out at p 1095 *j*, post

Notes

a For proceedings before the Employment Appeal Tribunal, see 16 Halsbury's Laws (4th edn) para 1045.

For the Sex Discrimination Act 1975, see 45 Halsbury's Statutes (3rd edn) 221.

For the EEC Treaty, see 42A ibid passim.

b **Appeal and application for costs**

Arthur Burton appealed to the Employment Appeal Tribunal against the dismissal of his complaint to an industrial tribunal that his employers, the British Railways Board, had discriminated against him, contrary to the Equal Pay Act 1970, as amended by the Sex Discrimination Act 1975, in rejecting an application by him for voluntary redundancy under a scheme operated by the board. On 16 January 1981 the Employment Appeal Tribunal referred certain questions as to the interpretation of art 119 of the EEC Treaty

c and EEC Council Directives 75/117 and 76/207 to the Court of Justice of the European Communities for a preliminary ruling under art 117 of the treaty. The European Court answered the questions referred to it in favour of the board and reserved the question of the costs of the board and of Mr Burton to the Employment Appeal Tribunal (see [1982] 3 All ER 537, [1982] QB 1080). The board applied to the appeal tribunal for an order for the payment of their costs of the reference. The facts are set out in the judgment of the

d appeal tribunal.

N E Beddard for the British Railways Board.
Anthony Lester QC for Mr Burton.

e

BROWNE-WILKINSON J. This is the final stage in the litigation *Burton v British Railways Board.* Mr Burton brought proceedings against British Rail under the Sex Discrimination Act 1975. His application was heard by an industrial tribunal, who treated the case as falling entirely under the 1975 Act although arguments related to a possible claim under art 119 and other provisions of the EEC Treaty were ventilated.

f   An appeal was then brought to this tribunal. This tribunal formed the view, which is not challenged by anybody, that important questions of European law did arise and, without opposition from British Rail, the case was referred to the Court of Justice of the European Communities. British Rail incurred costs on that reference.

On 16 February 1982 the European Court decided the points referred in favour of British Rail and against Mr Burton (see [1982] 3 All ER 537, [1982] QB 1080). The

g decision by the European Court was decisive of the case and the parties are today agreed that the case will be withdrawn by Mr Burton. However, the parties are not agreed as to the correct order for costs.

The Court of Justice of the European Communities reserved to this appeal tribunal the costs of the hearing before the European Court, it being the practice that costs incurred on a reference are to be treated as costs forming part of the proceedings before the

h national court. It is at that stage that the difficulty arises.

The jurisdiction of this court to award costs is contained in r 27 of the Employment Appeal Tribunal Rules 1980, SI 1980/2035. It provides that we can only make an order for costs—

j   'Where it appears to the Appeal Tribunal that any proceedings were unnecessary, improper or vexatious or that there has been unreasonable delay or other unreasonable conduct in bringing or conducting the proceedings.'

That rule is made pursuant to para 19 of Sch 11 to the Employment Protection (Consolidation) Act 1978, sub-para (1) of which gives the rule-making power; sub-para (2) provides:

'Except as provided by sub-paragraph (1), the rules shall not enable the Appeal Tribunal to order the payment of costs or expenses by any party to proceedings *a* before the Tribunal.'

This tribunal therefore has no jurisdiction to award costs save to the extent authorised by r 27.

British Rail are asking for an order that Mr Burton and the Equal Opportunities Commission (which was supporting and conducting his case) pay the costs of the reference to the European Court. Counsel for the British Railways Board, who has *b* presented the case on behalf of the board with great skill and candidness, accepted that it could not be said that the proceedings before the European Court were unnecessary, improper or vexatious, or that there had been unreasonable delay or other unreasonable conduct in relation to them. That being so, as a matter of jurisdiction, we cannot make any order for the payment of British Rail's costs.

However, we think that the facts of this case disclose a possible anomaly in relation to *c* the costs of a reference to the European Court. The rules as to costs are directed towards ordinary litigation before industrial tribunals and this tribunal. Where it becomes necessary or desirable to refer a case to the Court of Justice of the European Communities, the proceedings become quite different in scale and type. In some cases it may be unfair that no court will have jurisdiction to order the unsuccessful party on the reference to pay any or all of the costs of that reference. It may therefore be desirable that para 19 of *d* Sch 11 to the 1978 Act (and, consequently, the rule as to costs) might be modified to take account of the anomalous position that exists where there has been a reference. Until that happens, it may be that for the future, when this tribunal is asked to order a reference to the European Court, consideration should be given to making it a term of such reference that the parties should agree how the costs of the reference should be dealt with. If no provision can be made for costs, then, if the case is decided by the appeal *e* tribunal without a reference to Europe, there would be an appeal to the Court of Appeal. The Court of Appeal would then refer the matter to the Court of Justice of the European Communities. When the matter came back to the Court of Appeal, costs would follow the event in the ordinary way. It seems unfortunate, if other circumstances show a reference to be desirable, that the case has to be forced up to the Court of Appeal before any court can have jurisdiction over the costs of a necessary reference. Whether it is right *f* to require an undertaking as to the costs of a reference will depend on the circumstances of each particular case.

We dismiss the application for costs of the reference to the European Court.

The Equal Opportunities Commission, on behalf of Mr Burton, have now asked for an order against British Rail that they pay the costs of today on the grounds that the application for costs was an unnecessary procedure or, alternatively, unreasonable conduct *g* by the Railways Board.

Immediately after the decision by the Court of Justice of the European Communities, British Rail invited the Equal Opportunities Commission to withdraw proceedings subject to them paying the costs of British Rail. There followed some correspondence thereafter in which the Equal Opportunities Commission made it clear that they were not prepared to pay the costs and, indeed, pointing out that there was no power to order *h* them to pay the costs. Notwithstanding that, British Rail persisted in the application.

If there were previously any doubts in the matter, in a letter of 4 October 1982 the circumstances affecting the jurisdiction of this court to make an order for costs were spelt out in great detail to British Rail. British Rail were told that, if the board went ahead with their application for the costs of the European reference, the Equal Opportunities Commission would apply for the costs of today to be paid by British Rail. Notwithstanding *j* that, British Rail went ahead.

We hope we do not do counsel for the British Railways Board any injustice when we say that he was really unable to make any submission how we could have jurisdiction to order the costs of the European reference. All he could do, and he did it very eloquently, a was to point out the hardship to British Rail. However, that is not a matter that we can take into account as we have no jurisdiction to take it into account. Effectively, British Rail, with notice of the fact that they had no case, have forced the Equal Opportunities Commission to incur the costs of today. British Rail, having been put on notice of the Equal Opportunities Commission's attitude and even so persisting in making this application, have been guilty of unreasonable conduct. In our judgment it is an appropriate case in which we should make an order as to costs.

b   Costs to be taxed, if not agreed, on the footing that the case was appropriate to be dealt with by junior counsel.

Order accordingly.

Solicitors: *Elaine R Donnelly*, Manchester (for Mr Burton); *Michael G Baker* (for the British
c Railways Board).

K Mydeen Esq   Barrister.

d

Practice Direction

e FAMILY DIVISION

Child – Welfare – Welfare report – Independent welfare report – Use of independent welfare reports in matrimonial, wardship or guardianship proceedings.

f The Family Division of the High Court in matrimonial, wardship or guardianship proceedings or any divorce county court in matrimonial proceedings may entertain the evidence of an 'independent' reporter but the following points should be noted:

1. No person (other than the party who instructs the 'independent' reporter) is under any obligation to discuss the case with or to be interviewed by the 'independent' reporter.
g 2. Where the child is a ward of court, the 'independent' reporter should not interview the child without leave of the court.
3. The 'independent' reporter may not see a report by the court welfare officer if this is confidential to the parties and the court.
4. The court welfare officer may not discuss the case with the 'independent' reporter unless authorised by the court.
h 5. Where the court has ordered an inquiry and report from a court welfare officer the court should not depart from the usual practice of relying on that report or of ordering a further report by a different court welfare officer.

Practitioners will bear in mind that the party wishing to obtain the service of an 'independent' reporter may, if legally aided, need the authority of the area committee.

j Issued with the concurrence of the Lord Chancellor.

J L ARNOLD
President.

24 March 1983

Practice Note

QUEEN'S BENCH DIVISION
LORD LANE CJ, TAYLOR AND McCOWAN JJ
17 MARCH 1983

Practice – Long vacation – Queen's Bench Division – Judge in chambers and master – Service, filing and amendment of pleadings – Summonses issuable without leave returnable before master – Appeals – Marking of applications or appeals as fit for August or vacation – RSC Ord 3, r 3, Ord 18, r 5, Ord 64, r 3.

LORD LANE CJ made the following statement at the sitting of the court. Attention is drawn to the recent amendments to RSC Ord 3, r 3, Ord 18, r 5 and Ord 64, r 3 (see RSC (Amendment No 2) 1982, SI 1982/1111, and RSC (Amendment No 3) 1982, SI 1982/1786). Pleadings may now be served, filed and amended during the month of September, and time will run during that month.

1. *Queen's Bench masters*
    (a) Any type of summons may be issued before or during the long vacation returnable before a Queen's Bench master in the month of September.
    (b) A summons may, without leave, be issued returnable before a master in the month of August for any of the following purposes: to set aside writ, or service of writ; to set aside judgment; for stay of execution; for any order by consent; for judgment or leave to enter judgment; for approval of settlements or for interim payment; for relief from forfeiture; for charging order; for garnishee order; for appointment or discharge of a receiver; for relief by way of sheriff's interpleader; for transfer to a county court or for trial by master; for time where time is running in the month of August; originating summons.
    (c) In any case of urgency any other type of summons (that is other than those for the purposes in (b) above) may, with the leave of a master, be issued returnable before a master during the month of August.

2. *Queen's Bench judge in chambers*
    (a) Subject to the discretion of the judge, any appeal to a judge in chambers and any application normally made to a judge in chambers may be made in the month of September.
    (b) In the month of August, save with the leave of a judge, appeals to a judge in chambers will be limited to the matters set out in 1(b) above, and only applications of real urgency will be dealt with, for example urgent applications in respect of injunctions or for possession under RSC Ord 113.
    (c) It is desirable, where this is practical, that applications or appeals are submitted to a master or judge prior to the hearing of the application or appeal so that they can be marked 'fit for August' or 'fit for vacation'. If they are so marked, then normally the judge will be prepared to hear the application or appeal in August if it has been marked 'fit for August', or in September if marked 'fit for vacation'. The application to a judge to have the papers so marked should normally be made in writing, the application shortly setting out the nature of the application or appeal and the reasons why it should be dealt with in August or in September, as the case may be.

3. All previous notices and directions on these matters are revoked.

N P Metcalfe Esq   Barrister.

a   # R v Boundary Commission for England, ex parte Foot and others

COURT OF APPEAL, CIVIL DIVISION

SIR JOHN DONALDSON MR, SLADE AND ROBERT GOFF LJJ

12, 13, 17, 18, 19, 25 JANUARY 1983

b

Elections – Parliamentary – Redistribution of seats – Discretion of the Boundary Commission – Judicial review of commission's exercise of powers – Method employed in determining boundaries of recommended constituencies – Commission adopting policy of not crossing local boundaries in recommending new boundaries – Rules for redistribution of seats – Whether paramount objective of redistribution rules the attainment of electoral equality between constituencies – Whether

c   *commission entitled to adopt policy of not crossing local boundaries even though policy causing electoral disparity – Whether redistribution rules binding on commission – House of Commons (Redistribution of Seats) Act 1949, s 2(1)(a), Sch 2, rr 4, 5, 6 – House of Commons (Redistribution of Seats) Act 1958, s 2(2).*

d   Under s $2(1)(a)^a$ of the House of Commons (Redistribution of Seats) Act 1949 it was the duty of the Boundary Commission for England to make periodic recommendations to the Home Secretary regarding the boundaries of parliamentary constituencies, though the final decision regarding boundaries lay with Parliament. In formulating their recommendations the commission were required, under s $2(1)(a)$, to give effect to the rules for redistribution of seats set out in Sch 2^b to the 1949 Act. Rule $4(1)$ of those rules required that 'So far as is practicable' constituencies were not to cross county or London

e   borough boundaries. Rule 5 required, first, that 'The electorate of any constituency shall be as near the electoral quota as is practicable' (the electoral quota for each constituency being, at the material time, 65,753 electors) and, second, that the commission were permitted to depart from the strict application of r $4(1)$ if it appeared to the commission that a departure was desirable to avoid an excessive disparity between the actual electorate of any constituency and the electoral quota. Rule 6 gave the commission a discretion to

f   depart from the strict application of both rr 4 and 5 if geographical considerations appeared to render such a departure desirable. Section $2(2)^c$ of the House of Commons (Redistribution of Seats) Act 1958 expressly stated that it was 'not . . . the duty of [the] Boundary Commission . . . to aim at giving full effect in all circumstances to the [redistribution] rules' and then went on to require the commission to take account, so far as they reasonably could, 'of the inconveniences attendant on alterations of constituencies

g   . . . and of any local ties which would be broken by such alterations'. In recommendations which the commission intended to submit to the Home Secretary pursuant to s 2 of the 1949 Act, revised constituency boundaries led to a wide disparity in several constituencies between the actual electorate and the electoral quota. The size of the electorate in those revised constituencies ranged from 46,824 at one extreme to 94,768 at the other. In formulating their recommendations the commission adopted, in line with r 4, a general

h   policy of not crossing local boundaries when proposing constituency boundary changes while remaining free to use their power under r 5 to depart from that policy where appropriate. The applicants, who were members of a political party, considered that the commission had laid undue emphasis on the requirement in r 4 of not crossing local boundaries and had given insufficient emphasis to the requirement in r 5 of achieving equality of numbers in the electorates of constituencies. The applicants accordingly

j   applied to the Divisional Court for judicial review of the commission's recommendations by way of orders of prohibition or injunctions restraining the commission from submitting their recommendations to the Home Secretary, contending that r 5 was the paramount requirement, that the main purpose of the redistribution rules was to achieve

---

a   Section 2(1) is set out at p 1105 *e f*, post
b   Schedule 2 is set out at p 1105 *j* to p 1106 *j*, post
c   Section 2(2) is set out at p 1107 *b c*, post

electoral equality, that the commission had not achieved that purpose because of their
excessive regard to r 4 in not crossing local boundaries, and that in not producing equality   *a*
between electorates the commission had unreasonably exercised, or had failed to exercise
properly, their statutory powers. The Divisional Court dismissed the application. The
applicants appealed.

Held – The appeal would be dismissed for the following reasons—

(1) Although s 2(1)(*a*) of the 1949 Act, construed by itself, imposed a mandatory   *b*
requirement on the commission to give effect to the redistribution rules set out in Sch 2
to the 1949 Act, the effect of s 2(2) of the 1958 Act was to override that requirement and
to reduce the rules to the status of guidelines. Accordingly, the commission, although
required to have regard to the rules in formulating their recommendations, were not
bound to give effect to them in all circumstances and therefore even if r 5 and electoral
equality was the paramount requirement of the rules the commission were not bound to   *c*
observe that requirement in all constituencies (see p 1107 *d*, p 1108 *g* to p 1109 *b*, p 1117
fg and p 1118 *h*, post).

(2) Furthermore, on the true construction of the rules themselves, electoral equality
between constituencies could not be said to be the primary purpose of the rules since r 5,
in which that requirement was embodied, was expressly subordinate to 'the foregoing
rules' including r 4(1) and the requirement therein that constituencies should not cross   *d*
local boundaries. Moreover, the latter requirement was reinforced by the second part of
s 2(2) of the 1958 Act which imposed a mandatory obligation on the commission to take
into account, as far as they reasonably could, the inconvenience of altering constituencies
and the breaking of local ties in order to achieve electoral equality, and that obligation
underlined the importance placed by Parliament on the requirement embodied in r 4
that local boundaries were to be respected when boundary changes were considered (see   *e*
p 1107 *e* to *h*, p 1109 *c*, p 1116 *e*, p 1117 *fg* and p 1118 *h*, post).

(3) In any event, there were substantial obstacles to granting judicial review of the
commission's recommendations regarding constituency boundaries. Although in theory
the court had jurisdiction to review the commission's exercise of their powers, since the
commission's discretion in exercising those powers, although very wide, was fettered by
the redistribution rules, in practice it was difficult, if not impossible, to discharge the   *f*
heavy burden of showing that the commission had exercised their powers wrongly or
improperly, because (a) the rules themselves were no more than guidelines and the
commission were not bound to observe them in all circumstances, (b) if they did observe
rr 4 and 5 they could nevertheless decide subjectively what was 'practicable' in terms of
those rules and what was an 'excessive' disparity between the electoral quota and the
electorate of any constituency for the purposes of r 5, and (c) the commission were not   *g*
required to give reasons and therefore the court could not know what matters they had
taken into account or ignored in observing the rules (see p 1103 *b c*, p 1107 *j*, p 1108 *a* to
d, p 1109 *b c*, p 1110 *b c*, p 1111 *a*, p 1116 *e*, p 1117 *fg* and p 1118 *h*, post).

(4) It could not be said that no reasonable commission which had regard to the
redistribution rules could have made the recommendations which the commission had
decided on, because the numerical disparities between constituencies did not per se   *h*
establish error on the face of the recommendations on the part of the commission and
were within the limits of the commission's discretion under r 6 to depart from rr 4 and
5 for geographical reasons. Furthermore, it had not been shown that in adopting a
general policy of not crossing local boundaries the commission had misdirected
themselves, since that policy was merely a preliminary policy and was in any event
justifiable under the rules (see p 1112 *h* to p 1113 *d*, p 1114 *c* to *f j*, p 1115 *e f j*, p 1116 *d*   *j*
to *f* and p 1118 *g h*, post); *Associated Provincial Picture Houses Ltd v Wednesbury Corp* [1947]
2 All ER 680 applied.

Per curiam. If relief were to be granted on an application for judicial review of a
boundary commission's recommendations the appropriate relief would be a declaration
expressing the court's view of the legal position since an order of prohibition would
wholly preclude Parliament from considering the commission's proposals (see p 1116 *g*
to *j*, post).

Notes

a For the redistribution of seats at parliamentary elections, see 34 Halsbury's Laws (4th edn) paras 1087–1096.

For the House of Commons (Redistribution of Seats) Act 1949, s 2, Sch 2, see 11 Halsbury's Statutes (3rd edn) 535, 541.

For the House of Commons (Redistribution of Seats) Act 1958, s 2, see ibid 809.

b **Cases referred to in judgment and by the Appeal Committee**

Associated Provincial Picture Houses Ltd v Wednesbury Corp [1947] 2 All ER 680, [1948] 1 KB 223, CA, 45 Digest (Repl) 215, 189.

R v Secretary of State for Foreign and Commonwealth Affairs, ex p Indian Association of Alberta [1982] 2 All ER 118, [1982] QB 892, CA.

c **Appeal**

The appellants, Michael Foot, Michael Cocks, James Mortimer and David Hughes, applied, with the leave of McNeill J given on 29 November 1982, for judicial review by way of orders of prohibition or injunctions restraining the Boundary Commission for England from submitting to the Secretary of State for the Home Department pursuant to the House of Commons (Redistribution of Seats) Act 1949 as amended a report *d* containing the commission's recommendations for revised parliamentary constituency boundaries. On 21 December 1982 the Divisional Court of the Queen's Bench Division (Oliver LJ and Webster J) dismissed the application and affirmed the commission's decision to submit its recommendations to the Secretary of State on the grounds (1) that no case had been made out on the merits sufficient to justify the court's intervention in the exercise of its discretion with the commission's recommendations and (2) that in any *e* event the lateness of the application made it inappropriate for the court to grant the relief sought. The appellants appealed, seeking an order that their application for judicial review be granted. The facts are set out in the judgment of the court.

J Melville Williams QC and *Julian Fulbrook* for the appellants.
Simon D Brown and *John Mummery* for the commission.

f

Cur adv vult

25 January. The following judgment of the court was delivered.

g **SIR JOHN DONALDSON MR.** This is an appeal against the decision of a Divisional Court consisting of Oliver LJ and Webster J dismissing an application by the appellants for an order of prohibition or injunction restraining the Boundary Commission for England from submitting to the Home Secretary a report containing recommendations for revised parliamentary constituency boundaries of a nature which it is now expected that the commission intends shortly to make. This judgment is one to which we have all *h* contributed.

The parties

The appellants are all distinguished politicians. Mr Michael Foot is the member of Parliament for Ebbw Vale and the Leader of the Labour Party. Mr Michael Cocks is the member of Parliament for Bristol South and the Opposition Chief Whip. Mr James *j* Mortimer is the general secretary and Mr David Hughes the national agent of the Labour Party.

The respondents are all distinguished non-political lawyers. Sir Raymond Walton is the deputy chairman of the Boundary Commission for England (to which we will refer as 'the commission'), the Speaker of the House of Commons being the chairman. He is also a judge of the High Court. His Honour Judge Newey QC is a member of the commission and also a circuit judge. Mr William Ruff is a member of the commission and is also a solicitor with great experience of local government.

All parties, and indeed the members of this court, are electors in one parliamentary constituency or another.

The role of the Boundary Commission

Over a period of years the electorate of Great Britain must inevitably change both in terms of numbers and in terms of where they live. If there is to be fair representation in Parliament, it follows that constituency boundaries must also be changed, but there would be scope for embarrassment if politicians were to be required to redraw those boundaries without independent advice. Hen·e the creation of the Boundary Commissions, the membership of which is indeµ :ndent and non-political. Under the terms of the House of Commons (Redistributic of Seats) Acts 1949 to 1979, the Boundary Commissions are required to report to th Secretary of State from time to time on which changes, if any, they recommend. When ·he report is made, the Secretary of State is required to lay it before Parliament together, except in a case where the report states that no alteration is required to be made, with the draft of an Order in Council giving effect, with or without modifications, to the recommendations contained in the report. A Boundary Commission can make recommendations when particular local changes take place, but this appeal concerns a general review which has to be undertaken not less than 10 or more than 15 years from their last review.

A Boundary Commission would face considerable problems if they received no guidance on the principles to be applied in their reviews. However, that is not the case. Such guidance is provided by Sch 2 to the 1949 Act read with s 2(2) of the 1958 Act.

The role of the court

Since a very large number of people are interested in this appeal and since it is most unlikely that our decision, whether for or against the appellants, will meet with universal approval, it is important that it should at least be understood. In particular it is important that everyone should understand what is the function and duty of the courts. Parliament entrusted the duty of recommending changes in English constituency boundaries to the commission. It could, if it had wished, have further provided that anyone who was dissatisfied with those recommendations could appeal to the courts. Had it done so, the duty of the court would, to a considerable extent, have been to repeat the operations of the commission and see whether it arrived at the same answer. If it did, the appeal would have been dismissed. If it did not, it would have substituted its own recommendations. Parliament, for reasons which we can well understand, did no such thing. It made no mention of the courts and gave no right of appeal to the courts.

There are some who will think that in that situation the courts have no part to play, but they would be wrong. There are many Acts of Parliament which give ministers and local authorities extensive powers to take action which affects the citizenry of this country, but give no right of appeal to the courts. In such cases, the courts are not concerned or involved so long as ministers and local authorities do not exceed the powers given to them by Parliament. Those powers may give them a wide range of choice on what action to take or to refrain from taking and so long as they confine themselves to making choices within that range the courts will have no wish or power to intervene. But if ministers or local authorities exceed their powers, if they choose to do something or to refrain from doing something in circumstances in which this is not one of the options given to them by Parliament, the courts can and will intervene in defence of the ordinary citizen. It is of the essence of parliamentary democracy that those to whom powers are given by Parliament shall be free to exercise those powers, subject to constitutional protest and criticism and parliamentary or other democratic control. But any attempt by ministers or local authorities to usurp powers which they have not got or to exercise their powers in a way which is unauthorised by Parliament is quite a different matter. As Sir Winston Churchill was wont to say, 'That is something up with which we will not put.' If asked to do so, it is then the role of the courts to intervene and, in the interest of everyone concerned, to prevent this happening.

There are undoubtedly distinctions between the position of the commission and that
a of a minister or local authority taking executive action under statutory powers which
affects the individual citizen. The commission have no executive power. Their function
and duty is limited to making advisory recommendations. Furthermore the commission's
task is ancillary to something which is exclusively the responsibility of Parliament itself,
namely the final decision on parliamentary respresentation and constituency boundaries.
These are distinctions to which we will return when giving further consideration to what
b action should or should not be taken by the court in the circumstances of this case. At
the moment all that need be said is that it is common ground that in some circumstances
it would be wholly proper for the courts to consider whether the commission have, no
doubt inadvertently, misconstrued the instructions which they have been given by
Parliament and, if they have done so, to take such action as may be appropriate in order
to ensure that the will of Parliament is done.

c
The commission's instructions from Parliament and their method of working
Parliament has laid down certain 'Rules for Redistribution of Seats', which tell the
commission the basis on which they should formulate recommendations to the Secretary
of State. We shall set out the relevant statutory provisions, and in particular these rules,
later in this judgment. We shall also consider the proper construction to be placed on the
d rules, as to which there has been some argument. The rules indicate the number of
constituencies in each part of the United Kingdom, and point to certain basic
considerations, such as that constituencies shall, so far as practicable, not cross county or
London borough boundaries (r 4), that the electorate of each constituency shall be as near
as practicable to what is called the electoral quota (r 5), and the relevance of geographical
considerations (r 6). The manner of calculating the electoral quota for each constituency
e is also specified, and it is common ground that, for the purposes of the present review,
the electoral quota is 65,753 electors for each constituency. Some provision is made for
the procedures to be adopted by the commission. Thus they have to publish provisional
recommendations and, in certain circumstances, to cause local inquiries to be held to
investigate objections to those recommendations before making their report to the
Secretary of State. However, subject to these somewhat limited requirements, the
f commission are entitled to regulate their own procedure.

The commission have to report not later than 15 years after their last general report,
and they must begin their review in sufficient time to enable this to be done. In the
present instance the report is due not later than May 1984 and the commission decided
to begin their task in February 1976. Hence it is that the figure for the electoral quota
and the basic figures for the electorate are those for 1976. Having given formal notice of
g an intention to make a report, the procedure is as follows: the commission's first task is
to formulate provisional recommendations and publish them in the localities which may
be affected. Where they receive representations objecting to their proposals and the
representation comes from a local authority in the area concerned or from a body of
electors numbering 100 or more, the commission have to hold a local inquiry. These
inquiries are conducted by non-political lawyers appointed by the Home Secretary and
h known as 'assistant commissioners'. After each inquiry is concluded, the assistant
commissioner sends a written report to the commission and the commission then review
their provisional recommendations in the light of that report and any other information
or representations which have come to their attention. When this process has been gone
through for the whole of the territory concerned, in this case England, the commission
report to the Secretary of State.

j These are the formal procedural steps, but in addition it is the practice of the
commission to have informal meetings with the representatives of the political parties at
which there are discussions on general matters. To give an example which is not directly
material to the appeal, in November 1979 the commission and representatives of the
political parties discussed whether in principle it was practicable to have 'Polo Mint'
constituencies, i e a central urban constituency wholly surrounded by another and rural

constituency, the alternative being to have two constituencies each with urban and rural parts. The commission are in no way bound by the advice or representations which they receive, but it is clearly sensible and useful that they should have the benefit of the experience of the political parties and their organisers.

The appellants' complaints

Mr Foot in an affidavit put the complaint this way:

'Our first concern as a party with the Boundary Review was that it should reflect fairly in the seats the balance of votes between the parties at a General Election and should give us fair representation. To achieve this numerous representations were made to the local enquiries held up and down the country. It gradually became apparent that the way in which the Boundary Commission was operating itself led to disparities between the size of the electorates in different constituencies. At one extreme there is the Isle of Wight with 88,463 electors in 1976 and 94,768 now while at the other there is Surbiton with only 46,493 in 1976 and now 46,824. Neither of these seats is regarded as a Labour Party stronghold. This disparity offends against the principle of equal representation for all electors which is required by our modern system of Parliamentary representation. The purpose of periodic reviews of Parliamentary constituencies is to secure as far as possible equality between one constituency and another. That has not been done by the review chiefly because the Commission have chosen to ignore their power to cross county and borough boundaries.'

Mr Cocks in another affidavit said:

'From about 1979 onwards I received information about the proposals being made by the Boundary Commission for England pursuant to the General Review of Parliamentary Constituencies which started in 1979. During 1981 the pace of the review increased and it became apparent that there were many inconsistencies in the proposals being made and that these were not being cured by enquiries and reports of the Assistant Commissioners... From the middle of 1981 onwards because of the inconsistencies in the practice of the Commission and the disparities between different constituencies we have been examining closely the proposals of the Commission and the procedure and results of the enquiries. In the course of such examination it has become apparent that the Commissions' proposals are not achieving anything like the equality of representation which should be the aim of the boundary review and that this is caused to a large extent by the Commission's failure to use their power under Rule 5 to recommend constituencies crossing county boundaries. Indeed the way in which the Commission formulated their proposals county by county and district by district precluded consideration in many cases, as in Avon and Somerset, being given to the exercise of the power. In addition they have failed to apply properly the general requirements of Rule 5 to recommend constituencies as near to the electoral quota as possible. Of the 439 constituencies in England outside London recommended by the Commission 54 are more than 10% below the electoral quota of 65,753 and 36 are more than 10% above it, that is 20·5% of all proposed seats diverge by more than 10% from the quota. In London the situation is much worse with 30 constituencies more than 10% below and 10 constituencies more than 10% above out of a total of 84 seats. Thus in London 47·6% diverge by more than 10% from the quota.'

Mr Storer, who is the technical adviser in the national agents department of the Labour Party, makes the same point in his affidavit. The commission, he says, have concentrated on r 4 which requires the commission so far as is practicable having regard to rr 1 to 3 to ensure that no constituency crosses a county, county borough, metropolitan borough or county district boundary at the expense of compliance with r 5, which requires the electorate of each constituency to be as near 65,753 as is practicable, having regard to rr 1 to 4, but also provides that it may depart from the strict application of r 4—

a

'if it appears to them that a departure is desirable to avoid an excessive disparity between the electorate of any constituency and the electoral quota, or between the electorate thereof and that of neighbouring constituencies . . .'

Mr Storer, like Mr Foot and Mr Cocks, says that the failure to depart from r 4 and to recommend constituencies which cross boundaries has in fact produced serious disparities between the electoral quota and the size of the electorate for many of the proposed constituencies.

b

The relevant statutory provisions and their construction

Before we further consider these complaints and the application for judicial review, we must set out the relevant statutory provisions, and express our view of the construction to be placed on those provisions.

c

(1) *The statutory provisions*

The principal statutory provisions are contained in the House of Commons (Redistribution of Seats) Act 1949 and in certain rules set out in Sch 2 to that Act as amended and qualified by the House of Commons (Redistribution of Seats) Act 1958. These provisions have, however, to be read in the light of the Local Government Act

d 1972, which amended the rules to take account of substantial changes made by that legislation in the structure of local government.

Section 1 of the 1949 Act (later amended by s 1 of the 1958 Act) provides for the establishment of four permanent boundary commissions, one each for England, Scotland, Wales and Northern Ireland. Section 2(1) of the 1949 Act provides:

e

'Each Boundary Commission shall keep under review the representation in the House of Commons of the part of the United Kingdom with which they are concerned and shall, in accordance with the next following subsection, submit to the Secretary of State reports with respect to the whole of that part of the United Kingdom, either—(a) showing the constituencies into which they recommend that it should be divided in order to give effect to the rules set out in the Second Schedule

f to this Act; or (b) stating that, in the opinion of the Commission, no alteration is required to be made in respect of that part of the United Kingdom in order to give effect to the said rules.'

Section 2(2) provides for the minimum and maximum periods which may elapse between the making of reports by the commission, periods which were later varied by s 2(1) of the 1958 Act. Section 2(5) of the 1949 Act provides:

g

'As soon as may be after a Boundary Commission have submitted a report to the Secretary of State under this Act, he shall lay the report before Parliament together, except in a case where the report states that no alteration is required to be made in respect of the part of the United Kingdom with which the Commission are concerned, with the draft of an Order in Council for giving effect, whether with or

h without modifications, to the recommendations contained in the report.'

Section 3 of the 1949 Act contains provision for the manner in which Parliament shall deal with any draft Order in Council so laid before it, giving Parliament the alternatives of either approving or declining to approve the draft order. If approved, the draft order is to be submitted by the Secretary of State to Her Majesty in Council; if a motion for approval of the draft order is rejected, the Secretary of State may amend the draft and lay

j the amended draft before Parliament for approval.

It is therefore in Sch 2 to the 1949 Act that the rules are found to which the commission are required to give effect in making their recommendations under s 2(1) of that Act. These rules (as amended by the 1958 Act and two Local Government Acts) are in the following terms:

'1. The number of constituencies in the several parts of the United Kingdom set

out in the first column of the following table shall be as stated respectively in the
second column of that table—

Part of the United Kingdom.	No. of Constituencies.
Great Britain	Not substantially greater or less than 613.
Scotland	Not less than 71.
Wales	Not less than 35.
Northern Ireland	Not greater than 18 or less than 16.

2. Every constituency shall return a single member.

3. There shall continue to be a constituency which shall include the whole of the
City of London and the name of which shall refer to the City of London.

4.—(1) So far as is practicable having regard to the foregoing rules—(a) in
England and Wales,—(i) no county or any part thereof shall be included in a
constituency which includes the whole or part of any other county or the whole or
part of a London borough; (ii) [repealed by the Local Government Act 1972]; (iii)
no London borough or any part thereof shall be included in a constituency which
includes the whole or part of any other London borough; (iv) [repealed by the Local
Government Act 1972]; (b) in Scotland, regard shall be had to the boundaries of local
authority areas; (c) in Northern Ireland, no ward shall be included partly in one
constituency and partly in another.

(2) In paragraph (1) of this rule the following expression has the following
meaning, that is to say:—"area" and "local authority" have the same meaning as in
the Local Government (Scotland) Act 1973; "county" means an administrative
county.

5. The electorate of any constituency shall be as near the electoral quota as is
practicable having regard to the foregoing rules; and a Boundary Commission may
depart from the strict application of the last foregoing rule if it appears to them that
a departure is desirable to avoid an excessive disparity between the electorate of any
constituency and the electoral quota, or between the electorate thereof and that of
neighbouring constituencies in the part of the United Kingdom with which they
are concerned.

6. A Boundary Commission may depart from the strict application of the last
two foregoing rules if special geographical considerations, including in particular
the size, shape and accessibility of a constituency, appear to them to render a
departure desirable.

7. In the application of these rules to each of the several parts of the United
Kingdom for which there is a Boundary Commission—(a) the expression "electoral
quota" means a number obtained by dividing the electorate for that part of the
United Kingdom by the number of constituencies in it existing on the enumeration
date; (b) the expression "electorate" means—(i) in relation to a constituency, the
number of persons whose names appear on the register of parliamentary electors in
force on the enumeration date under the Representation of the People Acts for the
constituency; (ii) in relation to the part of the United Kingdom, the aggregate
electorate as hereinbefore defined of all the constituencies therein; (c) the expression
"enumeration date" means, in relation to any report of a Boundary Commission
under this Act, the date on which the notice with respect to that report is published
in accordance with section two of this Act.'

We shall refer to these rules as so amended simply as 'the rules'. Of the rules, we are
concerned in particular with rr 4, 5 and 6, the construction of which we shall consider in
a moment.

We should add that s 1(2) of the 1949 Act provides that the procedure of the Boundary
Commissions shall be regulated in accordance with Part III of Sch 1 to that Act.
Paragraphs 1 and 2 of Part III provide for meetings of the commissions. Paragraph 3
provides for the publication of provisional determinations to make recommendations
affecting any constituency. Paragraph 4 empowers the commissions to cause local

inquiries to be held in respect of any constituency or constituencies; though under s 4 of
a the 1958 Act, if a commission receive from an interested authority or from a body of
electors numbering 100 or more any representation objecting to a proposed
recommendation, a local inquiry must be held. Paragraph 5 makes certain provisions
relating to procedure at local inquiries; and para 6 provides that: 'Subject to the foregoing
provisions of this Schedule, each of the Commissions shall have power to regulate their
own procedure.'

b   Finally, s 2(2) of the 1958 Act provides as follows:

> 'It shall not be the duty of a Boundary Commission, in discharging their functions
> under the said section two, to aim at giving full effect in all circumstances to the
> rules set out in the Second Schedule to the principal Act, but they shall take account,
> so far as they reasonably can, of the inconveniences attendant on alterations of
> constituencies other than alterations made for the purposes of rule 4 of those rules,
c > and of any local ties which would be broken by such alterations; and references in
> that section to giving effect to those rules shall be construed accordingly.'

(2) *Construction of the statutory provisions*
(a) *Section 2(1)(a) of the 1949 Act*
    Under s 2(1)(a) of the 1949 Act, the commissions are required to submit their reports
d to the Secretary of State showing the constituencies in which they recommend that their
area should be divided 'in order to give effect to the rules set out in the Second Schedule
to this Act'. The requirement in this subsection to give effect to the rules is plainly
mandatory. We shall however have to consider in a moment the impact on this
requirement of s 2(2) of the 1958 Act.

e (b) *The relationship between rr 4 and 5*
    Turning to the rules themselves, rr 4, 5 and 6 are each concerned with separate matters.
Rule 4 is concerned with county and London borough boundaries; r 5 is concerned with
the size of the electorate of each constituency, considered in relation to the electoral quota
for that constituency; and r 6 is concerned with geographical considerations. It is clear,
in our judgment, that of these matters, although they may all be properly regarded as
f interlocking, the requirement in r 4 that 'So far as is practicable' constituencies shall not
cross county or London borough boundaries must be regarded as taking precedence over
the requirement in r 5 concerning the size of the electorate for each constituency. This
appears from the facts that (1) r 4 is on its face not qualified by reference to r 5, whereas
r 5 provides that the electorate of any constituency shall be as near the electoral quota as
is practicable having regard to the foregoing rules, which of course include r 4, and (2)
g the second limb of r 5 authorises departure from r 4 only in the circumstances there
specified.
    This point is not academic in the present case. Counsel for the appellants asserted in
argument that the primary purpose of the rules is to achieve electoral equality between
constituencies. On a true construction of the rules, this is not so. The requirement of
electoral equality is, subject to the second limb of r 5, subservient to the requirement
h that constituencies shall not cross county or London borough boundaries.

(c) *Construction of rr 4, 5 and 6*
    The requirements of rr 4 and 5 are qualified by the words 'So far as is practicable' or 'as
near . . . as is practicable'.
    Practicability is not the same as possibility. In part of his argument before us (and, it
j appears, also before the Divisional Court) counsel for the appellants came close to
suggesting, particularly in relation to r 5, that the two were the same. But this is plainly
not so. Practicability not merely connotes a degree of flexibility: it contemplates that
various matters should be taken into account when considering whether any particular
purpose is practicable, ie capable in practical terms of achievement. We can see no limit
to the matters which may be so taken into account, whether under r 4 or r 5, save that
they must be relevant to the particular question, having regard to the terms of the
relevant statutes and the rules themselves, of which rr 4 and 5 form part. It may be that

the test of what is or is not practicable is objective; but in relation to the requirement in
r 5 (with which we are primarily concerned) this is for present purposes theoretical, *a*
because the power to depart from the requirement in r 4 to respect local boundaries only
arises if, in the subjective view of the commission, such departure is desirable to avoid
any excessive disparity of the kinds specified (see the second limb of r 5). Exactly the
same comment can be made concerning the word 'excessive' itself in this context. It may
involve an objective, albeit flexible, standard, but whether it is to be treated as achieved
is dependent on the subjective judgment of the commission. Likewise the question *b*
whether there is to be a departure from the strict application of r 4 or r 5 by reason of
special geographical considerations is made, by r 6, dependent on the subjective view of
the commission whether such a departure is thereby rendered desirable. These
considerations obviously have an inhibiting effect on any judicial review of the kind
sought by the appellants. We add in parenthesis that, since the Boundary Commissions
are not subject to the provisions of the Tribunals and Inquiries Act 1971, they are not *c*
required to give reasons for their decision to make any particular recommendation. It
follows that it cannot usually be known whether, or if so to what extent, any such
decision has been affected by the matters referred to in r 4; or those in r 5; or those in
r 6; or, indeed, those referred to in the second limb of s 2(2) of the 1958 Act, to which we
will shortly refer. This consideration alone must make it very difficult, indeed usually
impossible to seek judicial review of the kind now sought on the basis that the *d*
commission have failed to construe or apply the rules properly.

(d) *Section 2(2) of the 1958 Act*
   Overriding these various points, however, there is, in our judgment, the impact of
s 2(2) of the 1958 Act. There was considerable argument about the construction of this
subsection, both before the Divisional Court and before us. For the appellants, counsel *e*
made two submissions, both of which (if accepted) would limit the impact of the
subsection. The first (which found favour with the Divisional Court) was that the first
limb of the subsection (discharging Boundary Commissions from the duty to aim at
giving full effect in all circumstances to the rules) was to be read subject to the second
limb of the subsection. On this construction the dispensation in the first limb is effective
only to take account of the two matters specified in the second limb, viz inconveniences *f*
attendant on alterations of constituencies, and local ties which would be broken by such
alterations. This argument found favour in particular with Oliver LJ in the Divisional
Court, because he felt that otherwise no weight would be given to the conjunction 'but'
which provides the link between the two limbs of the subsection. We have formed a
different view. We consider that the function of the first limb is to do just what it says,
viz to relieve commissions from the duty to give effect in all circumstances to the rules, *g*
with the result that, although plainly commissions must indeed have regard to the rules,
they are not strictly bound to give full effect to them in all circumstances. The word 'but'
has a role to play because it points the contrast between the dispensation in the first limb
of the subsection, and the mandatory requirement in the second limb, that Boundary
Commissions shall nevertheless take account of the matters specified in the second limb.
So read, we consider that effect is given to all parts of the subsection, whereas on the *h*
submission of counsel for the appellants, which we feel unable to accept, no weight is
given to the first limb which could, if he is right, for all practical purposes be deleted.
   Counsel for the appellants' second submission on the subsection related only to the
second limb. It was that Boundary Commissions were required thereby only to take
account of the specified inconveniences and local ties when considering *whether* to
recommend the alteration of a constituency; but that, once they had decided to *j*
recommend an alteration, they were not required to take these matters into account
when considering the *nature* of the alteration to be recommended. This submission,
which underwent some refinement in the course of argument before us, we are quite
unable to accept. We reject it as a matter of construction. Section 2(2) of the 1958 Act is
a statutory provision which modifies the duty placed on commissions under s 2(1) of the
1949 Act. The second limb of s 2(2) of the 1958 Act requires commissions to take account
of the specified matters, and this must mean that they are required to take account of

a them when making the recommendations which are the subject matters of a report to be submitted by them to the Secretary of State. If they are to take account of such matters for that purpose, they must plainly take account of them not only in deciding whether to alter a particular constituency, but for all purposes relative to their recommendations, which must include selection of the particular alteration which they decide to recommend. This view is, in our judgment, reinforced by the fact that we can see no practical sense in imposing any such restrictive meaning as that for which counsel for the *b* appellants has contended. For these reasons we are unable to accept his argument on this point.

The broad construction of s 2(2) of the 1958 Act which we prefer places yet another, very substantial, obstacle in the way of judicial review of a decision of a commission to make any particular recommendation in a report to the Home Secretary. For the practical effect is that a strict application of the rules ceases to be mandatory so that the rules, while *c* remaining very important indeed, are reduced to the status of guidelines. We also observe in parenthesis that the second limb of s 2(2) of the 1958 Act underlines (if this is necessary) the importance placed by Parliament on respecting the county and London borough boundaries mentioned in r 4, which will often also reflect local ties.

The course of the present review by the commission

d We have already described the general methods of working adopted by the commission in the light of their statutory obligations. For the purposes of their present review, the Boundary Commission for England gave notice on 5 March 1976 of their determination to make a report. That report has to be submitted before May 1984. Having given notice, the commission formulated proposals for the fixing of constituency boundaries. These were published at various times during the ensuing years; but the proposals relating to *e* all the London boroughs (except, for special reasons, Enfield) were published together on 31 July 1979. Before formulating and publishing their proposals, a meeting was held with the representatives of the main political parties in 1976; a further meeting was held in March 1978. At the second meeting, the representatives of all the political parties (including the representative of the Labour Party) expressed the opinion that none of the London borough boundaries should be crossed.

f After the publication of their proposals, and the receipt of objections and counter-proposals, the commission caused a number of local inquiries to be held, presided over by assistant commissioners. The commission decided that, where the proposed boundaries crossed district boundaries, one local inquiry should be held for both districts; where the proposed boundary did not cross district boundaries, it was decided that a separate local inquiry should be held for that district, unless counter-proposals had been received that constituencies should cross those district boundaries, in which event the same assistant *g* commissioner was engaged to hold the local inquiries for both districts involved. The various local inquiries have all been held, and the reports of the assistant commissioners have all been received by the commission. In every case, the commission intimated whether, in the light of the report so received, they intended to make any, and if so what, change in their original proposals; and the commission fixed the last date for the *h* submission of any further representations. In every case, that last date has now passed; the commission have carried out their final overall review of the various proposals, and are ready to submit their report to the Secretary of State as soon as there is no obstacle in their way. Against this background the appellants issued their application for judicial review, seeking prohibition against the submission by the commission to the Home Secretary of their report.

j
The decision of the Divisional Court

The Divisional Court (Oliver LJ and Webster J) dismissed the appellants' application substantially on two grounds, namely (1) that no case had been made out on the merits sufficient to justify the intervention of the court in the exercise of its discretion, and (2) that the lateness of the application made it in any event inappropriate for the court to grant relief in the exercise of its discretion.

Oliver LJ expressed the view that, in the circumstances of the case as disclosed by the evidence, the appellants had not been shown to have 'a sufficient interest' within RSC Ord 53 to give them a locus standi to make the application. Webster J, however, said that in his view, were they to have succeeded on the merits, the appellants would have established a locus standi.

The first point was developed in the two judgments, according to a number of its different facets. It is closely bound up with the extent of the powers of the courts to interfere with decisions of administrative bodies such as the commission. This is a question to which we now turn.

The powers of the court to intervene

We have already pointed out that the relevant legislation has provided for no appeal against the commission's recommendations. Furthermore, the discretion in carrying out their functions conferred on the commission by the legislature is a very wide one. However, it is not absolute and unfettered, in view of the existence of the rules.

A long line of cases have established that, if public authorities purport to make decisions which are not in accordance with the terms of the powers conferred on them, such decisions can be attacked in the courts by way of an application for judicial review; and furthermore that, even if such decisions on the face of them fall within the letter of their powers, they may be successfully attacked if shown to have been 'unreasonable'.

The situation of the commission differs from that of many other public authorities in that, even at the very end of their inquiries and deliberations, they make no final decision: they merely make a recommendation to the Secretary of State, who, after making any modifications to their report which he thinks appropriate, has to pass it on to Parliament for final approval or rejection. This distinctive nature of the function of the commission might well make the court in the exercise of its discretion more slow to intervene in regard to their activities than it would be in relation to those of many other public authorities. Nevertheless, it has not been suggested before this court, and in our opinion could not be correctly suggested, that the commission are above the law, in the sense that their activities are never susceptible to review by the courts.

In the present case, it has not been submitted that the commission have exceeded or are about to exceed the letter of their statutory powers. The complaint is more that they have unreasonably exercised or failed to exercise the various discretions conferred on them by statute. This submission necessitates a brief consideration of the meaning of 'reasonableness' in this context.

As Professor H W R Wade says in his work *Administrative Law* (5th edn, 1982) p 362:

> 'The doctrine that powers must be exercised reasonably has to be reconciled with the no less important doctrine that the court must not usurp the discretion of the public authority which Parliament appointed to take the decision. Within the bounds of legal reasonableness is the area in which the deciding authority has genuinely free discretion. If it passes those bounds, its acts ultra vires. The court must therefore resist the temptation to draw the bounds too tightly, merely according to its own opinion. It must strive to apply an objective standard which leaves to the deciding authority the full range of choices which the legislature is presumed to have intended.'

What then is this objective standard? The locus classicus on the subject is a passage from the judgment of Lord Greene MR in *Associated Provincial Picture Houses Ltd v Wednesbury Corp* [1947] 2 All ER 680 at 683, [1948] 1 KB 223 at 230 in which he stated what has become known as 'the *Wednesbury* principle'. Counsel for the appellants expressly accepted that this principle applies so as to govern and limit the powers of the court to intervene in regard to the activities of the commission. We need not cite the passage from Lord Greene MR's judgment verbatim. For present purposes it will suffice to say that the *Wednesbury* principle would or might in our opinion entitle the court to intervene if it was satisfied that the commission had misdirected themselves in law, or had failed to consider matters which they were bound to consider or had taken into consideration matters which they should not have considered. It would not, however, entitle it to intervene merely because it considered that, left on its own, it might (or indeed would) have made different recommendations on the merits; if the provisional

a conclusions of the commission are to be attacked on the grounds of unreasonableness, they must be shown to be conclusions to which no reasonable commission could have come. The onus falling on any person seeking to attack their recommendations in the courts must thus be a heavy one, which by its very nature may be difficult to discharge.

The issue on this appeal

b   In relation to the merits, therefore, the issue on this appeal is quite simply whether there is any sufficient evidence that the commission are intent on making recommendations which go beyond, or differ from, what any reasonable body of men in their position could properly make, exercising the best of their skill and judgment in the light of the instructions given to them by Parliament. If there is such sufficient evidence, it will or may be the duty of this court to intervene in order to ensure either that the commission's

c breach of duty is made known or, possibly, that it is remedied. If there is not it must be the court's duty to leave the commission to get on with the process entrusted to them, that being their business and not that of the courts.

The case for the appellants

In answering the appellants' case, counsel for the commission made it plain that, in

d addition to maintaining the objections to their case on its essential merits, which he and junior counsel for the commission put forward in the Divisional Court, they would seek to maintain the other submissions relating to locus standi and delay which were advanced in that court. Though strict logic might point to the adoption of another order, we prefer to follow the Divisional Court in considering first the appellants' case on its merits.

The essence of the appellants' case lies in the overriding importance which, as they

e submit, is to be attached to the first limb of r 5, which provides that 'the electorate of any constituency shall be as near the electoral quota as is practicable having regard to the foregoing rules . . .' This, the appellants say, is what the redistribution of seats is all about. This attitude is clearly reflected in their affidavits to which we have referred. That of Mr Foot, for example, refers to disparities in the numbers of the electorates of certain proposed constituencies as offending against what is there described as 'the principle of

f equal representation for all electors which is required by our modern system of Parliamentary representation'. Counsel for the appellants, in opening this appeal, similarly told us that the first main thrust of his argument would be that the commission had paid insufficient regard to the first limb of r 5. Whilst this provision, which is put forward as the key provision, is expressed to operate subject to rr 1 to 4, it is suggested of these earlier rules that only r 4 (which discourages the crossing of boundaries) can pose

g any real obstacle in the way of achieving something very near to equality with the electoral quota. And even this threat, it is suggested, is much less than it used to be because of the reduced number of boundaries which now have to be taken into account, in the light of recent changes in local authority boundaries and the amendments to r 4 made by the 1958 Act and the Local Government Act 1972. Any obstacle to electoral equality produced by r 4, it is suggested, is then reduced almost to vanishing point by

h the second limb of r 5, which permits departure from r 4 if compliance would produce any excessive disparity between the electorate of any constituency and the electoral quota or between its electorate and that of neighbouring constituencies.

The assertion of this paramount character of the first limb of r 5 is fundamental to the appellants' case. In concluding his opening of the appeal, counsel on their behalf summed up their complaint by saying that the commission have not achieved what he described

j as their fundamental purpose of proposing constituencies which are as near as practicable equal. He suggested that the commission have shown a quite excessive reverence for boundaries and districts and have demonstrably failed to pay sufficient regard to the discretion given to them by the second limb of r 5. Very broadly, these are the grounds on which he submits that their proposals or provisional proposals are open to attack on the *Wednesbury* principle. We now consider how he developed this attack as a matter of fact and law.

First, and we think foremost, he submitted that the draft proposals for a number of

constituencies reveal such wide disparities between many of the electorates and the
electoral quota that it is obvious *on the face of the proposals* that the commission must have   *a*
failed to observe the first limb of r 5, by failing to ensure that such electorates are as near
the electoral quota as is practicable having regard to the previous rules. He submitted in
effect that the disparities are so great that no boundary commission, properly instructed,
could reasonably have arrived at the same proposals, if they had had proper regard to this
first limb.

In the context of this attractively simple submission, counsel for the appellants referred   *b*
us to some interesting schedules and tables exhibited to an affidavit sworn by Dr E I
Marshall MP. These schedules and tables provide illustrations of wide divergences from
the electoral quota. They also provide substantial examples of what Dr Marshall describes
as the 'electoral gap' between the largest and smallest proposed constituency within any
county. We understand from him that one of the most extreme examples of the latter is
to be found in Staffordshire, where the figures of the proposed electorates for Stoke-on-   *c*
Trent North and South East Staffordshire respectively would be 76,180 (representing
15·86% over the electoral quota) and 51,602 (representing 21·52% under the electoral
quota). No useful purpose would be served by enumerating similar examples. We accept
that Dr Marshall's statistics reveal many instances of similar disparities.

We understand that, in the course of argument in the Divisional Court, counsel for
the appellants submitted that, if any given proposal results in an electorate for any   *d*
constituency which either exceeds or falls short of the electoral quota by more than 10%,
this by itself demonstrates that the commission have not complied with r 5 'so far as is
practicable'. In this court he expressly disclaimed the submission that there is any given
percentage of disparity which may never be exceeded. Nevertheless, he submitted that
there must come a point at which it is possible to say that in any given instance the
disparity between the electorate of a proposed constituency and the electoral quota is, on   *e*
the very face of it, obviously excessive. For example, by objective standards, in his
submission, the disparities of 15·86% and 21·52% in the case of Stoke-on-Trent North
and South East Staffordshire respectively are obviously excessive. In the case of these two
proposed constituencies, and many other similar proposed constituencies, where
substantial disparities of this nature are shown, the court can and must, in his submission,
inevitably conclude that the commission have failed to carry out their duties under r 5.   *f*
And, in his submission, the court can and should reach this conclusion without reference
to any evidence as to the particular circumstances which led them to make the relevant
recommendations.

We are prepared to accept the theoretical possibility that in a given instance the
disparity between the electorate of a proposed constituency and the electoral quota might
be so grotesquely large as to make it obvious on the figures that no reasonable commission   *g*
which had paid any attention at all to r 5 could possibly have made such a proposal. We
are prepared to accept that in such a hypothetical instance the court might be willing to
intervene.

For all this, the submission that the statistics on their face reveal an error on the part of
the commission seems to us totally unsustainable on the facts of the present case, for two
reasons if no others. First, as we have already pointed out, the guidelines designed to   *h*
achieve the broad equality of electorates, which are to be found in the opening limb of
r 5, have been deliberately expressed by the legislature in such manner as to render them
subordinate to the guidelines given by r 4, designed to prevent the crossing of boundaries
and *not vice versa*. With all respect to the appellants, we are not sure that this important
point has been fully appreciated by them, at least judging from their affidavits. Even if a
strict adherence to the principles of r 4 will produce what is prima facie excessive   *j*
disparity between the electorate of any constituency and the electoral quota, the wording
of the second limb of r 5 implicitly makes it clear that the commission are to be left with
a discretion *not* to depart from the strict application of r 4, if in all the particular
circumstances of the case they consider such departure undesirable. Any doubt about the
residual discretion of the commission in this context is removed by the first limb of s 2(2)
of the 1958 Act. From a bare reference to the statistics in the present case, we see no
reason to assume that the commission did not, consciously and on sufficient grounds,

conclude that departure from the strict application of r 4 was *not* desirable in any of the particular cases where 'excessive disparity' is alleged.

Second, and quite apart from this first reason, r 6 expressly confers on the commission a discretion to depart from the strict application of either r 4 or r 5 itself, if special geographical considerations, including in particular the size, shape and accessibility of a constituency appear to them to render a departure desirable. We are wholly unable to say that any of the discrepancies in the cases of Stoke-on-Trent North and South East Staffordshire, already referred to, or of the many other similar discrepancies, are so great that they could not have been justifiable simply by a conscious exercise of the commission's discretion under r 6 alone. There is no evidence that such discretion was not exercised.

In some of the constituencies proposed by the commission there would be disparities greater than those in the two constituencies to which we have just referred. In the passage from his affidavit which we have already quoted, Mr Foot has referred to two examples (Isle of Wight and Surbiton), which have not been particularly relied on by counsel for the appellants in argument but are at the top and bottom ends of the chart. Even having regard to them, however, for the reasons which we have already given, the statistical evidence is not by itself nearly strong enough to compel the conclusion that the decisions or proposals arrived at by the commission could not by any reasonable standards have been reached if they had properly carried out their duties. The statistics do not suffice to speak for themselves.

In these circumstances the burden of proof falls fairly and squarely on the appellants to show good grounds on the available evidence for saying that no reasonable commission, if properly instructed as to the relevant facts, could have arrived at the same decisions or proposals.

The Divisional Court apparently understood the submissions made to it on behalf of the appellants as including the submission that the commission erred on the grounds that, on the evidence, they *wholly failed* to consider whether they should exercise their discretion under the second limb of r 5 by proposing constituencies which crossed county or London borough boundaries. We did not understand counsel for the appellants to put such a far-reaching submission before us, but in any event we think it would be quite unsustainable on the evidence for the following reasons.

In an affidavit sworn on 16 November 1982 the deputy chairman of the commission said this:

'. . . in all our deliberations concerning the preparation of the report for submission to the Secretary of State for Home Affairs, the members of the Boundary Commission have given full and careful consideration to the application of the rules for the redistribution of seats set out in the Second Schedule to the 1949 Act as modified by section 2(2) of the 1958 Act. In particular, the members of the Boundary Commission have taken into consideration their power under rule 5 of the Second Schedule to depart from the strict application of rule 4 if it appears to them that a departure is desirable to avoid an excessive disparity between the electorate of any constituency and the electoral quota, or between the electorate thereof and that of neighbouring constituencies.'

The deputy chairman was not cross-examined on this affidavit before the Divisional Court and in this context Oliver LJ said in the course of his judgment:

'[Counsel for the appellants] has taken the perhaps unusual course of inviting the court to disbelieve this sworn testimony on the basis of the inferences which he asks the court to draw from the documents to which I have referred and from the fact that no cross-boundary constituency has yet been recommended.'

Before this court, counsel for the appellants indicated that in this context his submissions had been misunderstood by the Divisional Court and that he did not and does not seek to challenge the truth of these statements made by the deputy chairman, though he would seek to assert that the commission must have misdirected and did misdirect themselves as to the true effect of the rules. We are, of course, happy to accept this clarification by counsel of his submissions. If there was ever any doubt about it, this makes it quite clear that the appellants now accept that in every relevant instance the *a* members of the commission have taken into consideration their power under r 4, so that this point does not arise.

The next principal submission made on their behalf by counsel was substantially that the commission had *misdirected* themselves as to the true effect of the rules. The alleged misdirection is that, on the evidence, the commission, contrary to their duty to exercise a full discretion in the matter, had placed a rigid, self-imposed restriction on the exercise *b* of that discretion in regard to constituencies in London and the metropliten counties by adopting a fixed policy of following and not crossing existing borough or metropolitan district boundaries. The question whether the commission did or did not place a self-imposed restriction on the exercise of their discretion is a pure question of fact to be decided on the available evidence. It seems clear on such evidence that the commission in carrying out their functions have adopted a general policy of trying not to cross *c* London borough or metropolitan district boundaries, so far as they have considered this practicable and consistent with the guidelines given them by the rules. Thus far, however, we can see nothing objectionable about any such general approach, bearing in mind the nature of the primary guidelines under which the commission have to operate. Although metropolitan district boundaries are not mentioned in r 4, they may well reflect geographical considerations (r 6) and also local ties (s 2(2) of the 1958 Act).   *d*

In contrast we readily accept that it would have been objectionable if the commission had adopted a fixed and immutable policy in this context. The two members of the Divisional Court, however, having analysed the relevant evidence with great care and in detail, came to the conclusion in effect that no fixed and immutable policy of this nature had ever been adopted by the commission, but that the commission had done no more than adopt a preliminary and unobjectionable policy, which reflected the provisions of *e* the rules, and from which they consciously reserved liberty to depart in any cases which they regarded as appropriate: see the judgments in the Divisional Court of Oliver LJ and Webster J. Nothing in the argument that has been addressed to us on behalf of the appellants causes us in any way to doubt the correctness of this conclusion of fact. We therefore see no grounds for disturbing this conclusion.

However, we would draw attention to four points in this context. First, Mr Storer *f* expressly accepts in one of his affidavits that at least up to March 1978 it was the common view of all the political parties that boundaries should not be crossed; and indeed we think the evidence suggests that there was no serious suggestion to the contrary for many months later. Second, in 1979 the commission circulated to a number of assistant commissioners conducting inquiries both in and out of London a letter from a Mr Lodge, which expressly suggested the application of r 5 for the purpose of creating some cross- *g* boundary constituencies in London. This conduct, as Oliver LJ pointed out, is hardly consistent with the existence of a fixed and immutable policy of the nature suggested. Third, the statement in the affidavit of the deputy chairman sworn on 16 November 1982, which we have already quoted, the truthfulness of which is accepted by the appellants, seems to us quite inconsistent with the existence of a fixed policy of this nature. Fourth, the existence of such a policy is further negatived by a statement in a *h* further affidavit sworn by the deputy chairman, sworn on 6 December 1982, the veracity of which again is undisputed, and in which he says:

> '. . . I wish to make it clear that all provisional recommendations published by the Commission for Shire Counties, London Boroughs and Metropolitan Counties were reconsidered by the Commission in the manner explained in paragraph 4 of my previous affidavit after the Commission had received the reports of the Assistant *j* Commissioners and again after any further representations had been received and the final recommendation made by the Commission will be based on a full consideration of all such material.'

For all these reasons the submission that the commission have subjected their discretion to a self-imposed fetter of the nature suggested is in our opinion quite unsustainable as a matter of fact on the evidence and the Divisional Court was plainly right in so deciding.

The next submission of the appellants to which we should refer is one closely allied to
a the last. It is that in a number of instances the commission should have arranged, but
failed to arrange, the holding of joint local inquiries. Counsel for the appellants drew our
attention to certain specific instances in which he submitted that joint inquiries should
have been held. Thus, to mention a few instances, he said that there should have been,
but were not, joint inquiries for the whole of Yorkshire, for Barnsley and Sheffield, and
for Hillingdon and Harrow. The commission's failure to arrange for the holding of joint
b inquiries in cases such as these in his submission meant that they did not have the
necessary material before them to consider whether or not district or borough boundaries
should be crossed in particular instances in the exercise of their discretion.

Paragraph 4 of Part III of Sch 1 to the 1949 Act provides that—

'A Commission may, if they think fit, cause a local inquiry to be held in respect
of any constituency or constituencies.'

c

Paragraph 6 of Part III provides that, subject to the foregoing provisions of that
Schedule, each of the commissions 'shall have power to regulate their own procedure'.
The general procedure actually adopted by the commission in this regard has been
explained in the part of this judgment headed 'The course of the present review by the
commission'.

d We can see no possible grounds for an attack on this general procedure adopted by the
commission in the exercise of the power to regulate their own procedure conferred on
them by statute. It seems to us not only readily intelligible but prima facie sensible.
Furthermore, the fact that the commission had by no means closed their minds to the
possibility of holding joint inquiries in suitable cases is well illustrated by the fact that, as
Mr Pickersgill, a joint secretary of the commission has stated in an affidavit, they decided
e to hold one local inquiry for the whole county of Tyne and Wear, 'having regard to the
nature and relatively small number of representations received, which included several
counter-proposals for a different pattern of constituencies'. A contention that no
reasonable commission in the reasonable exercise of their discretion could have failed to
hold joint inquiries in any of the particular instances mentioned by counsel for the
appellants is in our judgment quite unsustainable.

f Counsel for the appellants made a wide variety of other submissions in his strenuous
and sustained attack on the commission's recommendations. Though we infer from the
judgments of the Divisional Court that his argument before that court followed much
the same lines as it has before us, one difficulty has been that it has traversed grounds far
wider than those stated in the appellants' formal application. Nevertheless, we believe
that we have referred to most of the main points of principle raised by counsel. The rest
g of his attack was chiefly directed to particular instances in which he contended that the
commission in making their proposals should have crossed district or borough boundaries
in order to achieve greater electoral equality. The proposals for the constituencies of
Blackburn and Ribble Valley, for example, produce a wide variation between the electoral
quota and the electorates of the two proposed constituencies, which could be reduced by
transferring two of the Blackburn wards to the Ribble Valley constituency. 'Excessive
h disparities' in his submission are also to be found among certain constituencies in Avon
and Somerset, where the commission should have crossed district borders, with a view to
achieving greater electoral equality. Similar submissions were made in relation to Oxford
and Wiltshire.

Though the relevant disparities are substantial in some of the instances relied on, they
are in no case so large as to point per se to the conclusion that the commission wholly
j failed to have regard to the provisions of r 5 relating to electoral equality; and indeed any
such conclusion is negatived by the undisputed evidence of the deputy chairman of the
commission to which we have referred. Nevertheless, for present purposes we are
prepared to assume that in all these instances, as the appellants contend, it would have
been 'practicable' for the commission's proposals to achieve greater electoral equality by
the crossing of district boundaries. On this basis counsel for the appellants submits in
effect that the relevant proposals cannot possibly be justified by the commission as a
proper exercise of their discretions.

The submission is, we think, once again founded on the premise that the overriding objective which must above all others guide the commission in their deliberations is the *a* achieving of electoral equality. In our observations on the construction of the rules we have attempted to make it clear that this premise is in our view an erroneous one. While the achievement of electoral equality is certainly a very important objective, the framework of the 1949 rules itself makes it plain that as a matter of general policy r 5 was to be regarded as subordinate to r 4 and not vice versa. Section 2(2) of the 1958 Act, while explicitly giving the commission a general discretion to depart from the rules in *b* formulating proposals, in effect placed a mandatory obligation on them to take account, so far as they reasonably could, of the inconveniences that would attend alterations of constituencies that might be made for the purpose of achieving electoral equality and of any local ties which would be broken by such alterations.

Though we have before us a number of reports of local inquiries, we do not have before us, and do not know, the totality of the evidence which the commission had *c* before them when they decided not to cross district boundaries in the various specific instances now complained of.

For example, for all we know, they may have considered that there were special geographical considerations, of the nature referred to in r 6, which compelled or justified a decision not to make proposals which involved the crossing of district boundaries. Alternatively, there may have been other relevant matters, not now in evidence, which *d* led them to exercise the wide general discretion vested in them, as confirmed by the opening words of s 2(2) of the 1958 Act. In the absence of evidence as to all the matters which the commission took into account and of any evidence that they misdirected themselves, we find it impossible to conclude that they have erred in any respect.

It cannot be emphasised too strongly that on this present application the onus does not fall on the commission to justify their proposals, either in general terms or in particular *e* instances, and either by evidence or otherwise. The onus of proof falls fairly and squarely on any person who seeks to challenge their proposals. Furthermore, the onus is a heavy one since the legislature has conferred no express right on any person to challenge the commission's decisions and any attack has to be based on the *Wednesbury* principle.

As in our judgment the appellants have not come near to discharging this onus, it follows that the Divisional Court was right to decide that the application failed on its *f* merits.

In these circumstances we find it unnecessary to express any opinion on the further questions whether the appellants have a sufficient locus standi to present this application and whether delay is by itself a bar to this claim. Indeed, we have not heard full argument on either of these points. Perhaps, however, we should say a very few words in relation to the form of relief claimed. Even though we have not heard full argument on this point too, our clear provisional view is that this would not have been an appropriate case *g* for the court in the exercise of its discretion to grant relief by way of prohibition, even if the appellants had surmounted all other hurdles. The effect of an order for prohibition would have been wholly to preclude Parliament from considering the proposals which the commission, after long and obviously careful consideration, were minded to place before it. Our present view is that, in the hypothetical contingency now under discussion, *h* the appropriate course for this court to take, in the exercise of its discretion, would have been simply to express its views as to the legal position in the form of a declaration, which would have been available for consideration together with the commission's report, both by the Secretary of State and in due course by Parliament.

As things are, however, these further matters do not arise for decision and we express no conclusion on them. *j*

Summary and conclusion

As our judgment has necessarily been long and somewhat detailed, it may assist those who are more interested in the broad basis of our decision than in the detailed legal arguments if we conclude with something in the nature of a summary.

a   Parliament and the courts are independent of each other and it is no part of the function or duty of the courts to review or intervene in any matter which pertains to Parliament itself. Thus the courts are not themselves concerned to draw or redraw constituency boundaries or to make any decision as to the basis of parliamentary representation. Those are matters for Parliament alone.

b   When it comes to advising Parliament and the Secretary of State on these matters, it is for Parliament and Parliament alone to decide what advice, if any, it requires and the nature of that advice. Parliament has thought it right to set up independent advisory bodies, the Boundary Commissions, to advise it and, in so doing, it has given the commissions instructions as to the criteria to be employed in formulating that advice. For good reasons, which we can well understand, Parliament has not asked the courts to advise it and it has not provided for any right of appeal to the courts from the advice or proposed advice of the commissions.

c   This does not mean that the courts have no part to play. They remain charged with the duty of helping to ensure that the instructions of Parliament are carried out. This is done by a procedure known as judicial review. Precisely what action, if any, should be taken by the courts in any particular case depends on the circumstances of that case including, in particular, the nature of the instructions which have been given by Parliament to the minister, authority or body concerned.

d   In the instant case we have had first to consider what exactly Parliament has instructed the commission to do and then to weigh the arguments of the appellants that the commission are bent on doing something different.

The appellants say that the commission were told to advise on how to produce a series of constituencies, the electorate of each of which was very nearly the same, that is to say numbering about 65,753, and that all other matters mentioned in their instructions,
e   such as respecting the boundaries of counties and London boroughs, were subordinate to that primary requirement. They then go on to say that the differences in the sizes of the constituency electorates proposed show clearly that the commission have misunderstood their instructions.

We do not read Parliament's instructions to the commission in the same way as do the appellants. Whilst we agree that Parliament attached great importance to each member
f   representing more or less the same number of electors, this was not the only matter which it considered to be important. Parliament has also said that in principle constituency boundaries should not cross the boundaries of counties or of London boroughs. It has no objection to their crossing metropolitan district boundaries as such, but it has said that account must be taken of local ties and geographical considerations such as the size, shape and accessibility of a constituency. These factors, which go to the
g   quality of representation, are often the very factors which led to the metropolitan district and other boundaries being where they are and may lead to a similar conclusion in relation to constituency boundaries.

It is important to realise that Parliament did not tell the Boundary Commission to do an exercise in accountancy: to count heads, divide by a number and then draw a series of lines around each resulting group. It told it to engage in a more far-reaching and
h   sophisticated undertaking, involving striking a balance between many factors which can point in different directions. This calls for judgment, not scientific precision. That being so, strict compliance with Parliament's instructions could result in several different answers. Indeed it must surely be the fact that it is possible to come up with many different answers to the problem of where constituency boundaries shall be drawn, all of which would be sensible, that has led Parliament to seek advice from the commission.
i   This is not to say that it is impossible for the commission to come up with a wrong answer, in the sense that it is one which could not possibly be given in the light of Parliament's instructions, properly understood. But it does mean that the mere demonstration that there is an alternative answer, which also could be put forward consistently with those instructions, tells us nothing. There being more than one answer, Parliament has asked the commission to advise on which, in their judgment, should be adopted.

First and foremost the appellants rely on the fact that many of the proposed constituencies would have electorates which are considerably, and in some cases very considerably, more or less than the arithmetical average figure of 65,753. They also rely on the number of cases in which a large, or very large, constituency in terms of the number of electors would be touching or near to a small, or very small, constituency.

It has to be remembered, and we are sure that Parliament and the commission have both had this well in mind, that you cannot, as a practical matter, draw constituency boundaries in such a way as to move a single elector or even a few electors from one constituency to another. The smallest unit of electors consists of those in a polling district, but polling districts are not permanent. They are changed to suit constituency boundaries and not vice versa. The smallest unit of electors for the purposes of the commission's deliberations is the ward and this can be a comparatively large unit, perhaps 5,000 to 10,000 electors. Indeed we were told that the Birmingham wards are as large as 17,000 to 20,000 electors. Since the commission can in practice only deal in this size of unit, moving it from one proposed constituency to another in order to achieve a balance, disparities between the electoral quota of 65,753 and the actual electorate of a proposed constituency may well be at least of this order.

However the other factors of which the commission have to take account may well lead the commission to conclude that a ward or even two wards should or should not be moved and, if this occurs, the variations in the sizes of proposed constituencies will become even larger.

Looking at the figures for the electorates of the proposed constituencies, we have no doubt that this is what has occurred. Undoubtedly the commission could have made different recommendations which would have produced constituencies whose electorates were more equal in size, but they could then have been criticised on grounds of a failure to take account of other factors, such as geographical considerations and the need to respect boundaries. We can see no grounds for thinking that the commission have misunderstood Parliament's instructions or have ignored them. It is intent on giving the Secretary of State and Parliament *their* advice (not ours or that of the political parties) and that is what they were instructed to do.

The appellants have one further complaint. They say that the commission organised the local inquiries in such a way as to prevent them having the materials on the basis of which it *might* (not *would*) have recommended different constituencies crossing various county, London borough or district boundaries and that they shut their mind to such a possibility. The evidence shows clearly that the commission did not shut their mind to this possibility. They organised the local inquiries in such a way as to give them the necessary materials for recommending constituencies crossing these boundaries in two categories of case. The first was where the commission themselves thought that this was a realistic option which they would have to consider. The second was where, in response to provisional recommendations, objectors specifically suggested the creation of such a constituency. This objection is therefore without foundation.

It is for the appellants to satisfy us that the commission are doing other than faithfully obeying the instructions of Parliament. This the appellants have completely failed to do. It follows that there are no grounds for us to intervene. The Divisional Court reached the correct conclusion when it dismissed the appellants' application and we should and do dismiss the appeal.

Appeal dismissed. Leave to appeal to the House of Lords refused. Injunction granted that boundary commission do not report for seven days. Liberty to apply.

11 February. The Appeal Committee of the House of Lords (Lord Diplock, Lord Fraser of Tullybelton, Lord Scarman, Lord Roskill and Lord Bridge of Harwich) heard a petition by the appellants for leave to appeal.

J Melville Williams QC and *Julian Fulbrook* for the appellants.
Simon D Brown and *John Mummery* for the commission were not called on.

LORD DIPLOCK. Their Lordships recognise the great public importance of this case.
a For that reason, as in the recent petition in the Canadian Constitutional case (*R v Secretary of State for Foreign and Commonwealth Affairs, ex p Indian Association of Alberta* [1982] 2 All ER 118 at 143, [1982] QB 892 at 937), they have constituted an Appeal Committee of five instead of the usual three. In their Lordships' unanimous view, no arguable ground has been shown on which an appeal to this House could possibly succeed. Accordingly their Lordships do not give leave to appeal.

b
Petition dismissed.

Solicitors: *Irwin Mitchell & Co*, Sheffield (for the appellants); *Treasury Solicitor.*

Diana Procter   Barrister.

c

Practice Note

d QUEEN'S BENCH DIVISION
LORD LANE CJ, TAYLOR AND McCOWAN JJ
30 MARCH 1983

Practice – Chambers proceedings – Queen's Bench Division – Chambers applications and appeals – Inter partes applications and appeals and ex parte applications – Listing – General list –
e *Special appointments – Procedure – Papers for perusal by judge – Affidavits in support of ex parte applications – RSC Ord 29, r 1.*

LORD LANE CJ made the following statement at the sitting of the court.

A. *Queen's Bench judge in chambers: special appointments*
f   1. A sharp increase in the volume of work listed to be heard by the Queen's Bench judge in chambers has led to unacceptable delays in the hearing of inter partes applications and appeals estimated to last more than 30 minutes. The following steps will be taken to reduce these delays.
2. All inter partes applications and appeals to the Queen's Bench judge in chambers will initially be entered in a general list. Whenever it appears or is agreed that any
g application or appeal is likely to last more than 30 minutes, it will in future be immediately and automatically transferred to a list of matters requiring special appointments. This will be a floating list and fixed dates will not be granted save on application to the judge, when special circumstances will have to be shown. The unavailability of counsel will not, save exceptionally, amount to a special circumstance. Every effort will be made to give at least seven days' notice before cases in this list are
h listed for hearing.
3. Cases for which fixed dates have already been given will retain those dates unless earlier dates acceptable to both parties can be granted. Any outstanding applications and appeals (estimated to last more than 30 minutes) not already entered in the special appointment list should be entered in it at once. *Counsel's clerks must take particular care to ensure that such outstanding applications and appeals do not remain in suspense.*
j   4. In order to ensure that a complete set of papers is available for perusal by the judge before hearing such applications and appeals it shall hereafter be required that, not later than five clear days before the date fixed for a special appointment (where a date has been fixed) and not later than 24 hours after a case in the floating special appointment list has been warned for hearing, (a) each party shall bespeak the affidavits already filed which it proposes to use, (b) each party shall lodge in room 128, Royal Courts of Justice, the exhibits to the affidavits referred to in (a), and (c) the appellant or applicant shall lodge in room 128 a bundle of the pleadings and previous court orders.

Except with the leave of the judge, no document may be adduced in evidence or relied on unless it has been bespoken or lodged as required.

a

B. *Queen's Bench judge in chambers: ex parte applications*

A large increase in the number of applications made ex parte to the Queen's Bench judge in chambers makes it necessary to introduce a new and clearly understood procedure, which will be strictly followed.

1. The standard procedure, suitable for all ordinary ex parte applications, will be:

b

(1) that the applicant shall lodge with the clerk to the judge in chambers by 3.00 pm on the day before the application is to be made papers which should include (a) the writ, (b) the affidavit in support and (c) a draft minute of the order sought;

(2) that the judge in chambers will hear the applications at 10.00 am on the following morning before embarking on his published list.

2. There will be some cases where the 3.00 pm deadline specified in para 1(1) *cannot*   *c* be met and where the urgency is too great to permit up to 24 hours' delay. Such applications should be dealt with in one or other of the three following ways:

(1) the applicant's advisers shall attend on the clerk to the judge in chambers at 9.50 am and lodge with him the papers listed in para 1(1) and also a certificate signed by counsel (or solicitor if counsel is not instructed) that the application is of extreme urgency. The application will be heard by the judge in chambers at 10.00 am;

d

(2) the applicant's advisers shall lodge the papers with the clerk to the judge in chambers by 12.30 pm (such papers to include all those specified in para 2(1)) and attend on the clerk at 1.50 pm. The application will be heard at 2.00 pm;

(3) in the very rare case where the application is of such urgency as to preclude any of the foregoing procedures, the applicant's advisers may give notice to the clerk to the judge in chambers and the judge in chambers will hear the application at once,   *e* interrupting his list if necessary. In such a case the applicant's counsel or solicitor must be prepared to justify taking this exceptional course.

3. (1) Attention is drawn to the provisions of RSC Ord 29, r 1, which ordinarily requires the issue of a writ or originating summons and the swearing of an affidavit in support of an ex parte application for an injunction before it is made.

(2) The affidavit in support should contain a clear and concise statement (a) of the facts   *f* giving rise to the claim against the defendant in the proceedings, (b) of the facts giving rise to the claim for the interlocutory relief, (c) of the facts relied on as justifying application ex parte, including details of any notice given to the defendant or, if none has been given, the reasons for giving none, (d) of any answer asserted by the defendant (or which he is thought likely to assert) either to the claim in the action or to the claim for interlocutory relief, (e) of any facts known to the applicant which might lead the court   *g* not to grant relief ex parte, (f) of the precise relief sought.

(3) Applicants for ex parte relief should prepare and lodge with the papers relating to the application a draft minute of the order sought. Such minute should specify the precise relief which the court is asked to grant. While the undertakings required of an applicant will vary widely from case to case, he will usually be required (a) to give an undertaking in damages, (b) to notify the defendant of the terms of the order forthwith,   *h* by cable or telex if he is abroad, (c) in an application of Mareva type, to pay the reasonable costs and expenses incurred in complying with the order by any third party to whom notice of the order is given, (d) in the exceptional case where proceedings have not been issued, to issue the same forthwith, (e) in the exceptional case where a draft affidavit has not been sworn, or where the facts have been placed before the court orally, to procure the swearing of the affidavit or the verification on affidavit of the facts outlined orally to   *j* the court.

The order should as a general rule contain provision for the defendant to apply on notice for discharge or variation of the order and for costs to be reserved.

N P Metcalfe Esq　　Barrister.

Care Shipping Corp v Latin American Shipping Corp

The Cebu

QUEEN'S BENCH DIVISION (COMMERCIAL COURT)
LLOYD J
26, 27 OCTOBER, 10 NOVEMBER 1982

Shipping – Time charterparty – Hire – Lien for non-payment of hire – Sub-freights – Charterparty giving owner lien on 'all sub-freights' for non-payment – Whether owner having lien over hire payable by sub-sub-charterer under time charter – Whether owner's lien limited to sub-freight payable under voyage charter.

By a time charterparty in the New York Produce Exchange form the shipowners' vessel was chartered to charterers, sub-chartered to sub-charterers, and sub-sub-chartered to sub-sub-charterers. Clause 18 of the charterparty provided that 'the Owners shall have a lien upon all cargoes, and all sub-freights for any amounts due under this Charter'. After a dispute arose between the owners and the charterers regarding the hire payable the owners sent a telex to the sub-sub-charterers purporting to exercise their right to a lien and requiring the sub-sub-charterers to pay to the owners direct any hire payable by them to the sub-charterers under the sub-sub-charter. The sub-charterers issued a summons seeking the court's determination of the question whether the hire due from them should be paid to the owners or to the sub-charterers. The sub-charterers contended (i) that cl 18 was only intended to give a lien on sub-freights earned by a voyage charter and did not apply to sub-hire earned under a time charter, (ii) that cl 18 only created a lien over sub-freights and not over sub-sub-freights and (iii) that in any event the lien could not be enforced by the owners against the sub-charterers since it was a contractual lien and there was no privity of contract between the owners and the sub-charterers.

Held – The owners had a lien over the hire payments payable by the sub-sub-charterers, for the following reasons—

(1) On its true construction cl 18 of the charterparty gave the owners a lien on any remuneration earned by the charterers from their employment of the vessel, whether by way of voyage freight or time-charter hire and entitled the owners to intercept all sub-freight, whether or not due directly to the charterers, including sub-freights due under any sub-sub-charter (see p 1123 *h j*, p 1125 *g h*, p 1126 *a* to *c* and p 1130 *b c*, post); dictum of Lord Blackburn in *Inman Steamship Co Ltd v Bischoff* [1881–5] All ER Rep at 444 applied; *Federal Commerce and Navigation Ltd v Molena Alpha Inc, The Nanfri, The Benfri, The Lorfri* [1978] 3 All ER 1066 distinguished.

(2) The absence of privity between the owners and the sub-charterers did not prevent the owners having a lien on payments due from the sub-sub-charterers to the sub-charterers since the owners could claim as equitable assignees not only hire due under the sub-charterparty, but also the rights which the charterers themselves held as equitable assignees of hire due under the sub-sub-charterparty (see p 1128 *d e g* to *j* and p 1130 *a* to *c*, post); *Hughes v Pump House Hotel Co* [1900–3] All ER Rep 480 and dictum of Kerr J in *Federal Commerce and Navigation Ltd v Molena Alpha Inc, The Nanfri, The Benfri, The Lorfri* [1978] QB at 942 followed; *American Steel Barge Co v Chesapeake and O Coal Agency* (1902) 115 F 669 and *Jebsen v A Cargo of Hemp* (1915) 228 F 143 considered.

Notes

For the liability of charterers for payment of freight, see 43 Halsbury's Laws (4th edn) para 707, and for the assignment of freight, see ibid paras 720–722.

For the shipowners lien, see ibid paras 687–695, and for cases on the subject, see 41 Digest (Repl) 495–505, 2672–2776.

Cases referred to in judgment

Aegnoussiotis Shipping Corp of Monrovia v A/S Kristian Jebsens Rederi of Bergen, The *a*
    Aegnoussiotis [1977] 1 Lloyd's Rep 268, Digest (Cont Vol E) 546, 48 2b(i).

Aluminium Industrie Vaassen BV v Romalpa Aluminium Ltd [1976] 2 All ER 552, [1976] 1
    WLR 676, CA, Digest (Cont Vol E) 520, 1128a.

American Steel Barge Co v Chesapeake and O Coal Agency (1902) 115 F 669.

Aries Tanker Corp v Total Transport Ltd [1977] 1 All ER 398, [1977] 1 WLR 185, HL,
    Digest (Cont Vol E) 557, 3481a.   *b*

Bond Worth Ltd, Re [1979] 3 All ER 919, [1980] Ch 228, [1979] 3 WLR 629, Digest (Cont
    Vol E) 521, 1128b.

Federal Commerce and Navigation Ltd v Molena Alpha Inc, The Nanfri, The Benfri, The Lorfri
    [1978] QB 927, [1978] 3 WLR 309; rvsd [1978] 3 All ER 1066, [1978] QB 927, [1978]
    3 WLR 309, CA; affd in part [1979] 1 All ER 307, [1979] AC 757, [1978] 3 WLR 991,
    HL, Digest (Cont Vol E) 109, 3036a.   *c*

Flint v Flemyng (1830) 1 B & Ad 45, 109 ER 704, 29 Digest (Reissue) 192, 1656.

Henriksens Rederi A/S v PHZ Rolimpex, The Brede [1973] 3 All ER 589, [1974] QB 233,
    [1973] 3 WLR 556, CA, Digest (Cont Vol D) 829, 3514a.

Hughes v Pump House Hotel Co [1902] 2 KB 190, [1900–3] All ER Rep 480, CA, 8(2) Digest
    (Reissue) 521, 226.

Inman Steamship Co Ltd v Bischoff (1882) 7 App Cas 670, [1881–5] All ER Rep 440, HL, 41 *d*
    Digest (Repl) 220, 476.

Jebsen v A Cargo of Hemp (1915) 228 F 143.

Mareva Compania Naviera SA v International Bulkcarriers SA, The Mareva (1975) [1980] 1
    All ER 213, CA, Digest (Cont Vol E) 331, 79b.

Molthes Rederi Akt v Ellerman's Wilson Line Ltd [1927] 1 KB 710, [1926] All ER Rep 417,
    41 Digest (Repl) 549, 3277.   *e*

Nova (Jersey) Knit Ltd v Kammgarn Spinnerei GmbH [1977] 2 All ER 463, [1977] 1 WLR
    713, HL, 3 Digest (Reissue) 75, 389.

Paul v Birch (1743) 2 Atk 621, 26 ER 771, 41 Digest (Repl) 499, 2710.

Steelwood Carriers Inc of Monrovia, Liberia v Evimeria Compania Naviera SA of Panama, The
    Agios Giorgis [1976] 2 Lloyd's Rep 192, Digest (Cont Vol E) 546, 482c.

Wehner v Dene Steam Shipping Co [1905] 2 KB 92, 41 Digest (Repl) 277, 948.   *f*

Interpleader summons

By an interpleader summons dated 6 April 1982 Itex Itagrani Export SA (Itex) sought the
court's determination, inter alia, of the question whether the balance of hire totalling
$US101,467 plus interest, paid into a joint bank deposit account pursuant to a consent
order dated 7 May 1982, and which was due and outstanding from Itex under a sub-sub-
charterparty between Itex and the defendants, Latin American Shipping Corp (LAMSCO), *g*
made on 30 July 1981 on the New York Produce Exchange form in respect of the vessel
Cebu was the property of the defendants or of the plaintiffs, Care Shipping Corp (the
owners). The plaintiffs, who as owners of the vessel had chartered it to Naviera Tolteca
on the same form, who had in turn sub-chartered it to the defendants also on the New
York Produce Exchange form, claimed a lien over the balance of hire pursuant to cl 18
of the head charterparty, which gave them 'a lien upon all cargoes, and all sub-freights *h*
for any amounts due under this Charter', following a dispute between the owners and
Naviera Tolteca as to the correct hire payable under the head charter. The facts are set out
in the judgment.

Bernard Eder for the owners.
Richard Siberry for LAMSCO.   *j*

Cur adv vult

10 November. The following judgment was delivered.

LLOYD J. In this case I have to consider the nature and extent of the shipowners

contractual line on sub-freights under cl 18 of the New York Produce Exchange form of
a time charter. There is a similar, though not identical, provision in cl 18 of the Baltime
charter. The question was described by Roskill LJ in *Mareva Compania Naviera SA v
International Bulkcarriers SA, The Mareva* (1975) [1980] 1 All ER 213 as one that had long
been a controversial matter. The point now arises directly for decision. It has been very
well argued on both sides.

b The plaintiffs are Care Shipping Corp. They are the owners of the Cebu. They
chartered her to Naviera Tolteca under a charter in New York Produce Exchange form
dated 18 October 1979 for what was described as a time-chartered trip lasting 17 to 20
months followed by a second period of 20 to 24 months, presumably at charterer's
option. She was delivered on 22 November 1979. The charterers had an express liberty
to sublet.

c By a second charter dated 3 March 1980, also on New York Produce Exchange form,
Naviera Tolteca sub-chartered the vessel to Latin American Shipping Corp, or, as I shall
refer to them, LAMSCO. The terms and conditions of the two charters are identical,
including the rate of freight. The only difference is that delivery under the sub-charter
did not take place until 29 March, 1980.

d By a third charter dated 3 July 1981, also on New York Produce Exchange form,
LAMSCO sub-sub-chartered the vessel to Itex Itagrani Export SA (Itex) for the period of
one time-chartered trip from Portland, Oregon, to Bandar Abbas with a cargo of grain.

Disputes arose between the owners and the head charterers, Naviera Tolteca. Those
disputes are the subject of current arbitration proceedings. The owners claim that at least
$US263,306 is due to them by way of unpaid hire, and possibly as much as $US1m.
Naviera Tolteca deny liability.

e On 25 September 1981 the owners sent a telex to Itex purporting to exercise their lien
under cl 18 of the head charter. They required Itex to pay them any hire which might
be due from Itex to LAMSCO under the sub-sub-charter. Very much later, they
purported to exercise a similar lien on any hire which might be due from LAMSCO to
Naviera Tolteca.

Itex, faced with this demand, wisely interpleaded. On 19 May 1982 Parker J ordered
that an issue be tried whether the balance of hire due under the sub-sub-charter belonged
f to LAMSCO or the owners.

The vessel was redelivered by Itex to LAMSCO on 17 October 1981. According to the
provisional final hire statement the sum then due to LAMSCO was $US101,467, and it is
that fund which has been paid into a joint bank account awaiting the outcome of these
proceedings.

If, in the arbitration, the owners fail against Naviera Tolteca, then it is conceded by
g counsel for the owners that their claim against the fund must also fail. In that event the
dispute in these proceedings would have proved academic. I inquired why these
proceedings could not wait. I was told, and I accept, that the exigencies of cash flow are
such that both parties wish to have the issue determined as soon as possible.

The owners' case is very simple. Clause 18 of the head charter provides—

h 'That the Owners shall have a lien upon all cargoes, and all sub-freights for any
amounts due under this Charter, including General Average contributions . . .'

According to the owners, these words mean what they say. They give the owners a
contractual lien on *all* sub-freights including sub-sub-freights due from Itex to LAMSCO.
Whatever be the correct legal analysis of the owners' contractual lien (a question to which
I shall have to return later), counsel submits that the intention of cl 18 is clear, and covers
j the present case.

Counsel for LAMSCO takes two main points. First, he submits that the lien is a lien
on sub-*freights*. In the present case what was due from Itex to LAMSCO was not freight,
but hire. Second, he submits that when cl 18 refers to sub-freights it means sub-freights,
ie freights due from LAMSCO to Naviera Tolteca, and not sub-sub-freights, ie freights
due from Itex to LAMSCO. Thus, counsel concedes, subject only to his first point, that
the owners are entitled to intercept hire payable by LAMSCO to Naviera Tolteca. But he

submits that nothing in the language of cl 18 entitles the owners to intercept hire payable by Itex to LAMSCO. Nor, if the language did purport to allow interception at that stage, would it be effective to produce that result.

Since it is agreed for the purpose of these proceedings that, if anything is due from Naviera Tolteca to the owners, then an equivalent sum is due from LAMSCO to Naviera Tolteca, and since it is conceded (subject to counsel for LAMSCO's first point) that the owners can intercept hire between LAMSCO and Naviera Tolteca, it may be thought pointless to investigate whether hire can be intercepted higher up the chain.

Once again I was told that it is cash flow which is all important. What matters most to these parties is the entitlement to the existing fund in the joint account. They cannot afford to wait, or at any rate do not want to wait, for the ultimate rights and wrongs to be sorted out. Moreover the right to intercept hire at the earliest possible stage could, it was said, be of crucial importance in other cases, if not in this one, should any of the intermediate parties become insolvent.

Against that background I return to the first of the two points relied on by LAMSCO. Does a contractual lien on sub-freights include a lien on sub-time charter hire? I doubt whether counsel for LAMSCO would have thought the point arguable but for the recent decision of the Court of Appeal in *Federal Commerce and Navigation Ltd v Molena Alpha Inc, The Nanfri, The Benfri, The Lorfri* [1978] 3 All ER 1066, [1978] QB 927.

I accept, of course, that freight in the strict sense means bill of lading freight or freight earned under a voyage charter.

But even in the nineteenth century the word 'freight' was frequently used in a wider sense to include what was called 'time freight' or 'time-chartered freight'. In other words, it covered any form of remuneration derived from the employment of a vessel. In *Inman Steamship Co Ltd v Bischoff* (1882) 7 App Cas 670 at 678; cf [1881–5] All ER Rep 440 at 444, where it was held that in a marine insurance context, a policy on freight covered loss of hire under a time charter, Lord Blackburn said:

'The construction of the policy remains that the underwriters are to make good any loss occasioned to the subject-matter of the insurance in this policy described as "freight outstanding". "Freight," says Lord Tenterden (*Flint* v. *Flemyng* ((1830) 1 B & Ad 45 at 48, 109 ER 704 at 705)), "as used in the policy of insurance, imports the benefit derived from the employment of the ship;" so that description covers the monthly hire of the ship for time.'

In the twentieth century there has been a progressive tendency to assimilate, so far as possible, the rules relating to voyage charters and time charters. This seems to me a sensible approach, particularly since the advent and rapid growth of the time-charter trip. No doubt the time-charter trip has many advantages over the voyage charter. For one thing it avoids the hideous complexities of demurrage. But it would be an odd consequence of the charterers opting to enter into a sub-time-charter trip that the owners should inadvertently be deprived of their security on sub-freights. I would hold, following Lord Blackburn in *Inman Steamship Co Ltd v Bischoff*, that the lien on sub-freights conferred by cl 18 includes a lien on any remuneration earned by the charterers from their employment of the vessel, whether by way of voyage freight or time-chartered hire.

Does the decision of the Court of Appeal in *The Nanfri* compel me to reach a different result? One of the many questions in that case was whether the charterers could make deductions from the hire due by reason of their various alleged cross-claims. In *Henriksens Rederi A/S v PHZ Rolimpex, The Brede* [1973] 3 All ER 589, [1974] QB 233 and in *Aries Tanker Corp v Total Transport Ltd* [1977] 1 All ER 398, [1977] 1 WLR 185 it had been held that no such deductions were permissible in the case of a voyage charter. Lord Denning MR distinguished those cases in *The Nanfri* [1978] 3 All ER 1066 at 1076–1077, [1978] QB 927 at 973) in the following passage:

'At one time it was common to describe the sums payable under a time

charterparty as "freight". Such description is to be found used by judges and
a textbook writers of great distinction. But in modern times a change has come about.
The payments due under a time charter are usually now described as "hire" and
those under a voyage charter as "freight". This change of language corresponds, I
believe, to a recognition that the two things are different. "Freight" is payable for
carrying a quantity of cargo from one place to another. "Hire" is payable for the
right to use a vessel for a specified period of time, irrespective of whether the
b charterer chooses to use it for carrying cargo or lays it up, out of use. Every time
charter contains clauses which are quite inappropriate to a voyage charter, such as
the off-hire clause and the withdrawal clause. So different are the two concepts that
I do not think the law as to "freight" can be applied indiscriminately to "hire". In
particular the special rule of English law whereby "freight" must be paid in full
(without deductions for short delivery or cargo damage) cannot be applied
c automatically to time charter "hire". Nor is there any authority which says that it
must. It would be a mistake to suppose that the House of Lords had time charter
hire and so forth in mind when they decided *Aries Tanker Corp v Total Transport Ltd*
or *Nova (Jersey) Knit Ltd v Kammgarn Spinnerei GmbH* [1977] 2 All ER 463, [1977] 1
WLR 713, or that anything said in those cases can bind this court. Many of us, I
know, in the past have assumed that the rule as to "freight" does apply; and some
d judges have said so. But now, after full argument, I am satisfied that the "freight"
rule does not apply automatically to time charter "hire"; and we have to consider
the position on principle.'

Goff LJ agreed with Lord Denning MR. Cumming-Bruce LJ took a different view. In
the House of Lords the point did not arise for decision (see [1979] 1 All ER 307 at 311–
e 312, [1979] AC 757 at 775–776 per Lord Wilberforce).
I recognise that the decision of the majority of the Court of Appeal in *The Nanfri*
provides some support for counsel for LAMSCO's argument. I accept that it goes against
the trend, noticed earlier, to assimilate so far as possible the rules relating to voyage
charters and time charters. Goff LJ in particular emphasised and relied on the distinction
between freight in the narrow sense, namely freight under a bill of lading or voyage
f charter, and freight in the wider sense which would include time-charter hire.
These are strong arguments. But it must be remembered that in *The Nanfri* the Court
of Appeal was faced with a rule relating to voyage charters which they clearly regarded
as somewhat anomalous. Goff LJ referred to the 'old rule' against deduction, or abatement,
in the case of carriage by sea. He suggested that it may have owed its origin to the need
of the master to receive freight in full at the end of a voyage, in order to pay off his crew
g and refit the ship for the return voyage. Such considerations no longer apply, or not to
the same extent. Whatever the origin of the old rule, it is now far too firmly established
to be overthrown in the case of voyage charters; but the majority of the Court of Appeal
saw no reason to extend the rule to time charters.
In *The Nanfri* there were therefore good reasons for drawing the distinction between
freight and hire. Ought those reasons to prevail here? I think not. As I have already said,
h I can see no sense in a construction which would make the owners' security depend on
whether the sub-charter is a voyage charter or a time-charter trip. In my view the parties
must be taken to have used the word 'sub-freight' in cl 18 to cover both. This is the view
expressed tentatively by the authors of *Wilford on Time Charters* (1978) p 222. I accept
and adopt that view. I would therefore reject the first argument of counsel for LAMSCO.
Counsel's second main argument for LAMSCO is that, even if cl 18 entitles the owners
j to intercept sub-freight in the form of hire, it does not entitle them to intercept sub-sub-
freights. The argument has two aspects. First, he submits that sub-freight does not
include sub-sub-freight as a matter of language. Second, he submits that there is no
privity of contract between the owners and LAMSCO. Accordingly, whatever may have
been intended between the owners and Naviera Tolteca, there is no way in which the
owners can attach hire due from Itex to LAMSCO. The contract between the owners and

Naviera Tolteca cannot impose a burden on LAMSCO, any more than the contract between Itex and LAMSCO can confer a benefit on the owners.

As for the meaning of sub-freights, I would hold that it includes *all* sub-freights, whether or not due to the head charterers direct. In *Aegnoussiotis Shipping Corp of Monrovia v A/S Kristian Jebsens Rederi of Bergen, The Aegnoussiotis* [1977] 1 Lloyd's Rep 268 Donaldson J held that 'all cargoes' in cl 18 'means what it says', ie all cargoes whether or not belonging to the charterers. True, he did not have in mind cargo carried under a sub-sub-charter. But if 'all cargoes means what it says' it seems to me that it must also, as a matter of language, include such cargoes. By the same token all sub-freights must include sub-freights due not only under the sub-charter, but also the sub-sub-charter. It is true that Mocatta J reached a different conclusion in *Steelwood Carriers Inc of Monrovia, Liberia v Evimeria Compania Naviera SA of Panama, The Agios Giorgis* [1976] 2 Lloyd's Rep 192. But I prefer the view of Donaldson J. It is more in accordance with the law as stated by Lord Hardwicke LC as long ago as 1743 in *Paul v Birch* 2 Atk 621, 26 ER 771. In that case a vessel was chartered at the rate of £48 a month. The charterers arranged for certain merchants to ship goods at the rate of £9 per ton. The charterers then went bankrupt. It was held that the plaintiff had a specific lien on the goods even though they did not belong to the charterers. True, he could not recover more than the freight due on those goods, ie £9 per ton. He could not recover the difference between £9 per ton and £48 a month; but that is a different point.

Finally, on this aspect of the argument, counsel for LAMSCO referred me to the corresponding clause in the Baltime form. The language, though similar, is different in one important respect. Clause 18 of the Baltime form provides:

> 'The Owners to have a lien upon all cargoes and sub-freights *belonging to the Time-Charterers* and any Bill of Lading freight for all claims under this Charter . . .' (My emphasis.)

Under a clause in that form it is clear that there is no lien on cargoes or sub-freights which do not 'belong to the charterers'. Is there any ground for construing cl 18 of the New York Produce Exchange form so as to produce the same result? I think not. I dislike narrow distinctions between different forms of charter as much as anyone. But here the different language justifies different conclusions. The words 'belonging to the Time-Charterers' are not to be found in the early forms of Baltime charter. They must have been introduced at some stage, perhaps in order to clear up what was thought to be an ambiguity. It would not be legitimate for me to imply those additional words in the New York Produce Exchange form. Certainly they are not necessary to give the clause business efficacy. The Baltime charter is often thought of as a form of contract which is particularly favourable to owners. But in this instance it seems less favourable to owners than the New York Produce Exchange form.

The second aspect of the argument is that, whatever may have been the intention, there is no way in which the owners can lawfully intercept sub-sub-freights due from Itex to LAMSCO. The legal machinery is simply not there.

The true explanation for the contractual lien on sub-freights has been the subject of much speculation, but there is little, if any, direct authority on the point.

There is, of course, no difficulty in relation to the common law lien for freight. It requires no explanation. The owners can exercise their lien for freight due on delivery independently of contract, though in practice there is usually a contract contained in or evidenced by the bill of lading.

Similarly, there is no difficulty where the master signs a bill of lading on behalf of the owners, even though there are one or more intervening charterers. In such a case the owner can exercise a 'lien' for charterparty freight by virtue of the contract between the owners and receivers contained in the bill of lading. I put 'lien' in inverted commas for two reasons: first, because ordinarily, at any rate, a lien in the common law sense is exercisable over goods or documents of another. It is difficult to envisage a lien in that sense over money due. A similar problem arises in relation to the so-called bankers lien: see *Paget on the Law of Banking* (8th edn, 1972) p 504.

Second, if the bill of lading is in truth a contract between the receivers and the owners,
a then lien is, in any event, the wrong concept. As Greer J pointed out in *Molthes Rederi Akt
v Ellerman's Wilson Line, Ltd* [1927] 1 KB 710 at 717, [1926] All ER Rep 417 at 421, you
cannot have a lien on your own property. The lien clause in the charterparty is needed to
give the owners a lien in those cases where the bill of lading freight is not due to the
owners but to the charterers, or where there is no bill of lading. Greer J said:

b   'It seems a misuse of words to say that a shipowner has a lien on the debt due to
       him under the contract made with him by the bill of lading.'

In passing I should say that it does not appear in the present case whether any bills of
lading ever came into existence, and if so whether they constituted contracts with the
owners or with Itex. Certainly there has been no attempt to exercise any lien on any bill
of lading freight.
c   The difficulty in the present case lies in the fact that the owners are seeking to claim
the benefit of a contractual lien against LAMSCO, with whom they have no contract. It
is a difficulty which was foreseen by Channell J in *Wehner v Dene Steam Shipping Co* [1905]
2 KB 92 at 98, where he said:

d   'In ordinary cases, where the charterparty does not amount to a demise of the
       ship, and where possession of the ship is not given up to the charterer, the rule is
       that the contract contained in the bill of lading is made, not with the charterer, but
       with the owner, and that will, I think, explain away and accounts for all the
       difficulties which would otherwise arise as to the existence of the shipowner's lien.
       When there is a sub-charterparty there is no direct contract between the sub-
       charterer and the owner, and if the contract in the bill of lading were made, not
       with the owner, but with the sub-charterer, how is the shipowner's lien to be
e   accounted for as against the holder of the bill of lading? It would be very difficult to
       deal with the question upon any logical or intelligible footing unless one starts with
       the proposition that the bill of lading contract is made, as it appears upon its face to
       be made, with the shipowner.'

It was unnecessary for Channell J to decide what happens in a case where there is no
f privity of contract between the owners and the sub-charterers. So far as I am aware, this
is the first case in which that question has arisen directly for decision.
       Counsel were agreed that in a simple three-party case, where owners are given a lien
on sub-freights, the owners can give notice to the sub-charterers, thereby compelling the
sub-charterers to pay freight to the owners, and not to the charterers. It was common
ground that the mechanism which produces this result is an equitable assignment of
g freight due under the sub-charter. There is some authority to support this view. In *The
Nanfri* [1978] QB 927 at 942, at first instance, Kerr J said:

       'I think that in the face of all these considerations the lien clause must give way
       and be construed restrictively. To do so does not by any means deprive it of all
       efficacy. As between the owners and charterers it still operates as something in the
       nature of an equitable assignment which can be perfected by giving the proper
h   notices if and when the charterers are in default in the payment of some sum due to
       the owners.'

When that case reached the House of Lords, Lord Russell said ([1979] 1 All ER 307 at
318, [1979] AC 757 at 784):

j   'The fact that cl 18 refers expressly to bill of lading freights appears to me to add
       nothing to the lien conferred by that clause on sub-freights belonging to the
       charterers, and serves only to distract the mind from the true scope of the lien. The
       lien operates as an equitable charge on what is due from the shippers to the
       charterers, and in order to be effective requires an ability to intercept the sub-freight
       (by notice of claim) before it is paid by shipper to charterer.'

In passing, I should mention that the lien clause in that case was in the Baltime form,

which explains the reference to bill of lading freights. In addition there is the passage in
Roskill LJ's judgment in *Mareva Compania Naviera SA v International Bulkcarriers SA* *a*
(1975) [1980] 1 All ER 213 at 216, where he refers to the 'legal or perhaps equitable right
which the shipowners may be entitled to have protected by the court'.

Although authority is slender, it was, as I say, common ground that in a simple three-
party case the so-called lien on sub-freights gives the owners the right to claim to be paid
sub-freights as equitable assignee. It would seem to me to follow (though this was not
conceded) that the owners can, if necessary, enforce that claim by exercising a lien on the *b*
cargo itself.

The core of the present dispute is whether the same reasoning can be applied to a four-
party case. Counsel for LAMSCO submits that it cannot. Naviera Tolteca could have
claimed sub-freights due from Itex to LAMSCO as equitable assignee. The owners can
still, if they wish, claim sub-freights due from LAMSCO to Naviera Tolteca as equitable
assignee. But there is no way of linking the two assignments. There is no way in which *c*
the owners can, as it were, bridge the gap and claim as assignee of sub-freights due from
Itex.

I do not accept counsel's argument. The real question, as it seems to me, is whether
Naviera Tolteca was capable of assigning to the owners the right which it had itself
received by way of equitable assignment from LAMSCO, and in particular the right to
claim freight due from Itex. So stated, I cannot see why the answer should not be Yes. *d*
Counsel for LAMSCO insisted that Naviera Tolteca's right to receive freight due from
Itex was only by way of security for the payment of sums due from LAMSCO, and could
not therefore be the subject of an assignment by Naviera Tolteca to the owners. I do not
agree. The fact that an assignment is by way of security does not prevent it being an
absolute assignment for the purpose of s 136 of the Law of Property Act 1925: see *Hughes
v Pump House Hotel Co* [1902] 2 KB 190 at 194–195; cf [1900–3] All ER Rep 480 at 482, *e*
where Mathew LJ, giving the leading judgment of the Court of Appeal, said:

> 'The learned judge appears to have been of opinion that the assignment was not
> absolute, but purported to be by way of charge only, because the object was that it
> should be a continuing security for such amount as might from time to time be due
> from the assignor to the assignees. But, if that were the true criterion, it might *f*
> equally well be argued that a mortgage is not an absolute assignment, because under
> a mortgage it may become necessary to take an account in order to ascertain how
> much is due; but, though a mortgage is only a security for the amount which may
> be due, it is nevertheless an absolute assignment because the whole right of the
> mortgagor in the estate passes to the mortgagee.'

So here, the equitable assignment by LAMSCO to Naviera Tolteca was effective to *g*
transfer to Naviera Tolteca the whole right of LAMSCO to receive freight due from Itex,
so long as there was anything due from LAMSCO to Naviera Tolteca. It seems to me that
Naviera Tolteca's right to receive that freight is a chose in action, like any other chose in
action, and equally capable as such of being assigned by Naviera Tolteca to the owners.
That is, as I think, precisely what happened here. On the true construction of cl 18 I
would hold that Naviera Tolteca has assigned to the owners by way of equitable *h*
assignment, not only sub-freights due to it as charterers, but also any sub-freights due
under any sub-sub-charter of which it is equitable assignee. In my view that is the clear
intention of the parties to be derived from the language they have used in cl 18. I can see
no reason why the law should not give effect to that intention by virtue of a chain of
equitable assignments such as I have attempted to describe.

The legal analysis might be different if the true nature of the lien on sub-freights were *j*
that it takes effect as an equitable charge only, as Lord Russell thought, and not as an
equitable assignment, or what is sometimes referred to as an equitable lien. But I need
not investigate that approach, since it was common ground between the parties before
me that in an ordinary three-party case the lien takes effect as an equitable assignment. I
inquired of counsel whether they wished to address any argument on the line of cases

following *Aluminium Industrie Vaassen BV v Romalpa Aluminium Ltd* [1976] 2 All ER 552,
a   [1976] 1 WLR 676. It seems to me that the decision of Slade J in *Re Bond Worth Ltd* [1979]
3 All ER 919, [1980] Ch 228, and in particular his comprehensive discussion of equitable
charges (see [1979] 3 All ER 919 at 936–955, [1980] Ch 228 at 245–268), might be very
relevant if this case were to go higher. But counsel did not take up my suggestion and it
does not seem right that I should express any view on that line of cases without having
had the benefit of hearing argument.

b   There is, as I have said, no English authority in which it has been held that an owner
can exercise a lien on freights under a sub-sub-charter. But there is one American
authority, *Jebsen v A Cargo of Hemp* (1915) 228 F 143, a decision of the District Court in
Massachussetts. In that case the shipowner, whom I shall refer to for simplicity as A,
chartered the vessel to B who sub-chartered to C. The vessel loaded a cargo of hemp
under a bill of lading on C's form. The hemp was consigned to D, and the freight under
c   the bill of lading was payable on delivery. C paid hire due under the sub-charter to B.
But B failed to pay hire due under the head charter to A. A thereupon sought to exercise
a lien on the bill of lading freight due from D to C. The owners' argument was
summarised by the district judge as follows (at 146):

d   'In effect he contends that he is entitled to have his loss, from the charterer's
        failure to pay, made good at the expense of the subcharterer; in other words, that
        under the terms of the charter and subcharter his right to the freight money in
        question is superior to that of [C].'

That is precisely the same argument as is advanced in the present case. The only difference
in the present case is that C, ie LAMSCO, has not paid B, ie Naviera Tolteca, or not paid
in full. That makes the present case stronger on the merits.

It was held in *Jebsen v A Cargo of Hemp*, following *Paul v Birch* (1743) 2 Atk 621, 26 ER
e   771, and an earlier United States decision of the First Circuit Court of Appeals in *American
Steel Barge Co v Chesapeake and O Coal Agency* (1902) 115 F 669 that A's lien, as shipowner,
was not confined to cargo shipped by B, and that A could recover freight due under the
bill of lading, notwithstanding C had paid B. The district judge said (at 148)—

f   '[C] must be deemed to have taken with notice of and subject to the reservation
        of the lien on the cargo for the charter money due to the owner, [A]; and the
        insolvency of [B], far from divesting [A] of the lien and entitling [C] by subrogation
        or otherwise to the benefit of it, furnishes occasion for resort by [A] to the security
        afforded by the lien which he expressly reserved, and which it is not contended that
        he has ever done anything to waive.'

The court went on to hold that payment by C to B did not create any equity in C's favour.
g   C knew of the existence of the head charter and was bound to inquire as to its terms: 'The
payment by [C] to [B] must, I think, be deemed to have been made at its risk.' Counsel
for LAMSCO criticised *Jebsen v A Cargo of Hemp* in so far as it held that C was bound to
inquire as to the terms of the head charter. This looks like the doctrine of constructive
notice, a doctrine which English courts are loath to apply in commercial cases. Be that as
it may, I do not find the decision of any great assistance. Although the court reached the
h   same conclusion as I have done, there is little or no discussion of the legal problems
involved.

In the earlier case of *American Steel Barge Co v Chesapeake and O Coal Agency* the decision
was put on the basis of subrogation. The Circuit Court of Appeals held (at 674):

j   'At the proper time, and under the proper circumstances, a libelant holding a lien
        on subfreight becomes subrogated to all the remedies of the charterer, which
        includes a proceeding in personam against the holder of the bill of lading, or against
        the cargo in the event the lien for freight has not been lost; but also, like the
        charterer, he could not properly institute this proceeding until there had been
        default in payment of the freight, unless under very peculiar circumstances, which
        do not arise in the case at bar.'

I confess that I do not fully understand the reference to subrogation in this context. The facts are too far removed from any which would fit our ordinary doctrine of *a* subrogation, based, as it is, on an underlying contract of indemnity. Counsel for the owners advanced an argument on what he called subrogation in a loose sense. But I prefer to put my decision, as already mentioned, on the basis of a chain of equitable assignments.

For the reasons I have given I reject both arguments of counsel for LAMSCO. I am glad to have reached the conclusion I have, for otherwise an unscrupulous charterer could *b* always defeat the owners' lien on sub-freights by the simple device of arranging an in-house charter at the same rate of hire. If the cargo were then carried on sub-charterers' bills of lading, the owners would have no security at all. The only way in which the owners could avoid that result would be by prohibiting the charterers from subletting. But the right to sublet is an essential requirement in the ordinary course of business. I hasten to add that there is no suggestion here that the charterers were adopting a device, *c* even though the charter and the sub-charter were the same rate of freight.

It follows, from the reasons I have given, that I would answer the question posed in the issue in favour of the owners.

Order accordingly. Leave to appeal.

d

Solicitors: *Holman Fenwick & Willan* (for the owners); *Coward Chance* (for LAMSCO).

K Mydeen Esq   Barrister.

e

Cheall v Association of Professional, Executive, Clerical and Computer Staff

HOUSE OF LORDS   *f*
LORD DIPLOCK, LORD EDMUND-DAVIES, LORD FRASER OF TULLYBELTON, LORD BRANDON OF OAKBROOK AND LORD TEMPLEMAN
21, 22 FEBRUARY, 24 MARCH 1983

Trade union – Membership – Termination of membership – No-poaching agreement between unions – Bridlington principles – Admission by union to membership of person recently belonging *g* *to another union – Failure of new union to inquire of former union if it objected to member joining new union – TUC disputes committee holding new union to be in breach of Bridlington principles and requiring new union to expel new member – Member concerned not allowed to make personal representations to disputes committee – Union's executive committee purporting to terminate membership without giving member opportunity to be heard – Committee terminating membership* *h* *under union rule giving it discretion to terminate membership where necessary to comply with decision of TUC disputes committee – Wether termination of membership valid – Whether disputes committee and union's executive committee acting in breach of rules of natural justice.*

The plaintiff was a member of a trade union (the first union) until May 1974, when he resigned because he was dissatisfied with the conduct of its affairs. He believed that having duly resigned from the first union he was free to join another union of his choice *j* and accordingly applied to join a rival union (the second union). The second union was aware of the plaintiff's recent membership of the first union and that under the code of conduct regulating inter-union relations (the Bridlington principles) it was required, before it accepted the plaintiff as a member, to inquire of the first union whether it objected to the plaintiff joining the second union. However, the second union failed to make any such inquiry before admitting the plaintiff to membership. The first union

lodged a complaint with the Trades Union Congress (the TUC) that the second union had
a acted in breach of the Bridlington principles. The TUC set up a disputes committee to
hear the complaint. The plaintiff, who had become an official of the second union,
attended the hearing as a member of the second union's team but was not regarded by
the committee as a party in his own right and for all practical purposes was not given an
opportunity to be heard on his own behalf, the committee taking the view that the only
parties to the dispute were the two unions. Having heard submissions from both unions
b the committee ruled in June 1977 that the second union had breached the Bridlington
principles, that it should exclude the plaintiff from its membership and that it should
advise him to rejoin the first union. On 30 June 1978 the executive committee of the
second union, without giving the plaintiff an opportunity to make representations,
purported to give him six weeks' notice terminating his membership of the union,
pursuant to r 14*ᵈ* of its rules under which the executive committee was empowered to
c terminate the membership of a member if that was 'necessary, in order to comply with a
decision' of a TUC disputes committee. The plaintiff brought an action against the second
union seeking a declaration that the notice was invalid and of no effect, and an injunction
restraining the union from asserting the validity of the notice. The judge dismissed the
action on the ground that the second union was entitled to terminate the plaintiff's
membership under r 14. On appeal by the plaintiff the Court of Appeal held that the
d notice terminating the plaintiff's membership was invalid. On appeal by the second
union the questions arose (i) whether on the construction of the union's rules, in
particular r 14, the second union was entitled to terminate the plaintiff's contract of
membership, (ii) if so, whether the second union was only entitled to terminate the
plaintiff's membership under r 14 for reasonable cause and if he had been accorded
natural justice at the disputes committee hearing of the TUC, and (iii) whether r 14 and
e the associated Bridlington principles were contrary to public policy.

Held – The second union's appeal would be allowed for the following reasons—
(1) On the plain and unambiguous construction of r 14 it was 'necessary' for the
second union to terminate the plaintiff's membership because that was the only way in
which the union could comply with the TUC disputes committee's decision. Furthermore,
f in order to rely on the principle that a party to a contract was not permitted to take
advantage of his own breach of duty the duty had to be one that was owed to the other
party under the contract; a breach of duty, whether contractual or non-contractual, owed
to a stranger to the contract did not suffice. It followed that the second union could rely
on r 14 to exclude the plaintiff from its membership and was entitled to do so even
though it had acted in conscious and deliberate breach of the Bridlington principles, since
g the plaintiff was not a party to those principles (see p 1133 *j*, p 1135 *a b* and p 1136 *f* to *j*,
post); *New Zealand Shipping Co Ltd v Société des Ateliers et Chantiers de France* [1918–19] All
ER Rep 552 explained.
(2) Although decisions that resolved disputes between parties, whether by litigation
or some other dispute-resolving process, might have consequences which affected persons
who were not parties to the dispute, the legal concept of natural justice did not require
h that such persons have the right to be heard by the decision-making tribunal before the
decision was reached. Accordingly, because the plaintiff was not a party to the disputes
committee's hearing nor was his conduct in issue before it the law did not require that
he be accorded a hearing at the disputes committee hearing (see p 1134 *h*, p 1135 *d* to *h*
and p 1136 *f* to *j*, post).
(3) Since freedom of association could only be mutual it was not open to an individual
j to claim that he had a right to associate with other individuals if they were not willing to
associate with him. The plaintiff could not therefore claim that the Bridlington principles
restricted his right to join and be a member of the union of his choice, since the union of
his choice, ie the second union as represented by the executive council, was not willing
to have the plaintiff as a member. Furthermore, there was no existing rule of public
policy which prevented trade unions from entering into arrangements such as the

---

a Rule 14 is set out at p 1133 *h*, post

Bridlington principles which they considered to be in the best interests of their members
in promoting order in industrial relations and enhancing their members' bargaining *a*
power with their employers, nor was it a permissible exercise of the court's power to
create a new rule of public policy to that effect (see p 1136 *c* to *j*, post).

Decision of the Court of Appeal [1982] 3 All ER 855 reversed.

Notes

For the rules of natural justice, see 1 Halsbury's Laws (4th edn) paras 64–65. *b*

For the rules of a trade union in regard to membership and expulsion, see 38 Halsbury's
Laws (3rd edn) 334–357, paras 612–615, and for cases on the subject, see 45 Digest (Repl)
545–546, *1230–1238*.

Cases referred to in opinions

Edwards v Society of Graphical and Allied Trades [1970] 3 All ER 689, [1971] Ch 354, *c*
[1970] 3 WLR 713, CA, 17 Digest (Reissue) 128, *273*.
New Zealand Shipping Co Ltd v Société des Ateliers et Chantiers de France [1919] AC 1, [1918–
19] All ER Rep 552, HL, 7 Digest (Reissue) 324, *2210*.

Appeal

The Association of Professional, Executive, Clerical and Computer Staff (APEX) appealed *d*
with leave of the Court of Appeal against the decision of the Court of Appeal (Lord
Denning MR, Slade LJ, Donaldson LJ dissenting) ([1982] 3 All ER 855, [1983] QB 126)
on 18 June 1982 allowing the appeal of Ernest Dennis Cheall, the respondent, against the
judgment of Bingham J ([1982] 3 All ER 855) dated 24 November 1981 and granting
the respondent a declaration in effect that the notice from APEX to the respondent
contained in a letter dated 30 June 1978 purporting to terminate his membership of *e*
APEX was invalid and of no effect. The facts are set out in the opinion of Lord Diplock.

Mark O Saville QC, Frederic Reynold QC and *Cherie Booth* for APEX.
George Newman QC and *Stephen Auld* for Mr Cheall.

Their Lordships took time for consideration. *f*

24 March. The following opinions were delivered.

LORD DIPLOCK. My Lords, the facts of this case, which has given rise to acute
conflict of judicial opinion in the courts below, are set out in considerable detail in the
judgment of Bingham J ([1982] 3 All ER 855). In the action the respondent, Cheall, *g*
sought a declaration that a letter dated 30 June 1978 addressed to him by the appellants,
APEX, the trade union of which he had been a member for the last four years, and
purporting to give him six weeks' notice terminating his membership, was invalid and
of no effect. Bingham J held the notice to be valid and effective. On appeal to the Court
of Appeal ([1982] 3 All ER 855, [1983] QB 126), Donaldson LJ in a dissenting judgment
agreed with Bingham J; but the majority (Lord Denning MR and Slade LJ), although not *h*
both for the same reasons, allowed the appeal and granted Cheall the declaration that he
sought.

For the purpose of disposing of the propositions of law, some of them far-reaching,
that have been advanced on Cheall's behalf at all three stages of this litigation, the
essential facts can be stated in summary form as follows, leaving the curious reader to
expand the summary if he so wishes by reference to the judgment of Bingham J. *j*

In the early 1970s Cheall was employed at the Vauxhall motor works at Luton as a
security officer. He was a member of the Association of Clerical, Technical and
Supervisory Staffs (ACTSS), a trade union which is itself part of the conglomerate trade
union, the Transport and General Workers' Union (the TGWU). Cheall was the secretary
of the local branch of ACTSS at the Vauxhall works. He became disenchanted with the

support that the branch was receiving from ACTSS and on 6 May 1974, together with a
a number of others, he resigned his membership of ACTSS. On 29 May 1974 he applied
to APEX to become a member of that trade union: APEX, who knew full well that Cheall
had until very recently been a member of ACTSS, accepted his application and he became
a member of APEX. By the express terms of his application form he agreed to be bound
by its rules.

In accepting Cheall into membership without first inquiring of ACTSS whether it
b objected, APEX was acting in breach of a code of conduct governing relations between
trade unions that are members of the Trades Union Congress (the TUC) that is known as
the Bridlington principles and is accepted as morally binding on constituent unions,
among which both ACTSS and APEX are included. Complaints by one trade union of
breaches of Bridlington principles which involve what is referred to as the 'poaching' of
its members by another union, if not settled by amicable agreement between the unions
c concerned, are referred to a disputes committee which is empowered to make an award.
ACTSS objected to APEX having poached Cheall and some 11 other former members of
ACTSS employed at the Vauxhall works; and after some considerable delay, in February
1976 the TGWU made a formal complaint to the TUC. The complaint came on for
hearing before a disputes committee on 17 May 1977. Cheall attended that hearing solely
for the purpose of assisting the representative of APEX who was presenting APEX's case,
d and not for the purpose of making representations on his own behalf so far as his personal
interests might differ from those of APEX. He was not invited, nor would he have been
permitted by the disputes committee, to do so.

On 20 June 1977 the disputes committee issued its findings and award, of which the
relevant part is—

> *e*   'that APEX should have made inquiries of the TGWU and by not doing so APEX
>   therefore acted in breach of Principle 2 of the TUC Disputes Principles and
>   Procedures. The Disputes Committee AWARD that APEX should exclude the eleven
>   named individuals and advise them to rejoin the TGWU.'

Non-compliance with this award would have exposed APEX to sanctions, including
suspension from membership of the TUC and the ultimate sanction of expulsion. These
f are risks which the executive council of APEX might reasonably think it would be
contrary to the interests of the general body of their members to run.

An award of a disputes committee on a poaching complaint which is upheld, has for
many years been in the standard terms adopted in the award in the instant case: the
offending union is required to exclude the poached members from membership and to
advise them to rejoin their former union. In order to enable it to comply with such an
g award APEX, like the great majority of trade unions that are members of the TUC, have
adopted a model rule recommended by that body in 1956 which forms r 14 of the rules
of APEX by which Cheall had agreed to be bound. It reads as follows:

> *h*   '14. *Decisions of T.U.C. Disputes Committee.*—Notwithstanding anything in these
>   rules the Executive Council may, by giving six weeks' notice in writing, terminate
>   the membership of any member, if necessary, in order to comply with a decision of
>   the Disputes Committee of the Trades Union Congress.'

It was under this rule that APEX terminated Cheall's membership.

The construction of the rule

My Lords, with great respect to Slade LJ who alone thought otherwise, the meaning of
j this rule as a matter of construction and its applicability to Cheall after the award of the
disputes committee of 20 June 1977 appear to me to be clear beyond argument. There
had been a decision of the disputes committee of the TUC; the only way in which APEX
could comply with it was by terminating Cheall's membership; it was therefore necessary
to do so in order to comply with that decision. There is in my view no room for
ambiguity about it.

Slade LJ, although he did refer to it 'as a matter of construction of the rule', relied on a principle that he considered could be extracted from the speeches in this House in *New a Zealand Shipping Co Ltd v Société des Ateliers et Chantiers de France* [1919] AC 1, [1918–19] All ER Rep 552, viz that—

> 'APEX cannot be heard to say that expulsion of Mr Cheall is "necessary in order to comply with a decision of the Disputes Committee of the Trades Union Congress" within the meaning of the rule, in a case such as the present where such necessity as there may be has arisen as a direct result of the conscious and deliberate breach by *b* APEX of the Bridlington principles in admitting him to memberhip.'

(See [1982] 3 All ER 855 at 896, [1983] QB 126 at 159.)

But this, with respect, is not construction; 'cannot be heard to say' is the language of estoppel; what Slade LJ is really saying is that there is some rule of law that prevents APEX from relying on r 14 as against Cheall. To the suggested rule of law I accordingly *c* now turn.

The supposed rule of law

My Lords, the *New Zealand Shipping* case, from which, it is contended, the supposed rule of law can be extracted, was an appeal on a case stated by an umpire in an arbitration on a phrase in a shipbuilding contract, 'thereupon this contract shall become void', where *d* the events to the occurrence of which 'thereupon' referred were of different kinds; some of them could only be brought about by some breach of the contract by the shipbuilder, others could happen without any breach of contract by either party. The umpire had found as a fact that the event relied on by the shipbuilder as bringing the clause into operation so as to render the contract void happened without any breach of the shipbuilding contract by either party, and the actual decision of this House was that the *e* shipbuilder was entitled to treat the contract as void. In the course of the speeches, which are not entirely consistent with one another, reference was made by all their Lordships to the well known rule of construction that, except in the unlikely case that the contract contains clear express provisions to the contrary, it is to be presumed that it was not the intention of the parties that either party should be entitled to rely on his own breaches of his primary obligations as bringing the contract to an end, ie as terminating any further *f* primary obligations on his part then remaining unperformed. This rule of construction, which is paralleled by the rule of law that a contracting party cannot rely on one event brought about by his own breach of contract as having terminated a contract by frustration, is often expressed in broad language as 'A man cannot be permitted to take advantage of his own wrong'. But this may be misleading if it is adopted without defining the breach of duty to which the pejorative word 'wrong' is intended to refer and *g* the person to whom the duty is owed.

The breach of duty which it is suggested disentitled APEX in the instant case to rely on r 14 as against Cheall was its duty under the Bridlington principles not to poach members from ACTSS. This duty, though moral only and not legally enforceable, it owed to ACTSS and the TGWU and, it may be, to other trade unions that are members of the TUC; but plainly it cannot have owed such duty to individual members of trade *h* unions, since only trade unions were parties to the agreement embodied in the Bridlington principles.

Since r 14 can only come into effect when there has been a breach by APEX of the duty owed by it to another trade union under the Bridlington principles, it is hopeless to argue that APEX is debarred from relying on the rule to terminate the membership of a poached member, merely because it acted in breach of the Bridlington principles in *j* poaching him. So counsel for Cheall felt constrained to introduce the concept of a distinction to be drawn between a 'conscious and deliberate' breach of the Bridlington principles and a breach that was merely inadvertent. The former, it was argued, disentitled APEX, as a matter of law, ever to rely on r 14 to terminate the membership of the person in respect of whom the conscious and deliberate breach was committed, while an inadvertent breach did entitle it to do so.

My Lords, I know of no principle of law which justifies this distinction. The *New*
a *Zealand Shipping* case, the only authority relied on for it, contains no hint that any such
distinction between deliberate and inadvertent breaches of duty is to be drawn in
applying the rule that was the subject of discussion in that case. To attract the principle,
whether it be one of construction or one of law, that a party to a contract is not permitted
to take advantage of his own breach of duty, the duty must be one that is owed to the
other party under that contract; breach of a duty whether contractual or non-contractual
b owed to a stranger to the contract does not suffice. I have no hesitation in rejecting the
argument based on the supposed rule of law.

Natural justice

It was contended on Cheall's behalf that the termination of his membership was also
void because the procedure which resulted in it constituted a denial to him of natural
justice. He was entitled, it was suggested, not merely to be present, as he was, at the
c hearing of the complaint against APEX by the disputes committee, but also to make
representations, written or oral, to the disputes committee explaining his reasons for
wishing to switch his membership from ACTSS to APEX and the consequences that an
award adverse to APEX would have on him personally.

This contention did not find favour with any of the judges in the courts below. The
d only parties to the dispute that was before the disputes committee were the trade unions
concerned. They, and they only, were entitled to make representations, written or oral,
to the committee. Decisions that resolve disputes between the parties to them, whether
by litigation or some other adversarial dispute-resolving process, often have consequences
which affect persons who are not parties to the dispute; but the legal concept of natural
justice has never been extended to give such persons as well as the parties themselves
rights to be heard by the decision-making tribunal before the decision is reached. If
e natural justice required that Cheall should be entitled to be heard, there could be no
stopping there; any other member of either union who thought he would be adversely
affected by the decision, if it went one way or the other, would have a similar right to be
heard. To claim that this is a requirement of 'fair play in action' (to borrow Sachs LJ's
description of natural justice in *Edwards v Society of Graphical and Allied Trades* [1970] 3
f All ER 689 at 701, [1971] Ch 354 at 382) would be little short of ludicrous.

Alternatively, though rather more mutedly, it was submitted that Cheall was entitled
to be heard by the executive council of APEX before they decided to comply with the
award, which was already more than one year old, by giving him notice of termination
of his membership under r 14. In his judgment Bingham J set out what had in fact
occurred before the executive council reached its decision to act under r 14 and Cheall's
own knowledge of it. That, in the judge's view, made it inevitable that the only way in
g which APEX could fulfil its duty to act in the best interests of its members as a whole was
by complying with the award of the disputes committee. His conclusion was that, in the
circumstances that he recounts, there was no legal obligation on APEX to give Cheall
prior notice of their decision or grant him an opportunity to be heard. 'To have done so',
said the judge, 'where nothing he said could affect the outcome would in my view have
h been a cruel deception.' My Lords, I can content myself with saying, 'I agree'.

Public policy

Finally it was argued that if all the submissions with which I have already dealt failed,
as in my opinion they plainly do, the Bridlington principles, which have been in
operation since as long ago as 1939, are contrary to public policy, since they restrict the
right of the individual to join and to remain a member of a trade union of his choice;
j and that any attempt to give effect to any such restriction would, on application by the
individual affected by it, be prevented by the courts.

This supposed rule of public policy has, it is claimed, always formed part of the
common law of England but it has now been reinforced by the accession of the United
Kingdom to the European Convention for the Protection of Human Rights and
Fundamental Freedoms (Rome, 4 November 1950; TS 71 (1953); Cmd 8969), of which
art 11 reads as follows:

'1. Everyone has the right to freedom of peaceful assembly and to freedom of association with others, including the right to form and to join trade unions for the *a* protection of his interest.

2. No restrictions shall be placed on the exercise of these rights other than such as are prescribed by law and are necessary in a democratic society in the interests of national security or public safety, for the prevention of disorder or crime, for the protection of health or morals or for the protection of the rights and freedoms of others. This article shall not prevent the imposition of lawful restrictions on the *b* exercise of these rights by members of the armed forces, of the police or of the administration of the State.'

My Lords, freedom of association can only be mutual; there can be no right of an individual to associate with other individuals who are not willing to associate with him. The body of the membership of APEX, represented by its executive council and whose best interests it was the duty of the executive council to promote, were not willing to *c* continue to accept Cheall as a fellow-member. No doubt this was because if they continued to accept him, they ran the risk of attracting the sanction of suspension or expulsion of APEX from the TUC and all the attendant disadvantages to themselves as members of APEX that such suspension or expulsion would entail. But I know of no existing rule of public policy that would prevent trade unions from entering into *d* arrangements with one another which they consider to be in the interests of their members in promoting order in industrial relations and enhancing their member's bargaining power with their employers; nor do I think it a permissible exercise of your Lordships' judicial power to create a new rule of public policy to that effect. If this is to be done at all it must be done by Parliament.

Different considerations might apply if the effect of Cheall's expulsion from APEX *e* were to have put his job in jeopardy, either because of the existence of a closed shop or for some other reason. But this is not the case. All that has happened is that he left a union, ACTSS, in order to join another union, APEX, which he preferred. After four years of membership he was compelled, against his will, to leave it and was given the opportunity, which he rejected, of rejoining ACTSS if he so wished.

My human sympathies are with Mr Cheall, but I am not in a position to indulge them; *f* for I am left in no doubt that on all the points that have been so ingeniously argued, the law is against him and that accordingly this appeal must be allowed and the judgment of Bingham J restored.

LORD EDMUND-DAVIES. My Lords, I am in entire agreement with the speech prepared by my noble and learned friend Lord Diplock in this case and would accordingly allow the appeal.
g

LORD FRASER OF TULLYBELTON. My Lords, I have had the advantage of reading in draft the speech prepared by my noble and learned friend Lord Diplock. I agree with it, and, for the reasons there stated, I would allow this appeal.

LORD BRANDON OF OAKBROOK. My Lords, I have had the advantage of *h* reading in draft the speech prepared by my noble and learned friend Lord Diplock. I agree with it, and for the reasons which he gives I would allow the appeal and restore the judgment of Bingham J.

LORD TEMPLEMAN. My Lords, for the reasons given by my noble and learned friend Lord Diplock, I too would allow this appeal.
j

Appeal allowed.

Solicitors: *John L Williams* (for APEX); *Boyle & Ormerod*, Aylesbury (for Mr Cheall).

Mary Rose Plummer   Barrister.

Banque de l'Indochine et de Suez SA v J H Rayner (Mincing Lane) Ltd

COURT OF APPEAL, CIVIL DIVISION
SIR JOHN DONALDSON MR, KERR LJ AND SIR SEBAG SHAW
6, 7, 17 DECEMBER 1982

Bank – Documentary credit – Irrevocable credit – Payment under reserve – Payment under reserve by confirming bank to beneficiary – Effect – Confirming bank alleging documents tendered not complying with terms of credit – Beneficiary disputing alleged discrepancies in documents – Confirming bank making payment under reserve – Issuing bank rejecting documents on account of discrepancies – Whether confirming bank immediately entitled to be reimbursed by beneficiary – Whether necessary for confirming bank to show that tender of documents defective – Whether confirming bank only having right to immediate repayment if issuing bank rejects documents for same reasons as confirming bank.

The sellers agreed to sell certain goods to the buyers. Payment was to be made by an irrevocable letter of credit issued by a bank and confirmed by another bank. The sellers tendered to the confirming bank documents purporting to comply with the letter of credit and requested payment. The confirming bank took the view that the documents did not comply with the terms of the letter of credit in certain material respects and that the discrepancies entitled it to refuse payment. However, when the sellers disputed the alleged discrepancies, the confirming bank offered to make payment 'under reserve'. The sellers accepted that offer and payment was duly made. The documents were then forwarded to the issuing bank which, acting on the buyers' instructions, refused to accept them because of some of the discrepancies alleged by the confirming bank. Thereupon the confirming bank demanded immediate repayment from the sellers of the amount paid to them under reserve. The sellers refused to repay the money, claiming that they were under no obligation to do so unless one or more of the specified discrepancies was proved to be a valid ground for refusing payment under the credit in the first place. The confirming bank brought an action against the sellers to recover the money, contending that once the tendered documents were rejected by the issuing bank because of the discrepancies it was immediately entitled to repayment of the amount paid under reserve irrespective of whether any of the discrepancies was a sufficient ground for refusing to make payment originally. The judge held that the mere fact that the payment had been made under reserve did not of itself entitle the confirming bank to demand its money back as soon as the issuing bank rejected the documents irrespective of whether the discrepancies were a valid reason for not making payment in the first place. The judge went on to hold that on the facts the alleged discrepancies were such that they called for inquiry and therefore entitled both banks to reject the documents and refuse payment. The judge accordingly ordered the sellers to repay the confirming bank the amount paid by it under reserve. The sellers appealed.

Held – The effect of the payment from the confirming bank to the sellers being made 'under reserve' was that the sellers were obliged to repay the money to the confirming bank on demand if the issuing bank rejected the tendered documents on its own initiative or on the buyers' instructions for the same reasons that the confirming bank had originally rejected them. Since the issuing bank had rejected the documents for reasons which included at least one of the discrepancies relied on by the confirming bank in making payment to the sellers conditional on the payment being under reserve, it followed that the confirming bank was entitled to demand repayment from the sellers as soon as the issuing bank rejected the documents. In any event, it had been established that at least two of the discrepancies alleged by the confirming bank were valid grounds for originally rejecting the documents. The sellers' appeal would therefore be dismissed (see p 1139 g to p 1140 d, p 1141 b to d, p 1143 g h and p 1144 a b and f to p 1145 a, post).

Per Kerr LJ. Semble. A term is to be implied into an agreement between a confirming
bank and a seller to make and receive payment under reserve that the confirming bank
is only entitled to demand repayment from the seller if the issuing bank rejects the
documents for reasons which include at least one of the reasons which caused the
confirming bank to make the payment to the sellers conditional on being made under
reserve in the first place (see p 1144 h j, post).

Decision of Parker J [1983] 1 All ER 468 affirmed on other grounds.

Notes
For commercial letters of credit, see 3 Halsbury's Laws (4th edn) paras 131–137, for the
stipulation for and tender of documents see ibid paras 140–141, and for cases on the
subject, see 3 Digest (Reissue), 665–670, 4121–4137.

Cases cited in the judgments
Bank Melli Iran v Barclays Bank (Dominion Colonial and Overseas) [1951] 2 Lloyd's Rep 367,
3 Digest (Reissue) 669, 4136.
Commercial Banking Co of Sydney Ltd v Jalsard Pty Ltd [1973] AC 279, [1972] 3 WLR 566,
PC, Digest (Cont Vol D) 789, 2124a.
Equitable Trust Co of New York v Dawson Partners Ltd (1926) 27 Ll L Rep 49, HL.
Golodetz (M) & Co Inc v Czarnikow-Rionda Co Inc, The Galatea [1980] 1 All ER 501, [1980]
1 WLR 495, CA; *affg* [1979] 2 All ER 726, [1980] 1 WLR 495, Digest (Cont Vol E)
550, 589a.
Hansson v Hamel & Horley Ltd [1922] 2 AC 36, [1922] All ER Rep 237, HL, 39 Digest
(Repl) 706, 1956.
Rheincold v Hanslow (1896) 12 TLR 422.

Cases also cited
Midland Bank Ltd v Seymour [1955] 2 Lloyd's Rep 147.
Rayner (J H) & Co Ltd and Oilseeds Trading Co Ltd v Hambros Bank Ltd [1942] 2 All ER 694,
[1943] 1 KB 37, CA.

Appeal
The defendants, J H Rayner (Mincing Lane) Ltd (the merchants), appealed against the
judgment of Parker J ([1983] 1 All ER 468) given on 21 July 1982 whereby the plaintiffs,
Banque de l'Indochine et de Suez SA (the confirming bank), obtained judgment against
the merchants in the sum of $US337,563·13, in respect of recovery from the merchants
of the sum of $US1,010,000 (plus interest thereon) paid to them by the confirming bank
under a letter of credit pursuant to an agreement between the confirming bank and the
merchants whereby because the confirming bank alleged that the documents tendered
by the merchants did not comply with the credit the payment was made 'under reserve'.
The facts are set out in the judgment of Parker J (see pp 469ff, ante).

Roger Buckley QC and *Roger Ter Haar* for the merchants.
Mark O Saville QC and *Michael G Collins* for the confirming bank.

Cur adv vult

17 December. The following judgments were delivered.

SIR JOHN DONALDSON MR. This is an appeal by sugar merchants from a
judgment of Parker J ([1983] 1 All ER 468) who held that the bank was entitled to the
repayment of money paid 'under reserve' to the merchants who drew on a letter of credit
confirmed by the bank. The facts and the reasons for the decision of the judge are
admirably set out in his judgment of 21 July 1982. Accordingly no useful purpose is
served by restating them in my own words.

The issues in the appeal were: (a) what was the agreement of the parties in paying and
a receiving the price of the sugar 'under reserve'; (b) whether the bank was under any
obligation to pay under the letter of credit in the light of three alleged discrepancies in
the documentation, namely (i) the absence of a steamship company certificate certifying
that the vessel belonged to a shipping company which was a member of an international
shipping conference; (ii) the clausing of the bill of lading 'not portmarked, vessel not
responsible for incorrect delivery. Any extra expense incurred in consequence to be
b borne by consignee', (iii) [numbered 4 in the judgment of Parker J] the difficulty in
relating the certificates of weight, quality and packing and certificates of origin and
EUR I certificates to the remaining documents and to the letter of credit; (c) the
consequences of decisions under (a) and (b) above.

'Payment under reserve'
c   It seems that it is not unusual for a confirming bank to be asked to pay on documents
which in its view do not fully comply with the terms of the letter of credit. The bank
then has to decide whether (a) to refuse payment, (b) to pay, taking an indemnity from
the beneficiary in respect of any loss or damage resulting from the deficiency in the
documentation or (c) to pay the beneficiary 'under reserve'. Which course is adopted
depends on the extent and importance of the deficiencies as perceived by the confirming
d bank, the likelihood of the bank at whose request the credit was opened (the issuing
bank) and that bank's customer refusing to accept the correctness of any payment to the
beneficiary and the creditworthiness and value attached by the paying bank to the
goodwill of the person seeking to draw on the letter of credit. It is a tribute to the
standing of J H Rayner (Mincing Lane) Ltd in the City of London that, notwithstanding
the bank's conviction that the documents were seriously defective, it paid them 'under
e reserve'.
    The use of the expression 'payment under reserve', as denoting the character of a
payment, is, we were told, widespread and would undoubtedly serve a very useful
purpose if it had a defined and generally accepted meaning. Unfortunately it seems that
it has not. If this is correct, banks will be most unwise to use it without at the same time
stating precisely what they mean by it. In the longer term the International Chamber of
f Commerce, who are the authors and guardians of the Uniform Customs and Practice for
Documentary Credits might like to turn their minds to this problem when undertaking
the next revision. Meanwhile we have to determine what the parties meant by the
expression when they used it on this occasion.
    It is common ground that it relates to the circumstances in which the beneficiary can
be called on to repay the money which he has been paid under the letter of credit. The
g competing submissions are that (1) the money is repayable on demand if the issuing
bank, in reliance on some or all of the deficiencies alleged by the confirming bank,
declines to reimburse the confirming bank or to ratify the payment, the beneficiary then
being left to sue the confirming bank, (2) the money is repayable if, but only if, the
circumstances in (1) exist and the beneficiary accepts that the documentation was
defective or this is established in a suit brought by the confirming bank against the
h beneficiary. If (2) is correct, the only effect of the qualification on the payment, albeit an
important effect, is that the beneficiary cannot resist an order for repayment on the basis
that the payment itself had been made under a mistake of law. This was the submission
accepted by the judge and his reasons appear in the judgment ([1983] 1 All ER 468 at
471–472).
    The point is clearly one of difficulty. Counsel for the confirming bank characterised
j the view of the judge as 'a lawyer's view' as contrasted with 'a commercial view' and I
think that this is right. It depends for its validity on the parties having had it well in
mind that money payable under a mistake of law is irrecoverable and wishing to do no
more than eliminate this defence. This seems to me to be an improbable premise when
the parties are a commercial bank and a commodity merchant. As I see it, the dialogue
to be imputed to the parties goes something like this:

'*Merchant*. These documents are sufficient to satisfy the terms of the letter of credit and certainly will be accepted by my buyer. I am entitled to the money and I need it. *Bank*. If we thought that the documents satisfied the terms of the letter of credit, we would pay you at once. However we do not think that they do and we cannot risk paying you and not being paid ourselves. We are not sure that your buyer will authorise payment, but we can of course ask.

Merchant. But that will take time and meanwhile we shall have a cash flow problem. *Bank*. Well the alternative is for you to sue us and that will also take time.

Merchant. What about paying us without prejudice to whether we are entitled to payment and then your seeing what is the reaction of your correspondent bank and our buyer? *Bank*. That is all right, but if we are told that we should not have paid, how do we get our money back?

Merchant. You sue us. *Bank*. Oh no, that would leave us out of our money for a substantial time. Furthermore it would involve us in facing in two directions. We should not only have to sue you, but also to sue the issuing bank in order to cover the possibility that you might be right. We cannot afford to pay on those terms.

Merchant. All right. I am quite confident that the issuing bank and my buyer will be content that you should pay, particularly since the documents are in fact in order. You pay me and if the issuing bank refuses to reimburse you for the same reasons that you are unwilling to pay, we will repay you on demand and then sue you. But we do not think that this will happen. *Bank*. We agree. Here is the money "under reserve".'

I now turn to the alleged defects in the documentation.

The conference line point

The letter of credit called for the presentation of documents covering shipment of 2,000 metric tons of sugar and were subject to the special condition 'shipment to be effected on vessel belonging to Shipping Company that is a member of an International Shipping Conference'.

This is an unfortunate condition to include in a documentary credit, because it breaks the first rule of such a transaction, namely that the parties are dealing in documents, not facts. The condition required a state of fact to exist. What the letter of credit should have done was to call for a specific document which was acceptable to the buyer and his bank evidencing the fact that the vessel was owned by a member of a conference. It did not do so and as, accordingly, the confirming bank had to be satisfied of the fact, it was entitled to call for any evidence establishing that fact. All sorts of interesting questions could have arisen as to what evidence could have been called for and what would have been the position if, contrary to that evidence, the vessel was not owned by a conference member. In fact it was so owned and the merchants produced the evidence required by the bank before the expiry of the credit. Accordingly no such questions arise.

On this point I am in complete agreement with the judge. As he pointed out ([1983] 1 All ER 468 at 473), this aspect of the dispute is of relatively little importance. At most it affects the date on which the merchants became entitled to be paid under the credit.

The bill of lading clause

The judge considered that this clause was not inconsistent with the credit because of the special condition:

'All charges outside Djibouti if any are to be paid by applicant—payment of costs additional to the freight charges . . . is strictly excluded and is not covered by this letter of credit. Their reference on shipping documents should be considered as null and void when negotiated or paid under the terms and conditions of this letter of credit.'

He considered that this condition recognised that charges 'outside' Djibouti might be incurred and, if incurred, were to be paid by the applicant (the buyer) and not under the

letter of credit. He might also have supported his view by reference to the Uniform
a Customs and Practice for Documentary Credits (1974 revision, International Chamber
of Commerce Publication no 290) art 16(d) of which provides:

> 'Banks will accept shipping documents bearing reference by stamp or otherwise
> to costs additional to the freight charges, such as costs of, or disbursements incurred
> in connection with, loading, unloading or similar operations, unless the conditions
> of the credit specifically prohibits such reference.'

b

However, in reaching this conclusion, I think that the judge overlooked the fact that
the credit called for documents covering shipment of sugar at a specified price 'Cost and
Freight liner out Djibouti'. It was common ground that this meant that the freight
covered all costs up to and including discharge at Djibouti. In my judgment this express
term would constitute a specific prohibition in terms of art 16(d). It is further,
c inconsistent with the special condition to which I have referred unless it is construed, as
I would construe it, equating 'outside' to 'beyond'. This is, I think, a permissible
construction, bearing in mind that the sugar was destined for the Yemen via Djibouti.
So construed, the documentation could have contemplated charges payable by the buyer
in respect of carriage beyond Djibouti, but not, as the portmarking clause provided,
additional charges for getting the sugar to Djibouti.
d   On this ground alone I would uphold the bank's rejection of the documents.

The linking of documents
Parker J held that on this point the bank was entitled to succeed (see [1983] 1 All ER
468 at 474–475).
e   I approach this aspect of the appeal on the same basis as did the judge, namely that the
banker is not concerned with why the buyer has called for particular documents
(*Commercial Banking Co of Sydney Ltd v Jalsard Pty Ltd* [1973] AC 279), that there is no
room for documents which are almost the same, or which will do just as well, as those
specified (*Equitable Trust Co of New York v Dawson Partners Ltd* (1926) 27 Ll L Rep 49),
that whilst the bank is entitled to put a reasonable construction on any ambiguity in its
f mandate, if the mandate is clear there must be strict compliance with that mandate
(*Commercial Banking Co of Sydney v Jalsard Pty Ltd*), that documents have to be taken up or
rejected promptly and without opportunity for prolonged inquiry (*Hansson v Hammel &*
Horley Ltd [1922] 2 AC 36, [1922] All ER Rep 237) and that a tender of documents which
properly read and understood calls for further inquiry or are such as to invite litigation
are a bad tender (*M Golodetz & Co Inc v Czarnikow-Rionda Co Inc, The Galatea* [1980] 1 All
ER 501, [1980] 1 WLR 495).
g   The starting point is therefore the mandate, read in the light of the Uniform Customs
and Practice for Documentary Credits (1974 revision). The mandate, so far as material to
this point, called for payment:

> 'Presentation of the following documents
> Signed Commercial Invoices in 5 copies
h Full set of clean on board bill of lading marked freight prepaid made out to the
> order of Banque de l'Indochine et de Suez Mer Rouge and notify Banque de
> l'Indochine et de Suez Mer Rouge and Marouf Aboubaker Belfakih et Freres Sarl
> P.O. Box 45 Djibouti
> Certificate of origin
> EUR 1 certificate
j Certificate of weight—quality packing
> Evidencing shipment from EEC port not later than 31 August 1981
> For transportation to: Djibouti port in Transit Yemen
> Transhipments are permitted
> This credit is valid until 21st September 1981 for presentation of documents in:
> London

Covering shipment: 2000 (two thousand) metric tons up to 5 percent more or less white crystal sugar category No. 2 minimum polarisation 99·8 degrees

Moisture maximum 0·08 percent at US Dlrs 505 (five hundred and five) per net metric ton net cost and freight liner out Djibouti packed in new polythene lined jute bags of 50 kgs net as per your telex dated 1/7/81.'

The sections of the Uniform Customs and Practice for Documentary Credits which are material for this purpose are:

'B. Liabilities and responsibilities

Article 7. Banks must examine all documents with reasonable care to ascertain that they appear on their face to be in accordance with the terms and conditions of the credit. Documents which appear on their face to be inconsistent with one another will be considered as not appearing on their face to be in accordance with the terms and conditions of the credit . . .

C.3 Commercial invoices

Article 32 . . . c. The description of the goods in the commercial invoice must correspond with the description in the credit. In all other documents the goods may be described in general terms not inconsistent with the description of the goods in the credit.

C.4 Other documents

Article 33. When other documents are required, such as Warehouse Receipts, Delivery Orders, Consular Invoices, Certificates of Origin, of Weight, of Quality or of Analysis etc. and when no further definition is given, banks will accept such documents as tendered.'

No complaint is or was made by the bank about the commercial invoice. The argument has turned on the other documents. It seems that the sugar came from two different sources. As a result some of the documents related to quantities smaller than the total contract quantity. Thus, whilst there was only one commercial invoice and one bill of lading, there were two certificates of weight, quality and packing, two certificates of origin and three EUR 1 certificates. The crux of the argument was the extent to which these documents had on their face to be linked to each other and to the commercial invoice.

Counsel for the merchants submits that in the light of art 33 it is sufficient if the various certificates purport to be certificates of the type called for, describe the goods at least in general terms and cover the full quantity of goods mentioned in the invoice. In particular, in the light of art 7, it is not necessary that the documents should on their face be linked one to the other, provided that they are not inconsistent with each other.

Counsel for the confirming bank submits that there must be sufficient linkage to prove that the documents, if accurate, all relate to the parcel of goods which are the subject of the commercial invoice. In support of this submission he referred us to *Rheincold v Hanslow* (1896) 12 TLR 422, where the certificate of quality did not mention that the bags concerned were marked with an 'F' and the bill of lading referred to bags so marked. The Divisional Court held that this was a bad tender, since there was no evidence that the bags shipped were those which were the subject matter of the certificate. He also relied on the decision of McNair J in *Bank Melli Iran v Barclays Bank (Dominion Colonial and Overseas)* [1951] 2 Lloyd's Rep 367 that a certificate that a number of vehicles were in new condition was defective in that it failed to identify the vehicles. From these authorities, the correctness of which has never been doubted, he sought to extract the principle that it is not sufficient to produce a certificate of quality or other supporting document called for by the credit, if that document is merely 'not inconsistent' with the other documents and, in particular, the commercial invoice. It must, he submitted, be consistent and *only* consistent if it is to render the letter of credit operative. For my part, I would accept this submission in a case to which the Uniform Customs and Practice does not apply. However that is not this case.

Article 7 undoubtedly supports the submission of counsel for the merchants and I do
a not consider that any of the documents produced were necessarily inconsistent with each
other. This is not surprising if, as I suspect is the case, the documents in fact relate to the
sugar concerned. His submission also gains support from the second sentence of art 32(c)
in that again I do not think that the description of the goods in any of the documents is
inconsistent with the description in the credit. Article 33 adds little. It entitles and
requires the bank to accept a document purporting to be a certificate of quality or
b whatever as being such a certificate. All the documents tendered purport to be documents
of the kind called for by the credit.

So far so good from the point of view of the merchants. But there is another obstacle
in their way. There is, in my judgment, a real distinction between an identification of
'the goods', the subject matter of the transaction, and a description of those goods. The
second sentence of art 32(c) gives latitude in description, but not in identification. For
c example, the EUR certificate or certificate of origin could identify 'the goods' by reference
to marks on the bags or by reference to a hold in the vessel which they occupied provided
that no other goods were in the hold. Having so identified 'the goods' they could then
describe them as 'sugar' simpliciter since this description is not inconsistent with 'EEC
White Crystal Sugar Category No. 2., Minimum Polarisation 99·8 degrees Moisture
Maximum 0·08 percent'. But however general the description, the identification must,
d in my judgment, be unequivocal. Linkage between the documents is not, as such,
necessary, provided that each directly or indirectly refers unequivocally to 'the goods'.
This seems to me to be the proper and inevitable construction to place on art 32(c) if the
specified documents are to have any value at all. It is here that the merchants are in
difficulties.

No problem arises with the commercial invoice or the bill of lading, the latter showing
e 40,000 polythene lined unmarked jute bags of white crystal sugar weighing 2,018·6
metric tons gross loaded on the mv Markhor at Antwerp bound for Djibouti in transit
for the Yemen. There are two quality certificates, which in total have the same gross
weight as that shown in the bill of lading and, by calculation from the net weights, the
same number of bags. However one refers to the sugar to which it relates as having been
loaded on the 'm/v Markhor or substitute'. Clearly this *could* be a different vessel and
f accordingly refer to a different parcel of sugar. There are two certificates of origin. One
refers to consignment by 'm/v Markhor or substitute', the other to 'Transports mixtes à
destination Djibouti Port' in Transit Yemen. The quantities are correct, but the certificates
might refer to two other parcels of sugar. There are three EUR 1 certificates. The total
quantities are correct, but one names Tate & Lyle for account their principals as
consignees, another Rayners for account their principals and the third Rayners simpliciter.
g Two give no indication of the method of transport, one says simply 'Fer'. One refers to
preferential terms between France and Djibouti and the other to France and Yemen
Nord. Clearly these certificates *could* relate to the goods, but they do not necessarily do
so. This will not do.

For these reasons I agree with the judge that the bank was entitled to reject the
documents on this ground as well as on that concerning the portmarking clause in the
h bill of lading.

Consequences

In the light of my conclusion the argument under this head does not arise. Counsel
for the confirming bank had submitted that if (1) the bank was entitled to repayment on
demand because it had only paid under reserve and (2) it was entitled to refuse payment
j unconditionally until it had received a certificate that the vessel was owned by a member
of a shipping conference, which only occurred after the payment under reserve, but (3)
thereafter the bank was bound to pay unconditionally, his clients were entitled to interest
on the money from the date when they demanded repayment until that on which the
merchants counterclaimed for payment. This was a considerable length of time. The
basis of this submission is that the merchants had no right to payment until, after having

provided proper documentation, they demanded payment. This submission earns full marks for ingenuity, but I should have required a lot of persuading before I was prepared to hold that merchants who have already been paid, albeit under reserve, must insist on being paid again unconditionally. However, as I say, this point does not arise.

I would dismiss the appeal.

KERR LJ. I agree that this appeal should be dismissed for the reasons given by Sir John Donaldson MR. I only add some comments of my own because it is said that the case is of considerable importance in relation to documentary credits.

Payment 'under reserve'

For the purpose of considering this point one must assume that, at the time when payment was agreed to be made and accepted 'under reserve', the confirming bank was convinced that the documents did not comply with the terms of the credit in all respects, but that the beneficiary was convinced that they did, and that the correct answer as a matter of law was uncertain. In this connection it is interesting that it appeared from the expert evidence at the trial that as many as two-thirds of presentations of documents against confirmed credits in London are thought to deviate from the terms of the credits in some respects, but in the great majority of cases this is somehow overcome by agreement.

When I read the judgment of Parker J ([1983] 1 All ER 468) for the hearing of the appeal, I had no doubt that he was right. In the course of the argument I reinforced that view by saying that the opposite conclusion would lead to the result that, since the confirming bank is legally bound to pay against correct documents, it cannot have been the intention that it should be absolved from a breach of this obligation by insisting on paying 'under reserve', in the sense of insisting on a right to have the money repaid on demand even if it should ultimately turn out that the beneficiary had been entitled to unconditional payment throughout. However, when counsel for the confirming bank came to deal with this point, he rapidly convinced me, to my surprise, that this approach is too legalistic and wrong. The commercial reality of the situation is that, while holding opposing views, both the bank and the beneficiary hope that, whichever of them is right, the issuing bank and the buyer abroad will raise no objection to the documents. It is therefore with this hope uppermost in its mind that the confirming bank agrees to pay, but only 'under reserve'. However, in agreeing to do so, the confirming bank cannot be realistically taken to have agreed to become involved in legal proceedings, if the documents are rejected, by having to sue the beneficiary to recover the money and establishing that the documents did not comply with the credit, or possibly by suing the issuing bank on the ground that they did, after all, comply with it. This would be the effect of the decision of Parker J, but on reflection I do not think that either party could have intended that this should be so. What the parties meant, I think, was that payment was to be made under reserve in the sense that the beneficiary would be bound to repay the money on demand if the issuing bank should reject the documents, whether on its own initiative or on the buyer's instructions. I would regard this as a binding agreement made between the confirming bank and the beneficiary by way of a compromise to resolve the impasse created by the uncertainty of their respective legal obligations and rights. For present purposes it is then unnecessary to go further and decide whether such a demand would only be effective if the grounds of the rejection included at least one of the grounds on which the confirming bank had relied in refusing to pay otherwise than under reserve. But I incline to the view that this should be implied, since the agreement to pay and accept the money under reserve will have been made against the background of these grounds of objection.

In the present case the issuing bank in fact rejected the documents on grounds which included at least one of the grounds of objection which had been raised by the plaintiffs (the confirming bank). It therefore follows that the judgment in favour of the plaintiffs must in any event be upheld. However, I also agree with Sir John Donaldson MR that a the plaintiffs were in any event entitled to refuse payment for all three reasons as stated by him.

SIR SEBAG SHAW. I agree.

Appeal dismissed. Leave to appeal to the House of Lords refused.

b Solicitors: *Clyde & Co* (for the merchants); *Durrant Piesse* (for the confirming bank).

Frances Rustin   Barrister.

c # Practice Direction

CHANCERY DIVISION

Practice – Chancery Division – Revision of system for listing causes and matters – Consolidation of former directions.

d [The purpose of this direction is to consolidate all the former directions relating to the Chancery lists, with minor revisions to indicate the present practice.]

1. *The lists*
    There are three main lists in the Chancery Division: the Witness List Part 1; the
e Witness List Part 2; and the Non-Witness List. Witness actions are allocated to Part 1 if the master's provisional estimate of duration exceeds three days; otherwise they are allocated to Part 2. Each list is in the charge of the judge named in the cause list.

2. *Responsibility for listing*
    The clerk of the lists (room 163, Royal Courts of Justice) is in general responsible for
f listing. All applications relating to listing should in the first instance be made to him. Any party dissatisfied with any decision of his may, on one clear day's notice to all other parties, apply to the judge in charge of the list, at a date and time to be fixed with the judge's clerk. Any such application should be made within seven days of the decision of the clerk of the lists.

g 3. *Lists of witness actions set down and warned*
    (1) By the beginning of each term the clerk of the lists will publish a list showing under separate headings the actions set down for hearing in each part of the Witness List, with the dates (if any) fixed for hearing.
    (2) By the beginning of each term, and subsequently on each Friday of term (and on such other days as may be appropriate), the clerk of the lists will publish a Warned List,
h showing the actions in each part of the Witness List that are liable to be heard during the following week (two weeks in the case of Part 2), and showing the dates, if any, fixed for hearing. Any action for which no date has been fixed is liable to appear in the list for hearing with no warning save that given by the next day's cause list posted each afternoon outside room 163.
    (3) With the written consent of all parties, the clerk of the lists may postpone a trial if
j an application to him is made within three days of the action first appearing in the Warned List. Any other application for a postponement must, after consultation with the clerk of the lists, be made to the judge in charge of the list as soon as possible after the action has appeared in the Warned List.
    (4) If an action is not ready for hearing when it is called on for trial it will be put at the bottom of the list unless the judge otherwise directs.

4. Witness actions: fixed and 'floating' dates

(1) Within 28 days after an action has been set down in Part 1 any party may give one clear day's notice to all other parties and to the clerk of the lists of his intention to apply for a fixed date for trial. Fixed dates are not normally given for actions set down in Part 2, but any party who claims that there are special circumstances which justify a fixed date being given may apply for one in the same way as for a case in Part 1.

(2) On an application for a fixed date, the clerk of the lists will consider the wishes of the parties, the circumstances of the case, and the state of Part 1 and Part 2 of the list. He may then either fix a date for the trial or else direct that the case shall be in the list for trial on or shortly after some specified date, depending on the state of the list then (a 'floater'). If he does neither, the action will be liable to appear in the Warned List for hearing at any time after 28 days from setting down, although it may appear earlier if this is agreed by the parties or directed by the court.

(3) The clerk of the lists may alter or vacate a date, whether fixed or 'floating' (a) on an application made by any party after giving one clear day's notice to all other parties or (b) of his own motion, if a revised estimate of duration or the state of the lists makes this necessary, or if circumstances arise which make it unlikely that there could be an effective hearing on the fixed or 'floating' date.

5. Estimates of duration

(1) Within ten days of an action being set down, the solicitor for each party separately represented must lodge with the cause clerk (room 163) a certificate signed by counsel stating the estimated length of the trial. A single certificate signed by all counsel should if possible be lodged. Certificates may be sent by post. Any undue delay in lodging the certificate may result in the hearing of the action being delayed.

(2) If the estimated length of trial is varied, or the action is settled, withdrawn or discontinued, the solicitors for the parties must forthwith inform the clerk of the lists in writing. If the action is settled but the parties wish the master to make a consent order, the solicitors must notify the clerk of the lists in writing, whereupon he will take the case out of the list and notify the master. The master may then make the consent order.

(3) Seven days before the date for trial, whether fixed or 'floating' (or, if there is no such date, within seven days after the action appears in the Warned List), the plaintiff's solicitor must inform the clerk of the lists whether there is any variation in the estimate of duration, and in particular whether the case is likely to be disposed of in some summary way. If the plaintiff is in person, this must be done by the solicitor for the first-named defendant who has instructed a solicitor. If a summary disposal is likely, the solicitor must keep the clerk of the lists informed of any developments as soon as they occur.

6. The Non-Witness List

(1) By the beginning of each term, and subsequently on each Friday of term (and also on such other days as may be appropriate), the clerk of the lists will publish a Warned List, showing the matters liable to be heard during the following week, and the dates (if any) fixed for hearing. Any matter for which no fixed date appears is liable to appear in the list for hearing with no warning save that given by the next day's cause list posted each afternoon outside room 163.

(2) Appeals from masters will appear in the Non-Witness List and will be heard in chambers. Such appeals (stamped £5) must be lodged in room 157. On being notified that the case has been set down, the solicitors should forthwith inform the clerk of the lists whether they intend to instruct counsel, and, if so, the names of counsel.

(3) An originating summons which is adjourned into court with witnesses will be put into the appropriate part of the Witness List, save that if the master considers that the hearing can be concluded within one day he may put the case into the Non-Witness List.

(4) The provisions for the Witness List as to fixing dates and giving estimates of duration (see paras 4 and 5 above) apply to the Non-Witness List, with any necessary modifications.

7. *Chambers summonses*

a   (1) Any chambers summonses adjourned to the judge will normally be heard at 10.30 am on a Monday morning fixed by the master.

(2) If the hearing is expected to last for more than about 15 minutes, the master will either put the matter at the end of the Monday morning list, or else adjourn it to a date and time to be fixed. In the latter case, the clerk of the lists will fix the hearing date.

b   8. *Short causes*

A motion for judgment on a notice that is marked 'short' and is accompanied by counsel's certificate that the hearing is unlikely to exceed ten minutes will usually be listed for hearing as a short cause on a Wednesday. If the notice is not marked 'short', or there is no certificate by counsel, the motion will be entered in the Non-Witness List.

c   9. *Short Probate List*

Applications for probate in solemn form made on affidavit evidence are entered in the Short Probate List. This is usually heard on a Monday morning after chambers summonses. When ordering trial, the master will specify the Monday for the hearing.

10. *Motions by order*

d   If a judge directs that a motion is to be a motion by order (as will usually be done if the hearing is likely to exceed two hours), the solicitors or the clerks to counsel concerned should apply to the clerk of the lists for a fixed or 'floating' date for the hearing. The motion will then be put into the cause list for hearing on the appropriate date.

11. *Practice directions revoked*

e   The following Practice Directions are now wholly revoked:

Practice Direction of 2 April 1954 relating to the Witness List ([1954] 1 All ER 946, [1954] 1 WLR 693)

Practice Direction of 18 April 1969 relating to listing of Chancery summonses ([1969] 2 All ER 1132, [1969] 1 WLR 1257)

Practice Note of 2 March 1970 relating to estimates of expected duration of Chancery *f*   causes and fixed dates ([1970] 1 All ER 904, [1970] 1 WLR 525)

Practice Direction of 5 May 1972 relating to the Witness List ([1972] 2 All ER 599, [1972] 1 WLR 723)

Practice Direction of 5 November 1974 relating to Chancery summonses ([1974] 3 All ER 880, [1974] 1 WLR 1659)

Practice Direction of 25 November 1974 relating to Chancery lists ([1975] 1 All ER 56, *g*   [1975] 1 WLR 75)

By direction of the Vice-Chancellor.

EDMUND HEWARD
Chief Master.

29 March 1983

R v Crown Court at Knightsbridge, ex parte Marcrest Ltd

COURT OF APPEAL, CIVIL DIVISION

WALLER, ACKNER AND PURCHAS LJJ

7, 8, 9, 13, 20 DECEMBER 1982

Gaming – Gaming licence – Fit and proper person to hold licence – Cancellation of licence by licensing justices – Unlawful granting of credit – Proprietors of gaming club accepting cheques from customers whose previous cheques had been dishonoured – Cheques not presented – Smaller amount later accepted in settlement of debt – Whether acceptance of cheques constituting a 'sham' – Whether acceptance of smaller amount in settlement of debt a 'release ... of any debt ... in respect of losses incurred ... in ... gaming' – Whether debt incurred in respect of gaming losses when cheque accepted – Whether proprietors fit and proper persons to hold a licence – Gaming Act 1968, s 16(1)(a)(b), Sch 2, para 20(1)(b).

From 1971 the applicants and their predecessors held a licence to run a London casino. In 1981 the Gaming Board and the police applied to the licensing justices to cancel the licence on the ground that the casino was being operated in a manner which seriously contravened the Gaming Act 1968. The board and the police alleged that the applicants accepted cheques signed by customers on 'house cheque' forms in circumstances which amounted to a sham because the applicants either knew that they were drawn on a bank at which the customer had no account or knew that they would be dishonoured. It was further alleged that the applicants accepted house cheques for very large amounts which they agreed not to bank and that they later accepted considerably smaller payments in full satisfaction of the debt owed. The board and the police claimed that the alleged transactions amounted to the unlawful granting of credit, contrary to s 16(1)[a] of the 1968 Act and were evidence that the applicants were not fit and proper persons to run a casino. The board and the police accordingly applied for the licence to be cancelled under para 20(1)(b)[b] of Sch 2 to the 1968 Act. The justices and, on appeal, the Crown Court found, inter alia, the allegations to be proved and cancelled the licence. The applicants applied to the Divisional Court for judicial review of the cancellation but the Divisional Court, while finding that the Crown Court had been in error on other aspects of the case, held that the Crown Court had not erred in finding that the applicants were not fit and proper persons to hold a licence. The applicants appealed to the Court of Appeal, contending, inter alia, (i) that the acceptance of cheques from persons whose previous cheques had been dishonoured did not amount to a sham, and therefore the unlawful granting of credit within s 16(1)(a), merely because the applicants knew from past experience that the cheques were likely to be dishonoured when first presented, and (ii) that the acceptance by the applicants of a sum less than the face value of the dishonoured cheques was not a 'release ... of any debt ... in respect of any losses incurred by any person in ... gaming', within s 16(1)(b). The applicants submitted that their acceptance of less than the face value of cheques made out to them was merely a compromise of the sum owing on the cheques and that, because cheques were accepted for tokens which the customer might or might not use for gambling or which he might use and then win, the cheques were not necessarily given in respect of 'losses' incurred in gaming.

Held – The appeal would be dismissed for the following reasons—

(1) Applying the principle that acts or documents were a sham if the parties had a

---

a   Section 16(1) is set out at p 1153 *fg*, post

b   Paragraph 20(1), so far as material, provides: '... the licensing authority may refuse to grant or renew a licence under this Act on any one or more of the following grounds, that is to say ... (b) that the applicant is not a fit and proper person to be the holder of a licence under this Act ...'

a common intention that the acts or documents were not to create the legal rights and obligations which they gave the appearance of creating, it was apparent from the course of dealing between the applicants and their customers over a long period and involving numerous cheques that the parties intended that there was to be no legal right to have a cheque honoured when it was presented. The function of the cheques was merely to record a loan of money or tokens to that value, and as such they were a sham for the purposes of s 16 of the 1968 Act, which contemplated that the only lawful cheque was *b* one in which there was a common expectation of payment on presentation within two days of acceptance (see p 1154 *e* to *g*, post); dictum of Diplock LJ in *Snook v London and West Riding Investments Ltd* [1967] 1 All ER at 528 applied.

(2) When a cheque was given by a customer to enable him to take part in gaming and the cheque was subsequently dishonoured, then prima facie a debt was incurred in respect of 'losses' in the gaming for the purposes of s 16(1)(*b*) of the 1968 Act, *c* notwithstanding that the customer might decide not to gamble after obtaining tokens by a cheque or might win, since until the customer proved that that was not the case the prima facie inference remained that the dishonoured cheque had created a debt in respect of losses which had been incurred in gaming before the cheque was dishonoured. It followed that the applicants' acceptance of lesser sums in satisfaction of amounts owing under dishonoured cheques amounted to the release of debts in respect of losses incurred *d* in gaming and was a prohibited act under s 16(1)(*b*) (see p 1155 *b c g* to *j*, post): *CHT Ltd v Ward* [1963] 3 All ER 835 distinguished; dictum of Lord Fraser in *Cumming v Mackie* 1973 SLT at 245 not followed.

(3) Although the Crown Court had erred in respect of certain aspects of the case the Divisional Court had been entitled to refuse an order for certiorari, since the Crown Court had a residual discretion whether to grant or refuse the licence and the evidence *e* that the applicants were not fit and proper persons to hold a licence was such that the Crown Court was entitled to exercise its discretion by cancelling the licence, notwithstanding its errors on other aspects of the case (see p 1157 *e f* and p 1158 *e* to *g*, post); *R v Crown Court at Knightsbridge, ex p International Sporting Club (London) Ltd* [1981] 3 All ER 417 considered.

f **Notes**

For regulations relating to the provision of credit in licensed club premises, see 6 Halsbury's Laws (4th edn) para 348.

For the Gaming Act 1968, s 16, see 14 Halsbury's Statutes (3rd edn) 710.

Cases referred to in judgment

g *CHT Ltd v Ward* [1963] 3 All ER 835, [1965] 2 QB 63, [1963] 3 WLR 1071, CA, 25 Digest (Reissue) 464, 4112.

Cumming v Mackie 1973 SLT 242.

R v Crown Court at Knightsbridge, ex p International Sporting Club (London) Ltd [1981] 3 All ER 417, [1982] QB 304, [1981] 3 WLR 640, DC.

R v Stafford Justices, ex p Stafford Corp [1940] 2 KB 33, CA, 16 Digest (Reissue) 400, 4421.

h *Snook v London and West Riding Investments Ltd* [1967] 1 All ER 518, [1967] 2 QB 786, [1967] 2 WLR 1020, CA, 26 Digest (Reissue) 755, 5168.

Stoneleigh Finance Ltd v Phillips [1965] 1 All ER 513, [1965] 2 QB 537, [1965] 2 WLR 508, CA, 10 Digest (Reissue) 863, 4977.

Yorkshire Rly Wagon Co v Maclure (1882) 21 Ch D 309, CA, 10 Digest (Reissue) 802, 4622.

j **Cases also cited**

Aziz v Knightsbridge Gaming and Catering Services and Supplies Ltd (1982) Times, 6 July.

Baldwin & Francis Ltd v Patents Appeal Tribunal [1959] 2 All ER 433, [1959] AC 663, HL.

Chief Constable of North Wales Police v Evans [1982] 3 All ER 141, [1982] 1 WLR 1155, HL.

Glynn v Keele University [1971] 2 All ER 89, [1971] 1 WLR 487.

Kavanagh v Chief Constable of Devon and Cornwall [1974] 2 All ER 697, [1974] QB 624, CA.

McDonald v Green [1950] 2 All ER 1240, [1951] 1 KB 594, CA.

Malone v Comr of Police of the Metropolis (No 2) [1979] 2 All ER 620, [1979] Ch 344.   *a*

Midland Bank Trust Co v Green [1979] 3 All ER 28, [1980] Ch 590, CA; *rvsd* [1981] 1 All ER 153, [1981] AC 513, HL.

O'Reilly v Mackman [1982] 3 All ER 680, [1982] 3 WLR 604, CA; *affd* [1982] 3 All ER 1124, [1982] 3 WLR 1096, HL.

Pearlman v Keepers and Governors of Harrow School [1979] 1 All ER 365, [1979] QB 56, CA.

R v Birmingham Justices, ex p Lamb (1982) Times, 4 December, DC.   *b*

R v Campbell, ex p Nomikos [1956] 2 All ER 280, [1956] 1 WLR 622, DC.

R v Crown Court at Knightsbridge, ex p Ladup (18 March 1980, unreported), DC.

R v Northumberland Compensation Appeal Tribunal, ex p Shaw [1952] 1 All ER 122, [1952] 1 KB 338, CA.

R v Orpin [1974] 2 All ER 1121, [1975] QB 283, CA.

R v Southampton Justices, ex p Green [1975] 2 All ER 1073, [1976] QB 11, CA.   *c*

R v Surrey Quarter Sessions, ex p Metropolitan Police Comr [1962] 1 All ER 825, [1963] 1 QB 990, DC.

Racal Communications Ltd, Re [1980] 2 All ER 634, [1981] AC 374, HL.

Sirros v Moore [1974] 3 All ER 776, [1975] QB 118, CA.

Smith Kline & French Laboratories' Patent, Re [1967] RPC 123, DC and CA.

Society of Medical Officers of Health v Hope [1960] 1 All ER 317, [1960] AC 551, HL.   *d*

South East Asia Fire Bricks Sdn Bhd v Non-Metallic Mineral Products Manufacturing Employees Union [1980] 2 All ER 689, [1981] AC 363, PC.

Steadman v Gooch (1793) 1 Esp 3, 70 ER 262.

Tatam v Reeve [1893] 1 QB 44, [1891–4] All ER Rep 391, DC.

Appeal   *e*

Marcrest Properties Ltd (Marcrest) appealed against the decision of the Divisional Court of the Queen's Bench Division (O'Connor LJ and Comyn J) on 22 October 1982 whereby the court dismissed an application for judicial review by way of an order of certiorari to quash the order made by the Crown Court at Knightsbridge (his Honour Judge Friend sitting with justices) made on 8 June 1982 dismissing an appeal from the decision of the gaming licensing justices for the South Westminster petty sessional division whereby on   *f* the application of the Gaming Board for Great Britain and the Commissioner of Police of the Metropolis the justices cancelled a licence held by Marcrest under the Gaming Act 1968 in respect of premises at 163 Knightsbridge, London SW7 and barred Marcrest from holding a gaming licence in respect of the premises for a period of three years on the ground that the appellants were not fit and proper persons to hold a licence. The facts are set out in the judgment of the court.   *g*

Gavin Lightman QC and *Jeffery Onions* for Marcrest.

Simon Tuckey QC and *Jeremy Nicholson* for the Gaming Board.

John Ryman for the Commissioner of Police of the Metropolis.

Cur adv vult   *h*

20 December. The following judgment of the court was delivered.

ACKNER LJ. On 9 December 1981, on the application by the Commissioner of Police of the Metropolis and by the Gaming Board, the gaming licensing justices for the South Westminster petty sessional division cancelled the gaming licence held by Marcrest   *j* Properties Ltd (Marcrest), in respect of the casino club known as the Knightsbridge Sporting Club at 163 Knightsbridge, London SW7. They also made an order of disqualification prohibiting a licence under the Gaming Act 1968 from being held in respect of the premises during a period of three years.

The justices made this decision after a hearing lasting some 20 days on the grounds that:

a '(1) Marcrest Properties Ltd is not a fit and proper person to be the holder of a licence under the Gaming Act. (2) If the licence were not cancelled the club would be managed by and carried on for the benefit of persons other than Marcrest Properties Ltd, who would themselves be refused the renewal or grant of a licence under the Act on the grounds that they are not fit and proper persons to be holders of such a licence. (3) That while the said licence has been in force, the premises have been used for unlawful purposes.'

Marcrest appealed to the Crown Court, but before 18 May 1982, when the hearing commenced, they had restructured themselves by the sale of the entire shareholding for a nominal £1,000 to a Mr Barnett, who nobody suggested was not a fit and proper person. This restructuring operation was carried out, no doubt in order to take advantage of the decision in *R v Crown Court at Knightsbridge, ex p International Sporting Club (London) Ltd* [1981] 3 All ER 417, [1982] QB 304, where the Divisional Court held that the question whether a company was a fit and proper person to hold a licence had to be considered in the light of any restructuring of the company which had occurred since the hearing before the justices. This tactical move eliminated the justices' second ground of decision referred to above.

The hearing before the Crown Court lasted some 14 days. The appeal was dismissed and the orders of cancellation and disqualification were confirmed.

Application was then made to the Divisional Court for judicial review, it being contended that the record disclosed at least four errors of law. The Divisional Court accepted that there was one error of law; it also held that the judgment delivered by the Crown Court was, in certain respects, slipshod, confused and mistaken, but that in the end the court had applied the right test. It concluded that Marcrest had suffered no injustice as a result of the error of law and, in the exercise of its discretion, it refused the application for an order of certiorari.

Marcrest now appeals to this court and counsel on its behalf contends: (1) the error of law which the Divisional Court found (and which is not contested by the Gaming Board or the Metropolitan Police Commissioner) entitled Marcrest to an order for certiorari, and the Divisional Court wrongly exercised its discretion in refusing to make such an order; (2) that there were two other errors of law made by the Crown Court which the Divisional Court should have found, and that these errors, or either of them, justified the grant of an order for certiorari; (3) that the judgment of the Crown Court was so unsatisfactory that, taken with the error of law which was established in the Divisional Court and/or the other error or errors of law which the Divisional Court should have found, justice demanded that its decision be quashed and a new hearing of the complaints ordered.

The error of law found by the Divisional Court

To appreciate the nature of the error, it is necessary to refer shortly to the history of this casino. In May 1971 Knightsbridge Sporting Club Ltd was granted a licence to operate this casino at 163 Knightsbridge. The licence was renewed annually, but allowed to expire in May 1978 for a purely technical reason. Where premises are enlarged a licence cannot be renewed. A new licence has to be granted. Such a new licence was granted in May 1978. On 22 January 1980 the licence was transferred to Marcrest. This licence was renewed in May 1980, but in 1981 the Gaming Board and the Metropolitan Police Commissioner applied for cancellation of the licence under para 36 of Sch 2 to the Gaming Act 1968, which application was duly referred to the licensing authority, who, by virtue of the powers conferred on them by para 42 of Sch 2, were entitled to 'cancel the licence on any of the grounds specified in paragraph 20 or paragraph 21 of this Schedule'. The Gaming Board and the commissioner alleged that Marcrest was not 'a fit and proper person to be the holder of a licence under this Act' (see ground (*b*) in para 20(1)) *and* that 'while the licence has been in force the relevant premises have been used for an unlawful purpose' (see ground (*e*) in para 21(1)).

There is no requirement for the provision of detailed particulars of the grounds for the application for the cancellation of a licence. Regulation 7 of the Gaming Clubs (Licensing) Regulations 1969, SI 1969/1110, provides that the application shall be made in writing in the appropriate form set out in Sch 2 of the regulations. The form (Form 43) provides that the application 'is made on the grounds specified in the statement, of which two copies are attached'. Marcrest were, however, left in no doubt as to the nature of the complaints made against them. They were provided with a 6-page statement of amended grounds and, in addition, they were furnished not only with copies of statements of witnesses to be called in support of the application, but even with the names and addresses of witnesses whom the commissioner or the Gaming Board did not propose to call, but who might be able to give relevant information. Marcrest had to meet a case of flagrant breaches of the requirements of the Gaming Act 1968, involving, inter alia, the unlawful granting of credit.

The totality of the material relied on was all relevant to establish that Marcrest were not fit and proper persons to be the holders of a licence under the 1968 Act, and in the amended statement of grounds the whole of the unlawful conduct of Marcrest from 1974 to 1980 was set out in six pages of particulars in support of the allegation that Marcrest were not fit and proper persons. At the end of the statement of grounds there was a further allegation that while the licences were in force the premises had been used for an unlawful purpose with a reference to the details already given.

In finding this latter complaint proved, the Crown Court (and for that matter the justices) undoubtedly relied on many of the incidents which occurred in 1975 and 1976 during the period of the *first licence*. It was never suggested, either to the justices or to the Crown Court, that they were not entitled so to do. However, in the Divisional Court, counsel on behalf of Marcrest, who had not appeared either before the justices or before the Crown Court, successfully submitted that 'the licence' in ground (*e*) in para 21(1) of Sch 2 of the 1968 Act refers to the licence of which renewal is sought, and he very properly supported this submission by reference to the definition of 'relevant premises' in para 2(2) of Sch 2 which reads: '"the relevant premises", in relation to a licence under this Act . . . means the premises in respect of which the licence is for the time being in force . . .' He accordingly validly submitted that quite clearly this was the second licence, namely the one granted in May 1978, and that it was wrong in law for the Crown Court to find that incidents before 1978 could be relied on as showing that the premises had been used for an unlawful purpose while the licence was in force.

Despite the highly competent representation on both sides, this simple point was overlooked until the hearing before the Divisional Court. We do not find this altogether surprising. The conduct which was alleged, and which both the justices and the Crown Court were fully satisfied had been established, did not lose its character of being unlawful because it occurred prior to the currency of the second licence. Nor did the fact that it took place prior to May 1978 disentitle the commissioner and the Gaming Board from relying on it in order to establish that Marcrest were not fit and proper persons. The point, if it had been taken, would merely have prevented any reliance being placed on this earlier conduct in support of the additional ground provided by para 21(1)(*e*). Thus, such earlier unlawful conduct, while fully capable of establishing, as indeed it did, that Marcrest were not fit and proper persons to hold a licence, could not be used additionally to support the further ground of the application.

We can fully understand that, if those then appearing for Marcrest had focused on this point, they might well have decided that tactically there was little or no merit in raising the point, because of its wholly technical nature in the circumstances of the dispute. They might well have thought that it was far better to concentrate on seeking to establish, as they strenuously attempted throughout the two lengthy hearings, that the allegations, all of which were relevant to the issue of unfitness, were unfounded.

Did Marcrest unlawfully grant credit to their customers?

In the amended statement of grounds for cancellation it was alleged that the premises were habitually used, during the years 1975 to 1977, for the unlawful purpose of granting a credit to enable players to take part in gaming at the club contrary to the provisions of s 16 of the 1968 Act. This unlawful granting of credit was alleged to have been done in several ways, as follows: (i) by accepting markers of IOUs on 'house cheque' forms which were never banked; (ii) by sending the cheques or markers to head office or Gramgas Securities Ltd to maintain a fiction that there was a compliance with the provisions of s 16(3) where there was none; (iii) by repeatedly accepting so-called cheques from persons

b whose previous cheques had been dishonoured in circumstances which amount to a 'sham' because the management knew that these 'cheques' would not be honoured on a first presentation; (iv) by allowing to mark on 'house cheque' forms signed by customers the name of a bank at which the customer did not bank so that these 'cheques' would be referred to drawer marked 'no account'; and (v) by allowing punters credit at the tables, in particular in the salon privé.

c The fourth reason gave nine examples of granting unlawful credit. It is sufficient to refer to two of them. In the first Sheikh Fahd Al-Tobaishi over a period of 15 months cashed 71 cheques totalling £966,000 all of which were referred to drawer in an unbroken sequence. In August and November 1976, after £175,000 had been accepted from him in discharge of a much larger debt in breach of the provisions of s 16(1)(b), cheques totalling £450,000 were accepted from him, and all were dishonoured.

d In the second, Dr Frangistas between 4 and 19 February 1976 signed 11 'house cheque' forms as markers for the total sum of £523,000. None were delivered to a bank for collection or payment within two days as required by s 16(3) of the 1968 Act, and in April 1976 a director on behalf of the licence-holder accepted the sum of £75,000 in discharge of this debt of £523,000 in breach of the provisions of s 16(1)(b) of the Act.

All these allegations were found proved by the justices and the Crown Court. However, it is in relation to Sheikh Al-Tobaishi that the first of the two questions of law raised by

e the appellants in the Divisional Court arise, and which, as previously stated, was decided adversely to the appellants.

It is contended that the repeated acceptance of cheques from persons whose previous cheques had been dishonoured, in circumstances in which the appellants knew those cheques would not be honoured on first presentation, did not amount to a sham, and accordingly did not amount to the unlawful granting of credit contrary to the provisions

f of s 16(1)(a) of the 1968 Act.

Section 16 of the 1968 Act provides:

'(1) Subject to the next following subsection, where gaming to which this Part of this Act applies takes place on premises in respect of which a licence under this Act is for the time being in force, neither the holder of the licence nor any person acting

g on his behalf or under any arrangement with him shall make any loan or otherwise provide or allow to any person any credit, or release, or discharge on another person's behalf, the whole or part of any debt,—(a) for enabling any person to take part in the gaming, or (b) in respect of any losses incurred by any person in the gaming.

(2) Neither the holder of the licence nor any person acting on his behalf or under any arrangement with him shall accept a cheque and give in exchange for it cash or

h tokens for enabling any person to take part in the gaming unless the following conditions are fulfilled, that is to say—(a) the cheque is not a post-dated cheque, and (b) it is exchanged for cash to an amount equal to the amount for which it is drawn, or is exchanged for tokens at the same rate as would apply if cash, to the amount for which the cheque is drawn, were given in exchange for them; but, where those conditions are fulfilled, the giving of cash or tokens in exchange for a cheque shall

j not be taken to contravene subsection (1) of this section.

(3) Where the holder of a licence under this Act, or a person acting on behalf of or under any arrangement with the holder of such a licence, accepts a cheque in exchange for cash or tokens to be used by a player in gaming to which this Part of this Act applies, he shall not more than two banking days later cause the cheque to be delivered to a bank for payment or collection ...'

The clear purpose of s 16 is to protect the punters against themselves. They are not to be given by the casinos so much rope that they may eventually hang themselves, figuratively or otherwise. The granting of all credit except cheques which comply with sub-s (2) is prohibited. This is clear from the very wide words of s 16(1), 'any credit', the only exception being limited to that which is provided for in sub-s (2). Parliament clearly intended that, if the conditions laid down in sub-s (2) were not complied with, then s 16(1) would be breached.

Were the Al-Tobaishi cheques a sham? Both counsel for Marcrest and counsel for the Gaming Board rely on the following observations by Diplock LJ in *Snook v London and West Riding Investments Ltd* [1967] 1 All ER 518 at 528, [1967] 2 QB 786 at 802:

'As regards the contention of the plaintiff that the transactions between himself, Auto Finance, Ltd. and the defendants were "a sham", it is I think necessary to consider what, if any, legal concept is involved in the use of this popular and pejorative word. I apprehend that, if it has any meaning in law, it means acts done or documents executed by the parties to the "sham" which are intended by them to give to third parties or to the Court the appearance of creating between the parties legal rights and obligations different from the actual legal rights and obligations (if any) which the parties intend to create. One thing, I think, however is clear in legal principle, morality and the authorities (see *Yorkshire Railway Wagon Co.* v. *Maclure* ((1882) 21 Ch D 309); *Stoneleigh Finance, Ltd.* v. *Phillips* ([1965] 1 All ER 513, [1965] 2 QB 537)) that for acts or documents to be a "sham", with whatever legal consequences follow from this, all parties thereto must have a common intention that the acts or documents are not to create the legal rights and obligations which they give the appearance of creating. No unexpressed intentions of a "shammer" affect the rights of a party whom he deceived.'

We agree with O'Connor LJ that the test propounded by Diplock LJ was fulfilled in the present case. Marcrest and the punters were intending to give to third parties or to the court the appearance of creating between them legal rights and obligations different from the actual legal rights and obligations (if any) which they intended to create.

The course of dealing between Marcrest and its customers over a long period and involving numerous cheques demonstrated that it was the intention of the parties that there was to be no legal right to have a cheque honoured when it was presented. The only lawful cheque contemplated by s 16(2) and (3) is one in which there is a common expectation of payment on presentation within two days. What was provided was a 'sham'; it was no better than, if as good as, a postdated cheque. As O'Connor LJ rightly commented, its function was merely to record a loan of money or tokens to that value.

Is the acceptance of a sum less than the face value of a dishonoured cheque a breach of s 16(1) of the Act?

This raises the second of the two points of law which counsel for Marcrest complains was wrongly decided against his clients in the Divisional Court. He contends that where a sum less than the face value of a dishonoured cheque is accepted this does not amount to the release of part 'of any debt in respect of any losses incurred by any person in the gaming'. He contends that it is but a compromise of a sum owing on the cheque or cheques. This raises the question: how can a debt in respect of losses incurred in the gaming arise? If a customer loses either cash at the tables or tokens that he has bought with cash, then he owes no debt to the casino. He has gambled with cash or the equivalent and he has lost cash or the equivalent. We agree with the Divisional Court that a debt to the casino can only arise where credit has been given by the casino to the customer. However, as previously stated, the only lawful credit that the casino can give is to accept a cheque to enable the customer to take part in the gaming. Again, as previously stated, such a cheque must comply with s 16(2) and (3). Thus the only way in which a debt in respect of any loss incurred in gaming can lawfully arise is if that cheque is dishonoured.

Counsel for Marcrest contends that when a casino issues tokens against a cheque there *a* is at that moment no debt in respect of any losses incurred by the customer giving the cheque. The customer might decide not to gamble and then to cash them in and walk out of the casino. Alternatively, he might gamble and win and cash in all the tokens and walk out of the casino. He thus contended that it did not follow that when the cheque was dishonoured there was any debt in respect of any losses incurred by the customer in the gaming.

b In our judgment, when the cheque is given by the customer to enable him to take part in the gaming, and is subsequently dishonoured, then prima facie a debt has been incurred in respect of losses in the gaming. Of course, if the customer can establish that he never used the cash or tokens purchased by means of his cheque, or that he in fact made no loss as a result of being enabled through the acceptance by the casino of his cheque to take part in gambling on their premises, then he will have destroyed the prima facie case that the cheque which was dishonoured had created a debt in respect of a loss *c* incurred by him on the occasion of their cashing his cheque.

Counsel for Marcrest has drawn our attention to *CHT Ltd v Ward* [1963] 3 All ER 835, [1965] 2 QB 63. He submits that it was to make provision for the situation revealed in that case that the release provisions in s 16 were enacted. He was unaware of this case when appearing in the Divisional Court, and he submits that had it been brought to that court's attention it would not have held that a person who gives a cheque to a casino in *d* return for tokens or cash for the purpose of gaming will only owe the casino money in the event of losing money in gaming. In that case members obtained chips from the proprietors of the club, who then debited the member's account for the total face value of the chips handed out. The normal practice was for a member who had finished playing to hand any chips remaining in his possession to the cashier, who then credited his account with the cash equivalent of the face value of the chips. Member's accounts with *e* the club were sent to them at their addresses for settlement on a weekly basis. This was therefore a plain case of granting credit. The old legislation did not make loans for lawful gaming illegal. The situation in that case is amply covered by s 16(1), which clearly prevents the running up of debts at the tables, or allowing a customer to game with chips not paid for. This case does not, to our mind, in any way help in the solution of the question: how can a lawful debt in respect of losses incurred in gambling arise?

f Our attention has also been called to the Scots case of *Cumming v Mackie* 1973 SLT 242. The case was concerned essentially with the Gaming Act 1710, but Lord Fraser did in the course of his judgment refer to s 16 of the 1968 Act. He said this (at 245):

> 'Clearly the provision of money against a post-dated cheque might amount, in substance, to lending money, but the implication of the section seems to be that the granting of money against a cheque which is not post-dated is not giving credit or
g making a loan.'

We cannot accept that this is the implication. The implication appears to us to be quite clear that the giving of a cheque which does comply with the conditions laid down by s 16(2) results in the lawful grant of credit. Both the facts and the statutes with which Lord Fraser were concerned were different from the present case and accordingly Lord *h* Fraser's finding in that case does not help us in this case.

The chips are purchased only for the purpose of enabling the purchaser to take part in the gaming. If they are used and a loss is incurred, that loss will arise before the cheque is in fact dishonoured.

Counsel for Marcrest forcefully urges that to make it unlawful for a casino to compromise a dishonoured cheque will, in practice, cause casinos to sustain on occasions *j* serious losses which might otherwise have been mitigated. We fully appreciate this fact. There may well be hard cases resulting from the casino being obliged to recover their debts in full or not at all. In our judgment, however, these commercial disadvantages cannot affect the proper construction of the section. Moreover, it seems to us to be fully consistent with the policy of the legislation, which is to ensure that licensees do impose realistic limits on the credit which they accord to their customers.

The defects in the judgment of the Crown Court

Counsel for Marcrest repeated before us the complaint he made in the Divisional **a**
Court, namely that in considering the effect of the restructuring of the appellant
company, referred to at the outset of this judgment (which took place before the appeal
was heard in the Crown Court), his Honour Judge Friend became hopelessly confused
when trying to apply the guidelines laid down by the Divisional Court in *R v Crown
Court at Knightsbridge, ex p International Sporting Club (London) Ltd* [1981] 3 All ER 417,
[1982] QB 304.   **b**

Before considering the deficiencies of the Crown Court judgment, it is right to bear in
mind that this was an extempore judgment, in which the reasons for the decision were
given in abbreviated or summary form, and that the circuit judge has been given no
opportunity to make any revisions that he might have thought necessary. It is surprising,
and regrettable, particularly since the judge had been previously criticised by the
Divisional Court in previous similar cases, that he did not take the trouble to reserve his **c**
judgment and ensure that his use of 'discretion' was not, as the Divisional Court very
properly described it, slipshod.

He says:

> '[Counsel] on behalf of the Gaming Board put forward certain submissions to us
> as being foundation for the grounds why we should not exercise our discretion and
> find them fit and proper persons or exercise our discretion in respect of the **d**
> appellants.'

The first reference to 'exercise our discretion' in that sentence is meaningless, and we
have no doubt that if the judge had made the effort to write out his judgment or been
given the opportunity to revise his oral judgment it would have been deleted.

On the same page there is the next reference to discretion. It is in these terms: **e**

> 'I am bound to say, having heard all the facts and circumstances of this case, we,
> in our judgment, say that what was submitted by [counsel for the Gaming Board]
> on that aspect of the case was right. For that reason (one of the reasons) we could not
> exercise our discretion, because of the past misconduct, and say that we would grant
> this licence.'
> **f**

The submission to which the judge was making reference was based on the observations
made by the Divisional Court in the course of its judgment in the *International Sporting
Club* case [1981] 3 All ER 417 at 426, [1982] QB 304 at 318, which had been set out
verbatim by Judge Friend in his judgment, namely:

> 'There may well be cases in which the wrongdoing of the company licence holder
> has been so flagrant and so well publicised that no amount of restructuring can **g**
> restore confidence in it as a fit and proper person to hold a licence; it will stand
> condemned in the public mind as a person unfit to hold a licence and public
> confidence in the licensing justices would be gravely shaken by allowing it to
> continue to run the casino.'

Counsel for the Gaming Board had submitted in substance that the evidence made it **h**
clear that the misconduct had been so bad that it was incapable of being cured by
reconstruction. In what sense the judge was using the words 'exercise our discretion' in
this second reference is by no means clear.

His third reference to 'discretion' is in these terms:

> 'He [counsel for the Gaming Board] said that even if we did find the company, as
> reconstructed, was a fit and proper person nevertheless the unlawful conduct in the **j**
> past was such that we should not exercise our discretion in allowing this appeal.'

No valid complaint can be made in regard to this reference.

Judge Friend concluded his judgment in these terms:

> 'I am bound to say that we find the unlawful use and purposes proved, we are

satisfied about that and we accept the submissions made by the Gaming Board why *a* we should not exercise our discretion in that respect. In the result we have come to the conclusion that the justices, as I say, were right in coming to the decision which they did and we are not now satisfied on the restructuring that the appellant company is a fit and proper person. We are also satisfied that the past misconduct which amounted to an unlawful purpose has been proved. We find no ground, on the evidence before us, why we should exercise our discretion and not cancel the *b* licence so far as that is concerned. We refer once again to what Griffiths LJ said. He said: "There may well be cases in which the wrongdoing of the company licence holder has been flagrant and so well publicised that no amount of restructuring can restore confidence in it as a fit and proper person to hold a licence ..." That is exactly this case. "... it will stand condemned in the public mind as a person unfit to hold a licence ..." Agreed in this case. "... public confidence in the licensing *c* justices would be gravely shaken by allowing it to continue to run the casino." There we are. We accept those and, as I say, for those reasons we are satisfied that this appeal must be dismissed. I have not gone into all the details of all the various arguments which have been put forward. It simply comes to this: we are satisfied the justices were right, with one or two qualifications about the premises not being used for an unlawful purpose because the unlawful purpose was done in South *d* Audley Street. We are not satisfied that the restructuring has cured this, particularly when the only restructuring that has so far occurred is that there has been some change in the staff: further cashiers have been brought in because it was thought there were not enough there already. No, we cannot exercise our discretion and we do not. In the result, the appeal is dismissed in all respects, that is to say the licence is cancelled and the disqualification remains for three years.'

e   We agree with the Divisional Court that the judgment as a whole shows that the Crown Court directed itself correctly on how it should approach the restructuring of the company which had taken place before the hearing. There was ample evidence to justify the Crown Court's decision that, despite the restructuring, the company were not fit and proper persons to hold the licence. We agree with the Divisional Court that this finding *f* was not reached as a result of any error of law.

Was the Divisional Court in error in refusing, in the exercise of its discretion, to grant the appellants an order for certiorari notwithstanding the error of law, referred to in the first heading, made by the Crown Court?

Counsel for Marcrest contends that the Crown Court, in having regard to the unlawful use of the premises under a previous licence to found a complaint under para 21(1)(e) of *g* Sch 2 to the 1968 Act, acted in excess of its jurisdiction. Accordingly, Marcrest are entitled to the remedy of certiorari ex debito justiciae and accordingly the Divisional Court was wrong in refusing to grant that order.

Counsel for the Gaming Board contends that the error was merely an error of law on the face of the record, it was an error made in the exercise of a lawful jurisdiction, and not an error of law in excess of jurisdiction. The same point arose in the *International* *h* *Sporting Club* case [1981] 3 All ER 417 at 426–427, [1982] QB 304 at 319, where the court stated:

'As we are of the view that the judgment forms part of the record and discloses error of law, it is not necessary for us to express our opinion on the alternative ground that the court exceeded its jurisdiction. To some extent the two points are *j* interrelated because if the judgment is part of the record it is not necessary for this court to seek by subtle reasoning to find excess or abuse of jurisdiction in order to enable it to do justice by quashing a decision founded on error of law. On this difficult question of jurisdiction we are at the moment divided.'

We propose to resist the temptation of deciding whether counsel for Marcrest or counsel for the Gaming Board is right because it is common ground that, even if the

Crown Court, by making the error referred to, acted in excess of its jurisdiction, there
still remains in the court a residual discretion to grant or refuse the order. There must, *a*
however, as Greene MR said in *R v Stafford Justices, ex p Stafford Corp* [1940] 2 KB 33 at
44, be something in the circumstances of the case which make it right to refuse the relief
sought. In this case the point of law which was successfully raised in the Divisional Court
was rightly said by O'Connor LJ to be 'technical and without merit'. This, as previously
stated, may well have accounted for the point being overlooked on all sides. The finding
of use of the premises for unlawful purposes was based on allegations which did not go *b*
outside the ambit of the material relevant to Marcrest not being fit and proper persons.
The Crown Court was merely permitted, by the failure of Marcrest to take the point, to
apply another, and technically incorrect, label to those selfsame allegations, namely
unlawful user while the licence (the current licence) had been in force. Had the point
been taken, it would have excluded none of the evidence relied on by the Gaming Board
and the commissioner to establish the unfitness of Marcrest and could therefore have *c*
made no difference to the finding that they were not fit and proper persons to hold a
licence.

Would it have made any difference to the exercise by the Crown Court of its discretion?
\. _ are quite satisfied the answer must be No. As was pointed out by the Divisional Court
in the *International Sporting Club* case [1981] 3 All ER 417 at 426, [1982] QB 304 at 319, if
the court concludes that, even at the date of the rehearing and taking into account the *d*
restructuring, the company is not a fit and proper person to hold a gaming licence, it is
difficult to see how it could exercise its discretion otherwise than by cancelling the
licence. The finding that the use, which was undoubtedly unlawful, was also a breach of
para 21(1)(*e*) adds nothing to the gravity of Marcrest's conduct, which was described in
the Crown Court as 'disgraceful'. The Divisional Court properly asked itself whether, in
the circumstances, Marcrest suffered any injustice as a result of the error of law and *e*
concluded that they had not. We would have reached the same conclusion, but that is
not the test. It was for the Divisional Court to decide whether or not to exercise its
discretion, and we can only interfere if it is established that that discretion was exercised
erroneously. We are quite satisfied that there is no basis for such a contention.
Accordingly, taking Marcrest's position at its most favourable, namely that the error of
law which the Crown Court made resulted in their exceeding their jurisdiction, a *f*
situation which we assume and do not decide, the discretion existed to refuse the order
applied for and that discretion was validly exercised against Marcrest.

While we accept that the order for disqualification for three years is a serious addition
to the penalty of cancellation, the Crown Court, which over a period of many days heard
the evidence, having reached the conclusion that Marcrest's conduct in the running of
the premises was 'disgraceful', was fully entitled to exercise its powers under para 49 of *g*
Sch 2 to the 1968 Act and make the disqualification order which it did. In our judgment
it is quite unreal to suggest that, if the technical point about unlawful user had been
taken, it would have refrained from imposing the additional penalty of disqualification.

Appeal dismissed. Leave to appeal to the House of Lords refused.

h

Solicitors: *Durrant Piesse* (for Marcrest); *Gregory Rowcliffe & Co* (for the Gaming Board);
D M O'Shea (for the Commissioner of Police of the Metropolis).

Sophie Craven   Barrister.

Tate & Lyle Industries Ltd and another v Greater London Council and another

HOUSE OF LORDS

LORD DIPLOCK, LORD KEITH OF KINKEL, LORD ROSKILL, LORD BRIDGE OF HARWICH AND LORD TEMPLEMAN

24, 25, 26, 27, 31 JANUARY, 1, 2, 3 FEBRUARY, 24 MARCH 1983

Water and watercourses – Riparian rights – Extent – Maintenance of depth of water – Obstruction of right of navigation – Plaintiffs owners of jetties on bank of river – Local authority building ferry terminals on river – Terminals causing siltation of river bed – Whether siltation interfering with plaintiffs' riparian rights – Whether jetties capable of attracting riparian rights.

Water and watercourses – Depth of water – Right to particular depth of water – Plaintiffs owners of jetties in river – Jetties used for loading and unloading vessels – Jetties used and maintained under licences granted by river authority – Local authority building ferry terminals on river with river authority's approval – Terminals causing siltation of river bed and preventing plaintiffs from using jetties – Whether plaintiffs having right under contract, negligence or private nuisance to particular depth of water in river – Port of London Act 1968, s 66(1)(b).

Water and watercourses – Navigation – Public right of navigation – Public nuisance – Interference with public right of navigation causing particular damage to plaintiffs – Whether interference with public right of navigation giving right of action in public nuisance.

Nuisance – Defence – Statutory authority – Action for damages arising out of construction of ferry terminals in river – Local authority constructing terminals under statute authorising it to 'execute . . . works' – Design of terminals causing 75% more siltation than necessary – Whether local authority able to rely on defence of statutory authority in action for nuisance – London County Council (Improvements) Act 1962, ss 17, 50(3)(a).

The plaintiffs owned and operated a sugar refinery on the north bank of the River Thames. In 1922 the plaintiffs were granted, pursuant to the Port of London (Consolidation) Act 1920, a licence by the Port of London Authority (the PLA) to construct a jetty (the refined sugar jetty) in the bed of the river adjacent to the plaintiffs' land. The depth of the water between the main shipping channel and the site of the jetty enabled small vessels to load sugar from the jetty. In 1964 the plaintiffs obtained a further licence to construct a second jetty (the raw sugar jetty) and to dredge a channel and berth between the main shipping channel and the jetty to enable raw sugar to be brought in by small vessels. Between 1964 and 1966 the predecessor of the Greater London Council (the GLC) and later the GLC, in exercise of the powers conferred on it by s 17[a] of the London County Council (Improvements) Act 1962 to 'execute . . . works' and with the approval of the PLA required by that Act, constructed two ferry terminals in the river. The terminals consisted of piers which jutted out of the north and south banks of the river and were designed to enable ferry boats to carry vehicles across the river. The terminals and the raw sugar jetty were both completed in 1966. The effect of constructing the terminals was to cause siltation of the bed of the river between the refined sugar jetty and the main shipping channel and siltation of the channel and berth dredged for the purposes of the raw sugar jetty. As a result vessels could not approach to load and unload at the jetties, and in order to enable the jetties to be operated the plaintiffs, with the consent of the PLA, carried out additional dredging at their own expense between 1967 and 1974. The plaintiffs subsequently brought an action for damages in respect of the additional dredging costs against the GLC and the PLA alleging

_____

a   Section 17, so far as material, is set out at p 1172 *a b*, post

negligence and/or nuisance and/or breach of duty in connection with the design and construction of the terminals and the maintenance thereafter by the GLC, with the approval of the PLA, which had caused excessive siltation of the river bed. The plaintiffs contended that it was reasonably foreseeable that, in order to carry on their business, they would be obliged to incur the additional cost of dredging if the terminals were not designed to cause the minimum amount of siltation in the river bed and foreshore in the neighbourhood of the plaintiffs' jetties. At the trial of the action, the judge held that the GLC should have realised that the terminals might cause substantial siltation and that if it had taken expert advice it could have used a different design for the piers which would have reduced the siltation by 75% thereby causing the plaintiffs only a quarter of the additional dredging costs actually incurred. The judge held that the GLC and the PLA were liable in damages to the plaintiffs. The GLC and PLA successfully appealed to the Court of Appeal. The plaintiffs appealed to the House of Lords, contending that they possessed a right to the maintenance of the depth of water existing before the terminals were constructed and that such right was vested in them (i) as riparian owners, (ii) by contracts constituted by the works licences granted by the PLA under the 1920 Act and continued by s 66(1)(b)[b] of the Port of London Act 1968, (iii) as members of the public suffering particular damage from interference with the public right of navigation on the River Thames. The plaintiffs submitted, inter alia, that, since their works were deemed under the 1968 Act to be licences granted under s 66(1)(b) of that Act to construct or retain works in, under or over land belonging to the PLA and to confer on them as holders of the licences 'such rights in, under or over [the PLA's] land as [were] necessary to enable the holder of the licence to enjoy the benefit of the licence', the effect of their licences to erect the jetties was to confer on them the right to a sufficient depth of water to operate the jetties, since without a sufficient depth of water they could not enjoy the benefit of the jetties. They further contended that the licences for the jetties and for the dredging of the channel and berth contained an implied term that the PLA would not allow any interference with the river which would cause siltation, or alternatively that the PLA derogated from its grant of the licences when it failed to prevent the erection of terminals which caused siltation. The GLC and the PLA contended that in constructing the terminals the GLC acted in pursuance of statutory authority under the 1920 and 1962 Acts which authorised interference with the public right of navigation caused by the construction of the terminals and that therefore there was no public nuisance. They further contended that even if they were guilty of creating a public nuisance they were nevertheless authorised by the 1962 Act to do so in order to construct the terminals. The GLC further contended that in designing the terminals its only obligation was to obtain the approval of the PLA under s 50(3)(a)[c] of the 1962 Act, and that, if its design did not protect the interests of the public and the plaintiffs, the 1962 Act nevertheless authorised it to construct the terminals strictly in accordance with the design approved by the PLA and therefore any duty to ensure that the design of the terminal did not cause unnecessary siltation lay on the PLA rather than the GLC.

Held – (1) The plaintiffs could not sue as riparian owners because a riparian owner had no power to object to an alteration to the depth of the water adjacent to his land which did not threaten to cause damage to his land or interfere with his acknowledged riparian rights or cause a nuisance to the occupier of his land. The effect of the siltation was to obstruct the passage of vessels between the main shipping channel and the plaintiffs' land which, although it constituted an interference with the public right of navigation, did

---

b   Section 66(1), so far as material, provides: '(a) The [PLA] may . . . on such terms as they think fit . . . grant to a person a licence to carry out . . . works, notwithstanding that the works interfere with the public right of navigation or any other public right. (b) A works licence granted under paragraph (a) . . . to carry out . . . works in, under or over land belonging to the [PLA] shall be deemed to confer on the holder of the licence such rights in, under or over land as are necessary to enable the holder of the licence to enjoy the benefit of the licence.'

c   Section 50(3), so far as material, is set out at p 1172 f and p 1173 e, post

not constitute an interference with the plaintiffs' riparian rights. The plaintiffs could not,
a as riparian owners, complain of a decrease in the depth of water merely because the
public right of navigation was obstructed. In any event, a jetty which was erected into
the River Thames from land adjoining the river under a works licence granted by the
PLA under the 1968 Act to the owner or occupier of the adjoining land was only a chattel
and not realty forming part of the bank belonging to the owner of the land and therefore
was not capable of attracting riparian rights (see p 1166 *f* to *h*, p 1167 *c d*, p 1169 *a b*,
b p 1176 *d* and p 1178 *f* to *j*, post); *Bickett v Morris* [1861–73] All ER Rep 778 considered.

(2) The plaintiffs had no cause of action in contract arising out of the jetty licences
granted to them by the PLA because neither the works licence nor the dredging licence,
expressly or otherwise, nor the associated right to moor, load or unload vessels at the
jetties conferred any right that a particular depth of water would be maintained around
the jetties. Furthermore, the effect of s 66(1)(*b*) of the 1968 Act was merely to enable the
c plaintiffs to exercise such rights over the bed and water of the river as were necessary for
the erection and maintenance of the jetties and did not extend to conferring on the
plaintiffs the right to a particular depth of water to enable them to enjoy the benefit of
the licences. Moreover, in the absence of a private right to a particular depth of water the
plaintiffs could not maintain an action in negligence or private nuisance (see p 1169 *d* to
f h j, p 1170 *a* to *c g*, p 1176 *d* and p 1178 *f* to *j*, post).

d   (3) (Lord Diplock dissenting) The plaintiffs were, however, entitled to maintain an
action in public nuisance because the River Thames was a navigable river over which the
public had the right of navigation, ie the right to pass and repass over the whole width
and depth of water in the river and the incidental rights of loading and unloading, and
the construction of the ferry terminals interfered with that public right of navigation on
the river between the main shipping channel and the plaintiffs' jetties by causing siltation
e on the bed and the foreshore of the river and in the channel and berth dredged by the
plaintiffs. Furthermore, the interference with the public right of navigation caused
particular damage to the plaintiffs because vessels of the requisite dimensions were
unable to pass and repass between the main shipping channel and the plaintiffs' jetties
(see p 1170 *h* to p 1171 *b* and p 1178 *f* to *j*, post).

f   (4) (Lord Diplock dubitante) The GLC could not rely on the defence of statutory
authority because, although the terminals were erected under the statutory authority of
the 1962 Act, the GLC could only claim immunity from any damaging consequences of
the terminals if it had paid all reasonable care and had regard for the interests of public
navigation and for the the interests of persons, such as the plaintiffs, who were liable to
suffer particular damage from any interference with the right of public navigation. In
particular the authorisation to 'execute ... works' in s 17 of the 1962 Act merely
g conferred immunity on the GLC in respect of siltation that was inevitable and not in
respect of additional siltation caused by the particular design for the terminals chosen by
the GLC. Furthermore, the requirement under s 50(3)(*a*) of the 1962 Act that the GLC
was to submit plans and particulars of river works to the PLA before commencing
construction did not transfer to the PLA the duty to ensure that the design of the
terminals did not cause unnecessary siltation, since the PLA was entitled to assume that
h the GLC had chosen a competent designer to ensure that the design did not have any
adverse effect. Nor did s 50(3)(*a*) in any way relieve the GLC of its elementary duties to
design and construct the terminals with all reasonable care for the interests of other
persons and to cause no more harm than was necessary. It followed (Lord Diplock
dissenting) that the GLC was liable to the plaintiffs in public nuisance and accordingly
the plaintiffs' appeal against the GLC would be allowed. On the measure of damages,
j since an alternative design would have caused one-quarter of the siltation that actually
occurred, and since one-quarter of the additional dredging costs was therefore an
inevitable consequence of the exercise by the GLC of its statutory power to construct the
terminals, one-quarter of the dredging costs was not recoverable by the plaintiffs (see
p 1172 *c* to *g*, p 1173 *a b j*, p 1174 *a*, p 1175 *a* to *d*, p 1176 *f g* and p 1178 *f* to *j*, post);
dictum of Lord Wilberforce in *Allen v Gulf Oil Refining Ltd* [1981] 1 All ER at 356
followed.

(5) There were no circumstances which should have alerted the PLA to the possibility that the terminals might cause the unforeseen and disastrous amount of siltation which took place, nor was there anything which would have justified the PLA in insisting on the design being submitted to further advice or subjected to tests to determine the possible effects of the terminals causing siltation. It could not be said therefore that merely because they approved the plans of the terminals the PLA continued or adopted or otherwise became liable for any nuisance created by the terminals. Furthermore, the PLA by giving approval to the plans did not thereby guarantee that the terminals would not interfere with the right of public navigation. The PLA was therefore not liable to the plaintiffs and the plaintiffs' appeal against it would be dismissed (see p 1172 *g h*, p 1174 *e f j*, p 1176 *a b* and p 1178 *f* to *j*, post); dictum of Viscount Maugham in *Sedleigh-Denfield v O'Callagan* [1940] 3 All ER at 358 considered.

Notes

For the general public right of navigation, see 39 Halsbury's Laws (3rd edn) 533, para 718, and for cases on the subject, see 47 Digest (Repl) 728, 727.

For the general public right of navigation on the Thames, see 39 Halsbury's Laws (3rd edn) 543, para 736.

For riparian rights generally, see ibid 514–524, paras 675–696, and for cases on the subject, see 47 Digest (Repl) 729–730, 739–740, 728–736, 814–817.

For the general powers and duties of the Port of London Authority, see 39 Halsbury's Laws (3rd edn) 618–621, paras 890–891, and for cases on the subject, see 47 Digest (Repl) 749–751, 890–898.

For the Port of London Act 1968, s 66, see 31 Halsbury's Statutes (3rd edn) 1057.

Cases referred to in opinions

A-G v Thames Conservators (1862) 1 Hem & M 1, 71 ER 1, 47 Digest (Repl) 747, 873.

Allen v Gulf Oil Refining Ltd [1981] 1 All ER 353, [1981] AC 1001, [1981] 2 WLR 188, HL.

Anns v Merton London Borough [1977] 2 All ER 492, [1978] AC 728, [1977] 2 WLR 1024, HL, Digest (Cont Vol E) 449, 99*b*.

Bickett v Morris (1866) LR 1 Sc & Div 47, [1861–73] All ER Rep 778, HL, 47 Digest (Repl) 645, 66.

Booth v Ratté (1890) 15 App Cas 188, PC, 47 Digest (Repl) 685, 364.

Chasemore v Richards (1859) 7 HL Cas 349, [1843–60] All ER Rep 77, 11 ER 140, HL, 47 Digest (Repl) 667, 257.

Donoghue (or M'Alister) v Stevenson [1932] AC 562, [1932] All ER Rep 1, HL, 36(1) Digest (Reissue) 144, 562.

Home Office v Dorset Yacht Co Ltd [1970] 2 All ER 294, [1970] AC 1004, [1970] 2 WLR 1140, HL, 36(1) Digest (Reissue) 27, 93.

Junior Books Ltd v Veitchi Co Ltd [1982] 3 All ER 201, [1982] 3 WLR 477, HL.

Kearns v Cordwainers' Co (1859) 6 CBNS 388, 141 ER 508, 47 Digest (Repl) 748, 879.

Lyon v Fishmongers' Co (1876) 1 App Cas 662, HL, 47 Digest (Repl) 739, 814.

Sedleigh-Denfield v O'Callagan [1940] 3 All ER 349, [1940] AC 880, HL, 36(1) Digest (Reissue) 486, 633.

Appeal

The plaintiffs, Tate & Lyle Industries Ltd (formerly Tate & Lyle Food and Distribution Ltd) (Tate & Lyle) and Silvertown Services Lighterage Ltd (Silvertown Services), appealed with leave of the Appeal Committee of the House of Lords granted on 28 July 1982 against the decision of the Court of Appeal (Cumming Bruce, Dunn and Oliver LJJ) allowing an appeal by the defendants, the Greater London Council (the GLC) and the Port of London Authority (the PLA), from the judgment of Forbes J given on 15 May 1980 on the issue of liability on claims by Tate & Lyle and Silvertown Services for damages for nuisance and negligence against the GLC and the PLA. (Following his judgment on the question of liability Forbes J gave judgment on the quantum of damages on 22 May 1981 ([1981] 3 All ER 716, [1982] 1 WLR 149). The Court of Appeal

did not refer to the judgment of Forbes J on 22 May 1981 (see [1982] 2 All ER 854n,
a [1982] 1 WLR 971n.) The facts are set out in the opinion of Lord Templeman.

Anthony Clarke QC and *Belinda Bucknall* for Tate & Lyle and Silvertown Services.
John Davies QC and *Charles Gibson* for the GLC.
Graeme Hamilton QC and *Christopher Purchas* for the PLA.

b Their Lordships took time for consideration.

24 March. The following opinions were delivered.

LORD DIPLOCK. My Lords, as I have the misfortune to differ in part from the
majority of the Appellate Committee I will ask my noble and learned friend Lord
c Templeman to deliver the first speech with which I understand the rest of your Lordships
concur.

LORD TEMPLEMAN. My Lords,

Introduction
d   Between 1964 and 1966 the first respondent, the Greater London Council (then called
the London County Council and hereinafter called 'the GLC'), in exercise of powers
conferred on its predecessor by the London County Council (Improvements) Act 1962
and with the approval, required by that Act, of the second respondents, the Port of
London Authority (the PLA), constructed two new terminals for the Woolwich Ferry in
the River Thames.
e   The new ferry terminals consisted of piers which jutted out of the north and south
banks of the Thames. The terminals were designed to enable ferry boats carrying vehicles
across the Thames to be end loaded. To achieve this object each pier assumed the shape
of a letter 'J' jutting out first at right angles to the bank and finishing parallel to the bank.
There were, however, alternative types of design for the piers and the design chosen by
the GLC caused an unforeseen and, as the trial judge Forbes J found, a largely unnecessary
f obstruction to the flow of the water in the river. This obstacle combined with the
configuration of the Thames in the area of Woolwich reduced the speed of the river flow
between the north bank of the river and the main shipping channel up-stream of the
terminals; that reduction of speed in turn caused sediment to be deposited and siltation
to take place which materially reduced the depth of water between the north bank and
the main shipping channel.
g   The first appellants, Tate & Lyle Industries Ltd, have for many years operated a sugar
refinery on the north bank of the Thames in Woolwich Reach up-stream of the Woolwich
ferry. In 1922 the PLA authorised Tate & Lyle to construct a jetty known as the refined
sugar jetty in the bed of the river adjacent to Tate & Lyle's refinery. The depth of the
water between the main shipping channel in the Thames and the site of the refined sugar
jetty enabled small vessels to come alongside the jetty and to load refined sugar for
h export.
     The raw sugar required at Tate & Lyle's refinery was discharged from larger vessels
lower down the river into barges which were then unloaded at wharves on the banks of
Tate & Lyle's land. In about 1964 Tate & Lyle conceived the idea of bringing the vessels
with raw sugar up the main shipping channel and thence by a dredged channel to a new
jetty to be constructed in the river bed adjacent to the bank of Tate & Lyle's land. To
j accommodate the required vessels at the new jetty it was necessary to dredge a berth six
feet below main channel depth. By the Port of London (Consolidation) Act 1920 Tate &
Lyle required a licence from the PLA for the construction of the raw sugar jetty and for
the dredging of the channel and berth. On 22 January 1965 the PLA authorised Tate &
Lyle to carry out the necessary dredging of the channel and berth and on 30 April 1965
the PLA authorised the construction of the raw sugar jetty.
     The terminals for the Woolwich ferry were completed for the GLC and the raw sugar

jetty was completed for Tate & Lyle in 1966. At the trial of this action Forbes J held, and it is not now disputed, that the effect of the terminals was to cause siltation of the *a* channels and berth dredged for the purposes of the raw sugar jetty and to cause siltation of the bed of the river between the refined sugar jetty and the main channel. In the result, vessels carrying raw sugar could not approach and be unloaded at the raw sugar jetty and vessels which had formerly loaded and departed with refined sugar from the refined sugar jetty could no longer do so. To enable both jetties to be operated Tate & Lyle, with the consent of the PLA, incurred additional dredging costs between 1967 and *b* 1974 of £344,998 to enable the raw sugar jetty to be kept in operation and £195,002 to enable the refined sugar jetty to be kept in operation, making total additional dredging costs of £540,000. Additional dredging ceased to be necessary after 1974 because the PLA made major alterations to the shipping channel of the River Thames which had the effect of putting an end to the siltation caused by the new terminals in the river bed between Tate & Lyle's jetties and the main shipping channel. *c*

The judge also held, and it is not now disputed, that the civil engineers who designed the terminals on behalf of the GLC should have realised that the terminals might cause substantial siltation and should have taken expert advice which would have resulted in a different design for the piers. This would have reduced the siltation caused by the terminals and only involved Tate & Lyle in 25% of the additional dredging costs which they incurred. *d*

In these preceedings Tate & Lyle claim £540,000, representing the total of the additional costs of dredging made necessary as a result of the construction of the Woolwich ferry terminals. Tate & Lyle claim against the GLC for causing the siltation and against the PLA for approving the plans for the terminals which were responsible for the siltation. The facts were exhaustively investigated at the trial; they were admirably elucidated by Forbes J in his judgment at first instance, when he found substantially in *e* favour of Tate & Lyle; the facts were subsequently summarised in the judgment of Oliver LJ in the Court of Appeal where the GLC and the PLA succeeded in obtaining a dismissal of all the claims put forward by Tate & Lyle. The question is whether on the established facts and on the true construction and effect of the London County Council (Improvements) Act 1962, the Port of London (Consolidation) Act 1920 and the Port of London Act 1968, the GLC and the PLA or either of them are liable to Tate & Lyle in *f* negligence or nuisance for the whole or part of the cost of the additional dredging made necessary by the effect of the Woolwich terminals on the flow of the River Thames in front of Tate & Lyle's land.

Negligence

The claim of Tate & Lyle in negligence was first put with engaging simplicity on the *g* grounds that the GLC and the PLA owed a duty to take reasonable care not to cause loss or damage to Tate & Lyle of a kind which the GLC and the PLA could reasonably foresee. It was reasonably foreseeable that in order to carry on their business, Tate & Lyle would be obliged to incur the additional cost of dredging if the terminals were not designed to cause the minimum amount of siltation in the river bed and foreshore in the neighbourhood of Tate & Lyle's jetties. *h*

The argument derives from the well-known passage in the speech of Lord Atkin in *Donoghue v Stevenson* [1932] AC 562 at 580, [1932] All ER Rep 1 at 11, namely that 'You must take reasonable care to avoid acts or omissions which you can reasonably foresee would be likely to injure your neighbour', that is to say, 'persons who are so closely and directly affected by my act that I ought reasonably to have them in contemplation as being so affected when I am directing my mind to the acts or omissions which are called *j* in question'. *Donoghue v Stevenson* was a case where it was assumed that injury to health had been suffered by a consumer as a result of a defect in a product supplied by a manufacturer.

In *Home Office v Dorset Yacht Co Ltd* [1970] 2 All ER 294, [1970] AC 1004 the Home Office was held liable in negligence for damage to the plaintiff's property caused by

absconding Borstal boys. Lord Reid said ([1970] 2 All ER 294 at 297, [1970] AC 1004 at
a   1026):

> '... there has been a steady trend towards regarding the law of negligence as
> depending on principle ... and the well-known passage in Lord Atkin's speech
> should I think be regarded as a statement of principle. It is not to be treated as if it
> were a statutory definition. It will require qualification in new circumstances. But I
> think that the time has come when we can and should say that it ought to apply
b   > unless there is some justification or valid explanation for its exclusion. For example,
> causing economic loss is a different matter; for one thing, it is often caused by
> deliberate action. Competition involves traders being entitled to damage their rivals'
> interests by promoting their own, and there is a long chapter of the law determining
> in what circumstances owners of land can and in what circumstances they may use
> their proprietary rights so as to injure their neighbours. But where negligence is
c   > involved the tendency has been to apply principles analogous to those stated by Lord
> Atkin.'

In *Anns v Merton London Borough* [1977] 2 All ER 492, [1978] AC 728 a local authority
which failed to exercise reasonable care in carrying out its statutory powers and duties in
the inspection and approval of the foundations of a house was held to be liable in
d   negligence to a subsequent purchaser of the house when the house suffered damage as a
result of defective foundations. Lord Wilberforce said ([1977] 2 All ER 492 at 498, [1978]
AC 728 at 751):

> '... the position has now been reached that in order to establish that a duty of
> care arises in a particular situation, it is not necessary to bring the facts of that
> situation within those of previous situations in which a duty of care has been held
e   > to exist. Rather the question has to be approached in two stages. First one has to ask
> whether, as between the alleged wrongdoer and the person who has suffered damage
> there is a sufficient relationship of proximity or neighbourhood such that, in the
> reasonable contemplation of the former, carelessness on his part may be likely to
> cause damage to the latter, in which case a prima facie duty of care arises. Secondly,
> if the first question is answered affirmatively, it is necessary to consider whether
f   > there are any considerations which ought to negative, or to reduce or limit the scope
> of the duty or the class of person to whom it is owed or the damages to which a
> breach of it may give rise ...'

In *Junior Books Ltd v Veitchi Co Ltd* [1982] 3 All ER 201, [1982] 3 WLR 477 a sub-
contractor was held liable to the owner of premises for damaging those premises by
g   installing a defective floor. Lord Roskill rejected the argument that the only remedy for
the owner of the premises was to sue the main contractor for breach of contract. He said
([1982] 3 All ER 201 at 213, [1982] 3 WLR 477 at 494):

> '... the proper control lies not in asking whether the proper remedy should lie
> in contract or instead in delict or tort, not in somewhat capricious judicial
> determination whether a particular case falls on one side of the line or the other, not
h   > in somewhat artificial distinctions between physical and economic or financial loss
> when the two sometimes go together and sometimes do not (it is sometimes
> overlooked that virtually all damage including physical damage is in one sense
> financial or economic for it is compensated by an award of damages) but in the first
> instance in establishing the relevant principles and then in deciding whether the
> particular case falls within or without those principles ... The first is "sufficient
j   > relationship of proximity", the second any considerations negativing, reducing or
> limiting the scope of the duty or the class of person to whom it is owed or the
> damages to which a breach of the duty may give rise.'

My Lords, in the cited relevant cases from *Donoghue v Stevenson* to *Junior Books Ltd v
Veitchi* the plaintiff suffered personal injury or damage to his property. In the present

case Tate & Lyle assert that they have suffered damage to their property caused by
interference with their right to use their jetties for the benefit of their sugar refining   *a*
business. But this assertion assumes that Tate & Lyle possess the right to use their jetties
in the sense that they are entitled to the maintenance of a depth of water in the relevant
parts of the Thames sufficient to enable vessels of the requisite size to load and unload at
the jetties. The question is whether Tate & Lyle possess any right to any particular depth
of water. If they have any such right then they will have a remedy for interference with
that right. But if they have no such right then interference with the depth of water   *b*
causing damage to Tate & Lyle's business constitutes an injury for which Tate & Lyle
have no remedy. The GLC caused siltation to the bed of the river which is owned by the
PLA. Tate & Lyle can only succeed if they establish that they were obstructed by the
GLC in the exercise by Tate & Lyle of rights over the river bed vested in Tate & Lyle.
   On behalf of Tate & Lyle it was submitted that the requisite rights over the river bed
are vested in Tate & Lyle firstly as riparian owners, secondly by contract constituted by   *c*
the licences granted by the PLA and thirdly as members of the public suffering particular
damage from interference with the public right of navigation on the Thames.

Riparian rights
   Tate & Lyle are riparian owners because they own part of the northern bank of the
Thames. As riparian owners Tate and Lyle are entitled to access to the water in contact   *d*
with their frontage, and to have the water flow to them in its natural state in flow, quality
and quantity so that they may take water for ordinary purposes in connection with their
riparian tenement including the use of water power. The siltation caused by the terminals
did not obstruct the access from Tate & Lyle's land to the water, did not constitute any
danger of damage to the land, and did not create any nuisance to the occupier of the land.
The siltation caused a decrease in the depth of water between Tate & Lyle's land and the   *e*
main shipping channel. Tate & Lyle claim that their riparian rights include the right to
the maintenance of the depth of water existing before the terminals were constructed. It
seems to me this argument confuses private riparian rights with the public right of
navigation. It is not clear to me whether Tate & Lyle's claim to the maintenance of the
status quo with regard to the depth of water extended to the whole of the river from Tate
& Lyle's bank on the north to the bank opposite on the south, or whether it was confined   *f*
to the depth of water between Tate & Lyle's bank and the main shipping channel, or to
some other area of the bed and foreshore of the Thames. On principle, I cannot accept
that a riparian owner has any power to object to an alteration to the depth of the water
which does not threaten to cause damage to his land or to interfere with his acknowledged
riparian rights or to cause a nuisance to the occupier of his land. The effect of the siltation
was to obstruct the passage of vessels between the main shipping channel and Tate &   *g*
Lyle's land. The obstruction constituted an interference with the public right of
navigation for which Tate & Lyle have a remedy but the obstruction did not constitute
an interference with Tate & Lyle's riparian rights. Tate & Lyle relied on general
statements of the rights of riparian owners to support their submission that as riparian
owners they can prevent any interference with the depth of water. In *Bickett v Morris*
(1866) LR 1 Sc & Div 47, [1861–73] All ER Rep 778 a riparian owner who owned part of   *h*
the bank of a non-navigable river also owned half of the land of the river from his bank
to the centre of the stream. He built a wall on part of his half of the bed of the river. The
riparian owner on the opposite bank obtained an injunction requiring the wall to be
removed. Lord Chelmsford LC said (LR 1 Sc & Div 47 at 55–56, [1861–73] All ER Rep
778 at 780):
                                                                                           j
   'The proprietors upon the opposite banks of a river have a common interest in
   the stream, and although each has a property in the *alveus* from his own side to the
   medium filum fluminis, neither is entitled to use the *alveus* in such a manner as to
   interfere with the natural flow of the water ... neither proprietor can have any
   right to abridge the width of the stream, or to interfere with its regular course; but

a

anything done *in alveo*, which produces no sensible effect upon the stream, is allowable.'

Lord Cranworth said that riparian proprietors have a common interest in the unrestricted flow of the water and may forbid any interference with it (see LR 1 Sc & Div 47 at 59, [1861–73] All ER Rep 778 at 782). Lord Westbury said that—

'though immediate damage cannot be described, even though the actual loss cannot be predicated, yet, if an obstruction be made to the current of the stream, that obstruction is one which constitutes an injury which the Courts will take notice of, as an encroachment which adjacent proprietors have a right to have removed.'

(See LR 1 Sc & Div 47 at 62, [1861–73] All ER Rep 778 at 783.)

In *Bickett v Morris* the court assumed that the wall of the defendant might cause damage to the riparian tenement of the plaintiff by erosion resulting from the diversion of the flow of water by the wall. The court will only interfere if there is 'an injurious obstruction' (see LR 1 Sc & Div 47 at 56, [1861–73] All ER Rep 778 at 780 per Lord Chelmsford LC). In my opinion *Bickett v Morris* is not authority for the proposition that a riparian owner can complain of a decrease in the depth of water when the only effect of that decrease is to obstruct the public right of navigation.

The distinction between private riparian rights and the public right of navigation is of great importance with regard to the River Thames because the PLA have statutory power to interfere and to authorise works which interfere with the public right of navigation provided that the PLA consider that the works are necessary or desirable in the general interests of improving the facilities furnished by the Thames. On the other hand, the PLA are not entitled by statute to interfere with established riparian or other private rights.

Section 9 of the Port of London (Consolidation) Act 1920 imposed on the PLA the duty—

'to take such steps from time to time as they may consider necessary for the improvement of the River Thames within the Port of London and the accommodation and facilities afforded in the Port of London and for these purposes'

the PLA were expressly authorised to construct jetties or piers and other works which, from their very nature, might cause some alteration to or interference with the public right of navigation in the neighbourhood of the works. Section 243 of the 1920 Act authorised the PLA to grant to any owner or occupier of any land adjoining the Thames a licence to make any pier, jetty, wharf or embankment wall or other work immediately in front of his land and into the body of the Thames, and again any such work by its nature might alter or interfere with the public right of navigation in the neighbourhood. If, in a bona fide exercise of its statutory powers, the PLA caused or authorised any work which interfered with the public right of navigation, then no action would lie in respect of that interference which was impliedly authorised by the statute. But s 307 of the Act provided that nothing—

'shall take away alter or abridge any right claim privilege . . . to which any owner or occupier of any lands on the banks of the Thames . . . or any person is now by law entitled . . . but the same shall remain and continue in full force and effect as if this Act had not been passed'.

Thus the owner of a riparian tenement can object to any work carried out by the PLA or by any licensee of the PLA, if the work interferes with his riparian rights. If Tate & Lyle's contentions are right, however, every work which interferes with the flow or depth of the water and creates an interference with the public right of navigation must also be an interference with riparian rights and will entitle a riparian owner to an injunction or damages. The authorities do not support this confusion between riparian rights and the public right of navigation.

In *Kearns v Cordwainers' Co* (1859) 6 CBNS 388, 141 ER 508, the Thames Conservators, who were the predecessors of the PLA, had licensed the erection of a jetty pursuant to *a* s 53 of the Thames Conservancy Act 1857, which corresponded to s 243 of the 1920 Act. The 1857 Act also contained a reservation of private rights in s 179 in terms similar to the provisions of s 307 of the 1920 Act. It was held that the Thames Conservators had power to license the jetty albeit that it might in some degree obstruct the enjoyment by adjoining owners of full and free navigation of the river.

In *A-G v Thames Conservators* (1862) 1 Hem & M 1, 71 ER 1, the court refused to *b* prohibit by injunction the erection of a pier licensed by the Thames Conservators, although the pier made more difficult the passage of vessels to and from the wharves of a neighbouring landowner. Page-Wood V-C distinguished between the private right of access which belonged to the landowner in respect of his wharves and the public right of navigation (see 1 Hem & M 1 at 31, 71 ER 1 at 14). The private right of access had not been taken away and no complaint could be made of interference with the public right *c* right of navigation.

In *Lyon v Fishmongers' Co* (1876) 1 App Cas 662, the Thames Conservators purported to exercise their undoubted power to license the construction of an embankment which interfered with the public right of navigation. The embankment, however, would have destroyed the plaintiff's frontage to the river and prevented him from obtaining access to the river. The plaintiff's private riparian rights were, therefore, injured. The *d* Conservators had no power to authorise any such injury and the defendants were restrained from constructing the embankment. Tate & Lyle rely on the passage from the speech of Lord Cairns LC (at 673–674) where he cited with approval the statement of Lord Wensleydale in *Chasemore v Richards* (1859) 7 HL Cas 382, [1843–60] All ER Rep 77 that—

> 'it has been now settled that the rights to the enjoyment of a natural stream of *e* water on the surface, *ex jure naturae*, belongs to the proprietor of the adjoining lands, as a natural incident to the right to the soil itself, and that he is entitled to the benefit of it, as he is to all the other natural advantages belonging to the land of which he is the owner. He has the right to have it come to him in its natural state, in flow, quantity, and quality, and to go from him without obstruction ... the riparian *f* owner on a navigable river, in addition to the right connected with navigation to which he is entitled as one of the public, retains his rights, as an ordinary riparian owner, underlying and controlled by, but not extinguished by, the public right of navigation.'

But there remains the distinction between private riparian rights and the public right of navigation. In *Lyon v Fishmongers' Co* the works in question interfered with private *g* riparian rights. The works could not be justified on the grounds that they also interfered with or improved the public right of navigation. In the present case the only interference which has been proved is interference with the public right of navigation. Tate & Lyle's land and Tate & Lyle's riparian rights are not affected.

The GLC and the PLA submitted in the alternative that in any event riparian rights do not attach to Tate & Lyle's jetties. Tate & Lyle claim that the jetties must be regarded as *h* extensions to Tate & Lyle's land, albeit that the jetties are structures erected on the bed of the river which belongs to the PLA and not to Tate & Lyle. I do not consider that riparian rights attach to the jetties.

The jetties were constructed pursuant to a licence granted by the PLA under s 243 of the Port of London (Consolidation) Act 1920. That section, to which reference has already been made, authorised the PLA to grant to any owner or occupier of any land adjoining *j* the Thames a licence to make a jetty immediately in front of his land and into the body of the Thames. In the case of the raw sugar jetty (and we are informed in the case also of the refined sugar jetty), the relevant licence authorised Tate & Lyle to construct a specified jetty in the River Thames off the refinery premises of Tate & Lyle subject to the express condition that Tate & Lyle would remove the jetty on seven day's notice. It seems to me

that a jetty thus erected on the foreshore of the Thames vested in the PLA was only a
a chattel and not realty forming part of the bank of the river belonging to Tate & Lyle, and
that such a jetty is not capable of attracting riparian rights. The Court of Appeal,
reversing Forbes J said, and I agree, that the jetties—

> 'are not part of the riparian tenement, although they are connected to it. They are
> artificial structures put into the stream under licence and built, not on the land of
> the riparian owner, but on that of the PLA. Riparian rights are rights attaching to
b the fee simple of the land ex jure naturae and it is not easy to see how, at common
> law, they can become attached to something which is not part of the fee simple and
> of which the riparian owner has nothing but a permissive and revocable enjoyment.'

Contractual rights
c   In default of riparian rights Tate & Lyle rely on contractual rights. They assert that the
PLA granted and the GLC infringed the right of Tate & Lyle to the maintenance of the
depth of water created by Tate & Lyle's licensed dredging which enabled the refined
sugar jetty and the raw sugar jetty to be operated for the loading and unloading of vessels.
In the licences granted by the PLA for the erection of the jetties, however, there was no
express grant of a right to use the jetties for loading or unloading vessels of any specified
d draught. The PLA granted a separate licence for Tate & Lyle to dredge a channel leading
to the jetties and to dredge a berth at the raw sugar jetty of a specified depth, but that
dredging licence was no more than a dredging licence, and did not grant Tate & Lyle any
rights in relation to the river bed, or to the river once the dredging had been carried out.
Tate & Lyle could not even remove any silt which subsequently to the initial dredging
by any means accumulated without a further licence from the PLA. Tate & Lyle had no
e right to any depth of water and no right other than the public right of navigation to
bring vessels from the shipping channel to their jetties. Tate & Lyle had the right to
moor, load and unload vessels at the refined sugar jetty and in the berth dredged at the
raw sugar jetty because Tate & Lyle were the owners of authorised jetties, but the right
to moor, load and unload did not confer any right or any guarantee as to the maintenance
of any specified depth of water for the accommodation of vessels of any particular size.
f   Tate & Lyle claim that their contractual rights were transformed by the Port of London
Act 1968 which replaced the Port of London (Consolidation) Act 1920. The licences for
the construction of the refined sugar jetty and the raw sugar jetty were granted by the
PLA to Tate & Lyle pursuant to s 243 of the 1920 Act. By para (*h*) of Sch 11 to the 1968
Act all licences issued by the PLA in force at the commencement of the Act on 26 July
1968 'shall continue in force and shall be deemed to have been made or issued under the
g appropriate provisions of this Act'. Power for the PLA to license jetties and other works
is contained in s 66(1)(*a*) of the 1968 Act. By s 66(1)(*b*), a works licence to construct or
retain works in, under or over land belonging to the PLA shall be deemed to confer on
the holder of the licence 'such rights in, under or over land as are necessary to enable the
holder of the licence to enjoy the benefit of the licence'. On behalf of Tate & Lyle it was
argued that the effect of s 66(1)(*b*) on the licences to erect the jetties was to confer on Tate
h & Lyle the right to a sufficient depth of water to enable Tate & Lyle to operate the jetties.
Without a sufficient depth of water, Tate & Lyle would not be able to enjoy the benefit
of the jetty licences. But the jetty licences only granted authority for Tate & Lyle to erect
and maintain the structures in the River Thames now known as the refined sugar jetty
and the raw sugar jetty. For the purpose of erecting and maintaining the jetties, Tate &
Lyle are entitled by virtue of s 66(1)(*b*) to exercise such rights over the bed and water of
j the river as are necessary to ensure that the jetties are installed and kept in good repair.
In my view, s 66(1)(*b*) did not confer on Tate & Lyle any rights to the maintenance of any
particular depth of water near or leading to the jetties.
    It was faintly argued that in the licences for the jetties and for the dredging of the
channel and berth in connection with the raw sugar jetty there must be implied a term
that the PLA would not allow any interference with the Thames which would cause

siltation. Alternatively, the PLA derogated from their grant of the licences when they
failed to prevent the erection of the terminals which caused siltation. In my opinion, the *a*
PLA had no statutory power to agree, and did not purport to agree, expressly or impliedly,
that no works would be allowed which affected the depth of water in the Thames
between the jetties and the main shipping channel.

I consider that Tate & Lyle cannot maintain an action in negligence because they did
not possess any private rights which enabled them to insist on any particular depth of
water in connection with the operation of their licensed jetties.   *b*

Private nuisance

An action in private nuisance must also fail if Tate & Lyle have no private rights in
connection with the depth of the River Thames. The siltation caused by the GLC did not
interfere with Tate & Lyle's use and occupation of the jetties but with Tate & Lyle's use
of the River Thames. Tate & Lyle rely on the decision in *Booth v Ratté* (1890) 15 App Cas *c*
188. In that case the plaintiff was a riparian owner who constructed a floating wharf and
warehouse moored to his bank of the river. The defendant operated a saw mill upstream
of the plaintiff's land and polluted the river with sawdust, bark and other refuse which
were deposited in front of the plaintiff's wharf and warehouse. The refuse resulted—

> 'not only in fouling the water, making it offensive both to taste and smell but *d*
> produce from the gas generated underneath the surface frequent explosions which
> are disagreeable and sometimes dangerous. It is thus proved that the plaintiff
> sustains special injury beyond the rest of the public by this unauthorised interference
> of the defendant's with the flow and purity of the stream. He is injured in the
> personal enjoyment of the property and the river, and he is injured in the business
> which he follows of hiring and housing pleasure boats'.
>   *e*

(See 15 App Cas 188 at 190.)

The only defence was that the plaintiff had no title to the wharf and boathouse. It was
held that the plaintiff was either the owner of part of the river bed on which the wharf
and boathouse were placed or was a licensee. Either title sufficed to enable the plaintiff
to maintain an action based on damage or threatened damage to the wharf and to recover
damages in private nuisance or public nuisance for damage to his business carried on *f*
upon his land, wharf and warehouse caused by smell and impurity of water. In *Booth v
Ratté* the plaintiff was claiming to be left undisturbed in the use and occupation of the
wharf and boathouse which he occupied. He was not claiming any rights over the river.
In the present case nothing has happened to disturb the possession by Tate & Lyle of their
jetties. Tate & Lyle complain of interference with their use of the bed of the River
Thames. They must prove some private right over the bed of the River Thames before *g*
they can complain that the siltation of the bed and consequent decrease of the depth of
the water constitute an actionable infringement of their private rights whether in
negligence or in nuisance.

Public nuisance

The Thames is a navigable river over which the public have the right of navigation, *h*
that is to say a right to pass and re-pass over the whole width and depth of water in the
River Thames and the incidental right of loading and unloading. The public right of
navigation was expressly preserved by s 210 of the Port of London (Consolidation) Act
1920 whereby—

> '(1) Subject to the provisions of this Act it shall be lawful for all persons whether
> for pleasure or profit to go and be, pass and re-pass in vessels over or upon any and *j*
> every part of the Thames through which Thames water flows . . .'

The construction of the ferry terminals interfered with the public right of navigation
over the Thames between the main shipping channel and Tate & Lyle's jetties by causing
siltation on the bed and foreshore of the river and siltation in the channel and berth
dredged by Tate & Lyle. This interference with the public right of navigation caused
particular damage to Tate & Lyle because vessels of the requisite dimensions were unable

a to pass and repass over the bed and foreshore between the main channel and the refined sugar jetty and vessels of the required dimensions were unable to pass and repass over the channel dredged by Tate & Lyle between the main shipping channel and the raw sugar jetty and could not be accommodated in the berth dredged by Tate & Lyle adjacent to the raw sugar jetty.

An individual who suffers damage resulting from a public nuisance is, as a general rule, entitled to maintain an action. In the present case the GLC and the PLA assert that

b in constructing the ferry terminals the GLC were acting in pursuance of statutory authority contained in the London County Council (Improvements) Act 1962 and the Port of London (Consolidation) Act 1920, and the combined effect of those two Acts was to authorise the interference with the public right of navigation which was in fact caused by the construction of the ferry terminals. There was therefore no public nuisance and Tate & Lyle have no cause of action in respect of any public nuisance.

c In the alternative, it is argued, Tate & Lyle's damages based on public nuisance must be limited to damages suffered in connection with the refined sugar jetty. The plans of the GLC for the ferry terminals were approved in 1964. The licences to Tate & Lyle granted by the PLA to construct the raw sugar jetty and to dredge the channel and berth required for the raw sugar jetty were not granted until 1965. Tate & Lyle, it is submitted, have no right of action in respect of the raw sugar jetty which was constructed after the

d plans for the ferry terminals were approved and contemporaneously with the construction of the ferry terminals.

Statutory authority

The GLC plead that if they were guilty of creating a public nuisance they are nevertheless excused because they were authorised by the London County Council

e (Improvements) Act 1962 to carry out the operations of which complaint is made. They were authorised by statute to construct the terminals in accordance with a design approved by the PLA and not otherwise.

The defence of statutory authority to an action for nuisance was summarised in the speech of Lord Wilberforce in *Allen v Gulf Oil Refining Ltd* [1981] 1 All ER 353 at 356, [1981] AC 1001 at 1011 as follows:

f 'It is now well settled that where Parliament by express direction or by necessary implication has authorised the construction and use of an undertaking or works, that carries with it an authority to do what is authorised with immunity from any action based on nuisance. The right of action is taken away . . . To this there is made the qualification, or condition, that the statutory powers are exercised without "negligence", that word here being used in a special sense so as to require the

g undertaker, as a condition of obtaining immunity from action, to carry out the work and conduct the operation with all reasonable regard and care for the interests of other persons . . .'

In the present case Parliament authorised the terminals and thereby granted immunity from the consequences of the terminals provided that the GLC paid 'all reasonable regard

h and care for the interests' of public navigation and for the interests of Tate & Lyle liable to suffer particular damage from any interference with the right of public navigation.

The GLC submit that in designing the terminals their only obligation was to obtain the approval of the PLA. If their design did not protect, so far as possible, the interests of the public and of Tate & Lyle, the 1962 Act nevertheless authorised the GLC to construct the terminals in accordance with the design approved by the PLA and not otherwise. If

j in constructing the terminals the GLC had themselves discovered some defect injurious to the GLC, the public or private individuals, the GLC would not have felt justified in completing the construction of the terminals without obtaining authority to amend the design. I would be reluctant to find that the 1962 Act had the effect of enabling the GLC negligently to inflict unnecessary damage on the public or on any individual provided the PLA negligently or without negligence approved a design which caused that damage.

Section 17(1) of the London County Council (Improvements) Act 1962 provided that the GLC—

'may, in the lines or situations and within the limits of deviation shown on the deposited plans and according to the levels shown on the deposited sections, execute the works described in subsection (2) of this section.'

Subsection (2) authorised—

'Work No. 10 A new pier of openwork construction partly on land and partly over the river Thames, commencing by a junction with Pier Road, North Woolwich . . . and terminating by a rising and falling stage or platform eighty-seven yards from the northern river wall.'

Work no 11 was described as 'A new pier of openwork construction over the River Thames . . . terminating by a rising and falling stage or platform eighty-seven yards northwards of the river wall . . .'

Section 17 does not expressly or by implication confer immunity on the GLC from an action based on public nuisance in respect of damage which was avoidable by 'all reasonable care and regard for the interests of other persons'. Section 17 gave immunity from an action in respect of the siltation which proved to be inevitable but not in respect of the additional siltation which resulted from the GLC's choice of a design which caused additional siltation, from the failure of the GLC to consider the effect of the design and failure to take available advice which could and would have resulted in an amended design fulfilling the objects of the GLC without unnecessary damage to Tate & Lyle.

The GLC rely on s 50 of the 1962 Act. That section is expressed to be 'For the protection of the [PLA] and river users . . .' The section was not therefore intended to confer any immunity on the GLC, least of all an immunity from any failure by the GLC to have 'reasonable regard and care for the interests of other persons'. Section 50 was intended as an additional and not as a substitute protection for river users. Section 50 provides that the section shall apply and have effect 'unless otherwise agreed in writing' between the GLC and the PLA. Parliament could not have intended that the GLC should be intentionally or accidentally relieved of liability to take reasonable regard and care by an agreement in writing with the PLA. Section 50(3)(a) requires that the GLC—

'Before commencing to execute any river works under the powers of this Act . . . shall submit to the [PLA] plans, sections and particulars of the river works for their reasonable approval (which approval may be given subject to such reasonable requirements as to the construction of works for the purpose of protecting navigation of the river as the [PLA] may make) . . .'

This requirement on the GLC did not transfer to the PLA the duty to ensure that the design of the terminal would not cause unnecessary siltation nor did it relieve the GLC of that duty. If, from the plans, sections and particulars it appeared to the PLA that some avoidable obstruction to navigation would result from the construction of the terminals, the PLA could require the GLC to make amendments or to provide adequate safeguards or take preventative measures. But the PLA were entitled to assume that the GLC had chosen a competent designer who would take care to see the design did not have any unnecessary adverse effect. The plans, sections and particulars might not alert the PLA to the danger that the design chosen by the GLC, as opposed to other possible designs, would cause unnecessary siltation. By s 50(3)(b) if the PLA did not, within 28 days of the submission to them of any plans, sections or particulars, intimate to the GLC their approval or disapproval they shall be deemed to have approved the same. This limitation on the powers of the PLA is another indication that s 50 was not intended to confer some new immunity on the GLC. Moreover, s 50(9) imposed on the GLC the duty to—

'bear and pay any additional cost to which the [PLA] may be put in dredging the river as a result of any accumulation of mud or silt which may occur in consequence of the construction by the [GLC] under the powers of this Act of any river work'.

The PLA could, therefore, in approving any plans submitted by the GLC take into consideration the fact that any siltation, whether siltation which was inevitable in any event or whether siltation attributable to the particular design chosen by the GLC, could be remedied at the expense of the GLC. Indeed, the present expensive litigation has only

a been caused by the adamant and unsuccessful contention by the GLC that it was a mere coincidence that the construction of the terminals was followed by substantial and continued siltation of the neighbouring bed of the Thames between Tate & Lyle's refinery and the main shipping channel.

In my view s 50 did not confer on the GLC any immunity from suit and in particular did not relieve the GLC of its duty to design the terminals 'with all reasonable care for the interests of other persons'.

b In the alternative, the GLC submit that the effect of s 50(3)(a) of the London County Council (Improvements) Act 1962 was to confer on the GLC all the immunity enjoyed by a licensee authorised to construct works by the PLA under s 243 of the Port of London (Consolidation) Act 1920. Section 243 of the 1920 Act, authorised the PLA—

c
> 'for a fair and reasonable consideration . . . and upon such terms and subject to such restrictions as they think proper grant to any owner or occupier of any land adjoining the Thames a licence . . . (1) For the making of any dock basin pier jetty wharf bank quay, or embankment wall or other work immediately in front of his land and into the body of the Thames . . .'

The terminals were not, in fact, constructed pursuant to a licence granted by the PLA under s 243. The terminals were constructed pursuant to the powers contained in the **d** London County Council (Improvements) Act 1962. But, it is submitted, by s 50(3)(a) of the 1962 Act, the terminals are deemed to have been constructed under a licence from the PLA given under s 243 of the 1920 Act. Section 50(3)(a) of the London County Council (Improvements) Act 1962 provides that the river works executed by the GLC—

e
> 'shall be deemed to be works upon the bed or shores of the river commenced or executed under the direction or with the licence, consent or permission of the [PLA] within the meaning of section 244 . . . of the Port of London (Consolidation) Act, 1920.'

Section 244 of the 1920 Act requires that—

f
> 'No works upon the bed or shores of the Thames shall at any time be commenced or executed under the direction or with the licence consent or permission of the [PLA] without such works having been previously approved of by the Board of Trade . . . or if such approval be not previously obtained without proper conditions being made to provide for the immediate removal of all such works upon notice from the Board of Trade . . . requiring the same to be removed.'

g Section 50(3)(a) of the 1962 Act therefore in practice made necessary the approval of the Board of Trade as well as the approval of the PLA to the plans for the terminals. On behalf of the GLC it was submitted that s 50(3)(a) had a wider effect and impliedly gave the GLC the immunity afforded by a licence granted by the PLA under s 243 of the 1920 Act. The authorities to which reference has already been made, in particular *Kearns v Cordwainers' Co* (1859) 6 CBNS 388, 141 ER 508, and *A-G v Thames Conservators* (1862) 1 Hem & M 1, 71 ER 1, show that no action will lie for an interference with the public **h** right of navigation caused by works licensed by the PLA under s 243.

In my opinion s 50(3)(a) is not apt to create a licence or to deem a licence under s 243 of the 1920 Act. Section 50(3)(a) of the 1962 Act sufficed to introduce and was intended to introduce s 244 of the 1920 Act, but is inconsistent with the introduction of s 243, which could have been expressly introduced if Parliament had wished to do so. Moreover, reading s 50 as a whole, and for the reasons already advanced, that section does not appear **j** to me either apt or intended to confer immunity on the GLC from actions based on public nuisance merely because the plans for the terminals required the approval of the PLA unless otherwise agreed.

The Court of Appeal held that there was 'no duty on the GLC to consider anyone else's interest in siltation' because s 50 of the 1962 Act contemplated that the PLA could inspect the design of the terminals and could nullify the effects of any siltation at the expense of the GLC. At the same time the Court of Appeal held that there was no duty on the PLA to ensure that the design of the terminals produced the minimum siltation, and no duty to nullify the effects of siltation. Thus the statute conferred immunity from unnecessary siltation causing unnecessary adverse effects on third parties such as Tate & Lyle. I decline   *a* to construe s 50 of the 1962 Act so as to relieve the GLC from any elementary duty to cause no more harm than was necessary.

The PLA

The action of Tate & Lyle against the PLA can only succeed if the PLA by their negligence bear some responsibility for the faulty design of the terminals.   *b*

The judge, Forbes J, appears to have assumed that the responsibilities of the GLC and the PLA were the same. He said:

> 'It is quite clear to me that, although the PLA gave some consideration to the possible effect on siltation at the time when the case for the 1962 Bill was being prepared, thereafter neither the consulting engineers nor the PLA gave any serious thought to what might happen to the river as a result of the intrusion of these   *c* structures into it . . . Although there was frequent consultation with the PLA during the design process this was, in my view, no more than one would expect to occur when designers have to obtain the approval of some authority for the work being designed, particularly where, as here, interference with navigation was obvious and the authority was a navigation authority.'
>   *d*

But 'interference with navigation was obvious' only in the sense that the terminals jutted out into the Thames and in the course of construction and after construction required warnings and other precautions against collisions.

'Interference with navigation was obvious' with regard to siltation only in the sense that any obstruction may cause siltation and that possibility was responsible no doubt for the inclusion in the Act of s 50(9) whereby the GLC assumed responsibility for any   *e* additional cost of dredging. Your Lordships were not, however, referred to any fact or circumstances which should have alerted the PLA to the possibility that the terminals might unnecessarily cause the unforeseen and disastrous amount of siltation which took place. There was nothing which would have justified the PLA in insisting on the design being submitted to further advice, or subjected to tests to determine the possible effects of the terminals on siltation. There was no reason for the PLA to suspect that the   *f* consulting engineers employed by the GLC had not produced a design which would only result in the minimum and inevitable amount of siltation. The judge thought the PLA were 30% to blame, but in my view, they are not liable to Tate & Lyle.

On behalf of Tate & Lyle it was submitted that the PLA had 'continued' the nuisance created by the terminals. In *Sedleigh-Denfield v O'Callagan* [1940] 3 All ER 349, [1940] AC 880, a culvert was laid by a trespasser on the defendant's land and caused flooding to the   *g* plaintiff's land. It was held that the defendant having acquired knowledge of the existence of the culvert in time to appreciate the danger involved and to take remedial action was liable for continuing the nuisance created by the culvert. Viscount Maugham said ([1940] 3 All ER 349 at 358, [1940] AC 880 at 894):

> 'In my opinion an occupier of land "continues" a nuisance if with knowledge or   *h* presumed knowledge of its existence he fails to take any reasonable means to bring it to an end though with ample time to do so. He "adopts" it if he makes any use of the erection, building, bank or artificial contrivance which constitutes the nuisance.'

In the present case the approval of the plans of the terminals by the PLA did not in my opinion continue or adopt or otherwise make liable the PLA for any nuisance created by the terminals. By approving the plans the PLA did not guarantee that the terminals   *j* would not interfere with the right of public navigation nor did they guarantee that the terminals would not interfere with the right of public navigation more than was necessary.

Measure of damages

The cost of the additional dredging required to remedy the siltation caused by the

terminals was £540,000. The judge found that an alternative design could, and should,
a have been adopted and that 'if such a design had been adopted it would have resulted . . .
in only one-quarter of the accretion' caused by the design which was in fact selected.
One-quarter of the cost of the additional dredging was the inevitable consequence of the
exercise by the GLC of its statutory power to construct the terminals; one-quarter of the
additional dredging costs is therefore not recoverable by Tate & Lyle.

On behalf of Tate & Lyle it was urged that the terminals as constructed created an
b unauthorised interference with the right of public navigation, and that the GLC are
responsible for all the consequences of that interference, and not only for three-quarters
of the cost of the additional dredging. I cannot accept that argument. To maintain the
public right of navigation, Tate & Lyle would have been bound to carry out some
additional dredging in any event, and their damages are the cost of dredging which
would have been avoided if the terminals had been designed to avoid siltation as much
c as possible. Tate & Lyle claim that if the design of the terminals had only caused one-
quarter of the siltation which in fact occurred, then the PLA might have undertaken the
additional dredging and recovered the cost from the GLC. This is speculation and the
fact is that the GLC adamantly maintained that the terminals were not responsible for
any siltation.

In these circumstances I am of the opinion that Tate & Lyle are entitled to recover
d from the GLC the sum of £405,000 representing three-quarters of the additional
dredging caused by the terminals.

The raw sugar jetty

The licences for the construction of the raw sugar jetty and for the dredging of the
channel and berth necessary to allow vessels to approach and unload at the jetty were
e issued after the PLA had approved the plans of the terminals. The raw sugar jetty and
the terminals were constructed at roughly the same time. The channel to the raw sugar
jetty was dredged to a depth corresponding to the depth of the main shipping channel,
and the berth was dredged to a depth of six feet below the depth of the main shipping
channel. Extensive siltation was caused by the coffer dams inserted in the river during
the course of the construction of the terminals, and siltation continued after the terminals
f had been completed. The siltation in the channel and berth caused by the terminals
involved Tate & Lyle in additional dredging costs between 1966 and 1974.

On behalf of the GLC it was submitted that Tate & Lyle could not recover the
additional cost of dredging required to keep the raw sugar jetty operational. Tate & Lyle
had themselves interferred with the natural flow of the water of the Thames when they
dredged the channel and berth and were not entitled to complain of interference with
g the artificial flow which they had themselves created. Alternatively, the dredging and
raw sugar licences were granted after the approval by the PLA of the plans of the
terminals. Tate & Lyle's licences were impliedly subject to the construction of the
terminals in accordance with those plants, and subject to any consequences flowing from
the construction of those terminals.

In my opinion these arguments fail. The channel and the berth dredged for the
h purposes of the raw sugar jetty were authorised works in the Thames which by statute
the PLA were entitled to sanction. The public right of navigation extended over the
channel and berth once they were dredged. The interference caused by the terminals, on
the other hand, was an interference with the public right of navigation which was not
justified by the statute under which the GLC erected the terminals. Tate & Lyle suffered
particular damage because vessels were prevented from plying between the main
j shipping channel and the raw sugar jetty. Tate & Lyle are entitled to damages for the
particular damage suffered by them as a result of the interference with the public right
of navigation unnecessarily caused by the terminals.

The PLA approved the plans of the terminals before they granted the raw sugar jetty
licences. But the terminals, so far as they caused more siltation than was necessary,
created a public nuisance. The GLC cannot escape the consequences of a public nuisance
merely because it was created before Tate & Lyle suffered damage.

Conclusions

It follows that the appeal of Tate & Lyle succeeds against the GLC but fails against the *a* PLA. The order of Forbes J against the GLC will be restored but varied, reducing the damages of £540,000 in respect of additional dredging costs to three-quarters of that sum, namely £405,000. Interest until judgment of £442,158 will be reduced by one-quarter to £331,618·50. The damages of £10,000 in respect of additional survey costs will stand. The second appellants, Silvertown Services Lighterage Ltd, are a subsidiary company of Tate & Lyle and provide lighterage and barge facilities for the refinery. They *b* were awarded by Forbes J £200 agreed damages and as against the GLC this award will be restored. All Tate & Lyle's claims against the PLA are dismissed.

LORD DIPLOCK. My Lords, in his speech my noble and learned friend Lord Templeman has given the reasons which lead him to the conclusion that the additional *c* silt deposited on the bed of the river between the jetty heads of Tate & Lyle's two jetties and the main navigational channel, as a result of the 'Husband design' to which the Woolwich ferry terminals were erected, did not entitle Tate & Lyle to any remedy in law against either the GLC or the PLA, based on breach of riparian or contractual rights or on negligence or private nuisance. I agree with his conclusions under these four heads. It is on the question of the GLC's liability to Tate & Lyle for the cost of additional dredging *d* at their raw sugar jetty, as particular damage sustained by them in consequence of a public nuisance, viz interference with the public right of navigation in the Thames (as to which Forbes J made no finding), that I am regretfully unable to associate myself with the conclusion reached by the rest of your Lordships.

The question whether the GLC could rely on statutory authority to cause such additional siltation as in fact resulted from the erection of terminals to the Husband *e* design rather than a Mouchel design turns on the effect of what qualifies for the description of a 'one-off' section in a private Act of Parliament. This is essentially a question of construction; it is one which I have found to be finely balanced and my mind both during and since the hearing has vacillated between the construction that has gained the support of the rest of your Lordships for the reasons given by Lord Templeman and the construction adopted by the Court of Appeal for reasons which are very persuasive *f* and, if right, would provide the GLC with a defence to the claim for the cost of additional dredging at the refined sugar jetty as well as the raw sugar jetty. In the end, however, I do not think my still lingering doubts justify my persisting in dissenting from your Lordships on a question of construction that is so narrow and so unlikely to recur as this.

There are, however, other reasons special to the raw sugar jetty why I think that the GLC are not liable to Tate & Lyle for the cost of the additional dredging there. These *g* reasons are based on the legal nature of the public right of navigation in the tidal waters of the Thames and are in my view of sufficient general importance to justify my stating shortly why I feel compelled to differ from your Lordships on this part of Tate & Lyle's claim.

(1) In order to succeed in a claim for particular damage caused to them by a public nuisance Tate & Lyle must first establish that the GLC by constructing the terminals *h* created a public nuisance, that is to say did an act of which *every* member of the public wishing to exercise his public right of navigation on the Thames at the place where the additional silting occurred could complain, and in respect of which the Attorney General, either ex officio or on the relation of such a member of the public, would be entitled to bring a civil action to restrain.

(2) A public right of navigation in navigable waters that form part of a port is a right *j* enjoyed by every member of the public to pass and repass over the whole of the surface of the water in vessels of such draught as the depth of water below any particular part of the surface permits and to keep such vessels stationary in the water for a reasonable time for navigational purposes in the course of a voyage (eg waiting for a tide) or for the purposes of loading, unloading or transhipping goods or passengers or waiting to do so.

a   (3) The concept that there is such a thing as a 'natural flow' of water that determines the configuration of the bed of a river with the consequence that it is, in law, a public nuisance to do anything that interferes with that configuration in such a way as to prevent vessels of a particular draught passing over a particular part of the surface of the water, can have no application to a navigable river like the Thames, whose bed, soil and shore are vested in a statutory authority whose functions include the control of all navigation on the river and which is empowered itself to do, and to authorise riparian

b   owners to do, acts on the bed of the river which inevitably affect the migration of silt from one part of the bed to another and cause changes in the former configuration of the bed.

(4) A member of the public wishing to exercise his public right of navigation over that part of the Thames adjacent to the jetty head of either of Tate & Lyle's jetties in a vessel of a particular draught would be entitled to find there such depth of water as was

c   from time to time permitted by the configuration which the bed of the river had assumed as a result of any dredging or of the erection of structures there or elsewhere in the river that the PLA had themselves undertaken or had licensed individual riparian owners to undertake. So changes in depth of the water at either of the jetty heads caused by the subsequent erection of some structure in the river, upstream or downstream of the jetties, if licensed by the PLA would not amount to an interference with the public

d   right of navigation and would not constitute a public nuisance. Accordingly, it would give no right of action to Tate & Lyle who suffered particular damage as a result.

(5) It is because your Lordships are prepared to hold that, on the true construction of s 50 of the London County Council (Improvements) Act 1962, the approval by the PLA of the Husband design for the ferry terminals does not confer on the terminals erected in accordance with that design the same status in law as structures in the river that the PLA

e   have licensed riparian owners to erect and maintain that the GLC cannot escape liability for the cost of the additional dredging adjacent to the refined sugar jetty where, prior to the construction of the terminals, no dredging was required to obtain the depth of water necessary to accommodate vessels of the draught used for the purpose of carrying away the refined sugar from that jetty.

(6) The raw sugar jetty differs from the refined sugar jetty in two respects which, in

f   my opinion, affect the public right of navigation at the jetty head and between the jetty head and the main navigation channel. The first is that the depth of water necessary to accommodate vessels carrying raw sugar to the jetty could only be obtained and maintained by dredging; and the second is that the licence to Tate & Lyle to erect the jetty was not granted until after the Husband design for the terminals had been approved by the PLA.

g   (7) Licences to deepen the bed of the river at any particular place by dredging are granted by the PLA for short periods only, which do not in practice exceed six months; if dredging is to continue after one licence has expired a fresh licence is required. So too, licences to riparian owners to erect and maintain structures on the bed of the river are terminable by the PLA on short notice requiring the licensee to remove the structure. Cessation of dredging at a particular place and removal of structures will inevitably affect

h   the configuration of the bed of the river; and since such cessation or removal may lawfully be called for by the PLA on short notice at any time, a member of the public wishing to exercise his public right of navigation over a particular part of the water of the Thames has no public right to continue to find at that place a depth of water greater than it would have been if no dredging of the river had taken place there or a licensed structure had not been removed.

j   (8) Before any construction work had started on the ferry terminals the depth of water at that part of the river where the jetty head of the raw sugar jetty was subsequently located was insufficient to permit of navigation by vessels of the draught that the raw sugar jetty was intended to accommodate; so at that time there could be no public right to navigate there in vessels of that draught. Dredging the bed of the river in that area to a depth sufficient to enable vessels of that draught to have access from the main

navigational channel to the raw sugar jetty head and to moor there for the purpose of
unloading raw sugar, whether such dredging was undertaken by the PLA themselves or
by someone else licensed to undertake it by the PLA, could not, for the reasons stated in
(7), give rise to any public right to the maintenance of that additional depth; and for the
purpose of any cause of action for particular damage sustained in consequence of a public
nuisance, which is the only cause of action to which your Lordships have held that Tate
& Lyle are entitled, they must as a condition precedent to that cause of action establish
that there has been an interference with a right of navigation to which every member of
the public is entitled. For this purpose the fact that the dredging was undertaken by Tate
& Lyle themselves and not by some stranger licensed by the PLA to undertake it, must
be ignored. On this ground I would hold that Tate & Lyle's claim for the cost of additional
dredging in the area of the raw sugar jetty fails.

(9) The second ground only arises on the assumption that the first ground fails and
the ferry terminals when erected did create a public nuisance in the vicinity of the raw
sugar jetty. In all the cases to which your Lordships were referred in which particular
damage sustained in consequence of a public nuisance has been recognised as giving rise
to a cause of action in civil law the particular damage has been caused by injury to
proprietary rights of the plaintiff in corporeal or incorporeal hereditaments that are in
proximity to the public nuisance; and I would accept that in principle where the injury
is to proprietary rights it is no defence to say that the plaintiff either created or increased
the particular damage that he sustained by the use to which he chose to put his property
after the public nuisance had come into existence, so long as such use was a lawful one.
But in the instant case your Lordships have held that *no* proprietary rights of Tate & Lyle
have been injured by the accumulation of additional silt at the jetty heads. When the
licence to erect the raw sugar jetty was granted by the PLA to Tate & Lyle the construction
of the ferry terminals to the Husband design had been already authorised. Assuming
that during its construction and after its completion it created a public nuisance by its
interference with the public right of navigation in the area in which Tate & Lyle chose
subsequently to obtain a licence for the erection of the raw sugar jetty head, it was that
choice which was the cause of their sustaining particular damage of a kind not suffered
by other members of the public who wished to exercise their public right of navigation
over that area. I do not think that particular damage arising from the choice of a person
as to how he uses his public as distinguished from his proprietary rights can, in principle,
give rise to a civil cause of action in damages against the creator of the public nuisance.

LORD KEITH OF KINKEL. My Lords, I have had the opportunity of reading in
draft the speech delivered by my noble and learned friend Lord Templeman. I agree
with it, and for the reasons he gives would allow the appeal against the GLC and dismiss
the appeal against the PLA.

LORD ROSKILL. My Lords, I have had the advantage of reading in draft the speech
delivered by my noble and learned friend Lord Templeman. I agree with it in all respects
and for the reasons he gives I would allow the appeal by Tate & Lyle against the GLC and
order them to pay damages and interest as he proposes. I would also allow the appeal of
the second defendants and award them the sum of £200. I would dismiss Tate & Lyle's
appeal against the PLA.

LORD BRIDGE OF HARWICH. My Lords, I have had the advantage of reading in
draft the speech delivered by my noble and learned friend Lord Templeman. I agree
both with his reasoning and his conclusions and accordingly concur in the orders which
he proposes.

Appeal against the GLC allowed. Appeal against the PLA dismissed.

Solicitors: *Ingledew Brown Bennison & Garrett* (for Tate & Lyle and Silverton Services);
R A Lanham (for the GLC); *Brian Golds* (for the PLA).

Mary Rose Plummer   Barrister.

a   # Swainston v Hetton Victory Club Ltd

EMPLOYMENT APPEAL TRIBUNAL
BROWNE-WILKINSON J, MRS D EWING AND MR S M SPRINGER
8 SEPTEMBER 1982

b
COURT OF APPEAL, CIVIL DIVISION
WALLER, WATKINS AND FOX LJJ
31 JANUARY, 10 FEBRUARY 1983

Industrial tribunal – Procedure – Complaint of unfair dismissal – Presentation of complaint to tribunal – Time limit for presentation of complaint expiring on day when tribunal office closed – Complaint presented to office on next working day – Whether complaint presented in time –
c *Whether complaint can be 'presented' by posting complaint through tribunal office's street letter box – Employment Protection (Consolidation) Act 1978, s 67(2).*

The complainant was dismissed from his employment on 7 September 1981. The three months period within which, under s 67(2)[a] of the Employment Protection (Consolidation) Act 1978, he had to present a complaint of unfair dismissal to an industrial tribunal
d therefore expired at midnight on Sunday, 6 December 1981. The local industrial tribunal's office was closed at weekends but there was a letter box in the office's door to the street through which communications could be posted when the office was closed. That box was cleared each Monday morning when the office reopened. The complainant did not present his complaint of unfair dismissal to the office until Monday, 7 December. At the hearing of the complaint the employers contended that the complaint was out of
e time because it was not presented within the prescribed time limit. The industrial tribunal held that the prescribed time limit was to be treated as not having expired until the next working day following Sunday, 6 December and therefore the complaint was presented in time. The employers appealed to the Employment Appeal Tribunal, which held that the presentation of the complaint was out of time. The complainant appealed to the Court of Appeal.
f

Held – Since presentation of a complaint to an industrial tribunal for the purposes of s 67(2) of the 1978 Act did not require any action on the part of the tribunal a complaint could be 'presented' within s 67(2) if it was communicated to the tribunal through a channel of communication held out by the tribunal as being an acceptable means of communication and receipt of a complaint. Accordingly, a complaint could be 'presented'
g to the tribunal if it was posted through a letter box in the door of the tribunal's office, and since the complainant could have presented his complaint to the tribunal in that manner on Sunday, 6 December 1981 he was out of time when he presented it on the following Monday. The appeal would therefore be dismissed (see p 1184 *c* to *g*, post).
    Dictum of Donaldson P in *Hammond v Haigh Castle & Co Ltd* [1973] 2 All ER at 291
h and *Post Office v Moore* [1981] ICR 623 followed.
    Pritam Kaur (administratrix of Bikar Singh (decd)) v S Russell & Sons Ltd [1973] 1 All ER 617 distinguished.
    Anglo-Continental School of English (Bournemouth) Ltd v Gardiner [1973] ICR 261 not followed.

j   **Notes**
For the time for presenting a complaint of unfair dismissal to an industrial tribunal, see 16 Halsbury's Laws (4th edn) para 637.
    For the Employment Protection (Consolidation) Act 1978, s 67, see 48 Halsbury's Statutes (3rd edn) 518.

---

a   Section 67(2) is set out at p 1183 *a b*, post

Cases referred to in judgments

Anglo-Continental School of English (Bournemouth) Ltd v Gardiner [1973] ICR 261, 20 Digest (Reissue) 414, *3394*.

Hammond v Haigh Castle & Co Ltd [1973] 2 All ER 289, [1973] ICR 148, 20 Digest (Reissue) 417, *3405*.

Hodgson v Armstrong [1967] 1 All ER 307, [1967] 2 QB 299, [1967] 2 WLR 311, CA, Digest (Cont Vol C) 955, *358a*.

Hughes v Griffiths (1862) 13 CBNS 324, 143 ER 129, 45 Digest (Repl) 268, *349*.

Mumford v Hitchcocks (1863) 14 CBNS 361, 143 ER 485, 45 Digest (Repl) 268, *358*.

Post Office v Moore [1981] ICR 623, EAT.

Pritam Kaur (administratrix of Bikar Singh (decd)) v S Russell & Sons Ltd [1973] 1 All ER 617, [1973] QB 336, [1973] 2 WLR 147, CA, Digest (Cont Vol D) 614, *277a*.

Appeal

Hetton Victory Club (the employers) appealed against the decision of an industrial tribunal sitting at Newcastle upon Tyne (chairman M Cohen) on 26 January 1982 whereby, on an application by Mr John Swainston claiming compensation for unfair dismissal against the employers, the tribunal held, on a preliminary point raised by the employers, that Mr Swainston's application had been presented to the tribunal within the time limit specified in s 67(2) of the Employment Protection (Consolidation) Act 1978 and that accordingly the tribunal had jurisdiction to entertain the application. The facts are set out in the judgment of the appeal tribunal.

T R H Sowler for the employers.
C F Chruscz for Mr Swainston.

BROWNE-WILKINSON J. This case raises yet again the question whether an application complaining of unfair dismissal has, or has not, been served within the time limit specified by the Employment Protection (Consolidation) Act 1978. Section 67(2) provides:

'... an industrial tribunal shall not consider a complaint under this section unless it is presented to the tribunal before the end of the period of three months beginning with the effective date of termination or within such further period as the tribunal considers reasonable in a case where it is satisfied that it was not reasonably practicable for the complaint to be presented before the end of the period of three months.'

The facts of the case are extremely simple. The effective date of termination of Mr Swainston's employment was 7 September 1981. The parties are agreed that the three months' period provided by statute expired at midnight on Sunday, 6 December 1981. In fact, the application was presented on Monday, 7 December 1981. Since 6 December 1981 was a Sunday the regional office of Industrial Tribunals at Manchester where the application was presented was closed on that day.

The industrial tribunal held that, since the regional office was closed on the Sunday, the case fell within the exceptional principle which permits a period of limitation to be treated as not expiring on the non-working day (the Sunday) but as expiring on the next working day thereafter, namely the Monday. The industrial tribunal, in a careful decision, therefore held that the application had been presented within time. The employers appeal against that decision.

Since the time limit of three months is prescribed by statute and excludes any jurisdiction in the industrial tribunal to extend the time save where it is satisfied that it was not practicable for the complaint to be presented within the three months' period, prima facie the three months expired on Sunday, 6 December 1981. It was conceded by the applicant that it was practicable to have served the application within the three

months; therefore, no question of the discretion arises in this case. Since the time limit
a is statutory, effect must be given to it, however harsh the conclusion may be in any
particular case.

In relation to the statute of limitations, the general rule is that the period expires on
the expiry of the relevant period notwithstanding that the last day is a non-working day.
However, in *Pritam Kaur (administratrix of Bikar Singh (decd)) v S Russell & Sons Ltd* [1973]
1 All ER 617, [1973] QB 336, the Court of Appeal held what where the limitation period
b expired on a non-working day a writ was issued within the period provided it was issued
on the next day on which the court offices open. In that case, the point under
consideration was the failure to issue a writ until the day after the statutory time limit
had expired, the statutory time limit having expired on a Sunday. It is clear from the
judgments of both Lord Denning MR and Megarry J, that the proposition they are laying
down is limited to cases where statute provides for an act to be done and that act can only
c be done if the court office is open on the day when the time expires, ie the issue of a writ
which is not the unilateral act of the complainant alone but involves co-operation or
action by the court or tribunal. The industrial tribunal applied that principle in the
present case.

As it seems to us, the relevant question is whether in the present case it was possible
for the complainant to present his application, within the meaning of the 1978 Act, on
d Sunday, 6 December 1981. If it could be done, then time expired on that day. If it could
not, then the principle laid down in the *Pritam Kaur* case would apply.

The industrial tribunal decided the case in the absence of information as to the position
at the Manchester regional office. We have ourselves made inquiries this morning of the
regional office as to the arrangements made there for the reception of communications.
The regional office is, as its address on its headed paper discloses, at Alexandra House,
e 14–22 The Parsonage, Manchester. Although many of its offices are on the upper floor
of that building, the floor on which it carries on its business is not indicated in its letter
heading. At ground floor level there is a door; during normal working hours the door is
protected by a security officer who is a member of the staff of the industrial tribunal.
There are three other government departments in the building. In the ordinary course,
when the offices are open, communications are delivered to the security officer and not
f direct to the offices of each of the departments. The door at street level is closed during
Saturday and Sunday when the offices are closed, but there is a letter box in the door
through which communications can be posted. That box is cleared by the security officer
when the offices are reopened on the Monday.

The question therefore is whether it was possible in this case for the complainant to
present his application on Sunday, 6 December. That involves consideration of what is
g meant by 'present'. The *Shorter Oxford English Dictionary* defines it as meaning 'to bring
or place a thing before or into the presence of a person, or put it into his hands for
acceptance;' alternatively, as meaning 'to deliver a document to the proper quarter for
acceptance or to be dealt with according to its tenor.'

In *Anglo-Continental School of English (Bournemouth) Ltd v Gardiner* [1973] ICR 261 the
National Industrial Relations Court held that the time limit was automatically extended
h by one day when the statutory time limit had expired on a Sunday. They based that
decision on the *Pritam Kaur* case. They stated that they took into account the fact that
some step was required by the tribunal in effecting a presentation of an application. In
the view of the National Industrial Relations Court the application could not be 'presented'
on a Saturday or a Sunday because it would not be presented until it had been opened by
an officer of the tribunal. That decision, if we should follow it, plainly justifies the
j decision of the industrial tribunal and would lead to the dismissal of this appeal.

On the other hand, in *Post Office v Moore* [1981] ICR 623 this appeal tribunal was
dealing with a case where the three months' period expired on a weekday and the alleged
presentation of the application consisted of the document being put through a letter box
on that weekday (the last day of the statutory period) but after normal working hours,
namely, at 10 pm. This tribunal held that by posting the application through the letter

box out of working hours the application had been validly presented within time. In doing so, they followed an opinion expressed by another division of the National Industrial Relations Court in *Hammond v Haigh Castle & Co Ltd* [1973] 2 All ER 289 which expressed the view that a claim delivered to the tribunal by post on a Saturday was presented on that day even though it was not registered until the following Monday. In *Post Office v Moore* this appeal tribunal chose to follow the *Hammond* case rather than the *Anglo-Continental* case and held that even though, in the case before them, the application had been put through the letter box outside working hours and had therefore not come into the hands of an officer of the tribunal until the following day, even so it had been 'presented'.

As it seems to us, there is no reconciling the conflict between the *Anglo-Continental* case and the *Moore* case. We therefore have to choose between them. With the benefit of much fuller argument than the industrial tribunal had, we have come to the conclusion that the *Moore* approach is to be preferred. As it seems to us, presentation is primarily a unilateral act to be carried out by the person who is presenting. However, it does require some form of collaboration by the person to whom the presentation is being made: an act of presentation cannot be completed unless it is either actually received by the person to whom the presentation is made, or has been placed or communicated through a channel which the person to whom the presentation is to be made has indicated as an acceptable means of communication and receipt. Therefore, it is only possible to say that presentation of the complaint was impossible so as to introduce the *Pritam Kaur* exception if it can be said that on Sunday, 6 December, there was no channel for receiving the complaint on that date. As it seems to us, if business is being carried on in a building which, when closed, has a door to which the public have access and that door contains a letter box held out as a means of communication, a document put through that letter box is in any ordinary sense 'presented' to the person carrying on that business when it is put through the letter box. We do not wish this case to turn on the exact details of the internal arrangements made in this particular regional office. As it seems to us, an application is presented if it is placed through a letter box or dealt with in some other way held out by the regional office as a means whereby it will receive communications.

For those reasons, and with respect to the careful and detailed decision of the industrial tribunal, we must differ from their conclusion and allow the appeal. We do so with regret since any case which cannot be heard on its merits because it is narrowly excluded by an artificial time limit is not a very acceptable form of justice. The legislature has been invited on a number of occasions (notably in the *Moore* case itself) to ameliorate the extreme rigour of the time limits imposed by the 1978 Act; but that has not, as yet, been done. For those reasons we must allow the appeal and hold that the application was out of time.

Appeal allowed.

Solicitors: *Swinburne & Jackson*, Durham (for the employers); *Berry & Berry Cocker Smith & Co*, Walkden (for Mr Swainston).

Appeal
Mr Swainston appealed to the Court of Appeal.

C F Chruscz for Mr Swainston.
T R H Sowler for the employers.

Cur adv vult

10 February. The following judgments were delivered.

WALLER LJ. This is an appeal from the Employment Appeal Tribunal raising the

question of the calculation of time for the presentation to the industrial tribunal of a
a complaint of unfair dismissal. Section 67(2) of the Employment Protection (Consolidation)
Act 1978, provides:

> 'Subject to subsection (4), an industrial tribunal shall not consider a complaint
> under this section unless it is presented to the tribunal before the end of the period
> of three months beginning with the effective date of termination or within such
> further period as the tribunal considers reasonable in a case where it is satisfied that
b > it was not reasonably practicable for the complaint to be presented before the end of
> the period of three months.'

It was agreed between the parties that the complainant's dismissal was on 7 September
1981 and that the end of the period of three months would be 6 December 1981. It was
further accepted that no help was available on the basis that it would not have been
c reasonably practicable to serve in time. The appellant contended that because 6 December
was a Sunday, and the industrial tribunal office was closed on Sunday, presentation on
Monday, 7 December was in time. The Employment Appeal Tribunal held in a full and
careful judgment that it was out of time, and this appeal is brought against that decision.

Under RSC Ord 3, r 4, where the time prescribed by the rules ends on a Sunday the act
shall be done within time if done on the next day. In *Pritam Kaur (administratrix of Bikar*
d *Singh (decd)) v S Russell & Sons Ltd* [1973] 1 All ER 617, [1973] QB 336, the Court of
Appeal held that where the limitation period expired on a non-working day a writ was
issued within the period provided if it was issued on the next day on which the court was
open. Lord Denning MR said ([1973] 1 All ER 617 at 620, [1973] QB 336 at 349):

> 'So I am prepared to hold that, when a time is prescribed by statute for doing any
> act, and that act can only be done if the court office is open on the day when the
e > time expires, then, if it turns out in any particular case that the day is a Sunday or
> other dies non, the time is extended until the next day on which the court office is
> open. In support of this conclusion, I would refer to *Hughes v Griffiths* (1862) 13
> CBNS 324, 143 ER 129. It was on a different statute, but the principle was enunciated
> by Erle CJ (at 333): "Where the act is to be done by the court, and the court refuses
> to act on that day, the intendment of the law is that the party shall have until the
f > earliest day on which the court will act".'

And Megarry J in the *Pritam Kaur* case ([1973] 1 All ER 617 at 626, [1973] QB 336 at
356) said:

> 'There are a number of cases which support the general rule that a statutory
> period of time, whether general or special, will, in the absence of any contrary
g > provision, normally be construed as ending at the expiration of the last day of the
> period. That rule remains; but there is a limited but important exception or
> qualification to it, which may be derived from a line of authorities which include
> *Hughes v Griffiths* (1862) 13 CBNS 324, 143 ER 129, *Mumford v Hitchcocks* (1863) 14
> CBNS 361, 143 ER 485, the judgment of Sellers LJ in *Hodgson v Armstrong* [1967] 1
> All ER 307, [1967] 2 QB 299, and the Scottish cases. If the act to be done by the
h > person concerned is one for which some action by the court is requisite, such as
> issuing a writ, and it is impossible to do that act on the last day of the period because
> the offices of the court are closed for the whole of that day, the period will prima
> facie be construed as ending not on that day but at the expiration of the next day on
> which the offices of the court are open and it becomes possible to do the act.'

j In *Anglo-Continental School of English (Bournemouth) Ltd v Gardiner* [1973] ICR 261 the
National Industrial Relations Court, following the *Pritam Kaur* case, held that the time
limit was automatically extended by one day when the statutory time limit had expired
on a Sunday. In the view of the National Industrial Relations Court the application could
not be 'presented' on a Saturday or a Sunday because it would not be presented until it
had been opened by an officer of the tribunal.

A different view was expressed in *Post Office v Moore* [1981] ICR 623, where it was held that posting through the letter box after the office had closed, but before midnight on *a* the last day, was presentation within the meaning of the section.

The *Shorter Oxford English Dictionary* defines 'present' as 'to deliver a document to the proper quarter for acceptance' or 'to bring a thing before or into the presence of a person or put it into his hands for acceptance'. And Donaldson P in *Hammond v Haigh Castle & Co Ltd* [1973] 2 All ER 289 at 291 said:

> 'Although it is immaterial to the present appeal, we have been asked to express *b*
> our opinion on the meaning of the word "presented". In our judgment, a claim is
> presented to a tribunal when it is received by the tribunal, whether or not it is dealt
> with immediately on receipt. Thus a claim delivered to the tribunal office by post
> on a Saturday is presented on that day, even if not registered before the following
> Monday. A claim is not, however, presented by the act of posting it addressed to the
> tribunal.' *c*

In my opinion it is difficult to say that presentation requires any action on the part of the body to which presentation is made. Delivery of a document to the proper quarter does not require action on the part of anybody at that proper quarter. Donaldson P in the passage quoted contemplates subsequent registration, but that is not part of the presentation. In my judgment the line of authorities of which *Pritam Kaur* *d* was an example depend on activity on the part of the other party, whereas presentation does not.

Counsel for the appellant argued that the interpretation adopted by the Employment Appeal Tribunal in this case would cause confusion in employment appeal cases because some industrial tribunals had post-box facilities when closed, whereas others had none when closed, and therefore different considerations would arise in different districts. I *e* am satisfied that no injustice would occur because a complainant or his solicitor who arrived at the industrial tribunal office and found no letter box might be able to show that it was not reasonably practicable for him to present the complaint within the relevant period. The Employment Appeal Tribunal in the present case, with whose judgment I entirely agree, concluded by saying: '. . . an application is presented if it is placed through a letter box or dealt with in some other way held out by the regional *f* office as a means whereby it will receive communications.' I agree with this and would dismiss this appeal.

WATKINS LJ. I agree.

FOX LJ. I agree. *g*

Appeal dismissed.

Solicitors: *Allan Jay & Co*, agents for *Berry & Berry Cocker Smith & Co*, Walkden (for Mr Swainston); *Swinburne & Jackson*, Durham (for the employers).

Sophie Craven   Barrister.

End of Volume 1